PLACE IN RETURN BOX to remove this checkout from your record.
TO AVOID FINES return on or before date due.

DATE DUE	DATE DUE	DATE DUE
JAN 1 1 2001	OCT 1 4 2004	

MSU Is An Affirmative Action/Equal Opportunity Institution

c:\circ\datedue.pm3-p.1

ENCYCLOPEDIA OF AMERICAN HISTORY

CONSULTING EDITORS

ENCYCLOPEDIA OF
American History

SIXTH EDITION

EDITED BY **RICHARD B. MORRIS**
GOUVERNEUR MORRIS PROFESSOR OF HISTORY
COLUMBIA UNIVERSITY

ASSOCIATE EDITOR **JEFFREY B. MORRIS**
ASSISTANT PROFESSOR OF POLITICAL SCIENCE
UNIVERSITY OF PENNSYLVANIA

1817

HARPER & ROW, PUBLISHERS, New York
Cambridge, Philadelphia, San Francisco, London,
Mexico City, São Paulo, Sydney

Five maps—Cold War Alliances; American Overseas Expansion to 1917; Western Indian Reservations, 1875; Immigration to the U.S. 1890–1917; and Triangular Trade Routes—are used with the kind permission of Rand McNally & Co., copyright by Rand McNally & Co., R.L. 74-S-38.

Library of Congress Cataloging in Publication Data
Main entry under title:

Encyclopedia of American history.

  Bibliography: p.
  Includes index.
  1. United States—History—Chronology. 2. United States—History—Dictionaries. I. Morris, Richard Brandon, 1904–   . II. Morris, Jeffrey Brandon, 1941–

E174.5.E52 1982	973'.03'21	81-47668
ISBN 0-06-181605-1		AACR2

82 83 84 85 86 10 9 8 7 6 5 4 3 2 1

CONTENTS

2. Topical Chronology

3. Five Hundred Notable Americans

4. Structure of the Federal Government

MAPS and CHARTS

HOW TO USE THIS BOOK
Foreword to the Sixth Edition

The speed with which America has been swept up in the Age of High Technology threatens to obliterate the past, with its collective memory of the political and cultural foundations, economic developments, and moral and social forces which shaped its traditions. History returns us to the roots and branches, and the facts which it records about the past enable us to evaluate our rapidly changing values and institutions. To aid such an evaluation this *Encyclopedia* aims to provide in a single handy volume the essential historical facts about American life and institutions. The organization is both chronological and topical. *Dates, events, achievements,* and *persons* stand out, but the text is designed to be read as a narrative.

The *Encyclopedia* is comprehensive in its coverage. There are four main divisions. Part I (Basic Chronology) presents the major political and military events in the history of the United States, introduced by an account of explorations, settlement, and colonial and Revolutionary problems. After reviewing the main political and constitutional developments in the original Thirteen Colonies, the focus is widened to encompass imperial and intercolonial issues. Thereafter the emphasis is upon national, federal, or major sectional problems rather than on localized and isolated occurrences—on the President, Congress, the Supreme Court, and the issues of war and peace.

Events are arranged in time sequence, with annual coverage beginning with the year 1763. For the purpose of clarity, however, as well as compression, many subjects are arbitrarily treated under the year in which they came to national attention; but, where feasible, the entire story is told only once even though it may be necessary to spread the net over more than one year. For instance, the removal of the federal government's deposits from the 2d Bank of the U.S. is treated under the year 1833 when it took place, but the censuring resolution of 1834 is thereunder included as well as the final expunging of that resolution in 1837. If, then, you do not find the entry under the year in which the event occurred, consult the Index.

The nonpolitical aspects of American life are examined in Part II (Topical Chronology), which organizes the facts about constitutional developments, American expansion, and demographic, economic, scientific, technological, and cultural trends. Much of this information has never been presented before in a general chronological framework. Needless to say, social and cultural events and contributions often do not lend themselves to close dating.

A special feature of the *Encyclopedia* is Part III (Biographical Section), which furnishes data on 500 notable Americans chosen for their outstanding achievements in major fields of activity. Elsewhere, the names of significant persons not included in this section are followed (the first time cited) by the dates of birth and death and in many cases by brief biographical information.

Part IV covering the structure of the federal government provides listings of Presidents, Cabinet heads, Supreme Court justices, as well as the texts of the Declaration of Independence and the Constitution of the United States.

Events Before 1752. The old Julian Calendar, in force in Great Britain and her colonies until 1752, overestimated the solar year by 11 minutes 14 seconds a year. Under that calendar the year technically began on 25 Mar. The New Style Calendar, which went into effect in 1752 (based upon the calendar ordained by Pope Gregory XIII in 1582), adjusted the errors in the old chronology by adding 10 days down through the year 1699 and 11 days beginning with 1700, and leaving 11 days out of the calendar in 1752 (3 Sept. became 14 Sept.). In addition, the new year once more began on 1 Jan. This chronology follows New Style usage for all dates prior to 1752. Thus, the Mayflower Compact, bearing the date of 11 Nov. 1620, was actually signed on 21 Nov. Under the Julian Calendar (Old Style), George Washington was born 11 Feb. 1731/2, but this book lists it as 22 Feb. 1732 (New Style).

Presidential Elections. Presidential and congressional elections were originally held on varying days. For convenience the day when the electors cast their ballots has been designated election day (the first Wed. in Dec. under the Act of 1 Mar. 1792; the Tues. following the first Mon. in Nov. under Act of 23 Jan. 1845).

Acts of Congress bear the date when they were signed by the president, although the dates of actual passage are indicated when deemed significant, as well as the division of the votes in Senate and House.

Sixth Edition. This revised, enlarged, and updated edition covers American historical events from the era of discovery and exploration to 15 December 1981. Headnotes to each subsection aim to organize and assimilate the discrete facts that follow and to furnish some sense of pattern and significance. Much more space is allotted to minorities, ethnic groups, and the role of women than in earlier editions. The domestic and foreign affairs chronologies have been completely reorganized for the period since 1945 and the content reassessed in terms of recent interpretive scholarship. Extensive changes are found throughout the

Topical Chronology, including under "Expansion of the Nation" sections on "Land, Natural Resources, and the Environment" and on "Indian Land Policy and Reform Since the Civil War." The section on "Population, Immigration, and Ethnic Stocks" includes a conspectus of black Americans since the Civil War, supplementing the updated coverage of Supreme Court decisions on desegregation. The Women's Movement and issues of gender discrimination are found in both the Basic Chronology and the Supreme Court sections. The section on "Indian Land Policy and Reform" covers issues and events through the Carter administration. "The American Economy" section has been extensively enlarged and reorganized, with more recent statistics included. Subsections on Film and Dance have been added to "Thought and Culture," and a new section, "Mass Media," covering the press, radio, and TV, has been incorporated in this edition, along with litigation on free press—fair trial issues (the latter to be found in "Leading Supreme Court Decisions"). Finally, the Biographical Section now provides compact accounts of 500 notable Americans, a compilation based on an extensive poll among historians and specialists in a variety of fields.

A concluding word about historical facts. The *Encyclopedia* endeavors to incorporate the results of the latest research. This often involves revisions of previously accepted data. For example, radiocarbon tests support very different datings for the crossing of the Bering Strait and the southward penetration into the Americas than had prevailed a generation ago, but one should be cautioned that much of the nonorganic objects uncovered lack evidence either of being man-made or of any links to human occupation. The extensive current publication programs of the writings of American statesmen are providing massive documentation of the authorship and dates of state papers, in some cases correcting previous information. We now know that John Jay wrote a first draft of the "Olive Branch Petition," whose final version has been correctly attributed to John Dickinson, while the latter's authorship of the "Declaration of the Causes and Necessities of Taking Up Arms" must now be shared with Jefferson, as Dr. Julian P. Boyd has conclusively demonstrated. Long-accepted birth dates for persons born in such different centuries as Peter Stuyvesant, Alexander Hamilton, and George Washington Carver have been revised on the basis of recent discoveries. This Sixth Edition incorporates the latest findings of *Historical Statistics of the United States: Colonial Times to 1970* (1975) brought up to date by the annual *Statistical Abstract*, including census figures for 1980.

For historians there is no quicksand more treacherous than a "first." In most cases "firsts" might more prudently be phrased as "earliest known." Particularly in the field of science and technology must the researcher seeking to establish priority of discovery and invention be on guard against pitfalls. Priority is often a matter of definition. Whether one accepts 1636 or 1786 as the year of the earliest known strike depends on what kind of work stoppage constitutes a "strike." With this problem in mind the *Encyclopedia* attempts to define terms with some degree of precision. Thus, Royall Tyler's *The Contrast* was the first *American comedy* to be produced by a *professional company*, but it was not the first native play. That distinction must be awarded to Thomas Godfrey's tragedy *The Prince of Parthia*. However, amateur performances of English plays had been given in the colonies as far back as 1665, more than 100 years earlier. Last, where the facts remain in the realm of conjecture (as in the Viking explorations and Polynesian contacts with South America), the *Encyclopedia* indicates how scholars still differ in interpreting the available evidence.

In the years that have elapsed since the preparation of the first edition of the *Encyclopedia,* which appeared in 1953, and in the preparation of five subsequent editions, this enterprise has incurred numerous debts to scholars and librarians, above all to Cass Canfield, who conceived the project. The editor has constantly enlisted his sagacious judgment and been sustained by his unfailing encouragement. Many others at Harper & Row have cooperated beyond the call of duty in the preparation of earlier editions, among them Daniel F. Bradley, Sidney Feinberg, and Beulah W. Hagen, as well as Corona Machemer, Nancy K. MacKenzie, and William B. Monroe. The list of the editor's obligations in the preparation of the previous revised editions and this Sixth Edition is extensive, starting with Henry Steele Commager and the other consulting editors. In the revisions of the opening section, "Original Peopling of the Americas," the editor enlisted the scholarship of Professor Helmut de Terra, formerly of Columbia University. In selections for biographical subjects in the categories of science, invention, and technology, the editor leaned heavily upon the sagacious counsel of Professor I. I. Rabi of Columbia University, and in the previous editions Arthur Dreifuss of Hollywood, Calif., was indispensable in revising and updating the subsections on theater, film, radio, and TV.

1
Basic
Chronology

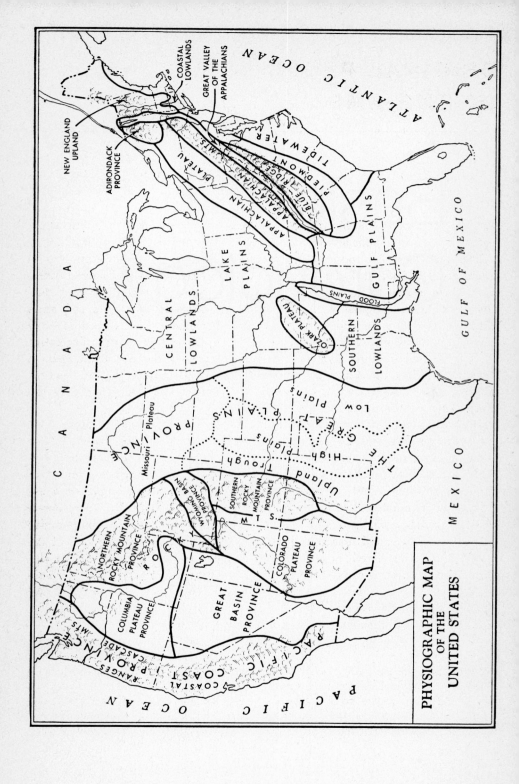

PHYSIOGRAPHIC MAP
OF THE
UNITED STATES

ORIGINAL PEOPLING
OF THE AMERICAS

As geologic time is counted, man is a latecomer to the New World, but as we record human events his arrival reaches back into remote antiquity, indubitably 10,000 years ago, and possibly as far back as 35,000 B.C. The aborigines of America, truly the first discoverers, came from northeast Asia and moved southward from Alaska to populate both continents. Since the waves of migration that brought the original settlers covered an enormous time span and since their settlements were widely scattered, the aborigines varied considerably in physical and cultural characteristics, speaking many different, often unrelated, languages. These cultural variances were most striking at the time of the Spanish occupation. Thus, the Aztecs in Mexico and the Incas in Peru had, by the time of Columbus, attained a cultural level of sophistication far higher than the North American Indian tribes.

In North America, notably the area that is now the United States, the European settlers and the Indians quickly came into cultural conflict. The white man spurned amalgamation with the Indians, and his farming practices and expansionist proclivities led to the expulsion or annihilation of great numbers of them. Until fairly recent times, when the Indian population has enjoyed some numerical recovery, the susceptibility of the Indians to epidemic diseases, notably smallpox and measles, brought by Europeans, compounded by military defeat and mass transplantation, led to an astonishing rate of depopulation of the native races in North America, extraordinary however disputed the population estimates may be. What happened after 1492 in Meso-America and North America was a demographic disaster with no known parallel in world history. Displaced, defeated, bypassed, and largely ignored, the Indian shared not at all in the affluence of white America.

c.50,000–8000 B.C. ASIATIC ORIGINS. The first human explorers entered this unpopulated region from northern Asia. Russian excavations since 1956 on the Chukchi peninsula at the easterly tip of Asia confirm the migration of man into America from that point over an ancient land bridge of what is now the Bering Strait. Despite differences among scholars over the exact date, it now appears

that the bulk of the early migration occurred during the last stages of the **Pleistocene glaciation** (the last **Ice Age**).
Physical tests based on the half cycle of
Carbon 14, which is present in all organic matter and disappears at a known
rate, indicate that the centers of population around the edges of the Arctic
Ocean, then a warm, open sea, began
shifting south in relatively heavy waves,
when c.11,000 years ago the Arctic froze
over, the Atlantic warmed, and the Ice
Age ended (Haynes, 1964). The crossing
of Bering Strait and the southward penetration of the Western Hemisphere introduced into this region Mongoloids,
traced to southeast and west-central Asia.
By 1492 this stock was dominant from
Cape Horn to Point Barrow. The very
early human remains found in archaeological deposits in the New World all belong to the modern human species, *Homo
sapiens,* although physical anthropologists disagree on nomenclature. It is
widely agreed that man did not evolve
in the New World and that no pre-*Homo
sapiens* ever existed here.

**LINGUISTIC STOCKS OF AMERI-
CAN INDIANS** are highly varied. Their
diversity is due to considerable variety
in stock and language among the original
immigrants for at least several millennia,
and to increasing differentiation once the
American Indians were in the New
World. By conservative estimate some
10 to 12 unrelated linguistic stocks or
families have been listed north of the
Rio Grande. A few links have been postulated between Eskimo and Chukchee,
and the Athapascan and Sino-Tibetan,
but in general few linkages between Old
and New World linguistic stocks have so
far been fully demonstrated, indicating a
considerable period of isolation.

**c.35,000–8000 B.C. EARLIEST SET-
TLEMENT.** Carbon 14 tests indicate
early-man sites in the Americas even
prior to the ending of the **Ice Age**, and
range in date from 35,000 to 8000 B.C.
The Folsom culture of the Lindenmeier
site in Colorado flourished **c.8820 B.C.**
(Haynes and Agogino, 1960) and a similar age is suggested for Tepexpan Man
from the Valley of Mexico (de Terra,
1958). Responsible opinion does not support the hypothesis of a considerably
earlier date for man's migration to the
Americas and casts doubt upon radiocarbon dates obtained for a Clovis-type
fluted projectile point near Dallas, Tex.
(Haynes,   1964);   the   basin-shaped
hearths on Santa Rosa Island off the
southern California coast and the Calico
site in California (Leakey, 1968) as being truly man-made; and the occurrence
near Pueblo, Mex., of fossil bone fragments bearing engravings of animals,
possibly both discoveries c.30,000 years
old. Despite current scientific controversy over early datings, no doubt exists
concerning the widespread dispersal of
early man in both Americas 10,000 years
ago, as suggested by radiocarbon dates
obtained from sites in Chile and southern Argentina. Tools fashioned either of
stone or bone and clearly recognizable
types were found in direct association
with extinct animals such as the mammoth, ground sloth, camel, and other
forms which have long since disappeared.

**HUMAN REMAINS OF EARLY MI-
GRATION.** Great faunal interchanges
took place between northern Asia and
North America in the closing stage of
the Pleistocene glaciation. Man was only
one of the many animals which moved
either west into Asia or east into North
America during such periods. Accurately
recorded ancient skeletal remains of these
early migrants are scarce and disputed.
The fossil-man discoveries include the
bones of the **Minnesota Woman** from
the dried-up bed of glacial Lake Agassiz;
the **Punin Calvarium** from fossil deposits
near Quito, Ecuador; the **Lagoa Santo**
skulls from coastal Brazil; the **Vero** and

Melbourne finds in Florida; the **Midland Man** (Midland, Tex., c.12,000–20,000 years old); and the **Tepexpan Man** from the Valley of Mexico. Racial admixture is indicated by the variety of the skulls.

c.9000–1500 B.C. EARLY KNOWN HUNTING AND GATHERING CULTURES. Archaeological research has demonstrated that these early human immigrants were in a simple hunting, fishing, and gathering stage of culture. Their formidable prowess as hunters is indicated by the fact that they killed great animals like the mammoth, mastodon, and large extinct species of bison. Cultural remains in the form of camps, hearths, stone and bone tools, and slain-animal remains indicate that they had no knowledge of horticulture. The earliest widespread pointed weapon is the "clovis projectile," found near the town of Clovis, N.M., at the Blackwater Draw No. 1 site. The site also contains blades, scrapers, hammerstones, bone shafts, and flakes as well as the bones of camels, horses, bison, and mammoths. The Folsom Fluted Points (8000 B.C.) developed from the Clovis form. The points were found underlying those of the Folsom culture (Sandia Cave, New Mex.) and even more prominently in the Lindenmeier location in Colorado. The people of the Folsom culture were hunters who used grooved, chipped darts with which they killed mammoth and bison. Remains of this culture have been found from Alaska south beyond the Great Plains. To the south, in Arizona and New Mexico, there were equally ancient peoples of the Cochise culture. Though the Cochise used grinding stones, remains of mammoths, horses, pronghorn antelopes, prairie wolves, and bison have been found, indicating the Cochise were both farmers and hunters. Traces of early hunters and gatherers have been found in Texas, the deserts of California, Oregon, Nevada, Utah, Washington, Iowa, Nebraska, and in Mexico, Peru, Chile, and Argentina. This prehorticultural period persisted through many millennia. In marginal or other regions unfavorable to farming, it survived up to and beyond the time of the European invasion. However, in the nuclear or heart regions of native American culture, primarily from Mexico south to Peru, it was gradually superseded by another mode of life.

c.3000–1000 B.C. EARLIEST AMERICAN FARMERS. The earliest evidences of extensive New World horticulture are based on recent discoveries. The **Huaca Prieta horizon,** 1946, revealed people who lived on seafood, simple farming, and gathering. They grew and twined or wove cotton and bast; cultivated beans and gourds, but did not grow maize (Indian corn) or manufacture pottery. Their stone industry was rudimentary. Farther north in **Chiapas** (S.E. Mexico), **Honduras,** and **Tamaulipas** (N.E. Mexico) evidences suggesting preceramic cultivators have since come to light. At Chiapas maize was grown even in this early period. The Chiapas area dates stratigraphically and with the aid of radiocarbon from 1500 B.C. to 1000 B.C. At Tamaulipas, a tiny primitive corn was first grown between 3000 to 2200 B.C., and pottery first produced about 1400 B.C. Still farther north, at **Bat Cave,** in central New Mexico, very primitive types of pod corn have been found in association with chipped stone tools, both below and intermixed with the remains of pottery. Carbon 14 tests at Huaca Prieta give estimates of dates back to 2307 B.C., at Bat Cave perhaps back to between 3000 and 2000 B.C., but such Carbon 14 datings may still require more adequate materials and further checking.

c.1000 B.C. FORMATIVE EPOCH. Based on this incipient farm pattern there developed in the Andean and Mesoamerican regions a series of Formative cultures sharing in common the **expansion of horticulture** (including cultivation of maize, squash, beans, and other plants), and in the later stages of this epoch developing **large settlements, irrigating systems,** and, in the Andean region, **metallurgy** based on gold, copper, and other minerals (save iron, which was never smelted in the aboriginal New World). Unlike the Old World, domesticated animals were few (dogs, turkeys in N. America, plus muscovy ducks in Mexico; in S. America, dogs, guinea pigs, and llamas), and neither utilitarian wheel traction nor the potter's wheel was known in these or later native American cultures. Many of these long-flourishing Formative cultures have now been identified in Peru, Honduras, and Mexico.

c.1 A.D.–900 A.D. **FLORESCENT, OR CLASSIC EPOCH IN MEXICO AND PERU.** In Meso-America and Peru this culture dates around 1 A.D.; in the Maya region of the Petén and Yucatán, stone stelae carved with the glyphs of an accurate calendrical system date the most elaborate of the Mayan temples, sculptures, and art forms from c.300–900 A.D. **Teotihuacán,** near Mexico City, the dead religious center with its huge pyramids and impressive mural paintings, belongs to this epoch as does the finest period **Monte Albán III,** in the vast ceremonial ruin in **Oaxaca.** The Monte Albán III period has exhibited evidences of monument art, hieroglyphics, numbers, and a calendar. Marked by great population, tremendous construction, and wide trade, this epoch constitutes the apogee of native American cultural progress and is comparable to that of the Bronze Age in the Old World which had flourished more than 3,000 years earlier in the Near East. On the northern coast of **Peru** the people of the **Mochica kingdom** built vast adobe-brick structures, made unsurpassed pictorial or modeled pottery, and practiced metallurgy; but unlike

Teotihuacán, the Peruvians did not have a system of writing or a calendar, but did have an art form absorbed in depicting warlike activity and rigid priestly and other class distinctions.

c.900 A.D.–1400 A.D. **EPOCH OF NATIVE EMPIRES.** In this period Meso-America and the central Andean region remained the major centers of cultural progress and military and political activity. Known as the **Militaristic** or **Epoch of Fusion,** this period in Mexico was marked by the **Toltec** rule at Tula (11th–12th centuries) and the Mexicanization of the Maya regions of Yucatán beginning in the 10th century, when Chichén Itzá was probably invaded by Mexican Toltecs. Following came the little-understood barbarian **Chichimec** invasion from the north, and then the rise of the short-lived but barbarically picturesque **Aztec Empire** (c.1325–1521). Similar conflict in Peru wiped out the Florescent Mochica, Nazca, and kindred cultures to be replaced by the so-called Tiahuanaco and related military conquerors. Finally, there emerged the far-flung **Inca Empire,** one of the most closely integrated totalitarian regimes of the pre-Columbian world. Zenith of Inca power: 11th to 15th centuries. After 1492 Spain pitted the small but desperately effective armies of Cortés and Pizarro against the more or less well organized native empires of the Aztecs (1518–21) and the Incas (1531–35), respectively, the latter then in the throes of bitter civil war.

c.1492. **CULTURES AND POPULATIONS OF NATIVE AMERICA NORTH OF MEXICO.** The regions north of the Rio Grande were occupied by largely unregimented native peoples, with strongly individualistic, if less complex, cultural patterns than the natives of the southern empires. On the basis of environmental and cultural similarities, the area now included within the United

States and Canada can, in late pre-Columbian times, be broken up into five major cultural and ecological areas: Southwest (in U.S.), Intermediate, Northwest coast, Arctic coast, Eastern-Northern. Estimates of the total population for this area vary between 1,025,950 for the late pre-Columbian period (Kroeber, 1939) to a figure between 9,800,000 and 12,250,000 for c.1492 (Debyns, 1966). The latter is based on a depopulation ratio of 20 to 1 for the lower figure, 25 to 1 for the higher total, both from the time of conquest to the beginning of population recovery.

1. SOUTHWESTERN CULTURE AREA is an arid and elevated region where farming tribes lived in close juxtaposition to hunters (a northern advance of Mexicanlike cultures) and gatherers (a southward extension of simpler hunting and gathering patterns to the north). In the northeastern plateau, a region of summer rains, farming is possible in selected areas, as the long archaeological record of the Anasazi or **Basket Maker–Pueblo** sequence clearly indicates. In the southwestern desert lowland farming was possible only in the flood plains of a few rivers or where irrigation was practiced. This region was the center of another ancient subcultural province known, archaeologically, as the **Hohokam.** Between these farming peoples were some other scattered tribes which eked out a living through gathering and hunting, much like the Intermediate area, below.

First to attract the notice of the Spanish explorers when they pushed north from Mexico were the **Pueblo,** or town-dwelling and farming peoples of the Anasazi province. In 1540 the Pueblos occupied some 70 towns scattered in the region of the present states of Arizona and New Mexico. Various linguistic stocks occupied this area, but, among the Pueblos, the Shoshonean-speaking

Hopi to the north, the central **Zuni,** and the **Keresan**-speaking and other Pueblos of the Rio Grande valley were outstanding. The mythical riches of the Zuni towns, under the name of the "**Seven Cities of Cibola,**" lured Coronado.

Pueblo Culture Pattern. The "Three Sisters," corn, beans, and squash, were the basic commodities of these skilled farmers, whose life was oriented around cultivating. Elaborate rituals were employed to bring the summer rains. Differing locally, Pueblo settlement patterns ranged from the contiguous stone masonry house of the Hopi, perched on top of high mesas, to the scattered adobe houses of the Rio Grande Pueblos. All were essentially town-minded, built no temples, but had underground **Kivas** or ceremonial rooms for their various clans and societies. The contiguous and sometimes several-storied buildings with roof entrances formed fortifications, further protected by their positions on high mesas or cliffs. The Pueblo government was theocratic; only the priests ruled. Each Pueblo group was a rule unto itself; no large tribal groups or confederacies existed. In the west the social unit was the **maternal clan;** in the Rio Grande region a **dual organization** was dominant. **Religious rites** included rain-making rites in both east and west, curing ceremonies in the east, and throughout the region procreative rites. Although unwarlike, the Pueblos through their town organization and fortifications strove to hold off the nomadic tribes, such as the **Apache,** which surrounded them. Archaeology indicates that their territory had been drastically cut down long before the arrival of the white man. Intensely conservative, the twenty-odd surviving pueblos today constitute the most viable and truly native culture pattern to be observed in the territory of the U.S. Their neighbors, the Athapascan-speaking **Navajo,** originally scattered nomads,

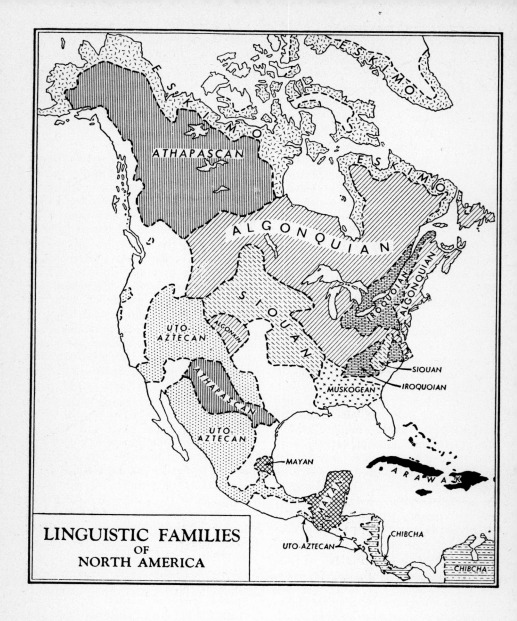

LINGUISTIC FAMILIES
OF
NORTH AMERICA

far surpass all present North American tribes in numbers, but the basic Navajo economic patterns, farming and sheep-herding, represent their respective debts, first to their Pueblo neighbor, and then to the white man.

2. **INTERMEDIATE CULTURE AREA.** North of the Southwestern area extends the arid intermontane Great Basin, and, to the north, the rugged Columbia and Fraser Plateau. These two regions, with that of central California across the Sierra Nevada range, represent a varied topographic but an essentially similar pre-Columbian culture pattern (Kroeber). (1) The **isolated**

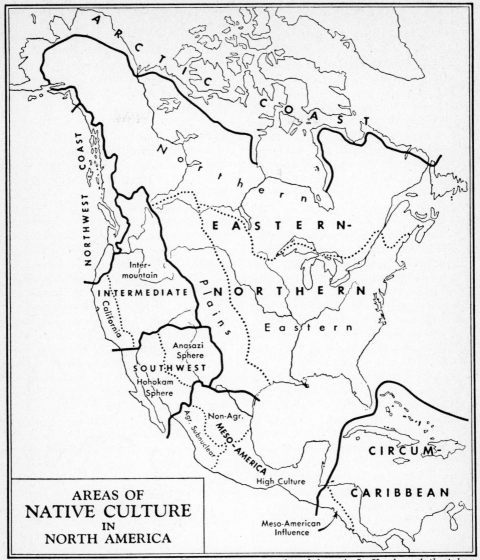

INTERMEDIATE

Inter-
mountain

California

NORTHWEST COAST

NORTHERN

Plains

Eastern

EASTERN-

ARCTIC COAST

Northern

Anasazi
Sphere

SOUTHWEST

Hohokam
Sphere

Agr. Subnuclear

Non-Agr.

MESO-AMERICA

High Culture

Meso-American
Influence

CIRCUM-

CARIBBEAN

AREAS OF
NATIVE CULTURE
IN
NORTH AMERICA

These two maps are adapted from A. L. Kroeber, *Anthropology*,
rev. ed., 1948, Harcourt, Brace and Co., Inc.

Great Basin proved one of the most unfavorable regions in North America for native culture; life based on intensive gathering of weed seeds, piñon nuts, insects, and small game; little leisure for activities unrelated to subsistence. (2) The **northern Plateau region** provided salmon runs that came up the great rivers which drained it, game, and access to the buffalo herds of the Great Plains after the white man brought the horse. (3) **Central California** abounded in a variety of oaks bearing acorns. The native, a balanophagist (acorn eater), supplemented his basic diet with deer and other game and locally abundant seafood. Aside from sporadic attempts to increase seed production, there was little plant cultivation in these three subareas.

Many **linguistic stocks** were represented in this region: Great Basin predominantly Shoshonean; Plateau largely Salish; Central California, a vast number of isolated languages and stocks. **Settlements** were small and scattered, brush shelters in the south, shelters and pit houses in the north. **Political organization** was based on small bands of bilateral family units, which, on the borders of the Great Basin and in the plateau, acquired some tribal polity when the horse was introduced. **Religion** was simple, primarily shamanistic, with some more elaborate cults among the central Californians, and certain Great Plains ceremonies adopted by the Plateau peoples after the introduction of the horse. **Warfare,** unimportant under native conditions, increased in the early 19th century with the advent of the horse. This area was among the last to feel the direct impact of U.S. expansion, but by the mid-19th century its effects were drastic. Tribal life had disappeared.

3. NORTHWEST CULTURE AREA (western British Columbia and Alaska) constituted a group of complex, competitive societies sustained without agriculture, dependent entirely on fishing (tremendous runs of salmon provided a food surplus), hunting, and gathering (abundant berries). The tribes of the Northwest Coast occupied a tortuous coast backed by the steep coast range located in a coniferous forest saturated but warmed by the Japan Current. Facing the sea, all life focused on the beach. ("When the tide is out the table is set," Nootka expression.) **Northern regions** (despite lack of plant domestication) were the most complex culturally just prior to the white invasion, with perhaps the greatest population density in native North America. At least **3 major linguistic stocks**—(1) most northerly: **Tlingit** and **Haida** of the Na-Dene stock; (2) central region: **Tsimshian** of Penutian stock and **Bella Coola** of Salish stock; (3) south: **Kwakiutl, Nootka** (Algonquian-Wakashan stock), and numerous other tribes in Puget Sound, western Oregon, and northern California.

Basic economy: salmon fisheries; secondary, whaling, sea fishing, berry gathering, and hunting. **Winter villages,** consisting of great plankhouses facing the beach, split from cedar and fir with fire, stone tools, and antler wedges, were often fortified or placed on protected points because of raiding parties. **Fishing stations** and **summer camps** located up the rivers were owned by individual families from time immemorial. Travel was by sea or along the fjords and rivers in great or small dugout canoes. **Northwest Coast art style,** highly symbolic: wood implements, particularly of cedar, characterized by a striking style of carved, painted, and shell-inlaid ornamentation, carried over into house facings, entrances, and especially the **totem poles,** or family crests, which marked the villages.

Organization was by independent villages, made up of graded groups of kinfolk and slaves, not tribally. North: local groupings crosscut by matrilineal clans and dual divisions, or moieties; Central region: both matrilineal and patrilineal groupings; South: patrilineal groupings predominant. **Class distinctions** emphasized: chiefs and nobles at the top; then commoners; last, slaves who were war captives or debtors. All rank rested on wealth, with an endless variation and shifting of grades. A comprehensive system of **private ownership** (embracing land, fishing stations, houses, masks, crests, names, etc.) carried prestige, and was acquired by inheritance, purchase, and sometimes warfare. At **potlatches** (ceremonies or feasts) rival chiefs, supported by their respective kinsmen and slaves of all degrees, competed in ostentatious display of wealth and property exchanges. "Gifts" between rival chiefs had to be returned with interest, default leading to social degradation. In the later periods the white fur trade made this society even more highly competitive by producing greater surpluses of exchangeable goods. With its class stratification resting upon validated wealth and ostentatious exchange and destruction of property, the Northwest Coast economy was **capitalist** in form, with a trading acumen which matched the Yankees who in the late 18th century traded along its coast for sea-otter fur.

Religion ranged from the belief in a supreme deity to pure shamanism; rich in display, complex in masks and other equipment, and sexual in character. The winter season was taken up with elaborate ceremonies held by the graded societies, of which the **hamatsa,** or cannibal society, and the animal societies were the most numerous. Like the potlatch, these society affairs were competitive, each trying to outdo the other in richness of costume and ferocity of act and aspect. **Warfare,** sporadic, chiefly for purposes of revenge, to secure slaves, and, occasionally, crests or property. As a result of the impact upon this culture of the Russians coming from the north (after 1741), the Spanish from the south (1774), and the Anglo-Americans from the east (1786), tribal life has been largely shattered.

4. ARCTIC COAST CULTURE AREA: THE ESKIMO. A relatively small population speaking related languages, the Eskimo-Aleut, occupied the long northern coast from the Aleutians all the way east to Greenland and southern Labrador. Present archaeological evidence indicates that the early Eskimoan groups entered western Alaska shortly before 1 A.D., with the last eastward migration reaching Greenland about the same time as the Norsemen arrived from the east (c.1000 A.D.). In **physical type** the Eskimo share most basic Mongoloid characteristics with the main Indian population, with certain minor, but distinctive, features. The Eskimo-Aleut language family falls into 2 divisions: the Eskimo and the Aleut. The Eskimoan **language** has two divisions: Western (Yupik) with perhaps two languages and Eastern (Ihupik), one language spoken from the Bering Strait to and including Greenland. **Occupations:** primarily hunters and fishermen, with numerous variations based on differences in water, temperature, and ice conditions along their extended coastal terrain. **Open, western Pacific:** Eskimos hunted large sea mammals in skin-covered **kayaks** and open boats, seasonally going inland after the caribou, but also eating fish, birds, foxes, and polar bear. Similar open-water conditions prevailed in Greenland and Labrador. **Central region** (where the sea freezes all winter, typically Eskimoan): Eskimos are ice hunters, living in block-built snow **igloos,** traveling by dog sledge, and securing the seal through the ice and the walrus along the floe edges; in summer moving to caribou-skin tents and hunting caribou and fishing salmon in the interior. **Settlement pattern:** villages attaining considerable size in western Alaska and southern Greenland, but composed of small, shifting family groups in the north-central regions. Tailored fur and leather clothing, elaborate hunting gear including toggle harpoons, floats, sleds, and dog traction in winter and **kayaks** in summer, all speak of long and skillful adaptation to Arctic conditions. Hence, the most successful Arctic explorers like Peary not only were accompanied by Eskimos but employed clothing, food, equipment, and methods of transportation of Eskimo origin. **Political organization:** loose; shifting family groupings dominant. **Religion:**

based in large part on fear of a hostile universe wherein many spirits dwell who must be propitiated. Contact with the supernatural is often attained through the **shaman,** who knows the speech of animals, and sends his soul away to treat with the recalcitrant spirits. The more elaborate ceremonies in western Alaska involve the use of masks, carvings, and equipment reminiscent of Northwest Coast culture. **Organized warfare:** rare or absent, although Indian-Eskimo conflicts were noted (by Samuel Hearne, 1771). Early European explorers, like Frobisher (1576–78) and John Davis (1585), were attacked by the Eskimos of Baffin Land. Today, a somewhat mixed Eskimo population of less than half the numbers estimated for the first contact period still survives in all but the southern limits of their former range. In the central Arctic, the old basic hunting pattern of life still continues in a few isolated places, but in general the Greenland, Canadian, and Alaskan Eskimos have today come under the influence of Euro-American culture although much of the native language, economy, and culture still persist.

5. EASTERN-NORTHERN CULTURE AREA comprises a great terrain which slopes east from the Rocky Mountains to the Atlantic Ocean. Variant but without drastic environmental or abrupt cultural breaks, this ecological area falls into 3 major subdivisions: (1) **Southeast,** (2) **Great Plains,** and (3) **Northeastern–Great Lakes** cultural provinces. From the palms of southern Florida to the dwarf-willow scrub of northern Labrador there is a gradual transition from tropical to subarctic conditions. Similarly, on the cultural plane, there is a gradual gradient from the elaborately class-structured society of the **Natchez** (Mississippi) to the wandering, classless **Naskapi** hunters (northern Labrador). The Great Plains to the west, due to the

introduction of the horse and firearms in post-Columbian times (c.1540–1880), became for a time somewhat unique, but the original cultural pattern was of the same fabric. **Ecologically,** the entire area is mainly woodland, deciduous trees predominating, with the addition of pine and spruce. Dominating the main regions were the hardwoods, thinning out into river-valley cover in the **tall-grass-prairie** regions from Illinois west, and, eventually, disappearing in the **short-grass** region of the **High Plains west of the 100th meridian** (westward from the 20-in.-rainfall line to the Rockies, an area of scanty rainfall which later offered greater inducements to cattlemen than to farmers). In the central regions the bison was important for food; to the north, deer, moose, and caribou. Native means of navigation over the great rivers and lake systems served as a means of intercommunication: the birchbark canoe, best developed in the Great Lakes region, like the dugout canoes and rafts on the lower rivers, and the "bullboats" of the Missouri, reminiscent of but not historically related to the Welsh coracle. Owing to the preoccupation with war, the natives failed to exploit the rich agricultural potential of this region.

Linguistically, the northeastern and Great Lakes regions were dominated by **Algonquian**-speaking tribes extending north to Labrador and as far south as the Carolinas. Splitting this distribution, from the Cherokee of Georgia north along the Great Lakes to the St. Lawrence, were a number of **Iroquoian**-speaking groups, most famous being the powerful **League of the Iroquois (Mohawk, Onondaga, Oneida, Cayuga, Seneca,** and, later, **Tuscarora**) in upper New York State. The southeastern subarea was dominated by **Muskogean**-speaking peoples, including the **Choctaw, Chickasaw, Creek, Seminole,** and the **Cherokee** (Iroquoian-speaking)—later known as the

"Five Civilized Nations"—and many others. Interspersed were peoples of **Siouan** and other smaller linguistic stocks. On the Great Plains to the west, tribes of the **Caddoan** linguistic stock stretched from Arkansas to the Dakotas, with many Siouan tribes along the west bank of the Mississippi and on both sides of the Missouri in both the tall-grass prairie and short-grass plains. Algonquian-speaking and other tribes were also interspersed throughout the Great Plains area. Most of these seem to have been latecomers, mainly after the advent of the horse, but some, like the **Blackfoot** (Algonquian), **Mandan** (Siouan), and **Pawnee** (Caddoan), appear to have been old residents. **Timetable of European settlement:** Southeast, by the French and Spaniards, beginning **1565**; the Northeastern Great Lakes and eastern Great Plains, by the French, beginning **1634** (Nicolet); the eastern maritime regions by the English, principally beginning **1607**. As in Meso-America, the Spanish encountered the most culturally advanced tribes.

Basic Economy. The aboriginal Southeast depended on the cultivation of **corn, beans,** and **squash,** supplemented by gathering, hunting, and fishing. Native farming by slash and burn methods soon exhausted the deciduous forest soil, causing villages to move frequently. Maize cultivation extended with lessening productivity north as far as the St. Lawrence River, and west along the river valleys of the Prairie-Plains. North and west of this area early frosts and drought prevented native farming. The extreme northern regions were dependent mainly on hunting the moose and caribou or fishing; the short-grass plains, primarily on the bison herds. The Great Lakes region had both farming and hunting, supplemented (in Wisconsin and Minnesota) by gathering "wild rice," which grows abundantly in shallow lakes. Because of farming, the southeastern subregion supported the larger population, while the forest and tundra of the northern subarea had a lower population density. Considering its rich agricultural food potential, even the eastern subarea seems underpopulated. Crude methods of cultivation, warfare, diseases, and disruption spread by the Europeans, limited population (Borah, Dobyns).

The **settlement pattern** in the Southeast, and north to the St. Lawrence river, at the time of first European penetration seems mainly to have been one of **villages** (generally larger in the south) often surrounded with **stockades. Architecture:** in the southeast with its Meso-American cultural cast, round, semi-subterranean "hothouses" for winter; loosely constructed, rectangular bark or "shake" houses for summer were the rule. These family units were arranged in a square ground pattern with an open plaza in the center often surrounded by artificial mounds of earth within which the ceremonial "Chunkey" game was played. To the north, the Iroquois and many of their Algonquian neighbors made "longhouses" out of bark and poles to house many families. To the west, arborlike houses of bark, matting, and poles were used. On the Great Plains even the earth lodge and the graceful skin **tipi** were employed. North of the St. Lawrence the conical **wigwam** covered with birchbark or caribou hide was most common. In the Southeast, the eastern prairies, and again north to the St. Lawrence, stockades, bastions, and firing platforms protected the villages. In the south-central area quite elaborate temple mound structures were in use, flourishing in the period 700 A.D.–1700 A.D., often located on top of large artificial earth mounds with ramps leading up to them. Some 100,000 mounds are estimated to exist in the U.S. The so-called ancient Indian "**Mound builders**" of the

Ohio region left remains of just such mound structures, often forming burial chambers, as De Soto, Bartram, and other white explorers found actually in use in what is now the southeastern U.S.

Political Organization: Confederacy. Beginning with the **matrilineal** system, family, or clan, political organization evolved into the **moiety** or dual division, then to the **tribal** group, and finally, to the **Confederacy,** or loose grouping of tribes, embodying certain concepts of the "state." In the south between **1836–40,** the **Creek Confederacy** included numerous tribes speaking a number of distinct languages in some 50 towns; the dominant one was Muskogee (Creek). Others, like the **Powhatan Confederacy** (c.1607) in Virginia—more like an incipient state —were smaller. One of the most famous was the **League of the Iroquois** (beg. c.1559–70) in New York. Founded for peace, the Iroquois Confederacy became a deadly instrument for war in the northeast. The unusual power exercised by the women in the latter tribes actually made or broke **sachems,** or chiefs. The northern peoples had a less complex political and social organization. Beyond the St. Lawrence it was based upon shifting family bands. To the west confederacies existed among the Caddoan peoples, matrilineal clans among certain Siouan peoples, and patrilineal and bilateral organizations among the bordering Plains tribes. Among some tribes on the lower Mississippi a true class system evolved; most celebrated was that of the **Natchez,** where by an imperative class-intermarriage system lineages passed from the top role of relatives of the sun to the lowest class of **"Stinkards"** within four generations.

Introduction of Horse. Archaeological research clearly indicates that the basic patterns of the eastern, or tall-grass-prairie, plains were horticultural and of a Southeastern semisedentary type (pre-

1540). With the advent of the European horse (post-1540), the pattern changed to equestrian, bison-hunting. Many border tribes then first entered the plains from north, east, and west, to overrun the older, more settled Caddoan and Siouan peoples such as the Arikara, Pawnee, and the Mandan respectively. The early Spanish pioneers from the south encountered the semisedentary native peoples; the later modern American westward migration met the equestrian bison hunters in their militaristic prime.

Religious and Ceremonial Activities were varied and complex (see J. R. Swanton, *Indians of the Southeastern U.S.,* Bur. Amer. Ethnology, *Bull. 137,* 1946). **Southeast:** temples and idols widely distributed, with a definite priesthood. Cultural climax attained by the **Natchez,** with their deified ruler representing the sun, living in a temple with sacred fetishes on top of a mound complex. Alongside supreme deities, a vast number of other deities, spirits, and sacred places were worshiped among the various tribes. Notable ceremonies: the **"busk"** or green-corn dance; and the **"new fire"** ceremony with its aim of "life renewal" and accompanying drinking of the "black drink," an emetic which led to purification. Ceremonies for both war and peace existed side by side. Evidence of a probable Meso-American cast to Southeastern culture exists in the pottery, special cemeteries, low conical or domed earthen mounds for burial, the cultivation of tobacco, and the use of tubular pipe. The 4-footed vessels seen early in Tchefuncte in the Southeast indicate more than any other form of pottery, possible Mexican influence (Jennings). **West:** basic in the religion of the Caddoan tribes were sacred bundles dedicated to agricultural pursuits. **North:** religion simpler and more shamanistic; great importance given to dreams in guiding all activity; the individual soul was identified with the breath. Among the most northeasterly Algonquians, the **Naskapi** combined an animalistic mythology, a shamanistic belief, with a native concept of a supreme deity associated with the caribou, the most important food animal.

WARFARE: SUBJUGATION OF TRIBES IN U.S. Warfare played a destructive role in the aboriginal Southeast, in the later phases of native life in the Iroquois region, and in the Great Plains, but to a much lesser extent in the northern areas. The fact that the eastern Indians cultivated less than 1% of the arable land available and achieved a population density of only 9 Indians per township in a region which today supports 400 persons per township is attributed by Kroeber to the "insane, attritional type of war" waged throughout the area, carried on incessantly by individuals for revenge, by small parties, towns, tribes, and confederacies. Warfare was highly ceremonialized, accompanied by elaborate torture rites (reaching a peak among the Iroquois), with war honors essential to almost every youth and the warpath the primary road to fame and honor. Aggressive behavior was somewhat canalized off in such ceremonial games as **lacrosse.** In addition, peace towns, moieties, and leagues were organized to maintain peace, but the eastern war pattern persisted to the end, latterly becoming blended with European war practices and weapons brought in by the new invaders. As a result of military defeat and white penetration native life as such has ended in most of the Eastern-Northern cultural provinces. The "Five Civilized Nations" were by 1838 moved over the "Trail of Tears" to the Indian Territory (Oklahoma); the Seminoles, after prolonged warfare with the U.S., suffered heavy losses while being deported to Indian Territory in 1842. Other eastern groups, like the Iroquois, were confined to reservations or else have blended with the modern white and Negro populations of the area. Only in the far north do the old hunting and fishing patterns still persist, along with fur trapping, which is post-Caucasian, but even these faint marginal manifestations decrease from year to year. In addition to the Oklahoma Reservation for the Five Civilized Tribes, various reservations in the Dakotas and elsewhere were assigned to the Sioux and other tribes. Resisting the advancing mining frontier and the federal government's reservation policy, the Indians of the West were finally overwhelmed by superior numbers and technology in a series of wars, 1861–68, 1875–90 (**Cheyenne-Arapaho War, 1861– 64; Red River War, 1874; Sioux Wars, 1862–67** and **1875–76; Nez Percé War, 1877; Apache War, 1871–87; Ghost Dance Uprising, 1890,** also pp. 611, 613– 615). For 20th-century issues and problems, see pp. 643–646.

THE ERA OF EXPLORATION

Pre-Columbian Exploration

Out of the mists of forgery and fact there is now emerging a somewhat clearer picture of when the Vikings came to America, where they made their landfalls, and why they discontinued their explorations. The Vikings lacked both the firepower of the later European invaders of North America and the manpower to defend themselves against the Indians, or Eskimos, in an area so far removed from the home base of Greenland, which in turn was abandoned after several centuries of occupation. With the freeze-over of the Arctic Ocean by the end of the fourteenth century, drift ice about Greenland, or between Greenland and Vinland, forced the abandonment of the old sea routes.

It remained for Columbus and Spanish and Portuguese navigators to inaugurate a whole new era for exploration and conquest. The first explorers for Spain were followed by the conquistadores, whose subjugation of the Aztecs in Mexico and of the Incas in Peru opened up vast treasures, brought Spanish and Roman Catholic culture to Central and South America and the borderlands that now form part of the United States, transformed Western society by vastly increasing the quantity of money in circulation, thereby unwittingly undermining the feudal structure and shaking the underpinnings of status, spurring capitalist activity, and arousing the cupidity of the have-not nations, notably of France, England, and Holland. In the late sixteenth and early seventeenth centuries the three latecomers staked out claims to largely unexplored and unsettled sections along the North Atlantic seaboard.

800–986. VIKING SETTLEMENT AND EXPLORATION. After occupying the Shetlands, the Faroes, and the Orkneys (by 800), the Vikings settled Iceland (874). **Eric the Red,** in exile from Iceland, after 3 years spent exploring the coasts of Greenland (982–85), led a group of settlers to the southwestern coast of that island, where the first Norse colony was planted (986). The discovery of the Narssaq Farm at the foot of Mt. Qagarsung in Greenland in 1953 confirms Eric's settlement in Greenland. **Bjarni Herjulfson** is credited with sighting the mainland of North America in 986 when blown off his course while seeking the new colony.

c.1000. LEIF ERICSON, the son of Eric the Red, either by accident (in 1000, according to the **Karlsevni Saga)**

or with forethought (in 1002, according to the **Greenland Saga**), explored the North American coast, naming the regions, as he voyaged southward, **Helluland** (land of flat rocks), **Markland** (forest land), and **Vinland** (wineland). Experts differ as to the identity of Vinland: Newfoundland (Hovgaard), mouth of the St. Lawrence (Steensby), Nova Scotia (Storm), northern New England (Thorvarson), Cape Cod (F. J. Pohl), Rhode Island (Rafn), New York (Gathorne-Hardy), middle Atlantic coast (Haugen), Virginia (Mjeldi). **Thorvald Ericson,** Leif's brother, explored the coast of the continent (1004–07), using Leif's headquarters in Vinland. A second brother, **Thorstein,** tried unsuccessfully to find Vinland (1008).

1010–13. Thorfinn Karlsevni, a trader from Iceland, with 3 ships and 160 men, mostly Greenlanders, sailed on an exploratory trip to the North American mainland. Despite similarity between the names used to designate the regions Karlsevni visited and those explored by the sons of Eric, enough differences in their geographical descriptions exist to raise some doubt that they were in the same area. The operations of the Ericsons, according to the prevailing view, were confined to the east coast of North America; but the possibility exists that Karlsevni, instead of coasting along Labrador or Newfoundland, sailed into Hudson's Bay. **Freydis,** Eric's daughter, believed to be a member of Karlsevni's group, is credited with making the last trip to the mainland described in the Sagas (1014–15).

Confirmation of Norse Voyages and Settlement. Discovery of the Vinland Map, executed before 1440, announced by Yale Univ. Press (1965), seemed to furnish circumstantial confirmation of Norse voyages. The map shows a large insular land mass west and southwest of Greenland, extending from c.47° N to c.67° N. An inscription attributes the discovery of the island (named Vinland) to Leif and Bjarni. Ink tests disclosed the map to be a forgery (1974). Recent archaeological discoveries by Helge Ingstad, 1961–68, confirm the Norse settlement of Vinland in the early 11th century as having occurred at L'Anse aux Meadows in Newfoundland. Most important among the artifacts found in excavation were: 8 house sites of a longhouse type similar to findings in Norway, Iceland, and Greenland; fireplaces, ember pits, a smithy, and boathouses, all with Norse characteristics; a stone lamp of old Icelandic type, a Norse-type spindle whorl of soapstone and a Viking-era type bronze ringheaded pin; 16 radiocarbon datings have confirmed the date of the house as c.1000 (Ashe). In addition, the North American mainland has yielded scores of Norse relics, most of which were either so patently spurious or found under such unverifiable circumstances that they have been dismissed by the majority of scholars. These repudiated findings include the **Newport Tower** (a round stone structure in Rhode Island, more likely built in the 17th than the 11th–12th centuries), the **Kensington Stone,** a slab with runic inscriptions dated 1362 (found in Minnesota, 1898), chiseled out apparently with a modern chisel and with runes and grammatical forms unknown to the 14th century; recent discoveries at Beardmore, in western Ontario, of a sword, axhead, and shield grip, definitely from the 11th century, but believed to have been brought to America in 1923 (Wallace).

1014–1415. DURATION OF NORSE SETTLEMENT. The Greenland Colony continued at least until the second decade of the 15th century, although its connection with Europe weakened during the 14th century. Its active role as a colony ceased with the sailing of the last royal ship to that island (1367). A party of Icelanders visited the colony, 1408, and a churchman appears to have sailed there in the second decade of the 15th century, but no further contacts are known.

1447–98. PORTUGUESE EXPLORA-TION. Under the impetus of **Prince Henry the Navigator** (1394–1460), third son of John I, expeditions were sent down the west African coast, and the Azores, the Canaries, and Madeira were occupied. **Bartolomeu Dias** reached the Cape of Good Hope, 1488, and **Vasco da Gama** completed a voyage around Africa to India and return, 1498. Portuguese claims to the discovery of the New World are based on a number of westward explorations. On the basis of a map of the Venetian Andrea Biancho (1448), in which a large island, **Ixola Otinticha** (authentic island), is shown lying a good distance southwest of Cape Verde, it has been suggested that the Portuguese already knew of the existence of South America. In 1452 Diogo de Teive and Pedro Vasquez sailed to the Azores, where they discovered two additional islands of that group (Corvo and Flores). After these discoveries they were blown northward, and the Portuguese scholars (particularly Cortesão) believe that they reached the Grand Bank of Newfoundland before returning to Portugal. Sometime before 1460 a Portuguese ship is said to have reached Antillia, identified by the Portuguese with the legendary **Ilha das Sete Cidades** (Island of the Seven Cities). A Portuguese document credits João Vaz Corte-Real and Álvaro Martins Homem with the discovery of **Tiera de los Bacalaos** (1472), a name applied to Newfoundland shortly after the voyages of Columbus. Lack of supporting data compels one scholar (Jansen) to place these explorers on a known Danish expedition as observers for the Portuguese Crown. In 1476 Fernão Teles sailed west in

search of Antillia. Fernão Dulmo received a patent from the King (3 Mar. 1486) to explore islands or the mainland of Ilha das Sete Cidades. After entering into partnership with João Alfonso de Estreito, he had his plans approved by the king (24 July and 4 Aug. 1486), but there is no mention of this expedition. Admitting the possibility that Portugal may have wished to keep her territorial discoveries secret, scholars are hesitant about accepting claims to New World exploration put forth in behalf of the explorers of that nation.

1473–81. DANISH AND ENGLISH ACTIVITIES. Diderik Pining and Hans Pothorst, German mariners, allegedly sailed on an exploratory trip to Greenland for King Christian of Denmark, 1472. Cartographical sources indicating that Scolvus, possibly a Pole, sailed to the northwest at this time point to the probability that he went on this Danish voyage as a pilot. Possibly Corte-Real and Homem were also in the party. In 1480 Thomas Lloyd of Bristol, England, sailed in search of the island Antillia. Further exploratory trips were made annually in Bristol ships both to this island and to Brasil, another small island shown on contemporary maps beginning in 1481 (Quinn).

OTHER POSSIBLE PRE-COLUMBIAN CONTACTS. African contacts with the New World, based on the alleged presence of Negroes in pre-Columbian America, have been postulated by Leo Weiner, but widely discredited. Claims have also been advanced that fishermen from the west coast of France sailed to the fishing waters off Newfoundland prior to 1492. Even had such trips been made, they failed to contribute to making Europeans aware of the existence of the New World. In fact, after the translation of Ptolemy's *Geography* (1410), and perhaps even before that date, such a possibility was suggested by available scientific knowledge. A connection between Inca and South Seas cultures has been argued by Thor Heyerdahl, who in 1947 sailed in an Inca-style raft in 101 days from the Peruvian port of Callao to one of the Tuamotu islands. Heyerdahl's thesis of a South American origin for Polynesian culture is disputed by Alfred Métraux (1957) and by Thomas S. Barthel's decipherment of the writing on the Easter Island statues, revealing that the people who made the mysterious statues spoke a Polynesian language. Hence, the evidence suggests rather a South Pacific westward cultural migration with the likelihood that contacts came after the development of Formative cultures on both sides of the Pacific. In short, there is no hard evidence for any pre-Columbian human introduction of a single plant or animal from the Old World to the New or vice versa (Riley).

Columbus and Subsequent Exploration

Improvements in navigation which gave impulse to exploration included (1) the **magnetic compass;** (2) the **astrolabe,** a device for determining latitude; (3) the use of **portolani,** the first practical hydrographic charts; and (4) the construction of the fast Portuguese **caravel,** a small vessel with broad bows, high narrow poop, and usually triangular lateen sails, which could sail against the wind more efficiently than earlier ships. The early explorations to the New World were largely shaped by geographical factors—winds and ocean currents determined the landfalls and guided the interior exploration. Since chronometers and watches were not in common use, it was difficult to determine longitude at sea. Mariners would first strike the desired latitude and continue on the course until their goal was reached. Thus, Columbus, sailing for the latitude of Japan and then heading west, was helped along by the **northeast trade winds** and by ocean currents. On his return trip he was aided by the **westerly winds.** Once North America was reached, penetration and occupation were determined by opportunities for profitable exploitation and by natural advantages for travel.

Thus, the accumulated wealth of Mexico and Central America repaid costly and laborious inroads and settlement, whereas similar expeditions from Florida and Mexico which ranged the lower half of the Mississippi Valley yielded nothing. The other two natural entries to the interior, the St. Lawrence–Great Lakes (with a branch by way of the Hudson River) and Hudson Bay, were first explored in vain as routes to Asia or to rich kingdoms, but remained unused until the North Atlantic fisheries stimulated a fur trade whose rapid drain of the supply drew traders along the waterways into the continent.

1451, c.25 AUG.–31 OCT. CHRISTOPHER COLUMBUS (It., **Cristoforo Colombo;** Span., **Cristóbal Colón**) was born in or near Genoa of a family of wool weavers. The fact that he could write only one modern language, Spanish, even before he went to Spain, combined with vagueness and inconsistencies in his earliest biographies (his 2d son Fernando's *Historie* and Bartolomé de Las Casas' *Historia de las Indias*), have cast some doubt on his Genoese birth. On the other hand, the records of that city present a wealth of substantiating evidence which no other location can offer, including references to his family as well as several to Columbus himself in various notarial papers (31 Oct. 1470; 20, 26 Mar. 1472; 7 Aug. 1473). Fernando's assertion that his father attended the Univ. of Pavia is not borne out by that institution's records. Columbus may have gone to sea in the service of René d'Anjou (1470–73), and made one or more trips to the island of Chios for the Centurione interests (1474–75).

1476–80. Following a naval battle off Cape St. Vincent between a Genoese fleet on which he was shipping and a Franco-Portuguese flotilla, Columbus arrived in Portugal (1476). Shortly thereafter (Feb. 1477) he made a trip to northern waters (possibly Iceland, but more likely England). Returning to Lisbon, he sailed (1478) once more for the Centurione, this time to Madeira. He married (1479 or 1480) Doña Felipa de Perestrello é Moñiz, daughter of the captain of Porto Santo, to which he moved (1480), the year in which his son Diego was born. Probably (1481–82) he made a trip to the Guinea Coast.

1484. Columbus asked King João II of Portugal to sponsor a western voyage to the island of Cipangu (Marco Polo's Japan). The plan was rejected (1485) either because of lack of confidence in Columbus' geographical knowledge or because the crown was licensing self-financed voyages with similar objectives (Fernão Dulmo, 1486–87). Columbus' stay at Lisbon is believed to have furnished him with opportunities for acquiring knowledge of geography and navigation. Portugal was the home of the most advanced geographers, including José Vizinho and Diogo Ortiz de Vilhegas; was visited by the great Nuremberg cosmographer, Martin Behaim. The court corresponded with the Italian geographer Toscanelli (1474), as did Columbus (c.1481).

1485–86. Columbus left Lisbon with his son Diego (his wife had died) and landed at Palos, Spain, where he was befriended by a Franciscan friar, Antonio de Marchena. After unsuccessful negotiations with Don Enrique de Guzmán, Duke of Medina Sidonia, Columbus turned to Don Luis de la Cerda, Count of Medina Celi, who arranged a meeting between Columbus and Queen Isabella (c.1 May 1486). The result was inconclusive. For the next two years Columbus received a small yearly stipend from the crown.

1488. Columbus attempted to reopen negotiations with King João II, and was in Lisbon to witness the triumphant return of Bartolomeu Dias. With India apparently within its grasp, Portugal was disinclined to back Columbus, who returned to Spain.

1490–92. Columbus' plan was twice rejected by the Castilian commission, but at the insistence of **Luis de Santangel,** Marrano treasurer of Aragon, the court, following the fall of Granada (2 Jan. 1492), marking the end of the reconquest of Spain from the Moors, agreed to sponsor his expedition. His voyage was financed by both the royal treasury and private sources. By the Capitulations of 17 Apr. and the Title of 30 Apr. 1492 Columbus was appointed Admiral of the Ocean Sea, Viceroy, and governor of whatever territory he might discover.

1492, 3 Aug.–1493, 15 Mar. 1ST VOYAGE. The 3 ships of Columbus' fleet (the *Niña,* commanded by Vincente Yáñez Pinzón; the *Pinta* by Martín Alonso Pinzón; and the *Santa Maria,* by Columbus), with a crew of 90, sailed from Palos. They arrived at the Canaries (12 Aug.), sailed west (6 Sept.), and during the first stage of the ocean crossing (9–19 Sept.) enjoyed favorable winds. With the next stage (20–30 Sept.) marked by unfavorable winds and calms morale dropped, with the crews at the point of

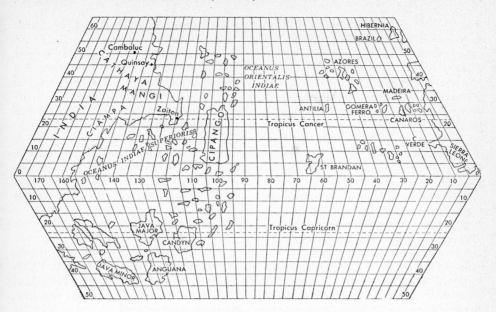

Reconstruction of alleged Toscanelli map (1474?)
reputedly used by Columbus on his first voyage

mutiny 2 days before land was actually sighted. Columbus first sighted (12 Oct.) **Guanahani** (probably **Watlings Island**) in the Bahamas, which he named San Salvador. He explored the Bahamas (14–26 Oct.), discovered and explored the northeastern coast of **Cuba** (27 Oct.–5 Dec.), then (6 Dec. 1492–15 Jan. 1493) the northern coast of **Hispaniola** (Santo Domingo), where the *Santa Maria* was wrecked (25 Dec.) and a post established (**La Navidad**). On the homeward journey (16 Jan.–15 Mar.) stops were made at the Azores (18–24 Feb.) and Lisbon (4–13 Mar.). News of the voyage had already reached the court in a letter written by Columbus off the Canaries (15 Feb.), addressed to Luis de Santangel, a substantial backer of the expedition. This was printed at Barcelona in the original Spanish shortly after its receipt; reprinted, Valladolid, with slight corrections.

1493–94. DIPLOMATIC CONSEQUENCES OF THE DISCOVERY. At the urging of the Spanish rulers Pope Alexander VI (Rodrigo Borgia) issued (3–4 May) two bulls, **Inter Caetera** (granting Spain all lands not under Christian rule) and **Inter Caetera II** (setting a demarcation line at 100 leagues west of the Azores and Cape Verde Islands, beyond which all future discoveries not held by a Christian prince on 25 Dec. 1492 would belong to Spain). By the **Treaty of Tordesillas** (7 June 1494) between Portugal and Spain the line of demarcation was moved to 370 leagues west of the Cape Verde Islands, Portugal to have exclusive rights to all land east of the line.

1493, 25 Sept.–1496, 11 June. 2ND VOYAGE. Columbus sailed from Cádiz with 17 ships and some 1,200 men (including his brother Diego). The fleet stopped at the Canaries (2–7 or 10 Oct.)

and reached the **Leeward Islands** (4 Nov.). After exploring the Leewards and **Puerto Rico,** Columbus anchored off La Navidad (28 Nov.), where he found his post destroyed. Columbus planted (2 Jan. 1494) **Isabela,** a second colony on Santo Domingo, which served as a base for inland exploration, and explored the southern coast of Cuba, the coasts of Jamaica, and the remaining coastline of Hispaniola (29 Apr.–29 Sept.). The Isabela settlement faced serious difficulties from the start owing to its unsuitable location, sparse gold resources, and the resentment of the natives to enslavement by the conquerors. It was abandoned, and the city of **Santo Domingo** founded 1496. Leaving in command of the island his brother, Bartholomeu, who had joined him in 1494, Columbus sailed for Spain (10 Mar. 1496) and reached Cádiz (11 June).

1498, 30 May–1500, 25 Nov. 3RD VOYAGE. Columbus, with a fleet of 7 ships, left the mouth of the Guadalquivir, touched at Madeira (7 June) and the Canaries (19 June), whence 3 ships proceeded directly to Santo Domingo and the remainder, with Columbus, took a more southerly route, touching the Cape Verde Islands (27 June–4 July) and reaching **Trinidad** (31 July). Columbus sighted South America (1 Aug.) at **Punta Bombeador,** explored the **Gulf of Paria** (1–13 Aug.), and sailed for **Santo Domingo,** where he arrived (31 Aug.) to find the colony in a state of rebellion. Some improvement in administration followed the granting of immunity to the rebel leaders (Sept. 1499), but news of unrest convinced the court of the need for a change in administration. The new governor, Francisco de Bobadilla, arrived 23 Aug. 1500, and the three brothers Columbus were sent home in chains (Oct.). They were ultimately restored to their honors but never to their old

authority in the Indies, which the crown henceforth retained.

1502, 11 May–1504, 7 Nov. 4TH AND LAST VOYAGE. Columbus with a fleet of 4 ships sailed from Cádiz, stopped at the Canaries (20–25 May), and hit land at **Martinique** (15 June). After stopping at Hispaniola Columbus sailed past Cuba to the mainland of Central America on the **Honduran coast** (31 July) and explored southward as far as **central Panama** (31 July 1502–15 Apr. 1503). En route to Hispaniola he was shipwrecked and marooned in Jamaica (25 June 1503–29 June 1504), and returned to Spain 7 Nov. 1504.

1506, 20 May. DEATH AND BURIAL PLACE. Columbus died in Valladolid after spending his final days trying to regain his old privileges. Until his death he insisted that he had skirted the shores of Asia. However, recognition that the territory he had charted was in fact a New World was already gaining ground. His remains were sent to Santo Domingo some time after 5 Nov. 1540 along with those of his son Diego (d.1526), and placed in the cathedral. As a result of the Treaty of Basel (22 July 1795), under which the Spanish part of Santo Domingo was ceded to France, the Spanish authorities removed certain remains from the cathedral in an unmarked lead casket and installed them in the cathedral at Havana. Bones were later removed to Seville and deposited at the cathedral in that city (1898). Meantime (10 Sept. 1877), a cask discovered on the Gospel side of the sanctuary of the Santo Domingo cathedral bore markings indicating that it held the Discoverer's remains. Authorities are divided on the authenticity of the find. Hence, two Columbus shrines at the present day—one at Seville, the other at Santo Domingo.

1497, 2 May–6 Aug. 1ST CABOT VOYAGE. John Cabot (b.c.1455, probably in Genoa), a resident (1461) and citizen (1472) of Venice, migrated to England (c.1484–90), where he lived chiefly in Bristol as a merchant or mariner. Henry VII issued (5 Mar. 1497) to the Cabots (John and his 3 sons, Lewis, Sebastian, and Sancio) a patent to discover for England regions to the east, west, and north (avoiding Portuguese claims). In return for a trade monopoly and customs exemptions the Cabots were to turn over to the crown 20% of all trading profits. John Cabot sailed from Bristol (c.20 May 1497) with a crew of 18, including some prominent Bristol merchants and possibly his son **Sebastian**, on a voyage of general reconnaissance. He sighted land (24 June), probably the northernmost tip of **Newfoundland**, took possession of the area for Henry VII, and then sailed southwest far enough to ascertain the direction of the coast, possibly reaching Maine before sailing for England (c.15 July), arriving at Bristol 6 Aug.

1498, EARLY MAY. 2D CABOT VOYAGE. Under new letters patent (3 Feb. 1498) Cabot left Bristol for Cipangu (Japan) and the Spice Islands via Newfoundland. From available evidence (La Cosa map, 1500, and the Hajeda patent, 8 June 1501), it appears that Cabot's company explored the coast of North America **as far south as the Delaware or Chesapeake Bay.**

1499–1501. SPANISH EXPLORATION AFTER COLUMBUS. Amerigo Vespucci (b.Mar. 1454 in Florence and employed by the Pier Francesco branch of the Medici, first in Italy, 1484–92, and then in Spain, 1492–99) sailed on an expedition commanded by **Alonso de Hajeda** (Ojeda), on which Juan de la Cosa, a member of Columbus' first and second expeditions, also participated. Before sighting land the party separated. Vespucci's company probably sighted land

south of **Cape Cassipore** (c.27 June), journeyed down the South American coast, possibly exploring the mouth of the Amazon and the Pará, thence southeastward, passing "Cabo de la Vela" (19 Sept., possibly near Camocim, Brazil). Meantime, the Hajeda–La Cosa group had already arrived at Hispaniola (5 Sept.). Vespucci returned (end of Nov.), and, after sailing around the Bahamas and visiting the Azores, he reached Spain (mid-June 1500) several months after Hajeda and La Cosa. Two other expeditions sailing under the Spanish flag left in 1499 for the New World: (1) Peralonso Niño (former pilot of the *Santa Maria* and *Niña*) and Cristóbal Guerra went on an expedition to the Pearl Coast (Venezuela) in June and returned to Spain (Apr. 1500) laden with pearls. Vincente Yáñez Pinzón (captain of the *Niña* on Columbus' first voyage) sailed in Nov. or Dec. and reached the coast of Brazil (20 Jan. 1500) at about 8°S and explored either the Amazon or the Marañón before returning to Spain (30 Sept. 1500). In 1500–01 Rodrigo de Bastidas explored the northern coast of South America from Maracaibo to the Gulf of Darien, and, possibly, Juan de la Cosa made another trip in 1501 (perhaps with Vespucci), in which he explored the Gulf of Darien and the Atrato River, where he found traces of gold.

1499–1501. PORTUGUESE VOYAGES TO NEW WORLD. João Fernandes, a small landowner of the rank of **Llavrador,** i.e., peasant, and a seaman of the Azores, under a patent from King Manoel of Portugal (28 Oct. 1499) reached Greenland, initially called by his rank (Labrador). Under a patent from King Manoel (12 May 1500) **Gaspar Corte-Real** sailed (June 1500) to the east coast of Greenland, down and around its southern tip, and up the west coast until he encountered icebergs. On a second trip (15 May 1501) to Greenland he crossed Davis Strait to present Labrador, coasted south to Newfoundland, dispatched 2 boats home, continued southward in a third, and was never heard from again. His brother, **Miguel,** sailed (10 May 1502) to Newfoundland, but was also lost. A Portuguese expedition to locate the missing brothers (1503) presumably visited Newfoundland, and out of these voyages the Portuguese fishery developed there. In addition to their activity in northern waters, the Portuguese made voyages to South America. Pedro Alvarez Cabral reached the coast of Brazil (1500). **Amerigo Vespucci,** having switched flags, sailed west for the Portuguese (13 May 1501). He made his landfall a short distance south of **Cape São Roque** (16 Aug.) and, after sailing to the cape, he coasted southward as far as **Porto di San Giulian** (Puerto San Julián, Feb. 1502) in **Argentina.** Upon his return to Lisbon he wrote a letter (1502) to **Lorenzo di Pier Francesco de' Medici,** his former employer and patron, setting forth his conviction that what he had seen was a new land and a continent. This letter, along with 2 others to de' Medici, are generally accepted as authentic. Two others, the first called **Mundus Novus** (Aug. 1504) and addressed to de' Medici, and the second, called the **Four Voyages** (Sept. 1504) and addressed to Piero Soderini, are held to be forgeries, spiced-up versions of authentic letters, but not without evidential value. On the basis of these dubious letters 4 voyages are ascribed to Vespucci. On the first (1497) he purportedly explored the Gulf of Mexico and voyaged north and eastward from Campeche, even reaching the Atlantic coast of the present U.S. The fourth voyage (1503) supposedly ended near Baía, Brazil. In 1507 Martin Waldseemüller, the geographer, proposed that the newly discovered world should be called "America, because Americus discovered it."

1501–04.   ANGLO-PORTUGUESE VOYAGES FROM BRISTOL. Under letters patent of Henry VII (19 Mar. 1501) a mixed group of 3 merchants from Bristol and 3 men from the Azores, including João Fernandes, are presumed to have made 2 transatlantic voyages. Under a patent (9 Dec. 1502) to an Anglo-Portuguese group known as the "Company of Adventurers to the New Found Lands," trips were made annually to the New World (1502–05), possibly as far south as the Middle Atlantic states.

1503–04. Binot Paulmier de Gonneville, a merchant of Normandy, left Honfleur (June 1503) for a voyage around Africa to the Indies, was blown off his course, and arrived off the coast of Brazil, where he stayed for 6 months before sailing (3 July 1504) for home.

1509. SEBASTIAN CABOT (b.Venice, c.1483) sailed north and west from England (c.1509), and then southwest, returning to England (after 21 Apr. 1509). In later years he claimed to have reached Hudson Bay.

1508–13. SPANISH EXPLORATION FROM CARIBBEAN. Hispaniola was the center from which the Spaniards directed their explorations. By 1512 that colony was sending annually to Spain almost $1 million in gold and was raising sugar cane (introduced by the Spaniards from the Canaries), cotton, and cattle. In 1508 Sebastián de Ocampo circumnavigated Cuba, proving that it was not part of the mainland. Vincente Yáñez Pinzón and Juan Díaz de Solís explored the coasts of Honduras and Yucatán (1508–09). The conquest of the Caribbean Islands was the first military problem. Puerto Rico (1508–09), Jamaica (1510), and then Cuba (1511) were subjugated. **Juan Ponce de León,** conqueror of Puerto Rico, sailed (3 Mar.

1513) to explore lands north of Cuba. Passing the Bahamas, he sighted **Florida** somewhere between St. Augustine and the St. Johns River, remaining a short time (2–8 Apr.). Thence he sailed north and, reversing his course, explored the entire eastern coast of Florida as well as the western shore as far north as Charlotte Harbor (23 May). In addition, he visited the Florida Keys and the Bahamas, and returned to Puerto Rico (21 Sept.). The Spanish set up temporary trading posts in present Venezuela and Colombia (at Santa Marta and Cartagena). From a third post, Santa Maria de la Antigua on the Gulf of Darien, **Vasco Nuñez de Balboa** pushed across the **Isthmus of Panama** to discover the **Pacific Ocean** (25 Sept. 1513). This discovery stimulated efforts to get around or through America.

1515–19. FURTHER SPANISH EFFORTS. Juan Díaz de Solís sailed from Spain (1515) and reached South America near present Rio de Janeiro, then sailed south to the mouth of the Río de la Plata (Jan. 1516). Francisco Hernández Cordoba and Antón de Alaminos explored Yucatán (Sept. 1517), while Juan de Grijalva explored the Mexican coast from Yucatán to the Panuco River (Tampico, 1518). Alvárez Pineda explored the Gulf of Mexico from Florida to Vera Cruz (1519).

1519–22. MAGELLAN'S CIRCUMNAVIGATION. Fernando Magellan (Port. Fernão Magalhães), a Portuguese, sailed under the Spanish flag from St. Lucar (20 Sept. 1519), skirted the coast of South America (29 Nov. 1519–end of Mar. 1520), and wintered at Puerto San Julián (Apr.–Aug. 1520). Sailing through the strait that now bears his name and thence north and westward, he reached the Ladrones (Marianas) and **Philippines,** where he was killed (27 Apr. 1521). After many vicissitudes the rem-

nants of his expedition returned to Spain (6 Sept. 1522). Permanent Spanish occupation of the Philippine Islands began with the expedition of Miguel López de Legaspi (1564).

1519–21. CONQUEST OF MEXICO. Hernando Cortés headed an expedition into the province of Tabasco, Mexico (Mar. 1519), defeated the Tabascan (25 Mar.) and Tlascala Indians (5 Sept.), but was amicably received by **Montezuma** (Moctezuma) in the Aztec capital of Tenochtitlán (Mexico City, 8 Nov.). After the death of Montezuma (30 June 1520), whom Cortés had imprisoned, the latter crushed an Aztec revolt at Otumba (7 July) and ended resistance by 13 Aug. 1521. This conquest opened to Spain the treasures of Mexico.

1521–30. SPANISH VOYAGES in these years include explorations of Francisco de Gordillo, along the Atlantic coast from Florida to South Carolina (1521); of Esteban Gómez, a Portuguese in Spanish service, from Nova Scotia to Florida (1524); of Pedro de Quexos as far north as 40°N (1524–25); and of Sebastian Cabot, sailing under the Spanish flag, to the Río de la Plata, exploring the Paraná and Paraguay rivers (1526–30).

1521–74. COLONIZING EFFORTS IN FLORIDA (see pp. 59–61).

1523, Dec.–1524, July. FRENCH EXPLORATION. French fishing vessels proceeded as far as Newfoundland (1504, p. 70). Efforts to find a route to the Indies through North America persisted.

GIOVANNI DE VERRAZANO (Fr. Jehan de Varrasanne), b. near Florence, was dispatched by Francis I of France as pilot on a ship commanded by Antoine de Conflans to find a route to the Indies. After leaving Dieppe (Dec. 1523) he sailed west from Madeira (17 Jan. 1524) and reached North America, probably the Carolina coast (c.19 Mar.), thence proceeding southward "fifty leagues" before reversing his course and coasting north, reaching **New York Harbor** (c.17 Apr.) and **Narragansett Bay** (c.21 Apr.–6 May), and continuing northward as far as **Nova Scotia** before returning to Dieppe. Copies of Verrazano's report to Francis I (8 July 1524) constitute the chief source of information about this voyage.

1527, 10 JUNE. The English crown dispatched two ships from Plymouth, the *Samson* and the *Mary Guildford*. The former probably foundered, but the latter explored the North Atlantic coast from Labrador south and arrived in the West Indies (19–26 Nov.).

1528–36. NARVÁEZ EXPEDITION. **Pánfilo de Narváez** sailed from Spain (1527) and landed near Tampa Bay, Florida (14 Apr. 1528) with a group of 400 colonists. They marched north and reached the village of Apalachee (25 June) near present Tallahassee. Unsuccessful in their quest for gold, they embarked, probably at Apalachee Bay, and sailed for Mexico (22 Sept.). As a result of shipwreck only 2 survived to reach Mexico City, Apr. 1536, one of whom was **Cabeza de Vaca**, whose account of the expedition popularized the notion that New Mexico (specifically, the Seven Cities of Cibola) was fabulously rich.

1534–43. INTERIOR EXPLORATION OF NORTH AMERICA: FRENCH. Jacques Cartier (b. St. Malo, Normandy, 1491), believed to have been on the Verrazano expedition, was granted (Mar. 1534) 6,000 livres by Francis I to proceed to Newfoundland in search of islands and countries where it was hoped to find gold and "other riches." After sailing from St. Malo to the **Strait of Belle Isle** (20 Apr.–10 June 1534), he continued down the west coast of Newfoundland and passed Prince Edward Island, Chaleur Bay, and Gaspé Bay, and returned to St. Malo (5 Sept.). On his

second voyage he sailed to Pillage Bay in the estuary of the St. Lawrence (19 May–9 Aug. 1535) and then proceeded up the river to **Quebec** (7 Sept.), where he left his ships and some men and went in small boats as far as **Montreal.** After wintering in Quebec, he returned home (6 May–16 July 1536). His last trip was organized for the conquest of the kingdom of Saguenay, which Indians had led him to believe possessed great treasure. He left St. Malo (23 May 1541), reached Quebec (end of Aug.), set up a post at nearby Cap Rouge. En route home he stopped off at St. Johns, Newfoundland, where a few days before (8 June 1542) **Jean François de la Rocque, Sieur de Roberval,** commissioned (15 Jan. 1541) by Francis I to direct the conquest of Saguenay, had already arrived. Cartier brought back to France a shipload of iron pyrites (fool's gold) and some quartz crystals he believed to be diamonds. Roberval led one, apparently fruitless, expedition up the St. Lawrence (6 June 1543) toward the kingdom of Saguenay, but he was back in France in the fall of that year.

1539, MAY 28–1543, 10 SEPT. INTERIOR EXPLORATION: SPANISH. Hernando de Soto, newly appointed governor of Cuba, landed with 600 soldiers on the Florida coast, either at Tampa Bay or Charlotte Harbor (28 May 1539), and, after exploring the western part of the peninsula, he wintered in Apalachee. The following spring he marched north to the vicinity of the Savannah River, thence west to the Blue Ridge Mountains, and southwest almost to the Gulf of Mexico near Mobile (17 Nov.), wintered (1540–41) probably in the Yazoo Delta country, and, proceeding north in the spring, crossed the **Mississippi** (May 1541) south of Memphis. He continued west through the Ozarks, wintered near the junction of the Arkansas and Canadian rivers in eastern Oklahoma, and returned to the Mississippi where he died of fever (1542). With Luís Moscoso de Alvarado as their leader, the survivors journeyed west to the upper reaches of the Brazos River, but returned to spend a last winter (1542–43) at the mouth of the Arkansas. They sailed down the Mississippi (July 1543) and reached Panuco (10 Sept.).

1539–42. NEW MEXICO. The Franciscan **Fray Marcos de Niza** headed an expedition from Mexico into the Zuni country, accompanied by Esteban, a Moorish or Negro companion of Cabeza de Vaca. Their discovery of a Zuni pueblo at Hawikuh in western New Mexico was magnified in Mexico. **Francisco Vásquez de Coronado** led a force into New Mexico to conquer the Seven Cities of Cibola. He left Compostela (23 Feb. 1540) and captured the first city (Hawikuh, named Granada-Cibola, 7 July), which served as a base for further expeditions. Don García López de Cárdenas, proceeded westward and discovered the Grand Canyon; Hernando de Alvarado, going east, reached the Rio Grande around Albuquerque (region called Tiguex) and, continuing past the upper reaches of the Pecos, pushed into the Texas Panhandle in search of Quivera, a mythical kingdom of gold. After wintering at Tiguex, Coronado marched to the upper Brazos River (26 May 1541) where, separating from his main force, he moved north and northwest across the Arkansas River near Ford, Kan. (29 June), into the district of the Wichita Indians, returning to Tiguez (20 Oct.), which he finally abandoned (Apr. 1542), and returned to Mexico City (before 13 Oct.).

1539–43. SPANISH WEST COAST EXPLORATION. Francisco de Ulloa sailed from Acapulco (8 July) into the Gulf of California, circled the southern tip of Lower California, and sailed up its western shore possibly as far north as 30°N, thereby establishing its peninsularity. Hernando de Alarcón, heading an expedition from Acapulco to support Coronado, sailed up the Gulf of California and into the Colorado River (c.25 Aug. 1540), proceeding to some point between the junctions of the Gila and Williams with the Colorado, but left shortly before a Coronado searching party, headed by Melchior Díaz, reached the same area. In an exploration of the west coast **Juan Rodriguez Cabrillo** sailed (27 June 1542) up the California coast to Drake's Bay and took possession of the country for Spain. He died on San Miguel Island (3 Jan. 1543), and his successor in command, **Bartolomé Ferrelo,** sailed north, possibly to the California-Oregon border (1 Mar. 1543). Permanent Spanish settlement of the California coast did not start until a system of presidios and missions (Franciscan) was established at San Diego (1769), Monterey (1770), and San Francisco (1776).

1577, 13 DEC.–1580, 26 SEPT. DRAKE'S CIRCUMNAVIGATION. Ostensibly on a voyage to Alexandria, Egypt, but actually to prey upon Spanish shipping in the Pacific (considerable following the conquest of Peru, 1530–32, by **Francisco Pizarro**), **Francis Drake** sailed through the Strait of Magellan and reached the Pacific (6 Sept. 1578). Raiding the west coast of South America—Valparaiso (5 Dec.), Tarapacá and Arica (4 and 5 Feb. 1579)—and capturing a rich treasure ship between Callao and Panama (1 Mar.), he continued north possibly to 40°N, then reversed his course, anchoring probably at **San Francisco Bay** (17 June). Upon taking possession of this territory in behalf of Queen Elizabeth he had a plaque struck commemorating the event. (A brass plate answering its description was uncovered [1936] in the San Francisco Bay district, but its authenticity is not definitely established.) On leaving California (July 1579), Drake sailed north apparently to 48°N in search of the western end of the Northwest Passage; then, heading westward across the Pacific, he completed his circumnavigation (26 Sept. 1580).

1576–1606. ENGLISH SEARCH FOR NORTHWEST PASSAGE. (1) **Martin Frobisher** sailed from England (June 1576) and pressed northwest after sighting Greenland until, at 62°N, he reached **Baffin Land** and entered **Frobisher Bay,** believing it to be a strait between America and Asia. To exploit his discovery (including ore [mistakenly believed to have gold content] brought back to England) the Company of Cathay was organized and Frobisher sailed under its auspices (May, 1577) both for further exploration and for mining operations, which he conducted in Baffin Land. He returned to Bristol (15 Oct.) with 200 tons of ore. On his third voyage (1578) for the purpose of shipping ore Frobisher reached **Hudson Strait,** which he now considered a more likely passage to Asia. His ore proved worthless. (2) **John Davis** made 3 trips in search of the Northwest Passage (1585–87). The first led him to Baffin Land via the west coast of Greenland and the strait now bearing his name; on the second he followed the north coast of Labrador but missed Hudson Strait, and on the third he reached 73°N in Baffin Bay. (3) **George Waymouth,** backed by the East India Co., sailed from Radcliffe, England (2 May 1602), reached Baffin Land, sailed south past Frobisher Bay and into Hudson Strait, where the mutiny of his crew forced him to return to England (autumn). (4) **John Knight,** sponsored by both the East India and Muscovy companies, explored the shores of Newfoundland and Labrador (1606).

1598–1610. SPANISH SETTLEMENT OF SOUTHWEST was begun in New Mexico by **Juan de Oñate** (1598),

who dispatched an expedition which explored from Kansas to the Gulf of California. **Santa Fe** was founded (1609–10).

1608–11. VOYAGES OF HUDSON. In 1608 **Henry Hudson** made a voyage for the Muscovy Co. in search of the Northwest Passage, reaching the Kara Sea. With the same goal in view he sailed from Amsterdam for the Dutch East India Co. (25 Mar. 1609), reached Nova Zembla (Novaya Zemlya), where he was forced back by calms and mutiny. Sailing westward, he passed Newfoundland (3 July), continued south to the Carolina coast, reversed his course, entered **Delaware Bay** (28 Aug.), and the **Hudson River** (13 Sept.), up which he sailed as far as **Albany** (19 Sept.). Hudson's last voyage (begun 27 Apr. 1610) was under private English auspices and to locate the Northwest Passage. He reached Resolution Island (end of June), but was forced south by ice. Proceeding through Hudson Strait, he entered **Hudson Bay** (3 Aug.) and coasted along its eastern shore to **James Bay,** where he wintered. On the homeward journey he was set adrift by his own men (23 June 1611).

1603–35. CHAMPLAIN'S VOYAGES. After having sailed with a Spanish convoy to the West Indies (3 Feb. 1599–2 July 1601), **Samuel de Champlain** (b.c.1567) made 11 trips to eastern Canada. On the first, sailing from Honfleur (15 Mar. 1603) as a geographer on an expedition sponsored by Aymar de Chastes, he reached **Tadoussac** on the St. Lawrence, already a trading station for furs and fish. He then explored the St. Lawrence as far as **Lachine Rapids.** On his return to France (20 Sept.), he wrote his first book, *Des Sauvages,* reporting his voyage. On his second trip (early June 1604–06) he sailed in the same capacity in an expedition to set up a fur-trading post for Pierre du Guast, Sieur de Monts, who had received the trading patent previously held by Aymar de Chastes. Unsuccessful attempts were made to establish a post at New Brunswick and Annapolis Basin in Nova Scotia, but Champlain made 2 trips as far south as Nauset Harbor on Cape Cod (20 July 1605) and Vineyard Sound (20 Oct. 1606). On his third voyage (13 Apr. 1608–15 Oct. 1609) he sailed in the service of de Monts, holder of a new monopoly. After erecting a fort at Quebec (8 July) and cementing friendly relations with the Indians (Algonquins of the lower St. Lawrence and Hurons and Algonquins of the Ottawa River), he voyaged up the Richelieu River into **Lake Champlain** (30 July 1609). On his fourth and fifth voyages (7 Mar.–27 Sept. 1610 and 1 Mar.–26 Sept. 1611) he devoted himself to the fur trade and Indian relations. On his sixth trip (6 Mar.–26 Sept. 1613) he pushed up the Ottawa River in quest of Hudson Bay (Northern Sea) above Waltham (7 June). On his seventh trip (24 Apr. 1615–3 Aug. 1616) he reached Georgian Bay via the Ottawa and Mattawa rivers and Lake Nipissing. **Étienne Brûle,** who had accompanied Champlain on the 1608–09 trip and had traveled in the Huron region, and **Le Caron,** a Recollect (Franciscan) missionary, preceded Champlain by a week. Champlain joined the Hurons in raiding the Iroquois and, crossing Lake Ontario, penetrated south to Lake Oneida. After unsuccessfully besieging an Iroquois stronghold (probably on Lake Onondaga), 10–16 Oct. 1615, he wintered with the Hurons. In a trip growing out of this campaign, Brûle traveled (Sept.–Oct. 1615) down the Susquehanna as far as Chesapeake Bay.

THE FOUNDING OF THE ENGLISH COLONIES, 1578-1732

★ ★
★

The English colonization of America was a phenomenon of extraordinary magnitude. Prompted by hunger, overpopulation, religious vision, mercantilist ambitions, and nationalist aspirations—drives that varied from colony to colony—the colonization movement shaped the future of a large part of the New World and affected the balance of power among the great nations of the Old. It involved both the transplantation from England and the European continent of many thousands of individuals and families as well as the grafting on the Atlantic beachhead of the institutions of local self-government of the mother country and the setting up of representative legislatures for each colony modeled after the Parliament of England. Some of the colonies, such as Virginia and Massachusetts Bay, were initiated by joint stock companies; others like Maryland, Pennsylvania, Delaware, and New York, for a short time after the conquest of the Dutch colony, were governed by proprietors, but the remainder were either from the start or in the course of time directly under royal control. In all the Thirteen Colonies governmental systems emerged without parallel among the contemporary colonies of other nations.

Settlement of the Tobacco Provinces

Virginia

1578–83. SIR HUMPHREY GILBERT obtained a patent (11 June) from Queen Elizabeth for discovery and colonization in northwest America. He made a voyage to the New World (1578–79), but his plan to establish a colony as a base against Spain had to await financial support. With meager funds raised in Bristol and Southampton, he sailed (June 1583) with 5 ships and 260 men, reached Newfoundland, and made exploratory trips, but his vessel was lost (Sept.) on the homeward journey.

1584–1602. RALEIGH'S COLONY. Sir Walter Raleigh, half brother of Gilbert and a member of his last expedition, was granted a virtual renewal of the Gilbert patent (25 Mar.). With the aid of Walsingham, Drake, Sidney, and the elder and younger Richard Hakluyt, he equipped an expedition which sailed (27 Apr. 1584) under the command of **Sir Richard Grenville** and **Ralph Lane,** both to explore the North American mainland and reconnoiter Spanish Caribbean defenses. After accomplishing the latter mission, the expedition entered Albemarle Sound on the North Carolina coast, landed on Roanoke Island (July), and returned to England (mid-Sept.). Raleigh named his discovery **Virginia** and dispatched a colonizing expedition (9 Apr. 1585) under the same commanders, which landed at Roanoke Island (27 July). Grenville left Lane in charge of settlement. As a result of Indian troubles and Spanish tension the colony was abandoned (June 1586) when Drake, stopping by after a raid on the Spanish West Indies, offered the settlers passage home. Returning with supplies a few weeks later, Grenville left 15 men at the deserted colony. A fourth expedition under **John White** (probably the painter whose watercolors of Indian life served as the conventional representation of the aborigines) sailed (8 May 1587), arrived at Roanoke Island (22 July), found no survivors of the Grenville expedition, but left a group of colonists. White sailed home to obtain supplies (25 Aug.) only a week after the birth of his grandchild, **Virginia Dare** (18 Aug.), the first English child born in the present U.S. His return to the colony was delayed by the threat and then the actuality of the Spanish Armada until 17 Aug. 1590, when he found no trace of the colonists, but noted the cryptic letters, CRO, cut in a tree and the word CROTOAN carved on a doorpost—apparently references to an island off the coast held by friendly Indians. Coincidental with the 350th anniversary of the colony's founding, a quartz stone was discovered in Chowan Co., N.C. (Sept., 1937), carved with

what purported to be a message from Eleanore White Dare, Virginia's mother, describing the slaughter of the entire colony save 7, presumably saved by friendly natives. This "find" was followed by 48 others, all seeming to corroborate the first (1937–39), but they were exposed as forgeries (by Boyden Sparkes, 1941). Raleigh dispatched a final expedition (Mar. 1602) in a futile search for survivors.

1605, 5 MAR.–1606, 18 JULY. GEORGE WEYMOUTH sailed under the auspices of the Earl of Southampton and the latter's Roman Catholic son-in-law, Sir Thomas Arundel, ostensibly to establish a colony for Catholics who found their position in England insecure (Catholic priests banished, 1604; Guy Fawkes' arrest, 4 Nov. 1605). The account of his voyage to Nantucket and the Marine coast, as narrated in James Rosier's *Relation,* prompted two interrelated groups of merchants, from London and Plymouth, to petition the crown (c.Sept. 1605) for a patent, which was conferred (20 Apr. 1606). Under its terms two **Virginia companies**—the **London** (or South Virginia) **Co.** and the **Plymouth** (or North Virginia) **Co.** were established. The former was authorized to settle in a region between 34°N and 41°N (present New York City); the latter between 45°N and 38°N (present Washington, D.C.), but neither was to settle within 100 miles of the other, in effect creating a neutral zone between the two colonies. Each was to receive all lands 50 miles north and south of the first settlement and 100 miles into the interior.

1606, 20 DEC.–1609, 23 MAY. SETTLEMENT OF JAMESTOWN. The London Co. dispatched 3 vessels, which reached Virginia (26 Apr. 1607), entered Chesapeake Bay, and disembarked at Jamestown (24 May). During the first 7 months famine and disease cut the number of settlers from the original

105 to 32 as the councilors chosen before sailing proved unable to cope with the situation. The arrival of 2 supply ships (Jan. and Apr., 1608), the compulsory work program instituted by Capt. **John Smith** (p. 1154) upon his election as president of the council (Sept.), and the emphasis upon self-sustaining agriculture, notably maize (1609), marked a turning point. Smith's capture by Powhatan, giving rise to the legend of Pocahontas' intercession, occurred when he left Jamestown (10 Dec. 1607) and ascended the Chickahominy to obtain provisions. He explored Chesapeake Bay (24 July–7 Sept. 1608). A new charter granted to Virginia (2 June 1609) vested control in a council to be selected by the company and extended the colony's boundaries north and south from Old Point Comfort 200 miles in each direction and from "sea to sea."

1609–19. Dissension marked the period preceding the delayed arrival of **Thomas Lord De La Warr** (16 June 1610). Smith refused to yield authority, but left the colony (5 Oct. 1609). The "starving time" ran through the winter of 1609–10. **Sir Thomas Dale** assumed control (23 May 1611) as deputy for De La Warr, whom sickness had forced from Virginia. The "Dale Code" (**Laws Divine, Morall, and Martiall**, London, 1612) imposed severe penalties to check internal disorder. Dale began construction of a fort at Henrico, 50 miles up the James, and a system of stockades. Both projects were completed under **Sir Thomas Gates** (governor from Aug. 1611 to early 1614). A third charter to the Virginia Co. (22 Mar. 1612) placed Bermuda under its authority. During the administrations of Gates, Dale (early 1614–Apr. 1616), and **George Yeardley** (acting governor, 1616–17), except for the misrule of **Sir Samuel Argall** (deputy governor, 1617–Nov. 1618), such constructive developments occurred as the

introduction of tobacco cultivation (credited to John Rolfe, 1612; first shipment to England, Mar. 1614; married Pocahontas, 14 Apr. 1614), individual allotments to tenant farmers (1613–14) supplementing the prevailing system of community labor, and fee simple grants (beg. c.1617).

1619–24. FINAL PERIOD OF COMPANY CONTROL. When, in 1618, **Sir Edwin Sandys** and the Earl of Southampton gained control of the company, reforms were introduced through **George Yeardley**, newly appointed governor (arrived Virginia 29 Apr. 1619). The harsh legal code was repealed. A **General Assembly**, comprising 22 burgesses (2 chosen by the planters from each town, hundred, or plantation) and the governor and council, met in Jamestown (9–14 Aug. 1619), constituting the first colonial legislature in the New World, although it also served in a judicial capacity. In this period a previously inaugurated system of granting land to subordinate corporations (Society of Smith's Hundred, 1617; Martin's Brandon, 1617; Martin's Hundred, 1618) was extended, with 44 patents issued between 1619 and 1623. Heavy mortality from disease continued. An Indian massacre (22 Mar. 1622) provoked a series of retaliatory raids. A break in 1619 between the Sandys-Southampton group and that of Sir Thomas Smith, previous treasurer, was followed by several years of unprofitable operations, to which the suspension (8 Mar. 1622) by the Privy Council of the lottery, authorized in the charter of 1612 as a fund-raising device, contributed. The company went into receivership and was placed under the management of the Privy Council (July 1623). The charter was revoked 24 May 1624, and Virginia became a **Royal Colony.**

1624–42. SIR FRANCIS WYATT, who had been company governor, 1621–

24, was appointed governor by James I (24 Aug. 1624). He in turn was superseded by **George Yeardley** (14 Mar. 1626). His successor, **Francis West** (Nov. 1627–5 Mar. 1629), was instructed to call a General Assembly, which convened at the end of March, 1628. Pending the arrival of his successor, **John Harvey**, Dr. **John Pott** controlled affairs down to the spring of 1630, acting thereafter as opposition leader. Harvey was finally replaced (Jan. 1639) by **Sir Francis Wyatt** (1639–41), who was instructed to convene the burgesses "once a year or oftener."

1642–52. BERKELEY'S FIRST ADMINISTRATION. Wyatt's successor, **Sir William Berkeley** (1606–77), introduced a number of reforms, including the abolition of the poll tax. An Indian uprising (18 Mar. 1644) by Opechancanough was suppressed. The Indians ceded all lands between the York and the James from the falls to Kecoughton, but retained territory north of the York. Peace lasted until 1675. On 30 Jan. 1649 Virginia announced its allegiance to the Stuart house after the execution of Charles I and gave refuge to prominent Cavaliers. In retaliation, Parliament passed an act (Oct. 1650) imposing a blockade on Virginia and subsequently dispatched 2 armed vessels with commissioners who received the submission of Berkeley and the council (12 Mar. 1652) upon liberal terms. Following a new election, the burgesses chose as governor **Richard Bennett,** one of the parliamentary commissioners. When the succeeding governor, **Samuel Matthews,** threatened to dissolve the burgesses (1658), he was temporarily removed as an object lesson, then reelected. With the collapse of the Protectorate and the death of Matthews (close of 1659) the burgesses asserted "supreme power" until lawful authority might be forth-

coming from England, and elected the royalist **Berkeley** governor (12 Mar. 1660). Upon the Restoration in England (29 May), Berkeley was commissioned by Charles II (31 July).

1660–75. DETERIORATING CONDITIONS. As a result of the Navigation Acts (p. 698) tobacco prices declined from 3d per lb. previously paid by the Dutch to ½d. (1667). To meet the crisis attempts were made to limit tobacco acreage and establish clothworks in each county. The Dutch Wars (1664 and 1672) caused severe losses to the tobacco fleet. The crisis was deepened by a cattle epidemic (1672–73), the reintroduction of the poll tax, and a number of servant uprisings (p. 760). Additional unrest was provoked by implementing the grant made by Charles II (1649) to Lord Hopton of a tract of more than 5 million acres between the Rappahannock and Potomac rivers (assigned to Lord Culpeper, 1689, on whose death proprietary rights descended to his grandson, **Thomas Fairfax,** 1693–1781, 6th Baron Fairfax of Cameron, who settled in Virginia, 1747), and by a grant of all Virginia (25 Feb. 1673) to Lords Arlington and Culpeper for 31 years. This claim was reduced to quitrents and escheats and ultimately assigned to the king in payment to Culpeper of £600 for 20 years (1684). Despite growing discontent, Berkeley had stubbornly refused to call another election since the last one (1662).

1675–76. BACON'S REBELLION: PRELIMINARIES. Bands of Susquehannock Indians fleeing more powerful tribes to the north crossed the Potomac and committed atrocities. A joint force of Marylanders (under Thomas Trueman) and Virginians (under John Washington) failed at Piscataway Creek (27 Sept.) to destroy the Indians, who now stepped up their attacks, killing in one

January (1676) raid 36 Virginians on a single day. Frontier settlers deserted their homes, but Berkeley, who was accused of protecting the fur trade in which he was personally involved, refused to allow a force under Sir Henry Chicherley to march against the Indians.

1676, 10 MAY–18 OCT. BACON'S REBELLION. Nathaniel Bacon (p. 977), a recent settler in Henrico Co. and a member of the council, marched without commission at the head of a force of frontiersmen to the Roanoke River, where he destroyed a body of Susquehannocks. Declared a traitor (26 May), he was arrested when he tried to take his seat in the burgesses, to which he had been elected, but was freed (5 June) on acknowledging his offense and pardoned by Berkeley. Returning to Henrico, he raised a force of 500 which he led unopposed into Jamestown (23 June), forcing Berkeley to sign his commission. The assembly now enacted a number of democratic reforms. Again Berkeley proclaimed Bacon a rebel (29 July), but, failing to raise a force against him, fled to the Eastern Shore. Meeting at the Middle Plantation (3 Aug.), the large planters took oath to support Bacon. Returning (13 Sept.) from an expedition against the Indians on the upper reaches of the Potomac and Rappahannock, Bacon drove Berkeley's force out of Jamestown (18 Sept.), which he burned the next day. He died suddenly (18 Oct.)

1676, OCT–1677, MAY. RESTORATION OF ORDER. The loss of its commander reduced the rebel army to a series of bands which were captured by treachery or surrendered piecemeal to Berkeley (Nov.–Dec.) under promise of amnesty. Commissioners John Berry and Francis Moryson arrived 29 Jan. 1677 to investigate the uprising, preceding by a few days Col. **Herbert Jeffreys**, sent to restore order. Jeffreys brought with him royal pardons for the rebels which Berkeley (10 Feb.) nullified. Executions totaling 23 continued until Jeffreys formally took over the government (27 Apr.) just prior to Berkeley's departure (5 May).

1677–89. REVOLUTION OF 1689 IN VIRGINIA. Jeffreys and his successors, Sir **Henry Chicherley** (9 Nov. 1678–May, 1680) and **Lord Culpeper** (10 May 1680–28 Sept. 1683), enjoyed comparatively peaceful administrations, but that of **Lord Howard of Effingham** (1683–89) was marked by a struggle between the governor and the legislature. A list of popular grievances was presented to James II (Sept. 1688), but before it could be acted upon William and Mary had landed in England. Their accession (13 Feb. 1689) and Howard's subsequent removal were hailed in Virginia.

Maryland

1620–32. PRELIMINARIES OF SETTLEMENT. George Calvert (c.1580–1632) became principal Secretary of State (1619), which office he resigned upon entering the Roman Catholic church (1625). By this act he did not lose favor with James I, who created him 1st **Lord Baltimore.** A member of the Virginia Co. (1609–20) and of the Council for New England (1622), Calvert bought from Sir William Vaughan (1620) the southeastern peninsula of Newfoundland, which he named Avalon. Because of the severity of the climate this colony did not prosper. After visiting Virginia (1628), Baltimore induced Charles I to grant him (1632) territory north of the Potomac River. The Maryland charter was granted (30 June) after his death. His son, Cecilius Calvert, 2d **Lord Baltimore** (c.1605–75), became its first proprietor. The charter recognized Calvert as **proprietor;** conferred upon him the authority of the county Palatine of Durham, subject to the limitations that laws be made with the consent of the freemen and agreeable to the laws of England. The charter did not forbid the establishment of churches other than Protestant, and Baltimore took advantage of this to settle his coreligionists. The northern boundary was finally settled at 40°N, the southern at the Potomac River (conflicting with Virginia's claims), with a line drawn east of the mouth of the Potomac constituting the southern boundary on the Eastern Shore.

1634–40. EARLY PROBLEMS. The first group of some 200 colonists, including 2 Jesuits and many other Catholics, sailed from Portsmouth (22 Nov. 1633), arrived in Virginia (27 Feb. 1634), and went up Chesapeake Bay to Blakiston's Island, erecting a cross and celebrating mass (26 Mar.) before finally settling at **St. Mary's** (Yoacomaco). The 2d Lord Baltimore never visited the colony himself, but governed by deputy. His brother, the first governor, **Leonard Calvert,** established the manorial government authorized by the charter, maintained friendly relations with the Indians, but came into conflict with Virginia. **William Claiborne** (c.1587–c.1677), a member of the Virginia Council, had established a trading post on Kent Island under royal license soon after the return of the 1st Lord Baltimore to England. Although this territory lay within Baltimore's patent, Claiborne refused to recognize his overlordship. His community sent representatives to the Virginia assembly, which supported his claim. The controversy culminated in sea fights between Claiborne's and Baltimore's vessels (23 Apr. and 10 May 1635). Claiborne visited England (1637) in a vain attempt to substantiate his claims, was attainted

by the Maryland assembly (3 Apr. 1638), the crown finally ruled against him (4 Apr.)

1640–60. UNDER LONG PARLIAMENT AND COMMONWEALTH. Baltimore's position in England grew increasingly insecure as Maryland suffered troubled times (1644–46). Claiborne proceeded to retake Kent Island and Capt. **Richard Ingle** (1609–c.1653), a Protestant tobacco trader, captured St. Mary's and plundered the colony, forcing Calvert to flee to Virginia. With the aid of Berkeley he recaptured the province, but Ingle, on return to England, almost succeeded (1647) in having the charter revoked. During the administration of **William Stone,** a Protestant, as deputy governor (1648–52) a **Toleration Act** was passed (21 Apr. 1649), granting religious freedom to all Trinitarians. When Stone left the colony (Nov. 1651) he designated **Thomas Greene,** a Roman Catholic royalist, as his deputy. The latter, by recognizing Charles II as lawful heir to the throne (15 Nov.), precipitated an investigation in England and the dispatch to the province of parliamentary commissioners, among whom was Claiborne. The commissioners ousted Stone (29 Mar. 1652), who still asserted his authority. William Fuller, designated governor by the commissioners, called an assembly (30 Oct. 1654), which repudiated the proprietor's authority, repealed the Toleration Act, and denied Catholics the protection of law. In the ensuing brief **Civil War** the Puritans were victors (25 Mar. 1655), Stone was wounded and imprisoned, and 4 of his supporters executed. Baltimore persuaded the Committee of Trade to restore his privileges (Jan. 1656) subject to the condition that **Josias Fendall** (who was actually chosen, 10 July) be governor in Stone's place. The new assembly (10 Mar. 1660) declared itself free of proprietary control. On accepting his commission from that body, Fendall was promptly ousted and **Philip Calvert** appointed in his place (Nov.). In turn, he was succeeded by **Charles Calvert** (1637–1715), who, upon his father's death (1675), became proprietor and 3d **Lord Baltimore.**

1661–81. INCREASING TENSION. The proprietary regime became increasingly unpopular as a result of the decline in tobacco prices, the restriction of the suffrage to freeholders (18 Dec. 1670), Indian raids, absentee proprietorship and official nepotism, and continued anti-Catholic sentiment. A short-lived uprising under William Davyes and John Pate (Sept. 1676) was crushed and the two leaders hanged, but in Apr. 1681, Fendall, enemy of the proprietary party, staged an unsuccessful "rebellion" and was fined and banished.

1684–95. REVOLUTION OF 1689 IN MARYLAND. Baltimore returned to England (May 1684) to settle boundary disputes with William Penn and the colony of Virginia and to answer charges of favoring Roman Catholics and interfering with the royal customs collectors. He was also called to account for the murder of Christopher Rousby (31 Oct. 1684), a collector, by the proprietor's nephew, **George Talbot,** acting governor in his absence. The charges of pro-Catholicism were dropped, Baltimore was fined £2,500 for obstructing the customs, and Talbot was taken to Virginia and sentenced to death (24 Apr. 1686), only to have this sentence commuted by the king to five years' banishment (9 Sept.). While the Maryland-Virginia Eastern Shore boundary had been settled (1668, 1671), Baltimore's claim to the entire Potomac was not settled for 200 years (1878), and the complicated border dispute with Penn also remained unsettled, until 1769, when the crown ratified the line defining the southern

boundary of Pennsylvania. A demarcation of the 2 colonies' boundaries, begun in 1763, was completed 4 years later by 2 English surveyors, Charles Mason and Jeremiah Dixon. Extended in 1784, the **Mason and Dixon Line** came to be known as the dividing line between slavery and free soil, as to its south lay Delaware, Maryland, and Virginia (incl. present W. Va.). During the absence of Baltimore (1684–89) and the disgrace of his lieutenant, Talbot, antiproprietary sentiment mounted. When Baltimore finally dispatched (1688) **William Joseph,** an advocate of divine right, to act as his deputy, the assembly (24 Nov.) voiced its disapproval, but took the oath (27 Nov.). Joseph then prorogued that body to meet in Apr. 1689, and again prorogued it until Oct. During the feverish period preceding the Glorious Revolution rumors were spread that the colony was to be turned over to the Roman Catholics. After the accession of William and Mary and the declaration of war with France (May 1689), an uprising led by **John Coode** (d.1709), with 250 recruits chiefly from Charles Co., marched on St. Mary's, where a surrender was signed by Joseph and 4 of his lieutenants (1 Aug.). The insurgent leaders (**Protestant Association**) called the assembly into session (22 Aug.). That body petitioned the crown to take over the province, and proceeded to elect **Nehemiah Blakiston** its president. The Lords of Trade made Maryland a **Royal Province** (27 June 1691), with Sir **Lionel Copley** as first royal governor, although Baltimore retained his property rights. In 1692 the Church of England was established, and in 1695 the capital moved from Catholic St. Mary's to Protestant Annapolis. With the death of Benedict Leonard Calvert (who had become a convert to the Church of England, 1713, and reared his children in his new faith) in 1715, leaving Charles, 4th

Lord Baltimore (1699–1751), as his heir, the government was restored to the proprietor (May 1715) and the charter of 1632 again put into force.

Settlement of New England

Plymouth

1606–20. EARLY ACTIVITIES OF PLYMOUTH COMPANY. The first expedition of the Plymouth Co. (dispatched Aug. 1606) was captured by the Spaniards in the West Indies. A second (Oct.) sponsored by Sir **John Popham** explored the coast from Maine southward and returned with extensive data on the coastal areas. Sir **Ferdinando Gorges** fitted out the *Gift of God* (under George Popham) and the *Mary and John* (under Raleigh Gilbert), which sailed separately (1 May and 1 June 1607) and dropped anchor off the Maine coast north of Monhegan (7 Aug.), then sailed to Popham Beach (14 Aug.) on the Sagadahoc River (lower Kennebec). There a fort was erected, within which were constructed other buildings. The colony failed owing to idleness and factionalism. After George Popham's death (5 Feb. 1608), the venture was abandoned (Sept.). Sir Francis Popham, son of Sir John, sent trading and fishing expeditions to the mainland and islands off Maine (1608–14) as did Dutch, French, and Spanish traders and fishermen, with fairly permanent posts established on the islands of Damariscove and Monhegan, and at Pemaquid Point. Capt. **John Smith** sailed for the New England coast (3 Mar. 1614). On his return (c.Sept. 1614) he pointed out to Gorges settlement possibilities of the area. Richard Vines, a former Gorges' agent, spent a winter at the mouth of the Saco (1616–17). The richness of the cod fishery in these waters revived the interest of the Plymouth Co. Through Gorges the company petitioned James I (3 Mar. 1620) for a charter according it privileges already granted the Virginia Co. A new charter, granted 13 Nov. to a **Council for New England** all land lying between 40°N and 48°N and from sea to sea.

1606–20. PILGRIM PRELIMINARIES. A group of separatists from the Church of England who had established a congregation at Scrooby, Nottinghamshire, emigrated to Amsterdam (Aug. 1608) and then removed to Leyden (1 May 1609). Although they enjoyed religious freedom in Holland, they found their children losing contact with English culture, were excluded from the local guilds, and feared the expiration of the 12 years' truce between Spain and the Netherlands (1609–21) would imperil their position and subject them to the rigors of the Inquisition. Leaders of the Leyden group—their pastor, John Robinson, and **William Brewster** (1567–1644)—sent agents to England (1616–19) to negotiate with the Virginia Co. for the right to plant a colony within its borders. Through the intervention of Sir Edwin Sandys they received a patent (19 June 1619) in the name of **John Wyncop**, an English clergyman. Pending royal approval, the Leyden group rejected an offer by the Dutch to settle under the States General (Feb. 1620). Meantime, **Thomas Weston,** a London ironmonger, in association with **John Peirce,** a London clothmaker, had received a patent from the Virginia Co. (20 Feb. 1620) and persuaded the Leyden group to join with them (July). Three groups were set up: (1) adventurers in England (70 in all) at £10 per share; (2) adventurer-planters, given 2 shares for each £10 in consideration of their settling; (3) planters, given 1 share each for their labor. Both capital and profits were to belong to the joint-stock for 7 years, at the end of which period they were to be divided proportionately.

1620, 22 July–9 Nov. VOYAGE OF THE PILGRIMS. Thirty-five members of Leyden group (known henceforth as **Pilgrims**), under the leadership of Brewster, left the Netherlands on the *Speedwell* (22 July) for England. When that ship proved unseaworthy, it was abandoned at Plymouth and the entire company crowded aboard the *Mayflower,* 180 tons burden, a ship provided by the adventurers. Sailing (16 Sept.), she carried, besides officers and crew, 101 persons (a majority non-Pilgrims, including Capt. **Miles Standish** [c.1584–1656], hired as their military leader), with 14 indentured servants and hired artisans. There were 35 from Leyden, 66 from Southampton and London. After Cape Cod was sighted (9 Nov.), decision was reached to land nearby despite the fact that this was outside the territory of the Virginia Co. This decision may have been inspired by a suggestion of Weston, who had reason to doubt the legality of their patent.

1620, 21 Nov. MAYFLOWER COMPACT. Fearing that the rebellious members of their company might prove even more untractable ashore, the Pilgrim leaders ("Saints") drafted an agreement which was signed in the cabin of the *Mayflower* by 41 adults. This preliminary plan of government, based on the social compact idea found in separatist church covenants, set up "a civil body politic" to frame "just and equal laws."

1620–24. PLYMOUTH, first sighted 11 Dec., was chosen as the site for the new settlement 25 Dec. The first winter

(1620–21) was mild, but disease carried off half the settlers the first year. The Indians, decimated by a plague (1616–17), proved peaceful. Deacon **John Carver** (c. 1576–1621), the first governor, was succeeded on his death (Apr. 1621) by **William Bradford** (p. 990), who held that office, with the exception of 5 years, down to 1656. A second **Peirce Patent,** obtained (1 June) from the newly organized Council for New England, vested title to land jointly in the adventurers and planters (100 acres for each person transported and 1,500 for public use) at a yearly quitrent of 2s. per 100 acres, but the colony's boundaries remained undefined. A party of some 50 men under **Andrew Weston** landed at Plymouth in June, moved to Wessagusset to establish a fishing and trading post, but failed because of Indian troubles and poor management (1623). Another colony was established (1623) by Capt. Wollaston at Passonagessit (Quincy). On Wollaston's departure within the year **Thomas Morton** assumed control at Mount Wollaston (Merrymount). The Pilgrims, outraged equally by his uninhibited life and his success at Indian trading, dispatched Miles Standish (June, 1628) to destroy the settlement and sent Morton back to England. **Robert Gorges,** son of Sir Ferdinando, sent out an expedition which moved into Weston's abandoned settlement at Wessagusset (end of Sept. 1623). Gorges abandoned the project (1624), but some settlers remained. In 1624 communal planting was modified and individual garden plots assigned. Meadow and pasture allotments were made (1632).

1626, 15 Nov. LIQUIDATION OF LONDON ADVENTURERS. Strengthened by a steady influx of settlers (since Aug. 1623), the Pilgrims were encouraged to make an agreement to buy out the London investors for £1,800 and assume the company's debt of

£ 600. Eight colonists underwrote the agreement in return for a monopoly of trade and a tax of 3 bu. of corn or 6 lbs. of tobacco per shareholder until the debt was paid (July 1627). This group established a trading post on the Kennebec (1628) and another on the Penobscot (c.1631).

1630, 23 JAN. NEW PLYMOUTH PATENT ("OLD CHARTER") granted by the Council for New England defined the colony's boundaries and confirmed title to land on the Kennebec.

1636. Adoption of a code, "Great Fundamentals," drawn up for the government of the colony established a General Court, comprising 2 deputies from each town chosen by the freemen together with the governor and assistants sitting as a single house.

Maine and New Hampshire

1622–31. On 10 Aug. 1622 the Council for New England granted **John Mason** and **Sir Ferdinando Gorges** all land lying between the Merrimack and Kennebec rivers. Special grants of 6,000 acres apiece were made to David Thomson (1622), who founded a plantation at the mouth of Piscataqua (Rye, 1623), and Christopher Levett (1623), who settled probably on an island at the mouth of Casco River (end of 1623). John Oldham and Richard Vines settled on the south side of the Saco (present Biddeford, 1623–24). In 1629 Mason and Gorges divided their northern holdings. Gorges received all land north of the Piscataqua; Mason all land to its south. A trading grant was conferred on Mason and Gorges (17 Nov.) of an indefinite area extending to Lake Champlain and the St. Lawrence. Under Walter Neale, settlements were made at present Portsmouth, c.1631, and present South Berwick, c.1632. After receiving a grant (2 Dec. 1631) of 24,000 acres on the Aga-

menticus (York) River, Gorges focused his colonizing activity in this area.

Massachusetts Bay

1624–26. DORCHESTER COMPANY planted a colony of Dorsetshire men on Cape Ann (present Gloucester). Proving ill-suited to both fishing and agriculture, most of the settlers returned to England, but the remainder (30–40) under Roger Conant removed to Naumkeag (Salem, 1626), where they set up a trading post.

1628, 19 MAR. NEW ENGLAND COMPANY. Rev. **John White**, a Dorsetshire nonconformist who had been active in the first Dorchester Co., formed a new association, the New England Co., which received a patent to land extending from 3 miles north of the Merrimack River to 3 miles south of the Charles River. The company's 90 members (largely but not entirely Puritan) included 6 from the old Dorchester group.

1628, 20 JUNE. JOHN ENDECOTT (c.1589–1665) sailed with a small group of colonists to Naumkeag (Salem). On arrival (6 Sept.) he served as governor (1628–30), handing over the administration to John Winthrop.

1629, 14 MAR. MASSACHUSETTS BAY COMPANY, successor to the New England Co., received a royal charter which specified no location for its annual meeting. This oversight made it possible to transfer the government to New England and transform the company into a self-governing commonwealth. The company dispatched its first fleet (Apr.), followed by 2 other ships (25 Apr. and mid-May). The Salem church was organized along separatist lines, and 2 freemen were sent home (Aug.) when they insisted on conforming to the Anglican ritual.

1629, 5 SEPT. CAMBRIDGE AGREEMENT. The position of the Puritans was becoming increasingly insecure after the dissolution of Parliament (10 Mar. 1629) and the growing influence of **William Laud** (Bishop of London, 1628), a zealous defender of conformity. In addition, the Thirty Years' War disrupted trade with the Continent and depressed the cloth industry. Twelve Puritan members of the Massachusetts Bay Co. signed the Cambridge Agreement, whereby they undertook to emigrate to America provided the charter and government were transferred thither. The company ratified the agreement (8 Sept.).

1630–40. EARLY COLONIZATION. The first 4 of 11 ships outfitted at Southhampton sailed (29 Mar. 1630) with **John Winthrop** (p. 1187), the newly elected governor. The remaining 7 sailed a month later; other emigrants embarked at Bristol and Plymouth (Feb. and Mar. 1630). The *Arbella,* first of the Southampton ships, entered Salem Harbor (12 June). The population settled along the Massachusetts coast north of Plymouth. Endecott moved to Mishawum (Charlestown); others went to Shawmut (Boston), Mystic (Medford), Watertown, Roxbury, and Dorchester. The elevation of Laud to the primacy in England, combined with the increasing economic difficulties, led to an influx of new settlers, beginning 1633, including such notable clergymen as **John Cotton** (p. 1007) from St. Botolph's Church, Boston in Lincolnshire (4 Sept.), and **Thomas Hooker** (1586–1647). In the first decade some 20,000 settlers emigrated to New England.

1630–34. CIVIL GOVERNMENT was rapidly established. The first meeting of the governor and assistants was held 2 Sept. 1630; the first General Court, 29 Oct. In addition to the 12 original freemen-settlers, 118 others were admitted to the freemanship (28 May 1631), but the freemanship was restricted to church members (in force until 1664), in viola-

tion of the charter. On 13 Feb. 1632 Watertown protested a tax levied by the Court of Assistants, and on 19 May the General Court regained the right of electing the governor and deputy governor. The freemen of each town were authorized to send deputies to the General Court (1634). Deputies and assistants (the latter elected by the freemen in a court of election) sat in one house until 1644, when, as a result of the "Sow Case" (*Shearman* v. *Keayne,* 1642–43), the legislature became bicameral.

1635. BANISHMENT OF ROGER WILLIAMS. Williams (p. 1185) arrived in New England (5 Feb. 1631), served in the Salem and Plymouth churches, and became pastor of the former (early 1635). He attacked the validity of the charter, questioned the right of the civil authorities to legislate in matters of conscience, and urged the Salem church to separate from the rest. The General Court (12 Sept. 1635) expelled the Salem deputies, seating them only when they had repudiated Williams. The court banished him (13 Sept.), but permitted him to remain over the winter. Fearing seizure and deportation to England, he fled from Salem (Jan. 1636) and wintered among the Indians. Joined by others in the spring, he first sought to settle at Plymouth, was warned off, and purchased land from the Indians at the site of the present Providence, which he founded (June 1636).

1635 MAY–1638, APR. ATTEMPTS TO REVOKE CHARTER. Thomas Morton, who went back to New England (1629), was arested by Endecott, had his house burned down, and was then deported, allied himself with Sir Ferdinando Gorges to secure revocation of the Massachusetts charter. On Gorges' complaint, the case came before the Privy Council (19 Jan. 1633). A Privy Council committee ("Lords Commissioners for the Plantations in General," known as "Laud Commission") ordered the recall of the charter on the ground that it had been surreptitiously obtained and unwarrantably overstepped (May 1635). Gorges was ordered to serve a writ of quo warranto on the Massachusetts officials, and the King's Bench ordered the charter canceled (3 May 1637). Meantime, Gorges' ship had broken in the launching, and he failed to secure the charter. Winthrop ignored a Privy Council order (4 Apr. 1638), but the outbreak of revolt in Scotland (signing of the Solemn League and Covenant, 28 Feb.) prevented the crown from taking further action.

1636–38. ANNE HUTCHINSON SEDITION TRIAL. Young Sir Henry Vane (1613–62), an aristocratic Puritan, elected governor (25 May 1636), the year after his arrival, came under the influence of **Anne Hutchinson** (p. 1065), along with most members of the Boston church including John Cotton. Her views, loosely called **"Antinomianism,"** stressed "grace" rather than "works," and her emphasis on personal revelation minimized the role of the orthodox clergy. When Rev. **John Wheelwright** (c.1592–1679), her brother-in-law, in a sermon in Boston (20 Jan. 1637) denounced the doctrine of works, he was tried for sedition and contempt, convicted, but his sentencing was postponed. On election day (27 May 1637) Winthrop's faction had the voting transferred from pro-Hutchinson Boston to Newtown (Cambridge). Winthrop defeated Vane, who returned to England (3 Aug.). A synod of 25 ministers convened at Newtown (30 Aug.) defined orthodox Puritan doctrine. On 12 Nov. the General Court banished Wheelwright and ordered Anne Hutchinson to stand trial for sedition and contempt. She was sentenced to be banished (17 Nov.). After an ecclesiastical trial (Mar. 1638), in which she was excommunicated, the

sentence was put into effect. With her husband and children she journeyed to Roger Williams' new settlement on Narragansett Bay. In cooperation with another Boston exile, William Coddington, she founded the town of Pocasset (Portsmouth, 7 Mar.). Upon her husband's death she removed to Long Island (1642) and later to the vicinity of Eastchester, where she and her entire household (except one daughter ransomed by the Dutch, 1651) were murdered by Indians (Aug. or Sept. 1643).

Expansion of New England, 1631–60

1631–60. FOUNDING OF CONNECTICUT. In the fall of 1632 Edward Winslow of Plymouth explored the Connecticut Valley probably as far north as Windsor. In support of their claim to the region the Dutch at New Amsterdam sent a ship up the Connecticut River (June 1633) and erected a small fort and trading post (Fort Good Hope, later Hartford). Although Winslow and Bradford sought unsuccessfully to organize a joint Plymouth-Massachusetts expedition to the Connecticut River (July), John Oldham of the Bay Colony took a small party overland (Sept.) and spent the winter (1634–35) at Pyquag (Wethersfield). Also in Sept. Lt. William Holmes, commissioned by Winslow, set up a trading post at Windsor above Hartford. Restlessness in Massachusetts seacoast towns where pasture lands were already proving inadequate caused a group from Dorchester (with perhaps a few from Newtown and Watertown) to settle in Windsor in defiance of Plymouth's claims (spring 1635) and a group from Newtown (Oct.) to settle around Hartford. Meantime, on 7 July a group headed by Lord Saye and Sele, who claimed rights to settle the region on the basis of a patent from the Council for

New England assigned by the Earl of Warwick (1631), authorized **John Winthrop the Younger** (1606–76), son of the Bay Colony's governor, to take control at the mouth of the Connecticut River. The settlers accepted Winthrop as governor (before Mar. 1636) and the Massachusetts General Court laid down a plan of government (13 Mar.) and placed final authority in the hands of the "inhabitants." After the arrival (Oct. 1635) of Rev. Thomas Shepard, who settled his followers at Newtown, Rev. **Thomas Hooker** departed with the remainder of his Newtown followers, and reached Hartford (31 May 1636). Hooker's democratic views were reflected in a sermon (31 May 1638), in which he declared that authority should rest upon the free consent of the "people." His views, as well as those of his associates, **John Haynes** and **Roger Ludlow** (founded Fairfield and Stratford, 1638), were reflected in the **Fundamental Orders** (24 Jan. 1639), a frame of government adopted by Hartford, Windsor, and Wethersfield. (Springfield under **William Pynchon** refused to join, and by 1649 deputies from that town sat regularly in the Massachusetts General Court.) The governor, who was to be of an approved congregation, and the magistrates were to be elected "by the vote of the country"; by this was meant the freemen, who were "admitted inhabitants" who had been selected for freemanship either by the General Court or by one or more of the magistrates. Voting in town affairs was open to "admitted inhabitants," i.e., Trinitarian male householders (after 1657 possessor of a £ 30 estate). In operation the franchise was as restricted as that of the Bay Colony. By 1662 (before the absorption of New Haven) 15 towns had been settled.

1636–56. RHODE ISLAND SETTLEMENTS. Roger Williams established his colony at Seekonk (**Providence**) on Narragansett Bay (June 1636) solely on the basis of an Indian deed. He was joined (Apr. 1638) by a band of Boston exiles under William Coddington, who bought the island of Aquidneck (**Rhode Island**) from the Indians, and, in collaboration with Anne Hutchinson, founded Pocasset (**Portsmouth**). Splitting with Mrs. Hutchinson, Coddington founded **Newport** (8 May 1639). These 2 Rhode Island colonies were joined (12 Mar. 1640). A fourth town, **Warwick,** was founded by Samuel Gorton (1643). Imperiled by the hostile New England Confederacy, Roger Williams left for England via New Amsterdam (Mar. 1643) to obtain a charter, which was granted him (24 Mar. 1644). Under its authority a general assembly composed of freemen from the 4 towns (Providence, Portsmouth, Newport, and Warwick) convened at Portsmouth (29–31 May 1647) and drafted a constitutional structure establishing freedom of conscience, separating church and state, providing for town referenda on laws passed by the assembly, and giving to towns as well as the assembly the right to initiate laws. William Coddington opposed the union, went to England (Oct. 1649), and obtained a separate charter for the island of Aquidneck (Mar. 1651), which Williams was able to have the Council of State revoke (Oct. 1652). Coddington finally accepted the authority of Providence Plantations (Mar. 1656).

1637–43. FOUNDING OF NEW HAVEN. Rev. **John Davenport** (1597–1670), a friend of John Cotton, sailed from England (Apr. 1636) with a group of followers, notably **Theophilus Eaton** (c.1590–1658), a London merchant, and, after stopping at Boston (26 June), established Quinnipiac (**New Haven**) as a colony and trading post. Land was purchased from the Indians, a town laid out on a modified grid pattern, and a government established which restricted the franchise to church members. In 1641 **Stamford** was founded and in 1643 the independent settlements of **Guilford** (6 July) and **Milford** (23 Oct.) joined New Haven colony. A General Court, comprising 2 deputies from each of the 4 towns, adopted (6 Nov.) a Frame of Government, established the Mosaic law as the basis of its legal system, and made no provision for trial by jury.

1636–37. PEQUOT WAR. A punitive expedition (24 Aug., led by John Endecott of Mass.) against the Pequots (who dominated the area between the Pequot [Thames] River and the present western boundary of Rhode Island, as well as eastern Long Island and Long Island Sound) in reprisal for the murder of a New England trader, John Oldham (20 July 1636), led to reprisals the following spring. A Connecticut force under Capt. John Mason destroyed the main Pequot stronghold near the present village of Stonington (5 June). The fleeing remnants were slaughtered near New Haven (28 July) by a combined force from Plymouth, Massachusetts, and Connecticut.

1638–43. NEW HAMPSHIRE. After John Mason's death (Dec. 1635) his lands and buildings were appropriated by his colonists. In Apr. 1638 **John Wheelwright,** banished from Massachusetts Bay, established the town of **Exeter.** His settlers signed (14 July 1639) the **Exeter Compact** (based on the Mayflower Compact). Portsmouth and Dover conceded the authority of Massachusetts (1641), and Hampton (1642) and Exeter (1643) followed, causing Wheelwright to withdraw to Maine rather than submit. Merrimack, Salisbury, and Haverhill were then united with the Piscataqua settlements.

1640–51. MAINE. Despite the attempt of Gorges to govern Maine through his cousin, Thomas Gorges, and the establishment of a provincial court at York (25 June 1640), Massachusetts persisted in its expansionist aims. Despite an appeal by the Maine government to Parliament (5 Dec. 1651), the Massachusetts General Court held that Maine was legally included within the boundaries of the Bay Colony (31 May 1652). Ligonia was annexed (4 July); Kittery (20 Nov.) and York (22 Nov.) capitulated.

1641–60. MASSACHUSETTS AS AN INDEPENDENT COMMONWEALTH. In response to criticism that too much discretionary authority was lodged in the magistrates, the General Court adopted (Dec. 1641) the **Body of Liberties,** a code drawn up by **Nathaniel Ward,** in preference to an earlier proposed draft by John Cotton, "Moses his Judicialls" (1636), which was published in England inaccurately as *An Abstract of the Lawes of New England* (1641). While less wholly drawn upon Mosaic law, the Body of Liberties based its criminal code on the Pentateuch. On 14 Nov. 1646 **Robert Child** and other remonstrants attacked the Bay Colony for its civil and religious discrimination against non-Puritans and for not observing the laws of England. Winthrop and other magistrates framed a reply, and the General Court declared: "Our allegiance binds us not to the laws of England any longer than while we live in England." A more extensive code was adopted in 1648, which was influential throughout the northern colonies with the exception of Rhode Island, whose code of 1647 adhered to the English common law. On 7 June 1652 the General Court set up a mint, and the "pine-tree shilling" was minted (down to 1684). On 29 Oct. Massachusetts, in defiance of Parliament, declared itself an independent commonwealth.

1643, 19 MAY. NEW ENGLAND CONFEDERATION. As a result of experience in the Pequot War, in which military action was not well coordinated, and the threat of Dutch expansion, representatives from Massachusetts, Plymouth, Connecticut, and New Haven, meeting at Boston, drew up 12 articles of confederation, which were ratified by the 4 colonies. The **United Colonies of New England** represented a union of the 4 colonies, each of whose territorial integrity was guaranteed. The government was a board of 8 commissioners, 2 from each colony, chosen annually by their respective general courts. The commissioners were empowered to declare both offensive and defensive war, the expenses for which were to be borne by the colonies in proportion to the number of their male inhabitants between 16 and 60. In addition, the commissioners were given jurisdiction over interstate quarrels, fugitive servants, fugitives from justice, and Indian affairs. Six votes were required for a decision. Annual sessions were held until 1664, occasional meetings prior to King Philip's War, which served as a basis for renewed activity. Thereafter operations virtually ceased, and the union was terminated in 1684.

1644–52. CONVERSION OF INDIANS. As a result of orders of the Massachusetts General Court (29 Nov. 1644 and 14 Nov. 1646), Rev. **John Eliot** (1604–90), pastor at Roxbury, who learned the Indian dialects and began to preach to the Indians at Nonantum (Newton), settled a group of converts at Natick (1651), followed by 13 other colonies of "Praying Indians," comprising more than 1,000 in numbers. His efforts resulted in the founding in London (19 July 1649) of the **Society for Propagating the Gospel in New England.** His work was largely destroyed by King Philip's War (1675).

1649–60. TREATMENT OF RELIGIOUS MINORITIES. The independent government of Maine, organized after the death of Sir Ferdinando Gorges (July 1649), passed an act (16 Oct.) granting all Christians the right to form churches provided "they be orthodox in judgment and not scandalous in life." On 18 July 1651 the Massachusetts authorities heavily fined and banished 3 Baptists. The first Quakers to arrive in Boston (July–Aug. 1656) were imprisoned, brutally treated, and expelled, a step which was ratified by the Federal Commissioners (17 Sept.). The Massachusetts General Court imposed penalties on Quakers entering the colony (24 Oct.), forbade Quaker meetings (29 May 1658), and imposed the death penalty for Quakers who returned in defiance of expulsion (Oct. 1658). Two returning Quakers (William Robinson and Marmaduke Stevenson) were hanged (27 Oct. 1659), and thereafter Mary Dyer, one-time follower of Anne Hutchinson (1 June 1660), and William Leddra (24 Mar. 1661) suffered the same penalty. Similar laws in Plymouth (1657–58) and New Haven (1658) were not as ruthlessly enforced.

New England Under the Restoration, 1660–75

1660–61. CHARLES II PROCLAIMED. The Restoration imperiled the position of the New England colonies. The Puritans were sympathetic with the cause of the Commonwealth, and New Haven harbored the regicide judges, Whalley and Goffe (1661). First to proclaim Charles II was Rhode Island (18 Oct. 1660), followed by Connecticut (14 Mar. 1661), New Haven (5 June), and Massachusetts (7 Aug.).

1661, Sept.–1662, 18 Oct. SUSPENSION OF QUAKER PERSECUTION. A royal order which reached Boston 9 Sept. 1661 commanded that all Quakers under sentence of death or corporal punishment be remanded to England for trial. Massachusetts released all imprisoned Quakers, permitting them to leave the colony rather than sending them to England for trial, and suspended (7 Dec.) the corporal punishment act of 1 June; but within a year (18 Oct. 1662) that penalty was revived.

1661–63. CONNECTICUT AND RHODE ISLAND CHARTERS. The Restoration threatened the independent existence of Connecticut (which had no charter) and Rhode Island (whose charter, 1644, now had no legality). Through the influence of Lord Saye and Sele, **John Winthrop, Jr.** (governor since 1657), obtained a royal charter for Connecticut (3 May 1662), whose boundaries were defined as Massachusetts on the north, Long Island Sound on the south, Narragansett Bay on the east, and the South Sea on the west. Since this grant included Providence, an agreement was entered into between Winthrop and John Clark, Rhode Island agent, to confine Connecticut's eastern limits to the Pawcatuck. The charter granted Rhode Island (18 July 1663) guaranteed religious freedom regardless of "differences in opinion in matters of religion." In implementing the charter provisions, the General Assembly (Mar. 1664) repealed the law requiring approval by the towns of laws of the General Court.

1662, OCT.–1665, 5 JAN. CONNECTICUT ANNEXES NEW HAVEN. Connecticut demanded that New Haven be incorporated within her territory in accordance with the Charter of 1662. Despite a vote of the freemen to maintain independence (4 Nov.), Southold voted to join Connecticut. Rather than come under the jurisdiction of the Duke of York, whose grant (12 Mar. 1664) included all land lying between the Connecticut and Delaware rivers, Stamford, Guilford, and part of Milford joined Connecticut (14 Dec.). New Haven formally submitted (5 Jan. 1665). Rather

than yield, a group in Branford left for Newark in East Jersey.

1664–66. KING'S COMMISSIONERS. The crown dispatched four commissioners to New England to secure aid in the war against the Dutch, investigate the governments of the colonies, settle boundary disputes, and see that the Navigation Acts were enforced. They laid down 4 conditions of compliance: (1) that all householders take an oath of allegiance to the crown, (2) that all men of competent estates be freemen, (3) that all of orthodox belief be admitted to existing churches or churches of their own choosing, and (4) that all laws derogatory to the crown be expunged. Plymouth (17 Feb. 1665), Connecticut (20 Apr.), and Rhode Island (3 May) agreed to comply, but Massachusetts, which had made a pretense of admitting nonchurch members to the franchise by qualifying all ratable at 10s (23 July 1664), refused further compliance (19–24 May 1665). Three out of the 4 commissioners recommended the cancellation of the Massachusetts charter. When, in 1666, the king commanded the Bay Colony to send representatives to England to answer charges, the General Court refused to comply.

1665–69. MASSACHUSETTS ANNEXES MAINE. The king's commissioners (following a regime set up, 1661, by commissioners of the Gorges' heirs) established a government in Maine which lasted from Oct. 1665 to May 1668. At a special convention at York the authority of Massachusetts was recognized (6 July 1668), and in May 1669 3 Maine deputies were seated in the Massachusetts General Court.

1674, 29 JUNE. A patent was issued to the Duke of York confirming his title to all lands between the Connecticut and Delaware rivers and (in Maine) between the St. Croix and the Kennebec. He proceeded to designate **Sir Edmund**

Andros (1637–1714) his governor general.

King Philip's War, 1675–76

1671, 10 Apr.–1675, 14 June. PRELIMINARIES. Five tribes which increasingly felt the pressure of the New England settlers' expansionist activities were (1) the **Wampanoags,** who had been pushed from the east coast to the eastern shores of Narragansett Bay; (2) the **Narragansetts,** whose lands between the Thames River and Narragansett Bay were threatened by a large land company, the Atherton Co. (organized 1659), which was attempting to foreclose a mortgage on most of this area (1662–76); (3) the **Mohegans,** occupying the hill country between the Connecticut and Thames rivers; (4) the **Podunks** to their north; and (5) the **Nipmucks,** who hunted in the country along the northern watersheds of the Thames and Pawtucket rivers. **Philip** (c.1639–76) son of the friendly sachem Massasoit, became chief of the Wampanoags on his brother Alexander's death (1662). At the request of the Plymouth authorities that he yield his arms, he made a token delivery (10 Apr. 1671). Accusations of conspiracy against the colonists brought against Philip resulted in the murder of the accuser and, in turn, the trial and execution of 3 Indians (8 June 1675).

1675, 20 June–6 Sept. START OF HOSTILITIES. When Philip attacked Swansea (20–25 June) a combined force of Plymouth and Boston troops attacked Mt. Hope, the Wampanoag stronghold on the Taunton River (28 June), but failed to destroy Indian forces. Philip now attacked the entire southern frontier, joined by the Nipmucks, who attacked Mendon (14 July) and Brookfield (2–4 Aug.). In turn, Lancaster (19 Aug.), Deerfield and Hadley (1 Sept.), and Northfield (2 Sept.) were attacked. The last was abandoned (6 Sept.).

1675, 9 Sept. NEW ENGLAND CONFEDERATION DECLARES WAR. Massachusetts was assigned a quota of 527 men; Connecticut, 315; Plymouth, 158. Indian victories at **Bloody Brook** near Hadley (18 Sept.) and attacks on Springfield (5 Oct.), Hatfield (16 Oct.), and other settlements followed.

1675, 2 Nov.–1676, Jan. NARRAGANSETT CAMPAIGN. A combined force under **Josiah Winslow** of Plymouth stormed the principal fort of the Narragansetts (present South Kingston, R.I.) on 19 Nov. Some 300 women and children were killed, but most of the warriors escaped. By the end of Jan. 1677 most of the tribe's women, children, and old men had been killed, while the warriors fled to the Nipmucks.

1676, 10 Feb.–30 Mar. INDIANS COUNTERATTACK. Driven by hunger the Indians attacked Lancaster (10 Feb. 1676), sacked the town, and took many captives, including **Mrs. Mary Rowlandson,** whose *True History* describing her captivity (ransomed, 2 May 1676) reveals the extent of Indian starvation. Attacks on Sudbury, Chelmsford, Medford, and Weymouth followed. Even Plymouth (12 Mar.) and Providence (29–30 Mar.) were attacked, as were Groton, Warwick, Marlboro, Sudbury, Rehoboth (all in Mar.), and Wrentham, Seekonk, Andover, Chelmsford, Scituate, and Bridgewater (Apr. and May).

1676, 18 May–28 Aug. COLLAPSE OF INDIAN RESISTANCE. A force of 180 under Capt. William Turner attacked a large body of Indians in the Connecticut Valley, near Deerfield, and destroyed many men and supplies, but subsequently were ambushed and annihilated. But the war of attrition stripped the Indians of offensive power. After Capt. John Talcott, with 250 men from the Connecticut Valley and 200 Mohegans, defeated the Indians at Hadley (12 June), chased the Valley tribes into the New Hampshire hills, and then, turning eastward, destroyed 250 Indians near Marlboro, Indians started surrendering in large numbers (410 from 16 June to 6 July). Philip, betrayed, was run down in the Assowamset Swamp and shot (12 Aug.), his wife and 9-year-old child were sold into West Indian captivity, and the last sizable surrender took place 28 Aug.

1675, 5 Sept.–1678, 12 Aug. WAR IN THE NORTH. Following a raid on Falmouth (12 Sept.), 80 Maine settlers were killed by 10 Dec. The resumption of warfare (11 Aug. 1676) caused the abandonment of the region between Casco Bay and the Penobscot. Indian raids were renewed in the spring of 1677. Sir Edmund Andros constructed a fort at Pemaquid (Aug. 1677), negotiated for a release of prisoners, and concluded peace with the Indians (12 Apr. 1678), by which they were to receive one peck of corn yearly for each family settled in Maine.

COST OF WAR. Some 600 English colonials were killed, £150,000 expended in prosecuting the war, 1,200 houses burned (including 12 towns completely destroyed and half of the New England towns suffering damage), and a probable 3,000 Indians were killed. With the exception of the tribes of Maine, the independent power of the Indians of New England was ended.

New England to the Glorious Revolution, 1676–89

1676, June. EDWARD RANDOLPH (c.1632–1703) arrived in Boston as special agent of the crown to convey royal instructions and check on the enforcement of the Navigation Acts. On return to England he submitted 2 reports (20 Sept. and 12 Oct.) charging Massachusetts with failing to enforce the Naviga-

tion Acts, putting English citizens to death for their religious views, denying the right of appeal to the Privy Council, and refusing the oath of allegiance.

1677. MASSACHUSETTS BUYS OUT GORGES HEIRS. The Lords of Trade upheld the title to Maine of the heirs of Sir Ferdinando Gorges. Through its agent, John Usher, Massachusetts proceeded to buy out the heirs for £1,250 (13 Mar.). Maine remained incorporated in Massachusetts until 1820 (p. 190–191).

1680, 4 Feb.–1686. ROYAL GOVERNMENT IN NEW HAMPSHIRE. By royal commission (Sept. 1680) New Hampshire was separated from Massachusetts. The administration of Governor John Cutt (1680–82) was comparatively peaceful except for the attempt of Robert Mason, John Mason's heir, to collect quitrents. Cutt's successor, Edward Cranfield (1682–85), ruled without an assembly when that body refused to pass his revenue bills (1683). Walter Barefoote, his deputy governor, succeeded him, pending arrival of the Dudley Commission. New Hampshire was part of the Dominion of New England (1686–89); its royal authority was reestablished (1692), after which date it had no connection with Massachusetts except that from 1698–1741 both provinces had the same governor.

1684, 21 June. ABROGATION OF MASSACHUSETTS CHARTER. Edward Randolph, appointed collector and surveyor of customs (1678), wrote a series of hostile reports to the home authorities (11 Apr., 7 Aug. 1682) and returned to England to aid in the prosecution against the Bay Colony (13 June 1683). The Court of Chancery annulled the charter (21 June 1684; final decree, 18 Oct.).

1685–88. DOMINION OF NEW ENGLAND AND ANDROS REGIME. Joseph Dudley (1647–1720), who had been sent to England to protest the threatened loss of the charter (1682), was appointed by James II (Sept. 1685) governor of Massachusetts, Maine, and New Hampshire. He was succeeded by **Sir Edmund Andros,** who arrived in Boston, 20 Dec. 1686, to assume the government of all the New England colonies (save Connecticut and Rhode Island) and to organize a Dominion of New England, to include New York, New Jersey, and Pennsylvania, for more effective military operations in the event of war with France and better enforcement of the Navigation Acts. Rhode Island was incorporated on 30 Dec., and Connecticut's government taken over (1 Nov. 1687), although the charter was successfully concealed in the **Charter Oak.** Other actions increasing his unpopularity were (1) his demand that Anglicans be permitted to share the Old South Meeting House (21 Dec. 1686), which he converted into an Anglican church (25 Mar. 1687); (2) his insistence that all land titles be reexamined and that the payment of a quitrent be a condition of regrants; (3) his imposition of assessments, which were resisted by an Ipswich town meeting (23 Aug. 1687), under the leadership of Rev. **John Wise** (1652–1725), arrested, tried, and fined £10 and costs; 4 others fined and disqualified from holding office; (4) an order limiting town meetings to one annually (17 Mar. 1688); (5) the placing of the militia under the direct control of the governor (24 Mar.). Rev. **Increase Mather** (1639–1723), president of Harvard, eluding detection, sailed for England to place the grievances of New Englanders before the Lords of Trade (10 Aug.).

1689, 10 Jan.–25 July. GLORIOUS REVOLUTION IN NEW ENGLAND. Andros received news of the impending landing of William of Orange while he was at Pemaquid, Me. (10 Jan. 1689), and returned to Boston in the middle of March. On 18 Apr. an armed uprising in Boston forced Andros to take refuge in the fort. A manifesto (largely the work of Rev. **Cotton Mather** [p. 1099]), excoriating the Andros regime and justifying the uprising on the grounds of fear of a French alliance and a Popish plot, was read to the populace. At the end of the day Andros surrendered and was lodged in jail. Also jailed were Randolph and Dudley. A "Council for the Safety and the Conservation of the Peace" was set up (20 Apr.). Deputies to a General Court were elected (6 June) before receipt of an order in council (25 July) for the return of Andros and his councilors to stand trial.

1691, 17 Oct. ROYAL CHARTER. Efforts to have the old charter restored proved unavailing; a royal charter was issued which formally incorporated Maine and Plymouth within Massachusetts' boundaries, provided for a governor to be appointed by the crown, a council elected by the General Court subject to the governor's veto, the substitution of a property for the religious qualification for voting, royal review of legislation, and appeals to the king in council. As a result of opinions of the attorney general (for Connecticut, 2 Aug. 1690; for Rhode Island, 7 Dec. 1693) that neither colony had been legally deprived of its charter, both colonies operated under their old charters until 1818 and 1842 respectively.

Settlement of the Middle Colonies

New Netherland

1610–18. INDEPENDENT VOYAGES. Following the voyage of Henry Hudson for the Dutch East India Co. (25 Mar.–4 Nov. 1609), several exploring and trading voyages under Dutch auspices were made to the area (1610, 1611, 1613–14). **Adriaen Block** (d. 1624) sailed to Manhattan (1613), braving the perilous passage named by him "Helle-gat" (Hell Gate), discovered the Housatonic and Connecticut rivers, Rhode Island, and Block Island (named for him). His map was the first to show Manhattan and Long Island as separate islands. A fort (Fort Nassau, later Orange) erected up the Hudson around this time (at Castle Island) was transferred (1617) to the west side of the river (present Albany). The 13 ship-owners engaged in trade with the New World organized the New Netherland Co. (1614), with a 3-year trading monopoly between 40° and 45°N. At expiration date the charter was not renewed.

1621, 3 JUNE. FOUNDING OF DUTCH WEST INDIA CO. Under the leadership of Willem Usselinx, a prominent merchant, the Dutch West India Co. was chartered by the States General, which participated in its financing. The charter conferred a trading monopoly and the right to colonize in the New World and along the west coast of Africa below the Tropic of Cancer. The company was organized into 5 chambers. The most important, that of Amsterdam, had immediate control of New Netherland (which province played a minor role in the vast trading activities of the company). The director-general of the colony, while chosen by the company, had to be confirmed by the States General. The Council of Nineteen (the company's executive body) adopted a resolution (3 Nov. 1623) authorizing the Amsterdam Chamber to dispatch 5 or 6 families to start a settlement and approved a **Provisional Order** (28 Mar. 1624), the first plan of government of the colony, based in large measure on the *Artikelbrief,* rules governing life aboard ship. Colonists were divided into 2 classes: (1) private colonists (*colonen*) who received transportation, seeds, cattle, and necessities of life for the first 2 years and free use of as much farmland as they could cultivate, upon agreeing to remain for six years; (2) *bouwmasters,* or head farmers, *bouwlieden,* or farmers, and *bouwknechten,* or farm laborers, who were required to work for a stipulated term on the company's own farms (*bouweries*) or on those of company officials. Trading with outsiders was prohibited, and the export trade confined to the company.

1624. FIRST PERMANENT SETTLEMENT. Some 30 families, mostly Walloons, sailed from Amsterdam (after 30 Mar. 1624) under the leadership of **Cornelis Jacobsen May,** a sea captain, named first director of the colony. On arrival in New York Bay, a small group was left at a fort on Nut (Governor's) Island, several families sent to the Delaware, where they established Ft. Nassau (now Gloucester, N.J.), and 18 families proceeded up the Hudson to the older Ft. Nassau. It is conjectured, but not established, that some members of this third group settled on Manhattan Island

and that other Walloons (at this time or somewhat later) crossed the East River to Long Island, settling at Wallabout (Walloon's Cove).

1625, JAN.-1626, SEPT. EARLY GOVERNMENT. Willem Verhulst, sent out as supercargo, became second director, with a council made up of available Dutch sea captains, a vice-director, and a vice-commissioner. As a result of his mismanagement the council ousted him (c.Sept. 1626), appointing in his place **Peter Minuit** (Pierre Minuyt, c.1580–1638), born Wesel on the Rhine of Dutch or Walloon ancestry. Minuit had arrived, 4 May 1626, on the *Sea-mew,* with a new group of emigrants who proceeded that summer to erect on Manhattan Island 30 houses. The same year he purchased Manhattan from native Indian chiefs for 60 guilders (c.$24) paid in trading goods, and changed its name to **New Amsterdam.** Settlement was reinforced by withdrawing settlers from Ft. Orange (leaving 16 men) and from the Delaware (completely abandoned by 14 June 1627).

1629, 7 JUNE. ESTABLISHMENT OF PATROONSHIPS. To promote farm settlement with a view to making the colony self-sufficient as well as a supply base for the expanding merchant marine of the company both in Brazil and the West Indies, the States General confirmed the **Charter of Freedoms and Exemptions,** under which the company was empowered to grant to those transporting 50 settlers estates fronting 16 miles along navigable rivers, and extending inland as far as settlement would permit. The grantees (*patroons*) were given feudal rights, including the right to hold courts as well as exemption from taxation for 8 years. By the end of Jan. 1630 5 patroonships had been granted along the Hudson, Connecticut, and Delaware rivers to directors of the company. Three were settled: **Pavonia,** across the North River from Manhattan, incl. Staten Island; **Swaanendael,** on the west side of Delaware Bay; and **Rensselaerswyck,** near Ft. Orange, the patroonship of **Kiliaen Van Rensselaer** (1595–1644), Amsterdam diamond and gold merchant, who ruled as an absentee proprietor. Rensselaerswyck was the only patroonship that succeeded. Its tenants held perpetual leaseholds. It was not until 1638 that Article 21 of the Freedoms and Exemptions, offering land to homesteaders, was implemented, and then to counter expansion of neighboring English settlements.

1629-37. UNDER MINUIT AND VAN TWILLER. Despite a generally constructive administration, Minuit was recalled by the company (1631) for being too liberal in granting trading privileges to the patroons. He was succeeded, temporarily, by Bastiaen Janseen Krol (Mar. 1632–Apr. 1633), who, in turn, was followed by **Wouter Van Twiller** (1633–38), nephew of Van Rensselaer, who was elevated from a clerkship in Amsterdam. Trade expansion was promoted by the construction of Ft. Good Hope (present Hartford), 8 June 1633, and by the ouster of a party of Virginians who had occupied the abandoned Ft. Nassau (Aug. 1635). A garrison was placed on the Delaware and the settlement of Long Island begun by grants of patents (1636) to Jacobus Van Curler, Wolfert Gerritsen, Director Van Twiller, and others in Flatlands and vicinity following purchase from the Indians. Although exports increased during his regime (45,000 guilders, 1626; 91,375 gldrs., 1634; 134,924 gldrs., 1635), Van Twiller was charged with illegal trading, incompetence, and hostility toward the Dutch Reformed Church, and was replaced (2 Sept. 1637) by **Willem Kieft** (1597–1647), an Amsterdam merchant.

New Netherland and Its Neighbors, 1638–64

1638–40. FOUNDING OF NEW SWEDEN. The New Sweden or New South Co. was organized (1633) as successor to a series of trading companies of which Willem Usselinx was the guiding spirit. The capital for the company was supplied by Dutch and Swedish investors in equal parts. Through the influence of Samuel Blommaert, who had a substantial interest in the patroonship of Swaanendael (destroyed by the Indians before 6 Dec. 1632), and Peter Minuit, who had now entered the Swedish service, the company was granted a charter for settlement on the Delaware (c.1637). Its first expedition sailed (31 Dec. 1637) under Minuit, arrived at the Delaware (mid-Mar. 1638), and, despite Dutch protests, built Ft. Christina (present Wilmington). Minuit was lost at sea on a return trip to Sweden (June), but the leaderless colony managed to survive until the arrival of a new expedition (spring 1640), bringing Peter Hollender Ridder, as governor; Rev. Reorus Torkillus, a Lutheran minister; and much-needed livestock. A group of Dutch settlers from Utrecht were planted 20 miles north of Ft. Christina (Nov. 1640).

1640, 19 JULY. NEW CHARTER OF FREEDOMS AND EXEMPTIONS, granted to promote peopling of New Netherland, reduced the size of patroonships, provided grants of 200 acres to those transporting 5 persons, liberalized commercial privileges, and provided for local self-government.

1640–45. DUTCH EXPANSION. New settlements were established at Vriesendael on Tappan Zee, Hackensack, and at Staten Island (1641). The movement of English colonists into Westchester (the Hutchinson, Throgmorton, and Cornell plantations) and on Long Island (Maspeth and Lady Moody's settlement at Gravesend) impelled Kieft to appoint a special English secretary (11 Dec. 1642). Confronted with expanding European settlements in the southern part of the province and Iroquois ascendancy in the north, the Indians of the lower Hudson Valley raided Staten Island and Manhattan (summer 1641). Kieft, who had levied tribute from the tribes, was accused by the settlers of provoking war. Twelve representatives of heads of families (**The Twelve**), called together by Kieft (21 Jan. 1642), agreed to a campaign against the Indians, which proved ineffectual (Mar.). A year's truce was arranged by Jonas Bronck, a settler on the Bronx River. The Twelve were dismissed (18 Feb.) when they requested representation on the council and courts to prevent taxes being levied without their consent. In Feb. 1643 the Mohawks, armed by traders at Rensselaerswyck and Ft. Orange, attacked the Indians of the lower Hudson, forcing them to seek refuge among the Dutch at Pavonia (New Jersey) and Manhattan. They were slaughtered by Kieft's men (25–26 Feb.), with resultant Indian reprisals throughout the area; Kieft was now (Sept.) forced to seek counsel from 8 men (**The Eight**). Despite reinforcements by a small English force under John Underhill of Connecticut (29 Sept.), the Dutch failed to prevent English plantations in Westchester (the Hutchinson, Throgmorton, and Cornell settlements) and Long Island from being destroyed (Lady Moody's at Gravesend was spared) as well as settlements on the west bank of the Hudson (17 Sept.–1 Oct.). Kieft's disastrous policy brought him into conflict with The Eight, who refused approval of excises (18 June 1644) and appealed to the Amsterdam Chamber for relief (Oct.). Peace with the Indians was finally established (9 Aug. 1645) through the intervention of the Mohawks, but only after most settlers south of Ft. Orange and Rensselaerswyck had retired behind the walls of Ft. New Amsterdam, on the southern tip of Manhattan (1644).

1644, 16 Nov.–1646. RESETTLEMENT OF LONG ISLAND. After Kieft purchased the western portion of Long Island (Coney Island to Gowanus), settlements were begun (Breukelen [northwest Brooklyn], 1646; Lady Moody's at Gravesend, chartered, 19 Dec. 1646), as well as English settlements at Heemstede (Hempstead, 16 Nov. 1644, and Flushing, 19 Oct. 1645). Meantime, the Dutch position on the Connecticut deteriorated with the expansion of English settlement in that area.

1646, 28 JULY–1664, 19 MAR. STUYVESANT'S REGIME. Kieft was succeeded by **Peter Stuyvesant** (p. 1162), commissioner in Brazil (1635) and governor of Curaçao (1643–44). On arrival at New Amsterdam (11 May 1647) he consented to an election (25 Sept.) by the Dutch householders of Manhattan, Pavonia (Jersey City), and Long Island of 18 men, from whom he and the council chose 9 (**The Nine**) to advise the governor and council and serve in a judicial capacity. The Nine soon complained to the States General (13 Oct. 1649), charging neglect by the company, and proposed reforms, including the establishment of local self-government. Stuyvesant was ordered by the Amsterdam Chamber to grant New Amsterdam a city government (Apr. 1652). The director-general proclaimed New Amsterdam a municipality, appointed the municipal officials, and retained the right to enact ordinances (2 Feb. 1653). By Dec. 1661 5 Dutch and 6 English villages were incorporated on western Long Island, as were the villages of Bergen and Esopus. After establishing municipal government for New Amsterdam, The Nine were disbanded, and most of their duties transferred to the magistrates of New Amsterdam. Stuyvesant called 5 assemblies of delegates from towns adjacent to New Amsterdam, 2 (Dec. 1653 and May 1654) during the Anglo-Dutch War; the other 3 while the colony was in its last crisis (July, Nov. 1663, Apr. 1664).

1647–63. END OF SWEDISH RULE ON THE DELAWARE. The Dutch members of the New Sweden Co. were bought out (1641) and the company reorganized (1642), with an increase of capital and an extension of control by the Swedish crown. **Johan Björnsson Printz** (1592–1663), a Swedish soldier of fortune, served as governor of New Sweden (1643–53). He erected a series of blockhouses at Varkens Kill (Salem Creek), Upland, New Gothenburg on Tinicum Island, 1643, and Ft. New Krisholm near the mouth of the Schuylkill (1647). Stuyvesant countered by building Ft. Beversrede across the river (at present Philadelphia, 27 Apr. 1648). Although the Swedes twice burned the post (May, Nov. 1648), the Dutch held the site until the establishment of Ft. Casimir (Newcastle, 5 Nov. 1651), controlling the approaches to New Sweden. This fort was captured by **Johan Classon Rising**, the newly appointed governor of New Sweden (1654), but Stuyvesant proceeded to retake the fort (26 Sept. 1655), thereby ending Swedish rule in North America. In payment of debts incurred as a result of this campaign, the Dutch West India Co. transferred to the city of Amsterdam all lands west of the Delaware from Cristina Kill to Boomtje's (Bombay) Hook. The city sent out 167 settlers, who, on arrival at Ft. Casimir (21 Apr. 1657), reorganized the settlement as **New Amstel**, under Jacob Alrichs as vice-director (succeeded, 1659, by Alexander d'Hinoyossa). As a result of the transfer to the city of Amsterdam by the company of all remaining lands on the west bank of the Delaware, as well as a tract 3 miles broad along the east bank (8 Feb. 1683), all authority in the area passed into the hands of d'Hinoyossa.

1650–64. ANGLO-DUTCH RELATIONS. Fearful of the encroachments of New Haven upon Westchester, Connecticut on Ft. Good Hope, and both colonies on Long Island, Stuyvesant at Hartford negotiated a boundary settlement (23–29 Sept. 1650) with the commissioners of the New England Confederacy whereby Long Island was divided by a line running north and south through Oyster Bay, and the mainland by a line 10 miles east of the Hudson (Ft. Good Hope to remain in Dutch hands). Although the English government never recognized this treaty, the boundaries were respected until shortly before the fall of New Netherland. During the **Anglo-Dutch War** (July 1652–Apr. 1654) the Confederacy refrained from declaring war on New Netherland, although Ft. Good Hope was seized (5 July 1653) by Connecticut and formally sequestered (Apr. 1654). In the spring of 1663 Connecticut dispatched Capt. John Talcott into Westchester and James Christie into Long Island. The former dismissed the magistrates and took an oath of allegiance from the settlers; the latter forced Stuyvesant to recognize English suzerainty over the English towns on Long Island (3 Mar. 1664) pending negotiations between England and the Netherlands.

1658, 31 MAY–1664, 16 MAY. INDIAN RELATIONS. Increasing hostility of the Hudson Valley Indians (beginning 1657) culminated in an attack on Wiltwyck, the village on the Esopus (7 June 1663). In 3 Dutch retaliatory expeditions (July, Sept., Oct.) 2 Indian forts were destroyed as well as most of their standing corn. On 16 May 1664 the Indians surrendered the whole of the Esopus Valley. Generally amicable relations with the Five Nations of the Iroquois, upon whom the Dutch were chiefly dependent for their furs, were marred by the activities of the *bosch loopers,* runners who intercepted Indians going to Ft. Orange to trade. Ordinances and prosecutions (June 1660) were instituted to end such illegal activities.

Establishment of English Rule

1661–64. CONQUEST OF NEW NETHERLAND. The English regarded the Dutch settlement as blocking westward expansion and interfering with the enforcement of the Navigation Acts through clandestine trade in tobacco. An open clash of national trading interests resulted from the chartering (1660) of "The Company of Royal Adventurers to Africa," with a monopoly of the African slave trade (reincorporated as the **Royal African Co.,** 1663; lost its monopoly, 1698). On 22 Mar. 1664 Charles II granted his brother, James, Duke of York, all of Maine between the St. Croix and Kennebec rivers and from the coast to the St. Lawrence, all islands between Cape Cod and the Narrows, and all land from the western boundary of Connecticut (Connecticut's claims west of the Connecticut River were recognized, 30 Nov. 1667) to the eastern shore of Delaware Bay, with power to govern, subject to the reservation that judicial appeals might be taken to the crown. On 2 Apr. the duke appointed Col. **Richard Nicolls** (1624–72) as chief of a commission to capture New Netherland and settle disputes in the New England colonies. A task force of 4 frigates reached New York Harbor (29 Aug.), and on 7 Sept. Stuyvesant, lacking support from the inhabitants, capitulated to Nicolls. Under the liberal surrender terms the Dutch were granted liberty of conscience, property and inheritance rights, and direct trade with Holland for 6 months (extended briefly, 1667; but canceled, 1668). Col.

George Cartwright, another commissioner, took the surrender of Ft. Orange without incident (20 Sept.) and the British assumed the place of the Dutch as allies of the Five Nations of the Iroquois (24 Sept.). But Delaware did not yield until Sir Robert Carr had stormed Ft. Casimir (10 Oct.).

1664, Oct.–1668, 21 Apr. ESTABLISHMENT OF ENGLISH RULE. Nicolls renamed New Amsterdam New York in honor of the Duke of York, but permitted the Dutch municipal officers to continue to function and even to name their own successors (2 Feb. 1665). Long Island, Staten Island, and Westchester were constituted as "Yorkshire," with three ridings (East, Suffolk Co.; West, Staten Island, Brooklyn, and northwest Queens; and North, Westchester and central Long Island). A meeting at Hempstead (11 Mar. 1665) of 34 deputies from 17 towns from Westchester and Long Island (13 English and 4 Dutch) approved the **Duke's Laws** (a compilation by **Matthias Nicolls**), which contained a civil and criminal code, based in part on New England codes, provided for the election of overseers and a constable in each town, set up a general provincial organization of the courts and the militia, and assured freedom of conscience. Initially, the code applied only to "Yorkshire," but it was later extended to the Delaware (21 Apr. 1668). In June, 1665, the offices of mayor, alderman, and sheriff in New York City, all appointed for 1 year by the governor, replaced the schout, burgomasters, and schepens. As a result of the **Second Anglo-Dutch War** (Dec. 1664–July 1667) Nicolls confiscated all property of the Dutch West India Co. (23 Feb. 1665) as well as the property of Dutch owners who had not taken the oath of allegiance to the British crown (10 Oct.). The **Peace of Breda** (21 July 1667) ending the war confirmed the English possession

of New Netherland. Pursuing the same general policy of conciliation, Nicolls' successor, Col. **Francis Lovelace** (1668–73), refrained from extending the Duke's Law to the predominantly Dutch areas of Kingston (Esopus, Wiltwyck), Albany, and Schenectady (settled 1661).

1673, 30 July–1674, 31 Oct. DUTCH REOCCUPATION OF NEW YORK. Following the outbreak of the **Third Anglo-Dutch War** (Mar. 1672), a Dutch fleet arrived at New York Harbor (7 Aug.), and after a brief exchange of fire (8 Aug.) the fort surrendered to the Dutch land force under Capt. **Anthony Clove,** designated governor general (12 Aug.). Esopus and Albany were speedily occupied (15 Aug.) and Dutch officials appointed for both the province and city of **New Orange** (New York, 17 Aug.). Western Long Island and settlements in New Jersey submitted, but the 5 towns of the East Riding (Suffolk) resisted. The province was restored to England by the **Treaty of Westminster** (19 Feb. 1674) and formally surrendered (10 Nov.) to **Sir Edmund Andros,** the deputy of the Duke of York to whom the province had been regranted by the king (9 July).

1674–87. STRUGGLE FOR REPRESENTATIVE GOVERNMENT. Andros confirmed the Duke's Laws, reappointed the previously ousted English officials, confirmed previous land grants, and secured the submission of towns on eastern Long Island which had claimed to be under Connecticut's jurisdiction. Despite popular demands for an assembly (as early as 1670), the duke (Jan. 1676) indicated his opposition on the ground that such a body would "prove destructive . . . to the peace of the government." By the "Bolting Act" (1678) New York City was given a monopoly on flour milling for export and its position was reaffirmed by Andros as the sole port of entry. Although exonerated of charges of illegal trading with the Dutch and corruption in office, Andros was supplanted by Col. **Thomas Dongan** (1634–1715), an Irish Catholic, who arrived in New York, 28 Aug. 1683. Pursuant to instructions from the duke he called a general assembly of delegates from each of the three ridings of Yorkshire and from New York and Harlem, Albany, Schenectady, Esopus, Martha's Vineyard, Nantucket, anad Pemaquid (eastern Maine), which proceeded to enact the **Charter of Liberties** (30 Oct. 1683), largely the work of the speaker, **Matthias Nicolls.** The charter, providing for a meeting at least once in 3 years of an assembly whose consent was necessary for the imposition of taxes, was approved by the duke, but after his accession as James II (6 Feb. 1685) he disallowed the legislation of the assembly (29 May 1686) and expressly empowered the royal governor to exercise full legislative as well as executive power in conjunction with the council. The assembly was dissolved (Jan. 1687), never to meet again. Dongan granted municipal charters to New York City and Albany (1683), taking the latter out of the hands of the patroon.

1689, 31 MAY–1691, 20 MAY. LEISLER'S REBELLION. Andros' commission as governor of the Dominion of New England included New York (7 Apr. 1687). His 42-man council appointed by the king included 8 New Yorkers (16 Apr.). Andros went to Boston (1 Oct.), leaving his lieutenant governor, Capt. **Francis Nicholson,** in charge of affairs. When news of the Boston rising and the outbreak of war between England and France reached New York (26–27 Apr. 1689), Suffolk, Queens, and Westchester ousted their officials and elected others in their place. Dongan, retired to Hempstead, was rumored to be the center of a Catholic plot, which included Nicholson as well. **Jacob Leisler** (1649–91) a trader who had come from Germany,

1660, in the employ of the Dutch West India Co., seized Ft. James (31 May 1689), and was left in control of the city when Nicholson fled (11 June). Leisler called upon representatives from counties and towns to join the government in New York (12 June), proclaimed William and Mary (22 June), and formed a Committee of Public Safety (26 June). Suffolk, Ulster, and Albany counties and a few isolated towns refused to participate in Leisler's first assembly (27 July–15 Aug.), and Albany elected its own officials (14 Oct.). A letter from William III's secretary of state addressed to Nicholson (20 July 1689), or "in his absence to such as for the time being take care for preserving the peace and administering the laws," was intercepted by Leisler and interpreted as applying to himself. The burning of Schenectady by a mixed force of French and Indians (9 Feb. 1690) impelled Albany to accept Leisler. Representatives from Massachusetts, Plymouth, Connecticut, and New York convened at Albany (1 May) voted to prosecute an invasion of Canada by 2 land forces (from New York and New England), and to dispatch a naval force up the St. Lawrence. The expedition proved a fiasco (summer 1690). Meantime, the Lords of Trade had recommended sending a new governor (31 Aug. 1689). Col. **Henry Sloughter** was commissioned (24 Nov.), but admiralty red tape and shipwreck delayed his arrival in the colony until 29 Mar. 1691. He was preceded by Maj. **Robert Ingoldesby,** who reached New York City with an English regiment (8 Feb.). Leisler refused Ingoldesby's request for the surrender of the fort on the ground that he lacked a royal commission as commander in chief or instructions from Sloughter to act as his deputy. Ingoldesby seized City Hall, and hostilities broke out (27 Mar.) just 2 days before the arrival of Sloughter. Leisler surrendered to Sloughter (30 Mar.). He was tried, along with 9 of his supporters (10–27 Apr. 1691), and with 7 others sentenced to death. Leisler and Jacob Milborne, his lieutenant, were hanged (26 May), while the 6 others were reprieved and eventually pardoned by the crown (15 Mar. 1694). Sloughter's commission had empowered him to call an assembly. Such a call was issued, 30 Mar. 1691, a date which marked the beginning of representative government in New York.

New Jersey

1664, 4 JULY–1665, 20 FEB. PROPRIETARY GRANT. The Duke of York granted to **John Lord Berkeley** and **Sir George Carteret** the region between the Hudson and Delaware rivers, bounded on the north by a line running from 41°N on the Hudson to the northernmost point of the Delaware. Technically, no governmental rights were conveyed, but the proprietors proceeded to issue their **Concessions and Agreements** (20 Feb. 1665), modeled on the Carolina Concessions, granting freedom of conscience, land on generous terms subject to quitrents, and the right of the freeholders to send deputies to a general assembly (first session 4 June 1668; last legal assembly until 1675 was held Nov. 1671). **Philip Carteret,** a distant relative of the proprietor (appointed governor 10 Feb. 1665), was accepted by the Dutch in the northern section (around present Bergen), but his authority was contested by English settlers under grants from Gov. Nicolls of New York.

1674–87. DEVOLUTION OF PROPRIETARY RIGHTS. Lord Berkeley sold his proprietary rights for £1,000 to **John Fenwick** (1618–83) and **Edward Byllinge,** fellow Quakers. On 8 Aug. 1674 the Duke of York then granted Sir George Carteret that part of New Jersey lying north of a line running from Barnegat Creek on the Atlantic to the mouth of Rankokus Kill on the Delaware. The province was divided (11 July 1676) between **East** and **West Jersey** by the **Quintipartite Deed** (between Carteret on one hand and Byllinge, William Penn, and two other Quakers on the other). The duke recognized the new proprietors of West Jersey, but substituted as a boundary between the two sections a line running from Little Egg Harbor (in the Barnegat region) to the northernmost branch of the Delaware (16 Aug. 1680). After Byllinge's death (1685) his heirs sold his share to Dr. **Daniel Coxe** of London. On the death of Sir George Carteret (1680), the trustee for his heir sold his rights in East Jersey (1 Feb. 1681) to William Penn and 11 associates, for the most part highly connected Quakers (who enlarged their numbers, 1682, to 24; confirmed by the duke, 14 Mar. 1683).

1674–88 GOVERNMENT OF EAST JERSEY. Philip Carteret, recommissioned governor (13 June 1674), resumed his post in the colony, but his authority was challenged by Gov. Andros of New York, who insisted on collecting duties on goods entering Jersey ports (5 Apr. 1679). Carteret was seized (30 Apr. 1680), tried in New York for illegally exercising governmental powers, but acquitted by a jury (May). Undeterred, Andros attended a session of the East Jersey assembly (2 June), which he dissolved when it refused to do his bidding, and continued in the exercise of executive powers (July–Aug.). Although Dongan's commission did not give him jurisdiction over East Jersey, he banned Jersey vessels from the Hudson (Aug. 1686) and proposed to the home authorities that the province be annexed to New York (19 Feb. 1688). James II had writs of quo warranto issued against the Jersey proprietors and secured the surrender of both Jersey charters (Mar.

1688), incorporating the area in the Dominion of New England. In the fall of 1692 the proprietors resumed control. **Andrew Hamilton,** a Scot, served as governor until his death (Apr. 1703), save for a period in 1698 when Jeremiah Basse, one of the proprietors, acted in that capacity.

1675–1701. GOVERNMENT OF WEST JERSEY. The first English settlement in the western portion of the province was established by Fenwick at Salem (1675). On charges of illegally assuming governmental functions Fenwick was arrested (8 Nov. 1676), brought to New York (Jan. 1677), fined £40, and released on parole. Despite warnings to desist (3 June 1678) he attempted to function as governor until Andros appointed his own officials (26 Oct.). Fenwick continued to make land grants until he had deeded most of his holdings to William Penn (1 Mar. 1682). On 13 Mar. 1677 the 4 proprietors of West Jersey issued the **Laws, Concessions, and Agreements,** largely the work of William Penn, providing for liberty of conscience, civil rights including trial by jury, and no taxation save with the consent of the representatives of the voters (proprietors, freeholders, and inhabitants). Byllinge, designated governor (1680), dispatched Samuel Jennings to serve as his deputy. The assembly, with its first session, 1681, continued to meet at **Burlington** until 1701. In 1683 that body challenged the proprietors' right to govern and chose Jennings as governor and its own councilors. On Byllinge's death Daniel Coxe, who had purchased his rights, including the title of hereditary governor, proceeded to function through deputies. Coxe sold his interest (1692) to a group of 48 (West Jersey Society, largely Anglicans).

1701–38. NEW JERSEY AS ROYAL PROVINCE. In 1701 the Board of Trade recommended that the crown resume control of private colonies. On 26 Apr. 1702 the proprietors of both Jerseys surrendered governmental authority to the crown. Until 1738 the governor of New York was also governor of New Jersey, but under a separate commission. Thereafter, beginning with **Lewis Morris** (1671–1746), New Jersey had its own royal governor. Despite the loss of governmental rights the proprietors retained their property interest. A Board of Proprietors of East Jersey (est. 1684, headquarters Perth Amboy) and a similar organization for West Jersey (est. 1688, headquarters Burlington) have continued in existence to the present day.

Pennsylvania

1680, 1 JUNE–1682, AUG. GRANTS TO PENN. William Penn (p. 1125), son of Admiral Sir William Penn, who had joined the Society of Friends, studied in France, then at Lincoln's Inn, received a charter from Charles II on 14 Mar. 1681, possibly in lieu of his father's claim against the exchequer for £16,000. Under its terms he was made absolute proprietor of an area between 43°N and 40°N, running west from the Delaware through five degrees in longitude. The ambiguity of the description left the lower Delaware undecided. The charter included specific limitations on his governmental powers: (1) laws had to receive the approval of an assembly; (2) the Navigation Acts were to be obeyed; (3) the Privy Council had the right to disallow all legislation within five years after passage; (4) the crown reserved the right to hear appeals from the courts of the province; (5) an ambiguous clause recognized the right of the king to impose taxes "by act of Parliament," an issue which remained academic until 1765.

1682–1704. PENN TAKES OVER DELAWARE. On 24 Aug. 1682 a grant to Penn of the region on the western shore of Delaware Bay, from New Castle to Cape Henlopen, was made by the Duke of York, who in fact lacked legal title to the area. These grants contained no rights of government. Hence, Penn's control over Delaware was of dubious legality. By the Charter of 1701 Delaware was empowered to have a government separate from Pennsylvania. On 22 Nov. 1704 the first independent assembly met at New Castle. Down to the Revolution both provinces were under the same governor, save that the king had to approve for Delaware.

1682–88. EARLY CONSTITUTIONAL DEVELOPMENTS IN PENNSYLVANIA. Penn's **Frame of Government** (5 May 1682) provided for a governor (proprietor or his deputy), council (in which proprietor had a treble vote; 72 members, later reduced to 18; one third elected each year), and assembly (200–500 members; reduced in 1683 to 32), elected by the freeholders. The council was to initiate laws, act in an administrative and judicial capacity, and try officials impeached by the assembly, which could merely ratify or reject legislation. The assembly's right to initiate legislation was recognized in 1696. The right to amend and alter (exercised by 1688) was the subject of controversy for many years. William Markham, dispatched (10 Apr. 1681) to inform the inhabitants (c.500 Dutch and Swedes) of the Penn proprietorship, was succeeded by 4 commissioners (Sept. 1681), and, in turn, by Thomas Holme, who (early 1682) laid out the site for Philadelphia. Penn arrived on the Delaware (27 Oct. 1682), received the territory from the Duke of York's agent (28 Oct.), and proclaimed in assembly (2 Nov.) that the Duke's Laws were to be in force until the people decided otherwise. At Upland Penn called a general court (8 Nov.) to consist of representatives from 6 counties (3 from present

Pennsylvania; 3 from present Delaware). The assembly (17 Dec. 1682) passed a declaration of liberty of conscience and placed the 3 lower counties under one administration. A new **Frame of Government,** reducing the size of council and assembly, was approved by a second assembly (12 Apr. 1683). Penn returned to England (16 Aug. 1684) to defend his southern boundary against Lord Baltimore, governing by deputy in his absence.

1682–83. EARLY SETTLEMENT. As the result of extensively publicizing his colonial venture in the British Isles, Holland, and Germany, immigration was sizable from the start. The first large contingent, Welshmen, arrived 13 Aug. 1682, settling on lands purchased from the Indians north and west of Philadelphia. Quakers from the Rhineland and lower Palatinate settled Germantown (fall, 1683), and groups of Irish and English Quakers established scattered settlements. Land grants were carelessly made; title quarrels were common. It remained for Penn's second son, **Thomas** (1702–75), on his arrival in the province, 1732, to organize the land system and straighten out the claims.

1688–94. GLORIOUS REVOLUTION IN PENNSYLVANIA. Because of the friendship between Penn and James II and the passive stand of the Pennsylvania Quakers toward participating in the war against France, the crown appointed Gov. Benjamin Fletcher of New York as governor of Pennsylvania (18 Mar. 1692). **Royal rule** lasted until 20 Aug. 1694, when the proprietary government was restored. Penn returned to the colony as a resident governor (1699).

1701, 8 Nov. CHARTER OF LIBERTIES, granted by Penn, remained the constitution of Pennsylvania down to the Revolution. Under its terms the legislature became **unicameral,** laws being passed by the governor with the consent of the assembly alone. Except in the appointment of a governor, proprietary rule, from a political point of view, virtually ceased. Penn returned to England (1701), leaving **James Logan** (1674–1751) as his agent. All but ruined by the chicanery of Philip Ford, a steward, Penn landed in the Fleet for debt, and had to mortgage the province to trustees (1708).

Settlement of Florida, the Carolinas, and Georgia

Early Spanish Colonizing Efforts

1521. PONCE DE LEÓN'S ATTEMPT. After a previous exploration of the Florida coast (1513, pp. 24–25), Ponce de León received a patent from the crown of Spain (27 Sept. 1514) to settle the "islands of Bimini and Florida." Sailing from Puerto Rico (20 Feb.) with 200 men, he landed, probably at Charlotte Harbor, where he was attacked by the natives, wounded, and forced to withdraw to Cuba, dying in May or June.

1526–27. DE AYLLÓN'S ATTEMPT. Lucas Vásquez de Ayllón received a patent similar to de León's (12 June 1523), sailed from Hispaniola (July 1526) with some 500 settlers for the Cape Fear region, whence he coasted south probably to the Pedee River to establish a settlement. He died shortly thereafter (18 Oct.) and the remnant of 150 who survived a difficult winter (1526–27) abandoned the site and returned to Hispaniola.

1528. NARVÁEZ EXPEDITION (p. 26).

1539. DE SOTO IN FLORIDA. Under a grant to settle the entire region north of the Gulf of Mexico, Hernando de Soto landed at Tampa Bay (May), and headed north (1 Aug.) for his long march into the interior (pp. 26–27).

1549. PIONEER MISSIONARY EFFORT. Fray Luis Cancer de Babastro, a Dominican, who had seen service in Guatemala (1535–38, 1542–46), sailed from Vera Cruz (spring) to convert the Florida Indians, coasted northward from Tampa Bay, then returned to that region where he was killed by the natives (26 June).

1558–61. SETTLEMENT FAILURES. In quest of Spanish treasure in the holds of ships wrecked along the Florida coast as well as for the conversion of the natives, **Don Tristán de Luna y Arellano** sailed from Vera Cruz (11 June 1559) with a party of 1,500 colonists with the immediate objectives of settling at Santa Elena and on the Gulf. Entering Pensacola Bay (14 Aug.), they failed to establish a permanent foothold, but explored the interior (northwest Alabama). Command passed to **Angel de Villafañe,** who made an unsuccessful voyage, possibly as far north as Cape Hatteras (27 May–9 July 1561) to establish a settlement. The entire project was abandoned that year. On 23 Sept. Philip II issued a cedula barring further colonizing efforts in Florida.

Struggle Between France and Spain for Control

1562–65. EARLY FRENCH ATTEMPTS AT SETTLEMENT. Gaspard de Coligny, Admiral of France, who had previously sent an unsuccessful expedition to Brazil (1555), dispatched 5 ships (16 Feb. 1562) under **Jean Ribaut** of

Dieppe to establish a Huguenot colony. Landing on the north Florida coast (30 Apr.), they settled in present South Carolina at Santa Elena, whose name they changed to **Port Royal**. Failing to receive supplies, the colonists abandoned settlement early in 1564. A second expedition of Huguenots under **René de Laudonnière** was established at Ft. Caroline (1564) near the mouth of the St. Johns River (commanding the homeward route of the Spanish treasure ships) and was reinforced by supplies and settlers brought by Ribaut (spring 1565).

1565–67. FOUNDING OF ST. AUGUSTINE AND OUSTING OF THE FRENCH. The new French threat impelled Spain to reverse its policy toward Florida and to dispatch **Pedro Menéndez de Avilés** (20 Mar. 1565) both to settle Florida and to expel the French. Sailing from Cádiz (28 July 1565) with a party of 1,500, he arrived at St. Augustine Harbor (28 Aug.), which he named, inspected the approaches to the St. Johns River (4 Sept.), returned to St. Augustine, where he disembarked the colonists (7–8 Sept.). To destroy the Spanish colony Ribaut left 240 men at Ft. Caroline and sailed (10 Sept.) with the major part of his force for St. Augustine, but a storm (13 Sept.) wrecked his fleet. Menéndez countered with a march to Ft. Caroline (17–19 Sept.), which he captured (20 Sept.), killing 132 French defenders in the first hour of the attack and massacring those taken prisoner save for a few who managed to escape to some French vessels anchored in the river. Renaming the fort San Mateo, Menéndez established a garrison, hunted down French survivors of the Ribaut expedition, set up forts on the Indian River (Nov.; removed to Santa Lucia, Feb. or early Mar. 1566) and at Santa Elena (San Felipe, Apr. 1566) and blockhouses at San Pedro and at the headwaters of the Broad River, as well as posts on the west coast at San Antonio (Charlotte Harbor, 1566) and Tocobago (Tampa Bay, 1567) and to the south at Tegesta near Miami (early 1567).

1567, 22 Aug.–1568, 2 June. FRENCH RETALIATION. Dominique de Gourgues sailed to the West Indies from France with 3 vessels (crew of 80 and 100 arquebusiers), finally landed on an island near San Mateo (c.Apr. 1568), enlisted Indian aid, marched on 2 blockhouses at the mouth of the St. Johns, which he captured (12 Apr.), then advanced upon San Mateo, which fell to him (16 Apr.), and massacred his prisoners, taking similar revenge on crews from captured Spanish vessels (6 June).

1566–72. JESUIT ACTIVITIES. Efforts of the Jesuits at converting the Florida Indians were launched (1566–68). Under **Fray Batista Segura** another group of Jesuits sailed from Santa Elena (5 Aug. 1570) to Axacan (Chesapeake Bay region), where all were murdered (in present Virginia, 14–18 Feb. 1571). As a result, all Jesuits were removed from Florida by the summer of 1572.

1576–81. FURTHER INDIAN AND FRENCH CONFLICTS. Indian unrest following the death of Avilés (1574) forced abandonment of the garrisons on the west coast of Florida, including San Felipe. **Pedro Menéndez Marqués,** acting governor, rebuilt the fort at Santa Elena (July 1577), burned a large Indian village (Cocopay, c.Apr. 1578), taking many captives, whom he traded for 12 Frenchmen previously captured by the Indians. In addition, French corsairs, including Nicolas Estrozi, were captured and killed (by early 1580). In a naval battle with a French force under **Gilberto Gil** at San Mateo (17 July), Marqués was the victor and Gil was killed. Another Indian uprising (4 Oct.) was quelled (by Jan. 1581).

1586, June–July. SIR FRANCIS DRAKE attacked and destroyed the fort and other buildings at St. Augustine and looted the settlement at Santa Elena.

Development of Spanish Florida

1577–1655. SPANISH MISSIONARY EFFORTS. Franciscan missionary activity under **Fray Alonso de Reynoso**, with the support of the crown, was attempted (1577–92) with conspicuous success. A more intensive effort was begun under **Fray Juan de Silva** (23 Sept. 1595) with the establishment of mission provinces: Timucua (north-central Florida), Apalachee (northwest Florida), Guale (Georgia coast), Orista (South Carolina coast), and Tama (interior Georgia). Despite Indian hostility in the Guale district 1,500 natives were converted (1595–96) and chapels were erected at San Pedro (Cumberland Island), Santiago de Ocone (Jekyll Island), Asao (St. Simon's Island), Tolomato (on the mainland above the mouth of the Altamaha River), and Tupique (north of Tolomato). As a result of attacks by the Guale Indians (1597–1600), all missions north of Saint Augustine were abandoned except Santa Elena. A punitive expedition out of St. Augustine (10 Oct.) destroyed Indian villages and supplies and forced the Indians to sue for peace (spring 1600). Thereafter (1603–06) Franciscan missions were established at San Juan and Santa Maria (below the St. Marys River), at San Pedro, Macoma, Talaxe (south bank of the Altamaha), and at Santa Catalina de Guale (on St. Catherine Island). In the period 1606–80 a chain of missions were pushed northward along the coast to Chatuache (Satuache, between the Combahee and Edisto rivers, by 1650), with subsequent activity among the Tamali (in the area between the junction of the Ocmulgee and Oconee rivers and the Guale, 1680). A second line of advance went west from St. Augustine across the northern neck of the Florida peninsula. Itinerant missionaries were active in Potano (1606–07), east of the Ocilla River, and at Apalachee (Oct. 1633), where (by 1655) 9 missions were established. Activity spread westward to the Chatot country around the Apalachicola River, where two missions (San Carlos de los Chacatos and San Nicolas de Tolentino) were established by 1674. Despite an Indian uprising (1647) 38 missions were established and some 26,000 Indians at least partly converted by 1655.

English in the Carolinas

1629–39. EARLY PATENTS. In 1629 Sir **Robert Heath** was granted a patent to settle the area between 31° and 36°N ("New Carolana"). On the basis of a conveyance from Heath (1630), **Samuel Vassal** and others made ineffectual efforts to explore and settle the area. In 1632 **Henry Lord Maltravers** is reputed to have been granted the "province of Carolana" by Heath, and by the Harvey Patent (1638), issued by Governor Sir John Harvey of Virginia, laid claim to land south of the James River to be called Norfolk County. But in neither area did did he effect a settlement.

1653–54. ALBEMARLE COLONY. Settlers from Virginia began to move across the Nansemond Valley and the Dismal Swamp into present North Carolina, settling (by 1653) north of Albemarle Sound between the Chowan River and the sea. This movement was encouraged by the Virginia assembly for the protection of its southern frontier with offers of land grants to the first settlers between the Chowan and Roanoke rivers (July) and by the expenditures of 2 Virginians, Francis and Argall Yeardley.

1655. FALL OF JAMAICA to England encouraged the belief that the Spaniards could be ousted from North

America and promoted English expansion along the southern frontier.

c.1660–63. CAPE FEAR COLONY. A group of New Englanders in association with London merchants organized the Cape Fear Co. and sent settlers from New England to the region around the Cape Fear River (c.1662), but the settlement was abandoned before the fall of 1663.

1663, 3 Apr.–1665, 10 July. CHARTERS OF THE CAROLINAS. As a result of a project formulated by Sir John Colleton, a Barbadian planter, Sir William Berkeley, former governor of Virginia, and **Sir Anthony Ashley Cooper** (later, 1672, **Earl of Shaftesbury**), an outstanding colonial promoter, Charles II granted to 8 proprietors—the 3 aforementioned prime movers as well as such high-ranking personages as the **Earl of Clarendon** (the king's chief minister), the **Duke of Albemarle** (General Monck), **John Lord Berkeley** (brother of Sir William and a high-ranking naval officer), the **Earl of Craven,** and **Sir George Carteret**—the area lying between 31° and 36°N and extending westward to the "south seas." Maltravers' heir, the Duke of Norfolk, and Samuel Vassal both countered by filing claims to this territory (10 June) and the Cape Fear Co. likewise challenged the validity of the charter (6 Aug.). However, the Privy Council declared all previous patents void (22 Aug. 1665), but claims continued to be urged until 1768, when the descendants of Daniel Coxe of New Jersey, to whom the Heath patent had been transferred in 1696, received from the crown a grant of 100,000 acres in New York in satisfaction of their claim. By a second charter (10 July 1665) the bounds were extended to include the northern end of Currituck Inlet (31° 30′N) and pushed south to 29°N to include the entire settled part of Florida.

1663, 23 May–1665. PRELUDE TO SETTLEMENT. From their first meeting the proprietors sought to promote settlement from New England and Barbados (considered overpopulated) and were encouraged by the favorable report (6 Feb. 1664) from Capt. William Hilton, who had recently explored the area. Sir William Berkeley, authorized to name a governor for the Chowan River settlement, designated (Oct. 1664) William Drummond as governor of the province of **Albemarle** (later North Carolina). For the government of the entire chartered area the proprietors drew up the **Concessions and Agreements** (1665)—the same as those adopted by Berkeley and Carteret for New Jersey 6 weeks later—granting freedom of conscience, generous terms of land distribution subject to a quitrent (½d. per acre), and an assembly of freeholders' representatives.

1669–70. FUNDAMENTAL CONSTITUTIONS. To supplant the inadequate Concessions and Agreements the proprietors issued (11 Mar. 1669) the Fundamental Constitutions, generally attributed to **John Locke** in collaboration with Sir Anthony Ashley Cooper. This elaborate scheme of government blended advanced concepts with an artificially contrived aristocratic society. Religious freedom was guaranteed, but, under the revision of 1 Mar. 1670, the Church of England was established. A popular, as opposed to a standing, army was authorized. At the apex of Carolina society was a hereditary nobility: the **proprietors** (each with a seignory of 12,000 acres in each county); next came the **landgraves** (with 4 baronies apiece, 48,000 acres in all), followed by the **caciques** (Spanish for Indian chief, 2 baronies, 24,000 acres). Below them stood **lords of manors** (3,000 to 12,000 acres) and **freeholders** (with 50-acre minimum requirement for voting). Land and rank were synonymous; the loss of one meant the loss of the other. The 8 proprietors in England constituted a **Palatine Court** which appointed the governor, disallowed laws, and heard appeals from the colony. The provincial assembly was to comprise the governor, hereditary nobility, and the deputies (holders of 500-acre freeholds), but ultimately that body became bicameral (by 1693). The governor's council came to be called the Grand Council. In all, 26 landgraves and 13 caciques were created. In a few cases the title descended to the second and third generations; in most they expired with the original holder. In fact, no seignory or barony above 12,000 acres was ever set up and no manors erected. The proprietors revised the Fundamental Constitutions (12 Jan. 1682); declared inoperative (1693); again revised in abridged form (1698); but they were never accepted by the assembly.

1669–80. FOUNDING OF CHARLESTON. A party of settlers under Joseph West left England (Aug. 1669), and finally settled at Port Royal Sound (by the end of Mar. 1670). Fear of the Spaniards caused them to move north to the Ashley, where at Albemarle Point their first settlement (Charles Town) was established (Apr. 1670, later called Old Charles Town). Subsequently (1680) this settlement was relocated at the junction of the Ashley and Cooper rivers, present site of Charleston.

1670, 18 JULY. TREATY OF MADRID between England and Spain, temporarily recognizing the principle of effective occupation in the New World, served as a basis for future boundary discussions involving the Carolina-Florida border area.

1671–74. EARLY GROWTH AND FACTIONALISM. As a result of arrivals from Barbados (including Sir John Yeamans), England, and New York the population of Charles Town colony was

close to 400 (by 1672). The first governor, William Sayle, was succeeded on his death (4 Mar. 1671) by Joseph West, who summoned the first assembly (25 Aug.). On 14 Dec. Sir John Yeamans claimed the right as sole landgrave resident in the province to be governor in place of West, a cacique whom he outranked. Yeamans, commissioned, reached the province Apr. 1672. He was supplanted by West (1674).

1671–83. INDIAN TRADE AND CONFLICT. A war against the Coosa, a tribe in the vicinity of Charles Town, who were believed to be conspiring with the Spaniards, resulted in their complete defeat (1671). Numerous captives were enslaved, marking the beginning of the experiment with Indian slavery. In May 1674 Dr. Henry Woodward was commissioned Indian agent to open trade with the Westos east of the lower Savannah in furs, deer hides, and slaves. Trade was also opened with the Kiowa to the north. A **Westo** uprising (Apr. 1680) was smashed by the end of that year and the natives along the Savannah persuaded to cooperate in trade with the western tribes.

1677–80. CULPEPER'S REBELLION. In protest against the arbitrary acts of Gov. John Jenkins at Albemarle, Thomas Miller, a leader of the "proprietary faction," undertook to combine the functions of governor and customs collector. The antiproprietary party set up a revolutionary government (3 Dec. 1677), and imprisoned Miller, who escaped to England and laid his case before the Privy Council. The rebels were defended before the proprietors by one of their leaders, **John Culpeper.** Through the conciliatory influence of Shaftesbury the proprietors decided that Miller had exceeded his authority and Culpeper, who was tried for treason before the king's bench, was acquitted.

1679, 10 OCT. An act passed in Virginia prohibiting the importation of Carolina tobacco made Carolinians increasingly dependent upon Massachusetts and Rhode Island sea captains and traders who carried their tobacco to New England and reshipped it to Europe in evasion of the Navigation Acts.

1682–86. PORT ROYAL COLONY. Under a patent from the Carolina proprietors (1682) a settlement of Scotsmen under Henry Erskine, Lord Cardross, was established (fall of 1684) at Port Royal on a site named Stuart's Town, despite the hostility of the Spaniards, who viewed this incursion as violating the Treaty of Madrid, and the antagonism of Charleston settlers, unwilling to divide their lucrative Indian trade with the Scotch Covenanters. As a result of the Westo War (1680) the Spanish authorities withdrew from their most northerly missions and sought to pull back their Indian allies. Rather than move south the Yamassees sought refuge among the English and Scots (the first Yamassee refugees arrived at Stuart's Town, Feb. 1685) and settled on former Westo lands. The Charleston authorities, who had ordered the arrest of Lord Cardross (5 May 1685) because of his refusal to submit to their control, now failed to heed appeals from Stuart's Town for aid against impending Spanish attack. The Spaniards, threatened in Guale, which they finally abandoned (1684–85), and outflanked by Carolina traders (who had reached the Lower Creeks on the middle Chatahoochee River by 1685), had previously erected a new mission at the junction of the Flint and Chatahoochee (1681) and engaged in raiding coastal settlements in southern Carolina. Stuart's Town was completely destroyed (Sept. 1686). Only a storm saved Charleston.

1683–96. POLITICAL UNREST IN THE CAROLINAS. The colonists of Berkeley Co. (Charleston area) rejected the revised Fundamental Constitutions of 1682. On orders from the proprietors Gov. Joseph Morton dissolved the assembly (20 Sept. 1685) and Gov. James Colleton (arrived Feb. 1687) refused to call an assembly (on orders, 1689). Under constant threat of Spanish invasion the colonists in this area made common cause with the corsairs who preyed on Spanish shipping, and juries acquitted those charged with violating the Navigation Acts. In the north Albemarle ousted (1689) its governor, Seth Southel (arrived c.1683), who went to Charleston and proceeded to oust Colleton, take over the government (Oct. 1690), and call an assembly. In Nov. 1691 he was suspended by the Palatine Court and charged with high treason. His death (1694) ended the controversy. The next three governors (Philip Ludwell, 1691–93; Thomas Smith, 1693–94; and John Archdale, 1694–96) attempted to restore harmony.

1706–29. SOUTH CAROLINA AS A ROYAL COLONY. After 1706 proprietary control steadily weakened, accentuated by the crises of the French and Spanish attack (1706) and the Yamassee War (p. 75). In Nov. 1719 the colonists set up a revolutionary government, ousted the last proprietary governor, Robert Johnson, and replaced him with James Moore as temporary governor. The crown then appointed **Francis Nicholson** (1655–1728), who had been governor or deputy governor of 3 other colonies (proclaimed 29 May 1721), thus formally incorporating South Carolina as a **royal colony.** The proprietary charter was surrendered (1729), and 7 out of the 8 proprietors sold their claims for £2,500 apiece. The eighth, Lord Carteret, exchanged his portion (1743) for a tract south of Virginia's southern boundary, which he retained until the Revolution.

1691–1729. NORTH CAROLINA AS A ROYAL COLONY. Albemarle, known after 1691 as North Carolina and governed by a deputy, was torn by sectionalism and unrest. The passage of the Vestry Act (1701), making the Church of England the established church, aroused intense opposition on the part

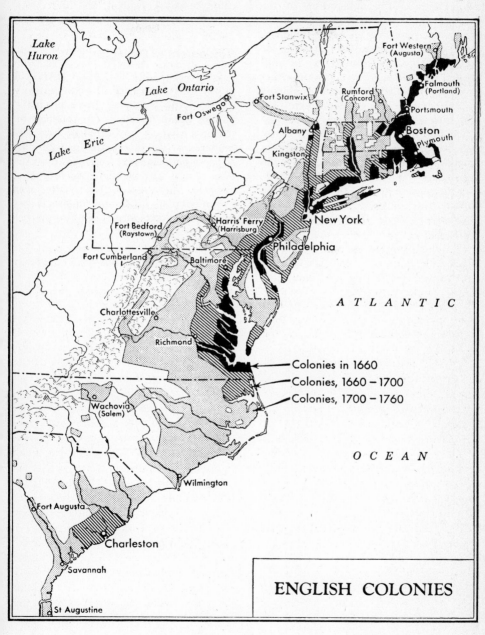

Colonies in 1660
Colonies, 1660 – 1700
Colonies, 1700 – 1760

ENGLISH COLONIES

of the Quakers and other dissenters. Though disallowed, a second Vestry Act (1704) was passed. In attempting to enforce the act, **Thomas Cary,** deputy governor, aroused the antagonism of the Quakers (now barred from office by a related act imposing an oath), who obtained from the proprietors an order for his removal. Cary refused to be supplanted by William Glover, chosen acting governor, rebelled, and was convicted of high crimes and misdemeanors. Escaping to Virginia, Cary was seized, dispatched to England, but allowed to return home. The crisis in the northern colony was further intensified by the **Tuscarora War** (1711–12), in which, after the massacre of 200 settlers, the Indians were defeated with the aid of Virginia and South Carolina. Remnants of the Tuscaroras removed to New York and joined the Iroquois as a sixth nation. In 1712 a separate governor was set up for North Carolina, with **Edward Hyde** the first incumbent. North Carolina became a **royal colony,** 25 July 1729, with the formal surrender of the charter.

Settlement of Georgia

20 JUNE 1732. ROYAL CHARTER granted to trustees for 21 years territory south of the Savannah River originally part of South Carolina, but retained by the crown when the Carolinas were surrendered by the proprietors in 1729, plus a one-eighth interest retained by Carteret at time of surrender, which he conveyed to the trustees. The charter was surrendered in 1752, when Georgia became a royal province. (See also p. 76.)

THE COLONIES AND THE EMPIRE, 1624-1775

It seemed an extraordinary paradox that the first British Empire, hailed by Englishmen both in the mother country and in the American colonies as a palladium of liberty, should have been dissolved in the acid bath of revolution. In an age of enlightened monarchs England was the only nation whose monarchy rested on a firm constitutional base, the only one where there seemed to be an effective check upon royal absolutism, the only one which had a functioning representative government in which monarchical, aristocratic, and democratic roles were blended.

The plan of government by which England ruled her empire had evolved empirically and unsystematically. Parliament always exercised some role in colonial rule, but during the century following 1660, that body confined its interest in the colonies largely to trade regulation, and refrained from imposing direct taxes on the colonists. With the Restoration the crown had assumed the main burdens of administering an empire numbering by the middle of the eighteenth century thirty-one colonies, extending from Hudson Bay to Borneo, from the Honduran logwood coast to the Bay of Bengal, acquired in bits and pieces over 150 years. Different mechanisms were improvised to meet special governmental problems as they arose, but by the middle of the eighteenth century a clear trend toward the setting up of royal provinces had emerged, colony after colony having been brought under the direct control of the crown, with a considerable measure of centralization achieved by 1696, when the Board of Trade was established. Authority over the colonies was divided among other departments and agencies as well, while the Privy Council reviewed legislation from the colonies and acted as the highest court of appeals for colonial lawsuits. The royal governors' authority came to be increasingly impaired by the colonial assemblies, which voted taxes, paid out or withheld salaries, and had by the middle of the eighteenth century exercised in fact much of the appointing power which the royal governor in theory possessed. The Second Hundred Years' War, waged between England and France, 1689–1763, eliminated France as a power in the New World and caused Great Britain to reshape her imperial policy, laying as much stress on strategic and military considerations as on direct benefits, while at the same time the expulsion of the French from North America liberated the colonists from fear of foreign aggression and loosened their sense of dependency upon the mother country.

Centralized Administration

1624, 24 MAY. REVOCATION OF VIRGINIA CO. CHARTER, making Virginia a royal colony (p. 32).

1634, 28 APR.–1641, AUG. LAUD COMMISSION. Under James I the Privy Council rather than Parliament had exercised control over trade and colonies. A Commission of Trade set up by Charles I (1625), subordinate to the Privy Council, considered the Gorges patent, and a special committee on New England Plantations (1632) served temporarily. On 28 Apr. 1634 there was set up as a subdivision of the Privy Council the **Commission for Foreign Plantations** ("Laud Commission" after its chairman, the primate, William Laud). Despite its broad powers, its 7 years of activity were marked by few achievements. Most supervisory activities were carried on by special Privy Council committees or occasional outside groups.

1643–59. PARLIAMENTARY COMMISSION FOR PLANTATIONS, comprising 18 members, assumed the functions of the Privy Council in colonial affairs. Save for the appointment of one governor, Sir Thomas Warner, for the Caribbean islands (1643) and the granting of the charter of Providence Plantations (1644), it was virtually inactive, and its functions assumed by the **Council of State** (14 Feb. 1649), which set up a standing committee to handle trade (17 Dec. 1651) and plantations (4 May 1652). The **Protector's Council** (16 Dec. 1653) directed plantation affairs, assisted by the Committee for Foreign Plantations (10 May 1655) and the Committee for America (15 July 1656). It was replaced by the **Council of State** (May 1659).

1660, 4 JULY–1695, 15 MAY. LORDS OF TRADE. The king in council appointed a Committee for Trade and Plantations of the Privy Council (Lords of Trade) to report to the council as a whole. A Council of Trade (7 Nov.) and a Council for Foreign Plantations (1 Dec.) were also subordinate to the Privy Council. When they ceased to function (1665), the Privy Council reappointed its own plantation committee (7 Dec. 1666), and on 31 Jan. 1668 a new standing committee was created similar to the Lords of Trade of 1660. It was assisted (1668) by a special Council of Trade and Plantations combining the functions of the two councils of 1660. These functions were again separated upon the revival (20 July 1670) of the **Council for Foreign Plantations,** but after considerable activity its commission was withdrawn (1674) and its functions assigned to the Lords of Trade (1675).

1696–1782. THE BOARD OF TRADE, commissioned by William III, comprised 15 members (7 high officials including Privy Councilors, 8 paid members, including a first Lord of Trade, president of the board), was empowered to supervise (1) trade and the fisheries, (2) care of the poor, (3) plantation affairs, (4) recommend appointments of colonial officials, and (5) review colonial legislation and report to the Privy Council. Its first 20 years were marked by exceptional activity, although its powers were curbed as early as 1704 when the Secretary of State for the Southern Dept. assumed the right to appoint governors (1704). With the accession of George I and the ascendancy of Newcastle the board declined, reaching its nadir during the presidency of Baron Monson (1737–48). It was revived under **George Mon-**

tagu Dunk, Earl of Halifax (11 Nov. 1748). Under an order in council (11 Mar. 1752) nominations to colonial offices were to be made by the board and transmitted (in the case of high officials) to the Privy Council or (in the case of lesser ones) to the Secretary of State. Nevertheless, the Seven Years' War marked a renewed decline of the board's activity. With Halifax's resignation (Mar. 1761) the board soon lost its right of nomination (22 May). The board's powers were subsequently curtailed by an order in council (8 Aug. 1766), and correspondence was henceforth channeled through the Secretary of State. With the appointment of Hillsborough as both Secretary of State and president of the Board of Trade (20 Jan. 1768), both offices were held by the same person until 1782.

1673–76. THE TREASURY BOARD'S colonial functions were greatly expanded as a result of the Navigation Laws (particularly the Act of 1673). Immediately subordinate to that body were the **commissioners of customs** with jurisdiction over the collectors, searchers, and surveyors of customs in the colonies. Naval officers to enter and clear vessels were appointed (as early as 1676 for Jamaica) to enforce the Acts of Trade, eventually 6 for each colony.

1697. ESTABLISHMENT OF VICE-ADMIRALTY COURTS. Under the Navigation Act of 1696 the Privy Council directed the Board of Trade to establish vice-admiralty courts in the colonies. Acting under commission the governors of New York, Massachusetts, Maryland, Pennsylvania, and Virginia designated judges and other officers of such courts. The vice-admiralty courts had jurisdiction over the Acts of Trade and ordinary maritime cases as well as prize (by act of 1708). In addition, the act of 1722 conferred jurisdiction over infringements on conserving timber—"broad-arrow pol-

icy" (p. 699). At first appeals lay to the High Court of Admiralty; after 1748 it shared appellate jurisdiction with the Privy Council, which assumed sole appellate jurisdiction (11 July 1766). But the new admiralty courts set up under the Townshend Acts (1767, p. 90) centered final control in America.

ROYAL DISALLOWANCE. The Board of Trade reviewed colonial legislation and made recommendations for disallowance where laws conflicted with imperial policy, were prejudicial to trade, or were in conflict with the law of England. Out of 8,563 acts submitted by the continental colonies (not including Pennsylvania prior to 1700 nor Maryland, 1691–1715), 469 were disallowed, with the highest percentage from Pennsylvania, 15.5 (E. B. Russell). Its application was more general in the first 2 decades (beginning 1691) than at any later time. The existence of such machinery of review undoubtedly affected the course of later legislation and prompted colonial evasion by passage of temporary acts.

1696–1783. JUDICIAL APPEALS TO THE PRIVY COUNCIL were taken from all the colonies in some 1,500 cases. Civil cases were chiefly taken from Rhode Island, Virginia, and Massachusetts (among the continental colonies); criminal appeals were largely restricted to the early years (chiefly from Barbados); and Chancery appeals to the British West Indies.

THE ROYAL GOVERNOR, chief representative of the crown in the royal colonies and executive head of the provincial government, was guided by **instructions** generally formulated by the Board of Trade and transmitted by the Secretary of State for the Southern Dept. His authority came in the course of time to be undermined both by the home government and by the colonial assemblies. By the middle of the 18th century the Secretary of State came to appoint an increasing number of provincial officials, including the naval officer responsible for enforcement of the Navigation Acts. In the conflict with the assemblies the governors gradually lost control over expenditures. The New York assembly forced the governor, Lord Cornbury (1701–08), to accept its own treasurer (1706). Under George Clarke, acting governor (1736–43), the assembly, by securing the right to pay salaries by name and amount, gained increasing control over

all appointments. Both governors Jonathan Belcher of Massachusetts (1730–41) and Lewis Morris of New Jersey (1738–46) failed to secure from the legislature other than temporary appropriations. In 1752 the Board of Trade instructed the governors to demand a **fixed civil list** (obtained nowhere except Jamaica) and in 1761 to appoint judges **during the pleasure of the crown** (a policy which aroused colonial antagonism reflected in the Declaration of Independence).

Anglo-French Colonial Rivalry to 1763

1497–1604. RIVALRY OVER FISH-ERIES. John Cabot (p. 22) and his English crew, first Europeans definitely known to have visited the Newfoundland coast since the Vikings, reported its waters as "swarming with fish." The French, who fished these waters as early as 1504, were in a dominant position by 1540, although after 1560 Portuguese and Spanish fishermen entered the area. Until 1578 England was dependent upon the Iceland fisheries. To free themselves of dependence on France and Portugal for their solar salt used in "green fishing" (i.e., salting fish aboard ship without drying), English fishermen introduced "dry fishing" (i.e., drying fish on land with a minimum amount of salt) in the Newfoundland area. Such fish found a ready market in Mediterranean ports (c.1580–1604). To compete, the French now sought land bases on which to dry their catch. Since the English had already preempted some of the best bases in Newfoundland, they chose Cape Breton and the Gaspé Peninsula.

1534–99. START OF FUR TRADE. Trade in furs developed virtually with the first contacts between the French and

the Indians (as far back as Cartier's voyage of discovery, 1534). As the French fishermen increased their land bases, the fur trade was expanded, notably at Tadoussac on the St. Lawrence (by the 1580s). European weapons hastened the extinction of the beaver, in immense demand for hatmaking, and drew the fur trade into the interior.

1598–1613. BACKGROUND OF FRENCH SETTLEMENT. Despite two unsuccessful attempts at settlement (under Baron de Léry, 1518, and Roberval, 1542–43, p. 26), the French crown granted (12 Jan. 1598) Troïlus du Mesgouez, Marquis de la Roche, a monopoly of the fur trade and settlement rights in Canada, Newfoundland, and adjacent lands. La Roche transported 2 shiploads of jailbirds (mostly beggars and vagabonds) to **Sable Island** off the coast of Nova Scotia and dominating Newfoundland, Acadia, and the Gulf of St. Lawrence, but, after an uprising, the settlement was abandoned. Another monopoly finally was assigned (1603) to **Pierre du Guast, Sieur de Monts,** who established a settlement at the mouth of the St. Croix River (June, 1604). This colony was moved across the Bay of Fundy to **Port Royal** (Annapolis Royal, Nova Scotia, Aug. 1607), but was abandoned when Monts' patent was canceled (1607), then reestablished (1610) with two subsequent stations set up on the west bank of the Bay of Fundy (by 1613).

1608–27. SETTLEMENT OF ST. LAWRENCE VALLEY. His monopoly restored for 1 year (7 Jan. 1608), Monts dispatched **François du Pontgravé** (5 Apr.) and **Samuel de Champlain** (c.1567–1635) (13 Apr.) to Canada. Champlain founded **Quebec** (3 July) and remained in charge of the new colony as lieutenant for a chain of successors of Monts as viceroys. However, stress on the fur trade discouraged permanent settlement and left the colony vulnerable to attack. With the outbreak of war between England and France (Mar. 1627), control was vested (25 Apr.) in **The Company of New France** (**The Hundred Associates**), a joint-stock company, which, in return for undertaking settlement, was given the fur monopoly.

1609–27. FRENCH-INDIAN RELATIONS. The entry of the French into the St. Lawrence challenged control of the area by the Five Nations of the **Iroquois.** The Montagnais (Saguenay Valley), the Algonquins of the Ottawa, and the Hurons (between the Ottawa and Georgia Bay) assured the French a steady flow of furs from the interior and sought to oust the Iroquois from the area. Before Champlain's arrival the Iroquois had been ousted from the St. Lawrence Valley, and Champlain undertook 2 expeditions (1609, with the Algonquins to Lake Champlain; 1615, with the Hurons into the Onondaga country), designed to push the Five Nations southward and protect the link with the friendly Indians. The arrivals of the Recollect friars (1615) and the Jesuits

(1625) served as another link between France and her Indian allies. Missions were established as far west as Georgian Bay (by 1616), while further campaigns against the Five Nations (1618, 1627 guarded the trade route from the west (Georgian Bay–Lake Nipissing–Ottawa River–St. Lawrence–Quebec).

1613–29. EARLY ENGLISH ATTACKS. After the French settlements on either side of the Bay of Fundy had been totally destroyed in a raid conducted by Capt. Samuel Argall (1613), the English crown granted the region (1621) to **Sir William Alexander,** who, in the course of the war between France and England (1627–29), was given a monopoly of the St. Lawrence fur trade. On 20 July 1629 Sir David Kirke, who had joined forces with Alexander, captured Quebec, unaware that peace had already been established (24 Apr.) by the Treaty of Susa. By the Treaty of St. Germain-en-Laye (29 Mar. 1632) England restored Acadia and the St. Lawrence to France.

New France to King William's War

1632–70. ACADIAN DEVELOPMENTS. Settlement of Acadia by the French began in earnest after the appointment of Isaac de Razilly as governor (10 May 1632), but was halted by factionalism and civil war. A small force collected in Boston under Maj. Robert Sedgwick, originally intended to attack New Netherland but diverted to Acadia to eliminate French competition with New England in fish and furs, easily reduced the area (c.1 July 1654). The English held the province for 16 years until its return to France (1670) under provisions of the Treaty of Breda (July 1667).

1632–35. NEW FRANCE UNDER CHAMPLAIN. Champlain's return to

Canada (22 May 1633), this time both as royal governor and company governor, inaugurated a period of expansion, with settlements founded at Beauport (near Quebec, 1634), Three Rivers (1634), and **Montreal** (14 Oct. 1641). Recollect and Jesuit missions were re-established among the Hurons (1634) and as far west as the Algonquin tribes at Sault Ste. Marie (by 1641). Exploration of the interior was pressed, notably by **Jean Nicolet,** who journeyed as far west as Green Bay and the Fox River Valley, possibly even reaching the Mississippi (1634–35).

1642–53. IROQUOIS WAR. The Five Nations, armed by the Dutch, who sought to divert the northern and interior fur trade of the Huron and Algonquin to their own posts, with the Iroquois as intermediaries, attacked the Hurons on the Richelieu (3 Aug. 1642) and even raided Montreal (30 Mar. 1644). A short truce (14 July 1645–18 Oct. 1646) was broken by the Iroquois, Ft. Richelieu (erected by the French at the mouth of the Richelieu River, 1642) was burned (1647), with raids deep into the Huron country which forced the Jesuits to abandon their last Huron mission (1650) and the Hurons to retreat as far west as Wisconsin, where they were joined by other fugitive tribes from the Ottawa Valley, the Ohio, and southern Michigan. Raids along the St. Lawrence penetrated to the Saguenay-Rupert River country (1652). Victorious, though dangerously overextended, the Iroquois signed a peace with the French (5 Nov. 1653).

1654–72. RENEWED FRENCH EXPANSION. Revival of the fur trade by the Algonquins began in 1654. **Médard Chouart, Sieur des Grosseilliers,** and his brother-in-law, **Pierre-Esprit Radisson,** set forth (Aug. 1659) for a journey into the interior to the western and southern shores of Lake Superior and into north-western Wisconsin. On Mazarin's death (1661) Louis XIV assumed personal rule. His finance minister **Colbert** pressed French colonization. A base and settlement were established at Placentia, Newfoundland (1662–63), and a resident governor appointed (1668). The government of Canada was placed under a governor, appointed council, and an intendant (the king's personal representative). During his terms in office (1663–68, 1670–72) **Jean Baptiste Talon** (1625–91), the "great intendant," dominated the government of New France. To guard the old Iroquois route to the St. Lawrence, forts were erected on the Richelieu River and at the head of Lake Champlain (1665–66). Renewed war against the Five Nations, now in alliance with England, was prosecuted, and the tribes were forced to sue for peace (1666). Despite the gradual return to their original homes of tribes dispossessed by the Five Nations, the French now continued direct trade with the Indians of Lake Superior and Michigan. To establish more permanent relations with the interior tribes, Talon sent Nicolas Perrot to the Wisconsin region (1668–69) and François Daumont, Sieur de St. Lusson, to Sault Ste. Marie. Missions were founded on the upper Michigan peninsula (c.1668) and on Green Bay and the Fox River (1670–72). **René Robert Cavelier, Sieur de La Salle** (1643–87), temporarily established amicable relations with the Iroquois and penetrated south of Lake Erie to present Ohio (1669–70).

1673–83. EXPANSION IN THE MISSISSIPPI VALLEY. When the English established trading posts on Hudson Bay (1670–83), tapping the continent's richest fur area, the French accepted the challenge, notably during the governorships of **Louis de Buade, Comte de Frontenac** (1620–98, gov. 1672–82) and Jacques René de Brisay, Marquis de Denonville (gov. 1682–88). Frontenac favored the Recollects (allied in France with the king in the struggle for temporal power) to check the Jesuits, supported by the papacy. In the beaver trade and the founding of missions the former outdistanced the latter in this period. **Père Jacques Marquette** (1637–75), a Jesuit missionary, and **Louis Joliet** (1648–1700), trader and explorer, set out from Mackinac Straits (17 May 1673), voyaged down Lake Michigan through Green Bay, up the Fox River, and, after a long portage, down the Wisconsin to the Mississippi (17 June), which river they paddled down as far as the Arkansas (17 July). Convinced that the Mississippi flowed into the Gulf of Mexico rather than the Pacific, they returned to Mackinac Straits by way of the Illinois River and Lake Michigan. La Salle, who wished to erect a government in the Mississippi Valley free of Jesuit control, sailed across the Great Lakes with **Father Louis Hennepin** (1640–1701?), who was the first to describe Niagara Falls, which they passed (Dec. 1678), for Green Bay, Wis., continuing by way of Mackinaw to the Illinois River, where he built Ft. Crèvecoeur (15 Jan. 1680). Hennepin, detached to accompany an expedition to explore the upper Mississippi, discovered St. Anthony's Falls (present Minneapolis, 1680). On a later expedition La Salle descended the Illinois to its mouth, embarked upon the Mississippi, paddling to its mouth (9 Apr. 1682), and took possession of the entire region, which he named **Louisiana.**

1668–88. EARLY STRUGGLE FOR HUDSON BAY. Radisson and Grosseilliers secured the backing of an English syndicate headed by **Prince Rupert,** cousin of the king, for a voyage to Hudson Bay (June 1668–Oct. 1669). The syndicate, now enlarged, was chartered by the crown (2 May 1670) as the **Governor and Company of Adventurers of England into Hudson's Bay.** To divert the fur trade from the St. Lawrence posts were erected at the mouths of the Rupert, Moose, and Albany rivers on James Bay and at the mouth of the Hayes River on the west side of Hudson Bay. After returning to French allegiance and capturing the governor of the Hudson's Bay Co. (1682), Radisson switched back to the company (1684). A French force under **Pierre le Moyne, Sieur d'Iberville** (1661–1706), captured the three James Bay posts (1686), leaving the English with lone posts at the mouth of the Hayes and the Severn. The French followed up their success with the setting up of two posts to the north, on Lake Abitibi (1686) and Lake Nipigon (1684).

1684–87. LA SALLE'S ATTEMPT TO SETTLE ON THE GULF. With a view to reaching the Spanish mines and establishing a base of operations against the Spaniards on the Gulf of Mexico (Spain and France were at war, Oct. 1683–Aug. 1684), La Salle sailed from France (July 1684) with a small fleet to the Gulf, failed to find the mouth of the Mississippi, landed at Matagorda Bay, Tex. (Jan. 1685), continued on foot in an attempt to reach Canada, and was murdered by his rebellious men on the banks of the Brazos (1687).

1684–89. RENEWED IROQUOIS HOSTILITIES. Encouraged by Gov. Thomas Dongan of New York, the Iroquois raided as far west as the Mississippi and across Lakes Erie and Ontario into the Huron country (1684), breaking the chain of trade that stretched along the lakes (by 1686). Nicolas Perrot conducted an ineffectual campaign against them (1687). In retaliation the Iroquois raided the St. Lawrence Valley (1688–89), slaughtering 200 at Lachine (Aug. 1689) and taking 90 prisoners.

The First Two Intercolonial Wars

FRENCH ADVANTAGES. (1) Centralized control, contrasted with colonial decentralization and lack of unity; (2) strategically placed forts; (3) an army considered the most formidable on the European continent; (4) Indian alliances, extending from the Abenakis in Maine to the Algonquin in Wisconsin and north toward Hudson Bay; (5) *coureurs du bois* familiar with forests and trails in the area of conflict.

ENGLISH ADVANTAGES. (1) Overwhelming numerical superiority (over 100,000 in New England alone contrasted with 12,000 in New France, 1688); (2) the Iroquois alliance; (3) marked naval superiority in combination with the Dutch; (4) trading and financial superiority.

1689, 12 May–1697, 20 Sept. KING WILLIAM'S WAR (WAR OF THE LEAGUE OF AUGSBURG). The European phase of the war broke out first when William III joined the League of Augsburg and the Netherlands (Grand Alliance, 12 May 1689) to resist Louis XIV's invasion of the Rhenish Palatinate (25 Sept. 1688). In America hostilities broke out between the English and French on Hudson Bay and between the Iroquois and the French in the area from the Mohawk to the St. Lawrence. The French under Frontenac (returned as governor, Oct. 1689) struck with their Indian allies along the northern frontier, with raids on Schenectady (9 Feb. 1690), Salmon Falls, N.H. (27 Mar.), and Falmouth (Portland, Me., 31 July), followed by Abenaki raids on Wells, Me. (21 June 1692), Durham, N.H. (23 June 1694), and Haverhill, Mass. (15 Mar. 1697). On the western frontier Frontenac attacked the Iroquois (1693–

96). On the part of the English the only successful colonial operation was the seizure of **Port Royal** (11 May 1690) by an expedition of Massachusetts troops under **Sir William Phips** (1651–95), recaptured a year later by the French. The 3-pronged attack on the St. Lawrence projected at the Albany Conference (p. 55) failed (3 Aug.–23 Oct. 1690). Iberville ousted the English from their Hudson Bay posts at the mouths of the Severn (1690) and the Hayes (1694), but the English recaptured the James Bay area (1693). The inconclusive **Treaty of Ryswick** (30 Sept. 1697) restored the *status quo ante* in the colonies and turned the Hudson Bay dispute over to commissioners, who reached no agreement (1699).

1698–1702. FRENCH SETTLEMENT OF LOUISIANA. Fearing an influx of English traders into the West following a French order (1696) closing the western posts (owing to a glutted fur market; rescinded, 1699), the French were determined to secure the Mississippi Valley. A Sulpician mission was established at **Cahokia** (near present East St. Louis, 1699) and a Jesuit post at the mouth of the junction of the **Kaskaskia** and the Mississippi (1703). To protect the route to this region forts were built at Mackinac (1700) and Detroit (1701). Iberville established Ft. Maurepas on Biloxi Bay (1699), but the colony was moved (1702) to Ft. Louis on the Mobile River.

1702, 4 May–1713, 11 Apr. QUEEN ANNE'S WAR (WAR OF THE SPANISH SUCCESSION). To prevent the close cooperation, if not the amalgamation, of France and Spain on the death of Charles II of Spain (1 Nov. 1700),

the Grand Alliance (7 Sept. 1701) declared war on France (4 May 1702). In
New England the war followed the pattern of the previous conflict. The Abenakis raided Maine settlements (10 Aug.
1703), destroyed Deerfield, Mass. (28–
29 Feb. 1704), and attacked Winter
Harbor, Me. (21 Sept. 1707). To eliminate the source of Abenaki supplies and
seize control of the Acadian fisheries, a
force of 500 New Englanders under Col.
Benjamin Church destroyed the French
villages of Minas and Beaubassin (1, 28
July 1704). After 2 unsuccessful sieges
of Port Royal (1704, 1707), a third expedition under Col. **Francis Nicholson**
and **Sir Charles Hobby** reduced that
stronghold (16 Oct. 1710). In **Newfoundland,** a mixed force of French and
Indians operating out of Placentia destroyed an English settlement at Bona-
vista (18–29 Aug. 1704), and as a result
of the capture of St. Johns (21 Dec.
1708) brought the eastern shore under
French control. In the **South** the Carolina assembly authorized (10 Sept. 1702)
an expedition to seize St. Augustine be-

fore it could be reinforced by the French.
A mixed force of 500 colonists and Indians seized, burned, and pillaged the
town (Dec.) after failing to capture the
fort. Another mixed force under former
Gov. James Moore destroyed all but one
of the 14 missions in the Apalachee
country (1704), opening the road to
Louisiana. But the Carolinians were unable to penetrate the Choctaw screen
protecting French Gulf settlements. By
the **Treaty of Utrecht** (11 Apr. 1713)
Newfoundland, Acadia, and Hudson Bay
were ceded to Great Britain, but France
retained Cape Breton Island and the
islands of the St. Lawrence. The failure
to define the boundaries of Acadia, Hudson Bay, and the interior of the continent left the door open to later conflict.
Great Britain was also accorded (26
Mar.) the **Assiento,** a contract allowing
the South Sea Co. (formed 1711) to
import into the Spanish colonies 4,800
Negroes a year for 30 years and to send
1 trading ship a year to the Spanish colonies.

Interlude Between Wars, 1713–39

**1718–29. FRENCH EXPANSION ON
MISSISSIPPI.** Prosperity in Louisiana
was supported by the profits of John
Law's Company of the Indies given royal
permission to develop the Mississippi
Valley. The founding of **New Orleans**
(Nov. 1718) by **Jean Baptiste le Moyne,
Sieur de Bienville,** brother of Iberville,
marked intensive French expansion. Forts
were erected at the mouths of the Kaskaskia and the Illinois (1720, 1726) and
on the north bank of the Missouri
(1723), and settlers from Canada relocated in the Illinois country (c.1735).
Following initial success with the Indians

in the South (Ft. Toulouse erected among
the Creeks on the Alabama River), the
French were on the defensive as the re-
sult of being outbid by Carolina traders.
The Yazoo and Natchez joined the
Chickasaws in attacking French settle-
ments (1729), ultimately confining the
French to the Louisiana Valley area.

**1715–28. THE CAROLINA FRON-
TIER: THE YAMASSEE WAR.** Pressed
by South Carolina settlers given large
coastal grants for cattle ranches, the
Yamassees joined the Lower Creeks, re-
sentful of Carolinian trading practices,
and raided the area northwest of Port

Royal, ultimately ousting the Carolina traders from the entire area west of the Savannah. With the aid of the Cherokee located at the headwaters of the Savannah, the Carolinians defeated the Yamassees (Jan. 1716) and by spring had almost eliminated the Creeks from their frontier. Forts were built at present Columbia and Port Royal (1718) and, as a defense against the French and Spaniards, on the Altamaha, the Savannah, and the Santee (1716–21) despite Spanish protests. A brief **Anglo-Spanish War** (Feb. 1727–Mar. 1728) served as a pretext for the Carolinians to stage a deep march into Florida to destroy a Yamassee village near St. Augustine (9 Mar. 1728).

1732–52. FOUNDING OF GEORGIA. James Edward Oglethorpe (p. 1117), a Tory member of Parliament (since 1722), concerned with the problems of pauperism, relief for imprisoned debtors, imperial trade, and naval supremacy, received, along with 19 associates, including John, Viscount Perceval (first Earl of Egmont), a charter (20 June 1732), conferring upon them as **trustees** for 21 years the right to settle the area between the Savannah and Altamaha rivers, originally part of South Carolina, but retained by the crown when the Carolinas were surrendered by the proprietors (1729). The charter granted liberty of conscience to all except Catholics and limited individual grants to 500 acres. Sailing with the first group of settlers, Oglethorpe founded **Savannah** (12 Feb. 1733). During the first year the trustees prohibited the importation or use of rum or brandy as well as slaves. Gradually the landholding restrictions were relaxed. Seven-year tenancies were permitted on new land, size of holdings increased from 500 to 2,000 acres (1740), original grants in tail male (inalienable and restricted to male heirs) to serve as military fiefs were enlarged

to fee simple (1750), rum importation permitted (1742), and, as a result of pressure from Carolinians settling in the province, the prohibition on slavery was repealed (1749). With the last meeting of the trustees (4 July 1752) control of the colony passed to the crown. In support of the project, which combined humanitarian and imperialist features, Parliament had by 1752 appropriated £136,608.

1733–39. MILITARY PREPARATIONS IN GEORGIA. Oglethorpe set about fortifying the southern frontier, erecting forts on St. Simon's, St. Andrew's, Cumberland, and Amelia islands (by 1739), and founding Augusta on the Savannah and Ft. Okfuskee on the Talapoosa (present Alabama, 1735). A notable achievement was his establishment of peace with the interior tribes, particularly the Creeks (1739).

1719–41. RIVAL PREPARATIONS IN THE NORTH. The powerful fortress of Louisbourg on Cape Breton Island (constructed 1720) secured the St. Lawrence approaches, guarded from the south by a new fort at Crown Point on Lake Champlain (1731). To protect the route to the Mississippi (Lake Erie–Maumee–Wabash) the French built Ft. Miami (1704) at the portage, Ft. Ouiataon on the Wabash (c.1719), and Ft. Vincennes (c.1724) on the lower Wabash. Ft. Niagara was built (1720) to secure the lower Great Lakes and serve as a base of operations against the Iroquois. The British countered by establishing Ft. Oswego on Lake Ontario (1725), and New Englanders built forts on the northern frontier against the Abenakis, who, as a result of Jesuit activities, remained loyal to France. In the West, **Pierre Gaultier de Varennes, Sieur de la Vérendrye,** French commander at Lake Nipigon, together with his 3 sons, readied both the Saskatchewan (1734) and the Missouri valleys (1738) for defense.

War of Jenkins' Ear and King George's War

1739–42. WAR OF JENKINS' EAR. Great Britain, aroused by tales of mistreatment of her merchant seamen (notably Robert Jenkins) and other hostile acts (provoked by British abuses of the Assiento and activities of her logwooders on the Honduran coast as well as by the unsettled Florida border), declared war on Spain (19 Oct. 1739). His western flank protected by the friendly Creeks, Cherokee, and Chickasaw, Oglethorpe invaded Florida, captured forts San Francisco de Pupo and Picolata on the San Juan River (Jan. 1740), and besieged St. Augustine (May–July), breaking off when his rear was threatened. A Spanish counterattack was crushed at the **Battle of Bloody Swamp** on St. Simon's Island (1742).

1740–48. KING GEORGE'S WAR (WAR OF THE AUSTRIAN SUCCESSION). The invasion of Silesia by Frederick II of Prussia (16 Dec. 1740) following the death of Emperor Charles VI (20 Oct.) touched off a series of continental wars with France, now allied with Prussia (5 June 1741), invading south-ern Germany. With the signing of the **Second Family Compact** (25 Oct. 1743) between France and Spain, France joined the war against England (15 Mar. 1744). Neither side prosecuted the war in America vigorously. The French made an unsuccessful assault on Annapolis Royal (Port Royal, Nova Scotia, 1744), and an expedition of New Englanders under **William Pepperrell** (1696–1759, Bt., 1746) in cooperation with a fleet under Sir Peter Warren captured Ft. Louisbourg (16 June 1745). The Maine towns were raided by the French and Indians (from Aug. 1745). In New York **William Johnson** (p. 1072), Mohawk Valley Indian trader and commissary of New York for Indian affairs (1746), succeeded in getting the Iroquois on the warpath, with resultant French retaliatory raids on Saratoga (burned, 28–29 Nov. 1745) and Albany. The inconclusive **Treaty of Aix-la-Chapelle** (18 Oct. 1748) restored the *status quo ante* in the colonies and returned Louisbourg to France.

Prelude to the Last War

1748–50. Although their area of effective control was confined to Nova Scotia the British claimed that Acadia included, in addition, present New Brunswick and the Gaspé Peninsula. To strengthen their hold on Nova Scotia Lord Halifax sent out 2,500 settlers (1749) to found the town of **Halifax.**

1744–54. WESTWARD MOVEMENT OF PENNSYLVANIANS AND VIRGINIANS. Ohio Valley traders from Pennsylvania, led by **George Croghan** (c.1718–82) and **Conrad Weiser** (1696–1760), rapidly expanded their posts in the Ohio area and as agents for the Pennsylvania legislature secured the alle-

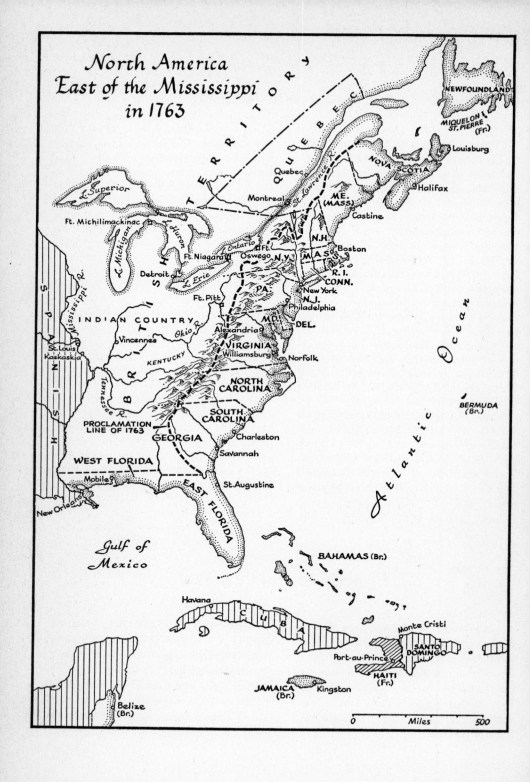

North America East of the Mississippi in 1763

NEWFOUNDLAND

MIQUELON ST. PIERRE (Fr.)

Louisburg

QUEBEC TERRITORY

Quebec

NOVA SCOTIA

Halifax

St. Lawrence R.

Montreal

ME. (MASS.)

Castine

L. Superior

Ft. Michilimackinac

L. Michigan

L. Huron

L. Ontario

N.H.

Ft. Niagara

Ft. Oswego

MASS.

Boston

Detroit

L. Erie

N.Y.

R.I.

CONN.

BRITISH TERRITORY

Ft. Pitt

PA.

New York

N.J.

Philadelphia

SPANISH

Mississippi R.

INDIAN COUNTRY

Ohio R.

MD.

DEL.

Alexandria

St. Louis

Vincennes

KENTUCKY

VIRGINIA

Williamsburg

Norfolk

Kaskaskia

Tennessee R.

NORTH CAROLINA

BRITISH

SOUTH CAROLINA

PROCLAMATION LINE OF 1763

GEORGIA

Charleston

Savannah

WEST FLORIDA

Mobile

EAST FLORIDA

St. Augustine

New Orleans

Gulf of Mexico

Atlantic Ocean

BERMUDA (Br.)

BAHAMAS (Br.)

Havana

CUBA

Monte Cristi

SANTO DOMINGO

Port-au-Prince

HAITI (Fr.)

JAMAICA (Br.)

Kingston

Belize (Br.)

0   Miles   500

giance of the Indians of the area (Aug. 1748). Virginians were equally interested in the area. The Ohio Co. (p. 590) obtained a huge grant on the upper Ohio and sent out **Christopher Gist** (1750) to explore the region. Erection of a trading house at present Cumberland, Md., and trail-blazing activities aroused the French to fortify present Toronto (1749), to divert trade from Oswego, to locate a post at Niagara portage, strengthen Detroit, and dispatch **Céloron de Bienville** to seize the Ohio Valley (1749). In the summer of 1752 the French attacked the trading post of Pickawillany and killed

its defenders, and erected Ft. Presque Isle (Erie, Pa.) and Ft. Le Boeuf at the portage to French Creek (spring 1753), and Ft. Venango at the junction of French Creek and the Allegheny. Lt. Gov. **Robert Dinwiddie** (?1693–1770) of Virginia dispatched 21-year-old **George Washington** (p. 1177) to protest these moves and to ascertain French intentions. He visited Ft. Venango and Ft. Le Boeuf (1753), reporting on his return (Jan. 1754) that the French planned to occupy the entire Ohio and could not be removed except by force.

The French and Indian War (Seven Years' War)

1754, 17 APR.–3 JULY. HOSTILITIES BEGIN. To forestall the French, Dinwiddie ordered construction of a fort at the Forks of the Ohio (junction of Allegheny and Monongahela, Feb. 1754), but the French seized the site and erected Ft. Duquesne. Dispatched with an advance party of 150 to occupy that post, Washington, following a successful skirmish with a French reconnaissance party (28 May), constructed Ft. Necessity at Great Meadows. Reinforced, he resisted a larger French force under Coulon de Villiers, but finally capitulated.

1754, 19 JUNE–10 JULY. ALBANY CONGRESS. Advised by the British authorities to make a treaty with the wavering Iroquois, delegates from New England, New York, Pennsylvania, and Maryland met at Albany. **Benjamin Franklin** (p. 1033), a Pennsylvania delegate, who had drawn up a plan of union (Mar. 1751), proposed (24 June) that the subject be considered. The "Plan of Union" finally approved (10 July) was based on Franklin's plan, with additions probably proposed by **Thomas Hutchin-**

son (p. 1065), a Massachusetts delegate. The plan called for a union of all the colonies (except Georgia and Nova Scotia) under a president general appointed and paid by the crown. A grand council elected by the colonial assemblies (each colony to have from 2 to 7 delegates, depending on its contribution to the general treasury) was to have legislative power subject to approval by the president general and the crown. President general and grand council were to have jurisdiction over Indian affairs, including new land purchases "not now within the bounds of particular colonies." The plan was rejected both by the colonies and the home government. The Board of Trade countered with a proposal (9 Aug.) for a single commander in chief and a commissary of Indian affairs.

1755, 14 APR.–9 NOV. CAMPAIGNS OF BRADDOCK AND SHIRLEY. Gen. **Edward Braddock** (?1695–1755) arrived in Virginia (14 Apr. 1755) as commander in chief of the British forces in America. At the head of 1,400 British regulars and 450 colonials under Lt. Col. Washington, he headed for Ft. Duquesne. On the Monongahela, about 8 miles below the fort, he was met by a mixed force of 900 French and Indians, surrounded, and defeated at the **Battle of the Wilderness** (9 July). With Braddock mortally wounded, Washington led the remnant back to Ft. Cumberland. Gov. **William Shirley** (1694–1771) of Massachusetts, replacing Braddock in command, was forced to postpone his campaign against Ft. Niagara owing to reinforcements which reached the French when their fleet slipped through a blockade established by Adm. Edward Boscawen (6–13 June). On 19 June Ft. Beauséjour was captured by a force of 2,000 New Englanders and a few British regulars under Colonels Robert Monckton (1726–62) and John Winslow (1703–74). By 30 June the Bay of Fundy area was completely in British hands. William Johnson, commanding a mixed force of 3,500 colonials, chiefly New Englanders, and 400 Indians, began constructing Ft. William Henry on Lake George in anticipation of a French attack. At the **Battle of Lake George** (8 Sept.) he defeated Baron Dieskau's mixed force of 1,400 French and Indian troops. But bad morale among the New England troops prevented Johnson from moving on Crown Point.

1755, JULY–8 OCT. EXPULSION OF THE ACADIANS. Fearing that a French attack would be supported by the Acadians acting as a fifth column, Col. Charles Lawrence, governor of Nova Scotia, announced that all who refused to take the oath of loyalty to the British crown would be expelled (5 Sept.). Embarkation began (8 Oct.). In all some 6,000 Acadians were exiled and distributed among the Thirteen Colonies. Villages at the head of the Bay of Fundy were burned to the ground, but many of the inhabitants escaped to the woods. A

sizable number eventually returned to Nova Scotia.

1756, 16 JAN.–29 AUG. WAR SPREADS TO EUROPE. The European phase of the war began following a new alliance between Britain and Prussia, on the one hand (16 Jan. 1756), and France and Austria, on the other (1 May), with a declaration of war by Great Britain on France (15 May). A British setback at Minorca, which fell 28 June, was matched by continued reversals in America.

1757–58. FURTHER BRITISH SETBACKS IN AMERICA. To command French forces in America **Louis Joseph, Marquis de Montcalm** (1712–59), arrived in Canada with reinforcements (11 May 1756). He was opposed by **John Campbell, Earl of Loudoun,** who arrived in America on 23 July. Montcalm took and destroyed forts Oswego and George (Aug.) and on 9 Aug. 1757 took and demolished Ft. William Henry, whose outnumbered defender, Lt. Col. George Monro, surrendered only to have his force treacherously set upon by the Indians. With 1,400 survivors he reached Ft. Edward. Under orders from Pitt to attack Louisbourg rather than Quebec, Loudoun assembled a large force at Halifax (30 June), but abandoned the attack on learning that the French navy had reached Louisbourg. Rear Adm. Francis Holborne proceeded to bottle up the French in Louisbourg Harbor, but a hurricane smashed the British fleet (24 Sept.). Loudoun's preparations had been hampered by failure to receive wholehearted cooperation from colonial assemblies.

1757. PITT'S WAR LEADERSHIP. French success in Europe continued, with Hanover overrun and three armies converging on Frederick II. With his advent to power in the **Pitt-Newcastle ministry** (29 June) **William Pitt** (1708–78, Earl of Chatham in 1766) committed the government to unlimited warfare, reinforcements in America, and subsidies to the continental allies, necessitating higher taxes and war loans.

1757, 30 Dec.–1758, 18 Sept. ABERCROMBY IN COMMAND. James Abercromby (1706–81) supplanted Loudoun in command, and assembled about 12,000 troops at Lake George (1 July 1758) for a march on **Ticonderoga.** Electing to defend a low ridge outside the fort, Montcalm, with a greatly outnumbered force of 3,000, threw up breastworks. Abercromby's frontal attack (8 July) was routed by withering fire. The British withdrew with great casualties (464 killed, 29 missing, 1,117 wounded). This disaster was counterbalanced by Maj. Gen. **Jeffrey Amherst** (1717–97), who, with Brig. Gen. **James Wolfe** (1727–59), a fleet of 40 ships, and a force of 9,000 British regulars and 500 colonials, took **Louisbourg** (26 July). Col. **John Bradstreet** (1711–74) took Ft. Frontenac (27 Aug.), and Brig. Gen. **John Forbes** (1710–59), marching along a new road he constructed southwest from Raystown, forced the French to blow up Ft. Duquesne (25 Nov.). With the turn of the tide, Abercromby was relieved of his command (18 Sept.) and Amherst named his successor.

1759. YEAR OF FRENCH DISASTER. Pitt outlined a 3-pronged campaign: (1) to capture Ft. Niagara and reinforce Oswego in order to sever the West from the St. Lawrence; (2) to strike through the Lake Champlain waterway to the St. Lawrence Valley; (3) to launch an amphibious attack against Quebec. **Ft. Niagara** fell (25 July) to a force of 2,000 regulars under Brig. Gen. John Prideaux (killed prior to the capitulation) and 100 Iroquois under Sir William Johnson. Meantime, Col. Frederick Haldimand had reinforced Oswego. Outnumbered by British attackers under Amherst the French blew up Ft. Carillon (**Ticonderoga,** 26 July) and Ft. St. Frederic (**Crown Point,** 31 July)—both refortified by Amherst—and retreated down the Richelieu. A combined force of 9,000 troops under Wolfe and a fleet under Rear Adm. Charles Saunders sailed up the St. Lawrence (16 June), anchoring off Bic and St. Barnabé, where Rear Adm. Durell landed a detachment of troops on the Île-aux-Coudres (28 May) and advanced to the Île d'Orléans to await the main force (25 June). Wolfe landed troops on Île d'Orléans (27 June); sent Monckton to occupy Pointe Lévis opposite Quebec, and Brig. Gen. George Townshend (1724–1807) to the north shore (9 July). After the failure of attempts by Montcalm to burn the British fleet (27 July) and by the British to storm the enemy position (31 July), Wolfe dispatched a force under Brig. Gen. James Murray (1719–94) to engage troops above Quebec. On their return (25 Aug.) he decided to attack. While the French were led to expect a major attack from the St. Lawrence, Wolfe moved his troops on the night of 12–13 Sept. upstream in small boats, landing before dawn on the north shore, and made a surprise ascent of the **Plains of Abraham,** a plateau about the city. Unwilling to await reinforcements by a force of 3,000 in the Cap Rouge area, Montcalm engaged the British with 4,500 troops. Superior discipline and arms won the day for the British, who lost only 60 killed and 600 wounded as against 200 killed and 1,200 wounded for the French. But these fatalities included both Wolfe and Montcalm. **Quebec** soon capitulated (18 Sept.).

1760. SURRENDER OF CANADA. Converging on Montreal, Amherst, striking from Lake Ontario, landed at Lachine (6 Sept.); William Haviland, marching north from Crown Point, captured Chambly (1 Sept.); and Gov. James Murray, pressing down from Quebec, made a junction with the others massed before Montreal, forcing Pierre François de Rigaud, Marquis de Vaudreuil, Governor of Canada, to surrender the entire province (8 Sept.). Maj. **Robert Rogers** (1731–95) took possession of Detroit and other Great Lakes posts (1760–61).

1761–62. INVOLVEMENT OF SPAIN. Apprehensive that a British victory would upset the balance of colonial power, Spain prepared to throw her weight on the side of France and Austria. Anticipating attack, Great Britain declared war (2 Jan. 1762). Martinique, principal French base in the lesser Antilles, fell to the British (15 Feb. 1762), followed by St. Lucia and Grenada, and, after a 2-month siege, Havana capitulated (12 Aug.). Manila fell (5 Oct.) to a second fleet operating in the Far East. To compensate Spain for her loss, France, anxious to end the war, ceded to her ally, by the secret **Treaty of Fontainebleau** (3 Nov. 1762), all her territory west of the Mississippi as well as the Isle of Orleans (ratified 13 Nov. 1762).

1763, 10 Feb. TREATY OF PARIS ended the west European and colonial phases of the Seven Years' War and the Treaty of Hubertusburg (15 Feb.) concluded its German phase. France ceded to Great Britain all claim to Acadia, Cape Breton, Canada, and the islands of the St. Lawrence, but retained fishing rights on Newfoundland's banks and was given the islands of St. Pierre and Miquelon. France further yielded all territory east of the Mississippi (including the port of Mobile) except the city of New Orleans. Pitt, preferring Canada to the French West Indies for reasons of military security as well as trade, returned to France Martinique, Guadeloupe, and St. Lucia, while St. Vincent, Dominica, and Tobago were restored to Great Britain. France agreed to evacuate her positions in Hanover, restore Minorca to the British, and to the *status quo ante* in India. Cuba was restored to Spain in exchange for East and West Florida, and the British agreed to demolish fortifications on the Honduran coast, but the rights of her logwooders to operate in that area were specifically recognized by Spain.

THE ERA OF THE AMERICAN REVOLUTION, 1763-89

★ ★
★

The issue of autonomous rule, articulated by the Albany Congress in 1754, for example, anticipated the rapid upsurge of antimonarchical sentiment on the very eve of the Revolution, sentiment which climaxed in the Declaration of Independence. When it came, the American Revolution was a movement of a colonial people for independence, a forerunner of the anticolonial movements in Latin America, Asia, and Africa. Second, it was a revolt against monarchy, which led to the establishment of a republic. Finally, it was a civil war, fought in each state, county, and village. Unlike later revolutions it was not fought along strictly class lines, as both Patriots and Loyalists recruited support from the landed aristocrats, the merchants engaged in transatlantic and Caribbean trade, the local shopkeepers, the professional people, the mechanics, and the laboring classes, while, in addition, the Loyalists had a following among tenant farmers and in certain frontier areas. The fact that the leadership of the American Revolution was upper class and moderate served to prevent conditions deteriorating to a state of terror, such as would blemish the subsequent revolution in France.

The American Revolution created a new nation conceived on republican principles, formulating new tenets governing the relation of men to government under the broad rubric of constitutionalism, inaugurating far-reaching democratic reforms, effective self-government, and acting as a spur to social and economic equality. It tested the establishment of a durable union spread out over a large extent of territory and governed along republican lines, one which would preserve to the states the powers of internal police but concede to the Congress the powers over war and peace and foreign affairs. The first formal constitution, the Articles of Confederation, attempted to define the relation of the whole and the parts in the new federal system. Its deficiencies spawned the movement for greater centralization of powers, without sacrificing the federal principle or jeopardizing the inherent rights of the people.

1763

7 Oct. PROCLAMATION OF 1763. The French and Indian War had revealed the insecurity of the frontiers against Indian raids. The first step in placating the Indians was the appointment by Gen. Braddock of **Sir William Johnson** as Indian Commissioner (Apr. 1755) and his reappointment as Commissioner for the North (spring 1756). Since land frauds were believed to lie at the root of Indian unrest Johnson's secretary, Peter Wraxall, urged (9 Jan. 1756) that henceforth land cessions require the approval of the Indian commissioners. By the **Treaty of Easton** (Oct. 1758) with its western Indians Pennsylvania agreed to make no settlements west of the Alleghenies. However, the abandonment of Ft. Duquesne (24 Nov.) and its occupation by the British resulted in an influx of settlers, compelling Col. **Henry Bouquet** (1719–65) to forbid settlement west of the mountains (13 Oct. 1761). The Earl of Egremont as Secretary of State for the Southern Dept. required royal approval for land grants in or adjacent to Indian territory (2 Dec.). To **William Petty, Lord Shelburne,** head of the Board of Trade in the Halifax-Grenville-Egremont ministry, was assigned the formulation of a policy for the newly acquired territory in North America resulting from the Treaty of Paris. Shelburne recommended (8 June 1763) that the Appalachians constitute the dividing line between the settlers and an Indian reservation save for a projected colonial settlement in the upper Ohio and some provision for Indian settlement east of that line. Out of the newly acquired territory 3 new provinces were to be created: (1) Quebec; (2) East Florida; (3) West Florida, with boundaries confined within modest limits in no way encroaching upon the Thirteen Colonies. News of an Indian crisis

reached the British ministry in August. Before the plan was put into effect Shelburne was replaced (2 Sept.) by the less-experienced **Earl of Hillsborough,** a close associate of Halifax, who prepared a proclamation which modified Shelburne's proposal by omitting provision for upper Ohio settlement and ordering colonists already settled in that area "forthwith to remove themselves." Purchases of land from the Indians east of the line were forbidden. Indian territory west of the line was placed under the control of the military commander in chief in America. English law was established in Quebec, a provision deemed unfair and anti-Catholic by French settlers. The proclamation was rushed through the cabinet and Privy Council and signed by the king (7 Oct.).

7 MAY–28 Nov. PONTIAC'S REBELLION. Following the surrender of Detroit to the English under Maj. Robert Rogers (29 Nov. 1760), the Indians demanded that the British authorities lower prices on trade goods and furnish them with ammunition. When these demands were not met at a conference at Detroit (9 Sept. 1761) the Indians grew increasingly restive, stirred up by the Delaware Prophet, a visionary living in the upper Ohio, and by his disciple, **Pontiac** (c.1720–69), chief of the Ottawa. After his plan to take Detroit by a surprise attack was betrayed (May), Pontiac took to open warfare. Within a few weeks every British post west of Niagara was destroyed (Sandusky, 16 May; Ft. St. Joseph, 25 May; Ft. Miami, 27 May; Ft. Ouiatenon, 1 June; Ft. Venango, c.16 June; Ft. Le Boeuf, 18 June; Ft. Presque Isle, 20 June), save for Detroit, which, under Maj. Henry Gladwin, resisted a 5-month siege, and Ft. Pitt, under Capt. Simeon Ecuyer. In retaliation Amherst proposed to Bouquet that "Small pox" be sent among the disaffected tribes, and the latter replied that

he would try to distribute germ-laden blankets among them, but, because of the danger of exposure to British troops, preferred hunting the Indians "with English dogs" (13 July). As a result of reinforcements which reached Detroit (29 July), Gladwin made a sortie against Pontiac and was repulsed at **Bloody Ridge** (31 July). Marching to the relief of Ft. Pitt, Bouquet defeated (with heavy British losses) and routed the Indians at **Bushy Run,** east of present Pittsburgh (2–6 Aug.), and relieved the fort (10 Aug.). In Nov. Pontiac raised his siege of Detroit. A number of tribes had already signed treaties with Col. John Bradstreet at Presque Isle (12 Aug. 1764). Pontiac finally submitted, concluding a peace treaty with Sir William Johnson at Oswego (24 July 1766). Subsequently he remained loyal to the British, but was murdered (1769) in Cahokia (Ill.), according to Parkman's version, by a Kaskaskia Indian bribed by an English trader.

5 Nov.–1 Dec. PARSON'S CAUSE. This case was the result of legislation in Virginia regulating salaries of Anglican ministers, which, from 1662, had by law been paid in tobacco, varying with the market value of that commodity. Owing to failure of the tobacco crop as a result of drought, the legislature (Oct. 1755) commuted such pay into currency at the rate of 2d. per lb.; reenacted, 1758. Acting on memorials from the Virginia clergy the Privy Council disallowed the act (10 Aug. 1759). As a result the clergy proceeded to sue for back salary even though the act had not been declared null and void *ab initio*. Most publicized was the case brought by Rev. **James Maury** in Hanover Co. Court. The bench held that the 1758 act was "no law," but a jury (swayed by the rhetoric of young **Patrick Henry** [p. 1057], who declared that by disallowing the act the king had broken the compact

between the governed and the ruler, thereby forfeiting "all rights to his subjects' obedience") returned a verdict of 1d. for plaintiff. The action of the General Court (10 Apr. 1764) in giving judgment against the clergy was affirmed by the Privy Council (3 Dec. 1766).

13–27 Dec. FRONTIER DISORDER IN PENNSYLVANIA: THE PAXTON BOYS. As a result of the insecurity of the frontier against Indian attacks (1754–63), a mob from Paxton and Donegal attacked the peaceful Conestoga Indians in Lancaster Co. The assembly, which had failed to respond to the demand of frontiersmen for protection, ordered that the "Paxton Boys" be arrested and brought to Philadelphia for trial. Instead, the frontiersmen marched east, but were persuaded by Franklin to forego battle, and issued a formal protest by which they obtained greater representation in the legislature.

1764

5 Apr. REVENUE FROM AMERICA. Faced by a large postwar debt, heavy taxes at home, and the necessity of supporting an army in America, the ministry of the Earl of Bute sought revenue from the colonies. When the debate on the 1764 budget opened in the House of Commons (9 Mar.), the Chancellor of the Exchequer, George Grenville, presented an American Revenue Act (generally known as the **Sugar Act**) to become the first law ever passed by Parliament for the specific purpose of raising moneys in the colonies for the crown. The act (1) extended the Molasses Act of 1733 but reduced the 6d.-per-gallon duty upon foreign molasses to 3d., the old rate on raw sugar was continued, and an increased duty levied on foreign refined sugar; (2) placed new or higher import duties on non-British textiles, coffee, and indigo, and on Madeira and Canary wines imported directly; (3) doubled the duties on foreign goods reshipped in England to the colonies; (4) added iron, hides, whale fins, raw silk, potash, and pearl ash to the enumerated list; (5) banned the import into the colonies of foreign rum and French wines. Grenville estimated that the act, if efficiently administered, would return c. £ 45,000 annually.

ENDING SALUTARY NEGLECT. More significant was Grenville's determination to enforce the trade laws by revitalizing the customs service (at that time the American customs returned little more than one fourth [£ 2,000] the cost of collecting them). A companion measure provided for tighter enforcement by (1) establishing a vice-admiralty court at Halifax with jurisdiction over all the American colonies and enabling prosecutors and informers to bring suit there at their option rather than in local colonial courts; (2) annulling the right of an accused to sue for illegal seizure; (3) placing the burden of proof upon the accused and obliging him to post bond for the cost of the trial; and (4) establishing stricter registration and bonding procedures for ships carrying nonenumerated as well as enumerated cargoes. Grenville ended the practice under which American customs officials were permitted to live in England and entrust their duties to a deputy in the colonies.

CURRENCY ACT widened the scope of colonial opposition as it affected the plantation as well as the commercial provinces. Aimed principally at Virginia, which had issued £ 250,000 of legal-tender paper money during the war, the act prohibited after 1 Sept. issues of legal-tender currency in all the American colonies (thereby extending the ban already operative in New England since 1751), as well as any extension of the recall date for outstanding issues. To guard against evasion, the act nullified all acts of colonial assemblies contrary to its terms and provided for a fine of £ 1,000 and dismissal from office (with ineligibility for any government position in the future) of any colonial governor who assented to legislative acts in defiance of the law.

COLONIAL OPPOSITION. To Americans already distressed by a marked postwar business decline, the Grenville program, by combining higher imposts and strict enforcement with the severe deflationary shock of the Currency Act, seemed calculated to ruin the colonial economy. Massachusetts led the way in protest. A Boston town meeting (24 May) denounced taxation without representation and proposed united action by the colonies in protest. The House of Representatives authorized a Committee of Correspondence (13 June) to contact the other provinces. In Aug. Boston merchants agreed to do without English lace and ruffles, an example which the town's mechanics followed (Sept.) in pledging to wear no leather work clothes not of Massachusetts make. By the end of the year **nonimportation** had spread to other colonies, notably New York.

1765

QUARTERING ACT. Requested by Gen. Thomas Gage, commander of the British forces in America, and not an integral part of the Grenville program, the Quartering Act added fuel to the rising fire of American resentment. Effective 24 Mar. for a 2-year term, the act required the civil authorities in the colonies to supply barracks and supplies for the British troops. A second act (1766) provided for quartering and billeting in inns, alehouses, and unoccupied dwellings.

22 MAR. STAMP ACT, the first direct tax ever levied by Parliament upon

America, was designed to raise £ 60,000 annually, which, together with the return from the 1764 imposts, would produce an American return equal to about one third the £ 300,000 upkeep of the colonial military establishment. The act (passed the Commons, 27 Feb., the Lords, 8 Mar., to become effective 1 Nov.) placed a tax upon newspapers, almanacs, pamphlets and broadsides, legal documents of all types, insurance policies, ship's papers, licenses, and even dice and playing cards. The receipts were to be paid into the royal exchequer for the defense of the colonies. With the sensibilities of the colonists in mind Grenville appointed Americans to be the stamp agents. Penalties for infringements could be imposed by courts of vice-admiralty (which had no jury) as well as by colonial common-law courts.

STAMP ACT CRISIS. Factors underlying the virtually unanimous opposition to the act were (1) the novelty of direct taxation by Parliament and the fear that this tax was to be but the first of many; (2) its all-inclusive character transcended sectionalism; (3) by affecting groups which carried great weight throughout the colonies (lawyers, printers, tavern owners, and land speculators as well as merchants and shipowners) the act broadened the base of the opposition; (4) the grant of jurisdiction to vice-admiralty courts raised fears of an assault upon the right to trial by jury; and (5) the imposition of the tax at a time of economic stagnation and currency stringency convinced many that Britain was deliberately aiming to weaken the colonies.

NEW POLITICAL THEORIES. In 1764 **James Otis** (p. 1120) had raised the issue of no taxation without representation. But the Stamp Act impelled other American writers to draw distinctions aimed at establishing the measure's il-

legality. Widely read and quoted was the argument advanced (*Considerations*) by Daniel Dulany, a Maryland attorney, conceding the right of Parliament to regulate trade, even when such acts produced a revenue, but denying its authority to impose internal taxes for revenue upon the colonists inasmuch as the Americans were not and by their situation could not be represented in Parliament. The same distinction was expressed more militantly in the Virginia Resolutions (29 May) introduced before the House of Burgesses by **Patrick Henry** with the "Treason" speech in which he warned George III to note the fate of Cæsar and Charles I. Asserting that the right of Virginia to govern its internal affairs had always been recognized by the crown, the resolutions claimed for the province's general assembly the sole power to tax Virginians. Upon further deliberation (30–31 May) the House rejected the more radical of these claims, contenting itself with stating that Virginians in the past had legislated respecting their own internal polity and approving the principle of no taxation without representation. Henry's complete set of resolutions were, however, published in the colonial newspapers.

SONS OF LIBERTY. During the summer of 1765 secret organizations known as the Sons of Liberty (the term had been used by Colonel Isaac Barré in a speech against the Stamp Act in the House of Commons) were formed in the provincial towns to organize the opposition to the Stamp Act. Often organized, sometimes personally led (as in New York City) by men of wealth and high position, these groups did not hesitate to resort to violence to force stamp agents to resign their posts and merchants to cancel orders for British goods. A notorious instance occurred in Boston on 26 Aug., when the records of the vice-admiralty court were burned, the home of the comptroller of the currency ransacked, and the elegant home and library of Chief Justice Thomas Hutchinson looted. The Boston stamp agent, Andrew Oliver (Hutchinson's brother-in-law), had been forced by mob violence to resign 15 Aug. Before the effective date of the Stamp Act (1 Nov.) all the stamp agents in the colonies had resigned.

7–25 Oct. STAMP ACT CONGRESS. Upon the motion of James Otis, the Massachusetts assembly resolved (6 June) to propose an intercolonial meeting to seek relief from the Stamp Act. A circular letter was dispatched to each colonial assembly (8 June) suggesting that a congress meet at New York City in Oct. South Carolina endorsed the proposal promptly (2 Aug.), followed by Rhode Island, Connecticut, Pennsylvania, and Maryland. The assemblies of New Jersey, Delaware, and New York failed to take formal action, but were represented by delegates chosen informally. The other 4 provinces failed to act, and were not represented when the Congress opened.

The moderate character of the Stamp Act Congress was clearly reflected in the "Declaration of Rights and Grievances" (19 Oct.), chiefly the work of **John Dickinson** (p. 1013). In 14 resolutions the delegates claimed all the rights and liberties of the king's subjects in Great Britain, stated that taxation without consent expressed personally or through representatives was a violation of these rights, pointed out that the colonists were not and could not be represented in the House of Commons, and concluded that no taxes could be constitutionally imposed on them but by their own legislatures. Specifically condemned was the provision in the Stamp Act giving jurisdiction to admiralty courts.

Separate petitions embracing these resolutions and demanding repeal of the Stamp Act and the measures of 1764 were prepared for submission to the king, the House of Commons, and the House of Lords before the 27 delegates disbanded. On 11 Feb. 1766 the Northampton, Va., County Court declared the Stamp Act unconstitutional.

ECONOMIC SANCTIONS. The passage of the Stamp Act gave a new impetus to **nonimportation.** In New York City leading citizens signed an agreement (28 Oct.) banning the purchase of European goods until the Stamp Act was repealed and the trade regulations of 1764 modified. Following suit were 200 merchants (31 Oct.), some 400 Philadelphia merchants (Nov.), and 250 Boston merchants (9 Dec.). Business throughout the colonies was generally suspended when the Stamp Act went into effect (1 Nov.), owing to the practically universal refusal to use the stamps. Except in Rhode Island, where Gov. Stephen Hopkins refused to execute the act, the courts also closed rather than use the stamps as the law required. Before the end of the year, however, business was renewed without the stamps in open violation of the act.

BRITISH DEMANDS FOR REPEAL. When the Stamp Act became operative a movement in Britain for its repeal was already well along. Grenville's ministry, which had fallen from power in a crisis over a regency bill (10 July), was succeeded by a government under the Marquis of Rockingham. The decline in British exports to America (from £ 2,-249,710 in 1764 to £ 1,944,108 in 1765) spoke more eloquently than colonial resolutions. A committee of merchants, organized to work for the Stamp Act's repeal, called upon some 30 towns in Britain to petition Parliament for repeal. The petition of the London merchants

(17 Jan. 1766) cited several bankruptcies resulting from shrunken American markets.

1766

18 Mar. REPEAL OF THE STAMP ACT. Parliament met on 14 Jan. and immediately debated the Stamp Act. Grenville demanded that the army be used to enforce it, while William Pitt, calling for repeal, commended the Americans for disobeying a tax framed by a body in which they were not represented. The colonial agents were called before the Commons sitting as a committee of the whole (beginning 3 Feb.) to give their views. The most telling testimony was given (13 Feb.) by **Benjamin Franklin** (p. 1033), agent for Pennsylvania. He stressed the heavy expenditures voted by the colonial assemblies during the French and Indian War (Pennsylvania spent £500,000, with a rebate of only £60,000 from the crown), pointed to the continuing expenses borne for prosecution of Indian wars, and declared that the Thirteen Colonies lacked sufficient specie to pay the stamp taxes for a single year. He warned that an attempt to carry out the Stamp Act by the use of troops might bring on rebellion, endorsed Dulany's distinction between internal and external taxes, and called for outright repeal.

A bill for full repeal was brought before the Commons by a vote of 275–167 (22 Feb.), passed the House (4 Mar.), and, as a result of pressure from the king, passed the Lords (17 Mar.). The repeal bill, effective 1 May, received the royal assent 18 Mar. America received the news (word reached New York 26 Apr.) with rejoicing. Nonimportation was immediately abandoned; the New York assembly voted statues to honor the king and Pitt (30 June).

18 Mar. DECLARATORY ACT. Generally overlooked in the rejoicing over the Stamp Act's repeal was a statement of Parliament's authority over America enacted into law on the same day as the repeal measure (couched in the same terms as the Irish Declaratory Act of 1719), and asserting that Parliament had full authority to make laws binding the American colonists "**in all cases whatsoever.**"

1. Nov. TRADE LAWS MODIFIED. The repeal of the Stamp Act was followed by another retreat on the government's part. The 3d. duty on foreign molasses imported by the colonists was now withdrawn (effective 1 Nov.) in favor of a uniform 1d.-per-gallon duty on all molasses, British as well as foreign, coming into the continental colonies. Export duties on British West Indian sugar were removed, thereby reducing its price on the American mainland. The act contained one notably unfavorable provision: all colonial products shipped to northern Europe henceforth had to clear through ports in Great Britain en route.

NEW YORK AND THE QUARTERING ACT CRISIS. Through Gov. Sir Henry Moore (1713–69) Gen. Gage requested (13 Dec. 1765) that the New York assembly make provision for quartering and supplying his troops in accord with the Quartering Act. The assembly, contending that his act weighed heaviest upon their province (New York was Gage's headquarters), refused full compliance (Jan. 1766). Tension mounted through the spring and summer. The destruction of a liberty pole by British soldiers (10 Aug.) led to a clash on the following day between citizens and bayonet-wielding redcoats in which **Isaac Sears** (c.1730–86), a leader of the Sons of Liberty, was wounded. On 15 Dec. the assembly refused any appropriations for Gage's forces and was prorogued (19 Dec.). Not until 6 June 1767 did the assembly vote £3,000. Ignorant of this step, Parliament suspended the assembly's legislative powers (effective 1 Oct. 1767), but due to the grant of 6 June the suspension was not carried out by the governor. On 7 May 1768 the Board of Trade sustained his decision by declaring invalid acts of the assembly after 1 Oct. 1767.

1767

29 June. TOWNSHEND ACTS. When the Chatham ministry came into office (Aug. 1766) Charles Townshend became Chancellor of the Exchequer. By the beginning of 1767, due to Lord Chatham's illness, Townshend was the actual leader of the government. In Jan., he attacked the distinction Americans (and Chatham himself, then William Pitt) had made between external and internal taxation and revealed that he was preparing a new revenue measure to free the administration of government in America from dependence on colonial assemblies. A reduction in the British land tax, carried in defiance of the ministry (27 Feb.), made it imperative to carry out this pledge, for that revision involved a cut of £500,000 in home revenue.

The Townshend Acts conformed to the American position of 1765–66: the taxes were all **external**: import duties on glass, lead, paints, paper, and tea. The estimated annual return of £40,000 could be used (according to the bill's preamble) not only for the defense of the colonies but also for "defraying the charge of the administration of justice, and the support of civil government" in America. To provide for efficient collection of the new duties this bill and a companion measure (1) clearly affirmed the power of superior or supreme court justices to issue writs of assistance; (2)

established new vice-admiralty courts; and (3) an American Board of Commissioners of the Customs at Boston, directly responsible to the British Treasury Board. The acts received the royal assent on 29 June and became effective 20 Nov.

28 Oct. REVIVAL OF NONIMPORTATION. Once more the colonists turned to nonimportation to force Parliament to retreat again. A Boston town meeting (28 Oct.) drew up a list of British products, chiefly luxury goods, which were not to be purchased after 31 Dec. In Providence a stringent nonimportation agreement was signed (2 Dec.) to become effective 1 Jan. 1768; Newport followed suit (4 Dec.); and a mass meeting in New York City (29 Dec.) appointed a committee to draw up a plan to promote domestic industry and employment.

5. Nov. FARMER'S LETTERS. The most significant statement of the constitutional basis for the opposition to the Townshend Acts was written by John Dickinson. First appearing in the *Pennsylvania Chronicle* (5 Nov. 1767–Jan. 1768), his 14 essays, entitled "Letters From a Farmer in Pennsylvania to the Inhabitants of the British Colonies," were widely reprinted in pamphlet form both in Britain and America during 1768. Dickinson conceded Parliament's authority to regulate trade, even if revenue was incidentally produced, but denied its right to tax in order to raise a revenue in America, declared the Townshend duties unconstitutional, and assailed the suspension of the New York assembly as a blow to the liberties of all the colonies.

1768

11 Feb. MASSACHUSETTS CIRCULAR LETTER, drawn up by **Samuel Adams** (p. 972) and approved by the Massachusetts House of Representatives, informed the assemblies of the other 12 colonies of the steps taken by the Massachusetts General Court, denounced the Townshend Acts as violating the principle of no taxation without representation, reasserted the impossibility of representing America adequately in the British Parliament, attacked any move by the crown to make colonial governors and judges independent of the people, and concluded by soliciting proposals for united action. Gov. Francis Bernard (1712–79) condemned the circular letter as seditious and on 4 Mar. dissolved the General Court. This view was shared by the Secretary of State for the Colonies, Lord Hillsborough, who, in a dispatch to the colonial governors (21 Apr.), denounced the letter and ordered that their respective assemblies be prevented, by dissolution if necessary, from endorsing it. This order came too late. By May the assemblies of New Hampshire, New Jersey, and Connecticut had commended the stand of Massachusetts, and Virginia had drafted its own circular letter advising support of Massachusetts. On 22 Apr. Hillsborough ordered Gov. Bernard to dissolve the new General Court should the House of Representatives refuse to rescind the circular letter. Bernard ordered the House to expunge the resolution embodying the letter from its journal (21 June), but after a protracted debate the representatives voted 92–17 (30 June) to defy this command. The court was then dissolved (1 July). The 17 "Rescinders" came under heavy attack by the Sons of Liberty; 7 lost their seats in the election of May 1769.

10 June. SEIZURE OF THE "LIBERTY." Meanwhile, the obstructionist tactics of the people of Boston had led the customs commissioners there to request an armed force to protect them in carrying out their duties (Feb.); repeated in a memorial to the ministry 28

Mar. From Halifax the frigate *Romney*, 50 guns, was dispatched to Boston. Its arrival (17 May) made the customs officials overconfident. When they were informed (9 June) that a wharf official had been locked in a cabin of John Hancock's sloop *Liberty* while Madeira wine was landed without payment of duty, they ordered the seizure of Hancock's vessel (10 June). The *Liberty* was towed from her wharf and anchored close to the *Romney*. A crowd assaulted the customs officials on the dock and demonstrated before their homes. The next day (11 June) the customs officials fled to Castle William on an island in the harbor and again (15 June) appealed for troops.

1 Oct. BRITISH TROOPS IN BOSTON. On 12 Sept. the Boston town meeting, on the alleged ground of an imminent war with France, called upon the people to arm and requested the governor to call the General Court into session. When he refused, 96 Massachusetts towns sent delegates to an informal provincial convention (23–28 Sept.), which broke up the very day British troopships arrived in the harbor. Despite threats of armed resistance made by the Sons of Liberty, 2 regiments of infantry with artillery landed without opposition (1 Oct.) and stationed in the town.

PROGRESS OF NONIMPORTATION. Boston merchants adopted (Mar.) a more stringent nonimportation agreement contingent upon similar action by New York and Philadelphia. In New York such an agreement was signed in Apr. (effective 1 Oct.), but meetings in Philadelphia (Mar.-June) failed to yield a similar compact. Thereupon the Boston merchants drew up their own plan (1 Aug.) barring the importation of the items bearing the Townshend duties from 1 Jan. 1769 until the duties were repealed, and of all but a brief list of British goods (mostly supplies for the fisheries) from 1 Jan. 1769 to 1 Jan. 1770. The merchants of New York countermanded all orders sent to Britain after 15 Aug. and agreed (28 Aug.) to import no British goods from 1 Nov. until the Townshend Acts were repealed. New York tradesmen pledged not to deal with any merchant who refused to join in this accord (5 Sept.).

1769

COURSE OF NONIMPORTATION. By the end of 1769 New Hampshire alone remained aloof from nonimportation. The Philadelphia merchants finally took concrete action (6 Feb.) and on 10 Mar. banned most British goods from 1 Apr.; Baltimore merchants followed suit 30 Mar.

16–18 May. VIRGINIA RESOLVES AND ASSOCIATION. On 16 May George Washington introduced in the Virginia House of Burgesses a set of resolutions framed by **George Mason** (p. 1098). Adopted unanimously, they asserted that the sole right of taxing Virginians lay with the governor and provincial legislature; censured by inference the British ministry for its denunciation of the Massachusetts and Virginia circular letters; condemned the Parliamentary proposal that American malcontents be brought to England for trial under an act of Henry VIII. An address to the king was drawn up by **Patrick Henry** and **Richard Henry Lee** (p. 1082) just before Gov. Botetourt (1718–70) dissolved the assembly (17 May). The burgesses met informally the next day in Williamsburg's Raleigh Tavern and adopted the Virginia Association, a nonimportation agreement banning the importation of British goods (except paper) upon which a duty was charged, of slaves (after 1 Nov.), and of a long list of European luxury goods.

June–Nov. SPREAD OF THE ASSOCIATION. A Maryland provincial convention meeting at Annapolis (22 June) drew up an association based on the Virginia model, augmented by a provision for boycotting those refusing to sign or keep the compact. South Carolina took similar action (22 July) and its agreement was copied by the citizens of Savannah, Ga. (19 Sept.). An informal meeting of the North Carolina assembly endorsed the Virginia Association (7 Nov.). In Delaware and Connecticut nonimportation pledges were drawn up in the port towns (June–Aug.). Providence merchants acted 24 Oct. In Newport a very weak agreement was signed (30 Oct.). Threats of boycott by New York and Philadelphia merchants forced a tightening of its terms later in the year. The New Jersey assembly endorsed (18 Oct.) the sanctions against British imports entered into by the merchants of New Jersey, Pennsylvania, and New York.

EFFECTS OF NONIMPORTATION. Colonial imports from Britain fell from £ 2,157,218 in 1768 to £ 1,336,122 in 1769; in New York and Philadelphia from £ 490,673 to £ 75,930 and from £ 441,829 to £ 204,978, respectively. Though these American trade losses were largely offset by a rising market in Europe for British goods, the ministry, now led by the Duke of Grafton, was disturbed. As early as 13 May the Board of Trade informed the governors that modifications of the Townshend duties were under consideration.

1770

12 Apr. TOWNSHEND DUTIES LIMITED TO TEA ALONE. The movement for repeal of the Townshend measures gained new impetus when **Lord Frederick North** became head of the government (31 Jan.). North believed that complete repeal might be interpreted as a sign of weakness; his stand for partial repeal was sustained in the cabinet by a 5–4 vote. In Commons (5 Mar.) he proposed a bill for the withdrawal of all the Townshend duties except that on tea and pledged that his ministry would lay no new taxes upon the colonists. The alteration in the Townshend duties received the king's consent 12 Apr. At the same time the Quartering Act was allowed to expire without renewal.

COLLAPSE OF NONIMPORTATION. Although most of the colonial nonimportation agreements had made repeal of all the Townshend duties a condition for dropping their sanctions against British goods, the withdrawal of all but the **tea tax** led to the abandonment of the program, despite Boston's attempt to hold the line (25 Apr.). Merchants in Albany, Providence, and Newport moved to abandon nonimportation (May); a house-to-house poll in New York City (7–9 July), which revealed that its inhabitants favored resuming imports of all but tea and other articles actually bearing a duty, led to an abandonment of the various associations, to which Philadelphia (12 Sept.), Boston (12 Oct.), South Carolina (13 Dec.), and finally Virginia (July 1771) bowed.

19 JAN. BATTLE OF GOLDEN HILL. The contest in New York over the Quartering Act had been renewed late in 1768 when the assembly once again refused to vote supplies (31 Dec.). This position was maintained by a new assembly (elected Jan. 1769) until 15 Dec. 1769, when an appropriation of £2,000 was voted. **Alexander McDougall** (1732–86), a leader of the Sons of Liberty in New York, issued a broadside criticizing the assembly, entitled "To the Betrayed Inhabitants of the City and Colony of New York" (16 Dec.). Clashes between citizens and soldiers broke out early in 1770. After one ineffectual attempt (13 Jan.) British soldiers succeeded in cutting down the town's liberty pole (17 Jan.). A countermove by Sons of Liberty to prevent the posting of broadsides by soldiers (19 Jan.) led to a riot on Golden Hill in which some 30 or 40 soldiers used bayonets against citizens armed with cutlasses and clubs. Several on both sides were wounded seriously, but there were no fatalities. McDougall was arrested (8 Feb.) and charged with authorship of the broadside. He refused to post bond and remained in prison until 29 Apr., when he entered a plea of not guilty and was released on bail. The case never came to trial owing to the death of the state's witness. However, McDougall was called before the assembly (13 Dec.) and imprisoned for contempt until 27 Apr. 1771.

5 MAR. BOSTON MASSACRE. Minor clashes between citizens and soldiers were common occurrences in Boston following the arrival of the troops (1 Oct. 1768). In Oct. 1769 a serious encounter was ended only when the troops fired a volley into the air. Early in 1770 collisions between town laborers and soldiers seeking employment in off-duty hours became frequent. A fist fight between a worker and soldier at Grey's ropewalk on the afternoon of 5 Mar. quickly became a small riot. That evening belligerent bands of both civilians and soldiers roamed the streets of Boston. The pent-up tension exploded about 9 P.M. when a beleaguered sentry in King St. near the State House called the main guard, led by Capt. Thomas Preston, to his aid. When the swelling crowd pressed upon this detachment, the soldiers, upon the command of a person never identified, fired into the mob, killing 3 outright and wounding 2 mortally. A general uprising was averted only when Lt. Gov. Hutchinson bowed to a demand by Sam Adams and withdrew the troops from the town to islands in the harbor. Preston and 8 of his men were arrested for murder by the civil authorities (6 Mar.). Two outstanding Patriot lawyers, **John Adams** (p. 971) and **Josiah Quincy** (1744–75), agreed to undertake the defense. At the trial (24–30 Oct.) Preston and 6 soldiers were acquitted, while 2 of the guard, found guilty of manslaughter, pleaded their clergy (were branded on the hand) and were released.

1771

LULL IN AGITATION. Despite exploitation of the "Boston Massacre" by Sam Adams as well as Paul Revere's engraving of the incident, tension relaxed between colonies and mother country. Compacts against the importation and use of dutied tea remained the sole significant vestiges of conflict.

16 MAY. BATTLE OF ALAMANCE. In interior North Carolina a group known as the **Regulators,** active as an organized body since 1768 (under the leadership of **Herman Husbands** [1724–95]), had taken the law into their own hands, protesting lack of representation for the Piedmont areas in the assembly and charging extortion and oppression by the eastern part of the province. Increasing disorders led to the passage of the Johnston Bill (the "Bloody Act"), which made rioters guilty of treason (15 Jan. 1771). Early in May Gov. **William Tryon** (1729–88) led a force of 1,200 militiamen into the heart of the Regulator country. On 16 May he met and crushed some 2,000 Regulators (many of whom had no firearms) at Alamance Creek near Hillsboro. One insurgent leader, James Few, was executed on the battlefield (17 May); 12 others were found guilty of treason (17 June) and

6 executed. The other 6 as well as some 6,500 Piedmont settlers were obliged to take an oath of allegiance to the government. The incident revealed deep-seated sectional differences, also reflected in South Carolina, where the grievances of a vigilante movement, also called Regulators, who had protested lawlessness on the frontier, were largely met in 1769 when courts were set up in the back country.

1772

9 JUNE. BURNING OF THE "GASPEE." On the afternoon of 9 June the customs schooner *Gaspee* ran aground on Namquit Point, 7 miles below Providence, while pursuing another vessel. After nightfall 8 boatloads of men from Providence led by merchant **John Brown** (1736–1803) attacked the schooner. Lt. William Duddingston, in command, was wounded. After the officer and crew were set ashore, the attackers set the *Gaspee* afire. A royal proclamation (26 Aug.) offered a £500 reward for the discovery of the culprits. On 2 Sept. Gov. Joseph Wanton (R.I.), the vice-admiralty judge at Boston, and the chief justices of Massachusetts, New York, and New Jersey were named as Commissioners of Inquiry. Those identified by the commissioners were to be sent to England for trial. Two sessions were held at Newport (Jan. and May 1773) but, in the face of open hostility by Rhode Islanders, neither turned up any tangible evidence. The commission finally adjourned June 1773.

13 JUNE. CRIPPLING THE POWER OF THE PURSE. The proposal to try the case of the *Gaspee* in England alarmed even the moderates. More threatening to local self-rule was the announcement by Gov. Hutchinson of Massachusetts (13 June) that henceforth he would receive his salary from the crown, followed in Sept. by a similar announcement relative to the Massachusetts judges. Thus executive and judiciary were at a stroke rendered practically independent of the General Court's power of the purse.

2 Nov. NEW COMMITTEES OF CORRESPONDENCE. Sam Adams issued a call (5 Oct.) to the towns to form associations to discuss this new threat. Over considerable opposition (led by John Hancock) within the Patriot circle, he succeeded (28 Oct.) in having a call issued for a Boston town meeting, at which (2 Nov.) he secured the appointment of a 21-man standing Committee of Correspondence to communicate Boston's position to the other towns in the province and "to the World" with the request that the other towns reciprocate. James Otis was made chairman of the Boston committee. On 20 Nov. 3 radical statements were reported from the committee to the town meeting, endorsed, and sent on to the other towns: Sam Adams' "State of the Rights of the Colonists," a "List of Infringements and Violations of those Rights" by **Joseph Warren** (1741–75), and a "Letter of Correspondence" by Dr. **Benjamin Church** (1734–76), later proved to be a British informer. The appointment of town Committees of Correspondence continued into 1773.

1773

EXPANSION OF COMMITTEES OF CORRESPONDENCE. Radicals elsewhere hastened to adopt the Massachusetts system. The Virginia House of Burgesses (12 Mar.) appointed an 11-man standing committee for intercolonial correspondence, including Patrick Henry, **Thomas Jefferson** (p. 1070), and Richard Henry Lee. By 8 July Rhode Island, Connecticut, New Hampshire, and South Carolina, in addition, had formed provincial committees, and by Feb. 1774 all but

North Carolina and Pennsylvania had taken action.

10 MAY. TEA ACT. By early 1773 the East India Co. was on the verge of bankruptcy, its stock down from 280 to 160 on the London exchange. With a vast surplus of 17 million lbs. of tea on hand in England, the company sought relief from a government predisposed to save it because of its valuable hold on India. A bill passed by the Commons (27 Apr.) provided for full remission (after 10 May) of all British duties on teas exported to the American colonies. The import tax of 3d. per lb. in America was retained, however. More important was the provision giving the company (obliged up to this time to sell its tea at public auction in England) the right to sell tea directly to agents or consignees in the colonies. With the drawbacks on the British duties enabling it to cut the price of its tea the company was now in a position, even with the handicap of the 3d. duty in America, to undersell there both the law-abiding colonial merchant who had bought tea through middlemen at higher prices and the colonial smuggler who bought his tea in Holland. The company, authorized (Sept.) to send half a million lbs. of tea to Boston, New York, Philadelphia, and Charleston, consigned the tea to a picked group of merchants.

TERRORIZING THE TEA CONSIGNEES. The American opposition to the Tea Act centered not upon the duty (now 6 years old) but upon the threat of monopoly. A mass meeting in Philadelphia (16 Oct.) condemned the act and appointed a committee to demand resignation of the Philadelphia consignees. The latter bowed to this demand. A Boston town meeting (5–6 Nov.) endorsed the Philadelphia resolves but was unable to secure the resignation of the Boston consignees, among whom were 2 sons and a nephew of Gov.

Hutchinson. In New York City, a broadside (10 Nov.) warned harbor pilots against guiding any tea ship up the harbor. A meeting of the Sons of Liberty (29 Nov.) branded tea importers enemies of America and pledged a boycott. The New York consignees resigned their commissions (1 Dec.).

16 DEC. BOSTON TEA PARTY. The *Dartmouth*, first of 3 tea ships, arrived in Boston harbor 27 Nov. Two mass meetings (29–30 Nov.) resolved that the tea must be sent back to England without payment of any duty. This Hutchinson refused to permit. He gave orders to the harbor authorities to allow the tea ships to pass outward only upon presentation of a permit certifying that the tea duties had been paid, a position he reiterated on 16 Dec. On the next day, in keeping with a 20-day waiting period under customs regulations, the tea aboard the *Dartmouth* became liable to seizure for nonpayment of customs duties. On the evening of the 16th some 8,000 people assembled in and near Boston's Old South Church heard Francis Rotch, the *Dartmouth's* owner's son, inform Sam Adams, chairman of the meeting, of the governor's final refusal. Thereupon, at a signal from Adams, a disciplined group of men disguised as Mohawk Indians rushed to Griffin's Wharf, boarded the tea ships, and, working through the night, dumped all the tea (342 chests) into the harbor. No other property aboard was damaged.

22 DEC. TEA LANDED AT CHARLESTON. Charleston's tea ship, the *London,* arrived 2 Dec. A mass meeting held the next day demanded and secured the resignations of the tea consignees. After the lapse of the 20-day period the customs officials, without opposition, landed the tea for nonpayment of the duties upon it. The tea was stored in government warehouses and remained there until the revolutionary government auctioned it off to raise funds (July 1776).

DEC. HUTCHINSON LETTERS SCANDAL. Late in 1772 Benjamin Franklin, as London agent for the Massachusetts House of Representatives, sent Speaker Thomas Cushing the originals of 6 letters written (1767–69) by Thomas Hutchinson (then chief justice) and 4 by Andrew Oliver (province secretary) to Thomas Whately, a member of the Grenville and North ministries. The letters were given to Franklin to show him that false advice from America went far toward explaining the obnoxious acts of the British government. Franklin sent the letters to Cushing, warning him that they were not to be copied or published but merely shown in the original to individuals in the province. But in June 1773 Samuel Adams read the letters before a secret session of the House of Representatives and later had the letters copied and printed. The House petitioned the king for the removal of Hutchinson and Oliver from office. When this petition reached London the affair of the letters became a scandal. Whately was now dead, but his brother William accused a John Temple of having stolen and released the letters. The pair fought a duel (11 Dec.), and when that was inconclusive plans were made for another encounter. Learning of this, Franklin announced (25 Dec.) that he alone was responsible for sending the letters to Boston.

1774

30 JAN. FRANKLIN DISCIPLINED. On 11 Jan. a committee of the Privy Council began hearings on the Massachusetts petition. Franklin was granted a postponement. Questioning was resumed on 29 Jan., by which date the news of the Boston Tea Party had reached London. Franklin disdained replying to a virulent attack by Solicitor General Alexander Wedderburn, who denounced Franklin as a man without honor and a thief. The committee's report to the Privy Council that the petition was based on false charges was approved (7 Feb.). On 30 Jan. Franklin was informed that he had been dismissed from his office of Deputy Postmaster General for America. In Massachusetts the House voted in Feb., 92-8, to impeach Oliver for accepting a salary from the crown, but before the case was tried Hutchinson prorogued (30 Mar.), and then dissolved the General Court.

MAR.–DEC. FURTHER TEA DISORDERS. March saw further Boston disorders. When a reckless private consignee elected to land a cargo of tea secretly in New York, Sons of Liberty disguised as Indians dumped the tea into the harbor (22 Apr.). A tea cargo brought into Annapolis aboard the *Peggy Stewart* (14 Oct.) was destroyed by fire along with the ship (19 Oct.). Flames consumed a shipment of tea (22 Dec.) temporarily stored at Greenwich, N.J.

31 MAR., 20 MAY. COERCIVE ACTS. Parliament met (7 Mar.) in an angry mood. Chatham and Edmund Burke failed to dissuade it from endorsing the king's personal wish that Massachusetts be punished for the Tea Party in particular and for its long intransigence in general. The first of the "Coercive" measures, the **Boston Port Bill,** passed the Commons 25 Mar. and received the royal assent 31 Mar. Effective 1 June, this act prohibited the loading or unloading of ships in any part of Boston Harbor. Exceptions were made for military stores and for shipments of food and fuel which obtained clearance from the customs officials henceforth to sit at Salem rather than Boston. The king was authorized to reopen the port to trade when the East India Co. and the customs had been

compensated for the losses incurred by the Tea Party.

Two months later more comprehensive measures were enacted. The **Administration of Justice Act** (20 May) was designed to encourage crown officials in Massachusetts by protecting them from major suits before hostile provincial courts. Upon the sworn statement of the governor that the act upon which an indictment for a capital offense was based had been committed in putting down a riot or in collecting revenue, and that a fair trial could not be obtained in Massachusetts, the trial could be transferred to Britain (the provincial council's assent to the move was stipulated).

Massachusetts Government Act (20 May) worked even more drastic changes, virtually annulling the Massachusetts charter. Effective 1 Aug., members of the Council, heretofore elected by the House of Representatives, were to be appointed by the king and hold office at royal pleasure. Effective 1 July, the attorney general, inferior judges, sheriffs, and justices of the peace became appointable and removable by the governor. The governor was also empowered to nominate the chief justice and superior judges for appointment by the king. Juries were to be summoned by the sheriff rather than elected by the people of the towns. Finally, in a move designed to deprive the radicals of their most effective medium, the town meeting, the act provided that meetings in addition to the annual election session could not be held without the prior written consent of the governor and, if approved, must be confined to the agenda which he approved.

20 MAY. QUEBEC ACT, though not a part of the coercive program, was regarded by the colonists as one of the "Intolerable" measures. The act provided a permanent civil government for Canada, ruled since 1763 by makeshift means. In keeping with the French tradition of the inhabitants the administration was made highly centralized. Legislative authority was vested in a council appointed by the crown. Its acts were subject to the royal veto and all but purely local taxation was specifically reserved to the British Parliament. Civil cases were to be tried without benefit of a jury. Catholics were granted religious toleration and civil rights; their church's privileges confirmed. American colonists looked askance at all these features so opposed to their own traditions. But perhaps the most objectionable feature of the Quebec Act in their eyes was the extension of Canada's boundaries to the Ohio River, an area in which Virginia, Connecticut, and Massachusetts had claims.

2 JUNE. QUARTERING ACT applied to *all* the colonies. It legalized the quartering of troops in uninhabited houses, out-houses, barns, and other buildings.

COLONIAL PROTEST. On 13 May Gen. Thomas Gage arrived in Boston to supplant Hutchinson as governor. On the same day a Boston town meeting called for new economic sanctions against Britain to force repeal of the Coercive Acts. The first of many public calls for an intercolonial congress came from Providence (17 May). Philadelphia (21 May) and New York City (23 May) sidestepped Boston's appeal for immediate nonimportation in favor of a congress at which common measures binding all the colonies might be framed. Massachusetts yielded. On 17 June the House of Representatives suggested that a congress be held in Sept. at Philadelphia. Boston's Committee of Correspondence, nevertheless, drew up a Solemn League and Covenant (5 June) which bound its subscribers to end all business dealings with Britain and stop consumption of British imports after 1 Oct. In the

other colonies provincial congresses or county conventions proceeded to name delegates to Congress (15 June–25 Aug.). Only in Georgia was the attempt (10 Aug.) to name delegates defeated.

5 SEPT.–26 OCT. 1ST CONTINENTAL CONGRESS. Twelve colonies (excepting Georgia) sent 56 delegates to the Congress, which opened in Carpenters' Hall. Among them were conservatives, such as **Joseph Galloway** (Pa., c.1731–1803), **James Duane** (N.Y., 1733–97), and **George Read** (Del., 1733–98), and radicals like the two Adamses (Mass.), **Christopher Gadsden** (S.C., 1724–1805) and **Patrick Henry** and **Richard Henry Lee** (Va.). **Peyton Randolph** (Va., c.1721–75) was elected president, and a nondelegate, **Charles Thomson** (Pa., 1729–1824), named secretary. The delegates decided to vote by provincial units, each having one vote, and pledged themselves to secrecy. On 17 Sept. the radical delegates succeeded in having the **Suffolk Resolves** endorsed by the Congress. These resolutions, the work of Joseph Warren, had been adopted by a convention in Suffolk Co., Mass. (9 Sept.), and carried posthaste to Philadelphia by Paul Revere. The resolutions (1) declared the Coercive Acts unconstitutional and hence not to be obeyed; (2) urged the people of Massachusetts to form a government to collect taxes and withhold them from the royal government until the repeal of the Coercive Acts; (3) advised the people to arm and form their own militia; and (4) recommended stringent economic sanctions against Britain.

28 SEPT. GALLOWAY'S PLAN OF UNION. The conservatives attempted to offset the endorsement of the Suffolk Resolves by uniting behind Joseph Galloway's "Plan of a Proposed Union between Great Britain and the Colonies" to regulate the "general affairs of America," each colony continuing to govern its internal affairs. The central administration would consist of (1) a president-general appointed by the king and holding office at the king's pleasure with a veto over the acts of (2) a grand council, whose members were to be chosen for 3-year terms by the assemblies of each province. The president and council would constitute an "inferior and distinct branch of the British legislature." Measures dealing with America might originate either with this body or the British Parliament, the consent of the other being required for a measure to become law. By a vote of 6–5 this plan was defeated, and subsequently (22 Oct.) expunged from the minutes of Congress.

14 Oct. DECLARATION AND RESOLVES adopted by the Congress denounced the Coercive Acts and the Quebec Act as unjust, cruel, and unconstitutional, and criticized the revenue measures imposed since 1763, the extension of vice-admiralty jurisdiction, the dissolution of colonial assemblies, and the keeping of a standing army in the colonial towns in peacetime. Ten resolutions set forth the rights of the colonists, among them to "life, liberty and property," and, of the provincial legislatures, to the exclusive power of lawmaking "in all cases of taxation and internal polity," subject only to the royal veto. Thirteen parliamentary acts since 1763 were declared to violate American rights and economic sanctions pledged until they were repealed.

18 Oct. CONTINENTAL ASSOCIATION, closely modeled upon a Virginia Association framed 1–6 Aug., constituted a pledge by the delegates that their provinces would (1) cease all importation from Britain effective 1 Dec.; (2) totally discontinue the slave trade 1 Dec.; (3) institute nonconsumption of British products and various foreign luxury products (1 Mar. 1775); (4) embargo all exports to Britain, Ireland, and

the West Indies effective 1 Sept. 1775. Notable were those clauses establishing extralegal machinery for enforcement. A committee was to be elected in each county, town, and city to execute the Association. Violators were to be punished by publicity and boycott. On the higher level, any province which failed to keep the Association was to be boycotted. By Apr. 1775 the Association was in operation in 12 colonies; even Georgia adopted a modified version (23 Jan. 1775).

26 Oct. ADJOURNMENT OF CONGRESS. After preparing an address to the king and to the British and American peoples, Congress adjourned, but (22 Oct.) resolved to meet again 10 May 1775 if by that date American grievances had not been redressed.

DOMINION THEORY. The delegates at Philadelphia had been influenced by the constitutional viewpoints of **James Wilson** (Pa., p. 1186) and young **Thomas Jefferson.** Wilson's *Considerations on the Nature and Extent of the Legislative Authority of the British Parliament* (17 Aug.) rejected Parliament's authority over the colonies in favor of allegiance to the king alone. Jefferson expressed a similar view in his *Summary View of the Rights of British America* (July), an appeal to George III to heed "liberal and expanded thought." After Congress adjourned John Adams expressed the "dominion theory" in his **Novanglus** letters (Dec. 1774–Apr. 1775) written to answer the Tory viewpoint of "Massachusettensis" (Daniel Leonard, p. 849). The colonies, Adams contended, were not part of the British realm and hence not subject to Parliament, for "Massachusetts is a realm, New York is a realm . . ." over which the king is sovereign.

WAR PREPARATIONS IN NEW ENGLAND. On 1 Sept. British troops from Boston marched out to Charlestown and Cambridge and seized cannon and powder belonging to the province. Thousands of militiamen flocked to Cambridge but hostilities did not break out. Gen. Gage set about fortifying Boston Neck (Sept.). On 7 Oct. the Massachusetts House, meeting in Salem in defiance of Gage, constituted itself a Provincial Congress, and named John Hancock to head a Committee of Safety empowered to call out the militia. Special groups within the militia (minutemen) were to be ready for instant call. On 14 Dec., warned on the 13th by Paul Revere of a plan to garrison British troops at Portsmouth, N.H., a band led by **John Sullivan** (1740–95) broke into Ft. William and Mary in Portsmouth, overpowered the small garrison without inflicting or suffering casualties, and carried away arms and gunpowder.

1775

27 FEB. LORD NORTH'S CONCILIATION PLAN. The petitions and Declaration of Congress were laid before Parliament on 19 Jan. The next day Chatham moved an address from the Lords to the king requesting immediate removal of the troops in Boston but was defeated by a 3–1 margin. Later (1 Feb.) he introduced a plan of reconciliation which embraced (1) a recognition of the Continental Congress, (2) a pledge by Parliament that no revenue measures would be levied upon America without the consent of the provincial assemblies, (3) American recognition of the "supreme legislative authority and superintending power" of Parliament, and (4) a plan by which the Continental Congress would vote a revenue for the crown. This measure was also rejected by the Lords. A declaration by both houses (9 Feb.) termed Massachusetts to be in rebellion. On 20 Feb. Lord North presented the ministerial plan for reconciliation which had George III's grudging consent. By its terms Parliament, with royal approval, would "forbear" to lay any but regulatory taxes upon any American colony which, through its own assembly, taxed itself to provide for the common defense and for the support of the civil government and judiciary within its own province. The Commons endorsed the plan 27 Feb.

30 MAR. NEW ENGLAND RESTRAINING ACT. On the same day (27 Feb.) a bill was introduced forbidding the New England colonies to trade with any nation but Britain and the British West Indies after 1 July and barring New Englanders from the North Atlantic fisheries after 20 July. Despite a brilliant speech by Burke (22 Mar.) the bill was passed and received the royal assent (30 Mar.). Soon afterward (13 Apr.) the provisions of the act were made to apply to New Jersey, Pennsylvania, Maryland, Virginia, and South Carolina, news of their ratification of the Continental Association having reached London.

CRISIS IN NEW ENGLAND. A second Massachusetts Provincial Congress met at Cambridge (1 Feb.), and under the leadership of Hancock and Joseph Warren framed measures to prepare the colony for war. On 26 Feb. British troops landed at Salem to seize military supplies, but were turned back without violence. On 23 Mar. Patrick Henry predicted in his famous "Liberty or Death" speech before the Virginia House of Burgesses that news of the outbreak of hostilities in New England could be expected momentarily. He proved to be a good prophet. On 14 Apr. Gen. Gage received a letter of 27 Jan. from Lord Dartmouth, Secretary of State for the Colonies, ordering him to use force if necessary to execute the Coercive and other acts, to strike at once, even if that meant bringing on hostilities, rather than permit the rebellious faction time to perfect their organization.

19 Apr. LEXINGTON AND CONCORD. Aware that Concord (21 miles from Boston by road) was a major supply depot for the militia organized by the Provincial Congress, Gage decided to strike quickly. On 14 Apr. he relieved the Light Infantry and Grenadiers from guard duty and had boats brought ashore from the transports (15 Apr.). On 18 Apr. Lt. Col. Francis Smith received secret orders to lead a force of some 700 men to Concord and destroy the supplies there the next morning. About 10 p.m. the troops marched to the edge of the Common and began embarking in boats for the short row across the Charles River to Cambridge. The Boston Committee of Safety, learning of their destination, sent **Paul Revere** and **William Dawes** (1745–99) to alert the countryside. Revere reached Lexington (5 miles from Concord) at midnight and warned Sam Adams and John Hancock, who were staying there. About 1 a.m. (19 Apr.) Revere, joined by Dawes and Dr. Samuel Prescott, left Lexington for Concord. On the way a British mounted patrol surprised them. Prescott escaped and got through to Concord; Dawes eluded the British but had to turn back; Revere was captured and brought back to Lexington before being released.

Smith's forces reached Lexington at dawn and found 70 armed Minute Men under Capt. **John Parker** (1729–75) drawn up on the Common. Upon the repeated commands of Maj. John Pitcairn, commanding the British advance units, the Americans had begun to file off (though without dropping their weapons as ordered) when a report from an unidentified firearm brought, without a command by Pitcairn, a series of volleys from the British platoons. Only a few shots were returned from the American ranks where 8 lay dead and 10

were wounded. Only one British soldier was wounded. Smith re-formed his men and marched on to Concord, where he destroyed some gun carriages, entrenching tools, flour, and a liberty pole. Late in the morning the steadily swelling American forces attacked a British platoon at Concord's North Bridge, inflicting 14 casualties. Smith left Concord for the return march to Boston shortly after noon and soon found the countryside swarming with militiamen who assailed his column from all sides. Only the arrival of reinforcements when he reached Lexington saved him from complete disaster. The relentless attacks continued until the expeditionary force reached Charlestown and the protection of the guns of the men-of-war in the harbor. Total British casualties for the day: 73 killed, 174 wounded, 26 missing. Almost 4,000 American militia saw action during that day; of these 93 were dead, wounded, or missing. The provincial forces closed in on Boston and began a siege which was to last until Mar. 1776. On 23 Apr. the Provincial Congress authorized the raising of 13,600 men, made **Artemas Ward** (1727–1800) commander in chief, and appealed to the other colonies for aid. By 20 May Rhode Island, Connecticut, and New Hampshire had voted to send 9,500 men to Cambridge, Ward's headquarters.

10 May. CAPTURE OF FT. TICONDEROGA. Late in Apr. the Massachusetts Committee of Safety authorized **Benedict Arnold** (p. 975) to raise 400 men in western Massachusetts and attack Ft. Ticonderoga on Lake Champlain, a strategic post rich in artillery and other military supplies. On 6 May Arnold learned that **Ethan Allen** (1738–89) was raising a force at Castleton, Vt., for an attack on Ticonderoga. Arnold hurried to Castleton and claimed command but without success. Nevertheless he accompanied Allen and was with the force of 83 men with which the latter crossed the lake (9 May). Early on the 10th the Americans surprised the British garrison of 42 men, which yielded, according to Allen, upon his demand "in the name of the great Jehovah and the Continental Congress." One wounded British soldier was the only casualty. On 12 May Crown Point north of Ticonderoga was also seized and St. John's, across the Canadian border, was occupied by Arnold on 16 May.

10 May. 2D CONTINENTAL CONGRESS. New figures at the 2d Continental Congress, convened in the State House (Independence Hall), Philadelphia, included Benjamin Franklin, John Hancock, James Wilson, and, later in the session, Thomas Jefferson. Missing were conservatives like Galloway (Pa.) and Isaac Low (N.Y.). **Peyton Randolph** and **Charles Thomson** were again chosen president and secretary, but on 24 May Randolph withdrew from the Congress and **John Hancock** was elected to succeed him. On 15 May Congress resolved to put the colonies in a state of defense and on 29 May adopted an address to the people of Canada asking them as "fellow-sufferers" to join with rather than against the 12 colonies (Georgia was not yet represented at the Congress officially).

20 May. MECKLENBURG COUNTY RESOLUTIONS, reputedly adopted by a convention in Mecklenburg Co., N.C., and sent to the North Carolina delegation at Philadelphia (but never presented to Congress), declared all laws and commissions deriving their authority from the king or Parliament to be annulled and the royal government of the provinces "wholly suspended" for the present. Henceforth all legislative and executive power within each colony would devolve upon the Provincial Congress. Within Mecklenburg Co. anyone accepting a royal commission was branded

an enemy and ordered to be apprehended. No original copy of the Resolutions has ever been found.

15 June. WASHINGTON NAMED CHIEF OF THE CONTINENTAL FORCES. On 10 June John Adams proposed that the Congress accept the forces besieging Boston as a Continental Army and appoint a general, hinting strongly that this appointment should go to **George Washington.** On 14 June Congress resolved to raise 6 companies of riflemen in Pennsylvania, Maryland, and Virginia to march to New England and named a 5-man committee to draft rules for the administration of the Continental Army. On 15 June Thomas Johnson (Md.) nominated Washington to be commander in chief; seconded by John Adams and carried by a unanimous vote. The next day Washington formally accepted the command and offered to serve without a salary. The proposed organizational plan for the army was adopted; **Artemas Ward, Charles Lee** (1731–82), **Philip Schuyler** (1733–1804), and **Israel Putnam** (1718–90) were appointed major generals (17 June). To support the army Congress voted (22 June) to issue $2 million in bills of credit with the "12 Confederated Colonies" pledged to share the burden of redemption in proportion to population.

17 June. BATTLE OF BUNKER HILL. During May both the British in Boston and the American forces surrounding the city built up their strength. Three major generals (**Sir William Howe, Sir Henry Clinton,** and **John Burgoyne**) arrived 25 May to assist Gage. British combat forces had increased from c.5,000 (1 Jan. 1775) to c.6,500 (15 June). By the middle of June the American strength was about 10,000 men. On 12 June Gage issued a proclamation which (1) imposed martial law; (2) declared the Americans in arms and those aiding them to be rebels and traitors; and

BATTLE OF BUNKER HILL
17 JUNE 1775

American forces
British forces

Scale of Feet
0   500   1000

Charlestown Neck

BUNKER HILL

PUTNAM

Mill Pond

GERRISH

CAUSEWAY

STARK

Fence

LIGHT INF.

GREN.

GREN.

PRESCOTT

BREED'S HILL

52nd

43rd

Redoubt

38th

GLASGOW

MARINES   47th   5th

GREN. LIGHT INF
43 RGT 52 RGT 5 RGT
38 RGT

Morton's Point

Landing

FALCON

MARINES   47th

Reinforcements landed here

LIVELY

Charlestown

C H A R L E S

R I V E R

SECOND POSITION OF LIVELY

SOMERSET

COPP'S HILL

(3) offered pardon to all those who returned to their allegiance with 2 exceptions: Sam Adams and John Hancock.

On 15 June the Committee of Safety learned that Gage intended to occupy Dorchester Heights on 18 June. The council of war decided upon an immediate countermove against the high ground on Charlestown peninsula overlooking Boston. After dark on 16 June 1,200 men moved onto the peninsula and began to construct a redoubt on **Breed's Hill**, nearer Boston than Bunker Hill, the site originally chosen for this fortification. The work party was discovered at dawn on the 17th and the American position was at once brought under fire from the British ships in the harbor. Gage decided on a frontal assault to dislodge the Americans, but had to await a favorable tide after noon for landing his troops on the peninsula. The immediate command of the assault force, 2,400 in number, was given to Gen. Howe. The main American position, the redoubt, was garrisoned by 1,600 men with 6 cannon, under the command of Col. **William Prescott** (1726–95). Twice Howe's troops, burdened by heavy packs and advancing in tight formation, moved up the hill only to be turned back by a murderous fire. Reinforced by Clinton for a third assault, Howe had his men drop their packs and ordered a bayonet charge. This time the fire from the redoubt slackened as the supply of powder gave out and the British seized the hill. Bunker Hill was then rapidly assaulted and won as the American retreat became a near rout. Howe decided against pressing on toward Cambridge and stopped the pursuit at the base of the peninsula. The British had won the field but at a cost of 1,054 casualties, a high proportion of them officers. The American losses, almost all of which were suffered after the fall of the redoubt, numbered 100 dead (including Joseph Warren), 267 wounded, 30 taken prisoner. Two weeks after the battle Washington reached Cambridge and took formal command of an army of 14,500 on 3 July.

5 JULY. OLIVE BRANCH PETITION, adopted by Congress and written by **John Dickinson** (largely discarding an earlier draft by John Jay), professed the attachment of the American people to George III, expressed their hope for the restoration of harmony, and begged the king to prevent further hostile actions against the colonies until a reconciliation was worked out. On 6 July Congress adopted another important resolution, written jointly by Jefferson and Dickinson, a "Declaration of the Causes and Necessities of Taking Up Arms," which rejected independence but asserted that Americans were ready to die rather than be enslaved. A significant phrase touched upon the possibility of receiving foreign aid against Britain. On 15 July Congress voted to waive the provisions of the Continental Association where war supplies were concerned and on 31 July rejected Lord North's plan for reconciliation. Before adjourning (2 Aug.) Congress assumed 2 additional functions of

an independent government: the appointment of commissioners to negotiate treaties of peace with the Indian tribes (19 July), and the establishment of a Post Office Department with Benjamin Franklin as Postmaster General (26 July).

28 AUG.–31 DEC. MONTGOMERY'S EXPEDITION AGAINST QUEBEC. On 27 June, having received word that Sir Guy Carleton, British commander in Canada, was recruiting a Canadian force for an invasion of New York, Congress authorized Gen. Philip Schuyler to seize any points in Canada vital to the security of the colonies. Schuyler assembled an expeditionary force at Ticonderoga and began his advance from there (28 Aug.) with about 1,000 men. Crossing into Canada, he laid siege to St. John's (6 Sept.), garrisoned by about 600 British and Canadian troops. Ill health forced Schuyler to leave the army (13 Sept.) in the command of Brig. Gen. **Richard Montgomery** (1738–75), to whom the garrison of St. John's capitulated (2 Nov.). Carleton withdrew the remnants of his small force toward Quebec, thereby uncovering Montreal, which the Americans occupied 13 Nov. Carleton was almost captured when his flotilla of 11 small ships surrendered (19 Nov.), but managed to escape to Quebec.

12 SEPT.–31 DEC. ARNOLD'S EXPEDITION AGAINST QUEBEC. Benedict Arnold recruited a force of about 1,100 volunteers at Cambridge with Washington's permission and set out for Maine (12 Sept.). From Gardiner he moved inland to Ft. Western (Augusta), from which base the main trek began (24 Sept.) through country few white men had seen. The difficult terrain and shortness of provisions led one of the expedition's 4 divisions to turn back (25 Oct.). With 650 men Arnold reached the St. Lawrence opposite Quebec (8 Nov.) and crossed the river on the 13th. On 3 Dec. he was joined by Montgomery with 300 men from Montreal. At 5 A.M., 31 Dec., a combined assault was launched against Quebec but ended in disaster. Montgomery was killed, Arnold wounded, almost 100 men killed or wounded, over 300 taken prisoner. With the remnants of his force Arnold maintained a weak cordon around the city throughout the winter.

12 SEPT. CONGRESS RECONVENES. The presence of a delegation from Georgia made Congress for the first time representative of all 13 colonies. On 9 Nov. news arrived that George III had refused to receive the Olive Branch Petition and had (23 Aug.) proclaimed the American colonies to be in open rebellion. (On 7 Nov. the House of Commons received the petition but a motion that it constitute a basis for reconciliation was defeated 83–33.) Congress answered the royal proclamation on 6 Dec., disclaiming any intention to deny the sovereignty of the king, but disavowing allegiance to Parliament. The breach was further widened on 23 Dec. when a royal proclamation was issued closing the colonies to all commerce effective 1 Mar. 1776.

13 OCT. CONGRESS AUTHORIZES A NAVY. On 2 Sept. Washington authorized Col. **John Glover** (Mass., 1732–97) to convert fishing vessels into armed ships. In Congress a committee was appointed (5 Oct.) to prepare a plan for intercepting 2 British ships known to have military stores aboard, and another (13 Oct.) authorized to fit out 2 ships of 10 guns each, an authorization increased to 4 ships (30 Oct.). Congress resolved to raise 2 battalions of marines (10 Nov.) and on 25 Nov. formally declared British vessels open to capture in retaliation for British raids on American coastal towns. "Rules for the Regulation of the Navy of the United Colonies" were adopted 28 Nov. and a marine committee appointed (14 Dec.) to carry

them out. On 22 Dec. Congress commissioned officers for the 4 Continental ships, naming **Esek Hopkins** (R.I., 1718–1802) commodore. Congress authorized privateering (19 Mar. 1776) and issued letters of marque and reprisal (23 Mar.).

29 Nov. CONGRESS LOOKS ABROAD. Congress appointed a 5-man Committee of Secret Correspondence with wide discretionary powers to get in contact with "our friends" abroad. An appropriation of $3,000 for the use of agents was voted 11 Dec. On the 12th the committee wrote to **Arthur Lee** (1740–92), agent for Massachusetts in London, requesting him to ascertain the attitude of the European powers toward America. Later that month a French agent, Achard de Bonvouloir, communicated with the Secret Committee and gave informal assurances that France would welcome American ships and might offer material aid to the colonies.

11 DEC. HOSTILITIES IN THE SOUTH. On 7 Nov. Gov. Dunmore (Va.) placed his colony under martial law, established a base at Norfolk, and began recruiting a Loyalist army. By a promise of freedom to those slaves who deserted their masters (17 Nov.) he raised a Negro regiment, but forfeited the support of almost the entire planter class. On 11 Dec. Dunmore was decisively defeated by a mixed force of 900 Virginians and North Carolinians at Great Bridge. He evacuated Norfolk, but on 1 Jan. 1776 landed there again and destroyed much of the town by fire. In Feb. the Americans reoccupied and completed the destruction of the town, rendering it practically useless as a base of operations.

1776

MILITARY BALANCE SHEET. The Patriots were favored by (1) campaigning on their own ground, (2) widespread acquaintance with firearms, (3) a great leader in George Washington, (4) the superiority (in both range and accuracy) of the American rifle over the British smoothbore musket, and (5) a significant number of officers and men with military experience gained against the French or Indians. Grave disadvantages: (1) lack of training and discipline; (2) short-term enlistments; (3) shortage of ammunition, food, clothing, and medical supplies; (4) the hostility or active opposition of perhaps one third of the colonial populace; and (5) the lack of an efficient naval arm.

British commanders in America possessed the advantages of (1) a well-equipped, trained, and disciplined force; (2) support of the British navy in landing and transporting troops and guarding communication and supply lines at sea; (3) a rich war chest which permitted the hiring of foreign troops to supplement their own forces; and (4) the cooperation of American Loyalists. Weighing against these advantages were (1) the distance of the theater of war from Britain; (2) its vast extent and varied nature; (3) a reluctance to adapt tactics to American conditions; (4) a disinclination to mobilize the Loyalists as an effective force; and (5) a tendency on the part of military and political leaders to underestimate the opponent.

9 Jan. "COMMON SENSE." The first clarion call for independence was voiced by **Thomas Paine** (p. 1120) in *Common Sense*, a pamphlet which appeared in Philadelphia. Paine attacked George III (the "Royal Brute") as chiefly responsible for the obnoxious measures against the colonies and flayed the monarchical form of government. His simple yet electric presentation converted thousands to the cause of independence.

Feb.–June. HOSTILITIES IN THE SOUTH. Gen. **Henry Clinton** arrived off Cape Fear, N.C. (Mar.), with a British expeditionary force. Clinton had originally planned to land in North Carolina and join forces with a Loyalist army, but scrapped these plans when he learned that the Loyalists had been crushed at the Battle of Moore's Creek Bridge near Wilmington (27 Feb.). After being joined by troops from Britain under Gen. **Cornwallis** (3 May) Clinton decided to attack Charleston, S.C., where defense preparations were well under way when the British appeared on 1 June. On 4 June Gen. **Charles Lee** arrived from New York to take command of the defense. On 28 June, the wind finally being favorable, the British warships under Sir Peter Parker moved against the main point of the American defenses, a palmetto log fort (later named **Ft. Moultrie** for its defender) on Sullivan's Island. Parker's fire was returned by the defenders with great effect, forcing him to abandon the attack at nightfall, with all his ships damaged and over 200 casualties. In the fort 10 were dead, 21 wounded. Clinton's troops likewise failed to achieve their objectives on the 28th and had to be withdrawn. The British failure at Charleston ended active operations by them in that theater for over 2 years.

17 Mar. BRITISH EVACUATE BOSTON. On 24 Jan. Gen. **Henry Knox** (1750–1806) reached Cambridge with 43 cannon and 16 mortars hauled laboriously overland from Ft. Ticonderoga. On 16 Feb. a council of war drew up plans for the seizure of Dorchester Heights, from which point Boston and most of its harbor would be within range of Knox's artillery. Under cover of a heavy cannonade the occupation was carried out by 2,000 men under Gen. **John Thomas** (1724–76) during the night of 4–5 Mar. Gen. Howe, who had succeeded Gage as British commander (10 Oct. 1775), gathered 2,400 men for an assault on the unfinished works on the 5th but heavy rains that day and the next forestalled the attack. On 7 Mar. Howe decided to evacuate Boston. By the 17th all his troops, plus some 1,000 Loyalists, were embarked on the troopships in the harbor. On 26 Mar. the fleet left for Halifax.

MAR.–MAY. FRANCE DECIDES TO AID AMERICA. On 1 Mar. the French foreign minister, Comte de Vergennes, wrote to the foreign minister of Spain, Grimaldi, asking his reaction to joint secret measures to provide help for Britain's rebellious colonists. Spain showed herself receptive. Thereupon Louis XVI ordered (2 May) that 1 million livres' worth of munitions be supplied the Americans through a fictitious company, Roderigue Hortalez et Cie., actually administered by secret agent **Pierre de Beaumarchais.** Charles III of Spain made a similar arrangement shortly afterward. From these sources the American armies were to receive over 80% of their gunpowder, to mention but one type of military supplies, throughout 1776–77. Meanwhile Congress, ignorant of these developments, voted (3 Mar.) to send **Silas Deane** (1737–89) to Europe to purchase war matériel. This action made inevitable the resolution of 6 Apr., an important forerunner of the Declaration of Independence, opening the ports of the colonies to the trade of all nations but Britain. Deane arrived in Paris 7 July.

APR.–JULY. RETREAT FROM CANADA. On 1 Apr. Gen. **David Wooster** (1711–77) arrived at Quebec with reinforcements for the Northern Army and to take over command from Arnold, but gave way to Gen. John Thomas on 1 May. Thomas had already decided to abandon the siege of Quebec when British reinforcements reached Carleton (6 May) and enabled the latter to turn an orderly American retreat into a rout. Thomas retreated to Chambly and died there of smallpox (2 June). Gen. Sullivan, who succeeded him, attempted a counterattack against **Three Rivers** (7 June) but was defeated. He then retreated to St. John's, was joined there by Arnold and the Montreal garrison, and continued his retreat to Ticonderoga early in July. With command of Lake Champlain the key to all strategy, both Arnold and Carleton set to work to collect and build ships for a fleet.

APR.–JULY. MOVEMENT TOWARD INDEPENDENCE. By the spring of 1776 sentiment for a break with Britain was clearly in the ascendant. On 12 Apr. the North Carolina Convention empowered its delegates in Congress to vote for a declaration of independence. Virginia followed suit (15 May). With this authorization Richard Henry Lee offered a resolution (7 June) that the United Colonies "are, and of right ought to be, free and independent States." While after some debate (7–10 June) it was decided to postpone a decision on the resolution until 1 July, a committee consisting of **Jefferson, Franklin, John Adams, Robert R. Livingston,** and **Roger Sherman** (p. 1151) was appointed (11 June) to prepare a declaration of independence. Within the committee it was decided that Jefferson should write the draft of the declaration. With a few changes by Adams and Franklin it was this draft which was presented to Congress on 28 June. Jefferson said he "turned to neither book nor pamphlet" in preparing the paper. He drew upon the prevalent "natural rights" political philosophy and compiled a long list of despotic "abuses and usurpations" by George III (Parliament received no direct mention) in asserting the right and the duty of the American people to dissolve their tie to Britain and declare the United Colonies free and independent States.

2 JULY. CONGRESS VOTES INDEPENDENCE. On 1 July Congress sat as a committee to debate the Lee resolution. When brought to a vote in com-

mittee the motion was carried, though
Pennsylvania and South Carolina were
in the negative and Delaware's vote was
divided. On 2 July Congress, now sitting
in formal session rather than as a committee, took the final vote for independence (12 for, none against). South Carolina shifted her vote, the arrival of a
third delegate from Delaware (Caesar
Rodney) threw the vote of that colony
for independence, and Pennsylvania
swung to the affirmative when John
Dickinson and Robert Morris purposely
absented themselves on the 2nd. The
New York delegation, advised (11 June)
by the New York Provincial Congress to
take no action for or against independence, abstained from voting.

Congress next debated the form and
content of the declaration prepared by
Jefferson (2–3 July), making several
changes. On 4 July the amended Declaration of Independence was approved
without dissent (New York again abstained) and signed by Hancock (president) and Thomson (secretary). Copies
were prepared (5–6 July) to be dispatched to all the states. The declaration was first publicly proclaimed in
Philadelphia (8 July) and was read before Washington and his troops in New
York City the next day. On 9 July also
the Provincial Congress of New York
voted to endorse the declaration, a decision of which Congress was informed
15 July. Congress then resolved (19
July) to have the "Unanimous Declaration" engrossed on parchment for the
signature of the delegates. On 2 Aug.
most of the 55 signatures were affixed.
One "Signer," Matthew Thornton of
New Hampshire (not a member of Congress when the declaration was adopted),
added his name as late as Nov.

**27 Aug. BATTLE OF LONG IS-
LAND.** After evacuating Boston, Howe
planned to use strategic New York City

as his base of operations. Anticipating
Howe's movement, Washington shifted
his army from Boston (21 Mar.–13
Apr.). On 2 July Howe landed unopposed on Staten Island with about 10,-
000 men. His brother, Adm. **Lord
Richard Howe,** arrived with a strong
fleet and 150 transports 12 July. Other
reinforcements reached Staten Island
throughout July and early August until
Gen. Howe had a command of 32,000
men, about 9,000 of whom were German
mercenaries. Between 22–25 Aug. he
landed about 20,000 troops on Long
Island. On the evening of the 26th he
led a wide flanking movement around
the left of the forces under Gen. Putnam
on Brooklyn Heights. On the morning of
the 27th Howe fell upon the rear of Sullivan's position, routed his forces, and took
the general prisoner. Gen. **William Alexander** (1726–83, who claimed the title
"Lord Stirling") fought a gallant delaying action to protect the escape route
of the American forces, but finally surrendered to the Hessian general, De
Heister. Howe cautiously halted the pursuit at the breastworks on Brooklyn
Heights after inflicting 1,500 casualties
upon an American force of about 5,000
at a cost of less than 400 of his own men.
On the 28th Howe began constructing
siege-works. Having decided against
making a stand in Brooklyn, Washington during the night of 29–30 Aug.
skillfully withdrew Putnam's entire force
to Manhattan Island unknown to the
British.

**11 Sept. STATEN ISLAND PEACE
CONFERENCE.** On 3 May Gen. and
Adm. Howe had been appointed peace
commissioners by the king with powers
to pardon and protect those Americans
who returned to their true allegiance,
but without authority to negotiate with
any colony until all extralegal congresses
and conventions had been dissolved.

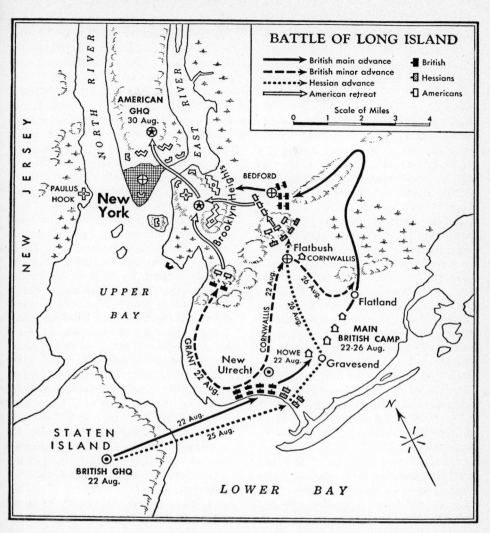

BATTLE OF LONG ISLAND

British main advance
British minor advance
Hessian advance
American retreat

■ British
⊟ Hessians
⊡ Americans

Scale of Miles

0   1   2   3   4

After the Battle of Long Island the Howes sent their prisoner, Gen. Sullivan, to Congress with a proposal that an informal peace conference be held. On 6 Sept. Congress appointed Franklin, John Adams, and Edmund Rutledge to confer with Lord Howe. The meeting took place on Staten Island and, although cordial, was fruitless. Howe's demand for a revocation of the Declaration of Independence as a necessary preliminary to negotiations for peace left no ground for further conversations.

15 Sept. BRITISH OCCUPY NEW YORK CITY. On 12 Sept. Washington decided to evacuate New York City rather than risk being trapped on lower Manhattan Island. The movement of his troops to hilly northern Manhattan was still under way when the British landed at Kip's Bay on the eastern side of the island (15 Sept.) and almost cut off a large section of the American army. Washington retreated to Harlem Heights, repulsed the British there (16 Sept.), and prepared new fortifications. Howe decided against an assault upon the American works and the next 3 weeks saw a lull in activity, marred by the great fire which destroyed almost 300 buildings in New York City (21 Sept.) and by the execution of **Nathan Hale** (1755–76) as an American spy (22 Sept.).

26 Sept. CONGRESS APPOINTS A DIPLOMATIC COMMISSION. On 12 June Congress appointed a committee to prepare plans for treaties of commerce and amity with foreign nations. The report of this committee (17 Sept.) was, after some alteration, adopted. On 26 Sept. 3 commissioners were appointed to negotiate treaties with European nations: **Silas Deane** (already in Europe), **Franklin,** and **Jefferson.** Jefferson declined the appointment and **Arthur Lee** (also in Europe) was named in his place. Franklin joined Deane and Lee in Paris on 21 Dec. Two days later Congress authorized the commission to borrow up to £ 2 million.

11 Oct. BATTLE OF VALCOUR BAY. The fleets which Arnold and Carleton had been gathering on Lake Champlain finally came to grips on 11 Oct. Arnold had placed his 83-gun fleet in the channel between Valcour Island and the western shore of Lake Champlain. Carleton's 87-gun fleet, manned by experienced sailors in contrast to Arnold's motley crews, attacked, and in a 7-hour battle crippled most of the American flotilla. That night Arnold's remaining ships slipped by the British. Another engagement at **Split Rock** (13 Oct.) resulted in the complete destruction of the American flotilla as a fighting force.

Carleton occupied Crown Point but then decided winter was too near at hand for a siege of Ticonderoga. He abandoned Crown Point (3 Nov.) and drew his forces back into Canada.

28 Oct. BATTLE OF WHITE PLAINS. In an effort to outflank Washington's strong position in northern Manhattan, Howe embarked the bulk of his army (12 Oct.), sailed up the East River and Long Island Sound, and landed on the mainland (13 Oct.) at Pell's Point. To meet this threat to his rear Washington evacuated his main force from Manhattan (23 Oct.) and moved northward to White Plains, leaving a strong garrison at Ft. Washington on the island. Howe moved against Washington (28 Oct.) and, in a sharp battle in which he suffered over 300 casualties and inflicted about 200, captured a key hill position. While Howe awaited reinforcements, Washington again slipped away (1 Nov.) to a new line 5 miles north at North Castle. On 16 Nov. Howe sent 13,000 troops against Ft. Washington, which capitulated. The British lost 458 in killed or wounded but took 2,818 prisoners. On 19 Nov. Howe sent Cornwallis across the Hudson with 4,500 men for an assault upon Ft. Lee. Gen. **Nathanael Greene** (p. 1046) evacuated the fort but was forced to abandon badly needed military supplies.

18 Nov.–20 Dec. RETREAT ACROSS NEW JERSEY. Greene and Washington joined forces at Hackensack and, with Cornwallis at their heels, retreated toward the Delaware River. After repeated commands from Washington, Gen. Charles Lee led the troops at North Castle across the Hudson (2 Dec.) and into Jersey. Washington crossed the Delaware into Pennsylvania 11 Dec. and 2 days later Lee was captured at Basking Ridge, N.J., by a British patrol. Sullivan took command of his troops and on 20

Dec. joined Washington in Pennsylvania. Congress, fearing a British attack on Philadelphia, fled from that city to Baltimore (12 Dec.) after vesting Washington with virtually dictatorial powers.

26 Dec. COUP AT TRENTON. Howe sent the bulk of his army back to winter quarters in New York (13 Dec.) but left garrisons at Trenton, Princeton, Bordentown, Perth Amboy, and New Brunswick. Informed that the Hessian garrison (c.1,400) at Trenton under Col. Johann Rall was ill-prepared to meet attack, Washington decided on an assault by 3 forces, only one of which—the main body of 2,400 under Washington himself—succeeded in crossing the ice-choked Delaware. Washington crossed 9 miles north of the town, split his force into 2 divisions, and at 8 A.M. drove into Trenton from the north and northeast. The surprise was complete. After an hour of confused street fighting in which Rall was mortally wounded, the garrison surrendered. Of the Hessians 918 were captured, 30 killed; while Washington suffered only 5 casualties. Washington recrossed into Pennsylvania with his prisoners and then once again crossed to the Jersey side and reoccupied Trenton (30–31 Dec.).

1777

3 Jan. COUP AT PRINCETON. Howe reacted to the news of the Trenton disaster with unusual celerity. On 1 Jan. he sent Gen. James Grant from New Brunswick toward Trenton and from New York dispatched a large force under Cornwallis to join Grant at Princeton. On 2 Jan. the British made contact with Washington's army of 5,200 men east of Trenton, but Cornwallis elected to wait until the next day for the attack which would "bag the fox." Leaving behind only enough men to give the illusion of an occupied camp, Washington stole around Cornwallis' flank that night and by dawn (3 Jan.) was close to Princeton. Near the town Patriot units under Gen. **Hugh Mercer** (c.1725–77) clashed with a British column under Col. Charles Mawhood marching to join Cornwallis. Mercer was killed and the American vanguard routed. Then Washington appeared with the main body and drove the British back with heavy losses toward New Brunswick. Cornwallis, hearing the sounds of battle to his rear, also fell back to protect the supply depot there. Washington drew his tired troops off to the northeast and soon established winter quarters in the hills around Morristown (6 Jan.). His victories had cleared all but easternmost New Jersey of the enemy and had an incalculable effect in restoring the shattered Patriot morale.

12 Mar. CONGRESS RECONVENES IN PHILADELPHIA. Congress returned to Philadelphia (4 Mar.), where it considered measures to obtain foreign aid. While at Baltimore Congress had resolved (30 Dec. 1776) to send commissioners to Austria, Prussia, Spain, and Tuscany. The commissioner to Spain was to be authorized to offer British-held Pensacola in Florida in return for a declaration of war by Spain against Britain. Similarly, the commissioners already in France were authorized to offer access to the Newfoundland fishing grounds and territorial gains as well if France would enter the war. On 1 Jan. Franklin was appointed to the Spanish, in addition to the French, mission, but on 1 May **Arthur Lee** was named to represent the U.S. at the Spanish court in his place. On 7 May **Ralph Izard** (1742–1804) was appointed commissioner to the Grand Duke of Tuscany, and on 9 May the Vienna and Berlin posts were assigned to **William Lee** (1739–95). Meanwhile, the Committee of Secret

Correspondence had been reconstituted by Congress as the Committee for Foreign Affairs (17 Apr.).

14 JUNE. STARS AND STRIPES. Congress resolved that the flag of the U.S. be "thirteen stripes alternate red and white, that the Union be thirteen stars white in a blue field. . . ."

RECRUITING FOREIGN OFFICERS. Congress had authorized Silas Deane to secure several European military experts for service in America, and by Mar. was swamped by applicants appearing in Philadelphia to claim commissions. On 13 Mar. Congress ordered that its agents send in the future only persons with the highest qualifications, including a knowledge of English. On 27 July two of the most famous foreign officers of the Revolution reached Philadelphia, 20-year-old **Marquis de Lafayette** (1757–1834) and veteran "Baron" **Johann de Kalb** (1721–80). Lafayette, who volunteered to serve without pay, was commissioned major general (31 July), as was De Kalb (15 Sept.). Foremost among the other foreign officers were **Thaddeus Kosciusko** (1746–1817), commissioned colonel of engineers (18 Oct. 1776), and **Baron Friedrich Wilhelm von Steuben** (1730–94), appointed inspector general 5 May 1778.

BRITISH PLAN KNOCKOUT BLOW. On 28 Feb. Gen. John Burgoyne, back in England, submitted to Lord George Germain, Secretary of State for the Colonies, his plan for a 3-pronged attack to isolate New England: (1) a main army of not less than 8,000 regulars to push southward down Lake Champlain and the upper Hudson; (2) an auxiliary force to operate from Oswego through the Mohawk Valley; (3) a strong force under Howe to move up the Hudson. Germain approved the plan; Burgoyne was given command of the main army to move from Canada; but Germain also approved (3 Mar.) Howe's plan for an attack on Philadelphia (by sea according to Howe's plan of 2 Apr.), hoping Howe could be finished in time to help Burgoyne.

23 JULY–26 SEPT. HOWE'S CAMPAIGN AGAINST PHILADELPHIA. On 23 July Howe embarked from New York with 15,000 troops, sailed up Chesapeake Bay, and landed at Head of Elk on 25 Aug. Washington, with about 10,-500 men, took up a defensive position barring the way to Philadelphia on the eastern side of **Brandywine Creek.** Howe attacked on 11 Sept., using a carefully planned flanking movement. The Germans under Gen. William von Knyphausen attacked the American center at Chad's Ford; Cornwallis routed Sullivan on the American right. Greene managed to turn the flight into an orderly if hard-pressed retreat, but the whole American army was forced back toward Philadelphia. Casualties: American, c.1,000; British, 576. The British scored again (21 Sept.), when a bayonet attack in the early hours of the morning routed a force under Gen. **Anthony Wayne** (1745–96) at Paoli. On 26 Sept. Howe occupied Philadelphia. Congress fled (19 Sept.) to Lancaster and then to York (30 Sept.).

4 OCT. BATTLE OF GERMANTOWN. On the night of 3 Oct. Washington began an intricate movement toward Howe's main encampment at Germantown. The battle began before dawn on the 4th with the Americans winning important initial successes. But the coordinated attack which Washington had planned did not materialize. Detachments became lost in a heavy fog and at one point American troops fired on each other. A retreat by several brigades forced the American detachments which had penetrated into the streets of Germantown to fall back. Again Greene distinguished himself in directing a stubborn retreat. Washington suffered almost

700 casualties and had 400 of his men taken prisoner against British losses of 534. The 400-man garrison of Ft. Mercer (on the Delaware below Philadelphia) repelled an attack by 1,600 Hessians (22 Oct.), but was forced to evacuate (20 Nov.) in the face of an assault by 5,000 men under Cornwallis. By 23 Nov. the Delaware as far north as Philadelphia was clear for British vessels. Washington meanwhile had withdrawn northwestward from Germantown and took up winter quarters at **Valley Forge** (mid-Dec.).

17 JUNE–17 OCT. NORTHERN CAMPAIGN: BURGOYNE AND ST. LEGER. On 17 June, with a force of about 7,700 British and German troops, Canadians and Indians, Burgoyne left St. John's with a huge baggage train and 138 pieces of artillery. By 30 June his army had reached Ft. Ticonderoga commanded by Gen. **Arthur St. Clair** (1736–1818). On 2 July the British seized Mt. Defiance, a strategic height south of the fort which the Americans had carelessly left unfortified and by 5 July had hauled cannon to the top, rendering the fort untenable. That night St. Clair evacuated, abandoning substantial supplies. Burgoyne, in pursuit, took Skenesborough and Ft. Anne, 6–7 July. Thereafter, his advance was slowed by the forested terrain and trees felled by Schuyler's forces. On 4 Aug. Schuyler was replaced in command by Gen. **Horatio Gates** (1727–1806).

Meanwhile a British force of 1,800, mostly Loyalists and Indians, advanced eastward from Oswego on Lake Ontario under the command of Col. **Barry St. Leger.** On 3 Aug. St. Leger reached and besieged Ft. Stanwix on the Mohawk River, garrisoned by 750 men under Col. **Peter Gansevoort** (1749–1812). On 6 Aug. 800 militiamen marching to the fort's relief under Gen. **Nicholas Herkimer** (1728–77) were caught in ambush

at **Oriskany** by a force of Indians and Loyalists led by the Mohawk chief **Joseph Brant** (1742–1807). Herkimer, badly wounded at the outset of the battle, drew his men together on high ground and fought back fiercely. The Indians, alarmed by firing from Stanwix, where the garrison made a sortie against the British camp, broke off the engagement. Herkimer retreated eastward with less than half his original strength. Schuyler now sent Arnold with a force of 1,000 volunteers to Gansevoort's aid. By a ruse the Indians were frightened off, and St. Leger abandoned the siege of Stanwix and retreated to Oswego (22 Aug.).

By early Aug. Burgoyne's supply problem became alarming. Learning that the Americans had quantities of military stores at Bennington, he detached some 700 men under the command of Lt. Col. Friedrich Baum to capture them (11 Aug.). At **Bennington** were some 2,600 American troops under Gen. **John Stark** (1728–1822), most of them raw militiamen now taking up arms in increasing numbers as news of atrocities by Burgoyne's Indians (particularly the murder of Jane McCrea on 27 July) spread through New England. Stark launched an attack on Baum on 16 Aug. Baum was mortally wounded and, except for the Indians (most of whom fled), almost his entire force killed or taken prisoner. The reinforcements for Baum under Lt. Col. Heinrich C. Breymann arrived too late and were in turn attacked by Stark, now reinforced by Col. Seth Warner (1743–84) leading 400 veteran Massachusetts troops. Breymann, with the loss of a third of his 650 men, was forced to fall back on Burgoyne.

Burgoyne resolved to press on to Albany, crossed to the west side of the Hudson (13 Sept.), and moved against the entrenched position Gates had prepared on Bemis Heights. Gates, reinforced, now had over 6,000 men, with

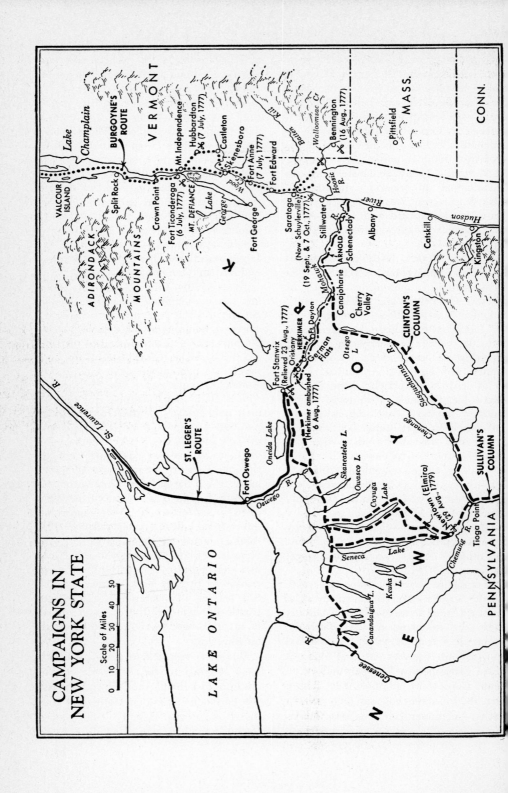

CAMPAIGNS IN NEW YORK STATE

Scale of Miles
0 10 20 30 40 50

LAKE ONTARIO

St. Lawrence R.

VALCOUR ISLAND
Split Rock
Lake Champlain

BURGOYNE'S ROUTE

Crown Point
Fort Ticonderoga (6 July, 1777)
MT. DEFIANCE
Mt. Independence
Hubbardton (7 July, 1777)
Castleton
Skenesboro
Lake George
Wood Creek
Fort Anne (7 July, 1777)
Fort George
Fort Edward
Saratoga (New Schuylerville)
(19 Sept., & 7 Oct., 1777)
ARNOLD
Stillwater
Hoosic R.
Walloomsac Cr.
Bennington (16 Aug., 1777)
Pittsfield

ADIRONDACK MOUNTAINS

VERMONT

MASS.

CONN.

Hudson River
Schenectady
Albany
Catskill
Kingston

ST. LEGER'S ROUTE

Fort Oswego
Oswego R.
Oneida Lake
Fort Stanwix (Relieved 23 Aug., 1777)
Oriskany
HERKIMER
(Herkimer ambushed 6 Aug., 1777)
Ft. Dayton
German Flats
Canajoharie
Cherry Valley
Mohawk R.
Otsego L.

CLINTON'S COLUMN

Skaneateles L.
Owasco L.
Cayuga Lake
Susquehanna R.
Chenango R.
Newtown (Elmira) (29 Aug., 1779)
Chemung R.
Tioga Point

SULLIVAN'S COLUMN

Seneca Lake
Keuka L.
Canandaigua L.
Genesee R.

O N E I D A
C O U N T R Y

PENNSYLVANIA

militiamen arriving daily. On 19 Sept. Burgoyne attempted to gain high ground on the American left but was checked short of his goal at **Freeman's Farm** by Gen. **Daniel Morgan** (p. 1106) and Col. **Henry Dearborn**. British casualties, c.600; American, 300. On 3 Oct. Gen. Clinton, commanding British troops in New York City, moved up the Hudson, taking Fts. Clinton and Montgomery on the 6th. Receiving an urgent appeal for help from Burgoyne on the 9th, he sent the fleet farther up the Hudson to Esopus (Kingston), which the British burned (16 Oct.), but felt too insecure to push on to Albany, and returned to New York for reinforcements.

Meanwhile Burgoyne had become desperate. On 7 Oct. he again ventured out of his lines toward the American left with 1,650 troops. A countermove by Gates, led by Morgan and Gen. Ebenezer Learned, repulsed the British. Then Benedict Arnold, though without a command that day, led a fierce assault which threw Burgoyne back upon **Bemis Heights**. The Americans continued to press on and carried the Breymann redoubt. That night, weakened by the day's toll of close to 600 (American casualties, c.150), Burgoyne withdrew northeastward about 1 mile and on 8 Oct. retreated to Saratoga. On 13 Oct., surrounded by a force now 3 times his own, he asked for a cessation of hostilities. On 17 Oct., by the terms of the **"Convention of Saratoga,"** the 5,700 men constituting the remnants of Burgoyne's army laid down their arms. They were to be marched to Boston, shipped back to England, and pledged not to serve again in the war against America.

25 SEPT.–23 DEC. "CONWAY CABAL." As a result of congressional antagonism to the military direction of the war **Gates** was named (27 Nov.) president of the Board of War and **Thomas Conway**, previously an Irish colonel in the French army, inspector general (14

Dec.). Earlier Conway had written Congress (25 Sept.) disparaging his own commanding officer, Lord Stirling, and on 11 Oct. had sent Gates a letter attacking Washington. The rebuke by Washington (9 Nov.) forced Gates to disavow any connection with the affair. Doubt exists whether there was in fact any organized plot to supplant Washington. Conway, who resigned from the army, was wounded in the summer of 1778 in a duel with Gen. John Cadwalader, and later apologized to Washington.

15 Nov. ARTICLES OF CONFEDERATION. When Richard Henry Lee offered his resolution for independence (7 June 1776), he also proposed that "a plan of confederation be prepared and transmitted to the respective colonies for their consideration and approbation." Congress appointed a committee headed by John Dickinson (12 June). On 12 July 1776 the committee's report, "Articles of Confederation and Perpetual Union," was presented to Congress. For over a year the Articles were debated intermittently. On 7 Oct. 1777 a vote was finally taken on the question of voting in the Congress under the Articles, 1 vote for each state winning acceptance. On 14 Oct. the apportionment of the expenses of the central government was settled on a basis of surveyed land in each state. Finally, on 15 Nov., the 13 Articles were formally adopted and on 17 Nov. sent to each state for prompt ratification. Complete ratification did not occur until 1 Mar. 1781.

17 DEC. FRANCE AND U.S. INDEPENDENCE. When Lord North heard the news of Burgoyne's surrender (early Dec.) he began preparing a new offer of reconciliation. A British agent, Paul Wentworth, was sent to Paris to confer with Deane and Franklin, but found they stood squarely for full independence (15 Dec.–6 Jan. 1778). Fearful that the Americans might come to terms with the British, the French informed the American envoys (17 Dec.) that the king's council had decided to recognize the independence of the U.S.

1778

6 FEB. FRANCO-AMERICAN ALLI-ANCE. After an unsuccessful attempt by the French to induce Spain to join in a tripartite pact against Britain, Comte de Vergennes informed the American commissioners (8 Jan.) that France was prepared to enter into an alliance with the U.S. Two treaties resulted from the negotiations of the next 4 weeks: (1) a treaty of amity and commerce, under which each nation was granted most-favored-nation status by the other; and (2) a treaty of alliance to become effective if and when war broke out between France and Britain. Article II of the latter declared its aim was to "maintain effectually the liberty, Sovereignty, and independence" of the U.S. The U.S. was given a free hand to conquer Canada and Bermuda; France, to seize the British West Indies, with mutual territorial guarantees and an agreement that neither would conclude a truce or peace with Britain without the other's consent. On 20 Mar. Franklin, Deane, and Lee were officially received by Louis XVI and within the week Conrad Gérard was named minister to the U.S. Congress received the news on 2 May, ratified the treaties unanimously on the 4th, voted (11 Sept.) to replace the commission in France by a minister, and elected (14 Sept.) Franklin to that post. Meanwhile, on 17 June a clash between French and British naval forces occurred; the two nations were at war.

12 APR. CARLISLE PEACE COMMISSION. To forestall U.S. ratification of the French alliance, Lord North introduced (17 Feb.) in Commons a series of bills for effecting reconciliation with America, proposing (1) repeal of the Tea and Coercive Acts; (2) a pledge that Parliament would impose no revenue taxes upon the American colonies; (3) appointment of a peace commission with powers to negotiate with Congress, and, if necessary, to agree to suspension of all acts passed since 1763. The bills passed the Commons 16 Mar. The Earl of Carlisle was appointed to head the commissioners (22 Feb.). William Eden, a member of the Board of Trade; George Johnstone, former governor of West Florida; and the Howe brothers, already in America, were the other members of the group (commissioned 12 Apr.). When Carlisle, Eden, and Johnstone reached Philadelphia (6 June), they learned Congress was cold to conciliation and had resolved (22 Apr.) that any man or group who came to terms with the commission was to be branded an enemy of the U.S. To a request (9 June) for a conference, Congress replied (17 June) that the only negotiations it would undertake would be for the withdrawal of British forces and the recognition of U.S. independence. The British evacuation of Philadelphia by Clinton (who succeeded Howe 8 May) forced the commissioners to move to New York. Before leaving Philadelphia, however, George Johnstone tried to bribe congressmen **Joseph Reed** (1741–85), **Robert Morris** (p. 1108), and **Francis Dana** (1743–1811). His attempt failed and its revelation led him to resign from the commission (26 Aug.). On 3 Oct. Carlisle and Eden appealed to the people over the head of Congress in a Manifesto and Proclamation which threatened a war of great destructiveness if the Americans did not abandon their French allies and make peace with Britain. On 27 Nov. the commissioners left New York for England, their mission a complete failure.

23 APR. JOHN PAUL JONES' RAIDS. The little squadron which Congress had put under Esek Hopkins' command late

in 1775 was too weak to operate as a fleet. A successful raid was carried out by Hopkins on Nassau (Mar. 1776), but thereafter the Continental Navy generally operated in single units whenever a captain could slip out to sea through the British cordon off the American coast. American privateers proved much more vexing to the British. The House of Commons was informed (Feb. 1778) that they had taken 733 prizes, but even their numbers declined from 143 in 1775 to a low of 73 in 1777. The revival of American naval operations in 1778 (115 privateers were in action in that year) was highlighted by the exploits of Capt. **John Paul Jones** (p. 1073) aboard the *Ranger.* Jones left Portsmouth, N.H., 2 Nov. 1777 and, after refitting at Nantes and Brest, sailed into the Irish Sea in Apr. He took 2 prizes (14–17 Apr.) and then on 23 Apr. landed at Whitehaven, England, spiked the guns of the fort, and set fire to a ship at anchor. That same evening he sailed to St. Mary's Island in Solway Firth, landing with the intention of kidnaping the Earl of Selkirk, who, in fact, was not on the island. Jones then crossed to the coast of northern Ireland, where, at Carrickfergus, he forced the British sloop *Drake* to strike after an hour's battle (24 Apr.) and took it to Brest (8 May).

28 JUNE. BATTLE OF MONMOUTH. The agony at Valley Forge ended for Washington on 19 June. Though the shrinking American army, desperately short of food, clothing, and military supplies, was but 20 miles from Philadelphia, Howe made no effort to disperse it during the winter. He was relieved by Clinton (8 May), who, concerned over reports of a French fleet heading for America, evacuated Philadelphia (18 June) and set out across New Jersey toward New York City. Washington broke camp at Valley Forge on 19 June and started in pursuit. Gen. Charles Lee (who had been exchanged and had returned to the army 20 May) was given command of a strong advance corps (26 June) with orders to press home at the first opportunity an attack on Clinton's extended column. On the 28th Lee attacked near Monmouth Court House. His orders to Lafayette and Wayne were vague and contradictory and early advantages were not followed up. As British reinforcements arrived, Lee suddenly ordered a retreat, a move which encouraged Clinton to engage his main army. Washington's arrival checked the flight of Lee's command and the discipline which Von Steuben had instilled at Valley Forge showed its worth when the Americans beat back Clinton's repeated attacks. The British, who stole away during the night, marched to Sandy Hook and boarded transports which took them to New York. Both sides had suffered about 350 casualties at Monmouth. After a court-martial suspended Lee from the service for disobedience and misbehavior (4 July), Washington led his army northward, crossed the Hudson, and on 30 July took up a position at White Plains above New York City.

3 JULY AND 11 Nov. WYOMING AND CHERRY VALLEY MASSACRES. On 3 July Sir John Butler led Loyalists and Indians in a sweep through Pennsylvania's Wyoming Valley. In New York a series of raids planned by Sir John Johnson and Guy Johnson and executed by Butler's Rangers and Bryant's Indians terrorized the outlying settlements from May through the culminating attack on Cherry Valley (11 Nov.) in which some 40 survivors were massacred after they had surrendered.

4 JULY. CLARK'S CAPTURE OF KASKASKIA. In the fall of 1777 **George Rogers Clark** (p. 1001), a militia leader at Harrodsburg, Ky., proposed to the Virginia authorities an expedition against the British, Indians, and Loyalists who, under the command of Col. Henry Hamilton (the "Hair Buyer"), lieutenant governor at Detroit, were raiding western settlements. Commissioned lieutenant colonel by Gov. Patrick Henry, Clark with 175 men moved (May) to the Ohio River, sailed down it almost to the Mississippi, and then struck northwestward. On 4 July he occupied Kaskaskia and, with the support of the French inhabitants, the other posts in the area within the next 6 weeks, organizing the territory as part of Virginia. On 17 Dec. Hamilton recaptured Vincennes with a force, more than half of which were Indians, numbering over 500. Clark gathered about 150 men at Kaskaskia, set out (6 Feb. 1779) across inundated plains for Vincennes, reached there 23 Feb., and by various ruses caused Hamilton's Indians to desert and Hamilton himself to surrender (25 Feb.).

29 JULY–29 AUG. FRANCO-AMERICAN ATTACK ON NEWPORT. On 11 July a French fleet of 17 ships under the **Comte d'Estaing** arrived off New York harbor, but the size of his ships made a crossing of the bar so hazardous that the plan of a sea-land assault on New York was abandoned (22 July) in favor of a joint operation against a British garrison of 3,000 men at Newport, R.I. D'Estaing arrived off that town on 29 July but it was 8 Aug. before the American land forces under Gen. Sullivan were grouped before Newport in sufficient numbers to begin the operation, by which date Howe's reinforced fleet was on its way to aid the garrison. D'Estaing moved out to meet Howe on the 10th and a decisive battle loomed when a fierce storm (11 Aug.) scattered both fleets. Without naval support Sullivan had to withdraw from Newport after an attack on the

garrison (29 Aug.) in which each side suffered about 250 casualties. D'Estaing left Boston (where he had gone for repairs) for the West Indies (4 Nov.).

29 DEC. FALL OF SAVANNAH. Clinton now shifted British operations to the South, anticipating aid from large numbers of Loyalists. On 25 Nov. a detachment of 3,500 men embarked for Georgia under the command of Lt. Col. Archibald Campbell, landed near Savannah (29 Dec.), crushed 1,000 militia under Gen. **Robert Howe** (1732–86), and occupied the town.

1779

6 JAN.–19 JUNE. BRITISH PROGRESS IN THE SOUTH. On 6 Jan. Ft. Sunbury fell to a force under Gen. Augustine Prevost which pushed northward from Florida; Augusta was seized by Campbell 29 Jan. The Americans were heartened by Moultrie's successful defense of **Port Royal**, S.C., (3 Feb.) and by Col. **Andrew Pickens'** victory over a Loyalist brigade at Kettle Creek, Ga. (14 Feb.). However, an attempt to recapture Augusta from the British failed when Gen. **John Ashe** (c.1720–81) lost over 350 men and inflicted fewer than 20 casualties at **Briar Creek** (3 Mar.). When Gen. **Benjamin Lincoln** (1733–1810) with a corps of Continental troops detached by Washington moved inland for another attempt against Augusta (23 Apr.), Prevost struck northward along the coast and reached Charleston (12 May), but pulled back. Lincoln attacked the British rear at **Stono Ferry** (19 June), but lost 300 men to 130 enemy casualties and failed to prevent Prevost from regaining Savannah. In isolated actions in the South during the spring a force of North Carolina and Virginia troops led by Col. **Evan Shelby** (1719–94) struck successfully at Chickamauga Indian villages in Tennessee (Apr.), while the British captured and set fire to Portsmouth and Norfolk, Va. (10 May).

31 May–15 Sept. WAR IN THE NORTH. On 31 May Clinton led 6,000 men up the Hudson and seized (1 June) 2 uncompleted American forts at Stony Point and Verplanck's Point. Another force under William Tryon, royal governor of New York, was sent to ravage (5–11 July) the Connecticut shore of Long Island Sound. On 15 July Gen. **Anthony Wayne** led 1,200 men in a night bayonet attack on **Stony Point** which bagged all but 1 man of the garrison of almost 700 at a cost of 15 killed, 83 wounded. Wayne dismantled the fort and evacuated it 18 July. While Clinton's attention was thus turned northward, Maj. **Harry Lee** (1756–1818) drove the British from their last major outpost in New Jersey, **Paulus Hook,** and took over 150 prisoners (19 Aug.).

More significant was the expedition led by Gens. **John Sullivan** and **James Clinton** (1736–1812) against the Loyalists and Indians who were ravaging the frontier settlements of Pennsylvania and New York. At Newtown (Elmira) a force of 1,500 Loyalists and Indians led by Sir **John Johnson** and **Joseph Brant** were defeated (29 Aug.). From Newtown, Sullivan moved northwestward meeting but scattered resistance. He destroyed 40 Seneca and Cayuga villages with their orchards and food plots and some 160,000 bushels of beans and maize. Sullivan turned back (15 Sept.) after penetrating as far as Geneseo (without pressing on to Ft. Niagara). His expedition had materially reduced the offensive threat from the Iroquois.

21 June. SPAIN ENTERS THE WAR. Fearful for her American possessions, Spain opposed American independence. When Britain refused to cede Gibraltar to her as the price of her neutrality or mediation, Spain delivered

an ultimatum (3 Apr. 1779), which, if accepted, would have sacrificed U.S. interests. On 12 April the secret **Convention of Aranjuez** between France and Spain provided for the entrance of the latter into the war if the ultimatum was rejected. When the British turned it down, Spanish and French fleets began joint operations in May. On 21 June Spain formally declared war on Great Britain, but refused to recognize U.S. independence or to pledge herself to fight on, as the French had, until that independence was secured. On 27 Sept. Congress appointed its president, **John Jay** (p. 1069), as minister to Spain, but he failed to obtain recognition, an alliance, or a substantial loan (he was able to borrow only $174,011) during his stay (Jan. 1780–May 1782).

14 Aug. CONGRESSIONAL PEACE TERMS. On 15 Feb. a report of a committee of Congress to propose peace terms (presented 23 Feb.) set forth as ultimata: independence, certain minimum boundaries, complete British evacuation of U.S. territory, rights to the fisheries, and free navigation of the Mississippi. Most of these terms were quickly approved by Congress, but those relating to the fisheries and the Mississippi occasioned long debate along sectional lines. Finally, on 14 Aug., Congress agreed on the instructions which were to guide the U.S. peace negotiator (still to be appointed). In these instructions the fisheries claim was removed from the list of ultimata, but that concerning the navigation of the Mississippi retained (4 Oct.). On 27 Sept., **John Adams,** who had replaced Silas Deane as one of the commissioners in Paris (8 Apr. 1778), was named to negotiate the peace treaty with Britain.

23 Sept. "BONHOMME RICHARD" AND "SERAPIS." In Jan. Jones (in France) was given command of a decrepit French ship, the *Duc de Duras*.

He refitted it, crowded 42 guns aboard, and renamed it the *Bonhomme Richard* in Franklin's honor. On 14 Aug. he sailed from L'Orient with 1 other American ship and 4 French ships. Two of the French ships soon turned back. On 23 Sept. Jones sighted a fleet of 39 merchant ships convoyed by the *Serapis* (44 guns) and the *Countess of Scarborough* (22 guns) off the east coast of England. Jones bore down on the *Serapis* and began action at close range. The early exchanges went heavily in favor of the *Serapis,* but a query as to surrender brought "I have not yet begun to fight" as Jones' reply. American marksmen in the rigging took a heavy toll on the enemy's deck, an American grenade touched off a powder explosion on the gun deck of the *Serapis,* and when its mainmast fell Capt. Pearson struck his flag. With the *Richard* in flames (it sank on the 24th) Jones transferred his 237-man crew, half of them casualties, to the *Serapis* and brought it to port 6 Oct. One of the French ships in Jones' squadron, the *Pallas,* took the *Countess of Scarborough* during the *Richard-Serapis* engagement.

3 SEPT.–28 OCT. FAILURE AT SAVANNAH. On 3 Sept., off Savannah, Adm. d'Estaing returned to the American coast with a French fleet of 35 ships and 4,000 troops. He captured 2 British frigates and 2 supply ships and then moved against Prevost's 3,000-man garrison in Savannah (15 Sept.). On the 23rd 1,400 American troops under Gen. Lincoln joined the French in besieging the city. The siege proceeded too slowly for d'Estaing's timetable; assault was pressed on 9 Oct. D'Estaing was wounded, Count **Casimir Pulaski** (1749–79) killed, and the Allies suffered over 800 casualties to 155 of Prevost's. With the withdrawal of d'Estaing's fleet (28 Oct.) the initiative again passed to the British. Clinton evacuated Rhode Island (11 Oct.) to permit an increased effort in the South and on 26 Dec. left New York with nearly 8,000 troops with Charleston as his target.

1780

11 FEB.–12 MAY. FALL OF CHARLESTON. Clinton arrived off the Carolina coast on 1 Feb. By 11 Apr. he had completed the investment of the city with 14,000 attackers. On 6 May Ft. Moultrie fell; Lincoln capitulated on the 12th. At a cost of only 255 casualties Clinton captured the 5,400-man garrison and 4 American ships, making this the heaviest American defeat of the war. On 29 May a force of cavalry under Col. **Banastre Tarleton** destroyed a Virginia regiment at **Waxhaw Creek.** On 5 June Clinton left for New York, satisfied that South Carolina was rewon for the crown, leaving Cornwallis with about 8,000 men to maintain, and if possible extend, control.

28 FEB. RUSSIA'S ARMED NEUTRALITY. The declaration of Catherine II that the Russian navy would be used against all belligerents to protect neutral Russian trade was a blow to British blockade efforts against France and Spain, for Russia refused to recognize naval stores (required by the Allies) as contraband. More significant was Catherine's invitation to other European neutrals to join in a **League of Armed Neutrality.** Denmark (9 July) and Sweden (1 Aug.) promptly accepted; the Netherlands, Prussia, Portugal, Austria, and the Kingdom of the Two Sicilies joined in the next 2 years. Britain went to war with the Netherlands (20 Dec.) and was able to shut off the clandestine trade between the U.S. and the Dutch island of St. Eustatius in the West Indies, center of contraband trade with the U.S. Although the League failed to aid the Dutch, its existence hampered

British naval measures against the Allies. On 19 Dec. Congress appointed Francis Dana as minister to Russia, but he was ignored at St. Petersburg.

25 MAY. MUTINY AT WASHINGTON'S CAMP. The condition of Washington's army during the winter of 1779–80 at Morristown, N.J., was even more critical than at Valley Forge, as supplies failed to arrive (Mar.) owing to the drop in value of Continental currency (40 [Continental] to 1 [Specie]). Rations were cut to one eighth of normal quantity during the next 6 weeks. On 25 May 2 Connecticut regiments paraded under arms to demand a full ration and immediate payment of their salaries, then 5 months in arrears, but were curbed by Pennsylvania troops.

11 JULY. FRENCH ARMY AT NEWPORT. Under the **Comte de Rochambeau** (1725–1807) 5,000 troops with a strong naval escort sailed from France on 2 May and arrived at Newport, R.I., 11 July. Washington planned to combine this army with his own for an attack on New York, but lacked adequate naval support. A British fleet under Adms. Marriot Arbuthnot and George Rodney blockaded Newport within a few weeks of Rochambeau's arrival.

16 AUG. BATTLE OF CAMDEN. The British hold on Georgia and South Carolina was not seriously challenged (guerrilla bands led by **Andrew Pickens** [1739–1817], **Francis Marion** [p. 1097], and **Thomas Sumter** [1734–1832] prevented consolidating British strength until Gates was commissioned by Congress [13 June] to lead a Southern Army with a core of Continental troops detached by Washington). Gates took over his command at Coxe's Mill, N.C. (25 July), and began a slow march against the British post and supply base at Camden, S.C. Cornwallis, with about 2,400 men, made contact with the Americans early on 16 Aug. north of that town. American troops broke when Tarleton's dragoons came crashing down upon their rear. Estimated U.S. losses: 800–900 killed (including Kalb) and 1,000 captured. Gates fell back to Hillsboro, N.C., 160 miles from Camden.

Defeat by Tarleton of an American force under Sumter at Fishing Creek, S.C. (18 Aug.), opened the way for a British invasion of North Carolina, begun by Cornwallis 8 Sept. On 7 Oct. a Loyalist force of about 1,100 led by Maj. Patrick Ferguson, screening Cornwallis' left flank, was caught atop **King's Mountain** on the border between the Carolinas by a 900-man force of American frontiersmen under Col. **Isaac Shelby** (1750–1826) and Col. **William Campbell** (1745–81). The marksmanship of the backwoodsmen prevailed over Ferguson's bayonet charges. The Americans lost 28 killed, 62 wounded in killing or capturing the entire enemy force. Cornwallis retreated back into South Carolina and established winter quarters at Winnsborough (14 Oct.). On the same day capable **Nathanael Greene** was named to succeed Gates in the southern command.

c.SEPT. 1780–JUNE 1781. RUSSO-AUSTRIAN COMEDIATION PROPOSALS. As the war spread without decisive results, neutral nations pressed for a negotiated peace. Count Nikita Panin, the Russian chancellor, proposed a general armistice to be followed by a peace conference to which delegates from the 13 separate American states rather than the Continental Congress would be invited. Austrian chancellor Prince Wenzel Anton von Kaunitz propelled himself by April 1781 into the role of comediator. While recognizing that the Panin-Kaunitz formula would mean the partition of America, Vergennes was prepared to accept it. However, in July 1781 John Adams reminded him that the authority to negotiate with foreign powers was the exclusive province of the Congress under the Articles of Confederation. Adams' timely intervention ended the comediation efforts.

21 SEPT. TREASON OF ARNOLD. As early as May 1779 Benedict Arnold, then under fire for his administration as military commander of Philadelphia, opened negotiations with Gen. Sir Henry Clinton in New York and by 23 May was sending him information on Washington's movements. Relations were broken off for a time when Clinton refused (late July) to pay £10,000 to Arnold for his services and indemnify him as well for any losses he might suffer if detected. But after a court-martial found Arnold guilty on 2 charges of misusing his powers at Philadelphia (26 Jan. 1780) and after Washington, in keeping with the decision of the court, reprimanded Arnold officially (6 Apr.), Arnold reopened negotiations with the British in May. On 15 June he informed them that he expected to be put in command of West Point and on 12 July wrote Maj. John André, Clinton's adjutant, that he desired a conference with a British officer to plan the "disposal" of that key fortress. Arnold took up command at West Point 5 Aug. and on 21 Sept. met André on the west bank of the Hudson near Haverstraw to deliver plans of the fort and inform the British of its weak points. On his way back to the British lines André doffed his uniform in favor of civilian clothes against Clinton's specific orders. On 23 Sept. he was captured by 3 New York militiamen near Tarrytown and the incriminating papers discovered. His captors, not suspecting Arnold's part in the affair, sent word of André's apprehension to him at West Point. When Arnold received this information (25 Sept.) he fled to the *Vulture,* a British warship in the Hudson. On 29 Sept. André was convicted as a spy, and executed on 2 Oct. For his treachery Arnold was commissioned a brigadier general in the British army and received £6,315 in cash, an annual pension of £500 for his wife Peggy (Shippen), army commissions for 3 sons by a previous marriage, and, beginning in 1783, pensions of £100 a year each for Peggy's 5 young children. Arnold led British raids against Virginia (Dec. 1780–Apr. 1781) and New London, Conn. (6 Sept. 1781).

1781

1 JAN. MUTINY OF THE PENNSYLVANIA LINE. The appearance of recruiting agents who paid $25 in coin to new enlistees provoked 1,500 out of 2,400 veterans of the Pennsylvania division to quit their quarters, seize arms and artillery, kill one and wound several officers who tried to stop them, and march off under their sergeants toward Philadelphia. On 3 Jan. they made camp at Princeton and elected negotiators to treat with the officials of their state. Joseph Reed, president of Pennsylvania's Executive Council, who opened negotiations (7 Jan.), made concessions which ended the mutiny, though over half the line left the service. When, on 20 Jan., troops of the New Jersey Line mutinied at Pompton, Washington dispatched Gen. Robert Howe with 600 men, some from West Point, others from Pompton vicinity, to put down the mutiny. Howe surprised the mutineers' camp (27 Jan.), forced them to parade unarmed, restored the officers to their commands, and had 2 men executed. Another outbreak among the Pennsylvania troops in May was similarly nipped by several executions.

20 FEB. ROBERT MORRIS MADE SUPERINTENDENT OF FINANCE. On 6 Feb. Congress resolved to establish a department of finance under a superintendent responsible to Congress. On 20 Feb. **Robert Morris** (p. 1108) was named. He took office on 14 May at a critical time. Despite subsidies and loans from France and Spain (totaling for the entire period of the war almost $9 million), American finances were close to collapse after 1779. By the beginning of 1780 Congress had issued $191,500,000 in paper money ("Continentals"). Additional millions were outstanding in quartermaster certificates (receipts given in payment by the army for supplies it requisitioned), close to $50 million in loan-office certificates, most paying 6% interest, and more debits in the form of certificates given soldiers for their back pay. An attempt had been made (Jan. 1779) to retire some of the paper money, but when the failure of the states to provide for the current expenses of the war resulted in new issues exceeding the amount retired by over $35 million Continental currency dropped precipitately. On 14 Jan. 1779 it stood at 8–1 with specie but by the end of the year was down to 40–1. On 18 Mar. 1780 Congress resolved to retire the bills in circulation by accepting them in payments due it from the states at one fortieth their face value. About $120 million in Continental bills was thus retired while the remaining $71 million was worthless by the end of 1780. When Morris took office his first proposal (21 May) was for a national bank, which Congress approved (26 May), but did not actually charter the Bank of North America until 31 Dec. In June Morris received authorization to supply the army by contract rather than by the inefficient and expensive system of requisition from the states. A timely subsidy from France (May) and French backing for a large loan from the Netherlands (5 Nov.) enabled Morris to make some progress toward returning the country to a specie basis by the end of the year.

1 MAR. RATIFICATION OF THE ARTICLES OF CONFEDERATION, before the states ever since November 1777, was delayed by Maryland's refusal to ratify until the states claiming western lands ceded them to the U.S. With the cession by Virginia (2 Jan. 1781, and p. 596), Maryland signed the Articles, 27 Feb. Congress then set 1 Mar. for final ratification and on 2 Mar. assumed a new title, "The United States in Congress Assembled." The president of the old Congress, **Samuel Huntington** (Conn., 1731–96), continued in office.

WAR IN THE CAROLINAS. After assuming command of the army in the South in Dec. 1780, Gen. Greene moved from North Carolina to Cheraw, S.C. Too weak to attack Cornwallis' main camp at Winnsborough, he detached Gen. **Daniel Morgan** with about 800 men for a sweep to the west and **Henry Lee** for guerrilla activity between Cornwallis and Charleston. Cornwallis ordered Tarleton to drive Morgan back against the main British force. But Morgan selected a position near **Cowpens,** disposed his force (now grown to 1,000) with great care, and met Tarleton's assault there on 17 Jan. By skillful handling of his militia and assisted by cavalry under Col. **William Washington** (1752–1810), Morgan won a smashing victory over the 1,000-man enemy force, suffering less than 75 casualties to Tarleton's 329, and capturing 600. Cornwallis now pursued Morgan into North Carolina. At Guilford Courthouse Greene and Morgan joined forces (9 Feb.) and retreated across the Dan River into Virginia. Lacking boats and supplies, Cornwallis was forced to discontinue the pursuit and withdrew into North Carolina. When reinforcements brought Greene's command up to 4,400 men he followed the British and offered battle at **Guilford Courthouse** (15 Mar.), where Cornwallis won the field but at a cost of almost 100 killed and over 400 wounded. Too weakened by these losses to continue the campaign, he retreated (18 Mar.) to

Wilmington to receive reinforcements by sea.

Greene now marched into South Carolina, and though defeated at **Hobkirk's Hill** (25 Apr.), failed in his siege of the British post at **Ninety-Six** (22 May–19 June), and lost again at **Eutaw Springs** (8 Sept.), he managed (aided by successes scored by Marion, Lee, and Sumter in capturing the smaller British posts in the state) by fall to narrow British control in South Carolina to Charleston and its immediate vicinity.

2 APR. "MARS" AND "MINERVA." In Apr. Capt. **John Barry** (1745–1803), returning from France on the *Alliance,* was attacked by 2 British privateers, the *Mars* and the *Minerva,* but soon had forced both to surrender (2 Apr.). On 29 May, while becalmed, 2 British men-of-war, the *Atalanta* and the *Trepassy,* attacked. Barry was badly wounded but held his rebellious crew to their guns until a breeze enabled him to drive between his attackers and force each to surrender. 1781 also saw a new high in the number of American privateers in action: 449. By the end of the war American privateers had accounted for about 600 British ships, worth, with their cargoes, over $18 million. The Continental Navy captured or destroyed 196 enemy ships during the war.

14 JUNE. U.S. PEACE COMMISSION. On 11 June Congress decided to entrust the peace negotiations to a commission rather than to John Adams alone. **John Jay** (13 June), **Benjamin Franklin, Henry Laurens** (1724–92), and **Thomas Jefferson** (14 June) were named in addition to **Adams.** On 15 June Congress modified the 1779 peace instructions. Only U.S. independence and sovereignty were deemed essential. Other matters were to be handled by the commissioners at their discretion without definite binding instructions. This change was made largely on the advice of the Chevalier de la Luzerne, French minister to the U.S., who was also responsible for that section of the instructions which directed the commission to take no action without the "knowledge and concurrence" of the French ministry and which bound them to "ultimately govern yourselves by their advice and opinion."

10 MAY–1 AUG. CORNWALLIS' CAMPAIGN IN VIRGINIA. Convinced that British control could not be restored in the Carolinas while Virginia remained as a supply and training base for the Americans, Cornwallis left Wilmington 25 Apr. with 1,500 men and marched northward into Virginia. At Petersburg (20 May) he joined his small force to a body of over 4,000 British troops which had followed up Arnold's expedition. Further reinforcements brought his strength to about 7,500, much superior to the small American forces under Lafayette and Von Steuben. He raided deep into Virginia (Tarleton almost captured Gov. Jefferson and the members of the legislature at Charlottesville, 4 June). But as Lafayette was reinforced by Anthony Wayne (10 June) and then joined by Von Steuben (19 June), Cornwallis turned back to the coast to establish a base from which he could maintain communication by sea with Clinton's force in New York. He picked Yorktown, where he arrived 1 Aug.

21 MAY. MEETING OF WASHINGTON AND ROCHAMBEAU. At a conference at Wethersfield, Conn., Washington secured Rochambeau's reluctant consent for a joint attack against New York supported by the French West Indian fleet under Comte de Grasse. Rochambeau left de Grasse free either to sail to New York or to operate against the British in Virginia. Meanwhile the French army moved from Rhode Island and joined Washington's above New York (5 July). Before a large-scale at-

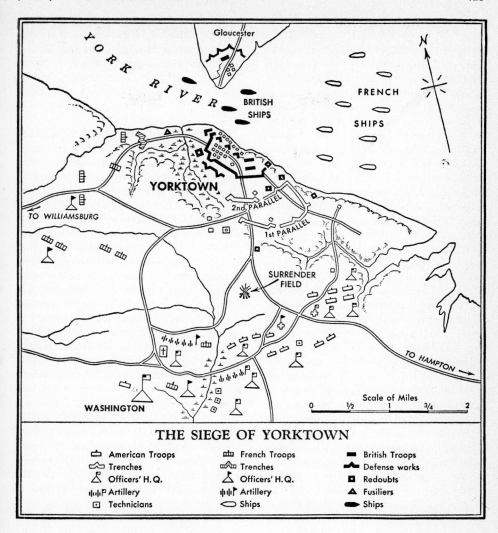

THE SIEGE OF YORKTOWN

⏛ American Troops	⏛ French Troops	▬ British Troops
⏝ Trenches	⏝ Trenches	⏞ Defense works
⏊ Officers' H.Q.	⏊ Officers' H.Q.	▣ Redoubts
⅋P Artillery	⅋ Artillery	△ Fusiliers
▣ Technicians	◌ Ships	◗ Ships

tack could be mounted, a letter from de Grasse reached Washington (14 Aug.) with news that he would leave the West Indies for Chesapeake Bay on 13 Aug. with 3,000 French troops and his entire fleet and would be available for operations in that area until mid-Oct. Washington immediately prepared to march both his and Rochambeau's troops to Virginia. Preserving the appearance of a movement against New York, the two armies crossed the Hudson (20–26 Aug.), feinted toward Staten Island, and then struck out southward across New Jersey.

30 Aug.–19 Oct. YORKTOWN CAMPAIGN. On 30 Aug. de Grasse arrived off Yorktown, set up a naval blockade of the garrison with his fleet, and landed (31 Aug.) his troops to join Lafayette's forces hemming in Cornwallis by land. On 5 Sept. the British fleet under Adm.

Thomas Graves appeared and de Grasse sailed out to give battle. A sharp action that day was followed by 3 days of maneuvering. On 9 Sept. the French were strengthened by the arrival of Comte de Barras with the French squadron from Newport and on 10 Sept. Graves drew off toward New York for repairs, leaving the French in command of the sea off Yorktown. Cornwallis' fate was now quickly sealed. De Grasse sent ships up Chesapeake Bay to bring the bulk of the forces under Washington and Rochambeau to Williamsburg (14–24 Sept.). From there the Allied army (about 9,000 American and 7,800 French troops) moved forward (28 Sept.) and began the siege of Yorktown. On 30 Sept. Cornwallis abandoned his outer line of fortifications, thereby permitting the Allies to bring up siege guns capable of hammering all parts of his inner line. These guns went into operation on 9 Oct. On 14 Oct. 2 redoubts on the left of the British line were taken in an assault in which Col. **Alexander Hamilton** (p. 1048) distinguished himself. A British counterattack on the 16th failed to regain possession of these key points. Cornwallis now regarded his position as hopeless and when a storm later that day forced him to abandon a desperate plan for escaping across the York River, he opened negotiations (17 Oct.) for the surrender of his army. The capitulation was signed on the 18th and on the 19th the British force of almost 8,000 men laid down their arms. Total Allied casualties were 262, against 552 British casualties (excluding prisoners). On 24 Oct. Clinton arrived off Chesapeake Bay with 7,000 reinforcements for Cornwallis, but put back to New York when he learned of the surrender. Washington now urged an attack on New York, but de Grasse, now overdue in the West Indies, refused to participate. Washington marched his army northward to resume the envelop-

ment of New York while Rochambeau's troops passed the winter in Virginia, returned to Rhode Island in the fall of 1782, and sailed from Boston for France 24 Dec.

1782

20 MAR. FALL OF LORD NORTH'S MINISTRY. With the capture of Cornwallis' entire army British hopes for victory in America collapsed. Defeats suffered at the hands of the French in the West Indies in 1781 and early 1782 further quickened Britain's desire for peace. The coercive policy of the North ministry was repudiated on 27 Feb. when the House of Commons voted against further prosecuting the war in America and passed a bill (5 Mar.) authorizing the crown to make peace with the former colonies. On 20 Mar. Lord North resigned. He was succeeded (22 Mar.) by Lord Rockingham, the minister who had secured the Stamp Act's repeal in 1766. The new ministry immediately decided to open direct negotiations with the American peace commissioners.

4 APR. SIR GUY CARLETON SUCCEEDS CLINTON. Carleton arrived in New York (9 May) to assume his new commission (4 Apr.) as British commander in chief. With plans for continuing the war abandoned, he set about concentrating all British forces on the seaboard at New York. Wilmington, N.C., had been evacuated (Jan.), Savannah (11 July), and finally Charleston (14 Dec.). A skirmish at Combahee River, S.C. (27 Aug.), was the last land action of the war on the seaboard.

12 APR. PEACE TALKS BEGIN IN PARIS. Richard Oswald, named by the Rockingham ministry to open peace negotiations with the American commissioners, began talks with Franklin (12 Apr.), at that time the only commissioner present in Paris. The British re-

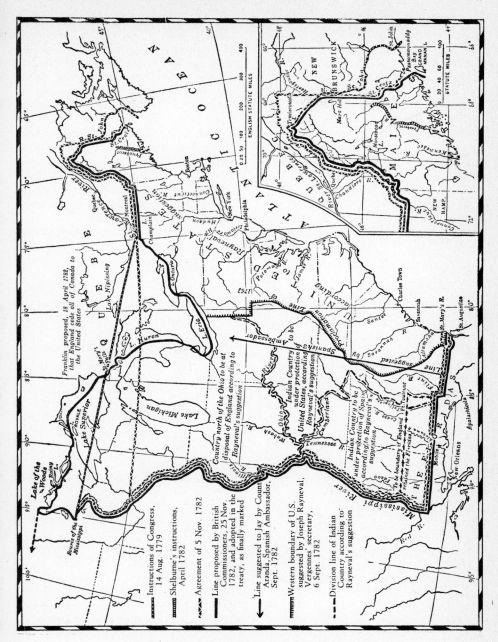

Boundaries proposed in the peace negotiations of 1782
between the United States and England

leased Commissioner Henry Laurens, whom they had captured (3 Sept. 1780) and imprisoned in England, and sent him to The Hague to sound out John Adams. Laurens arrived in time to congratulate the latter on obtaining recognition by the Netherlands of U.S. independence (19 Apr.). Before leaving for Paris, Adams followed up this success by obtaining a loan of about $2 million from Dutch bankers (11 June) and a treaty of commerce and friendship with the Netherlands (8 Oct.).

27 Sept. START OF FORMAL NE-GOTIATIONS. On 23 June, John Jay

arrived from Madrid to join Franklin in Paris. Adams arrived on 26 Oct. (Laurens took no part in the Paris discussions until the preliminary peace treaty was virtually completed in Nov., and Jefferson, the fifth commissioner named by Congress, did not serve.) Meanwhile, Rockingham had died and was succeeded by the **Earl of Shelburne** as head of the British ministry (1 July). On 19 Sept. Oswald was authorized to treat with the commission of the "13 U.S." (tantamount to recognition of American independence) and opened formal negotiations with Franklin and Jay.

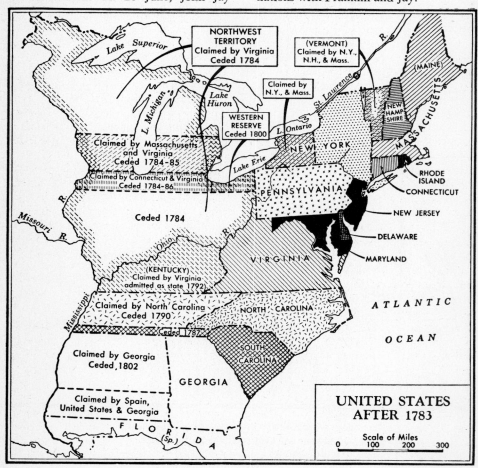

NORTHWEST TERRITORY
Claimed by Virginia
Ceded 1784

(VERMONT)
Claimed by N.Y.,
N.H., & Mass.

(MAINE)

Claimed by
N.Y., & Mass.

WESTERN RESERVE
Ceded 1800

NEW HAMPSHIRE

MASSACHUSETTS

Claimed by Massachusetts
and Virginia
Ceded 1784-85

Claimed by Connecticut & Virginia
Ceded 1784-86

NEW YORK

RHODE ISLAND

CONNECTICUT

Ceded 1784

PENNSYLVANIA

NEW JERSEY

DELAWARE

MARYLAND

(KENTUCKY)
Claimed by Virginia
admitted as state 1792

VIRGINIA

Missouri R.

Mississippi R.

Ohio R.

Claimed by North Carolina
Ceded 1790

NORTH CAROLINA

Ceded 1787

SOUTH CAROLINA

ATLANTIC OCEAN

Claimed by Georgia
Ceded 1802

GEORGIA

Claimed by Spain,
United States & Georgia

FLORIDA (Sp.)

UNITED STATES AFTER 1783

Scale of Miles
0   100   200   300

30 Nov. SIGNING OF PRELIMINARY ARTICLES OF PEACE. Jay's fears that France, in support of Spain, was determined to confine the U.S. within severe territorial limits and curtail her fishing rights were touched off by news (9 Sept.) that French undersecretary Gérard de Rayneval had gone on a secret mission to Shelburne. To counter this move, Jay dispatched to England a pro-American Englishman, Benjamin Vaughan, to press upon Shelburne the urgency of acknowledging U.S. independence as a precondition to any settlement. On 18 Sept. Shelburne persuaded the British cabinet to revise Oswald's commission in the manner Jay had requested. On Oswald's return to Paris, 27 Sept., with the new commission, negotiations moved forward rapidly. On 5 Oct. Jay presented Oswald with the draft of a preliminary treaty, to become effective when a similar treaty was signed by Britain and France. Upon the basis of these preliminary articles (which did not include an earlier demand by Franklin that Canada be ceded to the U.S.) negotiations continued. Oswald was joined by Henry Strachey (28 Oct.), Undersecretary of State in the Home Office. About 1 Nov. the 3 U.S. commissioners (Adams was now on the scene) decided to disobey Congress' instructions concerning full consultation with the French and to proceed on their own initiative. A new set of articles was agreed to on 5 Nov. With a few last-minute changes these constituted the preliminary treaty of peace signed by Oswald for the British and by Adams, Franklin, Jay, and Laurens for the U.S. Without a single change these articles became the definitive peace treaty signed 3 Sept. 1783. Its most important provisions: (1) Britain recognized U.S. independence; (2) boundaries: the St. Croix River dividing Maine and Nova Scotia; the St. Lawrence-Atlantic watershed divide, the 45th parallel, a line through the Great Lakes and their connecting waterways, and a line from Lake Superior to the Mississippi dividing Canada and the U.S.; a line through the middle of the Mississippi River south to the 31st parallel to be the boundary with Spanish Louisiana; and the 31st parallel and the Apalachicola and St. Mary's rivers as the boundary with Spanish Florida (Spain obtained Florida from Britain in the final peace treaty); (3) U.S. given the "right" to fish in their accustomed grounds off Newfoundland and Nova Scotia, and the "liberty" to dry and cure fish on any unsettled shore in Labrador, the Magdalen Islands, and Nova Scotia; (4) all debts due creditors of either country by citizens of the other were validated; (5) Congress was pledged to "earnestly recommend" to the legislatures of the states a full restoration of the rights and property of the Loyalists; and (6) hostilities were to cease and all British land and sea forces evacuated "with all convenient speed."

Vergennes, taken aback by the extremely favorable terms obtained for the U.S., criticized the commissioners (15 Dec.) for signing without consulting him. However, his own desire for a speedy settlement of the war and a tactful reply by Franklin (17 Dec.) prevented serious discord.

1783

20 JAN. EFFECTIVE DATE OF ARTICLES OF PEACE. The Anglo-American preliminary treaty was not to go into effect until Britain reached a settlement with France. On 20 Jan. preliminary articles of peace were signed between Britain and France and by Britain and Spain. Provisions were then made for a general armistice and on 4 Feb. Britain proclaimed a cessation of hostilities.

10, 12 MAR. NEWBURGH ADDRESSES. Early in Jan. a delegation of army officers memorialized Congress regarding grounds of their discontent: arrears in pay, unsettled food and clothing accounts, and Congress' failure to make provision for the life pension of half pay from the time of their discharge promised them 21 Oct. 1780. Their failure to obtain assurances of payment of sums owed officers and to secure a commutation of the pension for 6 years' full pay (rejected 25 Jan. by Congress) led to the first anonymous address to the officers of the army circulated at Washington's main camp near Newburgh, N.Y. Written by Maj. **John Armstrong** (1758–1843), the address attacked the "coldness and severity" shown by Congress, advised the officers to assume a bold tone and "suspect the man who would advise to more moderation and longer forbearance," and called upon them to meet the next day (11 Mar.) and draw up a "last remonstrance" which, if not well received by Congress, would justify the army in defying that body. Armstrong's call for pressure on Congress had the backing of Gen. Gates, Gouverneur Morris (1752–1816), and other civilian leaders who hoped to coerce the states into yielding more power to Congress. The address was well received by many of the officers, but Washington, with skill and tact, soon blunted the movement's force. On 11 Mar. he issued an order forbidding the unauthorized meeting called for by the anonymous address on that day, but went on to propose a regular meeting of the officers for the discussion of grievances on 15 Mar. A second anonymous address (also written by Armstrong) was issued on 12 Mar., expressing the opinion that Washington's action in calling for a meeting proved that he "sanctified" the claims of the officers. To the consternation of the plotters, Washington addressed the 15 Mar.

meeting in person, denounced the resort to immoderate measures, while promising quick redress for the officers' grievances. After Washington withdrew, the officers adopted resolutions, without dissent, affirming their patriotism, their confidence in Congress, and their disdain for the "infamous propositions . . . in a late anonymous address." Congress a week later granted the officers a sum equal to 5 years' full pay. Washington's stand is a historic precedent for the subordination of the military to civilian government.

15 APR. ARTICLES OF PEACE RATIFIED. On 13 Mar. Congress received the text of the provisional treaty from Paris. On 11 Apr. it issued a similar proclamation of the cessation of the war and on 15 Apr. ratified the provisional treaty after a debate in which the action of the commissioners in proceeding without consulting the French came in for considerable criticism. The treaty was signed in Paris 3 Sept., ratified by Congress 14 Jan. 1784, ratifications exchanged 12 May 1784.

26 APR. 7,000 LOYALISTS SAIL FROM NEW YORK, their departure made necessary by the impending embarkation of the British army. This group was among the last of the total of almost 100,000 Loyalists who left the U.S. for Europe or Canada. The early "test acts" passed by the revolutionary state governments in 1776–77 requiring a repudiation of loyalty to George III had been followed by more severe repressive measures. Nine states had passed acts exiling prominent Tories, 5 had disfranchised all Loyalists, and in most of the states Loyalists were expelled from all offices, barred from the professions, and forced to pay double or treble taxes. On 27 Nov. 1777 Congress recommended to the states that they appropriate the property of residents who had forfeited "the right to protection." By 1782 all the states had passed confiscation acts, some, in fact, antedating Congress' recommendation. New York obtained over $3,600,000 and Maryland over $2 million from the sale of Loyalist property. The British government established a commission (July) to which the Loyalists might present claims to cover their damages. The commission functioned until 1790, examined 4,118 claims, and authorized payment of a generous total of £3,292,452 in compensation.

13 June. ARMY DISBANDS. Congress voted (26 May) to give furloughs to soldiers who had enlisted for the duration until the signing of the peace treaty should permit their full discharge. Certificates for 3 months' pay were authorized for those furloughed. On 13 June, without waiting for these certificates to reach camp, most of Washington's army departed for their homes from the camps in the Hudson Highlands. On 18 Oct. Congress discharged all previously furloughed and on 3 Nov. discharged all other troops enlisted for the duration of the war. Only a small force of men serving time enlistments remained with Washington to await the evacuation of New York City by the British.

24 June. CONGRESS FLEES PHILADELPHIA. On 17 June about 80 soldiers began a march from Lancaster to Philadelphia to obtain justice from the state government and from Congress; they were joined (21 June) by an additional 200 from regiments in Philadelphia, and demonstrated before Independence Hall, where both the executive council of Pennsylvania and Congress were meeting. When the state authorities proved unwilling or unable to deal with the mutineers, President **Elias Boudinot** (1740–1821) changed the meeting place of Congress from Philadelphia to Princeton (24 June). Congress met there until 3 Nov., when it

adjourned to meet 26 Nov. at Annapolis, Md., under a plan (adopted 21 Oct.) calling for alternate sessions there and at Trenton until dual permanent seats for the government (authorized 7 and 17 Oct.) were established on the Delaware and Potomac rivers.

25 Nov. BRITISH EVACUATE NEW YORK CITY. On 21 Nov. the British drew back from northern Manhattan Island and from eastern Long Island into New York City and Brooklyn. Washington moved to Manhattan, taking up a position at Harlem Heights. Early in the afternoon of the 25th the last British troops left the docks of New York and Washington, accompanied by Gov. **George Clinton** (p. 1003), entered the city. By 4 Dec. the British had completed the evacuation of Staten Island and Long Island and were putting out to sea in their transports. On that same day Washington took leave of his officers at Fraunces' Tavern. After a triumphal tour to Annapolis where the Congress was in session, he appeared before that body (23 Dec.) to resign his commission as commander in chief and "take . . . leave of all the employments of public life."

SIGNIFICANT RESULTS OF THE REVOLUTION: (1) The 13 colonies became independent states and united under the Confederation of the U.S.; (2) the U.S. obtained title to a vast empire from the seaboard settlements to the Mississippi; (3) royal and proprietary colonial governments were replaced by republican state governments; (4) the overthrow of the royal and proprietary ruling class and the participation of men of all social levels in the Revolution brought a broader popular base to political life; (5) the confiscation of royal lands, proprietary estates, and Loyalist property, though chiefly designed as revenue-raising measures, brought, ultimately, a somewhat more democratic redistribution of property; (6) quitrents formerly collected by the crown and by colonial proprietors were abolished by the states; (7) entail and primogeniture, twin pillars of aristocratic land holding, were virtually abolished by state legislation, 1776–91; (8) the Anglican Church was disestablished in all colonies in which it had been tax-supported, 1776–86; (9) the slave trade was prohibited or heavily taxed in 11 states (1776–86), slavery abolished in Massachusetts (1780), in New Hampshire (1784), and gradual emancipation adopted by Pennsylvania (1780), Connecticut (1784), and Rhode Island (1784); (10) the reform of penal codes and prisons was advanced as well as the secularization and democratization of education.

1784

STATE CONSTITUTIONS. During the Revolution 11 of the 13 states drew up new constitutions. (Connecticut and Rhode Island continued to use the colonial charters of 1662 and 1663, merely deleting all references to the British crown.) Except in the case of Massachusetts, where a constitutional convention was called (1779) and its handiwork submitted to the people for ratification (1780), these new constitutions were the work of revolutionary congresses or conventions. Constitutions were adopted by New Hampshire, New Jersey, Pennsylvania, Delaware, Maryland, Virginia, North Carolina, and South Carolina in 1776; by New York and Georgia in 1777.

Main features: (1) **Bicameral legislature** (exceptions: Pennsylvania, with a unicameral legislature and plural executive—executive council of 13; and New Hampshire, with an executive council under 1776 constitution). (2) **Weak chief executive:** in 9 of 13 states his

term was for 1 year; in 7 his reeligibility was variously limited; in 9 a veto power denied him. In 9 out of 11 the executive shared appointing power with the legislature; governors with greatest power were found in Massachusetts and New York, elected by the people rather than by the legislature. (3) **Strong legislature:** elected executive in 8 states; shared appointing power in 6; lower house originated all money bills in 9. (4) **Frequent elections:** in every state except South Carolina (where both houses had 2-year terms) the lower house was elected annually, or semiannually (Rhode Island and Connecticut); upper house elected annually in 8 states for terms of 2 years (South Carolina), 3 years (Delaware), and 4 years (New York and Virginia). (5) **Property qualifications for office-holding** ranged as high as £10,000 for governor (South Carolina); £2,000 (North Carolina); £1,000 (New Jersey and Maryland) for the upper house; £500 (New Jersey and Maryland) for the lower. (6) **Property qualifications for voting** ranged from payment of a low poll tax (New Hampshire and Pennsylvania, where sons of freeholders were eligible to vote without payment of taxes) to Virginia's requirement of 25 acres of settled or 500 acres of unsettled land, with a shift from a freehold to a taxpaying qualification in evidence in numerous states. (7) **An appointive judiciary with tenure for good behavior** (8 states; annual appointment, Connecticut and Rhode Island; for 5 years, New Hampshire; for 7 years, New Jersey and Pennsylvania).

Innovations: (1) **Bills of Rights** (beginning with Virginia, 12 June 1776, drafted by **George Mason,** p. 1098) included in many constitutions; (2) **Council of Appointment** in New York, chosen annually from senate and assembly, exercised (with the governor, who had but one vote) appointive power; (3) **Council of Censors** in Pennsylvania, elected by the people every seventh year and empowered to investigate actions of the assembly and executive council and summon a convention to consider constitutional amendments.

23 Apr. JEFFERSON'S 1ST TERRITORIAL ORDINANCE. On 1 Mar., the day Congress accepted a revised version of Virginia's cession of her western lands, a committee headed by Jefferson proposed a plan for temporary government in the West, the division of the domain into states to enter the Confederacy on equality with the original members. Jefferson's proposal prohibiting slavery after 1800 in all parts was narrowly defeated. After amendments, the report was adopted 23 Apr. and, though never put into effect, served as the basis for the Northwest Ordinance (1787).

7 May. SECRETARY FOR FOREIGN AFFAIRS. In Dec. 1783 **Robert R. Livingston** (p. 1087) resigned as first Secretary for Foreign Affairs (named 10 Aug. 1781). After long delay **John Jay,** then about to return to America from Europe, was named to succeed him.

May–July. WYOMING VALLEY VIOLENCE. On 30 Dec. 1782 a 5-man court appointed by Congress (Aug.) held unanimously that the disputed title to the Wyoming Valley claimed by both Pennsylvania and Connecticut should be awarded the former, whose territory was contiguous. Without awaiting settlement of individual claims, the Pennsylvania Assembly approved a plan to oust the Connecticut settlers (1783). Militia actions against settlers were denounced by the Pennsylvania Council of Censors, which forced the assembly to enact measures (15 Sept.) restoring settlers to their lands under protection of a new commission (9 Sept.). After further violence in 1787, a Pennsylvania act of that year brought an equitable and conclusive settlement.

28 May. TREASURY BOARD. At his own request Robert Morris was replaced as Superintendent of Finance by a board of 3 commissioners—**Samuel Osgood** (1748–1813), **Walter Livingston** (1740–97), named 25 Jan., and **Arthur Lee** (27 July). The central government was still dependent upon requisitions on the states. Of an $8 million requisition (Oct. 1781) only $1,486,512 had been paid by 1 Jan. 1784. Late in 1783 Morris had been forced to overdraw his account in Europe to provide for the army's demobilization pay. Negotiation of loans by John Adams in Holland (1784) enabled Morris to pay off $230,000 in notes (outstanding 1 Jan.) and leave office (1 Nov.) with a surplus of $21,000.

30 Aug. OPENING OF CHINA TRADE. Independence brought freedom from the British Navigation Acts but also the closing to the U.S. of the British West Indies. A British order in council (2 July 1783) banned importation of meats, fish, and dairy products from the U.S. into the West Indies and closed the trade in all other products to all but British ships. As a result, American businessmen looked to new markets, notably to the Orient. On 22 Feb. the *Empress of China,* Capt. John Greene, sailed from New York by way of Cape Horn and reached Canton 30 Aug. The profit from the cargo of tea and silks which it brought back (May 1785) prompted merchants of Philadelphia, Boston, and Providence to fit out ships for China. Despite gains in trade with France and Holland, Britain was still the best customer of the U.S., in part the result of an order in council (26 Dec. 1783) permitting the importation of American manufactured goods (with a few exceptions) into Britain on the same favorable terms as in colonial days.

British exports to the U.S. amounted (1784) to £ 3,679,467 as against imports from the U.S. of only £ 749,345. The unbalance increased specie scarcity in the U.S. and led to overextension of inventories and credit.

23 DEC. NEW YORK TEMPORARY CAPITAL. Congress met in Trenton (1 Nov.) and voted (10 Dec.) to move from Trenton; on the 23rd it appointed commissioners to lay out a federal district on the banks of the Delaware and to move to New York until the federal city was ready.

1785

16 FEB. CONGRESS AND THE COMMERCE POWER. The weakness of the central government under the Articles of Confederation made it difficult to obtain commercial concessions from foreign nations. The British ambassador in Paris told Franklin, Adams, and Jefferson (26 Mar.) that Britain could hardly enter into a treaty with Congress when one state could render "totally fruitless and ineffectual" any such agreement, and proposed that they obtain authorizations from the individual states as well. Congress unsuccessfully appealed in 1784 for a 15-year grant of power to regulate foreign commerce. On 24 Jan. a committee headed by **James Monroe** (p. 1105) was appointed to consider a new appeal to the states. Its report called for an amendment to the 9th Article, which forbade Congress to enter into any treaty of commerce that deprived any state of its individual right to impose duties. No action was taken.

24 FEB., 10 MAR. MINISTERS TO BRITAIN AND FRANCE. On 31 July 1784, Jefferson reached Paris to serve with Franklin and Adams as commissioners to negotiate commercial treaties. On 24 Feb. Congress appointed John Adams minister to the Court of St. James

and granted Franklin's request to be replaced as minister to France, appointing (10 Mar.) Jefferson to succeed him. Jefferson was received by Louis XVI on 17 May and Adams by George III on 1 June.

8 MAR. HENRY KNOX SECRETARY OF WAR. In 1781 Congress replaced the cumbersome Board of War by a Secretary heading a War Department. Gen. Lincoln held that office until 1783. After a 2-year vacancy Knox was chosen to succeed him.

28 MAR. MT. VERNON CONFERENCE. Late in March 4 commissioners from Virginia, including Madison and Mason, met at Alexandria with 4 Maryland commissioners, including Samuel Chase (1741–1811), to consider problems relating to the navigation of Chesapeake Bay and Potomac River. On 28 Mar. the negotiators adjourned to **Mt. Vernon,** where Washington acted as their host but apparently took no direct part in the discussions. Swift agreement was reached concerning the jurisdiction of the Potomac and the apportionment of expenses for marking the channel through Chesapeake Bay. The commissioners then drafted an agreement recommending to their respective legislatures uniform commercial regulations and imposts, a uniform currency, and annual conferences on common commercial problems. A request was also drawn up that Pennsylvania be invited to join Virginia and Maryland in a pact to establish water communication between the Chesapeake and the Ohio River. The Maryland legislature not only endorsed this plan (5 Dec.) but proposed the addition of Delaware. At Madison's behest, the Virginia legislature invited (21 Jan. 1786) all the states to discuss commercial problems at a convention to be held at Annapolis (Sept.).

20 MAY. BASIC LAND ORDINANCE provided for rectangular surveys dividing the land into townships of 6 miles square. Townships were to be divided into 36 lots of 640 acres each (1 lot set aside for maintaining public schools; but an attempt to include another lot for the support of the religion of the majority of resident adult males narrowly missed passage) and sale of minimum lots (640 acres) authorized at $1 an acre.

23 JUNE–11 JULY. MASSACHUSETTS AND FOREIGN COMMERCE. As early as 1783 Maryland laid discriminatory rates and port fees on British shipping and South Carolina imposed a general duty of 2½% on foreign goods, with higher rates on specified articles. Pennsylvania, New York, and North Carolina acted in 1784. On 23 June Massachusetts banned the export of U.S. products in British ships and doubled the tonnage duty on all goods imported in other than American ships. New Hampshire took similar steps the same day. Earlier in June Rhode Island passed a high protective tariff to encourage domestic industry. On 11 July the Massachusetts legislature passed a resolution favoring a convention to revise the Articles of Confederation, but her delegates at New York failed to offer this resolution. Pennsylvania (20 Sept.) placed a discriminatory tonnage duty on ships of foreign nations which had no treaties with the U.S. U.S. imports from Britain totaled £ 2,308,023, a drop of £ 1,371,444 from the abnormally high figure of 1784, but exports to Britain rose from £ 749,345 (1784) to £ 893,594.

20 JULY. JAY-GARDOQUI NEGOTIATIONS. Spain refused to be bound by that part of the Anglo-American treaty which set the 31st parallel as the boundary between Spanish Florida and the U.S., claiming the territory 100 miles northward as far as the junction of the Yazoo River with the Mississippi (at 32°22′), and in 1784 refused to permit American shipping to pass freely through the lower Mississippi. On 15 May 1785 Don Diego de Gardoqui arrived as Spanish minister to the U.S. with specific instructions to make no concession on the navigation of the Mississippi. Congress authorized John Jay to negotiate with Gardoqui (20 July) and instructed him (24 Aug.) "particularly to stipulate the right of the United States to . . . the free navigation of the Mississippi. . . ." A year of fruitless negotiation followed. Finally, on 29 Aug. 1786, Congress authorized Jay to "forbear" American navigation rights for 25 or 30 years in return for a favorable commercial treaty with Spain. But the bitter debate on this authorization and the close vote (7–5) indicated the unlikelihood that 9 states (required by the Articles) would ratify the treaty. Hence, negotiations broke down, and the issues remained unsettled until the Pinckney Treaty of 1795.

10 SEPT. TREATY WITH PRUSSIA. John Adams negotiated (1784) with Baron Thulemeier, Prussian minister at The Hague, but was called to his English post before completing the treaty. Jefferson then sent his secretary, William Short, to complete negotiations. The treaty outlawed privateering and endorsed the principle of free ships-free goods.

30 NOV. NEGOTIATIONS WITH BRITAIN. In Britain Adams found that the inability of the U.S. to force the states to abide by those terms of the Treaty of Paris concerning the treatment of Loyalists and the removal of impediments to collection of debts to English creditors made it virtually impossible for him to obtain commercial concessions or British compliance with the treaty terms requiring them to evacuate Oswego, Niagara, Detroit, Michilimackinac, and other garrisons on U.S. soil. Adams' formal demand (30 Nov.) for the evacuation of the western posts brought the blunt reply (28 Feb. 1786) that the posts would be held until British creditors obtained payment from America. After 3 years, during which he pressed U.S. claims tenaciously but without success, Adams resigned and left for the U.S. (Apr. 1788).

1786

16 JAN. ADOPTION OF THE VIRGINIA STATUTE FOR RELIGIOUS FREEDOM. In 1779 an Ordinance of Religious Freedom written by Jefferson was proposed in the Virginia legislature and failed of adoption, but in Dec. 1785, virtually the same measure, now brought forward by James Madison, passed the House of Burgesses. Model for the 1st Amendment of the U.S. Constitution, the statute declared that no man could be compelled to attend or support any church nor suffer any discrimination because of his religious beliefs. Jefferson ranked his authorship of this act with the drafting of the Declaration of Independence and the founding of the Univ. of Virginia as his most significant accomplishments. Some months earlier Madison had drafted (June, 1785) his **"Memorial and Remonstrance"** against religious assessments, which successfully propagandized against a bill to have a general assessment levied for the support of religion and argued the inalienable right of individual freedom of conscience.

28. JUNE. TREATY WITH MOROCCO. With the removal of the protection of the British fleet, American commerce in the Mediterranean and off the coasts of Spain and Portugal suffered substantial losses from pirates from Algiers, Tripoli, Tunis, and Morocco. On 22 Feb. John Adams had an interview in London with the Tripolitine ambassador, Abdrahaman, who demanded £ 200,000 for the protection of U.S. commerce. Negotiations broke down.

Jefferson proposed a plan for an international expedition against the Barbary states, but Congress balked at contributing a frigate. On 28 June, Thomas Barclay, in direct negotiations with the Emperor of Morocco, obtained a treaty in exchange for gifts worth about $10,000. With Algiers, Tripoli, and Tunis, however, the U.S. was unable to reach agreements until 1795, 1796, and 1797 respectively.

JUNE–SEPT. LOW POINT OF DEPRESSION (p. 746). Imports from and exports to Great Britain dropped to £ 1,603,465 and £ 843,119 respectively compared to £ 2,308,023 and £ 893,594 (1785). Farm wages showed a decline of as much as 20% from the 1780 level. The combination of a money shortage, high taxes, and insistent creditors brought demands for relief through stay laws and paper money. The paper-money advocates succeeded in obtaining issues totaling £ 800,000 in Pennsylvania (Mar. 1785), South Carolina (Oct. 1785), North Carolina (Nov. 1785), New York (Apr.), Rhode Island (May), New Jersey (May), and Georgia (Aug.). In the remaining 6 states the pressure for similar action was greatest in Massachusetts. In Rhode Island the paper-money issue provided the background for the case of *Trevett* v. *Weeden,* in which the state's supreme court upheld the doctrine of judicial review propounded by counsel James Varnum in ruling (25 Sept.) that an act forcing a creditor to accept the paper money was unconstitutional.

7 AUG. PROPOSALS TO REVISE THE ARTICLES. On 26 June Congress debated a motion (3 May) by **Charles Pinckney** (S.C., 1757–1824) for a reorganization of the government. The debates and the proposed amendments submitted 7 Aug. by a special committee reveal the delegates' awareness of the weaknesses of the Articles of Confederation. One proposal would have set up a federal court of 7 judges with appeal jurisdiction from the state courts in cases involving foreign nations and federal matters; another would have given Congress power over foreign and domestic commerce; 2 others attempted to strengthen the requisition system to ensure payment of the state quotas. (The need for such measures had been highlighted when New Jersey flatly refused, 20 Feb., to pay the requisition voted by Congress in Sept. 1785.) Congress, apparently despairing of winning that unanimous approval necessary under the Articles for adoption of an amendment, never submitted these proposals to the states.

11–14 Sept. ANNAPOLIS CONVENTION. Virginia's invitation to an interstate commercial convention at Annapolis (issued on 21 Jan.) was accepted by 9 states. Georgia, South Carolina, Connecticut, and, oddly enough, Maryland took no action. The delegates named by New Hampshire, Massachusetts, Rhode Island, and North Carolina failed to reach Annapolis in time to participate. Hence, only New York, New Jersey, Delaware, Pennsylvania, and Virginia were represented. When the convention opened on the 11th John Dickinson, now a resident of Delaware, was elected chairman. The slim attendance convinced the 12 delegates that it would be useless to proceed to a study of interstate commercial problems. A committee was appointed, however, on 13 Sept. to prepare an address to the states, which the convention adopted 14 Sept. Drafted by **Alexander Hamilton,** a leading force at the meeting, the report called upon the states to send commissioners to a new convention at Philadelphia on the 2d Monday in May 1787, to discuss not only commercial problems but *all* matters necessary "to render the constitu-

tion of the Federal Government adequate to the exigencies of the Union." Congress referred this invitation to committee 11 Oct. Not until 21 Feb. 1787 was a cautious endorsement of the plan adopted. On that day Congress described as "expedient" a convention "for the sole and express purpose of revising the Articles of Confederation and reporting to Congress and the several legislatures such alterations and provisions therein." Five states (Virginia, New Jersey, Pennsylvania, Delaware, and North Carolina) had already named delegates to the Philadelphia convention.

Aug.–Dec. SHAYS' REBELLION. When the Massachusetts legislature adjourned on 8 July without heeding the petitions of the debt-ridden farmers for a paper-money issue or laws to stay the mounting number of farm and home foreclosures, discontent mounted. A town meeting of protest at Worcester (15 Aug.) was followed by a Hampshire Co. convention of some 50 towns at Hatfield (22–25 Aug.) The delegates condemned the Massachusetts senate, lawyers, the high costs of justice, and the tax system, and called for an issue of paper money. They also advised against violence, but mob action followed. On 31 Aug. armed men prevented the sitting of the court at Northampton and on 5 Sept. the court at Worcester was broken up. When similar mob actions occurred at Concord and Great Barrington, Gov. **James Bowdoin** (1726–90) sent 600 militiamen under Gen. **William Shepherd** (1737–1817) to protect the supreme court sitting at Springfield. About 500 insurgents gathered there under the leadership of **Daniel Shays** (1747–1825), a destitute farmer who had risen to the rank of captain during the Revolution, confronted the militia (26 Sept.), and obliged the court to adjourn. Shays' presence in Springfield, site of a federal arsenal, prompted Congress to authorize Gen. Knox to raise 1,340 men, mostly in Massachusetts and Connecticut, ostensibly for service against the Indians (20 Oct.). Actually, the federal forces never had to be used. The insurrection in eastern Massachusetts collapsed with the capture of Job Shattuck on 30 Nov. A greater threat to public order was posed in the western part of the state. At Worcester Shays gathered a force of about 1,200 men during Nov. and early Dec. On 26 Dec. he marched to Springfield to join forces with other insurgents led by Luke Day and threaten Shepherd's smaller force guarding the arsenal. The governor called for 4,400 men, enlisted for one month, to assemble at Boston and Springfield on 18–19 Jan. Command was given to Gen. **Benjamin Lincoln.**

1787

4 FEB. SHAYSITES ROUTED AT PETERSHAM. Shays and Day, their forces separated by the Connecticut River, planned to scatter Shepherd's force and seize the arsenal before Lincoln reached Springfield. On 24 Jan. Shays proposed a combined assault the next day. Day's reply that he could not attack until the 26th was intercepted, with the result that Shays went ahead confident of Day's cooperation. About 4 P.M. he led some 1,200 men toward the arsenal. When the insurgents approached to within 100 yards of the building (despite warnings), Shepherd opened fire with artillery. The Shaysites quickly broke and fled, leaving 4 dead. On 27 Jan. Lincoln arrived at Springfield and on the 28th moved on to Amherst, pushing Shays before him to Pelham and isolating Day, who fled to New Hampshire. On 3 Feb., in the midst of negotiations, Shays marched eastward to Petersham. Lincoln followed in a punishing night march and early on 4 Feb. surprised the insurgents, captured 150, scattered the rest, and sent Shays fleeing to Vermont. The uprising was completely crushed by the end of Feb. In Mar. the legislature offered a pardon to all Shaysites except Shays, Day, and 2 other leaders. Shays was finally pardoned 13 June 1788. The uprising had the effect of inducing the legislature not to impose a direct tax in 1787 and to enact laws lowering court fees and exempting clothing, household goods, and tools of one's trade from debt process.

FEB.–MAY. DELEGATES NAMED TO PHILADELPHIA CONVENTION. In addition to the 5 states that had already acted, 6 others (Massachusetts, New York, Georgia, South Carolina, Maryland, and Connecticut) named delegates. New Hampshire and Rhode Island were the only states that failed to act by the date set (14 May) for the opening of the convention. New Hampshire finally fell into line in June (its delegates reached Philadelphia 23 July) but Rhode Island ignored the convention.

25 MAY. OPENING OF CONSTITUTIONAL CONVENTION. On 14 May only the delegates from Virginia and Pennsylvania were on hand at Philadelphia's State House (Independence Hall). Not until 25 May was a quorum of 7 states obtained. From 81-year-old Franklin to 26-year-old Jonathan Dayton (New Jersey, 1760–1824) the delegates included outstanding public figures. Most respected and influential men were Washington and Franklin, while the actual leaders in the floor debates proved to be **Madison** and **George Mason** (Virginia), **Gouverneur Morris** and **James Wilson** (Pennsylvania), **Roger Sherman** (Conn.) and **Elbridge Gerry** (Massachusetts, 1744–1814). Of the 55 delegates 29 were college trained, over half were lawyers, while planters and merchants together with a few physicians and college professors made up the rest. When the convention opened Robert Morris nominated **Washington** as president; this won unanimous approval. **William Jackson** (Ga., 1759–1828) was elected secretary. (The journal kept by Jackson was meager; knowledge of the debates is derived very largely from notes taken each day by Madison. In keeping with the pledge of secrecy [29 May] these were not published until 1840, 4 years after his death.)

29 MAY. VIRGINIA PLAN. Edmund Randolph (Virginia, 1753–1813) proposed 15 resolutions comprising the "Virginia Plan" of Union, which went beyond revision of the Articles and favored a new national government. Outstanding features: (1) a bicameral national legislature, representing the states proportionally, with the lower house elected by the people, and the upper house by the lower house from nominees proposed by the state legislatures; (2) an executive chosen by the legislature; (3) a judiciary including a supreme court and inferior courts elected by the legislature; (4) a council of revision consisting of the executive and several members of the judiciary, with a veto over the legislature's acts. On 30 May the convention resolved itself into a committee of the whole and debated the Virginia Plan until 13 June. On that date 19 resolutions based on Randolph's proposals were reported to the convention.

15 JUNE. NEW JERSEY PLAN. Opposition to the Virginia Plan came chiefly from the small states and centered upon the provision for proportional rather than equal representation of the states in both houses of the proposed legislature. On 15 June **William Paterson** (New Jersey, 1745–1806) introduced 9 resolutions which stressed retention of the confederation but conferred upon Congress the powers to tax and regulate foreign and interstate commerce and to name a plural executive (without a veto) and a supreme court. U.S. treaties and acts of Congress were to be the supreme law in the states. The issue before the convention: whether to content themselves with amendments to the Articles or to draw up the framework of a new national government. After 3 days of debate (16–19 June) the convention voted 7–3 to work toward a national government as visualized in the Virginia Plan. The committee of the whole now debated the issue of equal versus proportional representation in the legislature.

13 JULY. NORTHWEST ORDINANCE. While the convention was debating a plan to supplant the Articles, the Congress of the Confederation registered its greatest achievement, the ordinance for the government of the territory north of the Ohio River. Based in part upon Jefferson's plan of 1784 and in part upon a committee report of 19 Sept. 1786, the Northwest Ordinance, largely written by Nathan Dane (Mass.), provided: (1) the territory to be governed initially by a governor, a secretary, and 3 judges appointed by Congress; (2) when there were 5,000 free adult males in the territory a bicameral legislature to be established; (3) ultimately, from 3 to 5 states to be created (a population of 60,000 free inhabitants was requisite for admission to the Union); (4) the new states to be "on an equal footing with the original states in all respects whatsoever"; (5) freedom of worship, right of trial by jury, and public support of education provided; and (6) involuntary servitude, save in punishment for crime, prohibited. On 5 Oct. **Arthur St. Clair** was elected first governor of the territory and **Winthrop Sargent** (1753–1820) named secretary.

16 JULY. CONNECTICUT COMPROMISE. A committee (appointed 2 July) reconsidered and rejected a proposal made on 11 June by Roger Sherman (Connecticut): representation to be proportional to population in the lower house and one vote for each state in the Senate. On 5 July the committee reported in favor of this plan. On 12 July the convention agreed that each state's representation in the lower house should be based on the total of its white population and three fifths of its Negro population. On 16 July it accepted as well the principle that in the Senate each state should have an equal vote. With this obstacle removed, the convention proceeded (19–26 July) to draw up 23 "fundamental resolutions" forming a rough draft of a constitution. On 26 July these were submitted to a 5-man committee of detail which drafted a constitution of 23 articles and submitted it to the convention 6 Aug.

6 Aug.–10 Sept. GREAT DEBATE. During the debates on the draft constitution, the specific provisions of the final constitution were hammered out: the 2-year term for representatives (8 Aug.); the 6-year term for senators (9 Aug.); the 4-year term for the president (6 Sept.); the power of Congress to regulate foreign and interstate commerce (16 Aug.); the prohibition of bills of attainder and ex post facto laws (22 Aug.); the prohibition for 20 years of congressional action forbidding the foreign slave trade, a compromise, like the three-fifths clause, revealing that below the surface deep divisions between North and South already existed over slavery.

17 Sept. FINAL APPROVAL. By 8 Sept. final agreement neared. A 5-man committee on style and arrangement was appointed with **William Samuel Johnson** (1727–1819) as chairman, and **Hamilton, Madison, Rufus King** (1744–1814), and **Gouverneur Morris** as members. The convention held its last day of debate on details 10 Sept. Johnson then assigned

Morris to prepare the final draft. Working with great speed, Morris had the constitution before Congress on 12 Sept. It was examined clause by clause and a few changes made (13–15 Sept.). Finally, on 17 Sept., each of the 12 state delegations voted approval. Three of the 42 delegates present refused to sign the engrossed copy: Gerry (Massachusetts) and Randolph and Mason (Virginia). When the 39 delegates had signed and a letter of transmittal to Congress had been prepared, the convention formally adjourned. By the terms of Article VII the Constitution was to become operative when ratified by 9 states.

28 Sept. CALL FOR STATE RATIFYING CONVENTIONS. On 20 September Congress received the proposed Constitution. Attempts were made (26–27 Sept.) to have Congress censure the convention for exceeding its authority, but on 28 Sept. Congress resolved to transmit the Constitution to the legislature of each state for submission to special ratifying conventions.

27 Oct. FIRST "FEDERALIST" PAPER. Advocates (Federalists) and opponents (Antifederalists) of the Constitution quickly unleashed a flood of propaganda pro and con. Outstanding were the 77 masterly essays signed by "Publius" which appeared in New York newspapers (27 Oct.–2 Apr. 1788). With 8 additional essays these appeared in 2 vols., entitled *The Federalist* (Mar.–May 1788). The work of Hamilton (who wrote c.51), Madison (29), and John Jay (5), the essays stressed the inadequacy of the Confederation, the need for a strong government, and the conformity of the Constitution with the best principles of republican government.

7–18 Dec. EARLY RATIFICATION. To Delaware went the honor of being first to ratify the Constitution. That action was taken by unanimous vote 7 Dec. Pennsylvania was next to approve but

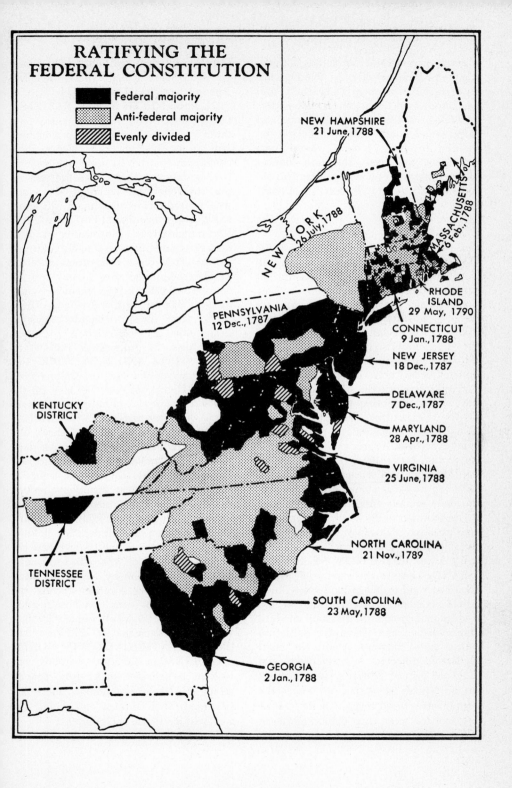

RATIFYING THE
FEDERAL CONSTITUTION

- ■ Federal majority
- ▨ Anti-federal majority
- ▨ Evenly divided

NEW HAMPSHIRE
21 June, 1788

NEW YORK
26 July, 1788

MASSACHUSETTS
6 Feb., 1788

RHODE
ISLAND
29 May, 1790

PENNSYLVANIA
12 Dec., 1787

CONNECTICUT
9 Jan., 1788

NEW JERSEY
18 Dec., 1787

DELAWARE
7 Dec., 1787

KENTUCKY
DISTRICT

MARYLAND
28 Apr., 1788

VIRGINIA
25 June, 1788

NORTH CAROLINA
21 Nov., 1789

TENNESSEE
DISTRICT

SOUTH CAROLINA
23 May, 1788

GEORGIA
2 Jan., 1788

opposition was considerable. In the convention, which met 21 Nov., the Federalist representatives from Philadelphia and the commercial towns defeated the Antifederalist moves for amendments and delays, and finally won on 12 Dec. by 46–23. In New Jersey, where Antifederalism was weak, the state convention required only a week's time to vote unanimously for ratification (18 Dec.).

1788

2 JAN.–6 FEB. FURTHER RATIFICATIONS. On 2 Jan., Georgia became the fourth state to ratify the Constitution and the third to do so unanimously. Connecticut was next to act favorably. Its convention met 4 Jan. and voted (9 Jan.) 128–40 for ratification. On that same day the Massachusetts convention met. Early estimates of Antifederalist strength gave opponents 192 votes against 144 for the Federalists, who reduced this opposition 30 Jan. by proposing that amendments to the Constitution be recommended along with ratification, a move which won over Sam Adams, and swung the convention for ratification. The Constitution was approved unconditionally (187–168) on 6 Feb. along with 9 recommended amendments, most significant, the reservation to the states of all powers not "expressly delegated" by the Constitution to the central government.

24 MAR. REJECTION BY RHODE ISLAND. Despite the failure of Rhode Island to send a delegation to the Philadelphia convention, the commercial and professional groups of the state made a determined effort to have the legislature call a state convention, but the rural legislators rejected a convention and proposed instead (Feb.) a popular referendum (held 24 Mar.), in which the Federalists refused to participate. Out of 2,945 of the more than 6,000 eligible to vote, only 237 voted in favor of the Constitution. Not until Jan. 1790 was a state convention called. On 29 May 1790 Rhode Island finally ratified (34–32).

21 JUNE. NINTH STATE RATIFIES. On 28 Apr. the Maryland convention ratified (63–11); South Carolina was next to act. Though the resolution for a convention passed by only one vote in the legislature (12 May), in the convention Antifederalist sentiment was much weaker, and ratification passed (23 May) by a large majority (149–73). With 8 states having ratified, one more was necessary for adoption of the Constitution. A New Hampshire convention, meeting 13 Feb., adjourned after a week until 18 June. The Federalists overcame an early majority against them and won by 57–47 on 21 June. Twelve amendments were proposed.

25 JUNE, 26 JULY. RATIFICATION IN VIRGINIA AND NEW YORK. Virginia's convention met on 2 June with Patrick Henry leading the foes of the Constitution and Madison in the vanguard of its supporters. The latter's logical arguments counteracted Henry's eloquence; the vote on 25 June showed 89 for, 79 against. Virginia attached to ratification proposals for a bill of rights of 20 articles as well as 20 other changes. In New York the convention met at Poughkeepsie on 17 June with Gov. George Clinton's Antifederalists holding a clear majority. Hamilton worked for delay, counting on the effect of news of affirmative action by New Hampshire and Virginia. His strategy turned the tide. A plan for conditional ratification was rejected (25 July) and on 26 July ratification was carried, 30–27.

2 AUG. RATIFICATION IN NORTH CAROLINA. In the North Carolina convention, which met on 21 July, despite strong Federalist sentiment, the view prevailed that ratification should be withheld until the incorporation of certain amendments, particularly a bill of rights. The submission of 12 proposed amendments to the states by the new Congress on 25 Sept. 1789 led to a second convention (16–23 Nov. 1789) at which ratification was carried (194–77) 21 Nov.

13 SEPT. CONGRESS PREPARES FOR THE NEW GOVERNMENT. On 2 July the president of Congress, Cyrus Griffin (Virginia, 1748–1810), announced that the Constitution had been ratified by the requisite 9 states. A committee, appointed to prepare the details for the change in government, reported (8 July), but not until 13 Sept. did Congress adopt an ordinance which set the site of the new government as New York and fixed the dates in 1789 for the appointment of presidential electors (7 Jan.), for the balloting by the electors (4 Feb.), and for the meeting of the first Congress under the Constitution (4 Mar.). On 2 Oct. the last Congress under the Articles was unceremoniously moved from its rooms in New York's City Hall in order that the edifice might be renovated as the capitol for the incoming government. On 10 Oct. Congress transacted its last official business. The only significant political action thereafter was the cession by Maryland (23 Dec.) of 10 square miles to Congress for a federal town, future site of the District of Columbia.

THE EARLY NATIONAL AND ANTEBELLUM PERIODS, 1789-1860

★ ★
★

In a scant dozen years of Federalist rule the Constitution was demonstrated to be a workable instrument of government. The chief executive determined the powers and traditions of the presidency, the cabinet system evolved, a federal judiciary was established, the taxing power was wielded audaciously and effectively, a national debt was created to strengthen the national authority and stimulate the economy. American credit was fixed at home and abroad on a firm foundation, and American territory cleared of British and Spanish interlopers. The coming of the French Revolution precipitated the rise of a two-party system, unanticipated by the founding fathers. Holding national survival as the central objective of foreign policy, the first two presidents prudently steered a neutral course.

In his old age Jefferson retrospectively hailed his election to the presidency in 1800 as a "revolution," but his eight years as president fell far short of accomplishing a root-and-branch change in the governmental system inherited from the Federalists. Much the same observation might be made of the next twenty years of Republican rule. Despite their rhetoric, the Republicans neither opposed private property nor sought to turn the country into a "mobocracy." Jefferson's aristocratic inclinations notwithstanding, he had the vision to identify himself with the cause of the common man, and if the substance of the Republican administration was not too different from its predecessors, the style sharply diverged. The sense of American nationality which emerged in this era was buttressed by great nationalist decisions of the Supreme Court, by huge territorial acquisitions—Louisiana Territory and Florida—by an inconclusive second war with Britain, and by the inauguration of extensive internal improvements.

With the accession of Andrew Jackson to the presidency the pace of change swiftened. It was a time of political ferment, when the elective franchise was broadened, popular participation in politics intensified, the spirit of reform was in the air, the railroads introduced a transportation revolution, and such issues as labor, banking, the tariff, and slavery impinged on national and local politics. It was a time of manifest destiny, in which the acquisition of Texas, the war with Mexico, and the settlement of the conflict over Oregon gave the United States in substance its present continental domain.

In the decades before the Civil War the movement to abolish or restrict slavery became the central national issue. By 1840 abolitionism was a political movement, touching off a vigorous response from the slaveholding states both ideologically and politically. While great unifying forces were at work, sectional differences, both economically and culturally, were if anything intensified, and these sectional tensions were strained to the breaking point by the issue of the extension of slavery to the territories. Neither the compromises of 1820 or 1850 nor the Kansas-Nebraska Act effected a durable resolution between the sections. "Bleeding Kansas," the Dred Scott decision, John Brown's raid, and the election of 1860 created an unbridgeable chasm between North and South, with the Southern states moving in a seemingly irreversible course toward secession.

1789

7 Jan. FIRST PRESIDENTIAL ELECTION. Presidential electors, chosen in all of the ratifying states with the exception of New York, were named either by the state legislatures or directly by the people. On 4 Feb., as elections of senators and representatives progressed in the various states, the presidential electors cast their ballots.

4 Mar. FIRST CONGRESS under the Constitution met in New York without a quorum (8 senators and 13 representatives present, the remainder still en route); 54 of the members of the first Congress had been members of the Federal Convention or state ratifying conventions; all but 7 had advocated ratification.

1 Apr. HOUSE OF REPRESENTATIVES organized, with 30 of its 59 members present. Frederick A. Muhlenberg (Pa.) was elected speaker, and on 8 Apr. the House began its deliberations.

6 Apr. THE SENATE, with 9 of its 22 members present, elected as temporary presiding officer John Langdon (N.H.), who counted the ballots cast by the presidential electors. **George Washington,** with 69 votes, was unanimously elected president; **John Adams,** receiving 34 votes, was chosen vice-president.

30 Apr. FIRST INAUGURAL. On 16 Apr. Washington set out from Mount Vernon for New York City, arriving there on 23 Apr. Adams, meanwhile, had taken his seat as vice-president on 21 Apr. In a ceremony held on the balcony of Federal Hall, at the corner of Wall and Broad streets, Washington was inaugurated as the first president of the U.S. The oath of office was administered by Robert R. Livingston, chancellor of the state of New York. The first inaugural address was delivered in the Senate chamber housed in Federal Hall.

9 Sept.–22 Dec. BILL OF RIGHTS. The Constitution, already ratified by 11 states, was ratified by North Carolina (21 Nov.) and Rhode Island (29 May 1790), whose delay pointed to the active strength of the Antifederalists. Five state ratifying conventions had stressed the need for immediate amendments to the Constitution; Federalist leaders had pledged themselves to changes in the Constitution; and in his inaugural address Washington had alluded to such alteration. Moreover, the Federalists wanted to forestall action on demands for a second constitutional convention.

Chiefly at the instigation of James Madison, the House of Representatives decided (9 Sept.) to recommend for adoption by the various states 12 amendments originally suggested by the state ratifying conventions (submitted to states 25 Sept.). Of these amendments, 10 were ratified by the states, and comprised a specific Bill of Rights. New Jersey was the first state to ratify these amendments (20 Nov.); Maryland followed on 19 Dec. and North Carolina on 22 Dec. On 15 Dec. 1791 the Bill of Rights became part of the Constitution.

EXECUTIVE DEPARTMENTS. The first executive department created under the new government was that of Foreign Affairs. Established on 27 July, it was officially redesignated (15 Sept.) as the Department of State. **Thomas Jefferson** was appointed (26 Sept.) to head the department, but did not take office until 22 March 1790. During the interim, John Jay handled the affairs of the State Department.

The War Department was set up on 7 Aug.; **Henry Knox** was named Secretary of War (12 Sept.). The Treasury Department was established on 2 Sept.; **Alexander Hamilton** was appointed Secretary of the Treasury (11 Sept.). The office of Postmaster General was created by Congress (22 Sept.); **Samuel Osgood** appointed to that office 26 Sept. The Post Office Department was established by Congress 8 May 1795.

24 Sept. FEDERAL JUDICIARY ACT made provision for the organization of the Supreme Court to consist of a chief justice and 5 associates, as well as 13 district and 3 circuit courts; and established the office of attorney general. On 26 Sept. **John Jay** became chief justice of the U.S. and Edmund Randolph became attorney general.

1790

HAMILTON'S FISCAL PROGRAM. The chief issue of Washington's first term was the fiscal program devised by Alexander Hamilton and submitted to the House of Representatives in a series of reports on the national and state debt, an excise tax, and a national bank. Controversy over these proposals ultimately led to the party cleavage between Federalists and Republicans.

14 Jan. FIRST REPORT ON THE PUBLIC CREDIT. Hamilton dealt with the debt inherited from the Confederation. The foreign debt, held chiefly by the French and Dutch, was set at $11,710,-379; the domestic debt, including arrears of interest and unliquidated claims and currency, was fixed at $40,414,086; state debts were estimated at $25 million. Hamilton recommended (1) funding of the foreign and domestic debt at par, enabling creditors to exchange depreciated securities for new interest-bearing bonds at face value; and (2) assumption by the federal government, to the extent of $21,500,000, of debts incurred by the states during the Revolution.

These measures had a double purpose: (1) to establish and maintain the public credit and thereby revive confidence in the government at home and abroad; (2) to strengthen and stabilize the central government by fostering a consciousness of national solidarity of interest among those business and commercial groups holding the greater part of the domestic debt.

While the proposal concerning the foreign debt was virtually unopposed, the plan to fund the domestic debt was bitterly attacked by debtor and agrarian groups compelled by necessity to sell their securities at a steep discount. James Madison's proposal to discriminate between original holders and subsequent purchasers was rejected (22 Feb.) by the House by almost 3 to 1.

Arousing even heavier opposition was the assumption scheme, which resulted in an approximately sectional alignment. The New England states, with the largest unpaid debts, generally favored assumption. But the Southern states, most of whom had made arrangements for discharging their indebtedness, were hostile to an immense increase in the national debt for which their inhabitants would be taxed. In addition, they feared that assumption would tend to aggrandize federal power at the expense of the states.

Virginia led the opposition to the plan, and her leading congressional spokesman, Madison, broke with the administration on this score. The assumption proposal was defeated in the House (12 Apr.) by a vote of 31 to 29.

SECTIONAL COMPROMISE. Hamilton's resourceful negotiations kept the assumption measure alive, and differences were finally settled by a compromise on the location of the permanent seat of the national government hammered out between congressmen from Pennsylvania and Virginia even before Hamilton, consulting with Madison at a dinner party (c.20 June) arranged by Jefferson, had agreed to exert his influence to secure enough Northern votes to assure location of the national capital along the Potomac (instead of Philadelphia) in return for Madison's pledge to obtain a sufficient number of Southern votes to effect passage of assumption.

The House, 32–29 (10 July), fixed the site of the projected national capital in a district 10 miles square along the Potomac, the precise area to be selected by the president. Philadelphia, where Congress assembled on 6 Dec., was named temporary capital until 1800. By 34–28 (26 July) the House adopted the assumption plan, and the funding provision for the debt became law on 4 Aug.

SOUTHERN FEARS. Despite the compromise, Southern apprehensions still remained, and found their voice in the Virginia resolutions (16 Dec.) framed by Patrick Henry. The Virginians protested that the assumption scheme established and perpetuated a moneyed interest, subordinated agricultural to commercial interests, and was inimical to republican institutions and the federal form of government, and that they could "find no clause in the constitution authorizing Congress to assume the debts of states!" Wrote Hamilton, privately: "This is the first symptom of a spirit which must either be killed, or will kill the Constitution."

1791

25 FEB. BANK OF THE U.S. On 13 Dec. 1790 Hamilton submitted to the House his report on a national bank. Before signing (25 Feb.) the bill chartering the Bank of the U.S., President Washington requested members of his cabinet to submit written opinions on the constitutionality of the measure.

Jefferson's opinion (15 Feb.) maintaining that the bill was unconstitutional advanced the doctrine commonly known as "strict constructionist." Jefferson took as his main ground the 10th Amendment (not yet adopted). The incorporation of a bank, he argued, was not among the powers specifically delegated to Congress.

Hamilton's opinion (23 Feb.) elaborated the doctrine of "implied powers" (the so-called "loose constructionist" view of the Constitution). He contended that the proposed bank was related to congressional power to collect taxes and regulate trade: a delegated power implied the employment of such means as were proper for its execution. He declared: "If the *end* be clearly comprehended within any of the specified powers, and if the measure have an obvious relation to that *end,* and is not forbidden by any particular provision of the Constitution, it may safely be deemed to come within the compass of the national authority."

Although Washington was not fully convinced of the weight of argument on either side, he favored Hamilton's view on the ground that in such instances presidential support should go to the cabinet officer whose department was immediately and directly involved.

3 Mar. WHISKY TAX. Hamilton's second report on the public credit (13 Dec. 1790) recommended an excise tax on the manufacture of distilled liquors as a means of supplementing revenue yielded by the traiff. This levy, imposing a heavy burden on backwoods farmers for whom distilling was the chief mode of disposing of surplus grain (owing to poor roads and high shipment costs), stirred keen discontent among those affected by it.

EMERGING POLITICAL ALIGNMENTS. Dissatisfied with the administration's fiscal policies, Jefferson and Madison made a tour (May–June) of New York state, with excursions into New England, where they appear to have sounded out Antifederalist sentiment (particularly among the Clinton-Livingston-Burr faction in New York) for the purpose of forming a coalition on national lines. The political breach was widened with the establishment (31 Oct.) of the *National Gazette,* an antiadministration organ under the editorship of Philip Freneau, which soon crossed swords with the Federalist *Gazette of the United States* edited by John Fenno (begun 15 Apr. 1789).

The emerging **Jefferson-Hamilton feud** later became a personal quarrel, but its essential significance lay in its origin: a conflict of principle over the nature and ends of society and government. Jeffersonian principles embraced (1) a democratic agrarian order based on the individual freeholder; (2) a broad diffusion of wealth; (3) relative freedom from industrialism, urbanism, and organized finance; (4) sympathy for debtor interests; (5) distrust of centralized government; (6) belief in the perfectibility of man; and (7) confidence in the view that the people, acting through representative institutions, could be left to govern themselves. Hamiltonian principles included (1) a balanced and diversified economic order; (2) active governmental encouragement of finance, industry, commerce, and shipping; (3) sympathy for creditor interests; (4) advocacy of a strong national government under executive leadership; (5) distrust of the people's capacity to govern; and (6) a belief that the best government was that of an elite.

These views generally reflected the doctrines associated with the two national parties (in each case a larger grouping of local coalitions) formed during this period: the Republicans, also known as the Democratic-Republicans, under the leadership of Jefferson; and the Federalists, under the leadership of Hamilton. Competent latter-day authorities differ over the approximate date of origin of these parties. Among the dates indicated for their definite emergence are 1787–88 (C. A. Beard), 1791–92 (J. S. Bassett; D. Malone), 1792–93 (N. Cunningham), and 1798 (O. G. Libby).

26 Nov. ORIGINS OF THE CABINET. As early as Oct. 1789 Washington consulted heads of departments on the advisability of his making a tour of the U.S. He continued to consult them individually on matters of policy. On 26 Nov. and 28 Dec. 1791 he met with department heads to consider foreign and military matters. At least 3 such meetings occurred in 1792. By the time Adams became president the practice of cabinet meetings was well established.

5 Dec. REPORT ON MANUFACTURES submitted by Hamilton proposed a system of tariffs for industry, bounties for agriculture, and a network of internal improvements under federal sponsorship. Hamilton's argument for encouraging manufactures made no marked impression at this time.

1792

21 Feb. PRESIDENTIAL SUCCESSION ACT (passed the House, 31–24, after passing the Senate 27–24) provided that in case of the removal, death, resignation, or disability of both president and vice-president, the president pro tempore of the Senate would succeed; if there was no Senate president, then the speaker of the House. The Federalists defeated Jefferson's effort to have the Secretary of State made next in line of succession, a proposal finally put into effect by the Act of 1886.

8 May. MILITIA ACT. To cope with the growing Indian menace in the Northwest Territory (Gen. Arthur St. Clair had been defeated by Ohio Indians 4 Nov. 1791; Gen. Anthony Wayne was commissioned Apr. commander in chief of army to move against Ohio Indians), the Militia Act authorized state enrollment and organization of all able-bodied free white citizens between the ages of 18 and 45.

21 Aug.–15 Sept. RESISTANCE TO THE EXCISE TAX was manifested in the South (especially in the central counties of North Carolina) and in the 4 Pennsylvania counties west of the Alleghenies. At a Pittsburgh convention (21 Aug.) a series of resolutions drawn up by a committee of which **Albert Gallatin** (p. 1037) was a member de-

nounced the excise tax and declared that legal measures would be used to obstruct collections of the tax. Washington issued a proclamation (29 Sept.) warning against unlawful combinations and stating that the excise provision would be enforced.

JEFFERSON-HAMILTON FEUD. Violent attacks upon Hamilton's fiscal policies appearing in the *National Gazette* provoked Hamilton to rejoinder with a series of anonymous articles (July–Dec.) in the *Gazette of the United States.* Hamilton asserted that Jefferson had been opposed to the Constitution and its adoption, that he did not support the program of the administration, and was responsible for political intrigue disparaging the government.

Letters written by Jefferson (13 May) and Hamilton (30 July) to Washington, prevailing upon him to serve as president for a 2d term, revealed the mutual animosity and distrust of the 2 cabinet officers. Washington intervened, and in letters to Jefferson (23 Aug.) and Hamilton (26 Aug.) sought to heal their differences. Their replies (9 Sept.) indicated that the quarrel was still in progress. Jefferson intimated his intention to retire after the close of Washington's 1st term. During a meeting with Jefferson at Mount Vernon (2 Oct.), Washington's attempt to mediate failed again.

5 Dec. PRESIDENTIAL ELECTION. Presidential electors cast their ballots. **Washington,** receiving 132 votes (with 3 abstentions), was reelected president; **John Adams,** with 77 votes, reelected vice-president. The Antifederalist opposition gave 50 votes to George Clinton (N.Y.) for vice-president.

1793

ATTACK ON HAMILTON. Rep. William Branch Giles (Va.) proposed a series of resolutions (23 Jan.) inquiring into the condition of the Treasury. The move climaxed the loose charges of corruption and mismanagement that had been made against Hamilton. In reports to the House (4, 13 Feb.) Hamilton made a detailed and factual defense of his official conduct. Giles and others submitted 9 resolutions (28 Feb.) censuring Hamilton's course, but none passed the House.

John Taylor of Caroline (Va., 1753–1824) published *An Examination of the Late Proceedings in Congress Respecting the Official Conduct of the Secretary of the Treasury.* An attack on the administration's fiscal measures, this pamphlet claimed that moneyed interests dominated Congress, and asked for a return to "genuine republicanism." Taylor wrote another pamphlet in a similar vein, *An Enquiry into the Principles and Tendency of Certain Public Measures* (1794).

IMPACT OF THE FRENCH REVOLUTION widened the cleavage between the Federalists and their antagonists, making party lines more definite. At its outset, the French Revolution had enlisted the sympathy of most Americans; but with the proclamation of the French Republic (21 Sept. 1792) and the execution of Louis XVI (21 Jan.), American opinion began to divide sharply. The French issue was injected into domestic affairs after France declared war (1 Feb.) on Great Britain, Spain, and Holland.

22 Apr. WASHINGTON'S NEUTRALITY PROCLAMATION. While both Hamilton and Jefferson desired to keep America neutral, Hamilton, unlike Jefferson, thought the occasion a good opportunity to repeal the treaties concluded with France in 1778. Hamilton's sympathies lay with Great Britain, those of Jefferson with France. Washington, however, steered an independent course. On 22 April he issued the Neutrality Proclamation (in which the word "neutrality" was not used) declaring that the U.S. was at peace with Great Britain and France and urging citizens to abstain from acts of hostility against any of the belligerent powers. Washington preferred Attorney General Randolph's draft to that of Chief Justice Jay, which used as a test for the recognition of new, revolutionary governments the extent to which they rested upon a popular mandate. Madison questioned the President's right to issue such a proclamation without Congressional concurrence.

CITIZEN GENÊT AFFAIR. On 8 Apr. **Citizen Genêt** (Edmond Charles Genêt), minister of the French Republic to the U.S., landed at Charleston, S.C., under instructions from the Girondist regime to win U.S. amity and negotiate a new treaty of commerce. Even before presenting his credentials, he commissioned 4 privateers and dispatched them to prey upon British vessels along the U.S. coast. He also took steps to organize on American soil expeditions against Spanish and British territories.

En route (18 Apr.–16 May) from Charleston to Philadelphia, Genêt received a warm ovation. President Washington, however, received him (18 May) with cool formality; and on 5 June Jefferson presented Genêt with a communication from the president stating that Genêt's grants of military commissions on American soil constituted an infringement of U.S. national sovereignty. Genêt was also notified that the privateers commissioned by him would have to leave American waters and could not send their prizes to U.S. ports.

Genêt promised to comply, but soon afterward authorized the arming of *The Little Sarah,* a prize that had been brought in by a French vessel and was being refitted as *La Petite Démocrate.* When Genêt was warned against dispatching the vessel, he threatened to appeal over the president to the people. In violation of a promise made to Jefferson, Genêt ordered the French privateer out to sea.

The newly established Democratic societies (from which the Democratic-Republican party took its name) and Antifederalist newspapers attacked Washington's neutrality policy. Hamilton, writing a series of articles under the pseudonym "Pacificus," defended the Neutrality Proclamation and the president's right to decide the matter. He was answered by Madison, who wrote under the signature of "Helvidius." But both Jefferson and Madison agreed that Genêt's conduct and poor judgment had harmed the Antifederalist cause.

The cabinet decided (2 Aug.) to demand Genêt's recall. Washington sent to Congress his full correspondence with the French minister, pointing out that Genêt's conduct had tended to involve the U.S. "in war abroad, and discord and anarchy at home." By this time the Jacobins had come to power in France. Genêt's successor, Joseph Fauchet, who arrived in 1794, carried orders for Genêt's arrest. Washington refused to extradite Genêt, who became an American citizen and married a daughter of Gov. George Clinton.

31 Dec. JEFFERSON'S RESIGNATION. President Washington, who had originally favored maintaining friendship with France, now veered toward the Federalists and henceforth tended to lean more heavily upon Hamilton for advice on foreign affairs. Jefferson submitted his resignation (31 July) as Secretary of State, but his withdrawal did not become effective until 31 Dec. He was succeeded (2 Jan. 1794) by Edmund Randolph.

POLITICAL OPINION split on the French issue. Most Federalists supported the British cause, regarding it as a bulwark against French anarchy and atheism. Most Republicans were in sympathy with the French, not so much from principle as from long-standing antagonism to the British.

1794

5 Mar. 11TH AMENDMENT, proposed by Congress to the states following protests from the legislatures of Georgia and other states against the Supreme Court decision in *Chisholm* v. *Georgia* (1793, p. 664), provided in effect that a state was not suable by a citizen of another state. It was declared ratified on 8 Jan. 1798.

5 June. NEUTRALITY ACT forbade U.S. citizens to enlist in the service of a foreign power and prohibited the fitting out of foreign armed vessels in U.S. ports. This reinforcement of the Neutrality Proclamation, however, did not entirely ease tension between the U.S. and Great Britain.

July–Nov. WHISKY INSURRECTION, the result of discontent over enforcement of the excise tax, broke out among the backwoods farmers of the Monongahela Valley in western Pennsylvania. President Washington issued a proclamation (7 Aug.) ordering the insurgents to return to their homes, and called for 12,900 militia from Virginia, Maryland, New Jersey, and Pennsylvania. Negotiations with the leaders of the insurrection proving fruitless, Washington issued a second proclamation (24 Sept.) ordering the suppression of the rebellion. Government forces under the command of Henry Lee, who was accompanied by Hamilton and President Washington (the latter going as far as Bedford, Pa., before returning to Philadelphia, marking the only occasion when a president took the field with his troops), quelled the demonstrations, as none of the "Whisky Boys" came forth to do battle. Of the insurgents tried for treason (May 1795), 2 were convicted, and were pardoned by Washington.

19 Nov. JAY'S TREATY. An old source of American grievance against England was the British refusal, despite the provisions of the peace treaty of 1783, to evacuate the Northwest military posts. The British justified their maintenance of garrisons on the ground that legal obstacles had been raised against the recovery of pre-Revolutionary debts owed to British merchants and Loyalist property confiscated by the states. Retention of the posts retarded Western settlement and kept the lucrative fur trade in the hands of the British. To assure their control of the posts and the fur trade, the British had encouraged the establishment of an Indian barrier state. American settlers in the Ohio country believed that Indian massacres of pioneers were instigated by the British.

Anglo-U.S. friction was intensified when the British issued orders in council (8 June, 6 Nov., 1793) interfering with neutral shipping. The enforcement of these orders resulted in the seizure of American vessels and the impressment and imprisonment of American crews. The two nations verged on war.

One of the leading motives behind the U.S. desire for a settlement was the maintenance of the fiscal structure. British exports to the U.S. were the chief source of tariff revenue, the main prop of Hamilton's fiscal system. For the negotiation of outstanding differences, President Washington named **John Jay,** chief justice of the U.S., as special envoy to Great Britain. Jay, whose nomination was confirmed in the Senate on 19 Apr., arrived in England in June. He was under instructions to make no commitment in violation of the treaties with France.

Jay's Treaty was signed on 19 Nov. The outstanding concession gained by the U.S. was the British withdrawal from the Northwest posts on or before 1 June 1796. The treaty also provided for (1) admission of U.S. vessels to British East Indian ports on a nondiscriminatory basis; (2) opening of the West Indian trade to U.S. vessels not exceeding 70 tons burden, on condition that Americans renounce their carrying trade in such staples as cotton, sugar, and molasses; (3) referral to joint commissions of the payment of the pre-Revolutionary debts (British claims settled at $2,664,000, 8 Jan. 1802), the northeast boundary question, and compensation for illegal maritime seizures; and (4) placing of British trade with the U.S. on a most-favored-nation basis. No provisions were made for impressment, the Indian question, the slaves removed by the British, or Loyalist claims.

When the terms of the treaty were made known (March 1795), the Republicans took the lead in whipping up popular opposition. Southern planters were chagrined by the treaty's provision for settlement of the debt (much of which was owed by Virginia) and its silence concerning the stolen slaves. Northern shipping and commercial interests as well as Southern Federalists attacked the treaty; even Washington and some Federalist legislators thought the treaty unsatisfactory. Hamilton entered the controversy with the publication (22 July 1795 *et seq.*) of his "Camillus" papers in support of the treaty.

The Senate ratified the treaty (24 June 1795) only after long debate and after suspension of that portion of Article XII pertaining to the West Indian trade. The Republicans in the House attempted to block the treaty by denying the appropriation for enforcing its provisions. The House request (24 Mar. 1796) for papers relating to Jay's Treaty was refused by Washington because the concurrence of the two Houses was not required to give validity to a treaty and "because of the necessity of maintaining the boundaries fixed by the Constitution." By asserting his executive prerogative, Washington thereby set an important precedent. The appropriation was approved on 30 Apr. 1796 by one vote, following a supporting speech (28 Apr.) by **Fisher Ames** (1758–1808).

1795

CABINET REORGANIZATION. Timothy Pickering (Mass.) was named (2 Jan.) Secretary of War. Hamilton resigned (31 Jan.) as Secretary of the Treasury and was succeeded by Oliver Wolcott, Jr., but continued as unofficial adviser on major policy decisions. Secretary of State Edmund Randolph resigned (19 Aug.) on suspicion of corruption, a charge for which he was never tried. Washington believed that Randolph had intrigued with the French minister, Joseph Fauchet, to block the ratification of Jay's Treaty. Some held that Randolph had been in the pay of the French (vindication of Randolph's conduct in Irving Brant's *Madison*, v. 3, 1950). Washington, although fearful that disclosure of letters and conversations with Randolph would damage relations with Britain and France, permitted Randolph to publish in his own defense "any and every private and confidential letter I ever wrote you; nay more: every word I have ever uttered in your presence." Randolph was succeeded by Pickering, and James McHenry became (27 Jan. 1796) Secretary of War. The cabinet as reorganized by Washington included only Federalists. After Adams took office as president, he retained Washington's cabinet. Pickering, McHenry, and Wolcott continued to be influenced by Hamilton.

29 Jan. NATURALIZATION ACT required 5 years' residence.

27 Oct. TREATY OF SAN LORENZO (PINCKNEY'S TREATY), signed at Madrid, 27 Oct. The failure of the Jay-Gardoqui negotiations (1785–86) to adjust differences between the U.S. and Spain left open the questions of the southern and western boundaries of the U.S. and the free navigation by Americans of the Mississippi from its source to its mouth. Negotiations for the U.S. were undertaken by **Thomas Pinckney** (1750–1828), U.S. minister to Great Britain. Spain recognized the boundary claims of the U.S. under the Treaty of 1783 (the Mississippi at the west, the 31st parallel at the south) and gave to Americans free navigation of the Mississippi and the right of deposit for their goods at New Orleans for 3 years and thereafter, if need be, at another point to be designated.

1796

8 Mar. *Hylton* v. *U.S.* (3 Dallas 171), a case involving the carriage tax imposed in 1794, in which the Supreme Court for the first time upheld the constitutionality of a congressional act.

17 Sept. WASHINGTON'S FAREWELL ADDRESS. Dated 17 Sept., it was first published (19 Sept.) in the Philadelphia *Daily American Advertiser*. Written with the aid of Madison (1792) and Hamilton (1796), it was never orally delivered before the public. The address (1) presented Washington's reasons for declining to stand for a 3d term; (2) deplored the dangers of a party system, particularly a division along geographical lines; (3) counseled that the public credit be cherished; (4) advised the nation to steer clear of *permanent* alliances with foreign nations and trust to "temporary alliances for extraordinary emergencies." Nowhere did it contain the phrase "entangling alliances" (used by Jefferson in his 1st inaugural).

7 DEC. PRESIDENTIAL ELECTION indicated the rising strength of the Democratic-Republican party, much of it due to dissatisfaction with Jay's Treaty. **John Adams,** Federalist candidate, received 71 votes and was elected president; **Thomas Jefferson,** Democratic-Republican, with 68 votes, vice-president. Among the other candidates were Thomas Pinckney (Federalist, 59 votes) and Aaron Burr (Democratic-Republican, 30 votes).

1797–1800

31 MAY. RELATIONS WITH FRANCE. The French Directory, angered by Jay's Treaty, interfered with American shipping and refused to receive **Charles Cotesworth Pinckney** (1746–1825) as U.S. minister to France when he arrived in Dec. 1796. President Adams appointed (31 May) a commission to France consisting of Pinckney and **John Marshall** (both Federalists) and **Elbridge Gerry** (Republican), who were instructed to secure a treaty of commerce and amity with France.

18 OCT. XYZ AFFAIR. The commissioners arrived at Paris (4 Oct.) and were unofficially received (8 Oct.) by the French foreign minister, Talleyrand, who found a pretext for delaying the opening of official discussions. The commissioners were visited (18 Oct.) by three agents of Talleyrand (Hottinguer, Hauteval, and Bellamy; later designated in the mission's dispatches as X, Y, and Z) who suggested a U.S. loan to France and a bribe of $240,000. The Americans refused to make concessions; Marshall replied firmly (17 Jan. 1798); and on 19 Mar. President Adams reported to Congress the failure of negotiations. Only Gerry remained at Paris, Talleyrand having intimated that if he de-

parted, a French declaration of war against the U.S. would ensue. On 3 Apr. 1798 Adams submitted to Congress the XYZ correspondence, which aroused American public opinion regardless of party.

UNDECLARED NAVAL WAR WITH FRANCE, 1798–1800. The prowar faction of the Federalists, headed in the cabinet by Pickering, wanted an immediate declaration of war against France. Adams, however, favored a peaceful course while strengthening national defenses: if war were to come, France would have to take the initiative. **Defense measures:** 20 Acts of Congress (passed 27 Mar.–16 July 1798) provided for consolidating the national defense. Washington was named (2 July 1798) commanding general; Hamilton, second in command, inspector general. On 3 May the Navy Department was established, and on 21 May Benjamin Stoddert named Secretary of the Navy. Congress repealed (7 July 1798) the treaties with France, and thus terminated the alliance. An undeclared naval war began with the capture of the schooner *Retaliation* by the French off Guadeloupe (20 Nov. 1798) and the engagement (9 Feb. 1799) between the *Constellation* (Capt. Thomas Truxtun, commander) and *L'Insurgente,* in which the latter was captured. On 1 Feb. 1800 the *Constellation* fought a drawn battle with *La Vengeance,* and on 12 Oct. Capt. George Little in the *Boston* captured the French ship *Le Berceau.*

CONVENTION OF 1800. A complete surprise to Hamilton's prowar faction was Adams' nomination (18 Feb. 1799) of **William Vans Murray** as minister to France, followed by publication of Talleyrand's assurance that a U.S. minister would be received with respect. Federalist pressure upon Adams to change his course failed, and the president appointed a commission to France consisting of Vans Murray, Chief Justice Oliver Ellsworth, and William R. Davie, governor of North Carolina (replacing Patrick Henry, who declined because of age). The negotiations bore fruit in the **Treaty of Morfontaine** (30 Sept. 1800, commonly known as the **Convention of 1800**), which superseded the treaties of 1778 and thus formally released the U.S. from its defensive alliance with France. The Senate ratified the convention on condition that the treaties of 1778 be not merely suspended but abrogated. The convention became effective on 21 Dec. 1801.

Adams' handling of the French crisis created a schism in the Federalist party. Adams finally concluded that he was the victim of a cabinet conspiracy, and that Pickering and McHenry, in conjunction with Hamilton, were working for his defeat in the presidential election of 1800. On 6 May 1800 he requested the resignation of McHenry (effective 31 May); on 10 May he asked for the resignation of Pickering (dismissed from office, 12 May). Pickering was succeeded in the State Department by John Marshall of Virginia (13 May).

1798

ALIEN AND SEDITION ACTS. Several of the leading Republican publicists were European refugees. The threat of war with France sharpened hostility to aliens and gave the Federalists an opportunity to impose severe restrictions:

18 June. Naturalization Act changed from 5 to 14 years the period of residence required for admission to full citizenship. It was repealed in 1802, when the naturalization law of 1795 was reenacted.

25 June. Alien Act authorized the president to order out of the U.S. all aliens regarded as dangerous to the public peace and safety, or suspected of "treasonable or secret" inclinations. It expired in 1800.

6 July. Alien Enemies Act authorized the president, in time of declared war, to arrest, imprison, or banish aliens subject to an enemy power.

14 July. Sedition Act made it a high misdemeanor, punishable by fine and imprisonment, for citizens or aliens to enter into unlawful combinations opposing execution of the national laws; to prevent a federal officer from performing his duties; and to aid or attempt "any insurrection, riot, unlawful assembly, or combination." A fine of not more than $2,000 and imprisonment not exceeding 2 years were provided for persons convicted of publishing "any false, scandalous and malicious writing" bringing into disrepute the U.S. government, Congress, or the president; in force until 3 March 1801.

The Sedition Act was aimed at repressing political opposition, and its enforcement, carried out in a partisan manner, resulted in the prosecution of 25 persons and the conviction of 10, all of them Republican editors and printers. (Most notable: **James Thomas Callender,** tried before Judge Samuel Chase, fined $200 and sentenced to 9 months' imprisonment; **Matthew Lyon,** imprisoned and fined $1,000; and Dr. **Thomas Cooper,** imprisoned for 6 months. When Jefferson became president he pardoned all those convicted under the act. Congress restored the fines with interest.) The Republicans attacked the Alien and Sedition Acts as unnecessary, despotic, and unconstitutional.

KENTUCKY AND VIRGINIA RESOLUTIONS. The Kentucky resolutions (in 2 sets, passed by the state legislature on 16 Nov. 1798 and 22 Nov. 1799) were drafted by Jefferson. The Virginia resolutions (passed by the state legislature 24 Dec. 1798) were framed by Madison. Both invoked the compact theory of the Constitution and maintained that the Alien and Sedition Acts were unconstitutional. The Kentucky resolutions, the more forthright of the 2, held that where the national government exercised powers not specifically delegated to it, each state "has an equal right to judge for itself, as well of infractions as of the mode and measure of redress." The Virginia resolutions pointed out that in such cases the states "have the right and are in duty bound to interpose for arresting the progress of the evil." The second set of Kentucky resolutions was enacted after several Northern states repudiated the doctrines set forth by Kentucky and Virginia and indicated that the federal judiciary was the exclusive arbiter of constitutionality. It was on this occasion that the Kentucky legislature added, as it restated the view that the states had the right to judge infractions of the Constitution: "That a nullification of those sovereignties, of all unauthorized acts done under color of that instrument, is the rightful remedy." Both states, however, declared their firm attachment to the Union and took no steps to nullify or obstruct the Alien and Sedition Acts.

14 Dec. 1799. DEATH OF WASHINGTON at Mt. Vernon; eulogized in Congress (26 Dec.) by Henry Lee as "first in war, first in peace, first in the hearts of his countrymen."

1799

30 Jan. LOGAN ACT made it a high misdemeanor subject to fine and imprisonment for any citizen to carry on correspondence with a foreign government in any controversy in which the U.S. was engaged. The act was prompted by a visit to France (June–Nov. 1798) by Dr. George Logan (1753–1821), a Philadelphia Quaker, who had gone abroad in an effort to preserve peace

between the 2 nations. The act is still on the statute books.

Feb. FRIES UPRISING. John Fries (c.1750–1818) raised several hundred men in Northampton, Bucks, and Montgomery counties, Pa., in opposition to the direct federal property tax established by acts of 9 and 14 July 1798 in anticipation of war with France. At Bethlehem he resisted the U.S. marshal. Convicted of treason, he was retried before Justice Samuel Chase, again convicted and sentenced to death, but pardoned by President Adams.

1800

4 Apr. FIRST FEDERAL BANKRUPTCY LAW enacted, extended only to merchants and traders; made possible the release of Robert Morris from prison; repealed 19 Dec. 1803.

17 Nov. Congress convened in Washington for first time.

3 Dec. PRESIDENTIAL ELECTION. Major campaign issues: (1) Alien and Sedition Acts, (2) increase by the Federalists of direct taxes occasioned by heavy defense expenditures, (3) reduction of trade with France, and (4) growth of anti-British sentiment over the impressment of American seamen. Federalist candidates: **John Adams** (Mass.) and **Charles Cotesworth Pinckney** (S.C.). Democratic-Republican: **Thomas Jefferson** (Va.) and **Aaron Burr** (N.Y.).

1801

20 Jan. One of Adams' last official acts was his appointment of **John Marshall** (p. 1097) as chief justice of the Supreme Court after John Jay had declined nomination and confirmation for a 2d term.

11–17 Feb. ELECTORAL TIE. When the ballot count (11 Feb.) in the electoral college resulted in a Jefferson-Burr tie (73 votes each; 65 for Adams, 64 for Pinckney, 1 for John Jay), the election was thrown into the Federalist-dominated House of Representatives. A deadlock followed; the Federalist caucus decided to back Burr; Hamilton, however, regarded Jefferson as the lesser evil, and used his influence to break the deadlock. It has been supposed that Jefferson made certain commitments to the Federalists, but there is no reliable evidence supporting this view. On the 36th ballot (17 Feb.) **Jefferson** was chosen president by 10 states (each state having 1 vote). **Burr** was elected vice-president.

The election demonstrated the inadequacy of the machinery provided by the Constitution for selecting the president. To prevent a similar situation in the electoral college, the **12th Amendment** was proposed by Congress (9 Dec. 1803) and was declared ratified on 25 Sept. 1804. It provided for separate balloting for president and vice-president.

13 FEB. JUDICIARY ACT reduced to 5 the number of Supreme Court justices, created 16 circuit courts (establishing a judgeship for each), and added to the number of marshals, attorneys, and clerks. In principle, the measure was justified, but it was exploited by Adams for political purposes, making under this law the so-called "midnight appointments" (3 Mar. until 9 P.M.) of Federalist judges and court officials.

4 MAR. Jefferson's inaugural was the first held at Washington, where the permanent capital had been officially established in the summer of 1800 (Congress assumed jurisdiction over District of Columbia 27 Feb. 1801; incorporation as a city 3 May 1802, its mayor to be appointed by the president). In his conciliatory inaugural address Jefferson stressed the need for a government of limited powers, economy in the national administration, support of state governments in all their rights, acquiescence in majority decisions, the preservation of civil liberties, and "peace, commerce, and honest friendship with all nations, entangling alliances with none."

8 DEC. Jefferson's first annual message to Congress broke the precedent, established by Washington and continued by Adams, of addressing Congress in person. Jefferson forwarded a written version to each house. This remained the custom until Woodrow Wilson reverted (1913) to the original practice.

TRIPOLITAN WAR, 1801–05. In order to buy immunity from interference with American commerce along the North African coast, Washington and Adams continued the custom, established by the British, of paying tribute to the pirates of the Barbary States (Algiers, Morocco, Tripoli, and Tunis). When the Pasha of Tripoli increased his demands for tribute and declared war (14 May 1801) against the U.S., Jefferson, although favoring economy and peace and opposed to a navy, decided to resist and dispatched warcraft to Mediterranean waters. In 1803 Commodore Edward Preble was named commander of the Mediterranean squadron, and on his orders Lieut. **Stephen Decatur** performed the most notable exploit of the war: the destruction (16 Feb. 1804) of the frigate *Philadelphia,* which had been captured and converted by the Tripolitans. A vigorous blockade brought the war to an end. A treaty of peace favorable to the U.S. was signed on 4 June 1805 (but the payment of tribute to other Barbary States continued until 1816).

1802

8 JAN.–29 APR. REPEAL OF THE JUDICIARY ACT OF 1801 was moved (8 Jan.) in the Senate at Jefferson's insistence; upon a deadlock, an adverse vote by Burr blocked the measure temporarily; but it was repealed 8 Mar. A new Judiciary Act, passed 29 April, restored to 6 the number of Supreme Court justices, fixed 1 term annually for the high court, and set up 6 circuit courts, each headed by a Supreme Court justice.

NEW FINANCIAL POLICY framed by Secretary of the Treasury Gallatin carried out Jefferson's pledge of retrenchment. It called for reduction of the national debt, repeal of all internal taxes (with a corollary cut in expenditures by the War and Navy departments), and a congressional system of appropriations for specific purposes. Between 1801–09 the national debt was reduced from $83 million to $57 million, notwithstanding the acquisition of Louisiana and the Tripolitan War.

16 Mar. U.S. Military Academy established by Act of Congress. On 4 July the academy was formally opened at West Point, N.Y.

1803

24 Feb. MARBURY v. MADISON (1 Cranch 137). The conflict between president and judiciary was brought to a head after Jefferson ordered Secretary of State Madison to withhold from William Marbury the signed and sealed commission of his appointment (2 Mar. 1801) by President Adams under the Judiciary Act of 1801 as justice of the peace of the District of Columbia. Marbury was joined in his suit for a writ of mandamus compelling delivery of the commission by 3 other Federalists, Robert T. Hooe, William Harper, and Dennis Ramsay, in the same situation. In dismissing Marbury's suit on the ground that the court lacked jurisdiction, Chief Justice Marshall employed a strategy calculated to avoid an open struggle with the executive branch responsible for enforcement of the writ. The case is remembered, however, as the first occasion

on which the high court held an Act of Congress unconstitutional: Marshall declared that Section 13 of the Judiciary Act of 1789, empowering the court to issue such a writ, was contrary to the Constitution and therefore invalid. This is the first case in which the Supreme Court held a law of Congress void; it did not do so again until the Dred Scott decision (pp. 263–264).

LOUISIANA PURCHASE. By the Treaty of Fontainebleu (1762) France ceded Louisiana to Spain, but by the secret Treaty of San Ildefonso (1 Oct. 1800) the province was returned to France. The transfer was made at the behest of Napoleon, who projected the revival of a French colonial empire in North America. The retrocession was confirmed (21 Mar. 1801) by the Treaty of Madrid; shortly afterward, Jefferson learned of the secret arrangement.

Jefferson was profoundly concerned over (1) the threat posed to American security by a neighboring imperial and aggressive power; (2) the possibility that the French possession of New Orleans would close the Mississippi to Western commerce. On 16 Oct. 1802, the Spanish intendant at New Orleans interdicted the right of deposit (restored 19 Apr. 1803). This action caused consternation in the West. In a letter (18 Apr. 1802) to the American minister at Paris, Robert R. Livingston, Jefferson declared: "The day that France takes New Orleans . . . we must marry ourselves to the British fleet and nation."

The president instructed Livingston to negotiate for a tract of land on the lower Mississippi for use as a port or, failing this, to obtain an irrevocable guarantee of free navigation and the right of deposit. On 12 Jan. 1803 James Monroe was named minister plenipotentiary to France and was given specific instructions for the purchase of New Orleans and West Florida with the $2 million provided by a congressional appropriation; if need be, he was to offer as much as $10 million. Even before Monroe arrived at Paris (12 April), Napoleon abandoned his scheme for a colonial empire. His decision to sell Louisiana and confine his sphere to the Old World was influenced by the costly French failure to suppress the slave revolt in Haiti (1794–1804), and by the impending resumption of hostilities with Great Britain. On 11 Apr. Talleyrand asked Livingston how much the U.S. was prepared to pay for the whole of Louisiana. With Barbé-Marbois, Napoleon's finance minister, acting for the French, Livingston and Monroe closed the negotiations. In sealing the bargain, the American envoys exceeded their instructions.

By the treaty of cession (signed 2 May, but antedated 30 Apr.), Louisiana was purchased by the U.S. for 60 million francs (approximately $15 million). The price for the territory itself was $11,250,000; the remainder covered the debts, owed by France to U.S. citizens, which the U.S. government assumed.

The purchase of Louisiana doubled the area of the U.S. by the acquisition of a tract of some 828,000 square miles lying between the Mississippi and the Rocky Mountains. The treaty, however, did not define exact boundaries. While the Gulf of Mexico was fixed as the line to the south and the Mississippi as that to the east, there was no clear understanding as to whether the cession included West Florida and Texas.

The Constitution made no provision for the purchase and assimilation of foreign territory, and the constitutional aspect of the purchase perplexed Jefferson, who, although in principle committed to strict construction, took a broad constructionist view on this issue, while the Federalists took an equally inconsistent strict constructionist stand. The substance of the Republican position—that the power to govern territory flows from the right to acquire it—was upheld (1828) by Chief Justice Marshall in *American Insurance Co.* v. *Canter* (1 Peters 511).

The Senate approved the treaty (20 Oct.) 24–7. On 20 Dec. the U.S. took formal possession of Louisiana. William C. C. Claiborne was formally installed (1 Oct. 1804) as territorial governor. In 1812 the state of Louisiana became the first to be admitted from the territory.

NORTHERN CONFEDERACY SCHEME, 1803–04. Behind the constitutional controversy over Louisiana lay Federalist fears that the states carved out of the Western territories would inevitably change the political balance of power in Congress, with the agrarian and frontier interests of the South and West gaining ascendancy over the commercial and industrial interests of the Northeast.

ESSEX JUNTO, a name first applied by John Hancock in 1781 to a group in Essex Co., Mass., who opposed the 1778 draft of the state constitution; later a propertied elite of anti-French Federalist extremists, some of whom under the leadership of Sen. **Timothy Pickering** (Mass.) considered establishment of a Northern Confederacy including the 5 New England states, New York, and New Jersey, but such extremists as George Cabot and Theophilus Parsons refused to associate themselves with the plan, which had considerable popular support. Hamilton's opposition to Pickering's scheme intensified when it became apparent that the disunionists were counting on Burr's election as governor of New York, a state held essential to the formation of the confederacy.

11 July 1804. BURR-HAMILTON DUEL. Hamilton, who played a decisive role in securing Burr's defeat in the New York election (25 Apr. 1804), was reported to have said (16 Feb. 1804) that Burr was "a dangerous man, and one who ought not to be trusted with the reins of government." Burr's demand for an explanation led to the Burr-Hamilton duel (Weehawken, N.J., 11 July 1804), in which Hamilton was fatally wounded. With Hamilton's death (12 July), the Burr-Pickering coalition disintegrated completely.

LEWIS AND CLARK EXPEDITION, 1803–06. In his message to Congress (Jan.) Jefferson asked for an appropriation for an expedition for the purpose of cultivating friendly relations with the Indians and extending the internal commerce of the U.S. Congress lent its approval. **Meriwether Lewis** and **William Clark** (p. 1084) were chosen to lead the expedition. On 31 Aug. the party began descent of the Ohio and on 14 May 1804 began ascent of the Missouri. They spent the following winter in a Mandan village, near present-day Bismarck, N.D. On 7 Apr. 1805, they began their ascent of a Missouri River fork which they named the Jefferson (others named Madison and Gallatin), crossed the Rockies, and came within sight of the Pacific Ocean on 7 Nov. 1805. The expedition, which returned to St. Louis on 23 Sept. 1806, proved the feasibility of an overland route to the Far West, added to scientific knowledge, and ultimately stimulated Western settlement and commerce.

1804

12 Mar. IMPEACHMENT OF PICKERING AND CHASE. Jefferson's conflict with the Federalist judiciary was carried forward by the impeachment as unfit of Judge John Pickering, federal district judge in New Hampshire, who was adjudged guilty by the Senate and removed from his post (12 Mar.), despite evidence at the trial establishing

that he was insane and hence not culpable of high crimes or misdemeanors. Contrariwise, **Samuel Chase** (Md., 1741–1811), associate justice of the Supreme Court, was impeached for his biased conduct in the trials of Fries and Callender and for an inflammatory anti-Republican charge to a Baltimore grand jury. His acquittal (1 Mar. 1805) discouraged subsequent administrations from using the impeachment device to remove politically obnoxious judges, while bringing to a close the Republican campaign against the Federalist bench.

5 Dec. PRESIDENTIAL ELECTION. The first regular caucus of members of Congress for the nomination of presidential candidates had (25 Feb.) unanimously nominated **Jefferson** for reelection and **George Clinton** as his running mate. **Thomas Jefferson,** opposed by the Federalist candidate **Charles Cotesworth Pinckney,** was reelected president, with 162 out of 176 electoral votes. Jefferson carried all the New England states except Connecticut. In the first election with separate ballots for president and vice-president, **George Clinton** was elected vice-president, 162 to 14 for Rufus King. The Republican party won undisputed control of Congress.

1805

9 Aug. PIKE'S EXPEDITIONS. Lieut. Zebulon M. Pike (p. 1128) was dispatched by Gen. James Wilkinson to explore (1805–06) the sources of the Mississippi. In a second expedition (1806–07) he explored Colorado and New Mexico. Named after him was Pikes Peak, Colo., which he sighted 15 Nov. 1806.

1806

25 Jan.–21 Nov. COMMERCE AND NEUTRAL RIGHTS. With the resumption (1803) of the Napoleonic wars, American neutrality faced new tests. Great Britain and France clamped further restrictions on the neutral carrying trade in order to deprive each other of the means of war. The overwhelming superiority of British over French naval power made its interference with American commerce the more serious invasion of neutral rights. There followed a renewal of the controversies with England over neutral trade, impressment, and blockade.

In a series of acts and orders (1804–05) the British evolved a West Indian trade policy calculated to destroy neutral commerce with French and Spanish colonies in America that furnished staples to Napoleon's armies. The "Rule of 1756," laid down by British courts during the Seven Years' War, to the effect that where a European nation has forbidden trade with its colonies in time of peace it shall not open it to neutrals in time of war, was enforced against U.S. neutral carriers (1793) after the outbreak of war between England and France. The latter had evaded this restriction by landing cargo at a U.S. port, passing it through the customs, and securing fresh clearance for a belligerent port. This principle of the "broken voyage" was upheld in British admiralty decisions in the cases of the *Immanuel* (1799) and the *Polly* (1800). Thereafter the large number of American vessels plying between the French West Indies and France enjoyed relative freedom. British policy was abruptly reversed by the decision (23 July 1805) in the *Essex* case, when the British judge, Sir William Scott, declared that American cargo was subject to seizure and condemnation unless the shipper could prove that he had originally intended to terminate the voyage in an American port. Failing that, the voyage could be regarded as a **continuous** one between enemy ports. As a

result of this decision, the seizures of American vessels increased sharply.

Madison's report (25 Jan.) on the British infringement of the rights of neutral commerce and the impressment of American seamen was followed (12 Feb.) by a Senate resolution attacking British seizures as "an unprovoked aggression" and a "violation of neutral rights." Great Britain took no heed. In retaliation, Congress passed the **Nicholson** (or first) **Non-Importation Act** (18 Apr.) prohibiting the importation from England of a long list of articles (including hemp, flax, tin, brass, and some classes of woolens) which could be produced in the U.S. or imported from other countries. It was to become effective 15 Nov.; upon the advice of Jefferson it was suspended (19 Dec.) and was not again operative until 22 Dec. 1808. On 16 May British foreign minister Charles James Fox declared a blockade of the European coast from Brest to the river Elbe. Napoleon answered with the **Berlin Decree** (21 Nov.) declaring the British Isles in a state of blockade, forbidding all commerce and communication with them, and authorizing the seizure and confiscation of vessels and cargo.

31 DEC. MONROE-PINKNEY TREATY. At the instigation of Congress, Jefferson dispatched (May) William Pinkney (Md.) as special envoy to London to join James Monroe in negotiating a treaty with Great Britain. His instructions called for (1) British abandonment of the impressment of American seamen, (2) restoration of the West Indian trade on the basis of the "broken voyage," (3) indemnity payments for seizures made after the *Essex* decision. Prolonged discussions with Lord Holland began 27 Aug.; as a bargaining point, the U.S. envoys used the threat of enforcing the Non-Importation Act. British refusal to make concessions finally moved

Monroe and Pinkney to violate their instructions. The treaty was a defeat for U.S. diplomacy. It made no reference to impressment or indemnities and constituted a slight compromise on the West Indian trade. Jefferson received the treaty in Mar. 1807. Deeply embarrassed over its terms, he never submitted it to the Senate, but instructed the U.S. envoys (20 May 1807) that the treaty serve as a basis for reopening discussions.

1807–09

7 JAN.–17 DEC. BRITISH AND FRENCH COUNTERMEASURES. The British retaliated against the Berlin Decree with an order in council (7 Jan.) barring all shipping from the coastal trade of France and her allies. The enforcement of Napoleon's Continental system nevertheless became more effective after his Tilsit agreement (25 June) with Czar Alexander I of Russia. The British struck back with new orders in council (11 Nov.) prohibiting commerce with Continental ports from which the British flag was excluded; only vessels which had first passed through a British port, and there paid customs duties and secured new clearances, were permitted to call at open ports on the Continent. Napoleon's **Milan Decree** (17 Dec.) declared that all vessels searched by the British or obeying the orders in council would be regarded as "denationalized" and subject to seizure and confiscation as British property.

19 FEB.–1 SEPT. AARON BURR "CONSPIRACY" AND TRIAL, 1804–07. Shortly after slaying Hamilton, Burr, his political career now at an end, asked money of Anthony Merry, British minister to the U.S., supposedly for the purpose of organizing a movement for separating the Western states from the U.S. The British never gave him funds; from the Spanish minister, whom he subse-

quently approached, Burr received a small sum. Whether Burr's aim was treasonable, or whether he was planning to lead a filibustering expedition against the Spanish dominions, is still a matter of dispute (Henry Adams, 1890, held that Burr plotted disunion; W. F. McCaleb, 1903, maintained that Burr, far from conspiring to commit treason, sought to build a Western empire through annexation of Spanish territories in the Southwest and Mexico). Burr is known to have conferred with Gen. James Wilkinson, commander of U.S. forces in the Mississippi Valley, during a tour (May–Sept. 1805) of that region. At the end of Aug. 1806, Burr went to Blennerhassett's Island, in the Ohio River, the home of Harman Blennerhassett, one of his chief associates. Here he made preparations for a military expedition, his force consisting of some 60 to 80 men and about 10 boats, and then left for Tennessee. Wilkinson and others warned President Jefferson, who issued a proclamation (27 Nov. 1806) warning citizens against participating in an illegal expedition against Spanish territory. Burr was apparently unaware of the proclamation by the time he rejoined his followers for the journey down the Mississippi. The expedition passed several American forts without interference; when the party reached a point some 30 miles above Natchez, Burr learned that Wilkinson, at New Orleans, had betrayed him. Burr fled toward Spanish Florida, but was arrested in Alabama (19 Feb.) and taken to Richmond, Va., where he was brought (30 Mar. 1807) before Chief Justice Marshall, presiding over the U.S. circuit court. Originally held for a misdemeanor in forming an expedition against Spanish territory, Burr was indicted (24 June) for treason. The trial (3 Aug.–1 Sept.), which ended in the acquittal of Burr and his associates, settled the U.S. law of treason, which Marshall strictly construed. In the course of the trial Marshall issued a subpoena duces tecum to President Jefferson for evidence in his hands. The president, while ignoring the subpoena, did in fact make the information in his possession available. Burr went into European exile to escape further prosecutions (for murder of Hamilton in New York and New Jersey and for treason in Ohio, Kentucky, Mississippi, and Louisiana).

22 June. CHESAPEAKE-LEOPARD AFFAIR. The U.S. frigate *Chesapeake,* commanded by Commodore James Barron, was hailed by the British frigate *Leopard* outside the 3-mile limit off Norfolk Roads. The British commander claimed that 4 men aboard the *Chesapeake* were British deserters, and demanded their surrender. When Barron refused to permit search of his vessel, the *Leopard* opened fire, killing 3 and wounding 18, and removed the 4 alleged deserters. The crippled *Chesapeake* returned to Norfolk. News of the incident aroused anti-British feeling. Jefferson issued (2 July) a proclamation ordering British warships to leave U.S. territorial waters. A British proclamation (17 Oct.) ordered a more vigorous prosecution of impressment of British subjects from neutral vessels. Discussions concerning reparations for the attack on the *Chesapeake* lasted until 1808, but satisfaction was blocked by the British demanding as a condition the withdrawal of Jefferson's proclamation. Not until 1 Nov. 1811 did the British present an offer of settlement which Secretary Monroe accepted (12 Nov.).

1807–09, EMBARGO. Jefferson decided to rely upon economic pressure to bring the belligerent powers to terms. While the Non-Importation Act had again become effective (14 Dec. 1807), its threatened use had already failed to move the British. Jefferson sent (18 Dec.) a message to Congress recommending an embargo. Federalist opposition failed to block speedy action on the measure. The bill was passed in the Senate (18 Dec.), 22–6; passage in the House (21 Dec.), 82–44, was supported chiefly by the South and West. The embargo became law on 22 Dec.

The **Embargo Act** interdicted virtually all land and seaborne commerce with foreign nations. It forbade all U.S. vessels to leave for foreign ports. U.S. ships in the coastal trade were required to post bond double the value of craft and cargo as a guarantee that the goods would be relanded at a U.S. port. While importation in foreign bottoms was not prohibited, it was almost outlawed by the provision that foreign vessels could not carry goods out of an American port. The law was supplemented by the **Embargo Acts** of 9 Jan. and 12 Mar. 1808.

Means were soon found for evading its provisions. A brisk smuggling trade was carried out by land and water, particularly across the Canadian border. U.S. ships which had been at sea when the act went into operation remained in foreign waters and continued their trade with the warring nations. The British government cooperated with merchants who violated the law. The effect upon the British economy was minor, as British shippers gained by the wholesale removal of U.S. competition, while their government was able to draw upon South America as a fresh source of supply. The French used the embargo to their own advantage. Under the pretext of aiding the U.S. to enforce the law, Napoleon issued the **Bayonne Decree** (17 Apr. 1808) ordering the seizure of all U.S. vessels entering the ports of France, Italy, and the Hanseatic towns. Napoleon justified this move by accepting the embargo as effective and declaring that any U.S. shipping in those ports must obviously be British vessels furnished with false papers. The strict enforcement of the Bayonne Decree resulted in French confiscation (1808–09) of some $10 million worth of U.S. goods and shipping.

Domestic opposition to the embargo was strongest in the mercantile areas of New England and New York, where Eastern Republicans made common cause with Federalists on this issue. Although the embargo stimulated New England industry, the benefits were outweighed by the heavy losses sustained by the carrying trade. Widespread economic distress brought the Federalists into power in the New England state governments after the elections of 1808. Popular hostility to the embargo was increased by the **Enforcement Act** (9 Jan. 1809), which provided for strict enforcement and authorized severe penalties for evasions of the act. Numerous town meetings attacked the embargo as a pro-French, anti-British measure, and state legislatures challenged its constitutionality. Resolutions drawn up by the Massachusetts legislature (Jan., Feb., 1809) characterized it as unjust and arbitrary. In his address to the Connecticut legislature (23 Feb. 1809) Gov. Jonathan Trumbull asserted that whenever Congress exceeded its constitutional powers, the state legislatures were in duty bound "to interpose their protecting shield between the rights and liberties of the people and the assumed power of the general government." Governors refused to furnish militia officers requested by collectors for enforcing the embargo. Timothy Pickering proposed a New England convention for nullifying the embargo.

Amid this flurry of states'-rights views, Chief Justice Marshall handed down his opinion (20 Feb. 1809) in *U.S.* v. *Peters* (5 Cranch 115). Although the case was not related to the embargo (it involved the annulment of a federal court order by the state of Pennsylvania), it was memorable for Marshall's pronouncement sustaining the power of the national over state authority. The embargo itself was upheld (1808) by a Federalist Judge John Davis in U.S. district court in Massachusetts, but appeal on the decision was never taken to the Supreme Court.

In Congress opposition came from (1) the Federalists, (2) the dissident "Quids," including a faction led by **John Randolph** of Roanoke (p. 1134), as well as other dissidents. Jefferson signed the **Non-Intercourse Act** (1 Mar. 1809) repealing the embargo effective 15 Mar. 1809, reopening trade with all nations except France and Great Britain, and authorizing the president to proclaim resumption of trade with France or Great Britain in the event either power should cease violating neutral rights. The British minister to the U.S., David M. Erskine, gave assurances to Secretary of State Robert Smith that the orders in council of 1807, as applicable to the U.S., would be revoked 10 June 1809. Unaware that Erskine had not been authorized to speak for his government, President Madison issued a proclamation (19 Apr. 1809) legalizing trade with Great Britain. British Foreign Secretary George Canning disavowed (30 May 1809) Erskine's arrangement and ordered him back to England. President Madison in turn issued a proclamation (9 Aug. 1809) reviving the Non-Intercourse Act against Great Britain.

1808

1 JAN. AFRICAN SLAVE TRADE. Congressional interference with the foreign slave trade before 1808 was forbidden under Art. I, Sect. 9 of the Constitution. In keeping with Jefferson's recommendation (2 Dec. 1806), Congress forbade (2 Mar. 1807) slave importations into U.S. on and after 1 Jan.

1808. The law provided a penalty of forfeiture of vessel and cargo, with disposal of the seized slaves to be left to the state in which the ship was condemned.

7 Dec. PRESIDENTIAL ELECTION. Confirming the precedent established by Washington, Jefferson refused to stand for a 3d term. As his successor in the "Virginia dynasty" he supported **James Madison,** who was nominated by a congressional caucus. Madison's nomination was opposed by 2 insurgent wings of the Republican party. The Southern "Old Republicans" (John Randolph–John Taylor of Caroline group) chose **James Monroe** (Va., who withdrew from the contest). The Eastern Republicans, smarting under the embargo, nominated Vice-President **George Clinton** (N.Y.). The Federalist candidates were **Charles Cotesworth Pinckney** (S.C.) and **Rufus King** (N.Y.). Madison received 122 electoral votes to 47 for Pinckney and 6 for George Clinton. **Clinton** received 113 for vice-president to 47 for Rufus King. The Federalists gained in the House, but did not secure a majority.

1810

1 May. MACON'S BILL NO. 2. Congress took its own course after the collapse of the Erskine agreement. Since the Non-Intercourse Act was due to expire at the close of the second session of the 11th Congress in 1810, a substitute measure introduced by Nathaniel Macon (N.C.), chairman of the Foreign Affairs Committee, authorized the president to reopen commerce with Great Britain and France, adding that in the event either nation should before 3 Mar. 1811 modify or revoke its edicts so as to cease violations of American shipping, the president could prohibit trade with the other. If at the end of 3 months the other power failed to withdraw its edicts,

the president was empowered to revive non-intercourse against it. The bill, which also excluded British and French naval craft from American territorial waters, passed the House 64–27, the Federalists voting solidly against it. The French regarded the act as discrimination in favor of Great Britain, whose naval power closed the sea routes to French shipping.

5 Aug.–2 Nov. NAPOLEON'S DECEPTION. Acting on the pretense of making reprisals against the Non-Intercourse Act, Napoleon issued (23 Mar.) the **Rambouillet Decree** ordering seizure and confiscation of all U.S. vessels entering any French port. The decree, published 14 May, was made retroactive to 20 May 1809. When Napoleon learned of Macon's Bill No. 2, he instructed (5 Aug.) his foreign minister, the Duc de Cadore, to notify John Armstrong, U.S. minister at Paris, that the Berlin and Milan decrees would be revoked after 1 Nov. on condition that the U.S. declare non-intercourse against the British unless the orders in council were withdrawn. Yet on the same day Napoleon signed the **Decree of Trianon** ordering sequestration of U.S. vessels that had called at French ports between 20 May 1809 and 1 May 1810.

In communicating Napoleon's order to Armstrong, the Duc de Cadore took liberty with his phrasing and declared that the Berlin and Milan decrees had been actually canceled. President Madison unsuspectingly accepted the French communication at face value and issued (2 Nov.) a proclamation reopening trade with France and declaring that commerce with Great Britain would come to a halt on 2 Feb. 1811. Non-intercourse against the British was sanctioned (2 Mar. 1811) by Congress. More than a year elapsed before the British revoked the orders in council. The delay proved costly. The immediate British response to the move was a renewal of the blockade of New York and a more vigorous impressment of American seamen.

Napoleon's duplicity was revealed after Joel Barlow, whom Madison had named minister to France, arrived at Paris (19 Sept. 1811) in order to seek clarification of the Berlin and Milan decrees. The Duc de Bassano, Napoleon's foreign minister, showed Barlow the Decree of St. Cloud, supposedly signed by Napoleon 28 Apr. 1811. It stated that his earlier decrees had been declared nonexistent in regard to U.S. vessels since 1 Nov. 1810. The decree had never been published and, despite French assurances, had never been communicated to the U.S. government. Barlow's death (24 Dec. 1812) in Poland, where he had gone to confer with Napoleon, brought his mission to an end. By this time, however, Napoleon's involvement in the Russian campaign had terminated his influence in American affairs, and the U.S. was at war with Great Britain.

27 Oct. ANNEXATION OF WEST FLORIDA. The Louisiana treaty of 1803 made no reference to the status of Spanish-ruled East and West Florida. Jefferson supported the view that Louisiana included that portion of Florida between the Mississippi River to the west and the Perdido River to the east. In 1810 Southern expansionists led a revolt in the Spanish dominion, captured the fort at Baton Rouge, and proclaimed (26 Sept.) the independent state of the Republic of West Florida. Madison issued a proclamation (27 Oct.) announcing U.S. possession of West Florida from the Mississippi to the Perdido and authorizing its military occupation as part of the Orleans Territory. Congress assembled in secret session and adopted a resolution (15 Jan. 1811) authorizing extension of U.S. rule over East Florida as well in the event local authority consented or a foreign power took steps to occupy it. On

14 May 1812 West Florida was incorporated by Congress into the Mississippi Territory. After the outbreak of the War of 1812, Gen. James Wilkinson took the Spanish fort at Mobile (15 Apr. 1813) and occupied the Mobile district of West Florida to the Perdido River. This was the sole territorial conquest retained by the U.S. after the War of 1812.

YAZOO LAND FRAUD. The Georgia legislature (7 Jan. 1795) sold to 4 land companies (whose shareholders were discovered to include Georgia legislators) 35 million acres in the Yazoo River country (Mississippi and Alabama) for $500,000. A new legislature rescinded (1796) this sale. When Georgia ceded (1802) to the U.S. her Western claims, the national government sought a final settlement by awarding 5 million acres to holders of Yazoo land warrants. With the support of other "Quids" John Randolph, who had already split with the administration over Louisiana, succeeded in blocking the bill (1804–05), which was not passed until 1814, when the claimants were awarded $4.2 million. Randolph's opposition precipitated a party schism and led to his removal as leader of the majority. The Yazoo affair was the subject of Chief Justice Marshall's opinion (1810) in *Fletcher* v. *Peck* (6 Cranch 87), in which he maintained that the judiciary could not inquire into the motives of legislators who made the original grant and construed the grant as a contract within the meaning of the Constitution and the rescinding law as impairing the obligation of the contract; hence void.

1811

24 Jan.–20 Feb. BANK DEBATE. The charter of the first U.S. Bank was due to expire 4 Mar. Petitions for extension of the charter had been made in 1808 and 1810, but congressional consideration was postponed because of the pressure of foreign affairs. Secretary of the Treasury Gallatin, lauding the management of the bank, endorsed renewal of the charter. Opposed to renewal were (1) "Old Republicans" who viewed the bank as the last survival of Federalist power, denounced it on constitutional grounds, and desired to drive Gallatin from office on the issue; (2) Anglophobes who pointed to the fact that two thirds of the bank stock was held by Britons and insisted that the measure would aid a potential enemy; (3) interests favoring the growth of state-chartered banks, which had increased rapidly, expanded their note issues, and were eager to share the profits of the bank. The recharter bill died in the House (24 Jan.). In the Senate, where William Henry Crawford (Ga.) led the fight for the administration bill and William Branch Giles (Va.) opposed it, the tie (17 to 17) was broken by Vice-President Clinton, who voted (20 Feb.) against renewal. The bank wound up its business and expired. Failure to recharter the bank deprived the government of urgently needed financial resources during the War of 1812.

16 May. "LITTLE BELT" AFFAIR. In May, British cruisers off New York Harbor resumed more freely their impressment of American seamen. The British 38-gun frigate *Guerrière* overhauled (1 May) off Sandy Hook the American brig *Spitfire* and impressed a native-born American. Capt. John Rodgers, commanding the U.S. 44-gun frigate *President,* was ordered (6 May) to cruise off Sandy Hook to give protection to American vessels. En route Rodgers sighted a ship he mistook for the *Guerrière* (actually the craft was the British 20-gun corvette *Little Belt*). Rodgers gave chase; the *Little Belt* refused to identify herself; and the pursuit ended in an evening engagement (16 May) off

Cape Charles. The broadsides of the *President* disabled the *Little Belt,* killing 9 and wounding 23 of her crew. On 1 Nov. the U.S. government informed the British minister, Augustus John Foster, that it was willing to settle the matter amicably, provided the orders in council were revoked.

31 July–8 Nov. TECUMSEH AND THE NORTHWEST. Along the frontiers of the Old Northwest the Shawnee chief **Tecumseh** (p. 1167) undertook the organization of a defensive tribal confederacy to resist the westward sweep of white settlement. The British governor in Canada, as well as the fur traders, were reputedly backing Tecumseh and his brother, the Prophet. When extensive Indian activity during the summer of 1811 created fear among frontier settlers, the people of Vincennes adopted resolutions (31 July) calling for the destruction of the Indian capital on Tippecanoe Creek. The settlers finally induced Gen. **William Henry Harrison** (p. 1053) governor of the Indiana Territory, to take the initiative against Tecumseh (who meanwhile had gone to the Southwest to seek support for his plan). Leading a force of some 1,000 men, Harrison set out (26 Sept.) from Vincennes for the Indian capital 150 miles to the north, near the confluence of the Tippecanoe and the Wabash. Ft. Harrison, about 65 miles above Vincennes, was established; on 28 Oct. the force resumed its march and encamped (6 Nov.) about a mile from the Indian village. In a surprise dawn attack (7 Nov.) the Indians descended upon the Americans. After a day-long battle, Harrison's men, despite heavy losses, beat back the Indians and razed the village (8 Nov.). The Americans then withdrew to Ft. Harrison. Westerners acclaimed the **Battle of Tippecanoe** as a great victory. Although the British authorities in Canada subsequently took steps to cut off aid to the Indians, the event increased anti-British sentiment along the frontier and resulted in louder demands for expelling the British from Canada. Indian raids broke out again (Apr. 1812) along the frontier, but Tecumseh chose to remain on the defensive. It was generally recognized that open war with the Indians would necessarily be part of a declared war against the British.

4 Nov. "WAR HAWKS." The prowar feeling that swept the country in 1810–11 left its mark on the congressional elections. The 12th Congress numbered even fewer Federalists and, in place of many of the cautious legislators who had enacted Macon's Bill No. 2, brought to the fore a new type of Republican who espoused nationalism and expansionism. Upon these war Republicans John Randolph bestowed the epithet: "war hawks." Among them were **Henry Clay** (p. 1002), **Richard M. Johnson** (Ky., 1780–1850), **John C. Calhoun** (p. 996), **William Lowndes** (S.C., 1782–1822), **Langdon Cheves** (S.C., 1776–1857), **Felix Grundy** (Tenn., 1777–1840), **Peter B. Porter** (1773–1844) from western New York. Notwithstanding their numerical minority the "war hawks" achieved a commanding position in the House. Clay was elected speaker; the Foreign Relations Committee came under the control of Calhoun, Grundy, and Porter; Cheves was named chairman of the Naval Committee.

Most of the "war hawks" came from the agrarian areas of the South and West whose people were hardly affected by maritime issues (although some Westerners claimed that the orders in council had crippled their markets for agricultural produce); yet they chose to view maritime seizure and impressment as outrages upon national rights and honor. Northern and Southern "war hawks" found common ground in expansionism (J. W. Pratt, 1925). Those from the Northwest, eager to destroy the frontier

Indian menace they attributed to British intrigue and incitement, equated security with land hunger and demanded the conquest of Canada. The Southerners wanted to wrest Florida from Spain, Britain's ally.

5 Nov. Despite expansionist pressures, the U.S. would not have been involved in war had it not been for maritime and commercial issues. Madison was no tool of the war party (see Theodore Clarke Smith, 1931), although he ultimately supported its program. The president's message to Congress attacked Great Britain, had no friendly words for France, but made no express reference to impressment. The president requested preparations for the national defense, pointing to the "evidence of hostile inflexibility in trampling on rights which no independent nation can relinquish."

1812

1–10 Apr. WAR PREPARATIONS. Madison's message to Congress (1 Apr.) recommending an immediate and general embargo for 60 days was regarded by the "war hawks" as a prelude to armed conflict. The bill passed in the House (70–41). In the Senate, where the vote was 20–13, moderate Republicans, anxious to prolong negotiations with Great Britain, amended the bill to extend the embargo to 90 days. The embargo became law on 4 Apr. On 10 Apr. the president was empowered to call up for 6 months' service 100,000 militia from the states and territories.

10 Apr.–16 June. FAILURE OF DIPLOMACY. Madison's persistence in maintaining that the Berlin and Milan decrees were not in force against the U.S. was countered by British denial that Napoleon had unconditionally revoked them. Refusing to annul the orders in council, the British affirmed their view in a note (10 April) sent by Foreign

Secretary Lord Castlereagh. Madison interpreted it as final notice of Britain's unyielding position, and toward the close of May drafted a message calling for an immediate declaration of war.

Under the impact of economic distress at home, the British government had begun to give way gradually, if reluctantly. The revival of non-intercourse, combined with the increased effectiveness of the Continental system, created severe hardships for English commercial and industrial interests. In 1810–11 factories and mills shut down; unemployment rose; the price of foodstuffs soared; and in one year alone (1811) British exports fell off by a third. Employers and workers joined in petitioning Parliament to consider repeal of the orders. Prime Minister Spencer Perceval stood in danger of losing his office on the issue when he was assassinated (11 May) by a deranged malcontent. The consequent delay in taking up the question was crucial. Lord Castlereagh announced (16 June) suspension of the orders in council (formally suspended 23 June). Across the Atlantic the U.S. Congress, unaware of the British concession, had already moved for war.

18 JUNE. DECLARATION OF WAR ON GREAT BRITAIN. Madison's message to Congress (1 June) listed 4 major grounds for war: (1) impressment of American seamen, (2) violation of U.S. neutral rights and territorial waters, (3) the blockade of U.S. ports, and (4) refusal to revoke the orders in council. The House (4 June) supported the declaration of war 79–49. In the Senate, where action was delayed by Federalist and "Old Republican" opposition, the vote (18 June) in favor of war was 19–13. The New England states (with the exception of inland Vermont) and other maritime and commercial states, such as New York, New Jersey, and Delaware, voted for peace. The vote of the Southern and Western states assured a declaration of war. On 19 June Madison proclaimed a state of war with Great Britain.

War of 1812 (1812–14)

THE BALANCE SHEET. U.S. advantages: (1) Great Britain's involvement in the Napoleonic wars prevented her from devoting her main resources to the war against the U.S.; (2) the U.S. had an initial advantage of proximity to the theater of war; (3) the U.S. population was overwhelmingly superior in numbers to that of Canada, the chief target of U.S. land operations; (4) the U.S. Navy, although numerically inferior to the British (it had but 16 seagoing craft), was manned by efficient and well-trained officers and crews. **U.S. disadvantages:** (1) a small and badly administered regular army composed of volunteers and raw militia with few experienced and capable commanders, and poorly equipped and supplied; (2) lack of united popular support, particularly in New England and New York, where the people spoke of "Mr. Madison's war" and accused the president of being a tool of the French; (3) lack of a national bank, which deprived the government of centralized financial machinery and compelled dependence upon borrowing by public subscription (a move that evoked a feeble response in the financial centers of the disaffected Northeast).

1812

MILITARY SETBACKS. The improvised U.S. plan of operations called for a 3-pronged drive into Canada. In the east, a force under Gen. **Henry Dearborn** (1751–1829) was to use the Lake Champlain route for an assault on Montreal. In the center, troops under Gen. **Stephen Van Rensselaer** (1764–1839) were to attack the Canadians along the Niagara River frontier. In the west, an expedition under Gen. **William Hull** (1753–1825) was to launch from Detroit an attack against Upper Canada. The U.S. forces were composed mainly of ill-trained militia.

16 Aug. Hull's Surrender. The Canadian campaign began with a series of disasters. The surrender (17 July) of the U.S. post on Michilimackinac Island, in the Strait of Mackinaw joining Lakes Huron and Michigan, led the Northwest Indians under Tecumseh to align themselves definitely with the British. The British gained valuable intelligence when Hull's personal baggage (containing official papers and plans) was seized (1 July) as it was being conveyed to Detroit. With a force of 2,200 men, Hull crossed the Detroit River into Canada (12 July) and occupied Sandwich, but withdrew to Detroit (8 Aug.), apprehensive that the Indians would cut his line of communication with Ohio and of the Canadian force of some 2,000 under Gen. Isaac Brock. Fearing an Indian massacre of women and children, Hull surrendered Detroit (16 Aug.) to Brock without firing a shot. The garrison of Ft. Dearborn (at the site of Chicago) was massacred (15 Aug.) as it evacuated the post, which was burned the next day. Hull's surrender left the British in control of Lake Erie and the Michigan country. A court-martial sentenced Hull to death for cowardice and neglect of duty (26 March 1814). The penalty was remitted because of Hull's Revolutionary War record but his name was dropped from the army roll.

13 Oct.–28 Nov. Niagara Campaign. Brock reached Ft. George on the Canadian side of the Niagara River (23 Aug.), where, facing the U.S. line under Van Rensselaer in New York state, he established a strong defense. Van Rensselaer took the offensive (13 Oct.) with the occupation of Queenston Heights (Gen. Brock was killed in the engagement). Opposed by a British force of 1,000, the 600 Americans on the heights were crushed when New York state militia failed to reinforce them on the ground that their military service did not require them to leave the state. Van Rensselaer retired from his command and was succeeded by Gen. Alexander Smyth, an indecisive regular army officer who made a feeble attempt (28 Nov.) to cross the Niagara River. As a result of his failure, Smyth was relieved of his command and his name dropped from the army roll.

19 Nov. Montreal Fiasco. Stationed at Plattsburg, under the command of Gen. Dearborn, was the largest force of Americans under arms. Projecting a synchronized movement with Smyth's operation at Niagara, Dearborn led his army (19 Nov.) to the Canadian frontier, at which point the militia refused to proceed further. On 23 Nov. Dearborn returned his army to Plattsburg.

The military disasters of 1812 revealed the need for well-trained regular troops and an overhauling of the army command. Madison's dissatisfaction with the War Department led to the replacement (13 Jan. 1813) of Secretary William Eustis by John Armstrong (N.Y.). Although he succeeded in invigorating the army command, Armstrong was tactless; upon his retirement in 1814, Monroe took charge of the War Department, remaining in that post until the appointment of William Henry Crawford (Ga.) in 1815.

NAVAL SUCCESSES. The skill and valor of U.S. seamanship were demonstrated in the engagement (19 Aug.) off Nova Scotia between the U.S. 44-gun frigate *Constitution,* Capt. **Isaac Hull** (1773–1843) commanding, and the British 38-gun frigate *Guerrière.* After a duel lasting about a half-hour, the *Guerrière* was so badly riddled and disabled that Hull had to abandon taking her as a prize and instead blew her up. The U.S. casualties numbered 14; the British, 79. News of the victory, coming hard upon reports of the fall of Detroit, helped to bolster sagging morale. The 18-gun sloop-of-war *Wasp,* Capt. Jacob Jones commanding, bested the British 18-gun brig *Frolic* in an encounter (17 Oct.) 600 miles off the Virginia coast. The U.S. losses, 10 killed or wounded; British, c.90. The 44-gun frigate *United States,* Capt. **Stephen Decatur** (p. 1011) commanding, subdued (25 Oct.) the British 38-gun frigate *Macedonian* off the Madeira Islands and brought her into New London as a prize. The *Constitution,* under her new commander, Capt. **William Bainbridge** (1774–1833), destroyed (29 Dec.) the British 38-gun frigate *Java* in a duel off the coast of Brazil (American loss, 12 killed, 22 wounded; British loss, 48 dead, 102 wounded). Her performance on this occasion earned for the *Constitution* the sobriquet "Old Ironsides."

PEACE FEELERS. At the instruction of Secretary of State Monroe, the U.S. chargé at London, Jonathan Russell, informed Lord Castlereagh (24 Aug.) that the U.S. was willing to negotiate an armistice provided the British would abandon impressment and paper blockades and agree to indemnities for maritime spoliations. On his own initiative, Russell added informally that the U.S. would renounce the practice of naturalizing British seamen. Castlereagh rejected (29 Aug.) both proposals. From Halifax, Adm. Sir John Borlase Warren sent to Washington an offer of armistice and negotiation (30 Sept.). Monroe replied (27 Oct.) that the U.S. would accept only on condition that the British suspend impressment. This peace overture also bore no result.

NEW ENGLAND DISAFFECTION. The declaration of war provoked sharp remonstrances in the Federalist stronghold. Gov. Caleb Strong (Mass.) issued a proclamation (26 June) declaring a public fast in view of the war "against the nation from which we are descended." The Massachusetts House of Representatives issued an "Address to the People" (26 June) terming the war as one against the public interest and asserting that "there be no volunteers except for defensive war." The General Assembly of Connecticut condemned the war (25 Aug.). The governors of Connecticut (2 July) and Massachusetts (5 Aug.) refused to furnish militia to the federal government. In New Hampshire the Rockingham memorial (5 Aug.) protested against "hasty, rash, and ruinous measures" and made veiled hints of disunion.

2 Dec. PRESIDENTIAL ELECTION. At a congressional caucus (18 May) where Southern Republican insurgents put aside their differences, **Madison** was renominated by unanimous vote. Vice-President **Clinton** having died in office (20 Apr.), **Elbridge Gerry** (Mass.) was chosen as vice-presidential candidate. The Federalist charge that Madison won renomination by truckling to **Henry Clay** (p. 1002) and the war Republicans appears to be without foundation. In New York state the antiwar Republicans nominated (29 May) **De Witt Clinton** (p. 1003) for the presidency. At a secret meeting (Sept.) in New York, the Federalists threw their support to Clinton, and both groups endorsed Clin-

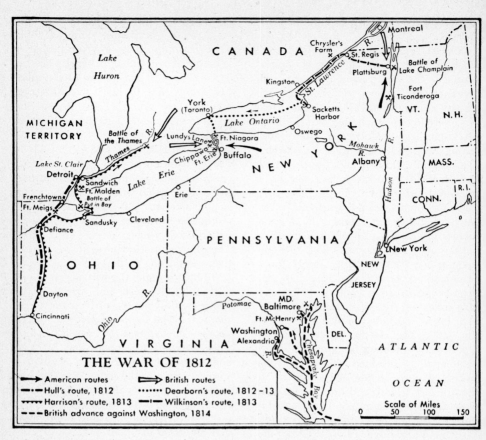

THE WAR OF 1812

→ American routes   ⇨ British routes
─·─· Hull's route, 1812   ······ Dearborn's route, 1812–13
∨∨∨∨ Harrison's route, 1813 ━•━ Wilkinson's route, 1813
─ ─ ─ British advance against Washington, 1814

Scale of Miles
0   50   100   150

ton's running mate, **Charles Jared Ingersoll** (Pa.), a moderate Federalist. The electoral vote: for president—**Madison, 128**; Clinton, 89. For vice-president—Gerry, 131; Ingersoll, 86. Madison carried the Southern and Western states. Clinton carried all of New England and the Middle States to the Potomac, with the exception of Vermont and Pennsylvania. The sweeping Federalist victory in the Northeast doubled the party's strength in the new Congress.

1813

BRITISH BLOCKADE. The blockade of Chesapeake and Delaware bays (announced 26 Dec. 1812) shut off commerce from those waters and was marked by British raids along the shores of the upper Chesapeake by a naval force under Rear Adm. Sir George Cockburn. The blockade was extended (26 May) to the mouth of the Mississippi and to the ports and harbors of New York, Charleston, Port Royal, and Savannah. Chesapeake Bay was used as a British naval station, and from the early months of 1813 until the end of the war the southern coast down to Georgia was kept in a constant state of panic. After the announcement (16 Nov.) of the blockade of Long Island Sound, only the ports along the New England coast north of New London remained open to neutral trade. The British hoped to exploit New

England disaffection. When the Northeast failed to fulfill expectations of disunion, and when the British decided to use a complete blockade as a support for general offensive operations in 1814, the blockade was extended to New England (25 Apr. 1814).

Despite many individual exploits by U.S. naval vessels, the blockade was highly effective. It created a scarcity of goods that stimulated domestic manufactures and led to widespread speculation and price inflation, with consequent hardships on farmers. The sharp reduction in customs receipts weakened the Treasury, helping to bring the government to near bankruptcy in 1814.

The Americans retaliated by dispatching cruisers to prey on merchant convoys. Until its capture (28 Mar. 1814) off Valparaiso, the 32-gun frigate *Essex,* Capt. David Porter (1780–1843) commanding, captured or destroyed more than twoscore merchant ships or whalers in the Atlantic and South Pacific. But such individual ship actions did little to lessen British naval superiority. The Americans also resorted to privateering. Ineffective in 1813, privateering did not become a powerful weapon until 1814, when the U.S. blockade of British coasts made it unsafe for enemy shipping to sail without convoy from the English to the Irish Channel. By the summer of 1814 Lloyd's listed 825 vessels as captured by Americans. But even these inroads did not affect the tight British blockade of the U.S. coast.

HARRISON IN THE WEST. The fall of Detroit and Ft. Dearborn (Aug. 1812) compelled the Americans to fall back to the Wabash-Maumee line. Westerners took alarm. Shortly after learning of Hull's defeat, a group of Kentucky officials and citizens (including Henry Clay) commissioned William Henry Harrison a major general of militia and appointed him to head an expedition to Detroit.

The move revived confidence along the frontier. When Madison and Secretary of War Eustis learned of Kentucky's action, they commissioned Harrison a brigadier general (17 Sept. 1812) and gave him command of the northwestern army (Harrison was nominated a major general on 27 Feb.). Harrison's orders were simply to retake Detroit. At his disposal he had 10,000 men. The first battle, at **Frenchtown** on the Raisin River, at the western end of Lake Erie, resulted in defeat (22 Jan.) for the Kentucky force led by Gen. James Winchester. Some 500 Americans were taken prisoner; another 400 were killed in action or massacred by the Indians. The British and Tecumseh failed in their siege (1–9 May) of **Ft. Meigs,** at the mouth of the Maumee, where Harrison commanded the defense. The British assault (2 Aug.) on **Ft. Stephenson,** on the Sandusky River, was repulsed by a stout defense led by Maj. George Croghan. Harrison could not move on Detroit as long as the British remained in control of Lake Erie.

1 JUNE. DESTRUCTION OF THE "CHESAPEAKE." The gloom that hung over the American cause in 1813 was darkened by news of the encounter between the U.S. 38-gun frigate *Chesapeake* and the British 38-gun frigate *Shannon,* 30 miles off Boston harbor. Acting against his better judgment, the commander of the *Chesapeake,* **James Lawrence** (1781–1813), accepted a challenge from Capt. P. B. V. Broke of the *Shannon.* Lawrence's sole advantage lay in the number of his crew (379) as against that of the *Shannon* (330), but the recently acquired American crew was ill-trained and poorly disciplined. Powerful broadsides raked the *Chesapeake* from stem to stern with unerring effect. A British boarding party of 50 men captured the disabled *Chesapeake* and brought her into Halifax as prize. The British suffered 83 casualties; the Americans, 146. It is said that the last order of the dying Capt. Lawrence was, "Don't give up the ship!" His words became the rallying cry of the U.S. navy.

10 SEPT. BATTLE OF LAKE ERIE. Lawrence's last order was inscribed on the battleflag of the *Lawrence,* flagship of the 28-year-old Capt. **Oliver Hazard Perry** (p. 1127) in the Battle of Lake Erie, the most important naval engagement on the Great Lakes during the war. Ordered from Newport (17 Feb.) to the Great Lakes, Perry reached Presque Isle (27 Mar.), where a flotilla of 2 brigs, a schooner, and 3 gunboats was under construction from materials (with the exception of timber) transported over land and water from Philadelphia by way of Pittsburgh. With the British evacuation of Ft. Niagara and Ft. Erie (27 May), Perry was able to remove 5 vessels from the navy yard at Black Rock (near Buffalo) and bring them to Presque Isle (5 June). During the temporary absence of the British blockading squadron (4 Aug.), Perry floated his heavier vessels over the harbor bar and brought them into deep water. He anchored off the island of Put in Bay, north of the mouth of the Sandusky River. The British squadron under Capt. Robert H. Barclay, consisting of 6 vessels (mounting a total of 65 guns), sailed for Perry's force (9 Sept.). Perry had at his disposal 10 vessels (mounting a total of 55 guns), improvised over the winter of 1812–13, but superior in tonnage and heavy armament. The engagement (10 Sept.), lasting more than 3 hours, was one of the bloodiest naval actions of the war, and resulted in a decisive defeat for the British. Perry's flagship was riddled to pieces, and 80% of her crew were casualties. British casualties: 41 killed, 94 wounded. Perry sent to Gen. Harrison, at Seneca on the Sandusky River, the message (dispatched 10 Sept., received 12 Sept.) containing the words:

"We have met the enemy and they are ours." Perry's victory placed Lake Erie under U.S. control and renewed the threat to Canada. It forced the British to evacuate Malden and Detroit and to fall back to a defensive line along the Niagara frontier.

5 OCT. BATTLE OF THE THAMES. Perry's triumph enabled Harrison to move his main force of about 4,500 infantry across Lake Erie to Middle Sister Island (20 Sept.) and to disembark them (27 Sept.) near Malden in Upper Canada. Meanwhile, against the protests of Tecumseh, Gen. Henry A. Proctor had evacuated Detroit (18 Sept.). The British, with Harrison in pursuit, withdrew from Malden (24 Sept.) and retreated northward by way of Sandwich. Harrison overtook the British and Indians at Moravian Town on the north bank of the Thames River, defeating them in a battle marked by the prowess of a Kentucky mounted regiment under Col. **Richard Mentor Johnson** (1780–1850). U.S. losses: 15 killed, 30 wounded; British: 12 killed, 36 wounded, 477 taken prisoner. The results of the battle were far-reaching. Tecumseh's death in this encounter brought about the collapse of the Indian confederacy and led the Indians to desert the British cause. The U.S. military frontier in the Northwest was made secure, and British power swept from that region (except at Ft. Michilimackinac, which the British occupied until the end of the war).

DRIVE ON UPPER CANADA. Despite their loss of Lake Erie, the British still maintained control of Lake Ontario. Their position was challenged by a combined military and naval action under Gen. **Henry Dearborn** and Capt. Isaac Chauncey, naval commander on Lake Ontario. Their plan was to gain U.S. control by seizing British naval craft at York (Toronto), capital of upper Canada. About 1,600 troops embarked (22

Apr.) from Sackett's Harbor and raided York (27 Apr.), garrisoned by about 600 British troops. The U.S. descent upon York resulted in its surrender and the destruction of 1 ship and capture of another. But 320 Americans (including Gen. Zebulon M. Pike) were killed or wounded by the explosion of a powder magazine; the bypassing of Kingston wrecked the plan to gain control of the lake; and the burning of the public buildings at York (including the assembly houses and the residence of the governor), put to the torch against Dearborn's orders, later gave the British their pretext for burning Washington in 1814.

The raiding force returned to Niagara (8 May), where, during Dearborn's illness, the troops came under the immediate command of Col. **Winfield Scott** (p. 1148), the general's chief of staff. Employing Chauncey's fleet, Scott moved a force of 4,000 men and attacked from the rear (27 May) the British force of 1,600 men stationed at Ft. George under command of Gen. John Vincent. Although the Americans failed to destroy the enemy body, the evacuation of Ft. George compelled the simultaneous withdrawal of the British from Ft. Erie to the south (opposite Buffalo), thus enabling Perry to liberate the vessels at the Black Rock navy yard.

A force of 2,000 Americans pursued Vincent. With only 700 men, Vincent attacked (6 June) at **Stony Creek**, 10 miles from Hamilton, compelling the Americans to fall back on Ft. George. Two American generals, William H. Winder and John Chandler, were captured by the British. The U.S. force at Ft. Erie withdrew (9 June), and that post was occupied by the British over the following winter.

The outstanding action in this sector was the **Battle of Sackett's Harbor** (28–29 May), in which Gen. **Jacob J. Brown** (1775–1828) repulsed a British landing force commanded by Sir George Prevost, governor general of Canada.

2D ATTEMPT TO TAKE MONTREAL. Dearborn was removed from his command (6 July) and replaced by Gen. **James Wilkinson** (1757–1825). The reorganization of the U.S. command also placed (3 July) Gen. **Wade Hampton** at the head of the force on Lake Champlain. Secretary of War John Armstrong, who arrived (5 Sept.) at Sackett's Harbor and established headquarters in the field, projected a combined attack on Montreal by Wilkinson and Hampton by way of the St. Lawrence. The strong Montreal position was supported by some 15,000 British troops in and around the city. Wilkinson's troops were to start from Sackett's Harbor and make the descent of the St. Lawrence; Hampton's force was to march northward from Plattsburg and effect a junction with them. The mutual dislike existing between the 2 generals made cooperation difficult.

Wilkinson left Sackett's Harbor (17 Oct.) at the head of 8,000 men and began (5 Nov.) the descent of the St. Lawrence. The flotilla stopped (10 Nov.) at Chrysler's Farm on the north bank of the river, about 90 miles from Montreal. Learning of an enemy force advancing from the rear, Wilkinson ordered Gen. John Parke Boyd to take the offensive. Boyd's 3 brigades of regulars (about 2,000 men) were virtually routed (11 Nov.) by a British force of 800 led by Col. J. W. Morrison. U.S. casualties: 102 killed, 237 wounded, more than 100 taken prisoner; British: 22 killed, 48 wounded, 12 missing. Informed (12 Nov.) that Hampton had abandoned the attack on Montreal, Wilkinson went into winter quarters (13 Nov.) at French Mills, along the Salmon River.

Hampton had marched his force of about 4,000 men to the Canadian line (19 Sept.) and, instead of proceeding north, had moved west (26 Sept.) to the Chateaugay River, where he awaited news of Wilkinson's progress. Ordered by Armstrong (16 Oct.) to move down the Chateaugay, Hampton established his force about 15 miles from the mouth of the river (22 Oct.). Although he theoretically menaced Montreal and British communications with upper Canada, Hampton had a numerically inferior force and lacked water transportation. His position was untenable. After attacking a smaller British force (**Battle of the Chateaugay**, 25 Oct.), Hampton, without consulting Wilkinson, abandoned the drive on Montreal and fell back on Plattsburg. His decision may have been influenced by his receipt (25 Oct.) of Armstrong's order indicating that the army was going into winter quarters on the American side. Before resigning from the army (Mar. 1814), Hampton presided over the court-martial of Gen. Hull.

29–30 DEC. BURNING OF BUFFALO. When Gen. Vincent dispatched a British force to retake Ft. George, that post was evacuated (10 Dec.) by George McClure, a brigadier general of New York militia. Before withdrawing, McClure burned the village of Newark and part of Queenston. In retaliation, a British force under Col. John Murray captured Ft. Niagara (18 Dec.), killing 67, wounding 11, and taking 350 prisoners. Then the British set loose the Indians, who ravaged Lewiston and the surrounding countryside. Leading a British force of 1,500 men, Gen. Gordon Drummond burned Buffalo and Black Rock (29–30 Dec.), destroying ships and supplies. Ft. Niagara remained in British hands until the end of the war.

RUSSIAN MEDIATION. The diplomatic mission of **John Quincy Adams** (p. 971), named minister to Russia (27 June 1809), benefited from the widening

gulf between Napoleon and Czar Alexander I. The Czar courted French hostility by interfering on behalf of U.S. commerce in Denmark, giving orders to release U.S. ships at Archangel, and issuing an imperial ukase (19 Dec. 1811) admitting U.S. goods to Russian ports. Following Napoleon's declaration of war on Russia (22 June 1812) the Czar learned (6 Aug. 1812) of the U.S. declaration of war on Great Britain, now Russia's ally, and took steps to end Anglo-U.S. differences in order to strengthen the Allied effort against Napoleon. Adams was notified (21 Sept. 1812) of the Czar's offer to mediate between the U.S. and Great Britain. Receiving Adams' communication (8 Mar.), Madison dispatched as peace commissioners James A. Bayard (Del.), a Federalist, and Secretary of the Treasury Gallatin. Bayard and Gallatin reached St. Petersburg on 21 July. In the meantime, however, Lord Castlereagh had declined mediation (5 July).

CASTLEREAGH'S PROPOSAL. Despite his resentment of the Czar's personal interference, Lord Castlereagh was becoming increasingly lukewarm toward the war with the U.S. British victories at Vittoria (21 June) and Leipzig (18–19 Oct.) were counterbalanced by reports of British defeats in the Lake Erie region. He sent (4 Nov.) an official letter to Monroe offering direct negotiation. The proposal was immediately accepted by Madison, who acted upon news of British victories on the Continent and the deteriorating U.S. military situation along the Niagara frontier and in the Lake Champlain region. The Senate confirmed (18 Jan. 1814) Madison's nomination of **J. Q. Adams, J. A. Bayard, Henry Clay,** and **Jonathan Russell** as peace commissioners. The addition of **Gallatin** to the commission was confirmed on 8 Feb. 1814 (Gallatin being replaced as Secretary of the Treasury by George W.

Campbell, Tenn., 9 Feb. 1814). The Flemish town of Ghent was designated as the meeting place, and discussions began 8 Aug. 1814. The British were represented by Lord Gambier, Henry Goulburn, and William Adams.

1814

WAR EMBARGO. New England and New York contractors supplied beef, flour, and other provisions to the British armies in Canada and to enemy vessels off the East Coast. In a special message to Congress (9 Dec. 1813), President Madison recommended an embargo to interdict trade with the enemy. The measure passed in the House 85–57; in the Senate, 20–14; and became law on 17 Dec. 1813. It was modified (25 Jan.) when its strict enforcement along the coast resulted in the near starvation of the people of Nantucket. But the border trade with Canada persisted. Madison gradually recognized that his entire system of commercial restriction had failed in its aim both at home and abroad. His message to Congress (31 Mar.) recommended repeal of the Embargo and Non-Importation Acts. The only significant protest against repeal came from Rep. Elisha Potter (R.I.), who spoke for newly developed manufacturing interests thriving under the exclusion of . imports and for commercial interests profiting from the high prices created by scarcity. New England as a whole, however, supported repeal. As a protective measure for U.S. manufactures, the repeal bill guaranteed war duties for 2 years after peace. The bill passed in the House (7 Apr.) 115–37; the Senate (12 Apr.), 26–4; and with Madison's approval (14 Apr.) commercial restriction came to an end. On 1 Sept. the British landed at the mouth of the Castine River in Maine, captured Castine, and advanced to Bangor. To the end of the war U.S. ships trading with the British paid out £13,-000 in duties to the royal customs officials at Castine.

CREEK WAR. In 1811 Tecumseh had visited the Creek Indians in the Alabama country, apparently attempting to enlist Creek support for his confederacy. A year after the outbreak of the War of 1812, a war faction of the Creeks known as the "Red Sticks," numbering some 2,000 warriors from the upper Creek country, took part in a general uprising along the frontier. A party of U.S. settlers clashed (27 July 1813) with some Indians at Burnt Corn, about 80 miles north of Pensacola. This led directly to the Creek War, which was opened by the Creek attack (30 Aug. 1813) on Ft. Mims, on the east bank of the Alabama River about 35 miles above Mobile. Of the 550 persons in the fort, 250 were massacred and many others burned to death. News of the affair reached **Andrew Jackson** (p. 1068) at Nashville. As major general of Tennessee militia, he called out 2,000 volunteers. Frontier armies were organized also in Georgia and in what later became the state of Mississippi, but the major engagements against the Creeks were fought by the Tennesseans under Jackson.

Tennessee militia under Gen. John Coffee, Jackson's chief subordinate, destroyed the Indian village of **Talishatchee** (3 Nov. 1813). Jackson surrounded and destroyed (9 Nov. 1813) **Talladega**, killing more than 500 Indian warriors. The Tennesseans were repulsed at **Emuckfaw** (22 Jan.) and **Enotachopco Creek** (24 Jan.), and suffered heavy casualties at **Calibee Creek** (27 Jan.). Jackson's major effort came in the early spring of 1814, when he penetrated to the heart of the upper Creek country. At the head of 3,000 men, Jackson and

Coffee attacked (27 Mar.) the fortified position built by the Creeks and their Cherokee allies at the **Horseshoe Bend** of the Tallapoosa River. An estimated 850 to 900 warriors were killed, some 500 Indian women and children were taken prisoner; U.S. casualties: 51 killed, 148 wounded. The campaign was brought to a close by the capitulation of the Creeks. Under the **Treaty of Ft. Jackson** (9 Aug.), signed by only part of the Creeks, two thirds of the Creek lands were ceded to the U.S. and the Indians agreed to withdraw from the southern and western part of Alabama. At almost the same time the Northwest Indians signed the **Treaty of Greenville** (22 July) restoring peace with the U.S. and requiring the Delaware, Miami, Seneca, Shawnee, and Wyandot Indians to declare war on the British. The treaty was signed for the U.S. by William Henry Harrison and Gen. Lewis Cass. Harrison had already resigned his army commission (11 May) and Jackson had been promoted to major general of the regular army (22 May).

BRITISH TAKE THE OFFENSIVE. The overthrow of Napoleon (6 Apr.) enabled the British to concentrate their resources on the war in North America. During the summer of 1814 some 14,000 British troops, veterans of the Duke of Wellington's Peninsular campaign, were sent across the Atlantic. The British planned concerted land and naval operations based on a triple thrust against Lake Champlain, Chesapeake Bay, and New Orleans. To support the general offensive, the blockade along the U.S. coast was enforced more rigorously.

U.S. MILITARY RESOURCES. While the U.S. military establishment was authorized at 58,254, the effective strength of the regular army (Jan.) stood at about 11,000. Under the law of 27 Jan., the army strength was authorized at 62,773; yet by 1 Oct. the regular army

had only 34,000 men. The administration's proposal to raise 100,000 men by conscription was never accepted by Congress. Whenever possible, the government used the militia only as a last resort. In other respects, the military establishment had been improved. Secretary of War Armstrong divided the country into 9 military districts and revamped (Jan.–Feb.) the army command. Incompetent generals were removed from active sectors. Wilkinson, who was relieved from his command (24 March) and acquitted by a court of inquiry, was replaced by Maj. Gen. **Jacob Brown,** who, with the newly promoted Brig. Gen. **Winfield Scott,** was responsible for operations in the Niagara sector. Also promoted to major general was George Izard (S.C.), who replaced Hampton at Plattsburg (1 May).

NORTHERN CAMPAIGN: Niagara. Between Long Point on Lake Erie and York on Lake Ontario the British Gen. Gordon Drummond had under him in the spring of 1814 less than 4,000 troops. The first considerable body of British reinforcements did not begin to arrive in that sector until late in July. In the meantime, Brown and Scott took the offensive and invaded Canada.

5 July. Battle of Chippewa. The U.S. army under Brown, consisting of about 3,500 effectives, crossed the Niagara River and seized Ft. Erie (3 July). Gen. Sir Phineas Riall established a British force along a defensive line on the north bank of the Chippewa River, 16 miles north of Ft. Erie, then, after routing the brigade under Gen. Peter B. Porter, he drew up his main force of 1,500 men on the Chippewa Plain about a mile from the river. He was engaged by Gen. Winfield Scott's brigade, called into action by General Brown as its 1,300 men were belatedly celebrating the 4th of July with a dinner and parade. The outnumbered Americans inflicted a severe defeat upon the British, whose lines crumbled after an action lasting a half hour. Scott's brigade lost 48 killed and 227 wounded; Riall's force lost 137 killed and 375 wounded. The Battle of Chippewa was the only one of the war in which approximately equal numbers of regular troops, neither enjoying the advantage of position, engaged in close combat in extended order. After Chippewa, no force of U.S. regulars was defeated by its British counterpart.

25 July. Battle of Lundy's Lane. In pursuit of Riall, Brown went as far north as Queenston (10 July). He requested (13 July) Commodore Isaac Chauncey, naval commander on Lake Ontario, to leave Sackett's Harbor and join his fleet with the army on the lake shore west of Ft. George, in order to work out a plan of operations for the conquest of upper Canada. Chauncey's failure to cooperate was a decisive factor in the subsequent U.S. retreat from the Canadian side of the Niagara frontier.

With 2,600 effectives at his disposal, Brown moved on the village of **Lundy's Lane,** near Niagara Falls. In the most sharply contested land action of the war, he engaged 3,000 British troops under Riall and Drummond in a 5-hour battle ending in a draw (although the Americans retired, leaving the British in possession of the field). U.S. losses: 171 killed, 572 wounded, 110 missing; British: 84 killed, 559 wounded, 193 missing, 42 taken prisoner.

2 Aug.–1 Sept. Siege of Ft. Erie. The U.S. army fell back on Ft. Erie. A British force of 3,500 under Drummond entrenched before Ft. Erie (2 Aug.) and brought up 6 siege guns from which they laid down a heavy fire (13 Aug.) before assaulting the fort. The attack was repulsed (15 Aug.) by Gen. Edmund Pendleton Gaines, causing heavy losses to the enemy. The British continued their bombardment of the fort, which held

about 2,000 Americans. Gen. Peter B. Porter led 1,600 men in a sortie (17 Sept.) that destroyed the enemy batteries and compelled Drummond to withdraw (21 Sept.). British losses: 609 killed, wounded, and missing; U.S.: 511 killed, wounded, and missing. Later in the year Ft. Erie was evacuated and destroyed by the Americans (5 Nov.) in final abandonment of the drive on Canada.

11 Sept. Lake Champlain and Plattsburg. The British offensive from Canada was planned as a joint land and water operation along the Lake Champlain route. The campaign was committed to Gen. Sir George Prevost, who had under him an army of 11,000 British veterans supported by a fleet of 4 ships and 12 gunboats (mounting a total of 90 guns and carrying about 800 men) commanded by Capt. George Downie. The Americans had at Plattsburg a mixed force of only 3,300 regulars and militia under Gen. Alexander Macomb, who took immediate command after Gen. Izard, with 4,000 troops, marched off for Buffalo (29 Aug.).

In order to meet the British attack, the U.S. required control of Lake Champlain. The naval commander on the lake was 30-year-old Capt. **Thomas Macdonough** (1783–1825), who had taken his post on 12 Sept. 1812, and by the spring of 1814 had at his command a flotilla of 4 ships and 10 gunboats (mounting a total of 86 guns and carrying about 850 men). Macdonough sought to use to full advantage his powerful short-range guns against the long-range pieces of the British. Choosing his position carefully, he anchored his fleet in the narrow channel between Crab Island and Cumberland Head, across the bay from Plattsburg. His vessels were so deployed that the enemy fleet would be obliged to enter a narrow stretch of water under a raking fire and meet him at close range.

Meanwhile, Sir George Prevost, leaving the St. Lawrence frontier (31 Aug.), marched along the western edge of Lake Champlain, driving Macomb's army to a heavily defended position south of the Saranac River, just below Plattsburg. Prevost halted his army (6 Sept.) and waited for his naval support to appear. Downie's fleet rounded Cumberland Head (11 Sept.) and deployed his vessels within 300 yards of Macdonough's fleet. The **Battle of Lake Champlain** lasted 2 hours, 20 minutes. For 2 hours the battle favored the British, but Macdonough won the victory by hauling about his flagship, the *Saratoga*, and bearing down with broadsides on the enemy flagship, the *Confiance*, which struck her flag. The British fleet received no support from Prevost's shore batteries at Plattsburg, at Macdonough's rear. The encounter resulted in the seizure or destruction of all of the British vessels except the gunboats. U.S. losses: 52 killed, 58 wounded; British: 57 killed, 72 wounded. The victory gave the U.S. undisputed control of Lake Champlain and compelled Prevost's army to retreat to Canada. Prevost left behind great quantities of supplies; many of his troops deserted. He was recalled to Canada and was replaced by Sir George Murray.

19–22 Aug. MARCH ON WASHINGTON AND BALTIMORE. A British force of 4,000 veterans commanded by Gen. Robert Ross left France (27 June) under instructions "to effect a diversion" on the U.S. coasts in support of the army in Canada. The instructions authorized quick descents upon selected points for the purpose of destroying naval and military property. The operation, as finally planned by Sir Alexander Cochrane, was in retaliation for York and for the unauthorized U.S. raid on Long Point on Lake Erie (15 May). Cochrane issued orders (18 July) directing his blockading squadron in Southern waters

"to destroy and lay waste such towns and districts upon the coast as you may find assailable." This order was still in effect when Cochrane's squadron and the transports bearing Ross' troops moved up Chesapeake Bay to the mouth of the Patuxent River (Md.) and were landed at Benedict (19 Aug.). The British expedition had 3 aims: to seize or destroy the flotilla of gunboats under Commodore Joshua Barney that had taken shelter in the Patuxent, to descend on Baltimore, and to raid Washington and Alexandria. At the approach of Rear Adm. Sir George Cockburn's fleet, Barney blew up his gunboats (22 Aug.) in order to prevent their seizure by the British.

24 Aug. Battle of Bladensburg. Without encountering resistance, Ross marched to Marlboro (22 Aug.). Meanwhile, hasty preparations were being made at the poorly defended capital, where the incompetent Gen. **William H. Winder** held the command of the Potomac District. From nearby states Winder received militia reinforcements and Commodore Barney brought his 400 sailors to Washington. At the head of a mixed force of about 7,000 men, of whom only several hundred were regulars, Winder took up his position at Old Fields, about 8 miles from Bladensburg, through which the British would inevitably pass. Learning that the British were advancing on Bladensburg (24 Aug.), Winder hastened there, followed by President Madison and most of the cabinet. The Americans, despite the advantage of position, were routed by 3,000 of the enemy and withdrew to Georgetown. Barney, with his 400 sailors and 5 24-pound guns, was left to cover the road about a mile from the village, on the District of Columbia line. The sailors offered stout opposition, holding their ground for a half hour against 4,000 invaders. U.S. losses: 26 killed,

51 wounded; British: 64 killed, 185 wounded.

24–25 Aug. Capture and Burning of Washington. The British marched unopposed to Washington (the panic-stricken U.S. army, together with government officers, had fled to Virginia) and encamped a quarter of a mile from the national capital. Detachments under Ross and Cockburn entered the town and set fire to the Capitol, the White House, all of the department buildings (with the exception of the Patent Office), several private homes, and the office of the *National Intelligencer*. The navy yard was destroyed by Americans at the order of Secretary of the Navy William Jones. The destruction (later estimated at more than $1,500,000) was completed on the morning of 25 Aug. A storm compelled the enemy to retire from the town. The British broke up their camp on the night of 25 Aug. and boarded their transports on the Patuxent. President Madison and some of his cabinet officers returned to Washington on 27 Aug. Denounced by an irate citizenry and militia, Secretary of War Armstrong announced (3 Sept.) his resignation. He had already been replaced by Monroe, who was named (27 Aug.) ad interim Secretary of War.

12–14 Sept. Attack on Baltimore. The British fleet under Cochrane sailed from the Potomac (6 Sept.) and reached the mouth of the Patapsco River, about 16 miles from Baltimore. During the British march on Washington, Baltimore had prepared a formidable system of defense works. Gen. Samuel Smith had under him about 13,000 regulars and militia. A mixed force of about 1,000 men held Ft. McHenry, where a line of sunken hulks barred enemy vessels from the harbor. Ross' army disembarked (12 Sept.) at North Point, about 14 miles from Baltimore, while the fleet moved up the river toward Ft. McHenry. The enemy land advance was opposed by 3,200 militia under Gen. John Stricker. The Americans fell back, but not before inflicting severe casualties on the British (Gen. Ross being mortally wounded), who were delayed until 13 Sept. When the enemy drew up within sight of the heavily defended heights, they halted. The British fleet's bombardment (13–14 Sept.) of Ft. McHenry was unsuccessful (inspiring a witness, Francis Scott Key, to write the verses of "The Star-Spangled Banner"). The invaders abandoned their attempt to capture the town and its shipping and made a rapid withdrawal to their transports. On 14 Oct. the British army left Chesapeake Bay and sailed for Jamaica.

8 Jan. 1815. BATTLE OF NEW ORLEANS. In May, Gen. **Andrew Jackson** was named commander of Military District No. 7, embracing the Mobile-New Orleans area and the U.S. army in the Southwest. He prepared an invasion of Spanish Florida and, disobeying Monroe's orders, seized Pensacola (7 Nov.). He then left Mobile (22 Nov.) for New Orleans, arriving there on 1 Dec. Jackson was unaware that a large British fleet carrying 7,500 veterans under Sir Edward Pakenham had sailed from Jamaica (26 Nov.) and was moving through the Gulf of Mexico for an assault on New Orleans. The British aim was to secure control of the Mississippi and its strategic river valley.

When he learned of the British move, Jackson established his main defense at Baton Rouge, 120 miles away, with a view to opposing an enemy attack by way of the Mississippi. But instead the British fleet of more than 50 craft entered Lake Borgne (13 Dec.), about 40 miles east of New Orleans. Jackson ordered (15 Dec.) his forces at Baton Rouge to speed to New Orleans, and proclaimed martial law in the city. Pakenham spent an entire week disembarking his troops. Without being detected, a British advance guard marched to 7 miles below New Orleans, where the U.S. had no troops or defense works.

Acting swiftly, Jackson led 5,000 troops, supported by the 14-gun war schooner *Carolina,* in a night attack upon the enemy force (23–24 Dec.), checking the British advance. During the delay in enemy operations, Jackson withdrew to a point 5 miles from New Orleans, where he utilized a dry, shallow canal to construct a line of breastworks between a cypress swamp and the east bank of the Mississippi. A furious artillery battle occurred on 1 Jan. 1815, in which the Americans outgunned the enemy. Pakenham waited for reinforcements and, on the morning of 8 Jan. 1815, attacked with his main force of 5,300 men. Behind Jackson's entrenchments were about 4,500 troops, many of them expert Tennessee and Kentucky marksmen armed with long rifles, and followers of French freebooter **Jean Laffite** (c.1780–c.1821). The British regulars, in close ranks, made 2 direct assaults in the face of a withering rifle and artillery fire. The British were cut down and driven back. The battle lasted about a half hour. Gen. Pakenham and 2 other British generals were killed. In this action, and in a tributary engagement on the west bank of the river, British losses: 2,036 men killed and wounded; U.S.: 8 killed, 13 wounded. The surviving British senior officer, Gen. John Lambert, withdrew his troops and reembarked them on 27 Jan.

The Battle of New Orleans, the last major engagement of the war, was fought 2 weeks after the signing of the peace at Ghent (24 Dec.). The greatest American land victory of the war, it had no effect upon its outcome, but acted as a powerful restorative to national pride and created Andrew Jackson a military hero.

MILITARY LOSSES. U.S.: 1,877 killed in action, 4,000 wounded. The total number of enlistments was 531,622 (a misleading figure, for numerous militiamen served or reenlisted as many as 10 times).

24 DEC. PEACE OF GHENT. The peace negotiations opened with the envoys of both nations firmly insisting on leading demands. The U.S. commissioners were under instructions to obtain satisfaction on impressment, blockades, and other maritime grievances (although Monroe's instructions of 27 July sanctioned the withdrawal of the impressment issue if such a concession became necessary). The British demanded the establishment of a neutral Indian buffer state in the Northwest and territorial cessions along the line from Maine to west of Lake Superior (amounting to about one third of the territory held by the U.S.). Neither nation pressed for the other to carry out disarmament on the Great Lakes.

The attitude of the British was governed by reports of the prevailing military situation. When the British learned (27 Sept.) of the burning of Washington, they affirmed the principle of *uti possidetis* (retention of territories held in actual possession). The U.S. supported the principle of *status quo ante bellum* (restoration of prewar territorial conditions). The U.S. commissioners rejected the British terms after receiving news (21 Oct.) of Macdonough's victory on Lake Champlain. The Duke of Wellington, proffered the Canadian command, replied to his government that their waning military fortunes on the Great Lakes did not entitle the British to demand a cession of territory. This consideration, combined with the depletion of the British treasury and Castlereagh's diplomatic embarrassments at the Congress of Vienna, led the British envoys to concede (26 Nov.) to the U.S. view.

The treaty restored the peace, but was silent on the issues over which Great Britain and the U.S. had clashed. No reference was made to impressment, blockades, indemnities, the right of search and visit, and other maritime differences. Nor did its clauses advert to military control of the Great Lakes or a neutral Indian barrier state. The treaty provided for the release of prisoners, a restoration of all conquered territory (although West Florida, taken from the Spanish, remained in U.S. hands), and for the appointment of an arbitral commission to settle the disputed northeastern boundary between the U.S. and Canada. By mutual understanding, the questions of the Great Lakes and the fisheries were left open for future negotiation.

News of the signing reached New York on 11 Feb. 1815. The treaty was unanimously ratified by the Senate (17 Feb. 1815) and was proclaimed by President Madison on the same day.

15 DEC.–5 JAN. 1815. HARTFORD CONVENTION. Early in 1814 numerous Massachusetts towns sent memorials to the state legislature calling for a convention of the New England states to discuss their "public grievances and concerns" and to propose amendments to the Constitution. The convention, called by invitation of the Massachusetts legislature (17 Oct.), assembled in secret session at Hartford, Conn., and was attended by Federalist delegates (26) from Connecticut, Rhode Island, Massachusetts, New Hampshire, and Vermont. Except for delegates from the last 2 states, chosen by local conventions, all were elected by their respective state legislatures.

The convention's proceedings and measures did not reflect the views of the extremist wing of the Federalist party. The Massachusetts delegation was headed by **George Cabot** (1752–1823), leader of the moderate element among the Federalists in the state. Cabot presided over the convention, and an influential role was played by his fellow delegate, **Harrison Gray Otis** (1765–1848). The report issued by the convention included a statement (echoing the states'-rights doctrine of the Kentucky and Virginia resolutions) that "in cases of deliberate, dangerous and palpable infractions of the Constitution, affecting the sovereignty of a State and liberties of the people; it is not only the right but the duty of such a State to interpose its authority for their protection, in the manner best calculated to secure that end."

The convention adopted a set of resolutions calling for (1) protection of the citizens of their states against military conscription unauthorized by the Constitution; (2) use of federal revenue collected within these states to provide for the defense of their territory; (3) an interstate defense machinery, independent of federal provisions, for repelling enemy invasion; (4) a series of amendments to the Constitution, including apportionment of direct taxes and representation among the states according to the number of free persons in each; (5) prohibition of all embargoes lasting more than 60 days; requirement of a two-thirds vote of both houses for declarations of war, restrictions on foreign commerce, and admissions of new states; (6) prohibition of the holding by naturalized citizens of civil office under federal authority; and (7) limitation of presidential tenure to one term. A committee of 3, headed by Otis, was appointed by the Massachusetts legislature to negotiate with the national government. News of Jackson's victory at New Orleans and the signing of the Treaty of Ghent brought an abrupt end to the work of the committee and made the Hartford Convention the butt of popular ridicule. That the convention had been conducted in secrecy gave its opponents a handle which they used for accusing the Hartford gathering of conspiracy, sedition, and treason (although there is no evidence supporting the charge).

1815

PEACETIME MILITARY ESTABLISHMENT. President Madison recommended a standing army of 20,000 men, but the House, by a vote of 70 to 38 (3 March), fixed the army strength at 10,-000. Congress ordered (27 Feb.) the navy's gunboat flotilla to be put up for sale, and the armed vessels on the lakes were stripped of their equipment and laid up. No further reduction was made in the naval establishment; henceforth most of its vessels consisted of cruisers. A 3-man Board of Navy Commissioners was authorized (7 Feb.) to carry out, under the Secretary of the Navy, general supervision of the department.

3 Mar.–30 June. DECATUR'S ALGERINE EXPEDITION. During the War of 1812 the Dey of Algiers renewed his plunder of American Mediterranean commerce. He dismissed the U.S. consul, declared war, seized American vessels, and enslaved U.S. nationals on the pretext that he was not receiving sufficient tribute. An act of Congress (approved 3 Mar.) authorized hostilities against the Dey. Capt. Stephen Decatur sailed from New York (10 May) with 10 vessels, seized the Algerine 44-gun frigate *Mashouda* (17 June), captured the 22-gun brig *Estido* (19 June), and sailed into the harbor of Algiers. He exacted a treaty (30 June) whereby the Dey renounced molestation of U.S. commerce and tribute, and agreed to release all U.S. prisoners without ransom. Decatur received similar guarantees from Tunis (26 July) and Tripoli (5 Aug.), both states making compensation for U.S. vessels which they had permitted Great Britain to seize as prizes. Decatur's action brought to a close the troubles with the Barbary States.

3 July. COMMERCIAL CONVENTION WITH BRITAIN ended discriminatory duties and admitted U.S. commerce to the East Indies without making specific concessions regarding the West Indies.

1816

10 Apr. 2D U.S. BANK. The wartime disorganization of the currency, bringing in its train a general suspension of specie payments, emphasized anew the need for a national bank. Secretary of the Treasury **Alexander J. Dallas** recommended (17 Oct. 1814) the creation of a bank capitalized at $50 million, under which the president would be empowered to suspend specie payments. His scheme was approved in principle by the House (24 Oct. 1814) by a vote of 66 to 40, but an emasculated compromise measure provided for a capitalization of $30 million and did not grant the bank authority to suspend specie payments and to lend up to 60% of its capital to the government. The bill passed in the House (7 Jan. 1815), 120–38; and the Senate (20 Jan. 1815), 20–14. Madison vetoed the bill (20 Jan.), basing his objection on practical considerations, but conceding the constitutional authority of Congress to enact such legislation.

Madison's annual message (5 Dec. 1815) noted that if state banks could not restore a uniform national currency, "the probable operation of a national bank will merit consideration." Congressional debate witnessed a Republican reversal of objections to the measure on constitutional grounds. The debate was also noteworthy for the leading role played by the triumvirate of **John C. Calhoun, Henry Clay** and **Daniel Webster** (p. 1179), to dominate House and

Senate proceedings until the decade before the Civil War.

The bill introduced by Calhoun (8 Jan.) followed in substance the recommendations of Dallas, and was supported by Clay, who in 1811 had maintained that the measure was unconstitutional. Calhoun backed the bill on the ground that it was necessary for the restoration of a sound and uniform circulating medium; for its constitutional sanction, he pointed to the power of Congress to regulate the currency. Clay, explaining his reversal, left the speaker's chair to assert that a change in circumstances made the bank an indispensable necessity, and that Congress had the "constructive power" to authorize the bank. Webster opposed the bill, arguing that no currency reform was required in view of the constitutional and statutory provisions for gold and silver currency. He maintained that the currency problem could be solved by congressional action against the note issues of suspended banks.

The bill, which passed in the House (14 Mar.) 80–71 (with 33 Republicans and 38 Federalists voting against it), and the Senate 22–12, created the 2d Bank of the U.S. with an authorized capitalization of $35 million, of which the government was to subscribe one fifth. In return for its charter privileges, the bank was to pay the government a bonus of $1,500,000. The president was empowered to name 5 of its 25 directors. The bank was authorized to act as a depository for government funds without paying interest for their use. In most other respects, the provisions followed the 1st Bank charter (1791). The central office remained at Philadelphia, and in time had 25 branches throughout the country. The bank began its operations on 1 Jan. 1817. Its first president was William Jones, whose inept management brought a congressional threat to repeal the charter (Jan. 1819). The bank management was reorganized and performed capably under Langdon Cheves, who was named president in 1819. Cheves was succeeded (1823) by **Nicholas Biddle** (p. 986), who served until the expiration of the charter in 1836.

A bill introduced by Webster and adopted by Congress stipulated that after 20 Feb. 1817 the payment of public dues would be collected in either legal currency or in bank notes redeemable in specie. This measure virtually compelled the resumption of specie payments by state banks and resulted in a contracted note issue.

4 Dec. PRESIDENTIAL ELECTION. At the Republican congressional caucus (16 Mar.) the younger element in the party supported William H. Crawford against **James Monroe.** Monroe won by a vote of 65 to 54, thus assuring the continuation of the "Virginia dynasty." **Daniel D. Tompkins** (N.Y., 1774–1825) was nominated for the vice-presidency. In the national elections, Monroe was opposed by the Federalist candidate, **Rufus King** (N.Y.). The waning strength of the Federalists, coupled with their popular discredit during the war years, gave **Monroe** an overwhelming victory. With 4 abstentions in the electoral college, he received 183 electoral votes, King 34. Monroe carried all of the states except Massachusetts, Connecticut, and Delaware. **Tompkins** was elected vice-president.

1817

3 Mar. BONUS BILL VETO. The rapid development of the West and the South created a need for adequate transportation facilities to link the outlying agricultural regions with the markets of the eastern seaboard, a need underscored by the military operations of the War of 1812. In his last annual message (3 Dec.

1816) President Madison recommended a federally subsidized network of roads and canals, but his misgivings about its constitutionality led him to indicate the necessity for a constitutional amendment.

Calhoun reported a bill (23 Dec. 1816) to create a permanent fund for internal improvements by setting aside the $1,500,000 bonus paid by the Bank of the U.S. and all future dividends from bank stock held by the government. Introducing the measure on 4 Feb., he declared that while the Constitution did not specifically authorize internal improvements, sanction could be drawn from the "general welfare" clause and from the power to establish post roads. Although Calhoun regarded the constituitional question as subsidiary to the value of internal improvements as a military necessity and a cement of national union, his argument showed the extent to which the Republican party had accepted the Hamiltonian doctrine of implied powers.

The bill passed in the House (8 Feb.), 86–84, and in the Senate, 20–15. Opposition to the bill was based on sectional rather than constitutional grounds. In the House, 34 opposing votes came from New England Federalists fearful of Western expansion; the South divided, 23 for, 25 against; the Middle States, 42 for, 6 against.

Performing his last act of office, President Madison vetoed the bill on constitutional grounds, stating that to draw authority from the "general welfare" clause for such a purpose "would be contrary to the established and consistent rules of interpretation, as rendering the special and careful enumeration of powers which follow the clause nugatory and improper."

4 Mar. Monroe's inaugural address revealed the Republican party's adoption of Federalist nationalist principles, including support of a standing army and an adequate naval establishment, and "the systematic and fostering care of the government for our manufactures."

ERA OF GOOD FEELINGS. During May–Sept. President Monroe toured the eastern seaboard north of Baltimore and visited the West as far as Detroit. The journey, undertaken ostensibly as an official tour of duty, soon became a popular symbol of the triumph of national feeling over party animosity. Enthusiasm, particularly marked in New England, where Federalists extended a warm welcome to the president, moved the Boston *Columbian Centinel* (12 July) to bestow upon the times the epithet "era of good feelings," a phrase commonly used to describe the state of the nation during Monroe's 2 terms in office (1817–25). The description is superficial and misleading. Although no formal political opposition existed during this period, new political factions and contenders were rising, as indicated by intra-cabinet controversies and by the circumstances attending the presidential election of 1824. During the same era, underlying sectional and economic issues were working basic transformations in the national life.

28–29 Apr. RUSH-BAGOT AGREEMENT. Among the sequels to the Treaty of Ghent was the arrangement for mutual disarmament on the Great Lakes effected by an exchange of notes between the British minister to the U.S., Charles Bagot, and Acting Secretary of State Richard Rush, although the agreement was almost wholly the work of Monroe and Castlereagh, and was the direct outcome of a threatened naval armaments race on the Great Lakes. The British and U.S. agreed to limit their naval forces on inland waters to 1 vessel each on Lake Champlain and Lake Ontario and 2 vessels each on the upper Lakes, none to exceed 100 tons or to have more than 1 18-pound gun. To allay British suspicion that succeeding U.S. administrations might not consider the arrangement binding, the Rush-Bagot agreement was submitted to the Senate, which gave it unanimous approval (16 Apr. 1818). The demilitarization of the Great Lakes, and the supposed extension of the principle to the land frontier, was thereafter regarded as an outstanding example of mutual disarmament. In reality, demilitarization of border fortifications and the equally important seaboard naval defenses was a lengthy and gradual process that did not produce genuine mutual disarmament until after the Treaty of Washington (1871).

1818

JACKSON AND THE FIRST SEMINOLE WAR. Ft. Apalachicola, on the river of that name in Spanish-held East Florida, had been built by the British during the War of 1812. After the war, the fort and the surrounding countryside occupied by Seminole Indians became a refuge for runaway slaves and hostile Indians. The threat to the Georgia border caused the U.S. government to dispatch an expedition which destroyed the fort (27 July 1816) and touched off armed conflict with the Negroes and Indians. A force led by Gen. Edmund P. Gaines was instructed to pursue hostile elements across the Florida boundary to the limits of the Spanish posts. On 26 Dec. 1817 command was transferred to Gen. Andrew Jackson, given similar orders. Upon receiving his instructions, Jackson wrote (6 Jan.) his **"Rhea letter"** to President Monroe, stating: "Let it be signified to me through any channel (say Mr. [congressman] J. Rhea) that the possession of the Floridas would be desirable to the United States and in sixty days it will be accomplished." No immediate action on the letter was taken at Washington by President Monroe and Secretary of War Calhoun. Jackson chose to regard their official silence as tantamount to approval of his subsequent course in Florida. The letter was revived during the political controversies of 1831 when Calhoun, during his break with Jackson, published the Seminole correspondence.

Jackson marched into Florida and seized St. Marks (7 Apr.) and Pensacola (24 May), even as Secretary of State Adams was conducting discussions with the Spanish minister, Luis de Onís, concerning a settlement of the Florida question. During the campaign Jackson captured and court-martialed 2 British traders, **Alexander Arbuthnot** and **Robert Ambrister,** both of whom were accused of aiding the enemy. Arbuthnot was hanged and Ambrister was shot. British public opinion was incensed, but Great Britain took no action. Jackson's raid also had domestic repercussions. His course met the disapproval of all cabinet members except Adams. Two of its members, Calhoun and Crawford, believed Jackson merited stern disciplinary action. A House report (12 Jan. 1819) condemned Jackson's conduct. Anti-Jackson forces in the House, with Henry Clay at their head, proposed a resolution of censure during a debate (18 Jan.–8 Feb. 1819) on the question, and a Senate committee submitted a report (24 Feb. 1819) unfavorable to Jackson. No proceedings were taken against him.

Popular approval of Jackson's Seminole campaign, which brought all of East Florida under U.S. military control, influenced Monroe's decision not to punish Jackson. Actually, Jackson's raid strengthened the administration's hand in foreign affairs. Adams' firm instructions (28 Nov.) to the U.S. minister at Madrid was virtually an ultimatum to the Spanish government. Accusing Spain of aiding and abetting hostilities against the U.S., Adams declared that the U.S. government had acted in self-defense. He defended Jackson's conduct and informed the Spanish government that it faced the alternatives of protecting and controlling Florida or ceding it to the U.S.

20 Oct. CONVENTION OF 1818. Another sequel to the Treaty of Ghent was the Convention of 1818, signed at London by Richard Rush, minister to Great Britain, and Albert Gallatin, minister to France. Under its terms, the northwest boundary between the U.S. and British North America was fixed along the 49th parallel from the Lake of the Woods to the crest of the Rocky Mountains (thus recognizing the northern line of the Louisiana Purchase). No boundary was established for the region west of the mountains, but the 2 powers agreed that the Oregon country was to be open to their subjects for 10 years, stipulating that such joint occupation would not be considered prejudicial to the territorial claims of either power in the Pacific Northwest. The convention gave U.S. nationals fishing privileges off sections of the coasts of Labrador and Newfoundland, and renewed the commercial treaty of 1815.

1819

PANIC OF 1819 was caused by commodity inflation, wild speculation in Western lands, overextended investments in manufacturing, mismanagement of the 2d Bank of the U.S., collapse of foreign markets, and contraction of credit. The last factor was a result of the congressional order (1817) for the resumption of specie payments, a move that strained the resources of state banks, caused many failures, and created hardships for debtors. The most severe effects of the panic were felt in the Southern and Western states. Many of the Western states, among them Missouri and Illinois, enacted legislation for the relief of debtors; in Kentucky such legislation led to the "**relief war**" (1823–26), a contest between the state legislature and judiciary over the constitutionality of replevin and stay laws. A more general result of the panic was widespread resentment against the national bank in rural areas, where it became known as "The Monster," an epithet originated by **Thomas Hart Benton** (Mo., p. 983).

CESSION OF EAST FLORIDA. The Spanish posts seized by Andrew Jackson in East Florida were returned to Spain, but Adams' vigorous instructions, coupled with Spanish colonial difficulties in South America, led the Madrid government to accede to the U.S. demands. The extended negotiations which Adams had conducted with the Spanish minister resulted in the **Adams-Onís Treaty** (signed at Washington, 22 Feb.) whereby Spain renounced all claims to West Florida and ceded East Florida to the U.S. The U.S. renounced its claims to Texas and assumed the claims of its own citizens against Spain to the maximum amount of $5 million. The treaty also defined the western limits of the Louisiana Purchase. The boundary was established from the mouth of the Sabine River on the Gulf of Mexico, proceeding in a broken northwesterly line along the Red and Arkansas rivers and the 42d parallel, from which it was drawn due west to the Pacific Ocean. In effect, the Spanish claims to the Pacific Northwest were surrendered to the U.S. It was stipulated that the Treaty of San Lorenzo (1795) was to remain in force, except as altered by the Adams-Onís Treaty. The Senate ratified the treaty (24 Feb.); because of delays created by the Spanish government, the Senate again ratified on 19 Feb. 1821. The exchange of ratifications became final on 22 Feb. 1821.

2 Feb. DARTMOUTH COLLEGE CASE. In 1816 the Republican-dominated New Hampshire legislature altered the royal charter (1769) of Dartmouth College under which the college had been established, and vested the administration of the institution in a board of trustees appointed by the state. The old board of trustees, asserting that the legislative act was unconstitutional because it impaired the obligation of contracts, sued William H. Woodward, secretary of the university, for recovery of the seal, the charter, and other documents. The state court upheld the action of the legislature, declaring that the body established under the Dartmouth charter of 1769 was a public, not a private, corporation; and that as such its charter was not a contract within the meaning of the Constitution.

The case was appealed to the Supreme Court (*Trustees of Dartmouth College v. Woodward*, 4 Wheaton 518), with Daniel Webster as counsel for the college. Chief Justice Marshall, for the court, held that a charter to a private corporation constituted a contract and was therefore protected under the contract clause of the Constitution against impairment by state legislatures and declared the New Hampshire law invalid.

The decision appeared to place charters of existing private corporations outside the scope of control by the states that had chartered them. While it encouraged business growth, it also led to abuses of corporate privileges. Important modifications of Marshall's opinion in this case were made in *Charles River Bridge* v. *Warren Bridge* (p. 667) in 1837, and in *Munn* v. *Illinois* (p. 671) in 1877.

6 Mar. M'CULLOCH v. MARYLAND. During the postwar period of financial disorganization, state banks took advantage of popular feeling against the 2d Bank of the U.S. to encourage legislation restricting its operations. A Maryland law provided that all banks not created by authority of the state were required to comply with restrictions concerning note issues or, in lieu of that, to pay an annual tax of $15,000. When the Baltimore branch of the National Bank ignored these provisions on the ground that the act was unconstitutional, the cashier of the branch, James W. M'Culloch, was sued by the state.

The case was appealed to the Supreme Court (*M'Culloch* v. *Maryland*, 4 Wheaton 316). The 2 leading points immediately at issue were the constitutionality of the act of Congress establishing the bank, and the constitutionality of the tax imposed by the state legislature. Daniel Webster was among counsel representing the bank, and the proceedings before the court included a notable 3-day argument by William Pinkney, senior counsel for the bank.

The opinion, delivered by Chief Justice Marshall for a unanimous court, ranks among Marshall's most important pronouncements, and is commonly regarded as his most vigorous and detailed exposition of the Constitution. Drawing liberally upon the Hamiltonian doctrine of implied powers, Marshall expounded the origin and nature of the federal union. The powers of the national government are derived from the people and are exercised directly on them, said Marshall; although the national government is limited in its powers, it is supreme within its sphere of action; and a government must be equipped with suitable and effective means to execute the powers conferred on it. He then proceeded to state the doctrine of "loose construction" based on Hamilton's opinion (1791) on the constitutionality of the 1st Bank of the U.S. "Let the end be legitimate," declared Marshall, "let it be within the scope of the constitution, and all means which are appropriate, which are plainly adapted to that end, which are not prohibited, but consist with the letter and spirit of the constitution, are constitutional." The act incorporating the bank was therefore constitutional. As for the power of the Maryland legislature to tax the branch bank, Marshall declared that no state possessed that right, denying it on the ground that "the power to tax involves the power to destroy." Accordingly, he held the act of the Maryland legislature unconstitutional and void.

Of all his other opinions, only that pronounced (1821) in *Cohens* v. *Virginia* (p. 665) compares with this forthright assertion of nationalist doctrine. *M'Culloch* v. *Maryland* set off a nationwide controversy, with declarations by several states against inroads on state power. Marshall himself entered the argument with a series of anonymously published articles answering the criticisms of Judge Spencer Roane of Virginia.

1820

3 MAR. MISSOURI COMPROMISE. At the close of 1819, when the applications of Missouri and Maine for admission to statehood were before Congress, there were 22 states in the Union, 11 slave and 11 free. The slave states: Virginia, Maryland, Delaware, Kentucky, Tennessee, North Carolina, South Carolina, Georgia, Alabama, Mississippi, and Louisiana. The free states: Massachusetts, Connecticut, Rhode Island, Vermont, New Hampshire, New York, New Jersey, Pennsylvania, Ohio, Indiana, and Illinois. The political balance between North and South had been maintained by admitting alternately (1802–19) slave and free states. But even with the three-

fifths ratio operating in their favor, the slave states had only 81 votes in the House of Representatives as against 105 votes held by the free states. In addition, the population of the North was growing at a more rapid pace (free states: 5,152,-000; slave states: 4,485,000). To preserve the sectional balance, the South looked to its equal vote in the Senate.

Late in 1819, the Missouri Territory embraced all of the Louisiana Purchase with the exception of the segments organized as the state of Louisiana (1812) and the Arkansas Territory (1819). The application of the Missouri Territorial Assembly (which had originally petitioned for statehood in 1817) raised the question of the legal status of slavery in Missouri and in the rest of the territory west of the Mississippi. In 1818 there were an estimated 2,000–3,000 slaves in the upper Louisiana country (where slavery went back to Spanish and French rule).

13 FEB. 1819. Tallmadge Amendment. When the enabling legislation for Missouri came before Congress at the outset of 1819, Rep. James Tallmadge (N.Y.) introduced an amendment (13 Feb. 1819) prohibiting the further introduction of slaves into Missouri and providing that all children born of slaves in Missouri after its admission should become free at the age of 25. The amendment set off a fierce debate. In the House, the first clause of the amendment was carried by 87–76 (16 Feb.) and the second clause 82–78 (17 Feb.); but the amendment was lost in the Senate (27 Feb.), 22–16 (1st cl.), 31–7 (2d cl.).

26 JAN. 1819. Taylor Amendment. When the organization of Arkansas Territory came before Congress, Rep. John W. Taylor (N.Y.) moved a proviso forbidding the further introduction of slavery. It was defeated (18 Feb. 1819), and Congress organized Arkansas as a territory (2 Mar. 1819) with its northern boundary at 36°30′ and with no restriction on slavery.

8 Dec. 1819–20 Mar. 1820. Missouri Debate. Sen. Rufus King (N.Y.) maintained that Congress was empowered to forbid slavery in Missouri and to make the prohibition of slavery a prerequisite for admission. Sen. William Pinkney (Md.) in reply asserted that the Union was composed of equal states and that Congress could not restrict Missouri's freedom of action.

17 Feb. 1820. Thomas Amendment. The 16th Congress, convened 6 Dec. 1819, faced the sectional issue with the presentation to Congress (8 Dec. 1819) of a memorial from the people of Maine petitioning for admission to statehood and the adoption (14 Dec. 1819) of a joint congressional resolution admitting Alabama as the 22nd state. A proposition to combine the bill for the admission of Maine with that of Missouri (without restriction on slavery) was passed in the Senate, 23–21 (16 Feb.). Sen. Jesse B. Thomas (Ill.) introduced a compromise amendment providing for the admission of Missouri as a slave state and for the prohibition of slavery in the Louisiana Purchase north of the line 36°30′. The Thomas amendment passed in the Senate (17 Feb.) 34–10. On 18 Feb. the Senate agreed to admit Maine to statehood on condition that Missouri enter as a slave state.

The Senate bill was rejected by the House (28 Feb.). By 91–82, the House passed its own bill prohibiting slavery (1 Mar.), a measure incorporating the restrictive amendment proposed (26 Jan.) by Rep. Taylor (N.Y.). Compromise elements arranged a conference and broke the deadlock. As a result, the Senate received the House bill, eliminated the Taylor amendment, and inserted the Thomas amendment. The Missouri bill was returned to the House,

which passed the compromise measure, 90–87 (2 Mar.). The compromise became final 3 Mar., when by a House vote, 134–42, Maine was admitted as a free state, Missouri as a slave state, and slavery excluded from the Louisiana Purchase north of the line 36°30′. The decisive vote was made possible only by the defection of Northern representatives (whom John Randolph described as "doughfaces"). The admission of Maine as the 23rd state became effective 15 Mar.

19 July. Missouri Constitution. On 6 Mar. Congress authorized the people of Missouri to adopt a constitution. The Missouri convention at St. Louis (12 June) incorporated in the constitution (19 July) a provision excluding free Negroes and mulattoes from the state. This clause provoked antislavery sentiment in Congress when the Missouri constitution was presented to the Senate (14 Nov.) and the House (16 Nov.). A compromise formulated by Henry Clay resulted in the so-called second Missouri Compromise (2 Mar. 1821) providing that the state of Missouri should not gain admission to the Union until the legislature gave assurance that the offending clause would never be construed as sanctioning the passage of any law abridging the privileges and immunities of U.S. citizens. This condition was accepted by the Missouri legislature (26 June 1821), which qualified its pledge by insisting that it had no power to bind the people of the state. On 10 Aug. 1821 President Monroe proclaimed the admission of Missouri as the 24th state.

15 May. AFRICAN SLAVE TRADE. Under the act of 3 Mar. 1819, a $50 bounty was granted to informers for every illegally imported Negro slave seized in the U.S. or at sea, and the president empowered to return to Africa slaves captured under such circumstances. Under the 1820 act the foreign slave trade was declared piracy. In addition to the forfeiture of vessels authorized by the act of 1807, the death penalty was provided for all U.S. citizens engaging in the importation of slaves.

6 DEC. PRESIDENTIAL ELECTION. Because of the poor attendance at the Republican congressional caucus called at Washington in Apr., no formal nominations were made. In the absence of old party distinctions, **Monroe's** candidacy for a 2d term went unopposed. Out of 235 electoral votes (with 3 abstentions), **Monroe** received 231. One dissenting vote by a New Hampshire elector went to John Quincy Adams. **Daniel D. Tompkins** was reelected vice-president, with 218 votes.

1821

5 MAR. The 4th of Mar. falling on a Sunday, Monroe postponed the inaugural exercises until the 5th, thereby setting a precedent.

28 AUG.–10 Nov. EXTENSION OF THE SUFFRAGE. The proposal to abolish the property qualification for voting in New York state, strenuously resisted at the New York Constitutional Convention by such conservatives as Chancellor James Kent (p. 1075) and Chief Justice Ambrose Spencer, carried the day. For extension elsewhere, see p. 762.

1822

4 MAY. CUMBERLAND ROAD BILL VETO. Construction of the Cumberland Road, more commonly known as the National Road or Turnpike, came to a halt with the panic of 1819. The road extended from Cumberland, Md., to Wheeling, on the Ohio River. A bill for the repair of the road, authorizing establishment of toll gates and collection of tolls, passed in the House (29 Apr.), 87–68, and the Senate, 29–7. In his veto

of the bill Monroe held that Congress did not have the right of jurisdiction and construction, but recommended a national system of internal improvements sanctioned by an appropriate constitutional amendment.

LATIN-AMERICAN REPUBLICS. The success of the independence movements in Spanish America after 1817 led Henry Clay to advocate (1818) recognition of the revolutionary governments. In 1821, at Clay's instigation, the House of Representatives adopted a resolution expressing sympathy with the Latin-American republics and indicating the willingness of the House to support the president whenever he should decide to recognize the republics. It was clear that such a move would antagonize the Spanish government, but this consideration became a minor one after the final exchange of ratifications (1821) of the Florida treaty. President Monroe sent to Congress (8 Mar.) a special message proposing recognition of the Latin-American republics. A House resolution (28 Mar.) called for recognition, and the Act of 4 May provided for establishment of diplomatic intercourse with those nations. The Republic of Colombia was formally recognized on 19 June and Mexico on 12 Dec. Chile and Argentina were recognized on 27 Jan. 1823, Brazil on 26 May 1824, the Federation of Central American States on 4 Aug. 1824, and Peru on 2 May 1826.

1823

RUSSIAN CLAIMS. The Czar issued an imperial ukase (4 Sept. 1821) extending Russian claims along the Pacific coast to north of the 51st parallel (which lay within the Oregon country) and closing the surrounding waters (of which the most important was Bering Strait) to the commercial shipping of other powers. The Russian claim was challenged by

Secretary of State Adams, who informed the Russian minister to the U.S. (17 July) "that we should contest the right of Russia to any territorial establishment on this continent, and that we should assume distinctly the principle that the American continents are no longer subjects for any new European colonial establishments." This principle regarding future European colonization in the New World was to become more familiar after its incorporation in the Monroe Doctrine. Under the treaty signed on 17 Apr. 1824, Russia agreed to a 54°40′ line and withdrew the maritime restriction. The U.S. renounced all claims to territory north of that line.

2 Dec. MONROE DOCTRINE. Great Britain was not sympathetic to the revolutionary governments in the former Spanish provinces; yet she was anxious to prevent the revival or extension of Spanish and French power in the New World, primarily in order to keep open to British commerce the rich markets of Latin America. This policy assumed a definite shape after George Canning became British foreign secretary (Sept. 1822).

At the Congress of Verona (Nov. 1822) the Quadruple Alliance (France, Austria, Russia, and Prussia) agreed to act to restore the authority of King Ferdinand VII of Spain, who in 1820 had been forced to accept a constitutional monarchy. The French were authorized to invade Spain, but no action was taken on the French request to intervene in South America. Canning protested against the Holy Alliance program of intervention and broke with the concert of European powers. Early in 1823, Canning attempted to obtain from France a promise barring the acquisition, either by cession or conquest, of any territory in Spanish America. France refused to make the pledge. (Authorities differ over the nature of the French

threat to the Spanish colonies: H. W. V. Temperley, 1925, holds it serious; Dexter Perkins, 1927, no genuine peril; C. K. Webster, 1938, holds that the French failed to formulate specific plans.)

Canning's break with the Holy Alliance was followed by a move to come to an understanding with the U.S., with whom Great Britain had experienced difficulties (1822–23) concerning Cuba. Canning followed up an informal proposal (16 Aug.) to Richard Rush, U.S. minister at London, with a note (20 Aug.) regarding the possibility of joint Anglo-U.S. action against intervention of the Holy Alliance in the New World. Rush was not authorized to commit the U.S., but he indicated (23, 26 Aug.) that this proposition might meet with the favor of his government if the British recognized the Latin-American republics. Rush referred the matter to Monroe, who turned to his unofficial advisers, Jefferson and Madison. Both voiced support of close cooperation with the British.

Secretary of State Adams took a different view. Adams believed that the U.S. should assert its strength and independence by acting alone, in order to create an "American system" in the Western Hemisphere, because (1) he was skeptical of Canning's apparently disinterested motives; (2) viewed the British proposal as a preliminary to exacting from the U.S. a pledge renouncing American designs on Cuba; and (3) felt that so long as the British maintained naval supremacy in the Atlantic, Russia's claims in the Pacific Northwest constituted a greater danger than possible French intervention in South America. Adams stated his position (7 Nov.): "It would be more candid, as well as more dignified, to avow our principles explicitly to Russia and France, than to come in as a cock-boat in the wake of the British man-of-war."

The U.S. government took no action on Canning's proposal. In the meantime, Canning secured his object in the **Polignac Agreement** (9 Oct.), whereby France renounced all intentions to conquer or annex the Spanish-American colonies. He did not resume his efforts to obtain a joint Anglo-American declaration.

The substance of Adams' views was adopted by Monroe and the cabinet. In preparing an announcement of U.S. policy, Monroe acceded to Adams' suggestion that the formulation of views concerning European affairs (such as Greek independence) should be toned down. Adams held that the declaration of policy would be stronger were it based on wholly American interest. However, Monroe rejected Adams' recommendation that the declaration should be embodied in diplomatic communications to the various governments. With the support of Calhoun, Monroe decided to make the announcement in his annual message to Congress (2 Dec.). That portion of the message relating to foreign affairs was largely the work of John Quincy Adams (on the question of substantive authorship, see W. C. Ford, 1902, and S. F. Bemis, 1949, both of whom attribute it to Adams; W. A. MacCorkle, 1923, Dexter Perkins, 1927, and A. P. Whitaker, 1941, ascribe it to Monroe).

The Monroe Doctrine contained 4 major points: (1) the American continents were no longer to be considered as subjects for future colonization by European powers; (2) there existed in the Americas a political system essentially different and separate from that of Europe; (3) the U.S. would consider dangerous to its peace and safety any attempt on the part of European powers to extend their system to any point in the Western Hemisphere; (4) the U.S. would not interfere with existing colonies or dependencies of European powers in the New World; she would not interfere in the internal affairs of European nations; nor would she take part in European wars of solely foreign interest.

At the time of its announcement the Monroe Doctrine drew scant attention from the great powers. In Commons Canning, defending his Latin-American policy, declared (12 Dec. 1826): "I called the New World into existence to redress the balance of the Old." Although the Monroe Doctrine had no standing in international law until the Senate ratified the Act of Havana in 1940, that pronouncement served as the classic definition of the U.S. role in international affairs. But its major significance emerged only after the middle of the 19th century. Over the course of the years, it was modified and extended to meet changing circumstances.

1824

30–31 Mar. "AMERICAN SYSTEM." In a speech defending the protective features of the Tariff of 1824, Henry Clay applied the phrase "American system" to a combination of the protective tariff and a national system of internal improvements as a means of expanding the domestic market and lessening U.S. dependence upon overseas sources.

30 Apr. INTERNAL IMPROVEMENTS. In 1818, William Lowndes (S.C.) submitted to the House 4 resolutions on internal improvements. The House (89–75) declared that Congress had authority to appropriate money for building military roads and other land routes, canals, and improved natural waterways. But following a debate on the constitutionality of these propositions, the House rejected all of them. Monroe's veto (1822) of the Cumberland Road Bill was sustained by both houses. The widespread demand, particularly from the West, for more and improved internal routes resulted in the introduction of the General Survey Bill empowering the president to initiate surveys and estimates of roads and canals required for national military, commercial, or postal purposes. By 115–86 (10 Feb.) the House passed the bill. The vote by sections: New England, 12 for, 26 against; the West, 43 for, none against; the South, 23 for, 34 against; the Middle States, 37 for, 26 against. The Senate passed the bill 24–18.

CABINET INTRIGUES. Between 1820 and 1822 political factionalism linked to presidential ambitions caused dissension within the cabinet. When the supporters of Secretary of War John C. Calhoun obtained his permission (28 Dec. 1821) to announce his presidential candidacy, Calhoun was attacked by the adherents of Secretary of the Treasury William H. Crawford. The political rivalry between Calhoun and Crawford extended even to the administration of government business. The Senate, dominated by Crawford's followers, called for retrenchment in Calhoun's War Department expenditures and refused to approve nominations of military officers made by President Monroe at the recommendation of Calhoun.

Suspecting that Crawford was intriguing against the administration and was also attempting to establish a new political party, Monroe asked Crawford for an explanation. Crawford denied that he opposed the administration program, and assured the president of his loyalty. Monroe sought to remain neutral during the contest for power within the cabinet, but the realization that he would soon be leaving office reduced his influence.

A direct outcome of factionalism at high levels was the "A.B." plot. Under the signature "A.B.," Sen. Ninian Edwards (Ill.) published a series of articles (1823) in the Washington *Republican,* the organ of the Calhoun forces. The articles attacked Crawford for malfeasance in office. It was widely believed that Edwards' object in accusing Crawford was to injure the latter's standing as a presidential candidate. Edwards, who was appointed minister to Mexico 4 Mar., was recalled to Washington to testify before a House investigating committee. On 19 Apr. Edwards preferred charges against Crawford, but the Secretary of the Treasury was exonerated (25 May) by the House committee.

PRESIDENTIAL CAMPAIGN. The dissolution of the old party distinctions, and a rising opposition to the congressional caucus as a means of choosing the presidential candidate, left most of the nominations to the state legislatures. **John C. Calhoun** announced his candidacy in 1821. The Tennessee legislature nominated **Andrew Jackson** (20 July 1822), who was also chosen (4 Mar.) by a state nominating convention at Harrisburg, Pa. The action of the Tennessee legislature, which followed its move by a formal protest against the caucus procedure (1823), was the signal for other state and local resolves. The Kentucky legislature nominated **Henry Clay** (18 Nov. 1822); **John Quincy Adams** was nominated by a meeting (15 Feb.) at Boston. The rump congressional caucus (attended by only 66 out of the 216 Republican representatives) that nominated (14 Feb.) **William H. Crawford** (1772–1834) was the last one to nominate a presidential candidate.

A paralytic stroke virtually eliminated Crawford (Sept. 1823). Calhoun withdrew and became vice-presidential candidate on the Jackson and Adams tickets. Adams held the strongest position; although he did not take part in trading for votes, he was to profit by the dissensions among the candidates from the

South and West. In addition, his support of the "American system" brought him close to Clay, who had strong differences with Jackson. Most of the candidates supported a protective tariff and internal improvements. To these issues, Jackson added his attacks upon "King Caucus," and supported the right of the people to choose their own president.

1 Dec. PRESIDENTIAL ELECTION. Jackson received 99 electoral votes; Adams, 84; Crawford, 41; and Clay, 37. **Calhoun,** receiving 182 electoral votes, was chosen vice-president. As no candidate had a majority (popular vote cast: Jackson, 152,933; Adams, 115,696; Clay, 47,136; Crawford, 46,979 [in 6 states the legislature cast the electoral vote]) the choice of the president was submitted to the House, which considered only the 3 leading candidates. Clay, eliminated, advised his friends (8 Jan. 1825) to vote for Adams; and the Kentucky representatives, acting under Clay's influence, disobeyed the instructions of their state legislature to vote for Jackson and instead cast their ballots for Adams. In the House vote (9 Feb. 1825), **Adams** received the votes of 13 states to 7 for Jackson and 4 for Crawford.

The charge that Clay had made a "corrupt bargain" by supporting Adams in return for the promise of the Secretaryship of State was made (Jan. 1825) by Rep. George Kremer (Pa.) in an unsigned letter to a newspaper. Clay demanded a congressional inquiry, but his accuser declined to appear. The charge received popular credence after Clay was appointed Secretary of State in the Adams cabinet, and was repeated by Jackson in 1827. Although no persuasive evidence exists in support of the charge, the accusation clung to Clay's name until the end of his career.

The election of Adams ended the succession of the "Virginia dynasty." Over the winter of 1824–25, the Republican party divided into two groups. The Adams-Clay wing became known as the **National Republicans,** while the "Jackson men" emerged as the **Democratic Republicans.**

1825

CIVIL SERVICE POLICY. In keeping with his declared aim to lend a nonpolitical character to his administration, Adams refused to employ against his opponents the principle of political rotation in federal appointive offices. He asserted that he would renominate any officeholder who did not warrant removal for official misconduct or incompetence (only 12 removals were made during his single term in office). Many of the incumbents were appointees of Crawford or John McLean (Jackson-Calhoun supporter) and used their influence against the president. Adams' deliberate refusal to have any connection with patronage cost him an essential means of building a political party.

AN OPPOSITION EMERGES. When the 19th Congress convened (5 Dec.) it soon became apparent that the forces opposed to Adams were beginning to coalesce. Adams' first annual message to Congress (6 Dec.) crystallized the opposition. Taking a broad nationalist view of constitutional powers, Adams recommended construction of roads and canals, a national university, an astronomical observatory, standardization of weights and measures, the exploration of the U.S. interior and the Pacific Northwest coast, and the passage of laws for the promotion of agriculture, commerce, and manufacturing and the encouragement of the arts, sciences, and literature. These proposals antagonized Southern adherents of states' rights.

There were other signs of opposition to the president. Calhoun, using the recently granted powers of the vice-president to appoint Senate committees, filled half of the important posts with senators who did not support the administration program. Adams, however, could count on the alliance of New England and the West based on common loyalty to the "American system"; so long as factionalism was rife in Southern politics, Adams still held the initiative.

1826

6 JAN. The first number of the *United States Telegraph* appeared at Washington, edited by Duff Green, a close friend of Calhoun and supported by senators and representatives opposed to the Adams administration.

PANAMA DEBATE. The first organized test of the Adams administration arose over the question of the mission to the Panama Congress. That assembly had been called for 1826 by Simon Bolívar, whose original invitation to the Latin-American republics (1824) had been extended by Colombia and Mexico to include the U.S. (1825). While not fully aware of the aims of the congress, President Adams, with the support of Secretary of State Clay, believed that the dominant position of the U.S. in the Western Hemisphere demanded representation at the congress. It was later revealed that the program of the congress looked to a union of the Latin-American republics against Spain or other unfriendly nations and the establishment of a general assembly equipped with full war powers binding upon the member countries, neither of which were actually provided. Following his reference to the congress in his annual message (6 Dec. 1825), Adams sent a special message to the Senate (26 Dec. 1825). He nominated 2 delegates to the Panama Congress and stressed the limited and consultative nature of U.S. participation.

The opposing coalition in the Senate, brought together on this issue by Calhoun and Sen. Martin Van Buren (N.Y.), attacked the message on the ground (1) that since the Panama Congress would have the status of a government, U.S. participation would sharply diverge from traditional concepts of national independence and neutrality; (2) that Adams had accepted the invitation without consulting the Senate. On this score, Sen. John Branch (N.C.) submitted a resolution affirming the authority of the Senate to pass upon appointments of ambassadors or other public ministers. Southern animosity was aroused on the slavery question. Adams' message had made no reference to slavery, but it was commonly known that the subject would enter into the proceedings at the Panama Congress, where some republics under the control of Negroes would be represented.

The Senate Committee on Foreign Relations reported unfavorably (11 Jan.) on the proposal, but the Senate approved the mission, 24–19 (14 Mar.), and the House approved the appropriation for it, 134–60 (25 Mar.). The U.S. was never represented at the congress. Of the 2 delegates, Richard C. Anderson died en route (24 July) and John Sergeant had not gone farther than Mexico City when the congress adjourned.

During the Panama debate John Randolph made his famous charge against the Adams-Clay "corrupt bargain." Randolph declared from the Senate floor (30 Mar.) that the administration was "the coalition of Blifil and Black George," the combination "of the puritan with the black-leg." Randolph's accusation was followed by a challenge from Clay. The duel, fought on the Virginia bank of the Potomac (8 Apr.), left both contenders unharmed.

4 JULY. Death of Thomas Jefferson at Monticello and of John Adams at Quincy,

Mass. on the 50th anniversary of the adoption of the Declaration of Independence (p. 107). Jefferson's death occurred a few hours before that of Adams. Shortly before he died, Adams is reported to have exclaimed: "Thomas Jefferson still survives."

1827

BROADENING OF DEMOCRACY. The movement against property-holding and taxpaying qualifications for voting was initiated before the War of 1812, with the abolition of those requirements in New Jersey (1807) and Maryland (1810), but even greater progress was made after 1815, with the admission of new Western states. The constitutions of Indiana (1816), Illinois (1818), and Alabama (1819) provided for white manhood suffrage; Maine, in 1820, made the same provision. The era of state constitutional revision between 1816 and 1830 saw a liberalizing of the constitutions of Connecticut (1818), Massachusetts (by amendments, 1821), and New York (1821), all of which abolished property qualifications. Religious qualifications for voting and officeholding were removed, as in Maryland (by constitutional amendment, 1826). There was also a trend toward apportionment on the basis of population rather than taxpayers, and an increase in popular elective offices. The selection of presidential electors was gradually transferred from the state legislatures to the people. By 1828 only 2 of the 24 states in the Union (S.C. and Del.) still chose electors through their legislatures.

REVIVAL OF THE TARIFF QUESTION. Dissatisfied with the Tariff of 1824 because it failed to eliminate British competition, the wool-growing and woolen textile interests of the Northeast attempted to obtain higher duties. A bill introduced 10 Jan. incorporated 3 minimum valuations for woolen goods and made the importation of those articles virtually prohibitive. The bill was passed in the House (10 Feb.), but was lost in the Senate when Vice-President Calhoun, aligning himself with the antitariff forces, cast the decisive vote.

The rejection of this bill touched off a move for higher duties generally. At the call of the advocates of protection, a convention, dominated by the woolen interests, met at Harrisburg, Pa. (30 July–3 Aug.), with 100 delegates from 13 states in attendance. It called for the establishment of the minimum-valuation principle on textiles and proposed additional duties on hemp, flax, hammered bar iron and steel, and other goods. The memorial of the Harrisburg Convention was presented to Congress (24 Dec.). Dependent upon a world market for the disposal of its agricultural commodities, the South opposed a protective tariff which meant higher prices for manufactured goods.

South Carolina, whose economy had suffered gravely under the exhaustion of cotton lands (in general the effects of the Panic of 1819 lingered in the South longer than the North), took the lead against protectionism. In a speech made at Columbia, S.C. (2 July), **Thomas Cooper** (1759–1839), speaking for a small minority, condemned the economic ambitions of the North as a menace to Southern equality within the Union, and declared that the South would have to calculate the value of the federal Union, for the "question is fast approaching the alternative of submission or separation."

1828

19 MAY. TARIFF OF ABOMINATIONS. The 20th Congress that convened on 3 Dec. 1827 witnessed the transfer of leadership from the administration forces to the "Jackson men." The protectionist scheme of the Harrisburg Convention having been rejected, the

Jacksonians decided to exploit the tariff issue to discredit Adams. Crucial in the impending national elections were the Middle States. Jackson supporters reasoned that in any case the vote of New England would go to Adams and the vote of the South to Jackson. The Jacksonians who dominated the House Committee on Manufactures planned their tactics accordingly. They would report a bill with such excessively high duties (particularly at the cost of New England interests) that no section would vote for it; the responsibility for the defeat would be attributed to Adams; and the protectionist interests of the Middle States would be alienated from Adams. The Jacksonians, without offending Southern free-trade adherents, would then assure the Pennsylvanians that they favored protection of their iron interests.

The House committee framed a bill imposing very high duties on raw materials, iron, hemp, and flax, and eliminated some of the protective features pertaining to woolen goods. The bill was introduced in the House on 31 Jan., and discussion began on 4 Mar. The alliance of the Middle States and the South engineered by Martin Van Buren and Calhoun voted down every attempt by the New Englanders to amend the bill, and confidently awaited its defeat. To the surprise of the Jacksonians, New England voted for the bill despite its deficiencies, supporting it on the ground that it embodied the protective principle. The bill passed in the House, 105–94 (23 Apr.); the Senate, 26–21 (13 May). The Jacksonians of the West and the Middle States voted for the tariff, thereby depriving the Adams-Clay forces of a campaign issue. John Randolph asserted that "the bill referred to manufactures of no sort or kind, but the manufacture of a President of the United States."

19 Dec. Resolves of South Carolina Legislature. The South Carolina legislature promptly adopted a set of 8 resolutions (19 Dec.) terming the tariff unconstitutional, oppressive, and unjust. The Georgia legislature also protested (30 Dec.), as did Mississippi (5 Feb. 1829) and Virginia (4 Feb.). The Carolina resolutions were accompanied by the *South Carolina Exposition and Protest*, written (but not signed) by Calhoun. A lengthy essay on the theory of state sovereignty and minority rights, the *Exposition* expounded the doctrine of nullification by a single state. With it, Calhoun formally abandoned nationalism and identified himself with the particularist views of his state and section.

PRESIDENTIAL CAMPAIGN. Nominated for the presidency by the Tennessee legislature (Oct. 1825), **Jackson** resigned from the U.S. Senate and began to build his political following for the election of 1828. His campaign was managed by a group of able editors and politicians including Amos Kendall, William B. Lewis, Duff Green, James Buchanan, and John H. Eaton. Jackson could count on the Southern vote, while in much of the West "Old Hickory" was acclaimed as a frontier military hero, a symbol of the common man, and a supporter of the "American system." **John C. Calhoun** was vice-presidential candidate on the Jackson ticket.

The National Republican Convention at Harrisburg, Pa., nominated **Adams** for a 2d term with **Richard Rush** (Pa.) as his running mate. The Jacksonians, now called Democrats, based their campaign on personal grounds, and their opponents retaliated in kind. The "corrupt bargain" charge was used against Adams and Clay with telling effect.

3 Dec. PRESIDENTIAL ELECTION. **Jackson** received 647,231 popular votes and 178 electoral votes; Adams 509,097 popular votes, 83 electoral votes. **Calhoun**, with 171 electoral votes, was re-elected vice-president. The crucial states of Pennsylvania and New York went for Jackson. The vote in New York was close: 140,763 votes (20 electoral) for Jackson; 135,413 votes (16 electoral) for Adams. New York had been swung into the Jackson ranks by Martin Van Buren and William L. Marcy, leaders of the powerful "Albany Regency" that had succeeded the old Republican machine in the state and maintained its power by exercising the "spoils system."

1829

4 Mar. In his inaugural address, Jackson pledged himself to economy in government, a proper regard for states' rights, a "just and liberal policy" toward the Indians, and a revamping of the federal civil service. The address contained no clear statement of policy on the tariff, internal improvements, the currency, or the Bank of the U.S. The boisterous reception at the White House, where Western frontiersmen mingled with Washington society, became a symbol of the common people's arrival at political power.

"KITCHEN CABINET." Shortly after taking office, Jackson suspended the practice of holding cabinet meetings. For advice on policy he drew upon a small group of unofficial political confidants whom his opponents called the "Kitchen Cabinet" (also known as the "Lower Cabinet"). Among them were **Amos Kendall, Isaac Hill, William B. Lewis, Andrew J. Donelson,** and **Duff Green.** Some of them held minor government posts: Kendall was fourth auditor of the Treasury, while Lewis served as second auditor. The "Kitchen Cabinet" was at the height of its influence between 1829 and 1831. With the reorganization of the cabinet (1831), Jackson relied upon the members of that body for counsel.

"SPOILS SYSTEM." The phrase, "to the victor belongs the spoils," was used (1831) by Sen. William Learned Marcy (N.Y.) during the course of a congressional debate. The "spoils system" refers to the use of patronage for party purposes. First president to use the system was Jefferson, who employed it with restraint. By 1829, it was entrenched in the political machines of several states, including New York and Pennsylvania. Although Jackson introduced the system into national politics on a scale hitherto unmatched, he did not make wholesale political removals. The peak of Jackson's so-called "clean sweep" was reached during his first year in office, when only about 9% of the officeholders were replaced. During Jackson's 2 terms (1829-37) not more than 20% of the officeholders were removed on political grounds.

WORKINGMEN'S PARTY (also p. 762) was organized in Philadelphia (1828). Its candidates were defeated, but the party continued to agitate for free public education and for the protection of mechanics against competition from prison contract labor. In New York the Workingmen's party was formed in 1829, under the leadership of Robert Dale Owen, Thomas Skidmore, Fanny Wright, and George H. Evans. The Jacksonians attempted to exploit the party for their own ends. Erastus Root, speaker of the assembly and an adherent of Van Buren, sought to win the Workingmen's nomination (16 Apr. 1830) for governor. In turn, Fanny Wright and Robert Dale Owen split the party and nominated (14 Sept. 1830) Ezekiel Williams for governor.

1830

19-27 Jan. WEBSTER-HAYNE DEBATE had its inception when Sen. **Samuel A. Foot** (Conn.) proposed a resolution (29 Dec. 1829) inquiring into the expediency of temporarily restricting the sale of public lands. The resolution, taken up on 13 Jan., came at a time when Jackson had not yet made any public announcement on the nullification stand taken by South Carolina. **Thomas Hart Benton** (Mo.) charged (18 Jan.) that Northeastern interests were attempting to check the settlement and prosperity of the West and was supported in this by **Robert Y. Hayne** (S.C.). In a speech (19 Jan.) invoking strict constructionist and states'-rights views against federal interference, Hayne asserted that "the very life of our system is the independence of the States, and that there is no evil more to be deprecated than the consolidation of this government." Hayne was answered (20 Jan.) by Daniel Webster (Mass.), who deplored the tendency of some Southerners to "habitually speak of the Union in terms of indifference, or even of disparagement."

From this point onward the debate became a contest between Webster and Hayne, and was eventually confined to the origin and nature of the Constitution and the Union. Hayne's first reply (21, 25 Jan.) advanced the doctrine of state sovereignty and nullification. Webster's reply to Hayne (26, 27 Jan.) was one of the most eloquent orations ever delivered in the Senate. Passing over the Southerner's expression of economic grievances, Webster denied the validity of the constitutional doctrines advanced by Hayne, and expounded the nature of the Union. The states are sovereign only so far as their power is not qualified by the Constitution, said Webster, but only the Constitution and the national government are sovereign over the people. In the event of disagreement between the states and the national government, the settlement of the dispute rested with the agencies provided for that purpose in the Constitution: the federal courts, the amending power, and regular elections. Attacking disunionist tendencies, Webster closed his oration with an eloquent per-

oration celebrating "Liberty *and* Union, now and forever, one and inseparable!"

Hayne's second reply to Webster (27 Jan.) included the statement that the federal government resulted from the compact between the states, and that each party to the compact was the rightful judge of infringements upon its rights. Questions of sovereignty, said Hayne, are not subject to judicial consideration; therefore the right of state interposition is "as full and complete as it was before the Constitution was formed." In his rebuttal (27 Jan.) Webster opposed Hayne's historical theory of the Constitution by attempting to show that the Constitution was not the result of a compact, but was established as a popular government with a distribution of powers binding upon the national government and the states.

13 Apr. "OUR UNION—" The Jefferson Day Dinner, held at Brown's Indian Queen Hotel in Washington, was arranged by Senators Benton and Hayne, ostensibly to align the Democratic party with Jeffersonian principles and to signify the alliance between the West and the South. Jackson gave much thought to the phrasing of his volunteer toast, given after he had heard 24 prepared toasts, many of them alluding to the propriety of state sovereignty and nullification. Jackson offered his toast: "Our Union: It must be preserved." Calhoun responded: "The Union, next to our liberty, most dear. May we always remember that it can only be preserved by distributing equally the benefits and burdens of the Union." At the request of Hayne, Jackson agreed to amend his toast for publication, to read: "Our Federal Union—." But the nullifiers could find only small comfort in this concession.

27 May. MAYSVILLE ROAD VETO. In his first annual message to Congress (8 Dec. 1829) Jackson referred to the constitutional objections that had been raised against internal improvements. He recommended the distribution of the surplus revenue among the states according to their congressional apportionment, the states to use the funds at their own discretion. Meanwhile, he had been heeding Van Buren's advice to put an end to congressional logrolling that resulted in the construction of internal improvements at federal expense. Van Buren had a political object: to strike at the Clay party.

The opportunity arose when Congress passed a bill authorizing a government subscription of stock to the amount of $150,000 in the Maysville, Washington, Paris, and Lexington Turnpike Road Co., for the construction of a 60-mile road in Kentucky. In his first veto, on expediency and strict constructionist grounds, Jackson declared that as the road lay within the limits of a single state and had no connection with any established system of improvements, it was not embraced by national jurisdiction. If federally subsidized roads and canals were thought desirable, said Jackson, they should be sanctioned by a constitutional amendment.

Jackson's concession to Southern states' rights was made without withdrawing his general support of internal improvements. Thus Jackson kept his Southern political support and did not antagonize the North and the West. His subsequent policy on internal improvements terminated sizable federal expenditures on roads and canals, although it did not materially affect the improvement of harbors and rivers. The only large landroute project he approved was the Cumberland Road Bill (31 May).

7 Dec. Publication of the first number of the *Washington Globe.* The growing gulf between Jackson and Calhoun led the president and the "Kitchen Cabinet" to arrange for the establishment of an administration newspaper. Francis P. Blair, Sr., of Kentucky, was chosen to edit the *Globe.* After the formal break between Jackson and Calhoun, Duff Green's *United States Telegraph* (with the aid of a loan from the Bank of the U.S.) became an antiadministration organ.

1831

JACKSON'S BREAK WITH CALHOUN. In the spring of 1830 Jackson learned that in 1818 Calhoun, as Secretary of War, had favored punishing Jackson for his conduct in the Seminole War. The letter containing this charge was written by William H. Crawford and was made known by William L. Lewis and others for the purpose of discrediting Calhoun. Jackson, who hitherto believed that Calhoun had supported him in 1818, requested an explanation. Calhoun's defense of his position did not satisfy the president. "Understanding you now," wrote Jackson, "no further communication with you on this subject is necessary" (30 May 1830). At Calhoun's direction, a pamphlet containing the correspondence on the Seminole affair was published (15 Feb.). It angered Jackson, completed the breach between him and Calhoun, and helped to confirm Jackson in his choice of Van Buren as presidential successor.

EATON AFFAIR. The split in Jackson's cabinet between the supporters of Calhoun and those of Van Buren as heir apparent to the presidency impinged upon a Washington social feud waged against Peggy O'Neale, a barmaid who had become (1829) the second wife of Secretary of War John H. Eaton. Jackson supported Mrs. Eaton, whose status in society soon became a political issue. Mrs. Calhoun and the wives of other members of the cabinet refused to receive Mrs. Eaton. Jackson's stubborn efforts to compel recognition met with little success; he encountered resistance even in the White House, where Mrs. Andrew J. Donelson withdrew as hostess rather than call on Mrs. Eaton. When he raised the issue at a cabinet meeting, the only cabinet member to support Mrs. Eaton was the widower Martin Van Buren, who thereby increased Jackson's favor for him.

Van Buren, who saw the Eaton affair as a liability to the administration, submitted his resignation, aware that this would precipitate a reorganization of the cabinet. When Eaton learned that Van Buren's resignation was impending, he offered his own.

CABINET REORGANIZATION. The resignations of Eaton (7 Apr.) and Van Buren (11 Apr.) were accepted by Jackson, who then requested and received those of Secretary of the Treasury Samuel D. Ingham (19 Apr.), Secretary of the Navy Branch (19 Apr.), and Attorney General John M. Berrien (15 June). Van Buren was named minister to England, and Jackson ended the Washington social war by appointing Eaton governor of Florida. A reorganized cabinet was formed with an eye to harmony: Levi Woodbury of New Hampshire, Secretary of the Navy (23 May); Edward Livingston of Louisiana, Secretary of State (24 May); Roger B. Taney of Maryland, Attorney General (20 July); Lewis Cass of Ohio, Secretary of War (1 Aug.); and Louis McLane of Delaware, Secretary of the Treasury (8 Aug.). The only cabinet member retained was Postmaster General William T. Barry.

JACKSONIAN DIPLOMACY. West Indian Trade. U.S. shipping interests suffered under the severe British restrictions on direct trade with the West Indies. The unsatisfactory results of the halfway measures adopted (1822–25) by the U.S. and Great Britain led both governments to make provisions (1826–27) for closing West Indian ports to

direct trade. After taking office, Jackson adopted a moderate approach on the issue, basing his application for a reopening of trade on the grounds of a new administration, a change in public opinion, and the restoration of privileges rather than rights. Congress authorized Jackson (29 May 1830) to take reciprocal action in the event British colonial ports were reopened. After some months of negotiation Jackson announced by proclamation (5 Oct.) that trade was reopened with the West Indian ports on the basis of reciprocal privileges.

French Spoliation Claims. Claims against the French for depredations on U.S. commerce during the Napoleonic wars had been pending since 1815. The negotiations lagged because of French counterclaims based on alleged U.S. violations of a commercial clause in the Louisiana Treaty. Jackson instructed William C. Rives, minister to France, to secure a satisfactory adjustment. A treaty was concluded (4 July) whereby France agreed to pay 25 million francs and the U.S. 1,500,000 francs for spoliations committed against the subjects of either nation in 6 annual installments. Delay in the French payment of the first installment caused Jackson to recommend (annual message, 2 Dec. 1834) reprisals on French property in the event no provision was made for payment. The French voted an appropriation (25 Apr. 1835) on condition that Jackson apologize for certain expressions in his message. Jackson replied in his annual message (7 Dec. 1835): "The honor of my country shall never be stained by an apology from me for the statement of truth and the performance of duty." In a special message to Congress (15 Jan. 1836) Jackson again recommended reprisals and an expansion of naval and coastal defenses, but at the same time made an adroitly phrased offer of conciliation. Great Britain's offer of mediation (27

Jan. 1836) was accepted, and on 10 May 1836 Jackson announced that the French had paid 4 installments. Other spoliation claims to the amount of $5 million based on depredations committed before 1800 were incorporated in a bill that passed the Senate (28 Jan. 1835), but did not receive House action.

ANTI-MASONIC PARTY. The mysterious disappearance in western New York of **William Morgan** (Sept. 1826), who had prepared an exposé of Freemasonry, led to a series of official inquiries and court trials (1827–31) that threw no light on the fate of Morgan but revealed that virtually all of the officeholders in New York State were members of the order. During the subsequent popular reaction against Freemasonry opponents of Jackson (who was a Mason) exploited the issue. In mid-1830 the Anti-Masons appeared in New York State as a political party opposed to Jackson. Anti-Masonry and antipathy to all kinds of secret societies spread to other states, and a national convention of Anti-Masons assembled at Baltimore (26 Sept.), nominating **William Wirt** (Md., 1772–1834) for president and Amos Ellmaker (Pa.) for vice-president. The Anti-Masonic party was the first third party in the U.S., the first to hold a national nominating convention, and the first to announce a platform. The party declined after the election of 1836 and was eventually absorbed by the Whigs.

ABOLITION MOVEMENT (p. 757).

13–23 Aug. NAT TURNER INSURRECTION (p. 757).

1832

INDIAN POLICY. Jackson's Indian policy was based mainly on the prospect of voluntary emigration to tracts west of the Mississippi set aside for permanent occupancy. Under the act of 28 May 1830 Congress made provision for re-

moval; the act of 30 June 1834 established a special Indian territory in the Arkansas country.

Under a series of treaties (1791 *et seq.*) concluded with the U.S., the Cherokee inhabiting the state of Georgia were recognized as a nation with their own laws and customs. However, Georgia settlers encroached upon the Cherokee as well as the neighboring Creek Indians. Alabama and Mississippi likewise violated federal treaties in annexing the lands of the Choctaw and the Chickasaw. Under a state law of 20 Dec. 1828, Georgia pronounced the laws of the Cherokee Nation null and void after 1 June 1830. After gold was discovered on the Cherokee lands (July 1829), the Cherokee sought relief in the Supreme Court. In an opinion delivered by Chief Justice Marshall (1831), an injunction against Georgia was denied on the ground that the court lacked jurisdiction because the Cherokee comprised a "domestic dependent" nation rather than a foreign state within the meaning of the Constitution (*Cherokee Nation* v. *Georgia*, 5 Peters 1).

A Georgia law (1830) ordered white residents in Cherokee country to secure a license from the governor and to take an oath of allegiance to the state. Samuel A. Worcester and Elizur Butler, both New England missionaries, refused to obey the law and were convicted and sentenced to 4 years at hard labor. On appeal to the Supreme Court Chief Justice Marshall (3 Mar. 1832) held that Indian nations were capable of making treaties, that under the constitution treaties are the supreme law of the land, that the national government had exclusive jurisdiction in the territory of the Cherokee nation, and that the law was unconstitutional because the Cherokee nation had territorial boundaries within which the laws of Georgia "can have no force." (*Worcester* v. *Georgia*, 6 Peters

515). Georgia defied the court and was supported by Jackson, who is reported to have said: "John Marshall has made his decision, now let him enforce it!"

Jackson pursued a broad policy of extinguishing Indian land titles in states and in removing the Indian population. During his 2 terms 94 Indian treaties were concluded under coercion. In the Old Southwest, the Creeks, Choctaw, and Chickasaw signed treaties of evacuation. By the end of 1833 only the Cherokee insisted on retaining their lands. Finally, under the treaty of 29 Dec. 1835 the Cherokee surrendered to the U.S. all their lands east of the Mississippi in return for $5 million, transportation costs, and land in Indian territory. A Bureau of Indian Affairs was established in 1836. Some Indians resorted to armed resistance. Seeking to reoccupy their ceded lands in Wisconsin Territory and Illinois, the Sac and Fox Indians fought the Black Hawk War (6 Apr.–2 Aug. 1832) along the upper Mississippi. They were beaten back. In Florida, the Second Seminole War broke out in Nov. 1835 and lasted until 14 Aug. 1842.

NULLIFICATION CONTROVERSY. In his annual message of 1830 Jackson affirmed the constitutionality of the Tariff of 1828 and protectionism. But to conciliate the South, he recommended tariff revision in his subsequent message.

During 1830–31, the nullification forces in South Carolina enlarged their following; but Union sentiment in the state was strong enough to prevent the calling of a convention. The Tariff of 1832, while somewhat milder than that of 1828, retained the protective principle. Its passage (14 July) encouraged the South Carolina nullifiers, who, under the leadership of Gov. James Hamilton, Jr., and Robert Barnwell Rhett, took a belligerent stand. The state elections (Oct.) resulted in a decisive victory for the nullification party.

Ordinance of Nullification. Meanwhile, Calhoun had reaffirmed and elaborated the doctrine of nullification in 2 important papers: the **Fort Hill Address** (26 July 1831), which contained the principle of the concurrent majority, and in a letter to Gov. James Hamilton, Jr. (28 Aug.) which defended nullification as a constitutional, conservative, and legitimate means of redress for acts deemed injurious to the state.

Gov. Hamilton called an extraordinary session of the legislature (22 Oct.), which promptly called for a state convention. The convention which assembled at Columbia (19 Nov.), attended by only a handful of Unionists, adopted (136–26) an ordinance nullifying the tariff acts of 1828 and 1832 (24 Nov.). The ordinance prohibited the collection of duties within the state, beginning 1 Feb. 1833; required a test oath for all state officeholders except members of the legislature; forbade appeal to the U.S. Supreme Court of any case in law or equity arising under the ordinance; and asserted that the use of force by the federal government would be cause for secession. The legislature (27 Nov.) passed laws for the enforcement of the ordinance. Among them were provisions authorizing the raising of a military force and appropriations for arms.

Jackson ordered the Secretary of War (29 Oct.) to alert the forts in Charleston Harbor. Maj. Gen. Winfield Scott was given the command of the army forces in South Carolina. Jackson's message to Congress (4 Dec.) again recommended downward revision of the tariff. On 10 Dec. he issued his **Proclamation to the People of South Carolina**, which was drafted by Edward Livingston and ranks as Jackson's most important state paper. The proclamation characterized nullification as an "impractical absurdity" and asserted the supremacy of a sovereign and indivisible federal government. No state, said Jackson, could refuse to obey the laws of the land, and no state could leave the Union. "Disunion by armed force is **treason**," Jackson concluded.

The South Carolina legislature adopted a series of resolutions (17 Dec.) replying to the Nullification Proclamation, and the newly installed governor, Robert Y. Hayne, issued a counterproclamation (20 Dec.). Calhoun resigned the vice-presidency (28 Dec.), having been elected (12 Dec.) U.S. senator in place of Hayne (121–28). A call by South Carolina for a general convention of the states to consider relations between the federal and state governments elicited a series of replies by various state legislatures unequivocally condemning nullification and secession.

Force Bill. Jackson asked Congress (16 Jan. 1833) for authority to enforce the revenue laws by the use of the military if necessary. The congressional battle against the so-called Force Bill was led by Calhoun, who was engaged by Webster in a notable debate on nationalism and states' rights. Meanwhile, Henry Clay had formulated a compromise tariff. Introduced on 12 Feb. 1833, it passed the House, 119–85 (26 Feb. 1833), and the Senate, 29–16 (1 Mar.). The Force Bill was passed in the Senate, 32–1 (20 Feb. 1833; Calhoun, Clay, and others abstained from voting), and passed the House, 149–47 (1 Mar.). The compromise tariff of 1833 and the Force Bill were approved by Jackson on 2 Mar.

Upon learning that a compromise tariff was in the making, South Carolina suspended the ordinance of nullification (21 Jan. 1833). Calhoun supported the compromise, although he did not participate in the proceedings of the state convention which met on 11 Mar. and adopted (153–4) a rescinding ordinance (15 Mar.). As a face-saving gesture the convention (132–19) adopted (18 Mar.)

an ordinance declaring the Force Bill null and void, and adjourned on the same day. The nullification episode was closed, with both sides claiming victory.

10 July. BANK VETO. The charter of the 2d Bank of the U.S. was due to expire in 1836. Under the conservative management (1823 *et seq.*) of **Nicholas Biddle** the bank had prospered and expanded. It aided business operations and reduced the threat of inflation posed by a disorganized currency. But there was a many-sided opposition to the bank. Biddle's policy of branch drafts, which compelled state and local banks to contract their note issues, made the bank unpopular among debtor groups, particularly in the South and West. Southern states'-rights groups questioned its constitutionality. State banks sought government deposits. Van Buren and his New York supporters disputed Philadelphia's financial leadership. Biddle's personal domination of the bank's policies, and his identification with conservative interests, ultimately made him a target for popular resentment against monopolies, corporations, and a moneyed aristocracy.

Jackson's first annual message (1829) questioned the bank's constitutionality and expediency, and asserted that the bank had failed to establish a sound and uniform currency. Jackson favored a government-owned institution with severely limited operations confined chiefly to deposit. When it became clear that Jackson was intent upon eliminating the bank, Biddle embarked upon a policy of opposition. Until early in 1832, however, he planned to defer his application for renewal of the bank charter until after the presidential elections.

Sen. Thomas Hart Benton launched an attack upon the bank in a speech (Feb. 1831). Biddle, alarmed, and at Clay's advice, decided to make immediate application for renewal of the charter, thereby forcing the bank issue upon Jackson.

A bill for recharter of the bank was reported in the House (10 Feb.) and in the Senate (13 Mar.). The measure passed the Senate, 28–20 (11 June), and the House, 107–86 (3 July). Jackson vetoed the bill (10 July). Although his message showed no firm grasp of banking and finance, it was an indictment of monopoly and special privilege, and accepted the challenge of the opposition to make the bank the major issue of the campaign of 1832. In referring to the Supreme Court's views on the constitutionality of the bank, Jackson made a notable definition of the character of the presidential office: "The Congress, the Executive, and the Court must each for itself be guided by its own opinion of the Constitution. Each public officer who takes an oath to support the Constitution swears that he will support it as he understands it, and not as it is understood by others. . . . The opinion of the judges has no more authority over Congress than the opinion of Congress has over the judges, and on that point the President is independent of both." The Senate vote of 22–19 (13 July) failed to override the veto.

PRESIDENTIAL CAMPAIGN. A National Republican Convention assembled at Baltimore (12 Dec. 1831), where its delegates nominated **Henry Clay** for president and **John Sergeant** (Pa.) for vice-president. The Anti-Masonic party had already nominated (26 Sept. 1831) **William Wirt** (Md.) for president and **Amos Ellmaker** (Pa.) for vice-president. The campaign of 1832 witnessed the adoption of the **national nominating convention** by the 3 parties in the field. The first platforms ever adopted by national conventions were by the Anti-Masons (Sept. 1831) and by a group of young National Republicans convened at Washington in May.

The first national nominating convention of the Democratic party (as it was now formally called) was held at Baltimore (21–22 May). It unanimously endorsed **Jackson** for a second term and named **Martin Van Buren** for the vice-presidency. Van Buren's nomination as minister to England had been rejected in the Senate 24–23 (25 Jan.). Calhoun, who had cast the deciding vote, thought the rejection would end Van Buren's political career; the move had an opposite effect. The convention adopted the **"two-thirds rule"** (which remained in force until 1936) requiring that "two-thirds of the whole number of votes in the convention shall be necessary to constitute a choice." No platform was adopted. The principal campaign issue was the bank question, which struck a wide response from agrarian and frontier prejudice against the bank and from Eastern feeling against privileged corporations. The National Republicans were identified with the conservative interests. Biddle printed and circulated campaign literature supporting Clay.

5 Dec. PRESIDENTIAL ELECTION was an overwhelming Democratic victory. **Jackson** won the electoral votes of 16 of the 24 states with 219 electoral votes (687,502 popular votes); Clay received 49 electoral votes (530,189 popular votes). William Wirt carried only Vermont (7 electoral votes). The South Carolina legislature cast 11 votes for John Floyd (Va.) and Henry Lee (Mass.). **Van Buren,** with 189 electoral votes, was elected vice-president (Pennsylvania having thrown its 30 electoral votes to Sen. William Wilkins, a native son).

1833

REMOVAL OF DEPOSITS. The Calhoun and Clay forces in the House united in adopting a resolution (2 Mar.).

stating that government deposits might be safely continued in the Bank of the U.S. Jackson, however, interpreted his reelection as a popular mandate to proceed against the bank. Biddle had already embarked upon a policy of tightening credit to bring the administration to terms.

Jackson asked (19 Mar.) the opinion of the cabinet on the regulation of deposits and the establishment of a new bank. **Attorney General Taney** (3 Apr.) supported removal of the deposits and their distribution among selected state banks (a policy which Amos Kendall and Francis P. Blair, Sr., had already recommended). Secretary of the Treasury McLane (20 May) opposed removal and supported the formation of a new bank. Jackson then reorganized the cabinet, appointing McLane Secretary of State (1 June) and William J. Duane (Pa.) Secretary of the Treasury. Upon receiving Jackson's instructions for removing the deposits, Duane replied with a letter (10 July) opposing the step.

On 10 Sept. Jackson submitted to the cabinet a report by Kendall indicating the availability of state banks, and announced that on 1 Oct. the government would discontinue the Bank of the U.S. as a depository. Taney and Woodbury supported Jackson; McLane, Cass, and Duane were opposed. Jackson read to the cabinet (18 Sept.) a paper drafted by Taney listing the reasons for removal. The document illuminated Jackson's concept of the role of the cabinet: namely, that it was the personal organ of the president.

When Duane persisted in his refusal to carry out the removal, he was replaced (23 Sept.) by Taney as Secretary of the Treasury. Taney announced (26 Sept.) that the public funds would no longer be deposited in the Bank of the U.S., and issued the first order for removal (effected by transferring the

funds). The Girard Bank of Philadelphia was the first state bank designated as a place of deposit. By the end of 1833, 23 state banks (popularly known as "pet banks") had been selected as depositories. By that time, too, Biddle's restrictions on credit had induced financial distress.

In his annual message (3 Dec.) Jackson assumed complete responsibility for removing the deposits, defending his action with the argument that the bank was attempting to influence elections. The Senate issued a call (11 Dec.) for a copy of the paper which Jackson had read to the cabinet. Jackson refused the request, declaring that "the executive is a co-ordinate and independent branch of the Government equally with the Senate, and I have yet to learn under what constitutional authority that branch of the Legislature has a right to require of me an account of any communication, either verbally or in writing, made to the heads of Departments acting as a Cabinet council."

Henry Clay introduced 2 **censuring resolutions** in the Senate (26 Dec.): The first, criticizing the action of the Treasury, was adopted 28 Mar. 1834, 28–18; the second, stating that "the President, in the late Executive proceedings in relation to the public revenue, has assumed upon himself authority and power not conferred by the constitution and laws, but in derogation of both," was adopted the same day, 26–20.

The Jackson supporters in the House pushed through 4 resolutions sustaining the administration's bank policy (4 Apr. 1834). Jackson made a formal protest (15 Apr. 1834), asserting that he had been charged with an impeachable offense but had been denied an opportunity to defend himself. On 21 Apr. 1834 he forwarded a supplementary message aimed at conciliating the Senate. By 27–16 (7 May 1834) the Senate rejected Jackson's power to question its authority and declined to enter the president's protest and message in the official record of its proceedings. In another move against Jackson, the Senate (24 June 1834) refused to approve Taney's nomination as Secretary of the Treasury. Through the repeated efforts of Sen. Benton, the resolution of censure was finally expunged from the Senate journal (16 Jan. 1837).

The Bank of the U.S., having failed to secure a new charter, obtained a state charter (Feb. 1836) and, upon the expiration of its national charter (1 Mar. 1836), became the Bank of the U.S. of Pennsylvania. Under the **Deposit Act** (23 June 1836) the Secretary of the Treasury was required to designate at least one bank in each state and territory as a place of public deposit, and the banks were assigned the general services previously rendered to the national government by the Bank of the U.S. The act also provided for the distribution of the surplus revenue in excess of $5 million among the states, as a loan subject to recall by the Secretary of the Treasury. It was never recalled.

1834

RISE OF THE WHIG PARTY. The union of the National Republican and Calhoun forces which secured the passage of the Senate censuring resolutions was the genesis of the Whig coalition on a national scale. The name "Whig" was formally adopted in 1834, after Clay mentioned it approvingly in a Senate speech (14 Apr.), but it had been in use for at least 2 years before that time. Gatherings of Northern and Southern opponents of the Jackson administration were held in the spring of 1834, apparently for the purpose of merging forces. By mid-1834 the Whig label was generally understood to refer to the coalition of the political groups led by Clay, Webster, and Calhoun, even though Calhoun preferred an independent course and acted with the Whigs when expedient. Included in this loose coalition: (1) National Republican supporters of Clay, Adams, and the "American system"; (2) states'-rights groups opposed to Jackson's stand on nullification; (3) former administration supporters alienated by Jackson's bank policy; (4) Southern planters and Northern industrialists; and, after 1836, (5) the remnants of the Anti-Masonic party.

1835

30 Jan. Attempted assassination of President Jackson. The assailant, Richard Lawrence, fired 2 pistols (both of which misfired) at the president as he was leaving the House chamber. Jackson was unharmed. Lawrence was adjudged insane and committed to a lunatic asylum.

ABOLITIONIST PROPAGANDA. The Southern states met abolitionist propaganda with regulatory or prohibitory laws. A Georgia code (1835) provided the death penalty for the publication of material tending to incite slave insurrections. Northern abolitionist editors and agents were expelled from the South. To the South Carolina legislature (1835) Gov. George McDuffie declared that "the laws of every community should punish this species of interference by death without benefit of clergy." At Charleston (29 July), a boatload of abolitionist tracts from New York impounded by the postmaster was seized by a mob and publicly burned. The Charleston postmaster, Alfred Huger, requested antislavery societies to discontinue their use of the mails; his appeal was rejected. When Huger's report reached Postmaster General Kendall, the latter replied that he had no official authority to bar abolitionist propaganda from the mails; unofficially he advised Southern postmasters to intercept such material, having already declared, "We owe an obligation to the laws, but a higher one to the communities in which we live."

In his annual message (2 Dec.) Jackson recommended a law to prohibit the circulation of antislavery publications through the mails. A Senate committee headed by Calhoun presented (4 Feb. 1836) a minority report on abolitionist publications, which supported Jackson's opposition to the dissemination of antislavery literature but took objection on states'-rights grounds to the recommended federal law barring circulation through the mails and offered a bill for the interception by postmasters of any publication prohibited by the laws of a particular state. The bill was defeated in the Senate, 25–19 (8 June 1836).

29 Oct. LOCO-FOCOS. The radical wing of Jacksonian Democracy, an urban faction that inherited the mantle of the Workingmen's party in New York, emerged (1834–35) as the Equal Rights party. Its followers, dividing with the Democratic regulars chiefly over banking and currency questions, regarded Jackson's banking policy as inflationary. Called the "Loco-Focos," this faction fought those financial interests which, with the aid of the regular Democratic party in the state, applied for bank and corporation charters from the legislature, and advocated abolition of monopolies and special privileges, hard money, elections by direct popular vote, direct taxes, free trade, and Jeffersonian strict construction. The radical wing found a voice in the New York *Evening Post*. The origin of the name "Loco-Focos" dates from a primary meeting (29 Oct.) at Tammany Hall when the regulars, over the protests of the Equal Rights men, declared the ticket carried and the meeting adjourned. The dissidents remained in the hall. To oust them, the Tammany stalwarts turned out the gas lights, whereupon the Equal Rights men furnished candles which they lit with the new self-igniting friction matches known as loco-focos, and proceeded to formulate their platform and nominate their own ticket.

1836

REPUBLIC OF TEXAS. The American settlement of Texas began when **Moses Austin** secured a charter (17 Jan. 1821) granting lands for colonization by 200 American families. The charter was obtained from the moribund government of New Spain, which soon became the independent state of Mexico. Upon Austin's death in Missouri (10 June 1821), his settlement scheme was carried forward by his son, **Stephen F. Austin** (p. 977), who arrived at Bexar, Tex. (12 Aug. 1821), to take possession of the land grants. In 1822–23 Austin visited Mexico, where by a decree of the Emperor Iturbide he secured confirmation of his concession. Renewal was made during the subsequent revolutions in Mexico and the establishment of a federal republic under the constitution of 1824. A law (7 May 1824) made Texas part of a state (Coahuila) in the Mexican republic, and a colonization law (24 Mar. 1825) threw Texas open to colonization. The success of Austin's venture attracted other *empresarios* who obtained charters or grants and brought in settlers to develop the rich lands. Both J. Q. Adams and Jackson negotiated unsuccessfully for the purchase of Texas.

A procession of revolutionary governments in Mexico finally resulted in restrictions on Texan colonization and a violation of what the settlers held to be their local rights. The Mexican Congress (8 Apr. 1830) enacted a law prohibiting the introduction of more slaves and the further settlement of Texas by immigrants from the U.S. The Texans remonstrated in petitions and memorials adopted (1 Oct. 1832) by a convention held at San Felipe; another convention held there (1–13 Apr. 1833) resolved to separate from Mexico. When Austin visited Mexico City to present the resolves to the new Mexican government under the Federalist party headed by **Santa Anna,** he was arrested (3 Jan. 1834) and imprisoned for 8 months. Santa Anna, who had used his Federalist connection only to secure office, turned rapidly toward the Centralist position of absolute rule over all Mexicans, including Texans, worsening relations between the settlers and the government.

A group of Texan colonists led by William B. Travis seized the Mexican garrison at Anahuac (30 June 1835), and in the fall of that year other armed clashes occurred. At conventions (Oct.–Nov. 1835) Texans endorsed the Federalist party's position opposing overcentralized authority, drafted plans for an army to resist Santa Anna, and named commissioners to solicit aid from the U.S.

23 Feb.–6 Mar. The Alamo. Santa Anna replied by establishing a unitary state (15 Dec. 1835) which abolished all local rights. Then raising an army of about 6,000 men he marched against the Texans. A convention assembled at Washington, Tex. (1 Mar.), adopted (2 Mar.) a declaration of independence and drew up a constitution based upon that of the U.S. A provisional government was established, and **Sam Houston** (p. 1062) was named commander of the army (4 Mar.). Santa Anna began (23 Feb.) his **Siege of the Alamo** at San Antonio. The assaulting force of 3,000 Mexicans was held off by 187 Texans until 6 Mar., when the garrison commanded by William B. Travis (and including Davy Crockett) was massacred. Santa Anna also massacred (27 Mar.) more

than 300 of the defenders of Goliad led by Capt. James Fannin. By mid-April the Mexicans had swept through many of the American settlements and reached Galveston Bay.

21 Apr. Battle of San Jacinto, fought on the western bank of the San Jacinto River at its junction with Buffalo Bayou, near Galveston Bay. The Texans under Sam Houston went into battle with the cry "Remember the Alamo!," defeated about 1,200 Mexicans, and captured Santa Anna. A treaty (14 May) pledging Santa Anna to secure the recognition of Texas was repudiated by the Mexican Congress. Sam Houston was installed (22 Oct.) as president of the independent republic of Texas.

Resolutions calling for the U.S. recognition of Texas were adopted by the Senate (1 July) and the House (4 July). While Jackson was sympathetic to the Texans, he believed that the U.S. must honor its obligations to Mexico and maintain a strict neutrality. He feared that recognition might disrupt the Democratic party and involve the U.S. in a war with Mexico. He finally yielded, however, by nominating (3 Mar. 1837) Alcée La Branche (La.) as chargé d'affaires to the Texas republic. Texas petitioned for annexation to the U.S. (4 Aug. 1837), but her formal offer was refused (25 Aug. 1837).

28 June. Death of James Madison at Montpelier, his Virginia estate.

11 July. SPECIE CIRCULAR. Inflation and land speculation were fed by the expanded issue of paper money accepted as legal tender (also p. 747). The use of "land-office money" (currency based on speculators' notes) pyramided land sales from $2,623,000 in 1832 to $24,877,000 in 1836. The financial disorder was abetted by the employment of federal deposits by the "pet" banks.

President Jackson ordered Secretary of the Treasury Levi Woodbury to issue the

Specie Circular (11 July, after Congress adjourned) that had been drafted by Sen. Thomas Hart Benton (whose resolution embodying the basic purpose of the circular had been rejected in the Senate on 22 Apr.). It provided that after 15 Aug. only gold, silver, and, in some cases, Virginia land scrip would be accepted by the government in payment for public lands, but permitted the receipt of paper money until 15 Dec. for parcels of land up to 320 acres purchased by actual settlers or bona fide residents of the state in which the sale was made. The circular declared that it was aimed at repressing "alleged frauds," withholding government approval or support "from the monopoly of the public lands in the hands of speculators and capitalists," and discouraging the "ruinous extension" of bank notes and credit.

The circular succeeded in reducing public-land sales in the West but taxed the inadequate resources of the "pet" banks, drained specie from the East, led to hoarding, and weakened public confidence in the state banks. The pressure on the deposit banks was increased by the scheduled payment (1 Jan. 1837) to the states of the first installment of the surplus revenue under the distribution provisions of the Deposit Act.

Jackson defended the circular in his annual message (5 Dec.), maintaining that it had "produced many salutary consequences" and strengthened the Western banks against the rising financial distress. He recommended that public land sales should be limited in quantity and confined to actual settlers. A Whig resolution for repeal of the circular was introduced in the Senate (12 Dec.). A House bill (reported 18 Jan. 1837) provided for government acceptance of the notes of specie-paying banks discontinuing note issues of less than $10 denominations. The bill was amended by Sen. William C. Rives (Va.) to

provide for rescinding of the Specie Circular. The measure passed the Senate, 41–5 (10 Feb. 1837), and the House (1 Mar. 1837), but was pocket-vetoed by Jackson. The Specie Circular was finally repealed by a joint resolution (21 May 1838).

PRESIDENTIAL CAMPAIGN. The Democratic Nominating Convention met at Baltimore (20 May 1835) and unanimously chose **Martin Van Buren** as presidential candidate and **Richard M. Johnson** (Ky.) as the vice-presidential. No formal platform was adopted, but an address formulated by a committee and published in the Washington *Globe* (26 Aug. 1835) was the equivalent of the party's first platform. In his letter of acceptance Van Buren pledged himself to "tread generally in the footsteps of President Jackson."

The Whig coalition, unable to agree upon a single candidate, adopted the strategy of nominating candidates with strong local followings in the hope of throwing the election into the House. In Jan. 1835, **Daniel Webster** was nominated by a Massachusetts legislative caucus. In the same month **Hugh L. White** was chosen by anti-Jacksonian Democrats in the Tennessee legislature; the nomination was supported by Illinois and Alabama. Supreme Court Justice John McLean was nominated by an Ohio legislative caucus, but withdrew in Aug. 1836. The Anti-Masonic party met at Harrisburg, Pa. (16 Dec. 1835), and nominated **William Henry Harrison** (Ohio) for president and Francis Granger (N.Y.) for vice-president.

7 DEC. PRESIDENTIAL ELECTION. Van Buren received 761,549 votes. The Whig candidates received 736,250 votes (Harrison, 549,567; White, 145,396; Webster, 41,287). **Van Buren** carried 15 of the 26 states, receiving 170 electoral votes, including 3 disputed Michigan votes; Harrison, 73; White, 26; Webster,

14; and South Carolina gave its 11 electoral votes to Willie P. Mangum (N.C.). Van Buren retired as vice-president (28 Jan. 1837) and Sen. William R. King of Alabama was chosen president *pro tempore* of the Senate. None of the 4 vice-presidential candidates received a majority of the electoral votes. The election, for the first and only time, was thrown into the Senate, which chose **Richard M. Johnson** by a vote of 33 to 16 (8 Feb. 1837).

1837

4 Mar. Jackson published his *Farewell Address* (drafted by Taney), a review of his 2 terms, which appealed for loyalty to the Union, condemned sectionalism, monopolies, paper currency, and speculation.

PANIC OF 1837 (also p. 747) resulted from reckless speculation. In the South the price of cotton fell by almost one half on the New Orleans market (Mar.). In New York there were demonstrations (Feb.–Mar.) by the unemployed. Protesting against high rents and the inflated prices of foodstuffs and fuel, a mob broke into the city's flour warehouses and sacked the supplies (12 Feb.). The New York banks suspended specie payments (10 May), and were followed by banks at Baltimore, Philadelphia, and Boston. The sale of public lands fell from 20 million acres (1836) to 3,500,000 (1838). The effects of the panic persisted until 1842–43, particularly in the Southern and Western states.

In a message to a special session of Congress (5 Sept.) Van Buren advocated a specie currency, criticized state-chartered banks, and alluded to a scheme to establish Treasury depositories independent of state banks. In every year between 1837 and 1841 (with the exception of 1839), the government had a deficit. Numerous bank failures aroused dissatis-

faction with the use of state banks as depositories for public funds and helped to develop sentiment for the Independent Treasury (1840). In 1841 Congress authorized the establishment of a bonded debt.

ABOLITIONIST CONTROVERSY IN CONGRESS. The steady flow of petitions to Congress requesting the abolition of slavery and the slave trade in the District of Columbia reached a crest in 1836. Up to that time such petitions were customarily referred to the standing Committee on the District of Columbia, and did not create serious dissension in either house of Congress. By 1836 the mounting apprehensions of the slave states had hardened the conviction of many Southerners that congressional discussion of slavery was inimical both to the slave system and to the comity of the Union.

The Gag Rule. The Senate adopted a relatively workable formula for disposing of the petitions. When Thomas Morris of Ohio (7 Jan. 1836) and James Buchanan (Pa.) presented (11 Jan. 1836) abolitionist petitions, Calhoun made a bitter attack upon the abolitionists and recommended the barring of future petitions. Calhoun's motion was defeated, 36–10 (9 Mar. 1836); but on the motion of Buchanan, the Senate, 34–6 (11 Mar. 1836), rejected the prayer of the petitioners. Thereafter the Senate adopted this as a regular practice. It enabled the abolitionists to exercise their constitutional right of petition, and at the same time gave the foes of the antislavery agitators an opportunity to register their firm disapproval.

The issue was more complicated in the House, where former president **John Quincy Adams** ardently defended the right of petition from the very outset of his 8 successive terms (1831–48) as representative from the Plymouth District, Mass. Adams held antislavery opinions, but was not sympathetic to the abolitionist cause. His view was that Congress had no authority to interfere with the institution in the slaveholding states, although he declared in a House speech (25 May 1836) that in the event those states ever became a theater of war, "the war powers of Congress [would] extend to interference with the institution of slavery in every way." His persistence in supporting the right of petition earned for him the sobriquet "Old Man Eloquent."

Adams' stubborn intention was one of the factors that led the House to establish (8 Feb. 1836) a special committee under chairman Henry L. Pinckney (S.C.) to consider the question. Pinckney recommended the so-called "gag resolution" (18 May 1836), providing that "all petitions, memorials, resolutions, propositions or papers relating in any way or to any extent whatever to the subject of slavery or the abolition of slavery shall, without being printed or referred, be laid upon the table and that no further action whatever shall be had thereon."

The resolution was 1 of 3. The "gag resolution" itself was adopted (26 May 1836), 117–68. The resolution stating that Congress had no power over slavery in the states was adopted, 182–9; the one holding that interference with slavery in the District of Columbia was inexpedient was adopted, 132–45. When Adams' name was called on the roll, he withheld his vote with the response: "I hold the resolution to be a direct violation of the Constitution of the United States, of the rules of this House, and of the rights of my constituents."

When the 2d session of the 25th Congress convened (4 Dec.), the "gag rule" was not immediately renewed (House rules required its renewal at each session). At this time Northern abolitionist feeling was inflamed by the murder (7 Nov.) of the abolitionist editor **Elijah P. Lovejoy** at Alton, Ill. Rep. William Slade (Vt.) took advantage of the temporary lull in the "gag rule" and presented abolitionist petitions. The move culminated in an angry debate and led Southern representatives to consider an amendment for protecting the institution of slavery or, failing to gain that, to declare the expediency of dissolving the Union. Nothing came of this gesture. In reply to the abolitionists, a combination of Southern and Northern Democrats adopted a stricter "gag resolution," 122–74 (19 Dec.).

In the Senate, Benjamin Swift (Vt.) presented (19 Dec.) the resolutions of his state legislature opposing the annexation of Texas or the admission of any new slave state to the Union, upholding the constitutional authority of Congress to abolish slavery in the District of Columbia and to prohibit the interstate slave trade, and requesting Vermont representatives and senators to use their influence to promote these ends.

Calhoun responded by introducing into the Senate a set of 6 resolutions (27 Dec.). They reaffirmed the compact theory of the Union, the reserved-powers doctrine as it pertained to Southern action against abolitionist propaganda, and the theory that the federal government, as the agent of the states, was bound "to resist all attempts by one portion of the Union to use it as an instrument to attack the domestic institutions of another"; declared that the institution of slavery was not to be attacked or interfered with; that the efforts to abolish slavery in the District of Columbia or the territories was a "direct and dangerous attack on the institutions of all the slave-holding States"; and denounced as detrimental to the Union interference with annexation which might expand slave territory. During the course of the discussion in the Senate (3–12 Jan.

1838) the first 3 of Calhoun's resolutions were adopted; the 4th and 5th were altered and adopted; the 6th tabled.

The House "gag rule" was renewed at each session of Congress between 1836 and 1844 over the opposition of Adams, Joshua Giddings (Ohio), and a small group of other Northern legislators. The "gag rule," by depriving the abolitionists of one of their civil rights, enabled the antislavery agitators to add this charge to their arsenal of indictments against the South. Finally, when Northern Democratic support was lessened, the "gag resolution" was rescinded (3 Dec. 1844) on the motion of Adams.

During the course of Senate debates on the slavery question, Henry Clay, with an eye to the presidential nomination in 1840, attempted to placate Northern and Southern conservatives who tended to identify the Whig party with abolitionism. In a speech delivered on 7 Feb. 1839 he condemned the abolitionist agitators, accused them of being ready to risk a civil war, and denied congressional authority to interfere with the institution of slavery where it was already established. It was in reference to this speech that Clay remarked to Sen. William C. Preston (S.C.), when the latter suggested that the speech might injure Clay's following among Northern Whigs: "I trust the sentiments and opinions are correct; I had rather be right than be President."

1838

ANGLO-U.S. TENSIONS. In the wake of the Panic of 1837, the default of American state governments and corporations on debts owed to British creditors revived Anglo-American differences, aggravated by numerous British travel accounts presenting the U.S. as a nation of boors and blusterers. A powerful voice was added by many of the 56 British authors whose memorial (1 Feb. 1836) asking for copyright protection in the U.S. had been ignored by Congress, and the literary war found the Americans replying in kind. The controversy was heightened by the addition of incidents involving disputed boundary claims and violations of neutrality.

Caroline Affair. With the failure of the insurrection led by William Lyon Mackenzie in upper Canada in the autumn of 1837, the rebel leader and some of his followers, aided by American sympathizers, took refuge on Navy Island on the Canadian side of the Niagara River. Furnished with recruits, provisions, and arms by their Anglophobe U.S. supporters, the insurrectionists proclaimed a provisional government and launched attacks against the Canadian frontier. A small American steamboat, the *Caroline*, was employed to transport supplies from the U.S. side to Navy Island. On the night of 29 Dec. 1837 a party of Canadian militia crossed the river to the American side, boarded the *Caroline*, set it afire, and then turned the vessel adrift. In the course of overpowering the crew, the Canadians killed Amos Durfee, a U.S. citizen.

The *Caroline* affair touched off patriotic indignation and violent Anglophobe sentiment in the U.S. President Van Buren issued a neutrality proclamation (5 Jan.) warning Americans to desist from hostile acts against Great Britain. Militia called out by the president were posted along the Canadian frontier, where Gen. Winfield Scott took immediate command of the U.S. forces. The Canadian rebels abandoned Navy Island (13 Jan.) and surrendered their arms to U.S. militia.

The British Foreign Office ignored the protests made by the State Department concerning the violation of U.S. neutrality. A number of incidents during the course of 1838 kept anti-British feeling at a high pitch. A group of Americans boarded and burned the Canadian steamer *Sir Robert Peel* on the American side of the St. Lawrence (29 May). Along the frontier Americans organized secret Hunters' Lodges for the purpose of overthrowing the British regime in Canada. The U.S. government adopted measures to prevent violation of the frontier. A few parties dispatched by the Lodges penetrated Canada (Nov.–Dec.), but were quickly repulsed or captured. President Van Buren issued a second neutrality proclamation (21 Nov.) and ordered swift action against Americans violating the neutrality laws.

Anglo-U.S. tension lessened during 1839–40, but was renewed by the **McLeod case**. In Nov. 1840, Alexander McLeod, a Canadian deputy sheriff, was arrested in New York state on the charge of having murdered Amos Durfee and participated in the burning of the *Caroline*. He was jailed at Lockport, N.Y., to await trial. The British minister to the U.S. asked (13 Dec. 1840) for McLeod's immediate release. Secretary of State John Forsyth replied (26 Dec. 1840) that the New York courts had exclusive jurisdiction over McLeod. Brought to trial at Utica, N.Y., McLeod was acquitted (12 Oct. 1841). Had he been found guilty, Gov. **William H. Seward** (p. 1149) was prepared to pardon him in order to forestall international complications.

Aroostook "War." The disputed northeastern boundary (between New Brunswick and Maine) had loomed as an Anglo-American issue since 1783, when the peace treaty incorporated a complicated and unsatisfactory provision. The Peace of Ghent did not touch on the question. Shortly after Maine became a state (1820), its legislature, together with that of Massachusetts, disregarded British claims in making land grants to settlers along the Aroostook River. The

U.S. and Great Britain submitted the boundary differences to arbitration by the King of the Netherlands (29 Sept. 1827). His compromise award (10 Jan. 1831) was accepted by Great Britain, but was rejected by the Senate, 21–20 (23 June 1832).

During the winter of 1838–39 Canadian lumberjacks entered the disputed Aroostook region and began lumbering operations. Gov. John Fairfield of Maine requested the legislature (Jan. 1839) to name a land agent and to provide a force for breaking up the Canadian camps. Rufus McIntire, who was appointed land agent with authority to expel the lumberjacks, was seized by the Canadians (12 Feb. 1839). His arrest, and the refusal of the Canadians to leave, marked the beginning of the so-called Aroostook war, an undeclared conflict without bloodshed. Maine and New Brunswick called out their militia. The Nova Scotia legislature made war appropriations. Congress authorized a force of 50,000 men and voted $10 million for a possible emergency.

President Van Buren dispatched Gen. Winfield Scott to the trouble zone. War might have broken out had it not been for the truce (Mar. 1839) Scott arranged between the governor of Maine and the lieutenant governor of New Brunswick. The British agreed to refer the dispute to a boundary commission, and the question was settled by the Webster-Ashburton Treaty (1842).

18 Aug. WILKES EXPEDITION (p. 1184).

1839

13 Nov. LIBERTY PARTY. The entry of the antislavery forces into politics was signalized by the establishment of the Liberty party, which held its founding convention at Warsaw, N.Y., and nominated **James G. Birney,** a native of Kentucky and a former slaveholder, for president, and Thomas Earle (Pa.) for vice-president. These nominations were confirmed at the party's first national convention at Albany (1 Apr. 1840). Liberty party conventions were subsequently held in Ohio and other states in the Northwest. The party was composed of moderate abolitionists who did not share Garrison's opposition to political action. Unlike Garrison, they professed loyalty to the Constitution and did not advocate secession or dissolution of the Union. By virtue of holding the balance of power, the party played an important part in the presidential election of 1844, when it was responsible for the defeat of Clay. In 1848 it combined with the Free-Soil party and helped to defeat the Democratic candidate, Lewis Cass. The party's chief political issue was its stand against the annexation of Texas. Among its leaders were Gerrit Smith (N.Y.) and Salmon P. Chase (Ohio).

1840

4 JULY. INDEPENDENT TREASURY ACT. Van Buren's scheme to establish federal depositories independent of state banks and private business, set forth in his message (5 Sept. 1837) to a special session of Congress, had the support of the cabinet and of his congressional managers, Sen. Silas Wright and Rep. Churchill C. Cambreleng, both of New York. The plan aroused the bitter opposition of the Whigs under the congressional leadership of Henry Clay and Daniel Webster. While Calhoun and his followers still remained aloof from the Democratic party, they were in agreement with the administration on the Treasury issue, out of fear of the nationalist tendencies of the Whigs.

The independent treasury bill (also known as the subtreasury or divorce bill) was introduced in the Senate, where it passed, 26–20 (4 Oct. 1837), with incorporation of Calhoun's legal-tender amendment. This proviso called for a gradual reduction in the acceptance of notes of specie-paying banks in payment of government dues until 1841, when all payments should be made in legal tender. The amendment was later dropped, and the Senate (with Calhoun voting against the measure) passed the bill, 27–25. The bill was tabled in the House, 120–107 (14 Oct. 1837), and was rejected by that chamber, 125–11 (25 June 1838). Its defeat was caused largely by the split in the Democratic ranks: the conservative Democrats united with the Whig opposition, while the Loco-Focos supported the Van Buren plan.

A technicality that enabled the Democrats to organize the 26th Congress virtually assured its passage. Its enactment witnessed the reunion of the Calhoun wing with the Democratic party. The bill passed the Senate, 24–18 (23 Jan.), and the House, 124–107 (30 June), with Southern states'-rights men joining Northern hard-money Democrats to effect its passage.

The Independent Treasury Act entrusted the government with the exclusive care of its own funds and required the progressive enforcement of the legal-tender clause until all government payments and disbursements should be made in hard money after 30 June 1843. Subtreasuries were established at New York, Boston, Philadelphia, St. Louis, New Orleans, Washington, and Charleston. The act was repealed in 1841.

PRESIDENTIAL CAMPAIGN. When the Whig National Nominating Convention met at Harrisburg, Pa. (4 Dec. 1839), the Whig leaders, under the guidance of Thurlow Weed of New York, were determined to unite on a single candidate. Henry Clay was the leading contender, but his position on some issues, notably the protective tariff, impaired his availability. **William Henry Harrison** of Ohio had no substantial qualifications as a public servant, but he had no important political enemies, enjoyed a reputation as a military hero, and had received an encouraging vote in 1836. Clay had already indicated that in the interest of "union and harmony" he would if necessary defer to another candidate, and it was as the "union and harmony" convention that the Whig gathering went down in history. The convention adopted a rough equivalent of the **"unit rule"** by which the vote of the majority of each delegation was reported as the state's vote. Although Clay led on the 1st ballot, the convention finally nominated Harrison for president and **John Tyler** (Va.) for vice-president. Tyler was a states'-rights adherent who had turned against Jackson during the nullification episode. No platform was adopted. The Whigs, still a coalition rather than an organized political party, counted upon common opposition to the Democrats for their basic appeal.

The Democratic Convention at Baltimore (5 May) agreed on **Van Buren's** renomination, but failed to unite on a candidate for the vice-presidency. Because of strong opposition to the incumbent, Richard M. Johnson, the choice of a vice-presidential candidate was left to the state electors. The Democratic platform declared adherence to strict constructionist doctrine, opposed congressional interference with slavery (thus formally introducing the slavery question into the platform of a major political party), opposed a national bank and internal improvements at federal expense, and affirmed the principles of the Declaration of Independence (as no succeeding Democratic national convention during the pre-Civil War era would do).

Eschewing clear declarations on all leading issues, the Whigs waged their campaign on the basis of personalities. Ammunition for the Whig camp was unwittingly provided by a Democratic newspaper, the Baltimore *Republican*, which derisively remarked (23 Mar.) "that upon condition of his receiving a pension of $2,000 and a barrel of cider, General Harrison would no doubt consent to withdraw his pretensions, and spend his days in a log cabin on the banks of the Ohio." The Whigs turned this remark against their opponents, using the cider and log cabin symbols to present the hero of Tippecanoe as a sturdy son of the frontier and a simple man of the people.

In the rollicking **"Log Cabin and Hard Cider"** campaign that followed, the Whigs cleverly utilized many of the devices that later election contests featured as familiar means of stimulating popular enthusiasm: placards, emblems, campaign hats, effigies, floats, huge rallies, and transportable log cabins with the latchstring hanging out and furnished with coonskins and barrels of cider. The campaign slogan came into use ("Matty's policy, 50 cts. a day and soup; our policy, $2 a day and roast beef"), as well as newspaper advertisements with a political slant. ("The subscriber will pay $5 a hundred for pork if Harrison is elected, and $2.50 if Van Buren is.") The Whigs sang their way through the campaign to the words of "Tippecanoe and Tyler too," with its refrain of "Van, Van is a used up man."

In contrast to the studied simplicity of Harrison, the Whigs pictured Van Buren as an aristocrat of extravagant taste living amid the luxury of "the Palace" (as the Whigs called the White House) and supping with gold spoons. The campaign quickly degenerated into an exhibition of abuse, evasion, misrepresentation, and irrelevancies on a scale unparalleled in U.S. history up to that time. Its special significance, however, lay in its signaling the maturation of the **second party system** in U.S. history.

2 DEC. PRESIDENTIAL ELECTION. Van Buren received 1,128,702 popular votes; **Harrison,** 1,275,017; and the 7,059 votes received by the Liberty party candidate, James G. Birney, were drawn from all of the free states except Indiana. Carrying 19 of the 26 states, **Harrison** won 234 electoral votes, as did **Tyler,** Van Buren, 60. The elections gave the Whigs a congressional majority. The Whig victory was the first time since 1800 that a diffuse coalition defeated an organized political party holding power.

1841

4 MAR. Inauguration of William Henry Harrison, 9th president; John Tyler, vice-president. Harrison's platitudinous inaugural address made it clear that the executive would defer to congressional leadership.

CABINET APPOINTMENTS. Named to office 5 Mar. were Daniel Webster, Secretary of State (a post that had been refused by Henry Clay); Thomas Ewing (Ohio), Secretary of the Treasury; John Bell (Tenn.), Secretary of War; George E. Badger (N.C.), Secretary of the Navy; and John J. Crittenden (Ky.), Attorney General. Francis Granger (N.Y.) was appointed Postmaster General (6 Mar.). All of the cabinet members except Webster and Granger were supporters of Clay.

4 APR. Death of President Harrison, caused by pneumonia. John Tyler became the 10th president, the first vice-president to succeed to that office. A Virginia Democrat of the "old Republican" school, Tyler differed with the Whigs on constitutional principles and practical measures. In the quarrel between president and Congress that ensued, the mi-

nority of Whigs that supported Tyler was contemptuously termed "the Corporal's Guard." Tyler issued (9 Apr.) an address to the people indicating his intention of securing changes in the government fiscal structure compatible with the principles of "the fathers of the great Republican school."

7 JUNE. Clay introduced a set of resolutions embodying the essentials of Whig policy. He called for repeal of the Independent Treasury Act, the incorporation of a bank, customs duties designed to provide adequate revenue, and the distribution of the proceeds from the sale of public lands.

9 MAR. AMISTAD CASE. The Supreme Court sustained the lower courts and freed Negroes who in the course of being transported as slaves in Spanish ships mutinied and were captured by a U.S. warship (1839) off Long Island and carried to New London (15 Peters 518).

13 AUG. REPEAL OF THE INDEPENDENT TREASURY ACT. In order to clear the way for the incorporation of a national bank, the Whigs repealed the Independent Treasury Act. For 5 years thereafter a Whig majority in Congress defeated efforts of Democrats to reestablish the subtreasury system. During this period the management of the public funds was left to the discretion of the Secretary of the Treasury, who used the state banks as depositories. Until 1846 the deposit system of the government was not regulated by law.

16 AUG., 9 SEPT. FISCAL BANK VETOES. The Whig program was launched with a bill for incorporating a fiscal agency in the District of Columbia under the name of the Fiscal Bank of the U.S. The projected institution was tantamount to a revival of the 2d Bank of the U.S. Introduced in the Senate (12 June), the bill called for a bank capitalized at $30 million and authorized to set up state branches with deposit and discount functions, but only after obtaining the consent of the individual states in which branches were established (to satisfy Tyler's strict constructionist views). But this provision was eliminated, and a substitute measure stipulated that the consent of any state would be assumed unless its legislature registered explicit disapproval. The bill passed the Senate, 26–23 (28 July), and the House, 128–97 (6 Aug.). Tyler vetoed the bill on the grounds of constitutionality and expediency. The Senate (19 Aug.) failed to override the veto.

A second bank bill was formulated to which Tyler, in an interview with Rep. A. H. H. Stuart, a Virginia Whig, lent his apparent approval on condition of certain changes. The bill which was introduced provided for a fiscal corporation capitalized at $21 million. The provision for the establishment of offices only with state consent (one of the conditions Tyler had supposedly indicated as essential) was not included in the bill that passed the House, 125–94 (23 Aug.) and the Senate 27–22 (3 Sept.). The measure was vetoed by Tyler on substantially the same grounds as his veto of the first bill. The Senate (10 Sept.) failed to override his veto.

19 Aug. 2D FEDERAL BANK-RUPTCY LAW permitted, with few exceptions, any person to become a voluntary bankrupt, but allowed creditors to proceed against traders; repealed 3 Mar. 1843. During its brief life 33,739 debtors availed themselves of the law; $441 million in debt canceled, while less than $47 million was surrendered by debtors.

11 Sept. CABINET RESIGNA-TIONS. Angry over what they regarded as a betrayal of faith, all the members of the cabinet except Webster resigned (11 Sept.). All of the departing members

(with the exception of Granger) made public statements charging that Tyler had committed himself to support the bank bill. The evidence on the circumstances attending Tyler's second veto is conflicting, but it tends to clear Tyler of charges of duplicity.

Named to the cabinet on 13 Sept. were Walter Forward (Pa.), Secretary of the Treasury; Abel P. Upshur (Va.), Secretary of the Navy; Hugh Swinton Legaré (S.C.), Attorney General; and Charles A. Wickliffe (Ky.), Postmaster General. Upon the death of Legaré (20 June 1843), John Nelson (Md.) was named Attorney General (1 July 1943). On 12 Oct. John C. Spencer (N.Y.) was appointed Secretary of War.

Tyler's administration witnessed frequent cabinet shifts. Spencer was replaced in the War Department by James M. Porter (Pa., 8 Mar. 1843), who in turn was replaced (15 Feb. 1844) by William Wilkins (Pa.). Webster retired as Secretary of State (8 May 1843) and was replaced (24 July 1843) by Abel P. Upshur (Va.), who was succeeded as Secretary of the Navy by David Henshaw (Mass., 24 July 1843). Henshaw was replaced by Thomas W. Gilmer (Va., 15 Feb. 1844). Upshur and Gilmer were killed (28 Feb. 1844) by the explosion of a gun on the warship *Princeton*. John C. Calhoun was appointed Secretary of State (6 Mar. 1844) and John Y. Mason (Va.) was named Secretary of the Navy (14 Mar. 1844). Calhoun's entry into the cabinet marked his final *rapprochement* with the Democratic party, and the rise of Southern influence in shaping Democratic policy.

1842

21–23 Mar. "CREOLE" CASE AND GIDDINGS RESOLUTIONS. The *Creole*, an American brig carying a cargo of slaves, sailed from Hampton Roads,

Va. (27 Oct. 1841), for New Orleans. During the voyage the slaves mutinied, killed a white crew member in taking possession of the ship, and forced the mate to proceed to Nassau in the Bahama Islands. The British authorities at Nassau freed all slaves except actual participants in the revolt, who were held on criminal charges. Secretary of State Webster protested and demanded the return of the slaves as "mutineers and murderers and the recognized property" of U.S. citizens. The British took no immediate steps to satisfy the demand, and the matter was not adjusted until 1855, with an award of $110,330 to the U.S.

Rep. Joshua R. Giddings, a Whig from the Western Reserve district of Ohio, offered a series of resolutions (21–22 Mar.) based on the *Creole* case and directed against slavery and the coastal trade in slaves. The resolutions angered Southern representatives. When a censuring resolution against Giddings was adopted by a substantial House majority (23 Mar.), he resigned from Congress. A majority of more than 3,000 voters returned him to his seat in a special election (Apr.).

9 AUG. WEBSTER-ASHBURTON TREATY. Soon after taking office as Secretary of State, Webster initiated resumption of negotiations with Great Britain for settlement of the northeastern boundary question. A conciliatory atmosphere was created by the replacement (Sept. 1841) of the British government under Lord Melbourne by that headed by Sir Robert Peel. As special minister, Alexander Baring, 1st Lord Ashburton, arrived at Washington in the spring of 1842 and began his informal discussions with Webster on 13 June. Commissioners from the states of Maine and Massachusetts, and, at one critical point, President Tyler, took part in negotiations eventuating in the Webster-Ashburton Treaty.

Under its terms, the controversial northeastern boundary provisions of the Treaty of 1783 were scrapped and the Maine-New Brunswick boundary was fixed along its present line. The U.S. received about 7,000 of the 12,000 square miles of disputed territory, somewhat less than the award made by the King of the Netherlands in 1831. The compromise enabled the British to retain their military route between New Brunswick and Quebec. The claims of Maine and Massachusetts were satisfied in part by a U.S. payment of $150,000 to each state. The boundary line along the northern frontiers of Vermont and New York and thence westward to the Lake of the Woods was based on pre-1774 surveys and adjusted about a half mile north of the 45th parallel, thus leaving the U.S. in possession of its military works under construction at the northern head of Lake Champlain. Provision was made for a boundary commission to survey and mark the line.

Other articles gave the U.S. navigation rights on the St. John River (important for Maine's economy); provided for mutual extradition in cases involving 7 specified nonpolitical crimes; for a cruising convention authorizing the maintenance of joint squadrons for suppressing the slave trade along the African coast. The British without any reciprocal concession agreed to a line between Lake Superior and the Lake of the Woods (which gave the U.S. the Mesabi iron deposits, not discovered until 1866). Through an exchange of notes, Lord Ashburton made an unofficial and carefully guarded apology that disposed of the *Caroline* affair and the McLeod case.

The treaty was approved by the Senate, 39–9 (20 Aug.), and promulgated in Nov. The acceptance of the treaty was accompanied in both the U.S. and Great Britain by the so-called battle of the maps, in which each government answered domestic opposition by pointing to separate and conflicting maps indicating that the concessions were more than fair.

DORR REBELLION. The popular movement within the states to abolish limitations upon the suffrage resulted in serious disturbances in Rhode Island, where the charter granted (1663) by Charles II that served as the state constitution restricted suffrage to freeholders and their eldest sons. This provision deprived more than half of the adult males of voting privileges. When petitions proved ineffective, a committee of the disfranchised called a convention at Providence (Oct. 1841) that framed the "People's Constitution" providing for white manhood suffrage. The instrument was ratified by a majority of the adult male citizens who voted on it (Dec. 1841). In a countermove, the state legislature called a convention at Newport for revising the constitution (Nov. 1841), but the convention's decision to extend the franchise was defeated when the "Landholders' Constitution" was submitted to the vote of the freeholders (Mar.).

Both factions conducted separate elections for the legislature and state officers in the spring of 1842. The opponents of the old constitution chose **Thomas W. Dorr** as governor (18 Apr.). Dorr and his supporters, who controlled northwestern Rhode Island, established a state government basing its authority on the power residing in the people. Dorr was inaugurated at Providence. The old charter party reelected Gov. **Samuel W. King,** inaugurated at Newport. The conservative legislature of the King regime declared the Dorr party in a state of insurrection, imposed martial law, and called out the state militia to sustain its authority.

With Rhode Island under a dual government, both Dorr and King called upon President Tyler for help. Tyler replied in a letter to King which, despite its conciliatory tenor, made it clear that the national government would intervene if necessary on behalf of the old charter government to enforce Art. IV, Sect. 4 of the federal Constitution.

When the Dorr party undertook military preparations, President Tyler issued instructions for the employment of federal troops in support of state militia if circumstances required such action. The rebellion crumbled after the Dorrites made an unsuccessful attempt (18 May) to seize the Rhode Island state arsenal. After fleeing the state, Dorr returned and gave himself up to the authorities. He was tried and sentenced (25 June 1844) to life imprisonment, but amnestied and released in 1845. Meanwhile, a new constitution incorporating liberalized suffrage provisions was adopted (Apr. 1843). The suit arising from the contest of the 2 governments within the state led to the Supreme Court opinion (1849) in *Luther* v. *Borden* (p. 668).

31 MAR. CLAY'S RESIGNATION. The defeat of the Whigs in the midterm congressional elections enabled the Democrats to take control of the House. With the failure of the Whig program in Congress, Henry Clay, the chief proponent of party policy, resigned from the Senate to devote himself to consolidating the Whig party in preparation for the campaign of 1844. Clay took leave of the Senate in a speech that ranks among his most memorable. He was succeeded by John J. Crittenden.

1843

BEGINNINGS OF POLITICAL NATIVISM (also p. 827). The **Native American Association** was formed at

Washington in 1837. In the 1840s a variety of causes, including intensified anti-Catholic feeling and the influx of Irish immigrants, led to the establishment (June) of the **American Republican** party at New York. Its platform stressed opposition to voting and office-holding privileges for Catholics and foreigners. Nativist elements in New York and elsewhere frequently combined with the Whigs against the Democrats. The controversy was heightened by the public-school issue in New York state, where the Catholic demand for public funds to aid their parochial schools resulted in a movement to restrict voting privileges. Protestant resentment was also stirred by Catholic opposition to the reading of the King James version of the Bible in the public schools. In the local elections in New York City (1844), the American Republican party formed a coalition with the Whigs and succeeded in electing a nativist mayor.

The culmination of nativist agitation during the 1840s came at Philadelphia, where an American Republican Association was formed in Apr. 1844. A series of violent armed clashes between Protestants and Catholics (6–8 May, 5–8 July 1844) resulted in the death of about 20 persons and the injury of about 100. State militia were called out to suppress the disorders. The nativists called their first national convention at Philadelphia (5–7 July 1845) and adopted the name **Native American** party. Its platform called for changes in the naturalization laws. Nativist agitation was revived in the 1850s, which saw the rise of the **Know-Nothing (American)** party.

1844

OREGON DISPUTE. The Anglo-American Convention of 1818, which established a 10-year joint occupation of the disputed Oregon country, was renewed (6 Aug. 1827) for an indefinite term with the stipulation that on a year's notice the occupation agreement might be unilaterally terminated. The Oregon country lay between the Rocky Mountains and the Pacific Ocean, and between the 42nd parallel and 54°40′. The treaties which the U.S. concluded with Spain (1819) and Russia (1824) narrowed the Oregon controversy to 2 parties: the U.S. and Great Britain. The disputed area was the region north of the Columbia River and south of the 49th parallel.

U.S. Claims were based on (1) explorations of Capt. Robert Gray, who in 1792 discovered and entered the mouth of the Columbia River, which was named for his vessel; (2) Lewis and Clark expedition (1803–06); (3) rights to the Pacific coast north of the 42nd parallel, under the treaty with Spain, and to the coast south of 54°40′, under the treaty with Russia; (4) the fur-trading post of Astoria, established (1811) at the mouth of the Columbia by **John Jacob Astor** (p. 976), head of the Pacific Fur Co., as the first permanent settlement along the lower Columbia; and (5) actual occupation by American settlers (including Methodist and Presbyterian missionaries), who after 1841 came to Oregon in growing numbers, establishing settlements in the Willamette Valley south of the Columbia River. By 1845 5,000 Americans were in the region below the Columbia River.

British Claims were based on (1) Nootka Sound Treaty (1790), under which Spain relinquished some of her claims; (2) voyage of Capt. Cook (1778); (3) explorations of Capt. George Vancouver (1792), who ascended part of the Columbia River shortly after its discovery by Gray, and of Sir Alexander Mackenzie (1793), who ascended part of the Fraser River; (4) fur-trading activities of the Hudson's Bay Co., which consolidated its power by absorbing (1821) the North West Co., an organization that earlier had amalgamated all British and Canadian fur-trading operations; and (5) establishment (1805) by the North West Co. of Ft. McLeod, the first settlement in the Oregon interior.

Beginning with the administration of John Quincy Adams, the U.S. government made repeated offers to fix the Oregon boundary along the 49th parallel. British refusal stemmed from unwillingness to sacrifice the trade of the Columbia River basin, access to a port on the Strait of Juan de Fuca, and the navigation of Puget Sound. The question did not cause serious controversy until the American population in Oregon began to increase rapidly.

A Senate bill introduced (16 Dec. 1841) by Lewis F. Linn (Mo.) provided for the militarization of the overland route from Missouri to Oregon and for land grants to male immigrants over 18 years of age. The measure, which was before Congress, 1841–43, never became law, but encouraged immigration to Oregon and increased British apprehensions. Petitions for the establishment of a territorial government were submitted to Congress by the people of Oregon and by state legislatures. A meeting of Oregon settlers at Champoeg (5 July 1843) adopted a constitution for a **provisional government** to serve until the U.S. extended its jurisdiction over Oregon. In the same month a Cincinnati convention held on the Oregon issue adopted a resolution calling for 54°40′ as the American line.

Great Britain responded to U.S. offers by indicating her readiness to make a boundary adjustment along the Columbia River line. By the close of 1844 the development of serious Anglo-U.S. friction was intensified by the injection of the Oregon question into the presidential campaign. Great Britain, rebuffed by the U.S. on an offer to reopen negotiations, took a more determined stand.

TEXAS QUESTION. Largely because of the opposition of the antislavery forces, the ambition of the Texas Republic under President Sam Houston for immediate annexation to the U.S. was not fulfilled. The abolitionists viewed the Texas settlements and revolution as a conspiracy of slaveholders. Northern Whigs opposed annexation from fear that several slave states would be carved from Texas territory. Resolutions calling for annexation adopted by Southern state legislatures were answered by opposing resolutions from Northern legislatures.

Rebuffed by the U.S., Texas formally withdrew its offer of annexation (12 Oct. 1838) and under **Mirabeau B. Lamar,** who succeeded Houston as president (Dec. 1838), proceeded to shape a foreign policy designed to assure its complete and permanent independence. Texas dispatched diplomatic agents to Europe, concluded treaties with France (1839), Holland and Belgium (1840), and Great Britain (1840), and secured loans for a program of commercial development. The British favored an independent Texas as a balance of power in North America, a buffer state against U.S. expansion, a valuable source of cotton production, and a duty-free market for British manufactured goods. In the lead of British public opinion supporting Texan independence were the abolitionists, who believed that Texas might accede to the abolition of slavery in return for a sizable loan and thus become a base of operations against the institution of slavery in the U.S. South.

Texas, however, never abandoned its willingness to become a part of the U.S. Its ends were furthered by British moves and American alarm after Houston returned to power (Dec. 1841). The Mexicans invaded Texas in 1842. In mid-

1843 the British and French ministers to Mexico arranged a truce between that country and Texas. Shortly afterward, Isaac Van Zandt, Texan minister at Washington, was instructed to inform the U.S. authorities that the Texans were no longer interested in discussing annexation. The prospect of a close understanding between Texas and the 2 European powers caused anxiety at Washington and stirred fresh interest in annexation. Southern misgivings were increased by the circulation of reports that the British intended to use their influence to abolish slavery in Texas.

On 23 Aug. 1843, President Santa Anna notified the U.S. that the Mexican government would "consider equivalent to a declaration of war against the Mexican Republic the passage of an act of the incorporation of Texas in the territory of the United States; the certainty of the fact being sufficient for the immediate proclamation of war. . . ." On 16 Oct. 1843 Secretary of State Upshur informed Van Zandt that the U.S. was prepared to reopen negotiations for the annexation of Texas. Houston proceeded with caution, aware that if the treaty met rejection by the U.S. Senate, Texas would risk losing the support of Great Britain. He accordingly declined Upshur's proposal, thereby spurring the Secretary of State to make further efforts. On 16 Jan. Upshur informed William S. Murphy, the U.S. chargé in Texas, that "a clear constitutional majority of two-thirds" of the Senate favored the measure, and instructed Murphy to convey this information to Houston.

ANNEXATION OF TEXAS. On the basis of such assurance, Houston decided to accept the U.S. offer on condition that after the signing of the treaty but before its ratification the U.S. would take steps to furnish military and naval protection along the Gulf of Mexico and the south-western border as a safeguard against a Mexican attack. With the death of Secretary Upshur, his successor, John C. Calhoun, successfully completed the negotiations. The treaty, signed 12 Apr., provided for the annexation of Texas "subject to the same constitutional provision" as other U.S. territories, the surrender by Texas of its public lands to the U.S., and the assumption by the U.S. of the Texan debt to a maximum of $10 million.

The treaty was submitted to the Senate (22 Apr.), accompanied by a message from President Tyler urging annexation on the ground of broad national interest. Tyler made brief reference to the security of the Southern states and to the abolitionist danger posed by British interference in Texas. These remarks, coupled with Calhoun's note (18 Apr.) to the British minister vigorously defending the institution of slavery, strengthened the forces opposed to annexation. The abolitionists pointed to Calhoun's letter as proof of a slaveholders' conspiracy and succeeded in arousing Northerners who had been indifferent to annexation. The Senate rejected the treaty, 35–16 (8 June). Tyler then made a move to incorporate Texas in the Union by a joint resolution of both houses of Congress, but the measure failed to come to a vote by the time Congress adjourned (17 June). Meanwhile, Tyler carried out his pledge to send naval vessels to the Gulf of Mexico and troops to the Texas border. On 12 Dec. **Anson Jones** succeeded Houston as president of Texas.

Texas annexation, together with the Oregon dispute, became the leading issue in the presidential campaign. The British continued to use their diplomatic resources to keep Texas out of the Union. But British success (May 1845) in winning Mexican recognition of Texan independence came too late, for by then the U.S. Congress had acted and the Texans had decided to enter the Union.

27 Apr. CLAY–VAN BUREN LETTERS. Tyler's alienation of the Democratic party and his firm opposition to the Whig program made him a president without a party, leaving him without vital political support for renomination. Van Buren, still the political heir of Jackson, loomed as almost certain choice for the Democratic nomination in 1844. In May 1842, Van Buren visited Clay at Ashland, Ky. It was generally surmised that the 2 rivals reached an agreement to bar the Texas annexation issue from the next presidential campaign.

Van Buren's Southern opponents, aware of his hostility to annexation, obtained a letter from Jackson (12 Feb. 1843) favoring the acquisition of Texas. The letter, published in the Richmond *Enquirer* (22 Mar.), posed an immediate and crucial test for Van Buren on the eve of the Democratic National Convention. Approval of annexation would cost him his Democratic following in the key state of New York, where a party schism had begun to develop over the slavery question; rejection of the policy would lose him the Southern vote.

On 27 Apr. Van Buren and Clay published separate letters opposing the immediate annexation of Texas. Van Buren's letter (dated 20 Apr.), which appeared in the Washington *Globe*, maintained that annexation would probably involve the U.S. in an unjustifiable war with Mexico. His declaration, which incensed Southerners and alienated Jackson, was instrumental in depriving Van Buren of the Democratic nomination. When Jackson learned of the letter, he indicated that the candidate "should be an annexation man" and should be "from the Southwest," and finally threw his support to James K. Polk.

Clay's **"Raleigh letter"** (dated 17 April) was published in the *National Intelligencer*. It declared that the annexation of Texas without the consent of Mexico would lead to war with that nation, and was "dangerous to the integrity of the Union . . . and not called for by any general expression of public opinion." After winning the Whig nomination for the presidency, Clay publicly qualified his position in the **"Alabama letters"** addressed to Stephen F. Miller of Tuscaloosa, Ala. In the first letter (1 July), Clay stated that while he was not opposed to annexation, he believed that the unyielding attitude of the abolitionists made the integrity of the Union the paramount consideration. His second letter (27 July) asserted that "far from having any personal objection to the annexation of Texas, I should be glad to see it, without dishonor, without war, with the common consent of the Union, and upon just and fair terms. I do not think that the subject of slavery ought to affect the question, one way or the other." His explanation further embittered Northern antislavery sentiment and, derisively quoted out of context, was used by the Democrats to picture Clay as an opportunist.

3 July. TREATY OF WANG HIYA negotiated by **Caleb Cushing** (p. 1008) with Commissioner Extraordinary Tsiyeng, representing the Emperor of China, opened 5 Chinese ports to American merchants, insured extraterritorial legal rights for Americans living in China, and gave U.S. most-favored-nation treatment.

PRESIDENTIAL CAMPAIGN. The national convention of the Liberty party met at Buffalo, N.Y. (30 Aug. 1843), and unanimously nominated **James G. Birney** for president and **Thomas Morris** (Ohio) for vice-president. Its platform, consisting of 21 planks based almost entirely on the salvery question, made no direct reference to the annexation of Texas, but denounced the extension of slave territory.

The Whig National Convention met at Baltimore (1 May) and unanimously nominated **Henry Clay** for president; **Theodore Frelinghuysen** (N.J.) was chosen for vice-president. The Whig platform, a general statement of party principles, advocated a single term for the presidency, made no reference to the Texas issue, and was silent on the question of a national bank.

The Democratic National Convention, which assembled at Baltimore (27 May), was the first convention whose proceedings were reported by telegraph (over a line connecting Baltimore and Washington). Van Buren led on the 1st ballot, but Southern insistence on the application of the "two-thirds rule" disposed of his bid. On the 9th ballot (29 May), and on the 2nd ballot after his name had been placed before the convention, **James K. Polk** (Tenn., p. 1130) was unanimously chosen as the presidential candidate. Silas Wright (N.Y.), a Van Burenite and antislavery man, was chosen for vice-president. He declined the nomination, and the convention chose instead **George M. Dallas** (Pa.). Polk, first "dark horse" nominee in the history of the presidency, had the support of Andrew Jackson. The suggestion for his nomination came from the historian George Bancroft, a member of the Massachusetts delegation, in consultation with Gideon J. Pillow (Tenn.).

Robert J. Walker (Miss.), chairman of the executive committee of the Democratic party, formulated an expansionist platform designed to appeal to Northerners and Southerners alike. Its main plank declared that "our title to the whole of the Territory of Oregon is clear and unquestionable; that no portion of the same ought to be ceded to England or any other power; and that the reoccupation of Oregon and the reannexation of Texas at the earliest practicable period are great American measures, which this Convention recommends to the cordial support of the Democracy of the Union." The Democratic slogan of "54°40′ or Fight" (variously attributed to Sen. William Allen [Ohio] and Samuel Medary, editor of the *Ohio Statesman*) was used to court Northern voters on the Oregon issue and to offset the Whigs' scornful query, "Who is James K. Polk?"

The Tyler Democrats also assembled at Baltimore on 27 May, to the rallying cry of "Tyler and Texas." Although the delegates represented every state in the Union, they had an estimated total following of only 150,000. **Tyler,** who had unsuccessfully attempted to establish a third party by the use of patronage, accepted (30 May) the nomination. When it became clear that he could not hope to win over the annexationist element, he withdrew (20 Aug.) after reaching an understanding with Robert J. Walker, and brought his supporters into the Democratic fold. Tyler thus became the first president who failed to stand for a 2d term.

4 Dec. PRESIDENTIAL ELECTION resulted in a close popular vote: **Polk,** 1,337,243; Clay, 1,299,068; Birney, 62,300. Polk's victory hinged upon the electoral vote (36) of New York, which Clay lost by 5,080 votes, and where Birney, by an accession of antislavery Whig strength in the western counties, received 15,812 votes. **Polk** received 170 electoral votes, carrying 15 of the 26 states; Clay 105 votes. Had Clay carried New York, he would have been elected president by 7 electoral votes.

1845

23 Jan. By act of Congress, the Tuesday following the first Monday in Nov. was designated the uniform election day for future presidential elections.

1 MAR. ANNEXATION OF TEXAS. When the 2d session of the 28th Congress convened (2 Dec. 1844), Tyler recommended that the Texas treaty be accepted by **joint resolution** of Congress. He made his plea on the grounds that (1) the presidential election had demonstrated that "a controlling majority of the States have declared in favor of immediate annexation," and (2) that strained relations between Texas and Mexico weakened both powers, to the advantage of interested foreign nations (i.e., Great Britain).

A joint resolution (demanding a simple majority in both houses and the signature of the president) obviated the necessity of the two-thirds Senate vote required for ratification. The annexation resolution was passed by the House (25 Jan.), 120–98 (112 Democrats and 8 Southern Whigs in favor, 70 Whigs and 28 Northern Democrats opposed). In the Senate, Thomas Hart Benton posed the constitutional objection that Congress was not authorized to admit a state carved from foreign territory. An amendment offered by Robert J. Walker (Miss.) empowered the president to negotiate a new treaty which might either be ratified by the Senate or adopted by a joint resolution. In this form the measure, which made no reference to securing the consent of Mexico, was passed by the Senate by 27–25 (27 Feb.) and the House (28 Feb.), 132–76, indicating a restoration of party lines. It was the first time that a joint resolution had been employed to approve a treaty or to acquire territory. The resolution provided that Texas was to be admitted to statehood without a preliminary period of territorial status; that, with the consent of Texas, not more than 4 additional states might be formed from its territory; that Texas was to retain her public lands, but pay her own debt; and that the Missouri Compromise line of 36°30' was to be extended to Texas territory.

Great Britain and France succeeded (Mar.–May) in inducing Texas and Mexico to sign the preliminaries of a treaty whereby Mexico would recognize the independence of Texas if the latter should promise to relinquish annexation. These negotiations were quickly abandoned by Texas after the Lone Star Republic received news of the congressional action. A special session of the Texan Congress voted for annexation (23 June); a convention (4 July) called by President Jones accepted the terms; and the act of the convention was ratified by the people of Texas (13 Oct.). Texas was admitted to the Union (29 Dec.). A state government was formally installed at Austin on 19 Feb. 1846.

3 MAR. President Tyler vetoed (20 Feb.) a bill that prohibited payment for some naval craft that he had ordered built. The Senate and the House passed the measure over his veto on the last day of his administration, the first time a presidential veto was overridden.

4 MAR. In his inaugural address, Polk reaffirmed the Democratic platform's declaration that the U.S. title to Oregon was "clear and unquestionable" and asserted that the question of Texas annexation belonged "exclusively to the United States and Texas" as the prerogative of 2 independent powers.

10 OCT. Formal opening of the "Naval School" at Ft. Severn, Annapolis, Md. Founded by Secretary of the Navy Bancroft, it became known (1850) as the U.S. Naval Academy.

"BARNBURNERS" AND "HUNKERS" were 2 factions (c.1843 et seq.) in the Democratic party in New York state whose electoral vote played a pivotal role in the presidential election of 1844. In alliance with the Loco-Focos of the cities, the "Barnburners" were the radical and reform wing of the party. Leaders: Martin Van Buren and his son, John; Silas Wright; Benjamin F. Butler (1795–1858); and Azariah C. Flagg. Because of their uncompromising determination, the "Barnburners" were thus characterized by their opponents after the Dutch farmer who burned his barn in order to destroy the rats. The conservative "Hunkers" were so called by their antagonists after a corruption of the Dutch word *hunkerer*, meaning a self-seeking person, with particular application to politicians who "hunkered," i.e., "hungered" or "hankered" after office. Leaders: William L. Marcy and Daniel S. Dickinson.

Their initial differences stemmed from local issues, such as internal improvements and the chartering of state banks (both favored by the Hunkers) and the distribution of patronage. After the election of Polk, these disagreements were colored by national issues. The Barnburners opposed the annexation of Texas and the extension of slavery into the territories.

An open political contest between the 2 wings occurred in 1845, when they ran separate candidates for the state legislature in many districts. In Sept. 1847, the Barnburners withdrew from the Democratic state convention at Syracuse after the Hunkers defeated their resolution declaring "uncompromising hostility to the extension of slavery into territory now free." In 1848 the Barnburners seceded from the Democratic national convention and joined the Free-Soilers, whose vote held the balance of power in the presidential election of 1848. The Barnburners later rejoined the Democratic fold, but their antislavery views led them into the Republican party in the mid-1850s.

ANTIRENT WAR, 1839–46, a culmination of agrarian unrest in upstate New York against the perpetual leases dating from the period of Dutch and English rule. The earliest serious disturbances connected with the Antirent War broke out (1839–40) in the manor of Rensselaerswyck in the Albany region when the heirs of Stephen Van Rensselaer precipitated tenant resistance by attempting to collect $400,000 in back rents. The ensuing "**Helderberg War,**" directed against the system of patroonships, was suppressed by militia called out by Gov. William H. Seward. Other revolts occurred in the area south of Albany, where farmers organized secret societies and, disguised as Indians, interfered with or attacked law-enforcement officers (a situation portrayed by James Fenimore Cooper in his novels *Satanstoe* [1845], *The Chainbearer* [1846], and *The Redskins* [1846]). The murder of a deputy sheriff (Aug.) caused Delaware Co. to be placed under martial law. Impact on state politics: Gov. Silas Wright called for legislation (1846) restricting the duration of farm leases and abolishing distress for rent in all new leases. The disturbances led to the adoption of the more liberal constitution of 1846. Perpetual leases were gradually replaced by fee-simple tenure.

2 DEC. "POLK DOCTRINE." In his first annual message to Congress, Polk recommended tariff revision, the restoration of the Independent Treasury, urged Congress to take measures to protect the U.S. claim to the whole of the Oregon country, and proposed abrogation of the convention for joint occupation. Especially significant was his elaboration of the Monroe Doctrine: (1) "The people of *this continent* alone have the right to decide their own destiny." (2) "We can never consent that European powers shall interfere to prevent such a union [of an independent state with the U.S.] because it might disturb the 'balance of power' which they may desire to maintain upon this continent." (3) "No future European colony or dominion shall with our consent be planted or established on any part of the North American continent."

"MANIFEST DESTINY." The earliest known appearance of the phrase occurred in an unsigned editorial article published in the expansionist organ, *The United States Magazine and Democratic Review* (July–Aug.). The article, subsequently attributed to the magazine's founder and editor, **John L. O'Sullivan,** declared that foreign governments were attempting to obstruct the annexation of Texas in order to check "the fulfillment of our manifest destiny to overspread the continent allotted by Providence for the free development of our yearly multiplying millions." The phrase came into vogue after use in an editorial in the New York *Morning News* (27 Dec.) on the Oregon dispute. Its first use in Congress supposedly dates from the speech (3 Jan. 1846) made by Rep. Robert C. Winthrop (Mass.). During the debate on the resolution for terminating the joint occupation of Oregon, Winthrop referred to "the right of our manifest destiny to spread over this whole continent."

BREAK WITH MEXICO. On 28 Mar., soon after the passage of the joint resolution for the annexation of Texas, Mexico broke off diplomatic relations with the U.S. and took steps (June) to increase its armed forces in order to resist annexation. Major grievances: (1) **Boundary disagreements** stemmed from Mexican insistence on the Nueces River as the southwestern line of Texas. Under the treaty of 12 May 1836, which had been rejected by the Mexican government, the Texans laid claim to the Rio Grande as their lower frontier. The view of the U.S. government, as shaped by Secretary of State Buchanan, was that the annexation of Texas had revived legitimate territorial claims west of the Sabine River held by the U.S. before the signing of the Adams-Onís Treaty (1819). (2) **Halting by Mexico of payments** (1843) of more than $2 million in **adjusted damages to U.S. nationals** authorized by the claims conventions of 1839 and 1843 and the commission award of 1840. (3) **Status of California,** where the Mexican government had issued orders for expulsion of U.S. settlers and exclusion of further immigrants. The U.S. government believed that the British were actively engaged in intrigues to take California. For its part Mexico regarded the U.S. annexation of Texas as evidence of insatiable land- and power-hunger, and regarded the Nueces, the Texas boundary when it was part of Coahuila province, as the correct boundary.

Gen. **Zachary Taylor,** in command of the U.S. forces in the Southwest, with headquarters at Ft. Jesup, La., was ordered (28 May) to maintain his troops (known as the "Army of Observation") in a state of readiness for an advance into Texas to be made upon his receipt of official information that it had been invaded after consenting to annexation. On 15 June he was ordered to occupy a point "on or near the Rio Grande" for the defense of the territory of Texas. Taylor advanced into Texas (26 July); established his base (31 July) on the south bank of the Nueces, near Corpus Christi, about 150 miles from the Rio Grande; and suggested (4 Oct.) that if the U.S. contemplated fixing the boundary line along the Rio Grande, an advantage would be secured by advancing to Point Isabel, on the Gulf of Mexico near the mouth of the Rio Grande. By mid-Oct. Taylor had under his command about 3,500 troops, approximately one half the U.S. army.

Taylor was ordered (13 Jan. 1846) to

advance from the Nueces to "positions on or near the left bank" of the Rio Grande, but did not receive his instructions until 3 Feb. and did not begin his advance until 8 Mar. Point Isabel was burned by the Mexicans before Taylor arrived there (24 Mar.). His second in command, Gen. William J. Worth, proceeded to the left (or north) bank of the Rio Grande, opposite Matamoros, where the Mexicans had about 5,700 men. Both sides spent the following month building fortifications. On 12 Apr. 1846, Gen. Pedro de Ampudia, in command of the forces at Matamoros, warned Taylor to retire beyond the Nueces; otherwise, "arms and arms alone must decide the question." Taylor refused to comply, and requested U.S. naval forces to blockade the mouth of the Rio Grande.

SLIDELL MISSION. In Aug. the U.S. received confidential information that the Mexican government was apparently willing to resume diplomatic relations. At the recommendation of Secretary of State Buchanan, President Polk appointed **John Slidell** (La., 1793–1871) to undertake a secret mission to Mexico for the purpose of purchasing Upper California and New Mexico, and adjusting the boundary line to run along the Rio Grande from its mouth to the 32nd parallel and thence westward to the Pacific. Polk, with the unanimous support of his cabinet, was prepared to pay from $15 to $40 million.

John Black, U.S. consul at Mexico City, reported (17 Oct.) that Manuel de Peña y Peña, foreign minister of the Mexican government under President José J. Herrera, had agreed (15 Oct.) to receive a "commissioner" authorized to discuss the Texas boundary issue, on condition that the U.S. squadron off Vera Cruz should be removed. The recall of the naval force was ordered by Commodore David Conner immediately after

he learned that the Mexicans had consented to negotiation.

President Polk and Secretary Buchanan agreed (7 Nov.) to dispatch Slidell at once. Despite the Mexican government's insistence on confining the discussions to the disputed Texas boundary, Slidell received amended instructions (10 Nov.) authorizing the purchase of New Mexico for $5 million and of California for $25 million, in return for Mexican approval of the Rio Grande as the Texas boundary. In addition, the U.S. would assume the claims of its nationals against Mexico. Slidell was accredited as envoy extraordinary and minister plenipotentiary. Meanwhile, Thomas O. Larkin, U.S. consul at Monterey, Calif., was appointed confidential agent (17 Oct.) with instructions to block the attempt by any foreign power to secure California. He was also informed that the U.S. policy envisaged the peaceful acquisition of California with the active support of the settlers, but in a manner that would not give the Mexicans cause for grievance.

When Slidell reached Mexico City (6 Dec.), the nature of his mission had already become known. After some delay caused by Herrera and his cabinet, who refused to accept responsibility in the face of a hostile public opinion, Slidell was informed (16 Dec.) that the Mexican government could not receive him for the following reasons: his mission apparently lacked the consent of Congress; his appointment had not been confirmed by the Senate; and the Mexicans had agreed to receive a commissioner authorized to negotiate the Texas question rather than a minister plenipotentiary empowered to discuss extraneous issues. When Slidell's report reached Washington (12 Jan. 1846), Gen. Taylor was ordered (13 Jan. 1846) to proceed to the Rio Grande.

Slidell's appointment was confirmed by the Senate (20 Jan. 1846). The Mexican government, however, persisted in its refusal to discuss any question other than the Texas boundary. Meanwhile, the Herrera government was overthrown (31 Dec.) by Gen. Mariano Paredes, who assumed the presidency (4 Jan. 1846) with a reaffirmation of Mexico's claim to Texas up to the Sabine River and a declaration of his purpose to defend all territory regarded by him as Mexican. Slidell informed Washington (6 Feb. 1846) that the inflexible attitude of the Mexicans was reinforced by their belief that the U.S. would become involved in war with Great Britain over the Oregon dispute. Upon Slidell's final inquiry (1 Mar. 1846), the Paredes government refused to receive him (12 Mar.), and late in Mar. he requested his passports and left Mexico.

1846

15 June. OREGON SETTLEMENT. In his first annual message to Congress (2 Dec. 1845) Polk claimed the whole of Oregon; recommended ending the Anglo-U.S. convention for joint occupation; called for extension of U.S. jurisdiction over the Oregon settlers, military protection of the Oregon Trail, and the establishment of an Indian agency beyond the Rocky Mountains. His unyielding attitude toward Great Britain was greeted by expansionist cries of "54°40′ or fight!" Strong support of his position came from the states of the Old Northwest, whose prominent Democratic voices in Congress included Sen. **Lewis Cass** (Mich., p. 999) and Rep. **Stephen A. Douglas** (Ill., p. 1015).

The resolution for terminating joint occupation was introduced in the House (5 Jan.) and, after lengthy debate (including a Senate filibuster), was passed

(23 Apr.) in the Senate, 42–10, and in the House, 142–46. The resolution, signed by Polk on 27 Apr., authorized the president to give the required year's notice at his discretion. Polk served notice on 21 May.

Meanwhile, Richard Pakenham, British minister to the U.S., requested (27 Dec. 1845) renewal of the U.S. offer of the 49th parallel as the boundary of Oregon and asked that the question be submitted to arbitration. Polk refused to renew the proposal. Secretary Buchanan (26 Feb.) then informed Louis McLane, U.S. minister at London, that discussions would be reopened if the British took the initiative. There was strong resistance in Great Britain to concession on this score, but a truce in British party politics enabled the new ministry under Lord Russell to adopt a conciliatory approach toward the U.S. Not less important in influencing the British attitude toward the U.S. was consideration of the economic ties between the 2 nations (British Corn Laws repealed 26 June). Lord Aberdeen, British foreign secretary, submitted his proposal in the form of a draft treaty that reached Washington 6 June. Almost at the same time, Aberdeen informed the British minister to Mexico that Great Britain was unwilling to interfere between the U.S. and Mexico.

Because of the uncompromising stand he had taken on the Oregon question, Polk deemed it proper (at the suggestion of the cabinet) to take the unprecedented course of laying the British proposal before the Senate (10 June) for its advice on the matter. The Senate, 37–12 (12 June), advised its acceptance, and ratified it, 41–14 (15 June). Opposition came from expansionist elements in the Old Northwest, who accused Polk of deception and betrayal.

The treaty provided (1) that the

THE OREGON BOUNDARY DISPUTE

Scale of Miles
0   100   200   300

RUSSIAN TERRITORY

NORTHERN LIMIT OF U.S. CLAIM – 54°40′

OREGON

VANCOUVER IS.

CANADA

ROCKY

LINE OF 1846 – 49°

PACIFIC

CRUX OF DISPUTE 1846

Astoria   Ft. Vancouver   Ft. Walla Walla
Columbia

OCEAN

Willamette R.

OREGON

Snake

MTS.

UNITED

STATES

Ft. Hall

R.

SPANISH-AMERICAN BOUNDARY OF 1819 – 42°   TRAIL

MEXICAN   TERRITORY

boundary between U.S. and British territory in Oregon should be an extension of the existing continental line along the 49th parallel to the middle of the channel between Vancouver Island and the mainland, and thence along a line running southward through Juan de Fuca Strait to the Pacific; (2) for free navigation of the channel and strait by both parties; and (3) free navigation by the British of the Columbia River below the 49th parallel. The water boundary, however, was not finally defined until the arbitration award of 1873.

6 Aug. INDEPENDENT TREASURY ACT. With the defeat of the Whigs in the election of 1844, the Congress organized by the Democrats proceeded to revive the Independent Treasury Act that had been repealed by the Whigs in 1841. The bill was in substance the act of 4 July 1840. Except for changes in the banking structure made during the Civil War, the act served without important change as the basis of the U.S. fiscal system until passage of the Federal Reserve Act (1913). The subtreasuries were not abolished until after the act of 1920.

24 APR.–3 MAY. OPENING SKIRMISH. Gen. Mariano Arista succeeded Ampudia (24 Apr.) as commander of the Mexican forces at Matamoros, where the Mexicans had established Ft. Paredes. On the opposite bank of the river, Taylor's troops had erected Ft. Texas. Arista had orders (4 Apr.) from the Mexican minister of war authorizing him to attack. Arista notified Taylor (24 Apr.) that he considered hostilities as already begun. Pointing out that he had not committed any actions that could be construed as hostile, Taylor replied that "the responsibility must rest with them who actually commence them."

Arista dispatched a force of 1,600 cavalry under Gen. Anastasio Torrejón to cross the Rio Grande above Matamoros (24 Apr.). A reconnoitering party of 63 dragoons under Capt. Seth Thornton sent out by Taylor on the evening of the same day was surrounded and attacked (25 Apr.). Eleven Americans were killed, 5 wounded, the remainder captured. Upon receiving news of the Mexican attack, Taylor reported to Washington (26 Apr.) that "hostilities may now be considered as commenced." He immediately called upon the governors of Texas and Louisiana for a total of 5,000 volunteers. Taylor marched (1 May) to the relief of his supply base at Point Isabel. The Mexicans crossed the Rio Grande in force (30 Apr.–1 May) and on 3 May laid Ft. Texas (Maj. Jacob Brown commander) under siege.

The War with Mexico, 1846–48

11 MAY. POLK'S WAR MESSAGE. Slidell, reporting to Polk, 8 May, urged prompt action by the U.S. Taylor's report of the skirmish near Matamoros reached Washington Saturday, 9 May. The cabinet, in an evening session, unanimously supported the adoption of war measures. President Polk prepared his war message on Sunday and delivered it at noon on Monday, 11 May. Asserting that the U.S. held legitimate title to the disputed territory beyond the Nueces, Polk declared: "Mexico has . . . shed American blood upon the American soil."

13 MAY. DECLARATION OF WAR ON MEXICO. By 174–14 (11 May) the House of Representatives (29th Congress, 1st sess.) declared that "by the act of the Republic of Mexico, a state of war exists between that government and the United States." All of the opposing votes were cast by Northern representatives. An amendment stating that nothing in the measure should be construed as approval of Polk's course in ordering the military occupation of the disputed territory between the Nueces and the Rio Grande was defeated, 97–27. The House authorized a call for accepting 50,000 volunteers and voted a $10 million appropriation. Voting against this measure were 67 Whigs, foreshadowing the opposition to the administration that would increase as the war progressed. During the discussion of the war measures, an outspoken Whig, Garrett Davis (Ky.), asserted: "It is our own President who began this war."

In the Senate, Calhoun took exception to the preamble of the war declaration. He maintained that while armed clashes had occurred, Congress had not yet recognized a state of war, and so war did not exist "according to the sense of our Constitution." The war declaration, including the preamble, passed the Senate (12 May), 40–2 (both Whigs), with 3 abstentions, including Calhoun.

8–9 MAY. FIRST BATTLES. Battle of Palo Alto. After hastening construction of the defense works at Point Isabel, Taylor, at the head of about 2,300 troops and 200 supply wagons, began (7 May) his return march to Ft. Texas to relieve the besieged force. Midway on the road to Matamoros, near the water hole of Palo Alto, he encountered (8 May) an enemy force of 6,000 placed across the route of march. The engagement began at 2 P.M. and lasted about 5 hours. U.S. infantry broke up a Mexican cavalry attack across the prairie, and the Mexicans were finally repulsed by the superior fire of the U.S. guns, which easily won an artillery duel against the antiquated Mexican pieces. The U.S. losses: 9 killed, 45 wounded; Mexican losses: estimated 300–400. The Mexicans retreated southward, to a natural strong point above Matamoros, in a sunken riverbed or ravine called the Resaca de Guerrero, where a dense growth of chaparral afforded an excellent defensive position.

Battle of Resaca de la Palma. Instead of waiting for reinforcements, Taylor decided to pursue Arista's numerically superior force. At about 2 P.M. on 9 May, U.S. troops advanced to the edge of the Mexican position and occupied a ravine called the Resaca de la Palma.

About 1,700 Americans faced some 5,700 Mexicans in this engagement. Late in the afternoon, the Mexican army collapsed, fleeing across the Rio Grande with the Americans in close pursuit. U.S. losses: 39 killed, 83 wounded; estimated Mexican: 262 killed, 355 wounded, and about 150 captured or missing (in addition to many others lost by drowning during the crossing of the river). News of the battle made "Old Rough and Ready" Taylor a popular hero.

On the evening of 9 May, the siege of Ft. Texas was raised. The position was renamed Ft. Brown in honor of the officer who had commanded its defense. The Mexicans under Arista evacuated Matamoros (17–18 May), Taylor crossed the Rio Grande (18 May) and occupied the town.

MILITARY BALANCE SHEET. Mexican. At the outset of the war, the Mexican army had an initial numerical superiority. Its forces consisted of about 32,000 men, but the troops were defective in training, discipline, and equipment (most of its artillery pieces were obsolete and unreliable). It is estimated that during the war the peak strength of the Mexican army never exceeded 36,000 men. The officers were of a generally low quality (except for the engineers, who showed great skill in building entrenchments and fortifications), with a superabundance of high-ranking officers. The Mexicans had the advantage of fighting on familiar ground where the great distances involved afforded them a high degree of mobility.

U.S. At the outset of the war, the authorized U.S. regular army strength was 8,613, but the actual strength was 7,365 (8 regiments of infantry, 4 of artillery, 2 of dragoons). To fill the ranks, the government relied chiefly on short-term enlistments by volunteers (highly undependable). Six- and 12-month volunteers were the rule, and not until 12 Jan. 1847 did Congress enact legislation authorizing 5-year enlistments. Total U.S. force employed during the war, including about 31,000 regulars and marines: c.104,000. Chief U.S. disadvantages: (1) inadequate transportation and communication (telegraph not yet applied to military purposes); (2) poor provisions for health and sanitation (percentage of deaths caused by disease was more than 10% of total enrollment); (3) friction among the generals, and between them and the administration. Both Taylor and Gen. Winfield Scott were Whigs, and did not have the full confidence of a Democratic president and his cabinet. Scott was commanding general of the army, but because of strained relations with Polk and Marcy, was not permitted to depart for Mexico until late in 1846.

The Mexican campaigns gave U.S. officers who had never handled units larger than companies or battalions an opportunity to work with regiments and brigades. The war was valuable for its schooling of junior officers who later saw service as army or corps commanders with either side during the Civil War. Among those who later held commands in the Union armies were Lt. Ulysses S. Grant, Lt. William T. Sherman, Lt. George G. Meade, Lt. Joseph Hooker, Lt. George B. McClellan, Lt. John Pope, Lt. George H. Thomas, Lt. William B. Franklin, and Capt. Samuel P. Heintzelman. Those who afterward served with the Confederate forces included Capt. Robert E. Lee, Lt. Thomas Jonathan Jackson, Lt. Pierre G. Beauregard, Col. Albert Sidney Johnston, Lt. Col. Joseph E. Johnston, Lt. James Longstreet, Lt. Braxton Bragg, Lt. Richard S. Ewell, Lt. Daniel H. Hill, and Capt. William J. Hardee.

CAMPAIGN PLANS. Despite months of tension preceding the outbreak of hostilities, no military plans had been drawn up by the War Department. Within 2 days after declaration of war, Col. (later Gen.) **Stephen Watts Kearny** (1794–1848), commanding a cavalry regiment at Ft. Leavenworth, was ordered to lead the "Army of the West" (consisting of his regular force and a body of Missouri volunteers) on an expedition to New Mexico and to occupy its capital, Santa Fe. Commodore **David Conner** was ordered to blockade the enemy ports on the Gulf of Mexico, while Commodore

John D. Sloat was ordered to blockade the Mexican ports on the Pacific and to seize and hold San Francisco Bay. Additional instructions (3 June) authorized Kearny to take possession of California in conjunction with anticipated naval support from Sloat.

President Polk, in conference (14 May) with Secretary of War Marcy and Gen. Scott, formulated a plan of campaign, with the first major blow to be struck against the sparsely populated northern provinces of Mexico. At the urging of Scott, and after delays caused by friction between him and the administration, agreement was reached (20 Oct.–18 Nov.) on a joint army-navy expedition against Vera Cruz as the chief military objective. Gen. Scott was placed in command of the operation, which called for a landing at Vera Cruz, a march through the Mexican interior, and the seizure of Mexico City.

7 JULY–6 DEC. MISSION TO SANTA ANNA. Col. A. J. Atocha, a U.S. citizen of Spanish birth and a friend of Santa Anna (in exile in Cuba), advised Polk (Feb.) that in return for $30 million Santa Anna would arrange that the U.S. would get the Rio Grande as the southwestern boundary of Texas and that the boundary line of California would run through San Francisco Bay. Santa Anna advised Commander Alexander Slidell Mackenzie (7 July) that he would cooperate with the U.S., even give military advice. Accordingly, he was permitted to pass through the blockade, arrived at Vera Cruz (16 Aug.), and then proceeded to denounce the treachery of former President Herrera in attempting to negotiate with the U.S. He replied (19 Sept.) unsatisfactorily to Secretary Buchanan's peace feeler (19 Sept.). On 6 Aug. Paredes was deposed, Gen. Mariano Salas became acting president, and Santa Anna led (28 Sept.) an expeditionary force northward from Mexico City to

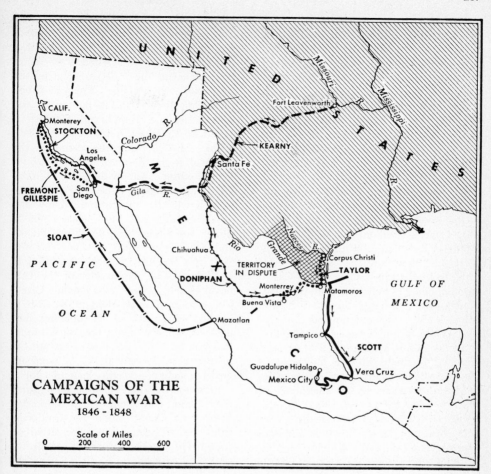

CAMPAIGNS OF THE
MEXICAN WAR
1846 - 1848

Scale of Miles
0   200   400   600

oppose Taylor. His election as president by the Mexican Congress (6 Dec.) ended hopes of early peace.

CONQUEST OF CALIFORNIA. Earlier History. Not until after 1840 did the American settlement of the Mexican province of California become numerically significant. The first important increase came with the colonization (1843) of the San Joaquin Valley. By the outset of 1846 there were approximately 500 American traders and settlers along the 500 miles of coast from Sonoma to San Diego, c.8,000–12,000 Mexicans of Spanish descent, and c.24,000 Indians.

The weak government of the province was made even more vulnerable by the conflict of authority between Pío Pico, provincial governor at Los Angeles, and Gen. José Castro, military commandant at Monterey. Acting on the mistaken belief that the U.S. and Mexico were at war, and that a British fleet was threatening to take possession of California, Commodore **Thomas ap Catesby Jones** proceeded from the Peruvian coast and landed a U.S. naval force at Monterey, where he seized the public buildings and raised the U.S. flag (20 Oct. 1842). Informed by Thomas O. Larkin, U.S.

consul at Monterey, that relations between Mexico and the U.S. were still
normal, Jones hauled down the flag (21
Oct. 1842). His act was disavowed by
President Tyler, and reparation and
apologies were made to the Mexican
government. On 17 Oct. 1845 Polk appointed Larkin confidential agent to
induce the California settlers to enter the
Union or establish an independent state
under U.S. protection. He learned of the
appointment 17 Apr. 1846.

10 JUNE–5 JULY. Bear Flag Revolt.
Leading his third surveying expedition
to the West (May 1845 *et seq.*), Capt.
John Charles Frémont (p. 1033) reached
Monterey (27 Jan.). With the apparent
permission of Castro, he established his
camp in the Salinas Valley. When Castro
warned him (3 Mar.) to quit the area,
his expedition erected breastworks atop
Gavilan Mountain and hoisted the U.S.
flag. In the face of a superior force, Frémont decided to withdraw (9 Mar.) and
marched to the north. He had reached
the edge of Klamath Lake, on the Oregon frontier, when he was overtaken (9
May) by Marine Lt. Archibald H. Gillespie, who conveyed to him dispatches
and correspondence. Whether Frémont
received from Gillespie secret verbal instructions to precipitate a revolt of the
American settlers against Mexican authority has not been established, but he
returned south and helped provoke resistance, at a time when the Pico-Castro
feud was brought to a head by news of
the revolution in Mexico (Dec. 1845)
that deposed Herrera and installed
Paredes as head of the government.
Castro announced (April) his support
of Paredes; Pico called a general convention (scheduled for 15 June at Santa
Barbara) to establish California as an
independent state under the protection of
a foreign nation. Castro retaliated by
dispatching an armed expedition to Los
Angeles, seat of the Pico regime.

A party of U.S. settlers in the Sacramento Valley attacked a section of Castro's expedition (10 June). Another
group, led by William B. Ide, seized Sonoma (14 June) and issued a proclamation declaring the independence of the
American settlements. This so-called
Bear Flag Revolt takes its name from the
standard of the "Republic of California"
raised at Sonama. Designed by William
Todd, this flag bore the name of the
republic, a grizzly bear, and a star, on a
field of white cloth. On 25 June, Frémont
arrived at Sonoma, where he identified
himself with the insurrection. A meeting
of the settlers (5 July) chose him to
direct the affairs of the "Republic of
California."

**7 JULY–17 AUG. Naval Expedition to
California.** The commander of the U.S.
naval force along the Pacific Coast,
Commodore **John D. Sloat** (1781–1867),
learned (17 May) of the opening skirmish of the war along the Rio Grande,
but took no action because of his written
instructions (24 June 1845) to avoid aggressive action and the lack of official
confirmation. When informed (7 June)
that Commodore Conner had blockaded
Vera Cruz, Sloat sailed for California
from the Mexican port of Mazatlán (8
June). He reached Monterey (2 July),
sent a force ashore (7 July), raised the
U.S. flag, and proclaimed California to
be a part of the U.S. On 9 July, under
Sloat's orders, Commander John B.
Montgomery seized San Francisco and
Lt. James W. Revere occupied Sonoma.
The Stars and Stripes replaced the Bear
Flag. Shortly afterward, a U.S. naval
party took possession of Sutter's Fort on
the Sacramento River.

In face of the common enemy, Castro
and Pico submerged their differences and
prepared their combined forces for a
stand at Los Angeles. Sloat, who was in
ill health, was replaced (23 July) by
Commodore **Robert F. Stockton** (1795–
1866), who issued a proclamation condemning Mexican resistance. The Cali-

fornia Battalion was organized (24 July) under Frémont, given the rank of major. Stockton's naval and military force occupied Santa Barbara and took Los Angeles (13 Aug.). Stockton issued a proclamation (17 Aug.) declaring the annexation of California by the U.S. and establishing a new regime with himself as governor. Frémont was named military commandant in the north and Gillespie in the south.

22–30 SEPT. Mexican Revolt. Immediately after Stockton reported to the Navy Department (22 Aug.) that "peace and harmony" had been restored in California, a Mexican revolt against the U.S. authorities broke out (22–30 Sept.), and the insurgents, under the leadership of Capt. José Maria Flores, drove the Americans from Los Angeles, Santa Barbara, San Diego, and other points. By 29 Oct., when Flores was installed as governor and military commandant, all of California south of San Luis Obispo was in the hands of the Mexicans. Meanwhile, the expeditionary force under Kearny, which had been reduced in the belief that the conquest of California had been consolidated, was headed toward San Diego.

2 AUG.–13 JAN. 1847. Kearny's Expedition. After a month's march from Ft. Leavenworth, the "Army of the West" under Kearny with a force of 1,700 reached Bent's Ft. (22–25 July) at the junction of the Arkansas River and the Santa Fe Trail, and he issued a proclamation (31 July) to the people of New Mexico declaring that he was entering the province "for the purpose of seeking union with and ameliorating the conditions of its inhabitants," and on 1 Aug. dispatched a letter to Gov. Manuel Armijo warning against resistance and pledging protection to those who cooperated. Kearny's force began (2 Aug.) its march through the desert country, proceeding along the Arkansas to the mouth of the Timpas and thence southwest to the mountains, where the troops negotiated the Raton Pass (elevation, 8,560 ft.). Kearny reached Las Vegas (15 Aug.) and proclaimed New Mexico to be part of the U.S. The estimated 4,000 Mexican troops assembled at the Apache Canyon dispersed without offering battle, thus terminating all enemy resistance in the province (an uprising by the Mexicans during the winter of 1846–47 was suppressed by troops commanded by Col. Sterling Price, who ended all organized resistance by investing Taos, 4 Feb. 1847). On 18 Aug., after marching 29 miles in less than a day, Kearny's troops occupied Santa Fe. Kearny issued a proclamation absolving the inhabitants of their allegiance to Mexico. After establishing a temporary territorial government under Gov. Charles Bent, Kearny left for California (25 Sept.) with 300 dragoons.

En route he encountered (6 Oct.) Kit Carson, bound for Washington with a dispatch from Frémont announcing the occupation of California. Kearny sent back 200 of his men. With the remaining 100 he crossed the Colorado (25 Nov.); entered Southern California, where the Flores insurrection against the U.S. occupation was in progress; and defeated (6 Dec.) a Mexican force at the village of **San Pascual.** U.S. losses: 18 dead, 13 wounded. Kearny reached San Diego 12 Dec. His subsequent operations under the command of Stockton secured the reconquest of California. Stockton and Kearny left San Diego (29 Dec.) with a mixed force of 559 dragoons, sailors, marines, and volunteers, and advanced northward across the plain to Los Angeles, which was taken (10 Jan. 1847) after 2 brief clashes with the enemy along and above the San Gabriel River (8, 9 Jan. 1847). These were the concluding hostilities of the war in California. The remnants of the Mexican forces, under Andres Pico in the San Fernando Valley, capitulated to Frémont and signed (13 Jan. 1847) the **Treaty of Cahuenga,** which gave them generous terms.

KEARNY-STOCKTON AFFAIR grew out of a conflict of instructions concerning the establishment of a civil government in California. Stockton, following to the letter the Navy Department orders to Sloat, contested Kearny's right to organize a new territorial government, suspended Kearny from all command other than that over his small force of dragoons, and appointed Frémont governor (16 Jan. 1847). Kearny, after warning Frémont that he was guilty of disobedience to his superior officer, returned to San Diego. The arrival of fresh instructions (13 Feb. 1847) gave Kearny the duty of establishing a new government. He issued a proclamation setting up a provisional government with its capital at Monterey. At Los Angeles, however, Frémont persisted in executing his authority as governor and refused to carry out orders from Gen. Kearny. The controversy was prolonged until Kearny named Col. Richard B. Mason governor of California and, together with Stockton and Frémont, started out (31 May 1847) for Washington.

Frémont was tried by a court-martial (Nov. 1847–Jan. 1848) on charges of mutiny, disobedience, and prejudicial conduct; found guilty on all counts; and sentenced to dismissal from the service. President Polk approved the sentence (except for the charge of mutiny) and remitted the penalty with instructions to restore Frémont to duty. Frémont, however, resigned from the army. The affair precipitated open opposition between the Polk administration and Frémont's father-in-law, Sen. Thomas Hart Benton.

8 AUG. WILMOT PROVISO. The prospect of acquiring additional territory as a result of the Mexican War precipi-

tated a far-reaching congressional debate occasioned by the Wilmot Proviso, introduced in the House as an amendment to the administration bill for a $2 million appropriation to facilitate negotiations with Mexico for territorial adjustments. Polk's request (known as the "Two Million Bill") was encouraged by the discussions with Santa Anna, which at that time seemingly augured a speedy peace settlement.

The Wilmot Proviso stated that "as an express and fundamental condition" to the acquisition of any territory from Mexico by the U.S. "by virtue of any treaty which may be negotiated between them, and to the use by the Executive of the moneys herein appropriated, neither slavery nor involuntary servitude shall ever exist in any part of said territory, except for crime, whereof the party shall first be duly convicted."

The proviso was drafted and introduced by **David Wilmot** (1814–68), a Democrat from northeastern Pennsylvania, previously a Polk supporter (some authorities credit the original proposal to Jacob Brinkerhoff [Ohio], a Van Buren Democrat).

Administration forces tried to amend the Wilmot Proviso by limiting its operation to territory north of the Missouri Compromise line. This attempt was defeated by a House vote, 89–54, and the proviso was adopted (8 Aug.), 87–64. The bill was lost in the Senate (10 Aug.) when discussion was terminated by the adjournment of the 1st session of the 29th Congress.

Polk's supporters in the House introduced a similar appropriation measure (8 Feb. 1847) raising the sum to $3 million. The more pronounced slavery-exclusion clause of a previous bill moved (3 Jan. 1847) by Preston King, a New York Democrat, was adopted and introduced by Wilmot in place of his original proposal. In this form, the Wilmot Proviso was passed as an amendment to the "Three Million Bill," 115–106, and the amended bill passed, 115–105 (15 Feb. 1847). In the Senate, which drew up its own bill, an attempt to add the Wilmot Proviso was defeated, 31–21, and the measure passed, 29–24 (1 Mar. 1847). The Senate bill was taken up in the House in committee of the whole, and was passed, 115–81 (3 Mar.).

In the heated debate in both houses Democrats defended the war as a just one; Whigs attacked it as an expansionist drive for territorial spoils, and accused the president of having initiated the war in violation of the Constitution.

19 Feb. 1847. Calhoun Resolutions. Southern Democrats and their Northern allies united in opposing the proviso as an unnecessary agitation of the slavery question and a threat to Southern rights. The defense of the Southern position was set forth by Calhoun in 4 resolutions on the slavery question (19 Feb. 1847). He asserted that the territories of the U.S. were the joint and common property of the states; that Congress, as the agent of the states, had no right to make any law discriminating between the states of the Union and depriving any of them of its full and equal right in any territory acquired or to be acquired by the U.S.; that the enactment of any law interfering with slavery would be a violation of the Constitution and states' rights, and inimical to the equality of the states within the Union; and that the people had an unconditional right to form and adopt their state governments as they chose, no condition being imposed by the Constitution for the admission of a state except that its government should be republican. Calhoun's remarks (19–20 Feb. 1847) forecast the position of the South: insistence on a positive protection of slavery; appeal to states' rights and constitutional-compact theory; the view of the section as the bulwark of conserva-

tism within the Union; attack upon the "aggressive measures" of the nonslaveholding states. Pointing out that the South was already becoming a political minority in the national councils, Calhoun warned that were the balance between North and South destroyed, it would herald the approach of "political revolution, anarchy, civil war, and widespread disaster." The South, he said, was acting defensively and restricting itself to "repelling attacks . . . all we ask is to be let alone; but if trampled upon, it will be idle to expect that we will not resist it."

The fundamental principle of the Wilmot Proviso reappeared in later congressional debates, and became a vital plank in the platforms of the Free-Soil and Republican parties.

25 Sept. CAPTURE OF MONTEREY. Taylor's army, increased (May–June) from 5,000 to 14,500 men, many being 3- and 6-month volunteers, and handicapped by lack of supplies and faulty transportation, began (6 July) its ascent of the Rio Grande from the advance base of Reynosa to Camargo, using a small fleet of river steamboats. Camargo, which the first troops reached 14 July, lay on the San Juan River, a branch of the Rio Grande, c.1,000 miles north of Mexico City. It became Taylor's base for his march on Monterey. With a force of 3,080 regulars and 3,150 volunteers, Taylor began (19 Aug.) his advance on Monterey, reaching its outskirts on 19 Sept. The major fortification in the city was the Citadel (or Black Ft.). To the west of Monterey, the Mexicans had well-fortified defenses on Independence Hill and Federation Hill. Taylor took immediate command of the troops attacking from the east, and dispatched a force under Gen. William J. Worth to make the assault from the west. The attack on Monterey began 20 Sept.

Worth advanced along the Monterey-

Saltillo road, took the redoubt on Federation Hill (21 Sept.), and seized Independence Hill (22 Sept.), thus securing control of the western approaches. In the east, the U.S. troops penetrated the town (21 Sept.), meeting heavy resistance in the fortified streets and houses. After a 4-day siege, during which the enemy fell back on the Citadel, the Mexicans capitulated (24 Sept.), the surrender being carried out 25 Sept. Estimated losses: U.S., 120 killed, 368 wounded; Mexican, 367 killed and wounded.

Taylor consented to an 8-week armistice, pledging that the U.S. forces would not penetrate southward beyond the mountains unless the armistice was disclaimed by either government. The armistice brought the disapproval of Polk, eager to press the war in order to exert pressure on the Mexican congress. The War Department's notification (13 Oct.) did not reach Taylor until 2 Nov. The disapproval of the armistice increased Taylor's suspicion that the administration was engaged in intrigues against him because he had been mentioned in June by the Whig leader, Thurlow Weed, as that party's presidential possibility.

Taylor informed Santa Anna (5 Nov.), who had reached San Luis Potosí (8 Oct.), that the armistice would be terminated effective 13 Nov. Taylor occupied Saltillo, capital of Coahuila (16 Nov.). Meanwhile, a force of about 3,000 troops under Gen. John E. Wool left San Antonio (23–28 Sept.) on an expedition against Chihuahua. Wool occupied Monclova (29 Oct.), but abandoned his march on Chihuahua under orders from the War Department approved by Taylor. Wool took Parras (5 Dec.), to the west of Monterey, and reinforced Taylor at Saltillo (21 Dec.).

12 Dec. TREATY OF NEW GRANADA. U.S. concern about Central America was revived by a growing interest in an isthmian transit route between the Atlantic and the Pacific, and by suspicion of British designs on the Caribbean area. The Republic of New Granada (Colombia) feared that Great Britain or some other foreign nation might take possession of the Isthmus of Panama. At the initiative of the New Granada government, Benjamin A. Bidlack, the U.S. minister, signed (12 Dec.) a commercial treaty which conveyed to the U.S. the right of way across the isthmus. In return, the U.S. guaranteed the neutrality of the isthmus and the sovereignty of New Granada. The Senate approved the treaty (3 June 1848) ratifications exchanged 12 July 1848.

WHIG GAINS. State and congressional elections indicated loss of support for Polk. In the state contests (Oct.–Nov.) the Whigs carried New York, New Jersey, Ohio, Maryland, Georgia, and Florida with strong gains in Pennsylvania. In the congressional elections (Nov.) the Whigs made capital of the war (although Polk's opposition to internal improvements and a high protective tariff were also under fire). The new House had a slim Whig majority.

7 Dec. NEW SESSION. The attack on Polk was resumed, with Whigs notably Senators Robert Toombs (Ga. 8 Jan. 1847) and Thomas Corwin (Ohio 11 Feb.), and antislavery Democrats joining forces. Nevertheless $5 million in war appropriations were voted (15 Feb. 3 Mar.) and Treasury notes to $23 million authorized (28 Jan.).

1847

Oct. 1846–1 Mar. 1847. DONIPHAN'S EXPEDITION. Before leaving New Mexico, Kearny ordered (23 Sept 1846) Col. **Alexander W. Doniphan** (1808–87), commander of the 1st Regiment of Missouri Mounted Volunteers, to lead an expedition to the province of Chihuahua in support of Gen. Wool. Late in

Oct. 1846, Doniphan's troops departed from Santa Fe on a march that was to take them through 3,000 miles of mountain and desert country. After signing (22 Nov. 1846) a treaty of peace with the Navajo chiefs assembled at Bear Springs, he left Valverde (14 Dec.) for El Paso, 90 miles to the south, marched through virtually waterless country, and defeated the enemy in the **Battle of El Brazito** (25 Dec. 1846). U.S. loss: 7 wounded; Mexican, 43 killed. Occupying El Paso (27 Dec. 1846), Doniphan left the town (8 Feb.) on a march across desert wastes toward the provincial capital of Chihuahua. After defeating a defending Mexican force in the **Battle of the Sacramento** (28 Feb.)—U.S. loss: 1 killed, and 11 wounded; estimated Mexican: 300 killed, 300 wounded—he entered Chihuahua (1 Mar.).

22–23 FEB. BATTLE OF BUENA VISTA. In the late fall of 1846 Polk, convinced that Taylor could not bring the war to a successful conclusion, agreed to Gen. Winfield Scott's plan for an expedition to Vera Cruz. When Taylor learned (14 Jan.) that Scott had ordered (3 Jan.) the transfer of 9,000 of Taylor's troops to the Vera Cruz expedition and instructed him to remain on a "strict defensive" on the line of Monterey, Taylor's suspicions of political and military intrigue against him were again aroused. Most of Taylor's troops joined the expeditionary force at Tampico after Taylor withdrew from Victoria (12 Jan.), the capital of Tamaulipas, which had been occupied on 29 Dec. 1846. The friction between Taylor and the administration was intensified with the publication (22 Jan.) in the New York *Morning Express* of Taylor's letter to Gen. Edmund P. Gaines, in which he defended his agreement to the 8-week armistice, criticized the administration, and discussed military matters.

Taylor disobeyed orders (dated 20 Dec.) to communicate with Scott, and took the offensive, advancing (5–14 Feb.) to Agua Nueva, 18 miles west of Saltillo. Meanwhile, Santa Anna massed about 20,000 troops at San Luis Potosí, with the aim of striking a decisive blow at Taylor's army. On 20 Feb., Santa Anna reached La Encarnación, 35 miles from Taylor's encampment. Because of his poor defensive position at Agua Nueva, Taylor withdrew (21 Feb.) to La Angostura, a mountain defile along the Saltillo–San Luis Potosí road, in a valley 6,000 ft. above sea level. Here, 3 miles north of the hacienda of Buena Vista, the U.S. forces (c.4,800 men, mostly untried volunteer infantry) entrenched along deep gullies and ravines.

Santa Anna, after leading more than 15,000 ill-trained men on an exhausting march, sent Taylor a demand for unconditional surrender. Taylor refused, and the ensuing battle ended in a hard-won U.S. victory, the retirement of Santa Anna's forces (23–24 Feb.), and termination of the war in northern Mexico. U.S. loss: 267 killed, 456 wounded, 23 missing; Mexican: estimated at 1,500, of whom at least 500 killed. Santa Anna returned to Mexico City, where he took the oath of office as president (21 Mar.).

Shortly after the battle, Taylor received from Secretary Marcy a reprimand (dated 27 Jan.) for the Gaines letter. For the next 9 months Taylor remained in command of the U.S. forces in northern Mexico. Relieved at his own request, he left for the U.S. on 26 Nov. and received a hero's welcome.

21 FEB.–29 MAR. SCOTT'S VERA CRUZ EXPEDITION. Influenced by the favorable progress of events in California, and finally yielding to repeated proposals made by Scott, Polk placed Scott at the head of an expedition to take Vera Cruz, at that time the most powerful fortress in the Western Hemisphere. From this point on the east coast of Mexico, Scott was to proceed along a direct but mountainous inland route to Mexico City. After a reconciliation with Polk (19 Nov. 1846), Scott was ordered (23 Nov. 1846) to take command of a force whose projected strength of 20,000 actually never exceeded 10,000. Scott left Washington (24 Nov. 1846) and reached Camargo (3 Jan.), where his progress was hindered by bad weather and inadequate water transportation.

Scott established headquarters at Tampico (18 Feb.) and, without express approval of the administration, issued **General Order No. 20** (19 Feb.). The order, which set up a system for dealing with crimes not defined in the Articles of War, was aimed at preventing the atrocities committed by some of Taylor's volunteer troops and at securing the cooperation of the native population along Scott's lines of communication. To an extent compatible with military necessity, local government was left to Mexican officials acting under army supervision. The order and the machinery for its execution constituted the **first civil affairs administration** of enemy territory occupied by U.S. military forces.

Scott massed an invasion armada and 10,000 troops at the Lobos Islands, where he arrived 21 Feb. From this point, 50 miles below Tampico, the fleet under Commodore Conner sailed (2–5 Mar.) to the final rendezvous at Antón Lizardo, 12 miles south of Vera Cruz. Here Scott's operation was delayed by a serious outbreak of smallpox among the troops. At the advice of naval officers, Scott decided to abandon his plan to take the fortress city by direct assault from the sea. The Mexicans had 5,000 soldiers in the city.

The landings (9 Mar.), made on the beaches south of Vera Cruz, were virtually unopposed. The first large-scale amphibious operation in U.S. military history was carried out with special landing craft assembled at Sacrificios Island. Two weeks were spent in securing and building up the position on the beach. The Mexicans rejected a demand for surrender (22 Mar.). After a siege from U.S. land and naval batteries that began 22 Mar., Vera Cruz, with its strongly fortified seaward castle of San Juan de Ulúa, surrendered to Scott (27 Mar.) and was formally occupied (29 Mar.). U.S. losses: 82, of whom 19 were killed; Mexican losses: c.80 soldiers, 100 civilians.

18 Apr.–20 Aug. CERRO GORDO TO CHURUBUSCO. The route of Scott's march through the interior lay across an initial 55 miles of lowland, which at the mountain pass of Cerro Gordo rises precipitously to slopes ultimately reaching a height of about 8,000 ft., and then cross a heavily populated plateau between Perote and Mexico City. Scott's immediate objective was Jalapa, 75 miles northwest of Vera Cruz and 4,250 ft. above sea level.

Battle of Cerro Gordo. Leaving Vera Cruz 8 Apr., Scott's force of about 9,000 men marched along the National Road. On 13 Apr. they encountered the outlying enemy defenses at Plan del Rio, just below Cerro Gordo. Santa Anna, leaving the Mexican capital (2 Apr.), had reached Cerro Gordo (9 Apr.) and designated it as the point for containing the U.S. advance. The Mexican force numbered about 13,000 men. A skillful reconnaissance of enemy positions along the canyon near Cerro Gordo was made by U.S. engineer officers (including Capts. **Robert E. Lee** and **George B. McClellan**), but its value was partly vitiated by a premature action (17 Apr.). In an enveloping operation that witnessed much hand-to-hand combat, the U.S. forces carried Cerro Gordo by assault (18 Apr.), routing Santa Anna and his staff officers, capturing 204 enemy officers and 2,837 men, and seizing 43 artillery pieces and 4,000 small arms. U.S. losses: 63 killed, 337 wounded.

Scott's troops occupied Jalapa (19 Apr.), Perote (22 Apr.), and reached Puebla (15 May), 80 miles from Mexico City. During this period Scott lost about one third of his effectives whose short-term enlistments had expired (7 regiments and 2 companies of volunteers). He was left with about 7,000 men, of whom some 1,000 were stricken with disease. Scott lacked money, supplies, and transportation; reinforcements from New Orleans were slow in arriving. Yet during a 3-month pause at Puebla, while the navy carried out operations along the southeastern coast of Mexico, Scott built up his force to 10,783 effectives. On 6 Aug. Gen. Franklin Pierce arrived at Puebla with 3,000 reinforcements.

Battles of Contreras and Churubusco. Scott began (7 Aug.) his advance from Puebla, cutting through the mountains and entering the Valley of Mexico at Ayotla, where he established his headquarters (11 Aug.). Santa Anna, who had again taken office as president (22 May) after some changes in the Mexican government, had about 20,000 men in the valley, concentrated in the vicinity of Contreras and Churubusco, along the roads leading to Mexico City. An American force of about 3,300 men stormed the Contreras position (19–20 Aug.) and routed the enemy, killing 700 and capturing 800 at a cost of 60 U.S. killed and wounded The fighting at Churubusco (20 Aug.), where the enemy had converted a church and a convent into powerful defensive positions, also resulted in a U.S. victory, but at a heavy price. U.S. losses in both battles: 133 killed, 865 wounded, 40 missing (about one seventh of force engaged). Santa Anna lost more than 7,000 killed, wounded, or captured (about one third of his army). Santa

Anna withdrew to Mexico City, now within 5 miles of U.S. lines, and requested an armistice. Negotiations were conducted (22–23 Aug.), and the armistice of Tacubaya went into effect (24 Aug.) to enable the Mexican government to consider the peace proposals that had been entrusted to **Nicholas P. Trist** (1800–74), confidential commissioner accompanying Scott's army.

26 Aug.–6 Sept. TRIST MISSION. With the fall of Vera Cruz, Polk renewed his efforts for a peace settlement. He decided, with the agreement of his cabinet, to dispatch a peace commissioner to Mexico. Chosen for the secret mission was Nicholas P. Trist, chief clerk of the State Department, who received his instructions from Polk and Buchanan (15 Apr.). The terms of the offer were essentially those that Mackenzie had made to Santa Anna, except that Trist was also authorized to negotiate for Lower California and the right of transit across the Isthmus of Tehuantepec. Trist's "confidential" mission became publicly known 4 days after he left Washington (16 Apr.).

Traveling under an assumed name, Trist reached Vera Cruz on 6 May. He was authorized, with certain reservations, "to enter into arrangements with the government of Mexico for the suspension of hostilities." There immediately ensued a controversy over Trist's authority, Scott regarding it as an invasion of his own and holding that an armistice was exclusively a military question. Relations between Trist and Scott were aggravated by an exchange of hostile correspondence. With the aid of the British legation in Mexico, a reconciliation was effected (25 June), and the armistice of Tacubaya was arranged by Scott. The negotiations (27 Aug.–6 Sept.) between Trist and the Mexican commission headed by former President Herrera ended with a

Mexican rejection of the peace offer. The armistice was terminated 7 Sept.

8–14 Sept. MARCH ON THE MEXICAN CAPITAL. Battle of Molino del Rey. Scott resumed his march at once. A force of 3,447 men under Gen. William J. Worth was ordered to carry out a diversionary raid on the gun foundry of Molino del Rey, just outside the gates of the city, where the enemy was supposedly casting church bells into cannon. Here, and at the adjoining Casa Mata and the walled park of Chapultepec, an estimated 12,000 Mexicans were entrenched behind massive fortifications. The U.S. attack opened 8 Sept., and what had been conceived as a minor raid developed into a serious day-long battle. Although the Americans took the position, they withdrew to Tacubaya at the day's end. U.S. losses: 117 killed, 653 wounded, 18 missing; Mexican: c.2,000 men killed and wounded, c.700 captured.

Battle of Chapultepec. For the final assault on the capital, Scott had 7,180 men as against an estimated 15,000 enemy troops in the city. Scott decided to storm the fortified hill of Chapultepec (c.200 ft. high) commanding the causeways leading to the San Cosmé and Belén gates at the western outskirts of the capital. On Chapultepec there were some 1,000 troops, supported by 4,000 in the immediate area. Following an artillery bombardment (12 Sept.), the divisions commanded by Gens. John A. Quitman and Gideon J. Pillow began their assault at 8:00 A.M. on the morning of 13 Sept. The storming parties scaled the rocky slopes with ladders and pickaxes. The summit was taken at 9:30 A.M. Gallant resistance was offered by "Los Ninos," about 100 boy cadets who defended the Mexican Military College on the crest of the hill. The Belén gate was taken at 1:30 P.M., and the San Cosmé gate by 6 P.M. U.S. losses: 130 killed, 703 wounded, 29 missing.

Capture of Mexico City. Scott immediately pressed on the capital (pop.: 200,000) with less than 6,000 effectives. Using picks and crowbars, the U.S. infantry hacked through the city walls and entered the capital during the night and early morning (13–14 Sept.). The U.S. flag was raised above the National Palace, where a battalion of U.S. Marines (authorized by Congress 10 Nov. 1775; formed into a corps by act of 11 July 1798) took guard over the "halls of Montezuma." After several days of disorder, the hostile population was brought under control. Gen. Scott reissued (16 Sept.) General Order No. 20; henceforth, military government became the chief function of his army. Scott remained in command until 18 Feb. 1848.

Even before the Americans occupied the capital, Santa Anna fled to the suburb of Gaudalupe Hidalgo, where he renounced the presidency (16 Sept.). At the head of about 8,000 men, he marched to Puebla, where the Mexicans under Gen. Joaquin Rea had begun a siege (14 Sept.) of the U.S. garrison (about 2,300 troops, mostly wounded and convalescent) under Col. Thomas Childs, who rejected a demand for surrender. Santa Anna left Puebla (1 Oct.) and the siege was raised (12 Oct.) by a relief expedition under Gen. Joseph Lane from Vera Cruz. Deposed as head of the army (7 Oct.), Santa Anna fled the country.

Pedro María Anaya was elected (11 Nov.) *ad interim* president of Mexico. The Anaya government informed Trist (22 Nov.) that it had named commissioners to negotiate peace on the basis of the original terms. Trist had received (16 Nov.) an order for his recall, but when the Mexicans pointed out that they had not received official notification of the withdrawal of his authority, Trist decided (4 Dec.) to remain in Mexico and negotiate a treaty.

1848

24 JAN. DISCOVERY OF GOLD in California by James W. Marshall, a New Jersey mechanic who was erecting a saw-mill for **Johann Augustus Sutter** (1803–80) on a branch of the American River in Eldorado County, in the lower Sacramento Valley, about 40 miles from present-day Sacramento. The news, announced by Marshall to Sutter (28 Jan.), soon spread and stimulated the great California gold rush. Impetus was lent by Polk's confirmation of the discovery in his annual message to Congress (5 Dec.). Adventurers came from all parts of the U.S. and from overseas places as distant as China and Australia. By the end of 1849, it is estimated, the California population had been swelled by 100,000. The influx of the "Forty-niners" continued for the next 2 years. In 1851 the annual output of gold rose to $55 million.

2 FEB. TREATY OF GUADALUPE HIDALGO resulted from the unauthorized negotiations between Trist and the Mexican commissioners begun formally 2 Jan., and the treaty was signed at the village just outside Mexico City. By that time, Peña y Peña had become (8 Jan.) acting president of Mexico. **Terms:** Mexico relinquished all claims to Texas above the Rio Grande and ceded New Mexico and California to the U.S. The territory (including the present states of Arizona, Nevada, California, and Utah, and parts of New Mexico, Colorado, and Wyoming) added with Texas 1,193,061 square miles to the national domain. In return for the territory, the U.S. agreed to pay $15 million and assume the adjusted claims of its citizens ($3,250,000) against the Mexican government. The U.S.-Mexican boundary was fixed along the Rio Grande to the southern line of New Mexico, thence westward and northward along the Gila and Colorado rivers, and thence along the line between Upper and Lower California to the Pacific.

The treaty arrived at Washington on 19 Feb. Polk, doubtful and hesitant because the treaty was unauthorized, submitted it to the Senate (23 Feb.), which ratified the treaty, 38–14 (10 Mar.). For: 26 Democrats, 12 Whigs; against: 7 Democrats, 7 Whigs. A motion to add the Wilmot Proviso was defeated, 38–15. The opposition to the treaty stemmed from Secretary Buchanan and those senators who, supported by a growing expansionist demand, wanted to annex all of Mexico. The Mexican congress ratified the treaty (25 May), ratifications were formally exchanged (30 May), and Polk proclaimed the treaty in effect (4 July). The final territorial adjustment under the treaty was made with the **Gadsden Purchase** (1853, p. 257).

A military armistice suspending hostilities had been declared on 29 Feb., and the last action of the war was fought at Todos Santos in Lower California (30 Mar.). The U.S. forces evacuated Mexico City (12 June) and the last U.S. troops left Vera Cruz 2 Aug.

WAR COST. U.S. casualties: 1,721 killed or died of wounds; 11,155 died of disease; 4,102 wounded. Military and naval expenditures amounted to more than $97,500,000.

19 JULY. SENECA FALLS CONVENTION, held at the Wesleyan Chapel, Seneca Falls, N.Y., under the leadership of **Lucretia Mott** (1793–1880) and **Elizabeth Cady Stanton** (p. 1156), adopted a group of women's-rights resolutions, including a demand for woman suffrage, and a diminution of discrimination in employment and education. A few months earlier the 2 feminist leaders had worked successfully for the passage of the New York Married Women's Property Act, modifying the common law by recognizing a married woman's right to her separate property.

14 AUG. OREGON BILL. In his annual messages (1846–48) Polk urged the establishment of a territorial government for Oregon, whose provisional laws excluded slavery. The ensuing debates raised the issue of the constitutional power of Congress to prohibit slavery in the territories. The Senate tabled a bill passed by the House (16 Jan. 1847) applying the restrictions of the Northwest Ordinance. Sen. Stephen A. Douglas (Ill.) offered a bill (10 Jan.) providing that the Oregon laws should remain valid until the territorial legislature should change them.

The House (9 Feb.) reintroduced its Oregon bill. Sen. Jesse D. Bright (Ind.), acting chairman of the committee on territories, introduced an amendment (27 June) extending the Missouri Compromise line through all newly acquired territory to the Pacific. Thus the Oregon bill raised anew the problem of the status of slavery in California and New Mexico. Under the Mexican laws of 1829 and 1837 slavery had been forbidden in those areas. Calhoun opposed Bright's amendment, denied (27 June) both the validity of Mexican laws in the conquered territories and congressional authority over slavery in the territories, and insisted that slavery was not subject to congressional or local action.

The Senate (12 July) referred the question of slavery extension to a committee headed by John M. Clayton (Del.). The "Clayton Compromise," adopted by the Senate, 33–22 (27 July), validated the provisional laws of Oregon insofar as they were compatible with the Constitution, but forbade the territorial legislatures of New Mexico and California to pass laws on slavery. The question of the status of slavery in those territories was referred to appeals from the territorial courts to the Supreme Court.

The Senate bill was tabled by the House (28 July), which by 129–71

passed its own bill (2 Aug.) for organizing Oregon with restrictions on slavery. The Senate amendment to the bill extended the Missouri Compromise line to the Pacific. The House refused to concur, and its bill incorporating the prohibition of slavery in Oregon was adopted by the Senate (13 Aug.). Despite Calhoun's view that the measure merited a veto on constitutional grounds, Polk signed the bill (14 Aug.) on the ground that it did not conflict with the Missouri Compromise because the territory in question lay north of $36°30'$.

PRESIDENTIAL CAMPAIGN. The slavery issue was injected into the Democratic National Convention at Baltimore (22 May) when the 2 factions of Barnburners (also known as the "Softs") and Hunkers (also known as the "Hards") from the key state of New York sent separate delegations. The anti-administration Barnburners were firm supporters of the Wilmot Proviso. When a compromise on seating the delegations failed, neither one took part in the convention; but the Hunkers, unlike their opponents, pledged their support to the nominees.

Polk, who in accepting the nomination in 1844 had pledged himself to a single term, declined to run for office. Gen. **Lewis Cass** (Mich.) was nominated for president and Gen. **William O. Butler** (Ky.) for vice-president. Cass, a conservative and an expansionist, had approved the doctrine of "squatter sovereignty" (local determination of the status of slavery) in a letter (29 Dec. 1847) to A. O. P. Nicholson of Nashville. While his selection indicated the Democratic party's desire to win the Western vote and promote sectional harmony, the principle of "squatter sovereignty" was not incorporated in the Democratic platform. The platform, in substance that of 1844, denied the power of Congress to interfere with slavery in the states and criticized all efforts to bring the slavery question before Congress. In a move to quell the agitation of the slavery issue, the convention voted down a minority resolution of the Southern delegates favoring noninterference with slavery in the territories.

When the Whig National Convention met at Philadelphia (7 June), the 3 contenders for the nomination were Henry Clay, Gen. Zachary Taylor, and Gen. Winfield Scott. **Taylor,** whose political following grew rapidly after the battle of Buena Vista, was chosen presidential candidate; **Millard Fillmore** (N.Y.), the vice-presidential nominee. A resolution affirming the power of Congress to control slavery in the territories was proposed by the antislavery Ohio delegation and voted down. Taylor's nomination was opposed by the antislavery delegations from New England and Ohio. The Whig platform was a recital of Taylor's military character and reputation.

The Barnburners, seceding from the Democratic convention, held their own convention at Utica, N.Y. (22 June), nominating **Martin Van Buren** for president and **Henry Dodge** (Wis.) for vice-president. Soon afterward the antislavery Democrats and Liberty party supporters joined with dissident New England Whigs (known as "Conscience Whigs" because of their opposition to slavery) in holding a national convention of the **Free-Soil party** at Buffalo (9 Aug.). It was attended by 465 delegates from 18 states (including the 3 slave states of Virginia, Maryland, and Delaware). The Free-Soil opposition to Cass and Taylor united on the common basis of the Wilmot Proviso. In return for Barnburner support of a "thorough Liberty platform," John P. Hale (N.H.), who had been nominated for president by the Liberty party convention at New York City (Jan. 1848), withdrew in favor of **Van Buren,** who was nominated for president. **Charles Francis Adams** (Mass., p. 970)

was nominated for vice-president. Among the prominent members of the party were **Charles Sumner** (Mass., p. 1164) and **Salmon P. Chase** (Ohio, p. 1001). The Free-Soil party was pledged to a "national platform of freedom in opposition to the sectional platform of slavery." It attacked the "aggressions of the slave power," upheld the substance of the Wilmot Proviso, and favored river and harbor improvements and free homesteads to actual settlers. For its slogan the party adopted "Free soil, free speech, free labor, and free men."

7 Nov. PRESIDENTIAL ELECTION (the first conducted on a uniform election day, in accord with the congressional act of 1845). Popular vote: **Taylor,** 1,360,101; Cass, 1,220,544; Van Buren, 291,263. Electoral vote: Taylor, 163 (carrying 8 slave and 7 free states); Cass, 127 (carrying 8 free and 7 slave states). While Van Buren failed to carry a single state, the Free-Soil party was instrumental in winning the election for Taylor by depriving Cass of New York's 36 electoral votes. In that state, Van Buren received 120,510 votes to 114,318 for Cass, thus splitting the Democratic ranks.

1849

22 Jan. "ADDRESS OF THE SOUTHERN DELEGATES." A caucus (22 Dec. 1848) of 69 Southerners in Congress considered steps to oppose legislation prohibiting the slave trade in the District of Columbia. Spokesman for the caucus was Calhoun, whose "Address" listed the "acts of aggression" committed by the North against Southern rights—including (1) exclusion of slaves from the territories, (2) impediments to the return of fugitive slaves—and reaffirmed the right of slaveholders to take their property into the territories. Two additional meetings of the caucus (15, 22 Jan.) were attended by about 80 members, but owing to Whig opposition only 48 signed the "Address" (2 of them Whigs).

3 MAR. DEPT. OF THE INTERIOR created as the sixth with cabinet status. Established at the recommendation of Secretary of the Treasury Robert J. Walker, it was originally called the Home Department, and brought under a single head diverse government bureaus, including the Office of the Census, the Office of Indian Affairs, and the General Land Office.

NEW CONGRESS. In the House of Representatives (31st Cong., 1st sess.) that convened on 3 Dec., there were 112 Democrats, 109 Whigs, and 13 Free-Soilers. The last group held the balance of power. The Democrats had a Senate majority of 10. The organization of the House revealed the bitter factionalism produced by sectional controversy. Southern Whigs under the leadership of Alexander Stephens and Robert Toombs opposed the Whig candidate for speaker, Robert C. Winthrop (Mass.), because the Whig caucus had refused to pledge opposition to the Wilmot Proviso. The Free-Soilers refused to support Winthrop on the ground that he had not given adequate recognition to antislavery spokesmen during his previous service as speaker. It took 3 weeks and 63 ballots before Howell Cobb (Ga.) was elected speaker (22 Dec.). The debates, marked by threats of disunion, widened the breach between the Northern and Southern wings of the Whig party.

CALIFORNIA AND NEW MEXICO. Polk's efforts to secure territorial organization for California and New Mexico failed. The stumbling block was the status of slavery in the newly acquired regions. With the influx of settlers into California after the discovery of gold, territorial organization became a pressing need.

It was Taylor's view that Congress ought not to pass on the question of slavery in California and New Mexico. The people of these territories, he held, had the right to adopt their own constitution and form of government without congressional authorization before applying for admission to the Union. The final decision would rest with Congress. Accordingly, he dispatched special messengers to California and New Mexico to inform the people that it was not necessary to await congressional action before establishing a government.

The Californians took steps even before Taylor's special agent arrived. A convention met at Monterey (1 Sept.–13 Oct.) and adopted a constitution prohibiting slavery. The constitution was ratified by the people (13 Nov.) and a state government went into operation on 20 Dec. Taylor recommended in his annual message (4 Dec.) the immediate admission of California, and urged that Congress "should abstain from the introduction of those exciting topics of sectional character which have hitherto produced painful apprehensions in the public mind." Referring to threats of dissolution that had been freely made during the year, Taylor asserted that whatever dangers menaced the Union, "I shall stand by it and maintain it in its integrity to the full extent of the obligations imposed and the powers conferred upon me by the Constitution." Southerners at once attacked Taylor's proposal. (In the Union at this time there were 15 free and 15 slave states, and the admission of California would upset the balance.) On 12 Mar. 1850 California applied to Congress for statehood.

1850

29 JAN.–20 SEPT. COMPROMISE OF 1850. Clay's Resolutions. Mounting sectional antagonism over territorial accessions alarmed moderates and conserv-

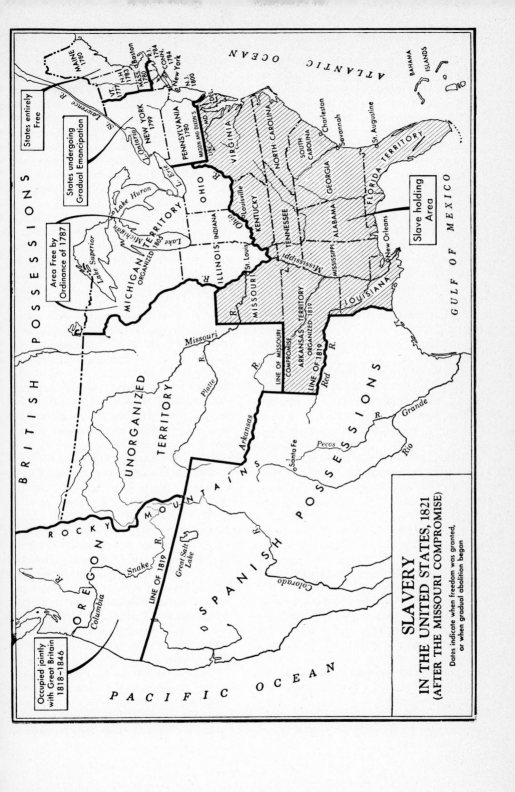

States entirely Free

States undergoing Gradual Emancipation

Area Free by Ordinance of 1787

Slave holding Area

Occupied jointly with Great Britain 1818-1846

BRITISH POSSESSIONS

ATLANTIC OCEAN

BAHAMA ISLANDS

MAINE 1780

N.H. 1783
VT. 1777
MASS. 1780
R.I. 1784
CONN. 1784
New York
N.J. 1800

St. Laurence R.

L. Ontario

NEW YORK 1799

L. Erie

PENNSYLVANIA 1780

MASON AND DIXON'S LINE

MD.
DEL.

VIRGINIA

NORTH CAROLINA

Charleston

SOUTH CAROLINA

Savannah

GEORGIA

St. Augustine

FLORIDA TERRITORY

Lake Superior

Lake Huron

Lake Michigan

MICHIGAN TERRITORY ORGANIZED 1805

OHIO

INDIANA

ILLINOIS

Louisville

KENTUCKY

TENNESSEE

St. Louis

MISSISSIPPI

ALABAMA

MISSOURI

New Orleans

LOUISIANA

GULF OF MEXICO

Missouri R.

UNORGANIZED TERRITORY

Platte R.

LINE OF MISSOURI COMPROMISE

ARKANSAS TERRITORY ORGANIZED 1819

LINE OF 1819

Arkansas R.

Red R.

R. Grande

SPANISH POSSESSIONS

Santa Fe

Pecos R.

Rio Grande

ROCKY MOUNTAINS

OREGON

LINE OF 1819

Snake R.

Great Salt Lake

Colorado R.

Columbia R.

PACIFIC OCEAN

SLAVERY
IN THE UNITED STATES, 1821
(AFTER THE MISSOURI COMPROMISE)

Dates indicate when freedom was granted,
or when gradual abolition began

atives. Returning to the U.S. Senate after a long absence, Henry Clay introduced (29 Jan.) a series of resolutions designed as a general formula for settling differences between North and South. These resolutions provided for (1) admission of California as a free state; (2) organization, without restriction on slavery, of the balance of the territory acquired from Mexico; (3) adjustment of the Texas-New Mexico boundary; (4) assumption by the U.S. of the Texas debt contracted before annexation, provided that Texas relinquished her claim to any part of Mexico; (5) noninterference with slavery in the District of Columbia; (6) prohibition of the slave trade in the District of Columbia; (7) more effective provision for the return of fugitive slaves; and (8) declared that Congress had no authority to interfere with the interstate slave trade.

The Great Debate. The Senate debate on the resolution, the greatest in congressional history, marked the last meeting of the senatorial triumvirate of Calhoun, Clay, and Webster. Clay's speech (5–6 Feb.) made an appeal for mutual concessions and warned that secession was not a rightful remedy for Southern grievances. Calhoun, enfeebled by his final illness (he died 31 Mar.), sat in silence as his speech (4 Mar.) opposing the compromise was read by Sen. James M. Mason (Va.). Calhoun maintained that the Union could be saved only by giving the South equal rights in the acquired territory, by halting the agitation of the slavery question, and by a constitutional amendment restoring "to the South, in substance, the power she possessed of protecting herself before the equilibrium between the sections was destroyed by the action of this government" (Calhoun did not elaborate on this last proposal; it was based on his doctrine of the "**concurrent majority**" expounded in his posthumous *Disquisition on Government*).

Webster's speech (7 Mar.) in support of the resolutions began: "I wish to speak today, not as a Massachusetts man, nor as a Northern man, but as an American. . . . I speak today for the preservation of the Union. 'Hear me for my cause.'" Contending that there was no necessity for congressional action on slavery in the acquired territory, Webster held that slavery had been excluded by virtue of soil and climate.

William H. Seward (N.Y.) opposed the compromise in a speech (11 Mar.) which held "all legislative compromises radically wrong and essentially vicious." He supported the Wilmot Proviso and appealed to "a higher law" justifying refusal of constitutional protection to slavery. Also opposing the resolutions were Jefferson Davis (Miss.), whose speech (13–14 Mar.) advocated congressional noninterference with slavery and upheld equal rights for the South; and Salmon P. Chase (Ohio), who asserted (26–27 Mar.) that it was the duty of Congress to prohibit slavery in the territories. Other opponents of Clay's proposals included Thomas Hart Benton (Mo.), John Davis (Mass.), and John P. Hale (N.H.). Prominent among Clay's supporters were Lewis Cass (Mich.), Stephen A. Douglas (Ill.), and Henry S. Foote (Miss.).

The resolutions were referred (18 Apr.) to a Senate select committee of 13 (of which Clay was chairman) consisting of 7 Whigs and 6 Democrats representing 7 slave and 6 free states. The committee reported 2 bills (8 May): (1) the "Omnibus Bill," covering the organization of the territories; and (2) a bill to prohibit the slave trade in the District of Columbia.

Compromise Measures. President Taylor was opposed to the immediate territorial organization of New Mexico and Utah. His death (9 July) brought to the presidency Millard Fillmore, who favored

Clay's compromise. The "Compromise of 1850" is a collective term of later origin applied to the 5 laws enacted (9–20 Sept.) after Clay and Douglas succeeded in coalescing Union sentiment in Congress. With the exception of California, the territory won from Mexico was divided at the 37th parallel into a northern half (Utah) and a southern half (New Mexico). The compromise included the following measures:

9 Sept. (1) Admission of California as a Free State. The bill passed the Senate, 34–18 (13 Aug.); the House, 150–56 (7 Sept.).

9 Sept. (2) Texas and New Mexico Act, which organized New Mexico as a territory without restriction on slavery, adjusted the Texas-New Mexico boundary, and provided for the payment by the U.S. to Texas of $10 million in return for the abandonment by Texas of all claims to New Mexico territory. It included the "popular sovereignty" provision that was the substance of the compromise: "That, when admitted as a State, the said territory, or any portion of the same, shall be received into the Union, with or without slavery, as their constitution may prescribe at the time of their admission." The bill passed the Senate, 27–10 (15 Aug.); the House, 108–97 (6 Sept.).

9 Sept. (3) Utah Act, which established a territorial government with identical provisions.

18 Sept. (4) Fugitive Slave Act amended the original law of 1793; placed fugitive slave cases under exclusive federal jurisdiction; provided for special U.S. commissioners who were authorized, following a summary hearing, to issue warrants for the arrest of fugitives and certificates for returning them to their masters. An affidavit by the claimant was accepted as sufficient proof of ownership. A feature of the law that abolitionists regarded as especially prejudicial

was the authorization of a $10 fee for commissioners when such a certificate was granted, and of only $5 when it was refused. The commissioners were authorized to call to their aid bystanders, or to summon a *posse comitatus*, when deemed necessary for enforcing the law. Fugitives claiming to be freemen were denied the right of trial by jury, and their testimony was not to be admitted as evidence at any of the proceedings under the law. Heavy penalties were provided for evasion or obstruction. Marshals and deputies refusing to execute warrants were liable to a $1,000 fine; and in cases where the fugitives escaped through official negligence, the marshal might be sued for the value of the slave. Citizens preventing the arrest of a fugitive, or aiding in his concealment or rescue, were subject to a fine of $1,000, imprisonment up to 6 months, and civil damages of $1,000 for each fugitive so lost. The bill passed the Senate, 27–12 (23 Aug.); the House, 109–76 (12 Sept.).

20 Sept. (5) An Act Abolishing the Slave Trade in the District of Columbia after 1 Jan. 1851, passed the Senate, 33–19 (16 Sept.); the House, 124–47 (17 Sept.).

Both North and South hailed the "finality" of the measures, although acceptance was in reality conditional. Most Northern Whigs and Democrats viewed it as a permanent settlement of the slavery question. Northern radicals, however, condemned the Fugitive Slave Act and hinted at their intention to obstruct its enforcement. That a majority of Southern voters regarded the compromise as a welcome alternative to disunion was indicated by the defeat of the secessionists in the Southern state elections of 1851, when the Unionists won by narrow margins over the Quitman-Davis faction (Miss.), the Rhett wing (S.C.), and the Yancey radicals (Ala.). Northern radicals, however, gained a signal triumph with the election (1851) of Charles Sumner (Mass.) to the U.S. Senate. The chief political effect of the compromise was its hastening of the breakup of the Whig party.

19 APR. CLAYTON-BULWER TREATY. U.S. interest in an interoceanic canal across the isthmian routes in Central America influenced Polk's foreign policy. Polk sent a special envoy, Elijah Hise, to Nicaragua to investigate British encroachments. The British, acting on the petition (1835) of the settlers of Belize (British Honduras), established a protectorate over the Mosquito Coast territory claimed by Nicaragua, drove the Nicaraguans from Mosquitia, and forced them (Jan. 1848) to renounce the area in the vicinity of the San Juan River, at the eastern terminus of the canal projected by the U.S.

Hise concluded with the Nicaraguans an unauthorized treaty granting the U.S. the exclusive right of way across the isthmus and the right to fortify the route, in return for the U.S. guarantee of the neutrality of the isthmus and the protection of Nicaraguan sovereignty. Polk never submitted the treaty to the Senate. A similar treaty was negotiated (1849) by E. G. Squier, an envoy sent by Taylor. Squier also obtained Tigre Island in the Gulf of Fonseca, at the western terminus of the projected canal. The island was seized (Oct., 1849) by British forces, who refused to leave despite Squier's contention that it belonged to the U.S.

Although the Taylor administration was anxious to reach an understanding with Great Britain, Secretary of State Clayton informed the British foreign secretary, Lord Palmerston, that the U.S. would not recognize the British protectorate over Mosquitia or its hold on the San Juan River. Clayton initiated discussions with the British minister to the U.S., Sir Henry Lytton Bulwer. The treaty was ratified by the Senate, 42–10, and ratifications were exchanged on 5 July. Terms: both nations (1) agreed never to obtain or exercise exclusive control over an isthmian ship canal, or to fortify it; (2) guaranteed the neutrality and security of the canal; (3) agreed to keep any future canal open to their nationals on terms of equality; and (4) pledged not to colonize, occupy, or exercise dominion over any part of Central America.

The British made the major concessions, but the treaty, unpopular in the U.S. with Anglophobes and expansionists, remained in effect until abrogated by the Hay-Pauncefote Treaty (1901). Anglo-U.S. friction was further allayed by cession (22 Nov. 1859) by Britain of the Bay Islands to Honduras.

10 JUNE. NASHVILLE CONVENTION. Early in 1850 Southern advocates of a separatist program took steps to consider their position on Clay's compromise and the larger question of Southern rights. At the instigation of Calhoun, a Mississippi convention (1 Oct. 1849) and the state legislature (6 Mar.) adopted resolutions calling a convention of the slave states, to meet at Nashville, Tenn., 3 June. The extremists, led by **Robert Barnwell Rhett** (S.C.), saw an opportunity to broaden their support for secession. Nine slave states were represented, but the moderates were in control. The convention adopted (10 June) a resolution calling for the extension of the Missouri Compromise line westward to the Pacific. A second convention, attended by a handful of delegates (11–18 Nov.), denounced the Compromise and asserted the right of secession.

9 JULY. Death of President Taylor at Washington, D.C., of cholera morbus. **Millard Fillmore** became the 13th president, taking the oath of office on 10 July.

13–14 Dec. GEORGIA PLATFORM.
Indicative of Unionist sentiment among
conservative Southerners was the Georgia
Platform drawn up by Charles J. Jenkins
and adopted by a state convention (10
Dec.) at Milledgeville. The resolutions
stated that while Georgia did not wholly
approve of the Compromise of 1850, it
would "abide by it as a permanent adjustment of this sectional controversy";
however, they warned that Georgia "will
and ought to resist, even (as a last resort)
to a disruption of every tie which binds
her to the Union," any future act of
Congress that would repeal or substantially modify the fugitive slave laws, the
suppression of the interstate slave trade,
and the abolition of slavery in the District of Columbia. The Georgia Platform
constituted the basis on which **Robert A.
Toombs** (1810–85) and his colleagues,
including the conservative Democrat
Howell Cobb (1815–68), formerly established the Union Rights party.

"SILVER GRAY" WHIGS. The impact of the Compromise of 1850 upon
the Whig party in the North was immediately reflected in the New York State
Whig convention that met at Syracuse
(Sept.). When the convention adopted
resolutions approving Sen. Seward's
radical position, 40 conservative delegates of the Fillmore wing left the hall.
They were led by Francis Granger, whose
gray hair lent the name "Silver Gray" to
the faction. The seceders held their own
convention at Utica (Oct.), condemned
Seward's policies and supported those of
Fillmore, and shortly after backed a fusion ticket that included Horatio Seymour, the Democratic candidate for governor. The "Silver Grays" lost their influence in the state Whig party and later
seized control of the American (Know-
Nothing) organization in New York.

FUGITIVE SLAVE RESCUES. Most
controversial aspect of the Compromise

of 1850 was the adoption and subsequent
enforcement of the Fugitive Slave Law.
Although the number of runaway slaves
was small (estimated, 1850, by the census of 1860 as only 1,000 out of c.3 million slaves, most of whom were ultimately returned to their masters), the
South regarded Northern interference
with the rendition of fugitive slaves as a
violation of a constitutional guarantee.
Sectional strife was increased by the further enactment of more stringent **"personal liberty"** laws in Vermont (1850)
and other free states during the decade.
Southern slaveholders who entered free
states to seize runaway slaves risked being mobbed, sued for false imprisonment,
or prosecuted for kidnapping. Outstanding rescues or attempted rescues of
fugitive slaves (some leading to riots
and loss of life): **James Hamlet** at New
York City (1850), **Rachel Parker** at
Baltimore, **Shadrach** and **Thomas Sims** at
Boston (1851), **"Jerry"** at Syracuse
(1851), the **Christiana** (Pa.) **affair**
(1851), **Anthony Burns** at Boston
(1854), and the **Oberlin** rescue (1858).

21 Dec. HÜLSEMANN LETTER.
While the Hungarian revolution of 1848
was still in progress, the Taylor administration instructed (1849) its special
agent, A. Dudley Mann, to give the
revolutionary regime discretionary assurance of U.S. recognition. Mann never
entered Hungary, but the offended Austrian government instructed Chevalier
Hülsemann, its chargé d'affaires in the
U.S., to register a firm protest against
interference in its affairs. Secretary Webster's reply to Hülsemann's letter defended the U.S. right to take an interest
in the European revolutions and asserted
that these "events appeared to have their
origin in those great ideas of responsible
and popular governments on which the
American constitutions themselves are
founded. . . . The power of this re-

public, at the present moment, is spread over a region, one of the richest and most fertile on the globe, and of an extent in comparison with which the possession of the House of Hapsburg are but as a patch on the earth's surface." Webster's letter received support in the U.S. Senate and was endorsed by both parties. U.S. sympathy with the revolutions of 1848 reached its height with the public reception (5 Dec. 1851) accorded **Louis Kossuth,** the Hungarian partiot.

1851

LOPEZ FILIBUSTERING EXPEDITIONS. Southern annexationists were involved in the armed expeditions undertaken against Cuba by the adventurer Gen. Narciso Lopez, a leader of Spanish refugees in the U.S. who claimed that Cuba was ripe for revolt against Spanish oppression. His first filibustering venture collapsed after President Taylor issued a proclamation (11 Aug. 1849) and federal authorities intervened. His second, manned by many Southern volunteers, failed after a landing was made at Cardenas, Cuba (19 May 1850). A proclamation by President Fillmore (25 Apr.) notwithstanding, Lopez sailed from New Orleans (3 Aug.) and landed (11–12 Aug.) about 60 miles from Havana. A Cuban uprising failed to materialize. Col. William L. Crittenden (Ky.) and 50 other Southern volunteers were captured (13 Aug.), tried and sentenced by a military court, and executed at Havana (16 Aug.). The news of the executions caused anti-Spanish riots at New Orleans (21 Aug.) and the wrecking of the Spanish consulate there. Lopez was captured (28 Aug.) and publicly garroted at Havana (1 Sept.). Nearly half his 162 supporters sent to Spain as prisoners were Americans. Their release was secured only after Congress voted a $25,000 indemnity for the damage at New Orleans.

1852

20 MAR. Publication in book form of *Uncle Tom's Cabin,* by **Harriet Beecher Stowe** (p. 1161), a work originally serialized in the antislavery newspaper, the *National Era* (Washington, D.C.). A sentimental novel directed against the brutality and injustice of slavery, it was inspired by the Fugitive Slave Act of 1850. By mid-1853 some 1,200,000 copies of the work had been published. As a stage play it was first presented 24 Aug. Mrs. Stowe wrote *Key to Uncle Tom's Cabin* (1853) in an attempt to show that she had relied on factual evidence.

"YOUNG AMERICA" was the name given to an amorphous movement that began in the mid-1840s identified with aggressive nationalism, manifest destiny, and sympathy with the European revolutions of 1848. The term is thought to have originated in an address (1845) made by Edwin de Leon. Most of its adherents were Democrats; most prominent, Stephen A. Douglas. Its chief spokesman was George N. Sanders (Ky.); its organ the *Democratic Review.* In 1852 the movement reached its high point when Sanders formulated a program of southward expansion, aid to republican elements in foreign countries, and free trade.

PRESIDENTIAL CAMPAIGN. The Democratic National Convention assembled at Baltimore (1 June) and nominated **Franklin Pierce** (N.H.) for president (49th ballot) and **William R. King** (Ala.) for vice-president on a platform accepting the finality of the Compromise of 1850, affirming opposition to attempts to renew congressional agitation of the slavery question, and endorsing the Kentucky and Virginia resolutions. The Whig National Convention met at Baltimore (16 June) and nominated Gen. **Winfield Scott** for president (53rd ballot) and **William A. Graham** (N.C.) for vice-president on a platform accepting the Compromise of 1850, condemning further agitation of the slavery question, affirming states' rights, and supporting river and harbor improvements. The Free-Soil convention met at Pittsburgh (11 Aug.) and nominated **John P. Hale** (N.H.) for president and **George W. Julian** (Ind.) for vice-president on a platform condemning slavery and the Compromise of 1850, and supporting free homesteads for "landless settlers" and unimpeded entry for immigrants.

2 Nov. PRESIDENTIAL ELECTION. Popular vote: **Pierce**, 1,601,474; Scott, 1,386,578; Hale, 156,149. Electoral vote: **Pierce**, 254 (27 states); Scott, 42 (4 states). The results indicated the further disintegration of the Whig party (the Unionists of the South having merged with the Democrats) and the decline of the Free-Soilers.

1853

4 MAR. Pierce's inaugural address (the first delivered by a president from memory) pledged full support to the Compromise of 1850 and favored new territorial acquisitions by peaceful means.

30 DEC. GADSDEN PURCHASE. James Gadsden (S.C., 1788–1858), named (19 May) to negotiate with Mexico a settlement of a boundary question arising from the Treaty of Guadalupe Hidalgo, signed a treaty whereby Mexico, for a payment of $15 million (later reduced to 10 million), ceded to the U.S. a rectangular strip of territory (area: about 29,640 sq. mi.) in the Mesilla Valley, south of the Gila River. The line established marks the existing boundary with Mexico. The region, which includes the southern part of present-day Arizona and New Mexico, was regarded as a desirable route for a southern railroad to the Pacific. The treaty was ratified on June 1854.

1854

31 MAR. PERRY'S REOPENING OF JAPAN. Since the early 17th century Japan had been virtually isolated from the Western world. U.S. concern about its shipwrecked nationals, and interest in the commercial potentialities of Japan, led the Fillmore administration to authorize (Jan. 1852) a special expedition commanded by Commodore **Matthew C. Perry** (p. 1126). He sailed from Norfolk (24 Nov. 1852) and reached Yedo Bay (later Tokyo Bay) on 8 July 1853. In the face of considerable distrust he presented (14 July 1853) Fillmore's letter to representatives of the Japanese emperor and then withdrew to give the government time to reach a decision. To forestall Russian maneuvers he returned to Japan (Feb.) with a fleet of 7 ships, and at a conference near present-day Yokohama (8 Mar.) he gave the authorities American presents (including a miniature telegraph and railroad) which the Japanese accepted as impressive evidence of the civilized arts of the Western world. Perry signed a treaty of peace, friendship, and commerce (**Treaty of Kanagawa,** 31 Mar.) that opened the ports of Shimoda and Hakodate to U.S. trade and made provision for shipwrecked U.S. seamen. Officially promulgated 22 June 1855, the treaty laid the foundation for future U.S. demands, pressed shortly thereafter by **Townsend Harris** (p. 1052), appointed (4 Aug. 1855) consul general to Japan, and resulting in agreements signed 18 June 1857 and 29 July 1858. The first opened Nagasaki to U.S. commerce; the second opened additional ports, granted Americans residence rights, and established diplomatic representatives at the respective capitals.

30 MAY KANSAS-NEBRASKA ACT.
The slavery extension issue was reopened
with the introduction (23 Jan.) by Sen.
Stephen A. Douglas (p. 1015) of a bill
for organizing the territories of Kansas
and Nebraska. (His first bill, introduced
4 Jan., provided for organizing the single
territory of Nebraska; the second authorized its division at the 40th parallel.)
The measure incorporated the "**squatter**"
or "**popular sovereignty**" principle originated by Lewis Cass and permitted the
admission of the territories with or without slavery. By implication, the bill repealed the Missouri Compromise (which
was expressly repealed in the bill's final
version) and thus formally established
the doctrine of congressional nonintervention in the territories. Passed after 3
months of bitter debate, the bill also
provided that in all cases involving
slavery, there might be appeal to the
territorial courts and the Supreme Court.

The "**Appeal of the Independent Democrats**," published 24 Jan., condemned
the measure as a "gross violation of a
sacred pledge" and the work of slaveholders' "plot," and maintained that the
Compromise of 1850 had specifically affirmed the Missouri Compromise. Signers
included Sens. Charles Sumner and Salmon P. Chase. Widely reprinted, the Appeal was partly responsible for the organization of the Republican party.

Among the motives attributed to
Douglas for sponsorship of the bill are
(1) his belief in the principle of self-
government; (2) his courting of Southern support for presidential ambitions;
(3) his conviction that by force of
geography and nature, the territories
would remain free soil; (4) his interest
in the building of a transcontinental railroad along a central route (as opposed
to a southern one advocated by Pierce
and Jefferson Davis) with Chicago as
its eastern terminus, inpelling him to take
steps to open to settlement the region
west of Iowa.

The Kansas-Nebraska bill passed the
Senate, 37–14 (3 Mar.), and the House,
113–100 (22 May). The Senate (25
May) approved the Clayton amendment
denying voting and officeholding privileges to aliens.

**26 APR. MASSACHUSETTS EMI-
GRANT AID SOCIETY** organized by
Eli Thayer (1819–99) of Worcester,
Mass., an adherent of "popular sovereignty." Reincorporated (21 Feb. 1855)
as the **New England Emigrant Aid Co.**,
it promoted the settlement of antislavery
groups in Kansas with the ultimate object of making it a free state. It founded
Lawrence and other Free State communities and was active in Kansas until 1857,
bringing some 2,000 settlers there. The
activities of the company led in turn to
the organization of secret societies in
Missouri for the purpose of establishing
slavery in Kansas.

**5 JUNE. CANADIAN RECIPROCITY
TREATY.** The prolonged Anglo-U.S.
dispute over fishing privileges granted by
the Convention of 1818 was settled by
the Reciprocity Treaty of 1854 signed
at Washington. The negotiations were
handled by Secretary Marcy and a special British delegation headed by Lord
Elgin, governor general of Canada. The
agreement gave the U.S. offshore sea-
fishing privileges along the inlets of
Canada, New Brunswick, Nova Scotia,
Prince Edward Island, and several adjacent small islands. The British were
granted fishing privileges along U.S.
shores to the 36th parallel. The reciprocity arrangement provided for the duty-
free entry of many articles, chiefly agricultural commodities. The treaty was to
remain in force for 10 years, and thereafter until terminated by either country.
It was abrogated by the U.S. on 17 Mar.
1866.

6–13 JULY. REPUBLICAN PARTY. Popular dissatisfaction with the Kansas-Nebraska Act caused realignment of political forces in the North and West. The immediate impact was felt in the Northwest, where "anti-Nebraska" men of all parties united on the common platform of opposing the extension of slavery into the territories. A coalition meeting of Whig, Free-Soilers, and antislavery Democrats held at Ripon, Wis. (28 Feb.), recommended the organization of a new party on this single principle and suggested the name "Republican." A state meeting of Michigan citizens held at Jackson (6 July) officially adopted the name. The Jackson platform called for the repeal of the Kansas-Nebraska Act and the Fugitive Slave Law and demanded the abolition of slavery in the District of Columbia. Similar meetings were held (13 July) in Ohio, Wisconsin, Indiana, and Vermont. By the end of the year the organization had begun to spread throughout the North. Among its leaders were radical antislavery men such as **Charles Sumner** and **George Julian;** Free-Soilers such as **Salmon P. Chase** and **Lyman Trumbull;** and conservative Whigs such as **Edward Bates** and **Orville H. Browning.**

KNOW-NOTHING PARTY. The anti-Catholic and anti-immigrant movement of the 1840s was revived on a national scale after the election of 1852, and by 1854 had emerged as an important political force. Officially called the American party, it was popularly known as the Know-Nothing party because of the password "I don't know" used by members of secret lodges that were active in nearly every state. These bodies stemmed from a clandestine organization, the Order of the Star Spangled Banner, established at New York in 1849. Its rise was symptomatic of the breakup of the 2 major parties over the slavery issue. The party program called for the exclusion of Catholics and foreigners from public office and for a 21-year residence for immigrants as qualification for citizenship. Internal divisions over the slavery issue ultimately weakened the party, which reached its zenith in 1854–55. Its disruption came after the election of 1856. The Republicans drew accessions of strength from its ranks.

18 OCT. OSTEND MANIFESTO. When the U.S. merchant vessel *Black Warrior* was seized and condemned by authorities at Havana (28 Feb.) for an error in her manifest, a clamor for war with Spain broke out among expansionists in Congress. **Pierre Soulé** (1802–70), U.S. minister to Spain, presented a claim for damages (8 Apr.) followed by an ultimatum demanding immediate satisfaction. Secretary Marcy checked Soulé and in 1855 the U.S. accepted a Spanish apology and reparation.

Soulé was instructed by Marcy (16 Aug.) to meet at Ostend, Belgium, with **John Y. Mason** (1799–1859) and **James Buchanan,** U.S. minister to France and Great Britain, respectively, for the purpose of shaping a policy on the acquisition of Cuba. The meeting (9 Oct.), with the approval of President Pierce, resulted in the Ostend Manifesto, sent as a confidential diplomatic dispatch from Aix-la-Chapelle (its common designation was of later origin). Declaring Cuba indispensable for the security of slavery, the ministers recommended that the U.S. should make every effort to buy Cuba; should Spain refuse, "then by every law human and divine, we shall be justified in wresting it from Spain, if we possess the power." The aggressive pronouncement of the document was the work of Soulé. The document brought Marcy's disavowal, and Soulé resigned (17 Dec.). Publication (3 Mar. 1855) of the manifesto aroused Northern feeling and intensified Spanish resentment of the administration's annexationist policy. The newly born Republican party pointed to the manifesto as proof that a Southern-dominated administration had surrendered to pressure for more slave territory; Buchanan's participation recommended him to Southern Democrats.

16 Oct. LINCOLN'S "PEORIA SPEECH." Speaking at Springfield, Ill. (4 Oct.), **Abraham Lincoln,** whose reputation as a politician and lawyer was still confined largely to Illinois, condemned the Kansas-Nebraska Act. The speech, delivered again at Peoria (16 Oct.), was Lincoln's first public denunciation of slavery. He denied that the Kansas-Nebraska Act was the result of a slaveholders' conspiracy. "I have no prejudice against the Southern people. . . . I surely will not blame them for not doing what I should not know how to do myself." He acknowledged the constitutional rights of the Southerners; with careful qualification favored gradual emancipation; and supported a fair and practical Fugitive Slave Law, but opposed slavery in free territory.

1855

"KANSAS QUESTION." The opening of Kansas to settlement under the "popular sovereignty" formula put that principle to a severe test. With congressional nonintervention a declared policy, control of the territorial government became a vital necessity. Armed contests between proslavery and antislavery settlers converted Kansas into a cockpit of civil war.

Proslavery Legislature. Andrew H. Reeder (Pa.), first territorial governor of Kansas, was appointed in June 1854. The election of **John W. Whitfield,** the proslavery candidate, as territorial delegate (29 Nov. 1854) was accompanied by fraud and violence, most of it the work

of about 1,700 armed men from western Missouri. Like methods were used by some 5,000 Missouri "Border Ruffians" in the election (30 Mar.) of a territorial legislature. Under armed intimidation, Reeder refused to declare the election fraudulent, and Kansas was organized with a proslavery legislature, which disregarded his conciliatory plea when it convened (2 July) at Pawnee and later (16 July) at Shawnee Mission, and enacted proslavery statutes providing severe penalties for antislavery agitation and authorizing a test oath for officeholders.

In convention at Big Springs (5 Sept.) the antislavery colonists repudiated the territorial legislature as illegal and asked admission to the Union under a free state constitution. Mass conventions (Sept.–Oct.) organized a Free State party. Arms poured in from the North. **James H. Lane** (Ind.) was appointed military commander of the Free State forces.

Antislavery Legislature. The **Topeka Constitution,** drawn up by a Free State convention (23 Oct.–2 Nov.), prohibited slavery. That the Free State colonists were not abolitionists was indicated by the ordinance prohibiting entry of Negroes which was submitted to popular vote together with the constitution. Both were adopted (15 Dec.) and a Free State governor and legislature were elected (15 Jan. 1856). Kansas now had dual government.

Meanwhile Reeder has been removed from office (31 July), ostensibly because of his implication in land speculation but actually because of his opposition to the proslavery legislature. He was succeeded by **Wilson Shannon** (Ohio), a proslavery man (arrived in Kansas 3 Sept.). On 9 Oct. Reeder was elected congressional delegate from Kansas Territory by the Free State men, while on 1 Oct. Whitfield had been reelected by proslavery men.

The so-called **"Wakarusa War"** (26

Nov.–7 Dec.), limited to a few shootings and brawls along the Wakarusa River near Lawrence, brought about 1,500 "Border Ruffians" into Kansas, who refrained from attacking Lawrence when they found that the town was heavily defended by Free State settlers. The "war" was terminated by the intervention of Gov. Shannon.

WALKER'S FILIBUSTERING EX-PEDITIONS. American filibustering in the Caribbean region was climaxed by the expeditions against Nicaragua (1855–57) led by the military adventurer **William Walker** (1824–60). Although his incursions received some support in the South, they were widely misinterpreted in the North as part of a slaveholders' "plot" to extend slavery southward. Actually, Walker was backed by U.S. isthmian-transit interests (the Accessory Transit Co.).

Walker, who had led an unsuccessful filibustering expedition against Lower California (1853), exploited a civil war in Nicaragua to his own end, subjugated the divided country (June–Oct. 1855), and set himself up as dictator. Though President Pierce issued a proclamation (8 Dec.) against the invasion of Nicaragua, his reception of Walker's emissary (14 May 1856) amounted to virtual recognition. Walker became president (July 1856) and issued a decree opening Nicaragua to slavery. His downfall was brought about by **Cornelius Vanderbilt** (now in control of Accessory Transit Co.), who promoted the formation of a coalition of neighboring republics that ousted Walker, who surrendered 1 May 1857 to the U.S. naval commander.

Acclaimed in the South as a hero, Walker raised a new expedition and landed (25 Nov. 1857) at Greytown, at the mouth of the San Juan River. By this time Walker had seriously embarrassed U.S. isthmian policy. His expedition was broken up by the U.S. navy.

Again, in Aug. 1860, he landed at Honduras at the head of a filibustering expedition, was captured, court-martialed, and executed (12 Sept.).

1856

"BLEEDING KANSAS." In a special message to Congress (24 Jan.) Pierce condemned the Topeka government as an act of rebellion and in effect recognized the proslavery legislature. Although he issued (11 Feb.) a proclamation warning both Free State men and "Border Ruffians" to disperse, it was now clear that Pierce was committed to support of the proslavery element in Kansas.

21 MAY–15 SEPT. Civil War. Skirmishes began in the spring of 1856, often between land speculators and would-be settlers rather than forces of slavery and freedom, or were started by unruly plunderers, instead of idealists on either side, who hoped to profit from the turbulence. By this time the Free State party had received from the East fresh shipments of arms (the Sharps rifles popularly known as "Beecher's Bibles"). On 21 May, Lawrence was taken and sacked, as "Border Ruffians" joined Kansas proslavery men (including Col. Jefferson Buford's company and the Kickapoo Rangers) in burning down the Free State Hotel, pillaging many homes, and destroying the offices and presses of *The Herald of Freedom* and *The Kansas Free State*. One man was killed. Exaggerated accounts of the Lawrence affair inflamed Northern antislavery sentiment.

In retaliation for proslavery depredations, the fanatical **John Brown** (1800–59), with 6 companions (4 of them his sons), carried out the Pottawatomie massacre on the night of 24–25 May with midnight executions of 5 proslavery colonists who lived near Dutch Henry's Crossing at Pottawatomie Creek. Free State men disavowed this act of terrorism, but the incident raised feeling to a pitch that caused both parties to alert their military forces.

Gov. Shannon issued a proclamation (4 June) warning all irregular armed bodies to disperse. The Free State party sized Franklin (13 Aug.), a proslavery stronghold. About 300 proslavery men attacked the town of Osawatomie (30 Aug.), which was defended by John Brown and about 40 other Free State men, drove off their opponents, and pillaged the settlement. Guerrilla warfare was now raging throughout the territory. The total loss (Nov. 1855–Dec. 1856) was estimated at 200 killed and $2 million in property destroyed.

Shannon resigned as governor (18 Aug.) and was replaced by Daniel Woodson, a proslavery man who became acting governor. Woodson issued a proclamation (25 Aug.) declaring Kansas in a state of open insurrection and called out the proslavery militia. **John W. Geary** (Pa.), appointed territorial governor by Pierce, assumed his official duties on 11 Sept. With the aid of federal troops, Geary intercepted (15 Sept.) an army of 2,500 "Border Ruffians" who were marching on Lawrence and persuaded them to return to their homes. By his intervention, Geary brought temporary peace to Kansas.

Congressional Reaction. The Topeka Legislature adopted (4 Mar.) a memorial requesting statehood and elected Lane and Reeder U.S. senators. Douglas introduced (17 Mar.) an enabling act for Kansas, providing for the election of a constitutional convention and the formation of a state government. He denounced the Topeka government and the New England Emigrant Aid Co. as lawless bodies.

The congressional opposition to Pierce and Douglas supported the admission of Kansas under the Topeka constitution. An amendment to the Douglas bill was

formulated by Robert Toombs (Ga.). Its substance provided for a free and open election for a constitutional convention. Introduced on 30 June, the Toombs amendment was approved in the Senate, 33–12 (2 July), but never considered in the House.

The House (19 Mar.) appointed a special 3-man committee to investigate the conduct of the Kansas elections. Its report, confirming the charges of fraud and violence, provided material for Republican electioneering. The House passed a bill (3 July) to admit Kansas under the Topeka constitution, but the measure was quashed in the Senate. The House (1 Aug.) refused to seat either the proslavery or Free State territorial delegate.

The Republicans held up an army appropriation bill (18 Aug.) by attaching a rider forbidding the use of the army in aid of the proslavery Kansas legislature. The bill was finally passed (30 Aug.) without the Kansas rider only after an extra session of Congress had been called. When Congress adjourned (30 Aug.), Kansas still had no settled government. The Democrats charged that the Republicans had deliberately left "Bleeding Kansas" to anarchy in order that they might exploit a catch phrase in the approaching elections.

19–20 May. "The Crime Against Kansas." During the congressional debates on Kansas, Sen. Charles Sumner delivered a speech that later became known by the title "The Crime Against Kansas." It was a bitter denunciation of the "Slave Oligarchy" and its "rape" of Kansas. Sumner's tirade included coarse and insulting aspersions upon the character of several senators, particularly the absent Andrew P. Butler (S.C.). In retaliation, Rep. Preston S. Brooks (S.C.), Butler's nephew, assaulted Sumner as the latter sat at his desk in the Senate chamber (22 May). Sumner collapsed under the heavy blows of a cane. House attempts to expel or censure Brooks failed. His act brought general approval throughout the South. Brooks resigned his seat (14 July) and was unanimously reelected by his district. In the North, news of the assault created widespread indignation that became even more inflamed when it was reported that Lawrence had been pillaged. The Brooks-Sumner affair was condemned as a gross violation of liberty of speech. Except for a single day in Feb. 1857, Sumner did not again attend congressional sessions until Dec. 1859. During that time his empty chair in the Senate remained a symbol of Northern opinion of the attack upon him.

PRESIDENTIAL CAMPAIGN. The National Convention of the American (Know-Nothing) party met at Philadelphia (22 Feb.) and nominated **Millard Fillmore** (N.Y.) for president and **Andrew J. Donelson** (Tenn.) for vice-president on a nativist platform. These candidates were also nominated by the Whig National Convention that met at Baltimore (17 Sept.) and adopted a platform eschewing specific planks and warning against the sectionalization of parties.

The Democratic National Convention at Cincinnati (2 June) nominated **James Buchanan** (Pa.) for president on the 17th ballot (Pierce and Douglas being rejected because of their close association with the Kansas issue) and **John C. Breckinridge** (Ky.) for vice-president. The Democratic platform affirmed the Compromise of 1850 and supported the Kansas-Nebraska Act as "the only sound and safe solution of the slavery question."

The Republican National Convention met at Philadelphia (17 June) and unanimously nominated Col. **John C. Frémont** (Calif.) for president and **William L. Dayton** (N.J.) for vice-president on a platform upholding congressional authority to control slavery in the territories. Other planks condemned the Ostend Manifesto and favored a railroad to the Pacific and the admission of Kansas as a free state.

The chief campaign issue was "Bleeding Kansas," as Republican electioneers called it. The American party split on the slavery issue and in the Northeast supported the Republicans. The Democrats and Fillmore supporters attacked the "Black Republicans" as a sectional threat to the Union.

4 Nov. PRESIDENTIAL ELECTION. Popular vote: **Buchanan**, 1,838,169; Frémont, 1,335,264; Fillmore, 874,534. Electoral vote (counted 11 Feb. 1857): **Buchanan**, 174 (14 slave and 5 free states); Frémont, 114 (11 free states); Fillmore, 8 (1 slave state, Md.). The election results forecast the speedy demise of the Whig organization and the hardening of sectional lines.

1857

4 MAR. Buchanan's inaugural address condemned the slavery agitation and supported the policy of noninterference with slavery in the states and "popular sovereignty" in the territories.

6 MAR. DRED SCOTT DECISION. Dred Scott, a Negro slave and the household servant of Dr. John Emerson, an army surgeon, was taken (1834) by his master from St. Louis, Mo., to Rock Island, Ill. (where slavery had been forbidden by the Ordinance of 1787), and later to Ft. Snelling, in Wisconsin Territory (where slavery was prohibited by the Missouri Compromise). Scott remained on free soil during most of the period 1834–38.

In 1846 Scott sued for his liberty in the Missouri courts, holding that he had become free because of his stay in a free state and free territory. A lower court's judgment in favor of Scott was overruled (1852) by the state supreme court, which had previously ruled that under such circumstances a slave became free upon his return to Missouri. The case was maneuvered into the federal district court and finally to the Supreme Court of the U.S. (*Dred Scott* v. *Sandford,* 19 Howard 393). Scott's nominal owner at this time was John F. A. Sanford of New York (whose name is misspelled in the official reports).

The case involved 3 leading issues: (1) whether Scott was a citizen of the state of Missouri and thus entitled to sue in the federal courts; (2) whether his temporary stay on free soil had given him a title to freedom that was still valid upon his return to the slave state of Missouri; and (3) the constitutionality of the Missouri Compromise, whose prohibition of slavery applied to Wisconsin Territory.

Each of the justices handed down a separate opinion (that of Chief Justice Roger B. Taney is customarily cited for the majority). The majority held that Scott (and hence all Negro slaves or their descendants) was not a citizen of the U.S. or the state of Missouri, and thus was not entitled to sue in the federal courts (on this point, only 3 justices explicitly denied such citizenship, while only 2 affirmed it). Having refused jurisdiction, the majority passed on other issues: (1) Scott's temporary residence in free territory had not made him free upon his return to Missouri, since his status was determined by the laws of the state in which he resided when the question of his freedom was raised (on this point, the decision was 6 to 3); and (2) the Missouri Compromise was unconstitutional on the ground that under the 5th Amendment Congress was prohibited from depriving persons of their property without due process of law (on this point, the decision was 6 to 3), a principle first enunciated as regards a state

law in *Wynehamer* v. *The People,* 13 N.Y. 378 (1856).

The dissenting opinions of Justices John McLean and Benjamin R. Curtis, both of whom are generally held responsible for introducing the thorny issue of the Missouri Compromise, maintained that free Negroes were citizens of the U.S. and that Congress was constitutionally empowered (Art. IV, Sect. 3) to regulate slavery in the territories. Curtis' opinion was subsequently used by Republican and abolitionist elements as one of their chief grounds for attacking the court decision.

Northern denunciation of the decision included charges of "conspiracy." Opponents pointed to the fact that Buchanan's inaugural had predicted that the slavery controversy would be "speedily and finally settled" by the court. It has been established that Justices Robert C. Grier and John Catron violated judicial ethics in confidentially advising the president as to the intention of the court; there is no substance to the charge of collusion. The decision, first since *Marbury* v. *Madison* (1803) in which the court declared an act of Congress unconstitutional, lowered the court's prestige among Northerners and widened the sectional cleavage.

19 Oct.–21 Dec. LECOMPTON CONSTITUTION. In Kansas, Gov. Geary's recommendations for a thorough revamping of the laws to assure free elections and genuine self-government were ignored by the proslavery legislature. Meeting at Lecompton (12 Jan.–14 Feb.), the legislature called for a census enumeration (Mar.) and an election (15 June) for delegates to a constitutional convention. No provision was made for submitting the constitution to a popular vote. Geary, whose sympathy with the proslavery party had been replaced by a desire for impartial justice, vetoed the bill, which was promptly passed over his objection. Geary's efforts to follow a nonpartisan course in Kansas failed to secure the support of the Pierce administration. He resigned (4 Mar.) and was succeeded (26 Mar.) by a Buchanan appointee, Robert J. Walker (Miss.).

Walker's inaugural address (26 May) made a plea for cooperation and pledged that any constitution adopted would be submitted to a fair vote. A Free State convention met at Topeka (15 July), but Walker finally persuaded its leaders to abandon their refusal to participate in the election of a new legislature. Walker's policy brought from the South demands that any constitution drawn up by the proslavery convention should go into force without being submitted to the people.

The territorial elections were held (5 Oct.) under fairly strict supervision. Walker and the territorial secretary, Frederick P. Stanton (Tenn.), threw out thousands of fraudulent votes cast by the proslavery party. The final results gave the Free State party a decisive majority in both houses of the legislature.

The Lecompton convention (19 Oct.– 8 Nov.) recognized that a proslavery constitution would be rejected if submitted to a fair vote. Instead of arranging to place the constitution as a whole before the people, the convention drafted a special article on slavery which alone was to be submitted to a popular vote. The article guaranteed the right of property in slaves. Should it be rejected (the "constitution without slavery"), slavery would exist "no longer," but the right of property in slaves already in the territory would not be abolished. This arrrangement gave the proslavery party an obvious advantage; in addition, the elections were to be conducted by officials named by the convention.

The Lecompton convention was denounced throughout the North. Walker, opposed to the Lecompton proposal, went to Washington to place the question before the president. Buchanan was anxious to preserve party unity and harmony; moreover, he was under the influence of his pro-Southern cabinet. He decided to reverse his earlier pledge to Walker, and upheld the Lecompton convention. Walker resigned (17 Dec.). Buchanan's fateful step precipitated a party crisis by placing Douglas (who had come out against the Lecompton constitution, 9 Dec.) in open opposition, and helped to bring on the disruption of the Democratic party.

The vote on the Lecompton constitution was held on 21 Dec. Free State men and others among its opponents refused to participate. Results: for the constitution with slavery, 6,226 (of these, 2,720 were later shown to be fraudulent); for the constitution without slavery, 569.

Rejection. The Free State party induced Stanton, now acting governor, to convene the territorial legislature on 7 Dec., in advance of its scheduled date. The legislature called another election, permitting unequivocal voting for or against the Lecompton constitution. The administration punished Stanton by removing him from office. The Kansas election was held on 4 Jan. 1858. Results: for the constitution with slavery, 138; for the constitution without slavery, 24; against the constitution, 10,226.

24 Aug. PANIC OF 1857 (also pp. 741, 748). The failure of the New York City branch of the Ohio Life Insurance and Trust Co. precipitated a commercial and financial panic.

"THE IMPENDING CRISIS." *The Impending Crisis of the South: How to Meet It*, by Hinton Rowan Helper (a native of N.C.), published at New York in mid-1857, sought to prove by statistics (drawn largely from the census of 1850) that slavery had degraded and impoverished broad sections of Southern whites. A compressed version of the book (the *Compedium*) was endorsed by 68 House Republicans (1859) and 100,000 copies distributed as electioneering material. The South banned the book on the ground that it was insurrectionary. In Dec. 1859, John Sherman (Ohio) was denied the House speakership because of his endorsement of the work. The Southern outcry against "Helperism" brought the publication of several rejoinders, among them *Helper's Impending Crisis Dissected,* by Samuel M. Wolfe.

1858

DOUGLAS AND LECOMPTON. In support of the Southern extremist position, President Buchanan submitted the Lecompton constitution to Congress (2 Feb.), recommending the admission of Kansas as a slave state. His policy stirred Douglas to open revolt. Taking his stand on principle, Douglas condemned the Lecompton constitution (3 Feb.) as a violation of "popular sovereignty" and a mockery of justice. The executive patronage was brought to bear against Douglas and his supporters. The Senate, 33–25 (23 Mar.), voted to admit Kansas under the Lecompton constitution.

1 APR. Crittenden-Montgomery Amendment, providing for resubmission of the constitution to popular vote, passed the House, 120–112.

4 MAY. English Bill, an administration compromise measure, sponsored by William H. English (Ind.), a moderate Democrat, was reported to both houses on 23 Apr. Designed to quell party upheaval, the English bill provided for a popular vote on the Lecompton constitution as a whole. In the event of ratification Kansas was assured of c.4 million acres of public land grants (Lecomptonites had requested 23½ million acres) and 5% of the net proceeds from about 2 million acres to be sold by the government in July. Rejection would delay admission to the Union until a census indictated that Kansas had a population (about 90,000) required for a congressional representative. By winning the votes of 9 anti-Lecompton Democrats, the compromise broke the House deadlock. In the Senate, Douglas wavered, but finally opposed the measure. On 30 Apr. the English bill passed the House, 112–103, and the Senate, 31–22.

16 JUNE. "A HOUSE DIVIDED." Abraham Lincoln (p. 1085), whose political reputation was still confined largely to the Northwest, in a speech before the Republican state convention at Springfield that nominated him for U.S. senator, took a radical stand on the institution of slavery, but scrupulously refrained from criticizing slaveholders. Lincoln asserted that under the Kansas-Nebraska Act the slavery agitation "has not only not ceased, but has constantly augmented. In my opinion, it will not cease until a crisis shall have been reached and passed. 'A house divided against itself cannot stand.' I believe this government cannot endure permanently half slave and half free. I do not expect the Union to be dissolved; I do not expect the house to fall; but I do expect it will cease to be divided. It will become all one thing, or all the other." Both as phrase and concept, the Biblical "house divided" passage was not new in the slavery controversy. It had been used, e.g., by Edmund Quincy, Theodore Parker, and the New York *Tribune*.

2 AUG. Lecompton Constitution rejected by Kansas voters (in favor, 1,926; against, 11,812). The decision to remain in territorial status brought the disturbances virtually to an end. Under the

Dred Scott decision slavery was legal in Kansas; practically, it was excluded because of Free Soil domination. Kansas did not enter the Union until 29 Jan. 1861, when it was admitted under the free-state **Wyandotte Constitution** (ratified 4 Oct. 1859). Political results of the Kansas controversy (1) gave the Republicans a powerful campaign issue; (2) encouraged Southern extremists; (3) lost Buchanan the support of Northern Democrats; and, by way of the Douglas-Buchanan feud, (4) disrupted the Democratic party.

21 Aug.–15 Oct. LINCOLN-DOUGLAS DEBATES. On 24 July Lincoln challenged Douglas, his opponent in the Illinois senatorial race, to a series of joint debates. Douglas accepted. Seven debates were held during the course of a state-wide campaign: Ottawa (21 Aug.), Freeport (27 Aug.), Jonesboro (15 Sept.), Charleston (18 Sept.), Galesburg (7 Oct.), Quincy (13 Oct.), and Alton (15 Oct.). The debates covered the ground of the slavery controversy and its impact on politics, law, and government. From them dates Lincoln's emergence as a national figure.

The most memorable debate was held at Freeport, where Lincoln asked Douglas how he could reconcile the doctrine of "popular sovereignty" with the Dred Scott decision. The question evoked from Douglas his formulation of what became known as the **"Freeport doctrine"**: the people of a territory could, by lawful means, exclude slavery prior to the formation of a state constitution. The right to admit or bar slavery existed despite the Dred Scott decision, "for the reason that slavery cannot exist a day or an hour anywhere, unless it is supported by local police regulations," which could only be established by the local legislature. The "Freeport doctrine" provoked a storm of Southern criticism, and, along

with his opposition to the Lecompton constitution, was instrumental in depriving Douglas of Southern backing for the presidential nomination in 1860.

The debates as a whole illuminated the sharp difference between Lincoln and Douglas: where Lincoln regarded slavery as "a moral, a social, and a political wrong" (Quincy, 13 Oct., although he avoided a radical position, and at Charleston, 18 Sept., rejected Negro equality), Douglas evaded the moral issue. Lincoln lost the election by a narrow margin, winning the larger popular vote but failing to carry the legislature, where the vote was 54–41.

It was during this campaign, between the 2d and 3d debates, that Lincoln is supposed to have said at Clinton (2 Sept.): "You can fool all of the people some of the time, and some of the people all of the time, but you cannot fool all of the people all the time."

25 Oct. "IRREPRESSIBLE CONFLICT." Speaking at Rochester, N.Y., Sen. William H. Seward, at that time the leading contender for the Republican presidential nomination, delivered a radical pronouncement on the sectional controversy: "It is an irrepressible conflict between opposing and enduring forces, and it means that the United States must and will, sooner or later, become either entirely a slaveholding nation or entirely a free-labor nation."

REPUBLICAN SUCCESS. The results of the autumn elections indicated the rapidly growing strength of the Republican party. The chief campaign issue was the Lecompton constitution. In some areas the Republicans also stressed the protective tariff (Pennsylvania, New Jersey, and New England) and the homestead policy (Western states). Except for Illinois (where the prestige of Douglas was an important factor) and Indiana, every Northern state election was carried by the Republicans, even Buchanan's own state, Pennsylvania. In New York, the Republicans and antiadministration Democrats won 29 of the 33 congressional seats. In all, the Republicans gained 18 seats in the congressional elections. With a dozen anti-Lecompton Democrats in the House, the administration lost control of that body.

1859

16–18 OCT. JOHN BROWN'S RAID. Obtaining money from a number of New England and New York abolitionists (including Theodore Parker, Thomas W. Higginson, Samuel G. Howe, and Gerrit Smith), John Brown formulated a plan for instigating a slave insurrection in Virginia, establishing a free state in the southern Appalachians, and spreading a servile rebellion southward. Collecting arms and equipment at the Kennedy farm in Maryland, across the Potomac from Harpers Ferry, Va., he led 18 of the 21 men in his band (including 5 Negroes) in an attack on Harpers Ferry. They seized the federal arsenal and armory and held some of the local citizenry as hostages. No slaves came to the aid of the attackers. After 2 days of battle, Brown and his surviving followers were taken prisoner by a force of U.S. marines commanded by Col. Robert E. Lee.

25 OCT.–2 DEC. Treason Trial. Brown was indicted for treason against the state of Virginia and criminal conspiracy to incite a slave insurrection. He was tried (25–31 Oct.) at Charles Town, Va., convicted, and hanged (2 Dec.). Four of his band were hanged on 16 Dec.; 2 others on 16 Mar. 1860. Brown's raid spread alarm throughout the South, which fixed responsibility not only on the abolitionists but also on the "Black Republicans." Conservative Northerners

deplored the raid, but antislavery groups mourned Brown as a hero and a martyr.

AFRICAN SLAVE TRADE. The **Southern Commercial Convention** at Vicksburg, Miss. (9–19 May), urged the repeal of all laws prohibiting the foreign slave trade. This move was in accord with the growing Southern view that the federal government's sole relation to slavery should be that of positive protection (on this score, Southern extremists were also demanding a federal slave code for the territories). Some Southerners, notably Jefferson Davis and William L. Yancey, condemned the slave importation act of 1820 as unconstitutional and called for its repeal.

The Buchanan administration was on the whole firmly opposed to the foreign slave trade. It increased the naval patrols off the African coast. In his message to Congress (19 Dec.), Buchanan declared that all lawful means would be employed to suppress the illicit traffic. But the administration also ordered that U.S. merchant ships were to be protected against detention or search, thus giving them immunity to the more effective British patrols. Under such circumstances, there was little recourse against non-American vessels which used the U.S. flag fraudulently.

1860

2 FEB. DAVIS RESOLUTIONS. The program of the Southern extremists was embodied in the set of resolutions introduced in the Senate by **Jefferson Davis** (p. 1010), asserted that (1) no state had a right to interfere with the domestic institutions of other states; (2) any attack on slavery within the slave states was a violation of the Constitution; (3) it was the duty of the Senate to oppose all discriminatory measures against persons or property in the territories; (4)

neither Congress nor a territorial legislature was in any way empowered to impair the right to hold slaves in the territories, and the federal government should extend all needful protection (i.e., a slave code) to slavery in the territories; (5) the territories might not decide on the question of slavery until admission to the Union; and (6) all state legislation interfering with the recovery of fugitive slaves was inimical to the constitutional compact. The resolutions, adopted 24 May, touched off an extensive Senate debate on the constitutional and political aspects of the slavery controversy, and widened the breach between the Northern and Southern wings of the Democratic party.

SECESSION THREATS. In the winter and spring of 1860 political leaders and state legislatures in the lower South openly avowed the right of secession and the idea of Southern solidarity. The more radical resolutions were adopted in South Carolina and Mississippi; in these states and a few others, the legislatures passed appropriations for raising military forces. Many of the states (e.g., Ala. and Fla.) asserted that the election of a "Black Republican" president would be considered just cause for dissolving the Union.

Prominent among the leaders who initiated an exchange of opinion on a course of future action was Gov. **William H. Gist** (S.C., 1807–74). However, the states of the upper South (notably Va.) did not support Gist's project for a convention on Southern rights. At this time public opinion in the upper South overwhelmingly believed that Southern grievances could be resolved within the Union. Even in the lower South (particularly Ga.) sentiment was divided.

. **27 FEB. LINCOLN'S COOPER UNION SPEECH.** Appearing before a distinguished audience at Cooper Union in New York City, Abraham Lincoln, still a virtual stranger to Eastern audiences, delivered a carefully weighed speech. refuting Douglas' "popular sovereignty" doctrine and examining Southern attitudes toward the North and the Republican party. Lincoln condemned Northern extremism and made an appeal for sectional understanding, but did not minimize the gravity of Southern disunionist threats and indicated that no compromise with principle on the slavery extension issue was possible.

PRESIDENTIAL CAMPAIGN. The disruption of the Democratic party was formalized at the national nominating convention at Charleston, S.C. (23 Apr.). The Southern Democrats, now under the dominant influence of the radicals, insisted on a platform supporting positive protection to slavery in the territories. The Douglas Democrats reaffirmed the party platform of 1856 approving congressional nonintervention, abiding by Supreme Court decisions, and acquiring Cuba. When the Douglas forces carried the convention, the delegations of 8 Southern states withdrew to meet in a separate convention. The Charleston convention adjourned (3 May), having failed to agree on a nominee after 57 ballots. The Democrats reassembled at Baltimore (18 June) and, following another session of Southern delegates, nominated **Stephen A. Douglas** (Ill.) for president (2nd ballot) and **Herschel V. Johnson** (Ga.) for vice-president.

The Charleston seceders, after meeting at Richmond (11 June), convened at Baltimore (28 June) and nominated **John C. Breckinridge** (Ky.) for president and **Joseph Lane** (Ore.) for vice-president on a platform supporting slavery in the territories, the admission of states into the Union on an equal footing with the rest, and the acquisition of Cuba.

The remnants of the Whig and American parties convened at Baltimore (9 May) and established the Constitutional

Union party, nominating **John Bell** (Tenn.) for president and **Edward Everett** (Mass.) for vice-president on a platform condemning sectional parties and upholding "the Constitution of the country, the Union of the States and the enforcement of the laws."

The Republican National Convention met at Chicago (16 May) and nominated **Abraham Lincoln** (Ill.) for president (3d ballot) after William H. Seward (N.Y.) had led on the first 2 ballots. Lincoln's "availability," as opposed to Seward's long political career and his identification with antislavery radicalism, was a prime factor in winning the nomination. **Hannibal Hamlin** (Me.) was chosen for vice-president.

The skillfully drawn Republican platform was calculated to win support in the East as well as the West, from conservatives as well as radicals. It reaffirmed the principles of the Declaration of Independence, the Wilmot Proviso, and the right of each state to control its domestic institutions. It supported internal improvements, a railroad to the Pacific, a homestead law, and a liberal immigration policy. Its reference to a tariff adjustment which would "encourage the development of the industrial interests of the whole country" was in-terpreted as support of a protective tariff (a leading issue in the doubtful states of Pa. and N.J.). The platform condemned attempts to reopen the African slave trade and denied the authority of Congress or a territorial legislature to give legal status to slavery in the territories.

6 Nov. PRESIDENTIAL ELECTION. The division among his opponents made Lincoln's election almost certain. The state elections (Sept.–Oct.), bringing Republican victories in Maine, Vermont, Indiana, and Pennsylvania, indicated the impending result. Popular vote: **Lincoln,** 1,866,352; Douglas, 1,375,157; Breckinridge, 847,953; Bell, 589,581. The electoral vote (Lincoln failing to secure a single Southern vote) demonstrated the sectional character of the contest: **Lincoln,** 180 (carrying 18 free states); Breckinridge, 72 (carrying 11 slave states); Bell, 39 (carrying 3 border slave states); Douglas, 12 (carrying Mo., and 3 N.J. votes). Had the Lincoln opposition combined on a fusion ticket (attempted unsuccessfully in several states), it would have changed the result only in New Jersey, California, and Oregon for a total of 11 electoral votes. Lincoln would still have had 169, a clear majority.

THE CIVIL WAR AND RECONSTRUCTION, 1861-77

★　★
★

The Civil War established for all time the supremacy of the Union over the states and ended the institution of slavery. In his noblest utterance President Lincoln declared that the war was a contest to insure that "government of the people, by the people, and for the people shall not perish from the earth." In addition, the Civil War marked the triumph of the industrial North over the agricultural South and forecast, if it did not promote, the enormously rapid industrialization of the nation which followed in its wake. If the industrial potential of the victor determined the outcome of the war, the record hardly supports the view that the nation would have gone to war over the issue of a tariff, a national banking act, or special grants for railroads, as none of these issues had precipitated such a conflict in the past.

Decisive though the Civil War appeared to be, it failed to come to grips with the basic problem of race relations which underpinned the institution of slavery. It provided technical freedom for the slaves without genuine equality, and it was responsible for transforming the race problem from one that was largely sectional to one that became national in scope and intensity. Indeed, the return of the seceded states to the Union became involved in a political struggle that turned the Reconstruction era into a time of bitterness and hatred. The legacy of Reconstruction cast a long shadow, and many of its unsolved problems persist to haunt American society.

1860, 13 Nov.–24 Dec. SOUTH CAROLINA SECESSION CRISIS. On news of Lincoln's election the South Carolina legislature by unanimous vote called for a state convention, which met at Columbia and passed (20 Dec.) without a dissenting vote an ordinance declaring that "the union now subsisting between South Carolina and the other States, under the name of the 'United States of America,' is hereby dissolved." The convention then issued (24 Dec.) a "Declaration of Immediate Causes" reiterating the arguments for state sovereignty and justifying secession on grounds of the North's long attack on slavery, the accession to power of a sectional party, and the election of a president "whose opinions and purposes are hostile to slavery."

1861

9 JAN.–1 FEB. EXTENSION OF SE-CESSION. South Carolina was followed by the other 10 states which ultimately formed the Confederate States of America. The 7 states of the lower South (S.C., 20 Dec.; Miss., 9 Jan.; Fla., 10 Jan.; Ala., 11 Jan.; Ga., 19 Jan.; La., 26 Jan.; and Tex., 1 Feb.) grounded secession on Northern aggression against their "domestic institutions." The 4 states of the upper South (Va., Ark., Tenn., and N.C.), though not seceding at this time, warned they would oppose any attempt of the federal government to coerce a state. In only 3 states (Tex., Va., and Tenn.) were the ordinances of secession submitted to the voters for ratification; elsewhere public opinion was registered through the election of delegates to state conventions. The votes in these 3 states: Texas (23 Feb.), 34,794 for, 11,255 against; Virginia (23 May), 96,750 for, 32,134 against; Tennessee (8 June) 104,913 for, 47,238 against (on 9 Feb. a call to consider secession was rejected, 68,282 to 59,449), but in all cases the referenda were held after the state governments had already committed themselves to the Confederacy. Sizable Unionist minorities existed in some areas (notably N.C., Va., and Tenn.), and some outstanding Southern leaders opposed secession, including **Alexander H. Stephens** (p. 1157, in a speech as late as 14 Nov. 1860), **Benjamin H. Hill** (1823–82), and **Herschel V. Johnson** (1812–80) of Georgia; **Benjamin F. Perry** of South Carolina; and Gov. **Sam Houston** of Texas.

BUCHANAN'S LAST DAYS. President Buchanan in his message to Congress (3 Dec. 1860) recognized the grievances of the slave states, deprecated the disruption of the Union, but announced the impotence of the federal government to prevent secession by force (relying upon an opinion of Attorney General Jeremiah S. Black). On 18 Dec. Sen. **John J. Crittenden** (Ky., 1787–1863) introduced a peace resolution which would have recognized slavery in territories south of 36°30′. This was unacceptable to Lincoln, who, through Thurlow Weed, advised its rejection. A Senate committee of 13 (appointed 20 Dec. 1860 to consider the Crittenden proposal) disagreed 31 Dec.

4 FEB. MONTGOMERY CONVENTION AND CONFEDERATE CONSTITUTION. Motivated by Southern nationalism and the need for united action, the seceding states called a convention which met at Montgomery, Ala., framed a constitution, and set up a provisional government (8 Feb.). The Confederate Constitution resembled the U.S. Constitution, with significant differences. It stressed "the sovereign and independent character" of each state while establishing a federal government and obliging state officers to swear to support the new constitution, which, together with the laws and treaties, was declared "the supreme law of the land." No specific provision was included for state secession, but that right was implied. Several clauses recognized and protected slavery, but Art. 1, cl. 1, sect. 9 prohibited "the importation of negroes of the African race from any foreign country." This clause was inserted to conciliate British and French opinion. The president was empowered to disapprove of specific appropriations in a bill which he signed.

4 FEB. PEACE CONVENTION, called at the urging of the Virginia assembly, met in Washington behind closed doors, with ex-president John Tyler as its chairman. Border and Northern states were represented as well as the South. On 23 Feb. the delegates called on president-elect Lincoln for a frank exchange of views. The convention failed to agree upon an acceptable compromise to save the Union.

9 Feb. JEFFERSON DAVIS (p. 1010) elected provisional president of the Confederacy; **Alexander H. Stephens** provisional vice-president; inaugurated 18 Feb. **Confederate Cabinet:** *State:* Robert Toombs (Feb.–July 1861), R. M. T. Hunter (July 1861–Mar. 1862), Judah P. Benjamin (Mar. 1862–Apr. 1865); *War:* Leroy P. Walker (Feb.–Sept. 1861), Benjamin (Sept. 1861–Mar. 1862), George W. Randolph (Mar.–Nov. 1862), Gustavus W. Smith (Nov. 1862), James A. Seddon (Nov. 1862–Jan. 1865), John C. Breckinridge (Jan.–Apr. 1865); *Navy:* Stephen R. Mallory (Feb. 1861–Apr. 1865); *Treasury:* Christopher G. Memminger (Feb. 1861–June 1864), George A. Trenholm (June 1864–Apr. 1865); *Attorney General:* Benjamin (Feb. 1861–Sept. 1862), Thomas Bragg (September 1861–Mar. 1862), Thomas H. Watts (Mar. 1862–Jan. 1864), George Davis (Jan. 1864–Apr. 1865); *Postmaster General:* J. H. Reagan (Mar. 1861–Apr. 1865). Until regular elections were held (6 Nov. 1861) the Montgomery convention acted as a provisional congress.

SEIZURE OF FEDERAL FORTS AND ARSENALS. On 28 Dec. South Carolina commissioners presented demands on President Buchanan for removal of U.S. troops from Charleston Harbor and delivery of forts within the state. Buchanan refused (31 Dec.), but on 30 Dec. South Carolina troops seized the U.S. arsenal at Charleston. Other seizures: 3 Jan., Ft. Pulaski by Georgia state troops; 4 Jan., Mt. Vernon arsenal and 5 Jan., Ft. Morgan and Ft. Gaines by Alabama troops; 6 Jan., Apalachicola arsenal by Florida troops; 10 Jan., Baton Rouge arsenal and barracks by Louisiana

troops; 24 Jan., Augusta arsenal by Georgia troops; 8 Feb., Little Rock arsenal by Arkansas troops; 16 Feb., San Antonio arsenal by Texas troops. On 18 Feb. Gen. David E. Twiggs surrendered to Texas U.S. military posts in that state.

Ft. Sumter. On 26 Dec. Maj. **Robert Anderson** (1805–71) commander of U.S. troops in Charleston Harbor, withdrew his garrison from Ft. Moultrie to the more formidable Ft. Sumter. On 5 Jan. President Buchanan ordered the dispatch to Sumter of the *Star of the West,* an unarmed ship with reinforcements and provisions. But on 9 Jan. the ship was repulsed with fire from South Carolina shore batteries and returned to New York. Buchanan's policy was to collect public revenues and protect public property "so far as . . . practicable under existing laws."

11–23 Feb. LINCOLN'S JOURNEY TO WASHINGTON. President-elect Lincoln took leave (11 Feb.) from his neighbors in Springfield, "not knowing when or whether I ever may return, with a task before me greater than that which rested upon Washington," and began his journey to the capital. In brief speeches en route (Indianapolis, Cincinnati, Columbus, Cleveland, Pittsburgh, Buffalo, Rochester, Syracuse, Albany, Troy, New York, Trenton, Philadelphia, Harrisburg) he avoided disclosure of plans and policies. Warned (22 Feb.) of an assassination plot in Baltimore, he was secretly put aboard a special train at night, arriving at Washington at 6 A.M., 23 Feb.

4 Mar. LINCOLN'S 1ST INAUGURAL was firm but conciliatory toward the South. He assured the South that the rights of that section would be protected and declared: "I have no purpose directly or indirectly to interfere with the institution of slavery in the States where it exists." On the other hand, secession would not be countenanced. "Physically speaking," he insisted, "we cannot separate. . . . No State, upon its own mere action, can lawfully get out of the Union." But there need be no violence "unless it be forced upon the national authority."

The Civil War, 1861–65

1–15 APR. FT. SUMTER AND THE CALL TO ARMS. Desirous of avoiding an overt act, Lincoln delayed a decision on Ft. Sumter. On 1 Apr. Secretary of State Seward proposed that Sumter be evacuated, but that the Gulf ports be reinforced and a strong stand adopted toward foreign nations in the interest of national unity. Lincoln, in reply, made clear that he intended to run his own administration. The president considered (4 Apr.) a proposal that Sumter be yielded in exchange for a loyalty pledge from Virginia, but rejected it as indicative of fatal weakness. When he decided to provision the fort he notified South Carolina (6 Apr.) that an expedition was on the way solely to provision the Sumter garrison. Fearing a ruse or prolonged federal occupation, South Carolina (11 Apr.) requested Maj. Anderson to surrender at once. Anderson's offer to surrender upon exhaustion of his supplies (a matter of a few days) was rejected by the state authorities, aware that provisions were on the way. At 4.30 A.M. 12 Apr. the shore batteries under command of Gen. **Pierre G. T. Beauregard** (1818–93) opened fire. The Civil War began. Anderson was forced to surrender at 2.30 P.M. 13 Apr., after 34 hours of intense but bloodless bombardment. **Lincoln's role:** Some historians (Masters, 1931; Ramsdell, 1937) charge that Lincoln deliberately maneuvered the South into the role of aggressor; others (Potter, 1942; Randall, 1945; Stampp, 1951) dispute the charge. The attack on Sumter galvanized the North to spring to defense of the Union. On 15 Apr. Lincoln declared that "insurrection" existed, and called for 75,000 3-month volunteers.

17 APR.–21 MAY. BORDER STATES. The outbreak of hostilities drove Virginia (17 Apr.), Arkansas (6 May), Tennessee (7 May), and North Carolina (20 May) over to the side of the Confederacy despite Unionist sentiment which had prevailed prior to the attempted reinforcement of Ft. Sumter. The declaration of Virginia's convention (17 Apr.) that the president's call for volunteers constituted a signal for the invasion of the South and its vote to secede (103–46) led to the resignation of some of the ablest officers in the U.S. army, including **Robert E. Lee** (p. 1082), who had been offered command of the federal forces, and **Joseph E. Johnston** (p. 1073). **Richmond** was chosen (21 May) as the new capital of the Confederacy; the government moved from Montgomery in early June.

West Virginia. The mountainous western section of Virginia, tied economically to the Ohio Valley and traditionally opposed to Tidewater and Piedmont, refused to recognize secession. A convention called at Wheeling (11 June) organized a Union government and elected Francis H. Pierpont governor (19 June). Ultimately the 50 western counties of Virginia were admitted into the Union as the state of West Virginia (20 June 1863), with a constitution providing for gradual emancipation of slaves.

3 June–11 Sept. Loyal Slave States: 4 slave states (Delaware, Maryland, Kentucky, and Missouri) remained loyal to the Union, but not without prolonged contests in the last 3. Delaware's legislature unanimously rejected secession (3 Jan.) and in Apr. raised troops to defend the Union.

Maryland, in a strategic position to cut the national capital off from the North, was divided. A majority opposed secession, but pro-Confederates were prominent, particularly in Baltimore, where a mob attacked the 6th Massachusetts Regiment 19 Apr. as it passed through the city en route to Washington (militia casualties: 4 killed, 36 wounded). To avoid repetition of the riot the Maryland authorities burned down the railroad bridges connecting Baltimore with Philadelphia and Harrisburg. Gov. Thomas Hicks, a Unionist, was opposed by a legislature ready to accept Southern independence or to remain "neutral" in the conflict (10 May). The federal government felt obliged to suspend habeas corpus in that state, followed, in the summer and fall of 1861, with arrest and imprisonment of numerous state and local officials. By the end of 1861 the state's position in the Union was assured. Maryland contributed 46,-000 men to the Union army.

Kentucky, native state of both Lincoln and Jefferson Davis, was economically oriented to the South but strongly nationalistic. The legislature resolved (20 May) to be neutral. Lincoln gave assurances that no troops would be sent into Kentucky provided it remained peaceful, and pointed out that the war was fought to preserve the Union, not to free the slaves. When on 3 Sept. Confederate forces crossed from Tennessee into Kentucky and occupied Hickman and Columbus, Gen. **Ulysses S. Grant** (p. 1044) countered by occupying Paducah (6 Sept.). The legislature demanded

(11 Sept.) the ouster of the Confederates, and on 18 Sept. took steps to expel them. Ultimately 75,000 Kentuckians served with the Union forces. In a convention held at Russellville (18 Nov.) the Kentucky soldiers in the Confederate army adopted an ordinance of secession.

Missouri became a theater of civil war. Attempts of Gov. Claiborne F. Jackson to lead the state out of the Union failed (22 Mar.). The state soon divided into opposed armed groups headed by Gen. Nathaniel Lyon, a Unionist, and Gov. Jackson, respectively. Two major battles were fought at **Wilson's Creek,** where Lyon was killed (10 Aug.), and at **Pea Ridge, Ark.** (6–8 Mar. 1862), a Union victory leading to Union control of the state. Guerrilla warfare thereafter necessitated the establishment of martial law. 109,000 Missourians joined the Union army; 30,000 fought for the Confederacy.

OPPOSING FORCES. The North was predominant in numbers and economic power. Population of 23 Northern and border states, 22 million, augmented by heavy foreign immigration during the war years (400,000 foreign-born served in the Union army). The North had the advantage of a **balanced economy** (advanced industrial development, prosperous agriculture, strong banking institutions), a **railroad grid** (an immense logistical advantage, with the Northeast closely bound to the Mississippi and Ohio valleys), a **merchant marine,** and **naval supremacy** which handicapped the South from the start of the war.

The South. The 11 seceded states numbered 9 million (with few immigrants), of whom 3,500,000 were Negro slaves. An **agricultural economy** (based on the staples: cotton, tobacco, rice, sugar cane, and naval stores), its industrial resources were stunted, in part due to lack of banking capital (one third that of the North) and in part to lack

of technological skills and equipment
(despite abundant resources in iron,
coal, and timber). An **inadequate railroad system,** despite expansion in the
1850s, progressively deteriorated during
the war. In addition, the Mississippi and
Tennessee rivers and the Great Valley
of Virginia offered invasion routes by the
Union armies. Its few good harbors
could be easily blockaded.

Calculated Risk. Despite preponder-
ant Northern strength the South risked
war as a result of underrating the North
and overestimating its own strength. Secessionists were convinced (1) that the
North would not fight to maintain the
Union; (2) if it did, Great Britain and
France, dependent on Southern staples,
would recognize Confederate independence and give material aid; (3) that the
South's control of the mouth of the Mississippi would swing the Great Valley to
the Confederacy (overlooking the new
East-West orientation resultant upon the
railroad building of the 1850s). Confederate optimism rested on (1) the fact
that it stood on the defensive; (2) it
could afford to lose battles and campaigns if only it could wear down the
Union in the process; (3) its men were
trained in arms and outdoor living and
predisposed toward military careers (182
general Confederate officers had begun
their careers in the U.S. army).

ENLISTMENTS (reduced to 3-years'
service equivalent and taking into
account desertions—Livermore): **Union,**
1,556,678; **Confederate,** 1,082,119, distributed as follows:

	Union	Confederate
July 1861	186,751	112,040
Jan. 1862	575,917	351,418
Mar. 1862	637,126	401,395
Jan. 1863	918,121	446,622
Jan. 1864	860,737	481,180
Jan. 1865	959,460	445,203

A relatively higher proportion of Southern than Northern men served in the

army. Considering the requirements of
offensive warfare, invasion, and maintaining long lines of communication, the
North had far less effective numerical
superiority than the figures would suggest.

WAR AIMS: The North: Originally,
the restoration of the Union; after 1862
freeing of the slaves became a secondary
objective. President Lincoln insisted that
only *individuals* not *governments* had
taken up arms in rebellion and that the
Union army was in effect an enlarged
sheriff's posse. Yet in proclaiming a
blockade of the South (19, 27 Apr.)
and forbidding trade with the seceded
states (16 Aug.), Lincoln in fact recognized the existence of a state of war.
The conflict was conducted in accord
with the rules of war—captured Confederate soldiers and privateersmen were
treated as prisoners of war; prisoners
were exchanged. **The South:** Recognition
by the North of the independence and
sovereignty of the Confederacy.

STRATEGY. The **major military operations** took place in 2 theaters: (1) east
of the Appalachians, particularly in the
vicinity of the rival capitals of Washington and Richmond; (2) between the
western slope of the Appalachians and
the Mississippi. **Lesser operations:** (1)
isolated trans-Mississippi region; (2)
amphibious operations along the coasts
and inland waters; (3) war on the high
seas waged by cruisers, privateers, and
blockade runners. **Northern military
strategy** aimed at (1) starving the South
by blockading her coastline; (2) dispatching an army to seize Richmond in
the East; and (3) another force in the
West, aided by gunboats, to capture the
Mississippi and Tennessee rivers and
divide and subdivide the Confederacy.
Then the 2 armies would join and crush
the South. **Confederate strategy** proposed to seize Washington and move
northward into Maryland and central

Pennsylvania, thus cutting the Northeast off from the Northwest and forcing the federal government to sue for peace. A large part of the Confederate forces were to be employed for defense only.

15 APR.–20 JULY. EARLY SKIRMISHING. Minor actions were fought in western Virginia, where 20,000 troops led by Maj. Gen. **George B. McClellan** (p. 1092), a West Pointer who had retired to railroad management in the 1850s but was recalled to service at the start of the war as commander of the Department of the Ohio, cleared the enemy from the Valley of the Kanawha, with a victory at Philippi (3 June).

21 JULY. 1ST BATTLE OF BULL RUN. Demand of press and politicians for a march on Richmond overruled the caution of General-in-Chief **Winfield Scott,** who wanted more time to train the green Union troops. Gen. **Irvin McDowell** (1818–85), in command of a force of 30,000, was ordered to advance from his position southwest of Washington against a Confederate force under Beauregard stationed at Manassas Junction, Va. Another federal force under Gen. Patterson was ordered to prevent Confederate general **Joseph E. Johnston** from bringing a force of 9,000 from the Shenandoah Valley. Patterson permitted Johnston to evade him and join Beauregard (20 July). Before dawn (21 July) McDowell attacked and by 3 P.M. seemed to have carried the day. Then the arrival of Confederate reinforcements and Gen. **Thomas J. Jackson's** (p. 1068) magnificent stand, which earned him the sobriquet of "Stonewall," turned an apparent Southern rout into victory. McDowell's men began an orderly retreat, which quickly became a confused, panicky stampede toward Washington.

24 JULY. McCLELLAN IN COMMAND. First Bull Run aroused the North to the peril to the capital and to the seriousness of the war and convinced Lincoln of the need for more thorough training for the army. McDowell was replaced by McClellan, who, upon retirement of Gen. Scott, became general-in-chief (1 Nov.).

NAVAL BLOCKADE. To enforce the blockade of the Confederate coast (proclaimed by Lincoln 19 Apr.) the Navy Department had to convert a small, and, for the main, obsolete, collection of ships into an effective force. Loss to the Virginia authorities of the Norfolk navy yard with its vast stores and the hull of the frigate *Merrimac* was a severe setback. A large naval construction program was launched (on 7 Aug. building of 7 ironclad gunboats by the engineer **James Buchanan Eads** [p. 1019] was authorized), but for immediate use ships of all types were purchased and assigned to blockade duty. By July the blockade of the 3,550 miles of Confederate coastline was well under way. The Confederates built numerous speedy ships to run the federal gauntlet, with Nassau in the Bahamas becoming a major supply port. About 800 vessels managed to evade the blockade in its first year of operation; by comparison, in 1860, last year of peace, 6,000 ships entered and cleared Southern ports. By Nov. 1861 the Union navy had set up bases on the Southern coast after the capture of Forts Clark and Hatteras, N.C. (28–29 Aug.), Ship Island on the Gulf (17 Sept.), and Port Royal, S.C. (7 Nov.). The Union gained control of Albemarle and Pamlico sounds when Gen. Burnside's naval and military expedition (Feb.–Mar. 1862) captured Roanoke Island (8 Feb.) and New Bern, N.C. (14 Mar.). With the fall of Ft. Pulaski (11 Apr.) commanding approaches to Savannah, Ft. Macon, N.C. (26 Apr.), and New Orleans (29 Apr.), the effectiveness of the blockade increased. Chances of capture were estimated as 1 in 10 (1861), later 1 in 3 (1864).

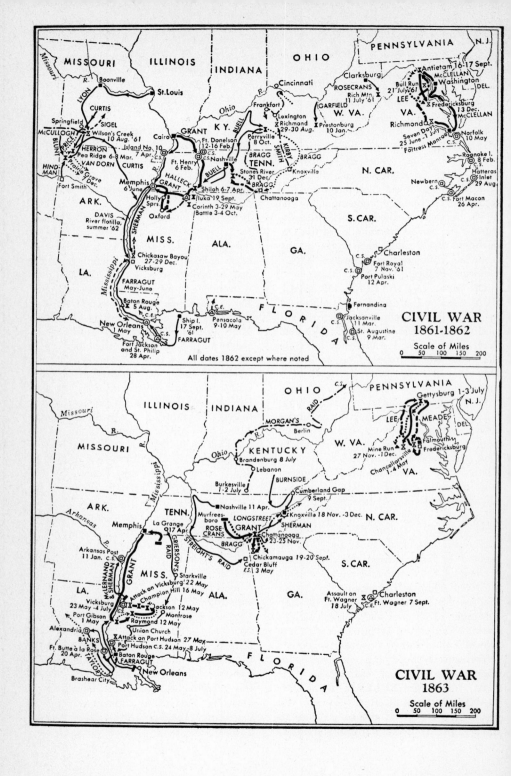

CIVIL WAR
1861-1862

Scale of Miles
0   50   100 150 200

All dates 1862 except where noted

CIVIL WAR
1863

Scale of Miles
0   50   100 150 200

CIVIL WAR
1864-1865

Scale of Miles
0   50   100   150   200

All dates 1864 except where noted

KEY TO ALL MAPS
SYMBOLS INDICATE VICTOR

Federal		Confederate	Federal		Confederate
——————	Major Advance	—·—·	O	Point taken by force	□
—————	Minor Advance	—··—··	⌣	Unsuccessful siege	⌣
— — —	Major Retirement	········	⌣	Successful siege	⌣
– – –	Minor Retirement	··········	F.S.	Surrender	C.S.
✕	Battle	✕	F.E.	Evacuation	C.E.
■	Point Occupied	□	◀▬ Continuation of troop movement ▭▶		
▲	Point occupied, later yielded	△	Confederate names and dates in italics		

EUROPE AND THE CIVIL WAR. The war divided British opinion. The upper class favored the Confederacy; the commercial interests, irked at the new high tariffs imposed by the Union, looked to the opening of a vast free-trade market in the Confederacy; British manufacturers and shippers expected to benefit from the defeat of their Northern competitors. The working class, however, and a large proportion of the middle class, favored the Union. A British declaration of neutrality (13 May) aroused the North by its mention of the belligerent status of the Confederacy. On 21 May Secretary Seward instructed U.S. minister **Charles Francis Adams** (p. 970), who arrived at Liverpool 12 May, that he should "desist from all intercourse whatever, unofficial as well as official, with the British Government, so long as it shall continue intercourse of either kind with the domestic enemies of this country." On representations to Lord John Russell, the latter replied that the British government had no intention of seeing the Confederate agents again (on 3 and 9 May Russell had received William L. Yancey and Pierre A. Rost, Confederate commissioners to Great Britain). On 1 June Great Britain forbade the armed ships of either side to bring their prizes to British ports, a heavy blow to Confederate privateering.

8 Nov.–25 Dec. "Trent" Affair. A second crisis with Britain arose when the U.S.S. *San Jacinto,* commanded by Capt. Charles Wilkes (p. 1184), stopped the British steamer *Trent* and removed James M. Mason and John Slidell, Confederate commissioners en route to England. News of the seizure provoked war fever in England, but war was abated when Secretary Seward ordered (26 Dec.) the release of Mason and Slidell on the ground that the 2 commissioners were "personal contraband" and, therefore, Wilkes had erred in not bringing the ship as well as the passengers to port for adjudication.

20 Dec. JOINT COMMITTEE ON CONDUCT OF THE WAR. As a result of growing dissatisfaction at the inactivity of the Union armies and a defeat at Ball's Bluff just above Washington (21 Oct.), a group of radical Republicans led by Sens. **Benjamin F. Wade** (Ohio, 1800–78) and **Zachariah Chandler** (Mich., 1813–79) and Rep. **Thaddeus Stevens** (Pa., p. 1158) pressed the administration for military action and emancipation of the slaves. Resentment at Lincoln's assumption of vast powers led Congress to set up the Joint Committee on the Conduct of the War, dominated by radical Republicans.

1862

15 Jan. STANTON AS WAR SECRETARY. The inefficiency and corruption of the War Department under Simon Cameron was ended when **Edwin M. Stanton** (1814–69) replaced him.

27 Jan. LINCOLN'S WAR ORDER NO. 1 set 22 Feb. for the launching of a general Union offensive. McClellan ignored this as well as subsequent orders.

WAR IN THE WEST. On 19–20 Jan. Union troops under Gen. **George H. Thomas** (p. 1168) decisively defeated the Confederates at the **Battle of Mill Springs,** Ky. A flanking movement by Union forces began in Feb. when Gen. **Ulysses S. Grant,** in conjunction with a gunboat flotilla under Commodore A. H. Foote, moved against Confederate positions on the Mississippi, Tennessee, and Cumberland. A joint attack captured **Ft. Henry** on the Tennessee (6 Feb.), but most of its garrison retreated to **Ft. Donelson** on the Cumberland, regarded by Confederate Gen. **Albert S. Johnston** (1803–62) as the major defense of Nashville. Another large Confederate force at Bowling Green, Ky., menaced by Gen. Don Carlos Buell from the north and by Grant from the south, retreated toward Tennessee to join the defense of Nashville and Ft. Donelson. After 4 days of siege Ft. Donelson surrendered to Grant (16 Feb.) with some 14,000 men. Johnston was forced to retreat from Kentucky and to evacuate Nashville, which fell 25 Feb.

6–7 Apr. SHILOH. Grant was prevented from striking a decisive blow against the main Confederate army of the East when his superior, Gen. Henry W. Halleck, given command of the armies in the West (11 Mar.), diverted part of the Union army under Pope to the task of expelling the enemy from the upper Mississippi. Pope, supported by Foote's fleet, besieged **Island No. 10** in the Mississippi (16 Mar.–7 Apr.). The Confederates surrendered, giving Johnston time to draw up his forces at Corinth, Miss., together with Beauregard's and Polk's. Grant marched to Pittsburg Landing just over the Tennessee border from Corinth, where he planned his attack without preparing suitable defenses. The Confederates struck (6 Apr.), and after a day of confused fighting in which Gen. A. S. Johnston was killed, the Union forces were close to defeat. During the night of 6–7 Apr. reinforcements from Gen. Buell's Army of the Ohio as well as Gen. Lew Wallace's division arrived. With the resumption of battle at dawn the tide turned. By evening the Confederates withdrew to Corinth, with the Union army too exhausted for pursuit. Heavy losses sustained on both sides: 13,000 out of 63,000 Union troops engaged; 11,000 out of 40,000 Confederates.

26 Apr. OCCUPATION OF NEW ORLEANS. Flag Officer (later Adm.) Farragut (p. 1026) ran the forts below New Orleans; bombarded the city (24–25 Apr.), which was occupied by Gen. **Benjamin F. Butler** (1818–93).

WAR IN THE EAST. Peninsula Campaign. Impatient with McClellan for his continued inactivity, Lincoln on 8 Mar. issued an order reorganizing the Army of Virginia into 4 corps. On 11 Mar. McClellan was relieved of supreme command except for the Army of the Potomac, and ordered to begin immediate operations against Richmond. McClellan preferred an advance by way of the peninsula between the James and York rivers instead of a frontal assault from Washington (Lincoln's preference). His opponents persuaded the president to withhold McDowell's corps in order to protect Washington.

9 Mar. "MONITOR" AND "MERRIMAC." The water route to Richmond up the James was guarded by the Confederate ironclad *Virginia* (formerly U.S.S. *Merrimac*), which on 8 Mar. had sunk the federal ship *Cumberland* and burned the *Congress* off Hampton Roads. The next day, when the *Virginia* sailed out to complete the destruction of the Union flagship *Minnesota,* which had run aground, she was met by the U.S.S. *Monitor,* another armored, raftlike craft with a revolving turret amidships. The ensuing 5-hour battle, the first naval engagement between ironclads, resulted in a draw, although the *Virginia* was driven back to Norfolk for repairs. The latter still closed the James and kept the federal fleet in Hampton Roads until burned by the Confederates to keep her from falling into Union hands when Norfolk fell 10 May.

17 Mar.–31 May. McCLELLAN'S ADVANCE. Embarkation of McClellan's army began from Alexandria, Va. On 5 Apr. McClellan began the siege of Yorktown, which he occupied 4 May. At a stubborn rear-guard action at **Williamsburg** (5 May) the Confederates frustrated McClellan's plans to come in contact with the main part of J. E. Johnston's army. By 14 May the Army of the Potomac had reached its advance base at White House on the Pamunkey River (20 miles from Richmond), where, despite overwhelming strength, McClellan awaited reinforcement by McDowell's corps.

23 Mar.–9 June. JACKSON'S VALLEY CAMPAIGN. "Stonewall" Jackson, in command in the Shenandoah Valley with some 18,000 men, kept 2½ times that many Union troops engaged and pinned down by the forces of Gens. Banks and Frémont. In late Mar. his cavalry attacked at Winchester; his main force hit Banks at Kernstown, forcing the Union general to bring his full forces back into the Valley. On 23 May he struck Banks at **Front Royal,** forcing him to retreat to **Winchester,** where Jackson again struck (25 May), routing the Union forces, who were forced to retreat across the Potomac. Stanton that same day telegraphed Northern governors to send militia to defend the capital. From McDowell's command 20,000 men were detached and rushed to the Valley.

28 Mar. BATTLE OF GLORIETA PASS was fought near Albuquerque, N.M., between a volunteer army of miners and trappers from Colorado and Confederate forces under Brig. Gen. George H. Sibley that had been advancing westward. Confederates were forced to retreat, ending last serious threat to Far West.

31 MAY–1 JUNE. BATTLE OF SEVEN PINES (FAIR OAKS). Mc-Clellan's lines were extended along both sides of the Chickahominy River in a great V, the upper arm stretching out along the north bank to meet McDowell, the lower reaching out to within 5 miles of Richmond, just beyond Fair Oaks Station. On 31 May Johnston attacked the 2 Union corps on the south bank isolated by the flooded river from the main part of McClellan's army. Only the fortuitous arrival of another corps which managed to cross the river prevented a disastrous Union defeat. Heavy losses were sustained on both sides: Union, under 6,000; Confederate almost 8,000, including Johnston, who was severely wounded. **Robert E. Lee** was given command of the Army of Northern Virginia (1 June).

26 JUNE–2 JULY. 7 DAYS' BATTLES. In an offensive move to drive McClellan off the peninsula, Lee sent Jackson to attack the Union right flank while he himself struck at McClellan's center. The Union army was alerted by a cavalry raid by **James E. B. ("Jeb") Stuart** (p. 1162) which misfired. McClellan withdrew to protection of Union gunboats on the James River. On 26 June Lee struck at the Union's extreme right at **Mechanicsville** and for 6 days attacked the smaller Union forces. At Mechanicsville (26–27 June), Gaines' Mill (27 June), Savage's Station (29 June), and Frayser's Farm (30 June) McClellan inflicted heavy losses on the Confederates while withdrawing across the Chickahominy to a new base at Harrison's Landing on the James. At Malvern Hill (1 July), supported by Union gunboats on the James, he withstood Lee's last desperate attacks. The next day the Confederates withdrew toward Richmond, marking the end of the Peninsula Campaign. Casualties of 7

Days' Battles: Union, killed 1,734; wounded 8,062; missing 6,053. Confederate, killed 3,478; wounded 16,261; missing 875.

11 JULY. Maj. Gen. Halleck was named general-in-chief of the U.S. army.

29–30 AUG. 2D BULL RUN. Halleck consolidated the Armies of Virginia under Gen. **John Pope** (1822–92), ordered Burnside north from Fortress Monroe to Falmouth, and directed McClellan to bring his army to Alexandria and join Pope for an overland march on Richmond. Determined to strike quickly, Lee moved his army toward the Valley. Jackson defeated Banks at **Cedar Mountain** (9 Aug.) and struck at Pope's rear (26 Aug.), destroying his headquarters and supply base at Manassas Junction. When Pope moved to attack Jackson in the belief that he was isolated from the main Confederate army, he was drawn into a trap. Maj. Gen. **James Longstreet** (1821–1904) forced Thoroughfare Gap (left practically undefended by Pope), struck at Pope's flank, and sent the Union army reeling toward Bull Run. Gen. **Fitz-John Porter** (1822–1901), who failed to throw his corps into battle the first day was made the scapegoat of Pope's defeat (cashiered 21 Jan. 1863). McClellan also had failed to get substantial forces to Pope in time.

14–15 SEPT. MARYLAND INVADED. Pope withdrew (3 Aug.) to the defenses of Washington, and was supplanted (5 Aug.) by McClellan as commander of the Army of the Potomac. The latter reorganized the army and moved to meet Lee, who had begun a general invasion in the hope of cutting railroad lines and isolating Washington, with Harrisburg as his probable ultimate objective. Overestimating Confederate strength, McClellan proceeded with his customary caution. Federal victories over Lee at **South Mountain** and **Crampton's Gap** (14 Sept.) did not come in time to save **Harpers Ferry,** which fell to Jackson (15 Sept.), with its 11,000-man garrison and immense body of equipment.

17 SEPT. ANTIETAM. The Confederates (40,000) were caught by McClellan (70,000) near **Sharpsburg, Md.,** the bloodiest day of the war. Union casualties, 2,108 killed, 9,549 wounded; Confederate, 2,700 killed, 9,029 wounded. McClellan failed to use his reserves, Lee held his lines, and the battle was a draw. But Lee pulled back to Virginia (18 Sept.), giving McClellan a technical victory. Although inconclusive from a military standpoint, Antietam had repercussions both at home and abroad. The British and French governments, on the verge of recognizing the Confederacy and intervening to force mediation (early Sept.), now held back. A crucial meeting of the British cabinet set for 23 Oct. was cancelled. French proposal (10 Nov.) for joint mediation including Russia was rejected (12 Nov.) by the British. The Union victory also enabled Lincoln to issue (22 Sept.) his **Preliminary Emancipation Proclamation,** freeing as of 1 Jan. 1863 all slaves in areas still in rebellion against the U.S. Lincoln had submitted the first draft of the proclamation to his cabinet on 22 July, but was persuaded to withhold it because of military reverses. On 1 Dec. the president appealed to Congress for passage of a constitutional amendment providing for **compensated emancipation,** but the border states opposed the plan.

8 DEC.–3 JAN. 1863. OPERATIONS IN THE WEST. Tied to Richmond by railroad, **Chattanooga** was the gateway to the nearer Southwest and a base to threaten Ohio and bar Union penetration of the lower South; while **Vicksburg** dominated the connections with the further Southwest and Texas, important supply sources. On 11 July Grant had been promoted to command the Army of West Tennessee. Gen. Braxton Bragg (successor to Beauregard), in an advance on Louisville from Chattanooga, was stopped by Gen. Buell's Army of the Ohio at **Perryville** (8 Oct.), but Bragg continued to dominate central Tennessee until forced to withdraw after the costly engagement with Rosecrans at **Murfreesboro** (31 Dec.–3 Jan. 1863). Casualties, Union, 1,677 killed, 7,543 wounded; Confederate, 1,294 killed, 7,945 wounded.

13 DEC. FREDERICKSBURG. The North, dismayed at Lee's escape at Antietam, was further shocked by McClellan's procrastination (Oct.), and by "Jeb" Stuart's daring cavalry raid around the Union army in Pennsylvania close to Gettysburg (10–12 Oct.). On 7 Nov. Lincoln replaced McClellan with Maj. Gen. **Ambrose E. Burnside** (1824–81). At Fredericksburg Burnside's overwhelming force (113,000 Union–75,000 Confederate) was shattered in a series of desperate attacks against the Confederate position, with losses of 1,284 killed, 9,600 wounded as against Confederate losses of 595 killed, 4,061 wounded. Burnside was replaced (25 Jan. 1863) by Gen. **Joseph Hooker** (1814–79).

17 DEC. CABINET CRISIS. A delegation of 7 Radical Republican senators demanded that Lincoln reorganize the cabinet, replace Seward by Chase, and fill the other cabinet posts with radicals. Lincoln confronted the committee with his whole cabinet (save Seward), who assured them that complete harmony existed. With the president declining the proffered resignations of Seward and Chase, the crisis was weathered.

1863

1 JAN. EMANCIPATION PROCLAMATION. To retain the loyalty of the border states Lincoln had resisted demands of the radical Republicans for abolition. **Military Action.** On 25 May 1861 Gen. B. F. Butler, in command of Fortress Monroe, Va., ruled that slaves escaping to his lines were "contraband of war" which he would not return to their masters. On 30 Aug. 1861 Gen. John C. Frémont issued a proclamation declaring that slaves of Missourians taking up arms against the U.S. were free. Lincoln modified this order (2 Sept.) to conform to existing law. On 9 May 1862 Gen. David Hunter proclaimed the emancipation of slaves in his Department (including Georgia, Florida, and South Carolina), but Lincoln disavowed this action 19 May. **Congressional Action.** The confiscation act of 6 Aug. 1861 provided for the emancipation of slaves employed in arms or labor against the U.S. A second confiscation act of 17 July 1862 liberated slaves of all persons who committed treason or supported the rebellion. Lincoln's plan of compensated emancipation was embraced by the act of 16 Apr. 1862 abolishing slavery in the District of Columbia, but no such compensation was provided in the act of 19 June 1862 abolishing slavery in the territories of the U.S. In vain Lincoln appealed to the loyal states to enact gradual and compensated emancipation. Aware of the public shift toward the radical position on slavery (as evidenced in Horace Greeley's signed editorial, "The Prayer of Twenty Millions," 20 Aug. 1862) and of the need to influence European opinion, Lincoln followed his Preliminary Emancipation Proclamation (22 Sept. 1862) with his Proclamation (1 Jan. 1863) declaring that all slaves in areas still in rebellion were "then, thenceforward, and forever free." The Proclamation actually freed no slaves; in fact, it went no further than Congress had already gone in legislation on the subject, for it applied *only* to areas over which the federal government exercised no control, specifically exempting all regions under federal military occupation.

RAISING THE ARMIES. Recruiting systems proved inefficient and inequitable. The state militia provided the bulk of the troops at the outbreak of war on a 3- to 9-month basis. Ill-trained and often poorly led by officers who were political appointees or elected by the men they commanded, the militia marched home when their terms expired, sometimes on the eve of important battles.

3 MAR. First Conscription Act made all men, 20–45, liable to military service, but service could be avoided by payment of $300 or procuring a substitute to enlist for 3 years. State quotas were fixed (proportionate to total population) and states given credit for previous enlistments. The draft was regarded as inequitable to the poor. The first drawings provoked serious riots in working-class quarters in New York City, culminating (13–16 July) in the **New York City Draft Riots,** 4 days of pillaging and Negro lynching, chiefly participated in by Irish-Americans, requiring the dispatch to New York of regiments detached from Meade's army sorely needed to pursue Lee after Gettysburg. Although there were 4 drafts in all, a very small proportion of the Union army was furnished through that means, although many "volunteered" under pressure (including **"bounty-jumpers"** who enlisted and deserted again and again).

Confederate Manpower Problems. The Confederacy first relied on enlistments; then, on 16 Apr. 1862, drafted into military service every white man (18–35) for 3 years. This first Confederate Conscription Act placed requisitions on the states but was administered and enforced by national authority. The lower classes denounced the long list of exempted occupations as well as the privilege of sending substitutes; many Southern leaders questioned the constitutionality of conscription; widespread fraud and evasion marked its administration. **Desertions** ran to about 10% in both Confederate and Union armies.

FINANCING THE WAR (also p. 734). An act of Congress (25 Feb.; amended 3 June 1864) established a **National Banking System,** requiring national banks to have one third of their capital invested in U.S. securities and authorizing them to issue notes up to 90% of such U.S. bond holdings. The imposition of a 10% tax (3 Mar. 1865) on state bank notes drove them out of circulation. Handicapped by inability to raise substantial loans abroad, by inade-

quate banking facilities, and opposition to taxation, the Confederate government resorted to **inflation.** Loans provided about $100 million (19 Aug. 1861) and an additional $15 million from abroad (authorized 29 Jan. 1863); taxation a similar sum, including the 10% tax "in kind" on the produce of land (24 Apr. 1863 and 17 Feb. 1864). On the other hand, over $1 billion in paper was issued by the Confederacy, beginning 9 Mar. 1861 with an authorization of $1 million in treasury notes. These notes, which were not legal tender, depreciated to 33 cts. in gold by 1863 and to 1.6 cts. by Appomattox. U.S. "greenbacks" (p. 734) dropped to a low of 39 cts. 11 July 1864.

UNION CONSCRIPTION AND ENLISTMENTS

	Draft of { 1863 July	1864 14 Mar.	1864 18 July	1864 19 Dec.
Number called for		700,000	500,000	300,000
Reduced by credits to		407,092	234,327	300,000
Names drawn	292,441	113,446	231,918	139,024
Failed to report	39,415	27,193	66,159	28,477
Examined	252,566	84,957	138,536	46,128
Exempted for physical disability, etc.	164,855	39,952	82,531	28,631
Exempted by paying commutation	52,288	32,678	1,298	460
Substitutes furnished by registered men		84,733	29,584	12,997
Substitutes furnished by draftees	26,002	8,911	28,502	10,192
Draftees held to personal service	9,881	3,416	26,205	6,845
Voluntary enlistments		489,462	188,172	157,058
Total number obtained		537,672*	272,463	187,092

* The excess, 130,579, credited to call of 18 July 1864.

HOME FRONT. The North enjoyed a war boom, as production, prices, and profits soared; only wages lagged. Between 1860 and 1865 prices rose 117%; wages 43%. A continuous flow of immigrants (almost 800,000 during the war) and the adoption of labor-saving devices by industry and agriculture compensated for the manpower drain by the armed forces. Passage of the **Homestead Act** (20 May 1862, p. 636) promoted westward agricultural expansion. Bumper crops met not only the increased home demand but also that from abroad occasioned by poor European harvests. Great Britain's dependence on **Northern wheat** counterbalanced her need for **Southern**

cotton. Dissension and subversion existed behind the lines. Some Northerners (mainly Democrats and known as "Copperheads") opposed the war. "Peace Democrats" like **Clement L. Vallandigham** (1820–71) of Ohio supported the secret Order of Knights of the Golden Circle. Their antidraft activities served to discredit the Democratic party.

The South, by diversifying her agriculture, raised sufficient food. Her supply of white manpower was depleted by the war, but women supervised farming and most slaves remained loyal and productive. But by 1863 the breakdown of the railroad system brought hardship and near starvation to some cities.

FOREIGN AFFAIRS. On 3 Feb. 1863 Napoleon III, through the French minister at Washington, proposed mediation of the conflict, but was rebuffed by Seward (6 Feb.) and by a concurrent resolution of Congress (3 Mar.) which branded as "foreign intervention" offers of mediation. The French emperor permitted French shipyards to build ships for the Confederates and forcibly intervened in Mexican affairs, occupying Mexico City with a French army (7 June) and placing Archduke Maximilian of Austria on the throne as emperor of Mexico (10 Apr. 1864). U.S. protests went unheeded until after the war (see p. 334).

4 APR. BRITAIN AND CONFEDERATE COMMERCE RAIDERS. In July 1862 the new raider *Alabama* had been permitted to slip out of Liverpool to join her sister ship, *Florida,* which had left England (Mar.), on a career of destruction of Union shipping. These and several other raiders destroyed 257 ships and impelled Union shipowners to transfer over 700 American vessels to foreign registries. The U.S. merchant marine did not recover from this blow for over half a century. Despite pro-Northern sentiment in Britain following the Emancipation Proclamation, the construction of Confederate naval vessels in British shipyards continued. When (Apr. 1863) it appeared that the *Alexandra,* another raider, would put to sea, the protest of U.S. minister Adams resulted in seizure (5 Apr.) of the ship by the British government. But the courts freed her and she put to sea.

2–4 MAY. CHANCELLORSVILLE. Following his victory at Fredericksburg, Lee clung to strong positions below the Rappahannock. Gen. Hooker crossed the river to attack (27 Apr.) with 130,000 men as against Lee's less than 60,000. Lee split his forces, sending Jackson through the Wilderness to hit the Union right, while he rolled up the Union center and left. Jackson struck on 2 May, completely surprising the Union troops under Howard and Sickles, who were sent reeling back in confusion. Gen. Pleasanton's stand prevented a Union catastrophe. On 5 May Hooker pulled his battered army back across the Rappahannock. Chancellorsville was the South's costliest victory: Confederate casualties, 1,665 killed (including Jackson, mortally wounded by his own men on 2 May), 9,081 wounded; Union, 1,575 killed, 9,594 wounded.

VICKSBURG CAMPAIGN. Failure had marked attempts to take Vicksburg by naval assault (May–June 1862) and by land (Dec.–early 1863). The river city, held by Gen. **John C. Pemberton,** was strongly fortified and protected by natural defenses. Most vulnerable were the approaches from south and east, remote from Grant's supply base at Memphis. Grant cut loose from his base (29 Mar.), crossed the Mississippi above Vicksburg, and marched down along the Louisiana shore of the river to a point south of the city where the fleet, which ran the Vicksburg batteries on the night of 16–17 Apr., ferried him across the river (30 Apr.). With 20,000 men he advanced northeastward on the rear of Vicksburg, living off the country. His 5 victories inside 3 weeks (**Port Gibson,** 1 May; Raymond; Jackson; **Champion's Hill,** 16 May; and **Big Black River,** 17 May) separated the armies of Johnston and Pemberton, driving the latter back into the Vicksburg perimeter.

22 MAY–4 JULY. Siege of Vicksburg. After 2 futile assaults (19, 22 May) Grant settled down to a siege. After a 6-week bombardment Gen. Pemberton surrendered the city and over 30,000 troops (4 July). Union casualties of the Vicksburg campaign (Oct.–July), c.9,000; Confederate, 10,000, not counting prisoners. On 9 July Gen. Banks, after a siege begun in mid-May, captured **Port Hudson**, La. The entire Mississippi was now under Union control and the Confederacy split.

27 JUNE–4 JULY. GETTYSBURG CAMPAIGN. Partly in the hope of winning foreign recognition, partly to encourage dissension and appeasement in the North, Lee decided to carry the war to the enemy. Early in June the Army of Northern Virginia began a move up the Shenandoah Valley. Confederate Gen. Richard S. Ewell crushed the Union garrison at **Winchester** (13–15 June), crossed the Potomac (17 June), and by 23 June neared Chambersburg, Pa. Hooker, preferring to stage a counterblow against Richmond, was ordered instead to follow on Lee's flank. On 25 June he crossed the Potomac, coming between Lee and his cavalry chief, "Jeb" Stuart, who was off on one of his audacious but costly forays, as a result of which Lee was deprived for 3 days of information about enemy movements. Hooker established headquarters at Frederick (27 June) before Lee (at Chambersburg) learned his whereabouts. The next day Hooker, at odds with Halleck, resigned the command, and Lincoln appointed Maj. Gen. **George G. Meade** (1815–72) to command the Army of the Potomac. An aroused North responded promptly to Lincoln's call (15 June) for 100,000 volunteers for 6 months' service. Carlisle and York fell 27–28 June, and the next day Ewell's cavalry came within 10 miles of Harrisburg.

1–3 JULY. Gettysburg. Lee took up a strong defensive position along the eastern slope of South Mt., near Cashtown. Meade planned to take a defensive position behind Pipe Creek. On 30 June a chance contact at Gettysburg of a part of Confederate Gen. Ambrose P. Hill's force in search of boots and saddles with John Buford's cavalry division drew both into that town, where the battle began. On the **1st day** (1 July), the Confederates drove the Union forces back through Gettysburg to strong defensive positions on Cemetery Hill and Culp's Hill. The Confederates occupied Seminary Ridge, a long, partially wooded rise running north and south parallel to the Union position. In the crucial battle that followed Meade enjoyed the advantage of a numerical superiority of 15,000, greater firepower, and a strong defensive position, with Cemetery Ridge and Culp's Hill heavily reinforced. Gettysburg was won and lost the **2nd day** (2 July). Lee attacked. Early was finally driven off Cemetery Ridge. Longstreet drove back Sickles' corps, but failed to take Little Round Top, which would have enabled him to enfilade the entire Union position. Ewell attacked Culp's Hill on the Union right; again on the **3rd day** (3 July), being repulsed. At Lee's insistence Longstreet reluctantly ordered a direct attack on the strongest part of the Union center, with Pickett's, Pettigrew's, and Trimble's divisions (15,000 strong). At 1 P.M. the Confederates opened up with an unprecedentedly heavy artillery barrage. As 3 gray lines of Confederate infantrymen approached Cemetery Ridge, they were mowed down by artillery fire and volleys of musketry. Less than a half company managed to reach the crest of Cemetery Ridge, only to be killed or captured. On 4 July Lee remained in position, but that afternoon retired to a position west of Hagerstown. There the flooded Potomac blocked his retreat. Lincoln and Halleck ordered Meade to attack, but rains stalled his reconnaissance; the river subsided, and Lee escaped into Virginia (13 July). Casualties: Union, 3,155 killed, c.20,000 wounded and missing; Confederate, 3,903 killed, c.24,000 wounded and missing. On 19 Nov. the cemetery at the Gettysburg battlefield was dedicated. The principal oration was delivered by Edward Everett, but Lincoln's brief remarks, in the course of which he referred to "a new birth of freedom," constituted the most memorable of all American addresses.

5 SEPT. Diplomatic Fruits of Gettysburg. The Union victories at Vicksburg and Gettysburg decisively tipped the diplomatic balance in favor of the North. On 5 Sept. U.S. minister Adams warned Russell that the ironclads under construction in England for the Confederacy (the "Laird rams") meant "war." Russell ordered that the rams be not permitted to leave Liverpool, and in Oct. the British government took over the ships. Similarly, Napoleon III ordered 6 naval vessels under construction for the Confederacy to be sold to European governments. The close of 1863 saw Confederate hopes for foreign recognition and aid irretrievably shattered.

19–20 SEPT. CHICKAMAUGA. Gen. William S. Rosecrans' Army of the Cumberland moved east from Murfreesboro at the end of June and maneuvered the unresourceful Braxton Bragg out of Chattanooga (9 Sept.), gateway to the East, without a battle. Alarmed at the loss of this key point, Davis rushed Longstreet and 11,000 troops from the East to reinforce Bragg. The armies clashed on the field of Chickamauga, northeast of Chattanooga, where the Union line cracked and broke, but Gen. **George H. Thomas,** who earned for himself the sobriquet "Rock of Chickamauga," used the bayonet to hurl back the Confederate attack until reserves saved the day. The Union forces retired into Chattanooga, and Bragg invested the city. Casualties: Union, 1,657 killed, almost 15,000 wounded and missing; Confederate, 2,312 killed, c.16,000 wounded and missing.

23–25 Nov. BATTLE OF CHATTANOOGA (LOOKOUT MOUNTAIN– MISSIONARY RIDGE). Grant, given command of the western armies (16 Oct.), replaced Rosecrans with Thomas; forced open communications with Chattanooga; and, reinforced by 2 corps under Hooker, prepared for the offensive. On 23 Nov. the armies came to grips. Hooker, Sherman, and Thomas drove Bragg off **Lookout Mountain** and the knolls south of Chattanooga, but Bragg concentrated his forces on **Missionary Ridge.** On 25 Nov. Thomas started a limited attack to clear the Confederates from the foot of the ridge, but continued to the crest, putting Bragg to rout. Casualties: Union, 753 killed, c.5,000 wounded and missing; Confederate, 361 killed, c.6,000 wounded and missing. The Union conquest of the Mississippi had split the Confederacy vertically. After Chattanooga, the Union armies of the West were poised to bisect the upper and lower South by marching across Georgia to the sea. On 3 Dec. Longstreet abandoned his siege of Knoxville, Tenn., and began a retreat.

1864

5–6 MAY. BATTLE OF THE WILDERNESS. Operations on the Virginia front bore little resemblance to the rapid movements of Sherman and Thomas. By comparison Grant's campaign before Richmond was slow and costly. Promoted (9 Mar.) to the newly revived rank of lieutenant general and given supreme command of the Union armies, Grant proposed to hammer away at Lee's army until it was decimated. The Army of the Potomac, over 100,000 strong, was assembled at Culpeper for its advance southward. Gen. Butler's Army of the James with some 36,000 men was to march up the south bank of the James and cut Lee off from the lower South. Maj. Gen. **Franz Sigel** (1824–1902) was to move up the Shenandoah Valley and seize Lynchburg. To meet Grant,

Lee had a force of 60,000, and was supported by Beauregard with 30,000 troops in the Richmond-Petersburg area. Grant and Meade crossed the Rapidan (4 May) and entered the Wilderness. Lee attacked Grant's right flank. In the ensuing indecisive 3-day battle Lee outmaneuvered his opponents, inflicting c.18,000 Union casualties (over 2,000 killed) to some 10,000 of his own men.

8–12 MAY. SPOTSYLVANIA. Disregarding losses, Grant futilely attempted to flank Lee at Spotsylvania Court House. Five bloody days of trench warfare followed. On 11 May Grant sent word to Halleck: "I propose to fight it out along this line if it takes all summer." Union losses, c.12,000, as Lee parried the Union blows. Heavy Confederate losses were never officially released.

1–3 JUNE. COLD HARBOR. At the Chickahominy, Grant again assaulted a well-entrenched foe, losing on 3 June alone 12,000 men. In one month ending 12 June Grant's losses amounted to nearly 60,000 (equal to Lee's total strength) as against Confederate casualties of c.25,000–30,000, but Lee's Army of Northern Virginia never really recovered from the heavy punishment.

15–18 JUNE. PETERSBURG. Grant decided to move his army south of the James to Petersburg, 20 miles below Richmond, approach the Confederate capital from the rear, and cut transportation connections with the South. Faulty generalship by Butler in his advance up the James prevented Grant from taking Petersburg, which withstood 4 days of battering and cost Grant 8,000 more men. Grant now dug in for a 9-month siege, longest of the war. On 30 July a huge mine was exploded in a costly but futile Union attempt to take the city.

2–13 JULY. EARLY'S RAIDS. Confederate Gen. **Jubal A. Early** (1816–94) who had defeated Sigel in the Shenandoah Valley (15 May) and driven

Hunter, Sigel's successor, into West Virginia (16–18 June), suddenly struck north into Maryland. Moving from Winchester (2 July), he crossed the Potomac, exacted tribute from Hagerstown and Frederick; then swung southeast and reached the District of Columbia, within 5 miles of Washington on 11 July. A thrust by Lew Wallace at Monocacy, Md., 9 July, slowed up Early and gave Grant time to assemble troops to defend the capital. Two divisions hastily returned from the Petersburg front helped drive Early back to Virginia on 13 July. Given command of the Army of the Shenandoah (Aug.), Gen. **Philip H. Sheridan** (p. 1150) defeated Early at **Winchester** (19 Sept.) and **Fisher's Hill** (22 Sept.), and rallied his men at **Cedar Creek** (19 Oct.), turning defeat into victory. Sheridan then proceeded to scorch the Valley as thoroughly as Sherman laid waste Georgia.

7 MAY–2 SEPT. SHERMAN'S MARCH THROUGH GEORGIA. With 100,000 men Gen. **William T. Sherman** (p. 1151) set out from Chattanooga (May 1864) and began his invasion of Georgia. Joseph E. Johnston, who had replaced Bragg after Chattanooga, faced Sherman with some 60,000 men, but fought a skillful series of defensive actions at **Resaca** (13–16 May), **New Hope Church** (25–28 May), and **Kenesaw Mountain** (27 June), where, momentarily forsaking his flanking movements designed to cut the enemy's communications, Sherman assaulted Johnston and was repulsed with 2,000 killed and wounded, compared with 270 Confederate casualties. On 17 July the Union army crossed the Chattahoochee River, only 8 miles from Atlanta. Davis, impatient at Johnston's masterfully executed Fabian tactics, replaced him with **John Bell Hood** (1831–79), who attacked Sherman in 2 pitched battles (20, 22 July), but, after suffering heavy losses, pulled back into Atlanta's

entrenchments. On 1 Sept. he was forced
to evacuate Atlanta; the next day Sherman occupied the city. The fall of Atlanta lifted Northern morale, staggered
by Grant's losses before Richmond, and
contributed to the Republican success in
the presidential campaign.

**14 Nov.–2 Dec. MARCH TO THE
SEA.** Changing his strategy, Hood decided to strike at Sherman's long lines of
communication stretching back to Tennessee. Dispatching Thomas to hold
Hood and protect Tennessee, Sherman
set out (14 Nov.) with 60,000 men in
his march to the sea. Before leaving Atlanta he destroyed or confiscated all supplies useful to the enemy. On his march
across Georgia his army cut a swath to
the sea, 300 miles in length, 60 miles in
width. Factories, cotton gins, warehouses, bridges, railroads, and some public buildings were systematically destroyed. His soldiers were ordered to
"forage liberally on the country," and
wild looting resulted. Sherman's advance
was virtually unopposed. On 10 Dec. he
reached Savannah, which fell (22 Dec.).

**15–16 Dec. BATTLE OF NASH-
VILLE.** In pursuit of Thomas, Hood
made contact with part of the Union
forces under Gen. John M. Schofield at
Franklin, Tenn. (30 Nov.), and was repulsed with heavy Confederate losses
(c.5,500 killed and wounded, as against
c.1,200 Union killed and wounded).
Schofield then joined Thomas at Nashville, where in a 2-day battle he all but
destroyed Hood's army. Mopping up operations against Confederate forces in
Tennessee were accomplished by Gen.
James H. Wilson's cavalry.

PRESIDENTIAL CAMPAIGN. On
7 June the Republican or National Union
Convention at Baltimore nominated **Lin-
coln,** with **Andrew Johnson** (Tenn.), a
War Democrat, as his running mate.
The Democratic National Convention at
Chicago nominated (29 Aug.) Gen.

McClellan for president and **George H.
Pendleton** (Ohio) for vice-president.
Under Copperhead influence the Democrats adopted a platform calling for immediate cessation of hostilities and the
restoration of peace "on the basis of the
Federal Union of the States." McClellan
repudiated the peace plank but sought
to capitalize on Northern defeatism. Pacifism and defeatism in midsummer made
the outlook for Lincoln's reelection seem
dark. On 4 July the president pocket-
vetoed the **Wade-Davis Bill,** a measure
for the Radical Reconstruction of the
South. A manifesto by the bill's authors
denouncing him was published by **Horace Greeley** (p. 1045) in the N.Y. *Tribune*
(5 Aug.). The Radicals covertly circulated a call for a new convention to
replace Lincoln with another nominee.
However, Sherman's success in Georgia
in Sept. changed the election outlook
and induced the Radicals to unite behind Lincoln.

**8 Nov. PRESIDENTIAL ELEC-
TION.** **Lincoln** was reelected by 212–21
electoral votes, but with a popular majority of but 400,000 out of 4 million votes.

1865

**LAST DAYS OF THE CONFEDER-
ACY.** The breakdown of transportation,
the blockade (tightened by the capture
of **Ft. Fisher,** N.C., 15 Jan., and the closing of the port of Wilmington, captured
22 Feb.), and federal occupation of important producing areas and devastation
of others spread hunger throughout
large sections of the South. Riots and
demonstrations against the Confederate
government or the food speculators broke
out in Southern cities. Army morale was
shattered by food and clothing shortages. Increasing desertions had forced
Davis to admit (Sept. 1864) that "two-
thirds of our men are absent . . . most
of them absent without leave." In desper-

ation he approved the **arming of the slaves** (7 Nov. 1864), but the Confederate Congress failed to authorize such action until 20 Mar. 1865, too late to take effect before the close of the war. The Richmond government tightened its laws against conspiracy and suspended habeas corpus with increasing frequency. Disunion tendencies appeared. South Carolina virtually nullified (23 Dec. 1864) an act of the Confederate Congress which had authorized the central government to impress goods and services.

16 Jan.–21 Mar. SHERMAN'S DRIVE THROUGH THE CAROLINAS. Sherman's corps fanned northward through South Carolina, wreaking even greater destruction than in Georgia. More than a dozen towns were burned in whole or part, including (17 Feb.) a large part of **Columbia,** the state capital. Whether Union soldiers (with or without orders) set the blaze or, as Sherman later claimed, retreating Confederates were responsible, has never been definitely established. The fall of Columbia led to the evacuation of Charleston, which fell to the Union (18 Feb.). Sherman advanced into North Carolina, his progress somewhat slowed by Johnston, whom Lee, now commander in chief of all Confederate forces, had restored to command. At **Bentonville** (19–20 Mar.) Sherman and Johnston met in their last battle. The smaller Confederate force was pushed back, but not crushed. Sherman entered Goldsboro (21 Mar.), where he joined Gen. Schofield.

3 Feb. HAMPTON ROADS CONFERENCE. Jefferson Davis, while agreeing to send Vice-President Stephens, R. M. T. Hunter, and J. A. Campbell to confer with Lincoln and Seward aboard the Union transport *River Queen,* stubbornly insisted on recognition of Southern independence. This was, of course, unacceptable to Lincoln, and the conference broke up.

4 Mar. LINCOLN'S 2D INAUGURAL. The president appealed to the nation to forget vengeance. "With malice toward none; with charity for all . . . let us strive on to finish the work we are in; to bind up the nation's wounds . . . to do all which may achieve and cherish a just and lasting peace."

2 Apr. PETERSBURG AND RICHMOND ABANDONED. On 25 Mar. Lee tried to break through Grant's besieging army by an attack on Ft. Steadman, east of Petersburg, but was badly beaten. Holding an advantage of 115,000 men to Lee's 54,000, Grant systematically battered the Confederate lines. On 1 Apr. Lee made his last assault of the war, hitting Grant's left flank at **Five Forks** near Petersburg, but was repelled by Sheridan, who arrived from the Valley. On 2 Apr. Lee evacuated Petersburg and Richmond and headed toward Lynchburg, whence he hoped to move by rail to North Carolina and join forces with Johnston.

9 Apr. SURRENDER AT APPOMATTOX COURTHOUSE. With Grant in pursuit of Lee, Sheridan's force took Burkesville, a railway junction, preventing Lee from moving south toward Danville. He then blocked Lee's path westward, and the Confederates were virtually surrounded. Lee's forces had now shrunk to less than 30,000, with few rations remaining. On 7 Apr. Grant requested Lee to surrender. Lee asked for terms. On 9 Apr. he met Grant at Appomattox Courthouse and quickly came to terms, by which Lee's soldiers were paroled to return home, officers were permitted to retain side arms, and all soldiers allowed to retain private horses and mules. All equipment was to be surrendered. 25,000 rations were issued by the Union army to the Confederates.

14 Apr. ASSASSINATION OF LINCOLN. The president visited Richmond on 5 Apr., then returned to Washington (where news of Appomattox arrived by noon 9 Apr.) and worked on plans for restoration of peace. In his last public address (11 Apr.) and at his final cabinet meeting on the morning of 14 Apr. the president repeated his plea for conciliation. At 10:15 P.M. that evening, as he was sitting in his box at Ford's Theater in Washington, watching a performance of *Our American Cousin*, he was shot by **John Wilkes Booth** (1838–65), carried unconscious to a lodging house across the street, and died there just before 7:30 A.M.

15 Apr. Vice-President Johnson took the oath of office as president 3 hours later. Simultaneously with the assassination of Lincoln, Secretary Seward was attacked and severely wounded at his home by Lewis Powell (alias Payne), a fellow conspirator of Booth. Booth escaped to Virginia, but was caught in a barn near Bowling Green. On his refusal to surrender, the barn was fired and (probably) he shot himself (26 Apr.). Of the 9 other persons implicated in the assassination 4 were hanged (7 July), 4 imprisoned, and a jury failed to convict the ninth suspect, John H. Surratt.

26 Apr.–26 May. FINAL CAPITULATION. Sherman drew closer to Johnston's army when he occupied Raleigh on 13 Apr. Despite Davis' plea for continued resistance, Johnston surrendered to Sherman (18 Apr.), with 37,000 men, and was granted liberal terms, including unauthorized political concessions disavowed by President Johnson. Final surrender terms along the lines of the Appomattox capitulation were agreed upon (26 Apr.) near Durham Station, N.C. Gen. Taylor surrendered the remaining Confederate forces east of the Mississippi to Gen. Canby at Citronelle, Ala., 4 May. Resistance ended (26 May) with the capitulation of Gen. Kirby Smith to Gen. Canby at New Orleans. Jefferson Davis was captured in Georgia on 10 May. The legal termination of the war was held by the Supreme Court in the case of *The Protector* (12 Wall 700), 1871, to have ended with presidential proclamations of 2 Apr. 1866 and 20 Aug. 1866.

WAR LOSSES. In the proportion of casualties to participants the Civil War was the costliest U.S. war, with casualties totaling between 33% and 40% of the combined Union and Confederate forces. Union dead, 359,528 (including 110,070 killed in battle or died from wounds); wounded, 275,175. Confederate dead, 258,000 (94,000 in battle or from wounds); wounded, 100,000 minimum. These figures take no account of the sufferings on both sides from imprisonment. Most notorious of the military prisons was **Andersonville,** operated by the Confederacy in Georgia (Feb. 1864–Apr. 1865). Bad rations, unsanitary conditions, inadequate medical services accounted for the deaths of some 13,000 out of 32,000 Union prisoners. In a war crimes trial (Aug. 1865) the prison's commander, Capt. Henry Wirtz, was found guilty by a military commission and hanged 10 Nov. 1865.

Reconstruction, 1865–77

1863, 8 Dec.–1865, 4 Dec. PRESIDENTIAL RECONSTRUCTION. Two constitutional issues were involved: (1) Were the rebellious states in the Union? (2) Was the president or Congress responsible for direction of Reconstruction

(involving both the status of the freedmen and the restoration to the Union of
the 11 Confederate states)? Lincoln consistently maintained that these states had
never left the Union, but was little concerned with the "pernicious abstraction"
of constitutional theory. In 1862 he appointed provisional military governors for
Louisiana, North Carolina, and Tennessee. On 8 Dec. 1863 he announced his
plan of Reconstruction: (1) amnesty,
with certain exceptions, to Southerners
taking a prescribed loyalty oath; (2)
executive recognition of state governments in cases where 10% of the 1860
electorate had taken the oath and where
the state agreed to emancipation. These
steps were taken by Arkansas and Louisiana in 1864, but Congress refused to
seat their representatives.

WADE-DAVIS BILL (4 July 1864),
purporting to represent the congressional
blueprint for Reconstruction, was enacted during absence of 5 key opponents
of the measure. It required a majority
of the electorate in each Confederate
state to take an oath of past as well as
future loyalty as a condition precedent
to restoration. Lincoln pocket-vetoed the
bill, and was excoriated by Radical Republicans, who considered him too lenient. Republicans of all shades feared a
revived Democratic party. In addition,
many in Congress resented the wartime
expansion of the executive power.

JOHNSON'S POLICIES. Andrew
Johnson quickly disabused the Radicals
of any idea that he favored their program. In fact, he adopted Lincoln's Reconstruction plan with minor changes.
During the recess of Congress he recognized the loyal governments of Arkansas,
Louisiana, Tennessee, and Virginia set
up by Lincoln.

**29 MAY–13 JULY. RECONSTRUC-
TION PROCLAMATION.** Johnson
granted amnesty to Confederates who
took the oath of allegiance, with several
excepted classes (among them holders
of taxable property exceeding $20,000)
who could petition him for special pardons. These he granted liberally. He
proceeded to organize provisional governments for the 7 remaining states.
Provisional governors were empowered
to convene conventions composed of
delegates elected by "loyal" citizens (including those pardoned by the president) to amend the state constitutions,
abolish slavery, and repudiate the state
war debt. By Dec., every Confederate
state except Texas had fulfilled these
requirements. Texas conformed 6 Apr.
1866. In his first annual message to
Congress (6 Dec.) Johnson announced
that the Union was restored; the delegates of the ex-Confederate states
awaited admission to Congress.

4 DEC. JOINT COMMITTEE OF 15.
When the 39th Congress convened it
refused to endorse Johnson's actions. Republicans secured the appointment of a
joint committee of 6 senators and 9
representatives to examine the issues of
suffrage and Southern representation in
Congress. Controlled by the Radicals,
this committee was dominated by **Thaddeus Stevens** (p. 1158), to whom, with
some exaggeration, tradition has attributed the exercise of almost dictatorial
powers both over the House and the Republican party.

**RADICAL THEORIES OF RECON-
STRUCTION.** To Stevens the ex-Confederate states were "conquered provinces"; to Sen. Charles Sumner (Mass.)
the seceding states had committed "suicide." Either interpretation put the
South under the control of Congress.
The joint committee declared that the
South had no state governments and that
Congress alone could restore them and
impose such conditions for readmission
as it deemed necessary.

18 Dec. 13TH AMENDMENT, abolishing slavery, ratified by 27 states, was formally proclaimed in effect.

1866

19 Feb. NEW FREEDMEN'S BUREAU BILL. Beginning with Mississippi (24 Nov. 1865), Southern state legislatures enacted "**Black Codes,**" a body of vagrancy and apprenticeship laws which bound the freedmen to the land. These codes varied in harshness; were notably lenient in Georgia, severe in Louisiana and Mississippi. To protect the Negro, Congress sought to enlarge the scope of the **Freedmen's Bureau** (est. 3 Mar. 1865) as a temporary bureau to care for the freedmen and the abandoned lands of the South. Congress sought to empower the bureau to try by military commission persons accused of depriving freedmen of civil rights. Johnson vetoed the bill on the ground that Congress had no power to legislate with 11 states unrepresented, and that the provisions for military trials violated the 5th Amendment. On 16 July the bill was passed over his veto.

9 Apr. CIVIL RIGHTS ACT, bestowing citizenship upon the Negro (legislation necessitated by the Dred Scott decision) and granting the same civil rights to all persons born in the U.S. (except Indians), was passed by Congress over Johnson's veto, which had condemned the measure as an unwarranted invasion of states' rights. The act enumerated rights including the right to make and enforce contracts, to sue, give evidence, to inherit, purchase, lease, and convey real and personal property. It was specifically amended in the House to exclude any application to state segregation statutes.

16 June. 14TH AMENDMENT was formulated by the joint committee of 15 because of widespread doubt as to the constitutionality of the Civil Rights Act. It passed Congress 13 June and was submitted to the states for ratification (16 June). Rejected by most of the Southern states, its ratification was made a condition of restoration to the Union (ratification announced 28 July 1868). The amendment for the first time defined national citizenship (to include Negroes) and threw the protection of the federal government around rights that might be invaded by the states. The charge has been made, with little support in fact, that the framers deliberately phrased the first section to protect property and the rights of corporations against state legislation. Subsequent judicial decisions did in fact so interpret the amendment. Section II abrogated the "three-fifths" clause, increasing Southern representation in the House by some 12 seats, but provided a proportionate reduction in representation when a state denied suffrage "except for participation in rebellion or other crime." This section has never been applied.

20 June. REPORT OF THE JOINT COMMITTEE OF 15 recommended that the Confederate states were not entitled to representation, and maintained the authority of Congress rather than the executive over the process of Reconstruction. Tennessee, under Radical control, ratified the 14th Amendment (19 July) and was restored to the Union (24 July). The other Southern states rejected the amendment, counting upon the approaching congressional election to repudiate the Radical program.

CONGRESSIONAL ELECTIONS. Johnson's abortive attempt to join all moderates in a new party at a National Union Convention meeting in Philadelphia (14 Aug.) convinced many Northerners that his supporters were primarily ex-rebels and Copperheads. Republicans also capitalized upon the president's maladroit speaking tour (28 Aug.–15 Sept.).

In contrast, the Radicals' skillful campaign stressed the connection between the Republican party and the Union cause. Race riots in New Orleans (30 July) and Memphis supported the Radical contention that the South was unregenerate. While Johnson failed to capitalize on the discontent of Western farmers, the Republicans were more successful in persuading industrial interests that a Democratic victory would lead to a reversal of policies favoring business. In the fall elections the Republicans captured two thirds of each house, giving the Radicals effective control of Reconstruction.

1867–68

2 MAR. 1ST RECONSTRUCTION ACT, passed over Johnson's veto, divided the South into 5 military districts subject to martial law. To achieve restoration the Southern states were required to call new constitutional conventions, elected by universal manhood suffrage, which were to establish state governments guaranteeing Negro suffrage and ratifying the 14th Amendment. Excluded from voting were ex-Confederates disqualified under the proposed 14th Amendment. Congress reserved to itself the power to review each case, end military rule, and seat representatives.

2 MAR. 3d FEDERAL BANKRUPTCY ACT allowed both voluntary and involuntary bankruptcy; amended 22 June 1874 to provide for composition of debts over a period of years; repealed 7 June 1878.

23 MAR., 19 JULY 1867; 11 MAR. 1868. SUPPLEMENTARY RECONSTRUCTION ACTS. On failure of the South to call new constitutional conventions, Congress passed the first supplemental act requiring the military commanders to initiate the enrollment of voters; then a second act giving the commanders broad powers to discriminate between voters and officeholders; and lastly, a measure declaring that a majority of votes cast was sufficient to put a new state constitution into effect, regardless of the numbers participating.

MILITARY RECONSTRUCTION. Despite doubts as to their constitutionality, President Johnson executed these laws, as to how conscientiously, contemporaries as well as later historians differ. He appointed military commanders who led 20,000 troops (as well as Negro militia) into the South. The governments previously set up by Johnson were supplanted. A total of 703,000 Negroes and 627,000 whites were registered as voters. In 5 states (Ala., Fla., La., Miss., and S.C.) Negro voters were in the majority. In other states a Negro-white coalition constituted Radical majorities. Southern whites allying with Radicals were called "scalawags"; Northerners who went South to participate in Reconstruction, "carpetbaggers."

1867, 4 DEC. GRANGER MOVEMENT. The Patrons of Husbandry, popularly called the Grangers, a secret association devoted to the promotion of agricultural interests, was organized in Washington, D.C. Typical of its objectives were the resolutions adopted at the Springfield, Ill., Farmers' Convention (2 Apr. 1873) attacking "all chartered monopolies," and urging laws "fixing reasonable maximum rates" for freight and passengers. The Declaration of Purpose of the National Grange (1874) stressed (1) cooperation, (2) reduction of the number of middlemen, (3) opposition to monopoly, (4) establishment of agricultural and technical colleges. Associated with this movement was the rise of independent farmers' parties, which, by 1874, had been organized in 9 prairie states and in Oregon and California under the leadership of **Ingnatius**

Donnelly (Minn., 1831–1901) and **Newton Booth** (Kan.). Their most effective supporters were not farmers, who were too thinly spread to be politically effective, but town merchants and small businessmen who suffered most from railroad price practices. First Granger legislation was enacted in Illinois (7 Apr. 1871), setting up a railroad and warehouse commission to fix maximum rates. Intrastate railroad freight rates were regulated by law in Wisconsin (11 Mar. 1874) and Iowa (23 Mar. 1874). For the early validation of Grange laws by the courts, see p. 671.

NEW SOUTHERN STATE CONSTITUTIONS. In late 1867 the Southern states voted to call conventions, which met in 1868 and established new constitutions. These conventions were Radical-dominated. Negroes participated in every such convention and formed a majority in that of South Carolina. The new constitutions were similar to those in effect in the North except for guarantees of civil rights for Negroes, universal manhood suffrage, and the disqualification of ex-rebels.

1868, 22–25 JUNE. OMNIBUS ACT. Seven states (Ark. [22 June] and Ala., Fla., Ga., La., N.C., and S.C. [25 June]) satisfied the requirements of the Reconstruction Acts and were readmitted by Congress. On 26 Feb. 1869 Congress proposed the **15th Amendment** forbidding any state from depriving a citizen of his vote because of race, color, or previous condition of servitude. By 1870 Mississippi, Texas, and Virginia, whose readmission had been held up by their refusal to approve the disfranchising clauses of the new constitutions, were restored to the Union following ratification of the 15th Amendment, proclaimed 30 Mar. 1870. Following restoration in 1868, Georgia was once more returned by Congress to military rule when, after withdrawal of federal military forces,

Negroes were expelled (Sept.) from the state legislature. With the return of troops, both the Reconstruction Acts and the 14th Amendment were enforced and the state (by act of Congress, 22 Dec. 1869) compelled to ratify the 15th Amendment and restore the expelled Negro members in order to gain readmission to the Union (15 July 1870).

1868

24 FEB.–26 MAY. IMPEACHMENT OF JOHNSON. The Radical sweep in the 1866 election resulted in their overriding Johnson's vetoes and enacting legislation curbing the power of the executive, who was prevented from appointing new Supreme Court justices (23 July 1866). Congress called itself into special session (22 Jan. 1867) and virtually deprived the president of Command of the army (**Command of the Army Act,** 2 Mar. 1867) by requiring that he issue all military orders through the General of the Army (U. S. Grant). An impeachment resolution was introduced (7 Jan. 1867) by Rep. James M. Ashley. The House Judiciary Committee reported 2 Mar. 1867 that further study of impeachment should continue in the 40th Congress, to begin 2 days later. The committee voted out a resolution of impeachment on 25 Nov., but the House of Representatives voted it down by a vote of 57–108 (7 Dec.). On 2 Mar. 1867 Congress passed the **Tenure of Office Act,** which prohibited the president from removing officials appointed by and with the advice of the Senate without senatorial approval. Johnson dismissed Secretary of War Stanton, 12 Aug., and named Grant Secretary of War *ad interim.* Johnson submitted his reasons for dismissing Stanton to the Senate when Congress reconvened (12 Dec.), but reinstated him (13 Jan.) after the Senate refused to concur with his action.

Challenging the Congress, he dismissed Stanton again (21 Feb. 1868). A resolution for impeachment, the **Covode Resolution,** was offered the same day, reported upon favorably by the Committee on Reconstruction 22 Feb., and the House impeached Johnson by a vote of 126–47 on 24 Feb. Subsequently the House drew up Articles of Impeachment encompassing 11 charges, including alleged violations of the Tenure of Office Act and Command of the Army Act and with attempting to bring disgrace and ridicule upon Congress.

4 MAR.–26 MAY. IMPEACHMENT TRIAL. The Managers of the House of Representatives presented the articles of impeachment to the Senate (4 Mar.). The president's attorneys filed an answer (23 Mar.) and the trial began with opening statements (30 Mar.). Chief Justice Chase presided over the Senate proceedings, and his insistence on the observance of legal procedure maintained some semblance of nonpartisanship. Johnson's counsel (Benjamin R. Curtis, William Maxwell Evarts [p. 1026], W. S. Groesbeck, and Henry Stanbery) disputed the evidence offered by the House managers (J. A. Bingham, G. S. Boutwell, B. F. Butler, J. A. Logan, T. Stevens, T. Williams, and J. F. Wilson). Voting (16 May) on the 11th article of impeachment as to whether the president was guilty of high misdemeanor as charged, the Senate voted 35 for conviction, 19 (including 7 Republicans and 12 Democrats) for acquittal, short by one vote of the two thirds necessary. On 26 May, 2 more ballots produced the same vote, and the Senate adjourned as a court of impeachment.

CAMPAIGN OF 1868. The Republican National Convention at Chicago nominated Gen. **U. S. Grant** for the presidency on the 1st ballot, with an Indiana Radical, **Schuyler Colfax** (1823–85) as his running mate (20–21 May).

The platform endorsed Radical Reconstruction, condemned Johnson and the Democrats, advocated payment of the national debt in gold, and equivocated on the tariff and Negro suffrage. The Democratic Convention, meeting in New York City (4 July), adopted a platform attacking Radical Reconstruction and endorsing Cong. **George H. Pendleton's** (1825–89) **"Ohio Idea"** (payment of the national debt in greenbacks). Their nominee for president on the 22nd ballot (9 July) was **Horatio Seymour** (1810–86), former governor of New York and a hard-money man. **Francis P. Blair** (Mo., 1821–1875) won second place. The Republicans made "the bloody shirt of the rebellion" their main campaign issue.

3 Nov. PRESIDENTIAL ELECTION. Grant captured 26 out of 34 states, with an electoral vote of 214–80, but a popular majority of only 306,000 out of 5,715,000 votes. A Negro vote exceeding 500,000 decided the election, in which 3 Southern states did not participate and 6 others were under Radical domination.

SUPREME COURT AND RECONSTRUCTION. In *ex parte Milligan* (Dec. 1866, p. 669) the court declared unconstitutional the resort to martial law where the civil courts were in operation. Nevertheless, the defiant Radicals made military tribunals a prominent feature of Reconstruction legislation. The court denied jurisdiction (*Georgia* v. *Stanton, Mississippi* v. *Johnson*) when 2 Southern states sought to enjoin executive enforcement of the Reconstruction Acts (Apr., May 1867). In Feb. 1868 the court agreed to consider *ex parte McCardle*. Fearing that a review of this case might invalidate Reconstruction measures Congress deprived the court of jurisdiction (27 Mar. 1868). In *Texas* v. *White* (1869) the court affirmed Lincoln's position that the Union was indissoluble, but at the same time upheld Congress' authority to reconstruct the states. In *ex parte Garland* and *Cummings* v. *Missouri* (1867) the court invalidated federal and state loyalty oaths which effectively barred ex-Confederates from pursuing their vocations.

1869

18 MAR. CURRENCY ISSUE. The Grant regime supported "hard" money. Congress, by the Public Credit Act, provided for payment of government obligations in gold, thus repudiating the "Ohio Idea." Bitter debate ensued over the question of whether the remaining $356 million in "greenbacks" still in circulation should be redeemed.

24 SEPT. "BLACK FRIDAY." In an attempt to corner gold **Jay Gould** (1836–92) and **James** ("Jubilee Jim") **Fisk** (1834–72), stock manipulators, induced Abel Rathbone Corbin, lobbyist brother-in-law of President Grant, to exert himself to prevent the government from selling gold. Despite Grant's refusal to agree, they spread the rumor that the president opposed such sales. With Grant's approval, Secretary of the Treasury **George S. Boutwell** (1818–1905) ordered the sale of $4 million in gold, and the gold price plunged from 162 to 135, with the ruin of many speculators.

1870–71

KU KLUX KLAN was founded at Pulaski, Tenn. (1866); constitution adopted May 1867. Ex-Confederate Gen. **Nathan Bedford Forrest** (1821–77) was the first Grand Wizard. Aimed to destroy Radical political power and establish white supremacy, the order was used as a cloak for lawlessness and violence and formally disbanded (1869), although its activities continued for some time after that date. Congress took cognizance of the order and similar secret societies,

such as the Knights of the White Camelia, by passing the **Ku Klux Klan Acts** of 31 May 1870 and 20 Apr. 1871, to enforce the 15th and 14th Amendments, respectively. A congressional committee sat during the summer of 1871 and took 13 vols. of testimony on conditions in the South. Certain sections of the Act of 1870 were declared unconstitutional (*U.S.* v. *Reese; U.S.* v. *Cruikshank*, 1876). In *U.S.* v. *Harris* (1883) the Supreme Court held part of the act of 1871 unconstitutional.

1871

1 JULY 1871. DEPARTMENT OF JUSTICE ESTABLISHED, with attorney general (1789) designated head of new department.

3 MAR. CIVIL SERVICE REFORM. Spoils politics and corruption led to a demand for civil service reform voiced by such leaders as **E. L. Godkin** (p. 1042) of the *Nation,* **Carl Schurz** (p. 1147), Sumner, and Lyman Trumbull. Grant appointed (4 Mar.) **George William Curtis** (1824–92) to head the first Civil Service Commission, authorized by act of Congress, which failed to make an appropriation, but he resigned (1875) when his recommendations were ignored, and the commission was discontinued.

8 JULY. TWEED RING. George Jones of *The New York Times* initiated his exposé of the regime of Tammany Boss **William Marcy Tweed** (1823–78) in New York City, where, through a new city charter creating a Board of Audit, he had seized control of the municipal treasury, which was systematically plundered to the extent of from $75 million to $200 million through faked leases, padded bills, false vouchers, unnecessary repairs, and kickbacks. Tweed was arrested 27 Oct., convicted (5 Nov. 1872), and died in jail. Others spent their plunder abroad.

1872

22 MAY. GENERAL AMNESTY ACT removed the disability to hold office (contained in Section 3 of the 14th Amendment) from all but the most prominent (c.500) ex-Confederates.

LIBERAL REPUBLICAN MOVEMENT represented a reaction from the Radical Republican policy toward the South as well as from the corruption of the Grant administration. It had its genesis in Sumner's break with Grant over Santo Domingo (p. 334) and in party division in Missouri. Leaders included **Schurz, Gideon Welles** (1802–78), **Charles Francis Adams** (p. 970), **Godkin,** and **Horace Greeley.**

4 SEPT. CRÉDIT MOBILIER. A New York *Sun* exposé charged Vice-President Colfax, vice-presidential nominee Wilson, Rep. James A. Garfield (Ohio), and other prominent politicians with accepting stock of the Crédit Mobilier (a construction company, organized 1864 by the promoters of the Union Pacific Railway to divert to themselves the profits from building that line) in return for political influence. An investigation which followed resulted in the censure (27 Feb. 1873) of Reps. **Oakes Ames** (Mass.) and **James Brooks** (N.Y.). Colfax escaped formal censure when the House Judiciary Committee recommended against impeachment on the ground that his alleged misconduct had been committed before he became vice-president, but he was ruined politically.

CAMPAIGN OF 1872. Convening at Cincinnati (1 May) the Liberal Republicans nominated **Horace Greeley,** protectionist and reformer, for president and **B. Gratz Brown** (Mo.), for vice-president, and adopted a platform favoring civil service reform, return to specie payments, and reservation of the public domain for the actual settler. The Greeley-Brown slate was also picked by the Democratic National Convention at Baltimore (9 July) despite Greeley's tariff views and long association with the Republicans, and by the Liberal Colored Republicans at Louisville, Ky. (25 Sept.). A "Straight" Democratic National Convention, meeting at Louisville (3 Sept.), nominated **Charles O'Conor** (N.Y.) for president and **John Quincy Adams, II** (Mass.), for vice-president. The Republicans at Philadelphia (5 June) renominated **Grant** on the 1st ballot and named **Henry Wilson** (Mass.) as his running mate. The Prohibition party (org. 1869) held its first national convention at Columbus, Ohio, 22 Feb. 1872, naming **James Black** (Pa.) for president and **John Russell** (Mich.) for vice-president. Labor Reform ticket, p. 765.

5 Nov. PRESIDENTIAL ELECTION. Grant was the victor, with 286 electoral votes to 66 for Greeley, and a popular majority of 763,000. As Greeley died 29 Nov. his electoral votes were cast as follows: Thomas. A. Hendricks, 42; B. Gratz Brown, 18; Charles J. Jenkins, 2; David Davis, 1.

1873

12 FEB. "THE CRIME OF '73," the **Coinage Act,** demonetized silver (omitting the standard silver dollar from the coinage) and made gold the sole monetary standard, despite the increase in U.S. silver production resultant upon new discoveries in the West (p. 611). The charge that this act was part of a "gold conspiracy" was without foundation, but was an article of faith of many Americans for 20 years. Gold-standard advocates had fears that silver presented at the Mint could feed inflation.

3 MAR. "SALARY GRAB" ACT doubled the president's salary to $50,000 a year and increased other government officials, including congressmen (from $5,000 to $7,500). Public indignation forced Congress to repeal the law (20 Jan. 1874) except for the increases voted the president and Supreme Court justices.

18 SEPT. PANIC OF 1873. Unbridled railroad speculation, notably in the field of construction, combined with overexpansion in industry, agriculture, and commerce weakened the U.S. financial structure, further shaken by the contraction of European demand for U.S. farm products after 1871. The failure (18 Sept.) of the powerful banking firm of **Jay Cooke** (p. 1005) precipitated a fall in security prices, ultimately affecting national income and leading to substantial unemployment (p. 751). As a palliative the government released $26 million in greenbacks (20 Sept.–15 Jan. 1874).

1875

14 JAN. RESUMPTION OF SPECIE PAYMENTS was recommended by President Grant on 6 Dec. 1869 and 7 Dec. 1874. The financial stringency resulting from the Panic of 1873 led to passage of a bill (14 Apr. 1874) to increase the issuance of legal tender notes to $400 million, which Grant vetoed (22 Apr. 1874). Instead, Congress (20 June 1874) placed a ceiling of $382 million on greenbacks in circulation, and by the Specie Resumption Act provided for the resumption of specie payments (by 1 Jan. 1879) and the reduction of greenbacks in circulation to $300 million. (For the **Legal Tender Cases,** see p. 670.)

1 MAR. CIVIL RIGHTS ACT (Sumner's Bill) guaranteed equal rights in public places (inns, public conveyances, theaters, etc.) without distinction of color and forbade exclusion of Negroes from jury duty. An attempt to include a school integration clause was defeated. (For the 5 cases involving the validity of the act, see p. 671.)

1 MAY. WHISKY RING. A conspiracy of revenue officials (chief among them John McDonald, a Grant appointee) and distillers, formed in St. Louis to defraud the government of the internal revenue tax, spread rapidly to other leading cities. As a result of an exposé by the *St. Louis Democrat,* Secretary of the Treasury **Benjamin H. Bristow** (1832–96) ordered an investigation, resulting in the indictment (10 May) of 238 persons, as well as Grant's private secretary, Gen. **O. E. Babcock** (indicted 9 Dec.), who was saved from conviction through the president's intervention.

1876

2 MAR. IMPEACHMENT OF BELKNAP. As a result of a House investigation disclosing that Secretary of War **William W. Belknap** (1829–90) had received bribes for the sale of trading posts in the Indian Territory, a resolution of impeachment passed the House. Belknap resigned the same day to avoid trial. Later (1 Aug.) he was aquitted by vote of the Senate, but 23 out of 25 senators who voted not guilty declared that they did so because they believed they had no jurisdiction over an official who had previously resigned.

PRESIDENTIAL CAMPAIGN. The Prohibition party meeting at Cleveland nominated Gen. Green Clay Smith (Ky.) for president and Gideon T. Stewart (Ohio) for vice-president. The National Greenback Convention at Indianapolis (18 May) nominated Peter Cooper (N.Y. p. 1006) for president and Samuel F. Carey (Ohio) for vice-president. The Republican National Convention at Cincinnati nominated (16 June) **Rutherford B. Hayes** (Ohio) for president on the 7th ballot and **William A. Wheeler** (N.Y.) for vice-president. Up to the final balloting the leading presidential candidate had been James G. Blaine, who had been discredited by testimony (31 May) before a House committee by James

Mulligan, a bookkeeper for Warren Fisher of Boston. Mulligan charged that Blaine had indirectly sold Little Rock and Fort Smith R.R. bonds to the Union Pacific and had borrowed from him and refused to return incriminating letters. On 5 June Blaine defended himself before the House, reading selected portions of the "Mulligan letters." The Democratic National Convention meeting at St. Louis (27–29 June) nominated **Samuel J. Tilden** (N.Y., 1814–86) for president and **Thomas A. Hendricks** (Ind.) for vice-president.

7 Nov.–6 Dec. DISPUTED ELECTION OF 1876. The presidential election gave Tilden a popular-vote margin of 250,000. More decisive, however, was the electoral vote. Tilden carried New York, New Jersey, Connecticut, Indiana, and, apparently, the South; but Republican headquarters refused to concede his election on the ground that the returns were in dispute in Florida, Louisiana, South Carolina, and Oregon (without these electoral votes Tilden, with 184, would be 1 short of the necessary majority). On 6 Dec. 2 sets of electoral returns were reported from the 4 disputed states (in the 3 Southern states Republican election boards threw out sufficient Tilden votes on the ground of irregularities to certify Hayes; in Oregon, which the Republicans had unquestionably carried, the Democratic governor, violating Oregon law, disqualified 1 Republican elector and certified a Democrat in his place).

1877

29 Jan. ELECTORAL COMMISSION. The Constitution offered no clear guide for the disputed election of 1876. It provided that "The President of the Senate shall, in the presence of the Senate and the House of Representatives, open all certificates and the votes shall

then be counted." But counted by whom? If by the Senate (Republican), the Hayes electors would be sustained; if by the House (Democratic since 1875), the Tilden electors. To break an alarming deadlock Congress set up an **Electoral Commission** consisting of 5 members of the House, 5 of the Senate, and 5 justices of the Supreme Court. Four of the justices were designated in the bill: 2 Republicans, 2 Democrats. The House selected 3 Democrats and 2 Republicans; the Senate, 3 Republicans and 2 Democrats. The 15th member, the 5th justice, was to be selected by the other 4 justices, with the tacit understanding that Justice David Davis, an independent, would be chosen. But owing to his election by the Illinois state legislature to the U.S. Senate, Davis was replaced by Justice Bradley, a Republican.

9–28 Feb. COMMISSION AWARD. Under pressure from Republican politicians Bradley, who had first written an opinion favoring Tilden, switched to the Hayes side. Deciding by a vote of 8–7 (along straight party lines) not to "go behind the returns" and investigate the count in each disputed state, the commission (9 Feb.) awarded the vote in Florida to Hayes, and later (16, 23, 28 Feb.) gave similar decisions for the 3 remaining states.

2 Mar. HAYES DECLARED ELECTED (185–184). Support by Southern Democrats for the Electoral Commission's decision was the result of Republican promises (1) to withdraw federal troops from the South, (2) appoint at least 1 Southerner to the cabinet, and (3) make substantial appropriations for Southern internal improvements. A lobby headed by Thomas A. Scott, president of the Pennsylvania R.R., and Grenville M. Dodge, chief engineer of the Union Pacific (1866–70), persuaded many Southern congressmen that the construction of the proposed route of the Texas & Pacific R.R. (chartered 1871) from East Texas to the Pacific coast was dependent on Republican victory. Hayes was inaugurated 5 Mar., after having taken the oath privately on 3 Mar. since 4 Mar. was a Sunday. On 5 Mar. he appointed David M. Key (Tenn.) Postmaster General, and in Apr. withdrew the last federal troops from the South.

10–24 APR. END OF "BLACK RECONSTRUCTION." The period of Radical control of the ex-Confederate states had been under attack for corruption, incompetence, and extravagance. Corrupt financial practices were notorious in South Carolina, where the public debt rose from $7 million (1865) to $29 million (1873); but in other states extravagant governments had raised tax burdens and increased state debts (in Ark., from $3.5 million, 1868, to $15.7 million, 1875—$115 per voter; in La., from $11 million to $50 million, 1875, and the state tax rose almost 5-fold, treble the N.Y. real property tax in 1870), while property values declined sharply. But maladministration and corruption were not confined to the South in that period. On the credit side, it should be pointed out that large sums were needed for rebuilding devastated areas and for essential public services in many cases hitherto not adequately provided, such as public education, hospitals, and asylums. By 1876 the constitution in nearly every Southern state contained provisions making tax-supported free public schools for both whites and Negroes mandatory.

In reaction against Radical rule the conservatives won control in Georgia, North Carolina, Tennessee, and Virginia (1869–71); and in Alabama, Arkansas, Mississippi, and Texas (1874–75). By the summer of 1876 only Florida, Louisiana, and South Carolina remained in Radical hands. On 2 Jan. 1877 carpetbag rule ended in Florida with the inauguration of George F. Drew, Democratic governor, and the Radicals also lost control in the 2 remaining states of the South. Federal troops were withdrawn from South Carolina (10 Apr.) and Louisiana (24 Apr.).

DOMESTIC ISSUES FROM HAYES TO WILSON, 1878-1918

★　★
★

Governmental leadership in the years immediately following Reconstruction was marked by timidity and complacency. Save for two nonconsecutive terms in the presidency of Grover Cleveland, a Democrat, the Republicans ruled the White House from 1869 down to the inauguration of Woodrow Wilson in 1913. The near monopoly of the office of the chief executive by the Republicans was countered by the fact that in Congress the two major parties were more or less evenly matched in strength, that until the presidency of Theodore Roosevelt, the initiative was retained by the Congress, and that trusts and monopolies expressed their will through the dominance of both political organizations and a relatively pliant Supreme Court. The trusts, hard currency, and high tariffs came to the fore as major issues, thus reflecting a pervasive grass-roots protest coupled with an awareness that the privileged constituted an ever-shrinking segment of the population. If the Populists alerted the nation to the perils of uncontrolled business leadership, the Progressives institutionalized the reform movement, gleaning a harvest of reform legislation in the states during the early years of the twentieth century and on the national level during the first Wilson administration, 1913–17.

1878

28 FEB. BLAND-ALLISON ACT. The demonetization of silver excited little controversy when adopted, but within a few years was characterized as the "Crime of '73" by Western silver-mine operators, among others. Chief factor in the agitation for resuming the unlimited coinage of silver was the discovery, during the middle 1870s, of new deposits in Nevada, Colorado, and Utah. The expansion of silver production coincided with a growing international trend toward adoption of the gold standard.

Declining market prices for silver bullion led Western mining interests to call for a return to bimetallism. The silverites found natural allies in inflationist-minded agrarian and labor groups who viewed an increase in the volume of circulating money as the best means of raising farm prices and industrial wages, while business interests were split over the issue. The House of Representatives, dominated by inflationist elements, passed a bill (13 Dec. 1876) sponsored by **Richard P. Bland** (Mo., 1835–99), providing for the free and unlimited coinage of silver at the ratio of 16 to 1. When the

Senate took no action, the House again passed the bill (5 Nov. 1877). Weakened by a Senate amendment introduced by Sen. **William B. Allison** (Iowa, 1829–1908), the bill was finally passed over President Hayes' veto.

The Bland-Allison Act required the Secretary of the Treasury to make monthly purchases of not less than $2 million and not more than $4 million worth of silver at the market price, such purchases to be converted into standard dollars. Thus, unlimited purchase and coinage, the original goal of the inflationists, was not attained. The act also provided for an international monetary conference (which met without achieving conclusive results).

The effect of the act was not inflationary because of the discretionary powers granted to the Secretary of the Treasury and his conservative use of them. Monthly purchases were made at the minimum amount authorized by law. A revival of prosperity beginning in 1879 staved off further agitation.

GREENBACK LABOR MOVEMENT. The labor unrest of 1877 helped to create labor support for the Greenback program. The Greenback Labor party, organized at the Toledo convention (22 Feb.) attended by some 800 delegates from 28 states, adopted a platform reflecting inflationist and labor viewpoints. The party denounced the resumption of specie payments, and called for the free coinage of silver on a parity with gold, the suppression of national bank notes, restrictions on the hours of industrial labor, and checks on Chinese immigration.

In the congressional elections of 1878, the Greenback party reached peak strength, with a total of 1,060,000 votes. Fourteen candidates won seats in Congress, where **James B. Weaver** (Iowa, (1833–1912) became the standard bearer

of the movement. In 1880 the party broadened its program by endorsing such issues as woman suffrage, federal regulation of interstate commerce, and a graduated income tax, but after that year declined in strength. In 1884 the Greenback Labor party ran its last independent presidential candidate, **Benjamin F. Butler** (Mass., 1818–93).

11 JULY. HAYES AND THE SPOILSMEN. By taking steps to separate the civil service from the domination of the Radical Republican machine leaders, President Hayes widened his differences with the Senate oligarchy. One of the most flagrant examples of corrupt patronage was the New York custom house, where appointments were controlled by the state political machine under Sen. **Roscoe Conkling** (1829–88). When Hayes asked for the resignations of **Chester A. Arthur** (p. 976), port collector of customs, and Alonzo B. Cornell (1832–1904), port naval officer, his request was ignored. The Tenure of Office Act prevented Hayes from removing them. Hayes' own nominations were blocked by the Senate Radicals (12 Dec. 1877), but soon after Congress adjourned in 1878, Hayes suspended Arthur and Cornell (11 July). Later, with Democratic support, Hayes secured confirmation of his appointments. This blow at the Conkling machine and the "Stalwart" faction within the Republican party weakened the Radical hold over the Senate and strengthened the executive, but it left Hayes without the support of a united party.

1879

1 JAN. RESUMPTION OF SPECIE PAYMENTS began, as authorized by the Act of 1875, with no wholesale attempt to reclaim greenbacks (now on a par with the national dollar). On 31 May

1878 Congress had enacted that the $346,681,000 outstanding in greenbacks should remain a permanent part of the currency. Because Secretary of the Treasury **John Sherman** (1823–1900) had accumulated a gold reserve of about $200 million, public confidence was restored in the government's ability to redeem the currency, reflected in the fact that on 17 Dec. 1878 greenbacks reached face value in gold, for the first time since 1862.

HAYES' "RIDER" VETOES. In 1879 the Democrats gained control of both houses of Congress. They attached to the Army Appropriation Act for 1880 a "rider" which in effect nullified the Force Acts of 1865 and 1874 authorizing the president to use federal troops in congressional elections. Hayes' veto (29 Apr.) invoked the constitutional principle of the equal independence of the various branches of the government. Hayes subsequently vetoed 4 other measures by which Congress attempted to repeal the Force Acts. In his avowal of the principle of military intervention in the South, Hayes drew the support of his party.

1880

PRESIDENTIAL CAMPAIGN. When the Republican National Convention met at Chicago (2 June), the field was open, for Hayes had earlier pledged not to run for a 2d term. There were 2 rival factions in the party—one headed by the supporters of James G. Blaine; the other by the "Stalwart" leader, Roscoe Conkling, who nominated Ulysses S. Grant. The Grant supporters failed in their effort to secure the adoption of the unit rule. Grant led on the 1st ballot, but **James A. Garfield** of Ohio, a "dark horse," was drafted on the 36th ballot (8 June) after the Blaine and Sherman

forces threw their support to him. The "Stalwart" faction was appeased with the nomination of **Chester A. Arthur** (N.Y.) for vice-president. The Republican platform advocated civil service reform, a protective tariff, veterans' legislation, and the restriction of Chinese immigration.

The Greenback Labor party met at Chicago (9 June) and nominated James B. Weaver (Iowa) for president and B. J. Chambers (Tex.) for vice-president. The Prohibition party met at Cleveland (17 June) and nominated Neal Dow (Me.) for president and A. M. Thompson (Ohio) for vice-president.

The Democratic National Convention met at Cincinnati (22 June) and nominated **Winfield Scott Hancock** (Pa., 1824–86) for president and **William H. English** (Ind.) for vice-president on a platform which, except for demanding a tariff for revenue purposes only, followed that of the Republican party.

The campaign indicated that the Republican tactic of "waving the bloody shirt" was losing its effectiveness, but the revival of prosperity favored the Republicans.

2 Nov. PRESIDENTIAL ELECTION. Popular vote: **Garfield,** 4,449,053; Hancock, 4,442,035; Weaver, 308,578; Dow, 10,305. Electoral vote: **Garfield,** 214; Hancock, 155. Victory in New York and Indiana decided the extremely close election for Garfield, whose plurality was under 10,000 out of over 9 million votes. The Republicans regained control of the House for the first time since 1874.

1881

23 Mar.–16 May. "HALF-BREEDS" AND "STALWARTS." Blaine's appointment to the cabinet as Secretary of State (5 Mar.) was regarded by the "Stalwarts" as a victory for the "Half-Breed" wing, and his prominent influence over the administration led to a reopening of political strife between the rival factions of the Republican party. The struggle, revolving about the spoils of office, came to a head when Garfield challenged Conkling's control of the New York patronage by naming (23 Mar.) a Conkling opponent, William H. Robertson, as collector of the port of New York over the protests of Conkling and Thomas Platt, junior senator from New York, who succeeded in blocking the appointment until May and then resigned (16 May) in protest. The New York legislature refused to reelect the pair. The result spelled Conkling's retirement from politics and the decline of the "Stalwart" faction. Garfield's determined stand was as much a victory for presidential power as it was for the "Half-Breeds."

2 JULY. ASSASSINATION OF GARFIELD. President Garfield was shot at the Washington railroad station by **Charles J. Guiteau,** a mentally unstable and disappointed office seeker who boasted that he was a "Stalwart" and wanted Arthur for president. Garfield died (19 Sept.) at Elberon, N.J. His assassin was tried (14 Nov.), convicted, and executed 30 June 1882. The murder of Garfield resulted in a strong wave of public opinion against "Stalwartism."

20 SEPT. Vice-President **Chester A. Arthur** took oath of office as president; 21st occupant of the office.

CABINET CHANGES. With Arthur's accession to the presidency, the "Half-Breeds" and independents left the cabinet. Arthur's choices, however, showed surprising caution and independence of the "Stalwarts."

1882

15 MAY–4 DEC. TARIFF COMMISSION. Congress authorized appointment by the president of a 9-man Tariff Com-

mission, which on 4 Dec. recommended substantial tariff reductions. (For tariff of 1833, see p. 713.)

1883

16 JAN. PENDLETON ACT. Public reaction to Garfield's assassination, combined with Democratic victories in the fall elections of 1882, impelled the outgoing Republican Congress to adopt civil service reform legislation. The Pendleton Act, drafted by **Dorman B. Eaton** (1823–99), secretary of the Civil Service Reform Association, and sponsored by Sen. **George H. Pendleton** (Ohio, 1825–89), provided for a bipartisan 3-man Civil Service Commission (of which Eaton was named head) for drawing up and administering competitive examinations to determine on a merit basis the fitness of appointees to federal office. A limited classified civil service list was set up, which the president was empowered to extend at his discretion. The act forbade the levying of political campaign assessments on federal officeholders and protected the latter against ouster for failure to make such contributions. Appointments were to be made on the basis of an appointment among the states according to population. The act immediately affected only larger units and about one tenth of the total number of federal employees. In addition, it governed only future appointments. Despite its weaknesses, the Pendleton Act enabled the chief executive to broaden the merit system and provided the foundation for the federal civil service in its present form.

1884

RESURGENCE OF AGRARIAN DISCONTENT. Five years of farm prosperity (1879–84) were followed by a decline in the prices of agricultural commodities that was to continue steadily until 1896, the result of overproduction and rising competition of foreign wheat-growing countries. The long drought (1887 *et seq.*) caused heavy damage and losses. (For other factors, see p. 693.) When attempts to revive the cooperatives of the Granger era failed to alleviate their plight, farmers banded together in state and regional organizations such as the **Agricultural Wheel,** the **Farmers' Union,** the **Texas State Alliance,** the **Farmers' Mutual Benefit Association,** and the **National Colored Farmers' Alliance.** There finally emerged 2 great regional bodies, the **Southern Alliance** and the **National Farmers' Alliance of the Northwest.** The farmers aimed their attacks against Eastern moneyed interests, the middlemen, the railroads, industrial monopolies, and advocates of the gold standard.

BIG BUSINESS STRIKES BACK. Reacting to popular sentiment against monopoly and privileged wealth, business leaders invoked the philosophy of individualism and laissez-faire, reinforced and elaborated by the teachings of **social Darwinism,** as expounded by the Englishman Herbert Spencer, who portrayed consolidation and combination as the inevitable result of the "struggle for the survival of the fittest." Exponents of social Darwinism ranged from intellectuals like philosopher-historian **John Fiske** (1842–1901) and social scientist **William Graham Sumner** (p. 1164) to business tycoon **Andrew Carnegie** (p. 998). These evolutionary views also served to underpin racism and expansionism, and supported a laissez-faire interpretation of the Constitution by the courts.

6 Oct. U.S. Naval War College established at Newport, R.I., with Commodore Stephen B. Luce (1827–1917) as first president. The first institution of its kind, it was founded to provide naval officers with postgraduate training in advanced naval science and warfare, international law, and history.

PRESIDENTIAL CAMPAIGN. The National Greenback Labor party met at Indianapolis (28 May) and nominated Benjamin F. Butler (Mass.) for president and A. M. West (Miss.) for vice-president. The Republican National Convention met at Chicago (3 June) and on the 4th ballot (6 June) nominated **James G. Blaine** (Me.) for president. **John A. Logan** (Ill.) was nominated for vice-president. The Republican choice alienated the Independent Republicans, a reform group that regarded Blaine as inimical to the cause of good government. Among the Independents, who were shortly dubbed "Mugwumps," were George William Curtis, E. L. Godkin, Carl Schurz, and Charles F. Adams, Jr. Valuing civil service reform above party regularity, the Mugwumps backed the Democratic candidate. The Democratic National Convention, meeting at Chicago (8 July), nominated **Grover Cleveland,** governor of New York, on the 2d ballot (11 July) and chose **Thomas A. Hendricks** (Ind.) for vice-president. The Prohibition party national convention met at Pittsburgh (23 July) and nominated John P. St. John (Kan.) for president and William Daniel (Md.) for vice-president.

The campaign promptly degenerated into one of the most scurrilous in American political history. The "Mulligan letters" (1876), illuminating Blaine's corrupt dealings during his service as speaker of the House, were fully exploited by the Democrats. The Republicans in turn charged that Cleveland, as a young bachelor in Buffalo, had fathered an illegitimate child. With characteristic honesty, Cleveland acknowledged the truth of the accusation.

The key state in the election was New York, where the Tammany machine headed by John Kelly opposed Cleveland. Shortly before election day, Rev. **Samuel D. Burchard,** leader of a delegation of clergymen who called on Blaine at the Fifth Avenue Hotel in New York (29 Oct.), referred to the Democrats as the party of "Rum, Romanism, and Rebellion." Blaine's failure to disavow the remark or to rebuke Burchard cost him many votes in the Irish-American stronghold of New York. Blaine later said it cost him the election.

4 Nov. PRESIDENTIAL ELECTION. Popular vote: **Cleveland,** 4,911,017; Blaine, 4,848,334; Butler, 175,370; St. John, 150,369. Electoral vote: **Cleveland,** 219; Blaine, 182. The Democrats carried New York by 1,149 out of a total of 1,125,000 votes. Cleveland was the first Democratic candidate since Buchanan to win a presidential election. The Republicans gained 18 seats in the House, but that body still remained under Democratic control (since 1882).

1885

25 Nov. Death of vice-president Thomas A. Hendricks at Indianapolis, Ind.

1886

19 JAN. PRESIDENTIAL SUCCESSION ACT, which replaced the statute of 1792, provided that in the event of removal, death, resignation, or inability, of both the president and vice-president, the heads of the executive departments, in order of the creation of their offices, should succeed to the duties of the office of the president. This law remained in effect until 1947.

TREASURY SURPLUS. The accumulation of a large federal surplus, most of it the result of the continuance of internal revenue taxes levied to finance the Civil War, began to loom as a major

political question. The revival of national prosperity in 1879 swelled the surplus (see p. 735), now attacked for withdrawing large sums from general circulation and promoting extravagant government spending. Cleveland referred to the problem in his annual message to Congress in 1886, and looked to a reduction of tariff duties as a means of dealing with it. The Republicans were unwilling to modify protectionism.

WHITNEY AND THE "STEEL NAVY." After the Civil War the U.S. Navy, consisting of obsolescent wooden ships, fell into disrepair. In 1880 the U.S. stood 12th among the world's naval powers. In 1881 a naval advisory board recommended the construction of steel cruisers. On 3 Mar. 1883 Congress, taking initial steps toward the creation of a modern navy, authorized the building of 3 steel cruisers; further shipbuilding authorized 3 Aug. 1886. Constructive reforms and advances awaited the reorganization of the Navy Department by Secretary **William C. Whitney** (1841–1904). He coordinated the bureaus, rid the fleet of antiquated vessels, and embarked on the rapid construction of modern steel ships incorporating advances in naval armament (22 such vessels had been built or authorized by the time Whitney left office, 1889). By insisting upon naval armor of American manufacture, Whitney encouraged the development of domestic steelworks capable of producing heavy ship plates and huge naval guns, thereby eliminating American dependence upon European steelmakers. Whitney's naval policy was continued by succeeding administrations. By 1900 the U.S. ranked 3d among world naval powers.

1887

3 FEB. ELECTORAL COUNT ACT, designed to prevent a disputed national election (as in the instance of the Hayes-Tilden election of 1876), made each state the absolute judge over appointment or returns, specifying congressional acceptance of electoral returns certified by a state in accordance with its own electoral law. Congress can intervene only if the state itself is unable to decide or has decided irregularly. In such cases, a concurrent vote of Congress is decisive, but should the 2 houses disagree, the votes of those electors whose appointment is certified by the governor shall be counted.

4 Feb. INTERSTATE COMMERCE ACT. Public resentment of abuses in railway transportation led to numerous bills and resolutions being placed before Congress. In 1874 a special Senate Committee headed by **William Windom** (Minn., 1827–91) had advocated competitive routes to the seaboard, development of waterways, and establishment of a statistical bureau; but this report failed to satisfy the demand of agrarian groups and businessmen for government regulation. The McCrary Bill, introduced in 1874, provided for the establishment of a federal commission empowered to fix maximum rates, investigate complaints, and call witnesses. The measure passed the House by a narrow margin, but was never considered by the Senate. The Senate likewise failed to act on the Reagan Bill (1878), which called for the prohibition of railroad pools, rebates, drawbacks, and discriminatory rates.

In the absence of federal legislation, the movement for railroad regulation within the states gained momentum during the 70s with the passage of the so-called **Granger laws,** which received judicial approval in the Supreme Court decision in **Munn** v. **Illinois** (1877, p. 671). However, the states were virtually stripped of their restraining power over the railroads by the Supreme Court decision in the **Wabash Case** (1886, p.

671). Continuing public dissatisfaction made itself felt through the Cullom Committee headed by Sen. **Shelby M. Cullom** (Ill., 1829–1914), which in 1885 conducted hearings throughout the country and submitted a report recommending the federal regulation of interstate commerce.

The result was the Interstate Commerce Act, which passed the House, 219–41, and the Senate, 43–15. Applying only to railroads passing through more than one state, the act provided that all charges made by railway must be reasonable and just (but did not authorize rate-fixing); prohibited pooling operations, discriminatory rates, drawbacks, and rebates; and made it illegal to charge more for a short haul than for a long haul over the same line. Railroads were required to post their rates, and could not change them until after a 10-day public notice. The act created the **Interstate Commerce Commission,** the first regulatory commission in U.S. history. The commission was authorized to investigate the management of railroads, summon witnesses, and compel the production of company books and papers, but its orders did not have the binding force of a court decree. However, it could invoke the aid of equity proceedings in the federal courts. The commission was empowered to require railroads to file annual reports of operations and finances and to adopt a uniform system of accounting.

At the outset, the railroads conformed to the law, but after 1890 difficulties in interpretation and application made the practical results of the act feeble and disappointing. Railroad operators used a variety of devices for circumventing the provisions of the act. The decisions of the commission met serious reversals at the hands of the Supreme Court, as in the Maximum Freight Rate case (1897) and the Alabama Midlands case (1897).

By 1898 the commission had been reduced to virtual impotence, and was active chiefly as a body for the collection and publication of statistics.

11 Feb. CLEVELAND'S PENSION VETOES. By the middle 1880s Union veterans on the pension rolls constituted a heavy drain on the national treasury. Veterans' appropriations increased markedly after the passage of the Arrears of Pension Act (1879), enacted under pressure from the Grand Army of the Republic. Cleveland, insofar as pressure of duties permitted, followed a policy of investigating individual claims and vetoing those which appeared to be fraudulent. While he approved more special pension bills than did any of his predecessors, he also vetoed more. In 1885, annual expenditures for pensions stood at $56 million; by 1888, they had increased to $80 million. Cleveland's vetoes earned him the bitter antagonism of the organized "old soldier" interests.

The climax came when Sen. Henry W. Blair (N.H.) introduced the **Dependent Pension Bill,** passed by Congress in Jan. 1887. This measure provided a pension for all honorably discharged veterans with at least 90 days' service who were then unable to earn their support and depended on manual labor for a living. It established a precedent for pensioning without regard to service-connected disability. Cleveland vetoed the bill (11 Feb.), declaring it would make the pension list a refuge for frauds rather than a "roll of honor."

2 Mar. HATCH ACT for the promotion of agricultural science provided federal subsidies for the creation of state agricultural experiment stations.

5 Mar. TENURE OF OFFICE ACT (1867), as amended in 1869, was repealed after Cleveland's contest with the Senate over appointments and removals from office. Cleveland's message to the Senate (1 Mar. 1886) had insisted that

under the Constitution the president had the sole power of suspension or removal. By his action, Cleveland strengthened the independence of the executive.

7–15 June. CONFEDERATE BATTLE FLAGS. Cleveland again incurred the enmity of the organized Union veterans' interest when he approved a War Department order (7 June) for the return of captured Confederate battle flags to the South. Even though the order was by way of executive routine, and had been initiated at the behest of Adj. Gen. Richard C. Drum, a Republican and a member of the Grand Army of the Republic (G.A.R.), it brought angry protests from Republican politicians and leaders of the G.A.R. Cleveland revoked the order (15 June). The flags were finally returned in 1905 during the administration of Theodore Roosevelt.

6 Dec. After long deliberation, and without consulting the leaders of his party, Cleveland devoted his entire annual message to a plea for a lowered protective tariff, pointing out that the existing rates had encouraged the creation of trusts and the maintenance of high prices. His advocacy of tariff reform alienated protectionist elements within the Democratic party.

1888

PRESIDENTIAL CAMPAIGN. The Union Labor party convention met at Cincinnati (15 May) and nominated Alson J. Streeter (Ill.) for president and C. E. Cunningham (Ark.) for vice-president. The United Labor party, also meeting at Cincinnati (15 May), nominated Robert H. Cowdrey (Ill.) for president and W. H. T. Wakefield (Kan.) for vice-president. The national convention of the Prohibition party met at Indianapolis (30 May) and nominated Clinton B. Fisk (N.J.) for president and John A. Brooks (Mo.) for vice-president.

The Democratic National Convention met at St. Louis (5 June) and nominated President **Grover Cleveland** for reelection and **Allen G. Thurman** (Ohio) for vice-president. The Republican National Convention met at Chicago (19 June) and nominated **Benjamin Harrison** (Ind.) for president and **Levi P. Morton** (N.Y.) for vice-president.

The Republicans made the high protective tariff the chief plank in their platform, and the campaign thus became the first in U.S. history waged on this issue. The Republicans also included a promise of generous pensions for Civil War veterans. A huge Republican campaign fund, which found ready contributors among the enemies of tariff reform, was employed to denounce Cleveland's stand on the tariff, his pension vetoes, and the Confederate battle flag order. On the eve of the election the Democratic cause was dealt a severe blow by the **"Murchison letter"** involving the British minister to the U.S., Sackville-West. The letter was written ostensibly by "Charles F. Murchison," a naturalized Englishman (in reality George A. Osgoodby, a California Republican) seeking Sackville-West's counsel on how to vote in the approaching election. The British minister's reply (13 Sept.) intimated that "Murchison" should vote for Cleveland. The correspondence was published (24 Oct.) by the Republicans and aroused public indignation against foreign interference in internal affairs. Sackville-West was handed his passports (24 Oct.), but the damaging political blunder cost the Democrats many Irish-American votes.

6 Nov. PRESIDENTIAL ELECTION. Popular vote: Cleveland, 5,540,050; **Harrison,** 5,444,337; Fisk, 250,125; Streeter, 146,897; Cowdrey, 2,808. Electoral vote: **Harrison,** 233; Cleveland, 168. Harrison carried the key states of New York and Indiana.

1889

11 FEB. Department of Agriculture raised to cabinet status. Norman J. Coleman (Mo.) named first Secretary of Agriculture.

22 FEB. OMNIBUS BILL provided for the admission of North Dakota, South Dakota, Montana, and Washington.

1890

19 JUNE. FORCE (or Federal Elections) BILL, reported in the House, provided for supervision of federal elections by the national government in order to protect Negro voters in the South against state measures designed to deprive them of the vote. It passed the House (2 July), but failed of adoption by the Senate.

27 JUNE. DEPENDENT PENSION ACT. Upon taking office, Harrison appointed as Commissioner of Pensions James "Corporal" Tanner, a past commander of the G.A.R., who declared, "God help the surplus!" During his 6 months in office, Tanner pursued a liberal private pension policy. The administration's debt to the "old soldier" vote was discharged with the passage of the Dependent Pension Act, which granted pensions to veterans of the Union forces with at least 90 days' service who were then or thereafter disabled because of physical or mental reasons (without regard to origin) and were unable to earn a livelihood by manual labor. The act, which inaugurated the principle of the service pension, also provided that pensions of varying amounts were to be granted to minor children, dependent parents, and widows who had married veterans before the passage of the act and had to work for a living. Between 1891 and 1895 the number of pensioners rose from 676,000 to 970,000. By the

time Harrison left office, the annual appropriation for pensions had increased from $81 million to $135 million.

2 JULY. SHERMAN ANTITRUST ACT. With the establishment of the first industrial combination, the Standard Oil Trust (1879), there followed in rapid succession other large combinations controlling such commodities as whisky, sugar, lead, beef, and linseed soil. In protest many Western and Southern states enacted antitrust laws, the first in Kansas in 1889. By 1893 similar legislation had been enacted in 15 other states and territories. Since such state laws were powerless to deal with trusts and monopolies engaged in interstate commerce, the demand for governmental regulation of national scope became insistent.

The result was the first federal measure that undertook to regulate trusts. Although the Sherman Antitrust Act was named for Sen. **John Sherman** (Ohio, 1823–1900), the bill was drafted by the Senate Judiciary Committee, the larger share of the work being credited to Sen. **George F. Hoar** (Mass., 1826–1904) and George F. Edmunds (Vt., 1828–1919). The act, consisting of 8 major provisions, declared: "Every contract, combination in the form of trust or otherwise, or conspiracy, in restraint of trade or commerce among the several states, or with foreign nations, is hereby declared to be illegal." The act authorized the federal government to proceed against a trust to obtain its dissolution, and invested federal circuit courts with jurisdiction to prevent and restrain violations of the law.

The most critical weakness of the act was its obscure and ambiguous phrasing, its failure clearly to define words like "trust," "combination," and "restraint." It was not clear whether the act was intended to apply to labor combinations and railroads as well as to combinations of capital. That its provisions embraced labor unions and railroads, respectively,

was the decision of the federal courts in *U.S.* v. *Debs* (1894) and in the Trans-Missouri Freight Association case (1897). In the case of *U.S.* v. *E. C. Knight Company* (1895), among the first in which the Supreme Court interpreted and applied the act, the effectiveness of the law was seriously limited. Between 1890 and 1901, the act was not vigorously enforced. During that period only 18 suits were instituted, 4 against labor unions. The existence of the statute did not prevent the continued growth of combinations and monopolies under other names. (See also p. 724.)

14 JULY. SHERMAN SILVER PURCHASE ACT. The Bland-Allison Act satisfied neither silverites nor gold standard advocates. Meanwhile, the steady decline in the market price of silver bullion (by 1890 it stood to gold at a ratio of 20 to 1), combined with the deepening economic depression, helped to increase the political strength of the silver and inflationist forces (reinforced by senators from the recently admitted Omnibus states [1889]). In the House, which still remained under the control of gold-standard men, the silverites gained new accessions from representatives voted into office by the Farmers' Alliances.

The prosilverite Senate passed a bill (June) for the free and unlimited coinage of silver, but the House blocked its passage. By threatening to vote against the McKinley tariff bill, Western interests were able to wrest a concession from conservative Easterners, and a compromise was arranged to permit a more liberal purchase policy. The Sherman Silver Purchase Act, while it did not provide for free silver, required the Treasury to purchase 4,500,000 ounces of silver each month at the prevailing market price and to issue in payment legal tender Treasury notes redeemable in gold or silver at the option of the Treasury. The amount of bullion specified was the currently estimated total U.S. production of silver.

The act had the effect of increasing the circulation of redeemable paper currency and weakening the federal gold reserve. Among Eastern business and financial groups it created a fear that the silver inflation might take the country off the gold standard. Nor did the act satisfy the demands of those who advocated free coinage and a bimetallic standard. Cleveland made his position clear. In a public letter (10 Feb. 1891) he attacked the "dangerous and reckless experiment of free, unlimited, and independent coinage."

4 Nov. Congressional elections in 39 states resulted in a Democratic landslide that cost the Republicans their control of the House. Public reaction against the McKinley Tariff of 1890 was blamed for the Republican defeat.

1892

PEOPLE'S (POPULIST) PARTY. The sectional struggle between debtor and creditor, intensified by the continuing agricultural depression, led the agrarian protest movement to take political action. Beginning in 1889–90, efforts were made to unite farmer and labor organizations on the basis of common objectives. The agrarian organizations of the West and South, together with labor, Granger, and Greenback representatives, held a meeting at St. Louis (Dec. 1889). In June 1890, the statewide People's party was formed in Kansas. In Dec. 1890, the Southern Alliance, the Farmers' Mutual Benefit Association, and the Colored Farmers' Alliance convened at Ocala, Fla., and drew up a list of grievances resembling the platform approved at St. Louis. These included cheap currency, the abolition of national banks, and the restriction of land ownership to American citizens. Labor men who at-

tended the Ocala meeting called for the establishment of a third party, but the Southern Alliance, fearing such a movement might bring the Negro into power, opposed independent action. The Alliance advised its members to support instead candidates of either major party who would pledge themselves to policies benefiting agriculture. In general, Southern agrarian leaders adopted the tactic of attempting to capture the Democratic machinery.

A national convention was held at Cincinnati (19 May 1891) to plan independent action. More than 1,400 delegates from 32 states adopted resolutions supporting a new party. The **People's Party of the U.S.A.** was formally organized at St. Louis (22 Feb.) and held its first national convention at Omaha (2 July). Present at Omaha were the outstanding leaders of the Populist movement, including **Ignatius Donnelly** (Minn.), **Thomas E. Watson** (p. 1178), **"Sockless Jerry" Simpson** (Kan.), **Mary Ellen Lease** (Kan.), **William A. Peffer** (Kan.), and **James Kyle** (S.D.). Only a small minority of the Southern Alliance backed the third-party movement.

The Populist convention nominated **James B. Weaver** (Iowa) for president and **James G. Field** (Va.) for vice-president. The Populist platform (4 July) demanded free and unlimited coinage of silver at 16 to 1, and an increase in the circulating medium of not less than $50 per capita; a national currency issued by the federal government only and without the use of banking corporations; government ownership and operation of all transportation and communication lines; a graduated income tax; establishment of a postal savings system; direct election of U.S. senators; adoption of the secret ballot, the initiative, and referendum; prohibition of the alien ownership of land; a shorter working day for industrial labor; and restrictions on immigration.

PRESIDENTIAL CAMPAIGN. The Republican National Convention met at Minneapolis (7 June) and on 10 June nominated President **Benjamin Harrison** for reelection and **Whitelaw Reid** (N.Y.) for vice-president. The party's chief plank was the high protective tariff. The Democratic National Convention met at Chicago (21 June) and nominated **Grover Cleveland** for president and **Adlai E. Stevenson** (Ill.) for vice-president. The straddling plank on the tariff, opposed by the radical wing of the Democratic party, was dropped in favor of a stronger declaration "that the federal government has no constitutional power to impose and collect tariff duties, except for purposes of revenue only." During the campaign, however, Cleveland took a moderate stand on the tariff. The national Prohibition Convention met at Cincinnati (29 June) and nominated John Bidwell (Calif.) for president and James B. Cranfill (Tex.) for vice-president. The Socialist Labor Convention met at New York and nominated Simon Wing (Mass.) for president and Charles H. Matchett (N.Y.) for vice-president.

Cleveland's unswerving position on the gold standard won him the heavy support of conservative Eastern financial and business groups. The Democrats kept the silver issue in the background except in those states where the inflationist forces were strong. Factors which militated against Republican success included public reaction to the McKinley Tariff of 1890 and the labor disturbances of 1892.

8 Nov. PRESIDENTIAL ELECTION. Popular vote: **Cleveland,** 5,554,414; Harrison, 5,190,802; Weaver, 1,027,329; Bidwell, 271,058 (peak of popular vote in a presidential election for Prohibitionists); Wing, 21,164. Electoral vote: **Cleveland,** 277; Harrison, 145; Weaver, 22. The Democrats secured control of both houses of Congress.

SOUTHERN POPULISM IN DECLINE. Despite Weaver's relatively strong showing for a third-party candidate Southern Populists mainly remained loyal to the Democratic party on the issue of white supremacy. Populism's decline in the South was accelerated when the Democrats took over their money plank. Southern Populism's collapse paved the way for the rise of demagogues like **"Pitchfork Ben"** Tillman (1897–1918) of South Carolina and **James K. Vardaman** (1861–1930) of Mississippi, who wooed the votes of the poor whites with an agrarian program carrying white supremacy overtones.

1893

PANIC OF 1893: U.S. GOLD RESERVE. U.S. fiscal conditions were adversely affected by (1) failure (Nov. 1890) of the British banking house of Baring Bros., causing British investors to unload American securities, with a resultant drain of gold from the U.S.; (2) a sharp decrease in U.S. revenues attributed to the McKinley Tariff Act; (3) depletion of government surplus by pension grants of the Harrison administration. The decline of the U.S. gold reserve below the $100 million mark (21 Apr.) helped precipitate the panic. On 5 May stocks on the New York Stock Exchange dropped suddenly, crashing 27 June (see also p. 748). By 30 Dec. the gold reserve fell to $80 million.

1 Nov. REPEAL OF SHERMAN SILVER PURCHASE ACT. To stem the drain on the gold reserve Cleveland summoned (30 June) an extra session of Congress to convene 7 Aug., requesting repeal of the Sherman Silver Purchase Act. The struggle over repeal, centered in the Senate, proved the grimmest of Cleveland's presidential career. Repeal passed the House, 239–108 (28 Aug.), and the Senate, 48–37 (30 Oct.), but the administration's victory split the Democratic party.

1894

25 MAR.–1 MAY. "COXEY'S ARMY." Over the winter of 1893–94 growing economic distress and mass unemployment brought the formation of scattered groups of jobless men into "armies" whose leaders were known as "generals." Of these, the best known was "Coxey's Army," led by the Populist **Jacob S. Coxey** of Massillon, Ohio. Coxey called upon the unemployed to march upon Washington and deliver to Congress their demands for relief. Although many small detachments of the "army" started out from various points throughout the country, only 400 reached the national capital (30 Apr.). Coxey advocated a public works relief program of road construction and local improvements financed by a federal issue of $500 million in legal tender notes. The program had a 2-fold purpose: to provide jobs and to increase the amount of money in circulation. "Coxey's Army" disbanded after its 3 leaders (Coxey, Carl Browne, and Christopher Columbus Jones) were arrested for trespassing on the Capitol grounds.

FREE-SILVER PROPAGANDA. *Coin's Financial School* (1894), by William H. Harvey of Chicago, which soon became the infallible guide of the bimetallists, was followed by similar tracts, including *The American People's Money* (1895), by Ignatius Donnelly. Among the magazines that served as a platform for the silverites were the *Arena* and the *National Bimetallist*.

1895

5 MAR. APPEAL OF THE SILVER DEMOCRATS. The broadening cleavage in the Democratic party between the gold and silver factions was indicated by the "Appeal of the Silver Democrats" framed by **Richard P. Bland** (Mo.) and **William Jennings Bryan** (Neb., p. 992), leaders of the silver bloc in the House. The appeal, signed by a minority of House Democrats, called for the immediate restoration of the free and unlimited coinage of silver at the ratio of 16 to 1. During the year a number of free-silver conventions were held in the South and West.

GOLD RESERVE. Repeal of the Sherman Silver Act failed to halt depletion of the gold reserve. Confronted by declining government revenues, the Treasury was compelled to use the gold reserve not only for redemption but also for meeting operating expenses. After unsuccessfully attempting to win congressional authority to sell bonds, Secretary of the Treasury Carlisle took steps to maintain a normal gold reserve. Invoking the unrepealed provisions of the Resumption Act of 1875 for borowing gold, he invited bids for a bond issue of $50 million (Jan. 1894), and in Nov. 1894 asked for a similar loan; but owing to lack of public response to the offerings, had to place the loans with New York bankers. Successive withdrawals finally caused the gold reserve to fall to $41 million early in 1895. Cleveland moved to cope with the Treasury crisis by calling J. Pierpont Morgan, the New York banker, to a White House interview (7 Feb.). The result was a third loan placed with a banking syndicate headed by Morgan and August Belmont. The arrangement called for the purchase of 3,500,000 ounces of gold, to be paid for in bonds. One half of the gold was to be purchased abroad. It is estimated that the bankers realized a profit of some $1.5 million on the $62 million loan. While the loan succeeded in relieving the Treasury emergency for a time, it was condemned by Populists and bimetallists. Upon the expiration of the Morgan-Belmont contract, the government was again compelled to resort to a loan when the reserve dipped to $79 million (Dec.), but this time the administration threw the $100 million loan open to the public (6 Jan 1896). Its quick subscription indicated a restoration of public confidence. But the Treasury had to resume withdrawal of gold to pay for bonds; consequently, by July 1896, the reserve fell below the $90 million mark. The situation was not serious because of the revival of business activity, but gold hoarding did not cease until after the election of 1896, when the future of the gold standard was assured.

1896

PRESIDENTIAL CAMPAIGN. The Prohibition National Convention met at Pittsburgh (27 May) and nominated Joshua Levering (Md.) for president and Hale Johnson (Ill.) for vice-president. A free-silver minority, organized as the National party, nominated Charles E. Bentley (Neb.) for president and J. H. Southgate (N.C.) for vice-president. The Republican National Convention met at St. Louis (16 June) and nominated **William McKinley** (Ohio, p. 1093) for president and **Garret A. Hobart** (N.J.) for vice-president on a platform upholding the single gold standard (although the Republicans promised to promote the free-silver policy by international agreement), the high protective tariff, and a vigorous foreign policy (calling for U.S. control of the Hawaiian Islands). The way for McKinley's nomination had been prepared by the maneuvers of the Cleveland industrialist and financier **Marcus A. Hanna** (p. 1049), named Republican party campaign manager. Adoption of the gold plank caused Western silver Republicans under Sen.

Henry M. Teller (Colo.) to bolt the party. Organized as the National Silver Republicans, they held a national convention at St. Louis (22 July) and endorsed the Democratic candidates. The Socialist Labor National Convention met at New York (4 July) and nominated Charles H. Matchett (N.Y.) for president and Matthew Maguire (N.J.) for vice-president.

When the Democratic National Convention met at Chicago (7 July), it was clear that the free-silver faction was in control of the party organization. The Democratic platform called for the free and unlimited coinage of silver at the 16 to 1 ratio; condemned trusts, monopolies, and the high protective tariff, as well as the use of injunctions against labor; and attacked the Supreme Court ruling in the income tax case. The dominant issue was the money question. In support of the adoption of the free-silver plan, William Jennings Bryan (Neb.) delivered his eloquent **"Cross of Gold"** speech (8 July), closing with this challenge to the advocates of the gold standard: "You shall not press down upon the brow of labor this crown of thorns, you shall not crucify mankind upon a cross of gold." **Bryan** was nominated for president and **Arthur Sewall** (Me.) for vice-president. The gold Democrats withdrew from the convention, organized the National Democratic party, and in convention at Indianapolis (2 Sept.) nominated **John M. Palmer** (Ill.) for president and **Simon B. Buckner** (Ky.) for vice-president on a platform supporting the gold standard. The People's (Populist) National Convention, meeting at St. Louis (22 July), endorsed Bryan's nomination and chose Thomas E. Watson (Ga.) for vice-president.

Supported by 3 parties, Bryan, the "Boy Orator of the Platte," waged a vigorous and strenuous campaign, traveling 13,000 miles in 14 weeks, making 600 speeches in 29 states. Against Bryan the Republicans, under Hanna's political generalship, and with a much larger campaign fund, pictured Bryan as an "anarchist" and a "revolutionist." McKinley staged a front-porch campaign from his home in Canton, Ohio. The campaign arrayed creditor against debtor, the moneyed East against the agrarian West and South.

3 Nov. PRESIDENTIAL ELECTION. Popular vote: **McKinley,** 7,035,638; Bryan, 6,467,946; Levering, 141,676; Palmer, 131,529; Matchett, 36,454; Bentley, 13,969. Electoral vote: **McKinley,** 271; Bryan, 176. The Republicans retained control of both houses of Congress which they had previously won in 1894.

1898

12 MAY. Louisiana adopted a constitution disfranchising Negroes under property and literacy tests and the "grandfather clause."

1 JUNE. ERDMAN ACT (p .767).

1 JULY. **FEDERAL BANKRUPTCY ACT** extended to traders and nontraders, allowed voluntary and involuntary bankruptcy, exempted wage earners or farmers from the latter, gave priority over other debts to wages, and provided for creditor participation and discharge of the debtor; amended by Act of 22 June 1938.

1900

14 MAR. **CURRENCY ACT (GOLD STANDARD ACT)** declared the gold dollar of 25.8 grains, nine tenths fine, the standard unit of value and placed all forms of money issued by the U.S. on a parity with gold. A gold reserve (fixed at $150 million and to be set apart from other funds), whose maintenance was authorized by the sale of bonds, was provided for the redemption of legal-tender

notes. Agrarian financial needs were partly satisfied by the authorization of national banks with a capital of not less than $25,000 in towns of under 3,000 population.

PRESIDENTIAL CAMPAIGN. The Social Democratic National Convention met at Indianapolis (9 Mar.) and nominated **Eugene V. Debs** (Ind., p. 1011) for president and Job Harriman (Calif.) for vice-president. The People's (Anti-Fusion) National Convention met at Cincinnati (9 May) and nominated Wharton Barker (Pa.) for president and Ignatius Donnelly (Minn.) for vice-president. The Socialist Labor National Convention met at New York (2 June) and nominated Joseph P. Maloney (Mass.) for president and Valentine Remmel (Pa.) for vice-president. The Republican National Convention met at Philadelphia (19 June) and nominated President **McKinley** for reelection and **Theodore Roosevelt** (N.Y., p. 1141) for vice-president on a platform upholding the gold standard, the administration's foreign policy, and a U.S.-built-and-controlled isthmian canal. The Prohibition National Convention met at Chicago (27 June) and nominated John G. Woolley (Ill.) for president and Henry B. Metcalf (R.I.) for vice-president. The Democratic National Convention met at Kansas City, Mo. (4 July), and nominated **William Jennings Bryan** (Neb.) for president and Adlai E. Stevenson (Ill.) for vice-president on a platform condemning imperialism and the Currency Act, and calling for the free coinage of silver. The Fusion Populists also endorsed Bryan. The Democrats made imperialism the "paramount issue"; the Republicans stressed the "Full Dinner Pail" as symbol of the administration's success.

6 Nov. PRESIDENTIAL ELECTION. Popular vote: **McKinley,** 7,219,530; Bryan, 6,358,071; Woolley, 209,166; Debs, 94,768; Barker, 50,232. Electoral vote: **McKinley,** 292; Bryan, 155. The Republicans retained control of both houses of Congress.

1901

6 SEPT. ASSASSINATION OF Mc-KINLEY. President McKinley, while attending a reception at the Pan-American Exposition, Buffalo, N.Y., was shot by Leon Czolgosz, an anarchist. McKinley died 14 Sept.

14 SEPT. Theodore Roosevelt took oath as 26th president.

27 Nov. ARMY WAR COLLEGE. The defects in the U.S. military structure, as revealed during the Spanish-American War, led Secretary of War **Elihu Root** (p. 1142, succeeded 1 Aug. 1899 Russell A. Alger, who resigned 19 July 1899 under public criticism) to undertake reorganization of the army. An initial step was to open the Army War College (Tasker H. Bliss, president) to advance the higher instruction and training of officers under a unified system.

1902

ROOSEVELT'S TRUST POLICY. The trend toward industrial mergers and combines (p. 724), culminating (1901) in the formation of the **U.S. Steel Corp.,** first billion-dollar company, and the **Northern Securities Co.,** a railroad holding company, was considered by Roosevelt in his first annual message to Congress (3 Dec. 1901), in which he recommended legislation to abolish abuses without destroying combinations. Failing to get congressional action, he directed Attorney General Knox to file suit (10 Mar.) for dissolution of the Northern Securities Co. On 19 Aug. Roosevelt left Washington on a tour of New England and the Middle West to bring the trust issue directly to the people. Demanding a "square deal" for all, he pledged strict enforcement of existing antitrust laws and called for stricter supervision and control of big business. "We do not wish to destroy corportions," he said, "but we do wish to make them subserve the public good." The adamant stand of the mine owners during the **anthracite coal strike** of 1902 (p. 768) created broad support for Roosevelt's program, which was strengthened by the Supreme Court decision in the government's favor in the **Northern Securities case** (1904, p. 673).

17 JUNE. NEWLANDS ACT (p. 638).

REFORM MOVEMENT IN THE STATES attacked the alliance between organized wealth and machine politics. An outstanding example was the **"Wisconsin Idea,"** a term applied to the legislative and administrative advances (including an **income tax** and a **railroad commission**) adopted in Wisconsin during the governorship of **Robert M. La-Follette** (p. 1079). In keeping with what became the Progressive ideal of returning government to the electorate, Wisconsin adopted the **direct primary** (23 May 1903), preceded only by Mississippi (1902). Oregon was the first state to adopt the **initiative** and **referendum** on a general scale (2 June 1902), and in 1904 instituted the **preferential primary.** The movement against municipal boss rule also gained impetus during this period, as exemplified in the reforms initiated by Mayor **Samuel** ("**Golden Rule**") **Jones** (1846–1904) of Toledo, who was elected in 1897, and by Mayor **Tom L. Johnson** (1855–1911) of Cleveland, who took office in 1901.

1903

MUCKRAKERS were a group of writers who aroused public opinion with exposures of dishonesty, greed, and corruption in machine politics and business and also attacked social evils like slums, juvenile delinquency, and prostitution. Magazines of wide circulation (*Collier's, McClure's, Cosmopolitan,* the *American,* and *Everybody's*) threw their pages open to disclosures, in time weakened by appeals to the purely sensational. One of the pioneer muckrakers was Ida M. Tarbell, whose *History of the Standard Oil Company* began in *McClure's* in 1903, although her exposé of that company was preceded by Henry Demarest Lloyd (1847–1903), whose *Wealth Against Commonwealth* (1894) had denounced monopolies, with Standard Oil as its chief target. Other noted exposures were Lincoln Steffens' *The Shame of the Cities* (1904), David Graham Phillips's *The Treason of the Senate* (1906), Thomas W. Lawson's *Frenzied Finance* (1902), Gustavus Myers' *History of the Great American Fortunes* (1910), Burton J. Hendrick's *Story of Life Insurance* (1907), Charles Edward Russell's *The Greatest Trust in the World* (1905; on the beef trust), and Ray Stannard Baker's "The Railroads on Trial" (*McClure's,* 1906). The muckraking impulse also appeared in fiction, most sensationally in Upton Sinclair's *The Jungle* (1906), exposing conditions in the Chicago stockyards and meat-packing plants. Muckraking literature reached its height between c.1904 and c.1910. Increasing stress on sensationalism led President Roosevelt (14 Apr. 1906) in a public address caustically to compare some of these writers to the man with the muckrake (in Bunyan's *Pilgrim's Progress*) who was so busy raking the filth off the floor that he could look no way but downward, and to suggest that constructive effort was more important than mere exposure.

11 FEB. EXPEDITION ACT, designed to expedite prosecution of federal antitrust suits, gave such proceedings precedence (at the request of the attorney general) on the dockets of the circuit courts.

14 FEB. DEPARTMENT OF COMMERCE AND LABOR established by act of Congress. It included a Bureau of Corporations empowered to investigate and report upon the operations of corporations (with the exception of common carriers) engaged in interstate commerce. The first Secretary of Commerce and Labor, George B. Cortelyou (N.Y.), was appointed 16 Feb.

14 FEB. Army General Staff Corps established by act of Congress at behest of Secretary of War Root. The move was part of the War Department reorganization based to some extent on Root's study of *The Military Policy of the United States,* by Emory Upton (1904). The act created a corps charged with the preparation and execution of military plans, and discarded the system of divided authority that had created conflict between the Secretary of War and the commanding general.

19 FEB. ELKINS ACT, aimed primarily at eliminating the rebate evil, reinforced the Interstate Commerce Act by defining unfair discrimination between shippers engaged in interstate commerce and by providing for the punishment of shippers and railway officials and agents, as well as railroad corporations, for the giving or receiving of rebates. The act made it a misdemeanor for railroads to deviate from published rates and invested the federal courts with the power to issue injunctions against violators.

1904

PRESIDENTIAL CAMPAIGN. The Socialist National Convention met at Chicago (1 May) and nominated **Eugene V. Debs** (Ind.) for president and Benjamin Hanford (N.Y.) for vice-president. The Republican National Convention met at Chicago (21 June) and by acclamation nominated President **Theodore Roosevelt** for reelection and **Charles W. Fairbanks** (Ind.) for vice-president on a platform shaped by party conservatives. The Prohibition National Convention met at Indianapolis (29 June) and nominated Silas C. Swallow (Pa.) for president and George W. Carroll (Tex.) for vice-president. The Socialist Labor National Convention met at New York (2 July) and nominated Charles H. Corregan (N.Y.) for president and William C. Cox (Ill.) for vice-president. The People's (Populist) National Convention met at Springfield, Ill. (4 July), and nominated **Thomas E. Watson** (Ga., p. 1178) for president and Thomas H. Tibbles (Neb.) for vice-president. The Democratic National Convention met at St. Louis (6 July) and nominated Judge **Alton B. Parker** (N.Y., 1852–1926) for president and **Henry G. Davis** (W. Va.) for vice-president on a platform which, at Parker's insistence, accepted the gold standard. The Democratic platform assailed the trusts and demanded supplementary powers for the Interstate Commerce Commission. The Continental Party National Convention met at Chicago (31 Aug.); its candidates were Austin Holcomb (Ga.) for president and A. King (Mo.) for vice-president.

8 Nov. PRESIDENTIAL ELECTION. Popular vote: **Roosevelt,** 7,628,834; Parker, 5,084,401; Debs, 402,460; Swallow, 259,257; Watson, 114,753; Corregan, 33,724; Holcomb, 830. Electoral vote: **Roosevelt,** 336; **Parker,** 140. The Republicans retained control of both houses of Congress. On the night of his election Roosevelt pledged that "under no circumstances will I be a candidate for or accept another nomination."

1906

29 JUNE. **HEPBURN ACT,** a compromise measure adopted after Roosevelt's demand for stricter railroad regulation met the opposition of congressional conservatives, reinforced the Interstate Commerce Act. The act increased the membership of the Interstate Commerce Commission from 5 to 7 and vested in that body the authority to fix just and reasonable maximum railroad rates and to prescribe uniform methods of accounting. The commission's jurisdiction was broadened to include express and sleeping-car companies, oil pipelines, ferries, terminal facilities, and bridges. Its orders governing carriers were made binding pending a court decision, thereby placing the burden of proof upon the carrier. The act restricted sharply the granting of free passes, and prohibited railroads from carrying any commodities produced by themselves or by companies in which they held an interest, with the exception of timber and other products necessary for railway operation. A serious limitation was the failure of the act to authorize the commission to fix physical valuations of railroads.

30 JUNE. **PURE FOOD AND DRUG ACT** forbade the manufacture, sale, or transportation of adulterated or fraudulently labeled foods and drugs sold in interstate commerce.

30 JUNE. **MEAT INSPECTION ACT,** aimed at discreditable and dangerous conditions in the meat-packing industry, provided for the enforcement of sanitary regulations in packing establishments and federal inspection of all companies selling meats in interstate commerce.

30 JUNE. **IMMUNITY OF WITNESSES ACT** required corporation officers to testify to company operations and conduct without invoking plea of immunity.

1907

PANIC OF 1907. Stock market drop (beg. 13 Mar.) and business failures in mid-1907 were followed by the suspension (22 Oct.) of the Knickerbocker Trust Co. in New York. In order to avoid a more serious decline, Roosevelt permitted (4 Nov.) the U.S. Steel Corp. to acquire the Tennessee Coal and Iron Co., with the understanding that no antitrust action would be instituted. The panic revealed flaws in the currency and credit structure, and was directly responsible for the passage of the Aldrich-Vreeland Act.

1908

13 May. WHITE HOUSE CONSERVATION CONFERENCE. (p. 638).

30 May. ALDRICH-VREELAND ACT, passed as an emergency currency measure, authorized national banks for a period of 6 years to issue circulating notes based on commercial paper and state, county, and municipal bonds. In order to limit bank note emission based on securities other than federal bonds, a graduated tax up to 10% was levied on such notes. While the act introduced some elasticity into the national currency, it provided no safeguards for the credit supply. The most important provision was the establishment of a **National Monetary Commission** authorized to investigate and report upon the banking and currency systems of the U.S. and European countries. The commission, consisting of 9 senators and 9 representatives, was headed by Sen. **Nelson W. Aldrich** (R.I., 1841–1915). Its report, submitted to Congress on 8 Jan. 1912, contained legislative proposals (notably, a national reserve association with branches throughout the country) later incorporated in modified form in the Federal Reserve Act of 1913.

PRESIDENTIAL CAMPAIGN. The People's (Populist) National Convention met at St. Louis (2 April) and nominated **Thomas E. Watson** (Ga.) for president and Samuel W. Williams (Ind.) for vice-president. The United Christian National Convention met at Rock Island, Ill. (1 May), and nominated Daniel B. Turney (Ill.) for president and L. S. Coffin (Iowa) for vice-president. The Socialist National Convention met at Chicago (10 May) and nominated **Eugene V. Debs** (Ind.) for president and Benjamin Hanford (N.Y.) for vice-president. The Republican National Convention met at Chicago (16 June) and nominated **William H. Taft** (Ohio, p. 1165) for President and **James S. Sherman** (N.Y.) for vice-president. Taft was largely the personal choice of President Roosevelt, who had announced his intention not to serve for a second elective term. The Republican platform pledged tariff revision, stricter enforcement of antitrust legislation, and a furthering of Roosevelt's conservation program. The Democratic National Convention met at Denver (7 July) and nominated **William Jennings Bryan** (Neb.) for president and **John W. Kern** (Ind.) for vice-president on a platform that condemned monopolies and unequivocally pledged a reduction in tariff rates. The Prohibition National Convention met at Columbus, Ohio (15 July), and nominated Eugene W. Chafin (Ill.) for president and Aaron S. Watkins (Ohio) for vice-president. The Socialist Labor Convention met at New York (24 July) and nominated August Gillhaus (N.Y.) for president and Donald L. Munro (Va.) for vice-president. The Independence Party Convention met at Chicago (27 July) and nominated Thomas L. Hisgen (Mass.) for president and John Temple Graves (Ga.) for vice-president.

3 Nov. PRESIDENTIAL ELECTION. Popular vote: **Taft,** 7,679,006; Bryan,

6,409,106; Debs, 420,820; Chafin, 252,-683; Hisgen, 83,562; Watson, 28,131; Gillhaus, 13,825; Turney, 461. Electoral vote: **Taft,** 321; Bryan, 162. The Republicans reained control of both houses of Congress.

1910

TAFT'S TRUST POLICY. Under Roosevelt, 44 antitrust suits were started; under Taft, 90 proceedings were initiated against monopolies. The Taft program was carried out by Attorney General **George W. Wickersham** (1858–1936). Taft proposed requiring federal incorporation of companies engaged in interstate commerce, and the establishment of a Federal Corporation Commission to supervise companies holding national charters, but Congress failed to act. The 2 major Supreme Court decisions of the Taft administration were the **Standard Oil Co.** case (1911, p. 674) and the **American Tobacco Co.** case (1911, p. 674). The suit for dissolution against the U.S. Steel Corp. (1911) had political overtones. The bill filed by the government charged that the Steel Trust had been strengthened by its absorption of the Tennessee Coal and Iron Co. during the panic of 1907, and alleged that the corporation had used misleading statements in order to secure Roosevelt's consent. The implication that Roosevelt had been hoodwinked served to widen the rift between Taft and Roosevelt after the latter's return from abroad in 1910.

COMMISSION ON EFFICIENCY AND ECONOMY. In his first annual message to Congress (1909), Taft stressed "economy in expenditures" and issued an executive order directing that all estimates must first be submitted to him. By this method the administration succeeded in saving more than $42 million during the fiscal year ending 30

June 1911 as compared to estimates for the preceding year. In June 1910, Taft secured a congressional appropriation of $100,000 to investigate federal spending, and appointed (Mar. 1911) a Commission on Efficiency and Economy to carry out a survey of administrative organization. Its members included Frederick A. Cleveland, William F. Willoughby, and Frank J. Goodnow. The reports of the commission pointed to outmoded business methods employed in numerous departments and recommended the establishment of a national budget. Partly because of the Taft-Roosevelt schism, partly because of patronage interests, the commission failed to secure congressional support and was finally dissolved. The detailed budget that Taft transmitted to Congress during his last year in office was ignored. Although Taft's attempt to establish a national budgetary system failed, it encouraged similar fiscal innovations in state and local governments; moreover, it paved the way for the Budget Act of 1921.

18 JUNE. MANN-ELKINS ACT, recommended by Taft, placed telephone, telegraph, cable, and wireless companies under the jurisdiction of the Interstate Commerce Commission. It gave the commission authority to suspend new rates pending a court decision and provided for effective enforcement of the long and short haul clause. The act created a federal Court of Commerce to pass upon appeals arising from rate disputes; this tribunal, however, was abolished in 1912.

25 JUNE. POSTAL SAVINGS bank system, recommended by Taft and established by act of Congress, authorized 2% interest on funds deposited at specified post offices.

25 JUNE. PUBLICITY ACT, recommended by Taft, required filing of statements concerning election campaign contributions for representatives. Previously state corrupt practices acts had been passed (beg. N.Y. 1890).

25 June. MANN ACT (WHITE SLAVE TRAFFIC ACT) prohibited interstate transportation of women for immoral purposes.

REPUBLICAN INSURGENCY. When Roosevelt left office, it was with the conviction that Taft, as his personally chosen successor, would carry forward the reform policies of the Roosevelt administration. Taft did not share Roosevelt's concept of the presidency as a stewardship of the public welfare, and early in his administration became involved in a party split that weakened his prestige and contributed to his break with Roosevelt.

During the Senate hearings and debates on the Payne-Aldrich Tariff (1909), open dissension within the Republican ranks emerged under the leadership of Sen. Robert M. La Follette (Wis.). Insurgent hostility toward Taft was hardened when he signed the tariff bill and then, in a speech at Winona, Minn. (17 Sept. 1909), termed it "the best bill that the Republican party ever passed." The Insurgents, most of whom came from the Midwest, later combined with the Democrats (1911–13) in enacting tariff revision measures which Taft vetoed.

19 Mar. REVOLT AGAINST "CANNONISM" in the form of an amendment (19 Mar.) to the House rules, offered as a resolution (17 Mar.) by George W. Norris (Neb.), deprived Speaker **Joseph G. Cannon** (Ill., 1836–1926) of his dictatorial power to appoint the Committee on Rules. This committee was made elective by the House itself and the speaker was barred from serving on it.

31 Aug. ROOSEVELT-TAFT SPLIT. In his "New Nationalism" speech at Osawatomie, Kan. (31 Aug.), Roosevelt, who had returned from Africa in June, attacked the Supreme Court's attitude toward social legislation and declared that the New Nationalism "maintains that every man holds his property subject to the general right of the community to regulate its use to whatever degree the public welfare may require it." The speech was interpeted as an assault upon the conservatism of the Taft administration.

BALLINGER-PINCHOT CONTROVERSY arose from charges made against the conservation policy pursued by Secretary of the Interior Richard A. Ballinger. Under the Roosevelt administration certain water-power sites in Wyoming and Montana had been withdrawn from sale by Secretary of the Interior James R. Garfield. Ballinger doubted the legality of the action and reopened the lands to public entry. Gifford Pinchot, chief of the U.S. Forest Service, publicly accused Ballinger of injuring the conservation program in order to aid corporation interests. Siding with Pinchot was **Louis R. Glavis,** a special agent of the Field Division of the Interior Department who, after being dismissed by order of Taft, charged in an article in *Collier's* (13 Nov. 1909) that Ballinger had favored the patenting of claims to Alaskan coal lands by interests alleged to include the Guggenheims. Taft upheld Ballinger. When a letter written by Pinchot in criticism of Ballinger's conduct was read to the Senate (6 Jan.) by Sen. Jonathan P. Dolliver (Iowa), an Insurgent Republican, Taft ordered Pinchot's removal from office (7 Jan.). A joint congressional committee was established (26 Jan.) to inquire into the administration of the Interior Department. While a majority of the committee exonerated Ballinger, the controversy had already become a major political issue that widened the breach between Taft and the Insurgent Republicans and ultimately contributed to the break between Taft and Roosevelt. Public feeling toward Ballinger was so unfavorable that he resigned (6 Mar. 1911) to relieve the Taft administration of political embarrassment.

8 Nov. MIDTERM ELECTIONS. The Democrats gained control of the House; the Senate, while nominally Republican, was actually under the control of a Democratic-Insurgent Republican bloc. In the state elections of 1910, the Democrats elected 26 governors, including **Woodrow Wilson** (N.J., p. 1187).

1911

21 JAN. National Progressive Republican League founded at Washington, D.C., by Insurgent Republicans under the leadership of Sen. Robert M. La Follette (Wis.). Sen. Jonathan Bourne (Ore.) was elected president of the organization, whose professed chief object was "the promotion of popular government and progressive legislation." Its platform: direct election of U.S. senators; direct primaries for the nomination of elective officers; direct election of delegates to national conventions; amendment of state constitutions to provide for the initiative, referendum, and recall; and a corrupt practices act. The Progressives sought to gain control of the Republican organization, block the nomination of Taft, and choose their own candidate, at this time, La Follette, whom they endorsed 16 Oct.

22 AUG. President Taft vetoed the joint resolution of Congress admitting Arizona to statehood, on the ground that the provision in its constitution authorizing the recall of judges was a blow at the independence of the judiciary. Arizona removed the offending clause and was admitted to statehood (14 Feb. 1912), but afterward restored the article.

1912

SOCIAL LEGISLATION IN THE STATES. By 1912, height of the Progressive movement, there had been enacted in the states a considerable body of social legislation relating to wages and hours, the employment of women and children, and safety and health conditions in factories. A few landmarks among state laws: the adoption by Maryland (1902) of the first state workmen's compensation law; the adoption by Oregon (1903) of a 10-hour law for women in industry (upheld by the Supreme Court in 1908, in *Muller* v. *Oregon*); the enactment by Illinois (1911) of the first state law providing public assistance to mothers with dependent children; the first minimum wage law in the U.S., adopted by Massachusetts (1912), which established a commission to fix wage rates for women and children (this and similar legislation in other states invalidated by the Supreme Court, 1923, in *Adkins* v. *Children's Hospital*).

ROOSEVELT ENTERS THE RACE. Early in 1912 the La Follette boom among the Progressives began to weaken. At the same time Roosevelt, whose alienation from Taft and the conservative Republican leadership had brought him close to the Progressive camp, decided (letter to William B. Howland, 23 Dec. 1911) to oppose Taft for the Republican presidential nomination. A Chicago meeting (10 Feb.) of Republican leaders sent Roosevelt a letter (signed by 7 Republican governors) declaring "that a large majority of the Republican voters of the country favor your nomination, and a large majority of the people favor your election as the next President of the United States." In an address (21 Feb.)

before the Ohio constitutional convention at Columbus, Roosevelt reaffirmed the principles of the New Nationalism and laid special emphasis on the recall of judicial decisions. The speech, which widened the gulf between Roosevelt and Republican conservatives, was followed by Roosevelt's reply (24 Feb.) to the Chicago letter: "I will accept the nomination for President if it is tendered to me, and I will adhere to this decision until the convention has expressed its preference." The Roosevelt boom gained pace during the preconvention campaign, with Roosevelt carrying 4 state conventions and the preferential primaries in 6 states.

PRESIDENTIAL CAMPAIGN. The Socialist Labor National Convention met at New York (7 Apr.) and nominated Arthur E. Reimer (Mass.) for president and August Gillhaus (N.Y.) for vice-president. The Socialist National Convention met at Indianapolis (12 May) and nominated **Eugene V. Debs** (Ind.) for president and Emil Seidel (Wis.) for vice-president. The Prohibition National Convention met at Atlantic City (10 July) and nominated Eugene W. Chafin (Ariz.) for president and Aaron S. Watkins (Ohio) for vice-president.

When the Republican National Convention met at Chicago (18 June), the party's national committee, under conservative control, excluded most of the Roosevelt support represented by contested delegations. As a result, President **Taft** was renominated (22 June). Vice-President **James S. Sherman,** also renominated, died at Utica, N.Y., on 30 Oct. The Roosevelt following met on 22 June, condemned the nomination of Taft as having been gained by fraudulent means, and called upon Roosevelt to assume the leadership of a third party. On 5 Aug. the Progressive ("Bull Moose") party met in national convention at Chicago and nominated **Roosevelt** for president and **Hiram W. Johnson** (Calif., 1866–1945) for vice-president. The Progressive platform, called "A Contract with the People," included demands for tariff revision; stricter regulation of industrial combinations; direct election of U.S. senators; nationwide preferential primaries for presidential candidates; the initiative, referendum, and recall; woman suffrage; recall of judicial decisions; prohibition of child labor; and minimum wage standards for working women.

When the Democratic National Convention met at Baltimore (25 June), the 2 chief contenders were **Beauchamp** ("Champ") Clark (Mo., 1850–1921) and **Woodrow Wilson** (N.J.). Clark held the initial lead, but partly because Bryan shifted his support, **Wilson** was nominated for president on the 46th ballot (2 July). **Thomas R. Marshall** (Ind.) was nominated for vice-president. The two major party platforms were almost alike in their support of conservation measures, a corrupt practices act, and banking and currency reform; but where the Republicans called for a stricter regulation of trusts and for a milder protective tariff, the Democrats asked for a virtual abolition of monopolies and declared in favor of a tariff for revenue only (pledging "immediate downward revision"). During the campaign Wilson shaped the creed known as the "New Freedom." It differed from Roosevelt's "New Nationalism" chiefly on the issue of monopoly control. Roosevelt believed that trusts were not harmful as long as they were subject to federal regulation; Wilson tended to view monopolies as positive evils inimical to the existence of free competition.

5 Nov. PRESIDENTIAL ELECTION. Popular vote: **Wilson,** 6,286,214; Roosevelt, 4,126,020; Taft, 3,483,922; Debs, 897,011; Chafin, 206,275; Reimer, 29,079. Electoral vote: **Wilson,** 435; Roosevelt, 88; Taft, 8. In point of the popular vote, Wilson was a minority president, but his electoral majority was the largest in U.S. presidential history up to that time. The Democrats gained control of both houses of Congress.

1913

25 Feb. 16TH AMENDMENT to the Constitution, proposed 12 July 1909, was declared adopted and in effect. This so-called **income tax** amendment authorized Congress to impose taxes on incomes, from whatever source derived, without apportionment among the states and without regard to any census or enumeration.

28 Feb. PUJO COMMITTEE REPORT. Charges of the existence of a "money trust" led the House (Feb. 1912) to authorize its Committee on Banking and Currency to inquire into the concentration of financial and banking resources. A subcommittee under Rep. Arsène Pujo (La.) began its investigations on 27 Apr. 1912. In the course of the inquiry prominent financiers, including J. P. Morgan, testified at the hearings. The committee's report stated that the concentration of money and credit was increasing. Cited among the methods that had been used to establish concentration were the consolidation of banks and trust companies; the acquiring of control through purchase of stock in competitive units; interlocking directorates; extension of control into insurance companies, railroads, public utilities, and industrial corporations; and joint arrangements for purchasing security issues. The report lent added cogency to the incoming Wilson administration's program of currency and banking reform.

1 Mar. PHYSICAL VALUATION ACT empowered the Interstate Commerce Commission to make thorough investigations of property held or used by railroads under its jurisdiction with a view to establishing cost and physical valuation as a basis for rate making and the fixing of a reasonable profit.

1 Mar. WEBB-KENYON INTERSTATE LIQUOR ACT, passed over President Taft's veto, forbade interstate shipment of liquor into states where sale was illegal.

4 Mar. Department of Commerce and Labor divided by act of Congress into 2 departments, each with cabinet status.

4 Mar. Wilson's inaugural address projected a broad program for the conservation of human and natural resources and the restoration of free competition.

8 Apr. Appearing in person before a special session of Congress to deliver his message on tariff revision, President Wilson broke the precedent set by President Thomas Jefferson in 1801. The last personal appearance of a president before the national legislature had been made by John Adams in 1800; since that time transmitted presidential messages had been read by clerks.

31 May. 17TH AMENDMENT to the Constitution, proposed on 16 May 1912, was declared adopted and in effect. It provided for the **popular election of U.S. senators.**

23 Dec. FEDERAL RESERVE ACT. Wilson asked Congress (23 June) for a measure that would create a government-controlled, decentralized banking system capable of assuring an elastic currency. The congressional debate lasted some 6 months, during which time banking interests fought to defeat the measure.

The **Owen-Glass Act** establishing the Federal Reserve system was the first thorough reorganization of the national banking system since the Civil War. The act provided for the establishment of not less than 8 and not more than 12 districts or regions with a Federal Reserve bank in each (12 centers were set up at Boston,

New York, Philadelphia, Richmond, Atlanta, Dallas, Kansas City, St. Louis, Chicago, Cleveland, Minneapolis, and San Francisco). At the apex of the system was a Federal Reserve Board consisting of 7 members (subsequently increased to 8) including the Secretary of the Treasury and the Comptroller of the Currency. This central board was authorized to raise or lower the rediscount rate prevailing at the district reserve banks, thus giving it direct control over the credit supply.

The district banks were to serve as bankers' banks, i.e., as depositories for the cash reserves of the national banks (which were required to join the system) and of state banks (whose membership was optional). Each Federal Reserve bank was to be governed by a board of 9 directors, 6 of them appointed by the Federal Reserve Board. A member bank was required to subscribe to the capital stock of its district Federal Reserve bank in an amount equal to 6% of its own capital and surplus. The Federal Reserve banks were empowered to rediscount the commercial and agricultural paper of member banks, and the system's currency was to be based upon approved rediscounted paper deposited by member banks. Against such paper the reserve banks could issue Federal Reserve notes (accepted as government obligations) as part of the circulating money supply. The amount could be expanded and contracted in keeping with the changing requirements of business activity. Each reserve bank was required to maintain a gold reserve of 40% against Federal Reserve notes outstanding, although it was specified that this provision might be suspended in time of emergency.

1914

8 May. SMITH-LEVER ACT provided for a system of agricultural extension work based on cooperation between the Department of Agriculture and the land-grant colleges. Federal grants-in-aid were to be matched by state appropriations in carrying out the program.

26 Sept. FEDERAL TRADE COMMISSION ACT, passed at Wilson's recommendation as part of his trust regulation program, was designed to prevent unfair methods of competition in interstate commerce. The Bureau of Corporations was eliminated, and in its place was established the Federal Trade Commission, a bipartisan body consisting of 5 members, authorized to demand annual and special reports from corporations, investigate the activities of persons and corporations (except banks and common carriers), publish reports on its findings, and issue cease and desist orders (subject to judicial review in the federal courts) to prevent unfair business practices. Among the practices which the commission subsequently singled out were trade boycotts, mislabeling and adulteration of commodities, combinations for maintaining resale prices, and false claims to patents.

15 Oct. CLAYTON ANTITRUST ACT, which supplemented and strengthened the Sherman Antitrust Act, was aimed at corporate methods hitherto not specified as illegal practices. It also contained provisions relating to labor and agricultural organizations. The act prohibited the following: price discriminations substantially tending to create a monopoly, tying contracts (i.e., contracts based on the condition that purchasers would not buy or handle the products of sellers' competitors), interlocking directorates in industrial aggregations capitalized at $1 million or more, and the acquisition of stockholdings tending to lessen competition. Officials of corporations violating antitrust statutes could be held individually responsible. The following remedies were provided whereby injured parties might secure relief: court injunctions, the issuance of cease and desist orders by the Federal Trade Commission, and civil suits for 3-fold damages in instances where the existence of price discrimination and tying contracts was established.

In regard to labor and agriculture, the act specified that "the labor of a human being is not a commodity or article of commerce; nothing contained in the antitrust laws shall be construed to forbid the existence and operation of labor, agricultural and horticultural organizations . . . nor shall such organizations or the members thereof be held or construed to be illegal combinations in restraint of trade under the antitrust laws." The act also forbade the use of the injunction in labor disputes unless the court decided that an injunction was necessary to prevent irreparable injury to property; made strikes, peaceful picketing, and boycotts legal under federal jurisdiction; and provided for trial by jury in contempt cases, except in instances where contempt was committed in presence of the court. Hailed by Samuel Gompers as labor's "Magna Carta," the act's labor provisions were substantially weakened by court interpretation.

1915

PREPAREDNESS MOVEMENT. Shortly after the beginning of World War I, the issue of military preparedness was introduced into public debate in the U.S. Private organizations and individuals pointed to occupied Belgium as an example of the fate in store for an unprepared nation, and undertook a campaign for strengthening the national defense. Among such organizations were the National Security League (est. Dec. 1914), the American Defense Society (est. Aug. 1915), the League to Enforce Peace (est. June 1915), and the Ameri-

can Rights Committee (est. Dec. 1915). Individuals prominent in the preparedness movement included **Theodore Roosevelt, Henry Cabot Lodge,** and **Henry L. Stimson.** The "**Plattsburg idea**" (military training camps for civilians) came into being at Plattsburg, N.Y., on 10 Aug. Preparedness was opposed by organized pacifist and antimilitarist groups who contended that the war did not involve vital U.S. interests. The most spectacular effort of the peace associations was Henry Ford's chartering of the "peace ship" *Oskar II*, which sailed for Europe (4 Dec.) in an ill-fated attempt to end the war by a negotiated peace. On 10 May Wilson in an address at Philadelphia declared: "There is such a thing as a man being too proud to fight. There is such a thing as a nation being so right that it does not need to convince others that it is right." But his opposition to a large standing army and advocacy of unarmed neutrality changed after the *Lusitania* incident (7 May, p. 359). On 7 Dec. he laid before Congress a comprehensive plan for national defense, and on 27 Jan. 1916 began a tour of the country to urge preparedness.

1916

10 FEB. Lindley M. Garrison resigned as Secretary of War. Garrison's advocacy of a volunteer force under direct national control, as opposed to the state-controlled National Guard units, was not accepted by Wilson, who feared loss of congressional support on the issue.

7 MARCH. Newton D. Baker (Ohio, 1871–1937) appointed Secretary of War.

3 JUNE. NATIONAL DEFENSE ACT, first major result of the administration's preparedness program, provided for expansion of the regular army to 175,000 men, and its further enlargement to 223,000 over a five-year period. It also authorized a National Guard of 450,000

men; established a Reserve Officers Training Corps at universities, colleges, and military camps; and made provisions for industrial preparedness.

17 July. FEDERAL FARM LOAN ACT provided farmers with long-term credit facilities similar to those made available to industry and commerce by the Federal Reserve Act. The country was divided into 12 districts under the general administration of a Federal Farm Loan Board consisting of the Secretary of Treasury and 4 members. In each district there was established a Farm Loan Bank (capitalized at $750,000) in which co-operative farm loan associations held membership. Farmers belonging to these associations could secure long-term loans (5–40 yrs.) on farm-mortgage security at interest rates (5%–6%) lower than those prevailing in commercial banks.

11 Aug. WAREHOUSE ACT authorized licensed and bonded warehouses to issue against specified agricultural commodities (including grain, cotton, tobacco, and wool) warehouse receipts negotiable as delivery orders or as collateral for loans. The measure assisted farmers in financing their crops.

29 Aug. COUNCIL OF NATIONAL DEFENSE established under the Army Appropriation Act. Organized (11 Oct.) under the chairmanship of Secretary of War Baker, this advisory body consisting of 6 cabinet members was charged with coordinating industry and resources for the national security and welfare. Its Advisory Commission, consisting of 7 civilian experts headed by Daniel Willard, was responsible for mapping preparedness plans in fields including transportation, munitions and manufacturing, labor, raw materials, supplies, engineering and education, and medicine and surgery.

7 Sept. SHIPPING ACT authorized the creation of the U.S. Shipping Board, a 5-man body empowered to build, purchase, lease, or requisition vessels through the agency of the Emergency Fleet Corporation, capitalized at $50 million.

PRESIDENTIAL CAMPAIGN. The Socialist Labor National Convention met at New York (23 Apr.) and nominated Arthur E. Reimer (Mass.) for president and August Gillhaus (N.Y.) for vice-president. The Socialist party held no convention; its candidates, nominated by a mail referendum, were Allen L. Benson (N.Y.) for president and George R. Kirkpatrick (N.J.) for vice-president. The Republican National Convention met at Chicago (7 June) and nominated Supreme Court Justice **Charles E. Hughes** (N.Y.) for president and **Charles W. Fairbanks** (Ind.) for vice-president. The Progressive National Convention, also meeting at Chicago (7 June), nominated Theodore Roosevelt for president and John M. Parker (La.) for vice-president. Roosevelt, however, declined the nomination, and gave his support to Hughes. Roosevelt's defection led to the rapid disintegration of the Progressive party. The national committee of the Progressive party endorsed (26 June) Hughes' nomination, but an Indianapolis conference of the Progressive party (3 Aug.) repudiated this step. The Democratic National Convention met at St. Louis (14 June) and renominated President **Woodrow Wilson** and Vice-President **Thomas R. Marshall**. The Prohibition National Convention met at St. Paul (19 July) and nominated J. Frank Hanly (Ind.) for president and Ira D. Landrith (Tenn.) for vice-president.

Wilson's supporters defended his record on neutrality and preparedness, waging the campaign with the slogan "He kept us out of war." The slogan was highly effective in attracting the support of women's groups, particularly in those Western states where the vote had been conferred on women. Some of the strongest opposition to Wilson came from Irish-American and German-American elements critical of his foreign policy. The Democrats, however, turned against Hughes his failure to repudiate (until late in the campaign) the support of these so-called hyphenate groups.

7 Nov. PRESIDENTIAL ELECTION. Popular vote: **Wilson,** 9,129,606; Hughes, 8,538,221; Benson, 585,113; Hanly, 220,506; Reimer, 13,403. Electoral vote: **Wilson,** 277; Hughes, 254. So close was the election that the final result was in doubt until it was definitely known that California had gone Democratic (by only 3,773 votes). The Democrats retained control of both houses of Congress.

1917

23 FEB. SMITH-HUGHES ACT provided for federal grants-in-aid, to be matched by the contributions of individual states, for promoting instruction in agriculture and the trades. It established a Federal Board for Vocational Education.

8 MAR. SENATE CLOTURE RULE, adopted by special session of Senate, permitted limitation of debate by two thirds of the senators present and voting. Rule 22 was amended (1949) to require two thirds of the entire Senate membership but modified (1959) to again require two thirds of the senators present. Cloture was successfully invoked to end filibusters only 8 times from 1919–70, and 16 times from 1971 through 7 Mar. 1975.

31 MAR. General Munitions Board established by Council of National Defense. Organized 9 Apr., it was responsible for coordinating the procurement of war materials for the War and Navy departments and for assisting them to acquire raw materials and manufacturing plants. Its purpose, however, was weakened by conflicting authority and by the board's lack of power to enforce its decisions.

14 APR. COMMITTEE ON PUBLIC INFORMATION, established by executive order of the president, was headed by the journalist **George Creel** (1876–1953) and consisted of the Secretaries of State, War, and Navy. Responsible for uniting American public opinion behind the war effort, the committee employed an elaborate nationwide publicity apparatus based on pamphlets, news releases, posters, motion pictures, and volunteer speakers.

24 APR. LIBERTY LOAN ACT, a war finance measure, authorized the issue of bonds to be sold by public subscription and provided for loans to the Allied powers to enable them to purchase food and war supplies. The Liberty Loan drives were as follows: 1st, June 1917 ($2 billion); 2d, Nov. 1917 ($3.8 billion); 3d, May 1918 ($4.2 billion); 4th, Oct. 1918 ($6 billion); Victory Loan, Apr. 1919 ($4.5 billion).

18 MAY. SELECTIVE SERVICE ACT provided for the registration and classification for military service of all men between the ages of 21 and 30, inclusive; as amended by the Man Power Act (31 Aug. 1918) it required the registration of all men between the ages of 18 and 45. The 1st registration (5 June) enrolled 9,586,508 men; the 2d (5 June 1918) added well over a million who had come of age; and the 3d (12 Sept. 1918) enrolled 13,228,762. Of the 24,234,021 registered during the war, 2,810,296 were called up for service in the army.

15 JUNE. ESPIONAGE ACT, aimed at treasonable and disloyal activities, provided severe penalties (up to $10,000 fine and 20 years' imprisonment) for persons found guilty of aiding the enemy, obstructing recruiting, or causing insubordination, disloyalty, or refusal of duty in the armed services. The act empowered the postmaster general to exclude from the mails newspapers, periodicals, and other material alleged to be treasonable or seditious. The constitutionality of the act was upheld in *Schenck* v. *U.S.* (1919).

28 July. WAR INDUSTRIES BOARD, established by the Council of National Defense as successor to the General Munitions Board, was directed to act as a clearing agency for the nation's war industries and to take steps to increase production and eliminate waste. A reorganization of the War Industries Board (4 Mar. 1918) placed at its head **Bernard M. Baruch** (1870–1965), who was given authority for all major controls. The board was endowed with wide powers over the determination of priorities, the conversion of existing facilities, the manufacture of war materials, price fixing, and the purchase of supplies for the U.S. and the Allies.

10 Aug. LEVER FOOD AND FUEL CONTROL ACT, effective for the duration of the war, empowered the president to make regulations and issue orders to stimulate and conserve the production, and control the distribution, of foods and fuels necessary to the war effort. The president was authorized to fix the price of wheat at not less than $2 a bushel (a provision effective until 1 May 1919; in practice, the guaranteed price was $2.20); to fix the price of coal, coke, and other commodities; to license producers and distributors; and to prohibit unfair trade practices. The act forbade the use of foodstuffs in the manufacture of distilled liquors, whose importation was also forbidden. **Herbert Hoover** was appointed Food Administrator (10 Aug.) and Harry A. Garfield named Fuel Administrator (23 Aug.). Among the other agencies employed in administering the act were the Grain Corporation (for the financing of wheat crops) and the Sugar Equalization Board (for stabilizing the price of sugar and regulating its distribution).

3 Oct. WAR REVENUE ACT, which made the income tax the chief source of revenue during the war, authorized a graduated income tax beginning at 4% on personal incomes of more than $1,000; raised the corporation tax to 6%; imposed a graduated excess profits tax of from 20% to 60% on corporations and persons; raised postal rates; and provided for sharp increases in excise taxes on luxuries, transportation, amusements, alcoholic beverages, and tobacco.

6 Oct. TRADING WITH THE ENEMY ACT forbade commerce with enemy nations or their associates and empowered the president to impose an embargo on imports and to establish censorship of material passing between the U.S. and any foreign nation. The War Trade Board assumed the task of licensing imports and halting commercial intercourse with the enemy. The act also created the Office of Alien Property Custodian to take possession and dispose of the property held in the U.S. by persons residing in enemy countries. **A. Mitchell Palmer** was named (12 Oct.) to the post.

18 Dec. PROHIBITION AMENDMENT. The war against Germany created wider support for the prohibition movement, which by the outset of 1917 had succeeded in establishing prohibition in 19 states. The **Woman's Christian Temperance Union** (est. 1874) spurred the founding (1893) of the **Anti-Saloon League,** which, along with spectacular crusaders like the hatchet-wielding Mrs. **Carrie A. Nation** (1846–1911), had long been agitating for a national prohibition amendment. With U.S. involvement in the war, there were added to the arguments of moral and social reformers the need for conserving food and the patriotic condemnation of individuals of German extraction prominent in the brewing and distilling industry. On 18 Dec. Congress adopted and submitted to the states an amendment to the Constitution prohibiting the manufacture, sale, or transportation of alcoholic liquors. This, the 18th Amendment, was declared ratified on 29 Jan. 1919 and went into operation on 16 Jan. 1920. It was repealed with the adoption of the 21st Amendment (1933).

26 Dec. U.S. RAILROAD ADMINISTRATION. An impending crisis in the national transportation system led President Wilson to place the railways under government operation. He named Secretary of the Treasury **William Gibbs McAdoo** (1863–1941) as director-general of the U.S. Railroad Administration, which controlled 397,014 miles of track operated by 2,905 companies. On 21 Mar. 1918 the **Railroad Control Act** provided for fixing compensation to the railroads during the period of government management (to end not later than 1 year and 9 months after ratification of a peace treaty), and established a regional system of administration. The U.S. Railroad Administration was subsequently authorized to control railway express companies and inland waterway systems.

1918

5 Apr. WAR FINANCE CORPORATION, created to finance war industries, was capitalized at $500 million and authorized to issue $3 billion in bonds and to make loans to financial institutions to cover commercial credits extended to war industries.

8 Apr. NATIONAL WAR LABOR BOARD appointed by President Wilson to act as court of last resort for labor disputes, Frank P. Walsh and ex-President Taft named cochairmen. On 8 June the **War Labor Policies Board** was constituted to standardize labor conditions, with Felix Frankfurter chairman.

10 Apr. WEBB-POMERENE ACT, authorized exporters to organize associations for export trade without becoming liable for violation of antitrust laws. Unfair methods of competition were prohibited.

16 May. SEDITION ACT, an amendment to the Espionage Act of 1917, provided severe penalties for persons found guilty of making or conveying false statements interfering with the prosecution of the war; willfully employing "disloyal, profane, scurrilous, or abusive language" about the American form of government, the Constitution, the flag, or the military and naval forces; urging the curtailed production of necessary war materials; or advocating, teaching, defending, or suggesting the doing of any such acts or things. The enforcement of the act was aimed chiefly at Socialists and pacifists, and resulted in the trial and imprisonment of the Socialist leaders Eugene V. Debs and Victor L. Berger. The case of *Abrams* v. *U.S.* (1919, p. 675) involved application of the Sedition Act.

20 May. OVERMAN ACT authorized the president to coordinate or consolidate executive bureaus, agencies, and offices in the interest of economy and the more efficient concentration of governmental operations in matters relating to the conduct of the war.

5 Nov. CONGRESSIONAL ELECTIONS gave the Republicans control of both houses of Congress. The result, coming after Wilson had appealed (25 Oct., p. 372) to the country to return a Democratic Congress, was interpreted as repudiation of the president.

THE UNITED STATES IN WORLD AFFAIRS, 1866-1918

★   ★
★

The Treaty of Washington of 1871 marked an end of an era of strained relations with Great Britain. After a century of miscalculation the British welcomed the United States not only as a full-fledged member of the family of nations but into the small circle of great powers as well. While the acquisition of Alaska in 1867 completed the continental expansion of the United States, it by no means spelled finis to the aspirations of imperialist-minded groups for overseas dominion—in the Caribbean to the Danish West Indies, Santo Domingo, Cuba, and an isthmian canal, and in the Pacific to Samoa and Hawaii. Against the deep-rooted instincts of many traditionally isolationist and anti-imperialist Americans, the nation between 1898 and 1917 found itself involved, first, with the fragments of the Spanish Empire in America, then in Pacific and Asiatic adventures, and finally in Europe. If entry into the Spanish-American War set the United States on a new path in world affairs, the fruits of that victory prompted a clamorous demand for withdrawal. World War I involved America even more directly in world affairs, and it remained for Franklin D. Roosevelt's "Good Neighbor" policy to bring about fundamental changes in our relationships with Mexico, which President Wilson's well-meaning intervention had exacerbated, and finally to extricate America's military presence, with occasional later exceptions, from Caribbean lands, to achieve commonwealth status for Puerto Rico, a changing status for the Panama Canal, and independence for the Philippines.

Despite earnest attempts to remain neutral for some three years, the United States entered World War I as a full participant, an involvment which put American isolationism to its severest test. It was a test, too, of the Wilsonian vision of a new international order in which the United States would, it was hoped, assume a role commensurate with its power, prestige, and influence.

1866

31 MAY. FENIAN UPRISING. The Fenians, a secret Irish brotherhood organized in the 1850s to achieve independence for Ireland, crossed the Niag-ara River with an army of several hundred and fought an engagement with Canadian militiamen ("Battle of Limestone Ridge") before fleeing back to New York. After the repulse of another Fenian attack (25 May 1870) under John

O'Neill, the leaders were arrested by the U.S. Marshal for Vermont.

1866-67

NAPOLEON III AND MEXICO. On 12 Feb. 1866 Secretary Seward delivered an ultimatum demanding French withdrawal from Mexico following the dispatch to the Mexican border under Gen. Sheridan of 50,000 U.S. troops. Napoleon withdrew his forces in the spring of 1867. Maximilian, Austrian Archduke, established on the Mexican throne as a result of the occupation of Mexico City by French forces (7 June 1863), was executed by Mexican partisans under Benito Juárez (19 June).

1867

ACQUISITION OF ALASKA. In Dec. 1866 Baron Edoard de Stoeckl, Russian minister to the U.S., was instructed to negotiate with Secretary Seward, an ardent expansionist, for the sale of Alaska, regarded by Russia as an economic liability. A treaty for the purchase of Alaska for $7,200,000 was submitted to the Senate (30 Mar.). With the aid of Sumner and a propaganda campaign, the treaty was ratified (9 Apr.), and formal transfer of "Seward's Folly" accomplished (18 Oct.). A similar campaign, aided by Stoeckl's judicious use of funds to buy votes, resulted in the adoption by the House of the necessary appropriation bill (14 July 1868).

24 Oct. DANISH WEST INDIES. Seward negotiated a treaty with Denmark for the acquisition of the Danish West Indies (now the Virgin Islands) for $7,500,000, but it died in the Senate.

1869-72

"ALABAMA" CLAIMS. The U.S. pressed claims against Great Britain for damage (estimated at 100,000 tons with cargoes) done to the Northern merchant marine by British-built Confederate raiders, including the *Alabama*. Seward negotiated the **Johnson-Clarendon Convention** (14 Jan. 1869) providing for adjudication of the claims, which the Senate, led by Sumner, rejected (13 Apr.). In the Grant administration Secretary Fish reopened negotiations. The **Treaty of Washington** (8 May 1871), which represented a triumph for Fish over Sumner, provided for the submission of all outstanding differences between the U.S. and Great Britain to an international arbitral tribunal (representatives from Italy, Switzerland, Brazil, and the interested parties). That tribunal decided (25 Aug. 1872) that Great Britain failed to use "due diligence" to prevent the Confederate raiders from going to sea, and awarded the U.S. $15,500,000. This amount was far below Sumner's demands (which included **collateral damage**, estimated at $2,125 million), but the tribunal refused to pass upon indirect claims.

1870

SANTO DOMINGO AFFAIR. Desirous of annexing Santo Domingo, Grant dispatched his secretary, Babcock, to survey the situation. On Babcock's return from the island Grant submitted a treaty of annexation to his cabinet, which was unanimously rejected. A more formal treaty was then drawn up and submitted to the Senate (10 Jan.). On 15 Mar. the Committee on Foreign Relations reported adversely on ratification and Sumner delivered his famous "**Naboth's Vineyard**" speech, a scathing denunciation of the Santo Domingo project, which cost him the chairmanship of that committee (deposed 9 Mar. 1871). Another opponent of ratification, Attorney General E. R. Hoar, was forced to resign from the cabinet. Despite Grant's insistence (31 May) that ratification would be "an adherence to the Monroe Doctrine," the treaty was defeated (30 June). On 14 July Secretary Fish submitted a memorandum upholding the no-transfer corollary (no territory shall be subject to transfer to a European power) as part of the Monroe Doctrine.

1873

CUBA AND THE "VIRGINIUS" INCIDENT. When revolt broke out in Cuba (1868) Fish persuaded Grant to abstain from recognition (1869). When Spanish authorities in Cuba captured (31 Oct. 1873) the arms-running ship *Virginius,* illegally flying the American flag, and summarily shot 53 of the crew (among them Americans) as pirates, Fish moderated U.S. demands and secured (29 Nov.) an indemnity of $80,000 for the families of the executed Americans.

1875

30 Jan. TREATY WITH HAWAII of commercial reciprocity signed, providing that no Hawaiian territory should be disposed to a third power. Senate approval 18 Mar.

1878

17 Jan. SAMOAN TREATY. U.S. interest in the Samoan Islands began as early as 1838 and was renewed after the Civil War. A U.S. naval officer, Commander Richard W. Meade, negotiated a treaty (17 Feb. 1872) with the Samoan chieftains giving the U.S. exclusive rights to a naval station at the strategic harbor of Pago Pago on the ilsand of Tutuila. The Senate failed to ratify the treaty. U.S. penetration was extended by Col. A. B. Steinberger, who, dispatched by President Grant as a special agent to the

islands (1873), became prime minister. During the brief period of his ascendancy Steinberger was regarded by the Samoans as an American governor. The U.S. and the native chieftains had a mutual interest in confining German influence in Samoa. Accordingly, a treaty of amity and commerce was signed (17 Jan.) and approved (30 Jan.) by which the U.S. was given nonexclusive rights to a naval station at Pago Pago.

1880

3 July. MADRID CONVENTION. U.S. joined European powers in restricting extraterritorial rights of Moroccans. Senate approval 5 May 1881.

17 Nov. CHINESE TREATY. Anti-Chinese agitation, chiefly on the Pacific Coast, led to pressure by Western interests on President Hayes for abrogation of the Burlingame Treaty (1868) giving the Chinese the right of unlimited immigration to the U.S. Hayes vetoed (1 Mar. 1879) a congressional measure restricting the number of Chinese passengers aboard U.S.-bound ships on the ground that it was equivalent to exclusion and hence violative of the Burlingame Treaty. Hayes dispatched a mission to China to consider the revision of the treaty. The result was the Treaty of 1880, giving the U.S. the right to "regulate, limit or suspend" but not absolutely to prohibit entry of Chinese laborers. On 6 May 1882 the Exclusion Act restricted such immigration for a 10-year period.

1881

BLAINE'S FOREIGN POLICY. Secretary of State James G. Blaine, the most influential figure in the Garfield administration, advocated closer commercial and cultural ties with Latin America. His program had a dual aim: to strengthen the competitive position of the U.S. ex-

port trade, and to increase U.S. prestige by attempting to arbitrate Latin-
American disputes threatening war or
European intervention. Blaine failed to
settle the War of the Pacific (begun by
Chile against Bolivia and Peru in 1879),
and made a fruitless attempt to intercede in the Costa Rica–Colombia and
Mexico-Guatemala disputes.

He invited (22 Nov.) the Latin-
American nations to a peace conference
at Washington scheduled for 22 Nov.
1882. Invitations had already been accepted by 9 countries by the time Blaine
left office (12 Dec.), but his successor,
Frederick T. Frelinghuysen, revoked
the invitations.

Blaine endeavored to secure British
consent to modification of the Clayton-
Bulwer Treaty. Hayes had asserted in a
message to Congress (8 Mar. 1880)
that since an isthmian canal would be
virtually part of the U.S. coastline, it
must on that account be under U.S.
control. In Apr. 1880, the House
adopted a resolution authorizing the
president to "take immediate steps for
the formal and final abrogation" of the
treaty. When Blaine learned of reports
that Colombia was sounding out several
European nations on assuming the guarantee of an isthmian canal, he invoked
(24 June) the U.S. "paramount interest" interpretation of the Monroe Doctrine. The British foreign secretary, Earl
Granville, dispatched a note (10 Nov.)
insisting on the finality of the Clayton-
Bulwer Treaty. The Frelinghuysen-
Zavala Treaty (1884), signed with
Nicaragua, violated the Clayton-Bulwer
Treaty, but died in the Senate.

1882

22 MAY. KOREAN–U.S. TREATY of
Commerce and amity signed; recognized
independence of Korea. Senate approval
13 Feb. 1883.

**26 JULY. GENEVA CONVENTION
OF 1862** for care of wounded proclaimed after Senate approval 16 Mar.

1884

**1 OCT.–1 NOV. INTERNATIONAL
PRIME MERIDIAN CONFERENCE,**
at Washington, recommended meridian
of Greenwich as basis for counting longitude and mean time.

**15 NOV.–26 FEB. 1885. CONGO
CONFERENCE** at Berlin, called by
Germany to consider commerce and
navigation in the Congo area and procedures for acquiring African territory,
was participated in by the U.S., which
had (22 Apr.) recognized the International Association of the Congo. The
U.S. was instrumental in bringing conference agreement on freedom of trade
and abolition of slave traffic in Central
Africa, but declined to ratify the general act. On 2 July 1890 the U.S. signed
an international agreement for suppression of the African slave trade; Senate
approval 11 Jan. 1892.

1887

20 JAN. PEARL HARBOR. The Hawaiian Reciprocity Treaty of 1875, which
had been renewed in 1884 but not approved by the Senate, was ratified when
it was amended to give the U.S. the
exclusive right to establish a fortified
naval base at Pearl Harbor, near Honolulu.

RIVALRY IN SAMOA. Mutual suspicion and consular intrigues marked the
activities of the U.S., Great Britain, and
Germany in the Samoan Islands after
1879. A tripartite agreement reached in
that year provided for a protectorate
over the municipal government of Apia
(an arrangement later extended to all of
the islands), but it never received Senate approval. A German-instigated revolt

brought the protest (19 June 1885) of Secretary of State Thomas F. Bayard, who proposed a 3-power meeting. Before discussions began at the Washington conference (25 June–26 July), the British and Germans came to an understanding whereby Britain supported Germany's ambition for a mandate over Samoa in return for German recognition of British interests in Africa and the Near East. The Washington conference terminated without reaching a decision. Germany then renewed her interference in Samoan affairs by deporting the resisting ruler and establishing a government under direct German influence. Tension rose after the new regime discriminated against U.S. and British commercial interests. By the close of 1888, warships of the 3 powers were stationed in Apia Harbor, and a conflict threatened.

1888

BAYARD-CHAMBERLAIN TREATY. Difficulties with Great Britain over the Canadian fisheries question arose after the U.S. served notice that beginning 1 July 1885 it would terminate the fishing clauses of the Treaty of Washington (1871). The Canadians then fell back on a narrow interpretation of the Treaty of 1818 and began seizing U.S. fishing vessels for technical violations. American resentment, especially in maritime New England, was aroused. On 2 Mar. 1887 Congress authorized President Cleveland to take retaliatory steps against Canada (by excluding her vessels from U.S. waters and halting the importation of Canadian products). A joint Anglo-American commission met at Washington (22 Nov. 1887). On 15 Feb. the Bayard-Chamberlain Treaty and a *modus vivendi* were concluded with Great Britain. The treaty was rejected (21 Aug.) by the Republican majority in the Senate, partly because it provided for a reciprocal tariff, partly because of anti-British feeling. But the *modus vivendi*, giving the U.S. privileges in Canadian ports, remained the basis for use of the fisheries until abrogated by Canada (1923) in retaliation against the Fordney-McCumber Tariff.

1889

BERLIN CONFERENCE ON SAMOA. Germany's policy of armed intervention in Samoa with the tacit approval of the British led President Cleveland to lay the question before Congress (15 Jan.). Terming the situation "delicate and critical," Cleveland asserted that the U.S. insisted upon the preservation of Samoan autonomy and independence. The threatened naval clash in Apia Harbor was averted by a hurricane (15–16 Mar.) that wrecked the U.S. warships *Trenton* and *Vandalia*, caused the *Nipsic* to be run ashore, and destroyed all of the German ships. Only the British *Calliope* escaped disaster. But even before the hurricane struck, President Harrison had already dispatched (14 Mar.) 3 American commissioners to the Berlin conference, which opened 29 Apr. The agreement, signed on 14 June, provided for the independence and autonomy of the Samoan Islands under a tripartite protectorate (the U.S., Great Britain, and Germany). The chief agents of the 3-power condominium were to be the chief justice and the president of the Apia municipal council. The agreement also provided for a foreign adviser to the Samoan king and a court for the settlement of land titles.

BLAINE'S LATIN-AMERICAN POLICY. Blaine's plan to call a Latin-American conference, which had been scrapped by his successor in the Department of State, finally won the approval of Congress, which on 24 May 1888 authorized President Cleveland to summon a conference for discussing measures for the promotion of the common peace and prosperity. Secretary of State Bayard issued invitations (13 July 1888); by the time the first International American Conference met at Washington (2 Oct. 1889–19 Apr. 1890), Blaine was again Secretary of State. Seventeen Latin-American nations were represented, Santo Domingo being the sole absentee. The major U.S. goal, to establish a customs union, was defeated by the opposition of the other delegates. The conference likewise failed to establish machinery for the arbitration of disputes, but set up the International Bureau of American Republics (later called the **Pan-American Union**), which served as a permanent agency for exchanging and disseminating information regarding each country; and paved the way for a U.S. policy of reciprocal tariff arrangements by executive agreement, as authorized by the McKinley Tariff Act of 1890.

1891

CONTROVERSIES WITH ITALY AND CHILE. Italy. The slaying (15 Oct. 1890) of the police chief at New Orleans, who had been investigating the activities of persons suspected of affiliation with the secret Mafia (Black Hand) Society, resulted in the trial and acquittal of the Italian suspects. A New Orleans mob broke into the jail (14 Mar.) and lynched 11 persons (3 of them Italian nationals). The Italian government demanded indemnity for the victims and punishment of the responsible parties. While Blaine deplored the action of the New Orleans mob, he refused to take action on the ground that the crime fell under state rather than federal jurisdiction. The Italian government withdrew its minister to the U.S. (31 Mar.),

and the U.S. took similar action, but there was no formal diplomatic break. President Harrison's annual message (9 Dec.) condemned the New Orleans lynching and assured the Italian government of the good faith of the U.S. government. The incident was closed with the offer (12 Apr. 1892) of a $25,-000 indemnity that was accepted by the Italian government.

Chile. Following the outbreak of civil war in Chile (1891), the rebel Congressionalist party sent a vessel, the *Itata*, to San Diego to take on a shipment of arms. The U.S.S. *Charleston* was ordered to pursue and seize the *Itata*. The rebel vessel was escorted back to San Diego but later released on the ground that there had been no violation of the neutrality laws. The incident gave the Congressionalists (who took over the Chilean government) reason for harboring resentment against the U.S. This hostility was brought to a head when a Valparaiso mob attacked (16 Oct.) sailors on shore leave from the U.S. cruiser *Baltimore*, killed 2, and injured 17. In his annual message to Congress (9 Dec.), President Harrison defended the conduct of the U.S. naval commanders. In reply, the Chilean foreign minister, M. A. Matte, sent a denunciatory telegram (11 Dec.), which aroused indignation in the U.S. Blaine's note to the Chilean government (21 Jan. 1892) stated that unless a retraction and apology were forthcoming, the U.S. would terminate diplomatic relations. In a special message to Congress (25 Jan. 1892) Harrison virtually asked for a declaration of war. The Chilean government submitted an official apology, and the incident was closed with the payment of an indemnity of $75,000.

1892

29 Feb. BERING SEA DISPUTE. The U.S. acquisition of the Pribilof Islands as a result of the Alaska purchase led to an Anglo-American controversy concerning jurisdiction over pelagic (i.e., ocean) sealing in the Bering Sea. The U.S., which exercised jurisdiction within the 3-mile limit, leased sealing rights to a private company. As the commercial value of sealskins rose, pelagic sealing vessels of other nations (principally Canada) began to operate in the waters beyond the 3-mile limit. The dispute was touched off when U.S. revenue cutters seized Canadian pelagic sealers in the Bering Sea (1886).

On 2 Mar. 1889 Congress empowered the president to take steps to protect U.S. rights and declared U.S. dominion over the waters of the Bering Sea. In a note to the British government (22 Jan. 1890), Secretary of State Blaine characterized its course as just short of piracy. In reply, British foreign secretary Lord Salisbury stated that Great Britain would hold the U.S. "responsible" for acts contrary to "established principles of international law." An Anglo-American arbitration treaty (29 Feb.) referred the question to a mixed international tribunal (French, Swedish, and Italian), whose decision (15 Aug. 1893) denied the U.S. claim to exclusive rights to a closed sea; provided for the assessment of damages against the U.S.; and prohibited pelagic sealing in a 60-mile zone around the Pribilof Islands for a specified period during each year. This protective regulation remained in force until 1908. The controversy was terminated with the payment (16 June 1898) of $473,151 by the U.S. to Great Britain.

1893

30 Mar. Senate confirmation of the appointment of Thomas F. Bayard as U.S. ambassador to Great Britain, first American to hold that rank.

HAWAIIAN QUESTION. The most vital links between the U.S. and Hawaii were the Hawaiian sugar planters, mostly Americans. The planters, ranged against native dynastic interests, brought off a revolution (1887) that succeeded in securing a liberal constitution and a government under their influence. However, they lost power in 1891. Meanwhile, the McKinley Tariff Act of 1890, which put imported sugar on the free list and authorized a bounty of 2 cts. a lb. for home-grown sugar cane, wiped out the reciprocity advantages hitherto enjoyed by Hawaiian sugar planters and broke sugar prices, with an estimated loss of $12 million.

Queen Liliuokalani, exponent of a firm pro-native policy, came to the Hawaiian throne in 1891. She revoked the liberal constitution of 1887 and by royal edict (14 Jan.) promulgated a new constitution giving her autocratic powers. The Americans under the leadership of **Sanford B. Dole** (p. 1014), had already established a revolutionary committee of safety to overthrow the native government, with the apparent support of the U.S. minister to Hawaii, the proannexationist **John L. Stevens** (1820–95). He ordered U.S. marines to be landed from the cruiser *Boston* (16 Jan.), ostensibly to protect American life and property. Aided by the marines, the committee of safety occupied the government buildings; and Stevens, without permission from the State Department, recognized the revolutionary regime (17 Jan.). On 1 Feb. Stevens raised the U.S. flag over the government buildings and proclaimed Hawaii a U.S. protectorate. Dole became president of the new government.

On 15 Feb. a treaty of annexation (signed 14 Feb.) drawn up by diplomatic commissioners of the Hawaiian provisional government was submitted to the U.S. Senate. Chiefly because of Democratic opposition, the Senate failed to act on the treaty by the time Harrison left office. President Cleveland withdrew the treaty (9 Mar.) and appointed ex-Cong. James H. Blount (Ga.) as special commissioner to Hawaii to conduct a thorough investigation. Blount ordered the withdrawal of the marines and the lowering of the American flag. After an inquiry lasting 4 months, he reported that Stevens' conduct had been improper; that the majority of Hawaiians were opposed to annexation; and that the Hawaiian sugar planters and their U.S. associates had been the chief force behind the revolution, hoping to secure the sugar bounty through annexation.

Independence of the provisional government was recognized when President Cleveland sent Albert S. Willis as the new minister to Hawaii. Willis was instructed to take steps to restore Queen Liliuokalani to power, with the proviso that she assume the obligations of the provisional government, grant amnesty to its leaders, and sustain the constitution of 1887. In return, the provisional regime was to abdicate. Queen Liliuokalani acceded to Cleveland's request on 18 Dec. President Dole, however, refused to surrender power, pointing out that the provisional government had received U.S. recognition and that the U.S. had no right to interfere in the internal affairs of Hawaii. Cleveland was unwilling to employ force to carry through his policy. In a special message to Congress (18 Dec.) he condemned the means by which the provisional government had been brought into power and stated he would not again submit the annexation treaty to the Senate. On 4 July 1894 the Republic of Hawaii was proclaimed, and on 7 Aug. 1894 Cleveland formally recognized the new government.

1895

VENEZUELAN BOUNDARY DISPUTE. The controversy between Venezuela and Great Britain over the boundary line of British Guiana went back to 1814 when the British took over that possession from the Dutch. In 1840 a survey made by Sir Robert Schomburgk, a British engineer, was rejected by Venezuela, and the dispute remained unsettled. With the discovery of gold in the contested region, Great Britain withdrew its offer of the Schomburgk line and claimed areas west of it. In 1887 Venezuela broke off diplomatic relations with Great Britain and asked the U.S. to arbitrate, but the U.S. offer to use its good offices was rejected by the British (1887). In his annual message to Congress in 1894 Cleveland declared that he would renew his attempt to bring about arbitration. A joint congressional resolution (20 Feb.) approved Cleveland's recommendation. Again Great Britain refused to arbitrate.

Largely under the influence of Secretary of State Richard Olney, Cleveland based the U.S. position on a broad construction of the Monroe Doctrine. Olney sent a note (20 July) to the British government stating that British pressure on Venezuela would be regarded by the U.S. as a violation of the Monroe Doctrine and that peaceful arbitration (with U.S. intercession toward that end) was the only way of settling the controversy. The belligerent tenor of the dispatch was evident in this: "Today the United States is practically sovereign on this continent, and its fiat is law upon the subjects to which it confines its interposition. Why? . . . It is because, in addition to all other grounds, its infinite resources combined with its isolated position render it master of the situation and practically invulnerable as against any or all other powers."

The reply (26 Nov.) of Lord Salisbury, the British prime minister and foreign secretary, asserted that the Monroe Doctrine was not applicable to the boundary dispute and rejected the U.S. offer of arbitration. The diplomatic correspondence was laid before Congress (17 Dec.) by President Cleveland, who affirmed the applicability of the Monroe Doctrine and recommended the creation of an independent commission to determine the boundary. "When such report is made and accepted," said Cleveland, "it will . . . be the duty of the United States to resist by every means in its power, as a wilful aggression upon its rights and interests, the appropriation by Great Britain of any lands or the exercise of governmental jurisdiction over any territory which after investigation we have determined of right belongs to Venezuela."

The American outburst caught the British off guard. In the eyes of Great Britain, whose imperial preoccupations lay elsewhere, the Venezuelan dispute was a relatively minor matter. Furthermore, her rivalry with Germany and other powers in Africa and the Near East made American friendship desirable. This became doubly clear when Kaiser Wilhelm II sent to President Kruger of the Boer Republic an indiscreet congratulatory telegram (3 Jan. 1896) that offended the British. On 25 Jan. the British colonial secretary, Joseph Chamberlain, publicly asserted that war between the U.S. and Great Britain "would be an absurdity as well as a crime. . . . The two nations are allied and more closely allied in sentiment and interest than any other nations on the face of the earth."

The Venezuelan boundary commission (created by Congress in 1895) was appointed on 1 Jan. 1896. Presided over by Associate Justice **David J. Brewer** (1837–1910), and also including **Chief Justice Fuller** (p. 1035), it held its first meeting on 4 Jan. 1896. The British aided the U.S. authorities by furnishing data. A treaty signed by Great Britain and Venezuela (2 Feb. 1897) through the good offices of the U.S. provided for submitting the dispute to a board of arbitration, on which Brewer and Fuller also served. The awards (3 Oct. 1899) were in substantial accord with the original British claims and placed the boundary roughly along the Schomburgk line (Venezuela, however, being awarded the mouth of the Orinoco River).

CUBAN QUESTION. American interest in Cuba declined after the U.S. attempt (1875–76) to terminate the Cuban rebellion (1868–78), but was revived following the outbreak (24 Feb.) of the native insurrection against Spanish rule. Added to Spanish oppression as a cause of revolt was the severe impact upon the sugar economy of the panic of 1893 and the high protective Wilson-Gorman Tariff of 1894. American sympathy favored the rebels. Financial contributions from Americans aided Cuban juntas (committees of revolutionists) in organizing filibustering expeditions on American soil, but these ventures were blocked by the U.S. navy and revenue service.

The revolutionists followed a policy of widespread and thorough destruction of sugar plantations and mills (in which American interests had extensive holdings), hoping by this method to induce U.S. intervention and to break the will of the Spanish rulers. The task of suppressing the uprising was assigned to Gen. Valeriano ("Butcher") Weyler, who established (after 10 Feb. 1896) concentration camps where he indiscriminately confined revolutionists, sympathizers, and neutrals, including women and children, many of whom became victims of disease, semistarvation, and ruthless treatment. American sympathy for the rebels was fanned by the "yellow press" (William Randolph Hearst's New York *Journal* and Joseph Pulitzer's New York *World*).

By concurrent resolution, the Senate (28 Feb. 1896) and the House (6 Apr. 1896) called for the U.S. to accord belligerent rights to the Cuban revolutionists and offer its good offices to Spain for the recognition of an independent Cuba. Spain declined the U.S. offer (22 May 1896).

1898

RELATIONS WITH SPAIN. The liberal Sagasta ministry, which came into power at Madrid (Oct. 1897), made important concessions on Cuban policy (25 Nov. 1897), including the recall of Gen. Weyler, a measure of autonomy, release of imprisoned U.S. nationals, and reform of the concentration camp policy. These concessions satisfied neither the insurrectionists nor the loyalists in Cuba. Loyalists at Havana held a violent demonstration (12 Jan.) condemning Weyler's recall and the grant of autonomy. The yellow press in the U.S. renewed its attack on Spain. Within the Republican party a group of younger politicians (including Theodore Roosevelt and Henry Cabot Lodge), who regarded Cuba as the key to domination of the Caribbean and favored expansionism, called for a firm attitude.

9 Feb. DE LÔME LETTER, written by the Spanish minister to the U.S., Dupuy de Lôme, was published (9 Feb.) in Hearst's N.Y. *Journal.* This was a private communication that had been stolen from the mails in Havana and released to the Hearst press by Cuban revolutionists in the U.S. Dupuy de Lôme called President McKinley "weak and a bidder for the admiration of the crowd, besides being a would-be politician who tries to leave a door open be-

hind himself while keeping on good terms with the jingoes of his party." De Lôme immediately cabled his resignation to the Spanish government.

15 Feb. SINKING OF THE "MAINE." After the Havana riot of 12 Jan., the U.S. battleship *Maine* was ordered to Havana harbor, ostensibly to protect American life and property. On 15 Feb. at 9:40 P.M. the *Maine*, while at anchor in the harbor, was destroyed by an explosion which killed 260 officers and men. The Navy Department appointed a court of inquiry (17 Feb.). Although the government urged the public to reserve judgment, the yellow press attributed the disaster to enemy agents and demanded U.S. intervention in Cuba. "Remember the *Maine!*" became a popular slogan. Congress without dissent voted a $50 million defense appropriation (9 Mar.).

The naval court of inquiry reported (21 Mar.) that the *Maine* had been destroyed by the explosion of a submarine mine, but was "unable to obtain evidence fixing the responsibility . . . upon any person or persons." Despite strong pressure from the public, Congress, and a prowar group within the Republican party, the McKinley administration followed an antiwar policy. The U.S. minister to Spain, Stewart L. Woodford, was instructed (27 Mar.) to notify the Madrid government that the U.S. had no territorial ambitions in Cuba and that it sought the following: a Cuban armistice until 1 Oct. and the revocation of the concentration camp policy. On the latter point, Spanish agreement came on 5 Apr., and on 9 Apr. the Spanish yielded to the U.S. demand for an armistice. This information was cabled to McKinley on 10 Apr.

11 Apr. McKINLEY'S WAR MESSAGE. Swayed by the powerful demand for war in and out of Congress, McKinley reversed his antiwar policy even before learning of the Spanish concessions. His message to Congress asked for the "forcible intervention" of the U.S. to establish peace in Cuba.

20 APR. WAR RESOLUTION. Congress adopted a joint resolution that (1) recognized the independence of Cuba; (2) demanded the withdrawal of the Spanish armed forces; (3) empowered the president to use the army and navy to carry out these demands; and (4) disclaimed any intention on the part of the U.S. to exercise sovereignty or control over Cuba, asserting that the government and control of the island would be left to its people after peace had been restored. (This last clause was the **Teller Amendment.**) McKinley signed the war resolution on 20 Apr.; and on the same day a formal ultimatum was served on Spain to the effect that if she did not grant Cuban independence and quit the island, the U.S. would take the necessary steps to carry the joint resolution into effect. On 21 Apr. Spain broke diplomatic relations with the U.S.; 22 Apr. the U.S. inaugurated blockade of Cuban ports; 24 Apr. Spain declared war against the U.S.; 25 Apr. formal U.S. declaration of war against Spain, made retroactive to 21 Apr.

The Spanish-American War, 1898

BALANCE SHEET. The opening of the war found the U.S. modern "steel navy" in an advanced state of readiness and efficiency. The navy consisted of about 2,000 officers and 24,000 men. The preparations of the Asiatic squadron, based at Hong Kong under the command of Commodore **George Dewey** (p. 1012), were enhanced by a secret order (25 Feb.) sent by Assistant Secretary of the Navy **Theodore Roosevelt,** who instructed Dewey to keep his fleet intact and to engage the Spanish fleet in the Philippines should war break out. In contrast, the U.S. army, consisting of about 2,100 officers and 28,000 men, was ill-prepared. Its high command, training, and equipment were inadequate, and it lacked proper supply and medical services for waging a tropical campaign. Congress authorized (22 Apr.) a volunteer force of 200,000 men, and approved (26 Apr.) an increase of the regular army to 60,000. The decisive battles of the war were naval engagements. On this score, the U.S. enjoyed the advantage, for the Spanish navy was outmoded in armament and had poorly trained crews.

1 MAY. BATTLE OF MANILA BAY. Dewey's Asiatic squadron at Hong Kong consisted of 4 cruisers (*Olympia, Boston, Baltimore,* and *Raleigh*) and 2 gunboats (*Petrel* and *Concord*). This force departed from Mirs Bay, China (27 Apr.), with orders to capture or destroy the Spanish squadron thought to be in Manila Bay under the command of Adm. Montojo. The U.S. squadron entered Manila Bay on the evening of 30 Apr. The Spanish fleet (consisting of 10 vessels, including cruisers and gunboats) lay off Cavite Point. Early on the morning of 1 May the U.S. fleet laid down a powerful broadside, methodically raking the Spanish line from end to end. The battle, beginning 5:40 A.M., was over in 7 hours. The Spanish suffered 381 men killed; all of the Spanish craft were destroyed, silenced, or captured. None of the American ships was damaged; U.S. casualties: 8 wounded.

13 AUG. FALL OF MANILA. Lacking the necessary support for land operations, Dewey imposed a blockade on

Manila Bay. Gen. Wesley Merritt was ordered (11 May) to the Philippines to support Dewey and take Manila. Merritt arrived at Manila Bay (25 July) with the final American contingent, bringing the total U.S. military strength there to 10,700 men. Dewey and Merritt sent (9 Aug.) the Spanish commander at Manila a formal demand for surrender. U.S. troops, reinforced by Filipino guerrillas under Gen. Emilio Aguinaldo, assaulted and occupied Manila (13 Aug.). On 14 Aug. Gen. Merritt received the Spanish capitulation and proclaimed the military occupation of the Philippines.

SPANISH FLEET IN CUBA. The blockade of Cuba was assigned to Rear Adm. **William T. Sampson** (along the northern shores) and Commodore **Winfield S. Schley** (along the southern shores). Sampson moved at once to hunt out the Spanish fleet; it was known that the enemy ships would have to recoal at Cuba or Puerto Rico after making the transatlantic voyage. Schley did not leave Key West until 19 May and did not arrive off Santiago de Cuba until 28 May. His delay gave the Spanish fleet its opportunity.

Commanded by Adm. Cervera, the Spanish force departed from the Cape Verde Islands (29 Apr.) and entered the harbor of Santiago de Cuba (19 May), where it lay under the protection of land batteries. Cervera's fleet of 4 cruisers and 3 destroyers was bottled up by Schley's force (29 May). Adm. Sampson arrived at Santiago (1 June) and assumed command of the blockading squadron. The capture or destruction of the Spanish fleet was the main task confronting the U.S. navy.

14 JUNE. CUBAN EXPEDITION. A land force of 17,000 regulars and volunteers, including the "Rough Riders" (the first U.S. Volunteer Cavalry Regiment under Col. **Leonard Wood** and Lt. Col. **Theodore Roosevelt**), was marshaled at Tampa, Fla., awaiting the end of the tropical rains before undertaking the invasion of Cuba. Commanded by Gen. **William Shafter,** this force was improperly trained, organized, and equipped. When the U.S. navy blockaded the enemy fleet at Santiago, Shafter was ordered to reinforce Sampson and seize the port. The expeditionary force sailed from Tampa on 14 June.

1 JULY. BATTLES OF EL CANEY AND SAN JUAN HILL. Shafter's force arrived off Santiago on 20 June and 2 days later began disembarking at Daiquiri and Siboney Bay, to the east of their main objective. Unloading operations were completed on 26 June; on 30 June the force began its march on Santiago. In the day-long battle of El Caney (1 July) about 7,000 U.S. troops took a strongly fortified village garrisoned by about 600 of the enemy. In the battle of San Juan Hill (1 July), in which the dismounted Rough Riders under Col. Theodore Roosevelt took part, the Americans seized the position under heavy fire. At a total cost of 1,572 casualties, the U.S. succeeded in winning command of the heights to the east and north of Santiago and were now in position to place the city and the Spanish fleet under artillery bombardment.

3 JULY. DESTRUCTION OF THE SPANISH FLEET. Sampson's blockading force outside Santiago harbor consisted of the battleships *Indiana, Iowa, Massachusetts, Oregon,* and *Texas,* and the cruisers *New York* and *Brooklyn.* Adm. Cervera, who was under orders not to surrender, decided to make an attempt to escape to the open sea. On the morning of 3 July the Spanish fleet left the harbor and tried to run the U.S. blockade. In a battle along the coast that lasted about 4 hours, the enemy fleet was destroyed by the superior fire of American guns. The Spanish losses, 474 killed and wounded, 1,750 taken prisoner; the

U.S. casualties, 1 killed, 1 wounded. The destruction of the Spanish fleet virtually terminated the war. Santiago and its garrison of 24,000 troops surrendered on 17 July.

7 JULY. ANNEXATION OF HAWAII. While Cleveland remained in the presidency, he checked all attempts to annex Hawaii. His successor, McKinley, favorably disposed to annexation, negotiated a new treaty of annexation (signed 16 June 1897), but Democratic and anti-imperialist Republican opposition in the Senate delayed its ratification. When the Japanese government protested against the treaty, McKinley pressed even harder for ratification. During the Spanish-American War Hawaii's use as a naval installation lent emphasis to its strategic value and brought increased demand for annexation. In order to preclude defeat under the rule requiring a two-thirds vote for ratification by the Senate, the treaty was accepted by a joint resolution of Congress, which required a simple majority vote (pp. 617, 1014).

4 AUG. Disease and food poisoning took such a high toll of U.S. troops in Cuba that the War Department instructed the Cuban expeditionary force to embark for Montauk Point, L.I. Such conditions, both in Cuba and in army camps in the U.S., were among those investigated by a commission appointed (8 Sept.) to inquire into the conduct of the war.

10 DEC. TREATY OF PARIS. On 26 July the Spanish government, making its approach through Jules Cambon, French ambassador at Washington, requested the U.S. to name peace terms. A protocol signed on 12 Aug. provided for a peace treaty to be concluded at Paris and terminated hostilities on the following terms: Spain was to relinquish Cuba, and cede Puerto Rico and one of the Ladrone Islands to the U.S.; and the U.S. was to hold and occupy Manila pending the conclusion of a peace treaty that would determine the disposition and control of the Philippines.

When the peace commission met at Paris (1 Oct.), U.S. policy on the Philippines was vague and divided. Guided by economic, strategic, and humanitarian considerations, McKinley decided to demand the cession of the Philippines. The demand, made by the U.S. commissioners on 1 Nov., encountered strong Spanish opposition; but with the conclusion of the treaty (10 Dec.), the Spanish agreed to cede the Philippines to the U.S. for a payment of $20 million. Spain surrendered all claim and title to Cuba and agreed to assume the liability for the Cuban debt amounting to about $400 million. As indemnity, Spain ceded Puerto Rico and Guam to the U.S. (pp. 622, 624).

WAR COST. Of the more than 274,000 officers and men who served in the army during the Spanish-American War and the period of demobilization, 5,462 died in the various theaters of operation and in camps in the U.S. Only 379 of the deaths were battle casualties, the remaining being attributed to disease and other causes. The total wounded was 1,604. The immediate cost of the war was about $250 million.

1899

TREATY FIGHT (pp. 619–620).

20 MAR. OPEN DOOR POLICY. Growing political and military weakness of China revealed during and after the Sino-Japanese War (1894–95) left her powerless to resist the demands of foreign powers for political and economic concessions in the form of leaseholds and spheres of influence. In 1898 and 1899 the British made overtures to the U.S. with a view to securing Anglo-American guarantees of equal commercial opportunity in China, but these proposals were rejected as contrary to the established U.S. policy of noninvolvement. But the U.S., despite the fact that its trade with China was relatively small, was disturbed by the possibility that the foreign powers might establish discriminatory tariffs and other commercial barriers in the Chinese regions under their influence.

The Open Door policy of securing equal commercial opportunity was more English than American in its origin. It was chiefly the work of Alfred E. Hippisley, a British citizen who had served in the Chinese customs service; and its fundamental idea had already been publicized in *The Break-up of China,* an influential book by Lord Charles Beresford, who visited the U.S. in 1899. Hippisley's views reached the U.S. administration through the offices of W. W. Rockhill, private adviser to Secretary of State **John Hay** (p. 1054) on Far Eastern affairs. Hippisley drafted a memorandum (17 Aug.) that was revised by Rockhill (28 Aug.) and accepted by Hay (5 Sept.). In his circular letter of 6 Sept., Hay instructed the U.S. embassies at Berlin, St. Petersburg, and London (and subsequently those at Paris, Rome, and Tokyo) to request formal assurances from each power as regards their respective spheres of influence in China: (1) that each power would in no way interfere with any treaty port or vested interests; (2) that the existing Chinese treaty tariff would apply to such spheres of interest, and the duties would be collected by the Chinese government; and (3) that no power would discriminate in favor of its own subjects regarding railroad charges and harbor dues. The various powers gave evasive and qualified replies, but Hay saw fit to construe their answers as approval of his proposals. He announced (20 Mar. 1900) that the acceptance of the Open Door policy was "final and definitive."

18 MAY–29 JULY. 1st HAGUE CONFERENCE, called at the invitation of Czar Nicholas II of Russia (24 Aug. 1898) to consider disarmament, the limitation of methods of warfare, and the creation of machinery for the arbitration of international disputes, was participated in by 26 nations, including the U.S. The conference failed to enlist the support of most of the nations on the prohibition of certain instruments of war (e.g., poison gas and balloon-launched missiles) or disarmament, but established the **Permanent Court of International Arbitration.** The U.S., which lent its weight to securing such a body, signed a convention (29 July) providing for the peaceful settlement of international disputes by the following means: mediation by a third party, international commissions, and the international tribunal at The Hague. It was stipulated, however, that arbitration was not to be compulsory and was not to extend to any question involving national honor or integrity. In addition, the U.S. delegation insisted on a reservation concerning disputes involving application of the Monroe Doctrine.

2 DEC. PARTITION OF SAMOA. Continuing differences among the U.S., Germany, and Great Britain after 1889 created dissatisfaction with the tripartite protectorate over Samoa which did not survive the outbreak of native warfare over succession which followed the death of King Malietoa in 1898. In the disorder which ensued, U.S. and British naval vessels bombarded Apia, landed sailors, and suffered casualties. In 1899 Germany proposed the partition of the islands. By the Anglo-German treaty of 14 Nov., the Samoan Islands were divided between the U.S. and Germany, with Britain surrendering her claims in return for (1) rights in West Africa and elsewhere in the Pacific, and (2) relinquishment by Germany of rights in certain areas of Samoa. Several islands, including Tutuila (with its harbor of Pago Pago), went to the U.S.; the islands of Upolu and Savaii went to Germany. This agreement was confirmed by a treaty signed (2 Dec.) by the U.S., Germany, and Great Britain, and ratified (16 Jan. 1900) by the Senate. (See also p. 626.)

1900

BOXER REVOLT. In the spring of 1900 an aggressively antiforeign group of Chinese revolutionists known as Boxers rose in revolt to expel the "foreign devils" from China. The Boxers occupied Peking and laid the foreign legations under siege. An international expedition that included U.S. troops relieved Peking (14 Aug.). Secretary of State Hay, fearing that the foreign powers would use the Boxer incident as a pretext to abandon the Open Door policy and carve up China, dispatched a circular letter (3 July) stating it to be the policy of the U.S. "to seek a solution which may bring about permanent safety and peace to China, preserve Chinese territorial and administrative entity [an elaboration of the Open Door], protect all rights guaranteed to friendly powers by treaty and international law, and safeguard for the world the principle of equal and impartial trade with all parts of the Chinese Empire."

The **Boxer Protocol** (7 Sept. 1901) provided a total indemnity of $332 million. The U.S. share was set at $24,500,-000, but the U.S. subsequently accepted $4 million to satisfy private claims, eventually remitting the unpaid balance for the purpose of educating Chinese students in the U.S.

1901

2 MAR. PLATT AMENDMENT. At the end of the Spanish-American War Cuba remained under the control of a U.S. military administration headed by Gen. Leonard Wood. Cuban finances were reorganized and a public health and sanitation campaign (in which Dr. **Walter Reed** [p. 1136] and Maj. **William C. Gorgas** [p. 1043] figured) succeeded in exterminating the yellow-fever menace. While the U.S., by the Teller Amendment (1898), had disclaimed all intention of exercising sovereignty over Cuba, it feared that rapid and complete withdrawal might jeopardize Cuban political stability and threaten American strategic and financial interests.

Gen. Wood was instructed to authorize the Cubans to call a constitutional convention. The convention met on 5 Nov. 1900 and ultimately adopted a constitution based upon that of the U.S., but made no provisions for continuing future relations with the U.S. At the behest of Secretary of War Root, Wood informed the convention that the withdrawal of American control was conditional upon the adoption of such provisions. These provisions, known as the Platt Amendment, were incorporated in the Army Appropriation Bill and sponsored by Sen. Orville H. Platt (Conn.), though most of the clauses were drawn up by Secretary Root. Its more important provisions: (1) Cuba would never enter into any treaty with any foreign power impairing Cuban independence; (2) the Cuban government would not contract any public debt in excess of the capacity of its ordinary revenues to discharge; (3) the U.S. was authorized to intervene to preserve Cuban independence and maintain law and order; and (4) Cuba agreed to sell or lease to the U.S. lands necessary for naval or coaling stations. In effect, the amendment gave the U.S. a quasi-protectorate over Cuba.

The Cuban convention appended the amendment to the constitution (12 June); the U.S. withdrew from Cuba (20 May 1902); and, to preclude its elimination by the amending power, the Platt Amendment was incorporated into a treaty between the U.S. and Cuba (22 May 1903). The amendment was abrogated on 29 May 1934 (p. 386).

18 Nov. HAY-PAUNCEFOTE TREATY. U.S. pressure for the modification of the Clayton-Bulwer Treaty to secure exclusive control over an isthmian canal resulted in the signing (5 Feb. 1900) of the first Hay-Pauncefote Treaty. Great Britain agreed to renounce all joint rights to a canal which the U.S. was to construct, control, and maintain. The U.S. pledged to maintain the neutrality of the canal and was forbidden to fortify it. The treaty was ratified by the Senate (20 Dec. 1900); an amendment permitting U.S. fortification as well as other changes proved unacceptable to the British (Mar. 1901). Because of mounting difficulties with Germany and Russia, Great Britain was anxious to remain on friendly terms with the U.S. Following negotiations in Apr., the second Hay-Pauncefote Treaty was concluded (18 Nov.) and ratified by the Senate (16 Dec.). It abrogated the Clayton-Bulwer Treaty; permitted the U.S. to construct and control the canal; stipulated that neutrality would be maintained under U.S. auspices; and provided that the canal was to be free and open to ships of all nations on equal terms. In a memorandum of 3 Aug. the British conceded the right to fortify the canal.

1903

22 Jan. HAY-HERRAN CONVENTION. With the ratification of the Hay-Pauncefote Treaty, Congress had to choose between Panama (then a province of Colombia) and Nicaragua as the route for the isthmian canal. At first, on the recommendation of the Walker Commission (16 Nov. 1901) the Nicaraguan right of way was favored, chiefly because the New Panama Canal Co., successor to the bankrupt De Lesseps venture, asked the exorbitant price of more than $109 million for its holdings and franchises. But when the Panama Co. (4 Jan. 1902) lowered its price to $40 million, the commission recommended (18 Jan. 1902) the Panama rather than the Nicaragua route. Congress passed the Spooner Act (28 June 1902), stipulating 2 conditions for the construction of a Panama Canal: (1) purchase of the property and rights of the New Panama Canal Co. (for which Congress made an appropriation of $40 million), and (2) a Colombian grant to the U.S. of perpetual control over the right of way. The act, which also established the Isthmian Canal Commission, authorized the president, if negotiations for the Panama route failed, to purchase the Nicaraguan route.

It was now necessary to obtain an agreement whereby Colombia would relinquish sovereignty over the proposed Panama canal zone. The Hay-Herran Convention provided that in return for a payment of $10 million and an annual rental of $250,000 the U.S. would receive a 99-year lease (with option of renewal) over a canal zone 6 miles in width. Under this arrangement Colombia was not to receive any part of the money paid to the Panama Co. The convention was ratified by the U.S. Senate; after much delay, it was rejected by the Colombian Senate (12 Aug.). The Colombians, who wanted at least $25 million, believed that by deferring action until after Sept. 1904 (expiration date of the New Panama Canal Co.'s charter), they could then receive the full price offered by the U.S. The Colombian Senate adjourned (31 Oct.) without having taken further action.

PANAMA REVOLT. Colombia's effective rejection of the Hay-Herran Convention aroused the strong displeasure of President Roosevelt, who for a time contemplated recommending the forcible seizure of Panama. On 3 Nov. the province of Panama rose in revolt and declared itself independent of Colombia. The revolution was accomplished by native groups and foreign promoters linked to the Panama Co. who acted with the tacit approval of the Roosevelt administration. Even before the revolution broke out, Roosevelt ordered (2 Nov.) U.S. warships to Panama to maintain "free and uninterrupted transit" across the isthmus, guaranteed by the Treaty of New Granada (1846). On 6 Nov. the U.S. recognized the Republic of Panama and on 13 Nov. formally received Philippe Bunau-Varilla (a onetime associate of the New Panama Canal Co.) as minister from Panama.

18 Nov. HAY–BUNAU-VARILLA TREATY granted to the U.S. in perpetuity the use and control of a canal zone 10 miles wide across the Isthmus of Panama, giving it full sovereignty (including the right of fortification) over that zone as well as all rights to the holdings of the New Panama Canal Co. and the Panama R.R. Co. The neutrality of the zone was to be maintained in conformity with the Hay-Pauncefote Treaty. The U.S. guaranteed the independence of Panama and agreed to pay $10 million and an annual fee of $250,000 beginning 9 years after the exchange of ratifications. The treaty was ratified by the Senate on 23 Feb. 1904 (p. 627).

ALASKAN BOUNDARY DISPUTE arose after the Klondike gold rush of 1896 showed that the Alaskan Panhandle (lying in U.S. territory) commanded the water routes to the goldfields. The Canadians invoked the Anglo-Russian Treaty of 1825 to support their contention that the shoreline ran in such a fashion as to give them practical control of the important harbors of the Alaskan Panhandle (the Canadians maintained that the boundary followed the outer edges of the promontories; the U.S. claimed it followed the heads of the bays and inlets).

The U.S. and Great Britain signed (24 Jan.) a convention providing for a joint tribunal of 3 Americans and 3 Britons to arbitrate the questions. When the tribunal met at London, its U.S. membership comprised ex-Sen. George Turner (Wash.), Sen. Lodge, and War Secretary Root (hardly an impartial trio); its British representation consisted of 2 Canadians and Lord Alverstone, the Lord Chief Justice of England. During the tribunal's deliberations (3 Sept.–20 Oct.) President Roosevelt intimated that if the U.S. did not receive satisfaction, it would employ military force in the disputed area. This was among the first demonstrations of "big stick" diplomacy (a term derived from a statement made by Roosevelt in 1900: "I have always been fond of the West African proverb: 'Speak softly and carry a big stick, you will go far.' ").

The U.S. claims were given a 4–2 majority when they were upheld by Lord Alverstone. The award ran a line excluding Canada from the ocean inlets of the Alaskan Panhandle.

1904

6 Dec. ROOSEVELT COROLLARY. During the rule of the dictator Cipriano Castro, Venezuela was plunged into heavy debt to European investors. Castro's unwillingness to meet these financial obligations led the European powers to consider taking forcible action, but they were mindful of the Monroe Doctrine, as indicated by the German memorandum to the State Department (Dec. 1901) disclaiming any intention of permanent occupation. At this time President Roosevelt did not regard such intervention as a violation of the Monroe Doctrine, for in his first annual message (1901) he observed that the U.S. did "not guarantee any State against punishment if it misconducts itself, provided that punishment does not take the form of acquisition of territory by any non-American power."

When Castro refused to submit the claims of the foreign powers to arbitration by the Hague Tribunal, Great Britain and Germany imposed a blockade (Dec., 1902) subsequently joined by Italian warships. Following the bombardment of Venezuelan ports and the destruction of Venezuelan naval craft, Castro asked Roosevelt to propose arbitration by the U.S. minister to Venezuela. This proposal was transmitted by Roosevelt (12 Dec. 1902) to Great Britain and Germany. Both powers accepted the principle of limited arbitration, and the matter was settled by the Hague Tribunal in 1904.

Similarly burdened by debts to European powers was the Dominican Republic, whose financial obligations were serviced chiefly by customhouse receipts pledged to various creditors (with the provision that default would permit the creditors to demand control of the customhouses). Political instability pointed to the likelihood of default by Santo Domingo. A proposal by Belgium (17 Oct. 1903) that the U.S. join in seizing all customhouses and provide for the governing of Santo Domingo by an international commission was refused by the U.S. A change in the Dominican regime brought into power a ruler (Gen. Morales) willing to accede to the U.S. administration of the customhouses.

The situation came to a head in 1904

when the debts payable to an American firm were given a preferred position over those owed to other creditors. The protests of European investors foreshadowed armed intervention, as in Venezuela. To forestall a threat to U.S. interest in the Caribbean, Roosevelt proclaimed in his annual message the dictum later known as the Roosevelt Corollary to the Monroe Doctrine (by which he transformed the doctrine from one of nonintervention by European powers to one of intervention by the U.S.): "Chronic wrongdoing, or an impotence which results in a general loosening of the ties of civilized society, may in America, as elsewhere, ultimately require intervention by some civilized nation, and in the Western Hemisphere the adherence of the United States to the Monroe Doctrine may force the United States, however reluctantly, in flagrant cases of such wrongdoing or impotence, to the exercise of an international police power."

The corollary was one of the outstanding examples of Roosevelt's "big stick" diplomacy. Santo Domingo signed an agreement with the U.S. (1905) providing for the U.S. administration of the customs and management of debt payments. Roosevelt carried out the protocol despite the fact that it was rejected by the Senate. A permanent treaty including the protocol in revised form was ratified (25 Feb. 1907) and on 31 July 1907 the U.S. withdrew from Santo Domingo.

1905

ROOSEVELT AND THE RUSSO-JAPANESE WAR. The Russo-Japanese War (10 Feb. 1904) jeopardized the Open Door policy. Roosevelt was perturbed by complaints of American commercial interests that the Russian advance into Manchuria endangered the Open Door. In a circular note (20 Feb. 1904) the U.S. asked the belligerents to respect "the neutrality" and "administrative entity" of China. However, each made its acceptance conditional upon the other's, and Russia went so far as to reject the proposed neutralization of Manchuria.

In Roosevelt's view, the complete defeat of either Russia or Japan was not desirable, since it would upset the balance of power in the Far East and endanger U.S. interests. On 25 Apr. Japan informed the U.S. that it would maintain the Open Door in Manchuria and restore that province to China. After the Japanese victory over the Russian fleet at the Battle of Tsushima Strait (27–29 May), the Japanese government formally asked Roosevelt (31 May) to take the initiative in acting as mediator. Roosevelt's proposal was accepted by Russia (6 June) and on 8 June he formally invited both powers to open joint negotiations.

In the interim, the secret Taft-Katsura Memorandum was concluded (29 July) by Secretary of War Taft, then on a mission to the Philippines, and the Japanese foreign minister. It stipulated that the U.S. would not interfere with Japanese ambitions in Korea in return for a Japanese promise to disclaim territorial conquest in the Philippines. This executive agreement was endorsed by Roosevelt (31 July) despite his earlier insistence on a Japanese pledge of support for the Open Door policy. The Japanese construed the Taft-Katsura Memorandum as U.S. approval of a Japanese protectorate over Korea (proclaimed 21 Dec.).

9 Aug. PORTSMOUTH PEACE CONFERENCE (held at the navy yard at Portsmouth, N.H.) was concluded by a Russo-Japanese peace treaty signed 5 Sept. Japan secured recognition of her dominant rights in Korea and, through the acquisition of Russia's Liaotung leasehold and the South Manchurian Ry.,

consolidated her economic and territorial position in Manchuria. Partly because of Roosevelt's opposition, the Japanese failed to obtain an indemnity and all of the island of Sakhalin (only its southern half was ceded to Japan). For his work as mediator, Roosevelt was awarded (1906) the Nobel peace prize.

1906

16 Jan. ROOSEVELT AND THE ALGECIRAS CONFERENCE. Since the turn of the century France had been engaged in securing agreements with Italy, Great Britain, and Spain looking toward the establishment of a French protectorate over Morocco, in return for recognizing the interests of these powers elsewhere in North Africa. German opposition to French ambitions and to the economic partition of North Africa grew stronger, particularly after the conclusion of the Anglo-French Entente (1904). Tension was heightened after Kaiser Wilhelm II made a speech at Tangier (31 Mar. 1905) proclaiming support of Moroccan independence.

Germany demanded an international conference on Morocco and asked Roosevelt to secure French participation. Although reluctant to intervene, Roosevelt feared that a Moroccan crisis might touch off a general European war. Through Roosevelt's efforts, France and Great Britain agreed to attend a conference at Algeciras, Spain, with U.S. delegates in attendance. Roosevelt was instrumental in securing German acceptance of the settlement (Act of Algeciras, 7 Apr.) affirming the independence and territorial integrity of Morocco, guaranteeing equality of commercial opportunity, establishing an international bank for the stabilization of Moroccan finances, and providing for the training and control of the Moroccan police by France and Spain. The Algeciras convention was ratified by the U.S. Senate (12 Dec. 1906) with the proviso that such approval was not to be construed as departure from the traditional U.S. policy of noninvolvement in purely European affairs.

RELATIONS WITH JAPAN. By the treaty of 1894 citizens of the U.S. and Japan were permitted mutual free entry, although both governments were empowered to protect domestic interests by legislating against excessive immigration of laborers. Because of American protests, Japan inaugurated a policy of voluntary limitation of emigration (Aug. 1900), but this move failed to halt the flow of emigrant laborers to Hawaii, Canada, or Mexico, whence entry to the U.S. could not be effectively controlled. The growth of anti-Japanese antagonism led West Coast labor to organize a Japanese and Korean Exclusion League (1905). Similar pressures, coinciding with the increasing fear of Japan as a military power ("the Yellow Peril"), resulted in a movement for the statutory exclusion of Japanese.

11 Oct. SAN FRANCISCO SCHOOL SEGREGATION. The San Francisco schools, disrupted by the earthquake and fire (18–19 Apr.), were reopened in July. On 11 Oct. the school board ordered the segregation of all Japanese, Chinese, and Korean children in a separate Oriental school. The Japanese government (25 Oct.) charged that the board's action violated the treaty of 1894. Faced with an impending international crisis, Roosevelt invited the San Francisco School Board to Washington for a conference (Feb. 1907), and effected an arrangement whereby the segregation order would be rescinded locally but the federal government take action on the immigration question. The result was an amendment to the Immigration Act of 1907 (20 Feb.) authorizing the president to exclude from the

U.S. immigrants holding passports to any country other than the U.S., any insular possession of the U.S., or the Canal Zone, and attempting to use such passports to enter the U.S. to the detriment of internal "labor conditions." By executive order (14 Mar.) Roosevelt put this authorization into effect.

"GENTLEMEN'S AGREEMENT" was embodied in a Japanese note (24 Feb. 1907) whereby Japan promised to withhold passports from laborers intending to migrate to the U.S., and recognized the American right to refuse admission to Japanese immigrants using passports originally issued for travel to any country other than the U.S. The San Francisco School Board order was formally rescinded 13 Mar. 1907. However, it was not until 18 Feb. 1908 that a Japanese note provided the basis for the effective restriction of immigration. To offset any Japanese surmises that the concessions extended by the U.S. in the Far East signified a fear of Japan, Roosevelt sent the bulk of the U.S. Navy on a world cruise (16 Dec. 1907–22 Feb. 1909) which demonstrated that the U.S. was now the 2d naval power in the world (Japan ranked 5th).

1907

15 June–15 Oct. 2D HAGUE PEACE CONFERENCE. Called by the Czar of Russia, this meeting, attended by 46 nations, was originally suggested by President Roosevelt in 1904 but had been postponed because of the Russo-Japanese War. The U.S. efforts for the establishment of a world court were unsuccessful. Of particular interest to the U.S. was the adoption by the conference of a revised version of the **Drago Doctrine** (reinforcing the Monroe Doctrine), which had been formulated (29 Dec. 1902) by Luis M. Drago, foreign minister of Argentina, during the dispute over the collection of the Venezuelan debts. The essence of the doctrine was that armed force must not be employed by a European power to collect national debts owed by American nations to foreign creditors.

PANAMA CANAL. Preliminary work on the Panama Canal was virtually halted in 1905 because of the heavy mortality rate caused by disease. In addition, opinion was divided over a sea-level canal as opposed to a lock canal. The sanitation program carried out under Col. **William C. Gorgas** of the U.S. Army Medical Department sharply reduced the deaths caused by malaria and yellow fever and enabled a long-term construction program under safe conditions. President Roosevelt signed a bill (29 June 1906) authorizing the construction of a lock canal. With the reorganization of the Canal Commission (1 Apr.), the entire project was placed under the direct authority of the Secretary of War. Appointed as chief engineer was Lt. Col. (later Col.) **George W. Goethals** (p. 1042) of the U.S. Army Corps of Engineers, under whose immediate direction the canal was built. The Panama Canal, 40.3 miles from shore to shore, links Cristobal, on the Caribbean, with Balboa, the Bay of Panama terminus. The total cost of original construction was more than $365 million. The canal was opened to traffic 15 Aug. 1914.

14 Nov.–20 Dec. CENTRAL AMERICAN PEACE CONFERENCE. The outbreak of war in Central America (19 Feb., involving Honduras, Nicaragua, and El Salvador, and dispatching of U.S. marines (Mar.) to protect American interests) prompted Secretary of State Root to propose, in conjunction with Mexico, the meeting of a peace conference in Washington under terms of treaty of peace signed by Central American nations 25 Sept. 1906. The participating powers were Costa Rica, Guatemala, Honduras, Nicaragua, and El Salvador. The U.S. was not a signatory party. The 8 conventions concluded by the conference included a general treaty of peace and amity and the establishment of a Central American Court of Justice (20 Dec.).

1908

30 Nov. ROOT-TAKAHIRA AGREEMENT, was an executive agreement concluded by an exchange of notes (30 Nov.) between Secretary of State Root and Ambassador Takahira. Carrying a step further the concession granted by the Taft-Katsura Memorandum, it provided that Japan and the U.S. would (1) maintain the "existing *status quo*" in the Pacific, (2) respect the territorial possessions belonging to each other in the Pacific, (3) uphold the Open Door policy in China, and (4) support by peaceful means the independence and integrity of China. The phrase "existing *status quo*," was interpreted by Japan as U.S. recognition of Japan's paramount imperialist influence in Korea and southern Manchuria.

1909

TAFT'S FAR EASTERN POLICY. President Taft and his Secretary of State, Philander C. Knox, reaffirmed the Open Door with a policy subsequently known as "**Dollar Diplomacy**"—increasing U.S. trade by supporting American enterprises abroad, and including Latin America as well as the Far East.

Shortly after Taft's inauguration an international consortium composed of French, British, and German bankers took steps to float a loan for building the Hukuang Railways in southern and central China. At the suggestion of the State Department an American banking group was organized to finance railroad concessions in China. The bankers' agent, Willard Straight, who played a dominant role in Far Eastern "Dollar Diplomacy," unsuccessfully asked the European interests for admission to the consortium. Only after Taft took the unprecedented step of making a personal appeal (15 July) to the Chinese regent, Prince Chun, was American participation permitted in a 4-power consortium agreement (signed on 20 May 1911). American bankers had already declined Straight's proposal (1909–10) to build a rail line in northern Manchuria. As a direct result of this attempted U.S. penetration of Manchuria, Russia and Japan concluded a treaty (4 July 1911) staking out spheres of influence in deliberate defiance of the Open Door. This treaty weakened U.S. prestige in the Far East. Japan's position in Manchuria was strengthened by the fact that France and Great Britain favored giving Japan a free hand there in order to safeguard their own spheres of influence elsewhere in the Far East.

Despite these setbacks, Secretary Knox encouraged the Chinese government to request (22 Sept. 1910) a large loan to underwrite currency reform in China and industrial development in Manchuria. Japan and Russia registered their opposition, and U.S. bankers announced that they would not be bound to participate in contracts objectionable to other powers. Although a 6-power consortium was established (20 June 1912), the final agreement was signed (26 Apr. 1913) without U.S. participation. Eager to avoid further commitments in China, American bankers informed President Wilson (5 Mar. 1913) that they would remain active there only under official pressure. Wilson withdrew U.S. support of the consortium (18 Mar. 1913) on the ground that its terms endangered China's "administrative independence." This step terminated the Taft-Knox pol-

icy in the Far East. The coming of World War I shifted U.S. interest to Europe and permitted Japan to expand at China's expense.

1910

7 Sept. NEWFOUNDLAND FISHERIES. The continuing controversy over the North Atlantic fisheries was finally resolved after the U.S. and Great Britain agreed (27 Jan. 1909) to submit the question to the Hague Tribunal. The decision was a compromise award upholding the Newfoundland claim to local regulation and authorizing the provisions of the rejected Bayard-Chamberlain Treaty (1888) pertaining to the definition of territorial bays. The award was confirmed by an Anglo-American convention (20 July 1912).

1911

U.S. INTERVENTION IN NICARAGUA. Nicaragua was the object of special U.S. interest because of the disturbing possibility that its canal route might fall under foreign control. In 1909 José S. Zelaya, an opponent of foreign penetration, was deposed as dictator of Nicaragua. The ensuing political turmoil brought to the presidency (1911) Adolfo Díaz, whose friendly policy toward the U.S. matured in the **Knox-Castrillo Convention** (6 June). This agreement gave the U.S. the right of intervention and provided for refunding of the national debt, payment to be secured by a customs receivership under U.S. protection. On 1 July the Nicaraguan government defaulted on a loan made by a British syndicate. Without waiting for the Senate to act, Knox persuaded a group of New York bankers to implement the treaty's provisions before formal ratification. The Senate adjourned without taking any action. Desperate for financial aid, the Nicaraguan government secured a loan of $1,500,000; in return, the U.S. bankers received control of the National Bank of Nicaragua and the government-owned railway. Customs receipts were pledged in payment, collection to be carried out under American auspices. The Knox-Castrillo Convention was rejected by the Senate, as was a similar one made with Honduras.

When native dissatisfaction with the agreement touched off a Nicaraguan revolt, the U.S. intervened. A force of marines was landed (14 Aug. 1912) to protect American interests. Knox then attempted to negotiate a treaty granting the U.S., in return for a payment of $3 million, the exclusive right of way for an interoceanic canal, a 90-year lease of the Great Corn and Little Corn Islands in the Caribbean, and a naval base on the Gulf of Fonseca. The Senate failed to act on this agreement. To insure the regular operation of the financial arrangements, a small detachment of marines remained in Nicaragua until 1925, and did not finally leave until 1933.

7 JULY. PELAGIC SEALING AGREEMENT. The controversy regarding pelagic sealing in the North Pacific persisted after Blaine's unsuccessful attempt to deal with it, and became acute as the steadily dwindling herds of seals were threatened with extinction. In 1911 a 4-power conference on the sealing industry was called at Washington and, participated in by the U.S., Great Britain, Russia, and Japan, agreed to a treaty, to continue in force subject to one year's notice, which outlawed for 15 years pelagic sealing north of the 30th parallel, established a U.S. monopoly of the catch, and authorized an allocation of profits to Great Britain and Japan in return for their withdrawal from pelagic sealing in the area. Japan abrogated the convention on 23 Oct. 1940.

CANADIAN RECIPROCITY. Anxious to forestall the breakup of trade with Canada, threatened in retaliation against the Payne-Aldrich Tariff of 1909, the Taft administration signed a reciprocity agreement (26 Jan.) providing for the reduction or elimination of duties on many Canadian items, chiefly agricultural commodities, and for reduced rates on U.S. manufactures. Because it involved fiscal matters, the agreement was subject to approval by both houses of Congress. The House approved, as did the Senate (22 July), despite opposition from Midwestern agricultural interests; but when Taft and several Congressmen publicly referred to the reciprocity agreement as a prelude to the U.S. annexation of Canada, national feeling was aroused in Canada. In the elections of 1911 the Liberal party, in favor of the agreement, was defeated by the antireciprocity Conservatives (21 Sept.), ending for the time being Canadian-American reciprocity.

ARBITRATION TREATIES. The arbitration treaties which Secretary of State Root negotiated (1908–09) with 25 nations, providing for the referral of controversies to the Hague Tribunal, were weakened by reservations concerning disputes involving national interests, honor, and independence. When Taft became president, he made efforts to obtain arbitration agreements of a more general character. The impetus was provided by the Anglo-Japanese Alliance, by which Great Britain was bound to aid Japan in the event of war. The U.S. was anxious to employ diplomatic means to restrain Japan. An opportunity arose with the renewal (13 July) of the Anglo-Japanese Alliance containing a proviso that neither nation would fight a third power with whom a general arbitration treaty was in force. The U.S. signed such treaties (3 Aug.) with Great Britain and France, but these agreements were vitiated by amendment in the Senate (which ratified them on 7 Mar. 1912), where Sen. Henry Cabot Lodge (Mass.) led the fight for reservations on matters involving Oriental exclusion and the Monroe Doctrine, and for determination by the Senate of the character of controversies before their submission to arbitration.

1912

2 Aug. LODGE COROLLARY. In 1911 it became known that a Japanese syndicate was conducting negotiations for the purchase of a large site near strategic Magdalena Bay, Lower California. The negotiations came to an end when the State Department registered its disapproval. A Senate resolution introduced by Lodge declared the U.S. viewed with "grave concern" the possession of strategically important areas "by any corporation or association which has such a relation to another Government, not American, as to give that Government practical power of control for national purposes." The Lodge Corollary extended the Monroe Doctrine's scope to non-European powers and to foreign companies as well as foreign nations.

1913

24 Apr. BRYAN'S "COOLING OFF" TREATIES. As early as 1905 William Jennings Bryan recommended that the U.S. take the initiative in establishing a system of arbitration providing for the referral of all international differences to a permanent court of arbitration. Shortly after becoming Secretary of State, he negotiated with 30 nations separate treaties (differing in detail, but similar in their broad features) providing for the referral of all international disputes, without exception, to a permanent investigating commission. Resort to armed conflict was prohibited until the commission submitted its report within a year. Twenty-one ratifications were finally exchanged.

MEXICAN REVOLUTION. Since 1877 Mexico had been almost without interruption under a dictatorship headed by President Porfirio Díaz, who had granted foreign investors liberal concessions for the development of Mexican resources including oil, mines, land, and railways. By 1913 a total of some $2 billion (of which more than half came from the U.S.) had been invested by foreign interests. A revolution led by the democratic reformer, Francisco I. Madero, broke out Nov. 1910. Americans were compelled to abandon their holdings and flee the country; some lost their lives. The revolution culminated in Díaz' resignation (25 May 1911) and the establishment of a liberal government.

The Taft administration recognized the Madero regime and embargoed the shipment of munitions to Madero's opponents; for the rest, the U.S. adhered to a policy of nonintervention. Madero was assassinated (22 Feb.) by agents of the reactionary Gen. Victoriano Huerta, who seized power and held it amid revolutionary upheaval. European powers recognized Huerta, but President Taft refused recognition despite pressure by American business interests.

When Wilson became president, he decided to follow a policy of cooperating with only such governments as rested upon the undoubted consent of the governed. In a speech (11 Mar.) he tacitly disapproved of Huerta and indicated the termination of Dollar Diplomacy with the announcement that the U.S. would not lend support to special interests. After a revolution headed by Venustiano Carranza gathered force, Wilson proposed an immediate armistice, to be followed by a free election in which Huerta should not be a candidate. In return the U.S. would encourage American bankers to extend loans to the Mexican government.

Huerta's refusal (16 Aug.) evoked from Wilson a policy of "watchful waiting" and the application of a strict arms embargo. Huerta dissolved the Mexican Congress (10 Oct.) and was elected president (26 Oct.). American business interests renewed their demand for intervention, but Wilson, in a speech delivered at Mobile, Ala. (27 Oct.), asserted that the U.S. "will never again seek one additional foot of territory by conquest."

Wilson applied sharper pressure in a note (7 Nov.) requesting Huerta's retirement from power. The Mexican ruler was further notified (24 Nov.) that it was the policy of the U.S. to isolate him from material aid and foreign sympathy, and to force him out of office. Early in 1914 Wilson lifted the arms embargo to permit munitions to reach the opponents of Huerta and stationed U.S. naval units off Vera Cruz to block the entry of European shipments of war materials to the Huerta regime.

1914

9–21 Apr. TAMPICO AND VERA CRUZ INCIDENTS. An unarmed party from the U.S.S. *Dolphin,* one of the vessels stationed in Mexican waters, went ashore at Tampico (9 Apr.) to secure supplies, and by error entered a restricted area. Despite the cover of the U.S. flag, they were arrested by Huerta's troops on the charge of violating martial law. Although they were released promptly, with apologies from a superior officer, Adm. Henry T. Mayo peremptorily demanded that the port commander apologize formally, promise to punish the responsible officer, and hoist

the American flag ashore, giving it a 21-gun salute. Mayo made these demands without consulting Washington, but the Wilson administration felt that he must be supported to preclude Huerta's exploitation of the incident. However, Huerta succeeded in evading the salute, despite a warning that a refusal would probably result in intervention.

Congress granted (22 Apr.) Wilson's request for permission to use force to uphold U.S. rights and secure redress of grievances. Meanwhile, U.S. forces had already landed on Mexican soil. Informed that a German ship was approaching with munitions, Bryan advised Wilson (21 Apr.) to use the navy to prevent delivery. On 21 Apr. the American forces bombarded Vera Cruz and occupied the city. Huerta promptly broke off diplomatic relations with the U.S. The incident united Mexican opinion behind Huerta and brought Mexico and the U.S. close to war.

20 May–30 June. ABC CONFERENCE. Wilson accepted the offer of the ABC Powers (Argentina, Brazil, and Chile) to mediate the dispute. At a meeting at Niagara Falls, Ontario, attended by representatives of the U.S., Mexico, and the ABC Powers, the mediators proposed the retirement of Huerta, establishment of a Mexican provisional government in favor of agrarian and political reforms, and no indemnity to the U.S. for occupation costs at Vera Cruz. This plan, agreed to 24 June, was rejected by Mexico, but its moral effect was instrumental in compelling Huerta to leave office (15 July). The U.S. occupation forces withdrew from Vera Cruz (23 Nov.) and on 19 Oct. 1915 the U.S. and several Latin-American nations recognized Carranza as *de facto* president.

15 June. PANAMA TOLLS ACT. On 24 Aug. 1912, Congress passed the Pan-

ama Canal Act, exempting U.S. coastwise shipping from payment of tolls, in
apparent contravention of the Hay-
Pauncefote Treaty provision that the
canal should be free and open to the
vessels of commerce and of war of "all
nations" on terms of entire equality. The
British protested on the ground that "all
nations" should include, rather than exclude, the U.S. American supporters of
the act (which was approved by both
major parties in the election of 1912)
maintained that the equality provisions
referred to uniformity of rates. Disturbed by the charges of bad faith
brought against the U.S., Wilson recommended (5 Mar.) repeal of the tolls
exemption. Repeal passed the Senate on
11 June. Settlement of the controversy
helped win British backing for the U.S.
course in Mexico. The Panama Canal
was officially opened to traffic on 15 Aug.

4 Aug. U.S. NEUTRALITY. With the
outbreak of World War I (Germany declared war on Russia 1 Aug., on France
3 Aug., and invaded Belgium 3 Aug.;
Britain declared war against Germany
4 Aug.), President Wilson issued a proclamation of neutrality. On 19 Aug. he
publicly appealed to Americans to be
"impartial in thought as well as in action."

**6 Aug. CONTROVERSY OVER
NEUTRAL RIGHTS.** Great Brtain justified her blockade of Germany by the
"unusual" conditions of warfare. Secretary Bryan asked the belligerents (6
Aug. 1914) to accept the Declaration of
London (drafted in 1909 and signed by
the leading powers but not ratified) as a
code of naval warfare. Because its guarantees gave the Central Powers their
only chance for large-scale trade with
neutrals, they promptly accepted, conditional upon enemy agreement. France
and Russia made acceptance conditional
upon Great Britain, whose position was

clarified by an order in council (20 Aug.
1914). The order, setting the pattern of
British trade regulation for the duration
of the war, accepted the declaration but
made exceptions to its contraband provisions, extending the list of conditional
contraband beyond the categories specified in the declaration.

A vigorous protest (26 Sept. 1914) by
the State Department was withheld at
the suggestion of Col. **Edward M. House**
(p. 1061), private diplomatic adviser to
President Wilson. The note sent instead
(28 Sept. 1914) stressed the evil effects
of British policy upon American public
opinion rather than neutral rights. When
the U.S. abandoned (22 Oct. 1914) its
efforts to make the Declaration of London effective, the British, in successive
orders in council (29 Oct., 23 Dec.
1914), further extended the contraband
list and revived the **doctrine of the continuous voyage** by proceeding to intercept neutral ships going to Germany and
to neighboring countries (Holland, Denmark, and the other Scandinavian nations,
which lay in the Baltic area under the
control of the German navy). This enabled the British to seize many goods
(especially foodstuffs) previously considered fair trade for neutrals. The British
declared (3 Nov. 1914) the North Sea
a military area and presently mined it
and proclaimed (11 Mar.) a blockade of
all German ports, with all merchant vessels bound for or coming from a German
port liable to seizure and confiscation.

**15 Aug. LOANS TO BELLIGER-
ENTS.** The U.S. government announced
that "loans by American bankers to any
foreign nation which is at war are inconsistent with the true spirit of neutrality."
This policy was modified (Oct.) at the
behest of **Robert Lansing** (1864–1928),
then counselor for the State Department.
Advised that the U.S. would not object to
short-term credits, the National City Bank

(4 Nov.) advanced $10 million to the French government. In Sept. 1915 Wilson reluctantly agreed to the floating of general loans by the belligerents, and on 25 Sept. 1915 a group of American bankers completed negotiations for a loan of $500 million to France and Britain. By Apr. 1917 U.S. investors had purchased $2,300 million in bonds from the Allies in contrast with only about $20 million in German bonds. U.S. trade with the Allies rose from c.$800 million (1914) to c.$3 billion (1916), while direct exports to Germany and Austria-Hungary dropped from $169,289,775 to $1,159,653.

1915

10 FEB. "STRICT ACCOUNTABILITY." The German government proclaimed (4 Feb.) the waters around the British Isles a war zone and announced that beginning 18 Feb. enemy merchant ships would be destroyed on sight in the forbidden area without provision for the safety of passengers and crew. Warning of the dangers resulting from the misuse of neutral flags and from the accidents of warfare, the German government declared that neutral craft entering the war zone would do so at their own risk. In contrast with the temporizing position on British interference with American rights on the high seas, the U.S. government registered a sharp protest (10 Feb.). The note stated that in the event American vessels or the lives of American citizens were destroyed by Germany on the high seas, the U.S. would view the act as "an indefensible violation of neutral rights" and hold Germany strictly answerable.

The German ambassador, Count Johann von Bernstorff, promptly urged the State Department to warn Americans against travel on belligerent ships, but his advice was not heeded. On 28 Mar. an American citizen perished in the sinking of the British liner *Falaba* in the Irish Sea. On 1 May the American tanker *Gulflight* was struck by a torpedo launched in a fight between a submarine and a British naval patrol off the Scilly Isles, causing the death of two Americans.

7 MAY. SINKING OF THE "LUSITANIA." The German embassy at Washington issued a warning (1 May) that Americans entering the war zone around the British Isles would do so at their own risk. On 7 May the British transatlantic steamer *Lusitania* was sunk off the Irish coast without warning by a submarine, with the loss of 1,198 lives, including 128 Americans. The ship's manifest subsequently revealed that the *Lusitania* carried some arms. The act precipitated a revulsion of public opinion against Germany.

13 MAY, 9 JUNE, 21 JULY. "LUSITANIA" NOTES. The first *Lusitania* note (13 May) was drafted by Wilson and signed by Bryan against his own inclination. It demanded that Germany abandon unrestricted submarine warfare, disavow the sinking of the *Lusitania*, and make reparation for the loss of U.S. lives. The note insisted upon the right of Americans to sail on the high seas and reiterated the "strict accountability" position. The German reply (28 May) excused the torpedoing on the ground that the *Lusitania* was armed and carried contraband (the vessel, in fact, was unarmed, but carried a shipment of rifles and cartridges). Wilson regarded the reply as evasive and unsatisfactory. A second note (also drafted by Wilson) took issue with the German contention that special circumstances imposed the necessity for unrestricted submarine warfare and demanded specific pledges. Bryan informed Wilson that he could not sign the note because he feared that it might involve the U.S. in war. His resignation, tendered on 7 June, was promptly accepted, and the second *Lusitania* note (9 June) was dispatched over the signature of Secretary Robert Lansing. The third note (21 July), virtually an ultimatum, warned Germany that a repetition of such acts would be regarded as "deliberately unfriendly."

24 July–1 Dec. GERMAN ESPIONAGE AND SABOTAGE. The U.S. Secret Service obtained possession of documents signed by Ambassador Bernstorff and Capt. Franz von Papen, revealing German sabotage activity in the U.S. Publication (beg. 15 Aug. in N.Y. *World*) led to the recall of the Austro-Hungarian Ambassador, Dr. Constantin Dumba (8 Sept.), and of the German attachés, Capts. Franz von Papen and Karl Boy-Ed (1 Dec.). On 30 July 1916 a munitions explosion on **Black Tom** Island, N.J., attributed to German sabotage, resulted in property loss of $22 million. On 11 Jan. 1917 an explosion wrecked the Canadian Car & Foundry plant at Kingsland, N.J. A Mixed Claims Commission (15 June 1939) found Germany guilty of both explosions, but Germany never paid the $55 million damage award.

19 Aug.–5 Oct. "ARABIC" CRISIS. Anxious to avoid the consequences of similar incidents, the German government privately instructed its submarine commanders (6 June) not to sink liners, even those under the enemy flag, without warning. When 2 American lives were lost in the sinking of the British steamer *Arabic* (19 Aug.), German Ambassador von Bernstorff rendered the so-called *Arabic* pledge (1 Sept.) on his own authority: "Liners will not be sunk by our submarines without warning and without safety of the lives of non-combatants, provided that the liners do not try to escape or offer resistance." During the remainder of 1915 the German U-boats concentrated on freighters in the Atlantic. The German government (5 Oct.) offered apologies and indemnity for the loss of American lives in the *Arabic* disaster, and this outcome was regarded as a diplomatic victory for the U.S.

INTERVENTION IN HAITI. A Haitian revolution raised Vibrun Guillaume Sam to power as president (5 Mar.), by which time Haiti's foreign debt had risen to c.$24 million. American financial interests held investments in the Haitian national bank and railroad, and the U.S., countering a Franco-German proposal (Mar. 1914) for joint customs, proposed a customs receivership. Following another revolution, resulting in the overthrow and assassination of President Sam (28 July), the U.S. marines, at Wilson's order, landed in Haiti (29 July) and imposed a military occupation. Sudre Dartiguenave, elected president (15 Aug.), signed a treaty (16 Sept.) by which Haiti became for all practical purposes a U.S. protectorate. The treaty, which went into effect for a 10-year period (with option of renewal) on 3 May 1916, stipulated that the Haitian public debt might not be increased, nor its tariff diminished, without U.S. consent.

1916

15 Mar. MEXICAN BORDER CAMPAIGN. Revolutionary opposition to Carranza was continued by a number of freebooting chieftains, particularly by **Pancho Villa** in northern Mexico. Villa was responsible for the deaths of Americans on both sides of the border. When 18 American engineers were invited by Carranza to return and operate the abandoned mines, Villa's band shot and killed them at Santa Ysabel (10 Jan.). Villa was also credited with repeated raids into Texas and New Mexico in the spring of 1916. A raid on Columbus, N.M. (9 Mar.), resulted in 17 deaths. Congressional pressure for intervention mounted, and Wilson was compelled to abandon his policy of "watchful waiting."

With Carranza's reluctant consent, Gen. John J. Pershing was ordered to head a punitive expedition of 15,000 men and pursue Villa into Mexico. Wilson called out 150,000 militia and stationed this force along the border. The pursuit of Villa (begun 15 Mar.) aroused the antagonism of Carranza and intensified anti-American feeling. Carranza refused to accept a proposal signed (24 Nov.) by joint commissioners of Mexico and the U.S. for withdrawal of U.S. troops and joint but independent guarding of the border. As war with Germany became imminent, Wilson finally withdrew the U.S. expeditionary force (Jan.–5 Feb. 1917). A new Mexican constitution was proclaimed (5 Feb. 1917), Carranza was elected president (11 Mar. 1917), and the U.S. extended *de jure* recognition to the new government.

LATIN-AMERICAN RELATIONS.

Nicaragua: Bryan-Chamorro Treaty (signed 5 Aug. 1914) perpetuated the Taft-Knox policy of Dollar Diplomacy. An unsuccessful attempt to insert Platt Amendment provisions delayed Senate ratification until 18 Feb. 1916. Nicaragua received $3 million in return for granting the U.S. exclusive rights to a canal route and a naval base. The U.S. secured a 99-year lease (with option of renewal) to the Great Corn and Little Corn Islands and to the Gulf of Fonseca. The treaty evoked the protests of Costa Rica and Salvador, both claiming that it infringed upon their territorial rights. An adverse decision of the Central American Court of Justice was disregarded by the U.S. and Nicaragua.

Intervention in Santo Domingo. The financial protectorate set up in Santo Domingo in 1907 temporarily relieved that country of political instability. But renewal of domestic disorders led to a further increase in the public debt. By Sept. 1912, revolutionary forces had seized 2 customhouses and laid 2 others under siege. The Dominican Republic accepted (June 1914) the temporary appointment of a new American official who exercised a check on expenditures; but when the U.S. minister again demanded (Nov. 1915) the acceptance of a financial adviser, the Dominican president was reluctant to comply. Internal disorder forced his resignation (May); partial occupation of the country followed; and U.S. officials began collecting internal revenue, putting the financial advisership into practical operation. Secretary Lansing recommended (22 Nov.) full military occupation of Santo Domingo. The occupation was proclaimed on 29 Nov. and an internal administration was established under U.S. naval officers, who remained in charge until 1924 (p. 381).

22 Feb. HOUSE MISSION AND MEMORANDUM. President Wilson, anxious to avoid U.S. involvement in the European war and concerned with the necessity of a negotiated peace, dispatched (Dec. 1914) his private adviser and close friend, Col. Edward M. House, as an unofficial emissary on a secret mission to the foreign offices of the major belligerent powers. House arrived in London (6 Feb. 1915), where he conferred with the British foreign secretary, Sir Edward Grey. These discussions were inconclusive, as were those held (Mar.–Apr. 1915) at Paris and Berlin. House again went to Europe and conducted (Jan.–Feb.) another series of discussions with British, French, and German statesmen. House proposed an understanding by which Germany would be granted

wider scope in colonial areas and overseas markets in return for a pledge to
reduce her naval construction. While the
scheme lacked precise formulation, it
proposed the following peace terms: the
restoration of Belgium and Serbia, the
cession of Alsace-Lorraine to France, and
of Constantinople to Russia. House's
conversations at London resulted in the
House-Grey Memorandum (22 Feb.),
which promised on Wilson's behalf that,
"on hearing from France and England
that the moment was opportune," the
president would summon a peace conference. Should Allied acceptance be followed by German refusal, the U.S. "would
probably enter the war against Germany." Wilson's endorsement (6 Mar.)
of the memorandum was communicated
to Grey 8 Mar. However, the Allies and
the Central Powers still believed that
they could break the military deadlock
by force of arms; hence, the U.S. proposal for a negotiated peace fell on deaf
ears.

**3–7 Mar. GORE-McLEMORE RESO-
LUTIONS.** A German declaration (8
Feb.) to the effect that all armed enemy merchant vessels would be sunk
without warning after 1 Mar. raised fears
in Congress that the further loss of
American lives on the high seas would
draw the U.S. into war and touched off
a revolt within Democratic ranks.

Rep. Jeff McLemore (Tex.) introduced a resolution (17 Feb.) requesting
the president to warn Americans not to
travel on armed vessels. At a stormy
White House conference with party
leaders (21 Feb.), Wilson made it clear
that he was adamant in his interpretation of U.S. rights. Construing the Mc-
Lemore resolution as a challenge to U.S.
sovereignty and a test of his presidential
leadership, Wilson informed the Senate
Committee on Foreign Relations (24
Feb.) that he could not "consent to any

abridgement of the rights of American
citizens in any respect. . . ."

Sen. Thomas P. Gore (Okla.) introduced a resolution (25 Feb.) to deny
passports to Americans seeking passage
on armed belligerent vessels and demanded protection of American trade
in noncontraband from the Allied restrictions. (In a direct challenge to the administration, this resolution was later
modified to read that the loss of American life because of the sinking of an
armed merchant vessel by Germany
"would constitute a just and sufficient
cause of war between the United States
and the German Empire"; by such a
positive declaration, the opponents of
Wilson's position hoped to embarrass the
administration.) Wilson decided (29
Feb.) to bring the fight over the resolutions to a head. Under pressure from
the White House, the Gore resolution
was tabled in the Senate (3 Mar.), 68–
14, and the McLemore resolution tabled
in the House (7 Mar.), 276–142.

24 Mar. "SUSSEX" AFFAIR. A secret German order (21 Nov. 1915) authorized submarine commanders to regard as troop transports that could be
sunk without warning all ships plying
the English Channel. A German submarine torpedoed (24 Mar.) the *Sussex,*
an unarmed French cross-channel passenger ship, causing injury to several
Americans. The U.S. regarded the attack as a violation of the *Arabic* pledge.
Secretary Lansing called for drastic action, informing President Wilson (27
Mar.) that he favored an immediate
severance of diplomatic relations with
Germany. Wilson resisted the pressure
for a break, and substituted an ultimatum (18 Apr.) that unless Germany
immediately abandoned its present
methods of submarine warfare, the U.S.
would sever relations. Germany agreed
(4 May) to the U.S. demands, but laid

down the countercondition that the U.S. compel the Allies to respect the "rules of international law." Wilson accepted the pledge, but refused (8 May) to accept the condition.

18 July. BRITISH BLACKLIST of 85 American individuals and firms (30 commercial firms) which because of suspected dealings with the Central Powers were to be denied the use of British banking, shipping, and cable facilities. Responding to U.S. public opinion, Wilson considered asking Congress to prohibit loans and cut exports to the Allies. Two retaliatory laws were passed. The **Shipping Board Act** (7 Sept.) empowered the president to deny clearance papers to any ship refusing to accept cargo from blacklisted firms. The **Revenue Act** (8 Sept.) authorized the president to withhold clearance or port facilities from any ship guilty of unfair discrimination against American commerce. However, these discretionary powers were never exercised, partly because the British government, under the pressure of this legislation, began to make concessions, and partly because Secretary of Commerce William C. Redfield reported (23 Oct.) that retaliation would invite counter-reprisals without guaranteeing the desired concessions. In addition, the naval appropriation of 1916, the largest in U.S. peacetime history to date, served as an implied warning to Great Britain.

2 Sept.–12 Dec. GERMAN PEACE OVERTURES. At the behest (2 Sept.) of Chancellor Theobald von Bethmann Hollweg, the German ambassador to the U.S., Count Bernstorff, inquired whether the good offices of the U.S. would be offered if Germany guaranteed the restoration of Belgium. Bernstorff was informed that President Wilson would not take any steps toward mediation until after the fall elections. By 25 Nov. Wilson had completed the first draft of his proposal for mediation and a program for an equitable peace, but the Allies were uncompromisingly hostile toward peace overtures. The fall of the Asquith cabinet in Great Britain (5 Dec.) and the accession of David Lloyd George as prime minister brought no change in policy. Before Wilson could release his peace proposal, the German government published a statement (12 Dec.) directed to all neutral powers announcing the willingness of Germany and the other Central Powers to enter immediately upon peace negotiations. The Allies declined the proposal because of the German refusal to state her peace terms.

18 Dec. WILSON'S PEACE NOTE to the belligerent powers was neither a peace proposal nor a mediation offer. It abandoned his proposed call for a general conference and put forward a simple request to both parties to state their war aims. The move was futile. The Germans refused a statement. An Allied joint reply (30 Dec.) rejected the German note of 12 Dec. In a joint note (10 Jan. 1917) to the U.S., the Allies outlined peace terms clearly unfavorable to the Central Powers: (1) the restoration of Belgium, Serbia, and Montenegro with appropriate indemnities; (2) the evacuation of the invaded territories of France, Russia, and Rumania with just reparations; (3) the restitution of territories or provinces taken from the Allies by force; (4) the liberation of Italians, Slavs, Rumanians, and Czecho-Slovaks from foreign domination; (5) the expulsion from Europe of the Ottoman Empire; and (6) the reorganization of Europe, guaranteed by a stable regime founded upon respect of nationalities and full security to all nations, great or small.

1917

17 Jan. PURCHASE OF THE VIRGIN ISLANDS. U.S. desire to annex the

Danish possessions in the Caribbean was heightened by fears that Germany had a long-standing ambition to use them as a naval base. By a treaty signed on 4 Aug. 1916, Denmark agreed to cede the Virgin Islands to the U.S. in return for $25 million (pp. 627–629).

22 Jan. "PEACE WITHOUT VICTORY." Shortly after receiving the Allied reply (10 Jan.) Wilson prepared his own program for a desirable peace settlement. In an address to the Senate (22 Jan.) he referred to the need for international organization as a guarantee of an enduring world peace and insisted upon "peace without victory."

1 Feb. RESUMPTION OF UNRESTRICTED SUBMARINE WARFARE. Early in 1917 the struggle between German civilian and military leaders over the unlimited use of the submarine came to a head. A conference at Pless (31 Aug. 1916) had agreed that the Supreme High Command of the German army should have the power to decide when the submarine campaign was to be opened. The leaders of the armed services agreed (Nov. 1916) that unless Germany's peace moves were successful, unrestricted U-boat warfare must be launched by the end of Jan. At a conference of political and military leaders, held (8–9 Jan.) at Pless, field headquarters of Gen. Paul von Hindenburg, Gen. Erich von Ludendorff supported the demand of the German admirals for resumption of unrestricted submarine warfare. Chancellor Bethmann Hollweg, spokesman of the civilian opposition, agreed reluctantly when it became apparent that the advantages likely to accrue (chiefly the destruction of the British means and will to fight) outweighed the dangers of U.S. entry into the war. Accordingly, Ambassador Bernstorff notified (31 Jan.) Secretary Lansing that, effective 1 Feb., submarine assaults against all neutral and belliger-

ent shipping would be renewed. The Germans specified that the U.S. would be permitted to send 1 ship to England each week, provided the vessel observed certain conditions set by the German government.

3 Feb. BREAK WITH GERMANY. The violation of the *Sussex* pledge made U.S. relations with Germany increasingly intolerable. On 3 Feb. U.S.S. *Housatonic* was sunk after warning. Wilson resisted (31 Jan.) Secretary Lansing's recommendation for a break, but soon made his own decision, and in an address to Congress (3 Feb.) announced the severance of diplomatic relations with Germany. He plainly implied that "actual overt acts" by the German government would bring positive steps by the U.S. A Senate resolution (7 Feb.) endorsed Wilson's action.

1 Mar. ZIMMERMAN NOTE was a code message (dated 19 Jan.) sent to Heinrich von Eckhardt, German minister in Mexico, by German foreign secretary Arthur Zimmermann. If war between Germany and the U.S. broke out, Eckhardt was to propose an alliance with Mexico on the following basis: "That we shall make war together and together make peace. We shall give generous financial support, and it is understood that Mexico is to reconquer the lost territory in New Mexico, Texas, and Arizona." Mexico was to urge Japan to switch to Germany's side. This message was intercepted and decoded by the British naval intelligence, and a copy given (24 Feb.) to **Walter Hines Page** (1855–1918), U.S. ambassador to Great Britain, who immediately transmitted it to the State Department, which, in turn, released it to the press (1 Mar.).

26 Feb.–13 Mar. ARMING OF U.S. MERCHANTMEN. Moving to prevent an overt act which would precipitate war with Germany, Wilson asked Congress (26 Feb.) for authority to arm American merchantmen in the hope of deterring submarines from attack. Publication of the Zimmermann note lent added force to his request. The House acted promptly (1 Mar.), passing the **Armed Ship Bill** by a vote of 403 to 13. In the Senate, however, a "little group of willful men" (as Wilson characterized these 7 Republicans and 5 Democrats) led by Robert M. La Follette filibustered the bill from 28 Feb. until the end of the session (4 Mar.). Wilson was then advised by Secretary Lansing (6, 8 Mar.) that under statute law he could arm merchant ships without the specific approval of Congress. The State Department announced (12 Mar.) that all American merchant vessels sailing through war zones would be armed. The Navy Department issued instructions (13 Mar.) authorizing such vessels to take action against submarines.

SUBMARINE TOLL. On 25 Feb., S.S. *Laconia* (British), with 2 U.S. dead, announced 26 Feb., day of Wilson's message to Congress; 12 Mar., S.S. *Algonquin*, unarmed, with warning; 16 Mar., sinkings reported of *City of Mem-*

phis, Illinois, and *Vigilancia;* 21 Mar., Standard Oil steamer *Healdton,* in safety zone off Dutch coast.

2 Apr. WILSON'S WAR MESSAGE. Secretary Lansing favored war with Germany, maintaining that U.S. participation would encourage the democratic elements within Germany and lend support to the new democratic government in Russia, where the March Revolution brought a provisional regime into power on the 12th. Wilson delayed his commitment. The unanimous advice of his cabinet (20 Mar.) for war was influential, and on 21 Mar. Wilson issued a call for a special session of Congress to convene on 2 Apr. In a message asking for a declaration of war Wilson condemned the German submarine policy as "warfare against mankind," stated that the U.S. was joining the fight for ultimate world peace, and declared: "The world must be made safe for democracy."

4–6 Apr. WAR RESOLUTION, which passed the Senate (4 Apr.), 82–6, was concurred in by the House (6 Apr.), 373–50.

The United States in World War I, 1917–18

6 Apr. U.S. DECLARATION OF WAR ON GERMANY. The joint congressional resolution declaring a state of war was signed by President Wilson. War against Austria-Hungary was declared on 7 Dec. During World War I the U.S. was not formally a member nation of the Allies. To the end of that conflict she was known as an "Associated Power" in a group of "Allied and Associated Powers."

MILITARY SITUATION. The U.S. entry into the war came when the prospects for an Allied victory had taken

a decided turn for the worst. The peak of the German destruction of Allied shipping (chiefly British) was Apr., when 881,000 gross tons were lost. Although the monthly losses declined thereafter, averaging about 200,000 tons a month over the following year, they still exceeded the Allied capacity for replacement. French failure in the Aisne and Champagne offensives (Apr.) caused a sharp drop in morale and led to mutinies in the French army. The Flanders offensive (June–Nov.) by the British was indecisive, and won little ground at the cost of enormous casualties. Brusilov's offensive (July), launched by the Russians, was smashed by the Germans; the defeat contributed to an upsurge of peace sentiment in Russia. Following the November Revolution (6–7 Nov.) the Bolsheviks negotiated a separate peace (**Treaty of Brest-Litovsk**, 3 Mar. 1918). Not only was Russia lost as a military ally, her defection enabled the release of masses of German troops for use on the Western Front. At the close of the year (Oct.–Dec.) the Italians suffered a crushing disaster in the Caporetto campaign, which gave northeastern Italy above Venice to the enemy. The Allies were reduced to defensive tactics, and the winter of 1917–18 saw a lull in military operations on the Western Front. At the outset of 1918, the balance of strength on land appeared to lie with the Germans. U.S. participation gave the Allies fresh resources of manpower, finances, raw materials, and munitions, and offset depressed morale.

U.S. MILITARY CONTRIBUTION. When war was declared, there were about 200,000 men in the army. During the war this number was expanded to 4 million. A total of 4,791,172 men served in the armed forces of the U.S. during World War I; of these, about 2,800,000 were inducted through Selective Service; 32 camps and cantonments, with facilities for 1,800,000 men, were built to carry out the training program. The number of American soldiers who went to France was 2,084,000. By May 1918, the U.S. had 500,000 men in France, and the peak of overseas movement was reached in July 1918, when 313,410 troops arrived in France. In all, 42 infantry divisions were sent to France (each division consisting of about 1,000 officers and 27,000 men). Of these, 29 took part in active combat (7 regular army, 11 national guard, and 11 national army), bringing to 1,390,000 the

number of men who saw active combat service.

AMERICAN EXPEDITIONARY FORCE (A.E.F.) was commanded by Gen. **John J. Pershing** (p. 1127). From June 1917 until 11 Nov. 1918, more than 4,400,000 tons of cargo were shipped directly to France for the A.E.F. Adm. **William S. Sims** (1858–1936) commanded the U.S. naval forces abroad. The navy, which had a wartime strength of about 50,000, convoyed troop transports, chased submarines, and aided the British fleet in keeping German craft out of the North Sea.

When General Pershing arrived at Paris (14 June) as commander of the U.S. overseas forces, his army was nonexistent (the first U.S. troops, units of the 1st Division, did not arrive in France until 26 June). Pershing's orders for cooperation with the Allied forces in operations against the enemy specified that the U.S. forces "are a distinct and separate component of the combined forces, the identity of which must be preserved." Against Allied opposition, Pershing vigorously maintained his demand for an integral U.S. army and a U.S. sector on the Western Front. He received the full support of Wilson to use his forces according to his own judgment. In July Pershing won Allied consent for concentrating the U.S. forces in eastern France, in the area east of Verdun known as the Toul sector. General orders issued on 5 July created the general staff of the A.E.F. On 1 Sept. Pershing established his general headquarters at Chaumont.

The first U.S. troops to go to the front were units of the 1st Division. They moved (21 Oct.) into the Toul sector, relieving French units holding the line. Pershing did not participate in the conversations (Nov.) that resulted in the creation (27 Nov.) of the Supreme War Council, on which civilian and military leaders served. This group, an inadequate attempt to unify the Allied military command, left the conduct and control of each army to its respective government. The Supreme War Council decided that it would be inadvisable to undertake an offensive until a sufficient number of U.S. troops arrived in France.

2 Nov. LANSING-ISHII AGREE-MENT. Japan joined (23 Aug. 1914) the Allies in the war against Germany and then attempted to expand her power in China and the North Pacific. Her policy of aggression was evident in the **21 Demands** on China (18 Jan. 1915). In revised form, these were embodied in a Sino-Japanese treaty (25 May 1915) by which Japan secured reluctant Chinese recognition of her position in South Manchuria and Shantung. This contributed to a renewal of U.S.-Japanese rivalry in the Far East and resulted in a U.S. note (11 May 1915) registering disapproval of the Japanese move and declaring that the U.S. would refuse to recognize any agreement impairing the political or territorial integrity of China, the Open Door policy, or the treaty rights of the U.S. in China.

The American position remained for some time the only foreign obstacle to Japan's realization of her objectives in China. To safeguard her territorial and economic ambitions, Japan took advantage of the submarine crisis and signed (1916–17) a number of secret treaties with the Allied powers designed to guarantee her succession to German rights in Shantung and the Northern Pacific islands. Her efforts to commit the U.S. to recognition of Japanese "paramount interests" in China resulted in the Lansing-Ishii Agreement.

Viscount Kikujiro Ishii was sent on a mission to Washington. Out of his discussions (6 Sept.–2 Nov.) with Secretary Lansing came an agreement by which the U.S. recognized that "territorial propinquity creates special rela-tions between countries, and consequently, the Government of the United States recognizes that Japan has special interests in China, particularly in the part to which her possessions are contiguous." Japan affirmed respect for the Open Door policy and the independence and territorial integrity of China.

Lansing viewed the agreement as a stopgap measure designed to prevent full recognition of Japan's position in China. But the terms of the agreement were ambiguous. According to the U.S. interpretation, Japan was conceded only an economic hold on China. The Japanese, on the other hand, construed the agreement as a political concession. When translated into Chinese the world "special" appeared as "paramount." Yet the agreement left the U.S. at the end of World War I as the only important nation holding reservations of this kind.

1918

8 Jan. 14 POINTS. The year 1917 was marked in Europe by a growing demand for a statement of war aims and a negotiated peace. In May the Kerensky government took office in Russia with a pledge to promote a peace based on the self-determination of peoples and without annexation or indemnities. Pope Benedict XV circularized (1 Aug.) the leaders of the belligerent powers, suggesting the following as a basis for a just and durable peace: renunciation of indemnities; disarmament; the substitution of arbitration for war; the evacuation of Belgium, and a guarantee for its complete independence; the evacuation of occupied territories; freedom of the seas; and the examination of territorial claims in a "spirit of equity and justice." The U.S. reply (27 Aug.) expressed the desire for a just peace but asserted that the word of the German government could not be accepted as a guarantee.

When, following the November Revolution in Russia, the Bolsheviks published the secret treaties concluded by the Allies and condemned these arrangements as evidence of imperialist designs, the need for a statement of Allied war aims became exigent. When an Interallied Conference at Paris (29 Nov.–3 Dec. 1917) was unable to agree upon such a statement, Col. House urged Wilson to issue a formulation. Lloyd George, in a speech (5 Jan.) before British labor representatives, announced his nation's war aims.

Addressing Congress (8 Jan.), Wilson set forth 14 points "as the only possible program" for peace from the U.S. standpoint. The address was based upon consultations with Col. House and a report furnished by a group of academicians and publicists called The Inquiry. **The 14 Points** were as follows: (1) open covenants of peace openly arrived at; (2) absolute freedom of navigation of the seas alike in peace and war, except as the seas might be closed by international action for the enforcement of international covenants; (3) removal, so far as possible, of all economic barriers and the establishment of equality of trade; (4) adequate guarantees that national armaments would be reduced to the lowest point consistent with domestic safety; (5) an absolutely impartial adjustment of all colonial claims, based on the principle that the interests of the population must have equal weight with the equitable claims of the government; (6) evacuation of all Russian territory and the independent determination by Russia of her own political development and national policy; (7) evacuation and restoration of Belgium; (8) evacuation and restoration of all French territory and return to France of Alsace-Lorraine; (9) readjustment of the Italian frontiers along clearly recognizable lines of nationality; (10) opportunity of autonomous development for the peoples of Austria-Hungary; (11) evacuation of Rumania, Serbia, and Montenegro, restoration of occupied territories, and free access to the sea for Serbia; (12) the Turkish portions of the Ottoman Empire to be assured a secure sovereignty, but the other nationalities under Turkish rule to be given free opportunity of autonomous development, and the Dardanelles to be permanently opened as a free passage to the ships of all nations under international guarantees; (13) establishment of an independent Poland, to include territories having an indisputably Polish population, with free and secure access to the sea; and (14) a general association of nations to be formed under specific covenants for the purpose of affording mutual guarantees of political independence and territorial integrity to great and small states alike.

21 Mar. GERMAN SPRING OFFENSIVE. The growing effectiveness of the British blockade and the lessening force of the U-boat campaign led the German military leaders to undertake a series of great offensives on the Western Front in the hope of decisively crushing the Allies before U.S. troops could arrive in force. The Germans enjoyed superiority of numbers in the West. The German assault, under the command of Gen. Ludendorff, was launched (21 Mar.) along a 50-mile front on the Somme battlefield, with the immediate objective of splitting the French and British armies at their junction point and breaking through to the vital rail center of Amiens and, ultimately, to the Channel ports. By 6 Apr. the Germans had smashed the lines of the British 5th Army and had penetrated the Allied lines to a depth of about 35 miles, advancing beyond Noyon and Montdidier and coming within 12 miles of Amiens with its vast stores of British supplies. In this action (also known as the Picardy offensive), approximately 2,200 U.S. troops served with the British and French.

The critical situation led the Allied statesmen and military leaders to confer (26 Mar.) at Doullens-en-Picardie, where Gen. **Ferdinand Foch** was assigned the task of coordinating the Allied armies on the Western Front. Wilson gave his approval (29 Mar.) to the Doullens agreement and on 14 Apr. Foch was formally appointed supreme commander for the Western Front. Although Gen. Pershing never yielded his intention of having a separate U.S. army with its own front, American units, at his decision (28 Mar.), were placed at the disposal of Foch and thrown into action wherever needed during the enemy spring offensive. However, the Beauvais agreement (3 Apr.) concluded by an Interallied Conference contained a reference to a separate U.S. army, which was endorsed at the conference (1 May) of the Supreme War Council at Abbeville.

9–29 APR. The attack upon Amiens had been only partly checked when the Germans struck again to the north in the Armentières sector and advanced for 17 miles up the Lys Valley; but the enemy was unable to exploit the wide gap in the British lines. About 500 Americans, serving with the British, participated in the Lys defensive.

27 MAY–5 JUNE. The next German drive was directed against the French front along the Chemin des Dames north of the Aisne. In this, the third battle of the Aisne, the line from Rheims to a little east of Noyon was forced back. Soissons fell (29 May), and the Germans reached the Marne (31 May) on a 40-mile front about 50 miles from Paris. At this critical moment the U.S. 2d Division and elements of the 3rd and 28th Divisions were thrown into the line. By blocking (3–4 June) the German advance at Château-Thierry, the Americans helped the French to stem the enemy drive.

6 JUNE–1 JULY. BELLEAU WOOD. The first sizable U.S. action of the war was fought when the 2d Division recaptured **Vaux, Bouresches,** and **Belleau Wood,** with the 4th U.S. Marine Brigade attached to the 2d Division playing a notable role. About 27,500 Americans were engaged in the third battle of the Aisne.

9–15 JUNE. The 3 enemy offensives established 2 salients threatening Paris, and the Germans now sought to convert them into one by a fourth massive blow delivered on a 27-mile front between Montdidier and Noyon. Even before the drive began the U.S. 1st Division demonstrated the fighting qualities of American troops by capturing (28 May) and holding the town of **Cantigny.** This first U.S. success reinforced the decision to permit Pershing to establish a separate army. In the Noyon-Montdidier offensive the French and Americans resisted firmly and the attack was halted after an initial German advance of about 6 miles. Throughout this operation the extreme left line of the salient was defended by the U.S. 1st Division. About 27,500 U.S. troops participated.

18 JULY–6 AUG. TURNING POINT: 2D BATTLE OF THE MARNE. On 15 July the Germans attacked simultaneously on both sides of Reims, the eastern point of the Aisne salient. To the east of Reims the Germans made slight gains; to the west they crossed the Marne, but made little progress. Stabilization of the Marne salient brought to an end the great German offensive. In this action some 85,000 American troops were engaged.

18 JULY–6 AUG. AISNE-MARNE OFFENSIVE. During the months of May and June more than 500,000 men were embarked from the U.S. for France, and in July the millionth American sol-

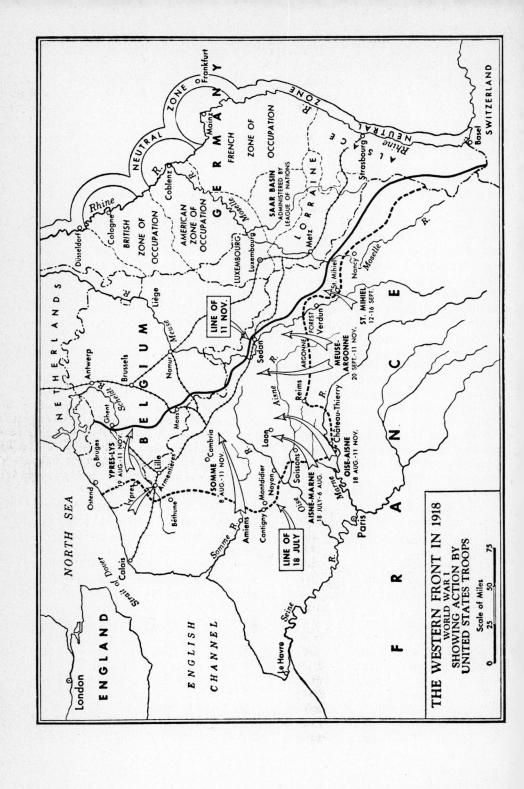

THE WESTERN FRONT IN 1918
WORLD WAR I
SHOWING ACTION BY
UNITED STATES TROOPS

Scale of Miles
0   25   50   75

dier arrived in France. The initiative passed from Ludendorff to Foch, who on 18 July launched his first counter-offensive, choosing as his point of attack the west flank of the German pocket from the Aisne to the Marne. About 270,000 U.S. troops, together with selected French units, were engaged in the Aisne-Marne offensive. When the operation was completed (6 Aug.), bringing to an end the 2d Battle of the Marne, the salient had been eliminated and the Allied line ran from Soissons to Rheims along the Vesle.

8 Aug. SOMME OFFENSIVE. The British, under Gen. Haig, struck at the Somme salient, initiating an offensive which, with intermittent lulls, lasted until 11 Nov. About 54,000 U.S. troops participated.

10 Aug. 1ST U.S. ARMY was organized, with Foch's consent, under the command of Gen. Pershing, who remained commander of the A.E.F.

18 Aug. OISE-AISNE OFFENSIVE was begun under Gen. Mangin, at the head of the French 10th Army. Starting from the Soissons-Rheims line, the French advanced by successive stages to the Aisne, to Laon, and on 11 Nov. were approaching the Belgian frontier. About 85,000 U.S. troops participated in the first stages of this advance, but by 15 Sept. all of these were withdrawn for the impending U.S. Meuse-Argonne offensive.

19 Aug. YPRES-LYS OFFENSIVE, launched by the British, lasted until 11 Nov. About 108,000 U.S. troops participated.

24 Oct.–4 Nov. BATTLE OF VITTORIO-VENETO on the Italian front ended in the rout of the Austrian army. About 1,200 U.S. troops participated.

12–16 Sept. ST. MIHIEL SALIENT. The first distinctively U.S. offensive was the reduction of the St. Mihiel salient, carried through largely by U.S. troops

and wholly under the command of Gen. Pershing. The Americans were aided by French colonial troops and by British and French air squadrons. St. Mihiel, on the right bank of the Meuse, was at the tip of a salient below Verdun (in French hands) to the northwest and Metz (in German hands) to the northeast. Within 24 hours after the offensive began, the salient had been cut off, and the completion of the operation removed a German threat of long standing. About 550,000 American troops were engaged at St. Mihiel; U.S. casualties: about 7,000. The Americans captured 16,000 prisoners and 443 guns. The operation demonstrated the ability of U.S. commanders and troops to plan and execute a major military undertaking.

26 Sept.–11 Nov. MEUSE-ARGONNE OFFENSIVE. After the St. Mihiel victory, U.S. troops were removed from the line and largely concentrated along a sector between the Meuse River and the Argonne Forest. Every available American division was employed. The goal of the American attack was the Sedan-Mézières railroad, main line of supply for the German forces on the major segment of the Western Front. Cutting this line would force a general retirement that would include German evacuation of the Briey and Longwy iron fields, which the enemy had been using to supplement its iron supply. The U.S. offensive, part of a larger advance planned by Foch to compel a general withdrawal by the Germans, involved 1,200,000 U.S. troops. Its first and middle stages comprised a battle of attrition. The final phase of the offensive began 1 Nov. Within a week, the Americans were in hot pursuit of the enemy east of the Meuse, while toward the north they reached the outskirts of Sedan and cut the Sedan-Mézières railroad, making the German line untenable. The armistice (11 Nov.) brought the offensive to a halt. The operation cost 120,000 U.S. casualties and resulted in the capture of 16,000 prisoners and 468 guns.

29 SEPT.–8 Nov. GERMAN PEACE MOVE. The rapid deterioration of the military position of the Central Powers during the summer of 1918 impelled Gen. Ludendorff, who foresaw imminent collapse, to press his government (29 Sept.) for an armistice. The situation became more critical with the surrender (30 Sept.) of Bulgaria. A new German regime headed by Prince Max of Baden took office on 2 Oct. and through Swiss auspices requested Wilson (6 Oct.) for an armistice preliminary to a conference which would use the 14 Points as a basis of peace. Austria made a similar request 7 Oct. Wilson spent about a month in negotiations. **Reasons for delay:** (1) Reluctance of the Allies to accept Wilson's war aims. The British pointed out that approval of the proposed armistice carried tacit acceptance of the 14 Points, and both the British and the French denied they had ever been asked to accept the 14 Points. However, a threat that the U.S. would take separate action finally compelled the Allies to accept (5 Nov.) the 14 Points as a basis for an armistice, but with 2 vital reservations. The Allies insisted upon reserving to themselves the unqualified right to discuss freedom of the seas in the peace conference, and they demanded that German restoration of evacuated territory include reparation for war damages to the civilian population. Wilson accepted these conditions and transmitted them to the German government (5 Nov.); thereafter responsibility for the truce was left to Gen. Foch. (2) Wilson's refusal to deal with a German government unless he was satisfied that it represented the German people. Following a mutiny in the German fleet that began at Kiel (3 Nov.), a revolution broke out (7 Nov.) in Bavaria. Austria had already

surrendered (4 Nov.). Kaiser Wilhelm II abdicated and fled from Germany (9 Nov.), and a German republic was proclaimed. Meanwhile, a German armistice commission met with General Foch in the Forest of Compiègne (8 Nov.).

11 Nov. ARMISTICE. Signing (5 A.M.) of the armistice brought the cessation of hostilities at 11 A.M.

The armistice terms were as follows: (1) German evacuation of occupied territory; (2) evacuation of the left bank of the Rhine and of the bridgeheads of Mainz, Cologne, and Coblenz; (3) reservation to the Allies and the U.S. of full right to make claim for damages; (4) surrender of submarines and internment of the German fleet; (5) abrogation of the treaties of Bucharest and Brest-Litovsk; (6) destruction of German aircraft, tanks, and heavy artillery; (7) maintenance of the Allied blockade until conclusion of the peace; (8) return of prisoners of war and deported civilians; and (9) 150,000 railway cars, 5,000 locomotives, and 5,000 trucks to be turned over to the Allies.

U.S. WAR COST. Total deaths for the U.S. armed forces (including army, navy, and marines) were 112,432—more than half caused by disease (chiefly the influenza-pneumonia pandemic that swept U.S. military camps). The battle casualties of the A.E.F. were 48,909 dead, 230,074 wounded. The total direct war expenditures (Apr. 1917–Apr. 1919), $21,850 million. (For loans to Allies, see pp. 379, 380, 383, 384.)

25 OCT. WILSON'S APPEAL TO THE ELECTORATE. Anxious that the position of the U.S. should not be weakened at the approaching peace conference, President Wilson decided to make the congressional elections a test of confidence in his policies. He issued an appeal to the voters to return a Democratic majority to both houses of Congress. The appeal evoked widespread disapproval the Republicans condemning it as a violation of Wilson's declared wartime truce on politics. The election (5 Nov.) resulted in the Democratic loss of the House by 50 seats and of the Senate by 2 seats.

REPUBLICAN OPPOSITION. Wilson's announcement (18 Nov.) that he would attend the peace conference provoked a storm of Republican criticism, as did the announcement that in addition to Wilson the U.S. peace commission would consist of **Col. House, Secretary Lansing, Gen. Tasker Bliss,** and **Henry White.** No member of the Senate was included, and the only Republican member was White. Wilson sailed for Europe 4 Dec. on the *George Washington.*

1918–20. U.S.–ALLIED INTERVENTION IN RUSSIA. Complicating the Allied problems of war and peacemaking was the abdication of Czar Nicholas II (12 Mar. 1917), the overthrow of the successor Provisional Government under Alexander Kerensky by the October Revolution (which began 7 Nov., or 25 Oct. by the old calendar), which led to Bolshevik control under **Vladimir Ilich Ulyanov,** known as **Nikolai Lenin** (1870–1924). The Bolsheviks signed a separate peace with Germany at Brest-Litovsk (3 Mar. 1918). In the winter of 1917–18 counter-revolutionary White armies began to form in peripheral areas of the former Russian empire. Fourteen Allied nations, including the U.S., originally sent forces to secure Allied war stores and to protect northern ports from possible German attack but later assisted anti-Bolshevik resistance groups. U.S. troops dispatched to areas in northern Russia near Archangel (2 Aug.) and Murmansk and to eastern Siberia (Vladivostok, 16 Aug.) were withdrawn from the former region in June 1919 and from Siberia 1 Apr. 1920 (while Japanese forces remained until Oct. 1922). Although Wilson refused to recognize the Soviet government, he induced the Allies to abandon their interventionist attempt. The Paris peace conference never dealt adequately with the problems posed by the Russian Revolution and the temporary vacuum of power in East Asia.

AMERICA BETWEEN TWO WORLD WARS, 1919-39

The twelve years following the close of World War I proved an age of isolation, as well as one of disillusionment and normalcy. It was marked by withdrawal from the responsibilities of world order, from America's commitments in the Pacific, and from political experimentation and reform at home. Emerging from World War I as the leading world power, the United States proceeded to dissipate that power. It withdrew from participation in the postwar settlement, refusing to join not only the League of Nations but the World Court as well. The era of negativism was followed by one of positive and dynamic leadership under the presidency of Franklin Delano Roosevelt. Before the recovery to which the New Deal was dedicated had been achieved, the shadow of totalitarianism fell across the land and lengthened with every passing day. Although an instinctive isolationist like Wilson, F.D.R. came to recognize that isolation was no longer a meaningful concept, but that the posture of the totalitarian forces threatened the free world and America's security. Reluctantly, during his second administration, Roosevelt began to shift gears, to move from a posture of neutrality, which had functioned with deplorable partiality, to some kind of intervention both in Europe and in Asia.

If the Republican ascendancy of the 1920s had been pervasively negative, that of the New Deal was overwhelmingly positive. "This nation asks for action, and action now," F.D.R. declared in his first inaugural address, and, beginning with 4 March 1933, action came thick and fast. "The Roosevelt Revolution" contained far less novelty than improvisation, as its program borrowed heavily from Populist-Progressive tenets, but the speed of improvisation was geared to the necessities of economic crisis and unprecedented unemployment. In fact, the six years from 1933 through 1938 marked a greater upheaval in American institutions than any similar period in the nation's history, save perhaps for the impact of the Civil War on the South. If the New Deal was not a new game, it was a necessitous reshuffle of the cards, too long stacked against labor, the farmer, the small businessman, the consumer, and the aged. It is a tribute to the staying power of New Deal reform that both parties in subsequent administrations have built upon without repudiating the fundamentals of the New Deal.

Foreign Relations

1919

18 JAN. BEGINNING OF THE PEACE
NEGOTIATIONS at Paris. All major
decisions were made by the "Big Four,"
Wilson, Georges Clemenceau (for
France), David Lloyd George (for Great
Britain), and Vittorio Orlando (for
Italy). Wilson's idealism was quickly
challenged. France and Britain were determined to punish Germany. France
wanted territorial concessions and reparations, as well as permanent military
security against Germany. In addition,
many of the provisions of the so-called
"Secret Treaties" entered into by the
Allies and known in broad outline to
American leaders shortly after America's
entry into the war ran counter to Wilsonian principles.

25 JAN.–14 FEB. DRAFT COVENANT
OF THE LEAGUE OF NATIONS.
Wilson insisted that the League must be
central to the peace negotiations, a position which the other Allies accepted only
after exacting serious concessions. On
25 Jan. the second plenary session voted
to include the League in the peace settlement. Beginning on 3 Feb., a commission, presided over by Wilson, worked
out a draft covenant submitted to the
plenary session on 14 Feb., based upon
the work of **David Hunter Miller** and
Lord Robert Cecil. Wilson then returned
to the U.S. on the *George Washington,*
arriving at Boston on 24 Feb. Opposition
was already mounting in the U.S. At a
dinner meeting between Wilson and
members of the Senate and House committees on foreign relations (26 Feb.)
the president was grilled by his Republican critics. On 2 Mar., 37 Republican
senators and 2 senators-elect signed a
senatorial **Round Robin,** proposed by
Henry Cabot Lodge (p. 1088) and
Frank B. Brandegee (Conn.), and
drafted by **Philander C. Knox,** which
rejected the League in its existing form
and opposed further consideration until
after the final peace settlement; read in
the Senate 2 days later. On 4 Mar. Wilson defiantly predicted in an address in
New York that it would not be possible
to "dissect the covenant from the treaty
without destroying the whole vital structure."

MAR.–APR. WILSON'S RETURN TO
EUROPE. French Demands. The president arrived at Brest on 13 Mar. The
next day he was presented in Paris with
a bill of particulars by Marshal Foch including (1) heavy but undefined reparations for German destruction of French
property; (2) either an Allied occupation
of Germany to the Rhine or the creation
of a Rhineland buffer state. A bitter
battle followed, in the midst of which
Wilson became ill (3 Apr.). On 7 Apr.
the president was reported to have ordered the *George Washington* to Europe,
presumably to take him home unless a
compromise could be worked out. The
French yielded to Wilson's threat and
agreed to a series of compromises. In return for a terminable occupation of German territory Wilson agreed to a treaty
binding Britain and the U.S. to defend
France against a future unprovoked German attack. This treaty was pigeonholed by the U.S. Senate.

Italian Demands. The Italians insisted
on territorial commitments of the Treaty
of London (26 Apr. 1915), by which
Italy was promised a strategic boundary
running to the Brenner Pass, including
some 200,000 Germans, as well as terri-

tory on the head and eastern shore of the Adriatic. In addition, Italy now demanded the port of **Fiume.** Wilson agreed to the Brenner line before his own experts had clarified this violation of his own principle of self-determination, but on 19 Apr. he informed the American delegation that he would stand fast against Fiume. When Italy's peace delegates, **Vittorio Orlando** and **Sidney Sonnino,** continued to press their claims, Wilson appealed directly to the Italian people (23 Apr.) to desert their leaders in favor of a peace of justice. The Italians quit the conference at once, but returned on 6 May. They were unsuccessful in their demand for Fiume. That port did not pass under Italian control until 1924. Under the Italo-Jugoslav Treaty of Rapallo (1920) it had been nominally independent.

Japanese Demands. Japan insisted on recognition of her right to **Shantung,** which she had occupied during the war. Defeated, 11 Apr., in her effort to obtain the passage of a resolution on **race equality,** Japan on 15 Apr. refused to agree to have German rights in Shantung turned over to the Allied powers. She rested her claim on the Secret Treaties of 1917, on agreements with China of 25 May 1915 and 24 Sept. 1918, and on the **Lansing-Ishii** Agreement with the U.S. (see p. 367). On 28 Apr. Wilson surrendered to Japan, but exacted a promise that Shantung would be eventually returned to China, with Japan retaining only economic concessions in the province.

Compromises on the League Covenant. In response to proposals of such pro-League Republicans as William Howard Taft and A. Lawrence Lowell, Wilson proposed amendments to the Covenant to overcome opposition in the Senate. These included: (1) permission of the U.S. to refrain from participating in the mandate system established to administer the conquered colonies; (2) restraints upon League interference with such matters as tariffs and immigration; (3) granting permission to a state to withdraw from the League upon 2 years' notice; (4) excepting "regional understandings like the Monroe Doctrine" from the League's jurisdiction.

7 MAY–28 JUNE. TERMS OF THE VERSAILLES TREATY. The treaty was presented to the Germans on 7 May; they signed on 28 June. Wilson returned to the U.S. on 8 July, and presented the treaty to the Senate on 10 July. The final treaty (1) forced Germany to admit her **war guilt** (**Art. 231**); (2) stripped her of her **colonies, Alsace-Lorraine, the Saar Basin** (its final disposition to be determined by a plebiscite in 1935), **Posen,** and parts of Schleswig and Silesia; (3) exacted reparations, later fixed at $56 billion; (4) substantially **disarmed** her. Attached to the treaty was the **Covenant of the League of Nations,** which provided for: (1) an **Assembly** in which all member nations had an equal voice; (2) a **Council** made up of representatives from the U.S., Great Britain, France, Italy, Japan, and 4 other nations elected by the Assembly; (3) a **Secretariat,** permanently located at Geneva. Members pledged themselves to (1) respect and preserve against external aggression the territorial integrity and political independence of all member nations (**Art. X**); (2) submit to the League all disputes threatening war; (3) employ military and economic sanctions against nations resorting to war; (4) reduce armaments; and (5) cooperate in setting up a **Permanent Court of International Justice.**

10 JULY–19 Nov. SENATE OPPOSITION. The Senate divided on the League issue into 3 groups: (1) Democratic supporters of Wilson who favored immediate ratification, led by **Gilbert M. Hitchcock** (Neb., 1859–1934), who succeeded Thomas S. Martin as minority leader when the latter died during the course of the Senate debate on the issue; (2) moderates, headed by **Henry Cabot Lodge,** chairman of the Senate Committee on Foreign Relations, who favored participation in the League with reservations to protect American interests; and (3) "irreconcilables," including **Hiram W. Johnson** (Calif., 1866–1945), **William E. Borah** (p. 989), and **Robert La Follette** (p. 1079), who advocated complete rejection of the Covenant. On 19 Aug. Wilson at a luncheon conference with the Senate committee agreed to accept interpretative reservations not requiring consent of the other parties to the treaty nor embodied in the resolution of ratification. This failed to satisfy the irreconcilables, who now launched a nationwide propaganda campaign against ratification, financed by Andrew Mellon and Henry C. Frick. Since 6 of the 10 members of the Senate committee were irreconcilables, action was held up until 10 Sept., when the committee proposed 45 amendments and 4 reservations to protect traditional American policies. Wilson took the case to the people in a 9,500-mile tour of the West, commencing 4 Sept., in the course of which he delivered 37 speeches in 29 cities. On 10 Sept. Sens. Johnson and Borah began a tour in opposition to the League and the treaty. On 25 Sept. Wilson collapsed at **Pueblo,** Colo., and was rushed back to Washington, suffering a stroke on 2 Oct. which incapacitated him during this crucial period. (Invalided for more than 7 months, Wilson was cut off from developments outside his sickroom except for information communicated to him by his second wife, Mrs. Edith Bolling Galt Wilson, and the White House physician, Dr. Cary Crayson. He never fully

regained his health.) A combination of Democrats and moderate Republicans voted down the reservations. On 6 Nov. Lodge reported a resolution of ratification accompanied by 14 reservations, which, while circumscribing somewhat American obligations under the Covenant, did not seriously impair the League. On 18 Nov. Wilson, in a letter to his supporters, expressed the view that the Lodge resolution "does not provide for ratification but, rather, for the nullification of the treaty," and urged its defeat. As a result, a combination of Wilson Democrats and irreconcilable Republicans defeated the resolution on 19 Nov. Had the Democrats voted for the Lodge resolution the League and the Treaty would have been carried, 81–13. Unconditional acceptance was defeated, by 38–53.

1920

JAN.–MAY. SENATE AND THE TREATY. A bipartisan approach to ratification was wrecked in January when Lodge yielded to threats by the irreconcilables and refused to modify his original reservations. On 9 Feb. the Senate voted to reconsider the treaty and referred it back to the committee, which reported it the following day with the reservations intact. Wilson remained adamant. In a message to the Jackson Day Dinner (8 Jan.) he insisted that the treaty must not be rewritten by the Senate, and again on 8 March reiterated his opposition to the Lodge reservations. On 19 March, 21 Democrats deserted Wilson to join the Republican reservationists in a vote on the Lodge resolution, which was again defeated, 49–35. When, on 20 May, Congress declared the war at an end by joint resolution, Wilson vetoed the action. Finally, on 2 July 1921, Congress, by a joint resolution, terminated war with Germany and Austria-Hungary, reserving for the U.S. any rights secured by the armistice, the Versailles Treaty, or as a result of the war. Separate treaties concluding peace with Germany, Austria, and Hungary were ratified 18 Oct.

JUNE–NOV. "SOLEMN REFERENDUM." Wilson urged the Democratic Convention which met in San Francisco on 28 June to endorse his views on the League. The party platform pledged unequivocal ratification of the Treaty of Versailles with only such reservations as should be found necessary under the U.S. Constitution. The party nominee, James M. Cox, publicly promised that as soon as possible after 4 Mar. 1921 the U.S. would enter the League. The Republicans were divided on the issue, Root, Taft, and Hughes, on the one hand, supporting the League, the irreconcilables opposing it. Hence, the Republican platform straddled the issue. It criticized the Covenant, but favored the formation of "an international association" to prevent war. Its candidate, Warren G. Harding, had no deep convictions either way. But when once in office, he promptly abandoned any attempt to bring the U.S. into the League, and retreated into what Wilson stigmatized as "sullen and selfish isolation." In his inaugural address Harding declared: "We seek no part in directing the destinies of the world." Again, in a special message to Congress on 2 Feb. 1923, he stated that the League "is not for us. Nothing could be more decisively stamped with finality."

1921

20 APR. A settlement reached between the U.S. and Colombia regarding the Panama episode (p. 348) when the Senate advised ratification of a treaty authorizing payment to Colombia of $25 million and the granting of special land transportation privileges.

1921–22

12 NOV.–6 FEB. 1922. WASHINGTON ARMAMENT CONFERENCE. On 14 Dec. 1920 Sen. Borah introduced a resolution requesting the president to call an international conference for the reduction of naval armaments. The resolution was appended to the Naval Appropriations Bill for 1921. In accordance therewith President Harding (11 Aug.) invited the principal powers, except Russia, to a conference to consider not only naval disarmament, but questions concerning the Pacific and the Far East. The American delegation included Secretary of State Charles Evans Hughes, Elihu Root, Henry Cabot Lodge, and Oscar Underwood. Hughes, who was designated chairman of the conference, proposed at the first session (12 Nov.) not only a limitation upon future naval building but also a substantial scrapping of ships already built or in construction. The U.S. offered to scrap ships amounting to 845,000 tons; Great Britain was asked to scrap 583,000 tons; Japan, 480,000 tons. This program was immediately accepted in principle. It was further agreed to fix the tonnage of capital ships (over 10,000-tons displacement or having guns larger than 8-in. cal.) at a ratio of 5 (U.S.)— 5 (Britain)—3 (Japan)—1.67 (France) —1.67 (Italy). France agreed to her ratio under pressure, but would not permit any limitation on cruisers, destroyers, or submarines, nor have land armaments placed on the agenda. As a result of the conference 9 treaties were drafted and signed: (1) a naval armaments treaty between the 5 powers (U.S., Great Britain, Japan, France, and Italy) providing for a 10-year naval holiday during which no new capital ships were to be built, and establishing a ratio of capital ships (6 Feb. 1922); (2) a 5-power treaty between the same nations restricting the use of submarines in war by the accepted

rules of naval warfare and outlawing asphyxiating gases; (3) a 4-power treaty (13 Dec.) between the U.S., Britain, France, and Japan, by which the signatories agreed to respect each other's rights over Pacific island possessions; (4) a 4-power treaty providing for consultation in the event of "aggressive action" in the Pacific (carrying with it the abrogation of the existing Anglo-Japanese alliance); (5) a 9-power treaty (6 Feb.) signed by all the states at the conference guaranteeing China's independence and territorial integrity, and reiterating the "Open Door" principle; (6) a similar treaty granting China greater control over her customs; (7) a treaty between Japan and China providing for the restoration of Kiachow and the Shantung peninsula to China (4 Feb.); (8) a treaty between Japan and the U.S. confirming American cable rights on the island of Yap; and (9) a 6-power treaty between the U.S., Britain, Japan, France, Italy, and China allocating the former German cable lines in the Pacific. The U.S. Senate ratified all the treaties, the 4-power treaty passing by the narrow margin of 4 votes, and with a reservation stating that "there is no commitment to armed force, no alliance, no obligation to join in any defense."

U.S. AND INTERALLIED WAR DEBTS. In addition to the war loans to the Allied governments, the U.S. also made loans after the armistice for relief purposes or as advances for the payment of surplus American war materials left in Europe at the close of the war:

To Allies	Total Indebtedness
Great Britain	$4,277,000,000.00
France	3,404,818,945.01
Italy	1,648,034,050.90
Belgium	379,087,200.43
Russia	192,601,297.37
Rumania	37,911,153.92
Greece	27,167,000.00
Cuba	10,000,000.00
Nicaragua	431,849.14
Liberia	26,000.00

To Countries Formed out of Allied Territory	
Estonia	13,999,145.60
Finland	8,281,926.17
Latvia	5,132,287.14
Lithuania	4,981,628.03

To Countries or Areas Formed Partially or Wholly Out of Enemy Territory	
Poland	159,666,972.39
Czechoslovakia	91,879,671.03
Yugoslavia	51,758,486.55
Austria	24,055,708.92
Armenia	11,959,917.49
Hungary	1,685,835.61

Total $10,350,479,074.70

As early as Dec. 1918 the British proposed to Wilson that they would agree to cancel debts due them from their Allies, virtually uncollectible claims approximating $10 billion, in return for the cancellation of British debts to the U.S. of about $4 billion. Wilson refused, insisting that the interallied debts were unrelated to German reparations. France also argued strongly for debt cancellation. To deal with this issue the World War Foreign Debt Commission, authorized by Act of Congress, 9 Feb. 1922, was set up to negotiate specific agreements. Based on their capacity to pay, the debtor nations accepted obligations of over $11.5 billion, payable over a 62-year period at an average interest rate of 2.135%. Under these agreements principal and interest totaled in excess of $22 billion. On 1 Aug. Great Britain (**Balfour Note**) agreed to remit, "as part of a satisfactory international settlement," both debts and reparations due herself, and in no case to ask more from her debtors than was necessary to pay her creditors. The U.S. remained adamant. President Coolidge continued the Harding policy. ("They hired the money, didn't they?") Finally, owing to the increasingly serious European financial situation, drastic reductions in principal were agreed to by the U.S. On 14 Nov. 1925 Italy's interest rate was reduced to .4% and 80.2% of the debt was canceled;

in Apr. 1926, the French interest rate was reduced to 1.6%, and 60.3% of the debt was canceled. Despite these concessions, the insistence by the U.S. on partial debt payments promoted anti-U.S. feeling in Europe, isolationism in America.

1922–23

1922, 4 DEC.–7 FEB. 1923. 2D CENTRAL AMERICAN CONFERENCE convened at Washington to settle issues between Nicaragua and Honduras. The U.S. and all Central American republics participated. The conference drew up a treaty of neutrality and provided for the establishment of a Central American court of justice and limitation of armaments.

1924

24 MAY. FOREIGN SERVICE ACT (Rogers Act) reorganized and consolidated the diplomatic and consular services and provided for initial appointment after examination, a period of probation, and promotion on merit.

15 DEC. 1923–9 APR. 1924. GERMAN REPARATIONS: THE DAWES PLAN. On 27 Apr. 1921 the Allied Reparations Commission set up under the Treaty of Versailles submitted a report fixing Germany's obligations at 132,000,000,000 gold marks. On 31 May 1922 the commission, to check the further collapse of the mark, granted Germany a moratorium for the remainder of the year despite protests from France. On 26 Dec. and, again, on 9 Jan. 1923, Germany was declared in default. Two days later French and Belgian troops began the occupation of the Ruhr. By 26 Sept., as a result of Germany's passive resistance, the mark had become worthless; the franc had depreciated 25%. On 15 Dec. 1923 President Coolidge announced that

Charles G. Dawes (1865–1951), Henry M. Robinson, and Owen D. Young would serve as experts on a commission to investigate German finances. The Dawes Plan, reported on 9 Apr. 1924, proposed (1) to stabilize German currency by reorganizing the Reichsbank under Allied supervision; (2) a schedule of payments for reparations, graduated from 1 billion gold marks in the first year (1924–25) to 2½ billion in the fifth year (1928–29). This plan was accepted by the Germans on 16 Apr. and adopted at a London conference (16 July–16 Aug.). Of a foreign loan totaling 800,000,000 gold marks to be advanced Germany under the plan, $110,000,000 was taken up in the U.S. To carry out the plan the Allied powers selected an American, S. Parker Gilbert (1892–1938), as Agent General of Reparations. At an Interallied Financial Conference at Paris (7–14 Jan. 1925) it was agreed that the U.S. should receive 2¼% of the annual payments made by Germany under the plan to satisfy American claims—$255,000,000 for American Army of Occupation costs, $350,000,000 for war damages.

U.S. AND THE LEAGUE. Although both Presidents Coolidge and Harding had favored entry into the League in 1920, neither took active measures to ratify the Covenant. On 11 Nov. 1929 Hoover declared that "public opinion will suffice to check violence" (similarly, on 14 Apr. 1930). Nevertheless, this period was marked by increasing U.S. participation in League affairs. On 17 Nov. 1924 U.S. delegates were represented at the International Opium Conference of the League, withdrawing on 6 Feb. 1925 when the U.S. proposal was not accepted. The U.S. participated in conferences on communication and transit (1926), in 3 conferences on the abolition of import and export prohibitions (1927), and in a conference on double taxation and fiscal evasion (1928). By 1931 212 persons had been officially appointed to represent the U.S. in more than 40 League conferences (Ellery C. Stowell), and the U.S. government maintained 5 permanent officials stationed at Geneva to represent American interests at the League (D. F. Fleming).

END OF DOMINICAN OCCUPATION. President Wilson directed (Dec. 1920) that preparations be made for ending military government in the Dominican Republic. An agreement on evacuation procedure was worked out by the State Department with a group of Dominican political leaders (30 June 1922). The military government delegated to a provisional president sufficient authority to permit the holding of elections. In July 1924 Gen. Horacio Vásquez was inaugurated as constitutional president and the U.S. marines withdrawn. A new treaty (27 Feb.) between the U.S. and the Dominican Republic superseded that of 1907.

1926

27 JAN.–JAN. 1935. U.S. AND THE WORLD COURT. The League Covenant provided for the establishment of a permanent Court of International Justice to consist of 15 members, to be elected by the Council and Assembly from a list of persons nominated by the Hague Court of Arbitration. The court was given jurisdiction over all international disputes submitted to it by states subscribing to the protocol, which was approved by the Council and Assembly in Dec. 1920. The U.S. had instructed its delegates to the 1st Hague Conference, 1899, and the 2d, 1907, to set up a permanent court of arbitration. On 17 Feb. 1923 Secretary of State Hughes wrote Harding urging U.S. membership in the World Court with the distinct understanding that such action would not involve any legal relation to the League. President Coolidge in 3 successive annual messages favored Senate action. On 3 Mar. 1925 the House supported a resolution of adherence by a vote of 303–28. Finally, on 27 Jan. 1926, the Senate approved adherence by 76–17, but attached reservations to safeguard U.S. interests. All were acceptable to members of the World Court except a reservation relating to advisory opinions. Since no agreement could be reached on this point, the U.S. did not join. In 1928 Hughes was chosen by the Council and Assembly to fill the vacancy in the World Court caused by the resignation of another American, **John Bassett Moore** (1860–1947). In Feb. 1929 Elihu Root sailed for Europe to join a commission to revise the statute of the court. His formula provided that the court shall not, without the consent of the U.S., render an advisory opinion touching any dispute to which the U.S. is a party, and reserved to the U.S. the right to withdraw from the court protocol if the interested parties insisted on an advisory opinion in the matter in which the U.S. claimed an interest. On 4 Mar. 1929 Hoover urged court membership in his inaugural address, and on 9 Dec. the U.S. chargé d'affaires in Switzerland, upon authorization of the president, signed the protocol of adherence with revisions agreed to both by the U.S. and the court members. Hoover submitted the protocol to the Senate on 10 Dec. 1930, but Sen. Borah blocked action. On 1 June the Senate Foreign Relations Committee finally came out for adherence. Involved in critical domestic affairs, President Roosevelt delayed risking debate on the issue until 16 Jan. 1935, when he urged ratification. Led by Huey P. Long (La.), the Senate rejected membership, 52–35. Although press opinion had favored the court, 3–1, the Hearst newspapers and the radio activities of Father Charles E. Coughlin kept the "irreconcilables" in line.

1927

20 June–4 Aug. NAVAL DISARMA-MENT: GENEVA CONFERENCE. On 10 Feb. President Coolidge called for a 5-power conference to be held at Geneva to consider limitations on the building of cruisers, destroyers, and submarines, not curbed at the Washington Conference. France and Italy refused to attend; Great Britain and the U.S. failed to agree on cruiser restrictions. The conference adjourned without accomplishment. In Feb. 1929 the U.S. authorized the construction of 15 cruisers of 10,000-ton displacement.

Mar.–27 Aug. 1928. OUTLAWRY OF WAR. As a result of conversations with Professor **James T. Shotwell** (1874–1965) of Columbia Univ. in Mar., French foreign minister **Aristide Briand** released 6 Apr. a proposal for the "outlawry of war" (a phrase attributed to Salmon O. Levinson). On 25 Apr. President **Nicholas Murray Butler** (p. 995) of Columbia Univ. revived the issue in a letter to *The New York Times.* On 11 June Secretary of State **Frank B. Kellogg** (1856–1937) made a formal acknowledgment. Briand submitted a draft treaty on 20 June. As a result of a conference with Sen. Borah, Kellogg substituted a **multinational** for a bilateral agreement in a note of 28 Dec. On 11 Jan. 1928 he published a draft treaty, which was brought to the attention of other powers on 13 Apr. On 27 Aug., 14 nations signed; eventually 62 nations signed. The sanctions of the **Kellogg-Briand Pact** rested on the moral force of world opinion.

31 Jan. 1917–26 Dec. 1927. MEXI-CAN-U.S. RELATIONS. The new Mexican Constitution of 1917 not only provided for radical political and social reforms but curbed foreign ownership of lands, mines, and oil fields. By a decree, 19 Feb. 1918, oil was declared an inalienable national resource, and titles to oil lands were to be converted into concessions. British and American companies promptly protested. Following the death of Carranza (21 May 1920) **Alvaro Obregón** was elected president (5 Sept.). He was recognized by the U.S., 31 Aug. 1923, upon an executive agreement (**Bucareli Agreement**) to respect subsoil rights acquired before 1917 and confirmed by some "positive act." After the election of **Plutarco Calles** in 1924, Secretary Kellogg warned Mexico (12 June) that the U.S. would continue its support "only so long" as Mexico "protects American lives and American rights." In retaliation the Mexican Congress passed 2 laws, to become effective 1 Jan. 1927, to implement the 1917 Constitution: the Petroleum Law, by which permanent foreign concessions were limited to 50 years and alien corporations required to waive their right of appeal to the home government (**Calvo Clause**); the Land Law, designed to break up the huge estates, restricted alien land ownership. A U.S. Senate resolution (27 Jan. 1927) unanimously recommended arbitration of the dispute with Mexico. In Sept. President Coolidge appointed **Dwight W. Morrow** (1873–1931) of J. P. Morgan & Co. as ambassador to Mexico. His conciliatory efforts quickly produced results. On 17 Nov. the Mexican Supreme Court declared the limitation on concessions under the Petroleum Law unconstitutional. On 25 Dec. the Mexican Congress granted unlimited confirmatory concessions to lands on which "positive" acts had been performed prior to 1 May 1917. Morrow's efforts to compose the differences between the Church and the Mexican government, growing out of the act of 11 Feb. 1926 nationalizing church property, were interrupted by the assassination of president-elect Obregón, 17 July 1928.

1927–28

NICARAGUAN RELATIONS. The U.S. refused to recognize the government of Emiliano Chamorro, which assumed power after a revolt on 25 Oct. 1925. After Chamorro became president (14 Jan. 1926), a Liberal insurrection was started by Gen **Augustino Sandino**. The U.S. landed troops and supported **Adolfo Díaz**, Conservative, as president. On 4 May 1927 President Coolidge sent Henry L. Stimson to bring the 2 factions together. Under an agreement Díaz was to complete his term, the rebels were to disarm, and the U.S. was to supervise the next election. When, 4 Nov. 1928, **José Moncada** (Liberal) was elected president, Sandino left the country. Again, in 1931, he started a revolt, which was suppressed by 1933. Under President Hoover **U.S. troops were finally withdrawn from Nicaragua in 1933.** Meantime, the U.S. had been impliedly criticized at the **Havana Conference**, opened by President Coolidge, 16 Jan. 1928, in a proposed resolution declaring that "no state has the right to intervene in the internal affairs of another." Charles Evans Hughes, heading the U.S. delegation, managed to block its passage. Immediately after his election on 6 Nov. Herbert Hoover embarked on a good-will tour (19 Nov.–6 Jan. 1929) of 11 Latin-American countries, where he received a cordial welcome.

17 Dec. 1928. CLARK MEMORANDUM of the U.S. State Department, drafted by **J. Reuben Clark** (1871–1961), defined the Monroe Doctrine as stating "a case of the U.S. v. Europe, and not of the U.S. v. Latin America," in effect **repudiating the Roosevelt Corollary.**

1929

YOUNG PLAN. German dissatisfaction with the operation of the reparations program resulted in a new series of negotiations. On 19 Jan. **Owen D. Young** (1874–1962) and J. P. Morgan were named as American experts on a Committee on German Reparations, which met in Paris (11 Feb.) to revise the Dawes Plan, and designated Young as chairman. The report aimed at a final settlement of German reparations. It reduced the amount due from Germany to **$8,032,500,000**, payable over **58½ years** at **5½% interest**; set up a **Bank for International Settlements** from the profits of which Germany's payments during the final 22 years should be made; and provided for a further reduction should the U.S. consent to scaling down the interallied war debts. In ratifying the debt settlement agreement with the U.S. (21 July) the French Chamber of Deputies resolved that the amounts paid to the U.S. should be covered by German reparation payments. At the **Lausanne Conference** (16 June 1932) **over 90%** of the reparations required to be paid under the Young Plan were **canceled.**

1930

21 Jan.–22 Apr. LONDON NAVAL CONFERENCE. On a visit to the U.S. (4–6 Oct. 1929) Prime Minister Ramsay MacDonald of Great Britain discussed with President Hoover the issue of naval disarmament. On 7 Oct. 1929 Great Britain issued a formal invitation to the other 4 major naval powers. The U.S. delegation was headed by Secretary of State Stimson, and included Charles Francis Adams, Secretary of the Navy, Dwight W. Morrow, Hugh Gibson, and Sens. David A. Reed (Rep.) and Joseph T. Robinson (Dem.). France refused to accept Italy's demands for parity with any continental power, and neither nation signed the more important provisions of the treaty. The U.S., Great Britain, and Japan adopted a program of cruiser limitation; an "escalator" or escape clause permitted Britain to start construction should France or Italy threaten her traditional policy of a navy equal to both continental powers. In cruisers Japan was restricted to a 10–6 ratio, but in other auxiliaries except submarines received a 10–7 ratio. In submarines parity at an upper limit of 52,700 tons was adopted. The capital-ship ratio remained at 10–10–6, but no new ships were to be built until 1936 (except French and Italian battleships authorized at Washington but not yet begun). As a result, 5 British, 3 American, and 1 Japanese capital ship were scrapped. The treaty's expiration date was **31 Dec. 1936.** President Hoover called a special session to secure favorable action by the Senate (21 July). **Further disarmament efforts** were continued by the League's Preparatory Commission on Disarmament. A general disarmament conference assembled at **Geneva, 2 Feb. 1932,** with U.S. participation. When the U.S. proposal for **abolition of all offensive armaments** failed of adoption, President Hoover countered with a proposal for a 30% overall reduction. The conference adjourned in July, resumed negotiations in Feb. 1933, adjourned from June until Oct. (by which time Germany had announced her withdrawal from the League), and broke up without accomplishment in the spring of 1934.

1931

20 June. HOOVER DEBT MORATORIUM. The deepening worldwide economic crisis made the payment of either reparations or war debts an impossibility. The repercussions of the New York stock market crash of Oct. 1929 were soon felt abroad. On 11 May 1931 the Austrian Credit-Anstalt failed. Foreign funds were hastily withdrawn from Germany. On 16 June the Bank of England, to stem the financial panic, advanced 150,000,000 schillings to the Austrian National Bank. On 20 June President Hoover proposed a **1-year moratorium** on both interallied debts and reparations. French opposition, delaying acceptance until 6 July, contributed to the closing of all the German banks by mid-July. The crisis seriously affected Great Britain, forcing the Bank of England off the gold standard on 21 Sept. The French position was presented to the U.S. by Premier Pierre Laval, who had a conference at the White House with the president, 23–25 Oct. As a result a statement was issued that, when the moratorium ended, some agreement on the interallied debts "covering the period of business depression," not merely the moratorium year, might be necessary.

1931–32

18 Sept. JAPANESE AGGRESSION IN MANCHURIA. In violation of the Washington treaties, the Kellogg-Briand Pact, and the League Covenant Japanese army leaders occupied major Manchurian cities, in effect launching an unofficial war between Japan and China. Military control of South Manchuria was completed by 4 Jan. 1932. On 15 Sept. 1932 Japan formally recognized the new puppet state of **Manchukuo.**

7 Jan. 1932. STIMSON DOCTRINE. Secretary Stimson addressed an identical note to Japan and China declaring that the U.S. does not "intend to recognize any treaty or agreement . . . which may impair . . . the sovereignty, the independence, or the territorial and administrative integrity of the Republic of China . . . or the Open Door policy. . . ." Instead of supporting Stimson, the British Foreign Office on 11 Jan. professed its faith in Japan's assurances regarding the Open Door. On 29 Jan. naval and military intervention by the Japanese took place at Shanghai, where the Chinese forces were expelled, 3 Mar. Stimson proposed to **Sir John Simon,** British foreign secretary, that a joint protest be made on the basis of the 9-Power Treaty of 1922, but the British government, preferring to work within the League, was unresponsive. On 23 Feb. Stimson, in a letter to Sen. Borah, chairman of the Senate Foreign Relations Committee, declared that the U.S. would stand by its treaty rights in the Far East, and urged other nations to follow the Stimson Doctrine of nonrecognition. On 11 Mar. the League of Nations Assembly unanimously adopted a resolution incorporating this doctrine. On 31 May Japan, bowing to world opinion, withdrew from Shanghai.

10 Dec. 1931–27 Mar. 1933. LYTTON REPORT. The League attempted to end hostilities in the Far East, formally inviting the U.S. on 16 Oct. 1931 to appoint a representative to sit with the Council in considering the Manchurian crisis. The U.S. accepted. **Prentiss B. Gilbert,** consul at Geneva, was authorized to participate in such discussions as related to U.S. obligations under the Kellogg-Briand Pact; otherwise to act as an observer. Meantime, a ground swell was developing in the U.S. for an economic boycott of Japan, which President Hoover opposed. When it appeared that the League might impose sanctions, Stimson, on 19 Nov., told Charles G. Dawes, American ambassador to Great Britain: "We do not intend to get into war with Japan." On 10 Dec. the League appointed the Lytton Commission, including Gen. **Frank Ross McCoy** (1874–1954), an American, to investigate the Manchurian crisis. The **Lytton Report,** 4 Oct. 1932, condemned Japan, but proposed a settlement recognizing Japan's special interest in Manchuria, which was to become an **autonomous** state under Chinese sovereignty but Japanese control. The report was adopted by the League on 24 Feb. 1933, and on 27 Mar. Japan gave notice of withdrawal from the League.

1933

4 Mar. GOOD NEIGHBOR POLICY. In his first inaugural Franklin D. Roosevelt declared: "In the field of world policy I would dedicate this nation to the policy of the good neighbor—the neighbor who resolutely respects himself and, because he does so, respects the rights of others." The implementation of this policy meant a further improvement in relations with Latin America. At the **Montevideo Conference** Secretary of State **Cordell Hull** (1871–1955) supported declaration: "No state has the right to intervene in the internal or external affairs of another." This pact was unanimously adopted, 26 Dec. "The definite policy of the U.S. from now on is one opposed to armed intervention," declared F.D.R. on 28 Dec.

12 June–27 July. LONDON ECONOMIC CONFERENCE. President Hoover had pledged American participation in this conference called by the League at the request of the Lausanne Conference. Between 4 Mar. and 12 June the U.S. had abandoned the gold standard. Hence, Roosevelt was disinclined to support a currency-stabilizing program supported by the gold-bloc nations (France, Belgium, the Netherlands, Italy, and Switzerland). Secretary Hull received instructions en route to the conference to limit participation to negotiating bilateral tariff treaties. On 2 July President Roosevelt, in a radio message, rebuked the delegates for concentrating on currency stabilization. Since the other participating nations would not agree to consider tariff reductions until *after* currency stabilization, the conference broke up without substantial accomplishment. Its failure marked a blow at international cooperation and signalized the American drift toward isolation.

16 Nov. RECOGNITION OF SOVIET RUSSIA. Following the overthrow of the Kerensky regime in 1917, U.S. administrations had refused to recognize the Soviet Union on various grounds, including Russia's refusal to assume the obligations incurred by former governments as well as her revolutionary program for the overthrow of capitalist nations. Roosevelt's communication of 16 May addressed to 54 heads of states, urging military and economic disarmament, was sent, among others, to **Mikhail Kalinin,** titular head of the Russian government. On 10 Oct. the president requested Kalinin to send an envoy to the U.S. **Maxim Litvinov,** Commissar for Foreign Affairs, arrived in Washington on 7 Nov. In a formal exchange of notes (16 Nov.) Russia promised (1) not to interfere with the domestic affairs of the U.S., including abstaining from propaganda; (2) to extend religious freedom to American citizens in the Soviet Union and to negotiate an agreement to guarantee a fair trial to Americans accused of crime in Russia; (3) to negotiate a settlement of mutual claims (no specific agreement on debts outstanding was ever made). The expected increase in American foreign trade failed to materialize, and the Soviet Union violated her pledge on propaganda and interference in U.S. internal affairs.

1933–38

DECLINE OF DOLLAR DIPLO-MACY. Cuba. As a result of the collapse of sugar prices in the 1920s Cuban economic conditions deteriorated and were further damaged by the Hawley-Smoot Tariff (1930). In Aug. 1931 dictator **Gerardo Machado** suppressed a revolt against his regime. To stabilize Cuban internal conditions President Roosevelt sent **Sumner Welles** (1892–1961) as ambassador to Cuba. Arriving in Havana on 1 June 1933, Welles served as mediator between the Cuban administration and various opposition groups. A general strike and an army revolt forced Machado out of office (12 Aug.). On 5 Sept. another army coup forced out his successor, Carlos Manuel de Céspedes, and a practical dictatorship was established under **Fulgencio Batista.** The radical government of President **Grau San Martín** was not recognized by the U.S. On 20 Jan. 1934 this regime was overthrown by Carlos Mendieta, favored by the U.S., Batista, and Cuban conservatives, who successfully negotiated a treaty with the U.S. **abrogating the Platt Amendment** (29 May) and removing limitations previously imposed on Cuban sovereignty. Chief credit for these negotiations belongs to Sumner Welles. On 25 Aug. the U.S. and Cuba signed a reciprocal trade agreement by which duties on sugar were reduced from 2.5 cts. to .9 cts. per lb. Cuban sugar production was finally stabilized by the **Jones-Costigan Sugar Control Act** (in effect 8 June).

Haiti. As the result of the restoration of order and the stabilizing of finances with U.S. aid, U.S. troops were withdrawn on 6 Aug. 1934.

Panama. As a result of a conference in Washington between President **Harmodio Arías** and President Roosevelt, a declaration was issued (17 Oct. 1933) that Panama should be permitted the commercial rights of a sovereign state in the Canal Zone. Negotiations between the two nations were soon entered into to secure a modification of the Hay–

Bunau-Varilla Treaty of 1903. The new treaty signed 2 Mar. 1936 was not ratified by the U.S. Senate until 25 July 1939, owing in part to opposition from U.S. military and naval authorities. The treaty incorporated a pledge of joint action in case "of any threat of aggression which would endanger the security of the Republic of Panama or the neutrality or security of the Panama Canal," allowed the U.S. to expand its canal facilities or to begin new construction, and increased U.S. annual payments to Panama from $250,000 to $450,000.

HEMISPHERE SOLIDARITY. Early Phases. The rise of fascist and totalitarian regimes in Europe underscored the need for unity among the nations of the Western Hemisphere. Three Pan-American conferences prior to the outbreak of World War II dealt with this new world peril: (1) The **Montevideo Conference,** which denied the right of any state to intervene in the "internal or external affairs of another" (26 Dec. 1933); (2) the **Buenos Aires Conference,** opened by President Roosevelt (1 Dec. 1936) in a speech in which he declared that non-American states seeking "to commit acts of aggression against us will find a Hemisphere wholly prepared to consult together for our mutual safety and our mutual good," and which adopted a pact pledging consultation whenever war threatened; (3) the **Lima Conference** (24 Dec. 1938), which adopted the **Declaration of Lima,** not only reaffirming the absolute sovereignty of the American states but expressing their determination to resist "all foreign intervention or activities that may threaten them." It provided for consultation where the "peace, security, or territorial integrity" of any state should be threatened. Actually, the Argentina delegation blocked an even stronger declaration desired by Secretary Hull, who headed the U.S. delegation.

Closer Ties with Brazil. As a result of radical unrest in Brazil, President **Getulio Vargas** was granted almost dictatorial powers, which were enlarged by a new constitution proclaimed 10 Nov. 1937. The U.S. refused to label Vargas' government as fascist, and moved quickly to supplant German influence in that strategic area. Largely as a result of the efforts of Sumner Welles, Brazil concluded a series of agreements with the U.S., 9 Mar. 1939, by which it obtained financial aid for economic development.

SETTLEMENT OF THE MEXICAN EXPROPRIATION CONTROVERSY. Under a 6-Year Plan launched by President **Lázaro Cárdenas** (inaugurated 11 Nov. 1936) numerous social reforms were introduced. Acting under authority of a statute passed in 1936, Cárdenas nationalized most of the properties of British and U.S. oil companies, valued at $450 million (18 Mar. 1938). Secretary Hull admitted the right of expropriation, but insisted on fair compensation (30 Mar.). On 1 Apr. the U.S. discontinued purchasing Mexican silver at a price above the world level, an act which threatened Mexico's financial stability. Certain aspects of the controversy were settled by a joint commission, and payments by the Mexican government began in 1939; other aspects were settled by agreement between the U.S. and President **Avila Camacho** (19 Nov. 1941). Mexico agreed to pay $40 million in settlements of agrarian claims; the U.S. to establish a $40-million fund to support the peso, to resume purchase of Mexican silver at a price above the world market, and to issue through the Export-Import bank a $30-million credit for Mexican highway construction. Each party agreed to appoint an expert to arrive at an equitable valuation of the U.S.-owned oil properties. On 18 Apr. 1942 a figure of $23,995,991 for subsoil rights was announced, in addition to $9,600,000 paid by Mexico in individual settlements with 2 U.S. oil companies.

ISOLATION AND NEUTRALITY.

As totalitarian regimes increasingly threatened the peace of Europe, the U.S. adopted a series of isolationist measures to avoid involvement in war. The **Johnson Debt Default Act** (13 Apr. 1934) prohibited loans to any foreign government in default to the U.S. Previously (June 1933) Britain, Czechoslovakia, Italy, Rumania, Latvia, and Lithuania had made token payments, their last on debts to the U.S. All formally defaulted on 15 June 1934. Only Finland continued to meet her payments in full. The new approach to neutrality, in part the result of the work of the **Nye Committee** (p. 411), sought to disentangle U.S. economic interests from foreign wars and constituted an abandonment of traditional concepts of neutral rights.

Neutrality Act of 1935. When Italy attacked Ethiopia (May 1935) the U.S. State Department drafted a bill which would have given the president power to embargo arms against one or all belligerents in future wars. Introduced in the House on 17 Aug., it was rejected by the Foreign Relations Committee, which substituted a resolution authorizing the president, after proclaiming the existence of a state of war, to prohibit all **arms** shipments and to forbid U.S. citizens from traveling on belligerent vessels except **at their own risk.** Yielding to the administration, Congress placed a 6-month limit on such embargo. Roosevelt signed the measure, 31 Aug., but characterized it as calculated to "drag us into war instead of keeping us out." The embargo did not include primary materials such as oil, steel, copper, easily converted to military use.

Neutrality Act of 1936. The Act of 1935 was extended on 29 Feb. 1936 to 1 May 1937, and forbade the extension of loans or credits to belligerents. On 14 Aug. 1936, in an address delivered at Chautauqua, N.Y., President Roosevelt pointed to the dangers of being drawn into war and declared: "I hate war."

Neutrality Acts of 1937. On 18 July 1936 the Spanish Civil War broke out, with a revolt of army chiefs in Spanish Morocco. Foreign powers soon intervened on both sides. Since the U.S. neutrality acts applied only to wars **between nations,** not to civil wars, new legislation was deemed necessary. On 6 Jan. 1937 Congress passed a joint resolution forbidding the export of munitions "for the use of either of the opposing forces in Spain." Under this act Roosevelt embargoed shipments to both sides. The embargo worked to the particular disadvantage of the Loyalist government in Madrid, as the rebels secured supplies from Italy and Germany. The deficiencies of each of the neutrality acts called for a more realistic and flexible measure, which was adopted on 1 May 1937. This act (1) authorized the president to list commodities **other than munitions** to be paid for on delivery (limited to 2 years); (2) made travel on belligerent vessels **unlawful.** Again, the ineffectiveness of the new act was demonstrated when, on 7 July 1937, fighting broke out between Japanese and Chinese troops near Peiping. The president declined to invoke the Neutrality Act of May 1937 on the ground that it would have worked to China's disadvantage. However, on 14 Sept. he forbade transport of munitions to China and Japan on U.S. government vessels, and notified private shippers that they acted at their own risk. Japan, with her large merchant marine, benefited by this ruling.

ROOSEVELT AND COLLECTIVE SECURITY: QUARANTINE SPEECH.

In complete disagreement with the isolationist trend of the neutrality legislation, President Roosevelt, in a speech in Chicago, 5 Oct. 1937, urged an international quarantine of aggressors as the only means of preserving peace. Roosevelt soon recognized that he had moved ahead of public opinion, although his address undoubtedly encouraged a widespread U.S. boycott against Japanese goods.

NAVAL EXPANSION. Japan, on 29 Dec. 1934, denounced the Washington Naval Treaty of 1922. The U.S. refused to grand parity to Japan at the discussions preliminary to the 2d London Naval Conference, from which Japan withdrew, 15 Jan. 1936. Great Britain, the U.S., and France signed (25 Mar.) a treaty providing for minor limitations, largely made ineffective by numerous "escape clauses." In 1938 Congress voted a billion-dollar naval-building program (see p. 424).

DETERIORATING JAPANESE RELATIONS. Panay Incident. On 12 Dec. 1937 Japanese planes bombed a U.S. river gunboat, the *Panay*. The vessel sank with a loss of 2 killed, 30 wounded. (For the Ludlow Amendment [14 Dec.], see p. 423). On 14 Dec. the U.S. formally demanded apologies, reparations, and guarantees against further incidents. On the same day Japan formally apologized and gave the necessary assurances. On 25 Dec. Secretary Hull acknowledged the reply. On 6 Oct. 1938 U.S. ambassador Joseph Clark Grew (1880–1965) protested against Japanese violations of the Open Door in China. The Japanese note of 18 Nov. declared that the Open Door was "inapplicable" to the conditions "of today and tomorrow." The State Department, in its reply of 31 Dec., refused to recognize the "new order."

1938–39

DETERIORATING EUROPEAN CONDITIONS. On 11 Jan. 1938 President Roosevelt proposed to the British government a program for a world conference to reduce armaments, promote economic security, and ameliorate the inhumane aspects of any war that might break out. Prime Minister Neville Chamberlain rejected this proposal. The German war timetable: 7 Mar. 1936, German reoccupation of the Rhineland; 17 Nov. 1936, Anti-Comintern Pact of Germany, Japan, and Italy against communism; Mar. 1938, annexation of Austria by Germany; Sept. 1938, the German-Czech crisis, which caused Chamberlain to intervene (at Berchtesgaden, 15 Sept.; at Godesberg, 22–23 Sept.). On 27 Sept. President Roosevelt appealed to Hitler and Mussolini for a peaceful solution of the issues. As a result of the Munich Conference and Agreement, 29 Sept., the Sudetenland and all vital Czech fortresses were yielded to Germany. Despite French and British guarantees of the new frontiers of Czechoslovakia, that nation came to an end in Mar. 1939, when Slovakia and Carpatho-Ukraine declared their independence, and Bohemia and Moravia became a German protectorate. On 23 Mar. Germany annexed Memel, and made stiff demands to Warsaw regarding Danzig and the Polish Corridor. On 31 Mar. Britain pledged Anglo-French aid to the Poles in case their independence was threatened, a pledge extended to Rumania and Greece on 13 Apr. Meantime, 7 Apr., Italy invaded Albania. On 15 Apr. President Roosevelt, in a letter to Hitler and Mussolini, asked assurances against attack on 31 nations of Europe and the Near East. Denying warlike intentions, Hitler, in reply, restated German grievances. On 22 May a military alliance was concluded between Germany and Italy. On 23 Aug. a Russo-German pact was signed at Moscow. This provided that (1) either party would abstain from attacking the other; (2) either party would remain neutral if the other were attacked by a third party. The next day President Roosevelt addressed an appeal to President Ignacy Moscicki of Poland, to Hitler, and to King Victor Emmanuel proposing direct negotiations between Germany and Poland, arbitration or conciliation. Poland accepted concili-

ation. On 31 Aug. the Poles decreed partial mobilization.

Domestic Issues

1919

28 Oct. NATIONAL PROHIBITION ENFORCEMENT ACT (VOLSTEAD ACT) was passed over President Wilson's veto (27 Oct.). Designed to provide the enforcement apparatus for the 18th Amendment, the act went into effect on 16 Jan. 1920. It defined as intoxicating liquor any beverage containing more than ½ of 1% of alcohol and placed the administration of the law under the Bureau of Internal Revenue, in which the post of commissioner of prohibition was created. A supplementary act (23 Nov. 1921) limited the use of liquor by medical prescription and extended prohibition to the Hawaiian and Virgin Islands. The **Jones Act** (2 Mar. 1929) increased the penalties for violation. Widespread evasion of the Volstead Act was evidenced by the growth of bootlegging (i.e., the illicit liquor traffic) on a vast scale during the 1920s, when the organized distilling and distribution of liquor fell under the control of criminal elements.

24 Dec. President Wilson announced that on 1 Mar. 1920 the railroads and express companies would be returned to private operation.

1920

13 Feb. Robert Lansing resigned as Secretary of State, at Wilson's request, after the president had charged him with holding unauthorized meetings of the cabinet following Wilson's physical collapse in 1919.

28 Feb. TRANSPORTATION ACT (ESCH-CUMMINS ACT) provided for the return of the railroads to private control on 1 Mar. and widened the powers of the Interstate Commerce Commission. The commission was authorized to draw up plans for the consolidation of all railroads into about a score of competing groups exempt from antitrust legislation; was empowered to make evaluations of the aggregate value of railroad properties, to set minimum and maximum rates, and to establish a fair return to stockholders; and was given jurisdiction over pooling, regulation of service and traffic, and new issues of securities. A recapture clause required carriers to turn over to the Interstate Commerce Commission one half of all net earnings in excess of 6%, these to be set aside as a revolving fund for the benefit of railroads handicapped by low income. **A Railroad Labor Board** was created for the adjustment of wage disputes.

5 June. MERCHANT MARINE ACT (JONES ACT) repealed emergency war legislation relating to shipping, reorganized the U.S. Shipping Board and extended its life, and authorized the sale of government-built ships to private operators, the proceeds up to $25 million to be used for loans to private owners for the construction of new craft. The Shipping Board was empowered to propose the establishment of shipping routes for the purpose of promoting mail and trade service and to operate the shipping service until private interests took over. The act provided that coastwise commerce was to be carried in U.S. vessels, as well as the mails where practicable.

10 June. WATER POWER ACT established a **Federal Power Commission** consisting of the Secretaries of War, Interior, and Agriculture, with an executive secretary directly responsible for its administration. The act applied to water power reserves on public lands of the U.S. (except reservations) and to navigable streams, including falls, rapids, and shallows. The commission was empowered to issue licenses, limited to 50 years, for the construction and operation of facilities (e.g., power houses, dams, reservoirs, and transmission lines) for improving navigation and developing and utilizing power. Upon expiration of the lease, the government reserved the right to take over and operate these facilities. The commission was authorized to regulate rates and security issues of licensees under its jurisdiction.

26 Aug. 19TH AMENDMENT to the Constitution, providing for **woman suffrage,** was declared ratified.

PALMER RAIDS AND THE "RED SCARE." Following the Bolshevik Revolution in Russia, the Soviets carried out an intensive propaganda campaign against the Western nations. In 1919 the Workers' (later the Communist) party was established in the U.S. Beginning in the fall of 1919, the Department of Justice under A. Mitchell Palmer made countrywide mass arrests of political and labor agitators. In instances where arrested persons were aliens, they were deported; on 22 Dec. 1919 the U.S. transport *Buford,* with 249 deportees aboard, including the anarchists Emma Goldman and Alexander Berkman, sailed for Russia. One of the largest mass arrests came on 2 Jan., when government agents carried out raids in 33 cities and took 2,700 persons into custody. The raids were terminated in May. Within individual states, criminal syndicalist laws were invoked against radicals.

PRESIDENTIAL CAMPAIGN. The Socialist Labor Party Convention met at New York (5 May) and nominated W. W. Cox (Mo.) for president and August Gillhaus (N.Y.) for vice-president. The Socialist Party Convention met at New York (8 May) and unanimously nominated Eugene V. Debs (Ind.) for president. Debs was then serving a 10-year sentence in federal prison for having engaged in seditious activity in violation of the wartime Espionage Act. Seymour Stedman (Ohio) was chosen as the Socialist candidate for vice-president.

The Republican Convention met at Chicago (8 June) and on the 10th ballot nominated Sen. **Warren G. Harding** (Ohio, p. 1050) for president. Gov. **Calvin Coolidge** (Mass., p. 1005) was nominated for vice-president on the 1st ballot. The Republican platform rejected the Covenant of the League of Nations and made a vague declaration favoring an "agreement among the nations to preserve the peace of the world." Harding waged a front-porch campaign; in a well-calculated appeal to the postwar temper, he called for a "return to **normalcy.**"

The Democratic National Convention met at San Francisco (28 June) and on the 44th ballot nominated Governor **James M. Cox** (Ohio) for president. **Franklin D. Roosevelt** (N.Y., p. 1141), Assistant Secretary of the Navy, was nominated for vice-president by acclamation. The Democratic platform unequivocally endorsed the Versailles Treaty and the League of Nations, but did not "oppose the acceptance of any reservations making clearer or more specific the obligations of the United States to the League associates."

The Farmer Labor Party Convention met at Chicago (11 July) and nominated P. P. Christensen (Utah) for president and Max S. Hayes (Ohio) for vice-president. The Single Tax party convention met at Chicago (12 July) and nominated Robert C. Macauley (Pa.) for president and Richard Barnum (Ohio) for vice-president. The Prohibition Party Convention met at Lincoln, Neb. (21 July), and nominated A. S. Watkins for president.

2 Nov. PRESIDENTIAL ELECTION. Popular vote: **Harding,** 16,152,200; Cox (D), 9,147,353; Debs, 919,799; Watkins, 189,408; Cox (S.L.), 31,175; Christensen, 265,411; Macauley, 5,837. Electoral vote: **Harding,** 404; Cox (D.), 127.

1921

BUSINESS RECESSION. The sharp deflation, 1920–21 (p. 751), was the result of stringent credit, a glutted domestic market and heavy inventories, and a sharp drop in the export trade. Wages dropped; about 20,000 business failures occurred in 1921; and some 4,750,000 persons were unemployed. The recession's impact upon agriculture was more lasting (p. 694).

10 June. BUDGET AND ACCOUNTING ACT, the first material step in the reform of the national budget, created a Budget Bureau in the Treasury Department, with a director appointed by the president. At each regular session of Congress the president was to submit to the legislators a budget including estimates of expenditures and receipts for the following year together with estimates for the current and last fiscal years. The president was also to present a complete statement of the government's financial condition and, when deemed advisable, recommendations for loans, tax revision, and other financial measures. Except on special request of either house of Congress, no financial recommendation or request for appropriations was to be made by any government officer except

through the budget. The act also created a General Accounting Office, under the Comptroller General of the U.S., for carrying out an independent audit of government accounts. **Charles G. Dawes** (1865–1951) was named (21 June) as first director of the Bureau of the Budget.

9 Aug. VETERANS BUREAU was established as an independent unit, directly responsible to the president, for assuming the administration of all forms of veterans' relief. Col. **Charles R. Forbes** was named as its head.

15 Aug. PACKERS AND STOCK-YARDS ACT related to livestock, livestock products, poultry, and dairy products. Its enforcement was vested in the Department of Agriculture. The act forbade unfair and discriminatory practices, the manipulation and control of prices, and other devices creating a monopoly and acting in restraint of trade. Operators of stockyards and other marketing facilities were required to register with the Department of Agriculture and to file their schedule of charges.

24 Aug. GRAIN FUTURES TRADING ACT was designed to regulate all contract markets authorized to sell grain for future delivery, in order to prevent market manipulation and monopoly practices. It discouraged speculative transactions by levying a prohibitive tax on grain sold for future delivery except by owners or certain authorized contract markets. The act was invalidated by the Supreme Court in 1922 and superseded by a second grain Futures Act (21 Sept. 1922) regulating trading under the interstate commerce power.

23 Nov. SHEPPARD-TOWNER ACT for the promotion of the welfare and health of maternity and infancy extended federal aid to states. The act authorized annual federal appropriations of $1 million. The act, which lapsed in 1929, was attacked as constituting federal interference in state affairs.

1922

18 FEB. COOPERATIVE MARKET-
ING ACT (CAPER-VOLSTEAD ACT)
exempted agricultural producers, cooperatives, or associations from the operations of antitrust laws and allowed
cooperative buying and selling by farmers
in interstate commerce. Administration
of the act was vested in the Department
of Agriculture.

22 SEPT. CABLE ACT granted married women U.S. citizenship independent
of their husbands' status.

1923

KU KLUX KLAN EXPOSÉS. The Ku
Klux Klan, a secret nativist organization
patterned upon the rituals of its post-
Civil War predecessor, and active against
minority groups (Negroes, Catholics,
Jews, and immigrants) as well as against
certain tendencies in modern thought
(e.g., birth control, pacifism, internation-
alism, Darwinism, and the repeal of prohibition), was revived at a meeting on
Stone Mountain, Ga., Nov. 1915. At
peak strength in the 1920s it was reported to have had 5 million members in
the North, South, and Midwest, with
political power in several states (including Ind., Okla., and Tex.). Exposés of its
activities appeared in 1923. The Baltimore *Sun* (7 Jan.) exposed the reign of
terror in Morehouse Parish, La., where
despite evidence of torture and murder
of marked victims, a grand jury refused
to indict. Concurrently the N.Y. *World*
exposed Klan activities in the North. In
Vincennes, Ind., Grand Dragon David C.
Stephenson was convicted on a charge of
murder in the second degree (21 Nov.
1925). By 1926 Klan membership was on
the decline. By 1930 it was estimated at
only 9,000.

4 MAR. INTERMEDIATE CREDIT
ACT was designed to facilitate loans for
crop financing by means of an intermediate credit system that liberalized the use
of short-term agricultural paper. It established 12 intermediate credit banks, 1 in
each federal reserve bank district, under
the jurisdiction of the Federal Farm Loan
Board. Each bank, with a capital of $5
million subscribed by the government,
was authorized to make loans (ranging
from 6 months to 3 years) to cooperative
producing and marketing associations.
The act also authorized the creation of
agricultural credit corporations by private
interests.

2 AUG. DEATH OF PRESIDENT
HARDING at San Francisco, while on a
return trip from Alaska. Embolism was
listed as the cause of death.

3 AUG. Vice-President Calvin Coolidge
took the oath of office as president at
Plymouth, Vt., becoming the 30th president of the U.S.

6 DEC. In his first annual message to
Congress, President Coolidge voiced his
support of U.S. adherence to a world
court, the tax reduction plan of Secretary
of the Treasury Andrew W. Mellon
(1855–1937), and prohibition enforcement. He opposed the cancellation of
Allied debts and the payment of a
veterans' bonus. His program called for
a scaling down of government expenditures, a minimum of government interference in business, and government aid
to industry and commerce.

1924

HARDING   ADMINISTRATION
SCANDALS. Early in 1924 congressional committees, acting upon persistent
rumors of graft and corruption in the
Harding administration, brought to light
scandals in the departments of Justice,
Navy, and the Interior, and in the Veterans Bureau and the Office of the Alien
Property Custodian. Col. Charles R.

Forbes, former chief of the Veterans Bureau, who had resigned in 1923, was indicted for fraud, conspiracy, and bribery, and sentenced (4 Feb. 1925) to 2 years in a federal penitentiary and a fine of $10,000. Col. Thomas W. Miller, the Alien Property Custodian, was also sent to prison (1927) on charges of conspiring to defraud the government.

The major scandals involved the lease of naval oil reserve lands by private interests and the influence over the Department of Justice wielded by the Ohio gang, a group of self-seeking politicians close to Harding. A Senate investigating committee disclosed that President Harding, acting with the approval of Secretary of the Navy Edwin Denby, had transferred (1921) to Secretary of the Interior **Albert B. Fall** (1861–1944) the administration of oil reserves at **Teapot Dome,** Wyo., and **Elk Hills,** Calif. During the Taft and Wilson administrations these reserves had been set aside for the use of the navy. The Teapot Dome reserve was secretly leased by Fall (7 Apr. 1922) to oil operator Harry F. Sinclair; the California fields were likewise leased (25 Apr., 11 Dec. 1922) to Edward L. Doheny.

The scandal came to light when a Senate committee headed by **Thomas J. Walsh** (Mont., 1859–1933) found that in 1921 Doheny had lent Fall $100,000 without interest or collateral, and that Fall, after retiring from the cabinet in March, 1923, had received a "loan" of $25,000 from Sinclair. A joint congressional resolution charged fraud and corruption. The government secured cancellation of the oil leases in 1927. Fall was indicted (30 June) for bribery and conspiracy, convicted of bribery, and sentenced to 1 year in prison and $100,000 fine. Sinclair and Doheny were acquitted of bribery; Sinclair sentenced to 9 months in prison and $1,000 fine for contempt of court.

An investigation revealed that Attorney General **Harry M. Daugherty** (1860–1941), acting in concert with members of the Ohio gang, had received payments from violators of the prohibition statutes. It was also disclosed that he had failed to prosecute for graft in the Veterans Bureau. Daugherty was tried for conspiracy, but acquitted (4 Mar. 1927). He resigned (Mar. 1924) at the request of President Coolidge.

The Supreme Court declared the Elk Hills lease invalid 28 Feb. 1927; the Teapot Dome lease, 10 Oct. 1927.

19 May. WORLD WAR ADJUSTED COMPENSATION ACT (SOLDIERS BONUS ACT). Shortly after the close of World War I organized veterans' groups, including the American Legion and the Veterans of Foreign Wars, initiated a demand for an ex-servicemen's bonus. The move was made on the assumption that veterans ought to be compensated for the differential between their service pay and the wages received by war workers who had remained in civilian life.

On 19 Sept. 1922 President Harding vetoed a bonus bill. Veterans' groups continued to exert pressure on Congress. On 18 Mar. a bonus bill was passed by the House, and on 23 Apr. it was approved by the Senate. It was vetoed (15 May) by President Coolidge, but was passed over his veto by the House (17 May) and Senate (19 May).

The act provided for the payment of adjusted compensation to all veterans (excluding officers above the rank of captain) on the basis of $1.25 a day for overseas service and $1 a day for service in the U.S. The bonus was made in the form of 20-year endowment policies on which ex-servicemen might borrow from the government up to about 25% of full value. Cash payment, which became a major issue in 1931–32, was finally authorized in 1936.

McNARY-HAUGEN BILL. The post-war depression in agriculture, deepened by a glutted market and a continuing slump in crop prices, and farm mortgages on expanded acreage, led spokesmen of farmer interests to consider basic legislation for coping with agricultural distress. The **Capper-Volstead Act** (1922) and the **Intermediate Credit Act** (1923) failed to satisfy agrarian discontent, mobilized by such organized groups as the American Farm Bureau Federation and the Farmers' National Council. A bipartisan agrarian bloc in Congress undertook to deal with the problem by 2 means: control of the surplus and stabilization of prices. The **McNary-Haugen Farm Relief Bill,** sponsored by Sen. **Charles L. McNary** (Ore., 1874–1944) and Rep. **Gilbert N. Haugen** (Iowa), was introduced in both houses of Congress (16 Jan.). The measure featured the equalization fee scheme, whereby a proposed federal farm board would purchase the annual surplus of specified commodities during years of large output and either keep it off the market until prices rose or sell it abroad at the prevailing world price. The equalization fee (i.e., the difference between the fixed domestic price and the free international price) was to be paid by producers of individual commodities in the event that the government suffered losses in selling at lower world prices. The bill was defeated in the House (3 June) when Western farm interests failed to muster adequate support. It suffered successive defeats in the House (21 May 1926) and Senate (24 June 1926). Passed by the Senate (11 Feb. 1927) and the House (17 Feb. 1927), it was vetoed by President Coolidge (25 Feb. 1927) on the ground that it incorporated a price-fixing principle and benefited special groups.

PRESIDENTIAL CAMPAIGN. The Commonwealth Land party (formerly the Single Tax party) met in convention (8 Feb.) and nominated W. J. Wallace (N.J.) for president and J. C. Lincoln (Ohio) for vice-president. The Socialist Labor Party Convention met at New York (11 May) and nominated Frank T. Johns (Ore.) for president and Verne L. Reynolds (Md.) for vice-president. The American Party Convention met at Columbus, Ohio (3 June) and nominated Judge Gilbert O. Nations (Washington, D.C.) for president and Charles H. Randall (Calif.) for vice-president. The Prohibition Party Convention met at Columbus, Ohio (5 June), and nominated Herman P. Faris (Mo.) for president and Miss Marie C. Brehm (Calif.) for vice-president.

The Republican Party Convention met at Cleveland (10 June) and nominated President **Coolidge** for reelection and Gen. **Charles G. Dawes** (Ill.) for vice-president. The Republican platform supported reduced taxes and retrenchment in government expenditures, the Fordney-McCumber tariff, the limitation of armaments, U.S. adherence to the World Court, and international action for the prevention of war.

The Democratic Party Convention met at New York (24 June) and, after a prolonged contest between the partisans William G. McAdoo (Tenn.) and Alfred E. Smith (N.Y., 1873–1944), nominated **John W. Davis** (W. Va., 1873–1955) for president on the 103rd ballot (9 July). Gov. **Charles W. Bryan** (Neb.) was nominated for vice-president. The Democratic platform favored a competitive tariff and endorsed disarmament and the League of Nations. It denounced the Ku Klux Klan and condemned the corruption of the Harding administration.

The Conference for Progressive Political Action, representing dissident agrarian and labor elements, met at Cleveland (4 July) and launched a new Progressive party that was endorsed by the Farmer Labor party, the Socialist party, and the American Federation of Labor. The Progressives nominated Sen. **Robert M. La Follette** (Wis.) for president and Sen. **Burton K. Wheeler** (Mont.) for vice-president. The Progressive platform called for government ownership of railroads and water power resources, the abolition of the use of the injunction in labor disputes, freedom for farmers and labor to organize and bargain collectively, ratification of the child labor amendment, limitation of judicial review, and tighter controls over futures trading in agricultural commodities. It denounced corruption in government, condemned the Mellon financial program, and attacked "the control of government and industry by private monopoly."

The Workers' (Communist) party met on 11 July and nominated William Z. Foster (Ill.) for president and Benjamin Gitlow (N.Y.) for vice-president.

4 Nov. PRESIDENTIAL ELECTION. Popular vote: **Coolidge,** 15,725,016; Davis, 8,385,586; La Follette, 4,822,856; Faris, 57,551; Johns, 38,958; Foster, 33,361; Nations, 23,867; Wallace, 2,778. Electoral vote: **Coolidge,** 382; Davis, 136; La Follette, 13. Both houses of Congress remained under Republican control.

1925

13 Feb. JUDGES' BILL. Continuing increase in the docket of the U.S. Supreme Court coupled with growing recognition of the value of the Circuit Courts of Appeals (created by Act of 3 Mar. 1891) led a committee of justices, Willis Van Devanter, James C. McReynolds, and George Sutherland, to draft a proposal for Congress. The bill became law, assisted by the lobbying of Chief Justice William Howard Taft, providing that most appeals from federal district courts would go directly to the Courts of Appeals. Appeals as of right by way of a Writ of Appeal from the Courts of Appeals and state courts to the Supreme Court were severely limited and the Supreme Court achieved substantial control of the cases it would hear through a *writ of certiorari* granted or denied at the discretion of the court.

10–21 July. SCOPES TRIAL (p. 829).

28 Oct.–17 Dec. "BILLY" MITCHELL TRIAL. Differences among military and naval authorities over the role of the airplane in warfare set the background for the court-martial of Col. William ("Billy") Mitchell (p. 1104) of the Army Air Service. A forthright critic of U.S. aviation policy, Mitchell publicly contended (5 Sept.) that the military high command was incompetent, criminally negligent, and almost treasonable in its administration of the national defense. An exponent of air power, he insisted that capital ships were vulnerable to air attack. Summoned to Washington, D.C., by the National Air Board, Mitchell advocated (29 Sept.) an independent department for aviation and a unified command of the armed services. A court-martial found him guilty of conduct prejudicial to good order and military discipline. He was suspended from the service for 5 years. Mitchell resigned from the service (29 Jan. 1926). He died in 1936. In 1942 he was posthumously restored to the service with the rank of major general.

1926

26 Feb. REVENUE ACT, in keeping with the Coolidge-Mellon fiscal program, reduced personal income and inheritance taxes and abolished a wide variety of excise imposts. It also repealed the publicity clause relating to income tax returns. Additional reductions were made in the Revenue Act of 29 May 1928.

2 Nov. CONGRESSIONAL ELECTIONS cut Republican majorities in both houses, with gains for Progressives.

1927

2 Aug. COOLIDGE'S WITH-DRAWAL. It was generally assumed that Coolidge would seek the presidential nomination in 1928. While on a vacation in the Black Hills of South Dakota, Coolidge issued the following statement to newspaper reporters at Rapid City, S.D.: "I do not choose to run for President in 1928."

SACCO-VANZETTI CASE. Nicola Sacco and Bartolomeo Vanzetti, 2 Italian anarchists, were arrested (5 May 1920) for having allegedly murdered (15 Apr.) a paymaster and guard at a shoe factory in South Braintree, Mass. They were convicted (14 July 1921) on what many regarded as insubstantial evidence. It was charged by liberals and radicals in the U.S. and abroad that Sacco and Vanzetti had been tried for their radical views rather than for any actual crime. During the 20s, when defense committees succeeded in securing a stay of the death sentence, the Sacco-Vanzetti case became a *cause célèbre*. Mass demonstrations for the convicted were held in the U.S., Latin America, and Europe. Under pressure of widespread protest that the convicted had not received a fair trial, Gov. Alvan T. Fuller (Mass.) appointed (1 July 1927) a commission (Pres. Abbott Lawrence Lowell of Harvard, chairman), which examined the evidence and conduct of the trial and sustained the verdict (27 July). Sacco and Vanzetti were put to death in the electric chair at the Charlestown State Prison (23 Aug.).

1928

FINAL DEFEAT OF THE McNARY-HAUGEN BILL. As the situation of the American farmer showed no sign of general improvement, agrarian spokesmen in Congress renewed efforts to enact the McNary-Haugen Farm Relief Bill. In a fifth attempt, the bill passed the Senate (12 Apr.), 53–23, and the House (3 May), 204–121, but was again vetoed by President Coolidge on the following grounds: that it sanctioned price fixing; was an improper delegation of the taxing power; would lead to overproduction and profiteering; and would antagonize overseas agricultural producers and thus invite retaliation. Coolidge's persistent opposition to this mode of farm relief was a leading issue in the presidential election of 1928.

15 May. FLOOD CONTROL ACT (p. 639).

22 May. MERCHANT MARINE ACT (JONES-WHITE ACT) was designed to encourage private shipping. It increased from $125 million to $250 million a ship construction loan fund from which private builders could borrow up to three quarters of the cost of constructing, reconditioning, or remodeling a vessel. It also permitted the sale of government-owned craft at low prices and liberalized long-term mail-carrying contracts.

PRESIDENTIAL CAMPAIGN. The Socialist Party Convention met at New York (13 Apr.) and nominated Norman Thomas (N.Y.) for president and James H. Maurer (Pa.) for vice-president. The Workers' (Communist) Party Convention met at New York (27 May) and nominated William Z. Foster (Ill.) for president and Benjamin Gitlow (N.Y.) for vice-president.

The Republican Party National Convention met at Kansas City, Mo. (12 June), and nominated Secretary of Commerce **Herbert C. Hoover** (Calif.) for president on the 1st ballot (14 June). Sen. **Charles Curtis** (Kan., 1860–1936) was nominated for vice-president. The Republican platform rejected the Mc-Nary-Haugen scheme for farm relief but supported the creation of a federal farm board authorized to promote the establishment of a farm marketing system and of farmer-owned and -controlled stabilization corporations or associations to pre-

vent and control surpluses through orderly distribution. The platform upheld
prohibition, the protective tariff, and the
Coolidge foreign policy. During the campaign Hoover made his "rugged individualism" speech at New York (22 Oct.),
in which he condemned the Democratic
platform as state socialism and upheld
free competition and private initiative as
the traditional American way.

The Democratic Party Convention met
at Houston, Tex. (26 June), and nominated Gov. **Alfred E. Smith** (N.Y.) for
president on the 1st ballot (28 June)
and Sen **Joseph T. Robinson** (Ark.) for
vice-president. The Democratic platform,
although not committed to the McNary-
Haugen plan, pledged that "farm relief
must rest on the basis of an economic
equality of agriculture with other industries," and advocated the creation of a
federal farm board with powers somewhat similar to those proposed in the
McNary-Haugen Bill. The platform
pledged enforcement of the prohibition
laws; and while Smith supported this
pledge, he called for repeal of the 18th
Amendment. His position cost him the
"dry" vote, particularly in the South.
Also favored by the Democratic platform
were collective bargaining for labor and
the abolition of the use of the injunction
in labor disputes, "except upon proof of
threatened irreparable injury"; the
stricter regulation of water power resources; and immediate independence for
the Philippines. Republican foreign policy was condemned.

The Prohibition Party Convention met
at Chicago (12 July) and nominated
William F. Varney (N.Y.) for president
and James A. Edgerton (Wash.) for
vice-president. The Farmer Labor candidate for president was Frank E. Webb.
The Socialist Labor party nominated
Verne L. Reynolds for president.

6 Nov. PRESIDENTIAL ELECTION.
Popular vote: **Hoover,** 21,392,190; Smith,

15,016,443; Thomas, 267,420; Foster,
48,770; Reynolds, 21,603; Varney, 20,-
106; Webb, 6,390. Electoral vote:
Hoover, 444; Smith, 87. In part because
of religious prejudice against Smith, a
Roman Catholic, the electoral vote of 5
Southern states went to Hoover. The Republicans maintained control of both
houses of Congress.

1929

15 APR. Special session of the 71st
Congress convened at call of President
Hoover to deal with farm relief and
limited revision of the tariff.

EXPORT DEBENTURE PLAN. The
agrarian relief scheme favored by the
congressional farm bloc differed fundamentally from that advocated by President Hoover. Exponents of the subsidy
principle, the farm bloc introduced in
the Senate the export debenture plan
initially advanced in 1926 and again in
1928. This scheme called for export
bounties on specified commodities. Equal
to one half of the tariff duties on such
commodities, these bounties were to be
added to the prevailing world price. Payment was to be made in the form of
debentures receivable in payment of import duties. Thus the difference between
the domestic and world price would be
met by the government out of customs
receipts. The proposal of this plan by the
farm bloc touched off a heated contest
between the Senate and House. The
House 3 times (25 Apr., 17 May, 13
June) rejected the debenture plan passed
by the Senate, and President Hoover
made it clear that he would veto the
measure. The Senate finally abandoned
the scheme.

**15 JUNE. AGRICULTURAL MAR-
KETING ACT** was an administration
measure which eliminated the subsidy
and price-fixing principle of the McNary-
Haugen and export debenture plans. The

act established a **Federal Farm Board** (consisting of 8 members and the Secretary of Agriculture) for promoting the marketing of farm commodities through agricultural cooperatives and stabilization corporations. It authorized a revolving fund of $500 million for low-interest loans to such agencies in the interest of the orderly purchasing, handling, and selling of surpluses of cotton, grain, livestock, and other specified commodities. The board was authorized to make agreements with cooperatives and stabilization corporations in order to prevent losses resulting from price fluctuations. As a means of maintaining an even level of staple prices, the Federal Farm Board created (1930 the **Cotton Stabilization Corps.**, the **Grain Stabilization Corp.**, the **Wool Marketing Corp.**, and similar bodies for the purpose of making purchases in the open market. However, the price support program did not succeed, partly because farmers were reluctant to reduce their acreage. In 1931 the board terminated its purchasing program; in 1933, after spending more than $180 million, it went out of existence.

PANIC OF 1929. (For the boom, 1922–29, fed by unprecedented securities speculation, see p. 751.) The Wall Street stock market crash (Oct.–Nov.) was the overt inception of the worldwide Great Depression. Severe breaks occurred on 24 Oct., when 13 million shares changed hands, and 29 Oct. (16 million shares traded). By 13 Nov. about $30 billion in the market value of listed stocks had been wiped out; by mid-1932 these losses had increased to c. $75 billion. (For the deepening depression, see p. 403.)

1930

3 JULY. VETERANS ADMINISTRATION ACT consolidated all federal functions for ex-servicemen's relief in a single agency known as the Veterans Administration.

4 Nov. CONGRESSIONAL ELECTIONS. In their first setback since 1916, the Republicans lost 8 seats in the Senate and their majority in the House. The vote on prohibition in states such as Rhode Island, Illinois, and Massachusetts pointed to lessening support for the 18th Amendment.

HOOVER RELIEF POLICY. Opposed to direct federal relief for unemployed persons suffering from genuine distress, President Hoover advocated a policy of decentralized work relief. In Oct. he formulated a relief program that called for federal leadership of a national voluntary effort by agencies operating on a self-help basis in state and local communities. His object was to "preserve the principles of individual and local responsibility." On 2 Dec. Hoover requested an appropriation of $100–$150 million for construction of public works. Hoover created national emergency relief organizations headed at various times by Walter S. Gifford, Newton D. Baker, and others. However, when early in 1932 unemployment rose to 10 million, Hoover approved the Relief and Construction Act (p. 400).

1931

19 JAN. WICKERSHAM REPORT. By 1929 it was clearly evident that the enforcement of the 18th Amendment had broken down, creating a set of serious social and political problems. An illegal traffic in liquor (rum-running and bootlegging) fostered powerful crime syndicates and such racketeers as "Scarface" **Al Capone** (1899–1947) who ruled the beer traffic and other rackets in Chicago, but was jailed on income tax evasion (1931). In May 1929, President Hoover appointed a Law Observance and Enforcement Commission headed by former

Attorney General **George W. Wicker-**
sham (1858–1936) to conduct a survey
to serve as the basis for formulating public policy on the 18th Amendment. In its
report the commission stated that effective enforcement was hindered by the
lucrative returns of the illicit liquor
traffic, by public antipathy or hostility,
and by the belief that enforcement of
the 18th Amendment ought to be the
function of the federal government alone
rather than a joint federal-state undertaking. The commission opposed repeal
of the Prohibition Amendment; a majority
of the commission, however, favored its
revision. In submitting the report to Congress (20 Jan.), President Hoover stated
that he did not favor repeal.

VETERANS' BONUS. As the depression deepened, veterans' groups demanded immediate enactment of a bill
authorizing a loan of 50% on the adjusted
compensation ("bonus") certificates provided for by the act of 1924. Congress
passed such a bill but Hoover vetoed it
(26 Feb.) on grounds that it would be a
blow to government economy and benefit
many veterans not actually in distress.
Congress passed the bill (27 Feb.) over
his veto. Later in the year Democratic
congressional leaders proposed that the
entire bonus be paid in cash. The pressure
for legislative approval resulted in the
"Bonus March" on Washington in 1932.

1932

2 FEB. RECONSTRUCTION FI-
NANCE CORP. President Hoover advocated an economic recovery program
based on the assumption that government
loans to banks and railroads would check
deflation in agriculture and industry and
ultimately restore the levels of employment and purchasing power. He proposed to Congress (8 Dec. 1931) the
creation of a government lending agency

with authority to issue tax-exempt bonds
and with wide powers to extend credit.
The Senate (11 Jan.) and the House
(15 Jan.) passed the measure establishing the Reconstruction Finance Corp.,
capitalized at $500 million and autho-
rized to borrow to the extent of $2 billion
to provide emergency financing for banking institutions, life insurance companies,
building and loan societies, railroads, and
farm mortgage associations. It was also
empowered to subscribe the capital for
government-owned corporations. The
measure was signed by President Hoover
on 22 Jan. The RFC was established on
2 Feb. with **Charles G. Dawes** as its
head. Within 6 months it had authorized
a total of $1.2 billion in loans to about
5,000 life insurance companies, agricultural credit corporations, and other financial institutions.

27 FEB. GLASS-STEAGALL ACT, a
credit expansion measure, broadened the
acceptability of commercial paper for rediscount by the Federal Reserve system
and made available for industrial and
business needs about $750 million of the
government gold supply hitherto used to
support the currency. This act was designed to counteract the contraction of
credit due to foreign withdrawals and the
domestic hoarding of gold and currency.

7 JULY. The House, 202–157, passed
the Wagner-Garner Bill to extend the
work of federal employment agencies to
states which did not sponsor such units.
The Senate passed it (9 July), 43–31.
President Hoover vetoed the measure
(11 July) on the ground that it would
interfere with state control over unemployment problems.

21 JULY. RELIEF AND CONSTRUC-
TION ACT extended the scope and
functions of the RFC and authorized it
to incur a total indebtedness of $3 billion.
The RFC was empowered to provide
$1.5 billion in loans for the construction

by state and local agencies of public works of a self-liquidating character, and to furnish $300 million in temporary loans to states unable to finance the relief of economic distress. The act also broadened the powers of the RFC to assist agriculture.

22 July. FEDERAL HOME LOAN BANK ACT, a measure recommended to Congress by President Hoover (8 Dec. 1931), established a 5-man Home Loan Bank Board and created a series of discount banks for home mortgages that provided for homeowners a service similar to that performed for commercial interests by the Federal Reserve discount facilities. It authorized the establishment of 8 to 12 banks set up in different parts of the country with a total capital of $125 million. Eligible for membership in the system were building and loan associations, savings banks, and insurance companies. The measure was designed to reduce foreclosures, stimulate residential construction (and thus increase employment), and encourage home ownership by providing the facilities for long-term loans payable in installments.

28–29 July. "BONUS ARMY." The demand for the immediate cashing of adjusted compensation certificates in full provided the impetus behind the "Bonus March" on Washington, D.C. About 1,000 ex-servicemen descended on the national capital (29 May) with the avowed purpose of remaining there until Congress authorized the cash payment. Other groups of veterans who arrived in June from all parts of the country brought the total number in the "Bonus Expeditionary Force" to an estimated 17,000. Many camped on the Anacostia Flats, on the edge of the city, and others made their homes in shacks and unused government buildings near the Capitol. The House (15 June) passed the **Patman Bonus Bill** providing for the issu-

ance of $2.4 billion in fiat money to pay off the remainder of the soldiers' bonus certificates. The Senate (17 June) defeated the measure. The government then provided funds for returning the veterans to their homes. Most of the ex-servicemen departed, but about 2,000 refused to disband. An attempt by the Washington police to evict them forcibly resulted in the death of 2 veterans and 2 policemen. President Hoover called out federal troops (28 July), who completed the removel of the veterans with the use of infantry, cavalry, and tanks.

PRESIDENTIAL CAMPAIGN. The Socialist Labor Party Convention met at New York (30 Apr.) and nominated Verne L. Reynolds (N.Y.) for president and J. W. Aiken (Mass.) for vice-president. The Socialist Party Convention met at Milwaukee (21 May) and nominated Norman Thomas (N.Y.) for president and James H. Maurer (Pa.) for vice-president. The Communist Party Convention met at Chicago and nominated (28 May) William Z. Foster (N.Y.) for president and James W. Ford, a Negro and native of Alabama, for vice-president.

The Prohibition Party Convention met at Indianapolis (5 July) and nominated William D. Upshaw (Ga.) for president and Frank S. Regan (Ill.) for vice-president. The Farmer-Labor Party National Committee met at Omaha (9 July) and nominated Jacob S. Coxey (Ohio) for president. The Liberty Party Convention met at St. Louis and nominated (17 Aug.) W. H. Harvey (Ark.) for president and Frank B. Hemenway (Wash.) for vice-president.

The Republican Party Convention met at Chicago (14 June) and renominated President **Hoover** (on the 1st ballot) and Vice-President **Charles Curtis.** The Republican platform called for a sharp reduction in government expenditures, a balanced budget, the maintenance and

extension of the protective tariff to stabilize the home market, U.S. participation
in an international monetary conference,
the gold standard, restriction of immigration, revision of the Prohibition
Amendment, and veterans' pensions for
service-connected disabilities.

The Democratic Party Convention met
at Chicago (27 June) and nominated
Gov. **Franklin Delano Roosevelt** (N.Y.)
for president on the 4th ballot (30 June)
and **John Nance Garner** (Tex., 1868–
1967) for vice-president. Breaking the
tradition that a presidential nominee
must await formal notification of his
selection, Roosevelt flew from Albany to
Chicago (2 July) and delivered an
acceptance speech stressing the need
for the reconstruction of the nation's
economy. "I pledge you, I pledge myself," he told the convention, "to a **new
deal** for the American people."

The Democratic platform advocated a
drastic cut in government spending, a
balanced budget, a competitive tariff for
revenue, unemployment and old-age insurance under state laws, a sound currency, U.S. participation in an international monetary conference, repeal of
the Prohibition Amendment, and veterans' pensions for service-connected
disabilities. It called for the "enactment
of every constitutional measure that will
aid the farmer to receive for basic farm
commodities prices in excess of the cost
of production." The platform advocated
banking and financial reforms including
the federal regulation of holding companies, of exchanges trading in securities
and commodities, and of the rates of
interstate utility companies. It supported protection of the investing public
by requiring full publicity and filing with
the government of all offerings of foreign
and domestic stocks and bonds.

During the campaign Roosevelt delivered numerous speeches in which he
set forth a program of economic nationalism and social reconstruction shaped by
him with the aid of a group of assistants
(including **Rexford G. Tugwell, Raymond Moley,** and **Adolf A. Berle, Jr.**)
known as the "**Brains Trust.**" Roosevelt's
appeal was made to the "forgotten man
at the bottom of the economic pyramid"
(a phrase he first used on 7 Apr., before
his nomination). In an address delivered
(23 Sept.) at the Commonwealth Club
of California, at San Francisco, he said
that the function of government was to
meet "the problem of underconsumption,
of adjusting production to consumption,
of distributing wealth and products more
equitably, of adapting existing economic
organizations to the service of the people.
. . ." However, such economic regulation was to be assumed "only as a last
resort."

Hoover condemned Roosevelt's philosophy of government as a "radical departure" from the American way of life
and called for the decentralization of
government to permit the free expansion
of private enterprise. Should the New
Deal come to power, Hoover warned (31
Oct.), "the grass will grow in streets of
a hundred cities, a thousand towns; the
weeds will overrun the fields of millions
of farms. . . ."

8 Nov. PRESIDENTIAL ELECTION.
Popular vote: **Roosevelt,** 22,809,638;
Hoover, 15,758,901; Thomas, 881,951;
Foster, 102,785; Upshaw, 81,869; Har-
vey, 53,425; Reynolds, 33,276; Coxey,
7,309. Electoral vote: **Roosevelt,** 472;
Hoover, 59. Roosevelt carried 42 states;
Hoover carried Maine, Vermont, New
Hampshire, Connecticut, Pennsylvania,
and Delaware. The Democrats secured
majority control of both branches of Con-
gress. The composition of the 73rd Con-
gress was as follows: in the Senate, 60
Democrats, 35 Republicans, and 1
Farmer-Laborite; in the House, 310
Democrats, 117 Republicans, and 5
Farmer-Laborites.

1933

6 FEB. 20TH AMENDMENT to the Constitution, sponsored by George W. Norris (Neb.) and proposed on 2 Mar. 1932, was declared ratified. This so-called "Lame Duck" Amendment provided that effective 15 Oct. 1933 Congress would convene each year on ·3 Jan. and that the terms of the president and vice-president would begin on 20 Jan. following the national elections.

15 FEB. At Miami, Fla., an assassin, Giuseppe Zangara, fired 6 shots at close range at president-elect Roosevelt and the party in the latter's open touring car. Roosevelt was uninjured, but several others were wounded, including Mayor **Anton Cermak** of Chicago, who died on 6 Mar. Zangara was put to death in the electric chair at Raiford, Fla. (20 Mar.).

ECONOMIC CRISIS. In the interim between the presidential election and the inauguration of President Roosevelt economic conditions reached gravely critical proportions. From Dec. 1932 to Mar. 1933 the index of industrial production dropped from 64 to an all-time low of 56. The nation's banking system revealed signs of alarming weakness as runs on banks became increasingly frequent and the hoarding of currency set in on a large scale. From 1930 until the eve of Roosevelt's inauguration, a total of 5,504 banks shut down. These banks had total deposits of $3,432,000,000. On 4 Feb. Louisiana declared a 1-day bank holiday. In Michigan, Gov. W. A. Comstock issued a proclamation (14 Feb.) calling for an 8-day bank holiday. By 2 Mar., 21 other states had suspended or drastically restricted banking operations. In New York, Gov. Herbert H. Lehman proclaimed (4 Mar.) a 2-day bank holiday. By Inauguration Day virtually every bank in the Union had been closed or placed under restriction by state proclamations.

4 MAR. In his inaugural address, Roosevelt affirmed that "the only thing we have to fear is fear itself," and called for vigorous national leadership.

5 MAR. President Roosevelt summoned the 73rd Congress to convene in special session on 9 Mar. Invoking powers granted by the Trading with the Enemy Act of 1917, Roosevelt prepared a proclamation, effective 6 Mar., declaring a 4-day national banking holiday suspending all transactions in the Federal Reserve and other banks, trust companies, credit unions, and building and loan associations. In order to permit the continuance of business operations, the use of scrip was allowed (e.g., clearing house certificates or other evidence of claims against the assets of banks). The proclamation also placed an embargo for a like period (6–9 Mar.) on the export of gold, silver, and currency, and ordered that gold and silver could be exported or withdrawn only on a license from the Treasury Department. During the first 3 days after the banking holiday, 4,507 national banks and 567 state member banks were opened (i.e., about 75% of all the member banks of the Federal Reserve system). Within 2 weeks stock prices rose 15%, with a return flow of hoarded currency and a rapid return of gold and gold certificates to the Treasury and the Reserve banks.

12 MAR. FIRST "FIRESIDE CHAT." Initiating a practice that became customary during his administration, President Roosevelt addressed the American people by nationwide radio broadcast. On this occasion he explained the steps he had taken to meet the financial emergency.

The New Deal

INAUGURATION OF THE NEW DEAL. The special session of the 73rd Congress that met on 9 Mar. was called

In

by the president to deal with the banking crisis, but Roosevelt decided to hold Congress in session to deal with unemployment and farm relief. By the time this session (later known as the "**Hundred Days**") ended its deliberations (16 June), it had enacted a comprehensive body of legislation affecting banking, industry, agriculture, labor, and unemployment relief. This was the initial phase of the "First New Deal" (1933–35), aimed primarily at **relief and recovery.**

9 MAR.–16 JUNE. "HUNDRED DAYS" produced the following body of legislation:

9 MAR. EMERGENCY BANKING RELIEF ACT, introduced, passed, and approved on the same day, confirmed all of the emergency steps taken by the president and the Secretary of the Treasury since 4 Mar. The Senate vote was 73–7; the House vote was unanimous. The act, affecting all national banks and Federal Reserve banks, gave the president broad discretionary powers over transactions in credit, currency, gold, and silver, including foreign exchange. Gold hoarding and export were forbidden. A maximum penalty of $10,000 fine and 10 years in prison was provided. The act permitted sound banks in the Federal Reserve system to open only under licenses from the Treasury Department; gave the Comptroller of the Currency authority to appoint conservators to care for the assets of insolvent national banks; authorized the Secretary of the Treasury to call in all gold and gold certificates in the country; enlarged the open-market operations of the Federal Reserve banks; and empowered the RFC to subscribe to the preferred stock of national banks and trust companies. This act, combined with the proclamation of 6 Mar., succeeded in checking the money panic.

20 MAR. ECONOMY ACT, requested by President Roosevelt on 10 Mar., was passed by the House (11 Mar.), 266–138, and by the Senate (15 Mar.), 62–13. It was designed to balance the budget of normal expenditures through (1) reductions of up to 15% in the salaries of government employees; (2) cuts in veterans' pensions and other allowances, particularly pension payments based on nonservice-connected disabilities; and (3) the reorganization of government agencies with a view to economy. Roosevelt estimated that the savings effected under this act would total $500 million. The amount actually saved was about $243 million.

22 MAR. BEER-WINE REVENUE ACT, aimed at securing additional revenue, amended the Volstead Act to legalize wine, beer, lager beer, ale, and porter of 3.2% maximum alcoholic content by weight, or 4% by volume, and levied a tax of $5 per barrel of 31 gallons. The act left to the states all regulatory and control measures, especially those relating to sale and distribution, and incorporated safeguards for states whose prohibition laws stipulated a lesser alcoholic content. The measure took effect on 7 Apr.

31 MAR. CIVILIAN CONSERVATION CORPS REFORESTATION RELIEF ACT, passed as an unemployment relief measure, established the Civilian Conservation Corps (CCC), authorized to provide work for 250,000 jobless male citizens between the ages of 18 to 25 in reforestation, road construction, the prevention of soil erosion, and national park and flood control projects under the direction of army officers. Work camps were established for those enrolled in the CCC; the youths received $30 per month, part of which went to dependents. Four government departments (War, Interior, Agriculture, Labor) cooperated in carrying out the program. CCC had as many as 500,000 on its rolls at one time; by end of 1941 had employed over 2 million youths.

APR.–MAY. BLACK-CONNERY-PER-KINS WAGES AND HOURS BILL was displaced on the legislative program by the **NIRA** (p. 407).

19 APR. The U.S. officially abandoned the gold standard, causing a decline in the exchange value of the dollar abroad and an increase in the prices of commodities, silver, and stocks on American exchanges.

12 MAY. FEDERAL EMERGENCY RELIEF ACT created the Federal Emergency Relief Administration (FERA) and authorized an appropriation of $500 million, allotting half this amount as direct relief to the states and the balance for distribution on the basis of $1 of federal aid for every $3 of state and local funds spent for relief. The FERA was based on the system of outright grants to states and municipalities, as differentiated from the loan policy initiated under the Hoover administration. The act left the establishment of work relief projects for employables to state and local bodies and authorized the RFC to supply the funds for distribution to the states through a relief administrator. **Harry L. Hopkins** (p. 1061) was appointed Federal Relief Administrator.

12 MAY. AGRICULTURAL ADJUSTMENT ACT was designed to restore the purchasing power of agricultural producers. The drastic decline of farm income between 1929 and 1932 had prompted a farmers' strike in the summer of 1932 organized by the Farmers' Holiday Assn., led by Milo Reno of Iowa, and reinforced by warnings in Jan. 1933 from the conservative American Farm Bureau Federation. The chief objects of the AAA were the elimination of surplus crops of basic commodities through curtailed production and the establishment of **parity prices** for enumerated basic commodities. Parity price was based on

the purchasing power of the farmers' dollar at the level of 100 cts. during the base period of 1909–14 for corn, cotton, wheat, rice, hogs, and dairy products; and the base period of 1919–29 for tobacco. The act incorporated the **subsidy principle**: in return for voluntarily reducing acreage or crops, farmers were to be granted direct benefit or rental payments. The funds for such payments were to be derived from levies on the processors of specified farm products. The act established the Agricultural Adjustment Administration (AAA). In 1934 the list of enumerated commodities was extended by the Jones-Connally Farm Relief Act and the Jones-Costigan Sugar Act.

The act relieved the credit situation by providing for the refinancing of farm mortgages through the agency of the Federal Land Banks. In addition, the Thomas Amendment to this act permitted the president to inflate the currency by the following means: devaluation of the gold content of the dollar, free coinage of silver at a ratio to gold determined by the president, and the issuance of paper currency to the amount of $3 billion. This last provision was never implemented by Roosevelt. The devaluation provision, however, enabled the president to make attempts to raise prices through control of the so-called "commodity dollar."

The processing tax and production control features of the Agricultural Adjustment Act were declared unconstitutional by the Supreme Court in *U.S.* v. *Butler* (1936, p. 677).

18 MAY. TENNESSEE VALLEY AUTHORITY. During World War I the national government, at a cost of $145 million, built a large hydroelectric power plant and two munitions plants at Muscle Shoals, on the Tennessee River in Alabama. During the 1920s the government unsuccessfully attempted to dispose of the Muscle Shoals facilities to private interests. Sen. **George W. Norris** (Neb., p. 1117) conducted a campaign to place the power resources of the Tennessee River at the service of the watershed's inhabitants, and to devote the World War I plants to the manufacture of fertilizer. On 25 May 1928 and again on 3 Mar. 1931 a group of legislators headed by Norris secured the passage of bills providing for government operation of Muscle Shoals, but the measures were vetoed by Presidents Coolidge and Hoover, respectively, on the ground that government operation would constitute governor of New York, Roosevelt sponsored and executed a statewide planning movement and helped to establish a state competition with private enterprise. As power authority. In Jan. 1933, he visited Muscle Shoals with a group of officials and experts. Before his accession to the presidency, Roosevelt envisioned for the Tennessee River drainage basin and adjoining territory a program embracing not merely power development but a plan of regional development based on the control and use of water resources. Aimed at furthering the general social and economic welfare of the region, the program contemplated flood control, land reclamation, the prevention of soil erosion, afforestation, the elimination of marginal lands from cultivation, and the distribution and diversification of industry.

The aims of Roosevelt and Norris were embodied in the act establishing the **Tennessee Valley Authority** (TVA), an independent public corporation with a board of three directors (the initial board consisted of Arthur E. Morgan, chairman; Harcourt A. Morgan, and David E. Lilienthal). The TVA was authorized to construct dams and power plants and to develop the economic and social well-being of the Tennessee Valley region (covering the states of Tenn.,

N.C., Ky., Va., Miss., Ga., and Ala.). It was authorized to produce, distribute, and sell electric power and nitrogen fertilizers to the industry and people of the region, and to sell explosives to the federal government. A "yardstick" for public utilities was embodied in the provisions for the construction of transmission lines to farms and villages not supplied with electricity at rates that were reasonable and fair, and for the selling of power to municipalities and other public bodies.

Between 1933 and 1944 9 main-river dams and many subsidiary ones were built along the water system. During World War II, TVA supplied the power facilities for the manufacture of munitions and aluminum and for the atom bomb plant at Oak Ridge, Tenn.

27 May. FEDERAL SECURITIES ACT was designed to compel full disclosure to investors of information relating to new securities issues publicly offered or sold through the mails or in interstate commerce. It required that with certain exceptions (e.g., federal, state, and municipal bonds; railroad securities; securities of religious, charitable, and educational bodies) all new issues were to be registered with the Federal Trade Commission by the filing of sworn statements placed on public file (in 1934 this function was transferred to the Securities and Exchange Commission).

5 June. GOLD REPEAL JOINT RESOLUTION, another move for making the abandonment of the gold standard effective, canceled the gold clause in all federal and private obligations and made contracts and debts payable in legal tender.

6 June. NATIONAL EMPLOYMENT SYSTEM ACT authorized a national employment system, established as the U.S. Employment Service, based on cooperation with states maintaining such agencies. It required matching of state appropriations for employment services.

13 June. HOME OWNERS REFINANCING ACT created the Home Owners Loan Corporation (HOLC), with a capital stock of $200 million and an authorized issue of $2 billion in bonds, to refinance home mortgage debts for nonfarm owners. Refinancing was accomplished by the exchange of HOLC bonds for mortgages and all other obligations (up to a total of $14,000), which were then converted into a single first mortgage. The HOLC was also empowered to furnish cash advances for taxes, repair, and maintenance up to 50% of appraised values on unencumbered properties. By the time the HOLC terminated its activities in June 1936, it had made loans covering 1 million mortgages.

16 June. BANKING ACT OF 1933 (GLASS-STEAGALL ACT) created the **Federal Bank Deposit Insurance Corporation** for guaranteeing individual bank deposits under $5,000. It also extended the open-market activities of the Federal Reserve Board to enable it to prevent excessive speculation on credit; permitted branch banking; divorced deposit from investment affiliates; and widened the membership of the Federal Reserve system to include savings and industrial banks.

16 June. FARM CREDIT ACT was designed to facilitate short-term and medium-term credits for agricultural production and marketing, thereby refinancing farm mortgages on long terms at low interest. On 27 Mar. President Roosevelt had by executive decree consolidated in a single agency, the Farm Credit Administration (FCA), the functions of all federal units dealing with agricultural credit (e.g., the Federal Farm Board, the Federal Farm Loan Board).

16 June. EMERGENCY RAILROAD TRANSPORTATION ACT, applying to carriers and subsidiaries subject to the Interstate Commerce Act, was designed to avoid unnecessary duplication of services and facilities; to promote financial reorganization of the carriers; and to provide for the study of other means of improving conditions pertaining to rail transportation. The act repealed the "recapture" clause of the Transportation Act of 1920, placed railroad holding companies under the supervision of the Interstate Commerce Commission, provided for a simpler rule of rate making, and created the office of Federal Coordinator of Transportation (a post to which **Joseph B. Eastman** was appointed).

16 June. NATIONAL INDUSTRIAL RECOVERY ACT (called the NIRA) was designed to revive industrial and business activity and to reduce unemployment. It was based on the principle of industrial self-regulation, operating under government supervision through a system of fair competition codes. The act created the National Recovery Administration (NRA) and formalized the fair trade codes that had been used by many industrial and trade associations in the period after World War I. Under the NIRA, fair competition codes drawn up by such associations and approved by the president were enforceable by law. The president was also empowered to prescribe codes for industries and to make agreements or approve voluntary agreements. Actions under codes and agreements were exempt from the operations of the antitrust laws. The courts could issue injunctions agains violators. When business pressure compelled the administration to abandon the Black-Connery-Perkins Bill, provision for labor was made in Section 7a of the NIRA guaranteeing labor's right "to organize and bargain collectively through representatives of their own choosing." Gen. **Hugh S. Johnson** (1882–1942) was appointed (16 June) head of the NRA, an

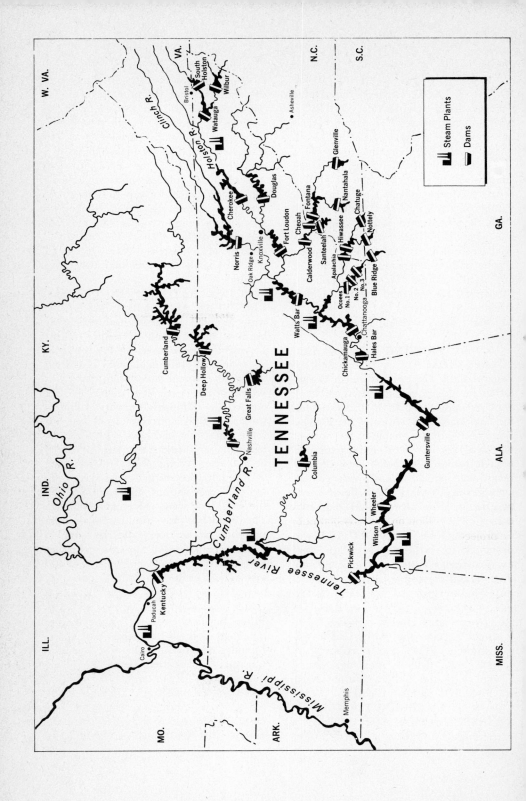

agency which ultimately affected about 500 fields and a total of 22 million employees. Sen. Robert F. Wagner (N.Y.) was appointed chairman of the **National Labor Board,** established (5 Aug.) by the president under NIRA to enforce the right of collective bargaining.

While the NRA was initially successful, code violations soon became increasingly frequent; complaints of cutthroat competition and unfair price fixing became numerous. The National Recovery Review Board, established on 19 Feb. 1934, reported (21 May 1934) that the NRA was encouraging monopoly and cartelization to the detriment of the small businessman. The Supreme Court held the NIRA unconstitutional in *Schechter Poultry Corp.* v. *U.S.* (1935, p. 676).

Title II of the NIRA established the **Public Works Administration** (PWA) for the construction of roads, public buildings, and other projects, for which a fund of $3,300 million was authorized. Secretary of the Interior **Harold L. Ickes** (p. 1065) was named (16 June) to head the agency. The PWA was created for the purpose of increasing employment and business activity by means of "pump priming" (i.e., the raising of popular consuming power). During its recovery phase, the PWA spent a total of more than $4,250 million on some 34,000 public projects.

16 June. Special session of the 73rd Congress adjourned.

18 Oct. COMMODITY CREDIT CORPORATION, an agency organized under the AAA with a capitalization of $3 million (increased in 1936 to $100 million), was authorized to use RFC funds for extending loans to farmers on their crops. Its purpose was to support farm prices by enabling producers to retain commodities. At the outset, loans were extended chiefly to cotton farmers; as a result cotton prices were bolstered.

22 Oct. "COMMODITY DOLLAR." President Roosevelt announced that he had authorized the RFC to establish a government market for gold newly mined in the U.S. and to buy and sell gold on the world market if necessary in order to enable the government to take "in its own hands the control of the gold value of our dollar."

The new gold policy was put into effect on 25 Oct., when the government set the price at $31.36 an ounce (as compared with $29.01 an ounce on the world market on 21 Oct.). The price was subsequently increased until it reached $34.06 on 18 Dec. The gold value of the dollar was set at 66 cts. This forced devaluation of the dollar, however, did not accomplish its object of raising farm commodity prices above the world level. Moreover, the measure provoked complaints from foreign nations (which feared that cheaper American goods gave U.S. exporters an unfair advantage in world trade); brought "sound money" elements in the Democratic party into open conflict with the administration; and ultimately led inflationist groups to increase their pressure for silver legislation.

8 Nov. CIVIL WORKS ADMINISTRATION (CWA) was established as an emergency unemployment relief program for the purpose of putting 4 million jobless persons to work on federal, state, and local make-work projects. **Harry L. Hopkins** was appointed (8 Nov.) as its administrator. Funds were allocated from FERA and PWA appropriations supplemented by local governments. The CWA was created to offset a drop in the business revival of mid-1933 and to cushion economic distress over the winter of 1933–34. The CWA was terminated in Mar. 1934, and transferred its functions to the FERA. Of the more than $933 million spent on 180,000 work projects, more than $740 million went directly into wages and salaries.

5 Dec. 21ST AMENDMENT to the Constitution, proposed on 20 Feb. 1933 and providing for the **repeal of the 18th (Prohibition) Amendment,** was declared ratified.

21 Dec. Acting under the Thomas Amendment to the Agricultural Adjustment Act, President Roosevelt ordered the Treasury to buy at 64½ cts. an ounce (21½ cts. above the prevailing market price) all the silver mined in the U.S. during the ensuing 4-year period.

1934

30 Jan. GOLD RESERVE ACT OF 1934 was designed to give the government full control over dollar devaluation and to increase commodity prices without relying on inflationary measures. The act empowered the president to do the following: to set the limits for devaluation of the dollar at from 50 to 60 cts. in relation to its gold content; to change the value within these limits from time to time, as deemed necessary by him; to impound in the Treasury the gold stocks held by the Federal Reserve banks; to assure to the government any profit that might accrue to the Treasury from an increase in the value of gold; and to use part of this profit to set up a fund (the Exchange Stabilization Fund) of $2 billion with which to stabilize the dollar. By proclamation (31 Jan.) Roosevelt fixed the value of the dollar at 59.06 cts.

31 Jan. FARM MORTGAGE REFINANCING ACT established the Federal Farm Mortgage Corporation (FFMC) under the Farm Credit Administration and authorized it to issue up to $2 billion in bonds guaranteed in principal and interest. The purpose of the FFMC was to further the refinancing of farm debts by exchanging its bonds for consolidated farm loan bonds and investing them directly in mortgage loans.

2 Feb. EXPORT-IMPORT BANK, established by President Roosevelt under powers granted to the RFC and NRA, was created to encourage the flow of overseas commerce by financing trade with foreign nations in the following ways: short-term credits in connection with the exportation of agricultural commodities, extension of longer-term credit to American firms desiring to export industrial manufactures, and loans to American exporters where foreign governments failed to provide their own nationals with sufficient exchange to permit them to meet dollar obligations. Two banks were set up, one to provide credits for trading with the Soviet Union, which had recently received formal diplomatic recognition by the U.S.; another (12 Mar.) to provide credit facilities for trading with Cuba and ultimately other foreign nations. Both banks were consolidated in a single bank in 1936.

15 Feb. CIVIL WORKS EMERGENCY RELIEF ACT authorized $950 million for use by the FERA until the end of the fiscal year 1935 for operating the program of civil works and direct relief. This program emerged (1935) as the Works Progress Administration (WPA). Under the Emergency Work Relief Program authorized by the Act of 15 Feb., a total of 2,500,000 unemployed were on the rolls by Jan. 1935, when direct relief was returned to state and local governments.

23 Feb. CROP LOAN ACT authorized the Farm Credit Administration to extend loans to agricultural producers in 1934 for crop production and harvesting. A fund of $40 million was set up for this purpose. Approximately $37,900,000 was loaned.

27 Mar. VINSON NAVAL PARITY ACT authorized the building of a full-treaty-strength navy within the limits set by the Washington Naval Limitations Treaty of 1922 and the London Naval Limitation Treaty of 1930. It provided for the construction of 100 warships and more than 1,000 airplanes over a 5-year period. Congress, however, did not appropriate sufficient funds, and until 1938 naval construction was carried out chiefly on a replacement basis.

28 MAR. INDEPENDENT OFFICES APPROPRIATIONS ACT represented the first defeat President Roosevelt sustained at the hands of Congress. The Senate and House passed (26 Mar.) the Independent Offices Bill restoring the cuts made under the Economy Act of 1933. It increased salaries of government employees by $125 million and the allowances of World War I veterans by $228 million. President Roosevelt vetoed the bill (27 Mar.) on the ground of economy. The House (310–72, 27 Mar.) and the Senate (63–27, 28 Mar.) overrode the veto.

7 APR. JONES-CONNALLY FARM RELIEF ACT extended the list of enumerated basic agricultural commodities subject to the Agricultural Adjustment Act, adding barley, flax, peanuts, grain sorghums, rye, and beef and dairy cattle.

21 APR. COTTON CONTROL ACT (BANKHEAD ACT) provided for the compulsory reduction of surplus cotton crops through the licensing of individual producers who in turn received benefit payments. The act, a departure from the voluntary principle of the AAA, authorized the fixing of a national limitation on the cotton crop and provided for the allocation of crops and marketing quotas for cotton-growing states, counties, and farmers. A tax of not less than 5 cts. a pound was authorized for production in excess of stipulated quotas.

27 APR. HOME OWNERS LOAN ACT guaranteed the principal and interest of the $2 billion in bonds authorized for the refinancing of home mortgages. From the funds made available as a result of the guarantee, the HOLC was enabled to extend further assistance for the repair and maintenance of homes and to provide funds to savings and loans associations operating under federal sponsorship.

9 MAY. JONES-COSTIGAN SUGAR ACT extended the list of enumerated basic crops subject to the Agricultural Adjustment Act to include sugar cane and sugar beets, and authorized benefit payments allocated from funds derived from a processing tax on sugar. It sought to stabilize the price of sugar by authorizing limitation on the national production of these sugar crops and empowered the Secretary of Agriculture to put all sugar imports on a quota basis. The decision of the Supreme Court in *U.S.* v. *Butler* (1936) invalidated the tax features of this act.

NYE MUNITIONS INVESTIGATION. The Senate voted (12 Apr.) an inquiry into the manufacture and traffic in arms in the U.S. Sen. **Gerald P. Nye** (N.D.) was appointed (23 Apr.) chairman of the Senate Munitions Investigating Committee, whose public hearings stressed the heavy profits made by American financiers and armament makers during World War I and sought to show, although without conclusive evidence, that the U.S. entry in World War I was due to the covert pressures they exerted. The activities of the Nye Committee, which continued until 1936, strengthened isolationist sentiment and set the domestic background for the neutrality legislation of 1935, 1936, and 1937 (see p. 388).

18 MAY. CRIME CONTROL ACTS. To counteract the widespread rise of racketeering, kidnaping, and other forms of crime, 6 new crime laws were enacted, among others empowering the federal government to punish persons assaulting, resisting, killing, or interfering with federal agents performing their law-enforcement duties and authorizing the death penalty for kidnapers taking their victims across state lines (the last as a result of the kidnaping and murder of the son of Charles A. and Anne Morrow Lindbergh (1 Mar. 1932). The federal criminal code was further strengthened by the Crime Prevention Compact Act (16 June) which permitted the states to enter into compacts for the prevention of crime and the enforcement of criminal laws.

24 May. MUNICIPAL BANKRUPTCY ACT permitted cities and other local government units to petition the federal courts for the ensuing 2 years to approve plans for readjusting their debt burden, providing that holders of 51% of outstanding obligations gave their consent.

6 June. SECURITIES EXCHANGE ACT provided for federal regulation of the operations of exchanges dealing in securities and for the correction of unfair practices in the securities markets. It established the **Securities and Exchange Commission** (SEC) and authorized that unit to license stock exchanges. It made trading in securities subject to the regulations of the SEC and prohibited price manipulation. It empowered the Federal Reserve Board to regulate the use of credit in financing trading in securities by prescribing regulations governing margin requirements (a move designed to curb speculation).

7 June. CORPORATE BANKRUPTCY ACT permitted the reorganization of corporations, provided that at least two thirds of their creditors consented, and stipulated that a petition for reorganization might be filed in court by a creditor or stockholder if approved by at least one fourth of other stockhold-

ers (10% where the corporation was not insolvent but unable to meet maturing obligations).

12 June. FARM MORTGAGE FORECLOSURE ACT authorized the Land Bank Commissioner to extend loans to farmers to enable the recovery of farm properties owned by them prior to foreclosure.

15 June. NATIONAL GUARD ACT made that military organization a part of the Army of the U.S. in time of war or during a national emergency declared by Congress.

19 June. COMMUNICATIONS ACT abolished the Federal Radio Commission and established the **Federal Communications Commission** (FCC) for the regulation of interstate and foreign communications by telegraph, cable, and radio. The act transferred to the FCC the authority of the Interstate Commerce Commission for control of communications, and imposed new regulations for the control of radio broadcasting.

19 June. SILVER PURCHASE ACT, a compromise measure passed to meet the demands for additional inflation voiced by farmer and silver interests in Congress, empowered the president to increase the monetary value of the Treasury's silver holdings until they should reach one third the value of its gold stocks; to nationalize silver stocks and purchases of domestic and foreign silver; and to impose a 50% profits tax on certain transfers of silver in order to preclude a windfall for silver speculators. By presidential order (9 Aug.) the Treasury was directed to buy all silver in the U.S. at 50 cts. an ounce, all newly mined silver at 64.64 cts. an ounce, and to pay for it with silver certificates at the rate of $1.29 an ounce (thereby placing silver on a 27–1 ratio with gold). This move benefited U.S. silver producers.

19 June. LABOR DISPUTES JOINT RESOLUTION established the National Labor Relations Board, replacing the National Labor Board, 1933.

27 June. RAILROAD RETIREMENT ACT OF 1934 was declared unconstitutional in *Railroad Retirement Board* v. *Alton R.R. Co.* (1935, p. 676).

27 June. CROSSER-DILL RAILWAY LABOR ACT (p. 768).

28 June. FEDERAL FARM BANKRUPTCY ACT (FRAZIER-LEMKE FARM BANKRUPTCY ACT), designed to prevent foreclosures, provided additional relief to farmers by enabling them to secure credit extensions. Provision was made whereby farmers could repurchase their properties at a newly appraised value with small annual payments, at an interest rate of 1%, distributed over a 6-year period. In the event creditors opposed such a settlement, farmers could retain possession on fair and reasonable terms for **5 years,** during which time bankruptcy proceedings were suspended. This act was declared unconstitutional in the case of *Louisville Joint Stock Land Bank* v. *Radford* (1935, 295 U.S. 555).

28 June. NATIONAL HOUSING ACT was designed to stimulate residential construction, promote improvement in housing standards, and create a sound system of home financing. It established the **Federal Housing Administration** (FHA) for the purpose of insuring loans made by banks, trust companies, building and loan associations, and other private lending institutions for new construction, repairs, alterations, and improvements. The act, which enabled the modernization of farm properties and of small business plants and equipment, increased the borrowing power of the HOLC to $3 billion.

28 June. TOBACCO CONTROL ACT (similar to the Cotton Control Act of 1934) authorized a compulsory production quota system for tobacco planters and subjected to an ad valorem tax producers who did not agree to crop reduction.

6 Nov. CONGRESSIONAL ELECTIONS gave the Democrats a gain of 9 seats in the Senate and 9 seats in the House. The 74th Congress was the first to convene (3 Jan. 1935) under the provisions of the 20th Amendment.

1935

4 Jan. SECOND NEW DEAL. In his annual message to Congress, President Roosevelt outlined a program of **social reform** that signalized the launching of the second New Deal, designating 3 major goals: security of livelihood through the better use of national resources; security against unemployment, old age, illness, and dependency; and slum clearance and better housing. He also recommended a national works program for absorbing the needy unemployed. The chief beneficiaries of the second New Deal were labor and the smaller farmers.

8 Apr. EMERGENCY RELIEF APPROPRIATION ACT signalized the withdrawal of the federal government from the arena of direct relief, which was left to the states and local communities, and provided for the establishment of a large-scale national works program for jobless employables, who were required to meet a means test in order to qualify for work relief. Established as the major agency of the program was the **Works Progress Administration** (WPA), which beginning in 1939 was called the **Works Projects Administration. Harry L. Hopkins** was appointed (6 May) administrator of the WPA. About 85% of the funds spent on WPA projects went directly into wages and salaries. Beginning in 1936 the "security wage" of WPA workers was based on the prevailing hourly rate, at reduced hours of work (the average monthly maximum schedule ranging between 120 and 140 hours). By Mar. 1936, the WPA rolls reached a total of more than 3,400,000 persons; after initial cuts in June 1939, it averaged 2,300,000 monthly; and by 30 June 1943, when it was officially terminated, the WPA had employed more than 8,500,000 different persons on 1,410,-000 individual projects, and had spent about $11 billion. While most of the projects were geared to the employment of manual labor, provision was made by way of arts projects for writers, actors, artists, and musicians. In addition to the WPA, other participating agencies in the national works program included the Public Works Administration, the Civilian Conservation Corps, and the National Youth Administration. During its 8-year history, the WPA built 651,087 miles of highways, roads, and streets; and constructed, repaired, or improved 124,031 bridges, 125,110 public buildings, 8,192 parks, and 853 airport landing fields. It operated community recreation and educational centers and carried out numerous surveys of federal, state, and local archives. The WPA was attacked on the grounds of inefficiency, extravagance, waste, and political corruption. Defenders pointed to its constructive achievements and to the rise in national purchasing power.

27 Apr. SOIL CONSERVATION ACT established the Soil Conservation Service as a permanent unit of the Department of Agriculture for the control and prevention of soil erosion.

1 May. RESETTLEMENT ADMINISTRATION (known as the RA) was established by executive order under powers granted by the Emergency Relief Appropriation Act of 1935. Undersecretary of Agriculture **Rexford G. Tugwell** was appointed administrator. The general objectives of the RA included the improvement of the conditions of impoverished farm families that had not been materially aided by the AAA, and the prevention of waste due to unprofitable farming operations and improper land use. The RA was authorized to administer projects involving resettlement of destitute or low-income families from rural and urban areas, or soil erosion, flood control, stream pollution, and reforestation; and to grant loans to enable the purchase of farm lands and equipment by smaller farmers, farm tenants, sharecroppers, or farm laborers. Among the activities of the RA were the establishment of subsistence homestead communities and the construction of suburban communities for low-income city workers—"Greenbelt towns," including Greenbelt (near Washington, D.C.), Greenhills (near Cincinnati), and Greendale (near Milwaukee). The functions of the RA were absorbed by the Farm Security Administration in 1937.

11 May. RURAL ELECTRIFICATION ADMINISTRATION (called the REA) was established by executive order under powers granted by the Emergency Relief Appropriation Act of 1935. Its purpose was to formulate and administer a program of generating and distributing electricity in isolated rural areas which were not served by private utilities. The REA was authorized to lend the entire cost of constructing light and power lines in such areas, on liberal terms of 3% interest, with amortization extended over a 20-year period. Priority was given to publicly owned plants distributing electricity.

22 May. VETO OF THE PATMAN BONUS BILL. The Patman Bill provided for the full and immediate payment in cash by issuance of $2,200 million greenbacks of the adjusted compensation certificates held by World War I veterans, which, under the act of 1924, were not due to mature until 1945. President Roosevelt, establishing a precedent by appearing before a joint session of Congress to deliver a veto message in person, rejected the bill, chiefly on the grounds that enactment of the measure would spur inflation and increase the national deficit. The House (322–98, 22 May) overrode the veto, but the Senate (54–40, 23 May) sustained it.

27 May. The NIRA was invalidated by the Supreme Court decision in the case of *Schechter Poultry Corp.* v. *U.S.* (p. 676).

7 June. NATIONAL RESOURCES COMMITTEE was created by executive order under powers granted by the Emergency Relief Appropriation Act of 1935 for the purpose of collecting and preparing plans, data, and information relating to the planned development and use of land, water, and other national resources. The successor to the National Resources Board set up on 30 June 1934, it later became known as the National Resources Planning Board and was entrusted with the preparation of long-range plans for the development of national resources and the stabilization of employment. It was terminated on 1 July 1943 upon failure of Congress to appropriate further funds.

26 June. NATIONAL YOUTH ADMINISTRATION (called the NYA) was established by executive order under powers granted by the Emergency Relief Appropriation Act of 1935. It was created as a part of the WPA and was placed under the direction of **Aubrey Williams**. The purpose of the NYA was to administer a work-relief and employment program for persons between the ages of 16 and 25, chiefly from relief families and no longer in regular full-time attendance at school, and to provide part-time employment for needy school, college, and graduate students to help them continue their education. By 1936, some 600,000 persons were engaged in NYA activities, with a peak in 1939–40 when about 750,000 students in 1,700 colleges and universities and more than 28,000 secondary schools received NYA benefits. In 1939 the NYA was transferred to the Federal Security Agency, and in 1942 became part of the War Manpower Commission. During 1941–43 it trained workers for national defense activities at an average rate of 30,000 a month. The NYA was terminated Sept. 1943.

5 July. NATIONAL LABOR RELATIONS ACT (WAGNER-CONNERY ACT) created a new National Labor Relations Board (NLRB) with power to determine appropriate collective bargaining units subject to elections it supervised at the request of the workers, to certify the duly chosen trade union, and to take testimony about unfair employer practices and issue cease and desist orders. Section 7 upheld the right of employees to join labor organizations and to bargain collectively through representatives of their own choosing. Section 8 defines unfair labor practices on the employers' part. The constitutionality of the act was upheld by the Supreme Court (Mar. 1937, p. 677). This legislation was soon complemented by state "Wagner Acts."

9 Aug. MOTOR CARRIER ACT placed buses and trucks engaged in interstate commerce under the authority of the Interstate Commerce Commission, which was empowered to regulate finances, labor, and minimum and maximum rates.

ANTI-NEW DEAL COALITION. Dissatisfaction with the social, fiscal, and other aspects of the New Deal led to the emergence of several organized antiadministration groups during 1934–35. The **Liberty League** (est. Aug. 1934), which drew its following from industrialists, financiers, corporation lawyers, conservative Democrats, and others, attacked the New Deal as a departure from the Constitution and actively opposed the passage of such measures as the Wagner-Connery Labor Relations Bill and the Wealth Tax Bill. The **Old Age Revolving Pension** scheme proposed by Dr. **Francis E. Townsend** of Long Beach, Calif., called for payments of $200 a month to persons 60 years of age and over, the pensions to be drawn from a national 2% tax on commercial transactions. The **Share-Our-Wealth** movement inspired by Sen. **Huey P. Long** (La., p. 1088) demanded that the federal government make "Every Man a King" by guaranteeing a minimum annual income of $5,000 to every family. Rev. **Gerald L. K. Smith** succeeded to Long's leadership of the Share-Our-Wealth clubs and formed an alliance with the Townsend movement, later to include Rev. **Charles E. Coughlin,** of Royal Oak, Mich., who in 1934 organized the **National Union for Social Justice.** Coughlin advocated a program of social reform that was specific in its support of silver inflation but vague on most other points. His radio speeches, directed against international bankers, Communists, labor unions, and the Roosevelt administration, attracted a national audience. The Smith-Townsend-Coughlin coalition gained in strength during 1935 and in 1936 emerged as a third-party movement. However, it never succeeded in uniting under a single and continuous leadership.

14 Aug. SOCIAL SECURITY ACT (an administration measure motivated in part by an attempt to win over the Townsend-Long following) created the Social Security Board as a general administrative agency and provided for the following in relation to unemployment compensation, old-age security, and various social services: (1) Establishment of a cooperative federal-state system of **unemployment compensation** designed to promote substantial uniformity of unemployment insurance plans among the various states and to invite the states to legislate in this field. The act levied a federal tax on total payrolls of employers of 8 or more workers (with certain exceptions, including agricultural laborers) equal to 1% in 1936, 2% in 1937, and 3% thereafter. Each state was to administer its own insurance system, and was to receive credit up to 90% of the federal tax. The act authorized grants to the states to enable them to meet administrative costs in providing unemployment insurance. (2) A tax for **old-age and survivors' insurance** to be levied in equal amounts upon all employers and employees (with specified exceptions) commencing at 1% in 1937 and gradually increasing to 3% in 1949. This part of the act was exclusively federal in scope and character. Out of the national fund created by these taxes the federal government was to pay to retired individuals 65 years of age and over a retirement pension (beg. 1 Jan. 1942) ranging from a minimum of $10 to a maximum of $85 per month, depending upon the number of working years during which the employee contributed. (3) Authorized money grants to states to help them meet the cost of **old-age pensions allowed under state laws** to aged persons in need of relief, the grants to match the amount contributed by the state, with a maximum federal contribution of $15 per month for each individual plus a small amount for administrative purposes. (4) Authorized money grants to the states to assist them in relief of the destitute blind and of homeless, crippled, dependent, and delinquent children, and in services such as public health work, vocational rehabilitation, and maternity and infant care. The tax features of the act were upheld by the Supreme Court in *Steward Machine Co.* v. *Davis* and *Helvering et al.* v. *Davis* (1937).

23 Aug. **BANKING ACT OF 1935** included the following provisions: (1) The title of the Federal Reserve Board changed to the Board of Governors of the Federal Reserve System, the board's ex-officio members were eliminated, and its membership increased from 6 to 7, with 1 member to serve as chairman for 4 years; (2) control over the regulation of credit vested in an Open Market Committee consisting of the Board of Governors and 5 representatives of the Federal Reserve banks; (3) purchase of government securities by the Federal Reserve banks confined to open-market operations; (4) Board of Governors empowered to increase the reserve requirements of member banks up to a limit of twice existing maximums; (5) Federal Reserve banks permitted to lend to member banks on time or demand notes with maturities not exceeding 4 months; (6) national banks authorized to make real estate loans.

28 Aug. **PUBLIC UTILITY HOLDING COMPANY ACT (WHEELER-RAYBURN ACT)**, designed to counteract the monopolistic public utility holding company device for controlling gas and electric operating companies, vested in the Federal Power Commission authority to regulate interstate transmission of electric power; in the Federal Trade Commission authority over gas; in the SEC authority over financial practices of such holding companies. The act restricted electric and gas holding companies to operations as single and concentrated systems confined to a single area, and called for simplification of the corporate structure of utility holding companies in order to eliminate pyramiding. The **"death sentence"** clause set a term of 5 years, at the end of which any holding company which could not demonstrate its localized, useful, and efficient character would be dissolved. In compliance public utility holding companies

had by 1952 divested 753 affiliates, with assets of $10.3 billion.

29 Aug. **FARM MORTGAGE MORATORIUM ACT OF 1935 (FRAZIER-LEMKE ACT OF 1935)** was passed following the Supreme Court decision invalidating the Federal Farm Bankruptcy Act of 1934. It provided for a 3-year moratorium against seizure for farmers who secured court permission, thus enabling debt-burdened farmers to keep possession of their properties by paying a fair and reasonable rental determined by the court.

29 Aug. **WAGNER-CROSSER RAILROAD RETIREMENT ACT** provided pensions for railroad employees after retirement and established a **Railroad Retirement Board** of 3 members appointed by the president to administer the law; amended and incorporated in the Railroad Retirement Act of 1937 (24 June).

30 Aug. **GUFFEY-SNYDER BITUMINOUS COAL STABILIZATION (or CONSERVATION) ACT**, popularly known as the "little NRA," created the **Bituminous Coal Labor Board** and the **National Bituminous Coal Commission** to administer production quota, price-fixing, and labor regulations based on the NRA soft coal code. The act sought to stabilize the bituminous coal-mining industry. A 15% tax based on the market value of coal was levied on producers, with 90% of the tax being remitted to producers complying with the code. The act was invalidated by the Supreme Court decision in the case of *Carter* v. *Carter Coal Co. et al.* (1936) and was succeeded by the Guffey-Vinson Act (1937).

30 Aug. **REVENUE ACT OF 1935 (WEALTH TAX ACT)**. In his message to Congress on tax revision (19 June), President Roosevelt declared: "Our revenue laws have operated in many ways to the unfair advantage of the few, and they have done little to prevent an un-

just concentration of wealth and economic power." His recommendations were embodied in the Revenue Act, which increased the surtax rate on individual incomes over $50,000 and affected individual estates of decedents over $40,-000. Taxes on individual incomes above $1 million were graduated steeply to 75% on income in excess of $5 million. Although an inheritance tax feature proposed by the president was eliminated from the bill, estate and gift tax rates were increased. In place of the existing uniform tax of 13¾%, income tax rates for small corporations were lowered to 12½%; rates on all corporation incomes above $50,000 raised to 15%; additional taxes of 6% were levied on profits in excess of 10%, graduated to 12% on profits in excess of 15%.

1936

6 Jan. The Agricultural Adjustment Act was invalidated by the Supreme Court in *U.S.* v. *Butler* (p. 677).

24 Jan. ADJUSTED COMPENSATION ACT. A bill calling for full and immediate cash payment of adjusted service (bonus) certificates held by World War I veterans demanding payment before the maturity date (1945) was passed by the Senate (20 Jan.) and the House (22 Jan.), but was vetoed by President Roosevelt (24 Jan.). Both branches of Congress immediately overrode his veto. The act authorized the issuance of 9-year interest-bearing bonds convertible into cash at any time. On 15 June more than $1,500 million in bonus bonds were distributed to some 3 million World War I veterans.

29 Feb. SOIL CONSERVATION AND DOMESTIC ALLOTMENT ACT, designed to replace the invalidated AAA, enabled the continued restriction of agricultural output, not by contracts with farmers for the control of crop production, but by **benefit payments** to growers who practiced soil conservation in cooperation with the government program. Farmers participating in the program through their county agricultural associations leased to the government land withdrawn from use for soil-depleting crops (such as corn, cotton, tobacco, wheat, and oats), and in return received compensation for their efforts to check wastage of fertility and erosion. Payments depended upon acreage withdrawn from soil-depleting crop production and turned over to soil-conserving crops. Provision was made whereby sharecroppers and tenants received part of the payments.

20 June. FEDERAL ANTI-PRICE DISCRIMINATION ACT (ROBINSON-PATMAN ACT), aimed primarily at chain stores engaged in interstate commerce, made illegal unreasonably low prices tending to destroy competition and empowered the Federal Trade Commission to abolish price discrimination tending to promote monopoly or reduce competition.

22 June. REVENUE ACT OF 1936 included among its provisions an undistributed profits tax on corporate income that added to the normal corporation income tax a scale of surtaxes ranging from 7% to 27%—attacked by business groups as penalizing the setting aside of corporate profits for expansion or as reserves for slack periods.

22 June. FLOOD CONTROL ACT (p. 639).

26 June. MERCHANT MARINE ACT OF 1936, substituted for the U.S. Shipping Board the **U.S. Maritime Commission,** an independent regulatory agency empowered to carry out a program to develop an American merchant marine through government aid. The act eliminated subsidies in the form of ocean mail contracts and provided instead outright subsidies based on differentials between foreign and domestic operating and construction costs. Other provisions of the act related to labor standards for seamen. As amended 23 June 1938 a **Maritime Labor Board** was established, primarily as a mediatory agency. In 1941 the board was shorn of its mediatory functions.

30 JUNE. WALSH-HEALY GOVERNMENT CONTRACTS ACT provided that all persons employed by a contractor dealing with the U.S. goverment shall be paid not less than the prevailing minimum wages as determined by the Secretary of Labor and shall not be permitted to work in excess of 8 hours a day or 40 hours a week; child labor (boys under 16, girls under 18) and convict labor barred in government contracts.

PRESIDENTIAL CAMPAIGN. The Socialist Labor Party Convention met at New York City (26 Apr.) and nominated John W. Aiken (Mass.) for president and Emil F. Teichert (N.Y.) for vice-president. The Prohibition Party Convention met at Niagara Falls, N.Y. (5 May), and nominated Dr. D. Leigh Colvin (N.Y.) for president and Claude A. Watson (Calif.) for vice-president. The Socialist Party National Convention met at Cleveland (23 May) and nominated Norman Thomas (N.Y.) for president and George Nelson (Wis.) for vice-president.

The Republican National Convention met at Cleveland (9 June) and on 11 June nominated Gov. **Alfred M. Landon** (Kan., 1887–   ) for president; on 12 June Col. **Frank Knox** (Ill.) was chosen for vice-president. The Republican platform condemned the New Deal, accused President Roosevelt of usurping the powers of Congress, and charged that regulated monopoly had displaced free enterprise and unconstitutional laws been passed. The platform called for return of responsibility for relief administration to nonpolitical local agencies, the protection of the rights of labor to organize and to bargain collectively, a balanced budget, farm subsidies, a revamped system of social security, opposed further devaluation of the dollar; but made no specific proposals for repealing New Deal legislation except for revising corporate and personal income taxation policies. During the campaign the Republicans were supported by conservative Democrats (including Alfred E. Smith, Bainbridge Colby, and John W. Davis) active in the Liberty League.

Rep. **William Lemke** (N.D.), a Republican, announced (19 June) that he would be presidential candidate on the Union party ticket and that the vice-presidential candidate would be Thomas C. O'Brien (Mass.). Lemke's candidacy was endorsed by Rev. Charles E. Coughlin, whose organization, the National Union for Social Justice, backed the endorsement at its first national convention, held at Cleveland (14 Aug.). The Union party platform, which denounced the New Deal, was drawn up with an eye to attracting the supporters of Coughlin, Townsend, and Gerald L. K. Smith.

The Democratic National Convention met at Philadelphia (23 June) and renominated President **Roosevelt** on 26 June and Vice-President **John N. Garner** on 27 June. The convention **abolished the two-thirds rule** for choosing candidates, in force since 1832, and restored the simple majority rule. In his acceptance speech (27 June), President Roosevelt attacked "economic royalists" who, he claimed, had "created a new despotism and wrapped it in the robes of legal sanction." The Democratic platform took its stand on the administration's record.

Labor's Nonpartisan League (which included the American Labor party in New York State) and the National Progressive Conference endorsed Roosevelt's candidacy.

The Communist Party National Convention met at New York City (24 June) and nominated Earl Browder (Kan.) for president and James W. Ford (N.Y.) for vice-president.

The campaign ranked among the most bitterly waged in U.S. political history. The Republicans attacked the New Deal as a bureaucratic, planned economy. About 80% of the press opposed Roosevelt. In defense, Roosevelt declared in his opening speech of the campaign (Syracuse, N.Y., 29 Sept.): "The true conservative seeks to protect the system of private property and free enterprise by correcting such injustices and inequalities as arise from it."

3 Nov. PRESIDENTIAL ELECTION. Popular vote: **Roosevelt,** 27,751,-612; Landon, 16,681,913; Lemke, 891,-858; Thomas, 187,342; Browder, 80,181; Colvin, 37,609; Aiken, 12,729. Electoral vote: **Roosevelt,** 523; Landon, 8. Roosevelt carried every state but Maine and Vermont, winning the most overwhelming electoral majority since Monroe's victory in 1820 and the greatest in any national contest in which there were 2 or more separate tickets. The election gave the Democrats majorities of 76–16 in the Senate and 331–89 in the House.

1937

20 Jan. Inauguration of President Franklin D. Roosevelt, serving his 2d term; John N. Garner, vice-president. Roosevelt was the first president inaugurated on this day, set by the 20th Amendment. In his inaugural address, Roosevelt reemphasized his objectives of social justice. The challenge to American democracy, he said, is the "tens of millions of its citizens . . . who at this very moment are denied the greater part of what the very lowest standards of today call the necessities of life. . . . I see one-third of a nation ill-housed, ill-clad, ill-nourished. . . ."

5 Feb.–22 July. SUPREME COURT FIGHT. The continued invalidation by the Supreme Court of major New Deal economic and social legislation led to the severest test of President Roosevelt's political leadership. On 5 Feb. Roosevelt submitted to Congress a plan for reorganizing the federal judiciary. His proposal included the following: (1) an increase in the membership of the Supreme Court from 9 to a maximum of 15 if judges reaching the age of 70 declined to retire; (2) addition of a total of not more than 50 judges to all levels of the federal courts; (3) sending of appeals from lower-court decisions on constitutional questions directly to the Supreme Court; (4) requiring that government attorneys be heard before any lower court issued an injunction against the enforcement of any act of Congress where the question of constitutionality was involved; and (5) assigning district judges to congested areas in order to expedite court business.

Announcement of the plan aroused widespread and bitter debate. The opposition concentrated on the proposal for increasing the Supreme Court membership. Roosevelt was accused of perverting the Constitution, and of attempting to "pack" the Supreme Court, to destroy judicial independence and integrity, and to aggrandize the power of the executive. Even administration adherents in and out of Congress who believed that the court plan had its merits insisted that the proper mode of making the change lay in a constitutional amendment. By early Mar. the bill had produced serious disunity in Democratic ranks in Congress. Sen. Burton K.

Wheeler (Mon.), a New Dealer, took the lead in campaigning against the measure. At the hearings which the Senate Judiciary Committee conducted on the proposal the weight of recorded opinion was against the plan. The opposition took heart from a personal letter (21 Mar.) which Chief Justice Charles E. Hughes sent to Sen. Wheeler pointing out that the Supreme Court was fully abreast of its work and needed no new justices.

When it became clear that the drift of congressional opinion was against the Judiciary Reorganization Bill, President Roosevelt took personal command of the campaign for the measure. In an address at the Democratic Victory Dinner held at Washington, D.C. (4 Mar.), he asserted that the "Personal economic predilections" of the court majority had rendered the national and state governments powerless to deal with pressing problems. In a fireside chat to the nation (9 Mar.), he declared that the courts had "cast doubts on the ability of the elected Congress to protect us against catastrophe by meeting squarely our modern social and economic conditions," and maintained that the purpose of the bill was to restore that balance of power among the 3 major branches of the federal government intended by the framers of the Constitution.

A number of developments contributed to the weakening of the claims for the urgency of the bill. The Supreme Court Retirement Act (1 Mar.), approved by Roosevelt, permitted Supreme Court justices to retire at the age of 70. The impending retirement of Justice Willis Van Devanter, a foe of the New Deal, was announced on 18 May. The death (14 July) of Sen. Joseph T. Robinson (Ark.), majority leader of the Senate fight for the reorganization plan, weakened further the administration forces. But even more compelling, the

Supreme Court in a number of leading decisions (29 Mar.–24 May) sustained important New Deal and state legislation, including the Washington state minimum-wage law for women, the Frazier-Lemke Farm Mortgage Moratorium Act of 1935, the Social Security Act, and the Wagner Labor Relations Act. These decisions, tantamount to judicial approval of the second New Deal, indicated that the court personnel was responsive to the national temper, and induced the administration to compromise. On 22 July the Senate (70–20) recommitted the original reorganization bill to the Judiciary Committee, where it died. On 26 Aug. President Roosevelt signed the **Judicial Procedure Reform Act,** a modified measure that reformed the procedure of the lower courts but made no provision for the appointment of new justices and judges.

Political costs of the court battle: (1) brought into the open a break on domestic policy in the Democratic ranks that, except for the liberal wing of the party, was never fully repaired and became especially evident in the congressional elections of 1938; (2) enabled Republicans and conservative Democrats to block other administration-sponsored legislation, such as the Executive Reorganization Bill (finally passed in 1939), whose merits were overlooked in the heat of feeling against the proposal for revamping the courts.

Although Roosevelt failed to secure provisions for adding new judges to the Supreme Court, he filled 7 vacancies on the court within the following 4 years. Among the justices appointed by him were Hugo Black (Ala.) in 1937, Stanley Reed (Ky.) in 1938, Felix Frankfurter (Mass.) in 1939, William O. Douglas (Conn.) in 1939, Frank Murphy (Mich.) in 1940, Robert H. Jackson (N.Y.) in 1941, and James F. Byrnes (S.C.) in 1941.

26 APR. GUFFEY-VINSON BITU-MINOUS COAL ACT reenacted all of the chief provisions of the outlawed Guffey-Snyder Act of 1935 with the exception of the wages-and-hours clause. It authorized the promulgation of a new code of fair competition for the bituminous coal industry (promulgated on 21 June), placed the output of soft coal under federal regulation, laid a revenue tax of 1 ct. a ton on soft coal, and imposed on noncode producers a penalty tax of 19½% of the sales price.

22 JULY. BANKHEAD-JONES FARM TENANT ACT, designed to cope with the steady decline in U.S. farm ownership and the rise of farm tenancy and sharecropping, established the **Farm Security Administration** (FSA), under which the Resettlement Administration was placed. The act authorized low-interest loans repayable in small installments over a 40-year period to farm tenants, sharecroppers, and farm laborers whose applications for the purchase of farms were approved by committees of local farmers. The act also authorized rehabilitation loans for operating expenses and educational assistance. The FSA, often against heavy opposition from Southern conservatives, developed a program of regulating the supply and wages and hours of migrant workers, of aid to migrants by way of sanitary camps and medical services, and of cooperative homestead communities.

18 AUG. MILLER-TYDINGS EN-ABLING ACT, reluctantly signed by President Roosevelt as a "rider" to an appropriations bill for the District of Columbia, amended the federal antitrust laws so as to legalize contracts made by producers or distributors for the resale price maintenance of branded nationally advertised goods traded in interstate commerce in states where such contracts, authorized by state laws, were illegal under existing federal statutes. The num-ber of states immediately affected was 42. The act was supported by influential trade associations on the ground it would end destructive competition brought on by price cutting.

26 AUG. REVENUE ACT OF 1937 was aimed at closing loopholes in the income-tax laws which permitted evasion of tax payments.

1 SEPT. NATIONAL HOUSING ACT (commonly known as the WAGNER-STEAGALL ACT), designed to alleviate housing conditions in low-income groups, established the **U.S. Housing Authority** (USHA) under the Department of the Interior, authorized to extend low-interest 60-year loans to local public agencies meeting at least 10% of the cost of low-cost slum clearance and housing projects, and to grant subsidies for setting rents geared to low-income levels in areas where local agencies provided an amount equal to 25% of the federal grant. By 1 Jan. 1941 the USHA had made loan contracts for 511 low-rent public housing projects containing a total of 161,162 dwelling units whose estimated development cost was $767,526,-000. During World War II the USHA was active in planning, constructing, and operating defense housing facilities.

15 Nov.–21 DEC. SPECIAL SESSION OF CONGRESS. On 12 Oct. President Roosevelt issued a proclamation calling Congress to convene in extra session on 15 Nov. On that date he submitted a message recommending the passage of legislation including a new agricultural program, wages-and-hours standards, reorganization of the executive branch, and planning for the conservation and development of national resources. During the 5-week session, Congress failed to enact any of the recommended measures, largely owing to the defection of Southern Democratic conservatives who joined with Republicans in blocking the administration's program.

1938

3 JAN. Although his annual message to Congress was for the most part concerned with domestic issues, President Roosevelt opened it with a reference to unsettled world conditions, declaring: "We must keep ourselves adequately strong in self-defense." On 28 Jan. he submitted to Congress recommendations for increased expenditures for armaments, including $8,800,000 for antiaircraft matériel, $6,080,000 for defense industry tools, and a 220% increase in the authorized naval construction program.

10 JAN. LUDLOW RESOLUTION. Beginning in 1935, the Ludlow Resolution for a national referendum on a declaration of war, sponsored by Rep. **Louis Ludlow** (Ind.), was introduced several times but failed of passage. The proposed resolution, in the form of a constitutional amendment, stated that except in the event of an invasion of the U.S. or its territorial possessions, the authority of Congress to declare war should not become effective until confirmed by a majority vote in a nationwide referendum. After the amendment was reintroduced in 1937, a national poll revealed that 73% of those polled favored a popular referendum of this type (however, the poll also showed that majority opinion favored a larger army and navy for defense). With the convening of the 2d session of the 75th Congress passage seemed assured. President Roosevelt sent a letter (6 Jan.) to Speaker William B. Bankhead asserting: "Such an amendment to the Constitution as that proposed would cripple any President in his conduct of our foreign relations, and it would encourage other nations to believe that they could violate American rights with impunity." The House (209–188) returned the resolution to committee. The vote for consideration of the resolution came from most Republican members and from most Democratic members from Western areas; opposed were representatives from the South and Northeast.

16 FEB. AGRICULTURAL ADJUSTMENT ACT OF 1938. When it became apparent that the Soil Conservation and Domestic Allotment Act of 1936 had proved unable to curb farm surpluses and price declines during the recession of 1937–38, that act was superseded by an administration-sponsored measure which revived the Agricultural Adjustment Act of 1933 in modified form. The processing taxes of the original AAA were eliminated, and financing provided out of the federal treasury. The act (1) empowered the Secretary of Agriculture to fix a marketing quota whenever it was determined that a surplus of any export farm commodity (such as cotton, wheat, rice, tobacco, and corn) threatened the price level; (2) authorized acreage allotments to each grower after two thirds of the farmers had by referendum expressed their approval of the marketing quota; (3) incorporated the **"parity payment"** principle and established the **"ever-normal granary"** arrangement by the following means: the Commodity Credit Corporation was authorized to make loans to farmers on their surplus crops at a level slightly below "parity" (a price based on the Aug. 1909–July 1914 level of farm purchasing power). Such excess crops were to be stored under government auspices, and the farmer was to repay the loan and market the surplus during crop failure years when the price was at "parity" or above. Since such disposal of surpluses would prevent the market price from rising too high above "parity," this arrangement stabilized agricultural prices and stored surplus crops without loss to individual farmer income.

The act also established the **Federal Crop Insurance Corporation** (FCIC) as an agency of the Department of Agriculture with a capitalization of $100 million, authorized to insure wheat crops only, beginning with the harvest of 1939, by accepting wheat in payment of premiums on insurance policies taken out against crop losses from unavoidable causes (such as drought, flood, hail, and plant diseases) ranging from 50% to 75% of the average yield.

14 APR. ROOSEVELT AND BUSI-NESS RECESSION. To combat the business recession under way since Aug. 1937, President Roosevelt sent to Congress a series of recommendations, which he outlined to the nation in a fireside chat the same day. They involved a reversal of the administration's deflationary policy, the expansion of WPA rolls from 1,500,000 to 3 million, a $3-billion recovery and relief program, "desterilizing" more than $3 billion in idle gold in the Treasury, "pump-priming" through RFC loans, and a "loose money" policy authorized by the Board of Governors of the Federal Reserve System. On 21 June the Emergency Relief Appropriation Act became law.

17 MAY. NAVAL EXPANSION ACT OF 1938 (also known as VINSON NAVAL ACT) authorized a $1,090,656,-000 expansion of a "2-ocean" navy over the ensuing 10 years and provided for a maximum increase of 135,000 tons in capital ships up to a tonnage of 660,000, a maximum increase of 68,754 tons in cruisers up to a tonnage of 412,500, and an increase of 40,000 tons in aircraft carriers up to a tonnage of 175,000.

26 MAY. HOUSE COMMITTEE TO INVESTIGATE UN-AMERICAN AC-TIVITIES, popularly known as the Dies Committee after its chairman, **Martin Dies** (Tex.), was established for the purpose of conducting investigations into Nazi, Fascist, Communist and other organizations termed "un-American" in character.

27 MAY. REVENUE ACT OF 1938, supported by Democratic and Republican opponents of the New Deal on the ground that tax concessions to business were necessary for the stimulation of the national economy, was passed by Congress on 11 May and became law without the signature of President Roosevelt. It repealed the progressive normal tax and undistributed profits tax authorized in 1936 and substituted a tax of 19% on corporations whose income exceeded $25,000, with the tax being reduced by a flat 2½% of dividends paid out of income subject to the tax (in effect it reduced taxes on large corporations and increased them on smaller firms). The measure also drastically modified the progressive tax provisions applicable to capital gains and losses.

16 JUNE. TEMPORARY NATIONAL ECONOMIC COMMITTEE (TNEC) was a joint legislative-executive body authorized by joint congressional resolution and established under the chairmanship of Sen. **Joseph C. O'Mahoney** (Wyo.), with **Leon Henderson** serving as executive secretary. Earlier, 29 Apr., President Roosevelt had submitted to Congress recommendations for curbing monopolies and the growing concentration of economic power. The TNEC conducted public hearings (1 Dec. 1938–26 Apr. 1940) to determine the effects of monopoly on prices, wages, profits, consumption, investment, cartels, patents, and many other aspects of the national economy with a view to improving federal antitrust policy and procedure. In its final report (31 Mar. 1941) the committee included the following among its recommendations: (1) amendment of the patent laws and revision of Patent Office procedure; (2) amendment of the Clayton Antitrust Act to lessen centralization of corporate resources; (3) prohibition of specified activities of trade associations tending to violate the antitrust laws; (4) legislation authorizing the Federal Trade Commission to forbid corporations from acquiring the assets of competing corporations over a certain size, unless it could be shown that such acquisition was in the public interest; (5) legislation to deal with the control exercised by foreign governments and their industry over American concerns through patent laws; (6) repeal of the Miller-Tydings Act of 1937; (7) allocation of defense funds in such a way as to eliminate monopoly control of basic products; (8) legislation prohibiting the use of "basing point" and other industrial pricing systems resulting in the elimination of competition; and (9) additional appropriations to strengthen the machinery for enforcing the antitrust laws by the Department of Justice and the Federal Trade Commission. Some antitrust suits initiated as a direct result of the TNEC's activities were suspended during World War II.

22 June. Chandler Act, amending **Federal Bankruptcy Act of 1898,** providing under Chapter XI procedures available to persons, partnerships, or corporations in financial distress, to voluntarily petition for the settlement, satisfaction, or extension of time of payment of unsecured debts, if acceptable to majority of creditors of each class affected, so as to avoid liquidation.

24 June. FOOD, DRUG, AND COSMETIC ACT, following enactment (21 Mar.) of **Wheeler-Lea Act** (broadening Federal Trade Commission's control over advertising of food, drugs, and cosmetics), superseded Pure Food Act of 1906. It prohibited misbranding of products; required manufacturers of foods, drugs, and cosmetics to list on their products' labels the ingredients used in processing; and forbade the use of false and misleading advertising claims dis-

seminated in more than 1 state. Enforcement of misbranding was left to the Food and Drug Administration; of advertising, to FTC, also given extended powers over unfair trade practices.

25 June. FAIR LABOR STANDARDS ACT (WAGES AND HOURS LAW), applied to enterprises which engaged in, or which affected, interstate commerce, with many occupations exempted (including farm laborers, domestic servants, and professional workers); established (1) a minimum wage of 40 cts. an hour (amended to 75 cts. an hour, 1949; to, most recently, $2.25, 1974) and (2) a maximum work week of 40 hours, to be put into effect, for wages, within 8 years beginning at 25 cts. an hour, and for hours, at 3 years beginning at 44 hours per week, with time and a half for overtime (750,000 workers received wage increases when the law went into effect in Aug.); (3) forbade labor by children under 16, and restricted to nonhazardous occupations those under 18. Constitutionality upheld by the Supreme Court in *U.S.* v. *Darby Lumber Co.* (1941, p. 678).

4 July. "THE NATION'S NO. 1 ECONOMIC PROBLEM." As a result of a request by President Roosevelt (22 June) to the National Emergency Council to prepare a report on the problems and needs of the South, the Conference on Economic Conditions in the South met at Washington. In a message (4 July) to the conference, Roosevelt declared: "It is my conviction that the South presents right now the nation's No. 1 economic problem." The findings of the conference, set forth in the comprehensive *Report on Economic Conditions of the South,* issued 12 Aug., pointed out that despite the South's good natural and human resources and potential untapped market, its people suffered from inadequate living standards.

8 Nov. CONGRESSIONAL ELEC-TIONS. To lessen the dependence of the New Deal domestic and foreign program on conservative Democrats (alienated from the administration over such issues as the Fair Labor Standards Act, the Anti-Lynching Bill [defeated by a Southern filibuster], and appropriations for the Farm Security Administration), President Roosevelt decided to participate actively in the Democratic primary campaign in order to effect the nomination of party liberals, with a fireside chat (24 June). The primary campaigns in selected districts in which Roosevelt made direct appeals included New York City, Georgia, Maryland, and Kentucky. Roosevelt's personal intervention fell far short of its intended goal. He failed to defeat Walter F. George (Ga.) and Millard F. Tydings (Md.), but scored a victory over Rep. John J. O'Connor of New York City. Although the Democrats retained control of both branches of Congress, the elections indicated the first Republican gains since 1928. The Democrats lost 7 seats in the Senate, 80 in the House. The composition of the 76th Congress was as follows: Senate, 69 Democrats, 23 Republicans, 2 Farmer-Laborites, 1 Progressive, 1 Independent; House, 261 Democrats, 164 Republicans, 4 others.

1939

4 JAN. In his annual message to Congress, President Roosevelt for the first time since taking office proposed no new domestic reforms, but stressed the dangers posed to democracy and international peace by the forces of aggression.

5 JAN. The $9-billion budget submitted to Congress by President Roosevelt for the fiscal year 1940 included $1,319,558,000 for national defense.

12 JAN. President Roosevelt urged Congress to pass additional appropria-

tions, amounting to $525 million, for an emergency program of national defense. He proposed that $300 million of this sum be used for military aviation to strengthen the air defenses of the continental U.S. and outlying possessions and territories, and suggested that the balance be devoted to the "2-ocean" navy, the training of civilian air pilots, the facilitating of matériel procurement, and the improvement and strengthening of the seacoast defenses of Panama, Hawaii, and the continental U.S. On 4 Mar. he requested further appropriations to increase the national defense, and on 26 Apr. signed an appropriations bill for $549 million. On 29 Apr. he submitted an additional request for defense appropriations.

3 APR. ADMINISTRATIVE REORGANIZATION ACT OF 1939. On 12 Jan. 1937 the report of the President's Committee on Administrative Management was submitted to Congress with President Roosevelt's recommendation for the enactment of most of its proposals. The Executive Reorganization Bill aimed to increase government efficiency by regrouping and simplifying the many federal agencies, boards, commissions, and other units that had come into existence since the turn of the century, and thereby reduce or eliminate overlapping and waste. In 1937, and again in 1938, the measure was not passed, largely owing to the fight over the reorganization of the judiciary and to opposition from conservative Democrats and Republicans, who charged that the bill would make Roosevelt a "dictator." Following the 1938 elections, there was little opposition to the measure, and the bill, in modified form, was approved.

Plans I and II for the regrouping of 50 government units were submitted to Congress by President Roosevelt on 25 Apr. and 9 May, respectively, and went into effect by presidential order on 1 July failing the passage of concurrent resolutions nullifying these plans. Under Plans I and II the president set up a **Federal Security Agency, a Federal Works Agency,** and a **Federal Loan Agency,** under all of which a total of 24 units was placed; and by transfer, consolidation, or abolition distributed among these 3 new agencies and the Executive Department the major independent establishments of the government. The Bureau of the Budget was transferred to the Executive Office of the President from the Treasury Department. By presidential order (8 Sept.) the reorganization of the Executive Office of the President established the following principal divisions: the White House Office, the Bureau of the Budget, the National Resources Planning Board, the Liaison Office for Personnel Management, the Office of Government Reports, and an optional office for emergency management (established 25 May 1940 as the Office for Emergency Management). The president was provided with 6 administrative assistants. Three additional reorganization plans were submitted in 1940 and became effective that year.

16 MAY. FOOD STAMP PLAN, a New Deal scheme established for the purpose of disposing of surpluses of agricultural commodities to persons on relief, was inaugurated in Rochester, N.Y. Recipients of relief were permitted to buy each week between $1 and $1.50 worth of "orange stamps" for each member of the family unit. For each $1 worth of these stamps the purchaser received gratis 50 cts. worth of "blue stamps" redeemable for foods officially designated as surplus commodities. By the end of 1940 the plan had been adopted in more than 100 cities. World War II forced its discontinuance (resumed 21 Sept. 1959 under "surplus food" plan).

CUT IN RELIEF EXPENDITURES. Although employment began to increase in Sept. 1938, it failed to reach the level of Sept. 1937. President Roosevelt requested (5 Jan.) a deficiency appropriation of $875 million for the Works Progress Administration. Congress reduced this to $725 million. Further requests by Roosevelt (7 Feb., 14 Mar.) for $150 million to avoid drastic reduction of WPA employment were scaled down by Congress (11 Apr.) to $100 million. The lack of sufficient funds necessitated a reduction of WPA rolls to 2,578,000 in June, 1939. On 27 Apr. Roosevelt recommended an appropriation of $1,477 million for the WPA for the fiscal year 1940. Although the Emergency Relief Appropriation Act of 1939 (30 June) allotted this sum, it abolished the Federal Theater Project, reduced the security wage, and set an 18-month limit for continuous WPA employment. (The act also changed the name of the Works Progress Administration to the Works Projects Administration.) The measure brought a nationwide strike of WPA workers and resulted in the dismissal of many.

2 AUG. HATCH ACT was passed chiefly as a direct result of alleged political malpractices involving the votes of WPA workers in the border states of Kentucky, Tennessee, and Maryland during the elections of 1938. The act prohibited federal officeholders below the policy-making echelon in the executive branch of the government to participate actively in political campaigns, to solicit or accept contributions from work relief employees, and to make use of official authority or favors in order to interfere with or influence the outcome of presidential or congressional elections. On 19 July 1940 an amendment to the act extended its scope to state and local government workers whose salaries were drawn in whole or in part from federal funds, and limited the annual expenditures of political parties to $3 million and individual campaign contributions to a maximum of $5,000. The constitutionality of the act was upheld in *United Public Workers* v. *Mitchell* (330 U.S. 75, 1947) and, after another challenge, again by the Supreme Court in *United States Civil Service Commission* v. *National Association of Letter Carriers* (413 U.S. 548, 1974).

4 Aug. RECLAMATION PROJECT ACT (p. 639).

10 Aug. SOCIAL SECURITY AMENDMENTS. Most of the improvements proposed by the Social Security Board in its report transmitted to Congress (16 Jan.) by President Roosevelt were embodied in amendments to the Social Security Act passed by the House (10 June) and the Senate (13 July). The amendments included the following provisions: (1) the date for starting monthly old-age benefit payments was advanced to 1 Jan. 1940; (2) supplementary old-age benefits provided for aged wives; (3) average wages replaced total wages as the basis for computing old-age benefits; (4) old-age insurance coverage extended to maritime workers, persons earning wages after they reached 65, and employees of federal instrumentalities, e.g., member banks in the Federal Reserve System; (5) the increased taxes to be paid by employers and employees postponed until 1943; (6) the maximum federal grant for each aged or blind person increased by $15 to $20 per month; and (7) the federal contribution toward state aid to dependent children increased from one third to one half the amount granted each individual. The **Social Security Act of 1950** raised employers' and employees' 1¼% payroll tax to 2% in 1954, 2½% in 1960, 3% in 1965, 3¼% in 1970, and extended coverage. By the **Social Security Act of 1952** (signed by President Truman, effective 1 Sept.) old-age and survivor insurance benefits were increased $5 per month or 12½% (whichever is greater), and beneficiaries permitted to earn $75 a month instead of $50. Liberalized and expanded by **Act of 1954** (1 Sept.), extending benefits to 7 million additional workers, including farm workers and household domestics, permitting retired persons over 65 to receive benefits while earning up to $1,200 per year; and by **Act of 1956** (1 Aug.), providing old-age and survivors' insurance benefits for totally and permanently disabled workers beginning at age 50 and reducing from 65 to 62 the age at which women are eligible for OASI benefits. **Act of 1958** (29 Aug.) increased benefits c.7% and raised earnings from $4,200 to $4,800; further liberalizations provided under **Acts of 1960, 1961, 1965, 1967, 1968, 1969, 1972, and 1974.**

THE UNITED STATES IN WORLD WAR II

The Nazi *Blitzkrieg* and Pearl Harbor together destroyed the myth that America could be insulated from European catastrophe or from the domination of Asia and the Pacific by a single nation. World War II committed the country to intervention in world affairs and a postwar isolationist reaction made less than expected headway. Unlike World War I, there never for a moment was any question where American sympathies lay in World War II: Hitler and Pearl Harbor had taken care of that.

World War II differed from all previous wars in its truly total character. With a few notable exceptions, it involved every great nation and most of the smaller ones as well. It was total in that it was fought in every quarter of the globe, even South America not being spared naval engagements, and on a dozen different fronts, on land, in the air, and at sea. It was total in that it affected every segment of society and the economy, making no distinction between combatants and civilians. It was almost total in its destructive character, ending with the first use of a terrible new weapon, the atomic bomb.

In contrast to World War I, the United States assumed leadership in building a grand alliance dedicated to victory and to the establishment of a postwar international organization for maintaining world peace and security. Especially close was the cooperation between the Americans and the British, but the relations between the Anglo-Americans and the Soviet Union must be viewed against a background of almost a generation of mutual mistrust and the paranoid leadership of the Soviet chieftain Joseph Stalin. For the most part the larger need of maintaining an unbroken Allied front against the common enemy prevailed, and only toward the very close of the war was it evident to Franklin D. Roosevelt that the wartime unity of the grand alliance was unlikely to survive the strains of postwar reconstruction and bitter ideological competition.

Prelude to Global War, 1939–41

1939

1 SEPT.–5 OCT. WAR BEGINS: PO-LAND CRUSHED. Germany invaded Poland (1 Sept.). Great Britain and France declared war on Germany; Belgium proclaimed its neutrality (3 Sept.). The Germans crossed the Vistula (11 Sept.), the San (16 Sept.), and demanded the surrender of Warsaw (17 Sept.). Soviet forces invaded Poland 17 Sept.). With the fall of Warsaw (27 Sept.) main organized resistance in Poland ended. Soviet-German partition of Poland (28 Sept.). Polish government-in-exile formed in Paris (30 Sept.). Last Polish forces east of the Vistula surrendered (5 Oct.).

3–21 SEPT. U.S. POSITION. In a fireside chat (3 Sept.) President Roosevelt declared: "This nation will remain a neutral nation, but I cannot ask that every American remain neutral in thought as well." On 5 Sept. the U.S. proclaimed its neutrality. Under the Neutrality Act of 1937 President Roosevelt prohibited the export of arms and munitions to belligerent powers. On 8 Sept. he proclaimed a limited national emergency, and on 21 Sept. urged a special session of Congress to repeal the arms embargo.

3 OCT. DECLARATION OF PAN-AMA, issued by the Inter-American Conference, announced sea safety zones in the Western Hemisphere, south of Canada. Belligerent powers were warned to refrain from naval action within these zones.

11 OCT. President Roosevelt was informed by **Albert Einstein** and other scientists of the possibilities of developing an atomic bomb.

14 OCT.–12 MAR. 1940. RUSSO-FIN-NISH WAR. On 14 Oct. Russia presented Finland with demands for military and territorial concessions, and invaded Finland 30 Nov. The war terminated with the signing of a treaty at Moscow 12 Mar. 1940.

4 Nov. NEUTRALITY ACT OF 1939 repealed the arms embargo and authorized "cash and carry" exports of arms and munitions to belligerent powers. The bill passed the Senate, 63–30 (27 Oct.), and the House, 243–181 (2 Nov.).

1940

26 JAN. U.S.-Japanese commercial treaty of 1911 expired. Secretary Hull notified the Japanese government that trade between the two nations would rest on a day-to-day basis.

9 FEB. WELLES MISSION. President Roosevelt announced that Under Secretary of State Sumner Welles would leave for Europe to gather information concerning the war aims of the belligerent powers and the possibility of a just and lasting peace. He reported to Roosevelt 28 Mar.

30 MAR. A Japanese-dominated government in China was established at Nanking under Wang Ching-wei.

9 APR.–11 JUNE. INVASION OF NORWAY. German troops invaded Denmark and Norway by sea and air 9 Apr. An Anglo-French expeditionary force which came (18–20 Apr.) to the aid of the resisting Norwegian troops was evacuated on 2 May. On 9 May British troops occupied Iceland. On 29 May the British announced the capture of Narvik, but withdrew on 11 June. A puppet regime

under Vidkun Quisling was established in Norway on 1 Feb. 1942.

17 APR. Secretary Hull announced that any change in the *status quo* of the Netherlands East Indies would be prejudicial to the peace and security of the Pacific area.

10 MAY–4 JUNE. FALL OF THE NETHERLANDS AND BELGIUM. Germany invaded Luxembourg, the Netherlands, and Belgium by land and air (10 May). British Prime Minister Neville Chamberlain resigned, and was succeeded (11 May) by **Winston Churchill,** who headed a coalition government. The Netherlands government fled to Great Britain (14 May) and the army capitulated on the 15th. On 27–28 May King Leopold III ordered the Belgian army to capitulate, thus forcing the withdrawal of the Anglo-French expeditionary force from Belgium. The **Evacuation from Dunkirk** of 338,226 British and French troops (28 May–4 June) was completed with the use of 861 vessels of all types.

16 MAY–3 JUNE. U.S. PREPAREDNESS AND AID TO BRITAIN. President Roosevelt, who in his annual budget message (3 Jan.) had requested $1,800 million for national defense, asked for new appropriations of $1,182 million and called for a production program of 50,-000 planes a year. On 31 May he requested an additional $1,277,741,170 for the acceleration and development of military and naval requirements. In response to Prime Minister Churchill's appeal for military supplies, the War Department (3 June) released to Great Britain surplus or outdated stocks of arms, munitions, and aircraft. More than $43 million worth was sent in the month of June alone.

5 JUNE.–10 JULY. FALL OF FRANCE. Battle of France opened (5 June) with German crossings of the Somme and the Aisne-Oise canal. Italy declared war on France and Great Britain (10 June) and Italian forces penetrated southern France. On 13 June Premier Paul Reynaud of France appealed to President Roosevelt for aid. Following a breakthrough at Sedan, German troops entered Paris (14 June), compelling transfer of the French government to Bordeaux. On 16 June France requested release from obligations under the Anglo-French agreement barring a separate peace, and Marshal Henri-Philippe Pétain succeeded Reynaud as head of the French government. On 17 June he asked for armistice terms. An armistice with Germany was signed at Compiègne (22 June); with Italy on 24 June. In London the French National Committee under Gen. Charles de Gaulle pledged (18 June) continued French resistance against Germany. On 2 July the Pétain government established its headquarters at Vichy; on 10 July Pétain was granted dictatorial powers.

15–22 JUNE. U.S. DEFENSE MEASURES. On 15 June President Roosevelt established the **National Defense Research Committee,** with Dr. **Vannevar Bush** (1890–1974) as chairman. In May 1941 this body was supplanted by the Office of Scientific Research and Development. The **Pittman Resolution** (16 June), designed to strengthen the military defenses of the Latin-American republics, authorized the sale of munitions to the governments of the republics of the Western Hemisphere. The U.S. notified Germany and Italy that it would refuse to recognize transfer of title from one non-American power to another of any geographic region of the Western Hemisphere. On 20 June **Henry L. Stimson** (N.Y., p. 1159) was named Secretary of War; **Frank Knox** (Ill., 1874–1944) Secretary of the Navy. On 22 June Congress adopted national-defense tax measures designed to yield $994,300,000 a year. The national debt limit was raised from $45 billion to $49 billion.

17 June. Soviet forces completed the occupation of Lithuania, Latvia, and Estonia, which were incorporated into the Soviet Union 25 Aug.

28 June. ALIEN REGISTRATION ACT (commonly called the **SMITH ACT**) strengthened existing laws governing the admission and deportation of aliens and required the fingerprinting of all aliens in the U.S. The measure, however, was designed primarily to check subversive activities. The act made it unlawful for any person to advocate or teach the overthrow or destruction of any government in the U.S. by force or violence, and to organize or become a member of any group dedicated to teaching such doctrine.

30 July. ACT OF HAVANA was unanimously approved by delegates of the 21 republics of the Pan-American Union gathered at an Inter-American Conference. It provided that the American republics, collectively or individually, might in the interest of the common defense take over and administer any European possession in the New World endangered by aggression. The measure was designed to prevent the transfer to Germany of European colonies in the Western Hemisphere.

4 Aug. Italian troops invaded British Somaliland and completed its occupation on 19 Aug.

8 Aug.–31 Oct. BATTLE OF BRITAIN. The Luftwaffe, with more than 2,600 operational fighters and bombers at its disposal, opened a vast air offensive against British shipping, RAF installations, factories, land transportation, and cities in the British Isles. The Nazi objective was to soften Great Britain in preparation for an invasion of England by sea and air. The Battle of Britain came to a climax on 15 Sept. when 56 German aircraft were destroyed (the original British claim was 185). Aircraft losses, 10 July–31 Oct.:

British fighters lost by RAF   915
Enemy aircraft actually destroyed
   (according to German records) 1,733
Enemy aircraft claimed by British 2,698

Defeat in this crucial battle compelled the Germans to abandon plans for the invasion of the British Isles.

18 Aug.–29 Oct. U.S. DEFENSE MEASURES. Meeting at Ogdensburg, N.Y. (18 Aug.), to discuss defense problems common to Canada and the U.S., Prime Minister W. L. Mackenzie King and President Roosevelt agreed to establish a **Permanent Joint Board on Defense.** On 27 Aug. Congress authorized induction of the National Guard into federal service. Initial units were called out 31 Aug. On 3 Sept. a defense agreement between the U.S. and Great Britain provided for the transfer of 50 U.S. overage destroyers to the British; in exchange, the U.S. acquired the right to take 99-year leases on naval and air bases in Newfoundland, Bermuda, the Bahamas, Jamaica, St. Lucia, Trinidad, Antigua, and British Guiana. On 16 Sept. the **Selective Training and Service Act** (the **Burke-Wadsworth Bill**) was approved. The first peacetime program of compulsory military service in the U.S., it provided for the registration of all men between 21 and 35, and for the training over a 1-year period of 1,200,000 troops and 800,000 reserves. The first registration (16 Oct.) resulted in a listing of 16,400,000 men; the first draft numbers were selected on 29 Oct.

May–July. PUBLIC OPINION IN THE UNDECLARED WAR. The policy of aiding the democracies set off a protracted debate. An important force in marshalling sentiment favorable to aid short of war was the Committee to Defend America by Aiding the Allies (est. mid-May), whose first chairman was a Republican editor from Kansas, William Allen White. To counter the interventionists Gen. Robert E. Wood, a Middle Western executive, organized in July the America First Committee, with its first public statement issued 4 Sept., one day after the president informed Congress of the Destroyer-Bases Agreement. Isolationists drew upon a wide spectrum of public opinion, including extreme reactionaries, moderate conservatives, and left-leaning pacifists.

4–27 SEPT. JAPANESE AGGRESSION. Secretary Hull advised the Japanese government (4 Sept.) that aggression against French Indochina would bring adverse reaction in the U.S. On 12 Sept. Joseph C. Grew, U.S. ambassador to Japan, warned Secretary Hull that Japan might interpret a drastic embargo on oil as sanctions and retaliate. On 22 Sept. Japan concluded with Vichy France an agreement giving the former air and troop maintenance bases in Indochina. On 27 Sept. Japan signed at Berlin a 3-power pact with Germany and Italy providing for a 10-year military and economic alliance. By this pact, which made Japan a member of the Axis, each of the signatories pledged mutual assistance in the event of war with a nation not then a belligerent. The pact was subsequently signed by other nations, including Bulgaria, Rumania, Hungary, and Yugoslavia. On 26 Sept. President Roosevelt proclaimed an embargo, effective 16 Oct., on exports of scrap iron and steel to all countries outside the Western Hemisphere except Great Britain. The ban was aimed at Japan. Ambassador Horinouchi protested the move as an "unfriendly act" (8 Oct.).

8–28 OCT. AXIS MOVES IN THE BALKANS. On 8 Oct. German troops began occupation of Rumania. On 28 Oct. Italy invaded Greece from Albania. British forces were landed on Crete and other Greek islands. Fighting between Greeks and Italians continued through the winter and spring.

PRESIDENTIAL CAMPAIGN. The Republican National Convention met at Philadelphia (28 June) and nominated **Wendell L. Willkie** (N.Y., 1892–1944) for president and Sen. **Charles L. McNary** (Ore.) for vice-president on a platform that attacked the New Deal administration but supported most of its major reforms. The Democratic National Convention met at Chicago (15 July) and received a message (16 July) from President Roosevelt stating that he had no desire to be a candidate for a 3d term. On 18 July **Roosevelt** was nominated for a 3d term; Secretary of Agriculture **Henry A. Wallace** (Iowa) was nominated for vice-president. Both major parties supported the national defense program, aid to Britain, and hemispherical defense, but opposed participation in foreign wars. Other presidential candidates: Norman Thomas (N.Y.), Socialist; Roger Babson (Mass.), Prohibition party; Earl Browder (N.Y.), Communist; and John W. Aiken, Socialist Labor.

5 Nov. PRESIDENTIAL ELECTION. Popular vote: **Roosevelt,** 27,244,160; Willkie, 22,305,198; Thomas, 100,264; Babson, 57,812; Browder, 48,579; Aiken, 14,861. Electoral vote: **Roosevelt,** 449 (38 states); Willkie, 82 (10 states).

20 JULY. President Roosevelt approved a bill authorizing a 2-ocean navy for the defense of the U.S. and the Western Hemisphere at a cost of $4 billion. The measure increased the authorized U.S. warship tonnage by 70% to a level of 3,500,000, and provided for the construction of about 200 warships, including 7 battleships of 55,000 tons each.

13 Nov.–8 FEB. 1941. BRITISH MEDITERRANEAN OFFENSIVE. British naval aircraft dealt a severe blow to the Italian fleet at Taranto (13 Nov.). Wavell's offensive began 9 Dec., with a surprise attack around the Italians' southern flank in North Africa. By 8 Feb. the British had occupied El Agheila, 500 miles from Matrûh, their starting point, and destroyed Marshal Rodolfo Graziani's army, capturing 133,000 prisoners.

20–29 DEC. U.S. DEFENSE PRO-DUCTION. The Office of Production Management, with **William S. Knudsen** (1879–1948) as director, was set up by President Roosevelt (20 Dec.) to coordinate defense production and speed all material aid "short of war" to Great Britain and other anti-Axis nations. On 21 Dec. Germany asserted U.S. aid to Great Britain was "moral aggression." In a fireside chat on national security (29 Dec.) Roosevelt stressed the Axis threat to the U.S. and called for an immense production effort that would make the U.S. "the great arsenal of democracy."

1941

6 JAN. "FOUR FREEDOMS." In his annual message to Congress President Roosevelt recommended Lend-Lease for the Allies and enunciated the "Four-Freedoms": freedom of speech and expression, freedom of worship, freedom from want, and freedom from fear.

27 JAN.–29 MAR. SECRET U.S.-BRITISH STAFF TALKS, held in Washington, produced a plan known as ABC-1, suggesting the strategy for war. In the event of Anglo-U.S. involvements in war with both Germany and Japan the concentration of force should be on **Germany first.**

FEB.–27 MAY. BATTLE OF THE ATLANTIC. Although the battle had assumed grim proportions as early as Nov. 1940, when the pocket battleship *Scheer* attacked a convoy and sank the *Jervis Bay,* it was at a critical stage at the time of the secret U.S.-British staff talks. In Feb.-Mar. the *Scharnhorst* and *Gneisenau* sank or captured 22 ships (115,000 tons). U-boats, using "wolf-pack" tactics, reached great effectiveness. To 9 Apr. 1940 total Allied and neutral shipping

losses had amounted to 688,000 gross tons. Between 10 Apr. 1940 and 17 Mar. 1941 losses amounted to 2,314,000 gross tons. On 11 Apr. Roosevelt informed Churchill that the U.S. would extend security zone and patrol areas to a line covering all North Atlantic waters west of about West Long. 26° (thereafter "the sea frontier of the U.S."). On 21 May the *Robin Moor,* an American merchant ship, was sunk by a German submarine in the South Atlantic, off the coast of Brazil. On 24 May the British warship *Hood* was sunk by the German battleship *Bismarck* in the North Atlantic. The *Bismarck* was sunk (27 May) while attempting to return to port.

5 MAR. The Republic of Panama agreed to permit the U.S. to extend air defenses beyond the limits of the Canal Zone. The agreement was limited to the duration of the war.

11 MAR. LEND-LEASE ACT approved by President Roosevelt. It was drawn up primarily to offset the exhaustion of British credits for the purchase of war supplies. The measure passed the Senate, 60–31 (8 Mar.), and the House, 317–71 (11 Mar.). Lend-Lease enabled any country whose defense the president deemed vital to that of the U.S. to receive arms and other equipment and supplies by sale, transfer, exchange, or lease. An initial appropriation of $7 billion was authorized. Total Lend-Lease aid during the course of the war amounted to $50,226,845,387. On 15 Mar. President Roosevelt promised increasing aid to the Allies for a total victory. Lend-Lease was terminated 21 Aug. 1945. Total Lend-Lease aid by U.S. (Mar. 1941–Sept. 1946) amounted to $50.6 billion; reverse Lend-Lease received by U.S., $7.8 billion.

24 MAR.–15 APR. ROMMEL'S COUNTEROFFENSIVE. A North African offensive by German and Italian forces under Gen. Erwin Rommel compelled the British (whose strength was drained by the dispatch of 60,000 troops to help Greece resist the Germans) to evacuate Bengasi and to withdraw to Egypt by the end of May. British troops aided by the Royal Navy held out at Tobruk.

6 APR.–1 JUNE. Germany invaded Greece and Yugoslavia (6 Apr.). The Yugoslavian army surrendered on 17 Apr.; Greek resistance ended on 23 Apr. The British withdrew from the Greek mainland (29 Apr.). German airborne troops landed in Crete (20 May) and by 1 June had conquered the island.

9 APR. GREENLAND. Signing of U.S.-Danish agreement pledging the U.S. to defend Greenland against invasion. In return, the U.S. was granted the right to construct, maintain, and operate in Greenland air, naval, radio, and other defense installations. President Roosevelt announced that the defense of Greenland was essential to the security of the Western Hemisphere.

13 APR. Mutual nonaggression pact signed at Moscow by Japan and Russia.

21–27 APR. U.S., Dutch, and British military planning officers met at Singapore and drew up a strategic plan for combined operations against Japan should the latter commit aggression against the U.S.

27 MAY–16 JUNE. President Roosevelt proclaimed (27 May) an unlimited national emergency and ordered (16 June) the closing of German and Italian consulates in the U.S. by 10 July. In retaliation, the German and Italian governments ordered the closing of U.S. consulates in European areas under Axis control.

22 JUNE. INVASION OF RUSSIA. Germany invaded the Soviet Union. Together with Finnish and Rumanian troops, the German forces penetrated Russia along a 2,000-mile front extending from the Arctic to the Ukraine. By mid-Aug. the Germans had overrun most of the Ukraine; by early Sept. they reached Leningrad; by mid-Nov. they had laid Sevastopol under siege and reached the outskirts of Moscow. Rostov fell on 22 Nov., but was retaken by the Russians on 29 Nov. In Dec. the Russians launched a counteroffensive.

24 JUNE–6 Nov. AID TO RUSSIA. On 24 June President Roosevelt promised U.S. aid to the Soviet Union. On 12 July Great Britain and Russia signed a mutual assistance pact at Moscow barring a separate peace with Germany. British and Soviet forces occupied Iran (25–29 Aug.). U.S.-British missions conferred in Moscow (29 Sept.) to determine Russian defense needs, and on 1 Oct. decided to grant Russian requests for matériel. The U.S. granted Lend-Lease credit of $1 billion to the Soviet Union (6 Nov.).

28 JUNE. OFFICE OF SCIENTIFIC RESEARCH AND DEVELOPMENT established by executive order, with **Vannevar Bush** (1890–1974), chairman, and **James B. Conant** (p. 1004) deputy. The OSRD became the principal agency for coordinating U.S. scientific effort, including radar, proximity fuse, sonar (antisubmarine warfare), and the **atomic bomb,** whose development was transferred to the army on 1 May 1943 and placed in charge of an administrative unit known for security reasons as the **"Manhattan District" project.** See also pp. 443, 452, 801.

7 JULY. ICELAND. By agreement with the Icelandic government, the U.S. landed forces in Iceland to prevent its occupation by Germany for use as a naval or air base against the Western Hemisphere. The agreement stipulated that the U.S. would withdraw following the close of the European war.

24 JULY–24 AUG. U.S.-JAPANESE RELATIONS. Japan occupied French Indochina (24 July). Two days later President Roosevelt froze all Japanese credits in the U.S., thus bringing Japanese-American trade to a virtual halt. Simultaneous action was taken by Great Britain. Japan ordered freezing of all U.S. and British funds. Roosevelt nationalized (26 July) the armed forces of the Philippines for the duration of the emergency, placing them under the command of Gen. **Douglas MacArthur** (p. 1090), who was named commander in chief of U.S. forces in the Far East. The Japanese ambassador to the U.S., Adm. Kichisaburo Nomura, was informed by Roosevelt that additional attempts to extend Japanese military control in the Far East would compel the U.S. to take immediate steps to protect American rights and interests. On 24 Aug. Prime Minister Churchill promised that Great Britain would come to the aid of the U.S. should the negotiations with Japan break down.

14 Aug. ATLANTIC CHARTER, a joint statement of principles issued by President Roosevelt and Prime Minister Churchill, formulated the broad postwar aims of the U.S. and Great Britain. The charter was not an alliance nor a binding legal commitment. It was drawn up at secret meetings (9–12 Aug.) that took place aboard the U.S. cruiser *Augusta* and the British battleship *Prince of Wales* at Argentia Bay off Newfoundland. Drafted by Roosevelt and Churchill with the aid of Sumner Welles and Sir Alexander Cadogan, the document included the following points: (1) renunciation of territorial or other aggrandizement; (2) opposition to territorial changes contrary to the wishes of the people immediately concerned; (3) support of the right of peoples to choose their own form of government; (4) support, with due respect for existing obligations, of the easing of restrictions on trade, and access to raw materials on equal terms; (5) support of cooperative efforts to improve the economic position

and social security of the peoples of the world; (6) freedom from want and fear; (7) freedom of the seas; and (8) disarmament of aggressor nations pending the establishment of a permanent peace structure. On 24 Sept. it was announced that 15 anti-Axis nations, among them the Soviet Union, had endorsed the Atlantic Charter.

18 Aug. SELECTIVE SERVICE EXTENSION. President Roosevelt approved a bill extending for 18 months the army service of draftees. The House vote (12 Aug.) on the extension of Selective Service was 203–202.

4 Sept.–30 Oct. WARFARE IN THE ATLANTIC. A German submarine attacked the U.S.S. *Greer,* a destroyer on duty in waters off Iceland (4 Sept.). On 11 Sept. President Roosevelt announced a "shoot-on-sight" order to U.S. naval forces in U.S. defensive waters, stating that German and Italian vessels would enter these areas at their own risk. Five days later the U.S. navy undertook merchant convoy duty as far as Iceland. On 9 Oct. President Roosevelt asked Congress to modify the Neutrality Act of 1939 to permit arming of U.S. merchantmen engaged in overseas commerce and their passage through combat zones. The U.S. destroyer *Kearny* was torpedoed and damaged by a German submarine in waters west of Iceland (17 Oct.), causing the loss of 11 American lives. On 30 Oct. the U.S. destroyer *Reuben James,* on convoy duty in waters off Iceland, was attacked and sunk by a German submarine, with about 100 American lives lost. The Senate, 50–37, approved repeal of restrictive sections in the 1939 Neutrality Act (7 Nov.), and the House followed (13 Nov.), 212–94. The measure, which became law on 17 Nov., authorized the arming of U.S. merchant vessels and permitted them to carry cargoes to belligerent ports.

18 Oct.–6 Dec. JAPANESE ATTITUDE HARDENS. On 18 Oct. the Japanese cabinet headed by Prince Fumimaro Konoye resigned. Gen. Hideki Tojo became prime minister. U.S. ambassador Grew warned Washington (17 Nov.) of the possibility of a sudden attack by the Japanese. On 20 Nov. discussions in Washington were opened between Secretary Hull and the 2 Japanese negotiators, Ambassador Nomura and a special envoy, Saburo Kurusu. Japan demanded that the U.S. abandon China; lift the orders freezing Japanese credits in the U.S.; resume full trade relations with Japan; exert pressure to aid Japan in securing supplies from the Netherlands East Indies; and bring a halt to U.S. naval expansion in the Western Pacific. On 26 Nov. Hull countered with a set of proposals that included the withdrawal of Japanese troops from China and Indochina and the conclusion of a multilateral nonaggression pact. The U.S. proposals restated the following principles: respect for the territorial integrity and sovereignty of all nations; support of the principle of noninterference in the internal affairs of other countries; support of the principle of equality, including equality of commercial opportunity; nondisturbance of the *status quo* in the Pacific except by peaceful means. In return, Hull promised to free frozen Japanese assets and to resume treaty based commercial relations. Asking for 2 weeks in which to study the proposals, Japan in the meantime, while recognizing the great danger in directly attacking U.S. territory, stepped up military and naval preparations in Asia and the Pacific. On 25 Nov. (Washington time) the carrier force that attacked Pearl Harbor left the Kurile Islands. The next day U.S. warned Great Britain of an impending Japanese attack. War and Navy Departments, believing it likely that the Japanese would strike in the Philippines or Southeast Asia, sent (27 Nov.) warnings of imminent war to commanders of U.S. forces in the Pacific. On 29 Nov. Premier Tojo publicly asserted that U.S. and British influence must be eliminated from Asia, and on 1 Dec. Japan publicly rejected the Hull proposals. The next day the U.S. requested an explanation by Japan for increasing its forces in Indochina, and on 6 Dec. President Roosevelt made a direct appeal to Emperor Hirohito, asking him to use his influence to preserve the peace and to withdraw troops from French Indochina.

7 Dec. ATTACK ON PEARL HARBOR. On the morning of Sunday, 7 Dec., Japanese naval and air forces made a sneak attack on the U.S. fleet at the Pearl Harbor naval base in Hawaii. On the same day (8 Dec., Far Eastern time) the Japanese launched assaults on the Philippines, Guam, and Midway Island, and on British forces at Hong Kong and in the Malay Peninsula. The air attack at Pearl Harbor began at 7:55 A.M. (local time; 1:20 P.M. Washington time) and continued until 9:45 A.M. Of the 8 battleships at Pearl Harbor, the *Arizona, California* and *West Virginia* were sunk; the *Nevada* was grounded; the *Oklahoma* capsized; others were damaged. Altogether 19 ships were sunk or disabled; 5 battleships were later raised; 4 restored to the fleet. About 150 U.S. planes were destroyed, 2,335 soldiers and sailors and 68 civilians were killed, and 1,178 were wounded. During the morning of 7 Dec., the official Japanese reply to the U.S. proposals of 26 Nov. arrived at Washington, with instructions to the Japanese envoys to present it to Secretary Hull at 1 P.M. (Washington time). Nomura and Kurusu, however, did not appear in Hull's office until 2:05 P.M., just as Hull received reports of the attack on Pearl

Harbor. On 24 Jan. 1942 a presidential commission headed by Supreme Court Justice Owen J. Roberts attributed the effectiveness of the Japanese attack to the failure of the naval and military commanders at Hawaii (Rear Adm. Husband Kimmel and Lt. Gen. Walter Short) to adopt adequate defense measures. Previously (17 Dec. 1941) **Chester W. Nimitz** (p. 1115) had suc-

ceeded Kimmel in command of the Pacific fleet.

8 Dec. With only 1 dissenting vote, the U.S. Congress declared war on Japan.

11 Dec. Germany and Italy declared war on the U.S., which then recognized a state of war with these nations.

19 Dec. Congress extended military conscription to men between the ages of 20 and 44.

The War in the Pacific and the Far East, 1941–45

1941

8–25 Dec. JAPANESE GAINS. Thailand and Malaya were invaded by the Japanese (8 Dec.). On 10 Dec. the British battleship *Prince of Wales* and the battle cruiser *Repulse* were sunk by Japanese torpedo planes in the South China Sea. This blow to Allied naval strength enabled the Japanese capture of Singapore and other enemy successes in Southeast Asia. The Japanese made landings on the Philippines (10–23 Dec.); took Guam (13 Dec.), Wake Island (22 Dec.), and Hong Kong (25 Dec.).

2 Jan. Supreme command for American, British, Dutch, and Australian forces in the Far East (ABDACOM), headed by Gen. Sir Archibald P. Wavell, with Maj. Gen. George P. Brett, deputy, was announced following a meeting at Washington.

1942

2 Jan.–6 May. BATAAN AND CORREGIDOR. Manila and Cavite fell to the Japanese (2 Jan.). Gen. MacArthur's forces retired to Bataan Peninsula, where MacArthur established headquarters at the fortress of Corregidor ("The Rock") in Manila Bay. On 17 Mar. MacArthur arrived in Australia after secretly leaving

Bataan Peninsula, and took command of the Allied forces in the Southwest Pacific. After resisting a siege of more than 3 months, Bataan fell 9 Apr. American forces under Gen. **Jonathan M. Wainwright** withdrew to Corregidor Island in Manila Bay. On 6 May Wainwright surrendered Corregidor and its garrison of 11,500 to the Japanese.

11 Jan.–3 May. JAPAN'S ADVANCE. Japanese forces occupied the Netherlands East Indies (11–31 Jan.). In the first major sea battle between the Allies and Japan, the Battle of **Macassar Strait** (between Borneo and Celebes), Allied sea and air forces inflicted severe damage on a large Japanese invasion convoy (24–27 Jan.). On 31 Jan. British troops withdrew from Malaya to Singapore and on the same day Vice-Adm. **William F. Halsey, Jr.,** carried out a bombardment of the Marshall and Gilbert Islands. Singapore and its British garrison unconditionally surrendered (15 Feb.). A naval battle was fought in Badoeng Strait (19–20 Feb.). On 24 Feb. the British withdrew from Rangoon, in Burma. Its occupation by the Japanese (9 Mar.) cut off supplies from the Burma Road. Mandalay fell 3 May. The **Battle of the Java Sea** (27 Feb.–1 Mar.), fought as a delaying action by the U.S. fleet under

Adm. **Thomas C. Hart,** resulted in the most severe U.S. naval losses since Pearl Harbor. On 6 Mar. Batavia, capital of the Netherlands East Indies, fell. By 9 Mar. the Japanese conquest of Java had been completed. On 8 Mar. Japanese troops landed at Lae and Salamaua in New Guinea. On 10 Mar. Lt. Gen. **Joseph W. Stilwell** ("Vinegar Joe") was made chief of staff of Allied armies in the Chinese theater of operations.

18 APR.–6 JUNE. STIFFENING ALLIED RESISTANCE. On 18 Apr. carrier-based U.S. army bombers (B-25s) led by Maj. Gen. **James H. Doolittle** raided Tokyo. On 7–8 May was fought the **Battle of the Coral Sea,** the first naval engagement in history in which surface ships did not engage enemy ships (all fighting was done by carrier-based planes). One Japanese carrier was sunk, 2 damaged, as well as a number of other ships. The U.S. carrier *Lexington* was lost in this engagement, which halted the enemy advance upon Australia by frustrating the Japanese attempt to seize Port Moresby in southern New Guinea in order to cut the Australian supply line. The naval and air **Battle of Midway** (3–6 June), in the Central Pacific, resulted in the first major defeat of Japanese naval forces. The attempted enemy seizure of Midway Island ended in failure, with the loss of 4 aircraft carriers and 275 planes. This action checked the Japanese advance across the Central Pacific, eliminated the threat to Hawaii, and restored the balance of naval power in the Pacific.

3–21 JUNE. The Japanese bombed Dutch Harbor and Ft. Mears, Alaska (3–4 June), and occupied the islands of Attu and Kiska in the westernmost Aleutians (12–21 June). On 21 June the Oregon coast was shelled. Previously (23 Feb.) an oil refinery near Santa Barbara, Calif., had been shelled by a Japanese submarine.

22 JULY. Japanese forces in northern New Guinea began an overland push against Port Moresby on the southern coast. After crossing the Owen Stanley Mountains they were halted by Australian forces who counterattacked from Port Moresby (29 Sept.) and crossed the Owen Stanley Range (10 Oct.).

7 AUG.–9 FEB. 1943. GUADALCANAL, 1ST MAJOR OFFENSIVE. Countering Japanese advances in the Solomons, U.S. marines landed at Guadalcanal (7 Aug.) and seized the airport, renaming it Henderson Field. Marines also landed on Tulagi, Florida, and other nearby islands. Two days later occurred the naval **Battle of Savo Island,** north of Guadalcanal, resulting in the loss of 4 heavy cruisers (3 U.S., 1 Australian), a Japanese victory which temporarily deprived U.S. forces on Guadalcanal of air and naval support. A 6-month fight for the island followed. A naval battle of the Eastern Solomons (23–25 Aug.) resulted in damage to Japanese carriers and cruisers by aircraft from the U.S. carriers *Enterprise* and *Saratoga.* On 26 Aug. Japanese landed at Milne Bay in New Guinea, but were defeated after a 2-week battle. The naval **Battle of Cape Esperance** (11–12 Oct.), in the Solomons, resulted in a U.S. victory over the Japanese, who lost 1 carrier and 4 destroyers. Strong Japanese attacks (21–25 Oct.) failed to take Henderson Field. The naval **Battle of Santa Cruz** (26–27 Oct.), in the Solomons, resulted in the sinking of 2 Japanese destroyers and damage to 8 other enemy warships. The naval **Battle of Guadalcanal** (12–15 Nov.), a decisive U.S. victory, prevented the Japanese from landing substantial reinforcements and made possible the conquest of Guadalcanal by U.S. troops. This action cost the U.S. 2 cruisers and 7 destroyers. The Japanese lost 2 battleships, 1 cruiser, 2 destroyers, and 10 transports. By 9 Feb. 1943 Japanese forces completed the abandonment of Guadalcanal.

1943

23 JAN.–16 SEPT. GAINS IN NEW GUINEA. Ground fighting ended in Papua (23 Jan.), with the Japanese cleared out. The air **Battle of the Bismark Sea** (2–3 Mar.), in the New Guinea area, resulted in the destruction of 12 Japanese troop convoys and 10 warships and the death of Adm. Yamamoto. On 16 Sept. U.S. forces under Gen. MacArthur took Lae in New Guinea, completing reconquest of Lae-Salamaua area.

24 MAR.–15 AUG. STRUGGLE FOR THE ALEUTIANS. Naval battle of the Komandorski Islands in the western Aleutians resulted in a U.S. victory. U.S. forces landed on Attu (11 May), in the western Aleutians. By 3 June all organized enemy resistance on Attu had ended. On 15 Aug. U.S. and Canadian troops reoccupied Kiska without resistance, the Japanese having already left the island.

30 JUNE–26 DEC. U.S. SOUTH PACIFIC OFFENSIVE began 30 June with the landing of U.S. troops on Rendova Island, in New Georgia. The naval **Battle of Kula Gulf** (6 July) was followed by other U.S. naval victories (Aug.–Oct.) which gave the Allies control of the waters adjacent to the central Solomons. On 1 Nov. U.S. marines landed at Bougainville, in the northern Solomons, in a thrust toward the bastion of Rabaul. The Japanese struck back, but naval **Battle of Empress Augusta Bay** (2 Nov.), off Bougainville, resulted in a decisive Japanese defeat and enabled the Allies to cut the supply lines to Rabaul, thus isolating all enemy forces remaining in the Solomons and securing the U.S. flank for an advance toward the Philippines. The next steps were landings by U.S. forces

at Arawe (15 Dec.) and Cape Gloucester (26 Dec.) in New Britain.

21 Nov. U.S. CENTRAL PACIFIC OFFENSIVE, under Adm. **Chester W. Nimitz,** commander in chief, and Adm. **Raymond A. Spruance,** commander, Pacific fleet, aimed at capturing islands "up the ladder" of the Solomons, the Gilberts and Marshalls, the Marianas, and the Bonin Islands to within effective bombing distance of Japan, began with landings on **Tarawa** and **Makin** in the Gilbert Islands. At Tarawa, which was not secured until 24 Nov., the direct assault on heavily fortified positions cost the U.S. 2nd Marine Division 913 killed and missing, and 2,037 wounded.

25 AUG.–21 DEC. Lord Louis Mountbatten was appointed (25 Aug.) supreme Allied commander, Southeast Asia. On 21 Dec. Gen. Stilwell began his campaign in northern Burma.

1944

31 JAN.–25 NOV. CENTRAL PACIFIC ADVANCE. U.S. forces invaded (31 Jan.) the Marshall Islands, taking Roi and Namur (3 Feb.), Kwajalein (6 Feb.), and Eniwetok (17–22 Feb.); landed on the air and naval base of Saipan (15 June), in the Mariana Islands, completing its conquest 9 July, on Guam (21 July), completing its reoccupation 9 Aug. The invasion of the Palaus began with the landing of U.S. marines on Peleliu (15–17 Sept.), finally taken on 25 Nov.

1 MAR.–22 APR. SOUTHWEST PACIFIC GAINS. U.S. troops invaded the Admiralty Islands (1 Mar.), completing their occupation on 25 Mar., and landed at Hollandia (22 Apr.), Dutch New Guinea, seizing enemy airfields.

17 MAY–3 AUG. BURMA CAMPAIGN. The capture (17 May) by Allied forces of Myitkyina airstrip in northern Burma

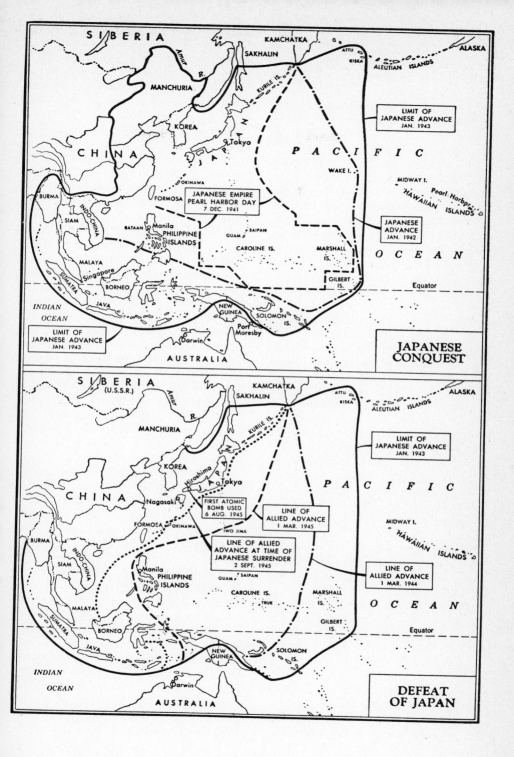

JAPANESE CONQUEST

LIMIT OF JAPANESE ADVANCE JAN. 1943

JAPANESE EMPIRE PEARL HARBOR DAY 7 DEC. 1941

JAPANESE ADVANCE JAN. 1942

LIMIT OF JAPANESE ADVANCE JAN. 1943

DEFEAT OF JAPAN

LIMIT OF JAPANESE ADVANCE JAN. 1943

FIRST ATOMIC BOMB USED 6 AUG. 1945

LINE OF ALLIED ADVANCE 1 MAR. 1945

LINE OF ALLIED ADVANCE AT TIME OF JAPANESE SURRENDER 2 SEPT. 1945

LINE OF ALLIED ADVANCE 1 MAR. 1944

gave them an air route to China. After severe fighting Myitkyina was retaken by Allied forces 3 Aug.

16 June. The U.S. air offensive against cities in the Japanese home islands was opened with an attack on Kyushu by U.S. Superfortresses (B-29s).

19 June–15 Dec. PHILIPPINES CAMPAIGN. Naval and air **Battle of the Philippine Sea** (19–20 June), fought entirely by carrier-based planes, cost the Japanese 3 carriers, 200 planes, and badly crippled its battleships and cruisers. On 18 July Premier Tojo resigned together with the entire Japanese cabinet, and was relieved as chief of staff. Gen. Kuniaki Koiso became premier. On 20 Oct. U.S. forces under Gen. MacArthur returned to the Philippines. Invading Leyte, in the central Philppines, they opened the drive for retaking the islands. The naval **Battle of Leyte Gulf** (23–25 Oct.), the last and greatest naval engagement of the war—in reality 3 separate engagements—resulted in decisive defeat for the Japanese. The battle caused the destruction of most of Japan's remaining sea power and gave the U.S. control of Philippine waters. After losing 2 battleships, 4 carriers, 9 cruisers, and 9 destroyers, the remnants of the Japanese fleet withdrew. On 15 Dec. U.S. forces landed on Mindoro Island in the Philippines.

28 Oct. Gen. Stilwell was recalled to Washington. Command of U.S. forces in China was assumed by Maj. Gen. **Albert C. Wedemeyer.**

24 Nov. Air offensive launched from Saipan in the Marianas began with Superfortress (B-29) attacks on Tokyo.

1945

9 Jan.–23 Feb. END OF PHILIPPINES CAMPAIGN. Landing at Lingayen Gulf (9 Jan.), U.S. forces invaded Luzon, main island of the Philippines, and took Manila (5–23 Feb.).

28. Jan. First convoy of trucks carrying war matériel over the Ledo (renamed Stilwell) Road across Burma from northeast India reached China.

10 Feb. Tokyo raided by 90 Superfortresses (B-29s).

19 Feb.–17 Mar. IWO JIMA. U.S. marines of the 4th and 5th Divisions landed on Iwo Jima, 750 miles from Tokyo. After bitter fighting, the U.S. forces took Mt. Suribachi (23 Feb.) and completed their conquest of the island on 17 Mar. Marine casualties: 4,189 killed, 15,308 wounded, 441 missing.

19 Mar.–21 June. BATTLE FOR THE RYUKYUS. U.S. carrier planes made extensive attacks on Japanese shipping and airfields in the Ryukyus (19–21 Mar.). On 1 Apr. the U.S. Tenth Army invaded **Okinawa,** main island of the Ryukyus, 360 miles southwest of Japan, completing their conquest on 21 June. Heavy air attacks by the Japanese, who used many suicide planes, made the campaign the costliest engagement of the war in point of losses in ships and sailors. The total U.S. casualties were 11,260 killed and 33,769 wounded.

5 Apr. Premier Koiso and the entire Japanese cabinet resigned.

30 Apr. The Fourteenth British Imperial Army in Southeast Asia, aided by U.S. and Chinese forces, completed the expulsion of Japanese armies from that sector.

May–Aug. AIR OFFENSIVE AGAINST JAPAN, the greatest in the Pacific and Far East war, was launched against the Japanese home islands by the U.S. Twentieth Air Force, supported by British and U.S. naval units which carried out attacks along the Japanese coast. On 5 July Gen. **Carl Spaatz** was appointed commander of the Strategic Air Forces in the Pacific. In accordance with the terms of the Cairo Declaration, the U.S., Great Britain, and China demanded

(26 July) that Japan surrender unconditionally. Japan formally rejected the Potsdam surrender ultimatum on 29 July. An **atomic bomb** with an explosive force of 20,000 tons of TNT was dropped (6 Aug.) on the Japanese city and military base of **Hiroshima,** the first time this weapon, until then held secret, was used for a military purpose. The bomb destroyed over 4 square miles of the city and brought death or injury to over 160,000 persons.

8 AUG. Russia declared war on Japan. Soviet armies invaded Manchuria.

9–15 AUG. An **atomic bomb** was dropped on the Japanese city and naval base of **Nagasaki.** On 10 Aug. the Japanese cabinet under Premier Suzuki offered to surrender on condition that Emperor Hirohito keep his throne. The Japanese accepted the Allied terms on 14 Aug. **V-J Day** (15 Aug.).

15 AUG. U.S. CASUALTIES (in the Pacific theater: 41,322 dead out of total casualties 170,596); in all theaters by 15 Aug.: 321,999 dead; 800,000 wounded, captured, or missing; 111,426 of the 124,079 captured returned to U.S. control. The ratio of fatalities per 100 wounded in World War II was less than one half the ratio of World War I, owing, among other reasons, to **penicillin,** the **sulfa** drugs, early use of **blood plasma,** and an efficient system of evacuation (much of it by air). Total maximum **enrollment** in all U.S. forces was 12,466,000 (army, 8,300,000; navy, 3,500,000; marine corps, 486,000; coast guard, 180,000).

27 AUG.–9 SEPT. U.S. forces began occupation of Japan (27 Aug.). The Japanese foreign minister and chief of staff signed the formal surrender on board the U.S.S. *Missouri* in Tokyo Bay, whereby home islands were to be under U.S. army of occupation, while the Emperor was to remain as head of state (2 Sept.). Surrender terms for Japanese forces in China were signed at Nanking (9 Sept.).

European and Mediterranean Theaters of War, 1942–45

1942

7 JAN.–29 JUNE. BRITISH VS. ROMMEL IN AFRICA. On 18 Nov. 1941 the British Eighth Army had opened its offensive in Libya, reached Agheila (7 Jan.), but held it for only 2 weeks. On 21 Jan. Rommel struck against the British and pressed them back in the neighborhood of Tobruk. A new offensive was launched in Libya by Rommel (26 May). Axis troops took Tobruk and Bardia (21 June), and Matrûh, in Egypt (29 June). The Axis advance was checked at El Alamein (29 June), 7 miles west of Alexandria.

20 JAN.–12 MAY. RUSSIAN COUNTERATTACK. The Russians retook Mozhaisk (20 Jan.), claimed Dorogobuzh (23 Feb.), advanced near Kursk (29 Apr.), and attacked near Kharkov (12 May).

26 JAN. U.S. forces arrived in Northern Ireland.

27 FEB.–19 AUG. COMMANDO RAIDS. Allied paratroopers raided Bruneval, France (27 Feb.); British commandos raided St. Nazaire (28 Mar.); and on 19 Aug. Dieppe was raided by about 6,000 British and Canadian troops and a small force of U.S. Rangers. About 3,350 invaders were killed, wounded, or taken prisoner.

30 MAY–17 AUG. ALLIED AIR WAR. First 1,000-bomber raid carried out by the British on Cologne (30 May), fol

lowed the next day by a 1,000-bomber raid on Essen and the Ruhr, and a 1,000-plane raid on Bremen (25 June). The first independent U.S. bombing attack in Europe was carried out (17 Aug.) by Eighth Air Force Flying Fortresses (B-17s) in raids on railroad yards near Rouen.

10 June. LIDICE, town in Czechoslovakia, laid waste by the Germans in reprisal for the assassination (27 May) of Reinhard Heydrich, Gestapo official.

28 June–13 Sept. GERMAN SUMMER OFFENSIVE AGAINST RUSSIA started from Kirsh (28 June). Sevastopol fell to the Germans (1 July) after an 8-month siege. The Germans took Voronezh (7 July), Rostov (24 July), Markov (9 Aug.), crossed the Don River (20 Aug.), and opened the siege of Stalingrad (22 Aug.). On 1 Sept. they crossed the Kerch Straits from the Crimea and invaded the south Caucasus. They entered Stalingrad (13 Sept.).

23 Oct.–24 Dec. ALLIED CAMPAIGNS IN NORTH AFRICA. British Eighth Army under Gen. Bernard L. Montgomery launched (23 Oct.) third Allied offensive in North Africa. British victory at **El Alamein** (4 Nov.) forced Rommel's forces to make a full retreat from Egypt by 12 Nov. The British took Bardia (12 Nov.), Tobruk (13 Nov.), Bengasi (20 Nov.).

8 Nov.–1 Dec. OPERATION TORCH. In the first major Allied amphibious operation in this theater, commanded by Gen. **Dwight D. Eisenhower,** with Adm. Sir Andrew Cunningham, naval commander, U.S. and British forces landed (8 Nov.) in North Africa. The main landings were made at Casablanca, Oran, and Algiers. On 10 Nov. fighting ceased at Oran. On 15 Nov. Allied troops advanced into Tunisia. Earlier, on 11 Nov., an armistice was arranged with Adm. Jean-François Darlan, Vichy representative in French North Africa, and the same day German forces entered Unoccupied France. Final agreement with Darlan was reached 13 Nov. On 27 Nov. the French fleet at Toulon was scuttled by its crews to prevent seizure of warships by Germans. With U.S. and British approval, Darlan became chief of state in French North Africa (1 Dec.), but he was assassinated in Algiers (24 Dec.), and Gen. Henri Giraud was appointed temporary administrator of North Africa.

19 Nov.–3 Mar. 1943. RUSSIAN COUNTEROFFENSIVE began on the Stalingrad front (19 Nov.), on Velikie Luki-Rzhev front (25 Nov.), and on Middle Don River (16 Dec.). On 18 Jan. 1943 the Russians raised the 17-month siege of Leningrad, the Germans at **Stalingrad** surrendered (2 Feb.), and the Russians retook Rostov (14 Feb.), Kharkov (16 Feb.), and Rzhev (9 Mar.).

1943

24 Jan.–13 May. END OF THE AFRICAN WAR. Tripoli fell to the British Eighth Army (24 Jan.). On 6 Feb. Gen. Eisenhower was appointed commander in chief of all Allied forces in North Africa. On 14 Feb. U.S. II Corps, commanded by Maj. Gen. Lloyd R. Fredendall, was thrown back by Rommel's Afrika Korps at **Kasserine Pass.** The Americans retook the position on 19 Feb. and by 23 Feb. had checked Rommel's drive. In March Fredendall was replaced by Maj. Gen. **George S. Patton, Jr.** (p. 1122). On 19 Mar. U.S. forces took El Guettar in Tunisia. On 21 Mar., from the east, Gen. Montgomery launched an offensive against Axis forces on the Mareth Line in Tunisia. The British breakthrough took place on 29 Mar. On 7 Apr. U.S. First Army and British Eighth Army joined lines near Gafsa, thus encircling the Axis forces in Tunisia. Tunis fell to the British, and Bizerte to the Americans (7 May). The main Axis forces under Gen. Jurgen

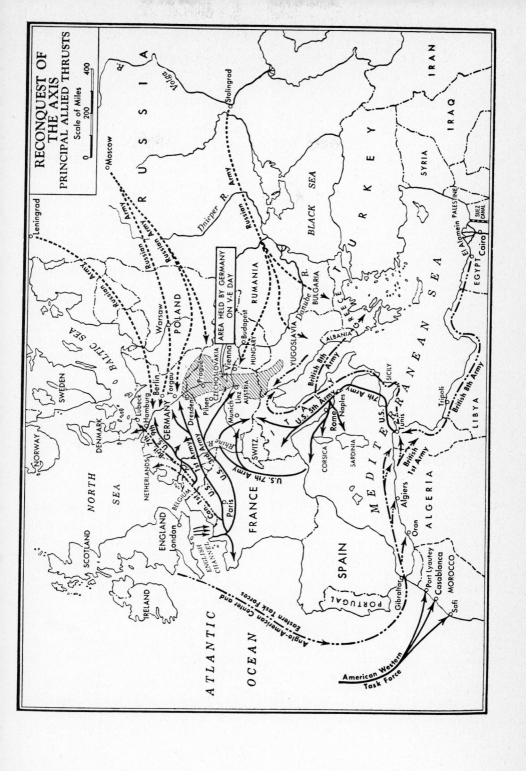

RECONQUEST OF
THE AXIS
PRINCIPAL ALLIED THRUSTS

Scale of Miles
0   200   400

von Arnim (Rommel having fled) retreated into the Cape Bon peninsula. About 250,000 Axis troops surrendered. 13 May marked the formal end of the North African campaign. Total U.S. casualties: about 18,500.

5 JULY–29 DEC. TURN OF THE TIDE IN RUSSIA. The German summer offensive in Russia, launched 5 July, made little headway. The Russians smashed back, retook Orel and Belgorod (4 Aug.), Smolensk (25 Sept.), cleared the German forces from the east bank of the Dnieper (29 Sept.), recaptured Dnepropetrovsk (26 Oct.), Kiev (7 Nov.), and broke enemy lines west of Kiev (29 Dec.), entering Poland on 3 Jan. 1944.

10 JULY–17 AUG. INVASION OF SICILY by air and sea was begun by Anglo-American forces (Operation HUSKY) on 10 July, under the immediate command of deputy commander Gen. Sir Harold R. L. G. Alexander, with British forces led by Montgomery and U.S. by Patton. Palermo fell to U.S. troops (24 July), Catania to British (5 Aug.). Fall of Messina to the U.S. (17 Aug.) completed the conquest of Sicily, assured greater safety to Allied shipping in the Mediterranean, and provided a springboard for attacks on Italy and Sardinia. U.S. casualties totaled about 7,400.

25–28 JULY. King Victor Emmanuel II announced (25 July) the resignation of Premier Mussolini and his cabinet. Marshal Pietro Badoglio became head of the Italian government. On 28 July Badoglio ordered the dissolution of the Fascist party.

17 AUG.–15 OCT. U.S. Eighth Air Force raided ball-bearing works at Schweinfurt and Regensburg (17 Aug.). On 15 Oct. U.S. Flying Fortresses (B-17s) bombed Schweinfurt.

3 SEPT.–2 DEC. ITALIAN CAMPAIGN. The British Eighth Army invaded Italy from Sicily across the Straits of Messina (3 Sept.)—Operation BAYTOWN. On 8 Sept. Italy accepted the Allied terms of unconditional surrender. Operation AVALANCHE was begun 9 Sept. when the U.S. Fifth Army under Gen. **Mark Clark** made amphibious landings at Salerno, about 30 miles below Naples. Strong German resistance at Salerno ended on 18 Sept. On 10 Sept. the Germans seized Rome. The bulk of the Italian fleet surrendered the next day. On 12 Sept. Mussolini, who had been placed under arrest by the Italian government, escaped with the aid of a raiding party of German paratroopers, and on 15 Sept. he proclaimed the establishment of a Fascist Republican regime in Italian areas under German domination. Allied crossings of the Volturno River (north of Naples) took place (12–14 Oct.) and by 25 Dec. an Allied front bisected Italy along the Garigliano and Sangro rivers. On 2 Dec. 1943 an air raid against Allied-held Bari resulted in the loss of 16 vessels. An Allied Control Commission for Italy was established 10 Nov.

9 OCT. Yugoslav partisans under Marshal Tito began assault against Axis forces near Trieste.

1944

11 JAN. ALLIED AIR OFFENSIVE. Strategic air offensive from the British Isles in preparation for Allied invasion of the Continent began 11 Jan., and reached its peak in Apr. and May. On 6 Mar. 800 U.S. planes bombed Berlin.

16 JAN. Gen. Eisenhower arrived in Britain to assume his duties as Supreme Commander, Allied Expeditionary Forces. He established **SHAEF** (Supreme Headquarters, Allied Expeditionary forces).

22 JAN.–4 JUNE. CAMPAIGN IN CENTRAL ITALY. On 22 Jan. Allied amphibious landings were made at Nettuno-Anzio beachhead 30 miles south of

Rome. The successful Allied assault on Cassino, in central Italy, a key position in the German Gustav Line, begun 15 Mar., ended 18 May. On 4 June Rome was liberated by the U.S. Fifth Army.

29 JAN.–9 MAY. FURTHER SOVIET GAINS. On 29 Jan. the Russians announced the Moscow-Leningrad area had been cleared of German troops. The Russians recaptured Odessa (10 Apr.) and Sevastopol (9 May).

22 MAR. German forces occupied Hungary.

6 JUNE. OPERATION OVERLORD. Allied forces concentrated in southern England invaded Europe on a 60-mile line along the coast of Normandy, from the mouth of the river Orne to the beaches near Ste-Mère-Église on the Cotentin Peninsula. The spearhead assault by a force of 176,000 troops was made with 4,000 invasion craft supported by 600 warships and an air cover of 11,000 planes, and was preceded by the descent of U.S. and British parachute and glider troops. The entire action was under the unified command of Gen. Eisenhower and was the largest amphibious operation of the war and all history. The ground forces (21st Army Group) were under the command of Gen. Montgomery. The American land contingent (U.S. First Army) was commanded by Gen. **Omar N. Bradley** (p. 991). The Germans countered (14 June) by initiating the bombing of southern England with jet-propelled pilotless aircraft (V-1s), launched across the Channel from special sites in France and Belgium, with London as chief target. The U.S. forces reached the west shore of the Cotentin Peninsula (18 June). On 27 June Cherbourg and its demolished harbor works were captured by U.S. forces. By 2 July the Allies had landed in Normandy about 1 million troops, 566,648 tons of supplies, and 171,532 vehicles. The British forces captured Caen (9 July); the U.S. forces took St. Lô (18 July), road center linking Normandy with Brittany. U.S. "breakout" from St. Lô (25 July) enabled powerful armored thrust toward Avranches and into Brittany, which by 10 Aug. had been overrun and cut off by the U.S. Third Army under Gen. Patton. The St. Lô action concluded the Allied offensive in Normandy and opened the **Battle of France.**

23 JUNE. The Russians opened their summer offensive along an 800-mile line south of Leningrad.

19 JULY. Leghorn taken by the U.S. Fifth Army.

20 JULY. Attempted assassination of Hitler and plot to overthrow the Nazi regime ended in failure.

2 AUG. Polish underground army in Warsaw area commanded by General Bor (Komorowski) opened fight against the Germans. The Polish forces surrendered on 2 Oct.

3–23 AUG. Allies closed the Falaise-Argentan pocket, causing heavy German losses.

12 AUG. Florence fell to British forces. German troops in Italy pulled back to the Gothic Line.

15 AUG. OPERATION DRAGOON. Allied forces, including the U.S. Seventh Army under Gen. **Alexander M. Patch,** landed in southern France, between Marseilles and Nice, and drove up the Rhône Valley.

25 AUG.–11 SEPT. LIBERATION OF FRANCE, BELGIUM, AND LUXEMBOURG. On 25 Aug. Paris was liberated. On 28 Aug. the U.S. Third Army reached the Marne. Brussels and Antwerp were liberated by British and Canadian troops (4 Sept.). By 5 Sept. the Allies had landed 2,086,000 men and 3,466,000 tons of supplies in Western Europe. Luxembourg was liberated 11 Sept.

7 SEPT. Germans fired first V-2 (p. 800) on London.

8 Sept. Bulgaria surrendered to the Allies.

12 Sept.–3 Dec. BATTLE FOR GERMANY. U.S. forces entered Germany near Eupen and Trier (12 Sept.). In an attempt to turn the flank of the Westwall and gain a bridgehead on the Rhine, the Allies landed 34,000 airborne troops in Holland (17–28 Sept.). The U.S. forces took Eindhoven and Nijmegen. The British were defeated at Arnhem. The Canadian First Army cleared the Scheldt Estuary (9 Oct.–9 Nov.), thus enabling the Allies to use the urgently needed port facilities of Antwerp. The U.S. First Army took Aachen (21 Oct.) after a battle that began on 2 Oct. and required penetration of the Siegfried Line. Aachen was the first large German city taken by the Allies. The U.S. Third Army entered Metz (22 Nov.) and Strasbourg (23 Nov.), and U.S. forces reached the Roer River (3 Dec.).

22 Sept.–29 Dec. SOVIET ADVANCES. Russians took Tallinn (22 Sept.) and entered East Prussia (20 Oct.). Russian and Yugoslav forces seized Belgrade (20 Oct.), and the Russians entered Budapest 29 Dec.

3 Dec. Civil war broke out in Greece and lasted until 12 Jan. 1945).

16–26 Dec. BATTLE OF THE BULGE. A German counteroffensive under the command of Gen. Karl von Rundstedt was launched in the Ardennes along an 80-mile front held by an inadequate number of U.S. troops, many of whom lacked battle experience. By this surprise attack the Germans hoped to split the Allied Armies and take Liège and Antwerp. After advancing 50 miles to a point near Dinant, within 4 miles of the Meuse, the German drive was checked, largely owing to the defense of ringed Bastogne, which was relieved on 26 Dec. The original Allied line in the Ardennes was not restored until 21 Jan. 1945. The Battle of the Bulge resulted in about 77,000 U.S. casualties, including 8,000 killed, 48,000 wounded, and 21,-000 captured or missing.

1945

12–23 Jan. Russians launched general offensive in Poland (12–15 Jan.), took Warsaw (17 Jan.), Lodz (19 Jan.), and reached the Oder River (23 Jan.).

8 Feb.–26 Apr. GERMANY CRUSHED. British offensive launched in Holland (8 Feb.); U.S. Third Army crossed the Saar River (22 Feb.). The Saar-Palatinate area was cleared of German troops by 25 Mar. U.S. forces penetrated the Ruhr Valley (23 Feb.) and reached the Rhine near Düsseldorf (2 Mar.). Cologne and Düsseldorf fell on 7 Mar.; on the same day U.S. forces captured the **Remagen Bridge** across the Rhine before the Germans could demolish it, and secured a bridgehead on the east bank. On 23 Mar. Allied forces crossed the Rhine between Rees and Wesel by water and air. The Ruhr was enveloped and reduced (24 Mar.–18 Apr.), with the surrender of 325,000 German troops. On 27 Mar. U.S. forces took Mannheim and Frankfurt am Main. The U.S. Ninth Army reached the Elbe (11 Apr.). The Russians launched (13 Apr.) a drive on Berlin, entering the city on 24 Apr. U.S. forces took Nuremburg (21 Apr.). U.S. and Russian troops met at Torgau, on the Elbe (25 Apr.). On 26 Apr. the British took Bremen.

3 Mar. Finland, which had quit the war against Russia 4 Sept. 1941, declared war against Germany.

28 Apr. Mussolini and his mistress, Clara Petacci, captured and killed by Italian partisans in the town of Dongo, on Lake Como, as he tried to flee to Switzerland. Allied forces invaded the Po Valley.

1 May–5 June. GERMAN CAPITULATION. On 1 May the provisional German government under Adm. Karl Doenitz announced Hitler's death. It was reported that he had committed suicide in Berlin. On 2 May Berlin fell and the German forces in Italy surrendered. The German forces in the Netherlands, Denmark, and northwest Germany surrendered 4 May. Field Marshal Jodl signed (7 May, 2:41 A.M. French time) the instrument of unconditional surrender of Germany in the Allied headquarters at Reims. 8 May, **V-E Day**—formal end of the war in Europe. The German surrender was formally ratified at Berlin (9 May). On 5 June Germany was placed under an Allied Control Council and divided into four occupation zones.

The United States and the Western Hemisphere, 1942–45

HEMISPHERE SOLIDARITY. On 12 Jan. 1942 the U.S. and Mexico established a joint defense commission. At the **Rio de Janeiro Conference** (15–28 Jan.) of American foreign ministers, delegates of all 21 American republics, under the leadership of Sumner Welles and Oswaldo Aranha, chairman, voted to recommend to their respective governments a break in diplomatic relations with the Axis powers. All of the governments involved, with the exception of Chile and Argentina, severed relations. Chile broke off relations with the Axis (20 Jan. 1943); Argentina not until 26 Jan. 1944. The U.S. revealed (19 Mar. 1942) establishment of air bases in Guatemala to defend the Panama Canal Zone. On 30 Mar. the Inter-American Defense Board held its first session at Washington, D.C. President Roosevelt and President Getulio Vargas of Brazil, in conference aboard a U.S. destroyer off Natal, Brazil, announced (28 Jan.) agreement on common defense aims. The friendly relations between the U.S. and Mexico were stressed at a meeting (21 Apr.) of Roosevelt and President Avila Camacho. On 16 Aug. 1944 the U.S. government froze Argentina's gold assets in the U.S. in retaliation against the Argentine government's refusal to cooperate fully against the Axis. On 29 Sept. Roosevelt expressed concern over the continuing spread of Nazi and Fascist influence in Argentina and accused its government of having failed to fulfill its "solemn inter-American obligations." The Inter-American Conference on Problems of War and Peace met (21 Feb.–8 Mar. 1945) at Chapultepec Castle, Mexico City. All of the American republics except Argentina were represented. The conference adopted (3 Mar.) the **Act of Chapultepec,** a regional security agreement binding for the duration of the war. It provided that aggression upon one American state by another would be regarded as aggression against all and specified the "use of armed force to prevent or repel aggression." On 27 Mar. 1945 Argentina declared war on Germany and Japan, was admitted to the Pan-American Union (4 Apr.), and recognized (9 Apr.) by U.S., other American republics, and Great Britain.

WAR MOBILIZATION. By executive order the 9-man **War Manpower Commission** (WMC) was established (18 Apr. 1942) for the more effective utilization of manpower resources. Federal Security Administrator **Paul V. McNutt** was named chairman. Later that year its powers were extended to include jurisdiction over Selective Service, the U.S. Employment Service, and other war recruiting and training agencies. Voluntary male enlistments in the military services were ended. All males 18–38 became subject to Selective Service (draft age lowered to 18, 13 Nov. 1942), with deferments limited to war industries, agriculture, hardship cases, and the clergy. After a trial, drafting of 38–45 was ended, but all males between 45 and 64 were registered (25 Apr.). Women were enlisted for noncombat duties in the Women's Auxiliary Army Corps (WAACS, by act of 15 May 1942), Women Appointed for Voluntary Emergency Service (WAVES), Women's Auxiliary Ferrying Squadron (WAFS), *Semper Paratus* Always Ready Service (SPARS), and the Women's Reserve of the Marine Corps. To deal with the labor shortage, President Roosevelt decreed (9 Feb. 1943) for the duration of the war a minimum work week of 48 hours, applicable immediately in U.S. areas where labor shortages prevailed, but specified time-and-a-half for the extra 8 hours. Following Roosevelt's "hold-the-line" order (8 Apr. 1943), the WMC adopted regulations to "freeze" 27 million workers in war jobs.

WAR PRODUCTION. On 13 Jan. President Roosevelt appointed **Donald M. Nelson** chairman of the **War Production Board** (WPB) with authority to mobilize the nation's resources for a total war effort. WPB was the principal agency in the field of production and supply. On 21 Jan. Nelson abolished the Office of Production Management, whose functions were absorbed by the WPB. On 8 Apr. the WPB halted nonessential residential and highway construction in a move to conserve materials for the war effort. On 14 Aug. 1944 Nelson issued orders permitting limited reconversion of industry from war to civilian output. Nelson resigned (30 Sept.) and was succeeded by Julius A. Krug. On 2 Nov. President Roosevelt appointed Nelson his "personal representative" and requested

him to organize war production in China. The WPB was terminated 4 Oct. 1945, and its functions transferred to the Civilian Production Administration. On 3 Oct. 1944 **James F. Byrnes** was named head of the newly established Office of War Mobilization and Reconversion.

STRATEGIC AND CRITICAL WAR MATERIALS. In June 1942 the WPB substituted for general priorities a classified system of specific allocations of all strategic materials. The problem was also tackled by other officials and war agencies. On 7 Jan. 1942 Federal Loan Administrator Jesse H. Jones announced a $4-billion program for increasing production of synthetic rubber. On 14 Apr. control of the U.S. stockpile of critical and essential materials was transferred to the **Board of Economic Warfare** headed by Vice-President Henry A. Wallace. On 15 Sept. William M. Jeffers, president of the Union Pacific R.R., was appointed **Rubber Administrator** with full authority over the entire U.S. rubber program. On 15 July 1943 President Roosevelt abolished the Board of Economic Warfare and created the Office of Economic Warfare (OEW), headed by Leo T. Crowley, which absorbed its predecessor's functions as well as the foreign subsidiaries of the RFC on 25 Oct. Other war agencies concerned with war materials included **Petroleum Administrator for War** (executive order, 2 Dec. 1942, preceded, 28 May 1941, by Office of Petroleum Coordinator for War, with the Secretary of the Interior as coordinator); **Solid Fuels Administrator for War** (established in the Department of the Interior by executive order, 19 Apr. 1943, with power over coal and certain other solid fuels, including supervision of operations when mines were placed under government control). Financing for war industries was facilitated by the RFC and the **Smaller War Plants Corp.,**

established by act of Congress, 11 June 1942 and terminated 27 Dec. 1945, when its functions were transferred to the RFC.

PRICE CONTROL AND RATIONING. The Emergency Price Control Act (30 Jan. 1942) established the **Office of Price Administration** (OPA) to fix price ceilings on all commodities (except farm products) and to control rents in defense areas. This federal agency was originally created (11 Apr. 1941) as the Office of Price Administration and Civilian Supply, with **Leon Henderson** as first Federal Price Administrator; succeeded (Jan. 1943) by Prentiss M. Brown, in turn by Chester Bowles (Oct. 1943), and by Paul A. Porter (Feb. 1946). **Rationing** began 27 Dec. 1941, with auto tires. The first war ration book (1942) provided coupons for sugar, then coffee, with separate books for gasoline (1 Dec.), and coupon sheets for fuel oil. Point rationing was started early in 1943 with meat, fats and oils, butter, cheese, and processed foods. Shoes were later added. At its peak 13 rationing programs were administered. Before the close of Nov. 1945 all rationing programs were ended except for sugar and rubber tires. Tire rationing ended 31 Dec. 1945; sugar, 11 June 1947. As compared with World War I considerable price stabilization was obtained. By V-J Day consumer prices had risen 31% as against 62% by the Armistice of 1918. (See also p. 751.)

LABOR CONTROLS. In Mar. 1941 the National Defense Mediation Board, a tripartite body, with **William H. Davis** as chairman, was given investigatory and mediatory powers to deal with labor disputes in defense industries. In Nov. 1941 it rejected the United Mine Workers' demand for a union shop in the steel companies' "captive mines." CIO members resigned and the board's usefulness was destroyed. It was replaced (12 Jan.

1942) by a 12-man **National War Labor Board** (NWLB), equally divided among public, employers, and labor representatives, with Davis as chairman (to 8 Mar. 1945), with authority to settle disputes by mediation and arbitration. In the **International Harvester Case** (15 Apr.) the board granted the union **maintenance of membership** on condition that a majority of union employees, voting in a secret election, approved; modified in June to provide a 15-day period when employees could resign from union membership, after which maintenance of membership would go into effect. The board tied wage increases to the rise in the cost of living since 1 Jan. 1941 (**"Little Steel" formula,** 16 July). On 8 Apr. 1943 President Roosevelt issued his "hold-the-line" order freezing prices, wages, and salaries; modified in effect (12 May). Because of a strike involving 450,000 soft-coal miners and 80,000 anthracite miners, Roosevelt ordered (1 May) Secretary of the Interior Harold L. Ickes to take over all coal mines in the Eastern U.S. Roosevelt placed responsibility for the stoppage upon **John L. Lewis** (p. 1083), who called off the strike on 2 May. The war **Labor Disputes Act** (**Smith-Connally Anti-Strike Act**), passed over Roosevelt's veto (25 June), broadened presidential power to seize plants where interference with war production was threatened by a labor disturbance; made illegal the instigation of strikes in plants seized by the government; and made unions liable for damage suits for failure to give 30 days' notice of intention to strike in war industries. By order of President Roosevelt (27 Dec.) the U.S. Army took temporary possession of all railroads in the U.S. in order to prevent a strike of railway workers. The railroads were returned to private management on 18 Jan. 1944. On 28 Dec. 1944 the U.S. army took possession of

Montgomery Ward establishments in Chicago and elsewhere following the firm's refusal to obey NWLB directives.

FEPC. The migration of Negroes from rural sections to industrial areas led to a demand for ending racial discrimination in war industries and the armed services. The **Fair Employment Practice Committee,** originally established (25 June 1941) to curb discrimination in war production and government employment, was strengthened by an executive order (27 May 1943) calling for the mandatory incorporation of nondiscrimination clauses in war contracts and subcontracts. Race riots broke out in Detroit (20–21 June). President Roosevelt ordered out federal troops to quell the disturbance. A strike in the transportation field in protest against the upgrading of Negroes occurred in Philadelphia 1 Aug. 1944, and the U.S. army quickly restored order and normal transportation facilities. In Feb. 1946 a bill for a permanent FEPC was killed in the Senate by a filibuster. Again in 1950 the Senate blocked passage, and a modified plan was blocked in 1952. By the end of 1946 5 states (N.Y., N.J., Mass., Conn., and Wash.) had enacted Fair Employment Practice acts.

OTHER WAR AGENCIES. Office of Civilian Defense (28 Jan. 1942), with Mayor **Fiorello H. La Guardia** (N.Y.) director; succeeded by James N. Landis. **Director of Economic Stabilization,** filled (4 Oct. 1942) by Supreme Court Justice **James F. Byrnes** (S.C.), who (28 May 1943) headed the **Office of War Mobilization** (OWM), established to unify the activities of federal agencies engaged in the production or distribution of civilian supplies. **Office of Scientific Research and Development** (28 June 1941). **Office of Lend-Lease Administration** (executive order 8 Oct. 1941). **Office of Censorship** (executive order 19 Dec. 1941), with Byron Price director until Nov. 1945.

Office of Defense Transportation (executive order 18 Dec. 1941). **War Shipping Administration** (executive order 7 Feb. 1942), with Rear Adm. **Emory S. Land** as administrator. **National Housing Agency** (executive order 24 Feb. 1942). **Office of Alien Property Custodian** (executive order 11 Mar. 1942). **Office of Foreign Relief and Rehabilitation** (by State Department order 4 Dec. 1942). **Office of Coordinator of Inter-American Affairs** (executive order 30 July 1941), **Nelson A. Rockefeller,** coordinator (1940–44). **Office of War Information** (OWI, executive order 13 June 1942), to consolidate in one agency the information activities, both foreign and domestic, of the government (Office of Facts and Figures, Office of Government Reports, Division of Information of the Office of Emergency Management, and the Foreign Information Service), **Elmer Davis,** director. **Office of Strategic Services** (executive order 13 June 1942), placed under the jurisdiction of the Joint Chiefs of Staff, to engage in intelligence operations abroad and in the analysis of strategic information; **William J. Donovan,** director.

ATOMIC BOMB PROJECT. The Manhattan Engineer District for the development of the atomic bomb was placed under the command of Brig. Gen. **Leslie R. Groves** (13 Aug. 1942). Construction was begun (Sept.–Dec.) on the 3 chief installations of the Manhattan District: the U-235 separation plant (Oak Ridge, Tenn.), the bomb development laboratory (Los Alamos, N.M.), and the plutonium production works (Hanford, Wash.). Scientists working on the Argonne Project at the Univ. of Chicago effected the first self-sustaining nuclear reaction (2 Dec.). The first atomic bomb was exploded (16 July 1945) in a test at Alamogordo, N.M.

GI LEGISLATION. The "state rights" soldier vote bill became law (31 Mar.

1944) without President Roosevelt's signature. Roosevelt approved (22 June) the "GI Bill of Rights" authorizing educational and other benefits for World War II veterans.

1942 ELECTION TREND. Congressional, state, and local elections (3 Nov.) indicated a swing toward the Republicans, who gained 46 seats in the House, 9 in the Senate. The Democrats, however, retained control of both houses.

RELOCATION AND ENEMY ALIENS. By order of President Roosevelt (19 Feb. 1942), the Secretary of War was authorized to prescribe restricted military areas from which persons might be excluded. About 110,000 Japanese-Americans living in California, Oregon, Washington, and Arizona were by 29 Mar. transferred to relocation camps in the U.S. interior. On 12 Oct. Attorney General Francis Biddle announced that, effective 19 Oct., 600,000 unnaturalized Italians in the U.S. would no longer be considered as enemy aliens. On 17 Dec. 1944 the U.S. army announced the termination, effective 2 Jan. 1945, of the mass exclusion from the West Coast of persons of Japanese ancestry.

INTERNAL SECURITY MEASURES. On 27 June 1942 J. Edgar Hoover, director of the FBI, announced the arrest of 8 Nazi saboteurs who had been landed from submarines on the Long Island and Florida coasts. Convicted by a secret military tribunal appointed by the president, 6 were electrocuted and the other 2 given long prison terms. On 23 July, 28 persons, including George Sylvester Viereck, William Dudley Pelley, and Gerald Winrod, were indicted as seditionists. In the course of their trial in 1944 Judge Edward C. Eichers died, and the indictments were dismissed (1946) by Chief Justice Bolitha L. Laws of the District Court for the District of Columbia, who rebuked the Department of Justice for "lack of diligence" in prosecution. On 15 May 1943 the third International (Comintern) was dissolved in Moscow. On 20 May 1944 the Communist party of the U.S. dissolved as a political party but was reconstituted as a supposedly nonparty group under the name of the Communist Political Association, headed by Earl Browder. Congressman Martin Dies' **Committee on Un-American Activities** was given permanent status by a House vote, 207–186 (3 Jan. 1945). The Dies Committee recommended dismissal of some 3,800 government employees; but after a Department of Justice investigation, only 36 were found to warrant dismissal. On 27 July 1945 the Communist Political Association voted to disband and to reconstitute the Communist Party of the U.S. On 29 July William Z. Foster replaced Earl Browder as head of the Communist organization.

PLANNING FOR PEACE: CONNALLY-FULBRIGHT RESOLUTION. On 16 Mar. 1943 Sens. Joseph Ball (Rep., Minn.), Harold Burton (Rep., Ohio), Carl Hatch (Dem., N.M.), and Lister Hill (Dem., Ala.) began a bipartisan movement to commit the U.S. Senate to participation in an international organization. On 21 Sept. the House of Representatives adopted the Fulbright Resolution (introduced by J. W. Fulbright [Ark.]) favoring "the creation of appropriate international machinery with power adequate to establish and to maintain a just and lasting peace," and U.S. participation "through its constitutional process." A similar resolution (introduced by Tom Connally [Tex.] was adopted in the Senate, 85–5 (5 Nov.), with the express stipulation that any treaty made to carry out its purpose would require a vote of two thirds of the Senate. On 21 July 1945 the Senate approved U.S.

membership in the United Nations Food and Agriculture Organization. On 28 July the Senate ratified the United Nations Charter by a vote of 89 to 2. President Truman signed the charter (8 Aug.).

PRESIDENTIAL CAMPAIGN OF 1944. The Republican National Convention met at Chicago (26 June) and nominated (27 June) Gov. **Thomas E. Dewey** (N.Y.) for president and Gov. **John W. Bricker** (Ohio) for vice-president. The Democratic National Convention met at Chicago (19 July) and on 20 July renominated President **Roosevelt.** Sen. **Harry S. Truman** (Mo.) was chosen as vice-presidential candidate. Minor party candidates: Norman Thomas (N.Y.), Socialist; Claude A. Watson (Calif.), National Prohibition; and Edward A. Teichert (Pa.), Socialist Labor. Both major parties backed U.S. participation in some form of postwar interna-

tional organization to maintain world peace and security. Organized labor took part in the campaign through the agency of the C.I.O. Political Action Committee (PAC), which claimed that its support helped to elect 17 candidates for the Senate and 120 for the House.

7 Nov. PRESIDENTIAL ELECTION. Included in the national vote were 2,691,160 soldiers' ballots. Popular vote: **Roosevelt,** 25,602,505; Dewey, 22,006,-278; Thomas, 80,158; Watson, 74,758; and Teichert, 45,336. Electoral vote: **Roosevelt,** 432 (36 states); Dewey, 99 (12 states). The Democrats retained control of both houses of Congress.

1945, 12 Apr. DEATH OF PRESIDENT ROOSEVELT. President Roosevelt died suddenly of a cerebral hemorrhage at Warm Springs, Ga. Vice-President **Harry S. Truman** took the oath of office as 33rd president of the U.S.

International Conferences, Declarations, and Agreements, 1941–45

1941

22 Dec. Prime Minister Winston Churchill arrived in Washington for a series of conferences with President Roosevelt. The fundamental basis of joint strategy was affirmed: to concentrate upon the defeat of the Axis in Europe (which was viewed as the decisive theater of war), and to follow a policy of containment in the Far East until military successes in Europe or mounting Allied resources permitted stronger blows against Japan. The last of this series of conferences was held on 14 Jan. 1942. The Declaration of the United Nations was drafted and the Combined Chiefs of Staff and the Munitions Assignment Board were set up.

1942

1 Jan. UNITED NATIONS DECLARATION was signed at Washington. Twenty-six nations, including the U.S., Great Britain, the Soviet Union, and China, affirmed the principles of the Atlantic Charter, pledged the employment of their full military and economic resources against the Axis, and promised not to make a separate armistice or peace with the common enemy.

27 Jan. Anglo-American Combined Raw Materials Board established at Washington.

6 Feb. Joint Anglo-American War Council established at Washington.

23 Feb. Master Mutual Lend-Lease

Agreement signed by the U.S. and Great Britain, Australia, and New Zealand.

29 APR. Hitler and Mussolini conferred at Salzburg.

26 MAY. Great Britain and Russia signed a 20-year mutual aid pact.

29 MAY. The Soviet foreign minister, Vyacheslav M. Molotov, arrived in Washington for conferences with President Roosevelt and other high U.S. officials. Among the results of the meetings was a new Lend-Lease protocol with Russia. The agreement provided that materials or data received from the U.S. would not be transferred to other parties without U.S. consent and that materials still available at the end of the war would be returned to the U.S. The new agreement went into effect on 1 July.

9 JUNE. U.S. and Great Britain established a Combined Production Resources Board and a Combined Food Board.

18–27 JUNE. Anglo-American conference at Washington discussed strategy problems. Roosevelt and Churchill participated, as did Russian and Chinese representatives.

JULY. The Combined Chiefs of Staff, meeting in London, decided to invade North Africa and to postpone a second front in Europe as well as the Pacific offensive.

12–15 AUG. 1ST MOSCOW CONFERENCE. Principal participants were Soviet Premier Joseph V. Stalin, Prime Minister Churchill, and W. Averell Harriman, who represented President Roosevelt. Churchill, with the support of Harriman, informed Stalin that it was not possible to open a second front in Europe in 1942.

9 OCT. U.S. and Great Britain announced they would abandon extraterritorial rights in China. A treaty incorporating this provision was signed by the U.S. and China on 11 Jan. 1943.

1943

14–24 JAN. CASABLANCA CONFERENCE was held in French Morocco. President Roosevelt and Prime Minister Churchill declared that the war would be fought until the "**unconditional surrender**" of the enemy had been secured. Agreement in principle was reached on a second front, but not on its location. U.S. officials favored an invasion of the Continent through France. The British urged an assault on the "soft underbelly" of Europe (i.e., Italy and the Balkans). A compromise was reached on the invasion of Sicily and Italy without prejudice to the ultimate invasion of Europe from the west. No agreement was worked out on the conflicting claims for leadership of Gens. Charles de Gaulle and Henri Giraud, who also attended the conference. Gen. Dwight D. Eisenhower was placed in supreme command of the North African theater.

25 APR. The Soviet Union broke off relations with the Polish government-in-exile.

12–25 MAY. ANGLO-AMERICAN CONFERENCE (TRIDENT) at Washington planned global strategy and the opening of a second front in Europe. President Roosevelt, Prime Minister Churchill, the Combined Chiefs of Staff, and many U.S. and British officials took part. The date (1 May 1944) for the Normandy invasion was definitely set and the seizure of the Azores authorized unless Portugal could be persuaded by negotiation to grant the use of bases on the islands. The conference also agreed to step up the quantity of aviation gasoline being flown over "the hump" from India to China.

18 MAY–3 JUNE. The United Nations Conference on Food and Agriculture met at Hot Springs, Va. It established the Food and Agriculture Organization (FAO) of the United Nations.

22 MAY. Moscow announced the dissolution 15 May of the Third International (Comintern).

31 MAY. In French Algiers, Gens. Charles de Gaulle and Henri Giraud announced their agreement on the formation of a French Committee of National Liberation, of which they were copresidents. The committee, which became (2 June 1944) the French Provisional Government-in-Exile, promised full support to the war against the Axis. On 23 Oct. 1944 the U.S., Great Britain, and Russia recognized the committee as the French provisional regime.

11–24 AUG. 1ST QUEBEC CONFERENCE (QUADRANT) attended by President Roosevelt, Prime Minister Churchill, and top-ranking advisers including the Combined Chiefs of Staff, reaffirmed 1 May 1944 as the target date for the Normandy invasion (OVERLORD), which was to be supplemented by landings in Southern France (ANVIL, later DRAGOON). Agreement was reached on stepping up military operations in the Far East, particularly in Burma, and a Southeast Asia Command was established, with Lord Louis Mountbatten as Supreme Allied Commander. The Chiefs of the Naval Staffs reported that the Battle of the Atlantic against the U-boat had turned in favor of the Allies.

19–30 OCT. MOSCOW CONFERENCE OF FOREIGN MINISTERS was the first Allied 3-power meeting of World War II. It was attended by Secretary of State Cordell Hull, Foreign Minister Anthony Eden, and Foreign Minister V. M. Molotov, together with U.S., British, and Soviet military officials. The most controversial point in the discussions involved the status of the Polish government-in-exile at London, which the Soviet Union refused to recognize. The U.S. and Great Britain assured the Russians that preparations for opening a second front in Europe were under way.

Stalin made an unconditional promise that after Germany's defeat Russia would enter the war against Japan. The conference established a European Advisory Commission for the purpose of formulating a postwar policy for Germany. The Moscow Declaration issued at the close of the conference recognized "the necessity of establishing at the earliest practicable date a general international organization, based on the principle of the sovereign equality of all peace-loving states, and open to membership by all such states, large and small, for the maintenance of international peace and security."

9 Nov. The United Nations Relief and Rehabilitation Administration (UNRRA) was established with the signing of an agreement at Washington by 44 nations. Its purpose was to aid liberated populations in war-devastated areas of Europe and the Far East. **Herbert H. Lehman** (1878–1963), former governor of New York, was named director general of UNRRA. By agreements of Mar. 1944 and Dec. 1945 the member countries contributed $4 billion. The U.S. paid 72% of UNRRA's operating expenses; 90% of all food and other supplies distributed were products of U.S. farms or factories.

22–26 Nov. 1ST CAIRO CONFERENCE. President Roosevelt and Prime Minister Churchill conferred with Generalissimo and Madame Chiang Kai-shek regarding the war in the Far East. The **Declaration of Cairo** (1 Dec.) affirmed that the 3 powers would prosecute the war against Japan until her unconditional surrender and that they had no desire for territorial expansion; that Japan should be deprived of all Pacific islands acquired since 1914, whether by capture or League of Nations mandate; that all territories which Japan had taken from the Chinese, such as Manchuria, Formosa, and the Pescadores, should be restored to China; and that the 3 powers were "determined that in due course Korea shall become free and independent."

At the **2d Cairo Conference** (4–6 Dec.) Roosevelt and Churchill held discussions with the president of Turkey, Ismet Inönü. This conference affirmed the alliance between Great Britain and Turkey and noted "the firm friendship existing between the Turkish people," the U.S., and the Soviet Union. As a result of military decisions taken at the second Cairo Conference, the command of the invasion of Western Europe was conferred on Gen. **Dwight D. Eisenhower.**

28 Nov.–1 Dec. TEHERAN CONFERENCE, held at the capital of Iran, was attended by President Roosevelt, Prime Minister Churchill, and Premier Stalin. It was the first 3-power war conference in which Stalin took a personal part. The chief subject of the meeting was the projected Anglo-American invasion of Western Europe, supported by a flanking invasion through Southern France, and the timing of this assault with the Soviet offensive against Germany. Stalin reaffirmed his promise to enter the war against Japan. The conference formulated a plan for an international organization to keep the peace.

1944

1–22 July. UNITED NATIONS MONETARY AND FINANCIAL CONFERENCE (BRETTON WOODS CONFERENCE), held at Bretton Woods, N.H., was attended by representatives of 44 nations. The conference established an International Monetary Fund of $8.8 billion (of which about 25% was contributed by the U.S.) for the stabilization of national currencies (it effected a general evaluation of the currencies of Western Europe late in 1949) and the

fostering of world trade. It also set up an International Bank for Reconstruction and Development with a capitalization of $9.1 billion (of which about 35% was supplied by the U.S.) for extending loans to nations requiring economic rehabilitation. By 1950 the bank had made loans of only $700 million. Russia refused to participate in these financial arrangements.

27 July. The Polish Committee of National Liberation, organized at Moscow, was recognized by the Soviet government. The committee, which later transferred its headquarters to Lublin, was entrusted with administrative control of Polish areas taken by the Red Army.

21 Aug.–7 Oct. DUMBARTON OAKS CONFERENCE, held near Washington, D.C., was attended by representatives of the U.S., Great Britain, the Soviet Union, and China (with the last 2 meeting separately, since Russia was still at peace with Japan). The conference discussed the draft of a charter for a permanent postwar international organization for maintaining world peace and security. The tentative proposals (known as the Dumbarton Oaks Plan) served as the basis for the Charter of the United Nations. Agreement on the veto issue could not be reached, Russia refusing to agree to bar a member of the Security Council from voting on a question to which it was itself a party.

11–16 Sept. 2D QUEBEC CONFERENCE, attended by President Roosevelt and Prime Minister Churchill, considered strategic plans for final victory over Germany and Japan. The chief subjects of the conference were the demarcation of the zones of occupation following the conquest of Germany and the policy governing the postwar treatment of that nation. The **Morgenthau plan** (sponsored by Secretary of the Treasury Henry Morgenthau, Jr.) for reducing Germany to an agrarian economy was tentatively approved at this conference, but was rejected by President Roosevelt a month later.

9–18 OCT. 2D MOSCOW CONFERENCE, attended by Prime Minister Churchill and Premier Joseph Stalin, divided the Balkans into spheres, Russia to predominate in Rumania, Bulgaria, and Hungary, Great Britain in Greece, with Yugoslavia to be shared. It was generally agreed that the Curzon Line should bound Poland on the east and the Oder River on the west. Roosevelt, who was not a party to these arrangements, let it be known that he would not be bound by them.

1945

JAN. Malta Conference. Combined Chiefs of Staff planned final campaign against Hitler.

4–11 FEB. YALTA CONFERENCE, held in the Crimea, was attended by President Roosevelt, Prime Minister Churchill, and Premier Stalin, together with their top diplomatic and military advisers. Most of the important agreements remained secret until the postwar period. In exchange for her pledge to enter the war in the Far East, Russia was given the Kurile Islands, the southern half of Sakhalin, and an occupation zone in Korea, and was granted privileged rights in Manchuria and in the Chinese cities of Dairen and Port Arthur. In addition, the U.S. and Great Britain agreed to recognize the autonomy of Outer Mongolia, which had severed its connections with China and come under Soviet influence. The U.S. and Great Britain also agreed to award eastern Poland to the Soviet Union. Poland's eastern border was fixed on the Curzon Line; and that nation was to receive territorial compensation in the north and west at the expense of Germany. Agreement was reached for reorganizing the

Polish (Lublin) government on a broader democratic basis. The Russian demand of $20 billion in reparation payments from Germany, to be taken out of current production, was referred to a reparations commission. The 3 powers reaffirmed the "unconditional surrender" formula and issued a Declaration of Liberated Europe pledging the Big Three to support postwar governments in the liberated states which would be representative of the popular will through free elections. The conferees announced they had worked out a formula for voting procedure in the Security Council and that a conference to elaborate the United Nations Charter would convene at San Francisco on 25 Apr. It was secretly agreed that the Ukraine and Byelorussia would be accorded full and equal membership in the United Nations organization on the footing of independent nations.

5 APR. The Soviet Union denounced its 5-year nonaggression pact with Japan.

21 APR. The Soviet Union concluded a 20-year mutual assistance pact with the Polish Provisional Government (the Lublin regime).

25 APR.–26 JUNE. UNITED NATIONS CONFERENCE ON INTERNATIONAL ORGANIZATION, attended by delegates of 50 nations, assembled at San Francisco to draft the Charter of the United Nations Organization (UNO). The Russians at San Francisco interpreted the Yalta voting formula to mean that a nation could use the veto to forbid the Security Council from even discussing questions which might require force in their settlement. Secretary of State Edward R. Stettinius, Jr., threatened that the U.S. would not participate in the organization unless the Russians yielded. The deadlock was broken when President Truman directed Harry L. Hopkins, then in Moscow, to take the issue to Stalin. The latter agreed that the veto should not be used to prevent discussion. Following the announcement (7 June) of this compromise, a draft charter was worked out. The charter of the United Nations provided for 6 chief organs: (1) a **General Assembly** of all member nations as the policy-making body, each nation to have a single vote; (2) a **Security Council** of 11 members in continuous session for deciding diplomatic, political, or military disputes, the Big Five (the U.S., Great Britain, the Soviet Union, France, and China) to have permanent seats, the other 6 to be held for 2-year terms; (3) an **Economic and Social Council** of 18 members elected by the General Assembly for the purpose of dealing with human welfare and fundamental rights and freedoms; (4) an **International Court of Justice** (sitting at The Hague) for dealing with international legal disputes, its 15 judges to be elected by the General Assembly and the Security Council; (5) a **Trusteeship Council** made up of states administering trust territories, the permanent members of the Security Council, and members elected by the General Assembly for a 3-year term; and (6) a **Secretariat,** headed by the Secretary-General, for performing the routine administrative work of the UNO, the staff to be selected from nations holding membership in the UN. The charter was unanimously approved on 25 June and signed on the following day. By charter amendments effective 31 Aug. 1965, Security Council membership was increased to 15; Economic and Social Council membership was increased to 27, and voting procedures were changed accordingly.

5 June. EUROPEAN ADVISORY COMMISSION established German occupation zones, assigning eastern Germany to Russia, dividing the south between the U.S. and France, and placing Great Britain in charge of the west.

Berlin, situated in the heart of the Soviet zone, was shared among the occupying powers, leaving all ground approaches dominated by the Russians. The administration of Berlin was entrusted to a military Kommandatura.

17 July–2 Aug. POTSDAM CONFERENCE, held near Berlin, was attended by President Harry S. Truman, Prime Minister Churchill (who after 28 July was replaced by the newly chosen British prime minister, Clement R. Attlee, head of the Labour government), and Premier Stalin. Also present, in addition to other top-ranking officials, were Secretary of State James F. Byrnes, Foreign Secretary Anthony Eden (who after 28 July was replaced by Ernest Bevin), and Foreign Secretary V. M. Molotov. The first declaration issued by the conference was the "unconditional surrender" ultimatum (26 July) presented to Japan. The chief questions before the conference were the plan for the occupation and control of Germany and the settlement of various European problems. A Council of Foreign Ministers, its members drawn from the Big Five, was established and entrusted with the preparation of draft treaties with Austria, Hungary, Bulgaria, Rumania, and Finland, and with the proposal of settlements of outstanding territorial questions. The council was also authorized to negotiate an agreement with a central German government whenever the latter should come into being. The occupation authorities were to conduct programs designed to denazify, decentralize, disarm, and democratize Germany, which was to be treated during the occupation period as a single economic unit. Provision was made for the trial of war criminals (shortly after the conference an International Military Tribunal was set up). Final delimitation of the Polish-German frontier was left to the peace treaty. The Soviet Union abandoned its $20-billion reparations de-

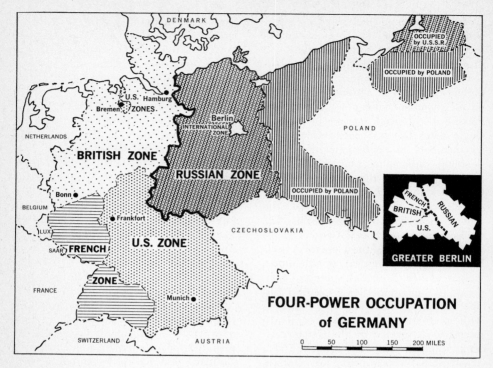

FOUR-POWER OCCUPATION of GERMANY

mand in exchange for a reparations schedule based on a percentage of useful capital equipment in the Western zone and materials in the Eastern zone. The conference agreed that Germany should make good for losses suffered at its hands by the United Nations. Provision was made for the mandatory transfer of 6,500,000 Germans from Hungary, Czechoslovakia, and Poland to Germany. Economic agreements were reached concerning German industry, foreign trade, finance, communications, and transportation. At the earliest practicable date the German economy was to be decentralized for the purpose of eliminating excessive centralization of economic power as exemplified by cartels, syndicates, and trusts. Primary emphasis in the German economy was to be given to the development of agriculture and peaceful domestic industries.

14 Aug. The Sino-Soviet treaty signed at Moscow formalized China's consent to the concessions granted to the Soviet at the Yalta Conference.

THE UNITED STATES AND THE BALANCE OF WORLD POWER, 1945-74

★ ★
★

With the close of World War II, the preponderance of power had moved to the periphery; the U.S. and the U.S.S.R. emerged as the two "superpowers" of the postwar era. Each interpreted the actions of the other as aggressive. Each championed an ideology antithetical to the other. Once the dynamic of the Cold War—the continuous confrontation between the "Free World" and the "Communist Bloc"—was set in motion, it tended to feed upon itself. The postwar era differed from all the others in one crucial respect—the power of the atom had been tapped. Although man could now destroy himself, paradoxically, the "balance of terror" kept conflict at conventional levels.

After nearly thirty years, the U.S. and the U.S.S.R. remain the two superpowers, but the bipolarity and the venomous climate of the Cold War era are slowly fading. The force of nationalism has exposed a degree of fragmentation in the Communist world; a huge number of uncommitted nations have emerged; other powers—Japan, China, West Germany—increasingly must be reckoned with by the U.S. and the U.S.S.R., along with the oil-rich states of the Middle East. In response, the United States did not retreat into isolation as it had after World War I, but the Vietnam War underscored the limits of power and the need to be more prudently selective in commitments overseas.

The Cold War: Opening Phases, 1945–52

1945

11 SEPT.–2 OCT. **LONDON CONFERENCE.** The first meeting of the Council of Foreign Ministers failed to bring agreement on treaties with Italy, Bulgaria, Hungary, and Rumania. The conference broke up over the issue of Chinese and French participation and revealed a cleavage between Russia and the West.

16–26 DEC. **MOSCOW CONFERENCE.** The second meeting of the Council of Foreign Ministers considered international control of atomic energy, a new 4-power control commission for Japan, trusteeship for Korea, and the drafting of European peace treaties by a 5-power conference for submission to a peace conference of the 21 Allied nations.

1945–49

WAR CRIMES TRIALS. Nazis. Acting under a charter adopted in London (Aug. 1945) to bring to trial the German and Japanese war criminals for crimes against (1) peace, (2) humanity, and (3) the laws of war, an International Military Tribunal at Nuremburg, Germany, tried 24 principal Nazi offenders (20 Nov. 1945–1 Oct. 1946). U.S. prosecutor was Associate Justice **Robert H. Jackson** (1892–1954). Twelve Nazis were sentenced to be hanged: Reichsmarschall Hermann Göring (committed suicide by poisoning on the eve of his execution), Martin Bormann, *in absentia*, and the 10 who were hanged 16 Oct. 1946: Joachim Ribbentrop, Field Marshal Wilhelm Keitel, Col. Gen. Alfred Jodl, Ernst Kaltenbrunner, Alfred Rosenberg, Hans Frank, Wilhelm Frick, Arthur Seyss-Inquart, Julius Streicher, and Fritz Sauckel; 3 were acquitted: Franz von Papen, Hjalmar Schacht, Hans Fritsche; 3 escaped trial: Martin Bormann, whereabouts unknown, Gustav Krupp because of advanced age and ill health, and Robert Ley, who committed suicide after indictment. In addition, the U.S. conducted a series of 12 trials, each centered on an occupation group. In all, 836,000 former Nazis were tried in the U.S. zone, of whom 503,360 were convicted, 430,890 fined less than 1,000 Rm., 27,413 sentenced to perform some community work, 7,768 given short terms in labor camps, 18,503 pronounced ineligible to hold office, and 20,865 suffered partial property confiscation.

Japanese war leaders were tried by an International Military Tribunal for the Far East (est. 19 Jan. 1946). Trials (3 June 1946–12 Nov. 1948) resulted in death sentences being meted out to former Premier Hideki Tojo and Gens. Seishiro Itagaki, Kenji Doihara, Heitaro Kimura, Iwane Matsui, and Akira Muto; on appeal the U.S. Supreme Court denied jurisdiction 20 Dec. 1948; the 7 were hanged in Tokyo 23 Dec. Adm. Shigetaro Shimada and Army Chief of Staff Yoshijiro Umezu and 14 others were given life sentences, former Foreign Minister Shigenoi Togo sentenced to 20 years, and former Foreign Minister Mamoru Shigemitsu 7 years (paroled Nov. 1950). In addition, a large number of high-ranking Japanese army and navy officers were tried before special tribunals in Japan and throughout the areas of Japanese military operations for offenses against the laws of war. As of 19 Oct. 1949, 4,200 Japanese had been convicted, 720 executed.

1947. "The MacArthur Constitution," originally drafted by the Occupation authorities, was subsequently redrafted, debated, and approved by the Japanese, and went into effect 3 May 1947. It launched a program of democratic reform, including dissolution of trusts (*zaibatsu*), support for the formation of political parties, labor unions, agrarian reform, and the emancipation of women.

1945–52

INDOCHINA. While criticizing French colonial policy in Indochina and advocating some kind of international trusteeship arrangement for the region, President Franklin D. Roosevelt was reluctant to risk a confrontation with the French—and the British—over the French desire to reclaim the area after the war. Upon Roosevelt's death U.S. policy toward Indochina was in a state of disarray. In Mar. 1945 the Japanese allowed Emperor Bao Dai to proclaim Vietnam's independence but when the Japanese occupation collapsed (Aug. 1945) Bao Dai abdicated, going into exile in France. The Viet Minh (the nationalist resistance organization, including the Indochinese Communist Party, established May 1941), led by Ho Chi Minh, set up its capital in Hanoi and proclaimed (2 Sept. 1945) Vietnam an independent democratic republic. By the end of 1945 the French army, which had returned to launch a campaign to reconquer Vietnam, had gained control of the south. Ho Chi Minh received no reply to a series of letters written (Oct. 1945–Feb. 1946) to President Harry S. Truman or the Secretary of State James F. Byrnes, appealing for U.S. and UN intervention against French colonialism. Large-scale hostilities erupted in North Vietnam in Dec. 1946. Driven out of Hanoi, Ho Chi Minh went underground to lead a guerrilla war. On 8 Mar. 1949 France and Bao Dai concluded an agreement by which France acknowledged the "independence" within the "French Union" of a unified, non-Communist state of Vietnam. Ho Chi Minh's Democratic Republic of Vietnam, which controlled a large part of the country, was recognized by Peking and Moscow in Jan. 1950. Fearful that Bao Dai was weak and tainted with French colonialism, the U.S. delayed recognizing Bao Dai's Saigon regime until 7 Feb. 1950. In response to a French request, the U.S. announced (8 May) it would provide economic and military aid to the French in Indochina, beginning with a grant of $10 million. On 27 June President Truman announced the dispatch of a 35-man military mission to Vietnam, followed the next month by an economic aid mission. On 23 Dec. the U.S., France, Vietnam, Cambodia, and Laos (the last 2, like Vietnam, "associated states" within the French Union) signed an agreement which "recognized the common interest" of the states in defending "the principles of freedom" and provided for U.S. aid. U.S. aid to the French effort in Indochina jumped to some $500 million in 1951 and increased annually thereafter. In the north, after the fall of major French outposts, French forces defended the Red River Delta while within France opposition to the war grew and within Vietnam Bao Dai's political support evaporated, leading to his withdrawal from the scene in Oct. 1952.

1946

INAUGURATION OF UNITED NATIONS ORGANIZATION. On 10 Jan. the first session of the UN General Assembly began in London. Trygve H. Lie of Norway was elected (1 Feb.) Secretary General. The Security Council convened the same month. The first complaint considered by the Security Council was raised (19 Jan.) by Iran and was directed against the U.S.S.R., alleging Soviet refusal to withdraw its troops from Iranian soil and interference in Iranian internal affairs. The Security Council considered the complaint despite Soviet abstention, but the issue was eventually resolved without official UN action (p. 465). In apparent retaliation, the U.S.S.R. complained (21 Jan.) of interference by British troops in the internal affairs of Greece. The developing cleavage between the West and the U.S.S.R., which would significantly affect the functioning of the UN, dimming hopes that the international organization would secure peace in the postwar world, soon became even more apparent.

The U.S.S.R. used the veto power for the first time 16 Feb., rejecting a U.S. proposal that Britain and France negotiate the withdrawal of their troops from Syria and Lebanon. Both the U.S. and the U.S.S.R. used the UN as a forum to propagandize against each other.

28 FEB. Secretary Byrnes declared that the U.S. would not and could not "stand aloof if force or the threat of force is used contrary to the purposes and principles" of the UN Charter.

15 MAR. "IRON CURTAIN" SPEECH. President Truman was in the audience when Sir Winston Churchill, in a speech at Fulton, Mo., observed that "from Stettin in the Baltic to Trieste in the Adriatic, an Iron Curtain has descended across the Continent." Noting the end of an era of hopeful wartime collaboration between the Western Allies and the U.S.S.R., Churchill called for closer Anglo-American cooperation to meet the new situation.

25 APR.–16 MAY, 15 JUNE–12 JULY, 29 JULY–15 OCT. PARIS PEACE CONFERENCE, attended by foreign minister of Great Britain, France, the Soviet Union, and the U.S., considered peace treaties for the Axis satellites, agreed (1 July) on terms of the treaties, and called a 21-nation conference to study the drafts. The 21-nation conference revealed increasing disagreement between Russia and the West, and the conference broke down when the Soviet Union objected to participation by the smaller powers.

4 NOV.–12 DEC. The Council of Foreign Ministers, at New York, completed peace treaties with minor Axis nations. Secretary Byrnes, supported in his firmer stand against the U.S.S.R. by President Truman's dismissal (20 Sept.) of Secretary of Commerce Wallace, who had opposed a "get tough with Russia" policy, succeeded in reaching agreement with Soviet Foreign Minister Molotov.

The treaties were signed for the U.S. in Washington by Secretary Byrnes (20 Jan. 1947), for the other powers in Paris (10 Feb.), and were ratified by the U.S. Senate on 4 June. **Italy.** The Republic of Italy (formed 14 July 1946) agreed to make reparations in kind to Yugoslavia ($125 million), the U.S.S.R. ($100 million), Greece ($105 million), Ethiopia ($25 million), and Albania ($5 million); to restrict its armed forces; to cede the Dodecanese Islands to Greece; to cede Fiume, the Istrian peninsula, and much of Venezia Giulia to Yugoslavia; and to set up Trieste provisionally as a free territory under UN guarantee. Italy renounced all claims to its former colonies. A UN Assembly resolution provided for a united and independent Libya (Cyrenaica, Tripolitania, and Fezzan), and Italian Somaliland was placed under Italian trusteeship for 10 years. **Hungary** agreed to pay reparations in kind to the Soviet Union of $200 million and $50 million each to Czechoslovakia and Yugoslavia. Northern Transylvania was returned to Rumania and the Carpatho-Ukraine became part of the Soviet Ukraine. **Rumania** agreed to make reparations to the U.S.S.R. ($300 million) and confirmed the cession of Bessarabia and northern Bucovina to the Soviet Ukraine and of southern Dobruja to Bulgaria. **Bulgaria** was required to pay in reparations $25 million to Czechoslovakia and $45 million to Greece. **Finland** agreed to pay reparations to Russia of $300 million and to cede to the Soviet Union the Arctic port of Petsamo, her part of the Rybachi peninsula west of Murmansk, and the Karelian peninsula, including the port of Viipuri. The U.S.S.R. gave up its lease on Hangö but took a 50-year lease on a naval base at Parkkala on the Gulf of Finland.

27 DEC. President Truman reported to Congress that settlements had been made with 7 nations (representing 70%

of U.S. Lend-Lease aid) including Great Britain (27 Mar.), but as yet not with the Soviet Union (received $11.1 billion; supplied about $2.2 million as reciprocal Lend-Lease). Coincident with settlement of the British agreement the U.S. granted Britain an additional loan of $3.75 billion payable at 2% in 50 annual installments beginning 31 Dec. 1951.

GERMANY. The U.S. announced 27 May it would suspend dismantling in its German zone, thus ending this mode of reparations payment in its occupation area. On 2 Dec. the U.S. and Great Britain agreed to merge their occupation zones.

IRAN. To prevent Nazi penetration of Iran and to protect a supply route from the Persian Gulf to the U.S.S.R., an Anglo-Soviet agreement (1941) provided for the stationing of British troops in the south and Soviet troops in the north. Under the agreement all troops were to be withdrawn within 6 months of the end of hostilities. The U.S.S.R. promoted the separatist revolts in the northern provinces of Azerbaijan and Kurdistan which began late in 1945. While British and U.S. troops—which had arrived after U.S. entry in the war to help move supplies to the U.S.S.R.—began to withdraw, Soviet troops remained (Dec. 1945), blocking the attempts of Iranian troops to put down the rebellion in Azerbaijan. After the U.S.S.R. announced (25 Feb. 1946) that its troops would stay beyond the 2 Mar. deadline set for evacuation, the U.S. sent (6 Mar.) a protest note to the U.S.S.R. calling for "immediate" withdrawal and repeated the demand in the UN Security Council. A Soviet-Iranian agreement was announced on 5 Apr., and on 4 May Iran reported that the withdrawal was complete. Since the first major crisis of the postwar period took place in the Near East, that region began to assume a larger place in U.S. foreign policy. By Nov. 1946 the U.S. was preparing to supply Iran with arms.

TURKEY. During 1945 the U.S.S.R. had begun to apply pressure on Turkey, demanding: (1) cession of several Turkish districts on the Turkish-Soviet frontier; (2) revision of the 1936 Montreux Convention, which provided for exclusive Turkish supervision of the Dardanelles, to provide instead for joint Soviet-Turkish administration; and (3) the leasing to the U.S.S.R. of naval and land bases in the strait to provide for the "joint defense" of Turkey and the U.S.S.R. U.S. responses designed to demonstrate support for Turkey included: (1) President Truman's warning, in an Army Day speech (6 Apr. 1946), that the U.S. would aid the UN with military power to protect nations in the Near East from "coercion or penetration"; (2) protest notes (21 Aug. and 11 Oct. 1946) rejecting Soviet demands; and (3) naval movements in the Mediterranean. Soviet pressure appeared to ease late in 1946.

GREECE. In Aug. 1946 a Communist-led rebellion against the right-wing government, elected 31 Mar., broke out in Greece, a continuation of the civil war which erupted after termination of the German occupation and was halted when the British effected a truce (p. 448). With their major activities in the north, the guerrillas gained support and sanctuaries from the neighboring Communist states of Albania, Bulgaria, and Yugoslavia. In Sept. the British, who had informed the U.S. in April of their desire to disengage their troops from Greece in the fall, confirmed their intention to begin at least partial withdrawals. Largely blaming the Athens regime for the political and economic chaos, the report (10 Oct.) of the Parliamentary Delegation that had surveyed conditions in Greece attached severe restrictions to future British economic aid.

In an initial move to support the Greek government, the U.S. granted Greece (11 Oct. 1946) $25 million in credits to purchase surplus U.S. military equipment in Europe.

INTERNATIONAL CONTROL OF ATOMIC ENERGY. On 24 Jan. 1946 the UN General Assembly created the UN Atomic Energy Commission (UNAEC), to study the international control of atomic energy. The State Department issued (28 Feb.) the **Acheson-Lilienthal Report** which, with some modifications, became the official U.S. proposal to the UNAEC. Presented (14 June) to the UNAEC by **Bernard M. Baruch** (1870–1965) and hence dubbed the "Baruch Plan," the proposal provided for an International Atomic Development Authority which would carry out its responsibilities (1) for ensuring the full exploitation of the peaceful potentialities of atomic energy; (2) for providing states with security against surprise attack by violators of the ban on atomic weapons by fully exercising—uninhibited by the veto power of any state —its capacities for ownership, management, research, licensing, and inspection. The plan was to be put into effect in stages, the crucial point being that the agency's control mechanisms should become fully operative and demonstrate their effectiveness *before* the U.S. would carry out its obligation to dispose of its atomic weapons, accept the prohibition on the manufacture or use of such weapons, and turn over to the agency all of its scientific and technological knowledge concerning atomic energy. The U.S.S.R. responded first (19 June) with a plan involving no international machinery for control or enforcement and later (11 June 1947) with a scheme which, like the first, embodied a reversal of U.S. priorities. The U.S.S.R. proposed that the U.S. abandon its monopolistic posi-

tion in atomic energy by destroying its weapons and accepting the prohibition of the manufacture or use of such weapons before establishing a system of international supervision, such international agency to function in subordination to the UN Security Council (hence the veto would be operative) and would lack the authority to own, operate, or license atomic facilities, possessing only limited inspection powers. The Baruch Plan was essentially accepted by the UNAEC in its first report (30 Dec. 1946), which was approved (4 Nov. 1948) by the General Assembly, but Soviet opposition prevented any progress toward its realization, and the UNAEC suspended its meetings 29 July 1949.

1 Aug. ATOMIC ENERGY ACT OF 1946. Sponsored by Sen. Brian McMahon (Conn., 1903–52), the act transferred full control over all materials, facilities, production, research, and information relating to nuclear fission from the War Department to an **Atomic Energy Commission** to be composed of 5 civilians nominated by the president and confirmed by the Senate.

1946–52

KEY ATOMIC EXPLOSIONS: fourth U.S. atomic explosion in tests with warships at Bikini Atoll, 1 July 1946; fifth, 25 July. New and improved bomb exploded in 3 tests at Eniwetok Atoll, Apr.–May 1948. On 24 Sept. 1949 it was disclosed that the U.S.S.R. had exploded its first atomic weapon. On 31 Jan. 1950 President Truman announced that the U.S. would undertake development of the **hydrogen bomb.** On 6 Apr. 1952 it was announced that the U.S. was manufacturing the H-bomb. On 3 Oct. Great Britain exploded its first atomic weapon in the Monte Bello Islands, off Australia.

On 1 Nov. 1952 the U.S. exploded its first hydrogen bomb, the most powerful bomb yet made.

1947

GERMANY. 10 MAR.–24 APR. MOSCOW CONFERENCE. Secretary Marshall and British Foreign Minister Ernest Bevin advocated a federal form of government for Germany, as opposed to Russia's demand for a centralized state, and rejected the Soviet claim for $10 billion reparations.

29 MAY. Secretary Marshall instructed Gen. **Lucius D. Clay** (1897–1978); military governor, U.S. Zone, to strengthen the bizonal organization in Germany and expedite upward revision of the level of bizonal industry. A directive of the Joint Chiefs of Staff to Gen. Clay (11 July) urged him to work toward "an increasing standard of living in Germany" and "a self-sustaining German economy." Under orders of U.S. and British commanders (29 Aug.) the maximum production was fixed at the 1936 level of German industry, thus increasing Germany's potential by one third over the 4-power level of Mar. 1946. A new level was introduced by the Allied powers on 3 Apr. 1951, and restrictions further relaxed.

25 NOV.–16 DEC. LONDON CONFERENCE. The fifth session of the Council of Foreign Ministers was marked by Soviet charges that the Allies had violated the Potsdam Agreement. The meeting adjourned without fixing a time or place for another meeting.

12 MAR. TRUMAN DOCTRINE. The British government informed the U.S. (21 Feb.) that because of Britain's economic crisis it could give no further financial aid to Greece or Turkey after 31 Mar. The U.S. moved into the breach, a pattern that had already begun to establish itself. Addressing a joint session of Congress to request authorization of a program of economic and military aid to Greece and Turkey, President Truman declared that U.S. policy must "support free peoples who are resisting attempted subjugation by armed minorities or outside pressures" and that U.S. assistance should be "primarily through economic and financial aid." Such a U.S. policy was deemed necessary because "the free peoples of the world look to us for support in maintaining their freedoms. If we falter in our leadership, we may endanger the peace of the world." Opponents argued that the Truman Doctrine would undercut the UN and could provoke a clash with the U.S.S.R. The Senate formally endorsed the Truman Doctrine 23 Apr. in a vote (67–23) on a bill to strengthen Greece and Turkey; the House followed 9 May (287–107). On 22 May President Truman approved an initial appropriation of $400 million in aid to Greece and Turkey—$250 million for Greece and $150 million for Turkey. U.S. military missions left for Greece and Turkey, 20 and 23 May, respectively.

Soviet Reaction. On 18 Sept. Andrei Y. Vishinsky, Soviet deputy foreign minister, attacked U.S. "warmongers" in the UN Assembly. On 5 Oct. Moscow announced formation of the Cominform, successor to the Comintern dissolved in 1943, and proclaimed its determination to block the Marshall Plan (p. 468). A *coup d'état* (25 Feb. 1948) gave the Communists control of the government of Czechoslovakia. The new regime was headed by Klement Gottwald. On 10 Mar. Czech Foreign Minister Jan Masaryk committed suicide in Prague.

In a report (28 Nov. 1949) to Congress, President Truman hailed the results of U.S. aid, indicating that the Truman Doctrine had led to "containment" of the Communists in Greece and "close cooperation between Turkey and the Western world."

18 JULY. President Truman signed an agreement naming the U.S. administering authority, within the UN Trusteeship System, of the Trust Territory of the Pacific Islands (p. 629).

JULY. CONTAINMENT policy concept articulated in "The Sources of Soviet Conduct," an article by "X" (**George F. Kennan,** 1904–   ) in the quarterly *Foreign Affairs.* Representing the newly formulated position of the U.S. government, the article stated: "It is clear that the main element of any United States policy towards the Soviet Union must be that of a long-term, patient but firm and vigilant containment of Russian expansive tendencies. . . . Soviet pressure against the free institutions of the Western world is something that can be contained by the adroit and vigilant application of counter-force at a series of constantly shifting geographical and political points."

2 SEPT. THE INTER-AMERICAN TREATY OF RECIPROCAL ASSISTANCE, signed in Rio de Janeiro by representatives of the U.S. and the states of Latin America, was the realization of a recommendation included in the Act of Chapultepec (p. 449). The first postwar defense system entered into by the U.S., it provides that "an armed attack by any State shall be considered as an attack against all American states." The treaty set up no machinery to implement its obligations but is complementary to the Charter of Bogotá (30 Apr. 1948), creating an organization of 21 American republics (p. 470).

1948

EUROPEAN RECOVERY PROGRAM. From V-E Day to the spring of 1947 the U.S. provided Europe with over $11 billion in the form of UNRRA aid, loans, etc. Opposition to UNRRA arose from the fact that the bulk of its relief supplies were distributed in Eastern Europe (ex-enemy countries were outside its functions; liberated countries in Western Europe had refused UNRRA assistance). A post-UNRRA Relief Bill (31 May 1947) appropriated $350 million relief for Austria, Greece, Italy, Hungary, and Poland.

On 8 May 1947, Under Secretary of State Dean Acheson speaking at Cleveland, Miss., revealed a "prologue to the Marshall Plan," outlining the rationale for U.S. participation in a European recovery program. The **Marshall Plan** was launched when, in an address at Harvard on 5 June, Secretary of State George E. Marshall proposed that the Europeans take the initiative in jointly drawing up a comprehensive recovery program for which U.S. support would then be provided. Marshall declared that U.S. policy was directed "not against any country or doctrine but against hunger, poverty, desperation, and chaos. Its purpose would be the revival of a working economy in the world so as to permit the emergence of political and social conditions in which free institutions can exist." Key participants in the formulation of the basic proposal included, in addition to Marshall and Acheson, Will L. Clayton, Under Secretary of State for Economic Affairs; Charles E. Bohlen, Special Assistant to the Secretary of State; George F. Kennan, director of the Department of State Policy Planning Staff.

The foreign ministers of Great Britain, France, and the Soviet Union met at Paris (27 June–2 July 1947) to consider Marshall's proposal of U.S. economic aid. On 2 July Soviet Foreign Minister Molotov walked out of the preliminary meeting, charging that the Marshall Plan was an "imperialist" plot for the enslavement of Europe. Great Britain and France invited 22 nations to join a Committee for European Economic Co-operation to draft plans for reconstruction.

The U.S.S.R. and its satellites did not attend the Marshall Plan Conference, which convened 12 July in Paris. Representatives of the 16 European nations which participated set up a Committee for European Economic Cooperation, which drew up a master plan for European reconstruction based on massive U.S. financial assistance. Its report (22 Sept.) estimated dollar aid needed for the next 4 years between $16.4 and $22.4 billion.

On basis of reports of the Krug Committee (9 Oct.), the House Select Committee on Foreign Aid (Herter Committee, 10 Oct.), the Nourse Committee (28 Oct.), and the Harriman Committee

(7 Nov.), a special session of Congress convened 17 Dec. to deal with aid to Europe as well as inflation, and enacted the Foreign Aid Act of 1947 providing interim relief for France, Italy, and Austria ($540 million), part to go to China. On 19 Dec. President Truman submitted to Congress a European Recovery Program which called for $17 billion in U.S. grants and loans over a 4-year period. Congress authorized the program 2 Apr. 1948 and **Paul G. Hoffman** (1891–1974) was confirmed (7 Apr.) as administrator of the Economic Cooperation Administration (ECA) which, independent of the State Department, ran the program. Inaugurated in mid-1948 with a virtually unmatched degree of bipartisan public support, the European Recovery Program, unlike earlier and subsequent aid programs, achieved its objectives at less cost and in less time than anticipated.

FOREIGN ECONOMIC AND MILITARY AID PROGRAMS: 1946–1973
[In millions of dollars. For years ending June 30]
(Source: *Statistical Abstract, 1974*)

Year	Total Economic and Military Aid[1]	ECONOMIC AID			MILITARY AID		
		Total	Loans	Grants	Total	Loans	Grants
1946–1973, total	163,694	101,520	34,313	67,207	62,175	3,698	58,477
1946–1952	34,670	31,186	8,519	22,668	3,483	—	3,483
1953–1961	47,411	24,054	5,850	18,203	23,358	165	23,193
1962	7,157	4,469	2,128	2,341	2,688	151	2,537
1963	7,234	4,372	2,124	2,248	2,862	123	2,739
1964	5,253	4,076	2,036	2,040	1,177	75	1,102
1965	5,373	4,121	2,059	2,063	1,251	110	1,141
1966	7,074	4,784	2,238	2,546	2,290	317	1,973
1967	6,883	3,942	1,662	2,281	2,941	323	2,618
1968	6,920	4,103	1,835	2,267	2,817	263	2,554
1969	6,772	3,524	1,340	2,185	3,248	281	2,968
1970	6,647	3,676	1,389	2,288	2,971	70	2,901
1971	7,705	3,442	1,299	2,143	4,263	743	3,520
1972	8,538	3,941	1,639	2,301	4,597	550	4,047
1973	8,363	4,118	1,391	2,726	4,245	550	3,695

— Represents zero.
[1] The figures for Economic Aid shown in this table represents total U.S. Economic Aid—not just the Aid under the Foreign Assistance Act.

17 Mar. BRUSSELS TREATY of collective self-defense signed by Britain, France, Belgium, Luxembourg, and the Netherlands. The treaty provided that if one of the signatories were attacked in

Europe the other parties would come to its aid with "all military and other aid and assistance in their power." The signatories of the Brussels Pact hoped that their alliance would attract U.S. backing. President Truman, addressing a joint session of Congress on the same date, hailed the 50-year defense pact and termed it "deserving of our full support."

2 MAY. ORGANIZATION OF AMERICAN STATES (OAS) established with the signing of the **Charter of Bogotá.** A regional association for the purpose of general cooperation and the promotion of peace, the OAS includes the U.S. and all the states of Latin America. The Charter of Bogotá, which complements the Rio Treaty of Reciprocal Assistance (p. 468), gave a permanent institutional framework to the loosely knit agencies, committees, and procedures of the Pan-American Union, which the OAS superseded, providing for: (1) an Inter-American Conference, to meet every 5 years; (2) consultative conferences of foreign ministers; (3) a Council, an executive body composed of 1 delegate from each state; (4) a Secretariat; and (5) various commissions. OAS headquarters were established in Washington, D.C.

CREATION OF ISRAEL. A special session of the UN General Assembly convened (28 Apr. 1947) to determine the future of the Palestine mandate. Largely because of U.S. influence, the General Assembly adopted (29 Nov.) a plan for Palestine's partition into Arab and Jewish states. When Israel proclaimed its independence, on 14 May 1948, the U.S. was the first country to recognize the new state, doing so within minutes. The Arabs rejected the partition and went to war against Israel. After UN mediator Count Folke Bernadotte of Sweden was assassinated in Jerusalem (17 Sept.), **Ralph J. Bunche** (1904–71) of the U.S. succeeded him as mediator and effected armistice agreements between Israel and its Arab neighbors. Israel was admitted to the UN, 11 May 1949. Attempting to bring stability to

the Middle East, the U.S. joined Britain and France in issuing a **Tripartite Declaration** (25 May 1950) in which they pledged that if either Israel or the Arabs broke the terms of the UN armistice they would act at once "both within and outside the United Nations to prevent such a violation." The declaration also opposed the development of an arms race between the Arab states and Israel.

11 JUNE. VANDENBERG RESOLUTION adopted (64–4) by the Senate. Sen. Arthur H. Vandenberg (Mich., 1884–1951), with the encouragement of the Truman administration, framed a declaration of U.S. foreign policy, introduced as S Res 239, supporting the principle of U.S. association with "regional and other collective arrangements" affecting national security, as permitted under Article 51 of the UN Charter. While having no legal force, the Vandenberg Resolution led to the opening of negotiations with the nations of Europe to construct a defense alliance on an Atlantic basis.

24 JUNE. BEGINNING OF BERLIN BLOCKADE AND AIRLIFT. Ministerial level 4-Power discussions on Germany having broken down (p. 467), the Western Powers continued to discuss the future of Germany without the U.S.S.R. The Soviets withdrew their representative from the Allied Control Council in Berlin 20 Mar. 1948. On 30 Mar. the Soviets refused to allow American, British, and French troop trains to go to Berlin without their inspection, beginning a graduated process of closing off various means of ground transportation to that city. On 7 June the Western Powers announced their intention to create a federal state in their zones, which would be consolidated. Currency reform, a major step in the economic rehabilitation of a unified West Germany, was inaugurated 18 June and extended to West Berlin when the Soviets introduced (23 June) a new mark in their own zone, including all of Berlin. On 24 June the Soviets clamped a total blockade on all land traffic between Berlin and West Germany (these land routes not having been guaranteed by the Potsdam Agreement or the Allied Control Council), charging that the Western Powers had violated the Potsdam Agreement. The Western Powers began the Berlin Airlift to supply 2,100,-000 residents of the blockaded area. The U.S.S.R. announced (1 July) that it would no longer participate in the meetings of the Berlin Kommandatura. Diplomatic discussions between the West and the Soviets (31 July–2 Sept.) proved fruitless and the Western Powers took the blockade issue to the UN Security Council (4 Oct.), where the U.S.S.R. vetoed a compromise proposal (25 Oct.) and boycotted discussions. In Feb. 1949 the U.S. and British forces set up a blockade to halt all traffic across the eastern boundaries of their respective zones. Secret and informal talks between the U.S. ambassador to the U.N., Philip Jessup, and the U.S.S.R. ambassador to the UN, Jacob Malik, begun in Feb. 1949, preceded the U.S.S.R.'s agreement to lift the blockade, the only condition being that the Council of Foreign Ministers convene to discuss questions relating to Berlin and Germany. A 4-Power communiqué (5 May) announced that the blockade would be lifted, effective 12 May, and the Council of Foreign Ministers would convene in Paris 23 May. During the Berlin Airlift, which lasted 321 days, American and British airmen made 272,264 flights and transported 2.3 million tons of food and other supplies. The Soviet blockade of Berlin not only failed to alter the direction of U.S. policy in Germany (and Europe) but accelerated its thrust.

1949

20 JAN. Point IV. In the fourth section of his inaugural address—hence the name **Point IV**—President Truman called for a "bold new program" of U.S. technical and capital assistance to the underdeveloped areas of the world. The president asked Congress (24 June) for authority to guarantee U.S. private investment in less developed areas and $45 million to start the program. On 27 Sept. 1950 $26.9 million were appropriated ($35 million had been authorized) to inaugurate the program.

4 APR. FOUNDING OF NATO. Following passage of the Vandenberg Resolution (p. 470), President Truman directed the State Department to discuss the question of regional security with Canada and the signatories of the Brussels Treaty (p. 469). Tentative agreement on a collective defense arrangement had been reached by Oct. 1948 when Denmark, Iceland, Italy, Norway, and Portugal were invited to join the negotiations. The 12 nations signed the **North Atlantic Treaty** in Washington, 4 Apr. 1949. Ratified by the Senate 21 July, the treaty became effective 24 Aug. By Article 5 of the treaty, each party agreed that an attack on any one of them would be considered an attack against them all, to be followed by the taking "individually and in concert with the other Parties, such action as it deems necessary, including the use of armed force, to restore and maintain the security of the North Atlantic area." The pact also provided for the establishment of a North Atlantic Treaty Organization (NATO), headed by a North Atlantic Council, to draw up plans for concerted action; called for intensified military self-help and mutual aid measures; and provided for the admission of new members by unanimous invitation. The U.S. was

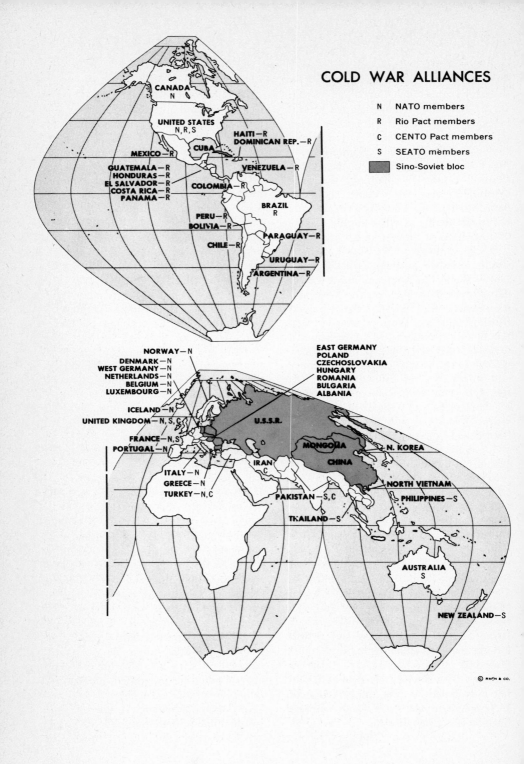

COLD WAR ALLIANCES

N   NATO members
R   Rio Pact members
C   CENTO Pact members
S   SEATO members
▨   Sino-Soviet bloc

CANADA
N

UNITED STATES
N, R, S

HAITI—R
DOMINICAN REP.—R

MEXICO—R   CUBA

GUATEMALA—R   VENEZUELA—R
HONDURAS—R
EL SALVADOR—R   COLOMBIA—R
COSTA RICA—R
PANAMA—R

BRAZIL
R

PERU—R
BOLIVIA—R

PARAGUAY—R

CHILE—R

URUGUAY—R

ARGENTINA—R

NORWAY—N

DENMARK—N
WEST GERMANY—N
NETHERLANDS—N
BELGIUM—N
LUXEMBOURG—N

ICELAND—N
UNITED KINGDOM—N, S, C

FRANCE—N, S
PORTUGAL—N

ITALY—N
GREECE—N
TURKEY—N, C

EAST GERMANY
POLAND
CZECHOSLOVAKIA
HUNGARY
ROMANIA
BULGARIA
ALBANIA

U.S.S.R.

MONGOLIA   N. KOREA
CHINA

IRAN
C

PAKISTAN—S, C

THAILAND—S

NORTH VIETNAM

PHILIPPINES—S

AUSTRALIA
S

NEW ZEALAND—S

© RMCN & CO.

for the first time committed to a European alliance in peacetime. Greece and Turkey joined NATO in Feb. 1952.

23 MAY–20 JUNE. PARIS CONFERENCE. The sixth session of the Council of Foreign Ministers failed to reach agreement on the German question. Russian proposals for German unification and withdrawal of Allied troops were unacceptable to the West. In turn, Russia rejected Western proposals for the extension of the Bonn Constitution to East Germany.

8 DEC. FLIGHT OF CHINESE NATIONALISTS TO FORMOSA. After the defeat of Japan, the U.S. took steps to reinforce the Nationalists under Chiang Kai-shek. Although by late 1945 the Nationalists controlled strategic cities in eastern and southern China, the Communists held large sections of the north, with full-scale civil war imminent. In Dec. 1945 Gen. **George C. Marshall** was sent to China as a special U.S. ambassador to promote a truce and the formation of a coalition government. Discussions between the 2 factions were undertaken and an uneasy cease-fire established (10 Jan. 1946). Mao Tse-tung, head of the Chinese Communists, demanded (24 June 1946) that the U.S. halt military aid to the Nationalists and that all U.S. forces leave. Abandoning his frustrating mission, officially terminated 7 Jan. 1947, Marshall returned to the U.S., denouncing both sides. Full-scale civil war ensued. Lt. Gen. **Albert C. Wedemeyer,** named (11 July 1947) to appraise the situation in China and Korea, condemned (24 Aug.) the use of force by the Chinese Communists and stressed the need for thoroughgoing political and economic reforms on the part of the Nationalists. Wedemeyer's recommendation that the U.S. provide the Nationalists with a comprehensive program of moral and material support was not accepted. While the Truman administration re-

fused fully to commit the U.S. to the Nationalists, the president signed (3 Apr. 1948) a foreign aid bill which earmarked $463 million, $125 million of which could be allocated for military purposes, to the Nationalist regime. Chiang requested (18 Nov. 1948) an immediate increase in material aid but Secretary of State George C. Marshall declared (24 Nov. 1948) that a large U.S. aid program might directly involve the U.S. in the civil war. With the war going decisively in favor of the Communists, who had taken control of Peking (Jan. 1949) and made it their capital, Congress authorized (14 Apr. 1949) the president to use unobligated funds until 15 Feb. 1950 to aid areas of China not controlled by the Communists.

A State Department white paper on China (*United States Relations with China; With Special Reference to the Period 1944–1949*), released 6 Aug. 1949, made the point that the Nationalists were on the verge of collapse because of the political, economic, and military deficiencies of the Chiang regime and that no greater amount of U.S. aid would have prevented the ultimate victory of the Communists. Secretary of State Dean Acheson observed in an accompanying letter that "the only alternative open to the United States was full-scale intervention on behalf of a government which had lost the confidence of its own troops and its own people." Powerful critics branded the white paper a "whitewash" of a policy by which the U.S. had "sold China down the river" and "lost" it to the Communists, allowing it to "pass into the Soviet orbit."

The Communist Chinese arrest (27 Oct. 1949) of U.S. Consul General Angus Ward in Mukden raised a storm of official and unofficial U.S. protest, making even less likely U.S. recognition of the Communist regime in the near future. Ward was released and deported with his staff in Dec. 1949.

The Communists challenged the right of the Nationalists to represent China in the UN and demanded (18 Nov. 1949) their ouster. The Soviet delegate boycotted (13 Jan.–1 Aug., 1950) the Security Council in protest of the continued presence of the Nationalists. U.S. policy toward China was ambivalent. While Britain, France, the U.S.S.R., and several other nations recognized the Chinese Communist government, the People's Republic of China, the U.S. continued to recognize the Nationalist regime on Formosa as China's legal government and to oppose any immediate change in China's UN representation. Yet in Jan. 1950 the U.S. refused to commit forces to Formosa's defense.

1950

11–14 May. LONDON CONFERENCE of foreign ministers of Great Britain, France, and the U.S. considered mutual defense problems and declared that Germany should "reenter progressively the community of free peoples of Europe."

1950–52

NATO DEFENSE PLANNING. The general strategic plan developed by NATO military planners, who began to meet Oct. 1949, was based on the following propositions: (1) the U.S. would assume responsibility, in case of hostilities, to use the atomic bomb in an air offensive against the aggressor; (2) ground forces on the Continent would blunt the enemy offensive; (3) U.S., British, and French fleets would secure control of the seas; and (4) Western European aircraft would be assigned to air defense and short-range tactical bombardment. While it was believed that

U.S. superiority in nuclear weapons—NATO's "sword"—would deter Soviet aggression for several years, NATO discussions began to focus on Europe's military capacity—NATO's "shield." This raised 2 crucial and interrelated problems: how to increase NATO's military strength in Europe and how to effect Germany's rearmament.

9 Sept. 1950. President Truman announced approval of "substantial increases" of U.S. forces in Europe (then consisting of 2 divisions in Germany) contingent upon European contributions to "our common defense."

15–20 Sept. 1950. The North Atlantic Council, meeting at New York, agreed to adopt a **"Forward Strategy."** In order to ensure the defense of all European members, any aggression was to be resisted as far to the east as possible. Such a strategy implied the defense of Europe on German soil and demanded forces far exceeding those available to NATO at the time (about 14 divisions on the European continent, compared to some 210 Soviet divisions). The council requested the NATO Defense Committee to plan for an integrated force, under a centralized command, adequate to deter aggression. The U.S. urged that Germany be rearmed while France insisted that German military participation in NATO be deferred until after the NATO allies had rearmed and an integrated defense force had been established.

26 Oct. 1950. In an effort to prevent creation of an autonomous German army, the French proposed the Pleven Plan, creation of a special, integrated European force of some 100,000 men in which German contingents at the battalion level would participate.

6 Dec. 1950. Under great pressure from the U.S., the French accepted a compromise on German rearmament. Under restricted conditions German forces would participate in Europe's defense under NATO and European planning for a European Army based on the Pleven Plan could go forward.

18 Dec. 1950. BRUSSELS CONFERENCE of foreign ministers of North Atlantic Pact nations approved plan for arming Western Europe. On 19 Dec. the conference agreed on Gen. **Dwight D. Eisenhower** as supreme commander of the North Atlantic Pact forces. He took formal command of SHAPE (Supreme Headquarters, Allied Powers in Europe) at Paris on 2 Apr. 1951, but resigned in the spring of 1952 to campaign for the Republican nomination for the presidency, and was replaced by Gen. **Matthew B. Ridgway** (1895–   ).

The **"Great Debate."** Prior to the dispatch of 4 additional U.S. divisions to Europe, signaled in President Truman's statement of 9 Sept., Republicans, led by former President **Herbert Hoover** and Sen. **Robert A. Taft** (Ohio, p. 1165), attacked the administration's military policies, opening the "Great Debate" of 1951. In a nationwide broadcast (20 Dec.) Hoover denounced the "rash involvement" of U.S. forces in "hopeless campaigns," arguing that the U.S. should cut off aid to Europe until those nations demonstrated a will to defend themselves. Meanwhile the U.S. should build up its own air and naval power, reinforce its Pacific bases and rearm Japan, thereby creating a "Gibraltar of Western Civilization." Taft, in a Senate speech (5 Jan. 1951), embraced Hoover's thesis, also charging the administration with having formulated policy since 1945 "without consulting Congress or the people." A fiery partisan debate ensued with the introduction (8 Jan.) by Senate Minority Leader **Kenneth S. Wherry** (Neb., 1892–1951) of a sense of the Senate resolution that no U.S. ground forces be sent to Europe "pending the adoption of a policy with respect thereto by the Congress." Gen. Eisenhower, ad-

dressing an informal joint session of Congress (1 Feb.), declared that because there was "no acceptable alternative" the U.S. had to assist Europe with troops as well as armaments. During public hearings of the Senate Foreign Relations Committee and Armed Services Committee in Feb., Secretary of Defense George C. Marshall disclosed that it was planned during 1951 to add 4 U.S. divisions to the 2 already in Europe and both he and the Joint Chiefs of Staff testified against any congressional limitation on U.S. troops for NATO. Govs. Thomas E. Dewey and Harold E. Stassen supported the administration's plans as being an "Eisenhower program." The Senate passed (4 Apr.) resolutions approving a "fair share" contribution of U.S. troops to NATO, asking the president to consult with Congress before sending troops abroad and declaring that no more than 4 divisions should be sent to Europe without Senate approval. Truman hailed the Senate's action as a "clear endorsement" of his troop plans but ignored the Senate's claim to a voice in future troop commitments—an issue which did not really arise again until the Vietnam War. The "Great Debate" served to confirm both the U.S. decision to defend Western Europe on the ground and the president's power to commit U.S. forces abroad without prior congressional approval.

20 Feb. 1952. The NATO Council in Lisbon agreed upon West Germany's financial and military contribution to mutual defense and set up permanent council headquarters in Paris.

27 May 1952. An agreement to create a **European Defense Community (EDC)** with a joint European army was signed in Bonn by France, Germany, Italy, and the Benelux countries. The EDC command would report directly to NATO. While Germany would remain outside NATO membership, her defense was guaranteed by NATO members in a protocol, signed the same day, which extended NATO defense commitments to Germany. In a separate "peace contract," consisting of 4 conventions signed by the U.S., Britain, France, and West Germany, the latter gained virtually complete sovereignty, the Allied occupation was ended, Allied military rights in Germany were reserved, and provision was made for German contributions to the cost of maintaining Allied forces in Germany. In addition, the U.S. and Britain gave France a separate pledge that their troops would remain in Europe indefinitely. The Senate ratified the peace contract and NATO protocol 1 July, 1952. The "peace contract" remained suspended pending French approval of EDC (p. 484).

1951

8 Sept. JAPANESE PEACE TREATY, signed at San Francisco by 49 nations (not including the U.S.S.R.), provided for withdrawal of occupation forces not later than 90 days after a majority of the signatories ratified and recognized Japan's "full sovereignty." Japan in turn acknowledged the independence of Korea and renounced all claims to Formosa, the Pescadores, the Kuriles, Sakhalin, and the Pacific islands formerly under her mandate, and agreed to UN trusteeship over the Ryukyu and Bonin Islands. By the **U.S.-Japanese Treaty** signed the same day at San Francisco Japan granted the U.S. the right to maintain armed forces in Japan. Previously, on 1 Sept., a **Tripartite Security Treaty** (U.S., Australia, and New Zealand) provided for mutual assistance. A similar pact was signed between the U.S. and the Philippines (30 Aug.), implementing the Philippines Trade Act (continuing free trade between the U.S. and the Philippines until 1954, with gradual imposition of tariff duties over a 20-year period thereafter), the Philippines Rehabilitation Act (both acts, 30 Apr. 1946), and the Philippines Military Assistance Act (26 June 1946).

1952

5–8 Jan. President Truman and Prime Minister Churchill reviewed the world situation in a conference at Washington and reported (9 Jan.) an agreement by which U.S. airbases in Britain would not be used for atomic bombing of Communist Europe without British consent.

The Korean War

1945–49. PREWAR CONDITIONS. As a result of the Second World War, Korea was "temporarily" divided at the 38th parallel into 2 zones, one occupied by the U.S. and the other by the U.S.S.R. On 1 Oct. 1946 Under Secretary of State Acheson reasserted U.S. intention to stay in Korea until it was united and free. On 17 Sept. 1947 the U.S. informed the Soviet Union of its intention to refer the question of Korean independence to the UN, which passed a resolution proposing free elections in the spring of 1948 in order to create a provisional government for the entire country. On 23 Jan. 1948 the Soviet government informed the UN that the UN Temporary Commission on Korea would not be permitted to visit North Korea. On 22 Mar. the U.S. military governor in Korea announced an extensive land-reform program. On 1 May the North Koreans announced adoption by a "North and South Korean Conference" at Pyongyang of a constitution for the "People's Democratic Republic of Korea" with jurisdiction over all Korea. On 10 May elections held in U.S.-occupied South Korea under the observation of the UN Temporary Commission were boycotted in North Korea. On 15 Aug. the Republic of Korea was proclaimed at Seoul, South Korea, with Syngman Rhee as president. On 9 Sept. a "People's Republic" claiming authority over the entire country was set up in North Korea. On 10 Dec. the Rhee government signed an agreement with the U.S. providing for a program of economic assistance to be carried out by the ECA and the War Department. In a speech on 12 Jan. 1949 Secretary Acheson omitted Korea from the U.S. defense perimeter, but added that the military security of other areas in the Pacific would be "the commitment of the entire civilized world" under the UN Charter. A Soviet veto (19 Apr.) blocked admission of the Republic of Korea into the UN. The U.S. completed withdrawal of its forces from Korea 29 June 1949, leaving only an American military advisory group numbering 500 men. The UN Commission on Korea reported 2 Sept. failure to settle differences between the Korean Republic and the North Korean Communist regime and stressed the danger of civil war. Both sides indicated their intention to achieve unification by force, if necessary.

25 June 1950. NORTH KOREAN AGGRESSION. North Korean Communist forces equipped with Soviet-made weapons invaded South Korea. The absence of a Soviet representative at the Security Council (p. 474) facilitated action. On 25 June the council ordered an immediate cease-fire and the withdrawal of North Korean forces. On the evening of 26 June President Truman decided to order the air force and navy to give support to the Korean forces, authorizing missions south of the 38th parallel, to order the 7th Fleet to prevent an attack on Formosa, and to increase aid to Indochina. On the next day the Security Council (27 June) called upon UN members to "furnish such assistance as may be necessary to the Republic of Korea to repel the armed attack and to restore international peace and security in the area." Truman the same day ordered U.S. air and sea forces to give the Korean government troops cover and support. Seoul fell to the North Koreans 28 June. On 30 June U.S. ground forces were ordered into the fighting and authorized to conduct missions above the 38th parallel. On 7 July the U.S. government announced that the draft would be employed to enlarge the army. The same day the UN voted for a unified UN command in Korea under a commander to be designated by the U.S. Gen. **Douglas MacArthur** was so designated 8 July. On 20 July President Truman proposed partial mobilization of U.S. resources to meet the Korean crisis and urged Congress to enact a $10 billion rearmament program. Future Security Council action was blocked by the return (1 Aug.) of Yakov A. Malik, Soviet representative.

MILITARY OPERATIONS. Battle of the **Pusan Beachhead** (6 Aug.–15 Sept.) in Southern Korea. Red offensive, which captured Pohang 6 Sept., failed to drive UN forces off the peninsula. Launching a counteroffensive (15 Sept.), UN forces made an amphibious landing at **Inchon** and began an eastward sweep across the peninsula. The operation was timed with the breakout of UN forces from the beachhead in southeastern Korea. On 26 Sept. Gen. MacArthur announced the capture of Seoul.

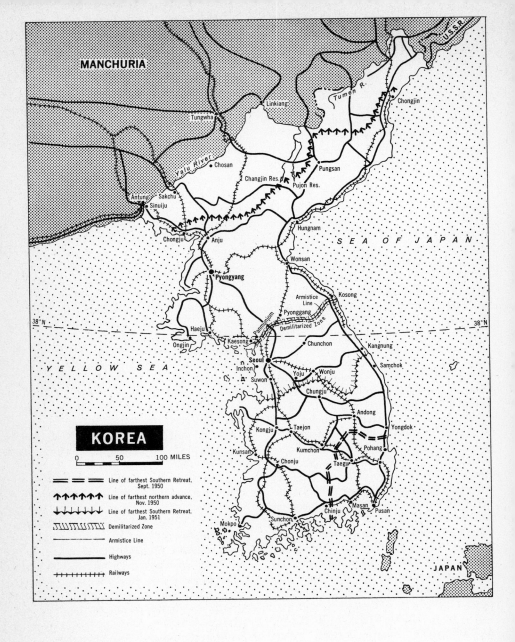

MANCHURIA

Tumen R.

USSR

Chongjin

Linkiang

Tungwha

Pungsan

Yalu River • Chosan

Changjin Res.

Pujon Res.

Antung Sakchu

Sinuiju

Hungnam

Chongju Anju

SEA OF JAPAN

Wonsan

Pyongyang

Armistice
Line

Kosong

Pyonggang

Demilitarized Zone

38° N

38° N

Haeju

Kaesong

Panmunjom

Chunchon

Kangnung

Ongjin

Seoul

Inchon

Suwon

Yoju

Wonju

Samchok

YELLOW SEA

Chungju

Andong

Kongju

Taejon

Yongdok

KOREA

Kumchon

Pohang

0   50   100 MILES

Kunsan

Chonju

Taegu

Line of farthest Southern Retreat,
Sept. 1950

Sunchon

Chinju

Masan

Pusan

Line of farthest northern advance,
Nov. 1950

Mokpo

Line of farthest Southern Retreat,
Jan. 1951

Demilitarized Zone

Armistice Line

Highways

Railways

JAPAN

Chinese Communist Intervention. On 30 Sept. Foreign Minister Chou En-lai implied that the Chinese government might intervene. U.S. forces crossed the 38th parallel, 1 Oct. On 7 Oct. the General Assembly laid down the objectives of the UN action in Korea as to "ensure conditions of stability throughout Korea" and called for "a unified, independent and democratic government" of Korea. On 11 Oct. Peking denounced the crossing of the 38th parallel and declared that China "cannot stand idly by." On 20–21 Oct. UN troops captured Pyongyang, capital of North Korea, and advanced toward the Manchurian border, reaching Chosan on the Yalu, 26 Oct. From 26 Oct.–24 Nov., troops identified as Chinese were fighting alongside the North Koreans. On 24 Nov. Gen. MacArthur ordered an "end-the-war" offensive. On 26 Nov. Chinese Communist forces opened a massive counteroffensive against UN troops in the **Yalu Valley.** The operation ended in a general UN retreat toward the 38th parallel and the abandonment (5 Dec.) of Pyongyang. A UN Security Council resolution (30 Nov.) calling for withdrawal of Chinese Communists and promising to safeguard Chinese border interests was vetoed by the Soviet delegate. On 3 Nov. the UN General Assembly adopted the **"Uniting for Peace" Resolution,** asserting its right to deal with any threat to the peace where failure of the permanent members of the Security Council to agree prevented the council from functioning. U.S. forces retreated (4 Jan. 1951) south of Seoul to the Han River. A counteroffensive (25 Jan.–21 Apr.) led to the retaking of Seoul (14–15 Mar.) and the recrossing of the 38th parallel (1 Mar.). On 1 Feb. the General Assembly passed a resolution condemning Communist China as an aggressor, but limiting UN objectives to a cease-fire and return to the status quo. A North Korean–Chinese offensive (22 Apr.–8 July) was turned back.

11 Apr. 1951. REMOVAL OF MACARTHUR. Disagreements over strategy between President Truman and Gen. MacArthur led to a meeting on Wake Island (15 Oct. 1950) which produced surface unity. But disagreements grew with Truman's refusal to accede to MacArthur's requests to expand the war by employing Nationalist Chinese troops to attack mainland China and by strategic bombing of China. Advised (Mar. 1951) that Truman intended to invite truce talks, MacArthur torpedoed the plan by publicly threatening the Chinese with expansion of the war. In a letter to House Minority Leader Joseph W. Martin (Mass.), disclosed 5 Apr., MacArthur declared that "there is no substitute for victory." Truman removed MacArthur from command (11 Apr.) but MacArthur was invited to address a joint session of Congress (19 Apr.). Closed hearings of the Senate Armed Services and Foreign Relations Committees began 3 May. No report was issued.

10 JULY 1951–26 JULY 1953. ARMISTICE NEGOTIATIONS. With U.S. troops just north of the 38th Parallel, Soviet representative Malik proposed a cease-fire and armistice along the parallel (23 June 1951). Acheson accepted in principle on 26 June. Truce talks began 10 July at Kaesong but were broken off 22 Aug. They resumed 25 Oct. at Panmunjom. During the following 2 years a stalemate prevailed, with heavy but limited military engagements. Eisenhower visited Korea (2–5 Dec. 1952) following his election. Stalin died 5 Mar. 1953, and a breakthrough in the armistice negotiations occurred 3 weeks later. On 17–18 June, South Korean guards allowed 25,000 North Korean prisoners to escape but the armistice was signed by the truce delegates in Panmunjom on

26 July 1953 and hostilities halted at 10 P.M. Under its terms a demilitarized zone of 4 kilometers separating the Communists from the Allies was set up; a neutral repatriation committee was to control the remaining prisoners, including those refusing repatriation, the strength of both sides was to be frozen, and the administration of the truce was to be entrusted to a military armistice commission consisting of 5 from each side. The armistice gave South Korea about 1,500 square miles more territory than it had before the fighting began, when the 38th parallel was the dividing line.

19 JAN. 1954. The Senate Foreign Relations Committee approved a U.S.–South Korean mutual defense treaty, with the stipulation that armed aid should be provided only in the case of "external armed attack" against the Republic of Korea. Ratifications were exchanged, 17 Nov., and the U.S., on the same day, agreed to expand its military and economic aid to Korea in 1955. On Oct. 26, 1958, China announced the withdrawal of the "Chinese People's Volunteers" from North Korea.

U.S. Casualties: 33,629 battle dead; 20,617 dead from other causes; 103,284 wounded.

Foreign Policy: Eisenhower-Dulles Years, 1953–60

1953

"CAPTIVE PEOPLES" RESOLUTION. On 27 Jan. Secretary of State **John Foster Dulles** (p. 1018) in a radio-TV talk held out to "captive" people behind the Iron Curtain a promise that "you can count on us." A resolution drafted by Dulles was introduced into both houses of Congress, 20 Feb., deploring "the forcible absorption of free peoples into an aggressive despotism" and denouncing Soviet interpretations of wartime agreements to "bring about the subjugation of free peoples." After the death of Stalin (5 Mar.), the administration, uncertain as to the future direction of Soviet policy, persuaded congressional leaders to shelve the resolution (HJ Res 200). The administration's essentially propagandistic intent was underscored, when, 18–24 June, strikes, arson, and rioting broke out in numerous East German cities, including Berlin, and Russian and East German

troops restored order only after shooting, but the U.S. made no move to intervene. Eisenhower told the press (1 July) that the U.S. planned no physical intervention in East Europe. However, on 30 Nov. Secretary Dulles declared the U.S. would not "confirm their captivity" by recognizing Russia's incorporation of Lithuania, Estonia, and Latvia.

26 SEPT. MUTUAL DEFENSE ASSISTANCE AGREEMENT WITH SPAIN signed, providing for development and maintenance of U.S. air and naval installations in Spain in return for U.S. military and economic aid. When the executive agreement, originally concluded for 10 years, was extended for 5 years (26 Sept. 1963), a joint declaration was issued which in effect committed the U.S. to Spain's defense. While favoring Spain's admission to NATO, the U.S. has not pressed the issue in view of opposition of other members to the Franco regime. From 1953–68 Spain received $1.2 billion in various forms of U.S.

military aid. The agreement was extended for 2 years (20 June 1969) and again for 5 years (6 Aug. 1971), providing Spain with an additional $385 million in various forms of military assistance in exchange for continuation of U.S. base rights.

8 Dec. "ATOMS FOR PEACE" proposal. The deadlock which had developed over international control of atomic energy, as well as the broader disarmament issue to which it was linked, prompted President Eisenhower to take a new tack and to stress new ways of devoting the atom to peaceful uses. Addressing the UN General Assembly, he proposed (8 Dec.) that the governments "principally involved" make contributions of uranium and fissionable materials from their stockpiles to an International Atomic Energy Agency (IAEA) which would be responsible for the protection and storage of these materials and would devise methods for their allocation to serve peaceful purposes. From 19 Mar.–23 Sept. 1954 the U.S.-proposed draft statute for the projected agency was rejected by the U.S.S.R., which stressed that the issues of disarmament and peaceful uses of atomic energy were inseparable. As the U.S.-Soviet impasse became apparent, the U.S. decided to proceed with the negotiation of a draft statute without the U.S.S.R., but without closing the door to Soviet participation. An 8-nation group (the U.S., Australia, Belgium, Canada, France, Portugal, South Africa, and Britain), meeting in Washington during the summer of 1954, prepared a first draft for the IAEA. Late in Sept. the U.S.S.R., in a sudden reversal, indicated its willingness to separate the issues of disarmament and the peaceful uses of atomic energy. The UN General Assembly unanimously adopted (8 Dec. 1954) a resolution calling for early establishment of an IAEA to promote the peaceful uses of atomic power. In Aug. 1955, the first draft statute was circulated to all UN members and specialized agencies and the efforts of the negotiating group were endorsed (3 Dec. 1955) by the General Assembly. Responding to pressure from the General Assembly, the U.S. decided to make the draft statute the subject of multilateral negotiations. Brazil, Czechoslovakia, India, and the U.S.S.R. were invited to join the original 8 in negotiations (27 Feb.–18 Apr. 1956), which produced a revised draft statute submitted in Oct. to a conference consisting of all members of the UN and the specialized agencies. This conference prepared and approved the **Statute of the IAEA,** signed (26 Oct.) by the representatives of 70 governments and entered into force 29 July 1957. The statute provides for an IAEA with a wide range of functions bearing on the peaceful use of atomic energy but it has not supplanted bilateral arrangements for making fissionable materials available for peaceful uses. On 30 Aug. 1954 President Eisenhower had signed the Atomic Energy Act of 1954, authorizing the exchange with other countries of information and material for the peaceful use of atomic energy.

1953–60

INDOCHINA. In Nov. 1953 the French occupied the key northern outpost, Dien Bien Phu. With the French military position in Vietnam deteriorating, a conference of the Big-4 foreign ministers met in Berlin, proposing (18 Feb. 1954) that a broader conference be convened 26 Apr. in Geneva to discuss the situations in Korea and Indochina.

Spring 1954. U.S. Twice at the Brink of Military Intervention. U.S. military aid had accounted for the bulk of the cost of the French war in Vietnam— 78%, according to a report (16 Mar. 1954) of the French National Assembly. The U.S. government was opposed to a negotiated settlement in Indochina under current conditions, projecting it would lead to the loss to Communism not only of Vietnam but of the whole of Southeast Asia: the "falling row of dominoes" theory, publicly supported (7 Apr.) by President Eisenhower. Secretary of State Dulles was among those urging a U.S. air strike to prevent the fall of Dien Bien Phu. After serious consideration such action was tentatively rejected on 4 Apr., when consultations (3 Apr.) suggested that the congressional support deemed necessary would not be forthcoming unless other nations, especially Britain, participated. Despite firm British opposition, after the fall of Dien Bien Phu (7 May) the U.S. again prepared for military intervention, but the French government became reluctant to initiate further military operations and, after continued deterioration of the French military position, the U.S. notified (15 June) the French that the time for intervention had passed.

26 Apr.–20 July. The Geneva Conference. The first plenary session concerning Indochina was held on 8 May. (The 19 nations failed to agree on a Korean settlement, ending their talks 19 June.) The U.S., France, Britain, U.S.S.R., Communist China, Cambodia, Laos, and the 2 Vietnam regimes participated in the discussions which led to the **Geneva Agreements** on Indochina of 20 July. These *inter alia* provided for: (1) armistices in Laos, Cambodia, and Vietnam; (2) partition of Vietnam by the fixing of a provisional military demarcation line at the 17th parallel with a 5-kilometer demilitarized zone (DMZ) on either side —Viet Minh forces to withdraw to the north and French Union forces to the south; (3) freedom of Vietnamese civil-

ians to choose whether to live in the North or the South; (4) prohibition of foreign bases in Indochina or of entry of any of the Indochinese states into military alliances; (5) establishment of an International Control Commission composed of Indian, Canadian, and Polish representatives; and (6) the holding of general elections throughout Vietnam in July 1956. Not associating itself with the Geneva Agreements, the U.S. took note of them and unilaterally declared that it would refrain from the threat or use of force to disturb them.

Aug. 1954–1960. Despite pessimistic U.S. intelligence estimates of the probability of a stable, civilian regime in South Vietnam, the National Security Council recommended direct U.S. military, economic, and political support for the government headed by Ngo Dinh Diem (became premier, June 1954). President Eisenhower approved (20 Aug.) the NSC policy paper by which the U.S. assumed the burden of defending South Vietnam. Even before this policy decision was taken, a CIA team headed by Col. Edward G. Lansdale began (June) covert operations against the Viet Minh. In a protocol to the SEATO pact (p. 484) the signatories extended their protection to Vietnam, Cambodia, and Laos. President Eisenhower promised Diem, in a letter 23 Oct., U.S. aid "in developing and maintaining a strong, viable state capable of resisting attempted subversion or aggression through military means." The first U.S. military advisers were dispatched to train the South Vietnamese army on 23 Feb. 1955. On 16 July, Diem, with U.S. backing, rejected the reunification elections provided for in the Geneva Agreements and on 26 Oct. he declared South Vietnam a republic with himself as president. In May 1956 the U.S. sent 350 additional military personnel to Vietnam on a "temporary" mission—lifting the number of

U.S. forces in South Vietnam above the 342 limit provided in the Geneva Agreements. In response to stepped-up Viet Cong (Vietnamese Communists) insurgency, the U.S. increased (May 1960) its military advisers in Vietnam to 685.

1954

JAN. 12. "MASSIVE RETALIATION" DOCTRINE ARTICULATED. Prompted by the Eisenhower administration's commitment to the reduction of federal spending and by advances in atomic weapons technology, the "New Look" in national security policy emphasized reductions in army manpower, the development of tactical nuclear weapons, and the buildup of strategic air power employing nuclear weapons—a "bigger bang for the buck." The complementary strategic doctrine was articulated 12 Jan. by Secretary of State John Foster Dulles. The capacity of the Strategic Air Command (SAC) to inflict "instant, massive retaliation"— always the primary deterrent against direct Soviet attack—would now serve "at times and places of our own choosing" as an explicit deterrent of lesser aggression. The doctrine of "massive retaliation" drew sharp criticism, both domestic and foreign; only after lengthy negotiations did Britain, Turkey, and Italy agree to the stationing of intermediate-range nuclear weapons on their soil (France refused, choosing instead to develop her own atomic force; and one of its major objectives, the withdrawal of U.S. troops from Europe, was never carried out, out of respect for America's NATO partners).

25 JAN.–18 FEB. BERLIN CONFERENCE OF FOREIGN MINISTERS. Agreement between East and West could not be reached on the reunification of Germany. The U.S.S.R. proposed a 50-year all-European security treaty, which would exclude the U.S. from the defense of Europe and make Red China and the U.S. equal "observers" of the pact's application. This proposal was rejected by Great Britain and France.

13 MAY. ST. LAWRENCE SEAWAY. The Wiley-Dondero Act authorized the U.S. to join Canada in construction of a 27-foot deep channel between Montreal and Lake Erie and established the St. Lawrence Seaway Development Corp. to finance and construct navigational improvements along the St. Lawrence in U.S. territory. This action reflected growing dependence of Midwestern steel mills on iron ore of the Quebec-Labrador region. St. Lawrence Seaway and St. Lawrence power project formally opened 26–27 June 1959. Seaway made possible the navigation of ships of 27-foot draft from Montreal to Lake Superior except in winter months.

GUATEMALA COUP. By the end of 1953 the U.S. regarded as threatening the spread of Communist influence in the regime of Guatemala's Jacob Arbenz Guzmán, elected president in 1950. At a meeting of the OAS in Caracas in Mar. 1954 the U.S. secured the adoption of a resolution calling for consultation on moves to head off Communist penetration in the Western Hemisphere. The arrival 15 May at Puerto Barrios of a vessel containing arms from Czechoslovakia was regarded (17 May) by the U.S. State Department as "a development of gravity." On 18 June an insurgent force under Col. Carlos Castillo Armas and, as later revealed, supported by the CIA, invaded Guatemala from Honduras. The UN Security Council (20 June) called for termination of the invasion and requested states to refrain from assisting the attackers. On 29 June the Arbenz Guzmán government was overthrown and an anti-Communist military junta installed. The meeting of OAS foreign ministers called for (26 June) by the OAS Council and projected for 7 July was canceled. On 1 Sept., with dissolution of the junta, Col. Castillo Armas became president. On 30 Oct. the U.S. promised Guatemala $6,425,000 in economic aid and on 18 June 1956 the U.S. and Guatemala signed a military assistance pact.

8 SEPT. The SEATO Pact, a U.S.-sponsored Southeast Asian collective defense treaty, was signed in Manila by the delegates of 8 nations: Australia, Great Britain, France, New Zealand, Pakistan, the Philippines, Thailand, and the U.S. The pact pledged joint action against aggression upon any member nation but, unlike NATO (p. 471), created no unified military command. Taiwan was excluded from the treaty region which was defined as "the general area of Southeast Asia . . . and the Southwest Pacific not including the Pacific areas north" of 21° 30′ N lat. In an addendum insisted upon by Secretary of State Dulles, the U.S. specified that America's agreement to "act to meet the common danger" applied "only to Communist aggression" and that in the event of "other aggression or armed attack" the U.S. would merely consult its allies. In a separate protocol, the signatories extended their protection to South Vietnam, Cambodia, and Laos—which the **Geneva Agreements** (p. 482) barred from joining any military alliance. The Senate ratified (82–1) the SEATO treaty 1 Feb. 1955.

27 SEPT. "DEW LINE." Supplementing the Pinetree Chain of radar stations extending across the continent north of the U.S.-Canadian border (work begun 1950) and the "Mid-Canada Line" 500 miles farther north (1953), the U.S. and Canada agreed in principle on establishing a third radar line, "Distant Early Warning" (DEW) Line, across Arctic Canada from Alaska to Greenland. DEW Line went into operation 1 July 1957.

TAIWAN STRAITS CRISIS. On 2 Feb. 1953, President Eisenhower announced his decision to lift the U.S. 7th Fleet's blockade of Taiwan, making possible Nationalist attacks against the Red Chinese mainland. On 11 Aug. 1954 Chou En-lai declared that Taiwan must be liquidated. President Eisenhower rejoined (17 Aug.) that "any invasion of Formosa would have to run over the 7th Fleet." Red China then turned attention to the Nationalist-held offshore islands, launching, 3 Sept., a bombardment of Quemoy and Little Quemoy. The Nationalists retaliated 7 Sept. against Amoy. At a meeting of the National Security Council on 12 Sept. the president rejected proposals for military action against Communist China because of the dangers of atomic war. On 2 Dec. 1954 the U.S. and Nationalist China signed a mutual defense treaty. While the treaty, which did not apply to islands along the Chinese mainland, was before the Senate, Communist China increased pressure on Nationalist China by seizing (18 Jan. 1955) Ichiang, 210 miles north of Formosa, and increasing attacks on Quemoy and Matsu. This situation led to the **Formosa Resolution**—requested by President Eisenhower in a special message (24 Jan.), passed by both houses and signed by the president 29 Jan. The Formosa Resolution authorized the president to employ the armed forces of the U.S. "as he deems necessary to defend Formosa and the Pescadores against armed attack, this authority to include the securing and protection of such related positions and territories . . . as he judges to be required or appropriate in assuring the defense of Formosa and the Pescadores." The imprecision regarding the offshore islands was intended to convey to the Communist Chinese the implication that U.S. forces might be used to repulse an invasion of Quemoy or Matsu while conveying to the Nationalist Chinese that the U.S. was not specifically committed to defending the islands, as such a commitment might encourage the Nationalist Chinese to attempt to regain the mainland. The **U.S.-Nationalist Chinese mutual security pact** was ratified by the Senate (65–6) on 9 Feb. 1955. The U.S. 7th Fleet helped the Nationalist Chinese evacuate 17,000 civilians and 25,000 troops from the Tachen islands during Feb. without Communist interference. On 1 Aug. Communist China released the 11 U.S. airmen (but not the 2 civilians) sentenced as spies Nov. 1954. Simultaneously, U.S. and Communist Chinese ambassadors began a series of secret talks, first in Geneva and then in Warsaw, which were to extend into the early 1970s.

1955

25 JAN. U.S. and the Republic of Panama signed a treaty of cooperation concerning the Panama Canal (p. 627).

AUSTRIAN PEACE TREATY. At the Moscow conference of foreign ministers (1947; p. 467) it was agreed to continue discussion of Austrian problems through a Treaty Commission. Agreement on a treaty, nearly completed by Dec. 1949, was blocked by the Soviets. Suddenly, in the spring of 1955 the U.S.S.R. invited the Austrian chancellor to discussions 11–16 Apr. in Moscow, where agreement was reached on a draft treaty. Accord was rapidly reached, and the U.S., Britain, France, the U.S.S.R., and Austria signed the Austrian State Treaty in Vienna 15 May. The pact reestablished Austria as a sovereign, independent, and democratic state with its pre-1938 borders, barred any economic or political union with Germany, provided no reparations would be paid but gave the U.S.S.R. certain oil concessions and refineries, provided for the withdrawal of all occupation troops by the end of

1955, barred Austria from owning or making atomic weapons or guided missiles, and declared Austria's military neutrality in perpetuity. The treaty was ratified (63–3) by the Senate 17 June.

BAGHDAD PACT. In an effort to block Soviet pressures on the northern tier of Middle Eastern states, the U.S. promoted formation of what became the Baghdad Pact—a mutual defense treaty which, by Apr. 1955, included Turkey, Pakistan, Iran, Iraq, and Britain. The U.S. declined to join formally, to avoid alienating Egypt by creating formal ties with Iraq. Egyptian President Gamal Abdel Nasser denounced Iraq for allying with the West and, in the fall of 1955, turned to the Soviets for military equipment in an attempt to gain a decisive military advantage over Israel. On 21–22 Nov. 1955 the Baghdad Pact Council held its first meeting in Baghdad with U.S. observers present. U.S. officials also participated in the defense and anti-subversion committees of the pact, formally joining the military committee June 1957. The U.S. provided military and economic aid to the members of the pact and (29 Nov. 1956) issued a declaration of support for the pact and the independence and territorial integrity of its members. On 5 Mar. 1959 the U.S. signed bilateral cooperation agreements with Turkey, Iran, and Pakistan in Ankara. On 24 Mar. Iraq announced its withdrawal from the Baghdad Pact, and canceled its military and economic agreements with the U.S. (30 May). The Baghdad Pact was officially changed to **Central Treaty Organization (CENTO)**, 18 Aug.

5 MAY. OCCUPATION OF WEST GERMANY ENDED. Despite the U.S. decision to proceed with German rearmament with or without French cooperation, the French National Assembly rejected (30 Aug. 1954) ratification of EDC (p. 475). On 3 Oct. agreement was reached in London on a new formula, devised by Prime Minister Anthony Eden, for meeting the problem of German rearmament and integration in NATO. With a protocol to the Brussels Treaty (p. 475) a new alliance, to be known as the Western European Union (WEU), comprising the 5 Brussels Treaty members plus Italy and West Germany, was created. The same protocol permitted German rearmament, with restrictions to reassure France. Adjoining the protocol establishing WEU was a revised "peace contract" giving the Federal Republic of Germany "the full authority of a sovereign state over its internal and external affairs" and in other ways somewhat more advantageous to the Germans than the original 1952 "peace contract" (p. 476). A protocol to the NATO pact authorized West Germany to join the organization once the other agreements were ratified. The various documents of the interlocking accord were signed in Paris (23 Oct.) and the Western deadlock on Germany was broken 30 Dec. 1954, when the French National Assembly approved the Brussels protocol and the other agreements. The protocols to the 1952 "peace contract" and the North Atlantic Treaty admitting Germany to the alliance were ratified (76–2) by the U.S. Senate 29 Mar. 1955. On 5 May the U.S., Britain, and France ended the occupation of West Germany and the Federal Republic of Germany formally joined NATO the next day. German rearmament proceeded slowly; the last of the 12 authorized divisions committed to NATO in 1965.

18–23 July. "SUMMIT" MEETING AT GENEVA. British Prime Minister Winston Churchill first suggested a "summit" conference of the heads of government of the U.S., Britain, France, and the U.S.S.R. in May 1953, but the Eisenhower administration, fearful that such a conference would interfere with plans to tie West Germany into NATO, was unresponsive. During 1954 British, French, and Soviet interest in such a meeting mounted but the U.S. insisted upon prior ratification of the Austrian treaty (p. 485) and progress on accords on Germany (23 Oct.). These conditions met, the 3 Western Powers proposed to the U.S.S.R. (10 May) that the 4 Powers meet soon to attempt to "remove sources of conflict between us." Attending the conference in Geneva were **President Eisenhower, British Prime Minister Anthony Eden, French Premier Edgar Faure,** and **Soviet Premier N. A. Bulganin.** Also present was **Nikita S. Khrushchev,** First Secretary of the Communist Party, who was emerging as the key figure in the Soviet hierarchy. On the agenda were 4 items: reunification of Germany, European security, disarmament, and improvement of East-West relations. The Western Powers gave first priority to German reunification, proposing that 3 safeguards surround a Germany reunited on the basis of free elections: a 5-Power mutual defense pact, an agreement as to the total forces and armaments permitted in Germany, and the setting up of a demilitarized zone between East and West. The Soviet Union gave first priority to European security, proposing again, as it had at the Berlin Conference of 1954 (p. 483), an all-European treaty of mutual defense, excluding the U.S. except as an "observer." On 21 July President Eisenhower made his "Open Skies" proposal: that each nation give the other "a complete blueprint" of its military establishments and that each permit the other freedom of photographic reconnaissance over its national territory. Although the conference ended with no agreements other than upon a directive to the foreign ministers of the 4 Powers to pursue matters on the agenda in Oct., it produced "the spirit of Geneva"—generally interpreted as a desire on both sides to avoid confrontation and seek accommodation. The foreign ministers of the 4 Powers met 27 Oct.–16 Nov. in Paris without reaching any agreement.

1956

SUEZ CRISIS. In response to Soviet arms shipments to Egypt in 1955–56, Israel stepped up military preparations. Israel's request to buy arms from the U.S. was rejected by President Eisenhower (7 Mar. 1956) on the ground that such sales would lead to an "Arab-Israeli arms race." On 17 Dec. 1955 the U.S. offered Egypt a loan of $56 million for construction of the Aswan High Dam, intended to increase Egypt's arable land and supply electric power. Britain followed with an offer of $14 million and the World Bank indicated willingness to lend another $200 million. Egypt accepted the offers (17 July), but Secretary of State Dulles, disturbed by Nasser's deepening ties with the U.S.S.R., announced (19 July) that the U.S. was withdrawing its Aswan loan offer. Britain withdrew its loan offer and the World Bank offer, contingent upon the others, automatically lapsed. In retaliation, President Gamal Abdel Nasser on 26 July announced that he was nationalizing the Suez Canal and would use the tolls to defray the expenses of constructing the dam. Nasser also refused to guarantee the safety of Israeli shipping. Conflicts over control of the canal were not resolved during 3 months of intensive negotiations, which included an international conference in London 16–23 Aug. On Oct. 29 the armed forces of Israel (whose borders with Syria, Jordan, and Egypt had been the scene of almost continuous fighting) invaded the Gaza strip and the Sinai peninsula, completing occupation of the Sinai peninsula to within 10 miles of the Suez Canal by 5 Nov. British and French aircraft attacked Egypt 31 Oct.–5 Nov. and an Anglo-French paratrooper force was dropped at the northern end of the canal 5 Nov. By 6 Nov. British and French forces controlled the canal. On 31 Oct. President Eisenhower declared himself opposed to the use of force as an instrument for settling international disputes. Yielding to U.S. pressure and Soviet threats of intervention (5 Nov.), the British, French, and Israelis accepted a cease-fire to become effective midnight 6 Nov. British, French, and Israeli troops withdrew as a **UN Emergency Force** (**UNEF**) was installed to act as a buffer between Egypt and Israel.

HUNGARIAN REVOLT. Antigovernment demonstrations in Budapest 23 Oct. 1956 forced a reshuffling of the government. Revolutionaries demanded that the government denounce the Warsaw Pact as well as seek the complete liberation of the country from Soviet troops. On 30 Oct. Moscow promised major concessions. The next day President Eisenhower hailed these developments as "the dawning of a new day" in Eastern Europe, but earlier, on 21 Oct., in connection with Polish uprisings, Secretary Dulles had made it clear that the U.S. would not give military aid. On 4 Nov. Soviet troops and tanks opened a violent assault on Budapest, and a new all-Communist government was set up. The revolt was crushed. It was revealed on 16 June 1958 that ex-premier Imre Nagy was executed following a secret trial. While making no effort directly to intervene in Hungary, the U.S. mounted a massive propaganda attack, in the UN and elsewhere, upon the Soviet actions.

1957

EISENHOWER DOCTRINE. After the Suez Crisis (1956), Secretary of State Dulles, concerned lest the Franco-

British setback prompt the U.S.S.R. to fill the Middle East vacuum, sought congressional support for presidential discretion in order to deter the Soviets. On 5 Jan. 1957, President Eisenhower, before a joint session of Congress, urged support for a declaration, immediately dubbed the Eisenhower Doctrine. The Eisenhower Doctrine, embodied in H J Res 117, introduced 5 Jan. and passed by Congress 7 Mar., authorized the president to extend economic and military aid to any Middle East nation requesting it, authorized the use of $200 million in Mutual Security funds for fiscal 1957, and declared that "if the President determines the necessity" the U.S. was "prepared to use armed forces to assist" any nation or group of nations in the Middle East "requesting assistance against armed aggression from any country controlled by international communism." The resolution failed to specify the nations to which it applied.

1958

27 APR.–15 MAY. Vice-President Richard M. Nixon made a goodwill tour of 8 South American countries, but encountered hostile demonstrations, particularly in Peru (7–8 May) and Venezuela (13 May). A precautionary movement of U.S. forces into Caribbean bases was ordered by President Eisenhower in view of the virulence of the demonstrations in Venezuela.

3 MAY. ANTARCTICA. The U.S. proposed to the other 11 involved nations that a treaty be formulated to preserve the present legal status of the continent. Political claims would be frozen, and the continent would remain a scientific laboratory for an indefinite period. At a conference in Washington (15 Oct.–1 Dec. 1959) attended by 12 nations (7 of which had made territorial claims in Antarctica; the remainder had conducted

scientific work there), a treaty was adopted and signed which reserved that continent exclusively for peaceful purposes and froze territorial claims for the duration of the treaty (34 years).

LEBANON. On 14 July a leftist coup, believed inspired by Nasser (heading the United Arab Republic, created by a merger of Egypt and Syria 1 Feb. 1958) and the U.S.S.R., ousted the pro-Western government of Iraq. Ongoing internal strife in Lebanon led President Camille Chamoun, fearing the effects of the Iraq coup, to appeal to the U.S. for support. President Eisenhower immediately ordered 5,000 U.S. marines from the 6th Fleet to land (15 July) in Lebanon to protect the Chamoun government while British troops were flown into neighboring Jordan (also under pressure from pro-Nasser elements) at King Hussein's behest. Citing the Eisenhower Doctrine (p. 487), the President in a message to Congress (15 July) declared Lebanon's territorial integrity and independence as "vital to U.S. interests" and found "indirect aggression from without." He also pledged to withdraw U.S. forces as soon as the UN was prepared to assume responsibility. Called into emergency session, the UN General Assembly approved a resolution putting the Lebanon-Jordan problem in the hands of Secretary General Dag Hammarskjold. As the political situation became more stable, U.S. forces —which had reached 15,000 but participated in no combat activities—were reduced and by 25 Oct. their withdrawal from Lebanon was completed.

TAIWAN STRAITS CRISIS. Following Soviet–Red Chinese discussions in Peking 31 July–3 Aug. 1958, bombardment of Quemoy and Matsu was renewed 23 Aug. In Sept. the U.S. 7th Fleet began to furnish naval escort to Nationalist convoys to the beleaguered garrison of Quemoy, but stopped 3 miles short of the objective to remain outside

Chinese territorial waters. A more cautious policy on both sides became evident. After Secretary Dulles criticized the concentration of large military forces on the off-shore islands, President Eisenhower (1 Oct.) noted that a cease-fire would provide "an opportunity to negotiate in good faith." A brief cease-fire was ordered by the Red Chinese on 6 Oct., and on 25 Oct. Red China announced that it would reserve the right to bombard the islands on alternate days of the month. This signaled the end of the acute phase of the Taiwan crisis.

BERLIN CRISIS. From 1949, when records began to be kept, to the end of 1958, some 2.9 million East Germans had fled into West Germany. Although by 1958 East German authorities had virtually sealed off the long frontier between the 2 Germanys, passage from East to West Berlin remained open. Meanwhile West Berlin had become a prosperous "showplace of democracy" and a symbol of Western commitment to resist Soviet pressure. The U.S., Britain, and France, refusing to recognize the German Democratic Republic (the Communist regime in East Germany), insisted on dealing with the U.S.S.R. in maintaining their positions in and access to West Berlin under the 4-Power occupation agreements. Accusing the West of violating those agreements by making Berlin a base for "subversive activity," Premier Khrushchev threatened on 10 Nov. 1958 to transfer Soviet responsibilities in Berlin to the East German regime, implying that the West would either deal with the German Democratic Republic or risk a land, water, and air blockade of West Berlin, and possible further escalation. The White House declared (21 Nov.) the intention of the West to "maintain the integrity" of West Berlin. On 27 Nov. the U.S.S.R. put a 6-month deadline on its transfer of authority to the German Democratic Re-

public, at the same time proposing that Berlin become a "free city." The U.S., Britain, and France, in similar notes to Moscow 31 Dec., formally rejected the Soviet position. While not leading to any forceful military gestures, the Berlin crisis dominated East-West relations in 1959, precipitating a flurry of diplomatic activity and travel by world leaders. Visiting the U.S. in Jan., Soviet Deputy Premier Anastas I. Mikoyan urged East-West talks on Berlin and related issues while playing down the ultimatum of Nov. President Eisenhower announced (3 Aug.) that he and Khrushchev would exchange visits that fall, after his own meetings with Chancellor Adenauer, Prime Minister Macmillan, and President de Gaulle in their respective capitals. Premier Khrushchev arrived in Washington 15 Sept., visiting New York, Los Angeles, San Francisco, Des Moines, and Pittsburgh before meeting with Eisenhower (25–27 Sept.) at the presidential retreat at Camp David, Md. It was agreed to hold a 4-Power summit conference soon to discuss Berlin and the problem of German reunification, and the Berlin ultimatum, in effect, was withdrawn.

1959–60

DETERIORATION OF U.S. RELATIONS WITH CUBA. After 3 years of guerrilla warfare, the resistance movement headed by **Fidel Castro** provoked the resignation (1 Jan 1959) and flight of the dictator Fulgencio Batista. As Castro proceeded to organize a broadly based social and economic revolution, anti-American in its nationalist assertions, relations with the U.S. rapidly deteriorated. At a meeting of OAS foreign ministers (Aug. 1959) the U.S. denounced Cuba as contributing to tensions in the Caribbean and urged an investigation by the Inter-American Peace Committee.

The final rupture between Cuba and the U.S. was precipitated when the Cuban government seized (29 June 1960) 3 U.S.- and British-owned oil refineries in Cuba after they refused to process 2 barge-loads of Soviet oil. Acting under a congressional authorization granted 3 July, President Eisenhower cut (6 July) the quota of Cuban sugar imported to the U.S. by 700,000 tons. Accusing the U.S. of attempting "to strangle the economy of Cuba," Premier Khrushchev warned (9 July) that any U.S. military intervention would confront Soviet rockets. Eisenhower replied (9 July) that the U.S. would not "permit the establishment of a regime dominated by international Communism in the Western Hemisphere." By decrees of July and Oct., the Castro government nationalized all big foreign and Cuban businesses. Spurred by the U.S., the OAS conference of foreign ministers condemned (28 Aug.) Communist intervention in the hemisphere. Further U.S. purchases of Cuban sugar were suspended and an embargo placed (20 Oct.) on most exports to Cuba. Threats made by Castro and members of his government against the continued U.S. occupation of the naval base at Guantanamo, held under the U.S.-Cuban treaty of 1903, prompted a White House announcement that it was "firm administration policy" to fight to defend the base. President Eisenhower ordered (17 Nov.) U.S. naval units to patrol Central American waters and shoot if necessary to prevent any Communist-led invasion of Guatemala or Nicaragua. On 2 Dec. Eisenhower announced that he had authorized the use of $1 million for the relief and resettlement in the U.S. of refugees from the "Communist-controlled" Castro regime. Beginning in July 1960, in various UN forums Cuba charged the U.S. with carrying on an interventionist policy and conspiring to commit aggression. In one

of his last official acts, President Eisenhower broke off U.S. diplomatic relations with Cuba (3 Jan. 1961) in protest against "a long series of harassments, baseless accusations, and vilifications."

1960

19 Jan. NEW U.S.–JAPAN SECURITY PACT signed in Washington. The U.S.-Japan defense treaty of 8 Sept. 1951, signed along with the Japanese Peace Treaty (p. 476), allowed the U.S. virtually a free hand in disposing of its armed forces in and about Japan. A Mutual Defense Assistance Agreement (8 Mar. 1954) provided for U.S. aid in developing Japan's self-defense forces. Negotiations looking toward a revision of the 1951 treaty to give Japan a larger voice in military arrangements on its territory began in Tokyo in Oct. 1958 and continued through 1959 with Ambassador Douglas MacArthur II representing the U.S. Removing remaining residues of Japan's postwar occupation status, the new treaty dropped old provisions forbidding Japan to grant military rights to a third power without U.S. consent and permitting the use of U.S. troops to put down disorders in Japan. The new pact committed the 2 parties to come to each other's defense only if either were attacked "in the territories under the administration of Japan," and affirmed U.S. rights to land, air, and naval bases in Japan, while making use of these bases for combat operations or any shifts in the deployment or equipment of U.S. forces conditional upon "prior consultation." Massive demonstrations and student riots failed to prevent ratification of the treaty (19 May) by the Japanese House of Representatives but renewal of anti-American demonstrations forced the Japanese government, on 16 June, to withdraw its invitation to President Eisenhower, who was in Manila preparatory to flying to Japan. His "good-will" tour aborted, Eisenhower returned to the U.S. On 18 June Japan's ratification became effective and Prime Minister Nobusuke Kishi, at whom the demonstrations had also been aimed, resigned. On 22 June the U.S. Senate ratified (90–2) the treaty, which was extended automatically and indefinitely on 23 June 1970 unless at any time thereafter either party wished to negotiate a revision or gave one-year notice that it wished to dissolve the pact.

MAY. U-2 INCIDENT. On 5 May the U.S.S.R. announced that an American U-2 (Lockheed high-altitude) plane used for photographic reconnaissance had been brought down (1 May) 1,200 miles inside the U.S.S.R. Previously, on 3 May, NASA released a CIA cover story of a lost weather research plane which might have been forced down inside the Soviet border owing to mechanical failure. On 7 May Premier Khrushchev announced that the pilot, Francis Gary Powers, was alive and had confessed to being a CIA agent. Secretary of State Christian Herter announced (9 May) that, at the president's direction, the U.S. had engaged in "extensive aerial surveillance" over the U.S.S.R. (the flights had begun in 1956), and President Eisenhower stated (11 May) that he himself had authorized the U-2 flights—an unprecedented avowal of espionage activities by a head of state. At the opening of the long-planned, 4-Power Summit Conference in Paris, Khrushchev censured (16 May) the "spy flight," demanded that the U.S. renounce flights over the U.S.S.R., called for postponement of the Summit Conference for "approximately 6 to 8 months," by which date a new U.S. president would have assumed office, and withdrew his invitation to Eisenhower to visit the U.S.S.R. The Summit Conference broke up 17 May. Powers

was tried (17–19 Aug.), found guilty of espionage, and sentenced to 10 years' loss of liberty. He was released (10 Feb. 1962) in exchange for the convicted Soviet spy Rudolf Abel. On 1 July the U.S.S.R. shot down a U.S. RB-47, a reconnaissance plane, on a flight to the Barents Sea; 2 surviving U.S. airmen were imprisoned, but released by the Soviet government 25 Jan. 1961.

14 DEC. UN DECLARATION ON COLONIALISM adopted by the 15th Session of the UN General Assembly. Virtually amending the UN Charter, Resolution 1514 proclaimed the rights of all peoples to self-determination and independence, calling for a "speedy and unconditional end" to colonialism "in all its forms and manifestations." The Declaration on Colonialism was passed 90–0 with 9 abstentions. The U.S.— along with Australia, Belgium, the Dominican Republic, France, Portugal, the Union of South Africa, and the United Kingdom—abstained. That U.S. policy toward the "Third World" was altered by the succeeding administration was dramatized by UN Ambassador Adlai E. Stevenson's statement (15 Mar. 1961) in the Security Council endorsing steps toward "full self-determination" in Angola, Portugal's African "province," and supporting creation of a UN committee to investigate disorders in that colony. The U.S. associated itself with the Declaration on Colonialism and (27 Nov.) voted for the establishment of a committee to implement it.

CONGO CRISIS. Following proclamation of the Congo's independence from Belgium (30 June), the army mutinied and the province of Katanga seceded. The U.S. refused to respond unilaterally to the Congo government's request for military aid. Subsequently the 14 July resolution of the UN Security Council directed the Secretary General, Dag Hammarskjold, to establish a UN force to restore order—which became known as **ONUC** (Force de l'Organisation des Nations Unies au Congo). During the 4 years of ONUC involvement, ending 30 June 1964, UN troops from a number of countries were involved in an anarchical situation of civil and tribal war. The U.S. supplied planes flown by ONUC and half of ONUC's financial support, promoting the cause of unity of the Congo. After the UN involvement ended, rebellion was renewed and Prime Minister Moise Tshombe (formerly leader of secessionist Katanga) requested U.S. military assistance, receiving (13 Aug. 1964) 4 transport planes, 3 helicopters, and 105 military personnel. U.S. planes also aided in the rescue of hostages from leftist rebels in Stanleyville (24 Nov.

1964). When the U.S.S.R. and other nations refused to pay special assessments for ONUC, the U.S. pressed for denial of the Soviet vote in the UN General Assembly, as specified in Article 19 of the UN Charter. At the 1964 General Assembly session potential dissolution was avoided by taking actions only by unanimous consent. A compromise arranged by the General Assembly's Special Committee on Peacekeeping Operations (18 Feb. 1965) provided that budget deficits would be made up by voluntary contributions. In 1967 3 U.S. planes were dispatched to the Congo again to aid the government of Joseph Mobutu against an uprising led by former Prime Minister Tshombe.

Foreign Policy: The Kennedy Years, 1961–63

1961

1 MAR. PEACE CORPS established on a temporary basis by executive order. On the same date President Kennedy requested legislation giving permanent status to the program which would send young American volunteers to other nations where, as educators, health workers, and technicians, they would help implement human resource and economic development programs. More than 13,000 Americans had already offered their services when the enabling legislation was signed 22 Sept. By executive order (effective 1 July 1971) the Peace Corps, VISTA (p. 529), and other volunteer programs were merged in a new agency, Action.

13 MAR. ALLIANCE FOR PROGRESS. Calling for a "decade of democratic progress" in Latin America, President Kennedy spelled out a 10-point

program of Inter-American cooperation. Chartered (17 Aug.) at the Inter-American Conference in Punta del Este, Uruguay, the Alliance for Progress program committed OAS members to a 10-year, $100 billion program, to which the U.S. pledged $20 billion (at least $1 billion per year in various forms of public spending). The *Alianza's* goals included: a 2.5% annual increase in GNP, a more equitable distribution of national income, industrial growth and increased agricultural productivity, price stability, agrarian and tax reforms, extension of education, improvement of public health and medical services, and increased low-cost housing. The uneven results have served in large part as testimony to the ambitiousness of the *Alianza's* proclaimed objectives. Despite the creation (Jan. 1964) of an Inter-American Committee for the Alliance, and the announced support of Presidents Johnson and Nixon for continued pursuit of the goals articulated at Punta del Este, from the U.S. standpoint the *Alianza* quickly became a foreign aid program based upon traditional bilateral negotiations between the U.S. and individual Latin-American nations.

17 APR. BAY OF PIGS INVASION. On 17 Mar. 1960 President Eisenhower had approved a CIA project involving the training and supplying of anti-Castro refugees to infiltrate Cuba. By Nov. the plans had escalated to a direct amphibious assault, in anticipation that such a landing would touch off a mass uprising against Castro. In spite of his own doubts about the operation, President Kennedy yielded to the combined advice of the CIA, the Joint Chiefs of Staff, and Secretary of Defense Robert McNamara, approving it early in April. Having ruled out any direct involvement of U.S. forces and confronted by persistent reports that the U.S. would furnish support for the expedition—an ill-kept secret—Kennedy publicly disclaimed (12 Apr.) "intervention in Cuba by the United States Armed Forces." Air strikes against Cuban airfields Apr. 15 by B-26 fighter-bombers piloted by Cuban exiles from bases in Nicaragua were perceived by Castro as "a prelude to invasion." A force of some 1,500 men, mostly Cuban exiles, landed 90 miles south of Havana at the *Bahia de Cochinos* (Bay of Pigs) on 17 Apr. As the result of faulty assumptions and poor planning, the invasion was crushed within 3 days. President Kennedy assumed responsibility for the fiasco, which resulted in worldwide denunciation of the U.S., while ordering an intensive review of CIA operations. Castro offered to exchange his 1,200 prisoners for 500 bulldozers, then demanded an "indemnity" of $28 million. The prisoners were finally exchanged for $52 million (privately raised) in food and medical supplies in Dec. 1962. The Bay of Pigs episode strengthened Castro—who pro-

claimed (2 Dec.), "I am a Marxist-Leninist and will be one until the day I die"—and increased U.S. concern about his efforts to "export revolution." At a meeting of OAS foreign ministers (22–31 Jan. 1962), at which Marxism-Leninism, alignment with the Communist bloc, and conduct of subversive activities were condemned, it was declared that by its acts the Cuban government had "voluntarily placed itself outside the inter-American system." Cuba's participation in the activities of the OAS (from which no state may be expelled) was thus suspended.

BERLIN WALL. Responding to the friendly overtures from the Soviets which followed the advent of his administration, President Kennedy agreed to meet Premier Khrushchev in Vienna, 3–4 June, for exploratory talks, after first meeting with Prime Minister Macmillan, Chancellor Adenauer, and President de Gaulle. At Vienna Khrushchev asserted that if the Western Powers failed to come to terms on a final German settlement he was determined to sign a separate treaty with East Germany "this year"—an ultimatum repeated (15 June) in an address in Moscow. Convinced that a demonstration of firmness was required, President Kennedy made statements (28 June and 19 July) indicating that the "real intent" of the Soviets was to force the Western Powers out of Berlin and then, on 25 July, he called for an extra $3.5 billion in defense spending—approximately one-half for immediate procurement of weapons and equipment—and an increase in U.S. and NATO forces. At the same time plans to more than double draft calls and call up reserve and National Guard units were announced. In response, Khrushchev threatened mobilization (7 Aug.) and, beginning 13 Aug., the Communists sealed off the border between East and West Berlin—first with a fence and then with a concrete wall topped with barbed wire. Kennedy ordered 1,500 troops to West Berlin to bolster the permanent U.S. contingent of 5,000 and sent Gen. Lucius Clay and Vice-President Lyndon B. Johnson to the scene as further symbols of U.S. commitment. An official end to the crisis came 17 Oct., when Premier Khrushchev, addressing the 23rd Communist Party Congress, backed away from his ultimatum by suggesting that the question of a deadline was of little significance if the West showed readiness to settle the German problem. While refraining from delivering another ultimatum, the Soviets continued to assert their intention of signing a separate pact with East Germany unless the West came to terms on a new regime for Berlin. The Berlin Wall was a scene of perpetual incident as East Germans risked Communist fire attempting to cross into West Berlin. With H Con Res 570 (10 Oct. 1962), Congress reaffirmed Western rights in Berlin and declared that the U.S. was determined to prevent "by whatever means may be necessary, including the use of arms, any violation of those rights by the Soviet Union directly or through others." Standing near the Berlin Wall, President Kennedy told a cheering crowd (26 June 1963) that the U.S. "will risk its cities to defend yours because we need your freedom to protect ours." He concluded by saying, *"Ich bin ein Berliner."*

FLEXIBLE RESPONSE DOCTRINE. At the time President Kennedy took office, NATO "shield" forces, though increasingly armed with tactical nuclear weapons, still fell short of goals. In military terms, NATO's combat forces stationed in Europe, not considered an effective "shield," had become a "trip wire" which would warn of, or precipitate, a full nuclear "exchange." President Kennedy and his advisers developed an alternative strategic theory based on a policy of "flexible response" to varying

levels of pressure. As flexible response required greater reliance on conventional forces, the U.S. urged that NATO forces in West Germany be increased to the level of 30 divisions (there were then 24) and be equipped to fight with both conventional and nuclear weapons. Strongly opposed to the proliferation of independent nuclear forces and concerned with the need to promote greater unity within the NATO alliance (the Summit Conference of 1955 [p. 486], by raising hopes of East-West detente, had opened an era of discord within NATO), the Kennedy administration advocated creation of a NATO nuclear force (approved in principle Dec. 1957 by the NATO Council). Most prominently discussed was the **multilateral nuclear force (MLF)**—a fleet of Polaris-armed vessels to be manned by mixed crews and integrated into the NATO command. However, the flexible response doctrine, as elaborated, necessitated a strategy of "controlled" or "graduated" nuclear response, which required a central command—meaning effective U.S. control over the firing of nuclear weapons. U.S. efforts to promote the controversial MLF concept were pressed during 1963–64, but lapsed thereafter. NATO officially accepted the flexible response doctrine in 1967. U.S. adoption of flexible response involved strengthening both U.S. strategic programs, to provide an invulnerable second strike capacity in the form of underground and mobile missiles, and conventional forces equipped to deal with a wide variety of contingencies.

1961–62

LAOS. After the Geneva Conference of 1954 (p. 482), indigenous Communists (Pathet Lao) continued to harass the neutralist government. In the developing triangular struggle between neutralist, Pathet Lao, and rightist elements, the Eisenhower administration supported the latter which, led by Boun Oum, regained control of the government on 16 Dec. 1960. In early 1961 the Boun Oum government was under fire by the other 2 factions. President Kennedy chose to press for a compromise. At the reconvened Geneva Conference the U.S. proposed (17 May) a revised neutrality program for Laos, involving a cease-fire and formation of a coalition government. When matters in Laos reached a head (Apr.–May 1962) Kennedy ordered 5,000 U.S. troops to Thailand to underscore U.S. concern while at the same time increasing pressures on Boun Oum to accede to a tripartite coalition. The 3 Laotian factions agreed (11 June) on the formation of a coalition government, paving the way for the signing, on 23 July, by 14 participants in the Geneva Conference, of agreements guaranteeing the neutrality, territorial integrity, and independence of Laos and specifying procedures for the withdrawal from the country of all foreign forces.

1962

22 Oct.–20 Nov. CUBAN MISSILE CRISIS. The increasing flow of Soviet military and economic aid, evident since midsummer, prompted increasing pressures on the Kennedy administration to take some direct action against Cuba. A new treaty, under which Cuba was to receive from the U.S.S.R. arms and technicians "to resist the imperialists' threats," was announced 1 Sept. President Kennedy, acknowledging Soviet missile deliveries to Cuba, described the weapons as short-range and defensive in nature but warned (13 Sept.) that if Cuba became an offensive military base "of significant capacity for the Soviet Union" the U.S. would do "whatever

must be done" to protect its security. Congress, modeling S J Res 230 (3 Oct.) after Kennedy's statement of 13 Sept., declared U.S. determination to prevent, with arms if necessary, the Cuban regime from extending its subversive activities to other parts of the hemisphere or the establishment in Cuba of an externally supported military capability threatening U.S. security. First shown "hard" evidence on 16 Oct. that the U.S.S.R. was building missile bases in Cuba with offensive capabilities against the U.S., President Kennedy announced on 22 Oct. that U.S. policy demanded their withdrawal, imposed "a strict quarantine of all offensive military equipment under shipment to Cuba," warned the armed forces to be prepared for any eventuality, and reinforced U.S. forces at Guantanamo. Calling for emergency meetings of the OAS Council and the UN Security Council, Kennedy appealed to Premier Khrushchev to eliminate the "reckless and provocative threat to world peace." Having secured (23 Oct.) the endorsement of the OAS Council to take action under the Rio Treaty of Reciprocal Assistance, Kennedy ordered the quarantine to take effect 24 Oct. As the first Soviet ship stopped (25 Oct.) was carrying only oil, it was allowed to proceed. By that time several Soviet-bloc ships heading toward Cuba 22 Oct. had reversed course. On 26–27 Oct. Kennedy received 2 communications from Khrushchev: one proposing removal of the missiles in exchange for a U.S. guarantee against Cuban invasion, another proposing removal of the missiles in exchange for U.S. dismantling of missile bases in Turkey. Choosing to ignore the more formal, second note, Kennedy responded (27 Oct.) to the first, proposing removal of the U.S. quarantine and a guarantee against invasion of Cuba in exchange for the withdrawal of Soviet missiles under appropriate UN supervision. With Khrushchev's letter of 28 Oct., agreement was reached on these terms. President Kennedy announced (20 Nov.) that the missile bases had been dismantled and lifted the quarantine.

21 Dec. President Kennedy and British Prime Minister Macmillan, meeting in **Nassau,** agreed that the U.S. would supply Britain with Polaris missiles—to replace the recently cancelled British Skybolt missiles—for which the British would supply both nuclear warheads and submarines. The resulting British nuclear force was, along with a comparable U.S. force, to be assigned to a NATO nuclear force if and when such a force were established. After the Nassau Agreement was published it was transmitted to French President Charles de Gaulle with an accompanying memorandum containing a U.S. offer to sell Polaris missiles to France on the same terms. France rejected the offer. The Nassau Agreement, underlining Britain's "special relationship" with the U.S., exacerbated problems involved in British entry into the European Common Market (EEC).

1963

20 June. "HOT LINE" agreement signed by the U.S. and U.S.S.R. in Geneva—a result of the Cuban missile crisis' demonstration of the need for a rapid communication line directly linking Moscow and Washington to avoid miscalculations during an emergency. Operative 30 Aug., the Hot Line was not used until the Six-Day War of 1967 (p. 506).

LIMITED NUCLEAR TEST BAN TREATY. Following a period of total stalemate, brought on by the Korean conflict and intensification of the Cold War, the UN Atomic Energy Commission (p. 466) merged with the UN Commission for Conventional Armaments (est. 13 Feb. 1947) to form (11 Jan.

1952) the UN Disarmament Commission. Thereafter disarmament talks were carried on in a variety of forums, most under the aegis of the UN, ranging in size from the full membership of the UN General Assembly to private talks of the U.S., U.S.S.R., and Britain. A 5-member (U.S., U.S.S.R., Britain, France, Canada) subcommittee of the UN Disarmament Commission, established 19 Apr. 1954 to conduct negotiations in private, separated from earlier package proposals for comprehensive disarmament certain partial, though usually interrelated, steps toward disarmament. Measures discussed in this context included: a nuclear test ban as a first step toward suspension of production of nuclear arms, establishment of inspection zones to guard against surprise attack, and agreed ceilings on conventional forces. These talks collapsed 6 Sept. 1957.

In the meantime, atomic weapons tests continued, accompanied by mounting fears of the dangers of atomic fallout and radioactive contamination. The detonation of an H-bomb "within the last few days," announced by the U.S.S.R. 20 Aug. 1953, was confirmed by the U.S. Atomic Energy Commission (AEC). The U.S. detonated its second H-bomb on 1 Mar. 1954 at Bikini Atoll in the Marshall Islands. The blast, in the megaton range, starkly revealed the peril of atomic fallout: of the 23 men on the Japanese fishing boat *Fukuryu Maru* (*Fortunate Dragon*), which was 80 miles away from the explosion, 1 died and the others all suffered serious injury from the radioactive ash, several Japanese fishing vessels, many of which had not come within 1,000 miles of Bikini, brought in radioactively contaminated catches. Widespread fallout was also reported from the Soviet nuclear weapons test series begun in mid-Sept. 1954. The UN Scientific Committee on the Effects of Atomic Radiation reported (10 Aug.

1958) that, while the relative danger from fallout varied from region to region, "even the smallest amounts of radiation are liable to cause deleterious genetic, and perhaps also, somatic effects."

On 31 Mar. 1958 the U.S.S.R. announced suspension of nuclear testing, reserving the right to renew if other nations failed to follow suit. The U.S. conducted an extensive nuclear weapons test series in the Marshall Islands Apr.–July 1958 and tested smaller-magnitude weapons in Nevada until 31 Oct. The U.S. AEC reported (7 Nov.) that the U.S.S.R. had exploded nuclear devices 1 and 3 Nov. President Eisenhower declared that, while the Soviet tests relieved the U.S. of any obligation to refrain from testing, it would observe a voluntary suspension for the time being. A voluntary moratorium on atomic testing was observed by the U.S., U.S.S.R., and Britain (France began tests in 1960) until 1 Sept. 1961, when the U.S.S.R. resumed atmospheric nuclear testing. The U.S. announced (5 Sept. 1961) resumption of underground and laboratory nuclear tests (begun 15 Sept.) and 25 Apr.–4 Nov. 1962 the U.S. conducted atmospheric nuclear weapons tests in the Pacific.

The Conference of Experts to Study the Possibility of Detecting Violations of a Possible Agreement on Suspension of Nuclear Tests met 1 July–21 Aug. 1958 in Geneva. The U.S.S.R. accepted (30 Aug.) the report of the technical experts and previously (22 Aug.) the U.S. invitation to negotiate a test ban under international controls. The U.S., U.S.S.R., and Britain began test ban talks in Geneva 31 Oct. 1958, which continued intermittently until 29 Jan. 1962. On 14 Jan. 1963 the U.S. and the U.S.S.R. began private talks in New York on a test ban treaty with the use of automatic recording devices to monitor underground tests—a system requiring "very few" on-site inspections. Britain joined these talks (22 Jan.), but an impasse was reached and the talks ended 31 Jan. The U.S., Britain, and the U.S.S.R. announced 10 June that high-level talks would be held in Moscow in July to seek agreement on a nuclear test ban. Opening 15 July, the 3-Power discussions of an uninspected test ban led to the Limited Nuclear Test Ban Treaty, signed in Moscow 5 Aug. The signatories pledged not to conduct nuclear weapons tests in the atmosphere, in outer space, or under water but were permitted to continue underground testing. When ratified (80–19) by the Senate (24 Sept.), 99 nations had already subscribed to the treaty, which went into effect 10 Oct.

The Vietnam War

U.S. TROOP LEVELS IN VIETNAM 1960-72
(Source: Department of Defense)

U.S. troop levels as of 31 Dec. of each year:

1960	900	1967	485,600
1961	3,200	1968	536,100
1962	11,300	1969	475,200
1963	16,300	1970	334,600
1964	23,300	1971	156,800
1965	184,300	1972	24,200
1966	385,300		

1961–63. BROADENING OF U.S. COMMITMENT. While U.S. involvement in Vietnam dated back to the Truman administration (p. 462), and, as the French withdrew, the U.S. government began directly to support the anti-Communist Saigon regime (p. 481), the U.S. commitment expanded markedly in

1961. On 11 May President John F. Kennedy dispatched to Vietnam 400 Special Forces soldiers (counterinsurgency specialists) and 100 additional military advisers, and authorized a campaign of clandestine warfare against North Vietnam to be conducted by South Vietnamese personnel trained and directed by the CIA and some Special Forces personnel. It was decided in Nov. to enlarge greatly the U.S. military advisory mission in Vietnam and, for the first time, to assign U.S. forces to combat support missions. The latter decision led to U.S. involvement in actual fighting and an increase in American casualties—from 14 in 1961 to 489 in 1963.

During 1963 Buddhist demonstrations became the focus for widespread Vietnamese political opposition to the Diem regime. In a TV interview (2 Sept. 1963) President Kennedy criticized the Saigon government and observed that the U.S. could play only a supportive role in Vietnam: it was "their war" to win or lose. With tacit U.S. approval, a military coup was launched 1 Nov., leading to Diem's assassination and a succession of military coups. Immediately following the Diem coup Viet Cong (South Vietnamese Communists) activity increased.

The Johnson Years

7 Aug. 1964. TONKIN GULF RESOLUTION. During the first 6 months of 1964, U.S. officials seriously considered and planned toward escalation of the war, focusing especially on initiation of bombing of North Vietnam. Major policy planners argued that a congressional resolution was needed before such action could be taken. On 1 Feb. Operation Plan 34A was inaugurated—a program of clandestine operations against North Vietnam significantly different from pre-viously covert operations: larger in scale and military in nature, controlled in Saigon by the U.S. Military Assistance Command. South Vietnamese naval commandos on a 34A mission raided, 31 July, 2 North Vietnamese islands, passing on their return the northbound U.S. destroyer *Maddox*. The *Maddox* was on a separate 34A mission, an intelligence-gathering patrol of the Gulf of Tonkin, but the North Vietnamese assumed it was part of the assault mission and, on 2 Aug., 3 North Vietnamese PT boats attacked her. On 3 Aug. 2 more 34A assaults took place and intelligence patrols were resumed by the *Maddox* and a companion ship, the *Turner Joy*. During the night of 4 Aug. the *Maddox* and *Turner Joy* radioed reports of combat—received in Washington, because of the time difference, starting at 9:20 A.M. Despite confusion as to whether an attack had actually taken place, President Lyndon B. Johnson informed congressional leaders (6:45 P.M.) that he had ordered reprisal air strikes against the North and would ask the next day for a congressional resolution. After brief hearings, in which the provocative nature of U.S. operations in the area was concealed, the Tonkin Gulf Resolution, declaring support for "the determination of the President, as Commander-in-Chief, to take all necessary measures to repel any armed attack against forces of the United States and to prevent further aggression," and affirming U.S. intentions to aid any member or protocol state of the SEATO pact "requesting assistance in the defense of its freedom," passed the House (414–0) and the Senate (88–2) on 7 Aug. Only Sens. Wayne Morse (Ore., 1900–74) and Ernest Gruening (Alas., 1887–1974) were opposed. Under Secretary of State Nicholas deB. Katzenbach testified before the Senate Foreign Relations Com-

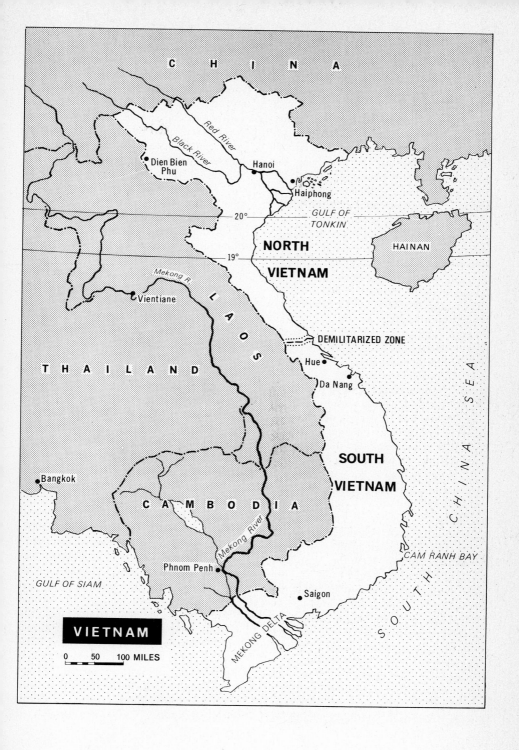

C H I N A

Red River

Black River

Dien Bien
Phu

Hanoi

Haiphong

20°

NORTH

VIETNAM

GULF OF
TONKIN

HAINAN

19°

Mekong R.

Vientiane

L A O S

DEMILITARIZED ZONE

THAILAND

Hue

Da Nang

SOUTH

VIETNAM

S O U T H   C H I N A   S E A

Bangkok

C A M B O D I A

Mekong River

CAM RANH BAY

GULF OF SIAM

Phnom Penh

Saigon

MEKONG DELTA

VIETNAM

0   50   100 MILES

mittee (Apr. 1967) that the resolution was the "functional equivalent" of a "declaration of war."

1965–67. ESCALATION. A Viet Cong attack 7 Feb. on a U.S. military advisers' compound at **Pleiku**, killing 8 Americans, triggered a presidential decision which for months had been the subject of serious planning efforts. On 8 Feb. President Johnson ordered a heavy reprisal air strike against the North and on 13 Feb.—after a Viet Cong attack (11 Feb.) on U.S. barracks at Qui Nhon had evoked a similar U.S. reprisal—Johnson ordered sustained bombing of the North, begun on 2 Mar.

The buildup of formal U.S. military units began (8 Mar.) when 2 battalions of Marines landed at Da Nang. On 1 Apr. Johnson, recognizing that sustained bombing had failed to move Hanoi to negotiate, decided to increase both U.S. military support forces and Marine combat forces, and to permit use of U.S. ground troops for offensive actions. There was no public acknowledgment of the crucial change of mission until it was admitted by the State Department on 8 June. The 13–19 May U.S. bombing pause was, according to the authors of the *Pentagon Papers* (p. 537), used to deliver to Hanoi a "demand for their surrender"—but appeared to be a peaceful gesture the failure of which could justify subsequent escalation. In late May the Viet Cong summer offensive began and in June U.S. troops participated in their first major "search and destroy" mission—the typical operation of the war, which usually lacked established battle lines. President Johnson announced on 28 July his decision greatly to increase U.S. combat forces—the U.S. commitment to an Asian land war had been made. The first major confrontation between U.S. and North Vietnamese forces, in the Ia Drang Val-

ley (Oct.–Nov.), demonstrated that, although they took heavy losses, the North Vietnamese army could maneuver in hostile country despite U.S. helicopters and planes and led the U.S. commander in Vietnam, Gen. William C. Westmoreland (1919–   ), to request vast increases in manpower.

A week after Ho Chi Minh declared that acceptance of Hanoi's peace plan was necessary to end the war, the U.S., ending a 37-day pause, resumed bombing (31 Jan. 1966). The 8 Feb. communiqué issued after the 2-day Honolulu meeting of President Johnson and South Vietnamese Premier Nguyen Cao Ky affirmed U.S. commitments to South Vietnam and stressed a new plan of combining military progress and civil reform. In Apr. the U.S. began using B-52s for raids on North Vietnam and, in a major escalation of the air war, on 29 June began strikes against oil installations in the Hanoi and Haiphong area. President Johnson met Premier Ky and the heads of the 5 other nations participating in the war—South Korea, Thailand, Philippines, Australia, New Zealand—in Manila (24–25 Oct.), where joint determination was pledged and a 4-point "Declaration of Peace" was issued. Escalation of the air war continued as B-52 sorties in the North increased from 60 to 800 per month in Feb. 1967. Sorties were aimed at lines of communications as well as such fixed targets as bridges, rail yards, troop barracks, petroleum storage tanks, and, for the first time, urban power plants—one located 1 mile from the center of Hanoi. On 3 Aug. Johnson announced U.S. forces in Vietnam would be increased to 525,-000 by June 1968 and requested a 10% income tax surcharge to finance the war —estimated (17 Jan. 1968) to be costing the U.S. $25 billion a year. In South Vietnam Nguyen Van Thieu was elected

(3 Sept. 1967) president—an office which the new constitution (effective 1 Apr.) granted sweeping powers.

1965–68. DOMESTIC DISSENT ESCALATES. While the Johnson administration stated that U.S. involvement in the Vietnam War was necessary to demonstrate that the U.S. kept its commitments, to halt Communist aggression, to assure the independence of South Vietnam, and to contain China; as U.S. participation in the war grew so did domestic opposition. In 1965–66 the war came under increasing congressional criticism from both "doves" who wanted to de-escalate the war and "hawks" who wanted greater military effort. Sen. **J. William Fulbright** (p. 1034), a leading "dove," used televised hearings (Jan.–Feb. 1966) of the Senate Foreign Relations Committee to call attention to the weaknesses of U.S. policy. Public dissent expanded rapidly from university "teach-ins" (1965) to massive demonstrations, notably the antiwar parades (15 Apr. 1967) sponsored by the Spring Mobilization Committee (New York City crowds—estim. 125,000–350,000; San Francisco—approx. 50,000); and the march (21–22 Oct.) from the Lincoln Memorial to the Pentagon, where some 55,000 protesters were met by solid lines of troops with fixed bayonets. After Secretary of Defense Robert S. McNamara reported (14 Oct. 1966) to the president that neither the "pacification" program (the drive to extend the South Vietnamese government's control to the countryside) nor the air war against the North was succeeding, doubts began to erode the administration's basic internal consensus. Sen. **Eugene F. McCarthy** (Minn., 1916–   ), a major antiwar critic, announced (30 Nov. 1967) his candidacy for the Democratic presidential nomination. In 1968, while protest demonstrations were widespread, debate over the war became a major issue in the Democratic primaries (p. 533).

1968. TURNING POINT.

Tet Offensive. Ignoring the week-long truce proclaimed for Tet (Lunar New Year), Viet Cong and North Vietnamese forces launched, on 30 Jan., a major 3-pronged offensive directed against: Saigon and all major cities and most important towns; U.S. forces at Khesanh and other outlying outposts; the countryside evacuated by government troops drawn back to defend the cities. Heavy fighting continued in Saigon through 20 Feb., and Hue, captured by North Vietnamese forces 31 Jan., was not retaken by U.S. and South Vietnamese (ARVN) forces until 24 Feb., when over 80% of Vietnam's cultural and religious center had been reduced to rubble. The 76-day siege of Khesanh was lifted 5 Apr. In the ferocious fighting U.S. forces sustained record casualties, though far less than Communist losses. The Communists suffered a military defeat but they demonstrated they could move at will, devastate major population centers, and disrupt the pacification program. The Tet offensive raised questions about the capacity of U.S. military force to end the war. Gen. Westmoreland's request (27 Feb.) for 206,000 new troops (to raise U.S. forces in Vietnam to 731,000) roughly half before 1 May, required a major call-up of reserves, which until then had been avoided, and vastly increased expenditures. President Johnson's decision (13 Mar.) that, in addition to the 10,500-man reinforcement already made, 30,000 more soldiers (reservists) would be sent to Vietnam, signaled an upper limit to the U.S. military commitment.

Peace Moves. Previously during the Johnson administration, U.S. bombing pauses, temporary truces, public and secret efforts by the U.S., other nations, and organizations—all had failed to bring about negotiations. President Johnson announced on 31 Mar., a unilateral halt of all U.S. air and naval bombardment of the North except in the area adjacent to the DMZ (effectively, up to the 20th parallel), and called upon Hanoi, which had indicated that a cessation of U.S. bombing was a precondition for peace talks, to begin negotiations. Hanoi agreed (3 Apr.) to the opening of a conference in Paris. On 7 Apr. bombing was stopped above the 19th parallel. Preliminary peace talks between the U.S. and North Vietnam began (10 May) in Paris. President Johnson announced (31 Oct.) U.S. cessation of "all air, naval and artillery bombardment of North Vietnam" as of 1 Nov. On 16 Jan. 1969 agreement was reached on the physical arrangements for expanded peace talks—to include the National Liberation Front (Viet Cong) and the Saigon regime.

The Nixon-Ford-Kissinger Years

1969. On 23 Feb. Communist forces launched a new general offensive in which U.S. troops—in Mar. at their peak level of the war, 541,500—took heavy casualties. President Richard M. Nixon secretly authorized intensive bombing raids over Cambodia (begun Mar.) to hinder Communist operations in Vietnam. After meeting (8 June) with President Thieu on Midway Island, Nixon announced the first U.S. troop withdrawal —25,000 men to leave Vietnam by the end of Aug. In a TV speech (3 Nov.) Nixon explained his administration's plan for the gradual withdrawal of all U.S. combat forces from Vietnam on a flexible timetable related to: (1) progress of the **"Vietnamization"** program— the intensified U.S. effort, launched in Mar., to train and equip South Vietnamese forces to assume major combat responsibilities; (2) progress in the Paris negotiations; and (3) levels of enemy activity.

Massive antiwar demonstrations resumed: millions, in cities and towns across the country, participated in "Moratorium Day" demonstrations on 15 Oct. and more than 250,000 gathered in Washington on 15 Nov. for a "March against Death."

16 Nov. My Lai Massacre first reported in the press. U.S. infantrymen gunned down (16 Mar. 1968) at least 450 unarmed South Vietnamese civilians —women, children, and old men. Lt. William L. Calley, Jr. was court-martialed (24 Nov.) and convicted, Mar. 1971, for premeditated murder of at least 22 Vietnamese civilians.

3 Sept. Ho Chi Minh died and control of North Vietnam was assumed by a group of Communist party leaders.

1970. On 18 Mar. Prince Norodom Sihanouk, Cambodia's neutralist chief of state, was overthrown by pro-West Lon Nol, who, alarmed by movements of Communist forces, appealed to President Nixon for extensive military supplies. Nixon announced 30 Apr. the **Cambodian Incursion**—a joint U.S.–South Vietnamese attack against Communist border sanctuaries in Cambodia, justified as "indispensable" for success of the U.S. troop withdrawal program in the context of the situation in Cambodia. Large caches of supplies were taken in the operation, which involved 32,000 U.S. and 48,000 ARVN troops and ended 30 June, but, alerted by military activities prior to 30 Apr., the Communists had already withdrawn most of their forces and some supplies from the sanctuaries. The operation spurred expansion of Communist-controlled areas in Cambodia.

May. Cambodia–Kent State Dissent. Demonstrations opposing the Cambodian Incursion took place on college campuses throughout the nation. Protests intensified after National Guardsmen shot to death (4 May) 4 students on the campus of Kent State Univ. (Kent, Ohio) during an antiwar demonstration and 2 students were killed by state police at Jackson State College, Miss. (14 May). A demonstration (9 May) attracted 60,000–100,000 to Washington. An intensive antiwar lobbying campaign focused on Congress. Counterdemonstrations by construction workers ("hard hats") occurred in New York City (8 May).

31 Dec. Congress repealed the **Tonkin Gulf Resolution** (p. 498) in a foreign military sales bill signed (13 Jan. 1971) by President Nixon, who did not view the resolution as necessary to justify U.S. involvement. Lengthy senatorial debate of measures to limit or end U.S. military involvement in Indochina (1969–72) demonstrated growing disillusionment with the war but, by approving each year the various defense and supplementary Vietnam appropriations, Congress set no effective limits on U.S. actions.

1971. On 8 Feb. the ARVN, with U.S. air support, launched a major drive into **Laos** aimed at North Vietnamese supply bases along the Ho Chi Minh trail, the main infiltration route into South Vietnam. The operation ended 24 Mar., earlier than projected, as the South Vietnamese took heavy losses. The operation fanned concern over a widening of the war. The heavily censored transcript of a Senate foreign relations subcommittee investigation (released 20 Apr. 1970) indicated the growth of U.S. involvement in Laos since the Geneva Agreements of 1962 (p. 495). Those activities brought to light included: covert military assistance of the Royal Laotian government in its war in northern Laos against Pathet Lao and North Vietnamese forces and the shift, after the cessation (1 Nov. 1968) of bomb-

ing North Vietnam, of U.S. air strikes to targets in Laos—both in the north and along the Ho Chi Minh trail in the southeast.

June. Publication of the **Pentagon Papers** (p. 537) helped further erode confidence in the government's conduct of the war.

3 Oct. President Nguyen Van Thieu was reelected in a controversial 1-man election in South Vietnam.

1972–73. ENDING OF AMERICAN INVOLVEMENT. On 25 Jan. 1972 President Nixon revealed that his National Security Adviser Henry A. Kissinger (p. 1077) had, since 4 Aug. 1969, held 12 secret negotiating sessions in Paris with Le Duc Tho, a member of Hanoi's Politburo, and/or Xuan Thuy, Hanoi's chief delegate to the formal Paris peace talks; disclosed the U.S. settlement proposal privately presented to Hanoi on 11 Oct. 1971; and accused Hanoi of refusing to continue the secret sessions which, unlike the formal talks, had "until recently . . . showed signs of yielding some progress." North Vietnamese troops launched a major offensive across the DMZ and from the west on 30 Mar. 1972. The U.S. provided heavy air support for the ARVN and resumed intensive bombing of the North —on 16 Apr. raiding Haiphong and Hanoi for the first time since 1968—as North Vietnamese troops advanced, gaining control of Quang Tri province by 2 May. On 8 May Nixon announced that to prevent delivery of war supplies to North Vietnam he had ordered: (1) the mining of Haiphong Harbor and all other North Vietnamese ports (mines to be activated 11 May); (2) a blockade of North Vietnam; (3) intensified bombing of rail and other lines of communication; and (4) continuation of air and naval strikes against military targets in the North. Cessation of these actions was linked to acceptance of a cease-fire and release of American prisoners of war (POWs) but, significantly, not to North Vietnamese withdrawal from the South. Despite continuing success of the North Vietnamese offensive, U.S. troop withdrawals continued—the last U.S. combat units left South Vietnam 13 Aug. Intensive U.S. air operations continued in both North and South and by the fall Communist military fortunes were beginning to decline. A breakthrough in peace negotiations occurred during private Kissinger–Le Duc Tho meetings 8–11 Oct. Kissinger met with President Thieu in Saigon (19–23 Oct.), unsuccessfully attempting to persuade him to accept the draft settlement upon which the U.S. and Hanoi were close to final agreement. President Nixon ordered (23 Oct.) a temporary halt of all bombing north of the 20th parallel. On 26 Oct. Kissinger announced that the U.S. and Hanoi were in substantial agreement on the 9-point settlement disclosed earlier the same day in a Hanoi broadcast. By the end of Nov. emergency deliveries to South Vietnam of some $1 billion of military equipment were completed. Private discussions between Kissinger and Le Duc Tho (20–25 Nov. and 4–14 Dec.) recessed with no final agreement reached. On 18 Dec. the U.S. resumed bombing attacks above the 20th parallel, including round-the-clock B-52 raids in the Hanoi-Haiphong area—the heaviest bombing of North Vietnam of the war. The White House announced 30 Dec. cessation of bombing north of the 20th parallel and resumption (8 Jan. 1973) of Kissinger–Le Duc Tho discussions. Negotiations concluded 13 Jan. and on 27 Jan. in Paris the U.S., North Vietnam, South Vietnam, and the Viet Cong's Provisional Revolutionary Government signed a 4-party "Agreement on Ending the War and Restoring Peace in Vietnam." In the afternoon the U.S. and North Vietnam signed the 2-party ver-

sion of the agreement, acknowledging the Provisional Revolutionary Government. The agreement *inter alia* provided for: release of all American POWs; withdrawal from South Vietnam of all U.S. forces and military personnel within 60 days; a cease-fire in status quo effective 27 Jan. to be supervised by a 4-nation International Commission of Control and Supervision; an end to foreign military activities in Laos and Cambodia and cessation of the use of the territory of either for military operations directed at Vietnam; receipt of military replacement aid and unlimited economic aid by the Saigon regime; formation of a tripartite National Council of National Reconciliation and Concord composed equally of members named by the Saigon regime and the Viet Cong, to promote implementation of the agreement and national reconciliation, and to organize elections in South Vietnam. By 29 Mar. 587 American POWs had been released and 23,500 U.S. troops withdrawn from South Vietnam.

1973–75. THE FALL OF SOUTH VIETNAM. The fragility of the Paris accords was revealed as the Control Commission was unable to prevent the continuation of hostilities and acrimonious disagreements blocked formation of the National Council of National Reconciliation and Concord. The number of North Vietnamese troops in the South increased. The Thieu government continued to receive substantial U.S. military (fiscal years 1973–74: $3,179.2 million) and economic aid. Two years of attacks by Communist and ARVN forces produced no major changes in territory.

The collapse of the Saigon regime began with the fall (9 Jan. 1975) of Phuoc Binh, capital of Phuoc Long Province. The capture (13 Mar.) of Ban Me Thuot (capital of Darlac Province) in the central highlands, 160 miles north of Saigon, prompted President Thieu to order a withdrawal of all forces from Pleiku and Kontum, bastions of the northern highlands, and a retirement to the coast of forces farther north. In the ensuing hasty retreat, which precipitated panic and refugee flights, Hue (26 Mar.), Da Nang (31 Mar.), and the coastal regions as far as the approaches to Saigon were abandoned. After fighting for 2 weeks at Xuan Loc, 40 miles east of Saigon, ARVN troops withdrew on 22 Apr. The Viet Cong announced their capture of the huge air base at Bien Hoa, 15 miles northeast of Saigon on 30 Apr.

On 21 Apr., in a speech carried on radio and TV, in which he accused the U.S. of breaking its promises of support and blamed the military debacle on U.S. cuts in aid, President Thieu resigned. Vice President Tran Van Huong took over, but on 27 Apr., with the concurrence of the National Assembly, he named General Duong Van Minh to become president and end the war. On 28 Apr. President Gerald Ford ordered the emergency helicopter evacuation of all Americans remaining in South Vietnam. U.S. helicopters removed (29 Apr.) approx. 1,000 Americans and 5,500 Vietnamese. (During the last 2 weeks of the war approx. 120,000 Vietnamese fled and were taken to the U.S.) On 30 Apr. President Minh announced the unconditional surrender of the Saigon government to the Provisional Revolutionary Government of South Vietnam.

1973–75. FALL OF CAMBODIA. By the time U.S. bombing in Cambodia ceased (p. 511), the Communist-led Khmer Rouge insurgents claimed approx. 90% of Cambodia's territory. Assisted by U.S. military (fiscal years 1973–74: approx. $519.3 million) and economic aid, the Lon Nol forces held until 1975, when Khmer Rouge forces blockaded the Mekong River, cut off all land access to Phnom-Penh and began closing in on the capital. Premier Lon Nol and his family left Cambodia on 1 Apr. and, Phnom-Penh's airport having been overrun, remaining U.S. citizens and American embassy personnel were evacuated (11 Apr.) by helicopter. On 17 Apr. the Phnom-Penh government surrendered to the Khmer Rouge forces.

MILITARY CASUALTIES (from 1 Jan. 1961)	KILLED	WOUNDED
United States	46,079	303,640
South Vietnam	184,546	495,931
Communist	927,124	unavailable
CIVILIAN CASUALTIES		
South Vietnam	451,000	935,000
REFUGEES		
South Vietnam		over 6.5 million
Cambodia		over 2 million
Laos		over 1 million
North Vietnam		unavailable

Foreign Policy: The Johnson Years, 1964–68

1965

DOMINICAN REPUBLIC INTERVENTION. A popular revolt, headed by civilian supporters of Juan Bosch (a liberal deposed by a military coup, 25 Sept. 1963) and some junior military officers, broke out 24 Apr. against the conservative, military-backed, civilian government of Donald Reid Cabral. Following Reid Cabral's resignation (25 Apr.), conflict between the military and the rebels escalated. On 27 Apr. President Johnson announced he had ordered the evacuation of U.S. citizens from Santo Domingo. A contingent of 400 U.S. marines landed (28 Apr.) and, as the result of decisions taken that day,

heavy reinforcements of U.S. troops followed immediately, reaching by 17 May
a total of 22,000. On 2 May President
Johnson justified the U.S. military intervention on the ground that a popular
revolution had been "taken over" by a
"band of Communist conspirators." According to the **"Johnson Doctrine"** then
enunciated, domestic revolution in the
Western Hemisphere ceases to be of
purely local concern when "the object is
the establishment of a Communist dictatorship." U.S. action was widely criticized in the U.S. and Latin America
both on grounds of the slim evidence of
Communist involvement in the rebellion
and because the U.S. had, contrary to
key provisions of the constituent documents of the OAS (the Rio Treaty of
Reciprocal Assistance and the Charter
of Bogotá), acted unilaterally. The
Council of the OAS was first convened
on the Dominican Republic situation the
evening of 28 Apr. and U.S. efforts to
"internationalize" its intervention resulted in an OAS resolution (6 May) authorizing creation of an Inter-American
Peace Force (IAPF). The IAPF (established 23 May and composed primarily
of U.S. troops, joined by small contingents from Brazil, Costa Rica, El Salvador, Honduras, and Nicaragua) remained in the Dominican Republic until
22 Sept. 1966. The state of civil war
ended with the establishment of a U.S.-
supported provisional government (31
Aug. 1965) which conducted free elections (1 Mar. 1966), in which Joaquin
Balaguer, a supposed moderate who had
served as premier during the dictatorial
regime of Rafael Trujillo, was elected
president.

1967

**16 Mar. U.S.–SOVIET CONSULAR
TREATY** ratified (66–28) by the Senate. Signed 1 June 1964, the consular

convention was the first bilateral treaty
between the U.S. and U.S.S.R. since
1917. Detailing the legal framework
and procedures for the operation of consulates in each country, it contained
2 key provisions, novel to such conventions, assuring full diplomatic immunity
to all consular officials and employees of
each country and prompt notification of
detainment of a citizen of either country
and access to him by his own consular
authorities. Because of Vietnam the
Johnson administration did not press for
ratification until 1967. Approval of the
pact, despite Vietnam War tensions, was
the first legislative endorsement of the
administration's policy of "building
bridges" to the U.S.S.R. and Eastern
Europe. President Johnson signed the
convention 21 Mar. and the U.S.S.R.
ratified it 26 Apr. 1968.

25 Apr. OUTER SPACE TREATY
unanimously approved by the Senate.
Besides establishing general principles
for the peaceful international exploration of outer space (including the moon
and other celestial bodies), the treaty
banned weapons of mass destruction,
weapons tests, and military bases in
outer space; suspended claims of national ownership or sovereignty in outer
space; and established measures for the
protection of astronauts. The treaty was
signed 27 Jan. 1967 by the U.S.,
U.S.S.R., Britain, and 57 other countries.

5–10 June. SIX-DAY WAR. War
broke out between Israel and the Arab
states as Israel reacted to removal of the
UN peace-keeping force, at Egypt's request, to Arab troop movements, and to
the closure of the Gulf of Aqaba to Israeli ships. Administration spokesmen indicated (5 June) that the U.S. was
"neutral," in the sense of not being a
belligerent, but this was "not an expression of indifference." The same day the
U.S. 6th Fleet was put on alert and 2
aircraft carriers and other vessels moved

east from Crete. Soviet Premier Aleksei N. Kosygin used the Hot Line (5 June) to inform the U.S. that the U.S.S.R. did not intend to intervene unless the U.S. did. By 10 June, when all parties had responded to the cease-fire called for (6 June) by the UN Security Council, Israel had driven 12 miles into Syria, seizing the Golan Heights; taken all of Egypt's Sinai peninsula and Gaza strip; and captured from Jordan the Old City of Jerusalem and all Jordanian territory adjoining Israel west of the Jordan River. Soviet efforts to have the UN Security Council and, later in June, the UN General Assembly adopt resolutions condemning Israel as an aggressor and ordering its withdrawal from all captured territories were rejected by the U.S. and failed to be adopted.

After the Six-Day War France, Israel's main supplier of jet aircraft, imposed an embargo on all arms sales to Middle East combatants, blocking delivery to Israel of 50 Mirages on order and already paid for. The U.S.S.R. decided immediately to reequip the devastated Arab air forces. Israel sought a new supplier of sophisticated combat aircraft and for the first time a U.S. administration was faced with the choice of either supplying Israel with aircraft or accepting at home the political responsibility for allowing Israel to lose military superiority. Israel had previously obtained U.S. surface-to-air Hawk antiaircraft missiles in 1962, Patton tanks in 1965, and, early in 1966, agreement was reached for the first sale of U.S. combat aircraft to Israel—48 A-4 Skyhawks (light fighter-bombers), to be delivered in 1968. After the Six-Day War the U.S. became Israel's chief supplier of sophisticated weaponry. The sale to Israel of 50 Phantom F-4s (supersonic jet fighter-

bombers) was announced 27 Dec. 1968.

23–25 JUNE. GLASSBORO CONFERENCE. President Lyndon B. Johnson and Soviet Premier Aleksei N. Kosygin met at the end of Kosygin's visit to the UN to present Soviet views on the Middle East crisis to the General Assembly. The impromptu "summit" held at Glassboro State College, N.J., a site midway between New York City and Washington, had nebulous results.

1968

23 JAN. "PUEBLO" SEIZURE. The 906-ton U.S. Navy intelligence-gathering ship which, according to U.S. officials, was in international waters 25 miles off North Korea was captured, along with its 83-man crew, by North Korea. North Korean officials contended that the "armed spy ship" had "intruded way into" their territorial waters. After the failure of initial U.S. diplomatic efforts to recover the *Pueblo* and its crew, President Johnson ordered (25 Jan.) the call-up of some 14,000 men in Air Force and Navy Air Reserve and Air National Guard. At that time U.S. military forces stationed in South Korea numbered approximately 56,000. U.S. and North Korean negotiators discussed the *Pueblo* incident at Panmunjom throughout the year. On 22 Dec. North Korea released the 82 surviving crew members and returned the body of the 83rd, who had died during the ship's capture, but retained possession of the ship. A North Korean draft statement assigning guilt in the incident to the U.S. was signed by a U.S. military officer, although U.S. officials rejected its "official" character, deeming it an expedient to secure release of the crewmen.

Foreign Policy: The Nixon-Kissinger Years, 1969–74

1969

13 MAR. NUCLEAR NONPROLIF-ERATION TREATY ratified (83–15) by the Senate. The product of more than 4 years of negotiations at the 18-Nation Disarmament Conference in Geneva, the treaty was signed (1 July 1968) by the U.S., U.S.S.R., and 60 other nations (not including France or the People's Republic of China) and submitted (9 July) to the Senate, but ratification was delayed in reaction to the Soviet invasion (20–21 Aug.) of Czechoslovakia. The treaty banned the spread of nuclear weapons (nuclear-weapons states pledged not to transfer them to non-nuclear states and states not possessing nuclear weapons pledged not to receive such devices); established safeguard procedures; and insured nondiscriminatory access to nuclear energy for peaceful uses. On 24 Nov. 1969 the treaty was signed by both President Nixon and Soviet President Nikolai V. Podgorny.

21 Nov. REVERSION OF OKINAWA TO JAPANESE ADMINISTRATION announced. Six months of intensive negotiations culminated in Premier Eisaku Sato's visit (19–21 Nov.) to Washington and the announcement that by the end of 1972 administration of the Okinawa (Ryukyu) and Bonin Islands would revert to Japan. Under the terms of the arrangement agreed upon, the provisions of the 1960 U.S.-Japan security pact (p. 490) would extend to U.S. bases on Okinawa. Both parties agreed on the need to retain extensive U.S. military facilities—a $2 billion complex, covering about 110 square miles

had been established—on Okinawa but in response to Japanese antinuclear sentiments the U.S. agreed to remove its nuclear weapons prior to reversion and to reintroduce them only after prior consultation with the Japanese government, as the 1960 pact provided. Prior to the reversion, completed 15 May 1972, Okinawa was the only U.S. base in Asia of which the U.S. had entirely free use.

1971

3 SEPT. BERLIN ACCORD signed by envoys of the U.S., U.S.S.R., Britain, and France, the first such settlement since the end of World War II. Endorsed by both Germanys, the accord, designed to improve communications between sections of the divided city and between West Germany and Berlin, became part of a comprehensive Berlin agreement signed 3 June 1972 in Berlin by the foreign ministers of the 4 Powers. The 1972 Berlin agreement, while not changing the city's legal status, recognized the existence of separate East and West German nations. On 4 Sept. 1974 the U.S. and East Germany established formal diplomatic relations.

1972

15 FEB. SEABED ARMS TREATY ratified (83–0) by the Senate. Prohibiting deployment of nuclear weapons on the ocean floor outside the 12-mile territorial limit, but not applicable to submarines anchored or resting on the seabed, the treaty had already been signed by 85 other nations, including the

U.S.S.R. and Britain, but not France or the People's Republic of China.

21–28 FEB. NIXON'S VISIT TO CHINA. After a week of private conferences, public banquets, and sightseeing tours, President Richard M. Nixon, the first U.S. President to visit China, and Premier Chou En-lai issued (27 Feb.) a joint communiqué indicating agreement on the need for increased contacts between the 2 nations. In the most controversial segment of the communiqué, the U.S. accepted Peking's contention that Taiwan was part of China, conceded that Taiwan's fate should be decided by the Chinese, and pledged ultimate withdrawal of U.S. military forces from Taiwan. In the same document the People's Republic of China claimed sovereignty over Taiwan and asserted that settlement of the Taiwan question was crucial to normal relations with the U.S. Nixon's visit, given heavy live coverage on U.S. television, dramatically marked the momentous change in U.S.-China policy set in motion by the Nixon administration. This reversal in policy had been foreshadowed in 1969 when, unilaterally and unconditionally, the U.S.: eased travel and trade restrictions (21 July), suspended the regular 2-destroyer patrol (7th Fleet) of the Taiwan Straits (Nov.), lifted the $100 limit on purchases of Chinese goods, and permitted foreign subsidiaries of U.S. companies to trade in non-strategic goods with mainland China (19 Dec.). After a 2-year lapse, U.S.-Chinese ambassadorial talks in Warsaw, the only official contacts between the 2 countries since 1955, resumed (20 Jan. 1970). The termination of all restrictions on the use of U.S. passports for travel to the People's Republic of China (15 Mar. 1971) and the lifting of the 20-year-old total embargo on U.S. trade with Communist China (14 Apr.) coincided with a Chinese invitation (6

Apr.) to the U.S. table tennis team to visit the mainland and their warm reception (14 Apr.) by Premier Chou En-lai in Peking. Following the secret meeting in Peking (9–11 July) between Chou En-lai and Dr. Henry Kissinger, Presidential Assistant for National Security Affairs, President Nixon announced (15 July) he would visit China before May 1972 "to seek normalization of relations between the two countries" and to exchange views on questions of mutual concern.

In a policy shift signaled (2 Aug. 1971) by Secretary of State **William P. Rogers** (1913–   ), the U.S. submitted (27 Sept.) a resolution to the UN General Assembly recommending that the Peking regime represent China in the Security Council while noting that Taiwan had a continued right to representation in the General Assembly. Despite U.S. efforts on behalf of the "2 China" policy, after a week of intense UN debate the General Assembly on 25 Oct. voted (76–35 with 17 abstentions) to admit Peking, seat it in the Security Council, and expel Taiwan from all UN bodies. The general thrust of U.S. China policy and the timing of Dr. Kissinger's second visit to Peking (20–26 Oct.) undercut the U.S. position in the UN.

The U.S. and China announced, 22 Feb. 1973, that they would set up liaison offices, not having embassy or mission status but with full diplomatic immunity, in each other's capitals. The U.S. office in Peking opened officially with the arrival (14 May) of veteran diplomat **David K. E. Bruce** (1898–1977).

22–30 MAY. MOSCOW SUMMIT. Richard M. Nixon, the first U.S. president to visit Moscow, returned to Washington (1 June) with 7 agreements he had signed with Soviet leaders, providing for: (1) the prevention of incidents between vessels and aircraft of the U.S. and Soviet navies at sea and in the air space over it; (2) cooperation in the fields of science and technology; (3) cooperation in health research; (4) cooperation in environmental protection; (5) cooperation in the exploration of outer space, with a joint-docking experiment contemplated for 1975; (6) the development of commercial and economic relations; and (7) arms control. Although the Johnson administration had begun to explore with the U.S.S.R. the possibility of some sort of freeze on strategic nuclear delivery systems, real progress on the question did not begin until the preliminary U.S.-U.S.S.R. **Strategic Arms Limitation Talks (SALT)** in Helsinki 17 Nov.–22 Dec. 1969. These established the framework for the full-scale SALT negotiations which opened 16 Apr. 1970 in Vienna and led to the 2 agreements signed in Moscow. The accords were based on 3 premises: (1) because the development of offensive weapons systems was markedly more advanced than that of defensive weapons systems, a freeze on both offensive and defensive systems would leave each side vulnerable to a first strike; (2) each side was confident that it could survive a first strike with sufficient capacity to destroy the other; and (3) the threat of nuclear obliteration—the "balance of terror" that had prevailed for a quarter century—was an adequate deterrent to all-out war. Signed in Moscow were: (1) a treaty limiting the deployment of antiballistic missile systems

(ABMs) to 2 for each country—one to protect the capital and one to protect an ICBM field; and (2) an executive agreement, to run for 5 years, limiting the number of offensive weapons to those already under construction or deployed. The Senate (88–2) ratified the ABM treaty (3 Aug.). The overwhelming majority reflected in part the reluctance with which the Senate had approved construction of the Safeguard ABM system to be located in North Dakota (key vote 6 Aug. 1969, when an amendment to block work on Safeguard was defeated 50–50). The offensive arms agreement did not require congressional action but was submitted (13 June) to both houses in the form of a resolution. After adopting amendments which, while not affecting the accord itself, indicated the uneasiness of Senate hard-liners, Congress completed action 25 Sept.

At Moscow U.S. and Soviet leaders professed a shared belief that the 2 nations should develop closer commercial and economic ties. The first major result was the Soviet agreement to buy at least $750 million in American grains over a 3-year period (p. 708).

13 JULY. $42.5 million were appropriated to the State Department for use by the president to help other nations and international organizations control narcotics traffic. The bulk of the funds was used for payments to Turkish farmers for ceasing opium poppy production and for enforcement of that effort. By the summer of 1974 the Turks had resumed opium poppy production.

1973

15 FEB. U.S.–CUBA ANTI-HIJACK PACT signed by Secretary of State William P. Rogers and Foreign Minister Raúl Roa. In the 5-year "memorandum of understanding" to curb hijacking of

OPERATIONAL U.S. AND SOVIET MISSILES

	1965 (Mid-Year)	1970 (Projected, End of Year)
Intercontinental Ballistic Missiles (ICBMs)		
U.S.	934	1,054
U.S.S.R.	224	1,290
Submarine Launched Ballistic Missiles		
U.S.	464	656
U.S.S.R.	107	300

aircraft and ships between the 2 countries, each agreed either to try hijackers for the offense or to extradite them. U.S. officials asserted that the agreement did not foreshadow improved U.S.-Cuba relations.

17–25 JUNE. BREZHNEV-NIXON SUMMIT II. Leonid I. Brezhnev, Secretary General of the Soviet Communist Party, repaid President Nixon's 1972 visit to Moscow. After his stay in Washington, where he met also with members of Congress and business executives, Brezhnev spent 2 days at the president's home in San Clemente, Calif. While several agreements were signed during the week, the main significance of the visit was symbolic: to demonstrate that the 2 superpowers had moved from a period of peaceful coexistence to one of détente. In addition to a declaration of principles intended to accelerate SALT and an agreement pledging each nation to avoid actions which could provoke a nuclear confrontation, the 2 leaders signed pacts initiating or extending cooperation in various scientific, cultural, and commercial fields.

CAMBODIA. Reacting against heavy U.S. bombing of Cambodia, where hostilities (p. 505) continued, Congress passed a $3.3 billion supplemental appropriations bill including an immediate cutoff of funds for the Cambodia bombing (vetoed 27 June by President Nixon). A compromise was reached when President Nixon assured Congress (29 June) that U.S. military activity in Cambodia would cease by 15 Aug. Legislation stipulating an end to all combat activities in Indochina by 15 Aug. was signed by the president, 1 July.

YOM KIPPUR WAR. War broke out 6 Oct. when Egyptian and Syrian troops crossed into Israeli-occupied territory in the Sinai peninsula and the Golan Heights. The U.S. announced 15 Oct. that it was resupplying Israel with military equipment to counterbalance the U.S.S.R.'s "massive airlift" to Egypt. On 17 Oct. 11 Arab oil-producing nations agreed to reduce their production and export of crude oil by 5% and to embargo its sale to nations deemed friendly to Israel. Saudi Arabia announced (20 Oct.) it was halting all oil supplies to the U.S. and all other Arab Persian Gulf producers followed suit (21 Oct.). A UN Security Council resolution (22 Oct.) calling for a cease-fire was accepted by Israel and Egypt (22 Oct.) and by Syria (24 Oct.), although sporadic fighting continued. What appeared to be a near confrontation between the U.S. and the U.S.S.R. was averted 25 Oct. when, reportedly in response to a Soviet threat unilaterally to move troops into the Middle East to supervise the truce, U.S. armed forces were placed on a worldwide alert in the early morning hours as a "precautionary" measure and, that afternoon, the U.S.S.R. agreed to creation of a UN peacekeeping force (UNEF) in which no big power would participate. On 7 Nov. Secretary of State Henry Kissinger met with Egyptian President Anwar el-Sadat in Cairo and the 2 countries announced that diplomatic relations, broken off during the Six-Day War of June 1967, would be resumed (resumption 28 Feb. 1974). A 6-point cease-fire agreement worked out by Kissinger was signed 11 Nov. by Egypt and Israel, leading to an exchange of prisoners of war and the lifting of the Israeli sieges of the city of Suez and of the Egyptian 3d Army, which after crossing the Suez Canal had had its supply lines broken by Israeli forces. The diplomatic efforts of Secretary of State Kissinger also led to the inauguration (21 Dec.) of Middle East peace talks in Geneva—participants including the U.S., U.S.S.R., and the UN. An Egyptian-Israeli accord (signed 18 Jan. 1974) providing for a mutual disengagement and pullback of forces along the Suez Canal and the establishment of a UNEF buffer zone was negotiated through the mediation of Kissinger, who shuttled (11–17 Jan.) between meetings with Egyptian and Israeli officials. On 18 Mar. 7 of 9 Arab oil-producing countries (all but Libya and Syria) agreed in Vienna to lift the embargo against the U.S.—an action explained as a response to a U.S. policy shift away from Israel.

1974

28 APR.–31 MAY. KISSINGER'S MIDDLE EAST "SHUTTLE" DIPLOMACY. Traveling back and forth between Middle Eastern capitals, Secretary of State Kissinger promoted a cease-fire and complex troop disengagement agreement between Israel and Syria, whose forces had regularly engaged in artillery duels on the Golan Heights since the end of the Yom Kippur War. The accords were signed (31 May) by Israeli and Syrian representatives in Geneva.

12–18 JUNE. NIXON'S MIDDLE EAST TOUR, including visits to Egypt, Saudi Arabia, Syria, Israel, and Jordan, symbolized recent changes in U.S. policy in the area and the success of Secretary of State Kissinger's efforts to bring greater stability to the region.

27 JUNE–3 JULY. NIXON–BREZHNEV SUMMIT III indicated the commitment of the 2 superpowers to détente. Only 2 minor accords on arms control were signed, underscoring the failure of SALT to produce agreement on terms limiting offensive nuclear arms. Several accords were signed promoting closer cooperation in technological and commercial areas.

DOMESTIC ISSUES AND NATIONAL POLITICS FROM TRUMAN TO REAGAN, 1945-81

★ ★
★

The postwar years brought Americans a continuing succession of problems. The nation's mood ran the gamut of hysterical suspicion, political apathy, bitter disillusionment, and exacerbated social and political divisiveness. The end of World War II, with its special problems of economic readjustment, was quickly followed by the Cold War, which on the domestic front fed a paranoiac search for traitors within. If the 1950s proved a time of complacency and political apathy, with such pressing problems as race relations largely deferred, the Thousand Days of Kennedy brought renewed vitality to the national government, a mood brutally shattered in Dallas. Although the U.S. attained its greatest degree of prosperity in the mid- and late 1960s, and achieved as well a series of notable reforms, both political and social, the Vietnam War cruelly divided the nation. Its conduct raised disturbing doubts about the credibility of the government and contributed to that revolution in mores and values which was sweeping the Western world. The Nixon administration assumed office in 1969 with the professed intention of "bringing us together," but a combination of misdirected leadership, double-digit inflation, and a cluster of high-level scandals revealed its incapacity to achieve its goals. Subsequent administrations have grappled with stagflation and mounting deficits. The presidential election of 1980 signaled a national reassessment of spending and welfare policies going back to the New Deal, with stepped-up programs for defense.

1945

WARTIME AGENCIES abolished by executive order included the Office of Censorship, Office of War Information, the Foreign Economic Administration, and War Production Board.

6 SEPT. RECOVERY PROGRAM recommended to Congress by President Truman consisted of 21 points, among them legislation toward full employment, an increase in the minimum wage, construction of 1–1.5 million homes annually, and a single federal research agency.

28 SEPT. TRUMAN PROCLAMATION asserted authority over the subsoil and seabed of the **Continental Shelf** (confirmed by international Convention on the Continental Shelf, 29 Apr. 1951).

19 Nov. COMPREHENSIVE MEDICAL INSURANCE proposed by President Truman in message to Congress.

1946

1946–53 ANTI-INFLATION MEASURES.

On 31 Dec. 1945 the National War Labor Board was abolished and replaced by the Wage Stabilization Board (WSB), which in turn was replaced (29 July 1952) by a new board with circumscribed powers. On 21 Feb. 1946 the Office of Economic Stabilization was established by executive order. **Chester Bowles** (1901–   ) was named director. Price control ended 30 June after President Truman vetoed a new measure, but was revived in modified form 25 July. On 15 Oct. meat price controls were ended and all other price and wage controls save on rents, sugar, and rice terminated 9 Nov. On 26 July 1948 Truman urged a special session of Congress to enact an inflation-control program calling for revival of excess profits taxes, priorities, and rationing. On 16 Aug. the **Anti-Inflation Act**, a compromise bill became law; on 17 Aug. the Board of Governors of the Federal Reserve System ordered curbs on installment buying. The **Defense Production Act of 1950** (8 Sept.) gave the president broad economic powers, including authority to stabilize wages and prices. On 21 Dec. **Charles E. Wilson** (1886–1961) was named director of the newly established Office of Economic Stabilization (26 Jan. 1951). On 30 June 1952 a compromise 1-year extension of the Defense Production Act with economic controls weakened was signed by Truman. Last price controls ended 17 Mar. 1953.

20 Feb. EMPLOYMENT ACT OF 1946

required the president to submit an annual economic report, created a 3-member Council of Economic Advisers to assist the president, a Joint Economic Committee of the Congress, and declared the continuing policy of the federal government to promote maximum employment, production, and purchasing power. The act did not endorse deficit spending and deliberately unbalanced budgets, but it was clear that this instrument of economic policy would be adopted.

2 Aug. LEGISLATIVE REORGANIZATION ACT

cut the number of standing committees from 48 to 19 in the House, from 33 to 15 in the Senate, and required regular meetings and records. The act provided for an annual legislative budget to complement the presidential budget and established the Legislative Reference Service as a special branch of the Library of Congress to provide Congress with information bearing on legislation. Title III, the **Federal Regulation of Lobbying Act,** required lobbyists to register and report their lobbying expenses. The legislative budget was abandoned in 1949. The elimination of standing committees led to proliferation of subcommittees of the Congress.

5 Nov. CONGRESSIONAL ELECTIONS

were marked by Republican victories, picking up 13 Senate seats, 56 House seats, thereby controlling the entire Congress for the first time in 14 years.

21 Mar. LOYALTY PROGRAM

established by Executive Order 9835 required the investigation of all government employees and all applicants for government jobs.

23 June. TAFT-HARTLEY ACT,

passed by Congress over President Truman's veto of 20 June: (1) banned the closed shop, which forbade the hiring of nonunion men; (2) permitted employers to sue unions for broken contracts or damages inflicted during strikes; (3) established a Federal Mediation and Conciliation Service, and required employers to submit a 60 day notice ("cooling-off" period) for termination of contract; (4) authorized the U.S. government to obtain injunctions imposing a cooling-off period of 80 days on any strike imperilling the national health or safety; (5) required unions to make public their financial statements; (6) forbade union contributions to political campaigns; (7) ended the "check-off system," in which the employer collected union dues; (8) required union leaders to take an oath that they were not members of the Communist party. The act was amended 22 Oct. 1951 to permit union-shop contracts without first polling employees.

7 JULY. HOOVER COMMISSION. Commission on Organization of the Executive Branch of the government was established with Herbert Hoover as chairman. The final reports (1949) proved influential: 116 of 273 recommendations were fully accepted, 35 mostly accepted, 45 partially accepted.

18 JULY. PRESIDENTIAL SUCCESSION ACT revised the law of 1886 and made the speaker of the House first and the president *pro tempore* of the Senate second in line of succession of president and vice-president, followed by the Secretary of State and other cabinet members according to rank.

26 JULY. NATIONAL SECURITY ACT coordinated the army, navy, and air force into a single national military establishment under the **Secretary of Defense** with cabinet status. Act also established a **National Security Council** and under it the **Central Intelligence Agency** (CIA) to correlate and evaluate intelligence activity relating to national security. Agency was denied internal security functions. Directors: Rear Adm. Roscoe Hillenkoeter (1947–50), Gen. Walter Bedell Smith (1950–53), Allen W. Dulles (1953–61), John A. McCone (1961–65), William A. Radford (1965–66), Richard Helms (1966–72), James R. Schlesinger (1973), William E. Colby (1973–77), Adm. Stansfield Turner (1977–81), William J. Casey (1981–).

1948

24 JUNE. SELECTIVE SERVICE ACT, passed after earlier act expired 31 Mar. 1947, provided for registration of all men between 18 and 25, with induction restricted to those between 19 and 25, for 21 months' service. On 30 June 1950 the draft was extended by law to 9 July 1951 and the president authorized to call out the National Guard and organized reserves for 21 months' active service. The draft was further extended (19 June 1951) to 1 July 1955 and the draft age lowered to 18½, paving the way for possible institution of universal military training.

30 JULY. EQUALITY IN THE ARMED SERVICES ordered by President Truman, following congressional failure to include ban in Selective Service Act of 1948. Truman established the President's Committee on Equality of Treatment and Opportunity in the Armed Services, whose report, *Freedom to Serve* (1950), coupled with the exigencies of the Korean War, largely wiped out segregation and discrimination in the armed forces. The report, *To Secure these Rights* (1947), of the President's Committee on Civil Rights, established by executive order (5 Dec. 1946), led to Truman message to Congress (2 Feb. 1948) recommending permanent civil rights commission, congressional committee on civil rights, a civil rights division of the Justice Department, federal antilynching law, a permanent FEPC, laws against discrimination in interstate transportation, and laws for protection of the right to vote. Truman banned discrimination in hiring of federal employees by executive order (26 July 1948) and established the Committee on Government Contract Compliance to effectuate nondiscrimination clauses in government contracts (3 Dec. 1951).

3 Aug. HISS CASE. Whittaker Chambers, admitted former Communist courier, testified at hearing of the House Un-American Activities Committee that Alger Hiss had been a member of the prewar Communist apparatus in Washington. A slander suit brought by Hiss against his accuser led to the production by Chambers of State Department classified documents or copies thereof allegedly turned over to him by Hiss. Rep. **Richard M. Nixon** (p. 1115) of the House Committee charged (6 Dec.) that the administration was more interested in concealing "embarrassing facts than in finding out who stole the documents." On 15 Dec. Hiss was indicted on 2 counts of perjury by a federal grand jury in New York. His first trial ended 8 July 1949 in a hung jury; he was found guilty at his second trial and sentenced (17 Nov.) to 5 years in prison.

PRESIDENTIAL CAMPAIGN. The Republican National Convention met at Philadelphia (21 June) and on 24 June nominated Gov. **Thomas E. Dewey** (N.Y.) for president and Gov. **Earl Warren** (Calif., p. 1077) for vice-president. The Democratic National Convention met at Philadelphia (12 July) and on 15 July renominated President **Harry S. Truman** and chose Sen. **Alben W. Barkley** (Ky., p. 979) for vice-president. Several Southern delegations walked out of the convention in protest against the strong civil rights plank and nominated Gov. **J. Strom Thurmond** (S.C.) for president on a States' Rights ("Dixiecrat") ticket. Other minor-party presidential candidates: Henry A. Wallace (N.Y.), Progressive; Norman Thomas (N.Y.), Socialist; Claude A. Watson (Calif.), National Prohibition; Edward A. Teichert (Pa.), Socialist Labor. Truman conducted his campaign against the "do-nothing" 80th Congress, which he called back into session (26 July). He rallied support on a 31,000-mile "whistle-stop"

barnstorming campaign to overcome divisions within his party and a large early Dewey lead.

2 Nov. PRESIDENTIAL ELECTION. Popular vote: **Truman,** 24,105,812; Dewey, 21,970,065; Thurmond, 1,169,-063; Wallace, 1,157,172; Thomas, 139,-414; Watson, 103,224; Teichert, 29,244; Dobbs, 13,613. Electoral vote: **Truman** 303; Dewey 189; Thurmond 39. The Democrats regained control of Congress, securing a majority of 12 in the Senate and 93 in the House.

1949

17 Jan. The trial began of 11 top leaders of the U.S. Communist party on charges of violating the Smith Act of 1940. They were convicted 14 Oct. and sentenced 21 Oct. to prison terms. Their conviction was affirmed by the Supreme Court in 1951 (*Dennis* v. *U.S.*, p. 679).

19 Jan. The president's salary was increased by act of Congress to $100,000 with a tax-free expense allowance of $50,000; salaries of vice-president and speaker of the House raised to $30,000.

20 June. REORGANIZATION ACT authorized the president to reorganize the executive branch of the government subject to veto by a majority of the full membership of either the House or Senate. In 1957 the act was amended to provide that plans could be vetoed by simple majority of either house. Act expired (1 June 1959), was reinstated early in 1961, and expired 1 June 1963.

10 Aug. NATIONAL SECURITY ACT renamed the National Military Establishment of the Department of Defense and reorganized it. A nonvoting chairman of the Joint Chiefs of Staff was set up, to which post President Truman named Gen. Omar N. Bradley (p. 991).

26 Oct. MINIMUM WAGE raised from 40 cts. to 75 cts. effective Jan. 1950.

1950

9 FEB. Sen. **Joseph R. McCarthy** (p. 1091) charged in a speech at Wheeling, W. Va., that 205 Communists (later revised to 57) were working in the State Department. McCarthy's charges gained wide public attention and led to investigation by special subcommittee of Senate Foreign Relations Committee, whose report (20 July) found the charges false.

7 MAR. Judith Coplon and Valentin Gubitchev, a Soviet consular official, were found guilty of conspiracy and attempted espionage against the U.S. Gubitchev was expelled from the U.S.

KEFAUVER INVESTIGATIONS. The Senate Special Committee to Investigate Interstate Crime, headed by Sen. Estes Kefauver (Tenn., 1903–62), attracted nationwide attention (1950–51) when its hearings were televised.

TRUMAN ADMINISTRATION CORRUPTION. Evidence of corruption among federal officials occurred during probe of Investigations Subcommittee of Senate Committee on Expenditures in the executive departments (Aug. 1949), where testimony suggested that officials were securing government contracts in return for a 5% commission ("five-percenters"). Truman aide Maj. Gen. Harry Vaughan admitted to accepting gift of a deep freeze (13 Aug. 1949). Secretary of the Treasury Snyder demanded the resignation of James P. Finnegan, St. Louis Collector of Internal Revenue (Aug. 1950), Finnegan finally resigning 24 Apr. 1951. On 31 July 1951 George J. Schoeneman, Commissioner of Internal Revenue, resigned. Collectors of Internal Revenue at Boston, San Francisco, and Brooklyn were removed along with 31 other Revenue Bureau officials as well as T. Lamar Caudle, Assistant Attorney General in charge of the Justice Department's Tax Division, and Charles Oliphant, chief counsel of the Revenue Bureau. President Truman appointed Newbold Morris (N.Y.) to ingestigate corruption among federal officials (1 Feb. 1952) but Morris was removed by Attorney General J. Howard McGrath (3 Apr.), who in turn was replaced (4 Apr.) by James P. McGranery.

28 AUG. **SOCIAL SECURITY AMENDMENTS** raised wage base to $3,600 per year with new payroll tax schedule, increased benefits approximately 70%, eased eligibility requirements for the aged, and extended system to bring in some 9.2 million workers—self-employed, domestic, agricultural, and in state and local government. Social security benefits were raised slightly in 1952.

23 SEPT. **INTERNAL SECURITY ACT OF 1950 (McCARRAN ACT),** passed over President Truman's veto, provided for registration of Communist and Communist-front organizations, and for the internment of Communists during national emergencies, and prohibited employment of Communists in national defense work. The act prohibited from entry into the U.S. anyone who had been a member of a totalitarian organization; but by amendment, 28 Mar. 1951, anyone who was under 16 when forced into such a group, or who joined to maintain his livelihood was not banned for that reason alone.

1 Nov. ASSASSINATION ATTEMPT. Two Puerto Rican Nationalists, Oscar Collazo and Griselio Torresola, attempted to assassinate President Truman at Blair House, Washington, D.C. Torresola was killed instantly; Collazo was tried and sentenced to death for the killing of a guard, but on 24 July 1952, the same day that Truman signed an act enlarging the self-government of Puerto Rico, he commuted the sentence to life imprisonment.

7 Nov. MIDTERM ELECTIONS. After a campaign during which a major issue was "softness on Communism,"

Republicans made wide gains in congressional and state elections, increasing their representation by 5 seats in the Senate and 28 in the House. The Democrats, however, maintained control of both houses.

29 Dec. CELLER-KEFAUVER ACT OF 1950 amended Section 7 of Clayton Act to prohibit corporate acquisitions where the effect may be to substantially lessen competition, thus granting power to cope with monopolistic tendencies in their incipiency.

1951

26 Feb. 22ND AMENDMENT made 2 terms the maximum for the presidency and barred election for more than 1 term of a person who held that office for more than 2 years of a term to which some other person was elected. The amendment did not apply to President Truman.

1952

8 Apr. STEEL SEIZURE. President Truman seized steel mills to avoid strike by steel workers. After Supreme Court ruled the seizure unconstitutional (2 June; *Youngstown Sheet and Tube* v. *Sawyer*, p. 679), Truman returned mills to owners. Ensuing strike was settled with wage and price increases (24 July).

30 June. McCARRAN-WALTER ACT codifying immigration laws (p. 658).

16 July. KOREAN GI BILL OF RIGHTS provided veterans with educational benefits, mustering-out pay, housing, business and home-loan guarantees, similar to those given to World War II veterans.

PRESIDENTIAL CAMPAIGN. The Republican National Convention convened at Chicago (7–11 July). Preceding the convention the National Committee ruled on disputed credentials of delegates from the Southern states, awarding most of the delegates from the crucial states of Georgia, Louisiana, Mississippi, and Texas to Sen. **Robert A. Taft** despite the claims of Gen. **Dwight D. Eisenhower,** whose backers carried the fight to the floor of the convention. In an initial test of strength the Eisenhower forces (658–548) secured adoption of a rule barring disputed delegates from voting on contested seats until their own credentials had been decided. Thereafter the convention sustained Eisenhower delegates in Georgia and Texas, and the General was the victor over Taft on the 1st ballot as a result of switch by Minnesota from Harold E. Stassen to Eisenhower. Vice-Presidential nominee was Sen. **Richard M. Nixon** (Calif.). The Republican platform attacked the stands of the Truman administration on China and Korea, advocated a balanced budget, reduced national debt, "progressive tax relief," retention of the Taft-Hartley Act, and federal legislation in the matter of discriminatory employment practices while conceding the right of "each state to order and control its own domestic institutions."

On 30 Mar. President Truman announced: "I shall *not* be a candidate for reelection," leaving the race for a Democratic nominee wide open for the first time since 1932. At the Democratic National Convention at Chicago (21–26 July) Gov. **Adlai E. Stevenson** (Ill., p. 1158), Truman's own choice, was nominated on the 3d ballot after trailing Sen. Estes Kefauver on the first 2. Stevenson, who did not seek the nomination, was the first presidential nominee to be drafted since Garfield (1880). A Southern bolt failed to develop after the convention permitted delegations from Virginia, South Carolina, and Louisiana to vote despite their refusal to take an oath to support the party's candidates. Sen. **John J. Sparkman** (Ala.) was nominated for vice-president. The platform endorsed the domestic and foreign policy of the New and Fair Deals; advocated repeal of the Taft-Hartley Act and federal legislation to secure civil rights.

Minor-party candidates: Progressive (and American Labor): Vincent W. Hallinan; Socialist Worker, Farrell Dobbs; Socialist, Darlington Hoopes; Christian Nationalist (in 5 states) and Constitution (2 states), Gen. Douglas MacArthur; Prohibition, Stuart Hamblen.

After disclosures that Sen. Nixon had been the beneficiary of a secret fund from California businessmen, Nixon defended his conduct in the emotional and effective "Checkers" speech on TV (23 Sept.). Eisenhower announced the following day that Nixon would remain on the ticket.

Eisenhower announced (24 Oct.) that he would make a personal trip to Korea after the election to try to facilitate the end of the war. He visited Korea 2–5 Dec.

4 Nov. PRESIDENTIAL ELECTION. Gen. **Eisenhower** scored a sweeping personal victory, with 442 electoral votes to Stevenson's 89. The Republican candidate carried 4 Southern states: Tennessee, Virginia, Florida, and Texas. Both candidates received the highest popular vote for a winner and loser respectively in U.S. history: Eisenhower, 33.9 million; Stevenson, 27.3 million; Hallinan, 140,123; Hoopes, 20,203; Dobbs, 10,312; Hamblen, 72,949; MacArthur, 17,205. The Republicans captured both houses by a slim majority: Senate, 48 Rep., 47 Dem., 1 Ind. (Wayne L. Morse, Ore.).

1953

7 Jan. BRICKER AMENDMENT. An amendment to the Constitution to limit the scope of international treaties to which the U.S. could be a party and to impose novel controls on the power of the president to negotiate treaties and executive agreements was proposed by Sen. John W. Bricker (Ohio). The amendment was opposed on 6 Apr. by Secretary of State John Foster Dulles as "dangerous to our peace and security." After extended debate the Senate (26 Feb. 1954) rejected the amendment, 60–31, one vote short of the two-thirds majority required.

25 Mar. McCARTHY ALLEGATIONS that Charles E. Bohlen, nominated ambassador to the U.S.S.R., ought to be disqualified from that position because of his close association with the foreign policies of F.D.R. and Truman did not succeed in blocking Bohlen, who was confirmed by the Senate 74–13 (27 Mar. 1953). McCarthy, chairman of the Senate Permanent Investigating Subcommittee of the Government Operations Committee, conducted (1953–54) a long series of hearings, public and secret, on the role of Communism in government and in other areas of American life. During the same period the Senate Internal Security Subcommittee under Sen. William Jenner (Ind.) investigated Communism in education, and the House Un-American Activities Committee, under the chairmanship of Rep. Harold R. Velde (Ill.), looked into Communist activities in the entertainment field. On 4 Feb. 1954 McCarthy set off on a Lincoln Week speech-making tour, whose theme, he announced, was the Democratic party's "twenty years of treason." McCarthy's tactics were denounced by President Eisenhower, who on 14 June 1953 assailed "the book burners," on 23 Nov. 1953 asserted the right of everybody to meet his "accuser face to face," and on 31 May 1954 attacked "demagogues thirsty for personal power and public notice."

After McCarthy's investigation (Dec. 1953–Jan. 1954) of alleged subversion in the Signal Corps Engineering Laboratories at Ft. Monmouth, N.J., the McCarthy subcommittee, with McCarthy appearing as a party rather than a member, held hearings on a controversy between Army Secretary Robert T. Stevens and 2 associates, and McCarthy and 2 aides. At issue were Army charges that McCarthy had attempted to secure preferential treatment for a former consultant, Private G. David Schine, and McCarthy charged that the army had tried to pressure him into calling off his Ft. Monmouth investigation; 35 days of televised hearings (22 Apr.–17 June) featured McCarthy and special army counsel Joseph N. Welch. McCarthy's attack (9 June) on a member of Welch's Boston law firm, Hale and Dorr, produced Welch's emotional reply, "Little did I dream you could be so reckless and so cruel as to do an injury to that lad. . . . Have you left no sense of decency?" The majority report of the 7-man subcommittee largely exonerated McCarthy from charges of "improper influence," although the 3 Democrats disagreed, and 1 Republican stated that he was convinced the principal accusation of each side was borne out.

On 2 Aug. the Senate established a select committee to study charges against McCarthy, with Sen. Arthur V. Watkins (Utah) as chairman. On 2 Dec. the Senate "condemned" by a vote of 67–22 McCarthy for contemptuous conduct toward the Senate Subcommittee on Privileges and Elections and for abuse of the Select Committee.

11 Apr. DEPARTMENT OF HEALTH, EDUCATION, AND WELFARE was created to take over functions of Federal Security Agency, by means of a presidential reorganization plan and a joint resolution of the Congress making it effective 10 days after presidential signature. Mrs. Oveta Culp

Hobby was sworn in as first Secretary (11 Apr.).

22 May. SUBMERGED LANDS ACT (p. 640).

19 June. ROSENBERGS EXECUTED in Sing Sing Prison. Klaus Fuchs, a German-born physicist, was sentenced 1 Mar. 1950 by a British court to a 14-year term in prison after being convicted of atomic espionage for the Soviet Union. His trial was followed by the arrest in the U.S. of his confederate, Harry Gold, sentenced to 30 years in prison (9 Dec. 1950), and by the trial and conviction (29 Mar. 1951) for atomic espionage of Julius and Ethel Rosenberg, who were sentenced to death, and of Morton Sobell, to a 30-year term.

1954

11 Jan. REPUBLICAN FARM PROGRAM. President Eisenhower in a message to Congress proposed to replace rigid, mandatory farm price supports with flexible supports based on "modernized parity" instead of the "old" parity (the 1910–14 relationship between prices farmers received for their products and prices they paid for the articles they bought). The bill finally enacted by Congress substituted 82½–90% of parity for rigid 90% props for wheat, cotton, rice, and peanuts; 75–90% for dairy products instead of prevailing 75% level; and gave the Department of Agriculture authority to barter surplus crops to foreign nations for strategic goods. Eisenhower signed the bill 28 Aug.

1 Mar. 5 Congressmen were shot on the floor of the House of Representatives by Puerto Rican nationalists; all recovered.

1 Apr. AIR FORCE ACADEMY. President Eisenhower signed a bill authorizing the establishment of an Air Force Academy, similar to West Point and

Annapolis; first class sworn in at Lowry Air Force Base, Denver, Colo., 11 July 1955, and academy moved 1958 to permanent site near Colorado Springs.

13 May. ST. LAWRENCE SEAWAY (p. 483).

17 May. BROWN v. BOARD OF EDUCATION OF TOPEKA (347 U.S. 483) reversed *Plessy v. Ferguson* (1896), with its "separate but equal" doctrine. In 1950 *McLaurin v. Okla. State Regents* (339 U.S. 637) and *Sweatt v. Painter* (339 U.S. 629) had struck down state laws for the higher or professional education of Negroes as failing to meet the requirements of equality. In the Brown case, involving elementary education, the Supreme Court (Earl Warren, Chief Justice) held unanimously that segregation in public education was a denial of the equal protection of the laws. The court (349 U.S. 294, 1955) directed the lower courts to admit Negroes to public schools on a racially nondiscriminatory basis "with all deliberate speed." Reactions ranged from compliance in some border states to hostile gestures toward the court. In response to the desegregation decisions of the Supreme Court, White Citizens' Councils, originating in Mississippi, 1954, spread to much of the South. This prosegregationist movement used economic pressures against proponents of desegregation, including mortgage foreclosures, withdrawal of credit, job dismissals, and business boycotts. On 19 Jan. 1956, the Alabama Senate passed a "nullification" resolution; the Virginia legislature adopted (1 Feb.) an "interposition" resolution asserting the right of the state to "interpose its sovereignty" against the decision of the court. On 11 Mar., 19 U.S. senators and 81 representatives issued a "Southern Manifesto" declaring their purpose to use "all lawful means" to reverse the desegregation decision. Spearheading the drive for de-

segregation was the National Association for the Advancement of Colored People (NAACP) with a membership of some 310,000 in 1956.

29 June. OPPENHEIMER CASE. Atomic Energy Commission upheld by vote of 4–1 the decision of a 3-man review board (1 June), which had voted 2–1, refusing to reinstate the security clearance of **J. Robert Oppenheimer** (p. 1119), wartime head of Los Alamos atomic laboratory.

2 Aug. HOUSING LEGISLATION. The Housing Act of 1954 authorized the construction over a 1-year period of 35,-000 houses to serve families displaced by programs of urban redevelopment, slum clearance, or urban renewal, increased the amount of the maximum mortgage on both sale and rental housing, lowered down payments, and lengthened amortization periods. Provisions were included to curb future abuses under FHA operations as a result of disclosures of irregularities in the administration of the FHA home-loan insurance program. An additional 45,000 public housing units for the next 2 years were authorized by the Housing Act of 1955 (11 Aug.). The Housing Act of 1957 (12 July) raised maximum permissible mortgage amounts in a number of FHA programs and cut required cash payments. As a result of the increase under the act of existing $900-million capital-grant authorization for urban renewal by another $350 million, urban renewal programs were sharply stepped up. The Housing Act of 1958 (1 Apr.) further liberalized minimum down payments and increased the funds available for home mortgages. Another housing bill providing $650 million for slum clearance and urban renewal was signed by President Eisenhower on 24 Sept. 1959 after his veto of 2 other bills had been sustained. A stopgap housing bill extending the FHA loan improvement program 1 year was signed 14 Sept. 1960.

16 Aug. INTERNAL REVENUE CODE OF 1954, a major tax reform, permitted (1) dividend credit and exclusion; (2) retirement income credit; (3) accelerated depreciation; (4) deductions for medical expenses; and (5) increased the maximum charitable deduction.

24 Aug. COMMUNIST CONTROL ACT deprived the Communist party of rights, privileges, and immunities, subjected Communists to penalties under the Internal Security Act, and provided that Communist-infiltrated organizations lose their rights under the National Labor Relations Act. On 11 Oct. the Civil Service Commission reported that 2,611 security risks had been dismissed from federal positions in the period 28 May 1953–30 June 1954, and 4,315 other civilian employees had resigned before determination was completed about "unfavorable" information in their files.

30 Aug. ATOMIC ENERGY ACT permitted private power companies to own reactors for production of electric power, to own nuclear materials, and to obtain patents on their own atomic inventions, which had to be shared with others for 5 years. In addition, the law authorized the release of certain information on atomic weapons to European allies and the sharing of information on the peaceful use of atomic energy with friendly nations.

1 Sept. SOCIAL SECURITY ACT AMENDMENTS raised benefits, raised the wage base to $4,200, created a new tax schedule, and added approximately 7.5 million workers to the program's coverage, largely self-employed farmers. Further Social Security amendments during the Eisenhower administration include those of 1 Aug. 1956, lowering the minimum age for benefits to women to 62, creating disability insurance for those 50–64 years of age who were permanently disabled, and slightly extending program's coverage; 28 Aug. 1958, increasing benefits and wage base to $4,800, and providing a new tax schedule; 13 Sept. 1960, eliminating the minimum age of 50 years for disability coverage.

2 Nov. CONGRESSIONAL ELECTIONS. Election marked by controversial role of Vice-President Nixon, who charged that Democrats were unfit to govern because of their record on Communism. Democrats narrowly regained control of Congress, with a 29-seat margin in the House, and a 1-seat margin in the Senate. The Democrats won 19 of the 36 gubernatorial contests, including the Maine election (13 Sept.) of Edmund S. Muskie.

1955

30 June. SECOND HOOVER COMMISSION on Organization of the Executive Branch of the Government (created 10 July 1953) filed final report with Congress with basic theme, "get government out of business."

11 July. DIXON-YATES CONTRACT. On 5 Oct. 1954 the AEC approved a contract under which the Middle South Utilities, Inc., and the Southern Co. (Dixon-Yates group) were to build a generating plant at West Memphis to feed power into the TVA system to supply Memphis, Tenn. The contract was an issue during the congressional elections of 1954, when the Democrats raised the cry of "Nixon, Dixon and Yates." In Feb. 1955 the Joint Congressional Atomic Energy Committee disclosed that Adolph H. Wenzell, Bureau of the Budget consultant, had participated in the Dixon-Yates negotiations, although he was also vice-president of the First Boston Corp., Dixon-Yates' financial agent. Following an announce-

ment that the city of Memphis had voted to build its own steam-generating plant, the contract was canceled by President Eisenhower 11 July. Generating capacity of TVA system rose from 2.9 million kilowatts (1950) to 11.3 million kilowatts (1960). On 15 Nov. 1960, TVA sold publicly an initial issue of $50 million bonds to be secured by net power revenues. TVA's expansion brought steam-generating projects of great magnitude, accounting in 1960 for 10% of all power production by the nation's utility systems, and servicing an area of 80,000 square miles in 7 states.

4 Aug. HELL'S CANYON. Proponents of public power were unable to secure passage in 1955 and 1957 of a bill providing for a single high federal dam at Hell's Canyon in the Snake River, about 100 miles below Weiser, Ida. The Federal Power Commission awarded, 4 Aug. 1955, a license to the Idaho Power Co. to build 3 small dams.

24 Sept. EISENHOWER'S ILLNESSES. President Eisenhower suffered a coronary thrombosis in the early hours of 24 Sept. on vacation in Colorado. He entered Fitzsimons Army Hospital near Denver, began to resume limited official activities 30 Sept., and returned East in Nov. On 10 June 1957 the president was seized by an attack of ileitis, was operated upon for removal of part of the intestinal tract, and entered a period of convalescence. In his 2d term he suffered a slight stroke on 25 Nov. 1957.

1 Dec. MONTGOMERY BUS BOYCOTT. A boycott by blacks of buses in Montgomery, Ala., began when Mrs. Rosa Parks, a 43-year-old seamstress, refused to relinquish her seat to white man. Mrs. Parks was arrested and fined $10 (5 Dec.). Under the leadership of Rev. Dr. **Martin Luther King, Jr.** (p. 1076) the boycott resulted in the bus company's loss of 65% of its normal income. Following a Supreme Court decision of 13 Nov.

1956 the boycott was ended and unsegregated bus service began (21 Dec.).

1956

17 Feb. NATURAL GAS BILL VETO. President Eisenhower vetoed bill to exempt independent producers of natural gas from federal utility rate control after Sen. Francis Case (S.D.) revealed he had been offered $2,500 campaign contribution by the oil interests.

11 Apr. UPPER COLORADO PROJECT (p. 641).

29 June. HIGHWAY ACT (p. 617).

PRESIDENTIAL CAMPAIGN. The Democratic National Convention convened at Chicago (13–17 Aug.). **Adlai E. Stevenson** was nominated on the 1st ballot with 905½ votes to 200 for Gov. Averell Harriman of N. Y., supported by ex-President Truman. Prior to the balloting Sen. **Estes Kefauver** (Tenn.) withdrew his name and asked his 200 delegates to support Stevenson. Sen. Kefauver was named for second place on the ticket, defeating Sen. John F. Kennedy (Mass.) by a narrow margin. The Republican National Convention, opening in San Francisco on 20 Aug., renominated **Dwight D. Eisenhower** and **Richard M. Nixon.**

Platform differences were not sharp. The Democrats asserted the right of all citizens to "equal opportunities for education"; the Republicans declared their approval of the Superior Court decision that segregation must be "progressively eliminated." The Democrats favored public as opposed to private development of water power; the Republicans advocated partnership among federal agencies, the states, and private enterprise. The Democrats supported 90–100% parity payments to farmers; the Republicans, the flexible parity payments.

In the ensuing campaign Stevenson proposed an international ban on the testing of H-bombs. Late in Oct. Marshal Bulganin impliedly endorsed Stevenson's position and was rebuked by Eisenhower. The latter stages of the campaign were marked by serious international crises in the Middle East and Hungary (p. 487).

6 Nov. PRESIDENTIAL ELECTION. Eisenhower scored a personal victory but the Republican party lost ground in Congress. Eisenhower secured a landslide electoral vote of 457–73, and a popular vote of 35,590,472 to 26,029,752 for Stevenson. Minor-party vote: T. Coleman Andrews (Constitution), 107,929; Enoch A. Holtwick (Prohibition) 41,973, Eric Haas (Socialist Labor), 44,300; Darlington Hoopes (Socialist), 1,763. One Democratic elector in Alabama voted for Walter P. Jones. The Democrats carried both the House, 232–199, and the Senate, 49–47, presaging 4 years of divided rule in Washington.

1957

21 Aug. NIAGARA POWER ACT authorized N.Y. State Power Authority to build a $532 million power project at Niagara Falls, N.Y. The Niagara project was put into operation in 1961. By 1963, the Niagara plant was the nation's second greatest hydroelectric generating plant, trailing only the Grand Coulee Dam on the Columbia River.

30 Aug. JENCKS ACT. In response to the decision in *Jencks* v. *U.S.* (353 U.S. 675; 1957), which had given the defendant in a federal trial the right to see all evidence in government files, new law provided that only material in FBI files relating to the subject of a witness' testimony at a trial might be produced in court after his direct examination.

9 Sept. CIVIL RIGHTS ACT OF 1957, first civil rights legislation since Reconstruction, established a 6-man Civil Rights Commission and a Civil Rights Division in the Department of Justice. Although an 1866 Civil Rights Law giving the president power to use troops to enforce civil rights laws was repealed, the new act prohibited attempts to intimidate or prevent persons from voting, and authorized the attorney general to seek injunctions in district court if a person was deprived of his right to vote. The longest personal senatorial filibuster on record, 24 hours 18 minutes, by Sen. J. Strom Thurmond (S.C.) on 28–29 Aug. failed to stop passage of the law.

24 Sept. LITTLE ROCK. Sporadic violence broke out in 1956 at such places as the Univ. of Ala., Mansfield, Tex., and Clinton, Tenn., when Negro students sought admission to all-white schools. In 1957, with the start of the fall term, the school integration issue erupted at Little Rock, Ark. A federal district judge nullified a state court injunction forbidding the school board to start integration beginning with the upper grades of high school. Gov. Orval E. Faubus on the eve of the school opening called out the National Guard to maintain order, although not a single case of interracial violence had been reported to the police. As a result the 9 Negro students were prevented from entering the high school. Despite a meeting of Gov. Faubus with President Eisenhower at Newport 14 Sept., the governor did not withdraw the troops until the federal court issued an injunction barring him from obstructing the Negro students' entry. Rioting broke out on 23 Sept. after the National Guard was withdrawn. On 24 Sept. the president dispatched 1,000 U.S. paratroopers of the 101st Airborne Division to Little Rock and put the Arkansas National Guard under federal command. The Negroes entered the guarded school 25 Sept. Gradually the troops were reduced. Elsewhere in the South integration made slow progress. A start was made in Sept. in North Carolina at Charlotte, Greensboro, and Winston-Salem, but in the lower South there was massive resistance. Of the border states, West Virginia, Maryland, Missouri, and Oklahoma had made the most progress by the fall of 1957; Kentucky, Delaware, Arkansas, and Tennessee the least. Token integration, begun in New Orleans schools 14 Nov. 1960, sparked rioting and heavy absenteeism. On 1 Dec. the U.S. Circuit Court of Appeals declared unconstitutional a series of segregation laws and interposition resolutions adopted by the Louisiana legislature.

1958

10 Feb. REGULATORY AGENCY SCANDALS. Investigations by the House Interstate and Foreign Commerce Legislative Oversight Subcommitee led to hearings about the firing (30 Jan.) of its own counsel, Prof. Bernard Schwartz, who had been discharged after he accused the committee of potential whitewash of FCC scandals. Hearings unveiled improper conduct of FCC Commissioner Richard A. Mack over award of Miami's Channel 10. Mack resigned 3 Mar. Later hearings revealed that Boston industrialist Bernard Goldfine had given Chief Presidential Assistant Sherman Adams a vicuna coat and an oriental rug and had in turn received preferential treatment before the FTC and the SEC. Adams resigned 22 Sept.

29 July. NASA. Soviet space achievements of 1957 (p. 801) inaugurated space race. Congressional hearings before Senate Preparedness Subcommittee, chaired by Lyndon B. Johnson, revealed agreement on need for larger and better coordinated research and development program. The National Aeronautics and Space Administration was established for this purpose, while the Department of Defense remained responsible for military activities in outer space.

6 Aug. DEFENSE REORGANIZATION ACT affirmed direction, authority, and control of Secretary of Defense over 3 "separately organized departments."

20–21 Aug. DEFEAT OF JENNER-BUTLER BILL and other bills attempting to limit aspects of jurisdiction of the Supreme Court and reverse or modify results of decisions in cases of *Watkins* v. *U.S.* (p. 680), *Pennsylvania* v. *Nelson* (p. 679), and *Yates* v. *U.S.* (p. 680) by the Senate by close votes.

25 Aug. A law granting pensions to ex-presidents of the U.S. became effective, the first ever enacted to provide pensions for former chief executives.

28 Aug. AGRICULTURE ACT modified price supports on basic crops for 1959 and 1960, giving farmers choice between modified price supports and increase of crop allotments. Supports on dairy products were raised 31 Aug. 1960.

28 Aug. LABOR PENSION REPORTING ACT required the reporting and disclosure of employee welfare and pension plans covering more than 25 employees, whether operated by unions, employers, or both in combination.

2 Sept. NATIONAL DEFENSE EDUCATION ACT provided $295-million loan fund to lend college students $1,000 at 3% interest over 10 years with 50% reduction if the student later teaches in an elementary or secondary school for 5 years after graduation. In addition, $280 million was voted for grants to state schools for facilities in sciences or modern foreign languages, with matching grants by states, 5,500 fellowships for graduate students planning to go into college or university teaching, c. $28 million for language study in higher institutions, and $18 million for utilization of TV, radio, motion pictures, and related media for educational purposes.

4 Nov. CONGRESSIONAL ELECTIONS strengthened the Democratic party's control of Congress by 15 seats in the Senate and 48 in the House, with a net gain of 6 governorships (including Alaska). Accountable in part for Democratic victories were the 1958 recession, farm opposition to the administration policy of lowered price supports for farm products, labor opposition to state right-to-work laws prohibiting union membership as a condition of employment, and dissatisfaction with administration leadership in foreign affairs. Sen. **John F. Kennedy** (Mass.) gained in political stature as a result of his re-election by a record margin of 860,000 votes.

1959

27 June. STRAUSS NOMINATION DEFEATED. The Senate refused by a vote of 49–46 to confirm **Lewis L. Strauss** (1896–1974) as Secretary of Commerce, the first cabinet nominee since 1925 to be rejected. Opposition to Strauss was based upon his role in denying J. Robert Oppenheimer security clearance, his involvement in the Dixon-Yates contract, and accusations that he had withheld information from the Congress while chairman of the AEC.

29 Aug. VETERANS PENSION ACT made major revisions in benefits of needy veterans for nonservice-connected disabilities, or of their widows and children.

14 Sept. LANDRUM-GRIFFIN ACT (Labor Management Reporting and Disclosure Act), designed to suppress gangsterism, racketeering, and blackmail in labor organizations, enacted a cluster of proposals, including the anticorruption, fair election, and trusteeship guarantees proposed by Sen. John F. Kennedy (Mass.), 15 Apr.; the "Bill of Rights" of Sen. Thomas H. Kuchel (Calif.), 22 Apr., setting criminal penalties to protect union members against unfair actions by their unions; and the amendment of Sen. John L. McClellan (Ark.), 24 Apr., revising the ban on secondary boycotts

under the Taft-Hartley Act to prohibit unions from inducing or coercing an employer or employee to stop doing business with another firm or handling its goods, and to extend the secondary boycott prohibitions to all unions.

1960

1 Feb. SIT-IN MOVEMENT began in Greensboro, N.C., where 4 black college students took lunch-counter seats in a Woolworth store in peaceful protest against "local custom" of refusing to serve a seated black person.

6 May. CIVIL RIGHTS ACT OF 1960 strengthened provisions of the 1957 Act for court enforcement of voting rights. Judges were authorized to appoint referees to help Negroes register and vote; voting and registration records were required to be preserved; criminal penalties were prescribed for bombing and bomb threats.

PRESIDENTIAL CAMPAIGN. The Democratic National Convention convened at Los Angeles (11 July). Sen. **John F. Kennedy** was nominated (13 July) on the 1st ballot, 806 to 409 votes for his nearest rival, Sen. **Lyndon B. Johnson** (Tex.), who won the nomination for vice-president. Despite a strong civil rights plank, the Southern delegates failed to walk out. The platform favored placing medical care for the aged under social security and criticized the administration's tight-money policy. At the Republican National Convention in Chicago **Richard M. Nixon** was nominated (27 July) on the 1st ballot, after Gov. Nelson A. Rockefeller had eliminated himself for consideration on the ticket. **Henry Cabot Lodge** (Mass.) was nominated for vice-president. Reaffirming the Eisenhower foreign policy, the platform pledged a health program "on a sound fiscal basis and through a contributory system," an expanded national defense program, and a strong civil rights bill, including enforcement of the right to vote and desegregation in the public schools.

PRESIDENTIAL DEBATES. Kennedy and Nixon appeared on 4 nationally televised hour-long programs (26 Sept.; 7, 13, 21 Oct.) in which newsmen questioned them and they were permitted to rebut each other's remarks. The debates were made possible by suspension by Congress of the "equal time" provision of the **Communications Act of 1934.** Result of debates was inconclusive, although probably of slight benefit to Kennedy.

8 Nov. PRESIDENTIAL ELECTION. In the closest presidential election since 1884, **Kennedy** was elected by just over 100,000 out of a record 68.8 million votes cast. Kennedy received 34,226,731 votes and Nixon 34,108,157. Minor-party candidates: Eric Haas (Socialist Labor), 47,522; Farrell Dobbs (Socialist Workers), 40,165; Dr. Rutherford B. Decker (Prohibition), 46,203; Gov. Orval Faubus (National States Rights), 40,165. Because of demands for recount in some of the close states, such as Illinois and Texas, and the role of unpledged electors from Mississippi, the final issue was in some doubt until the electoral college vote, 19 Dec., which gave **Kennedy** 300 (22 states); Nixon, 219 (26 states); Sen. Harry F. Byrd, 15 (unpledged electors in Ala. and Miss. and 1 Nixon vote in Okla.). Hawaii's vote was withheld at that time as a recount was still in progress. Official count, 6 Jan. 1961, gave Kennedy 303 (including Hawaii), Nixon 219.

1961

17 Jan. EISENHOWER FAREWELL message warned nation of military-industrial complex.

DEFENSE BUDGETS
Fiscal Years 1950–1973
(Source: House Appropriations Committee, 1960–1973; Congressional Quarterly, 1950–1959.)

Fiscal Year	[In Billions] Appropriation[1]
1950	$12.9
1951	13.3
1952	56.9
1953	46.6
1954	34.4
1955	28.8
1956	31.9
1957	34.7
1958	33.8
1959	39.6
1960	39.2
1961	40.0
1962	46.7
1963	48.1
1964	47.2
1965	46.8
1966	46.9
1967	58.1
1968	69.9
1969	71.2
1970	69.6
1971	66.6
1972	70.5
1973	74.3

[1] Above amounts exclude appropriations not made in the regular annual Defense Appropriation Acts.

20 Jan. KENNEDY'S INAUGURAL ADDRESS called for "a grand and global alliance" to combat tyranny, poverty, disease, and war, served notice on the world that the U.S. was ready to "pay any price" to assure survival and "the success of liberty," but also to resume negotiations with the Soviet Union to ease world tensions. "Let us never negotiate out of fear. But let us never fear to negotiate," the president declared. Kennedy urged his fellow Americans: "ask not what your country can do for you—ask what you can do for your country."

29 Mar. 23RD AMENDMENT gave citizens of the District of Columbia the right to vote in presidential elections with the number of electors equivalent to those possible if the District had Congressional representation. Amendment had cleared Congress 16 June 1960.

1 May. AREA REDEVELOPMENT ACT authorized loans, grants, technical assistance to industrial and rural redevelopment areas ("depressed areas").

5 May. MINIMUM WAGE increased in stages to $1.25/hour. Previous increase to $1/hour effective 1 Mar. 1956. The 1961 law brought the 23.9 million workers then covered to a wage of $1.14 (Sept. 1961), and $1.25 (Sept. 1963). For the 3.6 million newly covered workers, wages of $1/hour (Sept. 1961) increased to $1.14 (Sept. 1964), and $1.25 (Sept. 1965).

25 May. MOON COMMITMENT. In message to Congress Kennedy urged commitment to goal of "landing a man on the moon and returning him safely to earth" before end of decade.

30 June. HOUSING ACT OF 1961, most comprehensive since 1958, attempted to reduce urban blight, improve low- and moderate-income housing, and stimulate economy through increase in construction.

1962

26 Mar. *BAKER* v. *CARR* (p. 681).

10 Apr. STEEL PRICE INCREASES resisted vigorously by President Kennedy, who charged that they constituted "a wholly unjustified and irresponsible defiance of our public interest." Beginning 13 Apr. the companies responded by canceling their price increases.

31 Aug. COMMUNICATIONS SATELLITE (p. 802).

30 Sept.–10 Oct. MEREDITH CRISIS. Over the "interposition" of Gov. Ross Barnett, James Meredith, a black, was admitted under federal court order to the Univ. of Mississippi, not, however, without a riot in which 2 died and federal troops, along with the federalized National Guard, were called up. Meredith received his degree 18 Aug. 1963. On 11 Sept. 1963 Gov. George C. Wallace backed down from refusal to allow integration of Univ. of Alabama, after

President Kennedy federalized the National Guard.

11 Oct. TRADE EXPANSION ACT removed bars to world trade by giving the president authority to cut tariffs up to 50% below the 1962 level or raise them 50% above the 1934 level within the next 5 years, and to remove tariffs on products in which the U.S. and Western Europe account for 80% of free world trade.

6 Nov. CONGRESSIONAL ELECTIONS. The Democrats reversed the usual midterm trend by picking up 4 seats in the Senate, with minimal losses in the House. The Republicans won several important gubernatorial contests, including the reelection of Nelson Rockefeller in New York and the election of George W. Romney in Michigan, but former vice-president Richard M. Nixon was beaten in his campaign to unseat Gov. Edmund G. Brown of California.

1963

14 Aug. HIGHER EDUCATION FACILITIES ACT authorized 5-year program of federal grants and loans for construction or improvement of public and private higher educational facilities.

CIVIL RIGHTS. The Kennedy administration witnessed the most massive demonstrations by civil rights groups since Reconstruction and achieved a notable breakthrough in that area. Among the major accomplishments were the presidential support given to the *Brown* v. *Board of Education of Topeka* ruling and presidential commitment to integration of public facilities. Major administration efforts went into enforcement of the voting rights provisions of the 1957 and 1960 Civil Rights Laws. The Civil Rights Division of the Department of Justice, with the support of the president and his brother, Attorney General Robert Kennedy, and under the direction of Assistant

Attorney General Burke Marshall and his deputy, John Doar, brought over 50 suits in 4 states to secure the right to vote for the Negro. Among the most significant executive orders to end discrimination was that of 20 Nov. 1962, prohibiting racial and religious discrimination in housing built or purchased with federal aid.

THE 1,000 DAYS. The "New Frontier" brought to the public service a distinctive style together with some of the enthusiasm and intellectual vigor of "The Hundred Days" (9 Mar.–16 June 1932) without achieving a comparable legislative record. Able appointees, notably Secretary of Defense **Rober S. McNamara,** Secretary of Labor **Arthur J. Goldberg,** Secretary of the Interior **Stewart L. Udall,** and FCC head **Newton N. Minow,** revitalized their departments and agencies. On the legislative front, however, the results were modest. Congress defeated proposals for a Department of Urban Affairs, along with bills for housing, medical care for the aged, and federal grants for public school construction and teachers' salaries.

22 Nov. ASSASSINATION OF KENNEDY. While riding in a motorcade on a visit to Dallas, where he was seeking to heal a rift in the Texas Democratic party, the president was shot by **Lee Harvey Oswald,** a former marine and leftist. He was pronounced dead at 1 P.M., one-half hour after the shooting. Gov. John B. Connally (Tex.) was also shot. **Lyndon B. Johnson,** who also had been riding in the motorcade, took the oath of office from Federal District Judge Sarah T. Hughes in the presidential plane 2 hours after the assassination. Oswald, while in police custody, was shot and killed by **Jack Ruby,** Dallas nightclub owner (24 Nov.), an event which was recorded by TV coverage. Ruby was convicted of murder 14 Mar. 1964, and sentenced to

death. On 27 Sept. the 888-page report of the 7-man Presidential Commission, headed by Chief Justice Earl Warren, held Oswald to be the sole assassin.

1964

8 JAN. WAR ON POVERTY called for by President Lyndon B. Johnson in State of the Union Address. Subsequently the **Economic Opportunity Act** (30 Aug.) and other legislation was enacted for a coordinated attack on multiple causes of poverty—illiteracy, unemployment, and inadequate public services. $947.7 million authorized for 10 separate programs conducted by Office of Economic Opportunity including Job Corps, VISTA (Volunteers in Service to America), work-training programs, work-study programs, and small-business incentives.

23 JAN. 24TH AMENDMENT ratified banning the poll tax as a prerequisite for voting in federal elections. Submitted to the states by Congress 27 Aug. 1962.

26 FEB. TAX REDUCTION ACT. Personal income tax rates were reduced from 20–91% scale to 14–70% over 2-year period; corporate rates from 52% to 48%.

2 JULY. CIVIL RIGHTS LAW OF 1964. Mass civil rights demonstrations for equality in Birmingham, Ala. (beginning 3 Apr. 1963) attracted wide attention focused upon harsh treatment of demonstrators. President Kennedy announced commitment to equality in public accommodations (11 June 1963); 200,000 marched in Washington, D.C. (28 Aug. 1963) "for jobs and freedom." After a long legislative fight, the House passed the bill (10 Feb. 1964). Cloture was enforced by a vote of 71–29 to end a Senate filibuster (10 June 1964), the first time a filibuster had been ended on a civil rights bill. Senate passed bill 73–27 (19 June) and House the revised version (2 July, date of the president's signature).

Omnibus bill included provisions (1) to bar discrimination in public accommodations; (2) authorizing the attorney general to institute suits to desegregate schools or other public facilities; (3) outlawing discrimination in employment on the basis of race, color, religion, sex, or national origin; and (4) gave added protection to voting rights by making a 6th-grade education a rebuttable presumption of literacy and by prohibiting denial of registration due to immaterial errors in filling out registration forms. The public accommodations sections were upheld by the Supreme Court in *Heart of Atlanta Motel* v. *U.S.* (p. 681).

8 July. Senate Rules and Administration Committee Report on Robert ("Bobby") G. Baker, former Secretary to the Senate Majority Leader Lyndon B. Johnson, found him "guilty of many gross improprieties" but cited no specific violations of law.

9 July. URBAN MASS TRANSPORTATION ACT OF 1964 provided financial aid up to $375 million.

3 Sept. WILDERNESS PRESERVATION ACT (p. 642).

PRESIDENTIAL CAMPAIGN. The Republican National Convention, opening in San Francisco 13 July, nominated Sen. **Barry M. Goldwater** (Ariz.) for president and Rep. **William E. Miller** (N.Y.) for vice-president on the 1st ballot, in a triumph for the conservative wing of the Republican party. The platform pledged enforcement of the Civil Rights Law of 1964, affirmed presidential control over nuclear weapons, but the convention rejected a proposal denouncing the right-wing John Birch Society.

The Democratic Convention, held in Atlantic City 24–27 Aug., nominated **Lyndon B. Johnson** for president and Sen. **Hubert H. Humphrey** (Minn.) for vice-president, by acclamation. The latter was Johnson's declared choice.

3 Nov. PRESIDENTIAL ELECTION. In the biggest landslide of the century **Johnson** was elected, with 486 electoral votes (44 states and the District of Columbia) and 43.1 million votes (61%) to Goldwater's 6 states and 27.1 million votes (38.8%). Minor-party candidates: Eric Haas (Socialist Labor), 21,390; Clifton DeBerry (Socialist Worker), 10,934; Earle H. Munn (Prohibition), 18,227; John Kasper (National States Rights), 11,204. The Democrats strengthened their hold on Congress and lost but one governorship, retaining 33.

1965

4 Jan. STATE OF THE UNION. The president called for a vast program to achieve the "Great Society," including a massive attack on crippling and killing diseases, a doubling of the war on poverty in 1965, enforcement of the Civil Rights Law and elimination of barriers to the right to vote, reform of the immigration laws, an education program of scholarships and loans with a first-year authorization of $1.5 billion, and a "massive effort" to establish more recreational and open space areas. The Johnson budget (25 Jan.) called for an expenditure of $97.7 billion, less than 15% of the gross national product, the lowest ratio in 15 years, with an anticipated deficit of $5.3 billion.

JOHNSON'S LEGISLATIVE ACCOMPLISHMENTS. At the urging of the president the 1st session of the 89th Congress passed the most significant amount of legislation since the New Deal including:

11 Apr. Elementary and Secondary School Act, the first large-scale program of aid to elementary and secondary schools, granting $1.3 billion to school districts on the basis of number of needy children, including funds for parochial and private pupils disbursed under public school supervision.

30 July. Medicare providing medical care for the aged financed through the Social Security System (p. 816). Social security benefits were increased by 7%, the social security tax raised to 5.65%, and the income based to $6,600. Widows aged 62 became eligible for benefits. The tax and income base rose to 5.9% and $7,800 by law in 1967 and benefits were increased 13% by law, 2 Jan. 1968.

6 Aug. Voting Rights Act of 1965 suspended literacy and other voter tests and authorized federal supervision of registration in states and individual voting districts where tests had been used and where fewer than half of voting-age residents were registered or had voted. The Justice Department suspended literacy tests in 7 states (7 Aug.).

10 Aug. Omnibus Housing Act established new programs of rent supplements to low-income families and authorized federal funds to place low-income individuals into private housing.

9 Sept. Department of Housing and Urban Development (HUD) was established, absorbing functions and programs of Housing and Home Finance Agency (HHFA), and administering and coordinating federal programs. Robert C. Weaver was chosen first Secretary of HUD.

29 Sept. National Foundation of the Arts and Humanities established to provide financial assistance for painters, actors, dancers, musicians, and others in the arts.

2 Oct. Water Quality Act of 1965 (p. 640).

3 Oct. Immigration Laws were revised (p. 658), setting annual quotas of 120,000 for immigrants from the Western Hemisphere with no national quotas, and 170,000 from the rest of the world with a maximum of 20,000 from any one nation.

20 Oct. Air Quality Act amendments of 1965 (p. 641).

20 Oct. Higher Education Act provided the first federal scholarships to college undergraduates and other assistance. Other legislation passed during the session included a reduction of excise taxes by $4.7 billion over a 4-year period (21 June).

1965–66 RACIAL DEMONSTRATIONS. Rev. Martin Luther King, Jr., led a 5-day, 54-mile march from Selma to Montgomery, Ala. (21–25 March 1965). Stokely Carmichael, chairman of Student Non-Violent Coordinating Committee (SNCC), popularized "Black Power" as a slogan (14 May 1966); the slogan endorsed at the Congress of Racial Equality (CORE) National Convention (4 July) but rejected at the NAACP Convention (4–9 July). Dr. King's first Southern Christian Leadership Conference drive in the North was launched in Chicago (29 July 1966) for open housing. After violent opposition from lower-class whites, an agreement to end de facto housing segregation was reached with civic leaders and Mayor Richard J. Daley (26 Aug.).

1965–68. URBAN RACIAL RIOTING. Racial violence occurred in the "ghettoes" of almost all the nation's large cities. Among those affected were Los Angeles (11–16 Aug. 1965), where riots in the Watts area took 28 Negro lives and $200 million damages; Chicago (12–15 July 1966); Newark (12–17 July 1967); Detroit (23–30 July 1967), where 40 persons died, 2,000 were injured, and 5,000 left homeless by rioting, looting, and burning until 4,700 paratroopers dispatched by the president arrived. The **assassination of Martin Luther King, Jr.,** set off a wave of riots (4–11 April 1968) in 125 cities in 29 states.

"Poor People's Campaign" for reforms in welfare, employment, and housing policies, led in Washington, D.C. (29

Apr.–23 June 1968) by Dr. King's successor, **Dr. Ralph Abernathy,** as head of Southern Christian Leadership Conference. The president's 11-member National Advisory Commission on Civil Disorders headed by Gov. Otto Kerner (Ill.) stated, in a 1,400-page report on the 1967 riots (released 29 Feb. 1968) that: (1) the U.S. is "moving" toward separate and unequal societies, black and white, but it is possible to head off the division; (2) white racism is the chief cause of Negro violence and riots; (3) to reverse the situation calls for unprecedented levels of funding and performance.

1965–68. VIETNAM WAR DISSENT (p. 501).

1966

3 MAR. VETERANS EDUCATIONAL BENEFITS granted for all who served 180 days on active duty after 1955. Veterans pensions and educational allowances increased, 1967.

9 SEPT. NATIONAL TRAFFIC AND MOTOR VEHICLE SAFETY ACT required federal establishment of safety standards on all vehicles from 1968 model year and on used cars within 2 years, as well as federal standards for tires. The **Highway Safety Act,** enacted the same day, required each state to set up federally approved highway safety programs by 31 Dec. 1968 or face the loss of 10% of federal-aid construction funds. Impetus for the legislation came from the efforts of **Ralph Nader** (p. 1112).

23 SEPT. MINIMUM WAGE was raised for 30 million workers already covered from $1.25/hour to $1.40, effective 1 Feb. 1967, and to $1.60 effective 1 Feb. 1968. Coverage was extended to 9.1 additional workers in retail stores, restaurants, and hotels, as well as one third of nation's 1.2 million farm workers, and some service workers. Their minimum wage was to become $1 (1967) and rise to $1.60/hour by 1971 except for the farm workers ($1.30 by 1971).

15 OCT. DEPARTMENT OF TRANSPORTATION was created, including federal agencies dealing with air, rail, and highway transportation but not Maritime Administration nor the Corps of Engineers nor urban mass transit. The independent regulatory bureaus were left with their rate-making and regulatory functions. Alan S. Boyd was confirmed as first secretary 12 Jan. 1967; department began operation 1 Apr. 1967.

3 Nov. CLEAN WATER RESTORATION ACT OF 1966. (p. 640).

3 Nov. MODEL CITIES. Demonstration Cities and Metropolitan Area Redevelopment Act encouraged rehabilitation of slums, financed metropolitan area planning, provided land-development mortgage insurance over a 3-year period: 63 "model" or demonstration cities were chosen by HUD to draw up plans for the program (16 Nov. 1967).

8 Nov. CONGRESSIONAL ELECTIONS. The Republican party gained 3 Senate and 47 House seats, enabling a revived conservative coalition to slow down the Johnson legislative program in Congress. Republicans also won 8 additional governorships. **Black voting** increased from 28.6% of the 5 million persons of voting age in the South to 47.5% as registrations rose from 687,000 to 1,150,000 after the 1965 Voting Rights Act.

1967

10 FEB. 25TH AMENDMENT ratified, providing procedures for presidental succession and disability. Amendment had been proposed by Congress 6 July 1965.

17 OCT. UNIFIED BUDGET recommended by Presidential Commission on the Federal Budget to replace existing multiplicity of budgets, including administrative, consolidated cash, and national income accounts budget. The Unified Budget, which was adopted by President Johnson for the remaining years of his term, included in addition to previous items, transactions of federally administered trust funds, an accrual account system, and government loan operations.

7 Nov. PUBLIC BROADCASTING CORPORATION established to provide financial assistance for noncommercial educational TV and radio broadcasting.

1968

1 Apr. OPEN HOUSING LAW to prohibit discrimination in the sale or rental of 80% of all housing when fully in effect; not applicable to privately owned homes sold without the services of a real-estate agent. Act also included provisions making it a crime to cross interstate lines with intent to incite or take part in riot.

23–30 Apr. COLUMBIA UNIVERSITY student demonstrations paralyzed the campus. Student demonstrations occurred in May in many other institutions.

29 May. TRUTH-IN-LENDING ACT required disclosure to consumer of information about credit transactions in terms of the annual rate calculated under specified procedures.

19 June. OMNIBUS CRIME CONTROL AND SAFE STREETS ACT established Law Enforcement Assistance Administration (LEAA) in the Justice Department to administer program of grants to states to be spent for upgrading law-enforcement and criminal-justice operations. $100 million was authorized for fiscal 1969 and $300 million for fiscal 1970. In addition the act (1) permitted broad wiretapping by all levels of government while banning private wiretapping or electronic eavesdropping; (2) attempted to overturn by legislation Supreme Court decisions in *Mallory* v. *U.S.* (1957), *Miranda* v. *Ariz.* (p. 681), and *U.S.* v. *Wade* (p. 685) by providing that a confession would not be inadmissible solely because of a delay no more than 6 hours after arrest in bringing defendant before commissioner, nor because he was not informed of his constitutional rights, nor would testimony of eyewitness at lineup be inadmissible because defendant was denied counsel.

26 June. FORTAS NOMINATION. President Johnson nominated Justice Abe Fortas (26 June) as Chief Justice after Earl Warren had informed Johnson of his intention to retire, contingent upon the qualifications of a successor. Circuit Court of Appeals Judge Homer Thornberry was nominated to fill the Fortas vacancy. The Fortas nomination was withdrawn (4 Oct.) by the president at his request after the Senate refused to invoke cloture (45 for, 43 against; 59 votes needed) to end a filibuster.

28 June. TAX SURCHARGE of 10% on personal and corporate income taxes enacted.

1 Aug. HOUSING. A $5.3-billion, 3-year program designed to provide more than 1.7 million units of new and rehabilitated housing for low-income families including federal subsidies to help the poor buy their houses and rent apartments.

2 Oct. CONSERVATION measures included (1) scenic rivers bill to preserve stretches of wild and scenic rivers in their natural state; (2) law establishing a national system of trails; (3) the 58,000-acre Redwood National Park; and (4) the 1.2-million-acre North Cascades National Park.

PRESIDENTIAL CAMPAIGN. Following the unexpected success of antiwar candidate Sen. Eugene F. McCarthy (Minn.) in the New Hampshire primary

(12 Mar.) where he polled 42% of the vote against 48% for the yet unannounced candidate Johnson, Sen. Robert F. Kennedy (N.Y., p. 1075) also a major critic of U.S. involvement in Vietnam, announced his candidacy (16 Mar.). President Lyndon B. Johnson declared in a TV address: "I shall not seek, and I will not accept, the nomination of my party for another term as President" (31 Mar.). Vice-President Hubert H. Humphrey entered the race (27 Apr.). Sen. Kennedy was assassinated (5 June), the night of his victory in the California primary. His death (6 June) cast a shadow over the election year. Humphrey easily won renomination at the Democratic National Convention in Chicago (26–29 Aug.) after Sen. Edward M. Kennedy (Mass.), the brother of John F. and Robert F. Kennedy, refused to seek the nomination. The convention was marred by dramatic clashes between police and peace demonstrators in the streets of Chicago. Sen. Edmund S. Muskie (Me.) was nominated for vice-president.

Richard M. Nixon and Gov. Spiro T. Agnew (Md.) were nominated by the Republican Convention in Miami (8 Aug.). George C. Wallace and Gen. Curtis E. LeMay were the candidates of the American Independent Party.

5 Nov. PRESIDENTIAL ELECTION. In a dramatically close election, **Richard M. Nixon** was elected president with 302 electoral votes (1 elector later voted for George C. Wallace) and 31,785,480 (43.4%) votes to 191 electoral votes and 31,275,166 (42.7%) for Humphrey, and 45 (later 46) and 9,906,473 (13.5%) for Wallace.

Minor-party candidates: Hennings Blomen (Socialist-Labor), 52,588; Dick Gregory (New) 47,097; Fred Halstead (Socialist Worker), 41,300; Eldridge Cleaver (Peace and Freedom), 36,385; E. Harold Munn, Sr. (Prohibition), 14,-519; Charlene Mitchell (Communist and

Free Ballot), 1,075. The antiwar New Party placed Sen. Eugene McCarthy on the ballot in some states without his consent, receiving 25,858 votes, and received 1,480 votes in 3 states where no candidate was listed.

The Democrats maintained control of the Congress, 243–192 in the House, 58–42 in the Senate (later 57–43 due to a death). The Republicans gained a net of 5 governorships to dominate 31 of 50 statehouses (later 30, due to the resignation of Spiro Agnew as governor).

1969

17 JAN. Presidential salary increased to $200,000 annually; travel allowance of $40,000 (untaxable) and official allowance of $50,000 (taxable) remained. Vice-president's salary raised to $62,500, 7 Aug. Presidential retirement allowance increased from $25,000 to $60,000 and widow's pension from $10,000 to $20,000 (1970).

20 JAN. NIXON'S INAUGURAL ADDRESS stated that Americans "cannot learn from one another until we stop shouting at one another" and announced that the government "will strive to listen in new ways."

18 FEB. HOUSE COMMITTEE ON UN-AMERICAN ACTIVITIES changed to House Committee on Internal Security with mandate modified to authorize committee to investigate groups seeking to overthrow or change the form of the federal government by violence or obstruct the execution of internal security laws.

3 JULY. CIVIL RIGHTS POLICIES. Statement by Attorney General John N. Mitchell and Secretary of HEW, Robert H. Finch, on school desegregation guidelines insisted that dual school systems must end by Sept. unless "bona fide educational and administrative problems warrant delay." HEW and Department

of Justice argued in court (19 Aug.) that HEW-approved desegregation plans should be withdrawn and desegregation delayed. While Nixon administration efforts to secure compliance switched from lawsuits to HEW fund cutoffs, attorneys in the Civil Rights Division of the Department of Justice drafted protests against decision to delay desegregation in 33 Mississippi counties (26 Aug.). U.S. Supreme Court ordered end to all school segregation at once (29 Oct.; *Alexander* v. *Holmes Co.*, p. 682). Leon E. Panetta, chief of Civil Rights Office of HEW, strong advocate of desegregation, resigned because of political pressures (17 Feb. 1970) triggering letter to the president from over 100 members of the office expressing disappointment, as well as a memorandum from 1,800 members of the staffs of HEW offices to Secretary Robert H. Finch asking for an explanation of HEW's civil rights policy.

HAYNSWORTH-CARSWELL NOMINATIONS. Justice Abe Fortas resigned (14 May) after disclosure that he had accepted and belatedly returned installment on lifetime retainer from family foundation of convicted stock manipulator. Warren Burger, judge of the U.S. Court of Appeals for the D.C. Circuit (1956–69), nominated to succeed retiring Chief Justice Earl Warren, was confirmed by vote of 74–3 (9 June). The nomination of Clement Haynsworth, chief judge of the U.S. Court of Appeals for the 4th Circuit, to succeed Fortas was defeated 55–45 (21 Nov.) by the Senate, after debate over Haynsworth's sensitivity to the appearance of ethical improprieties, following disclosures that he had participated in cases where he held stock interests. A second Nixon nomination, G. Harrold Carswell, judge of the U.S. Court of Appeals for the 5th Circuit, was defeated 51–45 (8 Apr.

1970) after a debate over his racial views and intellectual caliber. Harry A. Blackmun, judge of the U.S. Court of Appeals for the 8th Circuit, was confirmed unanimously by the Senate (12 May 1970).

20 July. MOON LANDING (p. 803). Cost of civilian space program through 1969—$24.6 billion.

3 Nov. PRESS ATTACKS by Nixon administration gained wide attention with Des Moines, Iowa, speech of vice-president Spiro T. Agnew deploring the power of a "small band of network commentators." Agnew attacked the *New York Times* and *Washington Post* at Montgomery, Ala., 20 Nov. Later pressures on press encompassed federal and state subpoenas requiring reporters to testify before grand juries to disclose sources for stories about criminal activities, upheld by Supreme Court in *Branzburg* v. *Hayes* (p. 684); *Pentagon Papers* litigation (p. 537, 541, 684); and FBI investigation of CBS correspondent Daniel Schorr (1971).

4 Nov. Defense Department dismissed A. Ernest Fitzgerald, deputy for management systems in Office of Assistant Secretary of the Air Force, for disclosure of cost overruns on C-5A by Lockheed Aircraft (13 Nov. 1968). On 1 Aug. 1971 federal government guaranteed up to $250 million in bank loans for Lockheed Aircraft Corp., apparently near bankruptcy. Fitzgerald was reinstated in 1973.

1970

1 Jan. NATIONAL ENVIRONMENTAL POLICY ACT OF 1969 (NEPA) made the protection of the environment a national commitment (p. 642).

Jan. MILITARY SURVEILLANCE of civilian political activity during late 1960s described in *Washington Monthly* article by former Army Intelligence Capt.

Christopher H. Pyle. Hearings of Sub-committee on Constitutional Rights of Senate Judiciary Committee (Feb.–Mar. 1971) further explored army intelligence program which army announced had been abandoned.

3 Apr. WATER QUALITY IM-PROVEMENT ACT OF 1970 (p. 640).

May. CAMBODIA-KENT-STATE DISSENT (p. 502).

1 July. WHITE HOUSE REORGA-NIZATION PLAN created Office of Management and Budget, absorbing existing Bureau of the Budget (p. 392), with authority to oversee and evaluate all federal programs in 12 cabinet departments. A Domestic Council was created to evaluate and tie together interagency planning with presidential adviser John R. Ehrlichman chosen as executive director.

CRIMINAL LAWS recommended by Nixon administration enacted during 1970 included (1) **Organized Crime Control Act of 1970** providing for immunity for witnesses for use of testimony, special grand juries to investigate organized criminal activities, and limited disclosure of electronic surveillance evidence; (2) **District of Columbia Court Reorganization and Criminal Procedure Act of 1970** (29 July) modernizing the D.C. court system, and depriving the liberal U.S. Court of Appeals for the D.C. Circuit of jurisdiction over local criminal cases, as well as providing for stiff law-enforcement measures such as selective preventive detention, no-knock search and arrest warrants, and elimination of jury trials for juveniles; (3) **Omnibus Crime Control Act of 1970,** authorizing $3.55 billion federal aid to state and local law-enforcement agencies over a 3-year period: (4) **Drug Abuse Prevention and Control Act of 1970** unifying and revising federal narcotics laws, and providing expanded programs of rehabilitation.

12 Aug. POSTAL REFORM. Postal Reorganization Act replaced Post Office Department with an independent governmental agency and removed the Postmaster General from the cabinet.

5 Oct. URBAN MASS TRANSIT grants and loans up to $3.1 billion approved.

26 Oct. LEGISLATIVE REORGA-NIZATION ACT provided for public recording of roll-call votes in congressional committees and House committee of the whole, as well as liberalization of committee procedures.

3 Nov. CONGRESSIONAL ELEC-TIONS. Republicans suffered net loss, losing 9 House seats and 11 governorships (giving Democrats control of 29) but picking up 2 Senate seats. Basic compaign strategy of Republicans was to appeal to "silent majority" of "middle America" on issues such as the Vietnam War ("peace with honor") and "law and order." Vice-President Agnew's attacks on "radical-liberals" and vigorous rhetoric ("nattering nabobs of negativism") and tough presidential address of 2 Nov., were apparently answered effectively by televised reply for Democrats of Sen. Edmund Muskie (Me.).

25 Nov. Secretary of the Interior Walter J. Hickel was fired by President Nixon because "essentials of confidence" did not exist. Nixon and Hickel differed on approaches to the environment and the young.

30 Nov. AGRICULTURE ACT OF 1970 (p. 695).

29 Dec. OCCUPATIONAL SAFETY AND HEALTH ACT mandated that employers shall provide employment "free from recognized hazards to employees," provided for federal establishment and enforcement of safety and health standards for the protection of workers.

31 Dec. 1970 CLEAN AIR ACT (p. 641).

1971

22 JAN. NEW AMERICAN REVO-LUTION called for by President Nixon in State of the Union Address asking Congress to enact legislation to secure 5 of 6 great goals: (1) welfare reform, (2) environmental initiatives, (3) health insurance reform, (4) revenue sharing, (5) government reorganization. The 6th goal was full prosperity in peacetime.

1 MAR. Bomb exploded in restroom of Capitol, 30 minutes after a telephone warning in which the action was proclaimed a protest against U.S. involvement in Laos (p. 503), causing $200,000 damage.

23 MAR. D.C. NONVOTING CONGRESSIONAL DELEGATE, Walter E. Fauntroy, first since 1875 elected by citizens of Washington.

24 MAR. SST PROGRAM DEFEATED. The Senate by vote of 51–46 eliminated funding for 1,800 mph supersonic transport plane following a similar vote (18 Mar.) by the House.

1 MAY. AMTRAK began service (p. 618).

1 JULY. PENTAGON PAPERS, classified history of the policy decisions which led to U.S. involvement in Vietnam commissioned by Secretary of Defense Robert S. McNamara (1967), were first published in *New York Times.* Injunctions by Justice Department sought against *New York Times* (15 June), *Washington Post,* and other newspapers denied by U.S. Supreme Court 30 June (p. 684). Daniel Ellsberg, former Defense Department aide, was indicted (28 June) for theft of government property and violation of the espionage act in leaking classified documents (also p. 541).

30 JUNE. 26TH AMENDMENT. After the Supreme Court declared unconstitutional (21 Dec. 1970, *Oregon* v. *Mitchell,* p. 683) a section of the **Voting Rights Extension Act** (22 June 1970), which lowered the voting age to 18 in state and local as well as federal elections, Congress proposed 26th Amendment (23 Mar. 1971) lowering franchise to 18 in all elections. The court had early upheld the voting act as applicable to presidential and congressional elections. The amendment was quickly ratified. In addition, the **Voting Rights Extension Act** extended the **Voting Rights Act of 1965** and prohibited literacy tests as a qualification for voting, established uniform residence requirements for voting in presidential elections, and applied the act to Northern cities or counties where literacy tests had previously been required.

11 JUNE. PHASE 1 of Nixon Economic Policy (p. 752).

21 SEPT. SELECTIVE SERVICE extended draft for 2 years and increased military pay and benefits, a step toward all-volunteer army. The draft, based upon the **Universal Military Training and Service Act of 1951** had previously been extended in 1955, 1959, 1963, and 1967. With the expiration of the Act (30 June 1973), the armed forces were on an all-volunteer basis for the 1st time since 1948.

10 DEC. REVENUE ACT OF 1971 (p. 737).

12 DEC. DEVALUATION OF DOLLAR (p. 711).

1972

22 MAR. WOMEN'S RIGHTS AMENDMENT proposed by Congress and sent to states, providing "Equality of rights under the law shall not be denied or abridged by the United States or by any state on account of sex."

7 APR. FEDERAL ELECTION CAMPAIGN ACT effective. Signed 7 Feb., the act repealed the **Corrupt Practices Act of 1925** and limited the amount a candidate or his family could contribute to his own campaign. In addition, the act limited to 10 cts. per voter the amount that could be spent by candidates for Congress and the presidency for media advertising, strengthened the requirements for reporting of campaign receipts and expenditures, including names and addresses of all persons who made contributions or loans in excess of $100.

17 June. WATERGATE BREAK-IN (p. 539).

17 Oct. SUPPLEMENTAL SECURITY INCOME program established by 1972 Social Security Act Amendments replacing existing federal-state programs of assistance to the aged, blind, and disabled with a program fully financed and administered by the federal government, effective 1 Jan. 1974. Social security benefits continued to increase but so did the social security tax and the wage base for the tax.

18 Oct. FEDERAL WATER POLLUTION ACT, enacted into law as Congress overrode President Nixon's veto (p. 640).

20 Oct. REVENUE SHARING, a 5-year program to distribute $30,236,-400,000 of federal tax revenues to state and local governments as supplements to their own revenues, to use generally as they saw fit.

PRESIDENTIAL CAMPAIGN. Operating under reforms in delegate selection processes and convention procedures made by the Commission on Party Structure and Delegate Selection, headed first by Sen. **George McGovern** (1922–   ), the Democratic party held more primaries accounting for more convention votes than hitherto. Primaries were generally not "winner-take-all." Among other reforms were the opening of the delegate selection process to all enrolled party members, and the proportionate representation of minorities, women, and young persons.

Basing his campaign for the nomination primarily upon opposition to the Vietnam War, Sen. McGovern (S.D.) did unexpectedly well in primaries and profited by the new convention guidelines. **McGovern** captured the Democratic presidential nomination on the 1st ballot at the Democratic National Convention, Miami Beach, Fla. (10–13 July). The Democratic platform called for immediate withdrawl from Indochina, abolition of the draft, amnesty for war resisters, and guaranteed income above the poverty line.

Sen. **Thomas F. Eagleton** (Mo.), chosen by McGovern and the convention for the vice-presidential nomination, withdrew from the ticket (31 July) at McGovern's request after discovery by reporters that he had been hospitalized 3 times for psychiatric disorders. Nomination of **R. Sargent Shriver** (Md.), former director of the Peace Corps, apparently McGovern's 7th choice, was agreed to at a special meeting of the Democratic National Committee (8 Aug.).

The Republican National Convention, also meeting in Miami Beach (21–23 Aug.), renominated **Richard M. Nixon** and **Spiro T. Agnew.** The Republican platform supported presidential foreign policies, welfare reform, revenue sharing, governmental reorganization, national health insurance, and opposed amnesty for war resisters and the busing of children to correct racial imbalance in schools.

The American Independent Party nominated John G. Schmitz (Calif.) for president after potential nominee Gov. George C. Wallace, paralyzed as a result of gunshot wounds inflicted by Arthur Bremer at a political rally in Laurel, Md. (15 May), withdrew from the Presidential race after an impressive showing in Northern primaries.

Minor-party candidates included Benjamin Spock (People's Party), Earl H.

Munn (Prohibition), John Hospers (Libertarian), Louis Fisher (Socialist Labor), Linda Jenness (Evelyn Reed in some states) (Socialist Worker), Gus Hall (Communist).

Campaign was marked by a minimum of personal appearances by Nixon, who relied instead upon heavy expenditures, estimated at well over $50 million, and upon "surrogate campaigners," including cabinet officials. McGovern, whose campaign was poorly organized, assailed the Nixon regime as "the most corrupt administration in history," but failed to lure the president into debating the issue.

7 Nov. PRESIDENTIAL ELECTION. Nixon, 47,169,911 (60.8%); McGovern, 29,170,383 (37.5%).

Minor-party candidates: Schmitz (American), 1,099,482; Spock (People's), 78,-756; Munn (Prohibition), 13,505; Hall (Communist), 25,595; Fisher (Socialist Labor), 53,814; Jenness or Reed (Socialist Workers), 66,677.

Electoral vote: **Nixon,** 520 (49 states), McGovern, 17 (Mass., D.C.); 1 elector in Virginia voted for John Hospers (Calif.) and Theodora Nathan (Ore.). The Republicans, however, made a net gain of only 13 seats in the House, losing 2 Senate seats and one governorship.

1973

PRESIDENTIAL IMPOUNDMENTS. After Congress denied President Nixon's request for a $250 billion ceiling in fiscal 1973 outlays, Nixon impounded $12 billion in funds for the Department of Transportation ($2.9 billion, largely for highway construction), the Department of Defense ($1.9 billion), Agriculture Department (food stamp, REA loans), and other federal programs. In 1973–74 federal courts almost uniformly ruled that the actions were illegal; Congress est. procedures (12 July 1974) to override impounding.

12 Feb. DEVALUATION OF DOLLAR (p. 711).

10 Aug. AGRICULTURAL ACT ended farm subsidy system, setting target prices for wheat, feed grain, cotton. If farmers' average sales price fell below target, government to pay difference.

10 Oct. RESIGNATION OF SPIRO AGNEW as vice-president was followed within hours by his pleading *nolo contendere* to a single charge of federal income-tax evasion. As part of the plea bargain, publication of grand-jury criminal information against Agnew cited acceptance of payoffs from construction company executives while governor of Maryland and vice-president. Under the procedures of the 25th Amendment President Nixon nominated House Minority Leader Gerald R. Ford to succeed Agnew, 12 Oct. Senate confirmed Ford 27 Nov. by a vote of 92–3, and House of Representatives on 6 Dec., 387–5. Ford took oath of office the same day.

7 Nov. WAR POWERS ACT veto overridden by Congress. Act set 60-day limit on presidential commitment of troops to hostilities abroad or into situations where hostilities appeared imminent, unless Congress authorized continued action; 30 days more are permissible for safe withdrawal of troops.

1974

8 Apr. MINIMUM WAGE raised from $1.60 per hour to $2.00, effective 1 May 1974; to $2.10, effective 1 Jan. 1975; and to $2.30, effective 1 Jan. 1976. Minimum wages for farm workers were raised from $1.30 per hour to $2.30, effective 1 Jan. 1978. Coverage was extended to seven million more workers—state and local government employees and domestic workers. The Supreme Court held in 1976 that Congress could not under the commerce clause constitutionally determine the wages and hours of state employees. *National League of Cities* v. *Usery* (426 U.S. 833). (See also p. 557.)

9 Aug. NIXON RESIGNATION (pp. MINISTRATION created to fix gas allotments and develop import-export policies to deal with fuel shortages.

12 July. BUDGET REFORM. Congressional Budget and Impoundment Act of 1974 provided Congress with greater control over federal spending and programs, tightening legislative oversight. It permitted Congress to look at the budget as a whole and make decisions on budgeting priorities and fiscal power. The Act created (1) House and Senate Budget Committees to formulate

overall spending and tax goals; (2) Congressional Budget Office to provide technical information; (3) a series of deadlines for congressional action; (4) procedures to override impounding. The start of the fiscal year was shifted from 1 July to 1 Oct., beginning 1 Oct. 1976 (fiscal 1977).

25 July. LEGAL SERVICES program of Office of Economic Opportunity (OEO) transferred to independent Legal Services Corporation, run by eleven-member board of directors, to provide legal assistance for the poor in non-criminal proceedings.

9 Aug. NIXON RESIGNATION (pp. 543–544).

Watergate Chronology, 1972–75

17 June 1972. WATERGATE BREAK-IN. On the eve of the '72 presidential campaign the first glimmer of what would prove an unprecedented series of scandals reaching into the White House occurred when 5 men were apprehended in the act of burglarizing the offices of the Democratic National Committee located in Watergate, an apartment-hotel complex in Washington, D.C. Links between the accused and E. Howard Hunt, Jr., White House consultant (revealed 19 June), and G. Gordon Liddy, counsel to the Committee to Reelect the President (CRP, disclosed 22 July), coupled with evidence that the accused carried money traceable to CRP's finance committee, implied a tie-in between the burglary and the president's reelection campaign (1 Aug.).

19 June. EARLY WHITE HOUSE DENIALS. Press Secretary Ronald L. Ziegler referred to the break-in as a "third-rate burglary." President Nixon stated (29 Aug.) that no one in the administration was involved and that "tech-

nical violations" of the election law had occurred on both sides. Ex-Attorney General John N. Mitchell resigned as campaign chairman (1 July), citing family problems.

June–July. COVERUP. Early attempts at covering up the burglary included (1) destruction of documents in offices of H. R. Haldeman, White House Chief of Staff; (2) emptying Hunt's White House safe; (3) pressures on FBI to limit investigation to avoid compromising the CIA; (4) money raised to support burglary defendants (indicted 15 Sept.); (5) perjury before grand jury committed by Jeb Stuart Magruder, deputy director of CRP.

29 Sept. WASHINGTON POST reporters Bob Woodward and Carl Bernstein reported that John Mitchell, while attorney general, had personally controlled a secret fund to finance intelligence operations against Democrats. Woodward and Bernstein revealed (10 Oct.) that a secret fund had financed spying and sabotaging of Democratic primary campaigns encompassing such activities as (1) forgery of correspondence, (2) false leaks to the press, and (3) seizure of confidential campaign files. President Nixon's appointments secretary, Dwight L. Chapin, was accused of hiring Donald H. Segretti, who recruited agents. Ziegler accused the *Washington Post* of "character assassination" and of "the shoddiest kind of journalism."

8–30 JAN. 1973. TRIAL OF WATERGATE 7. Although Attorney General Richard G. Kleindienst indicated (28 Aug.) that the investigation would be the "most extensive, thorough and comprehensive since the assassination of President Kennedy," only the original 7 men stood trial. At the trial, **Judge John J. Sirica** (1904–   ), chief judge of the U.S. District Court for the District of Columbia, expressed dissatisfaction with the questioning of the prosecution and personally interrogated defense witnesses in order to get to the bottom of the scandal. Five defendants pleaded guilty and 2 were convicted by a jury. At sentencing (23 Mar.) Sirica read a letter from James W. McCord, a defendant and former security coordinator of CRP, charging that others had been involved, that defendants had been pressured to plead guilty, and that perjury had been committed at the trial.

28 FEB. GRAY CONFIRMATION HEARINGS before Senate Judiciary Committee. L. Patrick Gray, acting director of the FBI, nominee for director, produced FBI recordings indicating that John Dean, the president's counsel, had sat in on all FBI interviews and received FBI files, evidence suggesting a coverup by White House aides. Dean claimed executive privilege and refused to testify. Gray asked president (5 Apr.) to withdraw his nomination and resigned 27 April.

30 APR. HALDEMAN-EHRLICHMAN RESIGNATIONS. After the president announced (17 Apr.) that he had begun extensive new inquiries on 21 March, Ziegler indicated that all previous White House statements were "inoperative." The president announced (30 Apr.) the resignations of Haldeman, Ehrlichman (his adviser on domestic affairs), and Kleindienst, praising all 3 men, while dismissing Dean. In a later statement (22 May), Nixon conceded a White House coverup, but pleaded innocent of planning or knowledge thereof.

11 MAY. ELLSBERG CHARGES DISMISSED by Federal Judge W. Matthew Byrne, Jr. (Calif.) after receiving information that there had been a wiretap from late 1969 to early 1970 on Ellsberg's telephone, and that the government could not find the tape transcripts. Ellsberg and Anthony J. Russo were charged with espionage, theft, and conspiracy in connection with the Pentagon Papers (p. 537). It had been previously reported (27 Apr.) that Hunt and Liddy had burglarized the files of Ellsberg's former psychiatrist (3 Sept. 1971) with some assistance from the CIA. On 30 Apr. it was reported that Ehrlichman had met with Judge Byrne at the Western White House, San Clemente (5 Apr.), and again in Santa Monica (7 Apr), to inform him that he was being considered for the post of director of the FBI.

17 MAY–7 AUG.; 24 SEPT.–15 NOV. ERVIN COMMITTEE HEARINGS. By a vote of 70–0 (7 Feb.) the Senate established a 7-man Select Committee on Presidential Campaign Activities with Sen. **Sam J. Ervin, Jr.** of North Carolina (1896–   ) as chairman, and Prof. Samuel Dash as chief counsel. Televised public hearings brought the Watergate scandal high public visibility. Among the most significant testimony: (1) Magruder confessed to having committed perjury before the grand jury (14 June) and implicated Mitchell in planning the burglary; (2) Dean (25–29 June) asserted that the president had been party to the coverup for 8 months, implicated the president in offers of executive clemency to the burglary defendants and Haldeman and Ehrlichman in the coverup; he revealed the existence of a White House "Enemies List" of politicians, journalists, academicians, entertainers, and others, for potential harassment, including audits by the IRS, as well as information about the "Plumbers," a special White House program of wiretaps and other activities under a Special Investigations Unit, begun originally to plug press leaks; (3) Mitchell's statement (10–12 July) that "White House horrors" encompassed an attempt to forge State Department cables to implicate President John F. Kennedy in the assassination of Ngo Dinh Diem and therefore to besmirch his brother, Sen. Edward M. Kennedy; (4) Alexander Butterfield, former deputy presidential assistant, disclosed (16 July) that Nixon had tape-recorded all his conversations in the White House and Executive Office Building; (5) Herbert W. Kalmbach, formerly Nixon's personal attorney, admitted (16 July) to having raised $220,000 for the defendants; (6) Ehrlichman asserted (24–30 July) that the Ellsberg psychiatrist's burglary had been within the constitutional powers of the president.

APR.–OCT. COX INVESTIGATIONS. After Kleindienst resigned, **Elliot L. Richardson** was appointed attorney general (30 Apr.) and Prof. **Archibald Cox** (1912–) special prosecutor (18 May). Butterfield's revelations prompted Nixon to assert executive privilege and to refuse to release the tapes to either Cox (23 July) or to the Ervin Committee (17 July). Both then served subpoenas upon the president 23 July. Judge Sirica ordered Nixon to turn over the tapes to him (29 Aug.) (p. 543). After Sirica's decision was upheld by the U.S. Court of Appeals for the District of Columbia Circuit (12 Oct.), the president decided not to appeal to the Supreme Court.

Nixon offered a "compromise," written summaries of tapes whose accuracy would be verified by Sen. John C. Stennis (Miss.), but with Cox enjoined to seek no further presidential documents through the judicial process.

20 OCT. "SATURDAY NIGHT MASSACRE." After Cox turned down the compromise, Nixon ordered both Attorney General Richardson and William D. Ruckelshaus, deputy attorney general, to dismiss him. Both refused and resigned. Solicitor General Robert H. Bork, becoming acting attorney general, then fired Cox, and FBI agents sealed off the offices of Richardson, Ruckelshaus, and the special prosecutor. Adverse public reaction led (1) the president to agree (23 Oct.) to obey Sirica's order for the tapes; (2) to the introduction of 16 impeachment resolutions in the House of Representatives, sponsored by 84 representatives; (3) to the appointment of Sen. William Saxbe (Ohio) as attorney general (1 Nov.), and **Leon Jaworski** (1905–), Houston attorney, as special prosecutor (1 Nov.). Of 9 tapes included in Sirica's order, 2 were asserted by the White House (31 Oct.) never to have existed, and an 18-minute gap appeared on a third (26 Nov.). Court-appointed experts later found the gap to be the result of multiple manual erasures (4 June 1974).

RELATED WATERGATE "SCANDALS" included (1) **ITT,** suggesting a possible presidential involvement in settlement of an antitrust suit in 1971 favorable to International Telephone and Telegraph Corp., which later pledged to defer the cost of the Republican National Convention; (2) **campaign contributions** by major corporations made under CRP pressure; (3) **Milk Fund,** suggesting a connection between the president's decision to approve higher milk price supports (Mar. 1971) and a pledge from the dairy industry of large campaign contributions; (4) **Hughes gifts**—whether the president knew about large and secret gifts of cash, allegedly campaign donations (1969–70), from Howard Hughes, financier, to Charles G. "Bebe" Rebozo, the president's close friend; (5) **San Clemente—Key Biscayne**—whether the method by which the president bought his 2 estates was improper and whether he had profited illegally from government expenditures of above $10 million to secure the grounds; (6) **president's taxes** —whether the president committed fraud in the preparation of his 1969–72 tax returns; the Joint Committee on Internal Revenue Taxation of the Congress, reviewing the president's taxes at his request, reported (3 Apr. 1974) that he owed $476,531 in back taxes and interest, which the president announced he would pay. The report drew no conclusions as to fraud; (7) **Vesco case**—John Mitchell and Maurice H. Stans, the latter former Secretary of Commerce and finance chairman of CRP, were found innocent (28 Apr. 1974) after jury trial of conspiracy in soliciting a gift of $200,000 to the president's campaign fund from financier Robert Vesco in exchange for interceding with the SEC on his behalf. Stans and Mitchell were aslo acquitted of perjury and obstruction of justice.

IMPEACHMENT PROCEEDINGS. Impeachment resolutions were turned over to the House Judiciary Committee, which began preliminary investigations, 30 Oct. 1973, by granting broad subpoena power to the chairman, **Peter Rodino** (N.J.; 1909–   ). Closed hearings, directed by staff counsel John Doar commenced 9 May 1974. Although the president refused to comply with a committee subpoena for tapes (4 Apr.), the president released 1,200 pages of edited transcripts of 42 taped conversations (30 Apr.). Judge Sirica turned over to the Judiciary Committee, 26 Mar., the sealed grand jury report (1 Mar.), apparently citing the president as a co-conspirator in the Watergate coverup.

1974. UNITED STATES v. RICHARD M. NIXON (418 U.S. 683). Special Prosecutor Leon Jaworski subpoenaed tape recordings and other data involving 64 conversations of the president and his aides for use in the Watergate coverup trial of 6 former White House aides. The president refused to turn over the recordings, citing the doctrine of executive privilege. In the district court Judge John J. Sirica ordered the president to turn over the tapes. The Supreme Court heard appeals from Judge Sirica's decision on an expedited procedure bypassing the Court of Appeals. On 24 July 1974, the Supreme Court held unanimously in an opinion written by Chief Justice Burger (1) that Jaworski had standing to bring the action against his nominal superior; (2) that while certain conversations in the White House were undoubtedly privileged, especially where military and national security issues were involved, the president must surrender evidence for use in a criminal proceeding; (3) the Supreme Court rather than the president is the final judge of the Constitution (citing **Marbury v. Madison**). The court took no action on the president's request to expunge the grand jury citation of R. M. Nixon as a co-conspirator in the Watergate coverup.

NIXON RESIGNATON. After televised debate, the House Judiciary Committee voted 3 articles of impeachment. On 27 July the committee voted 27–11 to recommend impeachment of Nixon on the ground that he "engaged personally and through his subordinates and agents in a course of conduct designed to delay, impede, and obstruct the investigation" of the Watergate break-in; "to cover up, conceal, and protect those responsible"; and to "conceal the existence and scope of other unlawful covert activities." A second article passed (29 July) by a vote of 28–10 charging Nixon with a persistent effort to abuse his authority in violation of his constitutional oath. The president was accused of engaging in conduct "violating the constitutional rights of citizens, impairing the due and proper administration of justice in the conduct of lawful inquiries of contravening the law governing agencies of the executive branch and the purposes of these agencies." The committee passed (30 July) 21–17 a third article charging the president with unconstitutional defiance of committee subpoenas, thus impeding the impeachment process. That day the committee voted down by 26–12 articles accusing Nixon of usurping congressional war powers by the secret bombing of Cambodia and of demeaning his office by misconduct of personal financial affairs. Nixon released (5 Aug) the transcript of 3 tapes of 23 June 1972 which revealed that he had been aware of a "coverup" long before 21 Mar. 1973, and that he personally had ordered a halt to the FBI investigation. Most of Nixon's remaining defenders in the Congress, including all 11 Republicans who had voted against the first article of impeachment, considered this the "smoking gun," evidence sufficient to support the first article. Nixon announced his resignation 8 Aug., stating that he "no longer had a strong enough political base" to persevere. The resignation took effect 11:35 A.M. on 9 Aug. when delivered to Secretary of State Kissinger.

9 AUG. FORD ACCESSION. Ford took the oath of office from Chief Justice Warren E. Burger at 12:03 P.M. in a ceremony in the East Room of the White House and delivered "not an inaugural address, not a fireside chat, not a campaign speech" but "just a little straight talk among friends." Ford nominated **Nelson A. Rockefeller** (p. 1139) to be vice-president on 20 Aug.

20 AUG. HOUSE OF REPRESENTATIVES votes 412–3 to accept final report of impeachment inquiry.

8 SEPT. NIXON PARDON. Ford gave Nixon an unconditional pardon for all federal crimes that he committed or may have committed or taken part in. Nixon did not confess guilt but in a statement admitted to "mistakes." A concurrent agreement recognized Nixon's title to the tape recordings and ultimate right to destroy them but preserved them for a 3-year period for use in court. The pardon and agreement on the tapes were widely criticized. By statute, Congress placed the tapes and Nixon administration papers in the custody and control of the federal government, requiring explicit congressional authorization for destruction of any materials. President Ford testified personally (17 Oct.) before the House Judiciary Subcommittee on Criminal Justice, "There was no deal, period."

19 DEC. NIXON TAPES and papers placed in custody and control of federal government with procedures for public access to some items in future. The Presidential Recordings and Materials Preservation Act was upheld by the Supreme Court in *Nixon* v. *Administrator, General Services Administration* (433 U.S. 425), 1977. By a vote of 5–4 the Supreme Court denied claim of broadcasting and recording companies to copy and broadcast or market the tapes. *Nixon* v. *Warner Communications* (453 U.S. 589), 1978.

1 JAN.–17 APR. 1975. CONVICTION OF NIXON AIDES. Haldeman, Ehrlichman, Mitchell and former Assistant Attorney General Robert Mardian were convicted on all counts and Kenneth W. Parkinson, former lawyer for CRP, acquitted after a 64-day jury trial. Mitchell, Haldeman, and Ehrlichman were convicted of conspiracy, obstruction of justice, and perjury; Mardian of the conspiracy to obstruct justice in the original investigation of the Watergate break-in. Haldeman, Ehrlichman, and Mitchell were sentenced to 2½ to 8 years in prison by Judge Sirica (21 Feb.) and Mardian to 10 months to 3 years. Ehrlichman had previously been convicted (12 July 1974) with G. Gordon Liddy, Bernard Barker, and Eugenio Martinez, of conspiring to violate the civil rights of Daniel Ellsberg's former psychiatrist, Lewis J. Fielding, and of making false statements to the FBI and grand juries. The Supreme Court refused to review the convictions of Ehrlichman, Haldeman and Mitchell (23 May 1977). Mardian's conviction had been previously reversed by the Court of Appeals.

In a separate case, former Secretary of Commerce Maurice Stans was fined $5,000 after having pleaded guilty to 5 misdemeanor violations of federal campaign laws, including 2 counts of "non-willful acceptance" of illegal corporate campaign contributions. Four members of the Nixon cabinet were sentenced for crimes: Mitchell, Stans, Attorney General Richard G. Kleindienst, and Agriculture Secretary Earl L. Butz. Secretary of the Treasury John B. Connally, Jr., was acquitted of bribery charges.

1976. 8 JULY. Nixon disbarred from practicing law in New York State.

1977. 12 APR. Liddy's jail term commuted by President Carter from 20 to 8 years. Liddy paroled (7 Sept.), having been in prison since 30 Jan. 1973.

1978. 4 Nov. By law most papers of outgoing Presidents were made public property, except for personal and private political records; effective with Reagan administration.

1979. 19 JULY. John Mitchell, the last Watergate prisoner, was freed. 25 men had served terms ranging from 25 days to 52½ months.

Domestic Policy: The Ford Years, 1974–77

1974

21 AUG. ELEMENTARY AND SECONDARY SCHOOL ACT amendments authorized $25.8 billion through the 1978 fiscal year; increased funding for programs for the handicapped; prohibited court-ordered busing beyond a student's second nearest school unless constitutional rights of minority group children were being violated; encouraged bilingual, multicultural education. In *Lau* v. *Nichols* (414 U.S. 563), 1974, the Supreme Court held that, under the 1964 Civil Rights Act, school officials must provide non-English-speaking students with language skills through remedial English instruction, bilingual classes, or some other method. The **Elementary and Secondary School Act** was extended for five years (1 Nov. 1978).

2 SEPT. PENSION REFORMS. Employee Retirement Income Security Act (ERISA) set minimum federal standards for private pension plans, permitting individuals not covered to set up individual retirement accounts qualifying for special tax treatment.

11 OCT. ENERGY RESEARCH AND DEVELOPMENT ADMINISTRATION (ERDA) established, taking over nuclear development functions from Atomic Energy Commission (abolished) and energy research programs from the National Science Foundation, Department of the Interior, and Environmental Protection Agency.

15 OCT. CAMPAIGN FINANCE LAW built upon 1971 laws permitting taxpayer to contribute to a general public campaign fund for presidential elections, setting ceiling in media advertising, and requiring full disclosure of campaign contributions and expenditures. The 1974 law established (1) spending limits of $10 million per candidate for presidential primaries and $20 million per candidate in presidential general elections; (2) spending limits on senatorial primaries of the greater of $100,000 or eight cents per eligible voter, and in senatorial general elections of the greater of $150,000 or twelve cents per eligible voter; (3) spending limits of $70,000 for primaries for Representatives and $70,000 in House general elections. The law also (4) provided for voluntary public financing of presidential general elections and presidential primaries from federal income tax dollar check-offs (first established 10 Dec. 1971); (5) required strict disclosure of sources and uses of campaign money; (6) set spending limits of contributions of $1,000 per individual for each election; (7) created an eight-member, fulltime, bi-partisan Federal Elections Commission.

In *Buckley* v. *Valeo* (424 U.S. 1), 31 Jan. 1978, the Supreme Court invalidated on First Amendment grounds the limits on what a candidate for federal office could spend unless public financing was accepted; struck down the limits an individual candidate could spend of his own money; upheld the system of public financing and the requirements for public disclosure of campaign contributors; held unconstitutional the manner in which the Federal Elections Commission was set up.

Congress reconstituted the Commission (11 May 1976) as a six-member panel appointed by the President and confirmed by the Senate; set up new contribution limits; restricted the proliferation of political action committees and the Commission's investigatory powers; provided for one house veto of Commission regulations.

16 OCT. RAILROAD RETIREMENT SYSTEM bailed out over President Ford's veto by governmental assistance of $285 million annually until year 2000.

23 OCT. COMMODITY EXCHANGES regulated by establishment of independent **Commodity Futures Trading Commission.**

26 OCT. NO-KNOCK SEARCHES provided by **D.C. Court Reorganization Act** and **Drug Abuse Prevention Act** (p. 536) repealed by Congress.

5 Nov. CONGRESSIONAL ELECTIONS. Republicans lost heavily in a campaign dominated by Watergate and concern about economic decline. Democrats gained 43 seats in the House, three in the Senate and four new governorships, leaving the Republicans with 13. 40 House incumbents were defeated; 92 new Representatives were elected.

21 Nov. FREEDOM OF INFORMATION ACT OF 1974, passed over President Ford's veto, liberalized the 1966 Freedom of Information Act by (1) mandating deadlines for agency responses to requests for documents and (2) placing the burden of justifying classification of information upon the government. The **Freedom of Information Act** (FOI) of 4 July 1966 required federal government agencies to make available to citizens upon request documents and records, with certain exceptions, among them secret national security information, trade secrets, and law enforcement investigatory information.

26 Nov. MASS TRANSIT aid of $11.9 billion voted for construction and capital improvements, as well as for day-to-day operations. Highway Trust Fund was opened for mass transit projects by **Federal Aid Highway Act of 1973.**

6–8 DEC. Democratic Party holds first non-presidential party convention in Kansas City, Mo., adopting first major party charter, requiring affirmative action "in all party affairs" to involve women, blacks, Indians and young voters "as indicated by their presence in Democratic electorate."

21 Dec. ANTITRUST LAWS: (1) Antitrust Procedures and Penalties Act increased penalties for violating the anti-trust laws while placing constraints upon the use of consent decrees; (2) placed restrictions upon President's authority to grant antitrust immunity to voluntary agreements entered into by industrial competitors under national defense or preparedness situations (Act of 16 Dec. 1975); (3) **Parens Patriae Act** of 30 Sept. 1976 gave state attorneys general the right to sue companies which violated antitrust laws for damage on behalf of citizens of state harmed by those violations; required large companies to notify the government of planned mergers; strengthened federal antitrust investigatory powers. In *Illinois Brick* v. *Illinois* (431 U.S. 720), 1977, the Supreme Court held that only the first purchaser—not others in the chain of distribution—could sue under price-fixing laws, even if financial damages were shown.

31 Dec. PRIVACY ACT of 1974 permitted individuals to inspect information about themselves contained in federal agency files.

1974. SHICK v. REED (419 U.S. 256) upheld discretion of President in exercising power of pardon.

1974. FORD ECONOMIC POLICY. Ford's presidency began with high inflation rate and slowly rising rate of unemployment, a slowdown in real economic output, a large trade deficit, and a stock market which fell 28% (1974). Ford moved to bolster confidence in the economy by holding "domestic summit" conferences, consisting of regional meetings of economists, representatives of business, labor, agriculture, consumers and other groups, as well as a meeting in Washington (27–28 Sept.), which produced little consensus. Ford announced (8 Oct.) his WIN (Whip Inflation Now) Program of (1) tax and spending assistance to hard-pressed industries; (2) a five percent tax surcharge; (3) voluntary efforts to hold down energy consumption; (4) tight monetary policy; (5) reduced federal spending.

During 1974 unemployment grew from 5% (May) to 7.2% (Dec.); consumer prices rose 12.2%. Residential construction fell as the cost of borrowing money was high—12%. Due to energy concerns, price increases, and general economic uncertainty, automobile sales collapsed, with large-scale layoffs. Economy had a negative growth of minus 2% (1974); real economic growth, minus 5%.

1974–76. ACCESS TO COURTS cases. Supreme Court rulings tending to discourage use of federal courts: (1) *Stone* v. *Powell* (428 U.S. 465), 1976, holding that federal courts are not required to grant habeas corpus relief on grounds that illegally seized evidence was used in state trial; (2) *Eisen* v. *Carlisle and Jacquelin* (417 U.S. 156), 1974, holding that persons initiating a federal class action suit must notify at their expense all other persons in that class; (3) *U.S.* v. *Reservists Committee to Stop the War* (418 U.S. 208), 1974, holding that taxpayers do not have standing to bring a federal suit challenging the CIA budget; (4) *Paul* v. *Davis* (424 U.S. 693), 1976, holding that a person whose reputation is damaged by police action must sue for defamation in state courts rather than under the Civil Rights Act of 1871; (5) *Alyeska Pipeline Service Co.* v. *The Wilderness Society* (421 U.S. 240), 1975, holding that federal judges do not have the authority, unless expressly authorized by Congress, to order the losing side in a case to pay the other party's attorneys' fees; (6) *Rizzo* v. *Goode* (424 U.S. 362), 1976, holding that a federal judge acted improperly by ordering city officials to formulate and implement a plan for better handling of citizen complaints of police misconduct.

1974–78. IMMUNITY CASES. The

Supreme Court broadened the liability of government officials for their conduct in office: (1) *Scheuer* v. *Rhodes* (416 U.S. 233), 1974, holding that state officials are not shielded by the Eleventh Amendment from civil rights damage suits; (2) *Wood* v. *Strickland* (420 U.S. 308), 1975, holding that school officials are not immune from civil rights damage suits brought by students; (3) *Monnell* v. *Department of Social Services* (436 U.S. 658), 1978, holding that cities and city agencies are not exempt from civil rights damage suits; (4) *Butz* v. *Economou* (438 U.S. 478), 1978, holding that federal officials are not absolutely immune from citizen damage suits.

1974–80. SPACE FLIGHT. Major American unmanned flights: (1) Pioneer 11 (launched 5 Apr. 1973) flies within 26,000 miles of Jupiter (Dec. 1974); discovers 11th moon and two more rings of Saturn (6 Sept. 1979); (2) Viking 1 (launched 20 Aug. 1975) lands on Mars (26 July 1976); (3) Viking 2 (launched 9 Sept. 1975) settles on edge of Mars' polar ice cap (3 Sept. 1976); found no trace of life in over three years; (4) Voyager 1 (launched 5 Sept. 1977) discovers Jupiter's 15th and 16th moons (5 Mar. 1979); during Saturn flyby (12 Nov. 1980) discovers three moons and reports that planet is surrounded by a thousand rings; (5) Voyager 2 (launched 20 Aug. 1977) flew by Jupiter (9 July 1979) en route to Saturn, Uranus, and Neptune; (6) Pioneer Venus 2 (launched 8 Aug. 1978) carrying probes landing on Venus (9 Dec. 1978), reporting surface temperature of 900°F.

1974–80. GENETIC RESEARCH AND GENETIC RESEARCH REGULATION. Rapid advances were made in mapping human genes. By 21 Aug. 1975, 100 genes had been mapped, among them interferon, one of body's major defenses against virus infection. First completely synthetic fully functional bacterial gene created and then implanted in a living bacterial cell by MIT scientists led by Har Gobind Khorana (27 Aug. 1976). Scientists at City of Hope National Medical Center and Genentech Inc. announced creation of a synthetic gene for use in making human insulin. For NOBEL PRIZES for work in area of genetics, see p. 817.

Scientists' concern about genetic research, especially research on E [Escherichia] coli, dangerous as common intestinal bacterium (which is one of the most studied), led to a voluntary moratorium recommended by a National Academy of Science committee (1974) on certain forms of recombinant DNA research, and then to guidelines published 23 June 1976 by Recombinant Advisory Committee of the National Institutes of Health. Cambridge, Mass. became the first city to regulate recombinant DNA research (Feb. 1977).

1974–80. NOBEL PRIZES IN CHEMISTRY: 1974, Paul J. Flory for development of plastics; **1976, William N. Lipscomb, Jr.,** for fundamental discoveries about how molecules are held together working with boranes (compounds of boron and hydrogen); **1979; Herbert C. Brown** and **George Wittig** (of Germany) for their independent work in organic synthesis. For 1980 prize see p. 818.

1975–80. NOBEL PRIZES IN PHYSICS: 1975, James Rainwater (along with Aage N. Bohr and Ben Roy Mottelson of Denmark) for discovery of connection between collective motion and particle motion in atomic nuclei and the development of the theory of the structure of the atomic nuclei based on this connection; **1976, Burton C. Richter** and **Samuel C. C. Ting** for discovery of subatomic particle named psi or j; **1977, John H. Van Vleck, Philip W. Anderson** (and Sir Nevill F. Mott of Great Britain) for contributions to understanding of electrons in magnetic, non-crystalline materials; **1978, Arno A. Penzias** and **Robert W. Wilson** (with Pyotr Kapitsa of USSR) for discovery of faint electro-magnetic radiation permeating universe, which supported big bang theory of creation of universe; **1979, Steven Weinberg, Sheldon L. Glashow** (with Aldus Sulam of Pakistan) for independent work toward discovery of unified field theory; **1980, Val Fitch** and **James Cronin** for disproving the laws of symmetry by experiments with K_2 mesons.

1975–80. NOBEL PRIZES IN ECONOMICS. American winners: **1975, Tjalling Koopmans** (with Soviet economist, Leonid Kantovich) for contributions to theory of optimum allocation of resources; **1976, Milton Friedman** for achievements in the fields of consumption analysis, monetary history, and stabilization policy; **1978, Herbert A. Simon,** for theories on structure and decision-making with economic organizations; **1979, Theodore W. Schultz** (with British economist Sir Arthur Lewis) for work in developing-country economic problems; **1980, Laurence R. Klein** for research dealing with the construction and analysis of empirical models of business fluctuation.

1977–81. DEATH PENALTY AS A NATIONAL ISSUE. After *Furman* v. *Georgia* (p. 685), 35 states passed new death penalty statutes. Ten chose to make death the mandatory punishment for certain crimes; 25 chose a two-stage process—a trial determining guilt or innocence followed by a proceeding hearing evidence on whether to impose the death sentence. In 1974 the Congress made hijacking an airplane punishable by death under some circumstances.

In *Gregg* v. *Georgia* (428 U.S. 153), 1976, the Court refused to declare the death penalty unconstitutional in all circumstances, but held that it must be imposed fairly, not arbitrarily. The Georgia two-step procedure was upheld. The Court by a 5–4 vote struck down state laws making death the mandatory penalty for first-degree murder. *Woodson* v.

North Carolina (428 U.S. 280), 1978. Imposition of the death penalty for rape was held to be forbidden by 8th Amendment. *Coker* v. *Georgia* (433 U.S. 583), 1977. On 17 Jan. 1977 Gary M. Gilmore was executed in Utah, the first execution in U.S. in almost 10 years. As of 20 Oct. 1981, there were 891 prisoners on death row awaiting determination of this issue.

1973–81. THE ABORTION ISSUE. *Roe* v. *Wade* (413 U.S. 113), 1973 struck down state abortion laws as a violation of the right to privacy, grounded in 14th Amendment due process guarantee of personal liberty which protected a woman's decision as to whether or not to terminate her pregnancy. According to Justice Blackmun's opinion, government interference with abortion was unconstitutional during the first 3 months of pregnancy; during the next 3 months the state may regulate to the extent that bears reasonable relation to protection of maternal health; in the last 3 months the state could bar abortions. *Roe* v. *Wade* and liberalized state laws (pp. 817, 818) sparked a counter-movement led by the Moral Majority to amend the Constitution to ban abortions. By Nov. 1981 sides were lining up for and against the amendment proposal of Senator Orrin G. Hatch (R., Utah) to take the abortion issue away from the courts and give Congress and the states the right to make laws in that area. Cardinal Terence Cooke of New York, chairman of "pro-life" activities for the National Conference of Catholic Bishops, announced his support (6 Nov.), as did its president, Archbishop John Roach of Minneapolis. Spokesmen for Catholics for a Free Choice and the American Jewish Congress came out in opposition. Meantime Senators Jesse Helms (R., N.C.) and John P. East (R., N.C.) favored a bill on the Senate calendar that would define human life as beginning at conception.

1973. COMMITTEE FOR PUBLIC EDUCATION v. NYQUIST (413 U.S.

756) struck down reimbursement of tuition and tuition tax credits for parochial schools.

1973–77. SCHOOL DESEGREGATION DECISIONS. In *Keyes* v. *School District #1, Denver* (413 U.S. 189), 1973, the 1st case decided by the Supreme Court where there was school segregation which had not been imposed by law, the burden of proof was placed on school board to demonstrate that the schools were not intentionally segregated. By a 5–4 vote, the Court struck down a district court order attempting to equalize the racial composition of Detroit's public schools, by ordering the busing of black children to the suburbs, in absence of evidence that the suburban districts had intentionally segregated. *Milliken* v. *Bradley* (418 U.S. 717), 1974. In the 2d *Milliken* case, the district judge's new remedy of comprehensive counseling and guidance programs in the city schools (50% to be paid for by the state) was held to be an appropriate remedy. *Milliken* v. *Bradley* (433 U.S. 267), 1977.

1975

3 Jan. SPEEDY TRIAL ACT required defendants to be brought to trial within 100 days by 1 July 1980 after a phase-in period with tighter deadlines. On 2 Aug. 1979 Congress delayed implementation until 1 July 1981.

Jan. HOUSE INTERNAL SECURITY COMMITTEE, successor to **House Un-American Activities Committee** (p. 424) was abolished.

7 Mar. FILIBUSTER rule modified by Senate to permit sixty Senators (⅗ of membership) to invoke cloture except for debate on changes in Senate rules, which would continue to require a ⅔ vote. Cloture was successfully invoked fourteen times (8 Mar. 1975–23 Sept. 1976) and three times (1977–79). By Senate

action (22 Feb. 1979), final vote on a bill must occur within 100 hours of debate after cloture has been invoked.

29 Mar. TAX REDUCTION ACT provided $18.1 billion individual tax cuts through 10% rebate on 1974 taxes and other provisions; business tax cuts of $4.8 billion; 22% oil and gas depletion allowance was largely eliminated, although small producers were exempted. $1.9 billion countercyclical spending provided through Social Security bonus payments and additional 13 weeks of emergency unemployment benefits to jobless workers in nine states. Tax cuts were kept in effect beyond end of year.

4 June. SECURITIES LAWS revised to encourage development by Securities and Exchange Commission of integrated national system for buying and selling stocks.

17 June. MICRONESIA STATUS. Referendum in Northern Marianas resulted in 78.8% approval for commonwealth status. President Ford signed covenant (24 Mar. 1976) giving the Northern Marianas commonwealth status, control of domestic affairs, while U.S. retained control of foreign relations, defense, and the right to have military bases. President Carter approved **Constitution of Northern Marianas** (24 Oct. 1977). After elections governor and bicameral legislature took office (9 Jan. 1978).

U.S. negotiated arrangements for free association, permitting full self-government, with U.S. responsible for defense —separately with (1) the Marshall Islands; (2) Palau; (3) the Federated States of Micronesia (composed of Truk, Yap, Ponopae, and Kosrae).

21 July. SEX DISCRIMINATION. HEW regulations, based upon Title IX of the Education Amendments of 1972, barring discrimination in admissions, classes, financial aid, employment, and athletics by schools and universities receiving federal aid went into effect.

Private undergraduate single-sex schools were permitted to maintain their policies, while expenditures for sports did not have to be equal.

6 Aug. VOTING RIGHTS ACT OF 1965 (pp. 531, 537) extended for seven years and expanded to cover persons of Spanish heritage, American Indians, Asian-Americans, and Alaskan natives. Bilingual elections were mandated under some circumstances. Nationwide ban on literacy tests was made permanent.

5 Sept. ASSASSINATION ATTEMPT on life of President Ford. Lynette ("Squeaky") Fromme, age 26, pointed automatic pistol at Ford while he was shaking hands in Sacramento.

10 Sept. EDUCATIONAL FUNDING of $7.9 billion for all federal educational programs (fiscal 1976–77) passed over President Ford's veto.

22 Sept. SECOND ASSASSINATION ATTEMPT on life of President Ford. Sara Jane Moore, age 45, fired a shot at Ford as he was leaving St. Francis Hotel in San Francisco. Bystanders deflected the weapon and Ford was not hit.

1 Oct. Pay increase of 5% for members of Congress, top-level federal employees, and federal judges took effect.

16 Oct. COPYRIGHT LAW REVISION (first complete revision since 1909) extended copyright protection from maximum of 56 years to life of author plus 50 years; protected all unpublished and most published work of foreign origin; imposed copyright liability upon public broadcasters, cable TV systems, and jukebox operators; limited copying of protected works by schools and libraries; defined "fair use" —the free use of copyrighted material for certain purposes.

10 Nov. CONRAIL, federally subsidized corporation, established to rejuvenate northeast railroad companies; took over operation of Penn Central and 6 other bankrupt carriers. On 5 Feb. 1976 $6.4 billion was authorized by Congress for modernization and revitalization of railroads, of which $2.1 billion were loans for Conrail and $1.85 billion were loans to improve passenger service within Northeast Corridor. Interstate Commerce Commission regulation of railroads was eased.

29 Nov. RIGHTS OF HANDICAPPED. By law Congress required that by 1 Sept. 1980 states would provide free and adequate education to all handicapped children; 20% of extra cost was to be paid by federal government. 50% of 7.9 million handicapped children were receiving adequate education; 1.75 million were receiving no education at all (1974). The act required that, where appropriate, handicapped children be educated with non-handicapped children. On 17 June 1977 $1.1 billion was authorized for education of handicapped children. Congress expanded aid to the handicapped for jobs and research to $5 billion (6 Nov. 1978).

9 Dec. NEW YORK CITY BANKRUPTCY AVERTED by federal loans up to $2.3 billion. On 8 Aug. 1978 Congress authorized $1.65 billion in federal loan guarantees, including guarantees up to 15 years. Congress also passed the first major change in municipal bankruptcy legislation (8 April 1976), providing that cities could file for bankruptcy without approval of creditors, while continuing to borrow to maintain essential services.

22 Dec. ENERGY POLICY AND CONSERVATION ACT OF 1975 expanded authority of Federal Energy Administration to order major power plants to switch to coal; increased presidential authority to control flow of energy supplies and energy related materials; provided for creation of 1 billion barrel national strategic petroleum reserve; required that average fuel economy for cars manufactured or imported in any model year after 1977 be 18 mpg (1978), rising to 27.5 mpg (1985).

Dependence upon foreign sources of energy persisted despite Ford administration program to cut consumption and stimulate domestic production by higher fuel prices. By end of 1976 consumption was at 1973 levels; domestic production had decreased one million barrels per day to 8.2 million barrels; importation of foreign oil had increased one million barrels per day; and the percentage of imported oil from Arab nations had risen. Price of oil rose from $3.27 per bbl. (1973) to $13.40 per bbl.

1975. U.S. v. MAINE et al. (420 U.S. 515) upheld the federal government's exclusive rights to the continental shelf beyond the 3-mile limit along the Atlantic coast, denying the validity of the claims of 11 Atlantic states resting on colonial charters, and holding that the **Submerged Lands Act of 1953** "embraced" the paramount rights of the federal government.

1975. DECLINE OF BIRTH AND DEATH RATES to record lows: 14.8 deaths per 1,000 births; 8.9 deaths for every thousand Americans. Deaths by heart attacks, strokes, and traffic accidents declined; deaths by cancer, suicide, and murder increased.

1975–78. COMMERCIAL FREE SPEECH CASES. In *Bigelow* v. *Virginia* (421 U.S. 809), 1975, the Supreme Court held that an editor may not be punished for publishing a truthful, non-deceptive advertisement. The Court also held unconstitutional: (1) Virginia law preventing advertisements of prescription drugs, *Virginia State Board of Pharmacy* v. *Virginia Citizens Consumer Council* (425 U.S. 738), 1976; (2) ban on lawyer advertising, *Bates* v. *Arizona State Bar* (433 U.S. 350), 1977; (3) law forbidding corporations from spending money to influence votes in a referendum, *First National Bank of Boston* v. *Bellotti* (435 U.S. 765), 1978.

1975–78. ANTITRUST DECISIONS

OF SUPREME COURT: (1) lawyers are not exempt from federal antitrust laws; minimum fee schedules constitute price-fixing in violation of antitrust laws, *Goldfarb* v. *Virginia State Bar* (421 U.S. 273), 1975; (2) a local hospital is covered by federal antitrust laws because its business sufficiently affected interstate commerce, *Hospital Building Co.* v. *Trustees of Rex Hospital* (425 U.S. 738), 1976; (3) *Illinois Brick* v. *Illinois* (p. 547); (4) foreign governments may sue for treble damages for antitrust violations under the Clayton Act, *Pfizer Inc.* v. *Government of India* (434 U.S. 308), 1978; (5) cities are not exempt from federal antitrust suits, *City of Lafayette* v. *Louisiana Power and Light Co.* (435 U.S. 389), 1978.

1976

19 May. INTELLIGENCE ABUSES. Permanent Select Committee on Intelligence to monitor CIA, FBI, and other agencies established by Senate. Investigations by committees of both Houses of Congress included revelation of burglaries; FBI campaign to discredit Martin Luther King (p. 1076); 25-year harassment of dissident groups; political use of FBI back to Franklin D. Roosevelt administration.

After the death of J. Edgar Hoover (p. 1060), L. Patrick Gray served as Acting Director (May 1972–April 1973) until his nomination was withdrawn during confirmation hearings, which exposed link to Watergate (p. 540). William D. Ruckelshaus served as Acting Director until the appointment of Clarence Kelley (27 June 1973). On 15 Oct. 1976 the director of the FBI was by law limited to one ten-year term. Judge William H. Webster (1924–) of Missouri was named Director 19 Jan. 1978 and launched program to end past abuses and prevent new ones.

29 MAY. SUPERSONIC COMMER-CIAL AIR SERVICE began with 3 hr. 35 min. flight by Anglo-French Concorde from London to Dulles Airport, Washington. Concorde flights to JFK Airport, New York City, were delayed by litigation until 22 Nov. 1977.

4 JULY. BICENTENNIAL celebrated throughout U.S. President Ford spoke at ceremony at Independence Hall, Philadelphia, and joined est. 6 million observing **Operation Sail**, flotilla of hundreds of sailing boats, New York harbor, with 16 tall ships from all over the world.

24 JULY. ABORTION. House of Representatives passed by vote of 207–164 amendment introduced by Rep. Henry J. Hyde (Rep., Ill.) barring use of Medicaid funds to pay for abortions. Senate-House compromise outlawed federal funding for abortions except where continued pregnancy would endanger life of mother. 1973 Supreme Court decision, *Roe* v. *Wade* (p. 817), which held unconstitutional virtually all state abortion laws, led to sharp increase in legal abortions while triggering emotional national debate between "pro-choice" and "right-to-life" groups. The Supreme Court held 2 July 1976 that state could not constitutionally require consent of husband or parent prior to abortion in first trimester of pregnancy. *Planned Parenthood of Central Missouri* v. *Danforth* (428 U.S. 52).

On 9 Dec. 1977 Congress prohibited use of funds for abortions except in cases of rape or incest; unless pregnancy would endanger the life of the mother; or in the opinion of two doctors continued pregnancy would cause "severe and long lasting physical health damage." The growing strength of the right-to-life movement was demonstrated in 1979 when riders barring abortion were attached to six appropriation and two authorization bills. Riders provided that federal funding for abortions could only occur if there was rape or incest

promptly reported or where the mother's life was endangered.

In *Maher* v. *Doe* (432 U.S. 464), 1977, the Supreme Court held that, under the U.S. Constitution or the Medicaid Program, states were not required to fund elective abortions. In *Harris* v. *McRae* (100 S.Ct. 2671), 1980, the Court upheld the constitutionality of the Hyde Amendment by 5–4 vote.

26 JULY. COASTAL ZONE MAN-AGEMENT ACT amendments authorized $1.2 billion program of federal aid to coastal states to assist them in dealing with social, economic, and environmental effects of offshore gas and oil development. $150 million was authorized (17 Oct. 1980) over 5-year period to assist cities adversely affected by energy development and to revitalize urban waterfronts. The **Coastal Zone Management Act of 1972** (27 Oct.) had provided grants to set up coastal management programs to weigh conflicting demands on the shoreline, protect choice scenic areas and estuaries, and arrest loss of marine resources.

14 SEPT. NATIONAL EMERGENCY ACT provided for congressional review of national emergencies declared by the President, continuing oversight, and termination of four states of emergency dating back to 1933.

4 OCT. TAX REVISION restricted tax shelters, made first major changes in gift and estate taxation in 30 years, revised capital gains, and increased minimum tax on wealth to 15%. Congress, against President Ford's wishes, acted to stimulate the economy through public works program and countercyclical aid to state and local governments. Unemployment compensation extended to 8.5 million additional workers—state and local government employees and domestic workers (20 Oct.). Congress continued 1975 tax cuts.

1976. ECONOMIC SLOWDOWN: Inflation—5%; unemployment—7.3% (May),

8% (Nov.); gross national product grew 6.1%; prime rate (monthly average), 6.84%.

13 OCT. REVENUE SHARING program extended through fiscal 1980.

PRESIDENTIAL CAMPAIGN. By winning the Iowa caucuses (19 Jan.) and sweeping a string of early Democratic primaries (24 Feb.–27 Apr.), **Jimmy Carter** eliminated six other candidates including Sen. Henry M. Jackson and Gov. George C. Wallace. Carter demonstrated strength among Southerners, farmers, urban blacks, and blue-collar workers. Sen. Hubert Humphrey's decision not to run for President removed possibility of coalition forming to block Carter. Sen. Frank Church of Idaho and California's Gov. Edmund G. Brown, Jr., defeated Carter in later primaries, but Carter continued to accumulate delegates under proportional representation voting. Carter clinched nomination with a victory in Ohio's primary (8 June).

The Democratic National Convention was held in unaccustomed harmony in New York City. **Carter** was nominated on the first ballot (15 July) over Rep. Morris Udall (Ariz.) and Gov. Brown, and chose **Sen. Walter F. Mondale** (Minn.) to be his running mate. The platform, drafted after 13 public hearings with 500 witnesses, called for full employment, tax reform, and comprehensive national health insurance with universal and mandatory coverage.

President **Gerald Ford** won the early Republican primaries (24 Feb.–16 Mar.) but Ronald Reagan gained ground with a series of important victories in the South and Southwest. Reagan lost support with uncommitted delegates by announcing that Sen. Richard S. Schweiker (Pa.) would be his running mate. At the Republican National Convention in Kansas City, Mo., **Ford** was nominated on the first ballot (18 Aug.) by a vote of 1,187 to 1,070. As Nelson Rockefeller withdrew (Nov. 1975), **Sen. Robert Dole** (Kan.) was chosen by Ford as his running mate.

The Republican platform condemned inflation, deficit spending, and bureaucratic over-regulation, while emphasizing concern for family values. The platform indirectly criticized Ford and Secretary of State Kissinger for losing public confidence and making secret international agreements.

Carter's large lead after the Democratic Convention dissipated during his campaign as an outsider who would make government more responsive and efficient. Ford contended that he had restored public confidence in government and thwarted a free-spending Democratic Congress. Three TV debates between the presidential candidates were held (23 Sept., 6 Oct., 22 Oct.), and one between the vice-presidential candidates (15 Oct.). Each presidential candidate was limited to expenditure of $21.8 million during the campaign paid for by public funds.

2 Nov. PRESIDENTIAL ELECTION. Carter was elected President in a very close election with 297 electoral votes and 40,829,056 (50.1%) votes to Ford's 240 electoral votes and 39,146,006 (48%) popular vote. One state of Washington elector gave his vote to Reagan.

Minor party candidates: Eugene McCarthy (Independent), 756,631; Roger MacBride (Libertarian), 173,019; Lester G. Maddox (American Independent), 170,531; Thomas Anderson (American), 160,773; Peter Camejo (Socialist Worker), 91,310; Gus Hall (Communist), 58,992.

The Democrats retained control of the Congress, holding their 62–38 margin in the Senate and gaining one seat in the House of Representatives, which they controlled 292–143. Democrats won 9 of 14 governorships, holding a total of 37 state houses, to 12 Republican and one Independent. Democrats controlled both houses of the state legislature in

36 states; Republicans controlled both houses in but five states.

16 Dec. SWINE FLU inoculation campaign suspended. Discovery of influenza in Fort Dix, N.J. (Feb. 1976) led to $135 million campaign to inoculate entire population to ward off pandemic like that of World War I (p. 812). Moratorium was declared after suspected link to paralytic illness, Guillain-Barré syndrome. In fact, only a few isolated cases of swine flu were reported. The U.S. government accepted liability for vaccine-related illnesses.

1976. *Michelin Tire Corp.* v. *Wages* (423 U.S. 276). In a unanimous decision the Supreme Court held that the export-import clause of the Constitution did not bar states from imposing a property tax on imported goods stored prior to sale, so long as the tax does not discriminate against imported goods. Court overruled *Low* v. *Austin* (13 Wallace 29), 1872.

1976–77. HOUSING DISCRIMINATION CASES. The Supreme Court held that where public housing officials contributed to racial segregation in housing, federal courts had the power to order a remedy which included the metropolitan area. *Hills* v. *Gautreaux* (425 U.S. 284), 1976. The Court also held that a suburb could refuse to rezone land for low and moderate income persons, unless there was a showing that the decision was racially motivated. *Village of Arlington Heights* v. *Metropolitan Housing Development Corp.* (429 U.S. 252), 1977.

1977

4 Jan. House rules changes, adopted at recommendation of Democratic caucus, enhanced power of Speaker, increased committee privileges and powers, restricted quorum calls, and doubled the number of days House could deal with bills under suspension of the rules procedures.

Domestic Policy: The Carter Years, 1977–81

1977

20 Jan. CARTER INAUGURAL characterized by lack of formality. President Jimmy Carter and wife, Rosalynn Smith Carter, walked down Pennsylvania Avenue from the Capitol to the White House after inaugural ceremony.

2 Feb. EMERGENCY NATURAL GAS ACT, enacted within week of President Carter's request, gave President authority to order transfers of interstate natural gas to areas hard hit by severe winter, as well as authority (until 31 July) to approve sales of gas to interstate buyers at unregulated prices.

4 Feb. Senate committee system revised, limiting each Senator to a total of three committees (two major and eight subcommittees). The number of Senate committees was to be reduced from 31 to 23 by end of 95th Congress.

20 Feb. Pay raises for Vice President (from $65,000 to $75,000), Congressmen (from $44,600 to $57,500), federal judges, and top executive branch officials took effect.

10 Mar. MAJOR U.S. ASTRONOMICAL DISCOVERIES include discovery of rings around Uranus by Cornell University team; discovery of "miniplanet" circling Sun between Saturn and Uranus by Charles Kowal, Hale Observatories (Nov. 1977); establishment of existence of Charon, moon of Pluto, by James W. Christy, U.S. Naval Observatory.

6 Apr. GOVERNMENT REORGANIZATION. Reorganization Act of 1949, which expired April 1973, after having been extended seven times and lapsed four times, was reestablished, giving President authority to submit government reorganization plans for three years, subject to one house veto within 60 days.

11 Apr. SACCHARIN BAN. Food and Drug Administration (FDA), acting under 1958 Delaney Clause of **Food, Drug and Cosmetic Act,** banned saccharin in diet soft drinks, toothpaste, and other products, because of tests which demonstrated saccharin caused cancer in laboratory rats. Congress voted to delay ban 18 months, pending new studies.

18 Apr. CARTER ENERGY PROGRAM. President Carter proposed a broad energy program to prevent waste and damage from interruptions in overseas supplies. To cut consumption by taxing it, Carter proposed: (1) relaxing controls on price of domestic oil; (2) taxing domestic oil at the wellhead, but rebating that tax to some consumers; (3) retaining federal price control over natural gas interstate while obtaining new controls over intrastate gas; (4) tying the price of new natural gas to that of domestic crude oil; (5) ending price controls on gasoline; (6) a five cent per gallon tax per year starting in 1979 and increasing until reaching 50 cents per gallon; (7) a tax penalty on many cars for failing to meet existing federal mileage standards; (8) a new tax on industrial use of oil and natural gas; (9) continuation of clean air standards for coal burning plants; (10) tax credits for specific conservation efforts.

23 May. TAX REDUCTION of $34.2 billion, mainly to individuals. Carter withdrew his proposal for $50 tax rebate. Congress also passed $4 billion emergency public works package (13 May).

During 1977 inflation was at 6.5%; the trade deficit at $26.7 billion, mostly due to oil imports; stock market slump continued into 1978. Unemployment dropped to less than 7%.

1 June. RIGHTS OF HANDICAPPED. Department of HEW regulations, based upon 1973 Rehabilitation Act, prohibited recipients of federal funds, such as schools and hospitals, from discrimination against the disabled, rehabilitated alcoholics, and other handicapped persons. Recipients of HEW funding were required to make both existing and new buildings accessible to the handicapped.

June. AMERICAN PUBLIC HEALTH PROBLEMS ascribed by HEW Secretary Joseph A. Califano, Jr., to: (1) uneconomical and unfair distribution of health resources; (2) performance by doctors of services that could be performed by others; (3) stress on acute care over preventive medicine; (4) expensive and inequitable health insurance. $212.2 billion was spent on health care (1979), $943 per person, and 9% of gross national product (compared with 4.4% thirty years before). 43% of health costs were paid for by governmental entities.

13–14 July. New York power blackout leads to widespread looting. 3,200 persons were arrested.

3 Aug. STRIP MINING CONTROL AND RECLAMATION ACT set performance standards for environmental protection; provided for joint responsibility and enforcement by both the states and federal government; established a self-supporting abandoned mine reclamation fund; protected lands regarded as undesirable for surface mining; provided for mining and mineral research institutes.

4 Aug. ENERGY DEPARTMENT created through merger and abolition of the Federal Power Commission, Federal Energy Administration, and Energy Research and Development Administration, and by absorbing energy-related functions from five other agencies. A five-member independent Federal Regulation Commission was established within the

Department, with power to set oil and electricity prices, but the Secretary of Energy was given power to circumvent oil-pricing rules if President declared national emergency.

7 AUG. CLEAN AIR AMENDMENTS to 1970, **Clean Air Act** delayed implementation for two years of auto emission standards and extended deadline for cities to meet national air quality standards.

16 SEPT. EPISCOPAL CHURCH SPLIT. Anglican Church in North America established by opponents of liberal attitudes toward abortion, divorce, priestly ordination of women (Sept. 1976), and substantial revision of Book of Common Prayer.

1 Nov. MINIMUM WAGE raised from $2.30 per hour to $2.65 (effective 1 Jan. 1978), $2.90 (1 Jan. 1979), $3.10 (1 Jan. 1980), and to $3.35 (1 Jan. 1981). For the first time the minimum wage for farm workers covered under the law was the same as for other workers.

18–21 Nov. NATIONAL WOMEN'S CONFERENCE, funded by federal government, took place in Houston. The convention approved a 25-point plan, including recommendations for expanded day-care centers, federal programs for battered wives and abused children. Endorsement of the Equal Rights Amendment, legalized abortion, and lesbian rights led to walk-out by pro-life and pro-family groups.

PERCENT OF FEMALE POPULATION IN THE LABOR FORCE

Year	All women	Single	Married	Married, husband present	Widowed/ divorced
1940	27.4	48.1	16.7	14.7	32.0
1950	31.4	50.5	24.8	23.8	36.0
1960	34.8	44.1	31.7	30.5	37.1
1970	42.6	53.0	41.4	40.8	36.2
1978	49.1	60.5	48.1	47.6	40.0

Note: The percentage of women who work has gone up sharply since 1940 in all categories except widowed/divorced.
Source: *Statistical Abstract, 1979.*

20 DEC. SOCIAL SECURITY financing legislation raised taxes to finance Social Security System by increasing maximum annual tax paid by employee: 1977, 5.85% tax on first $16,500; 1981, 6.65% on $29,700; 1987, 7.15% on $42,600. Benefits rose faster than inflation. In Aug. 1979 there were 34,770,792 beneficiaries of Social Security and Disability payments. Average monthly benefits (Aug. 1979): for retired worker— $293; for disabled worker—$321.

1978

3 JAN. AMERICAN SAMOAN SELF-GOVERNMENT. Peter T. Coleman took office as first elected governor. A nonvoting delegate to Congress was elected in 1980.

11 APR. CARTER ANTI-INFLATION PROGRAM limited wage increases to government employees and postponed income tax cuts, but failed to curb budget deficit, restrict growth of money supply, or set price and wage controls. On 24 Oct. Carter announced new plan to reduce inflation from 8% to 6½% by voluntary wage increase guidelines (7%) and voluntary price increase limits (5.75%). Inflation averaged 9% in 1978.

3 MAY. "SUN DAY." President Carter ordered policy review by all departments to investigate how solar energy can become a part of everyday life.

6 JUNE. TAX REVOLT exemplified by adoption in California referendum of **Proposition 13,** constitutional amendment cutting local property taxes by more than 50%. On 6 Nov. an $18.7 billion federal tax cut, aimed at middle and upper income groups, partially offset increases in Social Security tax and inflation-indexed tax increases. Capital gains tax was also reduced, but the act did not include tax reforms advocated by Carter.

9 JUNE. Spencer W. Kimball, President of the Church of Jesus Christ of Latter-Day Saints (Mormons), announced that, upon divine revelation, ban on ordination of black males as priests would end.

15 JUNE. ENDANGERED SPECIES. In *TVA* v. *Hill* (437 U.S. 153) the Supreme Court barred completion of Tellico Dam project on Little Tennessee River, because it was only known habitat of snail darter, a three-inch fish. The **Endangered Species Act of 1973** protected endangered and threatened species of fish, wildlife, and plants by prohibiting federal agencies from carrying out projects which would destroy habitat critical to survival of the species. As of Sept. 1978 there were 177 endangered and 37 threatened animals as well as 15 endangered and two threatened plants on the endangered species list. A Cabinet-level board was established by law (30 Nov. 1978) to consider permitting construction of federal projects even though a species might be extinguished. On 25 Sept. 1979 President Carter signed a bill assuring completion of Tellico project. The floodgates opened 30 Nov. 1979. Snail darters were later found surviving in other waters.

28 JUNE. AFFIRMATIVE ACTION. Long awaited Supreme Court decision in *Regents of University of California* v. *Bakke* (438 U.S. 265) involved a special admissions program at a state medical school under which places were set aside for members of minority groups. Justice Lewis F. Powell, Jr., cast the swing vote in both parts of the 5–4 decision which held (1) that certain race-conscious programs to remedy proven past discrimination might be upheld under the Constitution; but (2) that the University program violated Title VI of 1964 Civil Rights Act, which barred any discrimination on the ground of race, color, or national origin in any program receiving federal financial assistance.

In *United Steel Workers of America* v. *Weber* (433 U.S. 193), 1979, the Supreme Court held by a 5–2 vote that an affirmative action program established

voluntarily by an agreement by management and union to remedy past discrimination did not violate Title VII of the 1964 Act, which prohibited discrimination in employment. In *Fullilove* v. *Klutznick* (100 Sup.Ct. 2758), 1980, the Court upheld a program established by Congress to redress racial discrimination by setting aside 10% of the public works program money for minority contractors.

1 JULY. POPULATION U.S. DEPENDENCIES. Est. pop.: Puerto Rico, 3,358,000; Trust Territory of the Pacific Islands, 128,000; Guam, 114,000; Virgin Islands, 96,000; American Samoa, 31,000; Northern Marianas, 17,000.

10 JULY. MARINE MAMMAL PROTECTION ACT. Congress authorized $47.1 million (fiscal 1979–81) to implement the Marine Mammal Act of 1972, which had declared permanent moratorium on most killings of ocean mammals and on importation of marine mammal products.

22 AUG. D.C. REPRESENTATION AMENDMENT proposed by Congress provided treatment of the District of Columbia as a state for purpose of representation in Congress, participation in presidential elections, and in ratification of proposed amendments to the Constitution. By the end of 1980, nine of the necessary 38 states had ratified the proposed amendment.

The District of Columbia had been given a non-voting delegate to the House of Representatives in 1970. Partial self-government, including the right to elect a mayor and City Council, was authorized in 1973, although Congress retained veto of acts approved by City Council and control over expenditures.

18 SEPT. OUTER CONTINENTAL SHELF LEASING LAWS, revising **Outer Continental Shelf Lands Act of 1953** to take account of East Coast states' concern for resort and fishing industries, tightened restrictions on drilling and production to protect the environment, fostered competition for leases on offshore public land, and increased state participation in federal leasing decisions. On 14 Aug. 1978 Texaco announced that it had struck gas about 100 miles from Atlantic City, N.J. An estimated 10–49 billion barrels of crude oil and 42–81 trillion cubic feet of natural gas are located on U.S. outer continental shelf (more than 3 miles from shoreland).

6 Oct. EQUAL RIGHTS AMENDMENT deadline for ratification extended by Congress from 22 Mar. 1979 to 30 June 1982. By 31 Dec. 1980, 35 states had voted to ratify ERA (of 38 needed) and five states had voted to rescind their ratification.

6 Oct. BANKRUPTCY LAW revision intended to give persons who had gone through bankruptcy a fresh start, while elevating the rank and status of bankruptcy referees to bankruptcy judges with fourteen-year tenure and enlarged jurisdiction. Personal bankruptcies jumped 82% during first year law was in effect, reflecting economic conditions, expanded resort to credit card and installment buying, the liberalized conditions for declaring bankruptcy, and advertising by lawyers. U.S. Supreme Court (9 Nov. 1981) agreed to consider the constitutionality of new federal bankruptcy courts.

13 Oct. CIVIL SERVICE REFORM created Senior Executive Services (SES) of 8,000 top federal managers and decision-makers, eligible for cash bonuses; established merit pay system for middle-level management; increased management flexibility in firing incompetent employees; established the right of federal employees to join unions and bargain collectively over certain personnel practices. Civil Service Commission was replaced by an **Office of Personnel Management** and a **Merit Systems Protection Board.**

Foreign Service Act (17 Oct. 1980) established new Senior Foreign Service modeled after SES; upgraded and modernized Foreign Service.

20 Oct. FEDERAL JUDGESHIPS created by Congress: 117 District Court positions added to existing 398; 35 Court of Appeals judgeships added to existing 97.

21 Oct. INLAND WATERWAY FEES imposed on barge industry.

24 Oct. DEREGULATION of regulated industries stressed during Carter administration to promote competition. Federal control over airlines was to be phased out over seven years, while guaranteeing air service for small communities. In 1980, regulations dating back 45 years were removed from the trucking industry, easing entry of new companies. Companies were given more freedom to set rates. The railroads were given (14 Oct. 1980) more price-setting flexibility, but lost some immunity from antitrust laws. Household movers were deregulated (15 Oct. 1980) by an act intended to give better protection to the consumer.

25 Oct. FOREIGN INTELLIGENCE SURVEILLANCE ACT required warrants for most foreign intelligence surveillance in U.S. and evidence of criminal activity before warrant can be issued for surveillance of U.S. citizen.

25 Oct. PUBLIC GRAZING RANGE-LANDS IMPROVEMENT ACT, first major revision of U.S. range management laws in 44 years, established new grazing fee system for ranchers whose livestock feed on federal rangeland, and set program to reduce overpopulation of wild horses and burros.

SAGEBRUSH REBELLION, movement to return national public lands to state control, gained strength in western states (1978–80).

26 Oct. GOVERNMENT ETHICS LAW required financial disclosure by judges, congressmen and members of executive branch; tightened rules governing return of government employees to private jobs; established **Office 'of Government Ethics;** set up mechanism for appointment of temporary special prosecutor to investigate criminal wrongdoing by President, Vice President, and top executive branch officials. The law was liberalized (22 June 1979).

27 OCT. FULL EMPLOYMENT AND BALANCED GROWTH ACT (Humphrey-Hawkins bill) set national policy of promoting full employment, increasing real income, balancing federal budget, increasing productivity, improving balance of trade, and achieving price stability.

1 Nov. DOLLAR STRENGTHENED by Carter pledge of massive intervention in currency markets; quintupling of gold sales; increase by Federal Reserve in discount rate from 8.5% to 9.5%; restrictions on expansion of bank credit. The New York Stock Exchange recorded its largest one-day gain ever in Dow-Jones average, 35 points. During 1978 the **price of gold** rose to over $400. The federal deficit (fiscal year ending 30 Sept. 1978)—$49 billion. The prime rate rose from 8% to 10¼% in 1978, reaching 11¼% in Nov.

4 Nov. CONGRESSIONAL ELECTIONS. Republican Party gained total of three Senate and twelve House seats, as well as six governorships, including Texas and Pennsylvania. Among the new Senators was Nancy Landon Kassenbaum, the first woman ever to have been elected to the Senate without having been preceded in Congress by her husband.

9 Nov. ENERGY PROGRAM. Five parts of the Carter energy program became law: (1) price of newly discovered natural gas permitted to rise 10% per year until 1985, when controls would be lifted; (2) new industrial and utility plants required to use coal or fuel other than oil or gas, while existing utilities had to switch over by 1990; (3) state utility commissions required to consider use of energy-saving measures; (4) $900 million appropriated for schools and hospitals to install energy-saving equipment; (5) tax credits to be given for installation of energy-saving devices.

10 Nov. NATIONAL PARKS AND RECREATION ACT, largest parks bill in history, authorized $1.2 billion for developing and expanding national parks, seashores, trails, wild and scenic rivers in 44 states.

18 Nov. Jonestown, Guyana, mass suicide-murder of 911 followers of People's Temple, U.S. religious cult, led by **Rev. Jim Jones.**

Rep. Leo J. Ryan (Calif.) and four of his party were murdered there after investigating complaints. During the 1970s cults using hardsell recruitment and conversion, featuring communal life, strict discipline, and gifts of all possessions to the church, flourished among the young. Parents filed lawsuits and hired persons to "kidnap" and de-program their children. One of most successful was Unification Church, founded by **Rev. Sun Myung Moon** (1954) which began full-scale missionary operations in U.S. (1973).

31 DEC. House Select Committee on Assassinations concluded that Lee Harvey Oswald fired three shots at President Kennedy, but a fourth shot was fired by second gunman; James Earl Ray responsible for killing Martin Luther King, with circumstantial evidence of conspiracy.

1978. *City of Philadelphia* v. *New Jersey* (437 U.S. 617). U.S. Supreme Court held unconstitutional a state law which prohibited importation of waste from outside the state, as violating the Commerce Clause.

1978. *Marshall* v. *Barlow's Inc.* (429 U.S. 1347). U.S. Supreme Court held that warrantless searches of businesses, authorized by the Occupational Safety and Health Act of 1970 (OSHA), were unconstitutional, but to obtain a warrant an inspector would not need to demonstrate probable cause.

1978. *Penn Central Transportation Co.* v. *City of New York* (438 U.S. 104). U.S. Supreme Court upheld landmarks preservation law as not a "taking of property."

1971–78. IMMIGRATION PAT-TERNS (by country of birth) showed increased proportion coming from North and Central America and Asia. 1,322,600 immigrants (37.8%) came from North America (Mexico, 528,500; Cuba, 246,200; Dominican Republic, 113,300; Jamaica, 103,400; Canada, 87,400). 1,208,500 immigrants (34.5%) came from Asia (Philippines, 276,700; Korea, 210,400; China [including Taiwan], 150,700; India, 134,400; Vietnam, 113,500). 19.1% (668,400) came from Europe (Italy, 118,500; United Kingdom, 94,100; Portugal, 88,900; Greece, 83,900). 209,400 (6.0%) came from South America; 64,500 (1.8%) from Africa. Estimated total immigration for decade 1971–80 appeared greatest since 1911–20.

IMMIGRATION TO U.S., 1973–78
(Statistical Abstract, 1980)

Year	No. of persons	Year	No. of persons
1973	370,478	1976	398,613[1]
1974	384,685	1977	462,315
1975	400,063	1978	601,442

[1] An additional 103,676 were admitted from 1 July to 30 Sept. 1976 as reporting year was altered from 1 July–30 June to 1 Oct.–30 Sept.

1978. HISPANIC POPULATION estimated at 19 million, including 7 million "undocumented" (illegal) aliens. Total immigration (legal and illegal) est. 1 million per year. Of 12,079,000 Hispanics legally in U.S., 7.2 million were Chicanos (of Mexican origin); 1.8 million, Puerto Rican; 700,000, Cuban. The Hispanic population was considerably younger than the national average and resided largely in California (29%); Texas (20%); Arizona, Colorado, and New Mexico (9%); New York (15%). 21% of Hispanic families lived below the poverty level—39% of Puerto Rican families; 19% of Mexican families; 15% of Cuban families—compared with national average of 9%.

1978. ILLEGAL ALIENS estimated by federal government as 8.2 million (90% of Hispanic origin). An est. 1 million illegal aliens arrived annually; 90% from Mexico. Carter administration proposed amnesty (4 Aug. 1977) for undocumented aliens who could prove they had arrived in U.S. prior to 1970; those arriving after 1970 would have received five-year temporary resident status.

1978. POLITICAL REFUGEES. Congress authorized $455 million for relocation and resettlement of Indo-China's war refugees (1975). Effective 28 Oct. 1977 refugees from Vietnam, Laos, and Kampuchea (Cambodia), physically present or paroled into the United States and present in U.S. for at least two years, were made eligible for permanent resident status. 176,300 Indochinese resettled in U.S. (1975–78); 95,962 Indochinese were admitted as permanent residents (1977–78).

Refugee Act of 17 Mar. 1978 tripled annual limit of refugees who could be admitted to U.S. to 50,000 with provisions for emergency admission. 96,284 Cubans were admitted under refugee status (1977–78). Due to economic hardships inside Cuba, Cuban President Fidel Castor permitted refugees safe conduct out of country. Cuban-Americans from South Florida engaged in a boatlift (5 Apr.–26 Sept. 1980). 125,000 Cubans admitted to U.S., 80,000 settling in Miami.

1979

28 Mar. THREE MILE ISLAND AC-CIDENT. Breakdown in cooling system of nuclear power plant near Harrisburg, Pa., raised fears that the plant's nuclear fuel could overheat and "meltdown," releasing radioactivity outside the nuclear plant. A commission, appointed by President Carter and chaired by John Kemeny est. probable cost of accident at $1–2 billion. It recommended abolition of Nuclear Regulatory Commission; that government regulation of nuclear power concentrate upon safety instead of licensing; that oversight of plant operations be upgraded; that nuclear plants be located in remote areas if feasible. Carter announced that he was removing NRC Chairman, Joseph M. Hendrie. By presidential reorganization plan, the NRC was reorganized to give more authority to the chairman for day-to-day operations, assisted by executive director of operations, but policy-making responsibility left with Commission.

Wide concern surfaced over an industry whose 72 reactors generated 12% of U.S. electricity (3.5% of all energy consumption). At the time of Three Mile Island accident 125 reactors were under construction. The NRC placed moratorium on issuing new construction permits or operating licenses for plants.

The U.S. Supreme Court held (3 Apr. 1978) that federal courts have only a limited role to play in reviewing NRC decisions regarding expansion of the nation's nuclear power capability. *Vermont Yankee Nuclear Power Corp.* v. *Natural Resources Defense Council* (435 U.S. 519). On 26 June 1978 the Supreme Court upheld ceiling of $560 million on liability of the nuclear power industry for damage from any accident. *Duke Power Co.* v. *Carolina Environmental Study Group* (438 U.S. 59).

5 APR. OIL PRICE DECONTROL announced by President Carter beginning 1 June. A windfall profits tax of from 30 to 70% of the windfall was placed on oil company profits (2 Apr. 1980).

11 JULY. SKYLAB I DISINTEGRATION. Debris from 77-ton U.S. space station launched 14 May 1973 (p. 804) scattered in the Indian Ocean and across Western Australia; no reported injuries.

15 JULY. DOMESTIC SUMMIT held at Camp David where for ten days President Carter met with 134 persons of varying backgrounds. Carter's televised speech on 15 July described national

"crisis of confidence," of paralysis, stagnation, and grief, and indicated that solution of energy crisis could "rekindle our national sense of unity, our confidence in the future." Carter outlined a ten-year, $140 billion national energy program. Within several days Carter reshuffled his Cabinet, forcing the resignations (21 July) of HEW Secretary Joseph A. Califano, Jr., Treasury Secretary W. Michael Blumenthal, and Transportation Secretary Brock Adams. Attorney General Griffin Bell and Energy Secretary James R. Schlesinger also resigned for personal reasons. Hamilton Jordan was named chief of the White House staff.

29 SEPT. AMTRAK SYSTEM reduced 16% by Congress (more than 4,000 miles).

6 OCT. ANTI-INFLATION PROGRAM. With inflation at 13.3% annual rate, Paul Volcker, chairman of the Federal Reserve Board, announced: (1) discount rate increase to 12%; (2) imposition of stiff new reserve requirements on bank deposits. Prime rate rose from 14.5% to 15.75% (mid-Nov.). As interest rates went higher than state usury laws, mortgages became impossible to obtain in some states. Savings and loan institutions began to feel acute pinch.

16 OCT. Jimmy Carter and brother Billy Carter were cleared by federal special prosecutor of criminal wrongdoing in connection with loans to family peanut business from bank which had been headed by Carter friend Bert Lance. Lance had resigned as Director of Office of Management and Budget (15 Sept. 1977) over other alleged improprieties while bank president in Georgia. Billy Carter was criticized by Special Senate Judiciary Subcommittee (2 Oct. 1980) for accepting payments from Libyan government.

17 OCT. EDUCATION DEPARTMENT created by transferring programs from Department of Health, Education, and Welfare (renamed **Health and Hu-**

man **Resources**) and other departments. Judge Shirley M. Hufstedler was sworn in as Secretary of Education, 6 Dec. On 4 May 1980 HEW officially went out of existence.

1970–79. ONE-PARENT FAMILIES increased 79%; nearly 6 million out of 30.4 million families with children were one-parent families. Among black Americans the proportion of one-parent families rose to 49%.

1973–79. HOUSING COSTS. According to 1979 Survey of HUD and Census Bureau, value of single-family homes increased 95% (1973–79). Number of homeowners increased 15% to 51.4 million, although proportion of homeowners remained *c.* 65%. Monthly cost of owning home rose 61% for those with mortgages; 59% for those without mortgages; but homeowners benefited by the inflation and tax breaks. Nationwide, owner-occupied condominiums increased 91% to *c.* 1 million. Proportion of renters paying more than 25% of income in rent increased.

1980

7 JAN. CHRYSLER BAIL-OUT. Chrysler, nations' 10th largest corp., reported net losses of $240.6 million (1978) and 465.5 million in 1st six months of 1979. Chrysler had 9.1% share of auto market. On 7 Jan. 1980 Congress authorized loan guarantees of $1.5 billion on condition that Chrysler obtain wage reductions from employees, bank credit, concessions from creditors, state and local aid or credit, aid or credit from dealers and suppliers. On 10 May Chrysler Loan Guarantee Board stated conditions had been met.

14 MAR. ANTI-INFLATION PROGRAM announced by Carter: tighter fiscal policy; wage and price recommendations; higher taxes on imported oil; 3% surcharge on discount rate and tough

monetary measures. Due in part to rising oil prices, inflation neared 20% (18.2%) during first quarter of 1980. As stagflation re-emerged, annual rate of inflation was 13.5% and unemployment ended year at 7.4%. By Dec. 1980 the prime rate had risen to 22.5%.

31 MAR. BANKING REFORMS. Depository Institutions Deregulation and Control Act of 1980: (1) phased out interest rate ceilings on savings accounts; (2) permitted payment of interest on checking accounts; (3) established uniform reserve requirements for all depository institutions; (4) overrode state usury limits on mortgages; (5) permitted savings and loan associations to make real estate loans to same extent as national banks.

1 APR. CENSUS. U.S. Population—226,504,825. Black Americans—26,488,218 (11.7% of population), [Est. undercount of blacks, 4.5–5.5% in 1980 compared with 7.7% (1970)] Americans of Hispanic origin—14,605,883 (6.4% of pop.). Population of sun belt (15 states in Southern third of country) rose by 7,265,000; 64% of overall pop. increase. Increase in sun belt, 13 Western states, and California reflected in estimated shift of 17 seats in House of Representatives from Northeast and Middlewest to South and West. New York was expected to lose five seats; Illinois, Ohio, and Pennsylvania two each. Major gains expected by Florida—4, Texas—3, California—2.

The census was challenged in court by cities such as Detroit and New York because of alleged undercount of minority groups, the poor, and illegal aliens. The Supreme Court declined to prevent Bureau of Census from certifying to the President census tabulations, as mandated by law on 31 Dec. 1980.

18 MAY. MOUNT ST. HELENS ERUPTION. $2.7 billion damage caused by eruption of volcano in southwestern Washington state. $951 million federal disaster relief was appropriated by Congress (8 July).

27 June. DRAFT REGISTRATION funding authorized, permitting President to register 19- and 20-year-old men. Exclusion of women held constitutional by Supreme Court (*Rostker* v. *Goldberg*), 1981. Draft had been suspended in 1973; draft registration suspended (1975).

30 June. SYNTHETIC FUELS DEVELOPMENT spurred by creation of U.S. Synthetic Fuels Corp., to use authorized $20 billion for development of synthetic fuels. Aim was to achieve production of 500,000 barrels per day by 1992. Congress defeated Carter proposal for Energy Mobilization Board to speed licensing of plants to produce synthetic fuels. On 6 June 1980 Congress overrode Carter's veto of legislation, which killed a $4.62 per barrel fee on imported oil to be passed on to consumer as ten cents per gal. surcharge on gasoline. Congress also declined to tax wellhead price of domestic oil, gas, or gas-guzzling automobiles.

During Carter administration, oil consumption declined from 18.8 billion bbls. (1978) to 16.9 billion bbls. (1980). Gasoline consumption declined as the domestic automobile industry improved fuel efficiency. Average miles per gallon: 1968, 13.79; 1973, 13.10; 1978, 14.06. Importation of crude oil and petroleum decreased to 6.7 million bbls. per day. U.S. gas reserves increased. The **Alaska Pipeline** was completed 30 May 1977; oil began to flow 20 June 1977. World price of oil jumped from $16 to $30 per bbl. in 1979 due in part to turmoil in Iran. Saudi Arabia increased output to replace Iranian oil and bought $1.2 billion in arms from U.S. Average price of gasoline: 1979, $1 per gal.; 1980, $1.25 per gal.

2 Oct. ABSCAM SCANDAL. Rep. Michael J. Myers (Dem., Pa.) was expelled from House of Representatives, first occurrence since 1861, after conviction for bribery and conspiracy. Sen. Harrison Williams (Dem., N.J.) and 6 other Representatives were linked to FBI investigation. Some members of Congress resigned; others were beaten for reelection, disciplined in the Congress, or sent to prison for a variety of pecuniary and sexual offenses (1974–81). In 1977 both Houses of Congress adopted ethics codes restricting earnings from honoraria and providing for disclosure of outside income and gifts.

15 Oct. JUDICIAL TENURE AND DISCIPLINE ACT established procedures for disciplining judges short of removing them from bench through impeachment. Authority was given to chief judge and councils of each judicial circuit to investigate complaints and impose sanctions other than removal from office.

16 Oct. Tax rules for reporting capital gains from the installment sale of real estate or personal property were simplified.

PRESIDENTIAL CAMPAIGN set new marks for length, with more primaries than ever before. Rep. Philip Crane (Rep., Ill.) declared candidacy 2 Aug. 1978. Florida preference (non-binding) conventions attracted press interest (17 Nov. 1979). First delegates were selected at Iowa caucuses (21 Jan. 1980); first primary, New Hampshire (26 Feb.).

After victories by George Bush in Iowa caucuses, Ronald Reagan won primaries in New Hampshire, Florida (11 Mar.), Illinois, and New York (25 Mar.) over a field that included Sen. Howard Baker (Tenn.), former Treasury Secretary John B. Connally, and Rep. John B. Anderson (Ill.). Bush won some later primaries, including Pennsylvania, but lacking sufficient delegates, withdrew from the race (26 May).

Reagan won nomination on first ballot at Republican National Convention in Detroit (16 July). After negotiations with Gerald Ford over his possible selection as running mate, Reagan chose **Bush** for the vice-presidential nomination. The

Republican platform called for a constitutional ban on abortion; appointment of judges who favored such an amendment; across-the-board tax cuts of ten percent per year for three years; and opposition to Salt II Treaty. Republicans abandoned longtime support of Equal Rights Amendment.

Carter and **Mondale** were renominated (14 Aug.) on first ballot of Democratic National Convention which met in New York City. Renomination was assured after close vote preventing release of pledged delegates. **Sen. Edward M. Kennedy** had faded in early primaries, when Carter, citing crises in Iran and Afghanistan, campaigned in Rose Garden. Kennedy then won primaries in New York and Connecticut, but could not recapture lost ground.

The Democratic platform supported the Equal Rights Amendment, federal funding of abortions, and a $12 billion jobs program.

After losing in Republican primaries while attracting substantial attention and support among students and upper-middle-class voters, Rep. **John Anderson** ran for the Presidency as an Independent, choosing former Wisconsin Governor **Patrick J. Lucey** (Dem.) as his running mate (25 Aug.). Carter refused to debate with Anderson; Reagan-Anderson televised debate, 21 Sept.

Reagan received the support of a wide coalition of conservative groups: (1) longtime leading conservatives such as William Buckley, publisher of the *National Review;* (2) big-business conservatives concerned about federal regulation, high taxes and federal spending; (3) intellectual neoconservatives concerned about USSR, third world, and affirmative action; (4) the "New Right," notably the Moral Majority, led by popular evangelists such as Rev. Jerry Falwell of Lynchburg, Va., opposed to abortion and equal rights amendment, and including groups supporting lower taxes; (5) supply-side economists, holding that lower tax rates would cause prosperity.

Carter posed as the peace candidate, while Reagan assailed Carter's economic and defense policies. Although the election appeared very close, Reagan gained sharply in the last week, which included a 90-minute nationally televised debate (28 Oct.) of three leading candidates. The election was held exactly one year to the day of the taking of the American hostages in Iran (pp. 574–575).

4 Nov. PRESIDENTIAL ELECTION. Reagan won unexpected landslide with 489 electoral votes from 43 states and 43,901,812 popular votes. Carter received 49 electoral votes from six states and the District of Columbia and 35,-483,820 popular votes. Anderson won 5,719,722 votes (6.6%).

Minor Party candidates: **Ed Clark** (Libertarian), 921,188; **Barry Commoner** (Citizens), 234,279; **Gus Hall** (Communist), 44,954; **John Rarick** (American Independent), 41,268; **Clifton DeBerry** (Socialist Worker), 41,145; **Ellen McCormack** (Right to Life), 33,327.

Total popular vote was 86,513,296 (54% of those eligible). Republicans captured control of the Senate, 53–46, with one Independent, with a net gain of 12 seats. Democrats retained control of House of Representatives, 243–192, but the Republicans gained 33 seats and the complexion was more conservative. Republicans picked up 4 governorships, giving them a total of 23. Blacks gained 2 House seats to number 15. 5 Hispanic representatives were reelected. 2 Japanese-American Representatives and one Japanese-American Senator were reelected. 5 new women were elected to Congress, for a total of 19 in the House of Representatives and 2 in the Senate.

5 Nov. STOCK EXCHANGE RECORD TRADING. Reacting to Reagan victory, Dow-Jones Industrial Average rose *c.* 16% as trading soared to 84.08 million shares.

2 Dec. ALASKA NATIONAL INTER-EST LANDS CONSERVATION ACT, affecting land area larger than California and Maine, withdrew land from disposal and mineral leasing by establishing or expanding units of the National Park System and the National Wildlife System. 56.4 million acres of mountain range and animal habitat were totally protected. 49 million acres were substantially protected, although some mining and timbering was to be permitted. President Carter had invoked the **Antiquities Act of 1906** to prevent mining, logging, and other commercial development on 56 million acres (1 Dec. 1978) until Congress could act.

11 Dec. TOXIC WASTE SUPER-FUND. $1.6 billion fund was established by Congress for cleanup of any toxic substance, although not for oil spills. The law permitted the U.S. government to act in emergencies, and then to sue those responsible. The legislation was a response to discovery in Niagara Falls, N.Y., that Love Canal subdivision had been built on top of chemical dump and was slowly poisoning residents. The Superfund would be raised by fees levied on chemical and oil industries (86%) and from general revenues (14%).

15 Dec. JUDGES' SALARIES. In suit brought by 13 district judges, Supreme Court held that Congress could cut cost-of-living increases for life-tenured federal judges, if it did so *before* the scheduled increases were to go into effect. However, to do so *after* the salary increase had taken effect would "diminish" the compensation of federal judges and thus be unconstitutional. *United States* v. *Will* (101 Sup. Ct. 471).

1980. *Diamond* v. *Chakrabarty* (100 Sup. Ct. 2204). In a case involving genetically engineered bacterium capable of breaking down multiple components of crude oil, U.S. Supreme Court held a man-made live organism to be patentable.

1981

14 Jan. CARTER FAREWELL SPEECH emphasized concern about the environment and nuclear war, and defended his administration's commitment to human rights.

Foreign Policy: The Ford-Kissinger Years, 1974–77

1974

16 Sept. VIETNAM WAR DRAFT EVADERS offered clemency by President Ford in return for oath of allegiance and up to 24 months of alternate service.

24 Nov. DÉTENTE. Better relations with Soviet Union typified by (1) **Vladivostok Accords,** signed by Soviet leader Leonid Brezhnev and President Ford on an eight-day trip to Japan, South Korea, and USSR, providing for exact equivalence between U.S. and USSR in *numbers* of offensive strategic nuclear weapons, but not in throw weight or number of warheads. The agreement limited the U.S. and USSR to 2,400 strategic weapons systems, which could be composed of a mix of ICBMs, submarine-launched ballistic missiles, heavy bombers, and air-launched ballistic missiles. Up to 1,320 missiles of the 2,400 could be equipped with multiple independently targetable re-entry vehicles (MIRVs) containing several warheads that could strike more than one enemy target. Neither the Soviet **backfire** bomber nor the U.S. **cruise missile** were covered by agreement. (2) On 1 Aug. 1975 the **Helsinki Accords,** an agreement of 33

European nations, including the USSR, and the U.S. and Canada, was signed in Helsinki by leaders including President Ford, who also visited West Germany, Poland, Rumania, and Yugoslavia on this mission. The Agreement concluded the **Conference on Security and Cooperation in Europe,** which had begun in Geneva (1973), by avowing principles for assuring permanent peace in Europe, including formalizing post-World War II territorial boundaries and providing respect for human rights and freer exchanges and travel by each nation's citizens. (3) On 25 Oct. 1975 the **Soviet-American Grain Agreement,** intended to prevent rise in American prices caused by Soviet purchases, provided for Soviet pledge to buy between 6 and 8 million tons of grain each year beginning 1 Oct. 1976. President Ford and Chairman Brezhnev (4) signed 28 May 1976 **Nuclear Explosion Treaty,** which imposed 150 kiloton limitation on underground explosion of single nuclear device for peaceful purposes; a total yield of up to 1,500 kilotons from a series of nuclear explosions; on-sight inspection if any explosion exceeded 150 kiloton level.

While détente was exemplified by such cooperation as joint missions in space (p. 568), Soviet-American relations were marked as well by tensions over the treatment of Jews and dissenters in the USSR. Prominent emigrés from the Soviet Union who settled in the U.S. included the writer **Aleksandr I. Solzhenitsyn** (expelled 13 Feb. 1974), **Mstislav Rostropovich,** cellist and his wife, the singer **Galina Vishnevskaya** (Soviet citizenship revoked 15 Mar. 1978) and dancer, **Mikhail Baryshnikov.** Political opposition to détente in U.S. deepened in 1976. President Ford stated that the word "détente" would no longer be applicable to U.S.-Soviet relations.

16 Dec. CHEMICAL WARFARE banned by unanimous Senate ratification of Geneva Protocol of 1925, which pro-

hibited the use of poison gas and bacteriological weapons in warfare. The protocol resolution included reservation permitting use of chemical weapons by U.S., if enemy did so first. The Senate also ratified **1972 Convention on the Prohibition of Bacteriological and Toxin Weapons,** which prohibited the production and stockpiling of biological weapons.

1974–76. CONGRESSIONAL ASSERTION OF POWER IN FOREIGN AFFAIRS. Post-Watergate, post-Vietnam War struggles between executive branch and Congress exemplified by (1) total, then partial, embargo on arms deliveries to Turkey, over use of American weapons in invasion of Cyprus (July 1974). Embargo was lifted at the urging of the executive by a vote of 208–205 in House of Representatives (1978) and U.S. reopened four vital defense installations in Turkey; (2) congressional refusal to approve emergency assistance for South Vietnam and Cambodia just prior to the collapse of those governments (April 1975); (3) congressional veto of U.S. military aid to factions fighting in Angola's civil war (1975–76); (4) five-year delay by Congress in constructing $13.8 million fleet-refueling base on island of Diego Garcia (approved 1976); (5) congressional refusal to approve military aid to Chile.

1975

3 Jan. TRADE ACT authorized President (1) to enter into trade agreements with other countries for purpose of reducing tariff and non-tariff barriers; (2) to eliminate tariffs on goods carrying duties of 5% or less and to reduce tariffs by up to 60%; (3) to take corrective action whenever the U.S. had a large and persistent balance of trade surplus (requiring him to act whenever there was a large balance of payments deficit); (4)

to increase tariffs by 20% of 1973 rates or 150% of 1934 rates, whichever was lower; (5) relaxed the criteria for industries to be eligible for relief from losses suffered from import competition; (6) eased the criteria for workers displaced by imports to qualify for adjustment programs; (7) authorized the President to take retaliatory action against unjustifiable or unreasonable import restrictions by foreign countries against U.S. goods and services.

The Trade Act (and the extension of the Export-Import Bank's authority to finance sale of U.S. exports) prohibited tariff preferences to members of the Organization of Petroleum Exporting Countries (OPEC) and linked trade benefits for the Soviet Union to liberal emigration policies for Soviet Jews. Secretary of State Kissinger announced (14 Jan. 1975) that the USSR rejected such terms for trade. Multilateral trade negotiations, launched at Tokyo (Sept. 1973) under GATT auspices, were continuing.

15 May. MAYAGUEZ RESCUE. Seized by Cambodian forces in the Gulf of Siam (12 May), the merchant ship *Mayaguez* and a crew of 39 were rescued by military action involving the bombing of Cambodian patrol boats, marine assault on the island of Koh Tang, and ground fighting. 41 Americans died as a result of the operation.

17–19 July. APOLLO–SOYUZ TEST PROJECT. Apollo 18, carrying Thomas P. Stafford, Vance D. Brand, and Donald K. ("Deke") Slayton, and Soyuz 19, with 2 cosmonauts, linked in space, conducted 5 joint experiments. On 3 Aug. 1977 the Soviets launched a satellite with 7 U.S. experiments. The Apollo 18 flight was the last U.S.-manned space mission of the decade.

11 Aug. U.S. VETO used to block admission of North and South Vietnam to the UN. Vietnam had been formally unified 2 July 1976 and was admitted as the 149th member of the UN (20 Sept. 1977).

4 Sept. SINAI ACCORD. Secretary of State Kissinger's shuttle diplomacy produced Israeli-Egyptian pact signed in Geneva, providing Israel's withdrawal from Sinai mountain passes and oil fields while Egypt opened Suez Canal to nonmilitary cargoes of Israel. U.S.-Israel Memorandum specified U.S. aid and political commitments, if accord broke down. Volunteer U.S. civilian technicians were authorized by law (13 Oct.) to facilitate early-warning system in the Sinai to monitor peace accord.

UN General Assembly adopted by a vote of 72–35, with 32 abstentions and 3 absent, resolution defining Zionism "as a form of racism and racial discrimination" (10 Nov.), prompting U.S. Ambassador to UN **Daniel P. Moynihan** to declare that the U.S. "will never acquiesce in this infamous act."

30 Sept.–14 Oct. Goodwill tour of U.S. by Japan's Emperor Hirohito.

1–5 Dec. FORD CHINA TRIP with Secretary Kissinger included 2-hour talk with Mao Tse-tung, but was largely ceremonial. Ford briefly visited Indonesia and the Philippines, and on return in Honolulu proclaimed Pacific Doctrine which encompassed (1) normalization of relations with Communist China; (2) partnership with Japan; (3) U.S. stake in stability and security of Southeast Asia; (4) American strength in Pacific; (5) resolution of outstanding political conflicts; (6) economic cooperation in region.

Dec. Foreign economic assistance separated from military assistance and sales program for budgetary purposes in Congress for first time in post-World War II foreign aid programs.

1975–77. CIA INVESTIGATIONS by congressional committees and presidential commission on CIA activities within U.S. (1975–76) headed by Vice President Nelson A. Rockefeller, disclosed that the CIA had (1) conducted massive illegal domestic intelligence operations during the Nixon administration; (2) intercepted and photographed more than 2.7 million envelopes to and from USSR and opened more than 200,000 pieces of mail in 20 years; (3) monitored international cable and telephone traffic (1967–73); (4) engaged in secret war in Laos; (5) possibly been involved in assassination plots aimed at Rafael Trujillo of Dominican Republic (assassinated 30 May 1961), Congo's Patrice Lumumba (death reported 12 Feb. 1961), and Fidel Castro; (6) covertly been engaged in Chilean elections campaign, attempted to foment military takeover to prevent Salvador Allende taking office as President, and spent $8 million to oppose Allende after his election: (7) clandestinely used journalists, professors and students.

In 1977 there were further revelations of (8) payments to foreign heads of state—Chiang Kai-shek, Syngman Rhee, Ngo Dinh Diem, and Jordan's King Hussein; (9) experiments on human subjects to develop methods of behavioral control through the use of drugs and other materials. On 19 May 1976 the Senate established a permanent intelligence committee over the budget and activities of the CIA.

1976

FEB. LOCKHEED BRIBES. Documents made public by Senate Subcommittee on Multinational Corporations linked Lockheed Aircraft Corp. to bribing of foreign officials. Lockheed admitted paying out at least $22 million. Former Japanese Prime Minister Kakuei Tanaka and Prince Bernhard, husband of Dutch Queen Juliana, were among those accused of receiving money. Exxon, Northrop, and Gulf Oil Corp. and United Brands Co. admitted similar activities.

APR. U.S. exclusive fishing zone extended from 12 to 200 miles. In 1966 U.S. had extended zone from 3 to 12 miles.

27 APR. SOUTHERN AFRICA POLICY announced by Secretary of State Kissinger in Lusaka, Zambia, declaring U.S. support for black majority rule in Rhodesia, an independent Namibia (South-West Africa), and an end to apartheid in South Africa.

11 Nov. U.S.-EAST GERMAN GRAIN AGREEMENT provided sale to East Germany of 1.5 to 2 million metric tons of grain per year through 1980. East German ships were to be permitted to dock at U.S. ports for first time since establishment of formal diplomatic relations (4 Sept. 1974).

Foreign Policy: The Carter Years, 1977–81

1977

21 JAN. VIETNAM DRAFT EVADERS granted full pardon by President Carter, so long as they had not been involved in violent acts.

24 FEB. HUMAN RIGHTS POLICY. During Carter administration U.S. foreign policy stressed concern about human rights violations throughout the world. Secretary of State Cyrus R. Vance announced (24 Feb. 1977) that U.S. aid to certain countries, such as Argentina, Uruguay, and Ethiopia, would be reduced due to their human rights violations. Certain strategically located allies such as South Korea and the Philippines were spared cuts for security considerations. Carter ended restrictions on travel by U.S. citizens abroad (9 Mar. 1977), bowing to human rights criticism. In addressing UN (17 May 1977), Carter chided it for letting its human rights machinery be ignored and politicized. With human rights now a major factor in U.S. bilateral relations, Brazil canceled defense treaty with U.S. and rejected further military aid.

U.S. criticism of Soviet human rights violations exacerbated relations. Carter wrote (17 Feb. 1977) Soviet physicist **Andrei Sakharov** (1975 Nobel Peace laureate), stating; "Because we are free, we can never be indifferent to the fate of freedom elsewhere." Brezhnev rejoined that it was "unthinkable" to normal U.S.-USSR relations for Carter to continue his support of Soviet dissidents. The U.S. sharply criticized Soviet nonobservance of Helsinki Accords (6 June 1977) and Carter cited USSR, along with Cambodia, Ethiopia, Chile, Nicaragua, South Africa, and Uganda for human rights violations (6 Dec. 1978).

30 June. WEAPONS SYSTEMS. President Carter canceled **B-1 Bomber** program, which would have cost $100 million per plane, in favor of **Cruise Missile.** Efforts to override Carter decision in Congress failed (Feb. 1978). Carter deferred production decision on building **Neutron bomb** (7 Apr. 1978), enhanced radiation warheads for 60-mile-range missiles and howitzers, whose radiation would be lethal over more than half-mile radius. Permitting equipment modifications to continue, Carter indicated that production of the bomb would depend on attitude of USSR. Carter vetoed defense weapons bill for fiscal 1979 (17 Aug. 1978), objecting to construction of $2 billion nuclear-powered aircraft. Carter also rejected plans for another 90,000-ton aircraft carrier, favoring production of smaller 60,000-ton carriers. Development of the **MX missile**—a $30 billion program deploying large missiles on roads and railroad tracks leading to underground shelters—approved by Carter

(7 June 1979). 12 Dec. 1979 Carter called for a 4.5% "real" increase in the military budget over next five years, compared with previous increases in real dollars of 3% annually during his first 3 years.

10 Aug. PANAMA CANAL TREATIES. U.S. negotiators, led by Ellsworth Bunker and Sol Linowitz, reached agreement with Panama after thirteen years of negotiations. President Carter and Panama Chief of Government, Gen. Omar Torrijos Herrera, signed the two treaties in Washington, D.C., 7 Sept., in the presence of representatives of 26 Western Hemisphere nations. The **general treaty,** which would expire at the end of 1999, provided for (1) repeal of Hay-Bunau-Varilla Treaty of 1903 (p. 349) and other agreements giving U.S. exclusive rights to the canal; (2) continued U.S. responsibility for operation, maintenance, and defense of the canal with increasing responsibility of Panama until full control transferred 31 Dec. 1999; (3) 65% of the Canal Zone, those lands and waters not vital to operation of the canal, were to revert to Panama immediately after treaty ratification; (4) U.S. to retain bases, canal operating areas, and housing for employees; (5) U.S. to pay $10 million annually for police and fire services, $10 million annually from canal operating revenues, and $10 million annually out of any canal revenues exceeding expenditures; (6) Panama to receive 30 cents out of each $1.29 toll per canal ton and a percentage of other revenue from the canal; (7) Panama assured $300 million in loans over several years from international banking institutions; (8) the two nations agreed to study jointly the feasibility of a new sea-level canal.

The second treaty, that of **permanent neutrality,** provided for transit of naval and merchant vessels of all nations at all times; that the U.S. and Panama would agree to maintain the neutrality of the canal. A later **Statement of Understand-**

ing by Carter and Torrijos interpreted U.S. right to defend the canal as the right to act against any aggression or threat directed against the canal, but not the right to intervene in the internal affairs of Panama, and construed the right of the U.S. war vessels to expeditious transit as granting them priority of passage through the canal.

Panama's electorate ratified the treaties by a two-thirds vote in a referendum (23 Oct. 1977). The Senate ratified the **Treaty Concerning the Permanent Neutrality and Operation of the Canal** by one vote, 68–32 (16 Mar. 1978) with three reservations: (1) that each country would retain responsibility for defending the canal against a threat to neutrality after the year 2000; (2) in an emergency, U.S. and Panamanian ships would be given priority; (3) that the U.S. could open the canal with troops, if closed by domestic turmoil. The **General Treaty** was ratified 68–32 (18 Apr. 1978), with a reservation added, giving the U.S. the right to use military force if necessary to keep the canal open, but not to interfere with Panamanian internal affairs or to violate its independence and sovereignty. Carter and Torrijos exchanged the instruments of ratification in Panama City (16 June 1978). Treaty took effect 1 Oct. 1979 and U.S. jurisdiction terminated over the Canal Zone.

1 Nov. U.S. withdrew from International Labor Organization (ILO), protesting politicization, exemplified by 1974 condemnation of Israel for racism and occupation of Arab lands.

1978

1 Feb. U.S. ARMS SALES reduced. To cut down worldwide traffic in conventional arms, Carter administration: (1) placed ceilings on exports; (2) pledged not to introduce new weapons systems into any region; (3) attempted to secure agreement from other major arms suppliers. Policy failed due to availability of other sources of arms and U.S. Middle East commitments.

3 May. U.S.-JAPAN RELATIONS. Bilateral summit meeting between Prime Minister Takeo Fakuda and President Carter produced Japanese agreement to reduce its trade surplus, stabilize the yen against the dollar, and achieve 7% growth rate.

13–18 July. U.S.-USSR RELATIONS continued to deteriorate. Talks in Geneva between Secretary of State Vance and Soviet Foreign Minister Andrei A. Gromyko (12–13 July) were inconclusive. Following harsh sentences meted out (13–14 July) to Soviet dissidents, Anatoly B. Scharansky, leader of Jewish emigration, and Aleksandr Ginzburg, President Carter decided (18 July) to cancel sale of Sperry Univac computer and place oil technology exports under government control. In 1978 Soviets deepened involvements in Vietnam, Ethiopia, and Afghanistan (p. 575).

17 Sept. CAMP DAVID ACCORDS between Israel and Egypt. U.S. and USSR tried unsuccessfully to reconvene Geneva Middle East peace conference, recessed since Dec. 1973, by joint declaration on principles for Middle East peace settlement (1 Oct. 1977). Egypt and Israel seized initiative, with Egyptian President Anwar el-Sadat's visit to Israel (19–21 Nov. 1977). Secretary of State Vance visited six Middle Eastern countries, finding support for new peace process. When Egyptian and Israeli representatives met in Cairo to discuss procedural issues connected with peace negotiations (19 Dec. 1977), U.S. and UN observers attended, but other Middle East nations boycotted the process. Begin and Sadat met again in Ismailia, Egypt (25–26 Dec. 1977).

Carter met with Sadat (4 Jan. 1978) at Aswan in Egypt. Sadat and Begin toured U.S., promoting peace initiatives and meeting with Carter (Feb.–Mar. 1978). By a vote of 54–44 the Senate refused to block sale of 60 F-15 fighter planes to Egypt, permitting Israel to buy 15 F-15s and 75 F-16 fighter bombers (with the right to purchase 20 more F-15s later on).

Carter met with Sadat, Begin, and their aides at Camp David (6–17 Sept. 1978) under a news blackout. The two nations agreed on two principal documents: "A Framework for the Conclusion of a Peace Treaty between Egypt and Israel" and "A Framework for Peace in the Middle East." The first document provided that Egypt and Israel would sign a peace treaty within three months; that thereafter the Sinai would be turned over to Egypt, in stages beginning within three to nine months and ending within two to three years; normal diplomatic relations would follow. The latter document provided a five-year transition period on the West Bank and Gaza; the withdrawal of Israel's military government; an intervening local government for Palestinians; negotiation between Egypt, Israel, Jordan, and elected Palestinian representatives on sovereignty. Palestinians were guaranteed the right to elect representatives, determine their own local government, and participate in decisions on their own future. The issues of Jerusalem and of Israeli settlements on the West Bank were not dealt with in the two Frameworks. On 22 Sept., 9 letters exchanged by Carter with Sadat and Begin were released dealing with controversial issues in the Accords.

After the 17 Dec. 1978 deadline for an Egypt-Israel Agreement had passed, both Sadat and Begin refused to meet jointly with Carter. Carter met alone with Begin (2–4 Mar.) and then conducted personal shuttle diplomacy in the Middle East, meeting with Sadat in Cairo (8–9 Mar.), with Begin in Jerusalem (10–13 Mar.), where he addressed the Knesset; and stopping over in Cairo (13 Mar.) on his way home, where he announced achievement of formula for peace treaty. The Knesset approved the pact (22 Mar.).

The treaty ending hostilities between Israel and Egypt was signed 26 Mar. 1979 on the lawn of the White House and provided for: (1) withdrawal of Israeli military forces and certain settlements from the Sinai phased over three-year period; (2) establishment of normal relations after nine months when two-thirds of the Sinai would be in Egypt's possession; (3) free right of passage for Israel through the Suez Canal; (4) the end of the Egyptian boycott of Israel; (5) Israeli right of purchase of Sinai oil; (6) commencement of negotiations on Palestinian self-rule within a month. U.S. gave Israel assurances in case the treaty fell apart and pledged $4.5 billion ($3.3 billion in loans for arms purchases) aid to Egypt and Israel for 1979–81.

A Begin-Sadat meeting in Cairo (2–3 Apr.) provided for installation of telephone hot-line and return of Sinai town, El-Arish, ahead of schedule. Israel made 2nd stage Sinai withdrawal 25 July. On 19 Sept. the U.S., Egypt, and Israel agreed on the monitoring of the peace pact. Egypt and Israel exchanged ambassadors (26 Feb. 1980).

Sadat's assassination in Cairo, 6 Oct. 1981, imperiled further implementation of Camp David agreement.

15 Dec. U.S.-CHINA FULL DIPLOMATIC RELATIONS announced, effective 1 Jan. 1979. U.S. broke formal diplomatic relations with Nationalist Chinese government and terminated with one year's notice the Mutual Defense Treaty with Taiwan, agreeing to withdraw remaining U.S. troops. The People's Republic of China agreed not to oppose continued American sales of arms to Taiwan or continued American interest. Visiting the U.S. (28 Jan.–5 Feb. 1979), Vice Premier Deng Xiaoping signed agreements with President Carter (31

Jan.) calling for cooperation in science and technology, including U.S. assistance for building nuclear particle accelerator, launching civilian communications satellite, and an exchange of consulates. Formal exchange of ambassadors occurred 1 Mar. 1979, with Leonard Woodcock serving as first U.S. ambassador. On the same day China agreed to settle $196.6 million in claims for U.S. property seized after the Communists came to power in 1949 for 41 cents on the dollar.

The U.S. Embassay in Taiwan officially closed 1 Mar., but U.S. established unofficial institute to maintain cultural, transportation, and trade links (10 Apr. 1979). U.S. Supreme Court (13 Dec.) dismissed a suit brought by Sen. Barry Goldwater and other members of Congress to block termination of the Taiwan Treaty, which was terminated 31 Dec.

Steps to closer relations occurred with: (1) agreement granting China most-favored-nation status (7 July); visit of Vice President Walter Mondale during which it was announced that U.S. would extend $2 billion in trade credits over five years (25 Aug. 1979); announcement during visit of Defense Secretary Harold Brown (Jan. 1980) that U.S. would sell ground station for satellite reception and certain military equipment (which could not be sold to USSR). President Carter and Chinese Communist Party Chairman, Hua Kuo-feng (Hua Guo-feng) met in Tokyo (8 July 1980) after attending memorial service for Japanese Premier Masayoshi Ohira.

1979

6 Apr. NUCLEAR NONPROLIF-ERATION. U.S. cut off aid to Pakistan because of covert construction of uranium enrichment facility. Administration opposition to export of nuclear technology and materials led to strains with Brazil. Strict nuclear export controls were set by Nuclear Non-Proliferation Act (10 Mar. 1978). Sale of enriched uranium to India's atomic power plant approved by Carter, deferring to treaty obligation (19 June 1980).

12 Apr. MULTILATERAL TRADE PACT resulting from Tokyo round of negotiations would gradually lower average U.S. industrial tariff rate from 8.3% to 5.7%, permitting countervailing duties against domestic or export subsidies if domestic industry harmed. Trade liberalization law carrying out agreement passed 26 July.

18 June. SALT II AGREEMENT signed during summit meeting in Vienna between President Carter and Soviet Chairman Brezhnev set ceiling of 2,250 long-range bombers and missiles and limited development to only one new land-based missile system for duration of treaty. Carter and Brezhnev also agreed that Soviet production of TU-22M (Backfire) bomber would not exceed 30 per year. After Soviet invasion of Afghanistan (3 Jan. 1980) Carter asked the Senate to defer action on ratification.

15 Aug. ANDREW YOUNG RESIG-NATION as U.S. ambassador to UN after revelation of unauthorized meeting with representatives of Palestine Liberation Organization (P.L.O.). Young symbolized sympathy with Third World concerns, but had been a controversial figure, often publicly at odds with U.S. policies. Young was succeeded by Donald F. McHenry. McHenry's vote in favor of Security Council resolution calling upon Israel to dismantle settlements on West Bank and Gaza was disavowed two days later by President Carter (1 Mar. 1980), claiming "failure to communicate." Disarray in foreign policy was also exemplified by differences between Secretary of State Vance's emphasis upon traditional diplomacy and National Security Advisor Zbigniew Brzezinski's harder line.

31 Aug. CUBAN BRIGADE. "Discovery" of 23,000-man Soviet combat

brigade in Cuba stirred controversy. Soviets insisted that size and funding had not changed since Cuban missile crisis (pp. 495–96). Carter countered by dispatching 1,500 marines to Guantanamo and increasing surveillance of Cuba. Relations with Cuba had deteriorated over Cuban troop involvements in Angola and Ethiopia, as well as its role in promoting instability in Latin America. Longtime dictator Anastasio Somoza Debayle of **Nicaragua** was overthrown by Sandinista guerrillas (July 1979). Civil strife intensified in **El Salvador** after murder of Archbishop Oscar Arnulfo Romero y Galdames (24 Mar. 1980).

1–7 OCT. POPE JOHN PAUL II's visits to Boston, New York City, Philadelphia, Iowa, Chicago, and Washington hailed by enthusiastic crowds. Pope reaffirmed the doctrine of a celibate, male clergy and denounced abortion.

4 Nov. HOSTAGE CRISIS. Shah Mohammed Reza Pahlevi fled Iran (16 Jan. 1979), after small-scale disturbances by Islamic fundamentalists beginning in 1977 led to revolt. **Ayatollah Ruhollah Khomeini** returned from exile (1 Feb. 1979) and established Islamic republic. When U.S. admitted Shah to receive medical treatment in New York (22 Oct.–2 Dec.), hundreds of students stormed U.S. Embassy in Teheran (4 Nov.), taking hostages. Prime Minister Mehdi Bazargan resigned (6 Nov.) and Khomeini turned power over to Revolutionary Council. 53 Americans were to remain in captivity for 444 days (one was released earlier due to illness).

Carter cut off U.S. imports of Iranian oil (12 Nov.), froze Iranian assets in U.S. (14 Nov.), and ordered review of visas of Iranian students. A naval task force was sent to the Indian Ocean (20 Nov.) and Carter announced in his State of the Union Address (23 Jan. 1980) that U.S. would go to war to protect oil supply routes in Persian Gulf region. Iranian diplomats were ordered out of

the country, but formal relations were not broken until 7 Apr. 1980. Further economic sanctions were taken 17 Apr. The Shah flew to San Antonio (2 Dec.), to Panama (15 Dec.), and died of cancer in Cairo (27 July 1980).

Efforts by the Security Council, UN Secretary General Kurt Waldheim, and special UN Commission failed to secure release of hostages, as did rulings of International Court of Justice. The hostage crisis dominated U.S. foreign policy for over a year. Saturation coverage by mass communications elevated hostage plight to central national concern. While bolstering President Carter's race for the Democratic presidential nomination, it ultimately contributed to his defeat for re-election (4 Nov. 1980), anniversary of the hostages' capture.

On 25 Jan. Abolhassan Bani-Sadr was elected President of Iran. Elections for parliament (Majlis) were held (14 Mar.; 9 May 1980) and the Majlis then elected Muhammed Ali Rajai, Prime Minister. Debate on the hostage issue deferred in Iran until 26 Oct.

U.S. military operation to free the hostages (25 Apr.) was aborted because of helicopter failure. 8 U.S. servicemen died in collision of helicopter and transport plane. Secretary of State Vance resigned (28 Apr.) over rescue mission.

On 12 Sept. Ayatollah Khomeini listed four conditions for release of the hostages: (1) unfreezing Iranian assets in American banks; (2) U.S. promise not to intervene in Iran's affairs; (3) cancellation of American claims against Iran; (4) return to Iran of the Shah's wealth. On 22 Sept. border hostilities between Iraq and Iran turned into war. The Majlis voted (2 Nov.) to release the hostages, if the U.S. accepted the four conditions. Indirect negotiations commenced through the Algerian government, directed by Foreign Minister Mohammed Benyahia. On 27 Nov. it was announced that the hostages had been turned over to the Iranian government. On 21 Dec. Iran demanded U.S. deposit of $24 billion in Algeria to guarantee return of Shah's assets. Negotiations led by U.S. Deputy Secretary of State Warren Christopher, Iran's Minister of Executive Affairs Bezhad Nabavi, and Benyahia, reached final stages (16–18 Jan. 1981). An agreement was announced (19 Jan.) but held up until 20 Jan., Inauguration Day. The aircrafts carrying the hostages left Teheran airport at 12:33 P.M. EST, just after Ronald Reagan completed his Inaugural Address. The hostages were greeted in Wiesbaden, West Germany, by Jimmy Carter, President Reagan's envoy. They arrived at West Point for reunion with families (25 Jan.), before welcome at the White House (27 Jan.) by President Reagan: "You are home and our hearts are full of gratitude." Return of the hostages evoked an outpouring of spontaneous emotion and national pride.

The Agreement between the U.S. and Iran provided for: (1) U.S. declaration of policy to refrain from interference in Iran's internal affairs; (2) out of $12 billion in frozen Iranian assets, U.S. at time of hostage release would turn over $7.9 billion, of which $3.7 billion would be used to repay loans of U.S. banks to regime of Shah and $1.4 billion was to be kept in escrow for loans made to Iranian governmental entities; (3) of the remaining $4 billion, $1 billion would be placed in escrow account to be used to pay off claims of American private firms to be determined by international arbitral tribunal; (4) the U.S. agreed to move in U.S. courts to terminate attachments and legal proceedings against Iran; (5) the U.S. also agreed to nullify claims against Iran for seizing the embassy; (6) trade restrictions against Iran were removed; (7) the U.S. froze the assets of the Shah and his family and recognized the decrees of Iran nationalizing the property. On 2 July 1981 the United States Supreme Court upheld President's authority to have U.S. firms' claims settled by international tribunal (**Dames & Moore v. Regan**).

27 DEC. AFGHANISTAN INVASION. On 27 Dec. 1979 Soviet troops were airlifted to Afghanistan to support a coup ousting and executing Premier Hafizullah Amin, USSR ally, with Babrak Karmal replacing him. By early Jan. 1980, invasion forces numbered 85,000 troops. In response, President Carter embargoed the sale of grain—limiting the Soviets to 8 million metric tons sanctioned by the 1976 trade agreement (preventing sale of another 17 million tons)—and of high technology to the USSR, curtailed Soviet fishing rights, and delayed commencement of new economic and cultural exchanges. Carter called for delay in ratification of Salt II Treaty (p. 510) and for a boycott of the 1980 summer Olympic games, to be held in Moscow. 81 nations participated in the games (opening 19 July), but 65 abstained, including U.S., China, Japan, and West Germany. Other consequences of the Afghanistan invasion and the Iranian hostage crisis: (1) announcement by U.S. (24 Jan. 1980) that it was willing to sell military equipment to China; (2) draft registration (p. 564); (3) U.S. bilateral negotiations with Oman, Kenya, and Somalia for access to military and naval bases; (4) expansion of U.S. Indian Ocean naval base Diego Garcia.

1980

3, 6 JUNE. FALSE ALARMS that Soviet missiles had been launched against U.S. triggered by faulty computer in U.S. defense network.

5 AUG. COUNTERFORCE STRATEGY against USSR's threat to U.S. land-based missiles announced in Presidential Directive 59. Strategy of mutual deterrence, massive destruction of cities and industries as strategic targets, was replaced by targeting military installations and command posts.

4 SEPT. ARAMCO NATIONALIZED. Saudi Arabia confirmed completion of takeover of Arabian American Oil Company, which had begun with purchase of 25% (1973).

2 DEC.–15 DEC. 1981. POLISH UNREST. Soviet pressures on Polish government to deal sternly with widespread moves for political liberalization led to U.S. warning against Soviet intervention. Unrest continued for months thereafter as workers under the banner of the Solidarity labor union led by Lech Walesa pressed demands, in effect forming an opposition party without precedent in Communist countries. To overcome the severe economic crisis and to end the continuing strikes curtailing production the Communist government considered (4 Nov. 1981) forming a Front of National Agreement. The Soviet Union avoided direct military intervention, but a Polish military government imposed martial law, 13 Dec., rounding up Solidarity leaders. U.S. suspends aid 14 Dec. (See also p. 582.)

Reagan Administration: Initial Year, 1981

20 JAN. REAGAN INAUGURAL ADDRESS, given for first time on West Front of Capitol, declared that "government is not the solution to our problem; government is the problem," and announced that "it is time to reawaken the industrial giant, to get government back within its means, and to lighten our punitive tax burden." The 52 American hostages were released from captivity 5 minutes after Reagan completed his addess. Shortly after he finished his speech, Reagan ordered a freeze on government hiring of civilian employees.

23 JAN.–4 NOV. EL SALVADOR CRISIS. U.S. suspended aid fund payments to Nicaragua because of alleged support of the guerrilla movement in El Salvador by the Sandinista government. On 1 Feb. U.S. Ambassador to El Salvador, Robert E. White, was relieved of his duties. White, an advocate of internal reforms instead of increased military aid, was replaced by Frederic I. Chapin, a career diplomat without Latin American experience, and drastic changes were made in the top echelon of the Bureau of Inter-American Affairs. U.S. charges that both Russia and Cuba were aiding the guerrillas was, as regards the former, officially denied by Moscow (14 Feb.). On 16 July the Reagan administration announced support for a political solution in El Salvador, pledging U.S. backing for free elections, while Assistant Secretary of State Thomas O. Enders stressed the need for more economic as well as military aid, although conceding that the "ultimate resolution" was a Salvadoran problem. With evidence mounting that a stalemate existed, France and Mexico in a joint statement (28 Aug.) recognized the guerrilla-led opposition as a "representative political force," having a right to participate in negotiations ending the conflict. On 15 Oct. the National Liberation forces blew up the Golden Bridge severing a direct route to the eastern third of the country and increasing the guerrillas' freedom to move in that area. By November, with military stalemate continuing and excesses from the right matching those from the left, Secretary of State Haig conceded that the U.S. was forced to reexamine its military options.

30 MAR. ASSASSINATION ATTEMPT. President Reagan was shot in the chest about 2:30 P.M. while emerging from the Washington Hilton Hotel.

The assailant was 25-yr.-old John W. Hinckley, Jr., son of a Colorado oil executive. Presidential Press Secretary James S. Brady was critically wounded, and one Secret Service officer and a police officer were also wounded in the attack. After surgery at George Washington University Hospital the President made a rapid recovery and was released from the hospital on 11 April. During Reagan's stay at the hospital Vice President Bush, in Texas at the time of the shooting, assumed his duties, but not before Secretary of State Haig had presided over a Cabinet meeting and made a televised announcement that "as of now" he was in control at the White House.

31 Mar.–4 Nov. HUMAN RIGHTS POLICY REVERSALS. In a speech before the Trilateral Commission Secretary of State Haig, reaffirming a position previously articulated by UN Ambassador Jeane J. Kirkpatrick, insisted that the U.S. "should distinguish between the so-called totalitarian and authoritarian regimes" as regards their treatment of human rights, indicating in effect a reversal of the Carter human rights' policy. In accordance with this new policy the Reagan administration proposed legislation to remove restrictions on military assistance to Chile and Argentina. However, the State Department in a memorandum (4 Nov.) approved by Secretary of State Haig modified the Reagan line by advocating a strong posture on political freedom and human rights in order to offer a credible alternative to the Soviet example and help stem the rising tide of neutralism, while the White House named Elliot Abrams to handle human rights in the State Department instead of the controversial Ernest W. Lefever, whose nomination had been withdrawn in deference to objections from the Senate Committee on Foreign Relations.

12 Apr. SPACE SHUTTLE COLUMBIA, the world's 1st reusable spacecraft, developed at a cost of $9.9 billion, was launched at 7:00 A.M. EST at Cape Canaveral, Fla., gliding to a perfect landing two days later at 10:21 A.M. EST at Edwards Air Force Base, Calif. Manning the craft were John W. Young and Navy Capt. Robert L. Crippen. A 2d flight, with the first working payload of scientific instruments, was successfully launched at 10:10 A.M. EST on 12 Nov., and landed safely at Edwards Air Force Base at 4:23 P.M. on 14 Nov. The latter space flight was manned by Air Force Col. Joe H. Engle and Navy Capt. Richard H. Truly. The trip was shortened by several days because of the failure of one of the three fuel cells.

12 May. SOCIAL SECURITY MODIFICATIONS. President Reagan proposed revising the Social Security system in an effort to return it to fiscal solvency by cutting some $46 billion of benefits over a 5-yr. period. Proposals included raising the retirement age for initial benefits to 67 from 65, taxing social security payments, and slowing cost-of-living boosts after 1985. Congress stalled in response to powerful grass-roots opposition.

15 June–9 Nov. INTERNATIONAL TERRORISM. The Central Intelligence Agency issued a report revealing that worldwide terrorist attacks had mounted dramatically, citing 6,714 international terrorist incidents between 1968 and 1980, with U.S. citizens, especially diplomats and businessmen, as prime targets. The report charged Libyan ruler Col. Muammar Qadaffi with directing assassination teams in the U.S., Europe, and the Middle East to move against Libyan expatriates and student dissidents. By the fall of 1981 evidence mounted that ex-CIA employees had been or were currently engaged in illegally exporting U.S. arms to Libya, providing that government with pilots for military moves against Chad, and training terrorists. Reported to be the chief operator of the program was **Edwin P. Wilson,** a fugitive from an indictment charging him with illegal dealings in explosives, who had worked for the CIA and the Office of Naval Intelligence from 1955 to 1976. In a CBS interview from Beirut (8 Nov.) ex-CIA agent Frank E. Terpil, a Wilson associate and fugitive under sentence in New York to 53 yrs. in prison, admitted that he and Wilson had made payoffs to a State Department employee and certain U.S. military and intelligence officials to facilitate illegal operations. The CIA (9 Nov.) denied "official" involvement.

4 Aug. ECONOMIC RECOVERY TAX ACT (ERTA), the first major program of the Reagan administration, provided budget and tax cuts, which, considering their size and scope, constituted a significant structural change in government policy. Acting in response to campaign pledges and in deference to supply-side economics, the package of tax and budget cuts was designed to reduce the size of the federal government and stimulate growth in the private sector. Its major features: (1) **Personal income taxes** cut 25% across-the-board over 33 months; eliminated distinction between earned and unearned income; dropped maximum tax on all income from 70% to 50% as of 1 Jan. 1982. Effective 1985, tax rates, personal exemptions, and standard deductions are to be indexed to reflect cost-of-living increases; provides penalty relief for two-earner couples; allows taxpayers who do not itemize to deduct a portion of their charitable contributions; allows child care deductions for persons earning no more than $10,000, dropping off proportionately for taxpayers earning at least $30,000; permits Americans working abroad to exclude the first $75,000 of income in 1982, as well as housing expenses, both credits to rise in later years.

(2) **Personal savings and investment incentives** include reducing the maximum tax on capital gains from 28% to 20% retroactive to 10 June 1981; authorizes banks and savings institutions to issue for a 15-month period, beginning 1 Oct. 1981, a one-yr. savings certificate that could pay up to 70% of the yield on one-yr. Treasury bills, with income earned on these certificates excluded from taxable income, up to $1,000 for single taxpayers, $2,000 for couples filing jointly. Effective 1 Jan. 1985 15% of savings interest income can be excluded, up to $3,000 for individuals, or $6,000 for couples filing jointly. Present temporary exclusion of $200 of interest and dividend income ($400 joint) would drop back to $100 ($200) in 1982. The act liberalizes deductions for contributions to individual retirement accounts, doubling maximum deductible contributions under Keogh to $15,000. Extended tax-free repurchase period for sellers of real estate to 2 yrs. from 18 mos., and one-time capital gains exclusion for people over 55 would increase to $125,000 from $100,000.

(3) **Estate and gift taxes.** Between 1981 and 1987 the amount excluded from estate and gift tax would rise from $175,000 to $600,000. The act eliminates taxes on transfers between spouses beginning 1 Jan. 1982; raises the present limit of annual gift exclusion from $3,000 per beneficiary to $10,000 on 1 Jan. 1982; and allows lower than previous valuations of farm land passed on to heirs at $500,000 below the "highest and best use" valuations; a spread widening in two steps to $750,000 by 1982.

(4) **Business taxes.** The act replaces complicated array of useful-life categories by four categories: (a) 3 yrs. for autos, light trucks and some special tools; (b) 5 yrs., all other machinery and equipment; (c) 10 yrs., certain public utility property now written off in 18–25 yrs. and some real estate now written off in 10 yrs. or less; (d) 15 yrs. for all other depreciable real estate and public utility holdings now written off in 25 yrs. Other changes in the business tax package include investment tax credits; 3-yr.

fast write-offs for research and development; raising current 10% credit for rehabilitation of buildings from 15% to 25% (historic buildings); increases investment credit on used equipment, and allows depreciation and interest tax credits to be passed on to the lessee.

(5) **Small business.** The act provides gradual reduction to 1983 of corporate tax rate on income up to $25,000; liberalizes depreciation for investments in the first year of purchase; raises from $150,-000 to $250,000 the amount of accumulated earnings that can be held tax-free; increases to 25 from 15 the number of shareholders that qualify as partnerships for tax purposes.

(6) **Oil taxes.** The act cuts the Windfall Profits Tax on "new" oil (discovered after 1 Jan. 1979) in half over 5 yrs. from 30% to 15%; exempts oil from "stripper" wells (production less than 10 bbls daily); liberalizes the exclusion from the windfall profits tax by oil royalty owners up to $2,500 in 1981; 2 bbls per day, 1982–84; 3 bbls per day, in 1985–86, when the exclusion is estimated to be worth up to $12,000 per annum.

(7) **Retirement Plans.** The act provides that active participants in an employer-sponsored qualified plan will now also be able to participate in an Individual Retirement Account (IRA). The IRA limit has been raised to 100% of earned income, up to a maximum of $2,000 each year; an individual with a non-working spouse, up to $2,250 to a combined spousal and individual IRA. The contribution is tax deductible up to the above limits, and earnings on an IRA are tax-free until withdrawn.

'82 Budget Cuts. Accompanying the tax cuts was a package of budget cuts sought by President Reagan as a part of his economic recovery program. Congress (31 July) pared $35.2 billion in spending, while increasing defense outlays by $12.3 billion for fiscal '82, out of a total proposed '82 budget of $695 billion. Although not as deep as the President and Director of the Office of Management and Budget David A. Stockman had requested, Congress imposed severe cuts on many social and cultural programs. Education was cut from 50 to 30 programs; synthetic fuel projects canceled, and appropriations slashed in environmental, health, housing, and urban aid programs as well as for the National Endowments for the Arts and Humanities and the Corporation for Public Broadcasting. $1.6 billion was slashed from food stamp program and sharp reductions made in federal subsidies for school meals.

A second round of cuts was initiated by the President and Stockman (9 Sept.), when estimates projected a sharp decline in tax revenues as a result of the sweeping tax cuts just enacted, a projected decline in business earnings attributed to the emerging recession, and higher interest rates as a result of the continued tight money policy of the Federal Reserve Board. On 24 Sept. Reagan announced plans to seek an additional $13 billion in budget cuts, along with a recommendation of $3 billion of additional tax revenues for the current fiscal year. Without further budget cuts and additional tax revenue the Office of Management and Budget projected an '82 budget deficit of $100 billion, with a $125 billion deficit for '83, and the '84 budget deficit soaring to $145 billion. In the face of economic and fiscal realities the President on 6 Nov. abandoned his long-stated goal of a balanced budget by fiscal '84, and almost immediately thereafter Secretary of Health and Human Resources Richard S. Schweiker, following the recommendations of the Interagency Entitlement Advisory Group, proposed fundamental changes in Medicare and Medicaid programs, including strict new limits on federal payments for hospital care and physicians' services, increase in Medicare premiums, and new payroll tax on federal employees that would generate money for the medical trust fund.

6 OCT. SADAT'S ASSASSINATION. The fatal shooting of President Anwar el-Sadat during the annual commemoration ceremonies marking the Egyptians' storming across the Suez Canal during the Yom Kippur War stunned the world and forced the U.S. to reconsider its options for Middle East peace. In an historic mission of mourning, ex-Presidents Nixon, Ford, and Carter represented the U.S. at the Egyptian leader's funeral. Ford and Carter stated in interviews that sooner or later the U.S. would have to deal with the PLO.

13 OCT. NEW MX MISSILE PROPOSAL. The most controversial element in the new $180 billion dollar defense program announced by President Reagan was his proposal to build 100 MX missiles (more powerful and accurate than Minuteman ICBMs) to be placed in hardened existing Titan silos in Arizona, Kansas, and Arkansas, with a decision on permanent basing deferred. This proposal meant scrapping the Carter plan to shift 200 MX missiles around 4,600 shelters in the desert of Nevada and Utah. While the plan was applauded in the West, it was sharply criticized in Congress and publicly questioned by Gen. David Jones, chairman of the Joint Chiefs of Staff.

22–24 OCT. CANCUN CONFERENCE. To deal with the yawning gap between the prosperous Northern Hemisphere and the impoverished South, leaders of eight industrial powers and fourteen developing countries met in Mexico in a conference co-chaired by President José López Portillo and Canadian Prime Minister Pierre Elliott Trudeau. President Reagan attended on condition that Cuba not be invited, while the Soviet Union and the Eastern bloc nations were conspicuously absent. Data was considered concerning the mounting third world debt (debt service costs rose from $8 billion, 1971, to $47 billion,

1979), the chronic hunger and malnutrition suffered by approximately one billion people, and the soaring cost of energy. The conference adopted a vaguely worded statement endorsing further economic negotiations, and also agreed on an agenda for the UN, with the understanding that the latter could not override decisions of the World Bank. On 9 Nov., over U.S. protests, the International Monetary Fund approved a $5.8 billion loan to India to ease its balance-of-payments difficulties resulting from higher prices for imported oil.

28 OCT. AWACS FOR THE SAUDIS. The Senate, after spirited debate and intense lobbying, rejected, 52 to 48, a resolution of disapproval, keeping intact the $8.5 billion sale of five Airborne Warning and Control System (AWACS) radar planes and other military hardware to Saudi Arabia. In mid-October the House had rejected the AWACS deal by a 3 to 1 margin. The proposal had seemed headed for defeat barely 48 hours before the Senate vote, but the tide was turned by personal pressures exerted by President Reagan and Senate majority leader Howard H. Baker. To mollify pro-Israeli supporters Presidential counsellor Edwin Meese 3d, in a subsequent speech to the American Jewish Congress, declared that the President was "absolutely committed" to "ensuring that Israel retains its qualitative edge in military superiority over any foreseeable combination of adversaries."

Coincidentally, Saudi Crown Prince Fahd proposed an 8-point plan as a substitute for the Camp David agreement. The plan called for Israeli withdrawal from all territory captured in the 1967 war, the establishment of an independent Palestinian state, while affirming the "right of states in the region to live in peace," but without defining Israel as a "state." Avoiding outright rejection of the plan, which the administration considered "interesting" with "positive aspects," the President earlier suggested (17 Oct.) that U.S. would be willing to talk to the PLO provided they were prepared "to recognize Israel's right to exist."

3 Nov. ELECTION TRENDS. The results of the gubernatorial and state legislative races offered few clues to national opinion on the Reagan administration's performance to date. Both the Virginia victory with strong black support of conservative Democrat Charles S. Robb, son-in-law of the late President Lyndon B. Johnson, and the extremely close contest in New Jersey between Republican Thomas H. Kean, the victor, and Democrat James J. Florio suggested that local rather than national issues were controlling.

Among significant state referenda may be mentioned: (1) The rejection of a proposed state constitutional amendment in Kentucky, which would permit state officials, including the governor, to succeed themselves in office, was considered a defeat for Democratic Governor John Y. Brown, Jr. (2) Voters in Washington, D.C. overwhelmingly defeated a referendum that would have established tax tuition credits of up to $1,200 for parents who chose private schools or public schools outside the District for their children, a proposal in line with President Reagan's own support for a nationwide tax-credit measure. (3) Voters in Washington state approved a ballot proposition that limits the right of municipalities to issue revenue bonds for power plants without voter approval. The voters' target was the system of five nuclear reactors that the Washington Public Power Supply System had under construction since 1973. Cost overruns had already forced the shutdown of construction of two of the five nuclear power plants, clouding the future of the ambitious Northwest energy program. On 3 Nov. also the startup of the Diablo Canyon nuclear power plant, located less than 3 mi. from the San Andreas Fault system and center

of environmental demonstrations, was halted because of design construction faults. Contrariwise, the Senate on 4 Nov. voted to appropriate $188 million for the Clinch River breeder reactor as well as $189 million to the Tennessee–Tombigbee Waterway in Mississippi and Alabama, designed to link the Tennessee River with the Gulf of Mexico. Both projects continued to be highly controversial.

4–7 Nov. NUCLEAR TACTICS RIFT. Following closely upon anti-U.S. demonstrations in leading NATO cities protesting President Reagan's August decision authorizing production of neutron warheads and a subsequent comment on the possibility of limiting a nuclear war to Europe, Secretary of State Haig told the Senate Foreign Relations Committee on 4 Nov. that an attack by Soviet conventional forces might bring into play a NATO option of setting off a "demonstration" nuclear weapon. Testifying the next day before the Senate Armed Services Committee, Defense Secretary Weinberger denied that this option existed in current NATO plans. Prompt statements by the White House, State, and Defense Departments seeking to reconcile the apparent disarray in the Reagan administration, coming in the wake of charges by Haig that a high-ranking White House official was waging a "guerrilla campaign" to drive him out of the government, created an impression of deepening confusion on foreign policy and defense objectives. Quick to respond to U.S. statements suggesting the feasibility of using nuclear weapons, Soviet Defense Minister Dmitri F. Ustinov in a speech (7 Nov.) at the annual Red Square military parade, denied that Russia sought nuclear superiority, while warning that it would never allow another country to gain superiority.

30 Nov. U.S.–ISRAELI ACCORD signed providing for strategic cooperation against Soviet and Soviet-controlled forces in Eastern Mediterranean.

**1 Dec. GENEVA ARMS REDUC-
TION MEETING.** Following President
Reagan's announcement (18 Nov.) that
U.S. was prepared to cancel deployment
of nuclear missiles in Europe if the
Soviets would dismantle their SS-20,
SS-4, and SS-5 missiles, and seek equality
at lower levels of conventional forces,
Leonid I. Brezhnev countered (23 Nov.),
offering to reduce number of Soviet
medium-range nuclear weapons in Europe, if U.S. suspended missile deployment during 2-power negotiations. Formal U.S.–Soviet talks began (1 Dec.)
with Paul H. Nitze, chief of U.S. team,
and Yuli A. Kvitsinsky heading Soviet
mission.

4 Dec. CURBS ON CIA LIFTED.
Presidential order expanding power of
U.S. intelligence agencies to collect foreign intelligence from U.S. citizens relaxed Carter ban of Jan. 1978 on covert
actions by C.I.A. at home. (See also p.
559.)

**10 Dec. DETERIORATING LIBYAN
RELATIONS.** Acting on reports that Col.
Qaddafi had dispatched terrorist squads
to assassinate the President and other
high U.S. officials, Reagan called on
Americans to leave Libya "as soon as
possible" and invalidated U.S. passports
for travel to Libya. "Other measures,"
including an oil embargo, were mentioned as under consideration.

**19 Dec. U.S.–ISRAELI STRATEGIC
PACT SUSPENDED** in response to Israel's annexation of the Golan Heights.

**28 Dec. FIRST U.S. "TEST TUBE"
BABY,** Elizabeth Jordan Carr, born at
Norfolk General Hospital, Norfolk, Va.
(See also p. 818).

**29 Dec. NEW ANTI-SOVIET TRADE
BOYCOTT.** Declaring that "the Soviet
Union bears a heavy responsibility for
the repression in Poland" (also p. 576),
President Reagan announced sharp cutbacks on Soviet-American trade and scientific exchanges: (1) suspended issuance
or renewal of export licenses for electronic equipment, computers, and other
high-technology items; (2) restricted access to American ports by Soviet ships;
(3) barred new licenses for oil and gas
equipment, including equipment for the
proposed natural gas pipeline from Siberia to Western Europe; (4) suspended
landing rights in U.S. for Aeroflot, the
Soviet government airline.

**31 Dec. CRACKS IN WESTERN
ALLIANCE.** Although some Western
allies of the U.S. condemned Soviet interference in Poland, none as of year's
end joined the Reagan boycott. Significantly, West German Chancellor Helmut
Schmidt adopted a policy of cautious
inaction, not even speaking out to condemn the military takeover in Poland.

2
Topical
Chronology

THE EXPANSION OF THE NATION

America's abundant natural resources made it possible to create almost from the start a society with few of the carryovers of European feudalism, one based upon freeholding farmers. These abundant resources were hospitable to population growth, rapid interior settlement, and an optimistic economic climate favoring investment and development. A nation of freeholding farmers was promoted by federal land policy. Initially intended for gradual sale at high prices to provide federal revenue, land was made available for credit on increasingly liberal terms. When the Panic of 1819 plunged the credit of farmers into disarray, cash payments were required instead, an action which spurred a reduction of land prices, culminating in the demand for free land and, finally, in the Homestead Act of 1862. Closely related to the revenue secured from the public domain was the movement for national programs for internal improvements, a movement which in the 1830s culminated in a program for the distribution of the revenues to the states, the precedent for the recent Revenue-Sharing program.

Down through 1867 (the Pacific island of Midway excepted) territorial expansion, acquired by purchase, conquest, or diplomacy, and fostered by notions of "manifest destiny," created a continental domain. In the decades that followed the argument was increasingly pressed that overseas expansion was needed for expanding markets, for enhancing national prestige, and for national security, aside from religious and humanitarian considerations. Whether or not broadening markets to slake the appetite of ever-expanding industrial capitalism proved the predominant consideration, the United States did by the turn of the twentieth century find itself in possession of an overseas empire. Imperialism, however, never sat easily on the American conscience. Cuba quickly acquired full sovereignty, the Philippines its independence after a much longer interval, and Alaska and Hawaii became states of the Union. The path that Puerto Rico, the Virgin Islands, Guam, and the Trust Territories will take is as yet unclear, although a third road is offered by Puerto Rico's Commonwealth status, to which some Indian groups are also aspiring.

The civil rights struggle of the 1960s brought with it a retrospective look at the immense costs by which the North American continent had been tamed, including the decimation of American Indian society through disease, war, and maladministration, and the long and shameful chapter of black slavery. Almost from the beginning the federal government exercised some degree of control over private land acquisition by providing lands for the support of educational and charitable institutions. The post-Civil War period saw the burgeoning of a conservation movement and the growth of a national park system. Recent decades have brought a growing awareness that the era of limitless abundance was rapidly drawing to a close, that, beyond the early conservation measures, orderly future growth, prosperity, and even survival dictated far sterner conservation measures than had been adopted in the past, and that ecological considerations be given a high priority in national planning.

Territorial Expansion, Transportation, and Communications

GEOGRAPHICAL FACTORS. English settlement was favored by a heavily forested coastal area abounding in good ports and river systems leading into the interior. For the first 150 years the English colonists were largely confined within a strip running from the Atlantic coast inland to the Appalachian Mountains. First to be settled was the southern Tidewater region and the northern coastal lowlands; second, the Piedmont area above the fall line, a rolling elevation extending to the mountain barrier. The French ascended the St. Lawrence and the Great Lakes, and by easy portages were able to settle the interior as far as the upper Mississippi long before the English. For the English colonists the chief natural passages across the mountain barrier were: **To Canada**—Hudson–Lake George–Lake Champlain–Richelieu River. **To the Ohio Valley**—(1) Mohawk–Lake Ontario; (2) Susquehanna-Monongahela; (3) Potomac-Monongahela; (4) Roanoke-Kanawha. **To the South**—Valley of Virginia–upper Tennessee–Cumberland.

STAGES OF FRONTIER EXPANSION. The **frontier** (usually defined as an area containing not less than 2 nor more than 6 inhabitants to the square mile, and actually a plurality of zones) was constantly pushing into the interior, and generally according to the following stages: (1) initial zone—hunters, trappers, fur traders; (2) cattlemen; (3) miners (less significant in the colonial period than later); (4) farmers; (5) town dwellers.

EARLY NORTHERN FRONTIER EXPANSION: 1630–77. Advancing New England settlements spread over the coastal lowlands and up river valleys, thus isolating Indian tribes that occupied the highlands of the interior. The natives struck back in 2 wars—the Pequot War (1636–37, p. 43) and King Philip's War (1675–77, pp. 46–47). In the latter the Wampanoags (east of Narragansett Bay), Narragansetts, and Nipmucks (between coast and Connecticut Valley) were virtually exterminated.

1677–1704. Indian defeat allowed peaceful expansion over the remaining river valleys and into the highlands of Massachusetts and Connecticut. When wars with French Canada (pp. 74–75) brought new Indian attacks (1689–

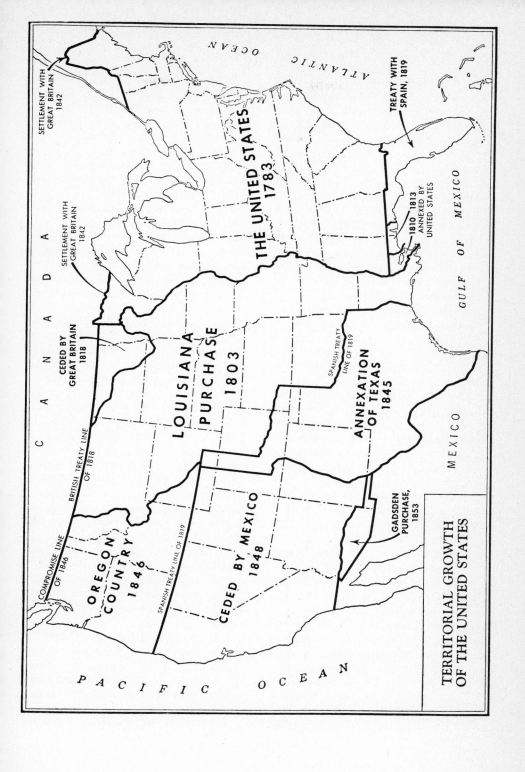

TERRITORIAL GROWTH
OF THE UNITED STATES

THE UNITED STATES
1783

LOUISIANA
PURCHASE
1803

OREGON
COUNTRY
1846

CEDED BY MEXICO
1848

ANNEXATION
OF TEXAS
1845

GADSDEN
PURCHASE,
1853

CANADA

MEXICO

PACIFIC OCEAN

ATLANTIC OCEAN

GULF OF MEXICO

SETTLEMENT WITH
GREAT BRITAIN
1842

SETTLEMENT WITH
GREAT BRITAIN
1842

CEDED BY
GREAT BRITAIN
1818

BRITISH TREATY LINE OF 1818

COMPROMISE LINE
OF 1846

SPANISH TREATY LINE OF 1819

SPANISH TREATY
LINE OF 1819

TREATY WITH
SPAIN, 1819

1810-1813
ANNEXED BY
UNITED STATES

1713), Massachusetts and Connecticut designated 19 towns as frontier forts, forming a fortified ring between York, Me., and Plainfield, Conn. Behind this the frontier advanced steadily.

1704–76. By 1750 the interior of Connecticut and Massachusetts was so well settled that expansion turned northward, where between 1750 and 1776 74 new towns were established in Vermont, 100 in New Hampshire, and 94 in Maine.

EARLY SOUTHERN FRONTIER EXPANSION SOUTHWARD: 1646–76. Settlement followed river valleys south and west. Indian attacks were prevented by granting 600-acre plots to adventurers who would establish forts on the western edge of the Tidewater.

1663–90. Establishment of the colony of Carolina, with centers of settlement at Albemarle Sound and Charleston (1670), pushed back the Spaniards who had been advancing northward from Florida.

1689–1713. Border warfare along the Carolina frontier, as part of the Intercolonial Wars (p. 75), resulted in the destruction of Spanish missions in southeastern Georgia and western Florida.

1713–32. Continued Indian warfare along the Spanish borderland, highlighted by the massacre of several hundred Carolinians by Yamassee Indians (1715), led to the founding of Georgia (p. 76) in 1732. This resulted in pushing the Spanish frontier back beyond the Altamaha River (1739–42).

EARLY SOUTHERN FRONTIER EXPANSION WESTWARD: 1650–76. Exploration of the Piedmont began in 1650 when Capt. Abraham Wood and Edward Bland explored to the forks of the Roanoke. A more important expedition under Thomas Batts and Robert Fallam (1671–73) followed the Staunton River through the Blue Ridge to emerge on the westerly-flowing New River. By 1673 the Yadkin River had

been explored, and a pass opened through the Carolina Blue Ridge.

1676. BACON'S REBELLION (p. 33), caused in part by failure to maintain a peaceful frontier with the Indians. The defeated rebels fled westward, stimulating the frontier advance.

1716. Governor Alexander Spotswood (1676–1740) of Virginia led an expedition up the James into the Shenandoah Valley, advertising the West.

1750. Engrossment of the Virginia and Carolina Piedmont by the mid-18th century, with 2 huge grants: (1) Lord Fairfax—"Northern Neck" of Virginia between the Rappahannock and Potomac rivers; (2) Earl of Granville—most of northern North Carolina. Hence, exploration and settlement of the West deemed imperative. In New York land system had discouraged settlement by small farmers in the western part of the colony. The settlement, Oct. 1710, of 3,000 Palatines near Livingston Manor, to produce naval stores, soon failed, some settlers moved into the Schoharie Valley, but could not get title. By 1750 all the river valleys and principal arable areas in New York had been engrossed by speculators and insiders, causing immigration to be deflected to Pennsylvania. But cheaper lands to the south drew immigrants (Germans and Scotch-Irish) into the Valley of Virginia (by 1727; Winchester settled 1731). In 1751 German Moravians purchased 100,000 acres near Yadkin River, N.C. Scotch-Irish settled the western fringes of the Appalachians and built outposts along the rivers of the upper Tennessee system.

EARLY INTERIOR TRANSPORTATION. River systems preferred to overland passage. Original roads were based on Indian trails. Intertown and intercolonial roads were developed in the first half of the 18th century.

1732. First stagecoach line for the

conveyance of the public opened between Burlington and Amboy, N.J. Connections made by boat from Amboy to New York and from Burlington to Philadelphia.

1756. Through stage, Philadelphia to New York, took 3 days (coach traveling 18 hours a day).

1760–76. Three roads to the West through western Pennsylvania had now been opened: **Forbes Road** (from Ft. Loudoun to Ft. Pitt), **Braddock's Road** (from Ft. Cumberland on the Potomac to Ft. Pitt), and **Gist's Road** (from Ft. Cumberland to the upper Monongahela).

c.1776. A continuous system of highways extended from Boston to Savannah, but no hard-surfaced turnpike existed, except for a hard-graveled road leading out from Portsmouth, Me. (c.1760).

1672–83. ORIGINS OF THE POSTAL SYSTEM. Temporary mail route opened between New York and Boston, 1672; discontinued upon recapture of New York by the Dutch, 1673. No organized postal system in early period. Massachusetts (1673) and Connecticut (1674) provided for transmission of official documents by riders. Massachusetts, by act of 1677, fixed a price for private letters and appointed a postmaster; similarly, Pennsylvania, 1683.

1691–1706. Colonial Postal System Under Proprietary Management. Thomas Neale granted a monopoly for 21 years; operation proved profitless, and Neale gave up patent before expiration date.

1707–75. Colonial Postal System Linked with Imperial System. By act of Parliament, 1710, the postmaster general of London was made postmaster general for the whole empire. Plan to extend postal system to Southern colonies blocked by Virginia until 1732 when ex-Governor Spotswood became postmaster general. The appointment in 1753 of Benjamin Franklin and William Hunter as joint postmasters general resulted in improving efficiency and increasing revenues. By 1758 newspapers were admitted to the mails at fixed rates. Franklin was removed from office in 1774 as a result of his release of the Hutchinson letters (pp. 96–97). In 1764 a second postal district was set up south of Virginia, including the Floridas and Bahamas, with headquarters at Charleston. Regular monthly packets were running to both New York and Charleston (by 10 Jan. 1769), and Suffolk, Va., was established as the transfer point between the 2 districts.

1774–75. William Goddard, publisher of the *Maryland Journal,* proposed (2 June 1774) that a "Constitutional Post Office" be set up to replace the "unconstitutional" British system. By 18 May 1775 all colonies to the north of the Carolinas had established their own postal systems. On recommendation of a committee headed by Franklin the Continental Congress approved a plan (26 July) establishing a postal system for the United Colonies with Franklin as postmaster general. All inland service of the British system came to a halt (25 Dec.). Plagued by wartime inflation, postal rates by 1779 rose to 20 times the '75 level. Rates again revised (12 Dec. 1780, 24 Feb. 1781). System reorganized in 1782; franking privileges curtailed. Within a year the service was flourishing, although foreign mails continued to be carried by British and French packets.

1745–49. LAND COMPANY RIVALRY. To contest the claims of Lord Fairfax, Virginia granted lands beyond the first ridge of mountains to such Tidewater families as the Carters, Beverleys, Pages, and Robinsons. By 1754 grants totaled 2.8 million acres. The latter phases of the Intercolonial Wars were marked by ambitious efforts of land

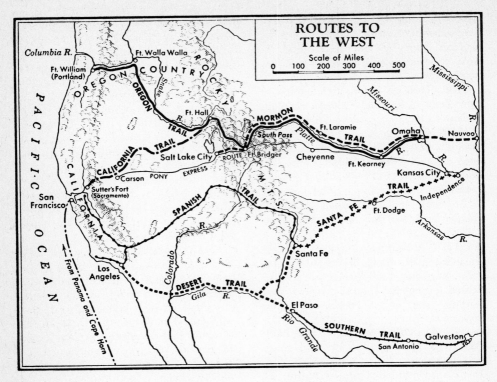

ROUTES TO THE WEST

Scale of Miles
0   100   200   300   400   500

speculators to exploit the trans-Appalachian area and by the formation of grandiose land companies. Early in 1747 the **Ohio Co.** was organized by Thomas Lee. Its traders under Hugh Parker and Thomas Cresap (c.1702–90) reached the Ohio country (by 20 Oct. 1748). On 16 Mar. 1749 the Privy Council granted the company 200,000 acres in the area bounded by the Ohio and Great Kanawha rivers and the Allegheny Mts., on condition they be settled and a fort built. Opposing crown grants of her territory Virginia granted (12 July) 800,000 acres to run west from the Va.-N.C. border to the **Loyal Co.,** formed by John Lewis (d. 1753) and Dr. Thomas Walker (1715–94), with the support of John Robinson (1704–66), president of Virginia Council, and son, John, speaker of the Burgesses. (See also p. 79.)

1750–53. Ohio Co. Developments. Christopher Gist (c.1706–59) explored the Ohio country as far west as Pickawillany for the company (31 Oct. 1750–51). The **Treaty of Logstown** between Virginia and the Iroquois and Delaware Indians (13 June 1752) ceded to Virginia lands south of the Ohio and authorized the Ohio Co. to build a fort and settle that area. Cutting a road over an old Indian route from the mouth of Wills Creek to the mouth of Red Stone Creek on the Monongahela (1753), Gist persuaded 11 families to settle near him on Red Stone Creek.

1744–54. ADVANCE OF PENNSYLVANIA TRADERS. The French who occupied the Ohio Valley resented the Ohio Co. intrusion, but were more alarmed by an influx of Pennsylvania traders under George Croghan and others. To protect the interior from this invasion, they decided to throw a line of forts across the back country of Pennsylvania. Ft. Le Boeuf at the French Creek portage and Ft. Venango at the junction of that stream with the Allegheny were built in 1753. **George Washington** was sent by Lt. Gov. Dinwiddie of Virginia (a member of the Ohio Co.) to warn away the French (p. 79). At the Winchester Conference (10 Sept.) the Indians abrogated the Treaty of Logstown. and moved into the French camp.

1754–63. FRENCH AND INDIAN WAR (pp. 79–82) at its outset brought a cessation of land grants as well as settlement in the West. French seizure of the forks of the Ohio (17 Apr. 1754) and the defeat of Washington at Ft. Necessity (3 July) and of Braddock at Ft. Duquesne (9 July 1755) drove the earliest settlers on the Monongahela back to the Atlantic watershed. To the north, the fall of Oswego (14 Aug. 1756) and the abandonment of the Mohawk by Gen. Webb (c.31 Aug.) forced the settlers to flee toward Schenectady and Albany. To the south, after suffering raids from Indians operating out of Ft. Duquesne (winter, spring 1755–56), the colonies, largely through the prodding of Washington, built a string of forts running from the mouth of Wills Creek on the Potomac (Ft. Cumberland) south along the south branch of the Potomac and the headwaters of the James and Roanoke rivers to Ft. Prince George in South Carolina. Ft. Loudoun on the Little Tennessee (completed summer 1757) served as an advance base to secure friendship of the Cherokee and Creeks. Cherokee raids on the Virginia frontier (spring 1758–Sept. 1759) and the retaliations of the frontiersmen led Gov. Lyttleton of South Carolina to make a treaty with the Cherokee (26 Dec. 1759) whereby the Indians agreed to surrender those guilty of disorders.

Lyttleton held some of the negotiators hostage at Ft. Prince George. Cherokee attacked the fort (19 Jan. 1760) unsuccessfully and turned to the westernmost settlements for vengeance. The slaying of the hostages (16 Feb.) brought a full-scale attack on the western forts, and Ft. Loudoun, isolated and reduced to starvation, surrendered (7 Aug.); its garrison slaughtered en route to Ft. Prince George (10 Aug.). The relief sent by Amherst (1 Apr. 1760) was ineffective, and war continued until Col. Grant, after a series of destructive raids, forced all the tribes to sue for peace (1761). After the abandonment of Ft. Duquesne by the French (24 Nov. 1758), settlers poured into the Monongahela and Youghiogheny valleys over roads built by Braddock and Forbes (p. 81) in spite of the Treaty of Easton (1758) and Col. Bouquet's proclamation (1761) forbidding settlement. By 1763 over 200 houses had been erected around Ft. Pitt alone. The recapture of Oswego and the fall of Ft. Niagara (1759) had a similar effect on the Mohawk Valley.

1755–62. Other Land Projects. Samuel Hazard, Philadelphia merchant, and Lewis Evans (c.1700–56), surveyor and mapmaker, proposed a new trans-Appalachian colony to include the Ohio and part of the Mississippi valleys. Franklin requested the crown to create two new colonies, one along the Scioto, the other south of Lake Erie (1756).

1762. Route for a canal from the Susquehanna at Middletown to the Schuylkill at Reading surveyed by Pennsylvania to prevent diversion of Western trade to Baltimore (settled, 1730); project postponed until 1791.

SUSQUEHANNA CO., under a charter from Connecticut, began the settlement of the Wyoming Valley over the protests of Pennsylvania.

1763. MISSISSIPPI CO., headed by **George Washington,** which had purchased military-bounty grants to the Virginia militia for a fraction of their value, petitioned the crown (9 Sept.) for 2.5 million acres at the junction of the Ohio and Mississippi to satisfy their claims.

7 May. Beginning of **Pontiac's Rebellion** (pp. 84, 85).

7 Oct. ROYAL PROCLAMATION OF 1763.

Dec. "**Suffering Traders,**" including **George Croghan** (c.1718–82), Sir William Johnson's deputy, and 2 Pennsylvania mercantile firms, Byanton, Wharton & Morgan and Simon, Trent, Levy & Franks, organized to seek compensation for losses suffered at the hands of the Indians. **Illinois Co.** (Mar. 1766) and **Indiana Co.** (1763–67) resulted from this group's activities.

1764, 10 July. Adoption by the Board of Trade of a plan by Croghan, Johnson, and Col. John Stuart (1718–98), Indian commissioner for the southern district, for subdividing the northern and southern districts and placing trade under the supervision of the commissioners. The plan broke down in the South owing to the refusal of the governors to curb illicit trade; in the North as a result of Johnson's order that all Great Lakes' trade be transacted at Detroit and Mackinac. Result: New York and Montreal traders and Frenchmen operating from beyond the Mississippi captured the fur trade. Peltry exports declined from £ 28,067 (1764) to £ 18,923 (1768).

20 July. Order in Council placed region west of the Connecticut River and north of Massachusetts (Vermont) within boundaries of New York. Patents had been issued (since 1750) by Gov. **Benning Wentworth** (1696–1770) of New Hampshire for 119 townships, or about one half the region.

1765. By a preliminary agreement with the Choctaw and Chickasaw, Stuart secured acceptance of the high-tide line as the boundary of the Floridas.

1766, 17 Apr. Opinion of R. Cholmondely, Auditor General of North America, that the Proclamation of 1763 did not void prior land grants encouraged speculators to press their claims both in England and the colonies.

1767, 11 Sept. Lord Shelburne (Secretary of State for the Southern Department) proposed abolition of the Indian Department, withdrawal of most troops from Indian territory, and creation of 3 new colonies (Upper Ohio, Illinois country, Detroit district) to be open for settlement. No action taken.

Fall. All licensed traders permitted by Johnson to operate north of Lake Superior and the Ottawa River.

1767–68. EXPLORATION OF KENTUCKY. Daniel Boone (p. 988), a frontiersman from the Upper Yadkin Valley, on his first trip into trans-Appalachian country (winter) proceeded along the present border of Kentucky and West Virginia without entering the bluegrass region. At least 4 parties of hunters had preceded him (1766), including **Benjamin Cutbird,** who had traveled along the Tenn.-Ky. border to the Mississippi, and thence south to New Orleans to market furs.

1768, Mar. Lord Hillsborough, first Secretary of State for the Colonies (since Jan.), secured cabinet acceptance of a new plan for the West: (1) Indian superintendents restricted to imperial affairs; (2) fur trade reverted to the colonies; (3) Proclamation Line to be moved west by treaties with the Indians.

MODIFICATIONS OF THE PROCLAMATION LINE. By the **Treaty of Hard Labor** (14 Oct.) between Stuart and the Cherokee the Virginia border was pushed west to a line running from Chiswell's mine to the mouth of the Big Kanawha on the Ohio. The Creeks agreed at Pensacola (Nov.) to have the South Carolina border run from Ft. Tryon south to the Savannah; Georgia's western border fixed at the Ogeechee River. By the **Treaty of Ft. Stanwix** (5 Nov.) between Johnson and the Iroquois the crown secured all land east of a line drawn near Ft. Stanwix, south to the Unadilla River, along that stream to the town of Unadilla, thence south to the Delaware near Hancock, N.Y., westward to Oswego, southwest to the west branch of the Susequehanna near Williamsport and along that river to its head, thence west to Kittanning on the Allegheny, and along that river and the Ohio west to the mouth of the Tennessee—including much of western New York, the region between the branches of the Susquehanna, and the area west of the Big Kanawha—beyond what the British ministry had proposed. Meanwhile, on 3 Nov. the Indiana Co., with Johnson's aid, purchased from the Iroquois 1,800,-000 acres southeast of the Ohio from an extension of the Mason-Dixon Line (southern boundary line of Pa.) to the Little Kanawha.

1769. VANDALIA. Samuel Wharton formed "Walpole group" (including Thomas Walpole, British banker; Lord Hertford, Lord Chancellor; and George Grenville), organized as **Grand Ohio Co.** (27 Dec.), to obtain a crown grant of 20 million acres under the Treaty of Ft. Stanwix. On 4 Jan. 1770 the Lords of the Treasury approved the grant, to be organized as the proprietary colony of **Vandalia.**

1769–73. SETTLEMENT AND SPECULATION. Pittsburgh land office stormed by purchasers (Apr. 1769). Population of western Pennsylvania, end of 1769, 5,000 families; 1771, 10,000 families. Other Western settlements: Lewisburg and Peterstown (W. Va.), 1769–70; along the Watauga (1768), Holston, and Nolichucky lower rivers (1769). Judge **Richard Henderson** (N.C., 1735–85) sponsored a hunting expedition led by **Daniel Boone** (with John Stuart and John Finley) which used the Cumberland Gap and crossed the Licking, Kentucky, Green, and Cumberland river valleys before returning (spring 1771). In Aug. 1771 a proprietary force failed to oust the Connecticut settlers from the Wyoming Valley, Pa.

PROCLAMATION LINE CHANGES. The **Treaty of Lochaber** between Stuart and the Cherokee (18 Oct. 1770) modified the line by pushing the border westward to a line running from a point near the forks of the Holston to the mouth of the Great Kanawha, adding 9,000 square miles to Virginia, including most of the lands claimed by the Greenbrier and Loyal Cos. In surveying this line John Donelson tripled the acreage acquired under the treaty by running it along the Kentucky River to its mouth (with the connivance of Indian companions). In addition, the transmission to Croghan (9 Apr. 1772) of the **Camden-Yorke opinion** (1757, by the British Attorney General and Solicitor General), with the omission of the word "Grand Mogul," encouraged land companies to interpret crown authorization of the purchase of lands from Indian princes without crown patents (applicable originally to India) as being applicable to America. Pennsylvania speculators immediately made capital of this interpretation: Wabash and Illinois land companies organized 1774, and the George Croghan-William Trent interests accumulated 6 million acres, chiefly in western Pennsylvania. **Watauga Association** was a squatters' agreement, 1772, to obtain from the Indians by lease a tract embracing the northeast corner of Tennessee, south and east of the south fork of the Holston River, and a second tract including the headwaters of the Nolichucky River and

Lick Creek. On 14 Aug. 1772 the crown approved the **Vandalia** grant in payment of £ 10,460 7s 3d; Board of Trade fixed boundaries and drafted charter (3 Apr. 1773), but actual title never conferred. The coming of the Revolution killed this project. By a treaty with the Creeks (1 June 1773) Georgia's boundary was moved west from the Ogeechee to the Oconee River.

1774, Jan.–10 Oct. LORD DUN-MORE'S WAR. In an effort to control the northwest, Virginia's royal governor, **John Murray, Earl of Dunmore** (1732–1809), seized western Pennsylvania, appointing John Connolly governor at Pittsburgh. This action, combined with the entry of colonial hunters into Kentucky, goaded the Shawnee and Ottawa into war (by 10 June). Neutralization of Cherokee, Choctaw, Chickasaw, and Creeks in South obtained by manipulations of Stuart and **James Robertson** (1742–1814), negotiator of Watauga lease; in the North by Johnson and Croghan. On 24 July Maj. Angus McDonald marched into the Muskingum Valley. In a 2-pronged attack, Col. Andrew Lewis descended the Great Kanawha while Dunmore led a column down the Ohio. **Chief Cornstalk,** Shawnee leader, attacked Lewis at Point Pleasant (W. Va.) and was defeated (10 Oct.) at the **Battle of Point Pleasant.** By the **Treaty of Camp Charlotte** the Indians yielded hunting rights in Kentucky and agreed to allow unmolested transportation on the Ohio.

20 May, Quebec Act (p. 97), which extended the boundaries of Quebec to the Ohio and Mississippi, antagonized colonies claiming Western lands under charters (notably Virginia) as well as speculators who had made purchases under the Camden-Yorke opinion (e.g., Wabash-Illinois and Croghan-Trent interests).

16 June. Harrodsburg, Ky., founded by **James Harrod** (1742–93). Burned during Lord Dunmore's War, it was rebuilt the following year.

1775. Transylvania Co. under Judge Richard Henderson (Jan.) sent out **Daniel Boone** (10 Mar.) to blaze a trail through Cumberland Gap to the bluegrass country of Kentucky (**Wilderness Road**). By the **Treaty of Sycamore Shoals** (17 Mar.) the Cherokee for £ 10,000 conveyed an area between the Kentucky River and the southern border of the Cumberland Valley, as well as a strip through Cumberland Gap. At the same conference the Watauga settlers converted their lease into a purchase (19 Mar.). **Boonesborough** founded by Boone (6 Apr.), where he was joined by Henderson (20 Apr.) and the first settlers. A second group under **Benjamin Logan** (c.1743–1802) founded St. Asaph's Station (Apr.). An offshoot of Henderson's emigrants settled at Boiling Springs Station (Mercer Co., Ky.). Delegates from these new settlements met at Boonesborough (23 May) under Henderson and set up a proprietary government for **Transylvania.** Delegates to Continental Congress were rejected (25 Sept.). Population, back country, Maryland-Georgia, est. 250,000.

1776–83. THE WEST IN THE AMERICAN REVOLUTION. In the early phases of the war British advantages in the West stemmed from (1) loyalty of the Indian commissioners, Stuart and Guy Johnson (succeeded his uncle, Sir William, 1774) to the crown; (2) traditional seaboard-frontier animosities; (3) superiority of British goods. American military achievements had sufficiently overcome these handicaps to permit (by 1779–80) a resumption of migration into Kentucky and Tennessee over the Wilderness Road. Land companies continued their activities and the states engaged in a struggle for control of the West. **Frontier Military Incidents:** The Watauga settlements, forewarned by Stuart, withstood Cherokee attacks at Eaton's Station at the forks of the Holston (20 July 1776) and at Ft. Watauga (21 July). North Carolina troops retaliated by burning the Middle Cherokee towns and, acting with South Carolinians, attacked the Lower Cherokee (Sept.–Oct.). In Nov. the Watauga settlements were incorporated into North Carolina. Dissatisfied with Transylvania Co. domination, Kentucky settlers at a conference (6 June) called by **George Rogers Clark** (p. 1001) petitioned Virginia for annexation. The area was organized as a county (6 Dec.) and formally incorporated into Virginia (early 1777). By the end of 1776 Kentucky settlers, as a result of Shawnee and Delaware raids, were concentrated in three main centers—Harrodsburg, St. Asaph's, and Boonesborough. George Rogers Clark, appointed (2 Jan. **1778**) by Gov. **Patrick Henry** of Virginia, surprised the British and captured their base at **Kaskaskia** (4 July) and **Vincennes** (20 July). By the middle of Aug. he was in control of the Illinois country; established as Illinois Co. by Virginia (9 Dec.), Vincennes was retaken by the British under Capt. Henry Hamilton (Dec.). Boonesborough withstood a Shawnee siege (7–16 Sept.) after being warned by Boone, who escaped captivity (winter to 16 June). **Joseph Brant** (1742–1807), a Mohawk chief, with 300 Iroquois, destroyed Cobleskill (30 May) and continued depredations down the Mohawk Valley. A second column under Col. **John Butler** (1728–96), moving farther south, slew 360 settlers in the **Wyoming Massacre** (3 June). Joining Brant, they raided **Cherry Valley,** N.Y. (11 Nov.), costing the defenders 30 killed, 71 wounded. For the Sullivan campaign, see p. 119. On 29 Jan. **1779** George Rogers Clark captured Hamilton's force at Vincennes. The neutralization of the southern Indians for the remainder of the war resulted from a combined Virginia–North Carolina attack under Col. Evan Shelby which destroyed 11 Chickamauga villages in the Tennessee Valley (Apr.) and the destruction of 6 more villages by a South Carolina force in the fall. Settlers now moved into the Tennessee and Kentucky area over the Wilderness Road and down the Ohio. Nashville founded by Judge Henderson and James Robertson (1779–80); Louisville now assumed an urban character. Population of Kentucky, 1780: 20,000. **Further Frontier Raids:** British force attacked the Illinois country; repulsed at Cahokia and St. Louis (May, **1780**). Marching over the Maumee-Miami route, Henry Bird captured the Kentucky posts of Riddle's Station (20 June) and Martin's Station (27 June) along the Licking River. **Battle of King's Mountain** (7 Oct., p. 121) ended Loyalist raids in the Carolina back country. Retaliatory raids upon the Cherokee conducted by the Watauga settlers under Col. **John Sevier** (1745–1815) led to further land cessions by the second **Treaty of Long Island** (26 July **1781**). The Mohawk Valley, virtually in British hands as far east as Schenectady (as late as Aug.) was cleared (Aug.–Oct.) by a force under Col. **Marinus Willett** (1740–1830). Open conflict between the Delaware Indians and frontiersmen broke out in May **1782** as a result of the unprovoked slaughter of 96 Christian Delawares at Gnadenhutten (early spring). Marching into the Ohio country to bolster the frontier, William Crawford was defeated on the Upper Sandusky (4 June). During 1782 Brant's raiders penetrated Pennsylvania as far east as Hannastown; others, operating from Detroit, pushed into Kentucky as far south as Bryant's Station, defeating a Kentucky force at the **Battle of Blue Licks** (19 Aug.). The situation was critical when news of peace talks reached the West (c.Nov.).

1776–83. CONTROVERSY OVER WESTERN LANDS. John Dickinson's draft of the Articles of Confederation (12 July **1776**) proposed limiting the western boundaries of the states; rejected by committee. **Land Bounties:** Congress granted land to British military deserters (12, 27 Aug.) and 100–500 acres, depending on rank, to all soldiers up to the rank of colonel who would serve in the Continental Army for the duration of the war or until discharged (7, 18 Sept.). Land bounties were granted generals under the same conditions (12 Aug. 1780; 850–1,100 acres). Larger grants were offered by the states (N.Y., 600 acres; Pa., 200–2,000; Va., 100–1,500; N.C., 640–12,000). Continental and state grants underscored the need for political organization of the West. In Aug. **1777** states whose charters gave them no western lands (Pa., N.J., Del., Md., N.H., R.I.) proposed that Congress be empowered to limit the western boundaries of the states. The motion failed, but over their protests, a clause was added to the Articles of Confederation (27 Oct.) providing that no state be deprived of western lands for the benefit of the U.S. By the **Treaty of DeWitts Corner** (20 May) the Lower Cherokee ceded their remaining land in South Carolina, and by the **Treaty of Long Island** (20 July) the Overhill Cherokee surrendered lands east of the Blue Ridge and the Watauga-Nolichucky region. On 4 Nov. **1778** the Virginia assembly voided all Indian sales within its charter limits, in effect curbing land engrossment under the Camden-Yorke opinion. On 15 Dec. Maryland, spurred on by speculators eager for western lands claimed by Virginia, announced its refusal to ratify the Articles of Confederation until western lands were ceded to Congress by the states. On 17 Dec. Virginia offered to provide western lands for soldiers of the Revolution, but Maryland remained adamant (6 Jan. **1779**). As a result of the activities of the Illinois and Wabash Cos., the Virginia assembly nullified all Indian purchases in the Northwest (May, June). On 14 Sept. the Indiana and Vandalia cos. petitioned Congress for a confirmation of land grants. In Nov. a committee of Congress recommended that Virginia make no further grants until the end of the war. On 1 Feb. **1780** the New York legislature ceded to the U.S. all claims to western lands (based on her overlordship of the Iroquois). Connecticut followed (10 Oct.), excepting a 3-million-acre tract in Ohio (the Western Reserve). On 2 Jan. **1781** Virginia ceded her claims north of the Ohio River (p. 123). On 30 Dec. **1782** the commissioners appointed under the Articles of Confederation awarded to Pennsylvania all lands claimed by Connecticut within the charter limits of the former colony. The conditional offer of land cession by Virginia was rejected by Congress (13 Sept. **1783**); a revised offer (20 Oct.) was accepted 1 Mar. **1784**, Congress agreeing to reserve as bounty land for Virginia a tract between the Scioto and Little Miami, along with a small tract opposite Louisville. By the **Treaty of Augusta** with the Creeks (1 Nov.) Georgia extended her northern boundary west from the Tugaloo to the Oconee River. As a result of dissatisfaction with this treaty the Creeks raised to "kingship" **Alexander McGillivray** (c.1759–93), a half-breed and implacable foe of land cessions, who (June 1784) accepted a Spanish colonelcy.

1784–86. INLAND NAVIGATION. Potomac Co. (organized, 1784, with charters from both Md. and Va. and a grant of £6,666 by each state; **George Washington,** first president) publicly raised £40,300 to build a route from the headquarters of the Potomac to the Cheat or Monongahela rivers (connecting the Potomac Valley with the West); constructed a canal by 1808 along the Potomac with the first water locks in the U.S., although the project was not a paying one. (For steamboat franchise to John Fitch, 1786, see p. 792; for **Annapolis Convention,** 11–14 Sept. 1786, p. 137.)

1784–88. ORGANIZATION OF THE WEST. On 20 Feb. **1784** Georgia created Tennessee Co. to include the region of the big bend of the Tennessee, with authority to grant land entrusted to 3 commissioners associated with a land-engrossing project launched (1783) by **William Blount** (1749–1800) of North Carolina. On 2 June the North Carolina legislature ceded its western lands (most of which had been disposed of to speculators, 1783–84), with the proviso that Congress accept within 12 months. Under the leadership of **John Sevier** the trans-Allegheny settlers, in convention at Jonesboro (Tenn., 23 Aug.), set up the independent state of **Franklin** (including a southwest fringe of Va.) and continued down to 1787 to seek admission to the Union. On 20 Nov. North Carolina repealed its cession law and attempted to reestablish control over Franklin. By the **2d Treaty of Ft. Stanwix** (22 Oct.) the Six Nations of the Iroquois ceded to the U.S. all lands west of the Niagara River (rejected by the Ohio tribes). On 21 Jan. **1785** the Wyandot, Chippewa, Delawares, and Ottawa at Ft. McIntosh ceded to the U.S. all the present state of Ohio except for a strip south of Lake Erie between the Maumee River and a line drawn along the Cuyahoga and Tuscarawas rivers. On 7 Feb. Georgia created the county of Bourbon on land

ceded by the Indians between the 31st parallel and the Yazoo, but in control of Spain, which ordered the Georgia commissioners to leave (10 Oct.). In 1788 Georgia repealed the act. Led by Col. McGillivray, the Creeks were defeated in a short war with Georgia (May–Nov.) and signed the **Treaty of Galphinton** (12 Nov.), recognizing the cession of the Treaty of Augusta and yielding a strip on the coast from the Altamaha to the St. Mary's. **Massachusetts–New York Controversy:** Massachusetts cession of western lands completed (19 Apr.), excepting claims in New York. By agreement with New York (**1786**) the western part of the state was divided by a line running north and south through Sodus Bay. New York retained sovereignty over the whole region, but Massachusetts was awarded land west of the line.

Land Ordinance of 1785 (20 May, p. 134).

Treaty of Dumpling Creek (May 1785) between "State of Franklin" and the Cherokee extended the former's borders south and west along the Holston to the watershed of the Little River; disallowed by U.S. commissioners at the **Treaty of Hopewell** (28 Nov.), which confirmed Cherokee rights to most of the land held in 1777. Dissatisfied with the Treaties of Augusta and Galphinton, the Creeks resumed hostilities (summer 1786). On 28 Feb. the British government notified the U.S. that it would refuse to comply with the Treaty of Paris (Art. 7) and give up posts in the Great Lakes region which were centers of Indian unrest (notably in Ohio) until the U.S. honored British debts (Art. 4). On 8 Mar. **1787** South Carolina ceded its narrow strip of western claim to the U.S., leaving only North Carolina and Georgia with western claims. On 15 July **1788** Congress rejected the Georgia cession of its western lands (1 Feb.). Such cessions were not completed until the acceptance (2 Apr. 1790) of the second North Carolina act of cession (22 Dec. 1789) and the ratification by the Georgia legislature (16 June 1802) of the Articles of Agreement and Cession (24 Apr. 1802) between U.S. and Georgia. On 20 June 1788 Congress granted 4,000 acres to each head of a family settling the Illinois country before 1783 (c.150 French families), a privilege extended to those at Vincennes and along the Wabash (1790), although, for the most part, the grants were not actually made. By making bounty warrants transferable (9 July), Congress eased operations for the big land companies.

1786–88. SETTLEMENTS IN OHIO. Formation in Boston (1 Mar. 1786) of a new **Ohio Co.**, organized by Gens. **Benjamin Tupper** (1738–92) and **Rufus Putnam** (1738–1824), to dispose of $1 million worth of stock in exchange for Continental certificates redeemable at par in exchange for public lands. In behalf of the company Rev. **Manasseh Cutler** (1742–1823) petitioned Congress (5–14 July 1787) for 1½ million acres at $.66⅔ an acre. In a deal with Col. **William Duer** (1747–99), secretary of the Board of Treasury, the Ohio Co. was authorized to act for a group of insiders with whom Cutler organized the **Scioto Co.** Under authority of Congress (23 July) the board sold (27 July) to Cutler 1,500,000 (actually 1,781,760) acres for $1 million with an option on another 5 million acres. The lands lay between the first 7 ranges of townships (already surveyed) and the Scioto River. By agreement the option was assigned to the Scioto Co. In Oct. **John Cleve Symmes** (1742–1814) of New Jersey petitioned Congress for land on similar terms; granted (1788) a 20-mile strip east of the Great Miami. The first auctions of land surveyed in Ohio (the 7

Ranges) brought in only $176,090 in inflated currency (Sept.–Oct.). To offset lawlessness and "facilitate the surveying and selling" of public lands Congress resolved (3 Oct.) to station troops on the frontier. On 7 Apr. 1788 **Marietta, Ohio,** was founded by settlers sent out by the Ohio Co.

1786–90. JAY-GARDOQUI TREATY (29 Aug. 1787) between Spain and U.S. (p. 135), while never ratified, aroused such discontent in the West that "Spanish Conspiracy" spread through Kentucky and Tennessee, led by **James Wilkinson** and **John Sevier.** Purpose: to separate lower Mississippi Valley from U.S. under Spanish protection. Separatism threat remained in the West until Pinckney's Treaty (1795, p. 153).

1787, 13 JULY. NORTHWEST ORDINANCE (p. 139).

1789. First Yazoo land grant (25,400,000 acres) to a group of speculating companies authorized by Georgia legislature; additional grant made in 1795; immediate settlement impeded by Indian wars and Spanish diplomatic intrigues.

1789–1829. EXTENSION OF POSTAL SERVICE. As late as 1792 Vermont, Kentucky, Tennessee, and the entire West had no post office, but the federal government rapidly expanded the mail routes. The Act of 1794 established additional post roads and provided for stage transportation; the Act of 1814 provided that mail service be arranged from the nearest post office to the courthouse of any county in any state or territory. As a result, many new mail lines were extended to outlying regions. Miles of post roads in operation: 1790–94, 5,001; 1825–29, 104,521. Postal rates, 1825–38 (about half the rate prevailing in 1815): up to 30 mi., 6 cts.; 30–80 mi., 10 cts.; 80–150 mi., 12½ cts.; 150–400 mi., 18¾ cts.; over 400 mi., 25 cts.

1790. Southwest Territory organized.

ACQUISITION OF THE TERRITORY AND PUBLIC DOMAIN OF THE CONTINENTAL U.S., 1781–1867

Year and How Acquired	Total Area (Acres)
1781–1802 State cessions	236,825,600
1783 Treaty of Paris with Gt. Britain	541,364,480
1803 Louisiana Purchase[1]	529,911,680
1803 Red River Basin[2]	29,601,920
1819 Cession from Spain	46,144,640
1845 Annexation of Texas	249,066,240
1846 Oregon Compromise	183,386,240
1848 Mexican Cession	338,680,960
1850 Purchase from Texas	78,926,720
1853 Gadsden Purchase	18,988,800
1867 Alaska Purchase	375,296,000

[1] Data exclude areas eliminated by the Treaty of 1819 with Spain. Such areas are included in figures for annexation of Texas and the Mexican Cession.
[2] Drainage basin of the Red River of the North, south of the 49th parallel, sometimes considered part of the Louisiana Purchase.

Settlement of Gallipolis, in the Ohio country, by French immigrants on lands fraudulently claimed by Scioto Co. promoters; some eventually resettled on the "French Grant" authorized by Congress (1795).

1790–95. EARLY TURNPIKES. Opening of the **Philadelphia-Lancaster Turnpike** (1790), completed, 1794. Its financial success encouraged considerable building of toll roads, especially in New England and the Middle States. Construction of the **Knoxville Road** (1791–95), linking the Wilderness Road to the Cumberland settlements. **Wilderness Road** opened to wagon traffic (1795), facilitating settlement in the lower Ohio Valley. In the same year the **Old Walton Road** was opened, connecting Knoxville and Nashville, serving as route for settlers in the Tennessee interior.

1791, 4 Nov. A mixed force of regulars and militia led by Gen. **Arthur St. Clair** (1736–1818), governor of the Northwest Territory, was defeated by Indians of the Maumee and Wabash rivers. St. Clair was replaced (5 Mar. 1792) by Gen. **Anthony Wayne** as commander of troops in the Ohio country.

Vermont admitted to the Union.

1792. Kentucky admitted to the Union.

Capt. **Robert Gray** (1755–1806), of the ship *Columbia* out of Boston, discovered and named the Columbia River.

1792–1800. EARLY CANALS. Western Inland Lock Navigation Co., chartered in New York, 1792, opened canal (1796) around the Little Falls in the Mohawk River. Santee Canal constructed (1792–1800), joining the Cooper and Santee rivers in South Carolina. Middlesex Canal constructed (1793), linking Boston with the Merrimack River.

1794, 20 Aug. BATTLE OF FALLEN TIMBERS, won by Gen. Anthony Wayne at the rapids of the Maumee, in northwest Ohio, hastened to a close Indian resistance in the area, secured the Northwest frontier, and gave added proof of the national government's stability.

19 Nov. By Jay's Treaty (p. 152) the British agreed to evacuate the Northwest posts by 1 June 1796. The securing of the military frontier encouraged steady settlement of the upper Ohio Valley and freed the Old Northwest from diplomatic intrigues and Indian threats until shortly before the War of 1812.

1795, 3 Aug. TREATY OF GREENVILLE, signed by 12 Indian tribes, set up a definite boundary in the Northwest Territory between Indian lands and those available to U.S. settlers.

27 Oct. Treaty of San Lorenzo, also called **Pinckney's Treaty** (p. 153), signed with Spain; its favorable commercial and boundary provisions allayed Western discontent and separatist feeling.

Organization of the Connecticut Land Co., which purchased the **Western Reserve** in northeast Ohio. Its general agent was **Moses Cleaveland** (1754–1806), who laid out and named the city of Cleveland (1796).

1796. Tennessee admitted to the Union.

U.S. Military Reserve laid out in the Ohio country; set apart for land bounties to Revolutionary veterans.

Congress authorized construction of **Zane's Trace,** first road running through Ohio. Connecting Wheeling and Limestone (later Maysville), it was one of the main routes taken by emigrants.

1796–1803. Holland Land Co. organized by Dutch bankers, to whom Robert Morris sold in 1792–93 the greater part of a tract west of the Genesee River, helped to advance the settlement of western New York and Pennsylvania.

1798. Establishment of the **Mississippi Territory** opened the Old Southwest to settlement, but large-scale colonization came only after the pacification of the Georgia Indians and the elimination of Spanish control of the West Florida ports.

1800. Liberal provisions of the Land Act of 1800 (p. 633) stimulated settlement of the Old Northwest.

Establishment of the Indiana Territory.

1803, 30 APR. LOUISIANA PURCHASE (p. 158) secured the Mississippi Valley against foreign economic and diplomatic pressures, ushered in period of Western settlement temporarily halted by the War of 1812.

7 JUNE. Treaty of Vincennes, signed by 9 Indian tribes of the Old Northwest, gave the U.S. title to disputed lands along the Wabash River, beyond the line established by the Treaty of Greenville.

Ohio admitted to the Union.

1803–06. LEWIS AND CLARK overland expedition to the Far Northwest (p. 160).

1804–05. Lower Red River and Ouachita River explored by government scientific expedition under **William Dunbar** (1749–1810).

1805. Creation of the territories of Louisiana and Michigan.

1805–06. Government expedition to the upper Mississippi led by Lt. **Zebulon M. Pike** (p. 1128), who also conducted an expedition to the Southwest (1806–07).

1806. Government expedition led by Thomas Freeman (d. 1821) produced first accurate map of the lower Red River.

1807. John Colter (c.1775–1813), one of the pioneer fur traders in the Far West, traveled through the country south of the Yellowstone River, penetrating the valley of the Big Horn.

17–21 AUG. New York-to-Albany and return voyage of the *Clermont,* designed by **Robert Fulton** (p. 1036); inaugurated era of successful steamboat navigation on a commercial basis.

1807–08. Encouraged by the achievements of the Lewis and Clark expedition, parties of trappers and traders penetrated the region of the Missouri and Yellowstone rivers; led to the organization of the Rocky Mountain fur trade, active until c.1840.

1808. Incorporation of the **American Fur Co.,** organized by **John Jacob Astor** (p. 976).

1809. Establishment of Illinois Territory.

Treaty of Ft. Wayne, signed with Indians of the Old Northwest, gave the U.S. title to large tract in southern Indiana.

Formation of the Missouri Fur Co.; declined after c.1812.

First successful sea voyage (New York to Philadelphia) by a steamboat made by the *Phoenix,* designed by **John Stevens** (1749–1838).

1809–11. Exploration of the Missouri River beyond the Mandan villages made by **Thomas Nuttall** (1786–1859), natural scientist, who later carried out explorations along the Arkansas and Red rivers (1818–20).

1811. Fur trading post of **Astoria** established at the mouth of the Columbia River by Astor's Pacific Fur Co. (1810).

7 Nov. BATTLE OF TIPPECANOE (p. 167).

Construction at Pittsburgh of the side-wheeler *New Orleans*, the first steamboat used on western waters; made voyage between Louisville and New Orleans. First voyage on the upper rivers made in 1815 by the *Enterprise*, from Brownsville on the Monongahela to New Orleans and return.

1811–18. TURNPIKES (or toll roads) rapidly proliferated. Construction of the **Cumberland Road** (also called the **Old National Road**), a paved highway connecting Cumberland, Md., with Wheeling on the Ohio River. Subsequent extensions brought it to Columbus, Ohio, and to its final terminus at Vandalia, Ill. One of the chief arteries of western colonization, it was later neglected, only to become a part of U.S. Highway No. 40 in the era of the motorcar. As early as 1810 some 300 turnpike corporations had been chartered in New England, New York, and Pennsylvania, but The **Turnpike boom** came to an end in the mid-1820s. By that date all major cities in the eastern and northern states were interconnected by surfaced roads, while the South lagged behind.

1812. Louisiana admitted to the Union.

Creation of the Missouri Territory.

1812–13. Expedition under the fur trader **Robert Stuart** (1785–1848) made eastward journey from Astoria to St. Louis over route virtually unknown to white men; discovered **South Pass,** later used by California and Oregon immigrants.

1812–14. War of 1812 (pp. 169–182) brought Western expansion to a tempo-

rary halt. The war has been attributed by some historians to have been in part a result of frontier expansionist sentiment (Southern ambitions to secure East and West Florida; Western "land hunger" for Canadian territory) and of Western desire for security against Indian attacks. In fact, political and nationalist considerations are now deemed the chief motives for U.S. entry.

1813. West Florida seized by the U.S. British and Indians defeated at **Battle of the Thames** (5 Oct.), breaking power of Indians of the Old Northwest and opening region to settlement.

1814. Battle of Horseshoe Bend (27 Mar.) ended in defeat of Creek Indians by force under Andrew Jackson, and led to drafting of **Treaty of Ft. Jackson** (9 Aug.) in which Creeks ceded large tracts in Mississippi Territory. These events ended Indian resistance in Southwest and opened region to pioneers after War of 1812.

1815. Treaties of Portage des Sioux terminated virtually all Indian resistance in the Old Northwest; enabled rapid settlement of the westernmost part of the upper tier of trans-Appalachia.

c.1815–50. End of the War of 1812 brought resumption of westward expansion and large-scale settlement of the Lake Plains, the Mississippi Valley frontier, the Gulf Plains, and the Southwest. The northern areas were settled chiefly by emigrants from the Northeast (although many Southerners emigrated to the lower tiers of Ohio, Indiana, and Illinois) and, after 1848, by immigrants from Northern Europe. The Gulf Plains and Southwest were settled mostly by emigrants from the Southern seaboard and Piedmont. This period witnessed the rapid expansion of the "**Cotton Kingdom**" in the deep South.

1816. Indiana admitted to the Union.

1816–18. First Seminole War ended

in defeat of Florida Indians by expedition under Gen. **Andrew Jackson** (p. 1068).

1816–21. Series of treaties with Indians of the Southwest encouraged settlement in middle Georgia and in western Alabama and Tennessee.

1817. Mississippi admitted to the Union.

Creation of Alabama Territory.

STEAMBOAT. The *Washington,* designed by Henry M. Shreve (1785–1851) and launched at Wheeling, made return voyage between Louisville and New Orleans, initiating successful commercial steam navigation on the Ohio-Mississippi route. Quickly following was the inauguration of steam navigation on Lakes Ontario and Erie. Technical developments, such as a more efficient high-pressure engine (by 1825), stimulated steamboat building and operation. **Rates of speed** of fastest steamboats: On Hudson, 30 miles an hour; on Mississippi, 25 miles downstream, 16 upstream. **Passenger fares** fell rapidly from high initial levels: New Orleans to Louisville before 1818, $100–$125; 1825, $50; 1830s, $25–$30. Pittsburgh to Cincinnati, 1825, $12; 1840s, $5. Middle Western cities served by the Mississippi steamboat system outdistanced others before 1850. **Population,** 1850: Cincinnati, 115,000; St. Louis, 78,000; Louisville, 43,000; New Orleans, 116,000. Great Lakes ports: Chicago, 30,000; Buffalo, 42,000.

1817–18. Exploration of southern Missouri and Arkansas by **Henry R. Schoolcraft** (1793–1864), geologist and ethnologist, who made pioneer studies of the North American Indians.

1817–25. Construction of the **Erie Canal,** extending from Albany to Buffalo and linking the Hudson River with Lake Erie; was authorized by an act of the New York legislature of 1817, and vigorously pushed by **De Witt Clinton** (1769–1828). Formally opened in Oct.

1825, the canal made Buffalo and New York entrepôts of Western commerce, quickly became the chief route for emigrants from New England to the Great Lakes country, and was instrumental in creating an agricultural boom in the West. Its success set off a **canal-building boom.**

1818. Illinois admitted to the Union.

1819. ADAMS-ONÍS TREATY (p. 188) provided for cession of **East Florida** to the U.S. and defined western borders of Louisiana Purchase.

Alabama admitted to the Union.

Creation of Arkansas Territory.

24 MAY–20 JUNE. The *Savannah,* first steamship to cross the Atlantic, made voyage from Savannah to Liverpool.

1820. Maine admitted to the Union.

Moses Austin (1761–1821) granted Spanish charter to settle 300 families in Texas; colonization scheme carried out by his son, **Stephen F. Austin** (p. 977).

Army expedition under Maj. Stephen H. Long (1784–1864) explored the region between the Missouri River and the Rocky Mountains. Its report strengthened the myth of the "Great American Desert," a misnomer for the Great Plains but originating with Pike's report (p. 1128).

Completion of **Jackson's Military Road,** connecting Florence, Ala., and the Gulf region near New Orleans.

1821. Missouri admitted to the Union.

1821–22. Opening of the **Santa Fe Trail** to the commerce of the Southwest. Although parts of the trail had been in use, it remained for **William Becknell** (c.1790–c.1832), a Missouri trader, to define the route that was soon plied by trade caravans.

1822. Organization of the trapping and trading business that later became known (1830) as the **Rocky Mountain Fur Co.,** which originated the rendezvous method (as distinguished from trading posts). It dominated the trade in

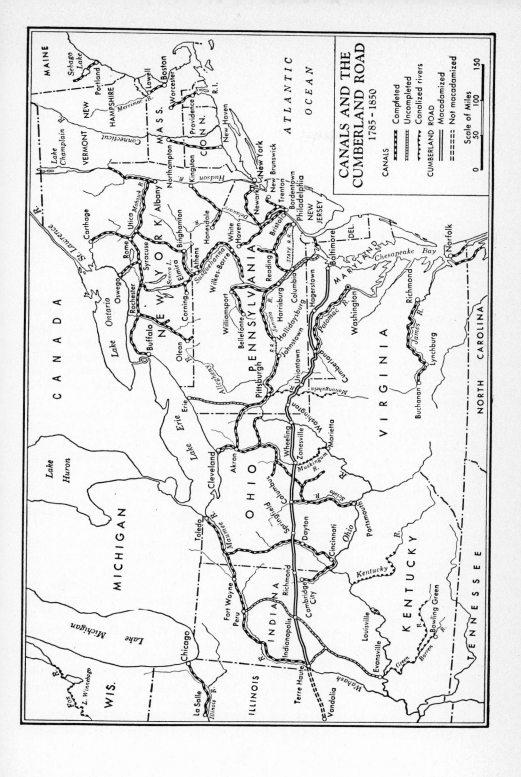

CANALS AND THE CUMBERLAND ROAD
1785 - 1850

CANALS
———— Completed
········· Uncompleted
–·–·–·– Canalized rivers

CUMBERLAND ROAD
———— Macadamized
= = = = Not macadamized

Scale of Miles
0   50   100   150

the central portion of the Rockies, finally yielding (1834) to the superior resources of the American Fur Co.

1822–23. Expeditions up the Missouri River to the Yellowstone led by **William H. Ashley** (c.1778–1838), one of the founders of the Rocky Mountain Fur Co.

1824. South Pass, at the lower point of the Wind River range of the Rockies, rediscovered by Thomas Fitzpatrick (c.1799–1854) and Jedediah Smith (1798–1831), active in the Rocky Mountain fur trade. It was later used by emigrants taking the Oregon Trail.

James Bridger (1804–81), fur trader and guide, credited with discovery of the Great Salt Lake. Another fur trader, **Peter S. Ogden** (1794–1854), for whom Ogden, Utah, is named, credited with being one of the first white men to explore the region of the Great Salt Lake.

Gibbons v. Ogden (p. 665), by ending private monopolies in interstate shipping, contributed to the expansion of steam navigation on Eastern rivers, harbors, and bays.

1824–50. CANALS TO TIDEWATER. Construction of the **Morris Co. Canal** across New Jersey (1824–32), connecting New York Harbor with the mouth of the Lehigh River, served as important route for Lehigh coal. Other canals between upcountry and tidewater included the **New Haven and Northampton** (1835, abandoned 1847); the **Delaware and Hudson,** connecting Honesdale, Pa., and Kingston, N.Y., and used chiefly for transportation of anthracite coal, reaching peak traffic, 1872; the **Lehigh** and the **Morris** in Pennsylvania and New Jersey; the **James River and Kanawha** from Richmond to Buchanan, Va., 1832–51; the **Chesapeake and Ohio Canal** (1828–50), linking Georgetown with Cumberland, Md., based on a route begun earlier by the Potomac Co., suffered heavily from the competition of

the B. & O. R.R., whose tracks paralleled its route; the **Pennsylvania Portage and Canal System** (Philadelphia to Pittsburgh, 1826–40), the eastern and western sections of which were joined by the **Allegheny Portage Railway** (1831–35), projected as a competitor of the Erie Canal in a bid for Western commerce, but burdened with high construction costs and strong railroad competition almost from the beginning.

1825. Definite adoption by U.S. government of **removal policy** providing for transfer of eastern Indians to trans-Mississippi regions in order to facilitate advance of white settlement and to fix a permanent Indian frontier beyond the 95th meridian. Originated by Secretary of War John C. Calhoun in 1823, the policy was announced by President Monroe (1825), and carried out on an extensive scale by President Jackson. Most of the Indians of the Old Northwest and Southwest were resettled in present-day Kansas and Oklahoma.

Treaties of Prairie du Chien established boundaries of Indian lands in Old Northwest. This division of tribal lands enabled the U.S. government to make individual treaties for land cessions.

Establishment of Ft. Vancouver by Hudson's Bay Co. on Columbia River solidified British control of the Oregon country.

1826. Treaty of Washington, signed by the Creek Indians, whose removal from Georgia to beyond the Mississippi was accomplished during 1827–29.

1825–56. WESTERN CANALS, linking the Ohio and Mississippi with the Great Lakes. The original **Welland Canal** around Niagara Falls, connecting Lakes Erie and Ontario, was built by Canada, 1829–33. Other interior canals included the Ohio Canal, connecting Portsmouth and Cleveland, 1825–32; Miami Canal (Cincinnati and Toledo, 1825–45); Louisville and Portland Canal around

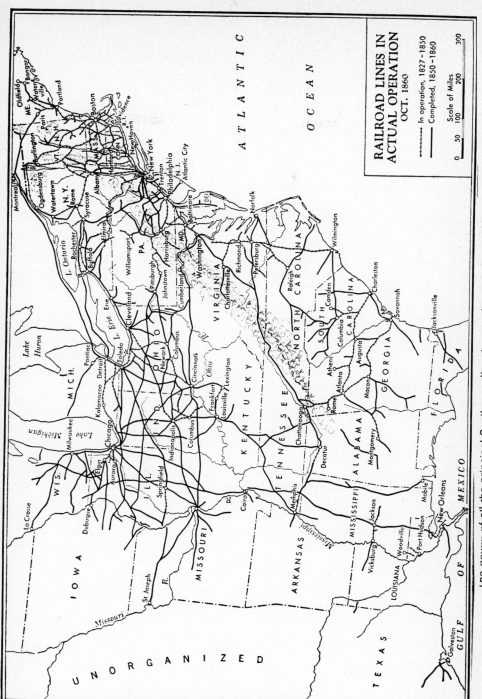

RAILROAD LINES IN
ACTUAL OPERATION
OCT. 1860

In operation, 1827-1850
Completed, 1850-1860

Scale of Miles
0   50   100   200   300

Ine gauge of all the principal Southern railroads was changed, June 1886, to 4 ft. 9 in. to conform to Northern railroads; previously it was generally 5 ft.

the falls of the Ohio River, 1826–31; the **Wabash and Erie Canal**, linking Toledo, Ohio, with Evansville, Ind. (452 miles), the longest canal in the U.S. (1832–56), helped open up northern Indiana, but was a financial failure; the **Illinois and Michigan Canal**, linking Lake Michigan and the Illinois River (1836–48), contributed to the rapid growth of Chicago (still in active use).

1826–40. EARLY RAILROAD ERA. In 1825 the Stockton and Darlington R.R. began operations in England. U.S. railroad building quickly rivaled European construction. Early efforts included **Mohawk and Hudson R.R.**, chartered in New York (1826), built in 1830; began operations (Albany to Schenectady) in 1831.

1827. Construction of short-line railway in Massachusetts from Quincy to the Neponset River, used for transporting granite; construction of the short-line Mauch Chunk R.R. in Pennsylvania from Carbondale to the Lehigh River, used for transporting coal; incorporation of the **Baltimore and Ohio R.R.**, the first passenger railway in the U.S. Construction began on 4 July 1828, lagged after the Panic of 1837, and was resumed in 1848. In 1853 the connection between Baltimore and Wheeling was completed. Chartering of the South Carolina Canal and R.R. Co., which by 1833 completed a rail link from Charleston to Hamburg, S.C.; later became the South Carolina R.R. Co.

1828. Philadelphia and Columbia R.R., chartered in New Jersey, opened 1834.

1829–57. Construction of the Memphis and Charleston R.R.

1830. Incorporation of the Boston and Worcester R.R., opened in 1835.

1830–32. Construction of the Lexington and Ohio R.R.

1832–52. Construction of the **New York and Harlem R.R.**

1833. Organization of the Western Railroad Corp., which built (1835–42) a connection between **Boston and Albany**; incorporation of the **Philadelphia and Reading R.R.**; formation of the **Central of Georgia R.R.**, which by 1843 linked Savannah and Macon.

1835–36. Chartering of the **Louisville, Cincinnati and Charleston R.R.**, projected by Southern interests to enable local centers to compete with Northern ports as entrepôts for the commerce of the Ohio and Mississippi valleys. Although state particularism and financial obstacles brought the venture to an end in 1839, the separate state roads built by local interests served as the foundation for the Southern rail network built in the 2 decades before the Civil War.

1836. Erie and Kalamazoo R.R. connected Toledo, Ohio, with Adrian in Michigan Territory; Richmond and Petersburg R.R. chartered by the state of Virginia, later the **Atlantic Coast Line R.R.** (1900).

1836–51. Construction of the Western and Atlantic R.R., connecting Atlanta and Chattanooga.

1837. As part of a state internal improvements program, Michigan projected 3 railroads: the Michigan Northern (Port Huron–Grand Rapids), the **Michigan Central** (Detroit–St. Joseph), and the Michigan Southern (Monroe–New Buffalo). Under separate private ownership, the Michigan Central and the Michigan Southern were completed to Chicago in 1852. Chartering of the **New Orleans and Nashville R.R.**, aimed at tapping the trade of the Tennessee and Cumberland regions; failed after the panic of 1837.

1840. Completion of the **Vicksburg and Jackson R.R.**, traversing central Mississippi.

U.S. had 3,328 miles of railroad; all Europe only 1,818.

1826–30. Explorations of California and the Pacific Northwest by **Jedediah Smith** (1798–1831).

1827. American Fur Co. absorbed the Columbia Fur Co.; thereafter dominated the upper Missouri trade.

1830. Congressional enactment of the **Removal Bill** empowering the president to transfer any eastern Indian tribe to trans-Mississippi areas.

Maysville Road Bill vetoed by President Jackson (p. 201).

1831–32. Expedition to the upper Mississippi led by **Henry R. Schoolcraft,** who discovered the source of that river to be a lake, which he named Itasca.

1832. Black Hawk War in the upper Mississippi Valley. The defeat of the Sauk and Fox led by the chieftain Black Hawk ushered in an active period (1832–37) of Indian removal to trans-Mississippi areas. By 1846 Indian removal from the Old Northwest had been completed.

Completion of the **Chicago Road,** a military highway facilitating the settlement of southern Michigan and upper Indiana.

1832–33. Treaties of Payne's Landing and **Ft. Gibson,** authorizing removal of the Seminoles from Florida to beyond the Mississippi, led to resistance culminating in the **Second Seminole War.**

1832–35. Rocky Mountain trapping and hunting expedition led by Capt. **Benjamin L. E. Bonneville** (1796–1878), subject of Washington Irving's *The Adventures of Captain Bonneville* (1837).

1833. Opening of the Black Hawk Purchase on the west bank of the Mississippi inaugurated large-scale settlement of Iowa country.

Organization of the village of **Chicago;** incorporated as a city in 1837.

1833–34. Expedition under the Rocky Mountain fur trader **Joseph R. Walker** (1798–1876) climbed the Sierra Nevada (believed to be the first ascent from the east made by white men), penetrated the Yosemite Valley, and on the return journey crossed the Sierra through the gap later called Walker Pass.

1834. With others, Rev. **Jason Lee** (1803–45), a Methodist missionary, explored the Willamette Valley and established the first mission and the first American agricultural settlement (near present-day Salem, Ore.) in the Oregon country.

Overland expedition to Oregon led by **Nathaniel J. Wyeth** (1802–56) from Independence, Mo., to Fort Vancouver. A member of this expedition was the ornithologist John K. Townsend (1809–51), who wrote *Narrative of a Journey across the Rocky Mountains to the Columbia River* (1839). Wyeth attempted to establish in the Pacific Northwest a project for exploiting the natural resources of the Columbia River region. His venture, the Columbia River Fishing and Trading Co. (1834–37), was unsuccessful due to the opposition of the Hudson's Bay Co.

The **Territorial Road,** a land route facilitating settlement in southern Michigan, opened to traffic.

1835. Treaty of New Echota ceded to the U.S. all Cherokee lands and provided for the transportation of the Cherokee Indians to areas beyond the Mississippi; removal completed by 1838.

Completion of the removal of Alabama Creek Indians to beyond the Mississippi.

Overland journey from St. Louis to the Green River under the leadership of Dr. **Marcus Whitman** (1802–47) and Rev. Samuel Parker (1779–1866), sponsored by the American Board of Commissioners for Foreign Missions. Whitman's next expedition from St. Louis (1836), the first party with women to cross the Rockies, reached Oregon, where Whitman established the Walla Walla mission.

1835–40. Final period of the Rocky Mountain fur trade.

1835–42. Second Seminole War ended with removal of most of the Seminole Indians from Florida to beyond the Mississippi.

c.1835–c.1841. State-assisted internal improvement programs in the states of the Old Northwest stimulated a **Transportation Boom,** particularly in Western canal building, resulting in heavy speculation in both lands and transportation facilities, many of the latter being built with funds from British investors. These elaborate programs collapsed after the **Panic of 1837,** burdening the states with heavy indebtedness. Between 1816 and 1840, about $125,000,000 was spent on canal projects alone. In the following decade some of the uncompleted projects were resumed by private interests, but railroad competition ultimately made canal operations unprofitable.

1836. Establishment of the independent **Republic of Texas** (pp. 210–211); recognized by the U.S. in 1837.

Arkansas admitted to the Union.

Territories of Iowa and Wisconsin organized.

1837. Michigan admitted to the Union.

1837–40. Opening of the **Lumbering Frontier** in northern Wisconsin and Minnesota, which in turn attracted farmers by creating a demand for foodstuffs.

1840–46. Father Pierre-Jean De Smet (1801–73), Jesuit missionary, founded Catholic missions in the Oregon country and the Great Plains.

1841, 4 Sept. Distribution-Preemption Act (p. 635).

Bidwell-Bartleson party inaugurated overland migration to California, opening California Trail through South Pass and across Humboldt region of Nevada; followed by numerous emigrants in next years.

1842. Exploring expedition to the Wind River range of the Rockies led by **John C. Frémont.** Second expedition (1843–44) took Frémont from the Missouri River to the Oregon country, thence to Pyramid Lake, into present-day Nevada, and across the Sierra into California. He returned to St. Louis by way of Nevada and Utah. The expeditions contributed valuable scientific observations and stimulated popular interest in the Far West, although Frémont saw no territory not previously explored by fur traders.

1842–43. Beginning of the "great migration" to the Oregon country as the "Oregon fever" spread throughout the Midwest, bringing settlers from Missouri, Ohio, Kentucky, and other states. The **Oregon Trail,** parts of which had been used by fur traders and explorers, became the main route for emigrants. The trail extended from **Independence, Mo.,** to **Astoria,** at the mouth of the Columbia River.

1844. First successful transmission of message by telegraph (pp. 794–795).

1845. ANNEXATION OF TEXAS (p. 225).

Texas and Florida admitted to the Union.

3 Mar. Postal Act reduced postage to 5 cts. a ½ oz. for 300 mi. and authorized mail subsidies for transatlantic steamers; discontinued in 1859.

1846. OREGON TREATY gave U.S. undisputed claim to Pacific Northwest south of 49th parallel (p. 232); stimulated migration to region.

Bear Flag Revolt in the Sacramento Valley; conquest of California by the Americans (p. 238).

Iowa admitted to the Union.

Pennsylvania R.R. chartered. Under the direction of **John Edgar Thomson** (1808–74) a link between Pittsburgh and Philadelphia was built; opened to passenger traffic, 18 July 1858, but the road's major expansion came after the Civil War.

1846–47. Donner party, a group of emigrants bound for California, suffered extreme hardships during winter at Donner Lake and Prosser Creek.

1847. First Mormon settlers arrived in the Salt Lake Valley after overland trek from Kanesville (now Council Bluffs, Iowa). Under the leadership of **Brigham Young** (p. 1190), Salt Lake City was founded (1847) and the State of Deseret established (Mar., 1849) with Young as governor.

Collins Line opened transatlantic steamship service between New York and Liverpool. Ocean Steam Navigation Co. opened similar service between New York and Bremen. These routes were abandoned after the reduction of federal mail subsidies in 1857–58.

Formation of the railway company later known (1851) as the Chicago and Rock Island R.R., the first to reach the Mississippi River (1854), across which it constructed the first bridge (1856).

Mobile and Ohio R.R. chartered; projected by Southern interests, it later received land-grant subsidies from Alabama and Mississippi.

Hannibal and St. Joseph R.R. (built 1851–59) incorporated in Missouri.

1847–51. Construction of the Hudson River R.R., connecting New York and Albany.

1848, 24 JAN. DISCOVERY OF GOLD in California by James W. Marshall on property of **Johann Augustus Sutter** (1803–80); announced by President Polk in farewell message to Congress (Dec.), starting **gold rush** (1849).

2 FEB. TREATY OF GUADALUPE HIDALGO gave U.S. large domain in the Southwest (p. 247).

Wisconsin admitted to the Union.

Oregon Territory established.

1848–49. Frémont's expedition explored railroad route across the Rockies; followed by similar venture in 1853–54.

1848–56. As part of a state program of internal improvements, the North Carolina R.R. was built from Charlotte to Goldsboro.

1849. Minnesota Territory established.

Pacific R.R. Co. (later the **Missouri Pacific R.R.**) chartered in Missouri. Built during 1851–56, it eventually linked St. Louis with Kansas City, and was the first railroad west of the Mississippi River.

Incorporation in Pennsylvania of the railway later known (1853) as the Delaware, Lackawanna and Western R.R.

1849–55. Consolidation of 4 railways in Illinois resulted in creation (1855) of the **Chicago, Burlington and Quincy R.R.**; furnished the Midwest with important connections to Eastern markets.

1850, 9 SEPT. California admitted to the Union.

TEXAS CESSION of all claims to New Mexico territory for $10 million (also p. 253).

Territories of Utah and New Mexico established.

20 SEPT. Congressional Act authorized land grants to Illinois, Mississippi, and Alabama, for railroad construction between Chicago and Mobile; permitted state grants to railways of tracts in the public domain in alternate sections not exceeding 6 miles. Between 1850–57 some 21 million acres were granted to subsidize the construction of railroads in the Mississippi Valley.

Louisville and Nashville R.R. chartered; completed in 1859.

1851. Chartering of the **Illinois Central R.R.**, the first land-grant railway. Completed in 1856, it linked Chicago, Galena, and Cairo. It received more than 2.5 million acres and, in the course of selling these lands in order to provide for construction costs, carried out extensive colonization work.

1853. Washington Territory organized.

GADSDEN PURCHASE (p. 257).

Consolidation of 3 New York railways connecting New York with Buffalo brought creation of the **New York Central Co.,** which in 1867 came under the control of Commodore **Cornelius Vanderbilt** (p. 1173).

The Cleveland, Columbus and Cincinnati R.R. joined with the Pittsburgh, Ft. Wayne and Chicago R.R. at Crestline, Ohio, to form the first rail connection between Pittsburgh and Cincinnati. Opening of the Cleveland and Erie R.R.

1854. Territories of Kansas and Nebraska organized; "popular sovereignty" principle inflamed issue of slavery in the territories (p. 258).

Assassination of James King, editor of *San Francisco Bulletin,* marked the apogee of desperado activity in California; led to setting up of **Vigilance Committee** utilizing quasi-legal process to restore order.

1854–57. War Department explorations for a railroad route to the Pacific constituted the federal government's first attempt at a comprehensive and systematic geographical examination of the West.

1855. Opening of the St. Marys Falls Ship Canal, linking Lake Huron with Lake Superior.

1857–58. Conflict of authority with the federal government resulted in dispatch of U.S. troops to Utah Territory; virtually bloodless "Mormon War" ended in compromise.

1858. Minnesota admitted to the Union.

Inauguration of mail service to California by the **Butterfield Overland Mail,** until 1861 active between St. Louis-Memphis and the Pacific coast.

Opening of the **mining frontier** following the discovery of gold in **Colorado, Nevada,** and **British Columbia; Pikes Peak gold rush** (1858–59). **Comstock Lode** (Virginia City) yielded $300 million in gold and silver in 20 years; continuous and profitable mining made possible by **Sutro Tunnel** (1869–79), built by **Adolph Sutro** (1830–98). Leadville, Colo., silver production peak 1880–93.

1859. Oregon admitted to the Union.

Establishment of the Leavenworth and Pikes Peak Express, a stage-line company operating between Leavenworth and Denver.

1860. Kansas territorial legislature chartered the Central Overland, California and Pikes Peak Express, to operate over the "Central Route" through South Pass between St. Joseph and Salt Lake City.

Establishment of the **Pony Express,** relay mail service between St. Joseph, Mo., and San Francisco; first run inaugurated on 3 Apr. 1860.

RAIL TRANSPORTATION ON THE EVE OF THE CIVIL WAR. Between 1840–60 an additional 28,000 miles were added to the U.S. railroad system, representing capital expenditures of close to a billion dollars. Originally, most of the railroads were extensions of existing lines of water transportation, but by 1855 New York was joined by a continuous line of rails to Chicago. The rapid expansion of East-West rail connections outpaced direct rail connections between North and South. As yet no direct rail connection existed along the coast between Washington, Charleston, and Savannah. However, the trunk lines from Chicago to New Orleans linked the South with the Middle West. The farthest western extension of the railroads by 1860 was to **St. Joseph** on the Missouri, but on the Pacific coast a short road near **Sacramento,** Calif., had already been built, signalizing the beginning of West-East construction.

Rail vs. Water-Turnpike Transportation by 1860: Rates per ton-mile ranged from about 15 cts. for turnpikes, 2 cts. for railroads, and from ¼ ct. to 1 ct. for canals.

TIME REQUIRED FOR FREIGHT SHIPMENTS FROM CINCINNATI TO NEW YORK CITY, 1815–1860, BY VARIOUS ROUTES AND METHODS*

Date	Route	Average Time Elapsed
1817	Ohio River keelboat to Pittsburgh, wagon to Philadelphia, wagon or wagon and river to N.Y.	52 days
1843–51	Ohio River steamboat to Pittsburgh, canal to Philadelphia, railroad to N.Y.	18–20 days
1852	Canal across Ohio, Lake Erie, Erie Canal, and Hudson River	18 days
1850's	Steamboat to New Orleans and packet to N.Y.	28 days
1852	All rail via Erie R.R. and connecting lines	6–8 days

* By permission of George R. Taylor, *The Transportation Revolution* (N.Y., Rinehart, 1951).

1860–64. MINING FRONTIER. Gold discovered (1860), in Humboldt and Esmeralda, Nev., intensified rush to mining areas. Government over these areas evolved through (1) mining camps; (2) vigilance committees providing a speedy trial for law-and-order offenders; (3) permanent government, territorial and state. In 1861–64 gold was discovered in Snake River Valley, **Idaho** (Clearwater and Salmon River gold fields; pop. Idaho City, 1863, 6,000). **Montana** gold rush (1863). Main camps: **Virginia City, Helena** (1864). Gang terrorism led by **Henry Plummer** put down by vigilantes, 1864.

1860–66. Pacific Telegraph Act, 16 June 1860, authorized the U.S. to construct a telegraph line from Missouri to San Francisco. The first telegraph message, San Francisco–Washington, D.C., was transmitted 24 Oct. 1861. The merger in 1866 of the **Western Union Telegraph Co.** (1856), controlling Western lines, with the American Telegraph Co. (1855) in control of the East, led to rapid expansion of telegraph service. **Postal Telegraph** organized, 1881.

1861. Kansas admitted to the Union. Colorado, Dakota, and Nevada organized as territories.

Merchandise admitted to the U.S. mails.

Beginning of the **Cheyenne-Arapaho War,** caused by the influx of miners into Colorado; climax in 1864 when Denver was isolated. On 28 Nov. the **Chivington Massacre** of 450 Indians took place, when Colorado militia under Col. J. M. Chivington attacked the main Indian encampment; submission of Indians by Oct., 1865.

1862–93. WESTERN RAILROAD BUILDING. (1) **Central Route:** Chicago to San Francisco via lowlands near South Pass. Pacific Railroad Act (1 July 1862) authorized the **Union Pacific R.R.** to build a line from Nebraska to Utah, where it was to meet the **Central Pacific** (organized, 1861, and directed by **Collis P. Huntington** [1821–1900] and **Leland Stanford** [p. 1155]) building east from California. Land grants of 10 alternate sections per mile on both sides of the entire distance were made (also p. 636). The route was completed, 10 May 1869, by a junction of the 2 lines at **Promontory,** Utah. Corrupt practices of **Crédit Mobilier,** Union Pacific's construction company, came into the open in Dec. 1867; scandal also attached to the operations of the **Crocker Corp.,** responsible for Central Pacific building. The latter used Chinese labor; the Union, Irish. In 1880 U.P. absorbed the Kansas Pacific and Denver Pacific, giving it access to Kansas City. By 1893 it had over 8,000 miles of track.

(2) **Northern Route: Northern Pacific R.R.** (chartered, 1864), to utilize route from Lake Superior to Portland, Ore., financed by **Jay Cooke** (p. 1005); reorganized, 1881, by **Henry Villard** (1835–1900); route completed, 1883. An additional northern route was started in 1878 by the St. Paul, Minneapolis, and Manitoba R.R. (reorganized, 1889 as **Great Northern R.R.**), as a result of the seizure of control of the bankrupt St. Paul and Pacific R.R. by **James J. Hill** (1838–1916). By 1893 the line reached the Pacific at Seattle, Wash. To compensate for the lack of a land grant Hill promoted farm settlement along the entire route to create traffic.

(3) **35th Parallel Route: Atchison, Topeka and Santa Fe R.R.**, promoted by **Cyrus K. Holliday** (1826–1900), received a land grant from Congress in 1863 of 3 million acres in alternate sections in Kansas. By 1872 the line reached Colorado. Over a combination of its own and leased tracks it ran to Los Angeles via Needles and Yuma by 1883, by which date the line had 7,100 miles of track, from Kansas City to the West Coast.

(4) **Southern Route** (32nd parallel) was granted the **Texas & Pacific R.R.** (organized, 1871), to build to California and meet the tracks of the **Southern Pacific R.R.**, a line operated by the controllers of the Central Pacific. Acquired by Jay Gould, 1879, T. & P. later shared track privileges with S.P. east of El Paso, which the latter railroad had reached in 1881, joining eastern lines in 1882 to complete a route to New Orleans.

1863. West Virginia admitted to the Union. Arizona and Idaho territories organized, the latter being separated from the Oregon Territory.

1863–73. Congress authorized, 1863, free-carrier mail service direct to ad-

dressee. By 1871, 51 cities had carrier service. In 1873 the **postal card** was introduced from Europe.

1864. Nevada admitted to the Union to ensure the ratification of the 13th Amendment.

Montana Territory organized.

Railway mail service, proposed by George B. Armstrong in 1862, inaugurated by Postmaster General Montgomery Blair (1813–83). **Money order** system went into operation 1864.

1865. Submission of the Indians marked the end of the **Apache and Navajo** wars and the establishment of reservations (1866–67). **First Sioux War,** caused in part by U.S. project to construct a road from Fort Laramie, Wyo., to Bozeman, Mont., ended on 29 April 1868, when Sioux agreed to accept permanent reservation in Dakota Territory.

CATTLE KINGDOM. Beginning of the "Long Drive" of cattle from Texas to railroads of Kansas and Nebraska. The transfer of cattle was caused by (1) a price decline in Texas, (2) scarcity and price rise in the Middle West, (3) the Civil War. Between 1865 and 1879, 4 million head of cattle were thus transported. A byproduct of the Long Drive was the "cattle towns"—**Abilene** (1867), Ellsworth, Newton (after 1872), and **Dodge City,** Kansas (after 1875). From these centers live cattle were shipped to slaughterhouses in Chicago. The **refrigerator car** (by 1875) delivered Western dressed beef to the East.

1867. Nebraska admitted to the Union.

30 MAR. ALASKA PURCHASE (p. 334).

Establishment by Congress of the **Oklahoma Reservation** for members of the Five Civilized Tribes (eventually settled by 75,000 Indians), of the Black Hills Reservation for the Sioux, and 5 smaller reservations.

Beginning of the extermination of the

buffalo. Hides worth $1 to $3 per head. By 1883, about 13 million buffalo had been killed.

1867–69. 4 GREAT WESTERN SURVEYS by the federal government: (1) by **Clarence King** (1842–1901), of 40th parallel (1867–78); (2) by Dr. **Ferdinand V. Hayden** (1829–87) of a geological survey of Nebraska and Wyoming (1867–78); (3) by Lt. **George M. Wheeler,** of the 100th meridian (1872–79); (4) by Maj. **John W. Powell** (p. 1132) of Utah, Nevada and Arizona (1869–78).

1867–1910. EASTERN RAILROAD CONSOLIDATION. Organization, 1867, of the **New York Central & Hudson River R.R.** by **Cornelius Vanderbilt** (p. 1173), subsequently adding the N.Y., West Shore, and Buffalo R.R. By 1885 control over the Michigan Central and the "Big Four" system (connecting Cleveland, Cincinnati, Chicago, and St. Louis) had been obtained. In 1898 the Boston and Albany R.R. was leased. The **Pennsylvania Co.,** a pioneer holding company (1870), was organized by the Pennsylvania R.R. for rail lines leased or controlled. Rapid expansion of lines to Pittsburgh, Cincinnati, Chicago, St. Louis, and to Baltimore and Washington followed. Having acquired terminal facilities on the west shore of the Hudson, it constructed a tunnel under the river and opened a terminal in New York City in 1910. By 1866 **Erie R.R.** was in control of stock manipulator **Daniel Drew** (1797–1879), who was associated with **Jay Gould** (1836–92) and **James Fisk** ("Jubilee Jim," 1834–72) in stock manipulations at the expense of Cornelius Vanderbilt, operations which threw the line into bankruptcy in 1875; reorganized by J. P. Morgan, 1894.

1868. Wyoming Territory organized. Beginning of first **Dakota boom.** By 1873, population of the Dakotas rose to 20,000.

1870. Beginning of the **Texas boom.** During the next decade the number of Texas farms increased from 61,125 to 174,184.

23 MAY. Start of the first transcontinental railroad trip from Boston to Oakland.

1871–86. Apache War in New Mexico and Arizona began 30 Apr. 1871 with the massacre of over 100 Apaches at Camp Grant, Ariz. The conflict ended with the capture of the Apache leader, **Geronimo,** in 1886, and the remnants of the tribe were assigned small reservations in the Southwest. Yeoman service in this and other campaigns was rendered by the "Buffalo Soldiers," the 9th and 10th Cavalry regiments authorized by Congress in 1866 to be formed of Negro troops.

1873. Passage of the **Timber Culture Act** (p. 637).

Panic of 1873 interrupted railroad construction. By that date the Rock Island R.R. extended to Council Bluffs (1869); the Chicago, Burlington & Quincy to south-central Nebraska; the Illinois Central to Sioux City; the Chicago, Milwaukee & St. Paul into Iowa; the Chicago & Northwestern across Minnesota and into the Dakotas; the Northern Pacific had reached Bismarck, N.D.; the Lake Superior & Mississippi had extended to Duluth; and the Santa Fe had completed the trans-Kansas line.

1873–1907. SOUTHERN RAILROAD EXPANSION. The Baltimore & Ohio completed its line to Cincinnati (1873); later extended its lines north to Lake Erie and west to Chicago, Cincinnati, and St. Louis. Chesapeake and Ohio crossed the Appalachians, reaching Asheville, N.C., 1892; Norfolk and Western extended to the Ohio Valley, 1892. In 1900 the Clinchfield completed crossing from North Carolina to Tennessee; in 1907 the Virginian completed the last Appalachian route. The main north-south route of the Southern Railway was completed to Atlanta, 1873; the Atlantic Coast Line consolidated more than 100 smaller lines, 1898–1900; Seaboard Airline, 1900. By the 1890s southern Florida was reached by the Florida East Coast. Another line from Atlanta to Cincinnati had been completed in 1880.

1874. The worst grasshopper plague in U.S. history spread devastation among Great Plains farmers from the Dakotas to northern Texas.

Joseph F. Glidden (1813–1906) marketed his first **barbed wire** and solved the problem of fencing the cattle range. Ultimately the American Steel and Wire Co. (U.S. Steel subsidiary) established a virtual monopoly of barbed wire based on the Glidden patents.

1875. Opening of the **Black Hills** area in South Dakota to gold seekers, after gold was reported (Aug.) by U.S. military expedition headed by Gen. **George A. Custer** (1839–76). By fall over 15,000 prospectors entered the region. Main camps: **Custer City** and **Deadwood** (the latter the scene of legendary lawlessness created by such residents as **James Butler** ["**Wild Bill**"] **Hickok**; actually only 4 murders and no lynchings marred its pioneer years). Ultimately the **Homestake Mining Co.** assumed control of operations in this area.

1875–76. Second Sioux War caused by (1) the gold rush into the Black Hills reservation; (2) extension of the route of the Northern Pacific R.R.; (3) corruption in the Department of the Interior. U.S. troops finally defeated Chiefs **Sitting Bull** and **Crazy Horse** (31 Oct. 1876), but not before Custer and a contingent of 264 men were annihilated at the **Battle of the Little Big Horn** (25–26 June).

1876. Colorado admitted to the Union.

1877. Passage of the **Desert Land Act** (p. 637).

Nez Percé War, fought in the Pacific Northwest. Nez Percé Indians under **Chief Joseph** were defeated (Oct.) and assigned a reservation in Oklahoma.

1877–1915. EARLY TELEPHONE EXPANSION. Operation in 1877 of the first practical intercity telephone lines— Salem to Boston (Bell), Chicago to Milwaukee (Gray)—led to establishment by 1880 of 148 telephone companies operating 34,305 miles of wire. These systems were ultimately consolidated by the **American Telephone & Telegraph Co.** By 1895 long-distance telephone lines were in operation between New York and Chicago; connections extended to Denver, 1911; to San Francisco, 1915. Number of telephones in the U.S.: 1900, 1,355,900; 1932, 17,424,406; 1952, 43,003,800; 1970, 120,155,000.

1878. Timber and Stone Act (p. 637).

1878–85. Second Dakota boom, promoted by entry of Northern Pacific R.R. and Great Northern into territory by 1882, followed by other lines. Peak in homestead grants in the Dakotas was reached in 1884 when 11,083,000 acres were granted to settlers. Population, 1890, 539,583; Montana, 142,924.

1879. "EXODUS OF 1879" in which between 20,000 and 40,000 Negroes from South sought homesteads in Kansas when word spread they would be welcome there, only to be turned back by lack of capital, inexperience, and white hostility.

1883. Four standard time zones established, facilitating railroad operations.

1883–86. Coeur d'Alene gold rush to northern Idaho. In 1885 the **Bunker Hill** and **Sullivan Mines** were discovered, eventually yielding $250 million in silver and lead.

1883–87. END OF THE CATTLE BOOM marked by big business control of ranching. In Wyoming 23 stock-raising corporations were organized with a total capital of $12 million. Overstocking the range was followed by serious drought, 1885–86, and a cold winter, 1886–87. Prices crashed in 1885. Result: the end of the open range and the introduction of fenced pastures and better cattle breeding.

1884. RAILROAD LAND GRANTS. Estimate of all public lands granted to railroads: 155,504,994 acres (Donaldson), almost the area of Texas (Union Pacific, 20 million; Santa Fe, 17 million; Central and Southern Pacific, 24 million; Northern Pacific, 44 million, sales of which by 1917 had brought the last-named railroad over $136 million). Western states also granted roads 49 million acres. Because of noncompletion of a number of projected roads, the final federal total: **131,350,534 acres** (U.S. General Land Office, *Ann. Rep.*, 1943). In addition, loans totaling $64,623,512 were advanced to 6 companies to build the Pacific routes, which were repaid with interest by 1898–99. In return, the land-grant railroads agreed to transport U.S. property and troops "free," a clause which was adjusted to **50%** of normal commercial rates. In 1940 Congress eliminated reductions on U.S. government's civilian passenger and freight traffic, but low rates continued during World War II for U.S. army and navy freight and personnel; discontinued 1 Oct. 1946.

17 MAY. Organic Act applied the laws of Oregon to Alaska after a period of government by the War Department.

1887. Dawes Severalty Act (p. 645). Interstate Commerce Act (p. 309).

1889. North Dakota, South Dakota, Montana, and Washington admitted to the Union (with Idaho and Wyoming admitted, 1890)—known as the **Omnibus States.**

22 APR. Since 1884 "Sooners" led by **David L. Payne** and **W. L. Couch** had been entering the **Oklahoma District,** a triangle of rich land in the center of Indian Territory owned by no one tribe, only to be dispersed by troops. Constant pressure led to the opening of the district to homesteaders, or "Boomers" as they were called, at noon. Within a few hours, 1,920,000 acres were settled under bedlam conditions (Oklahoma City by nightfall—population, 10,000).

1890, 2 MAY. Oklahoma Territory organized.

U.S. Census Director, in his report, announced that **"there can hardly be said to be a frontier line."**

The **Ghost Dance War** on the Black Hills Reservation arose when U.S. Army authorities sought to curb religious rites of the Teton Sioux; came to an end with an Indian massacre at the **Battle of Wounded Knee** (29 Dec.).

1891, 22 SEPT. Lands of the Sauk, Fox, and Pottawatomie in Oklahoma Territory (900,000 acres) opened to settlement.

1892. Opening of the Cheyenne-Arapaho Reservation of 3 million acres.

1893, 16 SEPT. Second major "Boomer" invasion of Oklahoma on 6 million acres of the **Cherokee Outlet.**

1896. KLONDIKE GOLD RUSH. Gold discovered 16 Aug. 1896 on Bonanza Creek, near Dawson, Canada, 50 miles east of Alaska border; followed by gold rush. Peak production, 1900, $22 million; total production, 1885–1929, exceeded $175 million.

Utah admitted to the Union.

Rural free delivery established.

1898. 7 JULY. Annexation of **Hawaii** (pp. 339–340, 345). On 30 Apr. 1900 Congress granted territorial status to Hawaii, the new government defined in the Organic Act becoming effective 14 June 1900.

1900. LAND SETTLEMENT. In the 30 years ending 1900, 430 million acres had been occupied; 225 million placed under cultivation. For the entire period,

1607–1870, 407 million acres occupied; 189 million improved.

1900–52. HIGHWAY CONSTRUCTION AND MOTOR TRANSPORTATION. Twentieth-century highway construction augmented the use of the automobile, the motor truck, and the bus as formidable competitors to railroad transportation. Asphalt roads had been introduced in New York City in the 1870s; Portland cement in the U.S. in 1894. Surface roads increased in mileage from 161,000 (1905) to 521,000 (1925), and 1,527,000 (1945). Most notable of numerous highway projects was the **Alaskan Highway (Alcan)**, work upon which was started on 12 Mar. 1942 and completed 1 Dec., 1,523 miles from Dawson Creek, B.C., through Canada and the Yukon Territory to Fairbanks, Ala. Constructed as a military supply route during World War II at a cost of $138 million, it was opened to tourists, summer 1948. **Passenger car registrations:** 1900, 8,000; 1913, 1,258,062; 1930, 26,545,281; 1951, 42,700,000. **Motor truck registrations:** 1904, 700; 1913, 67,667; 1952, 9,116,000. Regular route intercity passengers carried by **intercity bus** averaged 425 million (1944–48).

1906. Alaska permitted to elect a delegate to Congress.

1907. Oklahoma and Indian Territory admitted to the Union as 1 state.

1911–52. AIRPLANE TRANSPORTATION, following the first successful airplane flight by the **Wright brothers,** 1903, at Kitty Hawk (p. 797), made rapid strides in the U.S. The first air-mail service, New York to Washington, 1918; across the continent, 8 Sept. 1920. 15 Oct., first contracts for international air mail (Western Hemisphere) awarded to private operators. By the **Kelly Act** (1925) air-mail contracts were to be awarded on the basis of private bidding.

Factors promoting air transport in this period include (1) inauguration of regular night flying (Chicago to Cheyenne), 1923; (2) installation of radio beacons for aerial navigation (Washington, D.C.), 1925; (3) passage of the **Air Commerce Act,** 1926, which inaugurated a government program of aid to civil air transport and navigation, including the establishment of airports. Rapid expansion followed.

1927, 21 MAY. First nonstop flight, New York to Paris, by **Charles A. Lindbergh, Jr.** (1902–1974).

1 SEPT. Air express established by arrangement between American Railway Express Agency and airlines.

1934, 19 FEB. All domestic air-mail contracts canceled by Postmaster General **James A. Farley** (1888–1976) on the ground of collusion. U.S. Army Air Corps assumed operations pending new arrangements with private operators, who began to handle air mail by 8 May. The **Air Mail Act** of 12 June provided that the ICC was to determine "fair and reasonable" air-mail rates and to review them periodically, and reduced air-mail postage to 6 cts. an oz.

1935. Inauguration of transpacific air service (San Francisco to Manila) by Pan American Airways.

1938, 23 JUNE. Civil Aeronautics Act created **Civil Aeronautics Authority (CAA)** empowered to regulate rates of air transport and foster stability in the field.

1939. Inauguration of transatlantic air service (New York–Southampton) by Pan American Airways and Imperial Airways.

1947. First fully automatic (without pilot control) transport flight (U.S. Army C-54), Newfoundland to England. Airlines carried 12,890,208 **revenue passengers** that year as against 5,782 in 1926 and 1,365,706 in 1938.

1948–52. First U.S. jet-propelled commercial air transport—Consolidated Vultee Convair; first British DeHaviland Comet (1949); revised version ordered by several U.S. airlines (1952).

Domestic air routes in operation: 139,030 miles (1948) as compared with 8,252 miles in 1926 and 35,492 in 1938. **Domestic cargo,** exclusive of mail (estimated), 30,637,879 (ton-miles) for express, 69,023,000 for freight.

1912. New Mexico and Arizona admitted to the Union, completing the political organization of the West. Alaska given territorial status (population: 1920, 55,000, as against 30,000 in 1867).

1913. Establishment of **domestic parcel post** by Act of 24 Aug. 1912. Parcel post arrangements between the U.S. and the United Kingdom had been in existence since 1902

1919–50. EXPANSION OF RADIO COMMUNICATION SYSTEMS (pp. 798, 954–956).

1954, 13 MAY. ST. LAWRENCE SEAWAY (p. 483).

27 SEPT. "DEW LINE" (p. 484).

1956–78. HIGHWAY CONSTRUCTION AND MOTOR TRANSPORTATION.
29 June, the **Highway Act of 1956** authorized $32 billion over the next 13 years for construction of a 41,000-mile interstate system of highways and for completing construction of the federal-aid system of highways, the federal government to contribute 90% of construction costs for the interstate and 50% for the federal-aid system. The act also provided for new taxes on gasoline and other highway-user items for a **Highway Trust Fund** to finance the programs. By 1972 cost estimates has risen to $76.3 billion for a 42,500-mile interstate system and 1980 was considered a possible completion date; 33,796 miles of the interstate system were open to traffic.

Passenger car registrations 1978. 116,-600,000 as compared with 61,682,000 in 1960.

Truck and bus registrations 1978. 32,-200,000, as compared with 12,200,000 in 1960.

Intercity bus lines carried 338 million passengers in 1978 as compared with 366 million in 1960.

Motor vehicles transported 555 billion ton-miles of freight, 24.08% of domestic freight traffic in 1977, as compared with 285 billion ton-miles, 21.5% in 1960.

1958, 3 MAY. ANTARCTICA (p. 488).

1959, 3 JAN. ALASKA admitted to the Union as the 49th state. The first bill for Alaskan statehood was introduced in 1916 but the drive for statehood did not become sustained and serious until 1943. Partisan and sectional considerations figured importantly in congressional debates on statehood for the Democratic and pro-civil-rights territory. In order to demonstrate their readiness, Alaskans drafted and approved (24 Apr. 1956) a state constitution and elected (9 Oct.) to Congress 2 "senators" and a "representative." For Alaska to become a viable state it was considered necessary to give it an endowment of federal lands, which comprised more than 99% of its area. The Alaskan Statehood Act (7 July 1958) granted the state the right to select 102,-550,000 acres of vacant unreserved public lands and an additional 800,000 acres adjacent to communities.

21 AUG. HAWAII admitted to the Union as the 50th state. In 1903 the popularly elected Hawaii legislature petitioned for statehood, a request repeated at least 17 times. The first of a long series of Hawaiian statehood bills was introduced in 1919. The drive for statehood became significant in 1934 when it gained the support of the territory's economic leadership. Opposition in Congress to Hawaii's admission was based upon doubts about the wisdom of admitting a noncontiguous state, concern of Southerners as to the admission of pro-civil-rights congressmen, and fears of excessive Communist influence among unionized longshoremen and plantation workers.

1966, 15 Oct. DEPARTMENT OF TRANSPORTATION created (p. 532).

1968–74. RAILROAD REORGANI-ZATIONS. Pennsylvania and New York Central R.R. merger forming Penn Central R.R. was upheld by the Supreme Court 15 Jan. 1968 (p. 682). The New York, New Haven, and Hartford R.R. was absorbed into the Penn Central system (Dec. 1968). The Penn Central filed a petition in bankruptcy, 22 June 1970, but was the beneficiary of a law authorizing $125 million in federal loan guarantees (8 Jan. 1971). **AMTRAK,** a semipublic corporation created by the **Rail Passenger Service Act of 1970** to operate a nationwide passenger system, began service on 1 May 1971. The act enabled those railroads that wished to transfer all intercity passenger operations to the new corporation to do so. Travel was up 11% (1973) on AMTRAK, whose showpiece was the Washington, D.C. to New York City **Metroliner,** developed under the **High-Speed Ground Trans-portation Act of 1965,** which made its first run 16 Jan. 1969. Under the Rail Reorganization Act of 2 Jan. 1974 Congress provided for the reorganization of the Penn Central and 6 other bankrupt railroads in the Northeast and Midwest, established a federal agency to design a new rail system as a profit-making enter-prise, a corporation to run it and to issue up to $1.5 billion in guaranteed loans. The legislation also authorized the ex-penditure of $585 million and required construction of new electrified high-speed rail service in the Northeast Cor-ridor. The act was upheld by the Su-preme Court in the *Regional Rail Reorganization Cases* (419 U.S. 102), 1974.

Chronology of the States of the Union

1.	Delaware	7 Dec. 1787		26.	Michigan	26 Jan. 1837
2.	Pennsylvania	12 Dec. 1787		27.	Florida	3 Mar. 1845
3.	New Jersey	18 Dec. 1787		28.	Texas	29 Dec. 1845
4.	Georgia	2 Jan. 1788		29.	Iowa	28 Dec. 1846
5.	Connecticut	9 Jan. 1788		30.	Wisconsin	29 May 1848
6.	Massachusetts	6 Feb. 1788		31.	California	9 Sept. 1850
7.	Maryland	28 Apr. 1788		32.	Minnesota	11 May 1858
8.	South Carolina	23 May 1788		33.	Oregon	14 Feb. 1859
9.	New Hampshire	21 June 1788		34.	Kansas	29 Jan. 1861
10.	Virginia	25 June 1788		35.	West Virginia	20 June 1863
11.	New York	26 July 1788		36.	Nevada	31 Oct. 1864
12.	North Carolina	21 Nov. 1789		37.	Nebraska	1 Mar. 1867
13.	Rhode Island	29 May 1790		38.	Colorado	1 Aug. 1876
14.	Vermont	4 Mar. 1791		39.	North Dakota	2 Nov. 1889
15.	Kentucky	1 June 1792		40.	South Dakota	2 Nov. 1889
16.	Tennessee	1 June 1796		41.	Montana	8 Nov. 1889
17.	Ohio	1 Mar. 1803		42.	Washington	11 Nov. 1889
18.	Louisiana	30 Apr. 1812		43.	Idaho	3 July 1890
19.	Indiana	11 Dec. 1816		44.	Wyoming	10 July 1890
20.	Mississippi	10 Dec. 1817		45.	Utah	4 Jan. 1896
21.	Illinois	3 Dec. 1818		46.	Oklahoma	16 Nov. 1907
22.	Alabama	14 Dec. 1819		47.	New Mexico	6 Jan. 1912
23.	Maine	15 Mar. 1820		48.	Arizona	14 Feb. 1912
24.	Missouri	10 Aug. 1821		49.	Alaska	3 Jan. 1959
25.	Arkansas	15 June 1836		50.	Hawaii	29 Aug. 1959

1970, 12 AUG. POSTAL REORGANI-
ZATION ACT (p. 536). Pieces of mail
handled 1970 (estimated): 84.9 billion
as compared with 7.1 billion in 1900;
27.7 billion in 1940; 99.8 billion in 1979.

**1970–79. AIRPLANE TRANSPOR-
TATION.** On 22 Jan. a Boeing 747 carried 362 passengers on its first commercial flight, New York–London. By year's
end more than 100 of these **"jumbo jets,"**
capable of carrying up to 500 tourist-
class passengers, were in service on
domestic and international routes. Capable of carrying up to 400, the Mc-

Donnell Douglas DC-10 and Lockheed
10–11 followed the 747 into commercial
service.

Domestic revenue passengers carried
1979. 293 million as compared with 38
million in 1955 and 92 million in 1965.

Domestic ton-miles flown, express and
freight 1979. 3.465 billion as compared
with 228 million in 1955 and 943 million
in 1965.

Domestic ton-miles flown, mail 1980.
853 million as compared with 87 million
in 1955 and 226 million in 1965.

The American Empire

1858–1947 OVERSEAS EXPANSION OF THE U.S.

Year	Accession	Area, sq. mi.
1858	Johnston Atoll (Johnston and Sand Islands)	.5
1863	Swan Islands[1]	1
1867	Alaska	589,757
1898	Midway Islands	2
1898	Wake Island	3
1898	Hawaii	6,450
1898	Palmyra Atoll	4
1898	Philippines[2]	115,600
1898	Puerto Rico	3,435
1898	Guam	212
1899	American Samoa	76
1903	Panama Canal Zone[3]	553
1914	Corn Islands[4]	4
1916	Navassa Island	2
1917	U.S. Virgin Islands	133
1928	Roncador Cay, Serrano Bank, Serranilla Bank[5]	.4
1934	Howland, Baker, and Jarvis Islands	3
1934	Kingman Reef	.5
1939	Canton and Enderbury Islands[6]	27
1947	Trust Territory of the Pacific Islands (Micronesia)[7]	716

[1] Turned over to Honduras in accordance with treaty signed 22 Nov. 1971.
[2] Ceded by Spain in 1898, the Philippines consti-
tuted a territorial possession of the U.S. until
granted independence 4 July 1946.
[3] Under U.S. jurisdiction in accordance with treaty
of 18 Nov. 1903, with the Republic of Panama; jurisdiction ended 1 Oct. 1979.
[4] Leased from the Republic of Nicaragua for 99
years but returned to Nicaragua 25 Apr. 1971.
[5] Turned over to Colombia in 1973 under an agreement reached 8 Sept. 1972.
[6] Administered by the U.S. under a joint control
agreement with the United Kingdom.
[7] Former Japanese mandated islands, under UN
trusteeship with the U.S. as administering authority.
Ocean area approx. 3 million sq. mi.

1898–1946. The Philippines.

1899. TREATY FIGHT. As a result
of the Treaty of Paris (10 Dec. 1898;
p. 345), Spain ceded to the U.S. the
Philippines, as well as Puerto Rico and
Guam. Senate debate on the treaty
focused upon the Philippines—whose acquisition represented a major departure
from previous American experience—and
revealed the sharp division between the
imperialists and anti-imperialists. The
former, notably **Henry Cabot Lodge** (p.
1088) and **Albert Beveridge** (p. 985),
stressed national prestige, the civilizing
mission of the U.S., economic and strategic advantages, and the contention
that foreign powers active in the Far East
would establish a foothold in the Philippines if the U.S. withdrew. The anti-
imperialists, among them **George F.
Hoar, John Sherman, Thomas B. Reed,
Charles Francis Adams** (1835–1915), **Carl
Schurz,** and **F. L. Godkin,** maintained
that the acquisition of noncontiguous
areas peopled by alien stocks incapable
of assimilation was contrary to the traditional U.S. isolationism, inimical to the
Monroe Doctrine, and contrary to U.S.

principles of self-government. Democrats and Populists were generally opposed to the treaty, and were joined by a minority group of New England Republicans. The leader of the Democratic party, William Jennings Bryan, succeeded in influencing a sufficient number of opponents of the treaty to vote for it on the ground that it would end the war. The question of the independence of the Philippines, Bryan pointed out, could be left to the national election of 1900. The treaty was ratified (6 Feb.) by the close vote of 57–27 (thus securing confirmation by a 2-vote margin).

1899–1901. COLONIAL STATUS ISSUE. Imperialists contended that acquisition did not automatically incorporate the new possessions—including also Puerto Rico (p. 622) and Guam (p. 624) —into the U.S. and endow them with the constitutional privileges of U.S. citizens. Anti-imperialists argued that the "Constitution followed the flag," i.e., that territorial acquisition made these dependencies an organic part of the U.S., entitled to all constitutonal guarantees— a position based on legal arguments which tended to justify their position that annexation was an error. A middle group held that only "fundamental" constitutional guarantees, as distinguished from "formal" privileges, were applicable to the insular possessions. The anti-imperialists suffered another defeat when the constitutional status issue was settled by the Supreme Court in the so-called **Insular Cases** (1901 *et seq.*, p. 673).

1899–1902. PHILIPPINE INSURRECTION. At the outbreak of the Spanish American War the U.S. returned the insurrectionist leader **Emilio Aguinaldo** to the Philippines to direct the native uprising against the Spanish. Aguinaldo organized a Filipino army and on 12 June 1898 established a provisional government, proclaiming its independence of Spain. The Filipino rebels be-

lieved that the U.S. would grant freedom and independence to the islands. When Aguinaldo learned (4 Jan. 1899) that the Treaty of Paris gave the U.S. control of the Philippines, he called upon the people (5 Jan.) to declare their independence. On 4 Feb. the Filipinos broke out in armed revolt against U.S. rule. To suppress the uprising the U.S. employed a force of 70,000 men against a Filipino army almost as large. Organized Filipino resistance came to an end by the close of 1899 but guerrilla warfare that led to ruthless measures on both sides continued until mid-1902, despite the earlier capture (23 Mar. 1901) of Aguinaldo. Scattered resistance continued until 1906. The administration's Philippine policy was condemned by the Anti-Imperialist League, an organization established in June 1898 that included many influential citizens among its numbers.

1899. SCHURMAN COMMISSION. President McKinley appointed (20 Jan.) a Philippine Commission headed by Jacob G. Schurman, president of Cornell Univ., to study the situation in the islands and to submit a report to serve as a basis for setting up a civil government. In June the Schurman Commission recommended ultimate independence for the islands, but suggested the continuation of U.S. rule for an indefinite period, until the Filipinos were ready for self-government.

1900. TAFT COMMISSION. On 7 Apr. President McKinley appointed a second Philippine Commission, headed by Federal Circuit Judge William Howard Taft. The 5-man commission which, in accord with the Schurman Commission's recommendations, was directed to establish a civil government in the islands began to exercise legislative powers on 1 Sept. and, with the termination of military government (except in areas where rebellion persisted) became the civil government on 4 July 1901. (All military government was ended a year later.) As president of the commission, Taft became civil governor of the Philippines. Guided by specific instructions written by Secretary of War Elihu Root, the commission proclaimed guarantees essentially those of the U.S. Bill of Rights, organized municipal administrations, and by progressive steps created a government for the Philippines. Taft encouraged Filipino participation, ultimately adding 3 Filipinos to the commission.

1 July 1902. PHILIPPINE GOVERN-MENT ACT (also known as the Organic Act) passed by Congress constituted the Philippine Islands an unorganized territory. It confirmed the president's appointment of the Taft Commission, ratified the commission's reforms, and assured increased self-government—providing for establishment of a popular assembly (after peace was established and a census taken). The commission would then become the upper house of the bicameral legislature, its members retaining also their executive and ministerial functions. In the first general elections (1907) the Nationalist party, which stood for immediate independence, gained 58 of 80 assembly seats.

29 Aug. 1916. JONES ACT reaffirmed the U.S. intention to withdraw its sovereignty over the islands and to recognize their independence as soon as a stable government should be established. The act provided for male suffrage, established an elective Senate in place of the Philippine Commission, and vested executive power in the governor, to be appointed by the U.S. president. The governor was given veto power, subject to review by the president, but all appointments made by the governor were subject to confirmation by the Philippine Senate. From this time onward the Filipinos effectively controlled their domestic affairs. The Jones Act also provided for free trade between the Philippines and the U.S. (most U.S. duties and quotas on Philippine exports had already been removed). The U.S. maintained a virtual monopoly of Philippine trade as Philippine exports expanded.

PHILIPPINE INDEPENDENCE. Following the election of 1932 a movement gained ground to implement the promise of independence for the Philippines contained in the Jones Act. Joining forces to promote independence were U.S. beet-sugar and dairy interests seeking to bar Philippine cane sugar and coconut oil, respectively; organized labor favoring immigration curbs; and anti-imperialists. The immediate result was the **Hawes-Cutting Act**, passed by a Democratic Congress over the president's veto in the closing days of the Hoover administration, 13 Jan. 1933. The act provided for independence after 12 years, but reserved to the U.S. the right to military and naval bases, and to the U.S. Supreme Court the right to review the decisions of the Philippine courts. The Philippine legislature rejected the measure in Oct. on the ground that its real aim was to exclude Philippine products and labor from the U.S. To meet some of these criticisms, Congress (24 Mar. 1934) passed the **Tydings-McDuffie Act,** which substantially reenacted the Hawes-Cutting bill, but provided for the removal of U.S. military posts and the settlement by negotiation of the future status of U.S. naval bases. This act was unanimously accepted by the Philippine legislature (1 May). Under its authority a convention met on 30 July to frame a constitution, which President Roosevelt approved on 8 Feb. 1935. The constitution was ratified, 14 May, and the first president, **Manuel Quezon,** elected on 17 Sept. On 14 Apr. 1937 President Roosevelt appointed the Joint Preparatory

Commission on Philippine Affairs to recommend a program for economic adjustment. The committee proposed that the 75% of preferences existing on 4 July 1946 (the date when Philippine independence was to go into effect) be gradually eliminated by 31 Dec. 1960.

The Philippines became independent on the projected date, 4 July 1946. By an executive agreement embodying provisions of the Philippine Trade Act of 1946 (30 Apr. 1946), signed on that date, the Philippines received tariff concessions (duty-free entry until 1954 with duties to be gradually imposed over the following 20 years) but in return had to treat U.S. exports to the Philippines similarly and accept a "parity clause" guaranteeing U.S. businessmen equal rights with Filipinos to exploit Philippine natural resources and operate public utilities. The "parity clause" necessitated amendment (Mar. 1947) of the Philippine Constitution, which the U.S. had approved in 1935.

1898–1973. Puerto Rico.

After the outcome of the war with Spain had been decided in Cuba (p. 345), a U.S. force of some 3,500 under Gen. Nelson A. Miles landed in Puerto Rico—meeting only token military resistance and general popular acceptance (25 July 1898). After evacuation of the Spanish governor-general (18 Oct.) the U.S. took over complete authority. Spain's cession of Puerto Rico to the U.S. by the Treaty of Paris (10 Dec.; p. 345) was recognition of an accomplished fact. Puerto Rico was controlled by the military pending congressional establishment of civil government.

12 Apr. 1900. THE FORAKER ACT provided for the establishment of a temporary civil government in Puerto Rico, effective 1 May. The president was empowered to appoint, with senatorial con-

sent, the governor and the 11 members (at least 5 of whom were to be natives of Puerto Rico) of the executive council, which was to serve as the upper house of the legislature. Popular elections were provided for the lower house and a Resident Commissioner to speak for Puerto Rico in the U.S. House of Representatives (he could vote only in committee). Federal tariffs, at reduced rates, were applied to products of Puerto Rico—with the provision that their proceeds were to be returned to the insular treasury. (Taxes collected in the U.S. on Puerto Rican products were not actually paid to Puerto Rico until the provision was clarified in the Jones Act of 1917). Puerto Rico was also exempted from federal internal revenue taxes. Puerto Rican politicians were unwilling to undergo an indefinite period of tutelage under the Foraker Act—a majority demanding full territorial status and U.S. citizenship. A split began to emerge about 1909 between those who spoke of ultimate statehood and those who looked toward independence.

2 Mar. 1917. THE JONES ACT (also known as the Organic Act for Puerto Rico) made Puerto Rico an "organized but unincorporated" territory of the U.S. and granted Puerto Ricans U.S. citizenship. Regulation of the suffrage was left to the Puerto Rican government (male suffrage had become universal under the local discretion permitted by the Foraker Act) and a bill of rights essentially similar to that of the U.S. was established. The upper house of the legislature was made elective. The governor and the supreme court were to be appointed by the president, who would also appoint 4 of the 6 department heads.

1899–1952. ECONOMIC SITUATION AND MOVEMENT FOR REFORM. Included within U.S. tariff walls, Puerto Rico found a ready market for its agricultural products, particularly sugar.

Adoption of U.S. currency and unobstructed financial movement between the island and the U.S. mainland facilitated large capital investment—some $120 million during the first 3 decades of U.S. rule—which revolutionized sugar production. As sugar corporations absorbed the limited productive land which had sustained small farmers producing for local consumption, Puerto Rico was forced to import its foodstuffs. By the 1930s sugar production had expanded to more than 16 times what it had been under Spain but few Puerto Ricans lived above the subsistence level; poverty was widespread and unemployment high. Population pressure increased as the application of modern medical knowledge radically cut the island's death rate, causing the population nearly to double between 1899 and 1940 (1899: 953,000; 1940: 1,869,000).

In 1934 a commission of Puerto Ricans produced the first serious proposals for reform and development, the Chardón Plan, which stressed distribution of land to the cultivators and development of industry by essentially restrictive and protective measures. Established in 1935, the Puerto Rican Reconstruction Administration (PRRA)—successor to the New Deal Puerto Rican Emergency Relief Administration (PRERA)—was to have implemented the Chardón Plan but, to a large extent a victim of the politics of a colonial situation, the PRRA accomplished little. In answer to Nationalist violence (1935–36), the U.S. government fanned the status issue as serious consideration was given the Tydings Bill (1936). This punitive offer of independence under adverse economic conditions realigned Puerto Rico's political parties into pro- and anti-independence groups. The victorious pro-statehood coalition generally coincided with the forces opposed to economic and social reform.

Only temporarily sidetracked, the incipient political movement for reform took the form of the new Popular Democratic Party (PPD) led by **Luis Muñoz Marín** (p. 1097). Muñoz argued that immediate economic and social problems took precedence over the status issue. Appealing to the lower classes, the PPD won tenuous control over the legislature in 1940. The PPD's electoral success brought **Rexford G. Tugwell** (1891–1979)—a vigorous advocate of democratic planning—to Puerto Rico as governor in 1941. Tugwell and Muñoz established a cooperative relationship and the PPD undertook such reforms as land redistribution and establishment of an economic development program. Popular approval of the Muñoz-Tugwell program resulted in an overwhelming victory for the PPD in the 1944 elections. Gathering momentum after 1945, **"Operation Bootstrap"** gave marked impetus to industrial development by providing various incentives to investors in new or expanded industry and construction—notably 10-year tax exemptions (increased up to 17 years in 1963).

1952. ESTABLISHMENT OF THE COMMONWEALTH. In 1946 President Truman named Jesús T. Piñero as the first Puerto Rican governor. The Organic Act was amended (5 Aug. 1947) to provide for popular election of the governor. Advocating a commonwealth status (estado libre asociado), Muñoz was elected governor (2 Nov. 1948), decisively defeating advocates of both statehood and independence. U.S. sanction of a self-governing status for Puerto Rico was given with Puerto Rican Federal Relations Act of 1950, adopted "in the nature of a compact" and affirmed by a special election (4 June 1951). Accordingly, the Commonwealth of Puerto Rico was established by a constitution, drawn up by a Puerto Rican convention; approved in a referendum (3 Mar. 1952);

accepted with minor amendments in the Commonwealth Act (3 July); and, after acceptance of the U.S. amendments, proclaimed by Puerto Rico on 25 July 1952. The Puerto Ricans are free to modify the constitution so long as such changes do not conflict with the U.S. Constitution, the Puerto Rican Federal Relations Act, or the Commonwealth Act. The Puerto Rican constitution provides for popular election of a governor every 4 years with unlimited reelection permitted and a bicameral legislature in which the representation of minority parties is guaranteed. The judicial power is vested in one supreme court and lower courts but appeal to the federal court system is possible. Puerto Ricans elect a Resident Commissioner to the U.S. Congress. Puerto Ricans do not vote in U.S. presidential elections although emigrants on the U.S. mainland may do so.

1952–73. ECONOMIC DEVELOP-MENT. In 1956 a milestone was passed when income derived from industry began to surpass that derived from agriculture. By the 1970s income from manufacturing (textiles, apparel, leather goods, electrical and electronic equipment, chemicals, etc.) was more than 4 times that from agriculture—although sugar, tobacco, and rum were still produced and exported. The bulk of Puerto Rico's trade has been with the U.S. (80–90% of imports; approx. 95% of exports). San Juan became the center of an important tourism industry. After 1968 more than 1 million people visited Puerto Rico annually. By 1972 per capita income had increased to $1,713—the highest in Latin America but far below that of the U.S. Unemployment rarely dropped below 13%.

REEXAMINATION OF COMMON-WEALTH STATUS. The U.S.–Puerto Rican Commission on Status (estab. 24 Feb. 1964) reported that commonwealth, statehood, and independence were all theoretically open to Puerto Rico and urged a plebiscite. With statehood and independence advocates urging a boycott, 709,293 of the 1,067,349 eligible voted in the plebiscite of 23 July 1967. Results: commonwealth, 60%; statehood, 39%; independence, .06%. In the elections of 5 Nov. 1968 the New Progressive Party (PNP), which advocated statehood, won control of the House and the governorship (Luis A. Ferré). In the 1970s expressions of dissatisfaction with commonwealth status increased, taking the form of demonstrations and terrorist fires and bombings. A significant irritant was the navy's use of Culebra (a small island 22 miles off Puerto Rico, with a population of some 900) for bombing and target practice. On 24 May 1973 Secretary of Defense Elliot Richardson ordered such operations shifted, effective mid-1975, to 2 uninhabited islands off Puerto Rico. Leaders of the PPD, which regained control of the government in the elections of 7 Nov. 1972 (Rafael Hernández Colón, governor), argued that the commonwealth relationship needed to be improved and self-government broadened.

1898–1973. Guam.

During the Spanish-American War (pp. 343–345) the cruiser *Charleston,* convoying American troops en route to the Philippines, was ordered to stop and capture the Spanish island of Guam. This was accomplished (20 June 1898) without difficulty as the garrison did not know that Spain was at war. Spain ceded Guam to the U.S. (10 Dec. 1898) by the Treaty of Paris (p. 345).

By executive order (23 Dec. 1898) President McKinley made the Navy Department responsible for Guam's administration. In the absence of congressional action, the procession of navy governors assigned to Guam had virtually unlimited powers—which were usually exercised in the manner of a paternalistic caretaker. Through World War II indigenous Guamanians—an admixture of Chamorro, Spanish, and Filipino—played no important role in their own government. The Guam Congress was established as an appointive, advisory council in 1917 and became elective in 1931; but its development was not encouraged.

Guam was occupied by the Japanese from 13 Dec. 1941 to 9 July 1944 (pp. 438, 440). During the later stages of the War in the Pacific some 200,000 U.S. servicemen came to Guam and roughly 40% of the land was preempted for military purposes.

POST WORLD WAR II. At the request of President Truman, planning began (May 1949) for the transfer of administrative authority in Guam from the navy to the Department of the Interior. The transfer became effective 1 Aug. 1950.

Despite the change to civilian administration, the life and economy of Guam were dominated by the presence of the U.S. navy and air force. A tight security clearance system—established during the Korean War under the authority of the Guam Naval and Airspace Reservations (Executive Order 8683, 14 Feb. 1941) —inhibiting economic development by making it extremely difficult for any transpacific travelers (including Americans) to stay in Guam and by usually preventing reentry of aliens, was not lifted until 21 Aug. 1962 (Executive Order 11045). Guam became increasingly significant as a U.S. strategic military outpost. The Guam naval base became an important haven for Polaris submarines. During the Vietnam War Anderson Air Force Base served as a key takeoff point for American B-52s. U.S. military personnel and their dependents combined with resident "statesiders" and Filipinos outnumbered the indigenous Guamanians through 1970. The presence of the U.S. military transformed Guam's economy. Agriculture decreased in importance as a wage and service economy grew. As of 1970 the island imported approx. 96% of its essential goods, including foodstuffs.

Typhoon Karen (11–12 Nov. 1962) caused damages estimated at $60–$100 million. Designated a disaster area, Guam was allocated $16 million by the Office of Emergency Planning. Under the Guam Rehabilitation Act of 1963, as amended, Guam was authorized to receive $75 million in loans and grants to restore and improve public facilities—providing the basic infrastructure for economic development. Beginning in 1967, when regular commercial air service between Guam and Japan was first established, a substantial tourist industry began to be developed. In 1973 more than 90,000 tourists, mostly Japanese, visited Guam.

After World War II Guamanians requested U.S. citizenship, an Organic Act, and greater self-government. The Guam Congress was granted legislative authority in August 1947. Under the terms of the **Organic Act of 1950** (1 Aug.) those born in Guam became U.S. citizens, although not permitted to vote in national elections. The Organic Act provided for an appointive governor and a unicameral legislature. The act was amended (11 Sept. 1968) to make the governorship elective, beginning in 1970. As a result of local legislation, from 1965 to 1971, Guamanians elected a Washington representative who served as a liaison between Guam and the U.S. Congress. A U.S. law (10 Apr. 1972) gave Guam one delegate to the U.S. House of Representatives. The delegate could vote in committee but not on the floor of the House.

Population (1970): 84,996.

Status: organized, unincorporated territory of the U.S.

1899–1974. American Samoa.

U.S. interest in establishing a naval base and way station for ships trading with the Orient led to embroilment in struggles for authority in Samoa (pp. 335–337). With the partition of Samoa (2 Dec. 1899; p. 346), the U.S. acquired the island of Tutuila (with Pago Pago, one of the finest harbors in the Pacific) and all other islands of the Samoan group east of 171° W. Although the high chiefs of Tutuila and Aunuu ceded those islands to the U.S. on 17 Apr. 1900; the high chiefs of Tau, Olosega and Ofu ceded their islands to the U.S. on 14 June 1904; and U.S. jurisdiction was extended to Swain's Island (more than 200 miles north of Tutuila) in 1925; Congress did not formalize U.S. possession of American Samoa until 1929, when the islanders were granted the status of "nationals" of the U.S.

By executive order (19 Feb. 1900) President McKinley placed the Samoan islands assigned to the U.S. under control of the navy. While Pago Pago was developed as a naval station, the navy maintained a caretaker regime. Under a system of indirect rule village, county, and district councils continued to meet to manage local affairs and an assembly (*fono*) of chiefs (*matai*) from all of American Samoa, presided over by the naval governor, met annually, beginning in 1905. By executive order (effective 1 July 1951) administrative responsibility for American Samoa was transferred from the navy to the Department of the Interior. Since that time the Secretary of the Interior has appointed the territory's governor. In Dec. 1952 the territory's first general elections were held—for a reorganized House of Representatives. The new upper house, the Senate, was selected in accordance with Samoan custom. *Matai* continued to do well under the election system, but not to

the exclusion of others. The first constitution of American Samoa—drawn up by a committee chaired by the governor and ratified (27 Apr. 1960) by a convention of traditionally elected chiefs, became effective Oct. 1960. A bicameral legislature having a measure of competence (previous assemblies were solely advisory) was established. A new constitution, drafted by a constitutional convention, was approved in a territory-wide election (19 Nov. 1966). Powers of the legislature increased; e.g. for the first time it could appropriate funds raised from local revenues. Like its predecessor, the new constitution embodied various provisions designed to protect traditional customs and patterns of authority. In Nov. 1972 a proposal that the governor be elected was rejected by a 4 to 1 margin in a controversial referendum—the territory's governor, John Haydon, was found guilty of violating the Hatch Act (p. 427) but his removal from office was not demanded. A new constitution, providing for local election of the governor and lieutenant governor, was rejected by American Samoa's voters in Nov. 1973.

ECONOMIC DEVELOPMENT. In 1961 U.S. efforts to promote American Samoa's economic development began markedly to accelerate. **H. Rex Lee** (governor, 1961–67) inaugurated a 3-year "rehabilitation" program at the outset of his administration. Federal funding rose from $2.6 million in fiscal 1961 to $9.6 million in 1962. Programs were adopted to foster commerce and industry (e.g. tourism, tuna canning, watch assembly); improve education (educational TV system operative since 1964); and upgrade other public services. By fiscal 1973 the territory's budget was $27.5 million, of which $7.6 million were derived from local revenues. Subsistence farming and fishing remain major facets of economic life.

POPULATION (1970): 27,159.

STATUS: unincorporated, unorganized territory.

1903–74. Panama Canal Zone.

Since the signing of the Hay-Bunau-Varilla Treaty in 1903 (p. 349), the Panama Canal Zone has been in effect a U.S. government reservation. The Canal Zone Government and the Panama Canal Co. are the 2 operating agencies in the area (extending 5 miles on each side of the axis of the Panama Canal) in which the U.S. was granted perpetual sovereignty by the 1903 treaty with the Republic of Panama. Both agencies are headed by a single individual, appointed by the president. As governor of the Canal Zone he reports directly to the Secretary of the Army while as president of the Panama Canal Co., which operates the Canal and the Panama R.R., he reports to a board of directors appointed by the Secretary of the Army.

By a treaty signed 25 Jan. 1955, the U.S. agreed: (1) to increase from $430,000 to $1.93 million the annuity paid to the Republic of Panama; (2) to give Panama $28 million worth of buildings and real estate no longer required by the Canal Zone administration; (3) to guarantee equality of pay and opportunity to U.S. citizens and noncitizen employees in the Canal Zone; and (4) to construct a bridge over the Pacific entrance to the Canal to serve as a link in the Inter-American Highway. The bridge opened 12 Oct. 1962.

On 3 Nov. 1959 mobs attacked the U.S. embassy in Panama City and attempted to invade the Canal Zone. To allay Panamanian ill feeling, President Eisenhower ordered (7 Sept. 1960) that the Panamanian as well as the U.S. flag should henceforth be flown at certain sites. A later order (30 Dec. 1963) banned the flying of any flags in front of Canal Zone schools. Clashes (9–10 Jan. 1964) between U.S. troops and Panamanians were provoked when U.S. students attempted to raise the American flag over the Canal Zone high school. This outbreak of violence, which caused the deaths of 21 Panamanians and 4 U.S. soldiers, led to attempts to renegotiate the Canal Zone's status. After a change of government, Panama in 1970 rejected preliminary agreements reached in 1967 providing for the termination of exclusive U.S. sovereignty in the Canal Zone. At a UN Security Council meeting held in Panama (Mar. 1973), the U.S. vetoed a resolution calling upon the U.S. and Panama to negotiate a new treaty to "guarantee full respect for Panama's effective sovereignty over all its territory." On 7 Feb. 1974 the U.S. and Panama concluded an agreement on basic principles to guide the negotiation of a new Panama Canal treaty which would provide for the eventual transfer of sovereignty over the Canal Zone to the Republic of Panama.

POPULATION (1970): 44,189.

NOTE: normally some 11,000 U.S. military personnel are stationed in the Canal Zone.

1917–73. American Virgin Islands.

By a treaty signed on 4 Aug. 1916, Denmark agreed to cede to the U.S. St. Thomas, St. Croix, St. John, and approximately 50 small islets and cays in the Caribbean (p. 363). The U.S. took official possession on 31 Mar. 1917. The Act of 3 Mar., authorizing payment of $25 million for the Virgin Islands, also sanctioned the continuation of existing governmental institutions with only minor changes. In the governor, to be appointed by the president, were vested "all military, civil and judicial powers necessary to govern" the islands. The authority of the 2 local councils (St.

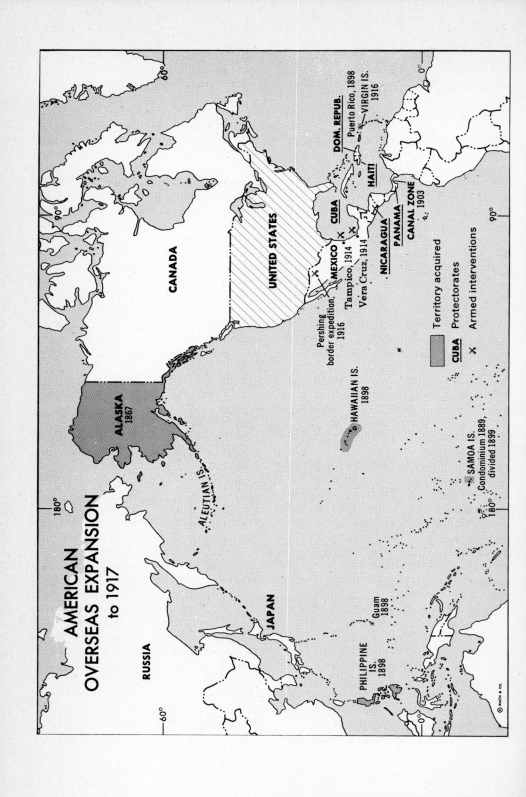

AMERICAN
OVERSEAS EXPANSION
to 1917

RUSSIA

JAPAN

PHILIPPINE
IS.
1898

Guam
1898

SAMOA IS.
Condominium 1889,
divided 1899

ALEUTIAN IS.

ALASKA
1867

HAWAIIAN IS.
1898

CANADA

UNITED STATES

Pershing
border expedition,
1916

MEXICO
Tampico, 1914
Vera Cruz, 1914

CUBA

DOM. REPUB.
Puerto Rico, 1898
VIRGIN IS.
1916

HAITI

NICARAGUA

PANAMA
CANAL ZONE
1903

Territory acquired

CUBA Protectorates

× Armed interventions

180°

180°

60°

60°

90°

90°

0°

0°

© RAND & CO.

Thomas and St. Croix) was limited and property or income requirements restricted the electorate to about 5.5% of the population, which was about 80% black. Naval governors administered the Virgin Islands until Feb. 1931, when administrative authority was transferred to the Department of the Interior.

The Virgin Islanders were granted U.S. citizenship by congressional acts of 1927 and 1932. The Organic Act of 22 June 1936 altered the political structure of the islands. Nearly universal suffrage was put into effect. The 2 local councils were to meet at least once a year as a territorial legislature. The governor was deprived of an absolute veto. The Revised Organic Act of 1954 designated the Virgin Islands an unincorporated territory (instead of an "island possession"); replaced the 2 local councils with a single, unicameral legislature; and provided for return of U.S. revenue collections on products of the Virgin Islands. A reform long sought by the Virgin Islanders was achieved in 1968 when the Organic Act was amended to provide for local election of the governor. Melvin Herbert Evans, a black physician, was elected to a 4-year term as governor in Nov. 1970. In 1972 a U.S. law gave the Virgin Islands one delegate to the U.S. House of Representatives; the delegate could vote in committee but not on the floor of the House. Tensions increased in 1972–73 with several murders which, apparently, were racially motivated.

ECONOMIC DEVELOPMENT. During the first 4 decades of U.S. administration, the economy of the Virgin Islands languished. In 1961, with the advent of the Kennedy administration and the appointment as governor of Ralph Paiewonsky (a white born in the Virgin Islands and an accomplished lobbyist and fund-raiser), a massive infusion of capital began. Increased federal development aid, much of it channeled through the Virgin Islands Corporation (a public body established in 30 June 1949 with a broad mandate to promote economic development), was accompanied by heavy private investment. The infrastructure for tourism was built and by 1969 over 1 million tourists per year were visiting the islands. St. Thomas was given over almost completely to tourism. The previously sugar-based economy of St. Croix was diversified to include—in addition to the production of rum—tourism, oil refining, aluminum and watch making.

POPULATION (1970): 62,468.

STATUS: Organized, unincorporated terr.

1945–74. Micronesia.

In the course of World War II the U.S. gained control of the Pacific Islands formerly mandated to Japan—the Marshalls, Carolines, and Marianas (p. 440): 2,203 islands or islets, approximately 716 square miles of land, scattered over an ocean area of 3 million square miles. After the Japanese surrender a navy military government of Micronesia was established. Conflict between those proposing outright U.S. annexation of Micronesia, to protect perceived U.S. defense interests, and proponents of U.S. support for creation of a strong UN trusteeship system led to development of the "strategic area" trust concept. A slot for Micronesia in the trusteeship system acceptable to the U.S. was provided by incorporating in the UN Charter drawn up at the San Francisco Conference in 1945 (p. 458) specifications that in the case of trust areas designated strategic ultimate UN authority would reside in the Security Council (where the U.S. would have a veto), rather than the General Assembly. Despite continued pressure for Micronesia's annexation, the U.S. submitted (26 Feb. 1947) a draft trusteeship agreement to the UN Security Council. With minor amendments

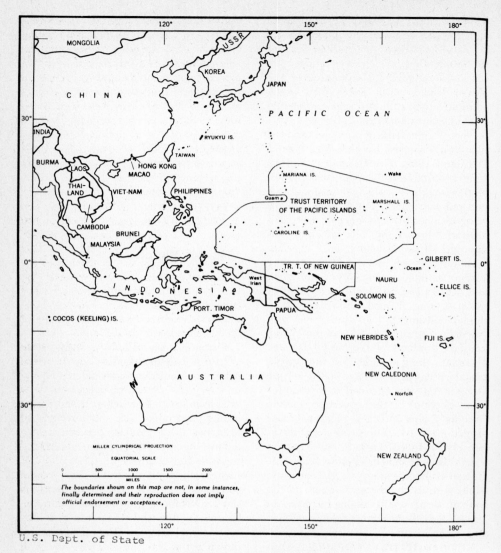

Trust Territory of the Pacific Islands

the U.S. proposal was unanimously accepted (2 Apr.) by the Security Council, approved by joint resolution of Congress and signed by President Truman on 18 July. Besides designating all of Micronesia—become officially the Trust Territory of the Pacific Islands (TTPI)—a strategic area, the agreement included provisions designed further to safeguard U.S. security interests—e.g. Article 13 provided that any part of the TTPI could be "closed for security reasons" by unilateral action of the U.S. and thus be excepted from the prescribed UN oversight procedures. The agreement also committed the U.S. to promote the educational, social, and economic advancement of the Micronesians and their development toward self-government or independence.

U.S. SECURITY OPERATIONS IN MICRONESIA. U.S. use of sites in the Marshall Islands for the testing of atomic weapons, begun in July 1946 at Bikini Atoll (p. 466), continued under the trusteeship administration. The Pacific Proving Grounds, established at Eniwetok Atoll (1947) and enlarged to include Bikini (1953), were closed to UN inspection. Experiments involving the explosion of nuclear and thermonuclear weapons were conducted in the Marshalls through 1958. The testing of nuclear weapons caused the displacement of more than 300 Marshallese from their ancestral homes. Fallout from the hydrogen bomb explosion of 1 Mar. 1954 caused significant short- and long-term medical problems for the 82 inhabitants of Rongelap. President Kennedy announced (8 Feb. 1962) that future atmospheric nuclear tests would be removed to sites outside the TTPI. Beginning in the 1950s Kwajalein Atoll (Marshall Islands) was developed from a naval station into a major facility for the testing of ballistic missiles.

CIVIL ADMINISTRATION. By executive order (18 July 1947) Micronesia's military government was succeeded by a civil administration under the temporary jurisdiction of the navy. President Truman transferred administrative responsibility for the TTPI to the Department of the Interior by executive order effective 1 July 1951. During the 1950s the TTPI was administered as a low-budget, caretaker operation. Cautious steps were taken to promote the development of Western democratic forms of local self-government. Partially in response to a severely critical UN Trusteeship Council report (27 July 1961), the Kennedy administration began to accelerate Micro-

nesian development programs. The $7.5 million ceiling on annual appropriations for civil administration (estab. 30 June 1954) was raised (19 July 1962) to $15 million for fiscal 1963 and $17.5 million thereafter. Federal subsidies for civil operations in the TTPI continued to increase, in 1972 reaching the level of approx. $68 million (compared to approx. $5 million in local revenues). Beginning in late 1966 Peace Corps Volunteers (p. 492) were sent to the TTPI, the only time they served in a U.S.-administered area. By the early 1970s efforts to improve education, public health, and other social services had met with greater success than those to foster a viable economy. A successor to earlier advisory councils, the Congress of Micronesia was established (12 July 1965) as a bicameral legislature with restricted powers—e.g. the U.S. Congress retained the power of appropriation of federal funds.

POLITICAL STATUS NEGOTIATIONS. Formal negotiations between U.S. officials and representatives of the Congress of Micronesia, led by Sen. Lazarus Salii, concerning Micronesian self-determination and the nature of Micronesia's political status after termination of the Trusteeship Agreement, began in Sept. 1969. By 1973 an impasse had been reached in attempts to define a relationship of "free association" between the U.S. and a self-governing Micronesia. Key problems related to: (1) U.S. security requirements; (2) possible Micronesian independence; and (3) the level of U.S. financial support under a free-association arrangement. Micronesia's potential for internal fragmentation became more salient as separate status negotiations between the U.S. and representatives of the Marianas District were opened (13 Dec. 1972). After their fourth round of negotiations (15–31 May 1974), agreement on a Commonwealth of the Northern Marianas was close to completion—an arrangement which would allow for U.S. development of a major air-naval base on the island of Tinian.

WAR CLAIMS. Impending Micronesian self-determination spurred U.S. action on an issue long of major concern to the Micronesians—war damage claims against both Japan and the U.S. The Micronesian Claim Act of 1971 (1 July) authorized: (1) payment of $5 million, to comprise the U.S. half of $10 million which the U.S. and Japan had agreed

(18 Apr. 1969) would be made available to the Micronesians as an *ex gratia* compensation for damages resulting from the hostilities of World War II; (2) payment of an additional $20 million to settle Micronesian claims against the U.S. for damages sustained after the U.S. secured the islands—the post-secure period ending 1 July 1951; and (3) creation of a Micronesian Claims Commission to handle both sets of claims.

POPULATION (1970): 102,250.

Land, Natural Resources, and the Environment

With the establishment of the national government, the disposal of the public domain was regulated under the Ordinance of 1785, which was accepted by the federal Congress but not recognized as binding. In practice, this conservative and orderly land policy favored the speculator at the expense of the actual settler.

New land legislation became urgent to meet both Treasury needs and the prospect of large-scale Western settlement. Wayne's defeat of the Northwest Indians

(1794) and the signing of the **Treaty of Greenville** (1795) gave the U.S. secure occupancy of the lands northwest of the Ohio River and encouraged Western pioneering.

Alexander Hamilton's "Report of a Uniform System for the Disposition of the Lands" (1790–91) had ignored the accurate and uniform survey procedure of the Ordinance of 1785 in favor of a modified system of indiscriminate location. His policy reflected the conservative

PUBLIC LANDS OF THE UNITED STATES
Disposition of Public Lands 1781 to 1970 (In acres)

Disposition by methods not elsewhere classified[1]	303,500,000	Granted to States for:	
Granted or sold to homesteaders	287,500,000	Support of common schools	77,600,000
Granted to railroad corporations	94,300,000	Reclamation of swampland	64,900,000
Granted to veterans as military bounties	61,100,000	Construction of railroads	37,100,000
Confirmed as private land claims[2]	34,000,000	Support of misc. institutions[6]	21,700,000
Sold under timber and stone law[3]	13,900,000	Purposes not elsewhere classified[7]	117,500,000
Granted or sold under timber culture law[4]	10,900,000	Canals and rivers	6,100,000
Sold under desert land law[5]	10,700,000	Construction of wagon roads	3,400,000
		Total granted to States	**328,300,000**
		Grand Total	**1,144,200,000**

[1] Chiefly public, private, and preemption sales, but includes mineral entries, script locations, sales of townsites and townlots.

[2] The Government has confirmed title to lands claimed under valid grants made by foreign governments prior to the acquisition of the public domain by the United States.

[3] The law provided for the sale of lands valuable for timber or stone and unfit for cultivation.

[4] The law provided for the granting of public lands to settlers on condition that they plant and cultivate trees on the lands granted.

[5] The law provided for the sale of arid agricultural public lands to settlers who irrigate them and bring them under cultivation.

[6] Universities, hospitals, asylums, etc.

[7] For construction of various public improvements (individual items not specified in the granting act) reclamation of desert lands, construction of water reservoirs, etc.

LAND OWNED BY THE FEDERAL GOVERNMENT (IN ACRES)

Agency (30 Sept. 1978)	Public Domain	Acquired	Total
Bureau of Land Management	478,082,433	2,368,000	480,450,433
U.S. Forest Service	160,299,670	28,608,064	188,907,734
U.S. Fish and Wildlife Service	26,893,001	4,256,719	31,149,720
National Park Service	20,177,356	6,353,878	26,531,234
U.S. Army	6,545,265	3,927,852	10,473,117
U.S. Air Force	6,923,865	1,361,075	8,284,940
Corps of Engineers	659,293	7,478,129	8,137,422
U.S. Navy	2,498,315	4,396,350	6,894,665
Water and Power Resources Services	4,741,482	1,940,843	6,682,325
Bureau of Indian Affairs	2,945,506	433,531	3,379,037
Energy Research and Development Administration	1,438,510	668,377	2,106,887
Others	756,328	1,495,341	2,251,669
Totals	**711,961,024**	**63,288,159**	**775,249,183**

(Source: Bureau of Land Management, U.S. Department of the Interior)

views of Eastern business interests desiring a check on the agricultural class and the systematic regulation of the labor supply. Its complete adoption would have meant the priority of revenue from sales to large speculators over actual settlement by cultivators.

1796, 18 May. After a lengthy House debate on land policy, Congress passed the **Land Act of 1796.** It provided for rectangular survey and public auction sales, but raised the minimum price from **$1 to $2 an acre,** payable within a year. The lands were to be divided into township units 6 miles square, and half of these were to be divided into single sections of **640 acres.** Intervening townships were to be disposed of in single sections, alternate townships in units of 8 sections. Land offices were established at Cincinnati and Pittsburgh. The attempt of frontier interests to secure an amendment for the sale of half of the 640-acre tracts in quarter sections (160 acres) was defeated in the Senate. Because of poor administrative machinery and inadequate credit provisions, only 48,566 acres were sold by 1800.

1800, 10 May. The needs of Western interests led to the adoption of a more liberal policy under the **Land Act of 1800** (also known as the **Harrison Land Act**). It retained the minimum price of **$2 an acre,** but authorized minimum purchases of **320 acres, a 4-year credit,** and a discount of 8% for cash payment. A frontier demand for the incorporation of the preemption principle was defeated. Land offices were established at Cincinnati, Chillicothe, Marietta, and Steubenville. This act served as the model for similar legislation until 1820. Sales under it began in Apr. 1800; by 1 Nov. 1801, 398,466 acres had been sold. Although its provisions were calculated to favor revenue rather than actual settlement, in practice the system encouraged the latter. The more important modifications of the act were:

OHIO ENABLING ACT (30 Apr. 1802). With the admission of the first public-land state, the federal government adopted the policy of retaining title to all ungranted tracts within state boundaries, except 1 section in each township set aside for educational purposes.

ACT OF 3 Mar. 1803. Provided for the survey and sale of ungranted lands in the Mississippi Territory.

LAND ACT OF 1804 (26 Mar.). Reduced the minimum cash payment to **$1.64 per acre** and authorized minimum sales of **160 acres.**

ACT OF 2 Mar. 1805. Provided for the determination and confirmation of Spanish and French land grants in Louisiana, extended the U.S. land surveys over the Louisiana Purchase, and authorized penalties for squatters illegal settlers).

INTRUSION ACT (3 May 1807). Authorized penalties for unregistered squatters; poorly enforced.

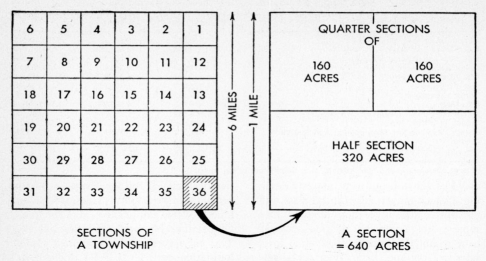

SECTIONS OF
A TOWNSHIP

A SECTION
= 640 ACRES

Public Land Survey System

ACT OF 25 APR. 1812. Established the General Land Office as a bureau of the Treasury Department. The central executive and administrative duties pertaining to public lands were transferred from the Secretary of the Treasury to a commissioner. In 1849 the Land Office was transferred to the Department of the Interior.

The liberal credit provisions of the Act of 1800 stimulated **widespread speculation,** weakened the national land system, and contributed to the Panic of 1819. Secretary of the Treasury W. H. Crawford reported that since 1789 the government had disposed of $44 million worth of land, but up to 30 Sept. 1819 had been paid only half that amount. By 1820 Congress had passed 12 relief acts for land purchasers. The precarious financial condition of the government after the War of 1812 made reform imperative.

1820, 24 APR. Under the **Land Act of 1820,** the **credit system was abolished,** but the minimum price was reduced to **$1.25 an acre** and minimum purchases were fixed at **80 acres.** In principle, this benefited the pioneer, but heavy and almost universal indebtedness made the full cash payment stipulation a hindrance to the actual settler and benefited the speculator.

1821–32. Eleven relief acts were passed by Congress to meet Western demands for (1) cheap land; (2) **preemption** (the legal confirmation of squatter claims on public lands as opposed to engrossment by nonresident purchasers). Except for some special instances, the national government had since its foundation opposed demands for granting preemption or donations to actual settlers.

After 1820 public-land policy was linked to (1) the maneuvering of North and South for sectional balance, and (2) the rise of the West as a distinctive section, with its own special interests. Sen. **Thomas Hart Benton** (Mo., p. 983), champion of the West, introduced (1824) his first bill providing for grading the price of land, whereby public lands would be sold at less than $1.25 an acre or even given away, after such tracts had failed to draw purchasers at the legal minimum price.

Western demands were echoed in urban areas. The Jacksonian era witnessed the rise in Northeastern centers of workingmen's groups supporting the agrarian program for more land. In New York City, labor publicists such as **Thomas Skidmore** denounced land monopoly, while another, **George Henry Evans** (1805–56, later the leader of the Land Reform movement), advocated free homesteads for Eastern surplus labor.

1829, 29 Dec. The Eastern conservative viewpoint was reflected in the resolution introduced by Sen. **Samuel A. Foot** (Conn., 1780–1846) proposing an inquiry into the advisability of temporarily restricting the sale of public lands (a proposal that touched off the **Webster-Hayne** debate, p. 200)—a resolution denounced by Western spokesmen.

1830. An alliance of South and West enabled the Senate to pass Benton's **Graduation Bill** (May), but the measure was tabled in the House. This sectional alliance, however, effected the passage of the **Pre-emption Act of 1830** (29 May), authorizing settlers who had cultivated land on the public domain in 1829 to enter as many as **160 acres** at the minimum price of **$1.25 an acre**. Although the act was adopted as a temporary measure, its substance was renewed at regular intervals (1832–40), and it remained in force until 22 June 1842.

1836, 23 June. HENRY CLAY'S SURPLUS REVENUE ACT provided for the distribution of the Treasury surplus in excess of $5 million as a **loan** to the states according to population. This was a modification of Clay's earlier proposals to distribute the proceeds of land sales to the states. However, the surplus disappeared in the Panic of 1837 and payments were discontinued. Western pressure caused the passage of further legislation combining the ideas of **Benton** (**preemption**) and **Clay** (**distribution**).

1841, 4 Sept. DISTRIBUTION-PRE-EMPTION ACT authorized settlers to stake claims on most surveyed lands and to purchase up to **160 acres** at the minimum price of **$1.25 an acre** (except for alternate sections of land grants to canals and railroads, which could be preempted at $2.50 an acre). The act, constituting a signal victory for the West, recognized (1) settlement before purchase was not illegal (making **permanent** the preemption feature of the Act of 1830); (2) actual settlement was now given priority in official policy over revenue. The distribution provisions authorized the grant of 500,000 acres to each new state for the construction of internal improvements; 10% of the proceeds of land sales were apportioned to the states in which the lands were located, and the remainder, minus administrative costs, to be divided among the states according to their representation in Congress. At the behest of the South, a stipulation was included that such apportionment was to be repealed in the event that the tariff should exceed the 20% level. The distribution provisions were repealed in Aug. 1842.

1854, 3 Aug. GRADUATION ACT marked the emerging sectional alliance of the Northeast and the West (against Southern opposition). It provided that all unsold lands on the market for **10 years or more** were to be sold at **$1 an acre**; 15 years or more, 75 cts. an acre; 20 years or more, 25 cts. an acre; **30 years or more, 12½ cts. an acre**. The provisions applied preemption to graduated lands but did not cover mineral lands and grants for internal improvements and railroads. As a result, 30 to 40 million acres were sold a year. Repealed, 2 June 1862.

1860. Land Reform movement (1840–60) gained ground with Eastern labor and by support from **Horace Greeley**. The program included free homesteads of 160 acres, homestead exemption from attachment for debts, and limitation on land grants to large interests. A Homestead Act that finally passed both houses was vetoed (22 June 1860) by President Buchanan. The Republican platform of 1860 included a homestead plank.

1862, 20 MAY. HOMESTEAD ACT offered any citizen or intending citizen who was the head of a family and over 21 years of age **160 acres** of surveyed public domain **after 5 years** of continuous residence and payment of registration fee ranging from $26–$34. As an alternative, land under the act could be acquired **after 6 months** residence at **$1.25 an acre.** Such homesteads were to be exempt from attachment for debt.

2 JULY. MORRILL ACT granted to each loyal state 30,000 acres for each senator and representative then in Congress for the purpose of endowing at least 1 agricultural college. Under its provisions **69 land-grant** colleges have been established.

1862–64. PACIFIC RAILWAY ACTS. By Act of 1 July 1862 a central transcontinental railroad was authorized with rights of way and 10 alternate sections per mile of public domain on both sides of the railway granted. A second act (2 July 1864) doubled the land grants and gave the government a second instead of a first mortgage on railroad property. The Northern Pacific, chartered by Congress 1864, was granted 20 sections per mile in the states, 40 sections per mile in the territories.

1862–1904. DISTRIBUTION OF PUBLIC DOMAIN. During this period 610,763,183 acres were acquired **by purchase** as against only **147,351,370** acquired **free** (except for fees). More acreage was patented under the Homestead Act **after 1904** than before that date, although most of these newer lands were inferior.

1864, 21 MAR. A homestead bonus provided for soldiers with 2 years' service, subject to a year's residence.

1866. Mining lands on public domain opened to occupation.

21 JUNE. SOUTHERN HOMESTEAD ACT, designed to provide free 160-acre farms in 5 Southwestern states to freed slaves. High costs of farm-planting and deliberate sabotage by plantation owners seeking to retain labor supply by keeping free Negroes at home made act ineffective; by 1872, when repealed, only 4,000 black families had received lands.

1870, 9 JULY. Congress authorized a survey of mineral lands to be sold at **$2.50 per acre.** Later amendment raised the price of land with lodes to $5 an acre, and reduced iron areas to the usual $1.25.

1871. Termination of land grants to railroads (also p. 611).

1872, 1 MAR. MINING LAW authorized prospectors who discovered gold, silver, iron, and certain other ores on public land to stake a claim for the land, mine it, and ultimately to obtain a patent (document of title) giving them the land and all its surface and subsurface resources in fee simple.

1872–1974. DEVELOPMENT OF THE NATIONAL PARK SYSTEM. Yellowstone was established (1 Mar. 1872) as the first National Park when Congress set aside a large tract of federally owned land in what became Montana, Idaho, and Wyoming, indicating that National Parks were to be created for the public's benefit and enjoyment, to preserve in as natural a state as possible areas of outstanding value in terms of natural scenery, recreation, and wildlife conservation. By 1974 Congress had established 38 National Parks, encompassing some 15 million acres. By the **Antiquities Act** (8 June 1906) the president was authorized to create National Monuments by withdrawing from the public domain and setting aside for preservation any lands with great natural or historic interest. By 1974 there were 85 National Monuments, encompassing some 9 million acres. The **National Park Service** was established by statute (25 Aug. 1916) to administer these areas. The National Park system has come also to include historical and commemorative areas—National Historic Parks, National Battlefields, National Military Parks, National Historic Sites, National Memorials, and National Cemeteries—and primarily recreational areas: National Seashores, National Lakeshores, National Recreation Areas, National Parkways, and National Scenic Riverways.

1873, 3 MAR. TIMBER CULTURE ACT authorized any person who kept 40 acres of timber land in good condition to acquire title to 160 acres thereof. The minimum tree-growing requirement was reduced in 1878 to 10 acres.

Coal Lands Act provided for sale of coal lands belonging to the U.S. Individuals could acquire up to 160 acres, associations, 320 acres, at $10–$20 an acre, depending on the distance of the land from railroads.

1877, 3 MAR. DESERT LAND ACT authorized individuals to acquire 640 acres at 25 cts. an acre, provided the land was irrigated within 3 years.

1878, 3 JUNE. TIMBER CUTTING ACT allowed bona fide settlers and miners to cut timber on the public domain, free of charge, for their own use. **Timber and Stone Act,** applicable to California, Oregon, Nevada, Washington, and later extended to all public-land states, provided for the sale of timber and stone lands unfit for cultivation at $2.50 an acre, with a limit of 160 acres.

1879, 3 MAR. Establishment of the U.S. Geological Survey, with **Clarence King** (1842–1901) as first director.

1885, 3 APR. Suspension by **William Andrew Jackson Sparks,** Land Commissioner, of all entries of titles where fraud was suspected, by this action preserving 2,750,000 acres for bona fide settlers. Sparks was dismissed in Nov. 1887, and the reforms were revoked.

1887–94. BEGINNINGS OF CONSERVATION. Early conservation measures included the establishment of the **Division of Forestry** (1887) in the Department of Agriculture and, shortly afterward, the survey of irrigation sites by Maj. **John W. Powell** (p. 1132) of the U.S. Geological Survey. The **Forest Reserve Act** (3 Mar. 1891) repealed the Timber Culture Act of 1873 and Timber Cutting Act of 1878 and authorized the president to set apart forest reserve lands in any part of the public domain. During Harrison's administration 13 million acres were set aside. The Pre-emption Act was repealed (3 Mar. 1891). The **Carey Act** (18 Aug. 1894) authorized the president to grant to each public-land state a maximum of 1 million acres within its boundaries for irrigation, reclamation, settlement, and cultivation. The surplus funds accruing to each state from this program were to be used for reclaiming other lands in the state.

1897. Publication of Capt. **Hiram Martin Chittenden's** (1858–1917) report on irrigation (*Reservoirs in Arid Regions*) served as the basis of later legislation, particularly the National Reclamation Act (1902).

The **Pettigrew Amendment,** a rider on an appropriation bill, permitted the president to change or revoke land reservations and excluded agricultural and mineral lands from reservations. Passed by the Senate and defeated by the House, a compromise was finally reached. The delegation of power to the president was held unconstitutional in *U.S.* v. *Grimond,* 1911.

1901–09. THEODORE ROOSEVELT'S CONSERVATION POLICY. In 1901, at the outset of his administration,

Roosevelt announced that the conservation of forest and water resources was a national problem of vital importance. The conservation program carried out under his leadership was instrumental in educating the country in the need for the planned protection and development of physical resources. During his incumbency more than 148 million acres were set aside as national forest lands and more than 80 million acres of mineral lands withdrawn from public sale. Also withdrawn were some 1,500,000 acres of water-power sites.

An important step in the conservation program was initiated with the appointment (14 Mar. 1907) of the **Inland Waterways Commission** for the study of such routes with a view to relieving transportation congestion. When the commission's first report indicated that water transportation was related to the general problem of natural resources, Roosevelt summoned the **White House Conservation Conference** (13 May 1908). Among those in attendance were members of the cabinet, the justices of the Supreme Court, congressmen, and the governors of 34 states. The conference succeeded in bringing wide public attention to the problem.

A direct outgrowth of the conference was the **National Conservation Commission** (8 June), of which **Gifford Pinchot** (1865–1946) was named chairman. The commission's systematic study of mineral, water, forest, and soil resources was supplemented by the work of local conservation commissions in 41 states. The commission's first report, submitted to President Roosevelt on 11 Jan. 1909, was the first attempt to inventory U.S. natural resources. The Commission urged repeal of the Timber and Stone Act of 1878, the valuation of land at title value instead of $1.25, and the repeal of the Desert Land Act. Organized later in 1909 was the National Conservation Association, a private body (Charles W. Eliot, president).

1901, 15 Feb. Congress passed an act establishing a licensing system for the use of water power on public lands.

1902, 17 June. NATIONAL RECLAMATION ACT (NEWLANDS ACT) set aside almost the entire amount of proceeds of public-land sales in 16 Western and Southwestern states to finance construction and maintenance of irrigation projects in arid states.

1904. KINKAID HOME ACT provided for grants of 640 acres of desert land in Nebraska after 5 years' residence and improvements valued at $800; extended, 1909, to the rest of the public domain.

1906, 11 June. FOREST HOMESTEAD ACT provided for the opening, at the discretion of the Secretary of Interior, of forest lands of agricultural value under the provisions of the Homestead Acts.

29 June. By executive order all coal lands were withdrawn from entry to permit their appraisal; later opened to buyers at from $35–$100 an acre.

1907, 19 June. A protest meeting against the land reservation policy, led by Western grazing interests, convened in Denver. A rider on an appropriation bill repealed the Forest Reserve Act of 1891. Before signing the bill, President Roosevelt added 21 reserves.

1909, 19 Feb. ENLARGED HOMESTEAD ACT, to satisfy Western cattle interests, increased the maximum permissible homesteads to 320 acres in portions of Colorado, Montana, Nevada, Oregon, Utah, Washington, Wyoming, and Arizona. Of these, 80 acres were to be cultivated. Timber and mineral lands were specifically excepted.

25 Aug. First National Conservation Congress convened in Seattle under the leadership of lumber interests.

1910, 25 June. An act of Congress

authorized the president to withdraw public lands subject to further legislation and prohibited the creation of further reserves in Oregon, Washington, Idaho, Colorado and Wyoming.

1916, 29 DEC. STOCK-RAISING HOMESTEAD ACT enlarged the maximum permissible homestead to 640-acre tracts of grazing or forage land not suitable for irrigation, and reserved mines and coal deposits.

1920, 25 FEB. MINERAL LEASING ACT, with later amendments, removed from the scope of the Mining Law of 1872 certain minerals—including oil, gas, coal, phosphate, and sulfur—making them available only on a discretionary leasing basis. The act required the Interior Department to use a system of competitive bidding for mineral leases for areas known to contain oil and gas and required the bidder to pay a royalty on his production in addition to the amount bid to obtain the lease.

1928, 15 MAY. FLOOD CONTROL ACT authorized $325 million for levee work in the Mississippi Valley over a 10-year period.

21 DEC. BOULDER CANYON PROJECT ACT, authorizing construction of Hoover (Boulder) Dam, marked effective beginning of federal government construction of large, multipurpose (water supply, irrigation, hydroelectric power, flood control, navigation) water projects. The **Reclamation Project Act of 1939** (4 Aug.) formalized this trend in planning of Reclamation Bureau (in Department of the Interior; established under Reclamation Act of 1902) water projects established during the New Deal, including giant Grand Coulee Dam (built 1933–42) on the Columbia River.

1933–36. NEW DEAL CONSERVATION PROGRAM, TVA, p. 405; Soil Conservation program of AAA, p. 423; Civilian Conservation Corps, p. 404; Conservation programs of FERA, CWA, PWA, pp. 405, 409, 410; Soil Conservation Service, p. 414; Resettlement Administration, p. 414. The **Taylor Grazing Act** (28 June 1934) provided for the segregation of up to 8 million acres (later raised to 142 million) for grazing purposes under the jurisdiction of the newly established Grazing Service in the Interior Department.

1935. President Roosevelt withdrew the remainder of the public domain for purposes of conservation. As of 1949, 455 million out of 1.9 billion acres were under federal ownership, or 23.89% of the total U.S. land area. By 1950 no less than 181.2 million acres were reserved in national forests. Mineral, water power, and oil reserves (mostly subsoil rights) affected another 47,948,454 acres; about 20 million acres under irrigation.

1936, 22 JUNE, FLOOD CONTROL ACT, for the first time asserted federal government responsibility for controlling floods in river basins all over the country. Major responsibility was assigned to the Army Corps of Engineers.

1946, 16 JULY. BUREAU OF LAND MANAGEMENT (BLM) created, uniting the functions of the former General Land Office and the former Grazing Service. The BLM was given responsibility for control and management of all the public lands of the U.S. and Alaska, including their surface and subsurface resources.

1947, 31 JULY. MATERIALS ACT, for the first time made it possible for the Secretary of the Interior to sell timber, sand, stone, gravel, clay, and certain related resources located on public lands without transferring title to the lands on which the materials were found. The materials had to be sold by competitive bidding where the appraised value exceeded $1,000.

1948–73. WATER POLLUTION became a cause of increasing public concern. The first major **Water Pollution**

Control Act (30 June 1948): (1) provided funding for sewage plant construction; (2) permitted the Justice Department to file suits to require cessation of polluting practices; (3) set up a Water Pollution Control Advisory Board; and (4) authorized pollution studies and research. The 1948 Act was amended (9 July 1956), authorizing $500 million over the next 10 years in federal grants for construction of sewage treatment works. As amended (20 July 1961) the act provided for higher grants and gave the Secretary of HEW authority to prosecute polluters without state government permission. Federal antipollution laws were significantly strengthened by the Water Quality Act of 1965 (2 Oct.), requiring states to establish by 30 June 1967, and enforce, water quality standards for all interstate waters within their boundaries. If states failed to take action or set standards considered too weak by HEW then the latter would set federal standards. The Clean Waters Restoration Act (3 Nov. 1966): (1) authorized $3.55 billion during fiscal 1967–71 for construction of sewage treatment plants, eliminating dollar ceilings on individual grants and permitting federal payment of up to 50% of construction costs if states contributed funds and set water quality standards for noninterstate waters; (2) authorized new programs of federal grants for research on industrial water pollution and advanced waste treatment and water purification measures; and (3) authorized federal grants to assist river basin planning organizations. According to a General Accounting Office report (4 Nov. 1969) the expenditure of $5.4 billion since 1957 on waste treatment facilities had accomplished little: efforts to combat pollution were inadequately financed, badly organized, poorly planned, and undermined by industrial and municipal pollution. The Water Quality Improvement Act of 1970 (3

Apr.), spurred by the Santa Barbara oil spills of 1969: (1) authorized the federal government to clean up disastrous oil spills with the polluter responsible for costs up to $14 million; (2) provided for absolute liability in cases of willful negligence or misconduct; (3) required compliance with water quality standards and the purposes of the act by all federal agencies engaged in any kind of public works activities; and (4) required builders of nuclear power plants to comply with state water pollution standards. The Federal Water Pollution Control Act Amendments of 1972 (enacted 18 Oct. over President Nixon's veto) initiated a major change in basic approach to water pollution control by limiting effluent discharges as well as setting water quality standards. The measure: (1) set a national goal of eliminating all pollutant discharges into U.S. waters by 1985; (2) made the discharge of any pollutant by any person unlawful except as authorized by a discharge permit; (3) authorized expenditure of $24.7 billion, including more than $18 billion in grants to states for construction of waste treatment plants; and (4) allowed citizens to sue polluters, the federal government, or the EPA (p. 642).

1953, 22 May. SUBMERGED LANDS ACT granted to the coastal states the rights then held by the federal government to a maximum distance of 3 geographical miles, subject to an exception for historic boundaries not over 3 leagues from the coast in the Gulf of Mexico. This exception has been ruled applicable only to Texas and Florida. U.S. v. Louisiana, 363 U.S. 1 (1960) and U.S. v. Florida, 363 U.S. 121 (1960). The Outer Continental Shelf Lands Act, 7 Aug. 1953, provided for federal administration of the Continental Shelf.

1955, 1 Aug. Repeal of the Timber and Stone Act of 1878.

1955–74. AIR POLLUTION became an increasing source of national concern as emissions from motor vehicles, basic industries (especially petroleum refineries, smelters, and iron foundries), power plants, home and office heating systems, and refuse incinerators caused health hazards and discomfort. Federal government involvement began (14 July 1955) with authorization of $25 million for fiscal 1956–60 for Public Health Service air pollution research. The **Clean Air Act of 1963** (17 Dec.) authorized $95 million for fiscal 1964–67 in matching grants to state, local, and interstate agencies to develop air pollution prevention and control programs and provided for a series of steps, culminating in legal action, which a state, locality, or the federal government could take to arrest air pollution. The **Clean Air Act Amendments of 1965** (20 Oct.): (1) directed the Secretary of HEW to establish emission standards for new motor vehicles; (2) authorized accelerated research to reduce sulfur oxide emissions from fuel combustion sources such as electric generating plants; and (3) initiated national research programs to develop new methods of solid waste disposal. The first standards for hydrocarbon and carbon monoxide exhaust emissions, published 29 Mar. 1966, were applicable to most new gasoline-powered motor vehicles beginning with the model year 1968. The **Air Quality Act of 1967** (21 Nov.) substantially enlarged federal responsibility: (1) authorizing $428.3 million for federal air pollution control efforts in fiscal 1968–70, $125 million earmarked for research on pollution caused by fuels combustion; (2) authorizing the Secretary of HEW to designate air quality control regions; (3) providing full federal financing for regional control commissions to be established by state governors; and (4) empowering the Secretary of HEW to enforce air quality standards in the control regions if the regional commissions failed to enforce an air pollution plan conforming to HEW guidelines. The **Clean Air Act of 1970** (31 Dec.) established a 3-year, $1.1 billion, comprehensive air pollution control program, including provisions requiring model year 1975 cars to emit 90% less carbon monoxide and hydrocarbons than did 1970 cars and specifying that 1976 cars must emit 90% less nitrogen oxides than 1971 cars. After twice refusing, EPA (p. 642) Administrator William D. Ruckelshaus granted (11 Apr. 1973) auto manufacturers the additional year they requested to meet the 1975 emission standards but imposed interim standards far stricter than the industry contended were feasible.

1956, 11 Apr. UPPER COLORADO PROJECT ACT authorized $760 million in initial costs for one of the largest and most controversial Reclamation Bureau multipurpose water projects.

1959, 23 June. RECREATION AND PUBLIC PURPOSES ACT AMENDMENTS, substantially increasing the acreage limitations of the 1954 Act (which had broadened the Recreation Act of 1926), authorized the sale or lease—to federal, state, and local agencies and nonprofit groups—of public lands to be used for recreational or other public purposes. Each state could receive up to 6,400 acres annually to establish state parks, and other agencies could receive up to 640 acres annually for recreation purposes. For nonrecreation purposes each state or other agency could receive an additional 640 acres annually.

1961, 23 Feb. PRESIDENT KENNEDY'S LAND POLICY. In his natural resources message, Kennedy, reflecting the basic development of public-land policy indicated by the Taylor Grazing Act of 1934 and evident in the postwar period, set forth the principle of **retention and multiple use:** public land was to be regarded as a potentially valuable natural resource which, rather than being disposed of, should be retained in federal ownership and administered under the principle of multiple use and sustained yield of surface resources. Kennedy's statement, together with Secretary of the Interior **Stewart L. Udall's** policy statement of 14 Feb., indicated that the BLM would not classify areas as open to homestead entry if they were especially valuable for some other public purpose, such as recreational development, and that the BLM would attempt to assure that all public lands, whether disposed of or retained by the government, would be used in a manner producing substantial benefits for the nation.

1964, 3 SEPT. NATIONAL WILDERNESS PRESERVATION SYSTEM established. 9.1 million acres of national forest lands which had been classified by administrative action as "wild," "wilderness," or "canoe" areas were immediately designated part of the system, to be safeguarded permanently (subject to existing rights) against commercial use and construction of permanent roads and buildings. However, new mining claims and mineral leases were allowed until 31 Dec. 1983 but not thereafter. Other federal lands were to be added after review by the executive branch and approval of Congress. Opposition from commercial mining, lumbering, and cattle-grazing interests slowed expansion of the system. By 1973 another 1.9 million acres had been added.

3 SEPT. LAND AND WATER CONSERVATION FUND ACT set up a special federal fund to help finance accelerated acquisition of outdoor recreation areas by federal and state agencies.

1970, 1 JAN. NATIONAL ENVIRONMENTAL POLICY ACT OF 1969 (NEPA) made protection of the environment a matter of national policy. NEPA also: (1) required all federal agencies to consider the effects on the environment of all major activities and to include in every recommendation for legislation or other significant actions an **impact statement**—a written analysis of those effects as well as alternatives to the proposal; (2) established in the Office of the President a 3-member Council on Environmental Quality; and (3) directed that the president submit to Congress an annual environmental quality report.

22 APR. "EARTH DAY" observed. In the late 1960s the warnings of such well-known environmentalists as Dr. Barry Commoner that industrial man was doing broad and perhaps irreversible damage to his surroundings began to evoke a wide popular response. Suggested by Sen. Gaylord Nelson (Wis.) as a means to focus national attention on ecological problems, Earth Day—when millions of Americans participated in environmental teach-ins, antipollution protests and various clean-up projects—marked the peak of national harmony on environmental issues. Thereafter enthusiasm for "saving the earth" began to diminish somewhat with realization of the multifarious economic costs of cleaning up the environment.

2 OCT. ENVIRONMENTAL PROTECTION AGENCY (EPA) created through executive reorganization. The EPA consolidated in a single agency, independent of existing departments, all major programs to combat pollution.

1971, 23 JUNE. The Public Land Law Review Commission (estab. 1964) in its 343-page report, *One Third of the Nation's Land,* recommended to the president and Congress that stringent controls over the environment be put into effect without delay on the 755 million acres of federally owned public land. The 19-member commission, headed by Rep. Wayne N. Aspinall (Colo.), in its more than 350 recommendations provided guidelines to aid Congress in overhauling outmoded laws and unsnarling often conflicting regulations governing the use and sale of federal lands.

1972, 21 Oct. FEDERAL ENVIRON-MENTAL PESTICIDE CONTROL ACT. A controversy over the dangers of pesticides was touched off by publication of *The Silent Spring* (1962) by **Rachel Carson** (1907–64). A study (1968) by the General Accounting Office showed that federal agencies took little action to enforce the Federal Fungicide, Insecticide and Rodenticide Act of 1947 requiring registration and proper labeling of pesticides. The 1972 act required that all pesticides be registered with the EPA (p. 642), which would control their manufacture, distribution, and use, and facilitated the banning of hazardous pesticides and the imposition of penalties for their improper use. On 14 June EPA Administrator William D. Ruckelshaus announced a ban (effective 31 Dec.) on almost all remaining uses of the pesticide DDT.

1973, 16 Nov. ALASKAN PIPELINE ACT. After 5 years of controversy between environmental groups and elements of the oil industry and their allies, construction of the huge pipeline—which ultimately could carry up to 2 million barrels of crude oil per day from Alaska's North Slope to the ice-free port of Valdez on the Gulf of Alaska, to be transported by tanker to the U.S.—was authorized. To prevent further court challenges by environmentalists—a ruling (9 Feb.) of the U.S. Court of Appeals, District of Columbia Circuit, blocking pipeline construction had been upheld (2 Apr.) by the Supreme Court—the act provided that all actions necessary for completion of the pipeline be taken without further delay under the National Environmental Policy Act of 1969 and restricted judicial review to constitutional grounds. The Aleyeska consortium, builders and operators of the pipeline, were held liable for the full costs of controlling and removing any pollution caused by the pipeline.

Indian Land Policy and Reform Since the Civil War

1869–94. INDIAN LAND CESSIONS. In less than a century following American independence the Indians, by a long series of treaties, ceded enormous tracts of land to the U.S. The old Indian Country on the Great Plains was reduced to the Indian Territory (later the state of Oklahoma) while the extinguishment of Indian titles proceeded rapidly from the Rockies to the Pacific coast. In 1869 a Board of Indian Affairs was created to exercise joint control with Interior Department officials over appropriations for Indian land cessions, to control the ceded trust lands not a part of the public domain, along with the reservations with

their valuable natural resources. In 1871 Congress ordered a cessation of treaty-making with Indian tribes. Between 1784 and 1894 a total of 720 Indian land cessions (often overlapping) were made (Royce), and up to 1880 the U.S. government had expended in excess of $187 million in goods or money to extinguish Indian titles, but huge amounts were quickly diverted to creditor traders.

1871, 3 Mar. INDIAN APPROPRIATIONS ACT rider declared no Indian tribe or nation to be recognized thereafter as an independent power with whom the U.S. could contract by treaty and established the policy that tribal

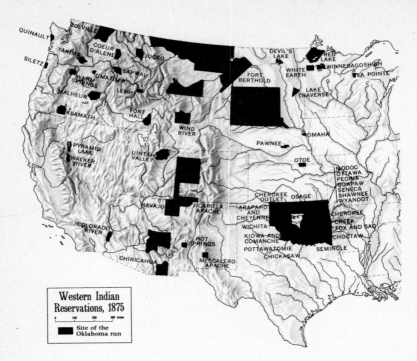

Western Indian
Reservations, 1875

Site of the
Oklahoma run

affairs could be managed by the U.S. government without tribal consent.

1881. Publication of Helen Hunt Jackson's *A Century of Dishonor* (1881) aroused new concern over Indian problems and sparked agitation by the Indian Rights Association, organized within a year.

1887, 8 Feb. DAWES GENERAL ALLOTMENT (SEVERALTY) ACT passed in response to reformers who believed reservation life fostered indolence and perpetuated customs which hindered assimilation. The act provided for the dissolution of Indian tribes as legal entities and the division of tribal lands among individual members—160 acres to each head of family and 80 acres to each adult single person. The government retained a 25-year trust patent; upon its expiration full ownership would devolve upon the individual and U.S. citizenship would be conferred. Reservation land remaining after distribution of allotments to living tribe members was declared surplus and could be opened to non-Indian homesteaders. The **Burke Act** (8 May 1906) speeded up allotment of lands to individual Indians by authorizing the Secretary of the Interior to waive the 25-year trustee period and issue patents in fee to Indians deemed competent to manage their own affairs. This procedure was further liberalized by the Commissioner of Indian Affairs in Apr. 1917. 118 reservations were thus allotted; Indians lost 86 million acres (62%) of land in Indian ownership prior to 1887. The undermining of Indian culture which resulted from the assault on communal organization basic to tribal organization did not automatically produce assimilation.

1924, 2 June. INDIANS AS CITIZENS. Defined by the Supreme Court, 1831 (p. 667), as "domestic dependent" nations, the Indians received piecemeal U.S. citizenship (Wyandots, 1855, Potawatomi, 1861, Kickapoos, 1862), a practice liberalized by the Dawes Act and extended, 1901, to all Indians in Indian Territory. By the **Snyder Act of 1924** all Indians born in the U.S. were admitted to full U.S. citizenship.

1924–34. INDIAN REFORMS. As a result of strong Indian protests, the **Fall Indian Omnibus Bill (Bursum Bill)** was defeated. In effect the bill would have transferred Pueblo title to white settlers. Under Act of 1924 a Pueblo Land Board was set up to fix compensation for lands; such compensation was awarded in 1933. Publication of Brookings Institution report *The Problem of Indian Administration* (1928) revealed deficiencies in federal administration. The **Indian Reorganization (Wheeler-Howard) Act (18 June 1934)** ended land allotments in severalty and provided for revestment to tribal ownership of surplus lands hitherto open to sale. Other provisions of the act encouraged tribal self-government and sought to improve Indian economic conditions.

1946, 13 Aug. INDIAN CLAIMS COMMISSION established to settle all outstanding Indian claims against the U.S. from the beginning of the nation until the date of the act (the U.S. Court of Claims to have original jurisdiction over Indian claims arising after 13 Aug. 1946 as well as appellate jurisdiction over the Indian Claims Commission). It was estimated that the commission's work would take 30 years with a final cost to the government of over $1 billion.

1953, 1 Aug. TERMINATION RESOLUTION. By concurrent resolution Congress adopted the policy of promoting termination: discontinuance of federal controls, restrictions, and benefits for Indians under federal jurisdiction. The withdrawal of federal services or trust supervision from 61 tribes or other In-

dian groups took place 1954–60, before opposition caused deceleration of the program—Indian tribes and such Indian organizations as the National Congress of American Indians condemned termination, advocating instead self-determination and a review of federal policies. During the 1960s federal aid greatly expanded and reservation governments were made eligible as sponsoring agencies for numerous federal economic opportunity programs.

1969, 20 Nov. CAPTURE OF ALCATRAZ ISLAND by 78 Indians, demanding that it be made available as a cultural center, signaled the rise of Indian activism. (The occupation, which had succumbed to media overexposure and indecision, was ended 11 June 1971 when the 15 remaining holdouts were removed without resistance by U.S. marshals.) The American Indian Movement (AIM), founded in 1970, soon emerged as the most militant spokesman for radical reform of federal-Indian relations—focusing public attention on the problems of the American Indian by occupying (2–8 Nov. 1972) the Washington, D.C. offices of the Bureau of Indian Affairs, demanding the rights and property guaranteed Indians by treaties with the U.S., and by occupying (27 Feb.–8 May 1973) the village of Wounded Knee, S. Dak., challenging the locally elected Oglala Sioux government and demanding general reform in Indian tribal government. Prosecution of AIM leaders for Wounded Knee affair was dismissed by federal court in 1974.

1970–72. LAND RESTORATIONS. By the Act of 15 Dec. 1970, 48,000 acres in the Blue Lake area of New Mexico were returned to the **Taos Pueblo Indians,** who considered the area a shrine whose religious value was destroyed when it was put to multiple use after being taken from them by the U.S. Forest Service in 1906. The **Alaska Native Land**

Claims Act (18 Dec. 1971) granted to the 53,000 native Eskimos, Indians, and Aleuts title to 40 million acres of federal lands and $962.5 million divided among native villages and regional corporations. The act was in answer to native claims that land had been illegally taken from them by the federal government through provisions of the Statehood Act (p. 617). By executive order (20 May 1972) some 21,000 acres of land in Washington were returned to the **Yakima Indian** tribe, for whom the area has religious significance. The land had been incorporated in the Mt. Rainier Forest Reserve in 1908 on the mistaken belief it was public land.

1970, 8 JULY. TERMINATION POLICY REPUDIATED expressly in President Nixon's message to Congress. Rejecting assimilation as a goal of federal policy and paternalistic approaches to federal support, the administration endorsed a policy of Indian self-determination.

1974. INDIAN SELF-DETERMINATION LAW provided administrative machinery to permit Indian tribes to assume control of federal programs carried out on their reservations for their benefit and provided for increased control by native Americans of their educational activities.

1975–76. NATIVE AMERICAN MILITANCY demonstrated by conferences of North and South American Indians, pressing for recognition and UN representation; formation of Council of Energy Resources Tribes that occupied land rich in coal and uranium.

1978. 6 MAR. U.S. Supreme Court held that Indian tribal courts could not, without express congressional authorization, try non-Indians for violating tribal law on reservation land. *Oliphant* v. *Suquamish Indian Tribe* (435 U.S. 191).

1980. 30 JUNE. In an opinion written by Justice Harry Blackmun, U.S. Supreme Court upheld an award totaling $107 million in damages and interest to Sioux Indians for illegal seizure (1877) of Black Hills of South Dakota. *U.S.* v. *Sioux Nation of Indians* (100 Sup. Ct. 2716).

1980. Western Shoshone tribe of Nevada charged U.S. government with violating 1863 Treaty of Ruby Valley by plan to requisition 10,000 sq. mi. of Shoshone land for MX missile system.

1980. 10 OCT. SETTLEMENT OF LAND CLAIMS. The claims of Penobscot, Passamaquoddy, and Maliseer tribes to Northern Maine, based upon the Indian Non-Intercourse Act of 1790, which had prohibited sale or disposal of Indian land without congressional approval, were settled for $81.5 million.

1981. U.S. Civil Rights Commission called upon federal government to (1) recognize Indian tribes on same basis as it recognizes states and other political subdivisions for purposes of distributing federal funds; (2) implement and enforce fishing rights; (3) negotiate settlement of land claims in the East; (4) enact legislation to allow tribes to exercise criminal jurisdiction over all persons within borders of reservation.

POPULATION, IMMIGRATION, AND ETHNIC STOCKS

★　★
★

Despite a population expansion from 1790 to 1900 running at a rate of from 25% to 35% per decade (slightly lower during the Civil War years), an increase in part the result of a constant flow of immigration, in part from large family formations, and in part the result of improved public health statistics, the United States never fulfilled Malthusian prophecies of population growth outrunning available food supply. Down to the end of the nineteenth century large tracts still awaited settlement, while revolutionary improvements in farm technology kept food production abreast of population. The deceleration of that earlier extraordinary growth rate is largely a twentieth-century phenomenon, traceable to the immigration restriction laws of the 1920s and to a decline in the birth rate, both in the depression years of the 1930s and again in the 1960s and 1970s. Starting with a large nucleus of settlers from England, the colonies and then the United States quickly became multi-ethnic. The character of non-English immigration shifted from Northern Europe in pre-Civil War days to Central-Eastern and Southern Europe after 1885, with Latin-American immigration playing an increasingly significant role beginning with the depression years of the 1930s. Accompanying this relative decline of migration from English-speaking countries was an increasing emphasis upon the values of cultural pluralism.

Internal migration has been associated in the public mind with the westward movement, but equally dramatic has been the shift of population from an overwhelmingly rural America of 1790 to the urban society of the 1970s. Notable in the movement has been the vast migration of blacks from the rural South to the urban North and West.

The civil rights movement of the 1960s not only reinforced black pride but also stimulated ethnic feelings among Mexican-Americans and led many different ethnic groups to a reexamination of their heritage, while a rising consciousness of ethnicity has raised questions as to the values of an evolving pluralist society.

Population

Figures prior to the first Census, 1790, are computed on the basis of militia, polls, taxables, families, and houses (Greene and Harrington).

1790. Regional Distribution of Population: New England, 25.7%; Middle states, 25.9%; Southern states, 48.5%.

AREA OF THE 13 COLONIES

1625	1,980	(Va., 1,800, Plymouth, 180)
1641	50,000	(English settlers)
1688	200,000	
1715	434,600	
1754	1,485,634	
1774	2,600,000	(Bancroft; 3,016,678, informal Congress poll)
1783	2,389,300	(Continental Congress)
1790	3,929,625	

ORIGINAL THIRTEEN STATES IN ORDER OF POPULATION

Virginia	747,610 (inc. W. Va.)
Massachusetts	475,199 (inc. Maine)
Pennsylvania	434,373
North Carolina	393,751
New York	340,120
Maryland	319,728 (inc. Dist. of Columbia)
South Carolina	249,073
Connecticut	237,655
New Jersey	184,139
New Hampshire	141,885
Georgia	82,548
Rhode Island	68,825
Delaware	59,096

URBAN POPULATION TRENDS TO 1790

	Phila. (1682)	N.Y. (1624)	Boston (1630)	Charleston (1680)	Baltimore (1730)
1730	8,500	8,500	13,000	c.4,000	
1750	13,400	13,300	15,731	8,000	c.100
1770	28,000	21,000	15,520	10,863	c.5,000
1790	42,444	33,131	18,038	16,359	13,503

URBAN POPULATION (8,000 INHABITANTS OR MORE) COMPARED WITH TOTAL POPULATION, 1710–1900 (A Century of Population Growth)

Year	% of Total
1710	2.5
1740	4.3
1790	3.3
1860	16.1
1900	32.9

Using the more recent reclassification of the Census Bureau (Urban Population, 2,500 inhabitants or more), the urban percentage, **1790**, was 5.4% as against 56%, **1940**.

LEADING U.S. CITIES SINCE 1790

	1820 (De Bow, Statistical View)		1860 (8th Census)
New York	123,700	New York	1,080,330
Philadelphia	112,800	Philadelphia	565,529
Baltimore	62,700	Baltimore	212,418
Boston	43,300	Boston	177,840
New Orleans	27,200	New Orleans	168,675

	1900		1980
New York	3,437,202	New York	6,800,000 (est.)
Chicago	1,698,575	Chicago	2,969,570
Philadelphia	1,293,697	Los Angeles	2,950,010
St. Louis	575,238	Philadelphia	1,680,235
Boston	560,892	Houston	1,554,492

CENTER OF POPULATION, 1790–1970
(Stat. Abstr. of the U.S., 1973)

1790:	23 mi. E. of Baltimore, Md.
1850:	23 mi. S.E. of Parkersburg, W. Va.
1900:	6 mi. S.E. of Columbus, Ind.
1950:	8 mi. N.–N.W. of Olney, Richland Co., Ill.
1970:	5.3 mi. E.–S.E. Mascoutah City Hall, St. Clair Co., Ill.

The 15-year period 1941–55 marked reversal of downward birth rate trend (*Stat. Abstr. of the U.S., 1949, 1951, 1969, 1973*). After that time the down trend set in again, accelerating during the decade 1961–70. Total yearly population growth (1961–70) was 1.3% compared with 2.2% for 1951–60.

POPULATION OF THE U.S. SINCE 1790

Year	Population (in thousands)	% Increase over Preceding Census
1790	3,929	....
1800	5,308	35.1
1810	7,239	36.4
1820	9,638	33.1
1830	12,866	33.5
1840	17,069	32.7
1850	23,191	35.9
1860	31,443	35.6
1870	38,558	22.6
1880	50,155	30.1
1890	62,947	25.5
1900	75,994	20.7
1910	91,972	21.0
1920	105,710	14.9
1930	122,775	16.1
1940	131,409	7.3
1950	150,697	14.5
1960	179,323	18.5
1970	203,212[1]	13.3
1980	226,505	11.4

[1] Population of U.S., Puerto Rico, and outlying areas was 183,285,009 (1960) up 22.1%, and 207,976, 452 (1970) up 13.5%.

	Birth Rate (per 1,000 population)	Death Rate (per 1,000 population)
1915	30.1	13.2
1936	16.7	11.6
1950	24.1	9.6
1960	23.7	9.5
1970	18.4	9.5
1978	15.3	8.8

LIFE EXPECTANCY, 1789–1970
(Historical Statistics of the U.S., to 1971; *Statistical Abstract, 1979*)

	At Birth		Age 20		Age 40		Age 60	
	Male	Female	Male	Female	Male	Female	Male	Female
1789 (Mass.)	34.5	36.5	34.2	34.3	25.2	26.9	14.8	16.1
1900–02	48.23	51.08	42.19	43.77	27.74	29.17	14.35	14.23
1945	64.4	69.5	48.6	52.9	30.6	34.4	15.4	17.8
1978	70.2	77.8	52.0	59.1	33.6	39.9	14.0[1]	18.4[1]

[1] 1979 life expectancy for both males and females at age 65.

INTERNAL MIGRATION WITHIN THE U.S., 1870–1940

	East-West Movement (Net gain of states west of Mississippi River)[1]	North-South Movement (Net gain of the North)[2]
1870	2,298,952	752,455
1880	3,300,378	639,018
1890	4,078,157	500,026
1900	3,993,554	274,403
1910	4,592,106	77,878
1920	4,188,945	430,200
1930	3,497,090	1,419,137
1940	2,731,002	1,381,500

[1] Excess of persons born east and living west of the Mississippi over persons born west and living east. [2] Excess of persons born in the South and living in the North over persons born in the North and living in the South.

1951–60. POPULATION SHIFTS. Final 1960 census returns brought the loss of 3 House of Representative seats for Pa.; 2 for N.Y., Mass., and Ark.; and 1 each for 12 other states. Chief gainers: Calif., 8; Fla., 4. Largest percentage population gains scored by Fla., 78.7; Nev., 78.2; Alaska, 75.8; Ariz., 73.7; Calif., 48.5; Del., 40.3. Losses: Ark., 6.5; W. Va., 7.2; D.C., 4.8.

1950 to 1979. MIGRATION TRENDS. Population shifts to South and West accelerated: South gained 25 million; West, 28 million; against a New England net gain, 1970–79 of 3.7%; the middle states, a decline of 1.4% and the East North Central states, a gain of only 2.5%.

1960–70. METROPOLITAN, URBAN AND RURAL POPULATION
(Stat. Abstr. of the U.S., 1973)

	Rural (millions)	Urban	Metropolitan[1]
1960	54.1	125.3	119.6
1970	53.9	149.3	139.4

[1] 243 SMSA's (Standard Metropolitan Statistical Areas) defined by Office of Management and Budget, generally conceived as an integrated economic and social unit with a large population nucleus. Each SMA contains one central city of 50,000 inhabitants or more, or a city of at least 25,000 which together with the population of contiguous places constitutes for general economic and social purposes a single community with combined population of at least 50,000.

1920–70. NATIVE BORN POPULATION (including Puerto Rico)

1920:	86.8%
1930:	88.4%
1940:	91.2%
1950:	92.8%
1960:	94.6%
1970:	95.3%

1967. 200 MILLION. The "population clock" of the U.S. Census indicated the presence of the 200-millionth American at 11 A.M., 20 Nov., although most demographers believed this figure had been achieved earlier.

1970. COMMISSION ON POPULATION GROWTH AND THE AMERICAN FUTURE, established by law (16 Mar.). Commission report received 5 May 1972.

1970. CENSUS UNDERCOUNT of about 5.3 million, 1.9 million of whom were black. The rate of underenumeration, 2.5% (1970) compared with 2.7% (1960), 3.3% (1950). Cities also claim undercount in 1980.

1970–80. POPULATION SHIFTS highlighted by new rural growth with nonmetropolitan areas growing faster than metropolitan areas, due in part to decentralization of manufacturing, growth or recreation and retirement areas located in warm climates, the environmental movement, and a leveling off of the loss of farm population. The western mountain states were repopulated due in part to a boom in coal, uranium, and oil.

1970. FAMILY PLANNING SERVICES AND POPULATION RESEARCH ACT (26 Dec.) set goal of making family planning sources and information available to every woman in U.S., creating Federal Office of Population Affairs to administer HEW responsibilities and authorizing $382 million for new and expanded sources and research programs for fiscal years 1971–73.

1972. ZERO POPULATION GROWTH. During first quarter of 1972 birth rate dropped below level of replacement rate, reflecting readier access to contraceptive services, changing sexual mores, later marriages, changing concepts of family size, changes in the economy, and the liberalization of state abortion laws (pp. 553, 817).

1970–79. One-Parent Families (p. 563)

1975. Decline of Birth and Death Rates (p. 552)

1978. LIFE EXPECTANCY (p. 649)

1980. CENSUS (p. 563)

1935–77. SOCIAL WELFARE EXPENDITURES UNDER PUBLIC PROGAMS
(Federal, State, Local)
(Stat. Abstr. of the U.S., 1973, 1980)

	Total ($ millions)	Social Insurance	Public Aid	Health & Medical Programs
1935	6,548	406	2,998	427
1940	8,795	1,272	3,597	616
1950	23,508	4,947	2,496	2,064
1960	52,293	19,307	4,101	4,464
1970	145,856	54,691	16,488	9,907
1977	361,553	160,867	52,895	20,438

1940–78. ILLEGITIMATE LIVE BIRTHS
(Stat. Abstr. of the U.S., 1980)

Year	Total	% All Births	Rate Per 1,000 Unmarried Age 15–44
1940	89,500	3.5%	7.1
1950	141,600	4.0%	14.1
1960	224,300	5.3%	21.6
1970	398,700	10.7%	26.4
1978	543,900	16.3%	26.2

1940–78. DIVORCES (inc. annulments) PER 1,000
(Stat. Abstr. of the U.S., 1980)

Year	Total (in thousands)	Rate per 1,000
1940	264	2.0
1950	385	2.6
1960	393	2.2
1970	708	3.5
1978	1,130	5.2

1960–78. CRIME RATE PER 100,000 INHABITANTS
(Stat. Abstr. of the U.S., 1979)

	Total	Murder & Nonnegligent Manslaughter	Robbery	Burglary
1960	1,187	5	60	502
1970	3,985	7.9	172	1,085
1978	5,109	9.0	191	1,424

Immigration of Non-English Stock

1624. Walloon settlement of New Amsterdam (p. 49).

1624–64. Dutch settlement of New Netherland (pp. 49–50); on the Delaware 1657–64 (pp. 51–53). Dutch cultural decline in New York City noted by 1763, when an invitation was extended to Rev. Archibald Laidlie, English-speaking Scottish minister, to preach in the Dutch Reformed Church. In Hudson and Hackensack valleys Dutch language persisted until 1835–41.

1637–55. Swedish settlement on the Delaware (p. 52).

1682. First Welsh settlement near Philadelphia.

1683–84. Settlement of **Germantown** (13 families from Crefeld, Germany) by Rhinelanders and Palatines under **Francis Daniel Pastorius** (1651–c.1720) and **Johann Kelpius** stamped Pennsylvania-Dutch settlement with cultural and linguistic persistence down to the 20th century.

1685. FRENCH HUGUENOT settlement following the revocation of the Edict of Nantes (18 Oct.), chiefly to New York (New York City and New Rochelle), Massachusetts (Boston, Salem, and Oxford), and South Carolina (Charleston and along Santee River).

1689. Beginning of sizable emigration from Scotland of Covenanters (opposing Anglican Church rule) and Jacobites (supporters of Stuart cause), and from Northern Ireland (Ulster) of Scotch-Irish Presbyterians (est., 1607–09); especially significant after Act of Parliament, 1704, barring Presbyterians from public office. English Navigation Act caused economic deterioration in Ireland and the exaction of tithes for the support of the Church of England was resented.

1709. Passage of Parliamentary Act of 1709 (Whig) extended the privilege of natural-born subjects to strangers who took the oath of allegiance and partook of the Sacrament (naturalizing German Protestant refugees); repealed by Tories, 1711. More liberal naturalization laws had been passed in the colonies beginning with the 17th century.

1710. GERMAN PALATINES, numbering over 3,000, given temporary refuge in England (1709) from devastations of War of Spanish Succession and severe winter, 1708–09, were transported to New York to produce naval stores in Hudson Valley. Unfavorable economic conditions caused their migration under **Conrad Weiser** (1696–1760) to Schoharie Valley (1713), then to the Mohawk Valley, and ultimately in some instances to Bucks (1723) and Berks counties, Pa. (1728–29).

Settlement of 650 Palatines by **Baron de Graffenried** at New Bern, N.C.; attacked and nearly destroyed by Indians in Tuscarora War, 1712, and colonists scattered throughout southeastern North Carolina.

1714–20. MAIN EXODUS OF SCOTCH-IRISH (including Jacobites after suppression of revolts of 1715 and 1745 on behalf of the 2 Stuart Pretenders) started, spurred by expiration, beginning 1717, of leases and increased rent demands by landlords in Ireland. A small portion went to New England but the bulk settled the counties of western Pennsylvania, between the Susquehanna and the Allegheny Mts., moving down the Shenandoah Valley (1732) into Virginia, the Carolinas, and Georgia. The famines, 1740–41, and the decline of the Irish linen industry, c.1771, assured the continuance of this emigration momentum.

1727–75. HEAVY GERMAN MIGRATION continued, including settlers from the German-Swiss cantons of Bern and Zurich, with substantial Pietist representation.

1735–53. MORAVIAN COLLECTIVIST EXPERIMENTS, under the leadership of **Augustus Gottlieb Spangenberg** (1704–92), at Savannah (1735), Bethlehem, Pa. (1744), and vicinity of Winston-Salem, N.C. (1753).

1740. Act of Parliament specifically provided for naturalization in the colonies, with 7-year residence provision, and the usual oaths not to be required of Jews or Quakers.

1768. 1,400 settlers from **Minorca, Leghorn,** and **Greece** established by **Dr. Andrew Turnbull** at New Smyrna, East Florida, the second-largest mass migration to the colonies. After an insurrection (p. 760), the colony was eventually abandoned (by 1777), and Turnbull lost his holdings.

IMMIGRATION TO U.S., 1790–1820 (8th Census, 1860, Prelim. Report, based upon a "survey of the irregular data previous to 1819"—a deduction of 14.5% for transients should be made from the following approximations): 1790–1800, 50,000; 1800–10, 70,000; 1810–20, 114,000.

1798. Alien and Sedition Laws (p. 155) providing for the deportation of subversive aliens.

1819–60. IMMIGRATION LAWS. State immigration laws, continuing colonial practices (Pa., head tax, 1729), generally required a bond upon entry of passengers deemed likely to be a public charge. Federal laws, 1819, 1847, 1848, 1855, were designed to protect immigrants from overcrowding and unsanitary conditions of the Atlantic crossing which had led to heavy mortality rate; largely ineffective.

1827–38. GREAT IRISH AND GERMAN MIGRATION to the U.S. began.

NATIONAL OR LINGUISTIC STOCKS IN THE U.S., 1790
(Based upon nomenclature, Census of 1790, as computed in Amer. Hist. Assn., *Ann. Rep., 1931,* I).[1]

State	Eng-lish	Scotch	Ulster	Irish Free State	German	Dutch	French	Swed-ish	Span-ish	Unas-signed	Total
Maine	60.0	4.5	8.0	3.7	1.3	0.1	1.3	....	....	21.1	100.0
New Hampshire	61.0	6.2	4.6	2.9	.4	.1	.7	....	....	24.1	100.0
Vermont	76.0	5.1	3.2	1.9	.2	.1	.4	....	....	12.6	100.0
Massachusetts	82.0	4.4	2.6	1.3	.3	.2	.8	....	....	8.4	100.0
Rhode Island	71.0	5.8	2.0	.8	.5	.4	.8	....	....	18.6	100.0
Connecticut	67.0	2.2	1.8	1.1	.3	.3	.8	0.1	....	26.4	100.0
New York	52.0	7.0	5.1	3.0	8.2	17.5	.9	.5	....	2.9	100.0
New Jersey	47.0	7.7	6.3	3.2	9.2	16.6	3.8	3.9	....	3.7	100.0
Pennsylvania	35.3	8.6	11.0	3.5	33.3	1.8	2.4	.8	....	3.9	100.0
Delaware	60.0	8.0	6.3	5.4	1.1	4.3	1.8	8.9	....	4.1	100.0
Maryland and District of Columbia	64.5	7.6	5.8	6.5	11.7	.5	1.6	.5	....	1.7	100.0
Virginia and West Virginia	68.5	10.2	6.2	5.5	6.3	.3	1.2	.6	....	.9	100.0
North Carolina	66.0	14.8	5.7	5.4	4.7	.3	1.5	.2	....	1.2	100.0
South Carolina	60.2	15.1	9.4	4.4	5.0	.4	1.7	.2	....	1.4	100.0
Georgia	57.4	15.5	11.5	3.8	7.6	.2	3.9	.6	....	1.1	100.0
Kentucky and Tennessee	57.9	10.0	7.0	5.2	14.0	1.3	2.3	.5	....	1.9	100.0
Area enumerated	60.9	8.3	6.0	3.7	8.7	3.4	2.2	.7	....	6.6	100.0
Northwest Territory	29.8	4.1	2.9	1.8	4.3	....	1.7	....	....	....	100.0
Spanish, United States	2.5	.3	.2	.1	.4	....	57.1	....	96.5	....	100.0
French, United States	11.2	1.6	1.1	.7	8.7	....	64.2	....	12.5	....	100.0
Continental United States	60.1	8.1	5.9	3.6	8.6	3.1	2.3	0.7	0.8	6.8	100.0

[1] W. S. Rossiter, *A Century of Population Growth* (1909), had previously estimated English and Welsh stock at 82.1% of total; Scotch and Irish, 8.9%, and the Germans, 5.6% (1790).

Causes included (1) cold winter, 1829–30; (2) restrictive legislation against German Jews; (3) economic distress in Northern Ireland; (4) increasing factionalism in Southern Ireland.

1843–82. "OLD IMMIGRATION": Scandinavian, Irish, and German. (1) **Scandinavian:** Although the settlement of 53 Scandinavians in western New York, 1825, marked the beginning of the inflow to the U.S., a more substantial Swedish inflow began c.1841 with a settlement of a small group at Pine Lake, Wis., and the main Scandinavian migration setting in, 1843, with a total of 1,777 in that year. The number rose to 4,106, 1852, and then leveled off until the post-Civil War period, with peak immigration, 1868–83 (1882, 105,326), again leveling off to 29,391 by 1914. Settlement primarily in Wisconsin and Minnesota. (2) **Irish:** Although substantial Irish immigration began in 1809 and was resumed at the close of the War of 1812, the main flow started in the 1820s,

representing 44% of the total immigration, 1830–40. Irish immigration (largely Roman Catholic) reached its peak after the great famine of 1846, constituting 49% of the total, 1841–50. Such emigration was in part assisted by British and Irish authorities. The immigrants were employed on canal and railroad construction projects. All-time peak year, 1851, 221,253. Highest post-Civil War year, 1883, 81,486. (3) **German** immigration amounting to 30% of the total, 1830–40, was augmented by bad farm conditions in the 1840s and by political refugees from the Revolution of 1848 (e.g., **Carl Schurz**), with German colonies formed in New York, Baltimore, Cincinnati, St. Louis, and a completely Germanized Milwaukee (by 1850). Peak German migration, 1853–54, 356,955 for the two years, with revival beginning 1866, reaching 149,671 in 1873, and setting a pre-World War I peak in 1882 of 250,630.

IMMIGRATION TO THE U.S., 1820–1972
(U.S. Bureau of the Census, *Historical Statistics of the U.S. to 1957; Statistical Abstract, 1958–73.*)

Year	No. of Persons[1]	Year	No. of Persons[1]	Year	No. of Persons[1]
1820	8,385	1871	321,500	1922	309,556
1821	9,127	1872	404,806	1923	522,919
1822	6,911	1873	459,803	1924	706,896
1823	6,354	1874	313,339	1925	294,314
1824	7,912	1875	227,498	1926	304,488
1825	10,199	1876	169,986	1927	335,175
1826	10,837	1877	141,857	1928	307,255
1827	18,875	1878	138,469	1929	279,678
1828	27,332	1879	177,826	1930	241,700
1829	22,520	1880	457,257	1931	97,139
1830	23,322	1881	669,431	1932	35,576
1831	22,633	1882	788,992	1933	23,068
1832	60,482	1883	603,322	1934	29,470
1833	58,640	1884	518,592	1935	34,956
1834	65,365	1885	395,346	1936	36,329
1835	45,374	1886	334,203	1937	50,244
1836	76,242	1887	490,109	1938	67,895
1837	79,340	1888	546,889	1939	82,998
1838	38,914	1889	444,427	1940	70,756
1839	68,069	1890	455,302	1941	51,776
1840	84,066	1891	560,319	1942	28,781
1841	80,289	1892	579,663	1943	23,725
1842	104,565	1893	439,730	1944	28,551
1843	52,496	1894	285,631	1945	38,119
1844	78,615	1895	258,536	1946	108,721
1845	114,371	1896	343,267	1947	147,292
1846	154,416	1897	230,832	1948	170,570
1847	234,968	1898	229,299	1949	188,317
1848	226,527	1899	311,715	1950	249,187
1849	297,024	1900	448,572	1951	205,717
1850	369,980	1901	487,918	1952	265,520
1851	379,466	1902	648,743	1953	170,434
1852	371,603	1903	857,046	1954	208,177
1853	368,645	1904	812,870	1955	237,790
1854	427,833	1905	1,026,499	1956	321,625
1855	200,877	1906	1,100,735	1957	326,867
1856	200,436	1907	1,285,349	1958	253,265
1857	251,306	1908	782,870	1959	260,686
1858	123,126	1909	751,786	1960	318,000
1859	121,282	1910	1,041,570	1961	271,000
1860	153,640	1911	878,587	1962	284,000
1861	91,918	1912	838,172	1963	306,000
1862	91,985	1913	1,197,802	1964	292,000
1863	176,282	1914	1,218,480	1965	297,000
1864	193,418	1915	326,700	1966	323,000
1865	248,120	1916	298,826	1967	362,000
1866	318,568	1917	295,403	1968	454,448
1867	315,722	1918	110,618	1969	358,579
1868	138,840	1919	141,132	1970	373,326
1869	352,768	1920	430,001	1971	370,478
1870	387,203	1921	805,228	1972	384,685

[1] From 1820–67, figures represent alien passengers arrived; 1868–91 and 1895–97, immigrant aliens arrived; 1892–94 and 1898 to present, immigrant aliens admitted.

1849–1950. MEXICAN-AMERICANS IN THE U.S.

The Treaty of Guadalupe Hidalgo (2 Feb. 1848) permitted Mexicans to continue to reside in the territories acquired thereunder by the U.S., including the right to acquire U.S. citizenship, guaranteed their property and the rights of U.S. citizens "according to the principles of the Constitution" (Articles VIII, IX). The period down to 1910 was marred by innumerable controversies over conflicting land grants and serious discrimination against Mexican-Americans, who served as the core of the labor force in the Southwest. After 1890 hundreds of thousands of Mexicans entered the U.S. illegally ("wetbacks"), enticed by American farm, railroad, and mining interests. Segregation was long practiced in California public schools under the law of 1885, amended 1893 (abolished since the 1950s), and ethnic clashes occurred sporadically—most notorious example the anti "Zoot-Suit" rioting in Los Angeles (June, 1943).

1854–68. Chinese immigrant labor (largely employed on transcontinental railroad projects, but in at least 1 case in a New England textile mill) totaled 75,000 in this period.

1865–85. CONTRACT LABOR. Office of Commissioner of Immigration established 4 July 1864; authorized to admit contract laborers under agreements based on a maximum of 12 months' labor for the immigrant's passage to the U.S.

1866. Most Southern states, notably South Carolina, attempted to attract European immigrants to take the place of Negro workers, but without success.

1868–82. CHINESE EXCLUSION. The Burlingame Treaty, 1868, gave Chinese the right to immigrate to the U.S., but anti-Chinese sentiment on the Pacific coast ("Sandlot Riots," San Francisco, July 1877) resulted in the enactment by Congress, 1879, of a bill abrogating the provision; vetoed by President Hayes, who appointed a commission to negotiate a new treaty. The result was the Treaty of 17 Nov. 1880 permitting the U.S. to "regulate, limit or suspend" but not to prohibit the entry of Chinese laborers. Chinese immigration in this period, 160,000, with 1882 the peak year,

IMMIGRATION BY COUNTRY OF ORIGIN, 1820–1950

(U.S. Bureau of the Census, *Hist. Stat. of the U.S., 1789–1945; Statistical Abstract*, 1946–50.)

(Figures are totals, not annual averages, and were tabulated as follows: 1820–67, alien passengers arrived; 1868–91 and 1895–97, immigrant aliens arrived; 1892–94 and 1898 to present, immigrant aliens admitted. Data below 1906 relate to country whence alien came; since 1906, to country of last permanent residence.)

Countries	1820–1900	1901–1910	1911–1920	1921–1930	1931–1940	1941–1950	1820–1950
Europe: Albania[1]	....	....	....	1,663	2,040	85	3,788
Austria[2]	1,027,195	2,145,266	453,649	32,868	3,563	24,860	4,172,104
Belgium	62,161	41,635	33,746	15,846	4,817	12,189	170,394
Bulgaria[3]	160	39,280	22,533	2,945	938	375	66,231
Czechoslovakia[1]	....	....	3,426	102,194	14,393	8,347	128,360
Denmark	192,768	65,285	41,983	32,430	2,559	5,393	340,418
Estonia[1]	....	....	....	1,576	506	212	2,294
Finland[1]	....	....	756	16,691	2,146	2,503	22,096
France	397,489	73,379	61,897	49,610	12,623	38,809	633,807
Germany[2]	5,010,248	341,498	143,945	412,202	114,058	226,578	6,248,529
Great Britain: England	1,824,054	388,017	249,944	157,420	21,756	112,252	2,753,443
Scotland	368,280	120,469	78,357	159,781	6,887	16,131	749,905
Wales	42,076	17,464	13,107	13,012	735	3,209	89,603
Not specified[4]	793,741	....	....	....	....	....	793,741
Greece	18,685	167,519	184,201	51,084	9,119	8,973	439,581
Hungary[2]	....	....	442,693	30,680	7,861	3,469	4,172,104
Ireland	3,873,104	339,065	146,181	220,591	13,167	25,377	4,617,485
Italy	1,040,479	2,045,877	1,109,524	455,315	68,028	57,661	4,776,884
Latvia[1]	....	....	....	3,999	1,192	361	4,952
Lithuania[1]	....	....	....	6,015	2,201	683	8,899
Luxembourg[1]	....	....	....	727	565	820	2,112
Netherlands	127,681	48,262	43,718	26,948	7,150	14,860	268,619
Norway[5]	474,684	190,505	66,395	68,531	4,740	10,100	814,955
Poland[6]	165,182	....	4,813	227,734	17,026	7,571	422,326
Portugal	63,840	69,149	89,732	29,994	3,329	7,423	263,467
Rumania[7]	19,109	53,008	13,311	67,646	3,871	1,076	158,021
Spain	41,361	27,935	68,611	28,958	3,258	2,898	173,021
Sweden[5]	771,631	249,534	95,074	97,249	3,960	10,665	1,228,113
Switzerland	202,479	34,922	23,091	29,676	5,512	10,547	306,227
Turkey in Europe	5,824	79,976	54,677	14,659	737	580	156,453
U.S.S.R.[8]	761,742	1,597,306	921,201	61,742	1,356	548	3,343,895
Yugoslavia[3]	....	....	1,888	49,064	5,835	1,576	58,363
Other Europe	1,940	665	8,111	9,603	2,361	5,573	28,253
Total Europe	17,285,913	8,136,016	4,376,564	2,477,853	348,289	621,704	33,246,339
Asia: China	305,455	20,605	21,278	29,907	4,928	16,709	398,882
India	696	4,713	2,082	1,886	496	1,761	11,634
Japan[9]	28,547	129,797	83,837	33,462	1,948	1,555	279,146
Turkey in Asia[10]	29,088	77,393	79,389	19,165	328	218	205,581
Other Asia	5,883	11,059	5,973	12,980	7,644	11,537	55,076
Total Asia	369,669	243,567	192,559	97,400	15,344	31,780	950,319
America: Canada & Newfoundland[11]	1,051,275	179,226	742,185	924,515	108,527	171,718	3,177,446
Central America	2,173	8,192	17,159	15,769	5,861	21,665	70,819
Mexico[12]	28,003	49,642	219,004	459,287	22,319	60,589	838,844
South America	12,105	17,280	41,899	42,215	7,803	21,831	143,133
West Indies	125,598	107,548	123,424	74,899	15,502	43,725	496,696
Other America[13]	....	....	....	31	25	29,276	29,332
Total America	1,219,154	361,888	1,143,671	1,516,716	160,037	354,804	4,756,270
Africa	2,213	7,368	8,443	6,286	1,750	7,367	33,427
Australia & New Zealand	19,679	11,975	12,348	8,299	2,231	13,805	68,337
Pacific Islands	7,810	1,049	1,079	427	780	5,437	16,582
Countries not specified	219,168	33,523[14]	1,147	228	....	142	254,208
Total all countries	19,123,606	8,795,386	5,735,811	4,107,209	528,431	1,035,039	39,325,482

[1] Countries added to list since beginning of World War I are theretofore included with countries to which they belonged. [2] Data for Austria-Hungary not reported until 1861. Austria and Hungary recorded separately after 1905. Austria included with Germany 1938–45. [3] Bulgaria, Serbia, Montenegro first reported in 1899. Bulgaria reported separately since 1920. In 1920, separate enumeration for Kingdom of Serbs, Croats, Slovenes; since 1922, recorded as Yugoslavia. [4] For United Kingdom. [5] Norway included with Sweden 1820–68. [6] Included with Austria-Hungary, Germany, and Russia 1899–1919. [7] No record of immigration until 1880. [8] Since 1931, U.S.S.R. has been broken down into European Russia and Siberia (Asiatic Russia). [9] No record of immigration until 1861. [10] No record of immigration until 1869. [11] Includes all British North American possession 1820–98. [12] No record of immigration 1886–93. [13] Included with "Countries not specified" prior to 1925. [14] Includes 32,897 persons returning in 1906 to their homes in U.S.

39,579. In 1882 a bill to prohibit the immigration of Chinese laborers for a period of 10 years received the signature of President Arthur. New treaty, 1894, recognized a 10-year exclusion period. Upon China's termination of this agreement, 1904, an exclusion act of 1902 was reenacted without terminal date. By Act of Congress, 17 Dec. 1943, Chinese immigration was permitted within the strict limitations of the quota system, with an annual quota of 105.

1882, 18 Aug. Federal act excluded criminals, paupers, the insane, and other undesirables, and imposed a head tax of 50 cts. upon those entering; subsequently raised to $2 (1903) and to $4 (1907).

1885, 26 Feb. CONTRACT LABOR ACT forbade the importation of contract laborers, but exempted professional, skilled, and domestic labor; modified, 1891, with respect to certain professional categories; again in 1907 and 1917.

1885–1914. "NEW IMMIGRATION" from Eastern and Southern Europe developed in the middle and late 1880s as prosperity dried up the source of German

immigration. Heavy inflow now developed from Russia, Russian Poland, Austria-Hungary, the Balkans, and Italy. The periodic persecution of the Jews in Russia also contributed to large migrations.

1901–05: from Italy, 959,763; Russia, 658,735; Austria-Hungary, 944,239; Germany, 176,995; Great Britain and Ireland, 385,469. Concentration of sizable foreign-born blocs appeared in the larger cities: Chicago (Poles, Bohemians, Hungarians), New York (Italians and Jews), Boston (Irish). **1905–14:** zenith of U.S. immigration, with the million mark exceeded in 6 separate years. In the peak year, 1914, 73.4% of the total immigrants came from Southern and Eastern Europe as against 13.4% from Northern and Western Europe.

1887. AMERICAN PROTECTIVE ASSOCIATION founded at Clinton, La. An anti-Catholic, anti-immigrant organization, peaking in 1896.

1903, 3 Mar. Act providing for U.S. inspection of immigrants at European ports of departure, with the U.S. government given the right to deport any

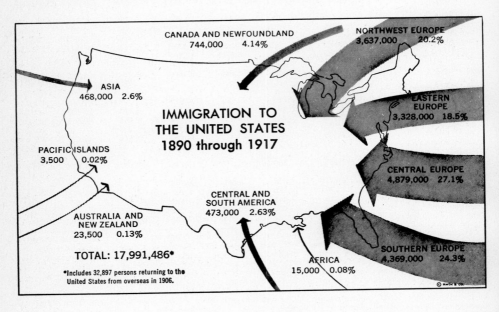

CANADA AND NEWFOUNDLAND
744,000   4.14%

NORTHWEST EUROPE
3,637,000   20.2%

ASIA
468,000 2.6%

IMMIGRATION TO THE UNITED STATES 1890 through 1917

EASTERN EUROPE
3,328,000 18.5%

PACIFIC ISLANDS
3,500   0.02%

CENTRAL EUROPE
4,879,000 27.1%

AUSTRALIA AND NEW ZEALAND
23,500   0.13%

CENTRAL AND SOUTH AMERICA
473,000 2.63%

TOTAL: 17,991,486*

*Includes 32,897 persons returning to the United States from overseas in 1906.

AFRICA
15,000 0.08%

SOUTHERN EUROPE
4,369,000 24.3%

immigrant illegally entering. Anarchists and prostitutes added to the list of excluded persons.

1906. Establishment of the Bureau of Immigration to keep records and statistical data.

1906–24. JAPANESE EXCLUSION. No significant Japanese immigration appeared until the decade 1891–1900, during which period 25,942 Japanese entered the U.S., a total which rose to a peak of 129,797 in the following decade. By the first "Gentlemen's Agreement" (Aug. 1900) Japan agreed to inaugurate a policy of voluntary limitation of emigration through refusal to issue passports to emigrant laborers. On 7 May 1905 the Japanese and Korean Exclusion League was organized on the West Coast. On 11 Oct. 1906 the San Francisco School Board ordered that Chinese, Japanese, and Korean children attend a separate public school. As a result of a conference with President Theodore Roosevelt the board rescinded this action (13 Mar. 1907), and in a series of notes, 1907–08 (the **"Gentlemen's Agreement"**), Japan affirmed her intention of stopping the emigration of laborers. This arrangement continued until superseded by the Immigration Act of 1924, excluding Japanese immigrants as "aliens ineligible to citizenship." Meantime, state laws, notably in California, had limited the right of the Japanese to own (1913) and then to lease (1920) farm lands; upheld by the Supreme Court, 1923. The result was "Humiliation Day" in Tokyo, 1 July 1924, marked by "Hate American" mass meetings.

1917–20. LITERACY TEST AND FURTHER BARS. Bills imposing a literacy test were vetoed by Cleveland (1896) and Taft (14 Feb. 1913). On 28 Jan. 1915 President Wilson vetoed such a bill on the ground that it constituted a fundamental reversal of historical policy without popular mandate. Again, on 29 Jan. 1917, Wilson vetoed a similar measure on the ground that it was "not a test of character, of quality, or of personal fitness." The act, passed over the president's veto, required aliens over 16 years of age to read "not less than 30 nor more than 80 words in ordinary use" in the English language or some other language or dialect. As a war measure, an act of 16 Oct. 1918 excluded alien anarchists and others advocating the overthrow of the government. An act of 10 May 1920 provided for the deportation of alien enemies and anarchists.

1921, 19 MAY. FIRST "QUOTA LAW" limited immigration in any year to 3% of the number of each nationality according to the **Census of 1910**, with a maximum quota of 357,000.

1924, 26 MAY. NEW QUOTA LAW halved 1921 quota (1923, 357,803; 1924–25, 164,447) and limited immigration in any year to 2% of the **Census of 1890** (in order to reduce quotas from Eastern and Southern Europe); to remain in force until 1927, when an apportionment on the basis of 1920 distribution of "national origins" would serve as the basis for a maximum quota of **150,000** per annum. Owing to opposition this law did not go into effect until 1 July 1929, since which date the annual quota of any nationality for each fiscal year has been a number which bears the same ratio to 150,000 as the number of inhabitants in 1920 having that origin bears to the total number of inhabitants in the U.S. in 1920. Under an act of 1929 consuls were empowered to refuse visas to all applicants who may become "public charges." The quota laws did not apply to immigration from Canada or Latin America, and provided a few minor exceptions for ministers, professors, and bona fide college students.

1945–52. DISPLACED PERSONS. Under directive of President Truman, 22 Dec. 1945, measures were taken to facilitate the entrance under quota of displaced persons. Under the directive 42,000 persons were admitted to the country. By act of 25 June 1948, visas were authorized for the admission of 205,000 European displaced persons, including 3,000 nonquota orphans; the number of visas authorized was increased by act of 16 June 1950 to 341,000 to be issued by 30 June 1951. Certain discriminatory provisions were eliminated and new categories of expellees and war orphans added with total visas of 54,744 and 5,000 respectively to be issued by 30 June 1952. By act of 28 June 1951, issuance of visas to displaced persons was extended to 31 Dec. 1951.

1951–65. IMPORTATION OF "BRACEROS." Under "temporary" laws Congress permitted controlled annual importation of farm workers (*braceros*) from Mexico (renewed 1951, 1956, 1958, but terminated 31 Dec. 1961). In Feb. 1962 the *braceros* became subject to the provisions of the minimum wage law, and in 1965 the importation of workers under the *bracero* program ended.

1952, 30 JUNE. McCARRAN-WALTER ACT, passed over the veto of President Truman (House vote, 278–133; Senate, 57–26), codified U.S. immigration laws and generally retained the provisions of the 1924 act on maximum immigration and the quota system, but removed the ban against immigration of Asian and Pacific peoples. Screening measures to keep out "subversives" and other undesirables were incorporated and the Attorney General empowered to deport immigrants for "Communist and Communist-front" affiliations even after they acquired U.S. citizenship.

1953, 7 AUG. REFUGEE RELIEF ACT provided for entry into the U.S., on an emergency basis outside regular immigration quota, of 186,000 escapees from Communist persecution, as well as selected persons in other groups up to a total of 214,000. Under accelerated procedure adopted late in 1956 to cope with a mass influx of refugees from Hungary into Austria, 21,500 Hungarian refugees were admitted into the U.S., with an emergency air- and sea-lift instituted by the Defense Department. Total displaced persons admitted, 1948–55, 406,028; refugees, 1954–59, 234,145.

1965. IMMIGRATION AND NATIONALITY ACT. The McCarran-Walter Act was revised (1 Dec.) and the national quota system substantially altered. Effective 1 July 1968, a limit of 170,000 was set for immigrants from countries outside the Western Hemisphere, with a 20,000 annual maximum for any one country. At the same time, an annual ceiling of 120,000 was set for the Western Hemisphere, on a first-come basis with no limitations set for a country.

1966. STATUS OF CUBANS. Effective 2 Nov. Cubans admitted or paroled into the U.S. after 1 Jan. 1959 and present in the U.S. for at least 2 years were made eligible for permanent resident status.

1951–70. CHANGING IMMIGRATION PATTERNS. The altered quota system, with special exceptions, was reflected in the changing immigration flow.

1951–60. Total (by country of birth): from **Europe**: 1,492,215 (Germany, 345,450; United Kingdom, 208,872; Italy, 187,904; Poland, 127,985); from **Asia**, 157,081; from **North America**, 769,147 (Mexico, 319,312; Canada, 274,926; Cuba, 78,330); from **South America**, 72,166 (Colombia, 17,581); from **Africa**, 16,569.

1961–70. Total: from **Europe**, 1,238,553 (United Kingdom, 230,452; Italy, 206,650; Germany, 199,980; Greece, 90,235); from **Asia**: 445,269 (Philippines, 101,656; China, incl. Taiwan, 96,702); from **North America**: 1,351,099 (West Indies, 519,499, incl. Cuba, 256,769;

Mexico, 443,301; Canada, 286,667); from **South America**, 228,475 (Colombia, 70,327; Argentina, 42,135); from **Africa**, 39,262.

1965–70. AWAKENING OF LA RAZA. A shift of Mexican-American population from the farms to the cities (80% by 1970), along with affirmative support for *La Raza* in a context of American cultural pluralism and militant organizing of migrant workers, opened up a new era for the Mexican-American. In 1965 the grape-pickers under **Cesar Chavez** (1927–   ), who had founded the National Farm Workers Association (1963), later transposed to United Farm Workers, struck against the growers of Delano, Calif. and called for an International Boycott Day (10 May 1969) of California table wines. In 1966 Cesar Chavez's force affiliated with the AFL-CIO, and on 29 July 1970 the 5-year-long strike was ended by a pact with the growers. By 1974, however, the UFW had suffered severe setbacks as the Teamsters sought to represent migrant agricultural workers. Other militant civil rights leaders have been Rodolfo ("Corky") Gonzalez, founder in Denver, Colo. (1965) of the Crusade for Justice, and Reies Lopez Tijerina, founder in the 1960s of the Alliance of Land Grants (later named Alliance of Free City-States), whose purpose was to reopen the question of Spanish and Mexican land grants.

1970. AMERICANS OF ASIATIC DESCENT in U.S. estimated as 591,000 of Japanese ancestry, 435,000 of Chinese ancestry, and 343,000 of Filipino ancestry.

1972. AMERICANS OF SPANISH DESCENT in U.S. estimated at 9,178,000, of whom 5,254,000 were of Mexican origin and 1,518,000 of Puerto Rican origin.

Black Americans Since the Civil War:
A Chronological Conspectus[1]

1865–77. BLACKS AND RECONSTRUCTION (see pp. 292–302).

1879. Start of black migration from South in large numbers, notably to the Middle West. Black population, Chicago, 1870, c.4,000; 1880, 7,400; 1890, 14,800.

1881. First Jim Crow law segregating railroad coaches passed by Tennessee; similarly, Florida, 1887; Texas, 1889.

Tuskegee Institute, headed by Booker T. Washington (p. 1117), founded.

1883. CIVIL RIGHTS CASES (p. 671).

[1] The role of blacks and the institutions with which they were associated is discussed at further length at appropriate places throughout this book. This section is intended to serve as a point of reference for major political developments.

1892. Lynching of blacks on the rise: 160 (1892); 1,400 since 1882.

1896. "Separate but Equal." See *Plessy* v. *Ferguson* (p. 672), upholding segregation in railroad carriages.

1898. Literacy tests and poll tax upheld in *Williams* v. *Mississippi* (170 U.S. 213).

"Grandfather clause" added by Louisiana to state constitution, waiving other voting requirements if a man's father or grandfather had voted on 1 Jan. 1867; also adopted by North Carolina (1900), Alabama (1901), Virginia (1902), Georgia (1908); upset by Supreme Court in *Guinn* v. *U.S.* (1915), (238 U.S. 497).

1903. General Education Board, endowed by John D. Rockefeller, supported improved preparation of teachers of black schools in the South.

1905. Niagara Conference, called by **W. E. B. Du Bois** (p. 1017), founded Niagara Movement, asserting equal political rights, economic opportunity, education, justice, and end to segregation.

1906–19. BROWNSVILLE AFFAIR touched off allegedly by riotous conduct of unidentified black soldiers in Brownsville, Tex., 13 Aug. 1906, resulting in dishonorable discharges of 167 privates and noncommissioned officers, 5 Nov. 1906. In 1972 the army cleared the soldiers of guilt and changed the discharges to honorable.

1909. NATIONAL ASSOCIATION FOR THE ADVANCEMENT OF COLORED PEOPLE (NAACP) founded; originally advocated extending industrial opportunity and greater police protection for blacks.

1910. National Urban League formed to aid adjustment of migrant blacks to cities, focusing on economic and social problems.

1911. Peonage declared unconstitutional, *Bailey* v. *Alabama* (219 U.S. 219 [1911]).

1920, Aug. Marcus Garvey (p. 1038) opens National Convention in Harlem of Universal Negro Improvement Association (UNIA); adopts bill of rights and advocates emigration of blacks to Africa.

Ku Klux Klan revival, with 100,000 members in 27 states (est. 4–4.5 million by 1924).

HARLEM RENAISSANCE, black cultural movement, continues for a decade.

1927. Texas law barring blacks from voting in the Democratic primaries invalidated in *Nixon* v. *Herndon* (273 U.S. 536). See also *Smith* v. *Allwright* (1944, p. 678).

1931. First Temple of Islam for **Black Muslims** founded in Detroit (p. 829).

1931. 25 Mar. Nine Scottsboro boys arrested in Alabama, charged with rape. Found guilty in 3 controversial trials; convictions reversed by U.S. Supreme Court, 1 Apr. 1935.

1935. 19 Mar. Harlem, N.Y., rioting with 3 killed, property damage est. $200 million.

1939. 2 Apr. Marian Anderson (1902–) gave concert on Easter Sunday at the Lincoln Memorial after having been denied Constitution Hall, Washington, due to racial policies of Daughters of the American Revolution. Anderson made her debut at Metropolitan Opera as Ulrica in *The Masked Ball* (7 Jan. 1955).

1941. 25 June. President Franklin D. Roosevelt issued Executive Order 8802, forbidding discrimination in employment in government and defense industries.

1941–60. BLACK MIGRATION. 43 cities outside the South doubled their black population as against 2 in the South, 1941–50. Black increase was greater in central part of cities, showing 48.3% increase, 1940–50, as against 10.1% for whites. Nonwhite population was 10% of central parts of cities (1940), 33⅓% (1950). In the period 1950–58, nonwhite population increased 21.9% in U.S. as against 14.2% for white, with greatest nonwhite percentage gains in Pacific (53.3%), Northeast (49.7%), East North Central (47.6%), Middle Atlantic (38.2%), and the lowest in the East South Central (4.9%). The South contained 6% less of the nation's nonwhite population in 1958 than in 1950.

1942. Congress of Racial Equality (CORE) founded by James Farmer.

1943. Spring. Race riots in Detroit, Mich., and Mobile, Ala., over employment of blacks. A Harlem riot (Aug.) left 5 persons killed, 400 injured, and property damage of some $5 million.

1946. 5 Dec. President Truman issued Executive Order 9802 creating Presidential Committee on Civil Rights; issued report, 1947, urging a civil rights section in the Department of Justice and a permanent Fair Employment Practices Commission (also p. 452).

1948. 30 July. President Truman's Executive Order 9981 barred segregation in armed forces, and a federal law (1949) barred discrimination in federal civil service positions (p. 515).

1951. 12 July. Cicero, Ill., riots over segregated housing led to calling out of National Guard.

1954. 17 May. *Brown* v. *Board of Education of Topeka* and other school and college desegregation tests (p. 679).

1955. 1 Dec. Montgomery bus boycott begins (p. 523).

1956. 11 Mar. Southern Manifesto (p. 521).

1957. 9 Sept. CIVIL RIGHTS ACT (p. 527).

Southern Christian Leadership Conference (SCLC) organized by Martin Luther King, Jr., Bayard Rustin, and others to achieve full citizenship rights for blacks and their integration in all aspects of life.

24 Sept. Little Rock desegregation incident (p. 527).

1960, 1 Feb. Sit-in at F. W. Woolworth lunch counter in Greensboro, N.C., set off a national movement of nonviolent protest.

15 Apr. Student Non-Violent Coordinating Committee (SNCC) formed at Shaw Univ., to win political power for Southern blacks.

1960–70. BLACK MIGRATION. U.S. Census showed for first time more than half the nation's blacks living outside the South, with 1,457,000 nonwhites moving from the South in the previous decade. Black migration, 1960–70: Mid-

dle Atlantic, 540,000; East North Central, 356,000; Pacific, 286,000; South Atlantic, 538,000; East South Central, 560,000; West South Central, 282,000. In official 1970 Census black population, 22,580,000, being 11.1% of total population, but apparently underestimation of 1.9 million. As of 1970 black population was located 39% in North, 53% in South, 8% in West; 16.8 million lived in metropolitan areas (74%) of which 13.1 million lived in central cities (58%).

1961, 4 May. Freedom Ride campaign initiated by CORE, testing integration by bus rides through the South.

1961–68. Civil rights under Kennedy-Johnson administrations, including Civil Rights Law of 2 July 1964 (pp. 528, 529).

1963, 12 June. Medgar Evers, state desegregation leader, fatally shot in Jackson, Miss.

1965, 21 Feb. Assassination in New York City of Malcolm X (b. 1925), founder of the Organization of Afro-American Unity and proponent of a philosophy of black unity.

7 Mar. Protest march from Selma to Montgomery, Ala., led by Martin Luther King, Jr.

1964–68. URBAN RACE RIOTING (p. 531).

1965–67. BLACK APPOINTEES to high federal positions, include **Thurgood Marshall** (p. 1098), Solicitor General of the U.S. (1965–67), justice of the U.S. Supreme Court (1967–   ); **Robert Weaver**, Secretary of Housing and Urban Development (1966–69), **Andrew Brimmer**, member of Federal Reserve Board (1966–74).

1966. The Black Panthers, a black revolutionary party, founded by Bobby Seale and Huey P. Newton. The Black Panthers subsequently were involved in many violent confrontations with the police and many of their leaders were killed or imprisoned.

JUNE. "Black Power" popularized as a slogan by Stokely Carmichael, leader of SNCC, during march to Jackson, Miss., led by James Meredith. Richard Wright authored *Black Power* (1954) writing about blacks on the Gold Coast of Africa, and Rep. Adam Clayton Powell, Jr., used the term at a Chicago rally (May 1965). The Black Power movement, rejecting the nonviolent, integrationist, coalition-building approach of traditional civil rights groups, advocated black control of black organizations—black self-determination.

1967. Carl Stokes elected mayor of Cleveland, Ohio, the first black mayor of a major U.S. city. Others included: Richard Hatcher (Gary, Ind., 1967); Kenneth A. Gibson (Newark, N.J., 1970); Thomas Bradley (Los Angeles, Calif., 1973); Maynard Jackson (Atlanta, Ga., 1973).

1968, 4 APR. Assassination of Martin Luther King, Jr., in Memphis, Tenn. (also p. 1076); SCLC leadership assumed by Rev. Ralph Abernathy.

2 MAY–24 JUNE. "Poor People's March" on Washington led by Rev. Ralph Abernathy.

5 Nov. Presidential election: 51.4% of registered nonwhites voted compared with 44% in 1964. Black registration, of voting-age black population, in 11 Southern states rose from 1,463,000 (1960) to 3,449,000 (1971), or from a total of 29.1% (1960) to 58.6% (1971).

1970–73. BLACK MIGRATION from North to South (198,000) outnumbered those moving from South to North (117,000), largely reflecting economic factors.

1971. The 13 black members of the

U.S. House of Representatives formed the Congressional Black Caucus.

1974–79. DESEGREGATION DECISIONS (p. 550)

1975. General Daniel ("Chappie") James, Jr., named chief of North American Defense Command, becomes first black four-star general. William T. Coleman, Secretary of Transportation under President Ford, was second black to hold cabinet office.

1977. Elected black officials rise from 1,469 (1970) to 4,311 nationally. 16 blacks were members of Congress, compared with maximum of 7 during Reconstruction.

1977–80. BLACK APPOINTEES to high federal positions include Patricia Roberts Harris (Secretary H.U.D., 1977–79; Secretary, Health & Human Services, 1979–81), Andrew Young (p. 573), as well as 28 black District judges and 9 black Court of Appeals judges.

1979–81. ATLANTA MURDERS of 28 black children stir national concern.

1980, 1 APR. CENSUS. Black population—26,488,218

17–19 MAY. RACIAL RIOTS in Liberty City neighborhood of Miami, Fla., triggered by acquittal by all-white jury in Tampa, Fla., of four Miami policemen, accused of fatal beating of a black man. In the rioting 18 were killed, 300 injured, and property damage est. $100 million. During visit to riot-torn area (7 June), President Carter was booed.

29 MAY. Vernon Jordan, Jr., President National Urban League, shot by unknown assailant in Fort Wayne, Ind.

1981. Samuel R. Pierce named secretary of Dept. of H.U.D.

LEADING SUPREME COURT DECISIONS

★ ★
★

The unanimous decision of the United States Supreme Court in *United States of America* v. *Richard M. Nixon* reminds us not only that almost all major issues of domestic policy arrive at the high court in the form of constitutional questions but also that it is a basic tenet of American governance that the Supreme Court is the final arbiter of the American Constitution. It is a remarkable paradox that the American republic refers some of its most difficult policy decisions to non-elected "wise elders" for resolution by interpretation of a document drawn up two centuries ago. Perhaps even more remarkable is the evolution of the court in the past thirty-five years as the most egalitarian branch of government and the one most protective of the individual citizen.

Although the docket of the court was light during its very first decade, the justices encountered cases raising substantial political controversy in their capacity as circuit justices. The first great era of the court was that dominated by John Marshall, who in thirty-four years left a heritage of broad nationalist decisions, laying the foundation for modern American federalism. Closer to his own time, those decisions assisted the growth of American capitalism. For the next three decades the able Roger Taney presided over a court which reconciled the approach of Marshall with the spirit of Jacksonian democracy.

The court rebounded rapidly from the tragic *Dred Scott* decision; from 1878 to 1937 it emerged as the protector of capital from most regulation of either the national or the state governments. Concurrently, the court strayed from the spirit of the 14th and 15th Amendments and ultimately, in *Plessy* v. *Ferguson,* sustained state-sponsored segregation.

Another great crisis, the court-packing fight of 1937, was triggered by the unwillingness of a majority of the Supreme Court, confronted by New Deal legislation aimed at pulling the nation out of the great depression, to depart from their constitutional gloss of sixty years. But once again the court was resilient, abandoning its role as chief economic arbiter, and assuming another, that of protector of civil liberties.

Remarkable indeed were the court's accomplishments under Chief Justice Earl Warren. Then the court struck down not only the segregation of schools but all state-imposed segregation, ordered the reapportionment of state legislatures and the redrawing of congressional district lines on the basis of "one man, one vote," and read into the 14th Amendment the protections of the Bill of Rights, greatly expanding the rights of the individual facing criminal prosecution.

Since then the Burger Court, responsive to growing public conservatism, has engaged in a partial retreat. It has, on the one hand, circumscribed the implementation of desegregation of Northern school systems and given freer rein to police procedures. On the other, it has invalidated all criminal abortion and capital punishment statutes then existing on the books; it resisted Nixon administration pressures by refusing to enjoin publication of the Pentagon Papers and by ordering the president to turn the Watergate tapes over to the lower federal courts.

1793. CHISHOLM v. GEORGIA (2 Dallas 419). The Constitution (Art. III, Sec. 2) gave the federal courts explicit jurisdiction over "controversies between a state and citizens of another state." As executors for a British creditor, 2 South Carolina citizens brought suit in the Supreme Court against the state of Georgia for the recovery of confiscated property. Georgia denied the court's jurisdiction, and refused to appear. The court decided in favor of Chisholm. Opinions of 4 majority justices (notably John Jay and James Wilson) elaborated on the sovereignty and the nature of the Union. Dissenting Justice James Iredell held that no constitutional sanction superseded the right (under English common law) of a sovereignty not to be sued without its consent. As a result of the decision, the 11th Amendment was proposed and ratified (p. 151).

1796. WARE v. HYLTON (3 Dallas 199). By the peace treaty with Great Britain (1783), no legal impediment was to be placed on recovery of debts owed by Americans to British creditors. In this test case, the court invalidated a Virginia statute (1777) providing for the sequestration of debts owed to British subjects before the outbreak of the Revo-

lution, on the ground that under the Constitution treaties are the supreme law of the land; hence paramount over state laws.

1796. HYLTON v. U.S. (3 Dallas 171) involved the question of whether a tax on carriages enacted in 1794 was an excise or a direct tax within the meaning of the Constitution. Holding that only land and capitation levies were direct taxes, the court ruled that the carriage tax was indirect and hence could be levied without apportionment among the states. This was the first time the court passed on the constitutionality of an act of Congress.

1798. CALDER v. BULL (3 Dallas 386). The court interpreted that provision of the Constitution (Art. I, Sec. 10) prohibiting state leigslatures from enacting *ex post facto* laws as extending only to criminal, not civil, laws.

1803. MARBURY v. MADISON (1 Cranch 137), p. 158.

1810. FLETCHER v. PECK (6 Cranch 87) involved the claims arising under the Yazoo land frauds (p. 166). The Georgia legislature, many of its members having been bribed by land speculators, granted large tracts along the Yazoo River to land companies

(1795). The grant was rescinded by the succeeding legislature on the ground that its enactment had been attended by fraud and corruption. Chief Justice Marshall rendered the opinion for a unanimous court, upholding the original grant on the grounds that (1) it was not within the province of the court to inquire into the motives actuating a legislature, and (2) the rescinding act impaired the obligation of contracts, Marshall ruling that the contract clause made no distinction between public and private contracts. This was the first time the court invalidated a state law as contrary to the Constitution.

1816. MARTIN v. HUNTER'S LESSEE (1 Wheaton 304) arose from the litigation over Virginia's confiscation of the Fairfax land grants and its statute prohibiting an alien from inheriting land, and involved the crucial question of the court's appellate jurisdiction over the decisions of state courts. The first court decision (1813), rendered against Virginia, stirred the defiance of the state court of appeals, which refused to obey the mandate and held that Sec. 25 of the Judiciary Act was unconstitutional. When the case was again brought to the Supreme Court, Justice Story vigorously affirmed the court's right to review decisions of state courts. Asserting the court's role as the harmonizer of decisions emanating from inferior courts, Story ruled that the constitutional grant of concurrent jurisdiction in specified cases did not deprive the Supreme Court of its appellate jurisdiction. The decision renewed the opposition of the Virginia Republicans led by Judge Spencer Roane and set off a lively pamphleteering war.

1819. TRUSTEES OF DARTMOUTH COLLEGE v. WOODWARD (4 Wheaton 518), p. 189.

1819. STURGES v. CROWNINSHIELD (4 Wheaton 122) involved the constitutionality of a New York statute (1811) relieving insolvent debtors of obligations contracted before the passage of the act. While Chief Justice Marshall held that state bankruptcy laws were permissible in the absence of congressional legislation, he declared that the New York statute impaired the obligation of contracts and was therefore unconstitutional. The decision served to restrict state action on bankruptcy during a period of financial chaos.

1819. M'CULLOCH v. MARYLAND (4 Wheaton 316), pp. 189–190.

1821. COHENS v. VIRGINIA (6 Wheaton 264) arose from the conviction of the Cohens for selling lottery tickets in violation of a state law. The larger issues involved were the constitutionality of Sec. 25 of the Judiciary Act, under which the Cohens had appealed to the Supreme Court, and the interpretation of the 11th Amendment, under which Virginia claimed exemption from federal jurisdiction in this instance. On the merits, the court decided in favor of Virginia, but Chief Justice Marshall issued a firm reply to the Virginia Republicans who denied that state court decisions were subject to court review. His comprehensive interpretation of the court's scope of jurisdiction was based squarely on the doctrine of national supremacy.

1823. GREEN v. BIDDLE (8 Wheaton 1). Ruling that the contract clause applied to contracts between 2 states as well as those between private persons, the Court nullified a Kentucky law pertaining to land titles on the ground that it impaired the obligation of contracts deriving from a political agreement that Kentucky made with Virginia when the former state was organized. The court also denied Kentucky's claim that agreement was invalid because Congress had not consented.

1824. GIBBONS v. OGDEN (9 Wheaton 1) involved a monopoly granted by the New York legislature

(1808) for the operation of steamboats in state waters. Aaron Ogden, successor to the exclusive right granted to Robert Fulton and Robert R. Livingston, sued Thomas Gibbons (who operated under a federal license) to restrain him from engaging in steam navigation between New York and New Jersey. The court invalidated the New York grant. The opinion of Chief Justice Marshall was the first broad construction of the nature and scope of congressional power under the commerce clause. Rejecting a narrow definition of commerce as "traffic" or simple exchange, Marshall construed it as embracing "every species of commercial intercourse," including navigation and other agencies of commerce. While he conceded that the regulation of wholly intrastate commerce was reserved to the state, he asserted that congressional power to regulate interstate and foreign commerce "does not stop at the jurisdictional lines of the several states." This curb on state authority, coming at a time when many states had granted similar monopoly privileges, freed transportation from state restraints.

1824. OSBORN v. BANK OF THE U.S. (9 Wheaton 738) involved the validity of a circuit court decree restraining an Ohio tax and outlaw act directed against branches of the U.S. Bank within the state, and was a direct result of the opposition to the court's decision in **M'Culloch v. Maryland.** The state auditor, Ralph Osborn, and other Ohio officials who seized bank funds were sued for damages. The court decision was in favor of the bank. Chief Justice Marshall held that the agent of a state, when executing an unconstitutional statute, was personally responsible for damages caused by his enforcement of the act, and that a state could not invoke the protection of the 11th Amendment.

1827. MARTIN v. MOTT (12 Wheaton 19). During the War of 1812 state authorities in New England employed various means for effectively denying the authority of the Congress or president to call out the state militia. Justice Story held that the president, acting under congressional authority, was the sole judge of the existence of those contingencies prescribed in the Constitution upon which the militia might be called out; that the president's decision was binding on state officials; and that state militia in federal service were subject to the authority of officers commissioned by the president.

1827. OGDEN v. SAUNDERS (12 Wheaton 213). The court ruled 4 to 3 that a New York bankruptcy law (1801) did not violate the obligation of contracts entered into *after* the enactment of the law. Justice William Johnson of the majority, anticipating the later doctrine of the state's police power, declared that "all the contracts of men receive a relative, and not a positive interpretation: for the rights of all must be held and enjoyed in subserviency to the good of the whole." But the majority also declared that a state insolvency law could not discharge a contract of a citizen of another state. This was the first time Chief Justice Marshall was in a minority on the interpretation of a constitutional provision. He and Justice Story dissented on the ground that the contract clause protected all contracts, future as well as past, from impairment.

1827. BROWN v. MARYLAND (12 Wheaton 419) invalidated a Maryland law requiring a special license for wholesalers dealing in foreign goods. Marking out the line between state and federal control of commerce, Chief Justice Marshall laid down the **"original package"** doctrine: imported goods which became "incorporated and mixed up with the mass of property in the country" were subject to the state taxing power, but those which remained "in the original form or package" (i.e., the property of the importer) were still imports and hence subject to congressional regulation.

1830. CRAIG v. MISSOURI (4 Peters 410). The court, 4 to 3, upset a Missouri law authorizing the issuance of loan certificates receivable in discharge of taxes and debts due the state. Marshall narrowly construed the constitutional clause prohibiting states from emitting bills of credit, while the dissenting justices held the law to be a justifiable use of the state's borrowing power.

1831. CHEROKEE NATION v. GEORGIA (5 Peters 1), p. 204.

1832. WORCESTER v. GEORGIA (6 Peters 515), pp. 204, 205.

1833. BARRON v. BALTIMORE (7 Peters 243). Chief Justice Marshall held that the amendments included in the Bill of Rights were protection against infringement by the federal government, but not binding upon the state governments.

1837. BRISCOE v. BANK OF KENTUCKY (11 Peters 257) upheld a Kentucky law creating a state-owned bank empowered to issue notes for public circulation on the ground that the state had not pledged the redemption of the notes but had established for this purpose a public corporation capable of suing and being sued; hence, the state bank notes could not be construed as bills of credit. Story dissented. The decision paved the way for increased state regulation of currency and banking.

1837. CHARLES RIVER BRIDGE v. WARREN BRIDGE (11 Peters 420). The Massachusetts legislature authorized (1785) the Charles River Bridge Co. to construct and operate a toll bridge over the Charles River, and in 1792 extended the charter to 70 years. The grant did not confer exclusive privileges. The charter of the Warren Bridge (1828) provided that the structure

(built a short distance from the Charles Bridge) should be turned over to the state upon the recovery of construction costs. The Charles River Bridge Co. brought suit for an injunction on the ground that the erection of the Warren Bridge constituted an impairment of the obligation of contracts. Rejecting the doctrine of vested rights invoked by the Charles River counsel, Chief Justice Taney ruled that the competing bridge was no such impairment, that a legislative charter must be construed narrowly, that no implied rights could be claimed beyond the specific terms of a grant, and that ambiguous clauses must operate against the corporation in favor of the public. Taney's first pronouncement on a constitutional issue, the decision substantially modified Marshall's earlier contract doctrines.

1837. NEW YORK v. MILN (11 Peters 102) upheld the constitutionality of a New York statute requiring masters of coastwise or transoceanic vessels entering New York to furnish prescribed information concerning all passengers brought in, as a legitimate use of the state police power for purposes of internal health and welfare, not in conflict with the federal commerce power. In a dissenting opinion, Story maintained that the statute infringed upon the exclusive congressional power to regulate foreign commerce.

1839. BANK OF AUGUSTA v. EARLE (13 Peters 519) was the chief of the 3 Comity Cases of 1839, which arose from the attempt of Alabama to exclude corporations chartered by other states. A citizen of Alabama refused to honor the bills of exchange of a Georgia bank, contending that a "foreign" corporation had no lawful right to enter into a contract within a "sovereign" state. Chief Justice Taney recognized the general right of a corporation to do business under interstate comity with other states, but also upheld the right of states to exclude corporations by positive action. Taney rejected the argument that a corporation possessed all the legal rights guaranteed to natural persons under the Constitution.

1842. PRIGG v. PENNSYLVANIA (16 Peters 539) involved the constitutionality of the federal fugitive slave law of 1793 and of a Pennsylvania "personal liberty" law of 1826 banning forcible seizure and removal of a fugitive. For the majority, Story held (1) the state law unconstitutional, and (2) the execution of the fugitive slave clause in the Constitution exclusively a federal power, hence no state was obliged to undertake the enforcement of the law. As a result, Northern states enacted a series of "personal liberty" laws forbidding state authorities from assisting in the return of fugitive slaves.

1847. LICENSE CASES (5 Howard 504). These 3 cases involved the legality of state laws restricting and taxing the sale of alcoholic liquors. The Massachusetts and Rhode Island statutes were upheld as not contrary to the "original package" dictum. The New Hampshire case, however, involved a tax upon liquor in the original and unbroken package. From the 9 opinions written by 6 justices emerged agreement on the view that a tax imposed as an exercise of the state police power is valid, even though the levy impinges on interstate commerce. Four justices (including Taney) indicated that in the absence of federal legislation the states had a concurrent right to regulate interstate commerce unless they came in conflict with a law of Congress.

1849. LUTHER v. BORDEN (7 Howard 1) arose from the Dorr Rebellion in Rhode Island (p. 222) and involved the validity of the declaration of martial law by the existing state legislature. The court decided that Congress

had power under Art. IV, Sec. 4 of the Constitution to guarantee republican government in the states and to recognize the lawful government; the president by Act of Congress must decide in case of an armed conflict within a state which is the lawful government. Neither decision could be questioned by the court as they turn upon "political questions."

1849. PASSENGER CASES (7 Howard 283). These 2 cases involved the legality of New York and Massachusetts acts authorizing a head tax on each alien brought into the ports of these states and directing the tax collections to be used for internal welfare. The court (5–4) held the acts unconstitutional on the ground that the power to regulate foreign commerce belonged exclusively to the federal government and could not be exercised even in the absence of congressional legislation. The dissenting justices maintained that the laws were a legitimate exercise of state police power. Taney contended that, failing positive congressional regulation, the states had a concurrent power in this domain.

1851. COOLEY v. BOARD OF WARDENS (12 Howard 299) upheld the validity of a Pennsylvania law regulating the employment of pilots in the port of Philadelphia. Justice Benjamin R. Curtis ruled that where commerce was national in character, the federal power was exclusive; but where local, the states had a concurrent power to legislate in the absence of federal action.

1857. DRED SCOTT v. SANDFORD (19 Howard 393), p. 263.

1859. ABLEMAN v. BOOTH (21 Howard 506). This case arose when the Wisconsin Supreme Court (1854) freed the abolitionist editor Sherman M. Booth, who had been convicted in federal district court of violating the fugitive slave law of 1850. U.S. District Marshal Ableman obtained a writ of error in the U.S. Supreme Court to review the state court's findings. In an opinion notable for its affirmation of national supremacy and its analysis of divided sovereignty, Taney denied the right of the state judiciary to interfere in federal cases and, in a brief obiter dictum, upheld the constitutionality of the fugitive slave law. His pronouncement led the Wisconsin legislature to adopt resolutions defending state sovereignty in the spirit of the Kentucky and Virginia resolutions.

1861. EX PARTE MERRYMAN (Fed. Cases No. 9487) involved military suspension of the privilege of the writ of habeas corpus, authorized in exceptional instances by President Lincoln. John Merryman, a Baltimore secessionist, arrested by military authority, successfully petitioned Chief Justice Taney (sitting as a circuit judge) for a writ of habeas corpus. That writ was rejected by the military commander. Taney, who cited the commander for contempt, filed an opinion denying that the executive had the power to suspend the writ, holding such power to be vested in Congress, and condemning the suspension of constitutional rights by military order. Lincoln justified his course in his message to Congress (July 1861).

1863. PRIZE CASES (2 Black 635). Before Congress recognized a state of war, neutral shipping was seized under Lincoln's proclamations (19, 27 Apr. 1861) which authorized a blockade of Confederate ports. The court (5–4) sustained the legality of the seizures, declaring that the president could not initiate war, but was fulfilling his lawful duties in resisting insurrection, and that insurrection was in fact war.

1864. EX PARTE VALLANDIGHAM (1 Wallace 243) involved arrests and trials of civilians by military commissions. Upon rejection of Vallandigham's petition for a writ of habeas corpus by a U.S. circuit court, his counsel appealed to the Supreme Court. The court refused to review the case on the ground that its authority did not embrace the proceedings of a military commission.

1866. EX PARTE MILLIGAN (4 Wallace 2) involving the trial and conviction of civilians by military commission at Indianapolis, unanimously held the military commission authorized by the president to be void and released Milligan. A majority held that neither Congress nor the president had legal power to institute a military commission to try civilians in areas remote from the actual theater of war, stating that the Constitution "is a law for rules and people equally in war and in peace, and covers with the shield of its protection all classes of men, at all times, and under all circumstances." Four justices argued in an opinion by Chief Justice Chase that Congress could have authorized the military commission under the war powers.

1867. TEST-OATH CASES: Cummings v. Missouri (4 Wallace 277), **Ex parte Garland** (4 Wallace 333). The **Cummings** case involved a Missouri constitutional (1865) provision requiring an oath of past allegiance from teachers, preachers, voters, and many others. The **Garland** case arose from a federal loyalty oath requirement (1865) demanded of attorneys practicing in the federal courts. Heard simultaneously, the court split 5–4 in both decisions. The majority held such tests of past fidelity ex post facto and bills of attainder. The dissenters maintained that such requirements were valid expressions of a government's right to protect itself by laying down certain qualifications of its officers and voters.

1867. MISSISSIPPI v. JOHNSON (4 Wallace 475) concerned an attempt by Mississippi to enjoin President Johnson from enforcing the 1867 Reconstruction Acts. Unanimously, the court refused the injunction on the ground that purely executive and political functions were not subject to judicial restraint, although mere ministerial acts might be. Similarly, a suit to enjoin the Secretary of War from enforcing these acts was dismissed as involving political questions over which the court had no jurisdiction; **Georgia v. Stanton** (6 Wallace 50).

1869. EX PARTE McCARDLE (7 Walker 506), p. 297.

1869. TEXAS v. WHITE (7 Wallace 700) involved the legality of financial actions of the Confederate government of Texas. The court held that, secession being inadmissible, the Confederate state authorities had never legally existed. Chief Justice Chase, for the majority, analyzed the nature of the Union and the theories of secession and Reconstruction in a manner consistent with the Union's constitutional arguments during the war. "The Constitution," he said, ". . . looks to an indestructible Union, composed of indestructible states." While refraining from passing on the validity of the Reconstruction Acts of Congress, the court declared that Congress had the duty to provide guarantees of republican governments in the states.

1869. VEAZIE BANK v. FENNO (8 Wallace 533) dealt with the prohibitive 10% tax levied by Congress on state bank notes to promote the national banking system initiated during the Civil War. Chief Justice Chase, for the majority, upheld the tax as a legitimate exercise both of Congress' taxing power and of its authority to provide for a sound national currency.

1870. 1ST LEGAL TENDER CASE: **Hepburn v. Griswold** (8 Wallace 603). By a 5–3 decision, the court held unconstitutional the Legal Tender Acts (1862, 1863), insofar as fulfillment of contracts made before their passage was concerned, as violating the obligation of contracts and due process clauses of the 5th Amendment. The minority held these acts to be legitimate exercises of the war power.

1871. 2D LEGAL TENDER CASE: **Knox v. Lee, Parker v. Davis** (12 Wallace 457). Two new justices, J. P. Bradley and W. Strong, appointed by Grant, joined the minority of the **Hepburn** case to reverse the latter ruling. Legal tender was validated as a justifiable exercise of the national government's powers in time of emergency, not limited to war. While there is no evidence that Grant "packed the court," he made no secret of his disapproval of the **Hepburn** decision, and was aware how his appointees stood on the issue.

1871. COLLECTOR v. DAY (11 Wallace 113). By an 8–1 decision, the court held invalid a federal income tax on the salary of a state official. From this decision there grew a large area of intergovernmental tax immunities, which was not ended until the **Graves** case (1939).

1873. SLAUGHTERHOUSE CASES (16 Wallace 36) were the first judicial pronouncement on the 14th Amendment. A monopoly grant of the Louisiana legislature was contested as a violation of the privileges and immunities clause of that amendment. By a 5–4 decision, the court upheld the grant. For the majority, Justice Miller distinguished between state and national citizenship. Only the rights deriving from federal citizenship were protected by the 14th Amendment, and those rights were narrowly defined. This interpretation placed the great body of civil rights under the protection of the state governments. The court refused to consider the due process clause as a general substantive limitation upon the regulatory powers of the states, and held that the equal protection clause applied solely to state laws which discriminated against Negroes. The dissenting jurists held that the 14th Amendment was a safeguard against state violations of the privileges and immunities of U.S. citizens, and that impairment of property rights by statute violated due process.

1877. GRANGER CASES: Munn v. Illinois (94 U.S. 113). This case (one of a group known collectively as the Granger cases) involved an Illinois law (1873) fixing maximum rates for grain storage. Chief Justice Waite, for the court, upheld the law as a legitimate expression of the state's police power in regulating **businesses affected with ". . . a public interest."** He declared that appeal was "to the polls, not to the courts," and denied that the due process clause was substantively violated or that state regulation of intrastate commerce impaired Congress' unilateral control over interstate commerce. In dissent, Justice Field asserted that procedural due process was insufficient protection for property rights.

1881. SPRINGER v. U.S. (102 U.S. 586) upheld the constitutionality of the federal income tax adopted during the Civil War on the ground that it was not a direct tax within the meaning of the Constitution, and did not require apportionment among the states in proportion to population.

1883. CIVIL RIGHTS CASES (109 U.S. 3) were 5 cases where Negroes had been refused equal accommodations or privileges, allegedly in defiance of the 1875 Civil Rights Act. That act was declared invalid for protecting social rather than political rights. The court held that the 14th Amendment prohibited invasion **by the states** of civil rights, but did not protect the invasion of civil rights **by individuals** unaided by state authority. This ruling virtually ended for 80 years federal attempts to protect the Negro against discrimination by private persons.

1884. JUILLIARD v. GREENMAN (110 U.S. 421). In issue was the 1878 Act of Congress which provided that Civil War legal tender notes should not be retired, but kept in circulation. Justice Gray for the court upheld the act on the ground that the power of Congress to make notes legal tender was derived from its constitutional authority to provide a uniform national currency and did not rest solely on the war power. Dissenting, Justice Field stressed the alleged dangers of a doctrine which gave to government ". . . the power to alter the conditions of contracts."

1884. KU KLUX KLAN CASES: Ex parte Yarbrough (110 U.S. 651) upheld Congress' power to punish as a crime against federal law private interference with the right of an American citizen to vote in a federal election. Such right, held Justice Miller, is dependent on the Constitution and laws of the U.S., and not exclusively on state law.

1886. SANTA CLARA CO. v. SOUTHERN PACIFIC R.R. CO. (118 U.S. 394). In 1882 in **San Mateo Co. v. Southern Pacific R.R. Co.** (116 U.S. 138), Roscoe Conkling, counsel for the railroad and ex-senator from New York, contended that in congressional committee the word "persons" in the 14th Amendment had been chosen to extend the protection of the due process clause to legal persons, i.e., corporations. In the **Santa Clara Co.** case Chief Justice Waite, for the court, by way of dictum, announced acceptance of this doctrine, and thereby encouraged the substantive interpretation of the due process clause as a defense of corporate property rights.

1886. WABASH, ST. LOUIS & PACIFIC R.R. CO. v. ILLINOIS (118 U.S. 557) involved the validity of an Illinois statute prohibiting long-short-haul clauses in transportation contracts. The court invalidated the law as an infringement on Congress' exclusive control over interstate commerce. The decision gravely weakened the ruling in the

Granger Cases (1877) and created a "twilight zone" where neither the states nor the federal government could operate.

1890. CHICAGO, MILWAUKEE & ST. PAUL R.R. CO. v. MINNESOTA (134 U.S. 418) invalidated a Minnesota law (1887) providing for a rate-setting railroad and warehouse commission, to have final rate-fixing powers without permissible appeal to the courts, on the ground that denial of recourse to the courts was, substantively, deprivation of property without due process of law. The decision posed the question of the possibility of judicial review of rates prescribed by legislative bodies rather than by quasi-judicial commissions.

1894. REAGAN v. FARMERS' LOAN AND TRUST CO. (154 U.S. 362) upheld the right of the courts to review the fixing of rates by a Texas commission, acting under state law. Justice Brewer declared: "It has always been a part of the judcial function to determine whether the act of one party . . . operates to divest another party of any rights of person or property."

1895. U.S. v. E. C. KNIGHT CO. (156 U.S. 1) involved the first judicial interpretation of the Sherman Antitrust Act. The government charged defendant with a near monopoly of sugar refining. In an 8–1 decision against the government Chief Justice Fuller, for the majority, drew a sharp line between commerce and manufacturing. "Commerce succeeds to manufacture," he asserted, "and is not a part of it." The Sherman Act was held inapplicable to intrastate manufacturing combinations. The effect of this decision was to impair seriously enforcement of the antitrust laws, and to place most monopolies beyond the reach of federal control.

1895. INCOME TAX CASES: Pollock v. Farmers' Loan and Trust Co. (157 U.S. 429, 158 U.S. 601). These cases involved the validity of the federal income tax clauses of the Wilson-Gorman Tariff Act (1894). In the first case the Court, 6–2, declared invalid that part of the tax statute imposing a tax on income from realty and municipal bonds. Such a tax, according to the court, was a direct tax, and must be levied by apportionment among the states, while its incidence on income from municipal bonds was held a tax on an instrumentality of a state. Since no decision resulted on the issue of whether the income tax as a whole was voided, a rehearing was held. By 5–4 the court invalidated the entire tax law, holding that taxes on personal property were direct taxes. As a result, the 16th Amendment was adopted to enable the federal government to enact the income tax.

1895. IN RE DEBS (158 U.S. 564). The 1894 Pullman strike resulted in an injunction under the Sherman Antitrust Act against the union leaders. Debs, president of the American Railway Union, was cited for contempt in violating that injunction, and sued out a writ of habeas corpus in the Supreme Court. The writ was denied. The court rested its judgment not on the Sherman Act, but on the broader ground that the relations of the federal government to interstate commerce and the transportation of the mails authorized the use of the injunction to prevent forcible obstruction.

1896. PLESSY v. FERGUSON (163 U.S. 537) upheld a Louisiana law requiring segregated railroad facilities. As long as equality of accommodation existed, the court held, segregation did not constitute discrimination, and the Negro was not deprived of equal protection of the laws under the 14th Amendment.

1897. U.S. v. TRANS-MISSOURI FREIGHT ASSOCIATION (166 U.S. 290). The court ruled (5–4) an association of 18 railroads which existed to fix transportation rates to violate the Sherman Antitrust Act. The counsel for the railroads pleaded the "rule of reason"—that only those combinations were illegal which were in unreasonable restraint of trade. Although rejected in this instance, this doctrine was later to rule the court.

1898. HOLDEN v. HARDY (169 U.S. 366) upheld (7–2) the validity of a Utah law (1896) limiting maximum work hours in mining industries as a reasonable exercise of the state's police functions. The right of freedom of contract must be modified when inequalities of bargaining power exist, the majority held. In addition, the court stressed the peculiarly hazardous nature of the mining industry. This case served as a precedent for state regulation of labor conditions.

1898. SMYTH v. AMES (169 U.S. 466) invalidated a Nebraska act of 1893 which had fixed railroad rates, on the ground that it constituted a deprivation of property without due process as guaranteed by the 14th Amendment. In order to be reasonable the rates fixed must yield a "fair" return on a "fair value" of the property involved. The rule was so vague as to leave to the courts for determination in each case the fairness of the rates contested.

1899. ADDYSTON PIPE AND STEEL CO. v. U.S. (175 U.S. 211) invalidated a market-allocation scheme as an infringement of the Sherman Act and as directly affecting interstate commerce. The ruling restored a degree of effectiveness to the Sherman Act, which had been impaired by the ruling in the **Knight** case (1895).

1901. INSULAR CASES: De Lima v. Bidwell (182 U.S. 1). The court ruled (5–4) that Puerto Rico ceased to be a foreign nation at the formal close of the Spanish-American War. Thus, duties could not be levied upon goods imported from Puerto Rico without congressional authority. **Dooley v. U.S.** (182 U.S. 222) held that U.S. goods shipped into Puerto Rico were free of duty. But **Downes v. Bidwell** (182 U.S. 244) asserted the principle that the Constitution did not automatically and immediately apply to the people of an annexed territory, nor did it confer upon them all the privileges of U.S. citizenship, but that it was for Congress specifically to extend such constitutional provisions as it saw fit.

1903. LOTTERY CASE: Champion v. Ames (188 U.S. 321) upheld (5–4) a federal law prohibiting the dissemination of lottery tickets through the mails under the commerce power, which, according to the majority, implied the power to prohibit as well as to regulate. For the minority, Chief Justice Fuller attacked the intent of the law as an infringement upon the police powers of the states under the guise of regulating interstate commerce. What was to become known as a "federal police power" was given judicial sanction by this case.

1904. NORTHERN SECURITIES CO. v. U.S. (193 U.S. 197) rejuvenated the dormant Sherman Antitrust Act and upheld (5–4) the government in its suit against the railroad holding company. The majority held that stock transactions constituting an illegal combination (whether reasonable or unreasonable) in restraint of interstate commerce came within the scope of the Sherman Act. Justice Holmes, in dissent, pleaded for the "rule of reason."

1905. SWIFT & CO. v. U.S. (196 U.S. 375) upheld unanimously the government's antitrust prosecution of the "Beef Trust." For the court, Justice Holmes expounded the "stream of commerce" concept, according to which certain local business agreements are regarded as integral parts of interstate commerce.

1905. LOCHNER v. NEW YORK (198 U.S. 45) involved the validity of a New York maximum-hours law for bakers. A bare majority of the court held the law invalid as an unreasonable interference with the right of free contract, and an excessive use of the state's police powers. In a notable dissent, Justice Holmes criticized the majority's decision as based ". . . upon an economic theory which a large part of the country does not entertain. . . . The 14th Amendment does not enact Mr. Herbert Spencer's Social Statics." He insisted that the Constitution "is not intended to embody a particular economic theory, whether of paternalism . . . or of *laissez-faire.*"

1908. ADAIR v. U.S. (208 U.S. 161). The Erdman Act (1898) prohibited railroads engaged in interstate commerce from requiring as a condition of employment an agreement ("yellow-dog" contract) by workers not to join a labor union. The court (6–2) invalidated this provision as an unreasonable violation of freedom of contract and property rights guaranteed by the 5th Amendment. Union membership, according to the majority, was not a subject of interstate commerce.

1908. LOEWE v. LAWLER (208 U.S. 274). This **"Danbury Hatters Case"** resulted in a unanimous decision by the court that a **secondary boycott** (initiated 1902) by a labor union was a conspiracy in restraint of trade within the meaning of the Sherman Act. This was the first time the act was applied to labor organizations.

1908. MULLER v. OREGON (208 U.S. 412) upheld an Oregon law limiting maximum working hours of women and denied that it impaired the liberty of contract guaranteed by the 14th Amendment. Notable was the use by Louis D. Brandeis, counsel for the state, of a brief (**"Brandeis Brief"**) which amassed statistical, historical, sociologi-

cal, and economic data to support his contentions, rather than traditional legal arguments.

1911. U.S. v. GRIMAUD (220 U.S. 506) upheld the validity of federal laws (1891, 1905) relating to the disposition and administration of public lands which vested the executive with a substantial measure of administrative discretion. The court distinguished between "administrative discretion" and outright delegation of legislative power (the latter declared unconstitutional).

1911. STANDARD OIL CO. OF NEW JERSEY ET AL. v. U.S. (221 U.S. 1) upheld the dissolution of the company, applying the "rule of reason" to the Sherman Act. Harlan, in dissent, denounced the ruling as judicial usurpation.

1911. U.S. v. AMERICAN TOBACCO CO. (221 U.S. 106) ordered the reorganization of the "tobacco trust" rather than its complete dissolution on the basis of the "rule of reason" (White).

1913. MINNESOTA RATE CASES (230 U.S. 252) sustained the validity of an order by a state commission setting intrastate railroad rates. The court held that, while Congress' authority over interstate commerce was exclusive, a state might properly act in a field where it did not conflict with federal laws.

1917. WILSON v. NEW (243 U.S. 332). Chief Justice White, for a bare majority of the court, upheld the constitutionality of the Adamson Eight-Hour Act (1916), which specified 8 hours as a day's work on railroads operating in interstate commerce. Despite the fact that this was in effect a wage-fixing measure, the court held that in an emergency Congress might establish a temporary standard.

1918. ARVER v. U.S. (245 U.S. 366), among the **Selective Draft Law Cases**, sustained the World War I conscription act. The power of a nation to secure military service from its residents was an incidence of sovereignty, the court found, as well as a direct result of the Constitutional authorization to Congress "to declare war . . . to raise and support armies" (Art. 1, Sec. 8). Similarly, in 1919, in the **War Prohibition Cases** (251 U.S. 146), the court upheld the wartime prohibition measure as a legitimate exercise of the war power of the government. Again in 1919, the power granted the president to seize and operate the railroads in wartime was upheld under the war power in **Northern Pacific Railway Co. v. North Dakota** (250 U.S. 585).

1918. HAMMER v. DAGENHART (247 U.S. 251). The Keating-Owen Child Labor Act (1916) forbade interstate shipment of products of child labor. The court split 5–4 on the issue of mutually restrictive areas of federal-state operations. Justice Day, for the majority, declared the act invalid as a regulation of local labor conditions rather than commerce. Holmes' dissent upheld Congress' right to regulate interstate commerce in unqualified terms, including the power to prohibit. **Bailey v. Drexel Furniture Co.** (259 U.S. 20), in 1922, involved the second Child Labor Act (1919), which levied prohibitive taxes upon the products of child labor in interstate commerce. Chief Justice Taft spoke for the majority of the court in holding the law invalid on much the same grounds as in the **Hammer** decision.

1919. SCHENCK v. U.S. (249 U.S. 47). For a unanimous court, Justice Holmes upheld the wartime Espionage Act as not violating the 1st Amendment. Applying the "clear and present danger" test, Holmes found that Schenck's pamphlets encouraged real resistance to the draft; that free speech is always under restraint, especially in time of war.

1919. ABRAMS v. U.S. (250 U.S. 616) upheld the 1918 Sedition Law. Applying the "bad tendency" test, Justice Clarke, for the majority, found pamphlets which criticized the U.S. expeditionary force to Siberia as falling within the scope of that act and held that the invoking of disaffection during wartime was not protected by the 1st Amendment. Holmes' dissenting opinion became a classic philosophical argument for freedom of speech ("the best test of truth is the power of the thought to get itself accepted in the competition of the market").

1920. MISSOURI v. HOLLAND (252 U.S. 416), involving the constitutionality of the Migratory Bird Treaty of 3 July 1918, which sought to enforce a convention between the U.S. and Canada, held (7–2) that a treaty conferred powers upon Congress which it might not possess otherwise. Holmes for the majority asserted that treaties are made under the authority of the U.S., while acts of Congress are enacted under the authority of the Constitution. By implication, the powers of the central government are almost limitless if written into a treaty.

1921. DUPLEX PRINTING PRESS CO. v. DEERING (254 U.S. 443), the first court pronouncement on the labor provisions of the Clayton Act, held that secondary boycotts were still enjoinable despite the anti-injunction provision of that act. As a result, the Clayton Act furnished meager protection for labor union practices held by the courts to constitute illegal obstructions to interstate commerce and violations of the antitrust laws. In **Truax v. Corrigan** (257 U.S. 312), 1921, the court invalidated a state statute forbidding the granting of injunctions against picketing as violating the due process and equal protection clauses of the 14th Amendment.

1923. MASSACHUSETTS v. MEL-LON (262 U.S. 447) involved the validity of the grants-in-aid provisions of the Sheppard-Towner Maternity Act, which the state attacked as coercion upon the states by the central government. While denying jurisdiction, the court (Justice George Sutherland) impliedly upheld the legitimacy of such grants. Since that date grants-in-aid have formed a vast complex of federal-state-municipal relationships.

1923. ADKINS v. CHILDREN'S HOSPITAL (261 U.S. 525) invalidated, as infringing upon the 5th Amendment, an act of Congress (1918) authorizing the Wage Board for the District of Columbia to fix minimum wages for women. In dissent Holmes stated: "The criterion of constitutionality is not whether we believe the law to be for the public good."

1923. WOLFF PACKING CO. v. COURT OF INDUSTRIAL RELATIONS (262 U.S. 522) restricted the concept of public interest to the narrow monopoly definition. A mere declaration by a legislature that a business is affected with a public interest is not conclusive of the question whether its regulation is justified, declared Chief Justice Taft. Holmes' dissent in 1927 in **Tyson and Bros. v. Banton** (273 U.S. 418), where the court invalidated a New York law regulating resale theater ticket prices, attacked the doctrine of public interest and insisted that the state legislature could do whatever it saw fit unless specifically restrained by the Constitution. By 1934, in **Nebbia v. New York** (291 U.S. 502), involving a state law fixing retail milk prices, the majority (Roberts) upheld the right of the state to correct maladjustments in industries subject to regulation in the public interest, following Holmes' view that there is no closed category of business affected with a public interest.

1925–1932. GITLOW v. NEW YORK (268 U.S. 652), 1925; **WHITNEY v. CALIFORNIA** (274 U.S. 357), 1927; **STROMBERG v. CALIFORNIA** (283 U.S. 359), 1931; **NEAR v. MINNESOTA** (283 U.S. 697), 1931; **POWELL v. ALABAMA (1ST SCOTTSBORO CASE** [287 U.S. 45]), 1932—all extended the 14th Amendment to cover the 1st as well as an uncertain number of the remaining sections of the Bill of Rights.

1935. GOLD CASES—Perry v. U.S. (294 U.S. 330), **U.S. v. Bankers Trust Co.** (294 U.S. 240), **Norman v. Baltimore & Ohio R.R. Co.** (294 U.S. 240), **Nortz v. U.S.** (294 U.S. 317)—involved the constitutionality of the congressional joint resolution of 5 June 1933 which nullified the gold clause in private and public contracts. The government's power to so act in private contracts was affirmed in the **Bankers Trust, Norman,** and **Nortz** cases. In the **Perry** case Chief Justice Hughes held that government bonds were contractual obligations of the U.S. government. Hence, the joint resolution was unconstitutional. But since the plaintiff had suffered no more than nominal damages he could not sue in the Court of Claims. In effect, the government was upheld.

1935. SCHECHTER v. U.S. ("Sick Chicken Case" [295 U.S. 495]) unanimously invalidated the NIRA on 3 grounds (Chief Justice Hughes): (1) the excessive delegation of legislative power to the executive, (2) the lack of constitutional authority for such legislation, and (3) the regulation of businesses wholly intrastate in character.

1935. RETIREMENT BOARD v. ALTON R.R. Co. (295 U.S. 330) invalidated (5–4) the Railroad Retirement Act as violating due process and the 5th Amendment and involving matters (pensions) outside the federal commerce power (Justice Roberts).

1936. U.S. v. BUTLER (297 U.S. 1) invalidated (6–3) the AAA on the ground (Justice Roberts) that the processing tax in issue was not really a tax but a part of a system for regulating agricultural production and not within the purview of the welfare clause. Justice Stone in dissent attacked the trend toward judicial legislation. By the Soil Conservation and Domestic Allotment Act (1936) and the Second AAA (1938) the court's objections were met.

1936. U.S. v. CURTISS-WRIGHT EXPORT CORP. (299 U.S. 304) upheld an embargo imposed on arms destined for nations at war in the Chaco (Paraguay and Bolivia) under authorization of a Congressional joint resolution. Justice Sutherland deemed the resolution a proper delegation of legislative power to the president, holding further that the power of the U.S. to conduct foreign relations did not derive from the enumerated powers of the Constitution, but that the transfer of external sovereignty had been effected by the American Revolution.

1936. ASHWANDER v. TVA (297 U.S. 288) upheld the dams built under the TVA as legitimate exercise of the federal government's power to control navigable streams and provide for adequate national defense.

1937. NEW DEAL CASES. During the struggle over President Roosevelt's court reorganization plan (p. 420) the court upheld a series of important New Deal measures. **West Coast Hotel Co. v. Parris** (300 U.S. 379) upheld (5–4) a Washington minimum wage law, overruling the **Adkins** precedent. The National Labor Relations Act was upheld (5–4) in **NLRB v. Jones and Laughlin Steel Corp.** (301 U.S. 1), where the majority stressed the broadest definition of the "stream of commerce" concept, and (5–4) in **NLRB v. Friedman-Harry Marks Clothing Co.** (301 U.S. 58), despite the local nature of the respondent's operations. The social security laws were upheld in **Steward Machine Co. v. Davis** (301 U.S. 548) and **Helvering v. Davis** (301 U.S. 619), by 5–4 in each instance. The **Steward** case upheld both the employer tax and the conditional federal grant-in-aid. Justice Cardozo found no coercion of the states involved in such grants. The **Helvering** case upheld the old-age and benefit provisions.

1937–43. CIVIL LIBERTIES CASES. De Jonge v. Oregon (299 U.S. 253), 1937, voided a conviction under an Oregon criminal syndicalist law by insisting that there was not a "clear and present danger" in a speech at an orderly meeting. **Herndon v. Lowry** (301 U.S. 242), 1937, reversed a Georgia conviction of a Communist organizer, with the court squarely applying the "clear and present danger" doctrine. The **Flag Salute Cases: The Gobitis Case** (310 U.S. 586), 1940, sustained a state flag salute law; but this decision was reversed in **West Virginia State Board of Education v. Barnette** (319 U.S. 624), 1943, where a state law was invalidated as infringing the 1st Amendment.

Palko v. Connecticut (302 U.S. 319), 1937, held that the 14th Amendment did not include the double jeopardy provision of the 5th Amendment (a state could retry a person on criminal charges after he had been found innocent), but opened the way for the court to investigate the scope of basic liberties which the states by the 14th Amendment were forbidden to infringe: (1) Peaceful picketing—**Thornhill v. Alabama** (310 U.S. 88), 1940. (2) Peaceable assemblage—**Hague v. C.I.O.** (207 U.S. 496), 1939. (3) the **Jehovah's Witnesses Cases** generally reaffirmed the right to disseminate religious literature without a license (**Lovell v. Griffin** [303 U.S. 444], 1938), and to solicit funds for religious ends (**Cantwell v.**

Connecticut [310 U.S. 396], 1940) and without being subject to a tax (**Murdock v. Pennsylvania** [319 U.S. 105], 1943).

1938. MISSOURI EX REL. GAINES v. CANADA (305 U.S. 337) upheld the "equality" of educational opportunity for Negroes in segregated Missouri, specifically the petitioner's right to be admitted to the law school of the state university in the absence of other provision for his legal training; reaffirmed in **Sipuel v. University of Oklahoma** (332 U.S. 631), 1948.

1939. GRAVES v. NEW YORK EX REL. O'KEEFE (306 U.S. 466) put an end to intergovernmental tax immunities, which had deprived federal and state governments of large potential sources of revenue, by holding that a state tax on federal employees was no unconstitutional burden upon the federal government.

1941. U.S. v. CLASSIC (313 U.S. 299) upheld the power of the federal government to regulate a state primary where such an election was an integral part of the machinery for choosing a candidate for federal office, reversing a previous decision that party primaries were private affairs.

1941. EDWARDS v. CALIFORNIA (314 U.S. 160) invalidated California's anti-"Okie" law designed to exclude indigent immigrants as a barrier to interstate commerce. In **Morgan v. Virginia** (328 U.S. 373), 1946, a Jim Crow law was voided as a barrier upon interstate commerce.

1941. U.S. v. DARBY (312 U.S. 100) unanimously overruled the **Hammer** case (1918) by upholding the Fair Labor Standards Act of 1938. Commerce was held a complete function, controllable by Congress to the point of prohibition. This decision repudiated the doctrine of mutually exclusive spheres of federal and state activities.

1943. HIRABAYASHI v. U.S. (320 U.S. 81) upheld military curfew regula-

tions on the West Coast under the war powers, but refused to consider the issue of Japanese exclusion from that area.

1944. KOREMATSU v. U.S. (323 U.S. 214) upheld the exclusion of Japanese from the West Coast. The dissenters (Roberts, Murphy, and Jackson) termed the relocation program unconstitutional. In **Ex parte Endo** (323 U.S. 283), 1944, however, it was held that the War Relocation Authority could not detain a person whose loyalty had been established.

1944. SMITH v. ALLWRIGHT (321 U.S. 649) involved the exclusion of Negroes from voting in a primary in Texas, where Democratic party membership was restricted to whites. The court held that in Texas political party membership was equivalent to suffrage; hence, exclusion from the party on grounds of race violated the 15th Amendment.

1947. FRIEDMAN v. SCHWELLENBACH (330 U.S. 838). The court here refused to review a lower court decision involving the dismissal of a federal civil servant on disloyalty charges, and in effect upheld the president's 1947 Loyalty Order authorizing such removal.

1947. U.S. v. CALIFORNIA (332 U.S. 19) rejected California's claim to the 3-mile marginal belt along its coast, Justice Black holding that protection and control of the belt was a function of national external sovereignty. Similarly, Louisiana's seaward claims were denied in **U.S. v. Louisiana** (339 U.S. 699), 1950, as well as those of **Texas** (339 U.S. 706), 1950, despite the latter's claim that it had enjoyed control over the marginal sea when it was an independent sovereign state. Such claims, the court held, were impliedly relinquished as a condition of statehood.

1948. ILLINOIS EX REL. McCOLLUM v. BOARD OF EDUCATION (333 U.S. 203) involved the "released time" plan (in this instance permitting public school students to receive religious instruction during school hours on school property but with private teachers). The court held this particular program violated the 1st Amendment prescribing separation of church and state, but left open the larger question of public aid to religious instruction. A New York released-time law was upheld (**Zorach v. Clauson,** 1952).

1948. SHELLEY v. KRAEMER (334 U.S. 1) held that a racially restrictive covenant violated the equal protection clause of the 14th Amendment.

1950. AMERICAN COMMUNICATIONS ASSN., C.I.O., ET AL. v. DOUDS (339 U.S. 382) upheld Sec. 9h of the Taft-Hartley Act (1947), requiring a non-Communist affidavit from labor union officers under penalty of denying to the union involved certain statutory privileges. The majority denied that the oath was ex post facto, a bill of attainder, or an abridgement of the 1st Amendment. Justice Black in dissent stigmatized test oaths as "instrument[s] for inflicting penalties and disabilities on obnoxious minorities."

1951. DENNIS ET AL. v. U.S. (341 U.S. 494) upheld the Smith Act (1946), which made it a criminal offense to advocate the forceful overthrow of the government. Implicit in the majority opinion of Chief Justice Vinson was a revival of the "bad tendency" test criticized by Holmes. Dissenting, Justice Black called for a return to the "clear and present danger" doctrine and declared the Smith Act violated the 1st Amendment, and Justice Douglas differentiated between a "conspiracy to overthrow" the government and the teaching of "Marxist-Leninist doctrine."

1952. SAWYER, PETITIONER v. YOUNGSTOWN SHEET & TUBE CO., ET AL. (STEEL SEIZURE CASE, [343 U.S. 579]) invalidated (6–3) the seizure of the steel companies by President Truman. Justice Black, for the majority, held that the president's power "must stem

either from an act of Congress or from the Constitution itself." Chief Justice Vinson, for the minority, argued that there was no statute prohibiting seizure "as a method of enforcing legislative programs."

1954. BROWN v. BOARD OF EDUCATION OF TOPEKA (347 U.S. 483) reversed **Plessy v. Ferguson** (1896), with its "separate but equal" doctrine. In 1950 **McLaurin v. Okla. State Regents** (339 U.S. 637) and **Sweatt v. Painter** (339 U.S. 629) had struck down state laws for the higher or professional education of Negroes as failing to meet the requirements of equality. In the Brown case, involving elementary education, the court (Warren, Chief Justice) held unanimously that segregation in public education was a denial of the equal protection of the laws. The court (349 U.S. 294), 1955, directed the lower courts to admit Negroes to public schools on a racially nondiscriminatory basis "with all deliberate speed." Reactions ranged from compliance in some border states to hostile gestures toward the court. On 19 Jan. 1956, the Alabama Senate passed a "nullification" resolution; the Virginia legislature adopted (1 Feb.) an "interposition" resolution asserting the right of the state to "interpose its sovereignty" against the decision of the court. On 11 Mar., 19 senators and 81 representatives issued a **"Southern Manifesto"** declaring their purpose to use "all lawful means" to reverse the desegregation decision. **Cooper v. Aaron** (358 U.S. 1), 1958, held that no scheme of racial discrimination against Negro children in school attendance can stand the test of the 14th Amendment if "there is state participation through any arrangement, management, funds or property."

1956. PENNSYLVANIA v. NELSON (350 U.S. 497) found Pennsylvania's antisubversive legislation, to the extent that it punished subversion against the U.S., to be unconstitutional, on the ground that Congress had preempted antisubversion enforcement. Since this is a field in which national interest is dominant, the federal system must be assumed to preclude enforcement of state laws on the same subject.

1957. WATKINS v. U.S. (354 U.S. 178) reversed a contempt conviction of a labor union official who had testified before the House Committee on Un-American Activities about his earlier activities with respect to the Communist party, but refused to name others on the ground that such questions were not relevant to the work of the committee. The court sustained Watkins on the ground of the lack of pertinency of the subject under inquiry and held that the resolution setting up the committee in 1938 was too vague and uncertain to give Watkins sufficient indication of the matter under inquiry.

1957. YATES v. U.S. (354 U.S. 298) held that the government had too broadly construed its powers under the Smith Act to prosecute Communist leaders. Since the **Dennis Case** (1951), nearly 100 convictions and many more indictments had been obtained for Smith Act violations. The court ruled that the Smith Act did not forbid advocacy and teaching of forcible overthrow as an abstract principle, divorced from any effort to incite action to that end.

1958. NAACP v. ALABAMA (357 U.S. 449). In reversing a contempt conviction by an Alabama court the Supreme Court held that the NAACP had a constitutional right to claim protection for its membership and to refuse to divulge its membership list.

1959. ABBATE v. U.S. (359 U.S. 187) and **BARTKUS v. ILLINOIS** (359 U.S. 121) held that neither the constitutional prohibition against double jeopardy nor the guarantee of due process prevented the federal and state govern-

ments from successively prosecuting the same man for the same criminal act.

1959. BARENBLATT v. U.S. (360 U.S. 109) upheld the conviction (under 2 U.S. Code 192) of a university teaching fellow who refused to answer questions on Communist affiliation asked by the House Committee on Un-American Activities on the ground that the balance of defendant's and the government's interest is struck in favor of the government, and that the conviction does not transgress the 1st Amendment. Contrariwise, 3 justices (Justice Black) held that the committee was improperly seeking to try, convict, and punish, powers denied a legislative body.

1960. BOYNTON v. VIRGINIA (81 Sup. Ct. Rep. 182) extended **Morgan v. Va.** (1946) in holding that a bus terminal operated as an "integral" part of interstate bus service may not segregate passengers who are on a trip across state lines.

1961–72. CRIMINAL CASES extended coverage of 14th Amendment to include: (1) Federal Exclusionary Rule (evidence secured by state officers through unreasonable search and seizure must be excluded from the trial): **Mapp v. Ohio** (367 U.S. 643), 1961, overturning **Wolf v. Colo.** (338 U.S. 25), 1949; (2) right to court-appointed counsel in state felony prosecution of indigent defendant: **Gideon v. Wainright** (372 U.S. 335), 1963, overturning **Betts v. Brady** (316 U.S. 455), 1942; **Gideon** extended by **Argersinger v. Hamlin** (407 U.S. 25), 1972, to all offenses potentially punishable by a jail sentence; (3) 5th Amendment protection against compelled self-incrimination: **Malloy v. Hogan** (378 U.S. 1), 1964; (4) statements obtained by the police when a suspect is in custody are inadmissible as evidence unless the suspect prior to interrogation is clearly informed (a) of his right to remain silent, (b) that anything he says may be used against him, (c) of his right to consult with an attorney, and (d) of his right, if indigent, to a lawyer appointed for him. Counsel may be present during questioning, **Miranda v. Arizona** (384 U.S. 436), 1966.

1962. ENGEL v. VITALE (370 U.S. 421), considering New York State Board of Regents' prayer, held that "it is no part of the business of government to compose official prayers to be recited as a part of a religious program carried on by government." Readings of the Lord's Prayer and daily Bible readings were struck down in **School Dist. of Abington Township v. Schempp** (373 U.S. 930), 1963.

1962–64. REAPPORTIONMENT DECISIONS. Baker v. Carr (369 U.S. 186), 1962, held that federal courts must consider on merits suits challenging apportionment of state legislatures as allegedly violating equal protection clause of 14th Amendment. In disposing of 14 such suits in June, 1964, the court held that those states did not meet the requirements of the clause; that both houses of the state legislature must be apportioned on basis of equal protection as nearly as possible (**Reynolds v. Sims** [377 U.S. 533]). Not even the electorate's approval by referendum of an apportionment plan can validate it if it is discriminatory (**Lucas v. Colo. Gen. Assembly** [377 U.S. 713]). Court also held that congressional districts must be equal in population "as nearly as practicable" (**Westberry v. Sanders** [376 U.S. 1], 1964).

1964. NEW YORK TIMES v. SULLIVAN (376 U.S. 254) held that public officials acting in their public capacity could recover in libel actions only by proof of publication of defamatory falsehood with actual malice. The rule was extended in later cases to encompass suits brought by public figures: **Curtis**

Publishing Co. v. Butts (388 U.S. 130), 1967, and to private persons, if the statements concerned matter of public interest: **Rosenbloom v. Metromedia, Inc.** (403 U.S. 29), 1971. In **Gertz v. Robert Welch, Inc.** (418 U.S. 323), 1974, the court moved away from *Rosenbloom,* refusing to apply the **New York Times v. Sullivan** rule to private individuals where an interest of general or public concern is involved.

1964. HEART OF ATLANTA MOTEL, INC. v. U.S. (379 U.S. 241) upheld constitutionality of Public Accommodations Title of 1964 Civil Rights Act.

1964. GRISWOLD v. CONNECTICUT (381 U.S. 479) held unconstitutional the Connecticut birth control statute, which banned the use of contraceptives and the giving of medical advice as to their use as a violation of marital privacy emanating from the 1st, 3rd, 5th, 9th, and 14th Amendments. **Griswold** was expanded by **Eisenstadt v. Baird** (405 U.S. 438), 1972, holding state ban on distribution of contraceptives violated equal protection clause.

1966. SOUTH CAROLINA v. KATZENBACH (383 U.S. 301) upheld the constitutionality of provisions of the Voting Rights Act of 1965 (p. 531).

1966. SHEPPARD v. MAXWELL (384 U.S. 333) reversed the murder conviction of Dr. Samuel Sheppard on grounds that he was deprived of a fair trial because of the massive prejudicial newspaper publicity which had taken place during the trial.

1966. A BOOK NAMED "JOHN CLELAND'S MEMOIRS OF A WOMAN OF PLEASURE" v. ATTORNEY-GENERAL OF MASSACHUSETTS (383 U.S. 413) continued the court's trend of hostility to the censorship of books by reversing the Massachusetts Supreme Judicial Court's holding that Cleland's *Fanny Hill* was obscene. The book was deemed not to be "utterly without redeeming social value," the test of **Roth v. United States** (345 U.S. 476), 1957.

1966–67. ANTI-MERGER CASES. Mergers and other centralizing business practices were attacked in a series of cases: (1) **U.S. v. Pabst Brewing Co.** (384 U.S. 546), 1966, where Pabst acquisition of Blatz Brewing Co. was held to have violated Sect. 7 of the Clayton Act. (2) **Federal Trade Commission v. Brown Shoe Co.** (384 U.S. 316), 1966, where the franchise program of the nation's largest shoe manufacturer was held to have violated Sect. 5 of the Federal Trade Commission Act barring unfair trade practices as well as sections of the Sherman and the Clayton acts. (3) **Federal Trade Commission v. Borden Co.** (383 U.S. 637), 1966, held that Borden's practice of marketing its milk under its own name and private brand names for customers was price discrimination tending to lessen competition substantially, thus violating Sect. 2(a) of the Robinson-Patman Act. (4) **Federal Trade Commission v. Procter & Gamble Co.** (386 U.S. 568), 1967, held that the acquisition of Clorox, a leading manufacturer of household liquid bleach, by Procter & Gamble might have substantially anticompetitive effects and therefore violated Sect. 7 of the Clayton Act.

1967. IN RE GAULT (387 U.S. 1) struck a blow at widespread juvenile court practices by finding that the Arizona Juvenile Court violated the 14th Amendment by failing to provide adequately for notice of hearings, right of counsel, right of confrontation, cross-examination of witnesses, and exercise of the privilege against self-incrimination.

1967. LOVING v. VIRGINIA (388 U.S. 1) held the Virginia antimiscegenation statute unconstitutional. Such schemes, said Chief Justice Warren, to prevent the marriage of persons solely on the basis of racial classifications violated the 14th Amendment.

1968. PENN CENTRAL & N&W INCLUSION CASES (389 U.S. 486) upheld the merger between the Pennsylvania R.R. Co. and the New York Central R.R. Co. and the inclusion of 3 small lines in the N&W system.

1969. STANLEY v. GEORGIA (394 U.S. 557) held unconstitutional statutes making it a crime to privately possess obscene material as a government intrusion into the privacy of one's home and an impermissible inquiry into what one might read or see.

1969. POWELL v. McCORMICK (395 U.S. 486). The House of Representatives voted to exclude Rep. Adam Clayton Powell, Jr. of New York from the 90th Congress (1 Mar. 1967) for misconduct. The Supreme Court held (1) that Powell had been improperly excluded; (2) that a suit was properly maintainable only against the employees of the House of Representatives as the representatives themselves were immune from suits for their legislative actions; (3) that the case did not present a "political question" as it required only a constitutional adjudication by the court. Powell was sworn in (3 Jan. 1969) at the beginning of the 91st Congress but fined $25,000. A later court decision refused to award Powell back pay or lost seniority.

1969–71. DESEGREGATION DECISIONS. Alexander v. Holmes County Board of Education (396 U.S. 19), 1969, turned down Nixon administration request for delay in desegregation of 33 Mississippi school systems holding that "the obligation of every school district is to terminate dual systems at once and to operate now and hereafter only unitary schools." **Swann v. Charlotte-Mecklenburg Board of Education** (402 U.S. 1), 1971, held that busing, balancing ratios, and gerrymandered school districts were all permissible methods of ending state-imposed segregation.

1969–72. ANTITRUST DECISIONS included (1) **Citizen Publishing Co. v. United States** (394 U.S. 131), 1969, applied to merger between advertising and circulation departments of newspapers where price-fixing, market control, and pooling of profits were involved: (2) **Federal Trade Commission v. Sperry and Hutchinson Co.** (405 U.S. 233), 1972, held FTC empowered to protect consumer and judge business practice against standards of fair competition; (3) **Flood v. Kuhn** (407 U.S. 258), 1972, held that Congress has acquiesced in exemption of baseball and its reserve clause from the antitrust laws; (4) **United States v. Topco Associates** (405 U.S. 596), 1972, held that territorial allocations among distributors are unlawful.

1969–73. POVERTY-WELFARE DECISIONS. The court generally expanded the rights of the poor in a series of decisions holding (1) that a state cannot constitutionally allow garnishment without prior notice and hearing: **Sniadach v. Family Finance Corp.** (395 U.S. 337), 1969; (2) state laws requiring residence for 1 year prior to eligibility for welfare assistance were held to violate right to interstate travel: **Shapiro v. Thompson** (394 U.S. 618), 1969; (3) a welfare recipient is entitled to full hearing prior to termination of welfare payments: **Goldberg v. Kelly** (397 U.S. 254), 1970; (4) summary seizure of goods sold on installment purchase without prior notice and hearing is unconstitutional: **Fuentes v. Shevin** (407 U.S. 67), 1972. However, in **Wyman v. James** (400 U.S. 309), 1971, court upheld right of a state to condition welfare assistance to dependent children upon on-site visits by caseworkers, and in **United States v. Kras** (409 U.S. 434), 1973, a $50 filing fee required for filing for bankruptcy was held not to violate due process or equal protection of the laws.

1970–72. JURY TRIALS. The court held in **Williams v. Florida** (399 U.S. 78), 1970, that states could use a 6-man jury in noncapital cases. In **Johnson v. Louisiana** (406 U.S. 356) and **Apodaca v. Oregon** (406 U.S. 404), 1972, the jury trial guarantee was held not to encompass jury unanimity, 4 justices dissented. State laws providing for verdicts by votes of 11–1, 10–2, and 9–3 were upheld.

1970. OREGON v. MITCHELL (400 U.S. 112) held that Congress had power to lower the voting age in federal but not state elections. Justice Black's opinion constituted that of the court, although 4 justices held that Congress had power to accomplish both objectives, and 4 justices held that Congress lacked the power to do either. The 18-year-old vote was subsequently achieved by the 26th Amendment (1971).

1970. WALZ v. TAX COMMISSION (397 U.S. 664) upheld property tax exemptions for church-owned land used solely for religious purposes as evidence of the "benevolent neutrality" of the states and not unconstitutional under 1st Amendment, as there was but a "minimal and remote involvement between church and state" which reinforced the desired separation.

1971. ABSTENTION. In a series of cases the doctrine of **Dombrowski v. Pfister** (380 U.S. 479), 1965, permitting federal injunctions where state officials threatened or were about to commence prosecution under statutes challenged as unconstitutional, was limited and the power of federal courts to enjoin state trials was limited to (1) great and immediate threat of irreparable injury; (2) where state law is flagrantly unconstitutional on its face; (3) where there has been official lawlessness: **Younger v. Harris** (401 U.S. 37), **Perez v. Ledesma**

(401 U.S. 82), **Samuels v. Mackell** (401 U.S. 66).

1971. PENTAGON PAPERS CASE. New York Times v. United States, United States v. Washington Post. (403 U.S. 713). In 1 *per curiam* and 9 separate opinions, the court by a 6–3 vote held that the government had failed to show sufficient justification for an injunction against the publication of the Pentagon Papers (p. 537). Justices Black and Douglas stated that all attempts to enjoin publication would violate the 1st Amendment; Justice Brennan argued that even temporary stays and restraining orders would be improper. Dissenting, Justice Harlan objected to the haste of the decision (one week) and Chief Justice Burger argued that the *Times* had the duty to return the purloined documents. The "swing" justices, White and Stewart, found no immediate and irreparable damage sufficient for an injunction but indicated that criminal prosecutions for the publication under the **Espionage Act of 1917** might be proper.

1971–79. GENDER DISCRIMINATION. During 1970s Supreme Court, while extending the guarantee of equal protection to victims of sex discrimination, did not view sex as a suspect category, so that gender-based laws were not strictly scrutinized under 14th Amendment. *Reed* v. *Reed* (404 U.S. 71), 1971, held unconstitutional an Idaho statute giving father preference over mother for administering estate of child, the Court finding no rational basis for law. A Utah law requiring divorced father to support sons to age 21, but daughters only to age 18, did not meet the standard of equal protection. *Stanton* v. *Stanton* (421 U.S. 7), 1973. Mandatory maternity leave policies were held unconstitutional in *Cleveland Board of Education* v. *La Fleur* (414 U.S. 632), 1974. In *Frontiero* v. *Richardson* (411 U.S. 677), 1973, four members of the Supreme Court stated that gender-based discrimination should be subject to stricter scrutiny, justifiable only by a compelling state interest. The Supreme Court held that Title VII of the 1964 Civil Rights Act, barring sex discrimination in employment, prohibited company policy of refusing to hire women with preschool-aged children while hiring men similarly circumstanced. *Phillips* v. *Martin Marietta Corp.* (400 U.S. 542), 1971. The Court upheld the **Equal Pay Act of 1963.** *Corning Glass Works* v. *Brennan* (417 U.S. 188), 1974. Private disability insurance plan excluding pregnancy from disability benefits plan providing general coverage was held not to be discriminatory. *General Electric Co.* v. *Gilbert* (429 U.S. 125), 1976. Laws granting veterans absolute preference for civil service jobs were upheld. *Personnel Administrator of Mass.* v. *Feeney* (422 U.S. 256), 1979.

1971. GRIGGS v. DUKE POWER CO. (410 U.S. 424). Interpreting Title VII of 1964 Civil Rights Act, prohibiting discrimination in employment, a unanimous Court held that artificial, arbitrary, and unnecessary barriers to employment must be removed, if unrelated to job skills and if there is discriminatory impact.

1972–80. PRESS RIGHTS. The Supreme Court generally upheld the right of the press to be free of any kind of restraint prior to publication, while denying claims for greater access to sources of information than the general public. In *Miami Herald Publishing Co.* v. *Tornillo* (418 U.S. 241), 1974, a statute requiring newspapers to grant political candidates equal space to reply to a newspaper's criticism was held unconstitutional. In *Nebraska Press Association* v. *Stuart* (427 U.S. 539), 1976, "gag rules" (judicial orders preventing newspapers from publishing certain information about court cases) could only be justifiable in extreme cases. In *Gannett* v. *DePasquale* (433 U.S. 368), 1979, the Court held that a judge could exclude press and public from pretrial hearings in criminal cases to avoid prejudicial pretrial publicity. A year later the Court held that the public and press could be barred from a criminal trial only under the most extreme circumstances. *Richmond Newspapers Inc.* v. *Virginia* (100 Sup. Ct. 2814), 1980.

The Supreme Court held that a newspaper does not have a right of access greater than that generally afforded to the general public (*Houchins* v. *KQED* [438 U.S. 1], 1978); that reporters were not constitutionally privileged to refuse to divulge their sources to grand juries investigating a crime (*Branzburg.* v. *Hayes* [408 U.S. 665], 1972); that the 1st Amendment does not protect the editorial process from scrutiny in a libel action (*Herbert* v. *Lando* [441 U.S. 153], 1979); that the police can search a newspaper for evidence of a crime (*Zurcher* v. *Stanford Daily* [436 U.S. 547], 1978).

1972. WIRETAPPING CASES. United States v. U.S. District Court (407 U.S. 297) rejected in a unanimous opinion written by Justice Powell the Justice Department claim of inherent power to wiretap without warrant domestic groups suspected of being subversive, as a reasonable exercise of the president's power to protect national security. The court held the surveillance violative of the 4th Amendment. Addressing the **Omnibus Crime Control and Safe Street Act** (p. 536), which authorizes court-approved electronic surveillance, and noting that the act does not delimit the president's constitutional power, the court held (1) that this did not constitute a grant of authority to the president to conduct warrantless national security surveillance; (2) that the 4th Amendment contemplates a prior judicial judgment; (3) that the president's domestic security role must be exercised in a manner compatible with the 4th Amendment. In an earlier case, **Alderman v. United States** (399 U.S. 165), 1969, the court ruled that the federal government must turn over for examination to a defendant all material obtained by illegal electronic surveillance even if the surveillance involved national security. **Olmstead v. United States** (277 U.S. 438), 1929, was reversed by **Katz v. United States** (389 U.S. 347), 1967, which held that any electronic surveillance not court approved ahead of time was unreasonable search and seizure, except in national security matters.

1972–77. DEATH PENALTY CASES. *Furman* v. *Georgia* (408 U.S. 234), a 5–4 decision, held unconstitutional the imposition of the death penalty in the cases before the court, and invalidated the death penalty throughout the nation as then imposed, sparing the lives of almost 600 condemned persons. There was a *per curiam* opinion for the court and one opinion for each of the 9 justices. Justices Brennan and Marshall argued that executions are *per se* cruel and unusual punishment in violation of the 8th Amendment prohibition. Justice Douglas stated that the discretionary application of punishment affected the "poor and despised" unequally and therefore violated equal protection of the laws. Justices Stewart and White found the system as then operating "so wantonly and freakishly imposed" as to be unconstitutional under the 8th and 14th Amendments. Chief Justice Burger's dissent emphasized that capital punishment laws which did not mete out death in a random and unpredictable manner might ultimately be held constitutional.

THE AMERICAN ECONOMY

Agriculture

Once America was a nation of farmers, with agriculture the most important economic activity. By the mid-nineteenth century, agriculture's share in the national product was steadily declining—from 69% (1839) to 49% (1879). Yet even as industry grew in the nineteenth century, by the 1880s replacing agriculture as the principal contributor to national product, farming also expanded. Farm employment reached an all-time high of 13.6 million persons in 1916. For the rest of the twentieth century, agriculture came to attract a decreasing number of persons. Agricultural employment had sunk to 3.5 million persons in 1972 (and the farm population was down to 9.5 million). Of the civilian labor force in 1972, only 4% were employed in agriculture. While farm employment was dropping, for a while the amount of land in farming continued to increase, peaking with 1,183 million acres in farmland in 1959; subsequently, this figure too has declined, and in 1972 American farmland comprised 1,114 million acres. From a labor-intensive activity, agriculture became highly capital-intensive. The application of mechanization and biochemical products as well as scientific and managerial methods sharply increased agricultural productivity. In 1916 a single farm worker provided food and farm products to 7 Americans; in 1972, each farm worker served 60 persons. Over the years, land tenure, ownership relationships, and the nature of the farm labor force have sharply altered. Crops have varied in importance, with tobacco and cotton showing relative declines and soybeans becoming in the post-World War II years a leading crop. Corn and wheat were important from the colonial period to the present. Americans have come to consume more meat relative to food grains and vegetables.

IMPACT OF LAND TENURE. The organization of farm production was determined not alone by soil, climate, technology, and labor, but also by land-tenure and land-grant policies. **Free and common socage** (the tenure of the English peasant proprietors) was generally established by colonial charters. Land was held in **freehold,** which by 1607 had come to mean for an indefinite period of time. In New Netherlands (later New York) and Maryland, where manorial systems were established, this tenure appeared in somewhat more feudalized form than in New England, but feudal services were generally limited to the reservation of a specific **quitrent** (in Pennsylvania, by 1775, 4s for 100 acres). Owing to the opposition to quitrents on the ground that they constituted a source of private income instead of being devoted to public purposes, they were abolished (Virginia and Pennsylvania, 1779; New York, 1786).

In New England and eastern Long Island grants of land were made to towns, generally 36 square miles (a figure later adopted for the rectangular surveys of the U.S. public lands of the Northwest), and group settlement was fostered (by the 18th century the descendants of the original grantees [proprietors] were generally able to acquire ownership of the undistributed lands [against the noncommoners]). Except in Rhode Island, New England land was inherited by the children equally, saving a double portion for the eldest son (held illegal by the Privy Council in *Winthrop* v. *Lechmere*, 1728; but reversed in *Phillips* v. *Savage*, 1737). New York, both under Dutch (patroonship of Rensselaerswyck [1630–37 and 1685], 1 million acres) and English rule, fostered large grants to proprietors and promoters, discouraging settlement. In the period, 1760–75, at least 6,000 tenant farmers dwelt in the colony, many of whom engaged in antirent demonstrations (1751–62), especially in Westchester, Dutchess, and Albany counties (culminating in the uprising under Pendergrast, Apr.–Aug. 1766). Although New Jersey followed a more democratic system of land distribution, uprisings broke out between squatters and proprietors (1745–48), finally quelled by 1755. The squatter problem was especially serious in western Pennsylvania.

In the Southern colonies large land accumulation was fostered by **headrights,** generally 50-acres per head to each person who transported an emigrant at his own expense. This system fostered land accumulation and speculation in land warrants which often raised the price of land beyond the means of servants who had worked out their time. As a result of modification of the system in 1705, after which date headrights were sold for cash, the system was in effect abolished and direct land purchases substituted.

Land accumulation in New York and the South was fostered by the **entail,** a legal device to make land inalienable (Georgia, 1750, enlarged all entails previously granted to absolute inheritances; Virginia, as a result of Jefferson's efforts, abolished entails, 1776; followed by the vast majority of states), and **primogeniture,** descent of land to the eldest son (abolished, Ga.; 1777; N.C., 1784; Va., 1785; Md. and N.Y., 1786; S.C., 1791; R.I., 1798, with the New England states and Pa. abolishing the eldest son's double portion). Two instances where huge land grants were conferred without rights of government (unlike Maryland and Pennsylvania) were the holdings of Lord Fairfax of 5 million acres between the Potomac and Rappahonnock rivers, Virginia, and of Lord Granville, North Carolina (1744); confiscated, 1777. The **confiscation of Loyalist estates** (p. 131) contributed eventually to the establishment of more moderate-sized farm holdings.

ABORIGINAL FARMING. Aside from hunting, fishing, and gathering, the Indians along the Atlantic seaboard generally engaged in hoe-type agriculture, utilizing natural clearings or clearing forest land by girdling, felling, or burning trees. Main products were **maize** (Indian corn), peas, and beans (cultivated in mounds—**hill culture**), squash, pumpkins, and tobacco. Fish was used as fertilizer along the Northern coast. The Indians lacked draft animals.

1607–1700. CEREAL CULTIVATION. European grains were initially unsuccessful. Because of its rapid ripening, its higher yield per acre (c.40% more), and its ease of cultivation (Indian-fashion) in stump-filled fields, **corn** quickly became the principal grain. **Wheat** was raised successfully in New Netherland by 1626, and by 1640 proved to be a close competitor to corn in the Connecticut Valley. The appearance of the wheat blast (black stem rust, 1660) served to check the introduction of the crop into other areas. **Rye,** better adapted to sandy soils, was successfully raised in eastern New England (1636), and by 1700 ranked second to corn. The Swedes and Finns on the Delaware preferred rye to wheat (from 1644), but later migrations into the area imposed a wheat culture (by 1680). Barley (for beer) was raised in scattered areas, and oats occasionally for feed (among the New Jersey Scots for human consumption). By 1696 a **rice** crop had been successfully raised in South Carolina from seed imported from Madagascar.

Livestock. Imported from Europe into Virginia, New Netherland, and Massachusetts, livestock was largely uncared for (especially in the South), with wild herds of cattle, horses, and swine roaming in droves, subsisting on roots and herbs. By 1682 cattle grazing had become a major economic activity in South Carolina, and early expansion southward along the coast was primarily to secure greater ranges. Since native grasses in the North (wild rye, broom straw) were not nutritious when dry, English grasses were introduced into New England by 1663 and spread to the Middle Colonies (direct importations from England to Pennsylvania, 1689).

1612–1700. EXPANSION OF TOBACCO CULTIVATION. After a short period of experimentation (1612–15), tobacco quickly became the cash crop of Virginia. Exports rose from 20,000 lbs. (1618) to 500,000 lbs. (1627). The crop was raised in Maryland shortly after settlement. By the 1680s tobacco exports from the 2 colonies averaged 28 million lbs.

Other Crops. Virginia experimented with viniculture (1612–22), silk culture (1613–22; bounties offered, 1658), hemp and flax (1611–21), indigo (c.1622), various exotic fruits, nuts, and spices (1609–21), as well as West Indies cotton (1607, 1611–12, 1622–23), without commercial success; although flax, hemp, and, to a lesser degree, cotton were cultivated for domestic consumption. Flax production, encouraged by Connecticut (1640), was inconsequential in this period. The cultivation of fruits from England and northern Europe, better adapted to the country north of Cape Hatteras, proved successful, especially apples, while peaches did well in the warmer coastal regions (particularly Virginia), where they were used to fatten hogs. European vegetables were introduced at settlement, with the largest varieties in New Netherland by 1650. However, pumpkins, squash, and native beans were still favored for human consumption. Potatoes were first introduced into Pennsylvania in 1685.

1701–75. SOUTHERN TRENDS. The farm economy of South Carolina and Georgia came to be based upon two staples, **rice** and **indigo** (especially after the successful experiments of **Eliza Lucas [Pinckney]** of St. Andrews' Parish, S.C., 1739–44, in producing indigo profitably with slave labor). Charleston rice exports mounted: 1699–1700, 1,800 barrels; 1734–35, 45,000 bbls; 1755–56, 90,000 bbls; 1772–73, 110,000 bbls.

Savannah shipments: 1755–56, 2,000 bbls; 1772–73, 24,000 bbls. With the introduction of irrigation in rice cultivation (c.1724), the crop, originally confined to the inland river swamps, was by 1750 introduced into the tidal swamps. Indigo, especially adapted to the sandy uplands of the coastal region (by 1744), made sensational gains as a Charleston export: 1747–48, 138,334 lbs.; 1756–57, 393,531 lbs.; 1772–73, 720,591 lbs.; 1774–75, 1,122, 218 lbs. (highest figure). Shipments from Savannah rose from about 5,000 lbs. (1755–56) to an annual average of 16,000 lbs. (1768–73). **Silk** production was constantly encouraged by bounties (South Carolina acts of 1736 and 1755; Georgia Trustees established a nursery of mulberry trees at Savannah and 4 public filatures). Results were meager: Virginia, 300 lbs. of raw silk exported (1730); South Carolina, 651 lbs., 1742–55. High point of Georgia exports, 1766–67, 1,087 lbs.; declined, 1772–73, to 485 lbs. **Tobacco** exports rose sharply: 1709, 29 million lbs.; 1744–46, 47 million lbs. (annual average); 1771–75, 100 million lbs. Production techniques showed no substantial change from the colonial period to the Civil War. Exhaustion of the soil (after 3 years fields generally turned over to other crops) required large holdings and the acquisition of newer acreage, with geographical shifts westward characteristic of tobacco farming. In some Tidewater areas grain displaced tobacco, but the substantial rise in grain exports (especially in wheat after 1742) in Maryland and Virginia was at least in part the result of the settlement of the Piedmont. **Livestock:** North Carolina became the chief Southern meat-producing colony. Swine and cattle were driven to Virginia and even as far north as Philadelphia to be fattened for slaughter (a practice introduced, c.1705, but not generally adopted in the South).

1701–75. NORTHERN TRENDS. Corn remained the chief cereal product of the North. **Wheat** cultivation shifted in New England from the eastern region and the Connecticut Valley to western Massachusetts. In the Middle Colonies the heavily fertilized (fish) lands on Long Island, the Hudson and Mohawk valleys, and the Delaware and Susquehanna regions became the chief wheat-producing centers. **Flax** became a commercial crop, first in New England, and later in New York (1740–60). The **plow** was used in grain growing, already having been introduced into corn cultivation in Connecticut (before 1700), with oxen extensively employed. **Livestock:** yellow oxen (Danish) and a hardy breed of red milch cattle had been introduced by 1700. The Conestoga horse was raised in Pennsylvania (by 1750) as a general work animal, and the Narragansett pacer was raised in Rhode Island, largely for the West Indies trade. By 1749 the practice of sowing grasses on tilled land had become widespread, with timothy widely adopted in the Middle Colonies. Sheep raising was general in New England, where there was an average of 7 to 10 sheep per farm, but the Narragansett country specialized in livestock raising. Along the Delaware, in northern New Jersey and around Hadley, Massachusetts (by 1750), stall feeding for the Philadelphia, New York, and Boston export markets had developed.

1789–1854. SCIENTIFIC AGRICULTURE. Although European scientific developments in agriculture had been called to the public's attention by **Jared Eliot** (1685–1763) with his *Essay upon Field Husbandry in New England* (1760) and by such agronomists as Jefferson and Washington, and modern techniques (rotation of crops, already practiced in eastern Pa., cultivation of legumes, use of fertilizer, and control of soil erosion) were already known, widespread adoption by American farmers proceeded slowly (rotation of crops in New England by 1800; in eastern N.Y., N.J., Va., and the older South by the 1840s). Public attention was called to the utility as fertilizers of lime, marl, gypsum, and other calcareous materials by **Edmund Ruffin** (1794–1865), Virginia planter, through his *Essay on Calcareous Manures*, published in 1831, and the columns of the *Farmer's Register* (1836–42). Publication (1841) of Liebig's *Chemistry in Its Application to Agriculture and Physiology* promoted soil chemistry studies in the U.S. A further stimulus was given by **agricultural societies** (Philadelphia Society founded 1785); by **fairs,** a movement sponsored by **Elkanah Watson** (1758–1842), beginning in Pittsfield, Mass., 1807, with an exhibit of Merino sheep; and by **farm journals** (*American Farmer,* established by John P. Skinner, 1819; *Cultivator,* founded at Albany by Jesse Buel, 1834, was the first to attain national circulation). In 1839 the U.S. Patent Office received an appropriation of $1,000 for work with agricultural statistics; budget increased to $35,000 by 1854.

1789–1860. SOUTHERN AGRICULTURE. Cotton: Sea Island or smooth-seed cotton was cultivated in South Carolina as early as 1767, but the importation of Bahama strains (1786–87) caused production to expand along the Carolina coast. Exports rose from 9,840 lbs. (1789–90) to 8 million lbs. (1800–01). Short-staple or green-seed cotton was also grown in scattered areas before the Revolution. Rising British cotton imports (1784, 12 million lbs.; 1800, 56 million) combined with the loss of the British indigo market turned South Carolina planters to this crop. The **invention of the cotton gin** (1793, p. 793) facilitated processing and encouraged extraordinary expansion. Out of the total national output of 100,000 bales (1801), South Carolina produced half; Georgia, a

quarter; with the remainder largely raised in North Carolina and Virginia. **Geographical Expansion:** Cultivation spread into the Yazoo delta region (by 1795), to Louisiana (by 1802), and to central Tennessee (by 1796). National production rose from 171,000 bales (1810), to 731,000 bales (1830), to 2,133,000 (1850), and reached 5,387,000 bales (1859). States in order of production (1859): Mississippi, 1,203,000 bales; Alabama, 990,000; Louisiana, 778,000; Georgia, 701,000; while Texas by 1860 already grew more cotton than South Carolina, as land values declined in the Southeast. The large **plantation system** developed in the rich lands along the Mississippi and in Alabama, with 2% of the planters holding estates of more than 50 slaves. However, the intermediate planter and the yeoman farmer were more truly characteristic of the Southern landholding class. In 1850 only 18% of the farms and plantations of the South could be described as "plantations." Even in the Black Belt of Alabama almost 80% of the nonslaveholding landowners, who in 1850 constituted 44% of the region's farm population, owned farms ranging up to 200 acres. The small planters and yeoman farmers of the Black Belt owned 75% of the landed wealth. **Rice** production remained stable during the period and was confined largely to the coastal districts of South Carolina and Georgia. **Cane sugar** production, after some experimentation (1791–95), rose from 20,-000 tons (1823) to 270,000 tons (1861), of which Louisiana produced 95%. **Tobacco** production, after reaching a new high (average of 110,000 hogsheads, 1790–92), stabilized until 1840, with exports rising on the eve of the Civil War to 160,000 hhds. Cultivation spread to Kentucky (by 1783) and Tennessee (by 1789), and receipts at New Orleans rose from 24,000 hhds. (1818) to 25,500 hhds. (1831–34), and an average of 74,-000 hhds. (1842–46). Virginia remained the chief tobacco state (1839, 75 million lbs.; 1859, 124 million), with Kentucky 2nd (1839, 53 million; 1859, 108 million). **Corn** was the only grain grown extensively in the lower South (274,-762,000 bu. out of U.S. total of 838,-793,000, 1859). The border states (including Missouri) produced c.25% of the nation's wheat, c.17% of its rye, 19% of its oats. In addition to a more varied grain economy, the border states raised livestock (especially mules and horses in Ky. and Mo.) for the Southern market, and participated actively in the improvement of American breeds.

1789–1860. NORTHERN AGRICULTURE AND WESTERN COMPETITION. During the first quarter of the 19th century New York and Pennsylvania led in **wheat** production, but a westward shift was taking place even within their borders. The Genesee country supplanted the Hudson-Mohawk Valley (1810–25), but by the 1830s lost ground to Ohio, which became an important wheat producer. By 1860 the top-ranking wheat states were Illinois, Indiana, and Wisconsin. During 1850–60 production in the Northeast remained stabilized (around 30 million bu.), while increasing from 43,842,000 bu. to 95 million in the North Central states. **Corn** production in the North Central states, occupying a belt directly south of the wheat region, doubled from 222,209,000 bu. (1850) to 406,167,000 (1860), or about 50% of the total crop. In 1840, Kentucky, Tennessee, and Virginia were the leading corn states; in 1860, Illinois, Ohio, Missouri and Indiana. The North Atlantic states expanded **dairy** production, and by the end of this period produced about 70% of the nation's cheese, 50% of its butter, and continued to lead the country in the production of the lesser grains (rye, over 60%; barley, c.35%, buckwheat, c.75%) as well as Irish potatoes (c.58%).

Cattle Raising and Meat Packing. Hog raising in the Middle West was closely related to corn production. By 1818 a meat-packing industry had been established at **Cincinnati** (founded 1788), which was the leading center until 1860, when it was surpassed by **Chicago** (established at Fort Dearborn, 1830). In 1833 Cincinnati firms packed 85,000 hogs; in 1848, 500,000.

1820–60. INTRODUCTION OF AGRICULTURAL MACHINERY (also pp. 793–795). The cradle was introduced in the North (c.1820) as a substitute for the sickle in reaping; in general use by 1840. The cast-iron plow replaced the wooden moldboard plow between 1825–40, and the steel plow (manufactured by **John Lane**, 1833, and **John Deere** [1804–86], 1837) replaced the iron plow on the prairies by 1845. The Hussey and McCormick reapers came into use in the East (c.1846) and the West (c.1848), and replaced the cradle by 1860. Mowing (patented 1844), threshing, and haying machines, as well as seed drills and cultivators, were widely adopted in the 2 decades before the Civil War. The first grain elevator was constructed in Buffalo, 1842.

1841–63. RISE OF PACIFIC AND MOUNTAIN STATES AGRICULTURE. The arrival of settlers in Willamette Valley (Ore.), 1841–43, opened the Pacific coast to the American farmer, and the settlement of the Salt Lake Valley, 1846, opened the Mountain States. The California gold rush (1849–50) created a demand for food products. Cattle increased from c.250,000 head (1849) to over 2 million head (1860). After being obliged to import 740,000 bags of grain (1853), California became self-sufficient by 1855, even producing a surplus the next year, while garden crops and viniculture expanded rapidly. The Pikes Peak rush (1859) had a similar effect on farm conditions in the Denver region.

1861–70. SOUTHERN AGRICULTURAL PROBLEMS. During the Civil

**PER ACRE MAN-HOUR REQUIREMENTS
IN WHEAT PRODUCTION
(U.S. Dept. of Agriculture, *Yearbook*, 1941)**

Date	Man-Hours 20 bu. per acre	Implements
1822	50–60	Walking plow, bundle of brush for harrow, hand broacast of seed, sickle harvesting, flail threshing
1890	8–10	Gang plow, seeder, harrow, binder, reaper, harvester, thresher, wagons, and horses
1930	3–4	3-bottom gang plow, tractor, 10-ft. tandem disk, harrow, 12-ft. combine, and trucks.

War, with the dislocation of foreign markets, cotton production dropped from an annual average of 4,500,000 bales (1859–61) to 1,597,000 (1862), reaching a low in 1864 of 299,000. Southern planters were further impoverished by the depreciation of Southern currency and securities, the wartime confiscatory policies of the federal government, the instability of the labor market, and the effects of 2 drought years (1865, 1867). In 1870 cotton production was only 51% of prewar figures, cattle and swine 60%, rice 40%, sugar under 50%. While average holdings in the Cotton Belt declined from 402 to 230 acres (1870–80), the holdings of sharecroppers and tenants were included in the census, distorting the nature of the breakup. By 1869 the gang labor system, the first approach to tillage under free labor, was largely superseded by **sharecropping** (a seasonal arrangement where the landlord determines the crop and arranges the market, with division of the proceeds: one third for labor, one third for land, one third for implements, seeds, fertilizer, etc.); **tenancy,** a leasehold arrangement; and the **crop-lien** system, under which the small farmer pledges his crop to be marketed by the merchant-creditor.

1862–1916. EXPANSION OF FEDERAL ACTIVITIES. The U.S. Department of Agriculture was established 15 May 1862 to expand and continue the activities of the agricultural division of the Patent Office. Chemical, entomological, statistical, and forestry divisions were set up (by 1881), and a Bureau of Animal Husbandry, 1884. Appropriations rose from $64,000 (1862) to over $1 million (1889). The commissioner was raised to cabinet rank (1889) and entrusted with the protection of national forests (1905), enforcement of the Pure Food and Drug Act (1906), Meat Inspection Act (1907), the inspection of dairy products for export (1908), and the Warehouse, Cotton Futures, and Grain Standards Acts (1916).

1866–1900. AGRICULTURAL EXPANSION. With the expansion of both domestic and foreign markets, the number of farms increased from around 2,660,000 to 5,377,000; total farm acreage from 493 million to 839 million (1870–1900).

**AGRICULTURAL EXPANSION
(in million acres)**

	corn	wheat	oats	cotton	hay
1866–75	40	22	11	9	20
1896–1901	91	47	30	24	42

**LIVESTOCK EXPANSION
(in million head)**

	cattle	milk cows	hogs	horses	mules
1870	24	8.9	25	7	1
1900	52	17	63	17	3

1870–90 GROWTH OF REGIONAL SPECIALIZATION. Rise of production (in million bu.) in west North Central States from 67 (1869) to 307 (1899) accounted for almost half of U.S. total **wheat** crop. Production in Pacific states rose from 19 to 72 and in Oklahoma and Texas to 33 by 1899. **Wool** production (in million lbs.) rose in the Mountain States from 1 (1869) to 123 (1899). **Corn** remained the most widely distributed of the grains, but the west North Central States produced over 40% of the national crop (1899), as well as 50% of the **barley** and over 95% of the **flaxseed.**

Illinois and Iowa produced over 35% of the **oats,** Pennsylvania and New York 70% of the **buckwheat,** Virginia and North Carolina 70% of the **peanuts,** and 4 states (Kentucky, North Carolina, Virginia, and Tennessee) over 70% of the **tobacco,** with Kentucky accounting for 35%. **Rice** production moved from South Carolina and Georgia to Louisiana, which by 1899 produced almost 70% of the national crop. Four states (New York, Wisconsin, Iowa, and Illinois) produced over 50% of the whole **milk,** with over 20% from New York.

1870–1900. TECHNOLOGICAL ADVANCES. Total value of farm implements and machinery increased from $271 million (1870) to $750 million (1900), or from $102 per farm to $130. Efficiency was promoted by the twine binder (1878), spring-tooth harrow (after 1877), disc harrow (after 1892 in the Prairie States), gang plow (after 1880 in the Pacific States), cotton seed planters and special plows (by 1900), corn shucking and fodder shredding machine (1890), corn binder (1892), and giant combine harvester thresher (1880s in Pacific States). The centrifugal cream separator (1879) became common in all dairy regions (40,000 in use, 1900). Consumption of commercial fertilizer increased from 321,000 short tons (1870) to 2,730,000 (1900).

1870–1900. FARM DIFFICULTIES. In the face of vast expansion the wholesale price index of farm products generally declined:

FARM PRODUCTS WHOLESALE PRICE INDEX
(Warren and Pearson)
(1910–14 = 100)

1866	140
1870	112
1876	89
1880	80
1882	99
1886	68
1890	71
1896	56
1900	71

Mortgages and Tenancy. Estimated average equity of farm operators in land they farmed was 62% (1880). This figure declined at an average rate of 4% each decade until 1935. In some prairie counties 90% of the farms changed hands during the 1890s; 11,000 foreclosures in Kansas (1889–93). Tenancy increased from 26% of total farms (1880) to 35% (1900), with marked rises in the cotton and wheat states.

GRANGER MOVEMENT (pp. 295, 313).

1900–14. AGRICULTURAL TRENDS. Agriculture stabilized in this period. Farms increased from 5,737,000 to 6,480,000; wheat acreage expanded from an average of 7 million bu. to c.8 million; and corn expanded gradually but steadily. Notable production gains were scored in (1) **cotton** (from 10 million bales, 1900, to 16 million, 1914), (2) **tobacco,** and (3) **citrus fruits;** while a sharp decline occurred in the exports of beef (352 million lbs., 1898, to 194 million, 1913) and bacon (from 650 million lbs., 1898, to 194 million, 1913), largely the result of increase in world production of these products.

1914. SMITH-LEVER EXTENSION ACT, providing for a nationwide extension of the county-agent system (p. 327).

1914–18. EFFECT OF WORLD WAR I. Wheat production rose to an average of c.870 million bu., although corn production was relatively stable. Beginning with 1918 grain production reached into the most arid sections of the Great Plains. Wholesale price index of farm products (Warren and Pearson; 1910–14 = 100) rose from 100 (1914) to 208 (1918) and continued to rise until 1920 (211).

1920–69. RISE AND DECLINE OF TENANCY. Tenancy rose during the farm depression: 38.1% of farm holdings (1920) to 42.2% (1935). World War II and postwar farm prosperity brought general declines: 24% (1954) to 12.9% (1969).

1920–39. SOME TECHNOLOGICAL CHANGES: (1) First hybrid corn involving inbred lines sold in 1921; (2) mills for extracting oil from soybeans first built about 1920; between 1930 and 1940, hybridization in breeding soybeans; (3) developments in livestock breeding: hogs with more meat, since lard was being replaced with vegetable oils; sheep-breeding; artificial breeding of cattle (first in New Jersey in 1938); and (4) increasing mechanization.

1921–33. FARM DEPRESSION. Wholesale price index of farm products dropped to 121 (1921), rising slightly to 138 (1923), but even in the prosperous years 1926–29 it never exceeded 149 (1928), and with the depression dropped to 68 (1932), lowest since 1899. Wheat hit an all-time low of 32 cts. per bu. Total farm receipts declined by 1932 to one third of the amount of 1918, while farm mortgage debt rose from $7,857 million (1920) to a high of $10,785 million (1923). Forced sales (bankruptcies, foreclosures, tax delinquencies) rose from an average of 12 per 1,000 (1921–24) to 21 per 1,000 farms (1926–30) and 54 per 1,000 (1933), and were exceptionally heavy in the Dakotas and Iowa. The estimated equity of farm operators in their farm land dropped from 62% (1880) to 39% (1935).

1924–32. FARM RELIEF. For the **Farm Loan Act** (1916), see p. 329. Under the **Agricultural Credits Act** (24 Aug. 1924) loans were granted dealers and cooperative groups to permit them to hold farm goods for domestic and foreign trade in an effort to prevent bankruptcies and dumping; $304 million loaned, 1924–32. For the **Agricultural Marketing Act** (1929), see p. 396.

1933–40. NEW DEAL FARM PROGRAM. By the **Agricultural Adjustment Act** (p. 405), the **Cotton Control Act** (p. 411), and the **Tobacco Control Act** (p. 413), the federal government sought to curtail farm production. Contributing to crop curtailment was a **severe drought,** even more severe than in the late 1880s, in the Prairie and Plains states (1934), as a result of which one third of the nation's grain crop was lost and "Okies" abandoned their Oklahoma farms to seek work in California. Total acreage in 52 major crops harvested fell from an average of 358 million (1929–32) to 321 million (1933–35). After these acts were declared unconstitutional (p. 676), the federal government continued its curtailment program through the **Soil Conservation and Domestic Allotment Act** (1936, p. 418), modified by the **2nd AAA** (1938, p. 423). Cash receipts for farm products rose from $4,743 million (1932) to $7,659 million (1935) and remained over $8 billion (1936–40). Wholesale price index of farm products (Bureau of Labor Statistics; 1926 = 100) rose from 48.2 (1932) to 86.4 (1936), then declined until World War II to 65.3 (1939). Farm mortgage debt declined from $8,466 million (1933) to $6,586 million (1940), and forced sales dropped from 54 per 1,000 farms (1933) to 16 per 1,000 (1940).

1940–52. WORLD WAR II AND POSTWAR EXPANSION. The index of gross farm production (1935–39 = 100) rose from 108 (1940) to 126 (1946), with a further high to 131 (1948), as cash receipts for farm products rose from $9,132 million (1940) to $22,286 million (1945). Value of farm implements and machinery rose from $2,153 million (1935) to an all-time high of $12,166 million (1950). Expenditures for fertilizer and lime in 1945 approximated $508 million, more than treble the 1934 figure. Farm prices soared in this period: No. 1 wheat, $.90 per bu. (1940) to a high of $2.88 (1948); cotton from an average of $.096 per lb. (1936–40) to

$.319 (1947) as production decreased. Beef cattle prices per 100 lbs. continued to soar in the postwar period: $7.46 (1940) to $23.30 (1950), as did hog prices: $5.39 (1940) to $23.10 (1948). The farm mortgage debt was reduced from $6,586 million (1940) to $4,681 million (1946), rose to $5,413 million (1950), but the ratio of mortgage debt to total farm value declined from 41.5% (1940) to 25% (1956).

1950–72. FARM POPULATION AND NUMBER AND TYPE OF FARMS.

The farm population declined sharply in absolute and relative terms from 23 million or 15.2% of the population in 1950, to 15.6 million or 8.7% (1960), to 9.7 million or 4.7% (1970), to 9.5 million or 4.5% (1972 prel.). So too, the number of farms decreased: 5.65 million (1950), 3.96 million (1960), 2.92 million (1970), to 2.83 million (1972 prel.). While many small farms remained, the trend was for existing farms to grow both larger and more specialized. Over the years, a larger percentage of the major agricultural products came from a smaller proportion of the farms. The corporate form came to farming. By 1969 1,586 farms had annual sales of more than $1 million. Of these, 239 were corporations with more than 10 shareholders, while 731 were "small" corporations, having fewer than 10 shareholders; 287 were partnerships and 300 were individual proprietorships.

1950–72. FARM INCOME, PRODUCTION, AND PRODUCTIVITY.

Gross realized income from farming rose steadily: $32.3 billion (1950), $38.1 billion (1960), $57.8 billion (1970), $68.8 billion (1972). But production expenses rose, so the net to the farmer actually went down in the 1950s: $12.9 billion (1950), $11.7 billion (1960), and then rose slowly in the 1960s and 1970s: $16.8 billion (1970), $19.7 billion (1972). Farm incomes did not increase as much as incomes in other sectors. Direct government payments supplemented farm income, rising from $283 million (1950) to $702 million (1960), $3,717 million (1970), $3,961 million (1972), as agricultural subsidies shifted further away from high price supports toward cash payments from the government to farmers. The **Omnibus Farm Bill** (5 Nov. 1965) utilized cash payments as incentives for the diversion of planted acreage of cotton, wheat, and food grains to conservation and other uses. The **Agricultural Act of 1970** increased direct payments to the farmer and gave him greater freedom in his planning decisions. Price support was not, however, abandoned; milk price supports increased 50% (1965–71). Quotas limited imports of sugar and thus supported high internal prices.

Despite fewer farmers and farms, farm production mounted. Based on 1967 = 100, indices of farm production rose from

FARM MECHANIZATION, 1930–73[1]
(Historical Statistics of U.S. to 1957; U.S. Dept. of Agric., Economic Research Service)

Year	Tractors	Motor Trucks	Grain Combines	Corn Pickers	Farms with Milking Machines
1930	920,000	900,000	61,000	50,000	100,000
1941	1,665,000	1,095,000	225,000	120,000	210,000
1950	3,394,000	2,207,000	714,000	456,000	636,000
1960	4,685,000	2,825,000	1,042,000	792,000	660,000
1970	4,618,000	2,984,000	790,000	635,000	[1965: 500,000]
1973 (prel.)	4,387,000	2,915,000	703,000	607,000	

[1] Declining numbers of farms and the acquisition of larger, more efficient machines were the principal reasons for the declines in the *number* of major machinery items 1960–73.

73 (1950) to 90 (1960), 102 (1970), 112 (1972 prel.); farm output per man-hour jumped from 35 (1950) to 93 (1960), 113 (1970), 122 (1972 prel.); while crop production per acre showed a less dramatic rise: 69 (1950), 88 (1960), 102 (1970), 116 (1972 prel.). These figures reflected the increasing efficiency of American agriculture. Contributing were mechanization; the use of fertilizer; superior seed; improved breeding stock; protection against insects, diseases, parasites, and weeds; irrigation and drainage techniques; better livestock

feeds; the application of electronic data processing; and more professional general management of equipment, skills, land, and livestock to obtain higher yields.

INDEX NUMBERS OF INPUTS—MECHANIZATION AND FERTILIZER (1967 = 100)

Year	Mechanical Power and Machinery	Fertilizer and Liming Materials
1930	40	11
1941	44	15
1950	79	32
1960	91	54
1970	102	113
1972 (prel.)	103	122

1950–78. PRINCIPAL CROPS

Year	Corn	Soybeans	Wheat	Production Oats	Cotton	Rice	Hay
	in million bushels[1]				in 000 bales	in 000 cwt	in 000 short tons
1950	3,075	299	1,019	1,369	10,014	38,820	103,820
1957	3,422	484	950	1,301	10,964	42,935	120,977
1978	7,082	1,843	1,799	601	11,000	138,000	142,000

[1] In *value* of production (in billions of dollars) in 1978, the principal four crops were **corn** ($14.9), **soybeans** ($12.2), **hay** ($6.6), and **wheat** ($5.3).

FARM PRODUCTION INDICES (1967 = 100)

Year	Total Farm Output	Meat Animals	Dairy Products	Poultry & Eggs
1950	73	74	93	56
1960	90	85	101	75
1970	102	102	100	106
1978 (prel.)	122	107	105	117

International Trade and Investment, Tariffs, Domestic Commerce

From being an exporter principally of raw materials in the colonial period, America became over time an exporter of manufactured products (although agricultural output still constituted an important part of U.S. exports); once an importer of manufactured goods, America became an importer of a range of raw materials (oil, copper, lead, zinc, iron ore) along with manufactured products. From the colonial period to 1875, America was in most years a net *importer* of goods; from 1875 to 1970 (with only two years excepted), America was a net *exporter*. In 1971–72, America was again a net importer (for the first time since 1893).

Until 1914, the United States was a debtor nation in international accounts (that is, we owed more than was owed to us); after 1914, America became the creditor nation of the world. In 1933, the dollar was overpriced relative to other currencies and gold, and in 1934, the dollar was set at $35.00 an ounce of gold (the former price was $20.67 an ounce). When the Bretton Woods international monetary system was established in 1944 the dollar was a foundation currency. After the United States had experienced about two decades of balance of payments problems, the dollar was again devalued, once in 1971–72 and again in 1973, emerging at $42.22 an ounce. The entire international monetary system as a consequence would need to be revised.

When America was part of the British empire, the colonies were subject to imperial, protectionist policy. After independence, out from under the British cloak, the U.S. developed national tariff policies. In broad terms, tariffs mounted until 1828, declined through 1857, rose from 1861 to 1897 to new heights, to be reduced in 1909 and 1913; from 1921 to 1930 rates increased, especially in 1930; since 1934 there has been an attempt at liberalization of trade policy and a tendency toward freer trade.

In the colonial period, domestic trade within, between, and among the colonies had begun, but transatlantic and West Indian trade was greater. After independence, as the nation became settled, internal transactions mounted and attention shifted to domestic commerce. Navigable rivers, roads, canals, railroads, and in the twentieth century, trucks and airplanes all contributed to the expansion of national commerce. Regional specialization increased trade. As products traded multiplied, so the outlets to sell these products became more numerous and over time their character changed.

International Trade and Investment

MERCANTILISM. The economic controls for the regulation of commerce, industry, and labor which were introduced into the English colonies were rooted in English experience and stemmed from a body of doctrine called "mercantilism," which had as its objective the creation of a prosperous and powerful national state or self-sufficing empire. Such prosperity and power were to be secured by (1) maintaining an adequate stock of precious metals; (2) protecting home industries against foreign competition; (3) making it possible for home industries to compete successfully in foreign markets through the assurance of necessary raw materials (from the colonies) and low production costs (subsistence labor). The **Acts of Trade and Navigation** (1650–1767) provided for the external regulation and control of foreign trade and the subordination of colonial interests to those of the mother country. The principal regulatory trade measures relating to the colonies:

1620. EARLY ATTEMPTS. Under the early Stuarts Parliament left colonial economic development to the crown. By agreement between the crown and the Virginia Co., in return for a duty of 1s. per lb. on tobacco, English tobacco growing was to be prohibited (carried out by proclamation 29 June 1620).

1650–60. LEGISLATION DURING THE INTERREGNUM. To liberate English trade from Dutch control Parliament (1) forbade foreign ships from trading in the colonies without special license (3 Oct. 1650); (2) enacted (9 Oct. 1651) that no goods from Asia, Africa, or America could be imported into England, Ireland, or the colonies except in ships of which the owner, the master, and the **major** part of the crew were English (including colonials); (3) that no European goods could be imported into England, Ireland, or the colonies except in **English** ships or ships of the **country of origin;** (4) prohibited foreign goods from being imported into England except from the place of production; (5) prohibited the importation of fish by aliens; and (6) excluded all foreign ships from the English coasting trade. These comprehensive acts depended for enforcement upon (1) informers and (2) colonial governors. Complaints arose of the hardships of enforcement owing to England's lack of shipping to replace the Dutch. The governors of Barbados and Antigua complained of supply shortages (1652, 1656) and the former colony petitioned for repeal of the Act of 1650. The Virginia Assembly declared that freedom of trade would be maintained and all merchants protected (1655), demanding bond of all sea captains not to molest foreign ship-

ping (Mar. 1660). Massachusetts (1655), Rhode Island (1657), and Connecticut (1660) publicly announced their intention of continuing trade with the Dutch.

1660. NAVIGATION ACT OF 1660, passed by the Convention Parliament, approved by the crown, 1 Oct. 1660, and confirmed by the first regular Restoration Parliament (27 July 1661), (1) provided that no goods or commodities, regardless of origin, could be imported into or exported out of any English colony except in English-built or owned ships (of which the master and **three fourths** of the crew were English); (2) required that **enumerated articles** (including **sugar, tobacco,** and **indigo**) of colonial growth and manufacture be shipped only to England or her colonies, with ships sailing from the colonies required to give bond that they would unload enumerated commodities in the realm.

1662. ACT OF FRAUDS provided that only **English-built** ships were to enjoy the privileges under the Act of 1660 (except ships bought before 1662).

1663. NAVIGATION ACT OF 1663 (passed to benefit English merchants) provided that, with the exception of certain specified commodities (salt for the New England and Newfoundland fisheries, wine from Madeira and the Azores, and provisions, servants, and horses from Scotland and Ireland), European goods destined for the colonies must be shipped from England and on English-built ships. Enforcement duties were placed upon colonial governors, who customarily delegated responsibility to a **naval officer** (in practice appointed in England).

1673. NAVIGATION ACT OF 1673 assessed duties at the **ports of clearance** upon enumerated products when shipped from one plantation to another (in order to prevent colonial shippers from evading English duties by stopping at a colonial port en route to Europe) and provided for the appointment of **customs commissioners** to collect the duties.

1696. NAVIGATION ACT OF 1696 (1) confined all colonial trade to English-built ships; (2) gave the provincial customs officers the same powers as in England, including the right of forcible entry; (3) required that bonds be posted on enumerated commodities, even where plantation duties were paid; (4) enlarged the direct responsibility of the colonial naval officer; and (5) voided colonial laws contrary to the Navigation Acts.

1699. WOOL ACT (passed to meet competition from Ireland and potential competition from the American colonies) restricted woolen manufacture in Ireland and forbade the export of wool products from any American colony either overseas or in the intercolonial trade.

1705. ENUMERATED ARTICLES (to be shipped only to English ports) expanded with the broadening of colonial economic activity: **rice** (now an established crop in Carolina) and **molasses,** mainstay of the West Indies economy; **naval stores,** not only enumerated but also given **bounties** per ton as follows: pitch and tar, £4; rosin and turpentine, £3; hemp, £6; masts, yards, and bowsprits, £1.

1709–74. FURTHER NAVAL STORES ACTS. Bounties continued for 11 years after expiration (1713) of Act of 1705; on hemp continued for another 16 years (1725); but on the other naval stores were allowed to lapse (1725–29). When renewed in 1729 the rates were changed per ton: pitch, £1; turpentine, £1 10s.; masts, £1; tar, £2 4s. Under this act the cutting of white pines was restricted to those standing on private property; of white pines 24 in. in diameter or greater was permitted only on lands granted before 7 Oct. 1692 (such a restriction had been included in the Massachusetts charter of 1692). Bounties

on naval stores were continued to 1774, except for hemp, which was allowed to lapse in 1741 (renewed 1764). Bounty payments totaled, 1706–74, £1,438,702.

1721. BEAVER SKINS, FURS, AND COPPER ENUMERATED and the duties on beaver skins lowered. Prior to this enactment 30–40% of New York's fur exports went to Continental Europe. In 1721 copper ore shipments had been made both to England and Holland from a newly opened New Jersey mine.

1730–35. Rice shipments were permitted from South Carolina to Europe south of Cape Finisterre (1730), and the privilege extended to Georgia (1735).

1732. HAT ACT. As a result of pressure upon Parliament from London felt makers, already suffering from French competition and fearing the effects of an expanding hat industry in the Northern colonies, Parliament (1) prohibited the exportation of hats from one colony to another; (2) limited the pursuit of this trade in the colonies to those who had served a 7-year apprenticeship and (3) the number of apprentices to 2 per shop; and (4) barred the employment of Negro apprentices. Enforcement sporadic.

1733. MOLASSES ACT, passed to protect the British West Indies planters from competition of the foreign West Indies, levied an almost prohibitive duty of 9d. per gallon on rum and spirits, 6d. on molasses, and 5s. per hundredweight on sugar imported to the continental colonies from the foreign West Indies. The act proved unenforceable.

1748–63. INDIGO BOUNTIES of 6d. per lb. granted to encourage production of a dye used in the woolen industry; lowered (1763) to 4d. Bounties paid to 1776 exceeded £185,000 (chiefly to Carolina and Georgia planters).

1750, 1757. IRON ACTS. To maintain the colonial supply of bar and pig iron for the iron and steel industry of the English Midlands but check the expansion in the colonies of the iron-finishing industry, Parliament (1) forbade the erection henceforth in the colonies of rolling and slitting mills, tilt-hammer forges, and steel furnaces; (2) allowed pig and bar iron to enter England free of duties under certain special conditions, which were removed (1757), after which date plantation iron was admitted free into England.

1764. SUGAR ACT (also p. 85) (1) forbade the importation of rum and spirits from the foreign West Indies into the continental colonies; (2) lowered the duties on molasses; (3) placed on the enumerated list hides and skins, pot and pearl ashes (a newly produced commodity), iron and lumber for Europe, and two minor products, whale fins and raw silk.

1767. ALL NONENUMERATED GOODS destined for any part of Europe north of Cape Finisterre were required to be first shipped to England. Only about 4.3% of colonial exports were affected by this act, for by 1770 it is estimated that, from the time of first enumeration, 96% of the tobacco exported from the colonies had been reexported from England, 79% of the rice, 40% of the indigo, 58% of the beaver skins, 95% of other furs, 26% of hides and skins, 13% of pot and pearl ashes. On the other hand, colonial naval stores (except for tar, 5% of which was reexported) and pig and bar iron were almost entirely utilized in English industry (L. A. Harper).

PATTERNS OF COLONIAL TRADE. Handicaps to Overseas Trade. In addition to (1) the **Acts of Trade,** which, while encouraging shipping, shipbuilding, and naval stores, were especially detrimental to the tobacco trade and to a lesser degree to certain branches of manufacturing, other obstacles existed, including (2) **piracy** (robbery committed upon ships of friendly nations). Under Act of 28 Hen. VIII, c.8 (1536), providing that pirates be tried in England before a commission specially named, the accused were sent from the colonies to England for trial. Most notable instance was the trial of Capt. **William Kidd** (c.1645–1701) for murder and piracy in Old Bailey (hanged 23 May 1701). By 11 Wm. III, c.7 (1699), pirates could be tried by commission in any colony. Under this act **Stede Bonnet** (S.C., 1718) was tried, convicted, and hanged. By proclamation, 1717, pirates who surrendered were pardoned (including a large contingent on Providence Island, Bahamas). **Robert Teach** ("Blackbeard") was killed in an attack by a Virginia expedition (1718). Thereafter a major hazard was (3) **privateering** (authorized attacks and seizures of enemy ships in wartime). (4) **Lack of Money and Credit Facilities:** Since the exportation of coin from Great Britain was forbidden, the colonists in the early period were dependent upon **wampum** (Indian shell bead money); **barter; commodity money** or "country pay" (notably tobacco crop notes [warehouse receipts] in Md. and Va. and rice crop notes in S.C.); **local coinage,** confined to the Massachusetts "pine-tree shillings" coined between 1652–84; **foreign coins,** which were consistently overvalued to attract importation (despite Royal Proclamation, 1704, limiting such overvaluation to 33⅓%, and the Parliamentary Act of 1704 providing a prison term and fine for violations); **bills of exchange** (especially those secured in trade with the British West Indies); and **paper money** (begun by Mass., 1690). In the early stages paper money was lawful only in **public** payments; after 1720 it was used as legal tender in all payments. Inflation arose, primarily in New England, 1730–50, as a result of the failure to support such

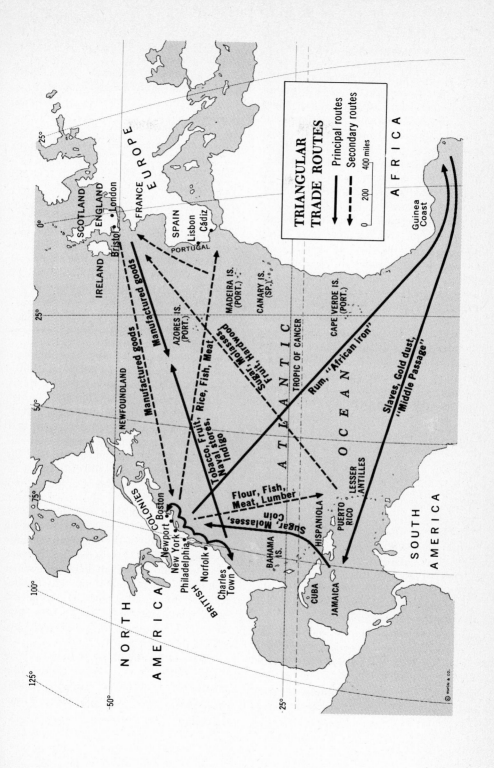

TRIANGULAR
TRADE ROUTES

Principal routes
Secondary routes

0   200   400 miles

issues by adequate taxes. In Massachusetts, 1740, a **land bank** was organized to issue £150,000 in bills secured by mortgages at 3% interest. In opposition the Boston merchants organized the Silver Bank, which issued notes based on silver. The operations of the land bank were declared illegal and void by Act of Parliament, 1741, which extended the Bubble Act, 1720, outlawing joint-stock companies operating without special authority of Parliament. By Act of 1751 Parliament prohibited the New England colonies from erecting new land banks and from making bills of credit legal tender except in times of war or other emergency, and by Act of 1764 (p. 86) forbade the further issuance of paper money throughout the colonies.

1621–1700. NORTHERN OVERSEAS TRADE. The "Triangular Trade" was in fact a series of geometrical patterns which were largely the result of the necessity of the Northern colonies (in the absence of English demand for their products) to raise enough money to pay England for imported manufactured goods (textiles and hardware). Among the "triangles": (1) New England (fish and lumber) or Middle Colonies (flour) to the English (or foreign) West Indies, in exchange for sugar, molasses, or rum, with a final haul to London or Bristol, returning with English goods; (2) New England to the West Indies for rum, shipped to West Africa for slaves, with numerous variations in these 2 patterns.

1607–1700. SOUTHERN OVERSEAS TRADE. Tobacco shipments from Virginia after 1616 increased rapidly: 1619, 20,000 lbs.; 1627, 500,000 lbs. With the spread of cultivation to Maryland and North Carolina, exports rose: 1663, 7,367,140 lbs.; 1669, 9,026,046 lbs.; and in the 1680s averaged 28 million lbs. Trade of the Carolinas (forest products and hides) was still at a low level and

in the hands of outsiders (chiefly New Englanders).

1701–74. EXPANSION OF THE COLONIAL OVERSEAS TRADE.

TRADE WITH GREAT BRITIAN
(Annual averages in thousands of £ sterling; D. Macpherson, *Annals of Commerce*)

Colony	Exports to England		
	1701–10	1731–40	1761–70
New England	37	64	113
New York	10	16	62
Pennsylvania	12	12	35
Md.-Va.	205	394	468
Carolinas	14	177	330
Georgia	—	—	36

Colony	Imports from England		
	1701–10	1731–40	1761–70
New England	86	197	358
New York	28	92	349
Pennsylvania	9	52	295
Md.-Va.	128	207	491
Carolinas	22	94	262
Georgia	—	3	40

Chief export to Britain was **tobacco** (c. £900,000 out of a total of £1,750,000 in 1770). Other principal exports in 1770 were **rice** (£170,000), indigo (£130,000), whale products, naval stores, pot and pearl ashes, furs and skins, and iron. In the years 1700–20 Virginia and Maryland accounted for about 75% of exports; 1760–70, 50%, with the proportion of the Carolinas and Georgia (rice, indigo, and naval stores) growing from less than 10% to over 35% in the same periods. The proportion of the export trade of the Northern colonies increased, 1770–75, as a result of heavier grain shipments. Philadelphia's wheat shipments increased from 52,000 bu. (1771) to 182,000 (1773), while all grain shipments from New York rose from 110,000 bu. (1766) to 350,000 bu. (1774).

Trade with the West Indies. In 1769 the Northern colonies provided the bulk of the exports (New England, c.40%; Middle Colonies over 30%). The importance of the foreign West Indies is indicated by the following figures for imports of gallons of **molasses** (Harper):

1768–70	From Foreign West Indies	From British West Indies
	9,625,426	853,229

The relative importance to Great Britain of the West Indies trade as compared with that of the continental colonies is evidenced by the fact that the annual average combined British imports and exports to the former, 1761–70, amounted to £3,406,000; to the continental colonies, £2,843,000. By 1772 Philadelphia was first in the overseas trade (in tonnage cleared), with Boston, New York, and Charleston rivals for second place.

1700–73. UNFAVORABLE BALANCE OF TRADE of the continental colonies with Great Britain is revealed by statistics of imports and exports showing excess of imports from England over exports rising from £50,680 (1700) to £754,000 (ann. av., 1761–70). While the sterling gap was greatest in the Northern colonies, all thirteen except the Carolinas had an unfavorable balance, 1761–70. For the period, 1700–73, the unfavorable trade balance amounted to £20,195,568.

1775–89. COMMERCE DURING THE REVOLUTION AND IN THE CONFEDERATION. During the war trade between Great Britain and the U.S., restricted generally to the area held by British troops, shrank to less than 5% of its former level. As a result of large-scale "dumping" of manufactured goods, imports from Britain, 1783–89, averaged only 10% less than the prewar level, while exports, on the other hand, amounted to only 50% of the prewar figure. The export industries lost their preferential treatment in the British market, and restrictions on trade with the West Indies (1783–1828) deprived the Northern states of a major outlet for their goods, only in part compensated for by direct shipments to the Continent of Europe; by the opening of the China trade (*Empress of China* entered New York from Canton, 1785); and by the beginning of trade between New England and the Pacific Northwest for fur products (then traded in China for Oriental goods), opened as a result of the voyage of Captain **Robert Gray** (1755–1806) to Oregon and China (1787–90).

1789–1815. FOREIGN TRADE. After averaging $20 million annually (1790–92), U.S. exports rose sharply, reaching $94 million (1801), and, after a temporary setback (1802–04), made a new high of $108 million (1807). Imports rose from $23 million (1790) to $110 million (1801) and, after suffering contraction along with exports, reached a new high of $138.5 million (1807). The rise, in large measure the result of the position of the U.S. as a major neutral shipping nation, represented in appreciable degree reexports ($6.5 million, 1794; $47 million, 1801; $60 million, 1806). The British Continental blockade, Napoleon's retaliatory acts, and the Embargo (1807) negated this advantage. Exports shrank to $22 million (1808), rising gradually until the War of 1812 (averaging $60 million annually, 1809–11). During the war exports sank to an all-time low of $7 million (1814) and imports to $13 million. **Cotton** exports, increasing throughout the period ($5 million, 1802; $15 million, 1810), surpassed tobacco as early as 1803. Lumber and potash replaced fur and naval stores as major forest products exported.

1789–1830. INTERNATIONAL INVESTMENT. America was a debter in international accounts. The country hoped to attract foreign capital. Alexander Hamilton sought to pay off foreign loans to establish national credit. Under the Jay Treaty (1794), the U.S. guaranteed payment to Great Britain, in sterling, of bona fide private debts incurred before 1783, and in 1802, the U.S. agreed to pay the British £600,000 sterling to settle private British claims. Foreign capital entered the U.S., investing in government securities, canals, and land. Both the First and Second National Banks had foreign stockholders. Some foreign investors profited, but many did not. In the years 1816–19, some $50 million in U.S. securities held by foreigners were in default. This retarded the entry of foreign capital in the 1820s.

NET LIABILITIES OF THE U.S. TO FOREIGNERS
1789–1830
(in millions of dollars)

Year	Amount	Year	Amount	Year	Amount
1830	75	1816	118	1802	74
1829	83			1801	81
1828	85	1815	80		
1827	74	1814	65	1800	83
1826	84	1813	56	1799	81
		1812	71	1798	96
1825	81	1811	50	1797	94
1824	88			1796	83
1823	89	1810	85		
1822	91	1809	92	1795	79
1821	83	1808	104	1794	66
		1807	87	1793	75
1820	88	1806	82	1792	77
1819	89			1791	69
1818	104	1805	75		
1817	109	1804	65	1790	61
		1803	77	1789	60

There were some U.S. investments abroad by traders and individual investors in commercial and producing activities, and by individuals in securities, but the total was small. The inflow of capital far exceeded the outflow.

1815–60. FOREIGN COMMERCE. Imports rose after the War of 1812 to an annual average of nearly $100 million (1815–20), declined to $72 million (1821–30), rising again in the following decades to $284 million (1851–60), with the greatest advances after 1850. Despite the growth of the domestic textile industry, **woolen and cotton manufactures** were the leading imports, amounting to 20% of the total, 1860, as against 29%, 1821, but rising in value from $12.7 million (1821) to $69.2 (1860). **Sugar** was the principal commodity imported, rising from 5% of the total imports (1821) to 9% (1860), with **coffee** in second place (6%, both years). **Exports** averaged $70 million (1815–20), remained steady during the next decade, but rose gradually to an average of $249 million (1851–60). **Cotton** remained the No. 1 export, rising in value from $321 million (1836–40) and 43% of exports to $744.6 million and 54% of total, 1856–60. Domestic manufactures amounted to 12% of total exports, 1856–60, wheat and flour 11%, while tobacco declined from 15% (1816–20) to 6% (1856–60). Beef and pork products rose from 2% of the total, 1812–20, to 6% (1856–60). **New York** and **New Orleans** shared first position among export ports, but 70% of imports entered New York. The bulk of exports went to the European market, with the West Indies declining in importance.

1830–60. INTERNATIONAL INVESTMENT. During the 1830s, British capital entered the U.S. in quantity, investing in canals, railroads, land, state bonds. That the U.S. government was able to pay off the national debt encouraged the inflow of British capital. The U.S. seemed a secure place for investment. But by the late 1830s, the British had become wary of U.S. investment. In 1841–42 there were U.S. defaults. Thus, America in the 1840s did not attract new investments. Its net foreign obligations were less in 1849 than in 1839. With the booming American economy in the 1850s, once again foreign (mainly British) capital entered the U.S.

There were U.S. direct and portfolio investments in foreign countries. The first "branch" plant of an American industrial company was started in England

NET LIABILITIES OF THE U.S. TO FOREIGNERS
1830–60
(in millions of dollars)

Year	Amount	Year	Amount
1860	377	1845	209
1859	384	1844	213
1858	358	1843	217
1857	381	1842	239
1856	364	1841	257
1855	352	1840	261
1854	337	1839	292
1853	295	1838	243
1852	239	1837	240
1851	223	1836	218
1850	217	1835	159
1849	188	1834	129
1848	191	1833	110
1847	189	1832	96
1846	208	1831	89

(Colt, 1852–53). The flow abroad of American capital was negligible compared with the influx of foreign capital into the U.S.

1789–1860. MERCHANT MARINE. U.S.-owned tonnage entering U.S. ports increased from 127,000 (1789) to 1,116,-000 (1807), but declined sharply during the War of 1812 to 60,000 (1814). Thereafter U.S. tonnage entering showed a steady growth (784,000, 1819; 1,577,-000, 1840; 5,921,000, 1860), but its proportion of the total tonnage of all vessels cleared in foreign trade declined from 90% (1821) to 71% (1860), reflecting rising U.S. shipbuilding costs and U.S. cost disadvantage in building **iron** ships. **Transatlantic packet lines** were inaugurated by New York merchants, 1818. By 1845, 52 transatlantic packets were sailing regularly from New York (three sailings weekly). Average time (Liverpool-New York), 1818–22, 39 days; 1848–52, 33.3 days (reflecting improved efficiency of ship design). **Clipper ships,** especially 1843–60, set numerous speed records: Boston to San Francisco, 89 days, 8 hrs. (*Flying Cloud*, 1854). **Steamboats** in transatlantic trade were used from 1838, but were not competitive with the packets until 1848. In 1840 a Canadian, Samuel Cunard, with the aid of a British government mail subsidy, established a steamboat line, Liverpool to Boston; challenged by Collins Line (U.S.) in 1850–57. Speed increased to 13 knots by 1860, but by that date steam navigation was largely in European hands. Factors leading to the decline of U.S. shipping: (1) reluctance of Americans to shift from sails to steam; (2) federal subsidies for mail carrying, inaugurated 1845, were less liberal than the British and were discontinued by Congress in 1858; revived 1862; (3) U.S. shops were unable to produce large iron frames and large steam engines.

1861–65. FOREIGN COMMERCE DURING THE CIVIL WAR. Value of exports declined from $400 million (1860) to an average of $248 million (1861–65), reflecting decline of cotton exports. Imports showed a much smaller decline, from $362 million (1860) to an average of $275 million (1861–65). Net tonnage of American vessels entering U.S. ports declined from 5,024,000 (1861) to 2,944,000 (1865), while foreign tonnage increased from 2,218,000 (1861) to 3,217,000 (1865).

1866–1914. EXPANSION OF FOREIGN TRADE. Value of exports more than trebled from $434 million (1866) to $1,499 million (1900), while imports more than doubled (from $445 million, 1866, to $929 million, 1900). **Chief Exports: Baled cotton** remained No. 1 export item ($192 million, 1860; $243 million, 1900), but its proportion declined from c.60% to c.17%. Meat exports rose to $176 million (1900) and exports of grain and grain products rose to $159 (1900). Both petroleum products and machinery ($84 million and $78 million respectively in 1900) became major exports during the period. Europe bought 80% of U.S. exports (1860) as against 76.7% (1901–05), while imports from Europe declined from 61.3% to 52.6% in the same period, during which exports to South America rose from 9.9% to 13.2% and to Asia from 8.3% to 14.6%.

The value of U.S. exports rose from $1.6 billion (1901) to $2.5 billion (1914); U.S. imports increased from $.9 billion (1901) to $2 billion (1914). Unmanufactured cotton continued as No. 1 export ($610 million, 1914).

In 1866, 72% of American exports were crude materials and crude foodstuffs; in 1914, 60% of U.S. exports were manufactured foodstuffs, semi-manufactures, and finished manufactures. In 1866, 75% of U.S. imports were manufactured goods; in 1914, 47% of U.S. imports were crude materials and crude foodstuffs (53% were manufactured goods).

1866–1914. U.S. MERCHANT MARINE. In 1860 American ships carried two thirds of U.S. ocean-bound commerce, but this figure declined to 10% in 1914. Decline was due to unfavorable cost differentials in ship construction, repair, and operation, and the American policy of limiting registration of the national merchant marine to American-built ships.

1866–1914. GROWTH OF INTERNATIONAL INVESTMENT. Foreign (in large part British) capital flowed into the U.S. (with reversals in the late 1870s and 1890s); a large amount of the funds went into financing U.S. railroads. Most British investment in the U.S. was in securities that did not carry management. Far more slowly, U.S. investment abroad also rose; U.S. foreign stakes were predominantly in direct investment that carried with the investment managerial

INTERNATIONAL INVESTMENT POSITION OF THE U.S. 1869 TO 1914
(in billions of dollars)

Year	Foreign Investments in the U.S.	U.S. Investments Abroad
1869	1.5	.1
1897	3.4	.7
1908	6.4	2.5
1914	7.2	3.5

control. Large American industrial corporations from their origins participated in international investment.

1914–45. FOREIGN TRADE FROM WORLD WAR I THROUGH WORLD WAR II. U.S. merchandise exports rose from 1914 to 1920 ($2.3 billion, 1914; $8.1 billion, 1920); they fell sharply with the recession of 1921 and fluctuated in the 1920s between a low of $3.8 billion (1922) and a high of $5.2 billion (1929); with the depression they sank to $1.6 billion (1932); then they rose slowly, reaching $3.3 billion in 1937, to decline in 1938, increase slightly in 1939; with World War II, U.S. exports once more soared (1940, $3.9 billion; 1941, $5 billion; 1942, $8 billion; 1943, $12.8 billion; 1944, $14.2 billion; 1945, $9.6 billion).

U.S. merchandise exports every year exceeded U.S. merchandise imports. But imports grew too from 1914 to 1920 ($1.9 billion to $5.3 billion); dropped in 1921 to $2.5 billion, and remained in the 1920s in the range of $3.1 billion (1922) to $4.4 billion (1926). 1930–32 saw a sharp dip in imports to a nadir of $1.4 billion (1932); slowly imports recovered, reaching $3 billion (1937), but then declining to $2 billion in 1938. Imports then moved slowly upward (1942 excepted), peaking in 1945 at $4.1 billion.

In 1914, America's principal exports had been crude materials (34% of U.S. exports); in 1945 finished manufactured goods accounted for 65% of U.S. exports (crude materials accounted for only 9%). In 1945 major exports by value were machinery, petroleum and petroleum products, and automobiles. In 1914 crude materials (including hides and skins, silk, and rubber) represented the largest single category of imports; in 1945, the largest single category of imports remained crude materials (raw materials of all kinds were imported to support the U.S. war effort).

In 1914 America's principal trading partner remained the U.K. Germany and Canada ranked second and third. 1945: Canada became America's key trading partner (taking $1,178 million in U.S. exports and sending the U.S. $1,125 million in merchandise, making a total trade of $2,303 million); the U.K. obtained from the U.S. $2,193 million in exports but sent the U.S. only $90 million in merchandise, making a total trade of $2,283 million.

1914–45. U.S. MERCHANT MARINE. Expansion of the merchant marine during World War I was the result of (1) the activity of the U.S. Shipping Board (est. by act of Congress, Sept. 1916); (2) seizure by the U.S. of German vessels (600,000 tons) upon U.S. entry into the war; (3) chartering by by Congress of the Emergency Fleet Corporation to build, own, and operate a merchant fleet for the U.S. government. Some 700 vessels (300 of them wooden) were completed by the armistice. Subsequently the Shipping Board disposed of c.1,100 vessels to U.S. citizens (for Merchant Marine Act [1920], see p. 390). In view of the decline of U.S. shipping from 18 million tons (1923) to 16 million (1928), Congress passed the **Jones-White Act** (1928, p. 397), providing for loans to private shipowners for new shipbuilding and for subsidies for mail carrying. The act failed to stimulate substantial ship construction, but $176 million in mail subsidies were paid out by 1937. The **Merchant Marine Act** (1936, p. 418) continued low-interest construction loans and inaugurated a policy of encouraging a merchant marine for national defense. The program expanded with the outbreak of World War II. U.S. tonnage entered rose to a record high (61,465,000) in 1945, but subsequently declined to 35,376,000 (1950).

1914–45. VICISSITUDES OF INTERNATIONAL INVESTMENT. America was a debtor nation in 1914; by 1919, America had become the greatest creditor nation in the world. In the 1920s, Americans made extensive direct foreign investments, carrying management, and also portfolio investments in foreign securities. U.S. foreign investments exceeded $15 billion (1929). In the 1930s, with the depression, Americans retreated from foreign investments; the devaluation of the dollar (1933) made foreign investment in the U.S. more attractive; in the late 1930s, Europeans were sending funds to the U.S. for safety. While the book value of U.S. investments abroad in 1940 was less than in 1929, foreign investment in the U.S. had risen 1934–40 and was higher in 1940 than in 1930.

During World War II, U.S. private foreign investment increased but not dramatically. The major element in the changing U.S. foreign investments related to the U.S. government's financing of the war effort. The Lend-Lease program (p. 434) involved a massive outflow of U.S. funds. The U.S. government became involved in international financial transactions as never before in history. In 1944, the U.S. participated in the **Bretton Woods Conference,** out of which emerged the **International Bank for Reconstruction and Development** (the World Bank) and the **International Monetary Fund** (IMF). The World Bank and later its associated agencies would play an important role in postwar development financing. The monetary arrangements set the basis for the free world monetary system for more than 25 years. The agreement that established the IMF provided for a pool of currencies and gold, drawn from member nations' reserves, to be available for aiding countries with short- and medium-term balance of payments problems.

Member currencies were valued according to a dollar-gold standard based on a fixed value of gold of $35 an ounce.

1945–73. FOREIGN TRADE. U.S. merchandise exports rose: 1945, $9.5 billion; 1950, $10.1 billion; 1960, $19.6 billion; 1970, $42 billion; 1972 (prel.), $47.4 billion. (The selected figures obscure periods of slumping exports, 1948–50, 1954, 1958–59.) U.S. imports rose more dramatically: 1945, $4.1 billion; 1950, $8.7 billion; 1960, $14.7 billion; 1970, $39.8 billion; 1972 (prel.), $54.4 billion. In 1971–72, for the first time in the 20th century, the U.S. had a deficit in its international trade accounts. America, once a large exporter of raw materials, became an importer of oil, copper, lead, and zinc. But America also became a leading importer of manufactured products. In fact, by the 1970s, the bulk of U.S. imports were manufactured goods.

FOREIGN TRADE 1960–70
(percentages by category)

	1960		1970	
	Exports	Imports	Exports	Imports
Food & beverages (incl. tobacco)	15.6	22.5	11.8	15.6
Crude materials (except fuel)	13.7	18.3	10.8	8.3
Mineral fuels & related materials	4.1	10.5	3.7	7.7
Chemicals	8.7	5.3	9.0	3.6
Machinery & Transport	34.3	9.7	42.0	28.0
Other Manu- factured Goods	18.7	30.3	17.9	33.3

In 1960 by value the 4 leading U.S. exports (in $ billions) were nonelectrical machinery (3.4), transporation equipment (2.5), grains and preparations (1.8), metals and manufactures (1.6); leading imports: petroleum and products (1.6), metals and manufactures (1.5), coffee (1.0), and ores and metal scrap (.8). In 1970 the leading exports: non-

electrical machinery (8.7), transportation equipment (6.2), electrical machinery (3.0), metals and manufactures (3.0); leading imports: transportation equipment (5.8), metals and manufactures (4.5), nonelectrical machinery (3.1), petroleum and products (2.8). In 1972 the leading exports: nonelectrical machinery (9.5), transportation equipment (8.2), electrical machinery (3.7), grains and cereals (3.5); leading imports: transportation equipment (9.6), metals and manufactures (6.0), nonelectrical machinery (4.4), petroleum and products (4.3).

1972, July–Aug. The Soviet Union made arrangements to buy U.S. grain, the largest order in U.S. history of grain exporting. The exports were U.S. government subsidized, under a wheat export subsidy that had been in effect since 1949. The size of the order pushed up domestic prices, contributing to inflation in the U.S.

1973. The 2 devaluations of the dollar (p. 711) improved the competitive position of U.S. exports and the U.S. trade balance once more became positive.

1945–72. Canada was U.S.'s key trading partner (1972: U.S. exports to Canada, $12.4 billion; U.S. imports from Canada, $14.9 billion). The U.K. ranked 2d through 1959; in 1960 Japan became the U.S.'s 2d most important trading partner (1972: U.S. exports to Japan, $4.9 billion; U.S. imports from Japan $9.1 billion). In 1961, the German Federal Republic surpassed the U.K. as the U.S.'s 3d most important trading partner (1972: U.S. exports to Germany, $2.8 billion; U.S. imports from Germany, $4.2 billion). In 1972, as a region, Western Europe was the major trading partner with the U.S. (1972: U.S. exports to Western Europe, $15.3 billion; U.S. imports from Western Europe, $15.4 billion).

1945–72. FOREIGN TRANSACTIONS OF THE U.S. GOVERNMENT.

From 1945 to 1947, the U.S. government participated in limited foreign aid programs; with the Marshall plan (p. 468) postwar foreign aid began on scale; in the 1950s U.S. foreign aid was shifted from Europe to less developed countries. By the 1960s and early 1970s, the U.S. was giving financial aid and technical assistance through the Agency for International Development (AID), the Export-Import Bank (p. 410), the Food for Peace Program, the Peace Corps (p. 492), and through contributions and subscriptions to such international lending organizations as the International Bank for Reconstruction and Development, the International Development Association, the Inter-American Bank, and the Asian Development Bank. U.S. foreign economic loans and grants (obligations and loan authorizations) averaged 1962–71 $4.7 billion per annum. 1972: Loans, $3.4 billion; grants $2.3 billion; total, $5.7 billion. In addition, unilateral outflows for military transactions were made by the U.S. government in connection with stationing of U.S. troops abroad, support to friendly governments, and fighting the Korean and Vietnam wars. The net outflow from the U.S. on military transactions was $.5 billion in 1946; it rose to $.8 billion in 1948 and declined in the next 2 years; with the Korean War the outflow increased and when the war was over the ascent continued; 1951, $1.3 billion; 1952, $2.1 billion; 1953, $2.4 billion; 1954, $2.5 billion; 1955, $2.7 billion; by 1958 it was up to $3.1 billion; then it declined slowly to reach a low of $2.1 billion in 1965, after which with the Vietnam War the figure moved steadily upward, peaking at $3.4 billion in 1970. A small decline in 1971 ($2.9 billion outflow) was offset when the outflow in 1972 reached a new all-time high of $3.6 billion.

1946–81. PRIVATE INTERNATIONAL INVESTMENTS.

American interest in foreign investment revived slowly after the war; by the mid-1950s, U.S. private foreign investment had started to accelerate. The bulk of the private foreign investment was by large U.S. corporations that developed and enlarged multinational operations. They built plants near their major customers around the world. Some of the private foreign investment involved overflow of funds from the U.S.; other investment involved the reinvestment of profits earned abroad.

U.S. DIRECT INVESTMENTS ABROAD
(book value at year's end—in $ billions)

1950	11.8
1960	31.8
1970	78.2
1979 (prel.)	192.6

The bulk of the U.S. direct investment was in industrial countries, for that was where the main markets were located. 1972 (prel.): $64.1 billion of the $94.0 billion total direct investment was in developed countries. The leading countries for U.S. direct investment abroad (book value at the end of 1972) were: Canada, which had $24.7 billion, the U.K., $9.0 billion, and Germany, $5.2 billion (prel. figures). Sales by U.S. multinational corporations abroad far exceeded U.S. exports.

Foreign investments in the U.S. also mounted, direct investments rising from $415 million (1965) to $6.294 billion (1979). By early 1980s Canadian, European, and Japanese firms had set up businesses in U.S. or were involved in takeovers.

1946–72. BALANCE OF PAYMENTS PROBLEMS.

In the immediate postwar period, Europeans were short on dollars; American aid gave Europeans the opportunity to buy dollar goods. Gold flowed into the U.S. U.S. gold stocks *increased* from $20.7 billion to $24.6 billion, 1946–49. After the devaluation of the pound sterling in Sept. 1949 (from $4.86 to $2.80), a change occurred: the U.S. began to run balance of payments deficits. In 1950, U.S. gold stock was down to $22.8 billion.

1958–60. Balance of payments and gold drain. As a result of a sharp decline in exports, 1958–59, higher spending abroad by U.S. tourists, increased U.S. private investment abroad, foreign economic aid, and U.S. military expenditures overseas, the U.S. lost over $4 billion in gold in 1958–60, with gold stock dropping below $18 billion by Dec. 1960. To stem the deficit in balance of payments President Eisenhower ordered (16 Nov. 1960) substantial reduction in total number of dependents of military personnel abroad, to go into effect 1 Jan. 1961, as well as cuts in staffs of civilian agencies abroad and purchases of foreign goods.

Kennedy administration efforts to stem the deficit in balance of payments included a rise in the rediscount rate (1963) from 3 to 3.5% by the Federal Reserve Board.

2 Sept. 1964. Interest Equalization Tax became law, designed to discourage U.S. investment abroad. Early in 1965, France decided to exchange $200 million of its dollar holdings for gold. President Johnson recommended new measures to cope with the now chronic balance of payments difficulties. He urged tourists to travel in the U.S. and called for voluntary curbs on foreign investments by bankers and businessmen.

Speculation in the dollar increased after the devaluation of the pound sterling by Great Britain (18 Nov. 1967) from $2.80 to $2.40 and with the concurrent rise in the interest rate to 8%. The Federal Reserve increased the dis-

count rate from 4% to 4.5% while banks raised the prime interest rate to 6% from 5.5%. President Johnson imposed mandatory curbs on most direct investments abroad by U.S. corporations (1 Jan. 1968) and ordered a 10% reduction in the overseas staffs of U.S. agencies (18 Jan.).

Following a wave of speculative buying in the world gold markets (1–14 Mar.), the U.S. and 6 Western European nations agreed to supply no more gold to private buyers, and established a 2-price system in gold, the official $35/oz. and a free-market fluctuating price (17 Mar. 1968). Congress eliminated the requirement that 25% of U.S. currency be backed in gold (19 Mar.), freeing $10.4 billion in gold reserves for use in meeting international demands for gold.

The U.S. payments position improved in 1968. Measured on a net liquidity basis the balance was less negative, while on an official reserve transactions basis there was a positive balance. The improvement was, however, temporary; the trade deficit in 1971 put new and more serious strains on the U.S. balance of payments. Confidence in the dollar deteriorated. From the start of 1971 to mid-August, the U.S. Treasury paid out over $3 billion in reserve assets—about 40% of this in early August. **15 Aug. 1971,** President Nixon announced new methods to curb inflation (p. 752), suspension of the convertibility of the dollar into gold, a 10% surcharge on goods imported into the U.S., and a 10% reduction in foreign aid.

With the suspension of convertibility, the dollar lost ground in relation to the major foreign currencies. The dollar had been the key currency in the international monetary system established at Bretton Woods in 1944. This system had served as a basis for international monetary transactions throughout the postwar

period. It had proved relatively successful, but since about 1965, with the dollar
under fire, the system had showed signs
of strain. There had been adaptations;
the introduction, for example, of Special
Drawing Rights (SDRs), first issued in
1970, had added a new reserve currency
and served to increase international
liquidity. Nonetheless, with the vast expansion of the world economy, a system inaugurated in 1944 clearly needed
major revisions in order to apply to the
1970s. **17–18 Dec. 1971,** meeting of the
Group of Ten (made up of representatives of major industrial nations) at the
Smithsonian Institution, Washington,
D.C. 18 Dec. Smithsonian Agreement included a new set of exchange rates (the
dollar would be devalued in terms of
gold to $38.00 an ounce, from $35.00 an
ounce); provisions were made for a wider
band that let market rates move to 2.25%
above or below the new central rates;
the U.S. agreed to lift the surtax on imports imposed on 15 Aug. The way was
opened for discussions of major modifications in the Bretton Woods system. **31
Mar. 1972,** the new price of gold at
$38.00 an ounce was signed into law in
the U.S.

In 1972, as the U.S. trade deficit
worsened, confidence in the dollar
weakened. **12 Feb. 1973,** after c.$6
billion of unwanted dollars flooded
Europe and Japan, the U.S. announced it
was again devaluing the dollar; the new
rate was set at $42.22 an ounce of gold.
22 Feb., the free market price of gold
reached $90 an ounce as speculators
dumped dollars. Despite steps taken by
the Group of Ten, confidence was not
restored. In June, Germany revalued the
Deutsche mark; the dollar declined in
value. In July the free market price of
gold reached a record $127 an ounce,
and then declined. Prospects of an improving U.S. trade balance—made possible by the devaluation—and the energy
crisis (p. 731) that affected Europe and
Japan more than the U.S. together served
to strengthen the dollar. **13 Nov.,** the
U.S. and 6 Western European nations
terminated their 1968 agreement prohibiting the sale of gold on the free
market by monetary authorities. The
gold price dropped, closing 14 Nov. at
$90 an ounce. By 1979 gold had risen to
$307.5, reaching a high above $800
(1980), and falling to c. $400 (1981).

U.S. BALANCE OF PAYMENTS 1960–72
(billions of dollars)

	1960–64 average	1965–69 average	1968	1969	1970	1971	1972
Net Liquidity Balance	−2.8	−3.4	−1.6	−6.1	−3.8	−22.0	−13.8
Official Reserve Transactions Balance	−2.2	*	1.6	2.7	−9.8	−29.8	−10.3

* Less than $.05 billion

U.S. Gold Stock
(billions of dollars)*

1950	1960	1970	1979
22.8	17.8	11.1	11.1

* U.S. reserve assets are greater than the gold
stock, since they include Special Drawing Rights
(as of 1970), convertible foreign currencies, and a
reserve position in the International Monetary Fund.

Tariffs

**1607–1789. COLONIAL PERIOD
AND THEREAFTER.** The American
colonies were subject to British imperial
rules (pp. 697–700) and were not
allowed to establish their own tariffs.

After the revolution, various states erected tariffs. The Constitution gave Congress the sole power to impose national tariffs; there could be no tariffs established by the states.

1789–1816. EARLY TARIFFS. Tariff of 1789 (4 July), designed chiefly for revenue, with moderately protectionist features, provided for (1) specific duties on 30 commodities including molasses, hemp, steel, and nails; (2) ad valorem rates (from 7½% to 15%, averaging 8½%) on listed articles; (3) 5% duty on all other goods (increased, 1792, to 7½%). A 10% reduction in duties was permitted on articles imported in U.S.-built or -owned shipping. Ad valorem duties rose to c.12½% (by 1812) and later (during War of 1812) to c.25%. **Tonnage Act** (20 July 1789) taxed U.S.-built and -owned vessels 6 cents per ton; U.S.-built but foreign-owned shipping, 30 cts.; foreign-built and -owned shipping, 50 cts.

1816–28. RISE OF PROTECTION. Tariff of 1816 (27 Apr.) placed a duty of 25% on most woolen, cotton, and iron manufactures (reduced, 1819, to 20%). Cheap cottons were virtually excluded by setting a minimum valuation on cotton cloth of 25 cts. a sq. yd. Ad valorem rate of 30% on certain goods including paper, leather, and hats; 15% on all other commodities. Chief opposition came from New England shipping interests. **Tariff of 1818** (20 Apr.) increased rates on iron manufactures; 25% duty on cotton and woolens was extended to 1826 instead of being reduced to 20% in 1819, as provided in Act of 1816. **Tariff of 1824** (22 May) increased protection for iron, lead, glass, hemp, and cotton bagging. The 25% minimum duty on cotton and woolens was increased to 33½%, but rates for raw wool advanced 15%. New England commercial and shipping interests joined with the South in opposition. In the **"Tariff of Abominations"** (19 May 1828) protection reached its highest

point before the Civil War. An ad valorem duty of 50% as well as a specific duty of 4 cts. per lb. were imposed on raw wool; 45% ad valorem on most woolen; duties on pig and bar iron and hemp sharply increased.

1832–60. LOWERING OF DUTIES. The **Tariff of 1832** (14 July) eliminated the features of the Tariff of 1828 objectionable to the manufacturers and commercial East; increased the duty on woolens, but admitted cheap raw wool and flax free. Hence, it was viewed in the South as a sectional measure. The **Compromise Tariff** (2 Mar. 1833) expanded the free list (including worsted goods and linens), and provided for a gradual reduction of all duties above 20% by removing, at 2-year intervals (from 1834 to 1842), one tenth from each impost in excess of that level. Chief opposition came from New England and the Middle States. The **Tariff of 1842** (30 Mar.), a Whig measure, returned the tariff to the level of 1832 with duties averaging (1842–45) between 23% and 35%. The **Walker Tariff** (30 July 1846), a Democratic measure, essentially for revenue, reversed the trend (since 1816) of substituting specific for ad valorem duties and dropped the minimum valuation principle. A few commodities were duty free. The **Tariff of 1857** (3 Mar.), another Democratic measure, reduced the tariff to a general level of 20%, the lowest rate since 1850, and enlarged the free list.

1861–97. TRIUMPH OF PROTECTION. The **Morrill Tariff** (2 Mar. 1861) once more substituted specific for ad valorem duties and raised duties generally from (5% to 10%). Subsequent revision (16 July 1862, 30 June 1864, 2 Mar. 1867, 24 Feb. 1869) increased duties to an average rate of 47%. The **Tariff of 1870** (14 July) reversed the trend, placing 130 articles, mostly raw materials, on the free list and provided for some small reductions in rates on other commodities. The **Tariff of 1872** (6 June) continued this trend, reducing by 10% the rates on all manufactured goods. Most of these reductions, however, were restored by the Act of 1875 (3 Mar.). The **Tariff of 1883** (3 Mar.), lowered schedules 5% but retained the protectionist principle. The **McKinley Tariff** (1 Oct. 1890) raised the average level to 49.5% and provided for reciprocal raising of duties to meet discrimination by foreign nations. Its successor, the **Wilson-Gorman Tariff** (28 Aug. 1894), which became law without President Cleveland's signature, put wool, copper, and lumber on the free list and lowered duties to the average level of 39.9%. The **Dingley Tariff** (7 July 1897) raised rates to a new high (average level 57%), imposed high duties on raw and manufactured wool, and restored hides to the dutiable list.

1909–21. PERIOD OF MODERATION. The **Payne-Aldrich Tariff** (9 Apr. 1909) lowered duties to c.38%. Its successor, the **Underwood Tariff** (3 Oct. 1913) lowered duties yet further to c.30% and put iron, steel, raw wool, and sugar (the latter in 1916) on the free list.

1921–34. RETURN TO PROTECTION. The **Emergency Tariff** (27 May 1921) reversed the downward trend of the Wilson administration by raising rates on most agricultural products. Its successor, the **Fordney-McCumber Tariff** (21 Sept. 1922) exceeded the rates of 1909 up to 25% on manufactured goods, with high duties imposed on farm products. The tariff introduced the "American selling price," a valuation of duties on chemical products based not on foreign market value but on the selling price of U.S. domestic output, which in effect increased the duties. The **Smoot-Hawley Tariff** (17 June 1930) raised rates upon agricultural raw materials from 38% to 49% and on other commodities from 31%

to 34%, with special protection given to sugar and textile interests. Under the Fordney-McCumber Act the president was authorized to change individual tariff rates on recommendation of the **Tariff Commission** (est. 1916), but such changes were limited to 50% of the congressional rates.

1934–60. TOWARD FREER TRADE. The **Trade Agreements Act** (12 June 1934) authorized the president to enter into agreements with other governments for the reduction of specific duties by as much as 50%. Such agreements (1) did not require congressional ratification; (2) were to be based on the unconditional most-favored-nation principle. By 1951 agreements had been concluded with 53 nations with which the U.S. did more than 80% of its normal foreign trade. The act was extended for 3-year periods down to 1951 and by Act of 16 June 1951 for a 2-year period, with certain restrictions imposed on the president's power to make concessions and the requirement that "escape clauses" be included in all agreements. On 1 Aug. President Truman proclaimed cancellation of tariff concessions to countries under Soviet control. Three major international tariff conferences were held after World War II: (1) **Geneva**, where, 30 Oct. 1947, a **General Agreement on Tariffs and Trade (GATT)** was concluded by 28 nations, with some two thirds of the trade items between the participating countries covered by concessions; (2) **Annecy,** France, 1949, where additional nations entered the Geneva Agreement and the U.S. granted concessions on about 400 items; (3) **Torquay**, England (Sept. 1950–Apr. 1951), where the U.S. received concessions on an estimated half billion dollars of 1949 exports. The effect of the Trade Agreements program had been to reduce U.S. tariffs from an average of 53%, 1930–33, to less than 15% by 1951.

Modifications of the New and Fair Deal tariff policy were introduced during the Eisenhower administration. On 21 June 1955 the Trade Agreements Act was extended for 3 years, with authority granted to the president to reduce tariffs 5% a year in return for foreign concessions, and on duties in excess of 50% ad valorem. On 20 Aug. 1958 the act extended the president's authority for 4 years, but also authorized increasing rates 50% above rates in effect on 1 July 1934 (instead of previously specified date of 1 Jan. 1945). Quota restrictions were proclaimed (22 Sept.) on imports of lead and zinc to 80% of average for preceding 5 years. Mandatory quotas on oil imports were imposed (Mar. 1959). Japan was encouraged to continue to extend its practice of establishing quotas on its shipment of certain items to the U.S.

1962. TRADE EXPANSION ACT (11 Oct.) contained unprecedented tariff-cutting authority for the president, authorizing him to reduce existing tariff of 1 July 1962 by 50% in 5 years. Further authority was granted to eliminate duties (1) on categories for which U.S. and European Economic Community together account for 80% of free world exports, (2) on selected agricultural commodities where such modification would assure some level of increase of U.S. exports of like goods, (3) on tropical agricultural or forestry products not produced in U.S. if EEC would reciprocate, (4) on articles for which ad valorem rate was 5% or less. Any industry, firm, or group of workers threatened with or experiencing serious injury as a result of tariff concession and increased imports can apply for assistance to be given in various forms such as loans, tax relief, technical assistance, unemployment allowances, and retraining or relocation allowances for workers.

1964–67. KENNEDY ROUND. Extensive negotiations began 1964 in Geneva among 50 countries accounting for 80%

of world trade for reduction of trade duties. The 6th round, under GATT, concerned itself with multilateral trade negotiations. Unlike the earlier negotiations, the Kennedy Round was conducted on a linear, across-the-board basis rather than item-by-item. It dealt with agricultural as well as industrial products, considered nontariff as well as tariff barriers to trade, and provided special negotiation procedures for developing countries. The principal result of the round was a tariff reduction of 50% by major participants on most industrial products and reductions of 30% to 50% on others. The average reduction of duties on industrial articles was about 35%.

1967–73. TARIFF AND TRADE POLICY. General U.S. policy continued to be toward freer trade; nonetheless, as imports rose (p. 708), protectionist sentiment grew. With the exception of the temporary 10% surcharge on imports (introduced 15 Aug. 1971 and removed 18 Dec. 1971), no new tariffs were imposed. But there were nontariff barriers to trade. The U.S. and Japan agreed that Japan would limit its steel and textile exports to the U.S. Until 1 May 1973 petroleum imports remained subject to quotas. Sugar, meat, and dairy products were under quantitive restrictions.

Efforts were made to stimulate U.S. exports, including: (1) extension of export credits; (2) under the Revenue Act of 1971, U.S. exporters could establish a Domestic International Sales Corporation (DISC); taxes on 50% of a DISC's income could be deferred indefinitely if 95% of DISC's receipts and assets were export-related; (3) attempts to increase East-West trade; and (4) most important, the devaluations of the dollar (pp. 710, 711).

1973 (12–14 Sept.). The 7th round of international trade discussions under the auspices of GATT opened in Tokyo, with 103 countries participating. The goal was to liberalize world trade still further, although developing nations were demanding preferential treatment. The U.S. sought to open European and Japanese markets to larger U.S. farm exports.

Domestic Commerce

1607–1775. INTERNAL AND INTERCOLONIAL COMMERCE. Aside from furs, the only frontier product that could bear the cost of overland haulage was **potash,** exchanged with the Middle Colonies for grain, primarily wheat (after 1720). Other New England ports depended on Boston for their European products, as did many Southern regions, notably North Carolina. Tonnage clearing Boston for the coastal trade (1714–17, 11,589) roughly equal that clearing for Great Britain. As late as 1769 Boston still led in the coastal trade, with New York and Philadelphia close rivals for 2nd place. In that year tonnage of vessels engaged in the coastal trade entering and clearing at colonial ports amounted to 213,000 tons as against 189,000 to and from Great Britain and Ireland, and 191,000 to and from the British and foreign West Indies.

1607–1789. RETAIL TRADE. Little specialization existed: in trade with Indians or settlers, in rural or urban areas, merchants handled a variety of staples, cotton and woolen cloth, gunpowder, kitchenware, sugar, rum, drugs, axes, and trinkets; this was true of the trading post, the peddler, and the general store. Exceptions related to goods produced by craftsmen (the blacksmith, for example). The reason for the typical lack of specialization lay in the small, segmented markets and sometimes in the shortage of money (barter was not uncommon and the retailer resold the goods obtained).

1789–1830. INTERNAL COMMERCE. The rapidly increasing popula-

tion of the Ohio and Mississippi valleys (150,000, 1790; 1 million, 1810) utilized the interior river systems for shipment of commodities to **New Orleans,** especially after 1803. Receipts at the Gulf port rose from $5 million (1807) to $10 million (1816) and $22 million (1830). **Cincinnati** (population 10,000, 1818) became a principal shipping point for provisions (grain and hogs) and **Louisville** for tobacco. The introduction of the steamboat on Western waters (*Enterprise,* 1815, also p. 602) proved a great boon to this trade, and by 1825 half the river traffic was carried on steamboats. The Great Lakes region, slower in development, tended to ship to Montreal. Land haulage from the West continued ($18 million from Pittsburgh to Philadelphia, 1820).

1831–60. DOMESTIC COMMERCE. The completion of the Erie Canal (p. 602) promoted the eastward flow of commerce. Ohio (by 1830), Indiana (by 1835), Michigan (by 1836), Illinois (by 1838), and Wisconsin (by 1841) shipped grain to the Erie Canal, and, later, to the Lakes termini of the railroads. Pork, lumber, copper (after 1845), and iron (after 1855) moved eastward. Chicago, drawing from more westerly farmlands from 1849), became the chief grain-shipping center (20 million bu. by 1858), and its meat trade surpassed Cincinnati (by 1863). Cincinnati's trade, still oriented toward the South as late as 1850, switched to the East (by 1860). Mississippi traffic continued to grow, with receipts at New Orleans rising from $50 million (1840) to $185 million (1860). Cotton was the chief commodity handled, with livestock and provisions for the cotton and sugar plantations major items of river traffic. The tonnage moved through the Erie Canal increased one fourth over 1856–60 as trade between the East and Midwest expanded.

Opening the way for the trade expansion was the growth of the railroad network (pp. 606, 610).

1800–60. RETAIL AND WHOLE-SALE TRADE. The general merchant continued in rural areas and on the frontier, but in cities specialization in retailing occurred. By the 1850s the general merchant had disappeared from the city and in his place were groceries, dry goods, hardware, house furnishing stores, as well as bookstores, hosiery stores, tobacco shops, and so forth. Small stores proliferated, each confined to a specialized line of merchandise. The retail and wholesale functions became clearly separable. But even as specialization occurred, the pendulum swung back, and certain retailers once again started to buy directly from the manufacturer, eliminating the middleman. Other innovations in retailing included (1) cash-only sales, adoption began c.1806 and (2) a one-price policy used by Arthur Tappan in the 1820s; Lord & Taylor by 1838; at least 2 Boston firms before 1850; R. H. Macy (1822–1877) in 1851.

1860–1900. INTERNAL TRADE. Canal and railroad traffic increased during the Civil War years. Subsequently, industrial and agricultural growth and specialization of era were accompanied by a great expansion of internal trade. The railway network expanded from 36,801 miles (1866) to 193,346 miles (1900). Railroad freight rose from c.39 billion ton-miles (1861) to c.142 billion (1900). Tonnage of vessels engaged in coastwise and internal trade increased from c.2,720,000 (1866) to c.4,286,000 (1900), Great Lakes tonnage alone from 408,000 (1870) to 1,446,000 (1900), including, in addition to grain shipments, the now expanded output of Lake Superior copper and iron mines.

1862–1900. WHOLESALE MARKETING TRENDS IN MANUFACTURED GOODS: (1) shift from general commission merchant to sales through brokers or manufacturers' agents (representing more specialization in wholesaling); (2) manufacturing companies often integrated forward into handling their own wholesale trade, thus bypassing wholesalers.

1860–1900. CHANGING RETAIL PATTERNS. (1) The **department store** was developed by **Alexander Turney Stewart** (1807–76) in New York (1862), by R. H. Macy and Lord & Taylor in New York (1860–74), by **John Wanamaker** (1838–1922) in Philadelphia (1876) and in New York (1896), and by **Marshall Field** (1834–1906) in Chicago (1865–81). (2) **Mail order houses:** Montgomery Ward & Co., opened in Chicago, 1872, to sell to the Grangers, and Sears Roebuck (1895) revolutionized rural retailing. (3) **Chain stores:** Great Atlantic & Pacific Tea Co. (1859); **Frank Winfield Woolworth** (1852–1919), who opened his first "5-and-10-cent" store in Utica, N.Y., 1879; United Cigar Stores (1892). (4) **Advertising:** Participation of nationally advertised brands began with patent medicines on eve of the Civil War; business consolidations in the postwar period promoted large-scale advertising.

1901–73. INTERNAL TRADE. Railroad mileage (first-line track) continued to expand until 1929 (260,570 miles); declined gradually, 230,169 miles (1960) to 222,164 miles (1969). Ton-miles of freight carried fluctuated as follows (in billions): 1920, 414; 1929, 450; 1931–35, 270 (annual average); 1936–40, 341; 1941–45, 655; 1960, 675; 1972, 800. Percentage of total freight traffic measured in ton-miles hauled by railroads declined from 62.34 (1939) to 44.73 (1960) to 38.64 (1971), during which period freight carried by water declined from 17.71 to 16.61 to 15.90%; motor vehicular freight percentage rose from 9.72 to 21.46 to 22.28, oil pipelines from 10.23

to 17.14 to 23.00, and airplanes from .002 to 0.06 to .18%. Rail passenger revenue dropped from wartime peak of $915 million (1944) to $412 million (1957) to $257 million (1972). In same period total domestic airline revenues rose from $160 million to $1,515 million to $11,163 million.

In terms of **ton-miles,** although their percentage of the business declined, railroads remained the chief freight carriers. Piggyback service (trailer-on-flatcar) in the 1960s was an exceptional innovation. **1960–73:** railroad mergers multiplied. **1966:** ICC approved merger of the Pennsylvania R.R. and the New York Central into the Penn Central. **2 March 1970:** merger of the Great Northern Railway Co., the Northern Pacific Railway Co., the Chicago, Burlington & Quincy R.R. Co.; these were the railroads separated in the Northern Securities Case of 1904 (p. 673). Railroad bankruptcies were frequent, the most spectacular being that of Penn Central in 1970. **21 Dec 1973:** Congress approved $1.5 billion in guaranteed loans to create a new system uniting 7 bankrupt railroad lines. While continuing to be important as freight carriers, rail passenger service declined drastically. **1971, May:** Amtrak (est. by Rail Passenger Service Act of 1971), a quasi-governmental corporation, began operating most intercity passenger trains. Trucks provided more flexibility than railroads in freight transportation. In terms of **operating revenues,** from 1967 motor carriers of freight had higher revenues than the railroads. Automobiles, buses, and airplanes captured passenger traffic from the railroads.

1901–73. CHANGING MARKETING PATTERNS. Wholesaling. (1) Wholesalers services changed from trading to distribution, as more manufacturers marketed trademarked goods and handled advertising. (2) Specialization increased

in wholesaling. The number of wholesale establishments rose (in thousands): 1929, 168; 1954, 252; 1963, 308; 1967, 311. The kinds of business engaged in changed in importance. Number of establishments in leading businesses, 1929 (in thousands): petroleum bulk stations (20), groceries, incl. meat (15), farm products (9), dry goods and apparel, (8); 1967: machinery, equipment, supplies (52), groceries and related products (40), petroleum, petroleum products (34), motor vehicles and automotive equipment (31). Wholesale trade, 1973, $357.8 billion (est.).

Retailing. Changes in retailing were related to the spread of the automobile and the spread of affluence. The automobile enlarged the consumer's trading area and changed the contents of his retail purchases. Affluence extended the demand for numerous differentiated consumer products. Related changes in retailing: (1) Chain stores: 1919, 4% of all retail sales; 1933, 27%. Chains with 11 or more stores increased their percentage of the retail trade from 18.2% (1951), 25.8% (1965), 30.7% (1972). Mail-order houses, Sears Roebuck (1925) and Montgomery Ward (1926), began to open retail stores. (2) Chain franchises: in the 1920s, automobile dealers to fast-food stands (A & W Root Beer began one of the earliest fast-food franchises in 1925). In the 1950s and 1960s, franchised retail outlets assumed even greater importance and came to include motels, car rentals, and other service industries. (3) Shift of country stores to towns: in the 1920s, as automobiles extended the trading areas; the trend accelerated in later years. (4) As suburbs grew, the suburban department store first appeared in the 1920s. (5) The supermarket developed in the 1930s: 6,175 food supermarkets (1940); 11,885 (1948); chain store organizations opened supermarkets. (6) Discount stores emerged in the 1950s and rapidly became incorporated in chain operations. (7) 1950–73. Expansion of suburban shopping centers, including both chain and independent stores. Supermarkets and discount stores were included in shopping centers. There was a move away from shopping in the central city. (8) 1972–73. a number of department stores accepted bank-issued credit cards, a major policy change. Large department store chains began to install computerized credit verification and automated point-of-sale cash registers, providing more detailed information, improved inventory control, and faster credit authorization. Total retail sales (in billions): 1929, $48.3; 1954, $170; 1959, $215.4; 1972, $448.4; 1973, $488.0 (est.). Number of retail establishments (in millions): 1929, 1.5; 1954, 1.7; 1967, 1.8. The figures indicate that the sales per retail establishment have grown substantially over the years.

Advertising expenditures rose steadily until 1929, slumped in the depression, and from 1933 onward generally moved upward. Expenditures (in billions): 1900, $.5; 1920, $2.9; 1929, $3.4; 1933, $1.3; 1940, $2.1; 1950, $5.7; 1957, 10.3; 1967, $16.8; 1973, $25.8 (est.). Brand names came to dominate many branches of retailing. Index of national advertising expenditures (1957–59 = 100): 19 (1940), 162 (1970); by media: magazines, 24 (1940), 162 (1970); network radio, 206 (1940), 104 (1970); network TV, 12 (1950), 249 (1970); newspapers, 20 (1940), 127 (1970); outdoor, 25 (1940), 109 (1970)

Consumer credit expanded, reaching $7.1 billion (1929) about one-half in installment credit and one-half in charge accounts, single-payment loans, and service credit; it equaled 9.2% of personal consumption expenditures in 1929. By 1980 consumer credit had mounted to a new high of $373.4 billion, of which $303.8 billion was in installment credit.

Industry

From a country with small-scale, mostly workshop or home manufacture, American industry in the nineteenth century moved into the factory. Steam began to replace horsepower, waterpower, and often manpower. Business ownership was primarily by individuals or partnerships. Gradually, in the nineteenth century in some industries mass production began, using standardized, interchangeable parts. In the late nineteenth and early twentieth centuries new sources of power emerged: electricity and the internal-combustion engine. Industrial enterprise grew in scale. The corporation became dominant in industry. The twentieth century saw new ways of organizing work. True mass production was realized with the assembly line; scientific management made production more efficient. By the 1920s, American industrial companies were becoming more diversified in their output, using technology based on science, becoming more international, and developing new methods to administer large-scale multiproduct industrial organizations. After World War II, new power sources for industry emerged, principally nuclear power plants.

Growth industries were science- and technology-related. Processes of production became more efficient with the use of automated techniques, particularly the application of computers. Business organization grew in complexity, with the rise of conglomerates and vast multinational operations; business management became more sophisticated.

Products in the colonial period related to basic needs—eating, clothing, housing, and transportation. Since then, the number of products has risen sharply. In the nineteenth century more producer goods (products used to produce other goods) came to be made; new consumer goods were presented (canned milk, fresh beef transported over distances, bananas, Coca-Cola, cigarettes, and also consumer durables such as sewing machines and washing machines). The twentieth century saw a multiplication of both producer and consumer products. Consumer durables such as telephones, automobiles, radios, and refrigerators—and later, TV sets and dishwashers—spread. Synthetic products were new to the 1920s, and numerous by the post-World War II years. Science-based industry created a panoply of both producer and consumer goods.

By 1900, American industrial production held world leadership, a leadership that began to be challenged in the 1970s by the growth of industry in Germany and Japan. In the 1970s unfamiliar concerns over the environment and sources of energy began to plague U.S. industry, while the early 1980s saw giant mergers in the energy field, including Du Pont takeover of Conoco (1981).

CAPITAL INVESTMENT to 1789. Both European and colonial sources furnished capital for industry. English capital financed the colonial fisheries, control of which soon passed into the hands of settlers; as well as a large part of the New England shipbuilding industry, the Lynn Iron Works (1643–44), the Principio Co. in Maryland (1715), and the projects in New Jersey and New York of Peter Hasenclever, Prussian-trained ironmaster (c.1764). Government subsidies in various forms also aided industry. Colonial capitalists (with considerable fortunes acquired between 1750–83) generally preferred more conservative investments—real estate or British government securities—to industrial risks. Notable exceptions at the end of this period were **Robert Morris** and **William Duer**.

FOREST INDUSTRIES TO 1775. (1) **Lumbering** (white pine abundant in New England) prospered despite royal conservation measures (p. 699). British navy sought a source of forest products to lessen dependence upon Baltic countries. (2) **Shipbuilding** (fostered by Navigation Act of 1660, p. 698): By 1760 one third of the total British tonnage (398,-000) was colonial-built; 1765–75, 25,000 tons built yearly in the colonies. Except during period of New England inflation (1730–50), ships were constructed in the colonies 20%–50% below European costs. (3) **Naval stores:** Tar, pitch, turpentine, and potash favored by British bounties (p. 699). Exports rose (1770) to 82,000 barrels of tar, 9,000 pitch, 17,000 turpentine (value £175,000).

MARITIME INDUSTRIES TO 1775. **Fishing.** From the presettlement period down to the present day, codfishing from New England to Labrador has been steadily pursued. There were three grades: (1) best—traded down the coast for flour and tobacco; (2) medium—sent to Southern Europe (Catholic) in exchange for salt and wine; (3) "refuse" —shipped to sugar isles to feed the slaves (H. A. Innis). **Whaling** flourished to supply demand for spermaceti (for important candlemaking industry begun in Rhode Island, c.1750, with attempted intercolonial monopoly and price-fixing agreements, 1761–75), sperm oil, whalebone, and ambergris (for drugs, confectionery, and perfumery). By 1774 a fleet of 360 ships collected 45,000 barrels of sperm oil, 75,000 lbs. of whalebone.

TECHNOLOGY AND ORGANIZATION TO 1789. (1) **Workshop crafts** made custom-made goods, with the leather and hat industries (beaver felt hats despite restrictions under the Hat Act [p. 699] outstanding examples), and with high standards obtaining among silversmiths (e.g., Jeremiah Dummer of Boston, Simeon Soumaine and Myer Myers of New York), cabinetmakers (Joshua Delaplaine of New York, William Savery, Philadelphia), and clockmakers (the Claggetts and Willards of New England). (2) **Domestic or putting-out system,** notably in weaving (chiefly homespuns), encouraged by the Nonimportation Agreements (pp. 88, 91, 99) and shoemaking (organized in Lynn, Mass., for wholesale operations by 1760). (3) **Mills and factories:** Flourmilling, especially in the vicinity of New York and Philadelphia, produced for export. Oliver Evans' mill elevator (p. 792), with its conveyor belt and labor-saving, cost-cutting features, was introduced shortly after 1783 by Ellicott brothers on the Patapsco River. Notable strides took place in **iron manufacture** despite restrictions of Iron Act of 1750 (p. 699), with **Henry William Stiegel** (1729–85) outstanding (after 1760) as an ironmaster and glassware maker (after 1764). In 1700 the colonies produced one seventieth of the world's iron supply; in 1775, **one seventh,** with pig and bar iron production exceeding England and Wales combined. Bar iron exports, 1771, 2,234 tons. Other outstanding ironmasters include, for the 17th century, John Winthrop, Jr. (1606–76), in Massachusetts (at Lynn, 1643) and Connecticut; for the 18th, Alexander Spotswood (1676–1740), who established iron furnaces on the Rapidan River (1714), Robert Carter (1663–1732), Peter Hasenclever (1716–93), John Jacob Faesch (1729–99), William Alexander ("Lord Stirling," 1726–83), Charles Carroll (1737–1832), and Philip Livingston (1716–78).

1789–1807. EXPANSION OF FACTORY PRODUCTION. Textiles. Samuel Slater, copying Arkwright machinery, first spun cotton by power, 20 Dec. 1790, at Pawtucket, R.I., a venture financed by **Moses Brown** (1738–1836), a Quaker merchant. By 1800, 7 Arkwright mills, containing 2,000 spindles, were in operation. Attempts to apply power carding and spinning to wool had proved abortive as late as 1801.

Arms Manufacturing. Eli Whitney (p. 1182), turning in 1798 to arms production for the U.S. government, succeeded in developing a system of interchangeable parts. **Simeon North** (1765–1852) of Connecticut devised tools and machinery for the production of interchangeable parts in the manufacture of pistols, 1799. Many of the ideas came from techniques already worked out in woodworking and reproductive metal industries. Cards and nails were manufactured in uniform shapes by automatic mechanisms in the 1790s. **Eli Terry** (1772–1852) and **Seth Thomas** (1785–1859) began the manufacture of clocks at Plymouth Hollow, Conn., and the basis of interchangeable parts and quantity production (1807–12). Seth Thomas Clock Co. organized, 1853.

1808–18. Nonintercourse and the War

of 1812 boomed domestic manufacturing. Gallatin's report (1810) listed 14 woolen mills and 87 cotton mills. By 1816 it was estimated that $12 million was invested in the woolen industry, which produced an annual product worth $19 million. The **Boston Manufacturing Co.** (also called the Waltham Co.), established at Waltham, Mass., 1813, was the first textile factory to conduct **all** operations for converting cotton into cloth by power under a single management (the "**Waltham System**"). Other features: large capital investment, recruitment of New England farm girls housed in dormitories, and the production of standardized coarse cloth requiring minimum skills of operatives.

1816–30. IRON INDUSTRY REORGANIZES. (1) The production of bar iron by **puddling and rolling** as a continuous process in western Pennsylvania (at Plumstock), 1817; soon adopted by the iron industry at **Pittsburgh.** (2) Introduction in urban rolling mills of coal for refining pigs while rural blast furnaces continued to use charcoal.

Machinery Production. Although the manufacture of machinery as a separate branch of industry dates back as early as 1803, when **Oliver Evans** (1755–1819) established a shop to fabricate steam engines (**Mars Iron Works**), a **specialization** trend is more decided in this period. Among the largest units were the Allaire Works, 1816; the Merrimac Co. (textile machinery), 1820; and the Novelty Works, 1830. By 1830, 9 textile machinery works existed in Worcester, Mass., alone, with the Lowell and Lawrence shops among the largest. The founding of mills at **Lowell,** Mass., the "Manchester of America," 1822, by Jackson and Lowell, marked the rapid extension of the Waltham System in cotton manufacturing. By 1830 belt transmission of power, dating back to the 1790s,

began to be widely employed in textile manufacturing.

Paper Manufacture. Thomas Gilpin is credited with manufacturing the first machine-made paper in the U.S. (1817) near Wilmington, Del. **Fourdrinier process** of paper manufacture was introduced into the U.S. c.1825; placed in large-scale operation at Holyoke, Mass. (1853), by Parson Paper Co.

1830–50. STEAM ENGINES AND STEAM POWER. As steam engines came into common use, locomotive building was transferred from general machine shops to specialized works—Baldwin Works (1832), Norris Works (1834). Steam power, however, was not widely introduced in manufacturing until 1850. The expansion of steam utilization as well as puddling and rolling created a demand for **anthracite coal.** Anthracite production rose from 215,272 tons to over 1 million tons by 1837. Although Frederick W. Geisenheimer conducted successful experiments in smelting iron ore with anthracite, 1830, and the hot blast was introduced, 1834, charcoal remained practically the sole fuel used for smelting.

Textiles. Power weaving and the Waltham System were extended in wool manufacture, beginning at Lowell, Mass. (1830), and at Lawrence, Mass. (1845). A loom for the manufacture of figured woolens was successfully demonstrated, 1840, by William Crompton (1806–91), and the process improved by his son, George (1829–86). As a result, hand weaving in New England practically disappeared, but in frontier areas household manufactures actually expanded down to 1830. During this period the cotton industry about doubled its capacity, the number of spindles exceeding 2,280,000.

1840–50. RAPID PROGRESS IN THE IRON INDUSTRY resulted from (1) substitution of mineral coal for charcoal, (2) replacement of open forge by reverberatory-type closed furnace, (3) advances in refining and rolling (heavy rails successfully rolled, 1845), (4) large-scale adoption of steam power, and (5) expansion of the railroad system. On 4 July 1840 David Thomas (1794–1884) made the first successful attempt to produce pig iron by the use of anthracite coal in hot-blast furnace of the Lehigh Crane Ironworks at Catasauqua, Pa. Output of anthracite quadrupled, exceeding 4 million tons.

Machine shop products multiplied in variety on the basis of standardized parts and quantity production: plows, threshing machines, harvesters, reapers (McCormick factory, Chicago, 1847), revolving pistols, stoves, metal clocks, sewing machines (first practical sewing machine produced by the Singer factory, 1850).

Textiles. Installation of steam power operation in textile mills at Salem and New Bedford, Mass., 1847, freed the industry from the limitations of water power.

Household manufactures throughout the U.S. declined: Per capita value 1840, $1.70; 1850, $1.18; 1860, $.78.

1850–60. In 1859 the value of the products of U.S. industry ($1,885,862,-000) exceeded for the first time the value of agricultural products. In gross value of products flour milling ranked first (first commercial flour mill began operations at Minneapolis, 1854), followed by the iron industry. Anthracite iron held first place, followed in order by charcoal iron, and bituminous coal and coke iron. Lake Superior ores were beginning to be used by 1860. In the 20 years ending in 1860 the consumption of raw cotton by the textile industry had almost quadrupled, and the number of spindles more than doubled (exceeding 5,235,000). In capital invested, labor employed, and net value of product, the cotton industry was first in the U.S. by 1860.

This period is also marked by the emergence of **machine toolmaking** as a separate industry. The manufacture of the **vernier caliper** (1851) by J. R. Brown of Providence (later known as Brown and Sharpe Mfg. Co.), making possible measurements in thousandths of an inch, inaugurated true precision manufacturing. The **turret lathe** manufactured by Robbins and Laurence at Windsor, Vt., 1854, proved essential to mass production techniques.

Expansion of Steam-Powered Factories. By 1860 almost one fourth of the Fall River spindles were steam-driven.

MANUFACTURING BY SECTIONS, 1860

Section	Number of Establishments	Capital Invested	Average Number of Laborers	Annual Value of Products
New England	20,671	$257,477,783	391,836	$468,599,287
Middle States	53,387	435,061,964	546,243	802,338,392
Western States	36,785	194,212,543	209,909	384,606,530
Southern States	20,631	95,975,185	110,721	155,531,281
Pacific States	8,777	23,380,334	50,204	71,229,989
Territories	282	3,747,906	2,333	3,556,197
Total	140,533	$1,009,855,715	1,311,246	$1,885,861,676

Phenomenal increase in manufacturing output since 1860: the result of technological developments which have revolutionized (1) **mineral production** through deeper mining (improved ventilation and air-conditioning) and deeper drilling of oil wells (made possible by rotary drill and steel alloys); improved blasting techniques; the pneumatic rock drill, increasing drilling speed; power shovels; the cyanide process in gold and silver mining; the electrolytic process in aluminum, copper, zinc, and lead refining; the open-hearth method in steel production (man-hour production in mineral industry, 1902–39, multiplied 3.67 times, in oil and gas 5-fold); (2) **chemical industry** (rayon, rubber, oil, leather, plastics); (3) **alloyed metals** production; (4) **electric power** and the **internal-combustion engine** (cheapening transportation and promoting farm production and marketing); (5) **large-scale organization** promoting industrial efficiency.

1861–65. IMPACT OF THE CIVIL WAR was variously felt, wool production expanding, cotton manufacturing being severely curtailed. The introduction of power-driven sewing machines in the manufacture of military uniforms and boots and shoes brought these industries into the factory system. Agricultural machinery output spurted, but locomotive production fell off sharply. Extensive use of condensed milk processed by **Gail Borden** (1801–74) on the basis of a patent (1856) encouraged development of food processing industry. Demands for iron for military use expanded, while curtailment was marked in structural iron and railroad equipment, in building construction, and in most types of raw-material production. The war encouraged technological developments by creating a demand for rolled-iron plates of considerable thickness. The Rodman process was successfully utilized in casting large cannon hollow, and progress was made in crucible steel.

1866–73. THE BESSEMER PROCESS IN MANUFACTURE OF STEEL started, 1864, at Troy, N.Y. (also p. 795), to meet demand for rails was principal achievement. By 1873, 115,000 tons of Bessemer rails were rolled, but as yet nearly 7 tons of iron rails were rolled for every ton of Bessemer rails. With **Bethlehem Steel Co.** beginning operations in 1873 and the Edgar Thompson Steel Works under construction, the Bessemer industry was on a firm basis by the end of this period. The **Lake Superior** region (U.S. government surveyors discovered ore deposits near Marquette, Mich., 1844) became the most important single source of iron ore, with annual shipments exceeding 1 million tons by 1873 (ultimately a number of ranges were opened up in Michigan and Minnesota, including the Menominee, Gogebic, Vermilion, Mesabi, and Cuyuna). While the Pittsburgh district continued to maintain its leadership, new establishments on a large scale were constructed on the Great Lakes with convenient access to the ore (notably at Gary, Ind., and Chicago district). Other trends: (1) **steam power** now surpassed water power as a source of industrial energy; (2) **coal production** almost doubled, with bituminous surpassing anthracite in physical output by 1870; (3) the **worsted industry** rapidly expanded.

1867–1911. PETROLEUM INDUSTRY AND STANDARD OIL. As a result of a scientific report by **Benjamin Silliman, Jr.** (1816–85), refining and drilling operations were begun in Pennsylvania. Oil was successfully drilled by **Edwin L. Drake** (1819–80) near Titusville, 1859, leading to an **oil boom,** as petroleum quickly ousted whale oil and burning fluids as an illuminant. After 1884 drilling became nationwide, with production in Ohio and West Virginia, in the 1890s in Wyoming, and by the early 1900s in Texas, Indian Territory (Okla.), Kansas, Louisiana, and Illinois. First oil pipeline completed from Pithole, Pa. (1866). **John D. Rockefeller** (p. 1138), concentrating on control of (1) **refining,** merged the interests of the Rockefellers, Harkness, and Flagler, organizing, 1870, the **Standard Oil Co. of Ohio** (capital $1 million). (2) By special **rate agreements** with Eastern railroads Rockefeller secured a competitive transportation advantage over rivals. (3) Control of **pipelines.** As a result of these 3 factors, by 1879 Standard Oil controlled 90–95% of the oil refined. Trust agreement, 1879; formally organized (1882) as one unit in Trust; Trust Jersey Standard became the leading Standard Oil Co.; trust broken by Ohio Courts (1892). **Standard Oil Co. of N.J.** became the leading Standard Oil Co.; acting as holding and operating company (1892, 1899); dissolved, 1911 (p. 674); since that date the business has been controlled by a number of corporations with competition appearing in the industry from Gulf Oil, Shell, Texas, as well as between the old Standard Oil companies.

1873–1904. CONCENTRATION OF ECONOMIC POWER. Devices employed: (1) **Pools** (1873–87), a combine of business units to control prices by apportioning markets; forbidden to railroads by Interstate Commerce Act, 1887 (p. 309), and by Supreme Court, 1897 (p. 672). For *Addyston Pipe and Steel Co.* v. *U.S.* (1899), which forbade pools among manufacturers shipping across state lines, see p. 673. (2) **Trusts,** a device whereby stockholders under a trust agreement deposit their stock with trustees—Standard Oil Co. (1879–82); "Cotton-Oil" Trust (1884); "Whisky Trust," "Sugar Trust," and "Lead Trust" (1887); illegal under the Sherman Act, 1890, p. 312; for Supreme Court interpretation, p. 672. (3) **Holding companies** (esp. 1892–1904) controlling stock in other corporations. Laws of states like New Jersey encouraged this device. The most notable example was the **U.S. Steel Corporation,** organized, 1901, by a group of financiers headed by **Elbert H. Gary** (1846–1927), Chicago, and **J. P. Morgan,** New York, who bought out **Andrew Carnegie's** (p. 998) interest in the Carnegie Steel Co. (resulting from a series of consolidations of iron and steel works, ore properties, and shipping facilities, 1874–99). Capitalized at $1.4 billion, U.S. Steel was for many years the largest holding company in the U.S. Holding companies were partially curbed by the dissolution of the Northern Securities Co., 1904 (p. 673); the dissolution of the Standard Oil Co. (p. 674) and the American Tobacco Co. (p. 674); and New Deal legislation (p. 417). **Operating companies** combined merged enterprises and on their own integrated horizontally and vertically. Often large companies acted as both holding and operating units. **International corporations:** most of the giant U.S. enterprises were interested in foreign business. Use of the **corporate form** became typical for industrial enterprises (p. 739).

1874–80. Bessemer plant capacity increased. By 1880 Pittsburgh blast furnaces produced 1,200 tons a week as against a maximum output of 600 tons in the previous decade. As a result Bessemer steel output exceeded 1 million tons for the first time, with pig iron production, 1880, attaining a new high of 4,295,000 tons, a one-third increase over the boom year, 1873. Other developments included (1) application of **refrigeration** to transportation, with the meat-packing industry now producing for a national market on a year-round basis; (2) expansion of machine manufacture of shoes, especially marked after the merger of firm established by Charles Goodyear (1833–96) with his competitor, Gordon McKay (1880).

1881–90. EXPANSION IN THE STEEL INDUSTRY. The **Open-Hearth Process** (introduced into the U.S. by **Abram S. Hewitt** at Trenton, N.J., 1868), removing sulfur and especially phosphorus, and consequently opening up a larger portion of the ore reserve of the U.S. (including scrap metal) than the Bessemer process, expanded its operatives 5-fold, especially after 1886. At the same time Bessemer steel ingots and castings rose from 1,074,262 to 3,658,871 long tons. By 1885 iron rails accounted for only 15,000 out of over 1 million tons, with the proportion devoted to other products constantly increasing. Structural iron, wire, pipe, tubes, and armored plate faced heavy competition from steel. Reflecting the marked growth in size per unit, the number of blast furnaces in Pennsylvania, chief U.S. producer, fell from 269 to 211. The northern Alabama and adjacent Tennessee district (center: **Birmingham**), with resources of coal as well as iron ore, spurted to second place in pig iron production. By 1890 iron ore production amounted to 4 million tons, or 25% of the national total, but this area did not keep up the pace, 1893–1914. Lake Superior ore shipments rose from 2 million to 9 million tons, accounting for 56% of the total U.S. output.

Other developments: (1) **rise of Southern textile production** (number of cotton spindles increased from 542,000 to 1,554,000, but in 1890 New England still accounted for 76% of total U.S. spindles); (2) **ready-made clothing industry** expanded as a result of the introduction of cutting machines and mechanical pressers, with the organization largely characterized by **subcontract system** and **sweat shops**; (3) **shoe industry** expanded, with annual output of Goodyear welt shoes amounting to 12 million pairs by 1890.

1891–1900. ELECTRIC POWER AND INTERNAL-COMBUSTION ENGINES. The introduction of steam turbines (1890) to drive dynamos for the generation of electric power and the development of the internal-combustion engine were the chief industrial developments. The Niagara Falls plant (1894) inaugurated the era of hydroelectric power. Utilization of such power was still in its infancy. By 1899 horsepower of electric motors run by purchased current amounted to merely 1.8% of the total installed primary power in manufacturing industries, while installed horsepower of internal-combustion engines amounted to 1.3%. The introduction (1891) of the electrolytic process of copper refining speeded up the complete displacement of steel wire by copper wire in the conduction of electricity. Other trends: (1) Southern cotton industry aided by the perfection of the Northrop loom (1889–95). By 1900, Southern mills consumed 1.5 million bales of cotton as against slightly under 2 million spun in Northern mills. (2) Meat-packing industry became centralized in the Middle West as receipts of live cattle in the East began to decline absolutely, beginning in 1890, and shipments of slaughtered cattle expanded. (3) Kerosene production declined relatively, amounting to one half of all petroleum refining in 1900 as against three quarters, 1890. During the same period petroleum output increased 40%. (4) Decline of relative importance of rails in the steel industry. By 1891 steel used for structural and other rolled products exceeded rails, with the ratio widening to 2–1 by 1896. In forging, hydraulic presses supplanted steam hammers. Open-hearth steel production outstripped Bessemer in rate of expansion. (5) American industrial output was the largest in the world by 1900.

1901–09. (1) Output of steel products rose from 10 million to almost 24 million tons, with open-hearth steel exceeding Bessemer output by 1908. In 1909 open-hearth accounted for 14,493,000 tons, Bessemer 9,330,000 tons. **Coke** (of major importance as a blast-furnace fuel after 1890) became the principal fuel in the steel industry. (2) Heavy chemical industry rapidly expanded as a result of the **Solvay** process and the electrolytic process. (3) Machine tool industry introduced electrically driven and high-speed cutting tools, power presses, heavy portable machine tools, and compressed air tools. (3) The **automobile industry,** not listed separately in the Census of 1900, rose rapidly by 1909, its output increasing 3,500% during the decade, with a corresponding increase in demand for alloys, glass, steel, rubber, and petroleum products. (4) Fuel oil production rose from 300 million gallons to 1.7 billion gallons. (5) Lagging industries included wheat flour milling, forest products (dropped 36%), and cotton and wool manufacturing, which kept pace with the population rise but not at the rate of knit goods and silk production.

1909–14. Steel Industry Trends. Bessemer production declined from 9.5 million tons to 6.2 million tons annually, while open-hearth steel totaled 21.5 million in 1914, setting a trend which continued through the first half of the 20th century. 1945: Bessemer, 3,844,034 long tons; open-hearth, 64,231,788 long tons. Ore from the Mesabi Range (about 100 miles long in N.E. Minn.) virtually supplanted ore from Wisconsin and Michigan fields, constituting over 70% of all Lake Superior region shipments in 1914.

Automotive expansion from 21st to 6th place in relation to value of output. In 1913–14 the **Ford Motor Co.** started reorganizing the assembly process, including the manufacture of its own motors and other important parts, and the utilization of "continuous flow production." A corresponding expansion was recorded in the rubber industry, largely due to a 4-fold increase in the value of tire and inner-tube production.

Textiles. Cotton manufacturing in the Southern Piedmont was accelerated by the utilization of hydroelectric power. By 1914 the South had almost 13 million spindles as against less than 11 million for Massachusetts. The former produced coarse cotton goods; New England specialized in finer cloth. Rapid advances were recorded in silk and knit goods. The value of silk products reached $254 million in 1914. The introduction of rayon in 1909 inaugurated a new **era of synthetics,** but production remained small in 1914.

Electric power installed in manufacturing rose from 1.7 to 3.8 million horsepower. By 1914 energy run by purchased current reached 17.3% of all installed primary power in manufacturing.

Scientific management ideas associated with **Frederick Winslow Taylor** (p. 1166), **Henry Lawrence Gantt** (1861–1919), and **Frank B. Gilbreth** (1868–1924) were introduced in certain industries; efficiency experts began to apply systems to plant management.

1914–19. WORLD WAR I increased the demands for alloys and accelerated the rise of the **aluminum industry.** To meet the needs for special alloys, electric furnace production increased conspicuously, rising from 27,000 long tons, 1914, to 511,693 long tons, 1918. In the tool industry electrically produced steel displaced crucible steel. During the war period total steel ingots and castings rose from 23,513,030 long tons (1914) to 45,060,607 (1917). Shipbuilding rose from $211,319,000 (1914) to $775,093,-000 (1918). The enlarged demands for munitions placed a premium upon the construction of **by-product coking ovens** to supply coal tar for explosives, the number of such ovens doubling by 1919, by which date by-product coke amounted to 56.9% of 44.2 million tons total. Installed primary power represented by purchased current more than doubled, reaching 9,347,556 horsepower, or 31.6% of total horsepower of manufacturing industries. New construction expenditures rose from $3.3 billion (1915) to $6.7 billion (1919). The **War Industries Board** (p. 331) supported increases in productive capacity, standardization and simplification of products and processes, and scientific management.

1920–29. RATE OF GROWTH IN MANUFACTURING. In terms of distribution of the national income and employment, manufacturing remained relatively constant, while advances were scored in aggregate physical output far greater than in nonmanufacturing industries. Rate of growth **uneven,** with a **recession** in older basic industries—coal, textiles, lumber, wheat flour milling. Expansion in steel and iron leveled off. **Marked expansion** in **automotive industry,** which now took 1st rank in terms of value of product as well as value added by manufacture, with 2,798,737 passenger cars manufactured in 1929. Output of tires and inner tubes doubled. Gasoline production increased 4-fold, accounting for 48% of all refined products, while fuel oil output doubled but declined from 52% to 42% of petroleum refining. **Chemical industry** expansion, given a fillip by World War I, made spectacular gains, especially in the fields of dyes (formerly imported from Germany) and synthetic fibers (rayon production rose from 3 million lbs., 1919, to 33 million lbs., 1929) and plastics. **Electrical equipment** manufacturing enjoyed boom conditions, with the value of heavy household appliances rising from $109 million to $268 million; portable household electric appliances, from $71 million to $106 million; **radios** and related apparatus, from $15 million to $338 million; and industrial electrical appliances, from $46 million to $976 million. By 1929 the rated capacity of horsepower equipment of motors run by purchased energy exceeded the rated horsepower capacity of all other prime movers in manufacturing. New construction expenditures rose from $6.7 billion (1919) to $12.1 billion (1926), declining to $10.8 billion (1929). Corporations grew in size, diversified their product lines, and frequently enlarged their business in foreign countries. Novel managerial methods were developed to administer multiproduct and, often, multinational companies. Enterprises emerged with central staffs and multidivisional structures (General Motors, Standard Oil of New Jersey, du Pont).

1929–39. DEPRESSION AND TRANSITION. The index of physical output of all manufacturing rose from 364 in 1929 to 374 in 1939 (1899 = 100; 1865 = 8.5), but in only 2 years of the entire decade was the 1929 output exceeded. Physical production rose 2.8%, while population increased about 6%, with one half of all industries declining absolutely and over one half declining in relation to population. New construction expenditures, $10.8 billion (1929), $2.9 billion (1933), $8.1 billion (1939). **Growth industries** included **chemicals** (plastics output rose from 50,000 tons, 1935, to 170,000 tons, 1939), **electrical equipment** (household refrigerator output rose from 890,000 units, 1929, to 2,824,000, 1937), and **petroleum** (gasoline production rose almost 50%, and the catalytic "cracking process" was developed). **Uneven trends** were marked in **textiles** (rayon used in the silk and rayon goods industry increased 4-fold, 1929–35, while silk consumption declined 50%, and by 1939 was relegated to full-fashioned hosiery only; cotton goods dropped from 22% of total physical output in textiles, 1929, to 16%, 1937) and in **clothing** (men's ready-made clothing showed a net rise in output of about 2%, while women's clothing advanced by almost 50%, 1929–37). Other trends: the introduction of cemented tungsten carbide (1928), followed by tantalum carbide, for cutting tools permitted "super-speed" cutting and practical cutting speeds on materials formerly unmachinable. Developments in synthetic abrasives, electric drive and control, hydraulic feed, and pneumatic accessories led to wide-spread redesigning of **machine tools.** Such processes as electrical welding and such substitutes for metal cutting as pressing, stamping, and punching were increasingly applied in the auto and other mass production industries and, during World War II, in the aircraft and ship-building industries. Purchased power used in manufacturing rose from 48% to almost 60% of total primary power utilized.

1938–52. ECONOMIC CONCEN-TRATION. By 1929, 69.2% of the products of manufacturing were pro-duced by firms doing a business in excess of $1 million as against 1.1% ($5,000–$20,000) by small firms (*Statistical Abstract*, 1933). The depression accelerated this trend, according to the TNEC *Hearings and Final Report* (p. 424). In 1935 less than 6% of the tobacco corporations owned 92% of the assets; 3% of the chemicals, 86%; 4% of the rubber con-cerns, 80%; 2% of the metal and metal products concerns, 74%. In 1937 one company produced 100% of the virgin aluminum (Aluminum Co. of América); 3 companies, 86% of the autos; and 4 companies, 58% of the whisky (1938). By 1938, 30 corporations had assets in excess of $1 billion. The leaders:

Corporation	Assets in Billion Dollars
Metropolitan Life Insurance	4.23
Amer. Tel. & Tel. Co.	3.99
Prudential Insurance Co. '	3.12
Pennsylvania R.R. Co.	2.86
N.Y. Central R.R. Co.	2.35
Chase National Bank	2.33
New York Life Insurance Co.	2.22
Standard Oil Co. (N.J.)	1.89
National City Bank of N.Y.	1.88
Guaranty Trust Co.	1.84
Equitable Life Assurance Co.	1.82
U.S. Steel Corp.	1.82
Allegheny Corp.	1.73
Southern Pacific R.R. Co.	1.67
General Motors Corp.	1.49
Consolidated Edison Co.	1.38
Bank of America	1.27

By 1952 the number of corporations with a billion or more in assets rose to 59 (24 industrial, utility, and railroad com-panies; 21 banks; 13 insurance com-panies; 1 finance company). Assets of Standard Oil Co. of N.J. rose to $4.7 billion; General Motors, to $3.67 billion; U.S. Steel, to $3.14 billion.

1940–52. WORLD WAR II, RECON-VERSION, AND COLD WAR. As a result of a shift from civilian to military production (military production rose from 2% of total national output, 1939, to 40%, 1944), plant expansion, and labor mobilization, industrial production rose from 100 (1935–39) to **239** by 1943, and durable manufactured goods to **360.** Mineral production rose to 148 (1942), fuels to 145 (1944). Steel ingots and castings reached a peak output in 1944 of 80,037,130 long tons, almost 50% above 1929 output ("turbo-hearth," new steelmaking technique, introduced, 1949). Most striking industrial gains oc-curred in (1) **alloys and light metals** (aluminum production increased 6-fold; magnesium output rose from 2,500 tons, 1939, to a peak of 170,000 tons, 1943); (2) **synthetics** (synthetic rubber produc-tion rose from 2,000 tons, 1939, to 930,-000 tons, 1945, meeting most of U.S. needs, and compared with prewar annual imports of natural rubber ranging from 550,000–650,000 tons); and (3) **plastics** (output expanded 5-fold as light-metal shortages developed, equaling by 1945 nearly one half the tonnage of aluminum produced. **U.S. government financed five sixths of the new plant** construction ($160 million through the Defense Plants Corp.). By the end of World War II the government owned 90% of the plants for synthetic rubber, aircraft, magnesium, and shipbuilding; 70% of the aluminum capacity; and 50% of the machine tool facilities. In addition, 3,800 miles of oil pipes ("Big Inch" and "Little Inch") were constructed by the government to carry petroleum to the East Coast.

The reconversion shift at the end of the war was virtually completed by mid-1947. Civilian production sought to meet shortages in **autos** (5 million units produced annually by end of 1948), **consumers' durable goods** (6,200,000 refrigerators, 14.6 million radios, and 7.4 million television sets manufactured, 1950), and **residential dwellings** (curtailed by high construction costs and material and labor shortages, with peak construction, 1950, $11,525 million). Production was further augmented by the European Recovery Program (p. 468). The Cold War, beginning 1949, curtailed industrial reconversion and led to restrictions upon civilian production (autos, one third from 1950 levels by 1952; radios and television sets, 40%) in favor of rearmament requirements. Nevertheless, peak output figures were achieved in this period. Iron and steel production rose to approximately 260 by 1951 (1935–39 = 100) as against 208, highest war year (1943); petroleum and coal products to 267 as against a record war output of 236 (1945); chemical products to 242 as compared with 228 (1943); and aircraft manufacturing was accelerated to reach, by July 1952, a production rate of 250 military planes monthly, considerably below earlier estimates.

Income originating from manufacturing (1949) amounted to $62.8 billion out of total national income of $216.8 billion as against $7.5 billion (manufacturing) out of $39.5 billion total national income in 1933.

1950–73. RATE OF GROWTH. Index of industrial production (1967 = 100) continued to rise from 45 (1950) to 66 (1960), 107 (1970), to 128 (Oct. 1973), with largest percentage increases in utilities output, 27 (1950), 158 (Oct. 1973). Overall, America's economic rate of growth (average annual increase in gross national product per capita in constant 1954 dollars), 1950–59, was 1.4%, considerably behind the rates of growth of Western Europe and the U.S.S.R. for the same period. In 1960–70, America's economic performance improved. The average annual increase in gross domestic product per capita (in constant dollars) was 3.3%, which nonetheless still compared unfavorably with the growth performance in the European Economic Community (4.1%), the U.S.S.R. (6.0%, net material product per capita), and Japan (9.7%).

1950–73. INDUSTRIAL TRENDS marked by greater regional diversification of industry. There was a relative decline of the Northeast and rise of Southern (esp. South Atlantic) and Pacific states.

VALUE ADDED BY MANUFACTURING
(percentage distribution by geographical area)

Area	1950	1963	1969
U.S.	100.0	100.0	100.0
New England	8.3	7.1	6.9
Middle Atlantic	26.2	22.7	21.3
East North Central	33.2	29.3	28.6
West North Central	5.7	6.1	6.5
South Atlantic	9.4	11.0	11.3
East South Central	3.8	4.8	5.5
West South Central	4.3	5.7	6.5
Mountain	1.2	1.8	1.8
Pacific	7.9	11.5	11.6

Technological innovation included (1) the spread of automation, aided by automatic high-speed computers; (2) development of computers (first production model of a large-scale general-purpose computer delivered to Census Bureau, 14 June 1951); IBM became the world leader in computers; by 1973 computers, serving a wide variety of functions, had become commonplace in American industry; 1972–73, mini-computers, developed for process and industrial controls, opened vast new markets for computers; as of summer 1973, est. 125,000 general- and special-purpose computers installed in the U.S.; (3) photocopying machines: the trademark Xerox entered the language; by 1973 over 1 million photocopiers in use; (4) TV sets became universal; by 1972, 99.8% of American households had TV sets; (5) the transistor (p. 801) came to substitute for the vacuum tube in radios, TVs, computers, etc.; (6) the electronics industry was stimulated by the development of defense and space industries, which encouraged research geared to military technology, notably in the fields of spacecrafts, electronics (guidance, control, and communication), instrumentation, along with expanded use of lightweight metals (beryllium, titanium, molybdenum) and the refractory metals; space missions made operational the fuel cell, a converter of the energy of hydrogen and oxygen into electricity; (7) electronics penetrated traditional industries, 1970s. Textiles: introduction of electronic knitting machines; electronic signals drive the needles; instead of taking 8 hours to change a pattern, the switch is made in minutes; production is one third more per day than by the mechanical counterpart; (8) electronic calculators appeared in the 1960s for office use and by 1972–73 for home use; (9) new chemical and petrochemical products related to agriculture proliferated: weed and brush killers, insecticides, fungicides, soil conditioners, mold inhibiters, fertilizers, synthetic hormones for animals; (10) chemical and petrochemical revolution in clothing, with acrylic and polyester fibers; durable press garments; new cleaning substances from detergents to solvents; (11) the chemical industry also presented new paints and pigments, new insulation materials, synthetic carpeting, heavy-duty construction materials, higher octane gasoline, new lubricants, nylontire cord, new plastics for the automobile industry, new synthetic rubber compounds, new tools and equipment, manmade industrial diamonds, new packaging materials (polyethylenes); (12) the electrochemical industries witnessed product and process innovations; (13) pharmaceuticals: new antibiotics, antihistamines, synthetic hormones, tranquilizers, vaccines, oral contraceptives; (14) processed food industry: new lines of frozen foods and premixed products; (15) the aircraft industry produced for civilian requirements a range of new planes; defense and space age industry had spinoffs for the aircraft industry; in the 1960s, the jet plane replaced the prop plane in commercial transportation; (16) automobile industry: cars grew in size and comfort; 1957–60, introduction of "compact" cars to meet rise in smallcar imports, with greatly expanded production as the energy crisis loomed (1973). 1972, Japanese Mazda car with Wankel (rotary) engine introduced in U.S.; G.M. declared it would bring out a car with a Wankel engine; energy crisis stimulated production and sales of compact cars while sales of larger cars dropped sharply; (17) other consumer durables: expanded output of refrigerators and freezers, washing and drying machines, dishwashers, self-cleaning ovens helped simplify the life of the housewife; (18) 1961–73, modernization of steel industry occurred due in part to competition from West Germany and Japan. Among the improved techniques were widespread adoption of the basic oxygen process of steel making (1972: 56% of raw steel output) by which steel of open-hearth quality is produced in a rotary oxygen converter using high phosphorus molten iron obtained from the blast furnace; continuous casting facilities, eliminating the ingot stage and **primary** rolling mill; new high-speed computer-controlled rolling mills; development of "ultrahigh strength" steels for space industry; (19) 1969–72, shipments of 1.9 million mobile homes equaled the number shipped in the previous 2 decades; (20) the construction industry boomed, from $33.6 billion of new construction (1950) to $123.8 billion (1972); (21) research and development expenditures by private business grew: $3.5 billion (1953) to $19.2 billion (1972 est.).

1950–73. ENERGY. Energy consumption expanded rapidly. Electrical energy production rose from 389 billion kwh (1950) to 1,747 billion kwh (1972 prel.). Production and consumption rose with affluence.

SELECTED APPLIANCES IN THE HOME

PERCENT OF HOUSEHOLDS WITH SELECTED APPLIANCES (1972)

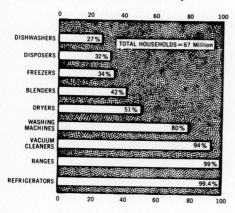

DISHWASHERS	27%
DISPOSERS	32%
FREEZERS	34%
BLENDERS	42%
DRYERS	51%
WASHING MACHINES	80%
VACUUM CLEANERS	94%
RANGES	99%
REFRIGERATORS	99.4%

TOTAL HOUSEHOLDS = 67 Million

SOURCE: Merchandising Week,
Bureau of Competitive Assessment and Business Policy

With the exception of the ranges (which used gas as well as electricity), these appliances typically used electricity.

Americans came to depend on oil to run their cars, to heat their homes, to produce electricity (in power plants), and for numerous other uses; oil exceeded natural gas and coal in energy consumption.

The U.S., once a net exporter of petroleum and petroleum products, by 1953 came on a regular basis to be an importer of oil. In an attempt to protect the domestic producer, from 1959 to 1 May 1973, the U.S. had quotas on imported oil. American oil reserves dropped, to be boosted only by the discovery of oil in commercial quantities in Alaska (Feb. 1968, Prudhoe Bay discovery announced). Alaskan oil did not, however, enter the U.S. market at once, for transportation was required. Fear about the impact on the environment delayed approval of the Alaska pipeline until 1973. Clean-burning natural gas—unlike oil and coal—does not pollute the environment; new use was made of natural gas; 1966–73, U.S. natural gas reserves decreased by one fifth; shortages began to develop. Despite abundant American coal, ecological and pollution considerations limited its use; states passed legislation requiring that coal operators restore land after mining; concern over the unpleasantness of burning high-sulfur coal curbed its consumption and added extra cost when employed. Fears over oil spills retarded the development of offshore oil resources. With import quotas, oil companies did not build refinery capacity to process large-scale crude oil imports. Widespread apprehension delayed the spread of nuclear power plants (in 1957, the Shippingport, Pa. Atomic Power Station was America's first nuclear power plant; 1973, Sept., 37 such plants in operation in the U.S.). After the 1973 Arab-Israeli war (6–22 Oct.), Arab nations embargoed oil shipments to the U.S. Embargo announced 17 Oct. President Nixon's energy crisis address (7 Nov.) presented temporary measures, involving personal, business, and government reduction in energy use and also long-run steps: the licensing of new nuclear plants, more utilization of coal relative to oil, increased oil production from naval

U.S. ENERGY SOURCES, 1979

Domestic production		Imports	
Crude oil	18.0	Crude oil[1]	13.5
Natural gas liquids	2.4	Refined petroleum products	4.1
Natural gas	19.2	Natural gas	1.3
Coal	17.4		
Nuclear power	2.8		
Hydropower	3.0		
Geothermal and other	.1		

[1] Imports rose from 483 mil. 42-gal. bbls. in 1970 to 2,332 mil.

reserves, approval of the Alaska pipeline, and greater energy research and development efforts, designed to make U.S. self-sufficient in energy resources by 1980. Nixon asked for authority to suspend environmental standards. States lowered speed limits to 50 mph. 16 Nov., Nixon signed the controversial Alaska pipeline enactment; 27 Nov., Nixon signed Emergency Petroleum Allocation Act, requiring president to establish a program for oil allocation. 14 Dec., Congress passed year-round daylight savings time (for 2 years) to save energy. Other measures of Nov.–Dec. to curb energy consumption included Sunday gas station closings, cutbacks in heating fuel deliveries, reductions in jet fuel deliveries. Plans were made for accelerated research on solar, geothermal, nuclear, and numerous other possible sources of energy.

1953–73. TRENDS IN BUSINESS ORGANIZATION. (1) **Conglomerate mergers.** The late 1960s saw more mergers than ever in U.S. history. The peak year was 1968, when 2,407 manufacturing and mining firms disappeared through mergers. Many mergers joined companies in unrelated industries. Among the leading conglomerates were Ling-Temco-Vought (originally in electronics and aircraft), the majority stockholder in Jones & Laughlin Steel Corp.; Litton Industries (typewriters to ships); ITT acquired Avis (car rentals), Sheraton (hotels), Levitt & Sons (home construction), and Hartford Fire Insurance, rising

from country's 80th (1955) to 8th ranking firm in terms of dollar volume of sales (1970). Because of antitrust action (controversial settlement announced 31 July 1971), ITT divested Avis and Levitt, but it retained Hartford Insurance and most other of its many acquisitions. Conglomerates appeared to reach their crest c.1970. The general decline of stock prices put them in a poor position to purchase new subsidiaries by offering own shares in exchange for those of smaller companies. (2) **Multinational enterprises.** Companies added production facilities worldwide. Industrial leaders at home, GM, Exxon (the old Standard Oil of N.J.), Ford, IBM, ITT took the lead abroad (p. 709, on distribution of foreign investments). (3) **Management.** In response to more diversified and more multinational corporations, management methods became more sophisticated. The central staff, multidivisional organization, an innovative structure in the 1920s, became a common means of organizing multiproduct, multiplant, multinational enterprises.

1965–73. ENVIRONMENT. The consequences of industrial and technological expansion concerned Americans as they worried about nuclear fallout; chemical products that resisted natural degradation and remained to pollute waters and countryside; chemical products that killed birds as they killed insects; and automobiles and smokestacks that dirtied the atmosphere (pp. 639–643 for legislation).

National Public Finance

From the origin of the U.S. federal government to the twentieth century, national public finance simply meant raising money to pay the expenses of government and paying those expenses. To meet special government needs, the government issued bonds; it was accepted that the public debt should be repaid. In 1836–37, for the only time in American history, there was no public debt. The principal source of federal government revenues until World War I was customs duties. Before the Civil War, typically over 50% of the expenditures went to the War and Navy departments; after the Civil War, veterans' benefits constituted an important part of government expenditures. Until well into the twentieth century, the total federal government budget was small—small relative to the national product as well as to later government budgets.

During the twentieth century the size of the federal budget grew. From World War I on, personal income taxes provided the most important single source of federal revenue. Government expenditures over the years became more diversified as they became more substantial. Until the 1930s, it was almost universally accepted that a balanced budget was desirable; from the 1930s onward, this idea—while it continued to be held—began to be replaced by the view that the budget should be used as an instrument of economic policy; deficit financing might be wise to spur recovery from depression and encourage economic growth. After World War II, as the government role expanded, budget deficits mounted, with the Reagan administration setting a balanced budget as a long-range target.

1789–1800. Hamilton's "Report on Public Credit" (9 Jan. 1790) placed the total public debt outstanding at **$77,-124,564** (foreign debt, $11,710,379; domestic debt, $40,414,086; state debts, $25 million, of which **$18,271,786** was actually assumed). Customs duties constituted the principal source of revenue, as a number of excise taxes and, in 1798, a direct tax on houses, land, and slaves apportioned among the states on the basis of population proved unproductive.

1791. Bank of U.S. chartered (p. 147).

1792, 2 Apr. Mint Act (1) provided for decimal system of coinage; (2) val-ued U.S. dollar at 24.75 grains of gold; (3) established bimetallism, with silver and gold legal tender at a ratio of 15 to 1; (4) established a mint at Philadelphia. New discoveries of Mexican silver resulted in silver being overvalued at this ratio.

1801–11. The Jeffersonian Republicans were committed to **retrenchment.** Increasing customs receipts made it possible to repeal all excises (1802), except tax on salt (eliminated 1807), and to reduce the debt of $83 million inherited from the Federalist administration by almost 50%.

1812–15. The War of 1812 undid the

economy moves of the preceding years. Heavy government borrowing (loans, c.$80 million; Treasury notes, c.$37 million) brought the debt to $127,335,000 ($15 per capita). Prewar annual expenditures of c.$11 million rose to $35 million, 1814, in which year Congress increased tariff rates; doubled the tax of 1813 on land, dwelling houses, and slaves; and increased items subject to internal revenue.

1816. Second Bank of U.S. chartered (p. 184).

1816–18. Large revenues permitted the retirement or funding into stock of Treasury notes outstanding and the removal by 1817 of most war taxes.

1819–21. Annual deficits handicapped Treasury fiscal operations.

1822–29. The accrual of surpluses was used to liquidate the public debt by the purchase in the open market of government securities. In 1826 a Senate committee complained of "the serious inconvenience of an **overflowing Treasury**."

1830–35. Land speculation made receipts from the sales of public lands an important source of government revenue. Reduced to only $7 million by 1832, the entire debt was paid off by Jan. 1835.

1834, 28 JUNE. Second Coinage Act authorized ratio of 16–1 between silver and gold and reduced weight of gold to 23.22 grains. Discovery of gold in California (p. 247) led to overvaluation of gold at this ratio.

1836. Income from land sales totaled $25 million, exceeding customs receipts for the first and only time. The government surplus exceeded $40 million.

11 JULY. Specie Circular (p. 211).

1837. $28 million of the surplus was distributed among the states in the form of a loan.

1837–43. Declining revenues brought deficits totaling $46.4 million. To finance

government expenditures, over $47 million of Treasury notes were issued.

1840. Independent Treasury system established (p. 217), discontinued 1841 (p. 219), reestablished 1846 (p. 233), continuing until merged with Federal Reserve System (1913, p. 326), and finally abolished (1921) by Act of 1920.

1844–46. Reappearance of annual surpluses.

1846–49. The War with Mexico was financed almost entirely by borrowing. The total deficits for the 3-year period amounted to $53.2 million. 1847 marked the record federal expenditure to date of **$57 million.**

1850–57. A period of large surpluses.

1853, 21 FEB. Coinage Act reduced silver in all small coins except the dollar and authorized coinage of $3 gold pieces.

1858–60. The Panic of 1857 was followed by annual deficits, annual expenditures increasing to $74 million in 1858, with government credit at low ebb.

1861–65. CIVIL WAR led to the introduction of a variety of taxes. An **income tax,** for the first time, was enacted, 5 Aug. 1861; its rates (3% on incomes in excess of $800) increased in succeeding years. 31 Dec. 1861 government suspended specie payments. Internal revenue surpassed customs duties as a source of government revenue. By 1865 the income tax produced almost 20% of the total federal receipts, and the manufacturers' and sales taxes amounted to some 23%. However, the major portion of the war expenditures was financed by paper money issues and loans. In Aug. 1865 the public debt reached a peak of $2,845,900,000 (in excess of $75 per capita), while some $450 million of U.S. legal tender notes or "greenbacks" had been issued (authorized Feb. 1862).

1866–70. With certain exceptions, excise taxes were gradually removed and the inheritance tax expired in 1870. Yet revenue exceeded expenditures by $133 million, 1867. Most of the debt was converted into long-term bonds, and the greenbacks outstanding were moderately contracted to c.$356 million.

1871–74. The U.S. Treasury issued $26 million legal tender notes by purchasing bonds. The income tax expired in 1872.

1873. Fourth Coinage Act ("Crime of '73"), p. 299.

1875. Specie Resumption Act. Under this act the dollar became convertible into gold in 1879.

1875–93. Every single year showed an excess of revenue over expenditures (1881, $145 million). The major source of government income was customs duties unrelated to fiscal needs. In order not to drain off currency by retaining in the Treasury the mounting surpluses, the government applied the surplus to debt reduction at an unprecedented rate, the net debt falling to $839 million and the bonded debt from about $1,800 million to less than $600 million.

1878–94. The struggle to monetize silver—bimetallism (pp. 303, 304, 312)—**Bland-Allison Act,** 28 Feb. 1878 (p. 303), **Sherman Silver Purchase Act,** 14 July 1890 (p. 312), repealed 1 Nov. 1893 (p. 314).

1894. Federal revenue failed to exceed expenditures (deficit $61 million) for the first time since the Civil War. Income tax passed 1894 (declared unconstitutional 1895, p. 672).

1895–99. Each year showed a deficit, which rose to $89 million in 1899. The war with Spain created no serious fiscal problem, although borrowing constituted the major source of government receipts, with the deficit rising to only $127 million for the war period.

1900. Gold Standard Act (p. 317).

1900–13. Government expenditures increased, but frequently lagged behind revenue, with surpluses in 6 years and deficits in 7 years. The gross national debt was slightly reduced and the per capita debt fell from $16.60 to **$12.27.**

1913. 16th Amendment to Constitution authorized Congress to impose taxes on income (p. 326); an income tax was included in the Underwood Tariff (3 Oct. 1913, p. 713).

1914–16. Slightly heavier spending for military purposes increased the annual deficit to over $62 million in 1915.

1917–20. U.S. entry into World War I brought drastic tax increases. The largest revenue producer was the excess profits tax, yielding over $2 billion in 1918, in which year income taxes amounted to $663.1 million. Of the c.$35.5 billion expended, including $9 billion loans to the Allies, approximately **25% was raised by taxes,** the rest by borrowing. Public debt rose from $1,300 million in Apr., 1917, to a peak exceeding $26 billion in Aug., 1919 (**$242** per capita).

1921–29. With "economy" the watchword of fiscal policy, tax reductions were effected, especially in the higher income brackets, and budgetary surpluses were applied to debt reduction. The national debt was reduced to $16 billion by 1930 (**$131** per capita). However, expenditures after World War I remained permanently higher than before the war, averaging in this period around $3 billion.

1931–32. Owing to falling revenues and declining incomes annual deficits occurred (1932, $2,529 million).

1933–36. In Mar. 1933 the gross national debt amounted to $20.9 billion. In 1936 it was in excess of $33 billion (**$263** per capita). Revenue rose ($3,100 million, 1934, to $4,115 million, 1936), but expenditures mounted even more rapidly (from $6 billion, 1934, to $8,600 million, 1936). Relief expenditures constituted the largest single item in the "emergency" budgets. For **abandonment of gold standard** (19 Apr. 1933), see p. 405; **gold devaluation** (25 Oct. 1933), p. 409; and **silver purchase proclamation** (9 Aug. 1934), p. 412.

1937. With recovery under way, President Roosevelt's budget message recommended sharp reductions in expenditures in the expectation of a balanced budget; but the acute business slump in the latter part of the year brought about a resumption of government spending to combat the down trend: 1937, $8,177 million; 1938, $7,238 million.

1938–40. The public debt rose from $37 billion to $43 billion (**$325** per capita), while the launching of an armament program in 1940 presaged larger deficits in the future.

1940–45. U.S. expenditures, 1 July 1940–30 June 1946, **$370 billion.** Despite the heaviest taxation in U.S. history revenue amounted to only $169 billion. The Treasury borrowed the remainder. The national debt exceeded $258 billion (**$1,852.74** per capita), and

annual interest payments to maintain the debt structure exceeded $5 billion.

1946, 20 Feb. Employment Act (p. 614).

1946–52. Slight surpluses were recorded in 1947–48, but military and diplomatic exigencies brought a return of deficits: $1.8 billion (1949), $3.1 billion (1950), $4 billion (1952), $9.4 billion (1953). As a result of continuing high tax rates (1951 record receipts, $48.1 billion) the national public debt remained virtually stabilized at peak levels, with per capita debt, 1951, **$1,693.80;** total public debt, 30 June 1952, $259.1 billion.

1953–60. Total **budget expenditures** in billions: 74.2 (1953), 67.7 (1954), 64.5 (1955), 66.5 (1956), 69.4 (1957), 71.9 (1958), 80.6 (1959), 77.2 (1960). **Deficits** were incurred in 5 out of 8 years, 1953–60, rising to record for peacetime of $12,427 million (1959). **Public debt** of U.S. subject to statutory debt limit rose to $286.3 billion (1960).

1961. With the Kennedy administra-

SOURCES OF FEDERAL REVENUE
(U.S. Treasury, *Annual Report*, 1945 and U.S. Bureau of the Budget)

1800	%	1836	%	1845	%
Customs	82.7	Customs	45.9	Customs	91.85
Int. Rev.	7.5	Public lands	48.9	Public lands	6.9
All others	10.8	All others	5.2	All others	1.25

1890	%	1925	%	1945	%
Customs	61.7	Customs	14.4	Individ. income	39.9
Liquor & tobacco	38.0	Tobacco	9.1	Corp. income	10.2
All others	3.0	Individ. income	22.4	Excess profits	23.3
		Corp. income	24.2	Liquor	4.8
		Foreign debt	4.9	Tobacco	1.9
		Estate and gifts	2.9	All others	19.7
		All others	18.4		

1960	%	1972	%
Individ. income	44.0	Individ. income	45.4
Corporate income	23.2	Corporate income	15.4
Social ins. & contributions	15.9	Social ins. & contributions	25.8
Excise tax	12.6	Excise tax	7.4
All others	4.2	All others	6.0

EXPENDITURES OF THE FEDERAL GOVERNMENT
(in percentages)

Purpose	1800	1836	1845	1890	1926
War Dept.	23.7	39.4	25.1	14.0	11.8
Navy Dept.	32.0	18.8	27.4	6.9	10.1
Interest on Public Debt	31.3	—	4.6	11.4	26.9
Veterans' Benefits*	.1	9.3	10.4	33.6	23.3
Other	12.9	32.5	32.5	34.1	27.9

	1945**	1960†	1972†
National Defense	82.5	49.8	33.8
International Affairs and Finance	3.4	3.3	1.6
Space Research and Technology	—	.4	1.5
Agriculture and Rural Development	1.6	3.6	3.0
Natural Resources and Environment		1.1	1.6
Commerce and Housing	4.0		
Commerce and Transportation		5.2	4.8
Labor and Welfare	1.1		
Community Development and Housing		1.0	1.8
Education and Manpower		1.4	4.2
Health			7.4
Income Security	***	20.3	28.0
Veterans' Benefits*	2.1	5.9	4.6
Interest on Public Debt	3.7	8.9	8.9
General Government	.9	1.4	2.1

* Includes only veterans' compensation and pensions 1880–90; all veterans' services and benefits 1926 +.
** Percentages do not add up to 100% because of rounding.
*** 1945 totals do not include transfer payments for social security, etc.; subsequent figures do.
† Percentages total over 100% because of intragovernmental transactions (−2.5% 1960; −3.4% 1970) and rounding.

tion economic growth became a prime object; a balanced budget was secondary.

1961–70. Unified Budget. Total budget receipts (in billions): $94.4 (1961); $99.7 (1962); $106.6 (1963); $112.7 (1964); $116.8 (1965); $130.9 (1966); $149.6 (1967); $153.7 (1968); $187.8 (1969); $193.8 (1970). Total budget outlays (in billions): $97.8 (1961); $106.8 (1962); $111.3 (1963); $118.6 (1964); $118.4 (1965); $134.6

(1966); $158.2 (1967); $178.8 (1968); $184.6 (1969); $196.6 (1970). With the exception of 1969, when the budget showed a surplus of $3.2 billion, in every year there were deficits, reaching $25.1 billion (1968), the largest deficit since 1943–45. The public debt of U.S. rose to $382.6 billion in 1970 (30 June).

Tax Reduction Act of 1964 (see p. 529) was designed to promote private demand and reduce unemployment, and it did so. The 10% tax surcharge of June 1968 was designed to slow spending and curb inflation but did not prove successful due in part to the overheating of the economy by high government military spending.

1971–73. Unified Budget. Budget receipts (in billions): $188.4 (1971); $208.6 (1972); $232.2 (1973). Budget outlays (in billions): $211.4 (1971); $231.9 (1972); $246.5 (1973). Deficits were recorded each year. Public debt rose (1973) to $458.1 billion.

Faced with high unemployment along with inflation (an unprecedented situation), **15 Aug. 1971,** President Nixon proposed tax changes designed to stimulate the economy, including repeal of the excise tax on automobiles, a tax credit on investment, and a reduction of income taxes on individuals. With some revisions, the president's proposals were enacted into law (1971, 10 Dec.). Nixon increased public spending. Fiscal policy continued to be expansionary in 1972, with the stimulus from rising expenditures. (See p. 752 for measures taken to try to cope with inflation.) **1972, 20 Oct.,** $5.2 billion **revenue-sharing bill** became law, providing for federal gov-

PER CAPITA NATIONAL DEBT

1790	(beginning of national govt.)	$19	1958	$1,630
1816	(after War of 1812)	15	1960	1,582
1866	(after Civil War)	78	1970	1,806
1919	(after World War I)	240	1973	2,177
1948	(after World War II)	1,720	1978	3,523

ernment grants to state and local governments. **1973:** expansionary fiscal policy
continued; 3 Dec. Bill extending the
debt limit to $475.7 billion (through
30 Dec. 1974) was sent to President
Nixon for signature. The former debt

ceiling of $465 billion expired midnight
30 Nov. and the ceiling had automatically reverted to $400 billion (the per-
manent statutory limit, set in 1971).
1981, 29 Sept. Debt ceiling raised above
$1 trillion.

Banking and Capital Markets

To mobilize capital the corporate form began to be used on a limited scale in
the colonial period. America's first private commercial bank appeared in 1781.
National banking began with the first national bank (1791). The first security
exchange was organized that year. From 1812 onward, life insurance companies
and savings banks also provided for capital mobilization. The second national
bank was chartered for 20 years (1816–36) and when the charter expired it
was not renewed. Meanwhile, state banks began to proliferate. The period
between 1836 and the Civil War was characterized by a laissez-faire approach
to banking, moderated by some state regulations. The national banking acts
of 1863–65 attempted to provide a safer and uniform currency.

The post-Civil War years witnessed the rise in investment banking houses.
These promoted mergers in railroads, utilities, and industrials and provided
capital resources for expansion. Commercial banking also flourished, although
there was a high rate of bank failures. In 1913, the Federal Reserve System
was established to correct the deficiencies in the national banking acts and
state banking legislation. The Federal Reserve Act created the basis for
modern banking, developing payments mechanisms that made dollars anywhere
applicable to payments of dollar debts across the nation, influencing credit
availability, and providing a means by which the national government could
attempt to use monetary policy to correct business fluctuations. Hopefully, the
Federal Reserve would provide effective supervision of national banking.

The 1920s witnessed a rapid expansion of the securities market, the growth
of investment trusts, and bank consolidations. Bank failures persisted. Industrial
corporations served as important mobilizers of capital. With the crash, 1929–33,
bank failures soared. New Deal measures attempted to reform the banking
system and the securities market. The U.S. government also came to play a
more direct role in the extension of credit, a role enlarged during the war years.

From 1945 to 1973 commercial banking expanded, and branch banking
increased in importance; the bank holding company in the late 1960s and early
1970s took on new significance. The growth of life insurance firms and savings
and loan associations was rapid. Pension funds became increasingly important

as holders of personal savings. The stock market did not play as significant a role in corporate financing as it had in the 1920s. For nonfinancial corporate business, internal sources of finance (profits and depreciation) were in every year—from 1951 onward—greater than all external financing. Throughout, the Board of Governors of the Federal Reserve System sought to employ monetary policy to avoid sharp economic fluctuations; the controls of the Federal Reserve over the entire banking system were extended.

1607–1810. CORPORATE form of organization developed very slowly. Early joint-stock companies (each member liable for the obligations of the joint enterprise) were principally **nonprofit** corporations for religious worship, philanthropy, education, or **land companies.** Commercial corporations make their appearance with a Connecticut trading corporation (1723), a Massachusetts wharf company (1772), a number of early fire insurance (notably Philadelphia Contributionship, 1768) and water supply companies, and the United Co. of Philadelphia (1775), organized to promote manufactures. For the Massachusetts Land Bank (1740), see p. 702. During the period 1783–89 numerous corporations were organized for building roads, canals, and bridges, and for banking (the **Bank of North America,** chartered by Congress, 31 Dec. 1781, the first private commercial bank in the U.S., and the **Bank of New York** and the **Bank of Massachusetts,** 1784). Such banks were localized and limited in scope (an exception was Aaron Burr's **Manhattan Co.** [1799], chartered as a water company but with broad enough powers to permit banking), paying out their notes on loans, with customers mainly merchants and bank stock subscribers.

1791. 1ST BANK OF THE U.S. (p. 147) opened its main office at Philadelphia, 12 Dec. 1791. Its 8 branches, located in the principal commercial towns, acted as clearing agencies. The bank acted as fiscal agent for the government, its notes had general acceptance, and its specie holdings made it a bank of last resort.

STOCK EXCHANGES. The first securities exchange was informally organized at **Philadelphia,** 1791, followed, 1792, in **New York.** Both dealt mainly in federal "stock." Most **domestic** enterprise was financed by **local capital.** Local merchants and storekeepers maintaining open accounts were still important sources of commercial credit. **Foreign commerce,** in large proportion, was financed by British merchants extending liberal credit.

1801–11. EXPANSION OF STATE-CHARTERED BANKING. The number of state banks rose from 30 to 88, while their total capital increased about 3-fold. In Feb. 1811, Congress failed to recharter the Bank of the U.S. State-owned banks ("mixed" enterprises in which private banks owned stock) started in Vermont (c.1800) and reached their highest development in Indiana, Ohio, and Virginia.

1811–60. EXPANSION OF CORPORATE DEVICE. Limitation of liability, almost invariably conferred in the early charters, was made general by judicial decisions and statutes limiting the risks of investors (Massachusetts between 1809–30, general acceptance by 1856). Beginning with the New York law of 1811 general incorporation laws were substituted for the previous practice of negotiating with the state legislature for a charter. After the restraints of the Jacksonian period had been lifted (in New York by the Constitution of 1846), general incorporation laws became increasingly loose (especially in Delaware, Maryland, and later Nevada). Down to 1860 only a minority of corporations were in manufacturing; in Pennsylvania over 60% chartered, 1790–1860, were in transportation. By 1900, however, two thirds of all manufacturing was done by corporations, a percentage which rose to 69.2%, 1929.

1812–15. WAR OF 1812 induced a banking boom (120 new banks chartered).

1812–60. LIFE INSURANCE AND SAVINGS BANKS. Pennsylvania Co. for Insurance on Lives and Granting Annuities, first company specializing in life insurance, incorporated Philadelphia, 1812. Rapid development of life insurance companies after 1843. By 1860, $160 million life insurance in force. First incorporated savings bank chartered, Boston, 1816; New York, Baltimore, and Philadelphia inaugurated policy of paying interest on deposits (1819). Total savings deposits: 1835, $7 million; 1850, $43 million; 1860, $150 million (278 savings banks).

1816–18. 2ND BANK OF THE U.S. (p. 184), chartered, Apr. 1816, as a result of the efforts of **Alexander J. Dallas, Stephen Girard** (1750–1831), and **John Jacob Astor** to aid government fiscal operations and support government securities, functioned, as did its predecessor, as a central bank. Under the direction of **William Jones** (1760–1831), a Republican politician, the bank was mismanaged and came close to bankruptcy.

1819–22. Administration of **Langdon Cheves** of South Carolina, second president of the Bank of the U.S., pursued a conservative and restrictive policy, restoring the bank to a sound condition.

1820–40. RAPID EXPANSION OF STATE BANKS to meet demand for loans of persons without capital or credit resulted in basic weaknesses: (1) lack of adequate specie reserve to redeem bank notes; (2) legal office for redemption purposely located in inaccessible spots ("wildcat banks").

1823–36. BIDDLE AND THE BANK. On the resignation (fall 1823) of Cheves, **Nicholas Biddle** succeeded to the presidency. During his regime the bank's operations and influence were aggressively expanded. Bank notes issued, 1823, averaged $4.5 million; 1831, $19 million. The bank advanced necessary loans to the U.S. government and made credit and currency more abundant in the West and South. The bank's expansion of operations in domestic exchange led to the rise of documentary bills rivaling the promissory note as a type of short-term commercial paper. Such short-term paper in effect provided the nation with an "elastic" currency. However, after 1832 the bank sought to check inflation and contributed markedly to the business contraction which occurred (pp. 213, 747). The bank's federal charter expired, 1836.

1825–40. "SUFFOLK SYSTEM," in full operation by 1825, by the Suffolk Bank, Boston (founded 1818), required country banks to keep deposits in the Suffolk Bank to insure honoring their notes. Result: discount on country bank notes disappeared. A similar system was set up by the Metropolitan Bank of New York (1851). However, this system of *de facto* clearing houses did not operate on a nationwide basis until the establishment of the National Banking System, 1863 (p. 285). In this period country banks began depositing surplus funds with correspondent banks in leading financial centers. In 1840 bankers' balances held by New York City banks reached nearly $8 million. These funds were increasingly concentrated (1857–72) in 6 or 7 out of a total of 50 banks (M. G. Myers).

1829. Safety Fund Act of New York, passed for the protection of bank creditors, established the principles of (1) insurance and (2) control by bank commissioners.

1830–40. NEW YORK'S FINANCIAL PREEMINENCE. New York Stock Exchange passed Philadelphia in volume of trading, beginning with the 1820s with the successful flotation of Erie Canal bonds. With the expiration of the Second Bank's charter, New York also supplanted Philadelphia in the commercial credit field. Other trends: Boston Stock Exchange, 1834, facilitated security transactions of New England manufacturing companies. The **Anglo-American merchant bankers,** a group of British houses led by Baring Bros. & Co., floated large issues of state bonds for internal improvements. Until the 1830s lotteries were also extensively used for this purpose; prohibited by state laws, 1821–33. By this period commercial credit dealing had become a major phase of banking, with rates on commercial paper quoted regularly in leading financial journals.

1837–48. PANIC OF 1837 (p. 213) and the wholesale failures of state banks with deposits of federal funds led to the establishment of the **Independent Treasury** on 4 July 1840; repealed 13 Aug. 1841, but reenacted in Aug. 1846. As a number of states repudiated their maturing obligations, American credit suffered abroad and foreign capital was curtailed.

1838. N.Y. FREE BANKING ACT introduced competition in the banking field by no longer requiring special legislation to obtain a charter. However, the state law required banks to keep a specie reserve of 12.5% against note

issues. Louisiana, 1842, and Massachusetts, 1858, introduced similar reserve requirements.

1841. Establishment by Lewis Tappan of the Mercantile Agency, the first credit-rating agency, which became Dun & Co., 1859; Bradstreet's est. 1855.

1847–48. U.S. government loans for the War with Mexico were handled by Corcoran & Riggs, Washington, D.C., outbidding New York firms.

1849–60. INVESTMENT OPERATIONS. Renewed foreign investments, particularly in railroads, raised U.S. foreign indebtedness (p. 734). Nevertheless, the U.S. money market had now become the chief source of capital funds. Out of a total exceeding $2 billion of corporate securities outstanding, 1860, **over three fourths** were owned by Americans. The expansion of security dealings led to the rise of "investment houses," particularly in New York, as well as brokerage firms, and firmly established the preeminent position in security trading of the New York Stock Exchange.

1853, Oct. Establishment of New York Clearing House formalized clearing operations. (Clearing houses also established at Boston, 1855; Philadelphia, Baltimore, and Cleveland, 1856.)

1857. PANIC OF 1857. Bankers' balances held in New York City surged from $17 million, 1850, to over $30 million. The withdrawal of balances during the fall, coupled with the failure of the Ohio Life Insurance and Trust Co., precipitated a panic (p. 265), during which specie payments were temporarily suspended.

1862. Employing new retail marketing techniques and stressing patriotic appeal, **Jay Cooke** successfully floated U.S. Civil War loan.

1863–65. National banking legislation (1863–64, p. 285) bore a striking re-

semblance to the New York Free Banking Act, but provided a safer currency.
With the first national bank organized at
Philadelphia by Jay Cooke, 20 June
1863, some 450 banks were established
by 1863, of which one third constituted
former state banks. The enactment,
1865, of a prohibitory tax on state bank
note issues (p. 285) forced an additional
700 state banks to become national
banks and brought about a **uniform currency** (national bank notes).

1869, 24 Sept. Black Friday (p. 298).

1873. The failure of Jay Cooke & Co.
contributed to the increased prominence
in the investment banking field of the
house of **J. P. Morgan** (associated with
the Drexels since 1871). The practice
now emerged of bankers demanding a
share in management control before
granting credit (financing of N.Y. Central R.R., 1879, although the general
practice was not conspicuous until the
1890s). Concentration of bankers' balances in a few New York banks continued (Sprague), making possible the development of the **call loan market.** For
Panic of 1873, see p. 748. Bank suspensions, 1873–75: 104 (17 national, 87
state).

1879–90. Investment bankers undertook a larger share of railroad financing,
as they began to exert influence on management and to promote combinations.

1891–1900. Investment bankers promoted consolidations in the railroad,
utility, and industrial field. Bank suspensions, 1893: 491 (69 national). State-
chartered **trust companies** rose from 251
to 290, with their investments increasing from $192 million to $326 million.

**1901–12. TRUST COMPANY EX-
PANSION:** number, 6-fold; capital,
4-fold; investments, $1.5 billion.

1907–8. Bank suspensions, which had
averaged 100 a year, rose to well over
200 in the years of the depression.

**1913. FEDERAL RESERVE SYS-
TEM** established (p. 326) to remedy
defects of the National Banking System:
inelasticity of the currency; need for a
"lender of last resort" to come to the aid
of commercial banks when there was a
drain on reserves (demonstrated by
Panic of 1907).

1914–18. Financing World War I. Investment market handled unprecedented
volume of securities, including loans to
Allies (nearly $2 billion by 1916), as
well as **Liberty Loans,** which encouraged widespread public acquaintance
with security issues.

1917–20. Modifications of Federal Reserve System: (1) Federal Reserve
banks authorized to issue Federal Reserve Notes on the basis of gold as well
as discounted paper; (2) gold reserves
of Reserve banks raised from approximately $600 million to nearly $1,300.
The effort of the Federal Reserve Board
to hold down interest rates had an inflationary impact.

1921–29. Corporations increasingly applied their earnings to satisfying capital
needs, adopting a conservative dividend
policy. The expansion of the securities
market and the rapid growth of **investment trusts** led to bypassing established investment bankers. The business
practices of reducing accounts outstanding, and stressing smaller inventories
and rapid turnover, left commercial
banks with idle funds. The volume of
call loans on security collateral dangerously expanded, and commercial banks
branched into other fields—real estate,
time-deposit banking, and investment
banking through investment affiliates.
This period is also noted for large banking consolidations and the spread of
branch banking. Bank failures totaled
5,411.

1929–33. Following the initial phase
of stock market decline and leveling off

of industrial production, European financial stringency (p. 384) led to large withdrawals from the U.S. of foreign bank deposits. Decline of agricultural prices led to farm mortgage deterioration, with rapid increase in the mortality of country banks in 1930 and the undermining of the whole rural credit structure, 1931–32. Liquidation of collateral by banks caused a demoralization of security values. **Bank suspensions, 1929–33: 9,765** (member, 2,391), or over a third of all banks.

1933–39. For New Deal reforms relating to banking and capital markets including deposit insurance, see pp. 404–411. New Deal banking legislation forced investment bankers to choose between deposit banking and underwriting. Between 1934–39, 20 New York City investment firms managed 78.6% of securities registered with the SEC, with **Morgan, Stanley & Co.** in first position. The U.S. government, especially through the medium of the RFC (p. 400) and various farm and mortgage credit agencies (pp. 401–422), became increasingly a supplier of capital funds for long and short terms, and Treasury officials largely supplanted the Federal Reserve Board as formulators of credit policy.

1940–45. The war years were marked by an enormous expansion of the government's role as supplier of capital needs. On 25 June 1940 the RFC was authorized to make loans for acquiring, producing, or stockpiling strategic raw materials and for constructing, expanding, and operating plants. Under an executive order of 26 Mar. 1942 the government began to guarantee or participate in loans made by banks to finance war production. By 31 Dec. 1945, Federal Reserve banks had executed 7,999 agreements for credits, totaling $9.9 billion, 80% of which were loans of $1 million and above. The Smaller War Plants Corp. was set up by the government to provide funds for small businesses with war contracts; its functions were taken over by the RFC in 1945. As a result of the government's desire to issue its securities at low interest, the Federal Reserve Board acted as an agency to support the bond market, and temporarily abdicated control over the money market.

1946–60. NEW INVESTMENT TRENDS. As a result of a marked increase in the assets of life insurance companies (500% by 1938 over 1910; by 1948, assets of legal reserve companies, $56 billion), such companies began to purchase whole issues of securities direct from the borrowing corporation in competition with investment bankers. Other corporations, owing to high taxes, proceeded to finance themselves out of profits in lieu of increasing dividends. In decade of 1950s investment companies, notably **mutual funds,** greatly expanded, with the number of shareholders exceeding 2.5 million (1960). Savings-bank deposits rose from $63.2 billion (31 Dec. 1952) to $100.8 billion (31 Dec. 1959); life insurance in force, $276 billion (1 Jan. 1953), $542 billion (1 Jan. 1960). Commercial banks in 1946 held 70% of the assets of the 4 major financial intermediaries—commercial banks, life insurance companies, savings and loan associations, and mutual savings banks; in 1955, they held only 54%. The competition from the so-called nonbank intermediaries was thus severe. 1956, 9 May, Bank Holding Company Act made it unlawful for any bank holding company to acquire bank stocks or take certain other actions without prior approval of the Federal Reserve System. Bank holding companies were required to divest themselves of interests in nonbanking organizations with certain specified exceptions.

Stock Market. Prices rose on the stock market; in 1954, the market passed its

1929 Dow-Jones high of 381.17; the bull market of the 1950s bore some resemblance to the 1920s market, *except* (1) with new margin requirements, stock trading was mainly in cash and thus the exchange was a relatively minor force in the money market and (2) since capital requirements of business were financed primarily from internal sources (profits and depreciation), the market did not play the role in corporate financing that it had in the 1920s. Mutual funds, trusts, pension funds, insurance portfolios, and foundations became important in the 1950s market; in 1949, such institutions held $9.5 billion in New York Stock Exchange securities; by the end of 1960 the figure was $70.5 billion; institutional holdings had risen from 12.5% to 20% of all equities.

Rising Interest Rates. To meet the record-breaking expansion of credit and bank loans (beg. fall 1950), the Federal Reserve Board increased bank reserve requirements (1951). 1951 accord between the Federal Reserve and Treasury gave the former independence in policy-making; the Federal Reserve was relieved of the responsibility to support government securities at a set price. U.S. government bonds sold below par for the first time in more than a decade, with long-term interest rates showing a tendency to rise. As an anti-inflationary step, bank rates on loans rose gradually in the 1950s—short-term business loans (average) from 2.7% (1950) to 5% (1959), the highest level in 28 years.

1960–73. TRENDS IN BANKING included: (1) Decline of the unit bank and increase in branch banking. 1960, the number of banks exceeded the number of branches (13,472 banks; 10,472 branches). 1966, branch bank offices accounted for almost 65% of total banking offices, and branch banks controlled almost 70% of the country's banking re-

sources. 1972, 31 Dec., 13,928 commercial banks, which had 24,414 branches and offices. (2) Increase in bank holding companies. In 1960 there were 42 bank holding companies and most of the major ones were organized between 1925 and 1930. They had 1,463 offices (6% of all commercial bank offices) and controlled c.8% of the deposits in commercial banks. The number rose in the 1960s, especially after a 1966 amendment to the Bank Holding Company Act of 1956. Then, under the authority granted by a 1970 amendment to that act, the Federal Reserve permitted bank holding companies to engage in a wider range of activities. 1972, 31 Dec., 1,607 bank holding companies owned 2,720 banks and 13,441 branches, a total of 42.1% of the nation's banking offices; they controlled 61.5% of total commercial bank deposits and 63.2% of total commercial bank assets; (3) commercial banks gave competition to nonbank intermediaries, offering full-service banking; (4) banking became more international, as banks established foreign branches, subsidiaries, and affiliates. 1968–73, American banks joined with foreign banks of industrial nations to participate in consortia, to create specialized institutions for Eurodollar lending, in part a response to the vast development of multinational industrial enterprises (p. 732). (5) The Federal Re-

LARGEST U.S. COMMERCIAL BANKS
(includes banks with deposits over $20 billion, 6/30/73)

Name	Deposits 6/30/73 (in billions)
Bank of America, S.F.	$36.86
First National City, N.Y.	29.55
Chase Manhattan, N.Y.	26.18

serve Board played an increasingly active role in monetary policy, concerning itself with the growth of the stock of money, with counter-cyclical responses to credit conditions, and with the outflow of gold (p. 710).

Interest Rates. Despite declines in 1960–61, 1967, 1970–72, the trend was upward. 3-month treasury bills, 1960, 2.9%; 1979 (Jan.–May), 9.44%; 3–5 year government securities issues, 1960, 3.5%; 1981, c. 14.5%; prime commercial paper, 4–6 months, 1960, 3.85%; 1979, 10.03% (the rate reached a new peak in May 1981, 20.5%). FHA mortgages, 1960, 6.2%; 1981, c. 17%, with high interest rates and inflation combined, the efficacy of monetary policy was subject to numerous questions.

Life Insurance and Pensions. Life insurance became a principal private absorber of savings. In 1972 total life insurance in force was $1,628 billion; assets of life insurance companies equaled $240 billion. The investments of such insurance companies included corporate securities ($113 billion), mortgages ($77 billion), and government securities ($11 billion). Private pension funds multiplied; unlike insurance companies, which were subject to state regulations, the pension funds were not regulated. In 1959 Congress passed the Welfare and Pension Fund Disclosure Act, which required pension funds to register with the U.S. Department of Labor; by 1972, 34,000 such funds had registered. The law established no rules or checks, or provisions for insurance and safety, of the pension funds. By 1972, c.$135 billion in assets had accumulated in private pension plans.

Stock Market. Sharp gyrations characterized the stock market, especially in 1962 and 1973. In 1960, the Dow-Jones range had been between 560 and 685; in 1962, the Dow-Jones index slumped to 535. 1973, 11 Jan., it reached a new high of 1,050, only to drop as low as 788 (5 Dec.). Between 26 Oct. and 5 Dec. the market fell 198¾ points—the largest point decline in any 3 months of market history. (But the drop was only 20.1% compared with the 193-point decline of 50.6% in 1929.) The decline was associated with the energy crisis and general economic uncertainty. In 1960–73, as in the 1950s, with capital requirements in large part—always over 50%—financed from internal sources (profits and depreciation) and with the margin requirements, the market gyrations did not have the economic consequences of the collapse of 1929. In 1960, est. gross proceeds from new corporate issues totaled $10.15 billion; in 1972, $41.96 billion. The early 1970s saw the small investor get out of the market; in 1970, an estimated 30% of U.S. families owned stock; in 1973, 21%. Down to mid-1980 institutions, pension funds, insurance portfolios, mutual funds, trusts, and foundations continued to dominate trading, although rising volume, 1979–80, pointed to a resumption of public buying, with Amex and O-T-C (because of energy and technology representation) advancing faster than N.Y. Stock Exchange shares. High interest rates blamed for failure of Dow-Jones to hold above 900 level to 1 Dec. 1981, as funds were siphoned from savings institutions to money market funds yielding high interest.

Business Cycles and Price Trends

Economic fluctuations (business cycles) have characterized American economic history. Each business cycle has a trough, a peak, and a trough. Until the depression of the 1930s, in the main market forces acted to correct the ups and downs of the economy. From the 1930s onward, the U.S. government played a major role in pursuing countercyclical policies (that is, in times of downturn to promote recovery; in times of inflation to try to dampen it). Countercyclical measures include fiscal, monetary, and incomes policies. In post-World War II years such policies were successful in that a downturn of the severity of the 1930s has not occurred; cyclical fluctuations have been moderated. On the other hand, the policies have not been effective in curbing the inflationary spiral. But the efficacy of government policies has been severely challenged during recession-inflation (stagflation) which began toward the end of 1972.

For most of U.S. history, prices have risen in wartime and then dropped; indeed, in 1790 and 1900, the price levels were about the same; the price level was actually higher in 1800 than in 1900. In the 20th century, prices rose during World War I, declined in the 1930s (but not below the 1900 level) and then climbed with World War II, the Korean War, the Vietnam War, and continued upward, with stagflation dominating the late '70s and early '80s.

1760. Peak of the French and Indian War boom. CP[1]: **79.**

1762–65. Low point of business slump early 1765. CP: 1762, **87;** 1765, **72;** 1766, **73.**

1768. Currency contraction precipitated a business slump, especially acute

DURATION OF MAJOR DEPRESSIONS
(Sachs-Thorp)

Years	Months' duration
1762–65	36
1768–69	12
1772–75	30
1784–88	**44**
1796–98	36
1802–03	24
1807–09	27
1815–21	**71**
1825–26	13
1833–34	9
1837–43	**72**
1857–58	18
1866–67	18
1873–78	**66**
1882–85	36
1890–91	9
1893–97	**48**
1907–08	12
1913–14	20
1920–21	18
1929–33	**42**
1937–38	10

1. CP represents commodity prices down to 1860, based on Warren-Pearson wholesale price index for all commodities, New York—1910–14 = 100.

in New York and Philadelphia. CP: **74.**

1770–71. The termination of nonimportation agreements, combined with rising prices and favorable exchange rates, fostered speculation and large importations of British goods. CP: 1770, **77;** 1772, **89.**

1772. The British banking crisis of the summer, with the ensuing credit contraction, brought widespread inventory liquidation and distress to colonial importers.

1773–75. Business sagged. CP: 1773, **84;** 1775, **75.**

1776–83. The American Revolution produced a business boom, with a sharp price rise caused in large measure by sizable emissions of paper money and deficit financing. CP: 1776, **86;** 1779, **226;** 1781, **216** (in depreciated currency the percentage rise was far greater).

1784–88. Excessive importations of British goods after the war, combined with an unstable currency and fiscal situation, set off a downturn, with the British banking crisis of 1784 precipitating a sharp deflation in the U.S. Although the business decline was arrested in the course of 1787, the drop in commodity prices was not halted until late 1788. CP: 1785, **92**; 1789, **86** (Bezanson, Philadelphia prices, puts decline at c.30% for same period).

1789–1800. While previous business fluctuations were mainly associated with external factors, cyclical factors inherent in business now became faintly discernible. Except for a minor recession, 1796–98, the period was one of substantial prosperity. The European wars created a large demand for U.S. farm commodities and shipping. Prices climbed steadily until 1797. CP: 1790, **90**; 1797, **131**; 1800, **129**.

1801–02. The peace of Amiens halted the war boom. CP: 1801, **142**; 1802, **117**.

1803–07. Another wave of prosperity followed renewal of the European war, only to be terminated by the Embargo Act, 22 Dec. 1807. CP: 1804, **126**; 1806, **134**; 1807, **130**.

1808–09. Depression spread inland, followed by revival, 1810–11. CP: 1810, **131**.

1812–14. The War of 1812 curbed foreign trade, but most other branches of economic activity enjoyed an uneven war boom, with manufacturing especially benefiting by the curtailment of British imports and the South depressed, 1813–14. Heavy government borrowing stimulated banking expansion. CP: 1813, **162**; 1814, **182**.

1815–21. Resumption of importations hurt U.S. manufacturing, but the downtrend was checked by European demand for American farm staples. As farm commodities soared and bank credit was liberalized, a wave of land speculation occurred. CP: 1815, **170**. However, with the collapse of foreign markets prices broke in the fall (1819) (CP: **125**), land values sank rapidly, and numerous banks and mercantile houses failed in

the **first major banking crisis** in U.S. history, with general business depressed until 1822. CP: 1821, **102**; 1822, **106**.

1823–34. Slow business recovery with minor fluctuations (downturns, 1825–26, 1833–early 34). CP ranged from **103** down to **95**. The recession of 1833 resulted from the removal of government deposits from the Second Bank of the U.S., with subsequent credit curtailment by the bank (pp. 213, 740).

1834–36. Brisk business activity returned by the spring of 1834. Land speculation was fostered by (1) a boom in canal and railroad building, (2) the transfer of U.S. deposits to state banks, (3) an inflow of foreign capital. The Specie Circular (July 1836, p. 211) resulted in a sharp downturn in land sales by the latter part of that year. CP: 1834, **90**; 1836, **114**.

1837. The collapse in real estate was followed in the 2d quarter of 1837 by a precipitate fall in stock and commodity prices and an acute banking crisis attributed to (1) Specie Circular; (2) distribution legislation of 1836, leading to government drafts on state banks; (3) high interest rates and calling in of loans by British bankers; (4) crop failures in 1835 and 1837; (5) mounting state debts; (6) unfavorable balance of trade which increased flow of specie to Europe. CP: 1838, **110**.

1838–43. The decline was briefly halted in 1838 as business activity appeared to be building toward a secondary boom, but a major break came in 1839 when the Bank of the U.S., now a Pennsylvania-chartered bank, closed its doors after an unsuccessful attempt to sustain cotton prices. The crisis was followed by a protracted depression, with its low point near Feb. 1843. CP: 1839, **112**; 1843, **75**.

1844–48. Gradual recovery with mild fluctuations. CP: 1848, **82**.

1849–56. A marked expansion of business fed in part by the inflow of foreign (particularly British) capital, which revived railroad building, and by the discovery of gold in California, which facilitated payments of international balances, stimulated foreign trade, and encouraged loans by domestic banks. Prosperity was briefly interrupted by a panic on the New York Stock Exchange in the fall of 1854. CP: 1850, 84; 1854, 108; 1855, 110; 1856, 105.

1857–58. The failure of the Ohio Life Insurance and Trust Co. (Aug.) touched off a sharp, though shortlived, financial panic, basically caused by overspeculation in railroad securities and real estate. CP: 1857, 111; 1858, 93.

1859–65. Recovery set in quickly, with prosperity continuing until the outbreak of the Civil War. Business wavered with the coming of war (1861), but heavy government spending and an inflationary price rise produced a war boom. The collapse of currency and finance in the Confederacy (Mar. 1865) brought temporary chaos to the South. CP[2]: 1861, 61.3; 1862, 71.7; 1863, 90.5; 1864, 116; 1865, 132.

1866–72. Postwar readjustment (1866–67) brought little distress to the North as a railroad boom steadily gained momentum; violent stock market fluctuations, mainly the result of speculative activity, had only a limited nationwide impact. Most spectacular incident was "Black Friday," 24 Sept. 1869 (p. 298). CP: 1868, 97.7; 1870, 86.7.

1873–78. The failure of the banking house of Jay Cooke and Co., 18 Sept. 1873, revealed the weakened speculative structure resultant upon overextension in railroad securities. With bankruptcies among banks and brokers multiplying, prices fell precipitately, as did national

income. CP: 1874, 81.0; 1879, 58.8. SP[3]: 1872, 39.8; 1877, 24.8.

1873–96. Economists not infrequently characterize this period as a "long-wave" depression. The price level declined steadily (CP: 1885, 56.6; 1896, 46.5), with only 8 partly or wholly prosperous years. Nevertheless, vigorous business upswings occurred, with enormous extension of investment in industrial plants and equipment. Recovery began in 1878 and continued until 1882, when a depression, 1883–85, primarily financial in origin, occurred, followed by quick recovery again, 1885–90, a short recession (1890–91), then a further upturn particularly in heavy industry (1892). The failure of the Philadelphia and Reading R.R. and the National Cordage Co. early in 1893 gave warning that the boom was over. Uncertainty over the status of the gold standard was a further depressing factor as foreign investors proceeded to sell U.S. securities, capital left the country, the reserve fell, and wholesale liquidation was set in motion. Before 1893 had ended, 491 banks and over 15,000 commercial institutions were reported to have failed. Before the turning point was reached by 1897, almost one third of the total railroad mileage was in the hands of receivers. SP: 1892, 43.9; 1896, 33.5.

1897–1914. Recovery followed rapidly, with relative continuing prosperity save for brief financial crises in 1903 and 1907, a recession, 1910–11, and a downturn on the eve of World War I (1913–14). CP: 1897, 46.6; 1900, 56.1; 1910, 70.4; 1913, 69.8. SP: 1897, 35.2; 1912, 75.5, with a decline, 1913–14, to 63.8.

1914–19. A financial reaction following the outbreak of war was succeeded by a war boom fed by Allied orders. The peak of business activity was reached

2. After 1860, CP is based on wholesale price index, all commodities, Bureau of Labor Statistics (1926 = 100).

3. Index of Common Stock Prices, all stocks (1926 = 100) U.S. Bureau of the Census, *Hist. Stat. of U.S., 1789–1945*.

EFFECT OF U.S. WARS ON WHOLESALE PRICES, 1770-1972*

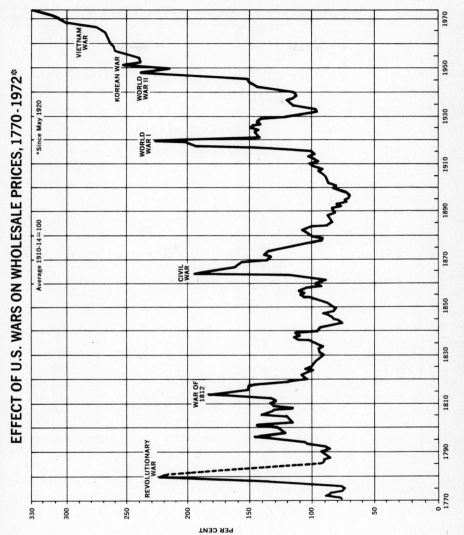

*From *Our National Debt*, prepared by the Committee on Economic Policy, copyright, 1949, by Harcourt, Brace and Company, Inc. and *Statistical Abstract*, 1960; *Economic Report of the President*, 1973.

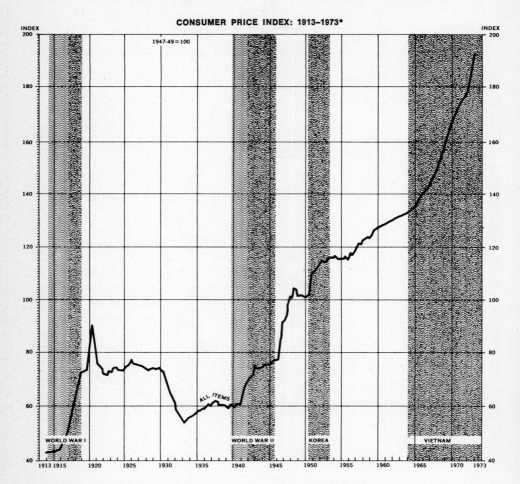

CONSUMER PRICE INDEX: 1913–1973*

1947-49 = 100

WORLD WAR I
ALL ITEMS
WORLD WAR II
KOREA
VIETNAM

* **1974–80.** Except for the years 1975–78, when consumer price rise ranged from 7–9%, the remaining years of the decade saw double digit inflation, exceeding 13% in 1979.

in 1916, and sustained by America's participation in the war. Temporary hesitation after the Armistice gave way to soaring prices, sales, and production, resulting from credit expansion and speculation in inventories. CP: 1916, **85.5**; 1917, **117.5**; 1918, **131.3**; 1919, **138.8**. SP: 1914, **63.8**; 1920, **64.2**.

1920–21. Sharp deflation after May 1920. CP: 1920, **154.5**; 1921, **97.6**; 1922, **96.7**.

1922–29. A rising tide of prosperity was sustained by conspicuous expansion of the consumers' durable goods industry. A boom in construction and real estate also developed (**Florida real estate boom** collapsed in 1926). By 1927 residential construction, auto output, purchases of consumers' durable goods, and new investment in producers' durable goods had begun to decline; but the boom continued, fed almost entirely by **unprecedented securities speculation not reflected in commodity prices.** CP: 1923, **100.6**; 1929, **95.3**, as contrasted with SP: 1922, **67.7**; 1929, **190.3**. The spectacular crash of stock prices occurred in Oct.–Nov. 1929.

1930–33. The depression deepened despite efforts to ease money market and extend credits (pp. 399, 727). Low point of depression: **Mar. 1933**, with industrial production rising 15%, July–Oct. 1932, but declining sharply by Mar. 1933 as the **banking crisis** deepened and bank holidays blanketed the nation. Industrial output almost halved, unemployment mounted to about 15 million, one third of the nation's railroad mileage was thrown into bankruptcy, and farm mortgage foreclosures were widespread. CP: 1930, **86.4**; 1931, **73.0**; 1932, **64.8**; 1933, **65.9**. SP: 1930, **149.8**; 1932, **48.6**.

1933–37. New Deal intervention to halt the downward spiral took a variety of forms (pp. 403–422), including **deficit financing.** Business activity and prices rose. SP: 1934, **72.4**; 1937, **111.8**.

1935–37. The business recovery was interrupted by a brief, but acute, recession, Aug. 1937. CP: 1935, **80**; 1937, **86.3**.

1938–39. Deficit financing on an increasing scale contributed to recovery. Yet in Aug. 1939, about 10 million persons were still unemployed. Based on 1929 national income of $81 billion, the estimated loss of national income, 1930–38, totaled $132,600,000,000 (TNEC *Hearings*). CP: 1938, **78.6**; 1939, **77.1**.

1939–45. The outbreak of World War II in Europe was followed by a sudden spurt in economic activity. The index of industrial production standing at **105** (1935–39 = 100) in Aug. 1939 leaped to **125** in Dec., with unemployment falling 10%. By 1940 the effects of the U.S. military program were being felt in government expenditures, industrial output, and national income. The entry of the U.S. into the war brought large-scale mobilization of manpower and resources, with economic activity making giant strides. Peak levels were attained by 1944–45. The index of industrial production by 1944 reached **235**, and national income increased 2½ times. Despite wartime price and wage controls (p. 451) wholesale CP rose from **78.6** (1940) to **105.8** (1945).

CURRENCY IN CIRCULATION
(Hist. Statistics of U.S.)

1932	$5,695,171,000
1940	7,847,501,000
1945	26,746,438,000
1957	31,081,913,000
1979	125,600,000,000

1946–60. The inflationary upturn was accelerated by the removal of government economic controls, deferred postwar demand, and financing (in part deficit) for defense and foreign expenditures.

BLS Consumers' Price Index (1935–39 = 100)

June 1950	177.8	(pre-Korean intervention)
Jan. 1951	184.7	(U.S. govt. price "freeze")
Sept. 1952	191.1	(all-time high to 1952)

BOOM AND RECESSION. Period of general business expansion interrupted by 4 recessions: (1) 1948–49, decline in gross national product from $259.4 billion (1948) to $258.1 billion (1949), chiefly as a result of shift in inventory accumulation; unemployment reached 3.4 million in 1949; (2) 1953–54, resulting from inventory liquidation and decline in federal expenditures for defense purposes, with 3.7 million persons unemployed by spring of 1954, and decline of gross national product from $364.9 billion (1953) to $356 billion (1954); (3) 1957–1958, resulting from overexpansion of plant capacity and drop in exports, with durable goods production chiefly hit; followed by rapid recovery until steel strike (15 July 1959); (4) beginning midsummer 1960, accompanied by falling off of demand for steel (below 40% capacity, Jan. 1961), autos, and appliances. Unemployment rose contraseasonally to 4 million (Nov. 1960) and est. 5.25 million (Jan. 1961). CP (1947–49 = 100) continued to rise, from 83.4 (1946) to 114.4 (1953) to 127.4 (Nov. 1960), with especially sharp increases in cost of housing, apparel, transportation, and medical care. (Care went from 90.6, 1947, to 155.0, Mar. 1960.)

Business cycle peak and trough dates (National Bureau of Economic Research): **troughs:** Oct. 1945, Oct. 1949, May 1954, Apr. 1958, Feb. 1961, Nov. 1970, Mar. 1975, July 1980; **peaks:** Nov. 1948, July 1953, Aug. 1957, Apr. 1960, Dec. 1969, Nov. 1973, Jan. 1980.

1961–68. PROSPERITY. Period of increasing prosperity and high employment marked by moderate price rises (1958–65) and balance of payments problems. The gross national product reached $864 billion (1968). Corporate

profits increased after taxes to $47.8 billion (1968). Profits before taxes, $87.6 billion (1968). The seasonally adjusted unemployment rate of 3.3% (Dec. 1968) was the lowest since the Korean War: 75.4 million employed, 2.45 million unemployed.

Balance of payments problems eased in 1968 (p. 710), although the surplus of exports over imports, $726 million, was the lowest since 1937.

The consumer price index rose 6% (1968) to 148.6 (1947–49 = 100), the worst inflationary year since the Korean War, as the high rate of federal spending overheated the economy. Wage increases in major industries (1968), involving 3.4 million workers, amounted to 7.5%, not including fringe benefits and cost of living increases.

1969–73. INFLATION. The inflationary spiral continued upward; at the same time, the rate of unemployment rose from 3.5% of all workers (1969), to 4.9% (1970), 5.9% (1971), and rose steeply by 1974 to 7.1%. Fiscal and monetary policy steps to curb inflation also tended to raise unemployment. In 1969, the administration, seeking to control inflation, attempted to hold back economic expansion. By the end of 1969 and early 1970, the rise in demand had slowed and output fell. Policy goals then aimed at expansion. Recovery was impeded by a long strike at General Motors at the end of 1970. 1971 saw output begin to mount. 1971, 15 Aug., Nixon imposed a 90-day freeze on prices, wages, and rents to try to halt inflation. The freeze was followed (14 Nov.) with **Phase II**, a broad, mandatory system of controls, directed by a Price Commission and a Pay Board, under the general coordination of a Cost of Living Council (CLC). Concurrently, Nixon took steps to stimulate the economy with an eye to increasing employment. 1972 was the first peacetime year in' American history of national, general price and wage controls; despite them, consumer prices continued to rise (see p. 750). Food prices that were excluded from the controls rose most rapidly. 1973, 11 Jan., the more permissive **Phase III** was announced; prices spurted upward and 5 months later (13 June) **Phase III½** — a new freeze was imposed; this lasted until 18 July, when **Phase IV** began with restraints in between those of Phases II and III. In Phase IV, companies could raise prices as long as the increase did not exceed the average rise set by the CLC. Prices continued to climb. Nov.–Dec.; the energy crisis created new higher prices.

1960–73. GROWTH OF MONEY STOCK.

CURRENCY PLUS DEMAND DEPOSITS (MI-A)
Averages of daily figures in billions of dollars

1960	$142
1970	$215
1980 (May)	$368

1972–81. STAGFLATION. The inflationary spiral accompanied slow growth, with inflation reaching 11.3% in 1979, but declining slightly in 1981, unemployment holding in the 7% range (1981–7.6%), and the Dow-Jones industrial stocks ranging between 923.9 (1973) and 817.2 (1978), temporarily crossing 1,000 several times down to 1 July 1981.

Labor, Slavery, and Social Reform

In preindustrial America the labor force comprised slaves, bound, and free labor. White bound labor gradually died out, in large part the result of insolvency and bankruptcy laws ending imprisonment for debt. The American Revolution proved a fillip to ending slavery, either immediately or by gradual stages, in most of the Northern states, but the "peculiar institution" remained the basis of plantation labor in the South as that region gradually shifted to cotton cultivation for a world market. While the Civil War and the 13th Amendment brought about the abolition of slavery throughout the United States, the black farm population, through sharecropping, tenancy, and peonage, remained for more than a generation thereafter in a semi-servile condition.

While sporadic strikes by free white labor took place in colonial and Revolutionary times, it was not until the post-Revolutionary and early National periods that more permanent trade unions appeared, notably in such skilled trades as the cordwainers, printers, and house carpenters. Moving from individual unions to city centrals in the Age of Jackson, the roots of national trade unions were nurtured in the 1850s, and assumed a large significance in post–Civil War industrial society.

Before the Civil War the amelioration of laboring conditions was closely tied to the reform movement. That movement pressed for an end to imprisonment for debt, prison reform, public education, temperance, women's rights, and a cluster of other issues, but, notably, its most sustained effort was directed toward abolition.

A landmark in the history of the labor movement was the organization in 1886 of the American Federation of Labor; its efforts were expended largely in behalf of craft unions and its objectives were chiefly business unionism. Its great rival, the Congress of Industrial Organizations, which concentrated on industrial workers and the organization of vertical unionism, came into being in 1935. Both labor organizations were beneficiaries of the New Deal reforms, the rivals finally merging in 1955.

For years, higher wages and shorter hours were the principal goals of labor unions; these goals broadened considerably in post-World War II years, to include job security, supplementary benefits, protection against inflation, and retirement pay. Union membership peaked at 35.8% of the nonagricultural labor force in 1945, and thereafter in percentages declined, although in recent years considerable attention has been devoted to organizing farm workers.

Real wages in America rose over time; income distribution tended to become more equitable. Although blacks shared in rising incomes, the gulf between the real incomes of white and black families remained wide.

Occupational shifts were dramatic. In 1820, only 28% of the labor force was in nonagricultural pursuits; by the twentieth century the bulk of the labor force was in nonagricultural activities. Employment in manufacturing gained vis-à-vis agriculture, but the service sector gained even more. In the years 1950–72, employment in the service sector (especially in trade, services, and government) witnessed substantial growth. In 1900 women constituted 20% of the labor force; in 1980, 47.8%.

Slavery to 1789

1619, Aug. First Negroes (20) imported into Virginia as **bound servants,** while in Spanish Florida, as in other Spanish colonies, black slavery had been long established.

1619–90. Importations of African Negroes continued on a moderate scale (only 3,000 Negroes estimated in Virginia, 1681), as white servants continued to perform bulk of farm labor.

1650–70. Judicial decisions and legislation in the tobacco provinces established slavery. Virginia act of 1661 assumed that some Negroes served for **life;** act of 1670 declared that "all servants not being Christian" brought in by sea were slaves for life, the issue following the status of the **mother.** Laws passed between 1667–71 authorizing conversion of Negroes to Christianity did not bring release from servitude. Black Code, 1705, severely restrained the mobility of slaves and forbade miscegenation under heavy penalties, evidencing a racial as well as a legal differentiation between Negroes and whites. Maryland, 1663, provided life servitude for Negroes.

1672–1760. SLAVE TRADE. Royal African Co., a reorganized trading company, was granted a monopoly of the English slave trade, 1672; but owing to the protests of independent traders, the monopoly was lost, 1698. In the 18th century New England traders were active in the slave trade, with **Newport, R.I.**, a principal port of entry. For the relation of the slave trade to the Triangular Trade (in which the trip from Africa to the West Indies was called the **"Middle Passage"**), see p. 702. Colonial legislatures imposed duties on slave importations, but royal instructions, 1731, forbade governors consenting to such acts. The action of South Carolina, 1760, in prohibiting the slave trade entirely was disallowed by the king in council. After 1690, slave importations mounted sharply. Virginia had 12,000 Negroes by 1708, with about 1,000 Negroes being imported annually for the 3 preceding years. By 1715, the total had risen to 23,000 Negroes, to 42,000 by 1743, 120,156 by 1756, and 259,230 by 1782. Slave importations to the continental colonies increased from an annual average of 2,500 (1715–50) to 7,450 (1760–70), with South Carolina averaging 2,800 (1753–73).

1712–40. NEGRO PLOTS AND INSURRECTIONS. Apr. 1712, the militia were called out to suppress a Negro insurrection in New York City; 21 Negroes executed. In 1739, 3 Negro uprisings broke out in South Carolina, most serious being the **Cato Conspiracy** (9 Sept.), which occurred at Stono, about 20 miles southwest of Charleston, with 30 white and 44 Negro fatalities. As the result of uncovering a Negro plot in Charleston, Jan. 1740, 50 Negroes were hanged. Beginning with a burglary committed in **New York City, 28 Feb. 1741,** followed by a series of fires, panic seized the city as rumors spread that Negroes and poor whites had conspired to seize control. Despite insufficient evidence, 101 Negroes were convicted (18 Negroes and 4 whites were hanged, 13 Negroes burned alive, and 70 banished).

1749. Trustees' prohibition against slavery in Georgia was repealed and a fixed ratio of 4 male Negroes to 1 white servant adopted. As early as 1741, settlers had hired slaves for 100-year terms.

1776. Slavery and the Declaration of Independence. Jefferson's attack on the role of the crown in the slave trade ("He has prostituted his negative for suppressing every legislative attempt to prohibit or to restrain this execrable commerce") was unacceptable to the Southern delegates at the Continental Congress and was stricken from the document.

1776–89. ANTISLAVERY AND MANUMISSION MOVEMENTS. (1) The first antislavery society in the U.S. was organized by the Quakers in 1775, but their fight goes back to Apr. 1688 when **Francis Pastorius** and the German Friends at Germantown declared that slavery was contrary to Christian principles. In 1696 the Yearly Meeting cautioned members against importing Negroes, and in 1755 ruled that all Friends who should thereafter import slaves would be excluded from the denomination. Antislavery societies spread in the Revolutionary era. (2) The New York Society for Promoting Manumission, with John Jay as president, was established in 1785, with other states from Massachusetts to Virginia following between 1788–92. The movement to manumit (free) slaves by will or deed continued in strength in the South during this period and down to c.1800. (3) The movement against the slave trade (prohibited in Maryland, 1783; curbed in North Carolina by imposing a heavy duty on every Negro imported; repealed, 1790) culminated in the antislave-trade provision of the federal Constitution (p. 570) as well as the provision relating to interstate fugitive slaves (p. 573). (4) Legislation was enacted, gradually abolishing slavery: Pennsylvania, 1780; Connecticut and Rhode Island, 1784; New York, 1785; New Jersey, 1786. By judicial decision, 1783, the Massachusetts Constitution of 1780, which held that "all men are born free and equal," was construed as having abolished slavery. In 1787 slavery was prohibited in the Northwest Territory (p. 139).

1790. POPULATION OF U.S. CLASSIFIED BY COLOR. White, 3,172,444; **Free Negro,** 59,557; **Slaves,** 697,624; **Total,** 3,929,625.

SLAVE DISTRIBUTION

Virginia	292,627
South Carolina	107,094
Maryland	103,036
North Carolina	100,783
Georgia	29,264
New York	21,193
Kentucky	12,430
New Jersey	11,423
Delaware	8,887
Pennsylvania	3,707
Southwest Terr.	3,417
Connecticut	2,648
Rhode Island	958
New Hampshire	157

In no state did the slave population exceed the white, but the ratio was higher in South Carolina, which had 140,178 white persons, and the highest average number of slaves per slaveholding family (12.1), as against 8.5 (est.) for Virginia and 7.5 for Maryland (W. S. Rossiter).

Slavery and the Negro, 1789–1860

1789–1831. MANUMISSION AND COLONIZATION PROJECTS. Chief impulse in this period for slavery reform came from the South. Out of 143 emancipation societies in the U.S. in 1826, 103 were in the South, including 4 abolition papers (1819–28). As far back as 1776, Jefferson proposed a plan for African colonization of the Negroes. Procolonization resolutions were passed by the Virginia Assembly (1800, 1802, 1805, 1816). As a result, the **American Colonization Society** was established in 1817, headed at various times by Monroe, Madison, and John Marshall, and supported by **Henry Clay.** Free Negroes were first sent to Sierra Leone, and finally in 1821 a permanent location was purchased at Monrovia (settled, 1822); established 1847 as independent Republic of **Liberia** (named by **Robert Goodloe Harper** [1765–1825]). The **Mississippi Colonization Society** (founded, 1831) set up a separate African colony for Negro emigrants from that state. The colonization movement declined in the South after 1831. Total Negroes colonized by 1860 estimated at 15,000, of whom 12,000 were transported through the efforts of the American Colonization Society.

1790, 11 FEB. First petition to Congress for emancipation (presented by the Society of Friends). Many such petitions were presented prior to 1820.

1793. Invention of the **cotton gin** by Eli Whitney, displacing the existing method of manual extraction of seed and increasing 50-fold the average daily output of clean short-staple cotton, promoted the rapid expansion of the **cotton kingdom,** firmly established the **plantation system** (also used for the cultivation of such staples as sugar cane, rice, and tobacco), and led to concentration of slaveholding. Of the more than 8 million whites in the South in 1860 only 383,637 were slaveholders. Of these, only 2,292 were large planters (holding 100 or more slaves).

1801, 30 AUG. GABRIEL PLOT in Richmond and elsewhere in Henrico County, Va., was suppressed by Governor Monroe; estimates of executions range from 16 to 35. Jefferson's comment: "We are truly to be pitied."

1808–60. SLAVE TRADE, FOREIGN AND DOMESTIC. Although Congress in 1808 prohibited the further importation of slaves, the illicit trade persisted, even after Congress declared it piracy (1820). Between 1854–60 every Southern commercial convention advocated reopening the trade. One estimate of the slaves brought into the U.S. illegally, 1808–60, places the total at 250,000. But the chief source of supply was the domestic slave trade, which by 1800 had already become regularized in response to the increasing demand for slaves. The upper South found that the sale of surplus slaves in soil-exhausted areas was more profitable than crop cultivation. Chief marketing and distribution points: Richmond, Louisville, Charleston, Mobile, and New Orleans. A substantial part of the domestic trade was in prime field hands, ranging from 18 to 30 in age. Next in order of demand were the full hands used for household and industrial tasks. As a rule slave prices rose continuously after the closure of foreign trade, but were subject to considerable fluctuation in periods of agricultural prosperity and depression. The approximate price of a field hand in 1795 was $300; in 1860 it ranged between $1,200 and $1,800. **Slave hiring** supplemented slave purchases, and made possible the seasonal use of slaves in iron, lead, and coal mines and in factories (notably in tobacco and textile mills). Slave-hiring wages (paid to owners, but bonuses and incentive payments to slaves in addition) rose from $100 (1800) to $500–$600 per annum for a skilled artisan (1860).

1820. Missouri Compromise (p. 190).

1821, Jan. Publication of the *Genius of Universal Emancipation,* antislavery journal edited by **Benjamin Lundy** (1789–1839), advocate of colonization, who published first in Ohio, then in Tennessee, and finally in Baltimore, where (1829) **William Lloyd Garrison** served as associate editor.

1822, 30 May. VESEY SLAVE PLOT in Charleston, S.C., led by a free Negro,

Denmark Vesey, and urban slave artisans, was revealed by an informer and crushed; 37 executed (18 June–9 Aug.).

1826. Nashoba, a Utopian community near Memphis, Tenn., established by **Frances Wright** for the training of Negroes and their eventual resettlement outside the U.S. It was active until 1828.

1831, 1 Jan. First number of *The Liberator,* edited and published by **William Lloyd Garrison:** the organ of the militant abolitionist movement. "I will not retreat a single inch—AND I WILL BE HEARD."

13–23 Aug. NAT TURNER INSURRECTION in Southampton County, Va., led by Turner (1800–31), a Negro preacher, in the course of which 57 whites—men, women, and children—were killed. Tracked down in a sensational manhunt (possibly 100 Negroes killed), 20 Negroes (including Turner) were executed after trials.

1831–32, Winter. VIRGINIA CONVENTION, after debates covering every phase of the slavery problem, defeated by a small majority various proposals for emancipation. These debates mark a turning point in the handling of the slave problem by the South. Immediately thereafter, beginning with North Carolina, and spreading to all the slave states, the **slave codes were tightened** to curb the mobility of slaves (through a strict system of patrols and passes), prohibit their attendance at meetings, curtail their education, drastically restrict manumissions, and impose special disabilities on free Negroes. By 1860, 10 states had constitutional provisions curbing either statutory or voluntary emancipation or both.

1832–40. Organization by Garrison of the New England Anti-Slavery Society, which, with a New York group led by **Arthur** (1786–1865) and **Lewis Tappan** (1788–1873), merchants and philanthropists, formed the **American Anti-**

slavery Society (1833). The Lane Theological Seminary debate at Cincinnati (1832) on colonization and abolition was followed by withdrawal (May 1833) of most of the students, led by **Theodore Dwight Weld** (Ohio, 1803–95), when the trustees ordered a halt to such discussions. After its organization (1833) Oberlin College (Ohio) was visited by Weld, who converted it into the center of Western abolitionism. The trustees of Oberlin, first college to admit women, voted (1835) to admit Negro students. Shortly afterward it became an important station on the Underground Railroad. In 1837 **James G. Birney** (Kentucky, 1792–1857) became secretary of the American Anti-Slavery Society. By 1838 a Garrisonian group in New England came out for passive resistance rather than physical force. With the Tappans and the **Grimké sisters** (Sarah Moore, 1792–1873; Angelina Emily, 1805–79), Weld launched the non-Garrisonian wing of the organized abolition movement—the **American and Foreign Antislavery Society**, which broke with the Garrison group in 1840.

1836. Adoption of the "gag rule" (p. 213).

1837, 7 Nov. A mob in Alton, Ill., attacked the office of **Elijah P. Lovejoy** (1802–37), an antislavery editor. In the ensuing battle Lovejoy was killed. Several persons were indicted, but found not guilty.

1839. *American Slavery As It Is,* by Theodore Weld and his wife, the former Angelina Grimké, was published. Consisting of extracts from Southern newspapers and the testimony of abolitionists who had seen slavery at first hand, this volume presented evidence of oppression. Additional eyewitness testimony was provided by a number of Negroes who participated in the abolition movement as speakers and agents, notably **Frederick Douglass** (p. 1015), who escaped from slavery in 1838, and was active in Negro conventions and the Underground Railroad.

Formation of the **Liberty party** (p. 216).

1840. UNDERGROUND RAILROAD, a secret and shifting network of hiding places and routes for helping fugitive slaves escape to the North or Canada, was well established by this date. Without formal organization, it is known to have existed as early as 1786 and to have flourished in the Western Reserve after the War of 1812, but its spread through 14 Northern states did not come until 1830. The name (originally "Underground Road") supposedly dates from the time (1831) the Kentucky master of a fugitive slave named Tice Davids unsuccessfully pursued him across the Ohio River at Ripley, Ohio, and remarked that Davids "must have gone off an underground road." At least 3,200 active workers have been identified (Siebert), outstanding among whom was the Quaker **Levi Coffin** (1789–1877) and the escaped slave **Harriet Tubman** (c.1821–1913), known as "Moses." At the most liberal estimate some 50,000 slaves escaped to freedom via the Underground Railroad, c.1830–60. A number of Northern states, including Pennsylvania, Connecticut, New York, Vermont, and Ohio, passed a series of "**personal liberty laws**" (1820–40) which impeded the enforcement of the federal fugitive slave law of 1793.

1848. "Free Soil" Convention (p. 249).

1850. COMPROMISE (p. 250) and **FUGITIVE SLAVE ISSUE**, 1850–58 (p. 255).

1852. *Uncle Tom's Cabin* (p. 256). *The Pro-Slavery Argument,* a collection of essays by **William Harper** (1790–1847), **Thomas R. Dew** (1802–46),

James H. Hammond (1807–64), and others, defended slavery as a positive good on the basis of (1) the Scriptures, (2) its role in the prosperity of the South, (3) the alleged biological inferiority of the Negro, (4) slavery as the foundation for a culture based on white supremacy, and (5) as an agency for the education and adjustment of a barbarian people.

1854. *Sociology for the South; or, the Failure of Free Society,* by **George Fitzhugh** (1806–81), who also wrote *Cannibals All! or, Slaves Without Masters* (1857), praised the slave economy and social order of the South as superior to the laissez-faire capitalism of the North.

Kansas-Nebraska Act (p. 258).

1857. Dred Scott Decision (p. 263).

1859. John Brown's Raid (p. 268).

GROWTH OF SLAVE SYSTEM, 1790–1860*

1790	697,624
1800	893,602
1810	1,191,362
1820	1,538,022
1830	2,009,043
1840	2,487,355
1850	3,204,313
1860	3,953,760

* Chief expansion was in the New South, where increase over 1810 was over 1,000% as against less than 100% in the Old South. Greatest increases: Ala., Miss., La., Tex., and Ark.

DISTRIBUTION OF SLAVES IN THE SLAVE STATES (1860)

Delaware	1,798
Maryland and Washington, D.C.	90,374
Virginia	472,494
West Virginia*	18,371
North Carolina	331,059
South Carolina	402,406
Georgia	462,198
Kentucky	225,483
Tennessee	275,719
Alabama	435,080
Mississippi	436,631
Louisiana	331,726
Arkansas	111,115
Missouri	114,931
Florida	61,745
Texas	182,566

* Comprises counties set off from Virginia to form West Virginia, 1863–66, demonstrating marked difference in the regions with respect to slavery.

Free and Bound Labor to 1789

Demand was met by (1) **free labor**, (2) **bound labor**, (3) **slaves**.

1621–1773. MAXIMUM WAGE AND PRICE CONTROLS, adopted in certain periods because of labor shortages.

1621–40. Tobacco Provinces. Virginia (1621–23) set specific wage and price scales. Maryland (Oct. 1640) authorized county courts to regulate wages; expired in 2 years.

1630–75. New England. Massachusetts set maximum wages in the building trades (1630); repealed, 1631; revived and extended to farm labor, 1633; turned over to towns, Oct. 1636. Proposals to reestablish sweeping wage scales, 1670, 1672, defeated; but act of 1675, passed at time of King Philip's War, authorized selectmen to impose double penalty upon takers of excessive wages. Similar legislation enacted in Connecticut (prior to 15 June 1640, and in 1641; repealed 1650; scales set in specific crafts, 1677) and New Haven (1640–41).

1671–1741. Rice and Sugar Colonies. In British West Indies **minimum** wage scales adopted to ensure adequate supply of white labor (e.g., Barbados, 1696); but **maximum** scales were drafted by South Carolina authorities, 1671, and in Georgia, 1739, 1741, for servants and laborers employed by the Trustees.

1690–1773. General wage scales and fees fell into disuse, but specific wages, fees, or prices were fixed by local authority in monopoly trades—carmen, porters, butchers, bakers, innkeepers, teachers, ministers, etc.

1774–83. REVOLUTIONARY WAGE AND PRICE CONTROLS. Congress and local committees set prices for scarce commodities as early as 1774. Major activity: **Providence, R.I., Convention,** 31 Dec. 1776, adopted sweeping wage and price regulations for New England states. **York, Pa., Convention,** Mar. 1777, failed to agree on schedules. **New Haven Convention,** Jan. 1778 (New England and Middle States), set up revised schedules. Subsequently town conventions in New England and Middle States continued to revise schedules to curb inflationary spiral (to 1780). Last regional convention, **Philadelphia,** 1790. Action of Congress, 18 Mar., fixing the value of Continental bills at not more than one fortieth of their face value (also p. 123), contributed ultimately to price and wage stabilization.

1636–1789. LABOR COMBINATIONS prior to permanent trade unionism fall into distinct categories: (1) **Combinations of master workers to maintain monopoly:** Massachusetts, shipbuilding guild, 1644; shoemakers, 1648; **New York,** coopers, 1675; Westchester, weavers, 1702; **Philadelphia,** cordwainers and tailors, 1718; **Carpenters' Co.,** 1724; **New York,** building-trades workers, 1747, 1769; ship carpenters, 1784. (2) **Combinations of white servants to redress grievances by strikes or insurrections:** Virginia, York Co., 1659, 1661; Gloucester, Sept. 1663 (4 executed for high treason); **Bacon's Rebellion,** 1676 (p. 33); **East Florida,** revolt of Minorcan immigrants at New Smyrna, 19 Aug. 1768 (2 leaders executed). (3) **Combinations of free white labor to bar their trades to Negroes:** Charleston, shipwrights, 1744; **North Carolina,** river pilots, 1773. (4) **Joint political action by workmen and employers, 1765–75:** Sons of Liberty (p. 87), Sons of Neptune (mariners); Boston Massacre, 5 Mar. 1770, p. 93; strikes of mariners on British transports, New York, 1768; of workers on British fortifications, Boston, 1774. (5) **Strikes by journeymen to secure better working conditions:** Rare prior to 1775, but occur at least as early as 1636 when fishermen struck on Richmond Island off the Maine coast. Boston

calkers, 1741, agreed not to accept notes in payment of wages; Savannah carpenters struck, 1746; New York tailors struck for higher wages, 1768; printers, 1778, for raise of $3 a week, successful; Philadelphia seamen, 1779.

1783–89: Increasing frequency of strikes and trade union organization: New York shoemakers, 1785; Philadelphia printers, 1786 (permanent organization by 1802); cordwainers, 1789 ("Federal Society," 1794).

WAGE SCALES. Statistics, fragmentary and without data on supplementary income derived by labor from farming, indicate that wages exceeded English scale—skilled workers by up to 100%, unskilled about 50%. Except during periods of inflation colonial real wages exceeded English by 30% to 100%. The differential was noted by Alexander Hamilton, "Report on Manufactures," 1791. High wage scale favored land purchases by labor, contributing to maintaining labor shortages in this period. **Per diem wages: Carpenters** (Massachusetts), 1701, 58.4–61 cts.; 1712, 83.3 cts.; 1735–40, 45.6 cts. (specie); 1743, 40 cts. (specie); 1751–75, 67 cts. **Common (unskilled) labor** (Massachusetts), 1752–57, 33 cts.; 1758–61, 25 cts.; 1762, 17.8 cts.; 1777, 22 cts.; 1779, 79 cts.

1619–1789. BOUND LABOR OR INDENTURED SERVITUDE, used principally in the Middle Colonies and the tobacco provinces, fell into 2 categories: (1) **voluntary,** (2) **involuntary.** The former were either (a) **redemptioners** or "free willers," white immigrants who, in return for passage to America, bound themselves as servants for from 2 to 7 years (4 years average), estimated at from 60% to 77% of total immigration down to 1776; (b) **apprentices,** minors who were provided training in return for services in specified trades (in addition, poor children were bound out by public authority—1619, London Common Council sent to Virginia 100 poor children as "bound apprentices"). The involuntary workers comprised (a) **British convict servants** transported to the colonies (principally Maryland, Virginia, or the West Indies) in commutation of death sentence—1655–99, 4,500 transported; 1750–70, 10,000 to Maryland alone. Total to continental colonies to 1775: approximately **50,000** (Butler). Terms of service fixed by Act of Parliament, 1718: **7 years** for lesser crimes within benefit of clergy; **14 years** for nonclergyable felonies (actually a number were transported for **life**). After the Revolution Britain continued convict dumping in the U.S. illegally as late as Aug. 1787, but eventually Australia replaced America for this purpose. (b) **Victims of kidnaping**, mostly cases of forcible detaining of prospective emigrants prior to taking passage for England committed by overzealous recruiting agents (called "spirits" or "crimps" in England; "newlanders" on the Continent). (c) **Servitude in satisfaction of criminal sentences imposed by colonial courts**, particularly for **larceny** (usually punished in the colonies by multiple restitution, as contrasted with England, where larceny from the person above 12d was capital) and **unlawful absence** from employer's service (punishable **10-fold** in Maryland by act of 1661); continued in Delaware to 1839 for whites; to 1867 for Negroes. (d) **Servitude for debt**, gradually eliminated by legislation abolishing imprisonment for debt, chiefly in the period, 1820–60 (below), with survivals in the form of post–Civil War **peonage**, or debt bondage, in the South.

Labor and Social Reform, 1789–1860

1794–1815. ORIGINS OF TRADE UNIONS. Federal Society of Journeymen Cordwainers, Philadelphia (1794–

1806), was the longest-lived of the early U.S. trade unions; struck, 1799. New York, printers struck (1794), cabinetmakers (1796); Pittsburgh, shoemakers (1809); Boston, printers (1809), and in other cities (1810–15). Objectives: higher wages, shorter hours, union control of apprenticeship, closed shop.

1806–15. CONSPIRACY CASES. Trade unions were prosecuted for strikes as illegal conspiracies at common law. Issue drawn between Federalists (anti-labor) and Jeffersonian Republicans (pro-trade unions). Major cases: Philadelphia Cordwainers (1806), New York Cordwainers (1809–10).

1817–48. DEBTOR RELIEF AND PRISON REFORM. New York legislature (1817) made $25 minimum debt for which a man could be imprisoned. Kentucky (1821) abolished imprisonment for debt; Ohio followed, 1828; Vermont and New Jersey, 1830; New York, 1832; Connecticut, 1837; Louisiana, 1840; Missouri, 1845; Alabama, 1848. Prison reform stems from prison societies (Philadelphia, 1787; Boston, 1825; New York, 1845). Auburn (N.Y.) Penitentiary instituted (1824) **Auburn System**—cell blocks, silence, group labor. Opposing **Pennsylvania System** (exemplified by Eastern State Penitentiary, erected 1829) provided completely solitary confinement and solitary labor. By 1840, 12 Auburn-type prisons erected in the U.S. For treatment of the insane and role of **Dorothea Dix**, see p. 1014.

1824. First recorded strike of women workers—Pawtucket, R.I., weavers.

1825. Establishment at **New Harmony**, Ind., by **Robert Owen** (1771–1858), British social reformer, of a short-lived collectivist colony.

1827. CITY CENTRALS, or central trade councils in cities, first established in Philadelphia with Mechanics' Union of Trade Associations. By 1836, 13 cities had centrals.

1828–34. LABOR PARTIES. Participation of workers in politics was accelerated by **removal of property qualifications for voting** (new Western constitutions and Connecticut, 1818; Massachusetts, 1820; New York, 1821; in Rhode Island not until 1843, after rebellion led by **Thomas W. Dorr** [1805–54]). First U.S. "labor" party organized in Philadelphia (May 1828); gained balance in the city council in the fall election. New York and Boston quickly followed. Leadership primarily not laborers but reformers and small businessmen. In Jacksonian period Eastern workers were divided in their allegiance. New York labor voted for Jackson; Philadelphia labor voted National Republican-Whig; Baltimore closely divided, as were the New Jersey towns. Jackson drew greater support from the small Eastern farmers than from industrial areas. Labor platforms demanded (1) 10-hour day; (2) abolition of imprisonment for debt (75,000 debtors in jail, 1829); (3) abolition of prison contract labor; (4) enactment of mechanics' lien laws (piecemeal extension beg. Pennsylvania, 1803; New York, 1830; Virginia, 1843; Maine, 1848); (5) abolition of discriminatory militia system; (6) curbs on licensed monopolies, particularly banks; (7) universal education. **Leadership:** New York: **Thomas Skidmore**, agrarian radical, and **William Leggett** (1801–39), editor and social reformer, as well as such extremists as **Robert Dale Owen**, son of Robert Owen, and Scottish-born **Frances Wright**, pioneer agitator in U.S. for women's rights, who coedited (with Owen) the *Free Enquirer*. Philadelphia: **John Ferral** and **William English.** New England: **Seth Luther**, labor agitator, **Charles Douglas**, and **George Bancroft**, historian, who feared the effects of industrialization on labor. By 1834 the "labor" parties were defunct, being absorbed by the 2 major

parties or reorganized as factions like **Loco-Focos** or Equal Rights faction, radical wings of the Democratic party in New York and Pennsylvania.

1834, 29 Jan. FIRST USE OF FEDERAL TROOPS to intervene in a labor dispute (closed shop). President Jackson ordered the War Department to put down "riotous assembly" among Irish laborers constructing Chesapeake and Ohio Canal near Williamsport, Md.

1834–37. NATIONAL FEDERATIONS. City central movement spread from Philadelphia to New York (14 Aug. 1833), Baltimore, Boston, Louisville, Pittsburgh, and Cincinnati, with emphasis on nonpolitical, trade-union objectives. In 1834, New York General Trades Union called a convention of delegates from other city centrals, which organized the **National Trades Union,** headed by **Ely Moore** (1798–1861), elected to Congress on Tammany ticket. A number of trades held national conventions during this period, but the movement was aborted by the Panic of 1837 (p. 213). Mounting number of strikes in this period. In the decade 1831–40, 126 strikes have been uncovered in Pennsylvania alone (W. A. Sullivan).

1835–42. In *People* v. *Fisher,* New York court declared strikes illegal; but in Massachusetts in *Commonwealth* v. *Hunt* (1842), Chief Justice Lemuel Shaw (p. 1150) ruled that trade unions were lawful and strikes for a closed shop legal.

1836–60. 10-HOUR MOVEMENT. Building trades workers in Eastern cities had obtained 10-hour day by 1834, and the Whig municipal government of Philadelphia had prior to 1836 put the 10-hour day into effect. As a result of a memorial to Congress by Ely Moore on behalf of the National Trades Union, and a local strike, President Jackson's Secretary of the Navy, Mahlon Dickerson, issued an order for a 10-hour day in Philadelphia Navy Yard (31 Aug.

1836). Executive order of President Van Buren, 31 Mar. 1840, extended "10-hour system" to all laborers and mechanics employed on federal public works. Average daily hours of factory workers in 1840 estimated at 11.4. New England Convention (Oct. 1844) urged 10-hour legislation; enacted: New Hampshire, 1847; Maine, 1848; Pennsylvania, 1848; Ohio, 1852; Rhode Island, 1853; California, 1853; Connecticut, 1855; no action in Massachusetts. Such laws were subject to evasion by contract. By 1860, the 10-hour day was standard among most skilled workers and common laborers, but had not yet been adopted in Lowell and Salem mills.

1840–52. SOCIAL REFORMS affected the labor movement, particularly the **Association** movement, an effort to draw men into cooperative programs: (1) Most notable example was the **Fourierist' system** inspired by a French reformer, Charles Fourier (1772–1837), and endorsed in the U.S. by **Albert Brisbane** (1809–90), who expounded his ideas in Horace Greeley's N.Y. *Tribune*. This system provided for the setting up of **phalanxes,** communities of about 1,500 persons devoted to an agrarian-handicraft economy based upon voluntarism. Goods produced were the property of the phalanx, but private property and inheritance were not abolished. More than 40 phalanxes were established, from Massachusetts to Wisconsin, all disappearing by 1860. Best known: **Brook Farm,** West Roxbury, Mass. (1841–47), established by **George Ripley** (1802–80), a Unitarian minister and Transcendentalist (p. 854), and numbering among its members Nathaniel Hawthorne, Charles A. Dana, and John S. Dwight; in 1845 it was converted into a Fourierist phalanx but failed to survive a major fire in 1846. The short-lived **Sylvania Phalanx** in Pennsylvania was organized, 1842, by Greeley and others. The

North American Phalanx near Red Bank, N.J., was established by Brisbane; disbanded, 1854. (2) **Owenite societies,** highly paternalistic collectivist communities, combining agriculture and factory production. In 1848 an Icarian community was settled in Texas by European workingmen under the leadership of **Étienne Cabet** (1788–1856), whose *Le Voyage en Icarie* (1840) projected a social order on communist principles. The Texas colony, like the one at Nauvoo, Ill. (1849), was unsuccessful. (3) **Cooperative societies** or protective unions (both producers' and consumers'). New England Protective Union, 1845, set up central agency to buy for retail stores; iron molders, Cincinnati, 1848; especially strong in New York City by 1851; more than 800 organized, 1845–60. (4) **Agrarian reform** agitated by the National Reform Association led by **George Henry Evans** (1805–56), editor of N.Y. *Working Man's Advocate* (1829–37, 1844–47), advocated free homesteads, exemption of homesteads from seizure for debt (p. 635), and foreshadowed Henry George's "single-tax" program (p. 1039). (5) **Temperance crusade,** with roots in the colonial period, was stimulated by the writings of Dr. Benjamin Rush, the preaching of Lyman Beecher, and popularized by Timothy Shay Arthur (p. 856), as well as by the activities of the General Conference of the Methodist Church (1780, 1816), the American Temperance Union (first national convention, 1836), and the Washingtonian Temperance Society (reformed drunkards, 1840). Under the leadership of **Neal Dow** (1804–97), Maine passed first statewide prohibition law in 1846; revision of 1851 served as model. Vermont, Rhode Island, and Minnesota Territory followed, 1852; Michigan, 1853; Connecticut, 1854; and 8 other states by 1855. (6) **Peace movement,** led by **William Ladd** (1778–

1841), who organized the American Peace Society (1828), and the "learned blacksmith," **Elihu Burritt** (1810–70), who founded the League of Universal Brotherhood (1846) and promoted the 2d Universal Peace Congress held at Brussels (1848).

1852–60. RISE OF NATIONAL TRADE UNIONS stressing business objectives: National Typographical Union, 1852; Hat Finishers, 1854; Journeymen Stone Cutters Assn., 1855; United Cigarmakers, 1856; Iron Molders (led by **William Sylvis** (1828–69) and Machinists and Blacksmiths, 1859. The weaker nationals were shattered by the Panic of 1857. In decade 1851–60 cost of living rose 12%; money wages rose 4%.

1860, 22 FEB. Strike of shoemakers in Lynn and Natick, Mass., for higher wages spread throughout New England and involved 20,000 workers, including women. Major demands won.

INDEX OF REAL WAGES
(Hansen)

Years	(Index 1913 = 100)
1820–29	46
1830–39	48
1840–49	56
1850–59	52

Labor and Occupational Trends Since 1860

1861–65. IMPACT OF THE CIVIL WAR. Few strikes during war years, although by 1865 real wages had declined **one third** from 1860 level. Expansion of **city centrals** and **national** organizations was countered by the organization of **employers' associations** (as in Mich., 1864; N.Y. Master Builders Assn., 1869). Louisville Convention, Sept. 1865, representing 8 city centrals, attempted unsuccessfully to form a national labor federation. **Consumers' cooperatives** multiplied, inspired by the **Rochdale** pioneers in England (1844).

1864, 4 JULY. Passage of the federal emigrant **contract labor** act, pledging wages of emigrants for terms not exceeding 12 months, resulted in the setting up of the **American Emigrant Co.** to import laborers.

1864–73. NATIONAL TRADE UNION MOVEMENT. Organization of 26 national unions, with 6 previously established. Total trade union membership, 1870–72: 300,000. Most influential national was the **Molders**. Defeated in its fight against organized employers (1867–68), that union organized **cooperative stove foundries**, but the cooperators quickly became "capitalists." **Railway brotherhoods** originated in this period: **Locomotive Engineers** (1863), **Railway Conductors** (1868), **Firemen** (1873). Widespread utilization of shoe machinery, 1861–70, led to displacement of skilled mechanics by unskilled labor and prompted the organization of the **Order of the Knights of St. Crispin** (7 Mar. 1867). By 1870 its membership was estimated at 50,000. Major objective: protection of members against competition of "green hands" and apprentices. By the end of this period the shoeworkers' union had already begun to decline in membership.

1866, 20 AUG.–1872. NATIONAL LABOR UNION organized at Baltimore. Original objective: the **8-hour day**, a movement led by **Ira Steward** (1831–83), a Boston machinist, and **George E. McNeill** (1837–1906). As early as July 1862, Congress had provided that the hours and wages of employees in federal navy yards should conform to those of private firms. Illinois, New York, and Missouri, 1867, enacted 8-hour day laws; not enforced; Wisconsin for women and children, but with loopholes. Failure of the 8-hour demands led the **National Labor Union,** under the presidencies of

Sylvis (1868) and **Richard F. Trevellick** (1869), head of Ship Carpenters and Caulkers Intl., to concentrate on **political reform.** In 1872 the federation was transformed into the **National Labor Reform party,** with Judge David Davis (Ill.) its nominee for president (22 Feb.). The withdrawal of Davis caused the collapse of both party and federation. The period 1868–72 was also marked by the establishment of numerous **producers' cooperatives** under union auspices.

1868. First federal 8-hour day enacted by Congress; confined to laborers and mechanics employed by or on behalf of the U.S. government.

1873–78. DEPRESSION AND LABOR TURBULENCE. National unions dropped from 30 to 9 (1877), and unionized labor from 300,000 to c.50,000. Knights of St. Crispin disappeared by 1878. Outstanding manifestations of labor unrest: (1) **Tompkins Square Riot,** New York City, 13 Jan. 1874, where police charged radical labor meeting. (2) **"Molly Maguires,"** a secret organization of miners, an outgrowth of the **Ancient Order of Hibernians,** organized in Ireland to oppose encroachments of landlords, promoted labor violence in eastern Pennsylvania, beg. 1862. As a result of prosecution instituted by Philadelphia & Reading R.R. and evidence gathered by a Pinkerton detective, 24 Molly Maguires were convicted (fall 1875), 10 hanged for murder, the others sentenced to jail terms of 2–7 years (1876), and the order was crushed. (3) **General Strike.** Railroad strikes, beg. 17 July 1877 on the B.&O. in protest against wage cuts, spread quickly to other lines east of the Mississippi and eventually to Western lines, with rioting in Baltimore, Pittsburgh, Chicago, and St. Louis. **President Hayes sent federal troops** to restore order at **Martinsburg,** W.Va., after strikers had repulsed militia (9 persons killed), and at **Pittsburgh,** where, after resisting Philadelphia militia in a pitched battle (21 July, 26 killed), a mob tore up railroad tracks and burned down machine shops, the Union Depot, and other property, with damage estimated at from $5–$10 million. As a result of strike violence legislatures revived conspiracy laws.

EUROPEAN REVOLUTIONARY LABOR PROGRAMS made their appearance in this period. Three major groups: (1) **Marxian Socialists,** who split in 1872 with (2) the **Anarcho-Communists,** followers of Mikhail Bakunin, and moved the headquarters of the **First International** to New York City, under the leadership of a lieutenant of Karl Marx, **Friedrich A. Sorge** (1827–1906); formed Workingmen's party, 1876; name changed to **Socialist-Labor party,** 1877; worked in the trade-union movement especially through the **Cigarmakers Union,** headed by **Adolph Strasser.** (3) **Lassallean Socialists,** mostly German immigrants, followers of Ferdinand Lassalle, who favored **political action.**

1878, Jan.–1893. KNIGHTS OF LABOR organized on a national basis. The Knights originated, 1871, as a **secret order** at a tailors' meeting in Philadelphia called by **Uriah Stephens** (1821–82), who headed the Knights until 1879, when he was succeeded by **Terence V. Powderly** (p. 1131), who held the post until 1893 (elected, 1878, mayor of Scranton on a labor ticket). The Knights was an **industrial union** headed by a General Assembly to which workers belonged as individuals, regardless of sex, race, or color. All gainfully employed persons, **including unskilled workers** (except certain professional groups) were eligible, but three fourths of each assembly were required to be wage earners. In the West farmers dominated; in the East trade unionists. Local assemblies rose from 484 (1882) to 5,892

(1886), with membership in excess of 700,000. Knights supported (1) 8-hour day; (2) boycotts and arbitration (rather than strikes); (3) various political reforms, including adoption of **graduated income tax;** (4) consumers' and producers' cooperatives (135 set up, including the ownership and operation of a coal mine). Hard times, 1884–85, led to widespread boycotts and strikes, notably by railway shopmen of Union Pacific and the Southwest System (1884), both successful, and against the Wabash (1885), forcing Jay Gould to negotiate with the Knights and agree to end discriminatory practices. Decline after 1886 peak due to (1) **failure of strike against Southwest R.R. System** (1 Mar.–3 May 1886) led by **Martin Irons,** which Powderly sought to terminate by negotiation, and to unsuccessful results of strike waves in the latter half of 1886, including **collapse of 8-hour-day general strike** at Chicago (begun 1 May 1886), and the packing-house lockout of 1887; (2) **Haymarket incident** (below). Agrarian control led to Powderly being replaced, 1893, by James R. Sovereign of Iowa.

1882, Sept. First Labor Day celebration held in New York City. By Act of Congress, 1894, first Monday in Sept. made an annual legal holiday. Two labor leaders, Peter J. McGuire and Matthew Maguire, share honors as cosponsors of the holiday.

1886, 4 May. HAYMARKET MASSACRE resulted when, after police broke up an Anarcho-Communist meeting at Haymarket Square, Chicago, a bomb exploded among the front rank of police, who then opened fire (7 police fatally injured; 70 wounded). The trial (19 June–20 Aug.) of **August Spies, Albert Parsons, Samuel J. Fielden,** and other radical agitators before Judge **Joseph E. Gary** resulted in convictions (7 sentenced to death; 1 to 15 years in prison). Conviction affirmed by Illinois Supreme Court, 14 Sept. 1887. As a result of petitions circulated by **William Dean Howells** (p. 1063), **Henry Demarest Lloyd** (1847–1903), and labor groups for commutation of the death sentence, 2 prisoners were commuted by Gov. Richard J. Oglesby to life terms. Remaining 4 executed on 11 Nov. 1887. Gov. **John Peter Altgeld** (1847–1902) freed 3 others, charging that the trial had been unfair (June 1893). The actual bomb thrower was never identified. The incident damaged the labor movement.

1886, 8 Dec.–1914. AMERICAN FEDERATION OF LABOR organized at Columbus, Ohio, by some 25 labor groups representing about 150,000 members. First president, **Samuel Gompers** (p. 1042), who, with Strasser, had reorganized the Cigarmakers Union (by 1879) and had participated at the founding of the **Federation of Organized Trades and Labor Unions** (Pittsburgh, Nov. 1881), formed to protect the legislative interests of trade unions. The A.F. of L. immediately declared war on the Knights and accepted members and locals also in the latter body. Recognizing the **autonomy of each trade,** it confined its objectives chiefly to **business unionism.** After the depression, 1893–97, large gains in trade union membership took place. Despite antiunion campaign of **National Association of Manufacturers** (org., 1895), the A.F. of L. claimed, 1904, 1,676,200 out of 2,072,700 union members. After a brief decline, 1905–09, union membership rose again, 1910–14, by which date the A.F. of L. claimed 2,020,671 out of 2,687,100 union members (Wolman)— the greatest gains among **coal miners, railroad workers,** and in the **building trades.** The bulk of the unskilled and semiskilled workers were still unorganized. A.F. of L. unions, 1900–14, (1) stressed "job ownership," (2) favored immigration curbs, (3) demanded relief from **technological unemployment,** (4) enactment of **labor legislation,** and (5) **collaboration** with employers, as evidenced by labor participation (with employers and the public) in the **National Civic Federation** (1900) to promote mediation of labor disputes (particularly effective between 1900–05).

1892, 6 July. HOMESTEAD MASSACRE occurred when strikers at the Carnegie Steel Co. plant at Homestead, Pa., fired upon 2 barges being towed up the Monongahela with 300 **Pinkerton detectives** engaged by the company's general manager, **Henry Clay Frick** (1849–1919); 7 killed. Strike, broken by strikebreakers as state militia took over on 12 July, ended 20 Nov. On 23 July **Alexander Berkman** (1870–1936), a Russian-born anarchist, shot and stabbed Frick, in an assault planned with **Emma Goldman** (1869–1940). Berkman was sentenced to 21 years. No effective steel union was organized until the 1930s.

14 July. Martial law declared in Coeur d'Alene silver mines in Idaho as result of violence between striking miners and strikebreakers. Federal troops dispatched to the area.

1894, 21 June–20 July. PULLMAN STRIKE called by **American Railway Union** (independent under **Eugene V. Debs**), with a boycott on Pullman cars. By the end of June the strike had tied up every Midwestern railroad. Attorney General Richard Olney had 3,400 men sworn in as special deputies to keep trains running. When violence broke out, railroad association appealed to **President Cleveland,** who (over the protest of Gov. **John Peter Altgeld,** p. 974) **sent federal troops** to restore order, safeguard the mail, and protect interstate commerce. On 2 July, a federal court issued an **injunction** forbidding interference with the operation of the mails or interstate commerce. Debs was jailed for contempt and the strike was smashed. The incident dramatized the increasing use of the

labor injunction (since 1883). Between 1901–28, 118 applications were officially reported for the federal courts; 116 unreported (Frankfurter and Greene)—most of which ended strikes before a final decree was needed. State injunctions were widespread, and the courts frequently circumvented curbs imposed by legislatures.

1898–1934. ADJUSTMENT OF RAILROAD LABOR DISPUTES. Although an act of Congress of 1888 provided for arbitration by special boards set up by the parties in interest and for a presidential commission to investigate and report where one of the parties refused the offer of the other to arbitrate, such machinery was ineffective in the Pullman strike. The **Erdman Act** (1 June 1898) provided for mediation by the chairman of the ICC and the commissioner of the Bureau of Labor, although neither official had legal power to initiate proceedings. Between 1906 and 1913, 61 railroad labor controversies were settled (26 by mediation). The **Newlands Act** (15 July 1913) created a Board of Mediation and Conciliation consisting of 4 members. Between 1913 and end of 1917 the board settled 58 out of the 71 controversies which came before it. The **Adamson Act** (3 Sept. 1916) provided for an 8-hour day and time and a half for overtime on interstate railroads. While the railroads were under federal operation during and after World War I, 3 national adjustment boards were established, representing management and unions, to settle grievances. Under the **Esch-Cummins Act** (28 Feb. 1920; p. 390) a Railroad Labor Board was established, comprising 9 members (3 each from the companies, the employees, and the public), whose authority stopped short of compulsory arbitration. Under the **Act of 1926** (20 May) the Labor Board was replaced by a Board of Mediation, an independent agency consisting of 5 members appointed by the president. By the **Railway Labor Act** of 1934 (27 June) a National Railroad Adjustment Board, with offices in Chicago, was established. The act upheld the right of employees to organize and bargain collectively through representatives of their own choosing.

1902. ANTHRACITE COAL STRIKE, called (12 May) by United Mine Workers of America (UMW) President John Mitchell, when mine owners declined offer of arbitration, led to intervention (3 Oct.) by President Theodore Roosevelt, who (16 Oct.) appointed a commission to mediate the dispute. The strike was called off on 21 Oct., and on 22 Mar. 1903 the commission awarded the miners a wage increase of 10% but refused union recognition.

1902–08. DANBURY HATTERS' CASE (p. 674).

1905, JUNE–1920. INDUSTRIAL WORKERS OF THE WORLD (I.W.W.), launched at Chicago convention, comprising Western Federation of Miners (1893) and the American Labor Union (org. 1898 as a rival of the AFL), emphasized revolutionary program: (1) **abolition of wage system,** and (2) **industrial unionism.** After eliminating the Socialist Labor faction headed by Daniel De Leon, the "Wobblies" stressed the organization in the West of **unskilled and migratory workers** in lumber, shipping, fruit growing, and textiles (largely the result of a successful strike at Lawrence, Mass., 1912). Most active organizer: **William D.** ("**Big Bill**") **Haywood** (1869–1928). Convicted in Salt Lake City on an allegedly trumped-up murder charge, and executed (1915), the Swedish immigrant **Joe Hill** became part of the movement's folklore. As a result of vigilante action and federal prosecutions, 1918–20, notably at **Centralia,** Wash., Chicago, Sacramento, and

Wichita, the I.W.W. was eliminated as an effective power in the Northwest.

1909–11. INTERNATIONAL LADIES GARMENT WORKERS UNION (ILGWU), organized in 1900, made notable strides in eliminating evils in sweatshops in the shirtwaist trade, particularly after the **Triangle fire** (25 Mar. 1911), with 146 fatalities (proprietors indicated, 11 Apr.; acquitted, 7 Dec.), which led to enactment in New York of a drastically revised and stringent building code and a revision of the labor laws.

1910–12. ARBITRATION, as a result of ILGWU's 2 successful strikes (1909–11), set up in **protocol** (1910) in New York cloak and suit industry (initiated by Louis D. Brandeis) and in agreement negotiated (1911) by Sidney Hillman of the United Garment Workers with **Hart, Schaffner & Marx,** Chicago; latter developed into **impartial chairman** machinery (1912).

1912. First minimum wage act for women and minors passed in Massachusetts.

1913. U.S. Department of Labor established.

1914. Clayton Act (p. 327).

1915. 4 MAR. La Follette Seamen's Act regulated conditions of employment for maritime workers.

1914–20. WORLD WAR I AND LABOR. Union membership increased by 2,350,000, with A.F. of L. gaining 2,068,000 (Wolman). Strikes were successful during the "seller's market." A.F. of L. strongly supported the war; the Socialist party and I.W.W. opposed U.S. entry. For prosecution of radicals, see p. 391. To maintain production schedules President Wilson set up a **Mediation Commission,** 1917, and the **National War Labor Board,** 8 Apr. 1918 (p. 332). Government agencies' general insistence that suppliers bargain collectively led to the rapid rise of company unions. After federal labor agencies ceased operations strikes increased, with the number of wage earners involved rising from 1,239,989 (1918) to 4,160,348 (1919). Most notable was the **steel strike**, 1919. The refusal of Judge **Elbert H. Gary** (1846–1927), chairman of the board, U.S. Steel, to confer with the strike leaders brought on a strike call by the A.F. of L. at the urging of radical labor organizer **William Z. Foster** (1881–1961). Strikers sought (1) union recognition, (2) collective bargaining rights, (3) abolition of the 12-hour day and (4) of company unions, (5) wage increases. The strike began 22 Sept. 1919 and was abandoned 9 Jan. 1920.

1916, 1 Sept. FEDERAL CHILD LABOR LAW (Keating-Owen Act) barred from interstate commerce the products of child labor; declared unconstitutional 3 June 1918; Act of 24 Feb. 1919 declared unconstitutional 15 May 1922; 2 June 1924, **Child Labor Amendment** to the Constitution was submitted to the states for ratification. By 1950 only 26 of the necessary 36 states had ratified. For **Fair Labor Standards Act**, 1938, restricting child labor, see p. 425.

1921–32. LABOR SETBACKS. The sharp recession of 1921–22, strong opposition by employer associations, and unfavorable decisions by federal courts weakened organized labor. Real wages and per capita income rose after 1923 (except in textiles and coal mining). Total union membership, 1929, 3,442,600 as against 5 million in 1921; A.F. of L., 2,961,096 against almost 4 million in 1921. Further drop by 1933 to 2,973,000, of whom 2,126,796 belonged to A.F. of L. **United Mine Workers** under **John L. Lewis** shrank from 500,000 to 150,000.

Communist Agitation (**Trade Union Education League** headed by W. Z. Foster) within trade unions (particularly the ILGWU, Furriers, Amalgamated Clothing, and United Mine Workers) resulted in dual unions and forced progressives into alignments with conservative leaders against Communists.

Judicial Setbacks: See pp. 675, 676.

Major Labor Gains: Railway Labor Act, 1926 (p. 767); **Norris–La Guardia Anti-Injunction Act**, 23 Mar. 1932, forbade injunctions to sustain antiunion employment contracts or to prevent strikes, boycotts, and picketing.

For A.F. of L. support of **La Follette** for president in 1924, see p. 395. **William Green** (1873–1952), of United Mine Workers, succeeded to the presidency of the A.F. of L. on the death of Gompers (1924), and kept the organization along **craft union** lines. **Company unions** expanded to over 400 by 1926, with a membership of 1,369,000, continuing to expand until 1935 to about 2,500,000. Chief violence occurred in textile strikes: Gastonia and Marion, N.C.; Elizabethtown, Tenn.; and Paterson, N.J.

1932. First Unemployment Insurance law in the U.S. enacted in Wisconsin.

1933–51. LABOR GAINS UNDER THE NEW DEAL AND FAIR DEAL. As a result of New Deal labor policies (pp. 415–425) total noncompany union membership approximated 4,400,000 in 1935, of which the A.F. of L. claimed 3,045,347. Further expansion was due in large measure to the **Wagner Act** (p. 416) and to the activities of industrial unions largely as the result of the formation, 9 Nov. 1935, within the A.F. of L. of the **Committee for Industrial Organization (CIO)**. In May 1938, leaders expelled from the A.F. of L. (**John L. Lewis** had resigned as vice-president of the A.F. of L., 23 Nov. 1935) set up a rival organization under the leadership of Lewis—spectacularly successful in increasing the membership of the United Mine Workers—and **Sidney Hillman** (p. 1058) of the

Amalgamated Clothing Workers. The CIO was reorganized, 1938, as the **Congress of Industrial Organizations. Philip Murray** (1886–1952) succeeded to the presidency of the CIO in Nov. 1940. By 1936 CIO began to organize the motor and steel industries. On 31 Dec. 1936 a few hundred workers seized a number of General Motors plants at Flint, Mich., staging a spectacular **sit-down strike** which lasted 44 days; involved 40,000 workers directly and 110,000 indirectly. Sit-down strikes spread to rubber, steel, textiles, oil refining, shipbuilding, and involved a half million workers. Following the Supreme Court decision in **Hague v. CIO,** 1939, declaring sit-down strikes illegal, this technique was discredited by organized labor.

1937, 30 MAY. MEMORIAL DAY MASSACRE. In the spring of 1937, the Steel Workers' Organizing Committee secured recognition by U.S. Steel as the bargaining agency, a wage boost of 10%, and a 40-hour week with time and a half for overtime. Other employers challenged the constitutionality of the Wagner Act (upheld by Supreme Court, 1937, p. 677). "Little Steel" under the leadership of **Republic Steel,** headed by **Tom M. Girdler** (1877–1965), was adamant. The issue came to a head when a group of union demonstrators before the gates of the Republic plant in South Chicago were fired upon by police, with 10 killed, 84 injured. Finally, in 1941, virtually all of the independent steel companies signed agreements with the CIO.

Dec. Publication of a report of a Senate subcommittee, headed by **Robert M. La Follette, Jr.** (1895–1953), disclosed antilabor techniques employed to fight unions (1933–37), including blacklists, espionage, vigilante groups to curb labor organizers (**Mohawk Valley formula**), recruiting of strikebreaking services, private armed forces, and private arsenals (in the possession of Youngstown Sheet and Tube Co. and Republic Steel Corp.). The report singled out terrorism in Harlan Co., Ky.

1938. FAIR LABOR STANDARDS ACT (p. 425).

LABOR IN WORLD WAR II (p. 449).

SMITH-CONNALLY ACT (1943, p. 451). For formation of CIO–PAC (1944), see p. 454.

UNION EXPANSION. A.F. of L. membership by 1943 had increased to almost 9 million; CIO claimed 5,285,000, with a total of 13 million union members in the U.S. by early 1944 out of a total employment of 54 million. By 1945 union membership rose to 14.8 million (35.8% of the nonagricultural labor force as against 11.5% in 1933). In percentage terms this was an all-time high.

1946, 20 FEB. Employment Act (p. 514) committed federal government to take steps to create and to maintain employment opportunities and to promote full employment.

1946, 1 APR. United Mine Workers' strike of 400,000 bituminous coal miners began. President Truman seized the mines; the government retained control when the operators refused to accept a contract with the union negotiated by federal authorities. A second strike call on 21 Nov. by John L. Lewis in defiance of a government injunction led to his being held in contempt of court by a federal district court (4 Dec.) and fined $10,000; United Mine Workers fined $3,500,000 (sustained by Supreme Court, 6 Mar. 1947, but fine subsequently reduced to $70,000). On 7 Dec. 1946 Lewis ordered the miners back to work.

1947, 23 JUNE. TAFT-HARTLEY ACT (p. 514).

1947–52. STRIKES AND WORK STOPPAGES increased in response to the inflationary cycle. By 1949 labor stressed pension plans and other "fringe" demands rather than higher wages. Work stoppages, relative to size of labor force, were lower in the postwar period (4,750 in 1945; 4,843 in 1950) than in 1903 (3,600) or 1917 (4,450), but were substantially higher than for the exceptional period, 1921–26 (c.1,500). When steel companies refused to abide by a Wage Mediation Board award (20 Mar. 1952) of higher wages to workers without rise in steel prices, President Truman under emergency powers seized the steel mills (8 Apr.). A preliminary injunction was granted 29 Apr. to nullify the seizure; on 2 June the Supreme Court ruled the seizure unconstitutional. The United Steel Workers Union called another strike, which was settled as a result of the intervention of President Truman (24 July), with the union obtaining a 16-ct. increase in wages, a rise of $5.20 per ton of steel, and a modified union shop.

1948. Mississippi became the 48th state to enact **workmen's compensation** legislation; first act, Maryland, 1902.

1952. Both A.F. of L. and CIO endorsed Adlai E. Stevenson, the Democratic party's unsuccessful candidate for president, who favored repeal of the Taft-Hartley Act.

Upon the deaths of William Green and Philip Murray, **George Meany** (p. 1101) and **Walter P. Reuther** (p. 1137) succeeded to the presidency of the A.F. of L. and CIO respectively.

1954. "**Right-to-work**" laws (outlawing union shop), on books of 13 states at beginning of year, adopted in Utah and Kansas, but new bills defeated in 31 states.

1955. GUARANTEED ANNUAL WAGE. Provisions for payments during layoff periods were obtained by UAW in a compromise settlement with Ford and General Motors; similar contracts were obtained by the CIO–Steelworkers.

5 DEC. MERGER OF A.F. OF L. AND CIO made official, with **George Meany** elected president. Under charter of the consolidated union, craft and industrial organizations were to have equal rank.

1957–73. RACKETEERING AND CRIME. A special Senate committee under the chairmanship of Sen. **John L. McClellan** to investigate racketeering in labor-management relations held hearings, largely concerned with the Teamsters Union and the activities of its president, **Dave Beck.** In May, Beck was expelled as vice-president of the AFL–CIO. He was convicted of embezzlement in a state court in Seattle, Dec. 1957. In addition, the Teamsters vice-president, **James R. Hoffa,** was also charged with misappropriation of funds and close connections with gangsters (and eventually jailed for jury tampering, 1967–71). The disclosure led to the adoption by the AFL–CIO of a Code of Ethics, the resignation of a number of union officials, and the suspension of several national affiliates in Oct. In Dec. the AFL–CIO convention expelled the Teamsters Union, the Bakery Workers Union, and the Laundry Workers Union. Previously, 22 Sept. 1954, the International Longshoremen's Association had been expelled from the A.F. of L. for refusing to rid itself of racketeering elements. Frank Fitzsimmons was elected president after Hoffa relinquished the office from prison (1971). Fitzsimmons and the Teamsters were among the leading labor supporters of President Nixon's reelection bid in 1972. Although granted clemency by Nixon (1971), Hoffa was prohibited from participating in union activity until 1980.

**1959, 14 SEPT. LABOR MANAGE-
MENT REPORTING AND DISCLO-
SURE ACT (LANDRUM-GRIFFITH),**
(p. 526).

15 JULY. Steel strike lasted until 7
Nov. when a federal court issued an
80-day injunction under the Taft-Hartley
Act, ordering the men back to work. The
strike was settled by year end at an estimated increase of 41 cts. per hour over
30 months. Previous steel strike of 1956
ended with a wage rise of c.50 cts. per
hour by 1958 and rise in steel prices.

**1929–59. TRENDS IN INCOME
DISTRIBUTION.**

PERCENTAGE OF INCOME AFTER FEDERAL TAX
(in percentages)

To:	1929	1941	1950–54	1955–59
Top 5%	29.5	21.5	18.0	18.0
Top 20%	54.0	47.0	43.0	44.0
Lowest 60%	26.5	30.0	34.0	34.0

Source: Department of Commerce

1960. UNIONS, concerned about unemployment and automation, stressed security in their bargaining. Under terms
of the 5½-year contract between the Pacific Maritime Association and the International Longshoremen's and Ware-
housemen's Union, the unions agreed to
relax work rules and accept labor-saving
devices. In return, the employers agreed
to reimburse workers for wages lost because of the effects of automation.
Supplementary wages and retirement
benefits were to be drawn from a $27.5
million automation fund supported by
the employers.

**1961–68. NATIONAL LABOR POL-
ICY.** The Kennedy and Johnson administrations attempted to combat unemployment by (1) increasing overall
economic activity without inflation and
(2) promoting manpower development
programs. Beginning in 1962 the Eco-

nomic Report of the President contained
"guideposts" for noninflationary wage
and price behavior—suggesting that
wage increases (including fringe benefits) in each industry equal the rate of
increase in productivity in the economy
as a whole. By 1966, a time of high
employment and inflation, a number
of major agreements exceeded recommended limits despite government pressures.

Manpower development programs
aimed particularly at the hard-core unemployed were stressed in such legislation as the **Area Redevelopment Act**
(1961), **Manpower Development and
Training Act** (1962), and the **Economic
Opportunity Act** (1964) and took the
form of programs such as the Job Corps
and Job Opportunities in the Business
Sector (JOBS). Outlays for such programs increased from $735 million
(1964) to an estimated $3.5 billion
(1970).

MINIMUM WAGE LEGISLATION.
The **Fair Labor Standards Act** (p. 425)
was amended to increase the federal
minimum wage to $1.25 per hour and
extended to cover 3,624,000 new workers (5 May 1961). The minimum wage
was increased (24 Sept. 1966) to $1.60
per hour (effective 1 Feb. 1968) with
the coverage extended to approximately
8 million more workers, for whom the
minimum of $1.60 was to be reached by
1971. The **Equal Pay Act** required equal
wages for equal work in industries engaged in commerce or producing goods
for commerce (10 June 1963).

1961–68. EMPLOYMENT. The size
of the civilian labor force rose from 69
million (1960) to 79 million (1968).
Unemployment rates for Negroes, teenagers, and the unskilled persistently were
higher than the national average (1967,
Oct.: Negroes, 8.8%; teenagers, 15.1%;
nonfarm labor, 9.2%).

1964. EQUAL EMPLOYMENT OPPORTUNITY.

Title VII of the Civil Rights Act of 1964 provided the first federal fair employment practices law, prohibiting discrimination on the basis of race, color, religion, national origin or sex by employers, employment agencies, and unions. An Equal Opportunity Commission was established to investigate and judge complaints.

1966–68. STRIKES.

Inflation, high employment levels, and the growth of corporate profits rose more rapidly than aggregate labor income in the early 1960s. In addition, the efforts of skilled workers to restore wage differentials, contributed to the increase in time lost because of strikes. Public service employees began to show increased willingness to strike or take other "job action." The first official strike in the history of the New York City transit system lasted 12 days (1966). Teachers unions displayed increasing militancy as did police and firemen. New York City schools were closed for 36 days (1968).

1969–74. UMW SCANDALS.

W. A. "Tony" Boyle won reelection as president of the United Mine Workers over reformer Joseph A. Yablonski in an election (1969) marked by intimidation and vote fraud. Yablonski and his wife and daughter were murdered (30–31 Dec. 1969) and Boyle found guilty (11 Apr. 1974) of first-degree murder in ordering the assassination. The election was set aside by federal court (June 1972) and when held in Dec. 1972 under Labor Department supervision, Boyle was defeated by Arnold Miller. Boyle was convicted (31 Mar. 1972) of illegal use of UMW funds in 1968 national elections. The union was held liable (1971, 1972) for $11.5 million for improper handling of its pension fund and Boyle ordered to step down as trustee of the fund.

1969–73. UNIONIZATION.

Unions attempted to organize the service trades (from college professors to government employees), Southern workers, Kentucky coal miners, and agricultural employees. After 5 years of strikes and nationwide boycotts, in 1970 (Apr.–July) grape workers obtained contracts from California grape growers, a victory for **Cesar Chavez**, head of AFL–CIO United Farm Organizing Committee; early 1973, when the contracts expired, the International Brotherhood of Teamsters signed with the owners and a dispute between the 2 unions ensued. **1973, Nov.**, Chavez called for a new boycott of grape and lettuce growers. Despite continued attempts at unionization, the U.S. labor force grew far more rapidly than the spread of unions. Union membership totaled 19.76 million in 1970, up slightly from earlier years, but as a percent of nonagricultural employment, union membership was 27.9%, a new low for the post–World War II years.

1969–73. STRIKES.

Man-days lost from strikes: 1969, 42,869,000; 1970, 66,414,000; 1971, 47,589,000; 1972 (prel.), 26,000,000. **1970, 15 Sept.**, 67-day General Motors strike began, which slowed nation's economic growth. Issues were pay, inflation protection, and early retirement; **12 Nov.**, UAW accepted contract with an est. 30% increase in wages and fringe benefits for 3 years. Major league baseball players struck for 2 weeks in 1972. **1973, Mar.** Major steel producers signed an innovative labor agreement with the steel workers, involving no strikes, no lockouts, binding arbitration, and at least a 3% pay rise per annum when the current contract expired.

1969–73. INFLATION.

Real spendable earnings dropped in 1969–70, but rose in 1971–72 (real spendable earn-

AVERAGE HOURLY EARNINGS IN MANUFACTURING

Year	Earnings
1909	$0.193
1919	0.477
1929	0.566
1933	0.442
1937	0.624
1945	1.023
1957	2.070
1972	3.810
1973 (Oct.)	4.130

PRODUCTIVITY AND COMPENSATION COMPARED (Private Nonfarm) (1967 = 100)

Year	Output per man-hour	Compensation per man-hour
1950	59.7	42.8
1960	88.6	73.9
1970	103.4	123.1
1972 (prel.)	112.1	140.3

SELECTED UNEMPLOYMENT RATES, 1961–70 (Percent)[1]

Group of Workers	1961–65 average	1966	1967	1968	1969	1970	1971	1972	1973
All workers	5.5	3.8	3.8	3.6	3.5	4.9	5.9	5.6	4.9
Sex and age:									
Both sexes 16–19 years	15.9	12.8	12.8	12.7	12.2	15.3	16.9	16.2	14.5
Men 20 years and over	4.4	2.5	2.3	2.2	2.1	3.5	4.4	4.0	3.2
Women 20 years and over	5.4	3.8	4.2	3.8	3.7	4.8	5.7	5.4	4.8
Race:									
White	4.9	3.4	3.4	3.2	3.1	4.5	5.4	5.0	4.3
Black and other races	10.4	7.3	7.4	6.7	6.4	8.2	9.9	10.0	8.9

Source: Statistical Abstract of the U.S.
[1] Percent of civilian labor force in specified group.

ings are calculated after social security and income taxes have been deducted as average weekly earnings in constant dollars in private nonagricultural businesses). By 1973, 40% of all workers under union contracts had escalator clauses in their contracts, which automatically increased their pay when the cost of living rose.

1969–73. GOVERNMENT POLICIES. With Nixon's **new economic policy** of 15 Aug. 1971 (p. 752) wage controls were imposed. Measures to stimulate the economy sought to reduce unemployment. New concern emerged to promote equality of opportunity for women. **1972. Equal Employment Opportunity Act** gave the Equal Opportunity Commission (est. 1964) enforcement power through the courts in sex-discrimination cases. Unemployment affected teenagers far more severely than those over 20, blacks to a far greater extent than whites, women more than men.

Government policies did little to solve the problems of the high teenage and black unemployment.

1946–72. UNEMPLOYMENT INSURANCE. The total unemployment insurance benefits paid was a function of the amount of unemployment and the extension of coverage. Total benefits paid under all programs was $2.9 billion in 1946; the figure declined in 1947–48; rose in 1949 ($2.3 billion); declined with the Korean War to a low for the entire period in 1951 ($.9 billion); the figure increased slightly in 1952–53, and with the end of the Korean War in 1954 was $2.3 billion. The sum declined again in 1955–56, rose moderately in 1957, and with the recession of 1958 reached a new high of $4.3 billion; in 1959, the figure dropped to $2.8 billion and then moved upward in 1960–61 (reaching $4.4 billion in 1961); from 1962 to 1966 benefits paid went down annually (1966: $1.9 billion); 1967–69, benefits were in the range of $2.2–$2.3 billion; they soared 1970–72 (1970: $4.2 billion; 1971: $5.5 billion; 1972 [prel.] $5.0 billion).

1947–71. FAMILY INCOMES.

MEDIAN FAMILY INCOMES
(in 1971 dollars)

Year	All Families	White	Black and Other Races
1947	$5,483	$5,714	$2,930
1950	5,594	5,811	3,142
1960	7,688	8,109	4,321
1970	10,289	10,674	6,806
1971	10,285	10,672	6,714

PERCENTAGE OF FAMILIES WITH INCOMES UNDER $3,000
(in 1971 dollars)

Year	All Families	White	Black and Other Races
1947	21.2%	18.4%	51.2%
1950	21.6	19.3	47.8
1960	14.6	12.5	34.8
1970	8.3	7.0	19.0
1971	8.3	6.9	19.4

OCCUPATIONAL TRENDS. Shift of population from rural to urban life (cf. p. 650) and technological progress were accompanied by far-reaching shifts in occupations:

LABOR FORCE STATUS
Number of Persons Engaged in Agricultural and Nonagricultural Pursuits
(1820–1970: 10 yrs. old and over)

(U.S. Bureau of Census, *Hist. Stat. of U.S., 1789–1945;* 1950–60: 14 yrs. and over, *Stat. Abstract, 1970:* 16 and over, Dept. of Labor.)

	Nonagri-cultural	%	Agri-cultural	%
1820	812,042	28.2	2,068,958	71.8
1860	4,325,116	41.1	6,207,634	58.9
1900	18,161,235	62.5	10,911,998	37.5
1940	42,985,704	82.4	9,162,547	17.6
1950	52,450,000	83.1	7,500,000	16.9
1960	59,702,000	92.9	4,565,000	7.1
1970	75,165,000	95.6	3,462,000	4.4

DISTRIBUTION OF GAINFUL WORKERS
(in thousands of persons)

	1870	1900	1940
All gainful workers	12,920	29,070	53,300
Agriculture	6,730	10,950	9,000
Forestry and fisheries	60	210	140
Mining	190	750	1,110
Manufacturing and hand trades	2,130	6,250	11,940
Construction	700	1,640	3,510
Transportation and other public utilities	580	2,020	4,150
Trade	850	2,870	7,180
Finance and real estate			1,550
Education	190	650	1,680
Other professional services	140	510	2,320
Domestic service	940	1,740	2,610
Personal service	270	1,020	3,100
Govt., not elsewhere classified	100	300	1,690
Not allocated	40	160	3,330

EMPLOYEES IN NONFARM ESTABLISHMENTS 1950–1972
(in thousands)

	1950	1960	1970	1972
Total Wage and Salary Workers	45,222	54,234	70,593	72,764
Manufacturing	15,241	16,796	19,349	18,933
Mining	901	712	623	607
Construction	2,333	2,885	3,381	3,521
Transportation and Public Utilities	4,034	4,004	4,493	4,495
Wholesale and Retail Trade	9,386	11,391	14,914	15,683
Finance, Insurance, and Real Estate	1,919	2,669	3,688	3,927
Services	5,382	7,423	11,612	12,309
Government (federal, state, local)	6,026	8,353	12,535	13,290

In the years 1870–1970, divided by sector, there were profound changes in employment patterns.

PERCENTAGE PARTICIPATION OF LABOR FORCE BY SECTOR 1870–1970

Year	Agriculture*	Manu-facturing**	Services***
1870	52	23	25
1970	4	32	64

* Includes forestry and fishing; ** includes mining and construction; *** includes all other activities not under agriculture or manufacturing.

As agriculture declined, manufacturing increased, but services expanded even more. In 1970, the service sector—augmented by the giant increase in government employment—was by far the most significant employer of American labor.

1900–72. The composition of the labor force changed as more women became employed.

WOMEN IN LABOR FORCE OR GAINFULLY OCCUPIED, 15 YRS. AND OVER

	Total No.	Married* No.	%
1890	3,712,144	515,260	13.9
1920	8,346,796	1,920,281	23.0
1940	13,840,000	5,040,000	36.4
1960	23,270,000	7,097,960	30.5
1972	33,320,000	13,827,800	41.5

* 1960, 1972 figures are for married with husband present. 1960: 14 yrs. and over; 1972: 16 yrs. and over.

WOMEN IN THE LABOR FORCE, SELECTED YEARS, 1900–72

Year	Women in Labor Force (thousands)	Women in labor force as percent of	
		Total labor force	All women of working age
1900	5,114	18.1	20.4
1910	7,889	20.9	25.2
1920	8,430	20.4	23.3
1930	10,679	22.0	24.3
1940	12,845	24.3	25.4
1945	19,270	29.6	35.7
1950	18,412	28.8	33.9
1955	20,584	30.2	35.7
1960	23,272	32.3	37.8
1965	26,232	34.0	39.3
1970	31,560	36.7	43.4
1972	33,320	37.4	43.8

Note.—Data for 1900 to 1940 are from decennial censuses and refer to a single date; beginning 1945 data are annual averages.
For 1900 to 1945 data include women 14 years of age and over; beginning 1950 data include women 16 years of age and over.
Labor force data for 1900 to 1930 refer to gainfully employed workers.
Data for 1972 reflect adjustments to 1970 Census benchmarks.
Sources: Department of Commerce, Bureau of the Census, and Department of Labor, Bureau of Labor Statistics.

WOMEN AS A PERCENT OF PERSONS IN SEVERAL PROFESSIONAL AND MANAGERIAL OCCUPATIONS, 1910–70
(Percent)

Occupational Group	1910	1920	1930	1940	1950	1960	1970
Clergymen	0.6	1.4	2.2	2.4	4.0	2.3	2.9
College presidents, professors, and instructors[1]	18.9	30.2	31.9	26.5	23.2	24.2	28.2
Dentists	3.1	3.3	1.9	1.5	2.7	2.3	3.5
Editors and reporters	12.2	16.8	24.0	25.0	32.0	36.6	40.6
Engineers	(2)	(2)	(2)	.4	1.2	.8	1.6
Lawyers and judges	.5	1.4	2.1	2.5	3.5	3.5	4.9
Managers, manufacturing industries	1.7	3.1	3.2	4.3	6.4	7.1	6.3
Physicians	6.0	5.0	4.4	4.7	6.1	6.9	9.3

[1] Data for 1920 and 1930 probably include some teachers in schools below collegiate rank. The Office of Education estimates the 1930 figure closer to 28 percent.
[2] Less than one tenth of 1 percent.
Note.—Data are from the decennial censuses. Data for 1910 and 1920 include persons 10 years of age and over; data for 1930 to 1970 include persons 14 years of age and over.
Source: Department of Commerce, Bureau of the Census.

SCIENCE, INVENTION, AND TECHNOLOGY

★　★
★

General Science

The discovery of the New World opened up a treasure-house of natural phenomena for scientific study and classification. The settlers of British North America, however, were more than mere collectors of data. From the seventeenth century on, they were members of the transatlantic scientific community, and some, notably Benjamin Franklin, made universally acclaimed contributions to theoretical science. But this promising start was cut short by the American Revolution. The ensuing cultural nationalism weakened the institutional base for scientific endeavor, threw open the field to gifted amateurs and hobbyists, and ushered in an exploitative economic order that set a premium on applied rather than basic science. In the mid-1870s the distinguished mathematician and astronomer Simon Newcomb, lamenting the state of science in America, contrasted its "beggarly and humiliating showing" to the progress of European science and asked: "Why, with our numerous educational institutions, and our great crowd of professors, should our contributions to the exact sciences be so nearly zero?" He detected "nothing worthy of the name of national science." Yet even as Newcomb delivered this harsh indictment, new and auspicious developments were visible.

The wave of scientific discoveries in the nineteenth century had a major impact upon America after the Civil War, when the rise of the modern research-oriented university, and its panoply of graduate schools, was accompanied by the rapid professionalization and specialization of the scientific community, the separation of religious and metaphysical speculation from the intrinsic concerns of scientific thought and inquiry, and increasing financial support for science from the private accumulations of wealth under the new industrialism, such as the large foundations. By 1910 American scientists were speaking confidently of "pure research." The role of science in the two great wars of the twentieth century endowed it with an unprecedented and even decisive importance in the affairs of mankind, and the increasing complexities of scientific knowledge stressed the necessity of cooperative investigation. Massive federal funding between 1950 and 1970 stimulated enormous progress in basic and experimental work, but also raised serious questions concerning the involvement of scientists with research and development goals laid down by the political and military establishment. Shaped in large measure by its relations with government and corporate enterprise, American science by the mid-1970s was marked by bureaucratic organization and increasingly centralized control seemingly at odds with the traditional patterns of self-directed basic research.

1665–1735. EARLY ASTRONOMY AND SEISMOLOGY. John Winthrop, Jr. (1606–76), probably the first colonial member of the Royal Society of London (Brasch), made the first systematic astronomical observations in the colonies (before 1665). Advanced astronomical knowledge was revealed by **Thomas Brattle** (1658–1713) in his *Almanack* (1678). His observations of Halley's comet (1680) were utilized and credited to him by Newton in his landmark *Principia mathematica* (1687). His account of a solar eclipse of 1694 was published in the *Philosophical Transactions* of the Royal Society (1704). He made significant observations of a later (1703) solar eclipse, 3 lunar eclipses (1700, 1703, 1707), and of variations of the magnetic needle (1708). **Thomas Robie** (1689–1729), Harvard astronomer and mathematician, described a meteor (1719) as a natural phenomenon. **Paul Dudley's** (1675–1751) report of an earthquake in New England (1727) and further data on such phenomena appeared in *Transactions* (1735).

1680–1725. NATURAL HISTORY. John Banister (c.1648–92) transmitted (1680) 52 species of American insects to Petiver, the English naturalist, and contributed a paper on American molluscs to the Royal Society (1693). His *Catalogus Plantarum in Virginia Observatarum*

(published in Ray's *Historia Plantarum*) is probably the first systematic paper upon natural history written in the colonies. **Cotton Mather** contributed 13 letters on natural history and biology to *Transactions* (1712) and was credited by Petiver (1717) with specimens of bones and dried plants. **Paul Dudley** contributed data on the swamp sumac, bees, and the rattlesnake to the *Transactions* (1720–23). Work on New England fruit trees (1724) established him as the first colonial horticulturist. His *Natural History of Whales* (1725), with its account of the source of ambergris, became a standard work.

1708–51. PHYSICS AND MATHEMATICS. James Logan (1674–1751) is generally credited with formally introducing Newton's *Principia* into the colonies (1708), although information was already available through the *Transactions*. Cotton Mather's *Christian Philosopher* (1721) contained the first lengthy explanation of Newtonian physics (in the colonies). The first colonial chair in philosophy and mathematics was filled (1717) at William and Mary by Rev. Hugh Jones (c.1670–1760). More significant was the endowment of a chair in mathematics and natural philosophy at Harvard (1727); the first incumbent, **Isaac Greenwood** (1702–45), offered a course in fluxions (calculus) and proposed (1727) to the Royal Society a plan for ocean charts, anticipating M. F. Maury's much later work.

1716–68. BOTANY AND ZOOLOGY. Cotton Mather wrote the earliest known account of plant hybridization (24 Sept. 1716)—hybridization of Indian corn and squash (Zirple); more details provided by **Paul Dudley** (1724). The correspondence between **John Bartram** (1699–1777) and Peter Collinson, English botanist, developed a channel for transmission of colonial plants and data abroad. Bartram, who established (1728) the first botanical garden in the colonies at Philadelphia, traveled widely through the colonies collecting specimens of rare plants and cultivating in North America plants received from abroad. He published (1751) his *Observations* of his trip to Lake Ontario. Together with his son, **William** (1739–1823), he explored the St. John's River, Fla., and there discovered the royal palm. William's list of 215 American birds (*Travels*, 1791) was the most complete published up to that time. Other pioneers in botany include **John Clayton** (1694–1773), best known for his *Flora Virginica*, revised and published by Gronovises (1739); **John Mitchell** (1680–1768), who pioneered in applying the Linnaean system of plant classification; **James Logan,** who performed the first colonial experiments in physiological botany—on the fructification of maize (reported 1734, 1736); **Cadwallader Colden** (1688–1776), whose work on the flora of New York was published in **Acts** of the Royal Society of Uppsala (1744); **Alexander Garden** (1728–92), who from 1752, collected the flora of South Carolina and discovered the mud iguana (1765) and the Congo snake (an eel, before 1775), correcting Linnaeus's classification of American flora and fauna; Rev. **Jared Eliot** (1685–1765), who published the first colonial work in the field of scientific

agriculture (1760), and **Adam Kuhn** (1741–1817), who offered (1768) the first course in botany as professor of materia medica at the College of Philadelphia.

1739–69. ASTRONOMY. John Winthrop IV (1714–79), who succeeded Greenwood as professor of mathematics and natural philosophy at Harvard, wrote papers on sunspots (1739), on a transit of Venus and a lunar eclipse (1740), and on Halley's comet (1759), with pioneer studies regarding the density of comets (1767) and the undulatory character of earthquakes (1756). He journeyed to Newfoundland to record the transit of Venus (1761; also transit of 1768), and observed the transits of Mercury (1740, 1743, 1769). **Ezra Stiles** (1727–95), applying Newton, calculated the true position of the sun and moon (1745). **David Rittenhouse** (1732–96), Philadelphia clock and instrument maker, built the first orrery in the colonies (1767); made notable observations of the transits of Venus and Mercury (1769), and of Lexell's comet (1770).

1743–71. AMERICAN PHILOSOPHICAL SOCIETY. Although Cotton Mather formed a group interested in natural history (1681) and Franklin organized the **Junto** (1727), the first truly scientific society was the American Philosophical Society, organized in Philadelphia, with Thomas Hopkinson (1737–91) as first president and Franklin as secretary. Its meetings were held irregularly until it was reorganized (1769) with Franklin as president (until his death, 1790). *Transactions* first published, 1771.

1746–52. ELECTRICITY. John Winthrop IV gave the first lectures on electricity in the colonies (at Harvard, 1746). **Benjamin Franklin** began his first experiments in electricity (1747), discovered the phenomenon of plus and minus charges (1747–48), suggested (1749) that thunder and lightning could be explained electrically, and performed an experiment proving the electrical nature of lightning (1752). His pamphlet, *Experiments and Observations on Electricity,* went through 11 editions (1751–76), 5 in English, 3 in French, 1 in German, 1 in Latin and 1 in Italian. **Ebenezer Kinnersley** (1711–78) refined and added to Franklin's electrical discoveries, noting (1762) that lightning and electricity melt metals by hot rather than cold fusion, while **James Bowdoin** corrected Franklin's notion that electricity was gathered into clouds of the sea (1756).

1746–56. MATHEMATICS. Cadwallader Colden's *Principles of Action in Matter* (1745–51), a highly original supplement to Newton, propounded the theory that gravitation was a force exerted by an elastic, contractive form of matter. Winthrop at Harvard is reputed to have been the first to teach a course in Newtonian fluxions (calculus).

1780–94. SCIENTIFIC SOCIETIES. American Academy of Arts and Sciences founded 1780 at Boston largely through the efforts of John Adams; published *Memoirs* (1785). New Jersey Society for the Promotion of Agriculture, Commerce, and Art (1781), with agricultural societies founded in South Carolina and Pennsylvania (1785), and the Chemical Society of Philadelphia (1792). Charles Willson Peale's Philadelphia Museum (1794) was the first independently established museum in the U.S.

1785. DESCRIPTIVE BOTANY. Publication of **Humphry Marshall's** (1722–1801) *Arbustrum Americanum,* a notable botanical essay based on the Linnaean system, and in the *Memoirs* of a paper by **Manasseh Cutler** (1742–1823), marked the beginning of systematic botany in New England.

1794–1860. DESCRIPTIVE ZOOLOGY. A paper on fish taken near Pisca-

taqua, N.H., by **William Peck** (1763–1822) is considered the first paper on systematic zoology published in America (Coe). **Samuel Latham Mitchill** (1764–1831), professor of natural history at Columbia (1792–1801), established himself as a foremost zoologist with his work on the fish of New York (1814). **Thomas Say** (1787–1834) published a paper (1817) and 2 books (1824–28) on entomology, followed by *American Conchology* (1830), both illustrated by Charles Alexander Leseur (1778–1846). **Constantine Samuel Rafinesque** (c.1783–1840) contributed papers on sponges, Western fishes, foxes, and on salivation of horses to Silliman's *Journal of Science* (1819–20). His *Ichthyologia Ohiensis* (1820) was notable in its field. **John D. Godman** (1794–1830) published his 3-vol. *American Natural History* (1826–28). With the encouragement of William Bartram, **Alexander Wilson** (1766–1813) began his *American Ornithology* (9 vols., 1808–13). **John James Audubon's** (p. 976) *Birds of America* began to appear in 1827; completed with publication of 5th vol., *Ornithological Guide* (1838). With John Bachman (1790–1874) he began work on the *Viviparous Quadrupeds of North America* (5 vols., 1842–54). **Louis Agassiz** (p. 973) became professor of zoology at Harvard (1848), founded the Museum of Comparative Zoology at Harvard (1859), and also established a pioneer marine station at Buzzard's Bay (1873).

1794–1860. CHEMISTRY. Arrival in U.S. of **Joseph Priestley** (1733–1804) stimulated interest in the field. First separate chair established at Princeton (1795) with **John MacLean** (1771–1814) as first incumbent. **Thomas Cooper** (1759–1839), as professor of chemistry and mineralogy at Dickinson College (1811–16), at the Univ. of Pennsylvania (1817–19), and the Univ. of South

Carolina (1819–34), acted as a missionary for the new chemistry of Priestley, Lavoisier, and Davy. **Benjamin Silliman** (p. 1152), first professor of chemistry and natural history at Yale (1802–53), discovered that carbon was vaporized in an electric arc (1822), prepared hydrofluoric acid for the first time in the U.S. (1823), and detected bromine in a natural American brine (1830), was also founder of *American Journal of Science and Arts* (1818), which he edited to 1846. Other advances in chemical analysis: detection of boric acid in tourmaline (1822) and of beryllium in chrysoberyl (1824) by **Henry Seybert**, and development by **J. Lawrence Smith** of a method for determining alkalies in minerals and destroying ammonium salts with aqua regia (1853). *Memoir on the Ammonia Cobalt Bases* (1857) by **Oliver Wolcott Gibbs** (1822–1908) and **Frederick A. Genth** (1820–93) constituted a solid achievement.

1797–1859.   PALEONTOLOGY. **Thomas Jefferson** described a fossil found in Virginia (1797) and in the remains of Proboscidea and other finds at Big Bone Lick, Ky. (1808). **Rembrandt Peale** wrote an account of the mastodon ("mammoth," 1802). **Edward Hitchcock** (1793–1864) pioneer in the detection of fossil footprints in the Connecticut Valley (1836), continued his work in his *Final Report on the Geology of Massachusetts* (1841) and *Ichnology* and *Supplement* (1858, 1865). The arrival in the U.S. (1846) of **Louis Agassiz**, followed (1847) by work on fossils by Hiram A. Prout and S. D. Culbertson, focused attention on the prairie regions. Other notable contributions include the series of papers on the paleozoic vertebrates (1849) by **Isaac Lea** (1792–1886) and *The Ancient Fauna of Nebraska* (1853) by **Joseph Leidy** (1823–91), based on the findings of an expedition sent out by Spencer F.

Baird (1823–87) of the Smithsonian Institution.

1798. BENJAMIN THOMPSON (Count Rumford, 1753–1814), a Loyalist exile who did all his scientific work abroad, reported the results of his experiments on the nature of heat as a form of motion. He endowed medals of the Royal Society (first awarded, 1802) and the American Academy of Arts and Sciences (first award, 1839) as well as the Rumford professorship of physics at Harvard (Jacob Bigelow, 1816, first incumbent).

1799. Publication of *Practical Navigator* by **Nathaniel Bowditch** (p. 990), still a standard work of reference for mariners. Bowditch translated Laplace's *Mécanique céleste* (1814–17) and made observations on a meteor (1815).

1799–1804.   WILLIAM DUNBAR (1749–1810) took the first important meteorological recordings in the Southwest and gave the first scientific account and analysis of the waters of Hot Springs.

1806–55.   BENJAMIN SILLIMAN founded (at Yale) a notable school of geologists, including Benjamin Silliman, Jr. (1816–85), who made valuable investigations into the uses and preparation of petroleum products and wrote a report on petroleum in Pennsylvania; **Edward Hitchcock**, who published notable reports on the geology of New England (1818, 1823); **Amos Eaton** (1776–1842), who published his *Index* to the geology of the North (1815); **Denison Olmstead** (1791–1859), whose report on the geology of North Carolina (1824–25) was the first official state geological survey in the U.S.; and, most notable, **James Dwight Dana** (1813–95), who, on his return from the Wilkes expedition (p. 1184) described for the first time 230 species of zoophytes and 636 of Crustacea, and published basic manuals on geology (1837, 1848, 1863). Other important geologists: **William Maclure** (1763–1840), whose

Observations on the Geology of the U.S.
(1809) contained the first geological map
of America; revised, 1817; **Thomas Say,**
the first American to point out the chro-
nogenetic value of fossils (1819). The
final integration of European and American chronologies was achieved through
the efforts of **Isaac Lea, T. A. Conrad**
(1803–77), and **James Hall** (1811–98).

1818–60. DESCRIPTIVE BOTANY.
Notable work in this period contributed
by **Gotthilf Muhlenberg** (1753–1815),
with his catalogue of 2,800 species of
North American plants (1813); **Thomas
Nuttall** (1786–1859), *Genera of North
American Plants* (1818); **John Torrey**
(1796–1873), on flora of North and Middle States (1824); **Lewis David von
Schweinitz** (1780–1834), on fungi
(1831). For the work of **Asa Gray** both
before and after 1860, see p. 1045.

1829–46. ELECTRICITY. Following
Franklin, electrical research was actively
pursued in Europe (Galvani, current
electricity, 1790; Volta, electric battery,
1800; Oersted, Ampère, Arago, electromagnetism, c.1820; Schweigger, galva-
nometer, 1820; Sturgeon, electromagnet,
1825). **Joseph Henry** (p. 1056) began experiments in electricity (1827); improved
the electromagnet (1829) and, independent of Faraday, discovered the method
for producing induced currents of electricity (1830–32); aided Morse in his
experiments in telegraphy; discovered the
oscillatory nature of electrical discharge
of Leyden jar (1842); and anticipated
later discoveries in radio and light waves
(to 1846).

**1831–61. METEOROLOGY. William
C. Redfield's** (1789–1857) pioneer observations (1831–37) and papers on
wind motion during storms (1842, 1846)
were challenged by **James P. Espy**
(1785–1860), whose *Law of Cooling of
Atmospheric Air* (1843) was one of the
great U.S. contributions to the field.
Further contributions in this field were

made by **James H. Coffin** (1806–73) and
William Ferrel (1817–91), who propounded (1856) Ferrel's Law, which
expressed the fact that on account of
the earth's rotation bodies on its surface
are deflected to the right in the Northern
Hemisphere and to the left in the Southern Hemisphere.

**1836–1902. ETHNOLOGY AND AN-
THROPOLOGY.** Earliest work in Ameri-
can ethnology directly related to the
study and classification of North American Indians by linguistic families. **Albert
Gallatin** (p. 1037) published pioneer contribution, "A Synopsis of the Indian
Tribes . . .," in American Antiquarian
Society *Transactions*, II (1836), drew
up first good ethnographical map of
North America, founded (1842) the
American Ethnological Society, and in its
Transactions (1845, 1848) published
important essays on the Indians of the
New World. Gallatin's writings prepared
the ground for an American science of
ethnology. **Henry Rowe Schoolcraft**
(1793–1864), an explorer and Indian
agent who lived among frontier tribes
for many years, compiled the monumental *Historical and Statistical Informational Respecting the . . . Indian Tribes
of the United States*, 6 vols. (1851–57).
Lewis Henry Morgan (p. 1106) published
in his account of the Iroquois (1851),
the first scientific study of an Indian
tribe; his analysis of Iroquois social and
political organization, as well as kinship
systems and marriage customs, constituted one of the significant steps in the
emergence of an American anthropology.
John Wesley Powell (p. 1132) founded
and served as first director (1879–1902)
of the U.S. Bureau of Ethnology of the
Smithsonian Institution, and in *An Introduction to the Study of Indian Languages*
(1877) and in a paper on North American Indian linguistic families (1891)
devised a system of nomenclature that
was later generally adopted for studies of

Amerindian languages. **Daniel G. Brinton** (1837–99) was one of the pioneers of American anthropology; although many of his hypotheses were subsequently discarded, his paper on the Mound Builders (1866) correctly identified them as Amerindian, while his *The American Race* (1891) was the first attempt to classify systematically the aboriginal languages of the New World Indians. He complied *Aboriginal American Authors and Their Productions* (1882–90). **American Anthropological Association** founded (1902) at Washington, D.C.

1840–59. ASTRONOMY. Astronomical observatory erected at Harvard (1840) by **William Cranch Bond** (1789–1859), its first director. With his son, **George Phillips Bond** (1825–65), he discovered 8th satellite of Saturn and first moon of Neptune, and invented electrochronograph for determining longitude. The Great Comet, which appeared in 1843, stimulated astronomical investigation. Notable work on the planet Neptune (discovered 1846) and the rings of Saturn done in this period by **Benjamin Peirce** (1809–80). **Maria Mitchell** (1818–89), of Nantucket, Mass., discovered a comet (1847) and became the first woman professor of astronomy in the U.S. (Vassar, 1865).

1846. SMITHSONIAN INSTITUTION founded by Act of Congress (1846), utilizing bequest (c. £ 100,000) of James Smithson, an English chemist and mineralogist; Joseph Henry named first director. **American Association for the Advancement of Science** organized, with William C. Redfield, president.

1847–56. HYDROGRAPHY AND OCEANOGRAPHY. Of great aid to worldwide exploration were the various *Wind and Current Charts* compiled by **Matthew Fontaine Maury** (p. 1100), appointed (1842) superintendent of Department of Charts and Instruments (later U.S. Naval Observatory and Hydrographic Office); cut sailing time from New York to San Francisco (by 1855) from 180 to 130 days, with similar reductions in many other parts of the world. His *Physical Geography of the Sea* (1856) was widely translated.

1864–1903. CHEMISTRY. M. Carey Lea (1823–97): platinum metals (1864); photochemistry (1865–93); discovery of photosalts (by 1880); notable work on colloidal suspensions, especially with silver (from 1889). Technics in volumetric analysis improved by **Josiah Parsons Cooke** (1827–94). Electrolytic analysis introduced by **Oliver Wolcott Gibbs** (1865) was improved by **Frank Austin Gooch** (before 1903) by the introduction of the rotating cathode. Completion by **Josiah Willard Gibbs** (p. 1041) of his *On the Equilibrium of Heterogeneous Substances* (1875), followed by a further paper (1877–78), established him as the founder of "chemical energetics." He extended the method of thermodynamics, applying it to chemical problems, and introduced the "phase rule." **Ira Remsen** (1846–1927), who founded U.S. graduate research in chemistry at Johns Hopkins (1876), obtained benzoic sulfinide (saccharin) and enunciated "Remsen's Law" determining the protection of methyl and other groups from oxidation.

1864–1903. GEOLOGY. California survey proved the presence of Upper Triassic (1864); found in Idaho (1877) and subsequently over most of the West. **F. V. Hayden** found marine Jurassic fossils in "Red Beds" of Rocky Mountain area, but it was not until the Jurassic strata were found in California (1885) that the outlines of this formation could be drawn. Work of **Robert T. Hill** (on Texas Cretaceous, 1887) and of **W. M. Gabb** and **J. D. Whitney** (on California Cretaceous, 1869) contributed to rounding out the geological map of the U.S. Glacial formations described by Hilgard (Miss., 1866), Stevens (Va., 1873), Hall

(Pa., 1876), and Rogers (Va. and N.C., 1876), with outstanding work (1873–82) by **Thomas C. Chamberlain** (1843–1928). **Grove K. Gilbert** (1843–1918) reported on extinct Lake Bonneville (1879). **William H. Dall** (1845–1927) made major contributions to stratigraphy (1885–1903). See also p. 613.

1864–1952. ASTRONOMY. Lewis M. Rutherfurd (1816–98) built astronomical camera and photographed the moon (1864), and invented micrometer to measure stars. **Henry Draper** (1837–82) obtained first successful photograph of the spectrum of a star (1872) and introduced photography of nebulae (1880). Using telescopes built by **Alvan Clark** (1808–87), **Asaph Hall** (1829–1907) discovered the moon of Mars (1877) and **James E. Keeler** (1857–1900) the composition of Saturn's rings (1886). **Samuel P. Langley** (1834–1906) devised the bolometer to detect temperatures and demonstrated a new way to test variations in surface temperatures of the sun (1881). **William H. Pickering** (1858–1938) discovered Phoebe, 9th satellite of Saturn (1898). As a result of prediction and research originated in 1905 by **Percival Lowell** (1855–1916), the planet Pluto was discovered (1930) by **Clyde W. Tombaugh** (1906–   ). **George Ellery Hale** (1868–1932) invented the spectroheliograph, with which he took the first successful photograph of solar prominence (1891). Through Hale's efforts the Mt. Wilson Observatory was opened (1906). Hale Telescope at Mt. Palomar opened in 1948. **Seth B. Nicholson** (1891–1963) discovered 9th,10th,11th moons of Jupiter 1914, 1938; 12th, 1952.

1866–1941. PALEONTOLOGY. Othniel Charles Marsh (1831–99), first professor of paleontology in the U.S. (Yale, 1866), led organized bone-hunting expeditions for Yale, and later (1881) for U.S. Geological Survey (discovered 500 new species, 225 new genera, 64 new families, 19 new orders). **Edward D. Cope** (1840–97) published 3 notable studies (1875, 1877, 1883) as a result of field expeditions he organized; his work on herpetology and ichthyology prepared the way for modern classification of North American reptiles, amphibians, and fishes. **Henry Fairfield Osborn** (1857–1935), professor of zoology at Columbia (1896–1910) and curator of vertebrate paleontology at American Museum of Natural History (1891–1910), popularized knowledge of the field. Dinosaur National Monument (Utah and Colorado) established (1915) to preserve area of great finds. The largest footprints yet found (4½ x 3 ft.) discovered in the Texas Big Bend country (1941).

1870–84. MATHEMATICS. At Johns Hopkins, **James J. Sylvester** (1814–97), the British mathematician, advanced the studies in this field and founded the *American Journal of Mathematics*. At Yale **Josiah Willard Gibbs** published his *Elements of Vector Analysis* (c.1881–84).

1881–1920. VELOCITY OF LIGHT. **Albert A. Michelson** (p. 1102) determined the velocity of light (1878–80) and invented the interferometer, by which length of standard meter was ascertained in terms of wave length of cadmium light (1887), and began investigations on existence of hypothetical ether (1881). Famous experiment with **Edward W. Morley** (1838–1923) in 1887 served as starting point for Einstein's Special Theory of Relativity (1905).

1902–60. ANTHROPOLOGY AND CULTURAL ANTHROPOLOGY. Franz Boas (p. 988) was the principal figure in establishing an American science of anthropology. He organized (1902) the Jesup Expedition to study the Indians of the Canadian Pacific Northwest; the expedition's reports on the Kwakiutl and other Indians reinforced the "culture-area" approach as distinguished from the geographical-diffusionist viewpoint. **Clark Wissler** (1870–1947), associated with the American Museum of Natural History, stressed the historical-diffusionist approach and was influential in defining Indian culture areas in the New World. Boas, who introduced cultural objectivity and scientific method into field work, and stressed the functional interconnection of group institutions, trained in his seminars at Columbia Univ. a number of anthropologists who made important contributions to theory and knowledge and were instrumental in shaping the direction of cultural anthropology in the U.S. Among his students were (1) **Alfred L. Kroeber** (1876–1960), who in 1902 received the first Ph.D. in anthropology awarded by Columbia. Kroeber studied the diffusion of tribal cultures in North and South America; gave standing to cultural anthropology in such books as *Handbook of the Indians of California* (1925), *Cultural and Natural Areas of Native North America* (1939), and *Configurations of Culture Growth* (1944); and, after Boas, was the major force in professionalizing anthropology in the U.S. and in fostering it as an academic discipline; (2) **Alexander A. Goldenweiser** (1880–1940), who wrote on totemism and contributed suggestive insights into theory and methodology in the study of magic, religion, and social organization, as in his *History, Psychology, and Culture* (1933); (3) **Robert H. Lowie** (1883–1957) wrote many monographs on North American Indians, especially the Crows (1912, 1935); his *Primitive Society* (1920) strongly influenced social organization theory, while his *Primitive Religion* (1924) expounded a diffusionist hypothesis; (4) **Edward Sapir** (1884–1939) drew links between personality and culture and wrote the innovative

paper "Time Perspective in Aboriginal American Culture: A Study in Method" (1916); he devoted much of his work to investigating American Indian languages and cultures, and was one of the trailblazers of an American science of linguistics; (5) **Ruth F. Benedict** (1887–1948), in her *Patterns of Culture* (1934), applied the findings of Gestalt psychology to the Kwakiutl, Pueblo, and Dubu societies. (6) **Margaret Mead** (1901–78) used the insights of Freudian psychoanalysis and made the relations between personality and culture the central theme of such works as *Coming of Age in Samoa* (1928), *Growing Up in New Guinea* (1930), and *Sex and Temperament in Primitive Societies* (1935). Other cultural anthropologists of note were **Ralph Linton** (1883–1953) and **Robert Redfield** (1897–1958). A trained anthropologist, **William Lloyd Warner** (1898–1970), used the techniques of the discipline in studying an American community (Newburyport, Mass.) in his "Yankee City" series (1941–59).

1909–26. STUDIES IN INHERITANCE. Thomas Hunt Morgan (p. 1107) at Columbia used the fruit fly (drosophila) to test Mendel's laws of inheritance; first to use "gene" (1909) to describe individual parts of chromosomes controlling particular characteristics; discovered the phenomenon of sex-linked characteristics (1910) and later (1911, 1913) characteristics of different linkages. His students elaborated work on mutants and the gene theory. Work by **R. A. Emerson** (1873–1947) on mutations in corn (from 1914) tended to confirm Morgan. **Hermann J. Muller** (p. 1111) found that with X rays he could artificially increase the rate of mutation in the fruit fly (by 1926). Confirmation of findings provided by experiments with barley by **Lewis J. Stadler** (1896–1954) and with tobacco by **T. H. Goodspeed** (1887–1966).

1910. Trivalent carbon discovered by **Moses Gomberg** (1866–1947).

1910–25. ROBERT A. MILLIKAN (p. 1104) announced (1910) he had measured the charge of an electron as a definite constant; elaborated results in his *The Electron* (1912; 2d ed., 1925). He succeeded in proving Einstein's hitherto unproven photoelectric equation and in evaluating Planck's Constant (h).

1911–70. LINGUISTICS. The major influence on linguistics in the U.S. in the 20th century was the concern of anthropologists with the indigenous languages of North America. The introduction by Franz Boas to *Handbook of American Indian Languages* (1911), a volume he edited, set forth a method of systematic description that challenged traditional grammatical theory by holding that each language had its own unique grammatical structure. This view, although not originated by Boas or restricted to him, became the point of departure for the "structuralist" approach with which the American school of linguistics has been associated. This school had 2 periods of development: (1) **1920–40.** The Linguistics Society of America was established in 1924. The professionalization of linguistics developed around the 2 seminal scholars of the period, **Edward Sapir** and **Leonard Bloomfield** (1887–1949), both of whom were initially trained in Germanic philology but turned to linguistics as a result of their studies of American Indian languages. Sapir, as an anthropologist, did field work in many American Indian languages, and produced 2 notable works: *Language* (1921), a discussion of basic principles that was destined to be influential for more than 2 generations; and the paper "Sound Patterns in Language" (1925), which set down the fundamentals of structural analysis for American linguistics. While insisting on the interdependence of linguistics with other disciplines, Sapir stressed the

autonomy of grammatical form. Emphasis on the autonomy of linguistics was reinforced by Bloomfield, whose *Language* (1933), embodying an approach based on the behaviorist psychology of John B. Watson, became a central work of the new structuralist school. Bloomfield established (1940) a department of linguistics at Yale that became a center of American linguistic scholarship. (2) **1940–70.** By 1945, linguistics was rapidly being distinguished from philology, and became generally accepted as an independent, scientific, and academic discipline. In this period a leading exponent of structuralism was **Zellig S. Harris** (1909–   ), of the Univ. of Pennsylvania, author of *Methods in Structural Linguistics* (1951), *Mathematical Structure of Language* (1968), and *Papers in Structural and Transformatinal Linguistics* (1970). His most gifted pupil, and the single most influential figure in American linguistics in this period, was **Noam Chomsky** (1928–   ), who since 1955 has been on the faculty of MIT. Initially a structuralist, Chomsky later rejected the mechanistic implications of the Bloomfieldian approach, and came to view linguistics as a branch of cognitive psychology. He has brought to the investigation of language a rigorous scientific method based on mathematics and logic. His chief contribution has been the formal syntactic theory associated with his universal models of generative and transformational grammar. Among his works are *Syntax Structures* (1957), *Aspects of the Theory of Syntax* (1965), *Cartesian Linguistics* (1966), and *Language and Mind* (1968).

1912–48. MEASURING THE UNIVERSE. Henrietta Leavitt (1868–1921) at Harvard announced her "period-luminosity" law; i.e., the period of fluctuation of brightness of a Cepheid star is directly proportional to its candlepower. **Harlow Shapley** (1885–1972), applying this law to globular clusters, was able (1917) to measure distances in the Milky Way. Data accumulated (by 1928) by **Vestro M. Slipher** (1875–1969), Lowell Observatory, on 43 spiral nebulae, using spectroscope and working with the "Doppler shift," showed that these nebulae were moving away from the earth at speeds increasing with distance. **Edwin Powell Hubble** (1899–1953), in conjunction with Milton L. Humason (1891–1972), at the Wilson Observatory, by adding the period-luminosity law to Slipher's technic (1929–43), worked out quantitative measurements of distance and speeds confirming Slipher.

1914–51. ATOMIC RESEARCH. Gilbert N. Lewis (p. 1083) set forth new theory of the structure of the atom (1916); expanded by **Irving Langmuir** (p. 1080) into the concentric shell theory (1919), which explained chemical activity of an element in terms of the completeness of its outer shell of electrons. **Theodore W. Richards** (1868–1928) at Harvard discovered an isotope of lead (1914, 2 isotopes of neon had been found in England, 1913). **William D. Harkins** (1873–1951), working on the problem of nuclei of atoms (1914–21), found that nitrogen bombarded by helium nuclei produced an oxygen isotope (atomic wt. 17) and predicted the neutron (1920), which was discovered in England (1932). **Arthur H. Compton** (p. 1004) discovered the Compton effect, which showed that X rays had a corpuscular structure (1923). **Clinton J. Davisson** (p. 1010) and **Lester H. Germer** (1896–1971) found that electrons shot against a nickel crystal were reflected in the same way as light waves, thus showing for the first time that matter has wavelike characteristics (1927). **Ernest O. Lawrence** (p. 1081) constructed the first cyclotron, which made possible the acceleration of nuclear particles to energies of millions of volts for smashing atoms (1930). **Harold C. Urey** (p. 1173) discovered hydrogen isotope of mass 2 (deuterium, or heavy hydrogen, 1931). **Arthur J. Dempster** (1886–1950) built improved mass spectrograph and isolated isotope uranium 235, later found to be the only natural fissionable element existing in relatively large quantities (1935). **Enrico Fermi** (1901–1954), **John R. Dunning** (1907–1975), and **George B. Pegram** (1876–1958) repeated uranium fission experiment of Otto Hahn and Fritz Strassman in Germany and Otto Frisch and Lise Meitner in Denmark, in which vast amounts of nuclear energy are released by the splitting of uranium 235 atoms with fast or slow neutrons, the discovery which led to the production of the atomic bomb and to the utilization of atomic energy. **Edwin M. McMillan** (p. 1094) and **Philip H. Abelson** (1913–) isolated neptunium (element 93), first transuranic element (1940). **Glenn T. Seaborg** (p. 1148) and **Emilio Segre** (1905–) produced plutonium, (element 94), first man-made fissionable element (1941). First self-perpetuating nuclear chain reaction, demonstrating practicability of atomic bomb and industrial atomic power, on 2 Dec. 1942. Electromagnetic and gaseous diffusion plants for separation of isotope uranium 235 built at Oak Ridge, Tenn., 1943–44. Nuclear reactors for producing plutonium built at Hanford, Wash., 1943–44. **First atomic bomb** designed and constructed at Los Alamos, N.M., 1945; tested at Alamogordo, N.M., 16 July 1945. McMillan announced discovery of principle of synchrotron (1945). Seaborg *et al.* produced americium, curium, berkelium, and californium, elements 95, 96, 97, and 98 (1944–50). First production of electric power from nuclear reactor, Arco, Ida. (1951). Cosmotron at Brookhaven National Laboratory generated 2,250 million volts (10 June 1952).

1916–53. ALBERT EINSTEIN (p. 1022), continuing (1933) his life work at the Institute for Advanced Study, Princeton, N.J., disclosed (30 Mar. 1953) formulas as last step in his quest for a Unified Field Theory, a single mathematical system embracing electromagnetism and gravitation in one universal law, and eventually uniting the Relativity and Quantum theories.

1921–51. COSMIC RAYS. Millikan, with **Ira S. Bowen** (1898–1973) began investigations in California on nature and origin of cosmic rays from outer space. **Arthur H. Compton** (p. 1004) organized worldwide study (1931). **Carl D. Anderson** (1905–) discovered the positron particle with mass of negative electron but with a positive charge of equal magnitude in cosmic rays (1932). Anderson with **Seth H. Neddermeyer** (1907–) discovered in the cosmic rays a new charged particle, intermediate in mass between the proton and the electron, which was named the meson (1936). **Jabez C. Street** (1906–) and **E. C. Stevenson** discovered same particle independently (1937). **Robert Marshak** (1916–) predicted on theoretical grounds the existence of heavier type of meson to account for nuclear forces, in accordance with earlier prediction by **Hideki Yukawa** of Japan (later at Columbia). Heavier meson, named pi-meson, later found in cosmic ray in British studies. Pi-meson produced artificially (1948) in giant synchrocyclotron at Univ. of California, marking first time that matter was created out of energy in accordance with famous Einstein formula ($E = mc^2$).

1941, 28 June. Office of Scientific Research and Development (p. 435).

1954–57. NEW ELEMENTS. 99 (einsteinium, atomic weight 247) and 100 (fermium, atomic weight 254)—AEC's Argonne National Laboratory and Univ.

of California (1954); 101 (mendelevium)—Univ. of California (1955); 102 (nobelium)—Nobel Institute and Argonne Laboratory (1957).

1955. Nobel prize awards in physics to **Polykarp Kusch** (1911–), Columbia, for precision determination of the magnetic moment of the electron, proving that energy level calculations of P. A. M. Dirac, British physicist, did not agree with experimental evidence, and to **Willis E. Lamb** (1913–), Stanford, for discoveries regarding the hyperfine structure of the hydrogen spectrum.

18 Oct. ANTI-PROTON, a new atomic particle, discovered by Emilio Segre and associates at Univ. of California.

1956. ANTI-NEUTRON identified at Bevatron Laboratory of U. of California.

1957. SPONTANEOUS GENERATION. Amino acids, the basic substance of proteins, produced by exposing mixtures of methane, ammonium, water, and hydrogen to electrical charges comparable to lightning in experiment performed by **Stanley L. Miller** of Columbia Univ. College of Physicians and Surgeons.

1957, July 1–1958, Dec. 31. INTERNATIONAL GEOPHYSICAL YEAR, an 18-month period of intensive study of the earth, the oceans, the atmosphere, and the sun. U.S. scientists participated, with an appropriation of $39 million from Congress to National Science Foundation.

1960–70. NEW ELEMENTS. 103 (lawrencium)—Lawrence Radiation Laboratory, Univ. of California, 1960; the Laboratory also created the heaviest known nucleus, the isotope mendelevium, 258 (1963); 104 (rutherfordium)—identified by Albert Ghiorso and others of the Lawrence Radiation Laboratory, 1969 (discovery disputed by Soviet scientists who claim precedence and named element kurchatovium); 105 (hahnium)—discovered in 1970 by A. Ghiorso and associates.

1960–73. NOBEL PRIZES IN PHYSICS: 1960, Donald A. Glaser (1918–) for invention of bubblebath chamber for photographing atomic particles; **1961, Robert Hofstader** (1915–) shared prize for providing evidence that the proton has complex structure; **1963, Eugene Wigner** (1902–) shared prize for formulation of the symmetry principles governing the interaction of nuclear particles in accordance with their direction of spin; **1964, Charles H. Townes** (1915–) for work on masers which helped produce lasers, light amplification by stimulated emission of radiation; **1965, Richard P. Feynman** (1918–) and **Julius S. Schwinger** (1918–) for their fundamental work in quantum electrodynamics with deepplowing consequences for the physics of elementary particles; **1967, Hans Bethe** (1906–) for his theoretical studies of the processes from which the sun devises its energy; **1968, Luis W. Alvarez** (1911–) for his work on subatomic particles and techniques for their detection; **1969, Murray Gell-Mann** (1929–) for his discoveries and contributions concerning the classification of elementary particles and their interactions; **1972, John Bardeen** (1908–), who shared a Nobel prize in physics, 1956, thus becoming the first laureate to win twice in the same field; **Leon N. Cooper** (1924–) and **John R. Schrieffer** (1931–) for joint research and development of the theory of superconductivity in ultracold metals, a property causing them to lose resistance to electric current; **1973, Leo Esaki** (1925–) and **Ivar Giaever** (1929–) for theories concerning "tunneling," or the superconducting behavior of electrons in solids, whose application underlies revolutionary progress in miniature electronics.

1960–72. NOBEL PRIZES IN CHEMISTRY: 1960, Willard F. Libby (1908–80) for inventing atomic time clock; **1961, Melvin Calvin** (1911–) for contributions to the discovery of the chemical reactions involved in photosynthesis; **1965, Robert Burns Woodward,** see p. 1188 for the synthesis of organic structures; **1966, Robert S. Mulliken** (1896–) for theoretical studies of the chemical bonds that hold atoms together in a molecule; **1968, Lars Onsager** (1903–76) for system of equations that show reciprocal reactions of activities such as the interaction of voltage and temperature in the transfer of heat (work done in 1931). **1972 prize** (p. 817).

1960–71. ELEMENTARY PARTICLE RESEARCH. Larger atom smashers such as the Brookhaven Synchotron (1960) and the Brookhaven High-Flux Beam research reactor (HFBR) (1965) and Stanford University's 2-mile, 20-billion-volt linear accelerator (1966) facilitated research into the atom or "nuclear zoo." Among the observed particles were the omega meson (1961, Lawrence Rad. Lab.); rho meson (1961, many labs); anti-xi-xero (1963, Brookhaven); omega minus (1964, Brookhaven); the anti-neutron (1965, Brookhaven team led by Leon M. Lederman); the phi-meson was confirmed (1963, Lawrence Lab. and Brookhaven). A team at Lawrence Radiation Laboratory identified (1971) the anti-omega-minus baryon, one of a basic group of subatomic particles comprising the principal constituents of atomic nuclei.

1962–74. DEVELOPMENTS IN ASTRONOMY spurred by space program. **Ranger 4** hit far side of moon 23 Apr. 1962. **Mariner 2** space probe (launched 22 Aug. 1962) discovered Venus temperature at 800° and indicated that there

was no break in the planet's cloud cover;
U.S. spacecraft **Ranger 7** took 4,316
photographs of lunar surface before hitting moon, 31 July 1964, discovering
more small craters and reporting the
slight depth of moon dust. Further lunar
photographs by **Ranger 8** (moon hit 20
Feb. 1965) and **Ranger 9** (24 Mar. 1964),
as well as **Surveyor 1** (2 June 1966).
U.S. lunar orbiter launched 14 Aug.
1966. Sun-orbiting **Pioneer 6** launched
16 Dec. 1965. **Mariner 4** spacecraft
photographs of Mars (15–24 July 1965)
after 7½ month flight detected no trace
of canals or seas. **Mariner 5** launched for
Mars 14 June 1967. **Surveyor 5** landed on
moon (10 Sept. 1967) and relayed analysis
of moon area consisting of basaltic materials, primarily oxygen and silicon, very
earthlike in composition. **Mariner 6**
(launched 24 Feb. 1969) and **Mariner
7** (launched 27 Mar. 1969) passed
within 2,000 miles of Mars on different
orbits and sent back many photos of the
planet's varied terrain; once more these
did not confirm the existence of canals
on Mars. Infrared spectrometer aboard
Mariner 7 detected features of the
southern polar ice-cap, found to consist
of frozen carbon dioxide. Information
was obtained on Phobos, one of the
planet's two moons. **Mariner 8** having
failed shortly after takeoff in May, 1971,
Mariner 9 was launched on 30 May 1971,
and entered orbit about Mars on 13 Nov.
1971. On 14 Nov. it began transmitting
the first of many thousands of photos,
resulting in the first systematic photo-
mapping of the planet's surface. An
infrared spectrometer measured the atmospheric and surface characteristics.
This information, in addition to the
photos, materially altered scientists' conceptions of Mars. It was indicated that
many of the surface formations are possibly of volcanic origin, and that liquid
water may have existed on the planet.

On 27 Oct. 1972 **Mariner 9,** after making
its 698th orbit around Mars and transmitting 7,329 photos, exhausted its
supply of altitude control gas, and the
mission was terminated. **Mariner 10,**
launched 3 Nov. 1973, provided views
of Venus (5 Feb. 1974) and first closeup
information on Mercury (closest approach, 29 Mar. 1974). **Pioneer 10,** a
nuclear-powered 570–pound unmanned
interplanetary probe, was launched from
Cape Kennedy, Fla. at 8:50 PM EST
on 2 Mar. 1972. Traveling faster and
farther than any other man-made object
(it attained speeds as high as 82,800
mph, or 23 miles per second), it was
the first to pass the orbit of Mars and to
journey safely through the asteroid belt.
On 3 Dec. 1973, after a voyage of 620
million miles lasting 21 months, Pioneer
10 flew within 81,000 miles of Jupiter;
the spacecraft's sophisticated communications enabled the first closeup inspection of the largest planet in the solar
system, and transmitted to earth color
pictures and scientific data on Jupiter's
radiation belts, magnetic field, atmosphere, satellites, and other features.
Accelerated by Jupiter's gravitational
force, Pioneer 10 sped toward Pluto,
continuing a voyage that in 1987 should
make it the first earth-launched spacecraft to leave the gravitational field of
the solar system and enter interstellar
space.

1962–73. QUASARS. Identification of
quasars (quasi-stellar radio sources) by
Allan R. Sandage (1926–   ), **Jesse L.
Greenstein** (1909–   ), and **Maarten
Schmidt** (1929–   ), led to discovery by
U.S. and other astronomers of approximately 200 of these extragalactic phenomena, generally considered to be more
distant (possibly 12 billion light-years)
than any other class of space object. One
hypothesis holds that quasars constitute
the "edge of the universe," and it is

believed by some that the basic assumptions of physics and cosmology may require radical revision to account for quasars. The enormous amount of infrared light emitted by quasars suggests that some of them may have energy ranging from an equivalent of 100 million suns to possibly 10 trillion suns.

Invention and Technology

The course of American technological development was set by the conditions of the colonial and early national period, during which the economic potential of an ever-expanding continental domain rich in natural resources was constrained by a sparse population in an underdeveloped country with a chronic scarcity of investment capital. A people largely devoted to agriculture and extractive industries in 1789, the Americans employed technology as an avenue to national power, social modernization, and a broader diffusion of abundance, prefiguring the road that other underdeveloped nations would take in the twentieth century. At first the United States borrowed its technology, chiefly from Great Britain. The British textile industry, the vanguard of the First Industrial Revolution, was quickly adapted and improved in the United States, where the social and economic climate was generally more receptive to technological innovation than in Europe. Between 1840 and 1890 the completion of the basic rail transportation network helped create a national market economy in which competitive advantage in the emerging large industries, among them oil and steel, came to depend more and more upon the cost-benefits yielded by technology. Moreover, the dynamic development of railroading, America's first example of big business, stimulated ancillary industries, and levied fresh demands for advanced technology.

The rise of an industrial economy based upon the intensive exploitation of technology gave impetus to the trend toward the integrated manufacturing enterprise and industrial consolidation and concentration in the late nineteenth century. At the same time, the first industrial laboratories came into existence; it is suggestive that the pioneer laboratory for the systematic "invention of invention" was set up in 1876 at Menlo Park, N.J., by the individualist inventor Thomas A. Edison. The period 1880–1914 saw the culminating result of the "American system" of manufacturing evolved by Eli Whitney and others in the early nineteenth century. Using a broad array of semiautomatic and automatic machine tools, of which Americans were the foremost makers by 1900, factories producing bicycles, typewriters, and other complex articles made from a multiplicity of diverse components, Americans gained rich experience in the manufacture of articles assembled from standardized interchangeable parts. The advent of the automobile, and the revolutionary innovation of the moving assembly line by Ford Motor Co. production engineers in 1913–14, opened the way for the central role of technology in the consumer economy of modern America. Not until the Great Depression of the 1930s, with its widespread unemployment, did public opinion begin to question the relentless pace of labor-saving industrial mechanization; but the technological feats that helped to bring a U.S. military victory in World War II, and the successive bursts of postwar prosperity marked by new or expanding industries like electronics and petrochemicals, restored a popular faith in the beneficence of technology. That faith would not be qualified until ecological concerns in the late 1960s pointed to the urgent need for restraining man's technological capability both to create his own environment and to alter, exhaust, or destroy the natural one.

1730–35. MARINER'S QUADRANT improved by **Thomas Godfrey** (1704–49), the mathematician. The theodolite, an instrument for measuring horizontal angles, improved by Roland Houghton (1735).

1730–40. LONG RIFLE (also Pennsylvania and, later, Kentucky Rifle) developed by Pennsylvania gunsmiths by elongating barrel, narrowing and improving the rifling of bore, and adding grease patch. Prototype was introduced by German immigrants (1710–20).

1742–52. BENJAMIN FRANKLIN invented Franklin stove (Pennsylvania fireplace), an adaptation of the German stove which permitted ventilation (1742), and the lightning rod (1752).

1750. FLATBOAT for inland navigation invented by Jacob Yoder (Pa.).

1750–60. CONESTOGA WAGON, adapted to frontier travel, made its first appearance in Pennsylvania.

1762. REV. JARED ELIOT (1685–1763) of Killingworth, Conn., developed a process for smelting iron from black magnetic sand (*Transactions*, 1762).

1775. DAVID BUSHNELL (c.1742–1824) built first American submarine, *American Turtle;* nearly succeeded in blowing up a British frigate in New York Harbor (1776).

c.1777–85. OLIVER EVANS (1755–1819) invented a card-making machine (c.1777–78) which could complete 150 pairs of cotton or wool cards from wire per day. During the same period he invented an **automatic flour mill** (cutting labor requirements by one half), which was first put into operation c.1785.

1781–87. STEAM ENGINES. First multitubular boiler (**John Stevens,** 1749–1838; patented, 1783). Noncondensing, high-pressure steam engine (**Oliver Evans,** 1787).

1783. Bifocal spectacles invented by Benjamin Franklin.

1785–87. FIRST STEAMBOATS. Steamboat invented by **John Fitch** (1743–89) franchised for New Jersey waters, 1786; launched on Delaware, 1787; patented, 1791. Second steamboat built by **James Rumsey** (1743–92), launched on Potomac, 1787; patented, 1791.

1790, 10 APRIL. FIRST PATENT LAW. A Patent Board consisting of the Secretary of State (who was entrusted with administering the law), the Secretary of War, and the Attorney General was given responsibility for granting patents on "useful and important" inventions. First federal patent, 31 July 1790, granted to **Samuel Hopkins** (Vt., 1721–1803) for a process for the manufacture of pot and pearl ash. Machine to cut and head nails in one operation invented by **Jacob Perkins** (Mass., 1766–1849). In the first 3 years (1790–92) 47 patents were issued. Under the patent law of 21 Feb. 1793, the system was changed. The duty of granting patents was conferred on the Secretary of State, and the requirement for investigating the originality and usefulness of inventions was discarded, thus substituting mere registration for evaluative examination. The term of a patent, as in the act of 1790, remained at 14 years.

1790–91. SAMUEL SLATER (p. 1152) reproduced Arkwright machinery, employing water power at Pawtucket, R.I.

1793–99. FARM INVENTIONS. Eli Whitney invented the **cotton gin,** cheapening the most costly process in refining cotton (1793). **Thomas Jefferson** invented the moldboard plow (1793). **Charles Newbold** patented the first cast-iron plow (1797). **Eliakim Spooner** invented a seeding machine (1799).

1798. Jig for guiding tools in operation invented by **Eli Whitney.**

1804–49. STEAM ENGINE ADVANCES. Steam dredge by **Oliver Evans.** Jacob Perkins embodied experiments with steam of high pressure (1823) in numerous inventions down to 1849, including bathometer (to measure depth of water), plenometer (to record speed of vessel through water), piezometer (to measure compressibility of water).

1805. ROBERT FULTON (p. 1036) built the first marine torpedo.

1807–08. PRACTICAL STEAMBOATS. Although **John Stevens** designed a screw propeller (1802) and with it operated *Phoenix* to Philadelphia by sea (1808, first steam vessel in the U.S. to navigate the ocean), **Robert Fulton** built the first successful steamboat (*Clermont* sailed, 17 Aug. 1807, New York to Albany, 32 hrs.). The first ironclad vessel was built by Stevens (1813).

1807–54. MACHINERY. Manufacture of tacks (Jesse Reed, Conn., 1807), screw-cutting machine (Abel Stowel, Mass., 1809), circular saw (David Melville, 1814), profile lathe (1818, **Thomas Blanchard,** Mass. [1788–1864]); commercial vernier caliper by Brown and Sharp (1851); turret lathe, Robbins and Lawrence (Vt., 1854).

1816–27. PRINTING PRESS IMPROVEMENTS. Hand printing press: George Clymer, Pa., 1816; with a toggle joint, Samuel Rust, 1827; improved, 1829.

1819–22. PLOW IMPROVEMENTS. Cast-iron 3-piece plow (standardized interchangeable parts), **Jethrow Wood** (N.Y., 1819); lock colter devised by John Conant (Vt., 1822).

1819. Breech-loading flintlock (John Hall).

1822. ARTIFICIAL TEETH. First patent to C. M. Graham.

1826–37. LOCOMOTIVE with multitubular boiler (John Stevens, 1826; first patent to William Howard (1828). **Robert L. Stevens** (1788–1856), son of John Stevens, invented the balance valve for steam engines and the T-rail (1830). Other railroad improvements included pilot truck and bogie and double-slide cutoff for locomotives. **Peter Cooper** (p. 1006) built first U.S. locomotive (1830). Swivel truck for locomotives devised by John B. Jervis (1831), equalizing lever by Joseph Harrison (1837).

1827–31. JOSEPH HENRY (p. 1056) insulated wire; invented multiple coil magnet; built first magnetic and acoustic telegraph.

1831–34. REAPER invented by **Cyrus H. McCormick** (p. 1092), 1831; patented, 1834; similar machine invented independently (1832–33) by **Obed Hussey** (1792–1860).

1833. STEEL-BLADE PLOWSHARE (John Lane, Ill.).

1834–39. ELECTRICAL MACHINERY. First actual electric motor invented by **Thomas Davenport** (1802–51), who also invented electric commutator (1835) and electric printing press (1839).

1835. REVOLVER patented by **Samuel Colt** (1814–62).

1836, 4 JULY. Inauguration of the **patent system.** A fundamental revision of the patent laws, the Act of 1836 reestablished the examination requirement for determining the novelty and usefulness of an invention. It created the Patent Office as a separate and distinct bureau in the Department of State, and placed it under a Commissioner of Patents. In 1849 the Patent Office was transferred to the Department of the Interior, and on 1 April 1925 was placed under the Department of Commerce. The term of a patent, as set under the act of 2 Mar. 1861, is 17 years. Since 1880 a model has no longer been required as part of the patent application.

1836–43. JOHN ERICSSON (b. Sweden, 1803–89) improved screw propeller for steamships (1836). Going to U.S. (1840), designed *Princeton,* first warship to have propelling machinery below waterline (1843). Other inventions in U.S.: telescopic smokestack, recoil mechanism for gun carriages, instrument for measuring distances at sea, gauges for fluids under pressure, alarm barometer, pyrometer, and self-registering deep-sea lead. For the *Monitor* (1861–62), see p. 281.

1837–40. FARM AND MILLING. Steel plow introduced (1837) in the U.S.

by **John Deere** (1804–86); thresher fanning mill (prototype of later improved threshers) built by Hiram A. and John Pitts (Me.).

1839. VULCANIZATION OF RUBBER discovered by **Charles Goodyear** (p. 1043); patented (France, 1844).

1840–44. ADVANCES IN IRON AND COAL TECHNOLOGY. Hot-blast iron furnace for anthracite coal (David Thomas, Conn.), anthracite coal breaker (Gideon Bast, 1840), roller and crusher for coal (J. and S. Battin, 1844).

1846–80. STEAM ENGINE IMPROVEMENTS. Valve gear and drop cut-off, central features of a 4-valve control system invented by **George H. Corliss** (1817–88), reduced condensation and enabled substantial fuel economies in the operation of reciprocating steam engines. Incorporating this and subsequent improvements constituting the most significant innovation in the art of the steam engine since that of James Watt, the Corliss engine was manufactured at the Corliss works at Providence, R.I., and was universally adopted. The spectacular 680-ton, 10-foot-stroke Corliss engine that provided the power for some 8,000 machines in Machinery Hall at the Philadelphia Centennial Exposition (1876) was one of the mechanical marvels of the age of steam.

1843–68. TYPEWRITER. Machine invented by **Charles Thurber** (Conn., 1843). First practical typewriter constructed, 1867, by **Christopher L. Sholes** (1819–90) in collaboration with Carlos Glidden and Samuel W. Soulé. Working alone, Sholes made numerous improved models and secured patents (1868); sold rights (1873) to E. Remington & Sons, who marketed it as Remington typewriter.

1844. TELEGRAPH. Samuel F. B. Morse (p. 1109) developed the first practical telegraph (1832), following a large number of experiments; put into operation (24 May 1844) with message from **Alfred Vail** (1807–59) in Baltimore to Morse in Washington, D.C. Morse invented Morse code (1838). Telegraphic printing technique invented by Vail (1844); patented by Royal E. House (1846).

1846–54. SEWING MACHINE invented by **Elias Howe** (p. 1063); improved (1849–54) by **Allen B. Wilson** (1824–88) and (1851) by **Isaac Merritt Singer** (1811–75), who, with the aid of Edward Clark, opened plant in New York City (1853).

1846. ROTARY PRINTING PRESS invented by **Richard M. Hoe** (p. 1058).

1847–64. FARM IMPLEMENTS. Revolving disc harrow (G. Page, 1847), agricultural binder (John E. Heath, 1850), chilled plow (**James Oliver,** 1855; improved by Marsh brothers, 1857), twine knotter (John F. Appleby, 1858), checkrower corn planter (John Thompson and John Ramsey, 1864).

1849. MODERN SAFETY PIN invented by Walter Hunt.

Pendulum press for can tops invented by Henry Evans.

1851–60. IRON AND STEEL ADVANCES. William Kelly (1811–88), Kentucky ironmaster, developed a process for converting pig iron into steel by directing a current of air upon molten metal (1851), independently of Henry Bessemer in England, who perfected the technic (1856). First Bessemer converter built at Troy, N.Y. (1864); Kelly process at Wyandotte, Mich., same year. Rival claims compromised 1866. Wrought-iron I-beams rolled (1860) by **Peter Cooper** at Trenton, N.J.

1852. ELISHA G. OTIS (p. 1120) invented first passenger elevator (making skyscraper possible).

1853. Sluicing process in mining perfected by E. E. Matteson.

1858–99. SHOE MACHINERY. Lyman R. Blake (1835–83) patented

(1858) a machine capable of sewing soles of shoes to the upper; promoted by **Gordon McKay** (1821–1903), who patented improved version (1862). The Blake-McKay machines were widely adopted by 1876. Charles Goodyear (1833–96), who acquired (1864–67) the welt-sewing machine, joined forces with McKay by 1880. Centralization of machine ownership brought about by formation (1899) of United Shoe Machinery Co.

1859. Successful **oil drilling** at Titusville, Pa., by **Edwin L. Drake** (1819–80).

1860. REPEATING RIFLE introduced by **Oliver F. Winchester** (1810–80).

1862. REVOLVING MACHINE GUN perfected by **Richard J. Gatling** (1818–1903).

1864. GEORGE M. PULLMAN (1831–97) built "Pioneer," first especially constructed sleeping car, and organized Pullman Palace Car Co. (1867).

1865. COMPRESSION ICE MACHINE invented by **Thaddeus Lowe** (1832–1913), who made first artificial ice in U.S., and in 1873 invented carbureted water-gas process.

1865–75. WEB PRINTING PRESS (using a web or role of paper) invented by **William A. Bullock** (1813–63). **Rotary press** (printing on both sides of a sheet at the same time) attributed to Andrew Campbell and Stephen D. Tucker (1875).

1868–72. AIR BRAKE patented by **George Westinghouse** (p. 1180); improved, 1872.

1869–99. CARPET SWEEPERS AND VACUUM CLEANERS. Suction-type vacuum cleaner patented by I. W. McGaffey (1869). Melville R. Bissell invented practical carpet sweeper (1876). First motor-driven vacuum cleaner patented by John Thurman (1899).

1869. ELECTRIC VOTING MACHINE invented by **Thomas A. Edison**

(p. 1021). First voting machine authorized for use, 1892.

1870–78. MOTION PICTURES: PIONEER STAGE. Experiments in depicting motion followed invention of zoetrope (designed in France, 1860), a series of pictures whirled on a drum to give effect of motion. Applying similar principle to magic lantern, Henry R. Heyl showed projected animated pictures (1870). Eadweard J. Muybridge set up a series of coordinated cameras to take successive photographs of a horse in motion (1878).

1871–74. TRANSPORTATION. Andrew S. Hallidie (1836–1900) invented cable streetcar (1871; in use in San Francisco, 1873). First electrically powered streetcar invented by **Stephen Dudley Field** successfully run in New York City, 1874. Railroad coupler patented by **Eli H. Janney** (1831–1912).

1872. CELLULOID. Commercial production developed by **John W. Hyatt** (1837–1920).

1872–85. CACULATING MACHINES. Edmund D. Barbour invented adding machine with printed totals and subtotals (1872). **Dorr Eugene Felt** (1862–1930) made first accurate comptometer (1884). First successful recording adding machine (1888) by **William S. Burroughs** (1857–1898).

1874. BARBED WIRE (p. 614).

1875–81. DYNAMOS. William A. Anthony (1835–1908) constructed first dynamo for outdoor lighting (1875, at Cornell Univ.); C. F. Brush (1876). Edison Machine Works constructed first successfully operating dynamo (27 tons, 1881).

1876–84. TELEPHONE invented by **Alexander Graham Bell** (p. 982) prior to 14 Feb. 1876; patent granted, 7 Mar.; first distinguishable conversation, 10 Mar.; outdoor transmission, 9 Oct.; first private home installation, 1877; New York to Boston, 1884.

1877–95. DISCOVERIES BY NIKOLA TESLA (p. 1168). Telsa dis-covered the principle of the rotary magnetic field, applying it in a practical form to the induction motor and making possible the alternating current motor and the transmission of power by such current, employing what became known as 2-phase, 3-phase, multiphase, and polyphase systems, particularly on long distance lines (later used extensively). Also p. 1168. Edison system of central power production introduced (1882) at New York City.

1878–83. ELECTRIC LIGHTING. Practical application of electric arc lamps (Philadelphia, 1878; Cleveland, 1879). Although Moses Gerrish of Salem had built an incandescent lamp as early as 1859, **Thomas A. Edison** invented the first practical incandescent bulb (1879); established factory (1880).

1878–1948. PHONOGRAPH patented by **Edison** (1878); practical machine made by firm of Bell and Tainter (1886). Electronic phonograph introduced 1924 by Western Electric Co., manufactured 1927 by RCA; 33⅓ rpm. microgroove record invented by Dr. Peter C. Goldmark, marketed 1948.

1879. CASH REGISTER patented by **James Ritty** (4 Nov.).

1880–88. CAMERA ADVANCES. George Eastman (p. 1020) patented first successful roll film (1880); perfected first "Kodak" hand camera (1888), resulting in popularization of photography.

1880–1931. RAZORS. Safety razor developed by Kampfe Bros., New York. First modern type with throwaway blades invented (1895) by **King C. Gillette** (1855–1932). Jacob Shick patented electric dry shaver 1928; marketed, 1931.

1882–1910. ELECTRIC APPLIANCES. Electric fan invented by **Schuyler Skaats Wheeler** (1860–1923). Patents granted for electric flatiron (1882, Henry W. Seely), electric stove (1896, William S. Hadaway), separable electric attachment plug (1904, Harvey Hubbell). Electric sewing machine developed

(Singer Mfg. Co., 1889). Completely self-contained electric washing machine developed (1907, Hurling Machine Co.).

1884. FOUNTAIN PEN perfected by **Lewis E. Waterman** (1837–1901).

1884–89. LINOTYPE MACHINE invented by **Ottmar Mergenthaler** (p. 1102); used commercially, 1886. **Monotype** machine patented 1887 by **Tolbert Lanston** (1844–1913).

1886. ELECTRIC WELDING MACHINE patented by **Elihu Thomson** (1853–1937), widely applied in auto industry and as a substitute for riveting in construction work; also patented cream separator, 1881.

Electrolytic process of refining aluminum discovered by **Charles Martin Hall** (1863–1914).

1890. PNEUMATIC HAMMER patented by Charles B. King.

1891. CARBORUNDUM (abrasive) discovered by **Edward G. Acheson** (1856–1931).

1893–1923. AUTOMOBILE. First successful U.S. gasoline-powered car, built by the brothers **Charles E.** (1862–1938) and **J. Frank Duryea** (1870–1967), was operated by the latter in its initial run (Springfield, Mass., 21 Sept., 1893). George B. Selden, of Rochester, N.Y., applied (1879) for first gasoline auto patent; granted 1895. Patent issued (1902) to Packard Motor Car Co. for "H" slot gearshift (sliding gear transmission); soon became standard on most American automobiles. Steering knuckle invented (1902) by Sterling Elliott; by allowing both front wheels to turn while axle remains stationary, it introduced steering wheel principle and led to replacement of tiller. Pneumatic tire (1892) followed by clincher-type tire (1899), standard quick-demountable tire rims (1904), the nonskid tire (1908), the cord tire (1910), and the balloon tire (1922). Automatic lubrication (1904); front bumpers (1906); first V-8 engine in production model

(1907 Hewitt, made by Hewitt Motor Co., N.Y.C.); left-hand steering (1908). Electric self-starter developed (1911) by **Charles F. Kettering** (p. 1076), introduced in 1912 Cadillac. All-steel automobile body (1912) by Edward G. Budd; 4-wheel hydraulic brakes (1918) by Malcolm Loughead (later Lockheed). Introduction of ethyl gasoline, 1923, developed by Thomas Midgley, Jr., and Charles F. Kettering.

1893–1953. MOTION PICTURES. Invention of photographic gun (E. J. Marey, France) and development of celluloid film (introduced by John Carbutt, 1883) led to invention of Edison's Kinetoscope (peepshow, 1893), which, employing a continuous roll of film, could be viewed by but one person at a time. Woodville Latham demonstrated the Pantoptiken (1895), a combination of the Kinetoscope with magic-lantern projection (simultaneously with the Cinematographe by the Lumières in France, the best projector at that time). **C. Francis Jenkins** (1867–1934) perfected the phantascope, modification of Edison's Kinetoscope, and with Thomas Armat demonstrated the Vitascope (1896), prototype of the modern motion picture projector. Cameraphone, first sound moving picture, developed by Edison, 1904. For later developments see p. 885. For wide screen processes see p. 891.

1896–1913. AIRPLANE. Orville and Wilbur Wright (p. 1189) made first heavier-than-air flight at Kitty Hawk, N.C., 17 Dec. 1903; previously, 8 Dec., Samuel P. Langley had made an unsuccessful attempt in a power-driven airplane. First American monoplane invented by Henry W. Walden (1909). **Gyroscope** stabilizer by **Elmer A. Sperry** (1860–1930) demonstrated on an airplane (1913), foreshadowing later instrument developments.

1897–1912. DIESEL ENGINES. Adolphus Busch (1839–1913) bought Diesel rights for the U.S. (1897); built first engine (1898); applied to submarine (1912, Vickers 4-cylinder).

1901. MERCURY VAPOR LAMP patented by **Peter C. Hewitt** (1861–1921).

1901–24. RADIO. Early American experiments in wireless communication were conducted (1866) by Dr. Mahlon Loomis (1826–86), Prof. Amos Dolbear (patent for "induction" system of wireless telegraphy, 1866), and Nathan B. Stubblefield (1892). Predicted by James Maxwell (1865), major research was undertaken abroad (Marconi, Fleming) until **Reginald A. Fessenden** (1866–1932) superimposed voice on continuous wave (1901). His improved transmitter, demonstrated 24 Dec. and 31 Dec. 1906 at Brant Rock, Mass., was heard by ships as far away as the West Indies. **Lee De Forest** (p. 1011) invented the 3-element vacuum tube (1906, triode amplifier) and applied the microphone (ordinary telephone-type mouthpiece, 1907) to broadcasting. **Irving Langmuir** (p. 1080) and associates developed the high vacuum tube for the General Electric Co. (1912–14). For **Edwin H. Armstrong's** regenerative circuit, 1912, and superheterodyne circuit, 1918, see p. 975. **Ernst F. W. Alexanderson's** (p. 974) high frequency alternator (1917), patented by General Electric, was supplanted by shortwave broadcasting, pioneered at Westinghouse and GE, 1923–24.

1902–10. SYNTHETICS AND PLASTICS. Rayon (cellulose ester) patented (1902) by **Arthur D. Little** (1863–1935), with William H. Walker and Harry S. York; same group patented artificial silk (1902). First commercial production by American Viscose Co. (1910). **Leo H. Baekeland** (p. 978) patented thermosetting plastic, 1909 (Bakelite).

1911. GYROCOMPASS patented by Elmer A. Sperry (another pat. abroad by Anchütz-Kämpfe, 1908), who also perfected the gyroscope (invented by Foucault, 1852) and invented the automatic steersman.

1913. X RAY. Development by William D. Coolidge of new X-ray tube capable of sustained operation at 140,000 volts (later designed for 200,000 volts) revolutionized making of radiographs.

CRACKING PROCESS for gasoline patented by **William M. Burton.**

1914–26. EARLY ROCKETS. Robert H. Goddard (p. 1041) patented liquid fuel rocket (1914), using liquid ether and oxygen; demonstrated lifting force of rockets (1920); directed first rocket flight (1926).

1916. THOMPSON SUBMACHINE GUN invented by **John T. Thompson** (1860–1940). **National Research Council** organized 20 Sept. 1916 to promote wartime research; perpetuated by order of President Wilson 11 May 1918 to stimulate scientific research, programs, and information.

1918–52. HELICOPTER. First to rise successfully from ground built by Peter C. Hewitt and F. B. Crocker (1918). Developments in U.S. largely due to **Igor Sikorsky** (1889–1972), who arrived in U.S. in 1918. Improved product (VS-300) produced by Vought-Sikorsky Aircraft (1939).

1922. TECHNICOLOR process successfully developed by **Herbert T. Kalmus** (1881–1963).

1922–26. TELEPHOTO. C. Francis Jenkins sent photos over telephone wires; transcontinental photo (1925); transatlantic service (1926).

1922–46. RADAR. Based on studies of Hertz (1888), radio detection was first developed by **Albert H. Taylor** (1879–1961) and **Leo C. Young** (1922) for the U.S. Navy. True radar detection, using pulse-ranging technic, employed by **Gregory Breit** (1899–) and **Merle A. Tuve** (1901–) for ionospheric research (c.1926), and for naval detection by

Taylor and Young (1930). Radar system developed by Naval Research Laboratory (1934–39) and U.S. Army Signal Corps (1936–38). By 1935 Great Britain had 5 radar detector stations in operation. Research accelerated under National Defense Research Committee (from July 1940). During World War II radar was employed both to direct artillery fire and to detect enemy submarines and aircraft. Radar signals sent to the moon and reflected back (from Belmar, N.J., 10 Jan. 1946).

1923–51. TELEVISION. Background work on television largely European (Senlecq, France; Nipkow and Braun, Germany; Rosing, Russia; Swinton, England) until **Vladimir Zworykin** (p. 1191) demonstrated for Westinghouse executives a partly electronic television system (Dec. 1923). In 1925 Zworykin invented the iconoscope, basis of the electronic television camera, and **C. Francis Jenkins** demonstrated television with the Nipkow system (1925). Philo Farnsworth patented dissector tube (1927). First transmission of television, New York City to Washington, D.C. (1927) by American Telephone and Telegraph. First televised drama (11 Sept. 1928), "The Queen's Messenger," the result of experiments of Ernst F. W. Alexanderson at Westinghouse. Radio Corp. of America demonstrated electronic transmission (using iconoscope and cathode ray tube, 1933). **Peter C. Goldmark** (1906–77) of Columbia Broadcasting System (CBS) demonstrated "sequential method" of **color television** (1940). CBS and RCA evolved independent systems by 1949. Hearings by FCC (1949–50) found CBS sytem sufficiently advanced to permit general transmission; production curtailed in interest of national defense (1951).

1926–57. AUTOMOBILE. Hypoid gears, introduced by Packard, 1926, facilitated design of lower-slung bodies. Carl Breer, Chrysler Corp., began work, 1927, on "Airflow" streamlined body design (introduced 1933–34). Aerocar (1929), first production-type house trailer. Free-wheeling, introduced by Studebaker, 1930, widely adopted for its gasoline economy, but subsequently abandoned after a number of states prohibited it as a safety hazard. Synchronized transmission, developed by Earl A. Thompson, offered by Oldsmobile, 1931. Independent front-wheel suspension (1939); tubeless tires introduced by Goodrich, 1948; puncture-sealing tires, 1950. High-compression V-8 engine (1949). Hardtop convertible introduced by Buick, 1949. Power steering, 1951. Improved sealed-beam headlamps became standard equipment, 1954–55; dual headlamps, introduced by Cadillac, 1954, became standard equipment in 1957–58. Seatbelts and padded dashboards first offered as optional equipment, by Ford (1955–56).

1927. MECHANICAL COTTON PICKER invented by **John Daniel Rust** (1892–1959) and **Mack Donald Rust** (1900–1966).

1928–34. AUTOGIRO first brought to U.S. from England (1928) by Harold F. Pitcairn; manufactured with closed cabin (1931) and applied to military uses (1934).

1930–31. TRACTORS. Diesel engine tractor manufactured (steam tractor, 1886; gasoline, 1892). Caterpillar tractor developed (1931).

1932. POLAROID GLASS invented by **Edwin H. Land** (p. 1080); polaroid camera 1947.

PARKING METER patented by Carl C. Magee.

1934. RAILROAD DEVELOPMENTS. First streamlined high-speed train (2 Mar.), followed by all-steel Diesel-motored train (11 Nov.) and streamlined steam locomotive (14 Dec.).

1934–39. FREQUENCY MODULA-TION. Early experiments by **Edwin H. Armstrong** (p. 975) led to patents (1933), public demonstration (Nov. 1935). Experimental 50,000-watt station W₂XMN built by Armstrong at Alpine, N.J. reached full power operation in 1939, and first regularly scheduled FM broadcast occurred 18 July 1939. Commercial operation of FM authorized by FCC, May 1940.

23 May. NYLON. Wallace H. Carothers synthesized a superpolymer; marketed (1938) by Du Pont as nylon.

1935. SPECTROPHOTOMETER patented by **Arthur C. Hardy** (1895–).

1935–39. SYNTHETICS. Casein fiber developed by **Earl O. Whittier** (1891–) and **Stephen P. Gould** (1897–1939); patented, 1938. **Nylon:** commercial production begun (toothbrush bristles, Du Pont, 1938; followed by nylon yarn, 1939). **Fiberglas** technics patented (1938) by **Games Slayter** (1896–1964) and John H. Thomas.

1940. XEROGRAPHY ("dry writing") patented by its inventor, **Chester F. Carlson** (p. 997), who developed this widely used duplicating process with the assistance of Roland M. Schaffert, a research physicist at the Batelle Memorial Institute. Utilizing electrostatics and photoconductivity, xerography produces an image by heat-fusing powder particles in the charged areas of a sensitized paper. In 1947 the Haloid Corp., Rochester, N.Y., was licensed to develop xerography commercially; it subsequently became the Xerox Corp., makers of the Xerox mechanized office copying machine. The first Xerox automatic copier was introduced in 1959. Xerography using different processes has also been developed by other companies.

1942–45. ROCKETS IN WORLD WAR II. "Bazooka," first U.S. rocket gun, developed by Capt. L. A. Skinner and C. N. Hickman; standardized, 1942.

Germans first used V-1, 250–400-mph pilotless aircraft, 12 June 1944, 6 days after D-Day; shot down by Allied gunners aided by radar, M-9 director, and proximity fuse. V-2 (long-range rocket, 3,400 mph) first struck London on 12 Sept. 1944. Rocket and guided-missile experiments pushed in postwar period. U.S. navy guided missiles reported used in combat in Korea (1 Sept. 1952).

1942–60. JET PLANES. Jet engine first produced by British inventor, Frank Whittle, 1937. Jets first tested in U.S., 1942. In June 1944 a Lockheed P-80 with jet motor flew over 500 mph. Jet-propelled fighters were ordered by U.S. air force (1947); bombers developed (1947). By 1952, U.S. had developed B-52 bomber, with 8 turbojet engines, ceiling 50,000 ft., speed c.600 mph.; B-47, c.700 mph. B-70 supersonic heavy bomber (designed for speeds exceeding 2,000 mph) program drastically restricted by government 1 Dec. 1959. Bell X-2 rocket-powered research airplane set speed record in excess of 2,100 mph (1956); North American X-15 rocket plane made first successful flight under own power 17 Sept. 1959. Commercial jet transport initiated 15 Aug. 1958 with Boeing 707 (transatlantic service by Pan American Airways, 26 Oct. 1958), followed by Douglas DC-8 (1959), and Convair 880 (TWA, 1961).

1944–51. ELECTRONIC DIGITAL COMPUTER. The "Automatic Sequence Controlled Calculator," known also as the Harvard Mark I, was built (1939–44) and operated at Harvard by the International Business Machines Corp. It was conceived principally by **Howard H. Aiken,** who in 1937, while a graduate student in physics at Harvard, distinguished between punched-card accounting machinery and the computer as required in scientific work, pointing out that the computer must be able to handle positive and negative numbers, use various mathematical functions, perform calculations in the natural sequence of mathematical events, and be completely automatic in operation. The Harvard Mark I was an electromechanical computer with external storage. Eight ft. high and 51 ft. long, it was slow and cumbersome by later standards, and, although not a true electronic computer, was nevertheless the pioneer information-processing device of the computer age. It could multiply two 11-place numbers at 3-second intervals. **1940–46. ENIAC** (Electronic Numerical Integrator and Computer), the first truly automatic electronic computer, was based mainly on the work of Dr. John Mauchly and Dr. John Presper Eckert, Jr., both of the Moore School of Electrical Engineering at the Univ. of Pennsylvania. Although large in size (ENIAC contained 18,000 vacuum tubes), its internal storage represented an important advance. It could multiply two 10-decimal numbers in less than three-thousandths of a second, and could complete 5,000 additions a second. **28 June 1946–16 August 1948.** Series of papers, "Preliminary Discussion of the Logical Design of an Electronic Computing Instrument," a report by **John L. von Neumann** (p. 1174), Herman H. Goldstine (1913–), and Arthur W. Burks (1915–), was the result of a project initiated by von Neumann in 1945 at the Institute for Advanced Study, Princeton, N.J., "to develop and construct a fully automatic, digital, all-purpose electronic calculating machine" controlled by orders formulated in a binary digital code and handling a wide range of problems at extremely high speeds. This landmark report became fundamental to the theory of computer logic and design; its conceptualization of stored programs and conditional transfer were later embodied in computer hardware. **1951. UNIVAC** (Universal Automatic Computer), a stored program computer made by the Eckert-Mauchly Corp. (later absorbed by the present Sperry Rand), was installed at the Bureau of the Census. The state of the art was subsequently improved by printed circuits, magnetic drums and magnetic-core storage, and the replacement of radio tubes by transistors. Miniaturized components made it possible to reduce the size of computers while increasing their information-handling capability.

1945–60. ATOMIC AND NUCLEAR DEVELOPMENTS. Atomic bomb completed and exploded (16 July 1945, p. 452). For **cyclotron,** see p. 1081; **cosmotron,** p. 787. First **atomic-powered submarine, U.S.S.** *Nautilus,* commissioned 30 Sept. 1954, made first undersea crossing of the North Pole (5 Aug. 1958), submerging near Point Barrow, Alas., 1 Aug. and sailing under 50-ft.-thick icecap for 96 hours before surfacing. Six days later submarine **Skate** covered same route from east to west. On 6 Oct. **Seawolf** surfaced after remaining submerged 60 days. Atomic-powered submarines were equipped (1960) with **Polaris** missiles, with nuclear warheads and range of 1,200 nautical miles. **Atomic-power projects,** p. 731. Controlled thermonuclear reaction created in Univ. of California laboratories, 3 Nov. 1960.

1948. TRANSISTOR invented at Bell Telephone Laboratories by Walter Brattain, John Bardeen, and William Shockley (p. 1151)—awarded Nobel prize in physics, 1956.

1954. SOLAR BATTERY developed by 2 different laboratories—Bell Telephone and the Air Research and Development Command, Baltimore, Md.

1955, 18 MAY. NUCLEAR REACTOR patent issued to **Enrico Fermi** (p. 1027) and **Leo Szilard.**

4 OCT. 1957. DAWN OF THE SPACE AGE. The world's first artificial satellite (Sputnik I) was launched as part of the Soviet participation in the International Geophysical Year 1957–58. On 3 Nov. a second artificial satellite (Sputnik II), carrying a dog, was launched. Sputnik III, a 2,925-lb. satellite, was launched 15 May 1958. In 1959 the U.S.S.R. launched 3 cosmic rockets: Lunik I, 2 Jan., reported 3 Jan. to have gone into permanent orbit around the sun as "first artificial planet"; Lunik II, 12 Sept., making contact with the moon 14 Sept.; and Lunik III, 4 Oct., which circled the moon. A photograph of the hidden side of the moon was released 27 Oct. Sputnik IV was launched 15 May 1960, and space ships 14 May, 1 Dec.

1958–60. U.S. SATELLITE, ROCKET, AND MISSILE EFFORT. The first U.S. artificial earth satellite (Explorer I) was placed in orbit by a modified Jupiter-C rocket, 31 Jan. 1958, followed 17 Mar. by the orbiting of a 3¼-lb. navy satellite (Vanguard I), and 26 Mar. by a 3¼-lb. satellite (Explorer III). On 11 Oct. an air force Pioneer rocket failed to go into orbit around the moon but achieved a penetration of 79,-173 statute miles into space. On 28 Nov. an Atlas intercontinental ballistic missile was successfully test-fired for a distance of 6,325 miles. On 18 Dec. an Atlas missile weighing c.8,700 lbs. was placed in orbit around the earth. In 1959 space exploration was achieved by Vanguard II (17 Feb.), Vanguard III (18 Sept.), Discoverer I (28 Feb.), and other Discoverer satellites (13 Apr., 13 Aug., 19 Aug., 7 Nov.).

1960–67. NONMANNED SPACE ACHIEVEMENTS include: (1) space probes taking photographs and performing other experiments (p. 790); (2) camera-bearing weather satellites: Tiros 1, Tiros 2 (1 Apr., 23 Nov. 1960), Nimbus 1 (28 Aug. 1964), Tiros 9 (22 Jan. 1965), Essa 1 (3 Feb. 1966), Essa 2 (28 Feb. 1966), replaced by Essa 3 (launched 2 Oct. 1966 in sun synchro-nous polar orbit); (3) orbiting Solar Observatory (3 Mar. 1962); (4) communications satellites: Telstar 1, Telstar 2 (7 May 1963); Syncom (26 July 1963), stationary above the earth; Early Bird (6 Apr. 1965); Lanibird (11 Jan. 1967), launched by International Telecommunications Satellite Consortium; (5) Biosatellite 2 (7–8 Sept. 1967), studying the effect of weightlessness on various kinds of activities under controlled laboratory conditions, discovered that seedlings grew faster in space.

1961–74. U.S. MANNED SPACE FLIGHTS: 5 May 1961, U.S. Navy Cmdr. Alan B. Shepard, Jr.; 21 July, Capt. Virgil I. Grissom; 20 Feb. 1962, Lt. Col. John H. Glenn, Jr. (3 orbits); 24 May, Lt. Cmdr. M. Scott Carpenter (3 orbits); 3 Oct., Cmdr. Walter M. Schirra, Jr. (6 orbits); 15 May 1963, Maj. L. Gordon Cooper (22 orbits).

Gemini Series, launched by Titan 2 rocket. Gemini 3 (23 Mar. 1965, Virgil I. Grissom and John W. Young; 3 orbits) showed spacecraft could be maneuvered for docking purposes. Gemini 4 (3–7 June 1965, James A. McDivitt and Edward H. White 2d; 62 orbits) marked by 20 minute space walk of White. Gemini 5 (21–29 Aug. 1965, L. Gordon Cooper, Jr., and Charles Conrad; 120 orbits) 8 days in orbit, displayed ability of astronauts to endure; apogee of 219 miles. Gemini 6A (15–16 Dec. 1965, Walter M. Schirra, Jr., and Thomas P. Stafford; 16 orbits) rendezvoused with Gemini 7 (4–18 Dec., Frank Borman and James A. Lovell, Jr.; 206 orbits). Gemini 8 (16–17 Mar. 1966, Neil A. Armstrong and David R. Scott; 6.5 orbits) achieved the docking of 2 vehicles in space. Gemini 9A (3–6 June 1966, Thomas A. Stafford and Eugene A. Cernan; 44 orbits) featured 2-hour 9-minute walk in space. Gemini 10 (18–21 July 1966, John W. Young and Michael Collins; 43 orbits) rendezvous with 2 targets. Gemini 11 (12–15 Sept. 1966, Charles Conrad, Jr., and Richard F. Gordon, Jr.; 44 orbits) record apogee of 851 miles. Gemini 12 (11–15 Nov. 1966, James A. Lovell, Jr., and Edwin E. Aldrin, Jr.; 59 orbits) photographs of 7 second total solar eclipse.

Apollo Program. Saturn 5 rocket and Apollo capsule. Crew of Apollo 1, Virgil I. Grissom, Edward H. White, and Roger Chaffee killed when a flash fire swept their craft, Cape Kennedy (27 Jan. 1967). First flight test of Saturn 5 rocket (9 Nov. 1967). Apollo 7 (11–22 Oct. 1968, Walter M. Schirra, Jr., Donn F. Eisele, R. Walter Cunningham; 163 orbits); Apollo 8 (21–27 Dec. 1968, Frank Borman, James A. Lovell, Jr., William A. Anders; orbiting of moon 10 times), "vast, lonely and forbidding sight"; live telecast from lunar orbit, Christmas Eve, 69.8 miles above moon. Apollo 9 (3–13 Mar. 1969, James A. McDivitt, David R. Scott, Russell L. Schweickart; 151 orbits) included test flight of the lunar module.

U.S. (13 Mar. 1969) led the U.S.S.R. in manned flights, 19 to 12; in moon orbital flights, 1 to 0; manned hours in space, 3,938 to 868; space "walks," 10 to 3; rendezvous missions, 8 to 3; space link-ups, 9 to 1.

Moon Landings. On 18 May astronauts Thomas P. Stafford, Eugene A. Cernan, and John W. Young descended in Apollo 10 to within 9 miles of the moon. Climaxing 8 years of manned space flight competition between the U.S. and the Soviet Union, U.S. astronauts Neil A. Armstrong and Col. Edwin E. Aldrin, Jr., taking off 16 July in Apollo 11, touched down on the moon with their lunar module. Armstrong's first step on the moon was taken 20 July at 10:56:20 AM, EDT. After taking rock and soil specimens, the pair successfully rendezvoused with Lieut. Col. Michael Collins, navigator of the Apollo craft,

and splashed down 950 miles S.W. of Hawaii, 24 July. Apollo 12 was launched 14 Nov.; Cmdrs. Charles Conrad, Jr., and Alan L. Bean in lunar module *Intrepid* landed on moon, 500 feet from Surveyor 3 spacecraft, 19 Nov., 1:54 AM, EST. After 31½ hours on lunar surface (2 moon walks), and 3 hours 20 minutes later, the *Intrepid* docked with command ship *Yankee Clipper*, Cmdr. Richard F. Gordon, Jr., pilot, at 12:45 PM, EST, 20 Nov. Splashdown in Pacific: 24 Nov., 3:58 PM, EST, 1,950 miles S.W. of Hawaii, less than 3 miles from target. Apollo 13, launched 11 Apr. 1970, was aborted 13 Apr. Apollo 14 launched from Cape Kennedy 31 Jan. 1971 at 6:30 PM EST, with astronauts Navy Capt. Alan B. Shepard, Jr., Navy Cmdr. Edgar D. Mitchell, and Air Force Maj. Stuart A. Roosa. It went into lunar orbit 4 Feb. In their lunar module *Antares*, Shepard and Mitchell landed on the target site at Fra Mauro, and remained on the surface of the moon for 33½ hours. They made 2 surface excursions lasting a total of some 9 hours, using a 2-wheeled cart, cameras, a magnetometer, hand tools, and a sample bag in which they collected corings and 97 pounds of rocks. The mission returned to earth at 1:37 PM EST on 9 Feb. Apollo 15 launched from Cape Kennedy 26 July 1971 at 9:34 AM EDT. Maj. Alfred M. Worden was at the controls of the command module *Endeavour* and Col. David R. Scott and Lt. Col. James B. Irwin, Jr., were in the lunar module *Falcon*. The target area was Hadley Rille, a deep canyon in the Apennine Mts., 465 miles north of the lunar equator. An innovation on this mission was the Lunar Rover, a 2-man, 4-wheeled, battery-operated vehicle which the astronauts used for exploring the surface for a distance of several miles from the touchdown area. In their 3 surface excursions, accounting for 21 of the 57 hours they spent on the moon, the crew covered more terrain than in any previous manned mission, making this the most productive of the Apollo flights. They obtained valuable data with special equipment that included an X-ray spectrometer, a gamma-ray spectrometer, and a TV color camera. The mission returned to earth at 4:46 PM EDT on 7 Aug. Apollo 16 launched from Cape Kennedy 16 Apr. 1972 at 12:54 PM EDT, with Cmdr. Thomas K. Mattingly 2d in the command module. Astronauts Capt. John W. Young and Lt. Col. Charles M. Drake, in the lunar module *Orion,* reached a landing site 45 miles north of the Descartes Crater on the Kant Plateau in the central lunar highlands. In 3 surface excursions lasting a total of 20 hours 14 minutes, they used an electric-powered Lunar Roving Vehicle to gather rock and soil samples that provided important data concerning the age and composition of the moon's surface. The astronauts spent about 71 hours on the moon, brought back 214 pounds of rocks, and returned to earth at 2:45 PM EST on 27 April. Apollo 17, launched from Cape Kennedy 7 Dec. 1972 at 12:33 AM EST, carried astronauts Capt. Eugene A. Cernan, Cmdr. Ronald E. Evans, and the civilian geologist Dr. Harrison H. Schmitt, the first scientist to journey to the moon. With Evans aboard the command module *America,* Cernan and Schmitt landed the lunar module *Challenger* in the Taurus-Littrow Valley, an area ringed by high mountains southeast of the Sea of Serenity. In 2 explorations that lasted a total of 7 hours 49 minutes, the astronauts used a 2-wheeled Lunar Rover with a wide array of equipment to gather data on geological formations, surface radiation, lunar gas, and gravity waves, and returned with a collection of rocks and soil samples. The discovery of soil containing iron oxide was especially significant, for it suggested that the moon's interior occasionally produced

water and gases. The astronauts returned to earth on 19 Dec. at 2:24 PM EST. Apollo 17, the 6th successful manned lunar mission by the U.S., concluded the $25 billion Project Apollo. President Richard M. Nixon announced (14 Dec.): "This may be the last time in this century that men will walk on the moon." Cernan was the 11th astronaut to walk on the moon, and Schmitt the 12th.

Skylab Program. The first U.S. space station project, Skylab cost $2.6 billion and was designed to test man's ability to live and work effectively in outer space for prolonged periods under conditions of weightlessness. The project consisted of 3 successive missions, each manned by a different crew of astronauts. **Skylab 1.** The 85-ton Skylab, an orbiting space laboratory and workshop, was launched from Cape Canaveral (formerly Cape Kennedy), Fla., on 14 May 1973 at 1:30 PM EDT. One minute and 3 seconds after its unmanned liftoff, Skylab was damaged. The loss of the micrometeoroid and thermal shielding caused overheating, and the jammed solar-power wings threatened loss of half of the space station's power capacity. On 25 May, at 9 AM EDT, 3 astronauts were launched in an Apollo spacecraft from Cape Canaveral, carrying 400 pounds of tools, heat-shielding devices, and other materials. Locking their spacecraft with Skylab, the astronauts made emergency repairs that cooled the interior of Skylab and salvaged the station. The crew members were Capt. Charles Conrad, Jr.; Cmdr. Joseph P. Kerwin, the first American M.D. to make a space flight; and Cmdr. Paul Weitz, an aeronautical engineering expert. The Skylab astronauts spent an unprecedented 28 days and 50 minutes in space, making 395 trips around the earth, performing scientific experiments, and taking 16,000 photographs of the earth and 30,000 solar telescope pictures of the sun. The 3 astronauts returned to earth in the Apollo spacecraft at 9:50 AM EDT on 22 June. **Skylab 2.** This mission was launched in an Apollo spaceship from Cape Canaveral at 7:11 AM EDT on 28 July 1973, bearing aloft astronauts Capt. Alan L. Bean, Maj. Jack R. Lousma, and Dr. Owen K. Garriott, a civilian solar physicist. Despite technical difficulties in their Apollo module, and severe motion sickness at the outset, the astronauts successfully completed their mission, spending a record 59 days and 11 hours in space, making 859 trips around the earth, and covering a total of 24 million miles. One of their accomplishments was a record 6 hour 31 minute space walk (6 Aug.). The Apollo spacecraft returned to earth on 25 Sept. at 6:20 PM EDT with a vast amount of scientific information, including 16,800 pictures and 18 miles of magnetic tape data on observations of the earth, 77,600 solar telescope photos of the sun's corona, samples of metals welded and shaped

in space, and biomedical specimens whose analysis promised to advance the knowledge of changes attributable to sustained exposure to weightlessness. **Skylab 3.** The final mission was launched in an Apollo spacecraft from Cape Canaveral at 9:01 AM EST on 16 Nov. 1973, carrying astronauts Lieut. Col. Gerald P. Carr, Lieut. Col. William R. Pogue, and Dr. Edward G. Gibson, a civilian scientist specializing in plasma physics. The longest manned space flight, it lasted 84 days; in addition to providing further information on the physiological and psychological adjustments required for protracted confinement to a space vehicle, the mission made observations and photographs of the comet Kohoutek. The astronauts returned to earth on 8 Feb. 1974 at 11:17 AM EDT.

1975–81. U.S. SPACE PROGRAM (p. 548).

1979. 28 MAR. THREE MILE ISLAND NUCLEAR REACTOR ACCIDENT (p. 561).

Medicine and Public Health

Epidemiology was the major concern of public health authorities in both the colonial and Revolutionary War years, with the decision to introduce smallpox inoculation truly a turning point in public health in that era. Prior to the introduction of medical education in some of the colleges in the late colonial period, physicians attained their education abroad, notably at Edinburgh, or by apprenticeship. In the nineteenth century American medical science kept abreast of European developments, and in the case of anesthesia and puerperal fever initiated important experiments and discoveries.

Since World War II vast advances in medical education, public health, vitamin research, chemotherapy, open heart surgery, and electronic devices for detection and diagnosis propelled the U.S. to the front rank in the fields of medicine and public health. As epidemic diseases declined in importance (notably with the recent development of vaccines for polio and measles) the principal areas of medical research came to be devoted to detecting the cause and treatment of cancer and circulatory diseases and in finding a cure for narcotics addiction. Birth control and abortion involved the medical profession in new ethical and moral issues, while spiraling medical costs posed the necessity of national health care, the need for paramedical training to supplement a shortage of physicians and hospital personnel, and raised the possibility of a complete transformation in the traditional goals of the profession.

1618–1776. EARLY EPIDEMICS. Smallpox: 1618–19, Mass. Indians, probably; 1631, 1635, 1638, 1648–49, 1666, N.E.; 1667, 1679–80, Va.; 1677–78, N.E.; 1689–90, Canada, N.E., N.Y.; 1696, Jamestown, Va.; 1702–03, 1721, Boston (over 50% infected, 1 in 7 deaths); 1730–31, Boston, N.Y., Phila.; 1737–38, N.E., Va., S.C.; 1746–47, Middle Colonies; 1751–52, Boston; 1756–57, Phila., Annapolis; 1758, N.Y.; 1759–60, Indians in S.C. and Ga.; 1760–61, 1764, N.E.; 1765, Md.; 1768, Reading, Pa. and Va.; 1774–76, throughout colonies. **Diphtheria:** 1659, N.E.; 1686, Va.; 1724, S.C.; 1735, N.H.; 1736–40, 1744–45, N.E., N.Y.; 1750–51, S.C.; 1754–55, N.E., N.Y.; 1763, Phila.; 1765, Boston; 1769, N.Y. **Scarlet fever:** 1702, 1735–36, Boston, Newport; 1764, Phila., N.C., S.C. **Measles:** 1657, Boston; 1687–88, N.E.; 1713–15, N.E. to Pa.; 1717, Va.; 1747–48, Conn., N.Y., Pa.; 1759, S.C., 1772–73, colonies generally. **Influenza:** 1647, N.E.; 1688, Va.; 1697–98, N.E.; 1722–23, colonies generally; 1756–57, 1761, 1767, 1770–72. **Pneumonia:** 1753–54, Mass. **Malaria:** 1658, 1668, 1683, N.E.; 1687, Va. Rising incidence in 18th cent., esp. in N.C. and S.C. **Dysentery:** 1669, N.E.; 1715, S.C.; 1731, Middle Colonies; 1751, S.C.; 1756, N.E.; 1757, Phila.; 1769, N.E. **Typhoid fever:** 1607, possibly, Jamestown; 1658, New Amsterdam; 1727, 1734, 1737, Conn. and Mass.; 1734, S.C.; 1741, N.E.; 1746, Albany, N.Y. By 1760 widely prevalent. **Typhus:** 1759, N.C.; 1764, 1766, Md. **Yellow fever:** first reported in Barbados,

1647; first clearly described in Phila., 1699, when it killed one-sixth of population; also Charleston; 1702, N.Y.; 1703, 1728, 1732, 1739, 1740, Charleston; 1741, Phila.; 1745, Charleston; 1747–48, Phila., Charleston; 1762, Phila.

1607–1750. EARLY PHYSICIANS, in addition to company physicians and ships' surgeons, included ministers like Revs. Gershom Bulkeley and Jared Eliot (Conn.) and emigrant physicians—**Cadwallader Colden, William Douglass** (c.1691–1752), the elder **John Moultrie** (d.1771), **Alexander Garden** (1730–91). Native physicians in this period received their training through apprenticeship.

1716–66. SMALLPOX INOCULATION (serum from mildly infected human patients) was advocated by **Cotton Mather** through readings of the *Transactions* (1714, 1716) and successfully put into practice (1721) by Dr. **Zabdiel Boylston** (1679–1766) prior to general acceptance in Europe (British royal children inoculated, 1722). Opposition led by **William Douglass** (died in smallpox epidemic, 1752), but practice spread to Philadelphia (1730) and South Carolina (1738). Results reported by Benjamin Gale (Conn.) in *Translations* (1766).

1735. First medical society in colonies founded at Boston.

First work describing lead poisoning from rum distilled with lead pipes published by **Thomas Cadwallader** (1708–79).

1736. First description of scarlet fever in the colonies by William Douglass.

1749–75. EUROPEAN MEDICAL

TRAINING. Starting with **John Moultrie,** the younger (1729–98), Americans began to study abroad, particularly at the Univ. of Edinburgh (41 colonials in period), at private London lectures, and at the universities of Leyden and Paris.

1752. EARLY HOSPITALS. Pesthouses were established at Boston (1717), Philadelphia (1742), Charleston (before 1752), New York (before 1757). A hospital for chronically ill patients was established at Charleston (1738). The first general hospital was established by **Thomas Bond** (1712–84) in Philadelphia (1752). New York Hospital, sponsored by Dr. **Samuel Bard** (1742–1821), was chartered 1771, but not opened until 1791. The first publicly supported mental hospital opened at Williamsburg, Va., 1773.

1754. *Opishotonus and Tetanus* by Lionel Chalmers (d.1777), the most important work on tetanus produced in the course of the century.

1765–68. MEDICAL SCHOOLS. Medical faculty of College of Philadelphia (1765, largely through efforts of **John Morgan** [1725–89] and **William Shippen** [1736–1808] and King's College [1768]).

1775. First surgical textbook written in the colonies by **John Jones** (1729–91), *Remarks on the Treatment of Wounds and Fractures.*

1778. First American pharmacopoeia published by **William Brown** (1748–92).

1783–1810. MEDICAL SCHOOLS. Massachusetts Medical School, 1783. Faculties at Dartmouth (1798), Transylvania (1799), and Yale (1810). College of Medicine (Md.) organized, 1807; associated with Univ. of Maryland, 1812. College of Physicians and Surgeons (1807) joined by the medical faculty of Columbia (1813); reorganized as Medical Department of Columbia (1860).

1786–91. DISPENSARIES. Philadel-phia Dispensary, opened, 1785, by Dr. **Benjamin Rush** (p. 1143); New York Dispensary, 1791.

c.1788–90. SURGERY. Dissection provoked serious rioting in New York City (1788). Dr. **John Jeffries** (1745–1819)—Loyalist physician who made a cross-Channel balloon ascension with François Blanchard, 1785—had his first public lecture on anatomy (on return to Boston, 1789) broken up by a mob.

1793, Aug.–Oct. YELLOW FEVER EPIDEMIC in Philadelphia, worst in history of any U.S. city, led to improvement of urban sanitary conditions and water-supply systems. Croton Aqueduct for New York City's water supply built 1837–42. **Other major epidemics:** cholera (New York City, June–Oct. 1832; South, 1849; Middle West, 1850); smallpox, typhoid fever, typhus (Northern cities, 1865–71); yellow fever, cholera, and smallpox (Southern cities, 1873).

1797–1820. MEDICAL PERIODICALS. *Medical Repository* (quarterly, edited by **Samuel Latham Mitchill** [1764–1831]), followed in this period by 11 journals, including *New England Medical Review and Journal* (1812, now *New England Journal of Medicine*) and *Philadelphia Journal of Medical and Physical Sciences* (1820, now *American Journal of Medical Sciences*).

1800–02. COWPOX VACCINATION introduced by Dr. **Benjamin Waterhouse** (Philadelphia, 1754–1846). Experiment by Boston Board of Health (Oct.–Nov. 1802) proved its efficacy and safety.

1808–20. PHARMACOPOEIAE. Massachusetts Medical Society published first official pharmacopoeia (1808; followed by New York Hospital, 1816). *U.S. Pharmacopoeia* prepared by representatives of state medical societies (1820), first to be nationally accepted.

1808. First work on **naval medicine** in U.S.: **Edward Cutbush's** (1772–1843) *Observations on the Means of Preserving* *the Health of Soldiers and Sailors.*

1809. First **ovariotomy** anywhere in the world performed by **Ephraim McDowell** (1771–1830) at Danville, Ky.

1810–40. MEDICAL EDUCATION. In this period 27 new medical schools were founded in U.S., foreshadowing later overexpansion. Middle Western pioneer was **Daniel Drake** (1785–1852).

1811. John Syng Dorsey (1783–1818) was the first in U.S. to ligate the external iliac artery for inguinal aneurism.

1812. *Diseases of the Mind* by **Benjamin Rush,** a pioneer work on mental disorders, earning for its author the sobriquet, "Father of American Psychiatry."

1817–50. CARE OF THE INSANE. Asylum opened at Frankford, Pa., 1817, and Boston (McLean) and New York (Bloomingdale), 1818, with general adoption by 1850. For work of **Dorothea L. Dix,** see p. 1014.

1829. Publication of first U.S. textbook on pathology, by **William E. Horner** (1793–1853).

1831. CHLOROFORM discovered by **Samuel Guthrie** (1782–1848) simultaneously with, but independently of, von Liebig in Germany and Soubeiran in France. First used as anesthetic in England (1847); popularized in U.S. (1863) by **Gardner Q. Colton** (1814–98).

1833. GASTRIC PHYSIOLOGY. Publication of experiments by **William Beaumont** (p. 982).

1837. Typhus and typhoid fever clinically differentiated by **William W. Gerard** (1809–72).

1839. PATHOLOGY. *Elements of Pathological Anatomy* by **Samuel D. Gross** (1805–84), first comprehensive work on the subject in English; also wrote significantly on intestinal lesions (1843), urinary bladder conditions (1851), respiratory organs (1854), and surgery (1859).

1839–41. DENTISTRY. *American Journal of Dental Science* (1839), College of Dental Surgery (Baltimore, 1840), American Society of Dental Surgeons (1840). Alabama introduced licensing of dentists (1841).

1842–46. ANESTHESIA. Although nitrous oxide (laughing gas) had been discovered by Joseph Priestley (1772) and its effects recognized by Humphry Davy and William Allen (1800), neither it nor ether (whose effects were observed by Faraday, 1818) was used in surgery until William E. Clarke, a medical student, administered ether for a tooth extraction by Dr. Elijah Pope (Rochester, N.Y., Jan. 1842). For the claims of Long, Wells, and Morton, see pp. 1109–1110.

1843. *Contagiousness of Puerperal Fever,* a paper by **Oliver Wendell Holmes** (p. 1058), anticipated Semmelweis in Vienna (1847; the latter's definitive report, 1861).

1844–47. NATIONAL MEDICAL ASSOCIATIONS. Assn. of Medical Superintendents of Amer. Institutions for the Insane (1844; now known as Amer. Psychiatric Assn.). Amer. Medical Assn. founded, 1847. Membership 1974, c.200,000).

1844–85. MEDICAL JOURNALS. *American Journal of Psychiatry,* first (1844) among others; *American Journal of Obstetrics* (1868) considered to be first specialized medical journal; *Annals of Surgery* (1885).

1846. LARYNGOLOGY introduced into the U.S. by **Horace Green** (1802–66) with his *Treatise on Diseases of the Air Passages.* Introduction into U.S. of laryngoscope (1858) by **Ernest Krackowizer** (1821–75) expanded field.

1849. James M. Sims (1813–83) devised original operative treatment of vesicovaginal fistula.

1849–55. WOMEN IN MEDICINE. Elizabeth Blackwell (1821–1910), first woman medical graduate in the world, received M.D. degree from Medical School at Geneva, N.Y. Women's Medical College of Pennsylvania, first school of medicine entirely reserved for women (1850); Woman's Hospital, New York (1855).

1850–54. ADVANCES IN PUBLIC HEALTH. Monumental *Report of Massachusetts Sanitary Commission* by **Lemuel Shattuck** (p. 1149). No action in Massachusetts until 1869 when a Board of Public Health was established; New Orleans, 1855. Daniel Drake's *Systematic Treatise* (1850–54) also aroused interest in subject.

1852. American Pharmaceutical Assn. founded.

1853. PEDIATRICS. Arrival in U.S. of **Abraham Jacobi** (1830–1919) promoted work in the field, as did **Job Lewis Smith** (1827–97) and **Thomas Morgan Rotch** (1849–1914).

1861. Kidney successfully removed by **Erastus B. Wolcott** (1804–80).

1867–68. ADVANCES IN ANESTHESIA. Gas inhaler covering nose and mouth introduced by S. S. White Dental Mfg. Co. (1867). **Edmund Andrews** (1824–1904) introduced use of oxygen with nitrous acid.

1869–72. PUBLIC HEALTH. First state board of health established in Massachusetts (1869). Amer. Public Health Assn. (1872) promoted work in field.

1872. Silas Weir Mitchell (1829–1914), pioneer U.S. neurologist, published his *Injuries of Nerves and their Consequences;* introduced "Weir Mitchell" treatment for certain types of nervous diseases. **Willard Parker** (1800–84) had distinguished (1856) between concussion of nerves and conclusion of nerve centers.

1873. NURSING. Bellevue Hospital (N.Y.) established school of nursing following principles of Florence Nightingale; rapidly spread: 15 schools by 1880; 432 schools by 1900.

1873–95. MEDICAL EDUCATION. From 1873–90, 112 medical schools were founded. Faculty distribution: Missouri first with 42; Cincinnati, 20; Chicago, 14; Louisville, 11. In an effort to raise professional level states tightened licensure; boards of examination by 1895 and the modern type in almost every state. Model was the Medical School at Johns Hopkins (founded 1893), with **William Henry Welch** (1850–1934) in pathology; **William S. Halsted** (1852–1922), surgery; Sir **William Osler** (1849–1919), the clinician.

1874–1930. OSTEOPATHY (emphasizing placement of bones in the body as key to health) founded by **Andrew Taylor Still** (1828–1917). Amer. Assn. of Advanced Osteopathy established, 1897. Three schools and 7,644 osteopaths in U.S. (1930).

1879–80. "INDEX MEDICUS" AND "INDEX-CATALOGUE." John Shaw Billings (1838–1913), curator of Army Medical Museum and Library, founded *Index Medicus* (1879), monthly list of newly published medical literature, and compiled great *Index-Catalogue to the Library of the Surgeon-General's Office* (1880), monumental bibliography of medical literature.

1884–99. ADVANCES IN ANESTHESIA. William Halsted injected cocaine into nerves to anesthetize peripheral regions (1884); **J. Leonard Corning** (1855–1923), using cocaine as spinal anesthetic, induced epidural anesthesia (1885) and used cocaine as local anesthetic (1887); spinal anesthesia used by Dudley Tait and Guido Caglieri in San Francisco and Rudolph Matas in New Orleans (1899).

1885–1913. ADVANCES IN SURGERY. Joseph O'Dwyer (1841–98) improved technic for intubation of the larynx in diphtheria (1885). Peroral endoscopy improved and modified by **Chevalier Jackson** (Philadelphia, 1865–1958). **Reginald Heber Fitz** (1843–1913) established "appendicitis" as a definite lesion (1886). First appendectomy following correct diagnosis of appendicitis performed by **Thomas George Morton** (1835–1903); technic improved by **John B. Murphy** (1857–1916), inventor of "Murphy Button" (1892), and **Charles McBurney** (1845–1913), who originated short incision. First successful removal in U.S. of brain tumor performed by **William W. Keen** (1837–1932; done in London, 1884). **William Steward Halsted** introduced the use of rubber gloves (c.1890), was the first to ligate the subclavian artery (1891), and perfected operations for hernia and breast removal. Founding of the **Mayo Clinic** (1889) at Rochester, Minn. by the brothers **William James Mayo** and **Charles Horace Mayo** (p. 1100) opened a new era in U.S. surgery, with stress on diagnosis as well as advanced technics. Advances in prevention of surgical shock and in operations for toxic goiter were made by **George W. Crile** (1864–1943). **Hugh H. Young** (1870–1945), urologist, devised a technic of prostatectomy. First thoracoplasty (1893) performed by **George Ryerson Fowler** (1848–1906). **American College of Surgeons** originated 1913 by **Franklin H. Martin** (1857–1935).

1885–1941. FIGHT AGAINST TUBERCULOSIS. Sanitarium at Saranac Lake, N.Y., founded (1884) by **Edward L. Trudeau** (1848–1915); established Saranac Laboratory for study of tuberculosis (1894). Early diagnosis aided by Roentgen's discovery of X ray (1895). For contribution of **Theobald Smith**, see p. 1155. National Association for Study and Prevention of Tuberculosis founded, 1904.

1889–1910. PREVENTIVE MEDICINE. Basic research in hog cholera,

swine plague, and Texas fever in cattle by **Theobald Smith. William Henry Welch** (1850–1934) discovered the bacillus of gas gangrene (1892). For the work in yellow fever of **Walter Reed** and associates, see p. 1136. Col. **William Gorgas** (p. 1043), applying technics worked out by Reed, eliminated yellow fever from the Panama Canal Zone (1904–06). **Howard Taylor Ricketts** (1871–1910) demonstrated (c.1910) that typhus fever was caused by a new class of organisms now known as Rickettsiae (including Rocky Mountain fever, by a tick; trench fever, by a louse).

1895. CHIROPRACTICS founded by **Daniel D. Palmer** (1845–1904), emphasizing position of joints (especially of the spine) as key to health. Illegal in some states, there were 21 schools and 16,000 practitioners by 1930. Its gradual rise to respectability is recognized by Medicare legislation (1973).

1896–1905. RADIUM AND X RAY IN THERAPY. X-ray treatment of breast cancer by **Emil H. Grube** (29 Jan. 1896) followed immediately upon publication of Roentgen's findings (5 Jan. 1896). Radium treatment for cancer used by **Robert Abbe** (1903); also first to treat cancer of womb with radium (1905).

1898–1927. HORMONES. Basic work on isolating adrenalin done by **John J. Abel** (1857–1938); completed by **Jokichi Takamine** (1854–1922) on basis of Abel's finding (1901). For isolation of thyroxine by **Edward C. Kendall**, see p. 1074. Work on insulin of Sir **Frederick G. Banting** and **J. J. R. MacLeod** (1922) utilized findings of **Moses Baron** on the pancreas. Isolation of substance in bull testes (later, androsterone and testosterone) accomplished (1927) by **Lemuel McGee.**

1901. ROCKEFELLER INSTITUTE OF MEDICAL RESEARCH founded. William W. Welch first head; succeeded, 1904, by **Simon Flexner** (1863–1946), who discovered (1905–07) serum for treating cerebrospinal meningitis and was first to transmit poliomyelitis to monkeys and to show it is caused by a virus (1909).

1906. "TYPHOID MARY," discovered by G. A. Soper, documented role of healthy carriers as sources of disease.

1908–50. MEDICAL EDUCATION. Report (1910) by **Abraham Flexner** (p. 1030) for the Carnegie Foundation exposed abuses in medical education and proposed reforms. Large grants for medical schools and centers to Duke, Vanderbilt, George Washington, and universities of Chicago, Rochester, and Iowa. Number of medical schools declined: 148 (1910), 76 (1932), 77 (1950). Number of graduates declined: Over 5,000 per annum (1900–06) to a low of 2,529 (1922), with a gradual rise to above 5,000 (1934–43). Number of physicians fluctuated slightly from 1 per 750 to 1 per 800. Studies abroad by many students (1,481 in 1931–32) cut off by World War II. Dental schools declined: 54 (1910), 39 (1945).

1909–52. PSYCHIATRY AND PSYCHOTHERAPY. Adolf Meyer (1866–1950), a founder (after 1892) of the mental hygiene movement in the U.S., enunciated the dynamic conception of dementia praecox, and with his associates discovered that serious mental disorders might yield to treatment involving introduction of malarial organisms into the blood stream. **Clifford W. Beers** (1876–1943) founded mental hospital movement (1909); **Elmer Ernest Southard** (1876–1920) made notable contributions in the field of neuropsychiatry and its social implications. Later U.S. psychiatrists (since 1930) confirmed European discovery that dementia praecox could be cured by insulin or other shock treatment. First concerned with treatment of persons in asylums and mental hospitals, psychiatrists broadened their scope to include the origin of criminal behavior (with pioneer work on juvenile delinquency by Dr. **William Healy,** 1869–

1962) and child guidance. Since 1940 considerable advances in psychotherapy and psychosomatic medicine have been achieved by **Franz Alexander** (1891–1964) and Dr. **William C. Menninger** (1899–1966) at the Menninger Clinic, Topeka, and as director of neuropsychiatry, Surgeon General's Office, U.S. Army, 1943–46. Lectures by **Sigmund Freud** and **Carl G. Jung** at Clark Univ. (1909) advanced psychoanalysis in U.S. *Psychoanalytic Review* established (1913) by **William Alanson White** (1870–1937) and S. E. Jelliffe. Recent psychoanalysis (since 1930) has emphasized social and cultural factors in neurosis and interpersonal aspect of analyst-patient relationship (**Karen Horney** [1885–1952], **Erich Fromm** [1900–80], **Harry Stack Sullivan** [1892–1947]).

1912–32. NEUROLOGICAL SURGERY. Contributions of greatest U.S. figure in field, **Harvey Cushing,** see p. 1009.

1913. **Bela Schick** (1877–1967) devised "Schick test," a skin test to determine susceptibility to diphtheria. Mass surveys, first in New York City, followed by immunization of Schick-positive children by inactive toxin, drastically cut incidence of disease.

1914–48. VITAMIN RESEARCH. Beginning 1888, early work was conducted abroad (Eijkmann, Dutch East Indies; Funk and Hopkins, England; Frohlich and Holst, Norway; Pekelharing, Holland; Lunin, Switzerland). Vitamin A discovered (1912–14) by **Elmer V. McCollum** (1879–1967); Vitamin B (1915–16); Vitamin D (1922). **Joseph Goldberger** (1874–1929), of U.S. Public Health Service, discovered (1915) that pellagra was a deficiency disease. **Harry Steenbock** (1886–1968) at the Univ. of Wisconsin and Alfred Hess at Columbia announced almost simultaneously (1924) methods for irradiating Vitamin D. Vitamin E isolated from wheat germ (1922) by **Herbert M. Evans** (1882–1958).

Vitamin C isolated by Dr. Charles G. King (1932). R. J. Williams reported pantothenic acid (1933). Vitamin K discovered (1934) by **Edward A. Doisy** (1893–   ), simultaneously with Dam and Schønheyder in Denmark; synthesized (1939). Medical use of niacin discovered by **Conrad Elverhjem** (1901–1962). Thiamin synthesized (1936); pyridoxine isolated (1938); biotin's complex structure determined (1942). Para-amino benzoic acid synthesized (1943), in which year folic acid was discovered. By 1941 vitamin B was shown to be a complex of at least 5 distinct vitamins. Vitamin B_{12} shown to be effective in treatment of pernicious anemia (1948).

1918–19. INFLUENZA PANDEMIC spread from Western Front, with estimated 500,000 deaths in U.S. alone.

1920–43. TREATMENT OF EPILEPSY. Phenobarbital (discovered by Hauptmann, Germany, 1911) introduced in treatment by **Julius Grinker** (1920). Work of **William G. Lennox** (1884–1960) and **Tracy J. Putnam** (1894–   ) led to dilantin being synthesized and applied (1936). Tridione synthesized at Abbott Laboratories (1940); applied (1943).

1923–34. ANESTHESIA. Ethylene demonstrated by Arno B. Luckhardt; Sodium Amytal used on animals by F. J. Fulton and on humans intravenously by Leon G. Zerfas (1923). Cyclopropane (by Neff, Rovestine, and Waters) and Nembutal (by R. H. Fitch, Waters, and Tatum) used as anesthetics (1930). Divinyl oxide, fastest yet devised, produced by Chauncey D. Leake (1930). Sodium Pentothal administered (1934) intravenously by John S. Lundy; also to permit free questioning by psychiatrists.

1927–28. IRON LUNG invented by Philip Drinker and Louis A. Shaw; used for poliomyelitis (1928).

1936–39. SULFA DRUGS. Perrin H. Long and Eleanor A. Bliss at Johns Hopkins proved the effectiveness of both prontosil (discovered by Domagk, Germany, 1932) and sulfanilamide (discovered by Fourneau and Trèfouëls, France) on peritonitis, scarlet fever, tonsillitis, blood poisoning, and impetigo. These drugs were displaced, first by sulfapyridine (proved effective in the Sudan, 1939), and later by sulfathiazole, sulfadiazine, and other sulfa compounds.

1939–52. ANTIBIOTICS. René J. Dubos (1901–   ) at Rockefeller Institute discovered tyrothricin in soil bacteria (effective in eye infections, ulcer, impetigo). **Selman Waksman** (p. 1175) discovered astinomycin (1940), streptothricin (1941)—both too destructive—and streptomycin (with Schatz, 1944; Nobel prize for discovery, 1952), the last effective in meningitis, tuberculosis, dysentery, and bladder and kidney infections. Other antibiotics followed: chloromycetin (Ehrlich *et al.*, 1947); aureomycin (Duggar, 1948); terramycin (Finlay *et al.*, 1950); magnamycin (Pfizer Lab., 1952).

1941–43. PENICILLIN. Discovered by Dr. Alexander Fleming in London (1929); experiments by Dr. Howard W. Florey (1938) led to use on a human patient (1941). At beginning of World War II production of penicillin transferred to the U.S. under the wartime direction of Dr. Chester Keefer. Due to findings of Robert D. Coghill, production rose to 300 billion units (c.15 lbs.) per month (1945). Tests made by Florey abroad, and by Keefer, Leo Lowe, and John Mahoney, revealed effectiveness in most sulfa-resistant streptococcus and straphylococcus infections, including syphilis and subacute bacterial endocarditis (1943). **Synthetic penicillin** developed in Beecham Laboratories, England (1959), and Bristol-Myers, U.S.; introduced in U.S., 1960.

1943–50. ANTIHISTAMINES. Paralleling work at Pasteur Institute, U.S. researchers began work in field (1943). Benadril discovered by George Rieveschl,

Jr. (1943); Pyrobenzamine (1946); Neohetramine (1948). Dramamine shown to be effective for control of seasickness (1948). Antihistamines used in treatment of allergies; promoted for common cold (1949–50), with debatable results.

1946–52. CORTISONE, a hormone of the cortex of the adrenal gland, synthesized by several groups (Sarett; Kendall, Mason, and Mattox; Julian; Gallagher, 1946; from carbon, oxygen, and hydrogen by Sarett, 1952). First used (1949) for rheumatic arthritis by Edward C. Kendall (p. 1074) and Philip S. Hench (1896–1965). ACTH, a hormone from the pituitary gland, was concentrated at Armour Laboratories and used by Hench *et al.* for rheumatoid arthritis.

1950–78. INDEX OF MEDICAL CARE PRICES
(U.S. Bureau of the Census, *Statistical Abstract*, 1973, 1978)

	Total Medical Care	Drugs and Prescriptions	Physician Fees	Dentist Fees	Hospital Daily Charges
1950	53.7	88.5	55.2	63.9	28.9
1960	79.1	104.5	77.0	82.1	56.3
1970	120.6	103.6	121.4	113.5	143.9
1978	236.3	140.6	240.7	212.4	363.9

1951–60. DRUG TRENDS. Tranquilizers: Miltown first synthesized 1950, in widespread use by 1955. Isolation (1952) of reserpine from old Indian shrub, along with introduction (1954) of thorazine, or chlorpromazine (synthesized in France), with dramatic effects in treatment of patients with mental disorders. **Steroids:** In addition to corticosteroids (for arthritis), research and development progressed rapidly in field of sex steroids for treating endocrine deficiencies, of applying steroids as an anabolic agent for reconstruction of body and muscle tissues, and as cardiovascular agents. Synthesis of polypeptide hormone, oxytocin, by **Vincent du Vigneaud** (1901–78), who also synthesized hormone vasopressin (1956), won him Nobel prize in chemistry (1955). ACTH equivalent synthesized (1960) by Dr. Klaus Hofmann and associates. **Diabetes control:** Introduction (1957) of a nonbactericidal sulfonamide (Orinase) for treatment of mild diabetes of old age. **Fat-reducing diets:** Rockefeller Institute announced (1956) liquid formula based on glucose and corn oil, which served as basis of proprietary products, widely marketed beginning 1959.

1953. CANCER AND CIGARETTE SMOKING. Increase of incidence of cancer of the lung due to cancer-producing factor in cigarette smoking reported 8 Dec. 1953 by Dr. Alton Ochsner; statistical confirmation by Drs. Evarts A. Graham and Ernest L. Winder, 2 Feb. 1954; by British government study, 12 Feb.; and by statistical report of American Cancer Society, 21 June.

1955, 12 Apr. SALK VACCINE. Widespread field tests of use of gamma globulin during polio epidemics in Utah, Texas, and Iowa, 1952, showed only short-term protection (c. 5 weeks). Earlier (1949) Drs. **John F. Enders** (p. 1025), **Thomas H. Weller** (1915–), and **Frederick C. Robbins** (1916–) of Harvard Medical School found that polio virus could be grown in clusters of non-nervous human and monkey tissues in test tubes, for which they were awarded the Nobel Prize in medicine and physiology (1954). This discovery paved the way for growth of the virus in quantities massive enough for use as vaccine. Using 3 strains of inactivated polio, Dr. **Jonas E. Salk** (p. 1145) of Pittsburgh Univ. Medical School reported (26 Mar. 1953) hopeful results from a vaccine he prepared. In the largest medical field test in history, 1,830,000 school children participated in program to evaluate Salk vaccine. Evaluation report (12 Apr. 1955) disclosed that active immunity was provided for at least 6 months, with more permanent protection by use of booster injections. As a result of a number of fatalities in the early stages, due to accidental inclusion of live virus in certain batches of vaccine, both the method of preparation and the strains of virus were modified for greater safety. The Poliomyelitis Vaccination Act (12 Aug. 1955) provided that the Public Health Service should allocate $30 million to the states to help them buy the vaccine, of which about 20% was given free. Rise and decline in U.S. polio cases: (annual average) 1938–42, 6,400; 1942–47, 16,800; 1947–51, 34,000; 1952, c. 60,000; 1955, 37,771; 1957–58, c. 5,700; 1960, 3,277 (lowest since 1938).

Building on the work of **Hilary Koprowski** (1916–), Dr. **Albert Sabin** (1906–) developed a live (attenuated) virus poliomyelitis vaccine during the late 1950s. Licensed in 1962, with the advantages of ease of administration, rapidity, and high degree of effectiveness, the oral vaccine has become widely used in the U.S. and the Soviet Union, largely supplanting Salk vaccine. Reported polio cases declined to 72 (1965), 21 (1971).

1957. Pandemic of "Asian flu," a new strain of Type A influenza, spread from northern China and reached the U.S. in June, where it quickly became epidemic, although death rate remained low.

1958–72. NOBEL PRIZES IN MEDICINE OR PHYSIOLOGY were dominated by American doctors: 1958, **Joshua Lederberg** (p. 1082) for discoveries concerning genetic recombination and organization of genetic material of bacteria, and **George Wells Beadle** (1903–) and **Edward Lawrie Tatum** (1909–) for discovery that genes act by controlling specific chemical reactions; **1959**, Drs. **Arthur Kornberg** (1918–), Stanford Univ., and **Severo Ochoa** (1905–), New York Univ., for the synthesis of nucleic acid; **1961, Georg von Békésy** (1899–1972), Harvard, for discoveries concerning physical mechanisms of stimulation within the cochlea

which opened the way for major advances in diagnosis and correction of damaged hearing; **1962, Dr. James Watson** (1928–), Harvard, shared the prize with British biophysicists Francis Crick and Maurice Wilkins for determination (1953) of the molecular structure of deoxyribonucleic acid (DNA), the device by which genetic information is transmitted from one generation to the next; 1964, **Konrad Bloch** (1912–) (shared with Feodor Lynen, of Germany), for research into the relation between heart disease and cholesterol and fatty acids; **1966, Charles B. Huggins** (1901–), Univ. of Chicago, for cancer research, and **Frances Peyton Rous** (1879–1970), Rockefeller Univ., for demonstrating in 1910 that animal cancer can be transmitted by virus; **1967, Haldan Keffer Hartline** (1903–), Rockefeller Institute, **George Wald** (1906–), Harvard, with Ragnar Granit of Sweden, for research into processes of the eye; **1968, Robert W. Holley** (1922–), Salk Institute, **Marshall W. Nirenberg** (1927–), National Institutes of Health, and **H. Gobind Khorana** (1922–), Univ. of Wisconsin, for "breaking the genetic code"; **1969, Max Delbruck** (1906–81), **Salvador E. Luria** (1908–), and **Alfred D. Hershey** (1912–) for work in the "replication mechanism and genetic structure of virus"; **1970, Julius Axelrod** (1912–) (shared with Bernard Katz, England, and Ulf Svante vol Euler, Sweden), for studies in the chemistry of nerve transmission; **1971, Earl Wilbur Sutherland, Jr.** (1915–74), for studies in the mechanism of hormones; **1972, Gerald Edelman** (1929–) (shared with Rodney Porter, England), for studies of the chemical structure of antibodies.

1960. KIDNEY DISEASE, treatment by transplantation and routine dialysis initiated.

1961–68. BIRTH CONTROL. Research on oral contraceptives ("the pill") began in the 1950s. Drs. **Gregory Good-**

win Pincus (p. 1128), **M. C. Chang,** and **John Rock** led in development of means of birth control dependent for the first time upon physiological action. A synthetic progesterone (hormonelike substance) suppresses ovulation. Believed to be 100 percent effective, the pill was first marketed in 1960. Initial popularity was later limited by side effects such as nausea and the gaining of weight, which were reduced by later research. By 1968 more than 6 million American women (nearly ⅙ of those of child-bearing age) had adopted the use of the pill, which was also credited with influencing changes in sexual mores.

A United States grant of $500,000 to the World Health Organization for research into human reproduction (1963) was the first official recognition of the need to provide technical assistance on population control to those nations requesting it.

1961–71. HEART SURGERY AND TRANSPLANTS. Dramatic advances were made in the treatment of abnormalities of the heart, blood vessels, and circulation. New instruments were employed for diagnosis, treatment, and observation; radioactive isotopes to estimate blood flow through the heart muscle; miniaturized "pacemakers" inserted to correct abnormal heartbeat; artificial pumps applied temporarily. First artificial heart surgery by Dr. **Michael E. De Bakey** (1908–) employing ventricle bypass pump to assist the heart. The discovery of new drugs effective in suppressing antibodies made possible the dramatic heart transplant operations. Dr. Christiaan N. Barnard, Groote Shur Hospital, Capetown, South Africa, performed the first heart transplant 3 Dec. 1967, the patient surviving 18 days. Dr. Barnard transplanted a heart for Dr. Philip Blaiberg (2 Jan. 1968), who survived over 19 months. The first American transplant, 6 Dec. 1967, was

performed by Dr. Adrian Kantrowitz (1918–), Maimonides Hospital Center, New York City; the patient surviving only a few hours. Dr. Norman E. Shumway (1923–), Stanford Univ., devised the standard transplant technique and Dr. Denton A. Cooley (1920–), St. Luke's Hospital, Houston, Tex., employed a streamlined technique, reducing the length of surgery from over 2 hours to about 25 minutes. Drs. Shumway, Cooley, and De Bakey, St. Luke's and Houston Methodist Hospitals, performed close to half of the 80 transplants which had taken place in 15 countries throughout the world as of Dec. 1968; 36 persons with new hearts were surviving (28 Nov. 1968). While heart transplants decreased by 1971, new techniques included completely artificial heart device inserted by Cooley (4 Apr. 1969) and patch booster, a partially mechanical heart driven by an air pump outside the body, inserted by Kantrowitz (11 Aug. 1971).

1962. Thalidomide Scare, caused by abnormal births to pregnant women taking drug in Europe (9 such births in U.S.), led to strong safety provisions of **Drug Amendments** of 1962 (10 Oct.) to assure that new drugs were safe and effective.

1963. Measles Vaccine. Vaccines against common ("red") measles introduced.

1964–67. CANCER AND CIGARETTE SMOKING. After 14 months of study, the U.S. Surgeon General's Special Advisory Committee on Smoking and Health reported that smoking was the chief cause of lung cancer (11 Jan. 1964). Although the causative role of smoking in coronary artery disease was not considered proven, risk of death from coronary artery disease was 70 percent greater for middle-aged men who smoked. A mandatory health warning on cigarette packages became effective 1 Jan. 1966 (bill signed 19 July 1965). Although numerous further studies, including *The Health Consequences of Smoking* by the U.S. Public Health Service (1967), reinforced and amplified the earlier warning, controversy over restrictions on cigarette advertising continued and smoking in the U.S. increased.

1965. Rubella Virus strain HPV-77 developed by Dr. Harry M. Meyer, Jr. and Dr. Paul D. Parkman of the National Institutes of Health, based upon isolation of rubella virus (1961) separately by Drs. Thomas H. Weller and Franklin A. Nevas of Harvard, and Drs. Parkman, Edward L. Buescher, and Malcolm S. Artenstein of Walter Reed Army Medical Center, led to rubella vaccine as developed by Drs. Maurice R. Hilleman and Eugene B. Buynak of Merck, Sharp, and Dohme (licensed 1969).

1965. MEDICARE. Social Security Amendments (30 July 1965), Medical Care for the Aged Program, were enacted more than 12 years after President Truman's Commission on the Health Needs of the Nation recommended a federal health insurance plan under social security. The Medicare program consists of (1) a basic hospital insurance program covering hospital and posthospital services for those 65 and over, paid for from a special contribution through social security, (2) supplementary (voluntary) medical insurance program providing payment for physicians' and surgeons' services, home health and other Medicare services for those aged 65 and more, (3) **Medicaid,** Title 19, a measure to assist the needy and disabled not covered by social security to meet expenses covered by the other two programs, plans to be implemented by individual states, with costs divided between the state and federal governments. 19.7 million persons were enrolled in the hospital insurance program (June 1968). By Jan. 1968, 30 states were participating in Medicaid programs.

1965–68. AIR AND WATER POLLUTION. Growing concern over air and water pollution was reflected in the increasing federal role (see pp. 639–643).

1966. L-DOPA, as a nonsurgical treatment of Parkinson's disease, introduced, proving highly effective in alleviating symptoms but not slowing the underlying progression of the disease.

1968. RH FACTOR. Reverse vaccination at the time of a woman's first delivery to ward off future Rh incompatibility crisis introduced.

1968–73. DEFINING DEATH AND MEDICAL ETHICS. Increasing transplantation of organs engendered concern over the definition of death. A new definition involving the use of the electroencephalograph was developed (1968) by a committee at Harvard Medical School in which the ceasing of brain function as detected by the electroencephalograph represented the death of the patient.

During the 1960s and reaching a high level of concern in the 1970s, physicians and society examined the ethics of medical practices. Noteworthy was the debate over defining informed consent for patients undergoing medical care and as subjects in experiments, the use of heroic measures to forestall death, and the treatment of the dying patient.

1969–72. MEDICAL SCIENCE AND GENETICS. 1972 Nobel prize in chemistry to Christian B. Anfisen (1916–   ), Stanford Moore (1913–   ), and William H. Stein (1911–   ) for studies in the composition and functioning of enzyme ribonuclease, the first synthesis of which was achieved by Merck, Sharp, and Dohme Research Laboratories and by the Rockefeller Institute. Isolation of a single gene by Harvard Medical School team (22 Nov. 1969) headed by Dr. Jonathan Beckwith. Major contribution to gene isolation also made by Dr. David Kohne of the Carnegie Institute. First synthetic gene by H. G. Khorana and group, Univ. of Wisconsin (1970).

Watson and Crick's detailed description of DNA as a double helix was confirmed by photographic evidence of Jack Griffith (1942–), Univ. of California, Berkeley.

Amniocentestis began to attract wide medical attention for prenatal diagnosis of Down's Syndrome and other inherited disorders characterized by chromosome abnormalities or enzyme deficiencies. The procedure involved piercing the uterus with a needle to withdraw some of the fluid surrounding the fetus and thus invading the hitherto sacrosanct uterine cavity for diagnosis during pregnancy.

1969–72. MEDICAL PROFESSION developments included (1) increasing interest in family practice, group practices, prepaid medical plans; (2) experiments in cutting one year from medical school; (3) postgraduate residencies in social medicine and in family practice; (4) employment of paramedics. New specialty, family medicine, announced by AMA, 10 Feb. 1969.

1969–73. DRUG USE AND ENVIRONMENTAL ISSUES. Society's alarm at the growing number of students taking drugs like marijuana, LSD, and dexedrine increased penalties for drug use and narcotics traffic (with life sentence being the enacted maximum penalty in New York state [1973]). Scientific studies expanded on the effect of certain drugs, particularly marijuana, on human beings.

In the face of increased concern about the quality of the American environment, the U.S. government banned the use of DDT in gradual stages, to be completely prohibited by 1971. President Nixon announced (1970) the establishment of the Council on Environmental Quality and the Environmental Protection Agency, but a number of programs were suspended as a result of the growing energy crisis beginning in 1973.

1970. LINUS PAULING'S (p. 1123) claim that vitamin C in massive amounts would ward off the common cold stirred considerable controversy in the medical profession.

1970–74. WOMEN STUDENTS in U.S. medical schools increased dramatically from 3,894 (1970–71) school year, 9.6% of total enrollment, to 7,824 or 15.4% (1973–74). Percentage first-year female medical students: 7.8% (1963–64), 11.1% (1970–71), 19.7% (1973–74).

1971. ACUPUNCTURE. Thaw in political relationship with Mainland China led to visits by doctors and journalists whose enthusiastic reports of the success of the ancient Chinese practice of inserting needles into various parts of the body as anesthetic and for relief of pain and cure of illness led to experimentation in U.S.

1970–72. ABORTION. Colorado was the 1st state to adopt liberalized model penal code abortion statute (1967). By 1970, 13 states had followed. The U.S. Supreme Court in *Roe* v. *Wade* (1972, p. 685) defined the rights of the mother and fetus in the case of abortion, striking down all existing state laws making abortion a crime. The decision followed several years of liberalized abortion laws in a number of states (1967–71). On developments, 1973–81, see p. 549.

1971–78 CARDIOVASCULAR DISEASE. Deathrate from strokes off 37%; from heart attacks, 25%. Among the causes: (1) better emergency treatment; (2) better hospital care and diet; (3) decline in cigarette smoking; (4) new diagnostic tools such as angiograms (X-ray pictures made by injecting a radiopaque substance into the heart), ultrasound imaging, nuclear scanning, positron emissions tomography; (5) new treatments such as unblocking arteries by balloon angioplasty; clot-dissolving streptokinase; implantable defibrillators, calcium blockers.

1972. 2 JAN. CIGARETTE ADVERTISING ban on radio and TV effective following 1970 act of Congress.

1973–81. GENETIC RESEARCH AND GENETIC RESEARCH REGULATIONS (p. 548).

1974–80. NOBEL PRIZES IN MEDICINE OR PHYSIOLOGY: 1974, **Albert Claude, George Emil Palade** and **Christian René de Duve,** first to examine intracellular structures and discover their separate functions; 1975, **Renato Dulbecco, Howard Temin,** and **David Baltimore** for discoveries concerning the interaction between tumor viruses and the genetic material of the cell; 1976, **D. Carleton Gajdusek** for work on slow-acting viruses, and **Baruch S. Blumberg** for work which led to development of experimental hepatitis vaccine; 1977, **Rosalyn Sussman Yalow** for development of radioimmunoassay, technique for measuring concentrations of biologically active substances, and to **Roger Guillemin** and **Andrew Schally** for research isolating and identifying TRH, hormone causing pituitary to produce hormone TSH; 1978, **Daniel Nathans, Hamilton O. Smith,** and Werner Arber (Switzerland) for discovery and application of enzymes which break molecules of DNA into manageable pieces; 1979, **Allan M. Cormack** and Geoffrey N. Hounsfield (United Kingdom) for computerized axial tomography, the CAT scan; 1980, **Baruj Benacceraf, George F. Snell,** and Jean Dausset (France) for their work in tissue typing and on the body's immune system.

1975. HOMOSEXUALITY. Classification of homosexuality as a mental disorder dropped by American Psychiatric Association.

1975. FIRST STRIKES by physicians occur in New York City and Chicago over hours and working conditions of interns and residents. Unionization of senior physicians accelerated.

1975. MALPRACTICE INSURANCE premiums increased sharply due to rise in successful malpractice actions and heavy damage awards. Southern California doctors protested 327% increase in premiums with 35-day work slowdown ending 5 Feb. 1976.

1976. RIGHT TO DIE. California became the first state (30 Sept.) to give terminally ill persons the right to authorize withdrawal of life-sustaining procedures when death believed to be imminent. New Jersey Supreme Court ruled (31 Mar.) that use of mechanical respirator could be discontinued for 21-year-old patient, Karen Ann Quinlan, in a coma for more than eleven months.

1976. LEGIONNAIRE'S DISEASE. 208 persons who attended convention of American Legion in Philadelphia were stricken with mysterious illness. 29 died. The disease was ultimately attributed to a hitherto unknown bacterium, housed in an air-conditioning cooling tower.

1976. SWINE FLU INNOCULATION CAMPAIGN (p. 555).

1977. Aug. First drug treatment of viral disease. Charles A. Alford and Richard J. Whitley of the University of Alabama employ drug Ara-A (vidarabine) against herpes encephalitis.

1978. TEST TUBE BABY. Birth in England (25 July) of baby resulting from implanting within the womb an egg fertilized outside it raised ethical issues. (Dr. Pierre Soupart, Vanderbilt University, had been the first researcher with proof of fertilizing a human egg in a dish [1972].) Ethics Advisory Board of HEW approved as ethically acceptable federally funded research in embryos so long as they were not kept alive beyond two weeks. U.S. effort was led by Drs. Howard and Georgeanna S. Jones at the In-vitro Fertilization Clinic, Eastern Virginia Medical School, Norfolk, Va.

1980. TOXIC SHOCK SYNDROME (TSS) linked by U.S. Center for Disease Control to use of tampons.

1980. NOBEL PRIZE IN CHEMISTRY shared by Americans **Paul Berg** and **Walter Gilbert,** along with Frederick Sanger (United Kingdom) mapping the structure and functions of DNA.

THOUGHT AND CULTURE

Religion

The fact that the American religious experience has been pluralistic has contributed substantially to the complete separation of church and state, while at the same time fostering religious liberty. Although the Roman Catholic faith had maintained an establishment on the North American continent some two centuries before the arrival of Protestantism, it was the latter, in diverse forms, which dominated the Thirteen English Colonies. Formally separating from the Church of England were the Congregationalists, Presbyterians, and Baptists, along with a number of more radical sects such as the Quakers, and to this latter group were added various Pietist sects that migrated to America from central Europe, starting in the 1680s. While the Church of England was established in the Southern colonies and in the 4 lower counties of New York, the Puritan Congregationalists effectively established their churches throughout New England save for Rhode Island.

Organized religion felt the thrust of the great revivals of the colonial period and the nineteenth century, with a quasi-establishment of evangelical Protestantism emerging, dominated by Methodists and Baptists, along with other indigenous groups, and the black churches having a separate and distinctive experience. More recently, the religious scene has responded to the powerful neo-orthodox impulse, with its thoroughgoing reconsideration of judgments rendered by a previous generation of liberal churchmen. Nineteenth- and twentieth-century immigration has given increasing prominence in numbers and influence to Roman Catholicism, Judaism, and the Eastern Orthodox churches, while mystical cults have recently emerged in response to youthful disillusionment and malaise.

c.1000. CHRISTIANITY IN THE NEW WORLD. According to the Icelandic *Saga of Eric the Red*, Leif Ericson (pp. 16, 17) introduced Christianity in Greenland and along the North American coast.

1492–1769. CATHOLICISM IN NEW SPAIN. Spanish explorers and conquistadores, supported by the church, introduced Catholicism into the Caribbean islands and the continents of North and South America as a culmination of a long campaign in Spain against Jews and Moors. In what is the continental U.S. the Catholic faith was spread by Spanish missions from Florida (1565), New Mexico (1598), Arizona (1680s), Texas (1690), and California, the last through the efforts of Father Junipero Serra (p. 27) starting in 1769. All these areas constituted borderlands of New Spain where Catholicism had been long entrenched.

1632–1774. CATHOLICISM IN NEW FRANCE. For the role of the Recollect and Jesuit missions, see pp. 72–73. For the treatment of the Catholic Church in Canada by the British government, 1763–1774, see pp. 97–98.

1609. CHURCH OF ENGLAND was established by law in Virginia. A statute (1610), reenacted when Virginia became a royal colony, but never rigidly enforced, provided for compulsory church attendance. The Anglican Church was also established in the lower counties of New York (1693), and in Maryland (1702), South Carolina (1706), North Carolina (nominally, 1711), and Georgia (1758). The first Anglican church in New York City, Trinity Church, was founded in 1697, with Rev. William Vesey as rector. In Massachusetts Anglican worship was introduced by Governor Andros (1686). In Pennsylvania Christ Church, Philadelphia, was organized in 1694 and gained ground following the Quaker schism. Anglicanism was introduced in New Jersey (1702) and in Connecticut (1706). The influence of the church was restricted by the predominantly mediocre quality of the colonial clergy, by oversized parishes, low salaries, neglect of discipline, and lay control. In the absence of a resident bishop confirmation and ordination could not be administered in the colonies. The latter served to discourage the growth of a native ministry. The **Bishop of London** was placed in charge of colonial churches

in 1635, and was represented in the colonies by **commissaries,** notably by **James Blair** (1655–1743) in Virginia, 1689–1743, and **Thomas Bray** (1656–1730) in Maryland. The latter founded (1701) the **Venerable Society for the Propagation of the Gospel in Foreign Parts** (S.P.G.), which engaged in missionary activities and founded churches (notably in the Carolinas). After the first quarter of the 18th century the Anglican Church gained ground as a result of a split among Calvinists. In 1722 a great defection from Yale College and the Congregational ministry to Anglicanism was led by **Samuel Johnson** (1696–1772), a follower of Bishop Berkeley's idealistic system of philosophy. Repeated agitation for an **American episcopate** (1700–70) failed because of the opposition of governmental officials, dissenters, and Southern laymen who insisted on the right to choose their own curates. The first bishop in America was **Samuel Seabury** (1729–96), consecrated in Aberdeen by nonjuring bishops (1784).

1620. THE CONGREGATIONAL CHURCH was introduced by the Pilgrims in Plymouth (1620) and by the Puritans in Massachusetts Bay (1630). The principal difference was that the former (Independents) repudiated the Church of England; the latter (Nonconformists) did not openly break with the Established Church. The Puritan theological system stressed 3 covenants—between God and man, between the church and its members, and between the state and its citizens. Since the church never controlled the state officially, Massachusetts never achieved a true theocracy, but rather a "Bible Commonwealth" in which the civil rulers, seeking to rule in accordance with the will of God, sought counsel of the divines (Calvinist "consociation"). Factors contributing to the decline of the church in New England were (1) the disappearance of the distinction in civil matters between the "elect" and all others, (2) gradual dispersal of the population on farms, and (3) the growth of rationalism. The **Halfway Covenant** (1657–62), which admitted to baptism the children of baptized persons who themselves had not experienced conversion, served to erase the distinction between the "elect" and all others, and marked an effort to return to the original New England way when evidence simply of purity of faith and life was required. Rationalist influences: (1) the revulsion against the **Salem witchcraft trials** (1692–93), (2) the ouster of the orthodox Increase Mather as president of Harvard College (1701); (3) the founding of the **Brattle Street Church** in Boston (1699), the first Puritan church not to require a public confession of faith for admission to communion. The religious monopoly of the Congregationalists was challenged by the Baptists under **Roger Williams** (p. 1185) and **Henry Dunster** (1609–59), who was forced to resign (1654) the presidency of Harvard College because of his opposition to infant baptism; by the Presbyterians, as evidenced in the remonstrance of Dr. Robert Child (1646), the later attempt of Increase Mather to Presbyterianize the church, resisted by Rev. **John Wise** (1710–17), and the **Saybrook Platform** (1708), by which Connecticut Congregationalists placed themselves under a Presbyterian-type government; and by the Quakers (p. 822); and was terminated as a result of the revocation of the old charter (1684).

1628. THE DUTCH REFORMED CHURCH (a Calvinist, Presbyterian group) was organized in New Amsterdam by Rev. Jonas Michaëlius (1628), placed under the jurisdiction of the Classis of Amsterdam, and established by the Freedoms and Exemptions (1640). A Coetus or synod of ministers and elders was formed in 1747. Between 1755 and 1771 a cleavage developed between the **Coetus** (demanding virtual self-government) and the **Conferentie** (conservative), which was settled by Rev. **John Henry Livingston** (1770–1825), with substantial independence for the Coetus. The organization of a General Synod, 1792, made the American church independent.

1633. THE ROMAN CATHOLIC CHURCH. The first group of Catholics to arrive in the English colonies came to Maryland, which had been founded (1632) to provide refuge for that denomination. Instructions from the proprietor, Cecilius Calvert, allowed freedom of religion to all Christians, and bid Roman Catholics to worship "as privately as may be." For the Toleration Act (1649) and its repeal (1654), see p. 35. The Revolution of 1689 in Maryland, leading to Protestant ascendancy, resulted in the passage of anti-Catholic legislation (1) imposing poll tax on Irish Catholic immigrant servants; (2) requiring that children of mixed marriages be reared as Protestants; (3) imposing a fine for sending children to Catholic schools abroad. Thenceforward to the American Revolution the Roman Catholic Church subsisted on a clandestine basis. In New York Roman Catholics enjoyed toleration under the administration of the Catholic Governor, Thomas Dongan (1682–88), but between 1691 and 1776 they were deprived of both political rights and religious freedom. In the beginning of the 18th century Rhode Island and Pennsylvania were the only colonies in which Roman Catholics enjoyed religious and civil rights. St. Joseph's Church, Philadelphia, 1733, was the first completely public Catholic church in the English colonies. For Protestant opposition to the Quebec Act, 1774, see p. 98. By 1775 public worship by Roman Catholics was confined to Pennsylvania (with Jesuit churches and chapels in Philadelphia, Conewago, Goschenhoppen, Lancaster, and Reading).

1639. BAPTISTS (opposed to infant baptism and stressing the separation of church and state) were organized as a church by **Roger Williams** (p. 1185) at Providence, R.I., followed by Newport (1644). Large gains were made in the Middle Colonies among the Welsh and as a result of the Quaker schism. In addition, their membership expanded as a result of (1) the Great Awakening and (2) the American Revolution, with substantive gains among the rural population of the South. Under such leaders as **Isaac Backus** (1724–1806) and **John Leland** (1754–1841), they were active on behalf of religious liberty and the separation of church and state.

1640. LUTHERAN CHURCH. Rev. **Reorus Torkillus**, first Lutheran minister to serve in the New World, arrived in New Sweden (spring 1640). In 1649 Dutch Lutherans organized a congregation in New Netherland. Large immigration of German Lutherans to New York began in 1708; after 1722, main stream flowed to Pennsylvania. The first synod was organized (1748) under Rev. **Heinrich Melchior Mühlenberg** (1711–87). The organization of the Ministerium of Pennsylvania led ultimately to the independence of the Lutheran Church in the U.S., with some 130 congregations, chiefly in Pennsylvania, at the outbreak of the Revolution.

1654. JEWS. Despite the efforts of Stuyvesant to deprive them of civil rights, the first group of Jews, arriving in New Amsterdam (1654) from Curaçao, induced the Dutch West India Co. (7 Jews were among the 167 stockholders) to permit them to reside and engage in wholesale trade (1655–56). In 1657 they were admitted to the retail trades. In 1685 they demanded the right of public worship, denied under Dutch rule, and a synagogue (Shearith Israel, "Remnant of Israel") was known to exist in New York City in 1695. In 1737 their right to vote for the N.Y. Assembly was denied. Admitted in Rhode Island to the freemanship (1665), they were later denied political rights (1728), which were restored by the state constitution (1777). Similarly, in South Carolina voting was confined to Christians (1721), but at least one Jew was elected to public office—Francis Salvador, Jr., to the first provincial congress. In Savannah, Ga., Jews held minor public office (1765–88), with David Emanuel elected governor (1801). The disqualification of the Maryland constitution of 1776, barring Jews from public office, was finally removed in 1826; in North Carolina, not until 1868. The Jews prior to 1789 were mainly **Sephardim** (of Spanish, Portuguese, and Dutch origin).

1656. QUAKERS (SOCIETY OF FRIENDS), founded by George Fox (1624–91), stressed "inner light," separation of church and state, opposition to war and oaths. Except in Rhode Island, they were persecuted in the period, 1656–70 (p. 44). Expansion of this sect is attributed to the visit of Fox to America (1671) and to Penn's "Holy Experiment" (1681, pp. 57, 1125). As a result of a schism in 1692 between Penn and **George Keith** (c.1638–1716), principal of the Penn Charter School, the latter founded a sect known as Christian, or Baptist, Quakers, or "Keithians," and then was ordained in the Church of England (1700).

1683. MENNONITES, led by **Francis Daniel Pastorius** (1651–c.1720), settled in Germantown, Pa. They advocated separation of church and state, religious liberty, adult baptism, a church of the elect, pacifism, refusal to take oaths, and drew up the first protest against slavery (1688). Most conservative of this group were the **Amish.** The Old Amish Order still uses the German language exclusively and is opposed to innovation.

1706. PRESBYTERIANS. The first presbytery was organized in Philadelphia by **Francis Makemie** (1658–1708); the first synod in 1718. The Adopting Act, the first constitution of American Presbyterianism, was adopted (1729). Expansion was due to the founding of "log colleges," especially the one by Rev. **William Tennent, Sr.** (c.1673–1746) at Neshaminy (1736), and by the establishment of the College of New Jersey (1746). Synod of 1786 provided for a General Assembly, the first meeting of which was held in Philadelphia (1789).

1721. Hollis Chair in Divinity, the first professorship in theology, was established at Harvard.

1723. DUNKARDS, OR GERMAN BAPTISTS, were organized under the leadership of **Alexander Mack.** Their distinctive features were triple immersion, pacifism, and agape feasts.

1726–56. GREAT AWAKENING, a series of revivals, usually dates from the preaching of Domine **Theodorus Frelinghuysen** (1691–1748), a Dutch Reformed minister in New Jersey, the establishment of Tennent's log college (1736), and the first visit of **George Whitefield** (p. 1181) to Georgia (1738) and his later itinerant preaching from Maine to Georgia (1739–40). In New England, undisputed leadership in the movement was assumed by **Jonathan Edwards** (p. 1021), beginning with his sermons of 1734. In Virginia it attained its peak, 1748–49, under Rev. **Samuel Davies** (1723–61). Stubal Stearns and Daniel Marshall spread the movement among the Virginia Baptists. The Methodist phase, under Rev. Devereux Jarrett, reached its climax, 1775–85. Among Presbyterians, the Great Awakening led to a schism between "New Side" (revivalists, who organized an independent synod, 1745) and "Old Side" (conservatives), which was healed in 1758. Among Congregationalists a similar division developed, with the more conservative joining the Anglican Church. The Awakening heightened back-country opposition to religious restriction, intensified the Protestant tradition to set limits to governmental power, and promoted the democratization of society.

1732. EPHRATA SOCIETY, an offshoot of the German Baptists, was founded by **Johann Conrad Beissel.** The group stressed the monastic life, chastity, and the 7th-day sabbath. For contributions to music, see p. 915.

1734. SCHWENKFELDERS, followers of the radical mystic Kaspar Schwenkfeld (1489–1561), made their first appearance in Pennsylvania, but lacked formal organization until 1782.

1735. MORAVIANS, OR UNITED BRETHREN, comprising Hussites and German Pietists, came to Georgia in 1735, under the leadership of **Augustus Gottlieb Spangenberg** (1704–92), to convert the Indians. Then, after impressing John Wesley with their pietist faith, they removed to Pennsylvania, where, under Count **Nikolaus Zinzendorf** (1700–60), they founded a settlement at Bethlehem (1741). Spangenberg was consecrated bishop of the Church in America (1744). In that year a semi-communistic General Economy was established at Bethlehem (at Winston-Salem, N.C., 1753), but was dissolved, 1762, when the crafts and trades returned to private management. Control was exercised from Herrnhut, Saxony. Not until 1857 was the American Church given a constitution with relative independence from German control. Renowned for church music, notably part-singing of congregations.

1747. THE GERMAN REFORMED CHURCH, organized by **Michael Schlat-**

ter (1716–90) as a subordinate body of the Dutch Reformed Church, made large gains among the Pennsylvania Germans. The church remained under Dutch control until 1793.

c.1750. RISE OF RATIONALISM. Influenced by John Locke (1632–1704), who applied the scientific method to problems of human understanding, the need for toleration, and the basis of government, were such seminal figures as Rev. Jonathan Mayhew (1720–66) and Charles Chauncey (1705–87), who, by stressing the function of reason apart from revelation (p. 847), laid the foundation for Unitarianism.

1766. METHODISM began in America, as in England, as a movement within the Church of England. It appeared first in New York City (1766) with the organization by **Philip Embury** (1728–73) of the John Street Church, and was expanded by the activities of itinerant preachers sent out by Wesley (1771), notably **Francis Asbury** (1745–1815). In Virginia, Rev. **Devereux Jarratt** (1733–1801), an Anglican minister, acted as unofficial chaplain to the Methodists. Centered first in Dinwiddie Co., Va., Jarratt (beginning in 1777) spread the Methodist faith through a dozen counties of Virginia and North Carolina, with a circuit some 500 miles long.

1774. SHAKERS, OR "MILLENNIAL CHURCH," a Protestant monastic group, first arrived in the colonies, led by Mother **Ann Lee** (1736–84). Settling at Watervliet, N.Y., they set up a socialistic Christian community. Scored gains in Kentucky and Ohio, with greatest growth, 1830–50.

1775–83. CHURCHES AND THE REVOLUTION. The Anglican clergy throughout the colonies were Loyalist, the Southern laity overwhelmingly Patriot. The Congregational and Presbyterian clergy took a Patriot stand. The Methodist missionaries were Loyalist.

Lutherans and Roman Catholics were divided in loyalty. The Quakers, officially neutral, leaned toward the Loyalists, as did the Shakers.

RELIGIOUS CENSUS, 1775 (Based on Rough Estimates—3,105 Religious Organizations and Congregations)	
Congregationalists	575,000
Anglicans	500,000
Presbyterians	410,000
Dutch Reformed	75,000
German Churches (incl. German Reformed, 50,000, and Lutheran in Pa., 75,000)	200,000
Quakers	40,000
Baptists	25,000
Roman Catholics	25,000
Methodists	5,000
Jews	2,000

1776–89. DISESTABLISHMENT. Under the leadership of Baptists and Presbyterians the movement for religious freedom and separation of church and state gained headway in Virginia in the Revolutionary period. Mainly the work of **George Mason** (1725–92) and **James Madison**, the Virginia **Declaration of Rights** (12 June 1776) advocated "free exercise of religion." An act of 1776 suspending payment of tithes (becoming effective 1 Jan. 1777) really disestablished the Church of England, although final steps were taken in Jefferson's Bill for Establishing Religious Freedom, passed through Madison's efforts (1785), and preceded by the latter's "Memorial and Remonstrance against Religious Assessments" (1784). Elsewhere the church was disestablished: 1776, Pa., Del., and N.J.; 1777, N.Y., N.C., and Ga. (partially, completely in 1789); 1790, S.C.; 1818, Conn.; 1833, Mass.

1780. UNIVERSALISTS. The first American Universalist church, built by Rev. John Murray (1741–1815) in Gloucester, Mass., favored separation of church and state. Its leading spokesman, **Hosea Ballou** (1771–1852), stressed Unitarian theology combined with evangelical conviction. "Winchester Program" adopted, 1803. General Convention, governing body, established 1833; incorporated, 1866; merged with Unitarians (1961).

1782. FIRST PAROCHIAL SCHOOL erected by St. Mary's Church, Philadelphia ("Mother School"). The system was officially sanctioned in Baltimore (1829). By 1840, there were 200 parochial schools in the U.S. In 1951, there were 236 colleges with 236,636 students, 1,628 high schools (diocesan and parochial) with 337,414 students, and 8,202 elementary schools (parochial) with 2,575,329 students.

1784. THEOLOGICAL SCHOOLS. The first theological college in the U.S. was established at New Brunswick, N.J. Other important seminaries were. Andover (founded to oppose Unitarian trends at Harvard, 1808), Princeton (1812), General (1817), Auburn (1818), Virginia (1823), Hartford (1834), and Union Theological (1836).

1784. Sixty **Methodist** preachers convened in Baltimore (Nov.) and organized an Episcopal Church independent from Anglicanism, with Francis Asbury (consecrated bishop, 1784) as its head. A schism led by James O'Kelley, who opposed Asbury's appointive powers, resulted in the organization of the Republican Methodist Church (1792). The Methodist Protestants seceded (1830).

1789. PROTESTANT EPISCOPAL CHURCH, depleted by Loyalist emigration, now independent of the Church of England, was organized at its first triennial convention in Philadelphia, and adopted canons along with revised prayers. By 1792 five bishops had been named.

1790. ROMAN CATHOLIC EPISCOPATE was established with the consecration of Rev. **John Carroll** (1735–1815); nominated, 1788; previously, 1784, appointed superior with power to administer confirmation. Political discrimina-

tion against Catholics continued until 1835 (N.C.).

1792. RUSSIAN ORTHODOX CHURCH began missionary activities in Alaska, wtih a resident bishop at Sitka, 1798. The episcopal see was moved to San Francisco (1872), and in 1905 to New York City.

1794. DEISM gained ground after the publication of Tom Paine's *Age of Reason.* Previously such views had been expounded in Ethan Allen's *Reason the Only Oracle of Man* (1784), but deism's most influential exponent in America was **Elihu Palmer,** ex-Baptist preacher, whose *Principles of Nature* (1797) attacked the orthodox tenets of Christianity. Deists established ties with pro-Jacobin democratic societies after 1794.

1797. GREAT REVIVALS began on the frontier with the preaching of **James McGready** (c.1758–1817). His camp-meeting movement was climaxed by the **Cane Ridge Meeting** (Aug. 1801). A schism among revivalists resulted in the organization of the Cumberland Presbyterian Church (1810). In Kentucky, the revival of **Barton W. Stone** (1772–1844) led to the New Light ("Stoneite") schism (1803; ultimately merging with Methodist and Baptist groups as the "Christian Church"). In New England the revival was led by the **Edwardseans,** centered at Yale under **Timothy Dwight** (1752–1817) and **Lyman Beecher** (1775–1863), and opposed by the rationalists and Unitarians.

1800. UNITED BRETHREN IN CHRIST, an Arminian group, was founded by **Martin Boehm** (1725–1812) and **Philip W. Otterbein** (1726–1813), first bishops; merged (1946) with the Evangelical Church, founded, 1800, by **Jacob Albright** (1769–1808).

1801. Adoption of the Presbyterian-Congregational Plan of Union to eliminate competition in regions where one or the other was already established.

1805. RAPPISTS, a group of German pietists led by **George Rapp** (1755–1847), was organized in Pennsylvania, founded New Harmony, Ind. (1815), sold to Robert Owen (1824), and then moved to Economy, near Pittsburgh. A celibate, authoritarian sect, it declined following Rapp's death, and its affairs were terminated (1905).

1810. Organization of the **AMERICAN BOARD OF COMMISSIONERS FOR FOREIGN MISSIONS** (Congregational), which became interdenominational (1812), marked the beginning of American missionary interest. The American Bible Society (1816), the Home Missionary Society (1826), and the American Tract Society (1825) followed. In 1814 the General Missionary Convention of the Baptists for Foreign Missions initiated home missions movement. In 1832 the Baptist Home Missionary Society was organized to operate in the South and West. American Board's missionary activity in Hawaii (beginning 1820) had profound cultural, economic, and political results. Foreign mission movements penetrated India, China, Japan, and Africa.

DISCIPLES OF CHRIST, a group of progressive Presbyterians opposed to closed communion, founded the Independent Church of Christ at **Brush Run,** Pa. Two groups, 1 founded by Rev. **Barton Warren Stone** (1774–1844) and the other by Rev. **Thomas Campbell** (1763–1854) and his son, Alexander (1788–1866) united at Lexington, Ky. (1832).

1813–17. BLACK CHURCHES. Large Negro groups formed independent churches, including African Methodist Episcopal Church (Philadelphia, 1816). The first Negro Baptist church was founded in Georgia (1773). In 1861 there were 200,000 Negro members of the Methodist Episcopal Church, South; 150,000 Negro Baptists.

1818. Connecticut constitution disestablished the Congregational Church.

1819. UNITARIAN CHURCH (stressing unity of God and denying Trinitarianism) founded by **William Ellery Channing** (p. 1000), but the transformation of Boston's King's Chapel from an Anglican to a Unitarian church occurred 18 Nov. 1787. The Dedham Case (Mass., 1820) allowed Unitarians, even though a minority, to retain church property they were occupying after a majority of orthodox had withdrawn, thereby strengthening the denomination.

1820–60. General Synod of the Lutheran Church held at Hagerstown, Md. (Oct. 1820). German (Missouri) Synod established 1847; Norwegian Synod, 1853, ultimately Norwegian Lutheran Church of America. Augustana, Swedish Synod, established 1860.

1824–50. REVIVALISM in Pennsylvania, New York, and Massachusetts led by **Charles G. Finney** (1792–1875), licensed to preach as a Presbyterian. The Broadway Tabernacle was established for him in New York City (1834). His followers withdrew from Presbyterianism (1836) and adopted Congregationalism. In the Middle West revivalism was led by such itinerant preachers as **Peter Cartwright** (1785–1872) and **James B. Finley** (1781–1856).

1827–28. Schism between **Orthodox** and **Hicksite** Quakers.

1828. Presbyterian schism between Old School (orthodox Calvinists) and New School (Western liberals).

1829–54. ANTI-CATHOLIC AGITATION, following the founding of the Society for the Propagation of the Faith (Lyons, France, 1822) and the Leopold Association (Vienna, 1829) to promote Roman Catholic missions in America (with Catholic laity increasing from 200,000 [1829] to 1.75 million [1850]— to which the Irish exodus after 1845 contributed substantially) resulted in such publications as *The Protestant* and *Priestcraft Unmasked,* of anti-Catholic sermons by Rev. **Lyman Beecher** and writings by **Samuel F. B. Morse** and of acts of violence, such as the burning of the Ursuline Convent at Charlestown, Mass. (11 Aug. 1834). For nativism and the Know-Nothing movement of the 1840s and 1850s, see pp. 223, 259.

1830. LATTER-DAY SAINTS, OR MORMONS, owe their origin to the publication of the *Book of Mormon,* based on a revelation claimed by **Joseph Smith** (p. 1154), followed by the founding of the church at Fayette, N.Y., the same year. As a result of opposition, the Mormons left New York (1831) for Kirkland, Ohio, and Independence, Mo. Expelled from Missouri, they settled at Nauvoo, Ill. Violence followed them, culminating in the lynching of Smith in the jail at Carthage. Driven from Nauvoo (1846), the Saints settled in the valley of the Great Salt Lake in Utah (1848) under the leadership of **Brigham Young** (p. 1190). Smith's pronouncement (1848) that polygamy was divinely sanctioned aroused intense opposition by non-Mormons; and led to the passage in Congress of anti-polygamy laws (1862, 1882, 1884). Finally, the church prohibited the practice (1890), and 6 years later Utah gained statehood.

1832–69. SLAVERY AND THE CHURCHES. The issue of abolitionism came to a head when Theodore Dwight Weld, a student at Lane Theological Seminary, Cincinnati, was dismissed from that institution when the trustees suppressed an antislavery society (1834). In the North abolitionism quickly became part of revivalism. The issue divided the Protestant churches. The Southern Baptists withdrew (1843) to organize the Southern Baptist Convention. The Methodist Church, South, set up a separate organization (1844). An abolitionist group of New School Presbyterians organized the Synod of Free Presbyterian Churches, Ohio (1847), followed by a major schism in the New School (1857), when the United Synod of the South was established. Old School Presbyterians split (1861), and the Presbyterian Church in the Confederate States was founded. The Ohio Synod and the New School Presbyterians united in 1862. In 1864 the Southern groups united as the Presbyterian Church in the U.S. The Northern groups united as the Presbyterian Church in the U.S.A. (1869). Division on this issue was avoided in the Protestant Episcopal Church.

1833. Massachusetts disestablished the church by constitutional amendment, ratified by popular vote of 32,234 to 3,273.

1840–60. REFORM AND CONSERVATIVE JUDAISM. Rabbis **Isaac Mayer Wise** (1819–1900), through *The Israelite,* established in Cincinnati, and **David Einhorn** (1809–79), in Baltimore (1855), transplanted from Germany the notion of reform (including vernacular worship, sermons, and hymns). In 1873 Wise organized the Union of American Hebrew Congregations, followed (1875) by Hebrew Union College in Cincinnati (merged with the Jewish Institute of Religion, New York City, 1948) and (1889) the Central Conference of American Rabbis. A conservative movement in opposition was headed by Rabbis **Isaac Leeser** (1806–68) and **Sabato Morais** (1823–97) of Philadelphia. The Jewish Theological Seminary (conservative) was founded (1886). Ashkenazi Orthodoxy reflected waves of immigration of Eastern European Jews from 1880s to World War I.

c.1840–60. GOSPEL OF INDIVIDUALISM, combining rationalism and evangelical Protestantism, was expounded by **Francis Wayland** (1796–1865), president of Brown University, and author of *Elements of Moral Science* (1835).

1843. MILLERISM, an Adventist movement, resulted from the preaching of **William Miller** (1782–1849), who prophesied the second coming of Christ between 1843–44. His followers founded the Adventist Church (1845). The **Seventh-Day Adventists** separated from the parent body (1846), with headquarters at Battle Creek, Mich. (1855), and later (1903) near Washington, D.C., where Ellen G. White (1827–1915) organized a united and rapidly growing movement, stressing legalism, Sabbatarianism, and strong views on health, medicine, and diet.

RISE OF THE BLACK CHURCHES. In the Revolutionary era black congregations appeared, notably the Baptists at Silver Bluff, S.C. 1773–75, with dozens of others, mostly Baptist, by 1800. By 1821 2 independent African Methodist Episcopal churches had been formed. The antislavery movement spurred Southern missionary activity, which sought to counter the antislavery movement. At the start of Civil War formal membership of Southern blacks (est.): Methodists, 225,000; Baptists, 175,000. After the Civil War blacks organized separate churches: Colored Primitive Baptists, 1866; National Baptist Convention, 1895; Colored Presbyterian Church, 1874; Methodists, 1870.

1847. THEOLOGICAL LIBERALISM was exemplified by the publication of Rev. **Horace Bushnell's** (1802–76) *Christian Nurture,* stressing mysticism, free will, and Christian nurture, rather than election, as the road to salvation.

1874. The publication of *Outlines of Cosmic Philosophy* by **John Fiske** (1842–1901), with its attempt to reconcile theism with Darwinian evolution, brought theological liberalism (advocated by

Rev. **Henry Ward Beecher** [p. 982], Rev. **Lyman Abbott** [1835–1922], **Washington Gladden** [1836–1918], Rev. **Phillips Brooks** [p. 992], **John William Draper** [1811–82], and **Andrew D. White** [1832–1918]) into open conflict with orthodoxy.

1875–86. Archbishop **John McClosky** became the first American cardinal. Archbishop **James Gibbons** (p. 1040) was elected to the same rank (1886). The Catholic Univ. of America was founded at Washington, D.C., by the third plenary council (1884).

1875–92. CHRISTIAN SCIENCE textbook, *Science and Health,* by **Mary Baker Eddy** (p. 1020), was published and the Christian Science Association organized. The first church was established at Boston, 1879; reorganized, 1892.

1876. SOCIETY FOR ETHICAL CULTURE established in New York by **Felix Adler** (1851–1933).

1880. SALVATION ARMY, evangelistic organization, after being first established by Gen. William Booth in England, was organized in the U.S.

1892. HIGHER CRITICISM resulted in several heresy trials, notably that of **Charles A. Briggs** (1841–1913), professor at Union Theological Seminary. Tried (1892) and acquitted, he was suspended from the Presbyterian ministry and subsequently entered the ministry of the Protestant Episcopal Church.

1898. ZIONISM. Following first Zionist Congress in Basel (1897), Zionism, a movement for Jewish colonization of the Bible homeland in Palestine, spurred Federation of American Zionists (1898), with Rabbi Stephen S. Wise (1874–1949) as secretary. Antisemitism of the 1930s served to advance Zionist cause in U.S., a movement culminating in the establishment of the state of Israel (1948).

1902. Five Years Meeting (a loose confederation) formed by 13 Yearly

Meetings of the Society of Friends. Kansas and Oregon have since withdrawn. Three Yearly Meetings from outside the U.S. have joined.

1905. The Federal Council of Churches of Christ in America, first major interdenominational organization, was founded; succeeded (1950) by the National Council of Churches of Christ in the U.S.A.

1907. SOCIAL GOSPEL. Publication of *Christianity and the Social Crisis* by **Walter Rauschenbusch** (p. 1135), with its criticism of capitalism and the industrial revolution and its stress on cooperation rather than competition. His views had been anticipated as far back as 1876 with the publication by **Washington Gladden** (1836–1918) of *Working People and their Employers,* and other works aiming to Christianize the social order.

1908. Home Missions Council established to direct noncompetitive missionary activity.

1909–25. FUNDAMENTALIST REACTION, inspired by such traveling evangelists as William Jennings Bryan (p. 992), William A. ("Billy") Sunday, and John Alexander Dowie, reached its climax at Dayton, Tenn. (10–21 July 1925), in the trial and conviction of **John Scopes,** a Tenn. schoolteacher, for teaching evolution contrary to a state law enacted 21 Mar. 1925 (Okla. first state to pass anti-evolution act [1923]). Scopes was opposed by Bryan; defended by Clarence Darrow and Dudley Field Malone.

1918. United Lutheran Church in U.S. formed, placing 45 synods on the same doctrinal basis.

1918. RECONSTRUCTIONISM, expounded at the Jewish Center (N.Y.) by **Mordecai M. Kaplan** (1881–   ), stressed the totality of Jewish civilization.

1931. BLACK MUSLIMS founded in Detroit, Mich., by Wali Farad, considered messenger from Allah to **Elijah Muhammad** (b. Elijah Poole, 1897–1975). Religion stressed black supremacy and separatism.

1931. JEHOVAH'S WITNESSES, under the leadership of Judge J. F. Rutherford (originating with the Russellites, incorporated by Pastor Charles T. Russell, 1884), were incorporated (1939) as The Watch Tower Bible and Tract Society. For Jehovah's Witnesses cases, see p. 677.

c.1935. NEO-ORTHODOXY, a synthesis of the socioeconomic liberalism of the Social Gospel and a rediscovery of Biblical theology, with stress on the fall of man and the judgment of God, secured a wide following among American Protestants under the leadership of **Paul Tillich** (1886–1965) and **Reinhold Niebuhr** (p. 1115).

1939. Methodist Episcopal Church, Methodist Episcopal Church, South, and the Methodist Protestant Church were reunited.

1952. Bible, Revised Standard Version (Natl. Council, Churches of Christ, U.S.A.), best seller; also Roman Catholic Confraternity translation, vol. I.

1950–60. PROTESTANT CHURCH UNITY TREND. National Council of the Churches of Christ in the U.S.A. formed 29 Nov. 1950 by 25 Protestant denominations and 5 Eastern Orthodox bodies embracing 37 million church members. Congregational Christian Churches and the Evangelical Reformed Church united (June, 1957) to form the United Church of Christ. Presbyterian Church in the U.S.A. and United Presbyterian Church joined 28 May, 1958 to form the United Presbyterian Church in the U.S.A. On 4 Dec. 1960 the chief executive officer of the United Presbyterian Church proposed a merger into a new church of the Methodist, Protestant Episcopal, and United Presbyterian

Churches and the United Church of Christ, with total membership of 12,-250,000 for the 4 churches.

1954–57. Evangelist **Rev. Dr. Billy Graham** (1918–   ), who began a series of popular evangelistic campaigns in 1946, toured Great Britain and western Europe in 1954–55, and conducted a 16-week campaign in New York City, culminating 27 Oct. 1957.

1960s–1970s. NON-WESTERN RELIGIOUS UPSURGE. Various mystical and occult cults gained in popularity, including **theosophy** (org. N.Y., 1875), and spread by Madame Helena Petrovna Blavatsky (1831–91) and Annie Wood Besant (1847–1933), with its concern for the Hindu and Buddhist tradition; **Vedanta,** with Transcendantal Meditation, spread by Maharishi Mashesh Yogi, a notable offshoot; and **Bahaism,** from a messianic sect of the Shiite Islam of Iran (beg. in U.S. 1893), centered at Wilmette, Ill. Similarly, **Zen Buddhism** enjoyed surging popularity among college students.

1960–74. ECUMENISM. Secular trends tended to undermine old confessional commitments and interchurch cooperation burgeoned. The Consultation on Christian Churches (COCU) proposed highly acceptable terms of reunion for 10 major Protestant denominations while Catholic-Protestant dialogue expanded. In Dec. 1973 the Anglican-Roman Catholic International Commission reported it had reached "basic agreement" on the nature of the Christian ministry. A joint commission of U.S. Roman Catholic theologians in a study issued 3 Mar. 1974 declared that papal primacy need no longer be a "barrier to reconciliation of their churches," the first time since the 16th century that the 2 creeds agreed on crucial aspects of papal authority, thus clearing the way for Christian unity. The U.S. Roman Catholic hierarchy was also engaged in separate

dialogues with 4 other Protestant groups as well as with the Orthodox churches. **Church affiliation in 20th century** rose from est. 43% (1910) to 62.4% (1970).

CHURCH MEMBERSHIP 1980
(1980 Yearbook of American and Canadian Churches)
(summary in millions)

Roman Catholic Church	49.6
Southern Baptist Convention	13.2
United Methodist Church	9.7
National Baptist Convention, USA	6.3
Church of Jesus Christ of Latter-Day Saints (Mormon)	3.2
Lutheran Church in America	2.9
Episcopal Church	2.8
National Baptist Convention of America	2.7
Lutheran Church-Missouri Synod	2.6
United Presbyterian Church in the USA	2.5
Churches of Christ	2.5
American Lutheran Church	2.4
Muslims	2.0
African Methodist Episcopal Church	2.0
Greek Orthodox Archdiocese of North and South America	2.0
United Church of Christ	1.8
United Synagogues of America (Conservative)	1.5
Assemblies of God (Pentecostal)	1.3

1960–74. CHALLENGES TO TRADITION. Reexamination of religious values and structures was sparked by such writings as **H. Richard Niebuhr's** *Radical Monotheism* (1960), **Gabriel Vahanian's** *The Death of God: The Culture of Our Post-Christian Era* (1961), **Peter Berger's** *The Noise of Solemn Assemblies* (1961), **Martin Marty's** *The Second Chance for American Protestantism* (1963), **Thomas O'Dea's** *The Catholic Crisis* (1968), and other provocative works giving a secular interpretation of the gospel, stripping the Bible of mythology, and laying bare the moribund state of religious institutions and traditions. Reaction to these critiques took a variety of forms. The United Presbyterian Church of the U.S., making the first major change in the Presbyterian position in 320 years, adopted a new confession of faith (1967). The widespread support for family planning, along with recently enacted liberalized abortion laws and judicial decisions in the U.S., prompted unprecedented resistance to Pope Paul's manifesto *Humanae Vitae* (July 1968), condemning artificial methods of birth control.

1963–77. AMERICAN SAINTS. Elizabeth Ann Bayley (**Mother**) **Seton** (1774–1821), founder of the Sisters of Charity of St. Joseph at Emmitsburg, Md., in 1809, was the first native-born American to receive beatification (17 Mar. 1963) and canonization (14 Sept. 1974). John Nipomucene Neumann (1811–60), fourth bishop of Philadelphia, was beatified 13 Oct. 1963 and elevated to sainthood 19 June 1977. Mother Frances Xavier Cabrini, a naturalized American, had been canonized in 1946.

1965. PAPAL VISIT. Pope Paul VI became the first Pontiff to visit the United States (4 Oct.). During his one-day visit to New York City, he spoke at the United Nations, talked privately with President Johnson, and conducted a mass at Yankee Stadium.

1967–73. Responding to the Six-Day Arab-Israeli War (1967) and the Yom Kippur War (1973) American Jews sent extraordinary aid to Israel, setting new records for U.S. private philanthropy.

1961–73. REFORM, ECUMENISM, AND SOCIAL INVOLVEMENT. Changing evaluations of the role of religious leaders contributed to the increased participation of clergymen in social and political conflicts. In 1960 the Southern Christian Leadership Conference (Rev. Martin Luther King, Jr.) and the Alabama Christian Movement for Human Rights (Rev. Frederick L. Shuttlesworth) were formed to act as Christian instruments for the promotion of better treatment of Negroes. As the civil rights movement gained momentum, the active participation of religious leaders of all faiths was enlisted. Religious leaders spoke out against the war in Vietnam and religious organizations acted to combat the problems of poverty. The Women's Movement was reflected in a steady pressure to ordain women in the ministry.

The church unification movement continued as the American, Evangelical, and United Evangelical Lutheran churches joined in 1960. The Methodist Church merged wtih the Evangelical United Brethren Church to become the United Methodist Church, the largest Protestant church in the U.S. (1966), while other religious reunions were spurred by the Consultation on Christian Union (COCU).

Within both Catholic and Protestant religious bodies there were reexaminations and protests against traditional structures of authority combined with reforms, reflecting in part the worldwide influence of Pope John XXIII and Vatican Council II.

1973–80. DEVELOPMENTS IN RELIGION (p. 560).

Education

The American educational tradition was the result of the confluence of four distinct streams of thought which had their sources in widely scattered parts of Europe and which reached America during the colonial and early national periods. Perhaps the widest stream flowed from the Protestant Reformation, with the Reformers' emphasis on education for religious and moral purposes. A second stream, with tributaries coming from Central Europe and England, introduced the utilitarian principle of education, the ideal of the Czech philosopher-educator-theologian John Amos Comenius and the English pioneer of the inductive method, Francis Bacon. The third stream had its origins in the Renaissance tradition and carried with it the ideal of the well-rounded gentleman scholar. The last stream, which joined the others somewhat later, came from John Locke and was to be replenished by French Enlightenment thought, stressing the role of education for civic and moral purposes. Until late in the nineteenth century, Renaissance and Reformation ideals dominated the colleges, but at the lower levels the other traditions proved far more influential.

Educational reform was the most popular and widely supported of all the reform movements of the period 1830–60. The reformers held that education was the responsibility of the community and that elementary education should be required of all children. As the fight for public schools was being won, reformers turned their attention to the conditions of the educational system itself, with such resultant innovations as the broadening of the school curriculum beyond the "three R's," the study of modern languages instead of Latin and Greek, and a gradual secularization of the ends of education.

After the Civil War public support and private philanthropy in combination stimulated an enormous expansion in higher education, with the enactment in 1862 of the Morrill Act, setting up the land-grant colleges, a major factor. New directions in education transformed the college curriculum. Notable among such reforms was the introduction of the elective system, associated with President Charles W. Eliot of Harvard, and the rise of graduate schools, modeled at the start largely on the German examples. By the third quarter of the twentieth century issues of desegregation, government support for private and parochial education, and a revolution in the career expectations of young people commanded increasing attention. Those who would reappraise the traditional role of teacher, student, and administrator and advocate for education a responsibility to be involved in community and societal problem solving were countered by traditionalists concerned with the decline of discipline and intellectual values.

1636–1775. ELEMENTARY SCHOOLS. Diversity in the 3 major regional systems was the result of (1) religious differences at the time of settlement and (2) divergences in the economic and social structure of the areas. **New England** (influenced by Calvinist emphasis upon individual responsibility for salvation and the concomitant necessity of each individual's reading the Bible) was committed to the **compulsory** maintenance program as developed in 2 Massachusetts laws:

1642. Act imposed fines for neglect of education.

1647. Act required all towns of 50 families to provide a teacher for instruction in reading and writing; all towns of 100 families to establish a Latin grammar school (already set up in Boston, 1636). The act made it optional whether the school was to be tax-supported or fee-supported, and imposed a penalty of £5 (raised in 1671 to £10) for noncompliance. Similar acts passed by Connecticut, 1650; Plymouth, 1671; New Hampshire, 1689; with Rhode Island only exception. Although historians disagree as to the extent of enforcement of this law, statistical evidence points to a higher degree of literacy in New England than elsewhere (1640–1700, 95% literacy [Shipton] as against 54%–60% for males in Virginia [Bruce]).

1692. Disallowance of Massachusetts statute reviving compulsory education laws resulted in adoption of policy whereby selectmen or overseers of poor were empowered to bind out as apprentices "any poor children."

1765. At least 48 out of the 140 Massachusetts towns with a population of 100 families or more were maintaining Latin schools.

The **Middle Colonies** adopted a **parochial school** program, both as a result of private and church efforts. New Amsterdam: 1638, first school under Adam Roelantsen, Dutch Reformed auspices but town-supported; 1659, classical school established. New York: despite act of 1702 to encourage a free grammar school in New York City, activity was left to the Venerable Society (S.P.G.), which in 1710 founded the Trinity School. Chief emphasis thereafter was upon charity and private schools. Pennsylvania: 1689, Friends' School, Philadelphia (chartered, 1697, later known as William Penn Charter School). In the Northern and Middle colonies **apprenticeship** generally imposed educational requirements, such as one quarter's schooling each year, necessitating the establishment in the 18th century of **evening schools** in the larger towns.

In the **South** apprenticeship was the leading method for educating the poor (in Virginia book education provided by

act of 1705), supplemented by the establishment of **pauper schools** (county pauper schools established in Maryland, 1723). Children of planters were educated by tutors or through private fee-supported schools.

1750–1860. ACADEMY (with a broader and more practical curriculum) came to supplant the Latin grammar school. Franklin's Academy (1751) had 3 curricula: English, mathematical, and classical; **Phillips Andover** (1778); **Phillips Exeter** (1783) 2 curricula: classical and English. Although especially popular in the South, the academy was by no means confined to that area (Massachusetts, 1840, had 112 chartered academies).

1636–1775. HIGHER EDUCATION. Nine colleges founded before the Revolution.

1636. Harvard (Congregational) established by bequest of John Harvard and a grant from the Massachusetts General Court.

1693. William and Mary (Anglican) through efforts of Rev. **James Blair** (1655–1743).

1701. Yale (Congregational), located at New Haven, 1716; named in honor of benefactor, Elihu Yale, 1718.

1746. College of New Jersey (Presbyterian); name changed to Princeton 1896.

1751. Franklin's Academy (originally nonsectarian), chartered 1754; reorg. as University of Pennsylvania, 1779.

1754. King's College (nonsectarian under Anglican control), largely suspended activities, 1776–84; reopened 1784 as Columbia College.

1764. Rhode Island College (Baptist); renamed Brown University, 1804, in honor of Nicholas Brown, benefactor.

1766. Queen's College (Dutch Reformed); renamed Rutgers, 1825, in honor of benefactor, Col. Henry Rutgers.

1769. Dartmouth College (Congregational), named for Lord Dartmouth, patron; originally Rev. **Eleazar Wheelock's** (1711–79) Indian school, established at Lebanon, Conn.; moved to Hanover, N.H., 1770.

1765–1817. PROFESSIONAL TRAINING was first provided in **medicine** by the College of Philadelphia, 1765 (affiliated with the Univ. of Pennsylvania, 1791), and by the medical department of King's College, 1767. The first **law** lectures were offered by Chancellor **George Wythe** (1726–1806) at William and Mary, 1779–89. In the post-Revolutionary period law schools were established by Judge Tapping Reeve at **Litchfield,** Conn. (1784–1833), and Peter Van Schaack at **Kinderhook,** N.Y. (1786–1830s), and law lectures at Pennsylvania (1790), Columbia (1797), and Transylvania (1799). A law faculty was organized at the Univ. of Maryland (1812) and a law school was opened at Harvard (1817).

1776, 5 Dec. Phi Beta Kappa (national scholarship fraternity) founded at William and Mary, Williamsburg, Va.

1779–86. Introduction by **Thomas Jefferson** of a school bill into the Virginia legislature containing the first definite proposal for a modern state school system (free tuition to all free children for 3 years, with attendance voluntary; outstanding students to be given grammar school education, with superior scholars furnished an additional 3 years at William and Mary). No action by the legislature.

1805–67. ORIGINS OF THE FREE PUBLIC SCHOOL:

1805. Establishment of Free School Society (later known as Public School Society) of New York, a private philanthropic body, opposed to the pauper school system. **De Witt Clinton** first president of board of trustees.

1806. First Bell-Lancastrian school in the U.S. (employing monitorial system of mass instruction) established at New York City; reduced teaching costs.

1834–67. Free School vs. Pauper School. Pennsylvania Free School Act, 1834, created school districts with option (supplanting act of 1802 for educating paupers at public expense); attempted repeal, 1835, blocked through efforts of **Thaddeus Stevens;** fully adopted, 1873. New York held two referenda, 1849–50 —cities (majority) favored having state assume rate bills by general tax; rural districts opposed. Result: a compromise (poor children entitled to free education with local option) adopted; in force until 1867, by which date public schools were free to all. Connecticut, Rhode Island, Michigan, and New Jersey followed by 1871.

1837–39. Major school reforms effected by **Horace Mann** (p. 1096), secretary of the newly established Massachusetts State Board of Education (first state normal school in U.S. established at Lexington, Mass., 1839) and by **Henry Barnard** (p. 980), appointed secretary of the Connecticut Board of School Commissioners, 1838.

1816–1902. EDUCATIONAL EXTENSION:

1816–73. Infant school introduced in Boston, 1816, and included in the public school system, 1818; admitted children at 4 years; New York, 1827. First German **kindergarten** (Froebel) introduced in the U.S. at Watertown, Wis., 1855, by Mrs. Carl Schurz; first English kindergarten at Boston, 1860, by **Elizabeth Peabody** (1804–94); first public school kindergarten by Susan Blow at St. Louis (1873) under sponsorship of **William Torrey Harris** (1835–1908), superintendent of schools (national Commissioner of Education, 1889–1906).

1821–27. First **high school** in U.S. established in Boston, 1821, with broad, liberal curriculum. Massachusetts act of 1827 required every town of 500 families to establish a high school.

1826–83. Josiah Holbrook (1788–1854) instituted adult education and self-improvement courses at Millbury, Conn., where he established the Millbury Lyceum No. 1, branch of the American Lyceum, thus inaugurating the **lyceum** movement. The National American Lyceum was organized at New York in 1831. By 1834 there were 3,000 town lyceums in 15 states. In 1874 Bishop **John H. Vincent** (1832–1920) and Lewis Miller organized the first **Chautauqua Assembly.** Home reading program established by 1878. **William Rainey Harper** (1856–1906, later president of the University of Chicago) appointed educational director, 1883; attracted outstanding lecturers. Young Men's Christian Assn. set up evening classes in the 1880s. In 1888 the New York City Board of Education established public lectures for working people. Other public lectures provided by Lowell Institute of Boston (inaugurated by Benjamin Silliman, 1839); Peabody Institute, Baltimore (1857); Cooper Union, New York (1857–59), endowed by **Peter Cooper** (p. 1006).

**1821–36. WOMEN'S EDUCATION:
1821.** The Troy (N.Y.) Female Seminary, the first women's high school in the U.S., established by **Emma Willard** (p. 1184).

1833. Oberlin College (Oberlin, Ohio) opened its doors to women, thus becoming the first coeducational college in the U.S.

1836. Mount Holyoke Female Seminary (later Mount Holyoke College), South Hadley, Mass., first permanent women's college, founded by **Mary Lyon.**

By 1902 women made up 25% of the undergraduates, 26% of graduate students, 3% of professional enrollment, with 128 women's colleges founded by 1901.

1789–1860. RISE OF STATE UNIVERSITIES. Univ. of North Carolina (1789) first state university to begin instruction (1795). Univ. of Georgia first state university to be chartered (1785), but not established until 1801. Other early state universities: Vermont, 1800; Univ. of South Carolina, 1801; Univ. of Virginia, 1819, a project conceived by Jefferson. Although the national government, beginning with Ohio, 1802, granted 2 townships to each new Western state for a university, there were only 17 state universities out of a total of 246 in 1860.

1862–1952. FEDERAL LEGISLATION. Morrill Act (p. 636) provided for grants of land to states to aid the establishment of agricultural colleges. Resulted in vast expansion of agricultural and engineering schools and served as the keystone of higher education in the Middle West and Far West. Extension of federal aid provided by Hatch Act (1887, p. 310), Smith-Lever Act (1914, p. 327), Smith-Hughes Act (1917, p. 330).

1944–66. "**G.I. Bill**" (Servicemen's Readjustment Act) of 1944 provided payments for tuition fees, books, and living expenses for up to 4 years of education for World War II veterans. Similar education benefit programs were provided (1952) for Korean War veterans and for post-Korean War and Vietnam War veterans (1966).

1861–1952. MAIN TRENDS IN HIGHER EDUCATION. Elective system fully in effect at Harvard under the administration of President **Charles W. Eliot** (p. 1023); swing to free electives accelerated, 1885–1918. Eliot's ideas supported by Presidents **Andrew Dickson White** (1832–1918) of Cornell, **James Burrill Angell** (1829–1916) of Michigan, **David Starr Jordan** (1851–1931) of Stanford, and **Arthur T. Hadley** (1856–1930) of Yale; opposed by Hadley's predecessor, **Noah Porter** (1811–92) and by **James McCosh** (1811–84) of Princeton. After 1918 free elective trend was checked, with emphasis placed upon a prescribed core of basic study for early college years. **Graduate study:** First Ph.D. degree in U.S. awarded at Yale, 1861. Graduate work organized at Yale and Harvard, 1870. In 1876 Johns Hopkins (under presidency of **Daniel Coit Gilman,** 1831–1908) opened as an institution of purely graduate study, followed by Clark Univ. (1887), Worcester, Mass., especially under the presidency of the eminent psychologist **Granville Stanley Hall** (p. 1047). Other leaders in the expansion of graduate instruction and research were **Charles Kendall Adams** (1835–1902) at Michigan, **John W. Burgess** (1844–1931) at Columbia, and Presidents **Frederick Augustus Porter Barnard** (1809–89) and **Nicholas Murray Butler** (p. 995) of Columbia. **General education,** with emphasis upon orientation courses, was established at Columbia 1918–19 with the course in Contemporary Civilization, and there were notable innovations in the Univ. of Chicago Plan, 1931.

1885–1974. PHILANTHROPY AND FOUNDATION SUPPORT FOR HIGHER EDUCATION. Among the more notable endowments were those of Stanford Univ. (1885), by Leland Stanford, of the Univ. of Chicago (1891) by John D. Rockefeller, and of Duke Univ. (1924, formerly Trinity College) by James B. Duke. Endowed institutions (notably in the South) have been the recipients of large grants from such foundations as the Peabody Education Fund, established by George Peabody (1795–1869); the Julius Rosenwald Fund (1917; dissolved, 1948); the Rockefeller Foundation (1913), including the Rockefeller Institute for Medical Research (University, 1965), the General Education Board, and the Laura Spelman Rockefeller Memorial; the Carnegie Endowment, including the Carnegie Institution of Washington (1902), the Carnegie Foundation for the Advancement of Teaching (1905), the Carnegie Endowment for International Peace (1910), and the Carnegie Corporation of N.Y. (1911); and the Commonwealth Fund, established by Mrs. Stephen V. Harkness (1918).

Foundations expanded rapidly after 1940, with only 600 reporting up to 1939 as against 3,564 reporting, 1940–55. They were the subject of an investigation by a special committee of the House of Representatives in 1954, and their policies subject to U.S. government control under the Tax Reform Act of 1969. A record educational grant of $550 million was made in 1955 by the Ford Foundation (chartered 1936) to 4,157 privately supported colleges, universities, and hospitals, to help raise salaries and improve services, with an additional $455.5 million granted in 1956, including $8 million for educational TV. Through 1973 Ford grants for educational and charitable projects totaled $4.5 billion.

1903–50. EDUCATIONAL TRENDS. Educational testing, the application of statistical measurement to mental and other human traits, developed in the U.S. notably by **Edward Lee Thorndike,** chiefly after 1902. **Progressive Education,** largely inspired by the instrumentalist philosophy of **John Dewey** (p. 1012), with emphasis on **problems** instead of rote learning (Progressive Education Association organized, 1918); opposed by National Council of American Education, Allan A. Zoll, director. **Modern School Plans** include the **Gary,** or platoon, school, first brought to public notice at Gary, Ind., by W. A. Wirt, 1908; the **Dalton** plan (individual instruction on laboratory plan), first used extensively by Helen Parkhurst at Dalton, Mass.

1920; the **Winnetka** plan (individual instruction supplemented by group activity), introduced by F. L. Burke of the San Francisco Normal School (1913) and C. W. Washburne at Winnetka, Ill. **Junior High School,** organized in Richmond, Ind., 1896, spread to Columbus, Ohio, 1908, and elsewhere. Numbers increased from 387 (1922) to 2,372 (1938). **Junior College,** organized by President Harper in Joliet, Ill., 1902. Numbers increased from 74 (1915) to 584 (1945). **Community colleges** multiplied in 1950s to meet postwar population bulge.

1929–74. INTERCOLLEGIATE ATHLETICS AS "ROMAN CIRCUS." In 1929 the Carnegie Foundation for the Advancement of Teaching reported that the college sports establishment was "sodden" with commercialism and professionalism. Reforms proved sporadic and ineffectual. Recruiting violations burgeoned in the 1970s as TV greatly increased the viewing public and superstadia attracted vast throngs to athletic events. A *New York Times* exposé (Mar. 1974) set off new calls for reform.

1946–74. FULBRIGHT PROGRAM. An amendment (1946) to the Surplus Property Act of 1944, sponsored by Sen. J. William Fulbright to establish educational exchange programs with funds in foreign currencies accruing to the U.S. from the sale abroad of surplus property after World War II, supplemented by enabling legislation authorizing the appropriation of dollar funds, led to the setting up of exchange programs with some 40 nations (by 1960). Under this program thousands of Americans have gone abroad to teach, study, or engage in research and an even greater number of foreigners have visited the U.S. A presidentially appointed Board of Foreign Scholarships supervised the program in Washington while binational foundations were responsible for the operation of the programs abroad. Among other fields, the program stimulated American studies abroad and foreign area studies in the U.S.

SCHOOL ATTENDANCE (% of population): 1910, 59.2; 1920, 64.3; 1930, 69.9; 1940, 70.8.

ENROLLMENT IN ELEMENTARY AND SECONDARY SCHOOLS, 1870–1972

	1870	1900	1972
% of total population— 5–17-yr.-olds	31.3	28.3	24.7
Pupils enrolled—% of population 5–17 yrs.	57.0	72.43	83.6

1970–78. ENROLLMENT DECLINE in elementary schools by 5.5 million.

1947–1969. ILLITERACY (persons unable to read or write any language). **1947:** total, 14 years of age and over: 2.7% of population (urban, 2%; rural nonfarm, 2.4%; rural farm, 5.3%), as compared with 20.0% (1870), 10.7% (1900), 4.3% (1930). **1959:** total 2.2% (white, 1.6%, black, 7.5%); **1969:** total 1.0% (white 0.7%; black 3.6%), figures documenting improving educational facilities for blacks.

1955, 28 Nov.–1 Dec. WHITE HOUSE CONFERENCE ON EDUCATION focused attention on educational goals as well as needs, teacher training and recruitment, and school financing, with the participants approving, 2–1, the proposition that the federal government should increase its financial participation in public education.

1957, 11 Nov. IMPACT OF SPUTNIK. U.S. Office of Education released 2-year study of Soviet educational system, revealing vast strides being made in secondary and technical education in U.S.S.R., with stress on science subjects; findings confirmed by government-sponsored study of Soviet education by U.S. educators, May–June, 1958, pointing out widespread teaching of foreign languages.

1958. NATIONAL DEFENSE EDUCATION ACT (p. 525).

1959–73. DESEGREGATION. The initial impact of *Brown* v. *Board of Education of Topeka* (1954) was slight and its implementation marked by sporadic violence (see pp. 521, 524). As of the 1962–63 school year, only .4% of black school children were attending integrated schools in the 11 states of the Deep South, with Alabama, Mississippi, and South Carolina still maintaining complete segregation except in colleges. The **Civil Rights Act of 1964** (p. 529), combined with massive new programs of federal aid to education, stimulated desegregation as each school district had to state its intention to integrate in order to share in federal funds for public schools. By Dec. 1966, 4,653 out of 7,072 school districts in 17 Southern states were "in compliance" with the federal regulations of the U.S. Office of Education; 965,000 black students (25.8% of black enrollment) were in schools with white students, with sharp gains continuing through 1973.

Outside the South efforts to end de facto segregation by busing school children to schools outside their neighborhoods or by redrawing the borders of school districts met with intense opposition. With a busing program begun Sept. 1968, Berkeley, Calif., became the first city with a population of over 100,000 to totally desegregate its school system. Racial imbalance and tensions contributed to the mounting problems of urban school systems. Attempts to begin the decentralization of the New York City school system resulted in a lengthy strike (1968).

1969–73. BUSING ISSUE. The directive of the Department of Health, Education, and Welfare restricting "freedom of choice" for school children if it had the practical result of maintaining a dual school system fueled the flames of controversy over the issue of busing to attain desegregation. While the federal courts and the U.S. Supreme Court (April, 1971) approved widespread busing to assure an integrated education for black children, President Nixon formally asked Congress (Mar. 1971) to call a temporary halt to all further court-ordered busing until 1 July 1973 or until broad legislation to control busing could be enacted. Congress agreed to prohibit the implementation of federal court orders for busing to achieve racial balance until all appeals had been exhausted or until the time for such appeals had expired, effective only until 31 Dec. 1973 (signed by the president, June 1972). In possible reaction to a rising tide of opposition to busing for integration the 4th U.S. Circuit Court of Appeals overruled (6 June 1972) a U.S. District Court order that would have required the merger of the Richmond, Va., city school system (70% black) with 2 suburban counties of Henrico and Chesterfield (each more than 90% white). As late as Feb. 1974 the New York City Board of Education admitted that the exodus of white residents to the suburbs was continuing de facto segregation in core areas of the city.

1961–71. EDUCATIONAL TECHNIQUES AND INNOVATIONS. Among the innovations in teaching methods and curricula at all levels were (1) the "new" mathematics, with greater emphasis on understanding of abstract concepts; (2) widespread application of team teaching, the nongraded primary unit, teaching machines (programed teaching), and audio-visual aids, including educational TV; (3) increased attention to both the gifted and the disadvantaged; (4) increasing regard for preschool education exemplified by the federally subsidized **Operation Head**

Start program, assisting environmentally deprived preschoolers; (5) bilingual programs, notably in Spanish-speaking areas (Florida, California, Texas, New York City); (6) **Open Classroom,** a British innovation, introduced in Watts section of Los Angeles, and in some schools in New York City and Atlanta, as well as in middle-class communities like Andover, Mass., and Culver City, Calif.; (7) multi-ethnic textbooks widely introduced to provide a more representative and positive image of blacks and other minorities; (8) "open admission" policies in colleges to encourage entry by minority groups.

1961–73. CHANGING ROLE OF FEDERAL, STATE, AND LOCAL GOVERNMENTS IN EDUCATION. Down through 1968 an unparalleled growth in federal support for education took place. Federal funds appropriated for education and related activities rose from $5,437.9 million (1963) to $12,-198.2 million (1967). As the revenue of public elementary and secondary schools increased from $14,747 million (1960) to $25,481 million (1966), the percentage accounted for by federal sources rose from 4.9% to 7.9%. Among the numerous legislative measures pertaining to education were the **Vocational Educational Act** (1963, with amendments 1968), the **Elementary and Secondary Education Act** (1965), the **Higher Education Act** (1965), and **Higher Education Act Amendments** (1968). The enactment in 1972 of the **Revenue-Sharing Bill** (p. 538) had the effect of shifting responsibility for certain funding for health, welfare, and education from the federal government to the states, and resulted in a substantial decline in government-supported funding for education. The **Education Amendments Act of 1972** (23 June) set up a new government-sponsored private corporation, the Student Loan Marketing Assn., but the funding proved inadequate and student loan funds increasingly difficult to obtain. The system of financing schools by local property taxes was ruled unconstitutional by the California Supreme Court (30 Aug. 1971) as constituting discrimination against the poor. However, the Supreme Court upheld such financing as a matter of U.S. constitutional law in *San Antonio Independent School District* v. *Rodriguez* (1973, p. 685). State reimbursement of tuition and tuition tax credits to parents whose children attended nonpublic schools held unconstitutional by Supreme Court, *Committee for Public Education* v. *Nyquist* (1973; p. 685).

1961–74. TRENDS IN SCHOOL ENROLLMENT. A reversal of expanding trends marked the latter portion of this period. Down to 1970 enrollments in institutions of higher education expanded rapidly from 3,570,000 (fall 1960) to 6,963,687 (fall 1967); 32% of all males 19 to 24 were enrolled in colleges (1967). Between 1960 and 1965 junior colleges and community colleges increased at an unprecedented rate both in number and size. By the start of the 1970s, however, a leveling of enrollments was evident. Total school enrollment declined from 56.4% of the population (1960) to 54.9% (1972). From a high of 34 million (1970) public school enrollment dropped to 31.5 million (fall, 1973), falling 1972–73 by 500,000, with private enrollment off 200,000. These figures, combined with tightened budgets and drastically reduced job openings for teachers, were reflected in declining enrollments in graduate schools, except in the fields of law and medicine.

1964–73. STUDENT RIOTS AND COUNTERMOVES. College campuses were swept by a wave of activism, demonstrations, sit-ins, strikes. Contributing to unrest were the size and impersonality of the multiversity, the impact of such issues as civil rights, the Vietnam War, and the quest by black and other minority students for recognition. The student upheavals gained national attention first at the Univ. of California at Berkeley (1964) and at Columbia (1968), with riots spreading to high schools, this time touched off by news of the assassination of Martin Luther King (4 April 1968). A student strike closed San Francisco State College for months, with bombings and loss of life at the Univ. of Wisconsin. Announcement by President Nixon (30 April 1970) of the movement of U.S. troops into Cambodia rekindled campus flames. Tragedies occurred at **Kent State Univ.** (Kent, Ohio), 4 May 1970, when the National Guard opened fire on activist demonstrators, with 4 students slain and 9 others wounded, and at **Jackson State** (Miss.), 14 May, when police fired upon a women's dormitory, with 2 students dead and 12 wounded. After the Jackson incident some 130 colleges suspended classes for a week, and some, like Princeton, for the remainder of the spring semester. The President's Commission on Campus Unrest headed by former Gov. William Scranton (Pa.) reported Sept.–Oct., condemning alike fanatical student tactics, complacent campus officials, and brutal law-enforcement officers. Following the Vietnam truce, the U.S. military withdrawal from that area, and the ending of the draft, order once more prevailed on American campuses (1973–74).

1967–74. GROWING MILITANCY OF TEACHERS. Teachers' unions displayed a new militancy, as some hundred strikes were called over both salaries and teaching conditions in 1968, a trend that continued in this period, with long stoppages of classroom activity in some of the nation's leading cities. Toward the end of this period the National Education Association and the American Federation of Teachers seemed poised for a power struggle to organize teachers nationwide.

1968–74. IMPACT OF WOMEN'S MOVEMENT. Teaching Patterns. 1968 survey revealed that 86% of teachers in elementary schools were women, 78% of the principals were men; in high schools, 47% were women, as against 95% male principals, while only 2 women held school superintendencies out of 13,000. A 1969 survey of women teaching in colleges and universities: instructors, 34.8%; assistant professors, 28.7%; associate professors, 15.7%; full professors, 9.4%, with salaries for women almost always less than those of their male counterparts. As a result of complaints of "patterns of discrimination" brought against numerous colleges and universities, combined with "affirmative action" directives of the Department of Health, Education, and Welfare, the teaching status of women in

1978–79. TOP UNIVERSITY ENDOWMENTS

Harvard	$1,457,700,000
Univ. of Texas	1,102,900,000
Stanford	586,800,000
Yale	585,000,000
M.I.T.	507,600,000
Columbia	504,000,000
Princeton	474,300,000
Rochester	328,700,000
Univ. of Chicago	311,200,000
Univ. of California	304,200,000

1972. TOP RECIPIENTS OF FEDERAL SUPPORT
(awards to individual institutions)

M.I.T.	$89,574,000
Univ. of Minnesota	72,534,000
Univ. of Michigan	60,881,000
Univ. of Wisconsin (Madison)	57,320,000
Univ. of Washington	56,535,000
Stanford	54,648,000
Harvard	54,037,000
Univ. of California (Los Angeles)	54,030,000
Univ. of California (Berkeley)	52,279,000
Columbia	52,219,000

colleges and universities showed some improvement by 1974. In addition, courses on women and even women's studies programs were widely initiated. Passing of the Education Amendments Act of 1972 (23 June) prohibited discrimination in all federally assisted educational programs, with some exceptions.

Coeducation. Beginning with 1968 coeducation at colleges accelerated, soon even penetrating the all-male citadels of "Ivy League" institutions, while the number of exclusively women's colleges declined sharply. Experiments in mixed dormitories were initiated in this period.

1971–74. REVIVAL OF TRADITIONAL APPROACHES spurred by results of testing, which showed a decline in achievement in fundamental subjects, prompted a reconsideration of reading and "new" mathematics programs as well as countermoves against informal "learning-through-joy" approaches and a reevaluation of "open admission" policies.

Literature

American letters during the seventeenth and eighteenth centuries were primarily records of the colonists' confrontation with a new continent and slavish imitations of European literature; the insularity of the first tradition and the derivativeness of the second prevented either from reaching an audience outside the United States. Histories of colonial settlements, chronicles of Indian tribes, and travel writings abound in the pre-Revolutionary era, but not much of it transcended its provincial heritage. On a slightly more formidable plane are the intensely Calvinistic documents of Puritan theologians such as Increase Mather, his prolific son Cotton, and Jonathan Edwards. Transcending parochial boundaries, however, was the Revolutionary political literature—notably the literary efforts of Thomas Jefferson and of that inspired pamphleteer Thomas Paine.

Side by side with such undeniably American work stand authors who are easily recognizable tintypes of the European masters of the period. In poetry this included the neoclassicist Philip Freneau and the pseudo-Augustan "Hartford Wits"; in the novel Charles Brockden Brown, a follower of Mrs. Radcliffe's school of gothic horror, is a good example. At the same time, a sui generis status must be accorded to Benjamin Franklin's *Autobiography*, with its plainspoken charms.

The real flowering of American literature came in the nineteenth century with the emergence of figures like Washington Irving, who brought a European narrative skill to his tales of headless horsemen and twenty-year slumbers. It was this fusion of Continental forms, philosophy, and technique with native American subject matter that accounted for such widely differing contributions as the nature poetry of William Cullen Bryant, the austere yet lyrical verse of Emily Dickinson, and the bardic chants of Walt Whitman. In the American novel this same amalgam was evident in the works of James Fenimore Cooper—a disciple of Walter Scott—whose *Leatherstocking Tales* chronicled the frontier; Nathaniel Hawthorne, whose New England romances were often a mating of English gothic formulas to Puritan themes and settings; Herman Melville, a post-Romantic who schooled himself on Byron and poured his lessons into *Moby Dick;* and Mark Twain, a journeyman in the racy, picaresque, colloquial tradition of Daniel Defoe. Even the Transcendentalism of philosophers like Henry David Thoreau and Ralph Waldo Emerson, derived from Rousseau and others, is given a characteristically (and memorably) American cast. Of the major American authors of the nineteenth century, only Edgar Allan Poe remained largely aloof from American experience, locking himself exclusively into the gothic mode.

The late nineteenth and early twentieth centuries brought a still more obvious European influence on American letters, the naturalism that Frank Norris, Stephen Crane, and others borrowed from Emile Zola. Concurrently, however, another American author had initiated a school of psychological realism that was to make him one of the prime movers of twentieth-century fiction. This was Henry James, whose *Portrait of a Lady* and *The Ambassadors* made their impact felt across the Atlantic with the force of Balzacian or Dickensian works. From this point on, American writing pulled abreast of its European rivals, especially in poetry, where T. S. Eliot and Ezra Pound—with their combination of traditionalism and experimentalism—literally rang up the curtain on modern verse. Other American poets who were leaders rather than followers were Wallace Stevens, Robert Frost, and Edwin Arlington Robinson. In fiction, the so-called Lost Generation, American expatriates centered in Paris, were also highly influential. The outstanding figures in this set were F. Scott Fitzgerald and Ernest Hemingway, the latter of whom created a whole new literary style. Even more substantial was William Faulkner, who, with his rich sagas of Southern life, captivated Europe long before his stature was fully recognized in America.

American literature since World War II has continued to produce works of interest, though it is too soon to make predictions about its durability. As poets have gradually faded from view, the works of Theodore Roethke and Robert Lowell have nevertheless continued to command respect. In fiction, some major devolopments have been the rise of black novelists like Ralph Ellison; the popularity of the "Jewish novel," particularly in the hands of such practitioners as Saul Bellow, Bernard Malamud, and Philip Roth; and the "new journalism," a mode of highly personalized reportage that makes use of fictional techniques (e.g., the works of Norman Mailer).

Pioneer Period, 1607–60

Best Seller: *Bay Psalm Book* (1640); reached 27 editions before 1750.

REPORTERS, ANNALISTS, AND HISTORIANS. 1608–29. Capt. **John Smith** (p. 1054), adventurer, explorer, and Virginia pioneer, 1607–09, published an account of the founding of Jamestown: *A True Relation of Occurrences in Virginia* (1608); subsequently recounted his exploring expedition along the New England coast in *A Descrption of New England* (1619) and *New England's Trials* (1620). His account of his rescue by Pocahontas first appeared in *The Generall Historie of Virginia* (1624), and its authenticity has been questioned. Despite embroidery, Smith's narration is unsurpassed for vivid and dramatic description of pioneer struggles. **1622–47. William Bradford** (p. 990) is generally believed to have collaborated with **Edward Winslow** (1595–1655) in compiling materials subsequently published in England (1622) by **George Morton** (1585–1624) and known because of its preface (signed "G. Mourt") as "Mourt's" *Relation*, a journal of events in Plymouth, 1620–21. Bradford's major historical work was his *History of Plimouth Plantation*, written 1630–47, but not published until 1856 (although drawn upon by **Nathaniel Morton** [1613–86] in his *New England's Memorial*, 1669). **Edward Winslow** (1595–1655) added further light on early New England history in his *Good News from New England*, 1624, and *Brief Narration*, 1646. **1630–49:** Comparable in importance for the early history of Massachusetts with the Pilgrim Bradford's *History* was the Puritan **John Winthrop's** (p. 1187) *Journal* (or *History of New England*), a diary record from Mar. 1630 to 1649, which remained unpublished until 1790 (subsequently revised,

1825, and again, 1929–31). In addition to accounts of the relations of the Massachusetts authorities with such major critics as Roger Williams and Anne Hutchinson, the *Journal* includes Winthrop's General Court speech, 1645, on the nature of liberty (which he maintained must be under authority and restraint). While en route to the Bay Colony, Winthrop wrote his *Model of Christian Charity* (1630), emphasizing self-denial and cooperation ("We must be knit together in this work as one man"). A leading critic of affairs in Plymouth and Massachusetts, **Thomas Morton** (1575–1647) satirized colonial policy in his *New English Canaan* (1637). **1654:** To counteract hostile reports of the Puritan colonization, which he considered a sacred crusade, **Edward Johnson** (1598–1672) wrote his *Wonder-Working Providences of Sion's Saviour in New England* (1654), an apologia for theocratic rule.

THEOLOGICAL AND RELIGIOUS WRITERS. "Chief stewards of the theocracy." **1638–40:** Thomas **Hooker** (?1586–1647), in his *Survey of the Summe of Church Discipline* (1648), postulated the principle of divine absolutism. This book and his orthodox Calvinist sermons reveal literary power and the author's conviction that it was his duty to "fasten the nail of terror deep" into the hearts of sinners. **1641–60:** Thomas **Shepard** (1605–49), "soul-melting preacher," whose *Sincere Convert* (1641) preached a gospel of love; *Theses Sabbaticae* (1649), Sabbath origin and observance; *Parable of the Ten Virgins* (1660). **1642–48:** John **Cotton** (1584–1652), major spokesman of theocracy, preeminent as scholar and theologian ("They could hardly believe God would suffer Mr. Cotton to err"— Roger Williams). His numerous writings include *The Keyes of the Kingdom of*

Heaven (1644), stressing consociation of church and state; *Milk for Babes, Drawn out of the Breasts of Both Testaments* (1646), for the religious instruction of children; and *The Bloudy Tenent, Washed and Made White in the Bloud of the Lamb* (1647), in refutation of Roger Williams and opposing freedom to "sinful error." **Minor figures** of the period include **Nathaniel Ward** (?1578–1652), author of the first Massachusetts Code of Laws, the Body of Liberties (1641), and a humorist and satirist (*Simple Cobbler of Aggawamm*, 1647); and **John Eliot** (1604–90), Puritan missionary, translator of the Bible into the Indian tongue, 1663, and author of *The Christian Commonwealth* (1659) and an Indian grammar (1666) and primer (1669).

Critic of the Established Order: Roger Williams (c.1603–83), radical in religious and political outlook; advocated separation of church and state as early as 1635; as ardent in polemics as his opponents. Writings include *A Key into the Language of America* (1643); *The Bloudy Tenent of Persecution for the Cause of Conscience* (1644), attack on the conservative ideas of Cotton. The latter's vindictive reply elicited from Williams *The Bloudy Tenent Made Yet More Bloudy* (1652). His *George Fox Digged out of his Burrowes* (1676) was a criticism of Quaker views.

POETS. 1641: *The Bay Psalm Book* (*The Whole Book of Psalms Faithfully Translated into English Metre*), the first book printed in the colonies,[1] was a translation of the Psalms purposefully sacrificing beauty to accuracy by **Thomas Welde, Richard Mather** (1596–1669), and **John Eliot,** an uninspired rendition. **1650:** Publication in London of *The Tenth Muse*, a collection of didactic poems by **Anne Bradstreet** (?1612–72),

[1] The first piece of printing was "The Freeman's Oath," followed by an almanac, both in 1639.

influenced by Spenser, Quarles, and Du Bartas. Emancipated from her literary models, she produced her most distinguished poem, *Contemplations*, written late in life (pub. 1678).

First Century of Native Literature, 1661–1760

BEST SELLERS BY COLONIAL WRITERS[2]

1640. *Bay Psalm Book*
1662. Michael Wigglesworth, *Day of Doom*
1682. Mary Rowlandson, *Captivity and Restoration*
1683? *New England Primer*, comp. and pub. by Benj. Harris (total sales estimated at 6 to 8 million)
1699. Jonathan Dickinson, *God's Protecting Providence*
1707. John Williams, *The Redeemed Captive*
1719. *Mother Goose's Melodies for Children*
1725–64. Nathaniel Ames, comp., *Astronomical Diary and Almanac*
1732–57. Benjamin Franklin, *Poor Richard's Almanac*
1741. William Penn, *No Cross, No Crown*

NARRATIVES OF INDIAN WARS AND CAPTIVITIES. c.1670: Capt. **John Mason** (1600–72) wrote *A Brief History of the Pequot War* (partly published by Increase Mather, 1677; completely, 1736). **1674: Daniel Gookin** (1612–87), *Historical Collections of the Indians in New England* (1792), a description of Indian mores, and *An Historical Account of the Doings and Sufferings of the Christian Indians* (completed 1677, published 1836), a vindication of their role in King Philip's War. **1676: Increase Mather** (1639–1723), *A Brief History of the War with the Indians* (1676). **1677: William Hubbard** (1621–1704), *A Narrative of the Troubles with the Indians* (hostile toward the Indians); also wrote *A General History of New England* (to 1680), not published until 1815. **1682: Mary White Rowlandson**

[2] Best-seller lists based upon A. D. Dickinson, *One Thousand Best Books* (1924); F. L. Mott, *Golden Multitudes* (1947); James D. Hart, *The Popular Book* (1950); Alice P. Hackett, *Fifty Years of Best Sellers* (1945; with *Supplement*, 1952). Best sellers' list hereinafter confined to works by American writers.

(c.1635–c.1678), captured by the Indians in a raid on Lancaster, 1676, wrote the most popular captivity account, *The Sovereignty and Goodness of God,* republished many times by its subtitle, *The Narrative of the Captivity and Restoration of Mrs. Mary Rowlandson.* **1699:** A straightforward, graphic account of captivity in Florida was told by an English Quaker merchant who later became chief justice of Pennsylvania, **Jonathan Dickinson** (1663–1722), *Journal, or God's Protecting Providence.*

1698: Gabriel Thomas. *An Historical and Geographical Account of the Province of Pennsylvania and West New Jersey,* a Quaker's humorous and favorable account.

TRAVELERS AND EXPLORERS. 1704: Sarah Kemble Knight (1666–1727), Boston schoolmistress, wrote a lively account of a horseback journey to New York (*Journal,* published for the first time, 1825), with refreshing sidelights on rural conditions. **1728–33: Col. William Byrd, 2d** (1674–1744) of Westover, a great Virginia estate owner, educated abroad, left a collection of manuscripts of absorbing interest, consisting of both travels and explorations (not published until 1841), and a shorthand diary, a frank and racy document, deciphered and published in part, 1709–12 (1941), 1739–41 (1942). His major work of exploration was *History of the Dividing Line Run in the Year 1728,* an account of experiences with a party surveying the Virginia–North Carolina boundary line. A satirical version, *The Secret History of the Dividing Line* (not published until 1929) is the most interesting and uninhibited travel book of the colonial period. His other works include *A Journey to the Land of Eden* (1732) and *A Progress to the Mines* (1736), published 1841. **1744: Dr. Alexander Hamilton** (1712–56), of Annapolis, whose *Itinerarium* describing his journey from Annapolis, Md., to Portsmouth, N.H., is one of the most entertaining and informative travel books of the colonial period. **1751: John Bartram** (1699–1777), the Pennsylvania botanist, published an account of a scientific expedition to western New York and Lake Ontario in 1751 (*Observations*).

REPORTERS, ANNALISTS, DIARISTS, AND HISTORIANS. 1666: George Alsop (1638–?), who served a term as an indentured servant in Maryland, wrote a colorful and humorous defense of that colony, *A Character of the Province of Maryland.* **1670: Daniel Denton** (d.1696), in his *Brief Description of New York,* provided a graphic account of a "terrestrial Canaan." **1673–1729: Samuel Sewall** (1652–1730) left the fullest diary of the period (1674–1729), with gaps 1677–85), invaluable for the social historian (not published until 1879–82). His tract *The Selling of Joseph* (1700) was an early antislavery appeal. **1676:** The *Burwell Papers,* attributed to **John Colton** (published 1814; revised, 1866), a spirited, if affected, account of the course of Bacon's Rebellion, closing with an eloquent eulogy of Bacon. **1676–93: Increase Mather** (p. 1099), president of Harvard, 1685–1701, upholder of the theocratic tradition of John Cotton, wrote *A Brief History of the War with the Indians in New England* (1676) and an uncritical compilation of other people's narratives of providential events, published, 1684, as *An Essay for the Recording of Illustrious Providences* (commonly known as *Remarkable Providences*). **1693–1702:** His son, **Cotton Mather** (p. 1099), the most prolific colonial author (over 400 published works), served as annalist of the Salem witchcraft episode (1692) in his book *The Wonders of the Invisible World* (1693). His apologia for the trial and execution of the accused was effectively answered by **Robert Calef** (1648–

1719), a Boston merchant, whose *More Wonders of the Invisible World* (1700) was publicly burned in the Harvard Yard upon order of Increase Mather. Cotton Mather's major work is his *Magnalia Christi Americana, or, The Ecclesiastical History of New England, 1620–98* (1702), which set forth the splendor of government by God's elect, combining accurate information with fable and gross misrepresentation. For his scientific contributions, see pp. 778, 806.

1697: Rev. James Blair (1655–1743), an Anglican clergyman, collaborated with **Henry Hartwell** and **Edward Chilton**, on a report, *The Present State of Virginia and the College* (published 1727).

1705: Robert Beverley (1675–1716), *The History and Present State of Virginia* (revised 1722), a lucid account of a land where "nobody is poor enough to beg or want food." **1724: Hugh Jones** (c.1670–1760), clergyman, *The Present State of Virginia*, a frank and factual account, with a dismal picture of educational standards at William and Mary College, where he was a teacher of mathematics.

1727–47: Cadwallader Colden (1688–1776), scientist and later lieutenant governor of New York, wrote a valuable account of the Iroquois tribes, *The History of the Five Indian Nations,* the most substantial colonial treatise on the Indians. **1736–56: Thomas Prince** (1687–1758), *Chronological History of New England,* arid but scholarly annals. **1740:** Patrick Tailfer's *A True and Historical Narrative of the Colony of Georgia,* a documented history attacking Oglethorpe. **1747: William Stith** (1689–1755), president of William and Mary, 1752–55, *History of the First Discovery and Settlement of Virginia* (from Jamestown to 1624), drew heavily upon Captain John Smith. **1748–53: William Douglass** (1691–1752), Scottish physician who settled in Boston, 1718, and

wrote innumerable pamphlets against religious revivalism, paper money, etc., produced a caustic, partisan, and disorganized *Summary, Historical and Political, of the First Planting, Progressive improvements and Present State of the British Settlements in North America.* **1756: William Livingston** (1723–90), educator, statesman, governor of New Jersey (1776–90), *A Review of the Military Operations in North America, 1753–56,* frank and significant history. **1757: William Smith** (1728–93), jurist and later Loyalist, *The History of the Province of New York* (to 1732), reprinted (1829) with his continuations to 1762, an able, if partisan, historical account, with valuable insights on contemporary New York society (supplemented by his massive unpublished diary in the New York Public Library).

THEOLOGICAL AND RELIGIOUS WRITERS. 1669–1717: Representative of the conservative theological tradition were **Increase Mather** and **Cotton Mather.** The former, a great pulpit orator, published 92 titles (1669–1723), mostly sermons. The latter, a child prodigy, published innumerable sermons and religious and moral tracts, one of the most notable being *Bonifacius* (1710), endorsing the performance of good deeds on business principles—a work which influenced Benjamin Franklin. Representative of liberalism and opposition to the Mather hierarchy was **John Wise** (1652–1725), minister at Ipswich, who, in addition to his notable fight against Governor Andros over the payment of unauthorized taxes, was the author of 2 pamphlets opposing the plan of the Mathers for reorganizing the churches along Presbyterian lines, and favoring democratic Congregationalism: *The Churches' Quarrel Espoused* (1710), and *A Vindication of the Government of the New England Churches* (1717).

1720–54: Jonathan Edwards (p. 1021),

pastor at Northampton, was a major writer on theological and moral questions, a logical thinker who devoted his energies to a regeneration of religious values, defended the "revival" as a legitimate device for quickening spiritual values, and opposed Locke's idealism with emphasis on mystical experience. His "Notes on the Mind" was a venture in Berkeleyan idealism. Typical of his later revivalist sermons emphasizing hell-fire and brimstone was *Sinners in the Hands of an Angry God* (Enfield, 9 July 1741). His greatest intellectual effort was *A Careful and Strict Enquiry into the Modern Prevailing Notions of Freedom of the Will* (1754), an exposition of his understanding of Calvinist predestination, followed 4 years later by the posthumous publication of *The Great Christian Doctrine of Original Sin Defended*. In his second dissertation, "Concerning the End for Which God Created the World" (written 1755), he returned to the mystic pantheism of his youth and foreshadowed Transcendentalism. Foremost opponents of revivalism were **Charles Chauncy** (1705–87), Boston Congregationalist pastor, whose notable sermon *Seasonable Thoughts on the State of Religion in New England* (1743), stressing divine benevolence assuring man a rational place in a world of free choice, dates the start of the controversy between the **New** and **Old Lights**; and **Samuel Johnson** (1696–1772), convert to Anglicanism and first president (1754–63) of King's College (Columbia), who became the chief exponent in the colonies of the doctrines of the English philosopher George Berkeley, as exemplified by *Elementa Ethica* (1746), republished by Benjamin Franklin in enlarged form as *Elementa Philosophica* (1752), stressing rationalism in religion and the concepts of the Enlightenment. Very different in form and spirit were the works of the New Jersey Quaker

John Woolman (1720–72), whose *Journal*, written 1756–72, published 1774, reveals his simplicity and purity. Sensitive to social injustice, he criticized the institution of slavery in *Some Considerations on the Keeping of Negroes* (1754–62), a plea for racial equality; and his *Considerations on the True Harmony of Mankind* (1770) revealed his concern about growing antagonisms between labor and capital.

POETS include **Michael Wigglesworth** (1631–1705), whose *Day of Doom* (1662), in jog-trot ballad measure, was a Calvinist version of the last judgment (unbaptized infants assigned to the "easiest room in hell"); **Edward Taylor** (c.1644–1729), English-born pastor of Westfield, Mass., whose sensuous poetry, rich in imagery, imaginative and dramatic, and the most inspired American verse of the 17th century, was discovered (1937) with the publication of some of his poems from MS.; the anonymous author ("Eben. Cook, Gent.") of *The Sot-Weed Factor* (1708) and *Sot-Weed Redivivus* (1730), satirical burlesques on the inhabitants of Maryland; and 2 Massachusetts Loyalists who produced poetry in the pre-Revolutionary era— **Mather Byles** (1707–88), an imitator of Pope (*Elegy addressed to Governor Belcher on the Death of his Lady*, 1732, and *The Conflagration*, 1744) and **Benjamin Church** (1734; lost at sea, 1776), whose *The Choice* (1757) was modeled upon a poem of Pomfret (1700), who also influenced the poetry of **William Livingston** (*The Philsophic Solitude*, 1747).

1696–1760. EARLY LIBRARIES. Dr. **Thomas Bray** (1656–1730), cofounder of the Society for the Propagation of the Gospel in Foreign Parts (1701), on becoming Commissary in Maryland (1696), established free circulating libraries in most of the 30 parishes in that province, beginning with Annapolis. Other libraries were established under his auspices in New York (Trinity Parish, 1698) and Charleston (1699). Although the largest libraries prior to 1789 were either those of private individuals (Cotton Mather, 3,000 vols.; William Byrd II, 4,000, 1788) or of colleges, the semipublic **subscription library** was the most common. Between 1731–60, 21 were founded, notably:

1731. Library Co. of Philadelphia, an outgrowth of the Junto, a debating society organized by Benjamin Franklin, 1727.

1747. Redwood Library, Newport, R.I. (Ezra Stiles librarian, 1755–75).

1748. Charleston Library Society.

1754. New York Society Library.

Revolutionary Generation, 1763–89

BEST SELLERS

1768. John Dickinson, *Letters from a Farmer in Pennsylvania*
1775–76. John Trumbull, *McFingal* (1st complete ed. 1782)
1776. Thomas Paine, *Common Sense*
1776–83. Thomas Paine, *The American Crisis*
1783. Noah Webster, *American Spelling Book* (*Blue-Backed Speller*—estimated total sale 70 million copies by 1883)
1787–88. Alexander Hamilton, James Madison, and John Jay, *The Federalist*

LITERATURE OF POLITICS: 1762: A year after his renowned arguments against the issuance of writs of assistance (24 Feb. 1761), **James Otis,** Boston lawyer, published his first political pamphlet, *A Vindication of the Conduct of the House of Representatives* (Mass.), in which he affirmed the privileges of the colonies under the British constitution. **1764:** His ablest effort, called forth by the Sugar Act, was *The Rights of the British Colonies Asserted* (July), in which he raised the argument of no taxation without representation. Other critics of the new imperial policy in-

cluded **Oxenbridge Thacher,** *Sentiments of a British American;* and Rhode Island's governor, **Stephen Hopkins** (1707–85), *The Rights of the Colonies Examined* (1765); answered by Martin Howard, a Newport lawyer, *A Letter from a Gentleman at Halifax*). **1765:** The Stamp Act prompted a series of articles by **John Adams** in the Boston *Gazette*, republished, 1768, in revised form, as *A Dissertation on the Canon and Feudal Law;* and 2 notable pamphlets, one by **John Dickinson** (1732–1808), *Considerations upon the Rights of the Colonists to the Privileges of British Subjects,* the other by **Daniel Dulany** (1722–97), a Maryland lawyer and later Loyalist, *Considerations on the Propriety of Imposing Taxes* (p. 87). **1766:** Most vigorous of the New England clergy in opposing parliamentary measures was **Jonathan Mayhew** (1720–66), a rationalist who anticipated later Unitarian doctrines. As early as 1750 in his *Discourse Concerning Unlimited Submission* he had asserted: "Britons will not be slaves." On the repeal of the Stamp Act he wrote his last published sermon, *The Snare Broken.* **1767–68:** The passage of the Townshend Acts prompted the issuance by Dickinson of a widely distributed pamphlet (at least 12 editions in the colonies and abroad), *Letters from a Farmer in Pennsylvania to the Inhabitants of the British Colonies* (p. 90). **1773:** The qualities of **Benjamin Franklin** as a political satirist are exemplified by his imaginary "An Edict of the King of Prussia" (*Gentleman's Mag.,* Oct.) and his renowned *Rules for Reducing a Great Empire to a Small One.* **1774:** The Loyalist argument was forcefully presented by Rev. **Samuel Seabury** (1729–96), later first bishop of the Protestant Episcopal Church in the U.S., in a series of four *Westchester Farmer* pamphlets attacking the aims and policy of the first Continental Congress (answered effectively by young **Alexander Hamilton**, in *A Full Vindication of the Measures of Congress* [1774] and *A Farmer Refuted*) and by **Daniel Leonard** (1740–1829), in a series of 17 letters to the newspapers under the pen name of "Massachusettensis," in which the unconstitutional character of the Revolutionary position was stressed. For **John Adams'** refutation, see p. 99. The plan of union proposed by **Joseph Galloway** (1731–1803; p. 1037) was published the following year in *A Candid Examination of the Mutual Claims of Great Britain and the Colonies.* The development of Patriot thinking by this date was best exemplified in **James Wilson's** (1742–98) *Considerations of the Nature and Extent of the Legislative Authority of Great Britain* (p. 99), and **Thomas Jefferson's** *A Summary View of the Rights of British America* (p. 99). **1776:** Most influential of all Revolutionary pamphlets was **Thomas Paine's** *Common Sense* (p. 106), which was followed by a series of 16 irregularly issued (1776–83) essays called *The Crisis*, designed to lift Patriot morale, the first words of the first number being "These are the times that try men's souls." **1782–87:** Thomas Jefferson's *Notes on Virginia*, a reply to a series of questions by the Marquis de Barbé-Marbois, is representative of his political thought. Written, 1782, it was first printed privately in Paris, 1785, then in London, 1787.

1787–88: The ratification of the Constitution was opposed in a considerable number of pamphlets, most notably by **Richard Henry Lee** (Va., p. 1082), (*Observations Leading to a Fair Examination* [1787] and *An Additional Number of Letters* [1788]) and **George Mason** (Va., 1725–92), (*Objections to the Proposed Federal Constitution*). Supporters of ratification included the lexicographer **Noah Webster** (1758–1843), *An Examination into the Leading Principles of the Federal Constitution;* the political economist **Pelatiah Webster** (1725–95), *The Weakness of Brutus Exposed;* **Tench Coxe** (1755–1824), political economist and industrialist, *An Examination of the Constitution,* and **John Dickinson** (*Letters of Fabius*); but most influential were the papers produced by **Hamilton, Madison,** and **Jay,** published as *The Federalist* in book form 1788 (p. 140).

FRANKLIN'S AUTOBIOGRAPHY. Ranking as an American classic is Franklin's *Autobiography* (covering the events of his life to the end of 1759), written between 1771 and 1789, published in part in France, 1791, and not in complete form until 1867, and exemplifying the Yankee-Puritan spirit which could accept the Enlightenment and follow the literary models of Defoe and Addison. For Franklin's journalistic enterprises, see p. 941; for his scientific contributions, p. 779. Franklin wrote for the amusement of his friends urbane bagatelles: *The Ephemera* (1778), *The Morals of Chess* (1779), *The Whistle* (1779), *The Dialogue between Franklin and the Gout* (1780).

HISTORIANS. 1764–67: Thomas Hutchinson (1711–80), lieutenant governor of Massachusetts, produced the major historical writing of the period. The 1st volume of *The History of the Colony of Massachusetts Bay* (1628–91) appeared in 1764; the 2nd (down to 1750) appeared in 1767; and the 3rd (1750–74) was published posthumously in 1828. The earlier volumes are marked by more detachment than the last, which is in part a defense of his own administration. Although an outstanding Loyalist he managed in the main to make judicious and objective valuations. **1780:** Another Loyalist, **George Chalmers** (1742–1825), published an account of colonial history down to 1763 (*Political Annals*) which largely reflects the official British attitude. **1782:** Chalmers' *Intro-*

duction to the History of the Revolt of the American Colonies was a legalistic and unsympathetic approach to colonial problems based largely on official records. **1784: Jeremy Belknap** (1744–98) wrote a scholarly *History of New Hampshire* (2nd vol. to 1790, pub. 1791) based upon prodigious research. **1788:** A more biased, but nevertheless notable, firsthand account of Shays' Rebellion was **George Minot's** (1758–1802) *History of the Insurrections in Massachusetts in the Year 1786*, a conservative's view of the issues and events.

MR. PENROSE: THE JOURNAL OF PENROSE, SEAMAN, a first-person picaresque narrative written by **William Williams** (1717–91) probably between 1745–75 and published posthumously in England (1815) is now credited as being the first American novel.

TRAVELERS. 1778: Jonathan Carver (1710–80), a New Englander, wrote a travel book based upon an exploring expedition to the Great Lakes and the Upper Mississippi, containing much information on natural history and Indian mores, *Travels through the Interior Parts of North America.* **1782:** A fresh recorder of rural life was **J. Hector St. John de Crèvecoeur** (1735–1813), born in France, served under Montcalm, traveled through the Great Lakes and Ohio Valley, and settled down on a farm in Orange Co., N.Y. (1769). His book of impressions of America, which attained wide popularity abroad, was published as *Letters from an American Farmer.* Crèvecoeur saw the American environment transforming the European from a peasant to a freeholder. To him the American was an amalgam of all nations, and his ultimate role in world affairs was dimly foreseen. **1784:** A Kentucky pioneer, **John Filson** (c.1747–88), prepared an account of *The Discovery, Settlement, and Present State of Kentucke,* to which was appended a pur-

ported autobiography of **Daniel Boone.**

POETS. 1776–88: The major poet of the period was **Philip Freneau** (1752–1832), whose poetry reflects 18th-century deism, love of nature, idealization of the "noble savage," the idea of progress, and hostility to tyranny. His more notable efforts include "The Beauties of Santa Cruz" (1776), lyric; "The House of Night" (1779), a powerful poem in the graveyard tradition; an elegy to the war heroes, "To the Memory of Brave Americans" or "Eutaw Springs" (1781); perhaps his most beautiful lyric, "To a Wild Honeysuckle" (1786); "The Indian Burying Ground" (1788); and a number of sea poems, including "The Memorable Victory of Paul Jones" and "The Battle of Lake Erie." For his pro-Jefferson paper, *National Gazette,* see p. 943.

1778: "The Battle of the Kegs," a satirical poem by **Francis Hopkinson** (1737–91), also the author of several satirical essays as well as musical compositions (p. 917), was one of the most popular poems of the war period.

CONNECTICUT (HARTFORD) WITS patterned themselves after the Augustan wits. Essentially conservative, opposing deism and egalitarianism and clinging to Calvinism and Federalism, they celebrated America's independence by extolling its history and society. Members included **John Trumbull** (1750–1831), *The Progress of Dullness* (1772–73), a Hudibrastic satire on education, and the enormously popular *McFingal,* an epic satire on the Tories (1775–82). **Joel Barlow** (1754–1812), land speculator, diplomat, and later an ardent democrat, whose most ambitious patriotic poem was *The Vision of Columbus* (1787), subsequently (1807) enlarged as *The Columbiad,* who is best remembered for his charming poem *Hasty Pudding* (1796). His volume of political essays, *Advice to the Privileged Orders* (1792), a radical defense of the

French Revolution, was proscribed by the British government. **Timothy Dwight** (1752–1817), a Congregational minister and president of Yale, 1795–1817, whose *Triumph of Infidelity* (1788) was a defense of orthodoxy, also wrote an important multivolume work on theology (1818–19) and a book of *Travels in New England and New York* (1821–22). Two of the minor Connecticut wits, **David Humphreys** (1752–1818) and **Lemuel Hopkins** (1750–1801), in collaboration with Barlow and Trumbull, pilloried New England radicals in the *Anarchaiad* (1786–87), a satire on mob rule, currency inflation, and other nostrums.

1789–1860

NOVELISTS. 1789: *The Power of Sympathy* by **William Hill Brown** (1765–93) is generally considered the seminal American novel. **1790: Susanna Haswell Rowson** (c.1762–1824), English-born actress, dramatist, novelist, and Boston schoolteacher, wrote an exceptionally popular sentimental novel, *Charlotte Temple*. **1789–1801: Charles Brockden Brown** (1771–1810) wrote a series of Gothic romances revealing some of the moral purpose of Godwin, the sentimentalism of Richardson, and above all the horrors of the school of Mrs. Radcliffe: *Weiland* (1798), an attack on superstition; *Arthur Mervyn* (1799), a realistic picture of the yellow fever epidemic in Philadelphia; *Ormond* (1799); *Edgar Huntley* (1799), crimes committed by a sleepwalker; *Clara Howard* (1801); and *Jane Talbot* (1801). His *Alcuin* (1798) was a treatise on women's rights. **1792–**

1815: Hugh Henry Brackenridge (1748–1816), editor and jurist, wrote *Modern Chivalry* (1792), a satire, realistically depicting frontier conditions and reflecting the influence of Cervantes.

1809–60. KNICKERBOCKER SCHOOL.

For some 2 decades after 1815 the foremost native literary figures were **Washington Irving** (p. 1066), **James Fenimore Cooper** (p. 1006), and **William Cullen Bryant** (p. 993). Irving and Bryant were identified with the Knickerbocker School of writers at New York, a group which took its name from Irving's satirical *A History of New York . . . by Diedrich Knickerbocker* (1809). Cooper's conventional association with the school is based almost wholly upon geographical circumstances.

Leaving the U.S. in 1815, Irving produced in 1819–20 *The Sketch Book,* which included such tales as "Rip Van Winkle" and "The Legend of Sleepy Hollow." His literary activity on the Continent resulted in *Bracebridge Hall* (1822), *The Life and Voyages of Columbus* (1828), *The Conquest of Granada* (1829), *Tales of a Traveller* (1829), and *The Alhambra* (1832). He returned to the U.S. in 1832 and maintained his popularity with *A Tour on the Prairies* (1835), *Astoria* (1836), and *The Adventures of Captain Bonneville* (1837), the U.S. army officer who led an expedition into the Rocky Mountain region. The most important of Irving's later works was the *Life of Washington* (1855–59), facilitated by the publication of *The Writings of Washington* (1833–39), edited by **Jared Sparks** (1789–1866).

Cooper's first novel, *Precaution* (1820), portrayed English society life. In *The Spy* (1821), the first of his works using an American theme and setting, Cooper displayed his capacity for picturing forest life and creating authentic American character. With *The Pioneers* (1823), Cooper inaugurated the *Leatherstocking Tales* for which he is best remembered, completing the series with *The Last of the Mohicans* (1826), *The Prairie* (1827, last in narrative order),

The Pathfinder (1840), and *The Deerslayer* (1841). Almost single-handed Cooper established the historical romance of the American scene and made American fiction's greatest statement about the clash between primitive and civilized values on the frontier. He is also noted for his sea tales, e.g., *The Pilot* (1823) and *The Red Rover* (1827–28), and his novels of social criticism, e.g., the Antirent series begun with *Satanstoe* (1845). Unlike Irving's continued popularity, Cooper's waned after 1833 when his aristocratic social ideals expressed in *A Letter to His Countrymen* (1834), *The American Democrat* (1839), and many novels antagonized his fellow citizens.

Bryant's fame began with the publication of "Thanatopsis" in the *North American Review* (1817, enlarged version in 1821), a poem notable for its handling of the theme of death and for its lyrical treatment of nature; and "To a Waterfowl" (1818), generally considered his masterpiece. In 1825 Bryant left Massachusetts and settled at New York City, joining (1828) the staff of the N.Y. *Evening Post,* of which he was editor (1829–78). He published *The Fountain* (1842), *The White-Footed Deer* (1844), and *A Forest Hymn* (1860), but his absorption in newspaper work weakened his powers as a poet.

Among the other members of the Knickerbocker School were **James Kirke Paulding** (1778–1860), author of *The Diverting History of John Bull and Brother Jonathan* (1812), the historical novels *Koningsmarke* (1823) and *The Dutchman's Fireside* (1831), and *The Book of St. Nicholas* (1836); **Fitz-Greene Halleck** (1790–1867), author of *Alnwick Castle, with Other Poems* (1827), who collaborated with another Knickerbocker writer, **Joseph Rodman Drake** (1795–1820), on the "Croaker Papers" (1819), a set of satirical verses; **Gulian C. Ver-**

planck (1786–1870), who divided his time between politics and literature; **Nathaniel P. Willis** (1806–67), writer of popular verse and travel sketches; and **Charles Fenno Hoffman** (1806–84), journalist and novelist.

1815–60. NEW ENGLAND RENAISSANCE. The community of thought which drew its vitality from New England Transcendentalism made the most fruitful and enduring contributions to American letters before the Civil War. After the War of 1812 the focal point of national literature gradually shifted to Boston, Cambridge, and the New England hinterland, where the successive ferments of Unitarianism and Transcendentalism gave to the nation that period later characterized as the "flowering of New England." Boston remained the intellectual capital of the country until after the Civil War. The **"Unitarian Controversy,"** which came to a climax in 1815 under the leadership of **William Ellery Channing** (p. 1000), was a spiritual revolt against the confinements of orthodox Congregationalism which exerted a potent liberating influence over the New England mind.

1836–50. When Unitarianism in turn fell into the ways of orthodoxy, it was challenged by **Transcendentalism,** whose doctrines received their most comprehensive exposition in *Nature* (1836), by **Ralph Waldo Emerson** (p. 1024). *Nature* appeared in the year when the Transcendental Club became active at Boston and Concord. Transcendentalism was a mood or cast of mind rather than a systematically articulated philosophy. Despite their diversity of outlook, the Transcendentalists agreed on the sacredness, uniqueness, and authority of the individual apprehension of experience. Man was of the divine essence. His insights, drawn from a conception of the mystic unity of nature, might enable the discovery of truth without reference to dogma and established authority. The self-reliance and self-determination exalted by Transcendentalism gave to American writers a freedom that vitalized the first great period in national letters.

Emerson was the seer of Transcendentalism. Between 1826 and 1832, when he held a Unitarian pulpit, he formulated the basic elements of his moral vision. His retirement from the church formalized his revolt against orthodoxy. After his journey to Europe in 1833 he became the spokesman of his generation. *The American Scholar,* delivered as the Phi Beta Kappa address at Harvard (1837), was an eloquent expression of the Emersonian creed of individualism, independence, and self-sufficiency. His address (1838) before the Harvard Divinity School challenged conservative Unitarianism. The luminous passages of the *Essays* (1841, 1844) contained the mature fruits of his thought. In the years before the Civil War, Emerson also expounded Transcendentalism from lecture platforms throughout the North and West. This period witnessed the publication of his *Poems* (1847), *Representative Men* (1850), *English Traits* (1856), and *The Conduct of Life* (1860).

In **Henry David Thoreau** (p. 1170) the individualism of the Transcendentalist movement reached its most intense and uncompromising form. Thoreau's views, molded by a long and extraordinary process of self-discipline, had already become confirmed principles by the time he went to live at Walden Pond in 1845. His 2-year sojourn was a criticism by example of the materialism of a social order that he regarded as a block to man's capacity for free development. Thoreau's first book, *A Week on the Concord and Merrimack Rivers* (1849), was received coldly by the public and by the few critics who noticed its appearance. *Walden* (1854) fared somewhat better, but general recognition of Thoreau came only after his death. Thoreau's literary artistry attained its high point in *Walden*. His philosophy of nature, supported by concrete instance, showed how man's rediscovery of himself could bring his freedom. The essay on "Civil Disobedience" (1849), which posed the sovereign rights of conscience against the claims of the state, was one of Thoreau's most moving utterances of an individualism grounded on high moral conviction.

Among the other members of the Transcendentalist movement were **Margaret Fuller** (p. 1035), editor of *The Dial;* **Bronson Alcott** (1799–1888); **Jones Very** (1813–80); **George Ripley** (1802–80); **Theodore Parker** (1810–60); **Orestes A. Brownson** (1803–76); **James Freeman Clarke** (1810–88); and **Christopher P. Cranch** (1813–92).

One of New England's most popular writers, and a leader of literary society in the Boston he christened the "hub of the Universe," was the Harvard medical professor **Oliver Wendell Holmes** (p. 1058). Mingled with his charming wit and light touch was a rationalism that appeared in his humorous parable of orthodox Calvinism, "The Deacon's Masterpiece; or, The Wonderful 'One-Hoss Shay,'" included (1858) in *The Autocrat of the Breakfast-Table* (1831–32 in the *New England Magazine* and 1857 as an installment in the initial number of the *Atlantic Monthly*). Holmes also published *The Professor at the Breakfast-Table* (1860), another collection of intimate and congenial essays; 3 psychiatric novels (including *Elsie Venner*, 1861); and poems ("Old Ironsides") and humorous ballads.

1837–52. HAWTHORNE, MELVILLE, WHITMAN, AND POE. The currents of Transcendentalism touched **Nathaniel Hawthorne** (p. 1053) and **Herman Melville** (p. 1101), although at a divergent angle. They did not share Emerson's optimism; for them the problem of evil was the most meaningful and enduring element in life.

Hawthorne's focus was relatively narrow, but it was intense. With a craftsmanship of the first order, he gave a somber portrayal of the Puritan mind of New England, searching out the play of evil and the ramifications of sin, guilt, and remorse. His finest achievement is embraced by *Twice-Told Tales* (1837), *The Scarlet Letter* (1850), *The House of the Seven Gables* (1851), *The Blithedale Romance* (1852), and *The Snow-Image* and *Other Twice-Told Tales* (1852).

Melville, who had been a sailor, set his great romances against the background of the sea. *Typee* (1846), *Omoo* (1847), and *Mardi* (1849) were based on experiences in the South Seas. *Redburn* (1849) drew upon his experiences on the Atlantic and in England. In *White-Jacket* (1850) and in *Billy Budd* Melville's portrayal of the brutality that prevailed aboard the warships of the Navy ranked with the revelation of stern treatment in *Two Years Before the Mast* (1840) by **Richard Henry Dana, Jr.** (1815–82). Melville's masterpiece was *Moby Dick* (1851), a novel of a whaling voyage allegorically conceived as a great tragedy imbued with philosophic significance.

Together with *Leaves of Grass* (1855; enlarged in successive editions to 1892) by **Walt Whitman** (p. 1182), *Moby Dick* was proof that American writers had shaped their own idiom. Whitman utilized a simple poetic style devoid of the ordinary usages of rhyme, meter, or ornament, and distinguished by a natural organic growth. Whitman had a profound belief in the perfectibility of man and in democracy. Among his later poems inspired by the events of the Civil War were "The Wound-Dresser" and 2 poems called forth by grief over Lincoln's death—"When Lilacs Last in the Dooryard Bloom'd" and "O Captain! My Captain!" (1865). His poetry is also marked by the frank though frequently symbolic treatment of sex—"Children of Adam" and "Calamus" (1860). His most important prose works were *Democratic Vistas* (1871) and *Specimen Days and Collect* (1882).

The greatest literary figure produced by the South during this period was **Edgar Allan Poe** (p. 1129), but his productive years were passed in Philadelphia and New York after 1837 and his art was independent of historical and geographical association. One of the most complex personalities in American letters, Poe is remembered as an innovator in fields as different as poetry and the detective story. He did pioneer work as a literary critic. His "The Philosophy of Composition," "The Rationale of Verse," and "The Poetic Principle" revealed his conception of poetic unity to be one of mood or emotion, with emphasis upon the beauty of melancholy. He preferred the short story to the novel on the same basis that he preferred the short poem to the long. These stories were either of horror or of careful reasoning. The latter set the standard for the modern detective story. Poe's aesthetic principles had a marked influence upon the French *Symbolistes* as well as upon such Americans as Ambrose Bierce and Hart Crane and such Englishmen as Rossetti, Swinburne, Dowson, and Stevenson. Among his works are *Tales of the Grotesque and Arabesque* (1840), "The Murders in the Rue Morgue" (1843), and *The Raven and Other Poems* (1845).

SOUTH. The representative Southern writers of the time concentrated on local themes. In *Swallow Barn* (1832), **John Pendleton Kennedy** (1795–1870) wrote a series of sketches portraying plantation life in Virginia. Working in a more realistic vein, **Augustus Baldwin Longstreet** (1790–1870) produced *Georgia Scenes, Characters, and Incidents* (1835), dealing with life in the backwoods. It was notable for its handling of dialect. The most prolific Southern writer was **William Gilmore Simms** (p. 1152), who published poetry, historical romances, history, and biography. His best works include *Guy Rivers* (1834), one of his Border Romances; *The Partisan* (1835), one of his Revolutionary Romances; and *The Yemassee* (1835), a panel in the series of romances dealing with the colonial period. In the first rank of the Southern poets of this period were **Henry Timrod** (1828–67) and **Paul Hamilton Hayne** (1830–86), both born in South Carolina.

1838–58. POETS. Henry Wadsworth Longfellow (p. 1089) was the most popular American poet of his day. Many of his lines, for all of their lack of originality and firsthand observation, quickly became American household favorites. His popularity was based on such works as *Voices of the Night* (1839), *Evangeline* (1847), the *Song of Hiawatha* (1855), and *The Courtship of Miles Standish* (1858). When **John Greenleaf Whittier** (p. 1183) did not turn his hand to antislavery agitation, as in *Poems Written During the Progress of the Abolition Question* (1838) and in individual pieces like "Massachusetts to Virginia" (1843) and "Ichabod" (1850), he produced ballads and narrative poems based on New England life and legend, as in "The Barefoot Boy" and "Maud Muller" (both 1856). **James Russell Lowell** (p. 1089) used Yankee dialect to good advantage in offering a Northern Whig's satirical view of the Mexican War in the *Biglow Papers* (1st series, 1848) and attacking slavery (2nd series, 1867). Other antislavery poems include "Prometheus" (1843), "The Present Crisis" (1845), and "On the

Capture of Certain Fugitives near Washington" (1845). Lowell characterized contemporary authors in *A Fable for Critics* (1848) and reached a wide audience with *The Vision of Sir Launfal* (1848).

1834–60. HISTORIANS. William Hickling Prescott (p. 1132), author of the *History of the Reign of Ferdinand and Isabella* (1838), *History of the Conquest of Mexico* (1843), *History of the Conquest of Peru* (1847), and *History of the Reign of Philip the Second* (1855–58), worked in the dramatic vein of William Robertson and Sir Walter Scott. **George Ticknor** (1791–1871), **George Bancroft** (p. 978), and **John Lothrop Motley** (p. 1111) were schooled in high standards of historical scholarship at German universities. Ticknor's *History of Spanish Literature* was published in 1849. In 1834 Bancroft brought out the first volume of his *History of the United States,* a work which ultimately ran to 11 volumes and concluded with the establishment of the national government. It was noteworthy both for its patriotic tone and its research in original materials. In 1856 Motley published *The Rise of the Dutch Republic.* Motley's concept of the vitalizing influence of Protestantism was shared by **Francis Parkman** (p. 1122), who began the grand design of his epic of France and England in North America to 1763 with the *History of the Conspiracy of Pontiac* (1851). Parkman did not write the bulk of his work until after the Civil War, but he had already won fame with his travel account, *The California and Oregon Trail* (1849). In conscious contrast to Bancroft's oratorical prose, **Richard Hildreth** (1807–65) employed a sparse, dry style in his *History of the United States,* whose 6 volumes covering the period 1492–1821 appeared between 1849 and 1852. Virtually ignored by contemporary readers, Hildreth's work has a high degree of factual accuracy and penetrating insights into economic interests. Two collections of source materials published at government expense were important in encouraging the writing of American history: the *Debates, Resolutions, and Other Proceedings in Convention on the Adoption of the Federal Constitution,* brought out between 1827 and 1845 under the editorship of **Jonathan Elliot** (1784–1846); and the *American Archives* (covering the years 1774–76), edited by **Peter Force** (1790–1868) and brought out between 1837 and 1853.

1848–60. REFORM NOVEL. The novel of propaganda, instruction and uplift flourished during this period of reform. *Uncle Tom's Cabin* (1852), by **Harriet Beecher Stowe** (p. 1161), was the most successful of the many tracts for the times largely because its publication coincided with the national impact of the antislavery crusade. Her second novel in this genre was *Dred, A Tale of the Great Dismal Swamp* (1856). Where *Uncle Tom's Cabin* (p. 256) fixed its attention on the evils of slavery as an institution, and was remarkably free from attacks upon Southerners, *Dred* sought to show the mark the institution left upon those who lived by it. Supposedly the first novels based on the antislavery theme were *Northwood, or Life North and South* (1827), by Sarah Josepha Hale (1788–1879), and *The Slave; or, Memoirs of Archy Moore* (1836), by Richard Hildreth.

Another reform impulse that was embodied in literature was the temperance movement, which reached its height in the 1850s. **Timothy Shay Arthur** (1809–85), best known for *Ten Nights in a Bar-Room and What I saw There* (1854), published some 100 tracts and stories of which 1,000,000 copies had been printed by 1860. Also popular as a temperance writer was Lucius Manlius Sargent (1786–1867), whose *Temper-*

ance Tales (1848) included such best-selling stories as "My Mother's Gold Ring" and "Groggy Harbor," originally issued between 1833 and 1843.

1840–60. POPULAR LITERATURE. The growth of the middle class, along with the extension of free public education, the establishment of subscription libraries, and the lyceum movement, had a direct influence on book publishing and literary standards. The mass audience widened the market for books of practical social instruction and sentimental novels of moral uplift. In addition to the best sellers listed above, etiquette books, juveniles (notably the moralistic *Peter Parley* juveniles, which sold approximately 7 million copies from 1827–60 and were written on a mass production basis by authors employed by **Samuel G. Goodrich** [1793–1860]), and anthologies were widely sold in this period. Two anthologist-editors, **Rufus W. Griswold** (1815–57) and **Evert A. Duyckinck** (1816–78), editor of the *Literary World*, had a substantial impact on reading taste. With **Park Benjamin** (1809–64), Griswold began in 1839 to serialize pirated fiction in *Brother Jonathan.* The first dime novel, *Malaeska* by **Ann Sophia Stephens** (1813–86), appeared in 1860. The last decade of this period is often called the "Feminine Fifties," a tribute to the number of women authors who wrote best sellers, easily outselling the works by Emerson, Hawthorne, Melville, and Whitman.

1802–60. BOOK PUBLISHING. Matthew Carey (1760–1839), Philadelphia publisher and economist, and founder of Carey and Lea (1785), promoted the American Co. of Booksellers, which managed 5 book fairs, 1802–06. More effective distribution was achieved by Harper & Bros. (est. New York City, 1817, as J. & J. Harper), with the adoption in 1830 of the stereotyping of plates

for "omnibus editions" of English reprints, and in the 1840s with the issuance of 25-ct. English novels. Carey & Hart (Philadelphia, 1829) followed suit. Scott, Dickens, and other foreign authors were printed in enormous pirated editions before the International Copyright Law (1891). Other major publishing houses included D. Appleton & Co. (1825); J. B. Lippincott & Co. (Philadelphia, 1836); Dodd, Mead & Co. (1839, 1870); the Boston firms of Little, Brown (1847), Houghton, Mifflin (1852) and E. P. Dutton (1852; moved to New York City, 1869); and Charles Scribner's Sons (Baker & Scribner, 1846).

1800–60. PUBLIC LIBRARY MOVEMENT. Library of Congress, Washington, D.C., established 1800 with the library of Thomas Jefferson as a nucleus. Its greatest expansion occurred under the librarianship of **Herbert Putnam** (1861–1955), 1899–1939. In 1951 its holdings totaled 9,400,000 books and pamphlets. **Beginning of Tax-Supported Local Libraries. 1803:** Founding of a childen's library in Salisbury, Conn., by a gift from Caleb Bingham, Boston publisher, supplemented by occasional grants of town money. **1833:** Under the leadership of Rev. Abiel Abbot a social library was established at Peterborough, N.H., supported by a small membership fee and a portion of the state bank tax set aside by the town to purchase books. **1850:** Public library at Wayland, Mass., established by gift of President Francis Wayland (1796–1865) of Brown University, matched by town donation and supported by regular tax funds. **1851:** Enactment in Massachusetts of a law permitting towns to tax inhabitants for the support of free libraries. Founding of the **Boston Public Library,** largely as a result of the activities of **Edward Everett** (1794–1865), orator, statesman, and scholar, and **George Ticknor,** with private book donations, money gifts, and a city appropriation.

Trends since 1860

BEST SELLERS

1862. William G. Brownlow, *Parson Brownlow's Book*

1863. Mrs. E. D. E. N. Southworth, *The Fatal Marriage**; Mrs. A. D. T. Whitney, *Faith Gartney's Girlhood*

1864. Mrs. E. D. E. N. Southworth, *Ishmael**

1865. Mary Mapes Dodge, *Hans Brinker and His Silver Skates**

1867. Horatio Alger, Jr., *Ragged Dick**; Augusta J. Evans Wilson, *St. Elmo*

1868. Elizabeth S. P. Ward, *The Gates Ajar**; Louisa May Alcott, *Little Women**

1869. Mark Twain, *Innocents Abroad**

1870. Bret Harte, *The Luck of Roaring Camp**

1871. Louisa May Alcott, *Little Men**; Edward Eggleston, *The Hoosier Schoolmaster**

1872. Edward Payson Roe, *Barriers Burned Away*; Mark Twain, *Roughing It**

1874. Edward Payson Roe, *Opening a Chestnut Burr*

1876. John Habberton, *Helen's Babies**; Mark Twain, *Tom Sawyer**

1878. Anna Katharine Green, *The Leavenworth Case**

1879. Henry George, *Progress and Poverty**

1880. Joel Chandler Harris, *Uncle Remus**; Harriet Lothrop (Margaret Sidney), *Five Little Peppers and How They Grew**; Lew Wallace, *Ben-Hur**

1883. James Whitcomb Riley, *The Old Swimmin'-Hole**; Mark Twain, *Life on the Mississippi** (chief sales in 1940's in pocket size)

1885. Mark Twain, *Huckleberry Finn**; Ulysses S. Grant, *Personal Memoirs*

1886. Frances Hodgson Burnett, *Little Lord Fauntleroy**

1887. Archibald C. Gunter, *Mr. Barnes of New York**

1888. Edward Bellamy, *Looking Backward**

1894. William Hope Harvey, *Coin's Financial School* (free-silver argument)

1895. Opie Read, *The Jucklins*; Stephen Crane, *The Red Badge of Courage**

1896. Harold Frederic, *The Damnation of Theron Ware*

1897. Charles Monroe Sheldon, *In His Steps** (sales c.8 million to 1945)

1898. Edward Noyes Westcott, *David Harum**

1899. Charles Major, *When Knighthood Was in Flower*; Winston Churchill, *Richard Carvel*; Paul Leicester Ford, *Janice Meredith*; Elbert Hubbard, *A Message to Garcia**

1900. Mary Johnston, *To Have and to Hold*; Irving Bacheller, *Eben Holden*

1901. George Barr McCutcheon, *Graustark*; Alice Hegan Rice, *Mrs. Wiggs of the Cabbage Patch*; Winston Churchill, *The Crisis*

1902. Owen Wister, *The Virginian**

1903. John Fox, Jr., *The Little Shepherd of Kingdom Come*; Kate Douglas Wiggin, *Rebecca of Sunnybrook Farm*; Jack London, *The Call of the Wild**

1904. Jack London, *The Sea Wolf**; Gene Stratton Porter, *Freckles*

1906. Zane Grey, *The Spirit of the Border**

1907. Harold Bell Wright, *The Shepherd of the Hills**

1908. John Fox, Jr., *The Trail of the Lonesome Pine*; Mary Roberts Rinehart, *The Circular Staircase*

1909. Gene Stratton Porter, *A Girl of the Limberlost*; Harold Bell Wright, *The Calling of Dan Matthews**

1911. Kathleen Norris, *Mother*; Gene Stratton Porter, *The Harvester*; Harold Bell Wright, *The Winning of Barbara Worth**

1912. Zane Grey, *The Riders of the Purple Sage**

1913. Eleanor Hodgman Porter, *Pollyanna*; Gene Stratton Porter, *Laddie*

1914. Edgar Rice Burroughs, *Tarzan of the Apes**; Booth Tarkington, *Penrod**; Harold Bell Wright, *The Eyes of the World**

1915. Gene Stratton Porter, *Michael O'Halloran*

1916. Edgar A. Guest, *A Heap o' Livin'**; Harold Bell Wright, *When a Man's a Man**

1918. Edward Streeter, *Dere Mable*; Henry Adams, *The Education of Henry Adams*; Zane Grey, *The U.P. Trail**

1920. Edward W. Bok, *The Americanization of Edward Bok*; Sinclair Lewis, *Main Street**

1921. Dorothy Canfield, *The Brimming Cup*

1923. Emily Post, *Etiquette**

1924. Edna Ferber, *So Big*

1925. John Erskine, *The Private Life of Helen of Troy**; Anita Loos, *Gentlemen Prefer Blondes*; Bruce Barton, *The Man Nobody Knows*

1926. Sinclair Lewis, *Elmer Gantry*; Will Durant, *The Story of Philosophy**; Thorne Smith, *Topper**

1927. Thornton Wilder, *The Bridge of San Luis Rey*

1929. Lloyd C. Douglas, *The Magnificent Obsession*; Robert L. Ripley, *Believe It or Not**

1930. Edna Ferber, *Cimarron*

1931. Pearl Buck, *The Good Earth**; Ellery Queen, *The Dutch Shoe Mystery**

1932. Ellery Queen, *The Egyptian Cross Mystery**

1933. Hervey Allen, *Anthony Adverse*; Erle Stanley Gardner, *The Case of the Sulky Girl**

1934. Erle Stanley Gardner, *The Case of the Curious Bride**; Ellery Queen, *The Chinese Orange Mystery**

1935. Lloyd C. Douglas, *Green Light*; Erle Stanley Gardner, *The Case of the Counterfeit Eye**

1936. Dale Carnegie, *How to Win Friends and Influence People**; Erle Stanley Gardner, *The Case of the Stuttering Bishop**; Margaret Mitchell, *Gone with the Wind**

1937. Erle Stanley Gardner, *The Case of the Dangerous Dowager**; *The Case of the Lame Canary**

1938. Marco Page, *Fast Company*; Marjorie K. Rawlings, *The Yearling*; Max Brand (Frederick Faust), *Singing Guns**; Erle Stanley Gardner, *The Case of the Substitute Face**; Damon Runyon, *The Best of Damon Runyon**

1939. John Steinbeck, *The Grapes of Wrath**

1940. Ellery Queen, *New Adventures of Ellery Queen**; Ernest Hemingway, *For Whom the Bell Tolls**

1942. Lloyd C. Douglas, *The Robe*; Marion Hargrove, *See Here, Private Hargrove*

1943. Ernie Pyle, *Here Is Your War*; Betty Smith, *A Tree Grows in Brooklyn*; Wendell Willkie, *One World*

1944. Ernie Pyle, *Brave Men*; Kathleen Winsor, *Forever Amber*; Lillian Smith, *Strange Fruit*

1945. Thomas Bertram Costain, *The Black Rose*; Betty MacDonald, *The Egg and I*; Samuel Shellabarger, *Captain from Castile*

1946. Joshua Loth Liebman, *Peace of Mind;* Frank Yerby, *Foxes of Harrow;* Taylor Caldwell, *This Side of Innocence*

1947. John Gunther, *Inside U.S.A.;* Laura Z. Hobson, *Gentleman's Agreement;* Sinclair Lewis, *Kingsblood Royal;* Samuel Shellabarger, *The Prince of Foxes*

1948. Frank Yerby, *The Golden Hawk;* Alfred C. Kinsey, *Sexual Behavior in the Human Male;* Frances Parkinson Keyes, *Dinner at Antoine's;* Thomas Costain, *High Towers;* Norman Mailer, *The Naked and the Dead*

1949. Lloyd C. Douglas, *The Big Fisherman;* Frank Yerby, *Pride's Castle*

1950. Henry Morton Robinson, *The Cardinal*

1951. Rachel Carson, *The Sea Around Us;* Herman Wouk, *The Caine Mutiny;* James Jones, *From Here to Eternity;* Gayelord Hauser, *Look Younger, Live Longer*

1952. Thomas B. Costain, *The Silver Chalice*; The Holy Bible: Revised Standard Version**

1953. Lloyd C. Douglas, *The Robe* (reissue); Catherine Marshall, *A Man Called Peter*

1954. Norman Vincent Peale, *The Power of Positive Thinking*

1955. Herman Wouk, *Marjorie Morningstar;* Anne Morrow Lindbergh, *Gift from the Sea*

1956. Edwin O'Connor, *The Last Hurrah;* Grace Metalious, *Peyton Place*;* Morey Bernstein, *The Search for Bridey Murphy*

1957. James G. Cozzens, *By Love Possessed;* Meyer Levin, *Compulsion;* Vance Packard, *The Hidden Persuaders*

1958. Robert Traver, *Anatomy of a Murder;* James Jones, *Some Came Running*

1959. Leon Uris, *Exodus;* Moss Hart, *Act One;* Harry Golden, *Only in America;* D. C. Jarvis, *Folk Medicine*

1960. Allen Drury, *Advise and Consent;* James A. Michener, *Hawaii*

1961. *The New English Bible: The New Testament*;* William Shirer, *The Rise and Fall of the Third Reich;* Irving Stone, *The Agony and the Ecstasy;* J. D. Salinger, *Franny and Zooey*

1962. Katherine Anne Porter, *Ship of Fools;* Dr. Herman Taller, *Calories Don't Count;* Allen Drury, *A Shade of Difference*

1963. Charles M. Schulz, *Happiness Is a Warm Puppy;* Morris L. West, *The Shoes of the Fisherman;* J. D. Salinger, *Raise High the Roof Beam, Carpenters* and *Seymour—An Introduction*

1964. American Heritage & UPI, *Four Days;* John F. Kennedy, *Profiles in Courage;* Terry Southern and Mason Hoffenberg, *Candy*

1965. Dan Greenberg, *How to Be a Jewish Mother;* James A. Michener, *The Source;* Saul Bellow, *Herzog*

1966. Norman F. Dicey, *How to Avoid Probate;* William Howard Masters and Virginia E. Johnson, *Human Sexual Response;* Truman Capote, *In Cold Blood;* Jacqueline Susann, *Valley of the Dolls*

1967. Eric Berne, *Games People Play;* Thornton Wilder, *The Eighth Day;* Jacqueline Susann, *Valley of the Dolls*

1968. Stephen Birmingham, *"Our Crowd": The Great Jewish Families of New York;* Leon Uris, *Topaz;* William Styron, *The Confessions of Nat Turner*

1969. *"Adam Smith," The Money Game;* John Updike, *Couples;* Arthur Hailey, *Airport;* Gore Vidal, *Myra Breckenridge*

1970. Joe McGinniss, *The Selling of the President;* Chaim Potok, *The Promise;* Philip Roth, *Portnoy's Complaint;* Mario Puzo, *The Godfather*

1971. *The New York Times* Staff, *The Pentagon Papers;* Dee Brown, *Bury My Heart at Wounded Knee;* Sylvia Plath, *The Bell Jar;* Frederick Forsyth, *Day of the Jackal*

1972. Larry Collins and Dominique LaPierre, *O Jerusalem!;* Roger Kahn, *The Boys of Summer*

1973. Richard Bach, *Jonathan Livingston Seagull;* Alex Comfort, *The Joy of Sex*

1974. James A. Michener, *Centennial;* Peter Benchley, *Jaws;* Carl Bernstein and Robert Woodward, *All the President's Men*

1975. E. L. Doctorow, *Ragtime;* Agatha Christie, *Curtain*

1976. Leon Uris, *Trinity;* Alex Haley, *Roots;* Robert Woodward and Carl Bernstein, *The Final Days*

1977. J. R. R. Tolkien, *The Silmarillion*

1978. James A. Michener, *Chesapeake;* Herman Wouk, *War and Remembrance;* Barbara Tuchman, *A Distant Mirror*

1979. Robert Ludlum, *The Matarese Circle;* William Styron, *Sophie's Choice;* Herman Tarnower and Samm Sinclair Baker, *The Complete Scarsdale Medical Diet*

1980. Kurt Vonnegut, *Jailbird;* Erma Bombeck, *Aunt Erma's Cope Book;* Robert Woodward and Scott Armstrong, *The Brethren*

---

* Also best sellers after their period, including cheap reprints (but not dictionaries, almanacs, manuals, textbooks, cookbooks, comic books, or government publications).

1865–1900. LITERATURE OF AMERICA'S REDISCOVERY.

The West: Samuel Langhorne Clemens (Mark Twain, also p. 1002), the great voice of the West of his generation, won a worldwide reputation by his defiantly American outlook, his uncompromising democracy (hostility to slavery, snobbery, and the tyrannies of chivalry), and his pungent colloquial style. Of all contemporary humorists (including John Phoenix [George Horatio Derby, 1823–61], Josh Billings [Henry Wheeler Shaw, 1818–85], Maj. Jack Downing [Seba Smith, 1792–1868], Bill Arp [Charles Henry Smith, 1826–1903], Petroleum V. Nasby [David Ross Locke, 1833–88], and Artemus Ward [Charles Farrar Browne, 1834–67]), Clemens alone created great literature. His experience on the frontiers in the Old Southwest and the Far West (the latter depicted in *Roughing It,* 1872) prepared him to use regional tall tales and realism with his own idiom, as in *The Celebrated Jumping Frog of Calaveras County* (1865), a brilliant reworking of a California folk tale. His frontier irreverence for ancient culture, displayed in *The Innocents Abroad* (1869), the first of several travel books, is in contrast to his enthusiasm in the first part of *Life on the Mississippi* (1883). *The Gilded Age* (1873), written with Charles Dudley Warner (1829–1900), was his first novel, marked like others by its episodic improvisation, but it lacks the distinction of *The Adventures of Tom Sawyer* (1876) and particularly *The Adventures of Huckleberry Finn* (1884), picaresque portrayals of regional character and frontier experience centered on the adventures of 2 boys. His later pessimism is seen in *The Man That Corrupted Hadleyburg* (1900) and *The Mysterious Stranger* (1916). The Western **Local-Colorists** (concerned with commonplace local scenes, utilizing regional dialects, and presenting character types) include **Bret Harte** (1836–1902), who, using stock characters and plots, created a romantic legendary view of California in stories and sketches (notably *The Luck of Roaring Camp*, 1870, called "the father of all Western local color stories," and *Mrs. Skagg's Husbands*, 1873), as well as poems, the most popular being the satiric comic ballad, "Plain Language from Truthful James" (1870), familiarly known under the pirated name "The Heathen Chinee." The vogue for vernacular Western poetry was further solidified by *The Pike County Ballads* (1871) of **John Hay** (p. 1054), whose prose works include *Castilian Days* (1871), an attack upon the Catholic Church; *The Bread-Winners* (1883), an antilabor novel; and, in collaboration with J. G. Nicolay, the classic 10-vol. *Abraham Lincoln: A History* (1890); and by **Joaquin Miller** (Cincinnatus

Hiner Miller, c.1839–1913). Miller romanticized some of his early experiences in *Life Amongst the Modocs* (1873), but in Oregon and California he was by turn horse thief, lawyer, newspaperman, and Indian fighter. His extravagantly romantic poems, e.g., *Songs of the Sierras*, were first hailed as products of a primitive, but he dwindled into a hack writer although the late *Songs of the Soul* (1896) includes his well-known "Columbus." Other balladists of the West: Will Carleton (1845–1912), *Farm Ballads* (1873), including the poem "Over the Hills to the Poor House"; **James Whitcomb Riley** (1849–1916), Indiana poet; and **Eugene Field** (1850–95), Chicago *Daily News* columnist, whose best-known poem was "Little Boy Blue." **Edward Eggleston** (1837–1902), in addition to writing pioneer historical works on American cultural history, notably *The Transit of Civilization* (1901), founded the **Hoosier School** with his novels of the middle border, notably *The Hoosier Schoolmaster* (1871), *The Circuit Rider* (1874), *Roxy* (1878), and *The Graysons* (1888).

The South: Joel Chandler Harris (p. 1052), creator of many "Uncle Remus" stories, a humorous animal legendary reflecting Negro folk life, furnished a memorable picture of the Georgia Negro under slavery and Reconstruction, notably in *Free Joe and Other Georgian Sketches* (1887), and of the "cracker" or "poor white" (*Mingo and Other Sketches in Black and White*, 1884). Other Southern Local-Colorists included **George Washington Cable** (1844–1925), with short stories (*Old Creole Days*, 1879) and novels of Creole life (*The Grandissimes*, 1880; *Dr. Sevier*, 1885; *Bonaventure*, 1888); **Thomas Nelson Page** (1853–1922), who idealized Tidewater Virginia of antebellum days (*Red Rock*, 1898, a study of the Negro problem); and **James Lane Allen** (1849–

1925), who used the central Kentucky plateau around his native Lexington for the locale of his novels (*A Kentucky Cardinal*, 1894; *Summer in Arcady*, 1896; *The Choir Invisible*, 1897; *The Reign of Law*, 1900).

New England: Regional fiction found its most accomplished exponent in **Sarah Orne Jewett** (1849–1909), who revealed social and psychological problems in the declining Maine seaport settlements, beginning with *Deephaven* (1877) and culminating in her masterpiece, *The Country of the Pointed Firs* (1896). Another exponent of the Local-Colorist School was **Mary Eleanor Wilkins** (Freeman) (1852–1930), whose early short stories (*A Humble Romance*, 1887, and *A New England Nun*, 1891) represent her most important work.

1865–1892. RISE OF REALISM. An early realist was **John William De Forest** (1826–1906), whose Civil War novel, *Miss Ravenel's Conversion from Secession to Loyalty* (1867), and story of a South Carolina feud, *Kate Beaumont* (1872), are frank accounts of the seamy, brutal, and corrupting aspects of life. Most popular exponent of the realists was **William Dean Howells** (also p. 1063), with his masterpiece, *The Rise of Silas Lapham* (1885), a sympathetic study of the *nouveaux riches*. Howells' novels provide a penetrating analysis of the post–Civil War American economy. His sympathy with socialism (by 1887) is evident in such novels of social protest as *A Hazard of New Fortunes* (1890). His critical theories are summarized in *Criticism and Fiction* (1891), in which he championed realism, whose sources he ascribed not only to science but to democracy. He insisted that art must serve morality. His economic novels showed the influence of the Utopian socialist novel of **Edward Bellamy** (1850–98), *Looking Backward, or 2000–1887* (1888). Howells' realistic

approach was adopted by Garland, Stephen Crane, Frank Norris, and Robert Herrick. **Hamlin Garland** (1860–1940), an advocate of "veritism," or honest realism (*Crumbling Idols*, 1894), wrote a number of propaganda novels of prairie life and agrarian conditions (1887–94). His major work was *Main-Travelled Roads* (1891), stories of the burdens of farm life. His autobiography, *A Son of the Middle Border* (1917), presents the everyday life of a group of migrating families to the prairies and the plains (1840–95).

1875–1941. HENRY JAMES AND THE NOVELISTS OF MANNERS. A detached observer contrasting American and European cultures and moral standards in relation to social conventions, James (also p. 1069) was a leader in psychological realism, a sensitive interpreter of subtle characters, and a master of a complex style and the formal architecture of fiction. His many novels of contrasting characters developed in subtlety from *The American* (1877) through *The Portrait of a Lady* (1881) to the later major period of *The Wings of the Dove* (1902), *The Ambassadors* (1903), and *The Golden Bowl* (1904). His short stories (e.g., "The Turn of the Screw," 1898) and his criticism (e.g., the prefaces to his revised collected novels and tales, 1907–09) are as distinguished as his longer fiction. James' most articulate disciple in portraying upper-class American society was **Edith Wharton** (1862–1937), whose major novels of New York's social elite include *The House of Mirth* (1905), *The Age of Innocence* (1920), and *The Old Maid* (1924). In *Ethan Frome* (1911), a tale of sordid misery in the New England hills, she produced a work of dignified simplicity. **Ellen Glasgow** (1874–1945) dealt with the ironies of a decaying Virginia society (*Barren Ground*, 1925; *The Romantic Comedians*, 1926; *In This Our*

Life, 1941), and **Willa Cather** (p. 1000) produced chronicles in which environment and character are deftly interwoven: *O Pioneers!* (1913), *My Antonia* (1918), *A Lost Lady* (1923), *Death Comes for the Archbishop* (1927), and *Shadows on the Rock* (1931).

1893–1949. NATURALISM AND THE PROPAGANDA NOVEL. 19th century theories of biological and economic determinism shaped the literary theory of naturalism, with its frankness, objectivity, determinism, and fatalism. Notable among the fiction writers of this school were **Stephen Crane** (p. 1007), **Frank Norris** (1870–1902), **Robert Herrick** (1868–1938), and **Jack London** (1876–1916). The influence of Zola was found in Crane's *Maggie: A Girl of the Streets* (1893), an impressionistic novelette; but his masterpiece was *The Red Badge of Courage* (1895), a lyrical and intense novel of the Civil War, influenced by both Zola and Tolstoi. Among his most successful short stories were "The Open Boat" and "Blue Hotel." *McTeague* (1899) by Norris was a major naturalistic American novel, a study in character disintegration under economic pressure. *The Octopus* (1901), the first of his "Epic of the Wheat" trilogy, a struggle between the wheat growers and the Southern Pacific Railroad, was followed (1903) by *The Pit* (Chicago grain market). *The Wolf,* last of the trilogy, was never written. Social protest against the forces of acquisitiveness found expression in Herrick's novels, notably in the *Memoirs of an American Citizen* (1905), *Clark's Field* (1914), and in *Waste* (1924), where the engineer, Thornton, finds "a sense of corruption working at the very roots of life." Most widely read in the U.S. and abroad of any of these writers was London, among whose 49 vols. of fiction, drama, and essays are *The Call of the Wild* (1903), the story of a dog in the far North who

escapes from civilization to lead a wolf pack; *The Sea Wolf* (1904), a ruthless captain of a sealing ship; *Martin Eden* (1909), a writer's struggle; and *The Valley of the Moon* (1913), in which economic problems are solved by a return to the land.

Other problem novelists of the period who diverged from the path of naturalism and produced straight propaganda novels include **Winston Churchill** (1871–1947), a middle-class progressive, who, in addition to historical romances like *Richard Carvel* (1899) and *The Crisis* (1910), wrote political and economic novels—*Coniston* (1900), *Mr. Crewe's Career* (1908), *A Far Country* (1915), *The Dwelling Place of Light* (1917); **Ernest Poole** (1880–1950), *The Harbor* (1915); **David Graham Phillips** (1867–1911), *The Great God Success* (1901) and *Susan Lenox: Her Fall and Rise* (written 1908, pub. 1917), an epic of slum life and political corruption; and **Upton Sinclair** (1878–1968), whose major novels include *The Jungle* (1906, corruption in meat packing and labor exploitation) and a series of expository and propagandist works: *The Profits of Religion* (1918), on the church; *The Brass Check* (1919), the press; *The Goose Step* (1923) and *The Goslings* (1924), on the schools; *Mammonart* (1925) and *Money Writes* (1927), on the arts. Other exposé novels include *Oil!* (1927), a story of corruption in the Harding era; *Boston* (1928), based on the Sacco-Vanzetti case; and the "Lanny Budd" series (1940–49), a personal interpretation of the two World Wars (1940–49).

1899–1901. FIN-DE-SIÈCLE RO-MANCE was exemplified in the works of **Paul Leicester Ford** (1865–1902), *Janice Meredith* (1899); **Mary Johnston** (1875–1936), *To Have and to Hold* (1900); and **Booth Tarkington** (1869–1946), *Monsieur Beaucaire* (1900).

Tarkington's best work dates from the end of World War I and includes *The Magnificent Ambersons* (1918) and *Alice Adams* (1921).

1900–25. NATURALISM OF THEODORE DREISER (p. 1016). *Sister Carrie* by Dreiser, the story of the realization of her own personality by a poor young girl (1900), remained largely unread until its 3d edition, 1912, a year after the appearance of *Jennie Gerhardt*, on a similar theme. Dreiser's preoccupation with Social Darwinism is given expression in the notable trilogy *The Financier* (1912), *The Titan* (1914), and *The Stoic* (1947), with the masterly character delineation of Cowperwood, prototype of worldly success. Another victim of social and biological forces is Clyde Griffiths in *An American Tragedy* (1925). Objective, amoral, Dreiser, despite lack of style and undistinguished language, achieved a powerful projection of reality.

1918–39. BETWEEN WORLD WARS. "Lost generation" was the name applied by **Gertrude Stein** (1874–1946) to the disillusioned intellectuals and aesthetes of post-World War I years. This group was typified by **F. Scott Fitzgerald** (p. 1029), whose *This Side of Paradise* (1920) is an expression of jazz-age cynicism, and *The Great Gatsby* (1925) of disillusion about quickly acquired riches. That cynicism and disillusionment were also reflected in the writings of **Sinclair Lewis** (p. 1084) in a revolt against small-town meanness (*Main Street*, 1920) and the dullness of the businessman (*Babbitt*, 1922). His writing is closer to caricature than to photographic realism. Other novels include *Arrowsmith* (1924), an exposé of the medical profession; *Dodsworth* (1929), a sympathetic portrayal of a retired American manufacturer; *It Can't Happen Here* (1935), concerned with a future fascist revolt in the U.S.; and

Kingsblood Royal (1947), a novel about race prejudice. Lewis became (1930) the first American author to be awarded the Nobel Prize for literature. This period was also marked by the literature of the **escapists**, including **James Branch Cabell** (1879–1958), with *Jurgen* (1919) and *Figures of Earth* (1921); **Joseph Hergesheimer** (1880–1954), with *The Three Black Pennys* (1917) and *Java Head* (1919); **Elinor Wylie** (1885–1928), poet and novelist; and **Thornton Wilder** (1897–1975), *The Bridge of San Luis Rey* (1927), *Ides of March* (1948) (also p. 879); and by experiments with words rather than ideas carried on by **Gertrude Stein** in many books written between *Three Lives* (1909) and *The Autobiography of Alice B. Toklas* (1933). The most powerful literary impact upon the new generation of American writers was that of **Ernest Hemingway** (p. 1055), with his plain, factual, but evocative style (*The Sun Also Rises*, 1926, a depiction of an expatriate group; and *A Farewell to Arms* [1929], the best American novel of World War I). Other writers of the period include **Sherwood Anderson** (1876–1941), with *Winesburg, Ohio* (1919), stories of small-town life, a naturalistic interpreter of America; and **Ring Lardner** (1885–1933), a sardonic humorist exposing foibles through conversational speech—*How to Write Short Stories* (1924), a collection; *What of It* (1925); *Round Up* (1929); *First and Last* (1934).

Bridging the decades of the 1920s and 1930s was **Thomas C. Wolfe** (1900–38), whose first novel, *Look Homeward, Angel* (1929), was a recognizably autobiographical account of his early years. In *Of Time and the River* (1935) he attempted to capture the variety and vastness of American life. His lyric passages, his brooding depths, and his mastery of satirical portraiture combine to give him a unique place in American letters. Other writings: *The Web and the Rock* (1939), *You Can't Go Home Again* (1940), and *The Hills Beyond* (1941).

The pervasive economic depression of the 1930s resulted in a revitalized social problem novel, as exemplified by such writers as **James T. Farrell** (1904–79), whose *Studs Lonigan* trilogy (1932–35) constitutes a naturalistic portrayal of squalor among the Chicago Irish; **Erskine Caldwell** (1903–   ), whose most popular novel, *Tobacco Road* (1932), recreates the contemporary Jukes and Kallikaks of the South; and **John Dos Passos** (1896–1970), whose outlook and style reached maturity in *Manhattan Transfer* (1925). His *U.S.A.* trilogy (1930, 1932, 1936), a Domesday Book of economic malpractices, employs several distinctive fictional devices, including a panoramic background, or "newsreel," and the "Camera Eye," the author's point of view toward his subject matter expressed in stream-of-consciousness passages. **John Steinbeck's** (1902–1968) *The Grapes of Wrath* (1939) is a memorable recreation of the economic dislocation of the Okies and the tragedy of the Dust Bowl. Other outstanding novels: *Tortilla Flat* (1935), *Of Mice and Men* (1937), *East of Eden* (1952). **William Faulkner** (p. 1026) wrote a series of novels constituting a bitter comedy of plantation family decadence (*The Sound and the Fury*, 1929, decadence as seen through the eyes of an idiot son; *As I Lay Dying*, 1930, psychology of a subnormal poor-white family with its use of naturalism to highlight the dominance of the irrational in human nature; *Sanctuary*, 1931, a sadistic horror story; *Light in August*, 1932, the ordeal of a pregnant girl; *Intruder in the Dust*, 1948).

1919–30. HARLEM RENAISSANCE. The post-World War I period brought an upsurge of black literary activity that culminated in the Harlem Renaissance of the 1920s. Under the influence of **W. E. B. DuBois** (p. 1017) and poet and novelist **James Weldon Johnson** (1871–1938), the movement was characterized by racial pride and interest in African culture and protest against bigotry and discrimination. **Langston Hughes** (1902–67), author of *Weary Blues* (1926), was the most popular poet, but equally accomplished verse was produced by **Countee Cullen** (1903–46) and **Claude McKay** (1889–1948). The latter also won renown as a novelist with *Home to Harlem* (1926), as did **Jean Toomer** (1894–1969), best known for his collection of rural sketches, *Cane* (1923).

1861–1950. CHANGING FASHIONS IN POETRY. Despite her individualism, the influence of **Emily Dickinson** (p. 1013), whose pieces were distinguished by sharp and unexpected imagery and poignant feeling, has been profound. Her metaphors made her seem to Amy Lowell a precursor of the Imagist School. Among the **conservative** poets of the earlier period were **Bayard Taylor** (1825–78); **Edmund Clarence Stedman** (1833–1908); **Thomas Bailey Aldrich** (1836–1907), editor of the *Atlantic* (1881–90); **Richard Watson Gilder** (1844–1909), reflecting the influence of Rossetti and other Pre-Raphaelites; **Edward Rowland Sill** (1841–87), whose *Poems* (1902) are marked by a classic finish and stoic idealism; **John Banister Tabb** (1845–1909), poet-priest whose poetry has been compared to Emily Dickinson and to the 17th-century English metaphysical poets; **Sidney Lanier** (1842–81), the outstanding Southern poet of the period, who attempted to produce in verse the sound patterns of music, revealing in his poetry exceptional melodic gifts and a fine rhythmical feeling ("The Song of the Chattahoochee,"

"The Symphony," and "The Marshes of Glynn"). Others in the period include **Richard Hovey** (1864–1900), whose poetry reveled in the joys of the open road (*Songs from Vagabondia,* 1894), **William Vaughan Moody** (1869–1910), best known for his verse dramas (p. 878), whose poetry combined lyrical treatment with attention to political questions treated along anti-imperialist lines; **Edwin Markham** (1852–1940), whose most popular poem, "The Man with the Hoe" (1899), was inspired by Millet's painting; and **Joyce Kilmer** (1886–1918), *Trees and Other Poems* (1914); **Paul Laurence Dunbar** (1872–1906), black poet whose verse suggested both apprehension and aggressive feelings about emancipation (*Lyrics of Lowly Life,* 1896).

The **revolt against traditionalism** was led by **Ezra Pound** (p. 1131), who served as an editor of *Poetry* (founded Chicago, 1912), a leader of the Imagists, and a sponsor of diverse authors. His disciplined metrical experiments, concern with a continuum of culture, and use of medieval and Chinese literature brought powerful new forces to play on modern poetry. His works include *Personae* (1926) and *Cantos* (1930–69). Pound's impact was especially notable in the work of **T.[homas] S.[tearns] Eliot** (1888–1965), American-born poet who became a British subject in 1927, with *The Waste Land* (1922), his major poetic effort, an epic compressed into 400 lines. In *Ash-Wednesday* (1930) he made clear his allegiance to the Church of England, and its value as a medium of social action is affirmed in *Murder in the Cathedral* (1935), a latter-day morality play. Eliot considered poetry as an escape from emotion and personality. His influence in turn was felt in the work of **Hart Crane** (1899–1932).

Other principal poets of the post-World War I period (many of whom published major works prior to 1914) include **Edwin Arlington Robinson** (p. 1138), heir to the New England tradition of Puritanism and Transcendentalism, who dealt primarily with ethical conflicts within the individual; **Amy Lowell** (1874–1925), a free-verse Imagist; **Robert Frost** (p. 1034), whose lyrics are marked by an intense but restrained emotion and a brilliant insight into New England character; **Vachel Lindsay** (1879–1931), known for his vivid imagery, vigorous rhythm, and dramatic conception (*Congo and Other Poems,* 1914); **Carl Sandburg** (1878–1967), also author of a monumental biography of Lincoln (1926–43), whose realism captures the American idiom; **Edgar Lee Masters** (1869–1947), *Spoon River Anthology* (1915), a bitter commentary on American urban standards; **Robinson Jeffers** (1887–1962), *Tamar* (1924), *Roan Stallion* (1925), poems of violence set in the headlands and valleys of California; **Conrad Aiken** (1889–1973), whose subjective poetry is marked by subtle musical rhythms; **Stephen Vincent Benét** (1898–1943), *John Brown's Body* (1928), a narrative poem of the Civil War; **Edna St. Vincent Millay** (1892–1950), whose *Renascence and Other Poems* (1917) exhibited technical virtuosity, freshness, and a hunger for beauty —her mastery of the sonnet form was demonstrated by *The Buck in the Snow* (1928) and *Fatal Interview* (1931); **Marianne Moore** (1887–1972), *Collected Poems* (1951); and **Wallace Stevens** (1879–1955), whose poems exhibit intensity, precision, and command of imagery; *Collected Poems* (1954); **William Carlos Williams** (1883–1963), who found a highly colloquial poetry in commonplace objects and everyday experience (*Patterson,* 1946); **John Crowe**

Ransom (1888–1974), whose hard, dry modern verse is typified by *Chills and Fevers* (1924); **Archibald MacLeish** (p. 1094), blank-verse drama, *Fall of the City* (1937).

1890–1970. LITERATURE AND SOCIAL CRITICISM. Chief critics of the period who considered literature from the point of view of social values were **Randolph Bourne** (1886–1918), *Youth and Life* (1913) and *Untimely Papers* (1919); and **Van Wyck Brooks** (1886–1963), who, in *The Wine of the Puritans* (1909), developed the thesis that the Puritan tradition crushed American culture, views which have been altered in later works, notably his 5 studies in cultural history, *Movers and Makers*, begun in 1936. His *America's Coming of Age* (1915) affirmed the prewar idealism of the younger generation. The most notable achievement in socioliterary criticism was *Main Currents in American Thought* (1927–30) by **Vernon Louis Parrington** (1871–1929). **Henry L. Mencken** (1880–1956), founder with **George Jean Nathan** (1882–1958) of *The American Mercury* (1924), which he edited to 1933, is best known for his aggressive iconoclasm toward American democracy and the cultural gaucheries of the American scene. His most important scholarly work is *The American Language* (1919–48). Leaders of **conservative criticism** were **Paul Elmer More** (1864–1937), **Irving Babbitt** (1865–1933), **Stuart Pratt Sherman** (1881–1926), and **William Crary Brownell** (1851–1928), with a neohumanist movement launched (1930) by **Norman Foerster** (1887–1972) and supported by More and Babbitt. Among the critics who rose to prominence in the 1930s were **Edmund Wilson** (p. 1186), whose wide-ranging interests were evident in works such as *Axel's Castle* (1931), and **Lionel Trilling** (1905–75), whose *The Liberal*

Imagination (1950) contained a number of seminal essays. Other important critical voices during this period were **Lewis Mumford** (1895–   ), **Kenneth Burke** (1897–   ), and **Allen Tate** (1899–1979).

1861–1951. HISTORIANS. The major impact on historical writing in the post-Civil War period derived from the "scientific school," as evidenced in the writings of **Henry Harisse** (1829–1910) and **Justin Winsor** (1831–97) and in the introduction of the seminar method in the universities by **Charles K. Adams** at Michigan (1869), by **Henry Adams** at Harvard (1871), and notably after 1880 at Johns Hopkins under **Herbert Baxter Adams** (1850–1901) and at Columbia under **John W. Burgess** (1844–1931). The founding of the American Historical Association, 1884 (with its *Review* appearing 1895), and the establishment of the *Political Science Quarterly*, 1886, were early evidences of the new trend. Major historians of the period include **Henry Adams** (p. 970); **James Ford Rhodes** (1848–1927), with his multivolume history of the U.S. since 1850; **John Fiske** (1842–1901), notable as well for his fight for Spencerian evolution (*The Outlines of Cosmic Philosophy*, 1874) as for his vitalizing early American history and stressing the European genesis of American institutions; **John Bach McMaster** (1852–1932), first of the important social historians; and a new group of objective analysts of (1) the colonial period: **Herbert Levi Osgood** (1855–1918), **George Louis Beer** (1872–1920), and **Charles McLean Andrews** (1863–1943), and (2) Reconstruction: **William Archibald Dunning** (1857–1922) and his disciples. But the chief impulse to the newer group of 20th-century historians came from the writing of **Frederick Jackson Turner** (p. 1172) and **Charles Austin Beard** (p. 980). In a paper entitled "The Significance of the Frontier in American History"

(1893) Turner pointed out that the frontier has been the one great determinant of American civilization, a point of departure from previous writers who stressed continuity of American institutions with Europe. Despite significant correctives of this thesis, it has had an exceptional impact upon the study of the roles of environment and geographical sections in U.S. history. The widest reading public in the post-World War period was achieved by Beard, whose major research was embodied in 2 early monographs, *An Economic Interpretation of the Constitution* (1913) and *The Economic Origins of Jeffersonian Democracy* (1915). *The Rise of American Civilization* (2 vols., pub. in 1927 with Mary Beard; vol. 3, *America in Midpassage*, 1939) revealed that Beard was no longer an economic determinist and stressed pluralism in historical causation. **James Harvey Robinson** (1863–1936) in *The New History* (1912) insisted that the historian had a duty to explain how things came to be as they are, to study all kinds of social facts, and to make "syntheses." Although Beard in later life distinguished between **history as actuality** and the **historical record** (involving selection and interpretation of the facts), and Robert L. Schuyler cautioned against the "present-mindedness" of recent historians, the prevailing trend down to the mid-century was to stress social, economic, and intellectual history and to relate historical data to contemporary problems.

In the 1930s and 1940s historical biography reacted from the earlier muckraking school, as well as from the critical and psychoanalytical studies of the 1920s (W. E. Woodward's Grant; Van Wyck Brooks, *Ordeal of Mark Twain*) to providing fuller and more sympathetic factual biographies (Carl Van Doren's Franklin, Douglas S. Freeman's Lee, Allan Nevins' Grover Cleveland, Carl

Sandburg's and James G. Randall's multivolume Lincoln, and Dumas Malone's Jefferson [6th vol., 1981]).

1861–1952. LIBRARIES: MAJOR TRENDS. System and Technique: In 1876 the American Library Association held its first convention; established *Library Journal*, 1876. The introduction of methods of business efficiency and cataloguing was largely the result of the efforts of **Melvil Dewey** (1851–1931), who founded the New York State Library School (1887) and originated the Dewey "decimal classification." **Free Library Movement:** in 1881 **Andrew Carnegie** (p. 998) made his original offer to donate buildings for public libraries provided that each municipality would establish and adequately finance such a library by annual tax appropriations. By 1900 there were 1,700 free libraries in the U.S. with over 5,000 vols.; by 1947 there were more than 7,100 public libraries and 4,200 libraries of other kinds. The free library movement was further accelerated by the enactment in 1893 of the first state law (in New Hampshire) requiring townships to create libraries. **Founding of the New York Public Library,** 23 May 1895, out of the consolidation of the Astor (1848) and Lenox (1870) Libraries, and the Tilden Trust created by the will of Samuel J. Tilden (d. 1886). By 1952 it had in excess of 5 million volumes and was the largest public library in the U.S. **Growth of University and Reference Libraries:** Among the largest university libraries at the end of the period were Harvard, 5,400,000 vols.; Yale, 3,980,000; California (including branches), 2,717,000; Illinois, 2,384,000; Columbia, 2,000,000. Notable among the specialized reference libraries: American Antiquarian Society, Worcester, Mass. (older newspapers); Henry E. Huntington Library and Art Gallery, San Marino, Calif. (English and U.S. literature and history); Smithsonian Institution (1846), Washington, D.C., scientific and learned societies publications; Library of the Surgeon General's Office, U.S. Army, Washington, D.C. (beg. 1818), medical science; Folger Shakespeare Library, Washington, D.C., English books, 1475–1640.

1861–1960. PUBLISHING TRENDS. Dime novels had a sensational vogue, 1860–1900, inspired by the success of the "penny dreadfuls" in England and published by such firms as Beadle & Adams and Street & Smith. The pen name "Nick Carter" was used by such writers as John Russell Coryell, Frederick William Davis, Frederick Van Rensselaer Day, and others. **Juveniles:** Conspicuously successful down to World War I were the works of **Louisa May Alcott** (p. 973); **Frances Hodgson Burnett** (1849–1924), *Little Lord Fauntleroy* (1886); and **Booth Tarkington,** *Penrod* (1914). Despite serious competition from comic books, juveniles came to command an increasing share of publishers' attention after 1940, constituting in 1950, after fiction, the largest single category. **Consolidation** among major firms took place throughout the period, notably in the formation, 1890, of the American Book Co. to publish school texts. Greater centralization of publishing in the New York area developed. Other firms founded prior to 1901 included Henry Holt & Co. (1866 as Leypoldt & Holt); Macmillan Co., 1870; Doubleday, 1900 (merged with Doran, 1927). Of considerable advantage to U.S. writers was the enactment, 3 Mar. 1891, of an international **copyright law** to prevent pirating the works of foreign authors; revised 4 Mar. 1909 (amended through 3 June 1949). New literary and distribution trends were encouraged by the rise of new publishing houses in the 20th century, notably B. W. Huebsch, 1905 (absorbed by Viking, 1925); Alfred A. Knopf, 1915, with emphasis

upon books by outstanding European authors; Boni & Liveright, 1917, with the moderate-priced "Modern Library" series (acquired by Bennett A. Cerf, 1925; since 1927 by Random House); Harcourt Brace, 1919; Simon & Schuster, 1924; Random House, 1927; and, in the field of scholarly and scientific works, by the establishment of **university presses,** notably Columbia, Harvard, Chicago, Yale, Princeton, and North Carolina. Two major distributing trends after World War I were the establishment of **book clubs** (Book-of-the-Month Club and Literary Guild both began distribution in 1926), with over 50 different clubs by 1947; and the successful distribution of reprints of popular books in the 25 ct.–35 ct. range, with Pocket Books (1939), Bantam Books (1946), and Signet-Mentor (New American Library) the 3 major organizations in the field by 1952.

1960 witnessed a rash of mergers in the book publishing business, including Henry Holt & Co. with Rinehart and Winston, the acquisition of Meridian by World, of the New American Library by the Los Angeles *Times-Mirror,* of Macmillan by Crowell-Collier, of Appleton-Century-Crofts by Meredith, and of Alfred A. Knopf, Inc., by Random House. Financing was chiefly done by public sale of stock, in most cases mergers being prompted by desire to expand in the textbook field.

1930–73. AMERICAN NOBEL PRIZE WINNERS in literature: Sinclair Lewis (1930), Eugene O'Neill (1936), Pearl S. Buck (1938), William Faulkner (1949), Ernest Hemingway (1954), John Steinbeck (1962).

1945–73. FICTION. Major novelists of the prewar era continued to produce work of merit, especially Faulkner (*Intruder in the Dust,* 1948), and Hemingway (*The Old Man and the Sea,* 1952). At a somewhat lower level, John

Steinbeck also remained productive (*East of Eden,* 1952).

Among the writers who established themselves with novels about World War II were **Norman Mailer** (p. 1095), with *The Naked and the Dead* (1948), and **Irwin Shaw** (1913–), with *The Young Lions* (1948). Simultaneously, the Southern school of writing continued to flourish with *All the King's Men* by **Robert Penn Warren** (1905–), *A Member of the Wedding* by **Carson Mc-Cullers** (1917–1967), both published in 1946, and the short stories and novels of **Eudora Welty** (1909–). In this school one might also mention **Flannery O'Connor** (1925–1964) and **Katherine Ann Porter** (1890–1980). Still other novelists who made their mark in this decade were **James Gould Cozzens** (1903–78) with *Guard of Honor* (1948), **Nelson Algren** (1909–81) with *The Man With the Golden Arm* (1949), and **Saul Bellow** (1915–) with *The Victim* (1947).

The 1950s produced diverse trends in American fiction, among them free-flowing picaresque narratives such as *The Catcher in the Rye* (1951), by **J. D. Salinger** (1919–) and *The Adventures of Augie March* (1953) by Bellow; the understated domestic tragedies of **John Cheever** (1912–) and **John Updike** ·(1932–), the most polished of which were, respectively, *The Wapshot Chronicle* (1957) and *Rabbit, Run* (1960); the anti-establishment "Beat" novels of **Jack Kerouac** (1922–1969), e.g., *On the Road* (1957); and the cold-eyed satires of the Russian émigré **Vladimir Nabokov** (p. 1112), of which *Lolita* (1958) was typical.

Most of these writers continued to produce fiction in much the same vein in the 1960s and 1970s, a period marked by 2 new schools of writing—"black humor" and "new journalism." The former, represented by such novelists as **Joseph Heller** (1923–), author of *Catch-22* (1961), was fiercely comic in its treatment of formerly serious or taboo subjects. Other "black humorists" who caught the critics' fancy were **Bruce Jay Friedman, Thomas Pynchon,** and **Donald Barthelme.** The new journalism stressed a loose, fictionalized approach to reporting, as in the later works of Norman Mailer (e.g., *Miami and the Siege of Chicago,* 1968). **Truman Capote**'s "nonfiction novel" *In Cold Blood* (1965), based on a set of murders in Kansas, seems to have been the most lucrative of these works.

Ethnic writing was also prominent at this time. Fiction by black authors had attracted a considerable national audience as far back as 1940, when **Richard Wright** (1908–60) published *Native Son.* The real outpouring came in the 1950s and 1960s, however, with **James Baldwin** (1924–) and **Ralph Ellison** (p. 1024) leading the way. Ellison's complex, subtly textured *Invisible Man* (1952) created a high standard of excellence for black writing. Some of those who attempted to equal this standard were Willard Motley, Ishmael Reed, and John A. Williams.

Jewish culture also received considerable attention in the postwar period. The best-known practitioners of the "Jewish novel" were **Bellow, Philip Roth** (*Portnoy's Complaint*) and **Bernard Malamud** (1914–), whose *The Magic Barrel* (1958) was widely praised.

The short stories and novels of **Joyce Carol Oates** (1938–) such as *Them* (1969) captured critical attention in the 1960s. Major contemporary novelists include **Thomas Pynchon** (*V,* 1963; *Gravity's Rainbow,* 1973) and **John Gardner** (*The Sunlight Dialogues,* 1972).

1945–1973. POETRY. Poetry in America has been generally less memorable than fiction since the war. Still, noteworthy contributions were made by

Robert Lowell (1917–77), **Theodore Roethke** (1908–63), and **Richard Wilbur** (1921–), all of whom abandoned the experimentalism of Eliot and Pound, creating instead a verse that followed traditional poetic forms. They were modest in their choice of subject matter, which was frequently personal and immediate, in contrast to the sweeping issues of cultural decline that occupied Pound and Eliot. Lowell's work is best exemplified in *Lord Weary's Castle* (1946) and *Life Studies* (1959), Roethke's in *Collected Poems* (1966), and Wilbur's in *Things of This World* (1957).

Simultaneously, senior American poets continued to produce work of some merit. Robert Frost's *In the Clearing* (1963) was a hard, crystalline, occasionally coy collection of verse. A naturalized American, **W. H. Auden** (1907–1973) brought out a number of volumes of highly uneven work, including *Collected Shorter Poems* in 1967. The same year saw the publication of Marianne Moore's *Complete Poems*.

Revolting against the "academicism" of poets like Lowell, the "Beat" poets tried to return to the colloquial, bardic manner of Whitman, whose influence they traced through William Carlos Williams to Charles Olson. Some followers of this school were Robert Duncan, Gregory Corso, and the flamboyant **Allen Ginsberg** (1926–), who produced the most publicized work of the movement, "Howl" (1955).

Though better known as a novelist, **Robert Penn Warren** has won praise for such poetic efforts as *Selected Poems* (1966). Of about equal stature is **John Berryman** (1915–72), whose rather obscure *Seventy-Seven Dream Songs* (1964) is his most substantial work. Later figures of note included a talented group of women poets such as Denise Levertov, Anne Sexton and, most memorably, **Sylvia Plath** (1932–63), author of the brilliant collection *Ariel* (1965).

Schools and trends were hard to discern in the 1960s and early 1970s, but there were many individual poets of ability, though rarely of genius. Robert Bly, James Merrill, and Robert Creely were typical figures. Among black poets, **Gwendolyn Brooks** (1917–), remained the most highly regarded; *In the Mecca* (1968) is representative of her racially oriented work. **Imamu Baraka** (LeRoi Jones), the black playwright, has also evoked a certain degree of enthusiasm for his poetry.

1951–74. HISTORIANS. Since World War II historians like Perry Miller (1905–63) and Richard Hofstadter (1916–72) have stressed intellectual history and ideological issues, while at the same time subjecting the Populist-Progressive historians to a critical reassessment. Stressing agreement rather than conflict, the "consensus historians" have argued that the American Revolution wrought no basic change in the life of the community (Daniel J. Boorstin), have stressed the divergence of the American from the European experience on the ground of the absence in America of feudal institutions and the relative freedom from poverty (Louis Hartz), have denied that the American Revolution was fought to achieve democracy, as a comparatively broad suffrage already existed (Robert E. and B. Katherine Brown), and have defended the constitutional and ideological arguments of the Whigs as sincerely held and not opportunistic (Edmund S. Morgan). To the "consensus historians" the Constitution was not the repudiation of the Revolution, as the Populist-Progressive historians viewed it, but the fulfillment of the aspirations of its leadership.

One of the major contributions of American historians since the 1950s has been the issuance of definitive editions of the writings of American statesmen and other figures (Julian P. Boyd's Jefferson; Leonard W. Labaree *et al.*'s Franklin; Lyman H. Butterfield's John Adams; Harold C. Syrett's Hamilton; William T. Hutchinson, William M. E. Rachal, Robert A. Rutland, *et al.*'s, Madison), editions published in accordance with the canons of modern scholarship. These editorial labors have rekindled a nationwide concern for collecting, preserving, and microfilming historical manuscripts and public records long neglected, a concern most appropriate to the commemoration of the Bicentennial of the American Revolution.

In the 1960s and 1970s a group of "New Left" revisionists, of whom William Appleman Williams may be considered a spokesman, have traced the roots of alleged U.S. neocolonialism back to post-Civil War years, while challenging the standard view of the origins of the Cold War, shifting the blame for obstinacy and myopia from Soviet to American leadership. "Cliometrics," the wedding of history and quantification, has been exemplified by a number of distinguished demographic and family monographs for the colonial period along with a notable, if controversial, analysis of the institution of slavery: *Time on the Cross: the Economics of Negro Slavery, I,* by R. W. Fogel and S. L. Engerman (1974).

1962–73. LIBRARIES: MAJOR TRENDS. University libraries pioneered in the adoption of new techniques, making use of developments in systems analysis, computers, data processing, xerography. The automation of bibliographic processing, catalog search, and document retrieval began. The National Library of Medicine employed computer process for *Index Medicus* (1963). Florida Atlantic Univ. opened (1964) with a computer-based library

operation involving (1) automated ordering, cataloging, and circulation, (2) methods of handling and disseminating information made possible by data processing but without an electronic information-retrieval system. The Univ. of Chicago Library received $500,000 from the National Science Foundation (1967) for development of integrated modular (building-lock) system of library data that will include bibliographic processing, catalog searching, and circulation control, while M.I.T. received $250,000 from the Council on Library Resources for Project Intrex, a study of remote access to centrally stored information.

Federal assistance to university libraries was expanded by the Higher Education Act of 1965, which authorized $70 million per year for 5 years for purchase of textbooks and materials to train students. By the period 1969–73, however, rising costs and declining federal support had left most American libraries in serious financial trouble. The New York Public Library, for example, reported a deficit of $1 million in 1972.

Other developments in the late 1960s and early 1970s included the opening of the Lyndon B. Johnson Library at the Univ. of Texas in Austin; a firm stand by the American Library Association against attempts by the government to obtain records of who had checked out books; a drive to unionize librarians; a U.S. court of claims decision (1972) prohibiting photocopying of copyrighted materials; an increase in the number of library schools offering accredited graduate programs to 57.

1960–73. PUBLISHING TRENDS. A sharp increase in book sales in the first part of this period was spurred in part by federal funds for education and library programs. The gross national book product jumped from $1 billion (1960) to $2.7 billion (1966); 28,762 new titles were published in 1967. By the early 1970s the book industry's gross was in excess of $3 billion, but the number of new titles had dropped to 26,000, while curtailment of funds for schools and libraries, along with a decline of leisure-time reading (from 21%, 1938, to 14%, 1974, according to a 1974 Gallup poll), combined with inflationary factors slowed sales of college and school texts, and were reflected in declining publishing profits.

Consolidation among major firms continued with the merger of Harper & Brothers with Row, Peterson, becoming Harper & Row (1962), and the purchase of G. & C. Merriam Co. by Encyclopaedia Britannica (1964). Publishing houses acquired by giant conglomerates included Random House, part of the RCA communications combine (1966); Bobbs-Merrill, which became an affiliate of ITT (1966); Holt, Rinehart and Winston, which was acquired by CBS (1967); American Book Co. and D. Van Nostrand Co., Inc., absorbed by Litton Industries (1968).

In the period 1968–73, sales in certain areas—notably fiction and textbooks—fell off markedly. Paperback titles soared but overall publishing experienced financial difficulties. University presses were especially hard hit, though a $2 million grant from the Mellon Foundation helped.

Technical breakthroughs in these years included the introduction of audiovisual cassettes, on which even the lengthiest literary works could be "recorded." One of the first of these to be undertaken in the new process was the 12-vol. *Oxford English Dictionary*. Posing a serious challenge to traditional school texts and library book sales were various types of "teaching machines," combining audio and visual materials, often supplanting and frequently supplementing the printed book in the elementary and secondary schools.

1974–80. AMERICAN NOBEL PRIZE WINNERS IN LITERATURE: Saul Bellow (1976); Isaac Bashevis Singer (Yiddish) (1978); Czeslaw Milosz (Polish) (1980).

Theater

Theatrical performances in America date from 1665, when *Ye Bare and Ye Cubb*, an English play, was presented in Virginia. A formal theatrical unit, the company founded by Thomas Kean and Walter Murray, existed as early as 1749 in Philadelphia, and the Hallam Company, formed in England, toured the colonies for two years (1752–54). The Revolution interrupted most activity on the stage, but it quickly resumed in the 1790s. Landmarks in the evolution of the American theater include the emergence of Negro minstrelsy (about 1799); the establishment of repertory companies in most major American cities during the early part of the nineteenth century; the creation of theatrical syndicates (especially the one founded by Charles Frohman in 1896, which controlled booking throughout the U.S. for a number of years); the "little theater" movement (1900–19), which sought to reduce the scale of stage productions and increase the quality; the Group Theater founded in New York City in the 1930s to bring social consciousness onto the American stage; and the off-Broadway movement of the late fifties and early sixties. The preeminence of the actor was established early in American theatrical history. Some of the notable stars of the past, with the dates of their debuts, are: Edwin Forrest (1820), Charlotte Cushman (1836), Edwin Booth (1849), Ethel Barrymore (1896), and Katherine Cornell (1917).

As one might expect, American playwrighting followed the English lead for some time, producing the comedies of Royall Tyler, the blank-verse tragedies of William Dunlap, and, later in the nineteenth century, the comparatively realistic dramas of Augustus Daly and Clyde Fitch. There was no work of lasting merit, however, until the arrival of Eugene O'Neill, whose gloomy but poetic family tragedies reach from *All God's Chillun Got Wings* (1924) to *Long Day's Journey into Night* (1956). After O'Neill, American drama at least became a distinct entity, rather than a facsimile of European work. Its entertaining, occasionally profound, efforts in different modes include the brittle sophistication of the Broadway team of George S. Kaufman and Moss Hart; the ambitious poetic dramas of Maxwell Anderson; the social realism of Clifford Odets; the earnest humanism of Arthur Miller; and the romanticized Southern dramas of Tennessee Williams. Despite repeated comments voiced in the sixties and seventies about the ill health of theater in America, specifically its declining audience appeal and the lack of major playwrights, new companies were still being formed (often with the help of foundations), and newer dramatists like Edward Albee and David Rabe indicated the continued vitality of the creative side of the American theater.

1665. *Ye Bare and Ye Cubb*, the first English play known to have been performed in the colonies, was written and produced by 3 amateurs of Accomac Co., Va.; prosecuted but acquitted.

1714. *Androborus*, a satirical farce by Gov. Robert Hunter (N.Y., d.1734), printed but not produced.

1716. First theater in the colonies was erected at Williamsburg. Foreclosed 1723, it became the Town Hall in 1745.

1749–50. First American acting company was organized in Philadelphia by Thomas Kean and Walter Murray. Staged Addison's *Cato.* The company opened in New York (1750) in *Richard III* with Kean in the title role. Fourteen other Shakespearean plays were produced in the colonies. In addition to *Richard III*, the most popular were *King Lear* and *Katharine and Petruchio* (*The Taming of the Shrew*). The Kean-Murray company's New York repertoire included 24 plays (by Addison, Cibber, Congreve, Dryden, Farquhar, Fielding, Garrick, Lillo, and Otway). The company also performed in Williamsburg, Fredericksburg, and Annapolis.

1752. HALLAM COMPANY, sent to America by William Hallam and headed by his brother, **Lewis,** opened at Williamsburg with *The Merchant of Venice.* This company had a repertoire of over 40 plays, chiefly from Elizabethan and Restoration dramatists. Played also in New York and Philadelphia; disbanded in Jamaica, 1754.

1758. David Douglass, organizer of the American Company, opened in New York with Rowe's *Jane Shore.*

1766. Southwark Theater in Philadelphia, the first permanent theater built in the colonies, opened with Shakespeare's *Katharine and Petruchio.*

Ponteach; or The Savages of America, by Maj. **Robert Rogers;** first tragedy written on a native subject; unproduced.

1767. *The Prince of Parthia,* a tragedy (written before 1763) by **Thomas Godfrey** (1736–63), pioneer American dramatist, performed at Southwark Theater, Philadelphia; first native play to be professionally staged.

1775–83. REVOLUTIONARY THEATER. During the war most theatrical companies moved to Jamaica. Resolutions of the Continental Congress (24 Oct. 1774 and 12 Oct. 1778) recommended legislation prohibiting public entertainments. However, regular performances were given by the British troops in occupied towns. Howe's Thespians, an amateur group directed by Surgeon General Beaumont, opened its season in New York in 1777 and in Philadelphia in 1778. Clinton's Thespians gave their first performance at the John Street Theater (built 1767), New York, and continued intermittently until 1782. A number of propaganda plays were written in this period. Tory plays included *A Dialogue between a Southern Delegate and His Spouse on His Return from the Grand Continental Congress* (anon., 1774), Jonathan Mitchell Sewell's *Cure for the Spleen,* and General Burgoyne's *The Blockade of Boston* (both in 1775). The Patriot playwrights included Mrs. **Mercy Warren** (1728–1814), whose first play, *The Adulateur,* a satire on Gov. Hutchinson (1773), was followed by *The Group* (1775), based on the revocation of the Massachusetts charter (neither play produced). Other Patriot plays included *The Fall of British Tyranny* (1776), attributed to John or Joseph Leacock (1776);

an anonymous farce, *The Blockheads* (1776); and 3 plays by **Hugh Henry Brackenridge** (1748–1816), *The Battle of Bunker's Hill* (1776), *The Rising Glory of America* (1771), and *The Death of General Montgomery* (1777).

1787. *The Contrast,* by **Royall Tyler** (1757–1826; later chief justice of Vermont), the first American comedy to be produced by a professional company, performed in New York.

1789–97. EARLY AMERICAN PLAYWRIGHTS of this period included **William Dunlap** (1766–1839)—*The Father, or American Shandyism* (1789), *The Fatal Deception* (1794; published, 1806, as *Leicester*) and *Fontainville Abbey,* a Gothic drama (1795); **Samuel Low**—*The Politician Outwitted,* Federalist satire, published 1789; **Susanna Haswell Rowson** (c.1762–1824)—*Slaves in Algiers* (1794) and *The Volunteers,* a play dealing with the Whisky Insurrection (1795); **John Daly Burk** (c.1775–1808)—*Bunker Hill,* patriotic drama (1797); **Royall Tyler**—*A Georgia Spec, or Land in the Moon,* based on the Yazoo land frauds (1797).

1797. The tragedy *Douglas,* performed at Washington, Ky., the first recorded performance of an English-language drama west of the Alleghenies.

1799. NEGRO MINSTRELSY. At the close of the 2d act of *Oroonoko,* a play produced in Boston, Gottlieb Graupner, said to have been made up in Negro character, sang "The Gay Negro Boy," accompanying himself on the banjo; one of the earliest known origins of Negro minstrelsy, subsequently developed and popularized by Andrew Jackson Allen, Thomas Dartmouth Rice, Bob Farrell, and George Washington Dixon.

1806–18. Leading American playwrights included **John Howard Payne** (1791–1852)—*Julia, or the Wanderer* (1806, at New York's leading theater,

Park Theater, built, 1798; destroyed by fire, 1820); Payne wrote 64 plays; including *Brutus, or the Fall of Tarquin,* a tragedy produced at the Drury Lane, London (1818; N.Y., 1819). **James Nelson Barker** (1784–1858)—*Tears and Smiles* (1807); *The Indian Princess,* first Indian play by a native American to be performed (Philadelphia, 1808); its production at the Drury Lane, London (1820), under the title of *Pocahontas,* made it the first American play performed overseas after initial production at home; *Marmion,* based on Scott's poem (1812).

1817–32. ACTING DEBUTS. Noah Miller Ludlow (1795–1886), a leading figure in the theatrical history of the West, embarked on his career as actor-manager (1817); **Edwin Forrest** (p. 1031), first native-born actor to attain top rank, made his debut at the Walnut Street Theater, Philadelphia, as Young Norval in the tragedy *Douglas* (1820); **Edmund Kean** (1787–1833), the English tragedian, made his American debut in New York as Richard III (1820); **Junius Brutus Booth** (1796–1852), English actor, made his American debut at the Richmond (Va.) Theater as Richard III (1821). **James H. Hackett** (1800–71) made his New York debut in *Love in a Village* (1826); **William Charles Macready** (1793–1873), English actor, made his American debut at the Park Theater, N.Y., in the role of Virginius (1826); **Fanny Kemble** (1809–93), British actress, made her American debut at the Park Theater, N.Y., as Bianca in *Fazio* (1832).

1823–35. Notable American plays of this period included *Clari, or The Maid of Milan,* by John Howard Payne (1823, Covent Garden, London; N.Y., 1823; included the song "Home, Sweet Home"); *Superstition,* James Nelson Barker's best play (1824); *Charles the Second, or the Merry Monarch,* a comedy by John Howard Payne in collaboration with Washington Irving (London and N.Y., 1824); *Metamora, or the Last of the Wampanoags,* a tragedy by **John Augustus Stone** (1800–34), N.Y., 1829; first surviving dramatization of Rip Van Winkle by John Kerr (1829); *The Triumph of Plattsburgh,* by **Richard Penn Smith** (1799–1854), a play celebrating McDonough's victory in 1814 (1830); *Pocahontas,* by **George Washington Parke Custis** (1781–1857), 1830; *The Gladiator,* by **Robert Montgomery Bird** (1806–54), a drama of democracy, including antislavery sentiments (1831); *The Broker of Bogota,* a domestic tragedy by Bird (1834); *Jack Cade,* a play by Robert T. Conrad, dealing with a Kentish peasant uprising in 1450.

1828. The minstrel character and song *Jim Crow* introduced in Louisville, Ky., by **Thomas Dartmouth ("Daddy") Rice** (1808–60).

1832. Publication of *A History of the American Theatre* by **William Dunlap,** a pioneer work.

1836. CHARLOTTE CUSHMAN (p. 1009), American tragedienne and first native-born actress to attain top rank, made her New York debut (1836) at the Bowery Theater (opened 1826) as Lady Macbeth.

1837–48. Notable American plays included *Bianca Visconti* (1837), tragedy by **Nathaniel P. Willis** (1806–67), and Willis' romantic comedy, *Tortesa the Usurer* (1839); *The People's Lawyer* (1839), by **Joseph Stevens Jones** (1809–77), with the central character the Yankee type, Solon Shingle; *Fashion* (1845), an outstandingly popular social comedy by Mrs. **Anna Cora Mowatt** (1819–70); *Witchcraft, or the Martyrs of Salem* (1846), historical drama by **Cornelius Mathews** (1817–89); *The Bucktails; or, Americans in England* (pub., 1847), a satirical play by **James Kirke Paulding** (1778–1860); *A Glance at New York* (1848), one of the first "city" plays, by **Benjamin A. Baker** (1818–90).

1842. PHINEAS T. BARNUM (p. 980) opened Barnum's American Museum at New York.

1843. Virginia Minstrels, a quartette that included **Daniel Decatur Emmett** (1815–1904), appeared at the Masonic Temple, Boston, in what is regarded as the first accurately dated public performance of a genuine full-length minstrel show. Among the popular minstrel companies of the following 2 decades were the Dixie Minstrels, the Columbia Minstrels, the Christy Minstrels, Bryant's Minstrels, White's Serenaders, the Congo Minstrels, the Kentucky Rattlers, and the Nightingale Serenaders.

1849, 10 May. ASTOR PLACE RIOT, which took lives of 22 persons and caused injuries to 36 others, occurred outside the Astor Place Opera House, New York City. A manifestation of revived anti-British sentiment, it involved the partisans of Edwin Forrest and William Charles Macready.

1849–60. Notable plays included *Calaynos,* a tragedy by **George Henry Boker** (1823–90), produced at the Sadler's Wells Theater, London (1849); in the U.S., 1851. Other plays of Boker: *The Betrothal,* a comedy (1850); *Leonor de Guzman,* a tragedy (1853); *Francesca da Rimini,* a tragedy and his most highly esteemed work (1855). In addition, *Uncle Tom's Cabin* (1852), dramatized by **George L. Aiken** (1830–76); *Ten Nights in a Bar-Room* (1858), a play by William W. Pratt based on the novel of Timothy Shay Arthur.

1849–60. NOTABLE DEBUTS. Edwin Booth (p. 989) at the Boston Museum as Tressel in Cibber's version of *Richard III* (1849); **Joseph Jefferson** (1829–1905) at the National Theater, N.Y., as Jack Rackbottle in *Jonathan Bradford* (1849); **Lola Montez** (1818–61), American debut in *Betty the Tyrolean* at the Broadway Theater, N.Y.; **Edward Askew Sothern** (1826–81), American debut at National Theater, Boston, as Dr. Pangloss in *The Heir at Law;* achieved fame as Lord Dundreary in *Our American Cousin* (1858); **Laura Keene** (c.1826–73), British actress, made her American debut at Wallack's Theater, N.Y.; subsequently became the first woman manager in the U.S. **Dion Boucicault** (1820–90), Irish actor-playwright, made his American debut at the Old Broadway Theater as Sir Charles Coldstream in his own farce, *Used Up;* several of his plays produced in this period, including *The Poor of New York* (1857), *The Octoroon* (1859), *The Colleen Bawn* (1860); organized the **road show** (1860). **Lotta Crabtree** (1847–1924) made her first stage appearance at the mining camp of Rabbit Creek, Calif.

1856. First copyright law passed protecting dramatists against literary piracy.

1861–1900. VOGUE OF DION BOUCICAULT. After 1860 his most important plays included *Arrah-no-Pogue* (London, 22 Mar. 1865), *The Shaughraun* (New York, 14 Nov. 1874), and the revision of Charles Burke's version of Washington Irving's *Rip Van Winkle* (London, 4 Sept. 1865).

1867–75. IMPACT OF (JOHN) AUGUSTIN DALY (1838–99), both as playwright and theatrical manager. His first play was *Leah the Forsaken* (1862). *Under the Gaslight* (a realistic drama of New York life) produced in New York 12 Aug. 1867. Original plays include *Divorce* (5 Sept. 1870), *Horizon* (25 Mar. 1871), and *Pique* (14 Dec. 1875). Daly organized a stock company (1867) and opened his own theater in New York,

1869, starring **John Drew** (1853–1927), Adelaide Neilson (1848–1880), and **Maurice Barrymore** (1847–1905).

1870–89. COMEDY OF MANNERS. The influence of the French drama was reflected in the popular plays of **Bronson Howard** (1842–1908), including *Saratoga* (21 Dec. 1870), *The Banker's Daughter* (30 Sept. 1870), *The Young Mrs. Winthrop* (9 Oct. 1882), *The Henrietta* (26 Sept. 1887), and *Shenandoah*, the first successful drama of the Civil War (9 Sept. 1887). Other exponents of the social comedy form were **Augustus Thomas** (1875–1934), whose most notable plays include *Alabama*, a romance of Reconstruction (1891); *In Mizzoula* (1893); *The Earl of Pawtucket* (1903); *Mrs. Leffingwell's Boots* (1905); *The Witching Hour* (1907), the first of his realistic dramas; *The Harvest Moon* (1909); *As a Man Thinks* (1911); and *The Copperhead* (1919), starring Lionel Barrymore; and **William Clyde Fitch** (1865–1909), with his first success, *Beau Brummel* (1890), written for Richard Mansfield. His 30 plays include *The Climbers* (1901); *The Girl with the Green Eyes* (1902), generally considered his best play; *Truth Again* (1907); *The City* (1909). Best known of his 17 adaptations was *Sappho*.

1872–79. THE WEST IN THE DRAMA. *Davy Crockett* (1872), a frontier drama by **Frank Hitchcock Murdock**; Daly's *Big Bonanza* (1875), satire on speculation; Bret Harte's *The Two Men of Sandy Bat* (1876); Joaquin Miller's *The Danites in the Sierras* (1877); Bartley Campbell's *My Partner* (1879).

1880–1930. ERA OF THE THEATRICAL MANAGER. Dramatist, actor, and producer, **David Belasco** (1854–1931) wrote or adapted 75 plays and made pioneer contributions to realistic staging. His successful plays include *The Darling of the Gods* (1902), *Madam Butterfly* (1900, in collaboration with John Luther Long), *The Return of Peter Grimm* (1911), and *The Girl of the Golden West* (1905). Coming to New York in 1880, he became stage manager of the Madison Square Theater, was later an associate of Daniel Frohman, and opened the Belasco Theater in 1902. Other notable theatrical managers of the period include **Charles Frohman** (1860–1915), who organized a stock company in 1890, opened the Empire Theater in 1893, and formed in 1896 the first theatrical syndicate, including Sam Nixon, Fred Zimmerman, Al Hayman, Marc Klaw, and Abraham Erlanger, which gradually extended its control throughout the U.S. From 1897 until his death (on the *Lusitania*) Frohman was the leading American manager, placing emphasis upon the "star system" (Maude Adams, Ethel Barrymore, and Otis Skinner) and the productions of established British dramatists. His brother, **Daniel Frohman** (1851–1940), opened the Lyceum Theater, N.Y. (1885), and was an exponent of the stock company. More commercialized was the impact of J. J., Lee, and Sam S. Shubert, who, beginning with the Herald Square Theater, N.Y., controlled some 70 theaters in N.Y. and other principal cities by 1924. During the period 1905–13 a **vaudeville empire** was erected by Benjamin F. Keith and Edward F. Albee, although the most conspicuously successful managers in that field were Oscar and William Hammerstein. Marcus Loew and William Fox rapidly accumulated theater chains.

1880–92. EARLY REALISM was exemplified in the plays of **James A. Herne** (1839–1901), notably his *Hearts of Oak* (1880), with David Belasco; *Margaret Fleming* (1890); and *Shore Acres* (1892).

1895–1913. Notable plays at the turn

of the century included **William Gillette's** (1855–1937) *Secret Service* (1895), a Civil War theme, and *Sherlock Holmes* (1899); **William Vaughan Moody's** (1869–1910) *The Great Divide* (1906); **Langdon Mitchell's** (1862–1935) *The New York Idea* (1906), critical of the marriage institution; **Eugene Walter's** (1874–1941) *The Easiest Way* (1909); and **Edward Sheldon's** (1886–1946) *The Nigger* (1909), *The Boss* (1911), and *Romance* (1913), with Doris Keane as Madame Cavallini.

1900–19. LITTLE-THEATER MOVEMENT. The first "little theater" in the U.S. was constructed (1900) for the Hull House Players, Chicago; the first in the academic world was **G. P. Baker's** (1866–1935) **47 Workshop** at Harvard (1912), later at Yale. Civic theaters developed rapidly, beginning (1919) with the Théâtre du Vieux Carré in New Orleans.

1908–48. MUSICALS. *The Black Crook* (1866) was the first long-run musical extravaganza produced in the U.S. **Florenz Ziegfeld** (1869–1932) originated a series of revues called the *Ziegfeld Follies,* featuring beautiful girls ("glorifying the American girl"), scenic invention, and comic sketches, and including such actors as W. C. Fields, Eddie Cantor, Fannie Brice, and Bert Williams. The **musical comedy,** a highly developed form in the U.S., combining opera, comedy, and ballet, flourished in the early 1900s with *The Merry Widow* and *The Chocolate Soldier,* but major innovations appeared in the 1920s largely as a result of the efforts of **Jerome Kern** (1885–1945), with his notable *Show Boat* (1928); **George** and **Ira Gershwin; Cole Porter;** and the team of **Richard Rodgers** and **Lorenz Hart** (beg. with *Garrick Gaieties,* 1925). An outstanding success was *Of Thee I Sing* (1931), book by George S. Kaufman and Morrie Ryskind. An innovation in

the field was *Pal Joey* (1941), a modern *Beggar's Opera,* music by Rodgers, lyrics by Hart, and book by John O'Hara. The most striking success was the presentation in 1943 of *Oklahoma!* by **Richard Rodgers** (p. 1140), and **Oscar Hammerstein II** (p. 1048), followed in 1949 by *South Pacific* (with Mary Martin and Ezio Pinza). The introduction of **ballet** by **Agnes De Mille,** dancer and choreographer, in such productions as *Oklahoma!, Bloomer Girl* (1944), *Carousel* (1945), and *Brigadoon* (1947) gave to the musical comedy of the 40s its major innovating feature.

1915–52. SCENIC DESIGN. Chief impact upon modern scenic design in the U.S. stems from 1915, with the designs of **Robert Edmond Jones** (1887–1954) for *The Man Who Married a Dumb Wife;* later *Hamlet* (1922), *Richard III, Othello* (1936), and *The Philadelphia Story* (1939). Other notable contributors in this field: **Norman Bel-Geddes** (1893–1958), *The Miracle* (1923), *Dead End* (1935); **Lee Simonson** (1888–1967), *Lilliom,* O'Neill's *Dynamo; Jo Mielziner* (1901–76), *Winterset* (1935), *High Tor* (1937).

1916–46. EUGENE O'NEILL (p. 1118), the most notable American playwright, whose works were first performed at the Provincetown Playhouse, New York (*S.S. Glencairn*), a group interested in experimental drama. His plays varied from the naturalism of *Anna Christie* (1921) to the expressionism of *The Hairy Ape* (1922), and from the symbolism of *The Great God Brown* (1926) to experiments in combining Greek tragedy and Freudian psychology, as in *Mourning Becomes Electra* (1931).

1919, 19 Apr. First production of the **Theater Guild,** Jacinto Benavente's *The Bonds of Interest,* at the Garrick Theater, followed by St. John Ervine's *John Ferguson.* Under the direction of **Theresa Helburn** the Guild, a subscription group dedicated to raising the level of the American stage, scored brilliant successes in the 20s with Du Bose Heyward's *Porgy,* Shaw's *St. Joan,* O'Neill's *Strange Interlude,* Molnar's *The Guardsman* (Alfred Lunt and Lynn Fontanne), and Sidney Howard's *They Knew What They Wanted.*

1924–48. POETIC AND IMAGINATIVE DRAMA. Maxwell Anderson (1888–1959), coauthor, with Laurence Stallings, of the most popular U.S. war play of the 20s, *What Price Glory?* (1924), wrote such notable tragedies as *Elizabeth the Queen* (1930), *Mary of Scotland* (1933), *Winterset* (1935), *Key Largo* (1939), *The Eve of St. Mark* (1942, war play), and *Joan of Lorraine* (1947). In addition, he wrote a romantic verse comedy, *High Tor* (1937), and a musical comedy, *Knickerbocker Holi-*

day (1938). Other exemplars of the imaginative drama were **Paul Green** (1894–   ), whose plays include *In Abraham's Bosom* (1926), *The Field God* (1927), *The House of Connelly* (1931), *Tread the Green Grass* (1932), *Roll, Sweet Chariot* (1934), and *The Common Glory* (1948); **Marc Connelly** (1890–1980), who, in addition to collaborating with **George S. Kaufman** (1889–1961) on satires and comedies (*Dulcy,* 1921; *Beggar on Horseback,* 1924), wrote *The Green Pastures* (1930); and **Thornton Wilder** (1897–1975), *Our Town* (1938), *The Skin of Our Teeth* (1942).

1924–39. TRENDS. Drawing-room comedy done with wit and craftsmanship was notably exemplified by **S. N. Behrman** (*The Second Man,* 1927; *Rain From Heaven,* 1934; and *No Time for Comedy,* 1939) and by **Philip Barry** (*Holiday,* 1928; *Animal Kingdom,* 1932; and *The Philadelphia Story,* 1939). **Sidney Howard** (1891–1939) contributed to realism with *They Knew What They Wanted* (1924), *Ned McCobb's Daughter* (1926), and *The Silver Cord* (1926). **Elmer Rice** (1892–1967), who had contributed an expressionistic play, *Adding Machine* (1923), wrote a naturalistic drama, *Street Scene* (1929). An individualistic approach is found in **William Saroyan's** (1908–81), *The Time of Your Life* (1940).

1935–39. WPA FEDERAL THEATER PROJECT, under the national direction of Mrs. **Hallie Flanagan** of Vassar College, brought back the theater to the road with low-priced productions of T. S. Eliot's *Murder in the Cathedral,* the Negro *Macbeth,* Orson Welles' and John Housman's *Doctor Faustus,* and *Pinocchio.* Most notable was its contribution of a new form to the American theater, the Living Newspaper, in which headlines were dramatized, including *Triple A Ploughed Under* (1936),

Power (1937), *One Third of a Nation* (1938).

1935–47. PLAYS OF PROPAGANDA AND SOCIAL CRITICISM were especially popular during the depression and in the early years of World War II. Representative were **Clifford Odets** (1906–63), *Awake and Sing,* 1935; *Waiting for Lefty,* 1935; *Golden Boy,* 1937; *Rocket to the Moon* (1938), **Lillian Hellman** (1907–   , *The Children's Hour,* 1934; *The Little Foxes,* 1939; *Watch on the Rhine,* 1941; *Another Part of the Forest,* 1947), and **Robert E. Sherwood** (1896–1955), *The Petrified Forest,* 1934; *Idiot's Delight,* 1936; *There Shall Be No Night,* 1940).

1951–60. OFF-BROADWAY THEATER continued its remarkable growth, stressing daring and experimental plays (*The Threepenny Opera* and the revival of O'Neill's *The Iceman Cometh*) and attracting performers of rank.

PULITZER PRIZE PLAYS, 1952–75

1952.   *The Shrike.* By Joseph Kramm
1953.   *Picnic.* By William Inge
1954.   *The Teahouse of the August Moon.* By John Patrick
1955.   *Cat on a Hot Tin Roof.* By Tennessee Williams
1956.   *The Diary of Anne Frank.* By Frances Goodrich and Albert Hackett
1957.   *Long Day's Journey Into Night.* By Eugene O'Neill
1958.   *Look Homeward, Angel.* By Ketti Frings
1959.   *J. B.* By Archibald MacLeish
1960.   *Fiorello!* By Jerry Bock, Sheldon Harnick, Jerome Weidman, and George Abbott
1961.   *All the Way Home.* By Tad Mosel
1962.   *How to Succeed in Business Without Really Trying.* By Abe Burrows and Frank Loesser
1965.   *The Subject Was Roses.* By Frank Gilroy
1967.   *A Delicate Balance.* By Edward Albee
1968.   No award
1969.   *The Great White Hope.* By Howard Sackler
1970.   *No Place to Be Somebody.* By Charles Gordone
1971.   *The Effect of Gamma Rays on Man-in-the-Moon Marigolds.* By Paul Zindel
1972.   No award
1973.   *That Championship Season.* By Jason Miller
1974.   No award
1975.   *Seascape.* By Edward Albee

1944–1962. IMPORTANT DRAMATISTS. O'Neill solidified his position as the preeminent American dramatist with *The Iceman Cometh* (1947) and the posthumous *Long Day's Journey into Night* (1957). After O'Neill, the most notable American playwrights were **Tennessee Williams** (p. 1185), whose poetic, heavily symbolic dramas included *The Glass Menagerie* (1944) and *A Streetcar Named Desire* (1947), and **Arthur Miller** (p. 1103), whose concern with ethical and moral dilemmas, particularly in family situations, found powerful expression in *Death of a Salesman* (1949) and *A View From the Bridge* (1955). The most highly regarded new dramatists to emerge in the 50s were **William Inge** (1913–73) and **Edward Albee** (1928–   ). Inge made his reputation with dramas of Midwestern sensibility, such as *Come Back, Little Sheba* (1950), a study of domestic conflict. Albee's masterpiece, *Who's Afraid of Virginia Woolf?* (1963), was also a story of marital strife. Some others who rose to prominence simultaneously or during the 60s were Jack Gelber, Arthur Kopit, Lorraine Hansberry, Murray Schisgal, Jack Richardson, and William Gibson.

1948–73. THE AMERICAN MUSICAL. The musical continued to flourish in this period. Among the most notable were *Kiss Me Kate* (1948), by **Cole Porter;** *The King and I* (1951), by **Rodgers** and **Hammerstein;** *Guys and Dolls* (1949), by **Frank Loesser;** *My Fair Lady* (1956), by **Alan Jay Lerner** and **Frederick Lowe;** *The Music Man* (1958), by **Meredith Willson;** and *West Side Story* (1958), by **Leonard Bernstein** and **Stephen Sondheim.** In the 60s and 70s the trend toward musicals with serious, even ponderous books was evident from *Fiddler on the Roof* (1964), *Man of La Mancha* (1965), *Cabaret* (1966), *Follies* (1971), and *A Little Night Music* (1973). Concurrently, however, shows like *The Fantasticks* (1960), *Man With a Load of Mischief* (1966), and *You're a Good Man, Charlie Brown* (1968) exhibited a lighter touch. Important also in this period was the emergence of a new permutation of the musical form, the "rock musical," commencing with *Hair* (1968), and including *Jesus Christ Superstar* (1970) and *Godspell* (1972).

1961–73. GROWTH OF COMMUNITY THEATERS. The appearance of regional theater throughout the country, though it was heavily dependent on foundation grants, was one of the healthiest signs in the American theater. The Association of Producing Artists (APA) became the first professional theater company backed entirely by university funds (subsidized by the Univ. of Michigan, 1962). The APA began Broadway seasons in 1966. By 1965, 24 cities other than New York had professional resident companies recognized by Actors Equity, including the Minnesota Theater Co. (1 May 1963) with Sir Tyrone Guthrie as director. Companies in 8 cities were aided by Ford Foundation grants. The Lincoln Center Repertory Co. opened with the premiere of Arthur Miller's *After the Fall* in the ANTA-Washington Square Theater, New York (23 Jan. 1964), moving (1965) to a permanent home, the Vivian Beaumont Theater in Lincoln Center for the Performing Arts. The American Conservatory Theater found a permanent home in San Francisco (1967). Among the major repertory successes were the APA's *You Can"t Take It With You* (1966), Minnesota's *The House of Atreus* (1967), based on the Greek *Oresteia* (1967), Arena Stage (Washington, D.C.), *The Great White Hope* by Howard Sackler (1967).

1964–72. PLAYS OF POLITICAL AND SOCIAL CRITICISM. A substantial number of plays offering a radical view of American life were produced during the 60s and early 70s. Barbara Garson's *MacBird* (1966), a blank-verse parody, took on the entire political establishment; Megan Terry's *Viet Rock*

(1966) questioned America's role in Vietnam; Jean Claude Van Itallie's *American Hurrah* (1966) satirized contemporary American mores; and Arthur Kopit's *Indians* (1969) promulgated a revisionist view of the American West.

New theater groups stressed political radicalism (peace, civil rights, sexual freedom) and dramatic radicalism (spontaneity, involvement of audience through dialogue and panel discussion, sensory communication, Eastern mysticism, and ritual). Among them were the San Francisco Mime Troup, the Living Theater, the Open Theater, and Cafe La Mama. The experimental new work of these groups soon became known as Off-Off-Broadway.

1967–73. CONTINUED GROWTH OF OFF-BROADWAY. In New York artistic hopes shifted from Broadway to the small Off-Broadway houses. The most exciting Off-Broadway producer in the 60s was **Joseph Papp** (1921–   ), whose New York Shakespeare Festival provided free Shakespearean productions during the summer at the Delacorte Theater; in 1967 it found a permanent home, the New York Public Theater. There it offered the works of provocative new dramatists such as David Rabe (1941–   ), e.g., *Sticks and Bones* (1971), and Jason Miller (*That Championship Season,* 1972). Papp assumed control of the 2 theaters at Lincoln Center in 1973.

1962–75. DECLINE OF BROADWAY. Broadway during this period suffered from ongoing financial woes and an increasing tendency toward slick, commercial offerings, especially grandiose musicals and lightweight comedies. The master of this latter mode was the phenomenally successful **Neil Simon** (1927–   ), of whose slight but entertaining work *The Odd Couple* (1966) is representative. However, several new theaters, including the Circle in the Square and the Uris opened in 1972–73, and Broadway was infused with new vigor during the 1974–75 season.

1964–72. BLACK PLAYS. The concerns of black Americans were brought to the attention of theatergoers in a series of plays by young black dramatists. *A Raisin in the Sun* (1959) by **Lorraine Hansberry** (1930–65) led the way and was soon followed by **James Baldwin's** *Blues for Mr. Charlie* (1964), **LeRoi Jones'** *The Toilet* and *The Slave* (1967), **Charles Gordone's** *No Place to Be Somebody* (1970) and **Joseph A. Walker's** *The River Niger* (1972). The cause of black theater was further advanced by the establishment of the Negro Ensemble Co. (1968) under the direction of Douglas Turner Ward.

1962–81. BRITISH IMPORTS. The '60s and early '70s were noteworthy for bringing a steady stream of British imports to America. *Oliver* (1962), a musical based on *Oliver Twist;* John Osborne's *Luther* (1963); Peter Shaffer's historical extravaganza *The Royal Hunt of the Sun* (1967); Harold Pinter's *The Homecoming* (1967); Tom Stoppard's *Rosencrantz and Guildenstern Are Dead* (1968); and *Amadeus* (1980)—a few of the many English works that made the Atlantic crossing successfully.

LONGEST RUN OFF-BROADWAY, *The Fantasticks,* opened 3 May 1960 with 8,802 performances as of 1 July 1981. (*The Drunkard* had 9,477 performances in Los Angeles, 6 July 1933–6 Sept. 1953.)

1972. OFF-OFF-BROADWAY ALLIANCE of 50 experimental companies, largely located in New York's Soho and Lower East Side, was formed and received financial assistance from the Theater Development Fund.

LONGEST RUNS ON BROADWAY
(Variety, 7 Jan. 1981)

Plays	No. of Performances
Grease	3,388
Fiddler on the Roof	3,242
Life with Father	3,224
Tobacco Road	3,182
Hello Dolly	2,844
My Fair Lady	2,717
Man of La Mancha	2,329
Abie's Irish Rose	2,327
Chorus Line	2,243
Oklahoma!	2,212
Pippin	1,900
Magic Show	1,859
Oh! Calcutta!	1,798
Harvey	1,775
Hair	1,742
South Pacific	1,694
The Wiz	1,666
Born Yesterday	1,642
Mary, Mary	1,572
The Voice of the Turtle	1,557

PULITZER PRIZE PLAYS, 1976–81

1976.	*A Chorus Line.* By Michael Bennett, James Kirkwood, Nicholas Dante, Marvin Hamlisch, Edward Kleban
1977.	*The Shadow Box.* By Michael Cristofer
1978.	*The Gin Game.* By Donald L. Coburn
1979.	*Buried Child.* By Sam Shepard
1980.	*Talley's Folley.* By Lanford Wilson
1981.	*Crimes of the Heart.* By Beth Hanley

Film

Motion pictures in America have continually manifested the extraordinary diversity of their origins—Yankee technology, theatrical tradition, the visual arts, and even European experimentalism. By common consent, the most significant film pioneer in the U.S. was D. W. Griffith, who revolutionized film technique with devices like montage. The "giants of the earth" like Griffith quickly gave way (c. 1920) to the "studio system," in which films were the result of group efforts and studio executives held (and exercised, often brutally) final control. The major studios—MGM, Warner Brothers, Paramount, etc.— quickly followed the example of the stage by creating a star system. Soon the financial fate of movies was tied to names like Rudolph Valentino, Gloria Swanson, Clark Gable, Gary Cooper, and Elizabeth Taylor. Competition from TV, spiraling production costs, and a new breed of independent producers dissolved the old movie empires. In their place, very frequently at least, were low-budget productions that ignored the importance of "name players."

In the absence of individual genius and high artistic goals, the most distinctive American film contribution during the first half-century was the "genre" film. At their best, though, these films were very good indeed, high-spirited and entertaining. American Westerns (*High Noon*), musicals (*Singin' in the Rain*), gangster melodramas (*Little Caesar*), and detective stories (*The Maltese Falcon*) attained worldwide popularity. The situation altered a good deal in the sixties and early seventies with the shift to a younger and more literate audience and the rise of independent producers. It became possible once more for American directors to experiment and to use films as a medium for personal expression. Some of the more striking examples of these new tendencies are Peter Bogdanovich's *The Last Picture Show* and Martin Scorsese's *Mean Streets*, and special effects films such as *Star Wars*.

The Silent Screen Period. 1889–1927

1889–1903. THE BEGINNINGS. Early efforts at developing moving pictures culminated in Thomas Edison's Kinetoscope, a machine with a light source and a peephole; pictures were produced by photographic film—a recent invention of George Eastman—which ran continuously in front of the hole.

1896. VITASCOPE, a mechanism for projecting film on a wall or screen, was developed by **Thomas Armat** of Washington, D.C. On 23 Apr. the first commercially exhibited motion picture was shown at Koster and Bial's Music Hall, New York. It used Armat's projector and Edison's Kinetoscope film.

1900. CINDERELLA, the first film to use "artificially arranged scenes" in progressive continuity, was produced by **George Méliès,** French producer.

1903. THE GREAT TRAIN ROBBERY, the first film narrative, was produced by **Edwin S. Porter.**

1905. NICKELODEON, an early movie house, was established in Pittsburgh by John P. Harris and Harry Davis. By 1908 between 8,000 and 10,000 were in operation, augmenting the need for expansion of film production facilities.

1909–14. EARLY STUDIOS. The pioneer film studios were Edison, Biograph, and Vitaphone, which, along with several others, formed the Motion Picture Patents Co. in 1909. However, a lawsuit by **William Fox** (1879–1952), independent distributor, broke the power of the monopoly. Subsequently, independent producers burgeoned, establishing Hollywood as the home of American movies.

1912. The first feature films to be shown in America, Italian spectacles, were imported by Adolph Zukor (1873–1976).

1913 SERIALS. *What Happened to Mary?* evidenced growing interest in serial films. Queens of the serial were Pearl White (*Perils of Pauline*) and Ruth Roland (*Ruth of the Rockies*).

1913–27. MAJOR FILM GENRES OF THE SILENT SCREEN.

Comedies. The earliest screen comedies were those of Mack Sennett, whose 2-reel films, featuring the Keystone Cops in a variety of burlesque situations, launched a new school of "slapstick" comedians. Sennet was soon transcended, however, by 2 of his protégés, **Charles Chaplin** (1889–1977) and **Buster Keaton** (1895–1966), who brought real genius to comedy of the silent period. Chaplin's "little tramp," a tragicomic small fry in baggy pants, endeared himself to the world in films like *Shoulder Arms* (1918) and *The Kid* (1921). Keaton's deadpan style, humanistic but unsentimental, was no less inspired and achieved equal popularity. *The General* (1927) and *The Playhouse* (1921) are among his best films. Other notable comedians of this era were **Fatty Arbuckle, Harry Langdon,** and the team of **Stan Laurel** and **Oliver Hardy**.

Westerns. From *The Great Train Robbery* (1903), the Western was one of Hollywood's liveliest and best-loved genres. The open spaces, the clear-cut conflicts, the heroic qualities had a wide appeal—even in Europe. The leading cowboy star in this period was **William S. Hart**, who portrayed a thin-lipped, 2-gunned protector of American virtues in such films as *The Return of Draw Egan* (1916). *The Covered Wagon* (1923), directed by **James Cruze,** was another highly successful Western of the silent era.

Swashbucklers. A mode perfected and dominated by **Douglas Fairbanks,** the swashbuckler brought the swaggering romance and excitement of Dumas and other adventure writers to the screen. Fairbanks was particularly famous for daring athletics, virile charm, and faint self-parody, qualities that he exhibited most brilliantly in *The Black Pirate* (1926) and *The Three Musketeers* (1921).

Sentimentalism. Producers of the silent era found a rich vein of popular interest in sentimental tales of lost waifs and pure-hearted farm girls. The leading player in this mode was **Mary Pickford,** "America's sweetheart," whose boyish figure and wholesome face became an international symbol of virginal innocence. Among her most popular films was *Pollyana* (1920).

Exoticism. A rage for movies with faraway settings and glamorously swarthy leading men brought 2 "Latin lovers" to the summits of fame—**Ramon Novarro** (1899–1968) and **Rudolph Valentino** (1895–1926). Valentino, whose films included *The Sheik* (1921) and *Blood and Sand* (1922), was perhaps the preeminent matinee idol of silent films.

1912–27. MAJOR CHARACTERISTICS OF THE SILENT FILM ERA.

Star System. From about 1912 on, producers gave greater and greater prominence to their leading players, who became household names throughout the world. The result was the "star system," in which the presence of a Chaplin or a Valentino was deemed a form of box-office security. Other silent film stars included **Lillian** and **Dorothy Gish, Gloria Swanson,** and **Greta Garbo**.

Directors. With his first film, *The Squaw Man* (1913), **C. B. DeMille** (1881–1959) established himself as an immensely skillful entertainer and held this reputation through a series of spectacles (*Ben Hur*, 1926; *King of Kings*, 1927) which employed a formulaic blend of sex, pomp, and piety. Far more talented was **D. W. Griffith** (1875–1948), almost universally regarded as the father of the American cinema. Using hackneyed Victorian melodramas, Griffith nevertheless managed to develop a set of revolutionary film techniques in such classics as *Birth of a Nation* (1915) and *Intolerance* (1919). **Erich von Stroheim** (1885–1957) was second only to Griffith as an innovator in the silent film period. His ambitious, experimental movies, often dealing with bizarre subject matter, included *Greed* (1923) and *Foolish Wives* (1922). Stroheim was one of a series of foreign directors who brought their imagination and intelligence to Hollywood in the 20s. Particularly influential were exponents of the "German school," which emphasized unnatural but poetic lighting and other expressionistic effects they had borrowed from the German stage. Ernst Lubitsch and F. W. Murnau (*Sunrise*, 1928) were 2 of these.

Technical Innovations. The best-known technical breakthrough of the silent era was montage, a method popularized by D. W. Griffith in which different shots were spliced together to achieve a dramatic effect. An approach diametrically opposed to montage, the "long take," in which continuous shots were used, was developed by the German school.

Although films were predominantly black and white until the 1930s, experimentation with color began as early as 1908, when Charles Urban and G. Albert Smith developed Kinemacolor. In 1915 Dr. Herbert Kalmus founded Technicolor Motion Corp., whose first film was *Toll of the Sea* (1922).

Early Critiques of Film. During the silent era, most serious critics of the arts regarded movies as strictly a form of popular entertainment and, as such, inherently vulgar and inartistic. The leading exception to this tendency was **Gilbert Seldes** (1893–1970), who wrote perceptively and sympathetically on the infant medium. The poet **Vachel Lindsay** also contributed an enthusiastic full-length work on the movies, *The Art of Moving Pictures* (1915).

Censorship. Regulation of movies became an issue as early as 1907 when the Chicago police department was invested with power to suppress offensive films. Other cities, such as New York and Boston, showed that they too regarded the supervision of movies as a municipal prerogative. To provide self-regulation of the industry, the Patents Co. founded the National Board of Censorship, renamed the National Board of Review in 1915. In the same year the Supreme Court held that moving pictures were not covered by the First Amendment. Later efforts at self-regulation were led by Will H. Hays, who organized Motion Picture Producers and Distributors of America (1922). For 23 years the "Hays office" policed movie morals.

Studio System. The studio system originated in Hollywood with the formation of the Famous Players Films Co. (reorganized as Paramount) in 1912 and innovated "block booking." Loew's (Metro-Goldwyn-Mayer, 1924) followed in 1920, Warner Bros. in 1923, Columbia in 1924, and Radio-Keith-Orpheum in 1928. Last of the major combines was 20th-Century-Fox (1935).

The Sound Era, 1927–74

SOUND FILMS were developed by Lee De Forest (p. 1011), transcribing sound waves into electric impulses which could be photographed on celluloid and, when passed around a photoelectric cell in a projector, transformed back into natural sound. De Forest's Phonofilms (1923) were commercially distributed. The Vitaphone system, which coupled a phonograph record synchronized to projector motors, was used by Warner Brothers in *Don Juan* (6 Aug. 1926), starring John Barrymore, to produce sound effects. *The Jazz Singer* (6 Oct. 1927), produced by Warner and starring Al Jolson, was the first movie in which singing and spoken dialogue were heard. Talkies quickly replaced silents and comparatively few of the silent screen idols succeeded in making the transition to the new medium. Such stars as John Gilbert, Emil Jannings, and Douglas Fairbanks saw their careers blighted overnight. The survivors included Ronald Colman and Greta Garbo.

MAJOR FILM GENRES OF THE SOUND ERA.

Social Protest. The most serious and ambitious films turned out in Hollywood during the 30s were in the area of social protest. *I Am a Fugitive From a Chain Gang* (1932) criticized the prison system in the South; *Black Fury* (1935) dealt sympathetically with the labor movement; *Fury* (1936) indicted mob violence; *The Grapes of Wrath* (1940) focused on the problems of migrant farm workers.

Social protest all but disappeared from American films during World War II, but the postwar era brought attacks on antisemitism (*Crossfire*, 1947) and racial intolerance (*Intruder in the Dust,* 1949). Exposés of racial injustice continued to appear throughout the 50s and 60s (e.g., *Island in the Sun*, 1957; *Guess Who's Coming to Dinner?*, 1967).

Escapism. For the most part, however, American studio heads seemed reluctant to test the endurance of a mass audience and were most successful at producing enjoyable escapism, with **Frank Capra**'s *It Happened One Night* (1934), starring **Claudette Colbert** and **Clark Gable,**

a highly popular example. Films that aspired to be serious drama tended to disintegrate into melodrama (*Detective Story*, 1951) or sentimentality (*How Green Was My Valley*, 1942). And even among the exceptions, most were taken directly from the stage (e.g., *A Streetcar Named Desire*, 1951).

The Musical. The only new genre of the sound era was the musical, but to many this represented Hollywood's major contribution to film culture. The first of these "all talking, all singing, all dancing" extravaganzas was *The Broadway Melody* (1929). In general, early musicals did little more than exploit the novelty of sound; revues (*The King of Jazz*, 1930), operettas (*The New Moon*, 1930), and Broadway shows (*Cocoanuts*, 1929) poured forth, nearly all of them clumsy and static. *Forty-Second Street* (1933) proved to be a major landmark, establishing the highly successful "backstage" formula, in which the characters were generally performers preparing a show. Later versions of this proven paradigm were *Gold Diggers of 1933*, *Dames* (1934), and *Babes in Arms* (1939). The outstanding innovator in this mode was the choreographer **Busby Berkeley** (1895–1976). Lasting popularity was achieved by *The Wizard of Oz* (1939).

A second musical tradition in the 30s was born when **Fred Astaire** and **Ginger Rogers** first appeared together in *Flying Down to Rio* (1933). Their intricate, swirlingly elegant dancing kept their fans entertained in *Top Hat* (1935) and *Swing Time* (1936), among other films. Yet another popular musical series in this decade was the operettas of **Jeanette MacDonald** and **Nelson Eddy**, commencing with *Naughty Marietta* (1935).

In the 40s, **Gene Kelly** became a dominant figure in musicals, introducing imaginative effects like animation (*Anchors Aweigh*, 1945) and extended ballet sequences (*American in Paris*, 1951). However, by the late 50s, original musicals had become virtually extinct, and only carefully packaged Broadway hits (e.g., *Oklahoma!*, 1955) were being produced. During the 60s even these dwindled, though a resurgence occurred with the remarkably lucrative *My Fair Lady* (1964), *Mary Poppins* (1964), and *The Sound of Music* (1965).

Gangster Movies. Though gangland subject matter had been seen in the silent period (e.g., *Underworld*, 1927), it did not become an important genre until the appearance of 3 classic efforts— *Little Caesar* (1930), *Scarface* (1932) and *Public Enemy* (1931)—which made their respective stars (Edward G. Robinson, Paul Muni, and James Cagney) world famous. These movies were fast, tough, laconic, and always reminded the audience that "crime does not pay." The host of imitations, all inferior to the originals, included *Manhattan Melodrama* (1934) and *The Roaring Twenties* (1939). The 40s brought *High Sierra* (1941) and *Johnny Eager* (1941), the 50s *New York Confidential* (1954) and the 60s *The Brotherhood* (1968), but these films lacked the fresh vigor of the first 3. *Bonnie and Clyde* (1967), *The Godfather* (1972), and *Godfather II* (1974) were among the few latter-day gangster films to be well reviewed and widely seen.

Westerns. The Western genre was well established by the time of sound movies, and such films as *The Virginian* (1929) and *In Old Arizona* (1928) perpetuated and amplified the traditions of pictorialism, simple frontier values, and ritualistic showdowns. A major plateau was reached with *Stagecoach* (1939), directed by **John Ford**, an archetypal Western that was copied for years afterward. The 40s brought a more psychological thrust to the prairie, particularly in *The Ox-Bow Incident* (1942), *Duel in the Sun* (1946), and *Red River* (1948). In the 50s this trend continued with the immensely successful *High Noon* (1952), though *Shane*, released the following year, was a return to the old heroic, legendary format. Since the early 50s, Westerns have evoked less critical praise, but they have never lost their hold on the public, as witnessed by the success of *The Professionals* (1968). One of the few to find general critical favor was *Ride the High Country* (1962).

Comedies. Of the major silent screen comedians, only Laurel and Hardy and Chaplin succeeded in talkies. The former retained their vast following with *The March of the Wooden Soldiers* (1934). Chaplin reached new heights in the 30s with *Modern Times* (1936), a satirical treatment of technology, and *The Great Dictator* (1940), a devastating burlesque of Hitler. Later Chaplin films included *Limelight* (1952) and *Monsieur Verdoux* (1947).

The 30s were perhaps Hollywood's richest era in comedy. The inspired nonsense of the **Marx Brothers** was displayed in such hilarious farces as *Duck Soup* (1933) and *A Night at the Opera* (1935). More restrained was the cynical and misanthropic **W. C. Fields,** whose movies (e.g., *You Can't Cheat an Honest Man,* 1939) took deadly aim at the cherished beliefs of the American bourgeoisie. Simultaneously, **Mae West** enjoyed a brief reign as the movie's leading comedienne (e.g., *I'm No Angel,* 1933) before her risqué jokes brought the wrath of censorship groups down on her.

Side by side with these comedians was a group of excellent light actors, whose films provided yet another facet of American screen humor, urbane and sophisticated comedy. Known as "screwball comedies," these movies included *Design for Living* (1933), *Trouble in*

Paradise (1932), and *My Man Godfrey* (1936). The "screwball" mode tended to focus on the foibles of the upper class and to utilize the same performers—among them, **Cary Grant, Melvyn Douglas, Irene Dunne,** and **Carole Lombard.**

On the whole, comedy in the 40s was blander and less creative, though there were a number of bright spots: *The Man Who Came to Dinner* (1942) with Monty Woolley; the lively teaming of Katharine Hepburn and Spencer Tracy (e.g., *The Woman of the Year,* 1941); the topical humor of *Mr. Blandings Builds His Dream House* (1948). Also of interest were the witty social satires of Preston Sturges—e.g., *Sullivan's Travels* (1941). In addition, the movies produced one major comedian in this decade, the versatile **Danny Kaye,** whose foremost screen successes included *Up in Arms* (1944) and *The Secret Life of Walter Mitty* (1947).

The 50s and 60s did little to improve the state of American comedy. Exceptions to the general mediocrity were *The African Queen* (1951), a comedy-adventure with **Humphrey Bogart** and **Katharine Hepburn,** and *How to Marry a Millionaire* (1953) and *Some Like It Hot* (1959), in which **Marilyn Monroe** graduated from a sex goddess to a talented comedienne. Stanley Kubrick's black comedy *Dr. Strangelove* (1963) commanded attention, as did *A Thousand Clowns* (1965) and *Mash* (1968).

Detective Movies. Another movie genre that came to fruition in the 30s was the detective film. *The Thin Man* (**Dashiell Hammett**) (1934) presented the sophisticated husband-and-wife team Nick and Nora Charles. The hardboiled school, created by the fiction of Hammett and **Raymond Chandler,** surfaced in the 40s with *The Maltese Falcon* (1941), in which Bogart played and immortalized the tough Sam Spade. Bogart, the epitome of the detective hero, was equally

tough as Philip Marlowe in *The Big Sleep* (1946). In the 50s, the detective tradition was carried on, not too memorably, in the Mike Hammer films (e.g., *I, the Jury,* 1953), from the popular novels by Mickey Spillane. However, by the end of the 50s this genre was more or less moribund.

War Movies. The first significant war film of the sound period was the celebrated *All Quiet on the Western Front* (1930), a powerful indictment of militarism in World War I. The gallantry of war was dealt with in 2 versions of *Dawn Patrol* (1930, 1938) and its boisterous, jovial aspects were featured in *The Fighting Sixty-Ninth* (1940). Not unexpectedly, production of war movies was particularly intense in the period 1941–45, when Hollywood turned out such morale-boosting efforts as *The Immortal Sergeant* (1943), *The Purple Heart* (1944), and *Back to Bataan* (1945). The most respected war film to emerge after World War II was probably *Paths of Glory* (1957), which was fiercely antiwar in its treatment of the French army during World War I. An interest in expensive, spectacular recreations of famous World War II battles during the 60s brought *The Longest Day* (1962) and *The Battle of the Bulge* (1965). In 1971 **George C. Scott** scored a great personal success in the title role of *Patton.*

Animated Films. Although some animated movies were produced in the silent era, they are primarily associated with the sound period. The giant in this field was unquestionably **Walt Disney** (p. 1013), who formed his own company in 1928 and brought out the first talking cartoon, *Steamboat Willie,* the same year. In addition to inventing such famous cartoon characters as Mickey Mouse, Goofy, and Donald Duck, Disney introduced feature-length animation in such films as *Snow White and the Seven*

Dwarfs (1937) and *Fantasia* (1940). Another important figure in the cartoon world was **Walter Lantz** (1900–), creator of Woody Woodpecker. Animation of a more offbeat, even avant-garde nature was produced by the UPA Studios.

1946–74. INDEPENDENT PRODUCERS. Hit hard by the rise of television in the 50s, the movie industry saw weekly attendance drop from an all-time high of 90 million in 1946 to a nadir of 40 million in 1960. Symbolic of the decline were RKO's sale of pre-1948 movies to TV and MGM's auction of sets and properties used in its most famous films. A new breed of independent producers began to appear, while simultaneously the role of the studios shrank to that of distributors and financial backers.

A positive outcome of the shattering of big-studio control was that American filmmakers suddenly found themselves with far more artistic freedom than ever before. The lifting of restrictions on content and treatment was evident from such independently produced, low-budget films as *Easy Rider* (1969), a savage attack on American conformity, and *Bonnie and Clyde,* an unorthodox biography of 2 bank robbers that impressed critics with its combination of humor and violence. Other attempts to deal honestly and intelligently with American life were *The Last Picture Show* and *Desperate Characters,* both 1972.

Black Films. One of the major phenomena of American films during the early 70s was the appearance of films created by blacks and aimed specifically at black audiences. Though damned by most critics, the financially successful *Cotton Comes to Harlem* (1970) and *Shaft* (1971) have given considerable impetus to this movement and created a place in the industry for black directors like **Ossie Davis** and **Gordon Parks.**

1946–74. THE DIMMING OF THE STAR SYSTEM. The star system continued to be a major factor in Hollywood after the advent of sound and the names of well-known players were generally billed over the title of the picture. MGM acquired the most impressive galaxy, boasting "more stars than there are in the skies." Prior to World War II most leading men were either rugged types cast in a heroic mold, such as Gary Cooper and John Wayne, or suave sophisticates like Melvyn Douglas and William Powell. These matinee idols often played opposite such equally glamorous actresses as Greta Garbo, Joan Crawford, and Ann Sheridan.

Following the war, a new acting style, called "method acting," developed in New York's Actors Studio, and spread to Hollywood. Stressing a more naturalistic approach to acting, it found its outstanding practitioner in **Marlon Brando,** whose studied inarticulateness and emotional turbulence became world-famous, especially through his powerful characterization of Stanley Kowalski in *A Streetcar Named Desire.* Other method actors who gained celebrity in the post-war era were Montgomery Clift, Rod Steiger, and the short-lived James Dean.

The star system declined somewhat in the 60s when many producers found themselves unable to afford expensive performers and had to rely on unknowns. The result was films like *Mash* and *Easy Rider,* which managed to turn a handsome profit without benefit of big-name actors. Frequently, however, graduates of these modestly produced ventures— e.g., **Elliott Gould**—became high-priced stars themselves.

DIRECTORS. American directors of the sound period were notoriously subject to the restrictions (and interference) of the studios they worked for. Still, the best of them managed to create films of imagination, energy, and beauty. None was more widely respected than **John Ford** (1895–1973), best known for his Westerns, beginning with *Stagecoach* and including *Wagonmaster* (1956). Of similar stature was **Orson Welles** (1915–   ), who at the age of 25 produced, directed, and starred in what many critics regard as the finest American film of the sound era—*Citizen Kane* (1941). Also highly esteemed were the versatile **John Huston** (1906–   ), director of *The Maltese Falcon* (1941) and *The African Queen,* and the clever satirist **Preston Sturges** (1898–1959). Another of the ablest products of the studio system was **Howard Hawks** (1896–1977), a superb craftsman who was at his best in the comedies *Twentieth Century* (1934) and *His Girl Friday* (1940) and in the Western *Red River.* Equally craftsmanlike but more sophisticated was **Fred Zinnemann** (1907–   ), whose feeling for character was evident in *High Noon* and *From Here to Eternity* (1953). As in the silent epoch, foreign directors of note brought their talents to America, among them the Englishman **Alfred Hitchcock,** whose long series of ingenious thrillers included *Foreign Correspondent* (1940) and *North by Northwest* (1959).

1934–73. CENSORSHIP. The early talkies made frequent use of fairly racy material and a storm of protest by concerned moralists frightened the Hays office into creating a highly restrictive code (1934) governing permissible language and subject matter in films. Eric Johnson succeeded Hays in 1945 and perpetuated the code. When Johnson was replaced by Jack Valenti in 1966, the old system of puritanical restraints was lifted from movies in favor of a rating system that labeled each film according to the frankness of its content (1968). The result was a marked increase in candor, obscenity, violence, and frank, even sordid, subject matter in American movies. In particular, pornography such as *Deep Throat* has thrived alongside attempts to deal maturely with formerly forbidden subjects (e.g., *Carnal Knowledge,* 1971).

In a landmark decision, the Supreme Court ruled that films are protected by the First Amendment (1952). A later (1959) high court ruling on a French version of *Lady Chatterley's Lover* established the principle that film material must be "utterly without redeeming social value" to be regarded as pornographic. However, in 1973 the more conservative Burger court decreed that local community standards were sufficient to determine whether censorship should be imposed, opening the way for more official, if highly inconsistent, suppression of films.

CRITICAL RESPONSES. The American film continued to receive little in the way of serious critical attention during the 30s and early 40s. A voice in the wilderness during this period was **James Agee** (1909–55), whose sensitive and impassioned critiques in *The Nation* are still looked on as the pinnacle of American movie criticism. Following World War II, critics writing in the French journal *Cahiers du Cinema* began to explore American films with great interest and enthusiasm. One of the most influential was **François Truffaut,** later a director of note, who helped originate the *auteur* theory of film criticism, which holds that a great director will impose his style and vision on his movies, even when working with poor actors or an inferior script. The auteur theory took hold in America, where its foremost proponent is **Andrew Sarris** (1928–   ), and helped to bring about a reappraisal of American films during the 60s and a recognition of movies as an art form. Among the critics who have helped to put them there are Stanley Kauffmann, Dwight Macdonald, and Pauline Kael.

1935–74. TECHNICAL INNOVA-TIONS. The major technical innovation of the 30s was the perfection and general adoption of color in American movies. Walt Disney's *Flowers and Trees* (1935) was the first picture to utilize successfully the 3-color process of **Technicolor,** while such films as *The Wizard of Oz* and *Gone With the Wind* (both 1939) brought the use of color to a high level of effectiveness. During the 50s, the crippling competition of TV sent the movie industry in search of splashy new techniques and it came up with various wide-screen processes, the first being *Cinerama* by Fred Waller (1952) and the most famous was CinemaScope, introduced by 20th Century-Fox in *The Robe* (1953). 3-D, a method requiring that the viewer wear special glasses to create a 3-dimensional effect, had its brief, spectacular day in films like *House of Wax* (1953).

SCREENWRITERS. Although for most critics, the director is the primary creative force behind a movie, the contribution of scenarists cannot be ignored. The most famous of these was undoubtedly **Ben Hecht** (1894–1964), author of *Nothing Sacred* (1937), *Gunga Din* (1939), and dozens of other films. Hecht, with his crisp, workmanlike approach, personified the smooth professionalism of Hollywood scenarists. Others who made important contributions were **Nunnally Johnson, Dudley Nichols, and Jules Furthman.**

ALL-TIME FILM LEADERS
(Estimated gross film rentals from U.S. and Canada, *Variety*, 14 Jan. 1981*)

Title and Release	
Star Wars (20th, 1977)	$175,685,000
Jaws (Universal, 1975)	133,435,000
The Empire Strikes Back (20th, 1980)	120,000,000
Grease (Paramount, 1978)	96,300,000
The Exorcist (Warner, 1973)	88,500,000
The Godfather (Paramount, 1972)	86,275,000
Superman (Warner, 1978)	82,500,000
The Sound of Music (20th, 1965)	79,748,000
The Sting (Universal, 1973)	78,963,000
Close Encounters of the Third Kind (Columbia, 1977)	77,000,000
Gone With the Wind (MGM/United Artists, 1939)	76,700,000
Saturday Night Fever (Paramount, 1977)	74,100,000
National Lampoon Animal House (Universal, 1978)	74,000,000
Smokey and the Bandit (Universal, 1977)	61,055,000
Kramer vs. Kramer (Columbia, 1979)	60,528,000
One Flew Over the Cuckoo's Nest (United Artists, 1975)	59,000,000
Star Trek (Paramount, 1979)	56,000,000
American Graffiti (Universal, 1973)	55,886,000
Jaws II (Universal, 1978)	55,608,000
Rocky (United Artists, 1976)	54,000,000

*The Birth of a Nation (Griffith, 1915), which may have grossed as much as $50,000,000, is omitted because of unrelaible data. Inflated box office prices distort recent rankings.

Fine Arts and Architecture

The American colonies produced no Rembrandt or Rubens, no Palladio or Sir Christopher Wren, but they did develop skilled craftsmen with integrity and imagination, and artists with a special gift for realistic portraiture. The earliest

American painters, the self-taught limners, whose portraits made up in qualities of innocence and vigor what they lacked in technique, were supplanted as the early eighteenth century began by European-trained artists, who spawned a school of painting that included such masters as Robert Feke and John Singleton Copley, and artists who used a broad historical canvas like Benjamin West and his protégé, John Trumbull. Romanticism in the early national period was exemplified by Washington Allston, and during the antebellum period an authentic native school of landscape painting emerged called the Hudson River School. In the post-Civil War years two expatriates, John Singer Sargent and James A. McNeill Whistler, attained international reputations by their facile brushwork and experimentation with light and color, while George Inness and Winslow Homer captured the American land- and seascape and Thomas Eakins demonstrated his profound mastery of the human form. The early twentieth century was marked by a revolt against the genteel tradition in the arts, signalized by the Armory Show (1913), and, by the 1920s, American artists were running the gamut of Cubism, Expressionism, and Abstractionism. The Federal Art Project of the New Deal era encouraged mural painting and provided the means of survival for a generation of talented painters, including Jackson Pollock, Willem de Kooning, and Mark Rothko, who were to make their mark as Abstract Expressionists.

Architecture in the colonies was influenced by the building style and techniques of the countries of the colonists' origin, and by the end of the seventeenth century prosperous planters and merchants reflected the affluent Renaissance taste of Europe. Dominating the east coast was the English Renaissance style, developed much earlier by Inigo Jones, and introduced by talented amateur architects like Thomas Jefferson and Peter Harrison, while French and Spanish architectural styles were introduced in areas under the control of these two powers. The early national and antebellum years were marked, first, by the dominance of the classical style in public buildings, then by the Gothic style, used not only for churches, but also for mansions, factories, and prisons. In the years 1860–1920 structural and mechanical developments made possible spectacular architectural advances, including the introduction of the steel skeleton, the elevator, and electricity. By the 1920s enthusiasm for the skyscraper became an obsession. In the 1930s the International style was in competition with the streamlined moderne, but the former dominated the urban scene for more than a decade after World War II, reaching its peak in the early 1960s, until such innovative architects as Louis I. Kahn and Robert Venturi broke away from the rectangular, International-style boxes, and founded the new movement of supermannerism, a rebellion against the stilted formality of the International style.

1650–1721. EARLY AMERICAN PAINTING. The limners, the earliest American painters, were probably self-taught. Their portraits are characterized by an excess of realistic detail and a refreshing naïveté (*The Mason Children*, c.1670; *Mrs. Freake and Baby Mary*, c.1674). Among the earliest known limners were John Foster (1648–81) and **Thomas Smith** (active c.1650–85), a sea captain, whose paintings shared the Puritan obsession with death. Later New England limners after 1700 reflect English influence more directly. The earlier rugged energy is replaced by shallow elegance and a looser technique (Pierpont limner, 1711; Nathaniel Emmons [d. 1740]; J. Cooper [active c.1714–18]; the Pollard limner, 1721). In New Netherland and New York the **patroon painters**, 1660–c.1710 (Stuyvesant limner, Provoost limner [c.1700]; *Grootje Vas*, 1723, possibly by Pieter Vanderlyn), portrayed the upper class in an attempted style of elegance after European models.

1708–17. German-born Justus Englehardt Kühn introduced at Annapolis a provincial translation of the European tradition of aristocratic portraiture (*Eleanor Darnall*, c.1712).

1729–50. NEW ENGLAND REVIVAL was inaugurated by **John Smibert** (1688–1751), who staged the first art exhibition in the American colonies in Boston, 1730. His severe middle-class realism, variant of the English portrait tradition (*Bishop Berkeley and his Entourage*), created a school that was to include the colonial masters **Robert Feke** (c.1705–c.1750) and **John Singleton Copley** (p. 1007). Feke, the first supposedly American-born painter of recognized talent, painted chiefly in Newport (R.I.), Boston, and Philadelphia, between c.1741 and c.1750. He was a skillful draftsman with a fine sense of color (*Isaac Royall*

and Family, 1741; *Rev. Thos. Hiscox*, 1745; *Mrs. Charles Willing*, 1746; *Charles Apthorp*, 1748), but no naturalist.

1740–74. In Charleston, S.C., the Swiss Jeremiah Theüs dominated local portraiture with his version of the "international" style derived from Lely and Kneller.

1760–63. BENJAMIN WEST (1738–1820) left Philadelphia for Rome to study, setting up his studio 3 years later in London.

1760–74. In Boston **Copley** painted his early realistic masterpieces (*Boy with Squirrel* [Henry Pelham], c.1765).

1761. John Hesselius (1728–78), son of the Swedish-born painter Gustavus Hesselius, painted *Charles Calvert and His Colored Slave;* had a wide patronage from Philadelphia to Virginia.

1765–81. In his famous London studio **West** played host to American artists, determining in large measure the character of American painting. His group included Matthew Pratt (1734–1805; returned to America, 1768), Earl, Charles Willson Peale, Copley, Stuart, and Trumbull. His romanticized characterization of *The Death of Wolfe* (1771), containing recognizable portraits, achieved wide popularity. In 1772 West became historical painter to George III.

1778–92. RALPH EARL (1751–1801), after whose paintings Amos Doolittle made popular engravings of 4 scenes of the early Revolution, went to London to study (probably with West); returned to the U.S., 1785. His mature portraits (*Chief Justice Oliver Ellsworth and His Wife*, 1792) are notable for the importance of placing setting and landscape in a personal relationship to his sitters.

1781–93. The highly successful London period of **Gilbert Stuart** (p. 1162). In this period also **Charles Willson Peale** (p. 1123) established himself at Philadelphia (*Benjamin Franklin*, 1787).

1792. Benjamin West succeeded Sir Joshua Reynolds as president of the Royal Academy.

c.1681–1789. EARLY SCULPTURE. Seventeenth-century efforts were chiefly in the field of gravestone carving in New England (Thomas Child, 1655–1706). Native sculptors were slow in appearing; 18th-century activity was chiefly the carving of ship figureheads (Senior Simeon Skillin, c.1741) and weathervanes (Sherm Drowne). **Patience Lovell Wright** (1725–86), a wax sculptress, was a U.S. secret agent in Great Britain during the Revolution (modeling George III, Queen Charlotte, and other notables), and her son, **Joseph** (1756–93), who studied under Trumbull and West, was commissioned to make a statue of Washington, but all that survived are 2 medallions based on a life mask (1783–84). Appointed (1792) diesinker of the U.S. Mint, he designed numerous coins and medals. When Franklin was commissioned by Congress, 1776, to find a sculptor to carve the memorial tablet to Gen. Richard Montgomery, he selected Jean-Jacques Caffieri; and Jefferson subsequently selected **Jean-Antoine Houdon** (1741–1828) to make a marble effigy of Washington, which he executed from a life mask (1785).

EARLY ARCHITECTURE. In their early architecture the colonists attempted to duplicate in their new homes the forms and atmosphere of those they had left, in areas with different materials and different climates. Three European countries provided the chief models—Spain, in Florida, later in the Southwest and California; France, in the Mississippi Valley; and England, along the Atlantic coast—with 3 diverging types developing: **Spanish** (Saint Augustine: Castillode San Marcos, 1672; the Cathedral [1793–97]; and a few early houses), **French** (New Orleans, planned 1721; Ste. Genevieve, early houses; Cahokia, Ill., *Courthouse*,

c.1737), and **English** (which eventually became the major influence).

1607–c.1640. EARLIEST ENGLISH HOUSES were shacks based either on Indian "wigwams" (round-roofed structures of oblong plan) or palisadoed dwellings (reconstruction of old Salem); but in Virginia timber-framed and even brick houses were built in urban fashion by 1612, and in the more northern areas permanent timber-framed houses were the rule by the 1630s or 40s. **Log cabins** (logs laid around **horizontally**) were unknown in England, and were introduced by the Swedes on the Delaware (*Lower Log House*, Darby, Pa., 1640); ultimately the Scotch-Irish made them the prevailing frontier dwelling.

1641–1700. Evolution of the "Colonial" Style. Seventeenth-century architecture remained largely medieval, a product of unsophisticated craftsmanship, but with variants from European standards, chiefly caused by the more severe climate. Characteristic clapboard or shingle-covered walls (found occasionally in southeastern England) were used, rather than typical English "half-timber" filled with brick or plaster, because they were more weather-proof. Windows were small leaded casements. Early examples of this type (upper story overhang, small windows, inconspicuous doorways, central chimney, and often characteristic "salt box" roof sloping to the rear) have survived in Connecticut, Rhode Island, and Massachusetts. The smaller houses of the less well-to-do settlers were frame structures of from 1 to 1½ stories, with relatively tall and simple gable or gambrel roofs. Roof slopes tended to become less steep in accordance with weather conditions.

The current English **Jacobean** style was introduced in details, especially in the South, notably in Bacon's Castle (c.1655), Surrey Co., Va., a good example of full Jacobean design, with its geometrical gables, clustered chimneys, and stair tower, and in **Fairfield,** or Carter's Creek, Va. (1692). The style was also found in Middleton Place, Ashley River, S.C.; in the old *Landgrave Smith Back River* plantation house; and in the *Peter Sergeant House* (*Province House*), Boston. *Malvern Hill,* Va., represents the transition from Jacobean to more classic Renaissance. Timber construction continued to prevail in New England; brick, stone, and wood were used in the Middle Colonies (with stone predominating in portions of Pennsylvania, New Jersey, and Delaware); and brick houses were generally constructed in the South (in Virginia as early as 1636), becoming the prevailing material for the better dwellings. The brick was sometimes stuccoed in Charleston; wood was more general in North Carolina).

1700–50. Increasing prosperity, greater numbers of skilled craftsmen, and the increased importation of architectural books and building details rapidly modified the earlier trends, and permitted a more sophisticated following of the fashions of the mother country. The English **baroque** style (of Wren and Gibbs) was now adopted for more pretentious homes, with symmetrical façades, the double-hung window (replacing the casement type), and the elimination of overhangs. Pediments and pilasters were added in the later period to embellish the central doorway. The better houses were in brick or stone, but wooden houses often imitated stone details.

c.1751–89. Growing national feeling and closer commercial and political contacts produced increasing similarities in colonial architecture and a greater freedom in using English precedent. An American architecture was being created. The term **Georgian** came to be applied to houses of 2 or 3 stories built upon a strictly rectangular plan, with windows regularly spaced, the use of dormers, with horizontal lines emphasized, the small entry, or porch, replaced by a spacious center hall, with 2 chimneys, one on each side of the hall, in place of the central chimney (*Hooper House,* Marblehead, 1745; *Longfellow House,* Cambridge, Mass., 1759).

In New York the earlier **Dutch** style of New Amsterdam and the Hudson Valley (stepped gables, *Widow Sturtevant House,* Albany) and the **Flemish** style (projecting roof curved or flared at the ends) of parts of Long Island and New Jersey were ultimately supplanted by the Georgian. Classicism was evident in *Johnson Hall,* Johnstown, 1762, and the *Morris* (*Jumel*) *Mansion,* N.Y.C., 1765. In the Hudson River Valley simple houses of stone masonry, long low rectilinear structures with chimneys at either end, were built after the English conquest (*Senate House,* Kingston, 1676–95; *Freer House,* New Paltz, 1720). Until 1750 the simple Quaker style dominated the Philadelphia area, but Georgian rapidly came into vogue (*Mt. Pleasant,* 1761, brick, stone, and stucco; *Woodford,* c.1750, brick, both with Doric doorways; *Cliveden,* Germantown, 1770, American Palladian style). **Pennsylvania-Dutch** architecture of the Upper Rhine Valley immigrants radiated from Bethlehem, Pa., down the Great Valley into South Carolina, with its generally stone construction and its square plan for a number of rooms clustered about a central flue (*Miller's House,* Milbach).

In the South the baroque style of colonial Georgian was adopted in such plantation houses as the *Hammond House,* Annapolis, 1770, designed by **William Buckland,** who came from England in 1755; in Virginia at *Stratford Hall,* Westmoreland Co. (c.1725), and at *Westover,* Charles City Co. (c.1730), with the Palladian influence notably present in *Mount Airy,* Warsaw (1755–58), and in *Mount Vernon* (1758–86).

Charleston's brick and stucco mansions adapted the West Indian style of long porches or piazzas, with houses often standing endwise to the street. The galleries (most existing galleries are post-Revolutionary additions) faced the gardens, rooms were high-ceilinged and spacious, and the ground-floor story was raised several feet above the ground, with curving wrought-iron stair rails. Outstanding examples: *Izard House* (before 1757); the *Miles Brewton House* (1765–69), with its double portico, Doric columns on the 1st floor and Ionic on the 2nd, evidencing the growing classical influence. The **Huguenot** type, based on French architectural styles, was also found in South Carolina, c.1690–1800 (*The Mulberry*, Berkeley Co., with its mansard roof; *Brick House*, Edisto Island, (c.1725).

Churches. Early churches were simple, in the South following English Gothic small parish churches (*St. Luke's*, Smithfield, Va., 1682); in the North, because of the Puritan religious-government system, taking the form of meeting houses—large rectangular structures with entrance on 1 long side, galleries on 3 sides, and the high pulpit on the long side opposite the entrance (*"Old Ship" Meeting House*, Hingham, Mass., 1681). By 1750, however, English influence, introducing the type of towered church developed by Sir Christopher Wren and James Gibbs, almost completely effaced the earlier types, even for dissenting churches (*St. Michael's Church*, Charleston, S.C., 1752–61, possibly the work of **Peter Harrison** [1716–75], patterned after James Gibbs' St. Martin's-in-the-Fields; Harrison's *King's Chapel*, Boston, 1749–54, also after Gibbs; and his *Touro Synagogue*, Newport, 1759–63, influenced by Inigo Jones and Gibbs).

Public Buildings were notably represented by the *Old State House*, Boston (1712–28); *Carpenters' Hall*, Philadel-

phia (1724); *Independence Hall*, designed by Andrew Hamilton, Philadelphia (1732–41); the *Pennsylvania Hospital* (1755); and the *Maryland State House*, Annapolis (1772), which helped to set the domed type which had become almost universal in state capitol buildings. The *Capitol* (1701–05) and the *College of William and Mary* (1695–1702) at Williamsburg (restoration begun 1927) show, in reconstructed and restored fashion, the most highly developed types; the latter was built from drawings supplied by Wren.

1793–1828. PAINTING. Portraiture. After his return from England in 1792 **Gilbert Stuart** was active in New York, Philadelphia, Washington, and Boston, producing a gallery of life-size bust portraits limning worthies of the Federal and Republican eras. His canvases, bearing the strong impress of the British tradition of Reynolds, Gainsborough, and Raeburn, possessed a high technical finish and a mastery of color tones. Among his portraits are many of *George Washington*, and those of *Mrs. Richard Yates, Mrs. Timothy Pickering, Mrs. Perez Morton* (c.1802), and *Nathaniel Bowditch*.

At Philadelphia, **Charles Willson Peale**, who had made his mark before 1789, finished *The Family Group* (1809) and also painted *The Staircase Group* (c.1795), *Exhuming the Mastodon* (1806), and *Self-Portrait in His Museum* (1824). These works were all innovations in American painting, possibly because Peale's interest in the Natural History Museum gave him an objective approach to nature. Because he believed anyone could learn to paint he taught many of his family to follow his trade, including his brother James (1749–1831) and his sons, Rembrandt (1778–1860) and Raphaelle (1774–1825).

Stuart's work helped make the life-size portrait bust in oil the favorite medium of the age. Active at New York were

Samuel Lovett Waldo (1783–1861) and William Jewett (1795–1874), and at Philadelphia, Thomas Sully (1783–1872).

c.1800–25. Miniature painters included Edward Green Malbone (1777–1807) and Benjamin Trott (c.1790–c.1841).

1830–50. Among portrait painters active near the midcentury, many of whom show the mark of their competition with **photography** from its rise, c.1840, were Henry Inman (1801–46), John Neagle (1796–1865), Charles Loring Elliott (1812–68), Thomas Hicks (1823–90), George P. A. Healy (1812–94), and Chester Harding (1792–1866). Mention should also be made of the Negro painter, Robert S. Duncanson (1821–71).

1790–1860. HISTORICAL PAINTING. The genres of historical, religious, and panoramic painting were developed about 1789. **John Trumbull** (1756–1843) painted *The Battle of Bunker's Hill* in West's studio in London in 1785 and *The Declaration of Independence*, one of the 4 murals in the National Capitol, between 1786–94. **John Vanderlyn** (1776–1852) painted the *Panorama of Versailles, The Death of Jane McCrea, The Landing of Columbus, Marius Musing Amid the Ruins of Carthage*, and his *Ariadne* (1810), one of the early nudes in American painting, and thought to be in such poor taste that it blighted his career. Edward Savage (1761–1817), who did a canvas of Washington's family, also painted a panorama of London. Henry Sargent (1770–1845) painted *The Landing of the Pilgrims* and *Christ Entering Jerusalem*. The versatile **William Dunlap** (1766–1839) painted *Calvary, The Bearing of the Cross*, and *The Attack on the Louvre*. Dunlap's *History of the Rise and Progress of the Arts of Design in the United States* (1834) was the first treatment of that subject.

Washington Allston (1779–1843) struck the first vibrant note of romanti-cism in American painting. His poetic-philosophic bent for religious themes was exhibited in the famous unfinished *Belshazzar's Feast, The Deluge, Uriel in the Sun*, and *The Dead Man Restored to Life by the Bones of Elijah*. A pupil of Allston was **Samuel F. B. Morse**, who made his mark as a portraitist before his association with the development of the telegraph. Among his portraits are those of De Witt Clinton, Lafayette, and President James Monroe. His *Exhibition Gallery of the Louvre* is a *tour de force*.

The school of historical painting that emerged by the midcentury included Robert Walker Weir (1803–89), *Embarkation of the Pilgrims;* John Gadsby Chapman (1808–89), *Baptism of Pocahontas;* James Walker (1819–89), *Battle of Chapultepec;* William Henry Powell (1823–79), *Perry's Victory on Lake Erie;* Emmanuel Leutz (1816–68), *Washington Crossing the Delaware* and *Westward the Course of Empire Takes Its Way;* Daniel Huntington (1816–1906), *Mercy's Dream* and *Pilgrim's Progress;* and Thomas P. Rossiter (1818–71), *Washington and Lafayette at Mount Vernon, 1776.* Perhaps the most deliberate of the historical-genre painters was George Caleb Bingham (1811–77), who recorded contemporary river and frontier life in *Daniel Boone Coming Through Cumberland Gap, Fur Traders Descending the Missouri, The Jolly Flatboatmen,* and *The Verdict of the People.*

1830–60. LANDSCAPE PAINTING. The early landscape painters included Alvan Fisher (1792–1863), Thomas Birch (1779–1851), James Hamilton (1818–78), and Robert Salmon (fl. 1800–40). A distinctive school of American landscape emerged only with the achievement of **Thomas Doughty** (1793–1856), the first American painter who made a successful career in this genre; **Asher Brown Durand** (1796–1886), and **Thomas Cole** (1801–52). These 3 pioneers were

the leaders of the **Hudson River School,**
which also included John W. Casilear
1811–93), John Frederick Kensett (1818–
72), the early work of **George Inness** (p.
1066), Jasper F. Cropsey (1828–1900),
Sanford R. Gifford (1823–80), Worthing-
ton Whittredge (1820–1910), Frederick
Edwin Church (1826–1900), Jervis Mc-
Entee (1828–91), William M. Hart
(1823–94), and James M. Hart (1828–
1901).

ANECDOTAL GENRE PAINTING.
The work of such early storytelling painters as Charles Cattron (1756–1819) and
John Lewis Kimmel (1789–1821) became more fully developed in the anecdotal paintings of William Sidney Mount
(1807–68), the first American to establish himself in this genre; also James
Henry Beard (1812–93), William Holbrook Beard (1824–1900), William Ran-
ney (1813–57), Tompkins M. Matteson
(1813–84), and David Gilmor Blythe
(1815–65). The life of the North American Indian and the Far West was recorded in the paintings of **George Cat-
lin** (1796–1872), **Alfred Jacob Miller**
(1810–74), Seth Eastman (1808–75),
John Mix Stanley (1814–72), Frank B.
Mayer (1827–99), and Carl Wimar
(1828–62). Among the most popular of
the later painters of Western scenes was
Frederic Remington (p. 1137).

In the field of art reproductions, **John
James Audubon** issued his superb aqua-
tint plates of the *Birds of America*
(1827–38). On a popular level, the
prints of Currier & Ives were based on
the work of such artists as George Henry
Durrie (1820–63) and Arthur Fitzwil-
liam Tait (1819–1905). The development of commercial lithography created
a wide market for art reproductions in
the medium of the "chromolith."

1789–1830. SCULPTURE. The work
of the early artisan carvers displays technical ingenuity and artistic integrity, notably William Rush (1756–1833), who

enjoyed a busy career as a woodcarver
of ships' figureheads, among them *The
Genius of the United States* and *Nature,*
both of which were mounted on U.S.
frigates. His Indian figures, e.g., the *Indian Trader* (on the ship *William Penn*),
were among his best works. Another
woodcarver, who later worked in marble,
was Hezekiah Augur (1791–1858), whose
best-known work is *Jephthah and His
Daughter.* John Frazee (1790–1852) began as a New Jersey stonecutter, was
wholly self-taught as a sculptor, and did
not carve his first marble bust until
c.1825. Among his marble portraits are
those of John Jay, John Marshall, and
Daniel Webster. Although the work of
John Henri Isaac Browere (1792–1834)
may be classified as life masks rather
than sculpture, his portraits of prominent
Americans are valuable as authentic historical records.

**1830–60. ITALIAN NEOCLASSI-
CISM.** In the 1830s U.S. sculptors began to pursue professional training
abroad (particularly in Italy). The first
American who deliberately chose sculpture as a profession was **Horatio Greenough** (1805–52), best known for the
heroic, half-draped statue of Washington
that stands on the Capitol grounds. Other
sculptors who performed all or most of
their work in Italy were William Wet-
more Story (1819–95) and Harriet G.
Hosmer (1830–1908). Among Story's
works were a statue of his father, Justice
Joseph Story, and *Saul, Moses, Cleopatra,*
and *Medea.* Those by Hosmer include
Beatrice, Zenobia, and the statue of
Thomas Hart Benton at St. Louis.

Hiram Powers (1805–73) shares with
Greenough the distinction of being the
first professionally trained native sculptor. He did many portrait busts of American statesmen in an age when the
marble bust predominated, but his best-
known work is the *Greek Slave,* which
created a sensation in its time. Powers

was the first American sculptor to win a European reputation.

Other sculptors noted for their busts and figures in white marble include Erastus D. Palmer (1817–1904) and Thomas Ball (1819–1911). Palmer is best known for *Indian Girl, White Captive,* and the bust of Washington Irving. Ball did the equestrian statue of Washington at the Boston Public Gardens and the *Emancipation* group at the national Capitol. William Rimmer (1816–79), whose works include *Falling Gladiator* and *Head of Saint Stephen,* was noted for his mastery of anatomical knowledge.

Thomas Crawford (1813–57) was one of the outstanding pioneers of American sculpture. Among his works are the statue of *Armed Freedom* on the dome of the Capitol, the group called *Past and Present of America* on the pediment of the Senate wing, and the *Washington Monument* at Richmond.

Henry Kirke Brown (1814–86) is best known for his equestrian statue of *Washington* in Union Square, New York City, where his statue of *Lincoln* also stands. **Clark Mills** (1815–83) made the first equestrian statue cast in the U.S., that of *Gen. Andrew Jackson* (erected 1853) which stands near the White House.

Randolph Rogers (1825–92) did the bronze doors of the Capitol rotunda and the *Genius of Connecticut* on the dome of the State House at Hartford, as well as *Nydia* and *Lost Pleiad.* **John Rogers** (1829–1904) gained wide popularity with his "Rogers groups," the mass-produced plaster statuettes that found their way into thousands of American homes. His folk artistry and sharp delineation are displayed in such representative works as *Checkers up at the Farm, Town Pump, The Fugitive's Story, Union Refugees, Council of War,* and *The Wounded Scout.*

1789–1860. ARCHITECTURE: CLASSIC REVIVAL. The American Revolution brought with it a demand (recognized by Jefferson in his *Notes on Virginia*) for a new American architecture, expressive of the new nation. Yet for some time the older building ways and the older dependence on England continued. Thus the **Adam** style continued as a major influence for 2 or 3 decades. Jefferson saw the source of inspiration for the new work in the ancient classic architecture of Rome and Greece, and eventually a **Roman Revival** (1789–c.1820) and a **Greek Revival** (c.1820–60) became dominant. One of the foremost practitioners in the persisting Adamesque manner was **Samuel McIntire** (1757–1811), who built houses and mansions for the Salem merchants, among them the Derbys and Crowinshields. Other adapters of this mode were **Asher Benjamin** (1773–1845), who worked at the beginning of his career in the Connecticut Valley and was the author of the popular handbook *The Country Builder's Assistant* (1797) and many other similar books; and **Charles Bulfinch** (p. 994), who embodied it in many distinguished houses in Boston. It was characteristic of the time that McIntire and Benjamin practiced as carpenter-builders rather than professional architects.

1789–c.1820. ROMAN REVIVAL saw the emergence of the professional architect in the U.S. Its vogue was due to (1) direct importation from Europe; (2) the analogy with the Roman Republic drawn by Americans of the early national period. Chiefly influential in this initial phase were **Thomas Jefferson** and **William Thornton** (1759–1828). Jefferson's design for the *Virginia Capitol* at Richmond (1785–89), the first American structure after the Roman style, was based on the ancient Roman temple at Nîmes, France, known as the Maison Carrée. His plan for the *University of Virginia* at Charlottesville, with its systematic use of the various orders, represents the high mark of the Roman Revival. Charles Bulfinch, among the first native professional architects, later shifted to the style of the Roman and, rarely, the Greek Revivals. In houses, the new classicism shows chiefly in the creation of a restrained, clear simplicity, with a diminution in decorative adjuncts. These are often called **Federal** in style. French influence appears occasionally. Perhaps the finest example of this type is the New York *City Hall* (1803–12), whose design was shared by **John Mc-Comb, Jr.** (1763–1853), and **Joseph F. Mangin** (fl.1794–1818).

1793–1830. NATIONAL CAPITOL expressed the idealism of the new nation. After Maj. **Pierre Charles L'Enfant** (1754–1825) had designed the Washington city plan, President Washington, as the result of a competition, selected **William Thornton** as architect of the Capitol. **Stephen Hallet** (fl.1789–65), who succeeded Thornton, shares the credit for the basic conception—the large central dome and the flanking Senate and House wings. Beginning in 1803, **Benjamin Henry Latrobe** (p. 1081) modified the somewhat impractical original design and used Greek inspiration in the details, working on the Capitol (which was burned by the British in 1814) until 1817. **Charles Bulfinch** brought Latrobe's plans to completion (1817–30). The architect of the **Executive Mansion** was **James Hoban** (c.1762–1831), who also designed the State House at Charleston, S.C. In the White House the east and west porticoes were built from Latrobe's designs. After the British burned the White House, Hoban rebuilt it with Latrobe's modifications.

c.1820–60. GREEK REVIVAL is attributable to the renewed Continental interest in classic forms, to the influx of foreign architects, and to American enthusiasm for the Greeks in their struggle for independence. This period saw the dominance of the carpenter-builder, when handbooks came into use, e.g., Asher Benjamin's widely reprinted *The Practical House Carpenter* (1830) and the 3 books by **Minard Lefever** (1797–1854): *Young Builder's General Instructor* (1829), *Modern Builder's Guide* (1833), and *Beauties of Modern Architecture* (1835), even more important in spreading the Greek Revival throughout the country. Many federal and state government buildings, merchants' exchanges, banks, and churches were designed in this style, generally a free inventive rendering of Greek forms based on such Greek structures as the Parthenon, the Erectheum, and the monument of Lysicrates. Among the prominent characteristics of the style were the use of the Greek orders, doors and mantels with creative versions of Greek inspiration, great variety in house plans, and, in public buildings, magnificent fireproof masonry-vaulted construction. Chiefly responsible for introducing the Greek Revival was **Benjamin Henry Latrobe.** The first Greek building in America was his Bank of Pennsylvania at Philadelphia, characteristic in its free adaptation of ancient precedent and in its fireproof vaulted construction. Two of his pupils were **Robert Mills** (1781–1855) and **William Strickland** (c.1787–1854). Mills, the designer of many houses, customhouses, and other federal buildings, is best known for the *Treasury Building, Patent Office,* and *Washington Monument* (begun 1836). Strickland built the *Merchants Exchange,* Philadelphia, and the *Capitol,* Nashville, Tenn. A pupil of Strickland was **Thomas U. Walker** (1804–87), who designed *Girard College,* Philadelphia, and brought the U.S. Capitol to final completion (1850–65). Others identified with this style include **Minard Lefever; Gideon Shryock** (1802–80); **Isaiah Rogers** (1800–69), who created the modern hotel concept in the *Tremont House* (Boston, 1828), and built the *Merchants Exchange* at New York; and **Alexander Jackson Davis** (1803–92), in partnership with **Ithiel Town** (1784–1844) until 1844, who designed the New York *Custom House* (1832) and several state capitols.

1840–60. BEGINNING OF THE GOTHIC REVIVAL. Groundwork was laid by **A. J. Davis; Richard Upjohn** (1802–78), first president of the American Institute of Architects, founded, 1857, who designed the new Trinity Church and Trinity Chapel; and **James Renwick** (1818–95), Grace Church, 1843–46, and St. Patrick's Cathedral, 1850–79, all in New York. The many-times-republished books of **Andrew J. Downing** (1815–52), dealing with landscape and rural architecture, had great influence in spreading the Gothic Revival, as well as in stimulating romantic gardens; he is also one of the fathers of the city park in the U.S. The eclecticism of the period did not go unchallenged. In 3 important works on architecture Horatio Greenough attacked current trends (*American Architecture* [1843], *Aesthetics at Washington* [1851], and *Structure and Organization* [1852]), anticipating by a half century Louis Sullivan's functional approach.

1861–1910. PAINTING. Portrait and Figure. Still active after 1860 were many of the portraitists, among them Daniel Huntington and Charles Loring Elliott, who before the Civil War shaped a technique of sober and almost photographic realism. The Lincoln theme made its early appearance in a series of studies by Francis Bicknell Carpenter (1830–1900), including *The Lincoln Family in 1861* and *The Reading of the Emancipation Proclamation*. Portraits of public figures

were a specialty of Alonzo Chappell (1828–87), whose pictures reached a wide audience through the medium of the steel engraving.

The absorption of Continental influences appeared in the work of a later generation: Gustave H. Mosler (1841–1920), Francis D. Millet (1846–1912), Frank Duveneck (1848–1919), William Merritt Chase (1849–1916), Wyatt Eaton (1849–96), and Kenyon Cox (1856–1919). The most successful portrait painter of the time was **John Singer Sargent** (p. 1147), who did most of his work abroad. His technical finish is evident in such characteristic portraits as those of *Ada Rehan, Ellen Terry, Mrs. John L. Gardner, Coventry Patmore, Madame X, The Four Doctors,* and *The Misses Hunter.* Another American portraitist who did virtually all of his work in Europe was **James A. McNeill Whistler** (p. 1180), whose work includes *Portrait of the Artist's Mother, Thomas Carlyle,* and *Miss Alexander.* Whistler's *Nocturnes* and *Symphonies* used color and mass with fresh inventiveness, and his etchings of Venetian and London waterside subjects exhibit a brilliant Impressionist technique.

Figure painting in the U.S. reached a new level with the work of Eastman Johnson (1824–1906), *Old Kentucky Home* and *In the Fields;* William Morris Hunt (1824–79), *The Bathers;* George Fuller (1822–84); Robert L. Newman (1827–1912); Abbott H. Thayer (1849–1921); Thomas Dewing (1851–1938); **Frederic Remington,** and John W. Alexander (1856–1915).

Historical, Mural, Anecdotal, and Still Life. The pre–Civil War tradition of historical painting was continued by Constantino Brumidi (1805–80), whose work at the national Capitol includes *Apotheosis of Washington;* and by William De La Montagne Cary (1840–

1922), Henry F. Farny (1847–1916), and John Mulvaney (1844–1906). Among the outstanding mural painters were **John La Farge** (p. 1078), who was also a prolific worker in stained glass; Kenyon Cox; Edwin Austin Abbey (1852–1911); Elihu Vedder (1836–1923); Edwin H. Blashfield (1848–1936); John W. Alexander; and Robert F. Blum (1857–1903). Anecdotal painters of the time included John George Brown (1831–1913), *The Music Lesson;* Thomas Waterman Wood (1823–1913), *The Village Post Office;* and Edward Lamson Henry (1841–1919), *The 9:45 Accommodation.* Among the still-life painters were George Henry Hall (1825–1913), Andrew J. H. Way (1826–88), William Michael Harnett (?1848–92), William Merritt Chase, John Frederick Peto (1854–1907), and John Haberle (1856–1933).

Landscape. Those who continued to produce repetitions or variations of the Hudson River School included William Rickaby Miller (1818–93), Frederick Edwin Church (1826–1900), **Albert Bierstadt** (p. 986), Samuel Colman (1832–1920), James David Smillie (1833–1909), Thomas Moran (1837–1926), George Henry Smillie (1840–1921), and Robert Swain Gifford (1840–1905). **George Inness,** who before the Civil War had been a follower of the Hudson River School, shaped a fresher idiom in such canvases as *Peace and Plenty, Autumn Oaks, Delaware Water Gap,* and *Home of the Heron.* Other landscape painters included Alexander H. Wyant (1836–92), *Falls of the Ohio and Louisville, Mohawk Valley,* and *An Old Clearing;* Homer D. Martin (1836–97), *View of the Seine* (best-known as *Harp of the Winds*); Ralph Albert Blakelock (1847–1919), *Brook by Moonlight;* and Abbott H. Thayer, *Monadnock.*

1860–80. TRANSITION TO OBJECTIVE REALISM: Homer and **Eakins.** American painting took on a greater power, resourcefulness, and maturity with the work of **Winslow Homer** (p. 1060) and **Thomas Eakins** (p. 1019).

Homer, who began as a magazine illustrator, first came to prominence in 1866 with *Prisoners from the Front,* a canvas based on his Civil War experience as a pictorial reporter; this reminiscent phase was continued in *Rainy Day in Camp* and *Sunday Morning in Virginia.* After 1880, when he began living in Maine, Homer abandoned illustrative and anecdotal subjects. Along the Maine seacoast, and during his stay in the Caribbean, Homer developed an original vein which appears in *All's Well, Winter Coast, Rowing Home, The Gulf Stream,* and *After the Tornado, Bahamas.* As a watercolorist, Homer is of the first rank.

Eakins brought to portrait and figure painting a strength and character based on a profound study of the human form and an intimate acquaintance with the work of the French and Spanish masters. His choice and treatment of subject signaled the rise of a new realism reflected in such paintings as *The Swimming Hole, The Agnew Clinic, The Gross Clinic, The Thinker, Max Schmitt in a Single Scull, The Concert Singer,* and *Katherine.*

1877. Opening of the first American Salon des Réfusés by the Society of American Artists (early exhibitors included La Farge, Inness, Ryder, and Eakins); amalgamated with the Academy in New York, 1906, to form the present National Academy of Design.

1880–1910. MYSTICISM. The poetic intensity of **Albert Pinkham Ryder** (p. 1144) produced canvases weighted with heavy yet luminous color and with strange masses and forms drawn from an imaginary world. A solitary worker during his lifetime, it was only after his death that Ryder won general recognition. Among his paintings are *Macbeth and the Witches, The Flying Dutchman, Jonah and the Whale, Toilers of the Sea,* and *Pegasus.*

1880–1910. IMPRESSIONIST MOVEMENT. French Impressionism, a school preoccupied with the subtle and iridescent play of light over forms, developed c.1871, *et seq.,* with the work of such painters as Claude Monet, Berthe Morisot, Camille Pissarro, and Alfred Sisley. American painting's first direct acquaintance with Impressionism began with **Mary Cassatt** (p. 1000), known for such characteristic pieces as *Caresse Maternelle* and *Mother and Child.* The only American invited to exhibit with the French Impressionists, she did all of her work abroad. It remained for Theodore Robinson (1852–96) to introduce Impressionism into America. The influence of Monet is apparent in Robinson's *Spring in Giverny.* Impressionism combined with American themes in the work of J. Alden Weir (1852–1919), *A Factory Village, Visiting Neighbors, Ploughing for Buckwheat,* and *Nocturne, Queensboro Bridge;* John H. Twachtman (1853–1902), *The White Bridge, Snowbound, Waterfall, Summer,* and *October;* and Childe Hassam (1859–1935), *Union Square in Spring, Church at Old Lyme, The 17th of October,* and *Central Park from the Plaza.* In 1898 Hassam, Twachtman, Weir, and others banded together as "Ten American Painters" and held the first exhibition of U.S. Impressionists.

1900–1910. REALISTS. In the early 20th century there emerged a group of painters who concentrated on homely incident, subject, and character, basing their content on direct observation and their technique on European masters such as Hals, Goya, Hogarth, and Daumier. Known as "The Ash Can School"

(and sometimes, with Maurice Prendergast [1859–1924] and others, as "The Eight"), this group included **Robert Henri** (p. 1056), *Martche in a White Dress* and *Boy with a Piccolo;* George Luks (1867–1933), *The Old Duchess, The Little Milliner,* and *The Spielers;* William Glackens (1870–1938), *Chez Mouquin* and *Roller Skating Rink;* John Sloan (1871–1951), *The Wake of the Ferry, Dust Storm, Election Night,* and *McSorley's Bar* (organizer of the Society of Independent Artists, 1917, in protest against the conservatism of the National Academy of Design); **George Bellows** (p. 983), *Stag at Sharkey's, Edith Cavell,* and *Day in June;* and Everett Shinn (1876–1953), best known for his treatments of stage subjects, as in *Revue* and *White Ballet.*

1913. ARMORY SHOW, which opened at the 69th Regiment Armory in New York on 17 Feb. 1913, was organized by the Association of Painters and Sculptors, whose president was Arthur B. Davies (1862–1928). It had a twofold purpose: to introduce to an American audience in coherent and integrated form the origins and evolution of the modern European art tradition, and to create a more favorable atmosphere for the reception of artists working outside the established academic tradition. In addition to exhibiting works by Ingres, Delacroix, Courbet, and the French Impressionists, the Armory Show included the post-Impressionists (Cézanne, Van Gogh, Seurat, and others), and Cubist and abstractionist painters like Picasso, Matisse, Duchamp, and Kandinsky. In the work of Brancusi, Maillol, and Lehmbruck, Americans saw new experiments in sculpture.

A landmark in the history of American art, the Armory Show signified a definite break in the hold exerted by the academic school and had a lasting influence over a wide range of media, including

interior design and advertising art. Its
notes were heard in the art criticism of
Willard Huntington Wright, Leo Stein,
and Walter Pach. The Armory Show
paved the way for the acceptance of a
new generation of American painters,
among them Louis M. Eilshemius (1864–
1941), Jerome Myers (1867–1940),
George ("Pop") Hart (1868–1933), Alfred Maurer (1868–1932), **John Marin**
(p. 1097), Eugene Higgins (1874–1958),
Kenneth Hayes Miller (1876–1962),
Maurice Sterne (1877–1957), Marsden
Hartley (1877–1943), Arthur G. Dove
(1880–1946), Walt Kuhn (1880–1965),
Max Weber (1881–1961), Rockwell
Kent (1882–1971), Edward Hopper
(1882–1967), Charles Demuth (1883–
1935), Charles Sheeler (1883–1965),
Guy Pène du Bois (1884–1958), and
Georgia O'Keeffe (1887–   ).

1861–85. SCULPTURE. The sculptors
of the post–Civil War era alternated between realism and classicism until c.1885,
when the influence of the Italian Renaissance began to make itself strongly felt
in monumental and ornamental sculpture.
The leading sculptors up to c.1880 included Launt Thompson (1833–94),
who executed *Rocky Mountain Trapper,*
the statue of *Abraham Pierson* at Yale
University, and the equestrian statues of
Gen. John Sedgwick at West Point and
of *Gen. Winfield Scott* at Washington,
D.C.; Larkin G. Mead (1835–1910),
Lincoln Monument at Springfield, Ill.,
the statue of *Ethan Allen* at the national
Capitol, and *The Father of Waters;*
George Bissell (1839–1920), statues of
Chancellor James Kent at the Congressional Library, *President Arthur* in Madison Square Park, New York, and *Chancellor James Watts* at Trinity Church,
New York; Franklin Simmons (1839–
1913), the *Naval Monument* at Washington, D.C., and statues of *Roger Williams* and *Gov. William King* at the nation Capitol; Martin Milmore (1844–

83), *Soldiers' and Sailors' Monument* on
Boston Common; and Olin L. Warner
(1844–96), known for his portrait busts
of *J. Alden Weir* and *William Crary
Brownwell,* the statue of *William Lloyd
Garrison* at Boston, and a series of relief
portraits of North American Indians.

1885–1938. American sculpture attained a new mark of craftsmanship and
conception with the work of the Irish-
born **Augustus Saint-Gaudens** (p. 1144)
and that of **Daniel Chester French**
(1850–1931) and **George Grey Barnard**
(1863–1938). Saint-Gaudens executed
the statue of *Lincoln* at Lincoln Park,
Chicago; the *Adams Memorial* (the
noted hooded figure sometimes called
Grief) in Rock Creek Cemetery, Washington, D.C.; the *Shaw Memorial* at Boston; the *Sherman* and *Farragut Memorials,* both at New York; *Amor Caritas;*
and *Diana* (the figure on the tower of
the old Madison Square Garden at New
York). Among French's many works are
The Minute-Man and *Ralph Waldo
Emerson* at Concord, Mass.; the statue
of *Lincoln* at the Lincoln Memorial,
Washington, D.C.; the statue of *John
Harvard* and the *Longfellow Memorial*
at Cambridge, Mass.; the statue of *Lewis
Cass* at the national Capitol; the massive
figure of *The Republic* at the World's
Columbian Exposition; *Gallaudet and
His First Deaf-Mute Pupil* at Washing-
ton, D.C.; the *Parkman Memorial* at
Boston; and *Death and the Young Sculp-
tor* at Roxbury, Mass. Barnard's works
include *The Two Natures, The Prodigal
Son, The Hewer,* the group at the state
Capitol at Harrisburg, Pa., and the uncompleted colossal World War I memorial.

Other leading sculptors of the period
were Frederick W. MacMonnies (1863–
1937), who executed *Civic Virtue,* formerly at City Hall Park, New York, the
site of his statue of *Nathan Hale; Bac-
chante,* at Boston; *Victory,* at West Point,

N.Y.; the *Soldiers' and Sailors' Memorial* at Grand Army Plaza, Brooklyn, N.Y., on which Thomas Eakins collaborated; the statue of *Shakespeare* at the Congressional Library; and the *Columbian Fountain* at the World's Columbian Exposition; Herbert Adams (1858–1945), best known for his polychrome portrait busts, including *Primavera, The Rabbi's Daughter,* and *Julia Marlowe;* Paul Wayland Bartlett (1865–1925), *The Ghost Dancer, The Bear Tamer, The Genius of Man,* and statues of *Michelangelo* and *Columbus* at the Congressional Library; Karl Bitter (1867–1915), *Carl Schurz Memorial* at New York, monumental reliefs at the Broad Street Station, Philadelphia, and *The Standard Bearers* at the Pan-American Exposition held at Buffalo; and James Earle Fraser (1876–1953), *End of the Trail, Alexander Hamilton* at the Treasury Department Building, Washington, D.C., group for the Theodore Roosevelt Memorial at New York, figures of *Thomas Jefferson* and *Lewis and Clark* at the Missouri State Capitol, and the statue of *Franklin* at the Franklin Institute, Philadelphia.

c.1861–c.1885. ARCHITECTURE. Rapid industrialization profoundly changed older ideas; cast iron came into wide use in commercial buildings, and glass in large sheets became available for the first time. New fortunes placed a premium on lavish, showy design. This period witnessed the first practical passenger elevators (p. 795), and the beginnings of the typical city office building as well as the large department store.

VICTORIAN GOTHIC (English), marked by an Italianate strain, appeared in numerous guises, ranging from the filigree jigsaw detail of "carpenter's Gothic" to polished careful designs that reflected the influence of John Ruskin. Used for public buildings and in many town and country houses, the style featured polychrome masonry, squat pointed arches, high ceilings, arcaded windows, and elaborate bays and oriels. Among the best examples: old *Boston Museum of Fine Arts* (1872–75), designed by **Russell Sturgis** (1836–1909; better known for his critical writings and *A History of Architecture,* 4 vols., 1906–15); library and *Memorial Hall* at Harvard University (completed 1874), designed by **William Robert Ware** (1832–1915) and **Henry Van Brunt** (1832–1903); and the *State House,* Hartford, Conn. (completed 1885), designed by **Upjohn.**

FRENCH RENAISSANCE REVIVAL was the architectural hallmark of the "Gilded Age." Among its prominent characteristics were mansard roofs, lavish and heavy ornamentation, coupled columns and pilasters, large cornices, and an undiscriminating use of the architectural orders. This style was employed in many types of buildings—churches, hotels, hospitals, schools, railroad stations, and public buildings. One of the most active exemplars was A. B. Mullett (?–1890), who as government architect designed the *State, War and Navy Building,* Washington, D.C., and the old *Post Offices* at Boston and New York. An important offshoot of this mode was the **brownstone-front house,** adopted on a wide scale in New York City during the 1870s and 1880s. The style achieved a fresh delicacy in the work of **Richard Morris Hunt** (1828–95), trained in Paris, designer of numerous houses for merchant princes at New York, Newport, R.I., and elsewhere, including those for the Vanderbilts.

COLLEGIATE ARCHITECTURAL EDUCATION began in the U.S. in this period. The first architectural school was opened at the Massachusetts Institute of Technology (1866) under the direction of William Robert Ware. Architectural courses were subsequently introduced at the University of Illinois (1870), Cornell (1871), Columbia (1883), and Harvard

(1890). The influence of the École des Beaux Arts in Paris, where many Americans were trained in the 1870s, was dominant in the majority.

1876. PHILADELPHIA CENTENNIAL EXPOSITION (U.S. International Exposition), with its 249 buildings occupying 465 acres of Fairmount Park, constituted a grandiose summation of the architectural styles of the period; its dominant modes were the Queen Anne variation of Victorian Gothic, French mansard, and Swiss châlet derivations. In it, however, the influence of new constructional ideas gave rise to a few prophetic and independent exteriors important as reflecting the new forms industrialized engineering might produce. Foreign art exhibits, particularly in the crafts, left a deep mark on public taste.

c. 1876–c.1894. ROMANESQUE REVIVAL. Although derived from the Romanesque of southern France, it was not based on any current European revival; its leading force was **Henry Hobson Richardson** (p. 1138), who received his training at the École des Beaux Arts. At the outset of his career he employed Victorian Gothic (design for the *Church of the Unity,* Springfield, Mass.), but turned to his own adaptation of French Romanesque in his plans for the *Brattle Square Church,* Boston. His integrated use of mass, space, and line, and his imaginative treatment of ornament, rank him among the foremost U.S. architects. His most famous work is *Trinity Church* at Boston (opened 1877). His other outstanding designs include *Crane Library,* Quincy, Mass.; the libraries at Malden, Mass., and Burlington, Vt.; the *Allegheny Courthouse and Jail,* Pittsburgh; the *Marshall Field Wholesale Store,* Chicago; the now demolished *Hay-Adams* houses at Washington, D.C.; and railroad stations for the Boston and Albany line. Especially influential in New England and the West, the Romanesque Revival

was frequently employed in the latter area by the partners, **Daniel H. Burnham** (1846–1912) and **John Wellborn Root** (1850–91), who designed the old *Chicago Art Institute* and the *Montauk, Phoenix, Rookery,* and *Rialto* buildings, all at Chicago.

1884–1914. COMING OF THE SKYSCRAPER. An indigenous American contribution, the skyscraper was made possible by cheap and abundant structural steel, the passenger elevator, inexpensive fireproofing, and resourceful solutions of the structural problems of foundations. Because its problems were new, the skyscraper induced architects to work out solutions based on function rather than style. Customarily accredited as the first tall structure embodying in part the basic principles of metal frame construction is the *Home Insurance Building* at Chicago (built 1884–85), designed by **William LeBaron Jenney** (1832–1907), who used cast-iron columns and wrought-iron beams. The first building erected completely of wrought-iron skeleton construction was the 13-story *Tacoma Building* at Chicago (built 1887–88), designed by Holabird and Roche. Precursors of the functional form were the *Wainwright Building* at St. Louis (1890), the characteristic nontraditional skyscraper design of the early 20th century, and the horizontal emphasis in the *Carson, Pirie, and Scott Building* at Chicago (1899), both by **Louis H. Sullivan** (p. 1163). Prevailing eclecticism governed architectural style at the turn of the 20th century. Characteristic of this style, all in New York City: *Singer Building,* by **Ernest Flagg** (1857–1947); *Metropolitan Life Insurance Co. Tower* (1906), by N. LeBrun & Sons; the *"Flatiron" Building* (1902), by Daniel H. Burnham; and the *Woolworth Building* (1911–13), with its overlay of Gothic motifs, by **Cass Gilbert** (1859–1934).

1893–1917. NEW CLASSICAL RE-VIVAL AND ECLECTICISM. The **Chicago World's Fair** (World's Columbian Exposition, 1893) provided the major impetus for the general adoption of Greek, Roman, and Renaissance forms and the gradual abandonment of the Romanesque. The Roman Classical mode for the grounds and buildings on 686 acres of Jackson Park, along Lake Michigan, was chosen by a group of architects working under the direction of Daniel H. Burnham, including Richard M. Hunt, McKim, Mead & White, and George B. Post. The most important building at the "White City" which did not bear the classic stamp was the *Transportation Building* by Sullivan. The classic-eclectic tradition of exposition architecture was continued at the **Pan-American Exposition** (1901) and the **Louisiana Purchase Exposition** (1904) at St. Louis. Among leading exponents of classic eclecticism was the firm of **McKim, Mead & White,** of which the most important members were **Charles F. McKim** (1849–1909) and **Stanford White** (1853–1906). Their work includes the *Henry Villard House* (1885), the *Century Club* (1890), *Low Memorial Library,* Columbia University (1893), the *Herald Building* (1894), the *J. Pierpont Morgan Library* (1906), all at New York City, and the *Boston Public Library* (1888). Other exemplars were Carrère and Hastings, who designed the *New York Public Library* and the *Senate* and *House Office Buildings,* Washington, D.C.; and **Cass Gilbert,** who designed the *Minnesota State Capitol,* the *U.S. Custom House* at New York City, the *U.S. Treasury Annex,* and the *Supreme Court Building,* Washington, D.C. Eclecticism marked the work of **Henry J. Hardenbergh** (1847–1918), who designed the old *Waldorf-Astoria Hotel* (1891–96) and the *Plaza Hotel* (1907), both at New York City, and the *Copley Plaza* (1910) at Boston; and the

work of **George B. Post** (1837–1913), who designed the *Pulitzer Building* (1889–92), the *New York Produce Exchange* (1881–85), the *New York Cotton Exchange* (1883–86), the *St. Paul Building* (1897–99), the *College of the City of New York* (1902–11), the *New York Stock Exchange* (1904), and the *Wisconsin State Capitol.* Gothic eclecticism found its most brilliant expression in **Ralph Adams Cram** (1863–1942), member of the firm of Cram, Goodhue & Ferguson. Among the structures which bear his distinctive mark are *St. Stephen's Church,* Cohasset, Mass.; major buildings at the U.S. Military Academy, West Point (1904); *St. Thomas's Church,* New York City (1911–13); *Calvary Church,* Pittsburgh (1907); and the *Fourth Presbyterian Church,* Chicago (1912). In his latter days **Bertram Grosvenor Goodhue** (1869–1924) broke with the Gothic style. His plan for the *Capitol* at Lincoln, Neb., marked a new expression of the classic tradition, with a free and daring use of decorative sculpture.

SULLIVAN AND WRIGHT. During the Classical Revival the quest for a functional, indigenous style was carried forward by **Louis H. Sullivan** and his disciple **Frank Lloyd Wright** (p. 1189). Sullivan was in partnership with Dankmar Adler at Chicago (1881–1900), and here Wright served his apprenticeship. Among Sullivan's most notable structures: *Chicago Auditorium* (1889), *Chicago Stock Exchange Building* (1894), *Bayard Building,* New York City (1898), and the *National Farmers Bank,* Owatonna, Minn. (1908). Toward the turn of the 20th century Wright began to develop his distinctive **"prairie house"** style in the Midwest. His first important commercial structure was the *Larkin Administration Building,* Buffalo, N.Y. (1904). One of his most successful suburban dwellings was the *Robie House,* Chicago (1908).

1914. World War I found U.S. architecture in a confused state. The brilliance of the planning in many of the great classic-eclectic monuments blinded many to the basic superficiality of its approach. Office buildings, department stores, mass housing, and factories of undreamed-of complexity and size constituted pressing challenges to which rational and beautiful answers were still rare. Industrial production of building materials was breaking down hand craftsmanship and curtailed building appropriations discouraged lavishness on the earlier scale. Only a completely new creative architecture, then only in its infancy, could provide the answer.

1905–73. GROWTH OF PHOTOGRAPHY AS ART. During this period, photography developed as an independent art form. Formalism, abstraction, and realism were approaches used by photographers who tried to capture on film the forms and textures of nature and the harsh social reality of the depression years. **Edward Steichen** (1879–1973), **Alfred Stieglitz** (p. 1159), **Edward Weston** (1886–1958), **Ansel Adams** (1902–
), **Paul Strand** (1890–1976), **Dorothea Lange** (1895–1965), and **Walker Evans** (1903–75) are among the earliest photographers to capture the concentrated sense of reality available through the medium of still photography. Most challenging of the photographic undertakings during these years was Steichen's notable exhibition, "The Family of Man" (1953), representing the work of 273 photographers and shown in more than 70 countries.

1914–29. REIGN OF PARIS ABSTRACTION. With the outbreak of World War I French artists (Gleizer, Picabia, and Duchamp) came to the U.S. and spread ideas of **cubism**, which in the period 1919–29 was changed into a purist style by Demuth, Sheiler, and Preston Dickinson (1891–1930). The mid-20s saw the apogee of Paris Abstractionism in the work of such artists as Weber, Maurer, and **John Marin** (p. 1097).

1914–60. DEVELOPMENT OF FORMALISM IN SCULPTURE. A revived interest in the archeotonic and expressive aspects of sculpture developed after 1914. Works displayed concern with the integrity of materials and questions of weight and balance as well as of texture and overall contour. Important work in direct carving and modeling was done by **Jacob Epstein** (1880–1959), U.S.-born expatriate who lived in London. **William Zorach** (1887–1966), *Mother and Child, Affection;* **Gaston Lachaise** (1882–1935), *Figure of a Woman;* and **Elie Nadelman** (1882–1946), *Seated Woman, Head in Marble,* simplified anatomical forms and captured a classical sense of monumentality and power in their work. In contrast to the rugged quality of Jo Davidson's (1883–1952) creations, *Gertrude Stein, Dr. Albert Einstein,* were the works of **Paul Manship** (1885–1966) reflecting Renaissance, archaic, and Oriental influences, *Centaur and Dryad, The Indian Hunter.* Outstanding for his animal sculpture was John B. Flannagan (1898–1942), *Chimpanzee.*

In general, concerns similar to those of the painters are reflected in the sculpture of this period. Abstract sculpture goes back to Cubism—**Max Weber,** *Spiral Rhythm* (1915); John Storrs (1885–1956), *Seated Gendarme* (1925). **Alexander Calder** (p. 995) created sculptures and suspended mobiles which owe much to the surrealists but break with the representational tradition. **David Smith** (p. 1153) created abstract sculptures of welded metal which bridge the gap between 2-dimensional and 3-dimensional art. Other sculptors, more concerned with shapes, voids, and masses than with representation were David Hare (1917–
), Seymour Lipton (1903–   ), Herbert

Ferber (1906–), Theodore Roszak (1907–81) and Richard Lippold (1915–). Richard Stankiewicz (1922–) and **Louise Nevelson** (p. 1113) used crude everyday "found objects" to construct their sculptures. Less affected by changing aesthetic style were such realists as William Zorach, Robert Laurent (1890–1970), José de Creeft (1884–), and Chaim Gross (1904–), who continued to work in their own respective styles throughout most of this period.

1918–60. SOME ARCHITECTURAL TRENDS. The confused state of taste in 1914 yielded to more creative tendencies, despite the widespread wave of "**colonialism**" in domestic architecture—final manifestation of eclecticism. Shortly after World War I strong influences from the new architecture of Europe (especially of France and Germany) were dominant. The form this new architecture took in the 1920s was primarily ascetic, geometrical, and antihistorical, even deliberately avoiding the use of traditional building materials and techniques. This is sometimes called the **International style.** It influenced domestic, school, and factory architecture profoundly, but its disregard of regional and national differences in materials, climate, and ways of living proved it too limited for wide U.S. application, although some of its basic ideals of truth to structure and material and its geometrical quality were absorbed into the U.S. tradition. The **Chicago World's Fair** (1933) and the **New York** and **San Francisco World's Fairs** (1939) were important chiefly as indicating public acceptance of the objectives of modern architecture. By 1940 its dominance was at an end. Instead, the best U.S. architecture sought much freer, though equally new and logical, solutions, using the traditional brick, stone, and wood in new ways, with marked regional differences (e.g., houses in Florida compared to California). In

this development the influence of **Wright,** who had always stood for a humane and nonmechanized ideal, was of primary importance.

In the 1950s, in protest against the neoclassicism of **Ludwig Mies van der Rohe** (1886–1964), with its stress on form rather than site (860 Lake Shore Dr., Chicago; Seagram Building, New York), new forms emerged—**Hugh Stebbins'** Congress Hall in Berlin, **Eero Saarinen's** (1910–61) auditorium for MIT and hockey rink for Yale; or texture was stressed—**Edward D. Stone's** U.S. Embassy at New Delhi and **Harry Weese's** U.S. Embassy at Accra. **Louis I. Kahn's** (p. 1074) Yale Univ. *Art Gallery* (1951) and *Richards Medical Research Laboratories* (1961), Univ. of Pennsylvania, gave the mechanical and service areas of modern buildings equal prominence with the other, more public, aspects of the structure. The use of exposed reinforced concrete as a building material became popular. Nevertheless, the boxlike curtain-wall office building became the most common form of urban architecture. The best example is *Lever House*, 1952, New York City, by Skidmore, Owings, and Merrill. These buildings have their roots in the International style but became popular due to their relatively low cost and easy method of construction.

1919–29. FROM REALISM TO SOCIAL REALISM. The influence of Robert Henri in emulating the work of Manet and Velasquez is found in the works of such students as **George Bellows** (p. 983), notable for his career as an illustrator and lithographer and for his prizefight scenes (*Dempsey and Firpo*, 1923); Edward Hopper, who classicized the facts of daily life in the U.S. (*Automat; The City; Compartment C, Car 293*); Edward Speicher (1883–1962; *Katharine Cornell, Graziana*); Alexander Brook (1898–1980; *Morning*); and Rockwell Kent, with his Alaskan and marine scenes. During the same period Georgia O'Keeffe and Charles Burchfield (1898–1967) painted objective records of the local scene.

1930–40. The social realism of the "Ash Can School" was intensified by the depression and by the organization in 1935 of the **WPA Federal Art Projects.** The newer artists, powerfully influenced by the Mexican school of muralists, divested slum scenes of poetry or sentimentality and used them as a medium of social protest. Robert Gwathmey (1903– ; *End of Day*) projected his message through complex semi-abstract types; Jack Levine (1915–) caricatured the privileged (*The Reluctant Ploughshare*); Mitchell Siporin (1910–) portrayed the heroes of the class struggle in allegorical groupings. Among the most effective exponents of social realism were William Gropper (1897–1977); *The Opposition*), Philip Evergood (1901–73); *Suburban Landscape*), and Ben Shahn (1898–1969; *Vacant Lot, Sunday Football*). A sympathetic treatment of working people was notably expressed in the work of the three Soyer brothers, Moses, Raphael, and Isaac.

1930–40. REGIONALISTS OR ISO-LATIONISTS. In reaction to the influence of Picasso, Matisse, and the Parisian school, a trio of U.S. artists stressed native Midwestern scenes, particularly after 1932: Grant Wood (1892–1942; *Dinner for Threshers, Return from Bohemia, American Gothic*), John Steuart Curry (1897–1946; *My Mother and Father, Baptism in Kansas, Roadworkers' Camp*), and Thomas Hart Benton (1889–1975; *First Crop*). Ultimately the trend ran its course and revealed its sterility.

1930–40. Abstract traditions were maintained by Stuart Davis (1894–1964), Karl Knaths (1891–1971), and Arthur G. Dove. When the **Bauhaus** closed in 1934, some of its leaders came

to the U.S. (Walter Gropius [1883–1969], Laszlo Moholy-Nagy [1895–1946], and Josef Albers [1888–1976]), as well as the expressionist George Grosz (1893–1959), and the American Lyonel Feininger (1871–1956).

1939–48. With the rise of fascism many European artists found refuge in the U.S. (Marc Chagall [1887–   ], Chaim Lipschitz [1912–   ], Pavel Tchelitchew [1898–1957], and Salvador Dali [1904–   ]). Socially conscious painting declined after the Nazi-Soviet pact (the American Artists Congress, a left-wing group founded in 1936, broke up in 1940), and abstractions and surrealist works enjoyed an increase in popularity (Peter Blume, *The Eternal City*). New experimentation appeared in the "magic realism" of Byron Thomas (1902–), *Night Ball Game*, and the abstractionism of German-born Max Beckmann (1884–1950). In addition, the WPA Index of American Design revived interest in U.S. primitives and encouraged self-taught artists, including in this period **Grandma Moses** (p. 1110), with her anecdotal detail, and the black artist **Horace Pippin** (1888–1946), *The Trial of John Brown.* A personal art form was still being developed by **Yasuo Kuniyoshi** (p. 1078).

1945–60. DEVELOPMENT OF AB-STRACT EXPRESSIONISM. The most significant aspect of the postwar period was the full development of Abstract Expressionism. American artists strove to create a new style, free of provincialism and the social preoccupation which marked much of prewar painting, and to find a form of expression different from that offered by the European movements of Cubism and Surrealism. **Ashile Gorky** (1905–48), *Agony* (1947), relied upon the biomorphic forms of the Surrealist tradition. **Willem de Kooning** (1904–), *Woman* (1950–51), used abstracted and torn-apart images of women in which the gesture and action of the painting process assumes great importance. The art of **Jackson Pollock** (p. 1131), *Mural on Indian Red Ground* (1950), broke new ground with his paintings made by dripping and splashing paint on canvas in order to create an all-over image free of recognizable subject matter and associations. The problem for painters became primarily to resolve the relationship of painted figures or forms to the ground of the canvas itself and to have the expressive content of the work carried by this relationship. **Franz Kline** (1910–62), *Ninth Street* (1951), and **Philip Guston** (1913–80), *Passage* (1957–58), are other artists who practiced "action painting." **Mark Rothko** (1903–70), *Tundra* (1950), and Adolph Gottlieb (1903–74), *Counterpoise* (1959), concentrated more on specific shapes and relationships of image masses to explore the same kinds of problems. These and other artists composed the New York School of painting and achieved international prominence to the point where American painting became trend-setting for the rest of the world. Other important Abstract Expressionists are Robert Motherwell (1915–   ), *At Five in the Afternoon* (1949), Hans Hoffmann (1880–1966), *Cathedral* (1959), Clyfford Still (1904–80), *1948-D* (1948), and Mark Tobey (1890–1976), *New Life (Resurrection)* (1957). At the same time, Andrew Wyeth (1917–   ) achieved great popularity through his evocative but highly representational paintings of subjects closely associated with rural America (*Christina's World*, 1948).

1959–73. EXPANDING INTEREST IN ART museums and galleries proliferated and established ones built new homes (Solomon R. Guggenheim Museum, 1959; Whitney Museum, 1966; Los Angeles County Museum of Art, 1964; Museum of Fine Arts, Houston, 1973). Numerous contemporary and retrospective exhibitions of importance were mounted; the volume of published art books skyrocketed. Paintings of both contemporary artists and recognized old masters sold for record prices (Rembrandt's *Aristotle Contemplating the Bust of Homer,* in 1961, for $2,234,000; Velasquez's *Juan de Parcja,* over $5 million [1970]) as museums competed for new acquisitions and private collectors speculated. American artists fetched record prices (Andrew Wyeth, Jackson Pollock, $2 million [1973]). Museum attendance figures shot up during the late 60s and museums became the center of social controversies as part of the protest movements of the times. Antiwar and antiestablishment attacks by artists extended to strikes and challenges to prevalent museum exhibitions and private collecting attitudes (sit-in at the Museum of Modern Art, 1970, the Art Workers Coalition). In the 70s attention was focused on the practice of paying high prices for works which had been surreptitiously exported from their place of creation or historic preservation (a portrait attributed to Raphael returned to Italy after purchase by the Museum of Fine Arts, Boston, 1971; controversy raged over the source of the Euphronios Vase purchased for over $1 million by the Metropolitan Museum of Art, 1972). The UN passed a resolution designed to restrict illicit traffic in art objects and archaeological artifacts (1973). Generally, museum operating policies became a matter of public concern as works of art were bought and sold for great sums of money, often works received as bequests.

The increased importance of art in public life was evidenced by the White House Festival of the Arts (14 June 1965), the reproduction of works of modern art on postage stamps (designed by Stuart Davis [1894–1964], 1964, and by Robert Indiana [1928–   ] 1973), the establishment of the National Foundation on the Arts and Humanities (1965), and the proliferation of state Arts Councils. The influence of American artists abroad became more firmly established as American art dominated the principal international art events such as the Venice Biennale and the Documenta held in Kassel, W. Germany. Showings of American sculpture occurred on a major scale in Paris for the first time in 1960, and the Tate Gallery, London, established an American wing in the same year. News magazines gave instant publicity to events in the art world and heralded each new artistic development: the creation of Pop Art, Self-destroying Art, Happenings, and Op Art. Auction prices shot up for American art and Madison Avenue art dealers and auction houses attained the stature of big business (Marlborough, André Emmerich; Parke-Bernet merged with Sotheby of London), while new galleries devoted to less well-established talents, sprung up in the SoHo (South Houston Street) district of New York City.

1960–73. PROLIFERATION OF STYLES IN PAINTING AND SCULPTURE. Abstract Expressionism began to wane as artists looked for new principles to govern their work. The emotional and subjective aspect of action painting was replaced by a carefully considered intellectual analysis of forms, colors, and subject matter. Owing something to Marcel Duchamp and the European tradition of Dada, **Pop** (popular) **Art** took advertising art and everyday objects and monumentalized them as if to draw attention to artistic qualities that could be found in mundane and commercial aspects of the environment. **Andy Warhol's** (1930–) Campbell's soup cans, **Roy Lichtenstein's** (1923–) blown-up comic-strip-like pictures, **Jasper Johns'** (1930–) *Pointed Bronze Beer Cans* sculpture, and **Claes Oldenburg's**

(1929–) *Hamburger with Pickle and Tomato Attached,* transformed objects commonly taken for granted. Other artists, such as **James Rosenquist** (1933–) and **Robert Rauschenberg** (1925–), whose work bridges the art of de Kooning with the Pop school, recombined everyday images into new compositions, which question assumptions about them. The sculptor George Segal (1924–), who made lifelike figures out of plaster and put these into actual settings, reminds one of the art of Edward Hopper, with nostalgic references to the 1930s, but in a very contemporary idiom. **"Happenings"** were events supposedly designed—or "allowed to happen"—to reveal the artistic significance of things that occur in experience (Al Hansen, Claes Oldenburg). Concern with more formal issues was evidenced by the **Op** (optical) artists who experimented with the perceptual process in combining and recombining colors in geometrically abstract shapes. This trend, which also has European precedents in the work of Victor Vasarely and Bridget Riely, develops from Josef Albers' experiments and studies. Gene Davis (1920–), Larry Poons (1937–), Richard Anuszkiewicz (1930–), and Nicholas Krushenick (1929–) associated with this movement and are also called "post-painterly abstractionists." The use of "hard edge" images is related to this style and relates as well to the concept of **"Minimal Art."** Minimal works, proceeding from the dictum that "Less is more," reduced the complexity of works to basic geometric shapes, subtle modifications of tone and brushwork or flat areas of color (Barnett Newman [1925–70], Ad Reinhardt [1913–67]). More lyrical color field paintings were made by Morris Louis (1912–62), *Saraband* (1962), and Jules Olitski (1922–). These involve the interaction of blended colors with each other to the canvas support and its edge. The paintings of Frank Stella (1936–) and Kenneth Noland (1924–) deal with the relationship of flat areas of color in geometric configurations to the rectangular or shaped picture surface. The analysis of picture making led to new media and to multimedia works such as shaped canvases in 3 dimensions (Charles Hinman, 1932–), the fluorescent-light works of Dan Flavin (1933–), neon works by Chryssa (1933–), painted wooden satirical sculptures by Escobar Marisol (1930–), kinetic art based on movement (*The Party*, 1965–66), laser-light-beam works, and those using a variety of other materials and processes. Earthworks and environmental constructions, too large to house in a museum or private home, were created in an attempt to treat new questions of scale, materials, and the definitions of art (Richard Serra [1939–], Ronald Bladen [1918–]). With the death (1965) of **David Smith** (p. 1153), whose large stainless steel sculptures (Cubi Series, 1961–65) culminate the line of development through Cubism and Abstract Expressionism to geometric abstraction, sculpture becomes more diverse. Surrealism survives in the work of Edward Kienholz (1927–) and Escobar Marisol, but it is transformed by modern concerns and realizations. Formalism continues in the work of Robert Morris (1931–) and Donald Judd (1928–). By the end of the 60s definitions between painting and sculpture had become indistinct and the arts overlapped considerably. Videotape (Keith Sonnier [1941–]) and movie film (Stan Brachage, Michael Snow) are 2 of the latest media being explored by artists.

1960–73. ARCHITECTURE. New materials were exploited for their expressive and structural potential. **Paul Rudolph's** (1918–) *Art and Architecture Building* at Yale (1963) was a harsh example of the power of raw concrete. **Eero Saarinen's** *TWA Terminal Building* (1956–62) at the John F. Kennedy International Airport, a concrete structure suggesting a bird in flight, while expressing the potential of this material, marks a triumph of style over convenience and function. **I. M. Pei** (1917–), **Skidmore, Owings, and Merrill,** and **Philip Johnson** (1906–) continued in the International style in major office buildings and public projects, and Edward Durrell Stone (1902–78) and **Minoru Yamasaki** (1912–) allude to historical types in a romantic or evocative manner. **Louis I. Kahn's** dramatic buildings for the Salk Institute for Biological Research, La Jolla, Calif., 1965, and for the Library at Phillips Exeter Academy, Exeter, N.H., 1972, achieve monumentality and classical harmonies through novel structural systems, giving full expression to the functional and mechanical realities of modern construction. By contrast, **Robert Venturi** (1925–), Yale's *Mathematics Building*, 1970, and **Charles W. Moore** (1925–) avoid monumentality as unsuitable to the modern age of mass production and economic necessity. With reference to the imagery of Pop Art, these architects rely upon humble vernacular building types and distinguish their structures by the use of signs and graphic decoration, their unorthodox approach often arousing storms of protest. Office buildings continued to dominate construction, as residential housing sharply declined in the early 1970s, the skyscrapers still conforming to the curtain-wall techniques evolved during the postwar period, with little if any regional variation. New heights were reached in the *Sears Tower*, Chicago, and the *World Trade Center*, New York City, but in brash disregard of demographic and environmental considerations.

Music

The colonial period was a time when song rather than instrumental music was the prevailing mode of musical expression. The colonists sang psalms, hymns, ballads, plantation work songs, sea chanteys, tavern songs, and, in the Revolutionary years, patriotic songs to English ballad tunes. What little professionalism existed was restricted to a few European performers and such religious groups as the Moravians. Versatile statesmen like Franklin, Jefferson, and Francis Hopkinson displayed a more than amateur interest in music, and by the early national period Americans were familiar with the works of such European giants as Handel, Gluck, and Haydn.

Professionalism took hold in the United States in the first half of the nineteenth century, with the founding of orchestras, choral societies, and music schools, with the distribution of sheet music by music publishers, and the manufacture of musical instruments on a large scale. Individual Europeans, notably Lorenzo Da Ponte at the start of the period, later Ole Bull, Jenny Lind, and Adelina Patti, provided a fillip to musical life, as did the immigration of many musicians as a result of the revolutions of 1848 in Europe. Theodore Thomas and other distinguished symphonic conductors played major roles in bringing the best European music and the most talented performers to the United States.

It was not until the twentieth century, however, that America's contribution both to popular and serious music gained wide recognition. Jazz, a distinctively American idiom, attained worldwide popularity, and its influence internationally has burgeoned with the years. As the quality of music conservatories improved so did the achievements of individual performers, symphonic orchestras, and opera companies. American composers have proliferated in numbers, performances of their music are less rare than in the past, and avant-garde experimentation has won a discriminating, if small, following.

Pioneer Period, 1640–1800

1640–1787. RELIGIOUS MUSIC. Psalmody, 1640–1764. *Bay Psalm Book* (also p. 844) published at Cambridge, Mass.; the first hymn book printed in the English colonies; adopted throughout New England and as far south as Philadelphia. This psalm collection was printed without tunes, leaving choice of psalmody to the individual congregation, with the result that psalm singing became a confused cacophony. The 9th edition (1698) included 13 tunes (first book with music printed in the colonies). **1712.** Rev. John Tufts of Boston published *A Very Plain and Easy Introduction to the Whole Art of Singing Psalm Tunes*, containing 28 tunes in 3-part harmony, the first instruction book on singing to be compiled in the colonies. **1721.** Rev. Cotton Mather of Boston published *The Accomplished Singer*, while his nephew, Rev. Thomas Walter of Boston, published *Grounds and Rules of Music Explained*. **1764.** Josiah Flagg of Boston published *A Collection of Best Psalm Tunes*, engraved by Paul Revere. **1771.** *New England Psalm Singer* published by **William Billings** (1746–1800), first New England composer, organizer of singing societies, composer of *Fuguing Tunes, Chester*, and numerous Revolutionary patriot songs.

Hymns, 1703–39. Hymns or hymnody began to replace psalmody as a result of the influence of the "singing dissenters." **1737.** John Wesley, influenced by Moravian hymn singing, was arraigned by the Savannah, Ga., grand jury, charged, among other counts, with introducing unauthorized psalms and hymns into the Anglican church service. The folk hymnody of the Methodists and Baptists on the frontier continued this tradition. **1739.** First American edition of Isaac Watts' famous *Hymns and Spiritual Songs* (pub. in England, 1707).

1720–30. EPHRATA CLOISTER, founded by German Dunkers, 50 miles west of Philadelphia. Women copied and illuminated hymn books. Hymns were sung in 4-, 5-, 6-, and 7-part harmony (while in the rest of the colonies congregations sang only in unison). *Ephrata Hymnbook (Gottliche Lieben und Lobes Gethöne)* published by Benjamin Franklin (1730). More than 1,000 of the hymns are attributed to **Johann Conrad Beissel** (1690–1768), reputedly the first composer in the colonies whose works were published.

1742. MORAVIAN MUSIC. First **singstunde** in **Bethlehem, Pa.** (settled, 1741, by Moravians). **Collegium musicum,** founded 1744; continued until 1820, when it was succeeded by the Philharmonic Society. Most notable among the Revolutionary generation of Moravian musicians was **John Frederick Peter** (1746–1813), a composer of chamber music as well as organist of the Moravian congregation.

1787. CATHOLIC HYMNS. First hymnal published for the use of Catholics in the U.S., *A Compilation of the Litanies and Vesper Hymns and Anthems as They Are Sung in the Catholic Church,* adapted to voice and organ by John Aitkin, Philadelphia (2 parts treble and bass; 3d part added later).

1627–1787. INSTRUMENTS. 1627. Pilgrims assembled by use of **drum. 1633.** Shipment of **recorders** and **hautboys** (oboes) received at New Hampshire plantations of Newitchwanke and Pascattaquack. **1635.** Shipment of **jewsharps** at Roxbury, Mass. **1638. Trumpet** used for assembly at Windsor, Conn. **1660. Viol** requested by Harvard College students. **1678.** Bequest of **bass viol** in Sudbury, Mass. **1694.** German Pietists settling in Wissahickon, Pa. (near Philadelphia) used **trombones** in quartets. **1699. Virginals** used and tuned in Boston. **1703–87. Organ.** First recorded use in a colonial church, Gloria Dei Church (Swedish) in present Philadelphia, accompanied by viols, oboes, trumpets and kettledrums. First organ built in the colonies was constructed by Dr. Thomas Witt of Philadelphia (1704). The first imported into New England was in 1711 by Thomas Brattle of Boston (still in existence in Portsmouth, N.H.). The first to be constructed (1745–46) by a native American was built by Edward Bromfield, Jr., of Boston. In 1756 the new organ constructed by Gilbert Ash was dedicated at City Hall, New York. A pipe organ was used for the first time in a colonial Congregational Church in Philadelphia, 1770. The first pipe organ west of the Alleghenies was built (1787) in Cookstown (now Fayette City), Pa., by Joseph Downer of Brookline, Mass.; instrument now at Carnegie Institute, Pittsburgh. **1716.** Shipment of **flageolets** and **flutes** advertised in Boston newspaper. Most of the previously named instruments were believed to have been in use by this time in the other colonies, including the **French horn** and bassoon. **1736. Harpsi-chord** used in recital given in New York by **Karl Theodore Pachelbel,** son of the famous organist (first European musician of note to visit Boston). **1761. Benjamin Franklin** invented his improved version of the glass harmonica, the **glassychord.** (Franklin is known to have played the guitar, harp, and dulcimer.) **1769–74. Spinet** and **pianoforte.** First American spinet made by John Harris in Boston; first pianoforte by John Behrent, Philadelphia.

1731–1800. PERFORMANCE. 1731–32. Early concerts. First authentic record in the English colonies of public concert at Mr. Pelham's (*Boston News-Letter,* 16, 23 Dec. 1731). First recorded concert in Charleston, S.C., a few months later.

1735–50. Ballad Operas. The ballad opera *Flora, or Hob in the Well* at the Courtroom, Charleston, S.C. (1735), the first recorded operatic performance in the colonies. *The Mock Doctor* (1750), the first performed ballad opera in New York, was followed that year by *The Beggar's Opera.*

1744. Collegium musicum founded by Moravians, credited with early performance of parts of oratorios, later of chamber music of **John Frederick Peter,** of Haydn quartets and symphonies, the first performance in America of *The Creation* and of Handel's *The Seasons.*

1752. First use of an orchestra in an operatic performance in the colonies: *The Beggar's Opera,* given in Upper Marlboro, Md., by the Kean and Murray Co.

1753. William Tuckey (1708–81), on arrival in New York, became organist and choirmaster of Trinity Church.

1754–69. Concert Halls and Outdoor Concerts. First concert hall in Boston opened by Stephen Deblois (1754). Ranelagh Gardens' series of open-air summer concerts announced in *N.Y. Mercury* (1765); continued for 4 years.

1757. Dr. Arnes' *Masque of Alfred* performed by students in Philadelphia. **1770.** Milton's *Masque of Comus* performed by Hallam Co., Philadelphia.

1761–87. MUSICAL SOCIETIES. St. Cecilia Society, oldest musical society, founded at Charleston, S.C.; continued until 1912; gave several concerts each year, including St. Cecilia's Day, 22 Nov. The orchestra was composed of "gentlemen performers," supplemented by professional musicians engaged by the season. **Harmonic Society,** New York, gave concert series (1773–74) presenting first French and Italian virtuosi. **Handel Society** (Dartmouth College, 1780), **Harmonic Society** (Fredericksburg, Va., 1784), **Musical Society of Boston** (1785–89) performed excerpts from Handel's works. **Stoughton** (Mass.) **Musical Society** organized by William Billings, probably the oldest singing society still in existence in the U.S.; held first singing contest in U.S. at Dorchester (1790), competing against First Parish of Dorchester. **Uranian Society** established (Phila., 1787–1800) to improve church music.

1763. EARLY MUSIC SCHOOL. James Bremner opened a music school in Philadelphia; subsequently active in city's musical life; pupils reputed to have included **Francis Hopkinson.**

1619–1800. POPULAR MUSIC. Black people's music, 1619–1776. First transported to Virginia as servants and later as slaves, black people from Africa introduced native African dances and songs into the colonies, to which were added elements borrowed from church and white folk music. Utilizing utensils and other materials at hand, they improvised primitive percussion, wind, and string instruments, invented the banjo (named "banjar" by Thomas Jefferson), and showed proficiency in the use of sophisticated European instruments. Notable performers included Sy Gilliat, a slave of Gov. Botetourt, and official fiddler at Williamsburg balls, and London Brigs.

c.1715. MOTHER GOOSE rhymes composed by "Mother Goose," mother-in-law of Thomas Fleet, Boston printer, who came to live with Thomas and her daughter Elizabeth after the birth of their baby, and sang to him. Fleet published the nursery rhymes under the title, *Songs for Nursery or Mother Goose Melodies for Children.*

c.1754–98. PATRIOTIC SONGS. "YANKEE DOODLE," attributed to Dr. Richard Schuckburg, a British army physician, whose original version written during the French and Indian War was a parody of the colonial soldier. It was set to a *Mother Goose* tune called "Lucy Locket Lost Her Pocket." It is mentioned in the first American comic ballad opera libretto, **Andrew Barton's** *The Disappointment, or the Force of Credulity* (Philadelphia, 1767; music by **James Ralph** [d. 1762]). First American printing, as part of an instrumental medley, in *Federal Overture* (1794), arranged by Benjamin Carr (1769–1831) and published by him in Philadelphia and New York (1795). First American edition to use words and music published by G. Willig (1798).

1767. *The Psalms of David,* the 1st book of music printed in the colonies from type (New York).

1768. John Dickinson wrote "American Liberty Song" to the tune of "British Grenadiers."

1775. Dr. Joseph Warren wrote "Free Amerikay" and Thomas Paine composed the ballad "Liberty Tree."

c.1776. "Chester" by **William Billings,** one of the most inspiring patriotic tunes.

c.1793. "The President's March," variously attributed to Philip Roth and Philip Phile.

1798. "Adams and Liberty," words by Robert Treat Paine; "Hail Columbia," words by Joseph Hopkinson, set to tune of "The President's March."

1759–88. SECULAR SONGS. First secular song by a native American, "My Days Have Been So Wondrous Free," music by **Francis Hopkinson** (1737–91), poem by Thomas Parnell. Hopkinson, a Philadelphian and the first native composer, was later a signer of the Declaration of Independence, a member of the Constitutional Convention, the first judge of the Admiralty Court of Pennsylvania, and author of many pamphlets and poems; his *Seven Songs,* 1788.

1781–96. EARLY AMERICAN OPERAS. *The Temple of Minerva,* libretto and music by **Francis Hopkinson,** 1st attempt at grand opera, performed in Philadelphia (11 Dec. 1781) in the presence of George Washington. *Tammany,* by **James Hewitt** (1770–1827), produced at New York under the auspices of the Tammany Society (1794). *The Archers, or the Mountaineers of Switzerland,* libretto by **William Dunlap,** music by **Benjamin Carr** (1768–1831); and *Edwin and Angelina,* libretto by Elihu H. Smith, music by Victor Pelissier (both New York, 1796).

1769–96. FOREIGN COMPOSITIONS IN AMERICA. John Gualdo (Italian immigrant, d. 1771), *Symphony,* Philadelphia, 1769; **Handel:** *Messiah,* first performance in colonies (overture and 16 numbers) at Trinity Church, New York, conducted and arranged by William Tuckey; **Gluck:** overture to *Iphigenie en Aulide,* performed by an orchestra of some 30 instruments, Charleston, S.C., 1796; **Haydn:** *Stabat Mater,* Charleston, S.C., 1796.

1791–94. EARLY SONG AND HAR-

MONY BOOKS. *Harmonia Americana,* by Samuel Holyoke (1791); *The American Harmony,* by Oliver Holden (1792), and Holden's *The Union Harmony* (1793), with first printing of "Coronation" (later the hymn "All Hail the Power of Jesus' Name"); *Rural Harmony,* by Jacob Kimball (1793); *The Continental Harmony,* by **Willam Billings** (1794).

Early National and Antebellum Years, 1800–60

1803–53. INSTRUMENTS. First authentic American **piano** made by Benjamin Grehorne of Milton, Mass. (1803). Firm of Stewart & Chickering, piano manufacturers, established at Boston, 1823. **Jonas Chickering** (1798–1853) patented first successful casting of a full iron piano frame capable of withstanding powerful tension without deflecting pitch. **Wilhelm Knabe** (1803–64) established at Baltimore the firm of Knabe & Co. (1837). Henry Steinway & Sons established by **Henry E. Steinway** (1797–1871), at New York (1853), exhibiting there (1855) a square piano with cross- or over-strung strings, and a full cast-iron frame.

1805. DA PONTE. Lorenzo Da Ponte (1749–1838), Italian poet who wrote the libretti for Mozart's *Don Giovanni* and *The Marriage of Figaro,* arrived in the U.S. (1805); held professorship of Italian literature at Columbia College; was active (1825–26) in establishing Garcia's Opera Co.; and backed the French tenor Montrésor in opening a season in New York with Rossini's *La Cenerentola* (1832). He also promoted the building of the Italian Opera House in New York (1833).

1810–50. MUSICAL PERFORMING GROUPS. Orchestras. Boston Philharmonic Society founded by **Gottlieb Graupner** (1767–1836); credited as the first genuine and regular orchestra in the U.S.; gave its last concert, 1824. Philharmonic Society of New York founded (1842) chiefly through the efforts of Ureli C. Hill, its first president; first concert 7 Dec. Chicago Philharmonic Society, 1850; disbanded c.1854.

1815–56. Choral Societies. Handel and Haydn Society, organized at Boston (1815) under the leadership of Gottlieb Graupner, Thomas Smith Webb, and others. Lowell Mason president and conductor beginning 1827. German Männerchor organized by Philip Wolsifer at Philadelphia (1835); oldest German singing society in the U.S. Chicago Sacred Music Society established 1842. Deutsche Liederkranz, New York, 1847. Milwaukee Musikverein, 1849. *Saengerfest* held at Cincinnati (1849) brought together for the first time the German singing societies of the Midwest. Chicago Männergesang-Verein (1852; disbanded, 1859). Arion Society, a German choral group (New York, 1854; merged, 1918, with the Liederkranz Society). Cecilia Society and Harmonic Society (Cincinnati, 1856).

1837. Harvard Musical Assn. founded by John S. Dwight.

c.1840. "Singing Family" Troupes (the Hutchinsons, Cheneys, Bakers, Harmoneons, and Father Kemp's Old Folks), group performers of popular choral and instrumental music.

1849. Ensembles. Mendelssohn Quintet Club, the first important string chamber music group in the U.S., established at Boston.

1825–60. MUSIC SCHOOLS AND EDUCATION. Musical Fund Society established a music school at Philadelphia (1825); first important institution of its kind in the U.S. Music school of Boston Academy of Music (established by Lowell Mason, 1832) introduced first significant advances in musical education in the U.S. First music school in Chicago, 1834. Lowell Mason introduced (1838) the teaching of music into the Boston public schools. Boston Music School established (1850) by Benjamin F. Baker; dissolved, 1868. Class system of pianoforte instruction begun (1851) by Eben Tourjée at Providence, R.I.

1827–35. MUSIC PUBLISHERS. Carl Fischer (New York, 1827); Oliver Ditson (Boston, 1835).

1800–81. MUSIC PERIODICALS. *American Musical Magazine* (Northampton, Mass., 1800; disc. 1801); *Boston Musical Gazette* (1838; disc. 1846); *Musical World* (N.Y., 1849; disc. 1860); *American Monthly Musical Review* (N.Y., 1850; disc. 1852); *Dwight's Journal of Music* (Boston, 1852; pioneered in musical criticism; disc. 1881).

1809–60* FOREIGN COMPOSITIONS IN AMERICA. Haydn: Haydn societies org. Phila., 1809; Cincinnati, 1819; first complete perf., *Creation*, Boston, 1819. **Handel:** *Messiah*, Univ. of Pa. (1801); 1st complete performance, probably HH (1818); oratorio, *Israel in Egypt*, Seguin Opera Co., N.Y. (1842). **Beethoven:** *1st Symph.*, MFSP (1821); *6th* (Pastoral) and *2nd* Boston (1842); *5th*, PS (1843); *Egmont Overture*, Boston (1844); *9th*, PS (1846); *3d* (*Eroica*) PS (1847); *7th Symph.*, MFSB (1859); *Leonore Overture*, No. 3 (Boston, 1850); *Egmont*, music complete (Boston, 1859). **Mozart:** *Jupiter Symph.*, No. 41, PS (1844); Mozart Society org., Chicago (1847); *G minor Symph.* (No. 40), MFSB (1850); *Requiem*, HH (1857); *E flat maj. Piano Concerto* (Boston, 1859); **Rossini:** *Stabat Mater*, HH (1843). **Mendelssohn:** oratorio, *St. Paul*, N.Y. (1838); oratorio, *Elijah*, HH (1840); *Hebrides Overture*, PS (1844); *Scotch Symph.*, PS (1845); Mendelssohn Festival, Castle Garden, N.Y. (1847); *Mid-*

* *Abbreviations*
HH   Handel and Haydn Society, Boston (1815)
MFSP   Musical Fund Society, Philadelphia (1820)
MFSN   Musical Fund Society, New York (c.1828)
MFSB   Musical Fund Society, Boston (1847)
PS   Philharmonic Society of New York (1842); now New York Philharmonic

summer Night's Dream, Germania Orch. (N.Y., 1848); *Italian Symph.* (Boston, 1851). **Schumann:** *1st Symph.*, MFSB (1841); cantata, *Paradise and the Peri*, Musical Institute, N.Y. (1848); *Symph. in D.*, PS (1857); *Manfred Overture*, PS (1857); *A minor Piano Concerto* (op. 54), PS (1859). **Berlioz:** *King Lear Overture*, PS (1846); *Roman Carnival Overture* (1857). **Donizetti:** *Il Poliuto*, performed as oratorio, HH (1849). **Schubert:** *C maj. Symph.*, PS (1851). **Wagner:** Overture to *Rienzi* played from manuscript by Germania Orch. (Boston, 1853); *Faust Overture* (Boston, 1857); Prelude to *Lohengrin*, PS (1857).

1819–59. FOREIGN OPERA. Rossini: *Barber of Seville* (English, N.Y., 1819; Italian, by Manual Garcia troupe, N.Y., 1825; 6 operas given at Italian Opera House, N.Y., 1833, including *La Gazza Ladra*). **Mozart:** *Marriage of Figaro* (Bishop's English version, N.Y., 1823; in Italian, N.Y., 1858); *Don Giovanni* (N.Y., 1825); *Die Zauberflöte* (Phila., 1832). **Weber:** *Der Freischütz* (English, N.Y., 1825); *Oberon* (Phila., 1827). **Meyerbeer:** *Roberto il Diavolo* (English, N.Y., 1834); New Orleans productions of *Les Huguenots* (1839), *L'Étoile du Nord* (1850), *Il Profeta* (1850). **Bellini:** *La Straniera* (N.Y., 1834); *La Sonnambula* (English, N.Y., 1834); *Norma* (Phila., 1841); *I Puritani* (N.Y., 1844). **Donizetti:** *L'Elisir d'Amore* (N.Y. 1838); *Lucia di Lammermoor* (New Orleans, 1841); *La Favorita* and *The Daughter of the Regiment* (New Orleans, 1843); *Gemma di Vergi* (N.Y., 1843); and 8 others by 1850. **Verdi:** Havana Opera Co. productions of *I Lombardi* and *Ernani* (N.Y., 1847); *Nabucco* (N.Y., 1848); *Attila* (N.Y., 1848); *Macbeth* (N.Y., 1850); *Luisa Miller* (Phila., 1852); *Il Trovatore* (N.Y., 1855); *La Traviata* (N.Y., 1856); *Rigoletto* (New Orleans, 1860). **Wagner:** *Tannhäuser* and *Lohengrin* (N.Y., 1859).

Halévy: New Orleans operatic season, 1858–59, probable first performances of *Jaquarita l'Indienne, La Juive,* and *Reine de Chypre.*

1845. AMERICAN OPERA. *Leonora,* an opera by **William H. Fry** (?1815–64), Phila., the first **grand opera** to be composed by a native American.

1847–52. OPERA HOUSES AND CONCERT HALLS. Astor Place Opera House opened in New York (1847). New York Academy of Music and Boston Music Hall (1852). Academy of Music, Philadelphia (1856).

1835–59. MUSICAL DEBUTS. Charlotte Cushman, actress, made her debut as a singer in *The Marriage of Figaro* (Boston, 1835). **Ole Bull,** Norwegian violinist (N.Y., 1843); **Jenny Lind,** Swedish soprano (Castle Garden, N.Y., 11 Sept. 1850); **Henriette Sontag,** German dramatic soprano (N.Y., 1853); **Louis M. Gottschalk** (1829–69), native-born composer and pianist (N.Y., 1853); **Marietta Alboni,** Italian operatic soprano (U.S. tour, 1853); **Adelina Patti** (in *Lucia,* N.Y., 1859).

1848. REVOLUTIONS OF '48 led to the migration of many musical artists to the U.S. The Germania Orchestra (N.Y., 1848) introduced Wagner's music into the U.S. Counterparts were organized at Boston, Philadelphia, and other cities. Among the composers and instrumentalists of the Germania group who later became well known were **Carl Bergmann** (1821–76), **Carl Zerrahn** (1826–1909), **Theodor Eisfeld** (1816–82), and **Otto Dresel** (1826–90).

1853–58. CONDUCTORS. American debut of the French conductor **Louis Antoine Jullien,** who toured the U.S. with his orchestra (1853–54), conducting 200 concerts, and directing a "Grand Musical Congress" made up of 1,500 instrumentalists and 16 choral societies performing oratorios and symphonies (1854). **Carl Zerrahn** named conductor

of the Handel and Haydn Society at Boston; later (1865–82) conducted the concerts of the Harvard Musical Assn. **Theodore Thomas** (p. 1170), who arrived in the U.S. from Germany in 1845, joined **William Mason** (1829–1908) in organizing a string quartet, which introduced music of Schumann and Brahms into the U.S.; Thomas named conductor of N.Y. Academy of Music (1858).

1814–60. POPULAR SONGS. 1814–43. Patriotic Songs. "Star-Spangled Banner." "The Defence of Fort McHenry," by **Francis Scott Key** (1779–1843), published (1814) in the Baltimore *Patriot.* This poem, based on the author's observation of the British bombardment of Ft. McHenry (13–14 Sept. 1814), was issued in handbill form almost immediately after its composition. On or about 19 Oct. 1814 the title was changed to "The Star-Spangled Banner," which by Act of Congress (1931) was designated as the national anthem. The tune, a familiar one in post-Revolutionary days, is that of "To Anacreon in Heaven," variously credited to the British composers Samuel Arnold and John Stafford Smith. Words of the national hymn "America" written by Rev. Samuel Francis Smith (1808–95); first performed at the Park St. Church, Boston (1831). The tune is that of the English national anthem, "God Save the King." "Columbia, the Gem of the Ocean" (1843) is usually credited to Thomas A. Beckett, but sometimes claimed for David T. Shaw.

1827–60. POPULAR SONGS. "The Minstrel's Return from the War," by John Hill Hewitt (1827). "Jim Crow" (1828) by Thomas Rice, Louisville, Ky., an international hit as well as the source of an unfortunate connotation implying racial segregation. "The Old Oaken Bucket" (1834), words by Samuel Woodworth, who wrote the poem in 1818. "Zip Coon" (c.1834, later known as "Turkey in the Straw"). "Woodman,

Spare That Tree" (1837), words by George P. Morris, music by Henry Russell. "Tippecanoe and Tyler, Too" (1840), political campaign song used by the Whig party; words by Alexander C. Ross to the tune of "Little Pigs." "We Won't Go Home Till Morning" (1842), words by William Clifton; based on the old French melody "Malbrouck." "Old Dan Tucker" (1843), generally credited to **Daniel D. Emmett** (1815–1904), also thought to be the composer of "The Blue Tail Fly" (also called "Jim Crack Corn," 1846). By **Stephen C. Foster** (p. 1032): "Oh! Susanna" (1848); "Ben Bolt" (1848), words by Thomas Dunn English; "De Camptown Races" (1850); "Old Folks at Home" (1851, often called "Swanee River"); "Massa's in de Cold, Cold Ground" (1852). Original version of "Frankie and Johnny" (1850); later reputedly sung at siege of Vicksburg (1863); more than 100 different versions uncovered, chiefly after 1899. "My Old Kentucky Home" (1853) by Foster. "Listen to the Mocking Bird" (1855), music by Septimus Winner (1826–1902). "Darling Nelly Gray" (1856) by Benjamin Russel Hanby. "Jingle Bells" (1857) by J. S. Pierpont. "Dixie's Land" (written 1859, commonly called "Dixie") by Daniel D. Emmett; first performed by Bryant's Minstrels (N.Y., 1859); played at the inauguration of Jefferson Davis, Montgomery, Ala., 18 Feb. 1861, it quickly became the symbol of the Confederacy. "Old Black Joe" (1860) by Foster.

Civil War and Postbellum Years, 1861–1900

1861–65. CIVIL WAR SONGS. "John Brown's Body," most widely sung Federal song, has been credited to Thomas B. Bishop, the musical adaptation of a Negro Carolina low-country melody to James E. Greenleaf. A ribald parody, beginning "Hang Jeff Davis on a sour apple tree," appeared in 1865. "Battle Hymn of the Republic," written by **Julia Ward Howe** (1819–1910) to the tune of "John Brown's Body" (pub. Feb. 1862). Next to Emmett's "Dixie" (1859), the most popular Southern marching song was "The Bonnie Blue Flag" (1862), words by Mrs. Annie Chambers-Ketchum, music by Henry McCarthy. "Maryland, My Maryland" (1861), by James Ryder Randall, sung to German folksong "O Tannenbaum." "We Are Coming, Father Abraham" (1862), by James Sloan Gibbons, abolitionist writer in answer to a plea to the states by Lincoln to raise "300,000 more" soldiers; musical settings by Orlando Emerson (1820–1915) and Stephen Foster. Walter Kittredge's "Tenting Tonight" (1862). "When Johnny Comes Marching Home" (1863), by **Patrick Sarsfield Gilmore** (1829–92). "Tramp, Tramp, Tramp" (1864), by George Root. "Marching Through Georgia" (1865), by **Henry Clay Work** (1832–84), who also wrote "Father, Dear Father, Come Home with Me Now."

1861–1900.* **FOREIGN COMPOSITIONS IN AMERICA. Verdi:** *Un Ballo in Maschera* (N.Y., 1861); *La Forza Del Destino* (1865); *Aïda* (1873); *Requiem Mass*, Italian Opera Co. (N.Y., 1875); *Don Carlo*, Havana Opera Co. (1877); *Otello*, Campanini, conduct. (N.Y., 1888); *Falstaff*, MO (1895). **C. P. E. Bach:** *Symph. in D maj.* (N.Y., 1862); *Symph. in C* (N.Y., 1866); **J. S. Bach:** *Toccata in F* and *Passacaglia*, Theo. Thomas (N.Y., 1865); *Suite in D*, PS (1869); *St. Matthew Passion*, in part, HH (1874), complete (1879); *Christmas Oratorio*, pts. 1 & 2, HH, with

* *Abbreviations*
BS   Boston Symphony Orchestra (1881)
CO   Chicago Opera Assn. (1910)
HH   Handel and Haydn Society, Boston (1815)
MO   Metropolitan Opera, New York (1883)
PH   Philadelphia Orchestra (1900)
PS   Philharmonic Society of New York (1842); now New York Philharmonic
SS   Symphony Society of New York (1878)

Emma Thursby (1877); *Mass in B min.*, Bach Festival, Bethlehem, Pa. (1900). **Beethoven:** *2nd Piano Concerto*, Brooklyn Philharmonic Society (1865); *Choral Fantasia* (1866); *Prometheus music*, Theo. Thomas (1867); *Grand Quartet* (op. 131), scored for full orchestra by Carl M. Berghaus, BS (1884). **Tchaikovsky:** frequent performances beginning with *1st Piano Concerto*, Hans von Bülow, soloist (Boston, 1875); *Romeo and Juliet Overture*, PS (1876). First complete performance of *Violin Concerto*, Maude Powell (N.Y., 1889); *4th Symph.*, SS (1890); *Nutcracker Suite*, Chicago Symphony Orchestra (1892); *1812 Overture*, Theo. Thomas (Chicago, 1893). **Wagner:** *Flying Dutchman music*, Theo. Thomas (N.Y., 1862); prelude to *Tristan*, PS (1866); "Ride of the Valkyries," Theo. Thomas (N.Y., 1872); "Wotan's Farewell" and "Magic Fire Scene" from *Die Walküre*, Thomas (Phila., 1865); "Centennial March," Centennial Exposition, Thomas (Phila., 11 May 1876); "Good Friday Spell" from *Parsifal*, SS (1883). *Die Meistersinger*, MO (1886); *Tristan*, MO (1886); *Der Ring des Nibelungen*, MO (1888). **Brahms:** *German Requiem*, N.Y. Oratorio Society (1877); *1st Symph.*, Damrosch and Thomas (1877); *2d*, Thomas (1878); *3d* (BS, 1884); *4th* (BS, 1886); *Academic Festival Overture*, Thomas (Boston, 1881); *2nd Piano Concerto*, PS, Rafael Joseffy soloist (1882); *Violin Concerto* (BS, 1889). **Gounod:** *Faust* (Phila. and N.Y., 1863). **Bizet:** *Carmen* (N.Y., 1878). **Johann Strauss:** *Die Fledermaus* (N.Y., 1885). **Leoncavallo:** *I Pagliacci* (N.Y., 1894). **Humperdinck,** *Hansel and Gretel* (English, N.Y., 1895). **Richard Strauss:** *F min. Symph.*, Thomas (N.Y., 1884); tone poem, *Don Juan*, BS, A. Nikisch (1891); *Tod und Verklärung*, PS, Thomas (1892); *Ein Heldenleben*, Chicago Symphony (1900). **Dvořák:** *Carnival* and *Otello* overtures at concert honoring composer's first U.S. ap-

pearance, National Conservatory of Music (N.Y., 1892); *New World Symph.*, PS (1893); *Concerto for Violin*, SS (1894). **Schubert:** Overture to *Fierabras*, Harvard Music Assn. (Boston, 1866); extracts from *Rosamunde*, Theo. Thomas (N.Y., 1867); *Unfinished Symph.*, Theo. Thomas (1867); *Octet for Strings; C maj. Symph.*, Theo. Thomas (N.Y., 1875). **Berlioz:** *Symphonie Fantastique*, N.Y. (1866); *Damnation of Faust*, N.Y. Symph. (1880). **Franck:** *D min. Symph.*, BS (1899). **Puccini:** *Manon Lescaut* (Phila., 1894); *La Bohème*, Royal Italian Opera (San Francisco, 1898).

1861–1905. PERFORMANCES OF AMERICAN COMPOSITIONS. John Knowles Paine (1839–1906); *Oratorio* (Portland, Me., 1873); *1st Symph.*, Theo. Thomas (Boston, 1876); *Spring Symph.* (Cambridge, Mass., 1880); symphonic poem, *An Island Fantasy*, BS (1889). **George W. Chadwick** (1854–1931): Overture to *Rip Van Winkle* (Boston, 1879); royalty of $13 by BS for performance of *2nd Symph.* (1886) established a precedent; *3rd Symph.*, BS (1894); *Judith*, choral work (Worcester, 1901); *Cleopatra*, symphonic poem, Chicago Orch. (1905). **George F. Bristow** (1825–98): *Arcadian Symph.*, PS (1874). **Arthur Foote** (1853–1937): Overture *In the Mountains*, BS (1887); *Suite for Strings* (1889). **Edward A. MacDowell** (p. 1093); *1st Piano Concerto* Theo. Thomas (N.Y., 1889); symphonic poem, *Lancelot and Elaine*, BS (1890); *Suite in A min.*, Worcester Festival (1891); *Indian Suite*, BS (N.Y., 1896). **Dudley Buck** (1839–1909): prize symphonic cantata, *Golden Legend*, Cincinnati Festival (1880); *Romance for 4 Horns and Orch.* (N.Y., 1891); *Star-Spangled Banner Overture* (N.Y., 1891). **Victor Herbert** (1859–1924): dramatic cantata, *The Captive*, Worcester Festival (1891); also composer of operas and numerous comic operas. **Charles M. T.**

Loeffler (1861–1935): *Concerto Fantastique*, BS (1894); *La Mort de Tintagiles* (1898). **Amy M. Beach** (Mrs. H. H. A.; 1867–1944): *Gallic Symph.*, BS (1896).

1862–1900. DEBUTS OF MUSICAL ARTISTS. Teresa Carreño, Venezuelan pianist (N.Y., 1862); **Carlotta Patti** in *La Sonnambula* (N.Y., 1862); **Christine Nilsson** (N.Y., 1870); **Anton Rubinstein,** pianist, and **Henri Wieniawski,** violinist (N.Y., 1872); **Hans von Bülow,** pianist (Boston, 1875); **Marcella Sembrich** as Lucia in *Lucia di Lammermoor,* MO (1883); gave violin, piano, and vocal concert 21 Apr. 1884; **Lillian Norton (Nordica)** as Margaret in *Faust* (N.Y., 1883); **Lilli Lehmann,** as Carmen in *Carmen,* MO (1885); **Maude Powell,** American violinist (Orange, N.J., 1885); **Josef Hofmann,** pianist (N.Y., 1887); **Francesco Tamagno** as Arnold in *William Tell,* MO (1889); **Adelina Patti** as Juliet in *Romeo and Juliet,* MO (1889); **Jean de Reszke** (tenor) as Lohengrin and **Edouard de Reszke** (bass) as King Henry in *Lohengrin,* MO (1891); **Emma Calvé** as Santuzza in *Cavalleria Rusticana,* MO (1893); **Nellie Melba** as Lucia in *Lucia di Lammermoor,* MO (1893); **Ernestine Schumann-Heink** as Ortrud in *Lohengrin* (Chicago, 1898); **Antonio Scotti** as Nevers in *Les Huguenots,* MO (1898); **Louise Homer** as Amneris in *Aïda,* MO (1900); **Ossip Gabrilowitsch,** pianist (N.Y., 1900).

1861–85. MUSIC PUBLISHERS. Beer and Schirmer took over C. Breusing; after 1866, G. Schirmer; Thomas B. Harms (N.Y., 1881), after 1922, Harms, Inc.; Theo. Presser (Phila., 1884); M. Witmark & Sons (N.Y., 1885).

1865–1900.   CONSERVATORIES. Oberlin Conservatory (1865); Boston Conservatory, New England Conservatory, Cincinnati Conservatory, Chicago Academy of Music (later Chicago Musical College)—all 1867; Illinois Conservatory of Music, Jacksonville (1871);

Northwestern Univ. (1873); Cincinnati College of Music, Theo. Thomas dir. (1878); Chicago Conservatory (1884); American Institute of Applied Music, Kate Chittenden (N.Y., 1885); American Conservatory of Music, J. J. Haffstaedt (1886).

1865–92. OPERA COMPANIES. Performance of 24 operas in San Francisco (1865); Crosby Opera House (Chicago, 1865); French *opéra bouffe* (N.Y., 1867), Offenbach's *La Grande Duchesse de Gérolstein* ran 180 nights); 6 nights of Russian opera given at Théâtre Française (N.Y., 1869); Col. Henry Mapleson's first operatic tour of U.S. (1878–79); opening of **Metropolitan Opera House** (23 Oct. 1883; destroyed by fire, 27 Aug. 1892; new opera house opened 1893); American Opera Co. (N.Y., 1886–87), Theo. Thomas conduct.; Tivoli Opera House (San Francisco, 1877); grand opera given in U.S. by Henry E. Abbey Co. (1883–84), with cast including Nilsson and Sembrich; Abbey and Schoeffel (1890), with cast including Patti, Nordica, Tamagno (1890). **Oscar Hammerstein** (1847–1919) opened first Manhattan Opera House (1892).

1862–95.   EXPANSION OF THE SYMPHONY ORCHESTRA. First concert by **Theodore Thomas'** own orchestra (N.Y., 1862); summer night concerts at Terrace Gardens, N.Y., begun by Thomas (1866); first of 22 annual tours by Thomas orchestra (1869). Germania Orch. (Pittsburgh, 1873). Symphony Society of N.Y., **Leopold Damrosch** (1832–85), conductor (1878); **Walter Damrosch** (1862–1950) succeeding his father (1885); merged with the N.Y. Philharmonic, 1928. Boston Symphony Orch., est. (1881) by Henry L. Higginson, with Georg Henschel conducting first concert; Chicago Symphony Orch. under Hans Balatka (1886), Frederick Stock, conduct., beg. 1905; Pittsburgh Symphony under Frederick Archer

(1893), Victor. Herbert conduct., 1898; Cincinnati Orchestra Assn., Frank von der Stucken, conduct. (1895).

1865–1900. FESTIVALS. Peabody concerts (Baltimore, Md., 1865); World Peace Jubilee, org. Boston (1869) by Patrick S. Gilmore, employed chorus of 10,000 and orchestra of 1,000 pieces; imported Johann Strauss to conduct *Blue Danube Waltz.* First annual Cincinnati Festival, dir. Theo. Thomas (1873); Bach *B min. Mass,* Bach choir, Bethlehem, Pa., as part of Bach Festival begun 1900.

1872–99. MUSICAL SOCIETIES. Mendelssohn Society (N.Y., 1863–72), Cecilia Society (Boston, 1874), Music Teachers National Assn. (1876). Society of American Musicians and Composers (1899).

The Twentieth Century

1900–45. POPULAR MUSICAL TRENDS. Ragtime, with catchy melodies, syncopated rhythm, played "hot," originated before the turn of the century with Scott Joplin's (?1868–1917) "Maple Leaf Rag" (c.1897), and was developed by **J. Rosamund Johnson** and his brother **James Weldon Johnson.** "Under the Bamboo Tree" (1902) was the most significant ragtime song before 1910. Ragtime attained its acme of popularity with **Irving Berlin's** "Alexander's Ragtime Band" (1911). **Blues,** sad words set to a special pattern (12 bars), using "blue" notes (off pitch, usually 3d and 7th notes), best exemplified by **W. C. Handy's** (1873–1958) "St. Louis Blues" (1914). **Jazz,** innovative dance music style, with varied instruments, individual solos, and syncopated ragtime melodies. Dixie Jass [*sic*] Band of New Orleans opened at Reisenweber's Cabaret, Chicago (26 Jan. 1917); jazz band reported in New York by *Variety* (2 Feb. 1917). **Paul Whiteman's** (1891–1968) concert

at Aeolian Hall, New York (1924), to bring artistic respectability to jazz, introduced **George Gershwin's** (p. 1039) *Rhapsody in Blue.* **Swing,** using large bands and "planned out" music, was the rage of the 1930s, exemplified by **Louis Armstrong** (1900–71), **Duke Ellington** (p. 1023), and **Count Basie,** with **Benny Goodman** (1909–   ), "King of Swing," giving a sensational concert at Carnegie Hall (1938). **Country Music,** commercial popular music favored in the hinterlands, has a remote origin. Accompanied in early times by dulcimer, fiddle, guitar, or banjo, country music in more recent times has utilized larger instrumental groups. Its great vogue dates from 1926, when "Grand Ole Opry," the leading country music program, began to broadcast from Nashville, Tenn., which still remains the center of the movement. Its leading exponents have been Johnny Cash (1932–   ) and Elvis Presley (1935–77).

1900–46°. NON-OPERATIC WORKS BY FOREIGN COMPOSERS. Bach: *Brandenburg Concerto,* F maj. (1901); *1st Violin Concerto,* BS (1902); *2d,* BS (1904). **Mahler:** *4th Symph.,* SS (1903); *5th Symph.* (*Giant*), Cincinnati Symph. (1905); *1st Symph.,* PS (1909); *8th Symph.,* PH with more than 1,000 performers (1916). **Rachmaninoff:** *2nd Symph.,* composer conduct., Russian Symph. Orch. (N.Y., 1909); *2nd Piano Concerto,* composer soloist, SS (1909); *Isle of the Dead* (tone poem), Chicago Symph. (1909). **Sibelius:** *2nd Symph.,* BS, 1904; *1st,* BS, 1907; *Finlandia,* BS, 1908; *Swan of Tuonela,* BS, 1911. On visit to the U.S. he conducted *Pohjala's Daughter, King Christian II, Swan of Tuonela,* Litchfield, Conn., Choral Union (1914). **Stravinsky** (p. 1161): *Feuerwerk,* Russian Symph. Orch., N.Y. (1910); BS (1914); Orch. suite from *Petrouchka,* BS (1920); *Le Sacre du Printemps,* PH

° For abbreviations, see footnote, p. 921.

(1922); *Symph. of Psalms* for orch. and chorus, BS (1930). **Schoenberg:** *5 Pieces for Orch.,* BS (1914); *Verklärte Nacht,* sextet, BS (1921). **Prokofieff:** *Concerto for Violin and Orch.,* BS (1924); *Concerto No. 3,* piano and orch., BS (1926); *Classical Symph.,* BS (1927); *Concerto No. 2,* piano and orch., BS (1930). **Ravel:** *Rhapsodie Espagnole,* BS (1914); *Daphnis et Chloë,* 1st suite, BS (1918); 2d suite, BS (1917); *Bolero,* Toscanini, PS (1929). **Hindemith:** *Nusch-Nuschi Dances,* PH (1924–25); *Concerto for Orch.,* BS (1926); *Konzertmusik for String and Brass Instruments,* BS (1931). **Milhaud:** *2d Orch. Suite,* BS (1921): *Le Carnaval d'Aix,* BS (1926). **Vaughan Williams:** *London Symph.,* N.Y. Symph. (1920); *Fantasia on a Theme by Thos. Tallis,* N.Y. Symph. (1922); *Norfolk Rhapsody No. 1,* BS (1926). **Shostakovich:** *1st Symph.,* BS (1928); *7th,* Toscanini, NBC Orch. (1942); *8th,* PS (1944); *9th* (Tanglewood, 1946).

1900–74. CONTINUED EXPANSION OF THE SYMPHONY ORCHESTRA. Leopold Stokowski (1887–1977) named conductor of Cincinnati Orchestra Assn. (1909); Fritz Reiner replaced (1922) Eugène Ysaye as conduct.; Philadelphia Orch., Fritz Scheel, conduct. (1900), succeeded by Stokowski (1914–36); St. Paul Symph., Walter Rothwell conduct. (1905); St. Louis (1907), Max Zach conduct.; Rudolph Ganz, 1921–27; Seattle, Michael Kegrizi conduct. (1908), Henry K. Hadley (1909); Kansas City, Mo., Carl Busch (1911); San Francisco, Henry K. Hadley (1911), reorg. under Alfred Hertz (1915); Baltimore, Gustav Strube (1915); New Orleans (1917); Detroit, Gabrilowitsch (1917); Cleveland, Nikolai Sokoloff (1918). Decade 1921–30 marked by **phenomenal increase** in professional orchestras, with notable conductors engaged: **Pierre Monteux** (1875–1964) to conduct Boston (1920), succeeded (1924) by **Serge Koussevitsky**

(1874–1951); **Willem Mengelberg** from Amsterdam as guest conductor of Bodanzky's National Symphony Orch. (1921), succeeding Josef Stransky when the N.Y. Philharmonic merged with Bodanzky's Symphony (1922); **Wilhelm Furtwängler** of Leipzig Gewandhaus and Berlin Philharmonic to conduct N.Y. Philharmonic (1925), with **Arturo Toscanini** (1867–1957) made regular conductor (1928–36), inaugurating the orchestra's most successful decade. Toscanini was organizer and conductor of National Broadcasting Co. (NBC) Symphony Orch., beg. 1937. **Eugene Ormandy** began his tenure as conductor and music director of the Philadelphia Orch. (1936–80). **Leonard Bernstein** (p. 985), who replaced (14 Nov. 1943) **Bruno Walter** as guest conductor of the N.Y. Philharmonic upon the latter's illness, succeeded Stokowski as conductor of the New York City Symphony (1945–48); became co-conductor with **Dimitri Mitropoulos,** 1957–58; music director, 1958–59; succeeded by **Pierre Boulez,** 1971. **Erich Leinsdorf,** music director, Boston (1962–69), succeeded by William Steinberg (1969–72); Seiji Ozawa (1972). **Georg Solti** named music director, Chicago (1968) and **Lorin Maazel,** Cleveland (1971) after the death of **George Szell. Henry Lewis,** first black to be named music director of a major orchestra, appointed to New Jersey Symphony, and in 1970 Dean Dixon became the first black to conduct New York Philharmonic.

1900–73. FESTIVALS. MacDowell Festival est. Peterborough, N.H. (1910). Music festival at Pittsfield, Mass., est. by Elizabeth Sprague Coolidge (1918), marking the beginning of her active participation in chamber music; Elizabeth Sprague Coolidge Foundation for sponsoring festivals of music at the Library of Congress est. 1925; first Festival of Chamber Music, 28 Oct. First Festival of

Contemporary American Music, Yaddo, Saratoga Springs, N.Y. (1932); first annual summer Berkshire Music Festival, Lenox (Tanglewood), Mass. (1934); Koussevitzky Music Foundation est. by Serge Koussevitzky (1942); first annual Festival of Contemporary American Music, sponsored by Alice M. Ditson Fund, Columbia Univ. (1945). American Jazz Festival began (1954) annual summer concerts at Newport, R.I. Pablo Casals moved to Puerto Rico (1956) and directed annual festivals at San Juan. During the 1950s other festivals, some long established, flourished, including Berkshire (Tanglewood, Mass.); Aspen, Colo.; Blossom (Cuyahoga Falls, Ohio); Caramoor (Katonah, N.Y.); Empire State (Ellenville, N.Y.); Eastman School (Rochester, N.Y.); Hollywood Bowl (Los Angeles, Calif.); Lewisohn Stadium Concerts (N.Y.C.); Marlboro, Vt.; Robin Hood Dell Concerts (Phila.); Ravinia Park (Chicago); Saratoga, N.Y.; Cincinnati Zoo; Central City, Colo. Woodstock rock festival (Bethel, N.Y.) drew more than 400,000 (1969); Newport Jazz Festival moved to New York City (1972); Watkins Glen, N.Y., festival (1973), attendance 600,000, largest on record.

1903–45. DEBUTS OF MUSICAL ARTISTS IN THE U.S. [*] Enrico Caruso as the Duke in *Rigoletto* (1903); **Geraldine Farrar** as Juliette in *Romeo et Juliette* (1906); **Feodor Chaliapin** as Mefistofele in *Mefistofele* (1907); **Emmy Destinn** as Aïda, Toscanini conduct. (1908); **Pasquale Amato** as Germont in *La Traviata* (1908); **Leo Slezak** as Otello in *Otello* (1909); **Alma Gluck** as Sophie in *Werther* (1909); **Lucrezia Bori** as Manon in *Manon Lescaut* (1910); **Luisa Tetrazzini** as Lucia in *Lucia di Lammermoor* (1911); **Frieda Hempel** as Marguerite in *Les Huguenots* (1912); **Giovanni Mar-**

[*] Metropolitan Opera for operatic performers unless otherwise indicated.

tinelli as Cavaradossi in *Tosca* (1913); **Amelita Galli-Curci** as Gilda in *Rigoletto,* Chicago Opera (1916); **Jascha Heifetz,** violinist (N.Y., 1917); **Rosa Ponselle** as Leonora in *La Forza del Destino* (1918); **Beniamino Gigli** as Faust in *Mefistofele* (1920). Last appearance of **Caruso,** *La Juive* (24 Dec. 1920; d. Naples, 2 Aug. 1921); farewell appearance of **Farrar** in *Zaza* (22 Apr. 1923). **Lawrence Tibbett** as Lovitsky in *Boris Godunov* (1923); **Yehudi Menuhin,** violinist, San Francisco Orch. (1923); PS (1926); **Lauritz Melchior** as Tannhauser in *Tannhäuser* (1926); **Ezio Pinza** as Pontifex in *La Vestale* (1926); **Vladimir Horowitz,** pianist (PS, 1928); **Lotte Lehmann** as Sieglinde in *Die Walküre* (1934); **Kirsten Flagstad** as Sieglinde in *Die Walküre* (1935); **Jussi Bjoerling** as Rodolfo in *La Bohème* (1938); **Leonard Warren** as Paolo in *Simon Boccanegra* (1939); **Jan Peerce** as Alfredo in *La Traviata* (1941); **Richard Tucker** as Enzo in *La Gioconda* (1945); **Robert Merrill** as Germont in *La Traviata* (1945).

1903–59. FOREIGN OPERAS IN AMERICA. Wagner: *Parsifal,* 1st performance in German outside of Bayreuth, Alfred Hertz, conduct., MO (1903). **Richard Strauss:** *Salome,* MO (1907), aroused storm of protest; barred for 27 years from MO repertory; banned in Boston (1909); *Elektra,* MO (1910); *Der Rosenkavalier,* MO (1913). **Puccini:** *Tosca,* MO (1901); *Madame Butterfly,* English, Washington, D.C. (1908); world premiere of *Il Tabarro, Gianni Schicchi,* and *Suor Angelica,* MO (Farrar, Easton, De Luca, 1918); *Turandot,* MO (1926). **Debussy:** *Pelléas et Mélisande,* Manhattan Opera (Mary Garden, 1908); *L'Enfant Prodigue,* Boston (1910). **Tchaikovsky:** *Eugene Onegin* in concert form, SS (1908); operatic version, MO (1910). **Mussorgsky:** *Boris Godunov,* MO (Anna Case, Louise Homer, 1913). **Prokofiev:**

Love for Three Oranges, Chicago Opera Assn. (1921). **Berg:** *Wozzek,* Philadelphia Grand Opera Co. (1931). **Gian-Carlo Menotti:** *Amelia Goes to the Ball,* Philadelphia (1937); MO (1938); *The Old Maid* and *The Thief* broadcast over NBC (1939), first stage performance, Philadelphia Opera (1941); *The Medium* and *The Telephone,* N.Y. (1947); *The Consul,* N.Y. (1950); *Amahl and the Night Visitors,* TV (1950). **Benjamin Britten:** *Peter Grimes,* Tanglewood (1946); *Billy Budd,* TV (1952).

1896–1952. OPERA BY AMERICAN COMPOSERS. Walter Damrosch: *Scarlet Letter,* Boston (1896); *Cyrano de Bergerac,* MO (1913); **Frederick Converse:** *Pipe of Desire,* first American opera to be performed MO, with entirely American cast (1910); **Victor Herbert:** *Natoma* (Phila., 1911), *Madeleine,* MO (1914); **Horatio T. Parker:** *Mona,* MO (1912, awarded $10,000 prize); **Reginald de Koven:** *Rip Van Winkle,* Chicago Opera Assn. (1920); **Deems Taylor:** *King's Henchman,* libretto by Edna St. Vincent Millay, MO (1927), *Peter Ibbetson,* MO (1931); **Howard Hanson:** *Merrymount,* MO (1934); **George Gershwin:** *Porgy and Bess,* setting of DuBose Heyward play, *Porgy,* with an all-Negro cast (Boston, 1935); **Douglas Moore:** *Devil and Daniel Webster* (1939), *Giants in the Earth* (N.Y., 1951); **Virgil Thomson:** *Four Saints in Three Acts,* based on text by Gertrude Stein, with Negro cast (Hartford, Conn., 1934), *The Mother of Us All* (1947); **Bernard Rogers:** *The Warrior* (book by Norman Corwin), awarded $1,500 Ditson prize (1946); MO (1947); **Leonard Bernstein:** *Trouble in Tahiti* (Tanglewood and TV, 1952).

1905–40. CONSERVATORIES. Institute of Musical Art (1905), Frank Damrosch, financed by a $500,000 bequest; Eastman School of Music (1918), est. by George Eastman as an affiliate of Univ. of Rochester (Howard Hanson, dir., 1924–64). Juilliard Graduate School est. (1924) with an endowment of $15 million, Ernest Hutcheson, dean. In 1926 the Institute of Musical Art became the preparatory school of the Juilliard. Curtis Institute of Music (Phila., 1924) by an endowment of $12,500,000 from Mrs. Mary Louise Curtis Bok (Josef Hofmann, dir., 1927). Berkshire Music Center org. at Tanglewood (1940) by Koussevitzky.

1906–74. OPERA COMPANIES. Second and better-known **Manhattan Opera House** opened by **Oscar Hammerstein,** 1906, with such artists as Melba, Nordica, Tetrazzini, and Garden, to become a serious rival of the Metropolitan; sold out to Metropolitan (1910). **Giulio Gatti-Casazza** (1869–1940) appointed manager of Metropolitan (1908). Boston Opera House (1909). Chicago Opera Co. (1910), Andreas Dippel, dir. Mary Garden (1874–1967) succeeded (1919) Campanini as impresario of the Chicago Opera, to become the first woman impresario; in turn succeeded (1923) by Giorgio Polacco. Edward Johnson, tenor, became manager MO (1935), and Rudolf Bing (1950). Schuyler Chapin named (1972) to succeed Goeran Gentele after latter's death in auto accident; Rafael Kubelik named music director; resigned (1974). New York City Center Opera Co. founded 1944; Julius Rudel named managing director (1957).

1907–52. PIONEER RADIO AND TV MUSICAL PERFORMANCES. Lee De Forest (p. 1011) transmitted (5 Mar. 1907) Rossini's *William Tell* overture by wireless from the Telharmonic Hall, N.Y., to the Brooklyn Navy Yard, the first broadcast of a musical composition. First broadcast from the stage of the Metropolitan (20 Jan. 1910), when portions of *Cavalleria Rusticana* and *Pagliacci,* both with Caruso, were picked up by radio amateurs. First major orchestral broadcast, BS over NBC (1926). First regular series of opera broadcasts from stage of Chicago Civic Opera (1927). In the same year concerts broadcast from BS and PS. Regular Sunday broadcasts inaugurated by PS (1929). First broadcast of a full opera from MO, *Hänsel and Gretel* (25 Dec. 1931). First opera written expressly for radio, *The Willow Tree*, by Charles W. Cadman, broadcast, NBC (1931); for television, Gian-Carlo Menotti's *Amahl and the Night Visitors*, NBC (Christmas eve, 1951; again 1952). First telecast of a major symphony concert, Ormandy, PH (20 Mar. 1948); Toscanini, NBC Orch., 1 hour later. Texaco sponsorship of MO broadcasts began with *Le Nozze di Figaro* (7 Dec. 1940). By conclusion of 35th season (19 Apr. 1975), 698 operas had been broadcast. **Milton Cross** (1897–1975) was announcer for over 34 years.

1913–41. MUSICAL SOCIETIES. Friends of Music Society (N.Y.), first concert 7 Dec. 1913; produced Schoenberg, Bloch, and Bach; disc. after 1931. Organization (1914) of American Society of Composers, Authors, and Publishers (ASCAP) by Victor Herbert, **John Philip Sousa**, Witmark, and others to protect musical copyright interests. Organization (1923) of League of Composers to promote contemporary compositions. New Friends of Music founded (N.Y., 1936), "to give the best in the literature of chamber music and lieder." Founding of the American Composers' Alliance (1938). ASCAP, after a struggle with radio networks and rival organization, Broadcast Music, Inc., over royalties, reached settlement (1941).

1935. FEDERAL MUSIC PROJECT of the WPA established to relieve unemployment among musicians, under direction of Nikolai Sokoloff; 1935–39, $50 million expended, 225,000 performances financed, 700 projects launched, 15,000 musicians employed. Among its most significant achievements was the estab-

lishment (1935) of the Composers' Forum-Laboratory devoted to the works of living American composers.

1919–49. PERFORMANCES OF AMERICAN COMPOSITIONS. Charles T. Griffes (1884–1920), *Pleasure Dome of Kubla Khan*, BS (1919); *Three Songs*, soprano and orch., PH (1919); *Clouds* and *White Peacock*, BS (1922). **Henry K. Hadley** (1871–1937): symph., *The Four Seasons* (Chicago, 1902); *The Culprit Fay* (Grand Rapids, Mich., 1909), *5th Symph.* (1949). **John Alden Carpenter** (1876–1951): orchestral suite, *Adventures in a Perambulator*, Chicago Symph. (1915); *Concertino* (1916). **Ernest Bloch** (1880–1959); came to U.S. 1917; naturalized, 1924): *Israel Symph.* and *Schelomo*, Society of Friends of Music (N.Y., 1916); *Three Hebrew Poems*, BS (1917); *Symph. in C sharp min.*, PS (1918); *Piano Quartet*, inaugural concert, League of Composers (N.Y., 1923); *America*, epic rhapsody, PS (1928). **George Gershwin** (p. 1039): *An American in Paris*, symphonic poem (N.Y., 1928). **Aaron Copland** (1900–   ): *1st Symph.*, SS (1925); *Concerto for Piano and Orch.*, BS (1927); *Symphonic Ode*, BS (1932); ballet, *Billy the Kid* (1938); *Appalachian Spring* (1945), *3rd Symph.*, BS (1946). **Douglas Moore** (1893–1969): *2nd Symph.*, Paris Radio Orch. (1946). **Charles Ives** (p. 1067): *3rd Symph.*, (1946). **Frederick Jacobi** (1891–1952): *Symph. in C*, San Francisco Symph. (1948). **Walter Piston** (1894–1976): *2nd Symph.* (1943), *3rd Symph.*, BS (1948). **Roger Sessions** (1896–   ): *1st Symph.*, BS (1927), *2nd Symph.*, PS (1951). **William Schuman** (1910–   ): *1st Symph.* (1936), *2nd Symph.* (1937), *3rd Symph.* (1938), *Symph. for Strings*, BS (1947). **Howard Hanson** (1896–1981): *Nordic Symph.* (1924), *4th Symph.* (*Requiem*) (1943), *Piano Concerto*, BS (1948). **Samuel Barber** (1910–81): *Adagio for Strings* and *Essay for Orch.*, NBC Orch., Toscanini (1938), *Symph. in One Movement* (Rome, 1936), *Violin Concerto* (1940), *2nd Essay for Orch.*, PS (1942), *2nd Symph.*, BS (1944), *Capricorn Concerto* (1944), *Concerto for Violoncello and Orch.*, BS (1946). **Virgil Thomson** (1896–   ): *Suite for Orch.*, PH (1948); **Lukas Foss** (1922–   ): *Song of Songs,* BS (1947), *Recordare,* orch. threnody, BS (1948). **David Diamond** (1915–   ): *2nd Symph.*, BS (1944), *Rounds for Orch.* (1944). **Roy Harris** (1898–1979): *3rd Symph.*, BS (1939), *6th Symph.*, BS (1944). **Leonard Bernstein** (p. 985): *Jeremiah Symph.*, PS (1944); symph., *The Age of Anxiety,* awarded $1,000 BS prize (1949). **William Grant Still** (1895–1978): *Afro-American Symph.* (1931), *Symph. in G min.* (1937). **Marc Blitzstein** (1905–64): *Airborne Symph.* (1946).

1945–74. POPULAR MUSICAL TRENDS. Bop, chamber jazz using thrumming "bop" sound, took hold in the 1940s, with such exemplars as **Charles "Bird" Parker** (1920–55), and **"Dizzy" Gillespie** (1917–   ). **Cool** marked the reaction to Bop and utilized French horns, trumpet, trombone, and tuba in dance bands, introduced (1948) by Miles Davis (1927–   ) with a 9-piece band. **Hard Bop,** which came out of folk music, using more traditional jazz forms, and **Funky,** more primitive and earthy, combining "blues" and "hot gospel," were in turn the reaction to Cool. An outstanding exponent of Funky was the black folk singer **Mahalia Jackson** (1911–72). Transforming "pop" music was **Rock 'n' Roll,** combining black beat and white sentiment, producing a great volume of sound. Among its most successful proponents were Fats Domino, Ray Charles, The Platters, Bo Diddley, and Bill Haley. The tremendously popular British group "The Beatles" made its U.S. debut (1964) using electrified instruments. Among the most popular figures in folk

music in the early 1960s were Pete Seeger, The Kingston Trio, Joan Baez, and Peter, Paul and Mary. **Folk Rock** took hold by 1965, popularized by **Bob Dylan** (1941–   ), composer and performer, whose return to the stage in 1974 after a long absence proved a sensational success. **Soul,** the black people's "pop," is perhaps best exemplified by such black singers as **Aretha Franklin** (1942–   ). Major trends (1965–71) were exemplified by (1) Hard Rock: "The Doors," "Jefferson Airplane"; (2) Folk Rock: "The Band," "Country Joe and the Fish"; (3) Blues Rock: "Blood, Sweat, and Tears," and Janis Joplin. Difficult to classify but enormously popular were "The Mamas and the Papas," with their distinctive harmonies, Simon and Garfunkle, "The Beach Boys," identified with the "California Sound." Most of these artists performed their own material.

1950–74. PERFORMERS. Debuts: **Cesare Siepi** as Philip II in *Don Carlo,* MO (1950); **Marian Anderson,** contralto, made her debut at MO as Ulrica in *Un Ballo in Maschera* (7 Jan. 1955), first black singer in its 71-year history. **Beverly Sills** as Rosalinda in *Die Fledermaus,* New York City Opera (1955), MO debut as Pamira in *The Siege of Corinth* (1975); **Renata Tebaldi** as Desdemona in *Otello,* MO (1955); MO debut of **Maria Callas** as Norma in *Norma* (1956); **Birgit Nilsson** as Isolde in *Tristan und Isolde,* MO (1959); **Sviatoslav Richter,** Soviet pianist, N.Y. (1960); **Joan Sutherland** in Handel's *Alcina,* Dallas Opera (1960); MO debut as Lucia (26 Nov. 1961); **Jon Vickers** as Canio in *Pagliacci,* MO (1960); **Leontyne Price's** and **Franco Corelli's** debuts as Leonora and Manrico in *Il Trovatore,* MO (27 Jan. 1961); American Symphony Orch., **Leopold Stokowski,** conductor (1st concert, N.Y., 15 Oct. 1962); Moscow Philharmonic, N.Y. (1965); **Montserrat Caballé** as Lucrezia Borgia in *Lucrezia Borgia,* N.Y. (1965), MO debut as Marguerite in *Faust* (1965); **Sherrill Milnes** as Valentin in *Faust*, MO (1965); Orchestre de la Suisse Romande, N.Y. (1966); Hamburg State Opera, N.Y. (1967); **Herbert von Karajan's** MO debut, conductor and director, new production of *Ring* cycle, *Die Walküre* (2 Nov. 1967); **Martti Talvela** as Grand Inquisitor in *Don Carlo*, MO (1968). European orchestras appearing in U.S. for first time in 1968 included Helsinki, Stockholm, Orchestre de Paris, English Chamber Orch.; in addition, Hamburg State Opera performed at MO (1967), Rome Opera (1968); **Placido Domingo** MO debut as Maurizio in *Adriana Lecouvreur* (1968); **Marilyn Horne** MO debut as Adalgisa in *Norma* (1971); **Kiri Te Kanawa** as Desdemona in *Otello*, MO (1974).

1954, 4 APR. TOSCANINI RETIRED as conductor of NBC Symphony Orch.; reorganized as Symphony of the Air, with first concert, New York (27 Oct.).

1955, 19 Nov. LEONARD BERNSTEIN named musical director of PS to succeed Dimitri Mitropolous; in Sept. his musical *West Side Story* opened on Broadway, followed by *Candide* (1956); presented TV shows on music (*Omnibus*, 1954–58).

1965. VLADIMIR HOROWITZ returned to concert stage (Carnegie Hall, 9 May) after 12 years of self-imposed retirement.

1950–73. PERFORMANCES OF AMERICAN COMPOSITIONS. Roger Sessions, *2d Symphony*, PS (1950); **Roy Harris:** *Symph. Fantasy* (Pittsburgh, 1954); **Darius Milhaud:** *6th Symph.*, BS (1955); **Walter Piston:** *5th Symph.*, BS (1955); *Concerto for Violin and Orch.* (1958); **Ives:** *He Is There*, Norwalk, Conn. (1959); *2d Symph.*, PS (1951), **Stravinsky:** *Canticum Sacrum* (Los Angeles, 1957), ballet score *Agon*, New York City Ballet (1957)—both on occasion of 75th birthday, *Threni*, Schola Cantorum, N.Y. (1959), *Movements for Piano and Orch.*, Columbia Symphony Orch., N.Y. (1960); *4th Symph.* (completed 1916), American Symphony Orch., N.Y. (1965), *Variations*, Chicago Symphony (1965), *Introitus: T. S. Eliot in Memoriam*, Chicago Symphony (1965); **Peter Mennin:** *Piano Concerto*, Cleveland Symphony, N.Y. (1958); **Barber:** *Toccata Festifa*, PH (1960); **Foss:** *Time Cycle, for Soprano and Orchestra*, PS (1960); **Vittorio Giannini:** *4th Symph.*, Juilliard School of Music, N.Y. (1960); **Carl Ruggles:** *Sun Treader* (composed 1933), BS at Festival of Carl Ruggles, Bowdoin College (1966); **Elliott Carter:** *Piano Concerto*, BS (1967), *Concerto for Orchestra*, PS (1970); **Louis M. Gottschalk:** *Montevideo*, American Symphony Orch., N.Y. (1969), *Concerto for Orchestra*, PH (1970); **Charles Wuorinén:** *Concerto for Amplified Violin and Orchestra*, BS (Tanglewood, 1972); **Alan Hovhaness:** *And God Created Whales*, PS (1970); **Louis W. Ballard:** *Devil's Promenade*, Tulsa Philharmonic (1973). **George Rochberg**, *Concerto for Violin and Orchestra*, Pittsburgh Symphony (1975).

1954–73. SOME EXPERIMENTAL TRENDS, including electronic music and mixed media, gained ground in this period. Pioneers include **John Cage** (1912–   ), who utilized tape recorder in *Imaginary Landscape No. 5* (duration 4 mins., 1952); **Otto Luening** (1900–   ) and **Vladimir Ussachevsky** (1911–   ), who collaborated on works for tape recorder and orchestra (1954); Lejaren Hiller and Leonard Isaacson used computer for producing music at Univ. of Illinois (1955); **Columbia-Princeton Electronic Music Center** est. (1959), produced Ussachevsky's *Creation-Prologue*. In the late 60s and early 70s music workshops and laboratories proliferated at such institutions as Hunter

College, Univ. of Illinois, Buffalo, etc. John Cage and Lejaren Hiller produced (1967–69) *HPSCHD* for 7 harpsichords and 52 computer-generated tapes. **Moog synthesizer,** invented by Robert A. Moog (1969), turned interest of "pop" enthusiasts toward Bach.

1953–74. NEW YORK PRO MUSICA, founded by Noah Greenberg, brought vitality to Medieval and Renaissance music.

1953–72. OPERAS BY AMERICAN COMPOSERS. Igor Stravinsky: *Rake's Progress,* MO (1953); **Aaron Copland:** *Tender Land,* New York City Opera Co. (1953); **Norman Dello Joio:** *Trial at Rouen,* NBC–TV (1956), *The Ruby* (N.Y., 1957); **William Bergsma:** *Wife of Martin Guerre* (N.Y., 1956); **Douglas Moore** and **J. Latouche,** *Ballad of Baby Doe,* New York City Opera Co. (1958); **Carlisle Floyd:** *Susannah,* Univ. of Florida, Tallahassee (1955), New York City Opera Co. (1959). **Leonard Kastle:** *Deseret,* NBC Opera Co., TV (1961); **Robert Ward:** *The Crucible,* New York City Opera Co. (1961); **Jack Beeson:** *Lizzie Borden,* New York City Opera Co. (1965); **Douglas Moore:** *Carry Nation,* Univ. of Kansas (1966); **Samuel Barber:** *Vanessa,* MO (1958), *Antony and Cleopatra,* first opera performed in new Metropolitan Opera House (16 Sept. 1966); **Martin David Levy:** *Mourning Becomes Electra,* Metropolitan Opera (1967); **Hugo Weisgall:** *Nine Rivers from Jordan,* New York City Opera Co. (1968); **Gunther Schuller** (John Updike, librettist): *Fisherman and His Wife,* Boston Opera Co. (1970); **Carlisle Floyd:** *Of Mice and Men* (based on John Steinbeck's novel), Seattle Opera Co. (1970); **Ezra Pound:** *Le Testament du Villon* (music written 1921–22), Western Opera Theater (1971); **Scott Joplin:** ragtime opera, *Treemonisha* (written 1907–11), 1 performance, Harlem (1911),

Morehouse College, Atlanta (1972), Carnegie Hall (1972); **Virgil Thomson:** *Lord Byron,* Juilliard, American Opera Co. (1972).

1953–71. PERFORMANCES OF FOREIGN COMPOSERS. Shostakovich: *10th Symph.,* PS (1954), *13th Symph.,* PH (1970); **Menotti:** *2nd Piano Concerto,* PS (1958); *Saint of Bleecker St.* (N.Y., 1954); *Maria Golovin,* NBC Opera Co. at Brussels World's Fair (1958); **Prokofiev:** *War and Peace,* NBC Opera Co., TV (1957); **Pablo Casals:** *El Pesebre,* San Francisco Symph. (1962), *Hymn to the United Nations* (UN, 1971); **Benjamin Britten:** *War Requiem,* BS, Tanglewood (1963); **Gustav Mahler:** *10th Symphony,* recons. by Deryck Cooke, PH (1965); **Krzysztof Penderecki:** *The Passion and Death of Jesus Christ According to St. Luke,* Minneapolis Symphony Orch., Minneapolis (1967), N.Y.C. (1969); **Hans Werner Henze:** *Essay on Pigs,* Los Angeles Philharmonic (1971).

1954–65. FOUNDATION GRANTS. Through a grant from the Rockefeller Foundation (Apr. 1953) the Louisville Orch. initiated (2 Jan. 1954) series of commissioned works by 65 American and foreign composers. Grants broadened to include other orchestras (1957). In spring of 1958 New York City Opera Co. presented 5-week season of 10 American operas under Ford Foundation grant. Four opera companies shared 1959 Ford grant to foster American opera, and in 1965 orchestras throughout U.S. shared $80.2 million in Ford grants.

1955–63 MUSICAL THAW IN COLD WAR. Exchange of visits of Soviet and American musicians included visits to U.S. of Emil Gilels and David Oistrakh (1955); Moiseyev Dance Co. (1958); Bolshoi Ballet; Soviet composers, including D. Shostakovich (1959); Moscow State Symph.; Leonid Kogan; Sviatoslav Richter (1960), Leningrad Kirov Ballet

(1961), Mstislav Rostropovich (1963). U.S. and U.S.S.R. signed a 2-year cultural exchange pact, 1962. U.S. artists who toured U.S.S.R. included Isaac Stern and Jan Peerce (1956), Boston Symphony (1956), New York Philharmonic (1959, 1960). In addition, Louis ("Satchmo") Armstrong (1900–71), Dixieland trumpeter and jazz-band leader, made a triumphal tour of the Middle East, Mediterranean countries, and Western Europe (1956) and of Africa (1960). **Harvey K.** ("Van") Cliburn, Jr., 23-year-old Texan, won first prize at International Tchaikovsky Piano Competition in Moscow (1958); on return to the U.S. he drew huge audiences at Chicago's Grant Park, Hollywood Bowl, and New York's Lewisohn Stadium.

1960–75. OPERAS BY FOREIGN COMPOSERS. Handel: *Hercules,* American Opera Society, N.Y. (1960); **Britten;** *A Midsummer Night's Dream,* San Francisco Opera Co. (1961), *The Burning Fiery Furnace,* Caramoor, N.Y. (1967), *The Prodigal Son,* Caramoor (1969), *Death in Venice,* MO (1974); **Berg:** *Lulu,* Santa Fe Opera Co. (1963); **Shostakovich:** *Katerina Ismailova,* New York City Opera Co. (1965); **Hans Werner Henze:** *Elegy for Young Lovers,* Juilliard (1965), *The Stag King,* Santa Fe Opera Co. (1965), *The Young Lord,* Santa Fe (1967); **Alberto Ginastera:** *Don Rodrigo,* New York City Opera Co. (1966), *Bomarzo,* New York City Opera Co. (1968); *Beatrix Cenci,* Opera Society of Washington (1971); **Janacek:** *The Makropulos Affair,* San Francisco Opera Co. (1966); **Schoenberg:** *Moses and Aaron,* Boston Opera Co. (1966); **Rameau:** *Hippolyte and Aricie,* Boston Opera Co. (1966); **Mozart:** *Lucio Silla,* Baltimore Opera Co. (1968); **Carl Orff:** *Ballad of Agnes,* Univ. of Missouri (1968); Richard Rodney Bennett: *Mines of Sulphur,* Juilliard (1968); **Penderecki:** *The Devils of Lou-*

don, Santa Fe Opera Co. (1969); **Luciano Berio:** *Opera,* Santa Fe Opera Co. (1970); **Villa-Lobos:** *Yerma,* Santa Fe Opera Co. (1971); **Berlioz:** *Les Troyens,* Boston Opera Co. (1972), MO (1973), *Benvenuto Cellini,* Boston Opera Co. (1975); **Delius,** *A Village Romeo and Juliet,* Opera Society of Washington (1972), New York City Opera Co. (1973).

1960–74. GOVERNMENT AND THE ARTS. Among the signs of the federal government's increasing interest in the arts were (1) the successful intervention as arbitrator of Secretary of Labor Arthur Goldberg after labor-management negotiations had broken down and the N.Y. Metropolitan Opera season had been announced as canceled (28 Aug. 1961); (2) a White House state dinner in honor of Luis Muñoz Marín (13 Nov. 1961), featuring a program by Pablo Casals, Alexander Schneider, and Mieczyslaw Horszowski; (3) the establishment of the National Foundation on the Arts and Humanities (29 Sept. 1965), whose appropriations increased to $81.5 million (fiscal 1973) and which announced, Mar. 1974, a grant of $1 million to Metropolitan Opera on matching basis.

1962–73. BURGEONING OF PERFORMING ARTS CENTERS. Lincoln Center for the Performing Arts, a $178 million project, includes Philharmonic Hall (opened 23 Sept. 1962), renamed Avery Fisher Hall (1973), home of New York Philharmonic; the New York State Theater (23 Apr. 1964), where New York City Opera Co. and New York City Ballet Co. are resident; and the Metropolitan Opera House (16 Sept. 1966). **The John F. Kennedy Center for the Performing Arts,** Washington, D.C., whose construction was funded in part by federal money, opened (8 Sept. 1971) with a performance of Leonard Bernstein's *Mass.* Other newly built performing arts centers included the Music Center, Los Angeles (fully opened 1967); Memorial

Arts Center, Atlanta, Ga. (1968), and Centers in San Antonio, Tex.; Jackson, Miss.; Garden State Arts Center in New Jersey (all in 1968), and at Indiana Univ. (1972), with new auditoriums for symphonic performance in Miami, Fla., and Norfolk, Va. (1972).

ALL-TIME SONG HITS, 1892–1980

Daisybelle (On a bicycle built for 2), w., m., Harry Dacre	1892
The Sidewalks of New York, w., m., Charles B. Lawler and James W. Blake	1894
The Stars and Stripes Forever, m., John Philip Sousa	1897
Sweet Adeline, w. Richard H. Gerard [Husch]; m., Harry Armstrong	1903
Kiss Me Again, w., Henry Blossom; m., Victor Herbert	1905
Shine on Harvest Moon, w., m., Nora Bayes and Jack Norworth	1908
Ah! Sweet Mystery of Life, w., Rida Johnson Young; m., Victor Herbert	1910
A Perfect Day, w., m., Carrie Jacobs Bond	1910
Alexander's Ragtime Band, w., m., Irving Berlin	1911
When Irish Eyes Are Smiling, w., Chauncey Olcott and George Graff, Jr., m., Ernest R. Ball	1912
St. Louis Blues, w., m., W. C. Handy	1914
Swanee, w., Irving Caesar; m., George Gershwin	1919
Yes, We Have No Bananas, w., Frank Silver; m., M. Irving Cohn	1923
Tea for Two, w., Irving Caesar; m., Vincent Youmans	1924
Dinah, w., Sam M. Lewis and Joe Young; m., Harry Akst	1925
Ol' Man River, w., Oscar Hammerstein 2nd; m., Jerome Kern	1927
Star Dust, w., Mitchell Parish; m., Hoagy Carmichael	1929
Dancing In The Dark, w., Howard Dietz; m., Arthur Schwartz	1931
Easter Parade, w., m., Irving Berlin	1933
Begin the Beguine, w., m., Cole Porter	1935
September Song, w., Maxwell Anderson; m., Kurt Weill	1938
God Bless America, w., m., Irving Berlin	1939
White Christmas, w., m., Irving Berlin	1942
Some Enchanted Evening, w., Oscar Hammerstein 2d; m., Richard Rodgers	1949
Don't Be Cruel, w., m., Otis Blackwell and Elvis Presley/Hound Dog, w., Jerry Lieber; m., Mike Stoller	1956
Mack the Knife, German w., Bertolt Brecht; English w., Marc Blitzstein, m., Kurt Weill	1959
Theme from A Summer Place, m., Max Steiner	1960
The Twist (re-released), w., m., Hank Ballard	1962
I Want to Hold Your Hand, w., m., John Lennon and Paul McCartney	1964
Hey, Jude, w., m., John Lennon and Paul McCartney	1968
Aquarius, w., James Rado and Gerome Ragni; m., Galt MacDermot	1969
Raindrops Keep Falling on My Head, w., Hal David; m., Burt Bacharach	1970
You Light Up My Life, w., m., Joe Brooks	1977
Another One Bites the Dust, w., m., John Deacon[1]	1980

[1] A projection, as time insufficient to determine all-time-hit status.

Dance

Social dancing and folk dancing have long been an important part of American life. However, widespread interest in dance as a serious art form is a relatively new phenomenon. The seminal forces in modern dance—Duncan, St. Denis, Graham, and Humphrey—were American. So are a substantial proportion of contemporary choreographers of modern dance. But it has been only the last ten years that have seen modern dance attract an audience of reasonable size.

The visits of great foreign performers, such as Pavlova and Nijinsky early in the century, as well as Diaghilev's Ballets Russes and the later Ballet Russe de Monte Carlo, laid a foundation for the tentative establishment of indigenous ballet companies in the 1930s which were to last. Later visits of stars, such as Fonteyn and Nureyev, and great companies, the Royal, Bolshoi, and Stuttgart, usually under the aegis of Sol Hurok, vastly expanded the size of the ballet audience in America. The past two decades have witnessed the rise to international stature of two American ballet companies, tremendous growth of regional companies, and the acclaimed choreography of Balanchine, Robbins, and others.

1607–1700. SOCIAL DANCING. Puritan laws discouraged dancing in New England except where instruction could teach coordination and poise. Despite the laws, people danced; dancing masters were common by the 1670s. Laws were less restrictive in other colonies. Dancing was considered an essential part of life among the aristocratic Southerners.

1701–1800. SOCIAL AND FOLK DANCING. Dancing masters, who generally taught country dances, jigs, cotillions, the minuet, courante, and other European imports were well established in the social life of the colonies. Toward the end of the century balls and assemblies were common in the large cities. Dancing was considered an important form of socializing on the frontier, where dances were less formal than in the Eastern cities and included versions of the square dance and the Virginia reel.

c.1727–94. BALLET. The first ballet performances in America were given by amateur and semiprofessional groups and by individual dancing masters. An English group, headed by Lewis Hallam, was the first truly professional company to dance in the colonies (c. 1750), performing harlequinades, spectacles, and incidental dances.

1767. John Street Theater opened in New York City for visiting European companies.

1774. First Continental Congress forbade theatrical activity in the colonies but Revolutionary War inspired patriotic pageants, which reawakened interest in the dance.

1785. Debut of John Durang, the first native American performer of repute, with the Hallam Company in Philadelphia. Durang's popularity increased throughout the 1790s.

c.1790. French Revolution stimulated the immigration of dancers from the continent who offered performances and instruction.

1794. *La Forêt Noire,* the first seriously regarded ballet in the U.S., performed in Philadelphia, featuring Anne Gardie and John Durang.

1801–1900. SOCIAL DANCING became increasingly popular in the 19th century. The rich continued to hold formal assemblies, cotillions, and society balls in larger cities and various organizations began to sponsor annual balls. Smaller cities and towns held public balls. The poor danced in concert saloons, beer gardens, and dance halls. On the frontier informal dancing such as the Virginia reel, country jigs, shakedowns, and plankdances, occurred at country fairs, logrollings, quilting parties, husking bees, and holidays. The Shakers, using a variety of movements in their religious services, structured and refined them into group dances. The waltz and polka were introduced from Europe (c. 1830). Other popular 19th-century dances included the cakewalk, the Washington Post, and the barn dance.

1801–1900. THEATRICAL DANCING, performed in musical variety shows and vaudeville, derived from many sources, a primary one being American Negro dance. By 1810 the singing and dancing "Negro Boy" (usually a blackened white man) was an established part of stage productions, dancing a jig or clog, accompanied by songs with allusions to Negroes. **Juba,** who imitated popular dancers and performed traditional Negro dances, became the first black to achieve fame as a stage performer (c. 1840). The black influence upon American dance forms included the buck-and-wing, tap dancing (a combination of the Irish clog and black shuffle dances), and the cakewalk. *Clorindy: The Origin of the Cake Walk* was performed on Broadway by a black company (1898).

1801–1850. POPULARITY OF BALLET led to increasingly frequent performances by visiting European artists.

1827. Mme. Francisque Hutin introduced Americans to the *pointe* footwork and multiple pirouettes of the romantic ballet.

1837. Debuts, in *The Maid of Cashmere,* Chestnut Street Theatre, Philadelphia, of American ballerinas **Mary Ann Lee** and **Augusta Maywood,** the first American to dance at the Paris Opera (1839), and as prima ballerina at La Scala.

1838. Debut of **George Washington Smith,** first American *danseur noble.*

1835–1887. FOREIGN BALLET PREMIERES IN AMERICA. *La Sylphide,* Philadelphia (1835) by M. Celeste; *La Fille Mal Gardée,* Park Theatre, New York (6 July 1839); *Giselle,* Howard Atheneum, Boston (1 Jan. 1846); *Coppélia,* Metropolitan Opera House (11 Mar. 1887).

1839–40. PERFORMANCES OF FOREIGN ARTISTS. Marius Petipa with Ballet Company of Madame Lacomte (1839); **Paul** and **Marie Taglioni,** Park Theatre, New York (21 May 1839); **Fanny Elssler,** New York (14 May 1840).

c.1855. Decline of ballet due to lack of major theaters, opera houses, state-supported schools, or other government subsidy.

1866. Premiere of *The Black Crook,* major dance phenomenon of Victorian Age, performed for forty years and featuring one ballet number in which performers danced almost nude.

1885–87. American Opera Co., formed in New York, made effort to present high-quality ballet.

c. 1890. Waning of popularity of ballet, with excessive emphasis upon technical virtuosity generating artistic stagnation.

1900–26. MODERN DANCE: THE BEGINNINGS. Modern dance in America developed as a reaction against the increasing sterility of classical ballet. The technical, mechanical, and elaborate aspects of the ballet were rejected for greater freedom of movement and emotional involvement. Subject matter of dances began to reflect contemporary interests as well as concurrent developments in art and music. Major concerns of dancers were simplicity, functionalism, and expressiveness. American choreographer-dancers dominated early developments; among them: **Isadora Duncan** (p. 1018), established the idea of dance as a means of personal expression; **Ruth St. Denis** (1877–1968) and her husband, **Ted Shawn** (1891–1972), established a school, Denishawn, which trained students in Eastern and other dance forms, introduced theatrical appeal and a religious mysticism, while creating new audiences. The Denishawn School produced **Martha Graham,** Doris Humphrey, and Charles Weidman.

1908–29. BALLET popularity revived with visits of leading European artists and companies. Major arrivals included **Adeline Genée** (1908), **Cid Fornaroli** (1910), and **Anna Pavlova** (1881–1931), whose debut occurred in *Cop-*

pélia, MO,* with Mikhail Mordkin (28 Feb. 1910). Pavlova toured the U.S. (1910–1925). **Serge Diaghilev's Ballets Russes** arrived, New York (1916), introducing **Vaslav Nijinsky** in *Le Spectre de la Rose* and *Petrouchka,* MO (12 Apr. 1916), **Michel Fokine, Léonide Massine** (1894–) and **Adolph Bolm.** 2d N.Y. season opened Manhattan Opera House with Nijinsky (*Tl Eulenspiegel*).

1910–29. SOCIAL DANCES attaining great popularity included the tango (introduced c. 1910) and the fox-trot, devised by **Harry Fox** for the *Ziegfeld Follies* (1913). **Vernon** and **Irene Castle** refined and popularized these dances, as well as the Boston waltz, the hesitation waltz, the turkey trot, and their own Castle Walk. Ragtime music inspired the grizzly bear and the bunny hug, popular in the 1910s. Dixieland jazz, whose roots were in African rhythms imported by slaves, was reflected in popular dances of the 1920s, especially the Charleston, noted for wildly flailing legs, the Black Bottom, with twisted contortions, and the Shimmy, with frenetic shaking.

1911–49. PERFORMANCES OF FOREIGN BALLETS.† *Les Sylphides,* New York (1911); *Swan Lake* (4 acts), MO (20 Dec. 1911); *Firebird,* BR, New York (1916); *The Rite of Spring,* Academy of Music, Philadelphia (11 Apr. 1930; danced by Martha Graham); *The Nutcracker,* MC, New York (17 Oct. 1940); *The Sleeping Beauty,* Philadelphia Ballet (12 Feb. 1937), Sadler's Wells' version, MO (9 Oct. 1949); *Les Patineurs,* BT, New York (2 Oct. 1946); *Symphonic Variations,* SW, MO (12 Oct. 1946).

* MO—Metropolitan Opera House, New York City
† *Abbreviations*
BR   Serge Diaghilev's Ballets Russes
BT   Ballet Theatre
MC   Ballet Russe de Monte Carlo
MO   Metropolitan Opera
SW   Sadler's Wells

1921. Fokine School opened in New York (1 Jan.).

1924–25. Pavlova and company make last American tour.

1926–63. MODERN DANCE. Martha Graham (p. 1043) gave her first independent dance recital, 48th St. Theatre, New York (18 Apr. 1926). Developing a nonballetic dance vocabulary expressive of inner tensions, Graham was the teacher of most of the important modern dancers-choreographers for five decades, including Merce Cunningham, Erick Hawkins, Donald McKayle, Glen Tetley, Paul Taylor, Anna Sokolow, and Pearl Lang. **Doris Humphrey** (1895–1958) based her style on "falls and recoveries," exploiting the drama of the falling body as well as the pressures and tensions of a balanced body in repose. More socially committed than Graham, Humphrey worked closely with choreographer **Charles Weidman** (1901–1975). Humphrey's major students included José Limon and Ruth Currier. Both Humphrey and Graham integrated the spoken word into their dances. **José Limon** (1908–72) was noted for symmetry in composition and a flair for theater, combining formal discipline with dramatic passion; *The Moor's Pavane* (1949) was one of the first modern dance pieces to enter the repertory of ballet companies. **Alwin Nikolais** (1912–) has developed a mass media theater where as choreographer-composer-designer he fuses sound, color, lighting, unusual props, music, and dance. A major work is *Imago* (1963). **Merce Cunningham** (1919–) works with dance-by-chance or random methods of composition, exemplified in *Suite by Chance* (1953), as well as in developing dance without either drama or music. **Paul Taylor** (1930–), who studied under Graham and danced under Balanchine, exemplifies a style close to ballet (*Aureole,* 1962), ofttimes spiced with humor. **Alvin Ailey** (1931–

) and **Donald McKayle** (1930–)
are black dancers—choreographers, who
successfully combine modern dance techniques with African and West Indian
dance elements. Ailey's *Revelations*
(1960) is perhaps the most popular
of all works of modern dance. *Cry*
(1971), written for Judith Jamison, is a
major solo. The Alvin Ailey City Center
Dance Theater is virtually unique in having a repertory embracing works of other
major modern dance choreographers including McKayle's *Rainbow Round My
Shoulder,* as well as works of Pearl
Primus and Janet Collins. Other major
creative figures in modern dance include
**Anna Sokolow, Pauline Koner, Erick
Hawkins, Ann Halprin, Lucas Hoving,
Katherine Litz, Pearl Lang, Glen Tetley,
Ruth Currier,** and **Katherine Dunham.**

1930–74. SOCIAL DANCING. Jazz
inspired the swing era of the 1930s and
dancing to the music of "big bands." It
led to the Lindy hop, which featured
gymnastics and wild footwork, as well
as other popular dances like the Big
Apple, the Shag, and Trucking. The
Lindy hop was the precursor of the jit-
terbug, which became the rage throughout the 1930s and was exported all over
the world by GIs in the 1940s. Group
dances became popular in the late 1930s.
The conga, in which a line of dancers
followed a leader, and the Lambeth walk,
a strutting dance, were imported from
England. Another phenomenon of the
1930s was the dance marathon in which
couples danced nonstop for days. In the
1940s Latin American dances such as the
samba, rhumba, and mambo became
popular. These rhythms inspired the ca-
lypso and cha-cha dances of the following
decade. The rock 'n' roll phenomenon
of the 1950s was another outgrowth of
American jazz. Couples danced to rock
'n' roll music but rarely established body
contact. The dances were open to a
great deal of individual improvisation.

In the 1960s, social dances such as the
twist, the monkey, and the frug encouraged individual expression.

**1933. BALLET RUSSE DE MONTE
CARLO,** outgrowth of disbanded Diaghilev troupe, toured U.S. (1st perf. St.
James Theatre, N.Y., 22 Dec. 1933),
under sponsorship of impresario **Sol
Hurok** (1888–1974) with Léonide Massine as chief choreographer. Repeated
tours increased the popularity of ballet.

1933. The Jooss Ballet makes U.S.
debut.

**1933–69. U.S. BALLET COMPA-
NIES. San Francisco Ballet Co.** (1933–
), founded by Adolph Bolm. **School
of American Ballet,** founded by **Lincoln
Kirstein** (1907–), E. M. M. Warburg,
and **George Balanchine** (1 Jan. 1934).
American Ballet, founded by Kirstein
and Edward M. M. Warburg, with a
repertory of ballets by Balanchine, gave
2-week season at the Adelphi Theatre,
New York (1935) and became resident ballet company at MO (1935–38).
Littlefield Ballet, Philadelphia, organized
(1935) by **Catherine Littlefield** (1904–
51), became the Philadelphia Ballet
(1936). **Ballet Caravan,** organized by
Lincoln Kirstein to tour U.S. and offer
opportunities to American artists (1936).
Ballet Theatre (since 1957, American
Ballet Theatre), founded by Lucia Chase
and Richard Pleasant (1st perf., Center
Theatre, N.Y., 11 Jan. 1940), encouraged
American choreographers **Jerome Robbins** (1918–), Michael Kidd, Agnes
de Mille, Antony Tudor, and Eliot Feld.
Ballet Theatre became first U.S. company
to dance at Covent Garden (4 July
1946). Lucia Chase and Oliver Smith
served as co-directors (1945–80), succeeded by Mikhail Baryshnikov (1980).
Ballet Society, created by Kirstein and
Balanchine for private subscription audience (1st perf., N.Y., 20 Nov. 1946) became **New York City Ballet,** resident
company of the New York City Center of

Music and Drama (1st perf., 11 Oct. 1948), and was recognized as a company of international stature after its performances at Covent Garden (1950). It moved to the New York State Theater of Lincoln Center for the Performing Arts (1964). Major companies founded in the 1960s included **Pennsylvania Ballet,** Philadelphia (1962); **City Center Joffrey Ballet** evolved from the Robert Joffrey Ballet with a well-balanced repertory combining revival of 19th and early 20th century works with contemporary multimedia ballets (1966); **Dance Theatre of Harlem,** combining classical training with black influences, established by **Arthur Mitchell** (1969).

1934–71. PERFORMANCES OF AMERICAN BALLETS.° *Serenade* (Balanchine-Tchaikovsky), School of American Ballet, Warburg Estate, White Plains, N.Y. (9 June 1934); *Orpheus* (Balanchine-Gluck, AB, MO (22 May 1936); *Billy the Kid* (Loring-Copland), BC, Chicago (16 Oct. 1938); *Pillar of Fire* (Tudor-Schoenberg), BT, MO (8 Apr. 1942); *Rodeo* (de Mille-Copland), MO (16 Oct. 1942); *Fancy Free* (Robbins-Bernstein), BT, MO (18 Apr. 1944); *Orpheus* (Balanchine-Stravinsky), BS, NYCC (28 Apr. 1948); *La Valse* (Balanchine-Ravel), NYCB (20 Feb. 1951); *The Cage* (Robbins-Stravinsky), NYCB (10 June 1951); *The Concert* (Robbins-Chopin), NYCB (6 Mar. 1956); *A Midsummer Night's Dream,* NYCB (17 Jan. 1962); *Les Noces* (Robbins-Stravinsky), ABT, New York (1965); *Astarte* (Joffrey-Syrcus), Joffrey, New York (1967); *Harbinger* (Feld-Prokofiev), ABT, New York (1967); *Dances at a Gathering* (Robbins-Chopin), NYCB (22 May 1969); *The*

° *Abbreviations*

AB	American Ballet
ABT	American Ballet Theatre
BC	Ballet Caravan
BS	Ballet Society
BT	Ballet Theatre
NYCB	New York City Ballet
NYCC	New York City Center
Joffrey	City Center Joffrey Ballet

River (Ailey-Ellington), ABT, New York (1970); *In the Night* (Robbins-Chopin), NYCB (29 Jan. 1970); *Trinity* (Arpino-Raph and Holdridge), Joffrey, New York (1970); *The Goldberg Variations* (Robbins-Bach), NYCB (27 May 1971).

1936–54. DANCING IN THEATER AND FILMS. Choreographers from ballet and modern dance contributed to the distinctiveness of the American musical theater as well as to the integration of dance and drama. Among the milestones were Balanchine's *On Your Toes* (1936), de Mille's *Oklahoma!* (1943), Jerome Robbins' *West Side Story* (1957). Modern dance choreographers who made major contributions to the stage musical include Hanya Holm, *Kiss Me Kate* (1948) and *My Fair Lady* (1956), Helen Tamiris, *Show Boat* (1928), and Jack Cole, *Man of La Mancha* (1965).

1930s film audiences were treated to the dance extravaganzas of Busby Berkeley (1895–1976). Fred Astaire and Ginger Rogers were an exceptionally popular dance team. Gene Kelly became the dominant dance figure in the films of the 1940s and 1950s.

1941–74. MODERN DANCE FESTIVALS of greatest influence were the Jacob's Pillow Dance Festival (Lee, Mass.), founded by Ted Shawn (1941) for presentation of modern dance, ethnic dance, and ballet, and the American Dance Festival at Connecticut College (New London, Conn.) (1948).

1949–81. POPULARIZATION OF BALLET. Annual tours by foreign companies attracted large audiences: **Sadler's Wells** (later **Royal Ballet**) (1st tour, 1949); **Royal Danish Ballet** (1st tour, 1956); **Bolshoi Ballet** (1st tour, 1959); **Leningrad Kirov Ballet** (1st tour, 1961); **Stuttgart Ballet** (1st tour, 1969); Maurice **Béjart Ballet of the 20th Century** (1st tour, 1971). Major foreign performers included **Dame Margot Fonteyn** of the Royal Ballet (debut 1949), **Erik**

Bruhn (debut, BT, 1955), **Maya Pliset-skaya** of the Bolshoi (1959), **Rudolf Nureyev** (debut Ruth Page Chicago Opera Ballet, 1962), Natalia Makarova (debut with ABT after defection, N.Y., 22 Dec. 1970), Mikhail Baryshnikov (1974). Nureyev made U.S. modern dance debut with Paul Taylor Company in *Aureole,* New York (14 Oct. 1974). Baryshnikov ABT debut in 1974 and with NYCB as Franz in Coppelia (Saratoga, N.Y., 8 July 1975); Soviet emigrées Valery and Galina Ragozina Panov American debut with Baltimore Symph. Orch. (Philadelphia, 1975); Panov's NY debut with Berlin Opera Ballet (July 1978).

1964. NEW YORK STATE THEATRE, part of Lincoln Center for the Performing Arts, designed esp. for dance, opens with NYCB performance of *A Midsummer Night's Dream* (23 Apr.).

1964–74. MODERN DANCE DEVELOPMENTS. Differences between ballet and modern dance began to disappear in some choreography. While some of ballet's technical elements, costumes, decor, and music became incorporated by modern dance, some of the freedom and emotionality as well as abstraction of modern dance were absorbed by ballet. Innovations in modern dance in the 1960s and 1970s have included the use of eurythmy, where dancers interpret a spoken or sung accompaniment; the use of film, slide, and light projections; the introduction of social and political protest in the dance, as well as nudity and homosexuality. Among major contemporary choreographers are Twyla Tharp, Meredith Monk, Yvonne Rainer, and Eleo Pomare.

Improved financing from government and foundations led to vast expansion of the number of performances. Audiences increased, seasons lengthened, and companies added artistic and administrative personnel.

1972–80. PERFORMANCES OF AMERCAN BALLETS. *Watermill* (Robbins-Ito), NYCB (3 Feb. 1972); *Chaconne* (Balanchine-Gluck), NYCB (22 Jan. 1976); *Ballo della Regina* (Balanchine-Verdi), NYCB (12 Jan. 1978); *Dybbuk* (Robbins-Bernstein), NYCB (16 May 1974); *The Leaves Are Fading* (Tudor-Dvorak), ABT (1975); *Vienna Waltzes* (Balanchine-J. Strauss; Lehar; R. Strauss), NYCB (23 June 1977); *Davidsbündlertanze* (Balanchine-Schumann), NYCB (1980).

1972–81. NEW YORK CITY BALLET FESTIVALS: Stravinsky Festival (18–25 June 1972) of 27 ballets, 20 of them world premieres; Ravel Festival (14–31 May 1975); Tchaikovsky Festival (4–14 June 1981).

1975. BROADWAY MUSICALS with significant dance materials include *Chicago* (Bob Fosse) and *A Chorus Line* (Michael Bennett).

1965–81. POPULARIZATION OF DANCE. In addition to major companies in urban areas, regional companies expanded. Books, magazines, and newspaper criticism proliferated in the late 1960s. Attention to dance was paid by cinema—*The Turning Point,* a film with Baryshnikov (1977)—and on TV over PBS's *Dance in America* (incl. Alvin Ailey, Eliot Feld, Paul Taylor), and *Live from Lincoln Center* series.

MASS MEDIA

Newspapers and Periodicals

Newspapers and pamphlets flourished on the eve of the Revolution and contributed to its genesis. During the first century after independence newspapers continued to boom, growing from 92 in 1790 to 3,725 in 1860, with the appearance of the penny newspaper a major factor in attaining a mass circulation. In the latter part of the nineteenth century intense competition between newspapers spawned such features as comics, photographs, and sensational reporting ("yellow journalism"), notoriously evident on the eve of the Spanish-American War.

Along with the growth of great newspaper chains and the wire services, the early twentieth century witnessed a concern for more factual and in-depth reportage. The economics of the industry had by the midcentury led to a monopoly situation, with most U.S. cities boasting but one newspaper and newspaper proprietors often owning local radio and TV stations. Magazines, once a flourishing industry, have been a victim of TV and economics, with recent casualties including *Life* and *Look*. News magazines, however, continue to be profitable, and a few journals low in circulation but high in quality continue to survive.

The polarization of the 1960s spurred openly subjective reporting, but more characteristic of contemporary trends in journalism is the investigative reporting of Seymour Hersh and Jack Anderson, and notably of Robert Woodward and Carl Bernstein, who contributed mightily to uncovering facts about the Watergate scandals.

Relations between the U.S. government and the press, despite First Amendment safeguards, have never been entirely free from friction, from the time of the Alien and Sedition Acts to the censorship of stories from the battlefield and the suppression or seizure of newspapers during the Civil War. Recent years have seen a heightening of tensions as a result of newspaper exposés of a credibility gap in administration statements during the Vietnam War, and relentless publication of the evidence in the Watergate scandal.

Issues in the '70s and early '80s of free press-fair trial are treated at pp. 546 and 552.

1690–1736. HARRIS TO ZENGER.
Public Occurrences (Boston; Benjamin Harris [fl.1673–1728]), suppressed by the government after 1 issue for critical comments on conduct of King William's war. First continuous colonial newspaper: Boston *News-Letter* (1704, John Campbell; discontinued, 1776), contained first illustration in colonial paper (19 Jan. 1708). Other papers: Boston *Gazette* (1719, William Brooker); Philadelphia *American Mercury* (1719, Andrew Bradford [1686–1742], employed Benjamin Franklin; .disc. 1749); *New England Courant* (1721, Boston, James Franklin; issued by brother Benjamin when editor jailed for criticizing government; disc. 1726); New York *Gazette* (1725, William Bradford [1663–1752]; sold to James Parker, 1743, and merged with New York *Post-Boy or Gazette*); *New England Weekly Journal* (1727, Samuel Kneeland; merged with Gazette, 1741); *Maryland Gazette* (1727, William Parker (c.1698–1750); disc. 1734; revived, 1745, by Jonas Green; cont. to 1839); *Universal Instructor . . . and Pennsylvania Gazette* (1728, Philadelphia, Samuel Keimer; bought by **Benjamin Franklin**, 1729, continued as *Pennsylvania Gazette;* David Hall proprietor after 1766; disc. 1815). *Weekly Rehearsal* (1731, Boston, Jeremy Gridley, forerunner of Boston *Evening Post;* disc. 1775 after pursuing neutral course); *South Carolina Gazette* (1732, Charleston, Thomas Whitmarsh with Franklin's support; later edited by Peter Timothy; became *Gazette of State of South Carolina*, 1777; then *State Gazette of South Carolina;* disc. 1802); *Rhode Island State Gazette* (1732, Newport, James Franklin, disc. 1773); New York *Weekly Journal*, 5 Nov. 1733, **John Peter Zenger** (p. 1190). For **Zenger Trial** (1734–35) in which Andrew Hamilton successfully argued that truth was a defense to seditious libel, see p. 1190. Boston *Post-Boy* (1734), leading Tory organ.

Virginia Gazette (1736), Williamsburg, William Parks; disc. 1750; succeeded by 4 other weeklies of this name, in order: Hunter, 1751–78; Rind, 1766–76; Purdie, 1775–80; and Dixon & Nicholson, 1779–80.

1739–78. FOREIGN LANGUAGE PRESS. The first foreign language newspaper in the colonies was the Philadelphia *Zeitung* (1732, Benj. Franklin); it quickly expired. The most lasting were the Germantown *Zeitung* (1739, **Christopher Sower**, 1693–1758, son 1721–1781, and Loyalist grandson, 1754–1799) and *Wöchentliche Philadelphische Staatsbote* (1762–79, Heinrich Miller).

1741–1775. EVE OF THE REVOLUTION. *American Magazine*, first magazine in the colonies (Jan. 1741, Philadelphia, Andrew Bradford; disc. Mar. 1741); *General Magazine and Historical Chronicle* (Jan. 1741, Philadelphia, Benjamin Franklin; disc. June 1741); *Pennsylvania Journal* (1742, Philadelphia, William Bradford, III; later *Patriot;* disc. 1793); New York *Post-Boy* (1743, James Parker; disc. 1773); Boston *Weekly Museum* (1743, Gamaliel Rogers and John Fowle, disc. 1743); *Christian History* (1743, a weekly to report Great Awakening, disc. 1745); New York *Evening Post* (1744, Henry DeForest; disc. 1752); *American Magazine and Historical Chronicle* (1746, Boston, Rogers and Fowle; disc. Dec. 1746); *Independent Advertiser* (1748, Boston, Rogers and Fowle); New York *Weekly Mercury* (1752, **Hugh Gaine** [1727–1807]; 2 editions published during Revolution—Loyalist in New York; Patriot in Newark, N.J.); *Independent Reflector* (1752, James Parker; disc. 1753). *Pennsylvania Gazette* carried first colonial cartoon (attributed to Franklin), depicting a cut-up snake and the caption: "Join or Die" (9 May 1754). Boston *Gazette* (1755, **Benjamin Edes** [1732–1803] and John Gill), leading Patriot organ, with such contributors as Sam and

John Adams, Josiah Quincy, Jr., and Joseph Warren. *Connecticut Gazette* (1755, New Haven, James Parker; disc. 1768); *New Hampshire Gazette* (1756, Portsmouth, **Daniel Fowle** [1715–87]), still published; *American Magazine and Monthly Chronicle* (1757, Philadelphia, William Bradford, III, with Rev. William Smith, provost of College of Philadelphia, as editor), first well-edited colonial magazine; disc. 1757. *New American Magazine* (1758, Woodbridge, N.J., Judge Samuel Nevill; disc. 1760); Newport *Mercury* (1758, James Franklin, nephew of Benj. Franklin), still published; New York *Gazette* (1759, William Weyman; merged with *Mercury*, 1768); *American Chronicle* (1762, New York, Samuel Farley; disc. July); Providence *Gazette* (1762, William Goddard; disc. 1825); *Georgia Gazette* (1763, James Johnston), Loyalist; published under British occupation during Revolution as *Royal Georgia Gazette,* 1779–82. New York *Pacquet* (1763, Benjamin Mecom; disc. Aug.); *Connecticut Courant* (1764, Hartford, Thomas Green, still published); New York *Journal or General Advertiser* (1766, **John Holt** [1721–84], Patriot organ published during Revolution in Kingston and Poughkeepsie; merged, 1793, with *Greenleaf's N.Y. Journal*); *Essex Gazette* (1768, Salem; removed to Cambridge 1775 as *New England Chronicle;* to Boston, 1776, as *Independent Chronicle;* cont. as *Semi-Weekly Advertiser,* 1840–76); New York *Chronicle* (1769, James Robertson; disc. 1770); *Massachusetts Spy* (1770, Boston, **Isaiah Thomas** [p. 1169]), Patriot; removed to Worcester, 3 May 1775, carrying story of Lexington and Concord; became Worcester *Gazette,* 1781). McDougall libel case (p. 93). *Pennsylvania Packet* (1771, Philadelphia, John Dunlap; disc. 1790); *Rivington's New York Gazetteer* (1773, **James Rivington** [1724–1802], Loyalist; disc. 1775, resumed,

1777, as *Loyal New York Gazette;* disc. 1783). *Royal American Magazine* (1774, Boston, Isaiah Thomas, Patriot; disc. Mar. 1775); *Pennsylvania Magazine* (1775, Philadelphia, Robert Aitken; **Thomas Paine** (p. 1020) editor, Feb. 1775–May 1776; disc. July 1776).

1775. POLITICS AND CIRCULATION. There were 37 newspapers in the colonies (23 Patriot, 7 Loyalist, 7 neutral or doubtful in loyalty). Average weekly circulation rose from c.600 (1765) to as much as 3,500 (1775, *Massachusetts Spy*). Price ranged from 2s. 6d.–6s. per quarter. Philadelphia *Evening Post* (1775, Benjamin Towne, later Loyalist; disc. 1784), first American daily, sold for 2d. an issue.

1776–89. New York *Packet* (1776, **Samuel Loudon** [1727–1813]; pub. at Fishkill, Jan. 1777; returned to New York, 1783; became daily; disc. 1792). New York *Evening Post* (1782, Christopher Sower *et al.;* became *Morning Post,* 1783; disc. 1792); *Boston Magazine* (1783, John Eliot, James Freeman, George R. Minot; disc. 1786); New York *Independent Journal* (1783, semiweekly; later a daily as *Daily Gazette;* published *Federalist Papers;* disc. 1795); *Mass. Centinel and Republican Journal* (1784, Boston, Benjamin Russell and William Warden, supported Constitution; as *Columbian Centinel,* beg. 1790, was a leading Federalist paper; disc. 1840). New York *Daily Advertiser* (1785; disc. 1806); *New Haven Gazette and Connecticut Magazine* (1786, Josiah Meigs and Eleutheros Dana; disc. 1789); *Worcester Magazine* (1786, Isaiah Thomas; disc. 1788); *Columbian Magazine* (1786, Philadelphia, ed. by Mathew Carey *et al.;* merged 1790 with *Universal Asylum;* disc. 1792); *Pittsburgh Gazette* (1786, John Sculland and Joseph Hall; first newspaper west of the Alleghenies; Federalist; cont. after merger [1927] as *Post-Gazette*); *American Museum* (1787,

Philadelphia, **Mathew Carey** [1760–1839]; disc. 1792; *American Magazine* (1787, New York, **Noah Webster** [p. 1179]; disc. 1788); *Gazette of the U.S.* (1789, New York; Philadelphia beg. 1790; **John Fenno** [1751–98]; leading Federalist organ; known, 1804–18, as *U.S. Gazette*).

1790–1860. NEWSPAPER GROWTH. There were 92 newspapers in U.S., 1790 —8 dailies, 70 weeklies, 14 semiweekly or at other intervals; 3,725 newspapers, 1860—387 dailies, 3,173 weeklies, 79 semiweeklies, 86 triweeklies.

1790–1804. FEDERALIST AND RE-PUBLICAN PRESS. *General Advertiser,* 1790, Philadelphia, **Benjamin F. Bache** (1769–98); later (1794) known as *Aurora,* succeeding *National Gazette* as leading Republican organ; later ed. by **William Duane** (1760–1835); disc. 1835. *National Gazette,* 1791, Philadelphia, ed. **Philip Freneau** (1752–1832), anti-Federalist; disc. 1793. *Massachusetts Mercury* (1793, Boston); known as *New England Palladium,* 1803–14. *New Hampshire Journal* (1793, Walpole, N.H.), best known beg. 1797 as *The Farmer's Weekly Museum,* a famous village weekly; **Joseph Dennie** (1768–1812) ed., 1796–99; shared literary column with **Royall Tyler** (1757–1826), beg. 1794; disc. 1810. *Centinel of the North-Western Territory* (1793, Cincinnati); first paper in present Ohio; later known as *Freeman's Journal;* merged with *Scioto Gazette* (Chillicothe), started by Nathaniel Willis; still published. *American Minerva* (1793, New York, **Noah Webster**), Federalist; became (1797) *Commercial Advertiser;* renamed *Globe and Commercial Advertiser,* 1904; absorbed by New York *Sun,* 1923. Dunlap and Claypoole's *American Daily Advertiser,* 1793, Philadelphia; became (1800) *Poulson's American Daily Advertiser;* absorbed (1839) by the Philadelphia *North American.* New York *Argus* (1795, Thomas Greenleaf, a Burr Re-

publican; name changed, 1800, to *American Citizen*). *Federal Gazette* (1796, Baltimore; disc. 1825); *Porcupine's Gazette and U.S. Advertiser* (1797, Philadelphia, **William Cobbett** [1763–1835], Federalist; disc. 1799). *Palladium* (1798, Frankfort, Ky., disc. c.1817). **Sedition Act** prosecutions, 1798 (p. 155). Baltimore *American* (1799). *Western Spy* (1799, Cincinnati; disc. 1822). Raleigh (N.C.) *Register* (1799, **Joseph Gales** [1761–1841]). *Washington Federalist* (1800, Georgetown; disc. 1809). Charleston (S.C.) *Times* (1800). *National Intelligencer* (1800, Washington, D.C.); purchased (1807) by **Joseph Gales, Jr.** (1786–1860); from 1812–60 by Gales and **William W. Seaton** (1785–1866); leading political organ (Whig); disc. 1869. New York *Evening Post* (1801), **Alexander Hamilton** *et al.,* Federalist; **William Cullen Bryant** (p. 993), editor in chief, 1829–78, supported Democratic party. Charleston (S.C.) *Courier* (1803); later as *News and Courier,* Unionist during Nullification. Richmond (Va.) *Enquirer* (1804), **Thomas Ritchie** (1778–1854) sole publisher in 1805; a leading Southern paper; disc. 1877. *Indiana Gazette* (1804, Vincennes) became (1807) *Western Sun;* later (1879) *Sun-Commercial.*

1804. CROSWELL LIBEL CASE. Harry Croswell, publisher of the Hudson (N.Y.) *Wasp,* convicted for a criminal libel upon President Jefferson. On appeal Alexander Hamilton, his counsel, reaffirmed and modified defense contention in Zenger case (p. 1190), arguing that truth published "with good motives and justifiable ends" was a defense. Although **James Kent** (p. 1075), then dominating the N.Y. Supreme Court, supported Hamilton, the motion for a new trial was denied by a divided court, but the prosecution was dropped. A New York act of 6 Apr. 1805 adopting Hamilton's formula (incorporated into constitutions of 1821 and 1846) served as a model for the press guarantees of many state constitutions.

1806–20. WESTERN EXPANSION. *Western World* (1806, Frankfort, Ky., Joseph M. Street) exposed Burr Conspiracy (p. 162); disc. 1810. *Democratic Press* (1807, Philadelphia; disc. 1829). *Argus of Western America* (1808, Frankfort, Ky., **Amos Kendall** [1789–1869] coeditor, 1816–29; disc. c.1838). *Federal Republican* (1808, Baltimore; plant destroyed by mob for opposition to War of 1812; resumed, 1816; disc. 1834). *Missouri Gazette* (1808, St. Louis; disc. 1822). *New Hampshire Patriot* (1809, Concord, **Isaac Hill** [1789–1851], Democrat; disc. c.1921). *Mobile Centinel* (1811, Fort Stoddert, first paper in present Alabama). *Ohio State Journal* (1811, Columbus; daily since 1837). *Niles' Weekly Register* (1811, Baltimore, **Hezekiah Niles** [1777–1839], Whig, with a nationwide influence; distinguished for factual reporting; disc. 1849). Albany *Argus* (1813), later organ of the "Albany Regency," disc. c.1894. Boston *Daily Advertiser* (1813, Whig; disc. 1929). *Illinois Herald* (1814, Kaskaskia); first paper in Illinois Territory. *Western Journal* (1815, St. Louis); later known as *Enquirer*, with **Thomas Hart Benton** (1782–1858) among early editors. *Ohio Monitor* (1816, Columbus); became (1838) *Ohio Statesman* Democratic. Detroit *Gazette* (1817), first successful paper in present Michigan; disc. 1830. *Texas Republican* (1819, Nacogdoches); first English-language paper in Texas. *Arkansas Gazette*, 1819, *Arkansas Post* (1822) removed to Little Rock. *National Gazette* (1820, Philadelphia; disc. 1842).

1820. Out of some 1,634 newspapers established between 1704 and 1820 only 4 had lasted 50 years or more.

1821–33. CONTINUED EXPANSION. Mobile *Register* (1821). Charleston *Mercury* (1822, Henry Laurens Pinckney ed., 1823–32; chief secessionist organ).

Richmond *Whig*, 1824, **John H. Pleasants** (1797–1846); disc. 1888. Boston *Courier* (1824, **Joseph T. Buckingham** [1779–1861]; disc. 1864). *National Journal* (1824, Washington, D.C.; disc. 1832). *U.S. Telegraph* (1826, Washington; **Duff Green** [1791–1875]; chief Jackson organ until c.1831; disc. 1837). New York *Morning Courier* (1827) became (1829) *Courier and Enquirer* (Whig) after merging with New York *Enquirer;* **James Watson Webb** (1802–84); merged with *World* (1861). Baltimore *Republican* (1827; actually Democratic; disc. 1863); Cincinnati *Daily Gazette* (1827; disc. 1883). *Journal of Commerce* (1827, New York, **Arthur Tappan** [1786–1865]). *Cherokee Phoenix* (1828, New Echota, Ga.), Indian newspaper printed in characters devised by Sequoyah (?1770–1843); disc. 1835. *Pennsylvania Inquirer* (1829; later *Philadelphia Inquirer*). Albany *Evening Journal*, 1830, **Thurlow Weed** (1797–1882), Whig; disc. 1925. *Evening Transcript* (1830, Boston, L. M. Walter, cultural organ; disc. 1941). Louisville (Ky.) *Journal*, 1830, **George D. Prentice** (1802–70); later (1868) merged with *Democrat* (1843) and *Courier* (1844) as *Courier-Journal*, ed. by **Henry Watterson** ("Marse Henry," 1840–1921). Washington *Globe*, 1830, **Francis P. Blair** (1791–1876); Jackson organ; disc. 1845. Boston *Morning Post* (1831; Democratic). Boston *Atlas* (1832; disc. 1861). *Pennsylvanian*, 1832, Philadelphia, ed. for a time by John W. Forney (1817–81); leading Democratic paper in state; disc. 1861. *Mercantile Journal* (1833, Boston); became *Evening Journal*, 1845; absorbed (1917) by Boston *Herald*. *Weekly Democrat* (1833, Chicago; disc. 1861). Green Bay *Intelligencer* (1833; first paper in Wisconsin Territory; disc. c.1836).

1828–34. EARLY LABOR PRESS. *Mechanics' Free Press* (1828, Philadelphia; first labor paper in U.S.; disc.

c.1835). *Working Man's Advocate,* 1829, New York, **George Henry Evans** (1805–56); disc. c.1851. *Man* (1834, New York, **George Henry Evans;** disc. 1835).

1834–56. GERMAN PRESS. New York *Staats-Zeitung* (1834, **Jacob Uhl**); tri-weekly, 1842; daily 1848; claimed largest German language circulation of any newspaper in the world. *Volksblatt* (1836, Cincinnati). There were 56 German newspapers in U.S., 1856.

1833–37. RISE OF THE PENNY PRESS. New York *Sun,* 1833, **Benjamin H. Day** (1810–89); first successful penny daily in the U.S.; celebrated "Moon Hoax" appeared in its papers in 1835; in 1868 purchased by **Charles A. Dana** (1819–97) and others; absorbed (1950) by New York *World-Telegram.* New York *Transcript* (1834; disc. c.1839). *New York Morning Herald,* 1835, **James Gordon Bennett** (p. 983); chief rival of *Sun;* pioneered in reporting crime and society news; following merger (1924), became *Herald Tribune.* Philadelphia *Public Ledger,* 1836; merged (1934) in the *Inquirer.* Boston *Daily Times,* 1836; merged (1857) with Boston *Herald.* Baltimore *Sun* (1837, Swain, Abell, and Simmons).

1835–60. ANTEBELLUM EXPANSION. *Telegraph and Texas Register,* 1835, San Felipe; later Houston *Telegraph;* disc. 1877. *Union* (1835, Nashville, Tenn.; supported Polk's candidacy; disc. 1875). Detroit *Free Press* (1835). New Orleans *Picayune,* 1836, **George W. Kendall** (1809–67); noteworthy coverage of War with Mexico; later the *Times-Picayune.* New York *Morning Express* (1836; Whig; disc. c.1864). Milwaukee *Advertiser* (1836; disc. 1841); Milwaukee *Sentinel,* 1837; became (1844) first daily in Wisconsin. Philadelphia *North American* (1839; Whig; disc. 1925). New York *Tribune,* 1841, **Horace Greeley** (p. 1045); Whig-Republican; *Weekly Tribune,* 1841, with wider circulation especially in Northern rural areas; merger

(1924) created *Herald Tribune.* Cincinnati *Commercial* (1843; disc. 1930). Springfield (Mass.) *Republican,* 1844, Whig, pioneer in independent journalism; est. as daily by **Samuel Bowles** (1826–77); previously a weekly since 1824; still published. *Plain Dealer* (1845, Cleveland, Ohio). New Orleans *Delta* (1845; disc. 1863). Rotary press invented by **Richard M. Hoe** (p. 1058) revolutionized newspaper printing; first used (1847) by Philadelphia *Public Ledger.* *Oregon Spectator* (1846, Oregon City; first newspaper on Pacific Coast; disc. 1855). *Californian* (1846, Monterey); first newspaper in California; became (1849) the *Alta Californian,* first daily in California; disc. 1891. *Republican* (1847, Santa Fe); first successful paper in present New Mexico. Chicago *Daily Tribune,* 1847; under **Horace White** (1834–1916) supported Lincoln in 1856 and 1860; came under control of **Joseph Medill** (1823–99) in 1874. Toledo (Ohio) *Blade* (1848). New Orleans *Crescent* (1848; disc. 1869). Organization of a group of New York newspapers later known as the **Associated Press** (1848). *Minnesota Pioneer* (1849, St. Paul; disc. 1875). *Deseret News* (1850, Salt Lake City). *Weekly Oregonian* (1850, Portland; became daily, 1861). New York *Daily Times,* 1851, **Henry J. Raymond** (1820–69); Whig-Republican; became (1857) *The New York Times.* *Missouri Democrat* (1852, St. Louis, later *Globe-Democrat*). *Columbia* (1852, Olympia, Wash.); later *Washington Pioneer;* disc. 1861. St. Paul (Minn.) *Daily Pioneer,* 1854; later (1875) *Pioneer-Press.* *Nebraska Palladium* (1854, Bellevue, Neb.); first paper printed in Nebraska; issued first number in Iowa. Chicago *Times* (1854; disc. 1895). *Kansas Weekly Herald* (1854, Leavenworth; disc. 1861). Two Free-Soil papers est. 1855 at Lawrence, Kan.: *Kansas Free State* and *Herald of Free-*

dom; latter disc. 1860. Proslavery *Squatter Sovereign* (1855, Atchison, Kan.); became (1858) *Freedom's Champion* and (1868) *Atchison Champion;* disc. 1917. San Francisco *Bulletin* (1855), **James King;** killed in 1856 for opposing lawlessness; later ed. by **Fremont Older** (1856–1935), who fought political machine; merged (1929) by **W. R. Hearst** with San Francisco *Call* (founded 1856). *Territorial Enterprise* (1858, Genoa, Nev.); later removed to Carson City and Virginia City; first newspaper in present-day Nevada; Mark Twain was reporter, 1862–63. Richmond *Examiner* (1859; disc. 1867); *Weekly Arizonian* (1859, Tubac; later removed to Tucson; disc. 1871). *Democrat* (1859, Sioux Falls, S.D.). Des Moines *Register* (1860). New York *World* (1860, Alexander Cummings); sold 1 July 1861 to August Belmont and Fernando Wood, with **Manton Marble** (1835–1917), as editor (to 1867).

1801–60. PERIODICALS. 1801: *Port Folio* (Philadelphia, **Joseph Dennie** [1768–1812]; a leading literary journal; disc. 1827). **1803:** *Massachusetts Baptist Missionary Mag.* (later *American Baptist Mag.,* Boston, disc. 1909). *Literary Mag. and American Reg.* (Philadelphia, **Charles Brockden Brown** [1771–1810]; disc. 1807). **1808:** *American Law Jl.* (Philadelphia; disc. 1817). **1813:** *Analectic Mag.* (later *Literary Gazette,* Philadelphia; disc. 1821). *Religious Remembrancer* (later *Christian Observer,* Philadelphia). **1815:** *North American Rev.* (Boston, **William Tudor** [1779–1830], a leading intellectual organ; other early editors included **Edward Everett** and **Jared Sparks;** disc. 1939): **1816:** *Portico* (Baltimore; disc. 1818); *Cobbett's American Political Reg.* (New York; disc. 1818). **1818:** *Methodist Mag.* (later *Methodist Rev.,* New York). **1819:** *American Farmer* (Baltimore; disc. 1897); *Universalist Mag.* (later *Universalist Leader*), Boston. **1821:** *Genius of Universal Emancipation*

(Mt. Pleasant, Ohio, antislavery monthly, **Benjamin Lundy** [1789–1839]; disc. 1839); *Saturday Evening Post* (Philadelphia, Charles Alexander and Samuel C. Atkinson); claims descent from *Pennsylvania Gazette,* founded, 1728; originally a newspaper, changed gradually to a weekly magazine by 1871. Bought 1897 by **Cyrus H. K. Curtis** (1850–1933). **1822:** *U.S. Catholic Miscellany* (Charleston; disc. 1832). *New England Farmer* (Boston; disc. 1846). **1823:** *Zion's Herald* (Boston); New York *Mirror* (a leading weekly; disc. c.1857); *Christian Examiner* (Boston; disc. 1869). **1825:** *Biblical Repertory* (later *Princeton Rev.,* Princeton, N.J.; disc. 1884). *New Harmony Gazette* (later *Free Enquirer,* New Harmony, Ind.; disc. 1835). **1826:** *American Journal of Education* (later *American Annals of Education,* Boston; disc. 1839). *Casket* (Philadelphia; disc. 1840); *Franklin Jl.* (later *Jl. of the Franklin Institute,* Philadelphia); *Christian Advocate* (New York). **1827:** *American Quarterly Rev.* (Philadelphia; disc. 1837). *Youth's Companion* (Boston; famous children's mag.; disc. 1929). **1828:** *Southern Agriculturalist* (Charleston; disc. 1846). *Southern Rev.* (Charleston; disc. 1832). **1829:** *American Jurist and Law Mag.* (Boston; disc. 1843). **1830:** *Lady's Book* (later *Godey's Lady's Book,* Philadelphia; most important of early women's mags.; disc. 1898). **1831:** *The Liberator,* 1 Jan., Boston, abolitionist organ, **William Lloyd Garrison** (p. 1038); disc. 29 Dec. 1865. *Biblical Repository* (Andover, Mass.; disc. 1850). *Spirit of the Times* (New York; disc. 1861). **1833:** *Knickerbocker Mag.* (New York; first popular monthly; **Lewis Gaylord Clark** [1808–73]; disc. 1865); *Parley's Mag.* (New York; disc. 1844). **1834:** *Southern Literary Messenger* (Richmond; leading Southern mag.; Poe, Simms, Matthew F. Maury among contributors; disc. 1864). **1837:** *U.S. Mag. and Democratic Rev.* (Washington, D.C.;

John L. O'Sullivan and Samuel D. Langstreet; later known as *Democratic Rev.;* jingoist; introduced term "Manifest Destiny" [p. 230]; disc. 1859). **1838:** *Pennsylvania Freeman* (Philadelphia, antislavery; disc. 1854). *Connecticut Common School Jl.* (Hartford; disc. 1866). *Common School Jl.* (Boston: disc. 1852). **1839:** *Brother Jonathan* (New York; disc. c.1845). *Merchants' Mag. and Commercial Rev.* (later *Hunts' Merchants' Mag.,* New York; disc. 1870). *Dial* (Boston; Transcendentalist organ; edited first by **Margaret Fuller** [p. 1035], then by **Ralph Waldo Emerson** [p. 1024]; disc. 1844). *Lowell Offering* (Lowell, Mass.; printed contributions by young women mill operatives; disc. 1845). *Graham's Mag.* (Philadelphia, **Edgar Allan Poe** lit. ed., 1841–42; disc. 1858). **1842:** *Pennsylvania Law Jl.* (later *American Law Jl.*), Philadephia; disc. 1852. *American Agriculturalist* (New York, now Ithaca; oldest farm jl. still published). *Peterson's Ladies National Mag.* (Philadelphia; close competitor to *Godey's;* disc. 1898). **1843:** *New Englander* (later *Yale Rev.*), New Haven, Conn. **1844:** *Brownson's Quarterly Rev.* (Boston; disc. 1875). *Littell's Living Age* (Boston; disc. 1941). **1845:** *American Rev.* (later *Whig Rev.,* New York; disc. 1852). *Harbinger* (Brook Farm, West Roxbury, Mass., **George Ripley** (1802–80), Fourierist; disc. 1849); *Scientific American* (New York). **1846:** *Commercial Rev. of the South and West* (later *De Bow's Rev.,* New Orleans; outstanding for economic coverage of antebellum South; disc. 1880). **1847:** *National Era* (Washington, D.C., **Gamaliel Bailey** [1807–59], antislavery jl.; disc. 1860). **1848:** *The Independent* (New York; disc. 1928). **1850:** *Harper's New Monthly Mag.* (later *Harper's Mag.*), New York; circulation 200,000 by 1860. *Waverly Mag.* (Boston; disc. 1908). **1851:** *New York Ledger* (**Robert Bonner** [1824–99], weekly; circulation 400,000

by 1860; disc. 1903). *Gleason's Pictorial Drawing-Room Companion* (Boston; first illustrated mag. in the U.S.; disc. 1859). **1852:** *American Law Reg. and Rev.* (later *Univ. of Pennsylvania Law Rev.,* Philadelphia). **1853:** *Putnam's Monthly Mag.* (New York; disc. 1857). *Country Gentleman* (Albany; now Philadelphia). **1855:** *Amer. Jl. of Education* (New York; disc. 1882). *Frank Leslie's Illustrated Newspaper* (later *Leslie's Weekly,* New York; disc. 1922). **1856:** *Jl. of Agriculture* (St. Louis; disc. 1921). **1857:** *Atlantic Monthly* (Boston, **James Russell Lowell** [p. 1089]). *Harper's Weekly* (New York, news weekly; disc. 1916).

1861–65. NEWSPAPERS: CIVIL WAR. The Northern press was divided in its support of the war. Only 5 out of 17 New York dailies were unquestionably loyal. To protect military secrets courtsmartial were authorized where news was released considered as aiding the enemy; telegraph wires from Washington were placed under State Department censorship. For open hostility to the war effort, the New York *Daily News* lost its postal privilege (Aug. 1861; suspended 18 months). The Columbus *Copperhead* (1861), the New York *Copperhead* (1863), and the Philadelphia *Evening Journal* were suppressed for support of Vallandigham, and the Chicago *Times* and Philadelphia *Christian Observer* were seized by the federal authorities.

1861–82. SYNDICATES AND PRESS ASSOCIATIONS. First newspaper syndicate organized (1861) by Ansell N. Kellogg of the Baraboc (Wis.) *Republic,* providing "readyprint" for local papers. United Press organized (1882); expired 1893. Second United Press founded (1907, below). McClure Newspaper Syndicate organized 1884 by **Samuel S. McClure.**

1864–96. NEWSPAPER CHANGES. St. Louis *Dispatch,* 1864; acquired by **Joseph Pulitzer** (p. 1132) in 1848 and combined with St. Louis *Post*, est. by John A. Dillon, 1875. San Francisco *Chronicle* (1865, Charles and Michael De Young). Atlanta *Constitution* (1868, W. A. Hemphill). New York *Sun* acquired (1868) by **Charles A. Dana** (1819–97). Its issue of 8 Nov. 1876 (Hayes-Tilden election story) had record sale of 220,000 copies. Sold to *World-Telegram*, 1950. *Public Record* (Philadelphia, 1870, W. J. Swain). Boston *Globe* (1872, Maturin Ballou; eve. ed. begun 1877). **Whitelaw Reid** (1837–1912) succeeded Horace Greeley (1872) as editor of New York *Tribune*. New York *Daily Graphic* (1873; featuring news pictures; disc. 1889). Chicago *Daily News*, 1876, **Melville E. Stone** (1848–1929). Washington *Post* (1877; sold to John R. McLean 1905). Kansas City *Star* (1880, W. R. Nelson). New York *Evening Post* sold (1881) to **Henry Villard** (1835–1900), with **Carl Schurz** (p. 1147) as editor. **Edwin L. Godkin** (p. 1042) became editor in chief, 1883. New York *Morning Journal* (1882, Albert Pulitzer); sold, 1884, to John R. McLean; **William Randolph Hearst** (p. 1055) became owner in 1895; merged with New York *Evening Journal* (1937) to become *Journal-American*. New York *World* acquired by **Joseph Pulitzer**. News coverage innovations, editorials, and 2-ct. price boosted circulation from 20,000 (1883) to 250,000 (1886). New York *Evening World* (1887, S.S. Carvallo; disc. 1931). Ownership of San Francisco *Examiner* (1865) transferred (1887) from George Hearst to his son, **William Randolph Hearst.** Emporia *Gazette* (1890); acquired, 1895, by **William Allen White** (1868–1944), whose editorials, e.g., "What's the Matter with Kansas?" (1896) were nationally read. **Adolph S. Ochs** (p. 1117) acquired (1896) *The New York Times*.

1880–1914. Daily circulation of German papers in St. Louis (1880) amounted to 21% of aggregate; in New York, 10%;

in Cincinnati, 28%, with 80 German dailies, 466 weeklies, and 95 other German periodicals. In addition: 13 Bohemian periodicals, 49 Scandinavian, 41 French, 26 Spanish, 4 Italian, 5 Welsh. *Jewish Daily Forward* (New York, 1897), ed. **Abraham Cahan** (1860–1951). There were 1,300 foreign language newspapers and periodicals in the U.S., 1914; 140 dailies (one third German). New York had 32 (including 10 German, 5 Yiddish, 3 Italian).

1897–1933. CHAIN NEWSPAPER ERA (paralleling trends in industry and merchandising) was inaugurated with the organization (1897) by Edward Wyllis Scripps and Milton Alexander McRae of the Scripps-McRae League of Newspapers; Scripps-McRae Press Assn., 1897. Together with the Publisher's Press (1904), it was the forerunner of the second **United Press** (1907). Between 1892–1914 the Scripps chain had a controlling interest in 13 newspapers, acquired principally by establishing new papers in smaller cities. With the addition of Roy W. Howard to the board in 1922 the organization became the **Scripps-Howard** chain. The **Munsey Chain** began (1901) with the purchase by Frank A. Munsey of the Washington *Times* and New York *Daily News*, followed by the acquisition of the Boston *Journal* (1902), the Baltimore *Evening News* (1908), and the Philadelphia *Evening Times* (1908). The **Hearst Chain** acquired 30 papers (1913–34) in addition to control of 2 wire services, the King Features Syndicate, 6 magazines, a newsreel, and the *American Weekly* (a Sunday supplement). The 5 other leading chains (1933, Patterson-McCormick, Scripps-Howard, Paul Block, Ridder, and Gannett) controlled 81 dailies, with combined total circulation of 9,250,000.

1897–1907. COMIC STRIPS appeared in the comic weeklies of the 70s and 80s; color sequence in New York *Sunday*

World (1894). Real origin dates from Rudolph Dirks' "Katzenjammer Kids" (New York *Journal*, 1897). First 6-days-a-week strip was H. C. "Bud" Fisher's "A. Mutt" (San Francisco *Chronicle*, 1907); later "Mutt and Jeff."

1898. SPANISH-AMERICAN WAR. New York *Journal* and *World* outdistanced all other "yellows" in agitating for U.S. intervention in Cuba as well as in coverage of the war.

1908–12. JOURNALISM SCHOOLS. School of Journalism est. at University of Missouri (1908; courses offered as early as 1878). Columbia University School of Journalism est. (1912) by a bequest from Joseph Pulitzer.

1917. PULITZER PRIZE awards inaugurated by the trustees of Columbia Univ., granted on recommendation of the Advisory Board of the Columbia School of Journalism. Awards have been made to newspapers for meritorious public service and to working newspapermen in various branches of journalism. In addition, awards are made for (1) novel, (2) drama, (3) U.S. history, (4) biography, (5) poetry, (6) music.

1918. The *Stars and Stripes* published by the American Expeditionary Force in France; disc. 1919; revived in Washington, D.C., 1919–26.

1919–24. TABLOIDS. The New York *Daily News* est. by the McCormick-Patterson chain. A tabloid featuring sensational news, crime, and sex stories, it attained the largest daily circulation in the U.S. in 1924 (1,750,000). By 1944, 2 million daily, 4 million Sundays. Its success led to the establishment in 1924 of New York *Daily Mirror* by W. R. Hearst and the *Daily Graphic* by Bernarr Macfadden.

1940. *PM* (New York, Marshall Field; disc. 1946).

1941. Chicago *Sun* (Marshall Field).

1942–45. ARMY PAPERS. *Stars and Stripes* est. as a weekly (17 Apr.; a daily

by 2 Nov.; coined phrase "GI Joe"). *Yank*, 24-page weekly tabloid est., with ultimately 21 editions in various war theaters.

1944, Nov. Thomas E. Dewey was supported for president by 796 newspapers (68.5% of total circulation); 291 (17.7% of circulation) supported F. D. Roosevelt (lowest press support since Bryan's campaign against McKinley, 1896). Similarly proportionate press support for Dewey v. Truman, 1948, and Eisenhower v. Stevenson, 1952.

1949, 1 Oct. There were 1,780 dailies with a circulation of 52,845,551; 546 Sunday papers with a circulation of 46,-498,968 (*Editor and Publisher*).

1862–1900. PERIODICALS. 1862: *The Old Guard* (New York, C. Chauncey Burr; Copperhead; disc. 1870). **1863:** *Army and Navy Jl.* (New York, William Conant Church, ed., 1863–1917). **1865:** *The Catholic World* (New York, Paulist Fathers). *The Nation* (New York, weekly jl. of politics, literature, science, the arts); first ed., **E. L. Godkin** (p. 1042), to 1881; later eds. include **Oswald Garrison Villard** (1918–32), **Joseph Wood Krutch** (1933–37), **Freda Kirchwey** (1933–55), and Carey McWilliams (1955–75). **1866:** *The Galaxy* (New York, monthly literary mag., William Conant Church and Francis Pharcellus; disc. 1878). **1867:** *The Southern Rev.* (Baltimore, Albert Taylor Bledsoe; disc. 1879). *Jl. of Speculative Philosophy* (St. Louis, **William Torrey Harris;** disc. 1893). *Harper's Bazaar* (New York, weekly women's mag.; Fletcher Harper; became monthly, 1901; purchased by Hearst, 1913). **1868:** *Overland Monthly* (San Francisco; California regional mag. **Bret Harte,** ed.; suspended 1876–82; cont. again until 1935). *Lippincott's Mag.* (Philadelphia, literary monthly; John Foster Kirk ed. until 1884; 1915 moved to New York as *McBride's Mag.;* merged with *Scribner's Mag.,* 1916). *Vanity Fair* (New York, ed. for a time by **Frank Harris;** absorbed by *Vogue,* 1936, a woman's fashion mag.). **1869:** *Appleton's Jl.* (New York, literary weekly; became monthly 1876; disc. 1881). **1870:** *Christian Union* (New York, "family mag.," Henry Ward Beecher and Lyman Abbott; name changed, 1893, to *The Outlook,* with more emphasis on political commentary; disc. 1935). *Scribner's Monthly* (New York, literary jl., ed., Josiah G. Holland); after absorbing *Putnam's* (1870), it was continued as the *Century* (1881); merged 1930 with *The Forum* (est. 1886), with **Walter Hines Page,** ed., a mag. of controversy; merged with *Current History* (1940). **1872:** *Publisher's Weekly* (New York, Frederick Leypoldt); *Popular Science Monthly* (New York, Edward L. Youmans). **1873:** *The Delineator* (New York, E. Butterick & Co., fashion mag.; later of general circulation; disc. 1937). *Woman's Home Companion* (Cleveland, originally a semimonthly under name of *Home Companion;* after 1897 a monthly). *St. Nicholas* (New York, children's mag.; ed. 1873–1905 by Mrs. Mary Mapes Dodge; disc. 1940). **1876:** *Frank Leslie's Popular Monthly* (New York, name changed, 1906, to *The American Mag.,* published by a group of muckraking authors including Ida Tarbell, Lincoln Steffens, *et al.*). **1877:** *Puck* (New York, a comic mag., Joseph Keppler and A. Schwarzmann; disc. 1912). **1880:** *The Dial* (Chicago, conservative rev.; became fortnightly 1892, when it was moved to New York as a radical jl. of opinion and chief of the "little magazines"; eds. included **Conrad Aiken, Randolph Bourne, Van Wyck Brooks;** disc. 1929). **1881:** *The Critic* (New York, weekly literary rev.; Jeannette and Joseph Gilder; disc. 1906). *Judge* (New York, comic weekly by authors and artists who seceded from *Puck;* disc. 1939). **1883:** *Ladies Home Jl.* (Philadelphia, monthly; **Cyrus H. K. Curtis;** popularized by its 2d ed., **Edward**

W. Bok [1863–1930], ed. 1899–1920). **1884:** *The Christian Century* (Chicago). *The Journalist* (New York; first professional mag. for journalists; consolidated 1907 with *Editor and Publisher*). **1887:** *Scribner's Mag.* (New York, literary jl.; purchased 1939 by *The Commentator* and renamed *Scribner's Commentator*). *The Cosmopolitan* (Rochester, a conservative family monthly; but removed to New York, 1887, and became popular mag.; after 1900 entered muckraking movement; purchased by Hearst, 1925). **1888:** *Collier's* (New York, weekly; under ed. of **Norman Hapgood** [1903–12] and **Mark Sullivan** [1914–17] was a leading liberal-muckraking publication). **1889:** *The Arena* (Boston, Benjamin O. Fowler; first muckraking periodical; disc. 1909). *Life* (New York humor mag., featuring **Charles Dana Gibson,** and his "Gibson Girl"; disc., 1936, when its title was acquired by a news weekly. *Munsey's Mag.* (New York, Frank A. Munsey; merged 1929 with *Argosy All-Story Weekly*). **1890:** *The Literary Digest* (New York, newspaper and mag. of comment; its straw poll erroneously predicting the election of Landon in 1936 contributed to its demise, 1938). *Smart Set* (New York, jl. of society; Mencken and Nathan, eds., 1914–24, when purchased by Hearst; disc. 1930). **1891:** *Review of Reviews* (New York, monthly of comments on events; **Albert Shaw** ed. from 1894; merged when *Literary Digest* 1937). **1893:** *McClure's Mag.* (New York, S. S. McClure; merged, 1929, with *New Smart Set*). **1899:** *Everybody's Mag.* (New York, absorbed by *Romance,* 1929). **1900:** *World's Work* (New York, monthly record of current events; **Walter Hines Page;** absorbed, 1932, by *Rev. of Revs.*).

1905–16. 1905: *Variety* (New York, theatrical trade jl., **Sime Silverman,** 1873–1933). **1911:** *Masses* (New York, proletarian monthly; superseded, 1918, by *The Liberator; New Masses,* 1926).

1912: *Poetry* (Chicago, **Harriet Monroe,** organ for new trends in poetry). **1914:** *New Republic* (New York, **Herbert Croly** and **Walter Lippmann,** p. 1086). *The Little Review* (Chicago, moving to New York and then Paris; best known for its serialization of Joyce's *Ulysses;* disc. 1929). **1916:** *Theater Arts Mag.* (New York, quality jl., cont. since 1924 as *Theatre Arts Monthly;* disc. 1964).

1922–36. 1922: *The Reader's Digest* (Pleasantville, N.Y., condensation of reprints of other periodicals, **De Witt Wallace;** circulation, 1944, exceeded 9 million, with another 4 million among its foreign editions). **1923:** *Time* (New York, news weekly, **Henry R. Luce** (p. 1090) and Brinton Hadden). **1924:** *American Mercury* (New York, critical and literary, **H. L. Mencken** and **George Jean Nathan).** *The Saturday Rev. of Literature* (New York **Henry Seidel Canby** ed. to 1936). **1925:** *The New Yorker* (New York, weekly humorous mag. for the "caviar sophisticates"; **Harold Wallace Ross** [1892–1951]). **1930:** *Fortune* (New York, monthly mag. of business, finance, and industry; **Henry R. Luce**). **1933:** *Newsweek* (New York, news mag.). *Esquire* (New York, monthly, short stories and humorous illustrations). **1936:** *Life* (New York, **Henry R. Luce,** news and feaures through photos).

1951, 30 June (period ending). INROADS OF COMICS revealed by the net paid circulation of leading U.S. magazines, (A.B.C. Publishers' statements):

Marvel Comic Group	11,057,832
Reader's Digest	8,500,000
National Comics Group	7,906,688
Harvey Comics Group	5,458,861
Life	5,301,331
True Story Women's Group	5,068,968
Ladies' Home Journal	4,458,219
McCall's	4,011,643
Woman's Home Companion	3,992,005
Woman's Day	3,866,062
Fawcett Comic Group	3,569,927
Archie Comic Group	3,569,927
Better Homes and Gardens	3,563,856
Look	3,260,927

1954, 27 Oct. Adoption of comic book code to be voluntarily enforced by 26 publishing firms to bar vulgar, obscene, and terror comics. By 1955, 13 states had passed laws to police comics.

1952–60 PERIODICAL TRENDS. While a few new periodicals quickly achieved success (*TV Guide, Confidential,* 1952; *Sports Illustrated, American Heritage,* 1954), the long-term trend was toward mergers and discontinuance. In 1956 *Collier's, American,* and *Woman's Home Companion* ended publication, followed (1957) by *Town Journal* (successor, 1953, to *Pathfinder*), *Omnibook,* and *Étude.*

1953, 28 Nov.–8 Dec. 11-day strike of photoengravers left New York City without a major daily newspaper for first time since 1778.

1958. United Press Assn. and International News Service merged to form United Press International.

1960–73 CONSOLIDATION. The number of daily newspapers serving many metropolitan areas decreased as economic difficulties led to mergers and to the demise of newspapers. New York City, with 15 major daily newspapers in 1900, was left with 3 in 1969. Philadelphia and Washington, D.C., had 3 newspapers; while Los Angeles, Detroit, and St. Louis had only 2 major dailies. In many cities, single corporations published both morning and evening newspapers, often the only major dailies operating in the area (i.e., San Francisco, after 1965).

There was a marked trend toward consolidation in the newspaper industry as major chains rapidly increased their holdings. Lord Thomson of Fleet, owner of 20 dailies, bought the entire Brush Moore chain (1967), 12 dailies and 4 weeklies, for $72 million, until then the biggest newspaper transaction in history. Already the largest chain in terms of circulation, the Hearst Corp. purchased the *Knicker-*

bocker News (Albany, N.Y.) in 1960, its first purchase in 32 years, and made several more acquisitions thereafter. Other evidence of consolidation was the purchase of the Montgomery *Advertiser* and the Atlanta *Journal* by the Scripps League News in 1969 and the acquisition of four Florida papers by the New York *Times* in 1972. The biggest merger, however, was brought off by the Los Angeles *Times*, which bought the Dallas *Times Herald* and its broadcasting interests for $91.5 million (1969), then taking over *Newsday* of Long Island, New York.

Concerned by this trend, the Anti-Trust Division of the Department of Justice brought suit against the Los Angeles *Times* which, in 1967, was forced to divest itself of the San Bernadino *Sun*, purchased in 1964. In further antitrust action, the Supreme Court prohibited (1970) cooperation in the production of newspapers, a practice used by 44 papers in 22 cities. Congress, however, counteracted the Court's decision with the Newspaper Preservation Act (1971).

In the magazine field, the pattern of consolidation was the same. McGraw-Hill bought *American Heritage* and *Horizon* in 1969, while simultaneously Curtis Publications was selling *Ladies' Home Journal* to Downe Communications, Inc. and Cowles was turning *Family Circle* over to the New York *Times*. In 1971 *Saturday Review* was sold to a syndicate headed by Nicholas H. Charney, who had successfully launched *Psychology Today* in 1967, but Norman Cousins reacquired *Saturday Rev.* in 1973. In the biggest of all sales and mergers, Cahners bought Conover-Mast Publications Inc. for $20 million.

The mortality rate for magazines was high in the period 1960–73. Among the most celebrated casualties were *Saturday Evening Post*, which died in 1969 after 148 years of continuous publication; *Look* (1971), which failed despite a circulation of 7 million; and *Life* (1972), which had dominated the field of photojournalism for 40 years. The causes of death were competition from TV, loss of advertising revenue, and steadily increasing postal rates.

1968–73. NEW PUBLICATIONS. Despite the problems besetting the journalistic world, new newspapers and magazines were created in the 60s and early 70s. In 1968 the Los Angeles *Times* established a new daily in Orange County, and the suburban Chicago area found itself with 2 new papers. There was far more activity, however, in the magazine world. In 1971 the *Saturday Evening Post* was reborn as a quarterly. Other notable births were *Change* (1969), an educational journal funded by the Ford Foundation; *Essence* (1970), a magazine appealing to young urban black women; *Liberty* (1971), the "Nostalgia Magazine"; and *Ms.* (1972), a feminist journal. The most successful of these new vehicles seemed to be *New York* (1968), one of a number of magazines aimed at a local audience.

Innovations and alterations were also evident among journalistic survivors. Losing circulation to *Newsweek*, *Time* toned down its splashy, hyperbolical style and exchanged its conservative stance for a liberal one.

1964–73. UNDERGROUND PAPERS. Spawned by the student uprisings of the 60s, underground newspapers numbered 600 by 1969 and boasted an estimated readership of 3 million. Generally they were short, economically produced, and technically inferior. They served as a conduit for radical political expression that was stifled by the mainstream press. Among the causes most commonly espoused were the movement against the war in Vietnam, the struggle for racial equality, the activities of Cesar Chavez' Farm Workers Union, the legalization of marijuana. Among the best-known of these publications were *The Berkeley Barb*, founded in 1964; the *Advocate*, a Los Angeles-based publication that first appeared in 1967; the *L.A. Free Press* (1968), modeled on New York's *Village Voice* and the most successful of all underground papers (circulation: 95,000); *Rat*, published in New York and run largely by a group of women who seized control in 1970. A group of environmentalist, how-to-do-it publications also flourished in the underground sphere, the most renowned of these being *The Whole Earth Catalog*, which was issued from 1969–71.

1967–73. UNDERGROUND COMICS. Underground comics (or "Comix") were another important journalistic phenomenon of the period. The fountainhead of this movement was Robert Crumb, who in 1967 conceived and published *Zap*, a comic book featuring off-beat artwork, unorthodox subject matter, radical politics, and a good deal of social criticism. Aimed at the counter-culture, *Zap* was quickly followed by an even more provocative series called *Feds 'n' Heads*, the brainchild of Gilbert Shelton. Typical of Shelton's work was the satirical treatment of superheroes embodied in a character named the "Wonder Wart-Hog." These and other underground comics were frequently obscene in their efforts to outrage bourgeois sensibilities and became the target of censorship attempts throughout the country.

1968. THE PRESS AND THE '68 CAMPAIGN. Press coverage of the tumultuous 1968 Democratic convention in Chicago confirmed the opinions of many Americans that the political process was breaking down and convinced others that newspapermen were slanting the news

and encouraging violence. In the course of the convention, 24 reporters and photographers were beaten by the Chicago police, while attempting to observe the events. A report by a presidentially-appointed analyst, Daniel Walker, accused the police of promoting disorder and exonerated the press.

1969–73. NIXON ADMINISTRATION AND THE PRESS (p. 535). For publication of the **Pentagon Papers**, see pp. 537, 541, 684.

1961–73. STRIKES. Issues related to automation precipitated a wave of major strikes, often accompanied by sympathy lockouts by unaffected publishers, causing total printed-news blackouts. The pattern of the long strike was set in Minneapolis (117 days, 1962). Two lengthy blackouts (113 days, 1962–63; 25 days, 1965) and a strike against 3 dailies (139 days, 1966) contributed to the demise of 4 major daily newspapers in New York City, including the New York *Herald Tribune* (1966). Other cities experiencing major shutdowns included Cleveland (129 days, 1962–63), Detroit (134 days, 1964), Baltimore (74 days, 1970), Pittsburgh (129 days, 1971).

1960–73. TECHNOLOGICAL ADVANCES. Coded tape signals sent by cable to activate typesetting machines in Paris produced the first international edition of the *New York Times* (20 Oct. 1960). The idea of an overseas edition, available the same day as the original, was immediately adopted by the *Herald Tribune*, whose international edition continued beyond the demise of its New York editions and outlived the international edition of the *Times*.

During the 60s and early 70s the replacement of lead type by offset type became commonplace. Other technological changes included development of varieties of photocomposition and composition by typewriter. Perforated tapes activating lead casting machines increasingly replaced human compositors while machines were programed to edit copy, justify lines (by memorizing syllable breaks), transmit tapes steadily from plant to plant, etc.

Radio and Television

A hobby at first and then a medium for entertainment, radio, by its capability of giving immediacy to distant events, helped revolutionize news reporting, perhaps best exemplified by Edward R. Murrow's wartime broadcasts from London. Its political impact was early recognized by Franklin D. Roosevelt, whose fireside chats became a national institution.

Although the entertainment potential of television may never have been fully realized, its popularity sharply altered the patterns of family life. Even more than radio, TV makes the viewer a part of an event, as was most tragically brought home in the few days following the assassination of John F. Kennedy. TV's potential in civic affairs has been repeatedly demonstrated, notably in the Kefauver hearings on organized crime, the Army-McCarthy hearings, and those of the Senate Watergate Committee, and its cultural potential especially by educational TV stations.

Enjoying less than rigorous government regulation, with little consistency in the enforcement of the "public interest" criteria by the FCC, radio and TV networks came under heavy fire during the Nixon administration, but the Watergate revelations undercut drastic regulatory proposals.

1901–24. RADIO: EARLY TECHNOLOGICAL DEVELOPMENTS (p. 798).

1907–16. RADIO: EARLY BROADCASTS. Early programs by individuals and small enterprises, heard by experimenters, ship operators, and a growing number of amateurs, included musical performances (p. 927), news bulletins, phonograph records, poetry readings, and presidential election returns (De Forest, 1916).

1912. RADIO ACT OF 1912 (13 Aug.) required operator's and station licenses to be awarded by the Secretary of Commerce and Labor (after 1913 Secretary of Commerce), who had power to assign wave lengths and time limits. Ship, amateur, and government transmissions were kept apart.

1914–21. EXPANSION OF RADIO COMMUNICATIONS SYSTEMS. Consolidation of radio industry was fostered by coordination imposed by Navy during World War I. In 1919 the **Radio Corporation of America** was organized by **Owen D. Young** (1874–1962), receiving the assets and operations of the Marconi Wireless Company of America. By 1921 two-thirds of RCA stock was held by General Electric, American Telephone and Telegraph Co., Westinghouse, and United Fruit, resolving patent struggles.

David Sarnoff (1891–1971) became general manager (1921), president (1930–47), chairman of the board (1947–71).

1920–29. GROWTH OF REGULAR BROADCASTING. The first station to begin regular commercial broadcasting was WWJ, Detroit, with a formal period of testing commencing 20 Aug. 1920. Election returns were broadcast by WWJ in Detroit, 31 Aug. 1920, and by WWJ and KDKA, Pittsburgh, Pa., 2 Nov. 1920, holding a special license to launch a broadcast service in order to stimulate radio receivers manufactured by Westinghouse. WJZ, Newark, N.J., broadcast the World Series, beginning 5 Oct. 1921. KYW, Chicago, began broadcasting with the Chicago Civic Opera, 11 Nov. 1921. 500 new stations began in 1922, many established by colleges, newspapers, churches, and department stores. The first municipally owned radio station was WNYC, New York (1924). The first commercial program was aired by WEAF, New York (later WRCA, WNBC), 28 Aug. 1922.

Programing in 1920s was dominated by classical music with both professional and amateur performers. The first radio drama broadcast, WGY, Schenectady, N.Y., 3 Aug. 1922; first news analysis, **H. V. Kaltenborn** (1878–1965), WEAF, New York (1921); first syndicated radio show, **Amos 'N Andy** (1928), established the possibilities of the radio serial.

SALES OF RADIO SETS AND PARTS
(millions $s)

1922	60	1926	506
1923	136	1927	426
1924	358	1928	651
1925	430	1929	843

1922. WASHINGTON RADIO CONFERENCES of representatives of regional and industrial interests was convened by Secretary of Commerce Herbert Hoover, 27 Feb. 1922, asking for advice concerning his regulatory powers. Conferees asked for government action to regulate airwaves. Second conference (1923) declared that Secretary could regulate hours and wave lengths where necessary in order to prevent interference detrimental to the public good. Hoover reallocated broadcast band (1923). After fourth conference (1925) Hoover refused to issue further licenses.

1922–32. CREATION OF NETWORKS. WJZ, Newark, N.J., and WGY, Schenectady, N.Y., joint broadcast of World Series (Oct. 1922) was earliest forerunner of network broadcasting. First network, a 6-station hookup by AT&T was established in 1923. Calvin Coolidge address on election eve (1924) estimated to have reached 20 to 30 million people. **National Association of Broadcasters** was founded in 1923 to oppose demands for royalties for songs which were broadcast. **National Broadcasting Co.** (NBC), incorporated 9 Oct. 1926, a subsidiary of RCA, General Electric, and Westinghouse, absorbed AT&T's interest in active broadcasting. Competition from NBC's 2 networks, "red" and "blue," led to a decline in local production. General Electric and Westinghouse withdrew from RCA and NBC (1932). **Columbia Broadcasting System** (CBS) was formed in Apr. 1927. William S. Paley (1901–) served as president, 1928–46, chairman of the board, 1946–).

1927. Car radios first produced by Philco.

1923–51. TELEVISION: EARLY TECHNOLOGICAL DEVELOPMENTS (p. 799).

1927. RADIO ACT (23 Feb.) provided ownership of airwaves by U.S., established a bipartisan 5-man Radio Commission for 1 year, licensing by a standard of public interest, convenience, or necessity, prohibited censorship except for obscenity. Broadcasters were required to treat rival candidates for public office equally. Later amendments extended the commission's life.

1930–39. RADIO PROGRAMING.
Comedy and variety programs with stars such as Eddie Cantor, Al Jolson, Rudy Vallee, George Burns and Gracie Allen, Jack Benny, and Ed Wynn dominated programing. Serials, *The Goldbergs, Just Plain Bill, Vic and Sade,* proliferated. Mystery and crime programs such as Eno Crime Club, Charlie Chan, and Sherlock Holmes were popular as were tales of romance and adventure. Among the quizzes and game shows was *Information Please* (1938). Major programs included Archibald MacLeish's verse drama, *The Fall of the City,* broadcast by CBS, 4 Mar. 1937; first NBC Symphony broadcast led by Arturo Toscanini (1937).

1933–39. PUBLIC AFFAIRS BROADCASTING. Franklin D. Roosevelt delivered first "fireside chat" 12 Mar. 1933. Political influence was wielded by broadcasts of Father Charles Coughlin and Sen. Huey Long. In the early days of the Spanish Civil War battle sounds were broadcast by shortwave to America by H. V. Kaltenborn as commentator on CBS. **Edward R. Murrow** (1908–65) broadcast news of the Anschluss by shortwave from Vienna on CBS, 13 Mar. 1938. During the Munich crisis (12–29 Sept.) CBS broadcast 151 pickups, NBC, 147.

1934–39. FREQUENCY MODULATION invented by Edwin H. Armstrong (pp. 800, 975).

1934, 19 June. COMMUNICATIONS ACT OF 1934 reenacted 1927 **Radio Act,** establishing 7-man Federal Communications Commission, with added telephone jurisdiction, was based upon obsolete premise that broadcasting was local responsibility exercised by individual licensees.

1938, 30 Mar. *The War of the Worlds,* narrated by Orson Welles, on CBS, triggered nationwide panic.

1939–45. WARTIME PROGRAMING. Edward R. Murrow's broadcasts from wartime London gained wide attention. Among other major news broadcasters during World War II: Howard K. Smith (CBS), Berlin; Charles Collingwood (CBS), England; Larry Lesueur (CBS), Moscow; Eric Sevareid (CBS), Paris; William Shirer (CBS), Berlin. Manufacture of receivers and recordings halted by war, 1942. Office of censorship created 16 Dec. 1941. Censorship was voluntary although news about troop movements and the weather was abandoned. **Voice of America** was launched (1942); placed within U.S. Information Agency (1953).

1939–41. TELEVISION: EARLY COMMERCIAL DEVELOPMENTS. Regularly scheduled commercial TV programs by NBC began formally 30 Apr. 1939 with program including Franklin D. Roosevelt. By May 1940, 23 stations were in operation. First coverage of election returns by TV, 5 Nov. 1940 (NBC and Dumont TV stations). Full commercial TV inaugurated 1941 but TV manufacturing and programing was severely curtailed by World War II.

1943, 12 Oct. FCC ordered the sale of NBC "Blue Network" and approved creation of American Broadcasting System (later, ABC).

1945–55. RADIO PROGRAMING. Major trends influenced by development of the tape recorder included the growth of disc jockeys on local stations playing phonograph records and giveaway shows. In addition, schedule dominance was maintained by comedians, drama series, serials.

1948–53. TV PROGRAMING. Among the early successes in programing was *Toast of the Town* (CBS, 1948)—later the long-lived *Ed Sullivan Show, Kukla, Fran, and Ollie, Texaco Star Theater* (starring Milton Berle), and *I Love Lucy.*

1950–73. TV NEWS COVERAGE on major political events included the Kefauver Crime Hearings (p. 517); Richard M. Nixon's "Checkers" Speech, 23 Sept. 1952 (p. 519); President Eisenhower's acceptance of B'Nai Brith's Anti-Defamation League award for contributions to civil rights (23 Nov. 1953), where he spontaneously asserted the right of everyone to confront his accuser "face-to-face" (p. 519); the Army-McCarthy Hearings (p. 520); Nikita S. Khrushchev's appearance on *Face the Nation* (CBS, 2 June 1957); the Nixon-Khrushchev "kitchen" debate (24 July 1959); Khrushchev's visits to the U.S. (1959, 1960); the Kennedy-Nixon debates (7, 13, 21, 26 Oct. 1960); live presidential press conferences (first, Kennedy, 25 Jan. 1961); the coverage of the Kennedy assassination and murder of Lee Harvey Oswald by Jack Ruby (22–25 Nov. 1963); news coverage of Vietnam (1964–72); the "Fulbright Hearings" on the Vietnam War (Feb. 1966, p. 501); coverage of the 1968 Democratic National Convention; and the Ervin Committee Hearings on Watergate (17 May–7 Aug.; 24 Sept.–15 Nov. 1973, p. 541).

1951, 18 Aug. First call placed over the microwave radio relay system, consisting of 107 steel and concrete towers, 30 miles apart, between New York and San Francisco, constructed at cost of $40 million.

1952. FCC freeze of TV licenses at 108 (1948) lifted, permitting increase in number of stations in the U.S. and territories from 108 to 2,051 by making maximum use of VHF band frequencies and opening UHF band. Two types of licenses were to be issued: for commercial stations (1,809) and for noncommercial stations (educational institutions and groups, 242). Processing of channel applications began July 1952. National Educational Television was established and supported by the Ford Foundation. First educational TV station in U.S., KUHT, operated by Univ. of Houston, Tex., began broadcasting 25 May 1953.

Amendments to Federal Communications Commission Act (16 July, 1952) prevented FCC from considering alternative applications for licenses in considering approval of sale of station.

1953–60. TV PROGRAMING encompassed (1) episodic series (*I Love Lucy, Dragnet, Gunsmoke*); (2) TV drama (*Philco Television Playhouse, Goodyear Television Playhouse, Studio One, Robert Montgomery Presents.*) with scripts by authors such as Paddy Chayefsky (*Marty,* 24 May 1953), Robert Alan Arthur, Gore Vidal, Rod Serling; (3) quiz shows (*The $64,000 Question,* 1955); (4) "spectaculars" (*Peter Pan* with Mary Martin); (5) films. Sale by RKO of pre-1948 films to TV (1955), for $25 million, followed shortly by other major companies, contributed to decline of "live" and original TV, replaced not only by movies, but by more situation comedies, quiz programs, and westerns. Difficult to classify but among the best critically-received shows of this period was *Omnibus* (1952–57), a Sunday-afternoon series, with Ford Foundation support. Influential documentaries included *See It Now* report on Sen. Joseph R. McCarthy (9 Mar. 1954). First colorcast of a commercial program: *Amahl and the Night Visitors* (NBC, 21 Dec. 1953).

1957–58. FCC PROBE produced links between applicants for TV licenses and politicians and FCC commissioners (p. 525).

1958. QUIZ PROGRAM SCANDALS. Revelations (Aug.–Dec.) that contestants on *Twenty-One* and *The $64,000 Question* had been given the answers to questions led to hearings (6–10 Oct. 1959) by House Special Subcommittee on Legislative Oversight of the Commerce Committee. Further probes brought out allegations of "payola" to disc jockeys (21 Nov., 4 Dec.). The result was the passage (30 Aug. 1960) of a federal law designed to curb payola and quiz-show rigging, which required radio and TV stations to announce whether they had received money or anything of value for broadcasting material and outlawed clandestine aid to contestants in purportedly bona fide contests, with maximum penalties of $10,000 fine and 1 year imprisonment fixed.

1957–69. MAJOR TV TECHNOLOGICAL DEVELOPMENTS included the videotape (employed 1957) leading to the "instant replay," used in sports coverage (1963). Due to the legislative requirement that all TV sets shipped in interstate commerce after 30 Apr. 1964 be capable of receiving all channels, 1–13 VHF, 14–83 UHF, 51 new stations, 26 of them educational, almost all UHF, went on the air in 1967, and the 11 million TV sets sold (1967) brought to 23 million (est.) the number equipped to receive UHF (1967). Videotape recorders were perfected and marketed for recording and playing back TV pictures in the home (1965). In 1967, CBS demonstrated EVR, a new electronic video recorder, invented by **Peter Carl Goldmark** (1906–77), that records picture and sound data originating from the TV camera, magnetic tape or motion picture films on very thin film by means of special electronic process, then converts it to radio-frequency signals to which EVR is directly connected. Color TV made rapid strides in sales and programing due to the introduction of new color studio cameras with improved resolution, definition, and more faithful color rendition. Sales of color TV sets outsold black and white for the first time in 1968.

1960–69. RADIO PROGRAMING reflected a heavy reliance upon phonograph records with stations aimed at spe-

cific audience groups. Other programing included telephone "call-in shows," and all-news stations.

1960–69. TV PROGRAMING was dominated by telefilm westerns, comedy series, shows with medical background, spy and science fiction, and shows of violence. Coverage of sports events claimed an increasing amount of time. CBS paid $28 million for TV rights for the National Football League games for 1964 and 1965. Late evening talk-shows (Johnny Carson, Dick Cavett) were also popular. Running out of feature films, networks entered their own feature film production (1967). Major TV documentaries included *Harvest of Shame* (CBS, 25 Nov. 1960) and *Hunger in America* (CBS, 1968).

1961–69. FEDERAL COMMUNICATIONS COMMISSION. FCC Chairman Newton N. Minow referred to TV as a "vast wasteland" in speech to National Association of Broadcasters (May 1961). "Network option" clauses, giving networks virtual control over blocks of time on affiliate stations, were banned (1963). U.S. Court of Appeals for the District of Columbia Circuit reversed FCC decision to renew on a 1-year basis without public hearings the license of WLBT and WJTV, Jackson, Miss., accused of ignoring black viewers (1964), and later held that the black listening audience had a right to intervene in the FCC hearing (*Office of Communication of United Church of Christ* v. *F.C.C.*, 1964, 1969). The FCC ruled (1968) that in the future a holder of an AM radio license could not acquire local TV or local FM license. In 1969 license renewal was denied to Boston channel WHDH.

1962. INTERCONTINENTAL LIVE TELECASTS became possible with the launching (10 July) of Telstar 1 satellite. Live transmissions were privately received (11 July 1962). The first public transatlantic TV broadcast occurred with the launching of Telstar 2 (7 May 1963). The opening ceremonies of the 1964 summer Olympic games were transmitted live from Japan via Syncom 3 (10 Oct. 1964). The first live coverage of the recovery of a space capsule occurred via the Early Bird satellite, launched by the Communications Satellite Corporation (COMSAT) (6 Apr. 1965), with the recovery of Gemini 9 (6 June 1966). The first global hook-up, a two-hour program, *Our World,* presented originations from 19 countries on 5 continents and was seen simultaneously in 39 countries by means of 4 satellites, 3 U.S. and 1 Russian (25 June 1967). Westar I, launched 13 Apr. 1974, was first U.S. domestic communications satellite.

1962–68. EXPANSION OF EDUCATIONAL TV. The Educational Television Facilities Act (1 May 1962) provided $32 million on a matching grant basis over a 5-year period for TV equipment for new educational TV station projects. The Ford Foundation continued its strong financial support; by Oct. 1966 it had given $100 million. The **Public Broadcasting Act** (7 Nov. 1967) set up a 15-man corporation to dispense federal and private funds for educational and cultural program production and networking. A fourth TV network started live programing (5 Jan. 1969) committed to noncommercial broadcasting, made possible by the cooperation of the non-profit Corporation for Public Broadcasting and ATT.

1963. Nov. Roper Poll found for first time chief source of news for Americans was TV.

1964–73. TV-GOVERNMENT TENSIONS. Indications of political hostility to TV newsmen surfaced at 1964 Republican National Convention and deteriorated during the Vietnam War. TV cameramen were clubbed by police during demonstrations outside the 1968 Democratic National Convention in Chicago. During Nixon's first term pressures were exerted to persuade networks to give a more sympathetic treatment to the administration, with public attacks by Vice-Pres. Spiro T. Agnew and other White House spokesmen. President Nixon accused networks of "outrageous, vicious, distorted reporting" (26 Oct. 1973). In addition, FCC regulatory measures were proposed to compel networks to divest themselves of stations and antitrust actions initiated by Department of Justice prohibited networks from producing their own entertainment shows or financing motion pictures (10 Apr. 1972).

1966–70. Publication of 3-vol. definitive *History of Broadcasting in the United States* by Erik Barnouw.

1967. TV profits (3 networks and 619 stations) reported at $2,275,000,000.

1968. Expenditures by political parties for radio and TV time continued to increase, exceeding $40 million as against $2,250,000 spent by the major parties for radio time in 1940.

1968. 24 Dec. Astronauts on Apollo 8 mission read from Genesis while in the vicinity of the moon.

1969–74. CABLE TV. By 1 Jan. 1969 there were approximately 1,900 community antennae or cable television systems operating in all 50 states. Founded (1949) in Lansford, Pa., such systems were confined originally to remote localities. By 1974 it was estimated that approximately 12% of the nation's 68 million homes were connected to cable systems.

The FCC (13 Dec. 1968) announced changes in the operation of CATV, permitting and requiring the origination of programs. At the same time, subscription TV (Pay TV) was authorized subject to severe restrictions.

1969. NATIONAL PUBLIC RADIO

incorporated to provide national program service for public radio stations. First programming, 1 Apr. 1971. By 1975 National Public Radio, with primarily educational, informational, and cultural programs, was composed of over 150 members operating over 175 noncommercial public radio stations with funds provided primarily by Corporation for Public Broadcasting.

1969. 20 JULY. Neil A. Armstrong's first steps and words ("That's one small step for a man, one giant leap for mankind") telecast live from the moon followed by split-screen conversation between Armstrong and Edwin "Buzz" Aldrin, Jr. and President Nixon.

1970–81. TV PROGRAMMING dominated by situation comedies (*Mary Tyler Moore Show; Rhoda; All in the Family; M*A*S*H*); action adventure (*Rockford Files; Charlie's Angels*); dramatic serials and comic serials (*Dallas; Mary Hartman, Mary Hartman*). The miniseries *Roots*, which appeared on eight consecutive nights (Jan. 1977), reached the largest audience in television history for non-news event (30 Jan.—36,380,000 households). Late-evening market was dominated by long-running shows (Johnny Carson) as was the children's market (*Sesame Street*). Among public television's most notable offerings were *Masterpiece Theatre* (serial dramatizations by BBC of literary classics), *Great Performances,* and *Live from Lincoln Center.*

1972. 2 JAN. Cigarette Advertising Ban.

1972–74. RADIO PROGRAM developments included both an increase of the one-dimension format—all news, all country music, all hard-rock stations—and "nostalgia" programming—the revival of recordings of serials from the 1930s and 1940s, such as *The Lone Ranger, The Shadow,* and *The Green Hornet.* Original radio dramas began to be broadcast again by the CBS radio *Mystery Theater* (Feb. 1974).

1974–81. CABLE TELEVISION services spurred by Supreme Court decision and 1976 copyright law (p. 551) which settled liability to pay broadcasters whose programs are picked up and delivered. Cable systems grew from 2,490 systems serving 4.5 million subscribers (1970) to 4,350 cable systems serving 18.6 million subscribers (Mar. 1981). By 30 Dec. 1979 there were 1,882 systems with pay-cable serving 5,731,000 subscribers.

In 1979 there were est. 79.3 million black-and-white televisions and 71.3 million color sets (88.9% of American homes) and 79.3 million radios (99.9% of homes). Average viewing time—29 hours/week.

1975–76. BICENTENNIAL PROGRAMS. Extensive American Revolution Bicentennial programming initiated by CBS-TV *Bicentennial Minute* (4 July 1974).

4 JULY 1976. Bicentennial programming included coverage of ceremonies at Liberty Bell, Operation Sail in New York City, and outdoor Boston Pops concert in Boston.

1978. PUBLIC TELEVISION FUNDING authorizations: $180 million (fiscal 1981), $200 million (fiscal 1982), $220 million (fiscal 1983) under legislation requiring public TV to raise $2 for each $1 of public money.

1981. RADIO DEREGULATON. FCC to offer broadcasting diversity eliminated restrictions limiting commercials and rules requiring "logging" of programming, surveys of communities by stations, and public affairs broadcasting.

3
Five Hundred Notable Americans

BIOGRAPHICAL SECTION

This Biographical Section, confined by reason of space limitations to 500 eminent figures, is meant to be used as a handy reference source. It underscores the contribution that men and women of different ethnic and racial origins have made to the building of the nation, from the settlement of Jamestown to the Nuclear Space Age. The 500 are representative of top-level achievement for their own time in a range of fields crowded with significant names.

Making selections involved some arbitrary choices. Thus, Nelson W. Aldrich has been chosen to symbolize the powerful clique that controlled the U.S. Senate in the late nineteenth century, while a more extended list would have included William B. Allison. In the steel industry Andrew Carnegie was selected in preference to either Henry Clay Frick or Charles M. Schwab, likewise substantial figures. In the areas of general science, of medicine and public health, and of invention and technology an effort has been made to give representation to earlier and less creative periods of American history, but the worldwide impact of American scientific achievement in the twentieth century justifies adequate recognition. Much technical knowledge and experiments by others contributed to the range of inventions covered herein, but the persons singled out for biographical treatment were those who developed, perfected, and usually patented their inventions.

To qualify as an American on the list of the 500 one must have spent a major portion of his career in the original Thirteen Colonies (exceptions being made for William Penn and James Edward Oglethorpe as founders of colonies) or, after 1776, made substantial contributions as citizens of the U.S. On this ground Charles Chaplin has been excluded as well as such expatriates as Benjamin Thompson (Count Rumford), the physicist, and T. S. Eliot. Exceptions have been made in the cases of Henry James, who became a British subject at the very end of his career, and Yasuo Kuniyoshi, whose entire professional life was spent in the U.S. Naturalized citizens are included as well as natural-born. All 39 presidents receive biographical treatments, but their relative historical importance is suggested by respective space allocations. Inclusion of such significant figures as Benedict Arnold and Aaron Burr does not imply value judgments, it goes without saying.

The table preceding the biographical articles lists the subjects for convenience by major fields of activity. A word of caution, however: the allocation by categories has been done rather arbitrarily. Men as versatile as Benjamin Franklin, Thomas Jefferson, Albert Gallatin, Increase and Cotton Mather, Samuel F. B. Morse, Theodore Roosevelt, and Benjamin Rush were conspicuous in more than one field. Natural and behavioral scientists like Louis Agassiz and G. Stanley Hall, who were perhaps more effective in the diffusion of knowledge than in original and creative work, appear in the table as Educators without necessarily reflecting on the originality and quality of their scientific contributions.

Finally, it should be pointed out that a great many notable Americans not herein included are referred to elsewhere in the *Encyclopedia* and appear in the Index.

THE PRESIDENTS (39)[1]

JURISTS and LAWYERS (31)

Hugo L. Black
Louis D. Brandeis
Benjamin N. Cardozo
Salmon P. Chase
Thomas M. Cooley
Clarence Darrow
Oliver Ellsworth
William Maxwell Evarts
David Dudley Field
Stephen J. Field
Felix Frankfurter
Melville Weston Fuller
Learned Hand
John Marshall Harlan
Oliver Wendell Holmes, Jr.
Charles Evans Hughes
John Jay
William Johnson
James Kent
Edward Livingston
John Marshall
Thurgood Marshall
Samuel Freeman Miller
Lemuel Shaw
Harlan Fiske Stone
Joseph Story
Roger B. Taney

Morrison R. Waite
Earl Warren
Edward D. White
James Wilson

STATESMEN and PUBLIC OFFICALS (86)

Dean Acheson
Charles Francis Adams
Samuel Adams
Nelson W. Aldrich
John Peter Altgeld
Stephen F. Austin
Nathaniel Bacon
Alben W. Barkley
Thomas Hart Benton
Sir William Berkeley
Albert Beveridge
James G. Blaine
William E. Borah
William Bradford
William Jennings Bryan
Aaron Burr
John C. Calhoun
Joseph S. Cannon
Lewis Cass
Henry Clay
De Witt Clinton
George Clinton
Caleb Cushing
Jefferson Davis
John Dickinson

---

1. Listed pp. 545–559. Cleveland, who served 2 nonconsecutive terms, is considered the 22nd and 24th president. Hence, Ronald Reagan is technically the 40th president, but in fact the 39th.

Sanford B. Dole
Stephen A. Douglas
John Foster Dulles
Hamilton Fish
Benjamin Franklin
J. William Fulbright
Albert Gallatin
Joseph Galloway
Alexander Hamilton
John Hancock
W. Averill Harriman
Townsend Harris
John Hay
Patrick Henry
J. Edgar Hoover
Harry Hopkins
Edward M. House
Sam Houston
Thomas Hutchinson
Harold L. Ickes
Sir William Johnson
Robert F. Kennedy
Henry A. Kissinger
Robert La Follette
Fiorello La Guardia
Richard Henry Lee
Robert R. Livingston
Henry Cabot Lodge
Huey Long
Joseph R. McCarthy
George Mason
Increase Mather
Robert Moses
Luis Muñoz Marín
George Norris
James E. Oglethorpe
James Otis
William Penn
Frances Perkins
Joel R. Poinsett
John Randolph of Roanoke
Samuel Rayburn
Nelson A. Rockefeller
Elihu Root
Carl Schurz
William H. Seward
Roger Sherman
Alfred E. Smith

Alexander H. Stephens
Thaddeus Stevens
Adlai E. Stevenson
Henry L. Stimson
Peter Stuyvesant
Charles Sumner
Robert A. Taft
Tecumseh
Samuel J. Tilden
Henry A. Wallace
Thomas E. Watson
Daniel Webster
John Winthrop

MILITARY and NAVAL FIGURES (28)[2]

Benedict Arnold
Omar Bradley
George Rogers Clark
Stephen Decatur
George Dewey
David G. Farragut
Nathanael Greene
Thomas J. Jackson
Joseph E. Johnston
John Paul Jones
Robert E. Lee
Douglas MacArthur
George B. McClellan
Alfred T. Mahan
Francis Marion
George C. Marshall
William Mitchell
Daniel Morgan
Chester W. Nimitz
George S. Patton, Jr.
Matthew C. Perry
Oliver H. Perry
John J. Pershing
Winfield Scott
Philip Henry Sheridan
William T. Sherman
J. E. B. Stuart
George H. Thomas

2. Other notable military figures are included with the presidents: Washington, Andrew Jackson, Taylor, Grant, and Eisenhower.

BELLES LETTRES (38)

Louisa May Alcott
Willa Cather
Samuel L. Clemens
James Fenimore Cooper
Stephen Crane
Emily Dickinson
Theodore Dreiser
Ralph Waldo Ellison
William Faulkner
F. Scott Fitzgerald
Robert Frost
Joel Chandler Harris
Nathaniel Hawthorne
Ernest Hemingway
Oliver Wendell Holmes
William Dean Howells
Washington Irving
Henry James
Sinclair Lewis
Henry Wadsworth Longfellow
James Russell Lowell
Archibald MacLeish
Norman Mailer
Herman Melville
H. L. Mencken
Edna St. Vincent Millay
Vladimir Nabokov
Thomas Paine
Edgar Allan Poe
Ezra Pound
Edwin Arlington Robinson
Carl Sandburg
William Gilmore Simms
Harriet Beecher Stowe
Henry David Thoreau
Walt Whitman
John Greenleaf Whittier
Edmund Wilson

HISTORY, PHILOSOPHY, and SOCIAL SCIENCES (24)

Henry Adams
George Bancroft
Charles A. Beard
Franz Boas
John Dewey
Ralph Waldo Emerson
William James
Simon S. Kuznets
Wassily Leontief
Lewis Henry Morgan
Samuel Eliot Morison
John Lothrop Motley
Allan Nevins
Francis Parkman
Talcott Parsons
Charles S. Peirce
William H. Prescott
Josiah Royce
Paul A. Samuelson
Lemuel Shattuck
William Graham Sumner
Frederick Jackson Turner
Thorstein Veblen
Lester Frank Ward

ARTISTS (27)[3]

John J. Audubon
George W. Bellows
Albert Bierstadt
Alexander Calder
Mary Cassatt
John Singleton Copley
Thomas Eakins
Robert Henri
Winslow Homer
George Inness
Yasao Kuniyoshi
John La Farge
John Marin
Anna M. R. Moses
Thomas Nast
Louise Nevelson
Isamu Noguchi
Charles Willson Peale
Jackson Pollock
Frederic Remington
Albert P. Ryder
Augustus Saint-Gaudens
John Singer Sargent

-----
3. Includes Photography.

David R. Smith
Alfred Stieglitz
Gilbert Stuart
James A. M. Whistler

ARCHITECTS (8)

Charles Bulfinch
Louis I. Kahn
Benjamin H. Latrobe
Frederick Law Olmsted
Henry H. Richardson
Eliel Saarinen
Louis H. Sullivan
Frank Lloyd Wright

THEATER and ALLIED ARTS (13)

George Balanchine
Phineas T. Barnum
Edwin Booth
Charlotte Cushman
Walt Disney
Isadora Duncan
Edwin Forrest
Martha Graham
D. W. Griffith
Oscar Hammerstein, 2d
Arthur Miller
Eugene O'Neill
Tennessee Williams

MUSICIANS and COMPOSERS (10)

Irving Berlin
Leonard Bernstein
Edward K. ("Duke") Ellington
Stephen C. Foster
George Gershwin
Charles E. Ives
Edward MacDowell
Richard Rodgers
Igor F. Stravinsky
Theodore Thomas

RELIGIOUS LEADERS (18)

Henry Ward Beecher
Phillips Brooks

William Ellery Channing
John Cotton
Mary Baker Eddy
Jonathan Edwards
James Gibbons
Anne Hutchinson
Cotton Mather
Dwight L. Moody
Reinhold Niebuhr
Theodore Parker
Walter Rauschenbusch
Joseph Smith
George Whitefield
Roger Williams
Issac Mayer Wise
Brigham Young

EDUCATORS (19)

Louis Agassiz
Henry Barnard
Nicholas Murray Butler
James Bryant Conant
Charles W. Eliot
Abraham Flexner
Daniel Coit Gilman
G. Stanley Hall
William Rainey Harper
Christopher C. Langdell
Mary Lyon
William H. McGuffey
Horace Mann
Benjamin Silliman
Edward L. Thorndike
Noah Webster
Andrew Dickson White
Emma Willard
John Witherspoon

SOCIAL REFORMERS and LABOR LEADERS (32)

Jane Addams
Susan B. Anthony
Clara Barton
John Brown
Peter Cooper
Eugene V. Debs

Dorothea L. Dix
Frederick Douglass
Neal Dow
W. E. B. Du Bois
Margaret Fuller
William Lloyd Garrison
Marcus Garvey
Henry George
Samuel Gompers
Sidney Hillman
Samuel Gridley Howe
Martin Luther King, Jr.
John L. Lewis
George Meany
Ralph Nader
Wendell Phillips
Terence V. Powderly
A. Philip Randolph
Walter P. Reuther
Anna Eleanor Roosevelt
Margaret H. Sanger
Elizabeth Cady Stanton
Lincoln Steffens
Norman Thomas
Booker T. Washington
Frances Willard

JOURNALISTS, EDITORS, and PUBLISHERS (12)

James Gordon Bennett
William Cullen Bryant
Herbert Croly
Edwin L. Godkin
Horace Greeley
William Randolph Hearst
Walter Lippmann
Henry R. Luce
Adolph Ochs
Joseph Pulitzer
Isaiah Thomas
John Peter Zenger

PIONEERS and EXPLORERS (10)

Daniel Boone
Richard E. Byrd
John C. Frémont

Meriwether Lewis and William Clark
Robert E. Peary
Zebulon M. Pike
John Wesley Powell
John Smith
Charles Wilkes

BUSINESS LEADERS (20)

John Jacob Astor
Nicholas Biddle
Andrew Carnegie
Jay Cooke
James B. Duke
Eleuthère Irénée du Pont
Cyrus W. Field
Marshall Field
Henry Ford
Daniel Guggenheim
Marcus A. Hanna
James J. Hill
Cyrus H. McCormick
J. Pierpont Morgan
Robert Morris
John D. Rockefeller
Samuel Slater
Leland Stanford
Cornelius Vanderbilt
Aaron Montgomery Ward

MEDICINE (incl. Psychiatry) and PUBLIC HEALTH (17)

William Beaumont
Alfred Blalock
Edwin J. Cohn
Harvey William Cushing
Arnold Gesell
William Crawford Gorgas
Alfred C. Kinsey
William J. and Charles H. Mayo
William T. G. Morton
Gregory Goodwin Pincus
Walter Reed
Benjamin Rush
Jonas Salk
Theobald Smith
Harry Stack Sullivan
Selman A. Waksman

GENERAL SCIENCE (33)

Benjamin Banneker
Norman E. Borlaug
Nathaniel Bowditch
George Washington Carver
Arthur H. Compton
Clinton J. Davisson
Albert Einstein
John Franklin Enders
Enrico Fermi
Josiah Willard Gibbs
Asa Gray
Joseph Henry
Edward C. Kendall
Joshua Lederberg
Gilbert N. Lewis
Fritz Albert Lipmann
Edwin M. McMillan
Matthew Fontaine Maury
Albert A. Michelson
Robert A. Millikan
Thomas Hunt Morgan
Hermann J. Muller
J. Robert Oppenheimer
Linus Pauling
I. I. Rabi
Henry A. Rowland
Glenn T. Seaborg
Wendell M. Stanley
Edward Teller
Harold C. Urey
John von Neumann
Norbert Wiener
Robert Burns Woodward

INVENTION and TECHNOLOGY (35)

Ernst F. W. Alexanderson
Edwin H. Armstrong
Leo H. Baekeland
Alexander Graham Bell
Chester F. Carlson
Wallace H. Carothers
Lee De Forest
James Buchanan Eads
George Eastman

Thomas Alva Edison
John Ericsson
Robert Fulton
Robert H. Goddard
George W. Goethals
Charles Goodyear
Richard M. Hoe
Elias Howe
Charles F. Kettering
Edwin H. Land
Irving Langmuir
Ernest O. Lawrence
Ottmar Mergenthaler
Samuel F. B. Morse
Elisha Graves Otis
Michael Pupin
John Augustus Roebling
William B. Shockley
Charles Proteus Steinmetz
Frederick Winslow Taylor
Nikola Tesla
George Westinghouse
Eli Whitney
Wilbur and Orville Wright
Vladimir Zworykin

Acheson, Dean Gooderham (b. Middletown, Conn., 11 Apr. 1893; d. Sandy Spring, Md., 12 Oct. 1971), statesman, was graduated from Groton (1911), Yale (1915), and Harvard Law School (1918). After spending 2 years (1919–21) as law secretary to Supreme Court Justice Brandeis he joined the Washington law firm now known as Covington and Burling, where he became a senior partner and practiced whenever he was not in the government. A Democrat, he was appointed Under Secretary of the Treasury in 1933 but was forced to resign 6 months later because he disapproved of President Roosevelt's plan to devalue the gold content of the dollar. Maintaining a good personal relationship with the president, he became an Assistant Secretary of State (1941–45)—helping to draft the Lend-Lease program and, as liaison with Congress, aiding in the development of the UN Food and Agricultural Organization, the UN Relief and Rehabilitation Administration, the World Bank, and the International Monetary Fund. As Under—Secretary of State (1945–47) and as Secretary of State (1949–53) he was a major architect of postwar U.S. foreign policy. His activities included development of the Marshall Plan for European economic recovery, NATO, the Truman Doctrine, and the policy of support of Nationalist China. A staunch anti-Communist, he pushed for strengthening the U.S. atomic arsenal and U.S. aid to countries on the perimeter of the Soviet bloc. After resuming his Washington law practice (1953), he exercised considerable influence, advising Presidents Kennedy, Johnson, and Nixon. His books include *Power and Diplomacy* (1958) and *Present at the Creation,* which won a Pulitzer prize in 1970.

Adams, Charles Francis (b. Boston, Mass., 18 Aug. 1807; d. there, 21 Nov. 1886), diplomat and statesman, son of John Quincy Adams and father of Henry Adams, was graduated from Harvard (1825), and admitted to the bar in 1829, establishing his practice at Boston. A member (1841–44) of the Massachusetts House of Representatives, he also served (1844–45) in the state senate. His growing antislavery convictions led him to establish the Boston *Whig* as an organ of opposition to conservative Whiggery, and in 1848 he was the unsuccessful Free-Soil candidate for vice-president on the ticket with Martin Van Buren. Elected to Congress as a Republican, he served from 4 Mar. 1859 to 1 May 1861, and in the months before the outbreak of the Civil War headed the Northern forces of concession and conciliation in the House of Representatives. He re-

signed from Congress to accept appointment by President Lincoln as minister to England, a post he held until 1868. During the first half of the Civil War, when British official sympathy for the Confederacy was at its height, Adams handled with exemplary tact and firmness vital diplomatic matters such as the *Trent* affair (p. 280) and the armored rams built by the Lairds for the Confederacy. (Adams to Lord Russell: "This is war.") In 1872 the Liberal Republicans considered him for a time as a likely candidate for the presidency. He brought out the *Works of John Adams* (10 vols., 1850–56) and the *Memoirs of John Quincy Adams* (12 vols., 1874–77).

Adams, Henry Brooks (b. Boston, Mass., 16 Feb. 1838; d. Washington, D.C., 27 Mar. 1918), historian and man of letters, grandson of John Quincy Adams. He was graduated from Harvard (1858), pursued postgraduate study in Germany, and during the Civil War served as secretary to his father, Charles Francis Adams, U.S. minister to England (1861–68). He returned to Washington (1868), was active as a journalist (1869–70), and from 1870 to 1877 was assistant professor of history at Harvard, meanwhile serving during most of his period at Cambridge as editor of the *North American Review*. He married (1872) Marian Hooper, whose suicide (1885) had a tragic impact on his life. While at Harvard and Washington, D.C., he brought out the following works: *Essays on Anglo-Saxon Law* (1876) and *Documents Relating to New England Federalism, 1800–1815* (1877), both of which he edited; *The Life of Albert Gallatin* (1879), *The Writings of Albert Gallatin* (1879); 2 novels, *Democracy* (1880) and *Esther* (1884), both of which were published anonymously; *John Randolph* (1882); and the *History of the United States During the Administrations of*

Jefferson and Madison (9 vols., 1889–91), a diplomatic, political, and military account that ranks as one of the landmarks in American historical writing. The latter part of his life was spent in travel in Europe and the South Seas. He is best remembered for *The Education of Henry Adams* (1907), which, with the writings collected in *The Degradation of the Democratic Dogma* (1919), sets forth his formulation of the dynamic theory of history and expresses his doubts that technological advance reflects progress. He also wrote *Mont-Saint-Michel and Chartres* (1904).

Adams, John (b. Braintree [now Quincy], Mass., 30 Oct. 1735; d. there, 4 July 1826), 2d president of the U.S., was graduated from Harvard (1755) and admitted to the Massachusetts bar in 1758. He attacked the Stamp Act in a series of articles in the Boston *Gazette* (1765), and after removal to Boston (1768) defended the British soldiers tried for murder in the "Boston Massacre" (1770). He served in the General Court (1770–71) and the Revolutionary Provincial Congress (1774–75), and his constitutional views were expounded in *Novanglus* (1774), written in reply to the Loyalist Daniel Leonard. As a delegate to the 1st and 2nd Continental Congresses (1774–78) he helped draft the petition to the king and the petition of rights, recommended Washington for command of the army, and defended the Declaration of Independence in its passage through Congress. He served as chairman of the Board of War and Ordnance and superseded Silas Deane as commissioner to France (1778). He was a delegate to the convention which framed the Massachusetts Constitution (1780), of which he was the principal author. With Franklin and Jay he negotiated the Paris peace treaty with Great Britain (1783), and was U.S. minister to Great Britain (1785–88). He was 1st vice-president of the U.S. (1789–97), casting votes in Senate ties no less than 20 times, and succeeded Washington as president (1797–1801). His feud with Hamilton, along with the Alien and Sedition Acts, for which he had no direct responsibility, contributed to his loss of popularity and the downfall of the Federalist party. In retirement he lived in Quincy and renewed his relationship with Jefferson.

Adams, John Quincy (b. Braintree [now Quincy], Mass., 11 July 1767; d. Washington, D.C., 23 Feb. 1848), 6th president of the U.S., eldest son of John and Abigail (Smith) Adams, studied in France (1778–79) and Holland (1780), and served as secretary to Francis Dana in Russia (1781) and to his father in Great Britain (1782–83). Returning to the U.S., he was graduated from Harvard (1787), admitted to the bar (1790), and practiced in Boston. Under Washington he served as minister to the Netherlands (1794–96) and, under his father, to Prussia (1797–1801). He was defeated for Congress in 1802, but elected to the U.S. Senate the following year. As a result of his support of the administration in the Embargo of 1807, which he favored as an alternative to war, he was forced to resign (1808). He served briefly as a professor of rhetoric at Harvard; was minister to Russia, 1809–14, chairman of the peace commission that negotiated the Treaty of Ghent (1814), and minister to Great Britain, 1815–17. Appointed Monroe's Secretary of State (1817–25), he obtained the cession of Florida (1819) and shared with Monroe credit for formulating the Monroe Doctrine (1823). In the presidential election of 1824, he was 2d to Jackson in electoral votes. In the House of Representatives Clay threw his support to Adams (resulting in an unsubstantiated charge of a "corrupt bargain") and Adams was elected president. During his administration he favored a broad national program of internal improvements, but refused to build up a personal political machine. Defeated by Jackson (1828), he was elected to Congress (1831–48). He opposed the annexation of Texas (1836) and the extension of slavery. Every year (1836–44) he opposed without success the adoption of the "gag rule," forbidding discussion or action in the House on antislavery petitions, until its defeat (1844). He was further identified with the antislavery cause by his argument before the Supreme Court vindicating the right to freedom of the *Amistad* captives (1841).

Adams, Samuel (b. Boston, Mass., 27 Sept. 1722; d. there, 2 Oct. 1803), Revolutionary patriot leader, 2d cousin of John Adams (1735–1826), was graduated from Harvard (1740); joined his father in the brewery business, which he later inherited and lost; and served (1756–64) as a tax collector. A member of the Boston "Caucus Club," he was by 1764 a power in local politics. He took a leading role in whipping up opposition to the Sugar Act (1764), the Stamp Act (1765), and the Townshend Acts (1767), was one of the organizers of the Non-Importation Association (1768), and played an important part in the agitation that culminated in the Boston Massacre (1770). He helped organize the Sons of Liberty (1765) and was a member (1765–74) of the Massachusetts House of Representatives, of which he served as recording clerk (1766–74). In writings for the press he enunciated many of the basic arguments that later became familiar Revolutionary doctrine, and kept the spirit of controversy alive during the period of comparative calm and conservative ascendency (1770–72). He initiated the Massachusetts committee of correspondence (1772), drafted

the Boston declaration of rights (1772), was the leading force behind the Boston Tea Party (1773), and with John Hancock was singled out by the British government for punishment. As a delegate (1774–81) to the Continental Congress, he favored immediate independence, proposed an intercolonial confederation of independent states, voted for and signed the Declaration of Independence, and opposed compromise with Great Britain. He was a delegate to the Massachusetts constitutional convention (1779–80) and to the state convention (1788) for ratifying the federal Constitution. He served as lieutenant governor (1789–93) and governor (1794–97) of Massachusetts.

Addams, Jane (b. Cedarville, Ill., 6 Sept. 1860; d. Chicago, Ill., 21 May 1935), humanitarian and social reformer. She was graduated from Rockford College (A.B., 1882) attended the Woman's Medical College in Philadelphia, and during a trip to England (1887–88) became interested in social reform. With Ellen Gates Starr, she founded (1889) Hull-House at Chicago, a settlement house devoted to the improvement of community and civic life in the slums, the most notable of its kind in the U.S. Active (1915–34) as a crusader against war, she was named chairman in 1915 of the Woman's Peace party and president of the International Congress of Women at The Hague. She served as president of the Women's International League for Peace and Freedom. In 1931 she was corecipient (with Nicholas Murray Butler) of the Nobel peace prize. Her writings on social reconstruction include *Democracy and Social Ethics* (1902), *Newer Ideals of Peace* (1907), *The Spirit of Youth and the City Streets* (1909), *Twenty Years at Hull-House* (1910), *A New Conscience and an Ancient Evil* (1912), *The Second Twenty Years at*

Hull-House (1930), and *The Excellent Becomes the Permanent* (1932).

Agassiz, Jean Louis Rodolphe (b. Canton Fribourg, Switzerland, 28 May 1807; d. Cambridge, Mass., 14 Dec. 1873), educator, zoologist, and geologist, studied at the universities of Zurich, Erlangen (Ph.D., 1829), Heidelberg, and Munich (M.D., 1830). After an early contribution to zoology (*The Fishes of Brazil,* 1829), he studied fossil fish under Cuvier in Paris (1831), publishing in that field *Recherches sur les poissons fossiles* (1833–44) and *Études critiques sur les mollusques fossiles* (1840–45). Professor of natural history at Neuchâtel Univ. (1832–46), he made extensive investigations of glacial phenomena in Europe (*Études sur les glaciers,* 2 vols., 1840). Coming to the U.S. (1846), he accepted (1848) the chair of natural history at the newly established Lawrence Scientific School at Harvard, where he founded the Harvard Museum of Comparative Zoology (1859). Interested in the natural history and geology of the western hemisphere (*Contributions to the Natural History of the U.S.,* 1857), he made extensive field trips to Brazil (1865) and to the U.S. West (1868, 1871), but his career in the U.S. was chiefly notable as teacher and lecturer and promoter of scientific study. His teleological view of natural history prompted him to take the leadership in the U.S. in opposing Darwinian evolution with its theory of natural selection, and his scientific reputation suffered as a result. He founded (1873) the Anderson School of Natural History on Penikese Island in Buzzard's Bay to train teachers of natural history.

Alcott, Louisa May (b. Germantown, Pa., 29 Nov. 1832; d. Boston, Mass., 6 Mar. 1888), author, daughter of Amos Bronson Alcott (1799–1888), was reared in Boston and Concord and received most of her education from her father. Her first book, written at the age of 16, was *Flower Fables* (1854). During the Civil War she served as a nurse in a Union hospital at Georgetown until her health was impaired. A volume of her letters, *Hospital Sketches* (1863), was followed by her first novel, *Moods* (1864). She became (1867) editor of *Merry's Museum,* a children's magazine. Her most popular work is *Little Women* (2 vols., 1868, 1869), whose familiar characters of Jo, Amy, Beth, and Meg were drawn from her family life. These books enjoyed a phenomenal sale. Among her later works are *An Old Fashioned Girl* (1870), *Little Men* (1871), *Aunt Jo's Scrap-Bag* (6 vols., 1872–82), *Work* (1873), *Eight Cousins* (1875), *Rose in Bloom* (1876), *Silver Pitchers* (1876), *Under the Lilacs* (1878), *Proverb Stories* (1882), *Jo's Boys* (1886), and *A Garland for Girls* (1888).

Aldrich, Nelson Wilmarth (b. Foster, R.I., 6 Nov. 1841; d. New York City, 16 Apr. 1915), statesman, attended public schools and the Academy of East Greenwich, R.I. Starting in the wholesale grocery business, he rapidly expanded his fortunes to include banking, sugar, rubber, gas, and electricity. As a Republican, Aldrich became state assemblyman (1875–76), a member of the U.S. House of Representatives (1879–81), and U.S. senator from Rhode Island (1881–1911). After 1890 he led a group of long-tenured Republicans including William B. Allison (Ia.), Orville H. Platt (Conn.), and John C. Spooner (Wis.) in dominating the Senate, the first effective leadership organization in the history of that body. This group dictated committee assignments, caucus positions, and decisions of standing committees. They succeeded in persuading the Senate to repeal the Silver Purchase Act (1893) and to pass the

Gold Standard Act (1900), forcing silver Republicans out of the party. Responsible for Republican administration legislation after 1897, this group forced President Theodore Roosevelt to modify the original Hepburn Rate Bill (1906) in order to stipulate how railroads could appeal rates set by the ICC to the circuit courts. Aldrich was considered a spokesman for big business and was a proponent of protective tariffs, such as the Wilson-Gorham Tariff (1894) and the Payne-Aldrich Tariff (1909). Successful passage of the latter tariff produced a split in the Republican party and a decline in the power of the leadership group. He shaped the Aldrich-Vreeland Currency Act of 1908 and headed the resulting National Monetary Commission which studied bank reform and produced a thorough and comprehensive report (8 Jan. 1912) which, although pigeonholed for a time, was to become—in modified form—the basis of the Federal Reserve Act (1913).

Alexanderson, Ernst Frederick Werner (b. Uppsala, Sweden, 25 Jan. 1878; d. Schenectady, N.Y., 14 May 1975), electrical engineer and inventor, was graduated (1900) from the Royal Institute of Technology, Stockholm, and pursued postgraduate studies at Berlin. Arriving in the U.S. in 1901, he joined the staff (1902) of the General Electric Co. at Schenectady, N.Y. His association with General Electric was unbroken for over 46 years except for service as chief engineer (1920–24) of the Radio Corp. of America, and after his retirement he became a consultant to GE. He was naturalized in 1908. The holder of patents for more than 300 inventions, many of which have revolutionized the field of radio communications, he is the inventor (1917) of the Alexanderson high frequency alternator, making worldwide wireless possible, and has also done pioneering work

in electric ship propulsion, radio electronics, railroad electrification, and television. Among his inventions are the tuned radio frequency receiver, the vacuum tube radio telephone transmitter, and the multiple tuned antenna.

Altgeld, John Peter (b. Nieder Selters, Germany, 30 Dec. 1847; d. Chicago, 12 Mar. 1902), governor of Illinois, reformer, came to Richmond County, Ohio, with his parents as an infant and was largely self-taught. Elected state's attorney for Andrew Co., Mo. (1874), he moved (1875) to Chicago, where he served as judge and chief justice of the Superior Court of Cook Co. (1886–91). Elected first Democratic governor of Illinois (1893–97), he outraged public opinion by pardoning (1893) the anarchists Fielden, Schwab, and Neebe, convicted of complicity in the Haymarket murders (1886). Conservatives were equally critical of his opposition on constitutional grounds to President Cleveland's use of regular army troops in the Pullman strike (1894). Supporter of free silver in the Democratic National Convention (1896), he was defeated that year for a 2d gubernatorial term by John R. Tanner. His treatise on crime, *Our Penal Machinery and Its Victims* (1884), expressed the view that the poor lacked equal opportunity before the law.

Anthony, Susan Brownell (b. Adams, Mass., 15 Feb. 1820; d. Rochester, N.Y., 13 Mar. 1906), social reformer and woman suffrage leader. Reared in a Quaker household, she was educated at her father's school and became a schoolteacher, serving (1846–49) as head of the Female Department of the Canajoharie (N.Y.) Academy. Abandoning education for reform activities, she devoted her first efforts to temperance, and was among the organizers of the Woman's

State Temperance Society of New York, the first body of its kind. She also took part in the abolitionist cause, being among the first to advocate Negro suffrage after the Civil War, but gradually shifted her main energies to the woman suffrage movement. She attempted to have inserted in the 14th Amendment a provision guaranteeing the franchise to women as well as to male Negroes. She was involved in a celebrated case that was touched off when she registered and voted at the Rochester city elections (1872) in a plan to test the legality of woman suffrage. She became president (1869) of the National Woman Suffrage Association and was president (1892–1900) of the National American Woman Suffrage Association.

Armstrong, Edwin Howard (b. New York City, 18 Dec. 1890; d. there, 1 Feb. 1954), engineer and inventor, studied at Columbia Univ. (E.E., 1913) under Michael Pupin (*q.v.*), succeeding him (1934) as professor of electrical engineering. His regenerative circuit (1912) won him engineering acclaim along with a patent controversy with Lee De Forest (*q.v.*). As a Signal Corps officer in World War I he developed the principles of his superheterodyne circuit (1918), basic to radio receivers. In 1920 he devised the super-regenerative circuit, used in 2-way police and aircraft radio systems. "Father of FM," Armstrong perfected (1939) his system of static-free radio through frequency modulation, widely adopted in the U.S., England, and Germany. At the time of his death by suicide he was involved in litigating claims against leading broadcasting and electronic manufacturing firms for patent infringement. In 1947 he was awarded the Medal of Merit for his contributions to military communications during World War II.

Arnold, Benedict (b. Norwich, Conn., 14 Jan. 1741; d. London, 14 June 1801), Revolutionary patriot and traitor, served in the French and Indian War, became a druggist and bookseller as well as active in the West India trade. Captain in the Connecticut militia, he undertook as colonel, with Ethan Allen of Vermont, the successful attack on Ft. Ticonderoga (1775). Heading an expedition across the Maine wilderness to Quebec, he was wounded in the assault on that city, but made brigadier general (10 Jan. 1776) for his conspicuous role. At Valcour Island he held up Carleton's invasion force on Lake Champlain (11 Oct. 1776), forcing the British to abandon the invasion of New York. Promoted major general as a result of actions at Ridgefield and Norwalk (1777), he played a leading role in frustrating Burgoyne's invasion of New York, raising the siege of Ft. Stanwix (1777), anticipated Burgoyne's movement to turn the American left at Freeman's Farm, and was wounded in a frontal assault on Breymann's redoubt at Bemis Heights. Military commander of Philadelphia (1778), he was court-martialed (1779) and found guilty of using military forces for his own private purposes. Gently reprimanded by Washington, his steadfast supporter, he was given command of West Point. Entering into treasonable correspondence with Sir Henry Clinton (in which his wife, Margaret Shippen Arnold, was involved) to surrender the key fort to the British, he was forced to flee to the British army when Major André was captured and the plot exposed. He received £6,315 for his treason and was made brigadier general of provincial troops by the British. He carried out a marauding expedition into Virginia (1780) and raided New London, Conn. (1781). He sailed for England Dec. 1781, and was held there in scorn.

Arthur, Chester Alan (b. Fairfield, Vt., 5 Oct. 1829; d. New York City, 18 Nov. 1886), 21st president of the U.S., was graduated from Union College (1848) and admitted to the New York bar (1853). An abolitionist, he was counsel for the state in the case of Jonathan Lemmon, securing a decision that slaves brought into New York while in transit between 2 slave states were thereby made free. During the Civil War he served as quartermaster general of New York, was appointed collector of the Port of New York by President Grant (1871), but was removed (1878) by President Hayes for violating an executive order (1876) forbidding federal officials from participating in party management and campaigns. Elected vice-president of the U.S. (1880), he became president following the death of Garfield (19 Sept. 1881). His administration continued the prosecution of the "Star Route" mail frauds (1882–83) and secured enactment of the Pendleton Civil Service Act (1883). In addition, he began the rebuilding of the U.S. Navy and vetoed a Chinese exclusion bill. He was denied renomination in 1884.

Astor, John Jacob (b. John Jakob Ashdour, Waldorf, Germany, 17 July 1763; d. New York City, 29 Mar. 1848), fur trader and merchant. Migrated to London, 1780; to the U.S., 1783; obtained a job in a fur store in New York City, mastered the business, and in 1786 opened his own establishment. The provisions of Jay's Treaty and the subsequent evacuation of frontier posts by the British (1796) enabled Astor to trade with the British North West Co. His business expanded rapidly; by 1800, when he had a fortune of $250,000, he was the chief factor in the fur trade. He became active in the shipping trade to the Far East and made prudent investments in New York City real estate. Fol-

lowing the acquisition of Louisiana and the Lewis and Clark expedition, he made plans for penetrating the West. He established the American Fur Co. (1808) and the Pacific Fur Co. (1810). With Montreal merchants as partners, he formed the South West Fur Co. (1811) for the purpose of supplying goods to both the British and his own fur companies free of customs duties. He established Astoria at the mouth of the Columbia River (1811) for transshipment of furs to Canton. He lost the post during the War of 1812, but managed to retain the South West and American Fur Cos. and to carry on trade with the British in the Great Lakes region throughout the conflict. After 1815, he established posts in the Mississippi Valley (old North West Co. posts) and expanded his fur-trading operations by establishing the Western Dept. of the American Fur Co. (1822). After absorbing the Columbia Fur Co. (1827), he held a monopoly in the upper Missouri territory, but after failing to eliminate the Rocky Mountain Fur Co., retired from business. At his death he was the richest man in America. He left a fortune of more than $20 million.

Audubon, John James (b. Les Cayes, Santo Domingo [now Haiti], 26 Apr. 1785; d. New York City, 27 Jan. 1851), artist and naturalist, pioneer American ornithologist. Taken to France in 1789, he was educated at Nantes and arrived (1803) in the U.S., where he began his ornithological studies in the Pennsylvania countryside. He made (Apr. 1804) the first experimental banding on the young of an American wild bird. Beginning in 1807, he made his home in Kentucky, where he was a merchant at Louisville and Henderson, and there continued his paintings and sketches of birds. Following a series of business reverses, he became (1820) a taxidermist at the Western Museum in Cincinnati. In 1826 he went to England and Scotland, where he secured the first subscriptions for the projected publication of his drawings and obtained the services of Robert Havell, Jr., a London engraver who brought out Audubon's monumental work, *The Birds of America* (1827–38), containing more than 1,000 life-size figures of about 500 species. After 1827 Audubon spent much of his time at Edinburgh, where he brought out his *Ornithological Biography* (with the assistance of William MacGillivray; 5 vols., 1831–39) and *Synopsis of the Birds of North America* (1839), and in 1842 made his home at the present site of Audubon Park, New York City. He collaborated with Rev. John Bachman on the *Viviparous Quadrupeds of North America* (2 vols. of plates, 1842–45; text, 3 vols., 1846–54). The Audubon Societies were founded in his memory.

Austin, Stephen Fuller (b. Wythe Co., Va., 3 Nov. 1793; d. Austin, Tex., 27 Dec. 1836), founder of Texas, moved with his parents to Missouri (1798), to which he returned (1810) after studying near New Haven, Conn., and at Transylvania Univ. He planted the first legal settlement of Anglo-Americans in Texas (1822), obtaining confirmation of his grant when Mexico achieved independence. Until 1828 he was executive, lawmaker, supreme judge, and military commandant, and kept a steady stream of emigrants coming into Texas. In 1828 he obtained the enactment of a contract labor law permitting the continued introduction of slaves as indentured servants. In pressing the claim of the convention of 1833 for a state government (against his own judgment), he was arrested and held by the Mexican government on the baseless charge of fomenting revolution in Texas and annexation to the U.S. He was released in July 1835. When the

War of the Texas Revolution broke out, Austin was called to command the army, then sent to Washington to negotiate a loan and enlist support. He returned to Texas (June 1836) and was defeated for the presidency of the Republic of Texas by Sam Houston, whose secretary of state he became for the brief period remaining until his death.

Bacon, Nathaniel (b. Suffolk, England, 2 Jan. 1647; d. Gloucester Co., Va., 26 Oct. 1676), colonial insurrectionist. Born into a wealthy and prominent family (he was a cousin of Francis Bacon), he attended Cambridge and studied law at Gray's Inn. Emigrating with his wife to Virginia (1674), he was appointed to the governor's council. Quickly at odds with the governor, his cousin, William Berkeley, Bacon sympathized with the country planters who complained of inadequate protection of the frontiers from Indian attack, a limited franchise, excessive taxation and unfair distribution of offices, tax and customs exemptions. In 1676, in defiance of Berkeley, Bacon led a small army against the Pamunkey, Susquehannock, and Occaneechee Indians. He asked the governor to summon an assembly with a wider suffrage to reform the colony's laws. Berkeley denounced Bacon as a traitor and had him arrested, but when Bacon confessed his guilt the governor quickly pardoned him and readmitted him to the council. Bacon soon assembled his supporters to form another raiding party. Again denounced by Berkeley, Bacon and his followers occupied Jamestown without a battle and the governor fled. While Bacon attacked the Pamunkeys, Berkeley returned to Jamestown, only to be forced out when Bacon and his forces, after a battle, captured Jamestown and burned it down. By this time in control of virtually all of Virginia, Bacon withdrew to Green Springs to consolidate his position, but his sudden death from illness led to the rebellion's rapid suppression.

Baekeland, Leo Hendrik (b. Ghent, Belgium, 14 Nov. 1863; d. Beacon, N.Y., 23 Feb. 1944), chemist, inventor, received his B.S. from the Univ. of Ghent (1882), where he taught until emigrating to the U.S. (1889) to serve as consultant to A. & H. T. Anthony (later Ansco) of New York City, a photographic firm. In 1888 he patented a dry plate which could be developed in water. Founding with Leonard Jacobi the Nepara Chemical Co. to produce a photographic paper (Velox) he invented, he sold his rights (1899) to Eastman Kodak for $1 million. Attacking the problem of chemical synthesis, he produced a plastic which he exhibited (Feb. 1909) as Bakelite, the first of a long series of resins to revolutionize modern economic and technological life. Organizer (1910) of the General Bakelite Co., Perth Amboy, N.J., he was president until 1939, when it was acquired by Union Carbon and Carbide Corp. He received the Franklin Medal in 1940. He wrote *Some Aspects of Industrial Chemistry* (1914).

Balanchine, George (b. St. Petersburg, Russia, 9 Jan. 1904–   ), choreographer. Born Georgi Melitonovitch Balanchivadze, son of composer Meliton Balanchivadze, at the age of 10 he entered the Imperial Academy of Dance (later the Soviet State Ballet School), graduating in 1921. He continued his studies at the Conservatory of Music and joined the Soviet State Dancers. While touring Europe with the ballet company he decided to remain in Paris (1924), where he joined (1925) Serge Diaghilev's Ballets Russes. It was Diaghilev who suggested the new name he then adopted. Until Diaghilev's death and the disbandment of his troupe (1929), Balanchine served

the company less as a performer than as ballet master and choreographer. During this period he choreographed, to music by Igor Stravinsky, *Apollo, Leader of the Muses* (premiere, 12 June 1928), his first masterpiece and, because of its innovations within the classical ballet tradition, his most influential and historically significant. He choreographed Cole Porter's *Wake Up and Dream* (1929) before becoming ballet master of the Royal Danish Ballet, Copenhagen (1930). He had helped organize (1932) the Ballet Russe de Monte Carlo when Lincoln Kirstein, an American philanthropist, intellectual, and balletomane, invited him (1933) to emigrate to the U.S., where they established (1934) the School of American Ballet in New York. Until 1948, when the New York City Ballet was established as a stable institution, with Kirstein as director, Balanchine was associated with the various emanations of the School of American Ballet—American Ballet Company, Ballet Caravan, and Ballet Society—and choreographed as a freelance as well. A seminal figure who has extended the vocabulary of classic ballet, he emphasizes visual patterns and movements drawn from the music. Prolifically inventive, he has choreographed more than 100 ballets, most of them plotless in the traditional sense. His ballets include *Agon* (1957), *Brahms-Schoenberg Quartet* (1966), *Bugaku* (1963), *Episodes* (1959), *Four Temperaments* (1946), *Jewels* (1966), *Serenade* (1935), *Square Dance* (1957), *Symphony in Three Movements* (1972), *Theme and Variations* (1947), and the *Nutcracker* (1954) —the last regularly performed each Christmas season. A full-length *Coppélia* (1974) was hailed by critics.

Bancroft, George (b. Worcester, Mass., 3 Oct. 1800; d. Washington, D.C., 17

Jan. 1891), historian, diplomat, and cabinet officer, was graduated from Harvard (1817) and in 1820 received the degrees of Ph.D. and M.A. from the Univ. of Göttingen. With Joseph Green Cogswell, he founded (1823) the Round Hill School at Northampton, Mass., but abandoned teaching in 1831 to begin research for his *History of the United States* (10 vols., 1834–76), covering the span between the discovery of America and the close of the Revolutionary War. Bancroft was active in the Jacksonian movement in Massachusetts in the 1830s; in 1844, when he was an unsuccessful candidate for the governorship of Massachusetts, he was instrumental in securing the Democratic Presidential nomination for James K. Polk. As Secretary of the Navy (1845–46), he established the U.S. Naval Academy at Annapolis, giving orders to Commodore John D. Sloat which upon the outbreak of the Mexican War facilitated early American success in the California area. As acting Secretary of War (May 1845) he signed the order which sent Gen. Zachary Taylor across the Texas frontier and brought on the clash with Mexico. Bancroft served as U.S. minister to Great Britain (1846–49) and Germany (1867–74), meanwhile tirelessly searching out materials in private and public collections for use in his *History*. In 1865 he wrote President Andrew Johnson's first annual message. In 1876 he brought out a revised edition ("Centenary Edition") of his history in 6 vols. His final revision (6 vols., 1883–85) included the *History of the Formation of the Constitution* (1882). He also wrote *Poems* (1823), *Literary and Historical Miscellanies* (1855), and *Martin Van Buren to the End of His Public Career* (1889).

Banneker, Benjamin (b. Ellicott's Mills, Md., 9 Nov. 1731; d. Baltimore, Md.,

25 Oct. 1806), mathematician and astronomer, was the son of free black parents and was taught to read by his maternal grandmother, Molly Welsh, who was originally an indentured servant from England. Son of a prosperous farmer, he was given an education, in which he quickly demonstrated his mechanical aptitude. Inheriting his father's farm, which he worked for many years, Banneker did not seriously turn to scientific pursuits until he was 41 years old, when some astronomical books were given him by his Quaker neighbor, the manufacturer Andrew Ellicott. Thereafter he read widely in geology, astronomy, and physics, observing the heavens with a makeshift telescope and accurately predicting an eclipse (1789). In that year he was named a member of the commission to survey the new Federal District (later D. C.). In 1791 he began issuing an annual almanac which, aside from his astronomical calculations which earned the approval of the renowned David Rittenhouse, contained his commentaries on social problems, and on bees and locusts, whose plague he calculated correctly as a 17-year cycle. On 19 Aug. 1791 Banneker forwarded a copy of his first almanac to Secretary of State Jefferson, accompanied by a letter denouncing the injustice of slavery. Jefferson courteously acknowledged the communication. In the 1793 edition of his almanac Banneker included "A Plan of a Peace Office for the U.S.," recommending what amounted to a department of the interior for the U.S. and a league of nations to achieve peace. He also came out against capital punishment. Two days after his death most of his manuscripts were accidentally burned.

Barkley, Alben William (b. Graves Co., Ky., 24 Nov. 1877; d. Lexington, Va., 30 Apr. 1956), statesman, attended rural schools and graduated from Marvin College in Clinton, Ky. (1897). After further study at Emory College and the Univ. of Virginia Law School, he was admitted to the bar (1901) and immediately began practicing law in Paducah, Ky. Barkley's political career began as prosecuting attorney for MacCracken Co., Ky. (1905–09) and he served there as judge of the county court (1909–13). He was elected in 1912 to the U.S. House of Representatives, where he served 7 successive terms. In 1926 he was elected to the U.S. Senate, to which he was reelected 3 times (1927–49). As Senate majority leader (1937–47), he was the main spokesman for the New Deal. A Democratic party regular, he vigorously fought for antilynching legislation and piloted the Lend-Lease Bill through the Senate (1941). A loyal supporter of President Roosevelt's foreign and domestic programs, Barkley broke with him briefly over his veto of a revenue law (Feb. 1944), resigning as majority leader. He was, however, unanimously reelected by his colleagues. A notable orator, he keynoted the Democratic conventions of 1932, 1936, and 1940. Truman's running mate in 1948, Barkley as vice-president cooperated closely with the president, was unusually active as congressional liaison, and participated in policy-making at cabinet meetings and on the National Security Council. Immensely popular, known as the "Veep," he sought the presidential nomination in 1952 but withdrew after labor refused support due to his age. He was reelected to the Senate (1954) and served until his death, while giving a speech at a mock political convention. He was the author of *That Reminds Me* (1954).

Barnard, Henry (b. Hartford, Conn., 24 Jan. 1811; d. there, 5 July 1900), edu-

cator. He was educated at the Monson (Mass.) Academy and at the Hopkins Grammar School in Hartford, was graduated from Yale (1830), read law privately and attended the Yale Law School (1833–34), and was admitted to the bar (c.1835). He was a member (1837–40) of the Connecticut General Assembly, where he sponsored legislation for the improvement of the common schools; secretary (1838–42) of the board of school commissioners in Connecticut; school commissioner (1843–49) of Rhode Island; superintendent (1850–54) of the Connecticut state schools; chancellor (1858–60) of the Univ. of Wisconsin; and president (1866–67) of St. John's College, Annapolis, Md. In 1867 he became the first U.S. Commissioner of Education, serving in that post until 1870. A leader in the public school movement, he published the *American Journal of Education* (1855–82) and founded the Connecticut *Common School Journal*.

Barnum, Phineas Taylor (b. Bethel, Conn., 5 July 1810; d. Bridgeport, Conn., 7 Apr. 1891), showman and promoter. Until 1834, when he came to New York City, he pursued a variety of occupations, including the editing of an abolitionist newspaper at Danbury, Conn. His career in show business began with his purchase and exhibition (1835) of Joice Heth, a Negress purported to be the nurse of George Washington and 161 years old (she was actually about 80 years old). He bought (1841) Scudder's American Museum and Peale's Museum, using their collections for his American Museum (opened at New York in 1842), where he exhibited the dwarf, Gen. Tom Thumb, and other freaks, and delighted the public with hoaxes. With Tom Thumb, Barnum made a successful tour of the Continent in 1844. In 1850 he brought the Swedish singer, Jenny Lind, to the U.S. for a concert tour, and in 1855 retired to Iranistan, his lavish home at Bridgeport, Conn. In 1871 he made his return as a showman, opening his circus ("The Greatest Show on Earth") at Brooklyn. In 1881 he combined forces with a rival to form the Barnum & Bailey Circus, and imported from the Royal Zoological Society at London the elephant known as Jumbo. One of the colorful aspects of his showmanship was the elaborate advertising he used to whet the public appetite for his bizarre exhibitions. In developing aquariums and menageries, Barnum stimulated the museum movement and popularized natural history.

Barton, Clara (b. N. Oxford, Mass., 25 Dec. 1821; d. Glen Echo, Md., 12 Apr. 1912), humanitarian. After teaching school in New Jersey, she went to Washington, D.C. (1854), where at the outbreak of the Civil War she organized supply and nursing services for sick and wounded Union troops. Without receiving compensation or accreditation, she performed her work behind the lines and on battlefields, including that of the Wilderness. In 1864, when she accompanied the Army of the James, she acted as superintendent of nurses under authority of Gen. Benjamin Butler. After the war she was in charge (1865–69) of a government-sponsored search for missing soldiers. During the Franco-Prussian War she was active in relief activities in association with the International Red Cross at Geneva. Upon her return to the U.S. she undertook a campaign to establish an American Red Cross, and it was through her efforts that a National Society of the Red Cross was organized (1881). Miss Barton served as its president until 1904. She was active in relieving suffering caused by wars and disasters, such as the Spanish-American War, the Boer War, and the Galveston flood (8 Sept. 1900), and was responsible for the introduction of the "American Amendment" at the Geneva International Conference (1884), specifying that in extreme peacetime emergencies the Red Cross should carry out humanitarian work similar to that assumed by it during wars.

Beard, Charles Austin (b. Knightstown, Ind., 27 Nov. 1874; d. New Haven, Conn., 1 Sept. 1948), historian, political scientist, was graduated from DePauw Univ. (1898), studied English local government at Oxford, and received his M.A. (1903) and Ph.D. (1904) from Columbia. Teaching history and politics at Columbia (1904–17), he resigned (1917) on an academic freedom issue, and cofounded (1919) the New School for Social Research. He was adviser (1922) to the Institute of Municipal Research in Tokyo. With James Harvey Robinson, he coauthored *The Development of Modern Europe* (1907) and an accompanying book of readings—pioneer text and source book offering a brilliant synthesis of political, social, and cultural history. *An Economic Interpretation of the Constitution* (1913), attributing the work of the Federal Convention to the self-interest of the Founding Fathers (in line with J. Allen Smith [1907] and Arthur F. Bentley [1908]) and introducing a strong element of economic determinism, had an enormous vogue. It was followed by *Economic Origins of Jeffersonian Democracy* (1915) and *The Economic Basis of Politics* (1910). He later repudiated such economic determinism in *The Republic* (1943), and more recent critics have challenged both his methodology and his evidence. With his wife, Mary Ritter Beard, he wrote *The Rise of American Civilization* (1927) and its sequels *America in Midpassage* (1939) and *The American Spirit* (1943), a notable and popular historical synthesis, stressing the Civil War as a second American Revolution. He also wrote *The Supreme Court and the Constitution* (1912) and *President Roosevelt and the Coming of the War, 1941* (1948), an isolationist critique.

Beaumont, William (b. Lebanon, Conn., 21 Nov. 1785; d. St. Louis, Mo., 25 Apr. 1853), army surgeon, pioneer in gastric physiology. He served his medical apprenticeship under Dr. Benjamin Chandler of St. Albans, Vt., was licensed (June 1812) by the Third Medical Society of Vermont, and was commissioned (13 Sept. 1812) a surgeon's mate to the 6th Infantry at Plattsburg, N.Y. After the close of the War of 1812, he resigned from the service and established a private practice at Plattsburg. He enlisted again (1820) and was assigned to Ft. Mackinac (in present-day Michigan) as a surgeon. It was there, on 6 June 1822, that Alexis St. Martin, a Canadian youth, was accidentally shot and suffered a powder-and-shot wound that left a portion of his stomach punctured and protruding from the abdominal cavity. St. Martin was brought to the military hospital for treatment. After a time a flap of the inner stomach closed the puncture, but the lid could be pushed back to expose the interior. Early in 1825 Beaumont undertook scientific studies in digestion, observing St. Martin's stomach temperature during digestion, the movements of his stomach walls, the relative digestibility of certain foods, and the workings of gastric juice under artificial conditions. These studies eventuated in the publication of *Experiments and Observations on the Gastric Juice and the Physiology of Digestion* (1833), revolutionary in its impact upon the existing knowledge and theories of the physiology of the stomach and the chemistry of gastric digestion, much of it still valid.

Beecher, Henry Ward (b. Litchfield, Conn., 24 June 1813; d. Brooklyn, N.Y., 8 Nov. 1887), clergyman and orator, son of Lyman Beecher (1775–1863) and brother of Harriet Beecher Stowe (*q.v.*), was graduated from Amherst (1834) and attended the Lane Theological Seminary, Cincinnati, in which city he began preaching as an independent Presbyterian. Called (10 Oct. 1847) to the Plymouth Congregational Church, Brooklyn, N.Y., he drew weekly audiences averaging 2,500, with notable sermons printed in pamphlet form and widely circulated. His influence was extended in editorials in the *Independent* (1861–64) and the *Christian Union,* which he edited 1870–81. An antislavery leader, he opposed interference in the slave states but counseled disobedience of the Fugitive Slave Law. In 1863 he visited England and defended the Union cause before hostile audiences. A modernist, he supported woman suffrage and civil service reform, accepted evolution, but clung to his belief in miracles. His Christianity stressed the love of God and the joy and glory of the religious life. His personal life became a public issue in the Beecher-Tilton adultery case (1874), in which his defense was upheld by a divided jury.

Bell, Alexander Graham (b. Edinburgh, Scotland, 3 Mar. 1847; d. Cape Breton Island, Nova Scotia, 2 Aug. 1922), inventor of the telephone and educator of the deaf. He was educated at McLauren's Academy in Edinburgh and at the Royal High School; became (c.1867) assistant in London to his father, Alexander Melville Bell (1819–1905), inventor of the Visible Speech System; accompanied his family to Canada (1870); and in 1871 began giving special instruction in his father's speech system to teachers of the deaf in cities throughout New England. He opened a normal training school at Boston (1872) and served (1873–77) as professor of vocal physiology and the mechanics of speech in the School of Oratory of Boston Univ. His work for the deaf and his interest in the science of acoustics were related to the experiments which he meanwhile pursued (1873–76) to invent a multiple telegraph and an electric speaking telegraph or telephone. These experiments led to his invention of the harmonic multiple telegraph (1874) and the telephonic telegraphic receiver (1874), in the course of which he gained a thorough knowledge of electrical wave transmission. His preoccupation with the idea of a machine for the electrical transmission of speech finally resulted in the first practical demonstration (at Boston, 10 Mar. 1876) of the first magneto-electric telephone. The Bell Telephone Co., the first organization of its kind, was founded in 1877, and thereafter the commercial development and application of the telephone proceeded rapidly. Bell became an American citizen in 1882. His career as an inventor did not interrupt his activities as an educator of the deaf. Among his other inventions were the photophone for the transmission of sound by light (1880), the telephone probe for locating metallic masses in the human body (1881), the spectrophone (1881), and the tetrahedral kite (1903). He was associated (1884–86) with the invention of the wax cylinder record for phonographs.

Bellows, George Wesley (b. Columbus, Ohio, 12 Aug. 1882; d. New York City, 8 Jan. 1925), painter, lithographer, and illustrator, was graduated from Ohio State Univ. (1903), studied painting in New York under Robert Henri (*q.v.*), and, in his early painting, was inspired

by city crowds (*42 Kids*, 1907) and prizefights (*Stag at Sharkey's*, 1907), following directly in the tradition of Eakins' realism. He taught at the Art Students League, beginning in 1910, and also at the Chicago Art Institute in 1919. His paintings show the influence of Goya and Daumier, and later of El Greco and Renoir, but are stamped with his own personality. Among his larger canvases are *Edith Cavell* (1918), with dramatic use of light and dark; *The Return of the Useless* (1918); and *The Pic-nic* (1924). Turning to lithography (1916), he soon became a master of that medium.

Bennett, James Gordon (b. Newmills, near Keith, Scotland, 1795; d. New York City, 1 June 1872), editor, emigrated to Halifax, Nova Scotia (1819), thence to Boston and New York, where he wrote for the press and acquired the *Sunday Courier* (1825). He was appointed associate editor of the New York *Enquirer* (1826) and coedited the combined *Courier & Enquirer* (1829). On 6 May 1835 he founded the New York *Herald*, a penny paper. Its sensational and comprehensive news coverage (in the Civil War it employed 63 war correspondents) and personalized editorial style raised its circulation to 100,000 (by 1864). Editorially, Bennett generally supported the Democrats, Douglas against Lincoln, and secession; but after Ft. Sumter, when a mob threatened him, he executed an about-face and backed the war, although he did not give Lincoln his full support until 1864.

Benton, Thomas Hart (b. Harts Mill, near Hillsboro, N.C., 14 Mar. 1782; d. Washington, D.C., 10 Apr. 1858), statesman, studied at Chapel Hill College (now Univ. of North Carolina) and the law department of William and Mary. Tennessee state senator (1809), he was admitted to the bar at Nashville (1806), served in the War of 1812 as aide-de-camp to Jackson, then removed to St. Louis (1815), where he practiced law and edited the *Missouri Inquirer*. In 1817 he killed Charles Lucas, U.S. district attorney in a second duel after wounding him in the first. Elected (1820) to the U.S. Senate, he was the first senator to serve 30 consecutive years (1821–51). Supporting Jackson (1828) as Senate floor leader in the war against the Bank and in his advocacy of hard money, "Old Bullion" secured a change in the ratio of gold and silver from 15 to 1 to 16 to 1. He sponsored the resolution to expunge from the Senate journal the resolution of censure of President Jackson. Advocate of free homesteads of 160 acres, anticipating the later Homestead Act, he opposed the annexation of Texas but supported the War with Mexico. Preferring compromise to war over the Oregon issue, he favored the 49th parallel, the boundary finally secured. Opposing Calhoun's pro-slavery resolution of 1850 as well as Clay's compromise, he lost his seat in the Senate, but in the House (1853–55) fought the Missouri Compromise repeal, which lost him his seat and his campaign for governor (1856). He supported Buchanan for president (1856) against his own son-in-law John C. Frémont (*q.v.*). He wrote a notable autobiography, *Thirty Years' View* (1854–56) and compiled *Abridgement of the Debates of Congress, 1789–1856* (1857–61).

Berkeley, Sir William (b. at or near London, 1606; d. England, 13 July 1677), colonial governor, received his B.A. (1624) and M.A. (1629) from Oxford. Knighted by Charles I (1639), he became royal governor of Virginia (1642), where he inaugurated vigorous and constructive policies. Heading an expedition (1644) against the Indians, he established a generation of peace and encouraged crop diversification and manufactures. Anglican and Royalist, he denied toleration to nonconformists, defied Parliament after the execution of Charles I, and, confronted by a naval force dispatched to Virginia by Parliament to establish its authority, worked out a compromise but yielded his own office. Back in office with the Restoration, his 2d administration, though continuing some of his constructive policies, was increasingly arbitrary, with no new elections of the burgesses called between 1660 and 1674. The unrest stemming from tax policies, bad crops, and Indian attacks, which Nathaniel Bacon (*q.v.*) exploited, found the governor obdurate. In the ensuing insurrection (1676) he was driven out of Jamestown, but on Bacon's death returned to power, rescinded recent reform measures, and despite royal promise of pardon hanged 23 rebels. Refusing to yield office to a royal investigating commission, he resigned on ground of ill health, returned to England, and, failing to obtain an audience with Charles II, died soon after.

Berlin, Irving [Isidore Baline] (b. Temun, Russia, 11 May 1888–   ), songwriter and composer, came to the U.S. in 1893, studied in the New York City public schools for 2 years, then worked as a song-plugger on the Bowery and as a singing waiter (1904). His first song hit, "Dorando," was published in 1909. Graduating to Broadway, he appeared in *Up and Down Broadway* (1910) and his "Alexander's Ragtime Band" (1911) quickly became a top hit. In 1912 he wrote the score for Ziegfeld's *Follies*. During World War I he became a U.S. citizen, and as an army sergeant he wrote an all-soldier show, *Yip-Yip-Yaphank*, while stationed at Camp Upton, Yaphank, L.I. Among his top hits was his musical comedy all-soldier revue *This Is* the Army, which opened on Broadway (1942), with Berlin singing "Oh, How I Hate to Get Up in the Morning," and wearing his World War I sergeant's uniform. For this show, the profits of which went to Army Emergency Relief, he was awarded the Medal of Merit, and for his song "God Bless America" (1917, but introduced in 1938) he received a congressional gold medal (1954). Other stage successes include *Annie Get Your Gun* (1947), *Call Me Madam* (1950, with Howard Lindsay and Russel Crouse), *Mr. President* (1962), and the film musical *Easter Parade* (1933). Lacking formal musical instruction, he played tunes in one key, F sharp, and used a piano adapted to change keys mechanically. Among his innumerable song hits are "Remember," "Always," "What'll I Do?," "All Alone," "A Pretty Girl Is Like a Melody," "Blue Skies," "White Christmas." He was married twice. His first wife, Dorothy Goetz, died 8 months after their marriage in 1913. In 1926 he married Ellin, daughter of Clarence H. Mackay.

Bernstein, Leonard (b. Lawrence, Mass., 25 Aug. 1918–), received his B.A. (1939) from Harvard, studying composition with Walter Piston, and at the Curtis Institute of Music, from which he was graduated (1941; piano with Isabella Vengerova and conducting with Fritz Reiner). Assistant to Serge Koussevitzky at the Berkshire Music Center (1943–44), he achieved fame overnight when in 1943 as Asst. Conductor he conducted the N.Y. Philharmonic upon the illness of Bruno Walter. Conductor of the New York City Symph. (1945–48), co-conductor of the N.Y. Philharmonic (1957–58) and its musical director 1958 to 1969, he has been outstanding as music educator and popularizer. He headed the conducting department of the Berkshire Music Center beg. 1948,

was professor of music at Brandeis Univ., 1951–56, a frequent music interpreter on TV (*Omnibus,* 1957; children's concerts), and inaugurator of the Thursday night previews of the N.Y. Philharmonic. His compositions include *Clarinet Sonata* (1942), *Symph. No. 1* (*Jeremiah,* 1942), *The Age of Anxiety* (1949), *Kaddish Symph.* (1963), *Chichester Psalms* (1965), *Mass* (1971), and *The Dybbuk,* a ballet score (1974). A musical virtuoso, he also wrote *Trouble in Tahiti,* a 1-act opera (1952); scores for musical shows *On the Town* (1944), *Wonderful Town* (1953), *Candide* (1956), *West Side Story* (1957); and the film score for *On the Waterfront* (1954). He conducted acclaimed revivals of *Falstaff,* Met. Opera (1963), and *Der Rosenkavalier,* Vienna State Opera (1968).

Beveridge, Albert (b. Highland Co., Ohio, 6 Oct. 1862; d. Indianapolis, Ind., 27 Apr. 1927), U.S. senator and historian, graduated from DePauw Univ. (1885) and was admitted to the Indiana bar (1887). After practicing law in Indianapolis and involving himself in politics for 12 years, Beveridge was elected as a Republican to the U.S. Senate (1899–1911). A nationalist and imperialist, Beveridge believed that "the trade of the world must and should be ours," supported the strengthening of the navy, and intervention in the Philippines. A leading progressive senator and strong supporter of President Theodore Roosevelt, he drafted the Meat Inspection Act (1906) which provided for the enforcement of sanitary regulations in packinghouses and for federal inspection of all companies selling meats in interstate commerce. Not against business *per se* but rather against big business, Beveridge supported Roosevelt's legislation regulating trusts and public utilities, and supported an income tax to curb "unhealthy fortunes." He was a leader in the campaign for national legislation against child labor, making the first important appeal (23, 28, 29 Jan. 1907) for action against an evil "as brutal and horrible in its humanity as anything the pen of Dickens ever painted." He was also a promoter of conservation. In the Republican split over the Payne-Aldrich tariff bill (1909), Beveridge strongly opposed the tariff as against the public interest, particularly attacking the tobacco schedule. After his defeat for reelection (1911), he became active in the new Progressive party, running unsuccessfully for governor of Indiana (1912), and for the Senate (1914, 1922) as a Republican. During an era when many politicians were also scholars, Beveridge produced major contributions to history. He is best known for his 4-vol. *The Life of Marshall* (1916–19), which remains the standard work on the Marshall court, in spite of a Federalist bias. At his death Beveridge was completing the first 2 vols. of a biography of Abraham Lincoln, which impressively placed the pre-presidential career of Lincoln in its historical setting (published posthumously, 1928).

Biddle, Nicholas (b. Philadelphia, 8 Jan. 1786; d. "Andalusia," near Philadelphia, 27 Feb. 1844), financier and editor, was graduated from the College of New Jersey (1801) and served abroad (1804) as secretary to John Armstrong, U.S. minister to France, and to Monroe, minister to Great Britain (1806). On his return to the U.S. (1807) he settled in Philadelphia and became associate editor (1807–12) of the *Port Folio* with Joseph Dennie and sole editor (1812). In collaboration with Paul Allen he prepared the *History of the Expedition of Captains Lewis and Clark* (1814). He served in Congress (1810–11) and in the Pennsylvania state senate (1814–18). Presi-

dent Monroe appointed him a government director of the 2d Bank of the U.S., of which he became president (1823) and served in that capacity until it closed its doors (1836) on failure to secure renewal of the charter. Following a conservative policy, Biddle made the Bank of the U.S. a paramount influence in the national economy, only to arouse the enmity of advocates of an "easy money" policy. His fatal error was to make the bank an issue in the presidential election of 1832. Jackson's overwhelming victory left no doubt about the issue. Under a charter from Pennsylvania Biddle continued to act as president of the bank, which finally failed (1841), although the creditors were fully paid.

Bierstadt, Albert (b. Düsseldorf, Germany, 7 Jan. 1830; d. New York City, 18 Feb. 1902), landscape painter. At the age of 2 he accompanied his parents to the U.S. and spent his childhood in New Bedford, Mass. After early exhibitions of his work in Boston (1851, 1853), he studied art in Germany and Rome (1853–57), with summer sketching tours of Germany and Switzerland. Returning to the U.S. in 1857, he went west with Gen. W. F. Lander's surveying expedition (1858–59). Thereafter his impressions of the scenery of the Rocky Mountains and the West, based on sketches made during this and subsequent visits, were recorded on canvas. One of his first Western landscapes was *Thunderstorm in the Rocky Mountains* (1859, Boston Mus. Fine Arts). Others include *Laramie Peak* (1861, Buffalo Acad. Fine Arts), *Looking Down Yosemite Valley* (1865, W. H. Cosby), *Estes Park, Colorado* (1877, Earl of Dunraven), and *Valley of Kern's River, California* (1875), bought for the Hermitage in St. Petersburg. He also produced historic landscapes such as *The Discovery of the Hudson River* (1875), which hangs in the Capitol, as well as 4 paintings (1887–88) treating Columbus' voyages, but his romantic landscapes of Western wilderness proved his most distinctive contribution.

Black, Hugo La Fayette (b. Harlan, Ala., 27 Feb. 1886; d. Bethesda, Md., 25 Sept. 1971), jurist, received his LL.B. (1906) from the Univ. of Alabama, practiced law in Birmingham (1907), where he served as police judge (1910–11) and later as solicitor of Jefferson Co. (1915–17). Democratic senator from Alabama (1927–37), he resigned to accept appointment as associate justice of the Supreme Court (1937). When appointed, considerable criticism was aroused by the revelation that he had once been a member of the Ku Klux Klan (1923–25), although his record in the Senate had been consistently progressive, notably in his investigation of the public utility lobby. His role as a liberal activist on the bench soon silenced some of his critics. Taking an absolutist position regarding much of the Bill of Rights, especially the 1st Amendment (*Bridges* v. *Calif.*, 1941; dissent in *Yates* v. *U.S.*, 1957), he opposed setting limits to the right to picket (*Milk Wagon Drivers Union* v. *Meadowmoor Dairies*, 1941). His dissenting opinion in *Conn. Gen. Life Ins. Co.* v. *Johnson* (1938) denied the right of corporations to claim protection under the 14th Amendment. In dissent in *Adamson* v. *Calif.* (1947) he asserted that the 14th Amendment extended to all the people the complete protection of the Bill of Rights. He upheld the right to distribute religious literature in a company town (*Marsh* v. *Ala.*, 1946), and in *Everson* v. *Bd. of Education* (1947) ruled that a N.J. law expending tax money for transportation to parochial schools did not constitute support of religion. Although he held that the exclusion order relating to Japanese-Americans during World War II was within the federal war powers (*Korematsu* v. *U.S.*, 1944), he invalidated the military courts set up in Hawaii during the war (*Duncan* v. *Kahanamoku*, 1946). His majority opinion held invalid President Truman's seizure of steel companies (*Youngstown Sheet & Tube Co.* v. *Sawyer*, 1952). He invalidated N.Y. State official school prayer (*Engel* v. *Vitale*, 1962), and upset inequitable congressional districting (*Westberry* v. *Sanders*, 1964). He refused to extend his 1st Amendment absolutism to symbolic speech (*Adderly* v. *Fla.*, 1966), and his 4th Amendment absolutism to cover electronic eavesdropping (dissent in *Berger* v. *N.Y.*, 1967). In his last major opinion he held that the U.S. could not enjoin publication of the Pentagon Papers (*New York Times* v. *U.S.*, 1971).

Blaine, James Gillespie (b. West Brownsville, Pa., 30 Jan. 1830; d. Washington, D.C., 27 Jan. 1893), statesman, was graduated from Washington College (1847); taught school (1848–54); studied law, moving to Augusta, Me., where he edited the Kennebec *Journal* (1854–57). While Republican state legislator (1859–62), he became speaker (1861–62). He served in Congress (1862–76) and was speaker of the House (1869–75). The "Mulligan letters" (1876), which accused Blaine of using his position as speaker for personal gain by giving a land grant to the Little Rock & Ft. Smith R.R., blasted his hopes for the presidential nomination that year. He again failed to secure the nomination in 1880. As Garfield's Secretary of State (1881) he planned the first Pan-American Conference and proposed to Great

Britain a modification of the Clayton-Bulwer Treaty. Republican nominee for president (1884), his defeat has been attributed in no small part to the indiscreet reference by one of his supporters to the Democratic party as the party of "Rum, Romanism, and Rebellion," which might well have lost the crucial state of New York. He supported Harrison (1888), and became Secretary of State (1889–92). His constructive achievements include the convening of the first Pan-American Conference (1889) and the settlement of the Bering seal dispute with Great Britain. He favored Hawaiian annexation.

Blalock, Alfred (b. Colloden, Ga., 5 Apr. 1899; d. Baltimore, Md., 15 Sept. 1964), surgeon, was graduated from Univ. of Georgia (B.A., 1918) and from Johns Hopkins (M.D., 1922), was on the medical faculty in surgery (1927–41) at Vanderbilt Univ. Medical School, and in 1941 became director of the department of surgery at Johns Hopkins Univ. and surgeon in chief of the Johns Hopkins Hospital. His most notable work was done in surgical shock and in regulation of the circulation. Testing a theory advanced by Dr. Helen Brooke Taussig (1898–   ), he operated (9 Nov. 1944) on a "blue baby," by-passing the pulmonary artery. As a result thousands of "blue babies" regained their health by the Blalock operation.

Boas, Franz (b. Minden, Westphalia, Germany, 9 July 1858; d. New York City, 21 Dec. 1942), anthropologist. He studied at Heidelberg and Bonn, received the degree of Ph.D. (1881) at Kiel, and as a member of a German Arctic expedition (1883–84) studied Eskimo life in Baffin Land. He served (1885–86) as an assistant at the Royal Ethnological Museum in Berlin and as *Privatdocent* in geography at the Univ.

of Berlin. Arriving in the U.S. in 1886, he was an editorial staff member (1886–88) of *Science* and instructor in anthropology (1888–92) at Clark Univ. In 1896 he was named lecturer in anthropology at Columbia Univ., where he became professor in 1899. He was curator of anthropology (1901–05) in the American Museum of Natural History; organized the Jesup North Pacific Expedition (1902), and edited its *Reports;* was president (1907–08) of the American Anthropological Society; and president (1910) of the New York Academy of Sciences. His numerous papers and studies, based upon the scientific fact-finding technique of the field survey, modified earlier concepts of cultural evolution. His publications on the Kwakiutl Indians are classics in their field. Among his writings are *Baffin Land* (1885), *The Central Eskimos* (1888), *The Mind of Primitive Man* (1911, 1938), *Anthropology and Modern Life* (1928), *General Anthropology* (1938), and *Race, Language and Culture* (1940) .

Boone, Daniel (b. near Reading, Pa., 2 Nov. 1734; d. near St. Charles, Mo., 26 Sept. 1820), pioneer. Becoming a hunter at the age of 12, he settled (1751) at Buffalo Lick in the Yadkin Valley of North Carolina; served as a teamster and blacksmith in Braddock's campaign (1755); made his first trip into Kentucky (1767–69), leading a party through Cumberland Gap over a trail later known as the Wilderness Road, living and exploring in central Kentucky with his brother-in-law John Stuart Finley and others, returning to North Carolina after his 2d trip (1769–71). Serving as the agent of Col. Richard Henderson of the Transylvania Co., he returned to Kentucky with a party of settlers (1775) and established a fort at what became the site of Boonesborough. Captured and adopted by the Shawnees (1778), he escaped. After Virginia repudiated Henderson's land titles and made Kentucky a county of Virginia, Boone served as lieutenant colonel of the Fayette County militia, and was chosen a delegate to the legislature, and was made sheriff and county lieutenant (1782). He moved to Maysville in 1786 and in 1788 left Kentucky, going to Point Pleasant in what is now West Virginia. Because of failure to make proper entry of his land holdings, he lost all of his claims. After being ejected from his last holding, he moved (c.1798) to present-day Missouri, where he received a land grant and continued his hunting and trapping. One of the folk heroes of American history, Boone is popularly credited with deeds, such as the discovery of Kentucky, which have no foundation in fact.

Booth, Edwin Thomas (b. near Bel Air, Md., 13 Nov. 1833; d. New York City, 7 June 1893), actor, son of Junius Brutus Booth (1796–1852), brother of John Wilkes Booth (1838–65). He made his debut (10 Sept. 1849) at Boston as Tressel in Cibber's version of *Richard III* and up to 1856 did most of his acting in California, where he emerged as an accomplished tragedian. Returning to the East in 1856, he scored a great success at Boston (20 Apr. 1857) in the role of Sir Giles Overreach. His appearances at New York and in the South and West established him as the leading American actor of his day. Among his favorite roles were Shylock, Hamlet, Romeo, and Othello. Between 1869 and 1874 he reached the peak of his career in performances given at Booth's Theater, built by him at New York City. Because of financial difficulties brought on by the Panic of 1873, Booth went into bankruptcy (1874) and for the remainder of his life was a roving player in the U.S. and Europe. He was the founder (1888) and first president of the Players' Club, to which he gave its present building on Gramercy Park, New York City.

Borah, William Edgar (b. Jasper Township, Ill., 29 June 1865; d. Washington, D.C., 19 Jan. 1940), statesman, studied at the Univ. of Kansas (1885–86), read law, was admitted to the bar (1889), and quickly gained prominence in Boise, Ida., as a criminal lawyer as well as counsel for timber and mining interests. Special prosecutor in the trial (1907) of William D. Haywood and others for the murder of Gov. Frank D. Steunenberg, he himself was unsuccessfully prosecuted (1907) for timber frauds. Elected to the U.S. Senate (1907), he served in that body until his death. Orator, reformer, and political maverick, he supported labor reform legislation and fought for the income tax and direct election of senators. Though a supporter of Theodore Roosevelt, he refused to follow him into the Progressive party in 1912. Opposing most of Wilson's progressive legislation, including women's suffrage, he favored national prohibition. Leader of the irreconcilables opposed to the League of Nations, he refused, with Henry Cabot Lodge, to compromise on that issue. Responsible for calling the Washington Disarmament Conference (1921) he exercised, as chairman of the Senate Committee on Foreign Relations (beg. 1924), enormous influence on U.S. foreign policy, favoring recognition of Russia but opposing U.S. intervention in Latin America as well as membership in the World Court. He induced Secretary of State Kellogg to substitute a multinational for a bilateral pact outlawing war (1928). He opposed Hoover's farm and tariff policies, supported much of the New Deal domestic program, but was an outstanding critic of the NRA and Franklin D. Roosevelt's Supreme Court bill. Supporting the Neutrality Act of 1935, he remained an isolationist to the end, advocating nonintervention in World War II.

Borlaug, Norman Ernest (b. Cresco, Ia., 25 Mar. 1914–   ), agronomist. The son of Norwegian immigrants, he grew up on a 56-acre farm. He received a B.S. in forestry (1937), M.S. (1940) and Ph.D. (1941) in plant pathology from Univ. of Minnesota. After spending 3 years as a pathologist for the du Pont de Nemours Foundation, studying how chemicals affect plants, Borlaug joined the Rockefeller Foundation's wheat improvement project in Mexico (1944). Borlaug has remained there ever since, directing a team of experts from 17 countries, experimenting with new, higher-yielding strains of wheat. Borlaug and the team's work began in 1944 when they planted 3 varieties of wheat—Japanese "Norin" dwarfs, Gaines, and Mexican—and found the only crop to resist rust was Norin. Then they crossed Norin with wheat from countries all over the world, until they developed a strain with good color and milling quality, rust resistance, high protein, a strong stem, and a very high yield. Planting seeds from Borlaug's strain of wheat, such countries as India and Pakistan have doubled their wheat production and Mexico quadrupled it. For his role in initiating the "Green Revolution," Borlaug received the Nobel peace prize (1970).

Bowditch, Nathaniel (b. Salem, Mass., 26 Mar. 1773; d. there, 17 Mar. 1838), astronomer, mathematician, was completely self-educated, learning algebra at 14 and studying Latin at 17 in order to read Newton's *Principia*. On his 5 sea voyages (1795–1803) as clerk, super-cargo, or master, he perfected his knowledge of mathematics and navigation. He corrected J. H. Moore's *The Practical Navigator*, and from the 13th English edition published (with his brother William's collaboration) the 1st American edition (1799). The 3d American edition, extensively altered, appeared under his name as *The New Practical American Navigator* (1802). Nine other editions of this classic appeared in his lifetime and at least 56 more since. *Bowditch's Useful Tables* were reprinted (1844) from the work. In addition, he published (1804–20) 23 important nautical and astronomical papers in the *Memoirs* of the American Academy of Arts and Sciences and translated the first 4 vols. of La Place's *Mécanique céleste* (1828–39). In addition to his numerous scientific honors he was president of the Essex Fire and Marine Insurance Co. (beg. 1804) and actuary of the Massachusetts Hospital Life Insurance Co. (1823–38).

Bradford, William (b. Austerfield, Yorkshire, England, 1590; d. Plymouth Colony, [now Mass.], 19 May 1657), Pilgrim leader. While still a boy he attended the Separatist group meetings held at William Brewster's house in Scrooby, and in 1609 accompanied the Scrooby congregation to Amsterdam and later to Leyden. He came to America (1620) in the *Mayflower* and was elected governor (1621) of Plymouth Colony following the death of John Carver. Between 1622 and 1656 he was reelected to the governorship in every year except 1633, 1634, 1636, 1638, and 1644, when he served as an assistant. The leading statesman of the Plymouth Colony, he exercised (1622–36) broad authority in governmental and religious matters. Plymouth Colony was placed on a firm economic footing when Bradford and other Pilgrim Fathers assumed (1627) the original investment of the merchant adventurers who had financed the settlement. Bradford took part in drafting (1636) a body of laws that endowed the office of governor with a quasi-constitutional status. Although he believed in maintaining the Plymouth Colony as a separate and compact settlement, Bradford cooperated in larger undertakings such as the Pequot War and the New England Confederation. He began (c.1630) writing his *History of Plimmouth Plantation,* completing it in 1651. It was not published in full until 1856.

Bradley, Omar Nelson (b. Clark, Mo., 12 Feb. 1893; d. New York City, 8 Apr. 1981), soldier. A graduate of the U.S. Military Academy (1915), he also received diplomas from the Army Infantry School (1925), the Command and General Staff School (1929), and the Army War College (1934). Commissioned a second lieutenant upon graduation from West Point, he served at various posts in the West and Midwest before becoming a professor of military science and tactics at South Dakota State College (1919–20). At the U.S. Military Academy he served as an instructor of mathematics (1920–24) and a training officer and instructor of military planning and tactics (1934–38). Promoted to brigadier general in 1941, his first combat service was in 1943, when he became a deputy to Gen. Patton (*q.v.*) in North Africa. After taking over command of the 2d Corps, in North Africa, he took part in the invasion of Sicily (1943). He was sent to England to begin planning for the invasion of Europe and to take over command of the 1st Army, which he directed during Operation Overlord (1944). Assuming command (Aug. 1944) of the 12th Army Group—composed of the 1st, 3d, 9th, and 15th armies, the largest force (1.3 million combat troops) ever to serve under a single American field commander

—he played a key role in engineering the offensive which led to Germany's defeat. Known as the "GI's General," he was respected for his tactical skill, courage, and refusal to waste troops. Promoted to full general (1945), after the war he served as head of the Veterans Administration (1945–47), Chief of Staff of the U.S. Army (1948–49), and the first chairman of the U.S. Joint Chiefs of Staff (1949–53). He was promoted to general of the army (1950). After his retirement (16 Aug. 1953), he pursued various business interests. He published his reminiscences, *A Soldier's Story* (1951).

Brandeis, Louis Dembitz (b. Louisville, Ky., 13 Nov. 1856; d. Washington, D.C., 5 Oct. 1941), jurist, studied in Germany (1873–75), was graduated from Harvard Law School (1878), and practiced in Boston until 1916. Because of his advocacy of public causes he came to be known as the "people's attorney." Attorney for the policyholders in the investigation of the Equitable Life (1906), he devised and secured enactment in Massachusetts of the issue of low-cost life insurance through savings banks (1907). His mastery of the facts and his firm grasp of economics were demonstrated in his pathmaking brief in *Muller* v. *Oregon* (1908), largely devoted to an analysis of the injurious effect of hard labor upon the physique of women. An opponent of bigness in business or government, his advice was sought by President Wilson on trust legislation, currency, and and labor problems. His appointment as associate justice of the U.S. Supreme Court (1916) was confirmed over strong opposition by the organized bar. Serving until retirement (1939), he was aligned in dissent with Holmes and (after 1932) with Cardozo and Stone. He cautioned the court against curbing social and economic experimentation by the states

(*New State Ice Co.*, 1932) and sought, in public-utility rate making, a measurement of value according to "prudent investment" (*Southwestern Bell Telephone Co.*, 1923).

Brooks, Phillips (b. Boston, Mass., 13 Dec. 1835; d. there, 23 Jan. 1893), Episcopal bishop. He attended Harvard; studied in the seminary at Alexandria, Va., where he was ordained a deacon (1859); and occupied his first ministry in the Church of the Advent in Philadelphia from 1859 to 1862. Here his eloquent and lofty preaching soon won wide attention. He served as rector (1862–69) of Holy Trinity in Philadelphia, and in 1865 made the prayer at the Harvard commemoration day. Brooks was rector (1869–91) of Trinity Church in Boston, where he brought into Episcopal preaching fresh currents of piety and conviction. His definition of preaching as "the bringing of truth through personality" was the central idea of the Lyman Beecher Lectures on Preaching given by Brooks at the Yale Divinity School (Jan.–Feb. 1877). In 1880, he preached in Westminster Abbey, winning the distinction of being the first American to preach before a crowned head in the Royal Chapel at Windsor. In 1891 he was elected and consecrated Bishop of Massachusetts, a post he held until his death.

Brown, John (b. Torrington, Conn., 9 May 1800; d. Charlestown, W. Va., 2 Dec. 1859), reformer son of an abolitionist and "underground railway" agent, Owen Brown, and Ruth Mills Brown (who died insane), had an unsuccessful business career as a tanner, land speculator, and shepherd in 10 different locations. Convinced of the need for a slave insurrection, he left Ohio in 1855 to join 5 of his sons in the Ossawatomie colony in Kansas, where he became captain of the local militia company. As Free-Soil crusaders, Brown and a party of 6 (4 of whom were his sons) planned and executed the massacre of 5 proslavery men (24 May 1856). "Old Ossawatomie Brown" and his company were eventually dispersed and the colony burned in retaliation. Supplied with arms and money by leading abolitionists, Brown and a band of 21 men, aiming to liberate the slaves, seized (16 Oct. 1859) the Harpers Ferry armory and bridges leading to the Ferry, a blow which inflamed the South. Forced to surrender to Col. Robert E. Lee, he was tried for treason to Virginia and speedily convicted. During and subsequent to the trial he conducted himself with dignity, protesting that his only desire was to free the slaves. Hanged at Charlestown, he was hailed as a martyr by antislavery elements.

Bryan, William Jennings (b. Salem, Ill., 19 Mar. 1860; d. Dayton, Tenn., 26 July 1925), political leader and orator, was graduated from Illinois College, Jacksonville, Ill. (1881), and from the Union College of Law in Chicago (1883); practiced law in Jacksonville (1883–87); and in 1887 moved to Lincoln, Neb., where he became active in Democratic politics. Elected to Congress in 1890, and reelected in 1892, he became a member of the silver bloc. An unsuccessful candidate for the Senate in 1894, he became editor in chief of the Omaha *World-Herald*, and at about this time began his long association with the Chautauqua lecture platform. Having already demonstrated in Congress his powers as an orator, he was much sought after as a public speaker advocating the free coinage of silver, and during 1894–95 went on speaking tours that augmented his reputation by the time the Democratic National Convention met at Chicago in 1896. His "Cross of Gold" speech (8 July 1896), his most famous oration, won him the presidential nomination. Conducting a brilliant and energetic campaign on the platform of the free coinage of silver in a sectional battle that saw the agrarian South and West aligned against the industrial and commercial Northeast, Bryan lost to William McKinley by 600,000 votes out of a total of 13,600,000. From 1896 until 1912 he was the virtually undisputed leader of the Democratic party. He advised Democrats in the Senate to approve the treaty of peace with Spain, but fought the presidential campaign of 1900 on the issue of anti-imperialism, receiving less votes than he had in 1896. In 1901 he established the weekly newspaper, the *Commoner,* which he edited and published until 1913, and in 1908 was again an unsuccessful presidential candidate. At the Democratic Convention of 1912, held in Baltimore, Bryan wielded considerable influence in securing the nomination of Woodrow Wilson on a liberal platform. As Secretary of State in Wilson's cabinet (1913–15) he adhered, after the outbreak of World War I, to strict neutrality. Differences with Wilson over the second *Lusitania* note led to his resignation from the cabinet (9 June 1915). A fundamentalist in religion, he drafted state legislation forbidding the teaching of evolution in public schools. When John T. Scopes, a teacher in Dayton, Tenn., was indicted for violating a state law of this nature, Bryan, on the prosecution staff, was subjected to withering examination by Clarence Darrow (*q.v.*), a defense attorney (1925).

Bryant, William Cullen (b. Cummington, Mass., 3 Nov. 1794; d. New York City, 12 June 1878), poet and editor, attended Williams College (1810–11); wrote the Federalist satire *The Embargo: or Sketches of the Times, a Satire; by a Youth of Thirteen* (1808); and in 1811 the first draft of the poem "Thanatop-

sis," first published in the *North American Review* in 1817. He studied law privately, was admitted to the bar in 1815, and finally established his practice at Great Barrington, Mass. He published *Poems* (1821), which included "The Ages," "To a Waterfowl," and "The Yellow Violet." His contributions (1824–25) to the *United States Literary Gazette* included "Monument Mountain" and the "Forest Hymn." By 1825 he had gained wide recognition as a poet. Abandoning his law practice, he moved to New York City in 1825 and for a year was coeditor of the *New York Review and Athenaeum Magazine.* In 1826 he was made assistant editor of the New York *Evening Post;* becoming its editor in 1829, he served in that capacity until his death. During his first decade as a newspaper editor he wrote relatively little poetry. A Jacksonian Democrat and a free trader, Bryant broke with the Democratic party in 1848, when he supported the Free-Soil ticket, and in 1856 became a Republican spokesman. During the Civil War, he took a radical stand on emancipation and the prosecution of the war, but afterward favored a liberal policy toward the South. He also published *Poems* (1832), *The Fountain, and Other Poems* (1842), and *The White-Footed Doe, and Other Poems* (1844). He ranks as one of the finest American lyric poets of nature.

Buchanan, James (b. near Mercersburg, Pa., 23 Apr. 1791; d. Wheatland, near Lancaster, Pa., 1 June 1868), 15th president of the U.S., was graduated from Dickinson College (1809), admitted to the Pennsylvania bar (1812), and practiced at Lancaster. Federalist state legislator (1815–16) and congressman (1820–31), he served as U.S. minister to Russia (1832–33), negotiating a commercial treaty, and was Democratic U.S. senator (1835–45). He entered Polk's cabinet as Secretary of State (1845–49), settled the Oregon dispute, and offered to purchase Cuba from Spain. Minister to Great Britain (1853–56), he joined with Mason and Soulé in drafting the "Ostend Manifesto" (1854). Democratic president of the U.S. (1857–61), he held slavery to be a moral wrong but urged acceptance of the Lecompton Constitution in Kansas (1858). Denying the right of states to secede, he failed to find the legal authority to meet secession and favored an amendment to the Constitution expressly recognizing slavery and the right to recover fugitive slaves. Although he endorsed Breckinridge in 1860, he supported the federal government during the Civil War.

Bulfinch, Charles (b. Boston, Mass., 8 Aug. 1763; d. there, 4 Apr. 1844), architect, was graduated from Harvard in 1781 and made a tour (1785–86) of England and the Continent, where, at Jefferson's suggestion, he studied the classical architecture of France and Italy that was to leave a lasting imprint on his style. He designed the old Hollis Street Church in Boston (1788), churches at Taunton and Pittsfield, the Beacon Monument (1789), the Boston Theater, the Massachusetts State House at Boston, and the State House at Hartford. His introduction of the Adamesque style (1792 *et seq.*), as in the Coolidge, Barrell, and Derby houses, led to a general adoption of that mode for New England residences during the early Federal period and influenced architect-builders such as Samuel McIntire and Asher Benjamin. Bulfinch also drew up plans for the Franklin Crescent (1793), the Harrison Gray Otis houses, India Wharf, the Boylston Market, additions to Faneuil Hall, the New South Church (1814), and the old courthouse, all at Boston; Christ Church at Lancaster (1816–17); the State Prison at Charlestown; the

Massachusetts General Hospital (1817–20); and the State Capitol at Augusta, Me. (1828–31). As chairman (1799–1817) of the Boston board of selectmen, he was largely responsible for the renovation and development of old Boston. He succeeded (1817) Benjamin H. Latrobe (*q.v.*) as architect of the Capitol Building at Washington, D.C., remaining in that post until the structure's completion in 1830.

Burr, Aaron (b. Newark, N.J., 6 Feb. 1756; d. Port Richmond, N.Y., 14 Sept. 1836), statesman, was graduated from the College of New Jersey (1772); studied theology briefly and then law. In 1775 he served in Arnold's expedition to Canada and, subsequently, on Washington's staff and then on Putnam's, becoming lieutenant colonel (1777). Admitted to the bar (1782), he moved from Albany to New York City (1783); became attorney general of New York (1789–91) and U.S. senator (1791–97). Defeated for reelection (1796), he served in the New York Assembly (1797–99). In the presidential election of 1800 he tied Jefferson. When the House of Representatives chose the latter, Burr became 3d vice-president of the U.S. He was defeated for governor of New York (1804). Provoked by published accusations made by his political foe, Alexander Hamilton, Burr mortally wounded Hamilton in a duel at Weehawken, N.J. (11 July 1804). He fled southward, but returned to preside over the impeachment trial of Supreme Court Justice Samuel Chase. In 1806 he became involved in a conspiracy which, whether to seize Mexico for the U.S. or to have the Western states secede from the Union, has never been clarified. Arrested by coconspirator Gen. James Wilkinson, he was brought before Chief Justice Marshall (30 Mar. 1807), sitting at Richmond in the U.S. Circuit Court. Acquitted both of treason and of high misdemeanor, he resided in Europe (1808–12) and then practiced law in New York City.

Butler, Nicholas Murray (b. Elizabeth, N.J., 2 Apr. 1862; d. New York City, 7 Dec. 1947), educator and author, was graduated from Columbia (A.B., 1882; A.M., 1883; Ph.D., 1884), studied at Berlin and Paris (1884–85), and served at Columbia as an assistant (1885–86), tutor (1886–89), and adjunct professor of philosophy (1889–90). In 1889 he established the *Educational Review,* of which he was the first editor (1889–1920). He was the organizer and first president (1886–91) of Teachers College and, as president of Columbia, from 1901 until his retirement in 1945, he was outstandingly successful in expanding the university's effectiveness and prestige. Active in public affairs, Butler was Republican vice-presidential nominee in 1912. He was appointed (1905) a trustee of the Carnegie Foundation for the Advancement of Teaching, served as president (1925–45) of the Carnegie Endowment for International Peace, and was chairman (1937–45) of the Carnegie Corporation. In 1931 he shared the Nobel peace prize with Jane Addams.

Byrd, Richard Evelyn (b. Winchester, Va., 25 Oct. 1888; d. Boston, Mass., 11 Mar. 1957), naval officer, explorer, was graduated from the U.S. Naval Academy (1912), entered the Aviation Service (1917); and was commander (July–Nov. 1918) of the U.S. air forces in Canada. He made a dirigible flight across the Atlantic (1921) and was commander (1925) of the aviation unit of the Navy-MacMillan Polar Expedition. With Floyd Bennett, he made an airplane flight (9 May 1926) over the North Pole, for which he was awarded the Congressional Medal of Honor. With 3 companions, he made a 4,200-mile flight from New York to France (29 June–1 July 1927). He made his 1st expedition to the Antarctic in 1928–30, flying over the South Pole (29 Nov. 1929) from his base at "Little America." In his 2d expedition to the Antarctic (1933–35) he recorded important scientific data near the South Pole and discovered and named Maria Byrd Land and the Edsel Ford Mountains, and on his 3d (1939) he made flights that resulted in the discovery of 5 islands, 5 mountain ranges, and 100,-000 square miles of land area. He commanded the U.S. Navy Expedition (1946–47) which explored 1,700,000 square miles, tested equipment, made weather observations, and carried out a geological survey of the South Pole region.

Calder, Alexander (b. Lawnton, Pa., 22 July 1898; d. New York City, 11 Nov. 1976), sculptor. Although the grandson and son (of Alexander Stirling Calder, 1870–1945) of well-known sculptors, Calder studied mechanical engineering, receiving a degree from Stevens Institute of Technology (1919) and worked at a variety of jobs, until he enrolled (1923) in the Art Students League of New York City, where he studied under John Sloan and George Luks, Kenneth Kayes Miller, Guy Pène du Bois, and Boardman Robinson. Du Bois, with his mannikinlike figures, and Robinson, with his background in journalistic illustrations, most directly influenced Calder. As an illustrator for the *National Police Gazette,* Calder came in contact with the circus (1925), attending performances frequently and drawing the animals and acrobats. He began to create a small circus of animals and performers out of wood and wire. In 1926 he set up a studio in Paris, displaying *Le Cirque Calder,* which was admired by Cocteau and Miro, among others. His sculptures of wood and metal (often just large sheets of steel), "stabiles," were first shown in 1931. His first "mobile," sections of wire and shaped sheets of metal in balance, suspended from a sphere, were shown the following year, and the first outdoor mobile designed in 1935. Mobiles were crafted for Martha Graham's *Panorama* at the Bennington (Vt.) School of the Dance and for other programs of hers. Calder designed the famous mobile *The Mercury Fountain* for the Spanish Pavilion at the Paris World's Fair (1937). Among his widely acclaimed mobiles are *The Whirling Ear* (Brussels Exposition, 1958), the hanging mobile for the John F. Kennedy Airport, the *Big Sail* at MIT. Among his major stabiles are *Ticket Window* (Lincoln Center, New York City, 1965) and his largest, *Man*, standing 70 feet high, at Montreal's Expo '67. Calder worked on toys, jewelry, opaque watercolors, tapestries, and book illustrations. His work was graceful and appealing, ofttimes humorous.

Calhoun, John Caldwell (b. Abbeville District, S.C., 18 Mar. 1782; d. Washington, D.C., 31 Mar. 1850), statesman, was graduated from Yale (1804) and admitted to the South Carolina bar (1807). After a term in the South Carolina legislature (1808–09), he was in Congress (1811–17), where he became a leader of the "war hawks" and supported nationalistic legislation after the War of 1812, including the protective Tariff of 1816. He served as Secretary of War under Monroe (1817–25), was a candidate for president (1824), but was elected vice-president of the U.S., serving first under John Quincy Adams (1825–29) and then under Jackson (1829–32). Charged with having improperly received profits from a contract while Secretary of War, Calhoun demanded (29 Dec. 1826) a House investi-

gation. He was exonerated by a Select Committee (1827). In his "South Carolina Exposition" (1828), written in opposition to the Tariff of 1828, he postulated the principles of states' rights and nullification. Breaking with Jackson over Peggy Eaton and nullification, he resigned as vice-president (1832). As U.S. senator (1832–43) he became the leading proponent of states' rights. While Tyler's Secretary of State (1844–45), he secured the annexation of Texas. Again senator (1845–50), he opposed the Mexican War, the admission of California to statehood (because its constitution forbade slavery), and the Wilmot Proviso. In his last speech, on the Compromise of 1850, read to the Senate by Sen. James Murray Mason of Virginia (4 Mar. 1850), he approved the purpose of the act but criticized it for its failure to provide the South with adequate guarantees. In his "Discourse on the Constitution," posthumously published, he proposed a dual Executive (from North and South), each armed with a veto.

Cannon, Joseph Gurney (b. Guilford, N.C., 7 May 1836; d. Danville, Ill., 12 Nov. 1926), political leader. Raised in Indiana, he studied law under John P. Usher and for 6 months at the Cincinnati Law School and was admitted to the bar in Illinois (1858). He practiced law in Danville, Ill., and served as state's attorney for the 27th judicial district (1861–68). First elected to the U.S. House of Representatives in 1873, he served in Congress for the next 50 years except for 2 terms (1891–93, 1913–15) when first the Populists and then the Progressives defeated him. Except for sponsoring a bill granting a low rate on 2d class mail and another starting the parcel post system (1874), he sponsored little legislation. As speaker of the House (1903–11), Cannon brought the power of that office to its peak, ruling dictatorially in the interest of his fellow "Old Guard" Republicans. He instituted few parliamentary changes but fully exploited those of his predecessors. Recognition was made entirely arbitrary; usually "Uncle Joe" recognized on the floor only those who had previously secured permission to speak. He made the Rules Committee an even more potent instrument of the speaker than it had been—its clearance was normally granted only for measures which Cannon approved and procedures were followed whereby "riders" added by him and his associates in committee stood little chance of defeat on the floor. He established a network of trusted lieutenants who were given key committee assignments. Cannon was shorn of his powers (1910) by a coalition of Democrats and insurgent Republicans. In the reaction, the speaker was barred from membership on the Rules Committee, the power of appointment to standing committees was transferred from the speaker to the full House, and the speaker's powers of recognition were limited to some extent.

Cardozo, Benjamin Nathan (b. New York City, 24 May 1870; d. Port Chester, N.Y., 9 July 1938), jurist, was graduated from Columbia (1889), admitted to the New York bar (1891), practicing law in New York until his election to the state supreme court (1913). Appointed to the state court of appeals (1917) and elected its chief judge (1927), he established that court's preeminent prestige and was the obvious choice to succeed O. W. Holmes on his retirement from the U.S. Supreme Court. Appointed by Hoover associate justice (1932), he aligned himself with the liberal wing (Brandeis and Stone) on social and economic issues. Although he vigorously concurred in the *Schechter Case* (1935)

in opposition to "delegation running riot," he just as vigorously dissented from the tendency of the majority to curb distasteful governmental policies (*Carter Case*, 1936), and upheld the Social Security Act under the general welfare clause (*Stevens Machine Co.* and *Helvering* v. *Davis,* 1937). His ideas of sociological jurisprudence and his position that adherence to precedent should be relaxed in the face of changing conditions were expressed in his writings (*The Nature of the Judicial Process,* 1921; *The Growth of the Law,* 1924; and *The Paradoxes of Legal Science,* 1928).

Carlson, Chester F. (b. Seattle, Wash., 8 Feb. 1906; d. New York City, 19 Sept. 1968), physicist and inventor. The son of a barber, Carlson supported his family from the time he was 12. Graduating from the California Institute of Technology (1930), he worked for a short time at Bell Telephone Co. and then took a job in the patent department of P. R. Mallory Co., an electronics firm in New York City. Finding it difficult to get copies of drawings of patents, Carlson started experimenting, using electrostatics to produce copies (1934). Working in a tiny one-room laboratory in Queens, he produced his first electrostatic copy, or Xerox, on 22 Oct. 1938, and received his first patent (1940). About the same time (1934–39) he studied law at night at New York Law School, and was admitted to the New York bar (1940). Four years later, after being refused by more than 20 companies, Carlson persuaded the Battelle Memorial Institute, a nonprofit research organization, to make Xerox copies. In 1947, the Haloid Co., a small company in Rochester, N.Y., later named Xerox Corp., bought the first commercial rights to Xerox. In 1958, the company introduced the first Xerox office machine, the

"914," whose widespread use revolutionized photocopying.

Carnegie, Andrew (b. Dunfermline, Scotland, 25 Nov. 1835; d. Lenox, Mass., 11 Aug. 1919), industrialist and philanthropist. Coming to the U.S. with his poverty-stricken parents (1848), he began his career in Allegheny, Pa., as a bobbin boy employed at $1.20 a week, then (1849) a messenger in the Pittsburgh telegraph office. At the age of 16 he became one of the first operators in the U.S. able to take messages by sound. In 1853 he became private secretary and personal telegrapher to Thomas A. Scott, general superintendent of the Pennsylvania R.R. Upon Scott's appointment (1860) as vice-president of the road, Carnegie was named superintendent of the Pittsburgh division; and when Scott was named assistant secretary of war (1861), Carnegie became superintendent of the eastern military and telegraph lines, performing notable services for the Union forces during the Civil War. Having reorganized the Keystone Bridge Works (1862), Carnegie resigned from the Pennsylvania R.R. (1865) to devote himself to the iron, oil, and other businesses. He established (1868) the Union Iron Mills, and beginning in 1873 concentrated solely on the steel industry. In the following 3 decades, during which the U.S. took the lead over British steel production, the rapid expansion of U.S. steel manufactures was largely his creation. Carnegie progressively added to his holdings by lease or purchase, and in 1888 took over the Homestead Steel Works. By 1900, the Carnegie Steel Co., which had been organized in 1899, controlled the bulk of U.S. steel production. After selling his company to the interests that formed the U.S. Steel Corp. (1901), Carnegie retired and devoted himself to philanthropy. He set up the Carnegie trusts and foundations, among them the Carnegie Institution of Washington (1902), the Carnegie Foundation for the Advancement of Teaching (1906), and the Carnegie Endowment for International Peace (1910). He endowed numerous libraries throughout the world. He wrote *The Gospel of Wealth* (1900).

Carothers, Wallace Hume (b. Burlington, Ia., 27 Apr. 1896; d. Philadelphia, Pa., 29 Apr. 1937), chemist, inventor, received his B.S. (1920) from Tarkio College, Mo., and his M.S. (1921) and Ph.D. (1924) from the Univ. of Illinois. His first independent papers, "Isosterism of Phenal Isocynate and Diazobenzene-Imide" (1923) and "The Double Bond" (1924), revealed his creativity in the field of theoretical organic chemistry. Instructor at Harvard (1926–28), he left to direct a fundamental research program in organic chemistry at E. I. du Pont de Nemours and Co. in Wilmington, Del. His interest in unsaturated compounds led to the production of a rubberlike polymer (1930) and to the commercial development of a synthetic rubber known as neoprene. The research of Carothers and his associates (1929–37) provided a general theory of polymerization processes, culminating (23 May 1934) in the synthesizing of a superpolymer, which led (1939) to the commercial production of nylon, the first completely synthetic fiber.

Carter, Jimmy [James Earl, Jr.] (b. Plains, Ga., 1 Oct. 1924–   ), 39th President of the U.S., studied at Georgia Southwestern College (1941–42), Georgia Institute of Technology (1942–43), and the U.S. Naval Academy (1943–46). Following sea service he was assigned to the Navy's nuclear submarine program (1951), and studied nuclear physics and engineering at Union College. After his father's death, Carter, then a lieutenant, left the Navy (1953) to take over the family businesses—raising peanuts, cotton ginning, and warehousing. Serving in the Georgia State Senate (1963–66), Carter was a progressive on most social issues, advocated fiscal restraint, and supported modest civil rights legislation. He was defeated for Governor of Georgia (1966), but won election (1970) in a campaign where he spoke out against federally imposed desegregation plans. As Governor (1971–75) he reorganized state government and supported an end to racial discrimination. Announcing his candidacy for President early (12 Dec. 1974), Carter won 18 of 31 primaries. As Democratic nominee he defeated incumbent Gerald Ford (1976). As President his foreign policy was highlighted by stress on human rights, negotiating the Camp David accords (1978), and the hostage crisis (1979–81). His style was open and unpretentious, but his administration was criticized for vacillation, and he was beaten for reelection by Ronald Reagan (1980).

Carver, George Washington (b. near Diamond Grove, Mo., c.1860; d. Tuskegee, Ala., 5 Jan. 1943), Negro agricultural chemist. Born of slave parents, illiterate until he was almost 20 he worked his way through high school and through the Iowa State College of Agriculture and Mechanic Arts (B.S., 1894; M.S., 1896), where he was head of the college greenhouse and of bacterial laboratory work in systematic botany (1894–96). In 1896 he became director of the department of agricultural research at Tuskegee Institute, Ala., where he remained for the rest of his life. Essentially a practical chemist, he used empirical methods in his work on the diversified utilization of common agricultural prod-

ucts, including the peanut, sweet potato, and soybean. His achievements exercised an important influence on the shift of the Southern agricultural economy from a single-crop basis to a diversified and more prosperous foundation. From the peanut and the sweet potato he developed more than a hundred different products, including plastics, lubricants, dyes, medicines, ink, wood stains, face creams, tapioca, and molasses.

Cass, Lewis (b. Exeter, N.H., 9 Oct. 1782; d. Detroit, Mich., 17 June 1866), soldier, diplomat, statesman, attended Exeter Academy. He set out on foot from Wilmington, Del., for the Northwest Territory in 1801; he studied law under Gov. R. J. Meigs in Marietta, Ohio, and was admitted to the Ohio bar (1802). In the Ohio legislature (1806), he was U.S. Marshal for Ohio (1807–12), when he resigned to enlist in the army. Colonel and brigadier general, he played an important role in Harrison's victories over the British and Indians in the War of 1812. Governor of Michigan Territory (1813–31), he concluded treaties with the Indians. Jackson's Secretary of War (1831–36), he directed the Black Hawk War. Minister to France (1836–42), he resigned because of differences with Secretary of State Webster over a 5-party treaty legalizing the right of search, which he opposed. In a bid for the Democratic presidential nomination, he urged (Hannegan Letter, 10 May 1844) annexation of Texas. A nationalist and expansionist, he backed Polk's Oregon policy and opposed the Wilmot Proviso as senator from Michigan (1845–48). He resigned to run as the Democratic nominee for president in 1848, suffering defeat by Taylor as a result of party defection in New York and Pennsylvania. Senator again (1849–57), he favored the Compromise of 1850. As Buchanan's

Secretary of State (1857–60), he re-signed 12 Dec. 1860 in protest against the president's decision not to reinforce the Charleston forts.

Cassatt, Mary (b. Allegheny City, Pa., 22 May 1844; d. Mensil-Theribus, France, 14 June 1926), painter. Having spent 5 years in Paris as a child (1852–57), she returned to the U.S. and stud-ied at the Pennsylvania Academy of Fine Arts (1861–62), but then returned to Europe where she studied the work of the old masters, especially Correggio. Her first major show was in the Paris Salon (1872). She made that city her home (1874). A disciple of Dégas, in-fluenced by Manet and by Japanese prints, Cassatt was the only American to exhibit her paintings in Paris with the Impressionists (1877–86). Outstanding Impressionist examples were *Little Girl in a Blue Armchair* (1878, Paul Mellon), *Dans la Loge* (1879, Paris), *The Boating Party* (1893, National Gallery, Washing-ton), and *La Toilette* (Art Institute of Chicago, 1894). Much of her work was done in pastels and she employed a richer and wider assortment of colors than other Impressionists. Her work was notable for simplicity and originality. Motherhood idealized was a major theme. While her visits to the U.S. were infrequent and Americans were slow to recognize her importance, she consid-ered herself American and was awarded the Lippincott prize by the Pennsylvania Academy of Fine Arts (1904) for *Caress* (1902, National Collection Fine Arts, Washington), the same year she received the chevalier of the Legion of Honor from France. Her work was included in the famous Armory Show (New York, 1913). Her eyesight began to fail (1900) and she ceased to work by 1914.

Cather, Willa Sibert (b. Winchester, Va., 7 Dec. 1876; d. New York City, 24 Apr. 1947), novelist, moved with her parents to Nebraska (1884) and graduated from the Univ. of Nebraska (1895). She taught school, did newspaper work in Pittsburgh, and published her first book of stories, *The Troll Garden* (1905). Editor, *McClure's Magazine* (1907–12), she resigned to devote herself to creative writing. Her novels, poignant recollec-tions of a pioneer past stressing the supremacy of moral and spiritual over material values, are economically con-structed and marked by a graceful, lucid style. They include: *O Pioneers!* (1913), *The Song of the Lark* (1915), *My An-tonia* (1918), *One of Ours* (1922, a Pul-itzer prize-winner), *A Lost Lady* (1923, often regarded as her best work), *Death Comes for the Archbishop* (1927), and *Shadows on the Rock* (1931).

Channing, William Ellery (b. Newport, R.I., 7 Apr. 1780; d. Bennington, Vt., 2 Oct. 1842), Unitarian clergyman. Graduating from Harvard in 1798, he was ordained and installed (1803) as minister of the Federal Street Church at Boston, a pastorate he held until his death. His humane and liberal theology touched off the "Unitarian Controversy" that saw Channing and his followers ranged against orthodox Calvinists. The controversy reached its height c.1815. Expressing the viewpoint of members of Congregationalist and other sects who were dissatisfied with Calvinist doctrine, particularly its emphasis on the deprav-ity of man, he preached the gospel of goodness and love, the dignity and per-fectibility of man, the validity of reason, and freedom of will and moral responsi-bility, but accepted the supernatural in Christianity. Channing became the ac-knowledged head of the Unitarians, whose formal emergence was precipi-tated by the sermon he delivered at Baltimore (1819) at the ordination of

Jared Sparks, an address in which he formulated the Unitarian creed. Channing organized the Berry Street conference of liberal ministers (1820), the predecessor of the American Unitarian Association (1825). After 1825 his influence spread beyond religious circles. His addresses on education, literature, slavery, and war attracted wide attention; some of them were published in pamphlet form, including *Remarks on American Literature* (1830), *Slavery* (1835), *The Abolitionist* (1836), and *Duty of the Free States* (1842). The moral and religious forces which he liberated were the bases of New England Transcendentalism.

Chase, Salmon Portland (b. Cornish, N.H., 13 Jan. 1808; d. New York City, 7 May 1873), statesman, was graduated from Dartmouth (1826), admitted to the bar (1829), and commenced law practice in Cincinnati (1830). Through his defense of fugitive slaves he became a leader of the antislavery movement, an organizer (1841) of the Liberty party, and a founder (1848) of the Free-Soil party. As U.S. senator (1849–55) he opposed the Compromise of 1850 and the Kansas-Nebraska Bill. Republican governor of Ohio (1855–60), he was again elected to the U.S. Senate (1860). Unsuccessful candidate for president in that year, he became Lincoln's Secretary of the Treasury, maintaining credit and funds to prosecute the Civil War and recommending the National Banking Act (1863). Opposing Seward in the cabinet, his resignation was finally accepted (June 1864), but in Dec. of that year Lincoln appointed him Chief Justice of the U.S. Supreme Court. He reorganized the federal courts in the South, presided over the trial of Jefferson Davis and favored quashing the indictment (1867), and over the Senate impeachment proceedings against President Johnson (1868). In the *Hepburn Case* (1870) he declared the opinion of the court invalidating the Legal Tender Act of 1862 making "greenbacks" (issued by him as Secretary of the Treasury) legal tender, and dissented from the reversal (1871). He stood with the majority of the court in decisions upholding the Republican policy of Reconstruction.

Clark, George Rogers (b. Charlottesville, Va., 19 Nov. 1752; d. Louisville, Ky., 13 Feb. 1818), conqueror of the Northwest, explored the Ohio (1772) and Kentucky rivers (1774), the latter as surveyor for the Ohio Co. Commissioned major in charge of the defense of the Kentucky area when the Revolution broke out, his plan for the conquest of the Illinois country was endorsed by Virginia's governor, Patrick Henry (*q.v.*). As lieutenant colonel he set out with a company of 175 men, capturing Kaskaskia and Vincennes (1778), soon lost to British counterattack. In a heroic winter march of 180 miles he recaptured Vincennes (1779), forcing Lt. Gov. Henry Hamilton to surrender. In 1780 he met a British threat to the Spanish outpost in St. Louis, was on the defensive in 1781, but held fast to the key bastion of Ft. Nelson on the Falls of the Ohio (1782). The close of the war found Kentucky in U.S. hands and much of Ohio and Illinois, and by the Treaty of Paris (1783) the Northwest was given to the U.S. In 1786 James Wilkinson made political capital out of Clark's seizure of Spanish goods at Vincennes (1786) in order to provision his garrison. Involved in 2 French projects (1793, 1798) to lead an expedition against the Spanish for the reconquest of Louisiana, he refused a U.S. demand to surrender his generalship in the French army, taking refuge in St. Louis. In later life he was interested in Indian history and archaeology.

Clark, William, see **Lewis, Meriwether, and Clark, William.**

Clay, Henry (b. Hanover Co., Va., 12 Apr. 1777; d. Washington, D.C., 29 June 1852), statesman, studied law in Richmond, was admitted to the bar (1797), and practiced in Lexington, Ky. Kentucky legislator (1803–06), he filled an unexpired term in the U.S. Senate (1806–07), became speaker of the state legislature (1807–09), and filled another unexpired term in the Senate (1809–10). While congressman (1811–21, 1823–25), he was speaker (1811–20 and 1823–25) and was a leader of the "war hawks." A commissioner to negotiate peace with Great Britain (1814), he urged recognition of South American republics by the U.S. (1817) and was influential in framing the Missouri Compromise (1820). As a candidate for president (1824), he was 4th in the number of electoral votes, throwing his support to John Quincy Adams, whose Secretary of State (1825–29) he became. Senator (1831–42 and 1849–52), Clay was the Whig candidate for president (1832), but was defeated by Jackson largely because of his support of the 2d Bank of the U.S. His "American System" was based upon tariff protection and federal aid for internal improvements. He sponsored the compromise Tariff of 1833, failed to secure the Whig nomination in 1840, and ran in 1844, losing because of his noncommittal stand on Texas. His sponsorship of the Compromise of 1850 earned him the title "The Great Pacificator."

Clemens, Samuel Langhorne [pseudonym **Mark Twain**] (b. Florida, Mo., 30 Nov. 1835; d. Redding, Conn., 21 Apr. 1910), novelist and humorist, was reared in Hannibal, Mo. (1839–53), where, at the age of 12, he was apprenticed to a printer. As a journeyman printer he worked (1853–57) in cities in the Old West and along the Eastern seaboard, and from 1857 to 1861 served successively as apprentice pilot and licensed pilot on Mississippi steamboats. In 1861 he became secretary to his brother Orion, who had just been named secretary to the territorial governor of Nevada. After an unsuccessful attempt at prospecting and mining, he became (1862) a reporter on the *Territorial Enterprise* in Virginia City, using for the first time the pseudonym Mark Twain (a river term indicating 2 fathoms deep), by which he is best known. This had been the nom de plume of Capt. Isaiah Sellers (d. 1863). Going to California in 1864, he wrote in the following year the humorous story "The Celebrated Jumping Frog of Calaveras County," which was reprinted in newspapers throughout the U.S. and served as the title of his first book (1867). After taking an assignment as a roving correspondent in the Sandwich Islands, he began (1866) his long career as a lecturer. A commission as a travel correspondent for a San Francisco newspaper took him to the Mediterranean and the Holy Land, a trip that provided the material for *The Innocents Abroad* (1869), a book that brought him a national reputation. He lived in Buffalo (1869–71), writing for the Buffalo *Express,* and married (1870) Olivia Langdon of Elmira, N.Y. His outstanding books include *Roughing It* (1872), *The Adventures of Tom Sawyer* (1876), *Life on the Mississippi* (1883), *The Adventures of Huckleberry Finn* (1884), *A Connecticut Yankee at King Arthur's Court* (1889), and *The Tragedy of Pudd'nhead Wilson* (1894). See also p. 860. *Mark Twain's Autobiography* was published in 1924.

A growing despair and bitterness toward the end of his life was reflected in *What Is Man?* (1906) and *The Mysterious Stranger* (1916). At his best, Twain raised to the level of universal human appeal the lusty humor of the frontier.

Cleveland, Stephen Grover (b. Caldwell, N.J., 18 Mar. 1837; d. Princeton, N.J., 24 June 1908), 22d and 24th president of the U.S., studied law in Buffalo and was admitted to the New York bar (1859). Assistant district attorney of Erie County (1863), elected Democratic sheriff (1869), mayor of Buffalo (1881–82), and governor of New York (1882–84), he was elected Democratic president of the U.S. (1885–89). He married Frances Folsom (1886) at the White House. His conciliatory attitude toward the South, his vetoes of over two-thirds of bills presented to him (mostly private pension bills), and his tariff reduction proposal (1887) contributed to his defeat by Harrison in 1888. Again elected president (1892), serving 1893–97, he took a "hard money" stand and had Congress repeal the Sherman Silver Purchase Act (1893) following the panic of that year. By sending troops into Illinois to break the Pullman strike and permitting Attorney General Olney to employ a railroad attorney as special counsel to the government (4 July 1894), he alienated labor. Cleveland intervened in the boundary dispute between Great Britain and Venezuela (1895). An anti-imperialist, he withdrew the U.S. treaty of annexation of Hawaii (1893), although he recognized the republic the following year.

Clinton, De Witt (b. Little Britain, Orange Co., N.Y., 2 Mar. 1769; d. Albany, 11 Feb. 1828), statesman, was graduated from Columbia (1786), studied law, was admitted to the New York bar (1788), and became private secretary (1790–95) to his uncle George Clinton, governor of New York. State assemblyman (1797–98) and state senator (1798–1802), he is credited with introducing the "spoils system" when serving on the Council of Appointment. In the legislature he sponsored relief for prisoners for debt, the abolition of slavery, and the promotion of steam navigation. Elected to the U.S. Senate (1802), he resigned to become mayor of New York City (1803–15, except for 1807–08 and 1810–11), in which office his record was outstanding. As chief organizer of the Public School Society (1805) and sponsor of the Lancastrian school system, he laid the foundation of the public school system in New York. Candidate of the New York Republicans (1812) in the presidential race of that year, he was defeated by Madison, 128–89. Appointed (1817) commissioner to examine and survey the route for the Erie Canal, he was chiefly responsible for its successful completion in 1825. Elected governor (1817) and reelected (1820), he retired from office in 1823 when the "Albany Regency" became supreme. Public reaction to his removal from office as canal commissioner (1824) led to his reelection as governor (1825–28).

Clinton, George (b. Little Britain, N.Y., 26 July 1739; d. Washington, D.C., 20 Apr. 1812), statesman, studied law under William Smith in New York City and returned to practice in Ulster Co. In the New York Assembly (1768) and the 2d Continental Congress (1775–76), as brigadier general of militia he unsuccessfully defended Ft. Montgomery against Sir Henry Clinton (1777). Seven-term governor of New York, serving from 1777–95 and from 1801–04, he may be considered the "father" of the state. Leader of the New York Antifederalists, he was outspoken in opposition to the Constitution, unwilling to surrender either his own power or any significant vestige of state sovereignty. As "Cato" his arguments in the N.Y. *Journal* against the Constitution were answered by "Caesar" (allegedly Hamilton) in the *Daily Advertiser*. His plan (1783) for a series of canals connecting the Hudson with Lakes Ontario and Champlain (1783) were later carried out by his nephew De Witt Clinton (*q.v.*). Elected vice-president (1804 and again 1808), he registered his old animosity against Hamilton and his contempt for Madison by casting (1811) the deciding vote against the bill to recharter the Bank of the U.S.

Cohn, Edwin Joseph (b. New York City, 17 Dec. 1892; d. Boston, Mass., 2 Oct. 1953), biochemist, was graduated from the Univ. of Chicago (B.S., 1914; Ph.D., 1917), held a National Research Council fellowship (1919–22) during his studies at the Carlsberg Laboratory in Copenhagen and at Cambridge Univ., and became (1922) assistant professor of physical chemistry at the Harvard Medical School, where he served (1935–49) as professor of biochemistry and head of the department of physical chemistry, and after 1949 as director of the physical chemistry laboratory at Harvard. His most notable researches have been made in the protein fractionization of blood, particularly the isolation of albumin. Serum albumin, as precipitated by Cohn and his associates, is a nontoxic, stable, and compact blood substitute better suited to emergency conditions than stored whole blood or dried plasma and widely used in the U.S. armed services after Pearl Harbor. Gamma globulin contains antibodies which help prevent or treat diseases like measles and jaundice. Other pure plasma proteins isolated by fractionization (such as thrombin and fibrinogen, in combination as a blood-clotting agency) serve a variety of uses in medicine and surgery. He wrote *Proteins, Amino Acids and Peptides* (with J. T. Edsall in 1943).

Compton, Arthur Holly (b. Wooster, Ohio, 10 Sept. 1892; d. Berkeley, Calif., 15 Mar. 1962), physicist and educator, was graduated from the College of Wooster (B.S., 1913) and Princeton (M.A., 1914; Ph.D., 1916); was an instructor in physics (1916–17) at the Univ. of Minnesota; research engineer (1917–19) for the Westinghouse Lamp Co.; research fellow (1919–20) at the Cavendish Laboratory, Cambridge Univ.; professor of physics (1920–23) at Washington Univ., St. Louis, and (1923–45) at the Univ. of Chicago. Chancellor of Washington Univ. (1945–53), he then became distinguished service professor of natural philosophy. His investigations (1923 *et seq.*) of the scattering of X rays by matter led to his discovery of the change of wave length known as the Compton effect. He also discovered the total reflection and (with C. H. Hagenow) polarization of X rays. With C. T. R. Wilson, he was the joint recipient (1927) of the Nobel prize in physics. He also did important work on cosmic rays, in which field he directed a worldwide study (1931–33) and showed the electrical composition of cosmic rays and their variation with altitude and latitude. As wartime director (1942–45) of plutonium research for the U.S. atomic bomb project, he guided the development of the first quantity production of plutonium.

Conant, James Bryant (b. Dorchester, Mass., 26 Mar. 1893; d. Hanover, N.H., 11 Feb. 1978), chemist, diplomat, educator, received his A.B. (1913) and Ph.D. (1916) from Harvard, where he taught chemistry (1916–33), with an interruption during World War I for service as lieutenant, Sanitary Corps, U.S. army, and major in the Chemical Warfare Service. He did notable research in the field of organic chemistry, specifically on the structure of chlorophyll and hemoglobin. President of Harvard (1933–53), he introduced significant reforms as regards admissions and curriculum. Chairman (1941–46) of the National Defense Research Comm., he had a key role in the production of the atomic bomb, was instrumental in the creation of the National Science Foundation (1950), and was a member of the general advisory committee, AEC (1947–52). He was high commissioner to West Germany (1953–55) and U.S. ambassador there (1955–57). He made extensive investigations of U.S. high schools (1957–62) and the education of American teachers (1962–63) under Carnegie grants, publishing several works including *The American High School Today* (1959), *Slums and Suburbs* (1961), *The Education of American Teachers* (1963), *Shaping Educational Policy* (1964), *The Comprehensive High School* (1967). He wrote numerous works in organic chemistry (1928) and *The Chemistry of Organic Compounds* (1933). He authored *My Several Lives* (1970).

Cooke, Jay (b. in present-day Sandusky, Ohio, 10 Aug. 1821; d. Ogontz, Pa., 16 Feb. 1905), banker and financier, was a clerk at St. Louis and at Philadelphia, where he entered (1839) the banking house of E. W. Clark & Co., from which he retired (1857) to participate in the general banking business. In 1861 he formed with his brother-in-law the banking house of Jay Cooke & Co. at Philadelphia, which during the Civil War acted as agent for the U.S. government in floating bond issues for meeting military requirements. In 1865 he was appointed fiscal agent of the Treasury Department. During the course of the war he floated $2,500 million worth of bonds at virtually no profit to himself. His firm

became financial agent for the Northern Pacific R.R. Its connection with that enterprise led to its failure (18 Sept. 1873), precipitating the panic of that year. Compelled to go into bankruptcy, Cooke later repaid his creditors and recouped his fortune.

Cooley, Thomas McIntyre (b. near Attica, N.Y., 6 Jan. 1824; d. Ann Arbor, Mich., 12 Sept. 1898), jurist, was admitted to the Michigan bar (1846) and practiced in Tecumseh and Adrian. He compiled the state statutes (1857), became reporter for the state supreme court (1858), and published his *Digest of Michigan Reports* (1866). Professor of law (1859–84) and of American history (1884–98) at the Univ. of Michigan, he was justice of the state supreme court (1864–85) and chairman of the ICC (1887–91), where he was largely responsible for turning it into a quasi-judicial body and for formulating ruling principles of rate regulation. His most important writings were on constitutional law. *The Constitutional Limitations Which Rest upon the Legislative Power of the States of the American Union* (1868), with its doctrine of implied constitutional limitations upon the state's legislative power, was the basis for widening the scope of the doctrine of judicial review, while his concept of due process provided the courts with authority to curb government intervention in the economic and social sphere. With Story, he ranks as the most influential commentator on the Constitution. Other works include *The Law of Taxation* (1876), *Treatise on the Law of Torts* (1879), and *General Principles of Constitutional Law in the U.S.* (1880).

Coolidge, Calvin (b. Plymouth, Vt., 4 July 1872; d. Northampton, Mass., 5 Jan. 1933), 30th president of the U.S., was graduated from Amherst (1895) and practiced law at Northampton (1897). Member of the Massachusetts General Court (1907–08), mayor of Northampton (1910–11), state senator (1912–15, serving as president of that body, 1914–15), and lieutenant governor (1916–18), he came into national prominence as governor (1919–20) through his suppression of the Boston police strike (1919). Elected Republican vice-president of the U.S., he became president on Harding's death (2 Aug. 1923), and was elected president (1924), serving 1925–29. He twice vetoed the McNary-Haugen Farm Relief Bill, refused to intervene in the general coal strike (1927); and did not "choose" to run for president in 1928. On 4 Dec. 1928 he told Congress: "The country . . . can anticipate the future with optimism." He left office before the 1929 crisis.

Cooper, James Fenimore (b. Burlington, N.J., 15 Sept. 1789; d. Cooperstown, N.Y., 14 Sept. 1851), novelist, historian, and social critic, was expelled from Yale, where he was a member of the class of 1806. He shipped before the mast (1806–07), was commissioned midshipman in the U.S. Navy (1808), and resigned from the service in 1810. From 1811 to 1822 he followed the life of a country squire. His first novel, *Precaution* (1820), was a conventional story with an English background that he wrote for his own satisfaction, but in *The Spy* (1821), where Cooper used a native setting for a theme drawn from the Revolutionary period, he showed signs of his powerful narrative gift. The novel enjoyed an international success. In 1822 Cooper moved to New York to follow a literary career. His most famous work, the Leatherstocking series, includes the following novels: *The Pioneers* (1823), *The Last of the Mohicans*

(1826), *The Prairie* (1827), *The Pathfinder* (1840), and *The Deerslayer* (1841). He also wrote *The Pilot* (1824) and *Lionel Lincoln* (1825) before going to Europe (1826), where he found the themes and settings for the novels *The Bravo* (1831), *The Heidenmauer* (1832), and *The Headsman* (1833). During his European stay he also published novels with an American background, such as *The Red Rover* (1828), *The Wept of Wish-ton-Wish* (1829), and *The Water-Witch* (1831), and gathered the material for the following travel accounts: *Sketches of Switzerland* (1836), *Gleanings in Europe* (1837), *Gleanings in Europe: England* (1837), and *Gleanings in Europe: Italy* (1838). Upon his return to the U.S. in 1833 he published *A Letter to His Countrymen* (1834) and *The American Democrat* (1838), forthright criticisms of the provincialism of his native land that precipitated a quarrel between Cooper and his public that lasted for several years. The same critical viewpoint was incorporated in novels such as *Homeward Bound* (1838) and *Home as Found* (1838), and, to some extent, in *The Monikins* (1835). After 1834, when Cooper lived at Cooperstown, he enjoyed his most productive period, including the writing of a scholarly *History of the Navy of the United States of America* (1839).

Cooper, Peter (b. New York City, 12 Feb. 1791; d. there, 4 Apr. 1883), manufacturer, inventor, and philanthropist. After brief formal schooling, he was apprenticed (1808) to a New York coachmaker, and later manufactured cloth-shearing machines of his own invention, glue, and isinglass. In partnership with 2 others, he established (1828) the Canton Iron Works at Baltimore. In 1830 he designed and constructed for the Baltimore & Ohio R.R. the first steam locomotive (popularly known as "Tom Thumb") built in America. In 1845 he established at Trenton, N.J., a rolling mill where the first structural iron for fireproof buildings was rolled (1854); and in 1856 became the first U.S. iron manufacturer to use the Bessemer converter. Cooper was the chief financial supporter of Cyrus Field's Atlantic cable project and was president of the New York, Newfoundland & London Telegraph Co. He founded (1857–59) Cooper Union, an educational institute at New York City "for the advancement of science and art." He was the presidential candidate (1876) of the Greenback party and outlined his position on currency and other matters in *Political and Financial Ideas of Peter Cooper with an Autobiography* (1877) and *Ideas for a Science of Good Government* (1883).

Copley, John Singleton (b. Boston, Mass., 1738; d. London, 9 Sept. 1815), painter, probably received his early training under his stepfather, the painter and engraver Peter Pelham, and at about the age of 18 became a professional portraitist. In the 1760s and early 1770s he painted many of the prominent personages of New England. In 1766, following the exhibition in London of Copley's *The Boy with the Squirrel,* he was elected a Fellow of the Society of Artists of Great Britain. In 1771–72 he held sittings at New York and in 1774, partly at the urging of Benjamin West, left Boston. He made the Continental tour and settled (1775) in London, where he painted portraits and also historical subjects, notably *The Death of Lord Chatham.* In 1783 he was elected a member of the Royal Academy. Among his many portraits are those of John Adams, Samuel Adams, Mr. and Mrs. Thomas Mifflin, and Mr. and Mrs. Isaac Winslow.

Cotton, John (b. Derby, Derbyshire, England, 4 Dec. 1584; d. Boston, Mass., 23 Dec. 1652), Puritan divine and author. He was graduated from Cambridge (A.B., 1603; A.M., 1606), was ordained deacon and priest (1610), and served as head lecturer and dean of Emmanuel College, Cambridge. In 1613 he received his divinity degree. While serving as vicar of St. Botolph's at Boston, Lincolnshire, he was attracted (c.1615) to Puritan tenets. A friend of John Winthrop, he preached the farewell sermon at Southampton when the *Arbella* departed for America (1630). In 1633 Cotton arrived at Boston aboard the *Griffin* and became teacher of the church at Boston. His change from liberalism to orthodox conformity is evidenced in the Antinomian controversy, during which his initial defense of Anne Hutchinson (*q.v.*) gave way to support of her excommunication and banishment from Massachusetts Bay. A prolific author, he prepared a code of laws for the colony, "Moses his Judicialls" (1636), which was not adopted, and wrote treatises on Congregationalism, such as *The Keyes of the Kingdom of Heaven* (1644), *The Way of the Churches of Christ in New England* (1645), and *The Way of the Congregational Churches Cleared* (1648). He also wrote *Milk for Babes* (1646), a children's catchism which long remained standard in New England. Cotton's controversy with Roger Williams (*q.v.*), which led the latter to write *The Bloudy Tenent of Persecution* (1644), brought in reply Cotton's *The Bloudy Tenent Washed and Made White* (1647).

Crane, Stephen (b. Newark, N.J., 1 Nov. 1871; d. Badenweiler, Germany, 5 June 1900), novelist and short-story writer, worked as a newspaper correspondent in Asbury Park, N.J., and attended Lafayette College and Syracuse Univ. (1890–91). He settled in New York City, where he was a reporter for the *Tribune* and *Herald*, and in 1892 published at his own expense his first novel, *Maggie: A Girl of the Streets*, a study of New York slum life that revealed Crane's strong bent for realism. His Civil War novel, *The Red Badge of Courage* (1895), brought him instant fame. In 1896 his adventures with a filibustering expedition bound for Cuba provided him with the substance of the short story "The Open Boat." As a war correspondent he covered the Spanish-American and Greco-Turkish wars. His last 2 years were spent in England, where he formed friendships with such authors as Joseph Conrad, Henry James, and H. G. Wells. He died of tuberculosis. Among his works are *The Black Riders and Other Lines* (1895, verse), *The Little Regiment and Other Episodes of the Civil War* (1896), *George's Mother* (1896), *The Third Violet* (1897), *Active Service* (1899), *The Monster* (1899), *War Is Kind* (1899, verse), *Wounds in the Rain* (1900), *Whilomville Stories* (1900), *The O'Ruddy* (1903), and *Men, Women, and Boats* (1921).

Croly, Herbert David (b. New York City, 23 Jan. 1869; d. Santa Barbara, Calif., 17 May 1930), editor, reformer, studied intermittently (1893–99) at Harvard with William James, Josiah Royce, and George Santayana, but did not receive his B.A. until 1910. Editor of the *Architectural Record* (1900–06), he gave up the editorship to write *The Promise of American Life* (1909), a Progressive classic. Combining a Hamiltonian belief in strong central government with advocacy of a positive program for social goals, it was a source of T.R.'s New Nationalism and of Wilson's New Freedom. Editor of the *New Republic*, founded 1914, he played a significant role in bringing about U.S. entry into World War I, but broke with Wilson

after publication of the Treaty of Versailles. His opposition to treaty ratification injured the magazine's circulation and influence. Other books include *Progressive Democracy* (1914) and *Marcus Alonzo Hanna, His Life and Work* (1912).

Cushing, Caleb (b. Salisbury, Mass., 17 Jan. 1800; d. Newburyport, Mass., 2 Jan. 1879), political leader and statesman. A prodigy, he was only 13 when he began studies at Harvard, where he graduated a member of Phi Beta Kappa and Latin Salutatorian (1817). After studying law (1817–19), he tutored mathematics and natural philosophy at Harvard (1819–21). He was admitted to the bar (1822) and practiced law, wrote political essays, and served intermittently in the state legislature before being elected to the U.S. House of Representatives (1834). During his 4 terms in the House (1835–43) he joined John Quincy Adams in opposing the "gag rule" which prevented the presentation of antislavery petitions on the floor, loyally supported President Harrison and, after his death, remained a Whig but chose to stand by President Tyler rather than to follow Henry Clay in his opposition program. Appointed by Tyler as minister plenipotentiary to China, Cushing negotiated the Treaty of Wang Hiya (3 July 1844), opening 5 Chinese ports to American merchants and ensuring extraterritorial legal rights for Americans living in China. Though out of office, he continued to be prominent in politics. An expansionist, he favored increased expenditures on defense and the acquisition of Texas, Oregon, and, later, Cuba. He served on the Supreme Judicial Court of Massachusetts (1852–53). He engineered the nomination of Franklin Pierce at the Democratic Convention of 1852 and served as President Pierce's attorney general (1853–57). He led the Democrats who nominated J. C. Breckinridge (1860) but supported Lincoln after secession convinced him that conciliation was impossible. He was a Republican thereafter. He acted as counsel for the U.S. at the arbitration of the Alabama Claims (1871–72) and was minister to Spain (1874–77). He was nominated by President Grant (1874) to be chief justice but his nomination was withdrawn after political opposition.

Cushing, Harvey William (b. Cleveland, Ohio, 8 Apr. 1869; d. New Haven, Conn., 7 Oct. 1939), neurological surgeon, specialist in brain surgery. He was graduated from Yale (A.B., 1891) and Harvard (A.M., M.D., 1895), was a practicing surgeon at Cleveland (1895–1902), and served as associate professor of surgery (1902–12) at Johns Hopkins, spending the years 1901–03 abroad studying under leading Continental surgeons. In 1912 he became professor of surgery at Harvard and surgeon in chief to the Peter Bent Brigham Hospital at Boston, holding these posts until 1932. During World War I he was senior consultant in neurological surgery to the A.E.F. He was Sterling professor of neurosurgery (1933–37) at Yale, where he was director in the history of medicine from 1937 until his death. During his service at the Peter B. Brigham Hospital he evolved a notable school of brain surgery based on experimental research in neurophysiology. He did important work on the operative treatment of facial paralysis, cerebral tumors, nerve block, and the intracranial hemorrhage of newborn babies; invented surgical instruments; pioneered in using the X ray and blood-pressure determination in the U.S.; and made contributions to endocrinology. He wrote the biography, *The Life of Sir William Osler* (2 vols., 1925), which was awarded the Pulitzer prize. Among his medical writings are

The Pituitary Body and Its Disorders (1912), *Tumors of the Nervus Acusticus* (1917), *A Classification of the Glioma Group* (1926), *Intracranial Tumors* (1932), *Pituitary Body and Hypothalamus* (1932), and *Meningomas* (1939).

Cushman, Charlotte Saunders (b. Boston, Mass., 23 July 1816; d. there, 17 Feb. 1876), actress. In 1835 she made her debut as an operatic singer, but while performing at New Orleans in that year abandoned opera for the dramatic stage, appearing as Lady Macbeth. She came to New York (c.1836) and appeared (8 May 1837) for the first time as Meg Merrilies in *Guy Mannering*, one of her best-known roles. She won acclaim as Nancy Sykes in *Oliver Twist* (1837), was stage manager (1842–44) of the Walnut Street Theater at Philadelphia, and made her London debut (14 Feb. 1845) as Bianca in *Fazio*. Emerging in England as a Shakespearean actress of the first rank, she toured the U.S. (1849–52), playing male as well as female roles, and was received as the leading actress of the American stage. She lived in England until 1857, but gave frequent "farewell performances" in the U.S., to which she returned in 1870.

Darrow, Clarence (b. Kinsman, Ohio, 18 Apr. 1857; d. Chicago, 13 Mar. 1938), lawyer and reformer, attended Allegheny College and spent a year at Univ. of Michigan Law School. Admitted to the Ohio bar (1878), he removed to Chicago (1887), where he was junior law partner of John Peter Altgeld (*q.v.*). Supporter of many reform movements and opponent of capital punishment, he won a reputation as a preeminent trial lawyer by his defense of more than 50 persons charged with 1st-degree murder, of whom only one, Robert Prendergast (1894), was lost to the executioner. His defense of Eugene Debs (*q.v.*) in the injunction proceedings and conspiracy charges resulting from the rail strike of 1894 gave him national prominence. He successfully defended Haywood, Moyer, and Pettibone (1907), charged with being accessories to the murder of Gov. Frank Steunenberg of Idaho. Undertaking the defense (1924) of Nathan Leopold and Richard Loeb, tried for the kidnapping and murder of Robert Franks, his introduction of psychiatric evidence and his masterly summation resulted in the prisoners receiving life sentences. In the Scopes evolution trial (1925) he had a celebrated courtroom encounter with William Jennings Bryant (*q.v.*), whom he subjected to a merciless cross-examination. Normally on the side of the underdog, he surprised his admirers by acting as defense counsel in the Massie case (1932), a sensational Honolulu trial for the murder and kidnapping of a Hawaiian, in which he secured for his clients a nominal sentence.

Davis, Jefferson (b. Todd Co., Ky., 3 June 1808; d. New Orleans, La., 6 Dec. 1889), president of the Confederacy, was graduated from West Point (1828) and served in the Black Hawk War (1832). Resigning his commission (1835), he married Zachary Taylor's daughter (who died within 3 months) and became a Mississippi planter (married Varina Howell, 1845). Democratic congressman (1845–46), he resigned to command the Mississippi Rifles in the War with Mexico and was wounded at Buena Vista. U.S. senator (1847–51), he resigned to run for governor (1851), being narrowly defeated by Henry S. Foote. As Pierce's Secretary of War he strengthened the army and coast defenses, directed surveys for the transcontinental Southern route, and urged the president to sign the Kansas-Nebraska Bill (1854). Again senator (1857–61), he resigned 21 Jan. 1861, when Mississippi seceded. On 18 Feb. 1861 he was inaugurated at Montgomery as provisional president of the provisional Confederate government, and was then elected for a 6-year term and inaugurated at Richmond (22 Feb. 1862). His autocratic methods and interference in military affairs aroused hostility among Confederate leaders. When Richmond fell he moved the executive offices to Danville, Va., and thence to Greensboro, N.C. At final cabinet meeting held at Charlotte (24 Apr. 1865), he conceded the end of the Confederacy. He was captured at Irwinville, Ga., and imprisoned at Ft. Monroe (1865–67). In 1866 he was indicted for treason; released on bail the following year, and the trial dropped. After travel abroad he made his home at Beauvoir, Miss., and wrote *Rise and Fall of the Confederate Government* (1881).

Davisson, Clinton Joseph (b. Bloomington, Ill., 22 Oct. 1881; d. Charlottesville, Va., 1 Feb. 1958), physicist, was graduated from the Univ. of Chicago (B.S., 1908) and Princeton (Ph.D., 1911); was an instructor in physics (1911–17) at the Carnegie Institute of Technology, Pittsburgh; and (1917–46) was a member of the research staff of the Bell Telephone laboratories (originally the engineering department of the Western Electric Co.) at New York. Beginning his researches on the electron in 1923, he discovered (1927, with Dr. L. H. Germer) the principle of electron diffraction (the exhibiting by electrons of wavelike as well as corpuscular properties). In 1928 he was awarded the Comstock prize for the "most important research in electricity, magnetism, and radiant energy made in North America" during the preceding 5 years. In 1937 Davisson and Germer discovered that the wave length of electrons depends on their velocity, confirming De Broglie's law (1932). He was awarded the Nobel prize in physics in 1937.

Debs, Eugene Victor (b. Terre Haute, Ind., 5 Nov. 1855; d. Elmhurst, Ill., 20 Oct. 1926), Socialist and labor leader. In 1870 he became a worker in the shops of the Terre Haute & Indianapolis R.R., subsequently becoming a locomotive fireman, and in 1875 took part in the organization of a Terre Haute Lodge of the Brotherhood of Locomotive Firemen, becoming secretary of the lodge. Debs was named (1880) national secretary and treasurer of the Brotherhood and editor of the *Firemen's Magazine*. An advocate of industrial unionism, he participated in the organization (1893) of the American Railway Union, of which he was made president. During the Pullman strike of 1894 he and other union leaders were held in contempt of court and sentenced to 6 months in jail. He emerged from his imprisonment a convert to socialism, and in 1897 founded the Social Democratic party of America, which in 1900 was formally united with a faction of the Socialist Labor party to form the Socialist party of America. He was 5 times a candidate for president on the Socialist ticket (1900, 1904, 1908, 1912, 1920). Sentenced to jail (1918) for 10 years on charge of violating the sedition provisions of the Espionage Act, he received during his confinement in the Atlanta penitentiary more than 900,-000 votes as Socialist candidate for the presidency. Debs was released (1921) by order of President Harding, but his citizenship was not restored. He was an editor of the *Appeal to Reason*, a Socialist weekly, and editor (1925–26) of the *American Appeal*, organ of Socialist and Progressive elements.

Decatur, Stephen (b. Sinepuxent, Md., 5 Jan. 1779; d. near Bladensburg, Md., 22 Mar. 1820), naval officer. During the naval war with France he was commissioned midshipman (30 Apr. 1798) and served in West Indian waters. He won fame during his service under Commo. Edward Preble in the Tripolitan War. On the evening of 16 Feb. 1804 Decatur and a boarding party recaptured the U.S. frigate *Philadelphia,* which had been stranded off Tripoli, and destroyed it, thus denying its use to the enemy. He was commissioned a captain and took part in the bombardments (3, 7 Aug. 1804) and subsequent assaults on Tripoli. He served (1808) as a member of the court-martial that suspended Capt. James Barron following the *Chesapeake-Leopard* encounter. During the War of 1812 he commanded the *United States* and the *President,* taking several valuable prizes, and was wounded in an engagement with the British blockading force off Long Island. In 1815 he commanded the squadron which compelled the Tripolitans to end their exactions of tribute and the other Barbary pirates to make compensation for damages inflicted by them during the War of 1812. Acclaimed as a hero on his return to the U.S., Decatur responded to a toast made at a dinner given in his honor: "Our country! In her intercourse with foreign nations may she always be in the right; but our country, right or wrong." He served (1815–20) on the Board of Navy Commissioners and was killed in a duel with Capt. James Barron.

De Forest, Lee (b. Council Bluffs, Iowa, 26 Aug. 1873; d. Hollywood, Calif., 30 June 1961), radio engineer and inventor, pioneer in the development of wireless communications, received his Ph.B. (1896) and Ph.D. (1899) from Yale, joined the experimental telephone laboratory of the Western Electric Co. at Chicago, and while engaged in working on wireless telegraphy for the Armour Institute of Technology at Chicago

(1900–02) designed the alternating current transmitter. He was the first to use the electrolytic receiver (a type of telephone receiver). He established (1902) the American De Forest (later United) Wireless Telegraph Co. at Jersey City, N.J., which installed at 5 U.S. Navy bases the first high-power naval radio stations. De Forest also developed several types of antennae, including the loop and direction antennae. His invention of the Audion amplifier (1905 et seq.), and in its improved form the 3-electrode vacuum tube, made possible transcontinental telephony after his telephone repeater rights were sold to the American Telephone and Telegraph Co. (1912). His invention of the oscillating Audion, first demonstrated in 1913, paved the way for the developments which earned him the sobriquet, "the father of radio broadcasting." The holder of more than 300 patents, he perfected the phonofilm method of sound recording, the glow-light recording of sound films, contributed to the development of television and high-speed facsimile transmission, and invented radio-therapy and the radio knife.

Dewey, George (b. Montpelier, Vt., 26 Dec. 1837; d. Washington, D.C., 16 Jan. 1917), naval officer, was graduated (1858) from the U.S. Naval Academy and became executive officer of the *Mississippi*, which was part of Farragut's fleet at the Battle of New Orleans (1862). Dewey became (1889) chief of the Bureau of Equipment in the Navy Department, and was appointed (1895) president of the Board of Inspection. He attained the rank of commodore and was ordered (Nov. 1897) to assume command of the Asiatic Squadron, which he led during the Spanish-American War. Learning (26 Apr. 1898) that war had been declared, Dewey led his squadron,

which he had been holding in readiness for such a contingency, from Mirs Bay to Manila, 600 miles away. He entered Manila Bay at dawn on 1 May 1898 and in 7 hours of fighting destroyed 8 Spanish warships, thus eliminating the enemy's naval power in the Far East. The victory assured the U.S. possession of the Philippines and made Dewey a national hero. Congress created for him the rank of admiral of the navy. He served (1900–17) as president of the General Board of the Navy Department.

Dewey, John (b. Burlington, Vt., 20 Oct. 1859; d. New York City, 1 June 1952), philosopher and educator, was graduated from Univ. of Vermont (B.A., 1879) and Johns Hopkins (Ph.D., 1884); taught philosophy at Univ. of Michigan (1884–88, 1890–94) and Univ. of Minnesota (1889); headed the philosophy department at Univ. of Chicago (1894–1904), where he was also director of the school of education (1902–04); and in 1904 joined the faculty of Columbia. As a philosopher, Dewey was the foremost exponent of the pragmatism of William James and evolved a view of environmental and functional reality called "instrumentalism" that has been widely influential in American social thought. In the field of education, he proved a major force in the development of progressive education. Among his many works are *The School and Society* (1899), *The Child and the Curriculum* (1902), *How We Think* (1909), *The Influence of Darwin on Philosophy and Other Essays in Contemporary Thought* (1910), *Essays in Experimental Logic* (1916), *Democracy and Education* (1916), *Human Nature and Conduct* (1922), *Experience and Nature* (1925), *The Quest for Certainty* (1929), *Philosophy and Civilization* (1931), *Art as Experience* (1934), *Ex-*

perience and Education (1938), *Freedom and Culture* (1939), and *Problems of Men* (1946).

Dickinson, Emily Elizabeth (b. Amherst, Mass., 10 Dec. 1830; d. there, 15 May 1886), poet, attended Amherst Academy and Mt. Holyoke Female Seminary (1847–48). Except for a trip to Washington and Philadelphia (1854) and 2 journeys to Boston (1864, 1865), she never left Amherst, where she gradually withdrew from society. She never married. During her lifetime only 2 of her poems were published. Her intense spiritual life was expressed in poetry whose directness of vision and vivid imagery are found in posthumously published works that include *Poems* (1890), *Poems: Second Series* (1891), *Poems: Third Series* (1896), *The Single Hound* (1914), *Further Poems* (1929), and *Unpublished Poems* (1936).

Dickinson, John (b. Talbot Co., Md., 8 Nov. 1732; d. Wilmington, Del., 14 Feb. 1808), statesman, moved with his parents in 1740 to Dover, where he studied privately under a tutor. In 1750 he began the study of law in the office of John Moland of the Philadelphia bar. After 3 years at the Middle Temple in London he returned in 1757 to Philadelphia, where he began to practice law and quickly rose to eminence in his profession. Elected to the Delaware assembly (1760–62) and the Pennsylvania assembly (1762–65 and 1770–76), he opposed Benjamin Franklin and defended the proprietary system. His pamphlet *The Late Regulations Respecting the British Colonies* (1765), showing the economic injury to the British business interests resulting from the Sugar and Stamp Acts, led to his designation by the Pennsylvania legislature as a delegate to the Stamp Act Congress in New York, where

he drafted the resolutions petitioning the king and Parliament for the repeal of the Stamp Act. His pamphlet *Letters from a Farmer in Pennsylvania to the Inhabitants of the British Colonies* (1768), written in opposition to the Townshend Acts, denied the authority of Parliament to tax the colonies in whatever form. It proved enormously influential in shaping colonial opinion. Thereafter he pursued an increasingly conservative course, opposing the use of force by the colonists. In the 1st Continental Congress from Pennsylvania he drew up the Petition to the King and the Address to the People of Canada; in the 2d Continental Congress as a Delaware member (1776, 1777, 1779, 1780), his 2d Petition to the King, or "Olive Branch Petition." Coauthor with Thomas Jefferson of the "Declaration of the Causes of Taking up Arms" (1775), he opposed the Declaration of Independence but stayed away from the final vote. In Congress he headed a committee which drafted (1776) the Articles of Confederation. Subsequently he served (1781) as president of the Delaware Supreme Executive Council and as president of Pennsylvania, 1782–85, and was a delegate and signer from Delaware to the Federal Convention. In the "Fabius" letters he advocated the adoption of the Constitution. His political writings in 2 vols. were published in 1801. He was a founder (1783) of Dickinson College, Carlisle, Pa., which was named for him.

Disney, Walter Elias (b. Chicago, Ill., 5 Dec. 1901; d. Los Angeles, Calif., 15 Dec. 1966), artist, film producer. He studied cartoon drawing at night at the Academy of Fine Arts, Chicago, left high school to drive an ambulance in France during World War I (1918), then worked as a cartoonist in Kansas City (1919–22). He organized his own company to make cartoons of fairy tales (1920) and moved it to Hollywood (1923), where he produced *Alice in Cartoonland* (1923–26) and *Oswald the Rabbit* (1926–28). These were the first motion pictures that combined animation with live action, a technique used successfully again in *Mary Poppins* (1964). The idea to use a rodent as a protagonist came to Disney on a train ride from New York City to Los Angeles (1927). First named Mortimer Mouse, then re-named Mickey, drawn by Ubbe Iwerks, it first appeared in *Plane Crazy* (1928), a filmed cartoon with sound track. In Mickey Mouse, Donald Duck, Pluto, Goofy, and other animated characters, he created the most popular of movie stars and the foundation of an entertainment empire. *Snow White and the Seven Dwarfs* (1937) was his first feature-length animated cartoon. It was followed by *Pinocchio* (1940), *Dumbo* (1941), *Bambi* (1942), *Cinderella* (1950), and *Alice in Wonderland* (1951). In 1943 he produced *Victory Through Air* to illustrate the importance of the airplane in modern warfare. During World War II he also produced a number of films for the government used for training in defense plants and the military. He achieved commercial success with "true-adventure" nature films (*Seal Island,* 1948; *The Living Desert,* 1953) and live-action adventure films (*20,000 Leagues Under the Sea,* 1954; *Swiss Family Robinson,* 1960). He was the first major movie producer to make shows for TV (1954). Disney was the creator of the world-famous amusement park Disneyland (1955) in Anaheim, Calif., termed "the greatest piece of urban design in the U.S. today," and of its successor, Disneyworld, near Orlando, Fla. (opened posthumously, 1 Oct. 1971). The appeal of his work is traceable in part to his evocation of simpler times, his combination of realism and fantasy, and

his ability to recreate "old-fashioned" beauty. During his career he received 29 Oscars, 4 Emmys, and the Presidential Medal of Freedom (1964). His work has captivated a new generation with the re-release of *Fantasia* (first shown, 1940) and a Disney retrospective at Lincoln Center (1973).

Dix, Dorothea Lynde (b. Hampden, Me., 4 Apr. 1802; d. Trenton, N.J., 17 July 1887), humanitarian. She operated the Dix Mansion at Boston (1821–34), a school for girls, went abroad for her health, and upon her return to Boston (1838) devoted herself to the reform of conditions in prisons, houses of correction, almshouses, and insane asylums. Her *Memorial to the Legislature of Massachusetts* (Jan. 1843), an indictment of prevailing conditions and treatment of the insane, was followed by similar investigations and exposés in other states. According to her own estimate, she visited in 3 years (c.1841–44) 18 state penitentiaries, 300 county jails and houses of correction, and more than 500 almshouses and other institutions, in addition to hospitals and houses of refuge. She was directly responsible for the enlargement or founding of state-supported hospitals for the insane in 15 states and in Canada and England. At the outbreak of the Civil War she offered her services to the surgeon general and was appointed (10 June 1861) superintendent of women nurses, in which capacity she was in charge of hospital nursing for the Union forces.

Dole, Sanford Ballard (b. Honolulu, 23 Apr. 1844; d. there, 9 June 1926), statesman, jurist, son of the missionary Daniel Dole, was educated in missionary schools, attended Williams College (1866–67), and studied law. Admitted to the Massachusetts bar, he returned to Hawaii to practice. In the legislature in 1884 and 1886, he supported the monarchy but advocated reforms. He was a leader in the revolution (1887) which ended the Gibson regime and forced King Kalakaua to grant a new constitution. Associate justice of the Hawaii Supreme Court (1887–93), he joined the 2d Hawaiian revolution aimed at overthrow of the monarchy, which failed to support the reforms, and annexation to the U.S. Heading the provisional government (1893), he refused, as minister of foreign affairs, to comply with Cleveland's demand (Dec. 1893) for the restoration of Queen Liliuokalani, denying the president's right to interfere in Hawaii's internal affairs but favoring ultimate union with the U.S. Declared president (1894) of the newly formed republic, he visited Washington (1898) in the interests of the newly negotiated annexation treaty. First governor of the Territory of Hawaii (1901), he resigned to become judge of the U.S. district court for Hawaii (1903–15).

Douglas, Stephen Arnold (b. Brandon, Vt., 23 Apr. 1813; d. Chicago, Ill., 3 June 1861), statesman. He attended the Canandaigua (N.Y.) Academy, and in 1833 set out for the Old Northwest, finally settling in Jacksonville, Ill., where he taught school and read law. Licensed to practice (1834), he became state's attorney (1835), state legislator (1835–37), secretary of state for Illinois (1840), and judge of the state supreme court (1841–43). During his 2 terms in the U.S. House of Representatives (1843–47), he was an expansionist on the Oregon issue, vigorously supported the Mexican War, and was chairman of the Committee on Territories. Elected (1847) to the Senate, where he served until his death, he was made chairman of the Committee on Territories. In the Compromise of 1850, he drafted bills providing territorial governments for Utah and New Mexico which left those governments free to enact laws concerning slavery. Known as the "Little Giant," he led the "Young America" wing of the Democratic party in the early 1850s and zealously championed sectional compromise. His principle of "popular sovereignty," an adaptation of "squatter sovereignty," was incorporated in his Kansas-Nebraska Bill (1854) and precipitated further sectional strife. Douglas was an unsuccessful contender for the Democratic presidential nomination in 1852 and 1856. In 1857–58, during the Senate debate over the Lecompton constitution, his denunciation of that constitution as a violation of the "popular sovereignty" principle led to a break between him and the Buchanan administration and alienated the proslavery wing of the Democratic party. In the Illinois campaign of 1858, he conducted with his opponent, Abraham Lincoln, a series of 7 joint debates commonly known as the Lincoln-Douglas debates, during the course of which he formulated the "Freeport doctrine," further angering Southern Democrats, with whom he finally broke in 1859. In 1860, when Douglas won the Democratic nomination for the presidency, the Southern faction withdrew and chose John C. Breckinridge as their candidate. The rift contributed to the election of Lincoln. In the closing days of the Buchanan administration, Douglas made further attempts at compromise, but upon the outbreak of the Civil War gave his complete support to Lincoln's measures to preserve the Union.

Douglass, Frederick (b. Tuckahoe, near Easton, Md., c.Feb. 1817; d. Washington, D.C., 20 Feb. 1895), Negro abolitionist, writer, and orator. The son of a Negro slave and a white father, he was originally named Frederick Augustus Washington Bailey, taking the name of

Douglass after he escaped to freedom from Baltimore (3 Sept. 1838), where he had learned to read and write while a house servant. Going to New York, and thence to New Bedford, Mass., where he supported himself by working as a common laborer, Douglass in 1841 attended a convention of the Massachusetts Antislavery Society at Nantucket. A speech he delivered there was so moving that he was immediately named as a lecturing agent of the society. Mobbed and assaulted in the performance of his duties, he became the leading figure in the "One Hundred Conventions" of the New England Antislavery Society and published a frank account, *Narrative of the Life of Frederick Douglass* (1845). To avoid possible reenslavement, Douglass stayed in Great Britain and Ireland (1845–47), where he collected enough money to buy his freedom upon returning to the U.S. He edited an abolitionist newspaper, the *North Star* (1847–64), at Rochester, N.Y., was active as a lecturer, and supported industrial education for Negroes and woman suffrage. One of the advisers of John Brown, he fled to Canada and then to the British Isles after Brown was arrested for the raid on Harpers Ferry. During the Civil War he assisted in raising Negro regiments and agitated for Negro suffrage and civil rights. He was secretary of the Santo Domingo Commission (1871), marshal (1877–81) and recorder of deeds (1881–86) of the District of Columbia, and U.S. consul general to Haiti (1889–91).

Dow, Neal (b. Portland, Me., 20 Mar. 1804; d. there, 2 Oct. 1897), temperance reformer, was a son of Quaker parents and reared according to the principles of the Friends, although he was eventually excluded from the Society because of his views on arms. At 24 he made his first temperance speech as a clerk of the Deluge Engine Co., opposing liquor at a company dinner. In 1838 he was instrumental in founding the Maine Temperance Union, committed to total abstinance and prohibitory legislation (1845). The first law (1846) proved inadequate, and Dow, elected mayor of Portland (1851), headed a committee urging more stringent legislation. With the passage of the "Maine Law" (2 June 1851) Dow achieved world renown for temperance reform, speaking on tours, serving (1853) as president of the World's Temperance Convention in New York City. In his 2d term as mayor (1855) the "June riot," led by antiprohibitionists, caused the repeal of the "Maine Law," but it was enacted again in 1857. As opposed to slavery as he was to liquor, Dow became colonel (1861), 13th Reg. of Maine Volunteers, during the Civil War and was commissioned brigadier general (1862). He was twice wounded at Port Hudson and imprisoned for 8 months in Libby Prison and at Mobile. He ran for president (1880) as a Prohibitionist.

Dreiser, Theodore (b. Terre Haute, Ind., 27 Aug. 1871; d. Hollywood, Calif., 28 Dec. 1945), novelist. Born into a poverty-stricken family, he was reared chiefly in Warsaw, Ind., attended Indiana Univ. (1889–90), and was a newspaper reporter (1892–94) in Chicago, St. Louis, and Pittsburgh. In 1894, when he settled in New York, he began a career as a magazine editor and free-lance writer that closed with his post as editor in chief (1907–10) of the Butterick Publications. His novels bear the deep impress of a deterministic philosophy drawn from his reading of Spencer, Huxley, Tyndall, and Haeckel. His view of life as a welter of blind, amoral forces was the underpinning of his first novel, *Sister Carrie* (1900), whose bold social realism (particularly its treatment of sexual mores) brought threats of censorship. The novel was withdrawn by the publisher; its reissuance was a victory for literary realism. Dreiser's naturalism and realism permeated his other novels: *Jennie Gerhardt* (1911); the trilogy based on the career of the traction magnate, Charles T. Yerkes, *The Financier* (1912), *The Titan* (1914), and *The Stoic* (1947); *The Genius* (1915); and the novel which found Dreiser's widest audience, *An American Tragedy* (1925). *The Bulwark* (1946) showed evidences of a return to religious conviction. In the years after World War I, Dreiser embraced socialism, writing *Dreiser Looks at Russia* (1928), *Tragic America* (1932), and *America is Worth Saving* (1941).

Du Bois, William Edward Burghardt (b. Great Barrington, Mass., 23 Feb. 1868; d. Accra, Ghana, 27 Aug. 1963), writer, reformer. Of slave descent, he received his A.B. at Fisk Univ. (1888), then 3 degrees at Harvard (A.B., 1890; A.M., 1891; Ph.D., 1895). Professor of history and economics at Atlanta Univ. (1896–1910), he devoted himself to Negro sociological and historical problems. Taking a militant position on race relations, as opposed to Booker T. Washington (*q.v.*), he helped launch (1905) the Niagara Movement for racial equality and became (1910) director of publicity and research of the NAACP, a post he held for 24 years. He organized the Pan-African Congress (1919) and called the first International Congress of Colored Peoples during the Versailles Peace Conference (1918). Heading the department of sociology at Atlanta Univ. (1933–44), he returned to the NAACP as head of a department of special research (1944–48). Candidate for senator in New York on the American Labor party ticket (1948), he subsequently served as vice-chairman of the Council on African Affairs (1949–54) and was prominent in organizations favoring friendlier postwar

relations with the U.S.S.R. He renounced his American citizenship (1961) and spent his remaining years in Ghana. Du Bois' numerous writings included *The Suppression of the African Slave Trade* (1896), *The Philadelphia Negro* (1899), *The Souls of Black Folk* (1903), *The Negro* (1915), and *Black Reconstruction* (1935). In addition he edited *Encyclopedia of the Negro* (1933–45), *Crisis* magazine (1910–32), and *Encyclopedia Africana* (1961–63).

Duke, James Buchanan (b. near Durham, N.C., 23 Dec. 1856; d. New York City, 10 Oct. 1925), industrialist and philanthropist. Shortly after the Civil War, he and his brother, Benjamin Newton Buchanan (1855–1929), helped their father put up packaged leaf tobacco which they sold on the road in North Carolina. The firm of W. Duke & Sons, of which he became a member in 1884, began in 1881 the manufacturing of cigarettes by hand and shortly thereafter turned them out by machine. In 1884 the Duke firm opened a branch factory at New York City and by adroit price and advertising policies commanded by 1889 half of the total U.S. production of cigarettes. The "tobacco war," a contest among 5 chief cigarette manufacturers, led to the organization (1890) of the American Tobacco Co., which merged the rival concerns. Named president, J. B. Duke was also president of the combination of plug manufacturers known as the Continental Tobacco Co. (formed 1898). In succession, he organized the American Snuff Co. (1900), the American Cigar Co. (1901), the Consolidated Tobacco Co. (1901), and the United Cigar Stores Co. In 1911, by which year Duke's various combinations controlled 150 factories capitalized at $502 million, the U.S. Supreme Court ordered the dissolution of the American Tobacco Co. as a combination in restraint of trade. Duke was also active in forming (1905) and developing the Southern Power Co. In 1924 he created a trust fund for Trinity College, subsequently renamed Duke Univ.

Dulles, John Foster (b. Washington, D.C., 25 Feb. 1888; d. there, 24 May 1959), lawyer, statesman, received his B.A. from Princeton (1908), studied at the Sorbonne (1908–09), and obtained his LL.B. from George Washington Univ. (1911). Beginning in 1911, he spent his entire legal career with Sullivan & Cromwell, which firm he headed from 1927. An outstanding international lawyer, he was chief counsel for U.S. bondholders of Kreuger & Toll, the international match trust. During World War I, in addition to service in the armed forces, he was special agent of the State Department in Central America (1917), assistant to the chairman, War Trade Board (1918), and counsel to the American Peace Commission (1918–19). Delegate to the San Francisco Conference (1945) and to the UN (1946–50), he also served as adviser to the Secretary of State at the Council of Foreign Ministers at London (1945, 1947). Appointed interim U.S. senator from New York (1949), he acted as adviser to the State Department (1950–53) and was the chief architect of the Japanese Peace Treaty (1951). Secretary of State (1953–59) in the Eisenhower administration, he was the major force in U.S. foreign policy in that period, personally engaging in innumerable missions abroad, traveling over 500,000 miles during his term. Holding Truman's policy of "containment" of Communism to be inadequate, he espoused "liberation" of Communist-controlled areas, held firm against Red Chinese threats to seize Quemoy and Matsu, forced Britain and France to abandon the Suez Canal attack (1956),

was responsible for the Eisenhower Doctrine (1957) designed to preserve peace in the Middle East, and committed the U.S. to hold West Berlin, if necessary by force (1958). Resuming his duties after an operation for abdominal cancer (1957), he died of that disease.

Duncan, Isadora (b. San Francisco, 27 May 1878; d. Nice, France, 14 Sept. 1927), dancer, quit school at the age of 10 to devote herself entirely to dancing, and with her sister, Elizabeth, taught a system of movements interpretative of nature, music, and poetry, which had some vogue in her native city. She made her first appearance in New York (1895) in the Augustin Daly company. Disillusioned by the formalism of dance in America, she left with her family for London on a cattle boat. Joining Loie Fuller's company on tour to Germany, she went on alone to Budapest, Munich, Vienna, and Berlin, taking them by storm. Failing in her attempt to build a temple of dance on a hill outside Athens, she opened (1904) a school of the dance on the outskirts of Berlin and returned to the stage, with tours of France, Germany, Russia, and the U.S. (1906–08). Performing barefoot and in flowing costumes, she was a notable interpreter of classical music and popularized the dance as an art in the U.S., awakening an enthusiasm upon which such later figures as Martha Graham (*q.v.*) and Agnes de Mille were able to build a more solid structure. Pagan in her advocacy of free love, she had one child by Edward Gordon Craig and another by "Lohengrin," a wealthy patron. The children were both drowned in an accident. In Moscow, where she established a dance school at the invitation (1921) of the Soviet government, she finally married Sergei Yessenin, later a suicide. A moment after saying, *"Je vais à la gloire,"* she came to a dramatic end when her long scarf caught in the wheel of a moving auto, breaking her neck.

du Pont, Eleuthère Irénée (b. Paris, 24 June 1771; d. Philadelphia, 31 Oct. 1834), manufacturer, son of the economist Pierre Samuel du Pont de Nemours, was given his baptismal name by Minister of Finance Turgot, his godfather. In 1788 Lavoisier, a friend of his father's, took him into the royal powder works at Essonne. He married at 20, fighting 2 duels over his fiancée. In 1797 the du Pont publishing business was suppressed, and the family left for the U.S. Here, Irénée investigated gunpowder manufacture and returned to Paris to procure machinery and designs for its manufacture in the U.S. He set up his works (1801) on the Brandywine River, near Wilmington, Del. In 1804 powder was ready for sale, and military orders, greatly increasing with the War of 1812, established the firm's position as the principal manufacturer of powder for the government. The plant also supplied South American governments. In 1833 he turned down a $24,000 cash order from the South Carolina nullifiers. In spite of opposition from his partner, Peter Bauduy, the company was called E. I. du Pont de Nemours & Co., the name by which it is still known.

Eads, James Buchanan (b. Lawrencebury, Ind., 23 May 1820; d. Nassau, Bahamas, 8 Mar. 1887), engineer and inventor. An autodidact, his formal education ended when he was 13. Using the knowledge of mechanics he gained as a purser on a Mississippi steamboat, he invented a diving bell which could retrieve sunken steamboats and their cargoes and became a partner (1842) in the first ship salvaging business on the Mississippi. He gave up this lucrative venture (1845) to start a glassworks in St. Louis but, soon heavily in debt, he returned to ship salvaging (1848) and within 9 years had acquired a fortune. He studied the geology of rivers and became a recognized authority on the Mississippi River system. At President Lincoln's request he developed (1861) plans for fortifying the Western rivers and was consulted on military operations in the region during the Civil War. At the outbreak of the war he proposed to build a fleet of ironclad, steam-propelled gunboats; the first was delivered within 45 days and the others followed rapidly. After a team of 27 leading engineers had been defeated by the project, Eads designed and constructed (1867–74) a bridge—with a center span of 520 ft. and a 50-ft. clearance—over the Mississippi at St. Louis, the largest bridge of any type built until that time and the first such bridge ever built almost entirely of steel. The bridge was a pioneering effort in the cantilevered method of constructing arches and marked the introduction in the U.S. of pneumatic caisson method of founding piers and abutments. An equally daring and successful feat was undertaken when he proposed (1874) to clear the mouth of the Mississippi. He devised and constructed (1875–79) a system of jetties which forced the river to dredge its own channel by carrying its sediment out into the Gulf of Mexico. His achievement made New Orleans an ocean port.

Eakins, Thomas (b. Philadelphia, 25 July 1844; d. there, 25 June 1916), artist and teacher, attended the Pennsylvania Academy of Fine Arts; was a student (1866–69) at the École des Beaux Arts in Paris, where he worked under Bonnat and Gérôme; in 1869 traveled in Spain, where his study of the realist painters, such as Velásquez and Goya, was influential in forming his style; and in 1870 returned to Philadelphia, where his study of anatomy at the Jefferson Medical College helped to make him a master of the human figure and resulted in two of his best compositions, *The Gross Clinic* and *The Agnew Clinic*. In 1873 he became a teacher (and subsequently dean) at the Pennsylvania Academy of Fine Arts, and also taught at the Art Students League. Among his paintings, both portrait and figure, are *The Writing Master, The Thinker, The Chess Players, Max Schmitt in a Single Scull, Whistling for Plover, Salutat, Between Rounds, The Concert Singer, The Swimming Hole,* and *Edith Mahon*. He also modeled sculpture, including 2 reliefs on the battle monument at Trenton, N.J.

Eastman, George (b. Waterville, N.Y., 12 July 1854; d. Rochester, N.Y., 14 Mar. 1932), inventor, manufacturer, philanthropist, became interested in photography at an early age. Patenting his invention of a dry-plate process in 1880, he began manufacturing dry plates in Rochester. Forming a partnership with Henry A. Strong, he invented a paper-backed flexible film (1884), soon put into production as roll film, and then a small box camera, the Kodak. Developing motion-picture film on the basis of patents he held jointly with Henry M. Reichenbach, the inventor, he formed the Eastman Kodak Co. (1892), recapitalizing and expanding its operations until by 1901 it was the world's largest industrial plant devoted to the manufacture of photographic supplies. Stressing research, Eastman's technicians constantly improved the firm's products and his welfare and profit-sharing programs built up a loyal labor force. His philanthropies by grant and bequest exceeded $100 million and included such institutions as the Univ. of Rochester, MIT, Tuskegee, and Hampton institutes, the establishment of a chair of American studies at Balliol

College, Oxford, and founding the Eastman School of Music in Rochester. Ironically, he preferred anonymity and was rarely photographed. He had no family, and leaving a note, "My work is done, why wait?" he took his own life.

Eddy, Mary Baker (b. Bow, N.H., 16 July 1821; d. Chestnut Hill, Newton, Mass., 3 Dec. 1910), founder of the Practice of Christian Science and of the Church of Christ, Scientist. She married (1843) George Washington Glover, by whom, a few months after his death, she had a son, George (born in Sept. 1844). In 1853 she married Dr. Daniel Patterson, a N.H. dentist and homeopathist, from whom she was separated in 1866 and divorced in 1873. She practiced intermittently (1866–70) a system of mental healing after undergoing treatment from Dr. Phineas P. Quimby (1802–66) of Portland, Me., in 1862. The principles later associated with Christian Science were formulated by her (c.1866), supposedly after making through "divine revelation, reason and demonstration" a remarkable recovery from a serious injury. Setting up a spiritual-healing practice at Lynn, Mass. (1870), she published *Science and Health with Key to the Scriptures* (1875, and numerous revised editions), in which she set forth the basic doctrines of Christian Science. She married (1877) Asa Gilbert Eddy, one of her disciples; he died in 1882. The Christian Scientists' Association, established in 1876, was chartered (1879) as The Church of Christ, Scientist. In 1881 Mrs. Eddy obtained a charter for the Massachusetts Medical College, a training institution for Christian Science practitioners. In 1883 she began publishing the *Journal of Christian Science*. She and 12 followers established at Boston (1892) The First Church of Christ, Scientist, the mother church of the national religious organization. In her last years she founded *The Christian Science Monitor*.

Edison, Thomas Alva (b. Milan, Ohio, 11 Feb. 1847; d. West Orange, N.J., 18 Oct. 1931), inventor. Taken out of school after a few months because he was a slow learner, he received his education at home from his mother. As a boy, he sold newspapers, candy, and other articles on trains; becoming acquainted with telegraph operators during his trips, he became one himself (1863), continuing in the meantime his keen interest in chemistry. In 1868, he joined the Western Union Telegraph Co. at Boston, patenting (1869) his first invention, an electrographic vote recorder. Moving to New York that year, he entered into partnership in the electrical engineering firm of Pope, Edison & Co. When the firm was bought out in 1870, Edison received $40,000 as his share, and with this money established his own business, early initiating his policy of hiring assistants capable of collaborating on inventions under his guidance. During the period 1870–75 he was active in the improvement of the telegraph. In 1876 he built an establishment at Menlo Park, N.J., and in 1887 transferred the Edison research laboratories to larger quarters at Orange, N.J. His ventures were ultimately combined into the Edison General Electric Co., later absorbed by the General Electric Co. In 1877 he produced one of his most important inventions, the phonograph. Beginning in 1879 he introduced improvements that made possible the commercial production of the incandescent electric lamp. During his work on this device he made his first and only significant discovery in pure science when he observed the "Edison effect," demonstrating that the incandescent lamp could be utilized as a valve admitting negative but not positive electricity. (In 1904 the principle of the "Edison effect" was employed by J. Ambrose Fleming, inventor of the electron tube.) In the field of motion pictures, Edison acquired and improved the projector invented by Thomas Armat (1895) and placed it on the market as the Edison Vitascope. Although Edison was granted a total of more than 1,000 patents, most of them were the fruit of collective effort in his research laboratories. Among the inventions or improvements produced at the Edison laboratories were the storage battery, dictaphone, mimeograph, district telegraph signal box, Sprague motor, ore separator, composition brick, compressing dies, electric safety lantern, electric dynamo, and electric locomotive.

Edwards, Jonathan (b. East Windsor, Conn., 5 Oct. 1703; d. Princeton, N.J., 22 Mar. 1758), Congregational theologian and philosopher. After his graduation from Yale (1720), he studied theology there, and in 1722 became minister of a Presbyterian church in New York, where he remained until 1723. He was a tutor at Yale (1725–26), and in 1727 became assistant pastor to his grandfather, Solomon Stoddard, in the church at Northampton, Mass. Edwards became its sole pastor in 1729. His preaching initiated the New England phase of the religious revival known as the "Great Awakening" (c.1730–50). At Northampton, Edwards expounded doctrines fusing rationalism and mysticism and aimed at stemming the rising tide of liberal thought. He stressed the rationality of Scriptural knowledge, the intuitive apprehension of spiritual experience, and the metaphysical concepts of understanding and will as moral agencies under the supreme and arbitrary power of God. In 1750, following a controversy over church doctrine and practices, he was dismissed from the Northampton pastorate. Edwards settled at Stockbridge, Mass., as pastor of the church and missionary to the Indians, and there wrote his most important treatises. In 1757 he was chosen as president of the College of New Jersey at Princeton, but died a few months after taking the post. For his principal works, see p. 847.

Einstein, Albert (b. Ulm Donnau, Germany, 14 Mar. 1879; d. Princeton, N.J., 18 Apr. 1955), physicist, was graduated (1900) from the Federal Institute of Technology at Zurich and received his doctorate (1905) at the Univ. of Zurich. His special theory of relativity (1905), his equation $E = mc^2$ (1905, keystone in the modern concept of the atom), and his contributions to quantum theory (1905) were followed by his general theory of relativity (1915) and work on the photoelectric effect of light, for which he received the Nobel prize (1921). He taught at the Federal Institute of Technology at Zurich (1912–14) and in 1914 assumed the post of director of the Kaiser Wilhelm Institute in Berlin. With the advent of Hitler he came to the U.S. (1932), accepted a post at the Institute for Advanced Study at Princeton (1933–45), and on 2 Aug. 1939 sent a historic letter to President Roosevelt stressing the urgency of research on the atomic bomb. His major work in the U.S. was his formulation (30 Mar. 1953) of a unified field theory, the mathematical expression of which appeared in 1950 as an appendix to *The Meaning of Relativity* (1922; Eng. tr., 4th ed., 1950). He also wrote *Relativity: the Special and the General Theory* (1918), and was active in the peace movement and in Zionism.

Eisenhower, Dwight David (b. Denison, Tex., 14 Oct. 1890; d. Washington, D.C., 28 Mar. 1969), 34th president of the U.S., soldier, spent his boyhood in Abilene, Kan.; was graduated (1915) from the U.S. Military Academy; served (1915–17) with the 19th Infantry at Ft. Sam Houston, Tex.; and during World War I, when he organized Camp Colt for the training of tank troops, attained the rank of captain. He was graduated (1926) from the Command and General Staff School at Ft. Leavenworth, Kan.; (1929) from the Army War College, Washington, D.C.; and (1932) from the Army Industrial College. He was named (1933) special assistant to Gen. Douglas Mac-Arthur (*q.v.*), then chief of staff, under whom he served (1935–39) as assistant military adviser to the Philippine Commonwealth. Promoted to lieutenant colonel in 1936, he returned to the U.S. in 1939 and was named (Feb. 1942) chief of the War Plans Division in the Office of Chief of Staff, subsequently became chief of the Operations Division, and in June 1942, was appointed commander of U.S. forces in the European Theater. He commanded the Allied invasion of North Africa that began on 8 Nov. 1942; was named (Jan. 1944) Supreme Commander of the Allied Expeditionary Force in Western Europe and set up his headquarters (SHAEF) near London. After the invasion of Europe (6 June 1944 *et seq.*) and the surrender of Germany (7 May 1945) he served as commander of the U.S. occupation zone of Germany. General of the army (Dec. 1944), he succeeded (Nov. 1945) Gen. George C. Marshall as chief of staff, became (7 June 1948) president of Columbia Univ., and took a leave of absence from Columbia to become (1951) Supreme Commander of the Allied Powers in Europe (SHAPE). He resigned that command in 1952 to campaign for the presidency, was the Republican nominee that year, and was elected with the largest popular vote to that time. Reelected (1956), he advocated personal top-level diplomacy, sought to contain Soviet expansion in the

Middle East, and to achieve a balanced budget. He was author of *Crusade in Europe* (1948), *Mandate for Change* (1961), *Waging Peace: The White House Years* (1965).

Eliot, Charles William (b. Boston, Mass., 20 Mar. 1834; d. Northeast Harbor, Me., 22 Aug. 1926), educator, was graduated from Harvard (1853), where he taught mathematics and chemistry (1854–63). After 2 years of study on the Continent, he was appointed (1865) professor of chemistry at Massachusets Institute of Technology. Early in 1869 he published in the *Atlantic Monthly* 2 articles on "The New Education: Its Organization," which drew wide notice, and in the same year was appointed and inaugurated president of Harvard, a post he held until his retirement in 1909. During his administration the elective system and sabbatical year were introduced at Harvard College; Harvard Univ. was expanded in enrollment and size to include units such as the graduate school of arts and sciences, applied science, and business administration; and the standards of the professional schools were raised. In 1892, as chairman of the National Education Association's Committee on Secondary School Studies, he prepared a report on the functions and curricula of public schools which led to the organization (1901) of the Board of College Entrance Examinations. He edited the *Harvard Classics* (popularly called the "five-foot shelf").

Ellington, Edward Kennedy (Duke) (b. Washington, D.C., 29 Apr. 1899; d. New York City, 24 May 1974), composer. His only formal musical education was a few piano lessons as a child and a few private music lessons as a teenager. His first composition, "Soda Fountain Rag," was written while working after school as a soda jerk. He formed his first band, The Duke's Serenaders, in 1917. A visit to New York (1922) gave Ellington the opportunity to hear the Harlem pianists Willie (The Lion) Smith, James P. Johnson, and Fats Waller, who influenced his own playing. Ellington brought his band, The Washingtonians, to New York (1923) and performed for over 4 years at the Kentucky Club and at the Cotton Club (1927–32), cutting 160 records between 1928–31 and making his first radio broadcast, introducing a signature theme, "East St. Louis Toodle Oo." During the 1930s he was associated with a large orchestra with fine sidemen, appearing in several films including *Check and Double Check* (1930). His band hit one of its peaks (1941–42) but by 1943 he was turning to extended compositions and concert presentations. *Black, Brown, and Beige,* a 50-minute work, received its first performance at Carnegie Hall (1953). The popularity of his band waned during the late 40s and early 50s when "bop" emerged and the big bands were no longer the leaders in the field. His triumph at the Newport Jazz Festival (1956) established his international reputation. For 15 years he performed throughout the world under State Department auspices. In 1965, he presented a concert of sacred music in Grace Cathedral, San Francisco, and gave sacred concerts of his compositions at the Cathedral of St. John the Divine, New York City (1968) and Westminster Abbey (1973). A prolific composer of thousands of pieces, Ellington's famous songs include "Solitude," "Sophisticated Lady," "I Got It Bad," "I Let a Song Go Out of My Heart." Short instrumental pieces include "Creole Love Call" and "Mood Indigo." As composer and arranger, his style was built upon the sounds of the instrumentalists in his band, among them Johnny Hodges, alto sax, Sam Nanton, trombone, and Bubber Miley, Cootie Williams, and Ray Nance, trumpets. His extended compositions include *Night Creatures* (1955), *Sweet Thursday* (1960), *My People* (1963). Among his film scores is *Assault on a Queen.* He also authored the theatrical score *Beggar's Holiday* (lyrics by John La Touche, 1947) and the ballet *The River* (1970).

Ellison, Ralph Waldo (b. Oklahoma City, Okla., 1 Mar. 1914–), author. While attending Tuskegee Institute (1933–36), where he studied musical composition, he visited New York and studied sculpture briefly, meeting Richard Wright, who inspired him to write. Ellison joined the New York City Writers' Program and began to contribute short stories, articles, and book reviews to a variety of publications and was a member of the editorial board of *The American Scholar. Invisible Man* (1953) has been described as a black American variation upon Dostoevski's *Notes from the Underground.* The theme of racial identity is prominent in this work which has been praised for its technical sophistication. The book won the 1953 National Book Award and was named the "most distinguished single work" published in the past 20 years by a *Book Week* poll (1965). *Shadow and Act,* a spirited, intellectual autobiography, was published in 1964. Ellison has been a lecturer on Black American culture and creative writing at Columbia, Princeton, Chicago, and Bennington, and Albert Schweitzer Professor in Humanities at New York Univ. (1970–79).

Ellsworth, Oliver (b. Windsor, Conn., 29 Apr. 1745; d. there, 26 Nov. 1807), jurist and statesman, attended Yale for 2 years; then the College of New Jersey, where he acquired an M.A. in 1766. Admitted to the Connecticut bar (1771), he soon gained prominence, serving as state's attorney for Hartford Co. (1777–85). Member of the Connecticut General Assembly and delegate to the Continental Congress (1777–83), he served on the latter's committee on appeals from state admiralty courts and the committee dealing with army supplies. Ellsworth was a member of the Governor's Council (1780–84), a position he left to serve first on the state's newly created Supreme Court of Errors (1784) and then on its Superior Court (1784–89). Influential at the Constitutional Convention, he helped shape the Connecticut Compromise and proposed the name "the government of the United States." His *Letters to a Landholder* urged ratification by Connecticut. As senator from Connecticut (1789–96), he was a major force in the early Congresses, drafting the Judiciary Act of 1789, reporting out the proposed first 12 amendments, helping to organize the census and the army, and proposing an economic boycott of Rhode Island, which induced that state to make its belated entry into the Union. A strong Federalist, he supported Hamilton's fiscal program. Appointed chief justice of the U.S. (1796), he served for 3 years, leaving no significant imprint. He retired for reasons of ill health (1800). With William R. Davie and William Vans Murray he served as envoy to France (1799–1800), negotiating the Convention of 1800 which helped to avert war.

Emerson, Ralph Waldo (b. Boston, Mass., 25 May 1803; d. Concord, Mass., 27 Apr. 1882), philosopher, poet, essayist, and lecturer, was graduated from Harvard (1821), where he was class poet, taught school at Boston and at Roxbury, Mass., and for a brief period in 1825 attended the Harvard Divinity School. Admitted (1826) as a candidate for the Unitarian ministry, he resigned his pastorate at the Second Church of Boston (1829–31) when he decided that he could not conform in the administration of the Lord's Supper. He made a tour of

England and the Continent (1832–33), meeting Coleridge, Wordsworth, and Carlyle, through whom he became acquainted with the doctrines of German idealism which, together with infusions from neo-Platonism and the sacred books of the East, influenced the molding of Transcendentalist thought. After his return to Boston, he resumed preaching, but gradually abandoned it for the lyceum and lecture platform. Settling at Concord in 1835, he formed friendships with Thoreau, Bronson Alcott, Margaret Fuller, and Nathaniel Hawthorne. His first publication, *Nature* (1836), was a fundamental exposition of Transcendentalism, a philosophical and literary reaction against Unitarian intellectualism. His address "The American Scholar," delivered as the Phi Beta Kappa oration at Harvard (1837), called for an indigenous national culture and defined the functions of the intellectual in the light of Transcendentalism. His "Divinity School Address," also delivered at Harvard (1838), indicted orthodox Christianity and brought attacks on Emerson from the ministery. With Margaret Fuller and other Transcendentalists, he edited *The Dial* (1840–44). The quarter century after 1840 constituted the period of his greatest activity as a lecturer in the North and the West. He published the *Essays* (1st series, 1841; 2nd series, 1844), which established his reputation in the U.S. and Europe; *Poems* (1847), including "May-Day," "Threnody," and "Concord Hymn"; *Addresses and Lectures* (1849); *Representative Men* (1850); and *English Traits* (1856). Active in the antislavery movement, he wrote *The Conduct of Life* (1860) and *Society and Solitude* (1870), gave a course of lectures at Harvard that was published as *Natural History of Intellect* (1893), and published *Letters and Social Aims* (1876). The *Journals* (10 vols., 1909–14) were edited by his son, Edward Waldo Emerson; the *Letters* (6 vols., 1939), by Ralph L. Rusk.

Enders, John Franklin (b. West Hartford, Conn., 10 Feb. 1897–   ), bacteriologist, received his B.A. (1920) from Yale and his M.A. (1922) and Ph.D. (1930) from Harvard, where he taught in the department of bacteriology and immunology (1929–   ), and served as chief of the research division of infectious diseases (1947–72), and chief of the Virus Research Unit (1972–   ), Children's Hospital, Harvard Medical School. Civilian consultant to the Secretary of War on epidemic diseases (1942–46), and member of the Commission on Viral Infections, Armed Forces Epidemiological Bd. (1945–49); he received the Nobel prize in medicine and physiology (1954) for culturing poliomyelitis virus in living tissue, laying the foundation for the production of the antipolio, measles, and mumps vaccine. He edited *Journal of Immunology* (1942–58).

Ericsson, John (b. Langbanshyttan, Sweden, 31 July 1803; d. New York City, 8 Mar. 1889), inventor and engineer, grew up in the midst of mining works, and at 11 designed and constructed a miniature sawmill. Adm. Count Platen, celebrated engineer, recognizing his ability, appointed him a cadet in the mechanical engineer corps. At 17 he enlisted in the Swedish army, where he was detailed to do topographical surveying. In London for 12 years, beginning in 1826, he made various marine inventions, and developed the screw propeller, which revolutionized navigation. Coming to New York in 1839, he furnished (1840) designs for the screw warship *Princeton* (which suffered an explosion on trials in 1844), the first ship to have its propelling machinery under water and out of firing range. In 1861 he designed and built for the Union the ironclad *Monitor* with a circular armored revolving turret. Following the victory of the *Monitor* over the *Merrimac* at Hampton Roads, Va. (9 Mar. 1862), he was kept busy designing and building other ironclads. He also made notable contributions to the improvement of the steam engine. After his death Ericsson's body was carried back to Sweden with great ceremony, appropriately in a new steel naval vessel.

Evarts, William Maxwell (b. Boston, Mass., 6 Feb. 1818; d. New York City, 28 Feb. 1901), lawyer and statesman, was graduated from Yale (1837), studied at Harvard Law School, and was admitted to the New York bar (1841). An assistant U.S. attorney for the Southern District of New York, 1849–53, and unsuccessful candidate for the U.S. Senate (1860), he argued in behalf of New York state the Lemmon slave case in dispute with Virginia (1860) and represented the federal government before the Supreme Court during the Civil War in asserting the right to treat captured vessels as maritime prizes. Among the preeminent leaders of the bar, he was President Johnson's chief defense counsel in the impeachment trial before the Senate (1868), winning an acquittal, and from 15 July until the close of Johnson's administration was U.S. attorney general. He was U.S. counsel in the Geneva Arbitration (1871–72) over the *Alabama* claims, chief counsel for Hayes in the presidential election dispute of 1876, and senior counsel for defendant in *Tilton* v. *Henry Ward Beecher* (1874–75). As Hayes' Secretary of State (1877–81) he asserted the "paramount interest" of the U.S. in an isthmian canal (1880). He was U.S. senator from New York (1885–91).

Farragut, David Glasgow (b. Campbell's Station, near Knoxville, Tenn., 5 July 1801; d. Portsmouth, N.H., 14 Aug. 1870), naval officer. Adopted (c.1808) by Cmdr. David Porter of the New Orleans naval station, he was appointed (1810) midshipman, and during the War of 1812 served aboard the frigate *Essex* in the Pacific. He saw duty in the Mediterranean (1815–20), and during the middle 1850s established the navy yard at Mare Island. Farragut was appointed (9 Jan. 1862) commander of the West Gulf Blockading Squadron with orders to open the Mississippi River and to attack and invest New Orleans. Departing from Hampton Roads aboard his flagship, the steam sloop *Hartford,* Farragut, with 17 ships and a mortar flotilla at his disposal, opened the Battle of New Orleans on 18 Apr. 1862. At his orders the Union warships ran by the Confederate defenses before they were reduced, destroying most of the Confederate fleet and thus hastening the fall of New Orleans (28 Apr.). In recognition of his achievement, Farragut was commissioned a rear admiral (30 July 1862), becoming the first to hold that grade. His victory (5 Aug. 1864) in the Battle of Mobile Bay, when to the warning of "Torpedoes ahead!" he replied, "Damn the torpedoes!" brought him the commission of vice-admiral (23 Dec. 1864), an office created for him, as was the commission of admiral (26 July 1866). He led the European Squadron on a goodwill tour (1867–68) of Continental ports.

Faulkner, William (b. New Albany, Miss., 25 Sept. 1897; d. Oxford, Miss., 6 July 1962), novelist and short-story writer, served as a pilot with the Canadian Royal Air Force in 1918 and attended the Univ. of Mississippi from 1919 to 1921. Most of his novels and stories comprise a saga of the Compson, Sartoris, Snopes, McCaslin, and other families living in imaginary Yoknapatawpha County, with its county seat of Jefferson, in northern Mississippi, a powerful narrative of decay and corruption portraying Southern life from early frontier days to the coming of modern industrialism. His works include *Soldier's Pay* (1926), *Mosquitoes* (1927), *Sartoris* (1929), *The Sound and the Fury* (1929), *As I Lay Dying* (1930), *Sanctuary* (1931), *These Thirteen* (1931), *Light in August* (1932), *Doctor Martino, and Other Stories* (1934), *Pylon* (1935), *Absalom, Absalom!* (1936), *The Unvanquished* (1938), *The Wild Palms* (1939), *The Hamlet* (1940), *Go Down, Moses, and Other Stories* (1942), *Intruder in the Dust* (1948), *Knight's Gambit* (1949), *Collected Stories* (1950), *Requiem for a Nun* (1951), *A Fable* (1954)—Pulitzer prize (1955), *The Reivers* (1962). In 1950 he was awarded the Nobel prize in literature.

Fermi, Enrico (b. Rome, Italy, 29 Sept. 1901; d. Chicago, 28 Nov. 1954), physicist, was graduated from the Univ. of Pisa (1922), taught physics at Florence (1924) and Rome (1926–38) before coming to the U.S. (1939). His early experiments in artificial radioactivity, using slow neutrons, led directly to the discovery of uranium fission and brought him the Nobel prize in physics (1938). In the U.S. he set the first atomic furnace into successful operation (2 Dec. 1942). The U.S. atomic bomb project was not only materially aided by his research abroad, but it benefited from his active participation in the project at Los Alamos. Professor of physics at Columbia (1939–45) and thereafter at Chicago, his numerous contributions to the new physics include his postulating the existence of an atomic particle (neutrino), his discovery of element 93 (neptunium), and his formulation of the theory of beta-ray emission in radiocativity. For work on the A-bomb he received the first Special Award

($25,000) of the AEC (1954). He wrote *Thermodynamics* (1937), *Elementary Particles* (1951).

Field, Cyrus West (b. Stockbridge, Mass., 30 Nov. 1819; d. New York City, 12 July 1892), financier, promoter of the first transatlantic cable, brother of David Dudley and Stephen Johnson Field. At the age of 15 he settled in New York City, where he became an errand boy in A. T. Stewart's dry-goods store. In 1837 he went to Lee, Mass., where he was assistant to his brother Matthew, a paper manufacturer, and about 2 years later organized his own paper mill at Westfield, Mass. Soon afterward he became a junior partner in the wholesale-paper-dealing firm of E. Root & Co. at New York. When this establishment failed (1841), he founded Cyrus W. Field & Co., and within 10 years paid all his debts and retired with a fortune of $250,000. His interest in the project of a transatlantic cable from Newfoundland was aroused when he met (1854) Frederick N. Gisborne, a Canadian engineer. Field vigorously promoted the idea and won the support of a group of New Yorkers who subscribed $1,500,000 for the project. After surmounting many disheartening technical and financial obstacles, the company completed the laying of the telegraph cable joining Valentia, Ireland, and Trinity Bay, Newfoundland (5 Aug. 1858). On 16 Aug. 1858 Queen Victoria sent over the line a message to President Buchanan. Soon thereafter, the cable stopped working. Field suffered heavy financial loss, but continued to press for support of the project. After the Civil War he secured the *Great Eastern,* at that time the largest steamboat afloat, and with it relaid an improved cable. Subsequent investments in railroad and elevated railway stocks cost him his fortune.

Field, David Dudley (b. Haddam, Conn.,
13 Feb. 1805; d. New York City, 13 Apr.
1894), lawyer and jurist, was graduated
from Williams College (1825), admitted
to the New York bar (1828), and practiced in New York City. A Democrat, he
opposed the extension of slavery and supported Frémont (1856) and Lincoln
(1860), returning to the Democratic
party in 1876, with 3 months service in
Congress. Although notable as a lawyer
(counsel for Milligan in *Ex parte Milligan*, 1867; for McCardle in a case involving the constitutionality of the
Reconstruction Act of 1867; for Jay
Gould and James Fiske in the Erie R.R.
litigation, 1869; chief counsel for "Boss"
Tweed, 1873–78; and counsel for Tilden
before the Electoral Commission, 1876),
his major contribution was as a law reformer and codifier. Appointed (1847)
to a commission for codification of New
York State laws and to another for reform
of procedure, he drafted a code of civil
procedure which was enacted by the legislature (1848). Codes based on his reforms were soon passed in many states,
notably in the West, and ultimately influenced English judicial reforms. Chairman of a new commission (1857) to
prepare penal and civil codes, a task
completed by 1865, his proposals were
opposed by James C. Carter (1827–
1905) and only the penal code became
law (1881). His *Draft Outline of an International Code* (2 vols., 1872) gained
recognition by the courts of many nations. He was a founder and first president of the Association for Reform and
Codification of the Law of Nations (now
International Law Association).

Field, Marshall (b. near Conway, Mass.,
18 Aug. 1835; d. New York City, 16
Jan. 1906), merchant and philanthropist.
His formal schooling ended when, at the
age of 17, he became a clerk in a dry-
goods store at Pittsfield, Mass. Moving

to Chicago in 1856, he became a clerk
and traveling salesman in the wholesale
dry-goods establishment of Cooley, Wadsworth & Co., of which he became general
manager (1861) and a partner (1862).
In 1865 the store became known as Field,
Palmer & Leiter, and in 1881 became
Marshall Field & Co., with Field as major
proprietor. He eventually bought out the
other interests in the concern. Field made
several pioneering innovations in retail
merchandising: the making of wholesale
purchases of goods in anticipation of consumer demand in order to improve his
position on the open market, the segregation of wholesale and retail departments in his store, the operation of
buying agencies throughout the world,
the purchase of the entire output of manufacturing plants, and the establishment
of his own factories as sources of supply.
Among his philanthropies were the founding of the Chicago Manual Training
School, the donation of the site of the
Univ. of Chicago, and the Columbian
Museum at the Chicago World's Fair
of 1893, a structure that was later converted, through a provision in his will,
into the Field Museum of Natural History.

Field, Stephen Johnson (b. Haddam,
Conn., 4 Nov. 1816; d. Washington,
D.C., Apr. 1899), jurist, was graduated
from Williams College (1837), admitted
to the New York bar (1841), and practiced in New York City with his brother,
David Dudley. He went to California
(1849) and was elected to the state legislature (1850), serving on the judicial
committee which reorganized the judicial
code of California along lines laid down
by his brother, and securing passage of
basic mining laws. Judge of the state
supreme court (1857–59) and chief justice (1859–63), he was appointed by
Lincoln associate justice of the U.S. Supreme Court (1863–97), serving 34

years and 7 months, the 2d longest term of any member of that bench. His most notable opinions were dissents, acting as a curb upon the centralizing tendencies of the majority. His dissents in the *Slaughterhouse Cases* (1873) and *Munn v. Ill.* (1876) forecast later recognized constitutional principles. He upheld Congress' paramount power over interstate commerce, even denying to the states the right to prohibit imports or exports of articles not recognized by them as legitimate subjects of commerce. With the majority in *Pollock* v. *Farmers' Loan* (1894), he opposed the income tax as an "assault upon capital." As presiding judge in his home circuit he courageously defied local sentiment on the Chinese question (*Chinese Immigration Case; Queue Case*).

Fillmore, Millard (b. Locke, N.Y., 7 Jan. 1800; d. Buffalo, 8 Mar. 1874), 13th president of the U.S., read law, was admitted to the bar (1823), practiced in East Aurora until 1830, and then moved to Buffalo. As a protégé of Thurlow Weed he was sent to the state assembly (1829–31) on the Anti-Masonic ticket. Congressman (1833–35 and 1837–43), he joined the Whig party (1834) and became its leader in the House. As chairman of the Ways and Means Committee he drafted the tariff bill of 1842. Defeated as Whig nominee for governor of New York (1844), he was elected vice-president of the U.S. (1848), having been nominated on the ticket with Zachary Taylor to placate the Clay wing of the Whig party. On Taylor's death he succeeded to the presidency (9 July 1850–4 Mar. 1853), signed the Clay Compromise of 1850, and sought to enforce the Fugitive Slave Act at the cost of much popularity in the North. He approved the Perry Treaty opening relations with Japan. Denied renomination in 1852, he was the nominee of the

American (Know-Nothing) party for the presidency in 1856, running a poor third.

Fish, Hamilton (b. New York City, 3 Aug. 1808; d. there, 6 Sept. 1893), statesman. Graduated from Columbia (1827), he was admitted to the New York bar (1830), and in 1842 was elected to Congress on the Whig ticket, serving 1 term. He was lieutenant governor (1847–48) and governor (1849–50) of New York, and served (1851–57) in the U.S. Senate, during which time he moved into the Republican party. During the Civil War he was a member of the Union defense committee of New York State and was a federal commissioner for the relief of prisoners. As Secretary of State (1869–77) under President Grant, he negotiated the Treaty of Washington (1871), which settled the *Alabama* controversy and other matters of dispute between the U.S. and Great Britain; handled the *Virginius* crisis that arose (Nov. 1873) with Spain; negotiated a treaty of commercial reciprocity with Hawaii (1875); and reached a general settlement with Spain (1876) concerning American claims in Cuba.

Fitzgerald, Francis Scott Key (b. St. Paul, Minn., 24 Sept. 1896; d. Hollywood, Calif., 21 Dec. 1940), novelist, lived between the poles of success and despair, much like the lost-rich characters of his novels. Entering Princeton in 1913, he left in 1917 to enlist in the army. His first novel, rewritten for the third time in St. Paul, *This Side of Paradise* (1920), depicted the younger generation of the "Jazz Age." On the strength of its financial success he married the beautiful Zelda Sayre, and they began the life of desperate gaiety which took a heavy toll of both. In 1922 he published *The Beautiful and Damned.* In 1924 he and his wife moved to Europe, where they hoped to live more cheaply, and remained there until 1930. Zelda Sayre suffered 2 mental breakdowns from which she never recovered, and Fitzgerald began drinking heavily. His most brilliant book, *The Great Gatsby* (1925), was a critical success but a financial failure, and *Tender Is the Night* was a critical failure as well (1933). He retreated to a small Southern town, where he wrote *The Crack-Up* (1936), and then left for Hollywood, where he wrote for the movies.

Flexner, Abraham (b. Louisville, Ky., 13 Nov. 1866; d. Washington, D.C., 21 Sept. 1959), educational administrator, was graduated from Johns Hopkins (A.B., 1886). After 19 years as secondary school teacher and principal he took graduate work at Harvard (M.A., 1906) and the Univ. of Berlin (1906–07). In 1908 he joined the research staff of the Carnegie Foundation for the Advancement of Teaching. His reports, *Medical Education in the U.S. and Canada* (1910) and *Medical Education in Europe* (1912), hastened much-needed reforms in American medical schools. Pamphlet, *A Modern School* (1916), led to the founding of the Lincoln Experimental School of Teachers College, Columbia. A member of the General Educational Board, 1912–25, he was influential in guiding philanthropies of the Rockefellers, the Carnegie trusts, and George Eastman. His *Universities—American, English, German* (1930) criticized abuses of the elective system in the U.S. and the trend toward noncultural subjects. As first director of the Institute for Advanced Study, Princeton, N.J., he profoundly influenced its plan, scope, and original membership. His other works include *I Remember: An Autobiography* (1940) and biographies of H. S. Pritchett (1943) and Daniel Coit Gilman (*q.v.*) (1946).

Ford, Gerald Rudolph [Leslie King, Jr.] (b. Omaha, Neb., 14 July 1913–   ), 38th president of the U.S. When he was 2 years old, his mother divorced his father and left Omaha for Grand Rapids, Mich. When she remarried, her husband, Gerald Ford, Sr., president of Ford Paint and Varnish Co., adopted the boy and gave him his name. Ford attended the Univ. of Michigan, where he was a star football player (A.B., 1935) and Yale Univ. Law School (LL.B., 1941). After 4 years in the navy (1941–45), he practiced law in Michigan. Elected to the House of Representatives as a Republican (1948), he served almost 25 consecutive years (1949–72). He was a member of the House Appropriations Committee (1951–65), elected chairman of the House Republican Conference (1963), and Minority Leader (1965), deposing Charles A. Halleck. His voting record in the Congress was conservative, opposing minimum wage bills (1960, 1966, 1973), the creation of the Office of Economic Opportunity (1964), and Medicare (1965). Ford supported Richard M. Nixon for the presidential nomination (1968). During Nixon's first term, he was a strong supporter of controversial administration policies such as construction of the supersonic transport plane. In 1970 Ford led the unsuccessful attempt to impeach Supreme Court Justice William O. Douglas. He was nominated vicepresident (12 Oct. 1972) by President Nixon in accordance with procedures of the 25th Amendment, two days after the resignation of Spiro Agnew. He took the oath of office the day the House of Representatives completed the confirmation process (6 Dec. 1972). While vicepresident, Ford staunchly defended Nixon's innocence of involvement in the Watergate coverup. He assumed the presidency (9 Aug. 1974) upon the resignation of Nixon. Ford's manner healed the wounds of Watergate, but his pardon of Nixon hurt his popularity. He was defeated by Jimmy Carter (1976). Ford declined to run for the Republican nomination in 1980.

Ford, Henry (b. near Dearborn, Mich., 30 July 1863; d. Dearborn, Mich., 7 Apr. 1947), industrialist. His formal schooling at Greenfield, Mich., ended in 1878, and in the following year he moved to Detroit, where he worked (1879–84) as a machine-shop apprentice and as a traveling repairman for a farm machinery firm. Ford became (1887) chief engineer of the Edison Illuminating Co. in Detroit. His first automobile was developed and built by 1896. For a time he was associated with the Detroit Automobile Co., manufacturers of custom-built vehicles. After manufacturing his first racing car, the "999," Ford organized (1903) the Ford Motor Co., which in 1909 produced the first "Model T" (popularly known as the "flivver"), a standardized vehicle turned out on a mass-production assembly line. The factory assembly methods evolved by Ford engineers made him a worldwide symbol of American industrial technique. Ford's victory in the suit (1903–11) brought against him by the Association of Licensed Automobile Manufacturers (the Selden Patent Suit) freed the industry from the hold of an agreement that threatened to retard the development of automobile manufacture. In 1914 Ford attracted national attention by introducing into his plants the 8-hour day with a minimum daily wage of $5. At the same time he inaugurated a profit-sharing plan for his employees. Late in 1915, Ford chartered the *Oscar II* (commonly known as the Ford Peace Ship), which took to the Scandinavian nations a group of pacifists, feminists, and other idealists in an attempt to halt World War I by neu-

tral mediation. During that war he manufactured a wide range of equipment for the U.S. government, including gun carriages and Liberty motors. In 1918 he was an unsuccessful candidate for U.S. senator from Michigan. He served as president of the Ford Motor Co. until 1919, when he was succeeded by his son, Edsel B. Ford; upon the death of the latter, he again became president (1943) and served until his death. The Ford Foundation was established by Henry and Edsel Ford in 1936. Its operations were conducted on a relatively modest scale until 1951, when with vastly increased assets the Ford Foundation undertook a diversified program in educational philanthropy and other fields.

Forrest, Edwin (b. Philadelphia, Pa., 9 Mar. 1806; d. there, 12 Dec. 1872), actor. He made his debut (27 Nov. 1820) at the Walnut Street Theater, Philadelphia, in the role of Young Norval, and subsequently was a member of a roving company on the frontier circuit. He played at New Orleans as a member of James H. Caldwell's company and supported Edmund Kean in an engagement at Albany (1825). He made his New York debut (23 June 1826) at the Park Theater as Othello and in the ensuing decade became a leading American actor, appearing in Shakespearean tragic roles and in plays such as John H. Stone's *Metamora* (1829) and Robert M. Bird's tragedy *The Gladiator,* both of which won prizes offered by Forrest to encourage plays by native dramatists. In 1834 Forrest went to Europe, where he was acclaimed as the first great American-born actor. His rivalry with the British actor Macready resulted in the Astor Place Riot (10 May 1849) at New York, in which 22 persons lost their lives. The last 2 decades of Forrest's life were darkened by domestic difficulties that took on the dimensions of public scandals, and by a growing personal bitterness and isolation. The house he bought at Philadelphia is now maintained as the Forrest Home for aged actors.

Foster, Stephen Collins (b. Allegheny City, Pa., 4 July 1826; d. New York City, 13 Jan. 1864), composer, for a brief period in 1841 attended Jefferson College. He worked (1846) as a bookkeeper for his brother at Cincinnati, where several Negro ballads composed by Foster, such as "O Susanna," "Away Down South," and "Uncle Ned," were used by a local publisher who brought out *Songs of the Sable Harmonists* (1848). Thereafter Foster devoted himself to songwriting, producing ballads and songs, most of them for Negro minstrels. He made an agreement (1851) with E. P. Christy giving first-performance rights to Christy's Minstrels and publication rights to himself. Among Foster's songs are "Nelly Was a Lady" (1849), "De Camptown Races" (1850), "The Old Folks at Home" (1851; also known as "Swanee River"), "Massa's in de Cold, Cold Ground" (1852), "My Old Kentucky Home" (1853), "Old Dog Tray" (1853), "Jeannie with the Light Brown Hair" (1854), and "Old Black Joe" (1860). Foster spent his last years in poverty.

Frankfurter, Felix (b. Vienna, Austria, 15 Nov. 1882; d. Washington, D.C., 22 Feb. 1965), jurist, came to the U.S. in 1894, received his A.B. (1902) from College of the City of New York and his LL.B. (highest honors, 1906) from the Harvard Law School. Assistant U.S. Attorney, southern district of New York (1906–10), he served as law officer in the Bureau of Insular Affairs (1911–14), and joined the faculty of the Harvard Law School in 1914, where he taught administrative law until 1939. During World War I he served as assistant to the Secretary of War, counsel to the president's Mediation Board (1917–18), and chairman, War Labor Policies Board (1918). He argued or filed briefs before the Supreme Court in *Bunting* v. *Oregon* (1917) and *Adkins* v. *Children's Hospital* (1923), and gained national prominence by his critique of the Sacco-Vanzetti trial (*The Case of Sacco and Vanzetti*, 1927). Close adviser to President Franklin D. Roosevelt, he was influential in recruiting personnel for the New Deal. Although officially neutral during the court-packing fight (1937), posthumous publication of his correspondence proves that he was a constant adviser to Roosevelt during the episode, remaining publicly silent at the president's request. Appointed associate justice of the Supreme Court (1939), he quickly assumed leadership in opposing the Black-Douglas position that the 1st Amendment rights were absolute, whereas he considered that amendment a generic provision requiring definition by present experience. The view that freedom is not absolute but must be weighed against legislative judgment he expressed in the *Gobitis Case* (1940), sustaining a state flag salute law. "One who belongs to the most vilified and persecuted minority in history is not likely to be insensible to the freedoms guaranteed by our Constitution," he declared in dissenting to the reversal in *W. Va. Bd. of Educ.* v. *Barnette* (1943). In setting boundaries to the right to picket (*Milk Drivers Union* v. *Meadowmoor Dairies* [1941]), he said: "Utterance in a context of violence can lose its significance as an appeal to reason and become part of an instrument of force." In the *Dennis Case* (1951) he repudiated the "clear and present danger" formula, holding that advocacy of overthrow of the government deserves little protection. He wrote numerous works in the field of constitutional and administrative law, including *The Commerce Clause under Marshall, Taney and Waite* (1937) and *Felix Frankfurter Reminisces* (1960, recorded by H. B. Phillips).

Franklin, Benjamin (b. Boston, Mass., 17 Jan. 1706; d. Philadelphia, 17 Apr. 1790), statesman, diplomat, editor, and scientist, attended school briefly; worked in his father's tallow shop and then in his brother's printing shop. In 1723 he went to Philadelphia and worked as a printer, acquiring an interest in (1729) and sole ownership of the *Pennsylvania Gazette,* which he edited until 1748, and publishing annually (1732–57) *Poor Richard's Almanack.* Leader in cultural movements, he founded the Junto, a debating club (1727) which developed into the American Philosophical Society (1743); a circulating library (1731); Philadelphia's first fire company (1736); and an academy (1751), nucleus of the Univ. of Pennsylvania. His international fame as scientist and inventor began with the invention of the Franklin stove (1742). The identity of lightning and electricity was demonstrated in France (1752) by methods he suggested, and he later confirmed it by his kite experiment. Clerk of the Pennsylvania Assembly (1736–51), he was a member of that body (1751–64), deputy postmaster at Philadelphia (1737–53), and, jointly with William Hunter, postmaster general for the colonies (1753–74). In this office he improved the postal service and placed it on a profitable basis. Delegate to the Albany Congress (1754), he drafted a Plan of Union which the Congress adopted but which both Great Britain and the colonies rejected for opposing reasons. He went to England (1757) to press the claims of the Pennsylvania Assembly to tax the proprietary estates, and acted as agent in England for Pennsylvania (1764–75), for Georgia (after 1768), and for Massachusetts (after, 1770). He was instrumental in securing the repeal of the Stamp Act (1766), but was publicly censured for allowing publication of the "Hutchinson letters" (1774). Returning to Philadelphia (1775), he was a member of the 2d Continental Congress and became the first Postmaster General (1775–76). He was one of 3 commissioners sent (1776) to secure the aid of Canada, helped draft the Declaration of Independence, and was a signer. One of the 3 agents dispatched to France (1776–85), where his fame preceded him, he secured loans and concluded a treaty of alliance (1778). He was one of the negotiators of the Treaty of Peace with Great Britain (1783). President of the Executive Council of Pennsylvania (1785–88), he was a member of the Constitutional Convention (1787), where he was influential in framing the compromise between the large and small states on the question of representation in the House of Representatives. His most famous book was his unfinished *Autobiography,* 1706–59 (written between 1771 and 1789).

Frémont, John Charles (b. Savannah, Ga., 31 Jan. 1813; d. New York City, 13 July 1890), explorer, politician, and soldier. He attended Charleston (S.C.) College, 1829–31, and in 1835 became an assistant engineer in the U.S. Topographical Corps, in which he was commissioned a 2d lieutenant (1838). In 1838 he assisted Joseph N. Nicollet in exploring the plateau between the upper Mississippi and Missouri rivers. He married (1841) Jessie Benton, daughter of Sen. Thomas Hart Benton (*q.v.*), who used his influence to further Frémont's expeditions. Frémont made 3 important explorations that earned for him the sobriquet "the Pathfinder": a scientific investigation of the Oregon Trail that took him to the Wind River chain of the

Rockies and through South Pass (1842); to the Great Basin between the Rockies and the Sierras (1843–44); and to the Sierra Nevada by way of the headwaters of the Arkansas, Rio Grande, and Colorado rivers. The 3d exploration was made on the eve of the Mexican War; when he reached the Pacific Coast, Frémont played a leading and controversial role in the conquest of California. His quarrel with Gen. Stephen W. Kearny resulted in a court-martial at Washington, D.C. (Nov. 1847–Jan. 1848), that found Frémont guilty of mutiny and disobedience. A 4th expedition (1848–49) to ascertain the practicality of Sen. Benton's proposed central route to the Pacific proved a disaster. Despite President Polk's remission of the sentence, Frémont resigned from the army. Returning to California, Frémont served a brief term as U.S. senator from that state and in 1853–54 made winter expeditions for a southern railway route to the Pacific. In 1856 he was the first presidential candidate of the newly organized Republican party on an antislavery platform, losing to Buchanan by about 500,000 votes. At the outbreak of the Civil War he was appointed major general in charge of the Department of the West, with headquarters at St. Louis. When his radical policy toward slaveholders brought him into conflict with the Lincoln administration, he was removed from his post and given a command in western Virginia, but resigned when he was placed under Gen. John Pope, with whom he was on unfriendly terms. After making unsuccessful attempts at railroad promotion, he served as territorial governor of Arizona (1878–83) and in 1890 was restored to the rank of major general with retirement pay.

Frost, Robert (b. San Francisco, Calif., 26 Mar. 1874; d. Boston, Mass., 29 Jan. 1963), poet. He attended Dartmouth and Harvard; worked in New England as a shoemaker, teacher, country editor, and farmer; and in 1912 went to England, where he brought out his first volume of poetry, *A Boy's Will* (1913). Following the publication of *North of Boston* (1914), he returned to the U.S. (1915), where he soon won recognition as a poet of the first rank; he was awarded the Pulitzer prize 4 times (1924, 1931, 1937, 1943). Most of his poetry is based on themes drawn from New England rural life. His works include *Mountain Interval* (1916), *New Hampshire* (1923), *West-Running Brook* (1928), *Collected Poems* (1930, 1939), *Selected Poems* (1937), *A Further Range* (1937), *A Witness Tree* (1943), and *The Gift Outright* (1961). Among his individual poems are "Mowing," "The Death of the Hired Man," "Home Burial," "Mending Wall," "Birches," and "Fire and Ice." He was the first poet to partcipate in a presidential inaugural ceremony (1961).

Fulbright, James William (b. Sumner, Mo., 9 Apr. 1905–   ), statesman, received his B.A. from the Univ. of Arkansas (1925), studied as a Rhodes scholar at Oxford, where he received a B.A. (1928) and M.A. (1931). He attended George Washington Univ. Law School and served as an attorney for the Justice Department's Antitrust Division. He taught law at the George Washington Univ. Law School (1935) and the Univ. of Arkansas (1939), and became president of the latter institution (1939–41). Elected to the U.S. House of Representatives (1942), Fulbright, the freshman congressman from Fayetteville, Ark., introduced the Fulbright Resolution (1943) ensuring active U.S. involvement in world affairs after the war and its entrance into the UN. He was elected to the U.S. Senate (1944) and served 5 consecutive terms (1945–74). He sponsored the Fulbright Act (1946), which established an educational exchange program between the U.S. and foreign countries. Although wary of Communist aggression during the Cold War, Fulbright opposed Gen. MacArthur's attempt to escalate the Korean War against Communist China. A close friend of Adlai Stevenson, he served as his adviser during the 1952 presidential campaign. Fulbright was one of the few senators to oppose U.S. atom bomb testing at Bikini Island (1946) and to vote against funds for Sen. Joseph McCarthy's investigations. As chairman of the Senate Foreign Relations Committee (1959–74), Fulbright was one of the first senators to oppose the Vietnam War, amplifying the national debate by holding televised hearings (1966). In his later years in the Senate he led the opposition to the manner and terms of U.S. foreign aid programs, and called for a less pro-Israel stance in the Middle East, and favored legislation curbing presidential warmaking powers. Fulbright was defeated in the Democratic party primary (1974) in his bid for a 6th term. His books— *Old Myths and New Realities* (1964) and *The Arrogance of Power* (1966)— were critical of U.S. foreign policy.

Fuller, Margaret [full name **Sarah Margaret Fuller;** title **Marchioness Ossoli**] (b. Cambridgeport, Mass., 23 May 1810; d. off Fire Island, N.Y., 19 July 1850), feminist, critic, and journalist. A precocious child, she received most of her education from her father and at an early age formed friendships with New England intellectual leaders such as James Freeman Clarke and Frederic Henry Hedge. She conducted (1839–44) her "conversations" at the Boston residence of Elizabeth Peabody, drawing her pupils from leading circles of the city. The material of her "conversations" appeared in her feminist work, *Woman in the Nineteenth Century* (1845). With Ralph

Waldo Emerson and George Ripley, she edited (1840–42) *The Dial,* Transcendentalist journal. Her book, *Summer on the Lakes, in 1843* (1844), drew the attention of Horace Greeley, who offered her a staff job with the New York *Tribune.* Her significant writings as literary critic of the *Tribune* from 1844 to 1846 were published as *Literature and Art* (1846). She went abroad in 1846 and while in Italy had a son (1848) by the Marquis Angelo Ossoli, whom she married in 1849. With her husband, an ardent follower of Mazzini, she took part in the Roman Revolution. She and her family died in a shipwreck while returning to America.

Fuller, Melville Weston (b. Augusta Me., 11 Feb. 1833; d. Sorrento, Me., 4 July 1910), chief justice of the U.S., graduated from Bowdoin College (1853). He studied law in the offices of his uncles (1853–54) and for 6 months at the Harvard Law School (1854–55), after which he entered practice in Bangor, Me. (1855). He became associate editor of *The Age,* a Democratic magazine (1855–56), and in 1856 became city solicitor and president of the Common Council of Augusta, Me. He soon moved to Chicago, where he established a reputation as an expert in commercial and real estate law, representing merchants and railroads. Active in politics, he was a member of the Illinois Constitutional Convention (1862), of the Illinois House of Representatives (1863–65), and a delegate to several Democratic National Conventions. As an advocate, Fuller appeared often before the U.S. Supreme Court. Fuller was appointed chief justice (1888) by President Cleveland and served on the court until his death. The Supreme Court during the period of Fuller's service developed new tools and concepts to protect property rights from government regulation—

among them substantive due process and liberty of contract. The Fuller court was noteworthy for its antilabor decisions. In *Pollock* v. *Farmers' Loan and Trust Company* (1895), a narrow majority of the court agreed with Fuller that the income tax law of 1894 was unconstitutional on the grounds that it was a direct tax, thereby reversing earlier decisions which the chief justice termed "a century of error." Fuller spoke for the majority in *United States* v. *E. C. Knight Co.* (1895), holding that sugar refining was manufacturing and not commerce, thereby drastically curbing the Sherman Anti-Trust Act. However, in the *Danbury Hatters Case* (1908) Fuller construed the Sherman Act so as to apply to labor. Believing that the Constitution followed the flag. Fuller was generally in the minority in the Insular Cases which followed the Spanish-American War. An excellent judicial administrator, he was responsible for calming tensions within the court and for persuading Congress to pass the Circuit Court of Appeals Act of 1891. Fuller declined Cleveland's offer (1892) to become Secretary of State but he did serve as arbitrator with Justice David J. Brewer of the Venezuela-British Guiana boundary dispute (1899).

Fulton, Robert (b. Little Britain, now Fulton, Pa., 14 Nov. 1765; d. New York City, 24 Feb. 1815), artist, civil engineer, and inventor, pioneer in steam navigation. During his boyhood he showed a talent for drawing and mechanical crafts, becoming an expert gunsmith in nearby Lancaster. Going to Philadelphia in 1783, he worked as an artist and draftsman; in 1786 he went abroad, where he remained for 20 years. Although his first years in London were devoted to painting, he soon shifted his interest to science and engineering. He invented an apparatus (the double inclined plane) for raising and lowering canal boats, a power

shovel for digging canal channels, a device for sawing marble, and a flax-spinning machine. His chief interest was in internal improvements, particularly inland waterways. In 1794 he settled in Paris, where he painted what is held to be the first panorama. He published *A Treatise on the Improvement of Canal Navigation* (1796), a comprehensive work of its kind, and submitted to the Board of Agriculture of Great Britain detailed plans and proposals (1796) for the construction of cast-iron aqueducts requiring simplified casting and building operations. One of these structures was later reared across the Dee near Chester. Fulton also proposed cast-iron bridges of his own design which were built at several points in England. For 9 years, beginning in 1797, he devoted himself to the development of the submarine mine and torpedo; failing to gain the financial support of the French government, he secured the aid of Joel Barlow and made short-lived experiments with a self-propelled submarine torpedo. In 1801, after Napoleon showed interest in Fulton's project, Fulton made successful experiments with his submarine boat, the *Nautilus;* but upon his failure to make a satisfactory demonstration under actual combat conditions, the French authorities quickly lost interest. In 1804 he placed his invention at the disposal of the British government, which finally refused to adopt it despite a successful test carried out in 1805. Returning to the U.S. (1805), Fulton continued the experiments with steamboats that he had begun along the Seine in 1803 with the assistance of the U.S. minister to France, Robert R. Livingston. Fulton designed the *Clermont*, a boat with 2 side paddlewheels. The *Clermont* was completed in the spring of 1807 and the Watt steam engine was installed later. During the course of its construction, he demonstrated in New York Harbor (20 July 1807) the effectiveness of his torpedo device. Starting out from New York on 17 Aug. 1807, the *Clermont* made its voyage to Albany and back in 5 days (62 hours of actual operating time). Until his death Fulton was active in organizing and managing steamboat lines. In 1814 he constructed for the U.S. government the *Fulton the First*, a huge paddlewheel steam warship, never tested in warfare.

Gallatin, Albert [full name **Abraham Alfonse Albert Gallatin**] (b. Geneva, Switzerland, 29 Jan. 1761; d. Astoria, Long Island, N.Y., 12 Aug. 1849), statesman, diplomat, and ethnologist. He was graduated (1779) from Geneva Academy; emigrated to Massachusetts (1780); settled in the Pennsylvania back country (1784), where he made unsuccessful ventures in land speculation; and as a member (1790–92) of the Pennsylvania legislature emerged as a leader of the nascent Republican forces in the western part of the state. He was elected (28 Feb. 1793) to the U.S. Senate, but a Federalist majority deprived him of his seat (28 Feb. 1794) on the ground that he had not been a U.S. citizen for 9 years. An opponent of the federal excise tax of 1791, he took a moderate stand during the Whisky Rebellion of 1794 and was instrumental in averting serious bloodshed. As a member of Congress (1795–1801), he became the recognized leader of the Republican minority in the House. His able grasp of finance and his criticism of the Federalist policy in the Treasury Department led to the creation of a standing committee on finance. As Secretary of the Treasury (1801–14) under Jefferson and Madison, he carried out a program of financial reform and economy which after 1807 was virtually destroyed by embroilments in the Napoleonic Wars and by the War of 1812. He was a member of the commission (1814) which negotiated the Treaty of Ghent, served as

minister to France (1816–23) and to England (1826–27), and from 1831 to 1839 was president of the National Bank at New York City. Called "the father of American ethnology," he wrote *Synopsis of the Indian Tribes . . . of North America* (1836) and founded (1842) the American Ethnological Society.

Galloway, Joseph (b. West River, Anne Arundel Co., Md., c.1731; d. Watford, England, 29 Aug. 1803), colonial statesman, studied law in Philadelphia, where he rose to eminence at the bar. Assemblyman (1756–76, except for 1764–65), he joined Franklin in attempts to tax the Penns' land, and eventually, with Franklin, petitioned the crown to substitute royal for proprietary government. An imperial statesman, he saw the need for a revenue for America, but opposed parliamentary taxation. Instead, he advocated a written constitution for the empire. In the 1st Continental Congress (1774) he proposed the Galloway Plan for an imperial legislature, defeated by a close vote. Refusing to be a delegate to the 2d Congress, he criticized its predecessor in *A Candid Examination of the Mutual Claims of Great Britain and the Colonies* (1775). Civil administrator of Philadelphia during Gen. Howe's occupation of the city, he left for London with the recapture of the city (1778), and became the spokesman for the Loyalists. His estates confiscated by Pennsylvania and his petition (1793) to return denied, he spent his last 20 years in exile.

Garfield, James Abram (b. Cuyahoga Co., Ohio, 19 Nov. 1831; d. Elberon, N.J., 19 Sept. 1881), 20th president of the U.S., was graduated from Williams College (1856), served as president of Western Reserve Electric Institute (later Hiram College), 1857–61, was admitted to the bar, and elected to the Ohio Senate as a Republican (1859). During the Civil War he distinguished himself in engagements at Middle Creek, Ky., Shiloh, and Chickamauga; was a member of the court of inquiry in the Fitz John Porter case (1862); and was on the staff of Gen. W. S. Rosecrans. Congressman (1863–81), his prestige as orator and parliamentarian made him Blaine's rival for influence with that body. Although charged, without proof, of corruption in connection with Crédit Mobilier, he was elected to the U.S. Senate (1880), and in that same year nominated and elected president. In the midst of involvements over appointments to office, prompting the resignation of Roscoe Conkling and T. C. Platt from the U.S. Senate, he was fatally shot in the Washington railroad station by Charles J. Guiteau, a disappointed office seeker.

Garrison, William Lloyd (b. Newburyport, Mass., 10 Dec. 1805; d. New York City, 24 May 1879), abolitionist. After brief schooling, he was apprenticed (1818) to the editor of the Newburyport *Herald;* became (1826) editor of the Newburyport *Free Press;* when that newspaper failed, he moved to Boston and became (1828) coeditor of the *National Philanthropist,* an organ devoted to reform causes. At about this time he met Benjamin Lundy, a Quaker antislavery writer and journalist, whom he joined at Baltimore (1829) as coeditor of *The Genius of Universal Emancipation.* Garrison's tirades in the columns of this paper resulted in his imprisonment for libel (1830), but he was released after the New York merchant and abolitionist sympathizer Arthur Tappan paid his fine. Returning to Boston (1830), he founded and published the *Liberator,* in which he was joined by his partner, Isaac Knapp. The first issue of this abolitionist paper, dated 1 Jan. 1831, announced the uncompromising attitude that henceforth characterized Garrison's crusade against slavery and slaveholders. He remained its editor until the last issue of the *Liberator* appeared 35 years later. Garrison demanded immediate and complete emancipation of slaves. He was one of the founders of the New England Antislavery Society (1831) and organized the American Antislavery Society (1833). Resentment in the North against the abolitionists was so strong that Garrison was dragged through the streets by a Boston mob and almost killed (21 Oct. 1835). His opposition to political action resulted in a split in the organized antislavery ranks in the late 1830s. During that period Garrison embraced disunionism, demanding that the North withdraw from a compact that sheltered slavery. Under his influence the Massachusetts Antislavery Society resolved (1843) that the Constitution of the U.S. was "a covenant with death and an agreement with hell." On 4 July 1854, before a gathering at Framingham, Mass., he publicly burned the Constitution, saying: "So perish all compromises with tyranny!" During the Civil War he gave his full support to Lincoln after the issuance of the Emancipation Proclamation. In the years after the war he was allied with reform causes, including prohibition and women's suffrage.

Garvey, Marcus (b. St. Ann's Bay, Jamaica, 17 Aug. 1887; d. London, England, 10 June 1940), social reformer. Largely self-taught, Garvey attended school in Jamaica until he was 14, and then worked for a printer, traveled in Central America, and lived in London (1912–14). After returning to Jamaica he established the Universal Negro Improvement and Conservation Association and African Communities League (UNIA, 1 Aug. 1914), whose aims were to instill racial pride, acquire economic power for blacks, and build a black-governed nation in Africa. In Mar. 1916 he arrived in Harlem where his oratory and natural leadership abilities drew thousands of blacks into the UNIA, making it the first important U.S. black nationalist movement. By 1919 there were 30 branches of the UNIA in the U.S., most in Northern urban ghettos. Garvey established (Jan. 1918) the *Negro World,* the official UNIA weekly, which was published until 1933 with an estimated circulation of from 60,000 to 200,-000. He presided over an international UNIA convention (1920), which promoted African nationalism and adopted a Declaration of the Rights of the Negro People of the World. The following year he proclaimed himself provisional president of an empire of Africa. Garvey was criticized by other black leaders, among them W.E.B. DuBois (*q.v.*) and A. Philip Randolph (*q.v.*), for his advocacy of racial purity and separatism and for his impracticality. A second convention in 1924 produced final plans for a "back-to-Africa" colonization program, which never received the necessary support from African nations. He supported an independent black economy within the framework of white capitalism and organized the Universal Black Cross Nurses, the Negro Factories Corp., as well as a chain of restaurants and grocery stores. His biggest project was the organization of the Black Star Line (1919), a steamship company owned, controlled, and operated by black people. In 1922 the line collapsed, due to faulty ships and mismanagement, and Garvey was tried, convicted, and sentenced to a maximum of 5 years in prison for using the mails to defraud shareholders. President Coolidge commuted his sentence and ordered his deportation as an undesirable alien (1927). Garvey moved the headquarters of the UNIA to London (1935) but he could never again build up a large following, and died in relative obscurity. Without Garvey the UNIA declined, but his ideas of racial solidarity and racial enterprise were revived by the Black Power movement of the 1960s.

George, Henry (b. Philadelphia, Pa., 2 Sept. 1839; d. New York City, 29 Oct. 1897), economist and reformer. After a brief period of formal schooling, he went to sea as a foremast boy (1855), became a typesetter (1856), was a prospector in the Pacific Northwest (1858), and until 1880, when he moved to New York, was a printer and newspaperman, chiefly at San Francisco. He published (1871) a pamphlet, *Our Land and Land Policy,* which set forth the basic elements of the single-tax theory elaborated by him in *Progress and Poverty* (1879). Holding that taxes should be confined to the economic rent derived from land, George asserted that the accumulation of such unearned increment tended to impoverish society, and that the single tax, by eliminating all other government levies, would enable the unimpeded and benevolent operation of the economic mechanism. After publishing *The Irish Land Question* (1881), he served as a correspondent in the British Isles for the *Irish World.* He was also active as a lecturer. In 1886, as the liberal and labor candidate for mayor of New York, he was defeated in a contest with Abram S. Hewitt and Theodore Roosevelt. In 1897 he was the independent Democratic candidate for mayor of New York, and died while campaigning for that office.

Gershwin, George (b. Brooklyn, N.Y., 26 Sept. 1898; d. Hollywood, Calif., 11 July 1937), composer, was educated in the New York public schools, studied the piano with Charles Hambitzer and harmony with Rubin Goldmark, and worked as a song plugger in Tin Pan Alley. His first song, "When You Want 'Em You Can't Get 'Em," was published in 1916; his first musical comedy score was written for *La, La, Lucille* (1919). Gershwin's use of the native jazz idiom in serious music first appeared in *Rhapsody in Blue* (1st performance given by Paul Whiteman and his orchestra at Aeolian Hall, New York City, 12 Feb. 1924). In this vein Gershwin also wrote *Concerto in F* (1925), *An American in Paris* (1928), *Second Rhapsody* (1931), *Cuban Overture* (1932), and the opera *Porgy and Bess* (1935). Among Gershwin's popular musical comedies were *George White's Scandals* (1920–24), *Lady Be Good* (1924), *Rosalie* (1927), *Strike Up the Band* (1927), *Show Girl* (1929), *Girl Crazy* (1930), *Of Thee I Sing* (1931; 1st musical comedy awarded the Pulitzer prize), and *Let 'Em Eat Cake* (1933). His best-known songs include "I'll Build a Stairway to Paradise" (1922), "Somebody Loves Me" (1924), "It Ain't Necessarily So" (1935), and "Summertime" (1935).

Gesell, Arnold (b. Alma, Wis., 21 June 1880; d. New Haven, Conn., 29 May 1961), child psychologist, received his B.Ph. from the Univ. of Wisconsin (1903) and his Ph.D. in psychology from Clark Univ. (1906). Meanwhile he taught history, German, and psychology in Wisconsin high schools (1899–1901), was principal of Chippewa Falls high school, Wis. (1903–04), and was a settlement worker on New York's lower east side (1906–07). While an assistant professor of education at Yale, he was a full-time student at the Yale Univ. Medical School, where he received his M.D. (1915). He first became interested in child psychology when he visited Dr. Henry Goddard's training school for mentally defective children in Vineland, N.J. (1909). Dr. Gesell was director of the Yale Clinic for Child Development from its inception (1911) to his retirement (1948); professor of child hygiene at Yale Medical School (1915–48); and a research as-

sociate at the Yale Child Vision Research Center (1948–50). He became a pioneer in studying the mental growth of babies from infancy until they went to school. *The Child from Five to Ten* (1946); *Youth: The Years from Ten to Sixteen* (1956); and *Infant and Child in the Culture of Today* (1943), all written with Dr. Frances L. Ilg, were Gesell's best-known works and were widely consulted by many American parents. Gesell considered these books only as broad guides and not as exact stipulations of normal child behavior, insisting that, while the mental growth of children reveals itself in consistent behavior patterns, each child is an individual at birth. His studies emphasized that parents should rear children with "discerning guidance," with neither excessive severity nor excessive laxity.

Gibbons, James (b. Baltimore, Md., 23 July 1834; d. there, 24 Mar. 1921), Roman Catholic prelate, was graduated (1858) from St. Charles College, near Baltimore, took advanced training for the priesthood at St. Mary's Seminary, Baltimore, and was ordained (1861). He took charge of St. Bridget's Church in the suburb of Canton and during the Civil War was chaplain at Ft. McHenry. Invited to take the post of secretary to Archbishop Martin J. Spalding, he became (1866) assistant chancellor of the Second Plenary Council of Baltimore and head of the newly established Vicarate Apostolic of North Carolina. Consecrated bishop of Adramyttum (16 Aug. 1868), he was at that time the youngest of all Catholic bishops. He served (1870) as the youngest member of the Ecumenical Council of the Vatican; succeeded (1872) to the bishopric of Richmond; was appointed (May 1877) coadjutor archbishop of Baltimore; and, upon the death of Archbishop James R. Bayley (Oct. 1877), became head of the See of

Baltimore. He organized and conducted the Third Plenary Council of Baltimore (1884), over which he presided as apostolic delegate. In 1885 he was named the second American cardinal and was formally installed at Baltimore (1886) and at Rome (1887), where he made a memorable pronouncement expressing his attachment to American institutions. Sympathetic to the cause of labor, he secured at Rome ecclesiastical assurances that the Knights of Labor would not be condemned in the U.S., and was instrumental in obtaining the removal of the hierarchical ban against that body in Canada. He laid the cornerstone of the Catholic Univ. of America at Washington, D.C. (1888), and served as chancellor until his death. In 1903 he was the first American to participate in the election of a pope.

Gibbs, Josiah Willard (b. New Haven, Conn., 11 Feb. 1839; d. there, 28 Apr. 1903), mathematical physicist. He was graduated from Yale (1858), where he received the degree of Ph.D. (1863), served as tutor at Yale, and in 1866 went to the Continent, where he continued his studies at Paris (1866–67), Berlin (1867–68), and Heidelberg (1868–69). He was appointed (1871) professor of mathematical physics at Yale, holding that post until his death. His chief contribution was his theory of thermodynamics, the basis for the major part of modern physical chemistry and chemical engineering. Among the papers he published are "Graphical Methods in the Thermodynamics of Fluids" (1873), "A Method of Geometrical Representation of the Thermodynamic Properties of Substances by Means of Surfaces" (1873), and "Electrochemical Thermodynamics" (1886). His most important single paper, "On the Equilibrium of Heterogeneous Substances" (1876), contained his formulation of the phase rule, one of the revolutionary laws of theoretical physics. Between 1880 and 1884 he evolved a system of vector analysis adapted to the needs of mathematical physicists, publishing papers such as "On the Role of Quaternions in the Algebra of Vectors" (1891) and "Quaternions and Vector Analysis" (1893). From 1882 to 1889 he devoted himself principally to theories of optics, developing an electromagnetic theory of light. In 1902 he published *Elementary Principles in Statistical Mechanics*. His *Collected Works* were published in 1928.

Gilman, Daniel Coit (b. Norwich, Conn., 6 July 1831; d. there, 13 Oct. 1908), educational administrator. He was graduated from Yale (1852), served as an attaché (1853–55) of the U.S. legation at St. Petersburg, and drew up the plan for the Sheffield Scientific School at Yale, where he served (1855–72) as librarian and professor of physical and political geography. With Eliot of Harvard and White of Cornell he was the chief maker of the modern American university, serving as president (1872–75) of the Univ. of California, and as first president (1876–1901) of Johns Hopkins, which he made into a leading center of creative study and research. He was instrumental in founding the Johns Hopkins Hospital (1889) and Medical School (1893), and raised the general level of medical training in the U.S.

Goddard, Robert Hutchings (b. Worcester, Mass., 5 Oct. 1882; d. Baltimore, Md., 10 Aug. 1945), physicist, "father of the modern rocket," attended the Worcester Polytechnic Institute (B.S., 1908) and Clark Univ. (M.A., 1910; Ph.D., 1911), where he became professor of physics (1919). In 1912 he began his work on rocketry, developing a general theory of rocket action, including the "optimum velocity" principle. Engaged in research during World War I, he developed a solid-propellant projectile which was used in World War II as the "bazooka." His paper "A Method of Reaching Extreme Altitudes" (1919) predicted the use of rockets to explore high altitudes and the lunar terrain. Other writings predicted interplanetary and intergalactic explorations. In 1926 he completed and successfully launched the world's first liquid-fuel rocket (prototype of the German V-2) and 4 years later fired a rocket to a height of 2,000 ft. at a speed of 500 mph. In 1935 one of his liquid-propellant rockets exceeded the speed of sound. During World War II he directed research in jet propulsion for the Navy.

Godkin, Edwin Lawrence (b. Moyne, County Wicklow, Ireland, 2 Oct. 1831; d. Brixham, England, 21 May 1902), editor. He was graduated (1851) from Queen's College, Belfast; worked in the London publishing house of Cassell, which brought out his *History of Hungary and the Magyars* (1853); was correspondent (1853–55) for the London *Daily News* during the Crimean War; and came to the U.S. in 1856. As the first editor (1865–1900) of the weekly *Nation,* and as editor (1883–1900) of the New York *Evening Post*, Godkin established new standards of American political journalism. An ardent exponent of civil service reform, he was an implacable foe of the spoils system. He pursued an independent liberal course in politics and in 1884 took a leading role in the Mugwump revolt against James G. Blaine.

Goethals, George Washington (b. Brooklyn, N.Y., 29 June 1858; d. New York City, 21 Jan. 1928), army officer and engineer, builder of the Panama Canal. He attended the College of the City of New York and was graduated from the U.S. Military Academy (1880). He

served (1882–1905) in the Engineer Corps of the U.S. army and (1903–07) on the Army General Staff. In the spring of 1907, when he held the rank of lieutenant colonel, he was appointed by President Theodore Roosevelt as chairman and chief engineer of the Isthmian Canal Commission. In this capacity, Goethals bore virtually sole responsibility for the successful administration of the canal project. His organizing ability overcame numerous serious difficulties involving engineering problems, employee grievances, housing and sanitation, and the establishment of a law enforcement system. He was made (1914) the first civil governor of the Panama Canal Zone, serving in that post until 1916, and was promoted to major general and received the thanks of Congress (1915). From Apr. to July 1917, he was general manager of the Emergency Fleet Corp. Although he was transferred to the retired list in 1916, he was recalled to duty (1917–19) as acting quartermaster general and director of purchase, storage, and supplies, responsible for the supply and transportation of all U.S. troops at home and abroad.

Gompers, Samuel (b. London, England, 27 Jan. 1850; d. San Antonio, Tex., 13 Dec. 1924), labor leader. Apprenticed as a cigarmaker in London, he arrived in the U.S. in 1863 and joined (1864) the Cigarmakers' Union, of which he became president in 1877. He was one of the main figures in the organization (1881) of the Federation of Organized Trades and Labor Unions of the U.S. and Canada, reorganized (1886) as the American Federation of Labor. Gompers was chosen president of the A.F. of L. and, with the exception of the year 1895, served in that capacity until his death. During that period he was the acknowledged head of the American labor movement. An exponent of craft unionism, Gompers stressed practical demands such as wages and hours, and was an avowed opponent of theorists and radicals in the labor movement. He was opposed to an independent labor party and eschewed political commitments by labor organizations to any of the existing parties. During World War I he organized a War Committee on Labor that was instrumental in maintaining national unity. Among his works are *Labor in Europe and America* (1910), *American Labor and the War* (1919), and *Seventy Years of Life and Labor* (2 vols., 1925).

Goodyear, Charles (b. New Haven, Conn., 29 Dec. 1800; d. New York City, 1 July 1860), inventor, pioneer of the rubber industry in the U.S. Until 1830, when he was declared bankrupt, he was in the hardware business at New Haven and Philadelphia. In 1834 he became interested in improving the process for curing India rubber. In the following years, despite poverty and time spent in debtors' prison, he experimented with raw rubber in an attempt to make a product that would not melt or decompose at high and low temperatures. He patented a process (17 June 1837) which he used in making articles such as shoes, tablecloths, and piano covers. From Nathaniel M. Hayward, who had devised a process that included the use of sulfur, Goodyear acquired a patent in 1839, and in the same year accidentally dropped a rubber and sulfur mixture on a hot stove, thus discovering the vulcanizing process. Borrowing a total of more than $50,000, Goodyear perfected the process and received a patent for it (15 June 1844). Financial obligations forced him to sell licenses and to establish royalties that were far less than the true value of the rights; consequently, the profits derived from his discoveries accrued to others. His subsequent years in Europe (1851–59) and America were marked by unsuccessful lawsuits and increasing debt.

Gorgas, William Crawford (b. Toulminville, Ala., 3 Oct. 1854; d. London, 3 July 1920), sanitarian, received his B.A. (1875) from the Univ. of the South. Unable to enter West Point, he was graduated from Bellevue Hospital Medical College (1879). After a year's internship at Bellevue, he was appointed (1880) to the U.S. Army Medical Corps. Surviving an epidemic of yellow fever at Ft. Brown, Tex., he was, due to his immunity, often assigned to posts where yellow fever was rampant. In 1898, following the occupation of Havana, he became chief sanitation officer of the city. Once the cause of yellow fever was established by Walter Reed, Gorgas succeeded in ridding the city of the disease by destroying the breeding places of the *Stegomyia* mosquito. Despite criticism, he introduced (1904) the same measures in the Panama Canal Zone, making Panama and Colón models of sanitation, and winning a worldwide reputation as a top sanitary expert. Appointed surgeon general of the army with the rank of brigadier general (1914), he was sent (1916) by the International Health Board to Central and South America on yellow fever missions. During World War I he served as head of the army Medical Service, and, when the war ended, on a yellow fever mission to the west coast of Africa. He wrote *Sanitation in Panama* (1915).

Graham, Martha (b. Pittsburgh, Pa., 11 May, c.1894–), dancer and choreographer, studied with Ruth St. Denis and Ted Shawn in Los Angeles and toured with their company. Her first professional appearance, with Shawn (1920), was followed by 2 years as solo dancer with the *Greenwich Village Follies* (1923–24). Her first recital with pupils came at the 48th Street Theater,

New York City (18 Apr. 1926). In 1930 Graham founded a Dance Repertory Theater. She taught at the Neighborhood Playhouse, the Juilliard School of Music, and founded Dance Studio (1928) which became the Martha Graham School of Contemporary Dance (1938). Graham was the first dancer to receive a Guggenheim Fellowship (1932). She enlarged the expressive possibilities of dance by her emotionality, her sense that movement is communicative, and by her strict technique with its distinctive vocabulary of contractions and contortions. She explored universal meanings in myth (*Alcestis*, 1960), religion (*Embattled Garden*, 1959), mystery (*El Penitente*, 1940), and in the conflicts of the individual psyche. She sought out as themes the basic forces of life—love, ecstasy, evil, and death—seen largely from the viewpoint of woman. She added to the theatrical possibilities of dance by employing dream sequences, flashbacks, symbolism, by collaborating with leading sculptors (Isamu Noguchi, *Seraphic Dialogue*, 1955), and by attention to costume and to color. A remarkable dancer, she starred in most of her own works and dominated the stage with a commanding "totemic" presence. Other major works include *Primitive Mysteries* (1931), *Letter to the World* (1940), *Appalachian Spring* (1944), *Night Journey* (1947), *Diversion of Angels* (1948), *Phaedra* (1962), *Clytemnestra* (1958). As a teacher, Graham's influence has been felt throughout contemporary dance. Her pupils have included Paul Taylor, Merce Cunningham, Erick Hawkins, Glen Tetley, and Anna Sokolow. Her company led off the Festival of Dance, 1968–69 (New York City), a turning point in the popular reception of modern dance. She retired as a dancer (1969) but reshaped her company to preserve her repertory and style. During her company's Broadway season (15 Apr.–4 May 1974) her 147th stage work, *Holy Jungle*, was premiered. The edited *Notebooks of Martha Graham* was published in 1973.

Grant, Ulysses Simpson (b. Point Pleasant, Ohio, 27 Apr. 1822; d. Mt. McGregor, near Saratoga, N.Y., 23 July 1885), 18th president of the U.S., was graduated from the U.S. Military Academy (1843). During the war with Mexico he served under Zachary Taylor and Winfield Scott (1845–48), being breveted captain for gallantry at Chapultepec. He served in California and Oregon until resigning from the army (1854), when he engaged in farming and real estate in St. Louis, Mo. (1854–60), and then clerked in his father's leather store in Galena, Ill. At the outbreak of the Civil War he was commissioned colonel, 21st Illinois Volunteer Infantry; then brigadier general of volunteers; and after capturing Forts Henry and Donelson (winning in the latter operation the sobriquet "Unconditional Surrender Grant"), he was promoted major general of volunteers (1862). Victor at Shiloh (Apr. 1862), he captured Vicksburg (4 July 1863) and won the Battle of Chattanooga (23–25 Nov. 1863). After driving the Confederates from Missionary Ridge and raising the siege of Chattanooga, he was given supreme command of the Union forces, with revived rank of lieutenant general (Mar. 1864). In a campaign of attrition (Wilderness, Spotsylvania, Cold Harbor, 5 May–3 June 1864), he wore down Lee's resistance and, finally, by capturing Petersburg forced his surrender at Appomattox, Va. (9 Apr. 1865). Commissioned general (1866), he was appointed Secretary of War ad interim (12 Aug. 1867–14 Jan. 1968). Republican nominee, he was elected and reelected president of the U.S. (1869–77). Among the constructive achievements of his administration were the funding of the national debt, the resumption of specie payments (1875), the inauguration of civil service reform, and the negotiation of the Treaty of Washington with Great Britain (8 May 1871). On the debit side were involvements in scandals, notably the Fisk-Gould attempt to corner the gold market (1869); Crédit Mobilier (1873); the resignation of Secretary of the Treasury W. A. Richardson (1874) to escape a vote of censure by Congress; the implication in the Whisky Ring of O. E. Babcock, Grant's private secretary; and the resignation of Secretary of War W. W. Belknap (1876) to escape impeachment for bribe taking. His administration also had to weather the severe depression which followed the Panic of 1873. After a world tour (1877–80) Grant lost his fortune through the bankruptcy of Grant & Ward (1884), but it was recouped by his writing his *Personal Memoirs* (1885), which earned nearly $500,000. In his later years he also served as president of the Mexican Southern R.R.

Gray, Asa (b. Sauquoit, Oneida Co., N.Y., 18 Nov. 1810; d. Cambridge, Mass., 30 Jan. 1888), botanist, received his M.D. (1831) from the Fairfield (N.Y.) Medical School, but soon he abandoned medicine for his study of plants and brought out his first independent publication, *North American Gramineae and Cyperaceae* (2 pts., 1834–35). He published his first botanical textbook, *Elements of Botany* (1836), and with John Torrey collaborated on *The Flora of North America* (2 vols., 1838–43). In 1842, when he published the first edition of his *Botanical Text-Book*, he was appointed Fisher professor of natural history at Harvard, a post he held until his retirement in 1873. The leading American botanist of his time, he was one of the founders of the National Academy of Science, president (1863–73) of the American Academy of Arts and Sciences,

and president (1872) of the American Association for the Advancement of Science. He made valuable contributions to the descriptive botany of North America, in which his most important work was *Manual of the Botany of the Northern United States* (1848 and subsequent editions). He also elaborated the botanical findings of the Wilkes Expedition in *United States Exploring Expedition during the Years 1838–42* (1854–57, 1874). It was to Gray that Charles Darwin wrote the letter (5 Sept. 1857) first outlining his theory of evolution. Gray became the chief American exponent of the Darwinian concepts, defending them against the attacks of Louis Agassiz (*q.v.*).

Greeley, Horace (b. Amherst, N.H., 3 Feb. 1811; d. New York City, 29 Nov. 1872), newspaper editor and reformer. He served his newspaper apprenticeship (c.1825–30) with the *Northern Spectator* at East Poultney, Vt.; arrived (1831) at New York City where he engaged in job printing and founded (1834) a weekly literary and news journal, the *New Yorker;* and edited and published 2 Whig journals, the *Jeffersonian* (1838) and the *Log Cabin* (1840). He founded (1841) the New York *Tribune,* which in its daily and weekly editions was influential in shaping political opinion in the Northern and Western parts of the U.S., and served as the vehicle for Greeley's social and economic views, including Fourierism, antislavery sentiment, temperance, women's rights, homestead legislation, and the protective tariff. He originated the phrase "Go West, young man." Until 1854 he maintained political alliance with William H. Seward (*q.v.*) and Thurlow Weed. One of the founders of the Republican party, he supported the nomination of Lincoln at the Chicago convention (1860), but during the war aligned himself with the radical antislavery faction and at times pursued an erratic course on the prosecution of the war. His attempt to bring about direct peace negotiations in the summer of 1864 ended in a fiasco. After the war he favored a liberal policy toward the South. In 1872, as the Liberal Republican candidate for the presidency, he made a poor showing against Grant.

Greene, Nathanael (b. Potowomut, now Warwick, R.I., 7 Aug. 1742; d. Mulberry Grove, near Savannah, Ga., 19 June 1786), Revolutionary general, served as deputy (1770–72, 1775) to the Rhode Island General Assembly, was appointed brigadier (May 1775) in charge of 3 regiments authorized by Rhode Island, and was named (22 June 1775) a brigadier general in the Continental army. He served through the siege of Boston, and after its evacuation by the British (Mar. 1776) was placed in command of the army of occupation. He was promoted (9 Aug. 1776) to major general in the Continental army, took part in the defensive operations in and around New York City, and played an important role in Washington's surprise assault on the British at Trenton (Dec. 1776). He participated in the Battle of Germantown (1777), went into winter quarters at Valley Forge, and was appointed (25 Feb. 1778) quartermaster general, in which capacity he reorganized and improved the supply system. He took part in the battles of Monmouth (1778) and Newport (1778). Difficulties with Congress and members of the "Conway Cabal" led to his resignation as quartermaster general. He was acting commander of the Continental army when Benedict Arnold's plot was brought to light, and served (1780) as president of the board of general officers which condemned Maj. John André to the gallows. Following the defeat of Gen. Horatio Gates at Camden, S.C. (1780), Washington chose Greene (14 Oct. 1780) to command the Revolutionary forces in the Southern theater. Carrying out an extensive program of reorganization and refitting, Greene assembled an army that included subordinate commanders such as Henry Lee and Francis Marion. To face Lord Cornwallis, he divided his forces. One division under Morgan defeated Tarleton at Cowpens (17 Jan. 1781). Cornwallis then turned upon Greene, who drained British strength at Guilford Court House, N.C. (15 Mar. 1781) and Hobkirk's Hill (26 Apr. 1781), forcing the British withdrawal from Camden. He defeated the British at the Battle of Eutaw Springs (8 Sept. 1781) and compelled the enemy to fall back on Charleston. The triumph of the Patriot forces in the South was largely due to his generalship.

Griffith, David Lewelyn Wark (b. La Grange, Ky., 22 Jan. 1875; d. Hollywood, Calif., 23 July 1948), motion picture director and producer. After being connected with the stage for almost a decade, he played his first movie role in *The Eagle's Nest*, made at the Edison Studio, and in 1908 joined the Biograph Co. as an assistant director, remaining with that unit until 1912. His first film was *The Adventures of Dollie*. Griffith won fame with *The Birth of a Nation*, which was made in 1914 and had its premiere at New York City on 3 Mar. 1915. Based on *The Clansman*, a novel by Thomas Dixon, Jr., *The Birth of a Nation* was produced on a $100,000 budget and earned approximately $48 million by the time Griffith died. Among the better known of the 500 pictures directed and produced by Griffith are *Intolerance* (1916), *Broken Blossoms* (1919), *Way Down East* (1920), *Orphans of the Storm* (1922), and *America* (1924). He was one of the founders of the United Artists Corp. in 1919, and retired in 1932. Among the foremost pioneers in the art of the motion picture,

Griffith introduced technical devices such as the fade-out and fade-in, cross-cutting, long shots for crowd scenes, high and low angle shots, soft focus, mist photography, the vignette, the vista backlighting and tinting. He did not introduce the close-up, but 1st used it for psychological and dramatic effects. His *Judith of Bethulia* was the first four-reeler.

Guggenheim, Daniel (b. Philadelphia, Pa., 9 July 1856; d. near Port Washington, N.Y., 28 Sept. 1930), industrialist and philanthropist, served his mercantile apprenticeship in Switzerland and upon his return to the U.S. (1884) became active in the copper mining and smelting business in which his father, Meyer Guggenheim (1828–1905), had made heavy investments. He soon became the leading figure among the 7 Guggenheim sons. It was largely due to his planning that the combination and integration of copper mining, smelting, and refining took place on a large scale. With his brothers, he took control (1901) of the reorganized American Smelting & Refining Co., of which he served as president or chairman of the board at different times between 1901 and 1919. Under his guidance the enterprise took shape as a vast industrial empire. It extended its activities to South America and Africa; developed nitrate fields in Chile, tin mines in Bolivia, and rubber plantations and diamond fields in the Belgian Congo; set up subsidiaries such as the Utah Copper Co., the Guggenheim Exploration Co., the Chile Copper Co., the Chile Nitrate Co.; and introduced mass production methods and technological improvements in mining and metallurgy. He established the Daniel and Florence Guggenheim Foundation and the Daniel Guggenheim Fund for the Promotion of Aeronautics; his brother, Simon (1867–1941), with his wife, the John Simon Guggenheim Memorial Foundation.

Hall, Granville Stanley (b. Ashfield, Mass., 1 Feb. 1844; d. Worcester, Mass., 24 Apr. 1924), psychologist, educator. He received his B.A. from Williams College (1867), and attended the Union Theological Seminary for a year before going to Germany, where he studied experimental psychology (1868–72). Returning to the U.S., he taught literature and psychology at Antioch College (1872–76), and English at Harvard (1876–77), where, studying under William James, he earned his Ph.D. (1878). After further studies in Germany, where he worked with L. F. von Helmholtz and Wilhelm M. Wundt, he became a lecturer in the new field of educational psychology at Harvard (1880–81). At Johns Hopkins, where he taught psychology and pedagogics (1881–89), he established one of the first psychology laboratories in the U.S. (1883). Applying the ideas of Darwin, Freud, Wundt, and others, his studies contributed to the development of the discipline. Among his many outstanding students were John Dewey (*q.v.*) and James McKeen Cattell. He founded and, at various times, edited journals which contributed to the growth of experimental psychology and child psychology in the U.S.: *American Journal of Psychology* (1887), *Pedagogical Seminar* (1891), *Journal of Religious Psychology and Education* (1902), *Journal of Applied Psychology* (1915). He was one of the organizers, and was first president of the American Psychological Association, founded in 1891. Author of some 490 published works, his major books include: *The Content of Children's Minds on Entering School* (1883), which gave great impetus to the new field of child psychology, *Adolescence* (1904), *Youth* (1906), *Educational Problems* (1911), *Jesus the Christ, in the Light of Psychology* (1917), and *Senescence* (1922). First president of Clark Univ. (1889–1920), he established there the first institute of child psychology in the U.S. and developed ambitious programs of graduate study in the fields of education and psychology.

Hamilton, Alexander (b. Nevis, B.W.I., 11 Jan. 1755; d. New York City, 12 July 1804), statesman. After clerking at St. Croix, left for New York in 1773, in which year he entered King's College, where he wrote pamphlets in the Patriot cause (1774–75). At the outbreak of the Revolution he organized an artillery company and gained Washington's attention by his skillful conduct in campaigns around New York City. With rank of lieutenant colonel he served as Washington's private secretary and aide-de-camp (1777–81). At his request he was given command of troops and fought at Yorktown (1781). Married (1780) Elizabeth, daughter of Philip Schuyler. After a year in Congress (1782–83), he began law practice in New York. As a delegate from New York to the Annapolis Convention (1786) he drafted report which led to the assembling of the Constitutional Convention (1787), where he advocated an extremely strong central government. He worked wholeheartedly for the ratification of the Constitution, writing some fifty-one of the *Federalist* papers (1787–88), and carrying the New York convention (1788) despite strong opposition. As first Secretary of the Treasury (1789–95), he devised the U.S. fiscal program (1790), recommending the funding of both the foreign and domestic debt at par, assumption by the federal government of Revolutionary state debts, and supplementing revenue from duties with an excise tax to bring national authority home to every citizen. He also recommended the creation of a national bank (1791), which he justified under the "implied powers" of the Constitution, and tariffs for industry, bounties for agriculture, and federally sponsored

internal improvements (1791). His policies ("Hamiltonian system") were supported by the Federalists and opposed by the Jeffersonian Republicans (1792). Resigning from the cabinet, he resumed law practice in New York, interrupted by assuming command of the army, second only to Washington, when war with France appeared likely (1798–1800). Federalist leader of New York, he was in opposition to President John Adams. By throwing support to Jefferson (1800) he thwarted Aaron Burr's ambitions for the presidency and killed his chances for the governorship of New York (1804). Challenged by Burr to a duel on account of his acrimonious comments, he was fatally shot at Weehawken, N.J., and died the following day.

Hammerstein, Oscar, 2d (b. New York City, 12 July 1895; d. Doylestown, Pa., 23 Aug. 1960), librettist, was graduated from Columbia (B.A., 1916), and quickly won acclaim for the books and lyrics he wrote, often in collaboration, for many Broadway musicals. Notable among his early productions were *Rose Marie* (music by Rudolf Friml, 1924); the *Desert Song* (1926) and *New Moon* (1928), for both of which Sigmund Romberg wrote the music; and his adaptation of Edna Ferber's novel *Show Boat* (1927) to Jerome Kern's score. His collaboration with Richard Rodgers (*q.v.*) established the musical comedy, employing serious plots and sometimes serious overtones, as a distinctively American contribution to the drama. Their first smash hit, *Oklahoma!* (1943, special Pulitzer award, 1944), was followed by *Carousel* (1945), based on Molnar's *Liliom;* the international success *South Pacific* (Pulitzer prize award for drama, 1949); and *The King and I* (1951). At the time of Hammerstein's death their last joint production, *The Sound of Music,* was playing on Broadway. The songs of Rodgers and Hammerstein quickly became American classics, among them "The Surrey with the Fringe on Top," "You'll Never Walk Alone," "Bali H'ai," "I'm in Love with a Wonderful Guy," "Do-Re-Mi."

Hancock, John (b. North Braintree, now Quincy, Mass., 12 Jan. 1737; d. there, 8 Oct. 1793), merchant and Revolutionary leader, first signer of the Declaration of Independence. He was graduated from Harvard (1754) and entered the shipping trade; became (1763) a partner in the leading Boston mercantile house of Thomas Hancock & Co., and its head in 1764. He took part in the protest (1765) against the Stamp Act and in 1768 was defended by John Adams in a *cause célèbre* involving the seizure by customs officers of Hancock's sloop *Liberty* on charges of illegal trading. He was elected (1769) to the Massachusetts General Court, became (1770) head of the Boston town committee, and thereafter took a leading part in the Patriot cause. Elected (1774) president of the Massachusetts Provincial Congress, he and Samuel Adams were singled out for punishment in Gov. Gage's proclamation (12 June 1775) and expressly denied amnesty. In 1775 he was chosen delegate to the 2d Continental Congress, of which he served as president (24 May 1775–29 Oct. 1777). Alone with Charles Thomson, secretary of the Congress, he signed the Declaration of Independence 4 July 1776. The other delegates affixed their signatures later. In 1780 he was elected the first governor of Massachusetts, serving (1780–85, 1787–93) in that capacity for 9 terms. Again elected president of the Continental Congress on 23 Nov. 1785, illness prevented him from serving, and he resigned on 29 May 1786. He presided (1788) over the Massachusetts convention for ratifying the Federal Constitution.

Hand, Learned (b. Albany, N.Y., 27 Jan. 1872; d. New York City, 18 Aug. 1961), jurist, was graduated summa cum laude from Harvard (1893); returned to secure his M.A. the following year, and his LL.B. from Harvard Law School (1896). Admitted to the New York bar (1897), he clerked or practiced in Albany (1897–1902), then moved to New York City (1902), becoming a member (1904) of the firm of Gould & Wilkie. U.S. District Judge, southern district of New York (1909–24), he ran unsuccessfully (1913) as a Progressive for the post of Chief Judge of the New York Court of Appeals. He served as Judge of the U.S. Circuit Court, 2d Circuit, from 1924 until his retirement (1951), rendering notable opinions in the fields of maritime law, taxation, banking, trademarks, and labor law. In the antitrust suit against the Aluminum Co. of America he declared: "Congress did not condone 'good trusts' and condemn 'bad' ones; it forbade all." He upheld (1950) the conviction of the 11 Communist leaders under the Smith Act, interpreting Justice Holmes's "clear and present danger" test to mean that the courts must ascertain "whether the gravity of the 'evil,' discounted by its improbability, justifies such invasion of free speech as is necessary to avoid the danger." A literary craftsman and master of epigram, he made numerous addresses, including his eloquent "The Spirit of Liberty," delivered (1944) at an "I Am an American Day" ceremony in Central Park, New York (pub. with other papers, 1952). Recognizing the values of detachment, skepticism, and nonconformity, he regarded the key to his philosophy to be epitomized in Oliver Cromwell's plea before the Battle of Dunbar: "I beseech ye in the bowels of Christ, think that ye may be mistaken."

Hanna, Marcus Alonzo (b. New Lisbon, Ohio, 24 Sept. 1837; d. Washington,

D.C., 15 Feb. 1904), businessman and politician, attended Western Reserve College for a brief time, entered the grocery and commission business at Cleveland, and in 1867 transferred his interests to the coal and iron trade in that city, becoming (1885) head of the firm of M. A. Hanna & Co. He also helped establish the Union National Bank, became owner of the Cleveland Opera House and the Cleveland *Herald,* and dominated the city's street railway system. Active in local politics, he was chosen a member of the Republican state committee and soon became a power in Ohio politics. A break between him and Joseph B. Foraker in 1888 led Hanna to support Congressman William McKinley, whom he backed for the Ohio governorship (1891, 1893) and groomed as a presidential candidate. In 1894–95 Hanna withdrew from business activity to devote himself to launching a McKinley boom. A skilled and astute political manager, Hanna conducted a preconvention McKinley campaign for which he paid most of the financial cost. McKinley was nominated on the first ballot at the Republican convention in 1896. In recognition of his political ability, Hanna was chosen chairman of the Republican national committee. Chiefly by levies on businessmen and corporations, Hanna raised the unprecedented sum of $3,500,000 for the Republican national campaign. He was elected (1897) to the Senate, where he defended large corporate enterprises and supported ship subsidies and the Panama route for an isthmian canal. He was an intimate adviser to Presidents McKinley and Theodore Roosevelt. Although Hanna became in the public mind almost synonymous with big business, he supported labor's right to organize and was chairman of the executive committee of the National Civic Federation. Shortly before his death there were signs that powerful Republican elements in the East were hoping to secure for him the presidential nomination in 1904.

Harding, Warren Gamaliel (b. Corsica, Ohio, 2 Nov. 1865; d. San Francisco, Calif., 2 Aug. 1923), 29th president of the U.S., attended Ohio Central College, Iberia (1879–82), studied law briefly, and (1884) became owner and editor of Marion *Star,* weekly, later a daily. He entered Republican politics as a protégé of Sen. Joseph B. Foraker, was elected to the state senate (1900–04), became lieutenant governor (1904–06), but was defeated in the gubernatorial election (1910). U.S. senator from Ohio (1915–21), he supported the 18th Amendment and the Volstead Act, and was known for his party regularity. At the Republican National Convention (1920) he was designated by the party leaders and nominated after a deadlock in the balloting between Gen. Leonard Wood and Frank O. Lowden. Straddling the League issue and pledging a "return to normalcy," he was elected by a landslide vote. Despite appointments to his cabinet of men of such standing as Hughes and Hoover, many of his choices were mediocrities (Attorney General Harry M. Daugherty of the "Ohio Gang" and Secretary of the Interior Albert B. Fall). The major achievement of his administration was the Washington Conference for naval limitation (1921–22). On a return trip from Alaska he died suddenly at San Francisco. Subsequent exposure of corruption in the Departments of Interior, Justice, and Navy, the Veterans Bureau, and Alien Property Custodian stamped his administration as both corrupt and incompetent.

Harlan, John Marshall (b. Boyle Co., Ky., 1 June 1833; d. Washington, D.C., 14 Oct. 1911), jurist, was graduated from Centre College (1850), studied law at Transylvania Univ. and was admitted to the Kentucky bar (1859). Adjutant general of Kentucky (1851) and judge of Franklin Co. (1858), he served in the Civil War as colonel, 10th Kentucky Infantry (1861–63). State attorney general (1863–67), unsuccessful candidate for governor in 1871 and again in 1875, he was appointed by President Hayes associate justice of the U.S. Supreme Court (1877–1911). A notable author of dissenting opinions, Harlan opposed the narrow interpretation of the federal commerce power in the sugar-trust cases (1895). He vigorously challenged the decisions holding the income tax unconstitutional (1895) and that invalidating a state maximum-hour law for bakers. Harlan was the sole dissenter from decisions holding that the Civil Rights Act did not reach invasion of civil rights by individuals (1883) and sanctioning state-sponsored racial segregation (1896). Harlan wrote the majority opinion rejuvenating the Sherman Antitrust Act (1904), maintained in the *Insular Cases* (1901) that "the Constitution followed the flag," and declared federal legislation barring "yellow-dog" contracts in railroad employment to infringe upon the 5th Amendment (1907).

Harper, William Rainey (b. New Concord, Ohio, 24 July 1856; d. Chicago, Ill., 10 Jan. 1906), educator and scholar, was graduated (1870) from Muskingum College where he taught Hebrew (1872–73), and in 1874, received a Ph.D. at Yale. He taught at Denison Univ., Granville, Ohio, from 1876 to 1879, when he became teacher of Semitic languages at the Baptist Union Theological Seminary in Chicago, and at Yale (1881–86), and was active in the Chautauqua movement, giving summer courses in Semitic languages and Biblical studies. In 1891 he assumed the presidency of the newly founded Univ. of Chicago, a post he held until his death. He introduced

such features as the university press, university extension, the summer quarter, and the division of the academic year into 4 quarters. He guided the Univ. of Chicago through the complex period of initial growth and was instrumental in assembling there a faculty that was among the most brilliant of its time. His work as a Hebraist produced *The Priestly Element in the Old Testament* (1902), *The Prophetic Element in the Old Testament* (1905), and *Critical and Exegetical Commentary on Amos and Hosea* (1905).

Harriman, William Averell (b. New York City, 15 Nov. 1891–), statesman and businessman, son of Edward H. Harriman of the Union Pacific R.R., graduated from Yale (1913). Vice-president of the Union Pacific and director of the Illinois Central (1915–32), he expanded his railroad inheritance—becoming chairman of the board of Merchant Shipbuilding Corp. (1917–25); founding (1921) the investment banking firm W. A. Harriman and Co.; and acquiring major interests in numerous other corporate enterprises. Originally a Republican, he became a Democrat when he supported Alfred E. Smith's presidential candidacy (1928). He first entered government service as a divisional administrator for the National Recovery Administration (1934–35). After serving as an official in the Department of Commerce (1937–40) he moved to the Office of Production Management and, after 3 months, was sent (1941) as a special representative of the president to Great Britain and the U.S.S.R. to coordinate the flow of U.S. military aid to those nations. He held the posts of ambassador to the U.S.S.R. (1943–46) and to Great Britain (1946)—relinquishing the latter after only 6 months to become Secretary of Commerce (1946–48). Resuming his diplomatic career, he was U.S. representative in Europe under the Economic Cooperation Act of 1948 (1948–50) and served as director of the Mutual Security Agency (1951–53). Entering electoral politics, he ran successfully for governor of New York (1954) but failed in his bids for the Democratic presidential nomination (1956) and for reelection as governor (1958). In 1961 President Kennedy appointed him Assistant Secretary of State for Far Eastern Affairs and 2 years later he was named Under Secretary of State for Political Affairs (1963–65). As ambassador-at-large (1965–69), he undertook a number of roving assignments—notably, that of chief negotiator (1968–69) at the Vietnam peace talks in Paris. Though never realizing his great ambition to become Secretary of State, he dealt with virtually every world leader prominent during his time and was highly respected as an effective negotiator.

Harris, Joel Chandler (b. near Eatonton, Ga., 9 Dec. 1848; d. Atlanta, 3 July 1908), journalist, author, became (1862) printer's devil for Joseph Addison Turner's *Countryman*. He worked for 6 months (1866) for the publisher of the New Orleans *Crescent Monthly*, but thereafter never left his home state except for brief trips. A growing reputation as a humorist earned him a position on the Savannah *Morning News*, and then with the Atlanta *Constitution*, His "Uncle Remus Stories," first published in the Atlanta *Constitution*, made that paper nationally famous. His first collection, *Uncle Remus, His Songs and His Sayings* (1880), was enormously popular, especially the "Tar-Baby" story (1904), and was followed by a series down to 1918. A master of dialect, he used folk tales, but the dialogue and characters of Uncle Remus and Br'er Rabbit (1907) and the world of animals were uniquely his own. In *Mingo and Other Sketches in Black and White* (1884) and *Free Joe*

and Other Sketches (1887), he captured the white Georgia cracker on printed page.

Harris, Townsend (b. Sandy Hill, N.Y., 3 Oct. 1804; d. New York City, 25 Feb. 1878), diplomat, was largely self-educated, beginning work in a dry-goods store in New York City at 13. Later he established a family partnership for importing china. Elected to the Board of Education as a Democrat (1846), he launched a ,vigorous campaign, against strong opposition, for a free city college, and carried through the necessary legislation to establish (1847) the College of the City of New York. Following his mother's death (1847), the bachelor Harris bought a trading ship and made trips in the Pacific and Indian oceans. In 1853 he applied for a consular post. First assigned (1855) to Ningpo, China, he managed, through the influence of Secretary of State William L. Marcy and Seward, to be named consul general to Japan (1855), a post resulting from ratification of the Perry Treaty. Responsible for the first U.S.-Japanese commercial agreement (17 June 1857) and the treaty of 29 July 1858, he exercised at Yeddo (Tokyo) great influence over the Japanese government. Resigning his post with Lincoln's election, he returned to New York and became a War Democrat.

Harrison, Benjamin (b. North Bend, Ohio, 20 Aug. 1833; d. Indianapolis, Ind., 13 Mar. 1901), 23d president of the U.S., grandson of William Henry Harrison, 9th president, was graduated from Miami Univ. (1852), admitted to the Cincinnati bar (1853), commenced practice in Indianapolis (1854), and was reporter of Indiana supreme court, 1860–62, and again, 1864–68, after service in the Civil War (commissioned 2d lt.; raised 70th Indiana Regiment and became its col.). Defeated as Republican candidate for governor of Indiana

(1876), he declined a post in Garfield's cabinet, having been elected to the U.S. Senate (1881–87), where he opposed Cleveland's pension vetoes and advocated civil service reform. Defeated for reelection, he was the Republican nominee for president (1888) and defeated Cleveland. During his administration (1889–93) the McKinley Tariff and Sherman Silver Act were passed, Civil War pensions were augmented, and imperialist policies pressed in the Pacific. Renominated (1892), he was defeated by Cleveland, and resumed his law practice, serving as chief counsel for Venezuela in arbitration of her boundary dispute with Great Britain.

Harrison, William Henry (b. Berkeley, Charles City Co., Va., 9 Feb. 1773; d. Washington, D.C., 4 Apr. 1841), 9th president of the U.S., attended Hampden-Sidney College (1787–90), studied medicine briefly at the Univ. of Pennsylvania, then entered the army, attaining a captaincy, resigning (1798) to accept appointment as Secretary of the Northwest Territory. He was elected its first delegate to Congress (1799) and was the drafter of the Land Act of 1800. Appointed by President John Adams first governor of Indiana Territory (1801–12), and as special commissioner to deal with the Indians he negotiated several boundary treaties. Confronted with Indian resistance under Tecumseh to further white encroachments, he won a nominal victory at Tippecanoe (7 Nov. 1811), and during the War of 1812, when he held the rank of major general, he decisively defeated both the British and the Indians at the Battle of the Thames (5 Oct. 1813). Congressman from Ohio (1816–19), state senator (1819–21), U.S. senator from Ohio (1825–28), he was appointed U.S. minister to Colombia (1828), but recalled by Jackson the following year. Retiring to North Bend, Ohio, he became clerk of the common pleas court of Hamilton Co. Candidate for the presidency on one of the Whig tickets (1836), with Anti-Masonic support, he was defeated by Van Buren, but was the successful Whig nominee (1840), staging his "log cabin and hard cider" campaign. He died of pneumonia a month after his inauguration.

Hawthorne, Nathaniel (b. Salem, Mass., 4 July 1804; d. Plymouth, N.H., 18/19 May 1864), novelist and writer of tales. Born of Puritan ancestry, he was graduated from Bowdoin College (1825) and returned to Salem, where he led a secluded life devoted to the mastery of his craft. He issued at his own expense the anonymously published novel *Fanshawe* (1828), and began publishing in the *Token,* an annual brought out by Samuel G. Goodrich, the stories later collected in *Twice-Told Tales* (1837; enlarged ed., 1842). He was editor (1836) of the *American Magazine of Useful and Entertaining Knowledge,* also published by Goodrich, for whom he compiled *Peter Parley's Universal History* (1837) and wrote children's books such as *Grandfather's Chair* (1841), *Famous Old People* (1841), *Liberty Tree* (1841), and *Biographical Stories for Children* (1842). With the aid of Franklin Pierce, whom he had known at Bowdoin, he secured a post as weigher and gauger (1839–41) in the Boston Custom House. He spent several months (1841–42) at Brook Farm, which furnished him with the setting for *The Blithedale Romance* (1852); was married (9 July 1842) to Sophia Amelia Peabody of Salem; settled in the Old Manse at Concord (1842–45); and was surveyor of the port of Salem from 1846 to 1849, during which time he published *Mosses from an Old Manse* (1846). His best-known novel, *The Scarlet Letter* (1850), dealt with the moral decadence of 17th-century New England Puritanism, and was followed by *The House of the Seven Gables* (1851), *The Snow Image and Other Twice-Told Tales* (1852), *A Wonder-Book for Girls and Boys* (1852), and *Tanglewood Tales for Girls and Boys* (1853). In 1850 Hawthorne moved to Lenox, Mass., where he became acquainted with Herman Melville, but in a few years returned to Concord. As a reward for writing a campaign biography, *The Life of Franklin Pierce* (1852), he was appointed (1853) U.S. consul at Liverpool, a post he held until 1860. The last books by him published during his lifetime were *The Marble Faun* (1860) and *Our Old Home* (1863). Among his other works are *Passages from the American Notebooks* (1868), *Passages from the English Notebooks* (1870), *Septimius Felton* (1871), *Passages from the French and Italian Notebooks* (1871), *The Dolliver Romance* (1876), *Dr. Grimshawe's Secret* (1883), and *The Ancestral Footstep* (1883). Among his better-known tales are "Ethan Brand," "The Great Stone Face," "The Maypole of Merrymount," "Dr. Heidegger's Experiment," and "The Ambitious Guest."

Hay, John Milton (b. Salem, Ind., 12 Oct. 1838; d. Lake Sunapee, N.H., 1 July 1905), statesman, was graduated from Brown Univ. (1858), admitted to the Illinois bar (1861), and practiced in Springfield, where he was drawn into the Lincoln circle. Accompanying Lincoln to Washington as assistant private secretary, he served until the president's death. Subsequently he was 1st secretary of legation at Paris (1865–67) and Madrid (1868–70) and chargé d'affaires at Vienna (1867–68). On his return to the U.S. (1870), he became an editorial writer on the New York *Tribune* (1870–75), then moved to Cleveland, returning to Washington as assistant secretary of state

under William M. Evarts (1879–81). McKinley's ambassador to Great Britain (1897–98) and thereafter, until his death, McKinley's and Theodore Roosevelt's Secretary of State (1898–1905), he supported the Open Door policy in China, and concluded the Hay-Pauncefote Treaty with Great Britain (1900–01) and the Hay-Herrán and Hay-Bunau-Varilla treaties with Colombia and Panama respectively. Poet and novelist, as well as historian, he published *Pike County Ballads* and *Castilian Days* (1871), the antilabor union novel *The Bread Winners* (anon., 1883), and, in collaboration with John G. Nicolay, *Abraham Lincoln: A History* (10 vols., 1890), and *Abraham Lincoln: Complete Works* (2 vols., 1894).

Hayes, Rutherford Birchard (b. Delaware, Ohio, 4 Oct. 1822; d. Fremont, Ohio, 17 Jan. 1893), 19th president of the U.S., was graduated from Kenyon College (1842) and Harvard Law School (1845); was admitted to the Ohio bar and commenced practice at Fremont (1845), removing to Cincinnati (1849). A Whig and then a Republican (from 1854), he was city solicitor (1858–61), resigning to become governor of Ohio (1868–72). Running on a "sound money" platform, he was elected for a 3d term (1875) and established himself as the logical candidate of the anti-Blaine forces at the Republican National Convention the following year, where he won the nomination. Although Tilden, the Democratic candidate, secured a larger popular vote, Hayes was adjudged by the partisan Electoral Commission to have obtained 1 more electoral vote (185–184). Despite party factional disputes and Democratic control of the lower house (1876) and of both houses (1878), his administration ended military reconstruction by withdrawal of federal troops from South Carolina

(1877) and made indecisive efforts toward civil service reform. On issues of labor and finance he was conservative, calling out federal troops to suppress the railroad strike (1877) and vetoing the Bland-Allison Silver Coinage Act (1878), which was passed over his veto.

Hearst, William Randolph (b. San Francisco, Calif., 29 Apr. 1863; d. Beverly Hills, Calif., 14 Aug. 1951), journalist. While at Harvard (1882–85), Hearst was financial editor of the *Harvard Lampoon*. He worked as a reporter for the New York *World* for several months and then took over his father's *San Francisco Examiner* (1887). In 1895 Hearst purchased the New York *Morning Journal*, where he boosted circulation by lowering the price and introducing sensational reportage of crime, society gossip, and comic strips in color. That newspaper's coverage of Spanish atrocities in Cuba sharply aroused the public and contributed to the Spanish-American War. Between 1885–1937, Hearst built a newspaper empire, publishing and personally editing during the latter year over 20 newspapers, including the New York *Evening Journal* (1896), *Chicago Examiner* (1902), and *Los Angeles Examiner* (1903). His papers took controversial positions, favoring reforms such as the 8-hour day, public ownership of utilities, and popular election of U.S. senators. Isolationist and anti-British, the newspapers were against U.S. entry into both world wars and into the League of Nations. Hearst also established King Features Syndicate (1914), published magazines including *Good Housekeeping* and *Harper's Bazaar*, and pioneered in movie newsreels (1913). He owned gold and silver mines and, at one time, was one of the leading real-estate owners in New York City, California, and Mexico. He moved permanently to his 240,-000-acre ranch at San Simeon (1927), where he amassed art and archaeological treasures. He served in the U.S. House of Representatives from New York City (1903–07) but ran unsuccessfully for the presidential nomination (1904), for mayor of New York City (1905, 1909), for governor of New York state (1906), and for Democratic nominee for senator (1922).

Hemingway, Ernest (b. Oak Park, Ill., 21 July 1898; d. Ketchum, Ida., 2 July 1961), novelist and short-story writer. After working as a reporter on the Kansas City *Star,* he went to France as a volunteer ambulance driver in World War I and then enlisted in the Italian army, winning 2 medals for battle actions in which he was wounded. After the war he served as a newspaper correspondent in the Near East for the Toronto *Star* and then settled in Paris, where he became associated with the expatriates of the "lost generation," whose leading spokesman he became. Hemingway spent most of his life abroad, chiefly in Europe and Cuba, and was a war correspondent during the Spanish Civil War and in France during World War II. His stories and novels, most of which are concerned with the disintegration of private values in a world between wars, are marked by a high level of craftsmanship and a terse prose style that has had a wide influence on writing in the U.S. and elsewhere. Hemingway's novels include *The Sun Also Rises* (1926), *A Farewell to Arms* (1929), *To Have and Have Not* (1937), *For Whom the Bell Tolls* (1940), *Across the River and into the Trees* (1950), and *The Old Man and the Sea* (1952). His volumes of short stories are *In Our Time* (1924), *Men Without Women* (1927), and *Winner Take Nothing* (1933), collected in *The Fifth Column and the First Forty-Nine Stories* (1938). *Death in the Afternoon* (1932) deals with bullfighting and *Green Hills of*

Africa (1935) is about big-game hunting. He was awarded the Nobel prize in literature in 1954 for *The Old Man and the Sea* (1952).

Henri, Robert (b. Robert Henry Cozed, Cincinnati, Ohio, 25 June 1865; d. New York City, 12 July 1929), artist and teacher, changed his name when his father became a fugitive from justice. He studied at the Pennsylvania Academy of Fine Arts (1886–88) under Thomas Anschutz and at the Académie Julien and the École des Beaux Arts in Paris (1888–91). Returning to the U.S., he enjoyed a distinguished teaching career at the Philadelphia School of Design for Women, beginning in 1891, and after 1899 at the New York School of Art, the Henri School, the radical Ferrer Center School, and the Art Students League. Rebelling against the narrow creed of "art for art's sake," but without abandoning technical excellence, Henri was a leading spokesman for better exhibition opportunities for newer painters. Henri was a member of "The Eight," or "The Ash Can School," a group of realists whom he encouraged to record the dramas of urban life. After the National Academy refused their canvases (1908), Henri withdrew his own pictures and organized the exhibition of "The Eight." Shocking the conservative art world, they protested also the excessive Europeanization of American painting. Although his work was exhibited at the Armory Show (1913), it was not in tune with some of his more radical contemporaries. His brushwork showed the influence of Hals and Monet, and in later years drew upon the color system of Hardesty Maratta. His work was not bloodlessly refined but healthy and vigorous. The subjects for most of his portraits painted during the years 1906–14 were men and women from all over the world, including Irishmen, Indians from New

Mexico, and Yankees. Some of his best known paintings are *Young Woman in White* (1904, National Gallery, Washington), *Himself and Herself* (both 1913, Art Institute of Chicago), *The Laughing Girl* (1910, Brooklyn Museum); and *The Spanish Gypsy* (c. 1906, Metropolitan). Henri inspired and motivated many students, including such notable ones as George Bellows, Stuart Davis, Edward Hopper, Yasao Kuniyoshi, Moses Soyer, and even Leon Trotsky.

Henry, Joseph (b. Albany, N.Y., 17 Dec. 1797; d. Washington, D.C., 13 May 1878), physicist. He attended the Albany Academy, where he became (1826) professor of mathematics and natural philosophy and carried out experiments in the magnetic fields created by electrical currents. In the course of these researches he improved William Sturgeon's electromagnet, increasing the magnetic condition of its core by an arrangement that is still the basis of the modern electromagnet. In a paper published in the *American Journal of Science* (Jan. 1831), Henry described his discovery of the quantity and intensity magnets, correctly predicting that the latter type would be used in the electromagnetic telegraph. His findings were indispensable to the commercial development of the telegraph. Another paper published by him on electromagnetic induction (July 1832) paralleled contemporaneous and independent researches by Faraday and led to Henry's important discoveries in self-induction (the modern practical unit of inductance, the henry, is named after him). In 1832 he was named professor of natural philosophy in the College of New Jersey, where his continued researches foreshadowed many of the developments in the modern science of electricity. He discovered (1842) the oscillatory nature of electrical discharge. In 1846 he was appointed the first secretary and director of the Smithsonian Institution at Washington, D.C.; his first report to its Board of Regents laid down the broad policies, particularly those relating to original research and the free diffusion of knowledge, that have since guided the Smithsonian. Henry introduced (c.1850) the system of transmitting weather reports by telegraph and using them for forecasting weather conditions, thus laying the foundation for the U.S. Weather Bureau. He also made valuable researches in fog signaling. One of the organizers of the American Association for the Advancement of Science, he was chosen its president (1849) and served as president of the National Academy of Science (1868–78).

Henry, Patrick (b. Hanover Co., Va., 29 May 1736; d. at his plantation, Red Hill, Charlotte Co., Va., 6 June 1799), Revolutionary patriot, orator, and statesman. After an early career as a storekeeper and farmer, he read law, was licensed to practice (1760), and soon became one of the leading lawyers in western Virginia. His fame as an orator began in 1763, when he appeared for the defense in the "parson's cause" and invoked the theory of mutual compact in making a plea against the royal disallowance of the "twopenny act" passed by the Virginia assembly. In 1765 he became a member of the House of Burgesses and emerged as a leader of the frontier and back-country elements in their contest with the conservative Tidewater interests. With the adoption of the Stamp Act, he proposed 7 resolutions (29 May 1765), one of which contended that Virginia enjoyed complete legislative autonomy, and in their behalf made the speech later reputed to have closed with the famous injunction: "Caesar had his Brutus—Charles the first, his Cromwell— and George the third—may profit by their example. . . . If *this* be treason, make the most of it." Under his leadership the

legislators gathered at Raleigh Tavern (27 May 1774), after Lord Dunmore dissolved the colonial assembly, and issued the calls for the Virginia convention and a Continental Congress. On 23 Mar. 1775, in a speech urging resistance to British policy and in advocating the establishment of an armed force, he declared: "Give me liberty, or give me death!" He was outlawed in a proclamation issued by Lord Dunmore (6 May 1775). Henry took his seat in the Continental Congress on 18 May 1775, helped draft the Virginia constitution of 1776, and as governor of Virginia (1776–79) dispatched in 1778 George Rogers Clark on a military mission to the Illinois country. After the war, Henry's political views changed sharply. He served again as governor (1784–86), but at the Virginia convention (1788) for ratifying the Constitution opposed its adoption as inimical to state sovereignty. A leader in the movement for the Bill of Rights, he wrote the Virginia appeal to the 1st Congress and the other states for amendments to the Constitution. In his closing years he was a Federalist.

Hill, James Jerome (b. near Rockwood, Ontario, Canada, 16 Sept. 1838; d. St. Paul, Minn., 29 May 1916), railroad builder, went to work at the age of 14 as a clerk in a village store, lost the sight of an eye by the accidental discharge of an arrow, and in 1856 became clerk in St. Paul, Minn., in a steamboat transportation firm. By 1865 he had gone into the forwarding and transportation business for himself, organized (1870) the Red River Transportation Co., and joined (1878) a syndicate that built the Canadian Pacific R.R. and purchased (1878) the St. Paul and Pacific R.R., which was expanded (1890) into the Great Northern R.R., from Lake Superior to Puget Sound. Without the aid of government land grants, Hill's line weathered financial storms. Together with J. P. Morgan, Hill was involved in a struggle with Edward H. Harriman and Jacob H. Schiff for control of the Northern Pacific R.R., which precipitated the stock market panic of 1901. The Northern Security Co., organized (1901) as a holding company of all Hill's interests, was dissolved by the U.S. Supreme Court (1904) as violating the Sherman Act. Because of his notable role in the development of the Northwest, Hill has been called the "empire builder."

Hillman, Sidney (b. Zagare, Lithuania, 23 Mar. 1887; d. Point Lookout, N.Y., 10 July 1946), labor leader, was educated at the Slobodka Rabbinical Seminary in Lithuania, and came to the U.S. in 1907, becoming a clothing worker with the Chicago firm of Hart, Schaffner, and Marx. The agreement which he negotiated with that firm (1911) formed the basis for the impartial chairman plan (1912), adopted by other industries. First president of the Amalgamated Clothing Workers (1914), he organized the New York, Rochester, Philadelphia, and Chicago industries and initiated such union activities as cooperative housing and banking. An advocate of industrial unionism, he quit the AFL (1935) to cofound the CIO, of which he became vice-president (1935–40) and headed the textile workers' organizing drive. Codirector of the Office of Production Management, later WPB (1940–42), he cofounded Labor's Non-Partisan League (1936) to support the reelection of Franklin D. Roosevelt and headed (1943) the CIO-PAC to support Roosevelt and congressmen sympathetic to labor. A central figure at the Democratic National Convention of 1944 ("Clear it with Sidney," F.D.R. told the party managers), he threw his support to Harry S. Truman for the vice-presidential nomination. Founder and chairman (1944–45) of the American Labor party, he was instrumental in setting up the World Federation of Trade Unions (1945).

Hoe, Richard March (b. New York City, 12 Sept. 1812; d. Florence, Italy, 7 June 1886), inventor and manufacturer. Educated in the public schools of New York, he entered (1827) the printing-press factory owned by his father, whom he succeeded in 1830. At about that time the Hoe Co. was manufacturing a single small cylinder press; in 1837 the double small cylinder press improved by Hoe was perfected and put into production; and during the same period Hoe designed and introduced the single large cylinder press, the first flat bed and cylinder press ever used in America. To meet the demands of newspaper publishers, Hoe invented and designed (1845–46) the rotary printing press, the first of which, capable of printing 8,000 papers an hour, was installed (1847) in the plant of the Philadelphia *Public Ledger*. This machine was the predecessor of the web press (1871) designed by Hoe and Stephen D. Tucker. First installed in the plant of the New York *Tribune,* the web press printed simultaneously from a continuous roll of paper both sides of a sheet at the rate of 18,000 papers an hour. Hoe also introduced the stop cylinder press (1853) and devised the triangular form folder (1881). The latter, in combination with the web press and the curved stereotype plate, is the foundation of the modern newspaper printing press.

Holmes, Oliver Wendell (b. Cambridge, Mass., 29 Aug. 1809; d. Boston, 7 Oct. 1894), author and physician, was graduated from Harvard (1829), studied law for a year, and then turned to medicine, graduating from Harvard Medical School (1836) and studying in Paris (1833–35). He commenced practice in Boston (1836); was professor of anatomy at Dartmouth (1838–40) and Parkman professor of anatomy and physiology at Harvard Medical School (1847–82) as well as dean (1847–53). His medical papers include "Homeopathy and Its Kindred Delusions" (1842) and, most notable, "The Contagiousness of Puerperal Fever" (1843), in which he demonstrated, statistically, that the disease was spread by contagion, a position which, despite criticism, was entirely vindicated by Semmelweis' study (1861). Accomplished as a poet ("Old Ironsides," 1830; "The Chambered Nautilus," "Wonderful One-Hoss Shay"), he was especially renowned as lecturer, conversationalist, and essayist, contributing extensively to the *Atlantic Monthly* after its founding (1857) and publishing *The Autocrat of the Breakfast Table* (1858), followed by *The Professor at the Breakfast Table* (1860) and *The Poet at the Breakfast Table* (1872). In addition, he published 3 novels of heredity and psychology (*Elsie Venner*, 1861; *The Guardian Angel*, 1867; and *A Mortal Antipathy*, 1885) and biographies of Motley (1879) and Emerson (1885).

Holmes, Oliver Wendell, Jr. (b. Boston, 8 Mar. 1841; d. Washington, D.C., 6 Mar. 1935), jurist, son of Oliver Wendell Holmes, was graduated from Harvard (1861) and served in the Civil War for 3 years, being wounded at Ball's Bluff, Antietam, and Fredericksburg, and attaining the rank of lieutenant colonel. On graduation from the Harvard Law School (1866) he practiced in Boston and became instructor in constitutional law at Harvard (1870–71), professor of law editor of the *American Law Review* (1870–73). Associate justice (1882) of the Massachusetts supreme judicial court, and chief justice (1899–1902), he was appointed by President Theodore Roosevelt an associate justice of the U.S. Supreme Court (1902), serving until his retirement at the age of 90 (12 Jan.

1932). The court's most notable dissenter and leader of its liberal wing, he sharply criticized the Sherman Anti-Trust Act (*Northern Securities' Case*), but his conception of a "current of commerce" (*Swift Case*, 1905) paved the way for increasingly broad interpretations of the commerce clause. In his dissent in *Lochner* v. *N.Y.* (1905) he declared that "the 14th Amendment does not enact Mr. Herbert Spencer's *Social Statics.*" His opposition to the rule in the *Adair* (1908) and *Coppage* (1915) cases foreshadowed later reversals by the court. He also dissented in *Hammer* v. *Dagenhart* (1918), where the majority invalidated the federal child labor law. In *Schenck* v. *U.S.* (1919) he enunciated the "clear and present danger" doctrine to govern the interpretation of the 1st Amendment, although in the *Abrams Case* (1919) he made an eloquent plea for "free trade in ideas." In later opinions he attacked wiretapping as "dirty business" (*Olmstead* v. *U.S.*, 1928) and denounced the use of the 14th Amendment to "prevent the making of social experiments" (*Truax* v. *Corrigan*, 1921). He refused to accept the common law as a fundamental all-pervasive set of principles and denied that it was "a brooding omnipresence in the sky." He edited the 12th edition of Kent's *Commentaries* (1873); his published works include *The Common Law* (1881) and *Collected Legal Papers* (1920).

Homer, Winslow (b. Boston, Mass., 24 Feb. 1836; d. Scarboro, Me., 29 Sept. 1910), painter and illustrator. After serving his apprenticeship under Bufford, a lithographer in Boston, he established his studio there (1857), drew illustrations for *Ballou's Pictorial* and *Harper's Weekly*, and in 1859 moved to New York, where he continued his training at the National Academy of Design. During the Civil War he drew battlefield scenes for

Harper's Weekly and recorded these impressions in such paintings as *Rainy Day in Camp, Sharpshooter on Picket Duty,* and *Prisoners from the Front.* He gradually abandoned magazine illustration and anecdotal painting, and after 1882, when he established his home at Scarboro, Me., began work on the long line of marine pieces that occupied the rest of his life. In Maine, and during his annual journeys to the Caribbean, he produced oil paintings and watercolors marked by original design, virile draftsmanship, and vivid color. His works include *The Life Line, Eight Bells, Sun and Cloud, Summer Night, The Fallen Deer, Northeaster, Cannon Rock,* and *The Wreck* (also p. 902).

Hoover, Herbert Clark (b. West Branch, Iowa, 10 Aug. 1874; d. New York City, 20 Oct. 1964), 31st president of the U.S., moved to Oregon and was graduated from Stanford Univ. (1895) as a mining engineer. After several years in the U.S. he engaged in mining operations abroad, first in Australia, then in China, Africa, Central and South America, and Russia. During World War I he was notably effective as chairman of the American Relief Committee in London, as chairman of the Commission for Relief in Belgium, and as U.S. Food Administrator. Appointed Secretary of Commerce (1921–28), he served in both the Harding and Coolidge cabinets, expanding the activities of that department and fostering trade associations. Republican nominee, he was elected president (1928). To deal with the economic collapse which occurred in the first year of his administration, he counted upon economic forces to bring about a revival and was hesitant to extend federal activities, although at the end of his term he signed an act creating the Reconstruction Finance Corp. (1932) to extend loans to banks and large business enterprises.

On 20 June 1931 he announced a 1-year moratorium on all intergovernmental debts. Renominated, he was defeated (1932) by Franklin D. Roosevelt. He served (1947–49, 1953–55) as chairman of the Commissions on Organization of the Executive Branch of the Government (Hoover Commissions). An isolationist prior to 1941, he advocated (1952) U.S. military withdrawal from Western Europe. His works include *Memoirs* (3 vols., 1951–52) and *The Ordeal of Woodrow Wilson* (1958).

Hoover, John Edgar (b. Washington, D.C., 1 Jan. 1895; d. there, 2 May 1972), public official, was a messenger in the Library of Congress while studying law at night at George Washington Univ. (LL.B. 1916; LL.M. 1917). Hired by the Justice Department as a file reviewer (1917), he became special assistant to the attorney general of the U.S. (1919–24) and was responsible for oversight of the "Red Scare" deportation cases, helping to put together 60,000 dossiers on radicals and anarchists, a prelude to the "Palmer Raids." Assistant director of the Justice Department's Bureau of Investigation (1921–24), he was appointed director (1924) and began its reorganization. Hoover remained director for 48 years, changing the bureau from an organization notorious for its apathy and corruption to the least corruptible and most sophisticated investigatory agency in the world. During his first year as director he set up the Identification Division, including the Central Fingerprint Repository. He established a crime laboratory (1932), the FBI Academy (1935), the same year the bureau became the FBI, and set up retrieval systems such as the National Fraudulent Check File, National Typewriter File, and National Automobile Altered Number File. In 1939, responding to presidential authorization, he inaugurated wartime internal-security and counterespionage programs. In later years Hoover and the FBI came under increasing attack for their concentration on finding Communists at the expense of enforcing civil rights laws and attacking organized crime. Hoover feuded with Attorney Generals Robert F. Kennedy (1961–64) and Ramsey Clark (1967–69) while maintaining close relations with President Lyndon B. Johnson and on Capitol Hill. A superadministrator and wily bureaucrat, he refused to cooperate with the Nixon administration's "Huston Plan" for domestic intelligence-gathering operations. He was the author of *Persons in Hiding* (1938), *Masters of Deceit* (1958), and *J. Edgar Hoover on Communism* (1962).

Hopkins, Harry (b. Sioux City, Ia., 17 Aug. 1890; d. New York City, 29 Jan. 1946), social reformer and statesman, graduated from Grinnell College (1912). As a social worker, Hopkins directed a boy's camp run by Christadora House, a settlement on the lower east side of New York City (1912), worked there for a year, and then took charge of fresh-air work and unemployment relief for the New York Association for the Improvement of the Conditions of the Poor. From 1915–17 he handled widows' pensions for the New York City Board of Child Welfare. During World War I and in the early 1920s he was chairman of the southern division of the American Red Cross in New Orleans. Brought to the attention of Franklin Roosevelt by Eleanor Roosevelt, he headed the New York State Temporary Emergency Relief Administration for Gov. Roosevelt (1931–33). When Roosevelt became president, Hopkins became director of New Deal relief agencies such as the Federal Emergency Relief Administration (1933), Civil Works Administration (1933–34), and Works Projects Administration (1935–40). Called the "world's greatest spender,"

Hopkins distributed over $10 billion both in dole and the work relief. A first-class administrator who fought for his agencies, Hopkins was radical in his willingness to experiment freely with social and economic reform. He attempted to end discrimination in the administration of relief funds. As Secretary of Commerce (1938–40) Hopkins supported Roosevelt's candidacy for a 3d term, after his own aspirations failed due to ill health. F.D.R.'s closest confidant during wartime, living at the White House (1940–43), "my house guest without portfolio," he was greatly admired by the president for his common sense, quickness, sympathy, and mixture of cynicism and idealism. Roosevelt's leading adviser during the war, he acted as buffer, communications line, and sounding board. As F.D.R.'s superadministrative assistant, Hopkins was given assignments without fixed boundaries in the conduct of the Grand Alliance. He was head of the Lend-Lease Program, member of the "Little War Cabinet," of the War Mobilization Committee, of the War Production Board, and a speechwriter for the president. He served as the president's special emissary to Churchill and to Stalin, making repeated trips abroad, and attending all of the major wartime conferences with the president. Although seriously ill, he made a last trip to Moscow to see Stalin (26 May–7 June 1945) at the behest of President Truman, insuring the holding of the Potsdam Conference and the success of the San Francisco Conference. He was author of *Spend to Save* (1936).

House, Edward Mandell (b. Houston, Tex., 26 July 1858; d. New York City, 28 Mar. 1938), statesman, attended Cornell (1878–79), took over his father's cotton plantation and bank after his death. Although he never ran for public office, he was active in Texas politics, advising a series of governors, one of whom made him an honorary colonel. In 1912 he influenced the Texas delegation to support Woodrow Wilson for the presidential nomination and planned strategy during the subsequent campaign. He became Wilson's most intimate friend (1912–19), called by the president "my second personality . . . my independent self." As Wilson's unofficial but most important adviser, he helped select his cabinet and performed an important role in political fence-mending. He was also a channel through which the captains of finance could get their needs and views relayed to the president. He was sent to Europe in 1914 by Wilson to attempt to prevent the outbreak of war and again for 4 months (1915) on a secret peace mission to England, Germany, and France. His 2d mission for negotiated peace (1916) resulted in the House-Grey Memorandum (22 Feb. 1916), suggesting U.S. commitment to the Allied cause. House was pro-Ally, believing that Allied victory was vital to American national interest. He represented the U.S. at the Inter-Allied Conference in Paris (Nov.–Dec. 1917) where the coordination of Allied resources against Germany was discussed. As early as Sept. 1917 House directed research on European social and economic conditions for use at the subsequent peace conference. He influenced Wilson's decision to issue a statement of war aims as well as the substance of those aims and it was his hint that the U.S. might make a separate peace (Nov. 1918) which precipitated the Allies into acceptance of those "14 Points." He was a delegate at the negotiations of the armistice and, with Wilson, a member of the 5-man U.S. delegation at the Paris Peace Conference, working especially on the Covenant of the League of Nations and the mandates system. Wilson apparently blamed him for U.S. concessions made during the president's brief return to the U.S. (Mar. 1919) and resisted House's advice for greater concessions to the Allies in order to achieve agreement on the League of Nations. Their friendship was strained during the peace negotiations, possibly because Wilson was ill, and House never saw Wilson again after the president left Paris (June 1919). After Wilson's stroke (2 Oct. 1919) House counseled compromise with the Senate in order to secure ratification of the League Covenant, and after Wilson persisted, urged his resignation so that vice-president Marshall could lead the fight (Nov. 1919). House's advice may never have been seen by the ill president. He advised Franklin D. Roosevelt during the 1932 campaign.

Houston, Samuel (b. near Lexington, Va., 2 Mar. 1793; d. San Antonio, Tex., 26 July 1863), soldier and statesman, removed to Blount Co., Tenn. (1807), clerked in a trader's store, left home, and lived nearly 3 years with the Cherokee. On return, he taught in a country school. In the War of 1812 he served under Andrew Jackson against the Creeks and was wounded at Horseshoe Bend (28 Mar. 1814). After assisting in the removal of the Cherokee from Tennessee to present Arkansas (1817–18), he resigned from the army, studied law in Nashville, and was admitted to the bar. Congressman, 1823–27, and governor of Tennessee, 1827–29, he resigned after his wife left him and was adopted into the Cherokee nation. Jackson sent him to Texas to negotiate a treaty with the Indians (1832) and he settled at Nacogdoches (1833). He was elected a delegate to the San Felipe constitutional convention, which petitioned for separation of Texas from Cohuila (1833). With the outbreak of the War for Texan Independence he became commander in chief of the Texan army (1835). He surprised and routed Santa Anna at San Jacinto (21 Apr. 1836), thereby achieving Texan independence. The newly founded (1836) city of Houston was named for him. Elected president of Texas (1836–38) and reelected (1841–44), he secured recognition of the republic by the U.S. After Texas was admitted to the Union (1845), he became one of the first 2 senators (1846–59). A Union Democrat, he opposed the Kansas-Nebraska Bill (1854). Elected governor of Texas (1859), he opposed secession, refused to espouse the Confederate cause, and was deposed (18 Mar. 1861).

Howe, Elias (b. Spencer, Mass., 9 July 1819; d. Brooklyn, N.Y., 3 Oct. 1867), inventor of the sewing machine. He was an apprentice (1835–37) in a cotton machinery factory in Lowell, Mass., and subsequently, while working in an instrument maker's shop in Cambridge, Mass., designed and constructed a sewing machine which he improved during the winter of 1844–45. The patent for the machine was issued on 10 Sept. 1846. Encountering indifference in the U.S., Howe marketed his machine in England to William Thomas, a London corset manufacturer, who also bought the English rights from Howe. After a quarrel that led to a break with Thomas, Howe returned to the U.S. to find that the English reputation of his machine had spread to his homeland. The lawsuits which Howe instituted against those (like Isaac M. Singer) whom he accused of infringing his patent lasted from 1849 to 1854 and ended in Howe's favor with the award of a royalty on every sewing machine that infringed his rights. His royalties for the period 1861–67 often amounted to $4,000 a week. He established (1865) that Howe Machine Co. of Bridgeport, Conn., whose perfected machine won the gold medal at the Paris Exhibition of 1867.

Howe, Samuel Gridley (b. Boston, Mass., 10 Nov. 1801; d. there, 9 Jan. 1876),

humanitarian, reformer, was graduated from Brown Univ. (1821) and received his M.D. from Harvard (1824). Drawn to the Greek cause like other romantics of his time, he spent 6 years fighting against the Turks, distributing food and clothing supplies, and aiding reconstruction. Appointed (1831) to run a Massachusetts school for the blind, he established it in his father's home and later in the Perkins mansion (Perkins Institution). His work with the blind demonstrated that the sightless could be economically and socially competent. During his 45 years with the school he trained a staff in educating the blind, visiting 17 states to advance this cause. He taught the deaf and blind child Laura Bridgeman, demonstrating to an incredulous world the values of such training, and promoted the oral, as against the sign, method for instructing the deaf. From 1865–74 he headed the Massachusetts State Board of Charities, the first of its kind in the U.S. With his gifted wife, Julia Ward Howe (1819–1910), whom he married in 1843, he coedited the antislavery paper *The Commonwealth* and aided and abetted John Brown. He backed Horace Mann's fight for better schools, helped Dorothea Dix in her campaign for care of the insane, and agitated for prison reform.

Howells, William Dean (b. Martin's Ferry, Belmont Co., Ohio, 1 Mar. 1837; d. New York City, 11 May 1920), novelist and critic, spent his boyhood in several Ohio towns, including Dayton and Ashtabula, had little formal schooling, and at the age of 9 began setting type in his father's printing office. He served (1856–61) on the editorial staff of the *Ohio State Journal*, in association with John J. Piatt published *Poems of Two Friends* (1860). After writing a campaign life of Lincoln (1860) he served as U.S. consul at Venice (1861–65) and published *Venetian Life* (1866) and *Italian*

Journeys (1867). Returning to the U.S. in 1865, he worked for the *Nation* and in 1866 became subeditor of the *Atlantic Monthly,* of which he was editor in chief from 1871 to 1881. During this period he formed his friendship with Henry James and gained an intimate knowledge of Boston and New England society. The novels published during this period were *Their Wedding Journey* (1872), *A Chance Acquaintance* (1873), *A Foregone Conclusion* (1875), *The Lady of the Aroostook* (1879), *The Undiscovered Country* (1880), *A Fearful Responsibility* (1881), and *Dr. Breen's Practice* (1881). After leaving the *Atlantic* he wrote serials for the *Century Magazine,* contributed (1886–91) influential critical writings to the "Editor's Study" in *Harper's Monthly,* and in 1891 moved to New York. After the Haymarket affair, Howells developed a deep interest in social and economic problems. During his middle and later period he wrote *A Modern Instance* (1881), *A Woman's Reason* (1883), *The Rise of Silas Lapham* (1885), *Indian Summer* (1886), *The Minister's Charge* (1887), *April Hopes* (1888), *Annie Kilburn* (1889), *A Hazard of New Fortunes* (1890), *The Quality of Mercy* (1892), *An Imperative Duty* (1893), *The World of Chance* (1893), *The Coast of Bohemia* (1893), *A Traveler from Alturia* (1894), *The Landlord at Lion's Head* (1897), and *Through the Eye of the Needle* (1907). His last novel was *The Leatherwood God* (1916). He also wrote works of reminiscence, such as *Boys' Town* (1890), *My Year in a Log Cabin* (1893), *My Literary Passions* (1895), *Impressions and Experiences* (1896), *Literary Friends and Acquaintances* (1900), *My Mark Twain* (1910), and *Years of My Youth* (1916). His critical works, among them *Criticism and Fiction* (1891) and *Literature and Life* (1902), helped pave the way for the acceptance of realism in the American novel. Howells gave encouragement to such realist writers as Frank Norris, Stephen Crane, and Hamlin Garland.

Hughes, Charles Evans (b. Glens Falls, N.Y., 11 Apr. 1862; d. Osterville, Mass., 27 Aug. 1948), 10th chief justice of the U.S., was graduated from Brown Univ. (1881) and received his law degree from Columbia (1884). His practice in New York City was temporarily interrupted by his professorship of law at Cornell (1891–93). He was counsel for the Stevens Gas Commission investigating utility practices in New York (1906) and attained nationwide reputation as counsel for the Armstrong Commission, which exposed abuses in the life insurance field (1906–07). Republican governor of New York (1906–10), his administration was notable for its reforms, including the establishment of a Public Service Commission. Appointed associate justice of the U.S. Supreme Court (1910), he resigned (1916) to accept the Republican nomination for president. His close defeat by President Wilson was attributed in no small measure to tactical errors he made during an electioneering tour of California, the loss of which state gave Wilson a majority in the electoral college. After a period of law practice, he served as Secretary of State in the administrations of Harding and Coolidge (1921–25), organized the Washington Conference on Naval Limitation of Armaments, and negotiated a series of multipartite treaties. Member of the Permanent Court of Arbitration (1926–30) and judge on the Permanent Court of International Justice (1929–30), he was chosen chief justice of the U.S. Supreme Court that same year, serving until his retirement (1941). In the alignment between liberals and conservatives, he, together with Associate Justice Roberts, occupied a middle ground and contributed to a cautious reshaping of the law to meet social change. He upheld civil liberties and the freedom of the press, curbed the judicial power of administrative agencies, spoke for a unanimous court in invalidating the NIRA (*Schechter Case*, 1935), but sustained the Wagner Act (1937). He effectively opposed President Franklin D. Roosevelt's court reorganization plan (1937).

Hutchinson, Anne (b. Alford, Lincolnshire, England, 1591; d. Eastchester, N.Y., Aug. or Sept. 1643), religious leader. Born Ann Marbury, she married (1612) William Hutchinson, and in 1634 came with her husband and family to Massachusetts Bay, where her openly avowed religious views provoked keen antagonism among the orthodox. She attacked the religious polity of the Massachusetts colony as a "covenant of works" and advocated a "covenant of grace" based on a direct personal apprehension of divine grace and love. Characterized as an Antinomian by her enemies, she was backed by Rev. John Cotton, Rev. John Wheelwright, and Gov. Henry Vane; but lost her support when Cotton recanted, Wheelwright was banished, and Vane departed for England. Brought to trial for sedition and contempt of the magistrates, she was sentenced to banishment and was later formally excommunicated from the church for heresy, after refusing to make a public recantation. With her family, she emigrated (1638) to the colony on the island of Aquidneck (now part of R.I.). For her subsequent career and death, see p. 41.

Hutchinson, Thomas (b. Boston, 9 Sept. 1711; d. Brompton, England, 3 June 1780), Loyalist statesman, received his B.A. (1727) and his M.A. (1730) from Harvard, and after serving in his father's business was elected to the Massachusetts House of Representatives (1737). Serving there (1737–49), he was speaker

(1746–48). An advocate of hard money, he opposed the Massachusetts Land Bank, and sponsored legislation to redeem the colony's bills of credit. Serving in the Council (1749–66), he represented Massachusetts at the Albany Congress (1754), where he collaborated with and supported Franklin in a plan of union. Lieutenant governor beg. 1758, he also served as chief justice from 1760. In the latter capacity he granted the writs of assistance (1761). His support of enforcement of both the Sugar and Stamp Acts marked him as the leader of the Court party. On 26 Aug. 1765 his home was sacked and his books and papers scattered in reprisal. Royal governor (1770–74), he argued for the supremacy of Parliament over the colonies. Publication in Boston (1773) of letters he sent to England urging the government to assert more vigorously its authority over the colonies created a sensation. His insistence that clearance papers would not be given to the tea ships until the tea was landed brought on the Boston Tea Party (1773). Reporting personally to George III (1774), he now advocated a conciliatory policy, but remained in exile, hopeful to the last of laying his "bones in New England." His most important writings were his notably objective *History of the Colony of Mass. Bay* (3 vols., 1764–1828) and *A Collection of Original Papers Relative to the History of Mass. Bay* (1769).

Ickes, Harold LeClaire (b. Frankstown, Pa., 15 Mar. 1874; d. Washington, D.C., 3 Feb. 1952), political leader. Ickes received his B.A. (1897) and LL.B. (1907) from Univ. of Chicago. He was a reporter on the *Chicago Tribune* and the *Chicago Record* (1897–1900), and later practiced law. An active and independent political campaigner, Ickes supported C. E. Merriam for mayor of Chicago (1911) and fought the influence of business interests in municipal government there. At first a Republican, he became leader of the Illinois Progressive party (1912–15), but returned to support Hughes for president in 1916. A delegate-at-large to the Republican National Convention (1920), Ickes opposed Harding's nomination and later endorsed the Cox-Roosevelt ticket. Partially because he campaigned for Franklin D. Roosevelt in the Middle West (1932) and because of his strong views on conservation, Ickes was Roosevelt's choice for Secretary of the Interior (1933), after he had trouble filling the position. As Secretary of the Interior (1933–46) Ickes was an outspoken opponent of big business, deeply concerned for the public interest, a supporter of conservation and of comprehensive national planning. As director of the Public Works Administration for 6 years (appointed 16 June 1933), established to provide employment and stimulate business by providing purchasing power, "Honest Harold" scrutinized each contract to determine whether the project was economically justifiable, satisfied engineering requirements, and was untainted by graft, corruption, and maladministration. Insuring incorruptibility, this procedure delayed the effect of the PWA in stimulating the economy. President of the Chicago NAACP in younger days, Ickes was, with Eleanor Roosevelt, the staunchest advocate of civil rights within the New Deal, hiring blacks, seeing that they received their share of the massive low-cost housing projects he supported, integrating the cafeteria of the Interior Department, and arranging for Marian Anderson to perform from the steps of the Lincoln Memorial when denied Constitution Hall by the Daughters of the American Revolution (1939). He advised Roosevelt to "purge" opposition congressmen (1938), attacked the Dies Committee (1938), and encouraged Roosevelt

to seek a 3d term (1940). An early and outspoken opponent of Hitler, during World War II Ickes also served as Petroleum and Solid Fuels Coordinator for National Defense. In 1943 he favored the immediate release of interned Japanese-Americans. President Truman accepted Ickes' resignation, an expression of Ickes' opposition to the appointment of Edward Pauley as Under Secretary of the Navy (1946). Both before and after his resignation, Ickes campaigned for civilian administration of U.S. islands in the Pacific. Pugnacious and honest to the point of bluntness, he wrote *The New Democracy* (1934) and *The Autobiography of a Curmudgeon* (1943).

Inness, George (b. near Newburgh, N.Y., 1 May 1825; d. Bridge of Allan, Scotland, 3 Aug. 1894), painter, received brief instruction in the studio of Régis Gignoux, New York City, but was virtually self-taught. He studied in Italy (1847, 1851, and 1871) and in France (1854), but did most of his painting in Medfield, Mass., and later in Montclair, N.J., and New York City. His early work was in the tradition of the Hudson River School, but his style broadened (*Delaware Meadows*, 1867) in the direction of lyricism and subjectivity, with a feeling for light and air achieved by his color patterns. Foremost American landscapist, his paintings are in the Art Institute, Chicago; the Metropolitan Museum, New York; and the National Gallery, Washington, D.C. They include *Peace and Plenty* (1865), *Coming Storm* (1878), *Sunset in the Woods* (1883), *Niagara Falls* (1884), and *March Breezes* (1885).

Irving, Washington (b. New York City, 3 Apr. 1783; d. Tarrytown, N.Y., 28 Nov. 1859), man of letters. He began reading law in 1798 and for a short time practiced law at New York, but soon abandoned this calling for writing and travel.

Beginning in 1802 he published in New York City journals "The Letters of Jonathan Oldstyle, Gent.," and in 1807–08 brought out a collection of essays, *Salamagundi: or, the Whim-Whams and Opinions of Launcelot Langstaff, Esq. and Others.* The spirit of these lively satirical pieces was carried over into his comic account, *History of New York . . . by Diedrich Knickerbocker* (1809), which gave its name to the Knickerbocker School of writers. In 1815 he sailed for Europe, remaining there until 1832. During his stay in England he wrote *The Sketch Book of Geoffrey Crayon, Gent.* (1819–20), which included essays such as "Westminster Abbey" and "The Mutability of Literature," and tales such as "Rip Van Winkle" and "The Legend of Sleepy Hollow." He also published *Bracebridge Hall* (1822). Leaving England in 1822, he went to Germany and France, and in 1826 went to Spain, where he served (1826–29) on the staff of the U.S. embassy. At Madrid, and in the Alhambra at Granada, he wrote *The History of the Life and Voyages of Christopher Columbus* (1828), *A Chronicle of the Conquest of Granada* (1829), and *The Alhambra: A Series of Tales and Sketches of the Moors and Spaniards* (1832). Irving served as attaché (1829–32) at the U.S. legation in London, and upon his return to the U.S. was hailed as the nation's leading man of letters. His travels to the West produced *A Tour on the Prairies* (1835), *Astoria* (1836), and *The Adventures of Captain Bonneville, U.S.A.* (1837). He settled at Sunnyside, near Tarrytown, N.Y., and, except for the years 1842–46, when he was U.S. minister to Spain, lived there until his death. Among his other works are *Tales of a Traveller* (1824), *The Crayon Miscellany* (1835), *Oliver Goldsmith* (1849), *Mahomet and His Successors* (2 vols., 1849–50), *Wolfert's Roost* (1855), and *Life of George Washington* (5 vols.,

1855–59). Irving was the first American to gain an international reputation as a man of letters and to make writing his full-time profession.

Ives, Charles Edward (b. Danbury, Conn., 20 Oct. 1874; d. New York City, 19 May 1954), composer. Son of George Edward Ives, a well-known musician and bandmaster in Gen. Grant's army, Ives took his first music lessons from his father, who encouraged him to adapt the disharmonies of village bands and country fiddlers to his compositions. At Yale he studied organ under Dudley Buck and composition under Horatio W. Parker. Upon receiving his A.B. (1898), Ives realized the impracticality of a musical career and chose instead to earn his living as an insurance executive. He remained in the insurance business retiring in 1930 as a millionaire. At the same time he was active as an organist and composer. By 1918, when illness forced him to curtail composition, he had composed 4 symphonies, 4 violin sonatas, 2 piano sonatas, 3 orchestral suites, 11 volumes of chamber music, as well as choral music and numerous pieces for organ. After 1915 he composed some 200 songs. His most famous compositions are the *Second String Quartet* (1896), the *Second Piano Sonata* ("Concord") (1909–15), the *New England Symphony* (1904–13), the *Fourth Symphony* (1910–16), and the *Third Symphony* (1901–04), which won the Pulitzer Prize in 1947. Ives' works are known for their complexity. He was one of the first to experiment with polyharmonies, polyrhythms, tone clusters, exotic scales, atonal systems, and quarter tone effects. His works often contain reference to American hymns, marches, and ditties. Because of the technical complexity of his music, the tendency of others to look to European models, and his fierce independence, Ives' work was largely ignored until well after his most productive years. Recognition came with the first complete performance of the *Concord Sonata* (Town Hall, New York, 20 Jan. 1939).

Jackson, Andrew (b. Waxhaw, S.C., 15 Mar. 1767; d. near Nashville, Tenn., 8 June 1845), 7th president of the U.S., served briefly in the American Revolution (1781), when he was taken prisoner by the British, studied law in Salisbury, N.C., was admitted to the bar (1787), and began practice in Martinsville. Appointed (1788) prosecuting attorney for western district of North Carolina (now Tenn.), he moved to Nashville. Married (1791) Mrs. Rachel Robards (née Donelson), mistakenly believing that she had already obtained a divorce (actually granted 2 years later). Member of state constitutional convention (1796), first congressman from Tennessee (Dec. 1796–Mar. 1797), U.S. senator (1797), he resigned and became judge of the Tennessee supreme court (1798–1804). In one of several duels he killed Charles Dickinson (1806). Personal feuds with President Jefferson (partly growing out of his attachment to Aaron Burr) and Gov. John Sevier (Tenn.) led to his temporary retirement from public life. As major general of militia he defeated the Creeks (1813–14). Commissioned major general in U.S. army, he decisively defeated the British at New Orleans (8 Jan. 1815) after the treaty of peace had been signed at Ghent. Commanding in the Seminole War, he invaded Florida (1818), captured Pensacola, and created an international incident by having 2 British subjects, Arbuthnot and Ambrister, executed for inciting the Creeks against the Americans. Military governor of Florida (1821) and U.S. senator (1823–25), he received the largest number of electoral votes for the presidency (1824), but, failing of a majority, was defeated in the House of Representatives, which elected John Quincy Adams (1825). He won easily 4 years later. His administration (1829–37) initiated the spoils system, set up a "Kitchen Cabinet" of intimate advisers (Amos Kendall, Duff Green, William Berkeley Lewis), and checked the program of federal internal improvements (Maysville veto, 1830). He reorganized his cabinet (1831) when Mrs. Calhoun and other wives of cabinet members refused to meet Mrs. J. H. (Peggy) Eaton. He finally broke with Calhoun on learning that the latter had favored censuring him for his conduct in Florida in 1818 and over the issue of nullification, which Jackson vigorously opposed, taking military measures to enforce South Carolina's respect for federal authority (1832). Favoring hard money, he warred on the Bank of the U.S., vetoed its recharter (1832), and ordered withdrawal of U.S. funds. His Indian policy consisted of relocation on lands west of the Mississippi. His administration is notable for expansion of the presidential power. After the inauguration of Van Buren, his choice for the presidency, he retired to his home, The Hermitage, near Nashville.

Jackson, Thomas Jonathan [commonly called "Stonewall" Jackson] (b. Clarksburg, Va., now W. Va., 21 Jan. 1824; d. Guiney's Station, Va., 10 May 1863), Confederate general, was graduated (1846) from the U.S. Military Academy; was breveted major during the Mexican War; became (1851) professor of artillery tactics and natural philosophy at the Virginia Military Institute, Lexington, Va.; and resigned from the army in 1852. He commanded the cadet corps at the hanging of John Brown (2 Dec. 1859). Commissioned (17 June 1861) a brigadier general in the Confederate forces, he earned his sobriquet "Stonewall" at 1st

Bull Run when his troops held off a strong Union assault (21 July 1861). Jackson was made a major general (7 Oct. 1861) and took command (5 Nov. 1861) of Confederate forces in the Shenandoah Valley. The Valley campaign (Mar.–June 1862) demonstrated Jackson's brilliance as a field tactician. Despite numerical inferiority, he defeated the Union force under Gen. Nathaniel P. Banks at Front Royal (23 May 1862) and Winchester (24–25 May 1862), and prevented the main enemy forces from uniting. During the 7 Days before Richmond, Jackson took part in the actions at Gaines' Mill (27 June 1862) and White Oak Swamp (30 June 1862). After destroying the Union advanced base at Manassas Junction (27 Aug. 1862), he helped defeat Pope at 2d Bull Run (30–31 Aug. 1862). He also took part in the battles of Antietam (17 Sept. 1862) and Fredericksburg (13 Dec. 1862). After forcing a Union retreat at Chancellorsville (2 May 1863), Jackson was accidentally wounded by the fire of Confederate pickets and died of pneumonia shortly afterward. His death deprived Lee of the greatest of his lieutenants.

James, Henry (b. New York City, 15 Apr. 1843; d. London, 28 Feb. 1916), novelist and essayist, son of Henry James (1811–82), the theologian, and brother of William James, was educated in France, entered Harvard Law School (1862), but turned to letters, contributing to the *Nation*, the *Atlantic*, and *Galaxy*. Returning to Europe for several visits in the 1870s, he finally settled in London (1876), becoming a British subject (July 1915). A master of the fiction technique, he established himself in the forefront of the analytical school of novelists with his subtle treatment of British and American society and his romanti-

cizing of aristocratic European culture. In his early works (*The American*, 1877; *Daisy Miller*, 1878; *The Bostonians*, 1886), his leading characters are Americans, although the scene is often abroad; but in his second period (*The Princess Casamassima*, 1886; *The Sacred Fount*, 1901), his novels are confined to English society. In his third period (*The Wings of the Dove*, 1902; *The Ambassadors*, 1903; *The Golden Bowl*, 1904; and his unfinished novels), he returned to his theme of the American abroad.

James, William (b. New York City, 11 Jan. 1842; d. Chocorua, N.H., 26 Aug. 1910), psychologist and philosopher, was educated abroad. After accompanying Agassiz on the Thayer expedition to the Amazon (1865–66), he entered Harvard Medical School, then pursued medical studies in Germany, and obtained a Harvard M.D. (1869). Harvard lecturer on anatomy and physiology (1872), assistant professor of physiology (1876), he transferred to the Department of Philosophy as assistant professor (1880), becoming a full professor (1885–1907). His works include *The Principles of Psychology* (1890), *The Varieties of Religious Experience* (1907), *A Pluralistic Universe* (1909), *The Meaning of Truth* (1909), and *Essays in Radical Empiricism* (1912). A radical empiricist, he evolved the method of pragmatism (the testing of truth by practical consequences), with its emphasis upon individuality, free initiative, spontaneity, and novelty. His conception of the world as one of changes, chance, and plurality largely anticipated trends in the physical sciences.

Jay, John (b. New York City, 12 Dec. 1745; d. Bedford, N.Y., 17 May 1829), first chief justice of the U.S., was graduated from King's College (1764), studied law, was admitted to the bar (1768), and practiced in New York. Secretary of the N.Y.-N.J. boundary commission (1773), he was a member of the 1st and 2d Continental Congresses (1775–76) and of the New York Provincial Congress (1776–77). Chairman of the committee which drew up the New York state constitution (1777), he became chief justice of New York in that year and also a member of Congress, becoming its president (10 Dec. 1778). Sent to Spain as minister plenipotentiary, his mission (1780–82) failed owing to Spanish hostility to U.S. independence. Member of the U.S. delegation to negotiate peace with Great Britain, he was instrumental in the decision to deal with Great Britain independent of France (1782). Secretary for Foreign Affairs (1784–90), his agreement with Gardoqui to settle differences with Spain (1786), which involved restricting U.S. use of the Mississippi, was defeated in Congress. Advocate of the new Constitution, he wrote 5 of the *Federalist* papers. Chief justice of the U.S. (26 Sept. 1789), he was sent to Great Britain (1794) to settle outstanding differences with that country. Jay's Treaty was denounced by Jeffersonian Republicans for its concessions to England, but it averted war at that time. His most important Supreme Court decision, *Chisholm* v. *Georgia* (1793), holding that a state could be sued by a citizen of another state, led to the 11th Amendment to the Constitution. He resigned from the court (1795) to accept the governorship of New York (1795–1801). Long an opponent of slavery, he signed (1799) the act for its gradual abolition in New York.

Jefferson, Thomas (b. Shadwell, Albemarle Co., Va., 13 Apr. 1743; d. Monticello, 4 July 1826), 3d president of the U.S., was graduated from William and Mary (1762), studied law, and was ad-

mitted to the bar (1767), practicing until 1770 and managing his estate. Sent to the House of Burgesses (1769–75), he published (1774) *A Summary View of the Rights of British Amercia*. A delegate to the Continental Congress (1775–76), he drafted the Declaration of Independence. Returning to the Virginia legislature, he supported measures providing "a foundation for a government truly republican"— abolition of primogeniture and entails, separation of church and state, establishment of a public school system. He also favored discontinuing the slave trade and gradual emancipation. Succeeding Patrick Henry as governor of Virginia (1779–81), he directed without conspicuous success resistance to British invasion. Returning to Congress (1783–84), he devised a plan for a decimal monetary system and drafted the Land Ordinance of 1784, the basis for the later organization of the territories. Succeeding Franklin as minister to France (1785–89), he published his *Notes on Virginia* (Paris, 1785) and witnessed the beginnings of the French Revolution. Washington's first Secretary of State, he supported Hamilton's funding and assumption plan on condition that the national capital be located on the Potomac. He served until 1793, when he resigned in protest against Hamilton's fiscal and centralizing policies. Leader in retirement of the Democratic-Republican party, he was vice-president under John Adams (1797–1801). Opposing the Alien and Sedition Acts, he prepared, with Madison, the Virginia and Kentucky Resolutions (1798), implying that a state could nullify congressional legislation. In the election of 1800 he tied with Aaron Burr in electoral votes and was chosen president by the House of Representatives with Hamilton's support. His administration (1801–09) was marked by simplicity and economy, the successful war against the Barbary pirates (1801–05), the

Louisiana Purchase (1803), the Lewis and Clark and Pike expeditions, the Burr treason trial (1807), and the Embargo Act (1807), adopted to preserve U.S. neutral rights, but repealed (1809). In retirement at Monticello, Jefferson founded the Univ. of Virginia (1819) and contributed notably to the revival of classical architecture in the U.S. A philosopher-statesman of the Enlightenment, he favored a society of self-sufficient free farmers and decentralized governmental powers.

Johnson, Andrew (b. Raleigh, N.C., 29 Dec. 1808; d. Carter Station, Tenn., 31 July 1875), 17th president of the U.S., was self-educated, becoming a tailor in Greenville, Tenn. Soon engaging in politics, where he came to stand for a more equitable land policy, he was alderman (1828–30), mayor (1830–33), Democratic member of the state's lower house (1835–37 and 1839–41) and of the state senate (1841–43); he was elected Democratic congressman (1843–53), served as governor of Tennessee (1853–57), and U.S. senator (1857–62) where he distinguished himself as the only Southern senator to support the Union during the Civil War. Appointed by Lincoln military governor of Tennessee with the rank of brigadier general (4 Mar. 1862), he was Lincoln's running mate (1864) on the Union-Republican ticket and was elected vice-president, becoming president upon Lincoln's death (1865). His attempt to carry out Lincoln's conciliatory Reconstruction policy led him into conflict with the Radical Republicans, who passed over his veto their own Reconstruction Act (1867) which enfranchised Negroes and disfranchised ex-Confederates. Johnson violated the Tenure of Office Act (passed 2 Mar. 1867 over his veto and declared unconstitutional by the Supreme Court, 1926), by dismissing Edwin M. Stanton, Secretary of War. Impeached by the House of Representatives, the Senate failed by one vote to convict him (May 1868, see p. 296). Reelected senator (1875), he died the same year.

Johnson, Lyndon Baines (b. nr. Stonewall, Tex., 27 Aug. 1908; d. Johnson City, Tex., 22 Jan. 1973), 36th president of the U.S., worked his way through Southwest State Teachers College, San Marcos, Tex. (B.S., 1930), and taught public speaking and debating in the Houston public schools (1930–32). He entered public service as secretary to Rep. M. Kleberg (1932–35). In 1934 he married Claudia Alta (Lady Bird) Taylor. State Director, National Youth Administration (1935–37), he was elected to fill a congressional vacancy, serving in the House of Representatives (1937–49), with a leave of absence for naval duty (1941–42). U.S. senator (1949–61), he was minority leader (1953–55) and majority leader (1955–61), cooperating closely with the Eisenhower administration. In 1955 he suffered a heart attack. Defeated by John F. Kennedy for the Democratic nomination for president (1960), he accepted the vice-presidential nomination. As vice-president (1961–63) he traveled extensively and served as chairman of the Presidential Committee on Equal Employment Opportunity, curbing racial bias by government contractors. Following the assassination of Kennedy (22 Nov. 1963), he succeeded to the presidency and secured the passage of such Kennedy legislation as a tax cut and the civil rights bill (1964). In 1964 he was elected to the presidency. His years as president were marked by extraordinary legislative accomplishment. Decisions he made to escalate American military efforts in Vietnam involved the United States in a lengthy, costly land war. The domestic unpopularity of the war led to his decision (announced 31

Mar. 1968) not to seek reelection. He wrote *The Vantage Point: Perspectives of the Presidency 1963–69* (1971).

Johnson, Sir William (b. Smithtown, County Meath, Ireland, 1715; d. Johnstown, N.Y., 11 July 1774), colonial official and diplomat, came to America in 1737, settling on the Mohawk, trading with the Indians, amassing a fortune as well as huge landholdings, and founding (1762) Johnstown. On intimate terms with the Six Nations, particularly the Mohawks, he was largely responsible for keeping them on the British side during King George's War. In 1746 he was made colonel and commissary of New York for Indian affairs, resigning the latter office in 1750. At the start of the French and Indian War, he attended, as a member of the New York Council, the Albany Congress (1754), helping to formulate Indian policy. In 1755 Braddock gave him command of the force against Crown Point and "sole management" of the Six Nations. Though he failed to capture Crown Point, he warded off the French threat to the northern colonies and was made (1755) a baronet for his achievements and superintendent of Indian affairs (1756). He advocated centralized control of the fur trade and a boundary line between white settlement and Indian hunting lands. Such a boundary he negotiated (1768) at Ft. Stanwix, opening up to settlement large tracts in New York, Pennsylvania, and Virginia. An imperialist, he secured by his policies the attachment of most of the Iroquois to the British side when the Revolution broke out (after his death).

Johnson, William (b. Charleston, S.C., 27 Dec. 1771; d. Brooklyn, N.Y., 4 Aug. 1834), jurist, graduated at the head of his class from Princeton (1790) and studied law in Charleston under Charles Cotesworth Pinckney. Admitted to the bar in 1793, Johnson was elected as a Republican member of the South Carolina House of Representatives (1794–98), serving as its speaker (1798). The legislature elected him to the South Carolina Court of Common Pleas (1799–1804). In naming Johnson to the Supreme Court of the U.S. (1804), President Jefferson expected that his appointee would counterbalance Chief Justice Marshall. These expectations were fulfilled only in part. Johnson did become the first major exponent of the dissenting tradition on the Supreme Court, opposing what were usually Marshall's majority views in 34 dissenting opinions and 21 concurring opinions during his 30 years on the court. Major dissents are exemplified by *Osborn* v. *Bank of the United States* (1824) and *Ogden* v. *Saunders* (1827). His Jeffersonian principles were reflected in his majority opinion in *U.S.* v. *Hudson and Goodwin* (1812), holding that the federal courts lacked the power to try offenses at common law—a decision which, however, terminated a criminal libel trial of 2 Federalist editors. His independence was revealed in his decision as circuit judge in *Gilchrist* v. *Collector of Charleston* (1808) declaring Jefferson's embargo illegal and asserting that "the officers of our government, from the highest to the lowest, are equally subject to legal restraint." He concurred with such typically Marshallian readings of the Constitution as *Cohens* v. *Virginia* (1821) and *Gibbons* v. *Ogden* (1824), where his interpretation of the commerce powers was even broader than Marshall's. As a justice, Johnson supported strong national powers and a powerful judiciary but not at the expense of Congress—as in *Anderson* v. *Dunn* (1821), upholding the contempt power—and looked to the states for economic and social regulation.

He vigorously opposed nullification in a pamphlet written under the pseudonym "Hamilton" (1828). He also authored *Sketches of the Life and Correspondence of Nathanael Greene* (1822) and *Eulogy of Thomas Jefferson* (1826).

Johnston, Joseph Eggleston (b. "Cherry Grove," Prince Edward Co., Va., 3 Feb. 1807; d. Washington, D.C., 21 Mar. 1891), Confederate general. Graduated (1829) from the U.S. Military Academy, he served in the Mexican War, in which he was wounded 5 times, and was promoted to lieutenant colonel in 1855 and brigadier general in 1860. With the secession of Virginia, Johnston resigned from the U.S. Army and was appointed (May 1861) brigadier general in the Confederate army. After turning back the Union forces at 1st Bull Run (21 July 1861), where he shared the field with Beauregard against Mc-Dowell, Johnston was commissioned a general and was wounded while commanding (31 May–1 June) at the Battle of Seven Pines (Fair Oaks). He was placed in command (Nov. 1862) of the Confederate forces in Tennessee and Mississippi, and after the fall of Vicksburg, which contributed to a worsening of Johnston's relations with Jefferson Davis, was assigned (Dec. 1863) to the Army of Tennessee, before Chattanooga. Late in the spring of 1864 Johnston fell back before Sherman's assault and was relieved from his command (17 July 1864) before Atlanta. The Confederate Congress passed a resolution asking his reinstatement. Restored (23 Feb. 1865), Johnston signed an armistice (18 Apr. 1865) with Sherman which the Union government rejected. When Johnston was ordered by Jefferson Davis to continue the war in the interior, he refused and surrendered his force to Sherman near Durham Station, N.C. (26 Apr.

1865). He served in Congress (1879–81) and was appointed (1885) a federal commissioner of railroads.

Jones, John Paul (b. Kirkbean, Kirkcudbrightshire, Scotland, 6 July 1747; d. Paris, France, 18 July 1792), naval officer. Until c.1773, when he arrived in America, he was known as **John Paul.** He was commissioned (7 Dec. 1775) a lieutenant in the newly organized Continental navy, captured 16 prizes as commander of the *Providence,* and in 1776 was promoted to captain. Appointed (14 June 1777) commander of the sloop *Ranger,* he carried out raids on British shipping, using Brest as a base of operations. Early in 1779 he was given command of an old East Indiaman which he christened the *Bonhomme Richard (Poor Richard)* in honor of Benjamin Franklin. On 14 Aug. 1779 he set out from L'Orient at the head of a small fleet to prey upon the British coast. On 23 Sept. 1779 there took place off Flamborough Head the naval engagement between the *Bonhomme Richard* and the larger and more heavily armed British warship *Serapis.* Although the *Richard* was sunk, the *Serapis* was captured by Jones, who on this occasion is reported to have said in reply to the British demand for surrender: "I have not yet begun to fight." He was made commander (26 June 1781) of the warship *America,* whose construction he supervised. When the navy was discontinued (1783), Jones went abroad. By unanimous resolve, Congress authorized (16 Oct. 1787) the presentation of a gold medal to Jones, the only Continental naval officer so honored. Late in 1787 Jones decided to enter the Russian naval service and, as a rear admiral, took command (26 May 1788) of a fleet on the Black Sea. He resigned from the Russian navy in 1789 and returned to Paris. In 1905 what are thought to be his remains were brought to the U.S. and now rest in the crypt of the chapel of the U.S. Naval Academy.

Kahn, Louis I. (b. Island of Saaremaa, Estonia, Russia, 20 Feb. 1901; d. New York City, 17 Mar. 1974), architect, came to the U.S. (1905), and graduated from the Univ. of Pennsylvania School of Architecture (1924). Though influenced by his training in the Beaux Arts tradition, Kahn was a fundamentalist who rethought the process and nature of architecture. Fitting into neither of the dominant schools of modern architecture (the abstract rationalism of the international style identified with Le Corbusier and Mies van der Rohe; the "organic" school of Frank Lloyd Wright), Kahn believed that both function and form should dictate a building's style. Rather than the modernists' steel and glass, he preferred brick, concrete, and stone. His work demonstrated an ability to create dramatic interactions of light and shadow and effective combinations of space and solid and of the grand and the intimate. Though he established his own firm in Philadelphia (1935) and was considered an excellent teacher at the Yale School of Architecture (1947–57), he did not receive recognition as a major architect until his Yale Art Gallery was completed (1951). His other major works include: the Richards Medical Research Laboratories of the Univ. of Pennsylvania (1961), the Salk Institute (La Jolla, Calif., 1965), the Kimbell Museum (Ft. Worth, Tex., 1972), and the Phillips-Exeter Academy Library (Exeter, N.H., 1972). At the time of Kahn's death, 2 major projects were under construction in Bangladesh: the capital area of Dacca, and the Institute of Ahmedabad. He was also professor of architecture at the Univ. of Pennsylvania (1956–71).

Kendall, Edward Calvin (b. South Norwalk, Conn., 8 Mar. 1886; d. Princeton, N.J., 4 May 1972), biochemist, was graduated from Columbia (B.S., 1908; M.S., 1909; Ph.D., 1910), where he was a Goldschmidt fellow. He served as a research chemist with Parke, Davis & Co. at Detroit (1910–11) and with St. Luke's Hospital at New York (1911–14). Head of the biochemistry section at the Mayo Foundation, Rochester, Minn., and professor of physiological chemistry under the Mayo Foundation at the Univ. of Minnesota (1914–52), and at Princeton (1952–72). His first notable achievement was to isolate thyroxine from the thyroid gland (1914); then he isolated glutathione from yeast (1929). For isolating and synthesizing the principal hormone of the adrenal cortex (cortisone), he won a Nobel prize in medicine and physiology (with Phillip Hench and Tadeus Reichstein).

Kennedy, John Fitzgerald (b. Brookline, Mass., 29 May 1917; d. Dallas, Tex., 22 Nov. 1963), 35th president of the U.S., son of Joseph P. Kennedy, banker and realtor, received his B.S. cum laude (1940) from Harvard, spending six months during his junior year working in the London embassy while his father was ambassador to Great Britain. His observations inspired *Why England Slept* (1940). In the navy (1941–45), he was awarded the Navy and Marine Corps Medals and the Purple Heart for action as commander of a PT boat. After a brief period as a news correspondent, he was elected Democratic congressman from Massachusetts for 3 terms (1947–53). His defeat of Henry Cabot Lodge in the senatorial race of 1952 was a major upset. His *Profiles in Courage*

(1956) was awarded the Pulitzer prize in biography (1957). He lost a close race to Estes Kefauver for the vice-presidential nomination in 1956, but was reelected to the Senate (1958) by a 875,000-vote margin. He won the Democratic nomination for the presidency (1960) on the 1st ballot. He became the first Catholic and youngest man to be elected president. His administration strongly resisted Communist threats in Berlin (1961) and Cuba (1962), entered into a nuclear test ban (1963), and was solidly committed to civil rights. His assassination, 22 Nov. 1963, by Lee Harvey Oswald caused universal grief.

Kennedy, Robert F. (b. Brookline, Mass., 20 Nov. 1925; d. Los Angeles, Calif., 6 June 1968), political leader, received his A.B. from Harvard (1948) and his LL.B. from the Univ. of Virginia (1951). During World War II, while at Harvard, Kennedy enlisted in the U.S. Naval Reserve, and served as a seaman on the destroyer *Joseph P. Kennedy, Jr.*, named for his elder brother who had been killed in battle. Admitted to the Massachusetts bar (1951), he began his legal career as an attorney in the Criminal Division of the Department of Justice (1951–52). In 1953 he served as assistant counsel to the Hoover Commission. Later that year he was appointed assistant counsel to the Senate Permanent Subcommittee on Investigations, whose chairman was Sen. Joseph Mc-Carthy. Kennedy served as counsel to the Democratic minority (1954) and as chief counsel and staff director of the committee (1955). He gained prominence by the vigor of his investigations of Teamster Union presidents Dave Beck and Jimmy Hoffa during his service as chief counsel to the Senate Committee on Improper Activities in Labor or Management (1957–60), writing *The Enemy Within* (1960). Campaign man-

ager for his brother, John F. Kennedy, during his 1952 senatorial and 1960 presidential campaigns, Robert Kennedy became attorney general of the U.S. (1961–64). In that position he continued the investigations of Hoffa and other union leaders. During his years in the Justice Department he actively supported reforms in criminal justice, fought for black civil rights, and strongly enforced federal voting laws. His brother's closest friend and adviser, Kennedy played a major role in deliberations during the Cuban missile crisis (1962). After the assassination of John F. Kennedy (1963), Robert Kennedy, grieving, sought his own political course. Rejected as a running mate by President Lyndon Johnson, Kennedy was elected U.S. senator from New York (1964). In the Senate he was among the earliest to oppose the Vietnam War and became increasingly associated with the causes of minorities generally lacking in power, such as migrant agricultural workers, American Indians, and Eskimos. A belated candidate for the Democratic presidential nomination in 1968, attempting to rally antiwar forces, Kennedy won major primaries in Indiana and Nebraska. He was assassinated by Sirhan Sirhan almost immediately after acknowledging his victory in the California primary.

Kent, James (b. Fredericksburg, N.Y., 31 July 1763; d. New York City, 12 Dec. 1847), jurist, was graduated from Yale (1781), admitted to the New York bar (1785), and practiced in Poughkeepsie until 1793 and thereafter in New York City until his elevation to the bench. Professor of law at Columbia (1794–98 and 1824–26), he became master in chancery (1796), justice (1798), and chief justice (1804) of the state supreme court, where he introduced much French civil law into the New York legal system as well as the practice of written opinions. Appointed chancellor (1814–23), his decisions, along with the work of Story, laid the foundations of equity jurisprudence in the U.S. His Columbia lectures, which followed the model of Blackstone, were expanded into *Commentaries on the American Law* (1826–30), called by Justice Story "our first judicial classic," and soon accepted as an authoritative exposition of the English common law in the U.S. and a standard interpretation of the Constitution. The most notable edition was the 12th by O. W. Holmes, Jr. (1873). A lifelong Federalist, Kent vigorously opposed universal suffrage at the New York Constitutional Convention (1821).

Kettering, Charles Franklin (b. Londonville, Ohio, 29 Aug. 1876; d. Dayton, Ohio, 25 Nov. 1958), inventor, received his E.E. degree (1904) from Ohio State Univ. He began work with the Star Telephone Co., Ashland, and then, with the National Cash Register Co., Dayton, he invented an electric motor for cash registers. In 1909 he organized the Dayton Engineering Laboratories Co. (Delco), and within 2 years made notable improvements in automobile ignition and lighting systems. His perfection (1911) of the self-starter, first installed in the Cadillac, enormously expanded the market for the motorcar. As general manager of General Motors' research laboratories (1925–47) he directed research on improving Diesel engines and the development of a nontoxic and noninflammable refrigerant. He also originated and guided researches resulting in higher octane gasoline, adding tetraethyl lead. In 1951 he developed a new high-compression engine. Founder and chairman of the Charles F. Kettering Foundation (1927), he directed research in the natural sciences, working on chlorophyll and photosynthesis, artificial-fever therapy, and cancer. He was cofounder of the Sloan-Kettering Institute for Cancer Research.

King, Martin Luther, Jr. (b. Atlanta, Ga., 15 Jan. 1929; d. Memphis, Tenn., 4 Apr. 1968), social reformer and clergyman, received his A.B. from Morehouse College (1948), his B.D. from Crozer Theological Seminary (1951), and his Ph.D. from Boston Univ. (1955). As pastor of the Dexter Avenue Baptist Church, he helped to direct the Negro bus boycott in Montgomery, Ala. (1955–56). His philosophy of nonviolent demonstrations, influenced by Gandhi (later expressed eloquently in *A Letter from Birmingham Jail* [1963]) was widely adopted in the rapidly growing civil rights movement. He founded (1957) and was president of the Southern Christian Leadership Conference, which first spurred voter registration activity and later helped to organize sit-ins and freedom rides. He was a leader of the demonstrations in Birmingham, Ala. (1963) which triggered Pres. Kennedy's decision to fight for a strong civil rights law. One of 8 leaders of the March on Washington by over 200,000 (28 Aug. 1963), he electrified the audience with his "I Have a Dream" address. His shrewd sense of strategy, eloquence, and moral courage proved major assets to the civil rights movement. King was awarded the Nobel peace prize (1964). He led a Freedom March from Selma to Montgomery, Ala. (1965), planned and led assaults on Chicago's de facto school desegregation (1965) and slum conditions (1966). He announced his opposition to the Vietnam War (1967). He was about to lead a nationwide campaign of the poor when assassinated in Memphis by James Earl Ray. He was the author of *Stride Toward Freedom* (1958), and *Why We Can't Wait* (1964).

Kinsey, Alfred C. (b. Hoboken, N.J., 23 June 1894; d. Bloomington, Ind., 25

Aug. 1956), sex researcher and zoologist, received his B.S. from Bowdoin College (1916) and his Sc.D. from Harvard (1920). He became a professor of zoology at Indiana Univ. (1929–56). Throughout the 1930s, Kinsey, an entomologist, studied the life and habits of the gall wasp, and his publications established him as a leading authority. Turning to research on sex (1938), he established, with financial support from the Rockefeller Foundation and the National Research Council, the Institute for Sex Research at Indiana Univ. (1942). Kinsey and 14 associates undertook the most ambitious investigation of sexual activity up to that time, interviewing 5,300 men and boys, and 5,940 women and girls. Using polling techniques, his interviews sometimes included as many as 300 questions on sex. The result of this research was the publication of *Sexual Behavior in the Human Male* (1948) and *Sexual Behavior in the Human Female* (1953). His controversial findings aroused wide national interest. Among the general conclusions, he found a wide divergence between moral codes and social mores; premarital intercourse more widespread among men and women than previously believed; a close relationship between social class and sex habits; potency among the male continuing far beyond age 60; and a far greater percentage of Americans engaged in homosexual activity than had previously been believed.

Kissinger, Henry Alfred (b. Fuerth, Germany, 27 May 1923–), statesman and scholar. Kissinger came to the U.S. (1938), becoming an American citizen (1943), and serving in the U.S. army (1943–46). He received his A.B. *summa cum laude* (1950) and his Ph.D. in government (1954) from Harvard. As professor of government at Harvard (1959–

69), Kissinger's scholarship included studies of diplomacy, nuclear strategy, and contemporary U.S. foreign policy. His Ph.D. dissertation was published as *A World Restored: Metternich, Castlereagh, and the Problems of Peace, 1812–22* (1957), and was followed by *Nuclear Weapons and Foreign Policy* (1957), *The Necessity for Choice: Prospects of American Foreign Policy* (1961), *The Troubled Partnership* (1965), and *American Foreign Policy, Three Essays* (1969). He was the founder and editor of the Harvard journal *Confluence* (1952), director of Harvard's Defense Studies Program (1951–69), and executive director of the Harvard International Seminar (1951–69). During this period Kissinger was director of the Special Studies Project of the Rockefeller Brothers Fund (1956–58), and director of Nuclear Weapons and Foreign Policy Studies of the Council on Foreign Relations (1955–58). He was consultant to the National Security Council during the Berlin crisis (1961–62), to the U.S. Arms Control and Disarmament Agency (1961–68), and to the Department of State (1965–69). As Assistant to the President for National Security Affairs (1969–74), and Secretary of State (1973–77), Kissinger was both a major architect and the key implementer of foreign policy during the Nixon administration. His performance, infused with energy, was characterized by personal diplomacy, secrecy, surprise tactics, and the conviction that in diplomacy momentum produces results. His major achivements were negotiating the opening of relations with mainland China and a peace agreement for Vietnam, promoting détente with the U.S.S.R. and, after the Yom Kippur War (1973), mediation in the Middle East. In 1973 Kissinger and Le Duc Tho of North Vietnam received the Nobel peace prize for their efforts toward ending the Vietnam War. After leaving office, Kissinger joined the faculty of Georgetown Univ. (1977–   ) and authored *White House Years* (1979).

Kuniyoshi, Yasuo (b. Okayama, Japan, 1 Sept. 1893; d. New York City, 14 May 1953), painter and graphic artist. He attended technical schools in Japan, emigrated to the U.S. at the age of 13, studied at the Los Angeles School of Art (1908–10), and in New York City at the National Academy of Design and the Robert Henri School (1910–14), the Independent School of Art (1914–16), and the Art Students League (1916–20). Throughout his school years, Kuniyoshi used his hobby, photography, as a means of support. His first 1-man exhibition came at the Daniel Gallery in New York (1922). When he visited Japan (1931–32), he gave 1-man shows in Tokyo and Osaka. In 1942 he had a 20-year retrospective for the United China War Relief Fund. Kuniyoshi taught at the New School for Social Research (1936–50) and at the Art Students League (1933–53). During World War II he created posters for the Office of War Information and broadcast to the Japanese. The first artist to have a 1-man show at the Whitney Museum of American Art (1948), Kuniyoshi was one of 4 artists to represent the U.S. at the 26th Biennale in Venice (1952). Among his notable paintings are *Mother and Daughter* (1945, Carnegie), *I'm Tired* (1938, Whitney), *Amazing Juggler* (1952, Des Moines). His paintings are distinguished by their iridescence, shimmering colors, witty sophistication, and inner meaning, combining Oriental sensitivity and Western sensuousness. His drawings and lithographs, like his paintings, revealed a gradual departure from his earlier soft-textured work to harshly powerful creations stressing fantasy·

Kuznets, Simon Smith (b. Kharkov, Russia, 30 April 1901–   ), economist. After emigrating to the U.S. (1922), Kuznets attended Columbia, where he was given advanced standing and graduated (1923). Continuing his studies in economics at Columbia, he received his M.A. (1924) and Ph.D. (1926). His first appointment as an economist was at the National Bureau of Economic Research (1926), just founded by his mentor, Prof. Wesley Clair Mitchell. There Kuznets worked on estimating and analyzing the U.S. national income, defining national income as the sum of earnings from wages, profits, interest, and rents. During the depression his work on national income and economic growth was spurred by the New Deal's need for economic statistics. He helped transform economics into a more exact science, and by developing the framework of national incomes accounting contributed much to the study of the problems of economic growth. His system eventually became the basis for the concept of gross national product. Kuznets was a professor of economics at the Univ. of Pennsylvania (1930–54) and at Johns Hopkins (1954–71). During World War II he was associate director of the Bureau of Planning and Statistics War Production Board. In 1971 Kuznets received the Nobel prize for economics for his work on national income accounting. Among his works are *National Income and Its Composition* (1941), *National Product Since 1869* (1947), *Shares of Upper Income Groups in Income and Savings* (1953), and *Economic Growth of Nations* (1971).

La Farge, John (b. New York City, 31 Mar. 1835; d. Providence, R.I., 14 Nov. 1910), artist and writer. He was graduated (1853) from Mount St. Mary' College at Emmitsburg, Md.; in 1856 went to Paris, where he worked briefly under the painter Couture and then made studies of the old masters during a tour of northwestern Europe; returned to the U.S. in 1858, studied under William Morris Hunt, and subsequently experimented with luminism in painting, anticipating the colorist treatments of the French Impressionists. From easel work he moved into mural painting, in which his outstanding achievements are decorations for Trinity Church at Boston, *The Ascension* in the Church of the Ascension at New York, panels for the Church of the Incarnation at New York, and lunettes at the State Capitol at St. Paul, Minn. La Farge also attained eminence as a worker in stained glass, reviving that field as a craft and an industry. He invented opaline glass and designed and manufactured hundreds of windows. With Henry Adams, he visited Japan and the South Seas in 1886, recording his journey in *An Artist's Letters from Japan* (1897) and *Reminiscences of the South Seas* (1912), illustrated by his paintings and sketches.

La Follette, Robert Marion (b. Primrose, Wis., 14 June 1855; d. Washington, D.C., 18 June 1925), statesman, was graduated from the Univ. of Wisconsin (1879), studied law privately and at the university law school, was admitted to the bar in 1880, and practiced at Madison, Wis. As a Republican, he opposed the regular political leaders of Dane Co., of which he was elected (1880) district attorney, and in 1884 was elected to Congress, where he served from 1885 to 1891. His fight against the political leadership of U.S. Sen. Philetus Sawyer led to an open break between La Follette and the party bosses. Although failing to win the Republican nomination for governor in 1896 and 1898, his fight against the entrenched political groups brought him (1900) nomination by acclamation. He took office as governor

(1901) with a program that soon became known as the "Wisconsin Idea" and served as a model of progressive government: opposition to political bosses, direct appeal to the people, and the employment of technical experts; and specific proposals for direct primary legislation, railroad control, and tax reform. The primary law was enacted in 1903; a railroad commission was set up in 1905. La Follette was reelected governor in 1902 and 1904, and in 1906 took his seat in the U.S. Senate, to which he was reelected 3 times. As a Progressive leader in the Senate, he opposed the Payne-Aldrich Tariff, advocated the physical valuation of railroads as a basis for rate making, and sponsored the La Follette Seamen's Act (1915). He established (1909) *La Follette's Weekly Magazine.* In 1911 he drafted the program for the National Progressive Republican League, campaigned for the Progressive nomination in 1911–12, but lost it to Theodore Roosevelt, partly as a result of a temporary breakdown (Feb. 1912) suffered in public. He opposed Wilson's foreign policy and early in 1917, as one of the "little group of willful men" (in Wilson's phrase), prevented passage of the armed merchant ship bill. He voted against the declaration of war on Germany, but supported most of the war measures. He opposed U.S. participation in the League of Nations and the World Court. A liberal leader in the postwar years, he was the author of a resolution for a Senate inquiry into the Teapot Dome and other naval oil leases made during the Harding administration. The Progressive candidate for president in 1924, he received nearly 5 million votes. He published his *Autobiography* (1913).

La Guardia, Fiorello Henry (b. New York City, 11 Dec. 1882; d. there, 20 Dec. 1947), congressman, mayor of New

York, reformer, received his early education in Arizona, where he wrote for the Phoenix *Morning Courier*. During the Spanish-American War he was a Florida correspondent for the St. Louis *Post-Dispatch*. He worked (1901–04) for the U.S. consular service in Budapest, Trieste, and Fiume, then for the U.S. Immigration Service at Ellis Island, N.Y. (1907–10) while studying law at New York Univ. (LL.B., 1910), and was admitted to the New York bar that year. Victor over Tammany, he was elected to Congress as a Republican (1917) and joined in the successful fight for the liberalization of the House rules, but resigned to command the U.S. air forces on the Italo-Austrian front in World War I. President of the board of aldermen (1920–21), he returned to Congress (1923–33), where he fought for labor reforms and cosponsored the Norris-La Guardia anti-injunction bill (1932). Elected Fusion mayor of New York (1933) and reelected (1937, 1941), the "Little Flower" (from his first name) proved indefatigable, incorruptible, and colorful in executing a vast program of reform and public works and bringing about the adoption (1938) of a new city charter. He served (1946) as director of the UN Relief and Rehabilitation Administration.

Land, Edwin Herbert (b. Bridgeport, Conn., 7 May 1909–   ), inventor. Even before attending Harvard (1926–27, 1929–32), Land experimented with a filter which would screen out all light not moving in parallel planes. In 1929 he successfully developed a plastic sheet —called Polaroid—capable of polarizing light passed through it. He left Harvard and, with a former Harvard physics instructor, opened Land-Wheelwright Laboratories (1932). They began producing polarizing filters for cameras (1935) and Polaroid lenses for sunglasses (1936). In 1937 Land organized the Polaroid Corp.—serving thereafter as president, chairman of the board, and director of research. During World War II Polaroid research teams worked for the U.S. army developing such optical devices as light-weight, stereoscopic range finders and searchlight filters used in signaling at night. In 1947 Land announced the invention of a camera that could produce a photograph with a minute of exposure. The Polaroid Land camera, a tremendous commercial success, was later refined to deliver color prints. Of special importance to cancer research was Land's development of a color-translating microscope (1948), which could produce full-color still and motion pictures of living cells.

Langdell, Christopher Columbus (b. New Boston, N.H., 22 May 1826; d. Cambridge, Mass., 6 July 1906), jurist and law teacher. He was graduated from Harvard (1851) and the Harvard Law School, practiced law at New York City (1854–70), and in 1870 was named Dane professor of law in the Harvard Law School, a post he held until 1900, as well as that of dean (1870–95). His fame rests on his introduction of the case method of teaching law, with its emphasis upon the formulation of legal principles from a study of specific court decisions, as expounded in his *A Selection of Cases on the Law of Contracts* (1871). He also wrote *A Summary of Equity Pleading* (1877) and works in the field of contracts.

Langmuir, Irving (b. Brooklyn, N.Y., 31 Jan. 1881; d. Schenectady, N.Y., 16 Aug. 1957), physical chemist, was graduated from the Columbia Univ. School of Mines (1903) and the Univ. of Göttingen (Ph.D., 1906), was an instructor in chemistry (1906–09) at Stevens Institute, and in 1909 joined the General Electric Co. as a research chemist and physicist. He was assistant (1909–32) and associate director (1932–51) of the General Electric Research Laboratory. In 1912 he developed a high-intensity tungsten electric lamp filled with nitrogen (later argon), a great improvement over the vacuum-type lamp. He did pioneer work in surface tension and with Gilbert N. Lewis formulated the Lewis-Langmuir theory of atomic structure and valence. He also carried out important investigations in colloid chemistry, the kinetics of gas reactions at low pressures, the production of artificial snow, the dissociation of hydrogen, acoustic devices for detecting submarines, and the vapor pressures of metals. In 1932 he received the Nobel prize in chemistry.

Latrobe, Benjamin Henry (b. Fulneck, Yorkshire, England, 1 May 1764; d. New Orleans, La., 3 Sept. 1820), architect and civil engineer. Educated in Germany, he took his professional training in England under the architect Samuel Pepys Cockerell and the civil engineer John Smeaton. He came to the U.S. in 1796; improved the navigation of the Appomattox and James rivers; designed (1797) the penitentiary at Richmond, Va.; and completed the façade of the Virginia State Capitol designed by Jefferson. The leading exponent of the Greek Revival in the U.S., Latrobe designed in that style the Bank of Pennsylvania at Philadelphia, where he also built (1799–1801) the city water works on the Schuylkill. He improved the navigation of the Susquehanna River, served as engineer of the Chesapeake & Delaware Canal, and constructed the Washington City Canal. In 1803 President Jefferson named him surveyor of

the public buildings, in which capacity Latrobe revised the plans for the national Capitol drawn up by William Thornton. He intermittently continued work on the Capitol, including its rebuilding after its destruction by fire in 1814, until his retirement from federal service in 1817. He also drew up plans for the Marine Hospital and St. John's Church, both at Washington, D.C.; the Baltimore Cathedral; the Bank of Philadelphia; the old Pennsylvania Academy of Fine Arts, the Markoe and Waln houses, and the 2d Bank of the U.S., all at Philadelphia; the Henry Clay house at Ashland, Ky.; and the Exchange (including the Bank of the U.S. and the Custom House) at Baltimore. In his last years he was engaged on the water supply system for New Orleans. Almost singlehanded, Latrobe raised architectural practice in the U.S. to the status of a profession.

Lawrence, Ernest Orlando (b. Canton, S.D., 8 Aug. 1901; d. Palo Alto, Calif., 27 Aug. 1958), nuclear physicist, inventor of the cyclotron, was graduated from the Univ. of South Dakota (A.B., 1922), the Univ. of Minnesota (A.M., 1923), and Yale (Ph.D., 1925), taught physics at Yale (1925–28), and after 1928 at the Univ. of California, where he directed the radiation laboratory beginning 1936. His major contribution was the development of the cyclotron, a mechanism which produces atomic transmutation through bombardment of matter with high-energy particles. Lawrence outlined the fundamental concept of the cyclotron as early as 1930 and, with his associates, constructed the first cyclotron in 1932, thereafter making improvements. In 1936 he transmuted other elements into gold. For his invention of the cyclotron, he was awarded (1939) the Nobel prize in physics. In World War II the cyclotron was used for separating U-235 from natural uranium during research on the atomic bomb, a project in which Lawrence took part. In 1957 he received the Fermi award given by the U.S. Atomic Energy Commission.

Lederberg, Joshua (b. Montclair, N.J., 23 May 1925–   ), geneticist, was graduated from Columbia (B.A., 1944), studied at the Coll. of Physicians and Surgeons (1944–46), receiving his Ph.D. at Yale (1947), where he worked with Dr. Edward L. Tatum (1909–75) on sexual reproduction in bacteria. He taught genetics at the Univ. of Wisconsin (1947–57) and became (1959) professor of genetics and biology at the Stanford School of Medicine. In 1958 he received the Nobel prize in physiology and medicine for his discoveries concerning genetic recombination and organization of the genetic material of bacteria. His work in virus breeding and cross-breeding is basic to research on the control of virus diseases.

Lee, Richard Henry (b. "Stratford," Westmoreland Co., Va., 20 Jan. 1732; d. neighboring "Chantilly," 19 June 1794), Revolutionary statesman, studied under private tutors, completing his education at the academy at Wakefield, in Yorkshire, England. Entering the House of Burgesses (1758), he opposed (1764) the Sugar Act and organized (1766) the Westmoreland Association, initiating the nonimportation association movement. With Henry and Jefferson, he originated (1773) the plan for intercolonial committees of correspondence. At the 1st Continental Congress (1774) he formed close personal and political ties with Sam Adams and backed the Continental Association. In the 2d Continental Congress he introduced (7 June 1776) the resolution calling for a declaration of independence, foreign alliances, and a confederation of the American states. To secure ratification of the Confederation he advocated the surrender by Virginia of her claims to western lands. He supported his brother Arthur in his dispute with Silas Deane, which divided Congress into 2 camps. President of Congress (1784–85), he declined to serve as a delegate to the Constitutional Convention. Leader of the opposition to ratifying the Constitution in Virginia, he urged in *Letters of the Federal Farmer* (1787) the need for a bill of rights and a more democratic lower house. Senator from Virginia (1789–92), his chief proposals were embodied in the first 10 Amendments.

Lee, Robert Edward (b. Stratford, Va., 19 Jan. 1807; d. Lexington, Va., 12 Oct. 1870), soldier, was graduated from the U.S. Military Academy (1829) and commissioned in the engineers. He married Mary Custis (1831), great-granddaughter of Martha Washington. Serving in the War with Mexico under Scott, he was superintendent of West Point (1852–53), and lieutenant colonel of cavalry on frontier duty in Texas (1855–61), with the exception of 2 years (1857–59) spent on leave at Arlington. He commanded the troops which put down John Brown's raid (1859). At the outbreak of the Civil War he declined field command of the U.S. army offered by Lincoln (18 Apr. 1861) but accepted command of Virginia's military forces, soon receiving the rank of general. When J. E. Johnston was wounded he was assigned to command the Army of Northern Virginia (1 June 1862), removing McClellan's threat to Richmond in the 7 Days' Battles (25 June–1 July 1862). He routed Pope at 2d Bull Run (29–30 Aug.), was checked at Antietam (17 Sept.), and defeated Burnside at Fredericksburg (13 Dec.) and Hooker at Chancellorsville (2–4 May 1863). His defeat and withdrawal at Gettysburg (1–3

July) constituted the turning point of the war. He opposed Grant (May–June 1864) in the battles of Wilderness, Spotsylvania, and Cold Harbor, and was appointed general in chief of all Confederate armies (Feb. 1865). He surrendered to Grant at Appomattox Court House (9 Apr. 1865) and advised the South to create a new and better section within the Union. After the war he accepted the presidency of Washington College (later renamed Washington and Lee Univ. in his honor).

Leontief, Wassily (b. Leningrad, Russia, 6 Aug. 1906–   ), economist. The son of a Russian economist, Leontief attended the Univ. of Leningrad (1921–25) and the Univ. of Berlin (1925–28), where he received his Ph.D. in economics. He became an economist for the Research Institut für Weltwirtschaft at the Univ. of Kiel, Germany (1927–28, 1930) and in 1929 he was an economic adviser to the Chinese government on railroad building. He emigrated to the U.S. (1931), working first for the National Bureau for Economic Research and then joining the faculty of Harvard (1935–75) where he held the Henry Lee Chair and directed the Economic Research Project. He became Professor and Director of The Institute for Economic Analysis, New York Univ. (1975–   ). Leontief received the Nobel prize for economic science (1973) for his development of the "input-output" method of economic analysis. By using the input-output method economists can predict how changes in one sector of an economy will affect the performance of other sectors. With the advent of the computer practical application of input-output analysis became feasible; it has been employed in economic forecasting by more than 50 industrialized countries—both Communist and non-Communist. Leontief has also worked with index numbers for prices

and quantities and has studied economic aspects of automation. Proud of his empirical methods, Leontief is openly critical of other economists for building theories and models little related to economic reality. His works include *Structure of the American Economy 1919–1929; An Empirical Application of Equilibrium Analysis* (1941), *Studies in the Structure of the American Economy* (with others, 1953), *Input-Output Economics* (1966), and *Collected Essays* (1966).

Lewis, Gilbert Newton (b. Weymouth, Mass., 23 Oct. 1875; d. Berkeley, Calif., 23 Mar. 1946), physical chemist. He was graduated from Harvard (A.B., 1896; A.M., 1898; Ph.D., 1899), attended the universities of Leipzig and Göttingen (1900–01), and taught chemistry at Harvard (1899–1906), the Massachusetts Institute of Technology (1907–12), and the Univ. of California (1912–46). During World War I he headed the defense division of the gas service of the A.E.F. One of the most versatile of American physical chemists, he evolved the "octet" theory of molecular structure, did important work on the absorption bands and phosphorescence spectra of dyes, improved thermodynamic methods by the concepts of "fugacity" and "activity," collaborated with Dr. Ernest O. Lawrence in inventing the cyclotron (atom-smashing machine), and with Dr. Irving Langmuir formulated the Lewis-Langmuir theory of atomic structure and valence. He wrote *Thermodynamics and the Free Energy of Chemical Substances* (with M. Randall, 1923), *Valence and the Structure of Atoms and Molecules* (1923), and *The Anatomy of Science* (1926).

Lewis, John Llewellyn (b. Lucas, Iowa, 12 Feb. 1880; d. Washington, D.C., 11 June 1969), labor leader, son of a

Welsh miner, joined his father as a laborer in a Lucas coal mine at the age of 16. As state legislative agent for District 12 of the United Mine Workers of America (1909–11), he secured the passage of workmen's compensation and mine safety laws in Illinois. Field and legislative representative of the AFL, he rose to the presidency of the UMW (1920), which post he held until his retirement (1960). A militant unionist and formidable bargainer, he called the crippling bituminous coal strikes of 1919 and 1922, scoring notable victories in each case. In a period of economic distress for the coal industry, he fought off (1930) an ouster move by insurgents. Vice-president of the AFL (1934), he resigned (1935) to form, with Sidney Hillman (*q.v.*) and David Dubinsky (1892–   ), the Congress of Industrial Organizations (later CIO), AFL's giant rival. With Hillman he organized (1936) Labor's Non-Partisan League, supporting the reelection of Franklin D. Roosevelt, with whom he later broke. His Apr. 1946 coal strike precipitated U.S. government seizure of the mines (21 May) and was ended by an injunction and a contempt conviction, although when the mines were returned to their owners (June 1947) Lewis secured all his demands.

Lewis, Meriwether (b. in Albemarle Co., Va., 18 Aug. 1774; d. in central Tenn., 11 Oct. 1809), and **Clark, William** (b. in Caroline Co., Va., 1 Aug. 1770; d. St. Louis, Mo., 1 Sept. 1838), explorers and territorial governors, leaders of the Lewis and Clark overland expedition to the U.S. Northwest (1803–06). Both were officers in the U.S. army, Clark being the brother of the Revolutionary soldier George Rogers Clark (1752–1818). In 1801 Lewis became private secretary to President Jefferson, who selected him as commander of an overland expedition to the Pacific. Lewis chose Capt. Clark as his companion officer, and they shared authority. The expedition was fitted out in Illinois during the winter of 1803–04 and was later transferred to St. Louis. Clark joined Lewis at St. Charles, Mo. Their party, consisting of 23 soldiers, 3 interpreters, and 1 slave, set out in the spring of 1804 and followed the Missouri River in a 1,600-mile journey to the Mandan villages in North Dakota, where it went into winter quarters near the site of present-day Bismarck, N.D. Resuming the journey on 7 Apr. 1805, the expedition reached the mouth of the Yellowstone (26 Apr.), the triple fork of the Missouri (25 July), and descended the Columbia, reaching the Pacific Ocean on 15 Nov. On the return journey (23 Mar.–23 Sept. 1806) to St. Louis, the party divided and, after exploring much of what is now the state of Montana, reunited below the mouth of the Yellowstone. The records of the Lewis and Clark expedition, including the diaries kept by both leaders and the maps and drawings made by Clark, constituted valuable scientific findings. Lewis, appointed governor of Louisiana Territory (1806), died either by suicide or killing. Clark, appointed superintendent of Indian affairs at St. Louis (1807) and governor of Missouri Territory (1813), concluded treaties with the Indians after the War of 1812.

Lewis, Harry Sinclair (b. Sauk Centre, Minn., 7 Feb. 1885; d. Rome, Italy, 10 Jan. 1951), author. He interrupted his studies at Yale (begun 1903) to join Upton Sinclair's utopian socialist community in Palisades, N.J. and to visit Panama to watch the canal construction. After graduating from Yale (1908), he pursued an unsuccessful career in journalism—at various times working as a reporter for the Waterloo (Ia.) *Courier,* the San Francisco *Bulletin,* and the Associated Press, and as editor for *Adventure* magazine and for the George Doran Co. He published several minor novels, but it was not until the appearance of his short stories in the *Saturday Evening Post* (1915) that his literary career began to blossom. His first major novel, *Main Street* (1920), an iconoclastic treatment of the American myth of the small town, was sensationally popular both in the U.S. and abroad. It was followed by such successes as: *Babbitt* (1922), *Arrowsmith* (1925), *Elmer Gantry* (1927), *Dodsworth* (1929), and *It Can't Happen Here* (1935). His works contributed to American thought the concept of "Babbittry"—complacent conformity to middle-class ideas, especially of material success. His social criticism and satire inspired much controversy. In 1926 he refused to accept the Pulitzer prize he was awarded for *Arrowsmith*. With *Babbitt,* he became the first American to win the Nobel prize for literature (1930). Lewis' oeuvre includes 23 novels and 3 plays.

Lincoln, Abraham (b. Hardin, Ky., 12 Feb. 1809; d. Washington, D.C., 15 Apr. 1865), 16th president of the U.S., moved with his parents (Thomas and Nancy Hanks Lincoln) to Spencer Co., Ind. (1816), then settled in southern Illinois (1830), where he clerked in a store at New Salem. He became captain of volunteers in the Black Hawk War (1832), but did not see action. He operated a store, practiced surveying, and served as postmaster at New Salem (1833–36) while he studied law and was admitted to the bar (1836). He moved to Springfield (1837), where he opened a law office and quickly obtained a reputation on the circuit as an outstanding jury lawyer. Whig state legislator (1834–42), he was elected to Congress (1846), but did not stand for reelection. In his

Peoria speech (1854) he denounced the Kansas-Nebraska Act. Joining the Republican party (1856), he ran for the Senate against Stephen A. Douglas (1858), accepting the nomination (17 June) with a speech in which he declared: "A house divided against itself cannot stand." In the course of 7 campaign debates with Douglas he forced the latter to announce the so-called Freeport Doctrine. Losing the election, Lincoln had established himself as a national figure. Although he won the Republican nomination for the presidency in 1860 because of his conservative views on slavery, his election was regarded in the South as forecasting an attack on the "peculiar institution." By 4 Mar. 1861, 7 states had already seceded. In his first inaugural Lincoln reiterated his constitutional doctrine that the contract between the states was binding and irrevocable. Against the advice of his cabinet, he ordered the provisioning of Ft. Sumter and when war began called out the state militia, suspended the writ of habeas corpus, proclaimed a blockade of Southern ports, and in other ways did not hesitate to use the dictatorial powers with which he was invested. He largely countermanded Frémont's proclamation (30 Aug. 1861) emancipating the slaves of rebels in Missouri and proposed his own plan for compensated emancipation (Dec. 1861, 12 July and 1 Dec. 1862). "My paramount object is to save the Union, and not either to save or destroy slavery," he stated (22 Aug. 1862). After Antietam he prepared a draft of emancipation, proclaimed formally 1 Jan. 1863. A diplomat in the handling of both his cabinet and his generals, his reelection in 1864, when he easily defeated McClellan, was assured by the military victories of Grant, Sherman, and Sheridan. His plan of Reconstruction (8 Dec. 1863) was based on the prompt restoration of the Southern states to "their proper practical relation with the Union." He pocket-vetoed the harsher Wade-Davis Bill (8 July 1864). He personally attended the Hampton Roads Conference (3 Feb. 1865) to discuss peace terms with Confederate leaders. His most notable speeches were his Gettysburg Address (19 Nov. 1863) and his second inaugural (4 Mar. 1865), in which he appealed to the nation to "finish the work we are in . . . with malice toward none, with charity for all." Shortly after Lee's surrender he was shot by John Wilkes Booth in Ford's Theater, Washington (14 Apr. 1865), and died the next day.

Lipmann, Fritz Albert (b. Koenigsberg, Germany, 12 June 1899–   ), biochemist, received his M.D. (1922) and Ph.D. (1927) from the Univ. of Berlin, became research assistant at the Kaiser Wilhelm Institute in the laboratory of Otto Meyerhof, where he began investigating the mechanism of fluoride effects and, from 1930–31, the field of tissue culture. Winner of a Rockefeller fellowship, he began work at the Rockefeller Institute (1931) on phosphorus mechanisms, then returned to Europe (1932), spending 7 years as research associate in the Biological Institute of Carlsberg Foundation at Copenhagen. Returning to the U.S. (1939) as a research fellow at the Cornell Univ. Medical College, he became (1941) senior biochemist at the Massachusetts General Hospital and professor at the Harvard Medical School. In 1957 he became a professor of the Rockefeller Institute. He became a U.S. citizen (1944). Experiments in 1937 started him on a series of investigations during which he developed the idea of phosphate bond energy. He isolated acetyl phosphate (1942) and with his coworkers synthesized it (1944). He received the Nobel prize in medicine and physiology (1953) for isolating and identifying coenzyme A (1945) as a crucial element in providing usable energy for the body-building process and demonstrating how coenzyme A brought forth the construction of fatty acids and steroids necessary to the body's renewal and growth. He later did research in the structure of cancer cells and investigated pantothenic acid and the action of the energy-regulating thyroid hormone.

Lippmann, Walter (b. New York City, 23 Sept. 1889; d. New York City, 14 Dec. 1974), journalist and author. After graduating from Harvard (1909) he did graduate work in philosophy there (1909–10). Joining Lincoln Steffens briefly on *Everybody's Magazine* (1910–11), he wrote *A Preface to Politics* (1913). With Herbert Croly he founded *The New Republic* (1914), a liberal weekly journal. During World War I he left the *New Republic* to serve as an assistant to Secretary of War, Newton D. Baker (1917), and as a captain in the U.S. Military Intelligence (1918), working on propaganda directed at persuading the Germans to surrender. President Wilson selected him to help formulate the Fourteen Points and contribute to preparations for the peace conference at Versailles, which he attended before rejoining *The New Republic* (1919). On the editorial staff of the *New York World* (1921–31), serving as editor the last 8 years, he wrote more than 2,000 editorials. In 1931 he began his column "Today and Tomorrow," which appeared regularly in the *New York Herald Tribune* and was syndicated internationally in at least 200 newspapers. The column, for which he won 2 Pulitzer prizes (1958, 1962), not only earned him a wide audience (more than 38 million readers) but established him as one of the foremost analysts of national and international affairs. In his commentaries on political, social, and ethical problems he sought to promote "liberal democracy" and warned against forces in society which he perceived as opposed to that end. He contributed articles to a wide variety of magazines, wrote 26 books, including 10 of political philosophy, among them: *Public Opinion* (1922), *The Phantom Public* (1927), *A Preface to Morals* (1929), *The Good Society* (1937), and *The Public Philosophy* (1955).

Livingston, Edward (b. "Clermont," Columbia Co., N.Y., 28 May 1764; d. "Montgomery Place," N.Y., 23 May 1836), jurist, statesman, and diplomat, was graduated from the College of New Jersey (1781), studied law in Albany,. and was admitted to the New York bar (1785). In Congress as a Jeffersonian Republican (1795–1801), he was U.S. district attorney of N.Y. (1801). Elected mayor of New York City (1801–03), he reformed the rules of procedure of the mayor's court. When a custom-house clerk misappropriated public funds, he sold his own property to meet the deficit and moved to New Orleans (1803), where he resumed law practice. Purchaser (1808) of the Gravier estate, he improved the *batture* (an alluvial deposit or river beach), was dispossessed on Jefferson's orders, but was the ultimate victor in a celebrated litigation. In the lower house of the Louisiana legislature (1820), congressman (1822–29), U.S. senator (1829–31), he was President Jackson's Secretary of State (1831–33) and wrote the Nullification Proclamation. U.S. minister to France (1833–35), he futilely endeavored to secure payment of U.S. spoliation claims. His fame rests upon his work as a codifier of the laws. After reading Bentham he drafted a code of procedure which was adopted by the Louisiana legislature (1805), the first real code in the U.S. At the request of the legislature he began his comprehensive criminal code (1820), completed (1824), and published (1833). Although not adopted in his own state, it was acclaimed abroad and became the model of state penal codes in the U.S., foreshadowing many later reforms in penology. Sir Henry Maine called Livingston "the first legal genius of modern times."

Livingston, Robert R. (b. New York City, 27 Nov. 1746; d. "Clermont," Columbia Co., N.Y., 26 Feb. 1813), Revolutionary patriot, jurist, diplomat, was graduated from King's College (1765). Admitted to the bar (1770), he practiced law briefly with John Jay (*q.v.*). In the Continental Congress (1775–76, 1779–81, 1784–85), he was on the committee which drafted the Declaration of Independence, but, owing to lack of instructions from the New York convention, neither voted for nor signed the document. Member of the committee which drafted the New York Constitution (1777), he was Chancellor of New York (1777–1801), administering the oath to Washington in 1789. First Secretary of Foreign Affairs (1781–83), he criticized the U.S. peace commissioners for their distrust of France, but supported the treaty they negotiated. With Hamilton and Jay, he was a leading supporter of the Constitution at the New York ratifying convention, but broke with the Federalists over the patronage and used his family and public influence to oppose Jay's Treaty. Defeated by Jay for governor (1798), he was appointed by Jefferson (1801) minister to France, where his most conspicuous achievement was the successful negotiation of the Louisiana Purchase (1803). Patron of the arts, he was interested both in scientific agriculture and technology, and financed Robert Fulton's (*q.v.*) experiments in steam navigation. The steamboat *Clermont* was named for his estate. With Fulton, he secured and maintained during his lifetime a monopoly of steam navigation on the Hudson, which involved him in litigation and was terminated by *Gibbons* v. *Ogden* (1824).

Lodge, Henry Cabot (b. Boston, 12 May 1850; d. Cambridge, Mass., 9 Nov. 1924), statesman and author, was educated at E. S. Dixwell's Latin School and Harvard, graduating in 1871. After a year in Europe, Lodge attended the Harvard Law School, graduating 1874, and was admitted to the bar (1875). He was assistant editor of the *North American Record* (1874–76), under Henry Adams (*q.v.*), and completed his Ph.D. in political science (1876), the first ever given at Harvard. He was lecturer in American History at Harvard (1876) and associate editor of the *International Review* (1879). Among his historical writings were biographies for the American Statesmen Series of *Alexander Hamilton* (1882), *Daniel Webster* (1883), and *George Washington* (2 vols. 1889), as well as *Life and Letters of George Cabot* (1877), a biography of his great-grandfather. He served in the Massachusetts House of Representatives (1880–83), but was defeated in an election for the U.S. House of Representatives (1884) before serving there for 6 years (1887–93). In the House he championed civil service reform and drafted and strongly supported the controversial "Force Bill," aimed at federal supervision of voting in the South to prevent discrimination. Serving in the U.S. Senate from 1893 until his death, Lodge, a Republican, helped to draft the Sherman Antitrust Law and the Pure Food and Drug Law. A thoroughgoing protectionist, Lodge also strongly opposed free silver. In the area of foreign affairs, he supported a strong navy and American imperialist ambitions, exercising a profound influence upon Theodore Roosevelt. As majority leader of the Senate and chairman of the Foreign Relations Committee, Lodge led the fight against ratification of the Versailles Treaty and the Covenant of the League of Nations (1919), publishing his account of the controversy as *The Senate and the League of Nations* (1925). He served as U.S. Representative at the Washington Conference (1921–22).

Long, Huey Pierce (b. near Winnfield, La., 30 Aug. 1893; d. Baton Rouge, 10 Sept. 1935), politician, worked as a traveling salesman before studying law (1914) at Tulane Univ. Admitted to the Louisiana bar (1915), he won a reputation as a poor man's lawyer by specializing in workmen's compensation cases. Elected and reelected railroad (later public service) commissioner (1921–26), as chairman he brought about telephone rate reductions and prevented streetcar fare rises. Defeated for the governorship (1924), he won election (1928), trouncing the New Orleans Democratic machine. An oil property owner himself and long known for his vindictive opposition to the Standard Oil Co., he pushed through the legislature a constitutional amendment to tax the oil interests and use the revenue for highways and education. Impeached by the lower house (1929) for bribery and gross misconduct, he rounded up enough state senators (the "Famous 15") to avoid conviction. Elected to the U.S. Senate (1930), he ruled Louisiana (1930–34) by alliance with the New Orleans machine, retaining the governorship and sponsoring a vast highway program and the expansion of Louisiana

State Univ. As U.S. senator, the "King-fish" failed to secure President Roosevelt's backing for his social program and organized (Jan. 1934) a Share-Our-Wealth Society, promising a homestead allowance of $6,000 and a minimum annual income of $2,500 for every American family. Meantime, to keep control in Louisiana, he reorganized the state government (1934–35), abolishing local government and creating a virtual dictatorship. Announcing his own candidacy for the presidency (Mar. 1935), he was fatally wounded on the steps of the Baton Rouge Capitol by Dr. Carl Weiss, who was shot and killed by Long's bodyguard. His death ended a threat to the New Deal of a 3d party, but his program, along with parallel proposals of Dr. Francis E. Townsend and Rev. Charles E. Coughlin, provided the impetus for the later New Deal social security legislation. Of all Southern demagogues Long posed the most serious threat to democracy.

Longfellow, Henry Wadsworth (b. Portland, Me., 27 Feb. 1807; d. Cambridge, Mass., 24 Mar. 1882), poet. He was graduated (1825) from Bowdoin College; studied modern languages in France, Spain, Italy, and Germany from 1826 to 1829; was professor and librarian at Bowdoin (1829–35); and served (1836–54) as Smith professor of modern languages and belles-lettres at Harvard. His first book of poetry was *Voices of the Night* (1839). His *Ballads and Other Poems* (1841) included "The Village Blacksmith," "Excelsior," and "The Wreck of the Hesperus." When he died he was the most popular American poet. Among other works of poetry by him are *Poems on Slavery* (1842), *Evangeline* (1847), *The Belfry of Bruges and Other Poems* (1845), *The Seaside and the Fireside* (1849), *Hiawatha* (1855),

The Courtship of Miles Standish (1858), *Tales of a Wayside Inn* (1863–74, which includes "Paul Revere's Ride"), *The Masque of Pandora* (1875), *Ultima Thule* (1880), and *In the Harbor* (1882). He translated *The Divine Comedy of Dante Alighieri* (3 vols., 1865–67).

Lowell, James Russell (b. Cambridge, Mass., 22 Feb. 1819; d. there, 12 Aug. 1891), author, editor, teacher, and diplomat. He was graduated from Harvard (1838) and from the Harvard Law School (1840), published *A Year's Life* (1841) and *Poems* (1844), and co-edited (Jan.–Mar. 1843) *The Pioneer: A Literary and Critical Magazine*. Through the influence of Maria White, whom he married in 1844, he became interested in the antislavery movement, and was an editorial writer (1845) for the *Pennsylvania Freeman* and a contributor and corresponding editor of the *National Anti-Slavery Standard*. He established himself as a writer with the following, all published in 1848: *Poems by James Russell Lowell, 2nd Series, A Fable for Critics, The Vision of Sir Launfal*, and *The Biglow Papers* (1st series), a satire on the Mexican War written in the Yankee vernacular. He succeeded. Longfellow (1855), as Smith professor of modern languages and belles-lettres at Harvard, was the first editor (1857–61) of the *Atlantic Monthly*, and joint editor (with Charles Eliot Norton) of the *North American Review* from 1864 to 1872. He was minister to Spain (1877–80) and to England (1880–85). His critical and other writings include *Fireside Travels* (1864), *Biglow Papers* (2nd series, 1867), *Under the Willows* (1868), *The Cathedral* (1870), *Among My Books* (1st and 2nd series, 1870, 1876), *My Study Windows* (1871), *Heartease and Rue* (1888), *Political*

Essays (1888), *Latest Literary Essays and Addresses* (1891), and *The Old English Dramatists* (1892). One of his best-known poems is "Ode Recited at the Harvard Commemoration" (1865).

Luce, Henry Robinson (b. Tengchow, Shantung Prov., China, 3 Apr. 1898; d. Phoenix, Ariz., 28 Feb. 1967), journalist and businessman. Son of a missionary in China, Luce came to the U.S. at the age of 15 and attended Hotchkiss School, Yale (1916–20), and then spent a year doing graduate work at Oxford. His educational career was briefly interrupted by service in the army (1918). At that time he and former classmate Britton Hadden planned a weekly news magazine. After serving as reporters on the *Baltimore News* (1920–23), Hadden and Luce put their plans into effect with the publication of the first issue of *Time* (3 Mar. 1923). With Hadden's death (1929), Luce assumed ownership of the successful enterprise. From the beginning *Time* was opinionated with a conservative slant. A staunch Republican, Luce defended free enterprise and big business and supported aggressive opposition to Communism. Originated by Hadden, *Time*'s unique style was "curt, clear, and complete." The magazine was known for its coining of new words such as "tycoon," from the Japanese "taik," "GOPolitics," "Freudulent," and "socialite." In 1930 Luce established *Fortune*, a monthly magazine for business executives, known for its artistic format and articles on technology. By 1954 Luce's magazine empire included *Time, Fortune, Architectural Forum* (1932), *Life* (1936–72), *House and Home* (1952), and *Sports Illustrated* (1954). The concept of *Life*, the first photojournalism magazine, was largely inspired by Clare Boothe Brokaw, editor of *Vanity Fair* and a playwright, who became Luce's second wife (1935). Luce is considered the key figure in the development of the modern news magazine and the concept of group journalism.

Lyon, Mary (b. Buckland, Mass., 28 Feb. 1797; d. South Hadley, Mass., 5 Mar. 1849), educator. She attended seminaries at Ashfield and Amherst, Mass., and in 1821 studied at the Byfield (Mass.) Seminary. She was a teacher (1821–34) at Ashfield and Ipswich, Mass., and at Londonderry, N.H. Between 1834 and 1837 she worked on a plan to establish a seminary for the education of girls of moderate means, raising the funds for the project and shaping the curriculum (which was based on that at Amherst College). Mount Holyoke Female Seminary (later Mount Holyoke College), of which she served as principal until her death, was opened at South Hadley, Mass., on 8 Nov. 1837. It was the first permanent institution devoted to the higher education of women. Miss Lyon made valuable contributions to educational theory and wrote *Tendencies of the Principles Embraced and the System Adopted in the Mount Holyoke Seminary* (1840).

MacArthur, Douglas (b. Little Rock, Ark., 26 Jan. 1880; d. New York City, 5 Apr. 1964), soldier. Graduated (1903) from the U.S. Military Academy, he saw service in the Philippines (1903–04) and Japan (1905–06), was aide-de-camp (1906–07) to President Theodore Roosevelt and served on the army general staff (1913–15, 1916–17). In Aug. 1917 he was named chief of staff of the 42d (Rainbow) Div., on 6 Aug. 1918 commanding general of the 84th Infantry Brigade, and in Nov. 1918 commanding general of the 42d Div. He took part in the major U.S. offensives of World War I and was twice wounded in action. He served (Nov. 1918–Apr. 1919) with the army of occupation in Germany, was

appointed (12 June 1919) superintendent of the U.S. Military Academy, and
was promoted to brigadier general in
1920. He served in the Philippines
(1922–25) as commander of the Manila
District, was promoted to major general
(1925) and general (1930), and in
1928 became commander of the Philippine Department. After serving as chief
of staff (1930–35) of the U.S. army, he
became (1935) director of the organization of national defense for the Philippine Commonwealth. Appointed (1936)
a field marshal in the Philippine army,
he retired (1937) from the U.S. army,
but was recalled to active service (26
July 1941) as commander of the U.S.
forces in the Far East, and subsequently
assumed his former rank of general. Following the Japanese attack on the Philippines, MacArthur led a skillful defense,
made a planned retreat to Bataan Peninsula, and set up his headquarters on
Corregidor. Appointed (22 Feb. 1942)
Supreme Allied Commander of forces in
the Southwest Pacific, he escaped to
Australia and commanded the Allied
campaigns against Japanese forces in
that area. He was made (Dec. 1944) a
general of the army, and in Aug. 1945
was appointed supreme commander to
accept the formal surrender of Japan,
where he subsequently served as commander of the occupational forces. Following the Communist invasion of South
Korea (25 June 1950), he was made
commander of the United Nations forces
fighting there. On 11 Apr. 1951 President Truman relieved him of his Far
Eastern commands.

McCarthy, Joseph Raymond (b. Grand
Chute, Wis., 14 Nov. 1909; d. Bethesda,
Md., 2 May 1957), U.S. senator, left
school at the age of 14. After working for
a short time, he returned to complete
4 years of high school in one year while
working as a grocery store manager and
movie theater usher in Manawa, Wis.
He received his LL.B. from Marquette
Univ. and was admitted to the bar
(1935). While practicing law in Sha-
waho, Wis. he became interested in
politics as a Democrat, but his first successful bid for elected office, as a state
circuit court judge, was as a Republican
(1939). He interrupted his term of office
during World War II to enlist in the
Marine Corps air force as lieutenant. He
was elected to the U.S. Senate from
Wisconsin in a surprising upset of incumbent Robert LaFollette, Jr. (1946).
Exploiting public fear of Communism,
engendered by Communist control of
China and Eastern Europe, McCarthy
had the distinction of being one of the
most popular and most hated men of his
time. In a speech delivered in Wheeling,
W. Va. (1950) he declared that he had
with him a list of card-carrying members
of the Communist party then employed
by the Department of State. After subsequent speeches, he testified before a
subcommittee of the Senate Foreign Relations Committee without producing
the name of a single Communist working for the State Department, although
he did list several "fellow travelers." Between 1951–54 McCarthy brought
charges of Communist membership or
leanings against civil servants, army officers, writers, actors, professors, and industrial workers. Among those accused
were Gen. George C. Marshall and Adlai
E. Stevenson. He charged previous administrations with "twenty years of treason" (1953) and later amended the charge
to include the first year of the Eisenhower administration. As chairman of
the Permanent Subcommittee on Investigations of the Senate Committee
on Government Operations, McCarthy
looked into disloyalty in the Voice of
America and reports of spying at the
Army Signal Corps installation at Ft.
Monmouth. The dispute widened to in-

clude Army Secretary Robert T. Stevens. Exposure to a national TV audience (Apr.–May 1954) sharply diminished the senator's popularity. An investigation of McCarthy's activities by a senate committee resulted in his formal condemnation by the Senate for refusal to explain a financial transaction and for abuse of other senators (Dec. 1954). His influence continually declined until his death.

McClellan, George Brinton (b. Philadelphia, 3 Dec. 1826; d. Woodstock, Conn., 29 Oct. 1885), soldier, studied at the Univ. of Pennsylvania (1840–42) and was graduated from West Point (1846) No. 2 in his class. He saw service during the Mexican War at Contreras, Chirubusco, and Chapultepec. Asst. engineer for the construction of Ft. Delaware (1851), he accompanied Capt. R. B. Marcy on an exploration to trace the source of the Red River (Ark.), then did river and harbor work in Texas, and commanded an expedition to survey a railroad route across the Cascade Mts. After a year in Europe observing the siege of Sevastopol (1855), he resigned from the army (1857) to become chief engineer of the Illinois Central R.R. and then (1860) president of the Ohio and Mississippi R.R. At the outbreak of the Civil War he was commissioned major general of the Ohio volunteers, and on 3 May 1861 appointed major general of the regular army in command of the Department of Ohio. He cleared western Virginia of Confederate troops and was given command of the Division of the Potomac, succeeding (Nov. 1861) Winfield Scott (*q.v.*) as general in chief. His Peninsular campaign ended in the bloody Seven Days' Battles (26 June–2 July 1862). His troops were detached from him and assigned to Gen. Pope's Army of Virginia, but after Pope's defeat at 2d Manassas,

he was called upon to defend Washington. Defeating Lee at South Mountain (14 Sept.) and Antietam (17 Sept.), he allowed the Confederates to withdraw across the Potomac. Criticized 13 Oct. 1862 by Lincoln for being "overcautious," he was removed from command 7 Nov. Democratic candidate for the presidency (1864), he was defeated by Lincoln, 212–21 electoral votes. After residing in Europe (1864–68) he served as chief engineer of the Department of Docks, New York City (1870–72), and governor of New Jersey (1878–81).

McCormick, Cyrus Hall (b. in Rockbridge Co., Va., 15 Feb. 1809; d. Chicago, 13 May 1884), inventor and manufacturer. He invented and patented a hillside plow (1831) and in 1832 designed and constructed a reaper which avoided the errors of the mechanism upon which his father, the inventor Robert McCormick (1780–1846), had been engaged for 2 decades. Successfully demonstrated in 1832, the reaper had the basic components of the modern reaper: the divider, reel, straight reciprocating knife, fingers or guards, platform, main wheel and gearing, and the front-side draft traction. McCormick added improvements to his machine during the 1830s and began its commercial manufacture (c.1840) at his birthplace. In 1847 he set up his own plant at Chicago. Despite widespread competition following the expiration of his patent in 1848, he developed a nationwide business by 1850. In 1851, on the occasion of the world's fair at London, he introduced the reaper into Europe; the machine won major prizes at London, Paris, Hamburg, Lille, Vienna, and elsewhere. Not less important than McCormick's achievement as an inventor was his contribution to modern industrial and business methods. He pioneered in the use of labor-saving, mass-production factory machinery, and in the use of field trials, cash and deferred payments, and guarantees and testimonials in advertising. His reaper increased the food output of the North during the Civil War, and made possible the export grain trade to Europe that helped to bolster the finances of the Union government; it tied agriculture even closer to the market economy, accelerated the settlement of vacant Western lands, and released manpower from the farms for industrial enterprises and urban settlement.

MacDowell, Edward Alexander (b. New York City, 18 Dec. 1861; d. there, 23 Jan. 1908), composer and teacher. In 1876 he went to Paris, where he studied with Marmontel and Savard; subsequently at Wiesbaden and at the Frankfort Conservatory; and in 1881 became chief piano teacher at the Darmstadt Conservatory. By the time he returned to America (1888), he had composed his 1st and 2d *Modern Suites,* 2 concertos, and a symphonic poem, *Hamlet and Ophelia.* From 1888 to 1896 he lived in Boston, where in addition to teaching and composing he gave recitals. During these years he wrote *Woodland Sketches, Sonata Eroica, Sonata Tragica, Twelve Virtuoso Studies,* and the 1st and 2d *Indian Suites* for orchestra. He became (1896) professor of music at Columbia, but resigned in 1904 after a conflict over policy. His health declined rapidly beginning in 1905. Among the works of his last active period are *Sea Pieces, New England Idylls, Norse Sonata,* and *Keltic Sonata.* After his death, MacDowell's farm at Peterboro, N.H., was established by his widow as the MacDowell Colony for artists, writers, and composers.

McGuffey, William Holmes (b. near Claysville, Pa., 23 Sept. 1800; d. Charlottesville, Va., 4 May 1873), educator and compiler of school readers, was graduated from Washington College (1826) and served (1826–36) as professor of languages, philosophy, and philology at Miami Univ., Oxford, Ohio. He was appointed (1836) president of Cincinnati College and was instrumental in securing the enactment of the law under which the common schools of Ohio were first established. He served as president (1839–43) of Ohio Univ., as professor (1843–45) at Woodward College, Cincinnati, and as professor of moral philosophy (1845–73) at the Univ. of Virginia. He is best remembered for his *Eclectic Readers* (commonly called McGuffey's Readers), 6 schoolbooks for elementary grades that were published between 1836 and 1857 and went through numerous editions that sold an estimated total of 122 million copies. The *Readers,* in part extracts from standard English writers, were an amalgam of entertaining literature, self-improvement themes, and patriotic and moral instruction.

McKinley, William (b. Niles, Ohio, 29 Jan. 1843; d. Buffalo, N.Y., 14 Sept. 1901), 25th president of the U.S., studied at Allegheny College; served in the Union Army during the Civil War, seeing action at South Mountain, Antietam, Winchester, and Cedar Creek (breveted maj., 1865); studied law in Albany, N.Y., and was admitted to the Ohio bar, 1867, commencing practice in Canton. Elected prosecuting attorney of Stark Co. (1869), he was Republican congressman (1876–90, excepting 1882). High-tariff advocate, he sponsored the McKinley Tariff (1890). Defeated on this issue (1890), he was elected governor of Ohio in 1891 and again in 1893. With the support of Marcus A. Hanna, he was Republican nominee for president (1896) on a protective tariff, sound money (gold standard) platform, defeating Bryan. His administration was marked by revision of the tariff upward to the highest rate in U.S. history (Dingley Tariff, 1897), the passage of the Gold Standard Act (1900), and the annexation of Hawaii (7 July 1898). After the blowing up of the battleship *Maine* (15 Feb. 1898), he yielded to press clamor for war and recommended intervention in Cuba (11 Apr.), despite a note received from Spain (10 Apr.) promising to order immediate cessation of hostilities on that island. The acquisition of Puerto Rico, the Philippines, and Guam (1899) as a result of the War with Spain established the U.S. as a world power. He again defeated Bryan for president (1900) in a "full dinner pail" campaign, but was assassinated (6 Sept. 1901) by an anarchist, Leon Czolgosz, on a visit to the Pan-American Exposition in Buffalo.

MacLeish, Archibald (b. Glencoe, Ill., 7 May 1892–   ), poet and public official, was educated at Yale (A.B., 1915) and Harvard (LL.B., 1919). He served from private to captain in World War I, then practiced law in Boston (1920–23), but left the law for poetry, studying in France (1923–28). Turning from personal and subjective poetry (*Poems, 1924–33* [1933]), he won a Pulitzer prize with his narrative poem of the conquest of Mexico, *Conquistador* (1932). In a radio verse drama, *The Fall of the City* (1937), as well as in prose writings (*The Irresponsibles* [1940], *A Time to Speak* [1941]), he spoke out on behalf of democratic values and against fascism. Librarian of Congress (1939–44), his appointment aroused criticism because of his lack of special training. He resigned this post to serve as Assistant Secretary of State (1944–45). During World War II he had also served as director of the Office of Facts and Figures (1941–42) and as-

sistant director of the Office of War Information (1942–43). In the postwar period he was active in UNESCO and became Boylston Professor at Harvard (1949–62). His *Collected Poems, 1917–52* (1952) won Pulitzer prize, Bollingen and National Book awards; *J.B.* (1958) dramatic verse adaptation of story of Job, also Pulitzer. Later works include *Poetry and Experience* (1961), *Herakles* (verse play, 1967), *The Magic Prison* (libretto, 1967), *A Continuing Journey* (prose, 1967); *The Wild Wicked Old Man and Other Poems* (1968), and *Scratch* (play, 1971).

McMillan, Edwin Mattison (b. Redondo Beach, Calif., 18 Sept. 1907–   ), nuclear physicist. He was graduated from the California Institute of Technology (B.S., 1928; M.S., 1929) and received his Ph.D. in physics at Princeton in 1932. In 1934 he joined the staff of the Radiation Laboratory (director since 1958) at Univ. of California, where he has taught physics. During World War II he worked on microwave radar and on sonar (underwater sound detection) at the Navy Radio and Sound Laboratory at San Diego, Calif., and was on the staff of the Los Alamos (N.M.) Atomic Bomb Laboratory. He has made important researches in nuclear physics, particularly in the field of artificial radioactivity. The discoverer of neptunium (element 93), he laid the foundation for the production of plutonium (element 94) by Glenn T. Seaborg and others. In 1951 he and Seaborg were joint recipients of the Nobel prize in chemistry for their discoveries in the chemistry of the transuranic elements. The construction of cyclotrons, such as the synchrotron, synchrocyclotron, cosmotron, and bevatron, with an atom-smashing potential exceeding that of earlier models, was made possible by his theory of phase stability.

Madison, James (b. Port Conway, Va., 16 Mar. 1751; d. Montpelier, Va., 28 June 1836), 4th president of the U.S., was graduated from the College of New Jersey (1771), was chairman of the committee of public safety for Orange Co., Va. (1775), and helped draft the state constitution in the Virginia Convention (1776). Member of the Virginia Council of State (1778–79), he served in the Continental Congress (1780–83), drafted instructions to Jay to demand of Spain free navigation of the Mississippi, and drew up the compromise plan whereby Virginia ceded her Western lands to the U.S. A member of the Virginia House of Delegates (1784–86), he was the author of the "Memorial and Remonstrance" (1784) in which he opposed taxation to support religious teachers, and secured the enactment of Jefferson's bill for religious freedom. Active in the call for the Alexandria and Mount Vernon conferences (1785), the Annapolis Convention (1786), and the Federal Convention (1787), he played a most influential role in the adoption of the Constitution, drafting the Virginia large-state plan presented by Randolph, and acting as reporter of the proceedings. Author of 29 of the *Federalist* papers, he was largely responsible for securing ratification in Virginia. Congressman (1789–97), he proposed the first 10 amendments to the Constitution, known as the Bill of Rights. Parting with Hamilton over debt assumption and later opposing his pro-British leanings, he became a leader of the Jeffersonian Republicans. He married Dolly Payne Todd (1794). He drew up the Virginia Resolves (adopted by the state legislature, Dec. 1798), condemning the Alien and Sedition Acts. While Jefferson's Secretary of State (1801–09), he was involved in controversies with France and Great Britain over neutral rights. President (1809–17), being elected over C. C. Pinckney (1808) and over De Witt Clinton (1812), he lost popularity largely as a result of his inept leadership of the War of 1812 ("Mr. Madison's War"), which the U.S. entered unprepared and disunited. His signing in his 2d administration of a bill chartering the 2d Bank of the U.S. and raising tariff rates marked a trend toward Hamiltonian nationalism.

Mahan, Alfred Thayer (b. West Point, N.Y., 27 Sept. 1840; d. Quogue, N.Y., 1 Dec. 1914), naval officer and historian, was graduated from the U.S. Naval Academy (1859) and an officer in the U.S. navy down to 1896, lecturer on naval history and tactics at Newport War College (1886), and its president (1886–89 and 1892–93). His monumental work, *The Influence of Sea Power upon History, 1660–1783* (1890), examined naval strategy and sea power, to which he gave pivotal importance. His *The Influence of Sea Power upon the French Revolution, 1793–1812* showed how British sea power nullified Napoleon's victories on the Continent. He also wrote *Major Operations of the Navy in the War of American Independence* (1913). His arguments in favor of a big U.S. navy, a strong merchant marine, naval bases, and colonial possessions had an enormous impact on U.S. political thought and were influential abroad, notably in Germany before World War I.

Mailer, Norman (b. Long Branch, N.J., 31 Jan. 1923–   ), author. He grew up in Brooklyn and, while at Harvard (1939–43), wrote for the *Advocate,* the undergraduate literary magazine, and, with "The Greatest Thing in the World" won *Story Magazine*'s college fiction contest (1941). After receiving a B.S. in engineering he served (1943–45) in the Pacific in the infantry. His first published novel, *The Naked and the Dead* (1948), a searing war story, brought him critical acclaim and was a best seller. The more philosophical and symbolic *Barbary Shore* (1951) suggested Mailer's hostility to both Communism and the authoritarianism he saw in the U.S. After a brief period as a scriptwriter in Hollywood he published *The Deer Park* (1955), a portrayal of a psychopathic Hollywood personality. With Daniel Wolf and Edwin Francher he cofounded *The Village Voice* (1955), becoming a frequent contributor to the weekly journal. His provocative essays also appeared in *Partisan Review, Commentary, Esquire, Dissent,* and other journals. He received the National Book Award (1969) and was cowinner of the Pulitzer prize for general nonfiction (1969) for *Armies of the Night*—a personal account of the 1967 march on the Pentagon by antiwar demonstrators. His other books include: *Advertisements for Myself* (1959), autobiographical and confessional essays; *The Presidential Essays* (1963), essays on President Kennedy, whom he much admired; *Cannibals and Christians* (1966), a collection of verse; *An American Dream* (1965), and *Why Are We in Viet Nam?* (1967), both allegorical novels; *Miami and the Siege of Chicago* (1969), on the 1968 presidential nominating conventions; *Of a Fire on the Moon* (1971), on the Apollo moon shot; and *Marilyn* (1973), a speculative biography of Marilyn Monroe. Mailer has also directed films—most notably *Maidstone* (1968)—and run for mayor of New York City (1967), conducting an unsuccessful Democratic primary campaign on the platform that the city should become the 51st state. Controversial, restless, turbulent, and very much a public personality, Mailer is recognized as a seminal figure in modern American literature.

Mann, Horace (b. Franklin, Mass., 4 May 1796; d. Yellow Springs, Ohio, 2 Aug. 1859), educator, pioneer in the improvement of the common school system. With little formal schooling up to his 17th year, he was graduated with high honors from Brown Univ. (1819), where he was a tutor in Latin and Greek (1819–21). He attended the Litchfield (Conn.) Law School, was admitted to the Massachusetts bar (1823), and practiced at Dedham (Mass.) and Boston until 1837, meanwhile serving in the Massachusetts house (1827–33) and senate (1833–37). He was active in humanitarian and reform movements and, as president (1836–37) of the state senate, signed the education bill (1837) providing for a state board of education. As secretary of the board (1837–48) he eliminated many of the evils of the decentralized state school-district system that had been in force for about a half century and instituted the following reforms: a minimum school year of 6 months, appropriations for public education more than doubled, about 50 new high schools established, public school-teachers' salaries increased, curriculum and methods of instruction revamped, the operations of local schools linked to a central authority, and professional training of teachers improved and regularized. During the period of his secretaryship Mann advanced the principle of nonsectarian education, established and edited the *Common School Journal,* and made illuminating surveys of existing conditions and needs in 12 annual reports that exercised a wide influence on the course of public education in the U.S. In 1839 he established at Lexington, Mass., the first state normal school in the U.S. His 7th annual report was devoted to a survey of European educational conditions made by him during a 5-month tour in 1843. He resigned his secretaryship (1848) to occupy the congressional seat made vacant by the death of John Quincy Adams. He was defeated (1852) as the Free-Soil candidate for the Massachusetts governorship, and from 1853 until his death served as president of Antioch College, Yellow Springs, Ohio.

Marin, John (b. Rutherford, N.J., 23 Dec. 1872; d. Addison, Me., 1 Oct. 1953), painter, studied at the Stevens Institute, then in an architect's office, at the Pennsylvania Academy of Fine Arts, the Art Students League, and in Paris. In 1906 he did an oil which was accepted by the Luxembourg. In New York his work was sponsored by Alfred Stieglitz (1864–1946). His annual 1-man shows of the sea (notably his Maine seascapes) and landscape, beginning 1909, brought to the attention of the art world an individual mode of painting, reflecting the influence of the Chinese school and the method both of abstract cubism and of expressionism. By 1932 he was producing important work in watercolor, and by 1936, when a 1-man show was assembled at the Museum of Modern Art, his reputation in the top rank of American artists was secure.

Marion, Francis (b. probably in St. John's Parish, Berkeley Co., S.C., c.1732; d. there, 26 Feb. 1795), Revolutionary soldier, popularly known as "the Swamp Fox." He took part (1759, 1761) in campaigns against the Cherokee; was elected to the South Carolina Provincial Congress of 1775; became a captain in the militia; and, as a lieutenant colonel of the Continental Line, commanded a regiment in the attack on Savannah (1779). When the Revolutionary forces under Gen. Horatio Gates were routed at Camden, S.C., Marion resorted to guerrilla warfare against British lines of communication, using Williamsburg as his base of operations and taking refuge

in the swamps when numerically superior enemy forces faced him. By also weakening Loyalist potential in South Carolina, Marion helped to wrest the initiative from the British in the South. In 1781, as a brigadier general of militia, Marion was instrumental in retaking South Carolina from the enemy. He served under Gen. Nathanael Greene at the Battle of Eutaw Springs (8 Sept. 1781), which forced the British to fall back on Charleston.

Marshall, George Catlett (b. Uniontown, Pa., 31 Dec. 1880; d. Washington, D.C., 17 Oct. 1959), soldier and statesman, was graduated from Virginia Military Institute (1901) and commissioned in the U.S. army (1902). With the A.E.F. (1917–19), he was detailed to the general staff, 1st Div.; was chief of operations, 1st Army; chief of staff, 8th Army Corps; and aided in planning the St. Mihiel and Meuse-Argonne offensives (1918). Aide to Gen. Pershing (1919–24), assistant commandant of the Infantry School, Ft. Benning, Ga. (1927–32), he was detailed to the general staff as chief of the war plans division (1938), and was appointed chief of staff with rank of general (1939–45), becoming general of the army (1944). As chairman of combined chiefs of staff he was the principal Allied strategist in World War II. Special ambassador to China (1945), he served as Secretary of State under President Truman (1947–49), responsible for the Marshall Plan (ERP) and in formulating the Truman Doctrine (Mar. 1947). In 1950–51 he served as Secretary of Defense, responsible for rebuilding U.S. armed forces and for overall military planning in defense of Korea. He was awarded the Nobel peace prize in 1953.

Marshall, John (b. Germantown [now Midland], Va., 24 Sept. 1755; d. Philadelphia, Pa., 6 July 1835), 3d chief justice of the U.S., served in the American Revolution (1776–79), first as lieutenant, then captain; attended law lectures at William and Mary (May–June 1780), was admitted to the bar, and began practice in Fauquier Co. and (1783) in Richmond. Member of the Virginia Assembly (1782–91 and 1795–97), delegate to the state convention which ratified the Federal Constitution (1788), he declined the attorney generalship offered by Washington (1795) and the post of minister to France (1796), but served as a member of the "X.Y.Z." mission to that country (1797–98). Federalist congressman (1799–1800) and then Secretary of State under John Adams (June 1800–Mar. 1801), he was in the meantime appointed chief justice of the U.S. Supreme Court (from 31 Jan. 1801). His 34 years on the bench established the prestige of the court. Taking upon himself the task of writing most of the important opinions, he used the court and the Constitution to curb interference by the states with vested rights. His major opinions include *Marbury* v. *Madison* (1803), with its assertion of the right of judicial review; *Fletcher* v. *Peck* (1810), the *Dartmouth College Case* (1819), and *Ogden* v. *Saunders* (dissenting opinion, 1827), sustaining the contract clause of the Constitution; *McCulloch* v. *Maryland* (1819), with its doctrine of implied powers; and *Gibbons* v. *Ogden* (1824), with its broad interpretation of the commerce clause.

Marshall, Thurgood (b. Baltimore, Md., 2 July 1908–   ), lawyer and jurist. The great-grandson of a slave, Marshall attended segregated public schools and worked his way through Lincoln Univ. as a grocery clerk and a waiter. Graduating from college in 1930, Marshall was ineligible because of his race to study at the Univ. of Maryland Law School. He was graduated first in his class from Howard Univ. Law School and was admitted to the Maryland bar (1933). During a brief period of private practice in Baltimore, Marshall successfully litigated a suit resulting in the admission of the first black to graduate study at the Univ. of Maryland (1935). Marshall came to New York to serve as assistant to the NAACP Special Counsel (1936–38), Counsel (1938–40), and then became head of the Legal Defense Fund, a separate litigating arm of the NAACP. Serving for 23 years as director-counsel of the NAACP (1940–62), Marshall coordinated attacks on discrimination in education, housing, public accommodations, and voting. Distinguished both as a legal strategist and as an advocate, Marshall won 29 of the 32 cases he personally argued before the U.S. Supreme Court. Among his notable victories was the decision holding unconstitutional the "white primary" (*Smith* v. *Allwright,* 1944), the decision invalidating segregation on interstate buses (*Morgan* v. *Virginia,* 1946), and the decision striking down state court enforcement of racially restrictive covenants (*Shelley* v. *Kraemer,* 1948). His most significant triumph occurred in *Brown* v. *Board of Education of Topeka* (1954, 1955), where segregation of schools was held impermissible under the Constitution. In 1961 President Kennedy appointed Marshall to the U.S. Court of Appeals for the 2d Circuit where he served until his appointment as Solicitor General of the U.S. (1965–67). On 2 Oct. 1967 Marshall became the first black justice on the Supreme Court, where he has since been recognized as a liberal and activist jurist.

Mason, George (b. near Pasbytanzy, Northern Neck, Va., 1725; d. "Gunston Hall," Va., 7 Oct. 1792), Revolutionary statesman, was educated by private tutors and studied law under John Mercer. He began his political association with Washington in the House of Burgesses (1759), joined with him in anti-Stamp Act activity (1766), and prepared the nonimportation resolutions, successfully proposed by Washington to the dissolved burgesses. Author of the Fairfax Resolves (18 July 1774), restating the colonial position toward the crown, he framed for the Virginia convention the Bill of Rights (12 June 1776), model for the first part of Jefferson's Declaration of Independence and basis of the first 10 Amendments to the federal Constitution, and the major part of the Virginia Constitution (29 June 1776). In collaboration with Jefferson, Patrick Henry, and George Wythe, he revised Virginia's legal system. Backer of George Rogers Clark's (*q.v.*) campaign, he also initiated the plan for the cession of Virginia's western lands and influenced Jefferson's first Territorial Ordinance (1784). A leading figure at the Federal Convention, he refused to sign the Constitution and campaigned against its ratification, insisting on the inclusion of a Bill of Rights and opposing especially the compromise on the slave trade, which he denounced as "disgraceful to mankind."

Mather, Cotton (b. Boston, Mass., 12 Feb. 1662; d. there, 13 Feb. 1727), clergyman, eldest son of Increase Mather and grandson of John Cotton and Richard Mather. He enrolled at Harvard at age 12, graduating in 1678. First a student of medicine, he turned to theology, receiving his M.A. from Harvard (1681). He was ordained (1685) and joined his father in the pulpit of Boston's 2d Church, where he remained for the rest of his life. While the elder Mather petitioned King James II in England for a new charter for Massachusetts, Cotton Mather led the colony's rebellion against the governor, Sir Edmund Andros. When a new charter was granted and a new governor, William Phips, appointed (1692), he became an adviser in the government (1692–95). His *Memorable Providences, Related to Witchcrafts and Possessions* (1689) contributed to the hysteria that led to the Salem witch trials (1692). Mather had advised the judges that executions would not be necessary; however, during the trials he did not criticize the mass executions, and in *Wonders of the Invisible World* (1693) he defended the verdicts of various trials. As colonial politics became increasingly secular his political influence waned. He tirelessly devoted himself to the cause of orthodox Congregationalism and to scholarly pursuits. A prolific writer—he published some 450 works—his best-known book, *Magnalia Christi Americana* (1702), is an aggregation of materials on the ecclesiastical history of New England. A Fellow at Harvard (1690–1703), he resigned when the college became less strictly Congregationalist in its policies and his hopes for the presidency were disappointed. He promoted the establishment of Yale as a new orthodox stronghold. He organized a school for Negro children and ministered personally to his parishioners. When a smallpox epidemic broke out in Boston (1721), he led an unpopular campaign promoting inoculation. Deeply interested in science, he was the first American elected to the Royal Society (1713).

Mather, Increase (b. Dorchester, Mass., 21 June 1639; d. Boston, 23 Aug. 1723), Puritan clergyman and political leader, was graduated from Harvard (1656), and received his A.M. from Trinity College, Dublin (1658). Before returning to Massachusetts (1661), he preached at Great Torrington, Devonshire, Gloucester, and on Guernsey. Teacher of the 2d Church in Boston (1664), he ultimately (1675) supported the Half-Way Covenant. Acting president of Harvard (1685) and rector (1686–1701), he supported the study of science and sought to maintain Congregational influence. He urged Bostonians (1683) to resist the royal authorities in the *quo warranto* proceedings against the Massachusetts charter. Representing the Congregational churches, he personally appealed (1688) to James II for renewal of the charter, which he finally obtained from William III. The charter, more liberal than the Puritans expected, gave the lower house the right to elect the Council, a unique feature. In 1692 he returned to Boston with William Phips, the governor whom he had nominated. Unlike his son and supporter Cotton Mather (1663–1728), most prolific of American Puritan writers, he took a cautious attitude toward the Salem witch trials. His *Cases of Conscience Concerning Evil Spirits* (1693), disapproving of spectral evidence, induced Phips to stop the execution of the convicted "witches." Other writings include *Wo to Drunkards* (1673), an early temperance tract, *A Brief History of the Warr with the Indians* (1676), and *Remarkable Providences* (1684).

Maury, Matthew Fontaine (b. near Fredericksburg, Va., 14 Jan. 1806; d. Lexington, Va., 1 Feb. 1873), oceanographer, naval officer, went to school in Tennessee. Becoming a midshipman (1825), he made 3 extended cruises in the following 9 years. In his leisure time he worked on navigation, publishing (1836) *A New Theoretical and Practical Treatise on Navigation*. In a series of anonymous articles in the Richmond *Whig* (1838) and the *Southern Literary Messenger* (1840–41) he criticized the

Department of the Navy and proposed reforms. Permanently lamed by a stagecoach accident (1839), he was appointed superintendent of the Dept. of Charts and Instruments of the Navy Dept. (1842), devoting himself to hydrographic and meteorological research, and publishing (1847) *Wind and Current Chart of the North Atlantic* and related works (1850–51). The uniform system of recording oceanographic data which he advocated was adopted at the Brussels International Congress (1853) for worldwide use by naval vessels and merchant ships. His charts reduced the time of passage from New York to San Francisco by 47 days (1855). His *The Physical Geography of the Sea* (1855) was the first text of modern oceanography. Dropped from active service (1855), but restored (1858), he resigned (1861) to accept a commission as commander in the Confederate navy, where he began experiments with electric mines. In England as special agent, he secured ships of war for the Confederacy. After the Civil War he was involved in an abortive colonization scheme to send ex-Confederates to Mexico. After a stay in England again, he returned to the U.S. (1868) to accept a professorship of meteorology at the Virginia Military Institute.

Mayo, William James (b. Le Sueur, Minn., 29 June 1861; d. Rochester, Minn., 28 July 1939) and his brother, **Charles Horace** (b. Rochester, Minn., 19 July 1865; d. Chicago, 26 May 1939), surgeons, sons of Dr. William Worrall Mayo (1820–1911), pioneer surgeon of the Northwest, both took medical degrees, William at the Univ. of Mich. (1883), Charles at the Chicago Medical College (1888). They gradually took over their father's large practice in Rochester, and father and sons constituted the medical and surgical staff of

St. Mary's Hospital, opened in 1889. Observing clinical and surgical practice in Europe and America, they incorporated the latest surgical techniques and originated much, William in abdominal surgery, Charles in surgery of the thyroid gland. Developing a cooperative group clinic, they added general practitioners, surgeons, and laboratory scientists. Out of this grew the Mayo Clinic, a group of some 200 doctors, each a specialist, engaged in cooperative practice. The first Mayo Clinic building was constructed in 1912, and in 1915 the brothers donated $1,500,000 (increased to $2,500,000 by 1934) to establish the Mayo Foundation for Medical Education and Research, which became an affiliate of the graduate school of the Univ. of Minn. During World War I they served as chief army consultants for surgical service, receiving the rank of brigadier general (1921). They published *Collected Papers of the Mayo Clinic and the Mayo Foundation* (1932).

Meany, George (b. New York City, 16 April 1894; d. Washington, D.C., 10 Jan. 1980), labor leader. Educated in New York City public schools, he became an apprentice plumber in 1910, was promoted to the rank of journeyman plumber in 1915, and practiced his trade in New York City. In 1922 he was elected business agent of Local 463 of the Plumbers Union, an affiliate of the American Federation of Labor, and he was subsequently elected to the New York City Central Trades and Labor Assembly, which was the main body of the AFL in the city. He was president of the New York State Federation of Labor (1934–39), and on 1 Jan. 1940 became secretary-treasurer of the AFL. When William Green died in 1952, Meany became president of the AFL. He was an architect of that organization's merger with the Congress

of Industrial Organizations. In 1955 he was elected president of the new AFL-CIO, a position he held until 1979. Under his direction the AFL-CIO conducted a campaign against corruption in organized labor, which culminated in the 1957 expulsion from the federation of 3 major unions, including the International Brotherhood of Teamsters. A political moderate who espoused the tradition of Samuel Gompers, Meany strongly supported legislation dealing with minimum wages, civil rights, public housing, aid to education and national health insurance. A strong backer of the Vietnam War, he was lukewarm toward Sen. George McGovern's presidential candidacy (1972). He led the AFL-CIO in its call for the impeachment of President Richard M. Nixon (1973–74).

Melville, Herman (b. New York City, 1 Aug. 1819; d. there, 28 Sept. 1891), author. His only formal schooling, which he received at the Albany Academy, ended at the age of 15. He worked as a bank and store clerk, farmer, and teacher, and in 1837 shipped to Liverpool as a cabin boy. In 1841–42 he made a voyage to the South Seas aboard the whaler *Acushnet*. Deserting at the Marquesas Islands, he lived among the natives, went to Tahiti, and in 1843 enlisted as an ordinary seaman on the frigate *United States*. He was discharged at Boston in 1844 and immediately set to work on the novels that were based on his adventures: *Typee* (1846), *Omoo* (1847), *Mardi* (1849), *Redburn* (1849), and *White-Jacket* (1850). Moving (1850) to a farm near Pittsfield, Mass., he formed here his friendship with Nathaniel Hawthorne and wrote his masterpiece, *Moby Dick* (1851). This was followed by a period of uneven achievement: *Pierre: or the Ambiguities* (1852), *Israel Potter* (1855), *The Piazza Tales* (1856), and *The Confidence Man*

(1857). In 1863 he moved to New York, where he worked as a customs inspector (1866–85) and lived in obscurity. His works of poetry date from this period: *Battle-Pieces and Aspects of the War* (1866), *Clarel* (1876), *John Marr and Other Sailors* (1888), and *Timoleon* (1891). The novelette *Billy Budd*, completed in his last year, was not published until 1924, following a revival of interest in Melville.

Mencken, Henry Louis (b. Baltimore, Md., 12 Sept. 1880, d. there, 29 Jan. 1956), journalist, literary critic, was graduated from Polytechnic Institute at the head of his class. Police reporter (1899), then city editor (1903) of the Baltimore *Morning Herald*, he joined the staff of the Baltimore *Sun* (1906). In the era following World War I, Mencken's vogue was enormous. Nietzschean iconoclast and debunker, he was critical of his age and cynical about democracy and the "Boobus Americanus." His literary criticism helped bring to the fore such writers as Dreiser, D. H. Lawrence, Ford Madox Ford, and Sherwood Anderson. With George Jean Nathan, he collaborated on *The Smart Set*, later (1924) on *The American Mercury*, of which Mencken was sole editor, 1925–33. His monumental *The American Language*, published in several editions (1919–48), is a more durable contribution to letters. His popularity waned during the depression, when his former admirers sought more constructive values.

Mergenthaler, Ottmar (b. Hachtel, Germany, 11 May 1854; d. Baltimore, Md., 28 Oct. 1899), inventor of the linotype. After serving his apprenticeship (1868–72) to a watchmaker at Bietigheim, he came to the U.S. in 1872 and was engaged in the making of scientific instruments in the establishments of August Hahl at Washington, D.C. (1872–76) and Baltimore (1876–82). During the early part of this period Mergenthaler worked on the improvement of a writing machine (originated by James O. Clephane and devised by Charles Moore) aimed at the lithographic reproduction of print. A full-scale model failing to operate successfully, Mergenthaler began experimenting with a machine that would eliminate typesetting by hand and supplant stereotyping with the lithographic process. Difficulties compelled Mergenthaler to abandon the project (1879); but shortly after he opened his own establishment (1883), he secured from Clephane an order to construct a typesetting machine capable of obtaining clean type from a matrix. When this device proved to be unsatisfactory, Mergenthaler devised a plan for the stamping and casting of type metal in the same machine; by July 1884, he had successfully incorporated this principle in the first direct-casting linotype. The machine was patented on 26 Aug. 1884, and for its manufacture he and Clephane organized the National Typographic Co. of W. Va.; a subsidiary, the Mergenthaler Printing Co., was established in 1885. By the time of his death Mergenthaler had made an aggregate of more than 50 patented improvements. The linotype revolutionized mass-circulation newspaper production.

Michelson, Albert Abraham (b. Strelno, Prussia, 19 Dec. 1852; d. Pasadena, Calif., 9 May 1931), physicist. Brought to the U.S. as an infant (1854), he was educated at Virginia City, Nev., and San Francisco, Calif., and was graduated (1873) from the U.S. Naval Academy, where he served (1875–77) as an instructor in physics and chemistry. He pursued postgraduate studies (1880–81) at Heidelberg, Berlin, and Paris; taught physics at the Case School of

Applied Science, Cleveland, Ohio (1883–89), and at Clark Univ. (1889–92); and in 1892 was made chief professor in the Ryerson Physical Laboratory and head of the physics department at the newly established Univ. of Chicago, where he served until his retirement in 1931. Virtually all of his experiments and researches lay in the field of optics and were marked by skillfully designed apparatuses for attaining precise measurement. His improvements of the Foucault apparatus for measuring the speed of light enabled him to determine the velocity of light with a margin of error of less than 1 in 100,000. He designed (1887) an interferometer with which he determined linear distances in terms of the wave length of light. Using the interferometer, he made (with Edward Williams Morley) the famous experiment (1887) designed to detect the relative motion of the earth through the ether. The findings of the Michelson-Morley experiment contributed much to the development of the theory of relativity. Michelson also determined the length of the meter in terms of the wave length of lines in the cadmium spectrum, was the first to measure the angular diameter of a star, devised the echelon spectrometer, and measured the tides in the solid earth. He was awarded the Nobel prize in physics (1907). He wrote *Light Waves and Their Uses* (1903).

Millay, Edna St. Vincent (b. Rockland, Me., 22 Feb. 1892; d. Austerlitz, N.Y., 19 Oct. 1950), poet, wrote her first long poem, "Renascence," at 19. Published in *The Lyric Year,* a prize anthology (1912), it won her critical acclaim. Her education at Barnard and Vassar (A.B., 1917) was financed by a woman admirer of that poem. Entering enthusiastically into Bohemian life in Greenwich Village, New York City, she published in that period *A Few Figs from Thistles* (1920)

and *Aria da Capo* (1921), an antiwar piece. In protest against the Sacco-Vanzetti trial, she wrote the poem "Justice Denied in Massachusetts" (1927) and was arrested for participating in the "death watch" demonstration outside the Boston State House. Recognizing the Nazi threat to Western civilization, she wrote *There Are No Islands Any More* (1940), a plea for U.S. aid to Britain and France, and *The Murder of Lidice* (1942). An advocate of sexual equality for women, her love poetry is characterized by an ironic poignance and a clarity of style. Her works include *Buck in the Snow* (1928); *Fatal Interview* (1931), a collection of sonnets; *Huntsman, What Quarry?* (1939); *Collected Sonnets* (1941). She was awarded the Pulitzer prize in poetry (1923).

Miller, Arthur (b. New York City, 7 Oct. 1915–), playwright, was graduated from the Univ. of Mich. (1938). Writing plays while at college, he later joined the Federal Theater Project in New York. In 1944 *Situation Normal* examined army conditions, and *Focus* (1945), a novel, dealt with anti-Semitism. His first Broadway play, *The Man Who Had All the Luck* (1944), was followed by *All My Sons* (1947; N.Y. Drama Critics Circle award). His Pulitzer prize-winning *Death of a Salesman* (1949), depicting the drama of a small man destroyed by an empty society, has been called the modern American tragedy. Other plays include *The Crucible* (1953), *A View from the Bridge* (1955), *After the Fall* (1964), *Incident at Vichy* (1964), *The Price* (1968), *The Creation of the World and Other Business* (1972). A collection of stories, *I Don't Need You Any More,* was published in 1967. Married to movie star Marilyn Monroe (1956; divorced 1961), he wrote a screenplay, *The Misfits* (1961), for her starring role. His sentence for contempt of Congress (1957) was reversed on appeal.

Miller, Samuel Freeman (b. Richmond, Ky., 5 Apr. 1816; d. Washington, D.C., 13 Oct. 1890), jurist, was graduated from the medical school of Transylvania Univ. (1838), practiced for 12 years, then turned to the law, and was admitted to the bar (1847). Becoming an abolitionist, he moved to Keokuk, Ia. (1850), and became a state leader of the Republican party. Lincoln appointee as associate justice of the U.S. Supreme Court (1862), he was a staunch supporter of the national authority. In his dissent in the *Test-Oath Cases* (1867) he upheld the loyalty oath. In the *Slaughterhouse Case* (1873) he denied that the 14th Amendment was applicable to business corporations, but restricted it to Negroes. In dissent in *Hepburn* v. *Griswold* (1870) he upheld the legality of the Legal Tender Act, and in *Ex parte Yarbrough* (1884) he upheld the authority of the federal government to supervise congressional elections in the states (1884). He voted with the Republican majority in the Electoral Commission (1876).

Millikan, Robert Andrews (b. Morrison, Ill., 22 Mar. 1868; d. Pasadena, Calif., 19 Dec. 1953), physicist. He was graduated from Oberlin College (A.B., 1891; A.M., 1893), received the degree of Ph.D. at Columbia (1895), and studied at Berlin and Göttingen (1895–96). He was a member of the physics staff (1896–1921) at the Univ. of Chicago, and in 1921 became director of the Norman Bridge Laboratory of Physics at the California Institute of Technology at Pasadena. He received the Nobel prize in physics (1923) for his determination of the exact values of the mass and charge of the electron. He also made important investigations in the laws of reflection of gas molecules, cosmic rays, the absorption of X rays, the polarization of light from incandescent surfaces, the effect of temperature on photoelectric discharge, and the velocities of electrons discharged from metals under the influence of ultraviolet light. He was the author of *Mechanics, Molecular Physics and Heat* (1901), *Electricity, Sound and Light* (1908), *The Electron* (1917), *Cosmic Rays* (1939), and others.

Mitchell, William Lendrum (b. Nice, France, 29 Dec. 1879; d. New York City, 19 Feb. 1936), military aviation officer and pioneer exponent of air power, popularly known as "Billy" Mitchell. He attended Racine College, Wisc., was graduated from George Washington Univ., enlisted as a private at the outbreak of the Spanish-American War (1898), and in the same year was commissioned an officer in the U.S. Army Signal Corps. He was graduated (1909) from the Army Staff College, served on the Mexican border (1912), and in 1913 became the youngest officer ever appointed to the army general staff. During World War I he was chief of air service for several units, including the U.S. 1st Corps and the U.S. 1st and 2d Armies, and after the war was promoted to the rank of brigadier general and named director of military aviation. As assistant chief of the Army Air Service from 1920 to 1924, Mitchell openly criticized national aviation policy and demonstrated his confidence in air power as a major arm of warfare by sinking target battleships with aerial bombs. He called for a unified command of the armed forces. In 1925, while serving as air officer for the 8th Corps Area, he accused the high military and naval command of "incompetency, criminal negligence, and almost treasonal administration of national defense." He was court-martialed, found guilty, and suspended for 5 years without pay or allowances. While President Coolidge upheld the suspension, he granted Mitchell half pay and restored his allowances; Mitchell, however, resigned from the service (1 Feb. 1926) and continued his criticism of official military aviation policy. He was posthumously restored to the service (1942) with the rank of major general.

Monroe, James (b. Westmoreland Co., Va., 28 Apr. 1758; d. New York City, 4 July 1831), 5th president of the U.S., left William and Mary (1774–76) to serve in the Continental army, fighting at Harlem Heights, White Plains, Trenton, Brandywine, Germantown, and Monmouth. He studied law under Jefferson (1780–83), and entered the Virginia House of Delegates (1782) and the Continental Congress (1783–86). In the Virginia convention (1788) he opposed the Federal Constitution. As U.S. senator (1790–94), he joined the Jeffersonian Republicans. Minister to France (1794–96), he was recalled for failure to allay resentment caused by the Jay Treaty. Governor of Virginia (1799–1802), he returned to France as envoy extraordinary (1802–03), joining R. R. Livingston with instructions to buy New Orleans from France and West Florida from Spain. Exceeding instructions, he acquired all Florida. Subsequently he served as minister to Great Britain (1803–06) and, with Charles Pinckney, went to Madrid (1804–05) in a futile effort to settle a boundary dispute. Again governor of Virginia (1811), he resigned to become Madison's Secretary of State (1811–17) and to serve for a time as Secretary of War (1814–15). Elected president (1816) and reelected (1820) with all but 1 electoral vote, his administration was characterized as an "Era of Good Feelings" following a quarter century of rivalry between Federalists and Republicans. He settled boundaries with Canada and eliminated border forts, acquired Florida (1819), and formulated with modifications suggested by J. Q. Adams, the Monroe Doctrine (2 Dec. 1823), which he decided to issue unilaterally.

Moody, Dwight Lyman (b. Northfield, Mass., 5 Feb. 1837; d. there, 22 Dec. 1899), evangelist, was admitted to membership in the Congregational Church at Boston (1856), but moved to Chicago, where he combined a career as a shoe salesman with church work. In 1860 he abandoned business to become an independent city missionary; in 1866, after having served with the U.S. Christian Commission during the Civil War, he was made president of the Chicago Young Men's Christian Association. He made his mark as a lay preacher dedicated to the saving of souls. In 1873–75, during his third trip to Great Britain, he and the organist and singer, Ira D. Sankey, conducted a series of revivalist meetings which were attended by an estimated total of 2,530,000 people and led to an almost unprecedented religious awakening in the British Isles. Upon his return to the U.S., he and Sankey conducted evangelistic campaigns (1875–76) in Philadelphia, New York, and Brooklyn, and between 1877 and 1881 preached in cities including Chicago, Hartford, Baltimore, St. Louis, and San Francisco. Subsequent evangelistic campaigns in Great Britain (1881–84, 1891–92) equaled the success of his British tour of 1873–75. Between 1884 and 1891 Moody was active as an evangelist in many small cities in the U.S. and Canada. He founded the Chicago Bible Institute (1889) and the Bible Institute Colportage Association (1894). The spiritual awakening he stimulated in American colleges led to the organization of the Student Volunteer Movement, a group devoted to foreign missionary service.

Morgan, Daniel (b. Hunterdon Co., N.J., 6 July 1736; d. Winchester, Va., 6 July 1802), Revolutionary soldier, ran away from home, worked as a farm laborer and teamster in the Shenandoah Valley in Virginia, was a lieutenant in Pontiac's War, and accompanied (1774) Lord Dunmore's expedition to western Pennsylvania. Commissioned (22 June 1775) captain of a company of Virginia riflemen, he traveled from Winchester to Boston in 21 days. On the march to Quebec with Benedict Arnold (*q.v.*), he took command after Arnold was wounded there, captured the first barrier, and penetrated to the lower city, but was forced to surrender to overwhelming odds. Released (12 Nov. 1776), he was commissioned colonel of a Virginia regiment and, rejoining Washington, organized a corps of 500 sharpshooters. His part at Saratoga was notable. At Freeman's Farm his riflemen checked the movement to turn the American left and at Bemis Heights he took his men on a wide circuit around the enemy's right and from the flank and rear of the British poured deadly fire on Lord Balcarre's troops. Sent (1780) by Nathanael Greene (*q.v.*) to harass British outposts, he inflicted a disastrous defeat upon Tarleton in the battle of Cowpens (17 Jan. 1781), a military classic and model for Greene at Guilford Courthouse and Eutaw Springs. In command of the Virginia militia (1794) he assisted in putting down the Whiskey Rebellion. He served 1 term in Congress (1797–99).

Morgan, John Pierpont (b. Hartford, Conn., 17 Apr. 1837; d. Rome, Italy, 31 Mar. 1913), financier. After being educated at Boston, he received further schooling at Vevey, Switzerland, and at the Univ. of Göttingen; entered (1856) his father's banking house at London; and came to New York (1857), where he established J. P. Morgan & Co. (1860), which acted as agent for his father's firm. During the Civil War he was engaged in foreign exchange and gold speculation. In 1864 he became a member of the firm of Dabney, Morgan & Co., and in 1869 won control of the Albany & Susquehanna R.R. from Jay Gould and Jim Fisk. In 1871 he established the New York firm of Drexel, Morgan & Co., which in 1895 became known as J. P. Morgan & Co. Together with its allied houses in London and Paris, this firm became one of the leading and most influential banking houses in the world. An exponent of combination, integration, and centralized financial control in the business and industrial world, Morgan played an important role in the reorganization of American railroads (1885 *et seq.*). After the Panic of 1893, the Cleveland administration called upon him to relieve the pressure on the Treasury. Morgan took part in the financing and organization of the United States Steel Corp. (1901) and the International Harvester Co. (1902). In alliance with James J. Hill, he became embroiled in a struggle with Edward H. Harriman for control of the Northern Pacific R.R. that ultimately came before the Supreme Court in the *Northern Securities Case* (1904). During the panic of 1907 he helped stabilize financial conditions. In 1912 he became the chief target of the Pujo investigation of the so-called Money Trust. Perhaps the leading private art collector of his time, he left at his death valuable collections of books, manuscripts, and art objects now housed in the Pierpont Morgan Wing of the Metropolitan Museum and in the Pierpont Morgan Library, both in New York City.

Morgan, Lewis Henry (b. Aurora, N.Y., 21 Nov. 1818; d. Rochester, N.Y., 17

Dec. 1881), ethnologist and anthropologist, was graduated from Union College (1840), studied law, and moved to Rochester, where he practiced in partnership with George F. Danforth. Member of the New York assembly (1861–68) and state senate (1868–69), he is best known for his work in ethnology and as the "father of American anthropology." His first research was an investigation of the customs and institutions of the Iroquois, inspired by his adoption (1 Oct. 1847) into the Hawk clan of the Seneca in appreciation of his services in defeating ratification of a treaty unfavorable to the Seneca. His *League of the Ho-dé-no-sau-nee, or Iroquois* (1851), written in collaboration with Ely S. Parker, was the first scientific account of an Indian tribe. In addition to his Iroquois research, he made ethnological investigations (1859–62) of the Prairie Indians and observed similarities between the kinship systems of the Iroquois and other Indian tribes in North America. These observations led to his *Systems of Consanguinity and Affinity of the Human Family* (1870), a comprehensive collection of the kinship systems of the world. In *Ancient Society* (1877) he formulated his social evolutionary scheme of culture as having developed in stages from savagery to barbarism and then to civilization. His postulate of unilateral evolution has been modified basically by later anthropology. He also wrote *Houses and Houselife of the American Aborigines* (1881). Although no Marxist, his work influenced Karl Marx and Friedrich Engles.

Morgan, Thomas Hunt (b. Lexington, Ky., 25 Sept. 1866; d. Pasadena, Calif., 4 Dec. 1945), biologist. He was graduated from the State College of Kentucky (B.S., 1886; M.S., 1888) and from Johns Hopkins (Ph.D., 1890), served as professor of biology 1891–1904) at Bryn Mawr College, was professor of experi-

mental zoology (1904–28) at Columbia, and in 1928 was named director of biological science at California Institute of Technology. After carrying out his initial researches in experimental embryology and regeneration, he made his more noted experiments and studies on heredity and mutation in the fruit fly (Drosophila). His findings made valuable contributions to the knowledge of the genes and the nature of mutations, and provided the basis for the development of the science of genetics. For his work in the phenomena of heredity, Morgan received the Nobel prize in physiology and medicine (1933). Among his publications are *Regeneration* (1901), *Evolution and Adaptation* (1903), *Heredity and Sex* (1913), *Mechanism of Mendelian Heredity* (1915), *Critique of the Theory of Evolution* (1916), *The Physical Basis of Heredity* (1919), and *The Theory of the Genes* (1926).

Morison, Samuel Eliot (b. Boston, Mass., 9 July 1887; d. there, 15 May 1976), historian, received his B.A. (1908), M.A. (1909), and Ph.D. (1913) from Harvard. Instructor at the Univ. of California (1914) and at Harvard (1915), Morison enlisted as a private in the army during World War I, afterward serving as an attaché to the Russian division of the Commission to Negotiate Peace, then returning to Harvard as a professor of history. An authority on early American history, Morison has also made a major mark as a naval historian. Denying previous theories, Morison's *Builders of the Bay Colony* (1930) portrayed the Puritans not as straitlaced individuals but as men and women with human strengths and weaknesses and motivated by deep-felt religious convictions. Morison's multivolume *Tercentenary History of Harvard College and University, 1636–1936* (1935, 1936) contributed significantly to an understanding of the development of American education. Morison's major textbooks include *The Growth of the American Republic* (with Henry Steele Commager, 1930) and the *Oxford History of the American People* (1965). A lieutenant commander of the naval reserve, who saw action at sea during World War II, Morison wrote a 15-vol. *History of the United States Naval Operations in World War II* (1947–62) as well as a short history of the U.S. navy in that war, *The Two Ocean War* (1963). He won Pulitzer prizes for *Admiral of the Ocean Sea* (1942), during the writing of which he had sailed 10,000 miles retracing Columbus' course, and for *John Paul Jones* (1959). Both Morison's love of the sea and his desire to make history come alive were exemplified by his research for *The European Discovery of America, The Northern Voyages, 1500–1600* (1971), for which, in his 80s, he coasted the eastern shores of the U.S. and Canada and flew at low altitude in a small plane along the north Atlantic seaboard to obtain a better comprehension of the challenges confronting the early explorers. *The European Discovery of America, The Southern Voyages, 1492–1616* was published in 1974.

Morris, Robert (b. at or near Liverpool, England, 31 Jan. 1734; d. Philadelphia, Pa., 8 May 1806), financier of the American Revolution. He received a brief schooling at Philadelphia, where he joined the shipping and mercantile house of Charles Willing, becoming partner of the latter's son Thomas (1754), under the firm name of Willing & Morris. Morris was not definitely committed to the Patriot cause until 1775. The Pennsylvania assembly named him (30 June 1775) a member of the council of safety. He also served on the committee of correspondence and was chosen (Nov. 1775) as a delegate to the Continental Congress, in which he served until 1778. He was a member of several committees, including the secret committee for procuring munitions. He was occasionally assigned banking business by Congress; meanwhile, he continued his private activities as a member of his Philadelphia firm in importing military supplies. Although he voted against the Declaration of Independence in July 1776 on the ground that it was premature, he signed it in Aug. When Congress fled from Philadelphia (Dec. 1776), Morris remained there to continue the work of the committee of secret correspondence to which he had been appointed in Jan. 1776. He borrowed money and purchased supplies that were of crucial importance to the weakened Revolutionary forces. During the critical financial period, 1780–81, Morris was appointed by Congress (20 Feb. 1781) as superintendent of finance. In this capacity, he wielded the powers of a financial dictator. He strengthened the public credit, instituted an economy program, and at times used notes based on his personal credit. He also served as marine agent for the government. His efforts contributed directly to the victory over Cornwallis at Yorktown. A loan he secured from the French enabled the organization (1781–82) of the Bank of North America. He resigned his government post on 24 Jan. 1783. Morris was a delegate to the Annapolis Convention (1786) and, as a delegate to the Federal Convention of 1787, supported a strong central government. He declined Washington's offer of the post of Secretary of the Treasury in the first administration, and served (1789–95) as U.S. senator from Pennsylvania. His involvement in various land speculations, including a large interest he held in the present site of Washington, D.C., brought his financial ruin. Confined to the Philadelphia debtors' prison (1798–1801), he never regained his fortune.

Morse, Samuel Finley Breese (b. Charlestown, Mass., 27 Apr. 1791; d. New York City, 2 Apr. 1872), artist and inventor. The son of the Congregational clergyman, Jedidiah Morse (1761–1826; known as the "father of American geography"), he was graduated from Yale (1810), and in 1811 accompanied the painter Washington Allston to England. Morse spent the next 4 years studying under Allston and at the Royal Academy in London. Returning to Boston (1815), he opened a studio, but the lack of sufficient portrait commissions compelled him to seek patrons elsewhere. He scored his first success at Charleston, S.C., where he passed the winters from 1818 to 1821, and in 1823 settled at New York. In 1825 he executed at Washington his 2 portraits of Lafayette. He was the chief founder of the National Academy of Design and served as its first president (1826–42). He went to Europe in 1829, and upon his return in 1832 was appointed professor of painting and sculpture in the Univ. of the City of New York (later New York Univ.). During the period 1832–35 he was active in the Native American movement and was its candidate (1836) for mayor of New York. Morse abandoned painting (c.1837) to devote himself to experimenting with the transmission of signals by electricity, an idea first broached to him during his return voyage from Europe in 1832; at that time Morse had set down his original conception of an electromagnetic recording telegraph. While working on the apparatus, which after many experiments was improved by the addition of Joseph Henry's intensity magnet, Morse devised a code of dots and dashes that was named after him (Morse code). Morse's most important contribution was his system of electromagnetic renewers or relays for the transmission of messages over great distances and through any number of stations and branch lines. In the development of the telegraph, he received financial support from Alfred Vail, who became his partner in 1837. Although Morse filed for a patent in 1837, he did not receive it until 1844. Congress appropriated (1843) $30,000 for an experimental line from Washington to Baltimore that was constructed by Ezra Cornell. On 24 May 1844 Morse transmitted over this line the message, "What hath God wrought!" When the government refused to buy the rights to the apparatus, Morse and his associates formed a company for the manufacture of the telegraph.

Morton, William Thomas Green (b. Charlton, Mass., 9 Aug. 1819; d. New York City, 15 July 1868), dentist and pioneer in surgical anesthesia. He was educated at academies in Northfield and Leicester, entered (1840) the College of Dental Surgery at Baltimore, Md., and in 1842 began his practice at Farmington, Conn. In 1842–43 he set up a joint practice at Boston with Dr. Horace Wells of Hartford, Conn., who in 1844 was to use nitrous oxide (laughing gas) in the extraction of teeth. When the partnership was terminated in late 1843, Morton remained in Boston. He matriculated (1844) at Harvard Medical School, but attended only for a brief period. At about this time, at the suggestion of Prof. Charles T. Jackson, a chemist, Morton employed ether in drops as a local anesthetic in filling a tooth. Jackson had also demonstrated that the inhalation of sulfuric ether induced loss of consciousness; it was this method that Morton used in experiments on animals and himself. He performed the painless extraction of an ulcerated tooth (30 Sept. 1846) after using ether inhalation on the patient. Following other successful painless extractions, Dr. John Collins Warren, a Boston surgeon, arranged for the use of Morton's discovery in an operation at the Massachusetts General Hospital. On

16 Oct. 1846, with Morton administering the anesthetic in the presence of physician spectators, Warren removed a vascular tumor from the neck of a patient. Formal announcement of the discovery was made on 18 Nov. 1846 in the *Boston Medical and Surgical Journal*. Morton patented his discovery under the name of "letheon" (12 Nov. 1846). When the French Academy of Medicine awarded a joint prize of 5,000 francs (1847) to Jackson and Morton, the latter did not accept his share, asserting that the discovery was his alone. Morton's claims led Dr. Crawford W. Long (1815–1878) of Athens, Ga., to publish accounts (1848, 1853) of independent discoveries he had made with sulfuric ether in 8 operations on human beings performed between 1842 and 1846. To Morton, however, goes the major credit for the discovery, for he was the first to make a public demonstration with assumption of full responsibility for the consequences.

Moses, Anna Mary Robertson (Grandma Moses) (b. Greenwich, N.Y., 7 Sept. 1860; d. Hoosick Falls, N.Y., 13 Dec. 1961), primitive painter. The daughter of a painter, from age 12 until her marriage (1887) she worked as a hired girl. The mother of 10 children, 5 of whom died in infancy, she took over their farm when her husband died. When she could no longer farm and when arthritis made it difficult for her to use a needle to make her woolen embroideries or "worsted pictures," she took up painting (1937). Using house paints and then oils she began by copying pictures from postcards. She became more imaginative, drawing scenes of her childhood from memory. In 1938 Louis J. Caldor, an art collector, saw 3 of her paintings in a drugstore in Hoosick Falls and bought all her existing work. After the Museum of Modern Art (New York City) hung 3 of her pictures in a show entitled "Contemporary Unknown

American Painters" (1939), her fame mounted, as did the price of her art. Acclaimed as the American Henri Rousseau, her works tell the story of skating, sleighing, picnics, weddings, wash days, and quilting bees. Reflecting craft tradition, her traditional American folk art was known for brilliant use of color as well as its humor, simplicity, realism, and emotional effectiveness. Altogether she held 250 exhibits and painted over 1,500 paintings, including 25 after the age of 100. Her works include *The Old Oaken Bucket* (1939), *Catching the Thanksgiving Turkey* (1943), and *From My Window* (1946).

Moses, Robert (b. New Haven, Conn., 18 Dec. 1888; d. West Islip, N.Y., 29 July 1981), urban planner, graduated from Yale (1909), earned B.A. and M.A. degrees from Oxford (1911, 1913) and a Ph.D. from Columbia (1914). Early involved in reform politics, Moses became closely associated with Gov. Alfred E. Smith, serving as Chief of State of the New York State Reconstruction Commission (1919–21) and Secretary of State for New York State (1927–28). Moses persuaded Smith to form the New York State Council of Parks from 11 isolated regional parks councils (1924). Appointed president of the Long Island Park Commission, he was chosen state chairman, serving for 39 years. His remarkable record of public service included the chairmanships of the Jones Beach State Parkway and Bethpage Authorities (1934–60), New York State Power Authority (1954–63), Triborough Bridge and Tunnel Authority (1946–68). He was also coordinator of construction for New York City (1946–60) and New York City Park Commissioner (1934–60). In 1959 Moses held 12 positions at once. He wielded more influence in public works construction in New York than any other man in the 20th century, supporting vast parkway construction, bridge building, and the creation of parks, beaches, and playgrounds. He employed the device of the public authority, which raised money by issuing its own bonds and collecting tolls and fees, thus providing a source of revenue and patronage outside traditional political processes. Moses believed in accommodating the automobile. His efforts fostered suburban growth, especially the development of Long Island. Moses' approach to urban renewal emphasized high-rise public and luxury housing. His achievements have been criticized for destruction of landmarks, harm to neighborhoods, for lack of interest in the problems of the poor, and for an unwillingness to address the need for mass transit. His preference for the use of parks for recreation rather than as islands of tranquility has been criticised by recent urban planners. Moses was defeated for governor of New York as a Republican candidate in 1934. He was president of the 1964–65 New York World's Fair Corp. from 1960–67. He is the author of *Public Works: A Dangerous Trade* (1970).

Motley, John Lothrop (b. Dorchester, Mass., 15 Apr. 1814; d. in Dorsetshire, England, 29 May 1877), historian and diplomat. He was graduated from Harvard (1831), studied at Göttingen and Berlin, and after returning to Boston wrote 2 novels, *Morton's Hope* (1839) and *Merrymount* (1849). He served (1841–42) as secretary of legation at St. Petersburg and in 1847 began work on the historical subject that was to occupy the rest of his life. To further his researches in archives in Germany and Holland, he went to Europe in 1851. *The Rise of the Dutch Republic* (3 vols., 1856) indicated the main lines of Motley's history and his point of view: his dramatic narrative treatment, his preoccupation with political and religious developments, and his studied contrast of liberty and absolutism. He also published *The History of the United Netherlands* (4 vols., 1860, 1867) and *The Life and Death of John of Barneveld* (2 vols., 1874). From 1861 to 1867 Motley was minister to Austria and from 1869 to 1870 minister to Great Britain.

Muller, Hermann Joseph (b. New York City, 21 Dec. 1890; d. Indianapolis, Ind. 5 Apr. 1967), geneticist, received his degrees at Columbia (B.A., 1910; M.A., 1911; Ph.D., 1916), and taught at Cornell, Rice Inst., Columbia, and the Univ. of Texas. Senior geneticist (1933–37) of the Institute of Genetics in Moscow, he was professor of Zoology, Indiana Univ. (1945–65). His genetics research was begun in 1911 and conducted mainly by breeding experiments in the fruit fly, Drosophila. Working with Thomas Hunt Morgan (*q.v.*), he established the principle of linear linkage, accounting for the inheritance of characteristics on the basis of a linear arrangement of genes. He made a special study of mutations leading to permanently altered, hereditary characteristics, and described the gene as probably a single molecule. For his discovery of hereditary changes or mutations produced by X rays, he was awarded the Nobel prize (1946). His writings include *The Mechanics of Mendelian Heredity* (with others, 1915), *Out of the Night* (1935), and *Genetics, Medicine, and Man* (with others, 1947).

Muñoz Marín, Luis (b. San Juan, P.R., 18 Feb. 1898; d. there, 30 Apr. 1980), statesman. The son of the Puerto Rican leader Luis Muñoz-Rivera, he attended Georgetown Univ. (1912–16) and then spent 2 years as secretary to the Puerto Rican Resident Commissioner in Washington. For the next few years he spent most of his time in New York City and was an author, contributing to magazines and editing *La Revista de Indias*, a journal focusing on Caribbean and Latin American culture. He returned to Puerto Rico, where he edited his father's daily newspaper, *La Democracia* (1925–27), and wrote "Puerto Rico, the American Colony," an argument for complete independence, which was published in *These United States* (1925). In 1927 he was sent to the U.S. as representative of the economic committee of the Puerto Rican legislature and, later, served as member of the Pan-American Conference in Havana (1928). He was elected to the Puerto Rican Senate (1932) on the ticket of the Liberal party. While a senator he was in contact with leading New Dealers, including President Franklin D. Roosevelt and Rexford Tugwell. In reaction to the punitive independence proposed in the Tydings Bill (1936), Muñoz began to search for a different solution to the status problem. Forced to withdraw from the Liberal party (May 1936), he founded (July 1938) the Popular Democratic party, dedicated to social and economic reform, and appealing to the working population as well as the landless *jíbaros*. The PDP won a majority of votes in its first campaign, Muñoz becoming president of the Puerto Rican Senate (1941–48). He worked closely with the newly appointed governor, Rexford Tugwell, on a program for economic and land reform. Serving four terms as Puerto Rico's first elected governor (1949–65), Muñoz was the chief architect of commonwealth status and supported Operation Bootstrap in which industrialization and capital investment were stimulated.

Nabokov, Vladimir (b. St. Petersburg, Russia, 23 Apr. 1899; d. Montreux, Switzerland, 2 July 1977), author. Born into a family of Russian nobility, he attended Prince Tenishev Gymnasium and, after his family left Russia (1919), earned his B.A. from Trinity College, Cambridge (1922). While living in Germany (1922–37) and France (1937–40) he wrote in Russian, his poetry, plays, short stories, and novels establishing him as a major post-1917 émigré author. Among his early novels later translated into English are: *Kamera Obskura* (1932, published in the U.S. in an altered version as *Laughter in the Dark*, 1938), and *Invitation to a Beheading* (1935, English, 1964). In 1940 he emigrated to the U.S., becoming a citizen in 1945. He taught at Stanford (1940–41), was a lecturer and professor of literature at Wellesley (1941–48), a professor of Russian literature at Cornell (1948–59), and a visiting lecturer at Harvard (1952). His novels written in English include *Bend Sinister* (1947), *Lolita* (1955), the controversial best seller which deals with the love of a middle-aged European man for a 12-year-old American girl, and *Pale Fire* (1962), which is considered to be the English work in which his intricate structural effects and verbal displays are at their peak. Although some have described him as a comic novelist, since his works display a magnificent wit and contain elaborate jokes and puns, his novels ultimately deal with a contemporary sense of loss and of society's disintegration, revealing a penetrating cultural and political awareness. Among his numerous other works are: *Nikolai Gogol* (1944), a critical evaluation; *Conclusive Evidence: A Memoir* (1950) and *Speak on, Memory* (1967), autobiographical works; *Look Back at the Harlequins* (1974), a mock autobiography. He has produced poetry (*Poems*, 1959), short stories, and translated Pushkin. A noted lepidopterist, he was a research fellow at Harvard's Museum of Comparative Zoology (1942–48).

Nader, Ralph (b. Winsted, Conn., 27 Feb. 1934–   ), social reformer, received his A.B. *magna cum laude* from Princeton (1955) and his LL.B. with distinction from Harvard Law School (1958), and was admitted to the Connecticut bar (1958). His book *Unsafe at Any Speed* (1965) portrayed the automobile industry as placing style, horsepower, comfort, and sales over safety, and attacked industry and government secrecy. Nader argued that additional safety features could save lives lost not by the "first collision" but immediately thereafter as victims collided with parts of their car or were thrown from it. Revelations (Mar. 1966) of industry surveillance and harassment of Nader brought Nader, his book, and viewpoint prominently to the fore. The National Traffic and Motor Vehicle Safety Act of 1966 (9 Sept.) is considered to be his achievement. As consumer advocate, Nader investigated health conditions in the coal industry, severely critcizing the Bureau of Mines (1968). His campaign led to legislation on matters as removed from one another as gas pipelines and the meat industry. Establishing the Center for the Study of Responsive Law (1969) with 5 full-time lawyers and 100 students hired for the summer, he inspired his "Nader's Raiders" in their investigations of the FTC, ICC, CAB, FDA, and the pesticide division of the Agriculture Department. He also organized the Public Interest Research Group, the Center for Auto Safety, Professionals for Auto Safety, and the Project for Corporate Responsibility. His study groups have produced works on old-age homes and water pollution. The Congress Project (1971–72) produced profiles of over 475 congressmen, encompassing their voting records, campaign financing, and personal behavior. Known for honesty, candor, incredible energy, and asceticism, Nader, with his modern brand of muckraking, has been the spearhead of consumer protection in the 1960s and 1970s.

Nast, Thomas (b. Landau, Bavaria, 27 Sept. 1840; d. Guayaquil, Ecuador, 7 Dec. 1902), artist and cartoonist, came to New York in 1846, studied art under Theodore Kaufman and at the National Academy of Design, and at 15 became draftsman for *Frank Leslie's Illustrated Weekly.* He was sent to London by the New York *Illustrated News* (1860), and accompanied Garibaldi as artist of the *Illustrated London News* and *Le Monde Illustré* (Paris). Returning to New York (1861), he became a staff artist of *Harper's Weekly,* with war drawings (*Emancipation,* 24 Jan. 1863; *Compromise with the South,* 3 Sept. 1864), which influenced public opinion. His fame rests largely on his dramatic cartoons exposing the Tweed Ring in New York City (1869–72), notably *Let Us Prey* and *Tiger Loose.* His adaptation of the tiger to represent Tammany proved a potent weapon of municipal reform. He also invented the elephant for the Republican party and popularized the donkey for the Democrats. The line and texture of his bold, graphic style lost none of their bite in being engraved in wood.

Nevelson, Louise (b. Kiev, Russia, 23 Sept. 1900–), sculptor. Nevelson emigrated to the U.S. (1905). From 1928–30 she studied at the Art Students League, New York City, then spent a year in Munich studying with the abstract painter Hans Hoffman. From 1932–33 she was an assistant to the Mexican muralist Diego Rivera. As part of a WPA project, Nevelson taught art at the Educational Alliance School of Art, New York (1937). She first exhibited her sculpture at a group show at the Brooklyn Museum (1935) and at a 1-man show in New York City (1940). Her works of the 1930s and 40s reflected the influences of cubism and Picasso, as well as Aztec, Mayan, and African art. Nevelson is most famous for her wood assemblages, bits of wood put together in an abstract form and usually painted in solid black, gold, or white. The earliest such assemblages, created in the 1940s, include *Circus*, *Menagerie*, and *Crowded Outside*. But it was not until the 1950s, after her series of exhibitions at the Grand Central Moderns Gallery (New York), that her wood assemblages first achieved fame. One of her most notable wood constructions of this period was *Sky Cathedral*, shown at the Albright-Knox Art Gallery, Buffalo, N.Y. (1958) and purchased by the Museum of Modern Art. Nevelson has also worked with terra cotta, stone, bronze, plaster, aluminum, and most recently, steel. In 1959 she won the grand prize of the New York Coliseum's "Art U.S.A.," and in 1960 the Logan Award of the Art Institute of Chicago. Since the 1960s Nevelson's style has become simpler and sparer, as reflected in her 1974 2-floor exhibit of collages, constructions, and etchings at the Pace Gallery, New York. A major retrospective took place at the Whitney Museum (Mar.–Apr. 1967).

Nevins, Allan (b. Camp Point, Ill., 20 May 1890; d. Menlo Park, Calif., 5 Mar. 1971), historian and journalist, author of more than 50 books, editor of another 175, and innumerable articles. Son of a farmer with a large library, Nevins early became interested in books. Graduating Phi Beta Kappa from the Univ. of Illinois (1912), he went on to receive his M.A. in English (1913). Up until 1930 he pursued a career as a journalist, working as an editor at various times on the *Nation*, the *New York Evening Post*, the *Herald*, the *Sun*, and the *World*. His first history books were written during this period, including his earliest work, *Life of Robert Rogers*, about a colonial frontiersman, written while he was still an undergraduate (1913), and the well-known *The Emergence of Modern Amer-*

ica (1927). Nevins began his second career in 1927 when he accepted an appointment as professor of history at Cornell. A year later he became associate professor history at Columbia, and in 1931 De Witt Clinton Professor of History. During his tenure at Columbia (1928–58) he was known as both a dedicated teacher and scholar. Although he never received a doctorate, he actively supported his Ph.D. candidates, backing them up during their oral examinations and dissertation defenses. An indefatigable worker, his writings were characterized by intense research, objectivity, imagination, engaging style, and the ability to make history come alive. Challenging Charles A. Beard's interpretation of American history, Nevins questioned whether the politics of American leaders had been influenced by economic self-interest. Nevins believed that America's economic leaders must be treated more objectively by historians, and appreciated for their contributions to American industrialization which allowed the U.S. to successfully engage in 2 world wars. He wrote numerous biographies of entrepreneurs, including *John D. Rockefeller: The Heroic Age of Enterprise* (1940) and *Ford: The Times, The Man, The Company* (with Frank E. Hill, 1954). He was awarded the Pulitzer prize in biography for his *Grover Cleveland* (1932) and a 2d time for *Hamilton Fish* (1938). During the last 30 years of his life, Nevins completed a 6-vol. definitive study of the U.S. through the Civil War, entitled *The Ordeal of the Union* (1947, 1952, the last 2 vols. posthumously). He pioneered tape-recorded interviews, founding Columbia University's Oral History Collection (1948). He was also one of the founders of *American Heritage*, a monthly magazine of popular history, and served as chairman of the Civil War Centennial Commission (1961).

Niebuhr, Reinhold (b. Wright City, Mo., 21 June 1892; d. Stockbridge, Mass., 1 June 1971), clergyman and theologian. He was graduated from the Yale Divinity School (B.D., 1914; A.M., 1915), was ordained (1915) as a minister in the Evangelical Synod of North America, and served as a pastor at Detroit (1915–28). In 1928 he became assistant professor of the philosophy of religion at the Union Theological Seminary, New York, where he was professor of applied Christianity (1930–60). Primarily concerned with social ethics and politically oriented, Niebuhr's theology combined the political liberalism of the Social Gospel with Biblical theology, stressing original sin and God's judgment. It differs from Continental Neo-orthodoxy (Karl Barth and Emil Brunner) in its refusal to consider man as having lost contact with God. Among his works were *Does Civilization Need Religion?* (1927), *Moral Man and Immoral Society* (1932), *Reflections on the End of an Era* (1934), *An Interpretation of Christian Ethics* (1935), *Beyond Tragedy* (1937), *Christianity and Power Politics* (1940), *The Nature and Destiny of Man* (1941–43), *Faith and History* (1949), and *The Irony of American History* (1952), *Faith and Politics* (1968). He was editor of *Christianity in Crisis* (1941–66).

Nimitz, Chester William (b. Fredericksburg, Tex., 24 Feb. 1885; d. San Francisco, 20 Feb. 1966), naval officer, was graduated from the U.S. Naval Academy (1905), and served as chief of staff to the commander of the U.S. Atlantic submarine fleet during World War I. In 1939 he was made chief of the Bureau of Navigation with the rank of rear admiral. After the Pearl Harbor attack he took over command of the Pacific Fleet from Admiral Husband E. Kimmel. Commander of the Pacific Fleet and the Pacific Ocean Areas with the rank of admiral, his initial strategy was to defend the Hawaiian approaches and the lines of mainland communication. Given much of the credit for the strategy of "island hopping," he began his offensive with the amphibious landing on Guadalcanal (7 Aug. 1942) and the decisive victory in the naval Battle of Guadalcanal (12–15 Nov.). In 1943 he pursued his offensive aimed at seizing the Solomons, the Gilberts and Marshalls, and the Bonin Islands to come within effective bombing distance of Japan. At the time of Japan's surrender he commanded 6,256 ships and 4,847 combat aircraft, the largest fighting fleet in history. Nimitz accepted the Japanese surrender in Tokyo Bay. He served as U.S. Chief of Naval Operations (1945–47). He headed (1949) the UN mediation commission in the dispute over Kashmir. He edited *Sea Power, A Naval History* (with E. B. Potter, 1960).

Nixon, Richard Milhous (b. Yorba Linda, Calif., 9 Jan. 1913–   ), 37th president of the U.S., graduated from Whittier College (A.B. 1934) and Duke Law School (LL.B. 1937), having been elected student body president of both schools. He practiced law in Whittier, Calif. (1937–42) and spent 6 months with the Office of Price Administration (1942) before service in the navy (1942–46) where he attained the rank of lieutenant commander. Elected to the 80th Congress, he served 2 terms as a representative (1947–51). A member of the House Un-American Activities Committee, he achieved national prominence for spearheading the investigation of Alger Hiss (1948–49). After a bitter election contest with Rep. Helen Gahagan Douglas, he was elected U.S. senator from California (1950). Reaching the Senate a month ahead of schedule, having been chosen to fill a vacancy, he served until 1953. As vice-president (1953–61), he served with restraint during the 3 major disabling illnesses of President Eisenhower (heart attack, 1955; ileitis operation, 1956; stroke, 1957). Traveling to 56 countries while vice-president, his unpopular reception in Latin America (1968) demonstrated the weaknesses of U.S.–Latin-American policies. On a goodwill trip to the U.S.S.R. (1959) to open the American National Exhibition, he engaged in an extemporaneous debate with Premier Nikita Khrushchev over merits of the rural economic systems. Nominated for the presidency in 1960 by the Republican party, he was defeated by John F. Kennedy in one of the closest elections of the century. Defeated by Pat Brown for the governorship of California (1962), he moved to New York City, where he practiced law (1963–68). Maintaining his activities in the Republican party by campaigning for Sen. Barry Goldwater (1964) and congressional candidates (1964, 1966), he was nominated again for the presidency on the 1st ballot and won a close election over Hubert H. Humphrey and George C. Wallace (1968). His 1st term as president was marked by major foreign initiatives, including the change of direction of U.S. policy toward mainland China, dramatically demonstrated by his trip there (21–28 Feb. 1972). Although he won an overwhelming reelection victory (1972), his 2d term was overshadowed by the Watergate scandals. Leading members of his staff and cabinet were indicted for offenses connected with covering up the Watergate break-in. Nixon cited the doctrine of executive privilege and refused to turn over to the special prosecutor's office, the courts, and the House Judiciary Committee, transcripts or tapes of White House conversations. After the Supreme Court ordered Nixon to turn over tapes to the lower courts, and the House Judiciary Committee voted 3 articles of impeachment, Nixon released transcripts which indicated that he had known of the Watergate coverup 9 months earlier than previously admitted and had ordered the FBI to stop its investigation. Faced with the loss of almost all support in Congress and with the imminence of impeachment and conviction, Nixon resigned on 9 Aug. 1974. He received a full and complete pardon from his successor, Gerald R. Ford, on 8 Sept. 1974. He is the author of *Six Crises* (1962) and *RN* (1978).

Noguchi, Isamu (b. Los Angeles, 7 Nov. 1904–   ), sculptor, studied for 2 years at Columbia as a premedical student, then switched to art, serving an apprenticeship in sculpture to Gutzom Borglum, then in Paris (1927–28) as assistant to Constantin Brancusi, an abstract sculptor, where he studied the works of Picasso and the constructionists. Experimenting with constructions, he used grooved joints held together by gravity or tension, and exhibited his creations in New York (1929). In 1930 he traveled to Peking, making brush and wash drawings, and then to Japan, studying Japanese traditional techniques, which have found expression in his later works in a feeling for landscapes and natural materials. After his model "Play Mountain" (1933), featuring sculptured earth, was rejected by the New York City Parks Department, he secured big commissions, including a 65-ft.-long relief sculpture in colored cement (Mercado Rodriguez, Mexico City, 1936) and a 10-ton stainless steel work for the façade of the Associated Press Bldg. in Rockefeller Center, New York (1938). During these years he also designed costumes and 20 "stagesets" for Martha Graham, creating a series of planes for dancers to move through. Widely employed as an interior designer of leading buildings, he is renowned as well for his courtyards and gardens (Yale Library, Chase Manhattan Plaza) and for his lamps and furniture. Basically a stone carver, he combines the abstract with a deep respect for nature. Among his best known creations is the 29-ft.-high bright red cube with a hole on one side standing in front of the Marine Midland Grace Trust Co. in New York. Widely exhibited internationally, Noguchi had a retrospective at the Whitney Museum (1968).

Norris, George William (b. Sandusky, Ohio, 11 July 1861; d. McCook, Neb., 2 Sept. 1944), statesman, was graduated in law (1882) from Northern Indiana Normal School (now Valparaiso Univ.), moved to Beaver City, Neb. (1885), and served 3 terms as prosecuting attorney of Furnas Co. and then as a district judge (1895–1902). As congressman (1903–18), he was a leader in the revolt against Speaker Cannon (1910). As a progressive Republican he supported the Bull Moose movement (1912), opposed U.S. entry into World War I as well as participation in the League of Nations, but endorsed U.S. participation in World War II. U.S. senator from Nebraska (1913–43), he was sponsor of the Norris-La Guardia Anti-injunction Act (1932) and of the 20th (Lame Duck) Amendment (1933); his most notable service was his fight for federal water power regulation and for public ownership and operation of hydroelectric plants. In 1928 he secured passage of a bill providing for government operation of the dam at Muscle Shoals, but it was vetoed by Coolidge. Another bill (1931) was vetoed by Hoover. The Tennessee Valley Authority (TVA) constituted the culmination of his efforts. Norris Dam (near Knoxville) was named in his honor.

Ochs, Adolph Simon (b. Cincinnati, Ohio, 12 Mar. 1858; d. Chattanooga, Tenn., 8 Apr. 1935), newspaper publisher. He received most of his schooling from his parents and during his boyhood served his apprenticeship in the newspaper business on the Knoxville (Tenn.) *Chronicle.* In 1878 he purchased the controlling interest in the Chattanooga *Times,* then on the brink of failure, and instituted a policy of full, accurate, and reliable reporting that characterized his subsequent career (1896–1935) as publisher of *The New York Times.* Taking over the *Times* when it was on the verge of bankruptcy, Ochs reorganized the newspaper according to the canons of responsible journalism in a day when the influence of the sensational press in New York City was at its height. By 1900 he had made the *Times* a profitable venture, and under his guidance it became known as the "newspaper of record" because of its extensive coverage of public events and its intelligent specialized reporting. His view of the responsibility of a free press is expressed in the motto he selected for the *Times:* "All the news that's fit to print."

Oglethorpe, James Edward (b. London, England, 1 June 1696; d. Cranham Hall, Essex, England, 1 July 1785), founder of the colony of Georgia. Oglethorpe studied at Eton and Corpus Christi College, Oxford. He held an army commission (1713–15) and in 1717 served as an aide-de-camp to Prince Eugene of Savoy in his campaign against the Turks. Elected to the House of Commons (1722) he served as the representative of Haslemere for 32 years. As chairman of Parliament's committee on prison reform he became concerned about the plight of the debtor classes. In his pamphlet *The Sailor's Advocate* (1728) he exposed the evils of impressment. Persuaded by Oglethorpe's arguments that a colony should be established as a refuge for imprisoned debtors and as a buffer against Spanish, French, or Indian encroachment on South Carolina, Parliament granted (1732) Oglethorpe and 19 associates a charter, to expire in 21 years, making them trustees of the colony of Georgia. With 116 carefully selected colonists, he reached Charleston, S.C. and went on to found (12 Feb. 1733) Savannah. Oglethorpe encouraged the immigration of Protestants being persecuted on the European continent and proved a benefactor to the German Lutherans, Moravians, Scotch Highland Presbyterians, and Jews who came. He developed a vigorous defense program, building forts and establishing a system of military training. In 1738 he persuaded Prime Minister Robert Walpole to send him a regiment of 700 men. After England declared war on Spain (1739), Oglethorpe led an unsuccessful expedition against St. Augustine (1740). When the Spanish attacked Frederica, Georgia's southern outpost, Oglethorpe defeated them in the Battle of Bloody Marsh (9 June 1742), thereby assuring Georgia's survival. A second unsuccessful assault on St. Augustine (1743) and increasing reports from malcontents led to his recall to England. Charges brought against him were dropped but he never returned to Georgia. Promoted a general (1765), Oglethorpe was offered the command of the British army in America (1775), but declined the position because he would not have had the power of concession and conciliation.

Olmsted, Frederick Law (b. Hartford, Conn., 26 Apr. 1822; d. Waverly, Mass., 28 Aug. 1903), landscape architect and author. He attended Yale (1842–43) and from 1847 to 1857 engaged in experimental farming in Connecticut and Staten Island. In 1850 he made an overseas tour, recording his observations in *The Walks and Talks of an American Farmer in England* (1852). His 3 journeys in the South (1852 *et seq.*) were described in as many volumes, comprising one of the most valuable factual records of Southern social and economic life on the eve of the Civil War: *A Journey in the Seaboard Slave States* (1856), *A Journey Through Texas* (1857), and *A Journey in the Back Country* (1860), all 3 of which were condensed in *The Cotton Kingdom* (2 vols., 1861). In 1857 he was appointed superintendent of Central Park, New York City, and in 1858, in collaboration with Calvert Vaux (1824–95), he won the prize competition for its new design. In 1858 he was named chief architect of Central Park, a pioneer enterprise of American municipal planning. In numerous commissions, most of them executed between 1865 and 1895, Olmsted laid the foundations of American landscape architecture and made the public park a significant factor in urban life. Among his works are Prospect Park, Brooklyn; Riverside Park, New York; the grounds of the national Capitol, Washington, D.C.; the park systems of Boston, Hartford, and Louisville; Mount Royal Park, Montreal; the grounds of the World's Fair (1893) at Chicago; Roland Park, Baltimore; Belle Isle Park, Detroit; and the grounds of Stanford Univ. and the Univ. of California.

O'Neill, Eugene Gladstone (b. New York City, 16 Oct. 1888; d. Boston, Mass., 27 Nov. 1953), dramatist. The son of the actor James O'Neill, he attended Princeton (1906) and, after a period of travel and adventure, was a student (1914–15) in the 47 Workshop of George Pierce Baker at Harvard. He became associated (1916) with the Provincetown Players, who produced (1916–20) 10 of his 1-act plays, including *Bound East for Cardiff* and *The Moon of the Caribbees*. With the Broadway production of *Beyond the Horizon* (1920), which was awarded the Pulitzer prize, O'Neill took his place as the foremost American dramatist of his day. He also won the Pulitzer prize for

Anna Christie (1921) and *Strange Interlude* (1928), both of which were later produced as motion pictures, and in 1936 was awarded the Nobel prize in literature. A resourceful and inventive dramatist, whose work passed through several stages of development including naturalism, expressionism, symbolism, romanticism, and a combination of Greek tragedy and Freudian psychology, O'Neill authored 45 published plays, including *The Emperor Jones* (1920), *Diff'rent* (1921), *The Hairy Ape* (1922), *All God's Chillun Got Wings* (1924), *Desire Under the Elms* (1924), *The Great God Brown* (1926), *Lazarus Laughed* (1927), *Marco Millions* (1928), *Mourning Becomes Electra* (1931), *Ah, Wilderness!* (1933), and *The Iceman Cometh* (1946). Unproduced before his death were *A Moon for the Misbegotten* (pub. 1952), *A Touch of the Poet* (1957), and *Long Day's Journey into Night* (1956), Pulitzer prize play, 1957. These late plays are the finest examples of the great drama O'Neil created from the stuff of his tortured spirit.

Oppenheimer, J. Robert (b. New York City, 22 Apr. 1904; d. Princeton, N.J., 18 Feb. 1967), physicist. He was graduated *summa cum laude* from Harvard (A.B., 1925), studied briefly at the Cavendish Laboratories in Cambridge under Lord Rutherford (1925–26) and at Göttingen (Ph.D., 1927) under Max Born. He was a National Research Fellow (1927–28) at Harvard and at the California Institute of Technology and continued postdoctoral studies as International Education Board Fellow (1928–29) at the Univ. of Leyden and the Technische Hochschule at Zürich. In 1929 he joined the physics faculties at both the Univ. of California, Berkeley, and the California Institute of Technology (1929–47), where he distinguished himself as a superb teacher. As a scholar

he made notable contributions to quantum theory (1926–27 with Max Born; 1935 with Melba Phillips), to the understanding of cosmic rays, of fundamental particles, and did work which later led others to explain quasars (1938–39 with George M. Volkoff and others). Because of his grasp of the entire range of nuclear and quantum physics he was appointed director of the Los Alamos Science Laboratory (1942), where he gathered together about 4,000 scientists and coordinated the effort to produce an atomic bomb by 1945. The successful effort was undoubtedly due in large measure to his administrative and diplomatic skills. For this he has been named the "father of the atomic bomb." In 1945 he resigned his position as director at Los Alamos but served as chairman of the General Advisory Committee of the Atomic Energy Commission (1947–52). He was the principal author of the Acheson-Lilienthal Report and of the Baruch Plan, proposals for international control of atomic energy. He also served on President Eisenhower's Scientific Advisory Committee and as an adviser to the Departments of State and Defense, and to the National Security Council. In 1947 he became director of the Institute for Advanced Study at Princeton, a position he held until his resignation in 1966. Because of his earlier associations with left-wing groups, his misrepresentation of a 1943 conversation with a friend regarding leakage of secret information to the U.S.S.R., and his cautious approach to the development of a hydrogen bomb, Oppenheimer became the subject of a security hearing in 1954. Thereafter, the Atomic Energy Commission permanently denied him security clearance (June 1954), although in 1963 it awarded him the prestigious Fermi prize for his "outstanding contributions to theoretical physics and his scientific and administrative leadership." In addition to several scientific papers, he was the author of *Science and the Common Understanding* (1954), *The Open Mind* (1955), and *Some Reflections on Science and Culture* (1960).

Otis, Elisha Graves (b. Halifax, Vt., 3 Aug. 1811; d. Yonkers, N.Y., 9 Apr. 1861), inventor and manufacturer. Educated in public school, Otis worked in construction (1830–35), the hauling business (1835–38), and owned a shop which manufactured carriages and wagons (1838–45). While operating a machine shop (1845–48) Otis built his first invention, a turbine waterwheel. In 1852, as supervisor of the construction of a bedstead factory in Yonkers, he invented a number of automatic safety devices for the installed elevator, preventing it from falling when rope or chain broke. Otis started manufacturing freight elevators. His business increased after his device was publicly exhibited at the Crystal Palace Exposition in New York City (1854). The first permanent passenger elevators were installed in the Haughwout Department Store (1857) and in the Fifth Avenue Hotel (1859). Otis' safety devices significantly increased the value of real estate by making it possible to reach towering heights by elevator and in fact underpinned the skyscraper. Demand for Otis and Sons elevators increased even further with the invention of the steam-run elevator (1861). Otis also invented railroad car trucks and brakes (1852), a steam plow (1857), a rotary oven for bread (1858), and an automatic wood-turning machine.

Otis, James (b. West Barnstable, Mass., 5 Feb. 1725; d. Andover, Mass., 23 May 1783), pre-Revolutionary leader, was admitted to the Plymouth Co. bar (1748), and 2 years later moved to Boston. He resigned his office as king's advocate general of the vice-admiralty court to appear on behalf of a group of Boston merchants to oppose (1761) as unconstitutional the issuance by the superior court of writs of assistance—general search warrants to aid the enforcement of the Sugar Act of 1733. Writing years later, John Adams asserted: "Then and there the child Independence was born." Although the court issued the writs, Otis took the battle to the general court, to which he was elected that year. Chief target of Otis was Thomas Hutchinson (*q.v.*), whose appointment as chief justice in place of Otis's father, James, senior, an active candidate, aroused the enmity of father and son. A vigorous pamphleteer, he expounded his constitutional views in *A Vindication of the Conduct of the House of Representatives* (1762) and most notably in *The Rights of the British Colonies Asserted and Proved* (1764). Participating in the Stamp Act Congress (1765), which had been summoned at his suggestion, he advocated colonial representation in Parliament and conceded the supremacy of Parliament (*A Vindication of the British Colonies,* 1765). By the time of the Townshend Acts he had become even more moderate in his political views, although he was increasingly abusive and unbalanced in personal behavior and was caned in a coffeehouse brawl by John Robinson, a customs officer. In 1771 his younger brother Samuel A. Otis was appointed his guardian, and he took no part in the Revolution. His death was dramatic; he was struck down by lightning in the Isaac Osgood farmhouse.

Paine, Thomas (b. Thetford, Norfolk, England, 29 Jan. 1737; d. New York City, 8 June 1809), Revolutionary propagandist. The son of a Quaker corsetmaker, he was engaged in a wide variety of occupations before coming to America in 1774. He settled at Philadelphia, where he contributed to the *Pennsylvania*

Magazine and wrote *Common Sense*, an anonymous pamphlet published on 9 Jan. 1776. In *Common Sense*, reputed to have sold 120,000 copies in 3 months and to have attained a total sale of 500,000, Paine advocated the immediate declaration of independence on both practical and ideological grounds. Joining the Revolutionary army, he took part in the retreat across New Jersey, writing at Newark the first of his *Crisis* papers (1776–83), of which the opening passage was: "These are the times that try men's souls. The summer soldier and the sunshine patriot will, in this crisis, shrink from the service of their country." The pamphlet, ordered read to the troops in the Revolutionary encampments, resolved by its eloquent patriotism the hesitation of many in and out of the army. In subsequent *Crisis* papers Paine favored a strong federal union and called for effective fiscal measures. He served (1777–79) as secretary to the committee on foreign affairs of the Continental Congress, and in 1779 was named clerk of the Pennsylvania assembly. After peace was concluded with Great Britain, he lived at New York and at Bordentown, N.J., until 1787, when he went to France and England. In *The Rights of Man* (1791–92), Paine defended republican government and the practical measures of the early phases of the French Revolution in reply to Edmund Burke's *Reflections on the French Revolution* (1790). *The Rights of Man*, which contained some seditious passages, was suppressed by the British government, and Paine, at that time in France, was tried for treason and was outlawed (1792). Made a citizen by the French Assembly (1792), Paine was elected to the Convention. He associated himself with the Girondist party; with the fall of the Girondins, he was stripped of his French citizenship and imprisoned (Dec. 1793). He remained in jail until Nov. 1794, when he was released through the intervention of the U.S. minister, James Monroe. While in jail he began work on *The Age of Reason* (1794–96), a deistic work, beginning: "I believe in one God, and no more; and I hope for happiness beyond this life." In his closing years, spent in New Jersey and New York, Paine lived in poverty and obscurity. He was buried on his farm in New Rochelle, N.Y.; in 1819 William Cobbett exhumed the remains and took them to England.

Parker, Theodore (b. Lexington, Mass., 24 Aug. 1810; d. Florence, Italy, 10 May 1860), clergyman, theologian, and author, graduated (1836) from the Harvard Divinity School, was ordained (1837) at the West Roxbury (Mass.) Church, and during the course of the Unitarian controversy supported the radical wing, enunciating his position in his sermon on "The Transient and Permanent in Christianity" (1841), which endorsed the views set forth by Emerson in the "Divinity School Address" (1838). His interpretation of Christianity as the high point of evolutionary progress, and his call for a new theology based on the immanence of God in human experience and in nature, appeared in *A Discourse of Matters Pertaining to Religion* (1842). His Transcendentalist views brought him into open conflict with the orthodox Unitarians and with the liberal clergy of the Boston Association of Ministers, and led to his resignation from the West Roxbury pulpit (1852) and to his installation as minister of the newly created 28th Congregational Society of Boston. An erudite scholar, Parker was also active in humanitarian and reform movements. He wrote *A Letter to the People of the United States Touching the Matter of Slavery* (1848), aided in the escape of fugitive slaves, and played a notable role in the defense of Anthony Burns (1854). He supported the New England Emigrant Aid Society and was a member of a secret committee that abetted John Brown's raid on Harpers Ferry (1859). His writings were collected in *Theodore Parker's Works* (14 vols., 1863–70).

Parkman, Francis (b. Boston, Mass., 16 Sept. 1823; d. Jamaica Plain, Mass., 8 Nov. 1893), historian. He was graduated from Harvard (1844), received the degree of LL.B. (1846) from the Harvard Law School, and in 1846 made the journey to the Far West which he recorded in *The California and Oregon Trail* (1849; commonly called *The Oregon Trail*). The strenuous expedition taxed his already impaired health and, soon after returning from the West, he suffered a physical and nervous breakdown. Although he was for the rest of his life a semi-invalid suffering from weak eyesight bordering on blindness and from a nervous disorder that prevented unbroken concentration, Parkman eventually won a place as the leading American historian of his time. His historical series dealing with the struggle of England and France for the domination of North America is based on a scholarly use of original sources, and is marked by a sweeping narrative power and vivid descriptive passages dealing with life in the wilderness. The volumes of his series are *History of the Conspiracy of Pontiac* (1851), *Pioneers of France in the New World* (1865), *The Jesuits in North America* (1867), *The Discovery of the Great West* (1869), *The Old Régime in Canada* (1874), *Count Frontenac and New France under Louis XIV* (1877), *Montcalm and Wolfe* (2 vols., 1884), and *A Half-Century of Conflict* (2 vols., 1892).

Parsons, Talcott (b. Colorado Springs, Colo., 13 Dec. 1902; d. Munich, West Germany, 8 May 1979), sociologist. He graduated from Amherst College (A.B., 1924), studied at the London School of Economics (1924–25), where he was deeply influenced by Bronislaw Malinowski, and received his Ph.D. from the Univ. of Heidelberg (1927). At Harvard he taught economics (1927–31) and sociology (1931–73 retirement), and helped to establish the Department of Social Relations and served as its chairman, 1946–56. In the 1930s he changed the focus of American sociology by introducing and emphasizing the broad theoretical works of Max Weber and Emile Durkheim. A structural functionalist in approach, he pioneered in constructing a complex general theory of society. Basic to his theory is the concept that a social system's structure is governed by the way it meets 4 basic needs: goal-attainment, adaptation, integration, and pattern maintenance. He is the author of numerous books, articles, and translations, including *The Structure of Social Action* (1937), *The Social System* (1951), and *Essays in Sociological Theory* (1947, 1954).

Patton, George Smith, Jr. (b. San Gabriel, Calif., 11 Nov. 1885; d. Heidelberg, Germany, 21 Dec. 1945), soldier. Upon graduation from the U.S. Military Academy (1909), he was commissioned a 2d lieutenant in the cavalry. After taking part in Gen. John J. Pershing's expedition into Mexico (1916), he sailed to France (May 1917) as a member of Pershing's staff. He organized and directed the American Tank Center at Langues and commanded a tank brigade at St. Mihiel and Meuse-Argonne. After World War I he promoted the new tank warfare methods and commanded the 304th Tank Brigade at Camp Meade, Md., before returning to cavalry duty. He served in the Washington, D.C. office of the Chief of Cavalry (1928–31), graduated from the Army War College (1932), and served with the 3d Cavalry at Ft. Meyer, Va. (1932–35). He became brigade commander (1940) and then commanding officer (1941) of the 2d Armored Division, which became known as the toughest outfit of the army. Promoted to commanding general of the 1st Armored Corps, he organized the Desert Training Center at Indio, Calif. Under Gen. Eisenhower he was in charge of the Task Force troops in the North African campaign (1942). He commanded the 7th Army in the successful invasion of Sicily and the rapid capture of Palermo (1943). During the Sicilian campaign a widely publicized incident—Patton had slapped a hospitalized soldier suffering from battle fatigue whom he suspected of malingering—brought Patton a reprimand from Gen. Eisenhower, cost him his command, and delayed his promotion to the permanent rank of major general until Aug. 1944. In the summer of 1944 he prepared the 3d Army for the surprise invasion of Normandy. His brilliant sweep across the base of the Breton Peninsula, liberation of Metz (3 Oct.–22 Nov. 1944), breaking of the "Bulge" (Dec. 1944–Jan. 1945), destruction of the Nazi forces in the Saar-Palatinate region, and surprise crossing of the Rhine (22 Mar. 1945) insured his place as one of the great tactical commanders. Relieved of his command of the 3d Army (2 Oct. 1945) for putting too little emphasis on denazification, he was assigned command of the 15th Army, a paper organization devoted to the study of tactical lessons to be learned from the war. He died from injuries suffered in an automobile accident.

Pauling, Linus Carl (b. Portland, Ore., 28 Feb. 1901–), chemist, received his B.S. from Oregon State College (1922) and his Ph.D. from the California Institute of Technology (1925), where from 1931 to 1964 he was professor of chemistry and director of the Gates and Crellin laboratories (1937–58). He was professor of chemistry at Stanford (1969–74). He is renowned for his theory of resonance in the molecular structure of organic chemicals, leading to a better understanding of certain properties of the carbon compounds, especially the aromatics, and for his contributions to immunology, notably on the nature of serological reactions and the molecular structure of antitoxins. With Campbell and Pressman he produced synthetic antibodies. He has also done important work in applying the quantum theory to chemistry, in crystal structure, and in the theory of electrolytes. He was awarded the Nobel prize in chemistry in 1954 for discoveries of forces holding proteins and molecules together, and became the first man to win a 2d complete Nobel award by receiving the prize for peace (1962, awarded 1963) for his intense campaign against nuclear testing. He has stirred controversy with his theory that large doses of vitamin C prevent or ameliorate the common cold.

Peale, Charles Willson (b. Queen Anne Co., Md., 15 Apr. 1741; d. Phila., 22 Feb. 1827), portrait painter, naturalist, was apprenticed as a saddler at 13. He began portrait painting at 20, studying with John Hesselius, then in Boston under Copley (q.v.) and in London (1767) in Benjamin West's studio. Lieutenant in the Philadelphia militia, he fought at Trenton, Princeton, and Germantown, and served 1 term (beg. 1779) in the Pennsylvania assembly. A naturalist as well as a painter, he opened (1802) Peale's Museum of Natural History Objects and Portraits (later the Philadelphia Museum) and founded (1805) the Pennsylvania Academy of Fine Arts. Renowned as the painter of Washington, he painted the first portrait of the Virginian in 1772, 7 additional ones from sittings, and a total of 60 in all. Of all Washington's portraits, Peale's are the most faithful and uncompromising. He painted other leading patriots, faithfully reproducing their dress and manner, but adding little character interpretation. He also painted *Christ Healing the Sick at the Pool of Bethesda* (1822). His sons, Raphael, Rembrandt, Titian, and Rubens, were painters and naturalists like their father.

Peary, Robert Edwin (b. Cresson, Pa., 6 May 1856; d. Washington, D.C., 20 Feb. 1920), naval officer and Arctic explorer. Graduating from Bowdoin College (1877), he became a county surveyor, entered the U.S. Coast and Geodetic Survey in 1879, and was commissioned a lieutenant (1881) in the U.S. navy corps of civil engineers. While on leave in the summer of 1886, he explored the west coast of Greenland, at that time still unknown territory, reaching the ice cap 100 miles inland at an elevation of 7,500 feet above sea level. After further tours of duty in Nicaragua and along the Atlantic coast, he secured support from scientific and geographical societies in the U.S. for another Greenland expedition, which he made (1891–92) in the company of 5 others, including his wife. Peary made a 1,300-mile return journey to the northeast coast of Greenland from his base on the northwest coast, determining the insularity of Greenland and the northernmost limit of the ice cap. The party returned to the U.S. with valuable scientific data. He made further trips (1893–95, 1896) in order to bring to the U.S. large meteorites discovered by him. In 1898 he made a voyage on the *Windward*, a vessel presented by Lord Northcliffe; reaching the shores of the Polar Sea, he marked the region of Smith Sound and made his nearest approach yet to the North Pole, returning to the U.S. in 1902. His next trip (1905–06), made in the *Roosevelt*, saw him come within 174 miles of the North Pole,

the closest approach made up to that time. Starting out again in the *Roosevelt* (1908), Peary, with his Negro servant Matthew Henson, 4 Eskimos, and 40 dogs, reached the North Pole by sledge on 6 Apr. 1909. Shortly before Peary's ship put in at Labrador, where he announced his discovery, a similar claim was made by Dr. Frederick A. Cook, who asserted he had reached the North Pole on 21 Apr. 1908. The bitter controversy which followed was finally resolved by the scientific world in Peary's favor.

Peirce, Charles Sanders (b. Cambridge, Mass., 10 Sept. 1839; d. Milford, Pa., 19 Apr. 1914), philosopher, logician, and scientist. The son of the Harvard mathematician and astronomer Benjamin Peirce (1809–80), he was graduated from Harvard (1859), where he also received the degrees of M.A. (1862) and Sc.B. (1863). As a staff member (1861–91) of the U.S. Coast Survey, he was the first American delegate to the International Geodetic Congress (1877) and made researches in pendulum work and geodesy. During the same period he was an assistant (1869–72) at the Harvard Observatory; the astronomical observations made there by him between 1872 and 1875 provided the material for the only book by Peirce that appeared during his lifetime, *Photometric Researches* (1878). He lectured on science and logic at Harvard (1864, 1869, 1870), the Lowell Institute (1866, 1892, 1903), and Johns Hopkins (1879–84). His most significant contributions were made in formal logic and philosophy. He laid the basis for the logic of relations in mathematical logic, and made vital contributions to the theory of probability, induction, and the logic of scientific methodology. Among the concepts developed by him were tychism (theory of the reality of absolute chance) and synechism (doctrine of continuity). Peirce is best known as the creator (1877–78) of the principle of pragmatism, as well as the term itself. The latter first appeared in print in 1898, when William James used it. Peirce's views, however, differed from those of James, and Peirce later called his doctrine "pragmaticism" to stress the distinction. Most of his voluminous papers remained unpublished until after his death. His studies covered a wide range of subjects including religion, philology, psychology, meteorology, and chemistry.

Penn, William (b. London, England, 14 Oct. 1644; d. Ruscombe, England, 30 July 1718), statesman and religious leader. The son of Adm. Sir William Penn, conqueror of Jamaica, he attended Christ Church College, Oxford, where he was expelled because of his Puritan beliefs (1662). Studying and traveling on the continent and then studying law at Lincoln's Inn (1665), Penn became a staunch member of the Society of Friends while holding office in Ireland (1667). During the next 10 years his sermons and pamphlets praising the Quaker faith led to periods of imprisonment, although it was his acquittal from charges of street preaching which led to *Bushnell's Case* (1670), a landmark in British law protecting the verdict of a jury. His pamphlet *The Sandy Foundation Shaken* led to his incarceration in the Tower of London for 8 months (1669), when he wrote *No Crosses, No Crown,* a moral tract, as well as political tracts. A wealthy man for much of his life, Penn was part owner of East Jersey and trustee of the colony of West Jersey, formulating its *Laws, Concessions, and Agreements* (13 Mar. 1677), a libertarian and democratic document. The idea of a colony where religious and political freedom could flourish came to him during a trip to the Continent (1677) with George Fox,

Quaker leader. Penn was granted proprietorship of Pennsylvania ("Penn's Woods") by charter of Charles II (14 Mar. 1681) as repayment for money owed by the crown to Penn's father. He acquired the "Lower Counties" (Del.) by charter (24 Aug. 1682) from his friend, the Duke of York (later James II). He arrived 27 Oct. 1682, after the first colonists, and after he had drafted the first *Frame of Government* (5 May 1682), which bore the stamp of his Quaker faith, humanitarian views, imperial vision, and proprietary aspirations. Remaining in America (1682–84), he made a peace with the Indians (1682) which built goodwill for generations, and assisted in laying out the city of Philadelphia. He returned to the court of James II (16 Aug. 1684) to press boundary claims against Charles Calvert, 3d Lord Baltimore. After the exile of James II (1688) Penn was accused of treason and the crown held his colony (1692–94). After Penn resumed his governorship (1694), he returned to Pennsylvania (1699–1701) and formulated a new constitution, *Charter of Liberties* (1701), which permitted greater internal autonomy and provided for the voluntary withdrawal of Delaware counties (1704), which nonetheless were governed by the governor of Pennsylvania until 1776. The first plan for unifying the British colonies under one government was proposed by Penn to the Board of Trade (1697). Penn's last years were unhappy due to his dissolute and profligate son and difficulties in the colony. He authored *An Essay Towards the Present and Future Peace of Europe* (1693), a significant early plan for confederation, arbitration, and peace.

Perkins, Frances (b. Boston, Mass., 10 Apr. 1882; d. New York City, 14 May 1965), social reformer and political leader. She received an A.B. from Mt.

Holyoke (1902), taught school, and did social work before resuming her studies at the Wharton School of Finance and Commerce, the Univ. of Pennsylvania, and at Columbia, where she received her M.A. in sociology and economics (1910). Executive secretary of the Consumers' League of New York (1910–12) and of the New York Committee on Safety (1912–17), she became an authority on industrial hygiene and safety. After the Triangle Shirtwaist Factory fire (1911), in which 146 died, she lobbied for state legislation on factory safety standards and, as director of an investigation for the State Factory Commission (1912–13), promoted legislation on hours and wages. On the New York Commission of Safety she worked for industrial and labor legislation, and in her lobbying became acquainted with New York political leaders such as Alfred E. Smith and Franklin D. Roosevelt. Perkins was largely responsible for the state legislation which lowered the 54-hour work week for women to 48 hours. She served as a member of the New York State Industrial Board (1922–26) and as its chairman (1926), as a member of the State Industrial Commission (1919–29), and as its Industrial Commissioner (1929–33). She was President Roosevelt's Secretary of Labor (1933–45), the first woman to serve in a president's cabinet. She influenced passage of national legislation establishing a federal floor on wages and a ceiling on hours, unemployment compensation, the Civilian Conservation Corps, and limiting the employment of children under 16. The Department of Labor's activities were greatly expanded during her tenure as the administration's interest in the problems of labor was unprecedented. Directly responsible for implementing New Deal labor legislation, particularly the Fair Labor Standards Act, she was often embroiled in controversy yet remained an efficient administrator. After resigning from the cabinet she became a member of the U.S. Civil Service Commission (1946–53). Thereafter she lectured on labor and industrial problems. She was the author of *The Roosevelt I Knew* (1946).

Perry, Matthew Calbraith (b. Newport, R.I., 10 Apr. 1794; d. New York City, 4 Mar. 1858), naval officer, brother of Oliver Hazard Perry. Entering the navy as a midshipman (1809), he served under his brother on the *Revenge* and took part in the War of 1812. After a varied tour of duty, he was named (1833) 2d officer of the New York navy yard, where he organized the U.S. Naval Lyceum, an educational body for naval officers, and served as its president. His plan for a naval apprentice system was adopted by Congress in 1837. Promoted to captain (1837), he took command of the *Fulton*, one of the first naval steam-powered vessels, aboard which he conducted (1839–40) the first American naval school of gun practice. He organized the first naval engineer corps and was appointed (1841) commandant of the New York navy yard. After another tour of duty that included the command (1843 *et seq.*) of the African Squadron for aiding in the suppression of the slave trade, service in the Mexican War (including command of the naval force that helped take Vera Cruz in 1847), and special duty at New York (1848–52) as superintendent of ocean mail steamship construction, he was chosen by President Fillmore to negotiate a treaty with Japan, which at that time barred all intercourse with the West. In command of the augmented Eastern Squadron, Perry anchored in Yedo Bay (8 July 1853), where he stayed 9 days; the Japanese officials, impressed with his show of naval strength, agreed to transmit Fillmore's proposals to high dignitaries. Perry sailed for China and returned to Yedo Bay (Feb. 1854), and concluded at Yokohama (31 Mar. 1854) a treaty that opened Japan to the Occidental nations. His official report is in *Narrative of the Expedition of an American Squadron to the China Seas and Japan* (3 vols., 1856).

Perry, Oliver Hazard (b. South Kingston, R.I., 20 Aug. 1785; d. along the Orinoco River, Venezuela, 23 Aug. 1819), naval officer, became a midshipman in the U.S. navy (1799), saw service in West Indian waters during the naval war with France, and was on tours of duty (1802–03, 1804–06) in the Mediterranean during the Tripolitan War. After the outbreak of the War of 1812, he was ordered (1813) to join Commodore Isaac Chauncey's force at Sackett's Harbor, N.Y., and was given command of the U.S. naval forces on Lake Erie. Perry went to Erie, Pa., where he spent the spring and summer constructing and equipping a fleet of 10 vessels, of which the largest were the *Lawrence* and the *Niagara*. The Battle of Lake Erie (10 Sept. 1813), in which Perry defeated the British fleet under Cmdr. Robert H. Barclay, was one of the decisive battles of the war. It gave the Americans control of Lake Erie and enabled Gen. William Henry Harrison (to whom Perry sent the message: "We have met the enemy and they are ours") to seize much of upper Canada. Perry was promoted to captain (1813), received the thanks of Congress (1814), and was acclaimed a national hero. He later took part in the operations against Detroit and in the Battle of the Thames. He commanded the *Java* on a Mediterranean tour (1815–16) and died of yellow fever after completing a diplomatic mission to the Venezuelan government.

Pershing, John Joseph (b. near Laclede, Linn Co., Mo., 13 Sept. 1860; d. Washington, D.C., 15 July 1948), soldier, commander of the A.E.F. in World War I, was graduated (1886) from the U.S. Military Academy, and served as a cavalry officer in operations (1886–90) against Indians in the Southwest and in South Dakota. He was a military instructor (1891–95) at the Univ. of Nebraska, from which he received the degree of LL.B. (1893), was an instructor in military tactics (1897–98) at the U.S. Military Academy, and served in the Spanish-American War. He was on a tour of duty in the Philippines (1899–1903), served on the army general staff (1903–05), was a military observer with the Japanese forces during the Russo-Japanese War, and was promoted (1906) from captain to brigadier general. He again served in the Philippines (1906–13), was named (1913) commander of the 8th Cavalry Brigade, with headquarters at the Presidio, San Francisco, commanded the Mexican border operations (1916), and was promoted (1916) to major general. He was appointed (May 1917) commander of the American Expeditionary Forces (A.E.F.), which he led in France during World War I. It was mainly through his insistence that the American forces operated as a separate command. He was promoted (Oct. 1917) to the rank of full general and received (Sept. 1919) the title of "General of the Armies of the United States." He served as army chief of staff from 1921 until his retirement from the service in 1924.

Phillips, Wendell (b. Boston, 29 Nov. 1811; d. there, 2 Feb. 1884), reformer, orator, obtained his B.A. (1831) and LL.B. (1834) from Harvard and practiced law briefly in Boston. In a speech at

Faneuil Hall (1837) he publicly identified himself with abolitionism, speaking out against the murder of Elijah P. Lovejoy, abolitionist editor. Frequent contributor to Garrison's *Liberator,* he was delegate from Massachusetts to the World Anti-Slavery Convention at London (1840) and was outspoken and uncompromising in his stand against slavery, opposing the annexation of Texas, the Mexican War, and Webster's stand on the Compromise of 1850. In the Civil War, he attacked Lincoln for his moderation on the slavery question and opposed his renomination. Succeeding Garrison (1865) as president of the American Antislavery Society, he kept it active until the adoption of the 15th Amendment. Phillips was sympathetic with the broad spectrum of reform, advocating the abolition of capital punishment, currency and Indian reform, votes for women, and the rights of labor. Gubernatorial nominee of the Labor Reform party and the Prohibitionists (1870), he drew up the Labor Reform platform (1871), advocating the overthrow of the profit system. An orator of the stature of Edward Everett and Daniel Webster (*q.v.*), although his style was easy and colloquial, his most popular lectures and orations include "The Lost Arts" (delivered over 2,000 times), "The Scholar in a Republic," and "Toussaint L'Ouverture." Two series of his *Speeches, Lectures, and Letters* were published (1863, 1891).

Pierce, Franklin (b. Hillsboro, N.H., 23 Nov. 1804; d. Concord, N.H., 8 Oct. 1869), 14th president of the U.S., was graduated from Bowdoin (1824), studied law, and was admitted to the New Hampshire bar (1827). In the state legislature (1829–32; as speaker, 1831–32), he became a Democratic congressman (1833–37) and U.S. senator (1837–42), when he resigned to resume law practice in Concord, N.H. In the War

with Mexico he became brigadier general of volunteers, serving under Winfield Scott. Democratic nominee (1852) on the 49th ballot over Buchanan, Cass, and Douglas, he defeated Scott. His administration was under proslavery influence. He extended the U.S. southern border through the Gadsden Purchase (1853), sent Perry to Japan (1853), signed the Kansas-Nebraska Act (1854), and recognized the Walker régime in Nicaragua. His "bleeding Kansas" policy lost him the support of Northern Democrats and the renomination (1856).

Pike, Zebulon Montgomery (b. Lamberton, now part of Trenton, N.J., 5 Jan. 1779; d. York, now Toronto, Canada, 27 Apr. 1813), soldier and explorer. Entering the army as a cadet (1794), he was commissioned (1805) by Gen. James Wilkinson to take an exploring party to the source of the Mississippi. His expedition, based at St. Louis, explored (9 Aug. 1805–30 Apr. 1806) the upper Mississippi region of the Louisiana Purchase, but did not find the true source of the river. Promoted to captain in 1806, Pike led a 2d expedition (1806–07) which explored what is now Colorado and New Mexico. He sighted but did not succeed in climbing the summit that was later named Pikes Peak. He explored the headwaters of the Arkansas and Red rivers; was arrested by the Spaniards in Santa Fe, but was soon set free; and published *An Account of Expeditions to the Sources of the Mississippi and through the Western Parts of Louisiana* (1810). After the outbreak of the War of 1812, he was commissioned a brigadier general (1813) and was killed in the explosion of a powder magazine while leading the assault on York.

Pincus, Gregory Goodwin (b. Woodbine, N.J., 9 Apr. 1903; d. Boston, Mass., 22 Aug. 1967), biologist. He received his

B.S. from Cornell (1924) and his M.Sc. and Sc.D. from Harvard (1927) and, as a National Research Council Fellow, did postdoctoral research at Harvard, Cambridge, and Kaiser Wilhelm Institute (1927–30). In 1930 he became an instructor in general physiology at Harvard and was an assistant professor there (1931–38). Having published some 70 research papers, he was already an authority on sex hormones and the sex of mammals when, in 1939, while a professor of experimental zoology at Clark Univ., he brought about the first fatherless mammalian birth by inducing parthenogenesis in a female rabbit. He fertilized the ovum in a test tube by using high-temperature hormone treatments and salt solutions and then implanted the fertilized ovum in the rabbit. In 1944 he founded, with H. Hoagland, the Worcester Foundation for Experimental Biology, where he was director of laboratories and later research director. In addition to his work at the foundation, he was research professor in physiology at the Tufts Medical School (1946–50) and research professor in biology at Boston Univ. (1950–67). In the late 1940s he focused his attention on the role of hormones in reproduction. His study of the properties of hydrocortisone, an adrenal hormone, involved use of progesterone, a female hormone secretion. Recognizing that progestins can inhibit ovulation, Pincus and Dr. M. C. Chang developed a synthetic progestin which prevented ovulation in laboratory animals. The development of the oral contraceptive for the human female, known as the Pill, was accomplished with the collaboration of Dr. John Rock and Dr. Celso-Ramon Garcia. After 4 years of experimentation with thousands of women, Enovid, a birth control pill, was first marketed in 1960. Believed to be 100% effective, the Pill is taken today by at least one fifth of all American women of childbearing age. Not only did the Pill revolutionize methods of birth control, it drastically altered the nature of the worldwide debate on the problem of overpopulation. Dr. Pincus also developed estrone, a hormone used in the treatment of breast cancer and pregnancy complications. His publications include: *The Eggs of Mammals* (1936), *The Control of Fertility* (1965), and *Steroid Dynamics* (1966).

Poe, Edgar Allan (b. Boston, Mass., 19 Jan. 1809; d. Baltimore, Md., 7 Oct. 1849), poet, short-story writer, and critic. Orphaned when he was about 3 years old, he was reared by a Richmond (Va.) tobacco merchant, John Allan, whose name he used as his middle name after 1824. He was admitted (1826) to the Univ. of Virginia, but left after 1 term because of gambling debts. His first volume, *Tamerlane and Other Poems* (1827), was published anonymously at Boston. Poe served (1827–29) in the U.S. army, was admitted (1830) to West Point, and was dismissed (1831) for gross neglect of duty. His second volume, *Al Aaraaf, Tamerlane, and Minor Poems* (1829), was published at Baltimore; *Poems by Edgar A. Poe* (1831) was published at New York. He first won public notice with "A MS. Found in a Bottle," which was awarded (1833) a prize by a Baltimore publication. He contributed to the *Southern Literary Messenger,* of which he became (1835) assistant editor. He married (1836) his 14-year-old cousin Virginia Clemm, and moved to New York City (1837), where he published *The Narrative of Arthur Gordon Pym* (1838). He moved to Philadelphia (1838), where he coedited (1839–40) *Burton's Gentleman's Magazine* and was literary editor (1841–42) of *Graham's Lady's and Gentleman's Magazine.* He published *Tales of the Grotesque and Arabesque* (2 vols., 1840) and won a prize (1843) for his story "The Gold Bug." He returned (1844) to New York, where he did freelance writing (the "Balloon Hoax" was published in the New York *Sun* on 13 Apr. 1844) and published his poem "The Raven," which brought him his first fame. He became (1845) editor and proprietor of the *Broadway Journal* and published (1845) *Tales* and *The Raven and Other Poems*. His chronic poverty, alcoholism, and poor health worsened after the death of his wife (1847). He returned to Richmond (1849) and died in Baltimore after being found semiconscious in a saloon. A lyric poet of the first rank, he exerted an important influence upon poetry in the U.S. and abroad, particularly on the French Symbolists; was one of the originators of the detective story genre; and made important contributions as a literary critic, notably in his essays "The Poetic Principle" and "The Philosophy of Composition."

Poinsett, Joel Roberts (b. Charleston, S.C., 2 Mar. 1779; d. Sumter Co., S.C., 12 Dec. 1851), statesman. After studying medicine at the Univ. of Edinburgh and attending Woolwich Military Academy in England (1797–99), Poinsett studied law in the U.S. (1800). Following 10 years of travel throughout Europe and Asia, he became special U.S. agent to Rio de la Plata and Chile (1810–14), investigating for President Monroe the conditions of countries struggling for independence. He encouraged the Carrera brothers' efforts to achieve Chilean independence. When the Carrera government fell, Poinsett returned to the U.S., where he served as a member of the South Carolina state legislature (1816–20) and U.S. representative (1821–25). As the first American ambassador to Mexico (1825–30), Poinsett sought to replace British with American influence in Mexico. However, he was regarded as an intriguer and imperialist with designs on Texas for the U.S. Mexico repeatedly asked for his dismissal. He introduced the U.S. to the Mexican flowering plant which is named for him— *poinsettia pulcherrima*. Poinsett aided his friend President Andrew Jackson during the nullification crisis as leader of the Unionist party in South Carolina (1830–33). As Secretary of War during President Van Buren's administration (1837–41) he organized a general staff and improved the artillery. He also removed 40,000 Indians to land west of the Mississippi and organized the war against the Seminole Indians in Florida. Poinsett founded the Academy of Fine Arts (South Carolina) and the museum of the National Institute for the Promotion of Science and the Useful Arts (Washington, D.C., 1840), which became a part of the Smithsonian (1862).

Polk, James Knox (b. Mecklenburg Co., N.C., 2 Nov. 1795; d. Nashville, Tenn., 15 June 1849), 11th president of the U.S., moved with his parents (1806) to central Tennessee, was graduated from the Univ. of North Carolina (1818), read law, was admitted to the bar (1820), and began practice in Columbia, Tenn. State legislator (1823–25), congressman (1825–39; served as speaker, 1835–39), he was governor of Tennessee (1839–41), but was defeated for reelection in 1841 and again in 1843. He was Democratic nominee (1844) on the 9th ballot when Van Buren failed of the necessary two thirds vote. He defeated Clay in the ensuing election. As president he accomplished all his major objectives; settled the Oregon question by a compromise on the 49th parallel (1846); achieved tariff reduction (1846) and the reestablishment of the independent treasury system originated under Van Buren. Dispute over the Texas boundary led to War with Mexico (1846–48). An expansionist rather than an imperialist, he approved the acquisition of Texas, California, and New Mexico, but opposed retaining Mexico by force. He did not seek reelection.

Pollock, Jackson (b. near Cody, Wyo., 28 Jan. 1912; d. Southampton, L.I., 11 Aug. 1956), painter, left Los Angeles high school at 17, receiving his formal training at the Art Students League, New York, under Thomas Hart Benton. On the Federal Arts Project (1939–42), he gave his first 1-man show in New York (1943). His work in his first period was characterized by violence and passion still under control (*Male and Female in Search of a Symbol, Wounded Animal*). In the mid-1940s he broke away from American realism to develop his own distinctive abstract style, abandoning the easel for drippings of color on canvas and creating "rhythmic labyrinths" or "dripped mazes" (*Sleeping Effort, Portrait with a Dream, Eastern, Totem, Scent,* and others simply given numbers). Before his death in an auto accident, he had become a leading figure among abstract expressionists, giving 1-man shows abroad, at Venice and Milan (1950) and Paris (1952). His paintings quickly acquired a phenomenal posthumous success.

Pound, Ezra Loomis (b. Hailey, Ida., 30 Oct. 1885; d. Venice, Italy, 1 Nov. 1972), poet, studied at Hamilton College (Ph.B., 1905) and the Univ. of Pennsylvania (M.A., 1906) and taught 4 months at Wabash College before leaving the U.S. (1907) to travel through Spain, France, and Italy, eventually settling in England. His *Personae* and *Exultations* (1909), followed by *Canzoni* (1911) and *Ripostes* (1912), demonstrated his poetic gifts. Leader of the Imagists, he edited (1917–19) the *Literary Review* (London) and was Paris correspondent (1920) for *The Dial.* He was a major influence upon

William Butler Yeats, whom he served as secretary and literary guide. He assisted T. S. Eliot in revising *The Waste Land* (1922), making it more intense and compact. He raised money for James Joyce and was responsible for the publication of *Ulysses.* His *Cantos* (1926–72), drawing upon legend, Oriental poetry, troubadour ballads, and modern jargon, constituted his most substantial work. Resident of Italy from 1924, he began (1941) broadcasting Fascist propaganda from Rome to the U.S. during World War II. Brought back to the U.S. on a charge of treason (1945), he was adjudged insane and hospitalized, but continued to write poetry. The award (1949) of the Bollingen prize for his *Pisan Cantos* (1948, part of the *Cantos*) evoked a storm of protest. Released from St. Elizabeth's Hospital (1958), he returned to Italy with his wife, Dorothy Shakespeare Pound, after treasons charges were dropped.

Powderly, Terence Vincent (b. Carbondale, Pa., 22 Jan. 1849; d. Washington, D.C., 24 June 1924), labor leader, reformer, attended school until 13, then worked on the railroad. Apprenticed to the machinist trade at 17, he worked at that trade until 1877. President of the Machinist and Blacksmith's National Union (1872), he was initiated into the secret order of the Knights of Labor (1874), became its Grand Master Workman (1879), and held that office until 1893. Heading the largest and most powerful labor organization of its day, he was basically a reformer, placing little stress on immediate demands for wages and hours, opposing strikes; but advocating producers' cooperatives, trust regulations, currency reform, and the abolition of child labor. He was instrumental in the passage of the alien contract labor law (1885). Elected mayor of Scranton on a Greenback-Labor ticket (1878), he was twice reelected (1880, 1882), but supported the Republican ticket beginning in 1894. Commissioner general of immigration (1897–1902), he was chief of the division of information in the Bureau of Immigration (1907–21). He wrote *Thirty Years of Labor, 1859–1889* (1889) and an autobiography, *The Path I Trod* (1940).

Powell, John Wesley (b. Mt. Morris, N.Y., 24 Mar. 1834; d. Haven, Me., 23 Sept. 1902), geologist and explorer, attended Illinois, Oberlin, and Wheaton colleges, and while still a youth made solitary botanizing trips on the Ohio and Mississippi rivers. He enlisted in the Union army at the outbreak of the Civil War, lost his right arm at the elbow as the result of a wound received at the battle of Shiloh (1862), and rose to the rank of major of artillery. He served as professor of geology in the Illinois Wesleyan College at Bloomington and as lecturer and curator of the museum of the Illinois Normal Univ. In 1869, on a grant from the federal government and the Smithsonian Institution, he led an exploring party along some 900 miles of the Green and Colorado rivers, being the first white man to make this expedition, and continued his Western explorations in 1871, 1874, and 1875. He became (1875) director of the 2d division of the U.S. Geological and Geographical Survey of the Territories, which in 1877 became known as the Survey of the Rocky Mountain Region, and in 1879 issued the *Report on the Lands of the Arid Region of the United States,* whose recommendations subsequently became a part of national land policy. When the western explorations were consolidated (1879) as the U.S. Geological Survey under Clarence King, Powell was placed in charge of anthropological investigations under the Smithsonian Institution. From 1880

to 1894 Powell served as director of the U.S. Geological Survey. His most important contributions in the field of physiographic geology were made in *Explorations of the Colorado River of the West and Its Tributaries* (1875; issued in 1895 in revised and enlarged form as *Canyons of the Colorado*).

Prescott, William Hickling (b. Salem, Mass., 14 May 1796; d. Boston, Mass., 28 Jan. 1859), historian. He was graduated from Harvard (1814), where an accidental blow blinded his left eye (1813); in 1815 an inflammation of his right eye virtually deprived him of his sight. In the research and composition of his histories, he was aided by a noctograph (a visual-aid device), by secretaries who read aloud to him, and by a tenacious memory. On the history of Spain and Spanish conquest, which he chose as his special subject, he wrote *History of the Reign of Ferdinand and Isabella* (3 vols., 1838), *History of the Conquest of Mexico* (3 vols., 1843), *History of the Conquest of Peru* (2 vols., 1847), and *History of the Reign of Philip the Second* (3 vols., 1855, 1858). His histories, narrative rather than analytical, and romantic in conception, are based on rigid standards of scholarship which justify the claim that he was the first American scientific historian. His stress on literary form popularized the reading of history by Americans.

Pulitzer, Joseph (b. Mako, Hungary, 10 Apr. 1847; d. Charleston, S.C., 29 Oct. 1911), journalist and newspaper publisher. Arriving in the U.S. in 1864, he served briefly in the Union army, became (1868) a reporter on the St. Louis *Westliche Post,* and in 1869 was elected to the Missouri legislature. He soon became a figure of some importance in St. Louis politics, served as a city police commissioner, and was active as a supporter of the Liberal Republican movement (1870–72). He was part owner (1871–73) of the *Westliche Post* and was admitted to the bar (1876) in the District of Columbia. He purchased (1878) the St. Louis *Post* and the *Dispatch,* combining them as the *Post-Dispatch,* a journal which under his leadership became one of the foremost organs in the Midwest. In 1883 he purchased the New York *World* from Jay Gould and, following a policy of sensational journalism that included recourse to large headlines, comic strips, and crime stories, converted the *World* into a profitable enterprise. The *Evening World* was established in 1887. During the period 1896–98 the *World* rivaled Hearst's *Evening Journal* in its "yellow journalism." Both newspapers shared responsibility for arousing public opinion for war against Spain. In subsequent years, however, the *World* became a responsible and politically independent journal that observed high standards. Pulitzer's announced intention (1903) to establish a school of journalism at Columbia resulted in the provision in his will of $2 million for the School of Journalism (1912) and for the Pulitzer prizes awarded annually in many fields of achievement.

Pupin, Michael Idvorsky (b. Idvor, Banat, Austria, 4 Oct. 1858; d. New York City, 12 Mar. 1935), physicist, inventor, grew up in an atmosphere supercharged with Serbian hostility to Hapsburg rule. He went to Prague (1873) to study, but left for the U.S. in 1874. He held odd jobs in Delaware and New York, picking up English, Latin, and Greek. Entering Columbia (1879), he obtained his A.B. degree and his U.S. citizenship papers in 1883. He then studied mathematics with John Edward Routh at Cambridge Univ. and physics with Helmholtz at Berlin

(Ph.D., 1889). Returning to New York, he taught mathematical physics and electromechanics at Columbia (1889–1931). Inventor of numerous electrical devices relating to long-distance telephony and multiplex telegraphy, his "pupinized" cable, transmitting sound over long distances, solved the problem of sound attenuation and distortion. He conducted research in X ray, was the first in the U.S. to obtain an X-ray photograph (1896), and discovered X-radiation. He was adviser to the Yugoslav delegation at the Peace Conference (1919). In addition to his Pulitzer prize-winning autobiography, *From Immigrant to Inventor* (1923), he wrote *Thermodynamics of Reversible Cycles in Gases and Saturated Vapors* (1894), *New Reformation* (1927), and *The Romance of the Machine* (1930).

Rabi, Isidor Isaac (b. Rymanow, Austrian Galicia, 29 July 1898–), physicist. He was brought to the U.S. in his infancy, was graduated from Cornell (B. Chem., 1919) and from Columbia (Ph. D., 1927), and as a fellow of the International Education Board took postgraduate study (1928–29) in Munich, Copenhagen, Hamburg, Leipzig, and Zurich. In 1929 he joined the physics faculty at Columbia, and in 1940 became associate director of the radiation laboratory at the Massachusetts Institute of Technology, where he was engaged in radar research (1940–45) during World War II. He was also wartime consultant to the Los Alamos atomic bomb laboratory. He has made notable advances in the study of magnetic properties of molecules, atoms, and atomic nuclei and in quantum mechanics, nuclear physics, and molecular beams, and was awarded the Nobel prize in physics (1944) for the general application of the resonance method to the magnetic properties of atomic nuclei. He was vice-president of the International Conference on Peaceful Uses of Atomic Energy at Geneva, 1955, 1958.

Randolph, Asa Philip (b. Crescent City, Fla., 15 Apr. 1889; d. New York City, 16 May 1979), labor and civil rights leader. He graduated as valedictorian from the Cookman Institute (1907), City College (1912–16) while working at various jobs. In 1915 he met Chandler Owen and together they studied socialism and working-class politics, joining the Socialist party in 1916. In 1917 they coedited *Hotel Messenger*, the monthly organ of the Headwaiters and Sidewaiters Society of Greater New York, but were fired after 8 months for exposing a kickback scheme. They began a successful, radical magazine, *The Messenger* (1917–28), which urged blacks to join unions, preferably the Industrial Workers of the World, and to endorse Socialist candidates for office. In his journal and in his numerous addresses to Negro workers, Randolph stated his conviction that only unionization would bring them equal treatment and recognition in industry and stimulate pride among members of their race. In 1925 Randolph founded and was elected president of the Brotherhood of Sleeping Car Porters, which became partially affiliated with the American Federation of Labor in 1929 (full membership in 1937). With almost no funds, the union struggled and dwindled in numbers until 1933, when the New Deal encouraged the formation of labor unions. Reenergized, the Brotherhood fought a successful battle for recognition by the Pullman Co. (1935) and finally won a favorable contract (1937). The Brotherhood gave impetus to the revival of a strong black mass movement in the next two decades. In 1941 Randolph threatened President Roosevelt with a mass march on Washington to protest the exclusion of Negroes from jobs in defense industries. The demonstration was called off when Roosevelt, by executive order (25 June 1941), established the Fair Employment Practices Committee to prevent racial discrimination in war production and government jobs. Randolph's advice spurred President Truman to issue the executive order by which the military was desegregated (1948). In 1955 Randolph was named a vice-president of the newly merged AFL–CIO. Regarded as the elder statesman of the civil rights movement, he was principal organizer of the March on Washington for Freedom and Jobs (28 Aug. 1963). The collapse of the railroad travel industry brought about the virtual demise of the once-powerful Brotherhood, and Randolph retired as president in 1968.

Randolph, John, of Roanoke (b. "Cawsons," Prince George Co., Va., 2 June 1773; d. Philadelphia, 24 May 1833), statesman, orator, studied at the College of New Jersey (1787) and at William and Mary (1792–93). A restless person, his education was casual and varied, but he was widely read. Elected to Congress in 1799 as a Jeffersonian, he became at 28 chairman of the Ways and Means Committee and administration leader under Jefferson. He mismanaged the prosecution in the impeachment trial of Judge Samuel Chase and was held responsible for the failure to convict. Heading a faction called the "Quids," he blocked the bill (1804–05) awarding land to holders of Yazoo land warrants, losing his party leadership thereby. Opposing the Embargo and Madison's candidacy in 1808, he was defeated for reelection (1813) as a result of his opposition to the War of 1812. Returning to Congress (1815), he opposed chartering the 2d Bank of the U.S. and the tariff. Maligning the Adams-

Clay alliance as the combination of the "puritan and the blackleg," he fought a duel with Clay (1826). In the Senate (1825–27) and again in the House (1827–29), he headed the opposition to President J. Q. Adams. Delegate to the Virginia Convention (1829), he sided with the conservative forces. U.S. minister to Russia under Jackson, he remained there only a month because of his health. Incomparable orator and master of invective, champion of lost causes and strict constructionist, he was, with his high soprano voice and increasingly unbalanced behavior, a figure both brilliant and pathetic.

Rauschenbusch, Walter (b. Rochester, N.Y., 4 Oct. 1861; d. New York City, 25 July 1918), clergyman, was graduated from the Gymnasium of Gütersloh, Westphalia (1883), received his A.B. (1884) from the Univ. of Rochester, and 2 years later was graduated from the Rochester Theological Seminary. Ordained a Baptist minister, he took charge of the 2d German Baptist Church, New York City, working with German immigrants. Studying economics and theology at the Univ. of Berlin (1891–92) and industrial conditions in England, he was influenced by the Fabian movement and by the work of the Salvation Army and the Consumers' Cooperatives. Succeeding his father, Rev. Augustus Rauschenbusch, to the chair of New Testament interpretation at the Rochester Theological Seminary (1897), he gained prominence as an advocate of the "social gospel," the application of Christian principles to social problems, by his *Christianity and the Social Crisis* (1907). This positive reaction to social Darwinism was also expounded in *Prayers of the Social Awakening* (1910), *Christianizing the Social Order* (1912), *The Social Principles of Jesus* (1916), and *A Theology for the Social Gospel* (1917).

Rayburn, Samuel (b. Roane Co., Tenn., 6 Jan. 1882; d. Bonham, Tex., 16 Nov. 1961), political leader. Raised on a farm in northern Texas, he received his early education in a 1-room schoolhouse, was graduated from East Texas Normal College (1903), studied at the Univ. of Texas Law School, was admitted to the bar (1908), and practiced law in Bonham Co. With the stated ambition of one day becoming speaker of the House, he entered politics as a Democrat and served in the Texas House of Representatives (1907–13), becoming speaker in 1911. First elected to the U.S. House of Representatives in 1912, he was reelected 24 times, serving a record 48 years 8 months. As chairman of the Interstate and Foreign Commerce Committee he shaped such New Deal legislation as the Securities Act (1933), the Securities Exchange Act (1934), and the Public Utilities Holding Company Act (1935). He became speaker of the House in 1940 and held that position a total of 17 years —a record. A master of the legislative process and the arts of persuasion, "Mr. Sam" was a strong speaker, respected for his integrity and fairness as well as for his skills. He was able to achieve his ends by maintaining personal friendships with key members of both parties, controlling Democratic committee assignments, and bargaining with individuals. If they followed his advice—"to get along, go along" —younger Democrats generally were rewarded. He was able to push through considerable legislation in the field of foreign relations as well as several significant domestic bills, including the civil rights acts of 1957 and 1960. He worked well with Presidents Roosevelt, Truman, Eisenhower, and Kennedy, and with his legislative counterparts in the Senate.

Reagan, Ronald [Wilson] (b. Tampico, Ill., 6 Feb. 1911–   ), graduated from Eureka College (1932). As a sportscaster with radio stations in Davenport and Des Moines, Iowa, he became widely known. Signing a film contract with Warner Brothers, Reagan made his debut in *Love Is on the Air*. Reagan's most notable film performances were as George Gipp in *Knute Rockne—All American* (1940), and Drake McHugh in *King's Row* (1941). Holding the commission of second lieutenant in the army reserve during World War II, he was disqualified for combat by poor eyesight, and made training films for the armed forces (1942–45). As President of the Screen Actors Guild (1947–52, 1959–60), Reagan fought Communist influence and changed from liberal to conservative. Among his major postwar screen performances were as baseball pitcher Grover Cleveland Alexander in *The Winning Team* (1952); *Bedtime for Bonzo* (1951) and *Hellcats of the Navy* (1957). Reagan acted as host and program supervisor for the General Electric Theatre (1954–62), and toured the U.S. as part of G.E.'s personnel relations program. He was host and performer in weekly TV drama, *Death Valley Days* (1962–65). Reagan campaigned for Eisenhower (1952, 1956) and Nixon (1960), but he did not register as a Republican until 1962. As Co-Chairman of California Republicans for Goldwater, his televised speech (27 Oct. 1964) gave him national political recognition. He defeated incumbent Edmund G. Brown for Governor of California with 57.6% of the vote (1966) and won reelection with 52.8% of the vote over Jesse M. Unruh (1970). His term as Governor was marked by cutting the welfare caseload while increasing benefits; limitation on increase of state employees; and hostility to student unrest. State taxes were raised during his administration, but were used to relieve local governments from welfare and education costs. Reagan's attempts to secure Republican presidential

nomination fell short in 1968 and 1976, but he succeeded in 1980. Defeating Jimmy Carter in the general election, campaigning against big government, high taxes, and for a stronger defense, he became the oldest person ever to begin office as President.

Reed, Walter (b. Belroi, Va., 13 Sept. 1851; d. Washington, D.C., 22 Nov. 1902), army surgeon and bacteriologist. He was graduated from the Univ. of Virginia (1869) and the Bellevue Hospital Medical School, New York City (M.D., 1870). In 1875, after having served on the boards of health in New York and Brooklyn, he entered the U.S. army Medical Corps as 1st lieutenant assigned as assistant surgeon. Ordered to Baltimore (1890) as attending surgeon and examiner of recruits, he studied at the Johns Hopkins Hospital and was attached to the pathological laboratory, where, under Dr. William H. Welch and others, he specialized in the then emerging science of bacteriology. In 1893, he was made curator of the Army Medical Museum at Washington, D.C., and named professor of bacteriology and clinical microscopy at the newly established Army Medical School. In the years immediately preceding the outbreak of the Spanish-American War he carried out researches in the bacteriology of erysipelas and diphtheria. In 1898 he was made chairman of a committee for investigating typhoid fever, at that time rife in the volunteer camps. The commission's report (1904) pointed to the importance of transmission by flies, dust, and other hitherto ignored agencies. In 1897–99 Reed and Dr. James Carroll disproved the theory propounded by Dr. Giuseppe Sanarelli of Italy concerning the causative agency of yellow fever. Named as head of the U.S. Army Yellow Fever Commission (1900), Reed and his associates (Carroll, Lazear, and Agramonte) carried out in Cuba experiments with soldiers and other volunteers which conclusively proved the theory of mosquito transmission of yellow fever (through the agency of *Stegomyia fasciata,* later classified as *Aëdes ægypti*). The commission's findings made it possible to control yellow fever and virtually eliminate the disease in the U.S. and Cuba. The general hospital of the army medical center at Washington, D.C., is named for Reed.

Remington, Frederic (b. Canton, N.Y., 4 Oct. 1861; d. Ridgefield, Conn., 26 Dec. 1909), noted painter, illustrator, sculptor, and writer on the American West and frontier. In between attending the Yale School of Fine Arts (1878–80) and the Art Students League (1880), Remington raised sheep and cattle out west. After graduating he traveled extensively through Germany, Russia, and North Africa. While a correspondent in Cuba during the Spanish-American War, he made sketches which were later used for his painting *Charge Upon San Juan Hill.* Remington's art first gained recognition with the publication of his drawings in Theodore Roosevelt's *Ranch Life and Hunting Trails* (1888). Thereafter, Remington was commissioned to make drawings for *Harper's Weekly* and for books by Longfellow, Francis Parkman, Owen Wister, and Hamlin Garland. The *Century* published his illustrated article on Indian life. The swift action and accurate detail revealed in Remington's paintings of frontiersmen, soldiers, Indians, and their horses, contributed a unique realism to American art. A skillful journalist, Remington also wrote and illustrated the books *Pony Tracks* (1895), *Crooked Trails* (1898), *Sundown Leflare* (1899), *Men with Bark On* (1900), *John Ermine of the Yellowstone* (1902), and *The Way of an Indian* (1906). Remington's sculpture *The*

Bronco Buster was exhibited at the Pan-American Exposition in Buffalo in 1901.

Reuther, Walter Philip (b. Wheeling, W. Va., 1 Sept. 1907; d. near Pellston, Mich., 9 May 1970), labor leader and social reformer. He quit school at age 16 to work as an apprentice at the Wheeling Steel Corp. but was discharged for mobilizing a protest against Sunday and holiday work. He went to Detroit (1926), where he became a tool and die craftsman and soon a foreman at a Ford Motor Co. plant. At the same time he finished high school and went on to complete 3 years at Wayne Univ. Laid off by Ford during the depression because, according to Reuther, of his union activities, he and his brother traveled around the world (1932–35), touring auto plants in England, bicycling across Europe, working in a Ford-built plant in Gorki, and continuing on through China before returning home. Back in Detroit he found work in a General Motors plant, helped organize United Auto Workers Local 174, and actively participated in the union's Flint, Mich., sitdown strike (1936–37) that led to the UAW's recognition by the major auto companies. Reuther soon became a major union organizer and a spearhead of the fight against Communism within the UAW. During World War II he helped keep auto workers in line on the no-strike pledge. He led the 113-day UAW strike (1945–46) of 200,000 workers against General Motors which ended with the union gaining significant pay increases. He was elected president of the UAW in 1946 and president of the Congress of Industrial Organizations in 1952. Shot in the chest and right arm by a would-be assassin (1948), never identified, he never recovered full use of his arm. In 1955 he led the merger of the CIO and the American Federation of Labor and served as vice-president and executive board members of the AFL–CIO, and as head of its industrial union department, but after years of disagreement with George Meany (president of the AFL–CIO) over the direction and structure of the organization, he took the UAW out of the AFL–CIO (July 1968) and joined the Teamsters in the Alliance for Labor Action (May 1969). An expert bargainer, he pioneered in achieving for his union pensions, pay increases based on the cost of living and productivity rises, supplementary unemployment benefits, profit-sharing, and early retirement. As a progressive, he sought to involve labor in industrial planning, the fight for a guaranteed annual wage, cooperative movements, production and pricing problems, civil rights, and politics. He died in an airplane crash.

Richardson, Henry Hobson (b. St. James Parish, La., 29 Sept. 1838; d. Brookline, Mass., 27 Apr. 1886), architect. Graduated from Harvard (1859) and admitted (1860) to the École des Beaux Arts in Paris, he made his early reputation with prize-winning designs for churches at Springfield and West Medford, Mass. With the Brattle Square Church at Boston he abandoned Victorian Gothic for the style that became his hallmark and reached its flower in Trinity Church, Boston, for which he was awarded the prize commission in 1872. Richardson was the leader in introducing the Romanesque Revival into the U.S. Adapted chiefly from the forms of Southern French Romanesque, this mode was widely used in the American Northeast and West until it gave way to the Classical Revival. Toward the close of his life Richardson was evolving a functionalist architecture, as in the John H. Pray Co. Bldg. at Boston (c.1886), that foreshadowed the modern-

ism of Louis H. Sullivan and others. For other outstanding designs, see p. 906.

Robinson, Edwin Arlington (b. Head Tide, Me., 22 Dec. 1869; d. New York City, 6 Apr. 1935), poet, attended Harvard from 1891 to 1893. His first volume of poetry, *The Torrent and the Night Before* (1896; reprinted with additions in 1897 as *The Children of the Night*), was published at his own expense. In 1899 he settled at New York, where poverty forced him to work as a timekeeper (1904) on the subway construction project. When his plight came to the attention of President Theodore Roosevelt, an admirer of Robinson's poetry, Robinson received (1905) a clerkship in the customs service at New York, a post he held until 1909. The following years brought him general recognition and fame in the U.S. and abroad. His poetry, which bears the stamp of his Calvinistic New England background, deals with traditional themes and reveals a masterly command of blank verse technique. His works include *Captain Craig and Other Poems* (1902), *The Town Down the River* (1910), *The Man Against the Sky* (1916), *Merlin* (1917), *Collected Poems* (1921), *Avon's Harvest* (1921), *Roman Bartholow* (1923), *The Man Who Died Twice* (1924), *Tristram* (1927), *Cavender's House* (1929), *Matthias at the Door* (1931), *Amaranth* (1934), and *King Jasper* (1935). He was awarded three Pulitzer prizes.

Rockefeller, John Davison (b. Richford, N.Y., 8 July 1839; d. Ormond Beach, Fla., 23 May 1937), industrialist and philanthropist, was educated in Cleveland, Ohio, where he worked as a clerk and bookkeeper and became a member of the firm of Clark & Rockefeller. Following the discovery of oil at Titusville, Pa. (1859), he became associated with

Samuel Andrews, inventor of a cheaper process of refining oil, and in 1865 joined his brother, William Rockefeller (1841–1922), in establishing the firm of William Rockefeller & Co. and the Standard Oil Works at Cleveland. The Standard Oil Co., organized in 1867 and incorporated in 1870 with John D. Rockefeller as president, became the largest unit in the American oil industry and the first great effective industrial combination of its time. By the mid-1870s it had absorbed or eliminated most of its rival concerns; by the end of that decade it exercised a virtual monopoly over oil refining and transportation. The company became known (1881) as the Standard Oil Trust, a unit that was outlawed by the Supreme Court of Ohio (1892) and dissolved in 1899. It was replaced by the Standard Oil Co. of N.J., which functioned as a holding company for the Rockefeller interests until its dissolution was ordered by the U.S. Supreme Court (1911). At about that time the active management of the business was handed over to his son, John D. Rockefeller, Jr. (1874–1960). The senior Rockefeller retired with a fortune estimated at $1 billion. The immense financial resources built up by him were devoted to a variety of philanthropies, including the endowment of the Univ. of Chicago (1892), the Rockefeller Institute of Medical Research (1901), the General Education Board (1902), and the Rockefeller Foundation (1913).

Rockefeller, Nelson Aldrich (b. Bar Harbor, Me., 8 July 1908; d. New York City, 26 Jan. 1979), statesman, was the third of 6 children of John D. Rockefeller, Jr., the grandson of John D. Rockefeller (q.v.) and Nelson W. Aldrich. Rockefeller was graduated from Dartmouth (1930) and served with family interests, including the

Chase Manhattan Bank, Creole Petroleum Co.—Venezuelan Exxon affiliate (1935–40), and Rockefeller Center, where he was president (1938–45, 1948–51). His career in government service began as coordinator of Inter-American Affairs (1940–44). He served as Assistant Secretary of State for Latin American Affairs (1944–45), chairman of the Development Advisory Board, where he helped to develop Point 4 aid for underdeveloped countries (1950–51), Under-Secretary of the Department of Health, Education, and Welfare, Special Assistant to President Eisenhower (1954–55) and chairman of the president's Advisory Committee on Government Organization (1953–58). Rockefeller was elected governor of New York as a Republican in 1958 and thereafter reelected 3 times. His gubernatorial career was marked by expansion of the State Univ. of New York, the building of the South Mall in Albany, considerable subsidization of the arts, development of a pure waters program as well as a land-use program for the Adirondacks, and the creation of the Urban Development Corp. to build new towns and neighborhoods. Rockefeller withdrew from active consideration for the Republican presidential nomination in 1960 and was defeated for the nomination in 1964 and 1968. He resigned as governor (Dec. 1973) to head his Commission on Critical Choices for Americans, but accepted Gerald Ford's nomination to the vice-presidency (20 Aug. 1974). He was confirmed and took office (19 Dec. 1974). He withdrew in 1975 from consideration for the 1976 vice-presidential nomination to placate conservative Republicans. Rockefeller's 4 brothers, known for their economic influence and interest in public service, were John D. 3d (1906–78), head of the Rockefeller Foundation; Laurance S. (1910–), business executive and conservationist;

David (1915–   ), president of the Chase Manhattan Bank; and Winthrop (1912–73), former governor of Arkansas. Nelson Rockefeller was a noted art collector, who served as president of the Museum of Modern Art (1939–41, 1946–53) and was the founder of the Museum of Primitive Art. He wrote several books including *Future of Federalism* (1962).

Rodgers, Richard (b. New York City, 28 June 1902; d. there, 30 Dec. 1979), composer, studied at Columbia Univ. (1919–21) and the Institute of Musical Art, New York (1921–23). He was the first Columbia freshman to win the competition for the annual varsity show, *Fly With Me*. As an outstanding composer for musical comedy, his greatest achievements were in collaboration with Lorenz Hart (1895–1943), whom he met in 1919, and, beginning in 1943, with Oscar Hammerstein, 2d (*q.v.*). He and Hart had their first musical hit with *Garrick Gaieties* (1925). They worked together on *The Girl Friend* (1926), *A Connecticut Yankee* (1927), *I'd Rather Be Right* (1937), *Pal Joey* (1940), and *By Jupiter* (1942), in which Rodgers collaborated on the script. Among their song hits of the 20s were "Thou Swell," "With a Song in My Heart," and in the 30s, "Bewitched, Bothered and Bewildered." His association with Oscar Hammerstein started with a signal success, *Oklahoma!* (Special Pulitzer award, 1944), and was continued with *Carousel* (1945), *Allegro* (1947), the Pulitzer prize-winning *South Pacific* (1949), and *The King and I* (1951). Their song hits quickly became American classics, among them "Oh, What a Beautiful Mornin'," "People Will Say We're in Love," "Some Enchanted Evening," and "I'm Gonna Wash That Man Right Outa My Hair." Rodgers also wrote film scores for numerous motion pictures, including *State Fair* (1945).

The Sound of Music (1959) was a great success on stage and screen. After Hammerstein's death (1960), he authored *No Strings* (1962) and *Do I Hear a Waltz?* (with Stephen Sondheim, 1965).

Roebling, John Augustus (b. Mühlhausen, Thuringia, Germany, 12 June 1806; d. Brooklyn, N.Y., 22 July 1869), engineer, bridge builder, and manufacturer. He was educated at Mühlhausen and at the Royal Polytechnic Institute at Berlin, where he received the degree of civil engineer (1826), and for the next 3 years worked on road construction in Westphalia, meanwhile making special studies of bridge construction. He came to the U.S. in 1831. After a period of unsuccessful farming in western Pennsylvania, he became a state engineer in the same year (1837) that he was naturalized. His work on the Allegheny Portage R.R. provided the stimulus for his manufacture at Saxonburg, Pa. (1841), of the first wire rope made in America. The factory, subsequently transferred to Trenton, N.J., is today known as the John A. Roebling's Sons Co. He built his first suspension bridge (1846) over the Monongahela River at Pittsburgh. After constructing other bridges, including the railroad suspension span at Niagara Falls (1851–55), Roebling suggested in 1857 the possibility of an East River bridge joining lower Manhattan and Brooklyn (Brooklyn Bridge). When the charter was granted, Roebling was named chief engineer, and his plans were approved by the bridge commission in 1869. Construction was about to begin when, as the result of an accident suffered by him at the bridge site (28 June 1869), he developed tetanus and died. The bridge was completed under the general supervision of his son, Washington Augustus Roebling (1837–1926). With James Buchanan Eads (*q.v.*) J. A. Roebling ranks as the greatest American bridge builder of the 19th century.

Roosevelt, Anna Eleanor (b. New York City, 11 Oct. 1884; d. there, 7 Nov. 1962), humanitarian, was educated in private schools, and married her distant cousin, Franklin D. Roosevelt (17 Mar. 1905). Active since World War I in educational and social reform, she participated in her husband's gubernatorial campaigns (1928 and 1930) and aided him in his campaign for the presidential nomination (1932). Her notable public career after entering the White House (1933–45) was unrivaled by any other president's wife. Lecturer and newspaper columnist, champion of the underprivileged and minority groups, she served the president as an invaluable source of public opinion. During World War II she served as assistant director, Office of Civilian Defense, and toured military bases abroad. After her husband's death she accepted appointment as U.S. delegate to the UN General Assembly (1945, 1949–52, 1961–62), and served as chairman, commission on human rights, Economic and Social Council (1946). In addition to her widely syndicated newspaper column, she continued political activity in the postwar years, supporting black civil rights, campaigning for Adlai Stevenson in 1956 and heading an unsuccessful draft movement for him at the 1960 Democratic National Convention. Author of several books, her most successful was *This I Remember* (1949).

Roosevelt, Franklin Delano (b. Hyde Park, N.Y., 30 Jan. 1882; d. Warm Springs, Ga., 12 Apr. 1945), 32d president of the U.S., was graduated from Harvard (1904), studied law at Columbia Law School, was admitted to the bar (1907), and practiced in New York. Democratic state senator (1911–13), he served as Assistant Secretary of the Navy (1913–20). James M. Cox's running mate on the Democratic ticket (1920), he was defeated in the Republican landslide of that year. Stricken with infantile paralysis (Aug. 1921), he recovered partial use of his legs and established the Warm Springs (Ga.) Foundation for those so afflicted. At the Democratic conventions of 1924 and 1928 he placed in nomination Gov. Alfred E. Smith, the "Happy Warrior." Elected governor of New York (1928) and reelected (1930), he was the Democratic nominee for president in 1932, defeating Herbert Hoover. His first inaugural, in which he exhorted that "the only thing we have to fear is fear itself" and promised "direct, vigorous action," keynoted his first administration, which was largely concerned with "New Deal" economic and social legislation to overcome the depression—relief and public works (resulting in deficit financing), labor legislation to implement collective bargaining (Wagner Act), and farm legislation to support agricultural prices. Largely responsible for U.S. aid to Great Britain after the fall of France (1940), he contributed notably to achieving interallied unity during World War II and conducted his own foreign relations. His "unconditional surrender" announcement (24 Jan. 1944) and his conferences with Allied leaders at Casablanca, Cairo, Quebec, Teheran, and Yalta determined the bases of the postwar world. First president to break the 3d term tradition (1940) by defeating Wendell L. Willkie, he was elected to a 4th term (1944), winning over Gov. Thomas E. Dewey. Three months after his 4th term had begun, and on the verge of victory against Germany and Japan, he was stricken with a cerebral hemorrhage and died.

Roosevelt, Theodore (b. New York City, 27 Oct. 1858; d. Oyster Bay, N.Y., 6 Jan. 1919), 26th president of the U.S., was graduated from Harvard (1880), read law briefly, and engaged in historical writing (*The Naval War of 1812,* 1882; *The Winning of the West,* 1889–96). After a term in the state assembly (1882–84), he lived on a North Dakota cattle ranch (1884–86). Returning to New York City, he was unsuccessful candidate for mayor (1886) and a notably effective U.S. civil service commissioner (1889–95) and president of the board of police commissioners of New York (1895–97). Assistant Secretary of the Navy (1897–98), he helped prepare the navy for the war with Spain. When war broke out he resigned and, with Leonard Wood, organized the 1st U.S. Volunteer Cavalry ("Rough Riders"), and as its colonel led the charge up San Juan Hill. Elected governor of New York (1898), his reform administration alarmed the political bosses, notably T. C. Platt, who arranged to have him nominated as McKinley's running mate (1900). On McKinley's death he became president and was reelected (1904), decisively defeating Alton B. Parker. Known as a trust buster, he dissolved the Northern Securities Co., but distinguished between "good" and "bad" trusts. His most notable achievements on the domestic front were his sponsorship of conservation of natural resources and of food inspection and railway rate legislation. Hastily recognizing the Republic of Panama, he secured the right to construct the Panama Canal (1903). For his successful intervention in the Russo-Japanese War (1905) he was awarded the Nobel peace prize. He supported his Secretary of War, William Howard Taft, as his successor; but after traveling abroad (1909–10), he reentered politics. Failing to secure the Republican nomination (1912), he was the nominee of the Progressive ("Bull Moose") party, losing in a 3-cornered contest to Woodrow Wilson. On an expedition to Brazil (1914) he explored the "River of Doubt," named Rio Teodoro in his honor. At the outbreak of World War I he favored the Allies and criticized Wilson's neutrality policy.

Root, Elihu (b. Clinton, N.Y., 15 Feb. 1845; d. New York City, 7 Feb. 1937), statesman, jurist, and diplomat, was graduated from Hamilton (1865) and in law from New York Univ. (1867). He began practice in New York, was U.S. attorney for southern district of New York (1883–85) and chairman of the judiciary committee of the state constitutional convention (1894). While Secretary of War under McKinley and Theodore Roosevelt (1899–1904) he created a general staff for the army, drew up a constitution for the Philippines, and formulated the Platt Amendment (1901) for the government of Cuba. As Secretary of State under Roosevelt (1905–09), he reorganized the consular service and negotiated the Root-Takahira Open-Door Agreement with Japan (1908). Republican senator from New York (1909–15), he served as chief counsel for the U.S. in the North Atlantic Fisheries Arbitration (1910) and was also, from 1910, a member of the Permanent Court of Arbitration at The Hague. In recognition of his services as president of the Carnegie Endowment for International Peace (1910–25) he was awarded the Nobel prize (1912). Advocate of U.S. entry into the League of Nations, he was a member of the committee of jurists at The Hague which devised the Permanent Court of International Justice (1920–21). He was a U.S. delegate to the Washington Conference on Limitation of Armaments (1921), and as a member of the commission to revise the World Court statute (1929), he devised a formula to facilitate U.S. entry.

Rowland, Henry Augustus (b. Honesdale, Pa., 27 Nov. 1848; d. Baltimore, Md., 16

Apr. 1901), physicist, was graduated as a civil engineer (1870) from the Rensselaer Polytechnic Institute at Troy, N.Y., where he taught physics (1872–75). In 1876 he became the first professor of physics in the newly established Johns Hopkins Univ., where he served for the remainder of his life. His achievements as a pioneer in the fields of optics, magnetism, the spectra of the elements, and the electron were marked by a combination of practical mechanics and mastery of theory. His researches into optics resulted in diffraction gratings which are still used in spectrum analysis. His work on the magnetic lines of force produced his paper "On Magnetic Permeability, and the Maximum of Magnetism of Iron, Steel, and Nickel," published in the *Philosophical Magazine* (1873), which served as the foundation for later researches into permanent and induced magnetization, and was essential to the design of transformers and dynamos. His experiments in electromagnetism (1875–76) in the Berlin laboratory of von Helmholtz made significant contributions to the modern theory of electrons. He made accurate measurements of the values which are still standard for the mechanical equivalent of heat, the wave lengths of various spectra and the ohm, carried out researches in the theory of alternating currents, and was consultant for the installation of equipment at the Niagara Falls power plant.

Royce, Josiah (b. Grass Valley, Nevada Co., Calif., 20 Nov. 1855; d. Cambridge, Mass., 14 Sept. 1916), philosopher and teacher, was graduated from the Univ. of California (1875) and in 1878 received the Ph.D. degree from Johns Hopkins. He taught English at the Univ. of California (1878–82) and in 1882, with the aid of William James, received an appointment at Harvard, where he taught philosophy for 34 years. His great-

est metaphysical work, *The World and the Individual* (2 vols., 1900–01), expounded his view that the life of an absolute purpose required the moral independence of the individual. His *Studies in Good and Evil* (1898) and *Outline of Psychology* (1903) provided the psychological basis for this theory. In *The Philosophy of Loyalty* (1908) and *The Hope of the Great Community* (1916) he established the metaphysical basis of loyalty.

Rush, Benjamin (b. Byberry, Pa., 24 Dec. 1745; d. Philadelphia, 19 Apr. 1813), physician, Revolutionary patriot, obtained his A.B. (1760) from the College of New Jersey, then studied medicine under Dr. John Redman (1761–66), completing his medical education at the Univ. of Edinburgh (M.D., 1768) and St. Thomas' Hospital, London (1768). Returning to Philadelphia (1769), he began the practice of medicine and served as a professor of chemistry at the College of Philadelphia, publishing (1770) the first American text on the subject. Member of the 2d Continental Congress and signer of the Declaration of Independence, he was surgeon general of the armies of the Middle Department (1777), but resigned in a dispute with Dr. William Shippen when he was not supported by Washington. In turn, he became a critic of Washington's military competence, favoring the general's replacement by Gates or Conway. With James Wilson, he led the successful fight in the Pennsylvania ratifying convention for the adoption of the Constitution, and was treasurer of the U.S. Mint (1797–1813). On the staff of the Pennsylvania Hospital from 1783, he established the first free dispensary in the U.S. (1786) and held chairs at the College of Philadelphia (1789) and the new Univ. of Pennsylvania (beg. 1792), in medical theory and practice, exercising an enormous influence as a teacher in medicine and clinical practice. Stoutly advocating the view that disease was due to spasms in the blood vessels, he favored extensive bleedings, which he practiced during the yellow fever epidemic of 1793 in Philadelphia, doubtless increasing the mortality rates. His principal works were *An Account of the Bilious Remitting Yellow Fever* (1794), where he stressed the need for sanitation, and *Medical Inquiries and Observations upon Diseases of the Mind* (1812), with its pioneer insights into mental healing and psychiatry.

Ryder, Albert Pinkham (b. New Bedford, Mass., 19 Mar. 1847; d. Elmhurst, N.Y., 28 Mar. 1917), painter. He took his early training at New York City under the painter William E. Marshall and, beginning in 1871, studied at the National Academy of Design. Although Ryder was a member of the Society of American Artists and was elected to the National Academy in 1906, he received scant recognition during his lifetime, most of which he spent as a recluse in New York. His paintings, the bulk of which were produced between 1873 and 1898, derived from an intense poetic vision and rank among the finest imaginative works of modern art. His works include *Toilers of the Sea, The Flying Dutchman, Moonlight at Sea, Death on a Pale Horse, Forest of Arden, Macbeth and the Witches, Jonah and the Whale, Ophelia, Temple of the Mind,* and *Pegasus.*

Saarinen, Eliel (b. Helsinki, Finland, 20 Aug. 1873; d. Bloomfield Hills, Mich., 1 July 1950), architect and city planner, graduated from Polytechnic Institute of Helsinki. From 1896–1907 he was associated with Herman Gesellius and Armas Lindgren, architects, designing the Finnish Pavilion at the 1900 Paris World's Fair, their own studio and

residence "Hvitträsk" (1902), the National Museum of Helsinki, and the Helsinki Railroad Station (1905–14). He published *Munksnas-Haga* (1915), a major work on city planning. Winning 2d prize in an international competition for a new office building for the *Chicago Tribune* (1922), Saarinen's design had a marked influence upon developing a more organic form for tall buildings. He came to the U.S. in 1923, and taught for a year at the Univ. of Michigan School of Architecture. After designing several art schools in Bloomfield Hills, Mich., he was named head of the Cranbrook Academy of Art. As a city planner he advocated greenbelts and satellite communities, and wrote the treatise *The City: Its Growth, Its Decay, Its Future.* His buildings were known for his ability to express the spirit of their environment. Major works include Kleinhaus Music Hall, Buffalo (1939), the opera and concert sheds, chamber music hall, and studios of the Berkshire Music Center (1941), and Christ Lutheran Church, Minneapolis (1950). He collaborated with his son **Eero Saarinen** (1910–61), also an internationally renowned architect, on the Tabernacle Church of Christ in Columbus, Ind. (1942) and other buildings. He won international prizes for city plans for Tallinn, Estonia; Riga, Latvia; Canberra, Australia.

Saint-Gaudens, Augustus (b. Dublin, Ireland, 1 Mar. 1848; d. Cornish, N.H., 3 Aug. 1907), sculptor. Brought to the U.S. in his infancy, he was apprenticed to cameo cutters during his boyhood at New York City. He studied drawing in night classes at Cooper Union and attended the National Academy of Design; went to France (1867), was admitted to the École des Beaux Arts in Paris; and then went to Rome, where he came under the influence of the Renaissance tradition and won his first commissions. His *Hiawatha, Silence,* and bust of *William Maxwell Evarts* were followed by *Admiral Farragut* (1881; in Madison Square, New York City), which demonstrated the forceful characterization and original design that appeared in later works such as *The Puritan* (1885), *Lincoln* (1887; in Lincoln Park, Chicago), the *Shaw Memorial* (1897) at Boston, the equestrian statue of *Gen. John A. Logan* (1897) at Chicago, and the equestrian statue of *Gen. William T. Sherman* (1903) in New York City. Among other works by Saint-Gaudens are *Diana* (1892; figure modeled for the tower of the old Madison Square Garden), *Amor Caritas,* reliefs of *Homer Saint-Gaudens* and *Bastien-Lepage,* the *Adams Memorial* (the figure sometimes called *Grief*) at Rock Creek Cemetery, Washington, D.C., and the *Parnell Monument* at Dublin.

Salk, Jonas (b. New York City, 28 Oct. 1914–   ), virologist, received his B.S. (1934) from City College, New York, and his M.D. (1939) from New York Univ. College of Medicine, where he carried on virus research under Thomas Francis, Jr. Joining Francis (1944) at the Univ. of Michigan's School of Public Health, he did research on influenza vaccine. He joined (1947) the staff of the Univ. of Pittsburgh School of Medicine and became director of its Virus Research Laboratory. With funds from the National Foundation for Infantile Paralysis, Salk began work on a polio preventive in 1951. Using a technique reported (1949) by Dr. J. F. Enders (*q.v.*) for growing polio virus in cultures of nonnervous tissues, he announced (1953) a trial vaccine against polio, made by cultivating 3 strains of virus separately in monkey tissue and killing the viruses in the vaccine with formaldehyde. Tested during a mass trial conducted by Francis in 1954, the vaccine was pronounced safe (1955) and 80–90% effective. First recipient (1955) of the Medal for Distinguished Civilian Achievement awarded by Congress, Salk served as director of the Salk Institute for Biological Studies, La Jolla (1963–75). He wrote *Man Unfolding* (1972).

Samuelson, Paul Anthony (b. Gary, Ind., 15 May 1915–   ), economist. The son of Polish immigrants, he received his A.B. from the Univ. of Chicago (1935) and his Ph.D. from Harvard (1941), where he studied under Prof. Alvin M. Hansen, at the time a leading spokesman for Keynesian economics. Upon graduating, Samuelson became a member of the faculty at the Massachusetts Institute of Technology, where, as institute professor of economics, he still remains. Samuelson's textbook, *Economics, an Introductory Analysis,* was first published in 1948. Since then it has been translated into almost every modern language, has gone through 10 revisions and has sold more than 3 million copies. Samuelson is also known for his theoretical contributions to the field of economics, his emphasis on the use of mathematics and scientific methods in economic analysis, and his willingness to discard a theory for another which proves more valid. Samuelson has proven the basic unity between such fields as international trade, production economics, consumer behavior, and business cycles. Criticizing laissez-faire capitalism as a system in which the wealthier sector of society can coerce the poorer, he believes that government in a capitalist society must be involved in regulating employment and distributing income. During the Kennedy and Johnson administrations he served as President Kennedy's economic adviser and as a consultant to the Council of Economic Advisers (1961–69). Samuelson has also

served as a consultant to the National
Resources Board (1941–43), the War
Production Board (1945), the U.S.
Treasury (1945–52, '61–), the RAND
Corp. (1948–75), and the Federal Reserve Board (1965–). Samuelson received the Nobel prize for economic
science (1970) for his work both in deriving new economic theorems and for
devising new applications of existing
ones. In addition to his textbook, his
other works include *Foundations of Economic Analysis* (1947), *Readings in
Economics* (1955), *Linear Programming and Economic Analysis* (1958),
and *Collected Scientific Papers* (1966).

Sandburg, Carl (b. Galesburg, Ill., 6
Jan. 1878; d. Flat Rock, N.C., 22 July
1967), poet, son of a Swedish blacksmith, left school at 13, enlisted in the
army, and saw active service in Puerto
Rico in the Spanish-American War. He
attended Lombard College in Galesburg
(1898–1902), but never graduated. He
served as a private secretary to the
mayor of Milwaukee (1910–12) and as
a newspaperman. First recognition as a
poet came to him in 1914, when *Poetry*
magazine awarded him the Helen Haire
Levinson prize. His *Chicago Poems*
(1915) established his reputation. In his
rugged poems Middle Western vernacular is mixed with lyric passages. His *Collected Poems* received the Pulitzer prize
for poetry (1951). A prodigious Lincoln
scholar, he published the first vol. of his
multivol. Lincoln biography, *The Prairie
Years* (1926), followed by *The War
Years* (1939), Pulitzer prize in history.
He wrote *Rootabaga Stories* for children
(1922). Collector and singer of American folk music, he edited his own collection, *The American Songbag* (1927).
Other works include *The People, Yes*
(1936); a novel, *Remembrance Rock*
(1949); his autobiography, *Always the

Young Strangers* (1953); *Harvest Poems*
(1960); *Honey and Salt* (1963).

Sanger, Margaret Higgins (b. Corning,
N.Y., 14 Sept. 1883; d. Tucson, Ariz.,
6 Sept. 1966), social reformer. She
graduated from the Nurses Training
School of White Plains (N.Y.) Hospital
(1902), and soon settled with her husband, William Sanger, in Hastings-on-
Hudson, N.Y. Tired of suburban living,
they moved back to New York City
(1912) and became involved in bohemian society. She became a Socialist
and developed a particular interest in
the sexual theories of Havelock Ellis,
Ellen Key, and Sigmund Freud. As a
visiting nurse for maternity cases on the
lower east side of Manhattan she saw
many women die of self-induced abortions. Renouncing her career in nursing
as merely palliative and futile, she began to devote herself to the cause of
birth control. She left her husband (from
whom she was divorced in 1921), and
went to France and Scotland (1913) to
study birth control conditions. Returning
to New York City, she launched (16
Mar. 1914) her magazine, *Woman
Rebel*, as the spearhead of her movement. While not the first in the U.S. to
advocate the use of contraceptives, she
coined the term "birth control" (1914)
and made the cause a worldwide movement. She was indicted (Aug. 1914) for
sending pleas for birth control through
the mails (under New York's Comstock
Act of 1873 contraceptive data was
classified as obscene). The indictment
was quashed (1916), but the interest in
the movement which it had aroused encouraged Mrs. Sanger to open the first
birth control clinic in the U.S. (Brooklyn, 16 Oct. 1916). Charged with creating a public nuisance, she served 30
days in jail, but a decision on appeal
enabled doctors to give contraceptive

advice "for the prevention or cure of disease." Although legal harassment continued, her work was increasingly accepted. An effective `organizer, she planned the first American Birth Control Conference (New York City, 1921), the International Birth Control Conference (New York City, 1921), and the World Population Conference (Geneva, 1927). She was the founder and first president of both the Margaret Sanger Research Bureau (1923) and the American Birth Control League (1921)—which became the Planned Parenthood Federation of America in 1946 and now includes more than 250 Planned Parenthood Centers in 150 cities throughout the U.S. She launched birth control programs in Europe, India, China, and Japan. Her numerous publications include *What Every Girl Should Know* (1916), *The Case for Birth Control* (1917), *Women, Morality, and Birth Control* (1922), *My Fight for Birth Control* (1931), *Margaret Sanger: An Autobiography* (1938).

Sargent, John Singer (b. Florence, Italy, 12 Jan. 1856; d. London, 15 Apr. 1925), painter, of American parentage, studied at the Academy of Fine Arts, Florence, and, when his parents moved to Paris (1874), at the École des Beaux Arts under Carolus Duran. After a first trip to the U.S. (1876), he returned to Paris, painting *Gitana* and exhibiting at the salons (1877–81). Following Spanish and Moroccan trips (1880) and a visit to Venice, he whipped up a storm of criticism in Paris by his *Madame Gautreau,* and at 28 established a studio in London. His triumphant *Carnation, Lily, Lily, Rose* (1884–86), first of a long series of pictures of children, brought him commissions in the U.S., where (1857) he painted Mrs. H. G. Marquand, Mrs. Charles Inches, and Mrs. John L. Gardner. Exhibiting in Boston (Dec. 1887), he made many visits to that city and was commissioned to do murals for the Boston Public Library (completed 1916), the Art Museum, and Harvard's Widener Library. A brilliant technician and a stylist both exotic and elegant, he was considered by contemporaries first of all as a portraitist (*Carmencita,* the Wertheimer family, and portraits of Theodore Roosevelt, Henry James, and Woodrow Wilson), but he did original and charming work as a painter of genre (*The Weavers, Neapolitan Children Bathing*), and his swiftly executed and luminous watercolors (*Melon Boats, White Ships*), painted during his later years, were to be considered his masterpieces. Declining a knighthood (1907) on the ground that he considered himself a U.S. citizen, he was sent to the front in northern France by the British government during World War I, where he painted *Gassed* (1919).

Schurz, Carl (b. Liblar, near Cologne, Germany, 2 Mar. 1829; d. New York City, 14 May 1906), soldier, statesman, diplomat, and author. Taking part in the unsuccessful German revolutionary movement (1848–49) while a student at the Univ. of Bonn, he emigrated to the U.S. (1852) and in 1856 settled at Watertown, Wis. He became active in politics, helped organize the Republican party in Wisconsin, and, as an antislavery man, actively supported Lincoln against Douglas in the Illinois senatorial campaign of 1858. He was admitted to the Wisconsin bar (1858) and practiced law at Milwaukee. As chairman of the Wisconsin delegation to the Chicago Republican Convention (1860) he backed Lincoln's nomination, was appointed (1861) minister to Spain, returned to the U.S. (1862), and was appointed brigadier general of volunteers. He commanded a division at 2d Bull Run (1862), was promoted to major general (1863), and in 1863 took part in the battles of Chancellorsville and Gettysburg. At President Johnson's request he made a survey (July–Sept. 1865) of the postwar South, was Washington correspondent (1865–66) of the New York *Tribune,* editor (1866–67) of the Detroit *Post,* and joint editor and owner (1867–69) of the St. Louis *Westliche Post.* An anti-Grant Republican, he served (1869–75) in the Senate as a member from Missouri and was one of the chief organizers of the Liberal Republican movement (1870–72). An exponent of civil service reform and of a liberal policy toward the South, he supported Hayes in 1876 and served (1877–81) as Secretary of the Interior, carrying out signal reforms in the treatment of the Indians. He lived in New York after 1881 and was an editor (1881–83) of the New York *Evening Post,* chief editorial writer (1892–98) for *Harper's Weekly,* and president (1892–1900) of the National Civil Service Reform League. He wrote *Henry Clay* (2 vols., 1887), a penetrating essay on Lincoln (1891), and *The Reminiscences of Carl Schurz* (3 vols., 1907–08).

Scott, Winfield (b. "Laurel Branch," near Petersburg, Va., 13 June 1786; d. West Point, N.Y., 29 May 1866), soldier, popularly called "Old Fuss and Feathers." He attended the College of William and Mary; served in the War of 1812, attaining the rank of brigadier general (1814) and performing gallantly at the battles of Chippewa and Lundy's Lane (1814), for which he was breveted a major general and acclaimed as a military hero. He served in the Black Hawk War and in the campaigns against the Seminole and Creek Indians, and in 1838, following the *Caroline* crisis in

Anglo-American relations, restored peace on the Canadian border. He became (June 1841) general in chief of the U.S. army, and in the Mexican War commanded the amphibious operation that took Vera Cruz (27 Mar. 1847) and led the overland advance over mountainous terrain, winning the battles of Cerro Cordo, Churubusco, Molino del Rey, and Chapultepec, and finally taking Mexico City (14 Sept. 1847). After the war his strained relations with Polk resulted in the preferring of charges against Scott; the charges, however, were withdrawn, and in 1852 Congress passed a resolution giving Scott the pay and rank of a lieutenant general. The Whig candidate for the presidency in the campaign of 1852, he was decisively defeated by Franklin Pierce. In 1859 he again acted as peacemaker between the U.S. and Great Britain, on this occasion averting serious trouble in the dispute over the possession of San Juan Island in Puget Sound. Despite his Virginian background, he remained loyal to the Union when the Civil War broke out, and as commander of the U.S. army made preparations for defending the capital. He retired on 1 Nov. 1861.

Seaborg, Glenn Theodore (b. Ishpeming, Mich., 19 Apr. 1912–), physical chemist. He was graduated (1934) from the Univ. of California, where he received the degree of Ph.D. in 1937 and became a full professor in 1945. With associates, including Dr. Edward M. McMillan, with whom he shared the Nobel prize in chemistry (1951) for their work in the transuranic elements, he discovered plutonium, which supplied the fuel for the atomic bomb. The researches of Seaborg and his associates on heavier-than-uranium substances led to the discovery of 8 other elements, including americium (95); curium (96); berkelium (97);

californium (98), produced by the alpha bombardment of americium and curium; einsteinium (99); fermium (100); mendelerium (101); and nobelium (102). The instruments and methods which were devised for the determination of these transuranic elements included the use of the Berkeley 184-inch cyclotron, and virtually created the new technique of ultramicrochemistry. Chancellor of the Univ. of California at Berkeley, 1958–61, he served as chairman of the AEC (1961–70).

Seward, William Henry (b. Florida, Orange Co., N.Y., 16 May 1801; d. Auburn, N.Y., 10 Oct. 1872), statesman, was graduated from Union College (1820), admitted to the bar (1822), and commenced practice in Auburn. Affiliated with the Anti-Masonic party, he was elected to the state senate (1830–34), but defeated for reelection (1832), and was unsuccessful Whig nominee for governor (1834). After election (1838) and reelection (1840) as governor, he resumed the practice of law with notable success in criminal cases and in the patent field. Elected to the U.S. Senate (1848) and reelected (1854), he took an advanced stand against slavery. In his speech of 11 Mar. 1850 attacking the Compromise of 1850 he enunciated "a higher law" than the Constitution. Opposed to the Kansas-Nebraska Bill, he declared at Rochester on 25 Oct. 1858 that the slavery struggle was "an irrepressible conflict" between North and South. Prominent in the new Republican party, he was unsuccessful candidate for president in 1856 and again in 1860, but entered Lincoln's cabinet as Secretary of State. His advocacy of a strong foreign policy to unify the country faced with civil war was fortunately not heeded by Lincoln. His most notable achievements were his negotiations with Great Britain

of the *Trent* affair and the *Alabama* claims. At the end of the war he forced France to agree to withdrawal from Mexico within a specified time limit. Coincident with Lincoln's assassination, he was wounded by Lewis Powell, coconspirator with John Wilkes Booth. On his recovery he continued in the cabinet of Johnson and supported him against the Radical Republicans. An expansionist, he acquired Alaska from Russia (1867) for $7,200,000 ("Seward's Folly"), negotiated a treaty for the purchase of the Danish West Indies which the Senate failed to ratify, and advocated the annexation of Hawaii.

Shattuck, Lemuel (b. Ashby, Mass., 15 Oct. 1793; d. Boston, Mass., 17 Jan. 1859), statistician. After briefly attending Appleton Academy, he taught school at Troy and Albany, N.Y., and then in Detroit. Returning to Concord, Mass., he set up a mercantile business at the age of 30 and, in addition, took a leadership role in reorganizing the school system of that town. Around 1836 he moved to Boston to become a successful publisher and bookseller, retiring at the age of 46 to devote himself to public service. A study of the local history of Concord (1835) and then a turn at genealogy suggested to him the value for vital statistics of birth, marriage, and death records. Founding the American Statistical Association (1839), he was instrumental in securing the passage in 1842 of a Massachusetts law requiring the registration of births, marriages, and deaths. Chosen to direct a census of the city of Boston in 1845, he made it one of persons rather than of families. He was instrumental in extending the scope of the U.S. Census of 1850, which marked a notable advance in information gathering. Chairman (1849) of the commission to make a sanitary survey of Massachusetts, his *Report* (1859) used newly gathered statistics for farsighted recommendations, which stamped the report a landmark in U.S. public health.

Shaw, Lemuel (b. Braintree, Mass., 9 Jan. 1781; d. Boston, 30 Mar. 1861), jurist, was graduated from Harvard (1800), was admitted to the bar (1804), and began practice in Boston. Representative in the General Court (1811–14, 1820, and 1829), he was also state senator (1821–22), and a member of the constitutional convention of 1820. He became chief justice of Massachusetts in 1830 and served for 30 years. On the bench he reshaped the state common law in accordance with changing industrial and social conditions, with especially notable contributions in the field of railway and public utility law. He invariably construed public grants in favor of the community and against private interests. His ruling (*Lombard* v. *Stearns*, 1849) that a water company was under an obligation to serve the public was a judicial landmark, as was his decision in *Comm.* v. *Hunt* (1842, p. 762), supporting legitimate trade union activity. On the other hand, in expounding the "fellow-servant rule," holding a company not liable when an employee was injured owing to the negligence of another employee, he materially delayed the expansion of workmen's compensation. Shaw presided (1850) over the trial of Prof. John W. Webster for the murder of Dr. George Parkman. Although personally opposed to slavery, Shaw upheld school segregation in Boston (*Roberts* v. *Boston*, 1849), and refused (1851) to release Sims, the fugitive slave, on habeas corpus.

Sheridan, Philip Henry (b. Albany, N.Y., 6 Mar. 1831; d. Nonquitt, Mass., 5 Aug. 1888), Union soldier, was reared in Ohio, had little schooling, clerked in a store at 14, and was appointed to West Point in 1848. Suspended a year for misconduct, he was graduated in 1853. He first saw service along the Rio Grande and against the Indians in the Northwest. When war broke out he was made captain in the 13th Infantry (1861), with service in the Corinth campaign, then (1862) colonel of the 2d Michigan Cavalry, and for his victory at Boonville, Mo., made brigadier general a little over a month later. Major general of volunteers (31 Dec. 1862), he commanded the 20th Corps, Army of the Cumberland, at Chickamauga, and his charge over Missionary Ridge at Chattanooga contributed largely to Grant's victory. Taking command (Apr. 1864) of the cavalry of the Army of the Potomac, he protected the flanks of Grant's army and attacked Confederate communications around Richmond. In Aug. 1864 he was given command of the Army of the Shenandoah, with orders to push the enemy south and destroy all supplies in the Valley. He defeated Jubal Early at Opequon Creek, Fisher's Hall, and Cedar Creek, making his renowned ride to the battlefield from Winchester 20 miles away to turn a near defeat into victory. Following this raid, he turned the flank of the Confederate army (1 Apr. 1865), forcing it to evacuate Petersburg and retreat to Appomattox. Military governor of the 5th Dist., Louisiana and Texas, with headquarters at New Orleans, he pursued stern policies and earned President Johnson's disapproval and transfer to the Dept. of Missouri, where he launched military operations against hostile Indians, whom he forced to settle on reservations allotted them. Lieutenant general (1869), he went to Europe (1870) to observe the Franco-Prussian War, and was made a full general (1888). He wrote *Personal Memoirs* (1888).

Sherman, Roger (b. Newton, Mass., 19 Apr. 1721; d. New Haven, Conn., 23 July 1793), jurist and statesman. Trained as a shoemaker by his father, Sherman nevertheless became surveyor of New Haven Co. (1745–58), studied law, and was admitted to the bar (1754). While a successful merchant, he served as justice of the peace for Litchfield Co. (1755–61) and for New Haven (1765–66), and as judge of the superior court (1766–67). As chairman of the New Hampshire Committee of Correspondence, Sherman backed a colonial boycott of English goods. By 1774, he denied Parliament's right to legislate for the colonies. A delegate to the Continental Congress (1774–81, 1783–84), he was a member of the committee which drafted the Declaration of Independence and the Articles of Confederation. At the Constitutional Convention (1787), Sherman introduced the Connecticut Compromise. Afterward he campaigned in the press for the Constitution's ratification under the pen name "A Countryman." He served in the first U.S. House of Representatives (1789–91). As U.S. senator (1791–93) he favored the federal government's assumption of state debts and opposed locating the capital on the Potomac. He was the only man to sign the Continental Association (18 Oct. 1774), the Declaration of Independence, the Articles of Confederation, and the Constitution.

Sherman, William Tecumseh (b. Lancaster, Ohio, 8 Feb. 1820; d. New York City, 14 Feb. 1891), soldier, was graduated from West Point (1840), served in the War with Mexico (1846–47), resigning from the army (1855) to engage in banking in San Francisco. After his bank failed, he practiced law briefly in Leavenworth, Kan., and then served as superintendent of the military academy at Alexandria, La. (1859–61). At the outbreak of the Civil War he rejoined the U.S. army, commanded a brigade at 1st Bull Run, was given command in Kentucky (Oct. 1861), promoted to major general for conduct at Shiloh (6–7 Apr. 1862), participated in Grant's final Vicksburg campaign, and, as commander of the Army of the Tennessee, in the Battle of Chattanooga. He succeeded Grant (Mar. 1864) in command of the military division of the Mississippi, set out from Chattanooga (May), and began his invasion of Georgia with a brilliant campaign against J. E. Johnston and later Hood. Taking Atlanta (1 Sept.), he made his "March to the Sea" with 62,000 men without supplies, capturing Savannah (21 Dec.). Under orders to live off the country and to destroy war supplies, public buildings, railroads, and factories, his army exceeded instructions by acts of pillage. In bringing the war home to civilians by destruction of goods rather than life, Sherman has been considered the first modern general. Turning northward, he marched through the Carolinas to join Grant in Virginia, receiving the surrender of J. E. Johnston at Durham, N.C. (26 Apr. 1865). In 1869 he succeeded Grant in command of the army, until his retirement (1884). His *Memoirs* (2 vols.) appeared in 1875.

Shockley, William Bradford (b. London, Eng., 13 Feb. 1910–   ), physicist and inventor, received his B.S. (1932) from the California Institute of Technology, and his Ph.D. from MIT (1936), in which year he joined the technical staff of the Bell Telephone Laboratories. During World War II he directed (1942–44) research at Columbia for the antisubmarine warfare operations program, and in the postwar period served as director of the research weapons system evaluations group, Department of Defense (1955–58). Known for his studies of semiconductivity and other aspects of solid-state physics, he shared with John Bardeen and W. H. Brattain the 1956 Nobel prize in physics for developing (1948) the transistor, a semiconductor and substitute for the vacuum tube. He is the inventor of the junction transistor (1951). He wrote *Electrons and Holes in Semiconductors* (1950) and edited *Imperfections in Nearly Perfect Crystals* (1952), *Mechanics* (with W. A. Gong, 1966). His recent exposition of alleged links between IQ, heredity, and race has aroused sharp controversy.

Silliman, Benjamin (b. Trumbull, Conn., 8 Aug. 1779; d. New Haven, Conn., 24 Nov. 1864), educator, scientist, was graduated from Yale (1796), studied law at New Haven, and was admitted to the Connecticut bar (1802), but abandoned law for chemistry and natural history. Professor of chemistry and natural history at Yale from 1802 to 1853, he was extraordinarily influential as a teacher and popularizer of science. His interest in geology was aroused on a trip to England and the Continent (1805). Utilizing the mineral collection of Col. George Gibbs, he introduced (1813) an illustrated lecture course in mineralogy and geology, and was one of the organizers of the Yale Medical School (1818). He began to give (1818) scientific lectures, utilizing experiments as demonstrations, open to the public of New Haven, and, responding to popular demand, lectured in New York, New England, and other parts of the country. He initiated the lecture series of the Lowell Institute (1839–40). He founded (1818) the influential *American Journal of Science and Arts*, which he edited for 20 years. In addition to many scientific papers, he wrote *A Journal of Travels in England, Holland and Scotland* (1810),

A Visit to Europe in 1851 (1853), and edited *The Elements of Experimental Chemistry* (1814).

Simms, William Gilmore (b. Charleston, S.C., 17 Apr. 1806; d. there, 11 June 1870), author, studied law privately and in 1827 was admitted to the Charleston bar. Writing in a Byronic vein, he produced 5 vols. of verse by 1832. Also active as a journalist, he was editor (1828–33) of the Charleston *City Gazette*. His first novel was *Martin Faber* (1833), a study of a criminal. With *Guy Rivers* (1834) and *The Yemassee* (1835), Simms inaugurated the series of romances based on South Carolina history and Southern frontier life by which he is chiefly remembered: The Border Romances, including *Richard Hurdis* (1838), *Border Beagles* (1840), *Beauchampe* (1842), *Helen Halsey* (1845), *Charlemont* (1856), *Voltmeier* (1869) and *The Cub of the Panther* (1869); and the Revolutionary Romances, including *Mellichampe* (1836), *The Kinsmen* (1841; published as *The Scout* in 1854), *Katharine Walton* (1851), *The Sword and the Distaff* (1853; published as *Woodcraft* in 1854), *The Forayers* (1855), and *Eutaw* (1856). A prolific writer who is the most representative of the men of letters of the Old South, he also wrote plays, a *History* (1840) and *Geography* (1843) of South Carolina, biographies of Francis Marion (1844) and Nathanael Greene (1849), and contributed to *The Pro-Slavery Argument* (1852).

Slater, Samuel (b. Belper, Derbyshire, England, 9 June 1768; d. Webster, Mass., 21 Apr. 1835), pioneer of cotton manufacture in the U.S. Apprenticed (1783) to Jedediah Strutt, a partner of Richard Arkwright in the development of cotton textile machinery, Slater became thoroughly skilled in all aspects of the business. At a time when the British government forbade the emigration of textile workers and the export of textile machinery or data, Slater memorized the details of the machinery made by Crompton, Arkwright, and Hargreaves, and, attracted by the bounties offered by American state legislatures, emigrated to the U.S. (1789). He met (1790) Moses Brown at Providence, R.I., and for the firm of Almy & Brown reproduced from memory Arkwright's cotton machinery, thus ushering in the American cotton industry. He became (1793) a member of the firm of Almy, Brown & Slater, which built a plant at Pawtucket, R.I. In 1798 he formed a partnership under the name of Samuel Slater & Co., which established plants at Pawtucket, Smithfield (later Slatersville), R.I.; East Webster, Mass.; Amoskeag Falls, N.H.; and Oxford (later Webster), Mass. In 1815 he began the manufacture of woolen cloth in his plants.

Smith, Alfred Emanuel (b. New York City, 30 Oct. 1873; d. there, 5 Oct. 1944), governor of New York, grew up on Manhattan's lower east side, attended parochial school, and worked in the Fulton Fish Market. Tammany assemblyman (1903–15) and majority leader of the assembly, he was identified with reform legislation, playing with Robert Wagner a leading role in the New York State Factory Investigation Comm., which secured the passage of safety laws after the Triangle fire (1911): Sheriff of New York Co. (1915–17) and president of the New York City Board of Aldermen (1917), he was governor of New York for 4 terms (1918–21, 1923–28). An outstanding state executive, he demonstrated exceptional talent for political administration and progressive legislation in the fields of labor, housing, and public works. Nominated for president by Franklin D. Roosevelt at the Demo-

cratic National Convention in 1924, he was opposed by William G. McAdoo, both withdrawing after 95 ballots, making possible the nomination of John W. Davis. First Roman Catholic nominee for president (1928) and advocate of the repeal of the 18th Amendment, he was defeated by Herbert Hoover. Failing to secure the Democratic nomination in 1932, he retired from politics and engaged in business. An organizer of the American Liberty League (1934), he aligned himself with the opponents of the New Deal.

Smith, David Roland (b. Decatur, Ind., 9 Mar. 1906; d. Albany, N.Y., 23 May 1965), sculptor, studied art at Ohio Univ. (1924), Notre Dame (1925), George Washington Univ. (1926), and at the Art Students League in New York City (1926–32). A summer job (1925) as a welder and riveter in the Studebaker plant, South Bend, Ind., gave him a feeling for industrial forms and for the handling of tools. Early sculptures (1930–39) reflected his interest in painting and his assimilation of European styles such as Cubism, Constructivism, and Surrealism (*Reclining Figure*, 1935), and specifically the influence of Picasso (*Head*, 1932) and Giacometti (*Head with Cogs for Eyes*, 1933). From 1934–40 he rented studio space at the Terminal Iron Works in Brooklyn. He participated in the art programs of the New Deal, first as technical supervisor in the mural division for the Treasury Relief Art Project (1937). Smith's first 1-man show occurred at the East River Gallery (1938). A period characterized by a unique symbolic and expressive style (1939–52) dates from *Medals of Dishonor* (completed 1940), an attack on war and social injustice. From this period are *Head of a Still Life* (1940), *Widow's Lament* (1942–43), and *The Cathedral* (1950). Beginning c.1951–52 and lasting until his death, he produced works (normally displayed outdoors) in a public, monumental sculptural style, the turning point coming with *Australia* (9 ft. high, 1951). He produced abstract sculpture in related series: *Agricola, Tank Totem, Verticals, Voltri-Bolton* (portraying the human figure in the flat planes of cubism), *Zig* (7 works, 1961–64), and his culminating achievement, the *Cubi* series (1961–65). He also produced landscape sculptures (*Hudson River Landscape*, 1951) and the lyrical *Study in Arcs* (1959). Smith's work was an amalgam of painting and sculpture. He would employ industrially fabricated units and raw materials of industrial construction (*Tank Totem*, 1955–56) or welded many small steel units together (*Raven*, 1957). Influential and prolific, Smith understood the sculptural possibilities of Cubism but developed them far beyond what Cubist sculptors had achieved. His mastery enabled the creation of a new monumental sculptural style.

Smith, John (b. Willoughby, Lincolnshire, England, c.1579; d. London, England, 21 June 1631), soldier of fortune, explorer and author, was apprenticed to a merchant, and then sought adventure as a soldier on the Continent, serving against the Turks. Returning to England (c.1604), where according to his own claim he participated in the organization of the London Co. (1606), he left for Virginia in Dec. 1606, as one of the party of 144 colonists aboard 3 ships and disembarked at Jamestown on 24 May 1607. He was made a member of the governing council, was active in exploration, and performed his most valuable services in securing food from the Indians for the hard-pressed colony. According to Smith's account in his *General Historie of Virginia* (1624), he was taken prisoner by the Indians, was condemned to death, and was saved by the intercession of Pocahontas, daughter of the chief Powhatan. When Smith returned to Jamestown (Jan. 1608), he found his enemies had seized control, was arrested and sentenced to hang, but was saved by the arrival of Capt. Christopher Newport with supplies and colonists from England. In the summer of 1608 Smith explored the Potomac and Rappahannock rivers and Chesapeake Bay. To Newport, who sailed for England in June 1608, he gave the manuscript of the account of Virginia's settlement brought out that year as *A True Relation*. Elected president by the council in late 1608, he governed the colony until 1609, returning to England in Oct. of that year. He published *A Map of Virginia* (1612). In Mar. 1614, he went on an expedition along the New England coast on behalf of London merchants. He returned with an excellent cargo of fish and furs, and in *A Description of New England* (1616), which fixed the name on that region, included a valuable map, and stressed the importance of fishing.

Smith, Joseph (b. Sharon, Vt., 23 Dec. 1805; d. Carthage, Ill., 27 June 1844), Mormon founder. Little is known about his childhood before 1820, when he claimed to have had a vision from God and then, 3 years later (21 Sept. 1823), to have been visited by the angel Moroni, who declared that the second advent was near and that Smith was to help God in these latter days. In a subsequent visit (1827), the angel directed him to buried golden plates (Palmyra, N.Y.) containing a history of the American Indians which described them as the lost tribe of Israel. With the aid of magic stones called Urim and Thummim he translated the text from "reformed Egyptian" and published it as *The Book* *of Mormon* (1830). Generally, scholars today regard the book as a combination of Indian legends, anti-Masonry, Biblical, and popular stories. Smith organized the Church of Jesus Christ of Latter-Day Saints on 6 Apr. 1830 at Fayette, N.Y., in order to restore primitive Christianity. Swelling numbers of converts followed Smith from New York to Ohio, Missouri, and Illinois, where at Commerce (renamed Nauvoo) he ruled his church of about 18,000 members and practiced polygamy (declared as a revelation 12 July 1843). Jailed for destroying the press of a heretical newspaper, he and his brother were fatally shot by an anti-Mormon mob. Smith is considered by the Church of Jesus Christ of Latter-Day Saints to be "seer, and translator, a prophet, an apostle of Jesus Christ, an Elder of the Church."

Smith, Theobald (b. Albany, N.Y., 31 July 1859; d. New York City, 10 Dec. 1934), pathologist and parasitologist. He was graduated from Cornell (Ph.B., 1881) and the Albany Medical College (M.D., 1883), and pursued postgraduate studies in biology at Johns Hopkins, Cornell, and the Univ. of Toronto. In 1884 he was named director of the newly established pathological laboratory in the Bureau of Animal Industry, Department of Agriculture. In 1886 he organized at the Columbian (later George Washington) Univ. the first department of bacteriology in any U.S. medical school, and was professor there from 1886 to 1895. With Dr. Daniel E. Salmon he made studies in the diseases of hogs, set forth in *Special Report on the Cause and Prevention of Swine Plague* (1891), and showed that the alarming mortality among pigs was caused chiefly by hog cholera and swine plague. He also demonstrated (1886) the practicability of immunizing man to cholera by injection of the filtered virus

of hogs. He published studies (1898, 1902) on the differentiation of the human and bovine types of the bacillus of tuberculosis. His researches in Texas fever of cattle resulted in the publication of *Investigations into the Nature, Causation, and Prevention of Texas or Southern Cattle Fever* (in collaboration with F. L. Kilborne, 1893), which set forth the discovery of the transmission of the protozoan parasite *Babesia bigemina* by the cattle tick *Boophilus annulatus,* a study which for the first time demonstrated the transmission of diseases by insect carriers. Smith served as director (1895–1915) of the pathological laboratory of the Massachusetts Board of Health, professor of comparative pathology (1896–1915) in the Harvard Medical School, and was director (1915–29) of the department of animal pathology of the Rockefeller Institute for Medicine. In 1933 he became president of the Rockefeller Institute. Among his many publications are *Studies in Vaccinal Immunity Towards Diseases of the Bovine Placenta Due to Bacillus Abortus* (1923) and *Parasitism and Disease* (1934). The debt of the American livestock industry to Smith is almost incalculable.

Stanford, Leland (b. Watervliet, N.Y., 9 Mar. 1824; d. Palo Alto, Calif., 21 June 1893), railroad builder, attended school at Clinton and Cazenovia, N.Y., entered an Albany law firm at the age of 21, and was admitted to the bar 3 years later. After the burning of his law office at Port Washington (1852), he followed his younger brothers to the Pacific coast, setting up in the merchandise business in El Dorado Co., and then Sacramento. Republican nominee for governor (1859), he was decisively defeated, but was elected in 1861 due to a split in the Democratic party. As governor he held California in the Union. Interested by

Theodore Dehone Judah (1826–63), engineer, in a transcontinental railroad, he joined with Mark Hopkins (1813–78), Charles Crocker (1822–88), and Collis P. Huntington (1821–1900) in organizing the Central Pacific R.R. (1861), which benefited by grants and other state assistance while he was governor. At the expiration (1863) of his term of office, he devoted himself entirely to railroad affairs, handling the financial and political interests of the Central Pacific, while Crocker took charge of construction and Huntington acted as chief railroad lobbyist back East. He was president and director of the Central Pacific R.R. from the beginning until his death and director of the Southern Pacific Co. (1885–93) and president (1885–90), as well as a shareholder in the railroad construction companies. His election as U.S. senator (1885–93) caused a break with Huntington, who succeeded in supplanting him as president of the Southern Pacific. He founded (1885) and endowed Stanford Univ. in memory of his son Leland Stanford, Jr. (d. 1884), and selected David Starr Jordan (1851–1931) as president.

Stanley, Wendell Meredith (b. Ridgeville, Ind., 16 Aug. 1904; d. Salamanca, Spain, 15 June 1971), biochemist. He was graduated from Earlham College (B.S., 1926) at Richmond, Ind., and from the Univ. of Illinois (M.S., 1927; Ph.D., 1929), where he was a research associate and instructor in chemistry (1929–30). As a National Research fellow he studied at Munich (1930–31) and was associated with the Rockefeller Institute for Medical Research (1931–48). He was professor of biochemistry and director of the virus laboratory at the Univ. of California (1948–69). He was the first to isolate and crystallize a virus (the tobacco mosaic virus) and has done notable work on the chemical na-

ture of influenza and other viruses, and in the fields of diphenyl sterochemistry and lepracidal compounds. In 1946 he shared the Nobel prize in chemistry with J. H. Northrop.

Stanton, Elizabeth Cady (b. Johnstown, N.Y., 12 Nov. 1815; d. New York City, 26 Oct. 1902), social reformer and militant feminist, was graduated (1832) from the Troy (N.Y.) Female Seminary, and in 1840 married the lawyer and reformer Henry Brewster Stanton. In 1840, while attending a London antislavery convention where Lucretia C. Mott and other American women were refused official accreditation because of their sex, Mrs. Stanton joined with Mrs. Mott in planning a women's rights convention in the U.S. This gathering, held at the Wesleyan Methodist Church in Seneca Falls, N.Y. (19–20 July 1848), ushered in the modern feminist movement. Mrs. Stanton was also active in the abolition and temperance movements, but devoted her chief efforts to the crusade for women's rights. After 1851 she worked in close cooperation with Susan B. Anthony. She was president of the National Woman Suffrage Association and its successor body, and was coeditor (1868 *et seq.*) of the *Revolution*, an organ of the feminist movement.

Steffens, Lincoln (b. San Francisco, 6 Apr. 1866; d. Carmel, Calif., 9 Aug. 1936), journalist, reformer, obtained a Ph.B. from the Univ. of California (1889), then studied abroad at Heidelberg, Munich, Leipzig, and the Sorbonne. Returning to New York (1892), he worked as a reporter for the *Evening Post*, covering the Lexow Committee's exposé of vice, and as city editor of the *Commercial Advertiser* (1897). Joining (1901) the staff of *McClure's Magazine*, which included Ida Tarbell and Ray

Stannard Baker, he wrote a series of articles, "Tweed Days in St. Louis" (1902), a pioneer "muckraking" article, focusing attention on municipal corruption in St. Louis, and following with an exposé of Minneapolis. His *Shame of the Cities* (1904) stressed the link between business and politics, maintaining that privilege was the enemy rather than the corruptionists. With Tarbell and Baker, he took over (1906) the *American Magazine,* which quickly became a major reform publication, but quit the following year to write as a freelance. He sponsored Walter Lippmann, whom he made his secretary, and John Reed, and after a trip to Russia (1917) he lectured in favor of a just peace. On the William C. Bullitt mission to Russia (1919), he met Lenin. ("I have seen the future; and it works.") His *Autobiography* (1931) evidenced disillusionment with the early reform efforts and a more revolutionary approach.

Steinmetz, Charles Proteus [Karl August Rudolf], (b. Breslau, Germany, 9 Apr. 1865; d. Schenectady, N.Y., 26 Oct. 1923), mathematician and electrical engineer, distinguished himself as a student in the sciences at the Univ. of Breslau, but owing to his Socialist activities was forced to flee Germany, emigrating to the U.S. in 1889 after a year in Switzerland. He worked with Osterheld and Eickemeyer Co. at Yonkers, N.Y., and, after its absorption by the General Electric Co. (1892), with G.E. at Schenectady, N.Y., serving as consulting engineer until his death, as well as professor of electrical engineering at Union College (1902–23). Concentrating on electrical engineering problems, he designed an alternating current commutator motor and determined the law of hysteresis mathematically from existing data, reporting his results in 2 papers

before the American Institute of Electrical Engineers (1892). This led to great progress in generator and motor design. He discovered a mathematical method of calculating the alternating current theory, which he presented to the International Electrical Congress at Chicago (1893), and published, with Ernest J. Berg, as a text, *Theory and Calculation of Alternating Current Phenomena* (1897). Expanded into several vols. (1901, 1911, 1916, 1917), this work established the universally adopted method in alternating current calculations which made a difficult subject more comprehensible to electrical engineers, and spawned major commercial developments. Steinmetz's work on lightning ("transient electrical phenomena," 1907–21) produced man-made lightning in the laboratory and the development of lightning arresters for the protection of electrical power lines. Steinmetz secured some 200 patents for improvements in electrical apparatus. Remaining a Socialist, he served as president of the Schenectady board of education (1912–23) and of the common council (1916–23).

Stephens, Alexander Hamilton (b. in present-day Taliaferro Co., Ga., 11 Feb. 1812; d. Atlanta, Ga., 4 Mar. 1883), statesman, author, and Confederate vice-president, was graduated (1832) from the Univ. of Georgia, admitted to the Georgia bar (1834), and practiced law at Crawfordville, Ga. He served in the state legislature (1836–42) and was a Whig (later Democratic) representative in Congress (1843–59). While he opposed the Mexican War, he resisted efforts to restrict slavery in the territory won from Mexico. In 1852 he entered the Democratic ranks. During the critical pre–Civil War years he advocated sectional moderation and conciliation, but became increasingly firm on the slavery issue. At the Georgia secessionist convention (Jan. 1861) he opposed immediate separation, but when the ordinance of secession was adopted he took part in organizing the new government and was elected (9 Feb. 1861) vice-president of the Confederate States of America. In his "cornerstone speech" delivered at Savannah (21 Mar. 1861), he termed slavery the basic foundation of the Confederate government. During the war his zeal for states' rights and civil liberties brought him into conflict with Jefferson Davis. He was head of the Confederate peace mission at the Hampton Roads Conference (1865). After the war he was held prisoner for 5 months at Ft. Warren in Boston Harbor. Although elected (1866) to the U.S. Senate, he was not permitted to take his seat. He was an editor and part proprietor (1871–73) of the Atlanta *Southern Sun,* served in Congress (1873–82), and in 1882 was elected governor of Georgia. He wrote *A Constitutional View of the Late War Between the States* (2 vols., 1868, 1870) and *The Reviewers Reviewed* (1872).

Stevens, Thaddeus (b. Danville, Vt., 4 Apr. 1792; d. Washington, D.C., 11 Aug. 1868), statesman, was graduated (1814) from Dartmouth College; moved (1814) to York, Pa., where he studied law; and after being admitted to the bar settled (1816) in Gettysburg, Pa., and practiced law, soon becoming one of the leading attorneys in his part of the state. His strong antislavery convictions led him to defend many fugitive slaves without fee. In 1826 he became a partner in the iron works of James D. Paxton & Co., which in 1828 became Stevens & Paxton. Elected on the Anti-Masonic ticket, he was a member of the Pennsylvania House of Representatives (1833–35, 1837, 1841) and served as a delegate to the state constitutional convention

(1838). In 1842 he moved to Lancaster, Pa. Elected (1848) to Congress on the Whig ticket, he served until 1853, becoming one of the leading antislavery spokesmen. He took an important part in the formation of the Republican party in Pennsylvania, and was elected (1858) as a Republican to the 36th and the four succeeding Congresses, serving from 1859 until his death. In 1860 he opposed concessions to the South. He was made chairman of the Ways and Means Committee, thus increasing his power in Congress; and during the Civil War became the foremost exponent of a stern policy toward the South, opposing Lincoln's plan of reconstruction in favor of harsh measures. As chairman of the House group of the Joint Committee on Reconstruction, he was the leader of the congressional Radical Republicans. He broke with President Andrew Johnson over the Freedmen's Bureau Bill (1866), imposed military Reconstruction on the South (1867), and was chairman of the managers appointed by the House in 1868 to conduct the impeachment proceedings against President Johnson, but was prevented by failing health from taking an important part in the trial.

Stevenson, Adlai Ewing (b. Los Angeles, Calif., 5 Feb. 1900; d. London, England, 14 July 1965), statesman, served in the U.S. Naval Reserve (1918) as apprentice seaman, was graduated from Princeton (A.B., 1922), attended Harvard Law School and received his law degree from Northwestern (1926), when he was admitted to the Illinois bar. He practiced law in Chicago (1927–41), except for the years (1933–35) when he served as special counsel to the new AAA (1933–34) and Asst. Gen. Counsel, Federal Alcohol Administration (1934). During World War II he was special assistant to the Secretary of the

Navy (1941–44). Assigned to the Foreign Economic Administration, he headed a mission to Italy (1943). Subsequently (1944) he returned to Europe for the War Department as a member of an Air Force mission. Special assistant to Secretaries of State Stettinius and Byrnes (1945), he was a member of the U.S. delegation to the UN Conference at San Francisco (Apr. 1945), Senior Adviser to the U.S. delegation to the UN (1946), and alternate delegate (1946–47). Elected Democratic governor of Illinois (Nov. 1948) by an unprecedented 572,067 plurality, he overhauled and reorganized the state administration, attacked gambling and corruption, introduced state economies, vetoed a loyalty oath bill, and fought unsuccessfully for a state FEPC. Democratic nominee for president (1952, 1956), he was defeated both times by Dwight D. Eisenhower. In 1961 he was made U.S. ambassador to the UN with cabinet rank.

Stieglitz, Alfred (b. Hoboken, N.J., 1 Jan. 1864; d. New York City, 13 Apr. 1946), photographer, studied at the College of the City of New York (1879–81) and the Berlin Polytechnic Laboratory (1881–90), where he experimented in new photographic techniques. Returning to New York (1890) after winning numerous photographic awards abroad, he edited a series of photo magazines, *American Amateur Photographer* (1892–96), *Camera Notes* (1897–1902), and *Camera Work* (1902–17), organ of the photo-secessionists. A master of the commonplace who used photographs to symbolize an extraordinary range of thoughts and feelings, he achieved for photography recognition as a fine art. Championing the newest art trends, Stieglitz, in his notable photographic and art galleries—291 Fifth Avenue (1905–07), the Intimate (1925–30),

and the American Place (1930–46)—introduced the works of Cézanne, Picasso, Matisse, Lautrec, and Brancusi, and was responsible for making known the works of such American artists as Max Weber, John Marin (*q.v.*), Charles Demuth, and Georgia O'Keeffe (1887–   ), whom he married in 1924.

Stimson, Henry Lewis (b. New York City, 21 Sept. 1867; d. Huntington, N.Y., 20 Oct. 1950), statesman, was graduated from Yale (B.A., 1888), Harvard (M.A., 1889), and the Harvard Law School (1889–90), and was admitted to the bar in 1891. He was in private practice in New York City until 1906, when President Theodore Roosevelt appointed him U.S. attorney for the southern district of New York, a post he held until 1909. The unsuccessful Republican candidate for the governorship of New York (1910), he was named (1911) Secretary of War by President Taft and served until 1913. As a delegate to the New York constitutional convention (1915), he was responsible for many of the principal reforms effected by it. During World War I he served with the A.E.F. in France as a colonel of field artillery. In 1927 he was named by President Coolidge as special representative to Nicaragua, where by arbitration he settled a political dispute that had brought on civil war. He served as governor general of the Philippines (1927–29), and as Secretary of State (1929–33) in President Herbert Hoover's cabinet was chairman of the U.S. delegations to the London Naval Conference (1930) and to the Geneva Disarmament Conference (1932). He formulated and announced the "Stimson Doctrine" (1931) of nonrecognition of territories and agreements obtained by acts of aggression. Resuming his private law practice in 1933, he supported many of President Franklin D. Roosevelt's foreign policy measures, and called for aid to Great Britain and for compulsory military training. Named Secretary of War (July 1940), he served through World War II and retired in Sept. 1945, when he resigned from Truman's cabinet. Stimson was the first American to serve in the cabinets of 4 presidents. He was the author of *American Policy in Nicaragua* (1927) and *On Active Service in Peace and War* (with McGeorge Bundy, 1948).

Stone, Harlan Fiske (b. Chesterfield, N.H., 11 Oct. 1872; d. Washington, D.C., 22 Apr. 1946), 11th chief justice of the U.S., was graduated from Amherst (1894) and Columbia Law School (1898), commenced practice in New York City, and joined the faculty of Columbia Law School (1899), serving as dean (1907 and from 1910–23, when he returned to private practice). Appointed attorney general in Coolidge's cabinet (1924), he reorganized the Federal Bureau of Investigation. As an associate justice of the U.S. Supreme Court (1925), becoming chief justice (1941), he was early identified with Holmes and Brandeis in dissents on social issues and after 1932 generally supported the New Deal program. In his dissent in *U.S.* v. *Butler* (1935), where the AAA processing tax was held unconstitutional, he declared: "Courts are not the only agencies of government that must be assumed to have capacity to govern." He sustained federal and state social security legislation. In a lone dissent in the *Jehovah's Witnesses' Case* (1940), he opposed state legislation compelling belief or expression violating religious convictions, but upheld restrictions imposed at the time of World War II upon U.S. citizens of Japanese origin as being within the war powers (1943). During the war he opposed the use of members of the court for nonjudicial activities.

Story, Joseph (b. Marblehead, Mass., 18 Sept. 1779; d. Cambridge, Mass., 10 Sept. 1845), jurist, was graduated from Harvard (1798), studied law under Chief Justice Sewall and later under Samuel Putnam, was admitted to the bar (1801), and practiced in Salem. A Jeffersonian Republican, he served in the state legislature (1805–08) and in the U.S. House of Representatives (1808–09), where he favored repeal of the embargo. Again in the state legislature (1811) he was appointed in that year by President Madison as associate justice of the U.S. Supreme Court. His decisions in admiralty and prize cases during the War of 1812 became classic expositions of international law. A nationalist along with Marshall, he went so far as to maintain that the power of Congress to regulate interstate and foreign commerce was exclusive (dissent in *N.Y.* v. *Miln,* 1837). He upheld the property rights of private corporations (*Terrett* v. *Taylor,* 1815) as well as the obligation of contracts, although outvoted by the Jacksonian majority in the *Charles River Bridge Case.* After Marshall's death (1835) he upheld, in dissent, the broad construction of the Constitution. His antislavery views were evident in the *Armistad Case* (1839), where he freed slaves as "property rescued from pirates," and in *Prigg* v. *Pa.* (1842), where he held that the enforcement of the federal fugitive slave laws vested exclusively in the national government. Appointed (1829) to the newly established Dane professorship of law at Harvard, where he taught until his death, he made a notable contribution both as a teacher and a writer on the law, particularly to the development of American equity jurisprudence (1836) and through his treatise on the conflict of laws (1834). He also published his *Commentaries on the Constitution of the U.S.* (3 vols., 1833).

Stowe, Harriet Elizabeth Beecher (b. Litchfield, Conn., 14 June 1811; d. Hartford, Conn., 1 July 1896), author, daughter of Lyman Beecher (1775–1863), sister of Henry Ward Beecher (p. 982). She was educated at Litchfield and Hartford, moved to Cincinnati (1832), where she produced her first published writings and developed antislavery sympathies, and married (1836) Calvin E. Stowe, professor of Biblical literature in the Lane Theological Seminary, of which her father was president. She left Cincinnati in 1850, when her husband became professor at Bowdoin College. The agitation over the Fugitive Slave Law of 1850 led her to write *Uncle Tom's Cabin, or Life Among the Lowly* (2 vols., 1852), originally published in serial form (5 June 1851–1 Apr. 1852) in the *National Era,* an antislavery newspaper brought out at Washington, D.C. The book sold 300,000 copies within a year, aroused deep hostility in the South, and won her an international reputation. She answered her critics in *A Key to Uncle Tom's Cabin* (1853). She wrote a second antislavery novel, *Dred; a Tale of the Great Dismal Swamp* (1856). Among her later works were *The Minister's Wooing* (1859), *The Pearl of Orr's Island* (1862), *Oldtown Folks* (1869), *Sam Lawson's Oldtown Fireside Stories* (1872), and *Poganuc People* (1878).

Stravinsky, Igor Fedorovitch (b. Oranienbaum, Russia, 17 June 1882; d. New York City, 6 Apr. 1971), composer. The son of an opera singer, Stravinsky started piano lessons at age 9, and although an apt pupil, was not thought to have extraordinary talent. From his earliest years he had shown a serious interest in composition, but his family having decided that he study law instead, he graduated from the Univ. of St. Petersburg (1905). Stravinsky came into contact with Rimsky-Korsakov at the university through the composer's son (1902) and a year later became his pupil. His early music such as *Symphony in E Flat* (1908) was of the traditional Russian nationalist school. It was with the music for the ballet that he achieved his first and most lasting fame—*The Firebird* (1910) and *Petrouchka* (1911) commissioned by Serge Diaghilev for the Ballets Russes—as well as *The Rite of Spring* (29 May 1913), which nearly caused a riot at its premiere, and was not recognized as a major work until Pierre Monteaux conducted an orchestral version almost a year later, again in Paris. *The Rite of Spring,* along with *Petrouchka,* opened the door to 20th-century music, offering complicated rhythms, severe melodies, polytonality, and wild dissonances. Among the other works in this style were *The Soldier's Tale* (1918) and, later, *Les Noces* (1923). In 1919 Stravinsky left his native country permanently and applied for French citizenship. With the ballet *Pulcinella* (1920) came a new phase of his work, a "neoclassical" period, utilizing past materials but aiming for clarity, brevity, and precision, thus moving from iconoclasm to formalism. Among his "neoclassical" compositions are the opera-oratorio *Oedipus Rex* (1926) and *Symphony of Psalms* (1930). Moving to the U.S. when World War II began (1939), he produced *Symphony in Three Movements* (1945), *Orpheus* (1947), and an opera, *The Rake's Progress* (1951). His music became more abstract and sparse with *Canticum Sacrum* (1956), *Agon* (1956), and *Movements for Piano and Orchestra* (1960), arriving at a "serial" technique, influenced by Webern and Schoenberg. His secretary (1947–71) and close friend Robert Craft is credited with influencing his later development, as well as assisting Stravinsky with the recording of his works, and with some of his books. Some of the latter are strictly about music, e.g. his *Poetics of Music* (1948), others are in a more personal vein, such as *Chronicles of My Life* (1956) and *Conversations with Igor Stravinsky* (1958). He became a naturalized U.S. citizen in 1945.

Stuart, Gilbert (b. North Kingston, R.I., 3 Dec. 1755; d. Boston, Mass., 9 July 1828), painter. He received his first professional training (c. 1769 *et seq.*) under Cosmo Hamilton, a Scotch painter at Newport whom he accompanied to Edinburgh. Returning to America after Hamilton's death (1772), he went to London (1775) and became the pupil (1776–c.1781) of Benjamin West. His *Portrait of a Gentleman Skating* (1782) brought him public notice, and thereafter Stuart enjoyed a wide patronage in London, where he won a place as a leading portrait painter and exhibited with the Royal Academy until 1785. In 1787 he went to Ireland to continue his success as a portraitist. He came to the U.S. (c.1793), set up a studio in New York City, and in 1794 opened a studio in Philadelphia, where he produced many notable portraits of women and his first 2 life portraits of George Washington. He moved to Germantown in 1796 and in 1803 went to Washington, D.C., where he painted his gallery of statesmen of the early republic, including Jefferson, Madison, and Monroe, by which he is best remembered. In 1805 he moved to Boston. Among his many portraits are those of Benjamin West, Colonel Isaac Barré, Rev. Joseph Stevens Buckminster, Gen. Henry Knox, James Sullivan, Joseph Story, Samuel Eliot, James Perkins, Oliver Wolcott, Albert Gallatin, Mrs. Perez Morton, John Trumbull, and John Randolph. These and many other lifelike and luminous paintings left him an unrivaled reputation in American portraiture.

Stuart, James Ewell Brown (b. Patrick Co., Va., 6 Feb. 1833; d. Richmond, Va., 12 May 1864), soldier, attended Emory and Henry College (1848–50), was graduated from West Point (1854), and joined the U.S. cavalry. He served with Lee in suppressing John Brown's raid at Harpers Ferry (1859). Resigning his commission at the outbreak of the Civil War, he was made a captain of Confederate cavalry (24 May 1861). At the 1st Battle of Bull Run he protected the Confederate left and was made brigadier general (21 Sept. 1861). He covered the Confederate withdrawal to the Chickahominy in the Peninsular campaign and rode completely around McClellan's army on reconnaissance. In a raid to the rear of Pope's forces he burned stores and captured headquarters documents disclosing the strength and position of the Union forces. Promoted major general (25 July 1862), he fought at the 2d Battle of Bull Run and in the Antietam campaign. He fought at Fredericksburg and Chancellorsville, and, after Jackson had been wounded, assumed command of the 2d Army Corps. His most controversial action took place in the Gettysburg campaign, where he allowed himself to be held up in interposing his cavalry between the Union army and Washington before attempting to make contact with Ewell, as a result of which Lee was deprived for 3 days of information about Union movements. At Yellow Tavern he turned off Sheridan's columns from the direct road to Richmond and was fatally wounded. A spectacular cavalry officer, "Jeb" Stuart was regarded by Lee as the "eyes of the army."

Stuyvesant, Petrus [Peter] (b. Scherpenzeel, Friesland, Holland, c.1610; d. New York City, Feb. 1672), colonial governor enrolled at the Univ. of Franeker (c. 1628), then pursued a military career followed (1635) by service with the Dutch West India Co., becoming governor of Curaçao (1644). His right leg was amputated as the result of an injury sustained in leading an expedition (Mar.–Apr. 1644) against the island of St. Martin. Commissioned (1646) director general of New Netherland, he arrived in Manhattan in 1647. His career was notable for its progressive measures and reforming zeal. He curbed the sale of liquor to the Indians, enforced Sabbath observance, and taxed imports to construct public works. He promoted intercolonial relations with the English, negotiating (1650) the Treaty of Hartford fixing a boundary line with Connecticut. He drove the Swedes from the Delaware (1655), which was incorporated into New Netherland. On the debit side, he was arbitrary and dictatorial, banished his critics, and, although instituting (1649) a Board of Nine Men to assist him, he only yielded (1653) under pressure to the demands of the burghers for municipal self-government in New Amsterdam. Devout Dutch Reformed adherent, he was intolerant toward other sects and, in a move aimed primarily against the Lutherans, forbade meetings by other religions. Reproved by the directors of the Company in Amsterdam, he was forced to back down, as he was in his efforts to bar the Jews from settlement and burgher rights (1655–56). On 6 Sept. 1664 he surrendered the colony to the English, but after returning to the Netherlands (1665) to defend his official conduct, he went back to New York (1667), living the remainder of his life on "Stuyvesant's Bouwery," the farm conveyed to him (1650) by the Company.

Sullivan, Harry Stack (b. Norwich, N.Y., 21 Feb. 1892; d. Paris, France, 15 Jan. 1949), physician and psychiatrist, worked his way through Chicago College of Medicine and Surgery (M.D., 1917). During World War I he served as a 1st lieutenant attached to the board of examiners for the Medical Corps, and after the war was medical executive officer, Federal Board for Vocational Education (1919–20), drafting policy and procedures for handling soldiers disabled by neuropsychiatric conditions. As psychiatrist, Public Health Institute (1921–22), and veterans' liaison officer at St. Elizabeth's Hospital (1922–23), where he worked in association with William Alanson White, he launched his career in psychiatry. As director of clinical research at Sheppard and Enoch Pratt Hospital, near Baltimore (1923–25), he pursued intensive studies of schizophrenic disorders. Convinced that psychoanalysis needed to be supplemented by consideration of the impact of cultural forces upon personality, he developed his theory of interpersonal relations. He taught psychiatry at the Maryland Medical School (1923–39) and became professor and head of the department at Georgetown School of Medicine (1939). Previously, he investigated schizophrenia and obsessional neurosis while practicing psychiatry in New York City, beginning 1931, and as head of both the William Alanson White Foundation (1933–43) and the Washington School of Psychiatry (1936–47). Coeditor and editor of *Psychiatry* (1938–49), he gathered a number of his papers in *Conceptions of Modern Psychiatry* (1940). During World War II he was consultant in psychiatry for the Selective Service System and medical adviser, personnel section, War Department General Staff.

Sullivan, Louis Henri (b. Boston, Mass., 3 Sept. 1856; d. Chicago, 14 Apr. 1924), architect. He attended (1872–73) the Massachusetts Institute of Technology, worked (1873) in the architectural office of William LeBaron Jenney at Chicago, and was admitted (1874) to the École des Beaux Arts at Paris. As a partner in the architectural firm of Adler and Sullivan (1881–95), he became the leading figure in the so-called Chicago school of architecture. His abandonment of the modes of Victorian Gothic and Romanesque Revival became evident in his plans for the interior of the Chicago Auditorium (built 1886–90), where he used the delicate ornamentation that became associated with his style. In his designs for the Wainwright Building at St. Louis (1890), the Schiller Building (1892) and the Gage Building (1898) at Chicago, and the Prudential Building at Buffalo, N.Y. (1895), he evolved resourceful solutions of the architectural and structural problems posed by the skyscraper, and was among the first to stress the vertical lines of steel skeleton construction. His root idea, "form follows function," established the basis of the modern organic architecture created by his disciple, Frank Lloyd Wright (q.v.). For his other notable designs, see p. 907.

Sumner, Charles (b. Boston, Mass., 6 Jan. 1811; d. Washington, D.C., 11 Mar. 1874), statesman, was graduated from Harvard (1830) and the Harvard Law School (1833). Admitted to the bar in 1834, he was appointed reporter of the U.S. circuit court and lectured at the Harvard Law School (1835–37). After a sojourn on the Continent (1837–40), he became active in the movement for outlawing war and in an address (1849) before the American Peace Society urged the establishment of a "Congress of Nations." An opponent of the Mexican War, he helped found the Free-Soil party (1848) and was the senatorial candidate of a coalition of Free-Soilers and Democrats. Following a prolonged contest in the Massachusetts legislature, he took his Senate seat in 1851, and was reelected as a Republican in 1857, 1863, and 1869,

serving until his death. An outspoken antagonist of slavery, he made a stirring indictment (1852) of the Fugitive Slave Law of 1850, opposed the Kansas-Nebraska Bill (1854), and helped organize the Republican party. After making "The Crime Against Kansas" speech (20 May 1856), Sumner was violently assaulted (22 May 1856) on the Senate floor by Rep. Preston Brooks (S.C.); the injuries he received compelled his absence from the Senate until 5 Dec. 1859. He became (1861) chairman of the Foreign Relations Committee; beginning late in 1861 he was an ardent exponent of emancipation; and in 1862 formulated the "state suicide" theory of Reconstruction, holding that the Confederate states had relinquished all rights under the Constitution. After the war, however, he gradually adopted a more sympathetic attitude toward the South. He championed equal suffrage for whites and Negroes. Differences with President Grant and Secretary of State Hamilton Fish led to his removal (1872) from the chairmanship of the Foreign Relations Committee.

Sumner, William Graham (b. Paterson, N.J., 30 Oct. 1840; d. Englewood, N.J., 12 Apr. 1910), economist, political and social scientist, and teacher, was graduated from Yale (1863), studied for the ministry in Germany and England, was a tutor at Yale (1866–69), and in 1869 was ordained a priest of the Protestant Episcopal Church. He remained in the ministry until 1872, when he was invited to occupy the newly established chair of political and social science at Yale, a post he held for the remainder of his life. An exponent of laissez-faire, he opposed trade unions, social legislation, and government regulation. As an economist, he favored free trade and opposed free silver and bimetallism. As a sociologist, he pioneered in establishing a general science of society based on the study and interrelationships of all social institutions, making his most illuminating contribution in *Folkways* (1907). Among his works are *A History of American Currency* (1874), *What Social Classes Owe to Each Other* (1883), *Protectionism* (1885), *The Financier and Finances of the American Revolution* (2 vols., 1891), *War and Other Essays* (1911), and *The Forgotten Man and Other Essays* (1919). The posthumously published *Science of Society* (4 vols., 1927) was completed by Albert G. Keller.

Taft, Robert Alphonso (b. Cincinnati, Ohio, 8 Sept. 1889; d. Washington, D.C., 31 July 1953), lawyer, statesman, son of President William Howard Taft, was graduated from Yale (1910) and studied law at Harvard (LL.B., 1913), practicing in Cincinnati with Maxwell & Ramsey, later (1923) becoming senior partner of Taft, Stettinius & Hollister. Member of the state House of Representatives (1921–26), he was elected U.S. senator from Ohio (1938) and served until his death. He consistently opposed the New Deal program, spearheaded the isolationist bloc in Congress, and fought the Lend-Lease bill, but later backed U.S. participation in the UN. Cosponsor of the Taft-Hartley Act (1947), he was 3-time candidate for the Republican presidential nomination (1940, 1948, 1952), supporting Gen. Eisenhower in return for the latter's acceptance (12 Sept. 1952) of most of Taft's program. After Eisenhower's election he became Senate floor leader.

Taft, William Howard (b. Cincinnati, Ohio, 15 Sept. 1857; d. Washington, D.C., 8 Mar. 1930), 27th president of the U.S. and 9th chief justice, was graduated from Yale (1878) and Cincinnati Law College (1880); practiced law in Cincinnati; and was assistant county prosecutor (1881–82, 1885–86), collector of internal revenue, 1st district of Ohio (1882–83), superior court judge (1887–90), and U.S. solicitor general under Harrison (1890–92). While federal judge for 6th Circuit (1892–1900), he was also dean of the Univ. of Cincinnati Law School. Appointed by McKinley president of the Philippine Commission (1900), he became the first civil governor (1901–04), credited with notable reforms, the restoration of peace, solving the problem of church lands, and establishing limited self-government. Theodore Roosevelt's Secretary of War (1904–08), he was the president's personal choice as Republican nominee (1908), defeating Bryan for the presidency. Although he continued a number of Roosevelt's policies, notably a vigorous enforcement of the antitrust laws (Standard Oil and American Tobacco trusts dissolved), he split with the progressives over the Payne-Aldrich Tariff (1909). Renominated (1912), he was defeated in a 3-cornered race with Theodore Roosevelt and Woodrow Wilson. Kent professor of law at Yale (1913–21), he was appointed by Harding as chief justice of the U.S. Supreme Court (1921–30). An intelligent conservative, he upheld the president's removal power (*Myers' Case*, 1926), and his dissent in *Adkins* v. *Children's Hospital* was later upheld by the court. However, his labor decisions curtailed the Clayton Act, permitted injunctions in secondary boycotts, made unions liable to be sued even though unincorporated, and invalidated the attempt of Congress to impose a tax on the interstate products of child labor.

Taney, Roger Brooke (b. Calvert Co., Md., 17 Mar. 1777; d. Washington, D.C., 12 Oct. 1864), 4th chief justice of the U.S., was graduated from Dickinson College (1795), read law, and was admitted to the bar (1799), practicing in Calvert Co. (1799–1801), Fredericksburg (1801–23), and Baltimore. Federalist state legislator (1799–1800), he broke with the Federalists (1812) and led a dissenting faction (the "Coodies"). State senator (1816–21), he supported Jackson (1824) and resigned his post as Maryland attorney general (1827–31) to enter Jackson's cabinet as U.S. attorney general. He drafted that part of Jackson's bank-charter veto message (10 July 1832) in which contention was made that the president was not bound by the interpretation placed upon the Constitution by the Supreme Court. When the Senate refused confirmation of his appointment as Secretary of the Treasury to succeed William J. Duane (1833), he was given a recess appointment to remove federal deposits from the 2d Bank of the U.S. and to set up a system of government depositories. On Marshall's death (6 July 1835) he was appointed chief justice of the U.S. Supreme Court over bitter Whig opposition. Reversing the court's nationalist trend, his most notable decision was the *Charles River Bridge Case* (1837), which curtailed the scope of the *Dartmouth College Case* and curbed the growth of monopolies. "We must not forget that the community also have rights," he declared on that occasion. His most fateful decision was the *Dred Scott Case* (1857), where, under cover of a discussion of jurisdiction, he declared invalid the Missouri Compromise and the Compromise of 1850, and furnished a major cause of the Civil War. In *Ex parte Merryman* (1861) he defended the rights of civilians in wartime.

Taylor, Frederick Winslow (b. Germantown, Pa., 20 Mar. 1856; d. Philadelphia, Pa., 21 Mar. 1915), efficiency engineer and inventor. After graduating from Phillips Exeter Academy (1874), Taylor became a patternmaker and machinist at Enterprise Hydraulic Works (1874–78), and afterward rose from a common laborer (1878) at Midvale Steel Co. to chief engineer (1884–90). During the same period he studied engineering at night at Stevens Institute of Technology, receiving his M.E. (1883). While at Midvale Steel Co., Taylor developed the concept of "scientific management." He believed that by scientifically studying the reasonable production capacity of man and machine, production could be raised and antagonism between worker and owner alleviated. Applying his concept, Taylor devised more powerful machinery and studied the amount of time involved in performing every operation at the plant. He was able to increase the output by 300% and pay by 25% to 100% at Midvale Steel. Co. In 1893 Taylor became the first scientific management consultant, and Bethlehem Steel Co. became one of his major clients. Taylor received patents for over 100 inventions, including his design and construction of the largest successful steam hammer ever built (1890). Convinced that earning beyond one's needs was dehumanizing, Taylor volunteered his services as a scientific management expert after 1900. Among his published works were "A Piece Rate System," in *Transactions of the American Society of Mechanical Engineers* (1895), *Principles of Scientific Management* (1911), and *A Treatise on Concrete: Plain and Reinforced* (1905).

Taylor, Zachary (b. Montebello, Va., 24 Nov. 1784; d. Washington, D.C., 9 July 1850), 12th president of the U.S., moved with his family to Kentucky, was privately tutored, and served as a volunteer in the Kentucky militia (1806). His commission as 1st lieutenant, 7th U.S. Infantry (1808), inaugurated 40 years service in the U.S. army. He successfully defended Ft. Harrison, Indiana Territory

(4–5 Sept. 1812); fought in the Black Hawk (1832) and Seminole (1837) wars, with a victory at Lake Okeechobee (25 Dec.); and commanded the department of Florida, 1838–40. Commanding the Army of Occupation on the Mexican Border (1845–46), his forces engaged in hostilities which precipitated war with Mexico (Matamoras, 25 Apr. 1846). Victor at Palo Alto (8 May) and Resaca de la Palma (9 May), he was appointed major general and, ignoring Polk's order to fight on defense, advanced into Mexico, capturing Monterrey (24 Sept.). Compelled to detach many of his best troops to reinforce Winfield Scott, he continued his invasion, decisively defeating Santa Anna at Buena Vista (23 Feb. 1847). "Old Rough and Ready," now a national hero, was the Whig nominee for President (1848) and was elected over his Democratic opponent, Lewis Cass (q.v.). Opposing appeasement of the South, he died suddenly in the midst of the struggle over the Compromise of 1850.

Tecumseh (b. nr. Oldtown, Ohio, Mar. 1768; d. Moravian Town, Canada, 5 Oct. 1813), Indian statesman and warrior, distinguished himself in the rout of Gen. Arthur St. Clair (4 Nov. 1791), one of the most disastrous defeats in the history of U.S. Indian fighting. He participated (1792) in an attack on the Cumberland settlement near Nashville, Tenn., by Creeks, Cherokees, and Shawnees, and later joined with Chickasaws in raids against Tennessee settlers. He directed Shawnee scouting of Maj. Gen. Anthony Wayne in Ohio (fall, 1793). Chief of the Shawnees, who were forced west by white settlements (1805–08), finding less and less game to hunt, Tecumseh conceived of a plan at once defensive and regenerative. He attempted to establish a confederation of Indian tribes of the Old West, the South, and the Eastern Mississippi Valley, believing that this could be a separate Indian nation which white men would respect. The confederation was based upon the principle that Indian land was held in common by all tribes and could not rightly be alienated by one tribe. An orator and diplomat, courageous, and endowed with organizational ability and leadership qualities, Tecumseh and his brother, the Prophet, encouraged Indians in the confederation to keep apart from white men, till their own soil, and give up liquor. Supplied with ammunition from England in increasing quantities (1803–11), he remained unwilling to wage war against the U.S. until the alliance was solid and the entire confederation in a state of readiness. While he traveled south to obtain the allegiance of the Creek nation, his brother, who had been warned, apparently found it difficult to resist the pressures of young braves, leading his troops into battle at Tippecanoe, Ind. (7 Nov. 1811) against troops led by the governor of the Indiana Territory, William Henry Harrison. Although not a defeat on the surface, the battle proved a disaster as food supplies dwindled and the confederation almost dissolved. Tecumseh joined the British during the War of 1812 as brigadier general and led a force of Indians in the siege of Ft. Meigs, covered the British retreat after Oliver H. Perry's victory on Lake Erie, and was killed, allegedly by Col. Richard M. Johnson (1780–1850), later vice-president, at the Battle of the Thames. His death brought about the collapse of the confederacy and Indian desertion from the British cause. Known for his chivalry, he opposed massacres and the torture of prisoners.

Teller, Edward (b. Budapest, Hungary, 15 Jan. 1908–   ), physicist, obtained his Ph.D. at the Univ. of Leipzig (1930), studied at Copenhagen with Niels Bohr, and left Germany when Hitler came to power. After lecturing at the Univ. of London, he came to George Washington Univ. as visiting professor (1935), collaborating on research with Dr. George Gamow. He worked on the A-bomb project (1941–45). Joining the physics department of the Univ. of Chicago (1945), he returned to work at Los Alamos Laboratory (1949). Following Russia's successful A-bomb test and the revelations (Jan. 1950) of Klaus Fuchs' atomic espionage, he became a leading proponent of a crash program for producing a thermonuclear weapon, and has been called "the principal architect of the H-bomb," although he himself had little to do with its actual building. Placed in charge of the new H-bomb laboratory of the AEC at Livermore, Calif. (1952), he brought the H-bomb issue to national attention by testifying before the AEC's Gray Committee in the Oppenheimer case (Apr. 1954). In subsequent international controversy over the dangers of H-bomb testing, he opposed cessation of tests and advised that a "clean" bomb, with little fallout, was practicable. He has coauthored *The Constructive Uses of Nuclear Explosives* (1968).

Tesla, Nikola (b. Smiljan, Lika, Austria-Hungary, 9 July 1856; d. New York City, 7 Jan. 1943), inventor. He was educated at Karlstadt and Gratz, where he specialized in mechanics, mathematics, and physics, studied philosophy at the Univ. of Prague, and in 1881 settled in Budapest, where he invented the telephone repeater and discovered the principle of the rotating magnetic field. He arrived in the U.S. in 1884, became a naturalized citizen, and for several years was associated with George Westinghouse and Thomas A. Edison. His best-known inventions are the alternating current motor (1888) and the Tesla coil

or transformer (1891). Principally known for his researches in alternating currents of high frequency and high potential, Tesla's discoveries and inventions include an arc lighting system (1886); incandescent lamps; an alternating current power transmission system (1888); an electrical conversion and distribution system based on oscillatory discharges (1889); high frequency current generators (1890); mechanical oscillators and generators of electrical oscillations (1894–95); radiations, material streams and emanations (1896–98); and a high-potential magnifying transmitter (1897). He worked (1897–1905) on a system of transmission of power without wires and subsequently devoted himself to the fields of telephony and telegraphy.

Thomas, George Henry (b. Southampton Co., Va., 31 July 1816; d. San Francisco, 28 Mar. 1870), soldier, often called "the Rock of Chickamauga." He was graduated (1840) from the U.S. Military Academy; during service in the Mexican War was promoted to brevet captain and major for gallantry at Monterey and Buena Vista; and was an instructor in artillery and cavalry (1851–54) at West Point. Despite his Southern ties, Thomas adhered to the Union cause at the outbreak of the Civil War. He was commissioned (17 Aug. 1861) brigadier general of volunteers; as commander, 1st Div., Army of the Ohio, won the Battle of Mill Springs (19 Jan. 1862); was promoted (25 Apr. 1862) to major general of volunteers; and was a corps commander at Stone River (31 Dec. 1862–3 Jan. 1863) and in the Tullahoma campaign (June–July 1863) in Tennessee. As commander of the XIV Corps of the Army of the Cumberland, Thomas withstood a fierce assault by Bragg and Longstreet during a general Northern rout at the Battle of Chickamauga (19–20 Sept. 1863). Promoted (27 Oct

1863) to brigadier general in the regular army, Thomas relieved Rosecrans as commander of the Army of the Cumberland and held Chattanooga against a siege. In the Battle of Chattanooga (24–25 Nov. 1863), his troops captured Lookout Mountain and Missionary Ridge. In the Atlanta campaign, the Army of the Cumberland under Thomas made up over half of Sherman's force. At Nashville (15–16 Dec. 1864) Thomas decisively defeated the Confederate army under Hood.

Thomas, Isaiah (b. Boston, Mass., 30 Jan. 1750; d. Worcester, Mass., 4 Apr. 1831), printer and publisher. He learned the printing trade at Boston during his apprenticeship to Zechariah Fowle, whose partner he became in 1770, and founded the *Massachusetts Spy,* a Patriot newspaper. He joined Paul Revere in warning the countryside (18 Apr. 1775) and as a Minuteman participated in the fighting at Lexington and Concord. Removing his printing plant to Worcester, he resumed publishing the *Spy* on 3 May, and quickly ranked as the leading publisher of the time, producing books distinguished for their typography and format. Also active as a bookseller, he maintained branches in Boston, Albany, Portsmouth, Baltimore, and elsewhere. He published the *Royal American Magazine* (1774–75), the *Worcester Magazine* (1786–88), and the *Massachusetts Magazine* (1789–96). Between 1771 and 1822 he published the almanac which, beginning in 1775, was known as *Thomas's New England Almanack.* He published the first dictionary (William Perry's) printed in America and the first English illustrated folio Bible in U.S. Included in his prolific output were editions of more than 100 children's books, including *Mother Goose's Melody* (1768). He wrote *The History of Printing in America* (2 vols., 1810), long a standard authority, and founded and incorporated (1812) the American Antiquarian Society, of which he served as first president.

Thomas, Norman (b. Marion, Ohio, 20 Nov. 1884; d. Huntington, N.Y., 19 Dec. 1968), social reformer and political leader. Son and grandson of Presbyterian ministers, he attended Bucknell for one year before transferring to Princeton, where he graduated at the head of his class (1905). He did settlement work in New York City traveled abroad before attending the Union Theological Seminary (1907–11). After receiving his divinity degree he was ordained in the Presbyterian Church (1911) and became pastor of the East Harlem Church (New York), where he worked among Italian immigrants. In his college days a self-described "progressive," Thomas had been influenced during his studies at the seminary by the writings of Dr. Walter Rauschenbusch (*q.v.*), who emphasized the Protestant churches' social responsibility. His work in the slums of New York City and his opposition to World War I converted him to Socialism. He joined (1916) the Fellowship of Reconciliation, a Christian pacifist group, and soon resigned his church post to work for the organization full-time, editing its monthly magazine, *The World Tomorrow* (1918–21). Joining the Socialist party (Oct. 1918), he lectured nationwide, often sponsored by the League for Industrial Democracy (the educational arm of the Socialist party), of which he was co-director (1922–37). He became active in the National Civil Liberties Bureau and helped found its successor, the American Civil Liberties Union (1920). He ran for office unsuccessfully as the Socialist party candidate for governor of New York (1924), for mayor of New York City (1925, 1929) and, as leader of the party after the death of Eugene

Debs (1926), for president in every election from 1928 to 1948. A brilliant orator and prolific writer, Thomas appealed to ethical values in his call for the reformation of American society. He stood for a mild brand of Socialism: public and democratic control of the means of production and long-term economic planning, denying the necessity of class conflict, and criticizing Communism and the Soviet Union. For over 40 years he effectively shaped the policies of the Socialist party and saw many of his proposals—e.g. 5-day work week, minimum wage, unemployment, accident and health insurance, old-age pensions, low-cost public housing, slum clearance—adopted by the major parties and enacted into law. He was a leading advocate of nuclear disarmament and, in his 80s, publicly assailed U.S. involvement in Vietnam. Among his 20 books are *Is Conscience a Crime?* (1927), *As I See It* (1932), *A Socialist's Faith* (1951), *Socialism Reexamined* (1963).

Thomas, Theodore [full name **Christian Friedrich Theodore Thomas**] (b. Esens, Germany, 11 Oct. 1835; d. Chicago, 4 Jan. 1905), musician and conductor. He received his musical training as a violinist under his father, arrived (1845) in New York with his parents, made a concert tour (1850) of the South, and played 1st violin (1853) with the American orchestra of Louis Antoine Jullien. He was made (1854) a member of the Philharmonic Society of New York; took part with William Mason in the Mason-Thomas chamber music concerts (1855) at New York, where he appeared (1857–58) as a violin soloist; and in 1860 became an operatic conductor at New York. He organized (1862) his own orchestra, which he took on frequent tours; became (1866) conductor of the Brooklyn Philharmonic Society; conducted the Philadelphia Centennial concerts (1876); and

was director (1878) of the College of Music in Cincinnati. He served as conductor (1877, 1880 *et seq.*) of the New York Philharmonic Society; became (1885) director of the American Opera Co.; was conductor (1891–1905) of the Chicago Symphony Orchestra and music director for the Chicago World's Fair (1893). Through his orchestral tours and astute program planning, Thomas advanced popular musical taste in America.

Thoreau, Henry David (b. Concord, Mass., 12 July 1817; d. there, 6 May 1862), poet and essayist, was graduated from Harvard (1837), taught school intermittently (1837–41), and from 1841 to 1843, when he lived in Emerson's home, became acquainted with the Transcendentalist circle. He lived at Walden Pond from 4 July 1845 to 6 Sept. 1847. His antislavery convictions led him to refuse the payment of the Massachusetts poll tax during the Mexican War, which he regarded as an expansionist scheme of the slave power. He was arrested and jailed, and later related his experiences in his essay on "Civil Disobedience," which subsequently became one of the leading works on passive resistance. Thoreau left Concord only to make his nature tours, or for lecture engagements, and toward the end of his life became an outspoken advocate of abolition. A poet-naturalist whose prose has a homely strength, Thoreau was also a social critic who believed in moral imperatives superior to the institutions fashioned by men. His works include *A Week on the Concord and Merrimack Rivers* (1849), *Walden* (1854), *Excursions* (1863), *The Maine Woods* (1864), *Cape Cod* (1865), and *A Yankee in Canada* (1866). Among his speeches and lectures are "Slavery in Massachusetts" (1854) and "A Plea for Captain John Brown," "The Last Days of John Brown," and "After the Death of John Brown" (1859).

Thorndike, Edward Lee (b. Williamsburg, Mass., 31 Aug. 1871; d. Montrose, N.Y., 9 Aug. 1949), educator, studied at Wesleyan, Harvard, and Columbia, then taught education at Western Reserve Univ. for a year before going to Teachers College, Columbia, where he taught until his retirement (1941). Starting with his early books (*Educational Psychology*, 1903; *Mental and Social Measurements*, 1904; *The Principles of Teaching*, 1905), he emphasized the application of scientific method in education, especially statistical techniques, and placed stress on practical education. His psychological testing methods employed in the U.S. army in World War I set the pattern for personnel, placement, and educational guidance. His doctrine of innate differences in the aptitudes of pupils constituted an important modification of the idea of equality of educational opportunity. His later views in educational psychology are embodied in *The Measurement of Intelligence* (1926).

Tilden, Samuel Jones (b. New Lebanon, N.Y., 9 Feb. 1814; d. Yonkers, N.Y., 4 Aug. 1886), governor of New York, reformer, spent one term at Yale (1834), studied at New York Univ. Law School (1838–41), and was admitted to the bar (1841), practicing law in New York City. Corporation counsel of the city (1843), he rose rapidly in the Democratic party, cofounding with John L. O'Sullivan the N.Y. *Morning News* to help Polk carry New York in 1844. In the subsequent party split Tilden joined the Barnburners opposing Marcy's Hunkers. Although Tilden was in the state legislature (1846), was prominent at the constitutional convention of that year, and ran unsuccessfully for attorney general (1855), his prominence in the pre-Civil War years was at the bar rather than in politics. The defense (1856) of Azariah C. Flagg

in a vote fraud case was one of his more sensational trial appearances, but more important was his huge railroad practice, which laid the foundations for his great fortune. During the Civil War he sought to build up the Democratic party as a "constitutional opposition" and supported Johnson's reconstruction policy. He gained national attention by his role as chairman of the Democratic state committee in ousting the "Tweed Ring" (1872), helping in prosecuting its members, securing legislation reforming the New York City government, and impeaching corrupt judges. Elected governor (1874) he introduced tax reforms and shattered the "Canal Ring." Democratic nominee for president (1876), he won a majority of 250,000 votes over Hayes, but lost the election when a partisan electoral commission awarded Hayes the electoral votes of all the contested states. He bequeathed the Tilden Trust, which after protracted litigation made possible the establishment of the New York Public Library.

Truman, Harry S (b. Lamar, Mo., 8 May 1884; d. Kansas City, Mo., 26 Dec. 1972), 33d president of the U.S., was educated in the public schools; operated the family farm near Independence, Mo. (1906–17); and saw service in World War I as 1st lieutenant and captain, 129th Field Artillery, 35th Div., participating in the Vosges operation and the St. Mihiel and Meuse-Argonne offensives. He studied nights at Kansas City School of Law (1923–25); was, with the backing of "Boss" Tom Prendergast, made judge of Jackson Co. court (1922–24) and presiding judge (1926–34), and was elected U.S. senator from Missouri (1934) and reelected (1940), where he achieved prominence as chairman of the Senate Committee to Investigate the National Defense Program. Franklin D. Roosevelt's choice as compromise running mate (1944), he was elected vice-president, succeeding to the presidency on the death of Roosevelt (12 Apr. 1945). With little preparation he was forced to make decisions for carrying the war to a successful conclusion (authorizing the use of the A-bomb against Japan) and for planning the postwar world (at Potsdam, July 1945). Losing control of Congress (1946), his sponsorship of the "Fair Deal," civil rights legislation, and repeal of the Taft-Hartley Act (1947), as well as his vigorous election campaign, won him a surprise victory over Gov. Thomas E. Dewey (1948). His 2d term was largely concerned with the Cold War against the Soviet Union, the Marshall and Truman plans, the resistance (after June 1950) to North Korean and later Chinese aggression in South Korea, the organization of the defense of Western Europe, and the negotiation of the Japanese (1951) and German (1952) peace treaties. He wrote 2 vols. of memoirs (1955, 1956).

Turner, Frederick Jackson (b. Portage, Wis., 14 Nov. 1861; d. Pasadena, Calif., 14 Mar. 1932), historian, received his B.A. (1884) and M.A. (1888) from the Univ. of Wisconsin and his Ph.D. (1890) from Johns Hopkins. Rebelling against the Johns Hopkins "germ theory" (holding that American institutions descended unchanged from their European ancestors) and responding to the universally held belief in environmental determinism, he delivered a seminal paper, "The Significance of the Frontier in American History," at a congress of historians held in connection with the World's Columbian Exposition at Chicago in the summer of 1893. In it he brilliantly advanced the hypothesis that the frontier experience had strengthened American democracy, individualism, and nationalism, and altered the character traits that distinguished Americans from

Europeans. Within a dozen years his thesis had transformed the nature of historical teaching and investigation as the "frontier influence" was used to explain all aspects of the nation's past. A second concept that he considered even more important—that "sections" bargained among themselves to shape the political history of the 19th century—was less favorably received. Turner published few books—the *Rise of the New West* (1906) and *The Frontier in American History* (1920) during his lifetime and *The Significance of Sections in American History* (1932) and *The United States, 1830–50* (1935; Pulitzer award) posthumously—but more than any other historian he convinced scholars to use interdisciplinary techniques to discover the underlyng economic and social forces shaping human behavior. His frontier thesis was violently attacked just after his death in 1932, but attracted renewed interest in the 1960s and 1970s. Turner taught at the Univ. of Wisconsin (1889–1910), and Harvard (1910–24), and spent his last years (1927–32) as research associate at the Huntington Library.

Twain, Mark, see **Clemens, Samuel Langhorne.**

Tyler, John (b. Greenway, Va., 29 Mar. 1790; d. Richmond, Va., 18 Jan. 1862), 10th president of the U.S., was graduated from William and Mary (1807), admitted to the bar (1809), and practiced in Charles Co., Va. State legislator (1811–16), he entered Congress as a Jeffersonian Democrat (1816–21), served as governor of Virginia (1825–27), and was U.S. senator (1827–36). He broke with Jackson over the Bank of the U.S., resigning his seat when ordered by the Virginia legislature to support Benton's resolution expunging Clay's censure of Jackson for removal of deposits from the bank. Joining the states' rights group cooperating with the Whigs, he was state legislator (1838–40) and was nominated vice-president on the Whig ticket with Harrison (1840) and elected in the "Tippecanoe and Tyler, too" campaign. He became president on Harrison's death (4 Apr. 1841). His veto of Clay's bank bill led to resignation of the entire Whig cabinet (12 Sept. 1841) except Daniel Webster, who also withdrew (May 1843) after negotiating the Webster-Ashburton Treaty. He reorganized his cabinet with both Whigs and Democrats, with Calhoun as Secretary of State (May 1844). The principal achievements of his administration were the Preemption Act (1841), a victory for the frontier, and the annexation of Texas through joint congressional resolution. Retiring to "Sherwood Forest," his Virginia home, he emerged briefly in 1861 as chairman of a peace convention at Washington, served in the Confederate Provisional Congress, and was elected to the Confederate Congress, but died before that body assembled.

Urey, Harold Clayton (b. Walkerton, Ind., 29 Apr. 1893; d. La Jolla, Calif., 6 Jan. 1981), physical chemist. He was graduated from the Univ. of Montana (B.S., 1917), where he was an instructor in chemistry (1919–21); received the degree of Ph.D. (1923) from the Univ. of California; and studied at Copenhagen (1923–24). He taught chemistry at Johns Hopkins (1924–29), Columbia (1929–45), Chicago (1945–58), and the Univ. of Calif. at La Jolla (1958–70). He was awarded the Nobel prize in chemistry (1934) for having been the first to isolate (1932) heavy water (deuterium oxide), which led to the discovery of the heavy isotope of hydrogen named deuterium. Research director (1942–45) of the Manhattan District project that produced the materials for the atomic bomb, he worked on the separation of uranium 235 and heavy water. Urey made contributions to atomic and molecular structure, absorption spectra, thermodynamic properties of gases, measurement of paleotemperatures, astrochemical research, and the geology of the moon.

Van Buren, Martin (b. Kinderhook, N.Y., 5 Dec. 1782; d. there, 24 July 1862), 8th president of the U.S., was admitted to the bar (1803) and practiced in Kinderhook (1807–16) and Albany. Surrogate of Columbia Co. (1808–13), state senator (1812–20), and state attorney general (1815–19), he headed a political organization known as the "Albany Regency." U.S. senator (1821–28), he supported Crawford in 1824 and Jackson in 1828. Governor of New York (1 Jan. 1829), he resigned (5 Mar.) to accept appointment in Jackson's cabinet as Secretary of State. After securing Great Britain's consent to opening direct trade with the British West Indies (1830), he resigned (Aug. 1831) to become minister to Great Britain, but returned from London when Calhoun blocked confirmation in the Senate. Vice-president under Jackson (1833–37), he was Jackson's choice for president, defeating Harrison (1836). His Independent Treasury policy reflected the views of the hard-money Democrats, but the Panic of 1837 undermined his popularity. Although nominated (1840), he was defeated by Harrison. His opposition to the immediate annexation of Texas cost him the nomination in 1844. Active among New York "Barnburners" opposing extension of slavery, he was the Free-Soil nominee for president (1848). He later returned to the Democratic party but opposed secession.

Vanderbilt, Cornelius (b. Staten Island, N.Y., 27 May 1794; d. New York City, 4 Jan. 1877), steamship and railroad promoter, financier, quit school after the age of 11, bought a small boat at 16, and began a freight and passenger service between Staten Island and New York. At 19 he married his cousin, Sophia Johnson, who bore him 13 children. During the War of 1812 he had a government contract to provision forts in New York harbor and in 1814 built a schooner for service to Long Island Sound. Working as a captain (1818–29) for Thomas Gibbons' shipping line, he moved to New Brunswick, where his wife ran "Bellona Hall," a stopping place for travelers between New York and Philadelphia. Competing aggressively with Daniel Drew in steamboat operations on the Hudson, he amassed over a half-million dollars by the age of 40. During the Gold Rush, he organized the Accessory Transit Co. and secured a charter from the Nicaraguan government to operate a passenger route (water and highway) across the isthmus, 2 days shorter than the Panama route, enabling him to cut the New York-San Francisco passenger fare. Selling out his Panama concern to rivals, he entered (1855) into competition for the Atlantic trade with the Cunard and Collins Lines. After the Civil War he turned his attention to railroads, winning control of the New York & Harlem R.R., then combining the Hudson River R.R. with the New York Central, and leasing the Harlem to the combination, creating a single line. At his death his fortune was estimated at $100 million. Late in life he gave $1 million to Vanderbilt (previously Central) Univ., Nashville, Tenn.

Veblen, Thorstein Bunde (b. in Cato township, Manitowoc Co., Wis., 30 July 1857; d. Palo Alto, Calif., 3 Aug. 1929), economist and writer. He was graduated (1880) from Carleton College, Northfield, Minn., and pursued postgraduate studies at Johns Hopkins, Yale (Ph.D., 1884), and Cornell. He taught at the Univ. of Chicago (1893–1906), at Stanford (1906–09), the Univ. of Missouri (1911–18), and the New School for Social Research, New York, N.Y. (1918–20). His first published book, *The Theory of the Leisure Class* (1899), an analysis of the pecuniary values of the business and middle classes, won him public notice. It was followed by *The Theory of Business Enterprise* (1904). A seminal social thinker, he conceived of the existing economic system as a price system, whose recurrent crises testified to its inability to adjust. As an alternative he suggested in his later works a system in which production and distribution would be controlled by the engineers, foreshadowing "Technocracy." Other works by him include *The Instinct of Workmanship* (1914), *Imperial Germany and the Industrial Revolution* (1915), *An Inquiry into the Nature of Peace* (1917), *The Higher Learning in America* (1918), *The Vested Interests and the State of the Industrial Arts* (1919), *The Engineers and the Price System* (1921), and *Absentee Ownership and Business Enterprise in Recent Times* (1923).

von Neumann, John (b. Budapest, Hungary, 28 Dec. 1903; d. Washington, D.C., 8 Feb. 1957), mathematician, studied at the universities of Berlin (1921–23) and Zurich (1923–25), obtained a Ph.D. from Budapest Univ. (1926), and came to the U.S. in 1930, becoming a citizen in 1937. He taught at Princeton and after 1933 was a member of the Institute for Advanced Study. Cofounder with Oskar Morganstern of the theory of games, a mathematical approach to the study of economic behavior, sociology, and military strategy, he also made important contributions to quantum theory. He worked on the A-bomb and the H-bomb projects and was a leader in the design and development of high-speed computers, notably MANIAC (mathematical analyzer, numerical integrator, and computer) developed at the Institute, and utilized in advanced government research projects, notably in building and testing the H-bomb. He was a member of the Atomic Energy Commission (1954–57).

Waite, Morrison Remick (b. Lyme, Conn., 29 Nov. 1816; d. Washington, D.C., 23 Mar. 1888), 6th chief justice of the U.S., was graduated from Yale (1837), studied law, and began practice (1839) in Maumee, Ohio, moving to Toledo (1850). Ohio state legislator (1849–50), he was, with William M. Evarts and Caleb Cushing, counsel for the U.S. before the *Alabama* tribunal in Geneva (1871–72) and president of the Ohio constitutional convention (1873–74). Appointed chief justice of the U.S. Supreme Court (1874), his most notable opinions were rendered in the *Granger Cases* (1877), where he stated that "business affected with a public interest" must be controlled by the public for the common good; upheld state legislation fixing rates; and declared that, until Congress acted, a state regulation of railroads was valid "even though it may indirectly affect those without." This position was reversed in the *Wabash Case* (1886), with Waite dissenting. He also laid the foundation for the modern interpretation of due process as a limitation of state power, insisting on reasonable regulation (*Stone v. Farmers' Loan*, (1886).

Waksman, Selman Abraham (b. Priluka, Russia, 22 July 1888; d. Hyannis, Mass. 16 Aug. 1973), microbiologist, came to the U.S. (1910), receiving his B.S. from Rutgers Univ. (1915) and his Ph.D. from the Univ. of California (1918) and becoming a citizen in 1916. Microbiolo-

gist at the New Jersey Agricultural Experiment Station (1921–24), he taught soil microbiology at Rutgers (1918–58). The discoverer of streptomycin (Nobel prize in medicine and physiology, 1952), an antibiotic—a term he coined—derived from a soil fungus and effective against tuberculosis, he turned over (1948) to Rutgers the funds accruing from the patent rights, making possible the establishment of the Institute of Microbiology at Rutgers. Its first director, he retired in 1958. His writings include *Streptomycin, Its Nature and Application* (1949), *Soil Microbiology* (1952), *My Life with the Microbes* (1954), *Neomycin, Nature and Application* (1958), *The Actinomycetes* (3 vols., 1959–62), *The Conquest of Tuberculosis* (1964).

Wallace, Henry Agard (b. Adair Co., Ia., 7 Oct. 1888; d. Danbury, Conn., 18 Nov. 1965), political leader. Son of Henry C. Wallace, magazine editor and Secretary of Agriculture under Harding and Coolidge. Upon graduation from Iowa State College (1910), he became associate editor of his family's magazine, *Wallace's Farmer,* and published *Agricultural Prices* (1926). When his father became Secretary of Agriculture he became editor (1921–33) of the magazine which, after a merger (1929), was known as *Wallace's Farmer and Iowa Homestead.* Shifting from the Republican to the Democratic party in 1928, he was Secretary of Agriculture (1933–41) under President Roosevelt, and responsible for the controversial Agricultural Adjustment Acts, aiming to stabilize farm income at parity levels and to bring about a more equitable distribution of income among farmers through storage of reserves, soil conservation, and government control of prices and production. His innovations, accepted by every subsequent administration, included the establishment of a federal food stamp plan for needy

people. He was also a principal spokesman for other aspects of the New Deal.
As vice-president during Roosevelt's 3d
term, he acted as goodwill ambassador
to Latin America and served as a member of the "war cabinet," chairman of
the Economic Defense Board and of the
Board of Economic Welfare. Passed
over for the vice-presidential nomination
in 1944 because of his ultraliberal views,
he served as Secretary of Commerce
(1945) but was forced to resign (1946)
because of differences with President
Truman over foreign policy. As the
presidential candidate of the newly
formed Progressive party he gained
more than 1 million popular votes but
no electoral votes (1948). He soon broke
with the Progressive party—whose machinery was largely controlled by elements of the far left—and returned to
private life. As a young man he had
developed successful strains of hybrid
corn and at the time of his death he was
conducting other significant agricultural
experiments. His other books include
America Must Choose (1934) and *The
Century of the Common Man* (1943).

Ward, Aaron Montgomery (b. Chatham,
N.J., 17 Feb. 1843; d. Highland Park,
Ill., 7 Dec. 1913), mail-order pioneer,
moved with his parents to Niles, Mich.,
where he attended public school until he
was 14, then worked in a barrel-stave
factory and later in a brickyard. His first
merchandising experience was in a general store in nearby St. Joseph, then,
about 1865, with Marshall Field's firm
in Chicago. As a traveling salesman for
a dry-goods wholesale house, he covered
the rural West and learned at first hand
the problems of farmers dependent upon
a general store for purchases. Recognizing the advantages of purchasing
direct from manufacturers and then selling for cash direct to the rural consumer,
he returned to Chicago, where he laid

his plans for a mail-order business. Although most of his savings were consumed by the Chicago fire of 1871, he
managed by the next year to scrape together $1,600, to which a partner added
$800, sufficient to set up a small mail-
order business. An original price list
soon became an 8-page and then a 72-
page catalog with enticing illustrations.
By 1884 the catalog had swollen to 240
pages and listed nearly 10,000 items.
Montgomery Ward, as the firm was
known, benefited by the support of the
Patrons of Husbandry, a farm organization which wished to eliminate the
middleman. The savings offered to
Grangers were soon extended to all
buyers. The consumer was wooed by
competitive pricing, ironclad guarantees,
and personal correspondence. Sales of
the firm reached $1 million by 1888 and
some $40 million by 1913. Active in the
civic life of Chicago, Ward was responsible for preserving for the public
Chicago's lake frontage. In turn, his
widow, the former Elizabeth J. Cobb,
made notable benefactions, especially to
Northwestern Univ.

Ward, Lester Frank (b. Joliet, Ill., 18
June 1841; d. Washington, D.C., 18 Apr.
1913), sociologist. He attended (1861–
62) the Susquehanna Collegiate Institute
at Towanda, Pa., enlisted (1862) in the
Union army, was wounded at Chancellorsville (1863), and was discharged in
1864. He served (1865–81) with the
U.S. Treasury Department at Washington, D.C., meanwhile attending Columbian College (later George Washington
Univ., A.B., 1869; LL.B., 1871; A.M.,
1872). He took posts as a geologist
(1883 *et seq.*) and paleontologist (1892
et seq.) with the U.S. Geological Survey;
served as president of the Institut
International de Sociologie (1900–03)
and first president of the American
Sociological Society (1906–07). In 1906

he was named professor of sociology at Brown Univ., where he served until his death. A pioneer of American evolutionary sociology, Ward stressed the role of mind and education in human progress and the necessity of intelligent and systematic planning for the furthering of rational social development, in opposition both to the laissez-faire school and to the evolutionary determinism of Spencer. His works include *Dynamic Sociology* (1883), *The Psychic Factors of Civilization* (1893), *Outlines of Sociology* (1898), *Pure Sociology* (1903), and *Glimpses of the Cosmos* (6 vols., 1913–18).

Warren, Earl (b. Los Angeles, Calif., 19 Mar. 1891; d. Washington, D.C., 9 July 1974), 13th chief justice of the U.S., received his B.L. (1912) and his J.D. (1914) from the Univ. of California, was admitted to the bar in 1914, and practiced in San Francisco and Oakland. District attorney of Alameda Co. (1925–39) and attorney general of California (1939–43), he was governor of California for 3 terms (1943–53), winning both the Democratic and Republican nominations in 1946. Republican nominee for vice-president of the U.S. in 1948, he resigned the governorship to become chief justice of the U.S. Supreme Court (Sept. 1953–June 1969). He proved adept at marshalling the court during one of its most activist periods, a time of libertarian reform. Among his most notable opinions were *Brown* v. *Bd. of Education of Topeka* (1954), abolishing the separate-but-equal doctrine and upholding desegregation in public education; *Reynolds* v. *Sims* (1964), holding that states must apportion both legislative houses according to equal population; *Miranda* v. *Arizona* (1966), holding that all arrested persons had a right to an attorney before questioning by the police and to be advised of that right. He served as chairman of the special 7-man presidential commission to investigate the assassination of President Kennedy (1963–64).

Washington, Booker Taliaferro (b. Hale's Ford, Franklin Co., Va., 5 Apr. 1856; d. Tuskegee, Ala., 14 Nov. 1915), Negro educator. The son of a Negro slave and a white father, he worked (c. 1865 *et seq.*) in a salt furnace and coal mine at Malden, W. Va., meanwhile attending school. He entered (1872) Hampton Institute, the Negro vocational school in Virginia, where he earned his board by working as a janitor, and graduated in 1875. He was a schoolteacher at Malden (1875–77) and a student (1878–79) at Wayland Seminary, Washington, D.C., and in 1879 returned to Hampton Institute, where he took charge of the Indian dormitory and night school. Chosen (1881) to organize at Tuskegee a Negro normal school that had been chartered by the Alabama legislature, Washington founded there the Normal and Industrial Institute for Negroes. He soon became the foremost advocate of Negro education and was active as a public speaker on race relations, stressing industrial education and gradual adjustment rather than political and civil rights. He wrote *The Future of the American Negro* (1899), *Sowing and Reaping* (1900), the autobiographical *Up From Slavery* (1901), and *Frederick Douglass* (1907).

Washington, George (b. Bridges Creek, Westmoreland Co., Va., 22 Feb. 1732; d. Mount Vernon, Va., 14 Dec. 1799), 1st president of the U.S. After his father's death (1743) he lived chiefly at Mount Vernon, and worked as a surveyor. He visited Barbados with his half-brother Lawrence (1751–52). Sent by Gov. Dinwiddie to warn the French from encroaching on land in the Ohio Valley (1753), he served in the French and Indian Wars (1754–58) with the rank of lieutenant colonel, was obliged to surrender Ft. Necessity (3 July 1754), distinguished himself in the engagement known as Braddock's Defeat (9 July 1755), and participated in the capture of Ft. Duquesne (1758). Inheriting Mount Vernon from Lawrence (1752), he married Martha Dandridge Custis (6 Jan. 1759), entering the Virginia House of Burgesses that same year. A leader in the movement for independence, he was a delegate to the 1st and 2d Continental Congresses. On 15 June 1775 he was chosen to command the Continental army and took up duties before Boston (3 July). When the British evacuated that city, he attempted to defend New York, but was forced to withdraw to Westchester Co. and thence into New Jersey (1776). Brilliant successes at Trenton (26 Dec. 1776) and Princeton (3 Jan. 1777) raised Patriot morale. Defeated at Brandywine (11 Sept. 1777), he evacuated Philadelphia, was thrown back at Germantown (4 Oct.) and endured a winter of semistarvation at Valley Forge (1777–78). The exposé of the alleged Conway Cabal (1777–78) to displace Washington left him secure in his command. His most brilliant achievement was his secret and rapid march from the Hudson to Chesapeake Bay, resulting in the surrender of Cornwallis at Yorktown (19 Oct. 1781), ending the war. He denounced the Newburgh Address (1783), which had hinted at monarchy, and took leave of his officers at Fraunces' Tavern, New York (4 Dec. 1783), retiring to Mount Vernon. Returning to public life, he supported the movement for more effective union and presided over the Federal Convention (1787) which adopted the Constitution. Unanimously elected first president, he was inaugurated in New York (30 Apr. 1789) and administered the office for 2 terms, during which Hamiltonian fiscal policies were followed, neutrality was observed

(1793), the Whisky Rebellion suppressed (1794), and Jay's Treaty (1795) upheld. Declining a 3d term as president, he advised his countrymen in his Farewell Address (19 Sept. 1796) "to steer clear of permanent alliances . . . [trusting] to temporary alliance for extraordinary measures." When war with France threatened (1798), he was called from retirement as commander in chief, but hostilities were averted.

Watson, Thomas Edward (b. Columbia Co., Ga., 5 Sept. 1856; d. Washington, D.C., 26 Sept. 1922), political leader and author. Following 2 years at Mercer Univ., Watson taught school and studied law (1874–76). Admitted to the Georgia bar (1875), he gained a reputation as a criminal lawyer and became a substantial property owner. As a state assemblyman (1882–83), Watson expressed distrust of "New South" leaders who were allying the South with the industrial North. In 1890 he was elected to the U.S. House of Representatives on a Farmers' Alliance platform calling for an alliance between the South and agrarian West (1891–93). A radical egalitarian, Watson favored a sweeping program of agrarian reform, a drastic shakeup in the Georgia penal system, and racial equality. He was the People's (Populist) party candidate for speaker of the House and a leader of the party (1890–92), supporting passage of the Rural Free Delivery Act. Although he opposed the fusion of Populists and Democrats with Bryan at the head of the ticket (1896), he reluctantly accepted the vice-presidential nomination on the Populist line. In 1904 and 1908 he ran for president as a Populist. He wrote a number of substantial histories, including *The Story of France* (1898), *Napoleon: A Sketch of His Life* (1902), *The Life and Times of Thomas Jefferson* (1903), and *The Life and Times of An-*

drew Jackson (1912). *Tom Watson's Magazine*, published in New York (1905), contained his reform editorials as well as articles by Gorky and Dreiser. After his defeats for president, Watson became reactionary and, in his appeals to tenant farmers and mill workers, anti-Negro, anti-Semitic, and anti-Catholic. His book *The Roman Catholic Hierarchy* (1910), virulently anti-Catholic, led to 3 indictments but no convictions. He used the Leo Frank case (1913) to attack all Jews. Watson opposed American entry into World War I and conscription. He was elected Democratic senator from Georgia (1920), with Ku Klux Klan backing, on a platform opposing the League of Nations but supporting the restoration of civil liberties.

Webster, Daniel (b. Salisbury, N.H., 18 Jan. 1782; d. Marshfield, Mass., 24 Oct. 1852), statesman and orator, was graduated from Dartmouth (1801), read law at Salisbury and Boston, and was admitted to the Boston bar in 1805. He moved (1807) to Portsmouth, N.H., where he engaged in politics as a Federalist advocate of regional interests opposing Jefferson's embargo. His "Rockingham Memorial" (Aug. 1812), a forceful condemnation of the War of 1812, led to his election (Nov. 1812) to Congress. Reelected in 1816, he opposed the protective features of the Tariff of 1816 as inimical to New England commerce and shipping, and in the same year moved to Boston. In the following years he devoted himself to his law practice, appearing before the U.S. Supreme Court in cases including the *Dartmouth College Case, McCulloch* v. *Maryland,* and *Gibbons* v. *Ogden,* and gaining a reputation as one of the foremost constitutional lawyers in the country. His standing as an orator was established by his Plymouth speech (22 Dec. 1820), his speech on Greek independence (19 Jan.

1824), and his Bunker Hill oration (17 June 1825). Elected to Congress from Massachusetts in 1823, he opposed the Tariff of 1824, and in 1827 was elected to the U.S. Senate. Reflecting the shift in the economic development of New England, Webster supported the Tariff of 1828 and thereafter was an ardent protectionist. A champion of nationalism, he made one of his great orations during the nullification controversy, when he engaged Sen. Robert Y. Hayne (S.C.) in the debate that stimulated Webster's utterance, "Liberty *and* Union, now and forever, one and inseparable!" Opposed to Jackson's financial policies, he supported a national bank and fought Van Buren's subtreasury proposal. In 1836 and 1840 he was an unsuccessful contender for the Whig nomination for the presidency. He served as Secretary of State under Presidents William Henry Harrison and John Tyler, negotiated the Webster-Ashburton Treaty of 1842, and resigned from the cabinet in 1843. Elected to the Senate in 1844, he served there until 1850. Although he consistently supported the Wilmot Proviso, he held the preservation of the Union as paramount and backed the Compromise of 1850, answering secessionists and abolitionists alike in his famous 7th of March speech: "I wish to speak today, not as a Massachusetts man, nor as a northern man, but as an American. . . . I speak today for the preservation of the Union. 'Hear me for my cause.' " As Fillmore's Secretary of State, he wrote the nationalistic "Hülsemann letter." With Calhoun and Clay, he comprised the great senatorial triumvirate; and to the conservatives of New England was known as "the god-like Daniel."

Webster, Noah (b. West Hartford, Conn., 16 Oct. 1758; d. New Haven, Conn., 28 May 1843), lexicographer, philologist, and journalist. After graduating from

Yale (B.A., 1778), he read law and was admitted to the bar at Hartford, but practiced for only a short period (1789–93). While teaching at Goshen, N.Y. (1782), he prepared the first part of what later became his *Spelling Book* (*Blue-Backed Speller*) for the use of school children. Published (1783) as *A Grammatical Institute of the English Language,* and completed with a grammar (1784) and a reader (1785), the work, designed to meet American needs, was influential in standardizing spelling and pronunciation in the U.S. as distinguished from prevailing British forms. The *Spelling Book* had an estimated printing of 15 million copies by 1837; by 1890 of more than 70 million. Webster wrote *Sketches of American Policy* (1785) and was later active as a Federalist pamphleteer and journalist, editing the *American Minerva* and *Herald,* both at New York (1793–1803). He abandoned journalism for lexicography and, moving to New Haven, brought out *A Compendious Dictionary of the English Language* (1806). This small work was succeeded by the scholarly *An American Dictionary of the English Language* (2 vols., 1828), which assured Webster's reputation in the U.S. and abroad as a pioneer in the science of lexicography.

Westinghouse, George (b. Central Bridge, N.Y., 6 Oct. 1846; d. New York City, 12 Mar. 1914), inventor and manufacturer. He served in the Union army until he was honorably discharged in 1864, and for the remainder of the Civil War was an engineer in the Union navy. Interested in mechanical inventions, he abandoned his education at Union College, Schenectady, N.Y., to enter his father's agricultural implement shop. In 1865 he obtained patents for a rotary steam engine and a car replacer, and in 1868–69 developed a railroad frog. In 1869, when he secured the first air-brake patent, he incorporated the Westinghouse Air Brake Co. This compressed air apparatus had a revolutionary impact on railroad transportation, making high-speed rail travel safe, and is still used as standard equipment. Westinghouse also invented an automatic air brake for long freight trains, and next turned his attention to railroad signaling by electrical controls. He organized (1882) the Union Switch and Signal Co. and later, after he became interested in natural gas and electrical power, formed the Philadelphia Co., the Westinghouse Machine Co., and the Westinghouse Electric Co. In the field of natural gas, he developed a long-distance transmission system. His interest in electrical inventions began in 1885, when he promoted the development and construction of transformers which enabled the introduction into the U.S. of high-tension systems using single-phase alternating currents. In 1886 he purchased the patents held by Nikola Tesla (*q.v.*) and developed a 2-phase system suitable for lamps and motors. Westinghouse held more than 400 patents, among them shock absorbers, marine steam turbines, a trolley car motor, and an electrical brake for subway cars.

Whistler, James Abbott McNeill (b. Lowell, Mass., 10 July 1834; d. London, 17 July 1903), painter and etcher. During his childhood he traveled with his parents in Russia and England; entered the U.S. Military Academy (1851), from which he was dismissed in 1854; served as a draftsman (1854–55) with the U.S. Coast Survey; and went to Paris (1855), where he took professional training and brought out his first etchings (1858). After c.1870 he did most of his work in England. The famous libel suit (1878) against John Ruskin, which resulted from the latter's excoriating comments on Whistler's *Black and Gold–The Falling Rocket,* ended with a 1-farthing verdict in favor of Whistler. The 2 dominant influences in his painting were Velásquez and Japanese art patterns. For Whistler, the essence of painting was arrangement in color. Among his works are the *Portrait of My Mother,* portraits of Thomas Carlyle, Theodore Duret, Rosa Corder, and Lady Meux, and a series of *Nocturnes* and *Symphonies* (such as *Battersea Bridge*) in which he experimented with color harmonies. A brilliant etcher, his etchings and dry-points of London river scenes and Venetian subjects show a complete authority in the medium. He wrote *The Gentle Art of Making Enemies* (1890).

White, Andrew Dickson (b. Homer, N.Y., 7 Nov. 1832; d. Ithaca, N.Y., 4 Nov. 1918), educator, diplomat, and historian. He was graduated from Yale (1853), served as an attaché (1854–55) to the U.S. legation at St. Petersburg, and in 1857, after taking his master's degree at Yale, became professor of history at the Univ. of Michigan, where he remained until 1863. He was elected (1863) to the New York senate and during his incumbency (1864–67) served as chairman of the committee on education, created the state system of normal schools, and was the leading spirit in planning and securing the charter for Cornell Univ., of which he became (1867) first president, serving in that capacity until 1885. At Cornell he introduced such innovations as the nonsegregation of the humanities, the natural sciences, and technical arts, and the employment of leading scholars as "nonresident professors." He also taught history at Cornell, and was one of the founders and the first president of the American Historical Association (1884).

He served as U.S. minister to Germany (1879–81), minister to Russia (1892–94), ambassador to Germany (1897–1902), and was president of the International Peace Conference at The Hague (1899). His works include *History of the Warfare of Science with Theology in Christendom* (2 vols., 1896), which accepted Darwinism, and *Autobiography* (2 vols., 1905).

White, Edward Douglass (b. Parish Lafourche, La., 3 Nov. 1845; d. Washington, D.C., 19 May 1921), 8th chief justice of the U.S., studied at Jesuit College, New Orleans, and at Georgetown, enlisted in the Confederate army at the age of 16, was taken prisoner at Port Hudson, La., and paroled. Admitted to the state bar (1868), he practiced in New Orleans, was state senator (1874 78), and judge of the state supreme court (1879–80). Democratic U.S. senator (1891–94), he was appointed by Cleveland as associate justice of the U.S. Supreme Court (1894) and made chief justice by Taft (1910). On the high court he followed a middle-of-the-road policy, taking a liberal position in his dissent in *Lochner* v. *N.Y.* (1905) and in *Wilson* v. *New* (1917), upholding the Adamson Act providing an 8-hour day for railroad workers, but he dissented in *Bunting* v. *Oregon* (1917), which upheld the Oregon 10-hour law. Dissenting in the *Northern Securities Case* (1904), he laid down the "rule of reason" opinion dissolving the Standard Oil Co. and the American Tobacco Co. (1911).

Whitefield, George (b. Gloucester, England, 16 Dec. 1715; d. Newburyport, Mass., 30 Sept. 1770), evangelist. He was graduated from Oxford, where he became associated with John and Charles Wesley and the Methodist movement. During the absence of the

Wesleys in Georgia (which Whitefield visited in May–Sept. 1738), he acted as the leader of the Methodist movement. When virtually all of the churches in England closed their doors against him, Whitefield took to preaching outdoor sermons, soon attracting large audiences and wide attention with his impassioned oratory and expert histrionics. In 1739 he returned to America, where he was the most important single influence in stirring the religious revival commonly called the Great Awakening. Upon his return to England (1741) Whitefield, who had become a Calvinist, broke with the Wesleys and assumed the leadership of the Calvinistic Methodist movement. He made subsequent visits to America in 1744–48, 1751, 1754–55, 1763–64, and 1769–70.

Whitman, Walt (b. West Hills, Huntington, Long Island, N.Y., 31 May 1819; d. Camden, N.J., 26 Mar. 1892), poet, worked as a printer's devil, taught school, and edited (1838–39) the *Long Islander*. From 1841 to 1848 he was associated with newspapers and magazines at New York, editing (1846–48) the *Brooklyn Eagle* and publishing a temperance novel, *Franklin Evans; or, The Inebriate, a Tale of the Times* (1842). He went to New Orleans (1848), where he worked for the *Crescent,* and after his return to Brooklyn wrote for the Free-Soil daily, the *Freeman,* during 1848–49, and edited (1857–59) the Brooklyn *Times.* He published *Leaves of Grass* (1855), which struck a new and indigenous note in American poetry, and to which many pieces were added in subsequent editions. During the Civil War, Whitman was a volunteer nurse at Washington, D.C., where he also worked as a clerk in the Department of the Interior. Following a paralytic stroke suffered by him in 1873, he moved to Camden, N.J., where he resided for the rest

of his life. Sometimes called "the Good Gray Poet," Whitman is the bard of democracy who, in celebrating his own identity, extolled both the average man and the uniqueness of the individual. Among his works are *Drum Taps* (1865), *Passage to India* (1871), *Democratic Vistas* (1871, prose work), *Specimen Days and Collect* (1882–83, prose work), and *Good-bye, My Fancy* (1891). Among his individual poems are "Pioneers! O Pioneers!" "The Song of the Broad Axe," "Once I Pass'd through a Populous City," "When Lilacs Last in the Dooryard Bloom'd," and "O Captain! My Captain!"

Whitney, Eli (b. Westboro, Mass., 8 Dec. 1765; d. New Haven, Conn., 8 Jan. 1825), inventor. As a boy and young man he became familiar with mechanical crafts in his father's metalworking shop. He entered Yale in 1789 and was graduated in 1792. While in the South, where he began his law studies on the Georgia plantation of the widow of Gen. Nathanael Greene, his attention was called to the tedious method of cleaning green seed cotton, at that time an unprofitable crop because of the costly manual process of separating the staple. Whitney designed a cotton gin and, after successive experiments, built a large and improved model (1793) with which a single slave could maintain a daily output of 50 lbs. of cleaned cotton. Before Whitney obtained his patent (1794), many imitations were placed on the market; in the various infringement suits he undertook, Whitney did not secure a favorable verdict until 1807, and most of the little money he made from the invention went for law costs. His cotton gin revolutionized the course of Southern agriculture and territorial expansion. In New Haven, Whitney undertook the manufacture of firearms. He obtained from the federal government a contract for 10,000 muskets (1798). For their manufacture he devised a system of interchangeable parts (1800), also devised independently (before 1808) by Simeon North (1765–1852), the Connecticut gunsmith. Whitney established a factory near New Haven, at the site of present-day Whitneyville, and designed and built the machinery for producing muskets with precision parts turned out by relatively inexperienced workmen engaged in simple operations.

Whittier, John Greenleaf (b. Haverhill, Mass., 17 Dec. 1807; d. Hampton Falls, N.H., 7 Sept. 1892), poet and abolitionist, published his first poems (1826 *et seq.*) in the Newburyport (Mass.) *Free Press,* edited by William Lloyd Garrison. He attended (1827–28) Haverhill Academy, became (1829) editor of *The American Manufacturer* at Boston, and edited (1831) the *New England Weekly Review* at Hartford, Conn. He published *Legends of New England in Prose and Verse* (1831) and *Moll Pitcher* (1832), and under the influence of Garrison became an active abolitionist (after c.1833). He served (1835) in the Massachusetts legislature, edited (1838–40) the *Pennsylvania Freeman,* and published *Poems Written During the Progress of the Abolition Question* (1838). He helped establish the American and Foreign Antislavery Society and ran for Congress on the Liberty party ticket. He became (1847) corresponding editor of the antislavery journal the *National Era.* His volumes of poetry include *Lays of My Home* (1843), *Voices of Freedom* (1846), *Songs of Labor* (1850), *The Chapel of the Hermits* (1853), *The Panorama and Other Poems* (1856), *In War Time and Other Poems* (1864), *Snow-Bound* (1866), *The Tent on the Beach* (1867), *Ballads of New England* (1870), and *At Sun-down* (1890). His best-known individual poems include "Maud Muller," "Barefoot Boy," "Massachusetts to Virginia," "Ichabod," and "Barbara Frietchie."

Wiener, Norbert (b. Columbia, Mo., 26 Nov. 1894; d. Stockholm, Sweden, 18 Mar. 1964), mathematician and philosopher. Son of Leo Wiener, Harvard's first professor of Slavonic languages, he was a child prodigy, with a B.A. from Tufts at age 14 and a Ph.D. from Harvard at 19. His graduate study also took him to Cornell, to Cambridge, England, where he studied under Bertrand Russell, to Göttingen Univ., and to Columbia. He lectured in mathematics at Harvard (1915–16) and at the Univ. of Maine (1916–17). From 1919 to 1960 he was a member of the mathematics department at the Massachusetts Institute of Technology. He formulated a theory of Brownian movement (1920) and made far-reaching discoveries about the flow of information along a wave (1925). Working for the government during World War II, he made major contributions to the development of radar, coding, antiaircraft fire-control and gun-aiming devices but, disturbed by the destructive potential of devices based on his investigations, he renounced (1947) military research. A pioneer in computer science, he recognized computers as constituting a second industrial revolution—one with great possibilities as well as great dangers, if through intellectual sloth man relinquished control to his mechanical creations. Though technical in nature, his *Cybernetics: On Control and Communication in Animal and the Machine* (1948), in which he summarized the results of his work in information control and communication, gained popular as well as scientific attention. He coined the term cybernetics —derived from the Greek for "steersman"—to define a new science which attempts to construct a theoretical framework for the comparative study of control and communications in machines and in living organisms. Cybernetics attempts to find the common elements in the functioning of automatic information-processing machines and of the human nervous system. Known as the "father of automation," his contributions altered the face of the modern world. The author of numerous articles and books (including detective stories written under a pseudonym, W. Norbert), his other works include *The Human Use of Human Beings* (1950), *Ex-Prodigy* (1953), *I Am a Mathematician* (1956).

Wilkes, Charles (b. New York City, 3 Apr. 1798; d. Washington, D.C., 8 Feb. 1877), naval officer and explorer, was commissioned midshipman in the U.S. navy (1818) and given charge of the Department of Charts and Instruments (1833), out of which developed the Naval Observatory and Hydrographic Office. In 1838 he was given command of the first national marine exploration and surveyed routes in the Pacific Ocean and South Seas frequented by American whalers. In Jan. 1840 he claimed discovery of the Continent of Antarctica, coasting along part of the Antarctic barrier from about 150°E to 108°E, subsequently named Wilkes Land in his honor. He supervised the preparation of the 19-vol. report of the expedition and personally prepared *Narrative* (1844), *Meteorology* (1851), and *Hydrography* (1861). Commanding the *San Jacinto* in the Civil War, he stopped the British mail steamer *Trent* in the old Bahama Channel (8 Nov. 1861) and seized the Confederate commissioners, James M. Mason and John Slidell, en route to Europe. Although thanked by Congress, his action was disavowed by Lincoln as a breach of international law, and Mason and Slidell were surrendered to Britain.

Willard, Emma Hart (b. Berlin, Conn., 23 Feb. 1787; d. Troy, N.Y., 15 Apr. 1870), educator. She attended the Berlin Academy, and from 1807 until 1809, when she married John Willard, was head of the Middlebury (Vt.) Female Academy. In 1814 she established the Middlebury Female Seminary, where she made innovations in women's education. She sent to Governor De Witt Clinton of New York *An Address . . . Proposing a Plan for Improving Female Education* (1819), in which she advocated educational equality for women. Although her proposals led the New York legislature to charter (1819) the Waterford Academy established by her, the state failed to provide financial aid. At the invitation of citizens of Troy, N.Y., she established there (1821) the Troy Female Seminary, the first U.S. college-level institution for women. It provided instruction in subjects such as mathematics and philosophy from which women had been traditionally excluded. Mrs. Willard wrote history and geography textbooks that were used in many schools and trained hundreds of teachers who spread her doctrines. She retired in 1838, thereafter devoting herself to the improvement of common schools. She was the author of a volume of poetry, *The Fulfilment of a Promise* (1831), which included "Rocked in the Cradle of the Deep."

Willard, Frances (b. Churchville, N.Y., 28 Sept. 1839; d. New York City, 18 Feb. 1898), reformer, was graduated from Northwestern Female College (1859) and settled in Evanston, Ill., where she began teaching (1860) and became president of the Evanston College for Ladies (1871–74). She resigned to join the temperance crusade and served as president (from 1879) of the National Women's Christian Temperance Union (WCTU) and of the World

Woman's Christian Temperance Union (from 1887). She helped organize the Prohibition party and participated in the women's suffrage movement.

Williams, Roger (b. London, England, c.1603; d. Providence, R.I., between 26 Jan. and 25 Mar. 1683), religious leader, founder of the Rhode Island Colony. Protégé of the lawyer Sir Edward Coke, who helped Williams secure his education, he was graduated from Cambridge (B.A., 1627), took holy orders in the Church of England (c.1628), and as chaplain to Sir William Masham became acquainted with Puritan circles. Immigrating to Massachusetts (1631), he antagonized the magistracy by his contentions that the civil government was not empowered to enforce the religious precepts of the Ten Commandments and that the royal charter illegally expropriated the land rights of the Indians. After serving in churches at Plymouth and Salem, he was tried by the General Court, which ordered his banishment (1635). With some of his followers he founded (1636) the earliest Rhode Island settlement at Providence, adopting a humane policy toward the Indians. Having already taken a position more radical than Separatism, he now viewed with skepticism all established churches. After a brief period as a Baptist, he became (1639) a Seeker, i.e., one who adhered to the basic tenets of Christianity but refused to recognize any creed. First champion of complete religious toleration in America, he also espoused a liberal political order in the Rhode Island colony, which was founded on the compact theory of the state and featured a democratic land association. To safeguard his colony against the encroachments of the New England Confederation, he went to England (1643) and secured a charter (1644). During his stay in England he wrote pamphlets on behalf of the liberal wing of Puritanism, including *Queries of Highest Consideration* (1644), which opposed the establishment of a national church, and *The Bloudy Tenent of Persecution* (1644), which advocated unqualified religious and political freedom. He returned to Rhode Island (1644) to find that William Coddington of Newport had organized opposition to Williams' plans for the union of the 4 Rhode Island settlements. With John Clarke, Williams again went to England (1651) where he succeeded in having Coddington's commission withdrawn. During this period he wrote *The Bloudy Tenent Yet More Bloudy* (1652) in reply to John Cotton's *The Bloudy Tenent Washed and Made White* (1647). Upon his return to Rhode Island, Williams served for 3 terms (1654–57) as president of the colony, which in 1663 obtained a new charter from Charles II.

Williams, Tennessee [Thomas Lanier] (b. Columbus, Miss., 26 Mar. 1911–   ), playwright, moved to St. Louis at 12, attended the Univ. of Missouri (1931–33), but left during the depression to clerk with a shoe company. After a year at Washington Univ., St. Louis (1936–37), he finished his college course at the Univ. of Iowa (B.A., 1938). A Rockefeller fellow in 1940, he quickly established a reputation as a talented and prolific playwright. His early plays include *Battle of Angels* (1940) and *The Glass Menagerie* (1945). His Pulitzer prize-winning *A Streetcar Named Desire* (1947) established his reputation. His plays, often concerned with the destruction of innocence by inexorable forces and with individual depravity, reached a broad audience through adaptation for the screen. Among his later plays are *The Rose Tattoo* (1948), *Cat on a Hot Tin Roof* (1955, Pulitzer prize), *Sweet Bird of Youth* (1959),

The Night of the Iguana (1962, N.Y. Drama Critics Circle award). Screenplays of importance are *Baby Doll* and *The Fugitive Kind.*

Wilson, Edmund (b. Red Bank, N.J., 8 May 1895; d. Talcottville, N.Y., 12 June 1972), author and critic. After graduating from Princeton (1916), where he began an association with fellow student F. Scott Fitzgerald (*q.v.*) which lasted until the latter's death, Wilson spent several months as a reporter on the New York *Evening Sun.* During World War I he served as private, a hospital attendant, and a member of the Intelligence Corps. As managing editor of *Vanity Fair* (1920–21) and associate editor of the *New Republic* (1926–31), he helped launch the careers of John Dos Passos and F. Scott Fitzgerald. His publication of *Axel's Castle* (1931)—a study of the writings of Yeats, Eliot, Pound, and Joyce in the context of the French Symbolist movement—and *American Jitters* (1932)—a collection of articles with a political bent—brought him acclaim as a critic. During the depression he called for a radical approach to the nation's ills and supported the Communist party's presidential candidate in 1932. His visit to the U.S.S.R. as a Guggenheim fellow (1935) led to his writing *To the Finland Station* (1940). At the conclusion of this scholarly survey of the revolutionary tradition—which focused on Vico, Saint-Simon, Taine, Marx, Engels, Lenin, and Trotsky—Wilson expressed doubt that Marxist theories would lead to a society without exploitation. The next year he published *The Wound and the Bow,* which explored the dualism of Dickens, Kipling, Casanova, Edith Wharton, Hemingway, and Joyce. Having mastered French, Italian, German, and Greek as an adolescent, he learned Hebrew, Russian, and Hungarian later in life. He wrote with authority

and elegance on a wide variety of topics, including the Dead Sea Scrolls (1955), the Iroquois (1959), the literature of the Civil War (*Patriotic Gore,* 1962), and the income tax (1963).

Wilson, James (b. Carskerdo, Scotland, 14 Sept. 1742; d. Edenton, N.C., 21 Aug. 1798), Revolutionary statesman, jurist, attended St. Andrews, Glasgow, and Edinburgh universities (1757–63). Leaving Scotland for America, he arrived in New York during the Stamp Act crisis and obtained a post as Latin tutor at the College of Philadelphia (1766). Studying law with John Dickinson (*q.v.*), he was admitted to the bar (1767), practiced in Reading (1768), and moved to Carlisle, where by 1774 he had amassed a huge practice. Heading a Committee of Correspondence at Carlisle (1774), he published in that year his notable *Considerations on the Nature and Extent of the Legislative Authority of the British Parliament,* denying Parliament's authority over the colonies and anticipating a British Commonwealth. Signer of the Declaration, he sought in the 2d Continental Congress to strengthen the national government. An opponent of the radical Pennsylvania constitution of 1776, he became leader of the conservative forces in Philadelphia, to which he moved in 1778. Incurring animosity for his defense of the Penn family and of profiteering merchants, he and his friends barricaded themselves against a mob (4 Oct. 1779). In Congress (1785–87), he played a leading role at the Federal Convention and successfully fought for adoption of the Constitution in Pennsylvania. Law lecturer at the College of Philadelphia (1789), he was associate justice of the U.S. Supreme Court (1789–98), and wrote a notable opinion in *Chisholm* v. *Georgia* (1793), upholding the national against the states' authority. Throughout his life a heavy land speculator, he fled to North Carolina to avoid arrest for debt and died under a cloud.

Wilson, [Thomas] Woodrow (b. Staunton, Va., 28 Dec. 1856; d. Washington, D.C., 3 Feb. 1924), 28th president of the U.S., was graduated from Princeton (1879), studied law at the Univ. of Virginia (1880), was admitted to the bar (1881), and, after opening a law office in Atlanta, entered the graduate school at Johns Hopkins (1883), where he completed his notable doctoral thesis, *Congressional Government* (1885). After teaching history at Bryn Mawr (1885–88) and Wesleyan (1888–90), he became professor of jurisprudence and political economics at Princeton (1890–1902), quickly establishing himself as a preeminent authority in his field and was in wide demand as a public lecturer. Appointed first nonclerical president of Princeton (1902–10), he became second only to Eliot of Harvard as an educational leader. Defeated in his plans for the graduate school, his position became untenable, and he resigned to accept the Democratic nomination for governor of New Jersey. His term (1911–12) was marked by reforms and a courageous fight against the Democratic political machine. Put forward as a conservative Democrat to defeat W. J. Bryan, he obtained the Democratic nomination for president (1912) and was elected as a result of a split in Republican ranks. His 1st administration was notable for such reforms as the Underwood Tariff, the Federal Reserve Act (1913), the Federal Trade Commission, and the Clayton Act (1914). He sent a punitive expedition across the Mexican border (1916) and sought to maintain U.S. neutrality after the outbreak of World War I despite infringement of American rights. Reelected president (1916) on the campaign slogan "he kept us out of war," he called for war (2 Apr. 1917) after Germany renewed unrestricted submarine warfare. "The world must be made safe for democracy," he then declared. On 8 Jan. 1918 he laid down 14 Points as the basis of peace and stated (27 Sept.) that the League of Nations was the "most essential part" of the peace settlement. Heading the U.S. peace delegation, he was given an unprecedented reception in Paris (14 Dec. 1918) and in other European capitals, but became involved in disputes with Allied leaders and was forced to compromise numerous of the 14 Points in order to save the League. When the Senate refused to ratify the Treaty of Versailles without reservations unacceptable to him, he set out from Washington (3 Sept. 1919) to carry to the people his case against "the little group of willful men." He collapsed at Pueblo (26 Sept. 1919) and never fully recovered.

Winthrop, John (b. Edwardstone, Suffolk, England, 22 Jan. 1588; d. Boston, Mass., 26 Mar. 1649), colonial Puritan statesman, first governor of Massachusetts Bay. He attended Cambridge, was admitted at Gray's Inn (1613), and practiced law in London, being admitted to the Inner Temple in 1628. A country squire, his Puritan convictions led him to take an interest in the Massachusetts Bay Co., of which he was chosen governor (1629). He signed the Cambridge Agreement (1629) by which 12 members pledged that if the charter and company could be legally transferred to New England they would go there with their families. He sailed from Southampton (1630) aboard the *Arbella,* part of a fleet transporting to Salem some 700 passengers, the first large contingent of the Puritan migration, and settled at the present site of Boston. Winthrop and his Puritan associates laid the foundation of the "Bible Commonwealth." He served as governor (1629–34, 1637–40, 1642–44, 1646–49) and was deputy governor for a total of ten years. As early as 1637 he advocated a New England Confederation, particularly for reasons of defense, and was the first president of the confederation when it was formed in 1643. The first 2 vols. of his manuscript *Journal* (1630–44) appeared in 1790, and it was published in full as *The History of New England* (2 vols., 1825–26).

Wise, Isaac Mayer (b. Steingrub, Bohemia, 29 Mar. 1819; d. Cincinnati, Ohio, 26 Mar. 1900), religious leader, entered (1835) a rabbinical school in Jenikau, then attended the Univ. of Prague for 2 years and the Univ. of Vienna for a year. Admitted to the rabbinate, he was elected (1843) rabbi of the congregation of Radnitz, but opposing government control and censorship, he left Bohemia for the U.S. (1846). Rabbi in Albany, N.Y. (1846–54), he accepted a call to the Bene Yeshurun Congregation in Cincinnati, where he was rabbi (1854–1900). His weekly newspaper, the *Israelite* (later *American Israelite*), advocated adjusting Judaism to American life and institutions, including the use of English in religious services and a simplification of ritual observances. Founder of Reform Judaism in the U.S. he appealed (1848) for a union of congregations, which saw fruition in the Union of American Hebrew Congregations (1873); founded the Hebrew Union College (1875), first native institution for training rabbis; and established a rabbinical organization, the Central Conference of American Rabbis (1889), of which he was president until his death. His writings include *History of the Israelitish Nation from Abraham to the Present Time* (1854), *The Cosmic God* (1876), and *Pronaos to Holy Writ* (1891).

Witherspoon, John (b. Yester, near Edinburgh, Scotland, 5 Feb. 1723; d. New Jersey, 15 Nov. 1794), religious leader, educator, and Revolutionary patriot. He received his divinity degree (1743) from the Univ. of Edinburgh, was ordained in the Presbyterian ministry in 1745, and held pulpits in Scotland until 1768, when he came to America to occupy the presidency of the College of New Jersey (now Princeton). As an educator, he revamped methods of instruction and the college curriculum, and was an exponent of the Scottish "common sense" philosophy. As a religious leader, he closed the factional breach between the "Old Side" and "New Side" Presbyterians in the colonies, was partly responsible for the rapid growth of the Presbyterian Church and was a staunch advocate of religious liberty. Delegate to the Continental Congress in 1776, he favored the Declaration of Independence, of which he was a signer. He served intermittently in Congress until 1782, and was a signer of the Articles of Confederation. He was a member (1783, 1789) of the New Jersey legislature and of the state convention that ratified (1787) the Federal Constitution, and was active (1785–89) in furthering the national organization of the Presbyterian Church. He coined the term "Americanism" in an article on language in the *Pennsylvania Journal* (1781). His *Works* (4 vols.) were published in 1800–01.

Woodward, Robert Burns (b. Boston, 10 Apr. 1917; d. Cambridge, Mass., 8 July 1979), chemist, obtained his B.S. (1936) from MIT and his Ph.D. a year later. Joining the Harvard faculty that year, he achieved, with Dr. William E. Doering, the first total synthesis of quinine (1944). His synthesis, with C. H. Schramm, of protein analogues (1947), materials resembling natural proteins found in animal and plant life, came closer than ever before to duplicating a natural growth process, and proved valuable in plastics, antibiotics, and medical research. First to synthesize a steroid (1951), he announced later that year the total synthesis of cortisone. He synthesized cholesterol (1951), strychnine (1954), chlorophyll (1960), and tetracycline (1962). He received the Nobel prize in chemistry (1965). In 1972, with Harvard colleagues, he completed the synthesis of Vitamin B-12, the most complicated molecule to have been made in the laboratory up to that date.

Wright, Frank Lloyd (b. Richland Center, Wis., 8 June 1867; d. Phoenix, Ariz., 10 Apr. 1959), architect. He studied civil engineering (1884–88) at the Univ. of Wisconsin and was a draftsman (1889–94) with architectural firms at Chicago, including Adler & Sullivan, for whom he worked on plans for the Transportation Building at the Chicago World's Fair (1893) and the James Charnley house at Chicago. In 1894 he established independent practice at Oak Park, Ill., and in 1911 moved to Spring Green, Wis., where he designed his own residences, Taliesin I and Taliesin II. His "prairie house" style appeared as early as c.1894 in the W. H. Winslow house at River Forest, Ill. A disciple of Louis H. Sullivan (*q.v.*), Wright became the foremost American innovator and exponent of an organic architecture based on the integration of form, function, building site, and materials, and on the subordination of style to human needs. His preoccupation with the social relations of architecture is expressed in his model for the projected community of Broadacre City. His designs have exerted a pervasive influence on modern European architecture. Among his works are Unity Temple, Oak Park, Ill.; the Larkin Ad-

ministration Bldg. and the Darwin Martin house, both at Buffalo, N.Y.; the Coonley Playhouse and Kindergarten, Riverside, Ill.; the Ward H. Willits house, Highland Park, Ill.; the F. C. Robie house, Francisco Terrace, and Midway Gardens, all at Chicago; the Aline Barnsdall house, Los Angeles, Calif.; the Imperial Hotel at Tokyo, which withstood the earthquake of 1923; Taliesin West at Paradise Valley, Phoenix, Ariz.; and the Kaufmann house (Falling River) at Bear Run, Pa. In 1956 he completed work on the Price Tower in Bartlesville, Okla. The Solomon R. Guggenheim Museum (New York) was completed posthumously (Oct. 1959).

Wright, Wilbur (b. Millville, near New Castle, Ind., 16 Apr. 1867; d. Dayton, Ohio, 30 May 1912), and his brother, **Orville** (b. Dayton, Ohio, 19 Aug. 1871; d. there, 30 Jan. 1948), aviation pioneers and inventors. The sons of Bishop Milton Wright of the United Brethren in Christ, they had only brief formal schooling, neither completing high school. In 1892 they established a bicycle shop at Dayton, where they began (1895) the manufacture of bicycles. Their interest in aviation having been aroused (c.1898), they read articles and books on aeronautics, built a biplane kite (1899), and conducted two man-carrying glider experiments (1900, 1901) at Kitty Hawk, N.C. Finding a relative paucity of scientific information in the field of aircraft design and construction, they built a wind tunnel (1901) in which they tested and verified the operation of some 200 wing and biplane surfaces. They worked out major innovations in aircraft control systems and, on the basis of their painstaking compilation of scientific data, began (Oct. 1902) the construction of a powered aircraft with a total weight of 750 lbs.

and carrying a 170-lb., 12-hp gasoline engine. This machine was completed at Kitty Hawk, where, on 17 Dec. 1903, Orville Wright made the first piloted flight in a powered airplane, remaining aloft for 12 seconds over a distance of about 120 ft. Of the 4 flights made on that day, Wilbur flew the longest one: 59 seconds over a distance of 852 ft. Returning to Dayton, the Wright brothers improved their machine. Toward the close of 1905 they made in it a flight of about 38 minutes over a distance of more than 24 miles around Huffman Field, Dayton. They obtained a patent for their aircraft on 22 May 1906. In 1908–09 Wilbur toured England, France, and Italy, setting records for altitude and distance. Their machine, after being subjected to tests at Ft. Myer, Va., was accepted by the U.S. Army (2 Aug. 1909). The commercial development and manufacture of the Wright airplane was begun in 1909 with the organization of the Wright Co.

Young, Brigham (b. Whitingham, Vt. 1 June 1801; d. Salt Lake City, 29 Aug. 1877), Mormon leader and colonizer. In his infancy he was taken by his family to the "burnt-over" district in western New York, a region of intense evangelical activity. After working as a house painter and glazier, he settled (1829) on a farm at Mendon, N.Y., about 40 miles from Palmyra, N.Y., where Joseph Smith (*q.v.*) published *The Book of Mormon* and founded the Church of Jesus Christ of Latter-Day Saints. Young became a convert to Mormonism (1832) and devoted the rest of his life to the upbuilding of the Mormon Church. In 1835 he became the 3d ranking member of the Quorum of the 12 Apostles, the administrative body of the church, and by 1838 was its senior member. During these years he was active as a Mormon missionary. Upon the death of Joseph

Smith at Carthage, Ill., he became head of the church. In this role Young demonstrated his brilliance, energy, and determination as a practical organizer. He led the Mormon mass migrations to the Valley of the Great Salt Lake and directed the settlement of Deseret, which in 1850 was organized by Congress as Utah Territory. Young was named territorial governor, and although removed from his post (1857) during the Mormon controversy with the federal government, remained the effective leader of the community. His lasting contribution was the shaping of an administrative machinery that enabled the survival and development of the Mormon Church. He adopted polygamy, had about a score of wives, and fathered 56 children.

Zenger, John Peter (b. in Germany, 1697; d. New York City, 28 July 1746), printer and journalist. He arrived at New York in 1710 and served his apprenticeship (1711–19) to the printer William Bradford, with whom he formed (1725) a short-lived partnership. In 1726 Zenger established an independent business. In 1733, after Gov. Cosby adopted arbitrary measures, Zenger became the editor and publisher of the *New-York Weekly Journal*, set up by him and prominent New Yorkers in opposition to the provincial administration and its organ, Bradford's *New York Gazette*. The polemical articles which appeared in the *Weekly Journal* were probably written by Zenger's associates; under existing law, however, the publisher was held responsible. In 1734 Zenger was arrested and imprisoned, and held incommunicado for about 10 months. Brought to trial (1735) for seditious libel, he was defended by Andrew Hamilton of Philadelphia. Despite the court's refusal to admit evidence establishing the truth of the libel, Hamilton succeeded in securing Zenger's acquittal. The case is a landmark in the history of the freedom of the press in America. Zenger became public printer for the colony of New York (1737) and the colony of New Jersey (1738).

Zworykin, Vladimir (b. Mourom, Russia, 30 July 1889–   ), electronics engineer, pioneer in the development of television. He was graduated from the Petrograd Institute of Technology (E.E., 1912), came to the U.S. in 1916, was naturalized in 1924, and served as research engineer (1920–29) with the Westinghouse Electrical and Manufacturing Co. He applied (1925) for the patent on the iconoscope (the essential basis of the electronic television camera), the first practical application and predecessor of modern television. He served as director of electronic research (1929–42) for the RCA Manufacturing Co., and was associate director (1942–45) of the RCA Laboratories, of which he was named director of electronic research (1946) and vice-president and technical consultant (1947). In 1933, employing the iconoscope and the cathode-ray tube, he made a successful demonstration of television over a radio-wave relay between New York and Philadelphia. He has also done work in the fields of electron optics and the electron microscope. He is the author of *Photocells and Their Applications* (1932), *Television* (1940), and *Television in Science and Industry* (1958).

4
Structure of the Federal Government

★

PRESIDENTS
AND THEIR CABINETS

Dates given below are when each individual assumed office

1st President	**George Washington**	**1789, 1793**
Vice President	John Adams	1789, 1793
State[1]	John Jay	1789*
	Thomas Jefferson	1790
	Edmund Randolph	1794
	Timothy Pickering	1795
War[2]	Henry Knox	1789
	Timothy Pickering	1795*
	James McHenry	1796
Treasury[3]	Alexander Hamilton	1789
	Oliver Wolcott, Jr.	1795
Post. General[4]	Samuel Osgood	1789
	Timothy Pickering	1791
	Joseph Habersham	1795
Atty. General[5]	Edmund Randolph	1790
	William Bradford	1794
	Charles Lee	1795

* ad interim.
[1] Dept. of Foreign Affairs est. 27 July 1789; redesignated Dept. of State 15 Sept. 1789.
[2] Est. 7 Aug. 1789.
[3] Est. 2 Sept. 1789.
[4] Est. 22 Sept. 1789.
[5] Est. 24 Sept. 1789, Dept. of Justice created 22 June 1870.

2d President	**John Adams**	**1797**
Vice President	Thomas Jefferson	1797
State	Timothy Pickering	1797
	Charles Lee	1800*
	John Marshall	1800, 1801*
War	James McHenry	1797
	Benjamin Stoddert	1800
	Samuel Dexter	1800, 1801*
Treasury	Oliver Wolcott, Jr.	1797
	Samuel Dexter	1801
Post. General	Joseph Habersham	1797
Atty. General	Charles Lee	1797
Navy[1]	Benjamin Stoddert	1798

* ad interim.

3d President	**Thomas Jefferson**	**1801, 1805**
Vice President	Aaron Burr	1801
	George Clinton	1805
State	John Marshall	1801*
	Levi Lincoln	1801*
	James Madison	1801

War	Henry Dearborn	1801
	John Smith	1809*
Treasury	Samuel Dexter	1801
	Albert Gallatin	1801, 1805
Post. General	Joseph Habersham	1801
	Gideon Granger	1801, 1805
Atty. General	Levi Lincoln	1801
	John C. Breckinridge	1805
	Caesar A. Rodney	1807
Navy	Benjamin Stoddert	1801
	Henry Dearborn	1801*
	Robert Smith	1801

* ad interim.
1 Est. 3 May 1797.

4th President	**James Madison**	**1809, 1813**
Vice President	George Clinton	1809
	Elbridge Gerry	1813
State	Robert Smith	1809
	James Monroe	1811, 1813, 1814,* 1815
War	John Smith	1809*
	William Eustis	1809
	James Monroe	1813, 1814, 1815*
	John Armstrong	1813
	Alexander J. Dallas	1815*
	William H. Crawford	1815
	George Graham	1816*
Treasury	Albert Gallatin	1809, 1813
	George W. Campbell	1814
	Alexander J. Dallas	1814
	William H. Crawford	1816
Post. General	Gideon Granger	1809, 1813
	Return J. Meigs, Jr.	1814
Atty. General	Caesar A. Rodney	1809
	William Pinkney	1812, 1813
	Richard Rush	1814
Navy	Robert Smith	1809
	Charles W. Goldsborough	1809,* 1813*
	Paul Hamilton	1809
	William Jones	1813
	Benjamin Homans	1814*
	Benjamin W. Crowninshield	1814

* ad interim.

5th President	**James Monroe**	**1817, 1821**
Vice President	Daniel D. Tompkins	1817, 1821
State	John Graham	1817*
	Richard Rush	1817*
	John Quincy Adams	1817, 1821
War	George Graham	1817*
	John C. Calhoun	1817, 1821
Treasury	William H. Crawford	1817, 1821
Post. General	Return J. Meigs, Jr.	1817, 1821
	John McLean	1823
Atty. General	Richard Rush	1817
	William Wirt	1817, 1821
Navy	Benjamin W. Crowninshield	1817
	John C. Calhoun	1818*
	Smith Thompson	1818, 1821
	John Rodgers	1823*
	Samuel L. Southard	1823

* ad interim.

6th President	**John Quincy Adams**	1825
Vice President	John C. Calhoun	1825
State	Daniel Brent	1825*
	Henry Clay	1825
War	James Barbour	1825
	Samuel L. Southard	1828*
	Peter B. Porter	1828
Treasury	Samuel L. Southard	1825*
	Richard Rush	1825
Post. General	John McLean	1825
Atty. General	William Wirt	1825
Navy	Samuel L. Southard	1825

* ad interim.

7th President	**Andrew Jackson**	**1829, 1833**
Vice President	John C. Calhoun	1829
	Martin Van Buren	1833
State	James A. Hamilton	1829*
	Martin Van Buren	1829
	Edward Livingston	1831, 1833
	Louis McLane	1833
	John Forsyth	1834
War	John H. Eaton	1829
	Philip G. Randolph	1831*
	Roger B. Taney	1831*
	Lewis Cass	1831, 1833
	Carey A. Harris	1836*
	Benjamin F. Butler	1836,* 1837*
Treasury	Samuel D. Ingham	1829
	Asbury Dickins	1831*
	Louis McLane	1831, 1833
	William J. Duane	1833
	Roger B. Taney	1833
	McClintock Young	1834*
	Levi Woodbury	1834
Post. General	John McLean	1829
	William T. Barry	1829, 1833
	Amos Kendall	1835
Atty. General	John M. Berrien	1829
	Roger B. Taney	1831, 1833
	Benjamin F. Butler	1833
Navy	Charles Hay	1829*
	John Branch	1829
	John Boyle	1831*
	Levi Woodbury	1831, 1833
	Mahlon Dickerson	1834

* ad interim.

8th President	**Martin Van Buren**	**1837**
Vice President	Richard M. Johnson	1837
State	John Forsyth	1837
War	Benjamin F. Butler	1837*
	Joel R. Poinsett	1837
Treasury	Levi Woodbury	1837
Post. General	Amos Kendall	1837
	John M. Niles	1840
Atty. General	Benjamin F. Butler	1837
	Felix Grundy	1838
	Henry D. Gilpin	1840
Navy	Mahlon Dickerson	1837
	James K. Paulding	1838

* ad interim.

9th President	**William Henry Harrison**	**1841**
Vice President	John Tyler	1841
State	J. L. Martin	1841*
	Daniel Webster	1841
War	John Bell	1841
Treasury	McClintock Young	1841*
	Thomas Ewing	1841
Post. General	Selah R. Hobbie	1841*
	Francis Granger	1841
Atty. General	John J. Crittenden	1841
Navy	John D. Simms	1841*
	George E. Badger	1841

* ad interim.

10th President	**John Tyler**	**1841**
Vice President	———	
State	Daniel Webster	1841
	Hugh S. Legaré	1843*
	William S. Derrick	1843*
	Abel P. Upshur	1843,* 1843
	John Nelson	1844*
	John C. Calhoun	1844
War	John Bell	1841
	Albert M. Lea	1841*
	John C. Spencer	1841
	John M. Porter	1843
	William Wilkins	1844
Treasury	Thomas Ewing	1841
	McClintock Young	1841, 1843,* 1844*
	Walter Forward	1841
	John C. Spencer	1843
	George M. Bibb	1844
Post. General	Francis Granger	1841
	Selah R. Hobbie	1841*
	Charles A. Wickliffe	1841
Atty. General	John J. Crittenden	1841
	Hugh S. Legaré	1841
	John Nelson	1843
Navy	George E. Badger	1841
	John D. Simms	1841*
	Abel P. Upshur	1841
	David Henshaw	1843
	Thomas W. Gilmer	1844
	Lewis Washington	1844*
	John Y. Mason	1844

* ad interim.

11th President	**James K. Polk**	**1845**
Vice President	George M. Dallas	1845
State	John C. Calhoun	1845
	James Buchanan	1845
War	William Wilkins	1845
	William L. Marcy	1845
Treasury	George M. Bibb	1845
	Robert J. Walker	1845
Post. General	Charles A. Wickliffe	1845
	Cave Johnson	1845
Atty. General	John Nelson	1845
	John Y. Mason	1845
	Nathan Clifford	1846
	Isaac Toucey	1848
Navy	John Y. Mason	1845, 1846
	George Bancroft	1845
	John Y. Mason	1846

* ad interim.

12th President	**Zachary Taylor**	**1849**
Vice President	Millard Fillmore	1849
State	James Buchanan	1849
	John M. Clayton	1849
War	William L. Marcy	1849
	Reverdy Johnson	1849*
	George W. Crawford	1849
Treasury	Robert J. Walker	1849
	McClintock Young	1849*
	William M. Meredith	1849
Post. General	Cave Johnson	1849
	Selah R. Hobbie	1849*
	Jacob Collamer	1849
Atty. General	Isaac Toucey	1849
	Reverdy Johnson	1849
Navy	John Y. Mason	1849
	William B. Preston	1849
Interior[1]	Thomas Ewing	1849

* ad interim.
[1] Est. 3 Mar. 1849.

13th President	**Millard Fillmore**	**1850**
Vice President	————	
State	John M. Clayton	1850
	Daniel Webster	1850
	Charles M. Conrad	1852*
	Edward Everett	1852
War	George W. Crawford	1850
	Samuel J. Anderson	1850*
	Winfield Scott	1850*
	Charles M. Conrad	1850
Treasury	William M. Meredith	1850
	Thomas Corwin	1850
Post. General	Jacob Collamer	1850
	Nathan K. Hall	1850
	Samuel D. Hubbard	1852
Atty. General	Reverdy Johnson	1850
	John J. Crittenden	1850
Navy	William B. Preston	1850
	Lewis Warrington	1850*
	William A. Graham	1850
	John P. Kennedy	1852
Interior	Thomas Ewing	1850
	Daniel C. Goddard	1850, 1850*
	Thomas M.T. McKennan	1850
	Alexander H.H. Stuart	1850

* ad interim.

14th President	**Franklin Pierce**	**1853**
Vice President	William R. King	1853
State	William Hunter	1853*
	William L. Marcy	1853
War	Charles M. Conrad	1853
	Jefferson Davis	1853
	Samuel Cooper	1857*
Treasury	Thomas Corwin	1853
	James Guthrie	1853
Post. General	Samuel D. Hubbard	1853
	James Campbell	1853
Atty. General	John J. Crittenden	1853
	Caleb Cushing	1853
Navy	John P. Kennedy	1853
	James C. Dobbin	1853
Interior	Alexander H.H. Stuart	1853
	Robert McClelland	1853

* ad interim.

15th President	**James Buchanan**	**1857**
Vice President	John C. Breckinridge	1857
State	William L. Marcy	1857
	Lewis Cass	1857
	William Hunter	1860*
	Jeremiah S. Black	1860
War	Samuel Cooper	1857*
	John B. Floyd	1857
	Joseph Holt	1861,* 1861
Treasury	James Guthrie	1857
	Howell Cobb	1857
	Isaac Toucey	1860*
	Philip F. Thomas	1860
	John A. Dix	1861
Post. General	James Campbell	1857
	Aaron V. Brown	1857
	Horatio King	1859,* 1861,* 1861
	Joseph Holt	1859
Atty. General	Caleb Cushing	1857
	Jeremiah S. Black	1857
	Edwin M. Stanton	1860
Navy	James C. Dobbin	1857
	Isaac Toucey	1857
Interior	Robert McClelland	1857
	Jacob Thompson	1857
	Moses Kelly	1861*

* ad interim.

16th President	**Abraham Lincoln**	**1861, 1865**
Vice President	Hannibal Hamlin	1861
	Andrew Johnson	1865
State	Jeremiah S. Black	1861
	William H. Seward	1861, 1865
War	Joseph Holt	1861
	Simon Cameron	1861
	Edwin M. Stanton	1862, 1865
Treasury	John A. Dix	1861
	Salmon P. Chase	1861
	George Harrington	1864,* 1865*
	William P. Fessenden	1864
	Hugh McCulloch	1865
Post. General	Horatio King	1861
	Montgomery Blair	1861
	William Dennison	1864, 1865
Atty. General	Edwin M. Stanton	1861
	Edward Bates	1861
	James Speed	1864, 1865
Navy	Isaac Toucey	1861
	Gideon Welles	1861, 1865
Interior	Moses Kelly	1861*
	Caleb B. Smith	1861
	John P. Usher	1863,* 1863, 1865

* ad interim.

17th President	**Andrew Johnson**	**1865**
Vice President	———	
State	William H. Seward	1865
War	Edwin M. Stanton	1865, 1868
	Ulysses S. Grant	1867*
	John M. Schofield	1868
Treasury	Hugh McCulloch	1865
Post. General	William Dennison	1865
	Alexander W. Randall	1866,* 1866

* ad interim.

Atty. General	James Speed	1865
	J. Hubley Ashton	1866*
	Henry Stanbery	1866
	Orville H. Browning	1868*
	William M. Evarts	1868
Navy	Gideon Welles	1865
Interior	John P. Usher	1865
	James Harlan	1865
	Orville H. Browning	1866

* ad interim.

18th President	**Ulysses S. Grant**	**1869, 1873**
Vice President	Schuyler Colfax	1869
	Henry Wilson	1875
State	William H. Seward	1869
	Elihu B. Washburne	1869
	Hamilton Fish	1869, 1873
War	John M. Schofield	1869
	John A. Rawlins	1869
	William T. Sherman	1869
	William W. Belknap	1869, 1873
	George M. Robeson	1876*
	Alphonso Taft	1876
	James D. Cameron	1876
Treasury	Hugh McCulloch	1869
	John F. Hartley	1869*
	George S. Boutwell	1869, 1873
	William A. Richardson	1873
	Benjamin H. Bristow	1874
	Charles F. Conant	1876*
	Lot M. Morrill	1876
Post. General	St. John B.L. Skinner	1869*
	John A.J. Creswell	1869, 1873
	James W. Marshall	1874
	Marshall Jewell	1874
	James N. Tyner	1876
Atty. General	William M. Evarts	1869
	J. Hubley Ashton	1869*
	Ebenezer R. Hoar	1869
	Amos T. Akerman	1870
	George H. Williams	1872, 1873
	Edwards Pierrepont	1875
	Alphonso Taft	1876
Navy	William Faxon	1869*
	Adolph E. Borie	1869
	George Robeson	1869, 1873
Interior	William T. Otto	1869*
	Jacob D. Cox	1869
	Columbus Delano	1870, 1873
	Benjamin R. Cowen	1875*
	Zachariah Chandler	1875

* ad interim.

19th President	**Rutherford B. Hayes**	**1877**
Vice President	William A. Wheeler	1877
State	Hamilton Fish	1877
	William M. Evarts	1877
War	James D. Cameron	1877
	George W. McCrary	1877
	Alexander Ramsey	1879
Treasury	Lot M. Morrill	1877
	John Sherman	1877

Post. General	James N. Tyner	1877
	David M. Key	1877
	Horace Maynard	1880
Atty. General	Alphonso Taft	1877
	Charles Devens	1877
Navy	George M. Robeson	1877
	Richard W. Thompson	1877
	Alexander Ramsey	1880*
	Nathan Goff, Jr.	1881
Interior	Zachariah Chandler	1877
	Carl Schurz	1877

* ad interim.

20th President	**James A. Garfield**	**1881**
Vice President	Chester A. Arthur	1881
State	William M. Evarts	1881
	James G. Blaine	1881
War	Alexander Ramsey	1881
	Robert T. Lincoln	1881
Treasury	Henry F. French	1881*
	William Windom	1881
Post. General	Horace Maynard	1881
	Thomas L. James	1881
Atty. General	Charles Devens	1881
	Wayne MacVeagh	1881
Navy	Nathan Goff, Jr.	1881
	William H. Hunt	1881
Interior	Carl Schurz	1881
	Samuel J. Kirkwood	1881

* ad interim.

21st President	**Chester A. Arthur**	**1881**
Vice President	—	
State	James G. Blaine	1881
	Frederick T. Frelinghuysen	1881
War	Robert T. Lincoln	1881
Treasury	William Windom	1881
	Charles J. Folger	1881
	Charles E. Coon	1884*
	Henry F. French	1884*
	Walter Q. Gresham	1884
	Hugh McCulloch	1884
Post. General	Thomas L. James	1881
	Timothy O. Howe	1882
	Frank Hatton	1883,* 1884*
	Walter Q. Gresham	1883
Atty. General	Wayne MacVeagh	1881
	Samuel F. Phillips	1881*
	Benjamin H. Brewster	1882
Navy	William H. Hunt	1881
	William E. Chandler	1882
Interior	Samuel J. Kirkwood	1881
	Henry M. Teller	1882

* ad interim.

22nd President	**Grover Cleveland**	**1885**
Vice President	Thomas A. Hendricks	1885
State	Frederick T. Frelinghuysen	1885
	Thomas F. Bayard	1885
War	Robert T. Lincoln	1885
	William C. Endicott	1885
Treasury	Hugh McCulloch	1885
	Daniel Manning	1885
	Charles S. Fairchild	1887
Post. General	Frank Hatton	1885

	William F. Vilas	1885
	Don M. Dickinson	1888
Atty. General	Benjamin H. Brewster	1885
	Augustus H. Garland	1885
Navy	William E. Chandler	1885
	William C. Whitney	1885
Interior	Merritt L. Joslyn	1885*
	Lucius Q. C. Lamar	1885
	Henry L. Muldrow	1888*
	William F. Vilas	1888
Agriculture[1]	Norman J. Colman	1889

* ad interim.
[1] Est. 11 Feb. 1889.

23rd President	**Benjamin Harrison**	**1889**
Vice President	Levi P. Morton	1889
State	Thomas F. Bayard	1889
	James G. Blaine	1889
	William F. Wharton	1892,* 1893*
	John W. Foster	1892
War	William C. Endicott	1889
	Redfield Proctor	1889
	Lewis A. Grant	1891*
	Stephen B. Elkins	1891
Treasury	Charles S. Fairchild	1889
	William Windom	1889
	Allured B. Nettleton	1891*
	Charles Foster	1891
Post. General	Don M. Dickinson	1889
	John Wanamaker	1889
Atty. General	Augustus H. Garland	1889
	William H. H. Miller	1889
Navy	William C. Whitney	1889
	Benjamin F. Tracy	1889
Interior	William F. Vilas	1889
	John W. Noble	1889
Agriculture	Norman J. Colman	1889
	Jeremiah M. Rusk	1889

* ad interim.

24th President	**Grover Cleveland**	**1893**
Vice President	Adlai E. Stevenson	1893
State	William F. Wharton	1893
	Walter Q. Gresham	1893
	Edwin F. Uhl	1895*
	Alvey A. Adee	1895*
	Richard Olney	1895
War	Stephen B. Elkins	1893
	Daniel S. Lamont	1893
Treasury	Charles Foster	1893
	John G. Carlisle	1893
Post. General	John Wanamaker	1893
	Wilson S. Bissell	1893
	William L. Wilson	1895
Atty. General	William H.H. Miller	1893
	Richard Olney	1893
	Judson Harmon	1895
Navy	Benjamin F. Tracy	1893
	Hilary A. Herbert	1893
Interior	John W. Noble	1893
	Hoke Smith	1893
	John M. Reynolds	1896*
	David R. Francis	1896
Agriculture	Jeremiah M. Rusk	1893
	Julius Sterling Morton	1893

* ad interim.

25th President	William McKinley	1897, 1901
Vice President	Garret Hobart	1897
	Theodore Roosevelt	1901
State	Richard Olney	1897
	John Sherman	1897
	William R. Day	1898
	Alvey A. Adee	1898*
	John M. Hay	1898, 1901
War	Daniel S. Lamont	1897
	Russell A. Alger	1897
	Elihu Root	1899, 1901
Treasury	John G. Carlisle	1897
	Lyman J. Gage	1897, 1901
Post. General	William L. Wilson	1897
	James A. Gary	1897
	Charles Emory Smith	1898, 1901
Atty. General	Judson Harmon	1897
	Joseph McKenna	1897
	John K. Richards	1898,* 1901*
	John W. Griggs	1898, 1901
	Philander C. Knox	1901
Navy	Hilary A. Herbert	1897
	John D. Long	1897
Interior	David R. Francis	1897
	Cornelius N. Bliss	1897
	Ethan A. Hitchcock	1899, 1901
Agriculture	Julius Sterling Morton	1897
	James Wilson	1897

* ad interim.

26th President	Theodore Roosevelt	1901, 1905
Vice President	Charles Warren Fairbanks	1905
State	John M. Hay	1901, 1905
	Francis B. Loomis	1905*
	Elihu Root	1905
	Robert Bacon	1909
War	Elihu Root	1901
	William Howard Taft	1904, 1905
	Luke E. Wright	1908
Treasury	Lyman J. Gage	1902
	Leslie M. Shaw	1902, 1905
	George B. Cortelyou	1907
Post. General	Charles Emory Smith	1901
	Harry C. Payne	1902
	Robert J. Wynne	1904, 1905
	George B. Cortelyou	1905
	George von L. Meyer	1907
Atty. General	Philander C. Knox	1901
	William H. Moody	1904, 1905
	Charles J. Bonaparte	1906
Navy	John D. Long	1901
	William H. Moody	1902
	Paul Morton	1904, 1905
	Charles J. Bonaparte	1905
	Victor H. Metcalf	1906
	Truman H. Newberry	1908
Interior	Ethan A. Hitchcock	1901, 1905
	James R. Garfield	1907
Agriculture	James Wilson	1901, 1905
Comm. & Labor[1]	George B. Cortelyou	1903
	Victor H. Metcalf	1904, 1905
	Oscar S. Straus	1906

* ad interim.
[1] Est. 14 Feb. 1903.

27th President	**William Howard Taft**	**1909**
Vice President	James S. Sherman	1909
State	Robert Bacon	1909
	Philander C. Knox	1909
War	Luke E. Wright	1909
	Jacob M. Dickinson	1909
	Henry L. Stimson	1911
Treasury	George B. Cortelyou	1909
	Franklin MacVeagh	1909
Post. General	George von L. Meyer	1909
	Frank H. Hitchcock	1909
Atty. General	Charles J. Bonaparte	1909
	George W. Wickersham	1909
Navy	Truman H. Newberry	1909
	George von L. Meyer	1909
Interior	James R. Garfield	1909
	Richard A. Ballinger	1909
	Walter Lowrie Fisher	1911
Agriculture	James Wilson	1909
Comm. & Labor	Oscar S. Straus	1909
	Charles Nagel	1909

* ad interim.

28th President	**Woodrow Wilson**	**1913, 1917**
Vice President	Thomas R. Marshall	1913, 1917
State	Philander C. Knox	1913
	Wm. Jennings Bryan	1913
	Robert Lansing	1915,* 1915, 1917
	Frank L. Polk	1920*
	Bainbridge Colby	1920
War	Henry L. Stimson	1913
	Lindley M. Garrison	1913
	Hugh L. Scott	1916*
	Newton D. Baker	1916, 1917
Treasury	Franklin MacVeagh	1913
	William Gibbs McAdoo	1913, 1917
	Carter Glass	1918
	David F. Houston	1920
Post. General	Frank H. Hitchcock	1913
	Albert Sidney Burleson	1913, 1917, 1918
Atty. General	George W. Wickersham	1913
	James Clark McReynolds	1913
	Thomas Watt Gregory	1914, 1917
	A. Mitchell Palmer	1919
Navy	George von L. Meyer	1913
	Josephus Daniels	1913, 1917
Interior	Walter Lowrie Fisher	1913
	Franklin Knight Lane	1913, 1917
	John Barton Payne	1920
Agriculture	James Wilson	1913
	David Franklin Houston	1913, 1917
	Edwin T. Meredith	1920
Commerce[1]	Charles Nagel	1913
	William C. Redfield	1913
Labor[2]	Charles Nagel	1913
	William Bauchop Wilson	1913

* ad interim.
[1] Est. 4 Mar. 1913, divided from Labor.
[2] Est. 4 Mar. 1913, divided from Commerce.

29th President	**Warren G. Harding**	**1921**
Vice President	Calvin Coolidge	1921
State	Bainbridge Colby	1921
	Charles Evans Hughes	1921

War	Newton D. Baker	1921
	John W. Weeks	1921
Treasury	David F. Houston	1921
	Andrew W. Mellon	1921
Post. General	Albert Sidney Burleson	1921
	Will H. Hays	1921
	Hubert Work	1922
	Harry S. New	1923
Atty. General	A. Mitchell Palmer	1921
	Harry M. Dougherty	1921
Navy	Josephus Daniels	1921
	Edwin Denby	1921
Interior	John Barton Payne	1921
	Albert B. Fall	1921
	Hubert Work	1923
Agriculture	Edwin T. Meredith	1921
	Henry C. Wallace	1921
Commerce	Joshua Willis Alexander	1921
	Herbert C. Hoover	1921
Labor	William Bauchop Wilson	1921
	James J. Davis	1921

* ad interim.

30th President	**Calvin Coolidge**	**1923, 1925**
Vice President	Charles G. Dawes	1925
State	Charles Evans Hughes	1923, 1925
	Frank B. Kellogg	1925
War	John W. Weeks	1923, 1925
	Dwight F. Davis	1925
Treasury	Andrew W. Mellon	1923, 1925
Post. General	Harry S. New	1923, 1925
Atty. General	Harry M. Dougherty	1923
	Harlan Fiske Stone	1924
Navy	Edwin Denby	1923
	Curtis D. Wilbur	1924, 1925
Interior	Hubert Work	1923, 1925
	Roy O. West	1929
Agriculture	Henry C. Wallace	1923
	Howard M. Gore	1924,* 1924, 1925
	William M. Jardine	1925
Commerce	Herbert C. Hoover	1923, 1925
	William F. Whiting	1928,* 1928
Labor	James J. Davis	1923, 1925

* ad interim.

31st President	**Herbert C. Hoover**	**1929**
Vice President	Charles Curtis	1929
State	Frank B. Kellogg	1929
	Henry L. Stimson	1929
War	Dwight F. Davis	1929
	James W. Good	1929
	Patrick J. Hurley	1929
Treasury	Andrew W. Mellon	1929
	Ogden L. Mills	1932
Post. General	Harry S. New	1929
	Walter F. Brown	1929
Atty. General	John G. Sargent	1929
	James DeWitt Mitchell	1929
Navy	Curtis D. Wilbur	1929
	Charles F. Adams	1929
Interior	Roy O. West	1929
	Ray L. Wilbur	1929

Agriculture	William M. Jardine	1929
	Arthur M. Hyde	1929
Commerce	William F. Whiting	1929
	Robert P. Lamont	1929
	Roy D. Chapin	1932,* 1932
Labor	James J. Davis	1929
	William N. Doak	1930

* ad interim.

32d President	**Franklin D. Roosevelt**	**1933, 1937, 1941, 1945**
Vice President	John N. Garner	1933, 1937
	Henry A. Wallace	1941
	Harry S. Truman	1945
State	Cordell Hull	1933, 1937, 1941
	Edward R. Stettinius	1944, 1945
War	George H. Dern	1933, 1937
	Harry H. Woodring	1936,* 1937
	Henry L. Stimson	1940, 1941, 1945
Treasury	William H. Woodin	1933
	Henry Morgenthau, Jr.	1934,* 1934, 1937, 1941, 1945
Post. General	James A. Farley	1933, 1937
	Frank C. Walker	1940, 1941, 1945
Atty. General	Homer S. Cummings	1933, 1937
	Frank Murphy	1939,* 1939
	Robert H. Jackson	1940, 1941
	Francis Biddle	1941, 1945
Navy	Claude A. Swanson	1933, 1937
	Charles Edison	1939,* 1940,* 1940
	Frank Knox	1940, 1941
	James V. Forrestal	1944, 1945
Interior	Harold L. Ickes	1933, 1937, 1941, 1945
Agriculture	Henry A. Wallace	1933, 1937
	Claude R. Wickard	1940, 1941, 1945
Commerce	Daniel C. Roper	1933, 1937
	Harry L. Hopkins	1938,* 1939
	Jesse H. Jones	1940, 1941, 1945
	Henry A. Wallace	1945
Labor	Frances Perkins	1933, 1937, 1941, 1945

* ad interim.

33d President	**Harry S. Truman**	**1945, 1949**
Vice President	Alben W. Barkley	1949
State	Edward R. Stettinius	1945
	James F. Byrnes	1945
	George C. Marshall	1947
	Dean G. Acheson	1949
War[1]	Henry L. Stimson	1945
	Robert P. Patterson	1945
	Kenneth C. Royall	1947
Treasury	Henry Morgenthau, Jr.	1945
	Fred M. Vinson	1945
	John W. Snyder	1946, 1949
Post. General	Frank C. Walker	1945
	Robert E. Hannegan	1945
	Jesse M. Donaldson	1947, 1949
Atty. General	Francis Biddle	1945
	Tom C. Clark	1945, 1949
	J. Howard McGrath	1949
	James P. McGranery	1952
Navy[1]	James V. Forrestal	1945
Interior	Harold L. Ickes	1945
	Julius A. Krug	1946, 1949
	Oscar L. Chapman	1949,* 1950,* 1950

Agriculture	Claude R. Wickard	1945
	Clinton P. Anderson	1945
	Charles F. Brennan	1948
Commerce	Henry A. Wallace	1945
	W. Averell Harriman	1946,* 1947,* 1947
	Charles Sawyer	1948, 1949
Labor	Frances Perkins	1945
	Lewis B. Schwellenbach	1945
	Maurice J. Tobin	1948,* 1949,* 1949
Defense[1]	James Forrestal	1947
	Louis A. Johnson	1949
	George C. Marshall	1950
	Robert A. Lovett	1951

* ad interim.
[1] Dept. of Defense est. 26 July 1947, incorporating Dept. of War and Dept. of Navy.

34th President	**Dwight D. Eisenhower**	**1953, 1957**
Vice President	Richard M. Nixon	1953, 1957
State	John Foster Dulles	1953, 1957
	Christian A. Herter	1959
Treasury	George M. Humphrey	1953, 1957
	Robert A. Anderson	1957
Post. General	Arthur E. Summerfield	1953, 1957
Atty. General	Herbert Brownell, Jr.	1953, 1957
	William P. Rogers	1958,* 1958
Interior	Douglas McKay	1953
	Frederick A. Seaton	1956, 1957
Agriculture	Ezra Taft Benson	1953, 1957
Commerce	Sinclair Weeks	1953, 1957
	Lewis L. Strauss	1958*
	Frederick H. Mueller	1959,* 1959
Labor	Martin P. Durkin	1953
	James P. Mitchell	1953,* 1954,* 1954, 1957
Defense	Charles E. Wilson	1953, 1957
	Neil H. McElroy	1957
	Thomas S. Gates, Jr.	1959,* 1960,* 1960
H.E.W.[1]	Oveta Culp Hobby	1953
	Marion B. Folsom	1955, 1957
	Arthur S. Flemming	1958

* ad interim.
[1] Est. 1 Apr. 1953.

35th President	**John F. Kennedy**	**1961**
Vice President	Lyndon B. Johnson	1961
State	Dean Rusk	1961
Treasury	C. Douglas Dillon	1961
Post. General	J. Edward Day	1961
	John A. Gronouski	1963
Atty. General	Robert F. Kennedy	1961
Interior	Stewart L. Udall	1961
Agriculture	Orville L. Freeman	1961
Commerce	Luther H. Hodges	1961
Labor	Arthur J. Goldberg	1961
	W. Willard Wirtz	1962
Defense	Robert S. McNamara	1961
H.E.W.	Abraham A. Ribicoff	1961
	Anthony J. Celebrezze	1962

36th President	Lyndon B. Johnson	1963, 1965
Vice President	Hubert H. Humphrey	1965
State	Dean Rusk	1963, 1965
Treasury	C. Douglas Dillon	1963, 1965
	Henry H. Fowler	1965
Post. General	John S. Gronouski	1963, 1965
	Lawrence O'Brien	1965
Atty. General	Robert F. Kennedy	1963
	Nicholas Katzenbach	1965
	Ramsey Clark	1967
Interior	Stewart L. Udall	1963, 1965
Agriculture	Orville L. Freeman	1963, 1965
Commerce	Luther H. Hodges	1963
	John T. Conner	1965
	Alexander B. Trowbridge	1967
	C. R. Smith	1968
Labor	W. Willard Wirtz	1963, 1965
Defense	Robert S. McNamara	1963, 1965
	Clark Clifford	1968
H.E.W.	Anthony J. Celebrezze	1963, 1965
	John W. Gardner	1965
	Wilbur J. Cohen	1968
H.U.D.[1]	Robert C. Weaver	1966
Transport.[2]	Alan S. Boyd	1967

[1] Est. 9 Sept. 1965.
[2] Est. 1 Apr. 1967.

37th President	Richard M. Nixon	1969, 1973
Vice President	Spiro T. Agnew	1969, 1973
	Gerald R. Ford	1973
State	William P. Rogers	1969
	Henry A. Kissinger	1973
Treasury	David M. Kennedy	1969
	John B. Connally	1971
	George F. Shultz	1972
	William E. Simon	1974
Post. General[1]	Winton M. Blount	1969
Atty. General	John N. Mitchell	1969
	Richard G. Kleindienst	1972
	Elliot L. Richardson	1973
	William B. Saxbe	1973
Interior	Walter J. Hickel	1969
	Rogers C.B. Morton	1971
Agriculture	Clifford M. Hardin	1969
	Earl L. Butz	1971
Commerce	Maurice H. Stans	1969
	Peter G. Peterson	1972
	Frederick B. Dent	1973
Labor	George P. Shultz	1969
	James D. Hodgson	1970
	Peter J. Brennan	1973
Defense	Melvin R. Laird	1969
	Elliot L. Richardson	1973
	James R. Schlesinger	1973
H.E.W.	Robert H. Finch	1969
	Elliot L. Richardson	1970
	Casper W. Weinberger	1973

[1] On 1 July 1971 the Post Office Department became the semi-independent U.S. Postal Service with non-Cabinet status.

H.U.D.	George W. Romney	1969
	James T. Lynn	1973
Transport.	John A. Volpe	1969
	Claude S. Brinegar	1973

38th President	**Gerald R. Ford**	**1974**
Vice President	Nelson A. Rockefeller	1974
State	Henry A. Kissinger	1974
Treasury	William E. Simon	1974
Atty. General	William B. Saxbe	1974
	Edward H. Levi	1975
Interior	Rogers C.B. Morton	1974
	Stanley K. Hathaway	1975
	Thomas S. Kleppe	1975
Agriculture	Earl L. Butz	1974
	John A. Knebel	1976
Commerce	Frederick B. Dent	1974
	Rogers C.B. Morton	1975
	Elliot L. Richardson	1975
Labor	Peter J. Brennan	1974
	John T. Dunlop	1975
	W. J. Usery, Jr.	1976
Defense	James R. Schlesinger	1974
	Donald H. Rumsfeld	1975
H.E.W.	Caspar W. Weinberger	1974
	F. David Mathews	1975
H.U.D.	James T. Lynn	1974
	Carla Anderson Hills	1975
Transport.	Claude S. Brinegar	1974
	William T. Coleman, Jr.	1975

* ad interim.

39th President	**Jimmy Carter**	**1977**
Vice President	Walter F. Mondale	1977
State	Cyrus R. Vance	1977
	Edmund S. Muskie	1980
Treasury	W. Michael Blumenthal	1977
	G. William Miller	1979
Atty. General	Griffin B. Bell	1977
	Benjamin R. Civiletti	1979
Interior	Cecil D. Andrus	1977
Agriculture	Bob Bergland	1977
Commerce	Juanita M. Kreps	1977
	Philip M. Klutznick	1979
Labor	F. Ray Marshall	1977
Defense	Harold Brown	1977
H.E.W.[1]	Joseph A. Califano, Jr.	1977
	Patricia Roberts Harris	1979
H.U.D.	Patricia Roberts Harris	1977
	Moon Landrieu	1979

[1] Divided 17 Oct. 1979 into Education and Health and Human Services.

Transportation	Brock Adams	1977
	Neil E. Goldschmidt	1979
Energy[2]	James R. Schlesinger, Jr.	1977
	Robert W. Duncan	1979
Health and Human Services[3]	Patricia Roberts Harris	1979
Education[4]	Shirley M. Hufstedler	1979

[2] Est. 4 Aug. 1977.
[3] Est. 17 Oct. 1979, divided from Education.
[4] Est. 17 Oct. 1979, divided from Health & Welfare.

40th President	**Ronald Reagan**	**1981**
Vice President	George Bush	1981
State	Alexander M. Haig, Jr.	1981
Treasury	Donald T. Regan	1981
Atty. General	William French Smith	1981
Interior	James G. Watt	1981
Agriculture	John R. Block	1981
Commerce	Malcolm Baldridge	1981
Labor	Raymond J. Donovan	1981
Defense	Caspar W. Weinberger	1981
H.U.D.	Samuel R. Pierce, Jr.	1981
Transportation	Andrew L. Lewis	1981
Energy	James B. Edwards	1981
Health and Human Services	Richard S. Schweiker	1981
Education	Terrel H. Bell	1981

PARTY STRENGTH IN CONGRESS

[Ad-Administration; AM-Anti-Masonic; C-Coalition; D-Democratic; DR-Democratic-Republican; F-Federalist;
J-Jacksonian; NR-National Republican; Op-Opposition; R-Republican; U-Unionist; W-Whig]

Congress	Year	President		Senate					House			
				Majority Party		Principal Minority Party		Others	Majority Party		Principal Minority Party		Others
1	1789–91	F	(Washington)	Ad	17	Op	9	0	Ad	38	Op	26	0
2	1791–93	F	(Washington)	F	16	DR	13	0	F	37	DR	33	0
3	1793–95	F	(Washington)	F	17	DR	13	0	DR	57	F	48	0
4	1795–97	F	(Washington)	F	19	DR	13	0	F	54	DR	52	0
5	1797–99	F	(J. Adams)	F	20	DR	12	0	F	58	DR	48	0
6	1799–01	F	(J. Adams)	F	19	DR	13	0	F	64	DR	42	0
7	1801–03	DR	(Jefferson)	DR	18	F	14	0	DR	69	F	36	0
8	1803–05	DR	(Jefferson)	DR	25	F	9	0	DR	102	F	39	0
9	1805–07	DR	(Jefferson)	DR	27	F	7	0	DR	116	F	25	0
10	1807–09	DR	(Jefferson)	DR	28	F	6	0	DR	118	F	24	0
11	1809–11	DR	(Madison)	DR	28	F	6	0	DR	94	F	48	0
12	1811–13	DR	(Madison)	DR	30	F	6	0	DR	108	F	36	0
13	1813–15	DR	(Madison)	DR	27	F	9	0	DR	112	F	68	0
14	1815–17	DR	(Madison)	DR	25	F	11	0	DR	117	F	65	0
15	1817–19	DR	(Monroe)	DR	34	F	10	0	DR	141	F	42	0

PARTY STRENGTH IN CONGRESS

[Ad-Administration; AM-Anti-Masonic; C-Coalition; D-Democratic; DR-Democratic-Republican; F-Federalist; J-Jacksonian; NR-National Republican; Op-Opposition; R-Republican; U-Unionist; W-Whig]

Congress	Year	President	Senate				House			
			Majority Party		Principal Minority Party	Others	Majority Party		Principal Minority Party	Others
16	1819–21	DR (Monroe)	DR	35	F	7	0	DR	156	F	27	0
17	1821–23	DR (Monroe)	DR	44	F	4	0	DR	158	F	25	0
18	1823–25	DR (Monroe)	DR	44	F	4	0	DR	187	F	26	0
19	1825–27	C (J. Q. Adams)	Ad	26	J	20	0	Ad	105	J	97	0
20	1827–29	C (J. Q. Adams)	J	28	Ad	20	0	J	119	Ad	94	0
21	1829–31	D (Jackson)	D	26	NR	22	0	D	139	NR	74	0
22	1831–33	D (Jackson)	D	25	NR	21	2	D	141	NR	58	14
23	1833–35	D (Jackson)	D	20	NR	20	8	D	147	AM	53	60
24	1835–37	D (Jackson)	D	27	W	25	0	D	145	W	98	0
25	1837–39	D (Van Buren)	D	30	W	18	4	D	108	W	107	24
26	1839–41	D (Van Buren)	D	28	W	22	0	D	124	W	118	0
27	1841–43	W (W. Harrison)									
		W (Tyler)	W	28	D	22	2	W	133	D	102	6
28	1843–45	W (Tyler)	W	28	D	25	1	D	142	W	79	1
29	1845–47	D (Polk)	D	31	W	25	0	D	143	W	77	6
30	1847–49	D (Polk)	D	36	W	21	1	W	115	D	108	4
31	1849–51	W (Taylor)									
		W (Filmore)	D	35	W	25	2	D	112	W	109	9
32	1851–53	W (Filmore)	D	35	W	24	3	D	140	W	88	5
33	1853–55	D (Pierce)	D	38	W	22	2	D	159	W	71	4
34	1855–57	D (Pierce)	D	40	R	15	5	R	108	D	83	43
35	1857–59	D (Buchanan)	D	36	R	20	8	D	118	R	92	26
36	1859–61	D (Buchanan)	D	36	R	26	4	R	114	D	92	31
37	1861–63	R (Lincoln)	R	31	D	10	8	R	105	D	43	30
38	1863–65	R (Lincoln)	R	36	D	9	5	R	102	D	75	9
39	1865–67	R (Lincoln)									
		R (Johnson)	U	42	D	10	0	U	149	D	42	0
40	1867–69	R (Johnson)	R	42	D	11	0	R	143	D	49	0
41	1869–71	R (Grant)	R	56	D	11	0	R	149	D	63	0
42	1871–73	R (Grant)	R	52	D	17	5	D	134	R	104	5
43	1873–75	R (Grant)	R	49	D	19	5	R	194	D	92	14
44	1875–77	R (Grant)	R	45	D	29	2	D	169	R	109	14
45	1877–79	R (Hayes)	R	39	D	36	1	D	153	R	140	0
46	1879–81	R (Hayes)	D	42	R	33	1	D	149	R	130	14
47	1881–83	R (Garfield)									
		R (Arthur)	R	37	D	37	1	R	147	D	135	11
48	1883–85	R (Arthur)	R	38	D	36	2	D	197	R	118	10
49	1885–87	D (Cleveland)	R	43	D	34	0	D	183	R	140	2
50	1887–89	D (Cleveland)	R	39	D	37	0	D	169	R	152	4
51	1889–91	R (B. Harrison)	R	39	D	37	0	R	166	D	159	0
52	1891–93	R (B. Harrison)	R	47	D	39	2	D	235	R	88	9
53	1893–95	D (Cleveland)	D	44	R	38	3	D	218	R	127	11
54	1895–97	D (Cleveland)	R	43	D	39	6	R	244	D	105	7
55	1897–99	R (McKinley)	R	47	D	34	7	R	204	D	113	40
56	1899–01	R (McKinley)	R	53	D	26	8	R	185	D	163	9
57	1901–03	R (McKinley)									
		R (T. Roosevelt)	R	55	D	31	4	R	197	D	151	9
58	1903–05	R (T. Roosevelt)	R	57	D	33	0	R	208	D	178	0
59	1905–07	R (T. Roosevelt)	R	57	D	33	0	R	250	D	136	0
60	1907–09	R (T. Roosevelt)	R	61	D	31	0	R	222	D	164	0
61	1909–11	R (Taft)	R	61	D	32	0	R	219	D	172	0
62	1911–13	R (Taft)	R	51	D	41	0	D	228	R	161	1
63	1913–15	D (Wilson)	D	51	R	44	1	D	291	R	127	17
64	1915–17	D (Wilson)	D	56	R	40	0	D	230	R	196	9
65	1917–19	D (Wilson)	D	53	R	42	0	D	216	R	210	6
66	1919–21	D (Wilson)	R	49	D	47	0	R	240	D	190	3
67	1921–23	R (Harding)	R	59	D	37	0	R	303	D	131	1
68	1923–25	R (Coolidge)	R	51	D	43	2	R	225	D	205	5
69	1925–27	R (Coolidge)	R	56	D	39	1	R	247	D	183	4
70	1927–29	R (Coolidge)	R	49	D	46	1	R	237	D	195	3
71	1929–31	R (Hoover)	R	56	D	39	1	R	267	D	167	1

PARTY STRENGTH IN CONGRESS

[Ad-Administration; AM-Anti-Masonic; C-Coalition; D-Democratic; DR-Democratic-Republican; F-Federalist; J-Jacksonian; NR-National Republican; Op-Opposition; R-Republican; U-Unionist; W-Whig]

Congress	Year	President		Senate			House		
				Majority Party	Principal Minority Party	Others	Majority Party	Principal Minority Party	Others
72	1931–33	R (Hoover)		R 48	D 47	1	D 220	R 214	1
73	1933–35	D (F. Roosevelt)		D 60	R 35	1	D 310	R 117	5
74	1935–37	D (F. Roosevelt)		D 69	R 25	2	D 319	R 103	10
75	1937–39	D (F. Roosevelt)		D 76	R 16	4	D 331	R 89	13
76	1939–41	D (F. Roosevelt)		D 69	R 23	4	D 261	R 164	4
77	1941–43	D (F. Roosevelt)		D 66	R 28	2	D 268	R 162	5
78	1943–45	D (F. Roosevelt)		D 58	R 37	1	D 218	R 208	4
79	1945–47	D (F. Roosevelt) D (Truman)		D 56	R 38	1	D 242	R 190	2
80	1947–49	D (Truman)		D 45	R 51	0	D 188	R 245	1
81	1949–51	D (Truman)		D 54	R 42	0	D 263	R 171	1
82	1951–53	D (Truman)		D 49	R 47	0	D 234	R 199	1
83	1953–55	R (Eisenhower)		R 48	D 47	1	R 221	D 211	1
84	1955–57	R (Eisenhower)		D 48	R 47	1	D 232	R 203	0
85	1957–59	R (Eisenhower)		D 49	R 47	0	D 233	R 200	0
86	1959–61	R (Eisenhower)		D 65	R 35	0	D 284	R 153	0
87	1961–63	D (Kennedy)		D 65	R 35	0	D 263	R 174	0
88	1963–65	D (Kennedy) D (Johnson)		D 67	R 33	0	D 258	R 177	0
89	1965–67	D (Johnson)		D 68	R 32	0	D 295	R 140	0
90	1967–69	D (Johnson)		D 64	R 36	0	D 247	R 187	0
91	1969–71	R (Nixon)		D 57	R 43	0	D 243	R 192	0
92	1971–73	R (Nixon)		D 54	R 44	2	D 254	R 180	0
93	1973–75	R (Nixon–Ford)		D 56	R 44	0	D 239	R 192	1
94	1975–77	R (Ford)		D 60	R 37	2	D 291	R 144	0
95	1977–79	D (Carter)		D 61	R 38	1	D 292	R 143	0
96	1979–81	D (Carter)		D 58	R 41	1	D 276	R 157	0
97	1981–	R (Reagan)		R 53	D 46	1	D 242	R 192	1

JUSTICES OF THE UNITED STATES SUPREME COURT

Name Chief Justices in italics	Service Term	Yrs.	Name Chief Justices in italics	Service Term	Yrs.
John Jay, N.Y	1789–1795	6	Henry B. Brown, Mich.	1890–1906	16
John Rutledge, S.C.	1789–1791	2	George Shiras, Jr., Pa.	1892–1903	11
William Cushing, Mass.	1789–1810	21	Howell E. Jackson, Tenn.	1893–1895	2
James Wilson, Pa.	1789–1798	9	Edward D. White, La.	1894–1910	16
John Blair, Va.	1789–1796	7	Rufus W. Peckham, N.Y.	1895–1910	14
Robert H. Harrison, Md.	1789–1790	1	Joseph McKenna, Cal.	1898–1925	27
James Iredell, N.C.	1790–1799	9	Oliver W. Holmes, Jr., Mass.	1902–1932	29
Thomas Johnson, Md.	1791–1793	2	William R. Day, Ohio	1903–1922	19
William Paterson, N.J.	1793–1806	13	William H. Moody, Mass.	1906–1910	4
John Rutledge, S.C.*	1795–1795	..	Horace H. Lurton, Tenn.	1910–1914	5
Samuel Chase, Md.	1796–1811	15	Charles E. Hughes, N.Y.	1910–1916	6
Oliver Ellsworth, Conn.	1796–1799	4	Willis Van Devanter, Wyo.	1911–1937	26
Bushrod Washington, Va.	1798–1829	31	Joseph R. Lamar, Ga.	1911–1916	6
Alfred Moore, N.C.	1799–1804	5	*Edward D. White,* La.	1910–1921	11
John Marshall, Va.	1801–1835	34	Mahlon Pitney, N.J.	1912–1922	12
William Johnson, S.C.	1804–1834	30	Jas. C. McReynolds, Tenn.	1914–1941	27
Henry B. Livingston, N.Y.	1806–1823	17	Louis D. Brandeis, Mass.	1916–1939	23
Thomas Todd, Ky.	1807–1826	19	John H. Clarke, Ohio	1916–1922	6
Joseph Story, Mass.	1811–1845	34	*William H. Taft,* Conn.	1921–1930	9
Gabriel Duval, Md.	1811–1836	25	George Sutherland, Utah	1922–1938	16
Smith Thompson, N.Y.	1823–1843	20	Pierce Butler, Minn.	1922–1939	17
Robert Trimble, Ky.	1826–1828	2	Edward T. Sanford, Tenn.	1923–1930	7
John McLean, Ohio	1829–1861	32	Harlan F. Stone, N.Y.	1925–1941	16
Henry Baldwin, Pa.	1830–1844	14	*Charles E. Hughes,* N.Y.	1930–1941	11
James M. Wayne, Ga.	1835–1867	32	Owen J. Roberts, Penn.	1930–1945	15
Roger B. Taney, Md.	1836–1864	28	Benjamin N. Cardozo, N.Y.	1932–1938	6
Philip P. Barbour, Va.	1836–1841	5	Hugo Black, Ala.	1937–1971	34
John Catron, Tenn.	1837–1865	28	Stanley Reed, Ky.	1938–1957	19
John McKinley, Ala.	1837–1852	15	Felix Frankfurter, Mass.	1939–1962	23
Peter V. Daniel, Va.	1841–1860	19	William O. Douglas, Conn.	1939–1975	36
Samuel Nelson, N.Y.	1845–1872	27	Frank Murphy, Mich.	1940–1949	9
Levi Woodbury, N.H.	1845–1851	6	*Harlan F. Stone,* N.Y.	1941–1946	5
Robert C. Grier, Pa.	1846–1870	24	James F. Byrnes, S.C.	1941–1942	2
Benj. R. Curtis, Mass.	1851–1857	6	Robert H. Jackson, N.Y.	1941–1954	13
John A. Campbell, Ala.	1853–1861	8	Wiley B. Rutledge, Iowa	1943–1949	6
Nathan Clifford, Me.	1858–1881	23	Harold H. Burton, Ohio	1945–1958	13
Noah H. Swayne, Ohio	1862–1881	20	*Fred M. Vinson,* Ky.	1946–1953	7
Samuel F. Miller, Iowa	1862–1890	28	Thomas C. Clark, Tex.	1949–1967	18
David Davis, Ill.	1862–1877	15	Sherman Minton, Ind.	1949–1956	7
Stephen J. Field, Cal.	1863–1897	34	*Earl Warren,* Calif.	1953–1969	16
Salmon P. Chase, Ohio	1864–1873	9	John Marshall Harlan, N.Y.	1955–1971	16
William Strong, Pa.	1870–1880	10	William J. Brennan, Jr., N.J.	1956–....	..
Joseph P. Bradley, N.J.	1870–1892	22	Charles E. Whittaker, Mo.	1957–1962	5
Ward Hunt, N.Y.	1872–1882	10	Potter Stewart, Ohio	1958–1981	23
Morrison R. Waite, Ohio	1874–1888	14	Byron R. White, Colo.	1962–....	..
John M. Harlan, Ky.	1877–1911	34	Arthur J. Goldberg, Ill.	1962–1965	3
William B. Woods, Ga.	1880–1887	7	Abe Fortas, Tenn.	1965–1969	4
Stanley Matthews, Ohio	1881–1889	8	Thurgood Marshall, N.Y.	1967–....	..
Horace Gray, Mass.	1881–1902	21	*Warren E. Burger,* D.C.	1969–....	..
Samuel Blatchford, N.Y.	1882–1893	11	Harry A. Blackmun, Minn.	1970–....	..
Lucius Q. C. Lamar, Miss.	1888–1893	5	Lewis F. Powell, Jr., Va.	1971–....	..
Melville W. Fuller, Ill.	1888–1910	22	William H. Rehnquist, Ariz.	1971–....	..
David J. Brewer, Kan.	1889–1910	21	John P. Stevens, Ill.	1975–....	..
			Sandra Day O'Connor, Ariz.[2]	1981–....	..

* Acting chief justice; the Senate refused to confirm nomination.

[1] The *First Judiciary Act* (Sept. 24, 1789) made provision for a Supreme Court to consist of 1 Chief Justice and 5 Associate Justices. The size of the court was decreased to 5 by the *Judiciary Act of 1801* (13 Feb.) but restored to 6 by their repeal of that Act (*Act of 8 Mar. 1802*). The size of the Supreme Court increased to 7 (*Act of 24 Feb. 1807*), to 9 (*Act of 3 Mar. 1837*), and to 10 (*Act of 3 Mar. 1863*). It was reduced to 7 (*Act of July 23, 1866*) but restored to its present size of 9 by the *Act of 10 Apr. 1869*.

[2] 1st woman named to the Supreme Court; sworn in 25 Sept. 1981.

THE DECLARATION OF INDEPENDENCE

★ ★
★

The unanimous Declaration of the thirteen United States of America.

WHEN, in the Course of human events, it becomes necessary for one people to dissolve the political bands which have connected them with another, and to assume, among the Powers of the earth, the separate and equal station to which the Laws of Nature and of Nature's God entitle them, a decent respect to the opinions of mankind requires that they should declare the causes which impel them to the separation.

We hold these truths to be self-evident, that all men are created equal, that they are endowed by their Creator with certain unalienable Rights, that among these, are Life, Liberty, and the pursuit of Happiness. That, to secure these rights, Governments are instituted among Men, deriving their just Powers from the consent of the governed. That, whenever any form of Government becomes destructive of these ends, it is the Right of the People to alter or to abolish it, and to institute new Government, laying its foundation on such Principles, and organizing its Powers in such form, as to them shall seem most likely to effect their Safety and Happiness. Prudence, indeed, will dictate that Governments long established should not be changed for light and transient causes; and, accordingly, all experience hath shewn, that mankind are more disposed to suffer, while evils are sufferable, than to right themselves by abolishing the forms to which they are accustomed. But, when a long train of abuses and usurpations, pursuing invariably the same Object, evinces a design to reduce them under absolute Despotism, it is their right, it is their duty, to throw off such Government, and to provide new Guards for their future Security. Such has been the patient sufferance of these Colonies; and such is now the necessity which constrains them to alter their former Systems of Government. The history of the present King of Great Britain is a history of repeated injuries and usurpations, all having in direct object the establishment of an absolute Tyranny over these States. To prove this, let Facts be submitted to a candid world.

He has refused his Assent to Laws the most wholesome and necessary for the public good.

He has forbidden his Governors to pass Laws of immediate and pressing importance, unless suspended in their operation till his Assent should be obtained; and when so suspended, he has utterly neglected to attend to them.

He has refused to pass other Laws for the accommodation of large districts of People, unless those People would relinquish the right of Representation in the legislature; a right inestimable to them and formidable to tyrants only.

He has called together legislative bodies at places unusual, uncomfortable, and distant from the depository of their Public Records, for the sole Purpose of fatiguing them into compliance with his measures.

He has dissolved Representative Houses repeatedly, for opposing, with manly firmness, his invasions on the rights of the People.

He has refused for a long time, after such dissolutions, to cause others to be elected; whereby the Legislative Powers, incapable of Annihilation, have returned to the People at large for their exercise; the State remaining in the mean time exposed to all the dangers of invasion from without, and convulsions within.

He has endeavoured to prevent the Population of these States; for that purpose obstructing the Laws for Naturalization of Foreigners; refusing to pass others to encourage their migrations hither, and raising the conditions of new Appropriations of Lands.

He has obstructed the Administration of Justice, by refusing his Assent to Laws for establishing Judiciary Powers.

He has made Judges dependent on his Will alone, for the tenure of their offices, and the amount and payment of their salaries.

He has erected a multitude of New Offices, and sent hither swarms of Officers to harass our People, and eat out their substance.

He has kept among us, in times of Peace, Standing Armies, without the Consent of our legislatures.

He has affected to render the Military independent of and superior to the Civil Power.

He has combined with others to subject us to a jurisdiction foreign to our constitution, and unacknowledged by our laws; giving his Assent to their Acts of pretended Legislation:

For quartering large bodies of armed troops among us:

For protecting them, by a mock Trial, from Punishment for any Murders which they should commit on the Inhabitants of these States:

For cutting off our Trade with all parts of the world:

For imposing Taxes on us without our Consent:

For depriving us, in many cases, of the benefits of Trial by Jury:

For transporting us beyond Seas to be tried for pretended offences:

For abolishing the free System of English Laws in a neighbouring province, establishing therein an Arbitrary government, and enlarging its Boundaries, so as to render it at once an example and fit instrument for introducing the same absolute rule into these Colonies:

For taking away our Charters, abolishing our most valuable Laws, and altering fundamentally the Forms of our Governments:

For suspending our own Legislatures, and declaring themselves invested with Power to legislate for us in all cases whatsoever.

He has abdicated Government here, by declaring us out of his protection, and waging War against us.

He has plundered our seas, ravaged our Coasts, burnt our towns, and destroyed the Lives of our People.

He is at this time transporting large Armies of foreign Mercenaries to compleat the works of death, desolation and tyranny, already begun with circumstances of Cruelty and perfidy scarcely paralleled in the most barbarous ages, and totally unworthy the Head of a civilized nation.

He has constrained our fellow Citizens, taken Captive on the high Seas, to bear Arms against their Country, to become the executioners of their friends and Brethren, or to fall themselves by their Hands.

He has excited domestic insurrections amongst us, and has endeavoured to bring on the inhabitants of our frontiers, the merciless Indian Savages, whose known rule of warfare, is an undistinguished destruction of all ages, sexes and conditions.

In every stage of these Oppressions, We have Petitioned for Redress, in the most humble terms: Our repeated Petitions, have been answered only by repeated injury. A Prince, whose character is thus marked by every act which may define a Tyrant, is unfit to be the ruler of a free People.

Nor have We been wanting in attentions to our Brittish brethren. We have warned them from time to time of attempts by their legislature to extend an unwarrantable jurisdiction over us. We have reminded them of the circumstances of our emigration and settlement here. We have appealed to their native justice and magnanimity, and we have conjured them by the ties of our common kindred, to disavow these usurpations, which, would inevitably interrupt our connexions and correspondence. They too have been deaf to the voice of justice and of consanguinity. We must, therefore, acquiesce in the necessity, which denounces our Separation, and hold them, as we hold the rest of mankind, Enemies in War, in Peace Friends.

We, therefore, the Representatives of the *united States of America,* in GENERAL CONGRESS assembled, appealing to the Supreme Judge of the World for the rectitude of our intentions, DO, in the Name, and by Authority of the good People of these Colonies, solemnly PUBLISH and DECLARE, That these United Colonies are, and of Right, ought to be *free and Independent States;* that they are

Absolved from all Allegiance to the British Crown, and that all political connexion between them and the State of Great Britain, is and ought to be totally dissolved; and that, as FREE and INDEPENDENT STATES, they have full Power to levy War, conclude Peace, contract Alliances, establish Commerce, and to do all other Acts and Things which INDEPENDENT STATES may of right do. AND for the support of this Declaration, with a firm reliance on the protection of divine Providence, we mutually pledge to each other our Lives, our Fortunes, and our sacred Honour.

John Hancock,

Josiah Bartlett, Wm Whipple, Saml Adams, John Adams, Robt Treat Paine, Elbridge Gerry, Steph. Hopkins, William Ellery, Roger Sherman, Samel Huntington, Wm Williams, Oliver Wolcott, Matthew Thornton, Wm Floyd, Phil Livingston, Frans Lewis, Lewis Morris, Richd Stockton, Jno Witherspoon, Fras Hopkinson, John Hart, Abra Clark, Robt Morris, Benjamin Rush, Benja Franklin, John Morton, Geo Clymer, Jas Smith, Geo. Taylor, James Wilson, Geo. Ross, Caesar Rodney, Geo Read, Thos M:Kean, Samuel Chase, Wm Paca, Thos Stone, Charles Carroll of Carrollton, George Wythe, Richard Henry Lee, Th. Jefferson, Benja Harrison, Thos Nelson, Jr., Francis Lightfoot Lee, Carter Braxton, Wm Hooper, Joseph Hewes, John Penn, Edward Rutledge, Thos Heyward, Junr., Thomas Lynch, Junor., Arthur Middleton, Button Gwinnett, Lyman Hall, Geo Walton.

THE CONSTITUTION OF THE UNITED STATES

Preamble

We the People of the United States, in Order to form a more perfect Union, establish Justice, insure domestic Tranquility, provide for the common defence, promote the general Welfare, and secure the Blessings of Liberty to ourselves and our Posterity, do ordain and establish this Constitution for the United States of America.

Article I

Section 1. All legislative Powers herein granted shall be vested in a Congress of the United States, which shall consist of a Senate and House of Representatives.

Section 2. The House of Representatives shall be composed of Members chosen every second Year by the People of the several States, and the Electors in each State shall have the Qualifications requisite for Electors of the most numerous Branch of the State Legislature.

No Person shall be a Representative who shall not have attained to the Age of twenty five Years, and been seven Years a Citizen of the United States, and who shall not, when elected, be an inhabitant of that State in which he shall be chosen.

Representatives and direct Taxes shall be apportioned among the several States which may be included within this Union, according to their respective Numbers, [which shall be determined by adding to the whole Number of free Persons, including those bound to Service for a Term of Years, and excluding Indians not taxed, three fifths of all other Persons.]¹ The actual Enumeration shall be made within three Years after the first Meeting of the Congress of the United States, and within every subsequent Term of ten Years, in such Manner as they shall by law direct. The Number of Representatives shall not exceed one for every thirty Thousand, but each State shall have at Least one Representative; and until such enumeration shall be made, the State of New Hampshire shall be entitled to chuse three, Massachusetts eight, Rhode-Island and Providence Plantations one, Connecticut five, New-York six, New Jersey four, Pennsylvania eight, Delaware one, Maryland six, Virginia ten, North Carolina five, South Carolina five, and Georgia three.

When vacancies happen in the Representation from any State, the Executive Authority thereof shall issue Writs of Election to fill such Vacancies.

The House of Representatives shall chuse their Speaker and other Officers; and shall have the sole Power of Impeachment.

Section 3. The Senate of the United States shall be composed of two Senators from each State, [chosen by the Legisla-

¹ Superseded by the Fourteenth Amendment.

ture thereof,][2] for six Years; and each Senator shall have one Vote.

Immediately after they shall be assembled in Consequence of the first Election, they shall be divided as equally as may be into three Classes. The Seats of the Senators of the first Class shall be vacated at the Expiration of the second Year, of the second Class at the Expiration of the fourth Year, and of the third Class at the Expiration of the sixth Year, so that one third may be chosen every second Year; [and if Vacancies happen by Resignation, or otherwise, during the Recess of the Legislature of any State, the Executive thereof may make temporary Appointments until the next Meeting of the Legislature, which shall then fill such Vacancies.][3]

No Person shall be a Senator who shall not have attained to the Age of thirty Years, and been nine Years a Citizen of the United States, and who shall not, when elected, be an Inhabitant of that State for which he shall be chosen.

The Vice President of the United States shall be President of the Senate, but shall have no Vote, unless they be equally divided.

The Senate shall chuse their other Officers, and also a President pro tempore, in the Absence of the Vice President, or when he shall exercise the Office of President of the United States.

The Senate shall have the sole Power to try all Impeachments. When sitting for that Purpose, they shall be on Oath or Affirmation. When the President of the United States is tried, the Chief Justice shall preside: and no Person shall be convicted without the Concurrence of two thirds of the Members present.

Judgment in Cases of Impeachment shall not extend further than to removal from Office, and disqualification to hold and enjoy any Office of honor, Trust or Profit under the United States: but the Party convicted shall nevertheless be liable and subject to Indictment, Trial, Judgment and Punishment, according to Law.

Section 4. The Times, Places and Manner of holding Elections for Senators and Representatives, shall be prescribed in each State by the Legislature thereof; but the Congress may at any time by Law make or alter such Regulations, except as to the Places of chusing Senators.

[The Congress shall assemble at least once in every Year, and such Meeting shall be on the first Monday in December, unless they shall by Law appoint a different Day.][4]

Section 5. Each House shall be the Judge of the Elections, Returns and Qualifications of its own Members, and a Majority of each shall constitute a Quorum to do Business; but a smaller Number may adjourn from day to day, and may be authorized to compel the Attendance of absent Members, in such Manner, and under such Penalties as each House may provide.

Each House may determine the Rules of its Proceedings, punish its Members for disorderly Behaviour, and, with the Concurrence of two thirds, expel a Member.

Each House shall keep a Journal of its Proceedings, and from time to time publish the same, excepting such Parts as may in their Judgment require Secrecy; and the Yeas and Nays of the Members of either House on any question shall, at the Desire of one fifth of those Present, be entered on the Journal.

Neither House, during the Session of Congress, shall, without the Consent of the other, adjourn for more than three days, nor to any other Place than that in which the two Houses shall be sitting.

Section 6. The Senators and Repre-

---

[2] Superseded by the Seventeenth Amendment.
[3] Modified by the Seventeenth Amendment.

[4] Superseded by the Twentieth Amendment.

sentatives shall receive a Compensation for their Services, to be ascertained by Law, and paid out of the Treasury of the United States. They shall in all Cases, except Treason, Felony and Breach of the Peace, be privileged from Arrest during their Attendance at the Session of their respective Houses, and in going to and returning from the same; and for any Speech or Debate in either House, they shall not be questioned in any other Place.

No Senator or Representative shall, during the Time for which he was elected, be appointed to any civil Office under the Authority of the United States, which shall have been created, or the Emoluments whereof shall have been encreased during such time; and no Person holding any Office under the United States, shall be a Member of either House during his Continuance in Office.

Section 7. All bills for raising Revenue shall originate in the House of Representatives; but the Senate may propose or concur with Amendments as on other Bills.

Every Bill which shall have passed the House of Representatives and the Senate, shall, before it become a Law, be presented to the President of the United States. If he approve he shall sign it, but if not he shall return it, with his Objections to that House in which it shall have originated, who shall enter the Objections at large on their Journal, and proceed to reconsider it. If after such Reconsideration two thirds of that House shall agree to pass the Bill, it shall be sent, together with the Objections, to the other House, by which it shall likewise be reconsidered, and if approved by two thirds of that House, it shall become a Law. But in all such Cases the Votes of both Houses shall be determined by yeas and Nays, and the Names of the Persons voting for and against the Bill shall be entered on the

Journal of each House respectively. If any Bill shall not be returned by the President within ten Days (Sundays excepted) after it shall have been presented to him, the Same shall be a Law, in like Manner as if he had signed it, unless the Congress by their Adjournment prevent its Return, in which Case it shall not be a Law.

Every Order, Resolution, or Vote to which the Concurrence of the Senate and House of Representatives may be necessary (except on a question of Adjournment) shall be presented to the President of the United States; and before the Same shall take Effect, shall be approved by him, or being disapproved by him, shall be repassed by two thirds of the Senate and House of Representatives, according to the Rules and Limitations prescribed in the Case of a Bill.

Section 8. The Congress shall have Power To lay and collect Taxes, Duties, Imposts and Excises, to pay the Debts and provide for the common Defence and general Welfare of the United States; but all Duties, Imposts and Excises shall be uniform throughout the United States;

To borrow Money on the credit of the United States;

To regulate Commerce with foreign Nations, and among the several States, and with the Indian Tribes;

To establish a uniform Rule of Naturalization, and uniform Laws on the subject of Bankruptcies throughout the United States;

To coin Money, regulate the Value thereof, and of foreign Coin, and fix the Standard of Weights and Measures;

To provide for the Punishment of counterfeiting the Securities and current Coin of the United States;

To establish Post Offices and post Roads;

To promote the Progress of Science and useful Arts, by securing for limited

Times to Authors and Inventors the exclusive Right to their respective Writings and Discoveries;

To constitute Tribunals inferior to the supreme Court;

To define and punish Piracies and Felonies committed on the high Seas, and Offences against the Law of Nations;

To declare War, grant Letters of Marque and Reprisal, and make Rules concerning Captures on Land and Water;

To raise and support Armies, but no Appropriation of Money to that Use shall be for a longer Term than two Years;

To provide and maintain a Navy;

To make Rules for the Government and Regulation of the land and naval Forces;

To provide for calling forth the Militia to execute the Laws of the Union, suppress Insurrections and repel Invasions;

To provide for organizing, arming, and disciplining, the Militia, and for governing such Part of them as may be employed in the Service of the United States, reserving to the States respectively, the Appointment of the Officers, and the Authority of training the Militia according to the discipline prescribed by Congress;

To exercise exclusive Legislation in all Cases whatsoever, over such District (not exceeding ten Miles square) as may, by Cession of particular States, and the Acceptance of Congress, become the Seat of the Government of the United States, and to exercise like Authority over all Places purchased by the Consent of the Legislature of the State in which the Same shall be, for the Erection of Forts, Magazines, Arsenals, dockYards, and other needful Buildings;—And

To make all Laws which shall be necessary and proper for carrying into Execution the foregoing Powers, and all other Powers vested by this Constitution in the Government of the United States, or in any Department or Officer thereof.

Section 9. The Migration or Importation of such Persons as any of the States now existing shall think proper to admit, shall not be prohibited by the Congress prior to the Year one thousand eight hundred and eight, but a Tax or duty may be imposed on such Importation, not exceeding ten dollars for each Person.

The Privilege of the Writ of Habeas Corpus shall not be suspended, unless when in Cases of Rebellion or Invasion the public safety may require it.

No Bill of Attainder or ex post facto Law shall be passed.

No Capitation, or other direct, Tax shall be laid, unless in Proportion to the Census or Enumeration herein before directed to be taken.[5]

No Tax or Duty shall be laid on Articles exported from any State.

No Preference shall be given by any Regulation of Commerce or Revenue to the Ports of one State over those of another; nor shall Vessels bound to, or from, one State, be obliged to enter, clear, or pay Duties in another.

No money shall be drawn from the Treasury, but in Consequence of Appropriations made by Law; and a regular Statement and Account of the Receipts and Expenditures of all public Money shall be published from time to time.

No Title of Nobility shall be granted by the United States: And no Person holding any Office of Profit or Trust under them, shall, without the Consent of the Congress, accept any present, Emolument, Office, or Title, of any kind whatever, from any King, Prince, or foreign State.

Section 10. No State shall enter into any Treaty, Alliance, or Confederation,

[5] Modified by the Sixteenth Amendment.

grant Letters of Marque and Reprisal; coin Money; emit Bills of Credit; make any Thing but gold and silver Coin a Tender in Payment of Debts; pass any Bill of Attainder, ex post facto Law, or Law impairing the Obligation of Contracts, or grant any Title of Nobility.

No State shall, without the Consent of the Congress, lay any Imposts or Duties on Imports or Exports, except what may be absolutely necessary for executing it's inspection laws; and the net Produce of all Duties and Imposts, laid by any State on Imports or Exports, shall be for the Use of the Treasury of the United States; and all such Laws shall be subject to the Revision, and Control of the Congress.

No State shall, without the Consent of Congress, lay any Duty of Tonnage, keep Troops, or Ships of War in time of Peace, enter into any Agreement or Compact with another State, or with a foreign Power, or engage in War, unless actually invaded, or in such imminent Danger as will not admit of delay.

Article II

Section 1. The executive Power shall be vested in a President of the United States of America. He shall hold his Office during the Term of four Years, and, together with the Vice President, chosen for the same Term, be elected, as follows.

Each State shall appoint, in such Manner as the Legislature thereof may direct, a Number of Electors, equal to the whole Number of Senators and Representatives to which the State may be entitled in the Congress: but no Senator or Representative, or Person holding an Office of Trust or Profit under the United States, shall be appointed an Elector.

[The Electors shall meet in their respective States, and vote by Ballot for two Persons, of whom one at least shall not be an Inhabitant of the same State with themselves. And they shall make a List of all the Persons voted for, and the Number of Votes for each; which list they shall sign and certify, and transmit sealed to the Seat of the Government of the United States, directed to the President of the Senate. The President of the Senate shall, in the Presence of the Senate and House of Representatives, open all the Certificates, and the Votes shall then be counted. The person having the greatest Number of Votes shall be the President, if such Number be a Majority of the whole Number of Electors appointed; and if there be more than one who have such Majority, and have an equal Number of Votes, then the House of Representatives shall immediately chuse by Ballot one of them for President; and if no Person have a Majority, then from the five highest on the List the said House shall in like Manner chuse the President. But in chusing the President, the Votes shall be taken by States, the Representation from each State having one Vote; A quorum for this purpose shall consist of a Member or Members from two thirds of the States, and a Majority of all the States shall be necessary to a Choice. In every Case, after the Choice of the President, the Person having the greatest Number of Votes of the Electors shall be the Vice President. But if there should remain two or more who have equal Votes, the Senate chuse from them by Ballot the Vice President.][6]

The Congress may determine the Time of chusing the Electors, and the Day on which they shall give their Votes; which Day shall be the same throughout the United States.

No Person except a natural born Citizen, or a Citizen of the United States,

[6] Superseded by the Twelfth Amendment.

at the time of the Adoption of this Constitution, shall be eligible to the Office of President; neither shall any Person be eligible to that Office who shall not have attained to the Age of thirty five Years, and been fourteen Years a Resident within the United States.

In Case of the Removal of the President from Office, or of his Death, Resignation, or Inability to discharge the Powers and Duties of the said Office,[7] the Same shall devolve on the Vice President, and the Congress may by Law provide for the Case of Removal, Death, Resignation or Inability, both of the President and Vice President, declaring what Officer shall then act as President, and such Officer shall act accordingly, until the Disability be removed, or a President shall be elected.

The President shall, at stated Times receive for his Services, a Compensation, which shall neither be encreased nor diminished during the Period for which he shall have been elected, and he shall not receive within that Period any other Emolument from the United States, or any of them.

Before he enter on the Execution of his Office, he shall take the following Oath or Affirmation:—"I do solemnly swear (or affirm) that I will faithfully execute the Office of President of the United States, and will to the best of my Ability, preserve, protect and defend the Constitution of the United States."

Section 2. The President shall be Commander in Chief of the Army and Navy of the United States, and of the Militia of the several States, when called into the actual Service of the United States; he may require the Opinion, in writing, of the principal Officer in each of the executive Departments, upon any Subject relating to the Duties of their respective Offices, and he shall have Power

[7] Modified by the Twenty-fifth Amendment.

to grant Reprieves and Pardons for Offenses against the United States, except in Cases of Impeachment.

He shall have Power, by and with the Advice and Consent of the Senate, to make Treaties, provided two thirds of the Senators present concur; and he shall nominate, and by and with the Advice and Consent of the Senate, shall appoint Ambassadors, other public Ministers and Consuls, Judges of the supreme Court, and all other Officers of the United States, whose Appointments are not herein otherwise provided for, and which shall be established by Law: but the Congress may by Law vest the Appointment of such inferior Officers, as they think proper, in the President alone, in the Courts of Law, or in the Heads of Departments.

The President shall have Power to fill up all Vacancies that may happen during the Recess of the Senate, by granting Commissions which shall expire at the End of their next Session.

Section 3. He shall from time to time give to the Congress Information of the State of the Union, and recommend to their Consideration such Measures as he shall judge necessary and expedient; he may, on extraordinary Occasions, convene both Houses, or either of them, and in Case of Disagreement between them, with Respect to the Time of Adjournment, he may adjourn them to such Time as he shall think proper; he shall receive Ambassadors and other public Ministers; he shall take Care that the Laws be faithfully executed, and shall Commission all Officers of the United States.

Section 4. The President, Vice President and all civil Officers of the United States, shall be removed from Office on Impeachment for, and Conviction of, Treason, Bribery, or other high Crimes and Misdemeanors.

Article III

Section 1. The judicial Power of the United States, shall be vested in one supreme Court, and in such inferior Courts as the Congress may from time to time ordain and establish. The Judges, both of the supreme and inferior Courts, shall hold their Offices during good Behaviour, and shall, at stated Times, receive for their Services, a Compensation, which shall not be diminished during their Continuance in Office.

Section 2. The judicial Power shall extend to all Cases, in Law and Equity, arising under this Constitution, the Laws of the United States, and Treaties made, or which shall be made, under their authority;—to all Cases affecting Ambassadors, other public Ministers and Consuls;—to all Cases of admiralty and maritime Jurisdiction;—to Controversies to which the United States shall be a Party;—to Controversies between two or more States;—between a State and Citizens of another State;[8]—between Citizens of different States,—between Citizens of the same State claiming Lands under Grants of different States, and between a State, or the Citizens thereof, and foreign States, Citizens or Subjects.

In all cases affecting Ambassadors, other public Ministers and Consuls, and those in which a State shall be Party, the supreme Court shall have original Jurisdiction. In all the other Cases before mentioned, the supreme Court shall have appellate Jurisdiction, both as to Law and Fact, with such Exceptions, and under such Regulations as the Congress shall make.

The Trial of all Crimes, except in Cases of Impeachment, shall be by Jury; and such Trial shall be held in the State where the said Crimes shall have been committed; but when not committed within any State, the Trial shall be at such Place or Places as the Congress may by Law have directed.

Section 3. Treason against the United States, shall consist only in levying War against them, or in adhering to their Enemies, giving them Aid and Comfort. No Person shall be convicted of Treason unless on the Testimony of two Witnesses to the same overt Act, or on Confession in open Court.

The Congress shall have Power to declare the Punishment of Treason, but no Attainder of Treason shall work Corruption of Blood, or Forfeiture except during the Life of the Person attainted.

Article IV

Section 1. Full Faith and Credit shall be given in each State to the public Acts, Records, and judicial Proceedings of every other State. And the Congress may by general Laws prescribe the Manner in which such Acts, Records and Proceedings shall be proved, and the Effect thereof.

Section 2. The Citizens of each State shall be entitled to all Privileges and Immunities of Citizens in the several States.

A Person charged in any State with Treason, Felony, or other Crime, who shall flee from Justice, and be found in another State, shall on Demand of the executive Authority of the State from which he fled, be delivered up, to be removed to the State having Jurisdiction of the Crime.

[No Person held to Service or Labour in one State, under the Laws thereof, escaping into another, shall, in Consequence of any Law or Regulation therein, be discharged from such Service or Labour, but shall be delivered up on Claim of the Party to whom such Service or Labour may be due.][9]

Section 3. New States may be admitted by the Congress into this Union;

---

[8] Modified by the Eleventh Amendment.

[9] Superseded by the Thirteenth Amendment.

but no new State shall be formed or erected within the Jurisdiction of any other State; nor any State be formed by the Junction of two or more States, or Parts of States, without the Consent of the Legislatures of the States concerned as well as of the Congress.

The Congress shall have Power to dispose of and make all needful Rules and Regulations respecting the Territory or other Property belonging to the United States; and nothing in this Constitution shall be so construed as to Prejudice any Claims of the United States, or of any particular State.

Section 4. The United States shall guarantee to every State in this Union a Republican Form of Government, and shall protect each of them against Invasion; and on Application of the Legislature, or of the Executive (when the Legislature cannot be convened) against domestic Violence.

Article V

The Congress, whenever two thirds of both Houses shall deem it necessary, shall propose Amendments to this Constitution, or, on the Application of the Legislatures of two thirds of the several States, shall call a Convention for proposing Amendments, which, in either Case, shall be valid to all Intents and Purposes, as Part of this Constitution, when ratified by the Legislatures of three fourths of the several States, or by Conventions in three fourths thereof, as the one or the other Mode of Ratification may be proposed by the Congress; Provided that no Amendment which may be made prior to the Year One thousand eight hundred and eight shall in any Manner affect the first and fourth Clauses in the Ninth Section of the first Article; and that no State, without its Consent, shall be deprived of its equal Suffrage in the Senate.

Article VI

All Debts contracted and Engagements entered into, before the Adoption of this Constitution, shall be as valid against the United States under this Constitution, as under the Confederation.

This Constitution, and the Laws of the United States which shall be made in Pursuance thereof; and all Treaties made, or which shall be made, under the Authority of the United States, shall be the supreme Law of the Land; and the Judges in every State shall be bound thereby, any Thing in the Constitution or Laws of any State to the Contrary notwithstanding.

The Senators and Representatives before mentioned, and the Members of the several State Legislatures, and all executive and judicial Officers, both of the United States and of the several States, shall be bound by Oath or Affirmation, to support this Constitution; but no religious Test shall ever be required as a Qualification to any Office or public Trust under the United States.

Article VII

The Ratification of the Conventions of nine States, shall be sufficient for the Establishment of this Constitution between the States so ratifying the Same.

done in Convention by the Unanimous Consent of the States present the Seventeenth Day of September in the Year of our Lord one thousand seven hundred and Eighty seven and of the Independence of the United States of America the Twelfth.

In witness whereof We have hereunto subscribed our Names.

Go. Washington, *President and deputy from Virginia; Attest* William Jackson, *Secretary; Delaware:* Geo. Read, Gun-ning Bedford, Jr., John Dickinson, Richard Bassett, Jaco. Broom; *Maryland:* James McHenry, Daniel of St. Thomas Jenifer, Daniel Carroll; *Virginia:* John Blair, James Madison, Jr.; *North Carolina:* Wm. Blount, Richd. Dobbs Spaight, Hu Williamson; *South Carolina:* J. Rutledge, Charles Cotesworth Pinckney, Charles Pinckney, Pierce Butler; *Georgia:* William Few, Abr. Baldwin; *New Hampshire:* John Langdon, Nicholas Gilman; *Massachusetts:* Nathaniel Gorham, Rufus King; *Connecticut:* Wm. Saml. Johnson, Roger Sherman; *New York:* Alexander Hamilton; *New Jersey:* Wil. Livingston, David Brearley, Wm. Paterson, Jona. Dayton; *Pennsylvania:* B. Franklin, Thomas Mifflin, Robt. Morris, Geo. Clymer, Thos. FitzSimons, Jared Ingersoll, James Wilson, Gouv. Morris.

[AMENDMENTS]

ARTICLES in addition to, and Amendment of the Constitution of the United States of America, proposed by Congress, and ratified by the Legislatures of the several States, pursuant to the fifth Article of the original Constitution.

[The first ten articles proposed 25 Sept. 1789; declared in force 15 Dec. 1791]

Article I

Congress shall make no law respecting an establishment of religion, or prohibiting the free exercise thereof; or abridging the freedom of speech, or of the press; or the right of the people peaceably to assemble, and to petition the Government for a redress of grievances.

Article II

A well regulated Militia, being necessary to the security of a free State, the right of the people to keep and bear Arms, shall not be infringed.

Article III

No Soldier shall, in time of peace, be quartered in any house, without the consent of the Owner, nor in time of war, but in a manner to be prescribed by law.

Article IV

The right of the people to be secure in their persons, houses, papers, and effects, against unreasonable searches and seizures, shall not be violated, and no Warrants shall issue, but upon probable cause, supported by Oath or affirmation, and particularly describing the place to be searched, and the persons or things to be seized.

Article V

No person shall be held to answer for a capital, or otherwise infamous crime, unless on a presentment or indictment of a Grand Jury, except in cases arising in the land or naval forces, or in the Militia, when in actual service in time of War or public danger; nor shall any person be subject for the same offense to be twice put in jeopardy of life or limb; nor shall be compelled in any criminal case to be a witness against himself, nor be deprived of life, liberty, or property, without due process of law; nor shall private property be taken for public use, without just compensation.

Article VI

In all criminal prosecutions, the accused shall enjoy the right to a speedy and public trial, by an impartial jury of the State and district wherein the crime shall have been committed, which district shall have been previously ascertained by law, and to be informed of the nature and cause of the accusation; to be confronted with the witnesses against him; to have compulsory process for obtaining witnesses in his favor, and to have the Assistance of Counsel for his defense.

Article VII

In Suits at common law, where the value in controversy shall exceed twenty dollars, the right of trial by jury shall be preserved, and no fact tried by a jury, shall be otherwise re-examined in any Court of the United States, than according to the rules of the common law.

Article VIII

Excessive bail shall not be required, nor excessive fines imposed, nor cruel and unusual punishments inflicted.

Article IX

The enumeration in the Constitution, of certain rights, shall not be construed to deny or disparage others retained by the people.

Article X

The powers not delegated to the United States by the Constitution, nor prohibited by it to the States, are reserved to the States respectively, or to the people.

Article XI [proposed 5 Mar. 1794; declared ratified 8 Jan. 1798]

The Judicial power of the United States shall not be construed to extend to any suit in law or equity, commenced or prosecuted against one of the United States by Citizens of another State, or by Citizens or Subjects of any Foreign State.

Article XII [proposed 12 Dec. 1803; declared ratified 25 Sept. 1804]

The Electors shall meet in their respective states, and vote by ballot for President and Vice-President, one of whom, at least, shall not be an inhabitant of the same state with themselves; they shall name in their ballots the person voted for as President, and in distinct ballots the person voted for as Vice-President, and they shall make distinct lists of all persons voted for as President, and of all persons voted for as Vice-President, and of the number of votes for each, which lists they shall sign and certify, and transmit sealed to the seat of the government of the United States, directed to the President of the Senate;—The President of the Senate shall, in the presence of the Senate and House of Representatives, open all certificates and the votes shall then be counted;—The person having the greatest number of votes for President, shall be the President, if such number be a majority of the whole number of Electors appointed; and if no person have such majority, then from the persons having the highest numbers not exceeding three on the list of those voted for as President, the House of Representatives shall choose immediately, by ballot, the President. But in choosing the President, the votes shall be taken by states, the representation from each state having one vote; a quorum for this purpose shall consist of a member or members from two-thirds of the states, and a majority of all the states shall be necessary to a choice. [And if the House of Representatives shall not choose a President whenever the right of choice shall devolve upon them, before the fourth day of March next following, then the Vice-President shall act as President, as in the case of the death or other constitutional disability of the President.][10] The person having the greatest number of votes as Vice-President, shall be the Vice-President, if such number be a majority of the whole number of Electors appointed, and if no person have a majority, then from the two highest numbers on the list, the Senate shall choose the Vice-President; a quorum for the purpose shall consist of two-thirds of the whole number of Senators, and a majority of the whole number shall be necessary to a choice. But no person constitutionally ineligible to the office of President shall be eligible to that of Vice-President of the United States.

Article XIII [proposed 1 Feb. 1865; declared ratified 18 Dec. 1865]

Section 1. Neither slavery nor involuntary servitude, except as a punishment for crime whereof the party shall have been duly convicted, shall exist within the United States, or any place subject to their jurisdiction.

Section 2. Congress shall have power to enforce this article by appropriate legislation.

Article XIV [proposed 16 June 1866; declared ratified 28 July 1868]

Section 1. All persons born or naturalized in the United States, and subject to the jurisdiction thereof, are citizens of the United States and of the State wherein they reside. No State shall make or enforce any law which shall abridge the privileges or immunities of citizens of the United States; nor shall any State deprive any person of life, liberty, or property, without due process of law; nor deny to any person within

[10] Superseded by the Twentieth Amendment.

its jurisdiction the equal protection of the laws.

Section 2. Representatives shall be apportioned among the several States according to their respective numbers, counting the whole number of persons in each State, excluding Indians not taxed. But when the right to vote at any election for the choice of electors for President and Vice President of the United States, Representatives in Congress, the Executive and Judicial officers of a State, or the members of the Legislature thereof, is denied to any of the male inhabitants of such State, being twenty-one years of age, and citizens of the United States, or in any way abridged, except for participation in rebellion, or other crime, the basis of representation therein shall be reduced in the proportion which the number of such male citizens shall bear to the whole number of male citizens twenty-one years of age in such State.

Section 3. No person shall be a Senator or Representative in Congress, or elector of President and Vice President, or hold any office, civil or military, under the United States, or under any State, who, having previously taken an oath, as a member of Congress, or as an officer of the United States, or as a member of any State legislature, or as an executive or judicial officer of any State, to support the Constitution of the United States, shall have engaged in insurrection or rebellion against the same, or given aid and comfort to the enemies thereof. But Congress may by a vote of two-thirds of each House, remove such disability.

Section 4. The validity of the public debt of the United States authorized by law, including debts incurred for payment of pensions and bounties for services in suppressing insurrection or rebellion, shall not be questioned. But neither the United States nor any state shall assume or pay any debt or obligation incurred in aid of insurrection or rebellion against the United States, or any claim for the loss or emancipation of any slave; but all such debts, obligations, and claims shall be held illegal and void.

Section 5. The Congress shall have power to enforce, by appropriate legislation, the provisions of this article.

Article XV [proposed 27 Feb. 1869; declared ratified 30 Mar. 1870]

Section 1. The right of citizens of the United States to vote shall not be denied or abridged by the United States or by any State on account of race, color, or previous condition of servitude.

Section 2. The Congress shall have power to enforce this article by appropriate legislation.

Article XVI [proposed 12 July 1909; declared ratified 25 Feb. 1913]

The Congress shall have power to lay and collect taxes on incomes, from whatever source derived, without apportionment among the several States, and without regard to any census or enumeration.

Article XVII [proposed 16 May 1912; declared ratified 31 May 1913]

The Senate of the United States shall be composed of two Senators from each State, elected by the people thereof, for six years; and each Senator shall have one vote. The electors in each State shall have the qualifications requisite for electors of the most numerous branch of the State legislatures.

When vacancies happen in the representation of any State in the Senate, the executive authority of such State shall issue writs of election to fill such vacancies: Provided, That the legislature of any State may empower the executive thereof to make temporary appointments until the people fill the vacancies by election as the legislature may direct.

This amendment shall not be so construed as to affect the election or term of any Senator chosen before it becomes valid as part of the Constitution.

Article XVIII [proposed 18 Dec. 1917; declared ratified 29 Jan. 1919; repealed by the 21st Amendment]

Section 1. After one year from the ratification of this article the manufacture, sale, or transportation of intoxicating liquors within, the importation thereof into, or the exportation thereof from the United States and all territory subject to the jurisdiction thereof for beverage purposes is hereby prohibited.

Section 2. The Congress and the several States shall have concurrent power to enforce this article by appropriate legislation.

Section 3. This article shall be inoperative unless it shall have been ratified as an amendment to the Constitution by the legislatures of the several States, as provided in the Constitution, within seven years from the date of the submission hereof to the States by the Congress.[11]

Article XIX [proposed 4 June 1919; declared ratified 26 Aug. 1920]

The right of citizens of the United States to vote shall not be denied or abridged by the United States or by any State on account of sex.

Congress shall have power to enforce this article by appropriate legislation.

Article XX [proposed 2 Mar. 1932; declared ratified 6 Feb. 1933]

Section 1. The terms of the President and Vice President shall end at noon on the 20th day of January, and the terms of Senators and Representatives at noon

[11] Superseded by the Twenty-first Amendment.

on the 3d day of January, of the years in which such terms would have ended if this article had not been ratified; and the terms of their successors shall then begin.

Section 2. The Congress shall assemble at least once in every year, and such meeting shall begin at noon on the 3d day of January, unless they shall by law appoint a different day.

Section 3. If, at the time fixed for the beginning of the term of the President, the President elect shall have died, the Vice President elect shall become President. If a President shall not have been chosen before the time fixed for the beginning of his term, or if the President elect shall have failed to qualify, then the Vice President elect shall act as President until a President shall have qualified; and the Congress may by law provide for the case wherein neither a President elect nor a Vice President elect shall have qualified, declaring who shall then act as President, or the manner in which one who is to act shall be selected, and such person shall act accordingly until a President or Vice President shall have qualified.

Section 4. The Congress may by law provide for the case of the death of any of the persons from whom the House of Representatives may choose a President whenever the right of choice shall have devolved upon them, and for the case of the death of any of the persons from whom the Senate may choose a Vice President whenever the right of choice shall have devolved upon them.

Section 5. Sections 1 and 2 shall take effect on the 15th day of October following the ratification of this article.

Section 6. This article shall be inoperative unless it shall have been ratified as an amendment to the Constitution by the legislatures of three-fourths of the several States within seven years from the date of its submission.

Article XXI [proposed 20 Feb. 1933; declared ratified 5 Dec. 1933]

Section 1. The Eighteenth article of amendment to the Constitution of the United States is hereby repealed.

Section 2. The transportation or importation into any State, Territory, or possession of the United States for delivery or use therein of intoxicating liquors, in violation of the laws thereof, is hereby prohibited.

Section 3. This article shall be inoperative unless it shall have been ratified as an amendment to the Constitution by conventions in the several States, as provided in the Constitution, within seven years from the date of the submission hereof to the States by the Congress.

Article XXII [proposed 24 Mar. 1947; declared ratified 26 Feb. 1951]

Section 1. No person shall be elected to the office of the President more than twice, and no person who has held the office of president, or acted as President, for more than two years of a term to which some other person was elected President shall be elected to the office of the President more than once. But this Article shall not apply to any person holding the office of President when this Article was proposed by the Congress, and shall not prevent any person who may be holding the office of President, or acting as President, during the term within which this Article becomes operative from holding the office of President or acting as President during the remainder of such term.

Section 2. This article shall be inoperative unless it shall have been ratified as an amendment to the Constitution by the legislatures of three-fourths of the several States within seven years from the date of its submission to the States by the Congress.

Article XXIII [proposed 16 June 1960; ratified 29 Mar. 1961]

Section 1. The district constituting the seat of government of the United States shall appoint in such manner as the Congress may direct:

A number of electors of President and Vice President equal to the whole number of Senators and Representatives in Congress to which the District would be entitled if it were a State, but in no event more than the least populous state; they shall be in addition to those appointed by the States, but they shall be considered, for the purpose of the election of President and Vice President, to be electors appointed by a State; and they shall meet in the District and perform such duties as provided by the twelfth article of amendment.

Section 2. The Congress shall have power to enforce this article by appropriate legislation.

Article XXIV [proposed 27 Aug. 1962; ratified 23 Jan. 1964]

Section 1. The right of citizens of the United States to vote in any primary or other election for President or Vice President, for electors for President or Vice President, or for Senator or Representative in Congress, shall not be denied or abridged by the United States or any State by reason of failure to pay any poll tax or other tax.

Section 2. The Congress shall have power to enforce this article by appropriate legislation.

Article XXV [proposed 6 July 1965; ratified 10 Feb. 1967]

Section 1. In case of the removal of the President from office or of his death or resignation, the Vice President shall become President.

Section 2. Whenever there is a vacancy in the office of the Vice President, the President shall nominate a Vice President who shall take office upon confirmation by a majority vote of both Houses of Congress.

Section 3. Whenever the President transmits to the President pro tempore of the Senate and the Speaker of the House of Representatives his written declaration that he is unable to discharge the powers and duties of his office, and until he transmits to them a written declaration to the contrary, such powers and duties shall be discharged by the Vice President as Acting President.

Section 4. Whenever the Vice President and a majority of either the principal officers of the executive departments or of such other body as Congress may by law provide, transmit to the President pro tempore of the Senate and the Speaker of the House of Representatives their written declaration that the President is unable to discharge the powers and duties of his office, the Vice President shall immediately assume the powers and duties of the office as Acting President.

Thereafter, when the President transmits to the President pro tempore of the Senate and the Speaker of the House of Representatives his written declaration that no inability exists, he shall resume the powers and duties of his office unless the Vice President and a majority of either the principal officers of the executive department or of such other body as Congress may by law provide, transmit within four days to the President pro tempore of the Senate and the Speaker of the House of Representatives their written declaration that the President is unable to discharge the powers and duties of his office. Thereupon Congress shall decide the issue, assembling within forty-eight hours for that purpose if not in session. If the Congress, within twenty-one days after receipt of the latter written declaration, or, if Congress is not in session, within twenty-one days after Congress is required to assemble, determines by two-thirds vote of both Houses that the President is unable to discharge the powers and duties of his office, the Vice President shall continue to discharge the same as Acting President; otherwise, the President shall resume the powers and duties of his office.

Article XXVI [proposed 23 Mar. 1971; ratified 1 July 1971]

Section 1. The right of citizens of the United States, who are eighteen years of age or older, to vote shall not be denied or abridged by the United States or by any State on account of age.

Section 2. The Congress shall have power to enforce this article by appropriate legislation.

INDEX